The
POSEN LIBRARY OF JEWISH
CULTURE AND CIVILIZATION

THE POSEN LIBRARY OF JEWISH CULTURE AND CIVILIZATION

A monumental project many years in the making, The Posen Library collects more than three thousand years of Jewish primary texts, documents, images, and cultural artifacts into ten encyclopedic volumes, with selections made by 150 internationally recognized scholars. When complete, the library will include the following volumes:

Volume 1: Ancient Israel, from Its Beginnings through 332 BCE, edited by Jeffrey H. Tigay and Adele Berlin

Volume 2: Emerging Judaism, 332 BCE–600 CE, edited by Carol Bakhos

Volume 3: Encountering Christianity and Islam, 600–1200, edited by Arnold E. Franklin

Volume 4: Late Medieval Era, 1200–1500, edited by Jonathan S. Ray

Volume 5: Early Modern Era, 1500–1750, edited by Yosef Kaplan

Volume 6: Confronting Modernity, 1750–1880, edited by Elisheva Carlebach

Volume 7: National Renaissance and International Horizons, 1880–1918, edited by Israel Bartal and Kenneth B. Moss

Volume 8: Crisis and Creativity between World Wars, 1918–1939, edited by Todd M. Endelman and Zvi Gitelman

Volume 9: Catastrophe and Rebirth, 1939–1973, edited by Samuel D. Kassow and David G. Roskies

Volume 10: Late Twentieth Century, 1973–2005, edited by Deborah Dash Moore and Nurith Gertz

The Posen Foundation's mission is rooted in the belief that Jewish education can make a meaningful difference in Jewish life, and should be available to all who are interested. To this end, the Foundation works internationally to promote Jewish learning, support academic research into Jewish history and culture, and encourage participation in Jewish cultural life

The Posen Library of Jewish Culture and Civilization

Deborah Dash Moore, *Editor in Chief*

VOLUME 8: CRISIS AND CREATIVITY BETWEEN WORLD WARS, 1918–1939

Todd M. Endelman and Zvi Gitelman, *Editors*

Yale UNIVERSITY PRESS   New Haven and London

The Posen Foundation   Lucerne

Yale University Press books may be purchased in quantity for educational, business, or promotional use. For information, please e-mail sales.press@yale.edu (U.S. office) or sales@yaleup.co.uk (U.K. office).

Designed by George Whipple Design for Westchester Publishing Services.
Set in Bulmer MT type by Newgen.
Printed in the United States of America.

Library of Congress Control Number: 2011043318
ISBN: 978-0-300-13552-7 (hardcover)

A catalogue record for this book is available from the British Library.

This paper meets the requirements of ANSI/NISO Z39.48-1992 (Permanence of Paper).

10 9 8 7 6 5 4 3 2 1

Contents

MEMOIR AND REPORTAGE

SCHOLARSHIP

VISUAL CULTURE

FICTION AND DRAMA

Advisory Boards

Project Staff

The Posen Library of Jewish Culture and Civilization, Volume 8

Editor in Chief	Deborah Dash Moore
Founding Editor	James E. Young
Volume Editors	Todd M. Endelman
	Zvi Gitelman
Executive Editor	Joyce Rappaport
Managing Editor	Rachel M. Weinstein
Senior Editor	Alison Joseph
Senior Editor	Maud Kozodoy
Senior Editorial Assistant	Avery Robinson
Editorial and Operations Assistant	Henry Rosen
Manuscript Coordinator	Marsha Lustigman
Text Permissions Manager	Melissa Flamson
Art Permissions Managers	Roberta Newman
	Fred Wasserman
	Elisa Frohlich Gallagher
Researchers	Amanda Burstein
	Alyssa Cam
	Claudia Lahr
	Flora Margolis
	Shannon Santiago
	Elena Stojic
	Jonathan Weiss

Posen Foundation

President and Founder	Felix Posen
Managing Director	Daniel Posen

Yale University Press

Executive Editor	Sarah Miller
Commissioning Editor	Jonathan Brent
Managing Editor	Ann-Marie Imbornoni
Editorial Assistant	Ashley E. Lago
Production Controller	Maureen Noonan
Project Management, Newgen North America	Charlie Clark

Acknowledgments

We would like to thank our student research assistants at the University of Michigan and elsewhere: Alyssa Cam, Claudia Lahr, Flora Margolis, Shannon Santiago, Elena Stojic, and Jonathan Weiss. They rendered excellent service over several years. Of the many translators whose names appear beneath the selections, we thank in particular Alexandra Hoffman and Vera Szabó for the multiple works to which they contributed. Our colleague Julian Levinson read a draft of our introduction. Over the years we have learned much from our Michigan colleagues Professors Mikhail Krutikov, Anita Norich, and Shachar Pinsker, who contributed their knowledge of Hebrew, Russian, and Yiddish literatures. We also had constructive exchanges with the editors of the ninth volume, Professors Samuel Kassow and David Roskies. To all we wish to express our deep appreciation.

Todd M. Endelman and Zvi Gitelman, Ann Arbor, Michigan

Introduction to The Posen Library of Jewish Culture and Civilization

Deborah Dash Moore and James E. Young

In 2003 Felix Posen had an audacious idea and the wherewithal to explore it. Born in Berlin, he subsequently abandoned the religious strictures of his youth in the face of the evil of the Holocaust. Then, in his fifties, he decided to learn about the antisemitism that had threatened his life. He began to read about it. "I learned; I listened; I attended lectures," he recalled. "I had the good fortune of befriending one of the world's greatest experts, Yehuda Bauer, who also happened to be the head of something I had never heard of—an Israeli movement in secular Judaism." Those years of reading and learning and that particular encounter ultimately prompted Felix Posen to convene a conference of prominent Jewish scholars and intellectuals. Having prospered in business, he possessed the wherewithal to establish the Posen Foundation to further Jewish education. Thus Felix Posen began a new life in philanthropy. He was able to underwrite not only a conference but also an ambitious project that imagined anchoring Jewish unity in the very multiplicity of the Jewish past. "Each generation must struggle to make sense of its legacy," he reflected. Out of that initial conference emerged a vision of an anthology of Jewish culture and civilization, one that would make more apparent Judaism's immense diversity over the centuries, extending far beyond the parameters of religious orthodoxy. In short, he came to share an understanding of Judaism articulated by the influential biblical scholar Israel Friedländer. In 1907 Friedländer, a recent immigrant to New York City, had observed that American Jews possessed the opportunity to return to Judaism's "original function as a culture, as the expression of the Jewish spirit and of the whole life of the Jews."

The idea of an anthology implicitly drew upon a long and rich Jewish history dating back to the Bible itself, the most influential of Jewish anthologies, including many classic Jewish texts, such as Mishnah and Talmud, as well as the prayer book. Anthologizing can be seen as a quintessential Jewish practice because of the ways it extends Jewish conversations backward and forward in time. Backward, because anthologizers must read and judge Jewish texts from previous eras, selecting some, rejecting others. And forward, because anthologizers seek to create new understandings that will shape the Jewish future, contributing to an ongoing dialogue. David Stern, editor of

The Anthology in Jewish Literature, argues that the anthology is a ubiquitous presence in Jewish literature—arguably its oldest literary genre. Jewish literature reflects what Stern calls an "anthological habit," that is, a tendency to gather together "discrete and sometimes conflicting stories or traditions." David Roskies dubs this Jewish predilection "the anthological imagination." *The Posen Library of Jewish Culture and Civilization* partakes of both "habit" and "imagination," with the latter often transforming the former. Unlike some past Jewish anthologies, The Posen Library makes no effort to weave together its varied components into a teleological whole.

During the Jewish Middle Ages, anthologies became primary mediums for recording stories, poems, and interpretations of classical texts. They also preserved and transmitted textual traditions across generations. For example, every year at Passover when Jews sat down to conduct a seder, they read from the Haggadah. This Jewish creation is a wonderful anthology that has been continually reinvented—illustrated, translated, modified—to reach new generations.

Yet even as *The Posen Library of Jewish Culture and Civilization* shares in a long and venerable anthological tradition, it also participates in its own moment in time. It is a product of the twenty-first century and the flowering of secular academic Jewish studies in Israel, the United States, and around the world. Its approach to Jewish culture and civilization reflects a new appreciation of Jewish diversity that, for example, embraces women alongside men. Unlike most previous Jewish anthologies, The Posen Library recognizes that both women and men created Jewish culture, although the contributions of women have largely been unacknowledged. The Posen Library's distinguished editorial board reflects contemporary Jewish diversity and includes many of this generation's leading scholars and thinkers in Jewish culture: Michel Abitbol, Robert Alter, Yehuda Bauer, Menachem Brinker (z"l), Rachel Elior, Moshe Halbertal, Paula E. Hyman (z"l), Sara Japhet, Yosef Kaplan, Nadav Na'aman, Fania Oz-Salzberger, Antony Polonsky, Jonathan D. Sarna, Anita Shapira, A. B. Yehoshua, and Steven J. Zipperstein.

Together with Felix Posen, this eminent editorial board invited James E. Young to serve as editor in chief of an ambitious anthology project dedicated to the collection of primary texts, documents, images, and artifacts constituting Jewish culture and civilization, from ancient times to the present.

In consultation with the editorial board, James Young prepared a working project outline and précis and appointed individual volume editors with special expertise in particular eras. The précis articulated three important criteria:

1. to gather into a single, usable collection all that the current generation of scholars agrees best represents Jewish culture and civilization in its historical and global entirety;
2. to establish an inclusive and pluralistic definition of Jewish culture and civilization in all of its rich diversity, an evolving amalgam of religious and secular experience;
3. to provide a working anthological legacy by which new generations will come to recover, know, and organize past, present, and future Jewish cultures and civilizations.

While this mandate appeared broad and compelling, the actual task of fulfilling it proved daunting. Gradually, the passing years revealed the immensity of *The Posen Library of Jewish Culture and Civilization* involving enormous challenges to find, select, translate, organize, conceptualize, and introduce artifacts and documents that constituted Jewish culture over the ages. The tasks involved produced changes in leadership. In 2016 James Young assumed the position of founding editor in chief, having launched The Posen Library, and Deborah Dash Moore accepted the responsibilities of editor in chief. Current editors of the ten volumes of *The Posen Library of Jewish Culture and Civilization* are Jeffrey H. Tigay and Adele Berlin (Volume 1); Seth Schwartz (founding editor), Carol Bakhos (Volume 2); Menahem Ben-Sasson (founding editor), Ora Limor and Israel Jacob Yuval (founding coeditors), Arnold E. Franklin (Volume 3); Ora Limor and Israel Jacob Yuval (founding coeditors), Yaacov Deutsch (past coeditor), Jonathan S. Ray (Volume 4); Yosef Kaplan (Volume 5); Elisheva Carlebach (Volume 6); Eli Lederhendler (founding editor), Israel Bartal and Kenneth B. Moss (Volume 7); Todd M. Endelman and Zvi Gitelman (Volume 8); Samuel D. Kassow and David G. Roskies (Volume 9); and Deborah Dash Moore and Nurith Gertz (Volume 10).

These volume editors invited specialists from across diverse genres and geographies in varied disciplines and eras to serve as members of their respective volumes' advisory boards. This collective of some 150 of the world's leading scholars of Jewish culture continues to cull examples of expressions of Jewish culture and civilization from around the world, from antiquity to the twenty-first century.

It is with great pleasure on behalf of all who are assembling *The Posen Library of Jewish Culture and Civilization* to present the third published volume of this massive anthology, *Crisis and Creativity between World Wars, 1918–1939*, coedited by Todd M. Endelman and Zvi Gitelman. Volume 8 joins Volume 10 and Volume 6 as the third of ten volumes comprising *The Posen Library of Jewish Culture and Civilization* to be published with Yale University Press.

The job of the anthologizer is far from easy. Not only does it involve sifting through many potential historical, philosophical, religious, legal, literary, exegetical, political, folkloristic, popular, and artistic documents, images, and artifacts that might be chosen and extracted. It also requires conceptualizing key themes that characterize each period under consideration. And that process introduces questions about the production of Jewish culture and civilization. Is Jewish culture global, or is it an aggregate of many local Jewish cultures, each of them formed and defined in the interaction between Jewish and surrounding non-Jewish cultures? Are there essentially Jewish qualities to Jewish culture or is Jewish culture itself a dialectic between "adaptation and resistance to surrounding non-Jewish cultures," as David Biale has suggested in his *Cultures of the Jews*? Or should Jewish culture be regarded as something that is produced mostly in relationship to itself, its own traditions and texts, as David Roskies argued in his review of Biale's volume of essays?

Each volume editor has proffered somewhat different answers to those questions. Some have stressed the experience of Judaism as a minority culture in constant contact and occasional conflict with majority civilizations. Others have emphasized the remarkable internal dynamic of Jewish creativity, responding to developments across time and space. Still others have noted the importance of geography and related political structures, dividing Jews from one another and fostering rather separate and even insular modes of cultural creativity. Historically, any number of distinctive and parallel Jewish civilizations have flourished, some sharing cultural practices and traditions, some with little in common beyond core religious laws and beliefs. Working answers to such fundamental questions as, What is

Jewish culture and civilization? are embedded in the multitude of entries selected by individual volume editors and their expert advisory boards. Each volume's extracts allow a reader to savor myriad juxtapositions of materials that often illuminate the familiar through the unfamiliar, or, conversely, introduce what is new and unexpected by placing it in conversation with what is well known. Insofar as any culture is itself a composite of multiple peoples, nations, languages, traditions, and beliefs, The Posen Library's volume editors have emphasized the heterogeneity of Jewish culture and civilization.

The Posen Library builds upon the efflorescence of university-based Jewish scholarship of the twentieth century, especially in Israel and the United States. It is heir to debates on the meanings of Jewish culture and Jewish civilization. In the United States, those debates often pictured culture as gendered female and civilization as masculine. Thus civilization evoked machines, work, politics, and technology often associated with cities. Culture suggested nonutilitarian activities, such as the arts, personal refinement, formal higher education, and religion. Nations produced civilizations; peoples nourished cultures. The fact that the title of The Posen Library references both culture and civilization indicates a critical openness to aspects of this binary formulation. It implicitly reflects a consciousness that Jews often had to struggle to gain recognition from others that they possessed a civilization. And it envisions a measure of reciprocity. The Posen anthology project aims for inclusivity and pluralism—"culture" understood both in its anthropological and in its literary senses, referring to products of everyday life as well as to religious and elite artistic and philosophical work. The inclusion of "civilization" refers to an interest in political, economic, and social dimensions of Jewish life. The Posen Library champions a perspective that is less hierarchical and more egalitarian, one that embraces multiple points of view.

Heterogeneous and pluralist, The Posen Library nonetheless presents Jewish culture and civilization in the English language, the lingua franca of our age. This means that in addition to being an exercise in Jewish anthologizing, it is an exercise in translation. As does anthologizing, translating has a long and distinguished Jewish history as a means of conveying sacred and secular texts to generations unfamiliar with their original source languages. As Anita Norich has observed in *Writing in Tongues*, "The need for translation in Western culture, and among Jews, is commonly traced to the familiar Tower of Babel story, which is to say that it is traced to the human desire to understand and interpret and the hubris implied in that desire." Translation has kept Jewish traditions alive as Jews have acquired new languages in the various parts of the globe where they have lived. In the twelfth century, the great Jewish scholar Maimonides, in a letter to his translator, Samuel Ibn Tibbon, wrote: "Whoever wishes to translate and purports to render each word literally, and at the same time to adhere slavishly to the order of the word and sentences in the original, will meet with much difficulty. This is not the right method." Rather, "the translator should first try to grasp the sense of the subject thoroughly, and then state the theme with perfect clarity in the other language." Creating a Jewish anthology in English means wrestling with the implications of translating Jewish sources into the current world's universal language.

Time, space, and genre are the fundamental organizational units of The Posen Library. These units reflect debates and a measure of consensus that emerged from conferences among the editors.

As much as all members of the editorial board admired the intellectual and interpretive insights into Jewish culture and civilization occasioned by a purely thematic organization of these volumes, most also agreed that consistency across all of the volumes, readability, and proper historicization required subordinating thematic interpretations to broad categories of chronology and genre, while taking into account the significance of the diasporic dispersion of Jews around the globe. As a means of "telling" history, thematic chapter heads are clearly the preferred modus of historian-authors. But as a means of "showing" what exists in its historical time and place, in the immediate context of other works in a given genre (e.g., art, literature, theater, architecture), thematic categories remain inadequate on their own. Such genres as literature, visual and material culture, and intellectual culture provide an immediate context for comprehension and can be found in all of the volumes. The Posen Library aims not to unify or homogenize Jewish culture. Rather, the anthology reflects as closely as possible multiple, even competing manifestations of Jewish culture and civilization as they existed in their own temporal and geographic contexts. It recognizes, for example, that while poetry as a genre exists across all of the many centuries of Jewish civilization, significant differences separate medieval Hebrew poetry from Yiddish poetry.

The volume editors' responsibility here is to research all that has been regarded as representative of Jewish culture over time, even as they may nominate new expressions of Jewish culture. Perhaps a particular editor thinks Soutine or Pissarro made Jewish art, or Kafka wrote Jewish parables, or Heine wrote Jewish poetry, or Freud or the Marx brothers or Al Jolson or any of the hundreds of others added to Jewish culture. However, editors also have to consider what the Jewish cultural worlds of museums, libraries, and other institutional and scholarly arbiters of culture have decided over time in their exhibitions, archives, and anthologies. As the editors of Volume 10 observed, "Jews make culture and make it Jewish in a variety of ways: through language, references, reception, uses." Texts chosen can reflect "a broad understanding of culture, including high and low, elite and popular, folk and mass." Examples can be "chosen as representative, illuminating, unusual, influential, or excellent." Accordingly, volume editors looked closely at how previous anthologizers arrived at their lists of Jewish literature, art, and philosophy in their particular times and places. Volume editors engaged in the anthological task in part by consulting other anthologies. Here is evidence of the anthological imagination at work.

How should the issue of non-Jews' participation and even creation of Jewish culture be answered? This challenging question remained in the hands of the volume editors and their advisory boards. For some members of the advisory board, it was obvious, as Yehuda Bauer insisted that Jesus' Sermon on the Mount is "so similar to a Jewish text that it is absolutely clear to [him] that this was a Jew speaking to Jews" and would have to be included, even if the original words were subsequently Christianized in the context of their redaction as part of the New Testament and depleted of Jewish meaning. Others, of course, disagreed. Or, consider adaptations that have moved the other way. When Jews employ the products of non-Jewish creativity for Jewish purposes—for example, illuminated Hebrew manuscripts, synagogue architecture, and headstone reliefs—these cultural works take their place as part of Jewish civilization and can be found in The Posen Library.

Thus The Posen Library presents a model for defining "national culture" as distinct from "nationalist culture." In this approach, a national culture defines itself by its differences and reciprocal exchanges with other cultures, whereas "nationalist culture" portrays itself as sui generis and self-generated. National cultures grow in reciprocal exchanges with others; nationalist cultures partake in a myth of self-containment and self-creation. Unfortunately, we know too well what happens when nations and cultures attempt to purge themselves of all supposedly foreign elements. They become small and sometimes so depleted of inspiration and imagination that they collapse inwardly like hollow shells. By contrast, national cultures continually reinvent and reinvigorate themselves, extending their creativity across new modes of expression.

"Our aim," write the editors of Volume 8, "was not to create a 'canon,' but to convey an awareness of and appreciation for the variety, breadth, and depth of Jewish cultural creativity in the tempestuous interwar period." This approach seeks to connect readers with conflicting and contrasting views of the era. It invites those who peruse The Posen Library to enter a conversation, one that was abruptly cut short through the violence of World War II, but which now is being renewed, often through the power of translation. It also reclaims voices that had been lost or neglected, restoring and contextualizing them. Some entries in this anthology include texts produced by Jews but not always with explicit Jewish content. Such documents warrant inclusion if they have been inspired by or placed in conversation with Jewish texts or experiences, or received by the Jewish world as Jewish texts, or codified and treated as Jewish writings. Here the stories of Franz Kafka might be regarded as parables for Jewish experience, as might Sigmund Freud's meditations on dreams and monotheism.

"No single volume can address the entire sweep of a multifaceted culture and hope to render it in full, in all its layered complexity and dynamism," writes the editor of Volume 6 with a compelling blend of modesty and insight. However, a volume can "trace a trajectory." Both individually and collectively, each volume "tells the tale of a people who refused to sit on the sidelines while others did the work of culture, be it literary, visual, material, musical, or intellectual." Recognition of such energies has inspired the editors of The Posen Library.

All of the editors agreed that visual culture constitutes a major part of Jewish culture and civilization and must be included throughout these volumes, in all of its forms. From early synagogue architecture and iconography of ancient texts, to later illuminated manuscripts and Haggadahs, Jewish visual culture in its many forms appears in every volume. It ranges from folk art to costume design and eventually encompasses painting, sculpture, photography, film, installation and performance art, television, as well as museum and synagogue architecture. In some cases, images may be used to illustrate nonvisual texts; but in most cases, they will be either the actual work (e.g., a painting) itself or images of objects and artifacts being anthologized.

As difficult and complex as it may be to select, extract, and translate every textual entry from its original language into English, or as expensive as it may be to secure the rights to reprint "flat art" images of paintings, sculpture, and architecture, it can also be said that the book form of the volumes itself made the compilation of these literary and visual expressions of culture possible. Unfortunately for The Posen Library, a traditional book excludes motion and sound, and therefore audiovisual works—whether orchestral, theatrical, performative, or cinematic—cannot be heard or seen. Reducing a musical composition to its score, or a theatrical presentation to its written script, or any kind of film or television performance to still-photos radically transforms these pieces into something they simply are not. As a consequence, The Posen Library represents audiovisual media with what amount to play-lists of music and titles of film, theater, and television presentations.

What strategic purposes animate this effort to collect in a ten-volume anthology all that this generation deems to constitute Jewish culture and civilization? First, The Posen Library seeks to restore consciousness of the diversity and richness of Jewish culture and civilization across many centuries in many lands. Second, it aims to democratize Jewish knowledge, facilitating readers' encounters with varied texts produced by Jewish thinkers, writers, and artists in dozens of languages around the globe. Third, The Posen Library implicitly demonstrates that like Jewish national and diasporic culture, other national and diasporic cultures consist of multiple, often competing constituent subcultures. Just as Jews express themselves in, participate in, and engage with cultures around the world, and just as these cultures bear the imprint of Jewish culture and experience, so too do many of these other cultures nourish and shape Jewish culture and civilization. Jewish literature and poetry, religious thought and Talmudic commentaries, and even treatises on what constitutes Jewish culture are written in many of the world's languages—in English, Arabic, French, German, Russian, Spanish, Italian, and Persian—as well as in Hebrew, Yiddish, Ladino, Aramaic, and Judeo-Arabic. Jewish culture and civilization lives in and is shaped by these cultural and linguistic contexts. Finally, The Posen Library offers otherwise disaffected and disengaged Jews opportunities to restore their cultural identifications as Jews. It demonstrates that Jews produced Jewish culture in part through struggles with Jewish identity and tradition, and not only through an embrace of Judaism.

How to Read This Book

This volume includes examples of Jewish cultural and intellectual creativity in the interwar years (1918–1939) from writers and thinkers throughout Europe, the Middle East, Africa, and the Americas. The selections appeared originally in more than a dozen languages—Hebrew, Yiddish, Ladino, Russian, Polish, Hungarian, Romanian, Czech, Serbo-Croatian, German, Dutch, French, and Italian, as well as English—and they are published here in English translation. The volume is organized by genre—social, political, and cultural thought; memoir and reportage; scholarship; religious thought; visual culture; fiction and drama; and poetry. Within each genre, the selections appear chronologically and then alphabetically according to the author's last name. Some of the authors, like Franz Kafka and Isaac Babel, are well known; many more are familiar only to specialists, and a few are so little known that the details of their lives cannot be recovered. Examples of performance and aural works—music and motion pictures—are included in lists following the textual sections. Readers may wish to read the selections sequentially within each genre, as they are presented, or, alternatively, they may wish to move back and forth between the different genres, selecting texts from a particular year or group of years. The former offers perspectives on how Jewish cultural and intellectual life developed over two decades; the latter samples Jewish cultural activity at a particular point in time in the major Jewish communities of the world, allowing for comparative perspectives.

This collection focuses on presenting the original works to the English-language reader in the most straightforward manner. Notes and other scholarly apparatus have been kept to a minimum. Editorial deletions are indicated by bracketed ellipsis points. A brief biography of each author accompanies each selection. Because a number of writers are represented by more than one selection, this biographical information appears only the first time a writer is included. The index lists page numbers to multiple selections by a writer, thus enabling readers to find any biography and read all the work by any given author. In addition, each biography ends with a short list of other works by the author. If a work has not been published previously in English, the title of the work is given in its original language with its date of first publication. If a work is available in English translation, the title of the translated work is given, along with the date of its appearance in English. Where multiple translations are available, the translation included is either the most recent or the most widely praised. We are obligated to accept the translations, spelling, and style of previously published works in English. That results in some inconsistencies in spellings and styles. The works that we commissioned for translation follow the style guidelines of The Posen Library.

Introduction to Volume 8

Todd M. Endelman and Zvi Gitelman

The Consequences of World War I

The outbreak of World War I in August 1914 ushered in more than three decades of upheaval and violence in Europe, the Middle East, and North Africa. Jews were caught up in international, regional, and multilateral conflicts. Jewish soldiers on both sides gave their lives for their countries. Jewish civilians faced death from starvation, as did many others, but they were victimized by a specific kind of mob brutality. Hundreds of thousands living amid the swirl of warring armies in Eastern Europe were uprooted from their homes, losing their possessions and livelihoods. In the aftermath of the war, another multilateral conflict went on for three or four years in the former Pale of Settlement: "Reds" fought "Whites"; Poles and Ukrainian nationalists fought Bolsheviks; anarchists fought everyone; robber bands pillaged indiscriminately. Pogromists wreaked havoc, killing, looting, and raping.

Although this volume focuses on Jewish culture from 1918–1919 to 1939, one must understand the experience of the war years (1914–1918) in order to comprehend how Jews made sense of their lives in the two decades that followed. Life in the trenches, in besieged cities and towns, and in flight from marauding armies and pillaging bands cast a very long shadow, one that darkened Jewish life and shaped ways of thinking about the Jewish future long after the shooting had ended.

Large numbers of Jews were swept up in the violence, certainly far more than in any previous pan-European conflagration, such as the revolutionary and Napoleonic wars a century earlier. More than one million Jews served in the Allied forces and about 450,000 in the armies of the Central Powers.[1] In Western and Central Europe, middle-class sons and fathers shared the patriotic frenzy of the hour. Unaware of the horrors ahead and anticipating a short war, they eagerly took up arms and marched off to fight, welcoming the opportunity to demonstrate their patriotism, courage, heroism, masculinity, and, above all, profound identification with their respective countries. French Jews enthusiastically embraced the spirit of the *union sacrée*, the sacred union of patriotism, harmony, and sacrifice among all classes, ranks, and religions. Rabbis preached jingoistic sermons, invoking divine backing for the military ventures of their various countries. In Vienna, Sigmund Freud yielded to the patriotic frenzy, declaring that for the first time in thirty years he felt himself to be Austrian: "All my libido is given to Austria-Hungary."[2] But enthusiasm for the war did not last long. As the conflict dragged on, the horrors of trench warfare sank in, the death toll on all sides mounted, and disillusion and despair set in.

In the tsarist empire, where Jews were officially disadvantaged, the deep sense of identification with the state that was the norm in Western Jewish communities gripped only a tiny portion of the Jewish population. Of the approximately half a million Jews who served in the Russian army (5 percent of Russia's armed forces),[3] most were reluctant conscripts; many tried to evade service. "Sons called to the army shortened their years as much as possible," wrote Chaim Hazaz in his Hebrew short story "Revolutionary Chapters" (1924), "violating their faces and shaving their whiskers very, very close every day, to remain boys, absolute youngsters, while the father added on years and grew older and older."[4] East European immigrants in the West—in Paris, London, and New York—were equally unenthusiastic about serving, especially since France and Great Britain were allied with the hated tsarist regime.

The main battles on the Eastern Front were fought in areas of concentrated Jewish settlement. In Galicia and other eastern Habsburg territories and in the westernmost provinces of the Russian Empire (the Pale of Settlement), armies advanced and retreated repeatedly, leaving death and devastation in their wake. Jews were victimized, both because they were in the way and because they were Jews. The impact was profound; the violence echoed in Hebrew and Yiddish poetry and fiction throughout the 1920s. As the Odessa-born writer Isaac Babel wrote in his story "Gedali," "The Pole [shot me] because he is the counterrevolution. And you shoot because you are the Revolution. But Revolution is happiness. And happiness does not like orphans in its house. [. . .] Who is going to tell Gedali which is the Revolution and which is the counterrevolution?"

Persistent fighting in areas of dense Jewish settlement uprooted tens of thousands of Jews and sent them streaming toward Vienna, Prague, Warsaw, and far beyond. Their arrival strained already-taxed communal relief agencies. The war also provided fertile ground for the expression of old hatreds, especially in Central and Eastern Europe. Anti-Jewish fears and suspicions surfaced, replacing Jews' feelings of solidarity, inclusion, and purpose that had marked the start of the war. In Germany, Jews were accused of being shirkers, profiteers, and defeatists. In Russia, the outbreak of revolution in February–March 1917, and the subsequent collapse of authority, inaugurated a period of unrest, disorder, and mayhem that lasted until the end of 1921 in some areas. After the Bolsheviks seized power from the Provisional Government in October–November 1917, their opponents exploited anti-Jewish sentiment, using the alleged link between Bolshevism and Judaism to target both the minority of Jews who ardently supported the new regime and the majority whose most pressing concern was staying alive. Military units and marauding bands attacked Jewish market towns. Pogroms in Ukraine, where civil war raged from 1918 to 1921, caused far more Jewish deaths than all the pogroms of the late-imperial period. Estimates of the number of Jewish casualties in the Civil War vary: at a minimum, fifty thousand died.[5] Although Red Army units were not blameless, more often than not they defended rather than victimized Jews. The willingness of the new regime to defend Jews from pogromists, despite their hostility to the Jewish religion and Jewish nationalism, was crucial in winning the tacit support of those who were not ideologically committed to building a socialist system.

Even more than the war years, the violence and pogroms of the Civil War period profoundly shocked Jewish writers and poets, who foregrounded brutality and cruelty in their work. Isaac Babel's Russian short story "My First Goose," which drew on his experience as a correspondent with Semen Budenny's (Bolshevik) First Cavalry in the Polish–Soviet War, is emblematic. In the story, the bookish, bespectacled Jewish protagonist wins the grudging acceptance of his battle-hardened Cossack comrades only when he crushes to death beneath his boot a goose that he wants for his dinner. Violence is even more pervasive in the short stories of the peripatetic Yiddish writer Lamed Shapiro. His story "White Challah" (1919) begins with the sharp edge of a broken bone piercing the skin of an abused stray dog and ends in a frenzy of cannibalism that evokes the sacrificial cult in the Temple. Decades before the Holocaust, horrific, unimaginable violence had become a staple of East European Jewish literature.

The Interwar Period

The new states that emerged in Europe and the Middle East from the collapsed German, Austro-Hungarian, Russian, and Ottoman empires were insecure, fearing their neighbors and their demands to change the borders created by the treaties ending World War I. They were suspicious of ethnic and religious minorities in their midst, including the Jews. With some exceptions, these states embittered Jews' lives in large and small ways. The collapse of the world economy in 1931, triggered by the earlier crash of the stock market in the United States, posed its own threats. One consequence was the continuing immiseration of the Polish Jewish community, the largest in Europe.

The suffering and insecurity of the Jews of Europe (and, to a lesser extent, the Middle East and North Africa) echoed in more secure parts of the Jewish diaspora, especially in the United States. North American Jewry, while not spared discrimination and stigmatization at home, rallied to provide material relief to the stricken communities of East Central Europe and slowly emerged as the richest and most influential Jewish community in the world. But with the passage of restrictive immigration laws in the early 1920s, the United States no longer served as a refuge for European Jews fleeing poverty and persecution. Indeed, as the Jews of Germany, Austria, and Czechoslovakia learned after the rise of Nazism, there were no longer any countries in the world that welcomed Jewish refugees.

Rapid, dramatic change characterized the short twenty-year interval between the two world wars (1918–1939). In Europe, economic crises after 1929, strident nationalist movements and militant radical parties, political polarization and the erosion of liberalism, and the slide from democratic to authoritarian norms undermined Jewish hopes for stability and security, especially in the new states that emerged in Eastern and Central Europe. In West European societies and in North America, the challenges were less dire but daunting nonetheless. However, despite the economic downturn of the 1930s, Western Jews (both native born and immigrants) continued to move into the middle class. In the United States, the Jewish community emerged as a significant influence in American and world Jewish politics. In Palestine, then under British control, the Jewish population grew rapidly, becoming more ideological and secular. If the fewer than 10 percent of European Jews who lived in Western democracies in the 1930s felt a sense of unease, then in Poland, Romania, Hungary, and Germany there was a palpable feeling of impending trouble, if not catastrophe. Aaron Zeitlin, a Polish Jew who published in Yiddish and Hebrew, sounded this alarm already in 1932, and by the end of the decade, a wide variety of writers—religious, secular, Zionist—did so as well.

Only in the Soviet Union, where "socialism was being built," did the government generate optimism and hope. In the late 1920s and the 1930s, large numbers of young people enthusiastically migrated to the Urals, Siberia, and other undeveloped areas to build cities and factories, break virgin soil, and try to propel the Soviet Union forward at breakneck speed, with tempos dictated by official "five-year plans." These efforts, which involved an explicit break with the past, were applauded in Soviet music, art, and literature, including in Yiddish works.

Before World War I, the Russian Empire had the largest concentration of Jews in the world, about 5.2 million. There were about 2.2 million Jews in the Austro-Hungarian (Habsburg) Empire. In 1918, the Jews in these empires became citizens of new or reconstituted states—the Baltic states, Czechoslovakia, Poland, Romania, Yugoslavia, Hungary, and what became the Soviet Union. Traditional trade patterns were disrupted; new political loyalties and, often, languages, had to be learned; and new ethnic policies confronted.

In the multilateral wars that occurred during and immediately after World War I, Jews were forced to choose between rival nations fighting for territory and sovereignty: Russians and Poles; Lithuanians, Russians, and Poles; Hungarians and Romanians; Germans and Czechs. Everywhere Jewish loyalty was suspect. The prominence of Jews in the early Bolshevik regime in Soviet Russia and their dominance in the short-lived communist regime in Hungary (1919) raised the specter of a communist–Jewish conspiracy to take over the world, despite the fact that nominally Jewish communists were disconnected from Jewish culture, let alone Judaism. Known as the *Żydokomuna* idea, the "Jewish-communist conspiracy" became an important element in domestic and foreign politics in nearly all countries of the region and was widely believed elsewhere.

The insecurity of the states created by the postwar peace treaties resulted in part from their neighbors' refusal to acknowledge their legitimacy. This was the case with newly created Czechoslovakia and Yugoslavia. Many borders were disputed: Romania–Hungary, Poland–Lithuania, Poland–Soviet Union, Germany–Czechoslovakia, and Bulgaria–Yugoslavia. The threat of subversion made majority nations suspicious of national and religious minorities, including the Jews, living within their borders. All states in the region, with the exception of Czechoslovakia, failed to sustain the democratic systems and nationality rights to which they had been pledged. They became "ethnic states," whose purpose was to serve the interests of one dominant nation, rather than "civic states," whose citizens were integrated around political ideas rather than ethnicity or religion. The Soviet

Union was exceptional in this regard, as it stood for "proletarian internationalism," but it was no democracy, and as its critics on the left pointed out, it became less of a "workers' state" and more a bureaucratic dictatorship. By the mid-1930s, significant fascist movements emerged in all of Europe, spurred on by Germany and Italy, which shared an interest with Hungary in revising the Versailles treaties. Even in the United States, there were vociferous pro-Nazi, antisemitic groups, as there were in Latin America. In the Middle East, some Arab leaders aligned themselves with Nazi Germany.

Worldwide economic depression in the 1930s fed a desire for radical solutions. Communist atheism and "internationalism," foundational values of the Soviet state, were abhorrent to the largely peasant, religious, and nationalistic populations of Eastern Europe. They were even more alienated by the Soviet collectivization of agriculture and forced rapid industrialization that were introduced in 1928. Fascism, invoking mythologized glorious national pasts and even more glorious futures, and committed to antisemitism and treaty revision, appealed especially to the unemployed, déclassé, and desperate. Conservative regimes felt as threatened by right radicalism as democratic ones, and both adjusted their foreign and domestic policies to head off right-wing revolutions.

Political unrest and violence roiled Germany, Austria, and Hungary, which had been allies during World War I, in the immediate postwar period. In 1922, Hungary passed a *numerus clausus* law restricting the number of Jews in higher education. A communist uprising was put down quickly in Germany, but the communist regime in Hungary, in which persons of Jewish origin were prominent, lasted more than four months and traumatized many Hungarians, instilling a deep fear of communism. In the 1930s, successive anti-Jewish laws were passed, but most Hungarian Jews, like their German coreligionists, remained highly patriotic.

For nonreligious and non-Zionist Jews in the late 1930s, the Soviet Union seemed to offer some relief from political instability, economic crisis, and social discrimination. True, it vigorously suppressed Judaism, Zionism, and Hebrew culture, but its Jews enjoyed unparalleled social and political mobility. They suffered no official restrictions, unlike in Poland, Hungary, and Romania, and were visible among the Soviet elite. In contrast, Polish Jewry, numbering some 3,350,000, was increasingly impoverished and discriminated against. It was internally divided into quarreling factions and unable to unite against antisemitism. The anti-Zionist, ultra-Orthodox political party Agudas Yisroel, for example, supported even antisemitic governments in return for their certifying that its religious schools fulfilled the demands of the compulsory-education law. Emigration, once a prominent solution to desperate situations, was nearly impossible, as in 1924 the United States had closed its doors to East European immigration, and the British imposed increasingly severe restrictions on immigration to Palestine.

Even without hindsight, the end of the interwar period loomed ominously for all of Europe, and especially for its Jews. German irredentism combined with Nazi racism and dreams of a thousand-year Reich, the economic crisis was prolonged, and neither stable democracies nor ethno-religious reconciliation was achieved.

However, it would be incorrect to characterize Jewish life in the interwar years in lachrymose terms alone. Although hardship and insecurity were the norm in much of East Central Europe, elsewhere in the Jewish world—Western Europe, the United States, the Soviet Union, and the Land of Israel (Mandatory Palestine)[6]—remarkable material and cultural changes were under way. In the liberal states of the West, especially in the United States, the children of pre–World War I immigrants from Eastern Europe—and in some cases the immigrants themselves—were entering the middle class, shaking off the poverty they had brought with them from the Old Country. In the newly created Soviet Union, Jews flocked to cities where their residence had previously been restricted. Many climbed the career ladders of the new society, finding employment as scientists, engineers, industrial managers and technicians, writers, artists, military officers, and government and Communist Party officials. In the Land of Israel, Jews created the social and political infrastructure for the sovereign state that arose in 1948, despite the resistance of the British Mandatory power, which worked to restrict immigration and dampen Jewish nationalism. Equally important, the Jews of Mandatory Palestine created a vibrant Hebrew-language culture that, whatever its linguistic debts to classical Jewish texts, was modern in content and form and that performed, in time, a critical integrative function for Jews whose mother tongue was Arabic, German, Hungarian, Polish, Russian, Yiddish, or some other language.

Indeed, the interwar years saw an explosion of Jewish creativity everywhere, not just in the Yishuv (the Jewish community in the Land of Israel). Regardless of the language in which they worked, groups of Jews embraced modernist trends in literature and art, produced middlebrow literature for popular consumption, and cultivated traditional forms of religious scholarship. In large numbers and with gusto they engaged in social and political commentary, historical research, and literary criticism. They painted, sculpted, and photographed, wrote poetry and philosophy, made movies, danced, and composed music. It would be difficult to identify another twenty-year period in any era of Jewish history in which Jewish cultural life was so effervescent. Undoubtedly, the many crises and challenges that confronted them during these years stimulated and stoked this outburst of creativity, in large part because the political, social, and economic issues of the day were so urgent. Jews were both consumers of and contributors to the rich general intellectual ferment of these years.

Soviet Exceptionalism

The situation of the Jews in the Soviet Union was different from that of Jews anywhere else. In line with their ideological commitment to create an atheist society with no racial, religious, or ethnic discrimination—all regarded as artificial constructs of the bourgeoisie designed to keep the proletariat divided—the Soviets repressed the practice of Judaism, along with other religions. They closed synagogues and religious schools, often transforming them into workers' clubs, gymnasia, theaters, and concert halls. The Soviet constitution guaranteed "freedom of religion" but forbade teaching religion to anyone under the age of eighteen. While many of the older generations clung to Jewish traditions, communist zealots embraced Soviet atheism enthusiastically. This did not mean rejecting Jewish culture, since a vibrant secular Yiddish—and, to a lesser extent, Hebrew—culture had developed, particularly in the nineteenth and twentieth centuries. Because the regime permitted the cultivation of Yiddish literature, at least until the late 1930s, and viewed Yiddish as the language of the Jewish proletariat, many of its ardent Jewish supporters attacked Jewish religious traditions using the Yiddish language. Itzik Feffer, a loyal communist who was to be shot as a traitor in August 1952, wrote in 1929:

> Who cares that I was circumcised
> and they made—as Jews do—a bris.
> The field winds scorched
> my drowsy pale feet. [. . .]
>
> After all, I'm no market trader
> Neither have I laid tefillin.

Other writers celebrated the demise of the shtetl and the acculturation of Jews to Soviet ways.

Demographic and Economic Dynamics in the Interwar Years

In the interwar period, about 1.7 million Jews lived in Western Europe, 70 percent of them in France, Germany, and Great Britain. They concentrated in the larger cities—about 90 percent of Austrian Jews lived in Vienna and nearly 70 percent of British Jews in London. There was considerable immigration from Poland to Belgium and France; in 1933, about 20 percent of German Jewry was foreign born. But West European Jewry's numbers were declining because of falling birth rates, rising intermarriage rates, and high conversion rates. In ten European countries in the early 1930s, Jewish birth rates were everywhere lower than the rates among the general population. In the early 1930s, one-third of Germany's half million Jews were married to non-Jews. Intermarriage rates in Hungary were the same and were even higher in western Czechoslovakia (Bohemia).

Italian Jews were highly acculturated, having lived in Italy for a millennium. A Jew became prime minister in 1910, twenty-six years before Léon Blum became head of the Popular Front government in France. Fifty Jews served as Italian generals in World War I. In 1930, Jews totaled 8 percent of all university professors. But religious observance declined sharply in the twentieth century. In 1938, fascist Italy enacted anti-Jewish laws. Some estimate that about six thousand Jews converted to Christianity at that point, just as about fourteen thousand Hungarian Jews converted at the same time to avoid anti-Jewish laws implemented by successive Hungarian governments.

After the rise of the Nazis in 1933, German Jews began to emigrate—130,000 by the end of 1937—and after the Kristallnacht pogrom (November 9–10, 1938) emigration accelerated until October 1941, when the Nazis prohibited it. Many more would have left if they had been able to gain entry visas to the United States, but the Johnson-Reed Act of 1924 initiated a period of immigrant restriction that lasted until well after World War II. Most other Western countries were also reluctant to accept Jewish refugees. Canadian immigration restrictions, for example, were much harsher than those of the United States. In the 1930s, Canada admitted only about 5,000 Jews. Mandatory Palestine, on the other hand, took in about 370,000 Jews, mostly from Europe, between 1921 and 1939, despite the obstacles raised by the British authorities in the late 1930s.

In East Central Europe there were wide variations in the socioeconomic profiles of the Jewish communities. Economic crisis and social and governmental discrimination limited the occupational and social mobility of Jews in Poland and Romania, and, after 1933 and 1938 in Germany and Austria, respectively. In contrast, in Hungary, before the *numerus clausus*, Jews accounted for half the lawyers and a third of all editors and journalists. Even in 1930, Jews owned more than 60 percent of the largest commercial firms in this largely rural country.

In Poland, Jews were about 27 percent of the urban population in 1931. Most were engaged in commerce, industry, and handicrafts. Of four hundred thousand Jewish salaried workers and wage earners, two-thirds were manual laborers. Only 7 percent of Jews who lived in urban areas were employers. Jewish proprietorship and employment in industry declined in the 1930s, but Jews still dominated the crafts: 80 percent of tailors were Jews, as were 40 percent of shoemakers and 75 percent of barbers. The number of Jewish students in higher educational institutions decreased from more than nine thousand in the early 1920s to four thousand in the late 1930s. Economic boycotts and antisemitism continued to take a toll right up to the German invasion of September 1939.

In the United States, Jews dominated the garment industry as both owners and workers, and they were prominent in printing, manufacturing leather goods and furniture, the scrap-metal business, baking, building, and the nascent mass entertainment field (movies, radio, and records). There was a substantial Jewish working class in the large cities, whereas Jews in smaller towns were most often storekeepers and small businessmen. Although many colleges and universities limited the number of Jews they admitted, some members of the younger generation were able to gain a college education at public institutions and then enter the civil service and the professions. The large-scale entry of Jews into higher education and the great migration from the cities to the suburbs did not occur until after World War II.

The most noteworthy demographic development in American Jewry was the emergence of New York as the largest urban concentration of Jews in history. By 1930, its Jewish population was approximately 1.5 million. This was greater than the Jewish population of Britain, France, Germany, Austria, Italy, or Hungary. The density of its Jewish population, New York's status as the country's cultural hub, at both the elite and the popular levels, and the avidity with which America's Jews embraced new and old forms of cultural expression led to an explosion of Jewish intellectual, literary, and artistic activity. The New York cityscape became an essential ingredient in the American Jewish imagination during this period and remained so for decades later.

In the Soviet Union, Jews experienced perhaps the most dramatic geographic and occupational mobility of any Jewish population. After the world war, the revolution, and the counterrevolution, the *shtetlekh* of the Pale lay in ruins. By 1939, almost 40 percent of the Jewish population that had once lived in the Pale had moved elsewhere. The Jewish populations of Moscow and Leningrad, which had been closed to most Jews before the revolution, grew rapidly. The number of Jews in

Moscow leaped from 86,000 in 1923 to 250,000 in 1939. On the eve of World War II, more than a million Jews lived in just five cities—Kiev, Odessa, and Kharkov in Ukraine, and Moscow and Leningrad in the Russian Republic.[7]

The New Economic Policy (NEP) period (1921–1928) allowed some Jews to return to private trade and artisanal crafts, while, under the slogan "with the face to the shtetl," Jews were encouraged to become farmers (they had been barred from owning land under the tsars). By 1930, there were about 134,000 Jews working the land. About 10 percent of all gainfully occupied Jews were farm laborers, the highest proportion ever recorded. However, with the launch of the ambitious industrialization drive (the "five-year plans"), the number of Jewish agriculturalists declined and the number of industrial workers increased exponentially. By 1935, there were more than a million Jewish wage and salary workers, a small majority of them manual laborers. Some Jews moved rapidly from worker to technician to engineer to manager or factory director.

The great cities where Jews lived were the centers of industry, administration, education, and science, areas from which they had been largely excluded before the revolution and to which they then had unfettered access. As a consequence, Jews were well represented in Soviet elites: they were 4.3 percent of the Communist Party (but 13 percent in Ukraine and an astounding 24 percent in Belorussia) and 19 percent of the NKVD (secret police)—at a time when they accounted for 1.8 percent of the population. In the 1920s, Jews were 2 percent of the military but 5 percent of those in senior positions. In 1927, they constituted 13 percent of all students in institutions of higher education. In fact, Soviet Jews had much easier access to higher education than their counterparts in the United States and, certainly, in any country in East Central Europe—and perhaps all of Europe. Toward the end of the period, their numbers in all these hierarchies declined as the educational levels of other nationalities rose.

Throughout this period, Jewish acculturation to Russian cultural norms and social habits proceeded apace. Migration to the Russian Republic and to larger cities, coupled with higher education, transformed the culture of Soviet Jews. In 1897, a total of 97 percent of the tsar's Jews told the census taker that their "mother tongue" was a Jewish one (Yiddish in most cases). In the 1926 Soviet census, the figure was 70 percent; and in the 1939 census, it was 40 percent (55 percent in Belorussia, 45 percent in Ukraine, but only 26 percent in the Russian Republic, where about one-third of the Jewish population lived—before the revolution only a very small number of Jews had been permitted to live there). Significantly, in 1939, only 19 to 21 percent of the Jews in Moscow and Leningrad declared a Jewish language as their "mother tongue." Urbanization and russification went hand in hand.

In the Soviet Union, marriage to non-Jews signaled not only acculturation but radical assimilation as well because the children of such marriages overwhelmingly registered their nationality as that of their non-Jewish parent. Soviet propaganda promoted interethnic marriage as a means toward the "drawing together" (*sblizhenie*) and fusion (*sliianie*) of Soviet peoples. The 1936 film *Seekers of Happiness* depicts the love and marriage of a Jewish woman and Russian man. Her parents object, but she prevails. As might be expected, by the late 1930s, Jews married non-Jews at a higher rate (about 40 percent) in the Russian Republic than in the old Pale areas of Belorussia and Ukraine, where the rates were about 11 to 18 percent. In the cities, divorce rates rose, fertility rates declined, and the number of people who did not marry also increased.

In the first Soviet census (1926), 2,672,499 people declared their nationality (ethnicity) as Jewish. In the less reliable 1939 census, about 3 million did so. Between September 1939 and June 1941, when the Germans invaded the Soviet Union, about 1.5 million to 2 million Jews from the territories annexed by the Soviet Union became Soviet citizens, so that in 1941, there were about 5 million Jews in the Soviet Union.

Poland had by far the largest Jewish population in the region, outside of the Soviet Union—by the end of the decade about 3.4 million Jews, 10 percent of the country's population but more than a quarter of the urban population. About 40 percent lived in cities with more than ten thousand Jews, mainly in the central and eastern parts of the country. Interwar Poland struggled economically. Government policy, especially after 1935, worked to limit economic opportunities for Jews, as most ethnic Poles believed that they, not Jews, should play the dominant role in the economy. Jews constituted fewer than 2 percent of Poland's civil servants but more than 20 percent of its professionals. Yet the "broad masses" lived in dire poverty. In 1934, more than a quarter of Polish Jews applied for Passover relief, and at the outbreak of World War II it was estimated that one-third of the Jewish population subsisted on welfare, none of it provided by the state and much of it coming from the Jewish diaspora.

The economic situation and the blatant antisemitism of the Polish state in the second half of the period helps explain the appeal of Zionism and left-wing, revolutionary politics. The Social-Democratic Jewish Labor Bund, the only Jewish party to have a Polish partner (the Polish Socialist Party), won a plurality of Jewish votes in the 1938 municipal elections in major cities. Thousands of would-be immigrants to the Land of Israel, encouraged by antisemitic cries of "Zydzy do Palestyny!" (Jews to Palestine!), were frustrated by British restrictions.

Ironically, oppression and restriction may have spurred Jews to turn their talents and energies inward. There were 40 Jewish daily newspapers, 30 of them in Yiddish, and 130 weeklies. Yiddish theater, Hebrew and Yiddish literature, and Jewish music, art, and dance flourished. Between 1930 and 1934, an average of 430 Yiddish or Hebrew books were published annually. There was a plethora of Jewish political parties, perhaps a source of political weakness, but also a manifestation of Jewish ideological commitment and creativity.

In Lithuania, which granted Jews cultural autonomy (1918–1925), Jewish cultural and political life was as vibrant as in Poland. This was true of Latvia as well. In Eastern Europe, there was a noticeable tendency toward secularization among the Jews. But in contrast to Western Europe, when Jews in the East distanced themselves from religion and even tradition, they tended not to embrace the dominant culture—although there were thoroughly polonized Jews—but to identify with explicitly Jewish secular culture and politics. The far-larger Jewish population of Romania (approximately 760,000) was more inclined to acculturation to Romanian language and culture, or, in Transylvania, to Hungarian. This second-largest Jewish population in East Central Europe was composed of culturally, socially, and economically quite different types of Jews. The Jewish communities of

Bessarabia and Bukovina were very poor; those of Wallachia, including the capital, Bucharest, were better off, and somewhat professionalized and acculturated. Throughout the interwar period, Romanian governments pursued antisemitic policies. In the 1930s, a powerful fascist movement, the Iron Guard, began to exert its power, forcing the conservative monarchy to confront and hound it. Jews in Transylvania were viewed as pro-Hungarian, and Jews everywhere were seen as radicals (although there were only three hundred Jews in the illegal Communist Party). Romanian Jewry was deeply divided along religious, linguistic, and class lines, weakening its ability to confront the severe challenges posed by the alliance between Romania and Germany, the Soviet annexation of previously Romanian Bessarabia and Bukovina (1940), and World War II.

Jewish Options

Whether they enjoyed the same rights as other citizens or whether their status was uncertain or imperiled, Jews everywhere worried about their collective fate and future. The "Jewish Question," as it was called in the nineteenth and early twentieth centuries, was as widely discussed as it had been in the decades before World War I. In Poland, Hungary, and Romania, the political status of Jews was still unresolved, despite the guarantees of the Minority Treaties signed at the Versailles Peace Conference. In Weimar Germany, widespread public debate raged about the incorporation of Jews into the cultural and social fabric of the German nation, as it had before the war. Although Jews there no longer faced state-mandated exclusion from high-status civil service positions, they still confronted the widespread stigmatization of Jewishness in social and cultural life. In more liberal societies in Western Europe and North America, where Jewish legal status was no longer debated, the morals and manners of Jews remained a target of adverse public and private comment, and their social integration and cultural accommodation a subject of ongoing discussion.

In the successor states of East Central Europe, the failure of democratic ideals and practices and flourishing exclusionary nationalism were largely responsible for the continued persistence of the "Jewish Question." In the West, where ultranationalist movements were weaker (though not absent), there was an additional factor. Integration and mobility carried unprecedented numbers of Jews into areas of life in which their presence previously had gone unremarked. Before World War I, the number of Jews in Western societies, while on the increase (largely because of migration from Eastern Europe), did not challenge the hegemony of traditional social elites. Most Jews were immigrants who lived and worked in socially self-contained communities. The number of native-born Jews who entered (or tried to enter) elite circles and institutions (such as city and country clubs, professional schools, and Ivy League and Oxbridge colleges) was relatively small. Establishment circles did not feel, on the whole, that Jews threatened the homogeneity and harmony of their world. This changed in the 1920s and 1930s. The state-educated children of the immigrants were not content to follow their parents into immigrant trades. Many aspired to be professionals, managers, civil servants, educators, and the like. They knocked at the doors of elite institutions and often gained admission. But whether admitted or not, Jews were somehow found in unprecedented numbers in places where their parents could not have entered.

The obstacles and threats Jews faced in the interwar years prompted them to reflect on their Jewishness and debate schemes and programs to resolve their predicament. Their responses to the persistence of the "Jewish Question" broke no new ideological ground, tending, rather, to repeat or elaborate on ideas first articulated in the nineteenth century: integrationism, radical assimilation, Zionism, Bundism, communism, socialism, immigration to a more welcoming country, and religiously traditional activism. What was different in the interwar period was the level of political sophistication and organization that Jews employed in pursuit of these goals and the number of Jews who were forced by circumstances to think long and hard about their collective fate. The unprecedented extent of political mobilization among Jews was in large part the outcome of dramatic political developments on the world stage. The Balfour Declaration and the establishment of the British Mandate for Palestine, on the one hand, and the Bolshevik Revolution and the establishment of the Soviet Union, on the other, meant that two responses to the "Jewish Question" were no longer speculative, utopian schemes. Second, the growing strength of fascism, ultranationalism, and authoritarianism—not just in the successor states—gave new urgency to questions about the Jewish future.

Most Jews in Western Europe and North America remained committed to a liberal, integrationist vision of Jewish life. They believed, to the extent that they thought consciously about these matters, that modernity had ushered in an age of religious toleration that allowed them to practice Judaism and, at the same time, identify with the nations among whom they lived and compete freely for society's glittering prizes. Thus, they pursued both acculturation and integration while simultaneously asserting a Jewish identity. Among themselves they also argued—sometimes publicly—about how much, in their quest for inclusion, they should tone down their distinctiveness, whether at home, in the synagogue, or in the street. They also wondered at times whether the price they paid for acceptance was excessive, that is, emotionally perilous and self-destructive.

A central theme in much of the fiction of the period was the desired extent of Jewish accommodation to the non-Jewish world, along with its successes and failures. While Orthodox leaders warned that Jews should remain a distinctive people and committed to Torah, Jewish writers in the United States, Great Britain, France, Germany, and Austria peopled their novels and short stories with ambitious, unobservant, acculturated Jews who erased or marginalized their distinctiveness. In Kurt Tucholsky's satirical sketches, the unreflective Herr Wendriner is the embodiment of the self-satisfied, successful German Jewish businessman who thinks he has shed his Jewishness. Often the protagonists in this literature experience an identity crisis and as a result begin to question the wisdom and efficacy of assimilatory behavior. In Betty Miller's novel *Farewell Leicester Square* (1935), the filmmaker Alec Berman angrily tells his Christian fiancée that she cannot begin to fathom how much he feels like a fish out of water in England, despite his worldly success and English manners: "You haven't—you can't possibly have—the slightest conception of the perpetual uneasiness in which a Jew lives—the terrifying lack of security: the sense that all one has yearned and striven for (the every-day happiness which any human being is entitled to) is entirely at the mercy of politicians, is challenged by every hostile word, look, gesture."

In extreme cases, Jews striving to advance socially voiced attitudes that reflected the antisemitism of the period. Some may have done so consciously, as a strategic move, to distance themselves from the stigmatized minority into which they had been born. Others did so unthinkingly, as a result of their immersion in social settings and cultural worlds in which anti-Jewish views were commonplace. Their acculturation and integration were so thorough that their thinking about Jews differed little from that of the non-Jews with whom they lived and worked. The philosopher Theodor Lessing described this phenomenon in his classic work *Jewish Self-Hatred* (1930). Although often crudely invoked in contemporary intra-Jewish debates about Israel, the term is still analytically useful to describe behavior and speech that were not uncommon in the interwar period. Most often, "self-hating" Jews were the subject of authorial scorn or satire. But some writers themselves embraced anti-Jewish discourse and filled their work with dark, grasping, hook-nosed Jewish characters. The Russian-born, French Jewish novelist Irène Némirovsky employed hoary anti-Jewish themes in her bestselling novel *David Golder* (1929). The Jewish characters in the novel are so morally abhorrent that later, after the Nazi seizure of power, she regretted the crude way in which she drew them. In any case, her efforts at radical assimilation, including eventually baptism, were unsuccessful. She was deported to Auschwitz in 1942.

A more common literary response in the West to the persistence of antisemitism was the time-hallowed recourse to apologetics, the effort to combat intolerance by explaining Judaism and Jews and thus defending Jews from anti-Jewish libels. In most cases, the urge to answer the enemies of the Jews did not lead Jewish writers to pen explicitly apologetic volumes, as in earlier periods (although defense organizations, such as the Anti-Defamation League in the United States and the Board of Deputies of British Jews, continued to sponsor them). Instead, they often introduced apologetic themes into works whose main subject was something else. For example, the novelist Jakob Wasserman's *My Life as German and Jew* (1921) is both a memoir and an overwrought apology, begging for understanding and stressing his "close inner relationship to [Germany's] soil, climate and people." Lay leaders in the West frequently responded to hostility by urging their communities to become more like their neighbors and to root out habits—ostentation, brashness, clannishness, and so on—that attracted adverse comment. The assumption underlying their pleas was that Jewish difference and misbehavior caused or, at a minimum, aggravated antisemitism. The American Zionist man-of-letters Maurice Samuel brilliantly satirized this view in his "Jews Be Nice" (1932), where he wrote that antisemitism, according to this way of thinking, was "the result of a lack of niceness in the Jew" and that Jews and Christians would live in harmony if only Jews would "temper their voices, their table-manners and their ties . . . be discreet and tidy in their enthusiasms, unobtrusive in their comings and goings, and above all reticent about their Jewishness." The thinking that Samuel targeted was not new, of course, the *maskilim* of Germany having launched this line of reasoning in the second half of the eighteenth century.

Samuel's ideological answer to the persistence of the "Jewish Question"—Zionism—attracted widespread support in Eastern Europe (outside the Soviet Union, where it was banned as "petit bourgeois nationalism") and in the West, especially as conditions in Central and East Central Europe deteriorated. To hundreds of thousands of Jews, contemporary events seemed to confirm Zionism's fundamental tenet that antisemitism was ineradicable. Ideologically committed Zionists, who were more common in Poland and the Baltic states than in the liberal states of the West, were prepared to abandon the lands of their birth and settle in the Land of Israel. While this was easier under the British than under the Turks, the obstacles were still daunting: obtaining an immigration certificate, whose numbers the British limited; learning modern Hebrew; equipping oneself to find employment; forsaking family and friends; and adjusting to a Middle Eastern climate and surroundings.

Much more common in the Zionist ranks, especially in liberal states, were Jews who saw their Jewishness as a national, ethnic, or racial bond (rather than as a religious tie) but who did not feel that antisemitism threatened their own well-being. For them, Zionism was a solution to the plight of Jews elsewhere whose situation was worse than their own. Still, whether they ever thought seriously of settling in the Land of Israel, Zionism addressed their existential predicament. It provided them with a way of thinking about their Jewishness that corresponded to how they and their Christian neighbors really imagined the Jews—that is, as a tightly knit collectivity. For European Jews, whether in the West or the East, who disapproved of and condemned assimilatory behavior, who saw it as unworthy, soul-destroying, and futile, Zionism was a comfortable ideological home. It connected them with a nation-building project that aimed to create a new kind of Jew who was neither passive nor weak. It was a militant, unapologetic, pride-enhancing ideological association that, ironically, allowed its adherents to feel comfortable while remaining in the diaspora. As Albert Einstein explained in a German Jewish periodical in 1921, he became a Zionist because Jewish nationality was a fact and because Zionism strengthened "Jewish dignity and self-esteem," which were critical for existence in the diaspora.[8] The English novelist Louis Golding captured the way in which Zionism aimed to "normalize" Jewish existence in his travel memoir *Those Ancient Lands* (1928). On a train in Palestine, he meets an English Jewish woman who has settled there and hears for the first time "the word 'Jew' as if it were not a thing to qualify, to temporise over, but to proclaim with not less pride than an Anglo-Indian colonel proclaims the word 'Englishman.'"

In Poland and the Baltic states, where collective Jewish politics flourished (in contrast to the Soviet Union), Zionism's chief opponent, Bundism, melded the economic radicalism of the socialist critique of capitalism with a Jewish cultural nationalism centered on Yiddish, the language of the Jewish masses. It shared left-wing Zionism's allegiance to Marxism but rejected the notion that creating a sovereign state in the Middle East would solve the plight of the Jews. Dismissing Zionism as bourgeois-nationalist and utopian, the Bund envisioned the Jewish future in terms of national-cultural autonomy within a classless society in territories where Jews were living in geographically compact communities.

Although not a consciously "Jewish" ideological response to the "Jewish Question," from its inception, communism attracted disproportionate numbers of Jews, even in nonindustrialized North African and Middle Eastern countries where capitalism was weak and proletarians were scarce. While the proportion of Jews among communists in Europe was greater than their proportion in the overall population, the proportion of communists among Jews was tiny. For example, there were about 2,700 Jews in the (illegal) communist parties in Poland around 1930, out of perhaps 10,300 communists. Thus, Jews were slightly more than one-quarter of the communists, although Jews

xlii INTRODUCTION TO VOLUME 8

accounted for only 10 percent of Poland's population. At the same time, these 2,700 Jews were but a tiny fraction of Poland's 3,350,000 Jews. Nevertheless, communism's appeal to Jews is not difficult to understand: it envisioned a classless society free of the inequities of the capitalist system, including ethnic, religious, and racial discrimination. It promised a society that would transcend the hostilities and divisions that capitalism purposefully generated, including, above all, the tensions between Jews and Christians (or Jews and Muslims in Iraq, Egypt, and Algeria). Communism's universalism, militancy, discipline, and intellectualism were attractive to a minority of Jewish workers and intellectuals. For those who found a home in the Communist Party, Judaism (as a religion) was no longer meaningful, whereas Jewishness more broadly was a marginal dimension of their identity, ceasing, in theory, to orient their behavior and lend meaning to their lives. But their rejection of religion and ethnicity did not mean that all Jewish communists broke with Jewish circles. Many communist groups in Europe and the United States bore a Jewish character by virtue of their ethnic composition. Some operated in Yiddish, even in the United States and France. In cities where the Party worked to mobilize Jewish workers, it was forced to use Yiddish in order to communicate with the Jewish proletariat. Thus, it contributed to the vibrancy of Yiddish-language cultural life in the interwar years, even if it did not ideologically endorse the persistence of Jewish distinctiveness.

At the opposite end of the political spectrum were Orthodox Jews, whose response to the challenges of the twentieth century was revitalizing Jewish observance and learning. Their Orthodoxy, however, amounted to more than clinging to millennia-old ways of thinking and behaving. In Western Europe, Poland, and Lithuania–Latvia, there was an activist Orthodoxy that, however firm its faith in divine providence, utilized the tools of modern politics—electioneering, journalism, coalition building, and lobbying—to promote its agenda. The chief organizational expression of political Orthodoxy in Poland, the Baltic states, and Mandate Palestine was Agudas Yisroel (Agudat Yisrael, or the League of Israel), a political party founded in Kattowitz, Poland (Katowice, in Polish), in 1912. "The Agudeh" included Jews from both the Hasidic and Misnagdic (non-Hasidic) streams of Orthodoxy and ran candidates in parliamentary and communal elections. It also had a presence in Central Europe and the United States, where it functioned as a pressure group rather than as a political party.

The dynamism of Agudas Yisroel in the interwar years is a reminder that traditionalism still characterized the majority of Jews in East Central Europe in those years. To be sure, radical secular ideologies (Zionism, Bundism, communism), along with hedonism and materialism, had eroded the religious commitments of many Jews and were becoming stronger. There certainly was a sense in Poland and elsewhere that the traditionalism of the nineteenth century was in decline. Keenly aware of this, the leaders of interwar Orthodoxy responded forcefully, if not always successfully, to the forces eroding their world. They may have been fighting a losing battle, but they could take comfort from the fact that the majority of Jews in Eastern Europe still spoke Yiddish, kept the dietary laws, and attended Orthodox synagogues, even if less consistently than before. Not all of them, of course, were enrolled in the ranks of Agudas Yisroel. A minority supported the Mizrahi, a religious-Zionist party with its own publications, school network, and *hahsharot* (training farms for settlement in the Land of Israel).

The young experienced the uncertainty and instability of the interwar years most acutely. Among Polish Jewish youth, there was a widespread sense that the ways their parents' generation faced the challenges of the time were outdated and unproductive, as the submissions to the YIVO youth autobiographies project in the 1930s reveal.[9] Their disillusionment with old measures pushed them to embrace radical solutions—Bundism, communism, and Zionism, including its militant "revisionist" variant—in which they found escape from the deprivations of home life. Twenty-year-old Khane wrote in her autobiographical submission to YIVO in 1932—the details of her life until then are unbearably bleak—that her love for her abusive mother cooled when Khane began devoting herself to politics, and that the movement became the most sacred thing in her life. "It even made the hard physical labor that I did seem easy."

Indeed, even in liberal states, radicalism won unprecedented numbers of young Jewish followers. This was the heyday of Communist Party appeal to Jews in Great Britain, France, Germany, Austria, Poland, and the United States. What is striking about the attraction of Polish Jewish youth to radicalism in this period is the fluidity of their allegiances. It was not uncommon, especially in Eastern Europe, for a young person to switch from one movement to another, often more than once, before landing permanently in this or that camp. Often, it was not ideology but friendships or romantic relationships that propelled changes from one movement to another.

In hindsight, the most effective response to the worsening plight of Jews in East Central Europe was migration to the Americas. With the exception of the few who chose the Land of Israel, this was a pragmatic rather than an ideological decision (and after 1933 even those who settled in the Land of Israel were as likely seeking a refuge as they were a homeland and an end to *galut* [exile and political servitude]). In the decades before World War I, when immigration controls were weak and international borders porous, more Jews chose to improve their lives by "voting with their feet" than by overthrowing the tsar or returning to Zion. Between 1871 and 1914, approximately 2,400,000 Jews fled the Russian and Austro-Hungarian empires.[10] Most sailed to the United States, but substantial numbers settled in Germany, France, Great Britain, Canada, South Africa, and Argentina. The Yiddish-language fiction from South Africa and Latin America included in this volume testifies to the growth of East European communities there. In contrast, less than 2 percent of Jewish migrants in that period headed to Palestine, an indication of both the weakness of Zionism before the Balfour Declaration and the challenges of settlement in Ottoman Palestine.

In the interwar period, mass migration was no longer an escape route from poverty and persecution. Leaving the Soviet Union was forbidden, except in rare cases. In the United States, swelling xenophobia and antisemitism led Congress to restrict immigration from Eastern and Southern Europe. Other Western countries also made immigration more difficult. Immigration to Mandatory Palestine was limited by the British government's control of the number of Jews permitted to settle there, while the Zionist movement lacked the wherewithal to finance the mass transfer of besieged and destitute communities.

Finding a refuge became even more difficult after 1933, when the Nazis seized power in Germany, and after 1938 and 1939, when they invaded Austria and Czechoslovakia, respectively. The United

States, Great Britain, and other countries beyond Germany's reach were reluctant to shelter Jews in acute distress. Although some countries took in a small number of refugees, most were indifferent and even hostile to them, thus unwittingly condemning hundreds of thousands to eventual death in Nazi camps. The American Yiddish poet Jacob Glatstein's "Good Night, World" (1938) registers the depth of despair and disillusionment that overcame many Jews at the time, as do the appeals of Rabbi Chaim Ozer Grodzensky of Vilna and the observations of Rabbi Moshe Neriah, included in this volume. For Glatstein and others, the "flabby" democracies offered only "cold compresses of sympathy." Vladimir (Ze'ev) Jabotinsky, ideologue of "Revisionist" Zionism, warned of an impending catastrophe in Europe, whose beginnings he was able to see before he died in 1940.

The most striking response to the persistence of the "Jewish Question" was the embrace of Jewish tradition or Jewish national or ethnic identity by persons who hitherto had been indifferent or hostile to the claims of Jewishness. While often allied with Zionist activism, this response was more than a shift in political outlook. It entailed a broad reorientation of values and attitudes and often led to a reworking of the individual's self-understanding. In the United States, the preeminent example is the literary critic Ludwig Lewisohn, who turned his back on radical assimilationism and became a passionate defender of Jewish self-affirmation. His novel *The Island Within* (1928) imagines the Jewish awakening of a young New York physician, whose initial feelings about his background mirror Lewisohn's youthful views. In Central Europe, Franz Kafka expressed disillusionment with the tepid Jewishness in which he was raised in his now-famous letter to his father, which he wrote in 1919 but never sent. The Czech writer Jiří Langer, who came from a Westernized, unobservant home, left his native Prague to live at the Hasidic court of Belz from 1913 to 1918. Even after abandoning Hasidism, he remained an Orthodox Jew. He also became a religious Zionist, a Hebrew poet, and a Freudian Judaica scholar. Needless to say, few Jews responded to the problematics of Jewishness in such radical ways.

One Central European variation on the return to Jewishness was a cult of the *Ostjuden* (Eastern European Jews). From at least the late eighteenth century, upwardly mobile, acculturated German Jews had looked down on Yiddish-speaking East European Jews as primitive, coarse, and benighted. German Jews viewed the East European immigrants in their midst as a threat to their own integration into German society, just as the German–American–Jewish establishment did in the late nineteenth and early twentieth centuries. During World War I, some young German Jews began to look at the *Ostjuden* in a new, more positive light. Influenced by cultural antimodernism and neoromanticism, they stood the previous caricature of the *Ostjude* on its head and discovered depths of spirituality and authenticity in the lives of their East European cousins, who, they believed, were uncontaminated by the soulless rationality of Western capitalism. The religious philosopher Martin Buber's romantic, tendentious accounts of Hasidism, enormously popular among German Jewish youth who thought they were rebelling against the values of their parents, are a prime example of this trend, as are the drawings of Hermann Struck.

However tempting, it is wrong to dismiss this kind of neoromanticism as late-adolescent posturing. Whatever emotional needs it fulfilled, it was also a critique of the lackluster state of Jewish practice and learning in Western countries, especially outside the immigrant communities in their midst. By the interwar period, the majority of native-born, middle-class Jews in the United States and Western and Central Europe were religiously indifferent. They attended synagogue rarely, observed domestic rituals haphazardly (if at all), knew little about Judaism or Jewish history and culture, and failed to pass on to their children the meager devotion and knowledge they had inherited. While Kafka's letter to his father is the classic expression of this critique, others in his cohort shared it. In his autobiography, *Witches' Sabbath*, completed in 1939 but not published until 1960, Maurice Sachs recalled that in his "free-thinking and fanatically republican" Paris home no one ever mentioned religion and that, before he was sent to boarding school, "I had never even been informed that there were different beliefs to be found throughout the world." Many Jewish protagonists in the fiction of the period are secular Jews, however aware of their Jewish descent and milieu. Soviet Yiddish poets often expressed their satisfaction with the abandonment of tradition. Still, there were some, such as the father and son Hillel and Aaron Zeitlin living in Poland, who were very much part of the "modern" East European literary scene but were also deeply religious and even inclined toward mysticism.

Some writers responded to the cacophony of Jewish proposals for universal and national salvation by proclaiming the folly, impudence, or irrelevance of all collective efforts to reshape the world. The fiction of Israel Joshua Singer, for example, casts a jaundiced eye on Jewish politics and turns inward. He also rejects romanticized, sentimental depictions of Jewish life. His psychologically incisive novel *Yoshe Kalb* (1932), for example, depicts Polish Hasidic life in relentlessly hostile terms. In New York, the Introspectivist (*In zikh*) Yiddish poets issued a manifesto in 1919 rejecting didactic or socially and politically situated poetry. They celebrated interiority and individuality. In the words of their manifesto, the poet "must really listen to his inner voice, observe his internal panorama—kaleidoscopic, contradictory, unclear or confused as it may be." Their poetry foreswore national uplift, social betterment, and political mobilization, and was self-consciously modernist in form and content.

In the Middle East and North Africa, where the clash between tradition and modernity came later and was less disruptive than in Europe, there were, nonetheless, stirrings of discontent in Jewish communities exposed to Western commercial and cultural influence. Teachers in the French-language schools of the Paris-based Alliance Israélite Universelle (AIU) in Morocco and Tunisia described, in reports to the AIU's central office, rampant spiritual and material decay. In 1929, a correspondent in Sousse, Tunisia, wrote of young people deserting the synagogues on Saturday and invading the cafés—to smoke, gamble, and talk business. He urged the AIU to provide moral guidance by expanding its network of schools, where Jewish children "would receive both a general education . . . and the moral and religious education of which they are currently almost totally deprived." Five years earlier, a teacher in Tangier bemoaned the fact that Jewish youth continued to enter economically marginal, "uncertain" occupations that perpetuated poverty, becoming "peddlers, porters, messengers, money changers, iron-mongers, pack-saddle makers, cobblers, etc." Echoing Enlightenment and Zionist adulation of agricultural labor, he urged the AIU to provide them with agricultural training and thus encourage them to pursue "a healthy life in the open air of the country."

What Are the Jews?

Undergirding the debate about the fate and future of the Jews was the fundamental question of who the Jews were and what bound them together collectively (if, indeed, they were a distinctive group in any sense). Were they a nation like other nations? Were they a race? A biologically diverse group whose primary ties were spiritual and liturgical? A spiritually elevated, "chosen" people, charged (by history or God) with a transcendent purpose? Were they the advanced guard of revolutionary universalism, destined to be absorbed in a not-yet-realized utopian future? These questions preoccupied Jewish writers and activists in the interwar years. This debate had been raging for more than a century, and those who took part in it in the interwar years offered little that was novel. What was different, perhaps, was its urgency and how it worked its way into so many public and private conversations.

In the Soviet Union, the Communist Party and the Soviet state decided the issue of who and what is a Jew; Jews themselves had little input in the matter. In 1913 Vladimir Lenin and Joseph Stalin explicitly rejected the idea that Jews were a nation, but in 1918 and thereafter Jews were granted the status of a *natsional'nost'*, or ethnic group. They were not a nation, Stalin had argued, because they had no common territory, economy, or language. In the Soviet Union, where ethnicity and religion were completely divorced, what bound Jews together, went the official doctrine, was not religion, but the Yiddish language, Jewish ancestry, and ethnic consciousness. Once Yiddish and self-consciousness would disappear in the common cauldron of ethnic rapprochement and fusion the Jews would disappear, as would all other ethnic groups. Some Jewish communists argued that as long as Jews remained ethnically conscious their cultural needs had to be served. Others said that the natural and inevitable process of assimilation should be actively encouraged. Probably a majority of Jewishly conscious communists remained "neutral," taking the position that only "history" would show whether the Jews would maintain their distinctiveness.

For secular Yiddishists, like Chaim Zhitlowsky, the Jews were a people, and any Jew who lived in the midst of his or her people was part of that people, whether he or she believed in God or not. Writing in 1927, when the majority of Ashkenazim in Europe and the Americas still spoke Yiddish, he declared: "When a Jew satisfies his spiritual-cultural needs in Yiddish, reads a Yiddish newspaper, . . . goes to a Yiddish lecture, to a Yiddish theater, discusses a Jewish or a general problem in Yiddish, listens to the Yiddish radio hour, sends his child to a modern Yiddish secular school, he is beyond doubt a Jew who belongs to the Jewish people."

Herzlian, left-wing, and Revisionist Zionists agreed with Zhitlowsky that the rites and doctrines of Judaism were not the essence of Jewishness. They, too, envisioned Jews in collective terms while assigning Hebrew, rather than Yiddish, cultural centrality. But those Zionists who settled or intended to settle in the Land of Israel imagined Jews as a collective whose ties transcended language and culture. Drawing on the conceptual world of romantic European nationalism, they emphasized the irreducible (and ultimately reason-defying) character of what made Jews, Jews. It was what remained after everything else was stripped away. Moreover, for them the national character of the Jews was rooted in their historical attachment to the Land of Israel and, in particular, its soil and landscapes, even if most Jews had not lived there for centuries. The future prime minister of Israel, David Ben-Gurion, writing in 1921, recalled that he did not sleep on his "first night in the Land, the dwelling-place of childhood and dreams celebrating its victory" (in 1906), that its smells, sounds, and sights made him drunk, and that he was "entirely swept away by happiness."

The most lyrical celebrants of the transcendent, life-giving, restorative character of the Land of Israel were the Hebrew poets who wrote there. They repeatedly invoked its flora and fauna, terrain, and climate, so radically different from those with which they were familiar in Eastern Europe, where they had been born. In "Toil" (1927), Abraham Shlonsky invests the Land with sacred qualities associated with the paraphernalia of Jewish prayer:

> My land is wrapped in light as in a prayer shawl.
> The houses stand forth like frontlets [*tefilin*];
>   and the roads paved by hand, stream down like phylactery straps.

Esther Raab, in "Upon Your Nakedness a White Day Celebrates" (1923), envisions the homeland as a naked woman's body on a blindingly hot summer day, "stretched and trembling," with a hill rising "like a round breast." For Saul Tschernikovsky, in "To the Sun" (1919), the Land is also feminine and, in this case, assumes a specifically nutritive character:

> The damp field suckled me: the smell, so near,
> Of crumbled clods, rose to my head.

This kind of sensibility was foreign to those Jews—both liberals and traditionalists—for whom the Jewish religion was the bedrock of Jewishness. To be sure, for traditionalists the Land of Israel was holy, but its sacredness derived from the redemptive acts that God had performed there in biblical times and would perform there again in the messianic age. The chief rabbi of Palestine, Abraham Isaac Kook, saw even antireligious Zionists as facilitating the coming of a messianic age. The uniqueness of the Land was not conceived in the quasi-pagan way in which secular Hebrew poets wrote about it. For liberal, and especially Reform, Jews in the West, however much they admired the pioneering efforts of East European Jews in Mandatory Palestine, Jews were not a nation—and thus not in need of a sovereign state in Palestine or anywhere else. While acknowledging that the Jews might have been a nation at one time (before the Roman conquest in 70 BCE or, according to some, before emancipation), they asserted that they were now citizens of the states in which they lived. Many German Jews imagined, until the Nazis told them otherwise, that they were "German citizens of the Mosaic faith." For them, Jewish nationalism, either in its Zionist or in its Bundist formulation, was a threat, for it reinforced the claim of the enemies of the Jews that they were fundamentally different from those among whom they lived in the diaspora and hence unassimilable and potentially disloyal.

In the interwar years, some liberal Jews began to soften the strictly religious interpretation of Jewishness that had been the hallmark of integrationist and Reform Jews in the nineteenth century. In Weimar Germany, leaders of the liberal defense agency the Centralverein deutscher Staatsbürger jüdischen Glaubens had been invoking terms of belonging that departed from a strictly religious definition of Jewishness since the end of the nineteenth century. They spoke of the Jews as a "community of fate" or "descent," a "tribe" bound together by "tribal consciousness" or an "ethnic soul."[11] In the United States, one unambiguous sign of this shift was the statement of principles adopted by the Central Conference of American (Reform) Rabbis meeting in Columbus, Ohio, in 1937. The Columbus Platform reiterated long-standing Reform views about the universality of Judaism, the continuous unfolding of revelation, and the mission of the Jewish people, but it also recognized a group loyalty that transcended religion and, in particular, a bond of unity with Jews who were estranged from Jewish practice and belief. It also acknowledged the importance of the Land of Israel not only as a refuge for the oppressed but also as "a center of Jewish culture and spiritual life." Indeed, two Reform rabbis—Stephen S. Wise and Abba Hillel Silver—were among the most prominent Zionist leaders in the United States in the interwar years, although others continued to vehemently oppose Zionism and raised the specter of "dual loyalty." The willingness of integrationist and Reform leaders to acknowledge publicly that Jewishness was not strictly a matter of religion reflected their awareness that concepts and terms forged in the age of emancipation were inadequate to understand the challenges facing world Jewry in the 1920s and 1930s. Both Nazism and communism, each in its own way, brought this home to millions of Jews.

The self-understanding of most Jews was not ideological in any systematic sense. Most would have been hard pressed to define exactly what made them Jewish, other than their descent. Still, many experienced a sense of collective belonging that transcended linguistic, cultural, and political borders. But it was difficult to find a term by which to call this amorphous sense of connection. Some would call it a sense of peoplehood or ethnicity (a term not in use at the time); we might even label it a kind of "soft" nationalism. One expression of this was the financial aid that the American Jewish community extended to East European Jews in the two decades following the devastation of World War I, largely through the relief programs of the American Jewish Joint Distribution Committee. Another was the support that non-Zionist Jews gave to strengthening education and public health in Mandatory Palestine. A literary manifestation of this sense of connection was Jewish travel literature, a body of writing that evoked simultaneously the difference and likeness of "exotic" Jews living elsewhere.

A minority of Jewish thinkers, most of them in Central Europe, embraced an even more rigorously essentialist definition of Jews and defined them as a race. In the light of the Holocaust, this can appear puzzling and perverse. Why would Jews have embraced a way of thinking that was so closely linked to antisemitism? The answer is that racial thinking was omnipresent in culture and science from the late nineteenth century to the rise of Nazism. It was difficult for educated Jews to avoid. Moreover, it was not inherently anti-Jewish. Many Jewish scholars and public figures used the term *race* to describe the Jews. The American educator and biblical scholar Israel Friedländer, for example, wrote in 1910: "The Jews have never regarded themselves otherwise than as a sharply distinguished *racial* [italics in the original] group, as a community which is knit together not merely by the bodies of faith, but also ties of blood. . . . The Jews have always *felt* themselves as a separate race, sharply marked off from the rest of mankind."[12]

It was also possible to divide humanity into races without ranking them hierarchically. The German-born pioneers of Jewish social science research, like Arthur Ruppin and Felix Theilhaber, accepted the biological determinism of racial thinking without celebrating "Aryans" and denigrating "Semites." One attraction of a racial definition of Jews to secular Jews like them was that it explained in scientific terms how and why the Jews remained a cohesive group in the West even after faith and observance melted away. Even rabbis and communal leaders in Western countries casually employed the language of race, peppering their writing and speech with references to the Jewish *race*, although they were not doctrinaire racists in any sense. The self-description of Jews as a "race" fell into disfavor with the intensification of Nazi persecution.

Scholarship

In the Soviet Union, ideology and state policy severely constrained Jewish scholarship. Because Jews were not a nation, Soviet Jews did not write about Jews elsewhere and concentrated on such themes as "class struggle in the Pale of Settlement." Nevertheless, some excellent work on Jewish economic history, linguistics, folklore, and music was produced. However, because they were vulnerable to charges of "nationalism and chauvinism," the state-sponsored research institutes in Minsk and Kiev and their staffs fell victim to the purges of the late 1930s. By the end of the decade, Jewish scholarship had effectively disappeared.

In Mandate Palestine as well, political ideology shaped research and writing on the history and culture of the Jews. Most intellectuals and scholars who settled there were ardent Zionists of one stripe or another. Their nationalist worldview not only led them to return to Zion; it also shaped the way they understood and presented the history and culture of the Jews. One way in which they did so was to identify *galut* as the primary condition of Jewish life since the destruction of the Second Temple in 70 CE. The historian of medieval Spanish Jewry Yitzhak [Fritz] Baer explored changes in the concept of exile through the ages in a short book, *Galut* (1936). He described the dispersion of the Jews as tragic and unnatural and Judaism's traditional messianic eschatology as irrelevant. The pioneer scholar of Jewish mysticism Gershom Scholem, who, like Baer, was born and educated in Germany, "rehabilitated" the false messiah Shabbetai Tsevi, explaining his often bizarre antinomian behavior as a revolt against the powerlessness and stagnation of exilic conditions. In doing so, he transformed this usually maligned character into a precursor of both modernity and Zionism. In a similar move, Ben-Zion Dinur, their colleague at the Hebrew University, dated the beginning of the modern period in Jewish history to the immigration to Ottoman Palestine in 1700 of one thousand Jews led by Rabbi Judah the Pious, whom he anointed "a prophet of redemption" and "a religious rebel against the *Galut*." This immigration was, in his view, "a portent for the future, a pointer to generations whose historical experience was largely one of mass revolts and mass migrations in search of national salvation." This kind of Palestino-centric nationalism was characteristic of history writing at the Hebrew University in the interwar years (often referred to as "the Jerusalem school" of Jewish historiography).

In the United States, too, Judaica scholarship registered the political climate. Economic turmoil, especially the Great Depression and the radicalism it fueled, led scholars to ask how economic institutions and structures shaped the fortunes of the Jews in earlier periods. In 1938 the rabbinics scholar Louis Finkelstein produced a two-volume study of the Pharisees with the subtitle *The Sociological Background of Their Faith*. In a chapter on the doctrine of resurrection and immortality, he explained its spread in Judaism as solace for "the hungry slum-dweller[s]" and "plebeian artisans and traders of Jerusalem." Historian Salo Baron emphasized the transformative power of early capitalism in shaping the emergence of modern Jewish societies. In his landmark essay "Ghetto and Emancipation" (1928) he launched the idea, more fully developed in later work, that the restrictions under which the Jews of premodern Europe labored (exclusion from agriculture and handicrafts) prepared them to flourish in the emerging capitalist economy. Increasingly, Baron insisted that Jewish history from the seventeenth century on could be understood only as part of general European history, a view rejected by the historians of "the Jerusalem school."

Secularist Rebellion

The interwar years were a period of bold experimentation for secular Jews who saw themselves as participants in European and American cultural life more generally. They expressed a strong desire to break free from the conventions and pieties of Jewish tradition and bourgeois society. Everywhere one looks one finds iconoclasm, a testing of limits, a repudiation of what had been held sacred. Novelists Mike Gold and Henry Roth wrote about sexual secrets in the tenements of immigrant New York. The brothers Israel Joshua Singer and Isaac Bashevis Singer peopled their fiction with psychotics, neurotics, narcissists, obsessives, and misfits of every stripe, focusing on the darker sides of human psychology. Jerome Weidman, in *I Can Get It for You Wholesale* (1937), and Meyer Levin, in *The Old Bunch* (1937), wrote about hard-driving, corner-cutting Jewish men and the ugly underside of business in New York and Chicago, respectively. The protagonist of Arnold Zweig's *De Vriendt Goes Home* (1932) is an Orthodox, anti-Zionist Dutch Jew living in Jerusalem who is sexually attracted to Arab boys; the protagonist of David Vogel's *Married Life* (1929) is a penniless Viennese intellectual who marries a sadistic, antisemitic aristocrat. A central figure in Simon Blumenfeld's provocatively titled *Jew Boy* (1935) is a young opportunistic East London Jew who sexually assaults the family's Christian servant girl on Yom Kippur while his parents are in synagogue. Few of these fictional characters lived within the "four cubits of halakhah"; none was intended to inspire enthusiasm for any religious or political stream within the Jewish world.

One flagrant effort to unsettle conventional Jewish pieties was the use of sacred Christian symbols in poetry, fiction, and art, especially the figure of Jesus of Nazareth. Before World War I, there were liberal religious thinkers in Great Britain and the United States who worked to present Jesus in the Jewish context of the late Second Temple period. In doing so, they judaized his person and teachings, thus appropriating him for Judaism while presenting him in ways that were critical of Christianity. In the interwar years, however, Jewish artists, scholars, and poets did more than reclaim Jesus for the Jews. They transformed him into a Jewish martyr, a symbol of Jewish suffering at Christian hands. Marc Chagall's *White Crucifixion* (1938), for example, calls attention to the persecution and suffering of European Jewry. It stresses the Jewish identity of the crucified Jesus by replacing his loincloth with a tallit, his crown of thorns with a head cloth, and the ministering angels with the patriarchs. On either side of the cross, Jews flee pillaged, burning buildings, desperately seeking refuge. In "The Madonna in the Subway" (1937), the Yiddish poet A. Glantz-Leyeles, one of the founders of Introspectivism, reimagines the mother of Jesus in naturalistic terms. She tells the poet sitting opposite her that she does not know who impregnated her, that it could have been "a soldier, a stranger, an angry man, a slave of a Caesar. / A fisherman, hands calloused from pulling his nets, / Or just a bum who happened to whisper: my God!" In the short story "Jesús" (1935), the Cuban Yiddish writer Pinkhes Berniker slyly describes a peddler, Joseph by name, who grows wealthy selling figurines of Jesus and Mary (called "idols" in the story) to peasant women. They are eager to buy from him because he so closely resembles the Jesus "idol." He even has a Cuban barber trim his blond beard to resemble that of Jesus. In a different register altogether, the Jerusalem historian Joseph Klausner devoted a book-length Hebrew-language study to Jesus (not included in this volume), in which he cast him as "the most Jewish of Jews." At the same time, however, he castigated Jesus for his "*exaggerated* Judaism," which Klausner believed was apolitical and indifferent to national statecraft, and thus "the negation of national life and of the national state," which, as a Zionist, he championed. In 1939, the Yiddish writer Sholem Asch published the first volume of his controversial trilogy on the origins of Christianity, *The Nazarene. The Apostle* appeared in 1943 and *Mary* in 1949.

Secularist essayists and scholars also reclaimed the radical philosopher Benedict Spinoza, whom the Amsterdam Jewish community put in ḥerem in 1656. The Harvard historian of philosophy Harry Wolfson not only devoted two volumes to explicating *The Latent Processes of His Reasoning* (the subtitle of his study) but also envisaged a chronological scaffolding for the history of Western philosophy that began and ended with two Jews—Philo and Spinoza. For nationalists like Joseph Klausner, who famously declared the 1656 ḥerem void in a dramatic speech at the Hebrew University in 1927, Spinoza's critique of revelation and repudiation of rabbinic authority were no barrier to his inclusion in the pantheon of Jewish thinkers.

In the visual arts, Jews were in the thick of modernist movements to establish new ways of painting and sculpting. Of course, not all Jews who embraced modernism identified themselves as Jews and not all of them chose recognizably Jewish subjects. But many did, trying to fashion a self-consciously Jewish modernism. Those who settled in Palestine often saw their work as part of a national project to create a new Jewish culture. In the West, the number of Jewish architects who built in the new international style was small, and the Great Depression severely curtailed communal building programs. Still, they produced a few notable modernist buildings, including Ignaz Reiser's ceremonial hall at the New Jewish Cemetery in Vienna (1928), Harry Elte's Rav Aron Schuster Synagogue in Jacob Obrechtplein in Amsterdam (1928), Fritz Landauer's Reform synagogue in Plauen, Saxony (1928–1930), and Eric Mendelsohn's Schocken Library in Jerusalem (1936). In the Soviet Union, Jews were among the leading architects who, in the 1930s, developed the grandiose "Stalinist" style that still is visible in major post-Soviet cities. Boris Iofan's monumental designs and Moisei Ginzburg's housing projects created new types of urban designs that were to reflect and promote a socialist aesthetic.

The cultural iconoclasm of the interwar years drew in part from the generational revolt that so dominated Jewish life at the time, especially in communities in economic and political peril. Jewish youth and their ideological mentors, whatever their affiliation, tended to view the wisdom and advice of their elders with skepticism and scorn. However, among the numerous Orthodox outside the Soviet Union, rabbinic leaders were still accorded great respect and were able to mobilize hundreds of thousands to strict obedience to their rulings. But in the eyes of many of the no-longer Orthodox, the conventional values and well-worn solutions of their parents' generation were incapable of addressing spiritual, cultural, economic, and political threats at home and abroad, and they dismissed them as bankrupt and sterile.

Their scorn for the failings of their parents and their generation was not limited to their political choices. It found expression in poetry, fiction, and the visual arts, as well. Franz Kafka's epistolary demolition of his father is a powerful and disturbing example of patricidal rage, fear, and guilt at work, and Irène Némirovsky's novelistic assault on her mother in *David Golder* an example of matricidal fury. The Central European Hebrew writer David Vogel dispatched his ineffective father in the poem "I Saw My Father Drowning" (1923). "His weak hand gave a last white flutter / In the distance— / And he was gone." The young men and women in Poland who submitted essays to the YIVO memoir contests in the 1930s repeatedly expressed their disappointment with their parents—their passivity, fatalism, and inability to help them make their way in the world. Their memoirs record their often difficult struggles to make their own lives on their own terms. On the other hand, the *yeshivot* of Lithuania, Poland, and Hungary were still filled with youth who followed as best they could the ways of their forebears and teachers, though people such as Rabbi Meir Shapiro of Lublin, sensing the drift away from the authority of *talmidei ḥakhamim*, attempted to modernize the physical surroundings of the *yeshivot*.

In part, a hunger for renewal—collective and individual, cultural and spiritual—drove this generational revolt. The *ḥalutsim*, the left-wing secular youth who pioneered reclamation and construction projects in the Yishuv, saw rebuilding the Land as a means as well for achieving their own personal redemption and wholeness. The yearning for renewal was also strongly felt in urban Central European intellectual circles, especially those that came under the influence of Martin Buber and other neoromantic critics of modernity. In his 1919 essay "Herut: On Youth and Religion," Buber wrote of the "depressing loneliness" of the youth of Europe, an affliction he attributed to their hypertrophic intellectualization and divorce from organic spirituality. He insisted, however, that there was no need to despair because youth was "a time of total openness . . . when every man is affected by the power of the unconditional" or "the All." If Jewish youth could not find meaning in "the official outward forms" of Judaism, then they needed only "descend into their own depths, to those ramifications of Jewish religiosity that, not having become dominant, still continue to live beneath the surface."

Emphasis on interiority—as opposed to the tyranny of convention—also manifested itself in avant-garde literary circles. Writers who positioned themselves in the forefront of cultural revolution, like Uri Zvi Greenberg, reveled in their dismissal of both the conventional *and* the conventionally experimental. In his 1922 "Proclamation," Greenberg contrasted writers like himself—"who are whole, with heavy heads ablaze and spirits horror-tested through expanses," whose "bodies convulse under the weight of the black global pain that they carry on their bare backs"—to the vulgar pseudo-expressionists and their "concealed falsehood of talentlessness" hiding "behind the sacred veil of modern poetry." He called, instead, for "free, bare, blood-seething human expression," of which apparently both bourgeois and "pseudo-expressionist" writers were incapable.

The cultural iconoclasm of the interwar period also included explicit and implicit challenges to conventional ideas about the place of women in Jewish life and their artistic and literary sensibility. Self-conscious, ideologically informed Jewish feminism was a post–World War II development, but women writers in the 1920s and 1930s offered alternative, frequently novel perspectives on Jewish life. First in Germany and then in Palestine, the bohemian modernist Else Lasker-Schüler wrote visionary poetry and fiction in German, often invoking wild orientalist fantasies. Gertrud Kolmar's German novel *A Jewish Mother from Berlin* (1931) and Esther Kreitman's Yiddish novel *The Dance of the Demons* (1936) feature the travails of abandoned or rejected women, poorly treated by their families and circumstances, who struggle to preserve their integrity. The protagonist of the Yiddish writer Celia Dropkin's "A Dancer" (1935), "agile, young and slender" in her youth, yearning to become a dancer, ages ungracefully, loses touch with reality, and takes refuge in dreams of flying. Eventually, she is institutionalized. Disappointment, frustration, lack of fulfillment, isolation, and weariness dog the lives of these and many other female characters in the fiction and poetry of Jewish women writers in this period. Their work registers the large gap between the aspirations of secular-minded women and the constraints imposed on them by culture and society.

Women writers also brought a heightened sense of sexuality to Jewish writing in these years, invoking needs and desires that were in tension with conventional notions of female sensibility and behavior. As she enters adolescence, the young woman in the above-mentioned Dropkin story takes pleasure in looking at her growing breasts when changing her clothes. In Dropkin's poem "The Circus Lady" (1935), the self-destructive character moves her "swaying, lissome body" among daggers "with their points erect," yearning to fall on them, her blood heating them "through and through." In the poem "Once I Was Young" (1929), the American Yiddish poet Anna Margolin writes as a pagan Greek male, a disciple of Socrates, who praises his male lover, the possessor of "the finest chest in Athens." Women writing in Hebrew, usually in the Yishuv rather than in Europe or America, also introduced the female body into verse, but in their case they often merged images of human sensuality with images of the Land's physical terrain. In the poem "My Heart Is with Your Dews, Homeland" (1923) Esther Raab imbues images, smells, and sounds of nature with pulsating sexuality, and in "Before Your Shining, Full Eyes" (1922) she compares her lover after intercourse to a eucalyptus tree after a storm—"tired, strong and still moving in the wind."

In Eastern Europe, the generational rebellion of freethinking writers and intellectuals was, in part, a testimony to the persistence, though not the hegemony, of the world of tradition. Although no longer an impregnable fortress (if, indeed, it had ever been), traditional Jewish culture—the world of the yeshiva, rabbinic authority, and halakhic norms—still commanded the loyalty of several million Jews. The world of Orthodoxy was not, of course, monolithic—there were divisions between Hasidim and Misnagdim, among the dozens of Hasidic sects, and between the modern Orthodox, who worked to embrace both Western culture and observance of the *mitsvot*, and the ultra-Orthodox, who disparaged Western learning and cultural accommodation. Nor did any of these groups, even the ultra-Orthodox, represent a stable, change-resistant Judaism untouched by time. In the United States and Western Europe, where Orthodoxy was more accommodationist than in Eastern Europe, university-educated modern Orthodox rabbis, like Alexander Altmann and Yehiel Yaakov Weinberg in Berlin and Leo Jung and Joseph Soloveitchik in New York, explored and presented Judaism in terms that drew on Western categories of thought and in ways that spoke to acculturated (but observant) middle-class Jews.

Not all Jewish writers, of course, were iconoclasts and experimentalists. Middle- and lowbrow writers, especially Yiddish writers, found large and appreciative audiences among the Jewish masses. The Yiddish theater, which began in Romania in the late nineteenth century and then spread to the Russian Empire and the New World, staged productions that ranged from *shund* (melodramatic trash and vulgar comedy) to translations of European theater classics and original Yiddish dramas by prominent authors. Actors moved across national borders and performed wherever Yiddish-speaking Jews concentrated. Some even made the transition from the stage to the screen. In 1919, the Soviet state set up the Moscow State Yiddish Theater; it toured abroad and its modernist productions became world famous (the Soviet authorities closed it in 1949). Its leading director and most celebrated actor was Shlomo (Solomon) Mikhoels, who during the war led the Jewish Anti-Fascist Committee but was murdered in a government-staged "accident" in 1948.

In interwar Poland, there were more than four hundred Yiddish theater companies. Polish troupes toured the world, performing in Berlin, London, New York, Paris, and Buenos Aires. The most famous of them were the Vilner trupe (Vilna Troupe) and the Warsaw Yiddish Art Theater. Among the leading lights of the Vilner trupe was Joseph Buloff, an actor who later made a career in New York's Yiddish Art Theater and on and off Broadway. The Warsaw Yiddish Art Theater, founded in 1924, was led by Zygmunt Turkow and Ida Kaminska, who resurrected Yiddish theater in Warsaw after World War II and became known in the West when she starred in the Czechoslovak film *The Shop on Main Street* (1965).

Yiddish theater in New York, which dated to the 1880s, flourished in the 1920s. At one point in the interwar period, there were a dozen Yiddish theaters in New York, concentrated along Second Avenue. Many other large cities had their own theaters as well. Actors such as Maurice Schwartz, Ludwig Satz, and the American-born actress Molly Picon became internationally famous, touring

Latin America and Europe. Major literary figures like Sholem Aleichem, H. Leivick, Sholem Asch, and Sh. An-ski wrote for the Yiddish stage. Some of its leading actors later appeared in Yiddish films, most of which were made in the 1930s in Poland. They addressed themes like acculturation and radical assimilation that were long-standing challenges to the vitality of Jewish life.

The Hebrew-language theater also began to flourish in the interwar years. The best-known company, Habima (The Stage), which was founded in Białystok in 1912, gained prominence under the tutelage of famous Russian directors in Moscow after the revolution. In 1926, while the company was touring outside the Soviet Union, some of its members decided not to return to Moscow because of the regime's hostility to Hebrew. They settled in the United States and in Erets Yisrael, where Habimah evolved into Israel's national theater.

The interwar period was also the "golden age" of cantorial music (*ḥazones*). It was heard not only in synagogue services but also in concerts, which attracted overflow audiences. While records popularized all forms of Jewish music, this was especially true for cantorial music. American-based cantors such as Yossele Rosenblatt, Mordechai Hershman, Yosele Shlisky, Zawel Kwartin, and many others enjoyed worldwide popularity through their records and their frequent concert tours. Among the most famous was Gershon Sirota, "the Jewish Caruso." He was based in Poland (where he was murdered in the Warsaw ghetto in 1943), but came to the United States regularly for the High Holidays.

The New Yishuv and Its Culture

The most remarkable experiment in fashioning a new page in Jewish history was the creation of a modern, Hebrew-speaking, largely secular society in the Land of Israel. It was called the "New Yishuv" to differentiate it from the "Old Yishuv"—those Jews, both European and Middle Eastern, who had "returned" to the Land over the centuries for religious rather than political reasons. The first immigrants committed to creating a Hebrew-based secular society began arriving there in the late nineteenth century. However, only after the overthrow of Turkish rule and the establishment of the British Mandate did Jewish immigration increase dramatically. At the start of World War I, about 60,000 Jews lived in the Land of Israel; in 1922, according to the first British government census, the number was about 84,000. By the time of the second government census, in 1931, it had jumped to 175,000, while the Arab population was about 850,000. Then, with the influx of Central European Jews fleeing Nazism, the Jewish population skyrocketed to about 450,000 in 1939. By 1941, the Jewish population numbered about 474,000.[13]

The commitments the British government made to the Jews in the Balfour Declaration in 1917 did not survive growing Arab militancy. Eager to placate Arab nationalists in Palestine and angry Muslims elsewhere in its far-flung empire, the British government gradually backtracked on its promise to create "a National Home for the Jewish people" (in the words of the Balfour Declaration) and imposed limits on Jewish immigration and land purchase. In response to the "Arab revolt" of 1936–1939, the government issued the White Paper of 1939, which all but brought an end to legal immigration. Its impact was devastating, as the number of European Jews who were desperate to escape Nazism climbed sharply in the late 1930s, following Kristallnacht and the German annexations of Austria and Czechoslovakia.

Despite the callous attitude of the British government toward the plight of European Jewry, the Mandatory administration in Palestine granted the New Yishuv wide-ranging internal autonomy, allowing it to create and nourish self-regulating cultural, economic, and educational institutions that became the foundations of the emerging Jewish society. Ideological differences among the Zionist parties engendered a lively debate about the character of these institutions and the structure of the new society. In the economic sphere, Labor Zionists created trade unions, whose reach extended to industrial enterprises, communitarian agricultural settlements, agricultural marketing cooperatives, health-care programs, and utility companies. For Labor Zionists like David Ben-Gurion, there was no conflict between the class needs and the national needs of Jewish workers. In "The National Mission of the Working Class" (1926), he denied any tension between the two. Workers who struggled to advance their class interests were simultaneously unifying and strengthening the nation, for their struggle "creates and conquers national positions in the land and paves the broad path for popular immigration." Marxist-Zionists, inspired by the writings of Ber Borochov, were committed to a more radical socialism combined with Zionism. They formed the Mapam Party, whereas the non-Marxists, whose ideology and institutions resembled those of the British Labor Party, formed Mapai. But the more capitalist-friendly Revisionists, under Vladimir (Ze'ev) Jabotinsky, branded the very notion of class warfare a chimera. As he wrote in "The Ideology of the Betar" (1934), the youth affiliate of the Revisionist Party, the New Yishuv was "in the initial stage of forming a social organism" and classes as such did not exist: "The proletarians are not proletarians and bourgeoisie are not bourgeoisie." Politically driven strikes to extend Labor Zionism's "baleful predominance of the economic life of the Yishuv," he believed, harmed rather than advanced the national cause.[14]

Beyond the question of the economic character of the new society loomed the equally vexing (and more abstract) question of its "purpose" or "mission." There was a consensus that the Jewish homeland should, at a minimum, shelter Jews who faced oppression or who wished to cultivate their Jewishness to the full, but there was no agreement among politicians and writers about whether the Jewish state-in-embryo required a universal justification as well, and, if so, what it should be. Some, like the "national poet" Chaim Nachman Bialik, imagined a state that would serve as "a light unto the nations." He concluded his essay "Jewish Dualism" (1922) with this uplifting vision of the Jewish state's destiny:

> here [in the Land of Israel] we are destined to fashion a culture sevenfold greater and richer than any we have heretofore created or absorbed. And who knows? Perhaps after hundreds of years we will be emboldened to make another exodus which will lead to the spreading of our spirit over the world and an assiduous striving toward glory.[15]

Others, viewing Jewish life in exile as unnatural and unhealthy, emphasized the normalizing function of the return to Zion and the building of a new society there. They believed that allowing Jews to develop freely in their own land and become a nation like all the other nations, with a character all its own, was sufficient to cure the harmful impact of centuries of diaspora existence. They did not believe the destiny of the Jewish people was to redeem, inspire, enlighten, or serve as an example for the rest of the world.

This aversion to ideological fervor found expression in fiction of the interwar years. The characters in Joseph Chaim Brenner's works are emotionally disengaged from the great tasks of the time, have trouble making sense of the world, and drift rather than navigate their way through life. Although they are Jews, they do not pursue communitarian "Jewish" goals or ruminate about the fate of the Jews. It is enough for them to keep their heads above water and survive. In this sense, they behave as if they were still living in the diaspora, where, of course, the Hebrew writers of the New Yishuv were born, raised, and educated. In some Hebrew fiction of the period—for example, in Chaim Hazaz's "Revolutionary Chapters" (1924), Avigdor Hameiri's *The Great Madness* (1929), and Yehudah Yaari's *When the Candle Was Burning* (1932)—political events are central to the narrative, but the events are those of World War I, the Russian Revolution, and their aftermath. Moreover, the attitude of the writers to the tumult and mayhem of these events is often ironic or detached. The events themselves are earthshaking, but the characters caught up in them are hardly heroic or larger than life, new Jewish men and women. Other writers, like Dvora Baron in her short story "In the Beginning" (1927), continue to draw on the world of the prewar East European shtetl for inspiration, although their treatment of shtetl life is markedly unsentimental. Perhaps the most profound literary encounter with the Old World from this period is the Nobel Laureate S. Y. Agnon's *A Guest for the Night* (1938), a meditative tale of a Galician Jew from Jerusalem who, on his return to his native town after World War I, finds that the world of his youth has vanished. Thus, when he enters the synagogue on Yom Kippur, he knows no one there: "The radiance that is wont to shine on the heads of the sacred congregation on the Eve of Atonement did not shine on their heads, and their prayer shawls shed no light."

For the most part, Jewish literary culture in the Mandate period only occasionally engaged with the presence of Arabs in the Land. Of course, political leaders were acutely aware of Arab opposition to Zionism. By the late 1930s, few had any illusions about the possibility of achieving a peaceful resolution to their competing claims to the Land. However, Arab anger and fear were not central to the Jewish cultural agenda of the New Yishuv. Jews under the Mandate lived within a social and cultural universe of their own making and were not compelled to confront, imaginatively and discursively, the presence of the native Arab population, as they were, say, after 1967. One exception to this was the writer Yitzhak Shami, an Arabic-speaking Syrian Jew from Hebron, whose novella *The Vengeance of the Fathers* (1928) is a tale of the physical and mental deterioration of an Arab chieftain from Nablus. Shami, however, was a cultural outlier—a Middle Eastern Jew who was at home in Arabic culture among writers whose background was Ashkenazi and East European.

The creation of a modern Hebrew-language culture was a remarkable achievement. There are no parallels to it in modern history. Although the use of Hebrew had never disappeared during centuries of diasporic life, it had served largely as the language of Jewish worship and religious scholarship. Beginning in the late nineteenth century and continuing into the 1920s and 1930s, it was transformed into a modern vernacular, capable of serving the needs of modern science, the arts, commerce and industry, and everyday life. What was not clear, however, at the time was its relationship to earlier forms of Hebrew (biblical, Mishnaic, and medieval). To what extent was it to draw on these earlier forms and to what extent was it to draw on contemporary Slavic, Germanic, and Romance languages? The greatest Hebrew writer of the period, Agnon, drew creatively on earlier forms of Hebrew to fashion a uniquely rich and learned language, but he was exceptional in this regard.

The Organization of This Volume

As with all anthologies, selecting the items to be included was an exhausting, often painful process. We devoted much time and effort to locating sources both known and unknown to English-language readers and to assessing their importance in the larger context of Jewish culture and its interaction with other cultures. No doubt some readers will be dissatisfied with our selections and wonder why we did not include texts that are important to them. All we can do, by way of response, is to explain our modus operandi.

In making our choices, we decided to include "longer" rather than "shorter" selections. We felt that this would allow readers to better appreciate the character, style, and tone of a text. We also believe that this enhances the teaching value of the volume. Our goal was not to create a "canon" but to convey an awareness of and appreciation for the variety, breadth, and depth of Jewish cultural creativity in the tempestuous interwar period. The omission or inclusion of a writer should not be interpreted as a judgment of his or her literary value, historical importance, cultural worth, or intellectual heft. A host of considerations guided the selection process. Because we were constrained by the size of the volume, we tended to choose short stories over novels. We also excluded works that, however important and influential in intellectual history, are not accessible to most readers because of their specialized and often abstruse language. A good example of this is Franz Rosenzweig's *Star of Redemption* (1921).

There were also more mundane considerations. Some heirs and copyright holders made unreasonable demands; others were simply uncooperative. As a result, we were unable to include the work of a few authors who would otherwise have found a place here. It may also appear that we have slighted Jewish communities in the Middle East, Africa, and Asia. However, it should be remembered that in the interwar years, 90 percent of the world's Jews lived in Europe and North America. Jews who traced their roots to lands in the orbit of Islam became demographically important only after the Germans destroyed the great centers of Ashkenazi life in Eastern and East Central Europe during World War II. It also should be remembered that the modernist cultural and intellectual currents that transformed Jewish creativity in Europe and North America in the interwar years touched the lives of fewer Jews living in North Africa, the Middle East, and Asia. In general, the selection of texts reflects the demographic realities, cultural practices, and social norms of the world's Jewish communities in the interwar period. Thus, there are more texts from Russia and Poland, for example, than France and Italy, whose small Jewish populations included many Jews who were distant from Jewish cultural and collective concerns. Not surprisingly, there are more texts by men than women, given the conventions that inhibited the full participation of women in cultural and political life in the interwar years. Perhaps future scholars will make available more materials by women and by Jews in non-Western communities.

The rabbinic sage Rabbi Tarfon, who lived in the period between the destruction of the Second Temple (70 CE) and the fall of Betar (135 CE), famously said, "The day is short, the work is considerable, the workmen are lazy, the reward is great, and the Master is pressing." He also said, "It is not your job to finish the task, but neither are you free to desist from it."

Notes

1. Derek J. Penslar, *Jews and the Military: A History* (Princeton, N.J.: Princeton University Press, 2013), 157.

2. Ernest Jones, *The Life and Work of Sigmund Freud*, 3 vols. (London: Hogarth Press, 1953–1957), 1:192.

3. Penslar, 157.

4. Unless otherwise noted, texts that are referred to or quoted from in this introduction come from works included in this volume.

5. John Klier, "Pogroms," *The YIVO Encyclopedia of Jews in Eastern Europe*, 2:1380.

6. The League of Nations awarded the formerly Ottoman areas that the British conquered during the war to Great Britain. It was to hold a "mandate" over this territory, known at the time as "Palestine," until its permanent character could be determined. Jews commonly referred to the area as "Erets Yisrael" (the Land of Israel) in Hebrew and Yiddish and as "Palestine" in English and other European languages. Today the term *Palestine* has other political connotations. Thus, we use the term the *Land of Israel* or *Mandatory Palestine* to refer to that territory in the interwar period.

7. Mordechai Altshuler, *Soviet Jewry on the Eve of the Holocaust* (Jerusalem: Centre for Research on East European Jewry, 1998), 12–13, 220.

8. Einstein, Albert, "How I Became a Zionist," in *Einstein on Politics: His Private Thoughts and Public Stands on Nationalism, Zionism, War, Peace, and the Bomb*, ed. David E. Rowe and Robert Schulmann (Princeton, N.J.: Princeton University Press, 2007), 142–145, 149–153.

9. Jeffrey Shandler, ed., *Awakening Lives: Autobiographies of Jewish Youth in Poland before the Holocaust* (New Haven, Conn.: Yale University Press, 2002).

10. "Population and Migration," *YIVO Encyclopedia*, 2:1427.

11. Donald L. Niewyk, *The Jews in Weimar Germany* (Baton Rouge: Louisiana State University Press, 1980), 103–106; Ruth Louise Pierson, "German Jewish Identity in the Weimar Republic" (Ph.D. diss., Yale University, 1970), chap. 1.

12. "Race and Religion," in Israel Friedlaender, *Past and Present: A Collection of Jewish Essays* (Cincinnati: Ark Publishing, 1919), 431–432.

13. These figures are drawn from Justin McCarthy, *The Population of Palestine: Population History and Statistics of the Ottoman Period and the Mandate* (New York: Columbia University Press, 1990); the British censuses of 1922 and 1931; and the Esco Foundation for Palestine, *Palestine: A Study of Jewish, Arab, and British Policies*, 2 vols. (New Haven, Conn.: Yale University Press, 1947), 1:46.

14. Vladimir Jabotinsky, "The Ideology of the Betar," in *From the Pen of Jabotinsky* (Cape Town: Cape Town Betar, 1941), 35–59.

15. Hayyim Nahman Bialik, "Jewish Dualism," in *Revealment and Concealment: Five Essays*, trans. Maurice Shudofsky (Jerusalem: Ibis Editions, 2000), 27–44.

Bibliography

Alter, Robert. *Defenses of the Imagination: Jewish Writers and Modern Historical Crisis*. Philadelphia: Jewish Publication Society, 1977.

Antler, Joyce. *The Journey Home: Jewish Women and the American Century*. New York: Free Press, 1997.

Bacon, Gershon C. *The Politics of Tradition: Agudat Yisrael in Poland, 1923–1939.* Jerusalem: Magnes Press of the Hebrew University of Jerusalem, 1996.

Beller, Steven. *Vienna and the Jews, 1867–1938: A Cultural History.* Cambridge: Cambridge University Press, 1989.

Bemporad, Elissa. *Becoming Soviet Jews: The Bolshevik Experiment in Minsk.* Bloomington: Indiana University Press, 2013.

Benbassa, Esther, and Aron Rodrigue. *The Jews of the Balkans: The Judeo-Spanish Community, 15th to 20th Centuries.* Oxford: Blackwell, 1995.

Brenner, Michael. *The Renaissance of Jewish Culture in Weimar Germany.* New Haven, Conn.: Yale University Press, 1996.

Cheyette, Bryan. *Constructions of "The Jew" in English Literature and Society: Racial Representations, 1875–1945.* Cambridge: Cambridge University Press, 1993.

Elkin, Judith Laikin. *Jews of Latin America.* 3rd ed. Boulder, Colo.: Lynne Rienner, 2014.

Endelman, Todd M. *The Jews of Britain, 1656–2000.* Berkeley: University of California Press, 2002.

———. *Leaving the Jewish Fold: Conversion and Radical Assimilation in Modern Jewish History.* Princeton, N.J.: Princeton University Press, 2015.

Feingold, Henry L., *A Time for Searching: Entering the Mainstream, 1920–1945.* Vol. 4 of *The Jewish People in America,* ed. Henry L. Finegold. Baltimore: Johns Hopkins University Press, 1992.

Gilman, Sander L., and Jack Zipes, eds. *Yale Companion to Jewish Writing and Thought in German Culture, 1096–1996.* New Haven, Conn.: Yale University Press, 1997.

Gitelman, Zvi Y. *Jewish Nationality and Soviet Politics: The Jewish Sections of the CPSU, 1917–1930.* Princeton, N.J.: Princeton University Press, 1972.

Glazer, Nathan. *American Judaism.* Chicago: University of Chicago Press, 1974.

Goldstein, Eric L. *The Price of Whiteness: Jews, Race, and American Identity.* Princeton, N.J.: Princeton University Press, 2006.

Gurock, Jeffrey S. *Jews in Gotham: New York Jews in a Changing City, 1920–2010.* New York: New York University Press, 2012.

Gutman, Yisrael, Ezra Mendelsohn, Jehuda Reinharz, and Chone Shmeruk, eds. *The Jews of Poland between Two World Wars.* Hanover, N.H.: University Press of New England, 1989.

Hart, Mitchell B. *Social Science and the Politics of Modern Jewish Identity.* Stanford, Calif.: Stanford University Press, 2000.

Hellerstein, Kathryn. *A Question of Tradition: Women Poets in Yiddish, 1586–1987.* Stanford, Calif.: Stanford University Press, 2014.

Hertz, Aleksander. *The Jews in Polish Culture.* Trans. Richard Lourie. Evanston, Ill.: Northwestern University Press, 1988.

Hoberman, J. *Bridge of Light: Yiddish Film between Two Worlds.* New York: Schocken, 1991.

Hyman, Paula E. *From Dreyfus to Vichy: The Remaking of French Jewry, 1906–1939.* New York: Columbia University Press, 1979.

Joselit, Jenna Weissman. *New York's Jewish Jews: The Orthodox Community in the Interwar Years.* Bloomington: Indiana University Press, 1990.

Kampf, A. *Chagall to Kitaj: Jewish Experience in 20th Century Art.* London: Lund Humphries, 1990.

Krämer, Gudrun. *The Jews in Modern Egypt, 1914–1952.* Seattle: University of Washington Press, 1989.

Laskier, Michael M. *North African Jewry in the Twentieth Century: The Jews of Morocco, Tunisia, and Algeria.* New York: New York University Press, 1994.

Levinson, Julian. *Exiles on Main Street: Jewish American Writers and American Literary Culture.* Bloomington: Indiana University Press, 2008.

Leydesdorff, Selma. *We Lived with Dignity: The Jewish Proletariat of Amsterdam, 1900–1940.* Translated by Frank Heny. Detroit: Wayne State University Press, 1994.

Lockhart, Darrell B. *Jewish Writers in Latin America: A Dictionary*. New York: Garland, 1997.

Malinovich, Nadia. *French and Jewish: Culture and the Politics of Identity in Early Twentieth-Century France*. Oxford: Littman Library of Jewish Civilization, 2008.

Mendelsohn, Ezra. *The Jews of East Central Europe between the World Wars*. Bloomington: Indiana University Press, 1987.

———. *On Modern Jewish Politics*. New York: Oxford University Press, 1993.

Mendes-Flohr, Paul. *Divided Passions: Jewish Intellectuals and the Experience of Modernity*. Detroit: Wayne State University Press, 1991.

Meyer, Michael A., ed. *Renewal and Destruction, 1918–1945*. Vol. 4 of *German-Jewish History in Modern Times*. New York: Columbia University Press, 1998.

Miron, Dan. *From Continuity to Contiguity: Toward a New Jewish Literary Thinking*. Stanford, Calif.: Stanford University Press, 2010.

Moore, Deborah Dash. *At Home in America: Second Generation New York Jews*. New York: Columbia University Press, 1981.

Mosse, George L. *German Jews beyond Judaism*. Bloomington: Indiana University Press, 1985.

Myers, David N. *Re-Inventing the Jewish Past: European Jewish Intellectuals and the Zionist Return to History*. New York: Oxford University Press, 1995.

Niewyk, Donald L. *The Jews in Weimar Germany*. Baton Rouge: Louisiana State University Press, 1980.

Pinkus, Benjamin. *The Jews of the Soviet Union: The History of a National Minority*. Cambridge: Cambridge University Press, 1988.

Polonsky, Antony. *1914 to 2008*. Vol. 3 of *The Jews in Poland and Russia*. Oxford: Littman Library of Jewish Civilization, 2012.

Segev, Tom. *One Palestine Complete: Jews and Arabs under the British Mandate*. New York: Metropolitan Books, 2000.

Shapira, Anita. *Land and Power: The Zionist Resort to Force, 1881–1948*. New York: Oxford University Press, 1992.

Shneer, David. *Yiddish and the Creation of Soviet Jewish Culture*. Cambridge: Cambridge University Press, 2004.

Shore, Marci. *Caviar and Ashes: A Warsaw Generation's Life and Death in Marxism, 1918–1968*. New Haven, Conn.: Yale University Press, 2006.

Shternshis, Anna. *Soviet and Kosher: Jewish Popular Culture in the Soviet Union, 1923–1939*. Bloomington: Indiana University Press, 2006.

Veidlinger, Jeffrey. *The Moscow State Yiddish Theater: Jewish Culture on the Soviet Stage*. Bloomington: Indiana University Press, 2000.

Wasserstein, Bernard. *On the Eve: The Jews of Europe before the Second World War*. New York: Simon & Schuster, 2012.

Wenger, Beth S. *New York Jews and the Great Depression: Uncertain Promise*. New Haven, Conn.: Yale University Press, 1996.

Whitfield, Stephen J. *In Search of American Jewish Culture*. Hanover, N.H.: University Press of New England, 1999.

Wirth-Nesher, Hana, ed. *The Cambridge History of Jewish American Literature*. New York: Cambridge University Press, 2016.

Wisse, Ruth S. *The Modern Jewish Canon: A Journey through Language and Culture*. New York: Free Press, 2000.

Zerubavel, Yael. *Recovered Roots: Collective Memory and the Making of Israeli National Tradition*. Chicago: University of Chicago Press, 1995.

Zimmerman, Joshua A., ed. *Jews in Italy under Fascist and Nazi Rule, 1922–1945*. Cambridge: Cambridge University Press, 2005.

Social, Political, and Cultural Thought

External and internal threats to Jewish well-being and continuity challenged Jewish writers to envision strategies of adaptation and survival. The texts in this section speak to these challenges and to the diversity of answers and strategies that politicians, rabbis, critics, social reformers, and men of letters produced in response. The texts address avant-garde currents in literature, the revival of Hebrew and its relationship to Yiddish, the Jewish labor movement in the diaspora and the Land of Israel, threats of acculturation and secularization, the complexities of Jewish identity, varieties of Jewish nationalism, settlement of the Land of Israel, the emergence of Jewish women into the public sphere, and the nature and extent of antisemitism. Although some of these texts address abstract cultural issues in appropriately abstract language, many more are impassioned pleas and biting critiques on issues of the day.

Agudas Yisroel

Established in 1912

Agudas Yisroel, the Aguda (Agudeh), Union of Israel, is an Orthodox Jewish political movement founded in Poland in 1912. Entering the modern Jewish political arena, Agudas Yisroel tried to create a universal Orthodox identity, having both Hasidic and non-Hasidic representatives. It opposed contemporary secular movements, the Zionist parties among them. Although the Aguda was active in Eastern and Western Europe, as well as in the United States and the Land of Israel, it was most influential in Eastern Europe during the interwar period, having representatives in the Polish Sejm and municipal governments, and also leading roles in some *kehilot* (Jewish communal governments) in Poland, Latvia, and Lithuania. The Aguda also created a school network of strictly Orthodox education, among them the Beys Yankev (Beth Jacob) girls' schools. In 1937, there were 818 schools of various kinds in the Aguda network, enrolling about 109,000 pupils. Aguda continues to be influential in Israel and the United States today.

Manifesto
1918

> *To the remnant whom Hashem calls Guardians of the Torah and Doers of His Word. May the Lord our God be with them and may they rise higher and higher*
> OUR BRETHREN GUARDIANS OF THE FAITH OF ISRAEL!

Our depressing situation, the difficult times and the great hardships that we are experiencing—may God, Blessed Be He, take pity on us—have led us to consult on how to strengthen and defend our position and the faith of our Holy Torah, and after taking into consideration all the details and reasons that have caused the humiliation of Judaism, we have realized the great necessity of following the positive commandments arising from the current situation, that all the Guardians of the Faith of Israel whom the fear of God moves—in every town and city they shall unite in one association under the banner of Mesorah—the Holy One Blessed be He, Israel, and Jewish Law—under the name of the Guardians of the Faith of Israel to watch over all matters of religion and faith and observance of the Holy Torah, and all of the associations shall be combined by a main center into one great and powerful body to take care of the Aguda's needs and to defend its rights.

And since the settlement of Erets Yisrael is one of the commandments of Hashem, the Aguda will in general act and seek, according to the ways of our Holy Torah, the welfare of the settlement of Erets Yisrael by desirable and concrete actions. And since this is a very important issue, it is worthwhile to establish in this association a special department called "Yishuv Erets Yisrael according to the Holy written Torah and the Mesorah," which will be responsible for all the details of the work in accordance with the approval of the great and holy rabbis of our generation.

And we explicitly state that all that the above-mentioned holy *geonim* have decided and proclaimed concerning the Zionists and Zionism is still fully valid and in force, and we must not depart from it, and this Aguda acts independently in all matters and has no connection with Zionism and its rebels.

And from now on we ask of all our brethren Guardians of the Faith of Israel: we beseech you, brothers, unite! Lend a hand to help this association. Each according to his strength and ability will bear the burden of the Aguda, will help and toil to increase the number of members and generally to be those who act and activate, and each will assist his neighbor and will explain the law to his brother, and thereby will remove the senseless hatred that caused all the exiles, and only reach agreement peacefully and lovingly so that the faith should be strengthened and the glory of the Torah, of Israel, and of our Holy Land shall be uplifted. And He whose name is Shalom, He shall establish peace, love, brotherhood, and friendship among all of us—and in our day may Judah be redeemed and may Israel dwell secure, and we shall see the redemption in the city where Hashem is present.

This proclamation was issued in the year (1918) with the addition of the signature of

Rabbi Mordechai Menachem Mendel from Otwock
Rabbi Shmuel Zvi from Alexander
Rabbi Meir Yehiel Halevi from Ostrowiec
Rabbi Avraham Mordechai Alter from Gur

Rabbi Pinchas Menachem from Warsaw
Rabbi Alter Azriel Meir Eiger from Lublin
Rabbi Alter Israel Shimon from Novominsk
Rabbi Yitshak Zelig from Kotzk, Av Bet Din Sokolov
Rabbi Menachem of Petrikov
Rabbi Mordechai Yosef Elazar Leiner from Radzin
Rabbi Shlomo Hanoch Hacohen Rabinowitz from
    Radomsk
Rabbi Natan David from Shidlowitz
On 8 Kislev . . . Warsaw

Translated by David Herman.

Abram Efros

1888-1954

Born in Moscow and educated at Moscow University's faculty of law, Abram Efros was a translator, poet, art historian, and critic. After 1917, he served on the commission for the protection of artistic and antique treasures in the Russian Soviet Republic, and on the boards of the Tretyakov Gallery, other art museums and installations, and the GOSET (Moscow State Jewish Theater). He edited art and literary journals and taught art and theater history, as well as museum studies, at universities in the Soviet Union. Efros translated the Song of Songs and other Hebrew biblical texts into Russian, as well as Petrarch, Dante, Michelangelo, and others. In the Stalinist purges of the late 1930s, Efros was arrested and exiled, and in the late 1940s he was ousted from his academic posts.

Lampa Aladdina
1918

His aged back bent under the burden of six decades, forever trying to crumple his weary countenance into furrows long since smoothed away, what possible kind of Aladdin is our old mutual acquaintance An-sky? And why do we of the Jewish artistic world, shallow-breathing folk who are permitted only just enough of our national reality to prevent us from stifling under the suffocating weight of what is termed "modern Jewish culture"—why do we, I ask, all of a sudden see Aladdin's lamp in the old man's grasp, and have such confident expectation that those wrinkled hands will reveal to us some sort of magic?

In the days of the early Renaissance, people in Italy used to walk on tiptoe, barely setting foot to ground, as

if afraid that by treading heavily, they might shatter the antique marble statues concealed in the earth beneath the narrow graveled streets of Verona and Padua, or the ploughlands of Campania and Tuscany. They knew that the soil of Italy was crammed with the products of a divine art, and that every builder excavating a foundation, every peasant digging a well, might at any moment strike against something white and clinking down below, and retrieve for them a damaged antique god. Ah! The joy of that encounter with great beauty, that which was lost, but is now found again.

So it is with us now. Something of that ancient fire touches us too. We are responding to Jewish folk art—to which An-sky is finally drawing widespread public attention with his truly historic collecting efforts—much as the vanguard of the *rinascimento* did to their statues. We are just as ardently impassioned and likewise strive to base our artistic activity on "beauty retrieved from the depths." In exactly the same way, we feel that what is created by the fledgling art of the Italian Renaissance, while unlike the beauty of the ancients, was wholly sustained by it. [. . .]

II

The "proud gaze of the gentile" will perceive and comprehend nothing in all this. Indeed how could it be otherwise? "Jewish artistic thought has encountered its own folk art and seeks to draw closer"—well, what of it? What is so novel or unusual about that? Put another way, why the noisy raptures—and public penitence—and bows to all four quarters?

The gentiles are right. There's nothing novel or unusual in it. It is a well-worn and familiar path. All these present-day cultures, which we extol and cluster round to this day have long since passed through this "neo-folk" stage in their art. They have already experienced that sudden revival through the powerful influence of grass-roots folk arts on the creative endeavours of the aesthetic pinnacles, the masters of palette and chisel. [. . .]

But we do not in fact dispute this. All that is the case. It's elementary. We are not suggesting that we have made some sort of revelation and we are not proposing to play an apostolic or, God forbid, messianic role. Oh, we know our place nowadays! Those times are gone when as the Chosen People, the elected tribe, the divine vanguard, we bore the revelation of the Lord-Yahweh to the peoples and the nations, spreading along all the meridians of the world. How should we describe what we have become since those days? We know, we know full well, and we nerve ourselves to speak out: we are the fashion-followers of world history. Jewry is always dressed in the latest style. Still, how could it be otherwise when it is always out visiting? A kind of millennium-long week-end in the world watering-place, with the thousand changes of attire that high society demands. In scientific language this attribute of ours is termed "national mimicry."

Verily, for those divine, apostolic wanderings so long ago we have paid a hundred times over: it is endlessly long since we were the leaders; but now we are certainly the led, preached at, dressed-up according to another's taste and at times, when feeling benevolent, voices praise us with cynical consistency: "I'd never have taken you for a Jew. Not a bit like, not a bit . . ." "Thank you," we reply, and surreptitiously wipe the tint of shame from our face and silently swallow our tears.

Is it clear now what it means for Jewish arts, neatly shaved and barbered, all of a sudden to discern beauty in ringlets and discover an aesthetic value in the lapser-dak [caftan]? Understood? Ah, dear gentiles: we are self-effacing, humbly self-effacing; we do not say: "We have seen a vision, follow after us, unheard-of beauty has been revealed unto us." We address one another only, and weep only before one another, and if we beat our chest publicly, that means publicly in the Jewish sense and does not concern you, because you are only *passers-by* skirting the square where we are repenting and going about our national business.

Truly, we lag behind and are the last to arrive at the aesthetic of folk art. It's also true that we feel considerable awkwardness in front of the assembled gentiles, for our popular-art enthusiasm has come very late, and in the world art market, apologetics on behalf of folk arts are obviously already becoming *démodé*. But therein lies the difference between what was and what is, between us as recent followers of fashion, tricked-out in the latest style, and us as present-day old clothes dealers clutching our rags lightly to our breasts, like that old lamp which seems like Aladdin's to us. In the guise of dandies, we are probably figures of fun in the eyes of the art world, with our parochial raptures, our jigging about almost like some pagan priest, in front of a popular print design or gingerbread decoration. However, we say that we respectfully hand back our admission ticket into good society, if keeping it means giving up our tears and raptures over the humble aesthetic,

a pinkas blossoming with patterns, or the astonishing swirling spiral of a tombstone; we say that our entire artistic future lies latent here; that we have been considered worthy to begin a new, unprecedented epoch in Jewish plastic arts, and that there is no price we would not pay, so long as we can cling on avidly, fiercely tenacious, to the world of national beauty that has been revealed to us. And if there is one thing more than another that we fear, it is that Jewish artistic thought, in its innocence, might, on hearing the inevitable street cry: "Who will exchange old lamps for new?" give up the precious old junk of Aladdin in exchange for some glittering fashionable utensil.

III

Either our national artistic renaissance will fail to take place at all, or it will flourish on the twin roots which underpin all contemporary world art—modernism and folk arts. The combination is astonishing and extraordinary in itself, but doubly so for Jewish art. The very latest, novel, forward-looking phrases and the most established, deeply-rooted tradition . . . Nor is this an idle whim of art history, nor, worse, some intricate paradox got up by art criticism. It is merely the abrupt manifestation of a link between art and reality that usually lies hidden. How many times has it been declared that art is the most sensitive barometer of the ills of the world; but let them say whether there has ever been a more graphic confirmation of that, positively eerie in its accuracy, than the present conjunction of the two most extreme artistic polarities of the day. The global crisis, the senseless cataclysm which is shaking the life of the world at the present time, cannot but see the simple reflection of what it has itself brought into being; for it is that crisis which has dislocated and shifted all the cultural strata so as to expose the most ancient layers of folk existence. Yet it is also the force which goes driving forwards, shaping the dynamic of history into completely novel "modernistic" "arch-left" nation-state and socio-economic alignments. [. . .]

Modernism and folk art! These two Janus faces summon every nation to a double and simultaneous task. The face of modernism is turned outwards, folk art—inwards. As they labour to pour the aesthetic programme of modernism into new artistic moulds, the futurists, cubists, abstractionists and . . . neo-classicists of all nationalities are working away world-wide at one *common* artistic task—like builders echoing the blows of hammer and spade in various parts of the edifice. Here artists, whatever their blood and mental attitude, coalesce, as it were, into one person. The community of their aims, methods, and results is stronger than the invention and efforts of each participating individual. The whole is greater than the sum of the parts.

But when each people returns home with the results of the day, and sets about its own private artistic activity, this levelling effect of world modernism becomes merely a pedestal and framework, and whatever springs upwards from it will start to blossom into strange complexities, impulses, even grimaces, with an inimitable combination of forms, through which sings the national blood and its artistic predilections. Thus folk art functions as the purest unadulterated crystallisation of national plasticity of forms, and becomes in our times the supreme regulator of artistic creation.

IV

We will not have to scurry around the world's art bazaars to lay in the necessary quota of modernism for *our* renaissance. Whatever else we lack, we have enough and to spare when it comes to that! Enough to splash about as we walk along. Our aesthetic "leftishness" is indisputable and ample. We have no need of An-sky's disciples here. We've been in the first ranks for ages. We can stand comparison with any one of our neighbours for "leftishness." Our own, Jewish part in the growth and spread of every extreme artistic "ism" has been enormous. "A-ooh!" we cry to all quarters—lo! the reply comes echoing back from brilliant names, familiar in every "salon," every studio and throughout the press. It becomes almost embarrassing to list them, vulgar and petty at any rate: it would not be seemly for us to rub in the celebrated roll-call of Jewish modern artists! [. . .]

No, there will be no shortcomings in this area. From paragraph to paragraph we will transfer all the discoveries of modernism to the assets of the approaching Renaissance—as well as a very experienced group of masters. The young generation of the start of the century has grown up by now; two more new generations have come to the fore—and everything remarkable in them, brimming over with talent and charged with power—everything has passed through the caustic fire of "left aesthetics," singed by those incessant explosions with which Paris has never wearied of shaking the artistic universe. The contemporary progressive artist can be recognized by one infallible indication—his pre-

dilection for *deforming* the objects being depicted. The artist of the future will *straighten* them up like the Lord God setting the fragmented world to rights in beauty and harmony. The proportion of analytics and synthetics, present-day and future masters, has been distributed in regular fashion throughout the Jewish art world. And that is the most consoling outcome one could wish for. We are not *freaks,* not outcasts from the world of contemporary art; we are equals among equals. And if so very many of us still wouldn't mind exchanging this modernistic abundance of ours for something a bit older and "steadier" then, naturally, this merely testifies to levity or a lack of comprehension when it comes to the contemporary historico-artistic process.

V

So we have an astonishing paradox, capable of troubling even us, accustomed as we are to the paradoxes of our existence, sometimes even glorying in them, since followers of fashion cannot help being snobs: Jewish *modernism* has created a *tradition* of its own, Jewish artistic *novelty* has established a solid continuity, Jewish *innovation* has taken on a kind of *aristocratic refinement,* and when we reflect upon this aristocratism of ours, we take it as our right and due and are practically ready to shout "About time, too!—it's half a century since the Israels and Pisarro [painters Jozef Israëls and Camille Pissarro] took upon Jewish shoulders the first cruel burden of the first cruel days of impressionism . . ."

"About time!" Half a century of tradition . . . There's wealth in the midst of poverty for you! There is a *tradition* of modernism but no tradition of folk art—we pride ourselves on five decades of work in the new art and ignore the vast disgrace of our age-old aloof indifference to the roots of folk creativity; we are bearing whole handfuls of the living seeds of modernism into the future, and as a bonus, a few archival pages of "artistic objects relating to the Jewish way of life" from such and such a province. And even today when we are contrite, bow down in prayer and walk about in noisy raptures, I am still not convinced, not convinced at all, that we shall reach the *living thread* of our folk art until we hand it over to the gate-keepers of the Renaissance and happily receive the right to utter "Boruch Schepitrani" [Barukh she-pitarani]—otherwise we shall hand over nothing besides intellectual, critico-aesthetic, museobookish admiration of it all. Because the point is not by any means that formerly the *mizrachim* and *pinkassim* were futile things to us and are now our great pride and joy. That's nothing—ah, how little that matters! If Jewry wishes to live an artistic existence and if it wishes to take care of its artistic future, then that inevitably predicates a *thorough-going* and *effective* bond with folk arts. Let it be stated plainly: at the present time it presupposes the *hegemony* of folk art, whatever the field of artistic endeavour; no picking and choosing, no laying down conditions, no accepting "insofar as it is possible." It's a simple matter, like being a pupil under a good teacher, of submitting to the task and carrying it out to the end. [...]

VII

[...] In probing the secret depths of folk art, we are compelled to extract from its agglomeration of elements and characteristics, the common structure of the folk aesthetic of forms and learn the *laws* governing Jewish line, colour, plane and space. And above all—carry out a process of selection, and cleanse the true folk material of alien accretions and borrowed embellishment.

I don't know, when all comes to all, whether we understand clearly, clearly enough, the sort of fire we are playing with. We talk lightly about *influences and borrowings* because we think that's the thing to do. We follow the rest in this. But we have to take full account of the powerful absorbent and imitative capacity of Jewry in order to understand how scrupulous and consistent must be our labour of purification. Of course, every folk art absorbs alien influences; however, the fact that Jewry has come to be clamped with the steel bonds of all the artistic influences of every nationality among whom it dwelt, is no coincidence. I would like Jewish artists to have seen the curiosity and bewilderment with which Russian art scholars perused An-sky's pages. It was in the highest degree instructive! "The eclecticism of it ... and yet it's Jewish." That summed up their opinion. Precisely: eclecticism, but still—Jewish. Are we to disagree? Even a kind of super-eclecticism: Russia, Galicia, Rumania, Poland, here Germany, there Italy, and, still further, the Muslim East and the ancient East—a dog's breakfast with every spice and seasoning.

But that's exactly the point—that the whole, here as always, is greater than the mere sum of the parts; putting all the component elements together, our folk art derives not only their sum but also a certain accumulated value. That is what converts *quantity* into *quality*. It is *that* which contains the secret and ultimate mean-

ing of our folk aesthetic. It creates that visual impact which no amount of ethnic analysis or resolution into elements can destroy. The secret of national artistic genius, it is not too much to say, lies in the *proportion* of the blending, the *methods* of combining, the *degree* of re-shaping of the identical elements they all hold in common. How otherwise can we differentiate for example the Russian iconostasis and the Byzantine, French and German Gothic, Japanese and Chinese painting, and so on and so forth? To understand the Jewishness in folk art is to comprehend the laws of its originality in *this* very area. *It is in this direction* that our conjectures and researches should be directed. And our present ecstasy, our present hope, the joy of recognition now overwhelming us—should be at *this* and this only, not the scrappy and garish patchwork of alien elements which now dazzles us.

Who knows, perhaps as a result of our long and meticulous labours over folk art, it will turn out that the pure essence of Jewishness will be found to be the tiniest of drops. Very well: the struggle for our artistic Renaissance will turn into a struggle for that droplet—for that and nothing more. In that case it will be our all in all. Our fanaticism, our pertinacity and perception, will be expended on discerning and extracting *that* out of the broad alien ocean. How many generations it will require I do not know—perhaps many, or perhaps we alone, the first, the pioneers, may suffice. Well, what difference does it make: one way or another, the Jewish droplet will be obtained.

And then the printing-press of the future will set its levers in motion: the first off-print—our "modernism," our leftishness, youth; the second—our "populism," our tradition, old age. But one scale will lie over the other and the colours will merge: before Jewry will stand forth her *Art*.

Translated by Ludmila Lezhneva and Alan Myers.

Other works by Efros: *Ėroticheskiye sonety* (1922); *Portret Natana Altmana* (1922); *Profili* (1930); *Risunki poeta* (1933); *Avtoportrety Pushkina* (1945).

Samuel Hugo Bergmann

1883–1975

A member of the Prague circle of German Jewish intellectuals before World War I, Samuel Hugo Bergmann was strongly influenced by Martin Buber's spiritual

Zionism and neoromantic religious philosophy. He settled in Jerusalem in 1920, where he served first as director of the National and University Library and later as professor of philosophy and rector at the Hebrew University. In 1925 he founded, together with Buber, Brit Shalom, a group that advocated the creation of a binational state in the Land of Israel.

Yavne and Jerusalem
1919

I. True Autonomy

We resist the penetration of capitalism and mercantilism into Palestine. How can we at this moment in history reconcile that with our conscience? Dare we burden this Zionist undertaking in addition to its thousand difficulties with the additional load of embodying a new economic order? And even if we dared—is the thing possible? Can we found a non-capitalistic island in the circumambient capitalistic sea? Will not the waves overwhelm us? Capitalism is still the law of the greater part of the economic system. How then shall we escape obedience to that law? It will be urged, then, that all anti-capitalistic talking and planning on our part is romanticism and utopianism. Worse still, it will be judged to be treachery against our leaders and those who are realizing our dream of Zion and a stab in their back.

I can hear the endless critical variations upon this theme. The so-called wholesome common sense of the majority will be aroused against us. We shall not yield to it. For we do not acknowledge any economic order to be necessary. Our law is that of our will. At this time when we see by the example of Zionism what miracles can be wrought by the will of a people, shall we let *them* lead us who do not yet see that every Utopia of yesterday *may* be the reality of tomorrow? Such is our historic fate that it can be tested only by a great act of willing. Gradually the societies to combat anti-Semitism became objects of ridicule. The idea of the Jewish state, on the contrary, became a practical political matter. Similarly now and here: The notion of realizing the Zionist hope through a merely capitalistic colonization is sure to fail. The problem will be solved by an economic attitude that is new and unheard-of in the Western World.

The practical people will protest in vain. Zionism is not a merely practical matter and is not to be justified on merely economic grounds. From a capitalistic point of view the Arab furnishes cheaper labor than the Jew and capitalistic industrialization will attract quite other elements than ourselves. Even before the war Christian Arabs began to come pouring in from Syria. If this kind of capitalism opens the land it will at the same time be closed to us.

And what attraction could a Westernized Palestine exert upon the Jews? . . . Only if Palestine offers great tasks will it attract the best among us. Mere capitalistic industry and trade will draw hungry people; the bearers of our ideal will remain estranged and cold. But let us imagine a Palestine in which a serious attempt is made to place human society upon a new foundation; let us imagine that Judaism, the ideas of which have hitherto always been confined to the cloudy realm of theoretical discussion, is now actually to be realized and that we are to make a truly Jewish land of Palestine! That is at least to dream greatly. Only so could the land once more become a holy land and the focus of our life.

Let it be admitted at once that we do not dream of returning to a pre-capitalistic economy. We are not so foolish as to resist the machine. Wherever capitalistic methods enable us to save on man-power, we shall use them. We are far removed from any reactionary romanticism. We are practical men in a world reality; only our reality is not that of today but that of tomorrow.

Precisely this sober facing of reality involves one demand: Palestine must become economically independent. We do not want to turn Palestine into an "economic bridge"; we must, above all things, be spared the quarrels of the capitalistic world and its conflicts over strategic security, foreign markets and trade routes. We desire to live unto ourselves and in peace, and by so doing we hope to make a modest contribution toward the liberation of all mankind from the curse of these conflicts. We must give the outer world as little opportunity as possible to mingle in our affairs and to assimilate our spirit to that of the West of this age. . . .

Hence our aims: economic independence and the founding of our entire economic structure upon an agricultural basis. By the most intensive cultivation a maximum must be wrung for our soil. This intensive culture is the central problem of our national existence. At the very beginning of our colonization Achad Ha'am criticized the cultivation of the vine where grain could be planted, since the exportation of wine would make us dependent upon foreign economic problems. The goal of our peasantry must be the product of the soil itself and not the money that can be obtained for it in foreign markets.

Hence what we resist is not capitalistic technique; it is the capitalistic spirit. Factories and machines do not constitute capitalism. It is the spirit that animates both industrialist and operative and in which the inhabitant of the country expects to enjoy the products of his work. For the operative thinks and feels capitalistically no less than the owner, when he has no inner relationship to his work, when it is indifferent to him whether he produces agricultural machinery on the one hand or wasteful trash or even armaments on the other; when, above all, he cultivates a class egoism, which would sacrifice the agriculture of his own country merely that he may buy cheaper bread baked of foreign wheat. In brief, capitalism not only alienates man from his work, but estranges man from his brother and substitutes for an unselfishly inspired folk-group the stark egoism of economic classes. . . . The conquest of capitalism will be achieved through the development of a new human type—a type that is firstly modest in its material demands, secondly, is consciously an organic part of its folk-group and which, finally, regards its own labor as a part of the creativity of its understanding that this group must leisure to enjoy the fruits of its total creativity. It is only an educational process which can produce this new human type.

Now this educational process is none other than that which Zionism desires to apply to the entire Jewish people. Palestinian colonization is not the innermost aim of Zionism. I am almost tempted to call it a pretext. The aim is the creation of a new type of Jew. In place of the Jew who is a victim of the merely material and who worships lifeless things a Jew is to appear whose life is rooted in the spirit, who is animated by love and sacrifice.

Our congresses and offices and committees must clarify their consciousness of the fact that there exists a specifically Zionist economic attitude. We are not to forget that in Hebrew there is only one word—*Avodah*—for work and worship. Our workers will, I hope, preserve the feelings for the difference between significant and meaningless work. . . . I nurse the hope that our workers will be concerned over other and deeper relationships in life. Those marvellous human beings who, even before the war, were agricultural labourers in Palestine have shown that Jewish workers can be prepared to risk their entire being for the creation of a new kind of human society. Our workers should be inspired by an ideology that will render them independent of capitalism. They will refuse to enter that mad witches' dance of capitalism whereby useless things are produced for which thereupon, through fashion and advertising, an artificial and wasteful demand is created, so that in the end great masses of people employ each other without any resultant enjoyment or true profit. . . . It is my hope that our workers will liberate themselves from the bonds of that insane fatalism which makes of men the mere objects of an economic order and will come to see that any economic order is the result of an active human will.

If such an economic ideology prevails it will save us from the class struggle which might so easily tear our young commonwealth asunder. . . . The mutual distrust which makes each man regard the other as his natural enemy is a fundamental characteristic of capitalism. It is only with the elimination of the capitalistic attitude that this distrust can be cleansed out of the soul and that our people can be united by the solidarity of their love for land and folk. There will remain conflicts among the classes, but not that hostility which grows out of regarding economic classes as fixed and fatal. Our millennial sufferings have forged us into one; a spirit of solidarity has become almost innate; it will be our task to transform this feeling from a mere passive "sticking-together" into a vital, ethical impulse toward mutual trust and coöperation. Life upon the soil of the homeland will make our people trustful and faithful. Let us be on our guard, therefore, against permitting the idea of the agricultural colonization of Palestine to be darkened by the hope of rapid conquest through industry and trade. Exaggerated urbanism would tend to emphasize all the unpleasant Jewish traits once more. . . .

Now when we say that we must be on our guard against excessive urban development and must not through the mere ambition for numbers risk a wound to the spirit of our community, we receive this customary answer: "Very well. But it is a political necessity that we shall constitute as soon as possible a majority of the population." There are those of us who regard this policy as wholly evil. We do not desire to enter the land as rulers. Our claim is not derived from numbers, but from the eternal yearning of our people for Palestine. Before the Areopagus of the nations the great Zionist cry of Yehuda Halevi constitutes a stronger right and claim than a few thousand more or less in Palestine on any given date. It is most true that we desire to animate the land with our very souls and to become its decisive spiritual power and representative. But that is not a quantitative question. If by an over-rapid colonization we drag the misery of European masses into Palestine; if, by exploiting the touristic possibilities of the country, we enter it as chafferers and advertisers and perhaps as chiefs and desecrate our holy places for tourists, we may within a brief period constitute a majority of the population, but Palestine will be none the less a wholly un-Jewish land and the smallest Chasidic *Klaus* in the remotest Polish village will be the depository of more true Judaism than all the so-called national institutions. . . . To all those finally who, dazzled by the momentary political constellation, are in mere haste and would deny the Zionistic spirit of our resettlement even for a moment we must say in all seriousness; for two thousand years the Jewish people has sustained its very life by the hope of some day leading a better, worthier, and purer life in Palestine. So long as we had not Palestine we were in the position of the sinner who can still hope and who can endure his degraded life because he can still say, "Tomorrow I shall lead a new life or day after tomorrow." Thus did we live in hope and thus were we able to bear the evil and the oppression and the corruption of exile. But the realization of our hope is also its end and Zionism will be either the triumph or the downfall of the Jewish people.

III. Pesach and the People of This Time

Throughout history there are certain eternal themes or ideas which always return or, rather, are reconquered in an ever-renewed conflict by successive generations. Wherever men strive whole-heartedly after such ideas the process of history liberates itself from space and time and becomes the permanent symbol of humanity. Such a theme is presented by Pesach, the feast of freedom.

But even as every age has its own Torah—a legend tells us that Moses heard Rabbi Akiba interpret his own teaching and could not understand the interpretation—so likewise every generation of Jews has its own *Hagadah*. The eternal theme of liberation appears to each age in a new light. It is a great word that has been handed down to us: each generation must feel as though itself had been brought forth out of Egypt. And to each generation the exodus symbolizes a different aspect. To one the symbol of its being may be the sudden miracle, to another the destruction of the enemy, to a third the

fortitude of the enslaved descendants of Jacob. What does the exodus mean to us?

In order to obtain a clear answer we must place Zionism where it belongs—within the total intellectual movement of this age. It is only one of the many waves that beat today against the shore of life. If anyone desires to grasp the movement which we Jews call Zionism in its universal significance, it would be just to define it as a striving for human renewal according to the spirit. When we have said that, we have sufficiently characterized the actual epoch in which we live and against which we fight—the epoch of the denial of the spirit, of materialism in its broadest sense.

There is a deeply moving passage in the Zohar in which it is said of the worshippers of the golden calf, that their sin consisted in substituting for the eternally hidden and eternally to be sought subject of the universe a mere visible and tangible object, an empirical "these" when they cried: "these be thy gods, O Israel!"

An exclusive faith in the sensuously tangible is the essential mark of our age. It reveals itself in a thousand forms. Let us illustrate the materialism of our age at the point which concerns us here: its relation to human action. For Pesach is the feast of the liberating deed.

Have you ever seen a billiard ball that rolls of itself? No, you must admit that the cue must strike it before it rolls. Hence—thus reasons the materialism of our time to which men are like billiard balls—hence it is not possible that man can determine his action from within and all that is called self-determination, freedom of action, is in truth nothing but a compulsion from without. It is something that happens to us. We do not act; we are acted upon. . . .

In brief, our time is obsequious before the successful deed but does not understand the deed itself. Where within our civilization there seems to be the strongest will toward rebuilding and conversion, namely in the labor movements, precisely there the theoretical folly of our time has substituted blind fatality for the human will. It is not the will of man that will bring about a better age; it is the "necessary action of economic forces"; it all works by itself. To the man of our time everything happens of and by itself. Just as the doctrine of evolution, that *deus ex machina* of all our thinking, succeeded all by itself in turning an ape into a man, so it will continue to take care of us. One fine day we shall awaken in Paradise.

That is, of course, an easy way. But our time has elevated the saving of time and trouble almost to the dignity of a moral law. The command to waste no energy has become a universal principle. Whoever still doubts that the so-called scientific period has been a wretched one for human beings as such has but to remember that at the beginning of the nineteenth century we had Kant's categorical imperative and that today we have the principle of the saving of energy even when it comes to thinking . . . I do not deny that the demand for an economy of energy can achieve much that is useful. Organizations are useful and so are charts and graphs and card-catalogues. But do you not see that all your card-catalogue wisdom will be self-annihilating? All that you register and prepare scientifically is in the end only human action. But action will cease if you choose the line of least resistance as your moral law. The fact that the science of our time can give the individual so pitifully little arises from its wrong relation to action. The cause is often sought for in overspecialization. But why have these manifold activities no unity? Because the spirit has been expelled. For all oneness has its source in the subject, call it reason, call it *logos*, call it what you will. But science has reached the point of seeing only objects in the world. It takes the world "as given." Scientists once knew that science is and can be nothing else than the spirit of man coming into a full consciousness of itself or, perhaps, the disengaging and redemption of mind from the world. Science once knew that. It has been forgotten. Do you want a crass example? Take the various phases of experimental psychology. It seeks to reduce the entire human spirit to sensation. Why? That has deeper roots than the psychologists themselves know. Because they want to turn the human soul itself into a thing, an object and so they select sensation as being the most object-like human characteristic, most accessible and tangible and—least experienced. And these are your Gods!

What has all this to do with Pesach and with Zionism? A great deal! A recent translator of the Upanishads has appealed to a light from the East against the intellectual distraction of our time. Now we who are people of this time which we must combat—we too must turn for light to the East, to our light from our East if we are to sustain ourselves against the allurements and the misguidedness of this present. And it is very alluring, for what is more comfortable than this life with its morality of intellectual sloth and irresponsibility?

Against this sodden comfort we appeal to our Judaism which is a will toward action. At the origin of our history we have placed a deed of liberation, even as at the origin of human history we have placed the free decision and choice between good and evil. Read once more the history of Moses and the people with its endless conflicts between the leader and the mass, and you will say: here is our conflict and our fight against sloth and self-sufficiency. There were the comfortable ones who infinitely preferred the making of bricks and the mixing of mortar, the sure trough of the slave to the dangerous and uncertain path of freedom. And there was Moses who brought to them the gospel of freedom and of action. In the first revelation that came to him the divine made itself known to him as an "I am." God is an "I," and man who is His image, who is to be like Him and to be holy must awaken the "I" within himself. And in the first commandment of the Decalogue God again reveals Himself as He who has been the liberator from the house of bondage. We must be very careful not to conceive of this liberation superficially. It is a question of something far beyond a political liberation; it concerns the struggle of action against rigid being and mere happening; it concerns the contradiction between willing and drifting, between decision and sloth, between daring and static cowardice. The conflict between Moses and the people is the conflict between spirit and matter.

Once more we stand within this conflict. Once more we must risk our lives in order to win them. And we are slaves even as we were in Egypt. Slaves of empirical, of compromise, of unveracity—men of this time. Will we stand the test that we must stand? Let us not forget that a good part of the mechanization of our life has been the work of Jews. The Jews by abandoning themselves, by shifting their centre of equilibrium to the world without, degraded themselves to billiard balls of which the fate is the cue's thrust. And after having depersonalized themselves as a people they used their Jewish energy to cooperate in making an alienation from the spirit the regnant view of life.

It is for this reason that Zionism—the struggle of those capable of spiritual decision against the slothful and the drifters—is an undertaking so eminently ethical in character. If it were possible to liberate the Jews from the cage of this period and teach them once more to bear responsibility and to act according to their inner monitions, then, I have faith to believe, the curse of this time will be taken from us.

Like all our fellow-men we are caught in a web of conditions and of opportunisms. Let us resist them and demand once more an unconditioned and a liberating deed by which we can be freed from the fetters of time and circumstance. . . .

Judaism is the will toward ethical action. Zionism is the form of Judaism which can save the Jews of this age.

Translated by Ludwig Lewisohn.

Other works by Bergmann: *Faith and Reason: An Introduction to Modern Jewish Thought* (1963); *The Philosophy of Solomon Maimon* (1967).

Jacob Glatstein, A. Leyeles, and N. Minkov

Glatstein, 1896–1971
The modernist Yiddish poet Jacob Glatstein was born in Lublin, Poland; in 1914, he moved to New York City, where he lived for the rest of his life. He was a regular contributor to the city's Yiddish dailies. He was among the founders of the Inzikhist (Introspectivist) movement in Yiddish poetry, which rejected metered verse and artificial lyricism and privileged the recording of inner emotional states. His own poetry was playful and inventive in form and made much of the sound of words. He also published two autobiographical volumes describing a trip to Poland in 1934 to visit his mother, in which he mixed memories of his childhood with accounts of contemporary Polish Jewish life.

Leyeles, 1889–1966
A. Leyeles was the pen name of the American Yiddish poet Aron Glanz. Leyeles was born and raised in Poland, where he received a modern Hebrew education. In 1905, he went to London and, in 1909, to New York. He worked in Yiddish education and, from 1914, was on the staff of the Yiddish daily *Der tog*. In 1919, he was one of the founders of the Introspectivist movement in Yiddish poetry, which extended and accentuated the aestheticism of the modernist group Di Yunge. Leyeles experimented with forms that were novel in Yiddish poetry and frequently did battle with critics who demanded more politically engaged, socially relevant verse.

Minkov, 1893–1958
The Yiddish literary critic and poet Nokhum Borukh Minkov was born and raised in Poland, where he spoke Russian and Polish at home and at school. He did not immerse himself in the Yiddish language until after he moved in his twenties to the United States and began moving in New York Yiddish literary circles. He was one of the founders of the Introspectivist movement in Yiddish poetry.

Introspectivism
1919

1

With this collection, we intend to launch a particular trend in Yiddish poetry which has recently emerged in the works of a group of Yiddish poets. We have chosen to call it the *Introspective Movement,* a name that indicates a whole range of individual character and nuance.

We know that introspective poems as such are nothing new. In all ages, poets have occasionally written introspectively; that is, they looked *into themselves* and created poetry drawn from their own soul and from the world as reflected in it. There are introspective poems in modern Yiddish poetry as well, even though the poets did not use this term.

The difference, however, between us and those other poets, both Yiddish and non-Yiddish, ancient and modern, is that we are dedicated to deepening, developing, and expanding the introspective method.

The world exists and we are part of it. But for us, the world exists only as it is mirrored in us, as it touches *us.* The world is a nonexistent category, a lie, if it is not related to us. It becomes an actuality only *in* and *through* us.

This general philosophical principle is the foundation of our trend. We will try to develop it in the language of poetry.

Poetry is not only feeling and perception but also, and perhaps primarily, the art of expressing feelings and perceptions adequately. It is not enough to say that all phenomena exist to the extent that they enter into an organic relation with us. The poet's major concern is to express this organic relation in an introspective and fully individual manner.

In an introspective manner means that the poet must really listen to his inner voice, observe his internal panorama—kaleidoscopic, contradictory, unclear or confused as it may be. From these sources, he must create poetry which is the result of both the fusion of the poet's soul with the phenomenon he expresses and the individual image, or cluster of images, that he sees *within himself* at that moment.

What does take place in the poet's psyche under the impression or impact of any phenomenon?

In the language of our local poets, of the "Young Generation" (*Di Yunge*), this creates a *mood*. According to them, it is the poet's task to express or convey this mood. How? In a concentrated and well-rounded form. Concentration and well-roundedness are seen as the necessary conditions, or presuppositions, that allow the poet's mood to attain universal or, in more traditional terms, *eternal*, value.

But this method, though sufficient to create poetic vignettes or artful arabesques, is essentially neither sufficient nor true. From our point of view, this method is a *lie*.

Why?

Because the mood and the poem that emerge from this conception and this method must inevitably result in something cut-off, isolated, something which does not really correspond to life and truth.

At best, such poems are embellishments and ornaments. At worst, they ring false, because the impression or the impact of any phenomenon on the poet's soul does not result in an isolated, polished, well-rounded, and concentrated mood. What emerges is more complex, intertwined with a whole galaxy of other "moods," of other feelings and perceptions. In the final analysis, concentration and well-roundedness of poetry symbolize the lie, the awesome contradiction between literature and life, between all of art and life.

We Introspectivists want first of all to present life—the true, the sincere, and the precise—as it is mirrored in *ourselves*, as it merges with us.

The human psyche is an awesome labyrinth. Thousands of beings dwell there. The inhabitants are the various facets of the individual's present self on the one hand and fragments of his inherited self on the other. If we believe that every individual has already lived somewhere in one incarnation or another—and this belief is often vividly sensed by each of us—then the number of inhabitants in the labyrinth of the human psyche is even higher.

This is the real *life* of a human being. In our age of the big metropolis and enormous variety in all domains, this life becomes a thousandfold more complicated and entangled. We Introspectivists feel the need to convey and express it.

In what form and shape does this complexity of moods appear?

In the shape of association and suggestion. For us, these two elements are also the most important methods of poetic expression.

Of course, poets of all times have used suggestion and association. The pre-Raphaelite Rossetti and the later Swinburne often used these elements in their work. Yet we want to make association and suggestion the poet's major tools because it seems to us that they are best suited to express the complex feelings and perceptions of a contemporary person.

So much about the introspective method. As for *individual* manner, it is perhaps even more important.

Because we perceive the world egocentrically and because we think that this is the most natural and therefore *the truest and most human* mode of perception, we think that the poem of every poet must first of all be *his own* poem. In other words, the poet must in every case give us what he himself sees and as he sees it.

Essentially, this should be self-evident as a prerequisite for any poetry. It should be but is not.

Indeed, most poems, not just Yiddish ones but the majority of non-Yiddish ones as well, lack the full individuality of the poet and hence of the poem, too. In most poems, the poet does not delve deeply enough to see what appears in his own psyche. Perhaps the fault lies with language, which generally works in our lives as a misleading and deceiving category. Be that as it may, we think that, in the great majority of all poetry, the poet is not sufficiently individual. He employs too many stock images and ready-made materials. When the poet, or any person, looks at a sunset, he may see the strangest things which, ostensibly, have perhaps no relation to the sunset. The image reflected in his psyche is rather a series of far-reaching associations moving away from what his eye sees, a chain of suggestions evoked by the sunset. *This*, the series of associations and the chain of suggestions, constitutes *truth*, is life, much as an illusion is often more real than the cluster of external appearances we call life. Most poets, however, will not even focus on what occurs inside themselves while they are watching a sunset but will paint it, search for colors, describe the details, etc. If, in addition, they are subjectively attuned, they will perhaps dip their brush into a drop of subjectivity, into a patch of color of their selves, make a comparison with their own lives, express some wisdom about life in general, and the poem is done.

For us, such a poem is not true, is a cliché. We insist that the poet should give us the authentic image that he sees in himself and give it in such a form as only he and no one else can see it.

If such a poem then becomes grist for the mill of Freudian theory, if it provides traces of something morbid or sick in the poet, we do not mind. Art is ultimately redemption, even if it is an illusory redemption or a redemption *through* illusion. And no redemption is possible in any other way but through oneself, through an internal personal concentration. Only a truly individual poem can be a means of self-redemption.

2

Both the introspectivity of a poem and its individuality must use suggestion and association in order to reach full expression. Now, the individuality of the poem has a lot to do with what is generally known as *form*.

In fact, form and content are the same. A poem that can be rewritten in another form is neither a poem nor poetry. They cannot be separated from one another. To speak of form and content separately is to succumb to the influence of a linguistic fallacy. And if we speak of form as a separate concept, it is merely for the sake of convenience, as is the case with many other linguistic fallacies.

The generally known aspect of form is *rhythm*. Every poem must have rhythm. Rhythm is the mystery of life; art which is no more than an expression of life obviously must also have rhythm. But what kind of rhythm must a poem have?

There is only one answer: it must have the only possible and the only imaginable rhythm. Each poem must have its *individual rhythm*. By this we mean that the rhythm of the poem must fit entirely this particular poem. One poem cannot have the same rhythm as any other poem. Every poem is, in fact, unique.

And if we see, in certain poets, how the most divergent poems are similar in their rhythm, this in itself is the best sign of their lack of productivity and creativity, and also of their lack of genuine sincerity.

We cannot understand how it is possible for a real poet to write one poem about the subway, another about the sand at the seashore in summer, and a third about his love for a girl—all in the same rhythm, in the same "beat." Two of the three poems are certainly false. But, more certainly, all three are false, because if a poet can write three poems in the same rhythm, this is proof in itself that he does not listen to the music in his own soul, that he does not see anything or hear anything with his own eyes and ears.

We demand individual rhythm because only thus can the truth that we seek and want to express be revealed.

This leads us to the question which has recently stirred the consciousness of poets in all languages and not least that of Yiddish poets, the question of *free verse*.

Free verse is not imperative for introspective poets. It is possible to have introspective poems in regular meter. Though regular meter may often appear as a hindrance, a straitjacket, free verse in itself is not enough. We Introspectivists believe that free verse is best suited to the individuality of the rhythm and of the poem as a whole; and for *that* rather than for any other reason, we prefer it to other verse forms.

Hence it is the greatest mistake, even ignorance, to claim (as many do) that it is easier to write free verse than to write in measured meters. If comparison here makes sense at all, the opposite is true. It is easier to write in regular and conventional meters because, after some experience, one acquires the knack and the poem "writes itself." But free verse, intended primarily for individual rhythm, demands an intense effort, a genuine sounding of the inner depths. Therefore free verse more easily betrays the non-poet, revealing the internal vacuum, if that is what is at stake.

When non-poets take on free verse, their situation is no easier than when they wrote iambs, trochees, or anapests. On the contrary, while in the latter case they can perhaps produce a certain musicality and thus create the impression that they are writing poetry, in the former case they are unproductive from the first or second moment, and their failure is exposed.

Only for the real poet is free verse a new, powerful means of expression, a new, wide world full of unexplored territories. For the non-poet, however, free verse is nothing but a mousetrap into which he falls in his first or second line. Let the non-poets beware of it!

We emphasize again that we are not against regular meters as such. Every true poet, Introspectivist or not, may sometimes feel that only in a regular rhythm, in a certain "canonical" meter, can he create a particular poem. It is more correct to say (for poets, it is a truism) that, inside every poet, including Introspectivists, *a certain poem will often write itself* in a regular meter. Then he does not fight it. Then he understands that it had to be like this, that in *this* case, this is the truth, this the individual rhythm.

If we prefer free verse, it is only for that reason. In general, we think that regular meter, the rhythm of frequently repeated beats, adapted itself perhaps to an earlier kind of life before the rise of the big city with its machines, its turmoil, and its accelerated, irregular tempo. That life was quiet and flowed tranquilly—in a regular rhythm, in fact—in beats repeated in short, frequent intervals.

Just as contemporary life created new clothing, new dwellings, new color combinations, and new sound combinations, so one needs to create a new art and new and different rhythms. We believe that free verse is best suited for the creation of such new rhythms. It is like fine, yielding plaster in which the inner image of the poet can find its most precise and fullest realization.

For the same reason, we are not against rhyme. Rhyme has its own charm and value. This is natural. The spirit of creative poets has used it for thousands of years as one of its poetic devices. This in itself is proof enough of its value. We say merely that rhyme is *not* a must. It often sounds forced or leads us on like a delusive, fleeting light. In such cases, rhyme is harmful and best avoided. Rhyme is good only when it is well-placed, when it is woven naturally into the verse. It is unnecessary to seek it, to make an effort to have rhyme at any cost, especially in our time when there is no need to learn poems by heart, when traveling poets do not have to recite their poems to amuse an ignorant or unpoetic audience.

Whenever a poet does feel the call of a wandering troubadour to recite his poems for a more primitive audience, as in the case of the American poet, Vachel Lindsay, the rhyme is well-placed and is good.

As with regular and irregular rhythm, many tend to assume mistakenly that writing without rhyme is easier than with rhyme. This is false. One can easily learn to make rhymes. And while one can sometimes cover with rhyme a trivial mood, which thus acquires the pretension to poetry, such a camouflage has no place in a rhymeless poem. There, one *must* be a genuine poet and a genuine creator. If not, the rhymeless poem will betray it much faster and easier than a rhymed one will.

The music of a poem—no doubt a desideratum—does not depend on rhyme. Rhyme is merely one element of its music, and the least important one at that. The music of a poem must also be purely individual and can be attained without rhymes, which necessarily produce a certain stereotype: after all, rhymes are limited in quantity and quality.

The *individual* sound combination is really necessary; indeed, because of our Introspectivism, we believe it to be unusually important. Not only do we not deny this element in poetry but we try to give it a new impetus, precisely through the individuality of the poem.

The musical and sound aspect of the Yiddish language has been generally neglected by most of our poets. Alliteration as a poetic device has remained almost untouched, although it is strongly represented in our language. As far as we can, we will try to remedy this neglect.

Individuality is everything and introspection is everything—this is what we seek, this is what we want to achieve.

When a certain phenomenon appears to a poet in the shape of colors; when an association carries him away to the shores of the Ganges or to Japan; when a suggestion whispers to him of something nebulous, something lurking in a fragment of his previous incarnation or of his hereditary self—all these are the roads and the labyrinths of his psyche. He must tread them because they are *he*, and only through the authentic, inner, true, *introspective* "I" lies the path that leads to creation and redemption.

3

Once this is accepted, it is self-evident that everything is an object for poetry, that for the poet there is no ugly or beautiful, no good or bad, no high or low. Everything is of equal value for the poet if it appears *inside* him, and everything is simply a stage to his internal redemption.

For us, then, the senseless and unproductive question of whether a poet "should" write on national or social topics or merely on personal ones does not arise. For us, everything is "personal." Wars and revolutions, Jewish pogroms and the workers' movement, Protestantism and Buddha, the Yiddish school and the Cross, the mayoral elections and a ban on our language—all these may concern us or not, just as a blond woman and our own unrest may or may not concern us. If it does concern us, we write poetry; if it does not, we keep quiet. In either case, we write about ourselves because all these exist only insofar as they are in us, insofar as they are perceived *introspectively*.

For the same reason, we do not recognize the difference between "poetry of the heart" and "poetry of the head," two meaningless phrases that belong to the same category of linguistic fallacies mentioned above. If the first phrase implies unconscious creativity and the second *conscious creativity*, then we say that neither we nor anybody else knows the boundary between conscious and unconscious. Certain aspects of the creative process are always conscious and cannot be otherwise. There is no tragedy in that. The modern poet is not, cannot, and should not be that naive stargazer who knows nothing but his little song, who understands nothing that goes on in the world, who has no attitude to life, its problems and events, who cannot even write a line about anything but his little mood, tapped out in iambs and trochees. The contemporary poet is a human being like other human beings and must be an intelligent, conscious person. As a poet, this is what is required of him: to see and feel, know and comprehend, and to see with his own eyes and be capable of expressing the seen, felt, and understood in his own internally true, introspectively sincere manner.

If conscious poetry means the expression of underlying thought in poetry, we see nothing wrong in that, either. A poet need not and must not be spiritually mute. A poet's *thought* is not a drawback but a great advantage. As a poet, as an artist, he must only be capable of expressing his thought in a proper form, of creating from it a work of art. And this depends on just one condition: that the thought should be his own, that it should be the true result of the fusion of his soul and life; and that he should express it in that form, in those very images, in the same true colors and tones as they take shape inside him, as they emerge and permeate him in the labyrinth of his soul. There is no boundary between "feeling" and "thought" in contemporary man or in the contemporary poet. Both are expressions of the same "I"; they are so closely intertwined that it is absurd to wish to separate them.

We make no distinction between intellectual poetry and poetry of feeling. We know of only one distinction: that between authenticity and falsehood, between true individuality and cliché. In the first case, poetry is born; in the second—"mood-laden" as it may be—merely licorice, vignettes, and false tones.

Our relationship to "Jewishness," too, becomes obvious from our general poetical credo.

We are "Jewish poets" simply because we are Jews and write in Yiddish. No matter what a Yiddish poet writes in Yiddish, it is ipso facto Jewish. One does not need any particular "Jewish themes." A Jew will write about an Indian fertility temple and Japanese Shinto shrines as a Jew. A Jewish poet will be Jewish when he writes poetry about "vive la France," about the Golden Calf, about gratitude to a Christian woman for a kind word, about roses that turn black, about a courier of an old prince, or about the calm that comes only with sleep. It is not the poet's task to seek and show his Jewishness. Whoever is interested in this endeavor is welcome to it, and whoever looks for Jewishness in Yiddish poets will find it.

In two things we are explicitly Jewish, through and through: in our relationship to the Yiddish language in general, and to Yiddish as a poetic instrument.

We believe in Yiddish. We love Yiddish. We do not hesitate to say that he who has a negative relation to the Yiddish language, or who merely looks down on it, cannot be a Yiddish poet. He who mocks Yiddish, who complains that Yiddish is a poor and shabby language, he who is merely indifferent to Yiddish, does not belong to the high category of Yiddish poets. To be a Yiddish poet is a high status, an achievement, and it is unimaginable that a person creating in Yiddish should spit in the well of his creation. Such a person is a petty human being and an even pettier poet.

As to Yiddish as a language instrument, we think that our language is now beautiful and rich enough for the most profound poetry. All the high achievements of poetry—the highest—are possible in Yiddish. Only a poor poet can complain of the poverty of the Yiddish language. The real poet knows the richness of our language and lacks nothing, can lack nothing.

Poetry is, to a very high degree, the art of language—a principle that is too often forgotten—and Yiddish poetry is the art of the Yiddish language, which is merely a part of the general European-American culture. Yiddish is now rich enough, independent enough to afford to enrich its vocabulary from the treasures of her sister languages. That is why we are not afraid to borrow words from the sister languages, words to cover newly developed concepts, broadened feelings and thoughts. Such words are also *our* words. We have the same right to them as does any other language, any other poetry, because—to repeat—Yiddish poetry is merely a branch, a particular stream in the whole contemporary poetry of the world.

We regard Yiddish as a fully mature, ripe, independent, particular, and unique language. We maintain that Yiddish separated long ago not only from her mother—German—but also from her father—Hebrew. Everything that ties Yiddish to Hebrew in an artificial and enforced way is superfluous, an offence to the language in which we create. Spelling certain words in Yiddish differently from other words because of their Hebrew etymology is false and anachronistic. All words in Yiddish are equal, it is high time to clean out the white basting of Hebrew spelling from certain Yiddish words.

We are not enemies of Hebrew. For us Yiddish poets, there is absolutely no language question. For us, Hebrew is only a foreign language, while Yiddish is *our* language. We cannot forget, however, that Hebrew and Hebraism have kept on disturbing the natural development of the Yiddish word and of Yiddish poetry. We know that, if not for the Hebraism of the Haskalah movement, which later branched out into Zionist Hebraism on the one hand and assimilationist anti-Yiddishism on the other, Yiddish poetry would stand on a much higher level than it does today. We know that if Yiddish poetry had developed normally and naturally from the poet Shloyme Etinger to now, if the natural course had not been interrupted by Hebraism and the Hebraists, there could be no language problem for anyone; it would perhaps never have arisen. The rich Yiddish literature would have nipped it in the bud.

We think, therefore, that one must finally have the courage to sever any tie between our language and any other foreign language. A time comes when a son must break away altogether from his father and set up his own tent. The last vestige of Hebrew in Yiddish is the Hebrew spelling of certain words. This must be abolished. As poets rather than propagandists, we solve the problem first of all for ourselves. We shall spell all Yiddish words equally, with no respect for their pedigree.

These are our views, these are our poetic aspirations in the various realms that must concern a poet in general and a Yiddish poet in particular.

4

Our emergence is not intended as a struggle against anybody or as an attempt to annihilate anyone. We simply want to develop ourselves and take our own road, which is, for us, the truest road.

We come at the right time, at a time when Yiddish poetry is mature and independent enough to bear separate trends and promote differentiation and diversity, instead of straying hesitantly in one herd.

By saying that we come at the right time we admit that everything that has come before us was also at its right time.

Mikhl Gordon, Shimon Frug, Morris Rosenfeld, Avrom Reyzin, A. Liessin, H. Royzenblat—they are all good in their own time, but only *in* their own time. All that was necessary for the development of Yiddish poetry, for its gradual progress was contributed by them and thus made our appearance possible. To this extent, we do not fight against them, we do not try to shout them down. On the contrary, we express our gratitude for their role in our emergence.

Only one representative of the older Yiddish poets has crossed the boundary of his time and is, for us, not merely a precursor but a fellow poet. This is *Yehoash*. In our view, he is the most important figure in all of Yiddish poetry today. He is a poet who does not stop searching, who has the courage and the talent—we do not know which is more important or more beautiful and greater—to sense at the very zenith of his creativity that this is perhaps not the way and to depart from the well-known path of scanned iambs and trochees to write in new forms and in different modes. Perhaps he should have been the initiator of a new trend in Yiddish poetry and perhaps also, at least in part, of our trend. He did not do this for understandable reasons, and we would like to note that we regard him as one who is close to us.

The development of a new group of Yiddish poets would not have been possible without certain intermediate steps. Art, like life, does not leap but develops gradually. On those intermediate steps, we find the so-called *Yunge* (the Young Generation).

Aynhorn, Menakhem, Mani Leyb, Zisho Landoy, Rolnik, Slonim, Schwartz, Ayzland, M. L. Halpern, B. Lapin—they are all good and good in their time. They have accomplishments, and not only do we not deny that but we understand and readily admit that only because of their work was a further development of Yiddish poetry possible, of which the Introspective trend is an expression.

All these poets led Yiddish poetry out onto a broader road. They brought Yiddish poetry, which was strongly akin to the verse of wedding jesters and rhymesters, closer to art and genuine poetry. In the case of poets like Rolnik or Mani Leyb, one could say that they made Yiddish poetry deeper, though as to the latter, it would be more correct to say finer. Slonim has the accomplishment of showing a sensibility for rhythm and, in part, also for individual rhythm.

The major contribution of the Young Generation, however, is with respect to language. They introduced a certain Europeanism into the language, a greater artistic authenticity, and raised the level of a Yiddish poem. They canceled Peretz's "my song would have sounded differently if I sang for Goyim in Goyish."

There it remained, however. As for content, even the deepest of them stayed on the surface and the finest hit a wall. With all his sensibility for rhythm, Slonim stopped where he should have, and perhaps could have, started. As for language, there too they came to a dead end. The refreshing, enriching, and refined became ossified and degenerated into a fruitless wasteland.

As with the older writers, here too there is an exception—namely, H. Leyvik.

Leyvik is only in part one of the Young Generation. From the first, he introduced so much that is individual—and even profound—that there can be no talk of his stopping, of his having already completed his poetic mission.

We regard him, too, as being close to us.

The Young Generation, as a whole, however—as a group—belong only to their own time. If one wants to characterize their contribution, which we consider finished, it is the contribution of an interim stage, of a bridge to a new poetry—a poetry more independent, courageous, profound, and authentic both in content and in form, to use an old formulation.

5

We would like to add a few comments on the mode of writing, points which can be found in most modern trends, such as, for example, in the American Imagists. We will also remark on the way in which this collection, which we consider the first in a series, was compiled.

Since we see our trend as an expression of a movement toward life, toward life as it is reflected in us—which is real life—we are in favor of making the language of our poems as close as possible to the spoken language in its structure and flow. We therefore abolish any possibility of "inversion," the contortion of the natural sentence structure for the sake of rhythm and rhyme. One cannot and under no circumstances should say "bird thou never wert" or "but not your heart away" or even worse barbarisms. One must write, "you never were a bird," "don't give your heart away," whether there is a rhyme or not, whether it scans or not.

We are against using expressions for their ostensible beauty. There can be no beauty without profound relationship and without authentic meaning.

We strive to avoid banal similes, epithets, and other figurative expressions. Their very banality makes them a lie and we seek, first of all, introspective honesty and individuality.

We try to avoid superfluous adjectives altogether, which add nothing and are merely an unnecessary burden. "Far distance" or "blue distance" or "snowing snow" do not make the distance or the snow different. Instead, it is always better to have an authentic, individual image.

It is always better to use the right word for the corresponding concept, even if it is not "beautiful" according to popular aesthetics. A word in the right place is always beautiful. If anyone has to look it up in the dictionary, this is none of the poet's business.

As to the composition of this collection, the initiative lies with the signers of this introduction. They invited others after agreeing on the tenets and goals of this trend. We have included here such poems as are more or less close to our position.

All these rules, as it were, were not formulated in advance of the poems. Should anyone think so, he is guilty of an absurdity. The rules, like the whole movement, grew out of poems already written. It cannot be otherwise. If in the process of writing new rules develop, even contradictory ones, we shall record that, too.

The poem creates the rule and not vice versa, and that is why no rule can be considered binding forever.

The number of poems included in this collection does not by any means indicate the relative importance of a poet. Neither does it have to do with whether the poet was one of the initiators. It indicates merely that someone has written more poems.

All participants are equally important.

We know that every poet develops better in solitude than in a group. The eight poets whose works are represented here are very different from each other. If we have decided to appear as a group with a particular name (which, by the way, should not be taken literally), it is because, through this collective separation and delimitation, we hope to enhance the individual development of each one of us.

We have been led to this collective step by the current internal situation of Yiddish poetry—chaotic, faceless, characterless, and increasingly an obstacle to further development.

Translated by Anita Norich.

Other works by Glatstein: *The Glatstein Chronicles* (1938, 1940); *Selected Poems of Yankev Glatshteyn* (1987); *I Keep Recalling: The Holocaust Poems of Jacob Glatstein* (1993).

Other works by Leyeles: *Labirint* (1918); *Rondos un andere lider* (1926); *A yid oyfn yam* (1947).

Other works by Minkov: *Masoes fun letsn shotn* (1936); *Idishe klasiker poetn: esseyn* (1937); *Baym rand* (1945); *Elyah Bahur un zayn bove-bukh* (1950); *Piyonern fun yidisher poezye in Amerika* (1956).

Berl Katznelson
1887–1944

Berl Katznelson was one of the central figures in the rise of Labor Zionism in the Land of Israel. Born in Bobruisk, Russia (now Babruysk, Belarus), the son of a member of Ḥovevei Tsiyon, he settled in Ottoman Palestine in 1909 and, as a firm believer in the redemptive character of physical labor on the land, worked in agriculture. He was a founder of the labor federation Histadrut, the consumer cooperative Hamashbir, the health plan Kupat Ḥolim, the Labor Zionist daily *Davar* (which he edited from its founding in 1925 until his death), and the Am Oved publishing house. He was outspoken in urging the Zionist movement to come to a peaceful agreement with the Arabs in Palestine.

On the Question of Languages
1919

We may assume that the executive committee of *Aḥdut Ha-Avoda* did what was necessary to explain our position to our allied organizations abroad, the exact situation of the question of language in Eretz-Israel, the essence of the decision of the Constituent Assembly, as well as the loss and disrespect revealed in the debate on the decision of the Constituent Assembly in the American Jewish press. That debate had only one purpose: under cover of "democracy," to sully Hebrew and the Hebrews in the eyes of their readers.

But, by presenting the decision of the Leeds Conference literally, the *Kuntres* found it necessary to accompany it with a few words addressed to its authors. A few, clear and sharp words:

In the world of the Hebrew worker in Eretz-Israel, the question of languages does not exist. Hebrew history gave our nation Eretz-Israel and the Hebrew language only one time. And the complete revival of the Jewish people lies in the regeneration of the life of the nation in its land and in its language, and in the renewal of a full, organic life. For us, there is only one practical question of language: how to hasten the complete revival of the language among the entire nation, how to make the treasures of Hebrew culture the property not only of exceptional individuals but of the entire nation, how to bring the masses of the nation as an active force into the making of the new Hebrew culture, how to implement this matter most decisively and effectively.

The decision of the Constituent Assembly requiring that those *elected* to the Assembly of Representatives know Hebrew was accepted not by pressure of outsiders but by general agreement. We workers of Eretz-Israel *participated in it and supported it*. This decision is not intended to deny the rights of anyone. The Assembly that made the election law did not deny any right of *the voters*. It was this assembly that gave voting rights to members of the Hebrew brigades from England, America, Argentina, and Canada, without asking whether they knew Hebrew. This decision which was accepted expresses our firm conviction—and we are sure that *this is* the conviction of the Hebrew people—that the Hebrew legislative body in Eretz-Israel has only one language: Hebrew. And this, our innermost conviction, will not be changed by all the powers of East and West. In fact, the accepted decision fits a minimal education requirement. It is not a requirement for "learning" and examinations but for an ability to speak the language. And a candidate, who has been in Israel no less than a year (before that, according to the law, he has no right to be elected) and has not learned the language of the people, that is, doesn't know the issues of the country, doesn't read what is written in books and newspapers, and won't understand what is said at meetings, including the Constituent Assembly itself—why should he be elected and what will his function be? Only one function remains for him—to obstruct Hebrew and to demand another language. Perhaps there is someone abroad who wants the Assembly of Representatives to be occupied with such issues. Here there isn't.

So this is the awful decision, the "decree" salted and peppered with some vain rumors,[1] which infuriated the Jewish press in America, caused grief for several innocent people, raised the scream: Hebrews upon you, Israel! And provided Jews with contempt and scorn for the language, the land and its workers, things reminiscent of the period of Territorialism, may it rest in peace.

And to our comrades abroad, let it be said: Stop the vestiges of national opportunism. The Socialist Zionist movement is a revolutionary movement in the highest sense. It triumphed over the concepts prevalent among the Jews, concepts of accommodation and socialization to the equal rights and the annulment of the Pale [of Settlement, in Russia]; it stood against the plague of rational and logical Territorialism. Should it give in to linguistic Ugandism? In the great Hebrew revolution, the revival of the Hebrew language takes its place. And, my brothers, please do not waste forces so necessary for the work of redemption in a war against us, *the vanguard that has advanced before you*. If this is not clearly understood by you in Diaspora, we promise you that, when you come to Eretz-Israel—you will listen and understand. Will you throw stones into that spring of blessing and redemption whose waters you will soon come to drink? The transition of the worker who comes to Eretz-Israel to our language is natural, the fruit of internal necessity—why burden it by compounding false concepts in Diaspora? It is natural for you there to do your educational work in whatever language the people understand. But the Jewish worker must be educated right away to recognize that here, the language of the nation, the only language, is revived. And this recognition will also make his own transition easy for him. You have accepted the decision about *He-ḥalutz* and about the preparation of pioneers by working the land and learning Hebrew. This is the way!

NOTES

Words in brackets appear in the original translation.

1. Like the lie that went around the world that soldiers aren't accepted for regular agricultural labor in Mikveh Israel unless they know Hebrew and that the gates are locked for the rest of them. In fact no knowledge is examined and no one was rejected in Mikveh because he didn't know Hebrew; on the contrary, scores who don't know Hebrew come there, and leave after two months speaking Hebrew.

Translated by Barbara Harshav.

Other works by Katznelson: *Kitvei B. Katsnelson*, 12 vols. (1945–1953).

Louis D. Brandeis

1856–1941

A native of Louisville, Kentucky, Louis D. Brandeis was a progressive reformer, a close adviser to President Woodrow Wilson, and a leader of American Zionism. He fought for good government, public control of utilities, worker rights, and a competitive economy. In 1910, while mediating the great New York garment workers' strike, he began to take an interest in his Jewish background. A few years later he became a Zionist and soon emerged as the leader of the American Zionist movement. He was associated with a school of Zionism that combined the return to the Land of Israel with American democratic ideals and organizational techniques. In 1916, Wilson appointed him to the Supreme Court, the first Jew to be so honored, where he earned a reputation as one of the greatest justices in the history of the court.

Efficiency in Public Service
1920

The opportunity for which we have been struggling has come. We have the opportunity of developing a Homeland, but nothing more than an opportunity. It is urgent that we enter upon the work, urgent because Great Britain and the other Governments expect it and require it, in order that we may establish our position in the Homeland. And the Jews, particularly the hundreds of thousands who are looking forward to relieving their present misery by going to Palestine, demand it. We must therefore act and act quickly. And yet everyone of you knows perfectly well that we are not adequately equipped in men, money or machinery to undertake that task.

So far as money goes, America, including of course Canada, has in the last two and one-half years contributed the money with which Palestine has been kept going. But we have not done anything else. All that we have done practically in this time is to pay the living expenses of the administration. And we have done it with very great difficulty. Except as through the Medical Unit we have made life a little more possible, we have not advanced a step towards developing the Homeland. And yet it is in the series of steps beyond keeping Palestine as it has been that our problem lies. . . .

There has been a tremendous amount of talk in the past, and properly, of the political question, of political Zionism. The political question will be important hereafter, but to my mind practically the whole of politics lies in proceeding efficiently in the building up of Palestine. That is the only political act which can effectively produce the result and make of our opportunity success instead of failure. Politics as such may now be banished; certainly politics may go into suspense. There is nothing that can be accomplished from this time on by ingenious political action, however great our diplomats and however wise the individual may be in manipulating this portion of the population or that, or this official or that.

We have come to the time when there are no politics that are valuable except the politics of action. We must be in a position to act in Palestine, and we have to be strong outside of Palestine. And it is not the strength which will come through any individual or his wisdom or his position. The strength must come through the strength of Jews organized together in large part in the Zionist Organization. Now, therefore, when we consider how we are going to make an efficient organization and accomplish our results, we have to see what the work is that is to be done. To my mind the work in the different countries of the Diaspora is no less important than the work in Palestine. Without that which will be done in the Federations of the several countries, our task is impossible of accomplishment.

Moneys must be given in several forms. A great deal will come by way of investment, and by way of quasi-investment. But it is absolutely necessary that a large part of the money which is going to develop Palestine is to come in the form of gifts from Jews throughout the world. There is no such thing as investment, in a proper sense of that term, unless there is either security or the prospect of a large return, which is the alternative in the investor's mind for security. You may run a risk if you have the prospect of a large return. That is good business, and it is not gambling. But if you have no prospect of a large return, you must have security or the approximation of security. On account of the nature and condition of the country there cannot be security in Palestine unless there is a margin created by the gifts of Jews throughout the world. And that is true for several reasons.

The first is that, unlike the land in other countries requiring development, the land in Palestine is not free. On the contrary, it is very expensive. The present price of the land in Palestine is, considered on a basis of producing power, far more than land of the same character in the world market anywhere else. And the land is in one way largely exhausted. Its trees had been cut off, and so there was produced the condition of swamps and consequent malaria. There must therefore be expended upon the land a very large amount of money before it can become properly productive. In other words we have to expend money to convert the raw material of

land into real productive land. We also have to build up the men who are going to use that land, because they are ignorant of agriculture and of the ways of the country, and they have to be educated.

Those are expenses that have to be borne in the first instance. In my opinion those expenses can ultimately become remunerative. The land can pay a return upon what we spend on it, and the country can pay a fair return in the sense of giving a living to those who go there. But there is no short cut in Palestine to earning a living there. It is difficult to earn a living there. It is more difficult in my opinion to earn a living in Palestine than it is in a large part of the world which is open to Jews. Therefore no investors can expect either security or a large return on a fairly conducted business unless there are done by us certain things which a state might do if it were ready, if it had great resources. This the state, Palestine, is not ready to do. It has not the resources. And it has an appreciable debt resting upon it which the land must return. Therefore, to do the things we want done, we have to raise a very considerable amount. And we have to raise men to go with the money; men who will administer the moneys that we send there. That can be done only by an immense development of the work in the several countries of the Diaspora, America of course included.

Insufficient as our work in America may have been, I think we can say that there are other countries in which it has been worse. And I think that attention cannot be too much directed to the fact that we cannot succeed in our attempt unless we have cooperation from all of these countries, notably Great Britain, where the prospects of successful work are even better than in America. British Jewry is a part of the mandatory, and it will feel, in a way, what Americans do not feel, an obligation and pride, and a sense of loyalty to England as well as of loyalty to the Jew, in working for Palestine.

I believe that any organization that we are to create now must recognize that the World Organization is in one way at least no more important than the Great Hinterland. The Hinterland is to be the great reservoir of money and of men, and must therefore be developed in every part. That, I think is the first proposition. We Americans must develop our organization and strength at home, and we must govern our action with that constantly in view. At the same time we must insist that all other countries, beginning with Great Britain and the British Dominions, must, to the very utmost of their ability, develop their possibilities, possibilities which I consider even more favorable, numbers and position considered, than our own in America. . . .

The only consideration which we are at liberty to regard is efficiency in that public service (to be rendered in Palestine), and not to pick men because of what they may have done in the past. The only proper test that can be applied in respect to the filling of these offices is fitness and efficiency. The man who is best fitted to perform a particular task must be selected. To my mind it is an insult to a devoted Zionist to appoint him to office only because of services which he has performed in the past. It is an insult to the intelligence, to the high-mindedness of the Jew, the Zionist Jew, to consider, in filling an office, whether a proposed incumbent needs or wants the compensation which comes from it. If there are men in Palestine or elsewhere who have served us well in the past and do absolutely need for their living certain means which they are not able to get by their own effort, the question properly arises whether we should create, either through private effort or through the Organization directly, a Pension Fund just as Governments and public bodies do. But I consider it no less than treason to our Cause knowingly to appoint any man to office for any other reason than that he can with the greatest fitness fill that office. We have no right, and it would be folly, to appoint any man to any office in Palestine or elsewhere, just as it would be, with the enemy at our gates in the most terrible of war times, to appoint a man general or colonel or captain, because he was popular or because he was poor or because we love him. We have a problem so difficult, that unless we set that standard for ourselves there is, to my mind, no possibility of our solving it. And, of course, not only must we get the fittest men, but we must do with the least possible number. We must abolish every unnecessary office. We must make every man do every bit of work that it is possible for him to do. We must make men understand that every penny which they waste in any way, either by an unnecessary office or by a salary of more than is necessary, that just to that extent they are obstructing the work which lies before us. What we can do in Palestine depends wholly upon the amount of money we can raise and what men we can get to administer it.

Waste of money raised will not only deprive us of the amount wasted. It will cost us ten and twenty and one hundredfold the amount wasted through its deterrent effect on possible contributions and investments. Men are willing to give, men can be made willing to give, when they know what they give, that whatever sacrifices they make, will result in some further approach to the end we have in mind. But every person who wastes a cent, whether it be in a cable, in a salary or in an unnec-essary letter, is postponing directly or indirectly to perhaps a hundred times that extent, the achievement of our aim. More Jews ought to understand this. We Jews have the intelligence to understand this. We must have character and high spirit enough to see that we may not allow our hearts and our love and our individual fancies or favors to guide us in the selection of the men who are to serve our organization.

When you consider the inter-relation of the work to be done in the Federations in the various countries, and the specific character of the work to be done in Palestine, you will see how essential it is to have an entire rearrangement of activities. To my mind, a large part of the men who have in the past occupied themselves in international activities can best serve the cause by going to their homes, with the knowledge which they have acquired from international action and experience, and particularly a knowledge of the necessities of the Cause and the character of those necessities, by going to their own people and making them understand that, unless that work is done in the Hinterland, success in Palestine is impossible. Make them understand the difficulties as well as the possibilities. Our undertaking is not a light thing. The time is past when jubilations are in order. There is a thing different from jubilation before us now. Great sorrow will follow the jubilation unless our people, in the different countries as well as in Palestine, are made to understand the real situation; unless they are made to understand the difference between the unreal and the ideal. Zionism has given a new significance to the traditional Jewish duties of truth and knowledge as the basis of faith and practice.

As for the work in Palestine and the large number of people engaged in administrative work there: I am not of course criticizing their motives in any respect. They performed very important things in the past which it is no longer necessary to perform. Unless our people recognize that the greatest public service they can perform in Palestine is to earn there an honest living and not be dependent upon the Organization, we shall not accomplish our work. The highest work that can be done for Palestine is to earn a living in Palestine; to put the Jewish mind and Jewish determination and Zionist idealism and enthusiasm into the problem of earning a living in Palestine; thus setting an example for others to earn a living. That is real patriotism. A young woman who was in Palestine some time ago said that to make a good soup in Palestine was a contribution to the cause. I agree with her. But it is not a contribution to have someone else make a soup for you. It is not a contribution to get paid for making plans for a good soup. What we have to do is to make it possible for men to earn a living in Palestine. That is a very difficult thing. It cannot be done by subsidizing people. It can be done only by the individual efforts of men actuated by the proper motives, guided in the proper ways.

Our organization can accomplish a few things to this end. In the first place, we can make it possible for people to work hard in Palestine. That is, we can overcome malaria. We cannot properly judge anybody's performance until we shall have done that. We cannot form an idea as to whether it is possible to develop any of our colonies or plantations unless we put people under conditions where they will work in health, that is, be as healthy as they are in other countries. The task is wholly one of eliminating malaria. Aside from malaria, the ordinary conditions in the country are conducive to the greatest physical wellbeing. We can, without pauperizing people, give them health if they are willing to live according to the rules essential to health.

We can also give to those who have not yet accustomed themselves to the peculiarities of the country, a certain amount of education in agriculture. We can let them have land practically free without exacting interest or returns for a considerable period, during the time of apprenticeship, while they are accommodating themselves to the new situation. . . .

Our task is to bring into Palestine, as rapidly as we can, as many persons as we can. That really comprises the whole work before us. Of course we want to do it in a way and under conditions that will allow the men and women we bring there to become self-supporting and self-respecting and enjoy proper social position. We, of course, take this matter for granted and it requires no reiteration.

Other works by Brandeis: *Other People's Money and How the Bankers Use It* (1914); *The Curse of Bigness: Miscellaneous Papers of Louis D. Brandeis* (1934).

Albert Einstein

1879-1955

Winner of the Nobel Prize in physics in 1921, Albert Einstein was the most renowned scientist of the twentieth century. He was recruited to the Zionist movement in 1921 by Chaim Weizmann. As the political climate in Europe deteriorated in the interwar years, Einstein increasingly devoted time to the fight against fascism, the refugee problem, and the Zionist cause. In 1952, he was offered, but declined, the presidency of the State of Israel.

Assimilation and Anti-Semitism
1920

When an intimidated individual or a careerist among my brethren feels inclined or forced to identify himself as a son of his forefathers, then he usually describes himself—provided he was not baptized—as a *"German citizen of the Mosaic faith."* There is something comical, even tragic-comical in this designation, and we feel it immediately. Why? It is quite obvious. What is characteristic about this man is not at all his religious belief—which usually is not that great, anyway—but rather his being of *Jewish nationality*. And this is precisely what he does *not* want to reveal in his confession. He talks about religious faith instead of kinship affiliation, of "Mosaic" instead of "Jewish" because the latter term, which is much more familiar to him, would emphasize affiliation to his kith and kin. Besides, the broad designation "German citizen" is ridiculous because practically everybody you can meet in the street here is a "German citizen." Then, if our hero is no fool—and that is rather rare indeed—there must be a certain intention behind it. Yes, of course! Frightened by frequent slander he wants to assert that he is a good and dutiful German citizen, even though all his life he has been bedeviled by "German citizens" because of his "Mosaic faith," and often not just a little.

For brevity's sake, I have used the term "Jewish nationality" above sensing that it could meet with resistance. Nationality is one of those slogans that cause vehement reaction in contemporary sensibilities, while reason treats the concept with less confidence. If somebody finds this word inappropriate for our case, he may choose another one, but I can easily circumscribe what it means in our case.

When a Jewish child begins school, he soon discovers that he is different from other children, and that they do not treat him as one of their own. This being different is indeed rooted in heritage; it is in no way based only upon the child's religious affiliation or on certain peculiarities of tradition. Facial features already mark the Jewish child as alien, and classmates are very sensitive to these peculiarities. The feeling of strangeness easily elicits a certain hostility, in particular if there are several Jewish children in the class who, quite naturally, join together and gradually form a small, closely knit community.

With adults it is quite similar as with children. Due to race and temperament as well as traditions (which are only to a small extent of religious origin) they form a community more or less separate from non-Jews. Aside from social difficulties, due to the changing intensity of anti-Semitism over the course of time, a Jew and a non-Jew will not understand each other as easily and completely as two Jews. It is this basic community of race and tradition that I have in mind when I speak of "Jewish nationality."

In my opinion, aversion to Jews is simply based upon the fact that Jews and non-Jews are different. It is the same feeling of aversion that is always found when two nationalities have to deal with one another. This aversion is a consequence of the *existence* of Jews, not of any particular qualities. The reasons given for this aversion are threadbare and changing. Where feelings are sufficiently vivid there is no shortage of reasons; and the feeling of aversion toward people of a foreign race with whom one has, more or less, to share daily life will emerge by necessity.

Herein lies the psychological root of all anti-Semitism, but by no means is it a justification for the agitation of the anti-Semites. A feeling of aversion may be natural, but to follow it unreservedly indicates a low level of moral development. A nobler individual will guide his actions by reason and insight and not by dull instinct.

But how is it with society and with the state? Can it tolerate national minorities without fighting them? There is no state today that does not regard tolerance and the protection of national minorities as one of its duties. Let us hope the state takes these duties seriously. This involves halting its practice of demanding that Jews in many cases abandon principle and abase themselves (baptism) in order to obtain government employment; it would be even more advisable to drop this custom as it creates a rather unfortunate selection.

The methods used by Jews to fight anti-Semitism are quite diverse. I have already characterized the assimilatory one, that is, to overcome anti-Semitism by dropping nearly everything Jewish and appealing to the civil rights of Jews. This method is not calculated to raise the reputation of the Jewish people in the estimation of the non-Jewish world; besides, it is useless and morally questionable. Another method of combating anti-Semitism, occasionally used by Jews who have

not yet broken with everything Jewish, is to draw a sharp dividing line between *East European Jews and West European Jews*. Everything evil blamed on Jews as a totality is heaped on the East European Jews and, thus, of course granted as an actually existing fact. The result of this not merely bad but also foolish procedure is, of course, just the opposite of what was intended. Anti-Semites have no intention of clearly distinguishing between East European and West European Jews as some West European Jews might wish; instead, they interpret this strange kind of defense as an admission and unfairly accuse those West European Jews of betraying their own people. It is not difficult to prove, in both general and individual cases, that most West European Jews are nothing but former East European Jews; and vice versa for all East European Jews. And since the major concern of anti-Semites is to prove that Jewish inadequacies and vices have not been acquired during a few generations, but can allegedly be shown to have existed through the entire history of the Jewish people, the inference from East European Jews to West European Jews appears logically justified. And here we do not even take into consideration that East European Jewry contains a rich potential of the greatest human talents and productive forces that can well bear comparison to the higher civilization of West European Jews—as is often admitted even by those who are by no means philo-Semitic.

It cannot be the task of the Jews to obtain "immunity" from the anti-Semites by accusing any part of their own people. This attitude reveals a severe misconception of both the law and of the significance of anti-Semitism, whose presumption of sitting in judgment on the Jewish people we will never accept. As Jews we know the faults of our people better than others do, and we alone are called upon and able to remedy this. This can only be achieved, however, if we follow our Jewish duty, which dictates that we always view the Jewish people as a living whole and that standing shoulder to shoulder with our brethren we work for a Jewish and human future for our people.

Translator unknown.

Chaim Ben-Kiki

1887–1935

A Sephardic intellectual and critic of Western intrusions into the Middle East, Chaim Ben-Kiki was born in Tiberias, the son of the chief rabbi of the Tiberias *bet din*. He lived and worked his entire life in Tiberias. Little is known about him. Many of his polemics appeared in *Do'ar hayom*.

On the Question of All Questions Concerning the Settling of the Land
1921

The Arab Question—with which the youngsters born in this Land have been familiar for many years, and because of which they were subject to disgrace and ridicule by the prominent men within the Yishuv—has now settled in the minds of the higher echelons of the Yishuv's leaders, who see it as most crucial. More are now of the opinion that the deliverance of the Yishuv is entirely dependent on the solution to this Question.

Before the War, the Nationalists viewed our Land as destroyed and deserted, awaiting our industrious hands. They believed that the Land's inhabitants, whether they wanted to or not, would have to accept us. The desolate Land must be built on. Humanism itself demands it! And we, only we—can carry out this task, and only we have the right to do so. No maligning or criticism could override this historical human claim. It did not occur to the leaders of the movement to consider the possibility that such criticisms could become so strong as to acquire a national value potent enough to impress the nations of the world.

True, before the Great War it was impossible to imagine that the Question would develop into such a complicated matter. But still, the natives of this Land felt that matters were not being well organized and that all the noise—accompanied with that ringing arrogant tone that came at us from outside—was inappropriate for both the time and the place. The Sephardic Yishuv, a community that came from the lands of the East to an Eastern country—whose soul was forged and formed along several generations with the Arab peoples—sensed that something unpleasant was taking place here, and that all this movement was not carried out decently. But the admonitions, criticisms, and warnings were considered meaningless. They stirred only ridicule and gave rise to accusations of assimilation. The new settlers say that any Jew who speaks the language of his native country is assimilating.

The leaders now see that the seed of evil that they have planted is beginning to produce fruit and thus see their mistakes. Mr. Itzhac Epstein thoroughly discusses this issue in *Do'ar Hayom* and describes and accentuates the danger to our hopes in this Land.[1] Epstein arrives at the same conclusions that were published in the journal *Ha-Herut* well before the War. He demands the establishment of an Arabic newspaper, the publishing of pamphlets in Arabic, the organization of concerts in Hebrew and Arabic, and the provision of moral and material support to the Arabs.

Although Epstein, the esteemed author, endeavors to encompass all aspects of the Question, we are still of the opinion that the main issue at stake remains unaddressed by him and is absent altogether from his writing. Epstein accuses the Yishuv of being negligent and for not initiating any action concerning the Arab Question. From his tone it seems that the settlers did all of this intentionally and maliciously—as if they were fully aware of all the bitter consequences—yet deliberately and wickedly ignored them. Yet neither we—nor, for that matter, Mr. Epstein himself—really consider such a claim to be true. We thus come to pose a most fundamental question: why did the leaders of the Yishuv ignore this crucial Question—a Question that today is seen as the single most dangerous one to all of our past, and future, work? Epstein did not touch on this at all. It is thus clear to us that the various elements in his essay do not fit together very well. We find his description of the danger powerful and riveting; his charge about our negligence does touch our heart. But we do not see that the remedies Epstein offers—at this point in our movement—are useful and practical, so that we can say with certainty that they will deliver us. From reading between Epstein's lines, we suspect that even the author himself is not certain about his own words and has doubts about the success of our project. But this is our duty and we cannot just rid ourselves of it.

What, then, is the reason that we thus far have not been able to understand the way our neighbors think and talk? This lack of understanding was intentional. Our expert diplomats—who flooded the world with their journals, speeches, interviews, and books, trying to show how just our cause is—were certainly not incapable of doing the same thing here, had they only found it necessary. But they deliberately ignored the necessity.

To begin with, they thought that the Arabs—who until recently were not the Land's de facto rulers—were not important enough to be considered. Second—and this is the crucial part—they thought that taking the inhabitants into account was not something that should be prioritized among the national and educational principles that the new literature and Zionism—with all its strands and concepts—sought to achieve. The failure lies in the fact that the settlers did not bring the Jew, as he is, to reside in the country, but placed him within the purgatory of exile and redemption and stuffed him with spiritual phrases about Judaism and its lofty and exalted ideals. These foggy ideals—that other people develop over generations—are the burden that the new settler has to bear. When we come here we do not want just to live in the country, cultivate its land, and be present in it. No, we want to carry out an entire national program so that all the Jews and all the nations of the world can see the new well-rounded Jew, who is complete in body and spirit and whose soul is not torn [. . .].

And what about the poor Arab who does not have all these nationalist ideologies? Who is he to place obstacles on the road to carrying out this program? When the new settler comes to the Land, he does not come to accommodate and adjust. The precise opposite is the case: he comes to make others adapt to him. He does not come to learn, but to teach. Our tragedy is that the guides of the Yishuv conceived of all aspects of the life of a free nation in its homeland and tried to implement them all at once in a single blow. They did not follow the path of historical development and move forward gradually—from the easy task to the harder one, from the simple to the complicated. All this new organization of life, which goes forth from the new literature, is a complete contradiction to Epstein's call for "descending to the culture of the natives of the Land." Epstein complains bitterly that we did not do anything in terms of utilizing popular diplomacy. With great agony he calls this behavior "social-political stupidity." But truly, no one is to blame for this—not politicos and not the committees. The problem is hidden within the foundation of the national movement itself. Paying attention to the mind of the Land's native residents and taking it into account is something that no one can imagine because it runs against the very basic general law of the national movement that considers such acts as assimilation.

Epstein is furious that "our diplomatic work is rotten" . . . Yet the actual fact is that our culture is rotten! The root of evil in our work that produced the rupture with the Arabs is that we deserted our Oriental culture, whose basis is Arab culture, and brought in Western culture in its place. This new culture is completely opposed to the culture and mind of the people of this country—it turns us into a foreign, alien element that threatens to destroy the foundations of their culture.

It is that which makes them angry. All the other complaints about occupation and domination are nothing but "politics," they are at best secondary. The principal condition for being good neighbors, as well as for mutual trust, before we come to propose to the Arab people what Epstein wants to offer to them (etc.), is one: return to our Oriental culture! [. . .]

In everything we do, we must think of building the country—creating a national Jewish home in this Land. We must neither think how this home should be, nor think who should dwell in it, whether these people or others. We need to do all that is easy and that will hasten the building of the country. We thus need to stir up a "pioneer movement" from the lands of the East—Turkey, the Balkans, Morocco, Tunisia, Algeria, and elsewhere. This Jewry is ready to respond to the first call to come to the Land, and there is no limit to the benefit that it would bring to it. The settling of such Jews costs considerably less money and would also cause a lot less noise. As many as these pioneers are, the Land's native residents will be immensely happy when they come. The Sephardim were the pioneers of the Old Yishuv, without which no one would have even imagined setting foot in the Land; they should likewise be the pioneers of the New Yishuv. We must help the Sephardi person to come, provide him with comfortable loans, and leave him by himself. He will enter the Land on his own without any supervision or care, and his presence alone will bring peace between the Hebrew Yishuv and the inhabitants. [The Sephardic person] will know how to pave the road that Mr. Epstein says is "long and hard" and even impossible; to him it will be easy.

One of the measures that would also pave the road to fulfill Epstein's proposals is to make room in the leadership for important elements from among the children of this Land. Not as clerks and panderers but as leaders and supervisors of departments dealing with settlement, or departments in charge of general projects that have public value or require direct contact with the Land's inhabitants in such domains as buying land, organization of *aliya*, etc. These leaders will be responsible for their actions in front of both the Yishuv's highest leadership and the public. Such forces exist in the country, and once we decide we need them, we will find them.

This road forward is easy and comfortable simply because it is natural. It fits the culture of the Land, and with simple, peaceful, and calm work our Yishuv shall grow and prosper and we will acquire a "national home" in the Land, walking a road that is free from any sense of enslavement—not of ourselves and not of others. This natural road is humanist and is nationalist without any artificial intention or program. It likewise does not require any "patience" because our actions will not look as if they are designed to change the conditions, norms, and customs. The great code for our work should not be "descending to the culture of the Land" but instead working with it.

NOTES

Words in brackets appear in the source document.

1. [Ben-Kiki is responding to the educator and activist Yitzhak Epstein (1863–1943), who encouraged relations with the Arab population.—Eds.]

Translated by Moshe Behar and Zvi Ben-Dor Benite.

Yeshurun

Established in 1921

Yeshurun was a Jewish community newspaper established in Baghdad in 1921, containing sections written in Hebrew as well as in Judeo-Arabic. The editorial included here is a manifesto to its readers. The publication saw only five issues.

The Voice of Yeshurun *to the Hebrews*
1921

Brothers, the great necessity and the significant need for the publication of newspapers in [any] state are well known in all countries. It is common knowledge. And you will not find one opposing opinion in the state wherein you find newspapers published, through which you value the culture of the people, their progress, knowledge and talents, thoughts and feelings. In a few words, the nation's character is imbodied in its newspapers.

The newspaper expresses the desires of the people, their will and their spirit. The newspaper is the heart of the people, their tongue and their weapons. Through the newspaper one party can triumph over another party. The newspaper is a general public creation and not a private one. The newspaper is like a mirror that reflects the position, appearance, and configuration of everything that faces it; the newspaper shows us the status of a nation, its level of education, and its various ideologies.

The general counselor of a state is the newspaper. The newspaper gives the people what a trainer gives

a trainee, it paves for the people the road for life, it is masculine and feminine, it influences and is influenced at the same time. So why should our share, we the Hebrews of the world, be missing?

Therefore, we felt obliged to edit a weekly called *Yeshurun*, half of which is in our forefathers' language while the other is in spoken Arabic. Let our brothers who live in Babylon hear the news of the world in general and the news of the Hebrew world in particular and understand the obligations of every Jew to act for his people and community.

Brothers, we know and realize the heavy responsibility that is more than we can take. We trust you and we are sure of your support. And because you know this enormous venture, you know this holy responsibility that applies to you too; and that we are your delegates and you will encourage us and help us financially and spiritually. Make efforts to expand the newspaper, its circulation among the Jews, so that Jacob [the Jews] will not be ashamed among the nations. And we will not future tire the dear reader and will end with these words: You will love your community.

You are Israel, run to the *Yeshurun*.

NOTE

Words in brackets appear in the original translation.

Translated by Lev Hakak.

Yaakov Zerubavel

1886–1967

Yaakov Zerubavel (also Vitkin) was a journalist, editor, activist in the Po'ale Tsiyon movement, and founder of the Mapam Party in Israel. Born in Poltava, Ukraine, Zerubavel was a fervent Yiddishist who sought to keep the language current in Israel. After living in Vilna and Lvov, and serving as editor of the *Yidisher arbeter*, he moved to Palestine in 1910, was arrested by Ottoman authorities during World War I, and spent time in the United States and Russia before returning to Palestine in 1935, where he served on the executive of the trade union organization Histadrut.

The Beginnings of the Jewish Social Democratic Workers Party, Po'ale Tsiyon
1921

The first Po'ale Tsiyon group in Poltava was born out of the theoretical battle between Zionism and the journal *Iskra* [the organ of the Russian Social Democratic Labor Party]. Up until 1905, [Dov Ber] Borochov still represented General Zionism. Earlier, in Yekaterinoslav, he had worked as a member of the broad social-democratic organization with workers in large industrial factories. He was dissatisfied, however. Especially after the Kishinev pogrom, he was faced with the burning questions of daily Jewish life; *Iskra* provided no answers and in general dismissed the national question. Borochov moved toward General Zionism, while still maintaining his general socialist worldview. However, he sought to apply it to the concrete conditions of Jewish life. As an agent of the Zionist organization, he traveled to Jewish cities and shtetls. His first works about Jewish issues belong to this period (published in the Zionist journal *Evreiskaia zhizn'* in February, June, July, August, September, and October 1905). At that time, the Uganda project was coming up for discussion, and Borochov took on the task of providing a broad and comprehensive justification for Palestinism. A large part of his Palestine research at the time also entered into his Po'ale Tsiyon agitation. As a Zionist, he was pessimistic about life in the diaspora, and spoke of *iskhod* [exodus], doubting the efficacy of "progress" as a resolution of the Jewish question. This view lasted only as long as he didn't see Jewish workers in front of him in their compact masses—only as long as he didn't feel the breath of their struggle.

On his trips through the Pale of Settlement, Borochov met the large Jewish proletarian masses. There he also encountered both the Bund and the theoreticians and activists of Po'ale Tsiyon. He went through an extended, long-lasting reevaluation of his values until he worked out his conception of Po'ale Tsiyonism, which had as its base the new socialist conception of the national problem. He reworked this last point, and in 1905 published his article "Class Elements in the National Question" (*Evreiskaia zhizn'*, December 1905). [...]

Our most important work at that time was to organize for self-defense and have our own printing press.

As we had lived through the events at Kishinev [the 1903 pogrom], the idea of self-defense was very popular. The illegal publications of the group *Vozrozhdenye* [Rebirth], the organ of Jewish revolutionary thought, were a major influence on our attitude. *Vozrozhdenye* exhibited unusual liveliness and a spirit of struggle. It was so new, fresh, and intimate that it affected both the mind and the heart. The Russian translation of Bialik's *Masa Nemirov* ["A Tale of Nemirov," later published in

Hebrew as "In the City of Slaughter"] made a similarly great impression on us, and included Jabotinsky's preface, which was a strong call to self-defense. It wasn't yet published at the time, but was circulating in manuscript form. [...]

The Poltava organization accomplished a lot in this matter. We had many weapons at our disposal, even dynamite and ready-made bombs. There were several attempts to start pogroms in Poltava, but we put a stop to them. Above all, it was thanks to the untiring work of Vladimir Korolenko, who personally went among the peasants, from group to group and from man to man, preaching to them. They knew that the railway workers, organized by the R.S.D. [Russian Social Democrats], would immediately come into the city to oppose the hooligans.

Translated by Ruth Bryl Shochat and Alexandra Hoffman.

Other works by Zerubavel: *Ber Borokhov: zayn lebn un shafn* (1926); *Draysik yoriker vikuah* (1930); *In onhoyb: artiklen, zikhroynes* (1938); *Barg ḥurbm: kapitlen Poyln* (1939); *Bleter fun a lebn* (1956).

Albert Avigdor

1893–1984

Albert Avigdor was born in Constantinople and immigrated to the United States in 1916. He was an exporter of chemical products to Latin America, which he visited frequently in the 1920s and 1930s.

A Sephardi Émigré Encourages Levantine Jews to Move to Mexico
1922

It is a great pleasure for me to have this occasion, offered to me by the serial *La Luz,* to inform readers of the current situation in the Republic of Mexico, and to mention some of the reasons why the Sephardim should consider Mexico.

In all the countries in which I have traveled, no other has left me with such a good impression as Mexico, due to the favorable conditions that this country offers Sephardi Jews who might want to establish themselves here. There are many reasons for this.

The first is that the Sephardim will encounter no difficulties in understanding the language spoken there, adopting local habits, or accustoming themselves to Mexican food.

The Spanish that is spoken in Mexico, although it contains some Indian words, quite possibly resembles our Ladino more than the modern Spanish spoken in Spain, since—it should not be forgotten—contemporary Mexican society began to form at nearly the same time that the Jews were expelled from Spain. My opinion is that Sephardi Jews of today, with three months of studying and reading, would be able to speak Spanish better than some Mexicans of the interior regions.

As I have said, it will be easy to adopt local customs, or better put, to maintain many of them because they resemble the customs of the Levant (Turkey, Greece, etc.). The people do not hurry in business, everyone takes time to roam around aimlessly. What can be done tomorrow is not done today. They are never content with the government, although they always bear it no matter how bad it is. Put simply, the country is not in the state of perfection [reached by] the great nations of Europe and America, [yet residents of] these nations suffer more from the state of things than does the Sephardi Jew, who is already accustomed to such things from the country of his birth.

In addition I should mention other facts [of life in Mexico] that are very favorable. Social life is much more active than in the United States, people are much more pleasant, more hospitable and possess a courtesy that at times seems exaggerated. The Sephardi Jew will not have difficulty in attaining these qualities because they already form a natural part of his character. In regard to the climate, I should say that it is quite varied in Mexico, such that while it is cold in one city, in another city several kilometers away, it is very hot. Mexico City itself is never either very hot or very cold, but rather, has ideal weather that makes this city one of the healthiest in the world.

The potential wealth of Mexico is incalculable. Aside from the numerous oil wells that have made many American millionaires rich and the large mines of gold and silver, copper and zinc, etc., the importance of agriculture (wheat, corn, chickpeas, coffee, cocoa, vanilla, rubber, etc.) has always been great, the raising of livestock (hogs, sheep, cattle) is also progressing by the day.

The current situation of Mexico is somewhat poor, partially as a result of the global economic situation. In spite of this, Mexico is [economically] more secure than many European states, including both France and Italy; the immigrants that come from these countries find a means of earning a livelihood almost immediately.

I am convinced that the Sephardi youth who have a bit of self-confidence and, especially those who have the idea of establishing themselves there [will succeed], because I am sure that today this country will provide them with a better opportunity for improving their lives than any other country in the world.

NOTE
Words in brackets appear in the original translation.

Translated by Devi Mays.

Menahem Salih Daniel

1846–1940

Menahem Salih Daniel was a prominent landowner, merchant, and philanthropist in Baghdad and a spokesman for the Jewish community in the early years of Iraqi independence. He was a delegate for Baghdad in the first Ottoman parliament in Istanbul in 1877 and a senator in the Iraqi legislature from 1925 to 1932. He was a supporter of both Jewish and Muslim charities and cofounder of the Red Crescent society in Iraq.

Letter to Chaim Weizmann
1922

The Secretary
Zionist Organisation
London
Baghdad, 8th September 1922

Dear Sir,

I have the pleasure to acknowledge receipt of your letter of the 20th July 1922. It is needless to say that I greatly appreciate and admire your noble ideal, and would have been glad to be able to contribute towards its realization.

But in this country [Iraq] the Zionist Movement is not an entirely idealistic subject. To the Jews, perhaps to a greater extent than to other elements, it represents a problem the various aspects of which need to be very carefully considered. Very peculiar considerations, with which none of the European Jewish Communities are confronted, force themselves upon us in this connection.

You are doubtless aware that, in all Arab countries, the Zionist Movement is regarded as a serious threat to Arab national life. If no active resistance has hitherto been opposed to it, it is nonetheless the feeling of every Arab that it is a violation of his legitimate rights, which it is his duty to denounce and fight to the best of his ability. Mesopotamia has ever been, and is now still more, an active centre of Arab culture and activity, and the public mind here is thoroughly stirred up as regards Palestine by an active propaganda. At present the feeling of hostility towards the Palestinian policy is the more strong as it is in some sort associated in the mind of the Arab with his internal difficulties in the political field, where his position is more or less critical. To him any sympathy with the Zionist Movement is nothing short of a betrayal of the Arab cause.

On the other hand the Jews in this country hold indeed a conspicuous position. They form one third of the population of the Capital, hold the larger part of the commerce of the country and offer [have] a higher standard of literacy than the Moslems. In Baghdad the situation of the Jew is nearly an outstanding feature of the town, and though he has not yet learnt to take full advantage of his position, he is nevertheless being regarded by the waking up Moslem as a very lucky person, from whom the country should expect full return for its lavish favours. He is moreover beginning to give the Moslem an unpleasant experience of a successful competition in Government functions, which having regard to the large number of unemployed former officials, may well risk to embitter feeling against him.

In this delicate situation the Jew cannot maintain himself unless he gives proof of an unimpeachable loyalty to his country, and avoid with care any action which may be misconstrued. This country is now trying to build up a future of its own, in which the Jew is expected to play a prominent part. The task will be of extreme difficulty and will need a strained effort on the part of every inhabitant. Any failing on the part of the Jew will be most detrimental to his future.

On the other hand, the large majority of the Jews are unable to understand that all they can reasonably do for Zionism is to offer it a discreet financial help. We have had, since Dr. Bension's arrival to this country,[1] a sad experience of the regrettable effects which an influx of Zionist ideas here may have. There was for some time a wild outburst of popular feelings towards Zionism, which expressed itself by noisy manifestations of sympathy, crowded gatherings and a general and vague impression among the lower class that Zionism was going to end the worries of life, and that no restraint was any longer necessary in the way of expressing opinions or showing scorn to the Arabs. This feeling it is needless to say was altogether unenlightened. It was more Messianic than Zionistic. To an observer it was merely the reaction of a subdued race, which for a moment thought that by magic the tables were turned and that it was to become an overlord. Very few stopped to think whether the Promised Land was already conquered, and if so how long it would take till all the Jews of Mesopotamia repaired to it, and whether any reasonable policy was in the meanwhile desirable. In this state of raving the Jews could not fail to occasion a friction with the Moslems, specially as the latter were then high up in nationalist effervescence, and a feeling of surprise and dissatisfaction ensued, which caused a prominent member of the Cabinet to remark to me reproachfully that after so many centuries of good understanding the Moslems were not at all suspecting that they had inspired the Jews with so little esteem for them.

During my first interview with Dr. Bension at a time when the internal political situation was particularly critical, I explained to him my anxiety as to the effect of the rather sonorous success of his mission on the political difficulty of the Jews at that juncture and requested him to postpone his mission, if possible till the political outlook should be more reassuring. I am not aware that he actually took any steps in this direction but the enthusiasm of the Jewish population has never abated since then.

In view of the above circumstances I cannot help considering the establishment of a recognised Zionist Bureau in Baghdad as deleteriously affecting the good relations of the Mesopotamian Jew with his fellow citizens. As stated above some misunderstanding has already occurred which if allowed to take root, might well lead to a breach, which will have for the Jews grave consequences. The Jews are already acting with culpable indifference about public and political affairs, and if they espouse so publicly and tactlessly as they have done lately, a cause which is regarded by the Arabs not only as foreign but as actually hostile, I have no doubt that they will succeed in making of themselves a totally alien element in this country and as such they will have great difficulty in defending a position, which, as explained above, is on other grounds already too enviable.

I hope you will fully understand the point of view which I have tried to set forth. I am the first to regret having to take it, because, I repeat, I have, on principle, great sympathy with your aims and warmly appreciate the devotion of your distinguished leaders of the Jewish cause. But you will realise that in practical policy the Jews of Mesopotamia are fatally bound to take for the time being a divergent course, if they are to have a sound understanding of their vital interests. I am not qualified to speak for them. The opinions expressed above are my own personal opinions. The Community is unfortunately too helplessly disorganised to have any co-ordinate opinion, and that is indeed why it is the more exposed.

For Dr. Bension personally I have nothing but high esteem, but I regret that his mission having had the practical consequences described above, I am forced to regard its development here with some misgiving. He is regarded both by Moslems and Jews as representing the Zionist Mission as nobody here, is realizing the distinction between that Mission and the Keren Yesod.

I again express to you my deepest regrets at being unable to respond to your call [to support Zionism], and at the unfortunate difficulty of our position vis-à-vis your Movement.

I am, Dear Sir,
Yours faithfully,

(SGD) [signed] Menahem S. Daniel

NOTES
Words in brackets appear in the original source document.
1. [Ariel Bension represented Keren ha-Yesod, the fundraising organization for the Land of Israel, in the Middle East.—Eds.]

Mikhail Gershenzon

1869–1925

Born in Kishinev, Russia, today Chisinau, Moldova, Mikhail Gershenzon received a traditional Jewish education and then studied at the Technical University of Berlin and at Moscow University. In the late 1890s, he began writing about Russian history and literature. Identifying with Russian culture, though never converting to Christianity, he was an antinationalist who rejected Zionism. In the early years of the Soviet regime, Gershenzon wrote about Pushkin and Turgenev and on

Jewish faith, literature, and history. He also served on the board of the People's Commissariat for Education.

Fate of the Jewish People
1922

The educated Englishman can live his entire life without ever once giving a moment's thought to his people's historical destiny or purpose. He knows instinctively that his people are alive and intact and that their historical path is unbroken. How is one to know where this path leads or whether it is correct? Obviously, the individual mind is incapable of comprehending phenomena on this scale. The face of a living people is like the fiery bright sun: it's visible to all, but no one can make it out clearly. Only cold suns, the dead faces of Egypt, Hellas, and Rome do we endeavor to view in their entirety, albeit without great success.

Nonetheless, there is not a single cultured people that would not occasionally attempt to understand itself through the minds of its thinkers. Observations of the past bring out a kind of linear scheme, a blueprint, the philosophy of a nation's history, and society greedily snatches at these conjectures because they satisfy the mind's insatiable need to see the diversity of a people's impulses and destiny as a speculative unity.

If comfortable peoples are prey to this impatience, then how is the modern Jew in particular to withstand the temptation? A believer has no need of rational hopes: his intact emotion allows him to draw consolation and hope from the idea of a benign Providence. When faith weakened in Judaism, a rationalistic philosophy of history inevitably came to take its place. First of all, the history of the Jews is too strange, with its striking dissimilarity to the history of other peoples; secondly, for the most part it is so hopelessly sad that the spectator cannot help but pull up short, amazed. The mind persistently seeks out the logic and meaning of this unusual spectacle. We know that many non-Jewish minds have also pulled up short at the puzzle of Jewish history; the Jew's hesitation is all the more understandable. Man is made in such a way that he seeks no grounds for his happiness and tranquility, accepting them as natural phenomena; his grief, however, he must invariably attribute to a cause. He must prove to himself the logical inevitably of his suffering; otherwise the world would appear to him as an absurdity and he would drown in despair. Why has the Jewish people been so severely punished by dispersions and persecutions? Does their past hold some fatal fault? Does their character hold some innate trait that inevitably gave rise to this outrageous succession of torments? This is the first question that naturally arises: the question of understanding. It gets asked because, unlike other living peoples, Jewry has in its Palestinian past its own frozen face, similar to the dead faces of Egypt, Greece, and Rome—a completed process that demands an explanation. Even more persistent is the second question, which is of practical importance. The people's past took shape spontaneously, but their future, at least their near future—can we really not bend it to our rational will? If Jewry were comfortable, the need for foresight would not be so acute. But even now Jewry is unlucky, disrupted, and homeless; fourteen million people who feel as one family are scattered across seventy countries; a people with their own culture are internally split among twenty heterogeneous cultures. A people that has forgotten its native language and speaks many foreign languages, a chameleon people, a shopkeeper people, estranged from nature, withering in the cities, everywhere, if not persecuted, then barely tolerated—where is the way out for such a people? The old faith did not dare ask about the future because the very question implied interference in God's intentions; on the other hand, unbelief by its very nature is doomed to predict and direct. But since one can only predict from past experience—otherwise the prediction is a chimera—then the question about the future comes down once again to the question about the past, and both together can be resolved only by a historical-philosophical hypothesis. This is why, for today's thinking Jew who has lost the faith of his fathers, there is no stronger temptation than the explanatory and guiding national myth. It is not hard to see that all the intellectual movements that have arisen among Jews in the last forty to fifty years have essentially been attempts at this kind of mythmaking. Possibly unaware of the sources of their inspiration, the actors themselves might have believed their program to be purely practical. Such, for example, were the assimilationists of the eighties. In reality, all their arguments were drawn from specific historical conclusions that were, however, only weakly conscious and so were never made into a system.

It would be extremely interesting to uncover the foundations of these teachings, to shell the philosophical nut of each one and then line up and connect all these hypotheses by both the time of their conception and their commonality of goal. I am convinced that careful research would reveal many related characteristics, in spite of their apparent dissimilarity, and would show that they all coincide both negatively, having as their common point of departure unbelief and historical rationalism, and positively, since all without exception are mere copies of various historical-philosophical theories that nineteenth-century European thought elaborated for its own needs.

But I am not going to do this. The assimilationists' doctrine and teachings about the Jewish people's religious or spiritual-cultural mission have outlived their brief time and are no longer attracting supporters. They have all been vanquished by the mighty movement of Zionism, which has been growing unstoppably for a quarter century and has now reached its apogee. Zionism, no longer an academic doctrine, has become the moving force behind the consciousness of hundreds of thousands of people; it has been transformed into an idea-feeling, an idea-impulse. If for now it may only excite minds and hearts and have yet to change very much in the world, then the enthusiasm it has aroused is a guarantee that, given favorable circumstances, it is destined to radically influence Jewry's destiny. Any day now, the principal external barrier will fall: Palestine will be given to the Jews, and a handful of ecstatic dreamers will rise up and lead the dark masses who, through their labor and their deprivations, will carry out an experiment in national rebirth. Only someone who knows unshakably the truth and strength of his intention can take on such a responsibility. Zionism believes zealously in its dream. Where does this confidence come from? From its worldview, its philosophy of history. Its concrete assertions have been wholly constructed, like a logical corollary, from a generally held idea. Anyone who wants to understand Zionism must seek its meaning not in the practical resolutions that have come out of the Basel or Helsingfors Congress but in the historical-philosophical theory that inspires Zionism and joins the separate parts of its program into a whole.

Meanwhile, it is this crucial aspect of Zionism that has been least illuminated. The same thing has happened to Zionism as can be observed in the history of any political party: its program has completely overshadowed its generating idea, turning that idea into dogma. No one debates the basic tenets of Zionism; they are safeguarded like a gold reserve to be presented *ad extra* when necessary. Since they were first formulated twenty-five years ago, no one has thought to reexamine them with the goal of verifying them or even for the sake of enriching and simplifying them. They have been repeated in countless magazines, articles, brochures, and books like immutable axioms, in the exact same complement, using almost the exact same words. Zionism's entire intellect has been swallowed up by its tactics, and all debates are conducted inside its program; even the most important schism in Zionism did not affect its core because even the spiritual Zionism of Ahad Ha-Am does not ask whether the ultimate goal has been correctly defined; it points only to another path to the same goal political Zionism set for itself. This universal accord is so ascendant that the voice of criticism might almost seem like blasphemy. If I am still determined to express my thought, then I take this daring from my respect for Zionism and my confidence that Zionists do not love their rightness as much as they treasure the truth and the good of the Jewish people. We are like a family at the crossroads. Ruin threatens our house. Where is the escape from this fateful crampedness? You Zionists have come up with a lifesaving method, and I have seen a mistake in your calculations, a mistake that threatens new disaster; and since I am a member of this family, my objection should not grieve you; we share the same love and the same concern.

Translated by Marian Schwartz.

Other works by Gershenzon: *Mechta i mysl' I.S. Turgeneva* (1919); *Mudrost' Pushkina* (1919); *Kleich very* (1921); *Perepiski iz dvukh uglov* (1921); *Golfstrem* (1922).

Uri Zvi Greenberg

1896–1981

The trailblazer of Yiddish and Hebrew modernist poetry Uri Zvi Greenberg was born in a Galician village into a Hasidic family, who moved to Lemberg (Austro-Hungary; Polish, Lwow; Russian, Lvov, today Lviv in Ukraine) when he was a young child. His first poems, in both languages, were published when he was sixteen. He was drafted during World War I, whose horrors he experienced firsthand. Following the war he almost lost his life in a pogrom in Lvov (Lwow, Poland) in November 1918. Both trench warfare and postwar anti-Jewish violence continued to echo in his work in the decades that followed. As early as 1919, he felt that European Jewry faced eventual annihilation. He lived in Warsaw and Berlin before emigrating to Mandate Palestine in 1923. He then shifted his writing

from Yiddish to Hebrew. In 1930, he joined Jabotinsky's Revisionist Party, whose maximalism found expression in his poetry. He spent much of the 1930s in Poland, representing the party, and was there when Germany invaded but was able to escape. He sat for Begin's Herut Party (the successor to the Revisionists) in the first Knesset and after 1967 campaigned for Israeli sovereignty over the West Bank.

Proclamation
1922

A bridge, four walls, and a rafter for the lone and homeless poets as they roam through foreign lands to the many centers of the Jewish people's exterritoriality. Literary diffusion.

I do not mean: mere talents, poets-in-the-making, or their publishable wares. Now is not the time for literary experiments. A generation is bleeding from the throat; puking from the mind. A lacerated age running or writhing in convulsions (winners' or diers' throes). Disruption in the depths. Smoldering on the plains. And the gifted ones are sparks, invisible in time of conflagration. They are but loners, confined in narrow places. Not to be confused with those whose spirit was nurtured in the Sturm und Drang and whose minds cleaved unto the universal: Man-You-Are-Numbered-in-the-Millions.

We proclaim the millionfold head-and-heart-individualism: the heroic Man of Wounds who stands in all his glory, as large as the earth, all eyes and ears and lips, with his 365 veins pumping into the life stream—deeper, deeper.

Individuals of this sort are the clearest manifestation of the paroxysm. Their bodies convulse under the weight of the black global pain that they carry on their bare backs. Glowing worldview. Idea-cluster. Man, world—in all the centuries' permutations.

And there *are* such among us. Poets who are whole, with heavy heads ablaze and spirits horror-tested through expanses. Poet-beings who out of their own bones carve the granite image of the caverned treasures of days and nights' experiences—hoarded on all the roads of the world.

The gates are thrown open to the Four Winds, whither the eternal pilgrims stream, sons of unrest, children of the pure union of universe and man. Albatrosses of Young Yiddish Poetry. Spiritual sustenance: their own flesh, veins, and nerves. Their drink, in goblets of their own marrow: pulsating blood. And black

Sabbath bread—our showbread—suffering. What else is missing in the kingdom of sacred poverty? We, the carousing caravan of God's paupers. Albatrosses. Poets . . .

Blessed be our sorrowful mothers who begat us in this world and in this age! Though woe to this world and to this age in the gaping mouth of infinity, whose tongue burns on the Saharan crossroad: Eldorado—Nirvana.

Renewal. Upheaval. Revolution of the spirit. Exaltation—and more. Of course. So it goes. With them and with us. All the literatures have been overrun in their classical stagnation. Idyllic daydreams and the poet's elegiac quietude have been devastated by a whirlwind: WHAM! A roar issued forth from the gaping-mouthed Colossus-Man with a million heads (according to Grosz: like a machine; technological age!). The fate of the old books—the fate of the Gothic churches and Roman towers: petrified pasthoods. Horrible to behold. *Even the roads pass them by in a run.* World and red century hurtling downhill. Optimists fix spectacles over their eyes trying to conjure up intuitively (for the time being) a glowing bit of new moon in some far-off horizon. Meanwhile, the sun is setting, and the world drags the red, creaking chariot of the bleeding century to its final rest. Downhill with the rotting heaps: generational excrement.

So it is. Whether we want it or not. We remain as we are—with gaping wounds, with veins exposed and bones undone after the howitzers and Hurrahs, after the gas attacks, the shells of bile, the opium, and surface water: nausea. With dusk foaming at the lips.

Thus: the brutality in the poem.
Thus: the chaos in the image.
Thus: the protest of the blood.

Cruel. Chaotic. Bleeding. It's nightfall. In our worldly towers, the tables are set with spiritual food for the losing generation, and a black Sabbath bread is our showbread. An age is celebrating a red feast marking the close of the world's black Sabbath at the feet of the Past. Behind their backs loom large black crosses. *Such songs must be sung.* Cruel. Chaotic. Bleeding . . .

Perhaps the song will be different following the birth of the new moon, and laurels shall yet rest upon the Albatross-heads of the poet-heroes. So far, however, we're naked. Disheveled. Exposed. A horror-and-shame evangel of veins and bones of the waste and wild generation that stands on the crossroads: Eldorado—Nirvana.

The proclamation came in seventy languages: down with the hackneyed—and especially—with limitations in the creative process. Introspective conception. Greater depth. Everywhere—and in our midst as well—spokesmen for free and naked human expression have sprung up, those who always await a crisis, then grab the bell cord of idolatry—and the air resounds with the news of a poetry styled in insanity.

These are sharp-witted, tricky creatures. "This kind of writing is called: modern?" "Fine. So we'll write modern." Scale the plaster! Down with the roof! Forward march over the sea on spider-web bridges! Sure thing! Why not? It sounds confused? That's just the point! Mankind! This is how *I* see it . . . And turning to the head, he says: Head, think up something truly weird. The more absurd, the better. Total impossibilities. Think, head: I have horseshoes on my feet. (Logically, then) I am a man-horse. (Logically, then) I pull. Whom do I pull? C'mon head, you can come up with something! Head thinks: a wagonload of iron . . . Sure thing! Why not?

And so on, and so forth. Imitation. Pseudoexpressionism. Cheapest imitation, sacrilege to one of us. One of us is hurt to the core. And the result: almost a whole generation of young people from the cities and towns is "suffering" from literariness. Suffering from modernism. Can you name an upstanding young man who does *not* carry around a pack of expressionist poems or ideas?

Ask any adolescent:

"What's expressionism all about?"

And the kid will answer with a laugh:

"You wanna know about expressionism? Expression, you see is . . . hmm . . . is when you write about craziness, you see . . . you can say anything you want . . . but not in any plain way . . . it's gotta sound strange . . . don't you see? . . . it's re-vo-lu-tion, you see."

In fact, you don't see a damned thing, except this: that from now on a table is a bed, a hand is a nose, a shoe is a cloak, and a stomach is a butcher's block—sure thing! And why not!

I want to put a stop to this anarchy once and for all. With every fever in my body's bones, I shall do battle against the desecration of an expressionism wrought in blood and marrow in seventy tongues. Against the vulgar imitation: pseudoexpressionism. Against the concealed falsehood of talentlessness that hides behind the sacred veil of modern poetry. Against a plethora of uninvited specialists stuffed full with their enlightened-heretical erudition: Such-and-such is new and such-and-such is not new.

Rather: for the free, bare, blood-seething human expression.

Translated by David G. Roskies.

Other works by Greenberg: *Kol ketavav*, 18 vols. (1991–2013); *Selected Poems* (2006).

David Horowitz

1899–1979

The Galicia-born economist David Horowitz was active in Ha-Shomer ha-Tsa'ir in his youth and moved to Palestine in 1920. He was a member of the executive committee of the Histadrut from 1922 to 1925 and secretary-general of Gedud ha-Avodah from 1925 to 1927. He then worked as a journalist for several years. Between 1935 and 1948, he headed the economic department of the Jewish Agency. He was director general of the Ministry of Finance in the newly established state and was the first governor of the Bank of Israel, a position he held from 1954 to 1970.

Our Cultural Work
1922

At the last council meeting of the Histadrut, the question of cultural work was on the agenda for the first time. This time it was impossible to discuss only the formal and technical aspects of our cultural work and be satisfied with organizing the institutions that deal with this work, without touching on the cultural direction of the new society in the Land of Israel. This time cultural issues stood out as one of the central questions of our life.

Almost all speakers emphasized the cultural decline in our movement, the Workers [Labor] Movement of the Land of Israel. The original and unique way of life of the community of workers, which has attracted thousands of young people to our land with its magnetic force, and has created new cultural values, has been blurred by the third wave of aliyah. Today our movement lacks its cultural character, which renews the entire extent of life, and cultural activity is also lacking. The living bond that unites the entire community of workers has been weakened, and this has caused the negation of consciousness of cooperation in our society, denying it the ability to produce a unifying and new project. The religious power of the movement has weakened, that which gave it the character of a new cultural phenomenon, of a revolutionary and creative flow of life.

Our great cultural mission was to unify the culture and the economy in the life of every human being and to integrate them. For the first time we would break through the wall to a new culture. The contradiction between culture and work might be the main cause of the present cultural crisis of Europe. We who are on the threshold of a new epoch may not be content with values that are being destroyed and built upon collapsing and weakening foundations.

Our cultural work has two main directions: to mediate between us and all the liberation movements in the world, to transmit cultural values that are produced from aspirations similar to ours, to heed the reverberations that herald innovation within the cultural chaos of our period, to attach us to the new cultural movement that is developing in the international labor movement. On the other hand, a far more difficult task is the challenge of creation: to conquer the new cultural elements in our movement, to register like a seismograph every cultural phenomenon that emerges within us and to activate it.

Our direction therefore is not only to serve as an intermediary but mainly to be creative.

The main tragedy of present culture is its fragmentation. Today no idea, no style exists to unify all cultural phenomena and to derive from them a single conception of life and worldview.

The cultural disintegration of our period has created a human type alienated from all cultural roots, wavering among contradictions, exploding life into thousands of fragments and directing them according to the moment without having any general comprehensive and unifying principle line. Life and culture have become a series of fragments with no inner connection, without the ability to see them as a single organic picture. Cultural consolidation in a single style of life is the expression of the most concentrated and intense cultural life, and it alone has the ability to create a new culture.

Culture is not a goal in itself, but it exists only for the sake of life. It must soak up within it all elements of life and penetrate it fully. It cannot exist as a solely intellectual and aesthetic phenomenon. Life in its essence is not only aesthetic and harmonious, but mainly tragic and dissonant, and this must be reflected in cultural creativity. The purpose of culture is not enjoyment, outside of gray everyday life, but it penetrates to the depths and gives it direction. From this assumption every current liberation movement in the world has found a connection to expressionist art and literature. This phenomenon is visible in the workers' movement in Russia and has made its mark on the cultural creativity of the youth movement in Germany. The existence and character of this cultural movement bring it close to every liberation movement; the direct connection with life, destruction of the pleasurable form for the sake of content. Most poets of the Russian Revolution are expressionists. Lunacharsky especially supported this movement during the first period of Soviet rule as an expression of revolutionary direction.

The workers' community in the Land [of Israel] is responsible for the fate of Hebrew national culture, because only within this community have renewed cultural values been created in the national and universal human sense: Brenner and Gordon lived within us and created and expressed the truth of Erets Israel life, cruel, wet with blood, and liberating.

Kibbutz Ha-Shomer ha-Tsaʻir, Sivan 5782
Translated by Jeffrey M. Green.

Other works by Horowitz: *The Economics of Israel* (1967); *Ha-etmol sheli* (1970); *In the Heart of Events—Israel: A Personal Narrative* (1980).

Henryk Erlich

1882–1942

Born in Lublin, Henryk Erlich received a traditional Jewish as well as a secular education at Warsaw University. As a student, he became active in the Bund, collaborating with Bronisław Grosser, and moving to St. Petersburg following the 1905 revolution. He married Sophia Dubnow in 1911 and, following the Bolshevik revolution, moved back to Warsaw with his family in 1918. There, he brought the Bund into the parliamentary political sphere and edited the Yiddish newspaper *Folks-tsaytung*. In 1931, through his efforts and after the party's suppression by the Soviet regime, the Bund became a member of the Labor and Socialist International. After the outbreak of World War II, Erlich went to the Soviet Union, where he was imprisoned, interrogated, and sentenced to death, but then released, to help establish what later became the Jewish Anti-Fascist Committee. He continued to use his networks to maintain a unified Jewish anti-Nazi front. He was soon rearrested, along with Victor Alter,

and again harshly interrogated. In 1942, Erlich hanged himself in his jail cell.

We Must Decide!

1924

On the Discussion Whether to Participate in the Kehilah Elections

After long deliberation, I concluded that we would be making a grave mistake if we did not participate in the upcoming *kehilah* elections. I came to this conclusion because in 1918 I was against involvement in the *kehilah* and because we all—both opponents and supporters—have a deep, well-founded aversion to and lack of enthusiasm for the *kehilah*.

But whether we boycott the elections or participate in them is not a matter of principles and political program but a tactical question that cannot be answered once and for all without considering the concrete circumstances of each particular moment.

Turning to the fundamental question, I have to note that I was rather dissatisfied with how the discussion about participation in the elections was conducted both by its opponents and its supporters. Comrades Rafalovich, E. Mus [pseudonym of Emanuel Novogrudski], and other opponents have been wasting too much energy on proving that the *kehilah*'s leadership is incompetent. And Mr. Khmurner [pseudonym of Yoysef Lestschinsky] occupies himself with a very unrewarding task when he tries to find a dry spot on the entirely wet clothing of the *kehilah*'s leadership.

I cannot detect even the slightest trace of any kind of positive socialist community work carried out by today's *kehilah* leadership.

For every bourgeois party the *kehilah* is a power position they are trying to exploit both on the Jewish street and in the general political arena. For the bourgeois parties the religious character and religious functions of the *kehilah* are not a drawback; on the contrary, it is a great advantage because religion is one of the most reliable tools in the hands of the reactionary bourgeoisie to maintain its influence on the Jewish masses, to counteract the natural process of social and political differentiation within Jewish society, and to preserve, as long as possible, so-called "Jewish unity."

We are interested in achieving exactly the opposite of this. But we are not going to reach our goal by only holding meetings and putting out calls. We have always held to the opinion—and still do so today—that we have to win the sympathies of the broad mass of the working people. Of course, the approximately 90,000 votes we received in the Sejm elections represent a fine achievement in comparison to all other larger election campaigns until now. But it is still not more than a quarter—or a third at best—of what the party of the Jewish proletariat has to and can achieve on the Jewish street.

Clerical reaction poses the greatest danger to us. Because of the Polish reactionary politics of national and religious oppression, clerical reaction among us Jews is even stronger than in Polish society. But in order to combat this danger it is not enough to agitate from outside. The clerical reactionary bourgeoisie turned the institution of the *kehilah* into a fortress, and we must break it open from within. We must infiltrate deep into the masses organized around the *kehilah*. We must reveal clericalism's class character and its hostility to the interests of the people every step of the way. We must break up the ground on which its rule stands. We must block attempts by the reactionary Jewish bourgeoisie to turn the *kehilah* into its own power position in political life. It will be much easier to do this from within, not standing outside.

We are not going to carry out "organic" work in the *kehilah*. We are not going to involve ourselves in the *kehilah* administration. [. . .] We are not going to elect rabbis and will not vote budgets for them. We will take advantage of every opportunity to "tear off the *shtrayml* [Hasidic fur hat]" and reveal the reactionary-clerical face of our seemingly progressive bourgeoisie.

In 1918 the general political prospects were different than now. Back then "the *shtrayml*" was still hiding in a mouse hole, whereas today it is self-confident and presumptuous. In 1918 we could afford the luxury of boycotting the *kehilah* elections, whereas today such a boycott would be a grave political mistake. If the political situation were to change radically, no one could force us to remain in the *kehilah*.

Translated by Vera Szabó.

Other works by Erlich: *In kamf farn revolutsyonern sotsializm* (1934); *Der "Forverts" un der "Bund"* (1935); *Der iker fun bundizm* (1935).

Horace M. Kallen

1882–1974

The social philosopher Horace M. Kallen was born in Silesia, the son of a rabbi, but came with his parents to the United States in 1887. He was educated at Har-

vard and taught there, at Clark University, and at the University of Wisconsin. In 1919, he helped to found the New School for Social Research in New York City, where he taught for the rest of his life. His best-known contribution to American thought was his theory of cultural pluralism. Rejecting Israel Zangwill's vision of the United States as "a melting pot," he compared American society to a symphony orchestra, to which each immigrant group contributed its own distinctive sound. He opposed efforts to force the homogenization of American society and urged immigrants to cultivate and take pride in their national origins. Not surprisingly, he was a supporter of Zionism.

"Americanization" and the Cultural Prospect
1924

I

That the image of these United States as a "melting-pot" might be a delusion and its imputed harmony with democracy a snare was not an idea which, prior to the Great War, seemed even possible to Americans, whether of the philanthropic or the academic or the business community. The spontaneous invincible egotism of the group was too impenetrable and the absorption in the autochthonous interests of the national enterprise—evangelism, industrial expansion, finance and the struggle of political parties—was too complete, either for self-observation or for comparison with others. The admitted, and lamented, cultural inferiority to Europe was held to be more than compensated for by the claim of political superiority. The patriotic sentiment, the appreciation of national character, was concentrated in the word "democracy," and in democracy the United States was still felt to be the nonpareil among nations, the paragon and avatar of a state of literally free and equal citizens, or at least, if not equal in fact, equal in opportunity for every man to become the same as his betters. The traits of these betters were envisaged as the traits of the essential American, and personified as Uncle Sam. The current leaders of the community were accepted as variants of him, and each in his turn—Bryan or Roosevelt, for example—was hailed as the "typical" American. Whoever failed to acknowledge and to conform to this type was somehow alien, a different order of being, not admissible to the benefits of democracy, and fit at best to be a hewer of wood and a drawer of water to the true Americans.

The historic name for this attitude and sentiment is Know-Nothingism. Know-Nothingism is not, of course, an American but a human trait. What differs from ourselves we spontaneously set upon a different level of value. If it seems to be strong it is called wicked and is feared; if it is regarded as weak, it is called brutish and exploited. Sometimes, as in the attitude toward the negro, the emotions interpenetrate and become a sentiment focalizing the worst qualities of each. Only watchful discipline, much suffering or rare sophistication enables us to acknowledge the equality in nature and peerage in the community of that which is different and strange, enables us to give its individuality understanding and its character respect. Otherwise, these are won from us by conflict, not yielded by good will, and most completely so among peoples, nations, states.

That the paragon and avatar of democracy should be an exception to this rule would have been morally proper but naturally impossible. The newcomers in the United States figured significantly, therefore, only as so much cheap labor-power, not as sentient men and women with temperaments, histories and hungers, settling down as neighbors in the house next door, to make a life as well as a living. As neighbors they were "undesirable," and over the barriers raised against them only a few of them could pass into the free intimacies of the neighborly life. On the whole and in the long run, they remained in their own communities, with their churches as the focus of the common life, and their "Americanization" consisted of their compenetration into the country's economic and political pattern, and of that alone. The residue of their being, where they were freest and most at home, remained continuous with their own old-worldly inheritance. As this inheritance did not enter into the overt contacts of economics and politics, it was ignored. Such attention as was given it, was given it as only an aspect of the struggles and rivalries in those fields of the national life, and then only to suit the occasion. Defeated parties had always the traditional animadversions to make on the political corruption and economic obstreperousness due to depraved aliens.

So, as in the new world the aliens grew in mass, number and articulation, they changed in the form and in the intensity of their consciousness. When, at last, interest was directed upon their peculiar status in the cultural complex of American life, and upon the qualities and implications of their communities for excellence and evil in American society, Europe was at war, and the hateful passions of that unhappy continent were echoing and swelling over the waters. Social intelligence,

never too keen in America, got beclouded by sharp partisanship and vague fears. Anxiety over the economic significance of the immigrant was reinforced by anxiety over his social significance. A turmoil of organization and fulmination ensued, with the late Colonel Roosevelt in his usual role of drum-major and prophet. Protecting the immigrant; restraining him; keeping him out; compelling him to conform to ourselves; doing at least something to the immigrant and especially talking all sorts of phantasies about him, became the order of the day. Only in very rare instances was any fundamental attempt made to discern the forces in American social life with which the immigrant was involved, and to analyze out their behavior and relationships.

And even in those cases the philosophical preconceptions and national eventualities of the ethnic, economic and cultural differences of the communities composing the complex and vivid pattern of American nationhood could not fail of contagion from the burning issues underlying the civil war in Europe. One publicist [Norman Hapgood], grown up in the tradition that equality and similarity were synonymous, had, in the course of his own reflection upon the character of civilization in the United States, come to the realization of the democratic significance and necessity of free diversification for groups no less than for individuals. He had grown distrustful of the uniformity and monotony imposed by the material conditions of modern life, and had reached the conclusion that diversity was not a menace to but a promise for democracy. Another, the late Randolph Bourne, saw his country over against the mêlée of national rivalries in Europe as a "transnational" America." The currents of modern life, he thought, rendered impossible tight geographical groupings of nationality. The world's population was once more adrift. Labor had been rendered unprecedentedly mobile. Groups were involved in temporary as well as permanent mixings, mixings in such wise that they could maintain their distinctive cultural individualities without special territorial sovereignties or political institutions. Thus, the great North American republic, with its free institutions and continental spaces, was a wonderful promise of the reconciliation without the destruction of the diverse races of Europe, one nation of many peoples. [. . .]

II

The mass feeling of the more or less native Americans found another and far more significant pattern of self-expression than that of government confusion and mob-turmoil. Like all deep and wide-ranging public emotion, it came to rest in an ideology, an orthodoxy of dogma to which all were to conform, whether freely or under compulsion. This orthodoxy was integrated and focalized in the term "Americanization." By means of it feeling was articulated in formula and restlessness drawn into a channel wherein it became policy. Between the indefinitely distensible formulae of Americanization and the restricted channels of possible execution there was a Rabelaisian contrast. For the formulae, being purely discharges of feeling unrestrained by fact, only served to make conspicuous the irrationality, the extravagance, and hysteria usual in such phenomena; while action, being, when it is sincere and not either politic of mad, of necessity relevant to fact, tended, wherever it really occurred, to deflate the formulae to dimensions of sanity and to convert them from devices for the salvation of the panic-stricken into descriptions of the machinery of group adjustment for the reasonable. [. . .]

Other works by Kallen: *Democracy versus the Melting-Pot* (1915); *"Of Them Which Say They Are Jews" and Other Essays on the Jewish Struggle for Survival* (1954); *Cultural Pluralism and the American Idea* (1956).

Hans Kohn

1891–1971

Born and educated in Prague, Hans Kohn was active in the Zionist student organization Bar Kochba. He was one of the first Zionist activists to recognize the challenge of Arab nationalism to the establishment of a Jewish state and, after settling in the Land of Israel in 1925, he cofounded Brit Shalom with Martin Buber, Robert Weltsch, and Hugo Bergmann, which advocated the creation of a binational state. After the 1929 riots, he left the Zionist movement, moving eventually, in the 1930s, to the United States, where he made a career in the academy and pioneered the study of the history of nationalism.

The Political Idea of Judaism
1924

The People of the Yoke

The character of a people, as of an individual, cannot be grasped in its totality. It is recognized by us ex-

clusively in that unfoldment and development in time which we call history. In this world of human history there arises and expands a unique psychical universe of which the willing, purposively acting individual is a member. In this universe, the character of which is made up of vital processes, such as striving and self-transcendence, there are no laws determined by any parallelisms in space; from the successive temporal stages of the process there arise corresponding directions of effort and corresponding tendencies. Tendency and trend take the place of the unity of law. We do not deal with successions of phenomena of one kind, but with series of unique phenomena which nevertheless tend in the same direction. Like all that pertains to life these tendencies of direction are never rigid, finished, or final; they are tensions and strivings and processes of becoming; their objective intellectual precipitations in the ideational world and culture of a people always appear in the nature of a task, never in that of a fulfilment.

Now in each people there exist, whether clear or blurred, the same universally human qualities. Every people has its share in the entire psychic world and wealth of humanity. But in different peoples different qualities, capacities and inclinations stand out in peculiar relief. A people, therefore, is not definable by the possession of definite characteristics, but by its tendency to emphasize certain characteristics. Again, as is true of all that pertains to life, the boundaries of these tendencies are fluid, nor can they be fixed by definition or convention. Transitions are possible in every direction. The essential tendencies of a people always occur interwoven with others and seek to affirm themselves in conflict with those. Everything is tentative; there are constant possibilities of losing the path or of seeking a new one; nor is the road ever completed. It is lost in the distance toward which it strives, not wholly to be grasped or defined. What, nevertheless, are the tendencies that determine the character of the Jewish people?

Two types of humanity stand in clean contrast facing each other—the peoples of *time* and of *space*, the auditives (to Anglicize the terms of Rémy de Gourmont), and the visuals. The Greeks were the people of the eye, of the sense for space, of the plastic arts. An eminent scholar once called them "the eye of the world." Their great gift was the gift of seeing; from it they derived their world significance; knowledge and seeing (not only in the etymology of δaιo) were but a single thing to them. Their philosophy no less than their art is plastic, commanding space, transforming into space. It is as though they sought to transform all that is fluid, time-conditioned, interwoven, and tangential into the sharp limitations of immobility in space and to capture the formless in the rigidness of visual form. At its highest point their philosophy becomes plastic and their symbolic instrument is the chisel. The verb ὁρίζειν means both "to limit" and "to form concepts." To the Greek thoughts became plastic images. Plato's ideas are primal images of the world, cleansed of the dross of becoming, reduced to the pure types of being. To the Greek the stone with which he builds is the symbol of space and seeing; to the Jew the stream in which he dips is the symbol of time and of becoming. "The tumultuous sea of the ages into which flows the river of becoming did not greatly impress the Greek. To his notion Athena always conquers Poseidon as the cliff does the sea; in his landscape the streams are lost amid the stones." The Greek turns the world into marble and takes it out of time.

The Jew lives within time. He does not see as clearly as he hears. His senses are less aware of the contours than of the inner flowing of the world. His excelling organ is the ear and his form the call. His life and the life of his race stand under that unique heavenly configuration from which he hears for evermore, and only he, the *voice* of God and under which his historians have placed from the beginning the entire meaning of his record: the succession of being called and of turning a deaf ear to the call. Being forever called causes the Jew to hold himself tense toward the self-consuming action; he wills and the deed is his expression. He is the untiring propagandist, the unwavering messenger. His experience of the divine never permits him, like the Greek, to attain the peace of contemplation, of θεωρία, of a consuming self-sufficiency. He hears the call and must in obedience undergo the suffering of the lonely preacher in the desert, of the leader and awakener. But the apostasy of deafness to the call (which none is spared in his hour of doubt and despair and of the terrible inner absence from God—not Moses or Jeremiah or Jesus) protects him from deeming himself a direct partaker of the divine which, nevertheless, is the historic goal of all his yearning, and plunges him back into the irrational tragedy of humanity. The message of the prophets is *massa*, a burden, to them, and Moses complains: "I am not able to bear you myself alone. . . . How can I myself alone bear your cumbrance, and your burden and your strife?" And not otherwise did Jeremiah speak in the deeply moving passage in which he curses his calling and the heavy burden of his being called: "O Yaveh, thou hast persuaded me, and I was persuaded;

thou are stronger than I and hast prevailed: I am become a laughingstock all the day, everyone mocketh me. . . . Cursed be the day wherein I was born: let not the day wherein my mother bare me be blessed."

Thus to this folk did God become a voice. Again and again sounds the command, "Hear!" When Elijah becomes aware of God he hears only a still small voice. Therefore the Jew never made himself an image of his God. It is the word, the λόγος, which to the Jew is the mediator between the infinite and the individual, and the word carries more of infinity within itself than the sharp form of the frozen image. The word of God is a creative word and the Jewish worker of wonders is "Master of the good Name."

Sight is the sense by which space is perceived as time is perceived by hearing. To the Greek only that which is limited in space is beautiful and perfect. Hence to him the most perfect of images is the circle. And what was true to the Greek in the sphere of aesthetics was equally true in the field of morals. It was the Jew Philo who first within the sphere of Hellenic thinking esteemed the infinite above the harmoniously finite. . . .

The Greeks were not only masters of the plastic arts, but created the drama from the inchoate spilth of song. But it has been remarked that they did not produce with equal greatness the poem conceived in solitariness. The psalm was, by contrast, the most characteristic form of poetry in Hebrew literature and to this day the Jew has remained a lyrist, master of the most fluid and subjective of forms which is farthest from the form of the chiselled stone.

The Jew, then, lives more awarely in time than in space. Henri Bergson made the living flowing continuity of time the substance of his philosophic vision and speaks of "time, concerning which we feel that it is the very stuff of which our life is made." And in Gustav Landauer's *Scepticism and Mysticism*, written in entire ignorance of Bergson's *Creative Evolution*, there is a chapter entitled "The World as Time," in which we read: "To express all spatial concepts in terms of time is perhaps one of the most important tasks of the humanity of the future. It were well once with the help of hearing to apperceive the world temporally and to say. . . . Time should be substituted for space." The world as time cannot disintegrate into multi-dimensionality; it is one-dimensional; there is the line into the past; there is the forward urge into the future; the tension of directions is abrogated in the oneness of fluidity. The world as time is a world of polarity; the tradition of the past weighs it down; the impulse toward the future strains it toward the uncertain distance. It is alien from the balance of the forces that develop in spatial parallelism and rest harmoniously there; it is in itself in the nature of a force (rather than of mere being), one and not manysided, inclined to extremes and averse from compromise, passionate after the infinite and so the foe of forms.

The human being who lives in this world, a world of becoming, will yearn as no one else does for a transcendence of this tension, for that unity in which all antinomies are resolved and this unity will, in fact, become both the aim and the task of his life. Martin Buber has called the Jew a phenomenon of polarity because in his character contradictories coexist in a state of extreme tension. Out of this polarity arises the striving after oneness. "Make my heart one!" cries the Psalmist. And Franz Werfel, a Jewish lyrist of our own day, prays in one of his poems:

Why gavest Thou me not oneness?
Cleanse and unite me, Eternal Fountain!
Behold Thy wiser children lament from of old
Continually concerning the number Two.

To the Jew God is the one, the only, He who has wrought oneness and so is the aim of the oneness in man. "Our God, make One Thy Name and build Thy kingdom," the liturgy has it in the daily evening prayer. The man at one and the One God belong together. In the Jew's chief prayer which he prays daily and which, first recorded in the fifth book of Moses, was pronounced by Jesus to be the central word, the unity of God is declared in a solemn invocation to the people. This invocation is followed here too by a demand made of mortals. Man is to be undivided, homogeneous, whole and entire; he is not to swerve but bind his contrary proclivities and inclinations up into oneness. "With *all* thy heart and with *all* thy soul and with *all* thy might," are the well-known words. God is the reconciliation of the many in the One; it is man's duty to forge a oneness of the manifoldedness of his soul. Here, too, a dynamic and volitional attitude prevails. An eminent philologist has interpreted the ultimate meaning of the root El-God as "striving toward an aim or goal." God is man's aim; life is the way to Him through the dynamism of action. God *is*—but He *becomes* real in the life of man by man's active bearing of witness. Fundamentally the Jew values action; to him faith is secondary. In post-Pauline Christianity faith is decisive and conditions salvation. It was the profession of the right

faith that bound Christians to each other. Judaism (including the Jew Jesus) however, emphasized the deed and the fulfilment of God's will through action. Judaism contained no binding dogmas of faith but the interpretation of God's will in respect of human action. The unity or integration of man is accomplished through action and concrete living, in the temporal continuance of spiritual struggle and in the tension of willing, not in cognitive vision. (The Greeks, on the other hand, did not doubt but what men would love virtue could they but awarely *see* it.) Nor has a Christian theologian failed to note how in Jesus the "centrifugal forces of his being were welded into a true oneness by the higher power of His overwhelming will." But the way of action leads through an uninterrupted series of decisions. The duty of decision constitutes both the burden and the nobility of our mortal fate. Choosing means tension, courage, danger. It is slackness, feebleness, sloth of the heart and cowardice that shrink from moral choice. This is the Jewish conception of sin. In fulfilment of the words of Genesis: "Ye shall be as God, knowing good and evil," the Deuteronomist reiterates: "Behold I set before you this day a blessing and a curse. . . . I have set before you life and death, blessing and cursing: therefore choose life." . . . And on the top of Carmel Elijah demanded of the people: "How long will ye limp to both sides? if Yaveh is God, follow Him; if Baal is God, follow *him*." "Ah, that thou wert either hot or cold," we hear in the Revelation of St. John. The One God requires man to be one, undivided, wholly dedicated to his task. This drive toward unity impels the Jew to make of unity the ideal of the world of man—and so to be the first among the peoples to conceive the notion of the oneness of humanity.

This Jewish thinking in terms of time produces its farthest-reaching result in the Jewish conception of history. It may well be, as Alexander von Humbold[t] maintained in his *Kosmos*, that the Jewish monotheistic view, which always regards the universe as indeed one and as directed by an undivided energy is important among the elements of human culture which, since the Renaissance, have inaugurated the modern observation of nature. To Jewish thinkers, however, nature was not the decisive element, but rather man and the actions of man, that is, history. Man introduced unity into the flow of time and significance into the running and drying up and springing forth again of events and his consciousness accepts these processes as one and homogeneous. The Jewish God is not a God in nature. In His solemn self-revelation he is not like Zeus νεφεληγερετα. He is the Lord of an historic event. "I am Yaveh, thy God, who brought thee out of Egypt, out of the house of bondage." The social ethic which God demands is no mere commandment nor is it grounded in reason; it is historical in character. "Ye shall not oppress the strangers, for ye know concerning the heart of the stranger, for ye too were strangers in Egypt." And it is this consciousness of history that binds the generations. "Guard thyself and take heed, lest thou forgettest these stories that thou hast seen with thine own eye and that all thy life long they leave not thy heart, but that thou speak of them to thy children and thy children's children." "When in days to come thy son asks thee: what are the witnessings and the commandments and the judgments that Yaveh our God has commanded, then thou shalt make answer to thy son: bondservants were we unto Pharaoh in Egypt, but Yaveh led us forth from Egypt with a strong hand." And to this day the Jews celebrate Pesach as though it were *they* themselves who had been saved from Egypt, as though the oneness of the generations merged above and within them, as though the historic past were not dead but a very living force within every hour of the present.

It is an historic consciousness of incomparable strength that animates this people, interpenetrates all its works and actions and gives it both a permanence and an inner certainty that are inexplicable otherwise. This people has established its home not in space but in time and in eternity and therefore time has no power over it. But on this account too every human action gains a new unheard-of value and a peculiar relationship to God. For history is the *path* of Yaveh. "I consider the deeds of Yaveh," the Psalmist sings, "I think of all Thy action and meditate concerning Thy great deeds." But God accomplishes his deeds through men. He has called and chosen them to be the bearers of the historic process. A gigantic responsibility rests upon them. By virtue of this fact men emerge from the context of nature and enter into that realm of history which, though spiritual and transcending nature, carries on its processes within nature. This is true of all men. For God's way is accomplished through all the peoples; all are his tools and building-stones and helpers. Once more from this point of view and only from this Jewish point of view we have the first vision of mankind as one—as humanity perceived and felt as such. Among the peoples Israel is elected in the sense that it is most powerfully aware of the meaning of history, of the burden of the calling of

God, of the presage of that end of things which its leaders have in all ages passionately yearned after as the goal of all mankind. For the way of God demands the ethical activity of man and human striving after perfection. It is terrifying to be torn out of nature into the storm of God. And nature and the natural instincts of man rebel again and again and apostasy takes place and courage faints. Since the exodus out of Egypt there goes through the Jewish people an eternal plaint after the flesh-pots of the life of nature and apostasy from God's way continually recurs.

The teachers of later ages sought—successfully but not without creating new dangers—to sanctify through ever more intricate regulations all the activities of life and thus constantly to relate them to God's will. They sought by this means to create security in place of the ever renewed necessity of moral decision and its danger. This method made the burden heavier and yet eased the bearing of it and simplified while it complicated. But the aim remained the same. The historic consciousness of the Jewish people establishes oneness within the happenings in time; since Amos the concept of world-history as a unified process is set into ever higher relief; the duty of man to be the ethically active embodiment of this process became a certainty upon the acceptance of the Law and the covenant under Moses and needed to receive from the words of the Prophets only its framing of universal history. The crown of this homogeneous historical process is its ultimate goal—God. His way (namely, human history) is the way to Him. . . .

Out of the primary elements of the Jewish character—its self-realization within time, its historical consciousness, its demand upon itself of ethical action—arose the Messianic yearning. To the Jew the world of the future is not a beyond, but the becoming and the coming time—*olam haba*. It is the time of oneness, of the becoming at one with himself of every human creature in that he is undividedly and with his whole self given over to God; it is the time of the union of all men in brotherly at-oneness and of the oneness of all nature in peace. This Jewish vision is the first vision of all mankind grown perfect; by virtue of it the passion of man embraced the struggle for the absolute and infinite, and a forever inextinguishable disquietude came into the world which through the instrument of Christianity communicated itself to the pagan peoples. The goal is set: the kingdom of God, the Messianic realm of the future. The way is found: to do the will of God, that is to say, to practice justice, to become perfect, even as

He is perfect, to sanctify oneself because He is holy and in order that He may be sanctified. All men strive after the kingdom. But the Jews as a people, from the time of their becoming a people onward, have been the heralds and forerunners of this striving. Despite apostasies they have through all their myriad martyrs and through all their leaders, through Moses and the Prophets, through Jesus and the Talmudic sages and the Baal Shem Tov and through the many millions who, unknown and forgotten, have lived for the sanctification of the Name and the coming of the kingdom—through all these they have been the people of the yoke, the folk of spiritual responsibility.

Translated by Ludwig Lewisohn.

Other works by Kohn: *Nationalismus: Über die Bedeutung des Nationalismus in Judentum und in der Gegenwart* (1922); *The Idea of Nationalism: A Study in Its Origins and Background* (1944); *Living in a World Revolution: My Encounters with History* (1964).

David Ben-Gurion
1886–1973

The Labor Zionist David Ben-Gurion was the dominant political figure in the Yishuv during the 1930s and 1940s and the first prime minister of the State of Israel, an office he held from 1948 to 1963 (with the exception of a brief period, 1953–1955). A conventional Marxist-Zionist when he moved to Palestine in 1906, he eventually came to privilege the nationalist side of his political outlook as his socialism became increasingly moderate. He was instrumental in forging the political power of the organized labor movement and in making Mapai the main political party in the Yishuv.

The National Mission of the Working Class
1925

The Hebrew worker did not come here as a refugee seeking shelter wherever it could be found, looking for any available means of survival. He went up into the land as an emissary of the nation, and as a pioneer in the great project of the Hebrew revolution he won his positions in labor, in the economy, and in Jewish settlement. In every deed, in every project, small or large, in his labor in the country or in the city, in building his agricultural or industrial unit, in the conquest of the language and the culture, in guarding and protecting, in the battle for his interests and rights in labor, in securing his class and national needs, in founding his institutions and his labor federation—the historical mission of the class to which he belonged and for whose establishment he had blazed a trail appeared before him: the historical mission of the working class on behalf of the revolution that will make labor rule over the life of the people and the land. The Hebrew worker included the cause of national redemption in the labor of his life, and in his struggle and class creation he bound together the entire content of the people's desires and historical needs.

In contrast to the representatives of other classes in the land and in Zionism, the worker was not confronted with the contradiction between his class needs and desires and national interests and aspirations. The worker who recognizes his class consciousness and is faithful to his historical mission fulfills two missions at the same time. These are: the class mission and the mission of the entire people. Every class effort of the worker in his economic and professional labor and his political and cultural work, to the degree that it is directed at the central and historical purpose, creates and conquers national positions in the land and paves the broad path for popular immigration. The class struggle of the workers in its principled breadth and in its concrete concomitants is aimed not at dividing the people and weakening it—but rather, on the contrary, at its true and complete unity, notable in its strengths and splendor.

However, the representatives of the other classes also advocate national interests, and to the degree that they fulfill a positive function in building up the land, they also are doing the work of the nation. However, this is the objective fate of all the other classes—their class interests must, sooner or later, conflict openly and in secret with the need of the people and immigration. Without mention of the parasites of "private initiative," who bring neither assets nor property to the country, but merely lust for lucre at the expense of the national wealth, of the national awakening, and of immigration, for even property-owners on every level, who help according to their ability in building up the land and enlarging the absorptive capacity of the Jewish settlement—are liable to rise up and hinder the needs of immigration and popular settlement, and not from ill will and malice, but by the force of the inner logic and the nature of private property, which seeks profit and exploitation. Increasing the cost of the necessities of life by commercial capital, raising rent by landlords, and making land more expensive by private purchase of land—all of these burden and hinder the absorption and assimilation of popular immigration and place difficult obstacles before national settlement. The private economy in cities and the countryside, which subsists through exploitation of hired labor, seeks, consciously or unconsciously, with and without malice, to reduce salaries and worsen the conditions of labor to the lowest level of the cheapest worker with few needs, thus endangering the Hebrew workers' possibility of subsistence and thwarting the immigration of working people.

Whose heart is so bold as to state that the quantity of private wealth in the Land of Israel increases proportionately with the needs of popular Hebrew immigration and the claims of the Hebrew worker? As for the "private capital" that has been invested so far in the Jewish economy that employs Hebrew workers—it is doubtful whether it is private so much as it is capital: and if it is really capital—how much it is private. Almost all of the "private" economy that exists in the country on the basis of Hebrew labor still draws upon national or quasi-national sources and depends on direct or indirect national support in one form or another. The capital invested in the factories of "Select," "Electricity," "Nesher [cement]," the grain mills, etc., is basically the fruit of voluntary contributions or national generosity, of institutions and companies that draw upon the Zionist will.

Moreover, in this country we have not yet seen a factory truly built on private capital that particularly seeks out Hebrew labor or especially makes use of the organized Hebrew worker, who has cultural needs and fights for the conditions of his work and his class rights, while the land and its neighbors offer plentiful cheap labor, easy to exploit and subject. And the few miserable workers who are employed outside of the factories, who stand beyond the sphere of influence and support of the national means, such as for the railroad, are forced to adapt to the conditions of work that are determined not according to their needs, but according to the needs of the workers who are not Jews.

Some individuals from the other classes are capable of rising above the concerns and interests of their class and recognizing the national need and to stand at its behest. However, these individuals are exceptional. These outstanding individuals become strangers to their class, and they do not have the power to change the nature of the economic and social reality that is impressed upon the class in general. At every time, in every country, the other classes were, as such, faithful to the needs of their people only to a degree, and as long as those deeds suited their particular egoistic needs. The working class is unique in *its objective conformity*

with the historical needs of the people, and it is unique in its ability and loyalty *and perseverance* on behalf of national interests, because in its hand is the key to the future of the nation, and upon it is incumbent the duty, through class struggle, to liberate the nation from class contradictions.

An individual or individuals from the working class are liable to deny their national mission, just as there are workers who are alienated from the needs of their class and lend a hand to their oppressors. However, those individuals are exceptional. The community of workers in general, among whom class consciousness has matured, that is to say, consciousness of the historical mission of their class, regard their needs and the needs of their people, their class interests and the national interests, as joined together and attached to each other, as a single unit, which cannot be sundered or dismantled.

The question that is sometimes asked, whether the workers must give preference to national needs or to class demands, merely demonstrates the ignorance of the questioner. This question can be asked of the representatives of other classes: their class interests often conflict with the interests of the entire people. Within the working class, which recognizes its historical mission, class interests go hand in hand with national interests. The organic identity of the national and class purpose of the workers' movement is imprinted in the social and economic essence of the working class, and this identity underlies class consciousness. This awareness sees the class oppositions within the people and also the way to abolish them—by class struggle within the nation.

Ignoring the class oppositions within the people in the name of the national idea and in the name of national unity makes a mockery of the national idea and deviation from the path that leads to the unity of the people. The government of property divides the people and tears it to shreds, and only the decisive victory of the working class will do away with the internal rifts and oppositions. Until the rule of labor has been achieved national unity will be nothing but an aspiration—the aspiration of the socialist movement of the working class. The war of liberation of the working class is also the war of liberation and unity of the nation. The road toward the realization of national unity is the road of class struggle.

Jerusalem, 24 Adar 5685

Translated by Jeffrey M. Green.

Other works by Ben-Gurion: *Rebirth and Destiny of Israel* (1959); *Israel: Years of Challenge* (1964); *Recollections* (1970).

Solomon Birnbaum
1891–1989

The son of the early Jewish nationalist Nathan Birnbaum, Solomon Birnbaum was a Hebrew paleographer, Yiddish philologist, and translator (from German to Yiddish and from Yiddish to German), first in Hamburg and then, after 1933, in London, where he taught at the School of Oriental and African Studies and the School of Slavonic and East European Studies. His major contribution to Hebrew scholarship was work on the evolution of Hebrew script.

Judaism and Yiddish
1925

"If God grant that the earth will be full of understanding, and everyone will speak the same language, Ashkenazic, then only (the form) Brisk will be written." That is how Meir ben Moses Hacohen, the father of Sabbatai Hacohen, wrote it. We infer that by "Ashkenazic" he meant Yiddish, since Brisk is the Yiddish name of the town that is called in Russian Brest. This quotation shows further that he took it for granted that the way Jews speak is a Jewish way—a simple truth which we have ceased to understand in recent times. His words about Yiddish have a warm ring, and the voice of this rabbi was the voice of the Jewish people.

Who is the Jewish people today, and who can be said to speak for it? There are very large parts of East Ashkenazic Jewry who live their whole life with a minimum of Jewishness on an alien soul-soil. Logically we would expect them also to abandon Yiddish, the language of those who remained faithful to the Jewish heritage. We would further expect that there would be such among the faithful who, fighting for their ideals, would stand up for Yiddish.

But we do not always find the facts accord with what appears to be logical. There is little thought given to Yiddish among the religious, while there is a whole section among the secularized to whom Yiddish is an ideal, in fact their whole ideal. How is that possible? Have we grown so weak, have we sunk so low in our own eyes that we can look on calmly while all that is ours is taken from us and we do not even realize that it is being taken from us?

Ours—for who created Yiddish? Did it grow out of modern theories? Out of the modern conception of what constitutes nationhood: land and language, and nothing more? No, the Jewish people of old, the people of Judaism and Jewishness created Yiddish. Neither of the two consecutive schools of the Maskilim, the Enlighteners, has a valid explanation for the rise of Yiddish, neither the assimilationists who ascribe it to the compulsory seclusion of Jews in the ghetto, nor their spiritual descendants, the nationalists, who attribute it to the "national distinctiveness" of the Jews.

For, on the one hand, the main emigration from Germany had taken place before the ghetto was instituted. And where was the element of compulsion in ghettoless Poland, which saw the great flowering of Yiddish? When they go on to say that Yiddish was born of misery, because the Jews were "thrust out from the general cultural life"—the assimilationists are very much mistaken when they think that the "general culture" of those times was like that of today, which keeps getting more irreligious, and where people to whom religion means nothing can live together in some sort of undifferentiated hash.

The "general culture" at that time was Christian, and the Jews, for their part, all lived as Jews should. So how can it be imagined that before the birth of Yiddish Jews and Christians had been living in a common cultural environment, and the Jews were expelled from it? They could not be expelled from the Christian culture, since they had a great and ancient culture of their own.

Nor, on the other hand, can the argument put forward by the nationalists be valid, that it was the national distinctiveness of the Jews which was responsible for the development of Yiddish. What do they mean by national distinctiveness? Do they mean the factor that derives from race? Even if this had some influence we have no way of detecting its effect, here or in any other language. If by national distinctiveness they mean the sum total of Jewish particularities—in other words, their culture—we would have to ask: What is the source of this culture and of its specific coloring?

The answer to this question is of course that Jewish culture grows on the soil of the Jewish religion.

With that we have discovered the cause that brought Yiddish into being; it was in the last analysis Judaism that fashioned a Jewish language out of Old German.

Yiddish is in fact in no way exceptional in this respect. The religions of other peoples, too, have been the creators of their cultures and so of new languages. Moreover, even in Jewish history the appearance of a language like Yiddish is not a unique phenomenon. This same creative process has occurred at various periods and in various places.

As far as their nature and function are concerned there is no difference between Yiddish, on the one hand, and the Aramaic of the Talmud, Judeo-Arabic or Spaniol on the other. But there is a great difference in actual fact, both quantitatively and qualitatively. The number of Yiddish-speakers had grown in our time to twelve million, a figure which had of course never been reached by any of the other Jewish groups. Furthermore, it embraced three quarters of the whole Jewish people, a ratio which had never existed since the Hebrew and Aramaic periods. Yiddish is the most distinctive of all Jewish languages: the others, including Hebrew, are considerably less differentiated from the non-Jewish parallel languages.

Where the influence of religion ends, there the culture-creating process ends, and with it the distinctive particularities and the essential barriers between peoples gradually disappear. History provides examples enough. But our Leftists did not and do not see this, and some of those who have made Yiddish their idol have used this creation of religion as a weapon in the war against Judaism.

This war—in which Hebrew too was usually one of the targets—did not mislead the people themselves, the Judaism people, into confusing their Yiddish with that of the Yiddishists, or their Hebrew with that of the Hebraists. They realized instinctively that Ivrit is not the Holy Tongue but just another instrument of secularization, of assimilation, annihilation as Jews.

They disregarded therefore the battle cry of the Hebraists, "Hebrew or Russian, not Yiddish!" and they held on to their mother tongue. It is characteristic—we come across press reports from time to time which tell us how in one synagogue or the other in the Holy Land, when someone wanted to address the congregation in Ivrit, the people protested, and insisted on Yiddish.

There were, however, some religious people who were misled into seeing only the dangers of Yiddishism, and not those of Hebrism. In their short-sightedness they overlooked the fact that basically there is no difference between the two, that both are manifestations of the same irreligious nationalism in a different guise. They did not see that the whole conflict "Yiddish versus Hebrew," "folk language versus national language" was only a quarrel between twin brothers.

Their attitude was rooted in the Jewish Enlightenment, combining both the influences of the earlier assimilationist and the present nationalist phase. They failed to realize that the fulfillment of God's command that we should be separated from the peoples is considerably facilitated by our having a vernacular of our own.

They not only overlooked the great practical value of Yiddish toward preserving the Jewish entity, but they failed to appreciate the importance of form in the whole structure of Jewishness—and this is one of the fundamental values of Yiddish.

Being under alien influences they stood blind-eyed before the facts, and nodded their heads in approval when they listened to such absurdities as "Yiddish is not really our language," "Yiddish is not beautiful," "Yiddish is a mixed language," "Yiddish is a corrupt German," "no other nation speaks Yiddish" (!)—all of which makes no sense from the point of view of scholarship and is equally indefensible from the Jewish angle.

Things went so far that the alien influence invaded the literary language of the religious Jews. The assimilationists had created an ugly, Germanized Yiddish, and the nationalists had on their part done nothing to make it more Jewish and to beautify it, though they did remove certain kinds of blatant Germanisms. The religious Jews did not bother to protect their traditional language from the disruptive power of secularized Yiddish—even in Bible translation. And when the scope of Yiddish for literary purposes was widened within the religious community, the writers and journalists simply took over the language of the secularizers—vocabulary, morphology and syntax, though it was all permeated by the spirit of assimilation.

We did not have the strength to build something of our own. The assimilationists introduced a Germanized, philologically stupid orthography. We have followed them in this, and we are holding on to it more tightly than they themselves are—for their descendants have replaced it by a number of brand-new spelling systems and, paradoxically, those among us who imitate them could truthfully say that the earlier modern system is even less Jewish than the new one. Who among us realized that our own traditional orthography was not so bad after all, and that it would have been easy to build on its basis a scientifically acceptable system which was not cut off from its Jewish roots? But we never thought of such a thing. Language . . . spelling . . . What does it matter!

This attitude remains. It does not occur to us that beauty should play a part in everything Jews do, including the language in which they think and write. It is not a matter of indifference whether the writers of Yiddish murder the language, or whether they use it with skill, and cultivate its beauty.

Some people may say that it requires philological training to attend to such matters, and that the subject is too dull for most people. First of all, nobody expects everybody to deal with this, and secondly, details are not dull if you realize their bearing on wider issues— and here the purpose is to shape, refine and beautify a medium which we use, among other things, in the service of God. God should be served with beauty.

This brings me to another value of Yiddish. The value of separation and the value of form, which I mentioned before, concern the community as a whole. When we stress the esthetic aspect our concern is more with the individual. A language that is the mother tongue has a direct impact—the conscious mediation of the intellect hardly comes into play. Rabbi Nachman of Bratzlav knew what he was doing when he left instructions that the originals of the tales (which he told in Yiddish and which were taken down by his disciple Nathan) must accompany the Hebrew translation when the book was published.

That explains also the fact that Chassidism increased the importance of Yiddish. The Chassidim sought new and even better ways of pouring out their souls to God, and they found them in the language which was on their tongue. That is how Rabbi Levi Isaac Berditchever came to sing in Yiddish.

But the role of Yiddish in religious life was not confined to the sphere where emotion plays the main part; it also extended to the intellectual fields. Yiddish was employed for literature—mainly translations, paraphrases, commentaries. There were whole sections of the people whose knowledge of Hebrew was quite inadequate and it was realized that they must not be left out in the wilderness. A whole people cannot all be scholars, and God's word, and also the teachings of our great men, had to be made accessible to them. It is important to remember that this part of the people included half the total number—women and girls. So translations were made of the Bible and of some of the literature. The number of translations, paraphrases and commentaries shows how well this need was understood.

The value of this literature is not sufficiently appreciated today. Who knows where we might now be if Isaac ben Jacob had not written his Tzenne Renne? It is all very well for some youngster to turn up his nose and call it "womanish stuff." But if it were not for the Tzenne Renne he might not now be studying his Talmud.

The most important intellectual function of Yiddish is oral: its use in the teaching and study of the Bible, the Talmud and the rest of the traditional literature. Thus it serves as a link both in life and in learning between the past and the present, between the smallest schoolboy and the greatest scholars.

We must not think that what appears in written form is all that counts. The vehicle of intellectual life is primarily the spoken Yiddish, even though what is thought and said in it may be written down later and published in the Holy Tongue.

This division of labor between the two languages continues into our own times. Here too there is room for an extension of the role of Yiddish. We can easily picture some outstanding scholar of today, or of the future, writing a new commentary in Yiddish, and to judge by the past, this would certainly not oust Rashi's Commentaries. Nor would there be any danger that the Holy Tongue would thereby lose any of its luster, sanctity or usefulness. On the whole, however, the functions of the two languages in the field of traditional learning are not likely to change.

But there is scope for the expansion of Yiddish through the creation of a modern *Jewish* literature, which would spread from end to end and cover every field of Jewish life and being. There are large numbers of people who must be given fiction, as well as the humanities and science, on the basis of Judaism—not popularization or trash, but works of high standards.

How have we met that need? Is it surprising that many of our people have turned to the secular literature in Yiddish and Hebrew—a European literature in a supposedly Jewish garb? We must also ask ourselves: Is it an accident that we have no poets today who sing in the service of God?

Let us not go on squandering that precious gift of God, a language of our own, a Judaism language. There is still hope, for there is still a people that sings the songs of Levi Isaac Berditchever, and there still are Jewish folksongs.

Let us remember the words of Bar Qappara who said that one of the four causes of Israel's redemption from Egypt was "that they did not give up their language."

Translated by Irene R. Birnbaum.

Other works by Birnbaum: *Praktische Grammatik der jiddischen Sprache* (1918); *The Qumran Scrolls and Paleography* (1952); *The Hebrew Scripts* (1954–1957).

Robert Weltsch

1891–1984

As did his cousin Felix Weltsch, Robert Weltsch grew up in a German-speaking Jewish milieu in Prague in the last days of the Habsburg Empire. He was a member of the Zionist student group Bar Kochba. From 1919 to 1938, he served as editor of the twice-a-week, Berlin-based Zionist newspaper *Jüdische Rundschau*. Because of his association in the 1920s and 1930s with Brit Shalom, which championed binationalism, he was a frequent target of criticism by mainstream Zionists. After fleeing Germany, he settled in the Land of Israel, where he worked for the prestigious daily *Haaretz*, serving as its London correspondent from 1945 to 1978. He was instrumental in establishing the Leo Baeck Institute, which promotes scholarship on the history, culture, and legacy of German-speaking Jews.

Our Nationalism: A Hanukkah Reflection
1925

The renaissance of the Maccabean festival, which began with the onset of modern nationalism, signified a great revolution in Jewish thinking. The Jew aspired to leave behind the unworthy life of exile in order to shape his destiny in terms of human and national dignity. Symbolic of this process was the legendary battle of those few who gathered around the banner of Maccabee in order to fight for the purity of the Jewish idea against a foreign, powerful civilization. A later, debased generation was able to rebuild its self-respect on the exemplary virtues of the Maccabees, who had relinquished the conveniences of living in slavery and even contemporary culture and who had fanatically dedicated their lives to the truth. The founding pillar of modern Jewish nationalism was the consciousness that we do not simply want to be like other peoples, imitating them like slaves. We rather want to ensure that we remain alert and do not bend to the pressures of generally accepted facts and conventions, but keep our freedom of conscience and our moral decisiveness. Decades have passed since this original mental revolution. The Maccabean festival has become permanently established. It has lost more and more of its original content and suc-

cumbed to the rules of habit. The spiritual tension of our national movement has faded—who would deny this? Our festivals become more and more cornerstones of self-inspection. Are we true to our idea, or have slackening and mechanization taken over? Let's be honest to ourselves: our nationalism has to be self-critical and not self-worshipping. Everywhere around us we see the damage done by nationalism when it does not appear as a moral force, but as disguised egoism, which enhances itself through the intoxication of self-righteousness. The modern nationalism of most peoples peaks in self-praise. It consists of a peculiar blindness and a will to hear only good things about themselves and bad things about their enemies. The truth quite loses out. Jewish nationalism, however, is unthinkable without the ideal of truth, which, like an all-consuming fire, turns even against its own people if it needs to. The great national heroes of Jewry are those who have held a mirror before the people, from the prophets to the lesser minds of our time. It made sense when Gorelik recently said that we should build a memorial to Otto Weininger in Palestine. Nationalism is a higher development of the nation. This, however, is unthinkable if one's own mistakes are not recognized, denounced, and hated. The comfortable sleep of oblivion has to be disturbed by the eternal, nagging voice of conscience. We Zionists know this. Our movement, which was called the conscience of Jewry, arose from dissatisfaction, nourished by holy anger at the ignobility of our own people. It might seem peculiar to many of our opponents that we Zionists criticize our own national movement fiercely. We do not dread the public, nor our prick-eared opponents, because we know that self-criticism is our greatest strength.

A peculiar celebration is to be held on this Maccabean festival in Jerusalem. The flag of the Jewish Legion, which fought in the war with the English army, is to be raised in Jerusalem's Great Synagogue in remembrance of the capture of the city by Lord Allenby eight years ago on the Hanukkah festival. That former members of the Legion feel the need to place their flag in the synagogue (although most of these fighters are not religious, to the best of our knowledge) is a debatable matter of taste. We would hardly engage in it. However, we heard that the plan is not to let this event proceed in silence as would be appropriate, but with great military pomp and demonstration marches in Jerusalem. Such a plan is politically shortsighted because it gives the impression that the Jews feel like the military lords of the land, holding military parades on every occasion. On Armistice Day they unfortunately couldn't refrain from such a spectacle either. Instead of shaping our policies to gain the trust of the Arab world, which is becoming more organized, we unnecessarily provoke the feelings of the Arabs. They will look at us like citizens of countries anywhere in the world would look at a people that holds military parades on their land. [. . .] More troublesome is the fear that our own nationalism could slide unnoticed and uncontrolled into empty, boastful theatricality, which we know from other people. We do not want to assess the political understanding of the organizers of this procession and conclude that they want to intimidate the citizens of Jerusalem. We rather believe that the decisive motive for this event is the need for display and self-intoxication. This, however, is dangerous because it corrupts the people. It masks its true worries and detracts its sense of responsibility from real problems. Such means are used everywhere in the world in order to addle the people. Who hasn't laughed heartily at the narrow-minded and inflated philistinism of war associations worldwide! Who hasn't felt how all nations unleash their worst instincts on such occasions, how they gloss over their human weaknesses with military celebrations? Should we not pause if we see that we are going off the rail in a similar way, our nationalism being diverted from its original holy essential core? We object to this kind of Hanukkah celebration in Jerusalem. We see it as a deviation from the idea of the Maccabees. We haven't yet cleansed the Temple, and we do not yet have a reason to celebrate a triumphal procession.

Jewish nationalism is a revolution of the Jewish soul. The awareness of belonging to our nation, and the moral obligations that come with it, cannot weaken once they have been experienced. Zionism is not only an awareness; it is above all a will; a will to build a better reality. Therefore our Zionist disposition is tightly tied to the work that is being done in our days in the land of the Maccabees. Our ideal is great, but we cannot conceal that our means are few, that reality is hard, that we are only humans, with the weaknesses and shortcomings of human beings. Zionism is characterized not by empirical facts, but by ideal ambitions. The ambition has to be big, strong, and unbroken. Facts change, and amidst the constantly unsettling daily struggle with its countless difficulties, our work manages at times better, at times worse. It moves forward, but it can only reach its goals if we stay strong enough in our souls to confront adamant criticism. We can claim without exaggeration that in Palestine much has been achieved in the process of the conquest of the land through labor. Previously unknown forces of the Jewish people have been exhibited, without which no results would have been achieved. This is not to say, however, that everything is good now and that every observer of the Palestinian reality is necessarily convinced of the correctness of Zionism. The correctness or incorrectness of our project cannot be judged according to the success of our efforts at this or that moment. Our propaganda cannot be built on the presentation of our own glory to the world and on the portrayal of Palestine as the land of the purest virtues and greatest achievements. In Palestine as well there is need for improvement; much evil that we would have liked to keep away has crept in because no human society exists without evil. We know, and every thinking person must know, that it cannot be otherwise. If an opponent uses this argument against us in political debate, he proves that he is not being honest, and that he is using whatever means he can in order to blacken the whole project. But we must not err by resorting to euphemisms or by denying badness on our side. Who would impudently claim to be doing such work without having anything bad creep in? The temptation is so strong, why shouldn't it be able to harm us? Badness is not dangerous as long as we do not approve it. That is why Zionism, alert nationalism, means self-control. We are the servants of a great work, but we have to be wary that the machine of our work will not defeat us.

Many Zionists are extremely sensitive to criticism of the situation in Palestine. They view a description of the mischiefs and dangers as an attack on Zionism, whereas it is the greatest service that can be done for us. In this respect, for instance, it is very interesting how much the latest article by [Arthur] Holitscher in the *Neue Rundschau* has upset some Zionists. They view him as damaging to Zionism. Now the article by Holitscher, as already mentioned in this publication, includes many debatable one-sided and superficial impressions. It is unfair in some aspects and disregards large problems that stand at the center of our work. Yet it also includes many truths, uncomfortable truths, which have repeatedly been published in one way or another in the *Jüdische Rundschau*. Zionism should hear and face them, not deny them. We will only recognize our task clearly if we keep the facts in mind as they really are. As Zionists, as real nationalists, we have to reject those compliments that put us to sleep and lull us into a false sense of security. We have to welcome the criticism that out of love for our idea of a new life shows the discrepancy between idea and contemporary reality. Holitscher's remarks, which show the enormous energy and concentration of creation in Jewish Palestine, should accordingly be evaluated in a positive manner. Our opponents, while far from being communists, use the communists' concern about the dangers facing the labor movement as an argument against us. Their hypocrisy should not scare us. Many of the causes for their accusations could have been alleviated if the Jewish people had been on the watch and hadn't frivolously abandoned the pioneers. Our task as Zionists is to do everything in order to alleviate the difficulty of the situation. We are far from having done everything. Yet even at best there always have to be crises and commotions. If the signs do not deceive us, we are facing such a crisis in Palestine today. Sooner or later the boisterously promoted developments of the last year will lead to a natural backlash. If we let ourselves be demoralized by such events or criticism, then we haven't yet understood the essence of Zionism. Certainly there are difficult times, and certainly people will also suffer. Some beautiful dreams will melt away, but only children and fools could have imagined the completion of a secular work of such extraordinary dimensions otherwise. Zionism is not dependent on whether in Palestine this succeeds today or that tomorrow. It is the fight for truth in Jewry, the fight for an idea that once the Maccabees illuminated. If our Maccabean festivals lull us into play and dance and bestow an undeserved atmosphere of sanctification on us, then they are a national mischief. However, if they manage to revolutionize our souls as they once did, making us look into the mirror of truth and making us aware of our national obligations, then they will be truthful stages on the way to our national redemption.

Translated by Sara Yanovsky.

Other works by Weltsch: *Deutsches Judentum* (1963); *Be-naftulei ha-zemanim* (1981); *Die deutsche Judenfrage* (1981).

World Sephardi Federation

Established in 1925

The World Sephardi Federation was founded in Vienna at an international gathering of Sephardim prior to the 14th Zionist Congress. The initiative for its establishment came from the leaders of the Sephardi and Mizrahi communities in Mandatory Palestine, who wished to give the Sephardi communities a larger voice in the Zionist movement and in the New Yishuv.

Is There a Need for a World Sephardi Federation? A Debate by Jewish Delegates in Vienna
1925

Rabbi Uziel:

My brothers and teachers: for some years, since I was enlightened by the luminous erudition of our pious forefathers, the rabbis in Babylon and the wise writers from Spain, my attention has turned to the present state of spiritual decline in the lands of our exile in the East. Turning my sights to our glorious past, and comparing it to our bleak present and future, two feelings stirred within me: on the one hand, a sense of national pride, and, on the other hand, a deep sense of shame and anxiety. . . .

Our exilic isolation tore us apart. It shredded us into pieces and turned us into divided entities—alienated and distant communities—disconnected and detached from the great nation building project . . . without any organic connection to unify us under a single public national leadership, or to consolidate us into a national body. With great hope and deep anticipation I have always craved that the spirit and power of God would revive our spirits and gather [our] scattered bones into a national body.

Unsettled in my heart, I wondered who would allow me to fly like a bird, who would bestow upon my hands the prophetic power to sound the horn of revival to all these communities, uniting them, consolidating them, and amalgamating them into one living party that includes all the communities from abroad. . . .

H. Z. Galuska:

I cannot put into words the utter delight that engulfs me at this moment, as I am surrounded by my Sephardi brothers who arrived here from their exilic homelands in order to discuss how and by what means we might protect Sephardi interests in particular and those of the Jews of the East in general. I apologize for not being able to attend all the sessions of this assembly. There are two reasons for my absence: (1) I am busy arranging issues vital to the Yemeni Council of the Zionist Congress that will commune in two days, and (2) Even if I attended all the sessions of this assembly it would be of no use, because to my great dismay I find that I am not familiar with the language with which you conduct this assembly—*Espanyolit*—used here because most of the participating members are not familiar with the Hebrew language.

On behalf of the Yemeni Council of the Land of Israel and the whole world I welcome this assembly heartily and wish it success in its endeavors to unify the Mizrahi communities of which we form a part, and I hope that this assembly will succeed in pursuing its demands at the Fourteenth Zionist Congress. I think it is about time that we merge our forces in order to reclaim our rights, which continue to be violated by the Ashkenazi communities of the land [of Israel]. Be courageous and brave, act and succeed, for your success is also ours. . . .

Dr. Saul Mezan:

The Sephardi Jew of Bulgaria has more in common with the Ashkenazi who resides in his village, as it is easier for him to unite with the Ashkenazi Jew than with the Moroccan Jew, the Jew from Manchester, or the Yemeni Jew. For this reason, there is no way to create a federation of these communities, which are only known by the [collective] label of "Eastern" Jews by accident. Judaism has been marked by various influences, such as German, Slavic, Latin, and Mizrahi traditions. A mix of all these influences can together create the new Jewish Hebrew. We thus reject the creation of the Council of Eastern Jews, due to the negative effects this council might produce.

Isaac Alcalay:

We, the Jews of Yugoslavia, have special needs. Yugoslavia is the last sphere that runs parallel to the Middle Eastern sea. It is there that the Sephardi flow ends and the Ashkenazi one begins. In Yugoslavia, Ashkenazim and Sephardim live together with strong ties. The Sephardim are the minority, numbering around thirty-seven percent; the remainder are Ashkenazim. To this day we have two central goals: on the one hand we have tried to strengthen the Sephardi element so that our sons would not be lost to the [Ashkenazi] majority. We have been concerned with educating our sons according to our tradition while on the other hand protecting our values as a minority within the general Jewish population of Yugoslavia. Through various organizations such as the Rabbinical Committee, the Rabbinical Assembly, and the Zionist Federation, Sephardim and Ashkenazim have worked together hand in hand. Now, after the recent establishment of the World Sephardi Federation, we are not sure how to respond. If we take the initiative and cease working with the Ashkenazim, the decision might not be perceived as an act of marginalization from a nationalistic point of view, yet from a local perspective it could be considered a divisive act. We are perplexed and unsure as to how to proceed.

I ask of the delegates from the Land of Israel that they clarify their views on the particular situation of the Jews from Yugoslavia. As we understand it so far, the [World] Sephardi Federation would be concerned with revival of the spiritual state of Sephardi Jews from a religious and educational perspective, as well as our relationship to practical Zionist actions. For part of this venture we are ready to join and offer all spiritual and material support for this endeavor; when it comes to practical Zionist action however, we will be able to express our views only after listening to debates on this topic. . . .

Moritz Levy:

The aims of the federation are not clear. We do not know whether the goals are educational and cultural, or political. . . . If the aims of this nascent federation are educational, or if the goals are to raise the cultural level of Sephardi Jews, then our response would be positive (although for us there is no need for a specific council for that purpose as we can achieve these aims through the organization of speakers, publications, and the publication of articles in the press). However if the aim of the federation is political, we would not support it. In that case we would therefore agree with the Bulgarian delegates who also disagree. . . .

Still I must admit that given the neglected state of several Mizrahi communities from North Africa and Syria, among other places, we need to request that the Zionist Council strengthen its interest in these centers. Additionally we need to ask that it pay closer attention to Sephardi immigrants [in Palestine].

[Moshe David] Gaon:

We are not of the opinion that the Zionist Committee discriminates against the Sephardim, but given the fact that Zionist work in the Land of Israel is conducted by humble people, without the guidance of great leaders, Sephardi issues are neglected. . . . For example, a group of immigrants from Bulgaria bought land near Acre, after which time other newcomers offered more for the land before the Bulgarians could sign their contract, thus stealing the land out from under them. Not a single voice stood up to defend their rights. [Similarly] a group of immigrants arrived to the land from Morocco but, lacking a counselor or guide, they returned to their place of origin. Fifty families from Salonica bought land together only to suffer from hunger, with no one offering financial or moral support. These families approached various foreign newspapers, disclosing their stories and describing their conditions. When we approached the Zionist Committee to sort out these matters, they claimed never to have heard of such an agricultural settlement. These events occurred because no single individual or organization was responsible for overseeing the Sephardi immigrants as they arrived, leaving them vulnerable to hustlers and swindlers.

Sephardi Jews donate great sums to the Jewish Colonization Association and other Zionist organizations, yet they are given no land on which to settle. In the *moshava* Givat Ezekiel, which was funded by a Sephardi donor, not a single Sephardi Jew resides.

The Sephardim could have helped to foster peaceful relations between [Jews] and our Arab neighbors, but so far we have not been used [for this purpose]. . . . We will continue our work. If the Bulgarians join us we will be pleased, if not, we will be disappointed, but our work will continue nonetheless.

NOTE
Words in brackets appear in the original translation.

Translated by Yehuda Sharim.

Peretz (Friedrich) Bernstein

1890–1971

The Dutch Zionist leader and Israeli politician Peretz Bernstein emigrated to Israel in 1935, where he was a prominent figure in the General Zionist and later Liberal parties. A member of the Knesset from its inception until 1965, he served as minister of commerce and industry in 1948–1949 and from 1952 to 1955. His pioneering study of antisemitism, first published in German in 1926, challenged the liberal assimilationist notion that education and the diffusion of knowledge would banish antisemitism. It also rejected the claim that the "negative" traits of insufficiently acculturated Jews in the diaspora encouraged antisemitism.

Antisemitism as a Group Phenomenon: An Essay in the Sociology of Judaeophobia 1926

I. The Sources of Human Hostility

It is necessary to remember that hatred is constantly in human society directed and discharged against persons who could not possibly have been guilty of causing it. . . .

We must disabuse ourselves of the common notion that feelings of hatred occur only as reactions toward injuries and are directed toward those who have inflicted them. We must remember that every human hurt or discomfort, no matter by whom it is caused or how, whether due to the guilt or the proper actions of another, whether caused by one's own fault or arising through no one's fault and through the action of no human agency, has the tendency to be transformed into an emotion of hostility, to be directed against fellow men and to express itself as enmity. . . .

All human pain is thus injected into human society in the form of hatred. *Enmity is pain projected upon fellow men.*

Let us now try to gain some precise insight into the mechanism of this process. The projection of hostile emotion upon people who are innocent of its origin offers no great difficulty. All that is needed is the illusory image of a guilt which the proposed objects of hatred may be feigned to have incurred. Whenever possible a fictive nexus is constructed between the origin of the human pain and a guilt on the part of the selected enemy. When this is not possible the faults of the putative enemy that have no relation to the pain or hurt in question can be used as motivation and occasion. But the illusion of the so-called guilt of the selected object of hatred can arise as readily without any objective basis, since the enemy, having once been picked, can easily be accused of evil traits and wicked intentions.

The expression in active form of the feelings of hostility is a good deal harder. He who hates must have the power to inflict hurt, but the possibility of reprisal must be reduced to a minimum. Now he normally possesses such power in a very small degree while at the same time the pain which he needs to project on others is of overwhelming intensity. In our civilization organized justice through the courts will sometimes assuage the deepest hurts actually suffered. But all pain that arises from impersonal sources gets no assuagement at all. . . . Hence the great mass of pain and hurt inwardly converted into hostility against life and society normally finds no way of venting itself and is morosely stored up.

Modern psychology has taught us that the human psyche contains instincts and inclinations that are held in leash below the threshold of consciousness. But their power is not broken and they tend always to reappear in the conscious life. Thus all the resentments against life that are transformed into hostility are held in a kind of reservoir. . . .

Popular psychology, though generally without logic or coherence, is often very precise in its observation of detail. It corresponds to the process in question when people say that So-and-so has had to "swallow" a great deal, that, therefore, he is "fed up to the eyes," that finally he can "hold in" no longer and that he has to "get rid" of his rage and hate. This picture of the psychical mechanism in question is pretty accurate. All pains and hurts, irrespective of their origin, have the tendency to be transformed into hatred, and this hatred can normally find only the mildest and most inadequate vent. Hence there are constantly present in man stored up masses of hostility which tempt him to wild and *random* expression of them so soon as a chance seems to present itself.

It goes without saying that this disposition differs in different individuals and that its intensity varies from epoch to epoch, even as sensibility to pain and the transformation of pain into emotion are not constant quantities. But the disposition itself is present in every human soul. Now let us assume that time and fate bring it about through abnormally high degrees of pain and rage and frustration that the feelings of hostility into which these are transformed rise so high in that inner psychical reservoir that none of the ordinary vents suffice and a catastrophic outburst and flood take place. What will take place then is this: that all hidden and irrational fears and hates will be hurled forth to the surface of the psyche and thus it comes about that extraordinary circumstances will bring into the light of day extraordinary quantities of unexpected and half-unknown enmities and bestial impulses.

Since—let this fact be emphasized—man always carries in his subconsciousness stored-up masses of hatred, these feelings can rarely if ever be adequately vented against the persons who have aroused them or who may be, however fancifully, in any true fashion connected with them. Thus the sudden possibility or overwhelming necessity for the expression of hatred will almost regularly direct that hatred toward objects used as mere pretexts or occasions. The nature of these pretexts and the character of the object can be explained without difficulty. But so much must be clear already: the expression of stored-up individual and group hatreds (transformed pains, hurts, humiliations, frustrations) almost never bears any direct relation to even its putative causes. It is for this reason that outbursts of group hostility normally seem aimless and perverse to those not affected by them, that they are dangerous since, being normally directed against the innocent, they arouse defensive hatreds, and that they are madly excessive since they are the result of long accumulations of repressed ferocities.

II. Racial Anti-Semitism

The conjunction of "racial" with "anti-Semitism" has been built up in the modern specifically anti-Semitic literature, the aim of which has been to establish the inferiority of the Semitic, specifically the Jewish, race in order to justify or rationalize its antecedent hatred. On this point the following observations are still to be made.

In all group antagonisms each group brands the other or hostile group as inferior. It has remained for the anti-Semites to extend this melancholy human characteristic into a pseudo-scientific system. But the phenomenon is not difficult to explain. For in spite of all collisions of taste or interest that may arise in the normal social contacts between Jews and non-Jews, little or no adequate cause for hostility ever arises from these. That is not true because the Jews are an abnormally excellent people; it is true because, being everywhere a feeble and defenceless minority, they are necessarily harmless and but moderately influential. Their uninterruptedly embattled situation, their complete dependence on such uncertain factors as the toleration of fickle and enormously preponderant majorities *forces* them as a rule to a peculiar circumspectness of conduct and an almost nervous adherence to the ethical demands of their environment. Their situation forces them to be careful of consciously giving offence. This fact does not in the least mitigate the hatred directed against their group, but serves rather to rob that antecedent hatred of normal and excusable outlets, and all hatred is intensified when its selected object will not supply it with any decent or tolerable motivation.

This is the reason why the accusations made against the Jews, having to be substituted for real delinquencies and grievances, assume a character so wildly fantastic and improbable and bear so constantly the stamp of a feeble but melodramatic imagination, such as, for instance, the charge of a universal Jewish conspiracy looking toward Jewish world-domination. That is the reason, too, why the ethnic inferiority of the Jews, proclaimed and reiterated with wild and lunatic cunning, has come finally to be the sole foundation and rationalization of anti-Semitic ideology. It follows, curiously enough, that anti-Semitic resentment finds difficulty in attaching itself either to the actions of the Jews or even to their highly supposititious vices, which are constantly negated by the test of experience, and has been forced to attach itself to the *external* traits of the Jew—his physiognomic type, his gestures, his manner of speech, to those characteristics, in brief, which are certainly Jewish but which cannot possibly be made the bases of an ethical valuation. Ethical condemnation is here supplemented by aesthetic repudiation. The majority naturally dictates all aesthetic norms; it supplies the group ideal of beauty; thus it stamps the abnormal, the *un*like, the nonconforming with the stamp of the unbeautiful, the repulsive, the ugly. This transferring of ethical to aesthetic devaluation is a *general* accompaniment of ethnic or group antagonisms. The physical type of the foreigner is felt to be ugly and is perceived as tolerable only in so far as it approaches the native type. The appearance of him who is hated is distorted in the perception of him afflicted with hatred into hatefulness of aspect. Thus during the World War the nations delineated their enemies in cinema pictures and cartoons with all the traits of bestial hideousness. This hideousness was, of course, subsequently accepted as the symbol of an inner and moral hideousness, since hostility on the basis of mere physical differentiation, felt as ugliness, was recognized as an insufficient motivation of hatred so murderous. By means of this insane but normal process the Jewish nose becomes the outer and visible symbol of a supposed Jewish insolence, the Jewish eye of an imputed disloyalty, the Jewish smile of an assumed treachery. Thus it is the *outwardness* of the Jew, which is both characteristic and perceptible by the senses, that is evaluated as inferior, gives offence and everywhere and always is used to activate the existent hatred. It is not for nothing that so many Jews have

sought to suppress or hide their racial physical traits and not without cause have they sought to assimilate at least the gestures and manners of the dominant majority. They have thus, of course, not in the least eliminated or enfeebled Jew hatred, but have merely sought by mimicry to escape its grosser effects. . . .

Racial enmities exist in the world in exact proportion to the number of recognizable ethnic groups. The enmity of such groups need not be sharper than among groups of other kinds. But the permanence of both peculiar physical and psychical traits renders fusion or absorption more difficult and in extreme cases forbids them altogether. Hence the ethnic group is peculiarly fitted to be a fighting unit; its characteristics are flags and insignia in themselves; the enemy is recognizable at a glance and desertion is next to impossible. . . . The difficulty of fusion or absorption tends to sharpen conflict and render its aim devoid of mercy: extermination or complete subjection are the alternatives. Subjection, even the completest, is only a substitute aim for extermination, but the latter is difficult in this period of universal news and interlocking human interests. Groups not affected by the conflict will accept it as an occasion of intervention and even the help given to the persecuted of an alien land is often used to intensify hostile attitudes which already exist.

It is these factors that determine the stubbornness of anti-Semitism, the deep irreconcilability of the antithesis which it expresses and the apparently stupid juxtaposition of trivial and tragic expressions of hatred. The complete extirpation of Jewish groups occurs but rarely. Pogrom waves are commoner. Commoner still are mass expulsions of Jewish groups from their dwelling-places. One gives them a chance to withdraw from sudden or slow destruction by flight. Yet even where these fugitives are received with benevolence at best, with condescending tolerance at worst, their condition will be one of more or less veiled subjection and enslavement. Out of this condition of moral enslavement there has arisen that hatred of so many Jews toward their own group which presents in both its grosser and its subtler forms so lamentable a picture.

III. Last Words

Certain ultimate conclusions from the entire situation should be soberly and clearly drawn.

Since the expression of enmity between groups corresponds to a primary psychical need and since the dark instinctive passion of this need creates freely, without any reference to reality, a devaluating and contorted image of the supposedly hostile group and utilizes the ever-present frictions of life as pretexts for its reiteration or even provokes new frictions in order to prove by means of them the evil character of the antithetical group—it follows that *no* significance whatsoever attaches to the character or the actions of this latter group and that they have *no* connection with the degree of "hostility or its expression. Conspicuous harmlessness or excellence only drives him who is impelled and determined to hate to find ever subtler and more fantastic pretexts for his hatred.

Hence the character of the Jews is utterly irrelevant; what they do or fail to do is equally so. Hence it is futile for them to seek to oppose anti-Semitism by any *kind* of human behaviour. If they seek to avoid the strictures of their foes by avoiding any imputed fault, their new attitude will be equally attacked because it is a Jewish attitude and they will be mocked in the bargain for assuming virtues that are not theirs. Under exceptionally favourable circumstances the Jew may temporarily hide from the results of hatred; he can never please his foes and the attempt to do so will only cause him to incur the last reproach of servile weakness.

And since it is not real lacks or vices that evoke anti-Semitism, it is an error to believe that a Jew can get the better of this hatred by personal qualities or achievements. Conspicuous success may occasionally be accepted as the price of entrance into Gentile society; anti-Semitism as such is diminished by no success, no virtue, and no achievement; it is like a tropic sun that sears the unjust and just Jew alike.

Thus it is of no avail to argue against anti-Semitic reproaches or imputations and to demonstrate their groundlessness; for anti-Semitism is not based on them, but uses them only as pretexts or rationalizations. If it happens that a given accusation is so clearly shown to be false that it cannot serve the anti-Semite's purpose—a rare occurrence on account of the irrelevant and fictive character of all such accusations—he will simply be forced to find new grounds for his hatred, and he *will* find them. We shall nevertheless continue to deny accusations, unmask slanders, and expose forgeries, but we should not do it without a conviction of the ultimate futility of all such measures.

Nor shall we fail to be indignant nor to cry out in our despair if tomorrow, even as today, Jews are murdered, tortured, robbed of their rights. We shall, as ever, appeal to the conscience of the peoples and demand of them an accounting for their evil deeds even as we desire to be *called* to accounting and to bear the weight of any responsibility that is our own. But we must not, therefore, suppose that our outcries or monitions will change human nature one jot or that our indignation or our anguish will alter the fact that the human psyche transmutes pain and frustration into enmity. A phenomenon like inter-group hatred, in brief, cannot be eliminated by moral appeals and any pacification that is anywhere achieved takes human nature as it is and not as we would have it be. . . .

This argument does not imply that the peculiar form of group enmity called anti-Semitism can *never* be destroyed. For it is with all its fatal consequences both for us and for our foes the consequence of an unhappy combination of circumstances that mark a given historic period. We cannot suddenly change human nature. We can hope, with reason or without, that in another three thousand years the world will be more in harmony with *our* yearning for peace among men and *our* dreams of moral perfection than it has been during the last three thousand years of Jewish history. But it is senseless to expect any sign of such amelioration within the first few centuries.

A regrouping of human masses offers a more realistic hope. Such regroupings can take place within reasonable periods. It is only because Jews live everywhere as scattered, weak, defenceless ethnic minorities that the normal group-hatred of mankind when directed against them assumes forms so cruel and so blasting. If one can end this specific situation, then, too, anti-Semitism which has made the life of the Jewish people for so long a veritable martyrdom, can be finally liquidated.

A Jewish people that lives in closed settlements in its own land will doubtless be exposed to the normal enmities of its neighbouring peoples and war will alternate with peace, as has been the way of the world for so long. But this enmity between the Jewish people and its neighbouring peoples will at least be a *normal* enmity and not that thrice-accursed one-sided hatred which has followed the fragments of a people for so long upon all the roads of earth.

This argument does not imply the certainty of success of the Zionist aspiration and attempt. The movement could well be shattered against obstacles of several kinds. Today the prospects of the plan seem reasonably favourable; time alone can teach us whether these hopes will come to full fruition. But that there is no other *possibility* of putting an end to anti-Semitism should appear as utterly irrefutable from the foregoing arguments.

Translated by Ludwig Lewisohn.

Other works by Bernstein: *Over joodse problematiek* (1935).

Moshe Beilinson

1889–1936

The Hebrew writer and journalist Moshe Beilinson was born in Veprika, Russia, and trained as a doctor. Initially a supporter of Russian socialism, he was won over to Labor Zionism by Zalman Shazar and Berl Katznelson. He moved to Italy after World War I and in 1924 settled in Petah Tikva. He wrote many articles on the problems of labor in the Yishuv and emerged as an important spokesperson for the labor movement. In 1925, Beilinson and Katznelson founded the Labor Zionist newspaper *Davar.*

Movements and Their Crises
1927

New and hitherto unknown words have entered our dictionary. These words can now be heard at gatherings, and even more in private conversations, and sometimes we read them in the press. And if, until fairly recently, these words characteristically expressed the general mood of the petite-bourgeoisie alone, in recent days they have been heard also here and there among the working-class community—the general mood—despair, and the words: "utter catastrophe." If this were simply a ruse to arouse the dormant forces among the Jewish people—this would not be so saddening. Then it would simply be a case of a misleading stratagem—misleading, since one must not think or hope that the Jewish people will be shocked to hear of the ruin of Erets Yisrael. After all, it witnessed in past times, and in the present as well, quite a few ruins, and greater than the unemployment of the seven thousand workers and the lack of income of several thousand craftsmen and shop owners. Possibly it will offer "charity" to these as well, just as it gives it everywhere where Jews go hungry, but we will not know what to do with this "charity"— and those same big forces, that same outstanding national effort that we expect and demand, will not be forthcoming for a situation of "utter catastrophe."

However, what is most distressing about these words is that it is not just a misleading stratagem, but a real feeling. And, indeed, in our economic and social situation there are enough elements that create and promote this feeling. Nevertheless, it is nothing but a memory lapse, a misunderstanding regarding the fate of the popular movements, shortsightedness, morbid impatience, if there are among us people who speak or think about "the utter catastrophe" of Zionism just because the movement is encountering difficulties and its prospects are not absolutely clear-cut.

The Zionist movement is unique in the manner of its realization, and yet other nations have experienced similar movements more than once. Neither Hess nor Pinsker nor Herzl was the first to utter these magic words: popular liberation, national and social liberation. On the contrary: they learned from others. Had we not been so impatient, we should have contemplated other movements a little and learned from them how many sacrifices and efforts their liberation cost them, and how many failures and how much despair they underwent before they realized their dream.

The French Revolution confronted humanity with the ideal of political freedom, and it took twenty years for the revolution to erupt. And in the year of the occupation of Paris by the united reaction it was as if nothing whatever remained of the effort to realize this ideal, and "the Holy Alliance" ruled unhindered in political as well as in intellectual Europe. And since then more than a hundred years have elapsed, and Europe has more than once seen its streets red with revolutionary blood—and even today the Constitution of 1793 still has not been completely implemented, whereas the man who has once felt the abomination of political subjugation has not given up his struggle, and no one doubts that tomorrow or the day after, political freedom will be established.

And the entire history of the socialist movement since the French Revolution, from its inception until today, is actually nothing but a long and painful sequence of failures and defeats—failures of thought and action and defeats due to coercion and harsh oppression as well as to lack of self-preparedness. The revolutions of 1830 and 1848, the disintegration of the Chartist movement, the fall of the Paris Commune, the failure of the First International, the decline of the Anarchist movement, the failure of the Second International, the World War, the failure of the Central European revolutions, the cruel form taken by the Russian

Revolution and its failure—the revival of the rule of exploitation in city and village—all of these are only major stages of the socialist downfall and the lesser stages are innumerable.

If we disregard abstract socialist thinking, and if we take into consideration the socialist movement alone, the mass movement, it too has existed for more than a century—and apparently has not been without its failures. Nevertheless, no man (and in their heart of hearts also the supporters of the current regime) doubts for a moment that man, once aroused to social injustice, will ever be reconciled with the regime that exists by exploiting the work of his fellow, and will not give up the fight for the rule of the worker and labor until the day of victory arrives.

The movements of national and popular liberation are still richer in defeats and failures than the political and social movements. In the history of each one of these movements are pages before which the reader must stop and ask himself: this nation waged a hard struggle for its liberation and now it has reached a point where the traces of this struggle have disappeared and no hint of it remains. All has been erased as if it had never existed, and this people has neither present nor future, no hope whatsoever. From where, nonetheless, did these people draw the strength and courage to continue their activities? On what did they base their calculations? And there are no answers to these questions—and yet victory comes. A hundred years ago, when the Italian liberation movement began, we ask which European statesmen did not mock the geographical concept alone of Italy, or shrug shoulders at the sight of a collection of young people—a few dozen of them—who took upon themselves the battle against the ten rulers of Italy, against mighty Austria, against the pope who at that time was really a world power? And the Italian movement experienced countless setbacks on a vast scale, and year in and year out they stood before an impenetrable wall, without prospects and without hope, and nevertheless liberation was achieved.

In what state was the Polish movement after the suppression of the 1830 uprising, after the suppression of the 1863 uprising, on the eve of the World War—when the Polish nation was torn into three pieces, and beside each one stood a formidable guard—Russia, Germany, Austria—when the dream of vanquishing them, and what's more all at once, was considered nothing more than pure folly? And nevertheless—Polish liberation was achieved.

What were the prospects and hopes of all the small nations in the Balkans and Central and Eastern Europe: the Czechs, Bulgarians, Southern Slavs, Greeks, Lithuanians, Estonians, etc.? What hopes had the Irish, the inhabitants of South Africa? What hopes do the peoples of the East have now in their struggle against the mightiest political powers in the world? And yet, the liberation of these peoples has either been achieved already or is in the process of being achieved, and nobody doubts that the day will come when each and every people will be the master of its own destiny.

And even if we consider such a tiny movement as our own—which is only thirty to forty years old—we shall discover that there were also times when it seemed that failure was total, and no wise man could foresee which path the movement would take toward its realization. This was the case after the failure of the Biluim, of the Hovevei Tsiyon, and of political Zionism (Uganda). Look at the Jewish newspapers and journals and see how frequently the death of the Zionist movement was proclaimed—not out of blind hatred, but out of awareness, sometimes out of deep and real pain, with facts and figures in hand. Nonetheless, the movement did not die, and precisely in the years after the war it knew both rejuvenation and success.

And there is still another side—apart from the endless failures—to all the popular movements: the disproportionate gap between efforts and their results. If we consider the history of nations from this standpoint, we shall be amazed to see how long—decades, hundreds of years—it took to achieve a victory that to us now seems so straightforward and taken for granted that it ought to have been achieved in a moment, with mutual agreement, and without any opposition. And, nevertheless, each step taken, even the smallest, the tiniest, in human advancement is fiercely fought at the cost of blood and tears and at a tremendous price. What could be simpler than the thought that no man is born to be the slave of his fellow man? And how many thousands of years passed until this awareness penetrated into the minds of human beings? What could be more understandable than the right of a person to pray to his god with his heart or to say simply and honestly what he has to say? And this "right" of freedom of belief and freedom of opinion—who can measure the blood spilled because of it, without our having achieved this freedom in its entirety even today. The Russian revolutionary movement has continued for more than a hundred years, and the finest sons of the Russian people have sacrificed themselves by the thousands, and Russia has undergone terrible years of civil war and starvation and despotic rule for the right of the peasant to work his plot of land. Thus history wills.

We complain about the indifference of our people, and in this indifference lies the very source of the despair. We don't see that same popular effort that we relied on and hoped for. The masses of the people are not standing shoulder to shoulder with their pioneering vanguard. However, if we agree for a moment that the Jewish people is in this territory a people like all the peoples of our day, and we observe the liberation movements of the other peoples, while we shall not cease complaining and demanding, we shall stop pinning all our hopes on the immediate awakening of the people at this precise moment, and we shall cease being amazed when it fails to respond.

Fifty years ago official history still loved to describe the popular movements as sudden or not sudden uprisings of "the entire people" from all walks of life: the giant rose up and with enthusiasm, self-sacrifice, and acts of bravery it severed its chains, overturned the royal throne, and expelled foreign despots. This historical philosophy described for us the nations in their sublime moments, when, dressed in their festive finery, our elders and perhaps also our forefathers really enjoyed themselves. It was a direct successor of the historical philosophy that preceded it and that also saw human history as one of brave deeds and self-sacrifice, although not of the peoples but of their rulers. Modern historians also recognize the prominent place in human history of Julius Caesar, Peter the Great, Lenin, and Kemal Pasha. And modern history also knows periods of determination when the oppressed people shakes off and severs its chains, and yet, as historians delved deeper in their material, and as human history became the history of the peoples in their humdrum daily existence, so, too, the great national figures and also the festive finery of the people were relegated to the background, and their place increasingly occupied by the people in its everyday garb. And ever since history abandoned its traditional path and adopted a critical stance and the courage to look reality in the face, even when this reality is not the most desirable or pleasant for the self-esteem of nations, a slightly different picture of national movements has emerged. While it is true that there were in the world Danton [. . .], Saint-Simon and Robert Owen, Marx and Lassalle, Garibaldi and Mazzini, Kościuszko and Mickiewicz [. . .], there were

people in the world who could not bear the shame, the hunger, and injustice prevailing around them, and who thought, acted, and lived in the name of freedom, and for this freedom incessantly appealed to their counterparts. And it is true that a large part of their dreams have been realized or are about to be realized. And it is also true that their dreams were realized by the same people that they summoned. However, they themselves did not know a single moment when they could truly say: here we have achieved what we wished for; the people—or at least a large part of the people—are with us and will never abandon us again. There was no such moment. Unending waves—a wave rises and a wave subsides. Sometimes it seems as if everything is already in their grasp, their thoughts and aspirations have already become the possession of the people. And acts of heroism already took place: here, barricades appear in the streets, it's all over! And you browse through one page, only a single page in the history book, and an entirely different picture is revealed to you—no mention of the barricades, the traces of the masses have been erased, the fire and enthusiasm have died down. Silence surrounds these people who once again have remained alone, a small handful—a few dozen, a few hundred, who maintain a solitary watch, which is liable to kill off even the strongest devotion and the most fervent faith. Historical researchers have calculated the number of volunteers who answered the call of Garibaldi and participated in the Polish uprisings. They estimated the sums that the Italians and Poles contributed to Mazzini and Mickiewicz for "national funds," and it appears that only small groups were prepared to sacrifice their lives, and property owners expended only meager sums from their pocket for the sake of the liberation of their nations. And when the social and political movements end, and the historians can rid themselves of every propaganda-driven thought and investigate only the unvarnished historical truth—the same picture will unfold. Already now we feel this from indications with which we are familiar.

All the peoples were indifferent in the process of their liberation. All the peoples responded derisively, with scorn and indifference to the prophets of their liberation. The history of every nation is full of faint-heartedness and betrayal. Nevertheless—their liberation is an established fact and their liberation was achieved by those same indifferent and treacherous masses. Were it possible to establish a formula for popular movements, it would be along these lines: an isolated group of the nation's pioneer vanguard, imbued with the will and destiny of the nation, together with knowledge and awareness of national responsibility, educates and constantly inspires the obtuse masses. It leads them and utilizes every opportunity; it exploits all events, both internal and external, in order to realize liberation. It, and it alone, pays the full and bitter price for liberation. Apart from a few exceptional moments, it is isolated and left on its own: that is its fate. It tastes victory at the time when it truly bears the responsibility of the nation, when it really concentrates within itself the will and destiny of the nation. Only when this force is manifest do the masses rise up at the crucial moment and join in the tremendous uprisings and build the barricades that afterwards obscure for decades the true face of the popular movements. Consequently, it is not pioneering spirit alone, nor mass movement alone, but the pioneering spirit that, in the course of a painful and at times destructive process, captivates the masses and overcomes the indifference of the nation. It is wrong to assume that only among us is the "internal problem" the crux of the problem as a whole. In the absence of any major external obstacles, the main obstacle in all the movements was the indifference of the people. [. . .] Fichte's *Addresses to the German Nation,* Mazzini's placards for Italian youth, were and remain to this day the classical documents of national movements. And also in social and political movements the truest and most powerful pages are not those that describe the tyranny of the rulers but those that describe the lack of power and self-respect of the oppressed.

Such is the picture in all the popular movements—and so it is with us. No movement has triumphed in a moment by dint of enthusiasm and sudden uprising. No movement was at the outset a truly mass movement. Nevertheless, no movement has vanished or failed to fulfill its historic role because "they abandoned it" or because "the people did not respond." Such abandoning occurred dozens of times in every living movement, and still they triumphed. Only two things are of vital importance: whether the movement truly reflects the will of the people and its destiny, and whether the pioneering camp has sufficient internal power to withstand any storm and overcome all obstacles—even the most formidable obstacle of all, the indifference of the people.

What has happened with us? If there is one outstanding and conspicuous example in all human history of the will and destiny of the nation being realized, then that is the will of the Jewish people to return to Erets Yisrael and its national destiny, which is forever bound up with Erets Yisrael. Nor is there today in our ranks anyone who doubts this. The nation has neither refuge nor respite—except in Erets Yisrael. And despite all the blows and disappointments, despite all the current difficulties and uncertainty of the prospects—with the same confidence of ten and of twenty years ago Zionism states and proclaims: here is the center of Israel's destiny—whether the masses acknowledge it or not. Has this land let us down in any sense when we returned to it from the lands of exile? Did we find here anything that we did not know of previously and would be liable to shake our confidence in the objective possibility of the realization of Zionism? This, too, is not the case since we were aware of all the difficulties, and neither the [Middle] Eastern nor the European complications, nor our own shortcomings, nor the poverty of the land were surprising for us. So what happened?

What happened was only that the same fate befell us as was the fate of every pioneering camp in every popular movement—the people did not respond when we hoped it would. And now comes the test for Zionism, to know whether this movement really does have the right to exist and can be certain of victory. This is our test and not that of the people because the fact that the people does not respond at all, after twenty to thirty years of education full of defects, is not a criterion, and the whole question of Zionism is now only whether the Zionists themselves—the pioneering vanguard among the people—will have the strength to withstand the cruelest test facing liberation movements.

And if the pioneering vanguard of the Jewish people will have this strength, then it will not speak either of utter catastrophe or despair. It will know that this is its destiny, not only to pave the way but also to remain isolated and forsaken in its difficult task. It will plough on doggedly in all conditions, undeterred by the fog of uncertainty. And if the handful of people who stand guard for Zionism will possess this strength, then it will also safely pass this test. And today or tomorrow, or the day after tomorrow, our victory shall come because it is with the pioneering vanguard, not with the distant masses and not with those who abandon the struggle, that the will of the nation and its destiny is bound up.

Translated by David Herman.

Other works by Beilinson: *Bi-yemei masah* (1930); *Bi-yemei teḥiyat Italyah* (1930); *Be-mashber ha-olam* (1940).

Joseph Klausner

1874-1958

The literary critic and historian Joseph Klausner was born in a small town near Vilna but moved to Odessa at age eleven. There he later became active in the circle of writers working to revive Hebrew. He studied in Heidelberg briefly and then moved to Warsaw, where he took over the editorship of *Ha-Shiloah* from Ahad Ha-Am. He moved back to Odessa in 1907 and taught modern Jewish history at the modern yeshiva there. In 1917, he settled in Jerusalem and was appointed to the chair in Hebrew literature at the newly opened Hebrew University (1925). In 1944, he was appointed to the chair in the history of the Second Temple period. A Revisionist Zionist, his scholarly work was imbued with a strong nationalist flavor.

The Jewish Character of Spinoza's Teaching
1927

Whoever reads Spinoza's *Theological-Political Treatise*, his letters, and even his Hebrew grammar, will recognize and avow that Spinoza was, relative to his times in Amsterdam, if not a great scholar, then, in any case, a learned [*talmid hakham*] Jew. Not only was he well versed in the *tanakh* in the original, which he knew by heart and cited in Hebrew from memory . . . but in Talmud too, which he often cites, . . . and in medieval Hebrew literature, which he often cites in Hebrew. . . . Roughly 80 percent of the *Theological-Political Treatise* deals with Jewish issues, and only 20 percent with Christian issues or universal human issues. Even the portion of discussions pertaining to Judaism and deriving from it in Spinoza's other works is not meager. . . .

Therefore, Spinoza does not belong only to humanity as a whole but, rather, especially, to Judaism. Had the *Theological-Political Treatise* been translated into Hebrew in its time, the sages of Israel would no doubt have argued against him at length, as they did with regard to Maimonides and Gersonides, Azariah de Rossi and Leone Modena. But, in spite of all its wrong and unjust statements regarding Judaism, this work, great and original by any account, would have then become—in spite of all its shortcomings—part of the canon of Hebrew literature. Its positive innovations and the objections to it would then have caused a powerful fermentation in the entirety of Hebrew literature. Even the *Ethics*, had it been written in Hebrew, or translated in its time into Hebrew, would no doubt have aroused no

more objection than did Gersonides' *Wars of the Lord*, whose detractors declared it to be a "war against the Lord" and which, nevertheless, was not excluded from Hebrew literature but rather greatly enhanced it. . . .

Spinozism is not Judaism in the pure theoretical sense. But Judaism is not only a religion, as it is not only a nation [*ummah*]. Judaism—that which the Jews created—is a national worldview [resting] on a religious-moral substratum. As this worldview stems from the multifaceted national life; and after this life had brought forth a unique religion and morality, from these [two] in unison, it necessarily has two characteristics. First, it changes according to time and circumstance on the basis of an unchanging national substratum. Second, it necessarily includes conflicts and contradictions—as does life itself and anything that derives from both reality and theory. . . .

[Klausner elaborates in great detail on what he takes to be the "Jewish" characteristics of Spinoza's philosophy.]

There is an amazing phenomenon in the history of [Jewish] philosophy. . . . The people of Israel have rejected, consciously or not, a long chain of philosophers of Jewish origin, all of whom were, consciously or not, Platonists. The first was Philo . . . the second Ibn Gabirol . . . the third Judah Abravanel . . . and the fourth Spinoza. . . . All were influenced by Plato, Plotinus, and the Neoplatonists of the late Renaissance. . . . Judaism either rejected them, as it did Spinoza, or ignored them, as was the case with Philo's works, [Gabirol's] *Fons Vitae*, and [Judah Abravanel's] *Dialogues Concerning Love*. This is [readily] understandable. So long as Judaism subsisted on religion alone, lacking territory and language and without a national foundation, it is possible that all those who wished to graft on to it a Platonic or Neoplatonic pantheism indeed endangered it.

Things have now changed. Judaism has ceased to be solely, or primarily, a religion (as Moses Mendelssohn and Hermann Cohen, who rejected Spinoza, conceived of it). Nor is it—now or ever!—a nation only. It will be a religion-nation in unison. It is beginning to acquire territory, a national language, and an earthly and political foundation. It is once again experiencing the sense of homeland. And in Spinoza's marvelous words, "Given the opportunity—such is the mutability of human affairs—[the Jews will] establish once more their independent state, and . . . God will again choose them" (*Theological-Political Treatise*, chapter 3 [C11, §6]). The former has already been partially fulfilled in our times, and we strongly hope that the latter will be fulfilled too. In such a situation, these four philosophers [hitherto] distanced from Israel can no longer be viewed as dangerous. They are not a danger but rather a source of support and strength to its spirit. Judaism will be enriched and augmented by all its great sons, even the lost and the estranged. But to Spinoza, nearly all of whose works have been translated into Hebrew in our generation, we call out, acknowledging the great sin that his people have sinned against him. [We do not deny] the not meager sin he has sinned against his people, but [we] recognize his human greatness and the Jewish character of his teachings. To Spinoza the Jew we call out nearly two hundred and fifty years after his death, from the heights of Mount Scopus, from within our mini-temple, the Hebrew University of Jerusalem: The *herem* is annulled! The sin of Judaism against you is removed, and your sin against [Judaism] is atoned! You are our brother! You are our brother! You are our brother!

NOTE

Words in brackets appear in the original translation.

Translated by Ari Ackerman and Menachem Lorberbaum.

Other works by Klausner: *Historiyah shel ha-sifrut ha-ivrit ha-ḥadashah*, 6 vols. (1930–1950); *From Jesus to Paul* (1943); *Ha-historiyah shel ha-bayit ha-sheni*, 5 vols. (1949–1951); *The Messianic Idea in Israel* (1955).

Chaim Zhitlowsky

1865–1943

Russian-born Chaim Zhitlowsky was a theoretician of Yiddishism, diaspora nationalism, territorialism, and revolutionary socialism. After 1908, he spent increasingly more time in the United States, where he eventually settled. There, he championed Yiddish language and culture, which he considered necessary for the continued health of the Jewish people. He was instrumental in the establishment of a network of Yiddish-language secular schools in the United States.

What Is Jewish Secular Culture?

1927

We take Jewish secular culture here in its modern shape, its language form, Yiddish. It is not the first expression of worldly or secular Jewish culture. In ancient times almost the entire cultural life of the children of Israel was secular, including their literary creations. It was only with the rise of the so-called sacred books, which are full of purely secular episodes and reflections, that we got the division into sacred books and outside books, which we would nowadays call secular books. Much later too the Hebrew wine and love songs, the elegies and the humorous writings of the Spanish-Arabic period, the poetry of Immanuel of Rome, and nearer our own day the neo-Hebrew literature of the Haskalah right up to the present time was and is purely secular, with no relation to any official religious belief.

Then there are the various branches of ordinary human activity among the Jewish people, economic and social, and where this was possible, political. Here the religious element played at times an important part, but not so great as to imprint its character on the whole of Jewish cultural and creative life.

So that Jewish secular culture is nothing new in our history. What is new is the modern secular culture in Yiddish. The language itself, Yiddish, is for the Jewish people holy, not as a language used for purely religious purposes and ritual, but as a secular, worldly language, used for all daily purposes. And the language itself was taken over from the outside world.

It doesn't mean that Yiddish wasn't used for religious purposes. Not only the women, blessing the Sabbath and Festival candles, with their "God of Abraham," their Techinas and their Ze'enu U'renus, not only the ordinary man of the folk who devoured the moralistic preachings of the Magidim in Yiddish, but also the Jewish Rabbinical scholarly world could not use the sacred tongue, Hebrew, for the entire cultural activity of the Jewish people in the German and East European countries, in education, in the Chedarim and the Yeshivas, in the sermons of the synagogue preachers, in Rabbinic discourses and learned writings, in Chassidic sayings and stories, in the wise words of the Tzaddikim, and in the Mussar books, the language used for religious education and exposition was and to a large extent still is Yiddish.

Yet despite the colossal part which Yiddish played and still plays in the religious life of generations of religious Jews, the language as such has not lost its secular character. The written Jewish religious culture is still most of it in the sacred tongue, Hebrew, and every Jewish religious work in the sacred tongue is a holy book, while the same religious book in Yiddish is a secular work, which only the religious women regard as holy. That is the new thing connected with the language itself, which was already established in the fifteenth century. When you compare our whole written culture in Hebrew and in Yiddish over our entire history you will see that in Hebrew the trunk and the main branches are religious, with the secular work only one of the branches, while in Yiddish it is the direct opposite—the trunk and the main branches are from the fifteenth century till today secular, and the religious works are only one branch of the tree, and even this branch because of its language claims no religious sanctity.

The new thing is the secularization of Jewish national and cultural life. It is a complete revolution. Previously for a Jew to live a Jewish life meant living within the framework of the Jewish religion, including the Jewish language. As the traditional religion began to lose its dominance over Jewish hearts and minds, as religion grew to be a private matter for each individual and Yiddish was able to satisfy the cultural needs which have nothing to do with the Jewish religious faith, the purely secular tree of Yiddish became stronger and firmer and spread its branches wide.

This is new and revolutionary in our national and cultural life. It is in accordance with the character of the new historic epoch into which our people has entered. Previously, both in the religious-national and in the progressive-assimilationist era, membership of the Jewish people was linked with adherence to the Jewish religion, to Judaism in one form or another. Leaving the Jewish religion meant leaving the Jewish fold, leaving the Jewish people. Now every Jew belongs to the Jewish people who lives in the midst of his people, and in its own field of Yiddish language, whether he believes in the Jewish religion or not, whether he believes in God at all, or is an atheist.

When a Jew satisfies his spiritual-cultural needs in Yiddish, reads a Yiddish newspaper, a Yiddish book, goes to a Yiddish lecture, to a Yiddish theater, discusses a Jewish or a general problem in Yiddish, listens to the Yiddish radio hour, sends his child to a modern Yiddish secular school, he is beyond doubt a Jew who belongs to the Jewish people. There are people of non-Jewish origin who live their life in a Jewish language sphere, and have become part of it, but their number is so small, and they are so exceptional, that we may leave them out of our calculation.

The great significance of this Yiddish culture sphere is that it has succeeded in building a "spiritual-national home," purely secular, which can embrace all Jews throughout the world, all our classes, parties, move-ments and levels of education, within which the language differences that had previously existed between men and women, between the scholarly class and the masses have been abolished. This gives individuals on the lower educational level the opportunity to rise to the highest heights of the cultural stage which the people can attain. At the same time the waters of the people's cultural reservoir can flow through channels and through irrigation pipes into the remotest corners, fertilizing its fields, and bringing new forces among the folk-masses into the cultural work. Thus the cultural sphere in Yiddish can expand on all sides, embracing all branches of human creation, and taking in all parts and all sections of the people throughout the world—which can't be done in the Hebrew culture sphere, nor in the other culture spheres among Jews in the different languages of their countries.

It means also that thanks to the rise of Yiddish secular culture we are beginning to be equal in our national-cultural character with all other cultural peoples in the world. A people is a culture-creating organism when it sits at its own loom weaving human culture according to its own pattern and form. The language—the threads of the soul that stretch from individual to individual and bind together all sections of the people. With these soul-threads, with the Yiddish folk language, which is at the same time the national language, the people sits at its own loom weaving its own culture, oral and written. As all other peoples do. This is the main significance of that national-cultural revolution which Yiddish secular culture introduces in our life.

We are beginning to achieve equality in this respect with the cultural nations of the world. But we still have a lot of leeway to make up. Because the new, the progressive-national epoch of our historic life has not yet completely sloughed the old skin of previous eras, because Yiddish secular culture still has so many enemies, and because the general condition of the people is so distorted and crippled, the conscious creators of secular culture in Yiddish faced problems that are strange to the nations of the world, because for them the answers to these problems are as easy as A B C, while to us they are intricate and complex, like the most erudite scholarship. The European nations, for example, lifted their folk-tongues centuries ago to the state of national languages, while with us this is still a matter of heated argument.

The French have a secular culture. Does anyone ask what the French content of French secular culture should be? But with us there is a constant saber-rattling over the question of what the Jewish content of our Yiddish secular culture should be. It is a very important question on the practical side, but theoretically it is a survival of the era when being a Jew was identified with belief in a particular religion. People couldn't understand our being an ordinary irreligious national entity, free to live and create, like all other peoples. This incomprehension was only fortified by our assimilationist intellectuals who became nationalist and Yiddishist penitents—why give up the rich cultural flesh-pots of the different Egypts to go out into the sandy wastes of the Yiddish language sphere? Just to enjoy Yiddish language form? If we and others like us have decided to go to the people and work for them, it is only for the sake of a serious Jewish content, which must be holy and dear to us, not merely for the language form.

I come to another point—the word "secular," which has become for many people a synonym for antireligious. Many of our active workers in this field have come to think that belief in God and longing for a religious life is a mortal offense, a sin against secularism, and must be eradicated root and branch. Other nations, whose secular governments, which may even contain atheists, help to maintain religious institutions, apparently see this problem differently. We still cling to the outmoded ideas of the doctrinaire radicals of the times of the "Yom Kippur Balls."

Actually, the terms "secularism" and "worldliness" never had anything to do with antireligion. Neither in France, nor in America or England, where cultural life is completely secular. The word secular has two meanings—one for the general affairs of the State, the other for the educational system and cultural activities generally, which is national in character. In the life of the State it means: Religion is a private matter, and antireligion is a private matter. No one may be discriminated against in his rights because he adheres to this or the other religion, or because he is fighting against any religious belief. In the educational field and in cultural activity secularism means excluding religious teaching from the State schools, excluding all that speaks in the name of a supernatural authority, and induces people to do what it wants in the expectation of divine favor or out of fear of divine punishment.

This and nothing else is secularism. Atheist materialism, which is often regarded as the essence of secularism, is only a certain trend in it, a trend which may be right or wrong. When someone comes along and says,

"God spoke to me and told me to say to you that you must do this," then his activity is religious-sectarian, and it must be excluded from secular education and from secular cultural activity. But if someone comes along and says, as some of us do, "According to my human understanding and feeling there is a Divine Power in the world, and it is good for man to believe in it, and in order to live within its sphere we must strive toward something that must be holy and dear to a man, as a man, whether he believes in God or not," then this does not fall outside the idea of "secularism." It is a metaphysical-idealist secular trend, the opposite of the other secular trend, which is atheist materialism.

Neither of these two trends should, in my view, be forced on the minds of the children in the lower educational institutions. They should both, however, be free and unhindered in the higher educational institutions and in secular cultural activity generally. And with the observance of religious festivals or even certain religious ceremonies.

For instance, if the Jewish Passover is kept because a people liberated itself from slavery and went out to seek a land in which to live its own life freely—though the whole story of the Exodus from Egypt is perhaps only a legend—the festival is of human, of great human significance.

Or if Christians keep Christmas, the birth of Jesus of Nazareth, because he was one of the greatest geniuses of moral teaching for mankind, who went to his death for his preaching—though the whole story of Jesus' life and work and death may be only a legend—the festival is of human, of great human significance.

On the understanding, of course, that there must be no supernatural elements introduced into the observance, nothing of confessional faith. The confessional celebration of these festivals must be left to the religious communities who can believe in the supernatural, super-worldly revelations.

Now the main problem—the content and form of Yiddish secular culture. The first thing to note is that there can be no content without form and no form without content. Content is the inner core, the essential; form is the outer garb. "Look not at the flask, but at what it contains," the Ethics of the Fathers teach us.

In every culture of every people in all times over the course of historical development there is only one single general content—human life and all its outbranchings and forms of expression, all its historic conflicts and struggles. Do our opponents believe that the life of our people is trivial to us, doesn't interest us? We fight for the Yiddish language form in our cultural life because we believe in the immensely important role it should play in the maintenance and progressive development of Jewish folk life. Thus the Yiddish language form becomes for us a content of great weight, a fundamental. It is form only in relation to the other contents of Jewish culture. The human life of the Jewish people and its past, insofar as it lives in the memory of generations, and its present, with all its battles and conflicts, and its future, as the various movements try to shape it, always was, is now, and always will be the main content of Jewish cultural life, as it always was and always will be the main content in every cultural sphere with every progressive people.

To show how content and form change places according to the different attitude, take the Prophet Micah's wonderfully beautiful declaration: "It has been told to you, O man, what is good, and what the Lord requires of you: Only to do justly, and to love mercy, and to walk humbly with your God." This is unique in Jewish culture. What here is content, and what is form? Let us assume that the Hebrew speech sounds here are the absolute form and that the content here is the special meaning of the Hebrew words. But when you consider the meaning you find that it falls again into content and form. You can say: the content here is religious, what God requires. This time it has clad itself in the form of a social-ethical ideal. Another time it may be in the form of a prohibition not to smoke on the Sabbath. And you may with the same right say the exact opposite—the content here is the social-ethical ideal of the love of man and the love of justice. The religious requirement from a supernatural Power, a God, is here the form in which the ideal has clad itself, thanks to the theological era in which all Jewish life found itself at that time. You can go further, and say that the content is in the final analysis the requirements and the needs of living a humane life, which found expression in a social-ethical ideal, and clothed itself historically in a theological-religious form.

This example, and all the others, teach us many things: first, the constant pairing of whatever content with whatever form; second, the relative character of these two conceptions; third, that "form" is not only language, and that national characteristics are forms, national ways of life are a form of living, unique strokes of talent are forms of national creative power. They teach us also of course that national form is not only language form.

And they give us that absolutely important realization that in the final analysis the content of a folk culture is always human life, past, present and future—human life with its needs and its requirements, problems and struggles, longings, yearnings and hopes, joys and sorrows.

We have seen that the secular culture in Yiddish, as a historical reality, as an oral culture for the whole people and as a written culture for the folk masses and also for the women of the scholarly Rabbinical strata goes back a good many centuries. But as a conscious aim, as a striving towards a revolutionary transformation of our national-cultural character, as the ideal of a "national-spiritual home" for all Jews throughout the world—it is of very recent date. This conscious Yiddish secular culture was born in the spiritual sphere of Jewish socialism and the Jewish labor movement. Later this same ideal was taken up also by the bourgeois elements who take a folkist standpoint. So the socialist stream on which I too am carried, became only one trend of it, which must struggle and fight to become the dominant trend in the life of our people, with the hope of one day becoming its one and only trend.

We hold that Yiddish must be the one and only language form of our culture; we want Yiddish to give us those national-psychic threads with which we as a people sitting like every people at its own loom should weave its own Jewish culture. Let us consider all other general human and national forms of manifestation in our folk life as "content." We have just seen that we have every theoretical right to this.

Then the question becomes: What should be the "content" of that Yiddish secular culture towards which we, as Jewish socialists, should strive? As Jewish socialists we are, so to say, citizens of five worlds, all bound up with each other. First, we are human beings, then we are Jews, after that we are socialists, then we are Yiddish secular Jews, and lastly, we are Yiddish secular socialists. All these five spiritual worlds have created cultural treasures. The true treasures are naturally found in the general human culture. This is an inexhaustible sea. Then come the rich culture treasures that the Jewish people created in its more than three thousand years of history. Then come the treasures of the general socialist culture sphere, which is almost as old as the Jewish culture sphere. Then come the valuable creations of the Yiddish secular culture and of its socialist trend, which too are not to be dismissed out of hand.

And if what we say is true, that the ultimate content of a folk culture is decent human living, not only in the present and in the striving for a better future, but also with the spiritual heritage of the past, we see how rich the content of the Yiddishist secular culture becomes, even if we only take over in our language form all the five heritages I have indicated. Even if we let them all drip down through the fine critical filter of the socialist spiritual outlook.

And this refinement through the delicate instrument of a proper human understanding should be applied to all the heritages, of general human culture, Jewish culture, and general socialist culture, in order to extract the gold from the historical dross. Yet the dross too, which will remain after refinement through the fire and flame of the socialist spiritual attitude will not be entirely lost. It will serve as material for that branch of culture which is called the science of history, which should explain to us the course of human development, as well as the historical life process of our own people.

The cultural heritage of the Jewish people is not all dross. It contains enough all-human and even socialist precious gold that deserves to be preserved always as a valuable element not only in our Yiddish secular but also in general human culture. Though much of this precious gold must be of greater value to us Jews than to any other people.

We must see to it now when we are trying to straighten out and equalize the national-cultural character of the Jewish people with that of all other progressive peoples, that the content of Yiddish secular culture, refined in the spiritual fire and flame of international socialism, and poured into the language form of Yiddish, should not be pushed into a corner within the four walls of the social-economic and social-political basis of general cultural life, but neither into the confines of purely Jewish national creative activity. All the heritages of the closely associated cultural spheres—the common human, the Jewish, the secular Yiddish, the general socialist and the Jewish socialist—must be poured into the basin of our culture in Yiddish, which will always have too as an ever-flowing new content, the running current life of the Jewish folk masses and the Jewish creative forces, with their struggles, hardships and sufferings, and so far but few and meager joys.

The basin will also have to be filled with the liberation efforts of the oppressed peoples and classes, and—in the first place—the social and economic liberation efforts of our own people, in accordance with our socialist ideals of labor, democracy, political and most es-

sentially spiritual liberty, cultural achievement, social justice, equality and international brotherhood.

Translated by Joseph Leftwich.

Other works by Zhitlowsky: *Der sotsyalizm un di natsyonale frage* (1908); *Gesamelte shriften*, 4 vols. (1912–1919); *Yidn und yidishkayt* (1939).

Moise B. Soulam
1890–1967

The Salonika-born Ladino journalist Moise B. Soulam settled in New York City in 1913. He was best known for an advice column he wrote, using the feminine pseudonym Tia Satula or Bula Satula, from 1913 to 1934. Sometimes entitled "Palavras de mujer" (Words of a Woman) and sometimes "Postemas de mujer" (Pet Peeves of a Woman), the column appeared intermittently in the Ladino newspapers *La Amérika, El Progresso*, and *La Vara*. Written in a popular style, the columns urged female readers to lead respectable, upright lives and to adopt American habits and customs.

We Speak and Write This Language against Our Will
1928

Dear *Vara* of my soul,

Wherever it may be, I am always hit in the face by a pet peeve, some vexation and angst, due to the misbehavior of certain of our women who still do not know whether they are in New York, in the city of the veritable Tower of Babel, where many languages are spoken, or whether they are living in the old Turkey, where our women used to speak not only shouting through the streets, but also moving their hands and feet.

Here it is the same with some of our women, who, without even knowing who is sitting by their side, in the car, elevated train, and subway, go around speaking to each other in Spanish, and shouting as if they were litigating.

If I write this to you, *Vara* of my heart, it is because on Monday, two Sephardi women living in . . . Harlem, were on the elevated, returning from downtown to their homes, speaking not only [by] shouting, but also gesticulating with their hands.

What was remarkable about the conversations that the women in question were having on the elevated was that one of them was speaking about matters between husband and wife. The woman speaking should have spoken to her friend either very softly or when they were alone in their homes.

Besides this they began to mock in Spanish a fat man who was sitting in front of them, and began to say things about him, both truths and untruths, ugly words that would make you want to block your ears.

Everything was going fine until the two women left the station at 116th Street, but as they walked down the stairs, they found themselves behind a Puerto Rican good-for-nothing, to whom they did not pay attention at first.

The women were walking on 116th Street, returning to their homes, and the Puerto Rican also continued to walk behind them.

The two ladies turned onto Park Avenue, when the Puerto Rican suddenly came to their side. After greeting them in Spanish, he invited the two to come to his house. . . .

You can well imagine that the two Sephardi women did not answer him, and the Puerto Rican continued to follow them. But seeing that he was not getting any response either to his greeting or to his inauspicious invitation, he ventured to speak a few dirty words to the two Sephardi women, who answered him brazenly, "What do you think we are? Get out of here before we call a policeman."

Upon hearing this the Puerto Rican told them:

"Excuse me, ladies, as I was sitting next to you on the elevated, I heard that you were speaking in Spanish some words that you will readily recall, and I thought that you two were—"

Thus saying, the Puerto Rican started walking rapidly or, better said, started running, before the two women could call a policeman. . . .

Don't ask me, dear *Vara*, how I came to know this, since my grandmother used to say, "do not pay money to learn a secret." This applies even more in this case because women cannot keep secrets. These two ladies told the story to their female neighbors, their female neighbors told their nieces, their nieces told their girlfriends, their girlfriends told their husbands, and before you could say "and the cat came and ate the kid, and the dog came and bit the cat," I also got a bite of this gossip. What I mean to say is that I came to know the matter and told it to you so that this may serve as a lesson for those women of ours who, finding themselves on the streets or in cars, on the elevated and in subways, be careful not to speak [by] shouting, because as I told

you before New York resembles the Tower of Babel. Here there are peoples and individuals who speak various languages, and without knowing or thinking about it we can be heard, understood, and accused by strangers, and the best thing of all is to behave yourself while talking.

NOTE

Words in brackets appear in the original translation.

Translated by Aviva Ben-Ur.

Arthur Ruppin

1876–1943

Arthur Ruppin was a pioneer in the sociological study of contemporary Jewry and the lead figure in purchasing land for Jewish settlement in the Land of Israel in the early twentieth century. Born in German-occupied Poland, he trained as a lawyer but from an early stage devoted his life to the Zionist movement. From 1902 to 1907, Ruppin headed the Bureau for Jewish Statistics and Demography in Berlin. In 1908, he moved to Ottoman Palestine to open and head the Palestine office of the World Zionist Organization. In this role, he was instrumental in the development of new, collective forms of Jewish agricultural settlement (kibbutzim and moshavim). In 1926, he founded the department of sociology at the Hebrew University of Jerusalem. Despite their frequently neoromantic and racial categories of analysis, his sociological and demographic surveys of world Jewry remain invaluable.

Palestine and World Jewry
1929

Palestine and the Jews

This will be the first of my addresses before the Zionist Congresses to deal not with the various questions involved in the upbuilding of Palestine but with the significance of this work for the future of Jewry. I regard it as essential that—at a time when we are entering upon a new phase of our work in Palestine—we recall anew the purpose and aim of Zionist activity.

Since the destruction of the Jewish State in Palestine there has been no age, I believe, whose importance in the shaping of the destiny of the Jewish people has been greater than that of the last three decades. They have been a period of both positive and negative events of enormous significance. The number of Jews has reached an unprecedented high mark, having increased from ten and a half to sixteen million in these thirty years. And great changes have taken place in the distribution of the Jews throughout the world: Almost three million Jews have emigrated from the East European countries during this period—to Central and Western Europe, to the United States and other trans-Atlantic lands; and most of them have risen from abject poverty to a state of at least comparative affluence. The United States, which sheltered only about a million Jews in 1900, now has four and a half million. The legal restrictions and unbelievable oppression which the six million Russian Jews suffered before the World War no longer obtain. The legal recognition of the equal rights of Jews is now—after fifteen hundred years of legal disability—a fact throughout the world. Since the World War international agreements for the protection of national minorities have brought the Jews of most East European countries recognition as such a national minority, thus enabling them to mould their cultural life in their own way. And the Balfour Declaration and Palestine Mandate have provided an international legal basis—which only fifteen years ago seemed a dream—for the realization of the century-old yearning of the Jews for Palestine.

Assimilation

From this point of view the structure of Jewry is more impressive to-day than ever before. Behind its splendid facade, however, destructive forces are at work, undermining its foundation—the Jewish sentiment of community whose basis was the common religion, race and destiny of the Jews. We style these forces assimilationist—a term which defines a tendency to abandon the traditional Jewish culture shared by all Jews to the end of the eighteenth century, and to adopt instead another culture which to the assimilationists seems higher than their own.

This cultural modification is the first step toward a change in nationality. Many, it is true, maintain that a Jew can change his nationality no more than a Negro can change his race. But the comparison is not apt. For race is a factor independent of the individual, while nationality depends largely upon external conditions in the choice and shaping of which each man has a share.

The menace of assimilation was evident even thirty years ago; but its degree was then not nearly as great as now. Because of the great part which religion has played hitherto in the Jewish feeling of community, Jewry has suffered more than other ethnic groups from the decline of religious life in the present day. In Central and Western Europe the community of Jewish interest has in many cases become a mere phrase devoid of all religious content.

Jewish organizations are making great efforts to check this desertion of Jewish tradition. In New York alone such organizations expended, in the course of 1928, about five million dollars for the religious education of children. Despite this, however, they succeeded in gaining only about a third of the Jewish schoolchildren of the city as regular attendants at Jewish religious classes. Similar conditions obtain in Central and Western Europe. The head of a large Italian congregation, indeed, complained to me that the Jews do not come to the synagogue even on Yom Kippur. When I inquired as to what connection with Judaism they retained he replied that they wish to be buried in a Jewish cemetery! The results of a recent investigation on the part of the Reform congregations of America showed that only fifty percent of the Jews attend the synagogue on Yom Kippur, but that ninety per cent of them still observe Jahrzeit. Thus the tie that binds many Jews to Judaism is not Jewish life, but the mystery of death.

Mixed Marriages and Conversion

A violent discussion is going on in Germany on the question of whether mixed marriages, conversion, and the decline of the birth-rate are heralds of the decline of German Jewry. To-day twenty per cent of the Jews of Germany—and in the larger Jewish communities, such as Berlin, Hamburg and Cologne, even twenty-five or thirty per cent—contract marriages with non-Jews. How great this percentage is can best be realized when one considers that fifty years ago, when such marriages were prohibited by law, practically none took place. In the matter of conversions the situation is similar. It is true that Germany has only one or two converts a year for every thousand Jews. In itself this proportion is small. But when we regard it from the point of view of the average life span we see that if this proportion is maintained it means that one out of every ten Jews abandons his religion. In Holland mixed marriages have become so common that last year some rabbis seriously considered excommunicating all Jews who entered into such marriages. Even in the United States, among whose East European immigrants intermarriage was unknown thirty years ago, the second generation frequently marries Italians and members of other immigrant groups and even persons of old American stock. As for those countries where a small number of Jews have lived and prospered for many years, such as Italy, Denmark, and Australia—there mixed marriages are no longer regarded as exceptional cases.

Decline in the Birth-Rate

Our losses through intermarriage and conversion present all the more serious a menace because they are accompanied by a very considerable decline in the birth-rate. In the period from 1841 to 1866—the generation of our grandfathers—the annual birth-rate of the Prussian Jews amounted to thirty-five per thousand. In 1926 this rate had fallen to twelve, while the figure among non-Jews was twenty-one. Thus the Jewish population, instead of increasing naturally, is suffering from a natural decrease—the equivalent of slow suicide. The Jewish birth-rate for 1927 was thirty-five, the death-rate thirteen and the natural increase twenty-two per thousand.

These developments arise from various causes. In Soviet Russia the Government is waging war upon all religion, which it regards as a narcotic for the drugging of the people. This persecution, together with the vastly different economic and political situation, has brought about the complete collapse of Russian Jewry, so that what was once the citadel of Jewish tradition is now but a waste field. Not only are the three million Jews of Soviet Russia now devoid of all influence upon world Jewry, but the latter also is unable to affect the life of the Russian Jews in any way. As a result, the extensive propaganda carried on by the Soviet Government among the youth is stripping the young Jews there of their Jewish consciousness and causing them to turn to other ideals. The clearest instance of this is the decline of the Jewish language and educational system, which together once formed the basis for the preservation of the Jewish individuality. In the other countries of Eastern Europe the situation also is entirely different from that of the pre-war period. The granting of civil rights to the Jews and the great cultural progress of these countries since the War has brought the Jews much closer to Christian culture than ever before. In Poland, where in 1897 ninety-seven per cent of the Jews still spoke Yiddish, the proportion had fallen to seventy-four per

cent by 1921. Before the World War the majority of the Jewish children of Poland attended Jewish schools; in 1925-1926 only twenty-two per cent of the Jewish children were enrolled in these schools, while the remaining seventy-eight per cent studied at public schools and high schools, so that their every-day speech has become Polish instead of Yiddish. Intermarriage and conversion—both exceedingly rare in Eastern Europe before the War—are becoming more common. In Soviet Russia, and particularly in its central part, mixed marriages are very frequent. In Poland the number of conversions is constantly increasing. The birthrate is decreasing and—in Roumania, Warsaw, and Lodz—is approaching that of Western Europe. As the death-rate is not falling as rapidly as the birth-rate, we must expect the growth of the Jewish population of Eastern Europe to proceed much more slowly in the future than in the past thirty years.

At the beginning of the nineteenth century practically all the Ashkenasic Jews were still living in Eastern Europe They spoke one language—Yiddish—and were homogeneous in their culture, religious tradition and occupation. To-day, however, this unified Jewry has not only become distributed through many new countries, but it has also split up into a great many cultural groups that differ widely in language, education, mores and religious forms. So little have these groups in common now that they often are unable to understand one another. This linguistic and cultural alienation has greatly weakened the old feeling of Jewish solidarity. To some extent that feeling still persists, as is testified by the generous aid which the Jews of the United States have given their brothers in Eastern Europe through the Joint Distribution Committee both during and since the War. But we cannot ignore the fact that assimilation of the Jews to the culture of the countries in which they live has brought the various groups farther and farther apart and has caused them to lose their feeling of community of destiny and interests.

Preventive Measures

To-day the front on which Jewry must fight is much more extensive and the foes whom it must combat are much stronger than formerly. Its old means of self-defence—such as the provision of religious education for children and the institution of regular religious services—are inadequate in the present struggle. In the course of the last hundred years the Jews of the entire world have derived their energies from the store accumulated by East European Jewry from the fifteenth to the nineteenth century through its concentration upon Jewish literature and through its inbreeding. Those Jews who emigrated from Eastern Europe took these energies with them into their new countries. But as the gates of the lands of immigration are being closed and as the East European reservoir of strength is threatening to become exhausted, the Jews of other countries are faced with the necessity of falling back upon their own resources. And it seems that these are not sufficient to ward off the danger, that the course of Jewry is sloping down toward final annihilation.

He to whom this means nothing, he who remains indifferent as he watches this disintegration of the Jews as a special ethnic group and their absorption by the rest of humanity—he will not understand the point we are making here. For he lacks comprehension of the significance of the Jewish people for the culture of the world now and in the future, and of the debt which each individual Jew owes to the whole of Jewry. Had not the Jews through their close inbreeding preserved and intensified all their inherent intellectual qualities they could not have provided mankind with so many outstanding figures in the scientific and economic worlds and would never have reached the high cultural and economic level they now occupy.

Actually, however, the number of Jews to whom the disappearance of their group is a matter of indifference is small. Much more numerous are those who do not see the full extent of the danger because they have had time to become accustomed to these phenomena and because they believe that something which did not deal Jewry a mortal wound in the past cannot do it fatal harm in the future. But the menace to-day is entirely different, both in degree and character, from that of former times.

And what can we do to ward off this danger? We Zionists see clearly that the Diaspora cannot alone and unaided produce the antitoxin to counteract the effects of assimilation. A Jewish life vigorous enough to overcome the influence of alien cultures and to infuse the Diaspora with a living Jewish spirit can arise only in a land far off the highway of Christian culture—the land to which we feel historically bound and which revives all the Jewish sentiments that have sunk down into our sub-consciousness, the land where the language of the Bible is the speech of our children and the moulder of their minds.

The Problem of Palestine

But the mere fact that we Zionists regard the establishment of a Jewish National Homeland in Palestine as the only means of obviating the peril provides no practical solution of the problem. The number of Jews in Palestine to-day is but a hundred and sixty thousand—only one per cent of all the Jews of the world. We can point with pride to the change in the status of Palestine, which three decades ago was merely the land of the Halukkah, a country ready to take but not to give. But it is manifest that if the active agent is only a little group of a hundred and sixty thousand Jews the achievements of Palestine cannot influence the rest of Jewry to as great an extent as is necessary.

For ten years I have repeatedly expressed my conviction that by a serious concentration of effort on the part of world Jewry it would be possible to increase the number of Jews in Palestine to half a million within the next ten or fifteen years, and to a million within another such period. If we succeeded in establishing a thousand families annually in agricultural colonies during the first few years—with the aid of the Keren Hayesod—and in gradually raising this figure to two or three thousand a year, we can have an agricultural colony of fifty thousand families, which will include a quarter of a million individuals, within the next twenty or thirty years. And if at the same time we support industry with credit we shall be provided with the fundament that will enable us to find economically secure places for a million Jews. It has been greatly to the disadvantage of our colonization work in Palestine that we have never been able to lay our plans far ahead because we have never been quite sure of the financial means at our disposal for even a year—not to mention a ten or fifteen year period. I hope that the removal of this disability will be one of the first steps taken by the enlarged Jewish Agency.

Another need that has become increasingly apparent in recent years and is universally understood by those who are interested in Palestine is that of a greatly intensified activity in the purchase of land through the National Fund. We must inaugurate a period of particularly energetic work in this field; for without it the expansion of our colonization is impossible. At the same time, however, I believe that we also need to organize this work of colonization anew. To repeat a demand I have made at previous Congresses: That work must be given over to a special colonization fund or bank which would be assured of a definite percentage of the annual budget of the Keren Hayesod. The situation now obtaining—that our agricultural colonization, the fundament of all our work, is a neglected step-child receiving only the crumbs left over after the so-called fixed expenditures have been covered—must be ended once and for all.

It may be objected that even a million Jews in Palestine would constitute only five per cent of the Jews in the world, so that ninety-five per cent would still remain in the lands of the Galuth. This, of course, is inevitable. No serious Zionist has ever thought that Palestine can absorb all the Jews of the world. Even in the days of the ancient Jewish State many more Jews lived in other countries than in Palestine itself; and we shall have to resign ourselves to the fact of a large Jewish Diaspora in the future also. But Palestine can cure the ill from which this Diaspora is now suffering. To-day the Jewries of the various countries are but scattered members that lack a central organ, a heart. Palestine can become their heart, the spiritual motive agent which will bring forth new and vital values from the well of Jewish community life in Palestine. Thus will the feeling of solidarity and of belonging to the Jewish people be revived in those dispersed groups.

But we must face another objection: In twenty or thirty years the number of Jews in Palestine, even if it shall have reached a million, will be less than the number of Arabs, which even to-day amounts to three-quarters of a million and which will rise to more than a million in thirty years because of the extraordinarily high natural increase in the Arab population. But aside from the fact that a Jewish population of a million need not be our final goal for all time this objection has significance only for those who believe that Arab domination of Palestine cannot be avoided unless the Jews form a majority. We must, however, take into consideration the solemn promise of the League of Nations that Palestine is to be so administered as to facilitate the establishment of a Jewish National Homeland. Our subjection to the domination of an Arab majority would be contrary to this promise. To my eyes the League of Nations provides a guarantee for the safe continuance of our work. We must bring as many Jews as possible to Palestine because an increase in our numbers heightens our economic and cultural power. It would be an excellent thing if we should become so numerous as to overbalance the Arabs. But the political relationship between the Jews and Arabs of Palestine should be so defined as to be independent, both now and later, of numerical preponderance on either side. We must avoid the erroneous view that prevailed in Europe for an entire century and which led to the catastrophe of the World War—the view that only one nationality can be sovereign in one state. Under the aegis of the League of Nations Palestine must become a political entity in which Jews and Arabs live side by side as two distinct nationalities enjoying equal rights and privileges. Neither is to rule—neither is to be enslaved. The right of the Jews to come to Palestine is as great as the right of the Arabs to remain there. This right we cannot and will not give up. For upon it depends the fate of a nation whose number is sixteen million, whose contribution to human culture is by no means negligible and which is destined to give much more to mankind in the future. But while we are fully conscious of our own important part in the cultural progress of humanity we do not want to minimize the worth and achievements of other peoples. We abominate chauvinism in other nations; we must combat it in our own.

Reconstruction

The success of our work in Palestine is largely dependent upon whether we succeed in gaining all classes of Jewry for peaceful co-operation in that work. The energies we fritter away in internal disputes are not available for creative activity. The majority of European Jews are independent; they are merchants, agents, artisans or industrialists; labour is represented by only a small percentage. But in Palestine, where most of the Jews will have to do productive work in agriculture or industry, the proportion of working-men will have to be much larger. A result of this difference in numerical relationship is that the working class asserts its ideals much more in Palestine than in the Jewish life of Europe. It is a characteristic of the Jewish worker—and a sign that he is a true son of the Jewish people—that he is not willing to remain a dumb cog in a great industrial organization but wants to take an active part in the development of the enterprise, that he refuses to content himself forever with a low standard of living but aims to better his situation. He wants to preserve his intellectual qualities though he is a workingman, and to enjoy his share of our cultural assets. But the Jewish worker brings two valuable qualities into Palestine: his dependability—speaking from a national point of view—and his intelligence. These lead him to avoid exaggerated demands and to realize that in this capitalist world Palestine cannot do without an influx of private capital. Palestine cannot have economic peace unless an understanding of the peculiarities of the Jewish worker is coupled with a comprehension of the international economic situation.

The European forms of capitalist economy have been moulded by a long course of historic development. We in Palestine have the advantage of finding no such rigid forms. We do not need to destroy existing institutions but are able, so to speak, to carve our economic system out of virgin rock. Even to-day Palestine shows the promising beginnings of an evolution toward new social forms. A large proportion of our land purchases has come into the possession of the Jewish National Fund, which administers its estates as the property of the Jewish people and wards off the danger of private speculation. Palestine is the only country where Jewish industries have introduced the eight-hour day and excluded child labour without government regulations to that effect. The number of co-operative organizations for the obtaining of credit, for buying and marketing, for public works and for agricultural enterprises is so great that Palestine may well be called the "land of co-operatives." Medical care among the workers is organized in exemplary fashion, although it receives no support whatever from the state. And when we consider that all this has been achieved in a very short time we feel justified in our expectation that the Jewish urge toward the creation of new social forms will bear fine fruit in Palestine in the future.

The New Social Ethics

More than two thousand years ago the Jewish prophets set up a high ethical ideal that has illuminated the road of mankind. And in their search for new and better forms of social organization the Jews of Palestine may contribute to the development of the new social ethics for which mankind is yearning. Thus would they give evidence that the spirit of the prophets is still living in their souls. I believe that only the hope for new and better social forms can keep alive in the broad ranks of our workers the enthusiasm without which our undertaking cannot possibly succeed. The enthusiasm of our colonists has been the most important factor in the gaining of friends for our work among both Jews and Christians. Indeed, non-Zionists—and real business men—have recognized that without the hope for a better social organization the enthusiasm of the great masses of our im-

migrants would run dry, and an asset of enormous value in our constructive work would be lost. As we progress beyond the pioneer period the spirit of economy must penetrate our life in Palestine more and more. But economy alone, unaccompanied by impetuous enthusiasm, will not build up a Jewish Palestine.

As the Jews of Palestine come from all countries and all sections of Jewry, their religious life reflects the dissension obtaining among the Jews of the Diaspora. But in Palestine religion is bound up much more closely with national sentiments and historic memories. No less a personality than Chaim Nachman Bialik is supporting the revival of religious customs with all his artistic creative power. And because this revival had its source not in the study but in the soul of the people, because it is not merely a subject for precepts but a part of actual life, its force of penetration is extraordinarily great. I firmly believe that sometime the current of our renewed religious life will flow into the Diaspora and infuse it also with a new religious spirit.

Nothing is as effective in bringing people close together as companionship in a struggle, as joint work at a difficult but lofty task. When Jews of all classes and lands take part in the upbuilding of Palestine they not only further the establishment of the Jewish National Homeland but also forge new bonds that will hold together even the Jews in the Diaspora.

The miracle of the resurrection of the Hebrew language in Palestine, the rise of a rich Hebrew literature, the Hebrew educational system headed by the Hebrew University—these will revive interest in Hebrew in the Diaspora also.

And thousands of Jews who will travel in Palestine or study at the Hebrew University will spread the gospel of the living Jewish nation throughout the Diaspora.

Palestine and the Galuth

In Palestine the Jews can build up a culture of their own on the foundation of the Hebrew language and of a national economy whose every branch is in Jewish hands. This culture will be a synthesis of the ancient lore of the Orient and the scientific knowledge of the Occident. And it may bridge the gap between these two worlds and thus solve a problem with which we have struggled in vain for centuries.

Anti-Semitism—which is a special case of group hostility, and arises not from the intellect but from dark recesses of instinct—will not disappear in the

Diaspora even though the Jews through their activity refute the accusation that they are not creative agents but only mediators in both the economic and intellectual realms. Once the groundlessness of this statement is established, anti-Semitism will invent some other proof of the racial inferiority of the Jew. The purpose of our upbuilding of Palestine is not the refutation of anti-Semitic arguments. But it will be a severe blow to anti-Semitism if the Jewish community in Palestine proves beyond question that Jews are able to perform all industrial and agricultural tasks from the simplest to the most complicated, that the research of Jewish scholars and the works of Jewish artists stand on a high plane.

But one may ask: If Palestine reaches a position of such supreme importance in Jewish life what functions will remain for the Jews of the Diaspora. To this we reply that, in the first place, the Diaspora will be Palestine's reservoir of human material and financial means for many decades to come. If it fails in this, the Jewish life of Palestine cannot flourish.

Moreover, the Jews of the Diaspora are an important cultural factor. They are endowed with an asset invaluable for their participation in the cultural development of their countries—their intellectuality, which they have acquired by purposeful breeding through many generations and which they will retain through the natural means of heredity as long as they remain a distinct ethnic group unmingled with the neighbouring peoples. Their share in the development of certain branches of culture in their lands is far greater than their numbers would lead one to expect. Thus the frequent occurrence of illustrious Jewish names in the fields of economics and science; I shall mention but a single one—Albert Einstein. The Jews gratefully pay back with interest what they have taken from the culture of the people about them.

But there is another great task which the future holds for world Jewry. The most significant event of our day—the only one which may possibly impart historic meaning to the senseless horror of the World War—is the founding of the League of Nations, whose purpose it is to abolish war and bring about peaceful co-operation among the nations. We Jews are the only people that is scattered throughout the world and that can gain through no war. For us the winning of a victory by one country means that we have suffered defeat in another. Thus we seem actually predestined to become the shield-bearers of the League everywhere and to work for international conciliation in all lands.

In closing let me express my hope that I have pointed out clearly the many perils and the great hope I see in Jewish life to-day. Looking back at our activity during the past three decades we may say with gratification that the tiny spark of Zionism has grown into a great flame which has become an essential element of Jewish life.

Other works by Ruppin: *The Jews of Today* (1904; rev. ed., 1911); *The Jews in the Modern World* (1934); *The Jewish Fate and Future* (1940).

Leo Löwenthal

1900–1993

The German-born sociologist of literature and mass culture Leo Löwenthal was associated with the Institute for Social Research in Frankfurt from 1926. With the rise of Nazism, he and its other members transferred the institute to New York. After the war he remained in the United States, where he taught at the University of California, Berkeley, from 1956. As a young man in Frankfurt, he was strongly influenced by Rabbi Nehemiah Anton Nobel and was active in the Freies Jüdisches Lehrhaus in its early years, but by the time he joined the Institute for Social Research he had drifted away from any serious engagement with Jewish themes.

Heinrich Heine
Late 1920s

[. . .] The Judaism into which Heine was born and with which he had to come to terms as a maturing man was the Judaism of the German reform. This was, to be sure, no longer the reform, creative in its way, of the generation of Moses Mendelssohn, but already in part the reform of the Sunday Jews. Heine hated these abuses growing out of the reform movement and he condemned them in the sharpest of terms. He found in them nothing other than a veiled, unacknowledged or unexpressed inclination toward the Christian. How he was able to ridicule that!

Others want an evangelical Christianity in a Jewish style and make themselves a talles [prayer shawl] from the wool of the Lamb of God, make themselves a jacket from the feathers of the holy dove of the spirit and underclothes from Christian love; and they go bankrupt. And the progeny calls itself "God, Christ & Co."

The path of radical reform was not the path of Heine the Jew. Certainly, he admired Moses Mendelssohn, but he also misunderstood him in part. In Mendelssohn he found a responsible, unsentimental and strong love for Judaism, which he frankly did not expect of David Friedländer and Eduard Gans. Heine's misunderstanding of Moses Mendelssohn is yet further proof of Heine's deep Jewish instinct. He was of the opinion that Moses Mendelssohn had done away, at least in Germany, with the Talmud—"that Jewish Catholicism." It is known that Mendelssohn did not want to do so, even if he perhaps helped to bring it about. In this connection, Heine thought that Mendelssohn wished to maintain the Jewish ceremonial laws for reasons of rational insight, rather than sentimentality. "As the kings of the material world, so must the kings of the spirit relentlessly oppose familial sentiment; nor on thought's throne may one submit to easy geniality." This principle, that what matters is knowledge, the sovereignty of thought, places Heine in the line of the most representative of Jewish thinkers. Such was, after all, also Maimonides' essential motive: to cleanse Judaism of all sentimentality, superstitions, atavisms, and psychological contingencies; and to establish forever as Judaism's duty the acknowledgment of the one, unknowable God. Without in any way making the risky suggestion of a comparison, one may say that Heine's hatred of all dogma and all religious fanaticism was shared by Maimonides, and it is in this context that the following takes on its deepest meaning:

> My devotion to the essence of the Jew has its roots simply in a deep antipathy for Christianity. Indeed, I, the despiser of all positive religions, will perhaps one day go over to the crassest rabbinicalism just because I view the latter as a proven antidote.

To be sure, it never went beyond this "perhaps," but Heine does in fact fall victim to the great historical error committed by the reform in identifying historical Judaism with Catholicism as respective expressive forms of dogmatic religion. Heine always knew only of the danger of legalistic Judaism, of its cumbersomeness and stiffness, and nothing of its vitality, nothing of its capacity for lively development. He completely overlooked the historical context internal to Judaism, the lively continuity between its oral and written lessons, between the Torah and the Halacha. For him, the Talmud belonged in the same historical context as Catholicism.

In fact, the Talmud is the Catholicism of the Jews. It is a gothic cathedral, overloaded, to be sure, with childish ornamentation, but which still astonishes us through its enormity reaching to the heavens. It is a hierarchy of religious laws, often concerning the most curious, ridiculous subtleties, which are nevertheless so ingeniously set over and under one another, which support and carry one another and work so terribly consistently together that they form a horribly defiant, colossal whole. After the decline of the Christian Catholicism, the Talmud must decline as well. For the Talmud will have then lost its meaning; it serves, namely, only as a bulwark against Rome.

This passage essentially echoes the same historical misperception that drove Heine to baptism, namely, the idea that Judaism could be periodized and classified without qualification alongside European cultural history and that, therefore, Jewish forms were definable and variable in accordance with a European point of view.

Yet the weakest point in Heine's ideas is simultaneously the strongest; for if he held false historical *theories*, he also possessed a deeper historical *intuition*. In his theories of the history of Judaism during the European middle ages, it sometimes appeared as if Heine subscribed to the views of modern Jewish nationalism which, in a grotesque lack of understanding, frequently makes of the history of Judaism from the destruction of the second temple up to the time of Pinsker and Herzl a *quantité négligeable*. But Heine is saved from such historical absurdities by his love for Judaism. Especially in his youth, he undertook diligent and loving historical studies of the Jews in the middle ages.

Following his love for life, the second great authentic Jewish trait in Heine was his historical consciousness of a Jewish nation. He loved Judaism, everywhere, in every shape, form, and custom, indeed, in every farce that was Jewish. It was no sentimental love, but a genuine open-eyed love. Works like the *Rabbi von Bacharach* and the *Hebräischen Melodien* are undying testimonies of Heine's love for historical Judaism.

Only a representative, vital Judaism could have saved Heine from regarding *minhag* [custom] as the central aspect of Judaism. Thus in his surroundings and in his historical sources he constantly saw only the deification of the commentary or customs. And to the extent that he loved Judaism, he was forced by the principle of reason and knowledge to reject it. But this love had made him a national Jew; in *Jehuda Halevy* Heine's version of national Jewishness found its suitable expression.

How Heine's national Jewishness was expressed is once again characteristic of his Jewish intuition. He sensed the cohesion of Jewish history in all periods and customs, and in this the secret longing for the promised land. We have already seen what Europe, France, and Germany meant to Heine. He affirmed Europe. He loved the Harz mountains and Parisian society; as a good continental European, he hated the English. All of this he took utterly seriously. And yet—here he distinguishes himself in principle from the Jewish reform (and not only from that)—he did not experience life in Europe as life in his allotted homeland. He did not dream of a life in Europe in harmonious agreement with the other peoples as the Jewish ideal, but experienced life among the other peoples as *Golus*. Jehuda Halevy, the splendid representative of occidental culture who lived in happy community among the Moorish peoples as a Jew, found no rest until he set out from the diaspora to his homeland on a journey which remains shrouded in mystery. In Heine, the European man of letters, there erupted over and over again—not in Jehuda Halevy's passionate determination to arrive at his goal, but in the melancholy brokenness of a poet—the longing for a home, the consciousness of homelessness.

Heine's love for Judaism found its most passionate expression in his relation to the Bible. Accustomed to making Jewish history of the middle ages the object of his conscious artistry, Heine increasingly withdrew as artist in those places where he spoke of the Bible. His poems demonstrate with what naivete and empathetic capacity he approached his Biblical material, but the older and more mature he grew, the more intimate and personal became his words about the Bible. His experience of the Bible is equivalent to that of the inadequacy of the artist. The longing for beautiful, genuine life that drove him to the baptismal, to France, into the arms of women, allowed him hope to find salvation and the meaning of life in artistic form. He was desperate, but also honest enough to understand that that could not succeed. As an artist he sensed that matters of artistic fact prevailed in the Bible, but he sensed as well that it was not artistic principles that had created them. The most flattering comparison that the artist Heine could bestow was the comparison of the Bible with Shakespeare, but in doing so, he did not lower the Bible into the sphere of art, but raised Shakespeare above it. Es-

sentially Heine found in Shakespeare—in accord with the gift, not the reality—a secret alter ego. Shakespeare, the man, used artistic means beyond a mere artistic purpose to see through and disdain all dogmatism and fanaticism incorruptibly and without bias. This unconditional, comparatively speaking, messianic type held the mirror before European humanity, as Heine understood himself to do in his moments of greatest purity. His comparison of Shakespeare with the Bible, a comparison of style of the sort the artist is allowed to draw, demonstrates its confinement within a legitimate frame.

> Only in one writer do I find something that recalls the immediate style of the Bible. That is Shakespeare. In him as well the word sometimes stands out with that terrifying nakedness that startles and unnerves us.

When Heine compares Moses Mendelssohn to Luther who, like him, repudiated tradition and declared the Bible to be the source of religion, does he not become a Karaite? Does he not remind us of the sect that denied the oral tradition and recognized solely the Bible, but whose members were fundamentally the most unJewish of people? No! Ultimately the Karaites loved their Judaism as little as their spiritual grandchildren, the Sunday Jews. Heine did love historical Judaism and its outward manifestations; it is simply that, as theoretician, he understood it wrongly or not at all. For the Karaites, the Bible was fundamentally an instrument of struggle against the nation of Jews that created for itself its living expression in the developing tradition. For Heine, the Bible was the quintessence of just that beloved people.

We began with Heine's position in relation to the reform and found that he too in part fell victim to that unhappy identification of Judaism with Catholicism. But what is decisive and significant for Heine is the appearance in those years of another conceptual pair which he distinguished cleanly and refined. I am speaking of reform and emancipation. In general, the reform conceived the emancipation of the Jews as liberation from unworthy living conditions and simultaneously as identification with the European ways of life. Heine took up the concept of liberation and understood it at first exactly as the reform understood it—as the liberation of the Jews from base servitude. But very quickly, this conception of Jewish, national liberation grew in him and became human liberation. If the great representatives of Judaism may be invoked once again in this connection, then one will remember the prophets, who formulated the concept of freedom as Judaism's central concept. Also recalled will be those who made of the national a social and universal human concept. As Heine writes:

> But what is this great task of our time? It is emancipation. Not merely the Irish, Greeks, Frankfurt Jews, West Indian blacks and other such oppressed peoples, but the emancipation of the entire world, especially of Europe, which has come of age and now tears itself loose from the iron reins of the privileged, of the aristocracy.

He was a critic of capitalism, but his criticism departed not from economic but from religious principles. Judaism was for him a symbol of liberation. To a symbol he was allowed to return, but not to a reality. He loved this symbol and suffered from it. For him Judaism was an illness, but it was an illness he affirmed.

The New Israelite Hospital in Hamburg

> A hospital for sick and needy Jews,
> For those poor mortals who are trebly wretched,
> With three great evil maladies afflicted:
> With poverty and pain and Jewishness.
>
> The worst of these three evils is the last one,
> The thousand-year-old family affliction,
> The plague they carried from the grim Nile valley,
> The old Egyptian faith so long unhealthful. . . .
>
> Will Time, eternal goodness, some day end it,
> Root out this black misfortune that the fathers
> Hand down to sons? And some day will the
>   grandsons
> Be healed and whole, and rational and happy?
>
> I do not know! . . .

(*The Complete Poems of Heinrich Heine*, translated by Hal Draper, Boston: Suhrkamp/Insel Publishers Boston, Inc., 1982, pp. 398–99.)

Thus did the baptized defendant become the Jewish accuser.

NOTE
Words in brackets appear in the original translation.

Translated by Donald Reneau.

Other works by Löwenthal: *Schriften in fünf Bänden* (1980–1987); *An Unmastered Past* (1987).

Berl Katznelson

On Matters of the Hour
1930

Now I want to talk about the approach to the Arab question. When I was discussing Brit Shalom [Covenant of Peace], I asked: Can there be a common position of Zionists and non-Zionists on this question? (By "Zionists" I mean people who believe that Zionism is the solution for the mass of Jews, satisfying their needs, the creation of a large settlement of broad expanse.) I deny that. A common point on Arab matters cannot be sought if there is no common point on Zionist matters, on social matters. This was even more evident to me when I read the pamphlet *The Brotherhood of Workers*. In the Land of Israel all sorts of attempts have been made by nonpartisan organizations. The Fraction began as a nonpartisan organization. They also invited members of Aḥdut ha-Avodah [The Unity of Labor, a political party] there, and they said, it is only a matter of the radicalization of the Histadrut [the umbrella labor union]. Dozens of other efforts like this will certainly be made. [. . .] All nonpartisan organizations degenerate: on the one hand, they are not transparent in the partisan manner, and on the other hand, they excel in all the activities of partisan existence and especially in all of its flaws. First, one must clarify for the public that it should seek a solution to the Arab question in a political framework: Zionist or anti-Zionist, socialist or bourgeois. [. . .] The possibility of speaking all of these things in a single chorus is, in my opinion, very dangerous and liable to create an atmosphere lacking all clarity of thought. Against this we must fight. And from this point of view I want to approach an analysis of ideas about the Arab worker among us.

It would seem sufficient for knowing the value of organizing the Arab worker if we started from the basic outlook shared by every workers' movement. If we said: we are socialists, we are workers, the worker's soul in us cannot accept the exploitation of the neighboring worker. [. . .]

Here I am trying to air a few questions about this subject, and not only in direct connection to the Arab worker in the Land of Israel. Let us look at workers' movements in the world, in countries where there are different nationalities in a single land. Has international organization in those lands ever served as a shield against pogroms against the Jews? True, we know from the history of revolutions that there were non-Jewish workers who fought in the ranks of self-defense against the rioters, who fought against the inciters. There were also a few like that among the intelligentsia and a few like that among the workers, but in general, they were not sufficiently active—and I am talking about the worker with class consciousness, the revolutionary worker—to prevent pogroms against us. If a worker did not take part in the pogrom himself, that was already a mark of his humanity. I don't think that many radical parties can state that their members did not take part in pogroms. No socialist may ignore this phenomenon, and it is impossible to say that it is the solution. This does not diminish the value of the socialist movement, and it should not prevent us from working within it, if necessary, but it is forbidden to say that it is a bulwark. In fact, it is possible to bring as an example in the Land of Israel, not only George Nassar, who kept faith with us and did not take part in the riots, but also Isma'il Tubasi, who was an important young man, who received party education in Poalei Tsiyon Left, and who nevertheless was an inciter in Jaffa. And it is important for the people among us to know that. I don't say this as a reproof. It is not my particular wish to reveal the beast in man, but this is an example that can refute the prevalent assumption that an international socialist party safeguards us against riots. It is known from the history of revolutionary movements that people, even great people, have moved from the revolutionary cause to the antisemitic camp. [. . .]

How do I see this question in the specific area of organizing the Arab worker? There is an evident distance between the two standards of living, Jewish and Arab, which perhaps is not at all possible to close with a leap, and although I have not found it written in books that two nations in a single country can belong to different economic circles, I have nothing before me except what my eyes see. There are three economic circles in the Land: the Hebrew economic circle, the *falah* [peasant farmer] economic circle, and the Bedouin economic circle in the Land and abroad. Each economic circle represents an entire political and cultural civilization. Anyone who thinks seriously about the Arab question and does not want to solve it effortlessly, by a parliament, etc., must see that these problems are inherent in the fact that we have Bedouin areas surrounding us. This is a source of all kinds of dangers, of all kinds of breakdowns, of falling wages, and of lack of security in the Land. For many years we will have to cope with

this circle with no solution in sight. The most successful organizing of the Arab worker might accomplish a certain aim, but it is impossible to withstand the danger of Bedouin civilization. For that reason, I cannot imagine that solely by dint of organizing—if not by government force—that it will be possible to close the Land to immigration from Trans-Jordan and Houran of people who [. . .] because they are natives, people of the desert, have no customs duties, borders, police stations. And if there is famine there, they'll come here, and no successful organization of those 15,000–20,000 Arab workers can prevent that. But at the same time, any cultural improvement of the Arab worker, any increase in his needs, is beneficial and facilitates and enables our immigration, in the sense that we will not have to lower our economic level. I also attribute some political significance to this. I assume that there will be elements among Arab workers, maybe a few, but some will accept what we say to them, who will say to themselves that there is some truth in it. There might be found Arabs who will see the larger political perspective inherent in our project, who will accept it from a socialist viewpoint, who will see that our immigration is not a danger to the Arabs; broadly speaking, this could happen. We also have to work in that direction. But we make that hope ridiculous if we see it as a mass hope. On the one hand, Comintern will not cease its work and will organize the Arab worker by various means, with idealism, at a cost, and it knows how to exploit various nuances. I have not the slightest doubt that the nationalist movement, which is supported both by Comintern and by government circles, and also perhaps by others, will try to establish an organization of Arab workers. Thus there will be various streams, and therefore there should also be a stream of our own. And with hard work we may end up with five hundred somewhat idealistic, honest Arab workers, with a certain political consciousness, not the consciousness of assimilation, but consciousness that our growth also helps them in the social sense and does not threaten their national future (I will speak about this later). They will recognize us as an important ally, from the perspective of the Arab nations in general. They will have a vested interest in this. It broadens life and creates conditions for mutual assistance, economic help, medical help. If we set for ourselves the goal of creating a group like that, it will have value, it will break the reactionary front. Comintern will not break the reactionary front because it will support every vision of persecution and pogroms. But a positive group that sees itself as our friend, though it will not mingle with us, can provide us with help and friendship and loyalty. But from the political view, I will never pin all the hopes of Zionism on this. The practical path that it is possible for us to take, in my opinion, is not that of labor unions, but clubs, in which the Jewish worker can meet the Arab worker. Just as with us organizing began with the health fund, here, too, there is a place for medical assistance, for mutual assistance, or a loan fund or joint cultural activity. Groups for specific purposes should be established everywhere that coming together is possible. It is also possible to help in economic tasks; if this does not lead to complications in the labor exchange, we can also be concerned in this area as well.

Three kinds of economy exist in the Land of Israel: mixed workplaces, the Jewish economy, and the Arab economy. In the mixed workplaces, like the railway, the postal service, etc., there are natural conditions for joint organizing. There is truly a single labor market, usually the conditions are equal, there is no national struggle, there is no push from our side, this is a place where it is possible to succeed. There is one other economy in which it is possible for us to work. Why not organize the Arab worker in the Arab economy? That doesn't harm us; there the Arab worker is in his natural surroundings, for example, in Migdal Gad [al-Majdal, the Arab city where Ashkelon now stands] or in Shekhem [Nablus]. We can go there and organize the Arab worker. The whole way of life there is natural for him. The complicated part for this question is mainly to find the place where the Arab worker and the Jewish meet in the Jewish economy. Here there is national competition, here is the question of the right to work, here is a complicated tangle of questions. And regarding this tangle I do not take the position of others among us. I say, we have a full moral right to the Hebrew economy, one hundred percent. We created that economy. It was created with our money, it was created with our blood, it has a specific function. One can demand the opening of the Jewish economy for Arab labor only if they open the Arab economy for Jewish labor. If they say there is no closed Arab economy, it must be open for us in the economic sense, not in the legal sense. Then we can sit and discuss this question. Maybe the matter will be worthwhile for us, too. Perhaps when there is a tariff in some country for my merchandise, I can impose a tariff on the merchandise of that country. I'm not talking about this as a matter of principle, as a matter of simple

calculation. Two nations cannot dwell in the Land, one next to the other, and one enjoy the privilege of having his economy closed to the other, while the economy of the second is open for him. As long as such a situation exists, we have an absolute right to demand a hundred percent of the labor in the Hebrew economy. Not only Jews will recognize this, but any honest tribunal must also acknowledge it. If it does not do so, we will fight for it, and my conscience will be at ease.

If we were to think seriously about joint organizing, we would start in the easiest places, but not in places where conflicts can develop. But among us we have reversed the order. They don't place the burning problem of organizing the Arab worker in the railroad, nor in the postal service, nor in Shekhem, nor even in Haifa, but in the Hebrew *moshavah*.

The organization of clubs of Arab workers with some consciousness, to which we could give resources and assist, might serve as a nucleus of extensive Arab action. I regard this as important, and it is worthwhile to devote resources to it. In this matter, our Histadrut shows some weakness, which is dangerous. Neither Brit Shalom nor the Brotherhood of the Worker is dangerous. All their activities are nourished by the inactivity of the Histadrut. This gives certain people exaggerated hopes. It creates a place where they can stake a claim: Look, we're doing something, and the others aren't. Why aren't we doing anything? Maybe because we want to do work that bears fruit immediately, and maybe because not many people are capable of it. This thing is liable to turn against us. If in easy places like the railroad, in the cities, there were groups of people who were devoted to this—it would be of great importance.

I will express another idea, even though it will be thought heretical. I attribute more importance to the question of the *felaḥin* than to organizing the Arab worker. I don't believe that our Arab action is genuine, that practical and important action can be taken from the center. Any central action can be beneficial and mend things, although in general we are dispersed in the land, and the true relations between us and the Arabs in the Land will not be determined by the center. They will be determined by a series of local actions and relations, and from there, perhaps, benefit may arise. I can list dozens of local moves, in relation to this kind of mutual assistance, that could be important. Formulas are not what it's important to find. It is an error to see the main thing as the organization of sections and their form. These are less important things. There is a need here to break a familiar pattern of life, to deepen roots in their life, or to acquire for ourselves the things that we lack: understanding, tact, a familiar conception, which can only be acquired over generations. The center only has to give pushes, to clarify things; the comrades, just as they create initiatives in the economy, so, too, they must take local initiatives in this matter.

Translated by Jeffrey M. Green.

Theodor Lessing

1872–1938

The German cultural historian, philosopher, literary critic, poet, and novelist Theodor Lessing was a disciple of Nietzsche. He converted to Protestantism in 1895 but reembraced his Jewishness at the turn of the century under the influence of Zionism. He was the first writer to examine the phenomenon of Jewish self-hatred, of which he himself had been an exemplar earlier in his life. Always controversial, he fled Germany in March 1933 and settled in Marienbad, Czechoslovakia, where Sudeten German Nazis assassinated him in August 1933.

Jewish Self-Hatred
1930

I

On the day I began writing this book on self-hatred, the Jews in the east groan under the burden of oppressive news. In Jerusalem, in the area of the Haram, a religious war has broken out before the Wailing Wall. It began as all wars in history have begun: because overwrought people cast senseless words at one another until from the senseless words there came forth senseless deeds. But a hatred stored up for a long time was released in these deeds. It can threaten the endeavor of the Jewish people.

"The endeavor of the Jewish people": the resurrection of our homeland seemed to have been secured! For even the sober experts—who in no way dream of an exodus of Israel to Palestine but consider themselves German, French, English, Italian, or whatever—had been won over to the thoughts of Zionism to the extent that they founded an executive organization, the so-called Jewish Agency, for the solution of the insoluble Jewish question. But then there transpired what could easily

transpire again in the future: the villages and farms newly constructed, wrung with sorrowful pains from the malarial land; the plantings in which every tree embodied the life of a *chaluz* [pioneer]; and the fields fertilized with sweat and tears went up in flames.

Artuf burned. Ataroth burned. Moza burned. Bands of Arabs set fire to the Jewish suburb of Talpioth and laid waste to the house of the poet [Shmuel Yosef] Agnon. The famous yeshiva in Hebron, the Talmudic school from Lithuanian Slobodka, was attacked. Unarmed young students, led by the son of the rabbi, fled into the oratory where they were slain one after the other as they pronounced their final prayer. And all of this happened under the eyes of the British Mandate authorities.

What does the world expect us Jews to do?

For thirty years and longer, since the Bilu movement of 1882, our noble elite has worked on the solution to the nationality question. Tired of ever-fresh outbreaks of mass hysteria, which no nobility of deed, of decorum, or of the heart has ever been able to reconcile; tired of the eternal either–or (either you give yourselves up or you get out of the country); tired of the centuries of reprimands, relocations, and regimentation—whether born of caprice or mercy; tired of all the insecurity and uncertainty, the oldest of all the peoples of the earth attempted to take its fate into its own hands.

It was said: "You are parasites on the property of others"—then we tore ourselves from the chosen homeland. It was said: "You are the middlemen among the peoples." Then we raised our children to be gardeners and peasants. It was said: "You are degenerating and will become cowardly weaklings." Then we went to battle and supplied the best soldiers. It was said, "You are only tolerated wherever you are." We responded: "We know no deeper desire than to escape from toleration."

But when we established ourselves on our own, we heard once again: "Have you still not learned that the tenacious self-preservation of the chosen people is a betrayal of the wealth of the universal human, of *trans*national values?" We answered, after a hundred deaths and wounds, by silently dissolving the Jewish Legion. We renounced self-defense and placed our due right under the protection of the European conscience. What is the answer?

Today, September 6, 1929, the answer seems to be: "Live or work however you can, you will be tolerated as long as you can be used." "Business people!" the Jews will be called. But when there is no more business to be done with the Jews, they will be dropped. The power most maniacally bent on exploiting the earth, the English–American, will also sacrifice Judaism for the next enterprise of colonial expansionism that comes along. Woe, however, to the defenseless: "*Niflad kidra al kefla, weile kidra. Niflad kefla al kidra, weila kidra. Wenkach, unwenkach, weile kidra!*" "If the pot falls on the stone, woe to the pot. If the stone falls on the pot, woe to the pot. Always, always, woe to the pot!"

What should the Jew do? The question is not to be answered. And because it is not to be answered, there arises a difficulty for one's conscience. How does one allay those difficulties?

They are allayed only in rare cases by confessing: "I am guilty." By far the majority of cases, however, attempt to attribute the *guilt* for the insufferable situation to the involuntary author of the condition. This is the law of "lending sense in retrospect." The fundamental law of all of history!

II

The events of human history, this endless chain of accidental transfers of power and acts of caprice, this ocean of blood, bile, and sweat, would be unbearable if it were not possible for people to read a meaning into all of these blind occurrences. They are not at all satisfied to discover the *original* meaning for all that happens; much more they want to find the *sensible* reason. And when they ask: "What is *responsible* for that?" they are already making a *moral* judgment.

Even if therefore the fate of peoples were "accidental" and if everything could also have come about differently, people would still, once it came about *as it did*, always undertake *to interpret* what happened in terms of its sense and ethics!

However, this *making sense* of all senselessness and nonsense can (as we already suggested) transpire in *two* ways. Either by attributing guilt to the "other" or by seeking the guilt in oneself.

Now it is one of the most profound and secure realizations of national psychology that among all peoples the Jewish people were the first, indeed perhaps the only people who have sought this responsibility for world events solely *in themselves.*

To the question "Why are we not loved?" Jewish doctrine has answered since ancient times: "*Because we are guilty.*" There have been great Jewish thinkers who have discovered in this formula, "Because we are

guilty," and in the experience of the collective attribution of guilt and collective responsibility of the people of Israel, the innermost core of the Jewish doctrine.

We may not go into more detail here concerning the significance of this religious collective guilt, but it is important that the reader sense that in this acknowledgment of guilt, emphasized in the mighty Judeo-Christian ethic, is also the key to the *pathology* of our national soul.

Very deep inside of every Jewish person there is a tendency to comprehend a misfortune that befalls him as atonement for a sin. If the reader should ask why this is so, I could only point here to the terrible fact that Jewish history over nearly three thousand years has been solely a *history of suffering.* And, indeed, a history of hopeless, irredeemable suffering.

To make sense and be bearable, however, such a condition of suffering permits only a single emergency exit: the person must believe that fate exercises a particular intention toward him. "God disciplines those he loves." With this understanding of his suffering as a *penalty,* the beginnings of the phenomenon of self-hatred are clearly given.

It is, however, different among the happy and victorious peoples. They have had no occasion, in self-analysis and self-torment, to endanger the healthy emotional relation to life and natural self-esteem. To the question: "Why does misfortune happen to us?" they answer with a forceful accusation against those who, in their opinion, are the "*cause* of the misfortune."

The situation of the Jewish person was thereby doubly endangered. Once because he himself responded to the question "Why are we not loved?" with the answer "Because we are guilty." Then, however, because now the other people could likewise respond to the question, "Why is the Jew unloved?" with the answer, "He says so himself. He is guilty."

Behind the sociological phenomenon designated as anti-Semitism (whereby an entire national type was characterized as *odium generis humani*), there is not merely bad will, the national egotism, or the envy and hate of the competition of peoples. There is a law behind it. A law of "lending sense to the *senseless.*" And this law of history arises out of an ultimate depth.

It is the same law that also sows discord into many an individual fate and leads to sundry enmities. For how often is it not the case that brothers and sisters, lovers, and friends estrange themselves forever because no one wants to look into himself and acknowledge *his* guilt, and instead everyone travels the easiest and most natural path: "Wherever I must introduce suffering into the life of another, I justify my action by the nature of the *other*." A few examples will suffice to illuminate the great significance of this simple fact.

III

All of us, in order to be able to live at all as people have to assume some guilt onto ourselves. We have, for example, to exterminate a world of animals, wonderful, perfect in itself, and originally superior to us. When we destroy the big beasts of prey, lions and leopards, then we conduct ourselves very badly. Therefore we say that the animal of prey is bad. When we exterminate the big snakes, we use much cunning in the task; therefore we say that snakes are cunning.

If I have ever cherished bad thoughts against another, then I have to *justify* these bad thoughts to myself precisely by way of the bad qualities in the other.

Whoever has once said, "God punish England," or "Germany must be humbled," from now on unconsciously cherishes an inclination to gather together and value highly whatever is expedient in the justification of his unfavorable prejudice. Ultimately it could even be that we do not hate something bad at all because it is bad; but rather that which we hate and must hate we *call* bad.

This procedure by which the hated is made hateful is further intensified when a secret feeling of sympathy has to be stifled and deadened. One finds this in such cases where a love or friendship is transformed into hate and persecution.

If I have esteemed or loved a person highly and feel disappointed and disillusioned, then as a rule I experience the disappearance of the old feelings in no way as my fault or as my error; rather I supply the motivation for the transformation of my emotions by saying that the other has changed. That is usually self-deception. It is not the other who has changed, but my inner attitude. But wherever people have to bear the weight of conscience and take responsibility for their actions, there we find beautiful words and ideals as well, in the name of which we can also recast our injustice as our good right.

Now to apply this universal law to the Jewish question:

The Jewish people have without a doubt been wrongly injured. Their unworthy being would have become a reproach to every one of the healthy peoples, among whom the sick people continue to vegetate, if there had been no historical formula thanks to which the wrong exercised upon the Jewish people had not been justified as a wrong, that is, as a *right*. To the Jews as well as to the non-Jews such sense-lending formulae were *necessary*. If one wants to exploit us in the future, then one will justify it with the insight that we were the exploiters of others. If one wants to push us out and reduce the vitality of our lives, then one will adduce everything that justifies exceptional determinations and particular laws. There is no wrong in history that cannot in retrospect be proven to have been justified or otherwise necessary. Wherever a group of people has been condemned to bear its cross on its back, there it will always be said: "They nailed the Savior to the cross."

What researcher into the human soul knows, however, whether the diminishing of souls over centuries does not actually transform the nature of those diminished as well, so that in the final reckoning all the wrongs of history actually become proven wrongs, that is, *become* true? For to change human beings into dogs, one only needs to shout at them long enough, "You dog!"

NOTE
Words in brackets appear in the original translation.

Translated by Donald Reneau.

Other works by Lessing: *Europa und Asien* (1918); *Geschichte als Sinngebung des Sinnlosen: oder die Geburt der Geschichte aus dem Mythos* (1919); *Einmal und nie wieder: Erinnerungen* (1935).

Felix Weltsch

1884–1964

Felix Weltsch—philosopher, journalist, and academic librarian—belonged to the Prague Circle of young Jewish intellectuals, whose members included Max Brod and Franz Kafka. A Zionist from his youth, he edited the main Zionist weekly in interwar Czechoslovakia, *Selbstwehr*. He fled Prague in 1939 and settled in Jerusalem, where he found a position in the Jewish National and University Library.

Antisemitism as Folk Hysteria
1931

Sociology and Psychology

To define the characteristics of antisemitism it is good to proceed on two fronts: i.e., to examine its development externally in a purely empirical manner and thereby find its sociological characteristics; and then to search internally for motives and reasons for its development with understanding and empathy, and thus to find its psychological characteristics.

First, the sociological characteristics: When, according to experience, does antisemitism arise?

To answer this question, it is useful first to ask the opposite: When does antisemitism not arise?

Here the following can be asserted: antisemitism is weaker in countries, populations, and social classes in which Jews do not substantially differ or hardly differ from the rest of the population, where they have largely given up their peculiarity and self-awareness (in Italy, in English high society, etc.).

It is also weaker where Jews are present in very small numbers (for example in Nordic countries).

This already results in two conclusions. Preconditions for the development of an antisemitic movement are

1. That Jews in the respective country differ notably from the rest of the population—in their appearance or habits, religion, worldview, economic activity, self-awareness, etc., and

2. That they are present in a certain percentage. Certainly statistical assessments could empirically determine a "threshold" of antisemitism that would have to be exceeded for antisemitism to develop.

To these two points we must add the most important:

3. Antisemitism arises or becomes strong when the respective group or people in the midst of whom the Jews live finds itself in an emergency situation. History has shown a clear increase in antisemitism after a defeat in war, economic depression, famine, epidemics, a civil war, and so on (in contemporary Germany after a lost war, in France after the war of 1870–71, in Poland in its economic crisis after the war, and indeed even recently in America during the great economic depression).

This last point needs to be remembered when approaching the core question, the question of the inner cause, the actual reason, the raison d'être of antisemitism.

This question has been contemplated sufficiently. It is not only the essential, but also the most obvious question. No wonder that a series of theories has been laid out as answers.

The most common theory in earlier times was the religious one: the Jews convicted Jesus—and therefore have been cursed. This theory was dominant for many centuries. Today it is well known that it is insufficient—although this motif might still play a part consciously or unconsciously. For the largest segment of our contemporary antisemites this theory is insufficient.

Another theory is the economic one: the Jews are creating economic competition as a result of their character, toughness, and speed of reaction. Therefore they are viewed with antagonism and because playing on their Judaism is such a good weapon, it is used willingly. Naturally, the question arises: Why is antisemitism such a good weapon in economic struggles? This again raises the underlying question. Moreover, the enmity of economic competition could never explain antisemitism's specific character of hatred.

There is also an aesthetic theory: the Jews incur hatred as a result of their flamboyant, noisy, and cheeky behavior. This theory does not explain anything either because the question has to be asked again: Why do people specifically perceive Jews' behavior as unpleasant? Why doesn't antisemitism develop against other peoples who are at least as noisy and vocal as the Jews? Moreover, there are enough Jews whose behavior is very modest, almost overmodest, who still don't escape antisemitism. Therefore, there has to be something behind it other than aesthetic sensitivity.

A widely prevalent theory is the cultural and racial defense theory. Antisemitism is nothing other than a defense against the contamination of race, culture, or ethics by the Jews. Every race and culture wants to protect itself from mixing with inferior elements. The superior race, the superior culture, defends itself against the influences of an inferior group. And so one fights against the judaisation of the press and the theater, literature and politics, science and philosophy. This theory is based on an error in reasoning: "being different" is perceived as "being worse." But why does the Jews' being different seem to the antisemite as "being worse"? This again can be explained only by antisemitism. Therefore the same cannot be explained with this theory. Besides, this defense theory is obviously a mental superstructure masking a much more deeply rooted motive. For group antisemitism and mass antisemitism can hardly be explained by reference to the more subtle troubles of racial and cultural purity.

There is certainly also a very simple theory that ascribes the hatred of Jews to instinctive aversion. Jews are hated just because they are disliked. What's the use of excessive deliberation? This is naturally not an explanation, but the renunciation of an explanation. Whoever still wants an explanation will have to ask again: What is the reason for this specific, instinctive aversion? Why are the Jews specifically hated in this particular way, and not other peoples as well, who also clearly differ from the rest?

The hitherto mentioned theories lead to the following conclusion: they are all somewhat accurate, but they do not explain the entire issue. They obviously do not get to the heart of the matter.

Now there is another approach to finding the actual raison d'être of the antisemitic movement. That is modern psychology, as manifested in the methods of psychoanalysis.

This new psychology offers a way to comprehend fully a particular fact. Its importance for the assessment of human circumstances is its awareness of indirect reaction.

Generally people do not react as directly, or logically, as one might naïvely assume, in a rational manner. This has been the reigning assumption so far.

A direct reaction would be, for example, if A is slapped by B in the face and reacts by doing the same thing to him right away. Now a person is rarely able to react in such a direct manner. He cannot immediately return the slap because the one who slapped him is not always right there, is too far away, is of higher standing. Often it is not clear whom one was slapped by—here we understand this in a figurative sense—for maybe there is no one who can be seen or at least recognized as the direct initiator of the slap. Yet there is a psychological desire to return the received slap, to deal with the suffered pain somehow. This means that someone will be hit, who is in no way the direct initiator of the slap and the pain but is well placed for some reason to receive the reaction. That is an indirect reaction.

We have learned this from psychoanalysis. A person's suffering from agoraphobia is not based on a reasonable fear that he could be harmed if he crossed the space, as we would believe if we followed the logical direct manner of reaction. It rather has a completely different motive, indirectly correlated to its effect, such as a distant childhood experience or a suppressed drive, etc.

If antisemitism is analyzed in this manner, one reaches much deeper insights into it than through hitherto existing theories.

Credit for having looked at antisemitism from this new perspective goes primarily to two men: Arnold Zweig, who wrote a particularly enlightening assessment about antisemitism in his essays in the publication Der Jude, which he later presented summed up in his book Caliban, and F. Bernstein, who offered an extremely wise and deeply immersing analysis of antisemitism in his book Antisemitism as a Group Phenomenon.

Both writers primarily use the term group. A group can be defined, for instance, as a number of people who feel that they belong together for a reason—because of their descent, kinship, common interests, or aims—so that a "we-consciousness" is developed. Therefore, a group is a people, a party, an association, a family, etc.

It becomes apparent, as these authors suggest, that such "groups" play an important and fatal role in the type of reaction that I called indirect.

The group expands the I and also expands the You. It also makes it easier to be vain. If I cannot easily be vain based on my I, then at least I can be vain based on a We, for instance as a member of an association, a party, or any other collective.

However, the group also lightens any feeling of responsibility. The individual doesn't feel that he alone is responsible, but only as part of a group, and therefore only needs to bear a fraction of responsibility for his actions.

Above all, the group also increases the circle of those people who can be given back the slap in the face, which leads back to our earlier example. There are a larger number of possibilities to let off steam through hatred for a misfortune that has hit us. It proves to be an element particularly suitable to be integrated into the mechanism of action and reaction. Thus, in this circumstance, Bernstein rightly sees the function of the group.

On this point, Zweig and Bernstein succeed in critically and stylistically quite different ways, but essentially achieve the same result, in explaining antisemitism as a reaction of a group to a minority.

It is not possible to retrace in detail these analyses in a short excerpt; here I refer explicitly to the two fundamental books.

The following section aims to offer a simplified analysis of antisemitism based on my view about "resistance" and "hysterical and inventive reaction." This analysis can essentially be seen as a supplement to and short summary of this new psychological outlook on antisemitism.

In the following sentence I formulate my basic concept of the essence of antisemitism:

Antisemitism is nothing but a hysterical reaction of a group to certain disturbances of its life tendencies.

Now I want to clarify this thesis.

All evolutions in human lives, as in the life of nature, show the following structure: All drives encounter resistance.

How does the human being react to resistances that block his drives?

There are four types of reactions: the negative, positive, hysterical, and creative.

1. The negative reaction: the person gives way to the resistance, gives up his will, and the drive is extinguished and driven back.

2. The positive reaction: the person overcomes the resistance and gets his way. The will is so strong, or the resistance so weak, that the will can become the master of itself.

3. There are, however, also resistances—including the majority of cases—that cannot be fought directly in a straight manner.

What happens there? The power of the drive or the will accumulates in the face of the resistance. This leads to a concentration, an aggregation, a strengthening of the will or the drive. This condition can now result in an explosive breakthrough, in a completely new direction. Arguably the resistance will not be removed, but a new path will be paved. Something new will be created, a third element that was not included in either the drive or the resistance. That is the creative reaction. I believe that all large cultural and intellectual formations are due to this: the human being cannot overcome his powerlessness in the face of nature and the world—but he creates religion. He cannot overcome the strangeness between people, the isolation of individuals—but he creates language. He cannot solve the mysteries of life—but he creates science. He can neither alleviate misfortune through lamentation, nor eternalize happiness by rejoicing—but he creates art. The living creature cannot overcome death—but it creates the spirit. That is creative reaction.

4. The accumulation of the drive in the face of the resistance can also be vented in another way. The kettle in which the steam is locked can explode in a weak spot. Any valve can open up and drain the accumulated drive. This I call the hysterical reaction.

In the case of the creative reaction, the tension is relieved through the creation of something new and valuable. In the case of the hysterical reaction, the tension is relieved through the valve of the weakest resistance. It not only creates nothing new but also acts in a destructive and damaging manner. It diminishes the health of the world.

I call this reaction hysterical because it corresponds to the mechanics of the formation of hysteria as set forth by psychoanalysis. Here a drive—namely the sexual drive or the power drive—is constrained by resistance. This constrained or suppressed drive is vented by the creation of a symptom of disease: stammering, agoraphobia, compulsive disorders, sleeplessness, etc.

This hysterical symptom in this case is just the path with the lowest resistance for the individual. What arises is in no way something valuable, but degrading that reduced the happiness and enthusiasm of the individual.

Even if I now call this reaction hysterical, I still want to distinguish it clearly from hysteria itself. I speak neither of a disease nor of an abnormal phenomenon. One refers to hysteria in its real sense if there is a symptom of disease, something that is in tension with the norms of life. However, what I call hysterical reaction is—unfortunately—quite normal. It is, so to speak, the hysteria of the healthy. It is the kind of reaction we are confronted with in life, and to which all the little troubles and hatred of the day, vanity and dissatisfaction, restlessness and nervousness, but also a large part of the "big" evil of the world can be traced back to.

Two typical cases from daily experience are presented here as examples. The boss, who had trouble at home, will vent his anger by tyrannizing his staff. Or a woman who is unsatisfied in marriage will take it out on the housemaid.

In both cases a drive accumulated through resistance is vented in the direction of the lowest resistance. This lowest resistance is the staff or the housemaid.

Antisemitism relies on the same mechanism.

Who offers people the lowest resistance? The people that, clearly distinct and sometimes conspicuous, lives among them, is everywhere the minority, nowhere sovereign, doesn't have a home anywhere and can be persecuted everywhere quite without punishment: the Jews.

We remember that in the sociological analysis we determined a state of emergency as a main principle for the emergence of antisemitism. Now we have found the explanation. This emergency is nothing else but resistance that stands in opposition to the natural development and evolution of the respective people. A people wants to live happily. If this drive is noticeably disturbed by some plight, it leads to the above described accumulation, which, in turn, leads to the hysterical reaction. One lets off steam, one sees a valve, a way out, the point of lowest resistance, a scapegoat, a housemaid. The suitable object of the lowest resistance, present everywhere and available everywhere . . . are the Jews.

That is the raison d'être of antisemitism.

If one now puts forward the question: Why are the Jews, in particular, such a suitable object for hysterical reaction? the answer lies in their already mentioned minority character. Zweig and Bernstein discuss this problem at length and in detail through the psychological principles of group functioning.

What does this theory of antisemitism mean as opposed to the other theories that have so far been put forward as an explanation?

They are—as opposed to our theory—either bare excuses, disguises, or cover-ups, even though they contribute partial answers and play a supportive role in explaining.

In the end, the housewife can cite a large number of shortcomings on the part of the housemaid. But the core of the issue lies elsewhere. And therefore people have also come up with all kinds of motives and theories about Jews. The Germans have established a whole science of antisemitism, but all that is just a superstructure. The core of the antisemitic reaction lies much deeper than its scientific explanation. It relies on a psychological principle anchored deeply and strongly in the soul of the human being as a member of a group, people, or even the mass.

And just as humanity owes everything great and good that it has accomplished to the possibility of creative reaction, so the largest part of evil in the world can be traced back to this hysterical reaction. It is the danger of human development. And if there is one great task in the moral education of humanity, then it is this: preventing hysterical reaction as much as possible, and promoting creative reaction as much as possible. As close as these two are related in their origins, as contrary they are in their effects.

Translated by Sara Yanovsky.

Other works by Weltsch: *Das Land der Gegensätze* (1929); *Das Wagnis der Mitte* (1937); *Teva, musar u-mediniyut* (1950).

Maurice Samuel
1895-1972

Romanian-born Maurice Samuel spent his youth in Manchester, England. He moved to the United States in 1914 and spent most of the rest of his life there, except for a few years when he lived in Palestine during the British Mandate. He wrote and lectured prolifically, mainly on Jewish matters, and was one of the best-known exponents of Zionism in the United States and Britain before 1948. The most popular of his books was *The World of Sholem Aleichem* (1943), which was instrumental in bringing Yiddish literature to the attention of English-speaking readers. In his delightful memoir *Little Did I Know* (1963), he recalled his youth in the Jewish immigrant community of Manchester.

Jews, Be Nice
1932

Chapter One

The Jews are probably the only people in the world to whom it has ever been proposed that their historic destiny is—to be nice. This singular concept has played such an important role in recent Jewish history that it almost characterizes an epoch.

As applied to an individual, the word *nice* indicates a pleasing absence of character. It is the best that a man can be without being anything. As applied to a people and to its historic role, the word rises to a sublime and solemn fatuity. For a people consisting of nice individuals and of nothing more is not a people at all; it is a loose association of fourth hands at bridge; it is a protracted Sunday afternoon call; it is a subdued cough in the Hall of Fame.

In the philosophy of many Western Jews niceness is something more than an ethical or aesthetic ideal; it is a historic force with a distinctive rationale. Its role among other peoples is not clear, but for the Jew it has a double function; it remedies the defect of his maladjustment and it gives spiritual content to his group existence.

According to this view, anti-Semitism is the result of a lack of niceness in the Jew. If the Jews would only temper their voices, their table-manners and their ties, if they would be discreet and tidy in their enthusiasms, unobtrusive in their comings and goings, and above all reticent about their Jewishness, they would get along very well. At the same time, Jews should have a mission in order to justify their almost unsuspected existence. They should espouse noble causes, not offensively, of course, but in a nice way. They should be social-minded, but never socialistic; they should stand for peace, without being pacifists; they should be intellectual, but not obviously clever. Having achieved a model citizenship through this combination of carefully moderated virtues they will not only be happy, but also liked by everybody.

Behind the ideal of niceness broods this tragic problem, the obsession of the modern Jew: "How can I get myself liked?" He sees the last twenty centuries of Jewish history as one long misunderstanding, hastiness on the side of the non-Jews, indiscretion on the side of the Jews. The time has come to do something about it.

Now it is true that the Jew has always had to walk warily. He has known the meaning of discretion ever since he left his own country. But he has known it as policy and not as *a* policy, as a necessity and not as an ideal. The Jew of the Middle Ages prostrating himself before the baron, the Jew of Poland prostrating himself before the Pan, paid the outer tribute of the physically weaker to the physically stronger. Nor can it be denied that the repeated gesture of submission at last affected the soul of the man. But there was a daily respite in his private life. The Jew never thought of getting himself liked, and he did not order all of his life to this strange, sycophantic end. He was content to get by. Whatever the stigmata produced in his soul by this perpetual dishonesty, he was at least not the dupe of his necessity; and therefore his moral and intellectual condition compares favorably with that of the nice Jew.

For the latter is in the curious position of the diplomat who does not say what he means, but has come to mean what he says. He has taken the gesture seriously and talked himself out of his soul. To win his point he has surrendered his purpose. He suffers all the discomforts of the old Jew, and has none of his relief. Nothing remains for a man in this desperate position but to surrender his identity too; and, consciously or unconsciously, this is the intention behind the theory of niceness.

But the conscious desire of an individual Jew to assimilate, to cease being a Jew, is strictly his own business. We may find it an intellectual absurdity. We may say that there is no such thing as an assimilated Jew, any more than there is such a thing as a digested cabbage. That is to say, in effect, that no Jew can assimilate; he can only arrange that his children should do so. And therefore one can talk of assimilating Jews, but not of assimilated Jews. "Assimilating" is then a transitive and causative verb: "I am assimilating my children," like "I am growing cabbages," meaning "I am causing cabbages to grow." (As we shall see further on, even this degree of assimilation is mostly illusory—but we let it stand now.) These aesthetic and intellectual reflections may be voiced in regard to the assimilating Jew, but we cannot go any further in discussing his case. No people has a moral claim on the loyalty or affection of its members; and the attempt to enforce such a claim is a form of mob brutality which is just as indefensible as a state-organized imposition of nationality.

But when Jews organize for purposes of assimilation, and issue a philosophy which hides that purpose from themselves and from others whom they pull into the stream, so that others find themselves involved in the same discomforts without having the same intentions, something like a moral element is involved. It then becomes legitimate to look into their statements and intentions. A man has the right to be wrong—in private. When he carries this privilege into the open, he becomes legitimate public game.

This interference is the more justified since the Jewish culture and Jewish group identity face, throughout the whole world, a combination of hostile forces which is new in form and effect. The genuine problems of the Jewish people, and of American Jewry—to which this book is more particularly addressed—have nothing to do with the problems raised by the assimilating group; and those who are lovers of Jewish cultural and intellectual values, and wish to see them perpetuated and developed, must first clear the ground of fake issues (always remembering that a fake issue is a real issue as long as it obstructs the view) and proceed to lay open the realities.

What truth is there, then, in the assertion that the manner and bearing of the Jews are responsible for most of their misfortunes; or even in the milder reproach that by their lack of the social graces the Jews exacerbate a dislike which might otherwise diminish and die out? Or in the still more subtle contention that whatever be the causes of anti-Semitism, we ought to be so nice that the anti-Semite would be baffled by the lack of a pretext, and just burst in impotence?

For years I made a collection at random of excerpts, wherever they occurred in my reading, of observations on Jews and the Jewish people. The sources range from Sir Thomas Browne and Gibbon and Voltaire, to Aldous Huxley, *Liberty* and *Vanity Fair*. I wondered whether it was not possible to establish for the majority of these allusions a certain general character; and I believe I have found it in their naturalness, their mechanical and unprovoked—almost rancorless—contempt. Why should Aldous Huxley have Richard Greenow, the hero of the story by that name, remark *à propos* of nothing at all, that he is quite sure that Jews stink? Mr. Huxley would not defend the thesis; he would not even assert, I suspect, that all the Jews he met, or the majority of them, stank. He is too scientific to believe in the *fetor judaicus*. Or why should the hero, in *Those Barren Leaves*, writing in his office, put down: "Why do I work here? In order that Jewish stock-brokers may exchange their Rovers for Armstrong-Siddeleys, buy the latest jazz-records and spend the week-end in Brighton?" Why Jewish stock-brokers? It does not appear from the story that the hero would be happy to be exploited by English or French or American stock-brokers. In both cases the allusion is set down just so—off-handedly and graciously. One cannot even take offense.

Why does someone, writing in *Liberty*, put these words into a short story: "Sid has been ranked with the pants-pressers, but he's the other kind of Jew?" Did the writer think that there are two kinds of Jews? In fact, did he think at all? I doubt it. The remark was not even meant anti-Semitically. It is merely the evidence of a general attitude, something worked into the cultural mind of the Western world. It is an accepted imagery: the donkey is supposed to be stupid (it is not); the ostrich is supposed to bury his head in the sand to hide from the hunter (it does not). In the same way the Jew stinks or lisps or presses pants psychologically out of business hours. One does not have to know Jews in order to make these remarks; as Shakespeare and Marlowe wrote long plays about Jews without having met one, so everybody makes literary allusions to them without thinking about them. It is in the folklore of the modern world.

Even the great make use of this general currency. Voltaire disliked Jews because, we are told, he had been swindled by one. Yet he must have been swindled, in the course of his long life, by a great many Frenchmen, and he never turned Gallophobe. Are we to assume that if the Berlin Jew in question had been nice to Voltaire, the latter would have turned philo-Semite, like his contemporary Lessing?

It must not be thought, however, that only Jews attribute their misfortunes to the absence of the Oxford and Harvard manner. Recently there appeared in New York a book, *The American Rich*, by Hoffman Nickerson. In the chapter on the Jews there is an astonishingly lucid sentence which indicates that Mr. Nickerson had thought about the Jewish problem. "The Jewish problem," he says, "is that of the friction caused by the present status of the Jew, deriving from the contrast between the legal fiction that no separate Jewish nation or people exists, and the fact of their actual existence." And yet the writer, to explain current dislike of Jews, solemnly quotes a piffling incident about a Jew who was too unctuously familiar during a business discussion.

I shall not discuss in this book the ancient riddle of the psychological difference between Jews and gentiles; and in speaking of anti-Semitism I shall devote myself to those causes which convert anti-Semitism from a sense of difference into an active hostility. But even from this point of view dislike of the Jew has nothing to do with his defects, much less his mannerisms. In fact, none of the anti-Semitic books or utterances that I have come across ever deals with the real defects of the Jews. An intelligent anti-Semitism, of the kind which might be useful to us by virtue of clear insight and sound advice, has yet to be created.

The philosophy of Jewish niceness must maintain a delicate balance between obtrusiveness and immediate self-obliteration. If the gentiles are to like us, they must know that we exist. Thus we have the inexhaustible stream of Jewish apologias issuing from the pulpit and the press, and the frequent though spasmodic efforts to "create a better understanding." At these public fraternizations, where Jews and gentiles foregather to tend the flame of their mutual affection and admiration, we may hear from both sides exposés of such virtues and such achievements as no people should ever be suffered to monopolize. The one great misfortune about these recitals is, however, that they seldom pass beyond circles where they are superfluous, and when they do, they are tacitly useless. There is little ground for the belief that anybody except a Jew is ever impressed by orations and books on Jewish contributions to civilization.

The anti-Semitically inclined do not care a rap about our achievements, aptitudes and geniuses; and the only reward we have reaped in Germany for playing a fantastically disproportionate rôle in the science and letters of the country is the additional charge that we are Judaizing the Teutonic spirit.

I trust that the foregoing will not be misinterpreted as an objection either to good manners or to the desire to be of some service to mankind. But we certainly shall not acquire the first or fulfil the second by living constantly on parade and replacing the will to create by the will to please. One cannot help wondering what the Bible would have looked like if the text, let us say, of Amos and Isaiah had been revised by a good-will committee. I once heard a Jewish judge of New York plead for more Jewish education on the ground that a study of Jewish prisoners in Sing Sing revealed the fact that children who had received a Jewish education did not join the criminal classes and consequently did not disgrace their people. Apart from the faulty sociology in the observation (Jewish children with a Jewish education must have come from better homes) there is a special inaccuracy and irrelevance about it. I do not know how much Jewish culture is needed to keep a Jew out of prison; judging from most Jews on the bench, precious little. But the relationship to the innate values of Jewish culture cannot be very important when the appeal is so roundabout. Also, if the numbers of Jews in prisons are increasing, I am less bothered about what the world will say than about the deeper question of what the devil is happening to us.

It is doubtful whether proving to the world that we have produced a great number of geniuses will make life more comfortable for us. It is probable, on the other hand, that an increase in the number of Jewish geniuses—unmanageable as they are, like all other geniuses—would upset the program of the nicer class of Jews. It was thoughtless of Einstein to turn Zionist and, on top of it, to propose revolutionary pacifism. In any case, Jewish genius is not likely to flourish in an atmosphere of anxiety to please. And perhaps what nice Jews really desire is to discover every hundred years that a hundred years ago we produced a great number of geniuses. They are safer at that distance. Nor will Jewish values—or any other kind—be produced by a people which orders its life with reference to the tastes of others.

It is the insistence on the production of Jewish values which is least sincere. For the formula of niceness may

be restated thus: "I'm going to be tolerated as a Jew if it costs me my last bit of Jewishness." Which is not unlike the desperate resolution of one of Sholom Aleichem's heroes: "I'll remain a millionaire if it costs me my last shirt."

It is an awful and ludicrous thing that a great human problem should be reduced to the level of Sunday-school babble. For it is really of the utmost importance that Jews should get along well with their neighbors, this being, in fact, one of the general problems of mankind. But it brings us no nearer a solution to suggest that the historic mission of the Jews is to keep their neighbors in good humor. It begs the question. It is, as Sir Toby Belch would say, to give a dog and, as a favor, ask to have the dog back. The commonest plea that one hears for "tolerance" between Jew and gentile is that there is no difference between them. But whether this is true or not, the plea is actually one for intolerance. For the virtue of tolerance is that it presupposes the existence of differences.

Other works by Samuel: *You Gentiles* (1924); *The Great Hatred* (1940); *Harvest in the Desert* (1944); *The Gentleman and the Jew* (1950); *Blood Accusation: The Strange History of the Beilis Case* (1966).

Isaac Bashevis Singer
1904–1991

Isaac Bashevis Singer was born into a strictly observant family in Leoncin, near Warsaw. During World War I, his mother moved the family to Bilgoraj, where his grandfather was a rabbi. As a young man, Singer followed in the footsteps of his older brother, Israel Joshua Singer, and moved to Warsaw to become a writer himself. Publishing in *Literarishe bleter* and *Undzer ekspres*, Singer began to use the pseudonym Yitskhok Bashevis. Together with Aaron Zeitlin, he founded in 1932 the monthly *Globus*, in the pages of which he attacked Jewish leftist aspirations. In 1935, he moved to the United States and became part of the *Forverts* staff in New York. After the Holocaust, he actively pursued the translation of his work into English and became perhaps the most read Yiddish writer, receiving the Nobel Prize in Literature in 1978. The corpus of his work translated into English far exceeds the corpus of his work published in Yiddish in book form.

Concerning the Question of Literature and Politics
1932

Hatred can never be good. (*Spinoza*, Ethics)

The spirit of politics has perhaps never before embraced people as tightly as today. There is an increase in social awareness. The class division of society is no longer an abstract concept. The war between world proletariat and fascism is drawing closer. The number of those who are still disoriented is declining. On the ideological front, the army of the impending world battle has already been mobilized. The production of mutual hatred—their spiritual ammunition—is in full swing. Cowardice and sentimentality are not in vogue these days. The streets have been flooded with knights.

Politicians on both sides, for whom people have never been the end, only the means, are already counting their flock and determining everyone's role in the upcoming bloodbath. Naturally, they have not forgotten about the writers. Writers, too, are being gradually pushed to the wall; they are asked more and more often and in an increasingly threatening tone: "Whom do you side with? Whom do you support?" "*Are you with us or with our enemies?*"

The proletariat is demanding clear answers to these questions, and global fascism is beginning to pose the same questions very explicitly, too. By nature, all politicians reject neutrality, and they deny even the possibility that neutrality as such can exist. The questions are simple and clear-cut, but the answers are far more complicated.

At this time, a small and insignificant number of writers have aligned themselves with either the right or the left, but the majority of writers of any worth have not yet taken any stand. Older writers in the capitalist countries are just hemming and hawing. The question is too difficult for them, apparently. They want to make it through the world neutrally, and it is very possible that they will succeed in doing so. Younger writers, those just beginning to emerge, are in a more difficult situation. They cannot escape the dilemma. Their answer must be clear and sharp as a knife, just like the question pointed at them. It is also clear that the sharpness of the question will increase proportionately with the sharpness of class struggle. The fact that the demands of the Proletkult[1] in the Soviet Union have been slightly reduced is a result only of the pacifist and con-

structive mood that temporarily dominates over there. But the moment the fight breaks out, they will demand categorically that the writer serve with his pen just as well and unambiguously as the soldier serves with his weapon. And the other side will, no doubt, voice the exact same demand. The writer had better not harbor any illusions, and look the truth straight in the eye.

Today's politician brings sharp accusations against the artist who attempts to ignore completely what is happening around him, at least to some degree. "Are you really planning to sit there shamelessly on your hands, look down from your Olympic height, and watch as the poor and the oppressed fight against their exploiters?" asks one side. "Is it possible that precisely you, the creator and carrier of culture, should look on as European culture is being destroyed, and not come to its defense with all your might?" asks the other side. And in fact, it is quite conspicuous that it is precisely they—the people who observe, delve, and inquire, those who notice even the tiniest detail and magnify it to an implausible size, those who undermine the existing world order, the spiritual revolutionaries—are the ones who have suddenly turned deaf and blind. Moreover, they seem to have deserted just at this critical time when some core issues are at stake, when the revolt, which they themselves ignited, is beginning to catch on and spread on a large scale. An ugly suspicion has been cast over the writer, society's ferment; namely, that he is a smooth talker, a phraseologue who is unable to pay his promissory notes, and probably never had the backing for them in the first place. People let themselves be fooled by his false pathos for nothing. The time has come when dreams could be turned into reality, and not only is he not the leader, but he comes up with all kinds of possible excuses for why he is not even willing to be the rear guard. This is what many embittered people must think, people who themselves go into the fight with devotion and resilience, and feel that there are no artistic works to give them wings, like in the olden days, when they still believed in the parity of word and blood.

Moreover, the politician does not settle for the role of prosecutor. He wants to be the judge, too, who sentences the writer and declares him bankrupt. He interprets the writer's neutrality as masked or mercenary opposition. He comes up with various accusations against the writer—sins that allegedly compromise the writer not just as a person but also as an artist. Then, the politician himself starts to "organize" art. Politicians are optimists by nature. If "Reuven" does not fulfill the hopes pinned on him, one must replace him with "Shimon" as soon as possible. It is always the complete or semi-graphomaniacs who can get their word in, those who are much more disciplined and much easier to understand. True, these people lack the forcefulness of the artist. But taste is something that can be corrupted with time. People will consume and enjoy the surrogate until they get used to it. When it comes to realizing generations-old ideals, people will do anything, apparently!

But let us see, what precisely does the politician demand from the writer? [. . .] There is no doubt that the task the politician wants to assign to the writer today is none other than *hatred between the classes*. Without hatred there is no fight. Hatred is the horse on which the politician rides. The last world war showed us not just the gruesomeness of killing but also the infernal image of hatred and incitement to hatred. Every possible resource has been mobilized to create the enormous hatred necessary in order to carry out such a bloodbath! But the class warfare that is now being prepared will definitely exceed the previous one, and the hatred-industry will have to grow proportionately. The press, the agitators, the entire hatred-spreading machinery—all this is not enough. All politicians—both on the right and on the left—decided that in order to achieve their goal, they needed to recruit the book, the artistic book. The number of readers and consumers of art is on the rise. They must see to it that art is "utilized" as soon as possible. Such a powerful tool should not be wasted. [. . .]

Immediately after the world war there were painful outcries against the bloodshed from everywhere. For a short while people [. . .] sobered up [. . .] and realized the senselessness of what had been committed. Peace, eternal peace, suddenly became everyone's slogan. [. . .] People were simply fed up with killing. The great old truth, that in a war neither side can win, flared up in everyone's mind for a second. But man was not destined to live in peace and quiet. The dead had not yet been buried when politicians and their followers already forgot about them. The eternal preachers of combat and revenge already raised their heads again. Now [. . .] the lust to fight has flared up again. The young generation, who has not felt the sharp edge of the knife on its own skin, is impatient. True, it is possible that the upcoming world war might develop into an open battle between the classes. But will it be less terrible because of this? Will the terrible killings and gruesome acts that we have seen with our own eyes, and about which we read in documents not be repeated?

People will again burn like torches; soldiers will again slaughter their captives with axes. Field-surgery—when feet are chopped off with the boots still on—will thrive again. True, the makers of politics do not think about this, they do not want to see this. [. . .] Another characteristic feature of people with no imaginative power is that they are convinced they will be victorious. But in a war, nothing is guaranteed. The only thing that a war guarantees is that all kinds of abominable acts will be committed; that all the dark forces will try to exploit it in order to achieve their ugly goals; that millions of innocent people will perish amidst great suffering, and millions will be crippled. There is a good reason why Remarque is detested today both by the right and the left. [. . .] Politicians do not want books like *All Quiet on the Western Front* these days. *They do not need books that bring people closer to each other. They demand books that incite people against each other.*

But can we imagine a work of art that strives to incite the reader? Is a work of art at all capable of eliciting hatred of a *community*? And can an artist even think in the categories of the politician?

Politician and artist—what a bizarre match! The politician does not remember and must not remember that his soldier (as well as the other side's, his enemy's soldier . . .) has a mother and a father, a wife and children; that the soldier has thoughts, feelings, and a will. The politician is blind, just as his weapon, hatred, is blind. [. . .]

The politician knows that character traits exist, but considers them irrelevant. He denies individuality, and this makes him a murderer. The politician—whether of today or of tomorrow—is not a one-time, accidental creature. His *character* is quintessentially the same in every generation. For thousands of years he has been setting new goals for himself, seemingly different ones, but they always require bloodshed. [. . .] In every period of time he aspired to please the community he represented (irrespective of its size) either by attacking [someone else], or by trying to protect the very same community [from some enemy]. This fight will be the last one! This victory will be final!—This is the slogan under which he has been marching perpetually, doing his work of slaughtering. [. . .] His victory has never been *final*, but he always put on a golden hat and decorated his chest with medals. Such a man was Alexander of Macedonia, such men were Genghis Khan and Napoleon, and such is the politician, regardless of whether he is the one sitting on the throne or the one who aspires to bring it down. Of course, he always knows which way the wind blows, and he can always exploit the weakness and stupidity of others. He always puts on a new, innovative mask and keeps changing his skin and his catchphrase so that the naïve do not recognize him. But he is still so similar to his old self! He just leaped off the pedestal of an old monument where he had been holding a rusty sword and scaring the birds with it.

The politician carries out what history commands—says the modern-day fool and bows down to Moloch. "History is on our side!" thunder Mussolini and Hitler. "History is on our side!" call out the [new] Dzerzhinskys in one voice. [. . .] These are the people who want to wed with the artist.

And who is the artist?

It happens occasionally that not only obtuse politicians are born to this world, but also people who are made of different stuff. These people might be cripples; they might be mistakes made by the world (or God). But they are here at all times. *Zeh leumat zeh asa elohim. The one no less than the other was God's creation.* Together with the bloodthirsty beast, sometimes the man of feelings is born, the person who finds the politician's method of counting bodies bizarre and disgusting. He does not see people as numbers or the means to achieve his ends, but as the end itself. Instead of armies he sees individuals who cannot be treated en masse. [. . .] These rare individuals are similar to each other in character—they are a character type, just like the politician. Whether they have appeared in the form of a Christian apostle or a Jewish prophet, a philosopher or a great poet—the similarity in their character is indisputable. All these people have one common trait: their eyes are always open, and they can see how much people suffer. [. . .] These people are the true artists, even though they have carried different names in various historical periods, and their modes of expression varied, too. Every one of them was, in his essence, perhaps an antithesis to the course and tendencies of history. They embodied the spirit of differentness. Their personal fate was and had to be terrible suffering and despair, because Her Majesty—History—was against them. Their screams did not scare off anyone, and their silence went unnoticed. But those who suffered and lived miserable lives found some solace in their words. Instead of saving the world, as they each had hoped, they were transformed into some sort of spiritual opium for the downtrodden. This is the maximum they have been able to achieve, swimming against the stream.

Yes, these people must be called Talents, as opposed to Virtuosos. The Virtuoso is the eternal *doppelgänger* of the Talent, and his phantom. History created the Virtuoso in order to correct the mistake it made by creating the Talent. Just like the true Talent, the Virtuoso knows the "craft" of the prophet, the writer, and the philosopher, but instead of being in opposition to the "makers of history" he endorses them. He always goes along with the politician, just as a dog always accompanies the hunter. This has been true in every historical period: he accompanied the nobleman and the knight; he sang songs of praise upon [their] victories and laments over [their] defeats; he was the one who incited one nation against another. [. . .] He has always been and still remains the darling of every politician. Among the politicians' enormous monuments we will occasionally find his statue, too. He has always been an important factor, no doubt. The Talent has become famous, too, but the hatred felt toward him only ceased when he became harmless to the politician of the time. [. . .]

It is quite ridiculous to hear politicians on all sides raise objections against the artists—that they are passive, that they do not conform, and other such complaints. The impertinence of the monster is so great that he wants to appropriate everything for his bloody game. He is blind, he does not see the absurdity of his demand. The true writer will never engage himself in the service of the murderer, as long as he lives. The artist loves people too much; he will not send them where the Politician wants to drive them away. [. . .] For the politician man is a simple thing, but for the writer—a precious work of art, an individual, something incomparable and irreplaceable. [. . .]

In vain do the Politician and his servant, the Virtuoso, jump on the writer and try to win him over peacefully or persuade him with gentle words or coerce him by threats. The writer will never become an inciter. *Not only will he refrain from inciting the rich against the poor, but he will also refuse to incite the poor against the rich.* The writer is by nature not a surgeon who has to choose between two bad options. Furthermore, he does not believe that good can ever come out of evil. [. . .] But all right, the Politician is strong enough to carry out his plan even without the help of a few sentimental, "illogical" people, although it is possible their number (also among non-artists) is much larger than one would think.

The writer may be forced to keep quiet, but he will never—remaining true to himself—lend a helping hand artistically to any fight that is conducted with prisons, bayonets, and field courts. He will never condemn the coward whom the war commanders on both sides hate so much; he will never turn into a spiritual field gendarme, not even if he is fully convinced that the Politician's way is the only possible way.

And maybe there is another way, after all . . . ?

This is a personal answer to the question. [. . .] It is clear that many *facts* contradict this thesis. Byron explicitly incited the Greeks, and he was a warrior. Mickiewicz incited against the Russians and he even wanted to fight against them with the sword. Dostoyevsky never missed an opportunity to talk badly about Jews, Poles, and Germans. [. . .] But people (including artists) are not one way *or* the other, but one way *and* another. [. . .] *When he hates, the writer does not function as a writer,* because at that time he is missing one of the main conditions that make writing possible: *seeing.* If we hate someone, we are blind to him. This tenet is true even of the *greatest spirits.* Jews, being the most hated nation in the world, are often reminded of this truth. . . .

It would be a noble task for a literary critic to prove the conclusion: in their hatred, great writers were not above the average citizen, and that their personality was revealed only then, when they related to their subjects with love.

NOTES

These excerpts do not represent the full text and were modified from the original Yiddish for clarity and brevity.

1. A radical cultural movement in the Soviet Union that advocated revamping culture according to a "proletarian esthetic."

Translated by Vera Szabó.

Other works by Singer: *Satan in Goray* (1935); *In My Father's Court* (1956); *The Magician of Lublin* (1960); *The Slave* (1961); *Gimpel the Fool and Other Stories* (1963).

Aaron Zeitlin

1898–1973

The poet, writer, playwright, essayist, and editor Aaron Zeitlin (Aharon; Arn Tseytlin) was the eldest son of Hillel Zeitlin (1871–1942) and the brother of Elkhonen Zeitlin (1902–1942). Born in Homel (then Russian Gomel, now Belarus), Zeitlin lived in Warsaw between 1907 and 1938. Beginning to write lyrical poetry as a child, Zeitlin was most prolific in interwar Warsaw. He participated in the debate on the role of Yiddish literature, attacking the politicization of Yid-

dish literature and developing an aesthetic of combining historical events with existential and mystical themes. He was the chair of the Yiddish PEN club from 1930 to 1934, and founded, with the help of Isaac Bashevis Singer, the literary monthly *Globus.* He moved to the United States at the beginning of World War II and continued to write and teach in New York City. Zeitlin was equally prolific in Hebrew and Yiddish.

Fliglman on the Left
1932

Warsaw, October 17, 1932[1]

Dear friend S. Niger,

When we speak about left and right, we should, first of all, enclose both words in thick quotation marks, and then we have to remember that true left and true right are both awfully rare. Their truths—however antagonistic the masks they wear—converge. It seems that this is precisely the reason that extremes unite in general. The extent to which the extremes are rooted in truth—in the unity of the world—that is the extent to which they are primarily no more than pretenses, and so the battle between them is often no more than a lovers' quarrel.

The poor water-carrier, the devout simpleton who picked up the word *tomeh* [impure] in the study house and prayed with this single word to God, remained steadfast to his notion, "impure," and no matter how many times the Kotzker Rebbe taught him to say *tahor* [pure], it all came to naught.

"It's useless," the rabbi finally relented, "Scream 'impure,' but at least do it with sincerity!"

I must tell you that to fight against the few who scream "impure" sincerely is perhaps futile. The "genuine coin of the left"—to the extent that it is genuine—has, or should have, value also for those who adhere not to the left side, but to the right. One only has to caution against the worn coin of the counterfeiters, against the "proletarian" liars, who have been *trained* to scream "impure!" and defile the pure *kavoneh* [intention] of the scream. And there are more than enough such people, not only among the "barely leftists" of the pseudo-literary and pseudo-proletarian *Vokhnshrift,* but also among those who are pursuing *true* leftism. They too—on *our* street and in *our* literature—are often just as far from the truth, that is, from *their* truth, as they are near that which I call "affected leftist style." They, too—again: on *our* street and in *our* literature—seem to me (why should I deny it?) very suspicious with regard to the final sincerity of their intentions. Not only because they, too (both among us, and also among you in America), keep producing scribblers who are somewhat or fully talentless, but primarily because the children of a people, whose course through history has always and primarily been marked by belief, belong now to the most unbelieving people among humans. And so I don't trust in the faith-competence of today's Jews, and I am prepared to accept that the "impure" is not "impure" to us, just as the "pure" is not "pure." Our truth, dear friend, is no longer with us. When Jews lost their truth—their God—they lost their psychic ability to believe in anything at all. And I don't find any faith, neither in an Aguda-Jew, who transformed the God of the prophets and mystics into a mere "G-d," nor in our ultra-leftist, who gets into maximal hysteria over minimal truth-fanaticism, an ocean of pathological cursing over a drop of sadness of human solitude. In neither of these two do I find that which our grandfathers called "a morsel of truth," that bit which has to be the glowing kernel of words and deeds.

The Jew of today lacks an "intellectual conscience," as Schopenhauer calls it. This doesn't mean that he is necessarily dishonest. It does mean, however, that the weight of his essential honesty is light. Even in places where honesty is beyond any doubt, its quality is such that one cannot take it too seriously.

In *this* sense, it's difficult for me to believe Dovid Bergelson, for example, when he—the typical non-mass-audience writer, the proclaimed representative of the (as you say) "subtle-art" in Yiddish prose, the ultra-individualistic detail-seer and detail-presenter—whenever he wants to convince the world (I mean the literary world, of course) of his absolute literary belonging to the "revolutionary toiling masses." With such an "attitude," it is not at all surprising that, in his Penek, you found the mere aggregate of poetry with proletarianism—an aggregate, as opposed to a synthesis. And the point is not the propaganda itself (propaganda, as you yourself note, can also be art, and even high art), but rather that the propaganda is external, superficial, light-weight. [. . .] [T]he "homo religiousus" within me was often comforted by the thought that the antireligious war that is being waged in the country of the Soviets, the war of the godless, may be a sign of living religiosity *à rebours*—a sign of the unextinguished

need for God (which does not stand, in my opinion, in any contradiction to the need for bread). When I read, however, that a *Jew* is waging that "campaign," a *Jewish* Bolshevik, I admit that I immediately lost all faith in the truth of that war. I may be exaggerating *in minus*; you can call it antisemitism if need be, but it's hopeless: I know that the Jew of today is capable of "celebrating" even blasphemy purely mechanically, for the sake of the party line, without any internal trembling, without any relationship to the object, without suffering, without that perverse religiosity of great heretics, who were able to talk about themselves using the language of Dostoevsky's protagonist: "*menya vsyu zhizn bog muchil*"—God, the question of God, has tortured me my entire life. . . .

We have few, very few who are capable believing in their own notions of "impure" or "pure" to the end, to the bitter end. And therefore, we have the empty (oh, entirely un-Gandhi-like) passivity of the contemporary Jewish intellectual, in whose mouth the word "fight" sounds most comical. Fliglman the fighter! Fliglman on the barricades of the world! Is it a wonder, then, that he is so busy writing *about* the revolution and . . . "literary criticism from a Marxist standpoint"? [. . .]

Yes, the ones who shape the *true* face of time don't enter into Fliglman's "world account." He is "modern" and is a "man of his time" only on the basis of externality—the very externality of the times. That which takes place in the *soul* of the time in which he lives remains foreign to him. And, in this sense, our Fliglman—today it's Fliglman on the barricades—is the anarchist in the world. He, the unpleasant, untragic impotent who longs for muscles, hates "soul" and "eternity," trembles before that which he calls mysticism, fear of death, and speaks today, for the sake of timeliness, about the fight and dictatorship. And it doesn't occur to him for a minute to think earnestly about those newly emerged, actualizing (and essentially eternal) ideas of the cosmos that are, that must be, almost obligatory for the thought and sensibility of a modern person, especially a person of the Einstein- and Bergson-time, or about those forms of struggle and dictatorship that attract the deepest attention of the entire current generation, aside from, of course, Fliglman's.

I mean, actually, again, the old man Gandhi with his dictatorship (yes, dictatorship!) of passive resistance.

Old man Gandhi! Yet again, he stood his ground and succeeded! When he goes to the sea to make salt, John Bull's soul gets salty! When he sits down to fast—[Ramsay] MacDonald's pressed trousers are shaking! And look: he is but one individual! And this one individual agitates the whole of India, the whole of England. This skinny, half-naked, ugly, old man with glasses!

We live in the age of the dictator because—our epoch is an epoch of the masses. The masses require a dictator. Isn't Gandhi—in *his* own way—a dictator?

Gandhi is a dictator. He imposes his will. He forces. He commands without commanding. Without doing anything miraculous, he performs miracles. He started the idea of passive resistance. He is, all and all, a great inventor. He discovered the active power of passivity. He discovered that passive energy is the most kinetic and real. This is a psychic rule, that the Mahatma not only made real theoretically but also demonstrated, showed its truth empirically.

I think that Gandhi did even more than that. He who, on the face of it, respects tradition, he, the venerable sanctifier of the cow—is actually the greatest innovator of Buddhism. He is Buddha's reformer. He demonstrated that Nirvana can make peace and coincide with *karma*. He found the connection between action and the ethical absolute. [. . .]

Gandhi? He is a Buddhist and much more—a Buddhist and something other than Buddhist. He is a doer. This second, different, braver Buddha doesn't run away from deed. He didn't escape it into a deep horrible angst, like Sakyamuni in days gone by. One has to—he said—shine through the deed. Let the deed be holy; let karma be sanctified. I would have said: in this way, he brought Buddhism closer to Jewishness. He elevated Buddhist melancholy to the level of the "joy of commandment." What is "commandment," really, if not deed in its brightness?

Through his brave fast, through his effective, *active* preparation for death, Gandhi not only united the Indian castes, and not only erased the boundary between the pariah and not pariah. He also traveled through the abyss between karma and Nirvana. He reformed Buddhism from the inside out. He replaced passivity, which is meant to lead to Nirvana, with a power that sanctified karma—a might that shines through the darkness of action. He had, in other words, instituted the most significant of all dictatorships: the dictatorship of passive resistance. He

gave a character of holiness to the darkest of all deed-forms—politics. Holiness. He, for whom the cow is holy, actually made holy the snake. . . .

But—what can all this "idleness" matter to our wingmen of all sorts? Don't forget that they, the arch-super-hyper-ultra-idlers, are the practical people, who speak day and night in the name of "real interests." And as soon as it is "real," it will never occur to them to ask: this hunger for bread—doesn't it have to do with the fact that a world of robbers—the world of capital, actually—has violently trampled on the *spiritual* bread of humanity? Oh, they will never grasp the causal connection between spiritual culpability and physical catastrophe. The horrible hunger of millions, the tempestuous abyss of human solitude—how should they know that it has to do with higher concerns?

They understand one thing only: the spirit is a "deviation" of sorts. The spirit is reactionary.

Yes, when it comes to "deviations," I respect them for the same reason that the proponents of the straight line fight against them. Here is Leivick, a "traitor" and a "deviationist." This grants him dignity. I also understand Leyeles when he doesn't want to go with the general stream of the "straight line" and has enough independence within him to be—as I had the opportunity to see from his articles in New York's "Yiddish"—a Trotskyite. Deviation means, after all: independence. And independence means: truth, *my* truth.

Oh, the general valid truths—what big piles of falsehood they are! Perhaps you can tell me, friend: where can one escape from these truths? Perhaps you know of such an island in a sea somewhere? I am ready and willing to make the true great deviation and to become a Robinson Crusoe if need be. . . .

Yours,
Aaron Zeitlin

NOTE
1. See Sh. Niger, "Fragn" [a letter about *Globus* and proletariat literature], *Globus*, Issue 3.

Translated by Alexandra Hoffman.

Other works by Zeitlin: *Metatron* (1922); *Shotns oyfn shney: lider* (1923); *Amerika: sipurim* (1927); *Brenner* (1929); *Brenendike erd* (1937); *Gezamlte lider* (1947–1957); *Lider fun ḥurbn un lider fun gloybn* (1967); *Gezamlte drames* (1974–1980).

Hannah Arendt
1906-1975

Born and educated in Germany, the political theorist Hannah Arendt fled to France after the Nazi seizure of power and then escaped to the United States in 1941, where she remained until her death. She taught at various American universities and won a reputation as an erudite and provocative writer on political, historical, and philosophical themes. While she worked for Jewish communal organizations in France and in New York before finding a university post, her relations with the Jewish community were often prickly as a result of her views on Zionism and Jewish responses to Nazi persecution.

Original Assimilation: An Epilogue to the One Hundredth Anniversary of Rahel Varnhagen's Death
1933

I

Today in Germany it seems Jewish *assimilation* must declare its bankruptcy. The general social antisemitism and its official legitimation affects in the first instance assimilated Jews, who can no longer protect themselves through baptism or by emphasizing their differences from Eastern Judaism. The question of the success or failure of assimilation is more urgent than ever precisely for assimilated Jews. For assimilation is a fact, and only later, in the context of defensive struggle, does it become an ideology; an ideology one today knows cannot maintain itself because reality has refuted it more fully and unambiguously than ever before. Assimilation is the entrance of the Jews into the historical European world.

The role of the Jews in this world can be unambiguously determined neither sociologically nor in intellectual-historical terms. Specifically modern antisemitism, the antisemitism directed against assimilated Jews and which is as old as their assimilation itself, this form of antisemitism has always reproached the Jews with being bearers of the Enlightenment. That basically was the charge of Grattenauer's vulgar polemic of 1802 as well as Brentano's consummately witty satire reflecting the antisemitism of the late Romantics, of the German Christian Table Society [*Tischgesellschaft*]. This polemic is not accidental. It is true that at least at the

beginning of the last century there was no unstructured assimilation. Assimilation always meant assimilation to *the Enlightenment*.

The Enlightenment promised the Jews emancipation and above all provided them with arguments for demanding equal human rights, hence almost all of them became Enlightenment advocates. But the *problem* of Jewish assimilation begins only *after* the Enlightenment, first in the generation that followed Mendelssohn. Mendelssohn could still believe himself in fundamental agreement with the Enlightenment avantgarde—which meant at the time the representatives of cultural Germany. But already his students found their appeals to reason and moral sentiment encountering resistance. Even Schleiermacher took the "Circular of Certain Jewish Household Fathers," written by David Friedländer, to be an example of "our earlier literary school." Initially the Jews could not understand the new historical consciousness that first emerged in Germany, because it provided them no further arguments for their demands.

That means: the Jews as a whole could no longer assimilate. Mendelssohn was still always able to speak in the name of "the" Jews, whom he wanted to enlighten and to free. He believed—like Dohm—that it was the Jews *as a whole* he would emancipate. The baptismal movement in the next generation shows that the Jewish question had become by then a problem for the *individual* Jew, had become the problem of somehow coming to terms with the world. That broad types of solutions can be discerned among what were in each case personal decisions does not refute the point. *The Jewish question becomes a problem of the individual Jew.*

II

Rahel, Henriette Herz, Dorothea Schlegel, and the Meyer sisters are examples of these "individuals." All they had in common was a desire to escape their Judaism, and all of them to some extent succeeded. Henriette Herz attempted it through scholarship. She mastered Latin, Greek, some Sanskrit, mathematics, and physics. The Christianity that Schleiermacher taught her became a self-evident cultural resource. She was respected, she was beautiful, she was much beloved. She developed a reputation for coldness because she remained untouched, nothing got through to her. With sound instincts she defended herself against every passion, against every serious engagement with the world.

She believed one could study the world; she hoped that one could bribe it through virtue. And the world confirmed this by respecting her.

Dorothea Schlegel, Mendelssohn's youngest daughter, abandoned her husband, a respectable Jewish merchant, for Friedrich Schlegel. She did not encounter the world, she encountered Schlegel. She assimilated not to Romanticism but to Schlegel. She was not converted to Catholicism but to Schlegel's faith. She wanted to "build [him] a temple." Her love was entirely unreflected, merely the shining expression of her enthrallment. What remains is the fact that she really did succeed in surrendering herself, in devoting herself to someone else completely and being pulled through the world by him. The world was nothing but the transient foil for her feelings, for the whole excited passion of her inner being.

Marianne and Sarah Meyer came from a rich family that provided them with "an aristocratic education and cultured instruction." Their intelligence, their education, were identical to worldly sophistication. Marianne married Count Reuss and after his death bore the title of Lady von Eibenberg. Sarah lived many years in a happy marriage with the Livonian Baron Grotthus. Both of them resided in the great world, surrounded by recognition and flattery. They were taken up by society, even if here and there they were suddenly turned away, if certain houses would not receive them, if Gentz said their society was almost "mauvaise société," and if Prince Ligne's quip that Baron Arnstein was "le premier baron du vieux testament" made the rounds all through Vienna. These petty insults they had to be prepared to confront at any moment provoked immeasurable vanity in Frau von Grotthus, and in Frau von Eibenberg the "misanthropic knowledge of human character." It also gave rise to intelligence, attentiveness, and the art of making "even boredom entertaining."

These are simply a few individual cases that could be supplemented at will. It is characteristic of all these women that they understood how to erase the traces they left behind, that they were able to enter into the social world, that they had no need even to emphasize: "one must escape from Judaism" (Rahel).

III

In light of its risks and its necessity, to ask whether or not assimilation succeeded seems idle. Nor is it possible to determine if Rahel succeeded at it. What is sure

is that she never was able to erase the traces, to deny practically her origins, although it was she who made the angriest and bitterest remarks about her Jewishness. Nonetheless she never attempted to compensate for the groundlessness of her existence with surrogates, and she understood how to pursue every despair, even that over her heritage, with the utmost consequence. Thus she has become exemplary—less through what she said than through the course of her life itself—for a situation that was not hers alone.

Rahel studied nothing. She stressed to Veit, the friend of her youth, her "ignorance" and that she could not change it; "one must use it as it stands." No tradition had passed anything on to her, no history foresaw her existence. Purely independent, because born into no cultural world, without prejudice, because it seemed no one had judged before her, as if in the paradoxical situation of the first human being, she was compelled to appropriate everything as if she were meeting it for the first time. She was dependent on unprecedence. Herder once demanded explicitly an absence of prejudice from "cultured Jews." For Henriette Herz, the freedom from all content passed over into freedom for anything at all. Everything could be studied. Her independence became a senseless aptitude for everything. Since Rahel insisted upon her ignorance, she actually documented the generosity and indeterminacy of a particular historically given world; this was the source of her striking way of describing things, people, situations. Everything presented itself to her as if for the first time. She never had a memorized formula ready. Her wit, which was already feared when she was a young girl, was but this entirely unburdened manner of seeing. She lived in no particular order of the world, and refused to study any order of the world; her wit could unite the most incongruous things, in the most intimately unified things it could discern incongruities. This her friends praised as originality, while her enemies found in it an absence of style, a disorder, an unmotivated pleasure in paradoxes. And perhaps her manner of expression truly was without style, for she had no model, no tradition, and no precise consciousness of which words belonged together and which did not. But she was genuinely "original": she never obscured a thing with a familiar expression. Despite all her originality, all her rapacity for conquest, Rahel demonstrated not only the absence of prejudice but also the vacancy of someone entirely dependent upon experience, who must marshal an entire life behind each opinion.

Entertaining an opinion in the alien world is an essential aspect of assimilation. For Rahel, this opinion derived from her life, depended upon the fact that human beings, destinies, occurrences did not leave her in the lurch, did not forget her, but met her. She could have escaped from this dependence upon her own life through senseless study or marriage. She attempted it once when she met Count Finckenstein, when he fell in love with her and she became his betrothed. She had enough influence over Finckenstein to have brought him to the altar. Even many years later it remained incomprehensible to her friends why she did not do so. The reason was quite simple: what could have been the history of her assimilation became her personal love story. She "surrendered to chance when she could have calculated everything." For only through chance could a world she found indeterminate meet her. She could have deceived herself into thinking that the chance that Finckenstein of all people was the first, *le premier qui a voulu que je l'aime*, made marriage necessary, and then she would have been sucked away like Dorothea Schlegel.

Having no social position that would render an orientation self-evident, the only possibility for Rahel to encounter the world was in her own life. That she relied on this life and its experiences was the precondition of her eventual success in breaking through to reality. But hardly more than the precondition. For in order to really enter an alien history, to live in a foreign world, she had to be able to communicate herself and her experiences.

IV

It is often remarked, doubtless correctly, that the most notable aspect of Rahel's assimilation, its test case, so to speak, was that she was among the very first truly to understand Goethe. But it must not be overlooked that this understanding was not a matter of any unusual cleverness or sensitivity but was rather the result of a predicament, the predicament of having to communicate and of needing for this communication a language. If her life was not to sink entirely into the void, she had to attempt somehow to transmit herself into history by communication. This attempt would have been completely hopeless and disoriented if she had not had in Goethe the "mediator" to whom she could attach herself and whom she could imitate.

Goethe was the great stroke of fortune in Rahel's life. "The poet accompanied me without fail through-

out my life." "Powerful and hale, he brought together in me what unhappiness and happiness had divided in me and what I was not able to hold visibly together." He taught her the connection: that happiness and unhappiness do not simply fall on a creature from heaven, but that there is only happiness and unhappiness within a life, and that this life as such can be their coherence. Happiness and unhappiness are formative elements in *Wilhelm Meister*. In Meister's life the question of happiness or unhappiness hardly has any meaning; so much is it the case that everything that occurs has meaning that there is barely a site where something simply destructive could break in. Chance itself is here an "educated man" (Schlegel). Initially, Rahel's life had no history and was exposed to pure destructiveness; but the folly of this other life let her understand; it taught her that love, fear, hope, happiness, and unhappiness were not simply blind terrors, but when they were specifically situated, emerging from a determinate past and passing into a determinate future, that they were able to mean something which human beings could comprehend. Without Goethe she would have seen her life only from the outside, its ghostly contours. She could not have fashioned a connection between it and the world to whom she had to recount it. "I made company with his largess, he was eternally my most single and certain friend"; for he was the only person whom she had so truly to love that her life's "measure [was] found not in me but in him." He compelled her at length to acknowledge the world of objects, that is, to cease being disproportionately and pointlessly original. Because she understood him, and understood herself through him, he could become for her something like a succedaneum for tradition. She converted to him, joined forces with him, and so has a place now in German history.

Rahel did not acquire from Goethe the "art of existing" (Schlegel), but she did master to the point of virtuosity the art of communicating her own life, of presenting herself. That she could properly invoke Goethe's authority, that through the invocation of Goethe she could be not merely understood by others but in solidarity with them, this Rahel owes to a peculiar congruence between her own situation and the larger environment: whether her life succeeded or failed depended upon whether or not she could break through to the reality of the world. For totally different reasons the whole generation, the generation of Humboldt, Schlegel, Gentz, and Schleiermacher, found itself in a similar circumstance.

V

The bearers of the Enlightenment, whose continuation is Romanticism, are the citizens. Citizens no longer belong to any social rank, they no longer represent anything. The citizen can only offer "what he has," if he wants to somehow "appear," then he is simply "laughable and tasteless." He cannot "present" himself, he is not a "public person" (*Wilhelm Meister*) but merely a private man. In representation such men had been visible. In the world of the citizen, which has to do without representation, once the social ranks have been dissolved there emerges the fear of not being seen, of having no endorsement of one's own reality. Wilhelm Meister attempts through education to learn how to present himself. If he succeeds in this, he becomes a "public person" and not just someone who "is only what he has." The people who are capable of self-presentation meet together in salons. This presentation is their conversation.

The "salon" is Rahel's social opportunity and justification. She finds in it the foundation upon which she can live, the space wherein she is socially recognized. The salon is her social reality. As long as this reality endures she has no need of marriage or of baptism. Only when the salon disappears after the unhappy war, or returns to the hands of those who had always belonged to good society, is she forced to seek another possible existence, another possibility not to be passed over by history and forgotten. In 1811 she marries Varnhagen and converts to Christianity. And Varnhagen devotes almost his entire life to preserving her life, her letters, her person, and handing them down to posterity.

NOTE
Words in brackets appear in the original translation.

Translated by James McFarland.

Other works by Arendt: *The Origins of Totalitarianism* (1951); *Rachel Varnhagen: The Life of a Jewess* (1957); *Eichmann in Jerusalem: A Report on the Banality of Evil* (1963); *On Revolution* (1963); *Men in Dark Times* (1968).

Henryk Erlich

No, We Are Not a Chosen People
1933

One of our greatest sins in the eyes of the Jewish bourgeoisie has been that in the course of the thirty-five years of our existence as a party we have not ceased to defend the simple idea that we, Jews, are not a chosen people, neither in the positive nor in the negative sense of the word, but a people just like any other nation, and that even though our history and the social-economic circumstances of our lives are unique, the same rules apply to us that regulate the lives of all other nations in the world. Our Jewish bourgeois opponents are especially enraged by our claim that there is a certain kind of Jewish nationalism that is just as ugly, just as disgusting as the nationalism of the other nations; and if Jewish nationalism, as a general rule, is not bloodthirsty, this is only out of necessity, not virtue; if an appropriate opportunity arose, Jewish nationalism would show its sharp teeth and nails no less than the nationalisms of other nations.

We live in times of mercilessly sharp contours. There is no place for halftones today. We live in a time of nationalistic bacchanalia. The high priests of nationalism in the holy temples of the capitalist world are preachers like Benito Mussolini and Adolf Hitler. In times like this, nationalism as such has been stripped naked and Jewish nationalism, too, has to show the world the ugliness of its face.

We need not talk much about Hitler's relationship to Poland. It should be enough to quote one of the favorite songs of the Hitlerite gangs beginning with the words, "we will beat all Poles to death and spread them like butter on bread."

What Hitler's rise to power means for Poland's state interests is a topic not worth wasting words upon. Eliminating the "Corridor," taking away from Poland its part of Upper Silesia, occupying Danzig—these are the first items on Hitler's program in the area of international politics; turning Poland into a German colony, into a "hinterland" of Germany—this is one of the subsequent points of the program.

One would think that Hitler's rise to power would make every "patriotic" heart in Poland shiver with fear, and especially the National Democratic [Endek] heart. After all, it was the National Democratic Party that always defended the idea that Poland has no greater enemy than Germany. In their fight against the "German enemy" they were even willing to make peace with the much hated Soviet Union.

We have written on more than one occasion about how the Endek's pope, Roman Dmowski, reacted to Hitler's rise to power, and how the ND's official organ, the *Gazeta Warszawska*, reacts to it every day.

But it would be a crime not to make note of the voice of the most openhearted and shameless member of the Endeks—Adolf Nowaczynski. What we have in mind is his latest article about [Josef] Goebbels.

Nowaczynski's article is a real hymn to Goebbels. The heart of the National Democratic camp's greatest cynic has begun to tremble with "pure" passion for the greatest cynic and bloodhound among all the cynics and bloodhounds surrounding Adolf Hitler: "He is not just one of the most interesting personalities—he is literally an extraordinarily agreeable person," exclaims with wonderment the Polish Goebbels.

"The Nazis are," explains Nowaczynski, "according to their program first and foremost anti-Jewish, and only secondarily anti-universal. They are 60 percent anti-Jewish, and due to the crazy and reckless stubbornness of revengeful world Jewry they managed to imbue all 90 million Germans in the world with the hatred of Jews."

This is what the spiritual countenance of Polish nationalism looks like in the infernal light of the Hitlerfire. And a similar formation has appeared on the Jewish street, too.

Not long ago we reported about a lecture held by a great revisionist on Hitlerism. The Hitlerite press concluded that "the whole lecture was not an accusation but a splendid defense of Hitler." We quoted an excerpt from an expressly Hitlerist article in [Vladimir] Jabotinsky's organ in Palestine. In it, one of Jabotinsky's adjutants complains about the "furor that has been raised recently by the Jewish public against National Socialism." [. . .] This revisionist hooligan "concludes" that Hitlerite Germany has not done "so much evil" to Jews as the Soviet Union, and he "cautions" the Jewish public not to discard the valuable, precious "anti-Marxist seed" of Hitlerism together with its antisemitic "skin."

To be sure, Jabotinsky is nothing more than a small-scale Hitler, a fascist clown. But this clown has devoured a significant portion, if not the majority of our very own [heymish] Zionism. The fascist hooliganism that Jabotinsky preaches suits the mood that enveloped a significant portion of the Jewish bourgeoisie and especially bourgeois Jewish youth. Of course, Jabotinsky's brown-shirt soldiers are nothing more than a tragicomic caricature of Hitler's SA people. But the only thing missing in order for them to become the same beasts is some muscle strength, some territory, and a political opportunity. In Berlin they have actually "bravely" joined the lines of the real brown-shirt bandits. And in

Palestine, too, they have demonstrated that they are not weaklings.

No, we are not a chosen people. Our nationalism is just as ugly, just as harmful, and has the same inclination to fascist debauchery as the nationalisms of all the other nations.

Translated by Vera Szabó.

Henryk Erlich

A Shtetl Is Starving to Death
1933

Not far from Łódź is a small town called Brzezhin. It has been a town of tailors from the beginning of time. When it was under Russian rule, Brzezhin was a center for manufacturing cheap clothes for the Russian market, especially for the Don Basin. After the establishment of independent Poland, production shrank in Brzezhin, but there was still work. Wages have always been very low there. The tailors of Brzezhin had to get used to the sweating system, but there was still enough work. Then came the crisis, and the tailors of Brzezhin could feel it just like everyone else in Poland. Work began to vanish slowly and working conditions worsened even more.

But then two years went by, and a miracle happened. In the middle of the crisis, when production was continuously decreasing everywhere, Brzezhin suddenly started to bloom. Production began to grow, and so did the number of employed workers. What happened? The answer is that Brzezhin started to work for the world market, for England and Belgium. The shrewd entrepreneurs of Brzezhin came to an agreement with the government and managed to get subsidies—"in the interests of the national production of Poland," of course. With these subsidies they shamelessly engaged in swindle. The subsidies were so high that the entrepreneurs could afford to sell the products abroad for a ridiculously low price, charging less for a man's suit in England and Belgium than the amount of state subsidy they got on each suit!

The Brzezhin entrepreneurs struck gold. Since there was a crisis, poverty and unemployment were on the rise in the entire Brzezhin region, and the entrepreneurs took advantage of the situation. Wages were very low, the working day very long, and working conditions in general were terrible.

That's how it was for some time. Brzezhin was working feverishly. After a while, however, the government realized that the Brzezhin entrepreneurs were swindling them, simply stealing from them. But they did not punish the entrepreneurs for this, God forbid. After all, swindle and theft are normal features of the capitalistic economy. They just reduced the amount of the subsidies. Thus, the great fortune of Brzezhin was suddenly over. If they cannot make lots of money fast, it is not worthwhile for the entrepreneurs to conduct business at all. Production began to decrease and unemployment started to grow again. Needless to say, working conditions also deteriorated even more.

And here lies in front of us a letter from Brzezhin, a desperate call for help, a terrible outcry of starving, suffering people. Seven hundred workers and one hundred small-scale pieceworkers [*khalupnikes*], along with their families, are literally fighting against starving to death. They have been in this horrifying situation for a year now, but in the last six months things have become even worse than they were during the war years. In addition, they were struck by a terrible influenza epidemic that was especially harsh among the starving population. Seeing a doctor or receiving medical care is beyond anyone's wildest dream.

The anguished workers are grinding their teeth as they watch the entrepreneurs, who acquired their riches here in the good years, now run from Brzezhin like rats. The desperate working-class population has been expecting help from the government—in vain, of course. There was no shortage of money for giving subsidies to the entrepreneurs, but for hungry workers and domestic manufacturers there are no funds, of course.

An entire town is about to starve to death. Moreover, Brzezhin is not the only town that is about to starve to death. And no one cares.

Translated by Vera Szabó.

Shmuel Niger

1883–1955

The Yiddish literary critic Shmuel Niger (Samuel Charney) grew up in fervently Hasidic surroundings in Belorussia, but at age seventeen, while studying for the rabbinate, he abandoned religious observance. At first he was attracted to radical socialist Zionism but from 1907 devoted himself exclusively to Yiddish literature, opposing those writers who harnessed their work to ideological movements. He wished to synthesize the Yiddish literary renaissance and Russian–Polish modernism to appeal to the emerging Jewish intelligentsia. Until 1919 he lived in Vilna, where he barely escaped death at the hands of the invading Polish army. He then sailed to New York City, where he remained until his death, writing for various Yiddish newspapers and journals.

Second Letter from New York to Warsaw
1933

Dear friend Aaron Zeitlin,

You write (in *Globus*, issue 4) that to fight against the truly leftist—or, as you express it, "against the few who scream 'impure' [*tomeh*] sincerely"—is perhaps futile. Perhaps! But it may also be that the work is *not* wasted after all. One has to try. [. . .]

We Jews—you seem to think—"belong now to the most unbelieving people among humans." And who is it that thinks like this, of all people? You, a person who knows that we Jews are "the children of a people, whose course through history has always and primarily been marked by belief"! If this is so, you must ask yourself: How could this happen? We are wondering, and cannot stop wondering, when we see that a person with a talent, let's say, for writing, suddenly becomes a mere scribbler. Faith is also a talent. (You yourself speak of the "psychic ability to believe.") This begs the question: Why should we, "whose course through history has always and primarily been marked by belief," why should we suddenly become so talentless in the religious sense? The question becomes even sharper when one is reminded that we are speaking about a people. An individual may fall silent or weakened for a while. But a people's spirit doesn't necessarily have to reveal itself in all its children. A people's spirit can speak to us through the mouth of Isaiah the prophet. . . . Did the Jewish people stop being a prophetic people when its sons were, as Amoz's son thought, "a brood of evildoers, children given to corruption" [Isaiah 1:4], and so forth, and so forth? No, it is precisely then that Jews became a prophetic people. Why? Because, like every creative force, a people is measured when it rises to its highest peak, not when it is at its nadir, because the people are not the numerous "children given to corruption," but the few Isaiahs, those who bring down the fiery whips of their words upon them, those who hold them together with their great, hefty girdle, through the magic and law of spiritual gravitation.

The folk imagination, which puts its faith in the thirty-six righteous people, is correct. In the loneliest moments, when one feels like, as you do now, "becoming a Robinson Crusoe, if need be," in times when one thinks that this is the end of the world, the world is actually safe, because it is being sustained by *concealed powers*, by the *hidden holy men*.

With an almost scientific precision, the folktale connects messianic time with a generation whose face is like the face of a dog [Sotah 9:15]. When insolence multiplies and "all hope is lost," then the anointed one, the chosen one, arrives. When a people, in other words, cannot live in its own right, it lives on account of a great individual, of the one who gathers within himself the secret, the power, the meaning of the people's existence. . . .

"We have," you say, "few, very few who are capable of believing in their own notions of 'impure' or 'pure' to the end, to the bitter end." . . . Dear friend, you intended to "curse," but you "bless" instead. You say that there *are* among us *a few of those* who are capable of faith. With this, you acknowledge that there are enough righteous people to rescue Sodom. . . .

I am going even further (in my optimism—or call it pessimism, if you'd like). I believe that we never actually had more than a "few, very few who are capable of believing in their own notions of 'impure' or 'pure' to the end, to the bitter end," and that was perforce enough. . . . Were all the former Hasidim like the Ba'al Shem Tov? Did all the Hasidic rabbis reach the level of *their* rabbi? Were some of them of the "blind follower" type? But regardless of the failures of Hasidism, we are ready to grant it its most beautiful ascent. And is the case only with Hasidism? Isn't it common in the history of humanity that one person knows what *holy* [*kodesh*] is, and all the rest bow and scrape, just jump *holy*? [the term *shpringn kodoish* refers to the custom of jumping slightly when reciting these words in the *kedusha* prayer].

Even if "those who are pursuing *true* leftism" are also, as you say, "often just as far from the truth, that is, from *their* truth, as they are near that which I call 'affected leftist style.'" Let's say that this is so (and it is so probably all over the world, not only among us); from this, however, it doesn't necessarily follow that there are no individuals who are *near to their truth*

and who believe in it to the end and who influence others with the power of their faith. I am sure that there are such individuals in our generation as well. But now is an age when the individual speaks in the plural.

In regard to the "lovers' quarrel" between the extreme left and the extreme right, what about those who fluctuate between "impure" and "pure"? There are those who do that. You cannot count them among the ones who have reached the "morsel of truth," or call them "counterfeiters," and you cannot ignore them, even though they lack substantial integrity. You demonstrated such a creative interest in your "The Sin and Death of De Haan, the Sick Jew," and you know very well that, to a greater or lesser extent, in one form or another, others also suffer from De Haan's "illness," from his dualism:

> The one among you who stones De Haan in disdain
> Does not yet fully fathom his own internal pain.
>
> It is perhaps our shared and common contradiction:
> Newspaper and the Bible, God and admonition.

And so we cannot rush to "stone in disdain" those who have two souls and two faces, and also those who seem to be without a soul and without a face. It just so happens that when a new Torah is carried in the air, it thunders, it flashes, "and the mountain blazes with fire" [Deuteronomy 4:11]—a mountain is in flames, and it descends on the people, on the masses, and lights them up and holds them together without their will, without their knowledge. Under such circumstances, "faith-competence," the "sincerity" you mention, is objective, so to speak. It is not in the people, but in the air that envelops the people. The faith-competent believe in the new commandment, and the nonbelievers—believe also. They believe that they believe. They can't help it. They may not know the meaning of "impure," which they shout; they wouldn't shout anything if they had a choice. But it is no longer their choice. It's not they who shout out to God. But something, someone is praying through their mouth, and this something, this someone cannot be waved aside. [. . .]

Truth be told, you have not convinced me, friend Zeitlin, that all our antireligious leftists celebrate "even blasphemy purely mechanically." I believe that there are those for whom "blasphemy" is actually a fulfillment, even if perverse fulfillment, of their "need for God," as you call it.

The Jewish God is, after all, no more than a "social being"—a God of righteousness. The metaphysics of "between man and God" has always been for us an extension of "between man and man" metaphysics. Gnoseology has never been important to us. Only kabbalists devote themselves to cosmology (*maasei bereshit*) and mysticism (*maasei merkavah*), and perhaps they are the only ones who have a religious *Weltanschauung.* Our sacred texts have always been, I think, a system of ethics more than a religion. Religion wants, above all, to know the truth—the truth about everything, not only about humanity. It seeks in its own way to recognize the *real*, to say what is, not only what should be. Its object is the cosmos. Our faith is one that is captivated by the human, and only by the human. Cosmology—when and how the sky and the earth and the light were created, and what is sky and earth and sun and stars and constellations— is important only to the extent that it is an introduction to the creation—and the lives—of Adam and Eve, Cain and Abel. Knowledge means knowledge of "good and evil," not *truth* in the objective sense of the word. [. . .] This is a difficult issue, and I am incapable of fully tackling it. I wanted to remind you, however, that since our religion as a whole is social ethics, every social-ethical (or antiethical) movement is—in the Jewish sense of the word—a religious (or an antireligious) movement. And when we see that Jews are attracted to the communist and socialist movements, it is usually assumed that they are sincerely attracted to it, not only "for the sake of the party line."

So why do many of them dedicate themselves to "writing *about* the revolution and . . . literary criticism from a Marxist standpoint"? The reason for this is not that for all Jews the revolution is only writerly, only *literature*, only "attitude." Rather, because there are so many Jews in all domains of revolutionary activity, they must *also* take up a respectable place in the domain of writing, of literature, of formal "attitude." . . . There are so many Jewish Don Quixotes (not Fliglmen!) in the world of revolution, that it is no wonder that there are also Sancho Panzas—and in a much larger number (the Sancho Panzas are *always* and *everywhere* in the majority; this is, by the way, one of the greatest dangers that lurk around every genuine democracy). [. . .]

And a few more things:

You write so wonderfully about Gandhism, you know, that the Mahatma's "passive resistance" is actually the highest and most real activity, and you consider him, rightfully, to be a great agent in our epoch, *an epoch of deeds.* So why shouldn't we add that we hear the language of today's epoch, the language of consequential and determined deeds, out of the mouths of other, not holy, dictators, as well?

[. . .] How can we make the dictator move from Stalin and Mussolini over to Mahatma Gandhi? Gandhi has learned in the West to activate *nirvana* and to sanctify *karma.* How can we make the West go and learn something from him, in the East? Learn that *action*, karma, when it isn't sanctified, is an abyss, Sodom? How can we achieve this? This is the problem of all problems. And you cannot escape it. It will follow you. It will not let you rest even in the most remote desert. . . .

Yours,
Sh. Niger

P.S. Read again through your letter and my comments on it, and I noticed that it wasn't leftism, but [. . .] we live in an epoch of black and white, or, more correctly, black and red. We find ourselves in an environment where we are constantly being asked for an echoing *yes* with a few exclamation marks, or a 100 percent *no.* Anything that is between *yes* and *no*, anything that is followed by a question mark, is scorned. So precisely *now* and precisely *here* it is necessary to come out with *questions*, to release the *silent doves* of thought, to let them fly—and to wait until they return with green leaves in their beaks, with news that the stormy waters of the flood are receding.

Translated by Alexandra Hoffman.

Other works by Niger: *Vegn yidishe shrayber* (1912); *I. L. Peretz* (1952); *Bilingualism in the History of Jewish Literature* (1990).

Walter Benjamin
1892-1940

Born into a wealthy business family in Berlin, the critical theorist Walter Benjamin went into exile in 1932 during the turmoil preceding the Nazi seizure of power. He committed suicide in 1940 while trying to escape from France, via Spain, to Portugal, where he hoped to sail to the United States. His essays on aesthetic theory, especially "The Task of the Translator" (1923) and "The Work of Art in the Age of Mechanical Reproduction" (1936), became foundational texts in university humanities departments in the late twentieth century.

Franz Kafka: On the Tenth Anniversary of His Death
1934

The Little Hunchback

Some time ago it became known that Knut Hamsun was in the habit of expressing his views in an occasional letter to the editor of the local paper in the small town near which he lived. Years ago that town was the scene of the jury trial of a maid who had killed her infant child. She was sentenced to a prison term. Soon thereafter the local paper printed a letter from Hamsun in which he announced his intention of leaving a town which did not visit the supreme punishment on a mother who killed her newborn child—the gallows, or at least a life term of hard labor. A few years passed. *Growth of the Soil* appeared, and it contained the story of a maid who committed the same crime, suffered the same punishment, and, as is made clear to the reader, surely deserved no more severe one.

Kafka's posthumous reflections, which are contained in *The Great Wall of China*, recall this to mind. Hardly had this volume appeared when the reflections served as the basis for a Kafka criticism which concentrated on an interpretation of these reflections to the neglect of his real works. There are two ways to miss the point of Kafka's works. One is to interpret them naturally, the other is the supernatural interpretation. Both the psychoanalytic and the theological interpretations equally miss the essential points. The first kind is represented by Hellmuth Kaiser; the second, by numerous writers, such as H. J. Schoeps, Bernhard Rang, and Bernhard Groethuysen. To these last also belongs Willy Haas, although he has made revealing comments on Kafka in other contexts which we shall discuss later; such insights did not prevent him from interpreting Kafka's work after a theological pattern. "The powers above, the realm of grace," so Haas writes, "Kafka has depicted in his great novel *The Castle*; the powers below, the realm of the courts and of damnation, he has dealt with in his equally great novel *The Trial*. The earth between the two, earthly fate and its arduous demands, he

attempted to present in strictly stylized form in a third novel, *Amerika*." The first third of this interpretation has, since Brod, become the common property of Kafka criticism. Bernhard Rang writes in a similar vein: "To the extent that one may regard the Castle as the seat of grace, precisely these vain efforts and attempts mean, theologically speaking, that God's grace cannot be attained or forced by man at will and deliberately. Unrest and impatience only impede and confound the exalted stillness of the divine." This interpretation is a convenient one; but the further it is carried, the clearer it becomes that it is untenable. This is perhaps seen most clearly in a statement by Willy Haas. "Kafka goes back . . . to Kierkegaard as well as to Pascal; one may call him the only legitimate heir of these two. In all three there is an excruciatingly harsh basic religious theme: man is always in the wrong before God. . . . Kafka's upper world, his so-called Castle, with its immense, complex staff of petty and rather lecherous officials, his strange heaven plays a horrible game with people . . . and yet man is very much in the wrong even before this god." This theology falls far behind the doctrine of justification of St. Anselm of Canterbury into barbaric speculations which do not even seem consistent with the text of Kafka's works. "Can an individual official forgive?" we read in *The Castle*. "This could only be a matter for the over-all authorities, but even they can probably not forgive but only judge." This road has soon led into a blind alley. "All this," says Denis de Rougemont, "is not the wretched situation of man without a god, but the wretched state of a man who is bound to a god he does not know, because he does not know Christ."

It is easier to draw speculative conclusions from Kafka's posthumous collection of notes than to explore even one of the motifs that appear in his stories and novels. Yet only these give some clue to the prehistoric forces that dominated Kafka's creativeness, forces which, to be sure, may justifiably be regarded as belonging to our world as well. Who can say under what names they appeared to Kafka himself? Only this much is certain: he did not know them and failed to get his bearings among them. In the mirror which the prehistoric world held before him in the form of guilt he merely saw the future emerging in the form of judgment. Kafka, however, did not say what it was like. Was it not the Last Judgment? Does it not turn the judge into the defendant? Is the trial not the punishment? Kafka gave no answer. Did he expect anything of this punishment? Or was he not rather concerned to postpone it?

In the stories which Kafka left us, narrative art regains the significance it had in the mouth of Scheherazade: to postpone the future. In *The Trial* postponement is the hope of the accused man only if the proceedings do not gradually turn into the judgment. The patriarch himself is to benefit by postponement, even though he may have to trade his place in tradition for it. "I could conceive of another Abraham—to be sure, he would never get to be a patriarch or even an old-clothes dealer—, an Abraham who would be prepared to satisfy the demand for a sacrifice immediately, with the promptness of a waiter, but would be unable to bring it off because he cannot get away, being indispensable; the household needs him, there is always something or other to take care of, the house is never ready; but without having his house ready, without having something to fall back on, he cannot leave—this the Bible also realized, for it says: 'He set his house in order.'"

This Abraham appears "with the promptness of a waiter." Kafka could understand things only in the form of a *gestus*, and this *gestus* which he did not understand constitutes the cloudy part of the parables. Kafka's writings emanate from it. The way he withheld them is well known. His testament orders their destruction. This document, which no one interested in Kafka can disregard, says that the writings did not satisfy their author, that he regarded his efforts as failures, that he counted himself among those who were bound to fail. He did fail in his grandiose attempt to convert poetry into doctrine, to turn it into a parable and restore to it that stability and unpretentiousness which, in the face of reason, seemed to him to be the only appropriate thing for it. No other writer has obeyed the commandment "Thou shalt not make unto thee a graven image" so faithfully.

"It was as if the shame of it was to outlive him." With these words *The Trial* ends. Corresponding as it does to his "elemental purity of feeling," shame is Kafka's strongest gesture. It has a dual aspect, however. Shame is an intimate human reaction, but at the same time it has social pretensions. Shame is not only shame in the presence of others, but can also be shame one feels for them. Kafka's shame, then, is no more personal than the life and thought which govern it and which he has described thus: "He does not live for the sake of his own life, he does not think for the sake of his own thought. He feels as though he were living and thinking under the constraint of a family. . . . Because of this unknown family . . . he cannot be released." We do not know the make-up of this unknown family, which is composed of human beings and animals. But this much is clear: it is this family that forces Kafka to move cosmic ages in his writings. Doing this family's bidding, he moves the mass of historical happenings as Sisyphus rolled the stone. As he does so, its nether side comes to light; it is not a pleasant sight, but Kafka is capable of bearing it. "To believe in progress is not to believe that progress has already taken place. That would be no belief." Kafka did not consider the age in which he lived as an advance over the beginnings of time. His novels are set in a swamp world. In his works, created things appear at the stage which Bachofen has termed the hetaeric stage. The fact that it is now forgotten does not mean that it does not extend into the present. On the contrary: it is actual by virtue of this very oblivion. An experience deeper than that of an average person can make contact with it. "I have experience," we read in one of Kafka's earliest notes, "and I am not joking when I say that it is a seasickness on dry land." It is no accident that the first "Meditation" was made on a swing. And Kafka does not tire of expressing himself on the fluctuating nature of experiences. Each gives way and mingles with its opposite. "It was summer, a hot day," so begins "The Knock at the Manor Gate." "With my sister I was passing the gate of a great house on our way home. I don't remember whether she knocked on the gate out of mischief or in a fit of absent-mindedness, or merely shook her fist at it and did not knock at all." The very possibility of the third alternative puts the other two, which at first seemed harmless, in a different light. It is from the swampy soil of such experiences that Kafka's female characters rise. They are swamp creatures like Leni, "who stretches out the middle and ring fingers of her right hand between which the connecting web of skin reached almost to the top joint, short as the fingers were." "Fine times," so the ambivalent Frieda reminisces about her earlier life; "you never asked me about my past." This past takes us back to the dark, deep womb, the scene of the mating "whose untrammeled voluptuousness," to quote Bachofen, "is hateful to the pure forces of heavenly light and which justifies the term used by Arnobius, *luteae voluptates* [dirty voluptuousness]."

Only from this vantage point can the technique of Kafka the storyteller be comprehended. Whenever figures in the novels have anything to say to K., no matter how important or surprising it may be, they do so casually and with the implication that he must really have known it all along. It is as though nothing new was being imparted, as though the hero was just being subtly invited to recall to mind something that he had forgotten. This is how Willy Haas has interpreted the course of events in *The Trial*, and justifiably so. "The object of the trial," he writes, "indeed, the real hero of this incredible book is forgetting, whose main characteristic is the forgetting of itself. . . . Here it has actually become a mute figure in the shape of the accused man, a figure of the most striking intensity." It probably cannot be denied that "this mysterious center . . . derives from the Jewish religion." "Memory plays a very mysterious role as piousness. It is not an ordinary, but . . . the most profound quality of Jehovah that he remembers, that he retains an infallible memory 'to the third and fourth, even to the hundredth generation.' The most sacred . . . act of the . . . ritual is the erasing of sins from the book of memory."

What has been forgotten—and this insight affords us yet another avenue of access to Kafka's work—is never something purely individual. Everything forgotten mingles with what has been forgotten of the prehistoric world, forms countless, uncertain, changing compounds, yielding a constant flow of new, strange products. Oblivion is the container from which the inexhaustible intermediate world in Kafka's stories presses toward the light. "Here the very fullness of the world is considered as the only reality. All spirit must be concrete, particularized in order to have its place and *raison d'être*. The spiritual, if it plays a role at all, turns into spirits. These spirits become definite individuals, with names and a very special connection with the name of the worshiper. . . . Without any scruples their fullness is crammed into the fullness of the world. . . . The crowd of spirits is swelled without any concern . . . new ones are constantly added to the old ones, and all are distinguished from the others by their own names." All this does not refer to Kafka, but to—China. This is how Franz Rosenzweig describes the Chinese ancestor cult in his *Star of Redemption*. To Kafka, the world of his ancestors was as unfathomable as the world of realities was important for him, and we may be sure that, like the totem poles of primitive peoples, the world of ancestors took him down to the animals. Incidentally, Kafka is not the only writer for whom animals are the receptacles of the forgotten. In Tieck's profound story "Fair Eckbert," the forgotten name of a little dog, Strohmi, stands for a mysterious guilt. One can understand, then, that Kafka did

not tire of picking up the forgotten from animals. They are not the goal, to be sure, but one cannot do without them. A case in point is the "hunger artist" who, "strictly speaking, was only an impediment on the way to the menagerie." Can one not see the animals in "The Burrow" or "The Giant Mole" ponder as they dig in? And yet this thinking is extremely flighty. Irresolutely it flits from one worry to the next, it nibbles at every anxiety with the fickleness of despair. Thus there are butterflies in Kafka, too. The guilt-ridden "Hunter Gracchus," who refuses to acknowledge his guilt, "has turned into a butterfly." "Don't laugh," says the hunter Gracchus. This much is certain: of all of Kafka's creatures, the animals have the greatest opportunity for reflection. What corruption is in the law, anxiety is in their thinking. It messes a situation up, yet it is the only hopeful thing about it. However, because the most forgotten alien land is one's own body, one can understand why Kafka called the cough that erupted from within him "the animal." It was the most advanced outpost of the great herd.

The strangest bastard which the prehistoric world has begotten with guilt in Kafka is Odradek [in "The Cares of a Family Man"]. "At first sight it looks like a flat, star-shaped spool for thread, and it really seems to have thread wound around it; to be sure, they probably are only old, broken-off bits of thread that are knotted and tangled together, of all sorts and colors. But it is not just a spool, for a small wooden cross-bar sticks out of the middle of the star, and another small rod is joined to it at a right angle. With the aid of this latter rod on one side and one of the extensions of the star on the other, the whole thing can stand upright as if on two legs." Odradek "stays alternately in the attic, on the staircase, in the corridors, and in the hall." So it prefers the same places as the court of law which investigates guilt. Attics are the places of discarded, forgotten objects. Perhaps the necessity to appear before a court of justice gives rise to a feeling similar to that with which one approaches trunks in the attic which have been locked up for years. One would like to put off this chore till the end of time, just as K. regards his written defense as suitable "for occupying one's senile mind some day during retirement."

Odradek is the form which things assume in oblivion. They are distorted. The "cares of a family man," which no one can identify, are distorted; the bug, of which we know all too well that it represents Gregor Samsa, is distorted; the big animal, half lamb, half kitten, for which "the butcher's knife" might be "a release," is distorted. These Kafka figures are connected by a long series of figures with the prototype of distortion, the hunchback. Among the images in Kafka's stories, none is more frequent than that of the man who bows his head far down on his chest: the fatigue of the court officials, the noise affecting the doormen in the hotel, the low ceiling facing the visitors in the gallery. In the *Penal Colony* those in power use an archaic apparatus which engraves letters with curlicues on the backs of guilty men, multiplying the stabs and piling up the ornaments to the point where the back of the guilty man becomes clairvoyant and is able to decipher the writing from which he must derive the nature of his unknown guilt. It is the back on which this is incumbent. It was always this way with Kafka. Compare this early diary entry: "In order to be as heavy as possible, which I believe to be an aid to falling asleep, I had crossed my arms and put my hands on my shoulders, so that I lay there like a soldier with his pack." Quite palpably, being loaded down is here equated with forgetting, the forgetting of a sleeping man. The same symbol occurs in the folksong "The Little Hunchback." This little man is at home in distorted life; he will disappear with the coming of the Messiah, of whom a great rabbi once said that he did not wish to change the world by force, but would only make a slight adjustment in it.

> When I come into my room,
> My little bed to make,
> A little hunchback is in there,
> With laughter does he shake.

This is the laughter of Odradek, which is described as sounding "something like the rustling in falling leaves."

> When I kneel upon my stool
> And I want to pray,
> A hunchbacked man is in the room
> And he starts to say:
> My dear child, I beg of you,
> Pray for the little hunchback too.

So ends the folksong. In his depth Kafka touches the ground which neither "mythical divination" nor "existential theology" supplied him with. It is the core of folk tradition, the German as well as the Jewish. Even if Kafka did not pray—and this we do not know—he still possessed in the highest degree what Malebranche called "the natural prayer of the soul": attentiveness.

And in this attentiveness he included all living creatures, as saints include them in their prayers.

Sancho Panza

In a Hasidic village, so the story goes, Jews were sitting together in a shabby inn one Sabbath evening. They were all local people, with the exception of one person no one knew, a very poor, ragged man who was squatting in a dark corner at the back of the room. All sorts of things were discussed, and then it was suggested that everyone should tell what wish he would make if one were granted him. One man wanted money; another wished for a son-in-law; a third dreamed of a new carpenter's bench; and so everyone spoke in turn. After they had finished, only the beggar in his dark corner was left. Reluctantly and hesitantly he answered the question. "I wish I were a powerful king reigning over a big country. Then, some night while I was asleep in my palace, an enemy would invade my country, and by dawn his horsemen would penetrate to my castle and meet with no resistance. Roused from my sleep, I wouldn't have time even to dress and I would have to flee in my shirt. Rushing over hill and dale and through forests day and night, I would finally arrive safely right here at the bench in this corner. This is my wish." The others exchanged uncomprehending glances. "And what good would this wish have done you?" someone asked. "I'd have a shirt," was the answer.

This story takes us right into the milieu of Kafka's world. No one says that the distortions which it will be the Messiah's mission to set right someday affect only our space; surely they are distortions of our time as well. Kafka must have had this in mind, and in this certainty he made the grandfather in "The Next Village" say: "Life is astonishingly short. As I look back over it, life seems so foreshortened to me that I can hardly understand, for instance, how a young man can decide to ride over to the next village without being afraid that, quite apart from accidents, even the span of a normal life that passes happily may be totally insufficient for such a ride." This old man's brother is the beggar whose "normal" life that "passes happily" does not even leave him time for a wish, but who is exempted from this wish in the abnormal, unhappy life, that is, the flight which he attempts in his story, and exchanges the wish for its fulfillment.

Among Kafka's creatures there is a clan which reckons with the brevity of life in a peculiar way. It comes from the "city in the south . . . of which it was said: 'People live there who—imagine!—don't sleep!'—'And why not?'—'Because they don't get tired.'—'Why don't they?'—'Because they are fools.'—'Don't fools get tired?'—'How could fools get tired?'" One can see that the fools are akin to the indefatigable assistants. But there is more to this clan. It is casually remarked of the faces of the assistants that they seem to be those of "grown-ups, perhaps even students." Actually, the students who appear in the strangest places in Kafka's works are the spokesmen for and leaders of this clan. "'But when do you sleep?' asked Karl, looking at the student in surprise. 'Oh, sleep!' said the student. 'I'll get some sleep when I'm finished with my studies.'" This reminds one of the reluctance with which children go to bed; after all, while they are asleep, something might happen that concerns them. "Don't forget the best!" We are familiar with this remark from a nebulous bunch of old stories, although it may not occur in any of them. But forgetting always involves the best, for it involves the possibility of redemption. "The idea of helping me is an illness and requires bed rest for a cure," ironically says the restlessly wandering ghost of the hunter Gracchus. While they study, the students are awake, and perhaps their being kept awake is the best thing about these studies. The hunger artist fasts, the doorkeeper is silent, and the students are awake. This is the veiled way in which the great rules of asceticism operate in Kafka.

Their crowning achievement is studying. Reverently Kafka unearths it from long-lost boyhood. "Not very unlike this—a long time ago—Karl had sat at home at his parents' table writing his homework, while his father read the newspaper or did bookkeeping and correspondence for some organization and his mother was busy sewing, drawing the thread high out of the material in her hand. To avoid disturbing his father, Karl used to put only his exercise book and his writing materials on the table, while he arranged the books he needed on chairs to the right and left of him. How quiet it had been there! How seldom strangers had entered that room!" Perhaps these studies had amounted to nothing. But they are very close to that nothing which alone makes it possible for something to be useful—that is, to the Tao. This is what Kafka was after with his desire "to hammer a table together with painstaking craftsmanship and, at the same time, to do nothing—not in such a way that someone could say 'Hammering is nothing to him,' but 'To him, hammering is real hammering and at the same time nothing,' which would have made the hammering even bolder, more determined, more real, and, if you like, more insane." This is the resolute, fanatical mien which students have when they study; it is the strangest mien imaginable. The scribes, the students, are out of breath; they fairly race along. "Often the official dictates in such a low voice that the scribe cannot even hear it sitting down; then he has to jump up, catch the dictation, quickly sit down again and write it down, then jump up again and so forth. How strange that is! It is almost incomprehensible!" It may be easier to understand this if one thinks of the actors in the Nature Theater. Actors have to catch their cues in a flash, and they resemble those assiduous people in other ways as well. Truly, for them "hammering is real hammering and at the same time nothing"—provided that this is part of their role. They study this role, and only a bad actor would forget a word or a movement. For the members of the Oklahoma troupe, however, the role is their earlier life; hence the "nature" in this Nature Theater. Its actors have been redeemed, but not so the student whom Karl watches silently on the balcony as he reads his book, "turning the pages, occasionally looking something up in another book which he always snatched up quick as a flash, and frequently making notes in a notebook, which he always did with his face surprisingly close to the paper."

Kafka does not grow tired of representing the *gestus* in this fashion, but he invariably does so with astonishment. K. has rightly been compared with the Good Soldier Schweik; the one is astonished at everything, the other at nothing. The invention of the film and the phonograph came in an age of maximum alienation of men from one another, of unpredictably intervening relationships which have become their only ones. Experiments have proved that a man does not recognize his own walk on the screen or his own voice on the phonograph. The situation of the subject in such experiments is Kafka's situation; this is what directs him to learning, where he may encounter fragments of his own existence, fragments that are still within the context of the role. He might catch hold of the lost *gestus* the way Peter Schlemihl caught hold of the shadow he had sold. He might understand himself, but what an enormous effort would be required! It is a tempest that blows from the land of oblivion, and learning is a cavalry attack against it. Thus the beggar on the corner bench rides toward his past in order to catch hold of himself in the figure of the fleeing king. This ride, which is long enough for a life, corresponds to life, which is too short for a ride—" . . . until one shed one's spurs, for there were no spurs, threw away the reins, for there were no reins, and barely saw the land before one as a smoothly mown heath, with the horse's neck and head already gone." This is the fulfillment of the fantasy about the blessed horseman who rushes toward the past on an untrammeled, happy journey, no longer a burden on his race horse. But accursed is the rider who is chained to his nag because he has set himself a goal for the future, even though it is as close as the coal cellar—accursed his animal, accursed both of them. "Seated on the bucket, my hands up on the handle, with the simplest kind of bridle, I propel myself with difficulty down the stairs; but once down below, my bucket ascends, superbly, superbly; camels lying flat on the ground do not rise any more handsomely as they shake themselves under the sticks of their drivers." There is no more hopeless vista than that of "the regions of the ice mountains" in which the bucket rider drops out of sight forever. From the "nethermost regions of death" blows the wind that is favorable to him, the same wind which so often blows from the prehistoric world in Kafka's works, and which also propels the boat of the hunter Gracchus. "At mysteries and sacrifices, among Greeks as well as barbarians," writes Plutarch, "it is taught that there must be two primary essences and two opposing forces, one of which points to the right and straight ahead, whereas the other turns around and drives back." Reversal is the direction of learning which transforms existence into writing. Its teacher is Bucephalus, "the new attorney," who takes the road back without the powerful Alexander—which means, rid of the onrushing conqueror. "His flanks free and unhampered by the thighs of a rider, under a quiet lamp far from the din of Alexander's battles, he reads and turns the pages of our old books."

Werner Kraft once wrote an interpretation of this story. After giving careful attention to every detail of the text, Kraft notes: "Nowhere else in literature is there such a powerful and penetrating criticism of the myth in its full scope." According to Kraft, Kafka does not use the word "justice," yet it is justice which serves as the point of departure for his critique of the myth. But once we have reached this point, we are in danger of missing Kafka by stopping here. Is it really the law which could thus be invoked against the myth in the name of justice? No, as a legal scholar Bucephalus remains true to his origins, except that he does not seem to be practicing law—and this is probably something new, in Kafka's sense, for both Bucephalus and the bar. The law which is studied and not practiced any longer is the gate to justice.

The gate to justice is learning. And yet Kafka does not dare attach to this learning the promises which tradition has attached to the study of the Torah. His assistants are sextons who have lost their house of prayer, his students are pupils who have lost the Holy Writ. Now there is nothing to support them on their "untrammeled, happy journey." Kafka, however, has found the law of his journey—at least on one occasion he succeeded in bringing its breath-taking speed in line with the slow narrative pace that he presumably sought all his life. He expressed this in a little prose piece which is his most perfect creation not only because it is an interpretation.

"Without ever boasting of it, Sancho Panza succeeded in the course of years, by supplying a lot of romances of chivalry and adventure for the evening and night hours, in so diverting from him his demon, whom he later called Don Quixote, that his demon thereupon freely performed the maddest exploits, which, however, lacking a preordained object, which Sancho Panza himself was supposed to have been, did no one any harm. A free man, Sancho Panza philosophically followed Don Quixote on his crusades, perhaps out of a sense of responsibility, and thus enjoyed a great and profitable entertainment to the end of his days."

Sancho Panza, a sedate fool and clumsy assistant, sent his rider on ahead; Bucephalus outlived his. Whether it is a man or a horse is no longer so important, if only the burden is removed from the back.

NOTE

Words in brackets appear in the original translation.

Translated by Harry Zohn.

Other works by Benjamin: *The Origin of German Tragic Drama* (1998); *The Arcades Project* (2006); *Berlin Childhood around 1900* (2006); *The Writer of Modern Life: Essays on Charles Baudelaire* (2006).

Milton Steinberg

1903–1950

Milton Steinberg was a well-known and influential Conservative rabbi in the United States in the 1930s and 1940s. Born in Rochester, New York, he received a Ph.D. in philosophy from Columbia University and was ordained at the Jewish Theological Seminary in 1928. After leading a congregation in Indianapolis for five years, he was appointed rabbi of the Park Avenue Synagogue in New York City in 1933, where he remained until his untimely death. He was greatly influenced by Mordecai Kaplan, although he was critical of Reconstructionism for its lack of philosophical attention to God. His historical novel *As a Driven Leaf* (1939), which examines tensions between religion and philosophy through the life of the second-century heretic Elisha ben Abuyah, has never been out of print.

The Making of the Modern Jew
1934

Chapter IX. Dissolution of Balance

For a half-millennium the Jew, rejected by the world, had secluded himself within ghetto walls, unconcerned with what lay without. But the day came when the world would no longer be denied, when it insinuated itself into his retreat, upsetting his balanced life and disturbing his peace. It hinted beguilingly of freedom and emancipation, of a fuller and richer existence. It beckoned and the Jew crept forth. He tasted of this strange thing called liberty, found it sweet and wanted more. And so he abandoned his ghettos for the pursuit of it. He stripped off the segregation which had protected his group being. Only when it was too late did he discover that the world had not been sincere. It had been playing with him, it had never intended fully to keep its promises of liberation. But for all that the modern world refused to receive him, it took advantage of his defenselessness. It bent and twisted his personality, thumped, kneaded and shaped him. He emerged from the mills of emancipation a new creature, scarcely akin to what he had been. He became the Jew as the world knows him to-day.

The story of the Jew in the modern world is then the history of the dissolution of an ordered ghetto into chaos, and of a fixed individuality into flux. It is a record formless and inchoate, for it describes not the purposeful stability of a healthy organism but its degeneration and decay. When a social system like that of the ghetto is alive, all its powers are concentrated upon intelligible, unifying objectives. It is then possible for the historian to describe its activities in terms of sweeping universality. Such was the character of our analysis of medieval survival. But when that organism disinte-

grates, conflicting energies play against each other in pointless confusion. No generalization possesses more than partial applicability. In this fact lies the root of the untidy incoherence of any account of the modern Jew and his group life. Unity has been displaced by mutually contradictory diversities. Henceforth every reference to the Jew will need to be taken with the traditional grain of salt, will demand the recognition that broad statements can involve only partial truth.

And it is a tale of pain, this process of the progressive emancipation of the Jew subsequent to the French Revolution. When an old world dies and a new world is not yet born, the soul of the individual is left homeless. It can no longer find rest in the order which is perishing. The new society in which it is to incarnate itself struggles toward birth but is not yet actualized. Such is the fate of all who are so unfortunate as to be born during an age of social transition. Such was the fate of the Jew during the nineteenth century when the ghetto at last collapsed, leaving him with a refuge neither in the old world nor in the new. The ghetto may have been chokingly confining, yet it was a dwelling-place for the soul. But now the ancient dwelling was no longer habitable, and the mansions of the world were still inhospitable. Torn by yearning for a peace that had vanished, without sure abode for his spirit, the modern Jew has moved restlessly from one to the other, finding surcease nowhere.

If the history of the Jew in the Middle Ages be an epic, the record of his modern life is a satirical comedy. For the essence of the epic is the heroic theme, and there is little heroism in recent Judaism. The act of renunciation may often be futile and unintelligent; it is always dignified. When the medieval Jew renounced the world, the light of martyrdom clothed him with something like majesty. The very gesture of self-sacrifice bred a tragic dignity that obscured his physical squalor. But the modern Jew is done with the renunciation of his fathers. From the very moment that he first tasted of liberty, he developed an insatiable appetite for it. The world, however, has been a grudging giver, it has liberated the Jew only bit by bit, it has always withheld more than it granted. As a result, the Jew has found himself a perpetual suppliant; he has been compelled to wheedle and flatter for additional favors; he must always beg for the portion of liberty which has been withheld. His posture is neither dignified nor graceful. An Achilles sulking in a tent is a fitting theme for a Homeric poet; an Achilles scrambling headlong after an ever elusive tortoise is a theme only for a comedian or a philosopher.

If the Jew was aware of the meanness of his pursuit, he placated his outraged self-respect by assuring himself that the end justified the means. If his emancipation entailed a loss of dignity, at least the game was worth the candle. But after he had played the game of self-humiliation long enough, he became oppressed with a sense of futility. This whole business of winning unreserved recognition from the world seemed discouragingly prolonged. It was like one of those nightmares in which one wanders through labyrinthine corridors hoping always to find a way out but never quite succeeding.

Did the Jew succeed in winning economic freedom, then he could not vote. When he had the right of ballot, he might not hold office. Was he guaranteed the right to stand for election, he discovered that his Jewishness made a political career difficult even in most liberal lands. When education was theoretically open to all regardless of race, religion or color, the Jew still experienced some difficulty in gaining admission to universities. He was always conscious of the fact that regardless of his merits, it was almost impossible for him to move freely toward academic advancement. When these bars had been lowered, entrance into certain professions still remained a virtual impossibility. Even when all formal obstacles had been eliminated, there was still the wall of social exclusion. There were always clubs into which Jews were not elected, societies that were by policy entirely Christian in membership, drawing-rooms where no Jew had ever sat. At each stage the world has held something back, at each step it has insisted—thus far and no farther.

For a time each generation of Jews engaged in wishful thinking. It believed, because it was more pleasant to believe it, that the whole evil would disappear if only certain trivial factors in the situation were modified. Now, the Jew told himself, the fault lay with himself: he was too clannish, too stubbornly loyal to his identity; perhaps he was not sufficiently urbane, not adequately cultured, not completely Americanized, Anglicized or Teutonized. Or else he might pin his hopes on changes in the scene external to the Jew. He assured himself that he would be accepted when some reactionary government was liberalized. He argued that the root of his difficulties lay in specific economic evils. He looked, in other instances, to the spread of democracy. Above all, he tended to lay responsibility for his lot to ignorance. He felt assured that when popular education had been universalized, when every Gentile had been taught to read and write, to enjoy music, art and fine literature, that then anti-Semitism would disappear like some evil mist before the rising sun of a tolerant intelligence. Assiduously he went about confusing causes and effects, symptoms with the disease.

The Jew remade himself, he dissolved his clannish bonds, he stripped himself of distinguishing Jewish marks. He became urbane and polished; he eliminated all ghetto crudities and eccentricities. Then he waited confidently for the word of welcome. To his pained surprise the world seemed to approve of him no more in his transformation than it had before. Meanwhile, the reactionary government fell, the economic evils he blamed were mitigated, democracy became an ideal widely accepted, and literacy attained to a delightful universality; Gentiles heard good music with keen appreciation, they read literature of unimpeachable nobility. Still salvation refused to come, acceptance was not complete. The old flies in the ointment had been removed only to reveal the presence of others hitherto unsuspected.

And then came the disillusionment of the last generation. Minority rights in Eastern Europe turned out to be scraps of paper. The German people under the Hitlerite frenzy turned against the Jew. Despite a century of Jewish emancipation, despite the refinement of the German Jew, his assimilating tendencies, and his contributions to Teutonic culture, the liberties attained by one hundred years of struggle have been blotted out. The unkindest cut of all, from the point of view of Jewish hopes, has been the betrayal by educated classes. That the ignorant masses should seek to submerge the Jew may be painful; it is at least excusable. But that universities and professors should, for all their culture, lead in the hymns of hate is too dreadful by far. For these were the corner-stone of the edifice of Jewish hope. To the Jews of Eastern Europe the German situation is pure despair. It tells them that full emancipation may never come to them. For the Jews of the Western world the savage episode of Hitler contains a chilling prophecy. What happened in Germany can happen elsewhere. If rights and liberties can be recalled in one land, there is no land in which they are secure.

The upshot of the whole process has been a progressive disappointment and disillusionment. No game is worth the candle if the game can never be won, or if the prize can be taken away in the very last inning. The Jew tends to feel resentfully that he has abandoned the dignity and serenity of the older way of life for mythical crocks of gold, located at the ever-receding feet of rainbows. Complementing the sense of futility goes a sense of disgust. The Jew to-day is likely to be ashamed of himself. The act of self-abasement is always painful. But when one has debased oneself in vain, the reaction tends to be nausea.

That out of the chaos, the pain, the ungraceful pursuit, the disillusionment, the Jew is now beginning to derive a new attitude of self-respect and a new philosophy for a tolerable existence in the modern scene we shall see later. Our immediate purpose is to set modern Jewish life in vivid opposition to the medieval. The elements of contrast between the two can be summarized in four antinomies and a conclusion.

1. On the *one* hand, the ordered homogeneity of a stable order; on the other, the formless, inchoate confusion of a society in disintegration.
2. A self-contained serenity as opposed to restless vacillation between two worlds.
3. The dignity of renunciation against the humiliation of persistent beggary.
4. An order rich in a satisfying culture and adequate ideology as contrasted with one impotent by lack of program and sicklied over by abstract alternatives of to be or not to be.

And the final crushing recognition that the tolerance of the world is an uncertain quantity, that final emancipation may never be conferred, that the Gentile is as likely as ever to suppress the Jew, that salvation must be won and can not be conferred.

The ghetto was gone, the life it sheltered went with it. Even before the process of emancipation was officially under way, the factors of medieval survival were beginning to lose their efficacy. Once the wild rush of liberating events was launched, degeneration proceeded with dizzy rapidity. A social organism which had lived for nigh on two thousand years, which had resisted violent attack and abuse, suddenly disintegrated. Age-old habits of life disappeared, hoary ideas and ideals dissolved, a whole society vanished in a puff of historic smoke.

That so solid a world should melt away so rapidly seems incredible. Not even the change in external circumstance quite accounts for it. The secret of the velocity of decay is to be discovered in the peculiar conditions of medieval Jewish stability. Equilibrium, whether physical or social, is an ambiguous word. It may denote merely inertia—the secure quiet of a book flat on a table. On the other hand, it may suggest the deceptive rest of a body in infinite motion. In that sense, the solar system is in a state of equilibrium. But the balance is unstable, it proceeds from the resolution of innumerable forces. Let one of these be withdrawn and the whole order collapses. The stability of the ghetto was that of a spinning top, it was the result of the interplay of social movement. It gave the illusion of firmness because the resolution of forces balanced exactly. Emancipation disturbed the stabilizing dynamism, the collapse of a society followed. [. . .]

THE NEGATION OF SOCIAL ISOLATION

By virtue of the emancipation, the Jew lost his protective segregation. The world and he both canceled their tacit compact of no intercourse. By that act, the ghetto and its internal life signed their own death warrant. The bulwark of isolation had been demolished. No longer was the Jewish way of life protected against alien and disturbing influences, it was now out in the open, exposed to contagion. As soon as the Jew stepped out of the ghetto, he became aware of the contrast between his own habits and those of the Gentile. Life on the Judengasse had possessed its own excellences, but polished refinement of manner had not been one of these. Existence for the Jew had been too dour and grim to allow for concern with external graces. The elegance of Gentile life intrigued the newly emancipated Jew with its novelty. He found himself imitating the non-Jew before he was aware of the fact.

Even had the ways of the world been hideous compared to his own, the Jew would have adopted them. For these were the patterns of the master class and newly liberated slaves are especially prone to ape the standards of those who sit securely in the seats of power. Besides, with the emancipation, the Jew ceased to seek outlets for his ambition within the Jewish group. He now looked for his laurels in a larger arena. But if he was to be successful in a world predominantly Gentile, he must show that he could behave like a Gentile, otherwise, he would be denied even an initial hearing. Most of all, the Jew imitated Gentile conduct because he hoped thereby to attain fuller emancipation. At each stage in the liberating process, some restrictions still persisted. The Jew felt naturally that once he had shown to the world that he was no strange monster, that in Rome he could do exactly as the Romans did, the world in turn would recognize that the Jew was indistinguishable from the non-Jew and treat him accordingly.

The integrity of Jewish social pressure crumbled under the strain. So long as every Jew lived under the ever-watchful eyes of the group, divergence from traditional practise was impossible. But now the individual was no longer a mere cell within a larger body. He was a footloose person struggling to make his way in a new order. He was free to do as he pleased. His interests encouraged him to do as did the Gentiles.

The new economic order, too, made its contribution to the dissolution of ancestral forms. In the ghetto, business had been regulated into conformity with Jewish group practises. With the emancipation, the Jew ceased to concern himself with an economy which was all his own. He eagerly availed himself of the opportunity to participate in the larger affairs of a larger world. But the economy of which he became part was Gentile. It had no respect for Sabbath or Holy Day. For the first time in two millennia, the Jew was compelled to choose between ancestral sanctities and economic advantage. The efforts made by many Jews to preserve traditional forms, often at the cost of their financial interests, were laudable. In the long run, they were doomed to failure. The wheels of industry continued to revolve sacrilegiously, grinding to destruction rite and ritual.

Some Jews resisted desperately the encroachments of the new economy upon Jewish practise; the vast majority decided that the observances of their fathers were no longer practicable. They kept the Jew from his shops on Saturday; they broke into the normal business day with numberless irrelevant interruptions; they erected a barrier of diet between him and his recently acquired Christian associates. The Jew cast about for some logical reason to justify all this troublesome inconvenience. He found none. The old rationale was no longer satisfying. He yielded to the demands of his interests and compromised.

The process of attrition, so long inhibited, now began in earnest. As a result of free contact with Gentile society, from considerations of personal advantage, out of the failure to find justification for Jewish practise, the Jew began quietly, imperceptibly, to depart from the practises of his fathers. There was generally nothing precipitate about the sloughing of Jewish habits; the automatisms of conduct rarely break sharply; they are worn away only gradually. But once the first concessions are made, a landslide has begun.

With the passage of time, the individual Jew yielded more and more, conformed less and less. With each successive generation the process of riddance went on with accelerating momentum. Of all the lands of the world it has moved most rapidly in the United States. For here, to the normal conditions which of themselves tended to encourage divergence, one unusual circumstance was added—the disruptive effects of migration. Millions of Jews were lifted from their setting, from familiar scenes and places suggestive of tradition, and deposited in a new world.

But whether slow or rapid, the progressive sloughing off of old forms goes on apace. Many a Jew now alive refused in his youth to violate the Sabbath. In his old age he transgresses with an untroubled conscience. Within the span of one generation, many a home once filled with Jewish ritualist symbols has been entirely emptied of them.

Contemporary Jewish practise is a crazy-quilt, a mass of contradictions and conflicts. In part, this is due to the difference in the tempo of emancipation. The Jew from Poland, fresh from the ghetto, is neighbor to the Jew who for a century has been subjected to the disintegration of freedom. Medievalism intact walks side by side with a shattered modernity; the full tradition rubs shoulders with its broken remnants. Another part of the explanation lies within the individual. Some few Jews there are, even in free lands, who have made no concessions, who know that *facilis descensus Averni*. There are others who have yielded in some things and not in others. And there are those who, in more than a dietary sense, have gone "the whole hog," whose lives are distinguished by not a single traditional form or practise. Toward that end the whole group slips relentlessly.

To Israel Zangwill we are indebted for the most apt characterization of this non-conformist chaos, of this ceremonial "catch as catch can." He puts into the mouth of an Irish maid employed in a Jewish household, this sage observation: "To-night being yer Sabbath, you'll be blowing out yer bedroom candle, though ye won't light it; Mr. David'll light his and blow it out too; and the old misthress won't even touch the candlestick. There's three religions in this house, not wan."

The Negation of the Culture

In one other realm did the new order shake the old society. It destroyed the scheme of learning, the tradition of a sanctified scholarship. For untold centuries the Jew found in his study courage in suffering, escape from a threatened insanity and a compensation for his lot. He cherished it with the intensity with which a mind threatened by degeneration clings to elements of lucidity. He trusted in its value, he was assured that no system of thought was so accurate, no literature so valid, and no culture so elevating as his. Then Western knowledge unfolded its ample page, rich with the spoils of time. The intellectual pride of the Jew turned to confusion. He discovered that his philosophy was obsolete, his science hopelessly mistaken. He awoke to the fact that his culture had none of the music and art which made Gentile civilization graceful. The tradition had been satisfactory as long as it had existed in a vacuum of isolation. It seemed ludicrously inferior when subjected to invidious contrast.

Elemental intellectual honesty compelled the Jew to turn his efforts from his own outdated culture to the thought of the new world. It was pure perversity to continue to study the Talmud when Shakespeare, Goethe and Gibbon were available for the asking. Maimonides seemed hopelessly antiquated in comparison with Kant and Hegel; Judah Halevi was only an interesting archeological survival compared to Schiller or Lessing. As rapidly as the Jew made intellectual contact with Gentile civilization, so rapidly did he turn his attention to the thought life which was now opened to him. Blinded by a novel brilliance, he gave scant attention to the quiet light of his native culture. He assumed that its outmoded exterior reflected an essential irrelevance.

While, in great measure, the abandonment of the tradition was nobly motivated, it was not without selfish and unworthy objectives. Not all Jews changed their intellectual allegiance on ideal grounds. As soon as the Jew was in the mills of emancipation, he developed a distinct sense of inferiority. He was not the equal of the Gentile politically, socially or economically. He felt inferior intellectually as well. The same imitative impulse which led him to adopt non-Jewish folk-ways, drove him to acquire an alien culture in preference to his own. He knew that the former was modern and fashionable, that it was a prime means of advancement in the world. If he and his children were to make their way successfully, they must be learned in that learning of which the world approved.

This combination of motives, selfish and unselfish, meant the end of the system of Jewish education. In the first stages of the emancipation, the old pedagogy managed to hold its ground. Traditional studies were maintained. Individual students supplemented them by teaching themselves modern languages, the sciences and literature. Many a student spent long days in the Yeshivah over the Talmud, and then, in secret, during the night (for at first such alien studies were forbidden) prepared himself for admission into some university. As the emancipation advanced, progressive Jews founded schools built on Gentile models, offering full curricula in modern subjects but including also courses of a specifically Jewish character. Before long, Jewish children were attending public schools and spending some time in a Jewish school after regular hours. But as Jewish allegiance disintegrated, this second education came to be regarded as a hardship on both the child and the parent. Then the Sunday-school appeared. The typical Jewish child to-day is given Jewish instruction one morning a week for one and a half to two hours.

This progressive abandonment of traditional learning was naturally not simultaneous in all lands. It ran parallel to the irregular movement of emancipation; it has gone farthest in those countries which most quickly liberated their Jews. It is least advanced where the emancipation is not yet really under way. There are still Jews in Eastern Europe and Asia to-day whose entire intellectual life has been traditional, who are completely innocent of any knowledge of Western thought. There is an ever-growing number of Jews in the West and East alike who are abysmally ignorant of the tradition of their own people.

The emancipated Jew to-day is in matters of Jewish culture pathetically uninformed. He knows nothing of it. His children, if possible, will know less. His knowledge of Jewish history is negligible; his understanding of his own past distorted and unintelligent. He presents a strange paradox to the world, a man who knows all literature except his own, all philosophies but that of his people, who reads books in all the seventy tongues but who generally can not construe a word of Hebrew.

Such is the story of emancipation and of how it canceled one by one each factor of survival. That during the nineteenth century the whole Jewish people did not disappear is due in part to certain external conditions, to the fact that at no time was emancipation full and complete, to the fact that liberation was so retarded in some lands as to provide constant reserves of human material. But much more was it due to elements internal to the Jewish scene. Somewhere, within this strange people lay unsuspected powers of resistance which drove them toward life. As soon as the tide of degeneration set in the Jewish will-to-persist set in motion creative vitalizing cross-currents. The old factors of survival disappeared, new ones were evoked. Before these can be examined and evaluated, the record of dis-integration must first be completed.

Other works by Steinberg: *A Partisan Guide to the Jewish Problem* (1945); *Basic Judaism* (1947).

Bertha Pappenheim
1859–1936

Bertha Pappenheim was the founder of the Jewish feminist movement in Germany. She grew up in a well-to-do religious home in Vienna and as a young woman was successfully treated by Joseph Breuer for psychological problems. Sigmund Freud's discussion of her case—as "Anna O."—immortalized her in the history of psychoanalysis. In 1889, she and her mother moved to Frankfurt, where she immersed herself in social work. In 1902, she created Weibliche Fürsorge, a Jewish social welfare organization for women run by women, and, in 1904, the Jüdischer Frauenbund. She was particularly active in the campaign against the international trade in Jewish women for prostitution. Unusually for the time, she combined a commitment to both traditional Judaism and feminism.

The Jewish Woman
1935

The position of the Jewish woman in Germany today cannot be ascertained from understanding the present alone. A brief look at the recent and distant past—perhaps even the long-distant past—is necessary, and it is useful to retrace this thread so that a contemporary woman might come to regard experience, memory, and tradition as background for keeping the image of the German Jewish woman in proper perspective.

Recent times have seen various attempts to paint Jewish womanhood with images of strong female types. In terms of numbers alone, these attempts, which have proceeded over the centuries, have yielded few highlights.

Apart from biblical women, Jewish women in the diaspora who achieved significance beyond a relatively small circle have been depicted over the ages only because of special circumstances.

Often mentioned and quite exceptional is Glückel of Hameln, who is significant in her appealing and admirable womanhood. She represented the Jewish German culture of her time, even though she did not influence

it. Her quite distinctive activities were entirely internal and limited to her—admittedly very large—family. If someone had not, for personal reasons, unearthed the memoirs of Glückel in the name of her humanity and thereby gained many friends for her, she would scarcely have enjoyed a resurgence outside a not-very-large circle interested in Jewish literary matters.

A rather long and empty span of time extends from Glückel to Jewish women of the more recent past. It includes famous women of the age of Romanticism who found their place in German literature but seem not to have played a decisive role in the development of German Jewish womanhood. These women certainly did not achieve a balance between their Jewish origins and the realm of German intellectuality in which they placed their fate. They might often have experienced their otherness—to use a modern word—with respect to the Christian culture-bearers among whom they moved disconcertingly, perhaps even disturbingly, but their baptism, which was the intellectual equivalent of the baptism of a person in a life-threatening situation, must, even though a strong plus, have never entirely counterbalanced the Jewish minus they experienced.

And yet a discernible confluence has long existed between Germanness and Jewish womanhood.

Naturally, in those former times of which I am thinking, it was not the case that the Jewish woman influenced the Christian world from her culture, but rather that the woman who remained entirely intact in her Jewish religious inwardness incorporated fragments of German culture into her general habitus.

Women's traditional dress and fashion were always—with the exception of religious demands on hairstyle and headdress—clearly influenced by national clothing conventions.

However, one finds the expression of German influence on Jewish womanhood most markedly in the subtlest and yet strongest factor of people's lives: their language.

Throughout the centuries, the "unknown Jewish woman," not mentioned in any chronicle, who lived on the moral plain of Jewish laws without achieving elevation, was the bearer of unbroken, self-evident Jewishness and at the same time was unconsciously the guardian of an ancient German linguistic inheritance. The women's Bible (*Tsene-rene*) and the *Maasse* books in their "women's German" (Yiddish-German)—and, I would almost like to add, the memoirs of Glückel of Hameln in classic form—are historical evidence of that.

Although this plain displays a considerably high ethical level, one can already detect here the germs of cultural discrepancy in the life of the Jewish woman, apparent within the customary view that women were to "be Jewish" but were not permitted to learn.

The People of the Book barred women from access to Jewish intellectual life and its sources; only in a piecemeal and truncated fashion were they to believe and act, and without knowing why.

No Bais Yakov school, no adult education can rectify the sin committed against the soul of the Jewish woman and thus Jewry in its entirety for withholding the Jewish meaning of life from the unknown woman. Her physical strength alone was recognized, and she was kept subservient to the man. A Jewish wife was permitted to carry the building blocks of family life as a beast of burden; she was to remain dull in her rhythm.

But how she was exalted and praised, the *Eshes ḥayil* (a love song with gefilte fish), how the male-human interpretations of the law turned against her, whose spirit was certainly also receptive and ready!!!

Having become sacrosanct, this attitude soon took a heavy toll. What one does not know—or knows only as something uncomfortable and burdensome, without recognizing its moralizing value—one does not regard highly, and I see logic and tragedy in the fact that the wives and mothers of the former age could no longer raise their children to respect the spiritual wealth of the tradition. The thread had been broken and thus the *empty house* was prepared, for which people today so readily and exclusively hold emancipation responsible.

But I also see a small intellectual rivulet from that time, stimulating the life of women and developing significantly, perhaps as natural compensation for the Jewish intellectual education that they were denied.

The German linguistic inheritance that was mixed with Jewish components, the women's German, is the narrow bridge into a world that, in the course of time, opened up to the Jewish woman. The very indifference with which women and girls learned (at a time of early marriage, girlhood in today's sense scarcely existed) contrasts with what boys and men were required to learn and know. This inheritance brought a steady and initially disregarded movement into the world of Jewish women.

The most visible expression of this centuries-old attitude and its shift appeared in one place indisputably and symptomatically: in attendance at the Baron de Hirsch schools in Galicia, where strictly Orthodox populations predominated. In the beginning, these schools were fiercely rejected by the heder; boys were not to attend them. (Admittedly, the administrations also made significant mistakes.)

What girls learned was not taken seriously; they attended the Baron de Hirsch schools, and frequently Polish schools as well, with great zeal and with growing rejection of their own families and those circles that seemed to them to be less "educated" in the religious and outward forms of life than the "young ladies," as even their parents respectfully called their daughters.

I have myself been able to observe how Yiddish-German, the women's German, developed over three generations in Austria, Hungary, Romania, Bohemia, Moravia, Poland, Galicia, and Russia. The middle generation did not cultivate its respective national language as much as the German language, scarcely becoming fluent or literate in it. (It is characteristic that in wealthy families the Jewish cook always spoke German, while the rest of the staff communicated in the national language.) Among Jewish women in particular, a strong distinctly German-tinged drive for education arose, and made new cultural elements accessible to bilingual—in higher classes (when French was added), often trilingual—women, though the importance of Jewishness diminished in form and content.

From the prominent figures of the Pressburg ghetto and their offshoots and influences, through the waiting room of the Rabbi of Sadagora and other bastions of classic Orthodoxy, to the circle of the families Schmelkes, Ringelheim, Ginsburg, Lilien, Buber, Nussbaum, Mandelstamm, and Motzkin, I observed with great awe the influence of the German language and German intellectual life, but at the same time saw Jewish consciousness fading among the women, who often already favored a newly awakening national consciousness in, for example, Hungary, Poland, and the Bohemian—today Czech—language regions.

Naturally, the women went to temple on the high holidays, the older ones on Saturday, too, but they could not follow the service properly. Here the break already began that in later decades led to the Liberal and the Reform liturgy. Would it not have been more sensible to educate the women—and, of course, not just the women—of the community to understand the service than to construct a service later that lacked historical and traditional foundation and was adapted to the failing understanding of the community?

But the fact remained: the majority of women understood neither the sermons in a mixed language interspersed with Hebrew quotations, nor the Torah reading, nor the literal meaning of the prayers, even though they could, usually without *kavanah* (devotion), outwardly follow the course of the service. I saw everywhere the old women with headband or *sheitl* sobbing bitterly over their thick books printed in Rashi script; the next generation chattering and already using prayer books printed in square script, mostly with a German translation, published in Rödelheim, Vienna, and Prague. I rarely saw Vilna, Amsterdam, and Kraków as the place of printing without *Tatsch* (German), though that might have been my own specific experience.

From my circle, to which I can only allude in this context, I must observe that the Jewish women of all classes and countries with whom I had occasion to speak were open to suggestions and ideas in the social realm. For the men, however, these were matters of indifference or discomfort.

The women with tradition in their blood and brains showed a readiness to put into practice the commandment to love their neighbor in a form adapted to the coming times. Thus, I recognized in the unknown Jewish woman, within Judaism, in the diaspora, the guarantor of the ability to perform great tasks ripe for development. I repeatedly took this conviction back to Germany with me from my travels, into my daily work, the radius of which I did not consider narrow.

To describe the development of the German Jewish woman from my own perspective, it was necessary in the above remarks to sketch the background on which, in my experience, this development was based.

I see three deep fissures in the mental life of the contemporary Jewish woman.

The first fissure is marked by the epoch in which, as a result of the changing times, the often thoughtlessly applied commandment of *mitsvah*, to help your neighbor, gave rise to the necessity to turn puffed-up philanthropy and blind almsgiving into meaningful, responsible action.

Fifty years ago, the community of Frankfurt am Main offered rich and challenging ground for such efforts.

It was therefore only a relatively small circle of unknown women (Orthodox as well as Liberal) who in Frankfurt recognized the need for female welfare activity in various areas, and who in humble, tireless, holy, painstaking work tilled the soil of the *kehilah kedoshah* in order to cultivate old cultures and plant new

ones. Let us remember with gratitude this first generation of women who willingly followed these lines of thought while the men stubbornly resisted them. It is interesting—despite the only sketchy picture—to note here the curious fact that within those fifty years male resistance to organization of social work turned into a hypertrophy of organization—to the point of being the idée fixe of an all-embracing "umbrella organization" lethal to any personal social effort.

This social work that took root in religious soil in Frankfurt would have achieved no significance beyond the bounds of the city had it not gained the impetus and support of the general German women's movement. From this new fusion of German cultural elements with Jewish cultural wealth, a mental substance developed that took on utmost significance for the German women's movement as well as for Jewish life.

The very Jewish women who at that time often had absolutely no desire to be such were in their social positions no longer "unknown." These women, who had no idea how Jewish they were in their deepest inherited mentality, proved themselves to be strong pillars of the German women's movement; that movement, in turn, brought to the timid, uncertain advance of Jewish women's aims a sureness of progress and purpose.

This confluence of two cultures cannot be discounted and can never be effaced from the lives of German and Jewish women. All women, whatever their position or inclination today, stand—unbeknownst to themselves—on the shoulders of these fighters for equal rights for women in all areas, beyond the limits of women's innate nature.

For the consciously and avowedly Jewish women who participated in social development, the experience of this convergence was a highpoint of their existence that became the psychological moment for the founding of the League of Jewish Women. Over the span of thirty years, the tendency of this league has unwaveringly remained religiously Jewish and culturally German. Today it is significant to note that the women who came together to lead the League of Jewish Women traced back their family origins as Germans living on German soil decades or centuries.

But not everything that the German women's movement and Jewish women yielded—albeit often only indirectly—was good and beneficial for us. Here the negative side of the mobility and adaptability of the Jewish spirit turned out to be to its own detriment. Slogans such as "new ethics," "century of the child," debates about the paragraph 218 birth control law, outgrowths of the youth movement, which were often taken up by the Jewish woman as a fashionable trend without due criticism and constraint, overshadowed for many women the significance of the achievements in all other intellectual and social areas.

Since then, time has again taught us to reevaluate many things. Nonetheless, we have experienced the ascent; we have learned to move intellectually in an atmosphere that would otherwise have been inaccessible to us. And if we had achieved and undertaken nothing but the movement for women's suffrage, that would have been enough.

The confirmation of the woman's right to codetermination, the conclusion that "nothing in religious law opposes it," we owe to Frankfurt Rabbi [Nehemia Anton] Nobel. May his memory be blessed with that of Rabbi Gershom, who introduced monogamy in the year 1000.

Another fissure in Jewish life of the late past is Zionism, though its increased influence on women is younger than the movement itself.

Because I have assumed the task of pursuing the formation of the modern Jewish female type, I suddenly find myself—as someone who consciously takes the keenest and most active interest in all manifestations and movements of Jewish life—faced with the need to account to myself for my distance from, lack of personal participation in, and even partial aversion to such a historic event as Zionism is for Judaism.

In a thorough examination of my conscience, I feel compelled to say that the deepest reason lies in the fact that, from the first expressions of the movement onward, the Zionists—not Zionism—treated as a *quantité négligeable* all the women's tasks that I recognize, propose, and defend as absolutely vital.

In addition, I knew that Theodor Herzl, the later Jewish national saint, acknowledged the role of his Jewishness at a relatively recent date.

Herzl was a journalist who usually served the Viennese their pleasant Sunday reading fare in the *Neue Freie Presse*.

In the circles from which I came, he was what people at the time did not yet call an "assimilated Jew" but was one who rejected his background. For me—perhaps for others, too—there was also the fact that Herzl's book *The Old New Land* appeared to be a direct imitation of *Looking Backward from the Year 2000* by Bellamy.

The fact that this book—it is important to underscore: this *German* book, which could be read by Pol-

ish and Russian Jews only by virtue of their Yiddish-German—was an inspiration for these Jews. That it brought them an idea of redemption was due to the horrible mental and physical constriction, the barbaric pressure, in which they lived.

Certainly the German journalist Herzl made the book, but the book, through a repercussion surprising even to him, also "made" the author. From his internal and external attitude at the time, the assimilated Viennese Jew could not have suspected that he had sounded a trumpet that would become a fanfare—and could have become a shofar, for, to use an old Jewish word, it all depends on the *mekabel* (the receiver).

At the time of the beginnings of Zionism, I moved a great deal in the countries today known as Eastern Europe, on behalf of the task that I had set myself, to help lift Jewish social life there out of decline, decay, and debasement. There, I saw in the subjective and objective view of the life of women a reason for this decline and decay and had for a moment thought, even hoped, that Zionism would help bring about a regeneration. Far from it! In endless heated debates with many unknown Zionists, I was repeatedly told that Zionism is a purely political movement, which should not be combined with social and religious matters; traffic in girls does not exist; prostitution is an international necessity; venereal disease is personal bad luck; and similar arguments. It was all devoid of culture: forms and tone, thoughtlessness and impiety in all expressions of life. I observed a congress in Vienna, a meeting in Karlsbad, and found no chance for me to feel supportive or sympathetic—nor did I find any later, when the Zionists interfered in German communal life with ever louder demands and disruptions and declared religion to be a private matter within the Jewish nation.

I resist the aroused temptation to further develop a reflection on "how I experience Zionism." Even if Zionism never ceased to stimulate thinking and observation for me, the influence of the movement on the German Jewish woman nonetheless happened entirely outside the sphere of my own interests. I could observe that women were only with hesitation accepted by Zionist men, and in special areas (mainly for collecting funds), that Zionist women's organizations developed intellectually and financially only slowly and with absolutely no autonomy, and that in my view they received their backbone and main strength from America.

However, it seems that it soon began to dawn on Jewish national circles that a nation—and especially a colonization—requires conscious, mature female will and action for securing its existence. It is hoped that in Jewish Palestine people will soon come to realize that collectivist procreation and childrearing are not promising bases for the survival of a "nation." I hope that the strong impression of the great German *aliyah* will have cultural influence in this respect. *Kindergarten* and *Krippe* [day care] are not only untranslatable German words, but are also pedagogical terms that should not be misused and misinterpreted. *Kindergarten* and *Krippe* are surrogates, which a healthy family should not use; nor should they be promoted as profitable institutions. The child belongs—to use a good German saying—at the mother's apron strings. Anything else is misfortune or a misguided social policy.

On the whole, however, it must be said that Zionism was a stimulating element for the German Jewish woman as well, to the extent that the propagandistic waves of Jewish nationalism *promoted* it, and that it also found a place—albeit not without a fight, but nonetheless entirely justifiably—in the League of Jewish Women. I could not discern great enrichment of mental life through the emergence of the Zionist women, and it was solely a matter of individual temperament—Zionist or non-Zionist—if they chose to engage in divisive, purifying, or pacifying activities.

Today, the failure of the German Jewish woman can be clearly seen in two places.

First of all, it is in Jewish social work, where it was organized to pieces. Women were frequently pushed out of their voluntary activity in favor of more experienced workers, who, already in a simply passive fashion, prevented social work from exerting its educational influence on wide circles of women—not only on the women themselves, but also, when it was not carried too far, on those around them. Voluntary social work as a means of instruction and education is one of the strongest moral powers of any community, but especially the Jewish one, through which it is possible to hark back to ancient abilities practiced in accordance with the commandments.

The evil of carrying out certain technical efforts less promptly and skillfully is the lesser one in comparison to the decline of the Jewish sense of duty and responsibility of voluntary women helpers. It is unwise for communities to forego moral training of their members and to mechanize what is a harmony of potentiated imponderables. There are in all enterprises positions that must be officially occupied, but the functionaries

(male and female) endowed with resemblance to God can tread every seed in the field of communal life and thereby cause even the taxpayers to lose interest.

We must demand the *Eshes ḥayil* in the community! Certainly, in the most recent past women too often lacked the aspiration and aptitude to fulfill such duties earnestly. Even where small paths had been trodden to that end, the women of the community and those admitted to organizations did not know how to give clear expression and carry out their special tasks as women. Where a middle class still lived in that era—albeit not in tradition, but in memory—what was deemed important was bobbed hair, a slim figure, and a sort of educational fad that I would like to call weekend *sekhel* (intellect). But just as with the utmost effort and great sacrifices of chocolate and potatoes women became thin and remained fat in the wrong places, so too did lectures and study groups make them clever in the wrong places, while in the other places they did not remain clever.

In an overall view, the exceptions are readily acknowledged, particularly where material concerns cast shadows and many women matured to quiet heroism. These invisible and inaudible women should be thanked for their attitude and dignity.

More far-reaching than the previously described events and formations—all portrayed from the standpoint of the life of women—is what the Jewish woman of our time accomplished as an educator and did not accomplish as an educator. The charge of failure, it must be made perfectly clear, does not apply to the woman alone, who is, after all, an educational product of the man (I wish to mention only in passing the consequences when a woman has no money at her disposal besides housekeeping money). The charge applies to Jews in general, and in the present context to German Jews in particular.

Ever since the influence of the lapidary commandments of the Jewish educator and pedagogue Moses lost the force of law in the life of the Jews, the moral atmosphere of the Jews has dissolved into nebulous form. There is no more education; there are no more educators. Every impropriety, every indecency, every immorality, every inanity, every immoderation, every lack of taste, every lack of tact, every inaction, every unscrupulous act is explained historically and psychologically. An explanation is turned into an excuse. Tradition is not revealed as a duty but is displayed in a cowardly and comfortable fashion as a backdrop of scenery. There are no demands, not of the man, not of the woman, not on husband and wife, not on children, on youth, whom one spoils instead of educates.

To educate, beyond the literal definition, means to demand: first of oneself, then of others. To demand with the goal of doing no wrong, tolerating no wrong, that is, putting defamation *in the wrong*. To teach to distinguish truthfulness and falsity, to see and cultivate beauty in nature and to practice art and love, which loves to the point of hate what is *wrong* and not loveable—all in the understanding, lenient-severe strictness of a divinely directed path.

"The path is everything, the destination is nothing."

People lament that there is no "communal idea," no ideal as an educational postulate for the youth! Is it then not a duty for a Jewish man and a Jewish woman to be upright, committed Jewish Jews, to represent world-bearing commandments in the world? Is that not a postulate, not an ideal to which it is worth devoting one's life? And particularly in the diaspora, for us in Germany, to whose German culture, *tarbut germanyah* we owe so endlessly much, so much that it would be stupidity and ingratitude to want to break away from it?

We could not even if we tried.

At this point, another word should be said about what today is understood by the watchword *attitude*. Though the distance from the unknown woman of the last two decades is not yet great enough to distinguish true contours from chance outgrowths, that is, to provide a completely accurate and just picture, the fast pace of the modern era nonetheless permits us, without becoming too superficial, to recall in the context of these comments the "attitude" of the Jewish woman. She is not blameless; she is not guiltless in the judgment and condemnation that has been visited on the Jewish community. Political and intellectual liberation have not led the Jewish woman to remain aware in all situations of her dignity and duty in narrower as well as broader circles—especially the careless woman sins. In questions of doubt, of uncertainty, the decision must always fall on the side of humility, restraint, quiet, and simplicity in appearance and life conduct.

We are responsible for each other, regardless of where the individual stands. We are bound to a common fate, and thus for us German Jews came the third fissure, the terrible blow on April 1, 1933. How it has struck us! How will we withstand it, how will we withstand the defamation, the misery?

By suicide of the individual? By suicide of the community? By obliteration of the memory of the past? By lament and renunciation, by migration and change of occupation, by waiting, by philosophy or frivolity?

May everyone, man and woman, out of their weakness or their strength, out of the depths and the great law of their fate—our fate—do what they must. Only we Jews should remember that from everywhere in the world, from the diaspora—and Palestine too is *golus* and diaspora—we can see the summit of Mount Sinai.

Translated from the German, edited by the volume editors.

Other works by Pappenheim: *Zur Lage der jüdischen Bevölkerung in Galizien* (1904); *Sisyphus Arbeit* (1924).

Viktor Alter

1890–1943

Viktor (Wiktor) Alter was born in Mława, Poland, and moved to Warsaw at the turn of the twentieth century. After studying engineering in Belgium, and fostering Bundist and socialist ideas there, Alter returned to Warsaw in 1912 and continued organizing for the Bund. After a short sojourn in postrevolutionary Russia, he returned to Poland to continue his work for the Bund, being disenchanted with the possibilities of collaborating with Bolshevism. Alter was a central figure in the Jewish trade unionist movement, and was influential, along with Henryk Erlich, in the Bund's decision to become a member of the Labor and Socialist International. Like Erlich, Alter was a victim of volatile and deadly Soviet politics. In September 1939, he was arrested by the Soviet police and was interrogated for months, sentenced to death in July 1941. He was then released in September 1941 and became one of the organizers of the Jewish Anti-Fascist Committee, only to be rearrested in December of the same year. He was executed by firing squad in 1943.

The Source of Our Belief
1937

A Good Catholic must believe that the Pope is infallible. A good communist must believe that Stalin is never mistaken. A good Bundist can and ought to ask himself at all times whether his party (together with himself) is on the proper course.

Every Bundist has the right to criticize the policy of his party. But the severest critic is reality itself. And let us, indeed, in the light of experience, verify the correctness or incorrectness of the fundamental political principles that have determined the policy of the Bund during the past twenty years. These twenty years constitute the second period of our party's history—from the victory of the Russian Revolution to the present day.

Unity

When the epidemic of splits in the labor movement erupted at the time of the emergence of the Comintern, the Bund, after some brief waverings, came down solidly on the ground of unity. It seemed to be a hopeless position at the time, when both the reformists and the communists contended that the split was unavoidable and—productive. The Bund adhered to the small minority in the labor movement that regarded the split as a misfortune and a source of weakness and setbacks.

And today? After the bitter experiences of twenty years, the whole labor movement has arrived at the conviction that the most important guarantee of success in the proletarian struggle is—unity. The supporters, on principle, of splitting have grown silent. And although unity has not yet been realized, the Bundist idea of unity has already been victorious. In this area, we were in the vanguard; life has justified our position. . . .

Splitting was and remains harmful. But unity can also vary. There is unity on the Stalin model, where intolerance and compulsion prevail with respect to every ideological minority. It is a unity that leads inevitably to new splits. And there is unity of the Bundist type, in which freedom of thought is coupled with discipline in the performance of deeds. This is the only loyal, fraternal, and lasting unity.

Democracy and Dictatorship

We have always been adherents of democracy. But we oppose those reformist supporters of democracy for whom parliamentarism and universal suffrage are sacred objects. We always counterpose true social democracy to formal political democracy, with its class character. . . .

Life has vindicated our position. How dearly the German workers are now paying for the reformist fetishism of formal democracy and for not having dared, when possessing the power, to infuse the democracy with a vigorous class content. And how dearly the masses in the Soviet Union and the actual communists there are paying for the character of the Soviet government, which has transgressed proletarian democracy. The autocracy of Stalin, drenched in blood, is a conse-

quence, after all, of the denial of democracy in the communist movement.

Hence we remain faithful to our position regardless of the fact that it is far from being recognized by the whole labor movement; to wit: 1) against personal dictatorship, including the Stalin kind; for proletarian democracy; 2) against formal democracy, which makes peace with the system of social class-oppression; for proletarian democracy that links political democracy to a radical transformation of the existing order. . . .

National Culture and Internationalism

For years we were criticized in the following terms: You are nationalists because you foster the national traits of the Jewish masses and consequently resist their joining forces with the non-Jewish population. We responded: There is no other way for the masses of various nationalities to join together in a dignified fashion than by building their national cultures. And life has shown that the Bundist path to nationalism is the only one that can attract not only individuals or small groups, but indeed broad masses. It is the only path where internationalism is coupled with human dignity.

The charge has been leveled against us that we wish to cram the Jewish masses into their backward and impoverished culture, thereby closing off their access to the modern and rich culture of the surrounding peoples. Life has demonstrated that the creative powers of the Jewish masses can best find expression precisely through their own cultural upsurge. Which is why the Bund, indeed, became one of the co-builders of the modern Jewish-socialist culture. And it is no coincidence, after all, that with respect to this question, all tendencies in Jewish proletarian life have adopted the position of the Bund.

The charge was leveled against us on the part of the bourgeois world that the Bund, while opposing traditional Jewish attitudes, customs, and ideals, jeopardizes the national survival of the Jewish people. If national survival is equivalent to nationalism, we are proud of our struggle against it. We have shown for a fact that it is possible to pour into the national form of Jewish culture the sincere international content that spiritually unites the Jewish masses with the militant, international proletarian army.

The Bund preaches to the Jewish masses both internationalism and the need for a feeling of personal and national dignity. We question the ostensible *mitzvah* of becoming similar to other peoples, just as we have denied the alleged socialist "theory" that in the socialist society everyone will be identical with everyone else.

But we—the Jewish labor movement—unwilling to artificially change our skin, have simultaneously endeavored to become better and more attractive. Together with the international labor movement, we strive within our milieu to lift both the individual and the group to a higher level in the material as well as the spiritual sense.

And the results of these exertions prove that the path is a correct one, and that the labor has been not in vain.

Conclusions

Of course we haven't exhausted all the fundamental principles of our movement. But the above-mentioned examples are sufficient to convince any objective person that the Bund, in general and on the whole, is able correctly to delineate the line of its policy. Our ideological position has passed the test under fire during the past twenty years with great success. This explains why the Bund, despite tremendous difficulties and the attacks of all its adversaries and foes, is today so influential and internally solid. It explains why the Bund has such power of attraction for Jewish working-class youth, which, like all youth, seeks a clear and honest answer to all the social questions that torment it. It explains why the Bund has celebrated its fortieth anniversary in a mood of faith in itself and its future.

Translated by Samuel Portnoy.

Other works by Alter: *Grund-printsipien fun der proletarisher kooperatsye* (1921); *Tsu der yidn-frage in Poyln* (1925); *Der sotsyalizm in kamf* (1927); *Gdy socjaliści dojdą do władzy . . . : (pierwszy etap rewolucji społecznej)* (1934); *Antysemityzm gospodarczy w świetle cyfr* (1937); *Człowiek w społeczeństwie* (1938).

Henryk Erlich

Manifesto of the General Jewish Workers' Union (Bund) in Poland
1937

Adopted at the Anniversary Congress in Warsaw, November 13, 1937

To the Jewish working men and working women.
To the rank-and-file of the Jewish people and working intellectuals!

At a difficult time, at an hour of destiny in your lives, the Bund turns to you.

There are people who say that the crisis is passed, that the situation has improved and has even become favorable. It is surely so for the wealthy, whether Jews or non-Jews; but not for you. The worker continues to be plagued by unemployment or low wages. The artisan and small tradesman live in poverty and want. The upcoming generation of workers has no prospect of employment, and the same calamity torments the working intellectual!

Yours is a hard and bitter struggle for economic survival, while at the same time all of the dark forces of the country have pressed down upon you. They wish to destroy you, to exterminate you, to drive you from Poland. All the hardships from which Poland is suffering stem from you, they say. All the afflictions from which other nations suffer are supposed to emanate from you as well! And here is the proof: Jews are being persecuted in Germany and Rumania; Jews are being beaten in Palestine. And the peddlers of venom, the incendiaries and cannibals in Polish society, do everything they can to poison your lives, to inflame in the country an infernal fire of hatred toward you.

Is it necessary to remind you of the frightful devastation which this fire has already succeeded in bringing about up to now? Need one total up the victims, enumerate the losses, make a survey of the ruins? No, it is not necessary.

Przytyk, Mińsk-Mazowiecki, Wysokie, Częstochowa, Brześć—these aren't all; they are merely the most painful stages along the road of martyrdom of the Jewish masses in Poland during the past year and a half.

But the cannibals continue to incite. They aren't satisfied with the boycott directed at the Jewish worker and working intellectual; nor are they satisfied with the economic extermination drive against the petty Jewish laborer. Physical force is not enough for them; they desire to degrade the human being in you, to trample upon your feeling of self-worth, to turn you into pariahs devoid of legal rights and dignity. For Jewish students they've introduced a ghetto in the universities; and their request is . . . to broaden the ghetto for the Jews to encompass the whole country. They fiercely demand exceptional laws for Jews on the model of Hitler Germany. They desire to place us beyond the bounds of social and political life, outside the law. They wish to deprive us not only of the right to live but also of the possibility of self-defense and struggle.

What Is the Way Out?

Jewish workers and common folk: Not a single one of you has asked during these dark days: What shall be done? Is there a way out of the situation, and where should one seek it?

The Jewish bourgeois parties attempt to provide answers to these painful questions while they themselves bear a great deal of responsibility for the present condition of the Jewish masses. As a part of the bourgeoisie in the country, they share in the responsibility for the economic misery of the common people in Poland. And as Jewish politicians, they have bowed all their lives before every holder of power and have been prepared to sell out the interests of the Jewish masses to all of them. At one time they concluded *ugodes* [unprincipled deals and agreements] with the Endeks. Later they placed themselves at the service of the Pilsudski forces. As recently as September 1935 they urged the Jewish masses on to the ballot boxes in order to elect to the Sejm the greatest anti-Semites. And to this day their representatives are ensconced in the present Sejm and Senate, bodies boycotted by the workers and peasants.

They have a simple answer to the questions that torment you.

Some of them—the zealous religionists, the Orthodox, declare:

"It is God's punishment. Jews committed sins. Hence the need to atone, to plead for mercy, to engage in fasting."

In short, it is not they who've sinned, but—you. Yet everyone knows, of course, that it is the poor, the needy, who suffer most from anti-Semitism. And if anti-Semitism is God's punishment for sins committed, then how account for the fact that the most bitter punishment has been meted out precisely to those who spend their days in heavy toil; who collapse from hunger thrice daily; who don't even have time to sin not only in deed, but even in thought. Why is God's punishing hand felt least of all precisely by idlers and the rich?

And the "secular" leaders—the Zionists—have their answer to your questions. They are bankrupt not only here but also there—in Palestine. They know already today, just as certainly as we, that Zionism is not a solution to the Jewish question. But they hold stubbornly to their position, and repeat along with all the Jew-haters:

"That's how it is; there is a law of some kind: 'gentiles' must hate Jews. There is no alternative. It is necessary to flee from here."

And in order to win the support of the overlords for the dissipated Zionist dreams, they approach those who are responsible for making our lives so bitter and declare:

"Correct, there is really insufficient bread for everyone in Poland. Correct, there is really a surplus of Jews in the country. So help us take the Jews to Palestine."

To which we reply:

Jewish workers and common folk: the answer to the questions that are tormenting you is an altogether different one. But if you wish to grasp it, you must briefly step out of the confines of your Jewish misery.

Look about you and you will see—the Jews are not the only ones who are suffering. The overwhelming majority in the country, whether Poles, Ukrainians, Jews, or others, is suffering from the economic crisis, from the difference between rich and poor. In the Polish, White Russian, or Ukrainian village, people live in a dismal state. Millions of others are scarcely able to eke out a daily existence. Hundreds of thousands of Polish workers are in deep despair under conditions of joblessness and, along with the landless peasants and the unemployed Jewish workers, exploring the possibility of migrating, of being able to earn by the sweat of their brows a piece of bread in the coal mines of Belgium and France or in the distant fields of Brazil or Paraguay.

Shift your gaze beyond the borders of Poland toward the wide world and you will see:

Seventy million people are languishing under the heavy boot of Hitlerism. Not only the 500,000 Jews—the whole German people has been transformed into a nation of slaves. After four-and-a-half years of Hitler rule, even fresh bread is an item of luxury in Germany. And instead of butter, the common people of Germany are fed guns.

Forty million Italians have been turned into a footstool for the "great" Mussolini. The Italian workers and peasants have long forgotten what eating a full meal is like. Which is why Mussolini is hurling their children from one battlefield to another; which is why Mussolini is calling on Italian women to bear children without letup so that there will be no lack of soldiers for his coming wars.

And just as in Germany and Italy, millions of working people in other, smaller countries which have become areas of reactions are sunk in privation and bondage. [. . .]

The Jewish worker grasped the message of the Bund. While the Jewish bourgeois elements sang words of blessing for the bloody Tsar; while the Jewish clericals preached humility as the response to all the evil decrees, and the Zionists promised the tsarist ministers, people dripping with workers' blood and Jewish blood, to lead the Jews out of Russia—Jewish workers, under the red banners of the Bund, fought for freedom in the front ranks of the revolution; the Bundist self-defense groups, with guns in hand, bravely defended the Jewish masses against the wild bands of tsarist *pogromshchiki*.

The Bund transformed the obsequious Jewish working man into a class-conscious proletarian, into a socialist, into a revolutionist.

That remained the spirit of the General Jewish Workers' Bund in Poland. [...]

The Heat of Struggle

[...] Then came the catastrophe. Germany was inundated by the filthy waves of Hitlerism, and their poisonous foam spread out far beyond the borders of Germany. Polish nationalism raised its head and grew frenzied. A terrible panic seized large parts of Jewish society. Stampeding emigrationism celebrated victories; and as always in times of political twilight, Zionism gave expression to its jubilation. As for the Communists, the political line, indeed, the whole ideology of communism, collapsed. A large section of the fellow-travelers of the labor movement began to waver, and together with it ... more than one socialist.

The Bund found itself in something like a besieged fortress. But the banner of consistent socialism did not for one moment grow shaky in its hand. Baited by Polish nationalism and scoffed at by Jewish nationalism, the Bund never grew tired of calling upon the Jewish masses; "Do not succumb to despair; do not surrender to any feeling of panic!" More than ever, the slogan remains valid:

"Ours is a life-and-death struggle against fascism, against every form of nationalism, and for socialism!"

Today, as always, and despite everything, the slogan remains in force:

"Salvation lies here and nowhere else, in untiring struggle for freedom, hand in hand with the working masses of Poland!"

We persevered. It took some time and the tide, slowly but surely, started to ebb. The working masses throughout the world gradually began to take hold of themselves. In Jewish society the sobering-up process developed more swiftly. The dream of Zion manifestly proceeded to come to an end. And with each passing day, the complete senselessness and criminality of the domestic policy conducted in Poland for years by the Jewish bourgeois parties became more glaring.

Then came Przytyk. It was a surge of electricity passing through Jewish society and shocking it from top to bottom. And when the Bund, in response to Przytyk and to the whole policy of which Przytyk was the symbol, proclaimed the general protest strike of March 17, 1936 and mobilized in that protest a significant part of the Polish working class and the whole proletarian public of the country, the overwhelming majority of the Jewish people, in a powerful, incomparable demonstration of struggle, responded to the call of the Bund.

Since then the Jewish population of both large and small cities of Poland has more than once found itself in grave danger. It was always the Bund which strengthened and encouraged.

And when the door was opened not long ago for a Nuremberg law in Poland through the edict concerning the Jewish benches in the universities, it was the Bund which demonstrated also this time, in the magnificent mass display of October 19 of this year, the readiness of the Jewish masses to defend their rights with tooth and nail. [...]

After Forty Years

[...] Therefore, abandon the hopeless and swampy roads of Jewish nationalism and forsake your passivity if you've hitherto been standing on the sidelines! And let all of us together—all the toilers among the Jewish people—constitute one great force which shall be capable, at the decisive moment, of throwing its weight onto the scale of events.

At this solemn hour, during the days commemorating the date when the Jewish working class broke down the walls of the spiritual ghetto and moved into the historic arena as an independent political force, we call upon you, Jewish working men and working women, Jewish toilers and laboring intellectuals, to enlist in the struggle—

Against anti-Semitism, against all manner of human hatred, against one's own and foreign nationalism!

Against fascism in all its forms!

Against capitalism!

For a free and democratic Poland!

For complete equality of all citizens!

For the right of free national-cultural development of the Jewish masses!

For a civic coexistence of all nationalities in Poland and the world!

For a workers' and peasants' government!

For socialism!

NOTE

Words in brackets appear in the original translation.

Translated by Samuel Portnoy.

Anna Rozental

1879–1940

Bundist leader Anna Rozental was born into a wealthy family in Volkovisk, Belarus, and raised at her family's rural estate, where she became conscious of class differences. She trained and worked as a dentist and grew increasingly politically active. Arrested for her Bundist activities, Rozental was exiled to Siberia in 1902 and returned to Vilna after the Russian revolution. In 1917, she became secretary of the Bund Central Committee, and also lived in St. Petersburg, Moscow, and Kiev. Rozental promoted day care and Yiddish schools and was elected to the Vilna City Council. Arrested when the Soviets entered that city, she died in prison.

Female Figures in the Bund
1937

Women have always played a noticeable role in the Bund movement. Even at the dawn of the Jewish labor movement they were distinguished by their number and activity. The mass movement in Vilna began with the strikes of female tobacco workers, stocking makers, and others. The passive female masses were roused and individual female workers proved capable activists and occupied responsible, dignified posts in the movement's leadership. Marie Zhaludski, Tsivie Hurwitz, Mirl Goldman, and others were strong personalities with sharp and clear heads, with ardent temperaments.

And a curious thing: the illegal movement attracted female activists more so than today, when the movement has emerged from the underground. How is this to be explained? Do female Bundists have a distinct inclination towards illegality? Surely not. There are deeper reasons.

Illegal work demanded a lot of faith, devotion, self-sacrifice. To work in a secret publishing house, dis-

tribute literature, appear at labor assemblies, ignite the masses with ardent feeling of enthusiasm—these were the tasks of the Bund's female activists. The legal movement demands speakers, writers, political activists, and wide-ranging organizers. Life has not prepared women of this kind in great numbers. Gradually, with effort, the masses of women are adapting to the new forms of the movement.

In the solemn days of our anniversary, I wish to talk about the past and cite the glorious female figures with which our party was so rich. A whole line of such women runs through my memory and it is hard to decide which of them should be immortalized in the pages of the anniversary edition. I wish to select those who were emblematic, representative, who embodied a whole school of thought. And may their sisters forgive me, both those who have passed away and those who are still living, if my choices are not objective: personal relations must influence my selection.

In chronological order, there proceeds out before my eyes a quiet, unassuming girl—Taybetshke Oshmianska—later Mrs. Zeldov. She came from Wilkomir, Kovno province—a city from which Avrom Mutnik, Sender Zeldov-Niemanski, Roza Levit, Sonia Leibowitz, and others also came. In that circle she became a fighter. She arrived in Vilna at the very beginning of the movement. Starved. Having educated herself, she gives workers lessons in reading and writing in the late evening hours, when they are freed from the fourteen- to sixteen-hour workday. She is always occupied with the movement, carries around literature to disperse, houses the storehouse at her own home, is constantly with workers, agitates, encourages, communicates with the center, relays decrees.

Such girls were in every city. Who remembers them? These are the unknown soldiers, whose names history did not even register.

Taybetshke died in 1935, in Leningrad. In her last years she worked as a dentist in a textile factory. Held the same wholehearted relations with female workers, who used to confide all their secrets and pour their hearts out to her. She remained a Bundist until her last breath.

Ludwig Börne exclaims in his article on Poland: "Hats off! I am going to speak of the Polish women!" In the Bund, people don't love fervor and tall phrases, but perhaps Börne's words would fit this name: Esther Riskind.

A legend was woven around her life and tragic death. A Hasidic daughter from Liady, the seat of the Hasidic Shneerson rabbis, a descendant of their dynasty, she was brought up as a kosher Hasidic daughter. At the age of sixteen—betrothed to a Hasid. On the eve of the wedding she runs away from home, arrives in Kharkov, learns a trade, and falls in with the circle of the propagandists, which was managed by Pavel Rozental-Anman, at that time still a student of medicine.

When Pavel settles in Białystok, she goes there as well and takes her first steps in the labor movement. Her entire physical appearance is original and enchanting. One is immediately struck by it—a tall, slender girl. B. Vladek writes about her:

> Esther was dark as a gypsy woman. Her eyes burned with a moving fire. Her dark countenance was set in a frame of pitch-black hair. And when she spoke, it seemed to me that she knew something more, something deep, secret, hidden.[1]

From the first day of her arrival in Białystok, she enters the movement heart and soul. A person with a strong intellect, with fine literary and aesthetic taste, she merges with the working masses. She soon becomes especially loved by the workers, lives a common life with them. She imparts Hasidic fervor to the movement. From Białystok, she travels to Warsaw, where she finds a broad field of work and can also satisfy her literary and artistic inclinations. She approaches the circle of young writers who gathered around [I. L.] Peretz. There, too, she becomes loved and respected. Avrom Reisen dedicates enthusiastic pages to her in his memoirs. Here is what he writes of his first acquaintance with her:

> Esther, a well-known Bundist, who around 1902 had just recently come to Warsaw, made an impression in our circles. . . . Before I met her myself, Nomberg told me of an interesting socialist activist, who possessed great intelligence and even had a refined taste for literature.[2]

In Warsaw she is arrested several times and sent off to Siberia. She escapes abroad. At the first thunders of the revolution of 1905, she returns. She works in Vilna, in Białystok, where she meets her dreadful and senseless death (August 1905).

As always and everywhere, her position is amid the crowd—in the most perilous places. At the exchange, on Surazher Street, the police are whipping up the crowd. The anarchists throw a bomb at a police patrol so clumsily that it strikes Esther and rips to shreds the most beautiful and glorious person that the labor movement had produced.

She left in everyone an impression of something violent and radiant, which had passed over the dark labor movement and was suddenly extinguished.

The female figure I will now present is perhaps not so dazzling and colorful, but no less deep and appealing, and her fate no less tragic. This is our beloved Rosa Levit-Frida.

If my lines should miraculously reach her, let her not be offended by my presuming to write about her. But miracles do not happen in our time and this grants me courage and boldness for the description.

Who of the elder generation of Bundists did not know Frida and who did not work with her? A few biographical notes:

She is from Wilkomir. Stems from wealthy parents, great aristocrats. The one daughter among several sons, she is raised and pampered as a cherished only daughter. She travels abroad to study and there she comes to be a ripe revolutionary. Despite her upbringing, she is a people's person, rapidly grows accustomed to life in the labor environment.

At that time, personal relationships with the workers played a colossal role. She is very gifted and full of revolutionary zest. She knows Yiddish well and writes proclamations, articles in the illegal press, translates. In 1907, in Vilna, she publishes *Der shnaider,* the organ of the needle-workers. Still, today, one cannot read the proclamations that came from beneath her pen without excitement, as, for example: "55 Casualties" published . . . after the trial of the followers of the Romanovs.

She is a good speaker. Her speeches inflame because she, herself, always burns with the holy fire of belief and enthusiasm. She works in all the great centers of the Bund movement. She knows people in Warsaw, Łódź, Vilna. She works as if intoxicated, runs from one assembly to another; nothing is too hard for her. She doesn't eat, doesn't drink, today spends the night here, tomorrow there. She is so busy, so absorbed in the movement, that she cannot, organically, think about conspiracy. Her briefcase is always full of little papers. Her whole being is so classically revolutionary that she immediately attracts the eyes of the spies and is often captured. As soon as she is released, she is instantly on the job somewhere once again. Her strongest defining trait is that she constantly strives for the most dangerous positions.

The revolutions of 1917 found her in Russia. From the year 1921 on, she is never free of Soviet prisons and exile. She remained a convinced Bundist. Such people do not bow.

(Comrade Leybetshke [Berman] gives a wonderful depiction of Comrade Frida in his book *In loyf fun yorn*.)

I want to end with a female figure of a different cut. A worker with a sharp intellect, a great deal of knowledge and of broad political scope. This is the one so unknown to many of us: Sora Fuchs.

A worker, a stocking maker, she educates herself. Travels abroad in 1909 (Switzerland, Germany), where she works in a factory and studies as well, becomes acquainted with the German labor movement. Returns with great intellectual baggage and a lot of experience. She works in the great centers—such as Łódź, Warsaw. In the war years we see her in southern Russia. The revolution sends her out to the front. At the tenth conference of the Bund, in April 1917, just after the revolution, she gives a lecture.

At the Jewish convention in Kiev of the same year, she is the only woman among hundreds of delegates, and how great is the terror and discomfit of the rabbis, when she appears on the stage! The petite, unassuming girl stands calm and self-assured, and she attracts the general attention of the audience with her logical and to-the-point presentation. She manages the election campaign for the city councils in Ukraine. She appears at assemblies attended by thousands and soon becomes enormously popular in Kiev, Berdichev, and other cities.

The Bolsheviks' October uprising cuts her activity short. She has a different view of the course of the revolution. In December 1918, she writes in a letter to a friend: "I do not imagine any social democracy without democracy and it becomes awful at the thought of what sort of a long hard road is still in store and if the S.D. will be able to begin anew."

She is sincere and straightforward. With disgust she observes how people rapidly conform, how they change their convictions, like gloves. She feels alone and useless in life. In the same letter she writes: "I know that people with opinions and spirits such as these will now be stoned or (in the best case scenario) spat upon. I know that there is no place among the living for people of my type, they are superfluous. . . ."

The last blow was her arrest. She, the revolutionary from head to toe, is accused—of "Counter-Revolution." She did not have any personal life; she devoted everything to the labor movement. Without it she couldn't

live and on 24 June 1919 she went to Kiev and threw herself into the Dnieper.

So lived and fought our elder generation of female Bundists.

NOTES

1. B. Vladek, *In lebn un shafn: Esther Riskind* (p. 111).

2. Avrom Reisen, *Epizodn fun mayn lebn*, second part, 64–65.

Translated by Maia Evrona.

Chaim Lieberman
1890–1963

Born in Ukraine, Chaim Lieberman was a prolific Yiddish essayist and literary critic. Lieberman wrote a regular column in the Yiddish daily *Yiddishes tageblat* and, as an active Labor Zionist, was a leading figure in the establishment of the secular Yiddish schools of the Jewish National Worker's Alliance (Yidish-natsyonaler arbeter farband) in the United States. In the 1930s, Lieberman become an Orthodox Jew and joined the religious Zionist movement, from which vantage point he began to attack left-wing Yiddish writers. He was a prominent critic of Sholem Asch's trilogy of Christological novels, which caused controversy in the American Jewish community.

In the Valley of Death
1938

1

Human wisdom has limits—stupidity has none.

God created a world with gifts and blessings for all: earth and water, sun and air in plenty, rye and wheat in abundance, a potato for everyone, a roof over every head, and thread enough to wrap around each body several times. God is with the people, if only the people were with God, too!

But the people turned the world they had received into a valley of death. [. . .] We are sixteen million Jews dispersed all over the earth; a web of sixteen million pairs of tear-soaked eyes, not a single one of them dry. [. . .]

Hatred has taken over the earth. Go and see for yourself how they live and die, and see our fate among them.

It happened in those days when the Nazi hordes descended upon Austria like locusts. They took the Jews, the finest and the best, the greatest Jewish sages, and deployed them to clean the sewers and toilets of Vienna. Just as in Egypt we were ordered to make bricks without straw, in Vienna we were ordered to clean toilets without equipment. The gentle hands that had woven the silver threads of Austria's fortune, the tender fingers that had spun its finest spirit were forcibly dipped in Austria's excrement and soaked in Nazi urine during Austria's last hour.

This is how Austria came to an end: the last spark of an empire has been flushed down the toilet, and a new empire rose amidst the stench. [. . .]

Whatever tragic and terrible can possibly happen to human beings already happened in that fateful hour in Vienna, only the Viennese did not realize it. They applauded the torturers and laughed at the tortured. Great was the shame.

But whose shame was it? Throughout their history Jews have known how to dissolve the enemy's worst anger, and how to turn around his slender arrow mid-air, back toward his own heart. Jews played a trick on their tormenters, a trick the tormentors may not have grasped at all. History, however, will understand it one day. They went to do lowly work dressed in fine Sabbath clothes; some even wore *talesim*. They cleaned toilets wearing talis and tefillin.

It was not about the work itself. There is nothing shameful about washing sewers and cleaning latrines. Work is work. It was the intention that mattered, the intention to shame and disgrace.

Jews accepted the work, but they turned around the intention. They turned shame into honor and disgrace into sanctity.

How easily spirit can transform the world! Creating spirit, however, is difficult. . . .

I would even say that this was *kiddush ha-shem*, the sanctification of God's holy name, if our generation were not atheistic. God's name can be sanctified anywhere, be it on the stake or in the sewer. His honor dwells all over the world. But maybe we should forge a new word to describe martyrdom in the age of nonbelievers: *kiddush ha-adam*, the sanctification of man. With their simple acts Jews proclaimed: *man cannot be humiliated!* [. . .]

2

[. . .] There are all kinds of nations in the world. Some embrace an idea and others do not. We are a peo-

ple embraced by an idea. [. . .] That is how Jews have always understood their destiny: the Torah existed before the Jewish people, and the Torah chose us. [. . .]

We are the product of an idea. An idea grabbed us by the hair and hurled us from one millennium to the next. We live within the heart of a miracle, enchanted. Miraculously, our forefathers kindled an inextinguishable fire in our hearts. The fire of Moses' burning bush smolders in our blood eternally. The flames rise up to the sky—no rain can extinguish them, and the wind will only fan them. And just as the prophet had to follow the divine calling, we cannot resist the mystical impulse. We had prophets because the entire people are prophetic. The entire people pushes somewhere, pulls—where? [. . .]

European culture with all its knowledge, beauty, and Christianity has been sitting in a house of cards that was toppled over by the first wind from the right. Its roof was blown off, and the rust was exposed. Its foundation rattled, and a dunghill was revealed. It did not stream forth from the fountain of the soul. It was just a little bit of spirit inlaid loosely in clay. When the clay was cracked, the spirit escaped. Their culture consisted of nothing but empty works, full of air; their morality—a matter of fashion. Books, books, books, newspapers, universities, churches, priests, and intellectuals—but it was all just a show, a theater performance, where conscience did not even get standing room. And even this was too much for them! "When I hear the word 'culture' I immediately reach for my revolver," said a Nazi leader. [. . .]

We brought a sacred book with sovereign grandeur, beauty, and marvel, philosophically the purest, the most human and most noble, clear as a children's story, sincere like God's heart, fresh as if it were written today. And what did they do with it? They took the true book and traded it for false, pagan casuistry; they stirred up the pure well and muddied its water. Our burning flame became ash in their hands. This is what they eat, this is what they drink, and this is what they live from. If you close the Bible, their homes will turn dark. If you take away the churches—what are they left with? Bourses and brothels, garrisons and prisons. Every chapel and every cathedral is a monument to our misunderstood genius. And yet they have decreed: no Jewish book, and no Jewish understanding! [. . .]

They think they serve God, but, in fact, they blaspheme him every day. Just listen to how they pray: "Forgive our sins, as we forgive those who sin against us." As do we—so should you! God should learn from man!

God should draw moral lessons from [Father] Coughlin and [General] Franco! [. . .]

Christians are two-faced creatures, and their rear face is toward Christianity.

That is why they received a terrible punishment, measure for measure. They played in masks, so they are now forced to wear masks—gas masks. A gas mask for each face. And when they put on the gas mask, they take the form of some wild, primordial monster. And this, in fact, is their true form in their civilization.

There are four great religions in the world and five continents. Of the four brothers Christianity is the crook, and of the five sisters Europe is the whore. The crook and the whore formed a diabolic union whose fruit is Fascism.

And when the son rose up against his father, the father was terrified; Christianity tried to reject Fascism but to no avail: it is his own son, his own flesh and blood. Christianity had waged war, blessed war, nurtured war, and was raised on war. And when, due to wartime shortage, they take down the church bells and melt them into cannons—that is when the Christian world reaches its most perfect harmony. [. . .]

Christianity has blood on its hands. It is rooted in blood, and it is drawn to blood. It likes wounds, it likes death. In every church the image of a murder occupies the most prominent place of honor. Jesus Christ with his five wounds is the center of the cult. Every day when people look up to the image of the Crucified their eyes are bathed in blood. In the midst of their deepest devotion they are immersed in human agony. Their most important dogma is redemption through death and their greatest sacrament eating God's flesh. [. . .]

Nazism has not invented anything new. Is it even capable of thinking? Nazism took everything from the Church's writings. It was the Church that declared us inferior, burned our books, then burned us and blessed the flames with an "Amen."

The crazy idea that everything is the Jews' fault comes from the Church, too. Remember Amalek! Remember the dogma that the world cannot come to final redemption and happiness as long as Jews are Jews and do not become Christians.

The fruit of Christianity's tree has finally ripened. The beastly nature of man has been revealed, just as a snake slithers from its skin. But humans are worse than beasts. Animals kill their prey before they devour them, but our flesh is torn to shreds while we are still alive. [. . .]

10

[. . .] Let someone point out where in all our literatures, in all the various languages, any evidence that we harbor hate for anyone. [. . .] We are a people with a long history and a short memory. We do not want to remember anything bad about people. Just imagine if we did want to hold on to all the bad! We would have to put a lock on the world and throw away the key. [. . .]

Did we bring up our suffering to Spain in its hour of need? The same way we will forget Germany, too. Germany forgot what compassion was. But the time will come when Germany will cry out for compassion, and we will be the first to respond before anyone else. [. . .]

Translated by Vera Szabó.

Other works by Lieberman: *Dos problem fun der idisher ertsihung* (1912); *Sholem Ash un kristentum: an entfer af zayneh misyonerishe shriftn* (1950).

Shmuel Niger

About Yiddish Literature
1938

There is a general rule that the environment makes the art. If you know the economic and social structure of a period you will also know the ideological and artistic superstructure. Now economically and socially the period which began with the Russian pogroms of 1881 was a period of suffering and misery. Where did the rays of light come from that illuminate the pages of the Yiddish literature of that period?

My answer is to put another question: Where do they come from now? For the darkness that surrounds us now is blacker and heavier than fifty years ago. For then we at least had illusions—and there were also genuine hopes. They strengthened our hands, and helped us to carry our load of troubles. "The western frontier," said an official Russian statement of the time, "is open." So people left Russia, and went to America. America was the Noah's Ark in that deluge. There were also dreams of going to the Land of Israel. Now all frontiers are closed, and the people behind them feel that they are in a prison, doomed to die there. We appeal to the conscience of the world; but the world is helpless or indifferent. We have our own ideas and plans, but nothing we can do can get out those masses of Jews who live behind those closed frontiers, without hope of escape.

We haven't even the consolation we had in times of former disasters, that these were the birth-pangs of Messiah. We have had such bitter disappointments that we no longer believe—and what are Jews without belief?

We are eaten up with doubt. And how can people live with doubt? So we envy our brothers of the eighties. There were some then too who despaired of "social progress" and of civilization generally. So they turned to the hope of national regeneration in the ancient Jewish land. But not all despaired. There were many who still believed in the realization of social justice for all. Both trends placed their hopes in the coming of salvation, and both were punished for it. Whether the ideal is Zionism or Socialism it cannot at this moment save the masses of Jews in Eastern Europe. Neither of them can now strike out of our life the vital sparks that set on fire the Yiddish literature of the nineteenth century.

No, there are no blazing social ideas in our present Jewish surroundings. Unless it is the Chalutzim ideal, which is intended however only for a small minority. The Yiddish literature in Soviet Russia is in a happier state. It has no need of its own well-springs from which to draw inspiration and enthusiasm. It has big Soviet plans to get excited about. Every five years a new plan. And the writers get optimistic, and sing songs of exultation. Pessimism is not allowed. Despair is forbidden. In the Soviet countries you are ordered to be happy. And who knows, perhaps those Yiddish Soviet writers really are happy. Perhaps they do believe, as they tell us they do, that "Forever gone is the sorrowful eye." I have no ground for suspecting Itzik Feffer's honesty. And he, like his colleagues, doesn't stop singing:

> Generations lived in darkness and fear.
> That darkness has gone.
> In every room there is Lenin's bright picture—
> Promise of eternal boon.
>
> In every room there is Stalin's bright picture—
> Greeting from the liberated sun.
> The roads that were full of fog and black sorrow
> Are now gay and bright for everyone.

Happy people! But what of those places where there is no sun and no boon? What is to inspire Yiddish literature there?

It would be hard to answer that question were it not for the fact that literature gives more than it takes from life, and often something quite different. It can absorb terror and give hope. It can be plunged into black despair and give light and faith. The Russian poet Sologub said that he took a drab piece of stuff and turned it into a legend.

Literature is not a slavish imitator that echoes unchanged the sounds of reality. It brings its own sounds to the great choir of life. And even the echo that rings from mountain to mountain as literature is more powerful than the original sound. It shows us not only what life is, but also where life is going and where it will reach. The Jewish legend says that on the day the Temple was destroyed Messiah was born. The day of destruction is also the day of salvation.

When did the bright classics of Russian literature flourish? In the dark days of Nicholas I. At the same time when the Russian serfs spurted blood under the knout Russian literature spurted light and justice. It was the same in Germany, where the greatest poets and thinkers grew up in the darkest period of the eighteenth and nineteenth century. They would have grown under Hitler too, if the ground hadn't been cut away under their feet.

In our Yiddish literature too our writers did not sit back doing nothing because of the hardships and miseries. Indeed, it was because of the cold chilling winds blowing at the time that Yiddish literature took heed of such calls as that of Dr. Kaminer, who wrote to Shalom Aleichem in 1888: "In the present freezing cold period of our history we must give our people more warmth. It needs a drop of wine too—poetry, imagination, hope— to give it strength." [. . .]

Peretz started writing his Chassidic tales to comfort his people. And Shalom Aleichem had before that written his *Jewish Stories* where he introduced, in his own words, "people who at first glance seem to be plain, ordinary people, but if you look at them properly you see that they are made of different stuff, with their souls elsewhere, in another world, a world of song." He wanted "the people to know what forces lie within it."

Mendele too had stopped writing so much about his "little people," and was trying to show that "The life of the congregation of Israel, though very ugly from outside, is lovely within. There is a powerful spirit in Jewish life, a divine spirit, so that when the wind blows it raises waves to wash away the filth. Under the dirt of the chedar, the Yeshiva and the Beth Hamedrash glows the flame of Torah, spreading light and warmth among the whole people."

Our Yiddish writers confronted our ordinary weekday Jews with a picture of "Sabbath Festival Jews."

They spread over our drab life the glow of sanctity and self-sacrifice. They said to the weak, "You are strong." And to slaves they said, "You are heroes." And when the great liberation movement started many of the slaves proved themselves heroes. When they read Peretz's stories about Jews ready to sacrifice their lives for God's sake, and about Jews who wanted eternal Sabbath on earth, they felt that Peretz was telling them not about things that were once upon a time, but about things that must be now. [. . .]

Why do I recall all this? To show how the coarser and more drab the surrounding life was, the more the creative word influenced the environment, instead of being influenced by it. The instrument of our creative literature, the Yiddish language, was refined and ennobled here in America. Was that a result of the environment? On the contrary, it was a result of resisting the environment. The more Yiddish was degraded and corrupted in America, the more the Yiddish word-artists purified and guarded it.

What they did for the language they also did for the ideas which are in Yiddish literature. These too were not the expression but the repudiation of the environment. The basic idea in the Yiddish literature in America was the idea of form, which was a revolt against the formlessness of immigrant life. And likewise there was the nostalgia for our cultural tradition, whose most monumental expression is Yehoash's Yiddish translation of the Bible, derived from the fact that we had been uprooted culturally. In going back to our patriarchal past we were seeking compensation for the drabness of our existence.

We saw the effect of war and extermination on literature generally. At first there was despair and anger, scorn and blasphemy. Young writers denied, became no-sayers to life, floundered in the bog of disbelief and despondency.

Then came the reaction. The older writers saw chaos spreading around them, and they drew back from the edge of the pit. The younger writers caught hold of the wings of imagination and lifted themselves out of the bog.

Yiddish literature, like general literature, has known simultaneously despair and hope. The nearer the army of deniers came, the stronger grew the host of the believers. Belief became the counterattack of creative man against the spirit of destruction. Imagination resisted reality. The awakening of religious energy in all its forms did not come, as some think, out of social defeatism, but on the contrary, out of the must to overcome this dangerous enemy. And there is no people to whom this must is more imperative than to us Jews, because no other people is faced with such dangers from outside and within. We have many times not been allowed to stay peacefully where we were, we were often expelled from our homes, we have frequently stood before closed doors, and when we knocked, no one opened to us. But now we are not allowed out—we are held in a vast prison. And if we are prisoners outwardly how can we keep ourselves from becoming prisoners inwardly as well? How in this confined space will we get air so that our souls can breathe?

We, more than others, need a literature which will not capitulate to reality, but will try to influence and to master reality, to subdue it to our will. Such a literature can't wait till it finds encouraging signs in the real life around us. We must find those signs in ourselves. Our literature has before this been a light in our darkness, and has led us out of terror into hope, out of Tohu-Bohu into new life. It must do this again. Our Yiddish literature must become more daring. It is already in process. Is this prophecy that I am saying? No, not prophecy, but observation, seeing what is going on, and will soon become clear and visible to all.

Translated by Joseph Leftwich.

Joseph Opatoshu
1886–1954

The Yiddish novelist and short-story writer Joseph Opatoshu was born in Poland but spent most of his life in the United States, where he settled in 1907. From 1910, he was associated with Di Yunge, a New York literary circle of young East European immigrants who were in revolt against the conventions of an older generation of writers. He was known for his long historical novels, his stories and sketches of immigrant life in America, and his sympathetic portraits of criminals, "loose" women, and other marginal figures. His most important work was the trilogy *In Polish Woods*, a narrative set in the nineteenth century, whose theme was the decline of Hasidism. His work was translated into many languages during his lifetime, and he achieved a fame that eluded most Yiddish writers at the time.

Yiddish and Jewishness
1938

The world is wicked. To us Jews—of course and of course. And if we are facing destruction, we must be ready, we must be armed against destruction. Fascism wants to exterminate us. It is a war on death and on life. Our time is comparable only to the crusades, to the expulsion from Spain, to the expulsion from Portugal. And, back then, Jews also did not surrender. They waged wars against the wicked world. And back then the war meant—to convert to Christianity, or not?

From the anonymous thousands and tens of thousands of Jews, those armed against downfall, who left Spain, left Portugal, left in search of a new place to settle, from them must we learn a lesson, although our war with fascism is, on the whole, against other enemies.

You have read how sixty Austrian Jews, who already had visas, who were ready to depart for South America, these Jews, before departing, converted of their own free will. They wanted to arrive in their new land as non-Jews. Here lies the peril. Our grandfathers, our great-grandfathers, whole Jews, responded to the wickedness of the Christian world, as one responds to dark forces of nature, as one responds to a flood, as one responds to a heavy rain, or even as one responds to a mad dog. Our grandfathers established this attitude miles above wickedness and this saved them from downfall.

Ask yourself: What sort of strength do we have, Jews of today, to oppose the wickedness of the world? The strength of religion? Of social justice? Of secularism? Of Jewishness? And the question arises: whose Jewishness?

And here it should be said: Jews all over the world feel disappointed, feel embittered, feel deceived, even. Voices are heard: *What has become of the great human ideals? Why is the democratic world silent? Have we really been sent deep into the ground? If so, we need not have any dealings with such a world. Jews have, thanks be to God, a place to hide. We can crawl back into the ghetto-walls.* And, at once, the voices are accompanied by singing. Such reasoning, which makes sense, is but decadence, an individual one, an inner decadence, which wants to vie with the external wickedness against us, Jews. [. . .]

All the ghetto-moods, all the back-to-the-synagogue moods, demonstrate how the average person is helpless in a time of trouble, how he is lost, how he grabs at every straw just to save himself. [. . .] In the time of the French revolution, Jewish schoolteachers threw into the fire: Siddurs, Pentateuchs, Gemoras. After the failure of the Russian Revolution (in 1906–1907), some Jewish poets and essayists saw salvation in putting on tefillin, in becoming Jews of the synagogue. Such moods always go hand-in-hand with personal weakness, with reaction. Here, the ideologues of the "Agudah" convene, with

a lot of representatives from Yiddish literature. These days, the Jewish "ghetto" is clearly fast becoming celebrated in songs. People see beauty in it, in the fur-edged hats worn by the Hasidim on holy days and the sabbath, in Jewish dress. But along the way, people forget that we alone chose the fur-edged hat with the long satin coat for ourselves, while we were wedged into the ghetto, as into a prison, against our will, where we have been held for over four hundred years. We were let out of the ghetto walls only so that we could conduct commerce, which was beneath lordly honor to engage in. Today, commerce is a genteel pursuit. The Jews are also being ousted from commerce. And to go of our own free will into the ghetto—means burying ourselves alive.

And from the ghetto it takes only a step to reach the synagogue. [. . .] It is laughable and detrimental, in just these times, to see our only salvation in the ghetto, between the four walls of the synagogue, in just these times, when Jewish life is on the balance, everything is tottering, everything is in jeopardy. For not only are we, Jews, being judged. The whole world is being judged. A world is on the verge of crashing. A new one: on the verge of being born. [. . .] As long as there are Thomas Manns, we are the Thomas Manns, we are the democratic people, we are with socialism, which extends from the prophets to Moses Hess. That must be our road, the only Jewish road.

And we, Jews, for all the blows that we have already been dealt and which we are yet to be dealt, we, Jews, will not be crushed. In us there is something of the legendary bird, which lives forever, only every thousand years the bird shakes off its feathers, burns up and, from its own ash, is born again. [. . .]

So what, then, is continuity? There, where there is hatred, where there is wickedness, there is no continuation. It's enough to surrender a little to introspection, enough to engage oneself, to realize that every man has, every now and then, experienced the sensation of continuation. Here, I will bring you an example from my own life. On the way home to Mlawa, in the year 1922, I was traveling on the *Aquitania* ship. On the third day of my journey, I went up to the highest deck after midnight. The night was full of stars. Above me: so much sky. Stars and sky. Around and around: water. And you, yourself, become so small, you become smaller still—a speck of dust in the middle of the ocean. And as I look like so into the sky, a star falls. A second crosses it, and in my mind a thought is born. A familiar thought. Thirty-something years ago my father traveled third class on this same ocean. Here—in the middle of the ocean—fifteen hundred miles from New York, fifteen hundred miles from Paris, my father cast out a thought, which he had inherited from his grandfather, from his great-grandfather: what is this, Jewishness? And the thought hovers between sky and water. For me, the thought is part of the ship, of the people, of all that is on the ship, part of the surrounding forces of nature. And my father, my grandfather, generations, generations speak through me: *What is Jewishness? And whose Jewishness? The prophets'? That of Maimonides, or Moses Hess and Yitskhok Leybush Peretz?*

And I say: Jewishness is all of this and something more. The "something more" is, however, hard to define. When Babylonia constructed its culture, built towers and skyscrapers, when the Egyptians constructed their culture, built sphinxes, we, Jews, devoted ourselves to God's word, to the divine utterance—*The world was created by means of ten divine utterances*—to the logos. [. . .]

It has taken generations, a thousand years, and the word—the fruitful, human word—has not just entered our blood, we have also imparted it to the Christian world, the Muslim world. And four hundred years ago when Europe was in the midst of falling apart, the Puritans, the pious Quakers, who had emigrated to America, had no need to pass away, like the ancient Greeks, Babylonians, and Egyptians, who could not drag into exile their towers, their colosseums, their sphinxes. Without their culture, they became extinct. The Puritans could easily shake off the culture of image and stone. They replaced that image-and-stone culture with the culture of the "word." They were able to place the New and Old Testaments between two book covers and bring their culture across to America. True, the European arrived in America naked, arrived only with the Christian Bible. The Bible, however, kept him from extinction. And that is our achievement, the great Jewish achievement.

Every Jew has been able to pack his entire culture into a tefillin pouch and journey with it all over the world. It was in the Jew's blood. Instead of Babylonian towers, instead of Egyptian pyramids, we had a movable ark. As it is written: they encamped and they set out. [. . .]

In the *word* lies our strength. And the word, whether it was once the divine word, whether it is today the fruitful human word, the word sustains us, it arms us against disappearance. [. . .]

This is the strength of culture.

And it occurred to me that this strength extends throughout our history. In the year 1937, I was standing in the Jewish pavilion in the Paris International Exposition. Opposite the Jewish pavilion was a section of the German pavilion.

What did Jews display in their pavilion?

Old manuscripts. Printing presses from 1600 and 1700. Old Yiddish literature, modern Yiddish literature, Chagall's paintings, Soutine's paintings, works from the modern Jewish school.

And the German?

The German displayed the newest artilleries, the newest rifles. So rifles were standing there, vying with the Jewish alphabet. And the Jewish alphabet was victorious. Even the Hitlerists were ashamed that they had displayed rifles opposite the Jewish alphabet and during the second week they took down the rifles.

And even though the Jewish pavilion was poor, I felt uplifted, I felt rich with the poverty. It took courage to stand between England, France, Germany, and Italy, to stand opposite a whole world with the sacred verses of the prophets, with Spinoza's ethics, with the truths of Moses Hess and Yitskhok Leybush Peretz.

Their truths, this folk-strength—this is Jewishness, this is Jewish culture. [. . .]

Only our intelligentsia has gotten lost, continues asking if we are not, indeed, in a state of downfall. The masses, whether they are workers or smalltime merchants, through all the persecutions and oppressions, through all the sacrifices, they have not been flustered. On the contrary, the nation [*folk*] has faith. And if one must: one rises up, one strikes the enemy back. In all failures, the worker still sees salvation in socialism. The pious Jew has his own socialism, which is made manifest in Reb Nachman of Bratslav's words: "For heaven's sake, Jews! Do not give up hope." [. . .] The ordinary person—whether he be a worker, a small merchant, or the Spanish Jew of four hundred years ago, who stood up to God and found a new place to settle—all these Jews are armed against downfall.

Translated by Maia Evrona, edited by Zvi Gitelman.

Other works by Opatoshu: *The Last Revolt: The Story of Rabbi Akiba* (1952); *A Day in Regensburg: Short Stories* (1968); *Romance of a Horse Thief* (1986).

Stephen S. Wise

1874–1949

Born in Budapest, the son and grandson of rabbis, Stephen S. Wise was brought as an infant to New York

City. He attended Columbia University and studied for the rabbinate privately. He served congregations in New York City and then Portland, Oregon. An outspoken progressive activist and Zionist, in 1907 he founded the Free Synagogue in Manhattan to ensure a pulpit free from the control of the congregation's board. Wise was prominent in national progressive politics and was among the founders of the National Association for the Advancement of Colored People in 1909 and the American Civil Liberties Union in 1920. In 1922, he established the Jewish Institute of Religion in New York City to train rabbis from all branches of Judaism. During the Nazi years, he led the effort to boycott German goods and to rally American opposition to German aggression.

Five Mournful Years for Jewry
1938

Five years have passed since that mournful 5th of March, which witnessed the so-called election of Hitler as Chancellor of the German Reich. It might long have been foreseen and perhaps even averted, had they been prepared, whose minds were under the moral obligation to be ready. Save for Labor and handsful of radicals who paid a terrible price, few resisted or even challenged the advent of the deadliest regime in a millennium. Least prepared were the Jews of Germany, about half a million, who had with most explicit insults been warned. At first some of the older and better circumstanced Jewish groups assented with incredible baseness to the diverting of anti-Jewish Nazi wrath to the newer East European emigrants who since war days had made their home in Germany. This was exactly as the Jews of Southern France more than a century earlier had attempted to burden their hapless Alsatian brother-Jews with the weight of putative Jewish iniquity.

Despite every escape mechanism, including cabled supplication to the leaders of the American Jewish Congress in our country, to desist from attack upon the new Nazi regime, what was threatened in pre-Nazi years has come to pass and German Jewry, which may no longer so style itself, lies prostrate and helpless beneath the iron heel of Nazi law and practice. In a review of five years of Nazism from the Jewish point of view, certain things stand out that justify special consideration. For years before Hitler's accession and for a time thereafter and in some part persisting to this day, certain groups of Jews have underestimated the gravity of the Hitler threat.

Again, it should be recalled that the German Jews took it for granted almost with unanimity that Hitlerism

or Nazism was a passing phenomenon. After declaring that his access to power was incredible, they crowned their blunder by assuming that he would speedily vanish. German Jewry made no preparations as against the advent of Nazism and indeed up to the recent mournful utterances of Dr. Stahl before the Jewish Community of Berlin, there had been no genuine and unafraid facing of ultimate and tragic facts by German Jewry. Such facing as came to light when the sagest of American Jews on March 13, 1933 a week and a day after the Hitler "election," declared "Jews must leave Germany." People scoffed at the impracticableness of this prediction rather than counsel. It is, alas, coming to pass. Had there, for example, been any concerted, wise facing of the facts by Jews in Germany, there never would have been one penny of foreign funds expended in Germany for relief to Jews. Moreover, every well-to-do family that migrated to Palestine should have been invited or even compelled to take a poorer Jewish family with it, so that instead of leaving funds in Germany or transmitting them elsewhere, instead of 50,000 German Jews going to Palestine, the number might have reached 100,000.

I do not hold that the German Jews should have been expected to foresee all the more tragic and the remoter consequences of the Hitler regime. Still a word must be said about those who, prior to March, 1933, maintained that the fulfillment would not be as evil as the promise. "The threat is grave but it cannot be carried out." The truth is that the fulfillment is a thousand times graver than any threat of the pre-Hitler days. I am reminded of that German official who, in 1918, was asked by an English diplomat, "And if you had conquered France, how would you have treated the inhabitants after exchanging a million of the French population with as many of the German?" His reply was *"dann haetten wir die Liebenswuerdigkeit tuechtig und gruendlich organiziert."* Verily the Nazis have in supremely thorough and competent fashion translated a campaign of hatred and vilification into the law and statute of their country. The Nuremberg Code stands as the incarnation of a nation's descent to the deeps of racial injustice and oppression of a minority.

What, of course, could not have been foreseen was that Germany would be permitted to disregard and to violate the Versailles Peace Treaty at every point, the most conspicuous example of such unchallenged violation being the surrender of Danzig to Nazism at its worst. Something more has happened within five years that is of moment not only to Jews in Germany but to

Jews everywhere and that is the spread through the devilish instrumentality of the Ministry of Propaganda and Enlightenment of Nazi propaganda in all the lands of Europe and indeed in Asia, Africa, North, Central and South America. Tragic as has been the cold "Anschluss," virtually unrebuked by the democratic powers which long stood as Austria's guardians, there has been something worse than the annexation of Austria over a period of five empoisoning years, namely, the permeation of Eastern and Central Europe by Nazi propaganda. The device of the "Ghetto Benches" would never have been urged had it not been for bribery by Nazi funds and empoisonment by Nazi propaganda. Even the temporary accession of a pair of desperate and dissolute creatures such as Goga and Cuza to power in Rumania could not have been had not Rumania been a prey of Nazism for some years.

One thing more requires mention. From the beginning, as that valiant anti-Nazi battler, Dr. Henry Leiper, has pointed out, the Christian communions of Germany imagined themselves to be secure and that Nazism was nothing more than yet another symptom of raging anti-Semitism. The writer of these lines predicted in the home of Harry Emerson Fosdick in October, 1933, that, even though anti-Jewish Nazism screened itself behind the mask of racialism, in time the Protestant and Catholic churches would become the victims of the Nazi scourge. For the most part there was unbelief on the part of those who took it for granted that Nazism could not, would not dare to touch either of the mighty Christian bodies of Germany. Needless to say, my prediction has come true. The Catholic and the Protestant churches alike of Germany are in danger of having their influence minimized by the new paganism which has the sanction not only of Alfred Rosenberg but of most of the leaders of Nazi Germany. In a word, Nazism is Aryan-racialism against Semitic Jews. With its protean capacity for hatred and injustice, it takes the form of a paganish revival against the great Christian church and communities of Europe.

Against the ever-growing might of Nazism in Germany, which unhappily has come into alliance with Rome and Tokyo, there has been no mighty uprising, whether political or religious or moral. Socialists and Communists and the free Labor Front of other countries such as England, France and America have uttered their imprecations, but there has been no union of the church bodies of the Western world against Nazi paganism. Individual Christian leaders have spoken with power and inspiration under the early leadership of the golden-tongued Parkes Cadman, but there has to this hour been no voluntary union of the religious forces of mankind against Nazi paganism—it may be because Jews were its first victims.

Even more disappointing has been the constant yielding of the democratic powers to Nazi Germany's demands. The last two days in the House of Commons witnessed the almost unchecked triumph of the Nazi-Fascist axis. A handful of us, who have not wholly lost faith in the triumph of decency in the world, have felt it our duty to unite in a boycott against Nazi goods and services, a boycott being a moral revolt against wrong, making use of economic instruments. Timorous Jews and queerish Christians seem to feel that we are not justified in boycotting the foes of the human race.

Out of it all emerges the truth that we Jews have been taught that, unless we choose to go down to dishonor and even death, we will have to rethink our problem through. We will have to face what Nazism means to ourselves. The world will not think or act for the Jewish people unless the Jewish people think and act for themselves. We are not minors who require non-Jewish guardianship and even if we required it, we would not have an effective, dependable saving guardianship outside of ourselves. It may yet be that good will come out of the Nazi plague, the good of a democratic awakening, the good of a Jewish renaissance. The democracies may yet conclude that they will either stay the power of Nazism and Fascism or be destroyed. Jews may yet come to understand that their position in the world is imperiled as never before in history. The alliance that alone might save them must be an alliance of the democratic forces challenging and battling against Nazism and Fascism, whether in Berlin, in Rome or in Tokyo, and Jews everywhere coming to understand that political tyranny anywhere means death, that political freedom and international justice alone can save them and make life worth saving for Jews and all peoples.

Other works by Wise: *The Great Betrayal*, with Jacob De Haas (1930); *Challenging Years: The Autobiography of Stephen Wise* (1949).

Sigmund Freud

1856–1939

The founder of psychoanalysis was a nonobservant, nonbelieving Jew whose closest social and professional colleagues in Vienna were other like-minded Jews. Although Freud took no part in the institutional life of the Jewish community, he always asserted and took pride in his attachment to the Jewish people. *Moses and Monotheism*, which he published late in life, was his only textual foray into the problematics of Jewish identity.

Moses and Monotheism
1939

IV. Application

Early trauma—defence—latency—outbreak of the neurosis—partial return of the repressed material: this was the formula we drew up for the development of a neurosis. Now I will invite the reader to take a step forward and assume that in the history of the human species something happened similar to the events in the life of the individual. That is to say, mankind as a whole also passed through conflicts of a sexual-aggressive nature, which left permanent traces, but which were for the most part warded off and forgotten; later, after a long period of latency, they came to life again and created phenomena similar in structure and tendency to neurotic symptoms.

I have, I believe, divined these processes and wish to show that their consequences, which bear a strong resemblance to neurotic symptoms, are the phenomena of religion. Since it can no longer be doubted after the discovery of evolution that mankind had a prehistory, and since this history is unknown (that is to say, forgotten), such a conclusion has almost the significance of an axiom. If we should learn that the effective and forgotten traumata relate, here as well as there, to life in the human family, we should greet this information as a highly welcome and unforeseen gift which could not have been anticipated from the foregoing discussion.

I have already upheld this thesis, a quarter of a century ago, in my book *Totem and Taboo* (1912), and need only repeat what I said there. The argument started from some remarks by Charles Darwin and embraced a suggestion of Atkinson's. It says that in primeval times men lived in small hordes, each under the domination of a strong male. When this was is not known; no point of contact with geological data has been established. It is likely that mankind was not very far advanced in the art of speech. An essential part of the argument is that all primeval men, including, therefore, all our ancestors, underwent the fate I shall now describe.

The story is told in a very condensed way, as if what in reality took centuries to achieve, and during that long time was repeated innumerably, had happened only once. The strong male was the master and father of the whole horde, unlimited in his power, which he used brutally. All females were his property, the wives and daughters in his own horde as well as perhaps also those stolen from other hordes. The fate of the sons was a hard one; if they excited the father's jealousy they were killed or castrated or driven out. They were forced to live in small communities and to provide themselves with wives by stealing them from others. Then one or the other son might succeed in attaining a situation similar to that of the father in the original horde. One favoured position came about in a natural way: it was that of the youngest son, who, protected by his mother's love, could profit by his father's advancing years and replace him after his death. An echo of the expulsion of the eldest son, as well as of the favoured position of the youngest, seems to linger in many myths and fairy-tales.

The next decisive step towards changing this first kind of "social" organization lies in the following suggestion: the brothers who had been driven out and lived together in a community clubbed together, overcame the father, and—according to the custom of those times—all partook of his body. This cannibalism need not shock us, it survived into far later times. The essential point is, however, that we attribute to those primeval people the same feelings and emotions that we have elucidated in the primitives of our own times, our children, by psychoanalytic research. That is to say, they not merely hated and feared their father, but also honoured him as an example to follow; in fact, each son wanted to place himself in his father's position. The cannibalistic act thus becomes comprehensible as an attempt to assure one's identification with the father by incorporating a part of him.

It is a reasonable surmise that after the killing of the father a time followed when the brothers quarrelled among themselves for the succession, which each of them wanted to obtain for himself alone. They came to see that these fights were as dangerous as they were futile. This hard-won understanding—as well as the memory of the deed of liberation they had achieved together and the attachment that had grown up among them during the time of their exile—led at last to a union among them, a sort of social contract. Thus there came into being the first form of a social organization accompanied by a renunciation of instinctual gratification; recognition of mutual obligations; institutions declared sacred, which could not be broken—in short, the beginnings of morality and law. Each renounced the ideal of gaining for himself the position of father, of possessing his mother or sister. With this the taboo of incest and the law of exogamy came into being. A good part of the power which had become vacant through the father's death passed to the women; the time of the matriarchate followed. The memory of the father lived on during this time of the "brother horde." A strong animal, which perhaps at first was also dreaded, was found as a substitute. Such a choice may seem very strange to us, but the gulf which man created later between himself and the animals did not exist for primitive man. Nor does it with our children, whose animal phobias we have been able to explain as dread of the father. The relationship to the totem animal retained the original ambivalency of feeling towards the father. The totem was, on the one hand, the corporeal ancestor and protecting spirit of the clan; he was to be revered and protected. On the other hand, a festival was instituted on which day the same fate was meted out to him as the primeval father had encountered. He was killed and eaten by all the brothers together (the totem feast, according to Robertson Smith). This great day was in reality a feast of triumph to celebrate the victory of the united sons over the father.

Where, in this connection, does religion come in? Totemism, with its worship of a father substitute, the ambivalency towards the father which is evidenced by the totem feast, the institution of remembrance festivals and of laws the breaking of which is punished by death—this totemism, I conclude, may be regarded as the earliest appearance of religion in the history of mankind, and it illustrates the close connection existing from the very beginning of time between social institutions and moral obligations. The further development of religion can be treated here only in a very summary fashion. Without a doubt it proceeded parallel to the cultural development of mankind and the changes in the structure of human social institutions.

The next step forward from totemism is the humanizing of the worshipped being. Human gods, whose origin in the totem is not veiled, take the place previously filled by animals. Either the god is still represented as an animal or at least he bears the countenance of an animal; the totem may become the inseparable companion of the god, or, again, the myth makes the god vanquish just that animal which was nothing but his predecessor. At one period—it is hard to say when—great mother deities appeared, probably before the male gods, and they were worshipped beside the latter for a long time to come. During that time a great social revolution had taken place. Matriarchy was followed by a restitution of the patriarchal order. The new fathers, it is true, never succeeded to the omnipotence of the primeval father. There were too many of them and they lived in larger communities than the original horde had been; they had to get on with one another and were restricted by social institutions. Probably the mother deities were developed when the matriarchy was being limited, in order to compensate the dethroned mothers. The male gods appear at first as sons by the side of the great mothers; only later do they clearly assume the features of the father. These male gods of polytheism mirror the conditions of patriarchal times. They are numerous, they have to share their authority, and occasionally they obey a higher god. The next step, however, leads us to the topic that interests us here: the return of the one and only father deity whose power is unlimited.

I must admit that this historical survey leaves many a gap and in many points needs further confirmation. Yet whoever declares this reconstruction of primeval history to be fantastic greatly under-estimates the richness and the force of the evidence that has gone to make it up. Large portions of the past, which are here woven into a whole, are historically proved or even show their traces to this day, such as matriarchal right, totemism, and male communities. Others have survived in remarkable replicas. Thus more than one author has been struck by the close resemblance between the rite of Christian Communion—where the believer symbolically incorporates the blood and flesh of his God—and the totem feast, whose inner meaning it reproduces. Numerous survivals of our forgotten early history are preserved in the legends and fairy tales of the peoples, and analytic study of the mental life of the child has yielded an unexpectedly rich return by filling up gaps in our knowledge of primeval times. As a contribution towards an understanding of the highly important relation between father and son I need only quote the animal phobias, the fear of being eaten by the father (which seems so strange to the grown mind), and the enormous intensity of the castration complex. There is nothing in our reconstruction that is invented, nothing that is not based on good grounds.

Let us suppose that the presentation here given of primeval history is on the whole credible. Then two elements can be recognized in religious rites and doctrines: on the one hand, fixations on the old family-history and survivals of this; on the other hand, reproductions of the past and a return long after of what had been forgotten. It is the latter element that has until now been overlooked and therefore not understood. It will therefore be illustrated here by at least one impressive example.

It is specially worthy of note that every memory returning from the forgotten past does so with great force, produces an incomparably strong influence on the mass of mankind, and puts forward an irresistible claim to be believed, against which all logical objections remain powerless—very much like the *credo quia absurdum*. This strange characteristic can only be understood by comparison with the delusions in a psychotic case. It has long been recognized that delusions contain a piece of forgotten truth, which had at its return to put up with being distorted and misunderstood, and that the compulsive conviction appertaining to the delusion emanates from this core of truth and spreads to the errors that enshroud it. Such a kernel of truth—which we might call *historical* truth—must also be conceded to the doctrines of the various religions. They are, it is true, imbued with the character of psychotic symptoms, but as mass phenomena they have escaped the curse of isolation.

No other part of religious history has become so abundantly clear as the establishment of monotheism among the Jewish people and its continuation into Christianity—if we omit the development from the animal totem to the human god with his regular (animal) companion, a development which can be traced without a gap and readily understood. (Each of the four Christian Evangelists, by the way, still has his favourite animal.) If we admit for the moment that the rule of Pharaoh's Empire was the external reason for the appearance of the monotheistic idea, we see that this idea—uprooted from its soil and transplanted to another people—after a long latency period takes hold of this people, is treasured by them as their most precious possession, and for its part keeps this people alive by bestowing on them the pride of being the chosen people. It is the religion of the primeval father, and the hope of reward, distinction, and finally world sovereignty is bound up with it. The last-named wish-phantasy—relinquished long ago by the Jewish people—still survives among their enemies

in their belief in the conspiracy of the "Elders of Zion." We shall consider in a later chapter how the special peculiarities of a monotheistic religion borrowed from Egypt must have worked on the Jewish people, how it formed their character for good through the disdaining of magic and mysticism and encouraging them to progress in spirituality and sublimations. The people, happy in their conviction of possessing truth, overcome by the consciousness of being the chosen, came to value highly all intellectual and ethical achievements. I shall also show how their sad fate, and the disappointments reality had in store for them, were able to strengthen all these tendencies. At present, however, we shall follow their historical development in another direction.

The restoration to the primeval father of his historical rights marked a great progress, but this could not be the end. The other parts of the prehistoric tragedy also clamoured for recognition. How this process was set in motion it is not easy to say. It seems that a growing feeling of guiltiness had seized the Jewish people—and perhaps the whole of civilization of that time—as a precursor of the return of the repressed material. This went on until a member of the Jewish people, in the guise of a political-religious agitator, founded a doctrine which—together with another one, the Christian religion—separated from the Jewish one. Paul, a Roman Jew from Tarsus, seized upon this feeling of guilt and correctly traced it back to its primeval source. This he called original sin; it was a crime against God that could be expiated only through death. Death had come into the world through original sin. In reality this crime, deserving of death, had been the murder of the Father who later was deified. The murderous deed itself, however, was not remembered; in its place stood the phantasy of expiation, and that is why this phantasy could be welcomed in the form of a gospel of salvation (evangel). A Son of God, innocent himself, had sacrificed himself, and had thereby taken over the guilt of the world. It had to be a Son, for the sin had been murder of the Father. Probably traditions from Oriental and Greek mysteries had exerted their influence on the shaping of this phantasy of salvation. The essence of it seems to be Paul's own contribution. He was a man with a gift for religion, in the truest sense of the phrase. Dark traces of the past lay in his soul, ready to break through into the regions of consciousness.

That the Redeemer sacrificed himself as an innocent man was an obviously tendentious distortion, difficult to reconcile with logical thinking. How could a man who was innocent assume the guilt of the murderer by allowing himself to be killed? In historical reality there was no such contradiction. The "redeemer" could be no one else but he who was most guilty, the leader of the brother horde who had overpowered the Father. Whether there had been such a chief rebel and leader must, in my opinion, remain uncertain. It is quite possible, but we must also consider that each member of the brother horde certainly had the wish to do the deed by himself and thus to create for himself a unique position as a substitute for the identification with the father which he had to give up when he was submerged in the community. If there was no such leader, then Christ was the heir of an unfulfilled wish-phantasy; if there was such a leader, then Christ was his successor and his reincarnation. It is unimportant, however, whether we have here a phantasy or the return of a forgotten reality; in any case, here lies the origin of the conception of the hero—him who rebels against the father and kills him in some guise or other.[1] Here we also find the real source of the "tragic guilt" of the hero in drama—a guilt hard to demonstrate otherwise. We can hardly doubt that in Greek tragedy the hero and the chorus represent this same rebel hero and the brother horde, and it cannot be without significance that in the Middle Ages the theatre began afresh with the story of the Passion.

I have already mentioned that the Christian ceremony of Holy Communion, in which the believer incorporates the flesh and blood of the Redeemer, repeats the content of the old totem feast; it does so, it is true, only in its tender and adoring sense, not in its aggressive sense. The ambivalency dominating the father–son relationship shows clearly, however, in the final result of the religious innovation. Meant to propitiate the Father Deity, it ends by his being dethroned and set aside. The Mosaic religion had been a Father religion; Christianity became a Son religion. The old God, the Father, took second place; Christ, the Son, stood in his stead, just as in those dark times every son had longed to do. Paul, by developing the Jewish religion further, became its destroyer. His success was certainly mainly due to the fact that through the idea of salvation he laid the ghost of the feeling of guilt. It was also due to his giving up the idea of the chosen people and its visible sign—circumcision. That is how the new religion could become all-embracing, universal. Although this step might have been determined by Paul's revengefulness on account of the opposition which his innovation found among the Jews, nevertheless one characteristic of the old Aton religion

(universality) was reinstated; a restriction had been abolished which it had acquired while passing on to a new carrier, the Jewish people.

In certain respects the new religion was a cultural regression as compared with the older Jewish religion; this happens regularly when a new mass of people of a lower cultural level effects an invasion or is admitted into an older culture. The Christian religion did not keep to the lofty heights of spirituality to which the Jewish religion had soared. The former was no longer strictly monotheistic; it took over from the surrounding peoples numerous symbolical rites, re-established the great mother goddess, and found room for many deities of polytheism in an easily recognizable disguise, though in subordinate positions. Above all it was not inaccessible, as the Aton religion and the subsequent Mosaic religion had been, to the penetration of superstitions, magical and mystical elements which proved a great hindrance to the spiritual development of two following millennia.

The triumph of Christianity was a renewed victory of the Ammon priests over the God of Ikhnaton after an interval of a millennium and a half and over a larger region. And yet Christianity marked a progress in the history of religion: that is to say, in regard to the return of the repressed. From now on, the Jewish religion was, so to speak, a fossil.

It would be worth while to understand why the monotheistic idea should make such a deep impression on just the Jewish people, and why they adhered to it so tenaciously. I believe this question can be answered. The great deed and misdeed of primeval times, the murder of the father, was brought home to the Jews, for fate decreed that they should repeat it on the person of Moses, an eminent father substitute. It was a case of acting instead of remembering, something which often happens during analytic work with neurotics. They responded to the doctrine of Moses—which should have been a stimulus to their memory—by denying their act, did not progress beyond the recognition of the great father, and barred the passage to the point where later on Paul started his continuation of primeval history. It can scarcely be chance that the violent death of another great man should become the starting-point for the creation of a new religion by Paul. This was a man whom a small number of adherents in Judea believed to be the Son of God and the promised Messiah, and who later on took over some of the childhood history that had been attached to Moses. In reality, however, we have hardly more definite knowledge of him than we have of Moses. We do not know if he was really the great man whom the Gospels depict or whether it was not rather the fact and the circumstances of his death that were the decisive factor in his achieving importance. Paul, who became his apostle, did not himself know him.

The murder of Moses by his people—which Sellin recognized in the traces of tradition and which, strangely enough, the young Goethe[2] had assumed without any evidence—has thus become an indispensable part of our reasoning, an important link between the forgotten deed of primeval times and its subsequent reappearance in the form of monotheistic religions.[3] It is an attractive suggestion that the guilt attached to the murder of Moses may have been the stimulus for the wish-phantasy of the Messiah, who was to return and give to his people salvation and the promised sovereignty over the world. If Moses was this first Messiah, Christ became his substitute and successor. Then Paul could with a certain right say to the peoples: "See, the Messiah has truly come. He was indeed murdered before your eyes." Then also there is some historical truth in the rebirth of Christ, for he was the resurrected Moses and the returned primeval father of the primitive horde as well—only transfigured, and as a Son in the place of his Father.

The poor Jewish people, who with its usual stiff-necked obduracy continued to deny the murder of their "father," has dearly expiated this in the course of centuries. Over and over again they heard the reproach: "You killed our God." And this reproach is true, if rightly interpreted. It says, in reference to the history of religion: "You won't *admit* that you murdered God" (the archetype of God, the primeval Father, and his reincarnations). Something should be added—namely: "It is true, we did the same thing, but we *admitted* it, and since then we have been purified." Not all accusations with which anti-Semitism pursues the descendants of the Jewish people are based on such good foundations. There must, of course, be more than one reason for a phenomenon of such intensity and lasting strength as the popular hatred of Jews. A whole series of reasons can be divined; some of them, which need no interpretation, arise from obvious considerations; others lie deeper and spring from secret sources, which one would regard as the specific motives. In the first group the most fallacious is the reproach of their being foreigners, since in many places nowadays under the sway of anti-Semitism the Jews were the oldest constituents

of the population or arrived even before the present inhabitants. This is so, for example, in the town of Cologne, where Jews came with the Romans, before it was colonized by Germanic tribes. Other grounds for anti-Semitism are stronger, as, for example, the circumstance that Jews mostly live as a minority among other peoples, since the feeling of solidarity of the masses, in order to be complete, has need of an animosity against an outside minority, and the numerical weakness of the minority invites suppression. Two other peculiarities that the Jews possess, however, are quite unpardonable. The first is that in many respects they are different from their "hosts." Not fundamentally so, since they are not a foreign Asiatic race, as their enemies maintain, but mostly consist of the remnants of Mediterranean peoples and inherit their culture. Yet they are different—although sometimes it is hard to define in what respects—specially from the Nordic peoples, and racial intolerance finds stronger expression, strange to say, in regard to small differences than to fundamental ones. The second peculiarity has an even more pronounced effect. It is that they defy oppression, that even the most cruel persecutions have not succeeded in exterminating them. On the contrary, they show a capacity for holding their own in practical life and, where they are admitted, they make valuable contributions to the surrounding civilization.

The deeper motives of anti-Semitism have their roots in times long past; they come from the unconscious, and I am quite prepared to hear that what I am going to say will at first appear incredible. I venture to assert that the jealousy which the Jews evoked in other peoples by maintaining that they were the first-born, favourite child of God the Father has not yet been overcome by those others, just as if the latter had given credence to the assumption. Furthermore, among the customs through which the Jews marked off their aloof position, that of circumcision made a disagreeable, uncanny impression on others. The explanation probably is that it reminds them of the dreaded castration idea and of things in their primeval past which they would fain forget. Then there is lastly the most recent motive of the series. We must not forget that all the peoples who now excel in the practice of anti-Semitism became Christians only in relatively recent times, sometimes forced to it by bloody compulsion. One might say they all are "badly christened"; under the thin veneer of Christianity they have remained what their ancestors were, barbarically polytheistic. They have not yet overcome their grudge against the new religion which was forced on them, and they have projected it on to the source from which Christianity came to them. The facts that the Gospels tell a story which is enacted among Jews, and in truth treats only of Jews, has facilitated such a projection. The hatred for Judaism is at bottom hatred for Christianity, and it is not surprising that in the German National Socialist revolution this close connection of the two monotheistic religions finds such clear expression in the hostile treatment of both.

NOTES

1. Ernest Jones calls my attention to the probability that the god Mithra, who slays the Bull, represented this leader, the one who simply gloried in his deed. It is well known how long the worship of Mithra disputed the final victory with Christianity.

2. *Israel in der Wüste*, Vol. VII of the Weimar edition, p. 170.

3. Compare in this connection the well-known exposition in Frazer's *The Golden Bough*, Part III, "The Dying God" (1911).

Translated by Katherine Jones.

Other works by Freud: *The Standard Edition of the Complete Psychological Works of Sigmund Freud*, 24 vols. (1953–1974).

Oskar Yeshayahu Wolfsberg

1893–1957

Oscar Yeshayahu Wolfsberg (Volfsberg; also Aviad) was a leader of religious Zionism, a writer who explored the history of philosophy, and a physician. He was born in Hamburg, served in World War I, and moved to Palestine in 1933. Active in the Mizrahi movement in both his native Germany (where he served as the organization's president and edited its journal) and in Israel (where he joined Ha-Po'el ha-Mizraḥi), Wolfsberg represented the state of Israel as a diplomat in Scandinavia and Switzerland.

Powers of Descent and Powers of Ascent
1939

1

[. . .] Why does the present Jewish fate appear so strongly connected to our entire past and to all that is currently unfolding before our eyes? At times it seemed that many distinct events stood almost isolated, and, moreover, that it was extremely difficult to connect them to other events, horizontally or vertically [over space or time]. Yet now the impression is clearly the opposite: what we are currently experiencing relates to the great lines of history and axes of our time. Most of all, it is difficult to interpret the wild stampede that has occurred over the last two to three decades and has driven us with such impetus into a sea of sorrows, to the extent that we have been unable to find our bearings. Suddenly, the apocalyptic riders have appeared before our eyes.

What does all this mean?

Realizing what is happening around us and trying to interpret the signs of the time—this gives the contemporary person something to grasp at, in particular when one is a Jew who has lived through the school of thought and faith. Thus we begin from the standpoint that thought has not lost its meaning, function, and power to illuminate events, however strangely wild they may seem, and that faith has not died. It is therefore our premise that the Jewish people and its spiritual and religious contents—everything the term *Yiddishkeit* encompasses—will also continue to exist, according to the will of history and our own will.

We are living through a time of reckoning in history. In hoping for the birth pangs of the Messiah, the pains of the footsteps of the Messiah, one may perhaps with a certain justification say, "He will come and I will not see him"—may he come and may I not see this. But when this time is upon us, there is no point in avoiding it. One must take up the heavy burden. And following all the difficult and senseless trials, there remains a powerful impression that finally, perhaps, from our dreadful situation history will truly show itself to be (as Lessing says) "making sense of the senseless." If there is a reason for our suffering, then one can justify accepting the pain with love—accepting torments lovingly. If the unity of history and goal shall shine forth out of the fear and darkness in our generation, then we, regardless of our pains and losses, shall merit one of the greatest revelations.

[. . .] Nothing taking shape presently does so by chance. While in other times we had to gather together with great effort from many periods, we now learn almost every day. Subjugations and wars almost always have a different character than in earlier times. Napoleon did not set out to enslave and violate peoples or individuals. Admittedly he was a "usurper" and his evil inclination was strongly set on subjugating and enslaving his opponents. However, following wars he set out many constructive aims: to unite Europe on the basis of a healthy administration and jurisdiction. His abilities to appreciate foreign geniuses (Goethe) and even to hold poetry in high esteem demonstrate that he was a constructive spirit.

Today everything has changed. The strongest motive behind the acts of the totalitarian great powers, in particular Germany, is not the positive aim of establishing an empire, a world power, as much as a negative desire to bring about the downfall of foreign governments, peoples—races—and enslave them. The fact that the concept of race has been introduced not into science, but rather directly into politics and life, is an externally recognizable sign of our times. The innovation lies not in the assertion that various races exist but rather in the dogma that one race, the Aryan, is supreme, the master, the superhuman, and that the remainder, especially the Semitic races, are inferior. From this dogma, the storm of National Socialism goes forth into the rest of the world that, as is known, is composed not only of kingdoms and races but also of ideas and spiritual and clerical institutions.

National Socialism is odious to democracy, the principle of goodness, Judaism, and many other things. Therefore, it is worthwhile to pay attention to two points. First, the effect of hate itself, its intensity and extent, and its general existence. It is not as much a reaction as something that grows from the inside, something primordial. It exists and seeks out its victims. [. . .] This is explicitly a fatalistic trait. The second point is its direction. It is directed against humanness no less than against humanity. More important than the tendency of hatred is its source. It stems from thinking too much of oneself, from making oneself divine.

The connection between our period and all of previous history is clear: the ideas entered the political arena. Never before has this happened with such a degree of power, with such a vehement resolve—at least on one side. Ideas are often drawn into the battlefield, or political arguments argue for or against one theory—Christianity, Islam, Reformation, freedom, or absolutism. However, never have the very foundations of human existence itself been brought into the arena. All preceding contradictions left a way out for most people: in the event that the opposing idea is victorious, they would, indeed, be restricted in their actions and declined many things, yet their simple life would not be taken away from them. With the victory of National Socialism, however, such a possibility will not remain. There will remain only a small number of masters—even without

nobility—and subjugated people possessing no right to free speech or free thought and no right whatsoever to any kind of human existence. The superhuman in the saddest form, Nietzsche's system in the ultimate degeneration—and an innumerable and inestimable group of slaves. [. . .]

National Socialism is not cynical, but it is an act of Satan, devilish in nature. It is the true heir of Amalek, that same figure that the Torah depicted with such unholy, symbolic strength, the new reincarnation of the same hellish people that stretched forth its hand against God's chair of glory. Perhaps for the first time we understand the Torah's positive commandment, "You shall blot out the memory of Amalek." We now understand the battle between the children of Israel and Amalek in Refidim, as it says in the Humash (Exodus 17:11), what is the meaning of the term *Refidim*? *Rifiyon-yadayim*— weakness of the hands. We know that only a person's elevated faith ensures him victory over this strength: "Then whenever Moses held up his hand, Israel prevailed; but whenever he let down his hand, Amalek prevailed." And the explanation of the Mishnah stands forever before us: "Do Moses' hands make war or break war? This means: when Israel would look up and devote their hearts to their father in heaven, they would win, and if not, they would fall" (Rosh Ha-shanah, chapter 3, mishnah 8). [. . .]

The insolent game of National Socialism is intended as an evil attempt to dismount God from His seat of glory [. . .]. Everything accomplished and prepared by National Socialism is a devastation and disfigurement of moral and holy values. It ridicules the concept of humanity that embraces all human children: this theory designates love and mercy as secondary values, yet in practice they are completely eliminated; feelings of honor and heroism, whose praises [the Nazis] sing, have been degraded because they do not believe that any other race is capable of possessing them (how often does Alfred Rosenberg refer to Jews and the Catholic Church as "dishonorable"!), and therefore they have been utilized for evil and ugliness. Honor and heroism reach a moral rank only when they are part of a system of ethical values, constructed upon the founding ideas of good, on its categorical imperative, and extended to all people. The restriction to one race, its birthright, is the clearest sign of the immorality of the National Socialist conception. [. . .]

It is difficult to know from where evil draws its strength. Is this the fault of humanity or is this part of history's plan? The generation which is entirely guilty[1]—did this [saying] really have to come to pass? And if it is indeed our fault—wherein lies the sin that resulted in this punishment? Is it in the form that we gave to economic life? [. . .] Is it in the half-measure of democracy or liberalism? Or is it in the political instability of the great nations, who know no limitations? Or is it in the unilateral nature of intellectual culture and the victory of the technique that has suffocated religious desire, the relationship with God, the words of calm and depth? It is enough to raise these many questions. It is not our task here to answer them. Yet perhaps we are leading to the absolutely critical situation which has overtaken us.

In this manner one can view the lines connecting today with the past. It is not hard to deduce from reality the connection between our Jewish fate and that of all humanity in the present time; it is not necessary to construe this relationship.

The attack of National Socialism is directed toward all powers that stand against its worldview. Peoples of other races, nations possessing some form of democracy, laws of humanity; religions, confessions, philosophies that refuse to renounce God and humanity, that regard the Bible as their holy book—this same hate is targeted at all of these. The Jewish people and its great traditions have merited to be the enemy of National Socialism—with a capital THE. Through this same hate, the Jews—completely against the will and the intention of the New Germany—are glorified into its most important opponents and the most valuable bearers of the best historical tradition. We must not forget what kind of recognition lies therein and how it once again highlights the Jewish people's mission in world history; even more—it elevates it to a level never before reached.

[. . .] However, what about the opposing side? Is the connection between democracy, religion, and the Jewish people sufficiently strong? The negative answer to this question directly reveals the tragedy of our period in its entirety. It is tragic that the greatest states of democracy have not understood the meaning of the historical process, have allowed the evil beast to grow, have abandoned the most valuable positions of freedom and dignified human existence, and also have not extended their hands to the Jewish people in the hour of deathly danger. No response to the problem of the refugees has been offered that accords with the scope of our misfortune, our historical role, or how this should constitute the exemplary answer to the evil attack upon humanity and upon us. And in that moment they did not allow

the free development of the Jewish national home in the Land of Israel.[2] Preventing our return to life in the Land of Israel, as affirmed by politics, which was pronounced in the White Paper is a blow not only to the historical logos, but also to moral obligation, which should have revealed itself now in an elementary fashion. And one can imagine the dimensions of the historical misfortune that results from this, when the devilishness of National Socialism is joined by the weakness and cowardice of others, who continuously step aside and in so doing make it [National Socialism] stronger.

No more has Christianity been able to awaken reason in the face of the metaphysical danger of the historical moment. Nowhere. The Catholic Church, as a whole, has not embarked on the battle in a way that would have brought it renown. Yet remarkable circles of Protestants and no less Catholic individuals—among them also clerics—have martyred themselves and in so doing awakened a long slumbering strength into a powerful belief. This is one factor that can help to initiate the change. Here we Jews have an ally, a friend to suffer for the same reason. This friendship is not only limited to the victim's pain but also binds together energies in a realization of a shared historical task. Thus, there presently exists a deep understanding between Christians and Jews. There is deep shock among earnest circles of Anglican Christianity, the events of the time have strongly kindled the moods and spirits among both thinkers and believers, and one sign of this revision is the clear movement toward our Bible—an answer to Hitler and Rosenberg and a greeting to us.

2

So appears the world around us. And what of within us and among us?

We are bleeding from a thousand wounds. The harshest blows landed on us, as a result of our history, our fate, our Torah and tradition, our culture, and we alone are, more than all other forces of good in the world, the witnesses for God and for His will in history. We have been immeasurably weakened, but not only through blood loss over the last years, which has reduced our physical material and moral strengths. We arrived at this time without thinking and were unprepared. Many of us did not believe the matter to be serious even as we found ourselves already in the midst of the misfortune. Only in November 1938 did the tip of the calamities open the eyes of the blind—that terrifying pogrom[3] that opened the final, and probably the longest, act of the tragedy.

Thus, the following calamities: the pain and need of the refugees and homeless, while the world demonstrated continuously less willingness to receive our people and give them a place to work; complications concerning the problem of the Land of Israel; the stubbornness of Western Jewry regarding the conception of assimilation—all this endows our sorrows with gigantic proportions. There is no reason to exaggerate and transform the mistakes of assimilation and emancipation into a sin beyond redemption. Nevertheless, we must provide an accounting and understand that the period of emancipation sapped from us our immense strength of resistance as a people. It spurred the process of disintegration and brought us no sympathy from the nations, serving only to sharpen the hatred of some, and among all creating wariness and an aftertaste. Emancipation inevitably led us to professions and cultural domains and to such activities within them that they considered an intrusion. The stranger, who is true to his group and remains tied to it, may be foreign and unsympathetic, but he knows his place. He, however, who breaks away from his roots, who links himself to a new circle, is suspect, and a conflict with him may erupt at any moment.

One hundred years ago, these thoughts could have appeared as an invented construction and a simplistic hypothesis, yet today they are [. . .] clearly and unambiguously characteristic. Likewise, we must not forget that in a range of countries that have not officially adopted racism, policies toward Jews are all the more hateful. Today we must look truth in the eye and see that even in those countries that are favorably inclined toward us, the positions of the Jews residing there have lost stability. Emancipation has been revoked—in principle; there is no reason to put it any other way.

We should not infer from this that we must throw off everything that the period of emancipation gave us. Such enduring historical stages, filled with so many events, always possess a relative significance. The closer contact of Jews with the surrounding world was not unfruitful, the participation of Jews in all aspects of life meant an exchange of riches, a give and take; after a long period of interiority, relations among Jews in various arenas brought invigoration and rejuvenation. [. . .] The emancipation of the individual was a false path, to which we should never have aspired. The emancipation of the collective—this would have been an important task. The Western nations and Western Jews thought differently—the prize was a dire one. We are almost atomized; we ourselves fractured our national structure, removed the mental strength of the col-

lective, and frivolously and willfully allowed our very culture to wither. The hour of need having arrived, we are unequipped to strengthen ourselves. Western Jewry has no national language, no natural cement for national sentiment, is almost without Torah, and lacks the rootedness provided by great faith. However, the East too finds itself in a stage of disintegration. This is the ledger sheet from the period of emancipation.

3

[. . .] The Jewish diaspora must assume a national character. The nineteenth- and twentieth-century version of emancipation cannot remain the form of life for Jews in the diaspora, and assimilation cannot continue to be the Jewish position. We must advance toward a form of autonomy. In the diaspora, too, the Jew must aspire to a center. [. . .] A social and cultural environment of a specific nature will prove to be a blessing. The Jew will necessarily return to the sources of his national spiritual energies, not only because other springs will be closed to him, but also because through contact with the roots of our spirituality the desired reanimation will nevertheless begin at some stage. [. . .]

Likewise, we will understand, endure, and overcome the great misfortune that has befallen us when we will descend deep into the Jewish character of religious brilliance, of the Torah and prophecy, and we will learn from the prophet Isaiah the secret of divine service. I cannot exhaust this theme, but I will not conclude before mentioning explicitly chapter 53 of Isaiah, in which the purpose of our nation's sufferings receives a universal interpretation, relevant to world history, and finally the peoples will acknowledge that which [. . .] they failed to understand for so long: how the nation "despised and shunned by men," beaten and afflicted, was chosen to be the bearer of the greatest mission. Today we truly stand before this sad picture. However, this will confirm our great appointment, our world-historical essence. Thus our misfortune will be a confirmation of our value and existence.

NOTES

1. [Sanhedrin 98a: the Messiah will come only in a generation which is entirely meritorious or entirely guilty.—Eds.]

2. [He refers to the restrictive immigration policy of the British Mandate over Palestine.—Eds.]

3. [Kristallnacht.—Eds.]

Translated by Rebecca Wolpe.

Other works by Wolfsberg: *Zur Zeit- und Geistesgeschichte des Judentums* (1938); *Judentum und Gegenwart*

(1941); *Ba-perozdor* (1943); *She'arim* (1948); *Iyunim be-ya-hadut* (1955); *Sefer Aviad: kovets maamarim u-meḥkarim le-zekher Dr. Yeshayahu Volfsberg-Aviad* (1986).

Leibush Lehrer
1887–1964

Leibush Lehrer was a beloved and prominent teacher, philosopher, writer, and pedagogical theorist in left-wing Yiddish-speaking circles, especially in the United States. Born in Warsaw, Lehrer immigrated to New York in 1919, teaching from that time until his death at the Jewish Teachers Seminary of the Sholem Aleichem Folk Institute. He was also deeply involved in the YIVO Institute's research programs, serving as secretary for the Section on Psychology and Education, member of the National Council for Jewish Education, and longtime principal of the Sholem Aleichem Secondary School. He is perhaps best remembered as the director of the Yiddishist children's summer retreat Camp Boiberik, a position he held for over four decades.

Jewishness (Yidishkayt) and Other Problems
ca. 1939

1

Our generation came to this country from lands where Jewish life had been lived within its own boundaries, and where our communal leaders had instilled in us a sense of responsibility to ensure that there is a Jewish tomorrow. These two elements—directing our own lives and exercising responsibility for our national future—constitute the substance of conscious Jewish existence. Thus, religious Jews have relied on their traditional way of life and anticipated the Days of the Messiah. Zionists and territorialists have nourished themselves with Jewish cultural values and the hope for a country of our own. Populists and socialists have been hoping for a free world where the continuity of Jewish existence would be guaranteed by autonomous organizations. Others, whose main consideration was the "free world," were still Jewish enough to have faith in a bright future without making specific plans. Once the world is liberated and the "sun of the socialists rises," all nations, including Jews, will be reestablished as a matter of course.

When we came to this country [the United States], the very foundation of our organized life was shaken, our language was threatened by the menacing force of assimilation, and our way of life began to crumble and break into pieces, as if its inner juices had dried up. We all started to live off the remnants of the good, bygone days, and those who had plans for the future and practical means to carry them out were the happiest. As for the present state of Jewish existence, we all had to content ourselves with the remaining torn-off fringes. The Jewishness of "Yiddish and Yiddish culture" did not provide any more security and strength to its proponents than various forms of strict religious observance to its adherents. And yet, everyone harbored grand illusions. This crafty, smart nation did not wake up to reality very fast.

The greatest losses were suffered by the national wing of the radical camp. They had been struck by a terrible blindness and were tragically duped—a blow that no other conscious segment of the [Jewish] people had suffered. I am referring to the Bolshevik revolution.

The messianic promise of the Bolshevik revolution regarding the national existence of the Jewish people sounded generous and definite: Jewish judicial courts, Jewish schools, Jewish theater, Jewish literature—and everything paid for by the government! True, Jewish life is not structured by centralized autonomous organizations, but this might even be for the better, after all. True, Jewish social life suffered terrible blows: the dictatorship eradicated every trace of a nationally conscious leadership; Zionism has been banned—and even broad-minded anti-Zionists can easily understand the national tragedy of such a legal ban. Soviet Jews have been forcefully cut off from the rest of world Jewry. But this, we were reassured, must be a temporary measure. Soon the revolution will subside a little bit, and everything will be all right. True, Hebrew has been relegated to the category of "counterrevolutionary"; Jewish history has been erased from the school curricula; the traditional Jewish way of life has not been banned legally, but, as a result of social pressure backed by state support, it was scorned and despised to such a degree that all past generations of Jews were almost considered criminals. All this is true, but ultimately this is just an expression of the fight against religion, people argued; why should we care about the Jewish religion? [. . .]

But when enough time has passed and the water is already up to our neck, then everyone will finally realize

where we stand in the world. The veil will be lifted revealing striking facts, and the terrible tragedy of Soviet
Jewry will stand naked in front of our eyes. The secular
segment of Polish Jewry has not brought us much Jewish joy either, and our cries for "Yiddish and Jewish culture" on this side of the ocean have become somewhat
hoarse too. We have detected some false tones in our
Judaism, some hollowness that brings fear. Claiming
that the Jewish religion is none of our concern, hiding
behind "secularism" has led us into a blind alley, and
there is no way out in sight. [. . .]

3

[. . .] We can see that Jewish tradition is a unique
system, and calling it the "Jewish religion" and thereby
putting it on the same page with all other religions only
obscures the picture. Professor M. M. Kaplan wants to
save himself from this mistake by talking about a Jewish "folk-religion" and argues that patriotism is nothing
but a modern form of "folk-religion." The fact is that
even though patriotism and religion do have, no doubt,
important similarities, these two experiences are usually not classified under the same rubric. The addition
of the word *folk*—even though it does bring us closer
to the ethnic structure of Jewish traditional life—does
not have the power to give us a clear picture because
the emphasis is still on the second word, *religion*. And,
indeed, Professor Kaplan's "religious-cultural conception of Judaism" wants to consciously lay the emphasis
on religious values.

Professor Kaplan concludes that, *"from the perspective of the religious-cultural program, everything that
helps produce creative social interrelations among Jews
belongs rightfully to the category of Jewish religion, because it contributes to the redemption of the Jew. [. . .]
A movement like spiritual Zionism, whose goal is to
keep world Jewry united and creative, is entitled to a
place in Jewish religion."* But if this is the case, then is
the movement for Yiddish, for Hebrew, for a world congress and many other things also religion? If everything
that strives "to keep world Jewry united and creative"
is religion, then this concept loses all its specificity and
loses its meaning. [. . .]

What term did our forefathers use to describe the
order according to which they lived? It is interesting
that the internationally widespread word *religion* was,
indeed, part of their Yiddish vocabulary, but they used
it only to describe the faith of the Christians among

whom they lived. When they described Jewish traditional life, they used a different word, a word that, in my
opinion, characterizes with firm folkloristic power and
exactness the central point of the Jewish way. Rather
than religion, they called it *yidishkayt*, Jewishness.

With this word at least three goals have been
achieved, the importance of which is clear in light of our
earlier considerations. First of all, this word originates
from the name of the people. This puts the emphasis
on the fact that we are not talking about life in general
and people in general, but about Jewish people's Jewish
life. This was the original idea behind the plan of this
cultural project. The entire building has been erected
with the aim of serving certain goals that grow out of
the social situation of an ethnic and historically interwoven group. Secondly, we have here one single word.
When we use a noun with a qualifying adjective, our
consciousness is automatically split into two directions.
When we say *Jewish religion*, we think of one branch
of a general tree. Jewish in this case is only one possible subdivision of religion in general. The single word
yidishkayt, however, does not allow such a split. It is a
particular unit that is an organism in itself, just like the
life it represents. Thirdly, this single abstract noun is
not a collective name for the numerous details of internal Jewish life; it synthesizes all shades and nuances of
the tradition in one quality, national wholeness. Just
like politeness, for example, expresses all possible ways
of being polite, the same way *yidishkayt* comprises all
forms of being Jewish. [. . .]

Regardless, *yidishkayt* has always been and to this
day remains a general folk culture and not a religious
system. This stood out especially in loud contrast to the
Christian religion that was the concrete religious model
of the surrounding society. [. . .]

Speaking of principles of faith reminds me of a story
a renowned Yiddish writer once told me. His father was
a famous rabbi, a pious Jew and an erudite scholar. He
could never reconcile himself to the Rambam's Thirteen Principles of the Jewish Faith. He considered
them essentially non-Jewish. For Jews it is much more
important that *yisrael af al pi she-ḥata, yisrael hu*, a
Jew who has sinned remains a Jew. Faith as such is not
an absolute requirement in *yidishkayt*. He used to say
to his son: "Whether you believe in God, that is your
business. The question is whether you pray—that is the
main issue." In other words: if you behave like a Jew
you will be part of the Jewish community. Theological
questions are of lesser concern. [. . .]

5

There are people today who feel aversion to *yidish-kayt* because it is a religion. A hundred years ago in Germany there were also people who spoke with hatred about traditional *yidishkayt* but they did so because in their eyes *yidishkayt* was *not* a religion, or not purely religion. I am talking about the reformers who were longing for a "German Jewish church," who truly wanted to have a real Jewish religion and decided to create it by way of "reforms" or by way of a cleansing process that the old Jewish way of life had to undergo. In their view, this way of life had to be broken up, cleansed, and changed until it was reduced to no more than a "Jewish religion." [. . .]

The Reform movement was the first and only one in the entire course of Jewish history—not counting the first Christians about whom we know so little—that attempted to create a Jewish religion, a religion in the sense of the word as it is understood in the entire Western world. I have often wondered why we, East European Jews—even the most radical freethinkers among us—feel so strange, cold, and alienated in a Reform temple. Even those who speak with admiration about the beauty of the Christian church as opposed to the shabbiness of the old-style *besmedresh* are disappointed by the Reform temple. The beauty of the architecture and decoration, the fine music, and the impressiveness of the quiet religious behavior cannot, it turns out, make up for the alienating coldness that an East European Jew feels when entering a Reform temple. [. . .]

Advocates of secularism also demanded that Yiddish should receive public and national acknowledgement as our language. Thus, *Yiddish* and *secular* became the slogans of a movement. However, we cannot say that these two slogans are logically connected in any way. They are very different in character and have different goals, too. Secularism is, after all, a primarily negative concept; it means renouncing the old forms of Jewish life that the so-called "Jewish religion" forced upon us. Yiddish, however, is a positive issue, both in terms of public acknowledgment and with regard to spreading and creating everything that can be expressed in the language. The goal of secularism is to eliminate from Jewish life something that is considered bad, to modernize it, to make [Jews] "equal with other peoples." Thus, it is a general human goal, not a specifically Jewish one. The goal of Yiddish, on the other hand, is national expression, national content, even if it is formu-lated in somewhat suspiciously shy words: "because the Jewish masses speak Yiddish."

In that sense there is really no direct connection between the two slogans, even though they are used together both in speech and in writing so often as if they were a conceptual unit. [. . .]

6

Secularism can only exist in opposition to religion. But, *yidishkayt* is not a religion. The secularists had to invent it in order to have logical grounds for their fight. Thus, Jewish secularism had to decide that the Tanakh was religion, that halakhah was religion, the holidays were religion, *bar-mitzvah* was religion, and yes, even the Hebrew language, Shabbat rest, and the Jewish calendar—all these were religious in nature. The only thing left was Yiddish. This is the only product of our traditional way of life—*yidishkayt*—that escaped the strict verdict passed by secularism against Jewish history and Jewish life. Why this happened we will see later, but my heart tells me that in this regard, just like in every other case mentioned earlier, external secularism was inspired by the custom of gentiles. [. . .]

In reality, secularism became a slogan for assimilation, even though this was definitely not intended. This concept came from foreign sources, it remained foreign, and it alienated itself from the very root from which every form of *yidishkayt* must grow out, from the desire to remain in the world as a national unit. The active and aggressive secularism that was represented by the workers' parties—the Bund, the communists—did not even have and did not want to allow any term that would express the above mentioned concept. Nationalism—which for Jews cannot mean anything else but the desire to remain a nation—became a sign of reaction. The term was given a foreign meaning, one it can only have in a ruling imperialistic nation. [. . .]

7

The idea of secularism was represented by several organized and nonorganized groupings in Jewish life. But the more extremely this idea was expressed, the weaker the national tone became in that group, and the looser the connection to the people, its values and hopes.

And what about Yiddish? Did Yiddish not come in to fill the empty hollow left by the expelled religion? Yes, it did, but this enterprise has not had great success. I am afraid that just as in the case of secularism, what we have here is a foreign-looking slogan taken over from foreign sources, which, for that reason, was unable to demonstrate much power.

It is worth emphasizing the fact that linguistic Yiddishism—considering Yiddish the only spiritual binding cord, according to Zhitlovsky's earlier mentioned definition—has not taken root in our life. Literature in Yiddish blossomed, a Yiddish school system has been created, Yiddish became a cultural language—but linguistic Yiddishism remained the theoretical property of a limited number of ideologues and a small number of conscious supporters. Large workers' parties helped cultivate Yiddish to a great extent, but they remained neutral and even hostile to the ideological conception of linguistic Yiddishism. As for the Orthodox, Yiddish is an intimate part of their lives, but the ideology has not touched them in any way. Other Jewish groupings are not even worth mentioning in this respect. [. . .]

The fate of Hebraism as a purely linguistic ideology has not been much brighter, either. The Hebrew language reverberated profoundly with the people; it inspired enthusiasm and energetic actions, but linguistic Hebraism left people cold. As we said before, the situation of Hebrew has been a little better, and we will soon see why. But the bottom line is that linguistic nationalism has not received such a warm reception by Jews as by other peoples. Why? For now, let us suffice to say just a few remarks that will help us understand our current problems.

Among the classical cultural nations, Jews are the only people who used a foreign language even while they were living in their own land and in the course of hundreds of years created grand cultural treasures in it. The Jewish people have shown a heartrending attachment to Hebrew to this day, but not to Hebrew as a language but as the Holy Tongue; Hebrew became some sort of a higher symbol of national-spiritual uniqueness, but this does not require that it should be used in the everyday functions of a language, that it should become the spoken language of daily life. [. . .]

9

Secularism is at odds with religion. It was secularism that declared *yidishkayt* a religion and, as a matter of course, a private issue (in reality a *foolish* and sometimes even a *criminal* private issue). Secularism has proved to be a terrible mistake for us Jews; it led to an attempt to uproot any connection to our history.

In its name people actually developed a revulsion for all ceremonies, celebrations, memorial days, and days of mourning—these healthy national cultural products with which the old *yidishkayt* illuminated our lives so beautifully. This went so far that Yiddishists who vehemently protested—and rightly so—against the persecution of Yiddish in Israel, looked neutrally—and to some extent with silent approval—at the anti-Jewish, antinational attitude to Hebrew in the Soviet Union.

By now it must be clear that if we think of *yidishkayt* as a religion, we are, as a matter of course, compelled to put the whole of Jewish spiritual life in the rubric of "religion." And if secularism requires that we relinquish it, what, then, remains? No more Jewish life, no more Jews. This is what it comes down to. [. . .]

If the spiritual life of the Jewish people is not cut off from its roots, as is done by Reformers and secularists, then we can see clearly the age-old web that unites us as a people, not just the individual binding cord. First of all, we are illuminated by the deeply rooted consciousness that we are a people and want to remain a people. We have a sense of age-old historical communality and share familial kinship with great personalities and great events in the Jewish past that we can see through the windows of history. We are all touched by the feeling of being connected to every Jewish community in the world and their historical fate, and we have a certain psychological readiness to feel their joys as if they were our own joys, and to soothe their pain in critical moments. We express the spirituality of our people by connecting to our grand historical drama through concrete symbols and rituals when things are serious, in times of festiveness, joyfulness, and mourning. In short, we all express the feeling of *betokh ami ani yoshev*, "I dwell among my people." [. . .]

Translated by Vera Szabó.

Other works by Lehrer: *Di moderne yidishe shul* (1927); *Shriftn far psikhologye un pedagogie* (1933).

MEMOIR AND REPORTAGE

While the memoirs in this section reflect the upheavals of the interwar period, they do so in personal terms, reflecting the subjective experiences of persons of vastly different backgrounds and temperaments in radically different circumstances. They display the multiplicity and complexity of Jewish lives in the interwar period and show how individuals made their way in the world. Travel accounts and journalistic reports in this section illuminate often-unknown corners of Jewish life but also reflect, at the same time, the personal sensibilities of those who wrote them. As a whole, they concentrate on the two great social and cultural experiments of the time—the efforts to fashion radically new societies in the Soviet Union and in the Land of Israel.

Franz Kafka
1883–1924

The tormented writer Franz Kafka was a literary original, the creator of dreamlike fables and tales featuring fantastic institutions and bizarre experiences. A native of Prague and a lawyer by training, he earned a living as a civil servant, working for the state-run workers' accident insurance company. He was close to several members of the Prague circle of Zionists, took an interest in Jewish affairs, and even talked of settling in the Land of Israel. He was diagnosed with tuberculosis in 1917 and spent long periods in sanatoria before his early death.

Letter to His Father
1919

[. . .] I found as little escape from you in Judaism. Here some measure of escape would have been thinkable in principle, moreover, it would have been thinkable that we might both have found each other in Judaism or that we even might have begun from there in harmony. But what sort of Judaism was it that I got from you? In the course of the years, I have taken roughly three different attitudes to it.

As a child I reproached myself, in accord with you, for not going to the synagogue often enough, for not fasting, and so on. I thought that in this way I was doing a wrong not to myself but to you, and I was penetrated by a sense of guilt, which was, of course, always ready to hand.

Later, as a young man, I could not understand how, with the insignificant scrap of Judaism you yourself possessed, you could reproach me for not making an effort (for the sake of piety at least, as you put it) to cling to a similar, insignificant scrap. It was indeed, so far as I could see, a mere nothing, a joke—not even a joke. Four days a year you went to the synagogue, where you were, to say the least, closer to the indifferent than to those who took it seriously, patiently went through the prayers as a formality, sometimes amazed me by being able to show me in the prayer book the passage that was being said at the moment, and for the rest, so long as I was present in the synagogue (and this was the main thing) I was allowed to hang about wherever I liked.

And so I yawned and dozed through the many hours (I don't think I was ever again so bored, except later at dancing lessons) and did my best to enjoy the few little bits of variety there were, as for instance when the Ark of the Covenant was opened, which always reminded me of the shooting galleries where a cupboard door would open in the same way whenever one hit a bull's eye; except that there something interesting always came out and here it was always just the same old dolls without heads. Incidentally, it was also very frightening for me there, not only, as goes without saying, because of all the people one came into close contact with, but also because you once mentioned in passing that I too might be called to the Torah. That was something I dreaded for years. But otherwise I was not fundamentally disturbed in my boredom, unless it was by the *bar mitzvah*, but that demanded no more than some ridiculous memorizing, in other words, it led to nothing but some ridiculous passing of an examination; and, so far as you were concerned, by little, not very significant incidents, as when you were called to the Torah and passed, in what to my way of feeling was a purely social event; or when you stayed on in the synagogue for the prayers for the dead, and I was sent away, which for a long time—obviously because of the being-sent-away and the lack of any deeper interest—aroused in me the more or less unconscious feeling that something indecent was about to take place.—That's how it was in the synagogue; at home it was, if possible, even poorer, being confined to the first Seder, which more and more developed into a farce, with fits of hysterical laughter, admittedly under the influence of the growing children. (Why did you have to give way to that influence? Because you had brought it about.) This was the religious material that was handed on to me, to which may be added at most the outstretched hand pointing to "the sons of the millionaire Fuchs," who attended the synagogue with their father on the high holy days. How one could do anything better with that material than get rid of it as fast as possible, I could not understand; precisely the getting rid of it seemed to me to be the devoutest action.

Still later, I did see it again differently and realized why it was possible for you to think that in this respect too I was malevolently betraying you. You really had brought some traces of Judaism with you from the ghetto-like village community; it was not much and it dwindled a little more in the city and during your military service; but still, the impressions and memories of your youth did just about suffice for some sort of Jewish life, especially since you did not need much help of that kind, but came of robust stock and could personally scarcely be shaken by religious scruples unless they were strongly mixed with social scruples. At bottom the faith that ruled your life consisted in your believing in the unconditional rightness of the opinions of a certain class of Jewish society, and hence actually, since these opinions were part and parcel of your own nature, in believing in yourself. Even in this there was still Judaism enough, but it was too little to be handed on to the child; it all dribbled away while you were passing it on. In part, it was youthful memories that could not be passed on to others; in part, it was your dreaded personality. It was also impossible to make a child, overacutely observant from sheer nervousness, understand that the few flimsy gestures you performed in the name of Judaism, and with an indifference in keeping with their flimsiness, could have any higher meaning. For you they had meaning as little souvenirs of earlier times, and that was why you wanted to pass them on to me, but since they no longer had any intrinsic value even for you, you could do this only through persuasion or threat: on the one hand, this could not be successful, and on the other, it had to make you very angry with me on account of my apparent obstinacy, since you did not recognize the weakness of your position in this.

The whole thing is, of course, no isolated phenomenon. It was much the same with a large section of this transitional generation of Jews, which had migrated from the still comparatively devout countryside to the cities. It happened automatically; only, it added to our relationship, which certainly did not lack in acrimony, one more, sufficiently painful source for it. Although you ought to believe, as I do, in your guiltlessness in this matter too, you ought to explain this guiltlessness by your nature and by the conditions of the times, not merely by external circumstances; that is, not by saying, for instance, that you had too much work and too many other worries to be able to bother with such things as well. In this manner you tend to twist your undoubted guiltlessness into an unjust reproach to others. That can be very easily refuted everywhere and here too. It was not a matter of any sort of instruction you ought to have given your children, but of an exemplary life.

Had your Judaism been stronger, your example would have been more compelling too; this goes without saying and is, again, by no means a reproach, but only a refutation of your reproaches. You have recently been reading Franklin's memoirs of his youth. I really did purposely give you this book to read, though not, as you ironically commented, because of a little passage on vegetarianism, but because of the relationship between the author and his father, as it is there described, and of the relationship between the author and his son, as it is spontaneously revealed in these memoirs written for that son. I do not wish to dwell here on matters of detail.

I have received a certain retrospective confirmation of this view of your Judaism from your attitude in recent years, when it seemed to you that I was taking more interest in Jewish matters. As you have in advance an aversion to every one of my activities and especially to the nature of my interest, so you have had it here too. But in spite of this, one could have expected that in this case you would make a little exception. It was, after all, Judaism of your Judaism that was here stirring, and with it also the possibility to enter into a new relationship between us. I do not deny that, had you shown interest in them, these things might, for that very reason, have become suspect in my eyes. I do not even dream of asserting that I am in this respect any better than you are. But it never came to the test. Through my intervention Judaism became abhorrent to you, Jewish writings unreadable; they "nauseated" you.—This may have meant you insisted that only that Judaism which you had shown me in my childhood was the right one, and beyond it there was nothing. Yet that you should insist on it was really hardly thinkable. But then the "nausea" (apart from the fact that it was directed primarily not against Judaism but against me personally) could only mean that unconsciously you did acknowledge the weakness of your Judaism and of my Jewish upbringing, did not wish to be reminded of it in any way, and reacted to any reminder with frank hatred. Incidentally, your negative high esteem of my new Judaism was much exaggerated; first of all, it bore your curse within it, and secondly, in its development the fundamental relationship to one's fellow men was decisive, in my case that is to say fatal.

You struck nearer home with your aversion to my writing and to everything that, unknown to you, was connected with it. Here I had, in fact, got some distance away from you by my own efforts, even if it was slightly reminiscent of the worm that, when a foot treads on its tail end, breaks loose with its front part and drags itself aside. To a certain extent I was in safety; there was a chance to breathe freely. The aversion you naturally and immediately took to my writing was, for once, welcome to me. My vanity, my ambition did suffer under your soon proverbial way of hailing the arrival of my books: "Put it on my bedside table!" (usually you were playing cards when a book came), but I was really quite glad of it, not only out of rebellious malice, not only out of delight at a new confirmation of my view of our relationship, but quite spontaneously, because to me that formula sounded something like: "Now you are free!" Of course it was a delusion; I was not, or, to put it most optimistically, was not yet, free. My writing was all about you; all I did there, after all, was to bemoan what I could not bemoan upon your breast. It was an intentionally long-drawn-out leave-taking from you, yet, although it was enforced by you, it did take its course in the direction determined by me. But how little all this amounted to! It is only worth talking about because it happened in my life, otherwise it would not even be noted; and also because in my childhood it ruled my life as a premonition, later as a hope, and still later often as despair, and it dictated—it may be said, yet again in your shape—my few small decisions.

For instance, the choice of a career. True, here you gave me complete freedom, in your magnanimous and, in this regard, even indulgent manner. Although here again you were conforming to the general method of treating sons in the Jewish middle class, which was the standard for you, or at least to the values of that class. Finally, one of your misunderstandings concerning my person played a part in this too. In fact, out of paternal pride, ignorance of my real life, and conclusions drawn from my feebleness, you have always regarded me as particularly diligent. As a child I was, in your view, always studying, and later always writing. This does not even remotely correspond to the facts. It would be more correct, and much less exaggerated, to say that I studied little and learnt nothing; that something did stick in my mind after those many years is, after all, not very remarkable, since I did have a moderately good memory and a not too inferior capacity for learning; but the sum total of knowledge and especially of a solid grounding of knowledge is extremely pitiable in comparison with the expenditure of time and money in the course of an outwardly untroubled, calm life, particularly also in comparison with almost all the people I know. It is

pitiable, but to me understandable. Ever since I could think I have had such profound anxieties about asserting my spiritual existence that I was indifferent to everything else. Jewish schoolboys in our country often tend to be odd; among them one finds the most unlikely things; but something like my cold indifference, scarcely disguised, indestructible, childishly helpless, approaching the ridiculous, and brutishly complacent, the indifference of a self-sufficient but coldly imaginative child, I have never found anywhere else; to be sure, it was the sole defense against destruction of the nerves by fear and by a sense of guilt. All that occupied my mind was worry about myself, and this in various ways. There was, for instance, the worry about my health; it began imperceptibly enough, with now and then a little anxiety about digestion, hair falling out, a spinal curvature, and so on; intensifying in innumerable gradations, it finally ended with a real illness. But since there was nothing at all I was certain of, since I needed to be provided at every instant with a new confirmation of my existence, since nothing was in my very own, undoubted, sole possession, determined unequivocally only by me—in sober truth a disinherited son—naturally I became unsure even of the thing nearest to me, my own body. I shot up, tall and lanky, without knowing what to do with my lankiness, the burden was too heavy, the back became bent; I scarcely dared to move, certainly not to exercise, I remained weakly; I was amazed by everything I could still command as by a miracle, for instance, my good digestion; that sufficed to lose it, and now the way was open to every sort of hypochondria; until finally under the strain of the superhuman effort of wanting to marry (of this I shall speak later), blood came from the lung, something in which the apartment in the Schönbornpalais—which, however, I needed only because I believed I needed it for my writing, so that even this belongs here under the same heading— may have had a fair share. So all this did not come from excessive work, as you always imagine. There were years in which, in perfectly good health, I lazed away more time on the sofa than you in all your life, including all your illnesses. When I rushed away from you, frightfully busy, it was generally in order to lie down in my room. My total achievement in work done, both at the office (where laziness is, of course, not particularly striking, and besides, mine was kept in bounds by my timidity) and at home, is minute; if you had any real idea of it, you would be aghast. Probably I am constitutionally not lazy at all, but there was nothing for me to do.

In the place where I lived I was spurned, condemned, fought to a standstill; and to escape to some other place was an enormous exertion, but that was not work, for it was something impossible, something that was, with small exceptions unattainable for me.

This was the state in which I was given the freedom of choice of a career. But was I still capable of making any use of such freedom? Had I still any confidence in my own capacity to achieve a real career? My valuation of myself was much more dependent on you than on anything else, such as some external success. *That* was strengthening for a moment, nothing more, but on the other side your weight always dragged me down much more strongly. Never shall I pass the first grade in grammar school, I thought, but I succeeded, I even got a prize; but I shall certainly not pass the entrance exam for the Gymnasium, but I succeeded; but now I shall certainly fail in the first year at the Gymnasium; no, I did not fail, and I went on and on succeeding. This did not produce any confidence, however; on the contrary, I was always convinced—and I positively had the proof of it in your forbidding expression—that the more I achieved, the worse the final outcome would inevitably be. Often in my mind's eye I saw the terrible assembly of the teachers (the Gymnasium is only the most integral example, but it was the same all around me), as they would meet, when I had passed the first class, and then in the second class, when I had passed that, and then in the third, and so on, meeting in order to examine this unique, outrageous case, to discover how I, the most incapable and, in any case, the most ignorant of all, had succeeded in creeping up so far as this class, which now, when everybody's attention had at last been focused on me, would of course instantly spew me out, to the jubilation of all the righteous liberated from this nightmare. To live with such fantasies is not easy for a child. In these circumstances, what could I care about my lessons? Who was able to strike a spark of real interest in me? Lessons, and not only lessons but everything around me, interested me as much, at that decisive age, as a defaulting bank clerk, still holding his job and trembling at the thought of discovery, is interested in the small current business of the bank, which he still has to deal with as a clerk. That was how small and faraway everything was in comparison to the main thing. So it went on up to the qualifying exams which I really passed partly only through cheating, and then everything stagnated, for now I was free. If I had been concerned only with myself up to now, despite the dis-

cipline of the Gymnasium, how much more now that I was free. So there was actually no such thing for me as freedom to choose my career, for I knew: compared to the main thing everything would be exactly as much a matter of indifference to me as all the subjects taught at school, and so it was a matter of finding a profession that would let me indulge this indifference without injuring my vanity too much. Law was the obvious choice. Little contrary attempts on the part of vanity, of senseless hope, such as a fortnight's study of chemistry, or six months' German studies, only reinforced that fundamental conviction. So I studied law. This meant that in the few months before the exams, and in a way that told severely on my nerves, I was positively living, in an intellectual sense, on sawdust, which had moreover, already been chewed for me in thousands of the people's mouths. But in a certain sense this was exactly to my taste, as in a certain sense the Gymnasium had been earlier, and later my job as a clerk, for it all suited my situation. At any rate, I did show astonishing foresight; even as a small child I had had fairly clear premonitions about my studies and my career. From this side I did not expect rescue; here I had given up long ago.

But I showed no foresight at all concerning the significance and possibility of a marriage for me; this up to now greatest terror of my life has come upon me almost completely unexpectedly. The child had developed so slowly, these things were outwardly all too remote; now and then the necessity of thinking of them did arise; but that here a permanent, decisive and indeed the most grimly bitter ordeal loomed was impossible to recognize. In reality, however, the marriage plans turned out to be the most grandiose and hopeful attempts at escape, and, consequently, their failure was correspondingly grandiose.

I am afraid that, because in this sphere everything I try is a failure, I shall also fail to make these attempts to marry comprehensible to you. And yet the success of this whole letter depends on it, for in these attempts there was, on the one hand, concentrated everything I had at my disposal in the way of positive forces, and, on the other hand, there also accumulated, and with downright fury, all the negative forces that I have described as being the result in part of your method of upbringing, that is to say, the weakness, the lack of self-confidence, the sense of guilt, and they positively drew a cordon between myself and marriage. The explanation will be hard for me also because I have spent so many days and nights thinking and burrowing through the whole thing over and over again that now even I myself am bewildered by the mere sight of it. The only thing that makes the explanation easier for me is your—in my opinion—complete misunderstanding of the matter; slightly to correct so complete a misunderstanding does not seem excessively difficult.

First of all you rank the failure of the marriages with the rest of my failures; I should have nothing against this, provided you accepted my previous explanation of my failure as a whole. It does, in fact, form part of the same series, only you underrate the importance of the matter, underrating it to such an extent that whenever we talk of it we are actually talking about quite different things. I venture to say that nothing has happened to you in your whole life that had such importance for you as the attempts at marriage have had for me. By this I do not mean that you have not experienced anything in itself as important; on the contrary, your life was much richer and more care-laden and more concentrated than mine, but for that very reason nothing of this sort has happened to you. It is as if one person had to climb five low steps and another person only one step, but one that is, at least for him, as high as all the other five put together; the first person will not only manage the five, but hundreds and thousands more as well, he will have led a great and very strenuous life, but none of the steps he has climbed will have been of such importance to him as for the second person that one, first, high step, that step which it is impossible for him to climb even by exerting all his strength, that step which he cannot get up on and which he naturally cannot get past either.

Marrying, founding a family, accepting all the children that come, supporting them in this insecure world and perhaps even guiding them a little, is, I am convinced, the utmost a human being can succeed in doing at all. That so many seem to succeed in this is no evidence to the contrary; first of all, there are not many who do succeed, and secondly, these not-many usually don't "do" it, it merely "happens" to them; although this is not that Utmost, it is still very great and very honorable (particularly since "doing" and "happening" cannot be kept clearly distinct). And finally, it is not a matter of this Utmost at all, anyway, but only of some distant but decent approximation; it is, after all, not necessary to fly right into the middle of the sun, but it is necessary to crawl to a clean little spot on earth where the sun sometimes shines and one can warm oneself a little.

How was I prepared for this? As badly as possible. This is apparent from what has been said up to now. In so far as any direct preparation of the individual and any direct creation of the general basic conditions exists, you did not intervene much outwardly. And it could not be otherwise; what is decisive here are the general sexual customs of class, nation, and time. Yet you did intervene here too—not much, for such intervention must presuppose great mutual trust, and both of us had been lacking in this even long before the decisive time came—and not very happily, because our needs were quite different; what grips me need hardly touch you at all, and vice versa; what is innocence in you may be guilt in me, and vice versa; what has no consequences for you may be the last nail in my coffin.

Translated by Ernst Kaiser and Eithne Wilkins.

Other works by Kafka: *The Complete Stories* (1971); *The Castle* (1998); *The Trial* (1998); *Amerika* (2008).

Hillel Zeitlin

1871–1942

Born in Korma, Belorussia, the Yiddish and Hebrew writer Hillel Zeitlin was raised in a Hasidic family but studied European literature and philosophy, later exploring the works of Spinoza, Schopenhauer, and Nietzsche. Zeitlin moved to Gomel and befriended the writers Joseph Chaim Brenner and Gershom Shofman. Zeitlin spent years in Vilna and Warsaw, editing journals in both languages, including the newspapers *Haynt* and *Der moment*. He was also an active Zionist, attending the Fifth Zionist Congress in 1901, and writing about cultural issues in the Jewish revival. Later in life he studied Kabbalah and Hasidism and experienced a personal religious revival. He was killed by the Nazis. Zeitlin's sons Aaron and Elkhonen were Yiddish writers and cultural activists.

Memorial to a Shtetl

1919

1

Far, far from the paved roads and broad ways, far, far from the ordinary shtetls, stood isolated villages that had a different sky over them and a different sun.

The God of heaven in His mercy made their faces glow, His sun shone more brightly and with splendor on their wooden roofs.

Their weekdays were different, and their holidays and Sabbaths were different.

The village of my youth! I see it while awake, I see it in a dream.

I raise my soul to you among the walls of the city, among the stone pavements, with my head teeming, among the streets lit with electric lights, and their shadow-people.

2

At night, every night, the dead come to pray in the high synagogue, ancient, in ruins. They bring Torah scrolls of fire with them. Our teacher Moses calls out: May Isaac, the son of Abraham, rise. . . .

At night, every night, the ancient, destroyed synagogue is full of saints, angels, and seraphim. The saints pray, the angels sing, and the seraphim say: Holy, holy.

At night, every night, when the burial society comes to pray, the birds accompany it.

And when the reader calls out: "May Isaac, the son of Abraham rise . . ." upon hearing about the bound son, and the crown the high angels placed on his head, the birds spread their wings and make a canopy over him.

And in reading about the Egyptians who drowned in the Red Sea and about the children of Israel who were redeemed—heaven and earth will rejoice, fathers will sing, birds will listen. [. . .]

Now the children [. . .] come to the nearby Hasidic house of study; there they will pray, there they will play music, there they will sing, there "they will cleave."

Now, next to one of the benches in the center of the house of study stands old Rabbi Jacob. He is all wrapped up in a prayer shawl. His face is not visible, his words cannot be heard. Just a soft sigh is heard. . . .

Now all the worshipers leave. Only a few chosen ones remain. Rabbi Jacob chants his Habad melody. His voice grows louder—

And now—a multitude of voices:

"The Lord your God is truth."

And the walls tremble:

Truth, truth, truth. . . .

And it is felt in everything—certainly, certainly, that is how it is, it is impossible otherwise—

Truth! . . .

And there, in a hidden corner in the second room, stands Rabbi Avremel and prays. He is a guest in our village.

His prayer is not in noise. He prays word by word and interprets everything.

Who covers the sky with clouds. [. . .] Why is it like that?

Because "He gives the animal its bread." [. . .]

And here in another corner stands a young scholar of average height, his face is black, his beard is round and black, his eyes are fire, wrinkles of thought; he is entirely immersed in "meditation."

Suddenly he leaps up as if a snake had bitten him: Ay, ay, ay! He runs from wall to wall, from one end of the house of study to the other, rests a little, stands, thinks a silent thought, returns to his place, once more sinks into meditation.

Behind the reading platform stands one of the worshipers, crying out bitterly, making strange contortions: he is fighting against some alien thought. He wants to eliminate it or to raise it up. For he is as one drowning in the sea, suspended between life and death, crying for help.

Near the eastern wall stands the singer himself. He, too, is a guest in our shtetl. He's an "influencer" [*mashpia*]. He "repeats" the "words of the Living God." He prays on the Sabbath until the fourth afternoon hour. Householders have already finished their meals, they stroll out of the village and return, coming inside to hear the prayer prayed by the "influencer," for himself.

He's not a cantor or the son of a cantor, but he stands there with his head bent to the side for whole hours without moving from his place and sings to the Lord.

He has endless melodies. He invents new ones every day. They are called up from the source of his soul. In them is both exalted joy and deep sorrow, yearnings, despair, weeping, torments of the soul, soaring to the heights and falling, the pleading of a child, the solace of a mother, redemptions and consolations from the upper worlds.

Next to one of the tables stand two scholars who have already finished their prayer. They are well-educated Hasidim: their speech is in fragments of sentences, in hints, in secret.

—In the end I don't understand, in what way the intelligent and informed soul at the hour when they are in potential—is it all one?

—Because then they are in "nothing," and in "nothing," everything comes in unity and simplicity.

—But after all then there is no intelligence, the intelligent and informed?

Next to another table two other scholars stand and speak humorously.

—What's the concern of a *misnaged*? In fact he's like that goy (not to compare them), who says: [in Russian in Hebrew characters] I didn't steal anything, I didn't murder, I'll go directly into paradise. The *misnaged* thinks: I prayed with a congregation, I didn't recite the *Shema* too late—all of paradise is mine!

Gradually the House of Study empties of those who came to pray late. In place of them come those who study Torah.

Here are the argumentation, the noise, the disputes on Jewish law, queries, answers, it's just the opposite, and let's compare the two—

And here the chants of the Gemara quaver.

Rava said: a lung has five lobes . . . five . . . five . . . two on the right and three on the left . . . well . . . once again: two on the right and three . . . three . . . three. [. . .]

And in the noise from one of the tables is a still small voice, the voice of a legend:

In the hour when Moses went up to heaven, he found the Holy One blessed be He was sitting and attaching crowns to letters—

And from the second table—:

In the hour when Moses went up to heaven, the attending angels tried to reject him: what is someone born of woman—immediately He spread a cloud over him—

From a third:

The Holy One, blessed be He, said: I set a fire burning in Zion. I must conclude the burning. . . .

Behold this—Sabbath in the shtetl.

3

When the "three days of restriction"[1] come, the children race about in the surrounding fields, climb the one tree in the village, and intend to strip it. It is a pear tree, and it belongs to Shimen the Chief (the biggest beggar in the village). Shimen's wife screams bloody murder. The children come down one by one, give the appearance of departing, then they come back, one with a stick, one with a stone, one with a piece or iron that he found, and they slowly approach the tree—and the fruit falls.

Shimen's wife sees it and curses; but who listens to her?

The war between her and the children grows fiercer. She grabs one of the children, hits him, takes off his hat, but while she's struggling with one, the other mischief-makers climb up the tree and make the pears fall to the earth.

From there the band goes to the river at the edge of the village, climb onto the bridge, look at the foaming water, and throw wood chips and stones, make their way up to the mill, come down from there to sail paper boats on the river below, wrestle, push one another into the water, roll about in the green grass, play wildly and race about.

They'll get tired of that too. The "white band" then turns to the other end of the village: there stands Mishke's mill, and the brick kiln.

There, in that place, there is an uncommon silence. A hush falls. The field is mute and broad, very splendid. No one is working there. The road is straight—and the distances. The windmill is not grinding. Mishke and his sons are absent. Ho, freedom, ho liberty!

True, Mishke's guards, two courageous dogs, were not displaced. But they're quiet, too, now, and don't harm anyone. They rest indolently. They only wag their tails—slowly, heavily—and grunt.

Then the gang climbs up to the mill, to Mishke's windmill. They try to move the wheels with their arms. Then they go down, and on their way down they go up on the roof of the neighboring house.

Others walk over to the brick kiln, where they go into the very inside of the lime box that stands in the center of the courtyard, and they dirty their faces and hands, until their features are whiter than white. They go down to where they fire the bricks, spend some time there, and come out disheartened.

Suddenly, one of the gang gets angry at the dogs because they are lying there so restfully. Look for yourselves! They aren't dogs at all!

The mischief-maker takes a stone up in his hand and throws it at one of the dogs so that it will notice. The dog growls a little and lies down again indolently.

Naturally things can't end up in that fashion. The boys throw a larger stone than the first one at the dog, and the dog challenges them now.

The gang sees that's how it is, and immediately one of them starts to throw his own stone at it, and then the dog becomes a proper dog; he leaps up, barks loudly, and runs after his enemies, and his friend—after him, and we all run for our lives in despair, with torn cuffs and drenched with sweat.

Some jump into a nearby pit, a lot run from the oppressor to the gentile cemetery, until the rage of Mishke's guards dies down.

After this holy war the gang goes elsewhere, and that's how things proceed until the stars come out.

Only toward evening does the gang remember that their parents are waiting, that they have to go to synagogue.

4

And here is the village on a holiday—and the holiday is the giving of the Torah.

The day is jubilant, and the young person tries to conquer the depth of the night. Through the window the sunrise is visible. In the vegetable garden next to the house, softly softly the plants move, plant after plant speaks and goes on, goes and tells the secrets of the night.

Now at last the first sunbeams move across them, and the plants prepare themselves to receive the splendor of the day's countenance.

The village's air is filled with a splendid fragrance from the nearby forests and fields. The sound of a shepherd's pipe is heard, the voices of Hasidim from the house of study, everything rises mixed together, song is in everything, melody is in everything.

The morning breeze flutters, the plants whisper, children, little Jews, are still reciting the *tikkun*.[2]

Very gradually the morning passes, the voices in the house of study grow stronger from minute to minute, the birds on the ancient synagogue have already begun singing their "psalm of the day."

Jews, small and grown up, come out of the house of study. Boys race in joy. The sun floods the roofs with its rays. Jews go to bathe in the river—

Pair by pair, they walk and talk, a Jew with a Jew, a silken scholar with a silken scholar. Pleasant conversations. Calm is spread over everything, the repose of the holiday holiness.

They talk about the giving of the Torah, about the influence of the Divine Presence, about the holy rebbes of past times, about the fresh air, and also about the month—the month of May. [. . .]

5

Jews of high lineage, learned Jews and Hasidim, stand on the eastern wall, and the sun pours its light on the ornaments of their prayer shawls. [. . .]

A gnarled Jew, short in stature, goes up to the prayer platform. He opens the prayer book, and he begins to sing the melody, steeped in joy and sorrow both together, of the *akdamot*.[3]

The congregation follows after him. The heads and selves of the worshippers are given over to the *akdamot*. Whoever doesn't understand [the Aramaic] looks at the commentary.

Like the pure wind of the morning, like a pure angel born of the holiday, the melody hovers.

The congregation immerses itself in the holy spirit as in deep water—"He leadeth me beside the still waters" [Psalms 23:2].

The whole congregation is full of joy, gaining pleasure because of the great honor that God has given His people of Israel, his chosen people, and because of honor that Israel will receive in the future.

For at the moment when the Israelites said, "we will do and we will heed" [Exodus 24:7], the exalted angels made crowns for them.

And when they heard the word uttered by the mouth of the Holy One, blessed be He, their souls flew up from them, and the Holy One, blessed be He, in His great mercy and love, brought dew down from heaven, which brings the dead back to life, and their souls returned to their bodies.

Angels bore them on their wings; they brought them to Mount Sinai, to the mountain that was burning with fire.

And the angels will serve them in the future, too, the Holy One, blessed be He, will give a banquet to the righteous, on chairs of gold they will be seated, and they will drink fortified wine to slake their thirst.

And now the prayer is coming to an end. Every man goes to his home—and his heart feels good.

After a dairy meal—young and old head to the fields.

In the fields, on a broad meadow, they will rest, speaking very slowly and at ease, and not all the Jews are equal:

The honored among them, the learned, and the pious among them, speak about Hasidism; ordinary Jews—are occupied with daily concerns. Boys are rowdy, and girls walk in pairs, setting their eyes on a boy, one or another—and lowering their eyelids.

6

Now it is a weekday in the shtetl.

Rows of low wooden houses, narrow streets, rows of wooden shops, and the market area in front of them, peasants stand next to their wagons, the horses are freed and eat the straw that's on the wagons, Jews approach, sniff, look in the wagons, ask the price of merchandise, bargain, make claims, buy and sell.

Women shopkeepers stand in the stores, their hands weigh the merchandise, wrap it, tie the bundles, and their mouths are full of words to seduce the buyers, sometimes with soft words, with requests and entreaties, and sometimes with harsh words (for a buyer who rebels or a competing storekeeper), and sometimes—with scraps of idle speech, with stories and jokes to win the buyer's heart, asking after his health and the health of his household, and his fruit and horses and everything he owns. At that time the men storekeepers help their wives, but their hands don't seem made for that. Their faces—the faces of scholars in the house of study, the faces of silken scholars. This is not their place. What can be done? Making a living!

Now a storekeeper is standing in his long coat, with his long, sharp nose, with his bent backbone and his sidelocks swinging back and forth. When the store is full of customers, male and female, and his wife rushes in a tizzy from corner to corner, from goods to goods, from speech to speech, from blessing to curse and from curse to blessing, he stands in a corner and recites the rest of the praises and exaltations that he didn't manage to recite during the hours he was sitting in the house of study, or the "portion" he didn't manage to finish there.

In another store an important store-keeping matron stands, with a double chin, a full and noble face, and she is of distinguished lineage. Her words are few and measured, and with her few words she does more than other women with their abundant words. It is restful here, and full of abundant blessing. In the corner of the store stands her husband, short of stature, his earlocks small and curly, from his eyes the splendor of purity is reflected, delicate features, a small beard, through the few whiskers of which the sharp chin can be seen. His head leans a bit to the side, and his lips murmur some *mishnayot* from the chapter he was studying.

Now a tall Jew is running in the market, his forehead high and broad, his darkened face sad, his eyes look toward a distance which is not now, his earlocks are scattered, his coat isn't buttoned, he grips one flap of it and waves the other flap back and forth, as though he wanted to test the strength of the wind, hurrying to a hay wagon that belongs to one of the peasants, asking the seller—what is the price, he doesn't hear the answer, he runs to another wagon full of straw, feels it, smells it also, exchanges words with the peasant.

The deal is done. The seller slowly brings the merchandise. Before he manages to take a few steps—the buyer is already sitting with a group of scholars, with whom he is studying the MAHARSHA on the topic of "exemption of damages. . . ."[4]

Because while he was standing with the peasant, in purchasing, in bargaining, his thoughts were on that passage in the MAHARSHA, and when he returned from the purchase—he began with the very word he had said before going to purchase, as though there had been no interruption, and as though his study had not ceased even for a moment.

And here is another Jew, his hat back on his head, his hands stretched before him, and he steps from group to group, discussing, arguing, and reasoning, proving with all sorts of sharp insights that the simple meaning in the matter of the wax, which he had given to someone else to sell, trusting him, and that "trustee" had gone bankrupt, and it is as he says—and not as the other says—and not as that trustee says, that he has an old debt with him. . . .

And there, next to the market area, two large stores compete with each other. Their owners deal in "fine things": in goods of wool and linen, silk and embroidery, cloaks, yarmulkas, lamps, all sorts of ornaments for brides and grooms. The two competitors are among the notables of the shtetl, but one is not like the other: one of them is an old, experienced merchant, composed, counting and weighing every word, walking heel to toe, never going to the market without a silk outer coat, his shoes always shined, his clothing from expensive material, clean and neat, his hat of silk, and he is all silk, speaking only with the select few, regarding himself as the "wise man of the state," secretly reading the books of RIBAL,[5] his snuffbox, from which he always sniffs, and which always lies with him in synagogue, is of silver, and his prayer shawl is decorated with silver. On the Day of Atonement he wears a yarmulka of white silk, enters the synagogue as though walking on tiptoe, bows courteously, steps to his place on the eastern wall, and does not move from there, with a splendidly bound Bible with commentaries lying before him, and while the Torah is read, he reads the portion and sings the Haftarah with a pleasant voice. He does not like to reason and argue, and when you ask him something—he answers with few words, as though doing a favor to the inquirer.

The other one is a scholar from head to foot: he buys in erudition and sells in erudition, argues fiercely and disputes with heat. Sparks fly from his mouth, and his hands grasp his disputant's button; in his youth he studied, along with the Talmud, the Turim and the

Shulḥan Arukh, the Guide of the Perplexed as well, and also RALBAG, and had there been another one like him in the shtetl, he would argue with him about "the necessity of reality," the way he now argues with the scholars of the village about the topic of "his fire is like his arrows."[6] His gait is always rushed, he speaks hurriedly and all of him is in a hurry. He knows neither pride nor humility. He is entirely given over to business, though he may close his store in the middle of the day, even on a market day, to consult a book in the house of study, if some severe difficulty won't give him rest.

And here are a few of the clumsy men of the village, here is the baker with the thick neck, and here are his sons, all of whom are stout fellows, who fight with a whole camp of young peasants and overcome them. And now he comes out to the market with his sons, and woe to anyone who dares to approach the wagon around which his sons are standing, and sets his eye on the merchandise they are buying. He would be risking his life.

And here is Moshe-Yitsḥak and his five sons, who conquered a place for themselves at the eastern wall without paying any price, and if they wished, they would take for themselves every third and sixth aliyah [the most prestigious—Eds.], and recite the *haftarah*, but there is honesty in their hearts, and they know that matters like that belong to those who know about "the black dots" [finer points—Eds.]. Woe to any man who dares to trespass on their place in the east [the eastern wall of a synagogue, the most prestigious], or who takes the merchandise they are considering.

And here are the village butchers, whom the tax collector fears more than he fears the policeman—and still both the slaughterer and the rabbi are not threatened by them because they fear sin as they fear death.

7

Behold, they are all before me, all the Jews of the village, as they pray, study, discuss matters of Torah, wrapped in their prayer shawls, weep, implore, sing, cleave to the infinite with their Habad melodies, are occupied with the commandments, turn to their business, work, trade. Preoccupied Jews, rushing, eating their bread in panic and running to learning or to earning—

Here are those very Jews before me in the circle of their family on the sabbath. Before me sabbath-Jews full of song and melody and yearning for the living God. Jews in silk and broad cloaks and new velvet yarmulkas,

sitting at the Sabbath meal, eating expansively, sitting and wiping their faces with handkerchiefs and enjoying the *tsholnt* [Sabbath stew] and making their wives happy, women who cover their hair with silk scarves, wear white robes and silver earrings, and gaze at their husbands and the fruit of their wombs, and derive pleasure.

And the song-Jews do what they do. They open up the "selections of the Torah" or the "Torah of Light,"[7] and after a melody of the ARI, and a little bim-bum, tapping with a finger and a slow tune, comes going deeply into the book, very slowly—and the transition to another world, exalted and holy. The porridges and kugels [. . .] are forgotten. Very slowly the wives and children who sit all around are also forgotten, and the brain is immersed in deep Habad thought, and the heart sings a Habad melody that comes on its own from the teaching of the angel. [. . .]

8

Thus I see in my mind's eye the shtetl of my childhood, which since then has been overturned ten times, and who knows whether the blood-soaked war, the world war of the last years,[8] has left a remnant or survivor. Where are you, my village? My heart yearns for you, the way a man's heart yearns for the mother of his childhood. What have they done to you from then till now, all sorts of intellectuals and all sorts of world reformers, and all sorts of battle-seekers, and bullies from left and right? And what has cruel chance done to you since I abandoned you, since time uprooted me and banished me to exile after exile and scattered me over and over, and stole my repose and shattered all hope?

Where are you, my shtetl? With a heavy spirit I returned to you. I have already returned to your God in truth and innocence. But you, where are you? Where are your low houses? Where are your fences, on which I climbed in my childhood, where is the great house of study and the many bookcases, and the books that I pondered for days and years? Where is the light-flooded house that stood in the middle of the market, where I once studied Torah? Where are the fields around you?—

Shtetl of my childhood! There was not much nature in you. Just one tree was in you, which belonged to Shimen "the Chief," and only a few vegetable gardens around a few houses. A living, pleasant fragrance reached you from the nearby fields, but it was hard for it to compete with the neglect in you and with the streets that were never cleaned.

Behold, a beautiful river was around you, and behold the courtyards of the landlords and the flower gardens around them, and here are woods around you and a meadow, that extends for many leagues. But you had very little interest and desire for the beautiful meadow and the beautiful tree, and especially—you had no free time.

For you were entirely given over to learning and earning, and whence could nature come to you? No planting hand was in you, and only seldom would a sowing hand appear in your gardens.

But *the light of God* was poured upon you, the light of the spirit, the light of Torah, the light of purity.

The angels of peace spread their wings over you, the glow and illumination of infinite light entered the hearts of your sons, awakened them, called them to the Torah and to repentance, wrapped the face of your great ones with the highest splendor, poured innocent grace on all who dwelled in you.

9

From time to time great pain attacks me, unbearable pain. Grief in my heart and longing for the village that no longer exists.

And when my heart is full of pain, I sometimes fall asleep and in a vision I see the shtetl of my youth, and it is enveloped not only with heavenly splendor, but also with earthly glory, with the glory of garden and vineyard, furrow and meadow.

Behold long avenues of tall trees, avenues shading the village. The whole village—as though drowned in the green of the trees. The streets are broad and very long. The houses are of one story, small and low, but carved with artistic skill. Around the houses—sculpted balustrades and finials and all sorts of enchanting decorations on top of them. A small vineyard to the right of every house, a small garden to its left, flower pots full of glorious flowers on the sill of every window. The windows are open on the broad avenue of trees. Boys and girls play among the trees. Tranquility not of this world is spread over the village. People discuss things, but everything is almost without saying words. Repose and silence virtually bear people's thoughts and wishes from one person to another. Abundance and happiness are all around. The people see one another's faces with

joy and love. The joy is of the soul, the happiness cannot be expressed.

And I wander in that dream-town. I know that it is the town of my youth, but where are my relatives and friends? I look for them with pain and eagerness, inquire and seek after them. It seems to me they are sometimes shown to me: here and there they are, but I can't find them. I look for my father and my mother and can't find them. I look for the house where I was born and where I spent my childhood, and I can't find it. I look for all the people I knew in my childhood—and I know that all the people of the village—there is no remnant of any of them. In their place—people who are strangers to me. I stand and wonder: where did all those people come from? Are they the children of the people I once knew? No. I mention the names of people who were known to me in my childhood, and they know nothing about them. The sons do not remember their fathers—and they know nothing. They are certainly total strangers. Where, then, are all those who used to be here? Did they die? Were they exiled? Lost? Did they all really die? But there were a lot of young people among them! Where did they all go? Where were they exiled to? . . .

I wander around the shtetl, walk around in the forests and villages, look for the mill, the brick kiln, the meadow, the hill. I meet people, ask them: where, tell me, good people, where is my village?—there, there it is. And where is the dwelling of my fathers? In such and such a house. I seek and I seek and I do not find my ancestors. I do not find any acquaintance. Everything is new and renewed. But this is my shtetl, and yet so distant, so distant and so exalted. . . .

I leave my shtetl, I stroll in a glade—the glade stands on the bank of the river. I wander among the trees, but the trees are not thick, they aren't dense, and they aren't close to each other. There is a great space between them. The walker sees the rushing river through them. I see the waves of the river, and I see steamboats borne on them, a large wheel on the boat, and on the wheel are carved dreadful and holy verses. They speak of great awe and great hope. . . .

Sometimes I myself am borne on that steamboat. Distant stars give signs from the high heaven, wave upon wave speaks from below. Where is the ship going?—

It comes to a bridge, whose beginning and end I cannot see. Multitudes and multitudes of people cross it, and they carry bundles with them, their worries and their sins; they bear with them their inherited suffering, the sins of their fathers; they bear with them high hopes and high longings; they bear with them the dreams of their youth and the images of their life of vanity.

Some of them cross restfully: they always strive for the other side. . . .

A new sun is seen in the distance. The sky opens. Cherubs burst out in song.

NOTES

1. [The three days before Shavuot, when the Torah was given.—Eds.]

2. [The collection of quotations from the traditional literature that is recited all night long on Shavuot.—Eds.]

3. [A hymn in Aramaic recited before the Torah reading on Shavuot.—Eds.]

4. ["HAMARSHA": Rabbi Shmuel Eliezer Edeles (1555–1631). Exemption of damages is discussed in the Babylonian Talmud, Baba Kama 29b.—Eds.]

5. [Isaac Baer Levinsohn, an early proponent of Haskalah in Russia.—Eds.]

6. [Reference to various halakhic treatises. RALBAG is Rabbi Levi Ben Gershon (1288–1344). The necessity of reality is a term of medieval philosophy.—Eds.]

7. [*Liqutei-Hatorah* and *Tora Or* are mystical biblical commentaries. The ARI was the founder of the mystical school of Safed.—Eds.]

8. [World War I.—Eds.]

Translated by Jeffrey M. Green.

Other works by Zeitlin: *Dos problem fun guts un shlekhts: bay yudn un bay andere felker: filozofish-historishe obhandlung* (1911); *Barukh Shpinozah: sefarav ḥayav ve-shitato ha-filosofit* (1914); *Al gevul shenei olamot* (1965); *Hasidic Spirituality for a New Era: The Religious Writings of Hillel Zeitlin* (2012).

Sh. An-ski

1863–1920

Sh. An-ski (Shloyme Zaynvl Rapaport) was born in Chashniki, Russia (today in Belarus) and was raised in Vitebsk. After attending heder, he studied Russian literature and criticism, then worked as a tutor and in the salt- and coal-mining industries. An-ski lived in Western Europe until 1905, serving as secretary to the radical philosopher Petr Lavrov and associating with the Bund. An-ski returned to the Russian Empire after the 1905 revolution, and in 1912–1914 he led an ethnographic expedition in Volhynia and Podolia (Ukraine), gathering thousands of photographs, folklore, historical documents, sacred objects, and wax-cylinder recordings of folk music from Jewish communities.

Using material from the expedition, An-ski drafted *The Dybbuk* in Russian in 1913. The play was first performed in Yiddish in 1920 by the Vilner Troupe in Warsaw. He fled to Vilna following the Bolshevik takeover and in 1919 he left for Warsaw.

The Enemy at His Pleasure: A Journey through the Jewish Pale of Settlement during World War I
1920

10

Before the war Bloyne was a rich and elegant Jewish town: wide streets, a large municipal park, several monuments, many tall buildings, large stores. But when the war came through, the town was passed from hand to hand; occupied by the Germans, then by the Russians, Bloyne was totally destroyed. At its center, the town hall, with its roof torn off and its walls riddled and shattered, looked like an ancient ruin. It symbolized the annihilation of Bloyne. Most of the houses and buildings had burned down. The rest were empty and desolate, their doors and windows ripped out; whole houses, especially Polish ones, had survived only in the side streets. Not a single large store endured; they were all deserted and their doors were gone. A few shops had been taken over by new proprietors, who sold bread, ham, cigarettes, paper, tea, and sugar. There was no other merchandise in town.

The large synagogue was unscathed. But all its contents were looted or smashed; the Torah scrolls were tattered and sullied. Now the building was used as a military hospital for cholera patients since the local city council had informed the army authorities that this would be the most appropriate site.

Ravaged as the town was, the streets were bustling and filled with nervous military movement. Baggage convoys and heavily loaded wagons rumbled incessantly; the artillery kept up its iron clatter; infantry and cavalry units slogged by one after another. They were all streaming toward Suchostow. The few terrified civilians hurrying along stood out against the gray military mass. They looked like useless, alien creatures entangled underfoot.

I traveled to Blonye [alternate spelling of Bloyne] with Dr. Berlin, our center's female physician. Upon arriving, we went straight to the city council, where we found one of its members, a Polish doctor. He told us that only four or five hundred people, one tenth of the population, were left—many of them refugees from the countryside. As for Jews, no more than ten or fifteen families had stayed put. The rest had scattered to wherever they could flee—mainly Warsaw. The city council, he went on, had organized a soup kitchen, which dispensed 150 to 200 lunches a day. The Zemstvo Alliance also had a free teahouse, which, however, didn't have enough manpower to take care of everyone. A second teahouse was needed. Tens of thousands of tired, thirsty soldiers were passing through town, and if they couldn't get tea they would drink plain water—sometimes even from the muddy street puddles, which caused epidemics.

"Who is your soup kitchen set up for?" I asked the Polish doctor.

"We don't discriminate," he answered. "Anyone who comes gets fed."

"I'm sure you know what I mean—Jews won't eat food that hasn't been specially prepared."

"Yes. . . . I know."

"And have you established a Jewish soup kitchen?"

"No. . . . There's little call for one. The few remaining Jews don't need free food. They're involved in business, and they're doing quite well."

"Why was the synagogue converted into a cholera hospital? Couldn't they find any other building?"

"That's none of our concern. It's a military matter," he responded dryly, apparently sensing my contentious tone.

"How did the Germans behave here?" Dr. Berlin asked.

"Some were very decent, courteous, and didn't touch anyone. They paid for everything. Others set houses on fire and committed the worst sort of atrocities. In a farm granary a mile from here, there were 192 wounded soldiers and patients with epidemic diseases. The Germans put straw around it and torched it. All the men were burned alive. The Germans did it to prevent the epidemic from spreading to the German army."

Dr. Berlin headed over to the Zemstvo Alliance's teahouse, while I walked through the town to find out what was happening to the Jews. I stepped into an old shop where an elderly woman was selling rolls, herring, and other cheap food. She confirmed that most of the Jews had fled.

"How many Jewish inhabitants were there?" I asked.

"Who counted them? Half the town was Jewish—like everywhere else."

"Why did they run away?"

"Not because they were doing so well here. There was something to run away from. Oh."

Her son came in, a young man with a bandaged head. He started to talk. "Before the Germans marched in, they shelled the town to bits. One girl was killed and about ten people came to the funeral. On the way back from the cemetery, they encountered a Russian patrol. The soldiers began firing and they killed two men. . . . But that wasn't the worst of it. The Jews ran away from lootings, beatings, from the lies. The Russians always assume that a Jew is a spy, and they arrest him."

The proprietor then said: "On an estate not far from here there was this tenant farmer. He was washing the dishes. . . . He was awfully dim-witted; he never understood anything; he didn't know his top from his bottom. And they suspected him of espionage. How could anyone mistake him for a spy? A spy has to have at least a little bit of gray matter. But try reasoning with them."

"How is the military treating the Jews now?"

"Now that there's nobody to beat up and nothing to plunder, everything's quiet, thank goodness," the woman replied with bitter irony.

"Well, to tell the truth," the young man explained, "ordinary troops don't do anything. They seldom bother anyone. The real problem is the Cossacks. The moment they ride in, they start looting and beating."

"Do you need a Jewish soup kitchen here?" I asked.

"No," the young man said. "The few Jews still here have stayed because they're earning a living. The poor ones have all gone to Warsaw."

Wandering through the town, I entered what had once been a dry-goods store. Now three men sat there, each at his own table, one sold bread, one ham, and the third, a Jewish youth, sold cigarettes. I introduced myself.

"I'm from Suchostow," he told me. "I had my own store there, and I had a nice income. When the Germans were approaching, the town was thrown into a panic. Then General Rennenkampf arrived, and he took his revenge. His men beat us and arrested us, and forced the best men to clean toilets—and of course they looted our property. Then they began expelling the Jews. Many had already scattered. I took off for Warsaw, but then I thought it over. How can I leave all my property? I rented a wagon for sixty rubles and drove back to Suchostow. Where was my store, what had happened to it? They had torn it to pieces. My merchandise was worth fifteen hundred rubles, and the stuff that was left, which my neighbors salvaged, was worth maybe one hundred rubles. So I brought it here and set up shop. In Suchostow they forced out the last Jews who came here. They were starving, exhausted, battered. A lot of them came barefoot; their shoes had been stolen on the way. One of the refugees was a young woman who gave birth as soon as she reached Blonye. She's lying in an empty store for now; we don't know where to put her."

I got hold of Dr. Berlin, and we went to find the new mother. On a pile of straw on the muddy floor of a small, empty shop lay a young woman covered with tattered clothes. Her feverish face was calm, but she was breathing heavily. Next to her, wrapped in dirty rags, lay the newborn infant. Two little boys, one four years old, one two, wandered aimlessly around the tiny room. Their oversized coats, hems dragging behind them, were covered with wet mud up to the collars. The children were scared, disoriented, and their bloodshot little eyes gaped at us. The instant I or the doctor moved toward the mother, the boys began wailing dreadfully.

The woman's elderly mother, careworn and embittered, stood off to the side. When I addressed her, she murmured with the deathly indifference of supreme despair.

We'd already gone through enough misery and horror. When the Germans came back to our town and began shooting at us, we hid in the cellars for five days without food or water. Somehow or other we managed to get by, but the thirst was unbearable. A father and mother went down to the river to get water and they never came back. Later on, we found their corpses. The day before yesterday, when the shooting fell off slightly, we ventured out of the cellars. The general ordered all Jews, including children, to assemble in the marketplace. There were sixty-eight of us. Thirty men were pulled out, arrested, and put in the trenches. We don't know what's going to happen to them. The rest of us were banished. We left on foot. Walking was terrible. It was raining. The road was covered with thick mud, and my daughter was pregnant, ready to give birth any moment—and we also had the two little boys. We dragged ourselves along for twenty-four hours.

At one point, my daughter asked me: "Mama, look! What's hanging from those trees?"

I looked. There were three Jews. I was afraid to take a closer look—I might know them. A few miles on, my daughter collapsed in exhaustion, and the children couldn't walk any farther. So we settled in the mud on the side of the road. A soldier riding by in a wagon— a Christian, mind you—felt sorry for us and offered us a lift. The moment my daughter climbed in, she went into labor, and she kept screaming in agony all the way. When we arrived in town, she gave birth right away. We didn't even have time to carry her to a home.

Dr. Berlin took the new mother and the entire family under her wing. She found them a place to stay and managed to obtain milk, eggs, barley, wine, tea, and sugar. We got all this from the only food center in Blonye. [. . .]

Translated by Joachim Neugroschel.

Other works by An-ski: *Khurbn Galitsye* (1920); *Gezamelte shriftn* (1922–1925); *The Dybbuk and Other Writings* (1992); *Pioneers: The First Breach* (2017).

Isaac Babel

1894–1940

Isaac Babel was born in Odessa to a middle-class Jewish family, and he studied in Kiev and in Petrograd. His prose explores Russian–Jewish relations, the loss and tensions involved in Jewish adaptation to life under the Soviet regime, as well as Jewish Odessan street life. From 1924 on, Babel lived in Moscow, while his mother and sister moved to Belgium and his wife to France. He adapted Sholem Aleichem's work into two screenplays in 1926. The same year, he published *Konarmiia* (Red Cavalry), based on his experiences as a correspondent with the Soviet army in the early 1920s. Babel's Odessa stories feature an array of vibrant Jewish characters, the gangster Benia Krik among them. Under the Stalinist regime, he was increasingly censored. He was arrested in 1939 and executed one year later.

1920 Diary
1920

August 25, 1920. Sokal

Finally, a town. We ride through the shtetl of Tartakuv, Jews, ruins, cleanliness of a Jewish kind, the Jewish race, little stores.

I am still ill, I've still not gotten back on my feet after the battles outside Lvov. What stuffy air these shtetls have. The infantry had been in Sokal, the town is untouched, the divisional chief of staff is billeted with some Jews. Books, I saw books. I'm billeted with a Galician woman, a rich one at that, we eat well, chicken in sour cream.

I ride on my horse to the center of town, it's clean, pretty buildings, everything soiled by war, remnants of cleanliness and originality.

The Revolutionary Committee. Requisitions and confiscation. Interesting: they don't touch the peasantry, all the land has been left at its disposal. The peasantry is left alone.

The declarations of the Revolutionary Committee.

My landlord's son—a Zionist and *ein ausgesprochener Nationalist*. Normal Jewish life, they look to Vienna, to Berlin, the nephew, a young man, is studying philosophy, wants to go to the university. We eat butter and chocolate. Sweets.

Friction between Manuilov and the divisional chief of staff. Sheko tells him to go to—

"I have my pride," they won't give him a billet, no horse, there's the cavalry for you, this isn't a holiday resort. Books—*polnische, Juden*.

In the evening, the division commander in his new jacket, well fed, wearing his multicolored trousers, red-faced and dim-witted, out to have some fun, music at night, the rain disperses us. It is raining, the tormenting Galician rain, it pours and pours, endlessly, hopelessly.

What are our soldiers up to in this town? Dark rumors.

Boguslavsky has betrayed Manuilov. Boguslavsky is a slave.

August 26, 1920. Sokal

A look around town with the young Zionist. The synagogues: the Hasidic one is a staggering sight, it recalls three hundred years ago, pale, handsome boys with *peyes*, the synagogue as it was two hundred years ago, the selfsame figures in long coats, rocking, waving their hands, howling. This is the Orthodox party, they support the Rabbi of Belz, the famous Rabbi of Belz, who's made off to Vienna. The moderates support the Rabbi of Husyatin. Their synagogue. The beauty of the altar made by some artisan, the magnificence of the greenish chandeliers, the worm-eaten little tables, the Belz synagogue—a vision of ancient times. The Jews ask me to use my influence so they won't be ruined, they're being robbed of food and goods.

The Yids hide everything. The cobbler, the Sokal cobbler, is a proletarian. His apprentice's appearance, a red-haired Hasid—a cobbler.

The cobbler has been waiting for Soviet rule—now he sees the Yid-killers and the looters, and that there'll be no earnings, he is shaken, and looks at us with distrust. A hullabaloo over money. In essence, we're not paying anything, 15–20 rubles. The Jewish quarter. Indescribable poverty, dirt, the boxed-in quality of the ghetto.

The little stores, all of them open, whiting and resin, soldiers ransacking, swearing at the Yids, drifting around aimlessly, entering homes, crawling under counters, greedy eyes, trembling hands, a strange army indeed.

The organized looting of the stationery store, the owner in tears, they tear up everything, they come up with all kinds of demands, the daughter with Western European self-possession, but pitiful and red-faced, hands things over, is given some money or other, and with her storekeeper's politeness tries to act as if everything were as it should be, except that there are too many customers. The owner's wife is so full of despair that she cannot make head or tail of anything.

At night the town will be looted—everyone knows that.

Music in the evening—the division commander is out to have some fun. In the morning he wrote some letters to Stavropol and the Don. The front will not tolerate the disgraceful goings-on in the rear lines. The same old story.

The division commander's lackeys lead his magnificent horses with their breastplates and cruppers back and forth.

The military commissar and the nurse. A Russian man—a sly muzhik—coarse and sometimes insolent and confused. Has a high opinion of the nurse, sounds me out, asks me all kinds of questions, he is in love.

The nurse goes to say good-bye to the division commander, and this after everything that's happened. Everyone's slept with her. That boor Suslov is in the adjoining room—the division commander is busy, he's cleaning his revolver.

I'm given boots and underwear. Sukhorukov received them and dealt them out himself, he's a super-lackey, describe him.

A chat with the nephew who wants to go to university.

Sokal: brokers and artisans—Communism, they tell me, isn't likely to strike root here.

What battered, tormented people these are.

Poor Galicia, poor Jews.

My landlord has eight doves.

Manuilov has a sharp confrontation with Sheko, he has many sins in his past. A Kiev adventurer. He came to us demoted from having been chief of staff of the Third Brigade.

Lepin. A dark, terrifying soul.

The nurse—twenty-six men and one woman.

August 27, 1920

Skirmishes near Znyatin, Dluzhnov. We ride northwest. Half the day with the transport carts. Heading to Laszczow, Komarow. In the morning we set off from Sokal. A regular day with the squadrons: we wander through forests and glades with the division commander, the brigade commanders come, sun, for five hours I haven't gotten off my horse, brigades ride past. Transport cart panic. I left the carts at a clearing in the forest, rode over to the division commander. The squadrons on a hill. Reports to the army commander, a cannonade, there are no airplanes, we ride from one place to another, a regular day. Heavy exhaustion toward evening, we spend the night in Wasylow. We didn't reach Laszczow, our target destination.

The Eleventh Division is in Wasylow or somewhere near there, pandemonium, Bakhturov—a tiny division, he has lost some of his sparkle. The Fourth Division is mounting successful battles.

August 28, 1920. Komarow

I rode off from Wasylow ten minutes after the squadrons. I am riding with three horsemen. Earth mounds, glades, destroyed farms, somewhere in the greenery are the Red Columns, plums. Gunfire, we don't know where the enemy is, we can't see anybody, machine guns are hammering quite near and from different directions, my heart tenses, and so every day single horsemen are out looking for their field headquarters, they are carrying reports. Toward noon I found my squadron in a ravaged village with all the villagers hiding in their cellars, under trees covered in plums. I ride with the squadrons. I ride into Komarow with the division commander, red hood. A magnificent, unfinished, red church. Before we entered Komarow, after the gunfire (I was riding alone), silence, warm, a bright day, a some-

what strange and translucent calm, my soul ached, all alone, nobody getting on my nerves, fields, forests, undulating valleys, shady roads.

We stop opposite the church.

The arrival of Voroshilov and Budyonny. Voroshilov blows up in front of everyone: "Lack of energy!" He gets heated, a heated individual, the whole army restless, he rides and yells, Budyonny is silent, smiles, white teeth. Apanasenko defends himself: "Let's go inside"—"Why do we keep letting the enemy get away?" Voroshilov shouts. "Without contact you can't strike."

Is Apanasenko worthless?

The pharmacist who offers me a room. Rumors of atrocities. I go into the shtetl. Indescribable fear and desperation.

They tell me what happened. Hiding in a hut, they are frightened that the Poles will return. Last night Captain Yakovlev's Cossacks were here. A pogrom. The family of David Zis, in their home, the old prophet, naked and barely breathing, the butchered old woman, a child with chopped-off fingers. Many of these people are still breathing, the stench of blood, everything turned topsy-turvy, chaos, a mother over her butchered son, an old woman curled up, four people in one hut, dirt, blood under a black beard, they're just lying there in their blood. Jews in the town square, the tormented Jew who shows me everything, a tall Jew takes his place. The rabbi has gone into hiding, everything has been smashed to pieces in his house, he doesn't leave his burrow until evening. Fifteen people have been killed: Hasid Itska Galer, 70 years old, David Zis, synagogue *shamas*, 45 years old, his wife and his daughter, 15 years old, David Trost, his wife, the butcher.

At the house of a raped woman.

Evening—at my landlord's, a conventional home, Sabbath evening, they didn't want to cook until the Sabbath was over.

I look for the nurses, Suslov laughs. A Jewish woman doctor.

We are in a strange, old-fashioned house, they used to have everything here—butter, milk.

At night, a walk through the shtetl.

The moon, their lives at night behind closed doors. Wailing inside. They will clean everything up. The fear and horror of the townsfolk. The main thing: our men are going around indifferently, looting where they can, ripping the clothes off the butchered people.

The hatred for them is the same, they too are Cossacks, they too are savage, it's pure nonsense that our army is any different. The life of the shtetls. There is no escape. Everyone is out to destroy them, the Poles did not give them refuge. All the women and girls can scarcely walk. In the evening a talkative Jew with a little beard, he had a store, his daughter threw herself out of a second-floor window, she broke both arms, there are many like that.

What a powerful and magnificent life of a nation existed here. The fate of the Jewry. At our place in the evening, supper, tea, I sit drinking in the words of the Jew with the little beard who asks me plaintively if it will be possible to trade again.

An oppressive, restless night.

Translated by Peter Constantine.

Other works by Babel: *Benia Krik* (1927); *The Complete Works of Isaac Babel* (2002); *Red Cavalry and Other Stories* (2005).

Alexander Benghiat

1863–1924

The journalist and translator Alexander Benghiat was born in Izmir (Turkey, also known as Smyrna) into a Ladino-speaking Sephardic family. He received a traditional Jewish education in a *meldar* there, as well as a modern Western education at an Alliance Israélite Universelle school. He belonged to a generation of young intellectuals seeking to advance the modernization of Sephardic Jews in the Ottoman Empire. He wrote for and edited a variety of Ladino periodicals, including his own Izmir weekly *El meseret* (The Joy), with its well-known literary supplement. He was also active as an adapter and translator, into Ladino, of European literary classics, most prominently Jonathan Swift's *Gulliver's Travels*, Victor Hugo's *Les misérables*, and Jacques-Henri Bernardin de Saint-Pierre's *Paul et Virginie*.

Memories of the Meldar: An Ottoman Jew's Early Education

1920

Did you go to a *meldar* as a child? Have any of you been so lucky and blessed? I am sure that, seeing these two questions, you will all object that you had no idea what a *meldar* was and that you went to a [modern] school. But I will forgive you this lie or truth and will tell you what a *meldar* is and what happened there.

A *meldar* was a room with a couch in a neighbor's courtyard. On the couch, some benches, and the floor, sixty or seventy children sat and crouched, one dirtier than the other, scratching their heads all day, putting their fingers in their noses and taking them out, pushing, pulling, pinching, or biting each other, until the teacher would see them and yell, "Scoundrels! Bastards! Rascals!"

In winter every child had to bring a couple of coals, because the teacher's wife would put a stove without fire in the middle of the *meldar*. And while the students were supposed to get warm by looking at the empty stove, the teacher, who was sitting in front of the burning stove, was busy heating his bread and roasting his cheese. Then he would scratch his chin, comb his beard, pick the hairs that had fallen out, and put them between the pages of a book. Having taken care of his face, he would begin teaching the alphabet to the youngest students by chanting the letters. . . . But all of this started very slowly with the young students, and since the others also enjoyed it, big and small children began chanting in unison and shouting at the top of their lungs. The Turks who passed by on the street, hearing this shouting and not knowing what was going on, asked each other, "Is this a mental asylum?" If it was winter and the teacher was cold, he would put his hands close to the fire and warm them. If it was summer and he was tired, he would recline and fall asleep. Sometimes when he was sleepy the teacher would leave us with his aide and go to a coffee house to have a coffee. . . . The *meldar* had a low window that faced the street. The teacher always kept an eye on it, and when he saw a Turk passing by with some chickens, he would call him, buy the chickens, and keep them tied up in the middle of the *meldar*. Once, Obadiayico Veisí's father, who came to scold his son, saw the chickens and asked the teacher about them. The aide, who was a real devil, immediately responded, "A Turk brought them and left them here as students so that they would learn to read."

"Shut up, you rascal! Don't you say another word!" yelled the teacher.

And the aide who, despite his impudence, was afraid of the teacher, immediately shut up, while the teacher went to wash his handkerchief at the well and then placed it to dry on the windowsill. A Turk passing by stole it, and we students cried over it.

On Thursdays the teacher's wife made dough, and we students put the pita on the stove. On Fridays older students mopped the floor and helped with other things, and Jamila, the teacher's elder daughter, would slip in her galoshes, fall down, and roll her eyes. On Shabbat there were no classes. On Sundays the teacher would be tired and irritated from not sleeping the night before, and we would not study much. . . .

A note: All the things you have just read about and many more happened in the *meldars* of Izmir, the interior [of the Ottoman Empire], Constantinople [Istanbul], Edirne, Angora [Ankara], Bursa, and everywhere in Bulgaria before the establishment of the Alliance Israélite Universelle schools. (Since Salonica had contacts with Vienna, that is to say with Europe, long before 1870, we cannot say how things were there.) The Alliance schools in our city saved us from this plague, may their unforgettable first directors, the late [David] Cazes and [Shemtov] Pariente, rest in peace. And may the venerable [Gabriel] Arié, who was the director before the present one and who adeptly headed his institution, leading it to great achievements, be blessed. But now with the current director the old plague has returned. To see what happens with [the students'] instruction, it is enough to test a student from the highest grade. And as proof of their level of education it is enough to stop in front of the door of the Alliance school at midday or in the afternoon while classes are in session . . . and you will find chaos and turmoil.

NOTE
Words in brackets appear in the original translation.

Translated by Olga Borovaya.

Other works by Benghiat: *Yosef y Reina: romanso gudio* (1903); *Unah familiyah de matadores* (1907); *Hasan-pasha el terivle: romanso istoriko* (1910); *Perlas del Talmud* (1921).

Alliance Israélite Universelle

Founded in 1860

The Alliance Israélite Universelle was established in Paris in 1860 to improve the legal and cultural status of Jews in Asia Minor, the Middle East, and North Africa. It promoted the Gallicization and Westernization of Sephardic and Mizrahi Jews in the Mediterranean world largely through an extensive network of elementary and vocational schools. By 1900, it was operating one hundred schools, primarily in Turkey, Tunisia, and Morocco, with a total enrollment of twenty-six thousand students. Highly centralized, like the French

government itself, its programs to transform traditional Jewish life often created tensions between the Paris headquarters and the traditional communities in which it established its schools.

Letters to the Central Committee of the Alliance Israélite Universelle from Tangier, Morocco; Sousse, Tunisia; and Tunis, Tunisia 1920–1938

Tunis, November 1920

Zionism still continues to make progress in Tunisia. In all the major cities of the Regency, Zionist committees have already been established. In Tunis itself there are three distinct Zionist groups which are at this time seeking to unite. Also in Tunis, we have five Zionist newspapers, three of which are published in French and two in Judeo-Arabic. But all of this movement seems to me to be superficial for the moment. It is a question of a few devoted militants and a good number of opportunists who are only using Zionism to forward their own personal interests. The majority of the population, although they are interested in the Zionist idea, do not yet have the faith that leads to action. Furthermore, none of the notables join any of the Zionist associations, and it is only, for the most part, the less influential who form these groups.

C. Ouziel

Tangier, 7 August 1923

An employee of the French government sees the current social status of the Moroccan Jew, his particularistic customs, the habits of his family life, and his code of ethics and judges him to be diametrically opposed to the European, tending to confuse the Jew with the Arab. This is not the case. The Arab has a plodding mind and is slow to comprehend; his religion and traditions make him a creature of habit and his ideas are desperately slow in changing. The Jew, on the other hand, now that he has been freed of the chains that had reduced him to the status of pariah through the ages, has suddenly taken flight. Yesterday he was wallowing in his ignorance and humiliation, and here he is today, a free man, capable of keeping step with the European in his dress, manners, and the development of his mind . . . He was able to make this transition smoothly and without trauma. The photograph that you published in the most recent issue of *Paix et Droit* is a striking testimony to this power of assimilation in the Jew. Those young girls in shorts preparing to run in a public event, what an impressive example! These are the children of those veiled women who, even ten years ago, did not dare to venture outside the *Mellah*, who lived a cloistered life of silence in their homes, and who in their ignorance and superstition fled at the sight of any foreigner . . . the Jew capable of such an awakening may well aspire to a full and complete education within the framework of a European life . . .

On the other hand, the Protectorate, which seeks to instruct and educate the Jew, is not considering that it might one day profit from him in the strengthening of its own political situation; the Protectorate wants the Jew to maintain his native status. In choosing this course of action, it remains haunted by what has quite mistakenly been referred to as the error of the Crémieux decree. The memory of this past is the dominating influence on policy concerning Moroccan Jews and Tunisian Jews alike. Those who govern us are afraid of the grumbling and protest to which the emancipation of the Jews might give rise. And yet, the patriotism demonstrated by the Algerian Jews should put their minds completely at rest. The Jew who has been given his freedom and raised in the French mentality becomes a true Frenchman; he becomes totally devoted to the development of the strength and power of his country.

In Morocco, where the Muslim population is more dense and more fierce and where the spirit of revolt and independence is stronger even than in Algeria, France must work toward increasing the number of French nationals. While proceeding with prudence and avoiding the displeasure of the Arab population, and even more that of the antisemitic colonies, France must work toward the eventual naturalization of the Jews. This would not happen immediately, of course, and not without certain trials and hardships. The Young Tunisians already create enough worry for the French administration; one need not have particular foresight to predict that in a few years a Young Moroccan party will be formed, a much more dangerous party. When this day comes, France should be able to look for support to the educated and completely liberated Jewish population.

Regarding education in the primary schools, it is the Alliance school that seems to us to be most capable of developing the intelligence and cultivating the awareness of the Jewish children; the teachers themselves are only recently emancipated. In their childhood memo-ries and in their understanding of the lives of their ancestors, they will find powerful reasons to open the hearts of their students and to create in their students the desire to be worthy of their past. Once the child has learned these lessons of pride, energy, and emulation at the Alliance school, he should go to the public secondary school so that he might share in the lives of children of other beliefs and might establish those solid bonds of friendship so rarely broken in later life. There he will also find access to the immense body of knowledge necessary for the modern man.

Y. D. Sémach

Tangier, 11 May 1924

. . . The Jew is not a native in the sense this term is used by the colonists. From the moment he started attending school, he was completely transformed; he has become a European and deserves to be treated as such. And when I say European, I am using . . . a general term in order to avoid offending certain sensibilities; I should say a Frenchman. The children in the Alliance schools acquire French ideas and learn to love France; their entire upbringing and all of their traditions lead them to look to the ideas of justice, equality, and freedom, and so naturally to a liberal and republican France . . .

I am convinced that France's policies in Morocco are governed by the belief that the Crémieux decree was, at the time, an error. And yet, the Algerian Jews have since demonstrated that they deserved the favor granted them. There should be some men today who can set superstition aside and who can see all that France has to gain by bringing the Jews of Morocco to her, by assimilating them over a more or less long period of time; granting no special favor for the moment but a just reward for duties accomplished and responsibilities accepted. All of the efforts of the administration, all of the work of the community leaders, and all of the ambition of the educators should be directed toward this goal: naturalization of the Jews. The day this goal is reached, what an impressive force there would be in the service of France. One hundred and fifty thousand, and perhaps more, active, intelligent, educated Jews spread throughout the empire would constitute an effective contribution to counterbalancing Muslim action. The more education the Muslims receive, the more they become conscious of their unity and isolate themselves in their fierce nationalism.

France should have adopted this policy toward the Jews thirty or forty years ago. If France, like Spain or Portugal, had widely granted French citizenship or protection to the Jews, the question of Tangier would have been more easily resolved in her favor today. France has come to the aid of the Jews each time they have been odiously persecuted; she has educated them and given them a feeling of dignity. But when they have asked her for political protection, she has refused them in order not to antagonize the Arab world! . . . How many Jews under foreign protection would have been happy to be French! The past must serve the present in developing a Jewish policy in Morocco.

Y. D. Sémach

The Importance of Agricultural Training: Morocco, 1924

Tangier, 4 June 1924

Agriculture. I am taking the liberty of bringing this question to your attention again. You tell me that this kind of undertaking has no chance of success when run by your organization. For the present I have asked you only to accept the idea in principle; possible means of putting it into practice can be discussed later.

But is it true that you have had so little success in this direction? Until now I had been given to believe that the Zionists themselves had recognized the validity of your efforts. Certainly the results you achieved were not equal to what you had expected. Still, it would be equally unjust to consider them negligible. You have broken new ground. When it is the enormous moral progress of a collectivity which is envisioned, the extent of the material sacrifice required must not be an issue.

That is not the question. You have proven the necessity of a return to the soil for a certain number of our fellow Jews; what you have accomplished or encouraged for Russian and Middle Eastern Jews would be equally beneficial to the Jews of Morocco. Here all of our fellow Jews, all of the students in our schools, have their eyes turned toward commerce. This is all the more the case as in the last few years several men have amassed rapid, outrageous fortunes. Therein lies the danger for the future; the danger of disappointment, of misery for the masses, of jealousy directed against individual successes provoking antisemitism. It is an accepted fact among the Europeans that the Jewish community of Tangier is enormously wealthy. There are twenty families in high standing; they have automobiles, travel in luxury, and indulge in their pleasures with no thought for the costs. Two thousand families struggle to earn their meager subsistence; no one takes any notice of them. And whenever I mention that our kitchens distribute more than five hundred free meals daily to our indigent students, the response is surprise and incredulity. People are unaware that there is such misery in our midst . . . This is why I feel that our Jewish youth must be rescued from those uncertain occupations which perpetuate instability and distress in the families. I believe we must decrease the number of peddlers, porters, messengers, money changers, iron-mongers, pack-saddle makers, cobblers, etc., and try to encourage our youth toward a healthy life in the open air of the country.

Y. D. Sémach

De-Judaization among the Jews of Tunisia and the Steps Needed to Fight It: Sousse, 1929

Sousse, 7 October 1929

After nearly half a century of French occupation, what have been the consequences? They are manifest and can only fill us with anxiety for the present and sorrowful concern for the future.

If I consider in particular the city of Sousse, whose community is the second largest in population in the Regency, what observations can be made?

Hebrew instruction for children, which was highly valued in the time preceding the arrival of the Alliance, can be said to be nonexistent. The *Keter-Torah* [the traditional Jewish school], which had been functioning there for about twenty years, is now completely deserted. Although it is true that on Thursdays and Sundays, as well as during the school holidays, a few children do wander in, they do nothing of value there. This has been attested by the very notables and members of the committee who belong to this society.

The children are ignorant of all that represents the beauty and uniqueness of our doctrine; they have no notion of biblical history or of Jewish history: they are totally unaware that a modern Jewish literature exists. How can these children love and practice their religion; how can they form a bond with their past?

I have observed the youth of Sousse in the temples on *Kipur*, which is the only day of the year on which they come to the temple in great numbers. They come only through habit or superstitious fears. Indeed, during the other feast days, on Saturdays, and for good reason on weekdays, only a very few faithful can be seen in the temple; these are usually old men in turbans. What I saw, then, on *Kipur* greatly enlightened me.

These young people come into the house of God. Wrapped in their *talits* [prayer shawls] they approach the tabernacle and, with devotion, kiss the cloth covering it. The father or grandfather who has seen his son or grandson gestures to him. The young man advances, takes the prayer book which is presented to him, and sitting, or most often remaining standing, he tries to follow the service . . . but as he cannot read as quickly as the officiant, and as he is not drawn to this fastidious reading, which speaks neither to his mind nor to his soul, he soon withdraws to the terrace adjoining the temple, where he finds other young people already gathered.

Finding the air in the room a little stifling, and also pushed by curiosity, I myself go out to the terrace for a moment. It is like entering a public meeting place. Everyone has closed his book, circles of people have formed, and there is chatting, yawning, jesting, laughing. In the evening, more than three-fifths of those attending services are gathered on the terrace. Those who remain in the place of prayer are elderly men. These men alone feel it their duty to follow the various services to their conclusion on this solemn day.

Let us consider the cafés on Saturdays. They are literally invaded by Jews. With few exceptions, all are smoking, gambling—often for large sums of money—at cards or at backgammon, or discussing business.

And let us consider a house in mourning where there is grief over the loss of a respected father or a beloved mother. We first hear a *drashah*, delivered by a rabbi who tries to inspire us with an avalanche of citations from the Bible or from the Talmud; the logic with which he strings them together is not always clear. After this, we see the sons form a circle around the preacher as they try to read, or rather mouth the words to, the required *Kadish*.

I could provide many more examples, but I have said enough to create a true picture of the situation. [. . .]

In short, there is a desertion of the synagogues, an almost complete ignorance of the religion and of the Jewish past, a lack of observance of religious practices, an extreme decline in sacred studies, a continual decrease in the number of doctors in the Law, and a decrease in the number of sacrificers and others who hold special functions in our faith.

Can we remain indifferent to these observations? Can we imagine the abyss into which our communities will have been swallowed twenty or thirty years from now if some superior strength is not to intervene energetically in reaction to those erring ways?

Already, mixed marriages are becoming common. The conversion to Protestantism of an entire family still living in Sousse has been registered (I shall not even mention those that have taken place elsewhere, especially in Tunis, Bizerte, and very recently in Sfax). Is it not to be feared that this detachment from old traditions and these apostasies will become ever stronger and ever more frequent, until one day we will see the collapse of that ancient edifice raised by the respectable ancestors of these lost Jews? [. . .]

What these failing communities need above all and without delay is the establishment of Alliance schools (for boys, girls, and younger children, as was discussed above). In these schools, where the facilities would be perfectly adapted to their needs, the young Jewish children would receive both a general education, in all respects as good as what they are currently receiving in the public schools, and the moral and religious education of which they are currently almost totally deprived.

The initiative must be forcefully undertaken to restructure these communities and to charge their welfare agencies, which currently handle only administrative issues, with the responsibility for the direction of centers of Hebrew education.

There is a need for the founding of *yeshivot* and for the encouragement of theological studies. To this effect, the seminary in Tunis should be reopened; if it is well organized and well directed, it will fill a crucial void in the community.

Finally, there is a need to create a rabbinical corps whose members, with an adequate modern education, would be seriously trained in the study of the Law so that they may become pastors whose voices are heard and respected.

This is a vast and complex program, but one of high moral aims. We must not be frightened by the extent and the diversity of the tasks to be undertaken. The very preservation of Tunisian Jewry, which now shows so many signs of degeneration, depends on this undertaking.

The tireless activity, constant involvement, and prodigious efforts of the Alliance have had a profound effect on the intellectual and moral development of the numerous generations it has educated and on the economic development of the principal communities of this country. It is the duty of the Alliance to lend its support in the accomplishment of this undertaking and in the restoration of Tunisian Jewry.

Only the Alliance has enough prestige to impose its views on those communities that are so lacking in organization and so often torn apart by internal struggles.

L. Loubaton

Tunis, 5 March 1938

Antisemitism and Zionism in Tunisia: How They Affect the School

. . . Yes, antisemitism exists in the Regency. The relations between Jews and Arabs are certainly satisfactory, but there are certain indications which do not escape the notice of those who are aware and which suggest that there are currents of discontent on the part of the Arabs toward the Jews. This discontent is especially caused by the jealousy of the Arabs when they see too many Jews succeeding in commerce and in the liberal professions (most of the businessmen, lawyers, and doctors in Tunis are Jewish) and little by little taking over the life of the nation. The Destourian movement serves only to increase and spread this discontent. They resent not only the French but also the Jews. Obviously, antisemitism does not figure directly in the program of the *Destour*, but it is implied. A violent spirit of chauvinistic nationalism and a call for "National Awakening" animate the Tunisian youth of today and dictate to them quite unfavorable sentiments toward the Jews. [. . .]

At the same time, it is no less certain that Zionism, too, exists and is rapidly developing. The Jewish daily newspapers, *La Nouvelle Aurore*, *Tel-Aviv*, and *La Semaine Juive*, regularly devote long articles to this topic. They comment at length on the activities of the Zionist movement, its efforts, its successes, the obstacles it faces in Palestine; they keep the public informed of the situation of the Jews in the various countries and show how that situation is daily growing worse. What is most distressing is that this movement is not simply a Zionist movement but rather a party with clearly Revisionist tendencies: often it is only a question of Mr. Jabotinsky and his projects. And this movement has grown even among the Boy Scouts. It is saddening to observe that

these troops of Jewish Scouts are becoming involved in politics. This is damaging not only to the Scouts themselves but to the entire population.

Thus the two movements growing stronger and stronger in Tunisia are Zionism and antisemitism. Are these two movements opposed? Should we believe that the former encourages the latter or that it is a remedy to it? Is it because of Zionism that antisemitism is developing? Is Zionism the solution to antisemitism? Are the Jews here justified in lending themselves to such a degree to political preoccupations of this nature?

Without trying to give a direct answer to such delicate questions, I will limit myself to applying these questions to what can be seen in the school. [. . .]

In general terms, all of our students, like most young people today—this is the *"mal du siècle"*—are taken with politics, and this is regrettable. Under the pretext of keeping informed, they scour the newspapers and become passionately involved in public and international issues. In this way, they waste a good portion of their time, often to the detriment of their studies and sound thinking. Indeed, through this kind of reading they acquire a mass of misguided opinions, which they take for Gospel and of which it is very difficult to rid them.

This is also true for my pupils, who are older adolescents preparing for the *brevet élémentaire*. Among them are several Muslims affiliated with the Destourian party . . . When I am giving my course on civics (in the second year of preparation for the diploma), there are always a few of them who point out certain so-called inequities or injustices which make them indignant. I cannot help but notice that the same idea is always behind these remarks: "make room for the Tunisians who are living in the streets and dying of hunger while scores of Frenchmen and Jews occupy all the respected positions."

Although I never allow myself to become involved in politics in the classroom and I do not tolerate the slightest allusion to this subject, I make it my duty to reply to these remarks, to analyze them, and to refute them. I believe that if these young people have been led astray in their circle of family and friends, it is up to us to show them the truth. Most often I succeed in convincing them and in disposing them toward higher sentiments and more just ideas.

The Jews live side by side with the Muslims, and on excellent terms. The Jews too, in their way, take an interest in politics. Obviously in their circle of family and friends, the sole topic of conversation is Zionism. How could they keep from talking about it, from discussing it at length, from considering all the possibilities and all the theories, and from enumerating all the solutions? Their minds are so steeped in these ideas that they cannot help but expose their personal sentiments, sometimes even in their compositions. Allow me to tell you about one case:

I had assigned the following topic (again it is a question of the students in the second year of preparation for the diploma), which is, as it happens, a regular topic in the program: "What emotions, what dreams does the word *partir!* [to leave] suggest to you?" A few spoke about Palestine and discussed the ideal of every Jew, to leave one day for the Holy Land. Thus far there could be nothing more legitimate and natural. But they did not stop there. "Why should I work for this ungrateful land?" I am quoting word for word from one composition, "Why pour out my efforts here while my country awaits me? I do not want to live in exile and sacrifice myself for foreigners. . . ."

Such ideas denote a special mentality. If the students speak about this even in their school compositions, that means that they certainly talk about this among themselves and with their Muslim friends. What might happen when these Muslims, strongly influenced by Destourian ideas (therefore nationalistic and antisemitic ideas), revolt and challenge their Jewish friends so full of misunderstood Zionist ideas? This is what will happen: the relations between them, which have been excellent up until now, will become more and more strained and will contribute to profound dissension between the two sections of the Tunisian population. On the one side, the Arabs will spread the word that the Jews are foreigners, who have only to leave, that this is not their home, and that they are living as parasites. On the other side, the Jews, continuing along these lines, will neglect even their most basic civic duties.

Such is, then, the precise state of mind of our students today, and such are the serious consequences in which it may result. [. . .]

How can we struggle effectively against such a situation? Should we systematically speak out against both the Destourian movement and Zionism? Is it wise to tell our students, even in an indirect and discreet manner: "You are both wrong; give up these ideas." In so doing, would we not risk shocking them and deeply wounding the sentiments they hold most dear?

It would appear that the solution lies elsewhere; this solution is twofold: 1. It is our duty to strengthen the civic and moral education of our students. They should understand that the first duty of the Jew is to the country in which he lives. Because they have the privileges accorded all citizens, it is right that they also accept the duties of citizens and carry them out fully. Even more than this: the Jews must always regulate their behavior and their lives in such a manner that they not become targets for those malicious minds who are always looking for faults and who never fail to generalize them. I would like to quote here a few of the noble words spoken by the Chief Rabbi of Geneva, Mr. Poliakoff, who visited our school when he was in Tunis and left an elevated moral teaching in the minds of our older students: "My dear children! Never forget that the Jews are closely bound together. The slightest fault, the slightest questionable affair on the part of one, is quickly generalized and attributed to all . . . We have a heavy burden to bear: for centuries the name Jew has been a synonym for coward, thief, usurer; this name represented all moral baseness. It is through our actions and our conduct that we can show the world the injustice that has been done to us and that we suffer still today. You must lead lives that are dignified, irreproachable, and exemplary from a moral, civic, and religious point of view. Then those who seek only to denigrate and belittle us, to deny us our very existence, will be able to find no fault in you. . . ."

And so the first duty of any Jew is to be a "good citizen," worthy of the country in which he lives and worthy of his glorious heritage.

2. But it is not enough to give the students a solid civic and moral base. They must also be turned away from politics, which is the source of contention, disorder, and so many fruitless, if not tragic, discussions. The mind of the adolescent, just beginning to awaken, has need of nourishment. He seeks it out, and because most often he is surrounded by discussions of politics, he turns to politics himself. But could not this active mind and this hunger for learning, which are typical of the adolescent, be put to other, more profitable use?

Since he has this passion for all that is new to him and for all that is capable of awakening, strengthening, and developing his most pure and noble sentiments, why not warn him against the wrong road and show him the right path, the path rich in positive results?

And what path could this be?

This path has just been discovered by the students at the *Lycée Carnot* in Tunis: they founded a paper, which they write, edit, and publish entirely on their own. All questions of politics are excluded; the paper treats topics in literature, the arts, the sciences, sports, and anything that has to do with daily life. The first issue has already come out, and to judge by the favorable opinion of the public and the encouragement offered by the authorities concerned, this paper promises to prosper for a long time to come.

Does not an initiative such as this deserve to be imitated? Could we not do something along those lines, obviously on a more modest scale, with some of our students? We could encourage the students in their French (a subject in which they are generally quite weak), lead them toward sound and instructive reading, introduce them to literary masterpieces rather than insipid serial novels, develop in them artistic taste and sensibility (some of them are gifted in this area; they have shown me their sonnets and their sketches, and they are quite good), talk with them about sports, which so fascinate them, and speak to them of friendship and brotherhood between Arab and Jewish classmates. And as we do all this, we would be stimulating a spirit of healthy competition, which could bring only good results. Is not this the most effective way to turn them away from politics completely and to channel their growing energy in a manner that is both instructive and enjoyable? . . .

These are the solutions resulting from my reflections on antisemitism and Zionism and their effects on the school.

M. Cohen

NOTE
Words in brackets appear in the original translation.

Translated by Aron Rodrigue.

David Ben-Gurion

In Judah and the Galilee
1921

> *Not fire and sun—but our blood will redden,*
> *Oh Zion, your mountains—*

Right after disembarking and finishing my business with the *numruk* [custom house], I hurried to Petah Tikva. My friends implored me to stay in Jaffa for a few days, but I couldn't curb my ardent desire to see a Hebrew *moshavah* [farming village], and toward evening on that day I reached the capital of our *moshavot*

in the Land of Israel. And that night, my first night on the soil of the homeland, is imprinted in my heart with the joy of victory. I was awake all that night—who could sleep on his first night in the Land, the dwelling-place of childhood and dreams celebrating its victory? Here I am in the Land of Israel, in a Hebrew village in the Land of Israel, a Hebrew village, whose name is "Gate of Hope."

The howl of the foxes in the vineyards, the braying of the donkeys in the dairies, the croaking of the frogs in the pools, the rich fragrance of the acacia tree, the distant murmur of the waves of the sea, the shadows of the orange groves in the darkness, the enchantment of the stars in the dark blue, the high, bright, dreamy heavens—everything made me drunk. It became a dream. I was entirely swept away by happiness, and everything was still surprising and strange, as though I was floating in a legendary kingdom. Was it so? I remember every detail of the journey; saying goodbye, sailing on the sea, approaching the shores of the Land—the entire transition from *there* to *here*. My soul was storm-tossed, and one feeling named "Here I am in the Land of Israel" was dominant within me—and still I thought: "Is it true?" But here was the Land of Israel, with every step and pace. I am walking on the soil of the homeland. Above my head, the heavens of the land and its host of stars—and I had not seen that sky and those stars until that day. All night long I sat and communed with the new sky.

The days in our land are beautiful, days washed with splendor and full of glow, rich in sights of mountains and sea. But seven times seven more marvelous are the nights; nights deep with secret, swooning in mystery. The blazing droplets of gold, trembling in the soft dome of deep blue, the pure darkness of crescent moon nights, the crystal hue of the transparent mountain air—everything is permeated with soulful longing, hints of yearning, the secret tumult, inspiring a mood of desire for what is not here, and you listen to the echoes of childhood in the stillness, and ancient legends and visions of the end of days are woven here on the shore, and they pour into your soul and sprinkle a dew of hope and nostalgia on your longing soul.

And if you are exiled from the Land and distanced yourself from this soil and these heavens, and you end up across distant seas, and you dwell on foreign soil, under an alien sky—you must take with you the memory of these nights—the legacy of your land—and you will never forget them.

I stayed to work in Petah Tikva. For about a year I worked in the *moshavot* of Judah—and more than I worked—I had malaria and went hungry. And all three—the work, the malaria, and the hunger—were new for me and full of interest because that was what I had come to the Land of Israel for. The malaria visited me with *mathematical* regularity once a week. It would stay for five or six days and go away. And I would always know the time of its arrival in advance, and I almost never made a mistake in my reckoning. The manner of its visit was also regular and unchanging. First it sent me a fierce chill, which would make my body tremble and shake it powerfully, but soon, half an hour later, the cold changed to burning heat, which would last for three or four hours.

Hunger was also a frequent visitor, and it would stay with me for a few weeks, and sometimes months at a time. During the day I would try to give it the slip in all sorts of ways—or at least to distract myself from it. But at night, in sleepless nights, the pangs of hunger grew stronger, they would pinch my heart, darken my head, suck the marrow of my bones, demanding and tormenting—and go away at dawn, when I would fall asleep, crushed and broken, and in the morning, when I washed, I saw that my hair was falling out.

And thus the days of work alternated with days of malaria and hunger, over and over, but my enthusiasm and joy were not weakened. Who paid any mind to malaria then? The few among us who didn't have malaria would be slightly ashamed before their friends. To come to the Land of Israel and not taste the taste of the malaria of the Land of Israel?!

That was ten years ago—during the time of the new aliyah. Every ship brought with it a stream of young people. Most of the new workers settled in Petah Tikva. And even though this was after the boycott of the farmers of Petah Tikva against the Hebrew workers—our numbers grew from week to week.

Young people came from every corner of Russia. People from towns and cities in Poland, Lithuania, Volhynia, southern Russia; students from houses of study and yeshivas came, students from state schools and gymnasiums. We left behind our books and inquiries, our logic-chopping and disputes, and we went up to the Land to redeem the soil of the homeland with our labor. We were still fresh. The dew of our first dreams had not yet dried up in our hearts. And the hardships of reality had not yet sobered the exaltation of our spirits. Merry, full of enthusiasm, and without worry, we were like travelers in a caravan that discovered treasures in an oasis. Each of us saw ourselves as though we had been born anew. We had left exile for redemption—for our own redemption. Far, far away we had left behind the narrow alleys and filthy streets—and now were living among gardens and orchards. Everything was new here—nature, life, labor. Even the trees here are new, different, not like the trees *back there*—here's an olive tree, an almond tree, a date palm, and a eucalyptus—and above all, oranges. And they were ours. We planted them and cultivated them. We were no longer sitting on school benches, struggling with books and sharpening our minds on vain issues—we were working. We were planting seedlings, picking oranges, grafting trees, hoeing, digging wells—we were tillers of the soil, and the soil was the soil of the homeland. And we were not working—we were conquering. We were conquering the Land. We were a camp of conquerors, and in the Land of Israel. What else did we need?

We worked and we conquered—we were merry with victory. And at night, after a day of labor or of malaria, we would gather in the workers' kitchen, on the sandy paths between the vineyards and the orchards, and we would dance and sing. Hand in hand, shoulder to shoulder in a circle . . . we danced and sang.

During our first honeymoon, everything looked new to us, "Land-of-Israelish." But when the inebriation of the first enthusiasm faded slightly, our gaze fell upon an old picture, which peeked out of a new frame—and the picture was one of the diaspora. The sky was new—the sky of the Land of Israel, and the land was new—the land of the homeland, but the people, the residents of the *moshavot*, were diaspora people, and their actions were diaspora actions. Like us, they too had come here in their youth with dreams of redemption and aspirations of conquest—but these first ones had turned into agents and storekeepers, who traded on the hopes of their people and sold the aspirations of their youth for pennies. And because of what they did, the graven image of the diaspora was brought into the temple of national resurrection, and the creation of the homeland was desecrated by "idol worship."

We grumbled about the desecration and challenged the pocketbook calculations that destroyed the resurrection to its foundations—and they wouldn't look us in the face. We were like a living protest, a reminder of injustice, from which there was no escaping in their eyes, and they regarded us with repressed hatred and open contempt. Between the old farmers and the new workers a deep gap opened.

The work itself, too, the constant work with a hoe, did not entirely satisfy me. It was too mechanical and monotonous. The smell of the factory wafted up from the constant banging of the hoes. I felt a thirst that was not slaked, an aspiration that did not find fulfillment—as if a vacuum had opened in my heart. I yearned for broad fields, for waves of grain, for the smell of grass, for the song of the plowman—so I decided to go up to the Galilee.

Judah and the Galilee have always been opposites. The residents of the plain were more cultured, spoiled, light in movement and soft in heart, and the mountain dwellers were coarse, simple, brave of heart and strong of soul and mingled with the clods of earth. Judah was richer and more cultured, and the Galilee—sturdier and sterner. The peasants of Judah are weak-handed, accept authority, and few of them bear arms. The peasants of the Galilee are strong of soul, experienced in robbery and battle and happy to take up arms. The mountains and boulders of the Galilee inspired those who lived there and infused them with a spirit of heroism and war.

The life of the Jews in the Galilee was also different from the life of the Jews in Judah. In the *moshavot* of the Galilee there are no "noblemen" farmers, owners of rich estates, who employ many workers. There are no vineyards and orchards, wells and irrigation machinery, and all the work is in the orange groves. But here in the Galilee there are sheep, goats, and cattle, chicken coops, and dovecotes, horses and plows, expanses of fields and grain. The Galilee farmer's holding is not rich—but it is moist with the sweat of his brow.

Ten years earlier, the Galilee had not yet donned its present form. The network of villages and farms that made the Tiberias district a small Hebrew state had not yet been built. On the site of [Kibbutz] Kineret dwelled the Bedouin of Sheikh Isa, in Migdal only the Germans had settled, Sharona—the ancient Sharon and the modern Rama—had not yet left the ownership of Sa'id Bek, on the land of Masha lived members of the tribe of Tsubiah, the hills of Poria and Mitspeh had been barren for centuries, and throughout the Jezreel Valley not a single Jewish plowman had been seen. The settlement of the Galilee was still at the start of its creation—only four small, feeble *moshavot*, founded three or four years earlier. At that time Sejera was the center of the Lower Galilee.

That *moshavah* was our young one, a *village* of Hebrew workers. Here began the new settlement of work-ing farmers who were not employers. Here the first effort was made at cooperative labor (then we called it a "collective"), and here Hahoresh [The Plowman] was founded, here the idea of Hebrew watchmen arose, and here on one of the green hills, the first graves of the fallen watchmen were dug.

From Judah I arrived at Sejera.

After Judah, Sejera was for me almost what Petah Tikva had been for me after the diaspora. Here I found the Land of Israel. The nature, the people, the labor—everything here was entirely different, more characteristic of the Land of Israel, and the scent of the homeland would burst out here from every foot of earth. Of ten measures of mountain beauty that came down to the Land of Israel, Sejera took nine. The mountains surround the *moshavah* on all sides and enclose it. On the east, within the vista of the other side of the Jordan, the mountains of Gilad and the Bashan are seen, enveloped in blue mists, and they look like blue waves of the sea that had risen upward and been frozen as they stood; to the west, on the boundary of the *moshavah*, lie the green hills of Nazareth; to the north rises the eldest of mountains, which is head and shoulders taller than all the rounded hills—white-haired Mount Hermon, fluttering with its white forehead and forelock and overlooking the entire Galilee; and to the south rises Mount Tabor in its arrogant isolation—the perpetual watchman over the Jezreel Valley. The *moshavah* itself is built on a slope—two rows of houses stand above one another, surrounded by a grove of eucalyptus trees and terebinths, and from a distance they look like rungs of a ladder leading to the top of the hill, and above, on the peak of the rocks, the farm is built.

Not only the nature around the village but the village itself stands out in the welter of its colors. Its small population was varied in hue and language. Among its fifty farmers and workers were broad-shouldered, tall Jews from Kurdistan, who are entirely uneducated, like their Kurdish neighbors; thin and gaunt Yemenites, excellent in their knowledge of Hebrew and traditional Judaism; young people from Russia, children of the Enlightenment and the Revolution; natives of the land, Ashkenazi Jews who had left the yeshivas of Safed and Tiberias to wield spade and plow; converts, Russian peasants from the banks of the Caspian Sea, who had become Jews and come to work in the homeland of their new religion; young Sephardic Jews, who had been educated in Alliance schools—and in that variegated crowd were heard: Hebrew, Arabic, Aramaic (the language of the *Targum* is still spoken by the Kurdish Jews), Jargon [Yiddish], Russian, French, and Spanish. But this was not the generation of the Tower of Babel. A firm and strong bond joined together this ingathering of exiles—the soil and labor. Sejera depended entirely—and at that time it was unique in the Land of Israel—upon Hebrew labor, the labor of the farmers and their families, and also on the farm that belonged to the Jewish Colonization Association only Hebrew laborers worked.

Sejera was divided in two: the people of the farm, the clerks and the workers, dwelt "above"—on the top of the hill, and the people of the village, the farmers, lived "below"—on the slope of the hill, but a covenant of peace was forged between those who dwelt above and those who dwelt below. Almost all the farmers had once been young workers at the farm who had become farmers and continued to work for themselves. And we, the workers, would meet with them often, in the field and at home, while at work and at rest. Here there was no sign of that gap that separated the farmers and the workers in Judah. On the Sabbath and on holidays we would come together and hold parties and festivals, and on weekdays we would meet in the field, each plowing beside his brother, and helping and assisting one another like comrades in labor.

Here, in Sejera, I found *the environment of the homeland* for which I had yearned so much. There were no more storekeepers and agents, foreign workers and idlers, living off the labor of others—all the people of the village worked and benefited from the labor of their hands. The men plowed, tilled the soil, and sowed. The women worked in the vegetable gardens and milked the cows, and the children herded geese on the threshing floor and rode horses out to their fathers in the field. They were countrymen. The smell of grain and manure arose from them, and their faces were suntanned. The work here also satisfied me more. There wasn't the same dryness, monotony, of working with a hoe in Judah. You walk behind the yoked animals and guide the plow, you turn over the clods of earth and open up furrow after furrow, and the earth that you plow and sow will soon be covered with greenery. It will bring forth produce before your eyes, and right after the rains are over, the wheat will ripen, and you will go out to reap and gather the harvest to the threshing floor. You see yourself as a partner in the Creation, and you enjoy your labor and take pleasure in it.

But here, too, the purity of our soul's desire was sullied—and a new flaw was revealed in the fullness of our lives in the Land of Israel. The soil of this mountain village was indeed worked entirely by Hebrew hands—but the guards were *alien* employees. In Judah we hardly noticed the alien watchmen, we hardly noticed the watchmen at all. The *moshavot* were large and well-populated, and the surrounding areas were quiet, and hardly any arms were to be seen in the Arab villages. There was great fear of the authorities, and the public order was hardly disturbed. That was not the case in the Galilee, among the hills. The *moshavot* were tiny and young. The surroundings were wild, and almost all the neighbors were experienced robbers and armed, "and the caves of the mountains and the clefts of the rocks are a shelter for all who seek revenge and for every hero among his people" [from "Poems of Exiles" by Tchernikhovsky]. Robberies and attacks were frequent—and the power of the government was negligible. In that environment, the safety and security of the *moshavah* depended on the watchmen. In the villages of Judah, the alien watchmen were swallowed up among the alien laborers and were barely felt to be present—but here, in Sejera, all the labor was ours, Hebrew labor and lively Hebrew youth all around—*and all of this was placed in the hands of foreigners?* Here, too, would we be in exile, *to hire strangers*, to watch over our property and protect our lives? We began to speak in earnest to the officials and the farmers, asking them to appoint Hebrew guards. But they looked at us as if we were dreamers and children. "Jewish guards—and the danger that involves?" At first they didn't believe that our demand was serious. Would it really occur to us to endanger the lives of young men for the sake of an "abstract principle"? Would there really be enough people who would agree to risk their lives? And wouldn't Hebrew guards be a huge danger for the safety of the *moshavah*? After all, the Arab guards, who knew all the secret places in the village, the ins and outs, would be the first to attack and rob, and we here were few and weak, surrounded on every side by strangers and enemies: the *falahin* of Lubia, the largest city in the Lower Galilee, were famous for their robbery and aggression; the Christian residents of Kfar Kama, who were full of venom and hatred for Semites; the people of the tribe of Tsubiah, who were encamped in the forest of Sejera intimidated all the surrounding area; the Circassians in Kfar Kama, who were outstanding in their pride and their courage. (Our neighbors from Kfar Kama, the Circassians, who had come to settle in the land by invitation of the Turkish government, occupied a special place among the *moshavot* of the Land of Israel. The government favored them and protected them against the rest of the inhabitants. Their sheikhs were appointed to important military posts, and their families acquired enormous influence among officialdom. However, the prestige of the Circassians and their aggressiveness depended not only on their political foundation, but also on their independent characters, and would it be at all possible for us to defy them under these conditions?). However, we stood by our opinion, and spoke out against the insult to our national honor, an insult to the honor of the work of resurrection. But our demands and protests were in vain.

We tried to convince the official in charge of the farm. He used to relate to us with respect and trust and gradually approached our worldview about the value of settlement and of national labor in the Land of Israel. He admitted that our principle was correct, but he did not dare to implement it in practice. The guards of the *moshavah* were then Circassians from Kfar Kama. They were diligent in their work, their economic situation was solid, and they were famous as experienced in war and excellent in their stalwart bravery. No *falah* and no Bedouin would dare to defy the Circassians. The *falahin* used to say: *fish akhbar min tsarkas*—no one is mightier than a Circassian. The center of their community was in Trans-Jordan, in the Kuneitra area of the Golan, and in the Lower Galilee, between Sejera and the Yama. They lived in good relations with the Jewish *moshavot* in their vicinity. They provided almost all the guards in the *moshavot* of the Galilee, and they guarded the farm, the forest, and the fields of Sejera. Our official did not dare to place Hebrew guards in the *moshavah* and arouse the envy of the Circassians. In the whole Galilee there was only one Hebrew guard. He was Shalom the Kurd, who guarded the courtyard of the farm in Sejera, but the official also discharged him that winter because one night he did not stand at his post and put a Circassian guard in his place.

We saw clearly that we could not conquer that fortress of foreign watchmen all at once—we had to do battle and fight, step by step, against every single watchman. We made up our minds to do battle right away and to start with the new Circassian guard.

We lay in wait for that Circassian guard for a few nights, and we saw that he did not come to stand at his post. He counted on his reputation to act as a guard in his place. That was also how the Arab watchmen behaved. They were known in the area for their courage and rapacity, and the guards were usually appointed from among the best-known robbers and thieves. They were sure that if the robbers only knew that they had been entrusted with guard duty, they wouldn't dare come and steal. And if some untoward event did take place, it would be easy for them, because of their close relations with the world of thieves and robbers, to discover the stolen goods and return them, of course not without a decent reward from the owner of the stolen property.

That was also how the Circassian guard acted. Instead of patrolling the fence of the *moshavah* all night and being alone in the darkness with the boulders and eucalyptuses that surrounded Sejera—he chose to go to the nearby Arab village and spend the night in the company of drunken companions.

In vain we protested to the official about the deceitful work of the Circassian guard and about the loss involved in that method of guarding; he paid no heed to our words. So we decided to prove in action that we were right. One dark night, after some of us had led the best mule away from the farm, we reported the theft to the official. The official rushed to the stable, and the mule was gone. He immediately blew his whistle to call the guard, but he whistled once, twice, thrice—and there was no sign that anyone was listening. He went out, walked around the wall, and the Circassian wasn't there. Messengers went to the Arab village to look for the Circassian—and they found him lying in a deathlike sleep. The official fired the Circassian and entrusted guard duty to Z. B.—one of our number.

The first stronghold had been taken.

We know that the Circassian wouldn't keep quiet, and indeed before long, one morning the official woke up and found the panes of his window smashed and his walls were studded with Martin bullets. A steady rain poured to the ground. The night had been stormy and windy. The sound of the shots had been swallowed by the roar of the storm, and the two watchmen had heard nothing. The intention of the attackers or attacker had been to threaten the Hebrew guards and make them abandon the watch. But their reckoning was mistaken.

Right after that night we decided to organize and stand on watch. Aside from the regular watchman and his assistant, we added a diversionary force of all the workers, a pair for two hours, from dusk till dawn. We lay in wait in the large barn next to the mill, with weapons at our side. Every pair, when their turn came, had to go out and wait in ambush in a cactus hedge or the clefts of rocks to be prepared for whatever trouble might come and to call for help from the others in time of need. It was the rainy season, and a storm, the likes of which had not been seen for many years, raged throughout the country for a week. In the *moshavot* of Judah the storm brought down almost all the oranges and caused an enormous loss to the owners of the orchards. In Sejera the storm was accompanied by steady rain, the darkness was great and thick, and it was impossible to see anything from a pace away. When my partner and I went out on watch, we were forced to hold each other's hand. The trees, the boulders, the houses—all of nature was black and dark. We could not even speak to each other. Our voices were snatched up by the storm, which didn't stop howling all night long. It seemed as if nature had joined forces with our enemies to test our strength.

The ambush continued for two weeks—until the attackers became convinced that their threats wouldn't keep us away from our posts—and they retreated.

We emerged from our first test with the upper hand.

That experience was a guide to the future. We soon saw that Hebrew guards were not enough. If the other workers were unable and unwilling to help guard in time of danger—there would be no value to Hebrew guarding, and it wouldn't last. The Hebrew guard couldn't depend on his reputation to serve as a barrier against thieves and attackers. He had to stay on watch all night long, without letting any oppressor or enemy enter the area he was guarding in the middle of the night. And to fulfill that task, not only faithfully but also successfully, there was a need for a constant reserve, who would help the guard and stand by him in emergencies. And such a reserve required two things: appropriate human resources and a decent supply of weapons.

The human resources were fine. We were prepared. But we lacked weapons. Only a few of us had pistols, and we looked at those fortunate ones with so much envy! We decided to demand weapons from the officials.

The official immediately accepted our demand. A special wagon was sent to Haifa to bring rifles from there. We waited impatiently for the wagon's return. Our one topic of conversation, by day and by night, was only about the weapons, and on the day when the wagon returned from Haifa—there was no limit to our joy. The rifles they brought were of the worst kind, cheap, crummy shotguns with two barrels. There were, in fact, decent guns in the official's house, Martins—

but the officials still didn't dare to give us "dangerous" weapons like those. But to our eyes, even the crummy guns were the height of perfection. Like little children we played with the guns and never let them out of our hands for a moment. Unwillingly we went to work the next day—we were forced to part with our guns for a whole day! As soon as we managed to return home and unhitch our horses and mules, we immediately hurried to our guns—and they didn't leave our hands until we fell asleep. We ate, hiked, washed, read, conversed—and our guns were in our hands or on our shoulders.

The large room in the caravanserai where most of the workers lived suddenly became a den of thieves. A person who entered there in the evening would see about twenty fellows sitting on their beds, and each was holding a gun! One was cleaning the barrel, and another was examining the ammunition, one was slipping the shells in and out, and another was filling his pouch—they compared the guns to each other, they listed the advantages and disadvantages of each of them, hung them on the wall and took them down, placed them on their shoulders and removed them—and so it was until it came time to sleep.

Once the farm, that is to say, guarding the farm, had come into our hands—we set our hearts on the *moshavah*. Here an incident came to our aid. One night the horses of farmer Y., a member of the *moshavah* council, were stolen. When the farmer noticed the theft, he rushed outside and found the watchman, who was returning from the field. It soon turned out that he had committed the theft. We decided to strike while the iron was hot, and we immediately turned to the *moshavah* council and offered to post Hebrew watchmen. This time they did not dare to reject our old arguments—and they agreed to Hebrew watchmen. Our victory on the farm sealed the lips of our few adversaries, and the responsibility for guarding the entire *moshavah* was given to us. That was the first *moshavah* to post Hebrew guards.

After conquering the guardianship of the farm and the *moshavah*, the way was open before us—to conquer the strongest stronghold of guarding—the "fourth season."

The fourth season begins in the second half of the rainy season: in the months of Shevat and Adar. At the end of Heshvan the *yoreh* falls, the first rain, and the hard earth, fissured from the dryness and heat of the sun for seven hot months, soaks the rains up thirstily. Then the farmer sets to work: he plows and sows, turns the earth over and tills the friable soil. The fields and the bald plots are covered with green, the grasses bloom, and when the plants in the forest reach a certain height—in the month of Shevat—the nightly pasturing begins, the fourth season. The horses and mules aren't taken to the stables after their work. The farmers gather all the cattle of the village, the oxen, the mules, the horses, and the donkeys, on the threshing floor, and from there they lead them to the pasture. For the nightly pasture is not like that of the daytime. Not just one or two herdsmen tend the flock. There is no "fourth season" without armed guards. Here, among the mountains, one mustn't abandon the flock in the darkness of night. A regiment of horsemen and foot soldiers, armed from head to foot, spreads out over the Emek, their ears are alert to every sound and movement, their eyes penetrate the darkness to catch every shadow, and their hands are steady on the rifles to greet an uninvited guest at any moment.

Guarding the flock is harder and more dangerous than guarding the *moshavah*.

In the *moshavah*, the guard has partners on his watch—iron locks on the stables and stone walls around the houses. Everything is shut tight. A stranger would not dare to enter after sundown. The place is private property, and if he just hears a suspicious noise, the guard gives the signal with his whistle and shoots his gun—and everyone in the village comes out to help him right away. But at the pasturage, he is far from the village. The road is public property. There is neither a wall nor a lock. Everything is open. The flocks wander freely in the forest and the valley, without reins or bridles. There is no hour more opportune than that for bold robbers to reach out to seize the flock. Many are the twisting paths and hiding places in the mountains—it is easy for the thieves to hide, to mislead the herdsmen and watchmen and hide the plunder without leaving traces.

To conquer the guarding of the fourth season—that was our third stop that winter.

Conquest of the guardianship of the *moshavah* and the farm prepared the soil for the new effort—and when the fourth season came, we managed to place some of our men among the guards of the flocks. To entrust the entire pasturage to us all at once seemed too risky to the official and to the *moshavah* council.

In that fourth season, for the first time the Hebrew watchmen were initiated into bloodshed, but fortunately things did not go so far as an instance of death.

Among the Hebrew shepherds was Dov Schweiger, who had arrived in Sejera a few weeks earlier. In a short time he managed to acquire not only the affection of all the comrades but also the confidence of the official, so that he entrusted such difficult and responsible work to him. Until then the fourth season, like the other branches of guarding, had been in the hands of the Circassians—and they never looked favorably upon their Jewish partners. Their pride and self-esteem was injured. Would these *walad-al-mit* [Arabic: doomed children] go out with them, with the brave Circassians, to the pasture at night? Young Hassan, the son of the sheikh of the Circassians, was particularly angry about the participation of Dov Schweiger, who was very young, almost still a boy. At first he thought that this soft Jew would not have the strength to do that hard work. But the nights passed, and "Berele" stood on watch, with diligence, with courage, like an experienced herdsman. Then Hassan started to provoke Berele, to mock and insult him. But Dov was not one to be insulted or one to trade insults. He would respond to every provocation and mockery with coarse words and sharp jabs, until finally Hassan couldn't restrain his spirit and he called out to Dov, "Yal'an-dinak" (curse your religion)—the strongest and must insulting curse in the eyes of the Arabs. Dov didn't say anything. He just raised his whip and slashed the Circassian's face with all his strength. Hassan was surprised by the Jew's insolence, that a *walad-al-mit* would dare to raise his hand against him, against the son of a Circassian sheikh! In fury he fell upon Dov—but he immediately felt two iron clamps grasping his arms. Dov gripped the Circassian, threw him onto the ground, and his whip rose and fell, rose and fell without cease on Hassan's back. True, Dov was also dealt some serious blows. But he stayed on his feet, and the Circassian lay on the ground. Dov didn't stop lashing with his whip until the Circassian lay helpless. He just managed to blow on his whistle to call his friends, and he fainted, bathed in his own blood. Ali, Hassan's friend, came quickly, and when he saw his friend bleeding, he wanted to attack Dov, for he was burning with the fire of revenge. But Dov aimed his gun at Ali and thundered out loud: "*Indak!*"—meaning, Don't move! And all night long the Circassian stood with his bleeding friend and didn't dare raise arm or leg—and Dov stood before him, also bleeding, with the gun in his hand.

Toward morning, when we were ready to go out to work, and we had prepared the courtyard for the return of the flocks—we were stunned by the horrifying sight. Dov came in, and we could barely recognize him: his face and his clothes were red. After him the Circassians bore Hassan.

When the official saw that Hassan was wounded and bleeding, he quaked with fear. "What did you do? The Circassians will take revenge against us," he whispered, and his face was as pale as a corpse.

We stood around Dov, and none of us said anything.

The official cast his eye on the band of workers—and he calmed down. The eyes that expressed courage and resolve gave him a sufficient answer.

The Circassians didn't take revenge. After that incident they began to seek our friendship more.

The guarding of Sejera was consolidated, and it had won a clear victory. After Sejera came Maskha and Yama as well, and we established Hebrew watchmen.

Sejera, which was the first of the guards, was also the first to see a casualty among the guards.

It happened a year later, during Pesah 5669 [1909]. All that winter the air of Sejera was full of the scent of gunpowder. Disputes broke out between us and the people of Kfar Kana about the borders of the land of Um-Jebel. Several times their plows went up onto our land, and we drove them out by force. The members of the Hatsbuah tribe, who were living in the Sejera forest, were also restive. Government soldiers had shot their sheikh, Hamadi. In Arab Sejera fights broke out between the Arabs and the Kurdish Jews, who were living there. The *falahin* from Lubia were extremely insolent and waylaid travelers who were going from Sejera to Tiberias. That was the first winter after the declaration of the [Ottoman] constitution, and the ignorant *falahin* interpreted the *Huria* in a special way: from now on there was no law and no judge. The government would no longer intervene, and everyone would do what he saw fit. And since the reins were loosened, acts of stealing and robbery increased in a shocking way, along with thieving and attacks.

A few days after Pesach a few attacks occurred in Sejera, drawing bloodshed in their wake—but that didn't prevent the workers of the Galilee from celebrating the Pesach holiday in this *moshavah*. Many guests also came from Judah, because on that Pesach the general assembly of the Organization of the Galilean Workers of Zion had been called in Sejera.

Although the mood was slightly depressed, on account of the frequent quarrels and attacks, we decided to celebrate the holiday and hold a communal seder as the year before.

The celebration was held in the upper caravanserai, in the courtyard of the farm. The large room, which had first been used as a stable for cattle and then as a dormitory for the workers, was decorated in honor of the holiday in Galilean fashion. The two long walls were covered with thick eucalyptus and pepper tree branches, so that it looked like a tree-lined boulevard. On the inner wall, opposite the date, were hung tools and weapons: plows, spades, tillers, and hoes were fastened on either side of the window, decorated with bunches of flowers, and above the window, interspersed, were rifles, pistols, swords, and daggers. The faces of the fellows sitting at the large table testified that those tools were not only ornamental.

We began the seder with song and wine, as usual. The sadness that had oppressed over us all that time gradually dispersed. All the worries and fears were swept away. With every new song, the joy increased, and from cup to cup the enthusiasm waxed—it was a mixture of Hasidic devotion and wild, Arab excitement, which prevailed in all the festivities of the workers of the Land of Israel. The songs were accompanied with dancing— wild dancing, without tempo or measure, accompanied by hand-clapping, like the Arab dances.

While we were singing and dancing, an angry voice reached our ears from outdoors. In a moment the dance stopped, and we were silent. An unfamiliar lad burst into the room, and with a trembling, broken voice, and a burning face, he told us about an attack that had just happened to him. He and an acquaintance had come from Haifa by foot. An Arab had escorted them along the way, and his donkey bore their belongings, which also included an expensive photographic apparatus. Toward evening they passed by Kfar Kama. After they left the village, from among the rocks three Arab robbers appeared before them. He alone, the one telling the story, was armed, with a Browning pistol—and he defended his life and that of his acquaintance, until the bullets in his pouch were used up. The robbers fell upon their Arab escort, beat him with murderous blows, and seized his donkey and everything that was on it. It seemed to him that one of the attackers was wounded. As they walked, they saw a trail of blood.

In a moment we took up our arms and rushed out. For a long time we looked for the robbers' footprints, but in vain. At the scene of the crime we found only spots of blood. A long line of blood twisted along the path then suddenly stopped and disappeared. Bitter and full of worry, we returned home.

The following day we heard that they had brought a mortally wounded Arab from Kfar Kana to the hospital in Nazareth. A few days later we learned that the Arab had died of his wounds. When they brought the wounded man to the hospital his friends reported that the wound had been self-inflicted. By chance he had fired a shot and the bullet had struck his body. However, while he was dying he admitted the truth, that a Jew from Sejera had wounded him. We sensed that something was about to happen, was knitting together in the air.

It was during the intermediate days of the holiday, when none of us was working. In one of the farmers' houses, at the foot of the hill, the assembly of the Galilean Workers of Zion gathered. The question of land was on the agenda, but our hearts were preoccupied by another, unspoken question. We were all armed. I was the chairman—but rather than listening to the course of the arguments and the theoretical discussion—my brain and heart were given over to the situation, and my hand did not leave the leather holster where my Browning was. Before the meeting we had placed a guard post on the top of the hill to warn us about anything that might be happening around the *moshavah*.

While we were pondering and arguing, one of the guards pushed in and announced that the Arabs had attacked the herd and stolen oxen and mules. The meeting stopped. The comrades who had come from other *moshavot* were sent to their houses right away to defend them in the emergency. We, the ones from Sejera, gathered in the caravanserai to discuss the situation. We decided as much as possible to avoid provoking the Arabs during the first seven days. The customs of blood revenge still existed among the Arabs. The victim's relatives were obligated to avenge the blood that was spilled, and the first seven days after the murder were the most dangerous. The blood avengers were permitted to plunder and rob then, and if anyone opposed them, his blood was on his own head.

We decided no longer to send the herd to graze in the forest far from the *moshavah*, but to graze them in nearby fields.

The next day, after the theft of the cattle, the Arabs once again attacked the fields in Shuk-al-Han, on the way between Sejera and Masha, and they harvested the barley that was ripening. The enemy was not seen in the *moshavah* itself, but all around the farm suspicious movements were noticeable.

From sunrise to sunset on the hilltops armed riders and footmen were seen. Two comrades who went to Tiberias to buy matzo encountered a band of Arabs, who attacked them, beat them bloody, and took their weapons.

A black shadow spread around us: the shadow of death lurking in secret. No one said it out loud—but every one of us knew in his soul and read in his friend's eyes: the avenging sword was suspended, and it would full on one of our heads. Fate would choose the victim. We were all prepared—and we waited.

On the last day of Pesach the lot fell, and not on one of us, but on two.

It was at about two in the afternoon. We were sitting at a gathering of a few friends in the pharmacist's house, a place where we used to spend our free hours. Israel Korngold, the guard of the farm, came in, fully armed: the Martin was on his shoulder, and an ammunition pouch was on his belt. The Browning was at his hip. Ordinarily he only walked about armed while he was on watch, at night. But in those days he went out on watch right after his afternoon nap.

When he came in, he told us that he had seen two unfamiliar Arabs sitting on the hill above the cemetery. They asked him something, but he didn't understand their language (Israel had only been in the Land for a short time, and his knowledge of Arabic was still slim), and he came to get someone who spoke Arabic back. "Now," he said to us with a laugh, "we'll drag them here by their ears."

A., a farmer from Sejera who was born in the Land, went out with him. We sat and waited. Half an hour later, a volley of shots came to our ears. We raced outside, and there was A., as pale as a corpse. "They shot Israel!" he shouted and fainted.

The bell of the *moshavah* sounded the alarm right away. We grabbed our guns and ran. Behind the hill, on the boundary of the *moshavah*, we found Israel dying. A small, dark red hole was in his chest. The bullet split his heart and went out his back. The gun was no longer on his shoulder. Just the ammunition pouch and the pistol remained.

Two comrades stayed at the side of the dying man, and the rest of the group dispersed among the hills to look for the killers. There were four attackers—but there are many hiding places among the rocks and caves of the hills of the Galilee, and our search was in vain. We returned despondent and eaten up with helpless rage and bitter despair. Israel hadn't brought the enemies to us alive—we had carried Israel dead to our house.

But that was not the end of the disaster—a second victim fell. On the way to Nazareth we all stood and looked toward the scene of the murder—toward Kfar Kana. Suddenly we saw three Arabs running and two of our comrades pursuing them. The Arabs had come from the hills of Tur'an and were running toward the Arab Sejera.

It was already evening. All the residents of the farm and the people of the *moshavah* had gathered near the caravanserai. Upon hearing about the calamity, all the farmers had left their houses on the slope and walked up to the farm. Among them was Shimon Melamed. He was a carpenter by profession, but he had come to the Land of Israel to work the soil, and when the JCA established a farm at Sejera to teach Hebrew workers how to run an agricultural unit, he had come there to learn the work. Since he was a good worker, the officials employed him in his profession for a few years, as a carpenter. But he found no satisfaction for his soul, though his salary was three times higher than that of an agricultural laborer, and even more than an independent farmer, but his sole aspiration was to stand on the soil. After five or six years of work at the farm, the officials obliged his request and gave him a plot of land to farm as a tenant in Sejera.

Shimon Melamed was the happiest man in the *moshavah*. The dream that he had borne in his soul for years had become reality.

His farmstead was one of the best kept and fertile in the *moshavah*. No farmer exceeded him in diligence and perseverance. Though he was still a beginner at farming, his harvest in the first year was no smaller than that of the more experienced farmers. That Pesach was the second Pesach in his life as a farmer, and his excellent work during the winter and the heavy rains promised him another fine harvest. As great as his diligence and his love of the soil was his courage. There was no incident of an attack or fight with his neighbors when Melamed was not among the first to defend the *moshavah*.

When disaster struck the farm, Melamed was sitting in his home at the end of the *moshavah*, on the slope. When he heard the shots, he rushed outside right away. In his haste he forgot to wear his hat and to take his gun, which was hanging on the wall of his room. His young wife took down the gun, rushed out after him, and handed him the gun. She went back home to watch over their child, and her husband went up to the farm. After him came the rest of the men of the *moshavah*.

When we saw the Arabs fleeing and our friends pursuing them, we decided to send a few of us to block the way of the escapees. Three of us went out: Y. S., a farmer from Sejera, Shimon Melamed, and myself. We rushed toward the Arabs and shot at them with our guns. The fugitives were hemmed in. Two of our comrades ran after them from behind, and we were in front of them. The Arabs from the village of Sejera saw that their brothers were in trouble. All the men of the village ran out toward the three of us. When our friends who remained back at the farm saw the danger threatening us, they called to us to return. But because of the whistling of the bullets, we didn't hear their voices. The Arabs of Sejera approached us. Our comrades rang the bell. We turned our heads—and all the men of the village were running toward us. Our comrades called to us to retreat, and we withdrew. One behind the other, at a distance of a few meters, we returned to the farm. We were already close to the place where all the men of the *moshavah* were standing. Suddenly I heard Shimon's voice: "They shot me!" He fell to the ground. I hurried to him. He was already dead. From behind the cactus hedge an Arab had shot him, and the bullet had struck his heart.

In the large room, where we had held the seder, the two of them lay all that night, wrapped in white sheets. The next day, after the holiday, instead of going to our work in the field, we stood in the cemetery and dug a grave—a single grave for two casualties, a grave for our two comrades.

Silently we removed them from the workers' dormitory, silently we bore them on our shoulders to the Sejera cemetery, and silently, without eulogies, we lowered them into the large grave.

They lived and died together in a Hebrew *moshavah*; there they dreamed the dream of their life, the dream of resurrection, and there they fell as casualties. Together they rest together—the guard and the farmer—in the earth, which they sanctified in their lives and with their death.

Translated by Jeffrey M. Green.

Beinish Michalevich
1876–1928

Beinish Michalevich (Yoysef Izbitski) was a leading figure of the Bund, and a member of the Tanners' Union. He met his wife, the Bundist leader Dina Blond, in

Vilna during World War I, and they settled in Warsaw. Michalevich, along with Henryk Erlich, Viktor Alter, and Vladimir Medem, worked to integrate the Bund into the Polish parliament. Michalevich was the first chairman of TSYSHO (the Central Yiddish School Organization), established in Warsaw in 1921.

Pioneers
1921

From the pioneer "intelligentsia" who lived in Vilna at the time, we must note Iulii Tsederbaum-Martov (people called him "Aleksey with the limp"), Arkadii Kremer (Aleksandr), Pati Srednitskaia (she later married Kremer), Polye Gordon, Shmul Gozhansky (Lonu), Tsemakh Kopelzon (Timofei), Lyuba Levinson (married Isai Aizenshtat-Yudin), Shmuel Pieskin, and Yoysef Mil (John). From later years we should mention Levinson (Vladimir Kossovskii) and Avrom Mutnik (Glieb). There was also a fairly large circle of so called "half-intelligentsia."

In 1893 this group came up with the idea that instead of spreading propaganda through circles they should employ the new "agitation" tactics. From the above-mentioned, Iulii Tsederbaum-Martov, Arkadii Kremer, and Shmul Gozhansky distinguished themselves.

Iulii Osipovich Tsederbaum (a grandson of Aleksander Tsederbaum, the editor of *Ha-Melits* and [*Dos yudishes*] *folks-blat*), who was a student at the time, was banished from St. Petersburg on account of some sin. He was one of the first and the most luminous representatives of early Marxism in Russia. A man with a sharp mind and great talent, he was the first to apply the general Marxist method to Russian politics and created social democratic tactics for Russia in general. Later, already abroad, he and Lenin together founded the *Iskra* [Spark], an organ of social democratic ideas and practice.

He occupied one of the most prestigious places in the social democratic movement and has remained to this day the leader and theoretician of the Russian Social Democratic Party (Mensheviks). Early on, he exhibited excellent theoretical understanding; he was the main "theoretician" of the group and was accepted widely both among the intelligentsia and the agitators.

Arkadii Kremer was a student at the Riga Polytechnic Institute. He was expelled for creating "unrest." He had an iron will and great organizational skills, and was very active. He was very embarrassed at assemblies and

larger circle meetings—always blushing like a bride, and not able to utter a single word.

Many years later, when Arkadii Kremer was the chairman of the Central Committee of the Bund, he would still keep quiet at large meetings. One time it was his official duty to give the first speech at a Bund conference—as its chairman, he had to open the conference officially. Aleksandr turned red up to his ears, mumbled something regarding what number conference this was, and concluded his speech.

Nevertheless, his contribution was not to be discounted at smaller meetings, in personal conversation with individual people, and in his practical work. In these settings his energy, initiatives, and practical sense literally bubbled forth.

In the 1890s he was the most energetic organizer of the social democratic group in Vilna and the most enthusiastic supporter of the "new" tactics. He wrote a booklet in Russian, "About Agitation," which was later published abroad. This is the only work he wrote in his whole life, but this brochure had a strong impact on social democratic tactics all over Russia. In it Kremer illuminates the importance of agitation for improving the economic situation of the working class from a political and socialist viewpoint, and he sheds light on how the agitator should approach the masses, how he can attract attention and win their approval.

In this work he also dissects phases of workers' enlightenment. First comes the economic phase, then the professional-political phase, and only then the socialist phase. This was a simplistic view of agitation, but it was where most socialists stood at the time. Later (in 1901), [Georgii] Plekhanov criticized this brochure in his work *Zaria*, exactly because of this deficiency. But Plekhanov knew who had written this brochure and held Kremer in high respect, as did all the other socialists of that time. He responded mildly to the brochure, with no trace of the venomous sarcasm that characterized all of his critical treatises.

Arkadii Kremer was the leader of the social democratic group in Vilna until the Bund was founded, and he later was the most active member of the Central Committee of the Bund and of the editorial board of the *Arbeter shtime* [The Workers' Voice]. He was arrested by [Sergei] Zubatov during the first round of arrests of Bund members and was imprisoned in Butyrki for a long time. Later he immigrated to London and then moved to Geneva. In Geneva a printing press was set up for the Bund where they printed brochures such as *Der yidisher arbeter* [The Jewish Worker], the organ of the Bund's committee abroad, and the *Letste nakhrikhtn* [Latest News] (in Russian and Yiddish). The financial resources of the organization were very meager; Kremer himself typeset the articles and did not let anything get in the way of publishing. In 1904 he came back to Russia and served as chairman of the Central Committee and was very active until 1908–1909. Later he went to France, completed his studies at the Polytechnic Institute of Bordeaux, and remained in France, working as an engineer.

Another person who distinguished himself in that period was Shmul Gozhansky. He was the only one in the group who knew Yiddish well and was thus able to adjust to the new ways of working with the masses. He completed his studies at the Teachers' Seminary in Vilna in 1888. Coming from a prominent Jewish bourgeois family in Grodno, he was very familiar with Jewish life. In fact, he was the author of brochures published by the group in 1895 and 1896: *Vegn skhires* [About Wages], *Der shtot-magid* [The Town Preacher], *A rede oyf Purim* [A Speech about Purim]. He also wrote "A Letter to the Agitators," in which he applies Arkadii Kremer's general ideas about agitation to the specific environment of Vilna and in which he polemicizes with those agitators who did not want to accept the new "tactics" and saw in them a reduction of their rights to education and a deterioration of the work in general.

Gozhansky had a fierce temper, excellent rhetorical talent, and a good pen. He did not pay much attention to economic-theoretical problems and was not particularly "picky" when it came to theories. For him, action, facts, and revolutionary work were more important than anything else. His constant enthusiasm and passionate concern for questions had a strong impact on his surroundings.

Translated by Vera Szabó.

Other works by Michalevich: *Zikhroynes fun a yidishn sotsialist* (1921–1923); *Geshtaltn un perzenlekhkaytn: gezamlte artiklen vegn denker un tuer fun der arbeter-bavegung* (1938); *Literatur un kamf: zamlung fun artiklen far shul un yugnt* (1939).

Jakob Wasserman

1873–1934

Although now largely forgotten, Bavarian-born Jakob Wassermann was one of the most widely read Euro-pean novelists of the first third of the twentieth century. His work frequently addressed Jewish themes, especially the failure of German and Austrian Jews to earn the unqualified respect of their neighbors, and he was always bitter that his novels were more respected in France, Britain, and the United States than they were in his native country. Although a champion of social justice, he often unthinkingly incorporated stereotypes of Jews in his writing, especially in his memoir.

My Life as German and Jew
1921

1

I was born and raised in Fuerth, a predominantly Protestant manufacturing city of Middle Franconia, with a large Jewish community consisting principally of artisans and tradesmen. The Jews formed about a twelfth of the total population.

Tradition has it that this is one of the oldest Jewish communities of Germany. Jewish settlements are said to have existed there as far back as the ninth century. Probably, however, they began to increase and flourish only at the end of the fifteenth, when the Jews were expelled from the neighboring city of Nuremberg. Later another stream of refugees—Jews driven out of Spain—came across the Rhine into Franconia. Among these, I believe, were my maternal ancestors, who for centuries lived in villages in the valley of the Main, near Würzburg; my ancestors on my father's side lived in Fuerth, Roth am Sand, Schwabach, Bamberg and Zirndorf.

Thirty or forty decades of living in this country must have given those Jews a close inner relationship to its soil, climate and people—a relationship which must have been bred in their very bone, even though they resisted this influence and formed a distinctly alien element in the national organism. Until the middle of the nineteenth century oppressive restrictions were in force; the registry law, inability to live wherever they pleased without paying special taxes, the prohibition of free choice as to trade or profession. My mother's father, a cultured man of noble gifts, was destroyed by these restrictions. And, of course, they provided constant nourishment for sinister religious fanaticism, for ghetto obstinacy and ghetto fear.

When I was born, two years after the Franco-Prussian War, the day of civil rights had already dawned for the German Jews. The liberal party in the parliament was even fighting for the admission of Jews to government positions, a presumptuous demand which aroused the indignation of even the most enlightened Germans. Thus Theodor Fontane wrote to a friend: "I like the Jews, but I refuse to be governed by them."

No yoke of serfdom, therefore, weighed upon my youth. One side had adapted itself, the other had become accustomed to the foreign element. Economic progress was favorable to tolerance. I remember my father's words, uttered in a tone of happy satisfaction on some occasion: "We live in an age of tolerance!" I often thought about that word *tolerance*. It filled me with awe; and although I did not grasp its meaning I was suspicious of it.

As far as clothing, language and mode of life were concerned, adaptation was complete. I attended a public government school. We lived among Christians, associated with Christians. The progressive Jews, of whom my father was one, felt that the Jewish community existed only in the sense of religious worship and tradition. Religious worship, fleeing the seductive power of modern life, became concentrated more and more in secret, unworldly groups of zealots. Tradition became a legend, and finally degenerated into mere phrases, an empty shell.

My father was a small merchant who could not, however he tried, succeed in gaining wealth as most of his coreligionists were doing. He was unfortunate in business. Something of a dreamer, he always had an *idée fixe* that robbed him of the flexibility of the money-makers. He dreamed of great speculations and large enterprises; but whatever he attempted was a failure. His spirit was sentimentally liberal, an indifferent descendant of the March revolution, whose milk-and-water tendencies had been carried over into the new empire. I remember hearing, as a child, an excited dispute between him and one of his cousins about Ferdinand Lassalle, of whom he spoke as of the very devil. But I also remember that sometimes he would play moving songs on the guitar in the evenings. That was in the good days, before worry had broken his spirit. He loved Schiller, and greatly esteemed Gutzkow. On one of his trips, in a Thuringian bathing resort, he had dined at the same table as Gutzkow; this incident he often related with great pride. In later years, angry at my literary struggles, he once told me, in order to discourage the overweening ambition to which he felt I had fallen prey: "What are you thinking of? You'll never become a Gutzkow!"

In the eighties he founded a small factory, with a tiny capital the borrowing of which had been very difficult, but with great hopes. A few years later he went bankrupt, and then became an insurance agent. But despite his indefatigable efforts he barely succeeded in keeping himself and his family afloat; and he always felt that his life was a failure. All his life he worked hard. When I, at the age of thirty, was able to invite him, then fifty-six years old, to be my guest for a few weeks, he seemed in a state of constant and silent amazement. And when he left he told me: "It was the first vacation I ever had!" Eight days after his return home he died.

My mother died when I was nine years old. She was beautiful, blonde, very gentle, very silent. I was often told that strangers in the city, their curiosity aroused by reports of her beauty, would ask to see her. I was also told that her first love had been a Christian, a master mechanic of Ulm. I still have some letters of hers, full of a child-like, simple melancholy, the poetry of sadness. I remember well the general dismay at her unexpected death, and how half the city followed her coffin to the cemetery.

Although my parents differed greatly in nature and character they had one trait in common: they were not suited to their time. Both were children of romanticism. My father was its late spiritual descendant; my mother's soul was subdued and saddened by it. It revealed itself in my mother's nature and gave her a tragic attitude toward life; and it affected all my father's actions, and was accompanied by an unfounded optimism that veiled the actual state of affairs in disastrous fashion, brought him disappointment after disappointment and destroyed his courage and strength.

2

The hostility I encountered in my childhood and early youth because of my Jewishness did not affect me deeply, as I remember. For I felt that it was directed against the community rather than against me personally. A sneering appellation on the street, a venomous glance, a scornfully appraising look, a certain recurrent contempt—all this was the usual thing. But I noticed that outside the community—that is, whenever my affiliations were unknown—I encountered almost none of these stings and malicious thrusts. As the years passed this became more and more evident. My features were not Jewish, nor my manner or speech. My nose was straight, my demeanor quiet and modest. This argument sounds primitive; but people who have not had this experience cannot imagine how primitive non-Jews are in their estimation of what is Jewish or in their idea of Jewish characteristics. Their instinct is silent when it is not confronted by a caricature. I have always found that the race prejudice into which they talk themselves, or of which they let themselves be convinced, is fed by the most external things, and that as a result they are quite falsely informed as to where the real danger lies. In this those who nursed the greatest hate were also the most stupid.

Of these things I had only an intimation at the time. As for the community, I felt no inner relationship whatsoever with it. Religion was a study, and not a pleasant one. A lesson taught soullessly by a soulless old man. Even today I sometimes see his evil, conceited old face in my dreams. Curiously enough I have seldom heard of a kindly or lovable Jewish religious teacher; most of them are bleak zealots and half-ridiculous figures. Mine, like the rest, thrashed formulas into us, antiquated Hebrew prayers that we translated mechanically, without any actual knowledge of the language; what he taught was paltry, dead, mummified. Only from the reading of the Old Testament did we derive positive gain, but there, too both the subject and its interpretation lacked true illumination. Events and characters were effective singly, unconnectedly, but the whole seemed rigid, frequently absurd, even inhuman, and was not ennobled by any loftier outlook. At times a ray broke through from the New Testament, like a gleam of light through a locked door, and curiosity blended with a vague dread. Those eternal images and legends enriched my imagination only after my relation to them had become private, psychological, so to speak. That process gave them individuality, rendering them spiritual in the intellectual, or material in the romantic sense, as the case might be; in any event, withdrawing them from their connection with religion.

Religious services were even worse. A purely business-like affair, an unsanctified assembly, the noisy performance of ceremonies become habitual, devoid of symbolism, mere drill. The progressive section of the community had built a modern synagogue, one of those quasi-Byzantine edifices to be found in most German cities, but whose upstart magnificence cannot disguise the fact that the faith has no power over the hearts of men. To me it all was but empty noise, death to religious devotion, abuse of great words, lamentation obviously groundless because it contradicted patent well-being and hearty worldliness; all was presumption, clericalism, zealotry. The only relief came in the German sermons of a very stately blond rabbi whom I admired.

The conservative and orthodox Jews conducted their services in the so-called *shuls*, tiny places of worship, often only little rooms in obscure, out-of-the-way alleys. There one could still see heads and figures such as Rembrandt drew, fanatic faces, ascetic eyes burning with the memory of unforgotten persecutions. On their lips the austere prayers, appeal and malediction, grew real. Their bowed shoulders bespoke generations of humility and privation, they observed the venerable customs with the utmost faithfulness, with resolute devotion, and they retained their belief, though it was dulled, in the coming of the Messiah. Their souls too were incapable of flight, they too lacked sympathy and cordiality and radiance and humanity and joy, but conviction and passion were theirs invariably.

To such a *shul* I, a boy of nine, had to go for a year after my mother's death—every morning at dawn, every evening at sundown, and on Sabbath and holy days every afternoon also—to recite before the congregation the *Kaddish* prayer for her whose first-born I was. For this purpose ten men over thirteen years of age had to be assembled; as a rule they were old men, ancients, relics of a bygone day. On frosty, snowy winter mornings, on summer mornings when the sun rose at five or even earlier, it was hard to fulfill a duty that had been forced upon me, whose significance I neither understood nor wanted to understand. No one took the trouble to show me the beauty of this custom, and thus to obviate the danger that its apparent cruelty might cause the image of my mother to become clouded, even if only temporarily. Moreover, there was no religious atmosphere or education in my father's house, especially after his second marriage. Certain superficial observances were carried out, but not so much because of an inner urge or to express solidarity as because of public opinion and our relatives; out of fear and habit. Feast and fast days still were holy, the Sabbath retained something of its ancient quality, the culinary regulations still were kept. But as the struggle for bread grew keener, as the spirit of the new age penetrated more and more, these commandments too were neglected and the domestic arrangements approached those of our non-Jewish neighbors. Not that the chains were cast off entirely; that would have been too daring. We still acknowledged membership in the religious community, though hardly any traces remained of either community or religion.

Precisely speaking, we were Jews only in name and in the hostility, remoteness or aloofness of the Christians about us, who, for their part, based their attitude only on a word, a phrase, a deceptive state of affairs. Why, then, were we still Jews, and what did it mean? This question became ever more urgent for me; and no one could answer it.

A cloud stood between me and all matters spiritual and commonplace. At every step forward I collided with barriers and concealing screens; the road was clear in no direction. When I said that no yoke or serfdom weighed upon me it was, of course, only the legal framework of life to which I referred, the individual feeling of security within which is set all that each man does or neglects to do. Once these two factors are stated and granted incomparably greater importance attaches to the question of the individual's attitude toward society and society's attitude toward the individual. His awareness of his life's work derives from this, and, varying with the decision, the strength for its accomplishment. It was at this point that my sufferings began.

3

The Jewish God was a mere shadow for me, both as the Old Testament figure implacable in wrath and inexorable in chastisement and as the opportunistically subtilized concept of the modern synagogue. In the minds of the strictly orthodox the divine image was terrifying, but as outlined by the half-renegades, the uncertain professors of the faith, it was meaningless.

When I sought to grasp the God-concept through my childishly philosophic speculations, in solitary thinking and later in talks with a friend, there arose a pantheistic being without distinctive countenance or character or depth, the product of current phrases, evoked only by the desire for a sustaining idea. As this idea proved more and more unsatisfactory—whether because of its mediocrity or because I had an inkling of its triteness—I fell into an equally cheap and fluid atheism that was in even greater consonance with the times, that age of hopeless shallowness and debilitation, which gave idolatrous worship to science, understood and misunderstood, and by means of education debased its entire intellectual plane.

No hand reached forth to guide me, no leader or teacher. I became lost in many respects; I sought support in situations in which the true man can dispense with it. I had to adjust myself to an order that had lost both its soul and its power of sensuous perception. Such a state of affairs demands expediency to the point of cold cerebral intoxication, or else the imagination grows inflatedly active and the soul loses its focal point. Had not my questioning received lasting discouragement in my early youth, I should have been able to find connecting roads and bridges. Conventions would have become important, formal rules would have commanded respect, imposing no burden. But my mother had disappeared too early from our circle, daily cares and the anxious struggle for life robbed my father of the broader outlook. He could hardly tolerate the gaze of his children; for he was deeply ashamed of the fact that constant toil had brought him no success, and thought himself the only one so unrewarded. He always looked as if tormented by a bad conscience. We were actually forbidden to ask questions, and disobedience sometimes received severe punishment. So that in my soul weeds grew freely.

I remember that I suffered from morbid fears: fear of ghosts, of people, of things, of dreams. In everything about me lay a sinister sorcery, always baneful, always boding disaster and always confirmed. I was often invited to an old house where lived an old couple. The husband was a scholar; in his room stood a bookcase behind whose glass door were numerous editions of the works of Spinoza; and these had a curious fascination for me. When, one day, I asked the mistress of the house to give me a volume she told me, in a tone of sibylline gloom, that whoever read these books must become insane. For years the name of Spinoza was associated in my mind with the sound and sense of her words. More or less the same thing happened with everything gay and playful and festive that tried to reach me or that I tried to reach. All these things were thrust aside, suspected, made joyless. Pleasure was forbidden.

After the death of my mother we had a loyal maid who was fond of me. In the evenings she used to sit before the fireplace and tell us stories. I recall that one night, when I had listened with particular raptness, she took me in her arms and said: "You could be a good Christian, you have a Christian heart." I also recall that these words frightened me. First, because they contained a tacit condemnation of being Jewish, and thus provided further material for the brooding to which I already was addicted; and secondly, because at that time the idea of a Christian still alarmed me, and, partly for atavistic reasons, partly because of my dread of life, represented a focus of hostile elements.

The same feeling seized me when I passed a church or a crucifix, a churchyard or a Christian priest. Unconfessed attraction strove against unconscious experience that lay in the blood. To this were added the overheard utterances of adults, tales of complaint and criticism and outlawing, the expression of recurrent typical experience, danger-signals in speech and in everyday events. From the other quarter, again, a searching glance sufficed, a shrug of the shoulders, a disdainful smile, an expectant gesture or attitude—sufficed to impose caution and to recall the unbridgeable gulf.

But just what constituted the unbridgeable gulf I could not discover. And later, when I grasped its essential nature, my first reaction was to reject it for my own person. In childhood my brothers and sisters and I were so closely bound up with the daily life of our Christian neighbors of the working and middle classes that we had our playmates there, our protectors, our refuge in hours of desolation. We went in and out of the houses of the gold-beaters, the carpenters, the cobblers, the bakers; on Christmas eve we were invited, and received presents also. But watchfulness and a feeling of strangeness persisted. I was only a guest, and they were celebrating festivals in which I had no share.

My nature, however, was such that I yearned to be not merely a guest, to be regarded not as a stranger. Not as an invited guest, nor as one tolerated out of pity and kindliness, nor, worst of all, as one admitted because his hosts have consented to ignore his race and descent. The longing to become merged with a certain fullness in the humanity about me was innate in me.

Not only was this longing not appeased, but with the years the gap between my impetuous demand and its realization yawned ever deeper. I would have become lost, would ultimately have had to give up all hope, had not two saving phenomena entered into my life: the landscape and the word.

Translated by S. N. Brainin.

Other works by Wasserman: *Caspar Hauser* (1928); *The Maurizius Case* (1929); *The Dark Pilgrimage* (1933).

David Zaslavsky

1880–1965

Born in Kiev, David Zaslavsky was expelled from Kiev University in 1901 for participating in student riots. He became a Bundist in 1903, and published in and edited socialist Yiddish and Russian publications, including the *Arbeter shtime* and *Den'*. Zaslavsky moved to Moscow in 1921 and, after avowing loyalty to the Soviet regime, wrote for *Izvestiia* and *Pravda*. He continued to write in Yiddish, publishing in *Der emes* and *Eynikayt*. He was spared the fate of most members of the Jewish Anti-Fascist Committee, continued to write satire, and was active in the persecution of other Soviet Jewish writers.

On the History of the Bund in Kiev
1921

In the mid-1890s some socialist circles already existed among Jewish workers. The primary proponents of socialist democratic propaganda were first and foremost Jewish workers. In 1897, proclamations in both Russian and Yiddish were disseminated in Berdichev. The first strikes that attracted the notice of the police took place in tailors' workshops, among Jewish workers. This was not yet, however, a Jewish workers' movement; the movement carried no national character. While the work of the Bund had already been felt in Berdichev as well as other Ukrainian cities, the Bund was still largely unknown in Kiev. [. . .]

Students who took part in socialist democratic circles stood apart from the student revolutionary community, where the popular Union Council was in charge. The Union Council was a nonpartisan revolutionary student organization with great reserves of political radicalism, but very vague socialist sympathies. It maintained contact with the "semi-intelligentsia" socialist democratic circles.

The pioneers of the Jewish national movement in Kiev were Zionists, and their semi-legal gatherings in synagogues and private homes drew attention to the Jewish question. Zionist circles emerged among the student youth. Machover, Rosengart, and Fridland were the first zealous propagandists of Zionism; L. Motzkin and Y. Buchmil would come to Kiev, and there were very animated discussions at Dr. Mandelstam's house. The socialist members of the Jewish student population related to Zionism not so much with hatred as with indifference. Zionism was outside their circle of interests. The national question was entirely dominated by cosmopolitanism in its outdated form, a "naïve cosmopolitanism," according to the formulation of Otto Bauer. This disposition was similarly shared by socialist workers. While workers attended Zionist meetings in synagogues, the Jewish socialist workers' circles had no interest in Zionism. Additionally, there were no "purely" Jewish workers' circles. There were simply socialist democratic circles; they appeared very Jewish, though. [...]

Zionism played a definitive and quite commanding role in developing a national movement among Jewish students. Truthfully, Zionism did not attract many followers. The more active groups remained detached from it. It did, however, disrupt the until-then entirely cosmopolitan *Weltanschauung*. National radicalism repelled those who were pursuing political radicalism when it came to socialist questions. However, the fact that the national question was radically posed within Zionism had the advantage of awakening new thought. We were not Zionists—that was clear to us. But the ideology of assimilation, which in its basic form was nihilistic, also could not satisfy us. We were Jews—we understood this very clearly. Who were we in terms of what we believed? We had no real answer to this question. We had striven to imbue our political radicalism, our socialist ideals, with a vague national consciousness. At the same time, part of the student body that had been captivated by Zionism, but had not found within it answers to their political and social aspirations, took great pains to combine their Zionism and socialism.

However, Zionism was only an ideological stimulus. Much more palpable were motives of a different sort. At the end of the 1890s, antisemitism in governmental policies had intensified; especially and most significantly, this was felt in the sphere of middle and higher education for Jews. Quotas were reduced to the lowest degree. Students were confined to study circles, while at Kiev University in the center of the Pale of Settlement, a quota of 2 percent was planned. That meant that for all intents and purposes, Jews were no longer admitted to the university.

Exactly at that time, the children of the petty bourgeoisie were drawn to diplomas and, following in the footsteps of Jewish city-dwellers, shtetl-dwellers also began to be attracted to university education. The class interest of the Jewish intelligentsia lay in receiving a diploma; they regarded this as the only means of getting ahead in the world and of gaining financial independence. The awakening of Jewish youth had naturally taken on revolutionary colors. The best segments of the Russian student body were very sympathetic. They were prepared to protest and mentioned the quotas in their proclamations. For Russian students, however, the quotas were not a horrendous personal affront; they were just an aspect of the detested regime, and not even the most terrible aspect of the general system. Jewish students, however, felt this deeply, often morbidly. Zionism was trying hard to sharpen and exasperate this feeling of discontent. The Jewish socialists understood that the reasons were rooted in the general system of government politics, but they also understood that general words and general methods in the struggle for political freedom were not enough, and that Jews needed to solve the Jewish question separately, through their own words, from their own energies. Our thinking was moving in this direction, feeling our way toward an answer. [...]

Many Zionists were in the Jewish student organization, but they did not hold leading positions. The organization saw as its task the protection of Jewish students' interests. The Union Council accepted the organization, but not without reservations. Strong opposition came from Jewish students who were true assimilators. The arguments of the representatives of the Jewish student organization were akin to the later arguments of the Bund in defending its political independence. The Union Council was not as strict as Iskra; it already included representatives of Ukrainian students (Hromada) and of Polish students (Kolo).

At the head of the Jewish organization stood students with names that held weight in the general student community, Faynberg and Diksheyn. They played a very important role in the Union Council as well. Despite the protestations of S. B. Ratner and Y. Ribakov, the organization was accepted into the Union Council. Its first representative—the *khaver-yid* [Comrade Jew] in official terminology—was Faynberg and the second was Zaslavskii. Diksheyn was elected chairperson. The organization had great success among the Jewish students in Kiev and even at the beginning had up to fifty members, which for that time was an immensely large number. [...]

Translated by Ruth Shochat and Alexandra Hoffman.

Other works by Zaslavsky: *Kadety i evrei* (1916); *Where the Workers Are in Power* (1931); *Evrei v SSSR* (1932); *The Face of Hitler's Army* (1943); *In New Poland* (1946); *F. M. Dostoevskii kritiko-biograficheskii ocherk* (1956).

Menahem Mendel Rosenbaum

1869–1954

Raised in a Hasidic family, Menahem Mendel Rosenbaum was influenced by the Bolshevik Revolution and subsequently worked with Lenin. Ultimately imprisoned, he made his way to the United States and Israel, where he was a founder of Kibbutz Na'an.

Memoirs of a Socialist-Revolutionary
1921–1924

Volume I. Chapter 1

[. . .] In the summer of 1903 I traveled to Russia, where I was to meet with the heads of the socialist revolutionary groups in various cities in south Russia and on the Volga. One of my principal tasks was to find people who could take the illegal literature which I would smuggle into Russia from Galicia. I was helped in this by Ruthenian peasants who were sympathetic to the Russian liberation movement. I was also to meet some members of the Central Committee to deliver a special mission from the foreign committee to them.

This time I traveled under the name of Hobson, an Englishman. [. . .] As usual in my travels to Russia I did not travel empty-handed. Between the double walls of my suitcases were packed the latest publications from the party, principally the most recent edition of *Revolutsionaya Rossiya*.

In order to look more like an Englishman and at the same time change my appearance, which was not unknown to the Russian police (they had me in their paws in the years 1898–1899), I sacrificed my beard and even my moustache on the altar of the fatherland, which previously I had greatly pampered: beforehand they were very useful to me, when I would travel to Russia from Germany and endeavored to appear as much as possible like a German traveling salesman.

In those times the Russian police were still polite to foreigners, in particular to the English. At the border I was treated with particular courtesy and my luggage was briefly inspected only to fulfill their duty. I was even permitted to keep the pair of English newspapers I had laid on top in one of my cases, without censorship. I spoke with the gendarme officer who took my pass in French, which was good enough for an Englishman. However, with the other officials at the customs

house and the porters, who understood no French, the situation demanded that I speak a few Russian words. I tried to speak a broken Russian, bad enough for an Englishman. Experiences of speaking Russian badly I had already had in the past. One female comrade, with whom I once had the opportunity to speak such a language, complimented me by saying that I speak Russian badly better than I speak it well.

My English Russian did not provoke any laughter, but rather evoked a certain respect. I remembered that a few years beforehand, when I traveled across the same border with a Jewish passport and with a *tallis* and *tefillin* in my suitcase rather than English newspapers, my broken Yiddish-Russian provoked mockery and contempt.

In Kamenets Podolsk there awaited me a large pack of literature I had sent with "Dyed" [grandpa]. This "Dyed" was an old Ruthenian peasant with a long gray moustache, who helped me more out of sympathy for the Russian revolutionary movement than for the small payment he received. I paid him to travel there to take forbidden books and newspapers.

Everything went like clockwork. I found the materials at the appointed inn and I conveyed them to the towns where we kept our stockrooms. [. . .]

I knew of a Jew in Kovno, a certain Levin, who had a business making Russian provincial government passports. For a little "thanks" he would report as missing the internal passport of the person in question (who meanwhile was living calmly somewhere out there) at one of Kovno's police stations, receive the necessary papers from the police, and thereupon have the foreign passport issued from the provincial administrative office, where he was well known.

He would make provincial government passports "wholesale," as they say in America. He would take a very small profit for himself—two or three roubles—and through him one could obtain a foreign passport much more quickly and even more cheaply than via "legal" channels. Therefore it was no wonder that people from various towns would send internal passports to Levin, which he would transform into foreign ones. In this way he made a good living and the Kovno regional police superintendents and the clerks of the regional administrative office had a nice addition to their small salaries. The police archives of those years regarding Levin's activities would show that twice as many residents from Kovno traveled abroad than really lived there [. . .]

Volume I. Chapter 3

We arrived in Odessa a day before the ship was scheduled to leave the port. We stopped in two places, with sympathizers who were not "compromised." The next day I went to the administrative offices of the municipal government in the morning and, without difficulty, received on my passport the confirmation that there were no hindrances whatsoever to my—rather, Mr. Hobson's—departure from Russia—an authorization that every foreigner was required to display on his passport before leaving the country. [. . .]

I met with a friend, Miss Becker, the daughter of a rich Jewish merchant with whom I had studied in Bern. She was one of our sympathizers. The ship was due to depart first at 6 o'clock in the evening and so, as I had the entire afternoon free, I spent it with the Beckers, at their summer home on the Black Sea. They gave me a present in honor of my departure—a large bouquet of wonderful irises, which with great pleasure I took with me, first because I love flowers and second because I always considered flowers a good means to divert the attention of the Russian policeman. I hired a closed coach and with the magnificent bouquet of irises in my hand traveled to the babushka. On this occasion she had dressed up in holiday clothes and even consented to buy a new hat.

We traveled to the port and on the little boat. Since I had purchased two first-class tickets to Constanza, I ordered the waiter to bring to the common room a jug with water for the flowers, which I placed on the table. On the same table I started to lay out a packet of English newspapers I had purchased at a restaurant in Odessa. In general I acted as though the entire ship belonged to me—as is fitting for an Englishman. [. . .]

A police under-officer came to us shortly, a fat, good-natured Ukrainian, and asked for our passports. The babushka did not interrupt the lively French conversation, taking out her passport from her handbag and presenting it to him. I took out Mr. Hobson's pass from my breast pocket. The gendarme went away with the passports.

After a quarter of an hour, which was not, as we thought, made up of fifteen minutes but rather fifty hours, he came back and gave us the passports with a polite "Please." Our hearts became lighter. But the ship still stood in the Odessa port and I waited with impatience for it to sail on the free waves of the Black Sea. [. . .]

When I think about the great events in Russia before the last years, I always return to the conviction that a significant portion of the tremendous sorrows, which are always bound up with a great historical upheaval, could have been avoided had the socialists worked together in harmony. However, the Socialist Revolutionary Party unfortunately had no leaders great enough to carry out this colossal task. And I think to myself that had [Grigory] Gershuni lived, perhaps he would have risen to the task in the great moment.

Although I believe in the impact of creative figures on the course of historical development, I am not so naïve as to think that one person, however great he may be, could change the course of history. I believe that the entire development of humanity leads to socialism and that, with more or less victims, a few years earlier or later—from an objective historical standpoint these are insignificant trivialities—humanity will achieve its aim. However, subjectively for us dead people often have a great importance for historical trivialities.

Just as in a deciding battle sometimes a brilliant strategic plan devised by a high commander can lead to the victory of his forces, so too at a critical historical moment a strong person can have a great influence on the current events. And I think that Gershuni was strong enough to be able to have an effect at the critical moment for Russian history after the revolution of 1917.

If all the auspicious possibilities had been realized, Gershuni would have, with body and soul, worked for the rebuilding of Russia and probably would not have been able to devote himself to the special Jewish interests. However, this was not because he was cold to the pain of his people but rather because he was concerned with the colossal work in Russia that was also of great importance for the Jews.

From all my encounters with Gershuni I received the impression that he was a warm Jew. All Jewish questions were very close to his heart. Therefore, I think to myself, had he not devoted himself to unifying the socialist forces in Russia and had the events not happened in the way they are unfolding now, perhaps he would have thrown himself into the national socialist Jewish movement with all his energy.

I am certain that Gershuni would not have agreed with the Bolshevik tactics. And he certainly would not have been able to work as a blind tool under the Soviet regime. However, I have absolutely no doubt that he would have thought it a foolish crime to fight together with the reactionary elements against the Soviet regime.

He would also have recognized that it would not be expedient to begin an independent fight for democratic socialism. Such an energetic battle temperament as Gershuni's could not, however, sit with idle hands and wait until circumstances would change. Therefore it is reasonable to think that in the present moment when, on the one hand, the sorrows of the Jewish people have taken on unheard-of proportions and, on the other, opportunities are opening for greater construction work in the Land of Israel, that Gershuni would throw all his seething energy into the work of saving his people.

And when I think about that possibility the sorrow of the loss by his death is doubled.

Volume II. Chapter 1

My revolutionary activity began in Vilna around 1887. The work consisted mainly of spreading socialist propaganda among students and Jewish workers. At that time we began to disseminate the Marxist philosophy of history in our circles. Only a tiny minority, I among it, adopted a critical position toward the new trend.

In 1892, I had to leave Russia and when, in that same year, I arrived in Zurich the battle against orthodox Marxism was already in full swing. The Marxist Social Democrats, to which the majority of the Russian colony then belonged, gathered around Pavel Axelrod, his brother-in-law Kalmanson, Krichevsky, and Luba Axelrod, who later began to write under the pseudonym "Orthodox."

Axelrod, the oldest of them, was a fiery Social Democrat. Karl Marx and Friedrich Engels's every word was holy to him, as the Bible and Talmud are holy to a religious Jew. He considered anyone who dared to criticize the slightest point of Marx's philosophy of history an enemy of socialism and he would attack him just as a Jew of deep faith assails a heretic who denies God and His Torah.

He was not a brilliant debater. However, his honesty and strong faith often served to enrapture his listeners. When he could not refute the arguments of his anti-Marxist opponent he would instead offer scientific proof of his opponent's impudence in criticizing the greatest German scholar and genius of political economics, the founder of scientific socialism, and the father of the powerful German Social Democrat Party.

Kalmanson was a much better speaker. He had a good head and was very learned. He would often come to Axelrod's aid and, with stinging sarcasm, using cold facts and logical proofs, endeavored to destroy the arguments against historical materialism.

At that time Chaim Zhitlowsky, who was the first in Switzerland to begin a systematic polemic against Marxism, left Zurich for Bern. His criticism caused a commotion among the entire Russian colony in Zurich and, as I was told, over the course of five to six months there raged a stormy debate in Zurich that lasted twenty-six nights! I say nights and not evenings, since the discussions for the most past lasted until three or four o'clock in the morning.

Zhitlowsky strove to prove that so-called scientific Marxism was not a scientific system but metaphysical conjecture, that socialism was not necessary for the theory of economic materialism, and that, therefore, one could be a good socialist without being a Marxist.

In his beliefs, Zhitlowsky was close to the Narodniki [Narodovoltses, Yiddish Populists], but he also understood the great significance of socialist propaganda among the urban proletariat. And when he came from Berlin to Zurich—I believe in 1888—he proposed to the Narodniki that they should publish a series of brochures for workers together with him. [. . .]

The Narodniki rejected Zhitlowsky's proposal. The Social Democrats, who then organized a group with the aim of creating a socialist workers' literature, proposed to Zhitlowsky that he work with them on this task. Zhitlowsky agreed, but he stipulated that the brochures provide pure socialist propaganda without attacking the Narodniki. [. . .]

Volume II. Chapter 2

[. . .] When I came to Zurich, I found there my old teacher, colleague and friend Chonen [Charles] Rappoport, who later was one of the founders and significant activists of the Union of Russian Socialist Revolutionaries.

Here I will present [. . .] his biography, which is characteristic of many of the Jewish socialist activists.

Rappoport was the only son of a scholar and merchant in the Lithuanian shtetl, Dūkštas. As a boy he was renowned as a prodigy in Talmudic learning and his father hoped that he would grow to be a great man in the Jewish nation. But Hebrew Haskalah literature led Chonen from the "right path" and at fourteen he ran away to Vilna. Living in hunger and poverty, within a year he prepared for the exams and entered the fifth class of the gymnasium.

When I got to know him he was one of the best students of the seventh class. He was well educated in Russian and German literature, knew a great deal of history, political economics and philosophy, and had a great influence on his fellow students at the gymnasium. Together with his friend Yaakov Yodelievsky, he founded secret self-education societies among the gymnasium students and the technical high school, at whose meetings members read and discussed the works of the famous Russian critics Pisarev, Dobroliubov, and Belinsky, as well as the *Historical Letters* of Mirtov (a pseudonym of Piotr Lavrov), Louis Blanc's history of the French Revolution—books that although printed in Russia were forbidden to gymnasia students.

Rappoport also established a group that aimed to produce teachers to educate the many young men who tore themselves away from the repressed atmosphere of the study house and chose light and erudition. This group offered financial support to the young men who had lost their "eating days" because they had been caught with *treyf-posl* [nonkosher books]. Rappoport, who in Vilna was known as an extraordinarily good teacher and made great sums of money from private lessons (at one time sixteen to seventeen roubles per hour!), lived very frugally and was almost thrown out of the gymnasium for his torn shoes and worn-out uniform. He used to give his salary to poor youths who thirsted for education.

Rappoport quickly became acquainted with Dembo and other Narodovoltses in Vilna and became a fervent socialist.

Chonen Rappoport had a great influence on my spiritual–intellectual development. He converted me to socialism and brought me into the group of the last Narodovoltses in Vilna. When he finished gymnasium he went to Paris. However, this did not interrupt our friendly relations and we frequently sent each other lengthy letters. This correspondence, which continued the entire time, greatly strengthened our friendship. Our meeting in Zurich gave both of us great joy.

In Paris Rappoport studied Marxist literature and became a Social Democrat. However, with his critical and original mind he understood Marxism much more deeply than most of the Russian Social Democrats and he did not see that economic materialism contradicted in any way the belief in the great role that critical-thinking personalities play in history. [. . .]

At that time in Russia there was a terrible famine, one of those chronic famines that were a direct result of the peasants' economic situation and the oppressive political regime, which flayed the skin of the village population and sought to keep them ignorant. The situation in Russia was terrible. Thirteen million peasants were simply dying of hunger. Foreign socialists founded a society to fight the hunger. The Social Democrats also joined the society, but half-heartedly. Their position on the terrible event was ambivalent: on the one hand they felt that a party dedicated to fighting for the exploited and downtrodden could not stand by while the masses of the people were in such an unfortunate situation; on the other hand, they considered the peasantry a reactionary petit-bourgeois mass and at every opportunity repeated Friedrich Engels's idea that socialism cannot penetrate a peasant's thick head.

They claimed that in order to be primed for socialism, the peasantry must first be transformed into a proletariat. Such was the process of the all-dominating economic development that the faster the villager would be torn from his little portion of land, the better for the general program. However terrible the hunger might be, at the same time this occurrence helped the program, as it would drive the peasant from the village to the ranks of the urban proletariat, the sole bearer of the conscious class war and socialism.

Translated by Rebecca Wolpe.

Mordechai Alpersohn

1860–1947

Mordechai Alpersohn was born in Ukraine and received a traditional religious education. He immigrated to Argentina and established one of the first agricultural settlements there. His *Thirty Years in Argentina: Memoirs of a Jewish Colonist*, published in three volumes over the period 1922–1928, was a bestseller everywhere in the Yiddish-speaking world. In contrast to the idyllic tone of Albert Gerchunoff's *The Jewish Gauchos* (1910), it was highly critical of the administrators of Baron de Hirsch's Jewish Colonization Association, which sponsored the settlements. Alpersohn also wrote plays, short stories, and novels.

Memoirs of a Jewish Colonist
1922

I. Of Pimps, Prostitutes, and Other Seducers

We saw some ten richly-dressed women, accompanied by fat-bellied men in top hats, standing at the green metal gate of the immigrants' hotel. Through the iron railing of a fence, they began pleading with our wives and offering chocolates and other candies to our children. One by one they approached the guard with muttered requests. He kept shaking his head and waving "no" with his hands. I realized that under no circumstances was he about to let them in.

Some of those individuals, who to judge by their accent were Polish Jews, recognized relatives and other acquaintances among the immigrants. They started sobbing, and their tears gushed onto the iron railings. It was hard to say whether those were tears of joy or sadness.

Through gestures, I attempted to ask the guard at the gate why those ladies and gentlemen were not allowed in. He gave me a strange little wink, grinned, turned his head of curly, black hair, and roguishly intoned, "No, no, no!"

Thereupon arrived a red-headed, freckle-faced young man, carrying a stack of papers under his arm. He identified himself as Baron Hirsch's agent. Respectfully, the guardian opened the gate for him. Speaking for Dr. Loewenthal, the young man announced that in a few days we would be sent to the tracts of land that Baron Hirsch had acquired for us. "We have to formalize the purchase through the government," he said to us in a confidential tone, "and you're off!"

The young man then launched into a speech, wherein he lamented that the committees in Galicia and Germany had rushed things by sending us over too soon. He enjoined us to avoid contact with the Jewish ladies and gentlemen who stood at the gate and by the railings. "They are impure!" he stated emphatically. "Don't let your wives and daughters take to the street!"

The young man continued: "There are hardly any decent Jews here, just those impure souls, the dregs of humanity. Because of them, the few Sephardic and English Jews one finds are ashamed to acknowledge their religion." He then spoke with the hotel employees, before departing.

No sooner had he crossed the threshold than a hubbub arose. A little Jew—who had earlier warned us to avoid eating a certain dish, lest it contain horse meat—chimed in with others, supposedly as honorable as he. They began inciting those assembled. "We've been hoodwinked!" they shouted. "They've bought no land at all! The whole colonization scheme is a swindle!"

"They're missionaries," screeched the little Jew, whose pointed beard waggled to and fro. "They want to baptize and convert us!"

From the other side of the gate, the "impure" poured oil on the fire. They brought their colored silken handkerchiefs to the corners of their eyes as they commiserated with the immigrants.

A few Jews with experience sneaking across borders had used false papers to smuggle some pimps and prostitutes into the hotel courtyard among us. These creatures used their whorish lips to paint our predicament as blackly as possible. The more naïve women among the immigrants broke out crying. Several of us protested, chasing out the interlopers. We came to blows, and the guard—who had apparently been bribed—failed to stop the fighting. They managed to trick some pious Polish Jews, wearing traditional fringed garments, into taking their wives, grown daughters, and all their earthly possessions over to the other side, never to return. Then the excitement died down.

The following morning, Dr. Loewenthal came to the immigrants' hotel. In my entire life, I shall never forget the figure cut by that tall, stately Jew with the mesmerizing black eyes, whose gaze none of us could bear for more than an instant. Each and every one of us went out to the courtyard, surrounding him. He simply waved his hand, and an awesome silence ensued.

"My children!" he said, speaking to us plainly, in Yiddish. "The good-hearted baron has sent Sir Cullen and me in search of refuge, in a free country, in some corner of the wide world, to establish a home for you and all of our oppressed brethren. The Argentine republic—a great, free, and fertile land—seemed to us best suited for that purpose. We have bought property enough to settle you as farmers in this secure and vibrant country. True, the committees in your homelands rushed things a bit. We have not had time to prepare housing for you; in fact, besides the earth itself, we have purchased nothing. But the fault lies not with the committee members. You came in droves, and the authorities in both Galicia and Prussia demanded that we ship you off, before . . . ," his tone turned bitter, as he took a deep breath, "before they deported you as undesirables!"

Throwing a penetrating glance over those assembled, he now spoke mildly: "You have already seen why it is impossible to keep you here in the city, while we acquire permanent housing and farming equipment. Decent families must remain far from those who would defile and corrupt them. Yesterday, some of you went down a path leading into a terrible abyss. My conscience impedes me from detaining you here much longer. I have sent forty young men out to the country to find shelter for you, and in a few days you will travel there. I beg of you to be patient, to employ the forbearance with which our people has been blessed. If you endure the first unavoidable difficulties that colonization demands, you shall attain peace and tranquility on your own plots of land. Believe me, brothers, you shall reap the benefits! The baron is guided by a great and noble ideal, born of his love for you. Remain steadfast and do not deviate from the proper path!"

"Send us, doctor! We shall go! Hurrah! Long live the baron!" These cries resounded from all sides.

Dr. Loewenthal departed contentedly. We began repeating his words, offering elaborate interpretations. We prepared for the trip to peace and tranquility on our own plots of land. All was optimistic commentaries and general satisfaction, until the Sabbath.

On Saturday morning arrived a red-headed gentleman, around thirty-five years old, wearing a high top hat similar to a coachman's. A swarthy young man accompanied him respectfully. They were greeted with reverence by the hotel employees. The gentleman in the top hat introduced himself as the rabbi of the local Western European Jews: Frenchmen, Germans, Englishmen and Belgians. Since he spoke only English and Spanish—languages none of us knew—the swarthy young man, who was his sexton and spoke Yiddish, served as the interpreter. We were invited to attend a synagogue service. Some ten of us followed them to a mud- and trash-filled alley. In a narrow, dark room stood a Holy Ark, a lectern, and a few benches strewn with prayer-books.

Such was their synagogue in those days. Now they have a magnificent temple with a cantor and an organ.

Cards were distributed to call us by order to the lectern, according to whether we were Cohens, Levites, or just plain Israelites. The sexton led the prayers and blessed the new month of Elul in the Hebrew year 5651. Besides the newcomers, only the rabbi, the sexton, and a few old men were in attendance.

The red-headed rabbi quickly decamped, whereupon the sexton shared with us some sad tales. Rabbi Henry Joseph, as was his name, lived with a Christian woman; his sons were uncircumcised; they were complete gentiles. The sexton confirmed what we had heard earlier: the Jews here were ashamed to reveal their identity, because the Poles and Galicians among them, who had arrived earlier, were active in prostitution rings. What is more, some of the Russian and Polish families whom Leizer Koifman had tricked into coming had

deserted the agricultural colonies at Palacios and Monigotes. Most of them now lived in town. If they themselves did not actually run the brothels, they worked in them as menservants, cooks, and maids.

"And that's the Jewish community of Buenos Aires!" he lamented. "Most of the year we can't even assemble a *minyan*. Only on Rosh Hashanah and Yom Kippur do the pure and impure elements come together to pray. I myself was one of those whom Koifman brought over three years ago."

A shudder went through me as I heard those words. "So you're one of Koifman's immigrants?" I asked in surprise. "Perhaps you know the Weiner family, who came over with Koifman, the Jewish official. Where are they? How are they doing?"

"What's your connection to them?" he asked. "Are you related?"

"Yes. Mr. Weiner is my wife's uncle. For eighteen years they lived in a village, until they were expelled by Ignatyev's infamous decree of 1881. They joined the hundred families who emigrated with Koifman to a prosperous settlement here."

"Your uncle Hirsch Weiner and his son Abraham Elijah are among the lucky ones!" he answered. "In Monigotes they found a mason who pays them a peso a day. They transport mud and bricks to earn their daily bread. Your aunt and her daughter-in-law make around eighteen cents a day doing laundry. But if it had not been for the misfortune that befell the little children of Monigotes, the misery there would not be so great." He stopped speaking, and sighed deeply.

We begged him to tell us all he knew about Koifman's colony. "After all, we're going to settle here. Let us at least be forewarned."

"God forbid something like that should occur again! It simply cannot happen to you!" the young sexton assured us. "Koifman was hoodwinked! But it wasn't for naught that the immigrants wanted to kill him!"

"Tell us! Tell us!" we implored in one voice. And he told us.

"In the villages and small towns, life had become unbearable for Jews under Ignatyev's decrees. In 1887, three delegates were sent to Paris and London. They beseeched Jewish millionaires to arrange for transport of their coreligionists to the United States, Canada, and Palestine. Two of them—Leizer Nisenzon and Moses Hendler from Kamenetz-Podolsk—wandered for one long year, knocking at the doors of Jewish philanthropists. They returned empty-handed. The third delegate, Koifman, was so unfortunate as to meet an individual who claimed to be an emissary of the Argentine republic and who promised everything: land, cattle, equipment, and financial aid for the first period of settlement. Entranced by such largesse, Koifman gathered some hundred families and set off for Argentina, only to find misery. All the promises turned out to be false; it was one gigantic swindle. The families were dumped on the train line between the Palacios and Monigotes stations, without food or shelter. Within one month, more than three hundred children perished from hunger and cold. Many of those families set off by foot to Buenos Aires. Their wives and daughters ended up in brothels. Some of the families stayed in the country, where they suffer unspeakable deprivation. Now word has it that Dr. Loewenthal is going to take them under his wing and settle them in the new colony. They shall finally be rewarded for their suffering!"

We heaved a deep sigh, wiped the tears from our eyes, and returned in sadness to the immigrants' hotel.

That same Sabbath, in the afternoon, we were taken to the train station and sent off to our settlement. That episode was the first link in a chain of woes that would weave through the next thirty years: nearly a third of a century replete with struggle, desperation, humiliation, with rarely a day of happiness. Few of the original settlers attained the "peace, tranquility, and their own plots of land" as promised by Dr. Loewenthal—unless we count those murdered by gauchos and those who died of natural causes, working on their farms. But we are getting beyond ourselves . . .

A streetcar, drawn by a pair of horses more dead than alive, came to the immigrants' hotel. The red-headed agent from Baron Hirsch's office ordered us to board the streetcar for the train station. No matter how intently the pious Jews implored him, "Let us go by foot! It is a sin to ride on the Sabbath!" he responded: "You must take the streetcar. Otherwise, you will miss the train." That turned out to be a bald-faced lie. The train did not arrive until nine o'clock that evening.

The cattle- and poultry-slaughterer Gedaliah Weiner, who was one of our number then, tried to run after the streetcar. His strength was soon at an end. One by one, the pious Jews, with heavy hearts and tears in their eyes, climbed onto the streetcar. They recited by way of excuse the words of the Talmud: "God pardons those forced to sin."

None of this surprised me. Throughout the whole trip I had noticed that the Jewish emigration and colonization officials systematically chose the Sabbath for us to travel or undertake difficult tasks.

Facing the train station, on a field of grass where *Plaza II* now stands, we sat and waited contentedly, as befits pioneers who are going off to settle their own plots of land. The young people sang Eliakim Zunser's "The Plow." The women bought oranges and bananas for next to nothing, after they had exchanged their Russian kopecks for shiny new ten-cent pieces. For five kopecks they got ten cents, but one hundred rubles brought in a full two hundred ten pesos! The general mood was one of excitement.

The sun shone so brightly that day, and it was pleasantly warm. Leaves were green, flowers bloomed, and we were thrilled. "What do you think of our Argentinean winter?" a young woman called out to those assembled. "Father in Heaven! What a country! What a surprise! Long live the baron and the great land to which he has brought us!"

"Hurrah! Long live Baron Hirsch!" The cry resounded in Yiddish and Russian.

At nine o'clock the train moved, and we were off.

Translated by Alan Astro.

Other works by Alpersohn: *Goles* (1929); *Di kinder fun der pampa* (1930); *Af argentiner erd* (1931).

Julius Martov

1873–1923

Born Iulii Osipovich Tsederbaum in Constantinople, Julius Martov grew up in Odessa and St. Petersburg. His grandfather Aleksander Zederbaum was a highly influential publisher of Jewish periodicals in Hebrew, Yiddish, and Russian. In the 1890s, Martov collaborated with Vladimir Lenin and Aleksandr Potresov to found the Union for the Emancipation of Labor and create the journal *Iskra*. He became a leading Menshevik in the Russian Social Democratic Workers' Party (RSDWP). During the Second Congress of RSDWP in 1903, he opposed the Bund's demand for autonomy, and his confrontation with Lenin was a factor in the split between Bolsheviks and Mensheviks. He died in Berlin.

Notes of a Social Democrat
1922

The time has come for me to touch upon the people of the Vilna leadership. When Iosif Mil was away and

I joined it, the acknowledged leader was my acquaintance A[rkady] Kremer ("Aleksandr"). His balanced, somewhat phlegmatic personality and great clarity of mind, his clandestine restraint and other qualities of a capable organizer of underground work lent him the essential authority for his role as leader. At meetings, he spoke little but with gravitas. He did not possess an agitator's gifts, nor do I think his personal inclinations attracted him to the agitator role. An engineering student in the past, in the late 1880s he was implicated in some political affair in Riga, served time in Kresty [prison], and since then had been under surveillance in Vilna. Finding himself in the same position was I. L. Aizenshtat (Yudin), who was the best-educated Marxist theoretician in our circle. A former student at the Yaroslavl lyceum, back in 1887 he landed in prison and after serving his sentence settled in Vilna. Having been subsequently in prison and exile several times, I. L. to this day remains one of the Bund's leaders. His wife, Liubov Levenson, who passed away in America in the late 1890s, was a very capable propagandist, enjoyed great popularity among the workers, and brought a seething energy to her relentless work. She served one of the longest and hardest prison terms. A former student at a Swiss university, she was arrested at the border while crossing into Russia because they found on her clandestine letters from Vera Ivanovna Zasulich. She was sent to a remote prison where for a year and a half she was subjected to extremely harsh treatment that undermined her health and shattered her nerves. After this, she was also given, by way of punishment, another year and a half of prison. Distinguished by no less activism but a less nervous and more joyful personality was M. D. Srednitskaia, known as "Pati." She was made of the kind of stuff from which female organizers of the Red Cross and committee secretaries at all stages of our revolutionary movement have been shaped, i.e., individuals who had to maintain practical relations with dozens of people, be able to deal with them and to hold permanently in their head hundreds of clandestine details and do ten different jobs at once. Frail, always ailing, but always lively and for the most part cheerful, M. D. Srednitskaia during her daily hours at her dentist's office dealt with many clandestine matters involving passing, receiving, and arranging for the safekeeping of illegal literature, organizing new circles, and seeking out leaders for them, and in the evenings she would run to meetings of circles or cashier representatives. If Kremer was the organization's head, then "Pati" was its soul.

Kopelzon the dentist ("Timofei," subsequently known in the Swiss emigration as "Grishin"),[1] who was also under surveillance and had been exiled from Warsaw, was engaged primarily in clandestine organizational affairs—relations with other organizations, relations which were fairly regular, especially in the towns of Lithuania and Poland, as was the transport of people and literature. Refugees from Russia usually sought out the "border" through the Vilna group, and Vilna received what were then the very few shipments of foreign literature organized with the help of Vilna natives living in Warsaw and Łódź who had maintained ties with the mother country.

The outstanding force in the actual propaganda and organizational work was S. Gozhansky, called "Teacher." His nickname was not terribly clandestine, for Gozhansky actually was a teacher in an official Jewish institute. A legal man compared with us and an official in the civil service as well, on the outside he had to be extremely secretive in order not to attract attention from his superiors, coworkers, and the parents of his pupils, who, for the most part, were those very same petty bourgeois in whose shops and workshops we "engaged in sedition." Capable and with major interests in general questions of theory, although with a highly paradoxical frame of mind that often led him to contradictory constructs, Gozhansky was greatly concerned with making the circle's propaganda systematic. The professional pedagogue in him was always manifest. Later, during the period of intensive economic agitation, he played a leading role in that internal organizational struggle of the Vilna movement over new methods of work. Subsequently he, together with L. Levenson and several workers, moved to Belostok [Białystok] and in that major proletarian center of "Liteh" laid the foundations of broad agitational work; soon after, he was arrested and exiled to Yakutia with L. Levenson. There, at one time, he wavered toward "Makhaevshchina," which was fashionable among exiles in the late 1880s; later he worked for a long time in the Bund (I met him at the party's London congress in 1907, when he was one of the congress secretaries); during the war he was a defensist; and after the October coup he suddenly turned into a communist and was a commissar in Tula.

The group's youngest member was Revekka Liass, who had graduated from the local grammar school. As a propagandist, she enjoyed the love of the workers.

Later, in my time, the group took in Tobias ("Maks") and the teacher Minna Volk, and later also two people under surveillance: A. Mutnikovich ("Gleb"), who had been exiled from Germany back in 1889 for his ties to German social democracy under the "exception law," and his friend V. Levenson (Kossovsky). Both, particularly the latter, played a guiding role in the Bund's activities. Kossovsky was one of that party's principal theoretical and literary forces.

Grouped around this tight circle were dozens more intellectuals closely linked to it, although not all of them participated regularly in our work. First and foremost among the young people from secondary educational institutions were some who were so trained in the party way that, except for individual assignments of an illegal nature, we entrusted them sometimes with conducting workers' circles. Such were the Realgymnasia students Eliashberg, A. Tropovsky (later a well-known translator and correspondent for major newspapers), M. Lurie (who for a long time played a prominent role in the Bolshevik Party, which he later left), Seliber, the grammar school students V. Goldman (now known as Gorev) and A. Shtessel, L. Bernshtein (translator and journalist under the pseudonym L. Borisovich),[2] Tsemakhovich, I. Rozenberg, Zeldov (subsequently, in the late 1890s, a member of the Bund CC [Central Committee]), Paikes, a prominent worker in the Iskra [Spark] organization and the Menshevik faction up until the October coup, when he became a communist and something like a state inspector. [. . .] Later, and down to the present day, Portnoy ("Noiech") honorably discharged his position as a member of the Bund CC, living for a long time as an illegal, while Goldevsky and P. O. Gordon in the early 1900s did a lot of work in the Iskra and Menshevik organizations of Southern Russia [Ukraine].

In my time, the governing group did not include a single worker. According to our views at the time, participation in this group assumed a certain rather high level of theoretical development and significant clandestine experience. In essence, the few workers who more or less satisfied this requirement were the most senior members of the self-development circles, who had spent eight years and more in these circles. However, as indicated above, these most senior members of the circles either came out of the apprentice "estate" and, having set themselves up as independent masters, had moved away from the general mass of workers, or else, not wishing to undergo this evolution, settled abroad (mostly in America). Of the rest, the most politically mature "senior" workers were organized by us later, in

1894, into a central workers' group, which included A. Kremer as the representative from our center and which was supposed to play a role with lesser rights in the organizational hierarchy, more of a consultative "Second Chamber." The most influential members of this workers' center were the most senior member of the workers' circles: the elderly butcher Solomon (I don't know his surname), a sullen and extremely powerful person; the female glove-maker Ts. Gurvich, later a member of the Bund CC and to this day in the RSDWP [Russian Social Democratic Workers' Party]; the tailor Tsilia Volk; and a few other workers. With her decisive and direct personality and political sense, Tsivia Gurvich stood out in this group and, besides the above-mentioned Solomon, was the most influential figure in the workers milieu after its more "intellectualized" proletariat, who had agitated back in the early part of the decade, [. . .] had left the stage.

NOTES

1. Plekhanov used his letters, as a defender of "economism," in a famous polemical pamphlet, "Vademekum" [Vademecum], aimed against the editors of *Rabochee Delo* [Worker's Cause].

2. Who now, as I have learned, has sold out to Wrangel and is a comrade-in-arms to Bursev in Common Cause.

Translated by Marian Schwartz.

Other works by Martov: *The State and the Socialist Revolution* (1938).

Vladimir Medem

1879–1923

The Bundist leader Vladimir Davidovich Medem grew up in Latvia and Minsk, in a family that had converted to Christianity. After joining the Russian Social Democratic Workers' Party and the Bund, he was repeatedly jailed, lived in exile in Bern, and spent time imprisoned in Warsaw. Opposing communism, Medem moved to New York in 1920. As a theorist of nationalism, Medem proposed that the state protect minorities by granting them national-cultural autonomy. He mastered Yiddish, advocated the establishment of Yiddish schools, and fought for the rights of Jewish workers. The Medem Sanatorium for patients of tuberculosis, in Międzeszyn, near Warsaw, was named in his honor, as is the Medem Library, the Yiddish resource in Paris.

My Life
1923

Chapter XLVI. Iskra [1901]

The leader and the soul of *Iskra* was Lenin. And although he was surrounded by a group of brilliant writers and first-class leaders (indeed, all enjoyed equal rights in a formal sense), he already placed on the whole enterprise—even at that time—the emphatic stamp of his personal character.

When I saw him for the first time (it was, I think, at the beginning of 1902) I was not impressed by him. Externally he failed to make a good impression. From what I had previously heard about him, I envisaged a towering revolutionist, both important and imposing—one of the "big guns." But what I saw before me was a little animated individual, short of stature (he is actually not short at all but of medium height; the broad shoulders make him appear short) with a small flaxen beard, bald head, and tiny brown eyes. A clever face but not an intelligent one. He was reminiscent of—the comparison came instantly to mind—a crafty Russian grain dealer. Such was my impression of him then.

Lenin was giving a lecture in Bern at the time. He spoke smoothly and with a quiet, dogged forcefulness; duty, without embellishments and without enthusiasm. Incidentally, this is worth noting: there was one subject about which he used to deliver inspired speeches and evoke great enthusiasm among the listeners, it was (most characteristically) the Paris Commune.

In later years I had occasion to meet Lenin numerous times, and I shall have more to say about him in subsequent chapters. For the moment I am concerned with the features of *Iskra*, and in this connection it is important to identify two qualities in Lenin's character. These are, first, the imperious will and second, the pronounced distrust of people.

Lenin is a man of iron. He has the ability to rule and the desire to rule. He knows what he wants. And when he wants something, he goes after it. He stops at nothing. When he wishes to carry out a decision and finds himself in the minority, this fazes him very little. He hits on what to do: he hurls himself upon his opponents with unrestrained fury and pulls the crowd over to his side; now he has his majority. Or if he cannot bring this off, he doesn't shrink from recourse to a few "innocent" tricks by which a majority is created even when it is in fact non-existent. . . . And if this too proves unavailing he resorts to splitting, and then he has a completely free field. One way or another, his will prevails. And in this sense Lenin is really a born dictator.

And the second thing: he doesn't believe you. When you speak to him he looks at you with his small eyes—eyes directed at you from somewhat of an angle—and with a cunning, devilish smile, as if to say: "There's not a word of truth in what you're saying! Oh well, go on; me you won't deceive."

This person believes no one and confides in no one but himself. Yet with Lenin this is no case of self-love, no conspicuous display and dangling about of the ego—something quite apparent in many others. Lenin is the precise opposite of Trotsky in this respect; the latter is an "I" person. From Lenin's lips one never hears the pronoun "I." Still he believes no one, and when he has the power to rule alone—he rules. Not because of his ambition, but because that's just the way it works out.

These two traits of Lenin's character were strikingly reflected in the spiritual face of *Iskra*. The lack of faith in the working masses, the wish for a firm hand that should lead them lest they lose themselves in a bog—that was Lenin; [. . .]

Chapter LXXV. The London Congress [1907]

The electoral campaign ended. Immediately afterwards we were forced to cease publication of our weekly. The reason was most prosaic: inadequate funds. The Yiddish daily—*Di Folks-Tsaitung* (The People's Press)—also had a substantial deficit; and the very limited financial means at the disposal of the Central Committee did not permit us the luxury of two newspapers. Accordingly, we were compelled to dissolve our editorial staff. A few days after we left Kovno, the police staged a raid on the house in which we had lived. But they made a small mistake. They went to the floor above and arrested an innocent person, someone who had no connection at all with the editorial staff or with the Bund.

I left for a brief visit to Moscow. (I had even managed to avail myself of a few days there at the time the paper was being published.) Now I had enough free time for a leave of several weeks, during which politics was set aside and the time devoted to private life. It was only by coincidence that I met a number of Russian comrades on several occasions. A large Russian publishing house run by the Granat brothers had decided at that time to issue an extensive *History of Russia During the*

Nineteenth Century—a collective product. The leading collaborators were two well known Bolshevik writers—the *privot dozenten* from Moscow—Rozhkov and Pokrovsky.

Through my former editorial-staff colleague Heilikman, who lived in Moscow, I was invited to take charge of the Jewish section. I agreed to do it, and was asked to meet with Pokrovsky for a discussion of the details. I went to see him. He was a congenial, serious, modest individual (if I'm not mistaken, he is presently working with Lunacharsky in the Commissariat of Education), and we quickly agreed on terms. While I was with Poktovsky, two other comrades came in whom I had not previously known. One of them was a young man of moderate height, with blond hair and a round little beard—the picture of a Russian *intelligent*. I later met him abroad. He was one of the few Bolsheviks whom I found personally quite affable. Despite his typically Russian face, he was a Jew. He is the present Chairman of the Moscow Soviet and one of the most important Russian leaders—Kamenev. [...]

While we were sitting at Pokrovsky's and chatting, the conversation turned to that very *History of Russia* in the publication of which I was to participate.

[...] Some time later, after having prepared a portion of the material, I received word at the editorial office that the various articles had expanded greatly and that space had grown scarce. There was not enough room. Who gets thrown out? Naturally, the Jews. I was even assured that the Jewish section would be included in a second compilation, *The History of the Twentieth Century*. But this second compilation has not yet seen the light of day.

Though I had no direct connection with the local movement my life in Moscow was anything but placid. Anyone living there illegally will have his troubles in any case. As usual, I had not reported to the authorities. I was staying at my brother's house, although he himself had already left Moscow and moved to Kovno. But my sister and her husband (my brother-in-law Zhaba) were still there. I lived quietly for a few days, bothered by no one. Then one evening a relative of my brother-in-law—a boy of sixteen and a conspicuous ne'er-do-well—suddenly came rushing over and informed me that he had an acquaintance who was serving . . . in the secret police and that the acquaintance had allegedly spoken to him about me. He knew I was here in Moscow and was looking for me. Well, I had no confidence in this lad and even suspected that it was no more than bluffing on his

part. But what if it were true after all? I therefore went to an acquaintance (in fact, it was to Heilikman) and stayed with him for a few days. Meanwhile everything was calm at my brother's house. The house was located on a small quiet street, and any suspicious individual loitering there would have been noticed. No one appeared so I went back. Some days elapsed. Everything was in the best of order. I used to visit the large Moscow library daily to gather material for my Jewish history. Once, while sitting quietly in the library reading a book, I chanced to look up. There directly across from me at the same table, sat . . . my brother-in-law. I gazed at him. What could have brought him here? Something must have happened. He wrote a note and slipped it to me. I read: "The police have interrogated our *dvornik*. They want to know who's living at our place." Trouble again. In the light of such information I could not go home, of course. So I spent a few days with other acquaintances, after which I left directly for the station and departed from Moscow.

It was the end of April. The Congress of the Russian Social Democratic Labor Party was scheduled to open in Copenhagen at the beginning of May. Without returning to Vilno, I went straight from Moscow to the Congress.

I had already prepared myself in advance with a foreign passport. It was assembled in Vilno. How such passports were made at that time is quite interesting. As previously noted, my "internal" passport was a "belletristic" one, fashioned by myself with a fictitious name. But Vilno had—as did every city in the Pale presumably—a Jew who was known as the "Governor-General." This person was an "operator," with ready entree to "high places" and access to various administrative offices, where he would consummate all manner of shady transactions. Thus, with such a *fal'shivka* (spurious passport) in hand he would bring it to the administrative office of the Governor and have it exchanged for a foreign passport. The *fal'shivka* would remain at the Governor's as security, and in its place one would obtain a genuine, legitimate foreign passport—with a fictitious name. This was the kind of passport I acquired; and with it I crossed the border in both directions. [...]

After crossing the border without incident I arrived in Berlin, where I met Liber. The two of us left for Copenhagen together. We registered at a large, attractive hotel, met other delegates. Trotsky, for one, was staying at the same hotel. He soon came into our room. I had

not seen him for several years; he had changed considerably during the interval. Trotsky had lived through
a great deal in the course of a few years. In 1905 he left
Switzerland for Russia, played a significant role in the
St. Petersburg Soviet, was arrested and exiled to Siberia. He had only recently escaped and returned abroad.
He was still weary from the journey, emaciated and
pale. He had also changed inwardly: grown more mature, solid. In the old days, when I used to see Trotsky
abroad, there was still much about him that was boyish.
[. . .]

Trotsky generally gave the impression in those days
of someone with little sense of responsibility, someone exceedingly pompous and in pursuit of the pretty,
pungent phrase. The humorous and acerbic Riazanov
tagged him at the time with the nickname "Balalai-
kin." Another nickname that he gave Trotsky because
of his attitude at the Congress was *Leninskaya dubinka*
(Lenin's little cudgel). But as already noted, Trotsky
had changed markedly. He had matured, and it seemed
to me that he had grown calmer and more serious. He
moved far from Lenin and broke with Bolshevism. He
did not actually become a Menshevik, but occupied a
middle position that was close to the political position
of the Bund. He wanted to form a faction of his own
in the Party and evidently counted on the support of
the Bund. Thus he began a rather strong flirtation with
the Bund and the "Bundovtses," which continued for
years. In earlier years he had been a bitter opponent of
the Bund; at the Congress in 1903 Trotsky had engaged
in the sharpest clashes with Liber. But the situation
changed and he endeavored to establish with us a relationship of some considerable amicability.

Personally, I had never believed in the sincerity of
this new friendship. From the first moment that I set
eyes on Trotsky, he became distasteful to me. And as
far as I know, his attitude toward me was precisely the
same as mine toward him. This was confirmed, incidentally, on the very first morning after our arrival in
Copenhagen. Here is what happened. During the time
we were publishing *Nashe Slovo*, I had written an article for it on the political situation, and touched on
the reasons why the revolution was not yet victorious.
I stressed, in particular, the significance of the Russian
peasantry. Trotsky was in prison at the time. There he
occupied himself with literary work, in the course of
which he happened to express himself along the same
line. When he came into our room in the Copenhagen
hotel, he immediately asked Liber: "Say, which of your

people is Vinitsky?" (That article had been signed by
this pseudonym of mine.) From the tone of the question
it was apparent that the article had strongly appealed to
him and that he was prepared to look upon the author
as a kind of partner. Liber replied: "That's Medem."
"Really!" rejoined Trotsky, and grew silent. It was clear
from his demeanor that he was not especially delighted
with this revelation.

We spent a few days in Copenhagen awaiting the arrival of the other delegates. Suddenly one morning we
received a piece of bad news. The Danish government
notified us that it could not tolerate a Russian socialist congress on its soil, and we were directed to leave
"hospitable" Copenhagen promptly. It was a severe
blow. Everything had already been arranged; the delegates were present—and they represented no small
host—about 300 persons had arrived. But we had no
alternative. It was decided to shift to the one and only
European city in which it would be certain we would be
left alone—London. And it was there, in fact, that this
large and interesting Congress took place, a Congress
that ran for weeks.

The surface aspect of the Congress was interesting
and noteworthy in itself. Our sessions were held in a
church. (London has very few large public halls for
the holding of mass meetings; hence the recourse to
churches.) Some sort of liberal "Brotherhood" (I have
forgotten its name), with a church of its own, had placed
its church facility at our disposal. The arrival of Russian revolutionists was known in the city. The newspapers had learned of our "Expellees Congress" and
of our shift over to England. Reporters with cameras
would stand at the entrance to the church. They had
succeeded in photographing a few female delegates,
whose pictures appeared in the newspapers accompanied by fantastic inscriptions. A policeman was also
posted at the gate—to see to it that we were safe from
any assault. It was the first time in history that a congress of Russian revolutionists took place under the
protection of the police.

The church was not particularly spacious, but there
was ample room for the 300 delegates. It also contained a gallery to which selected guests were admitted. The delegates seated themselves according to factions. The Bolsheviks sat on one side, the Mensheviks
on the other; in the middle were the three nationality
factions—the Bund, the Letts, and the Poles. It was a
real parliament. Each faction was tightly organized and
led by a forceful faction-committee, and fairly strict

discipline prevailed. A formal decision of the Polish faction, for instance, had affirmed that everyone was obligated to vote as a solid unit. No such formal compulsion was operational in our faction, but in point of fact, it turned out that way on virtually every vote. The Bolshevik and Polish factions had special "conductors" who indicated to the people how to vote, since not all the delegates had sufficiently oriented themselves to what was happening at the Congress. A large number of Polish delegates had not even understood—or had poorly understood—the Russian language. So, with each vote, the conductor would mount the dais and announce, "our faction votes such-and-such a way." And the people knew how to raise their hands. As a consequence there could be no question of one side convincing the other. There was actually discussion aplenty— but the result was a simple arithmetical calculation: how many votes from this faction, how many from that, how many another, etc. [. . .]

The endless series of series of sessions had begun. Russian congresses had the habit of forever starting with A–B–C. Accordingly, the first item on the agenda was the point about the current political situation. Then came other general questions. Only at the very end— after several weeks of hairsplitting and theorizing—did the Congress get around to more practical questions. And all the while an embittered, stubborn battle was being fought between the Bolsheviks and the Mensheviks. Only the Bundists and the "neutral" Trotsky would, from time to time, introduce a third voice into the duet. They constituted the center. [. . .]

Chapter LXXXVII. Smolensk

This much I know—and it may have something to do with my ability to adapt to any situation, even the harshest: when it was a matter of spending a substantial length of time in one place (I mean, in one prison), I could become accustomed to things and feel reasonably well even under the most adverse conditions. One learned somehow to adjust. In the final analysis, one managed even to cope with the worst prison overseers. They too were human beings, after all. To be sure, there were types among them who by nature had the souls of hangmen, or whose prison "work" had literally developed in them a morbid, sadistic inclination to derive pleasure from tormenting prisoners. But these were obviously the exceptions. The majority were simple Russian peasants, soldiers who had served their time, family people who suffered from an abundance of poverty and who were themselves greatly dissatisfied with their condition. With such people it was possible to get by. After an extended period of closeness, one established rather friendly ties with them. One became something of a "native," an intimate. Hard as it is to believe, it was so: one began to feel almost at home in prison.

But when the journeying started—the moving to places of interior exile by the *étape*—things became quite different. As soon as the *starshiy* (chief overseer) entered the cell and proceeded to read from the roster the names of those being banished to some distant location—as soon as one heard the shouted command: "Line up for the *étape*! Quickly! Now! This very instant!"—one lost one's human character, was reduced to a speck of dust, a grain of sand, a tiny portion of a huge agglomeration—devoid of significance, voiceless, without personality. One became a minuscule element in the vast pile of gray human dust, human waste, human refuse. As if by a gigantic steam shovel, this dust pile was scooped into an amorphous heap, cast off somewhere else, dispersed, congealed again, shoved into filthy prison cars, expelled once again, swept apart, and once more lumped together in a new pile. And so it continued, relentlessly, without limit and without end. Gone all pity and all humanity and all humans. The wheels of a cold, dead, savage machine rolled on. Its terrible iron tips grasped the puny, utterly inconsequential individual, hurled him into its deep cauldron, choked and pressed and chewed him, and ground him to bits with its heavy millstones. And when the machine had done its little job and spat him out somewhere, thousands of miles away, the human being found himself shattered and devastated physically as well as morally. Such was movement "by the *étape*."

And when, on top of everything, the machine tended to grow rusty and grind to a halt—when the driving could only function by fits and starts, with delays; with stoppages and breakdowns—well, nothing worse could be imagined. That's just how it was. The war was responsible for blocking roads, holding up the movement of trains, throwing the machinery out of kilter, bringing confusion into the whole apparatus. And it simultaneously hurled into the iron cauldron thousands upon thousands of new people, a wholly new and fresh mass of human material; and the rusted, clogged, overflowing machine proved incapable of digesting all the material. It was choking and suffocating; and each turn of the giant, ponderous wheels cost human lives.

No single individual was to blame; everything was confusion; it was the war's doing. But woe to those who fell beneath the terrible massive wheels. And I was one of them.

I shall relate the story in sequence.

I found myself meanwhile in Orel—in the miserable, filthy, solidly-packed cell. How truly fortunate, I pondered, was the individual who had the opportunity to draw enough clean, fresh air into his lungs each day. I was not among those fortunates. True, conditions were fairly tolerable for the moment: it was autumn, and the windows could still be kept open during the day. Happily this was not forbidden. But they had to be shut at night because it would have been too cold for the many of us sleeping on the floor. It was then that it became terribly stifling. And what would it really be like, one wondered, with the onset of winter?

The thought struck me: would it be possible to take a whole winter of this and still come out alive? It seemed to me at the time as if that would be quite impossible. And yet—the winter passed; and another; and even a third. People simply stayed and stayed in prison. . . . Indeed no one was actually compelled to say farewell to life.

Then all at once there arrived a piece of news: I was being returned to Warsaw—to stand trial. The trial would take place shortly. It was necessary to get ready for the trip.

Very well. I set to work. A sack was sewn together, and into it I stuffed my bit of underwear (the comrades from Paviak did have their things, and shared them with me), along with a piece of bread, some tea and sugar, a teakettle, a pot, and a wooden spoon. Finished. Then we began our journey—my five comrades and I, all involved in the same trial.

We were led out into the corridor. It was a scene of bustling activity. The soldiers were already on hand. Our names were called. We were searched. Rough soldier hands crept into our pockets, felt around our clothing, our underwear, our bodies. First one individual, then another, was forced to strip completely naked. Anything suspicious was thrown aside. "Suspicious," items however, included such things as tobacco, matches, toothpowder, or toothpaste. It was a time when one was not permitted to take along even soap.

We lined up. The hand manacles were locked on and we began the march to the train. Then once again the squalid prisoner cars pulled up. Again a new prison, a new filthy hole; and again soldiers, again the foul shakedown, again hand manacles. A new train, a new prison—on and on. Journeying by the *étape* often lasted weeks, sometimes whole months.

This was the customary routine. But as already noted, it was now war time and entirely new and special obstacles had accumulated. We no sooner arrived at the first *étape* station—it was the city of Smolensk—than we received a sad bit of intelligence: we could not proceed any further. The reason? All trains headed for Warsaw were occupied by the military. Movement by the *étape* had come to a halt.

How long would it last? The overseer smiled: "Yes, my friends, you will in all likelihood have to be patient until the end of the war. The Germans are on the outskirts of Warsaw!"

So we were going to remain in Smolensk. And when we stepped into our new "home" and gazed upon the scene that opened before us, we were appalled. We had stumbled into a veritable hell.

We were conducted into a long corridor, grimy and dark as a coal pit. Then a door opened on one side and our nostrils were assailed by a gush of stifling, nauseating, damp-warm air. We were placed inside. The door was shut. And we stood there staring at each other.

We were in a cell—eight paces long and the same in width. The space was almost completely filled by two large wooden pallets, long boards nailed on to thick wooden legs. The pallets extended the length of the wall on both sides, allowing for a narrow passageway between them. And on top of, between, and beneath the pallets, human bodies filled every space: standing, sitting, lying in a weird jumble. Squeezed together, filthy, sweating, bedraggled—disgusting! And as if to add its own mockery, a sign next to the door read "Room for 9 People." But there were easily twenty-five; and that, moreover, was a lucky day. Later on the number reached as high as thirty-five. . . .

With regard to sleeping—that took place on bare boards, without a bit of straw. But attaining even such a bed, on a couple of boards the width of two or three hands, involved a stroke of particular good fortune. The ones who had no such good fortune were obliged to sleep beneath the pallets, on the cold asphalt floor. For a pillow, one individual would have recourse to a broom; another, to a pair of old boots—or his own fist. A blanket of any kind was out of the question.

Fifth, stench, vermin. . . . Some of the prisoners had been lying about for months without a single change of underwear; without having once undressed, without having once held a piece of soap. Bedbugs by the million clung to the walls, lay on the floor, pressed into corners in thick black clumps. They used to descend upon the pallets at night and attack the people with savage ferocity.

I set up this kind of "agenda" for myself: twice a day I would go "hunting." The procedure involved stripping from head to toe and conducting a precise and systematic examination of each item of underwear. A slaughter was carried out. But to what avail? The disgusting creatures would lay thousands of fresh eggs each night and the routine would have to begin anew the following day. Alas, it was all in vain. During the pleasurable "hunt," I used to dispatch about forty or fifty specimens each time—i.e., twice a day. (My concern with "statistics" may seem laughable, but for me the matter was deadly serious at the time.) Then, after a few hours, they would be back again.

Of the individuals languishing there, more than one had succumbed so thoroughly to self-neglect as to lapse into a kind of dull indifference. Such persons submitted without resistance to the supremacy of the parasites. They would lie there and allow themselves to be consumed. But others did embark on the "hunt" from time to time, which invariably drew from one of the onlookers the quip beloved of the prisoners: "You're not being selective, brother! You're not going after the stubborn ones! Keep hammering away! Don't just dabble!" And the hammering would in fact go on continuously, in systematic fashion and with philosophic sedateness. After all, time we had aplenty.

We were constantly hungry. The food was poor and scanty. Whenever the bowls were brought in, the people lunged at them like starving animals; and in a minute all was gone. Whoever lacked the ability to gulp down the hot soup with extra swiftness was compelled to go practically without lunch. Six, eight sometimes as many as fifteen men would eat from a single pot—and among the eaters there were more than enough sick people.

The air . . . it would not even be accurate to say the air was bad; there simply was no air. The "common" Russian fears the cold more than anything else. One need not dwell on the matter of how the people were dressed: it was pathetic. And no one would agree to having the window open at night. And on top of that—there was the historic *parasha* standing in the corner. . . . The clearing of our lungs—the daily walk—lasted all of . . . fifteen minutes!

The guards treated us literally like cattle. A deluge of curse words rained down upon us constantly. What can I say? One gets used to it. Is there any alternative? We were nothing more than *étape*-prisoners—the most miserable among the miserable, the most deprived of the deprived. No longer the privileged, no longer the "politicals." Nobody knew we were politicals. And when we said we were, nobody believed us. So we were treated like common *brodyagi* (tramps). What could one do? One could only grit one's teeth and keep quiet. The price for failing to do so was not infrequently a kick in the side, a slap in the face. Hence one kept quiet. But even silence was no assurance against rudeness and vilification. Someone falling ill and seeking, for instance, the services of the *feldsher* [medical assistant]—a physician was out of the question—would elicit from the guard a perfunctory response coupled with an endearing Russian expression. Or the overseer would offer this rejoinder to someone wishing to make a request: "There's no need for you to write any request." "But . . ." "Hold your tongue." And once more a couple of familiar Russian expressions.

Such was the countenance of the lovely institution into which we had stumbled. We used to lie on the hard pallets and ask each other what there was to do. Money we didn't have; it was forbidden, of course, to take money along on the *étape*. As far as our relatives were concerned, we had disappeared; no one knew where we were. Notify them? Precluded. Writing letters was not permitted. Moreover, where would one obtain the seven kopecks for a stamp? We were thus confined, without help and without strength, and with a single prospect to die like animals in the filthy, miserable hole.

We would lie about and think. (One who has never been so situated cannot begin to imagine how trivial, how insignificant thoughts and ideas can become under such conditions.) A beautiful, a glorious "ideal" restricted solely to the realm of dreams was—for me—my "cozy" cell . . . in the Tenth Pavilion, in the Warsaw fortress. What would I not have given, I used to say at the time—and in all seriousness—just to be sitting in my fortress cell. But even that was too audacious a dream. My desires were generally far more modest. When I ate my supper (it consisted of a piece of black bread) I would dream about how delightful it would be if, along with it, I could have just a small piece of salami. Not to eat my fill; no—heaven forbid. I envisaged actually a small slice of salami—the size, let us say, of a two-kopeck coin. Just to inhale its odor and . . . perhaps take it to my mouth and hold it there while I chewed my hard piece of black bread. . . .

These were all trifles. Over and above such petty and inconsequential cravings, there always lived and ceaselessly echoed the single, deep, overriding wish-refrain: to hold out at all costs!

That I really did succeed in holding out and not falling apart was a real miracle.

Translated by Samuel Portnoy.

Other works by Medem: *Di legende fun der Yidisher Arbeter-Bevegung* (1938).

Egon Erwin Kisch
1885–1948

The journalist and essayist Egon Erwin Kisch was born and educated in Prague but worked in the interwar period for newspapers in Germany until he was arrested and deported to Czechoslovakia in 1933. He is often credited with elevating journalism to literature. Long concerned with the lives of the poor and the grittiness of urban life, he was radicalized by his wartime service in the Austrian army and became a communist in 1919 and later an operative of the Comintern. His party membership complicated his search for a refuge when war broke out, and he had to spend the war years in Mexico before returning to Prague in 1946.

Yiddish Literary Café
1924

The puritanically strict observance of the closing hour in London, the lack of continental-style coffeehouses, and perhaps also the isolated situation of the by no means untroubled British Isles may account for the fact that the network of the international coffeehouse bohème, which extends from the lily castle of the prince of Parisian poets, Paul Fort, to the various literary cafés of Berlin, Munich, Vienna, and even to the other bank of the Seine as far as the great boulevards, did not find its way across the English Channel. Out in East London, however, in the midst of every conceivable kind of poverty, there exists a haunt of literature. It bears a national stamp: the people there speak only Yiddish, that mixture of Middle High German, a few Hebrew words, and Slavic phrases that is written in Hebrew letters.

In order to tell the passerby that Jews from Galicia, Bukovina, Ukraine, and Palestine congregate here, the place is called "New Yorker Restaurant." A low, vaulted room, on the ground level. The aroma of baked fish wafts pleasingly from the buffet to the noses of all the customers to whom the aroma of baked fish is pleasing. Manuscripts are generated at two or three tables; uncompromisingly huge, black ties are the decided fashion here. A few smooth-shaven faces with the typical mime's wrinkles around the mouth stand out conspicuously in this full-bearded section of the city. They belong to actors from the Yiddish Pavilion-Theater on the opposite side of the street.

Even the proprietor of the café has literary inclinations; he is the amateur dramaturge of the theater, sometime collaborator with the Saturday supplement of newspapers, and "Ezesgeber"—that is, literary adviser to the Yiddish publishing house. The worst thing about him is his association complex. If he hears about the newest offense of the suffragettes, or an amusing street debate, or God knows what else, he's always ready to recite a fable of Krylov, the Russian Aesop, one, he believes, that perfectly fits the situation.

Everyone greets the gentleman with the goatee when he comes through the door, but only a few can tell you his name. People know him just as "Avroymele"; this is the pseudonym he uses to sign his satirical articles. His résumé is paradigmatic for the settlement of intellectuals in Whitechapel. He is the son of a timber merchant from Bobruysk and had to complete most of his secondary-school studies with private tutors because the existing quota for Jewish pupils in Russia had been exceeded. Hence no assimilation was possible for him in his youth. He went to Berlin as a medical student, got engaged to the tragedienne Klara Bleichmann, who made guest appearances with her parents' Yiddish troupe in the Pulhmann Theater on Schönhauser-allee and in the Concordia Theater on Brunnenstrasse. So as not to have to wait years for the delivery of his Russian identification papers, he married in London and remained in Whitechapel.

The Yiddish literary historian at the next table, of whom we can see just his neck with two boils, is drinking his "nut brown." He discovered in the library of the British Museum the four-act Yiddish drama of an author named Wolfsohn that appeared in 1796 in Posen, and is now doing a study of it when not here drinking his "nut brown."

We cannot deny the owner and director of the Pavillon Theater, Mister Joseph Kessler, our approval of his production of Gordin's drama *Di Yiddisher Koenig*

Lear. This doesn't surprise the general manager at all, since he's used to it; serious critics acknowledge daily that the actor Mister Hochstein is an advantage and that the actress Mistress Wallerstein has a lovely face. He regrets that we saw Mister Hamburger, the comic, only in a tragedy; he's apparently preferable in a comedy. We agree that the orchestra conductor is gifted: in the intermission and in melodramatic places he played the harmonium with one hand while attempting to control the orchestra with the other. The audience expressed its sympathy in the middle of the leading scenes through sincerely admiring whistles.

We talk about the theater and they ask us about Osip Dymov, Rudolf Schildkraut, and Sholem Asch. And if we knew Adolf Ritter von Sonnenthal, and if he was really as splendid as they say.

In no time we meet all the regulars, those for whom writing is an excuse, and those for whom it is a lucrative way of earning a living. A pockmarked, burly colleague—his head rests like a cube on a prismatic neck—is introduced to us. They make jokes about his laziness and say that he discovered the Yiddish distich in order to write just two lines. Urged by a Yiddish publisher to write an essay about Israel Zangwill, he began with the words: "Zangwill is a Catholic writer through and through . . ." From that time on he has not been burdened with any more requests.

The spindly local composer of songs is there as well. His specialty is rhyming Yiddish and English words, as for example in the refrain of a couplet about a buttonhole maker:

I am a yiddisher
Buttonhole-finisher . . .

All of Whitechapel sings his song about the "unfortunate worker:"

Fun de kindheit, fun dei yugend
Finsterst ob dein welt in shop,
Und kein heim dos hostu nit,
Mied dei herz, dei kopp.
Oi! seh! men behandelt dich punkt wie a hund.
Fun dei schwere horewanie leben reiche in paleste

　　. . .

(From childhood, from youth, /Your whole life is spent in a dark shop, /And you don't have a home you can call your own. / Ah! See! People treat you like a dog. / From your hard labor rich people live in palaces.)

A nineteen-year-old lad has run away from the Lodz Seminar; he doesn't want to be a "bocher" and doesn't want to become a rabbi. Instead, he wants to create, to conquer the world, to write books, to "become a second Max Brod."

There are three Yiddish dailies in Whitechapel that come out in the large format of the London newspapers: *Die Zeit*, *Yiddishes Journal*, and *Express*. They all differ in their political orientation, but join forces in fighting vehemently against anti-Semitism and the agitation of the well-represented missions houses, and for the amendment of the immigration law. One of the many Yiddish weeklies, the anarchistic *Arbeiterfreund*, is edited by a German Christian, an honorable book printer from Mainz who learned Yiddish expressly for the purpose of agitating in this ethnic neighborhood of London for Tolstoy and Luccheni, for philanthropy and direct action, for mutual help and political assassination. In the English anarchy described by Mackay, Prince Peter Kropotkin, now quite old and living reclusively in nearby Brighton, plays no greater a role than Karpovich, who provided the impetus to the Russian Revolution of 1917 with his fatal shooting of Minister of Culture Bobolepov and now leads a faultless bourgeois existence as a London masseur. On the occasion of the centenary of Bakunin's birth, great-grandfather Cherkesov spoke at an anarchists' meeting and told about his youth, about the revolution, and how—in 1848—he had fought alongside Bakunin on the barricades of Dresden.

The Yiddish corner café on Whitechapel Street also has regular Christian guests, among them journalists sent here from Fleet Street like foreign correspondents representing the big London papers to cover the life of the Whitechapel ghetto.

The bohemian café couldn't do without its literary waiter. To be sure, he doesn't have an army of newspapers at his disposal, but that is why, in the circle of the self-educated, "Waiter Jow" is a respectable personality, an authority in matters of learning. For Master Jow is a university-educated man. He studied philosophy in Bern, came to London in order to continue his studies, had no money, became a waiter, and remained one. And nobody in Whitechapel's Café Megalomania can tell if he despises or envies those of his guests who combine the historical restlessness of the Jews with the nervous rootlessness of the Bohemian.

Translated by Harold B. Segel.

Other works by Kisch: *Tales from Seven Ghettos* (1934); *Australian Landfall* (1937); *Sensation Fair* (1941); *Egon Erwin Kisch, the Raging Reporter: A Bio-Anthology* (1997).

Zvi Hirsch Masliansky

1856-1943

Zvi Hirsch Masliansky was born in Slutsk, Russia, today Belarus. He received a traditional Jewish education but was also attracted to Western ideas. Following the pogroms of 1881, he joined the Ḥibat Tsiyon movement and became a spellbinding, impassioned orator on its behalf, touring Jewish communities in Poland and Russia. He and his family immigrated to the United States in 1895 after tsarist officials threatened to jail him for his political activities. Settling in New York, he continued to preach Zionism to immigrant audiences, especially in his Friday-evening sermons at the Educational Alliance. A beloved figure in the immigrant community, he was known as *ha-matif ha-leumi* (the nationalist preacher).

Memoirs: An Account of My Life and Travels 1924

Mother and Son Meet

A man over eighty is seated at his desk, looking up at an old picture, one more than fifty years old. His eyes meet with those of a beautiful old woman, a woman who was born a hundred and twenty years earlier, lived eighty years and passed away over forty years ago. Their glances unite and a sea of images and visions rushes through their minds bearing a flood of memories, of unfulfilled hopes and aspirations, of age-old scenes deleted by time, few of which, still alive and existent, emerge from the dust of days long gone.

My mother Rivka, may she rest in peace, was beautiful and wise, renowned in the city of Slutsk for her wisdom and mathematical talent, which earned her the name "Rivka the Wise." She was born in the city of Mir, daughter of Rabbi Pinchas Popov, who served as a *Dayan* [judge of Rabbinical Law] in that city his entire life, descendant of the Harkavi family of Novogrudok.

People who have heard me speak were amazed to learn that "the National Preacher" was mute as a child

till the age of five—mute but not deaf. This is indeed an aberration of nature—a future preacher and speaker who was mute in his childhood and could not even say "Mama and Papa." I heard everything said to me with my own ears, understood everything, but I could not utter one word. My father, of blessed memory, who was a great pedagogue and could explain anything, taught me to read Hebrew orally, without pronouncing the words, and all the worshipers at the synagogue were astonished to see me going through the prayer book, turning its pages with the congregation without moving my lips.

My good mother told me that when I reached the age of five I suddenly started to talk and the first words I uttered were: "Mama, I want to go to the *Heder* with all the children!" You can imagine how happy my parents were to hear their son Hersheleh the mute speaking out clearly like all the children of his age. . . . My desire was fulfilled immediately, my father wrapped me in his large *Tallith* and my mother carried me in her arms to the *Melamed* in the *Heder*.

I remember being frightened at first when I saw thirty boys in one room, with two youngsters, "assistant teachers," supervising them as they all repeated the lesson together out loud. The teacher, a tall thin and bony man with a long yellow beard split in two, seated me at a long table; some twenty boys sat around the table on long benches made of simple wooden beams with no back support, and seemed as though they were floating in the air of the room. The teacher brought a large wooden tablet on which the letters of the Hebrew alphabet were printed. He held a long slender wooden stick in his right hand, pointed to the first letter "aleph" and ordered me to read out loud after him: "aleph, aleph, aleph." I, who could already read Hebrew fluently, read the entire alphabet from beginning to end, aleph to tav, in a single breath. The *melamed*, shocked, stared amazed at my mother, and she, full of happiness and satisfaction [*nachas*], could not contain her feelings and started to cry.

The image of this threesome—the beautiful woman, my mother, her face all lit up; the lean yellow man, the teacher; and I, the little boy—looms clearly before my eyes even now, seventy-six years later. [. . .]

When I was twelve years old I heard my late father speaking to my mother early in the morning, unaware of the fact that I heard his words: "Thank God, he has a complete knowledge of the Bible, also of two tractates of the Babylonian Talmud, and is capable of studying on his own, without a teacher. Rabbi Aharon, the son of Rabbi Mendele, has told me that none of the youngsters in the town are his equals, except Haimke the Rabbi's son (Rabbi Haim Soloveichik, the Rabbi of Brisk) and the prodigy of Rotgatchove; but our son needs an advanced *Yeshivah* [religious academy] and will then be ordained in a few years time. Let us send him to Mir, your native town, where your relatives live, where he won't, God forbid, go hungry and would be able to study in comfort."

My kind mother listened to my father's words attentively; she accepted his advice, but wiped her eyes in silence. My father spoke and my mother acted. She summoned Yoseph the tailor and Ber the shoemaker. The former prepared a suit of clothes for me and the latter made me new shoes. My mother prepared a white sack of good cloth for my possessions: three pairs of woolen socks for the winter, and three linen ones for the summer, three shirts and two undergarments with fringes, half a loaf of bread, dry cheese and six hard-boiled eggs. Above all these she placed my favorite prayer book. The sack was full—my mother tied it on the top and her lips murmured in silence: "May this be a blessed hour for my son, and may the angels of the Lord escort my son along the way." She then lifted me in her arms and covered my face with kisses.

"Go in peace, my son, and write about everything that happens to you there," my mother cried out in a tearful voice.

"No, no," my father interrupted her. "Write only once a week, so as not to neglect your studies."

I will never forget the image of my dear mother in those moments of separation. She looked like an angel of mercy and the tears in her shining eyes seemed like pearls.

Twenty-eight years passed since that day. During that time my father died and my mother was widowed. At the age of fifteen I carried the heavy burden of supporting my mother and my brother, the orphaned child. I became both a teacher and a student. I taught my students during the day and studied diligently at night. I married, became a national preacher, traveled to various towns and countries, sacrificed my life and talents for the sake of the triple revival—that of the people, of the Land [of Israel] and the [Hebrew] language; I was imprisoned ten times, locked up in the jails of Czarist Russia. I became "disgusted with my life" and decided to become naturalized in America. And before leaving the land of blood I traveled to my native town of Slutsk to say farewell to my kind mother and weep at the graves of my father and the family.

My final parting from my mother was a dreadful experience; my eighty-year-old mother hugged me without uttering a word. Her entire body trembled as she cuddled in my arms like a little girl, looking at me intensively while deeply absorbed in her thoughts. I too said nothing. Our last glances came together before we separated forever. [. . .]

Europe

CHAPTER 1

From my earliest childhood I was irresistibly drawn to the pulpit. One Saturday afternoon—when I was seven years old and already familiar with the whole Bible—I brought my friends into our courtyard and as usual we played various games. Suddenly I thought of a new game: I entered the house silently; I removed the snow-white cloth from the table and wrapped it around myself like a *tallith*. Dressed m this manner I came out to my friends and began preaching to them. I spoke with great heat, with the enthusiasm and innocence of a child, and cast a spell of terror over my audience who were all children of my age.

This was during the first nine days of the month of Av [days of mourning for the destruction of the Temple] preceding *Tisha B'Av*. The adults were not exactly in mourning but much more grave and serious than during the rest of the year. You could already feel the mood of the destruction in the air. I preached to my friends on the subject of the destruction of the Temple. I began with the last chapter of The Second Book of Kings depicting the destruction of the First Temple. I drew powerful pictures of the siege of Jerusalem by King Nebuchadnezzer and his army and of the increasing famine in the streets of Jerusalem. I remember, as if it were today, how clearly I described the enormity of the tragedy and the ravages of hunger. My friends burst into tears and I wept with them.

When I came to Nebuzaradon, the chief of the guards, who smashed the golden pillars, Yachin and Boaz, causing the whole Temple to totter and fall, my listeners wept so loudly that my father was awakened from his Sabbath afternoon nap. My father, who was a great scholar, a rationalist and a "complete *Mitnagged*" [opponent of the Hasidic movement], emerged from the house furious, drove out my audience and punished me doubly—for disturbing his rest and for uncovering the table which resembled an altar.

When I grew older, I would attend every sermon of the preachers who would visit Slutsk. When I got home I would repeat their speeches miming their movements and rhythms. People in the know prophesied that I would become a preacher in Israel. The greatest preacher of his generation, my relative Rabbi Zvi Hirsch Dainow, the Slutsker *Maggid*, said, when he heard me repeat his words and saw me imitate his motions, that I was destined to take his place.

But many years passed before their prediction was fulfilled. When I went out into the world—and my world then was the city of Pinsk—I became a teacher of Hebrew. During those years I was busy teaching and I had no opportunity to step on a pulpit. But every Saturday I would deliver a lecture on the Psalms before a large audience, for no remuneration, of course. But this was the occupation of a Rabbi not of a preacher. I lived as a teacher during the week and a Rabbi on Saturdays until 1881.

In that year I had an experience that I cannot explain to this day. And it was this experience that determined the course of my life.

It happened on a mid-summer Saturday after the assassination of Czar Alexander the Second and the ascension of his son Alexander the Third to the throne. The terrible pogroms against the Jews were beginning and Ignatiev, the Minister of the Interior, was issuing his evil decrees against Israel. The first pogroms broke out in Yelisavetgrad [later, Kirovograd, now Kropyvnytskiy, Ukraine]. When I read the headlines, "Slaughter of Jews in Yelisavetgrad" a fire was kindled in me and I had a burning desire to speak to an audience. I could not rest. I ran from synagogue to synagogue to find an audience until I came to the big Synagogue of the Tailors where the well-known preacher, Rabbi Aaron David, was speaking. The synagogue was full and the preacher had just finished his address. With tears in my eyes I ran to him and implored him to give me permission to go up on the pulpit and address a few words to the congregation. Rabbi Aaron David took pity on me and granted my request. I ascended the pulpit and delivered a passionate speech on Zion and the Land of Israel. The weekly portion from the Prophets, the *Haftarah*, was "But Zion said, 'The Lord hath forsaken me'" and it served as the keynote of my sermon. I preached with such passion that the whole congrega-

tion was moved to tears and even Rabbi Aaron David, that cold critical analyst, wept with them. [. . .]

CHAPTER 2

A new world was opened to me in the beautiful city of Odessa—"A new heaven, a new earth" and new people, renowned men with fine manners and refined customs. I was entranced by the sight of wide streets, large buildings and people full of life and joy, well-dressed and living in truth "like God in Odessa." I was especially impressed by the boulevard, which adorned the shore of the Black Sea. [. . .]

I remained in Odessa several weeks and preached in seventeen synagogues. My speeches had a great impact upon all segments of the population, old and young, rich and poor, orthodox and free thinkers. The Russian papers wrote about me practically every day as I was preparing to speak in the remaining synagogues; it was this publicity that forced me to leave the city. [. . .]

CHAPTER 3

After Odessa I visited a few cities in Bessarabia [today Moldova]. To tell the truth, I must confess that I traveled to these cities with no great desire.

Bessarabia was never particularly beloved in Lithuania. The Lithuanian Jews, who prided themselves on their learning and evaluated everyone by that standard, looked down on the Bessarabian Jews. They considered the Bessarabians to be physically strong with broad shoulders and red faces, crude persons, whose world began and ended with eating mamaliga and drinking wine. Should I travel to such Jews and speak of Zion and Jerusalem, of the exile of Israel and its future? The heart was full of fear and trembling and the question "what if they do not listen to me?" naturally arose. Perhaps my words would not penetrate the hearts of the listeners? Perhaps they would not pay attention to such "abstract and spiritual" themes.

But when I came to the cities and began to know these people and became acquainted with their customs, my fears were completely dissipated. I found many cultured people among them, many learned men who were profoundly interested in the *Hibbat Zion* movement and completely devoted to it. Their strong physique and upright posture conferred a special grace on them and further endeared them to me. Even the common people, who were far removed from culture and learning, took pride in their Lithuanian origins, and those who could claim a Rabbi in some town or a *schochet* [ritual slaughterer] in some village as a relative, were considered members of the aristocracy and came into their own when a son or daughter reached the age of marriage. [...]

Then I came to Kishinev [today, Chisinau, Moldova].

It was in Kishinev that I found the new movement of those days in full bloom. This new movement, in its time, was a strong competitor of *Hibbat Zion* and led to strife and dissension. This was the "Argentina" movement.

This movement was founded in the capital city by Baron de Hirsch's agents, Sonenthal and Feinberg, and spread like wildfire throughout the Jewish Pale of Settlement. Baron de Hirsch suddenly became a new redeemer, his picture adorned the walls of Jewish homes, and his name was blessed by all. Argentina, that distant country, whose name had never been heard of by the Jews of the Pale, suddenly became "a land flowing with milk and honey." Rumors spread that Baron de Hirsch wished to remove all the Jews from Russia and to give each and every one fields and vineyards in the fertile and blessed land of Argentina—all this to be a gift from the Baron. Later thousands of pamphlets were circulated among the people, telling of the merits and fruitfulness of that country and the great happiness to be found in it. These pamphlets were read at home and in public, in synagogue and house of study, and Argentina became the dominant topic for Jews of the Pale. There were Jews who neglected their trade and business and circulated all day in the market places and streets and knocked on the doors of the Baron's men to find out when the first caravan was leaving, so that they might join it. The agents did all in their power to inflame the people, heaped praise on the Baron, and painted the most glowing pictures of the treasures of this new Land of Israel, in which the order of creation was reversed—day becoming night and winter summer, a land blessed by the Lord, where there was no sickness or disease. There were those who demonstrated by specific proofs from the Bible and the *Midrash* that this was the end of the Diaspora and the true redemption. The Biblical text: "Behold, I am creating a new heaven and a new earth" and the statement that "The Land of Israel will in time spread into all countries" did not "cease from their lips." This was a time of a new false Messianic movement like that of Sabbtai Zevi. Kabbalists and students of *gematria* did not sit idly by, and daily brought proofs of the end of the dispersion.

Deeds soon followed the initial fervor. In many cities offices were opened, committees were formed and potential emigrants were enrolled. A strong desire to emigrate seized all the Jews. All those who were impoverished and disadvantaged rushed to enroll to be among the first to leave for the land of happiness. Special emissaries were sent by the committees to enroll all who wished to emigrate. Those enrolled would pay thirty kopeks a week, which were regularly collected. The desire to emigrate grew daily. Even well-to-do merchants neglected their affairs and added their names to the lists.

The only ones who opposed this movement were the *Hovevei Zion*. They saw in it not only the negation of their ideal but also the complete denial of the hopes of the people of Israel and the Land of Israel. If Jews were going to leave Russia in order to settle on the land and to become farmers, it was clear that the country should be the Land of Israel and not some other country. There were those who predicted that the Jewish settlement in Argentina would not succeed—which actually turned out to be the case. The *Hovevei Zion* tried with all their strength, by word of mouth and in writing, to open the eyes of the people to the danger involved in a mass exodus to a distant and uncultivated country. This opposition was frowned upon by those who favored Argentina and saw it as the redemption of Israel. Thus, the Jews were split into two camps, "Palestinians" and "Argentineans." The dissention between the two groups was so great that it led to continual quarrels and even to blows. Eventually it became known to the government, which favored the "Argentineans" because of the wealth of Baron de Hirsch. Alexander III authorized the Argentinean Movement and this authorization was signed on *Tisha B'Av*. This fact too served as propaganda material for the two groups. The proponents of *Hibbat Zion* [another name for Hovevei Zion] termed it "The Third Destruction," relating it to *Tisha B'Av* just as historians did with the Expulsion from Spain four hundred years ago. The false prophets of the "Argentines" demonstrated by statements from the *Midrash* that "the beginning of redemption" would date from *Tisha B'Av*. The two groups battled each other with hatred and rancor and the poor suffering Jewish community stood between two fires. [...]

In the course of my sermons I dealt with the Argentine issue and condemned it strongly. With all the fire at my command I explained to my large audience the dangers inherent in this movement and the great dif-

ference between the Land of Israel, our historic homeland, saturated with the blood of our forefathers, and a
strange and uncultivated country which our fathers and
their ancestors had never heard of.

These words of mine aroused the anger of the "Argentineans," and they began to seek ways to remove me
from their path.

They sought and they found.

One day certain individuals appeared before the
Governor of the Province and informed him that I was
inciting the Jews to oppose Argentina and to refuse to
emigrate from Russia. And since the Argentine movement was government sponsored as a result of the contract between Baron de Hirsch and the Czar I was a traitor, a political criminal, no more and no less.

The Governor did his duty and ordered me to be
arrested.

I sat in jail three whole days. During that period
Kishinev was boiling over. Influential persons and the
leaders of *Hovevei Zion* attempted to have me released,
but to no avail. Obviously my crime was too great and it
would not be easy to get me out.

An angel of deliverance then appeared—General
Blumenfeld, a nationally minded Jew, who was the chief
physician of the Province. He visited the Governor several times until he was able to influence him to release
me. The governor finally agreed on the condition that
I would translate for him the contents of my speeches.

I did this and explained in detail my reasons for
opposing the Argentine movement. I saw in it a great
danger to all the Jews of Russia and it was my duty as a
preacher to warn the people.

The Governor ordered me to leave Kishinev and all
Bessarabia and said to me: "Forget oratory! You would
be better off selling onions rather than being a preacher.
Know that Russia is the land of silence and not of
speech!" [. . .]

CHAPTER 14

From Bialystok I traveled to Warsaw.

Leaving Bialystok and the separation from the elite
of *Hovevei Zion* and its leading activists was difficult for
me; the trip to Warsaw, however, was even more difficult. Even before I visited Warsaw, the great metropolis
of Polish Jewry, I was aware of the confusion and chaos
that prevailed there in the communal life of the Jews.
That great sage Rabbi Yoshe [Joseph] Ber Soloveichik
had described that city very aptly: "Warsaw is not a

great city, but rather several towns in the same vicinity
called by one name."

The Jews of Warsaw are split into groups and there is
no unifying factor.

The first group is comprised of the natives, the Poles
of the Mosaic Persuasion. They are assimilationists who
have nothing to do with the people of Israel, its literature, its language, its culture and traditions. The fate of
millions of their brethren means nothing to them. They
are devoted in mind and spirit to the Polish nation and
are ready to sing the Polish national anthem until they
lose their voices. Anything that bears the Polish imprint
is sacred to them.

The second group is that of the Hasidim who consider
their Rabbis divine beings. They present themselves at
the Rabbi's court every holiday and festival. They thirst
for his blessings and live by his grace from the cradle to
the grave. They are dressed in the fashion of the middle
ages—long kaftans, flat shoes, long stockings and short
pants. They have big beards, long and curled side-locks
and wear small velvet hats. They speak Yiddish in a
peculiar accent, which is very difficult to understand.
They educate their sons in their own way, an old fashion
way with no system or order. Their daughters study in
Polish schools and *gymnasia* and get a European education while Judaism is foreign to them. Most of them are
pretty and it is easy to understand what problems arise
in the marriages of the young, rude Hasidim to these
pretty and cultivated young women. The young men
travel to the Rabbi for retreats, communion and devotion and the young women visit Carlsbad, Marienbad
and Franzbad [spas in what is now the Czech Republic].
Quite a few comedies and tragedies take place between
these daughters of Israel and the Russian and German
officers whom they meet at these spas. While this phenomenon is to be lamented we should not be surprised
by it. The root of the evil lies in the education of the
young women. They find more interest and satisfaction
in the company of young and cultured officers than they
do with their husbands, who are uncultivated and who
avert their eyes when they do speak with their wives. In
the world of the Hasidim stories are told even about the
daughters of leading Rabbis that would furnish much
raw material to writers of romances.

The third group is that of the Lithuanian Jews whom
fate uprooted from their native places and cast into
Poland. The Lithuanian feels himself lonely and isolated between the two other groups. Neither the Polish
aristocrats nor the Hasidim have any love for him. To

the former he is a wild fanatic while to the latter he is a heretic, who believes in the Creator of the World, but does not share their faith in the Rabbi. Even in death the Lithuanian does not find peace and quiet in the Warsaw cemetery. He is taken across the river to Praga. For these reasons the Lithuanians must be considered a separate group.

Before I reached Warsaw I knew that I would not have access to the Polish Jews and to the Hasidim. In the eyes of the first group my speeches on nationalism and *Hibbat Zion* would be "treason" against their native land, while to the second group they would be ranked "heresy." Only among the few Lithuanian Jews would I find attentive ears.

My first sermon was held in the Synagogue, *Ohel Moshe*, named after the great Sir Moses Montefiore. I saw before me a large and variegated audience, with many famous writers and young intellectuals among them and I was satisfied. I saw that the great idea of *Hibbat Zion* was making converts, reviving the spark of hope among those who had been far removed from the camp of Israel, and was destined with its strength eventually to penetrate the hearts of its opponents both of the Right and the Left.

While I was in Warsaw I felt that it was my pleasant duty to visit the local scholars and writers. As was only proper I paid my first visit to the oldest of the group, Chaim Selig Slonimski. When I came into his house I found him sitting by a table reading a book. His large white beard, his broad wrinkled forehead and his long eyebrows conferred upon him the dignity of old age and patriarchal splendor. At that moment he resembled an old Rabbi, sitting and studying Torah. He received me graciously and immediately began a conversation with me on Hebrew literature, or more exactly on the polemic of "The Flask of Oil," which still raged over since the day he published his famous article. He was extremely bitter at his opponents, who fought him with taunts and abuse, and not in the civilized fashion one might expect from scholars and writers.

"All my life," he complained to me, "I was engaged in study. I attempted to teach knowledge and science to my brothers; and now in my old age I am publicly reviled!"

These words came right from his heart, the aching heart of an old man.

The conversation finally turned to the *Ha-Tsefirah*, the subject that was closest to his heart. *Ha-Tsefirah* at that time was edited by Nahum Sokolov, who had made

it over into a lively and interesting newspaper. Slonimski who had founded *Ha-Tsefirah* for the publication of articles on the telegraph, magnets, and comets—the popularization of scientific knowledge, couldn't bear to see his brainchild converted into a daily paper. But the vigorous Sokolov, carried out his own policy. Slonimski still hoped that the time would come when the *Ha-Tsefirah* would once more become the scientific journal it once had been.

The old man's words awakened mixed feelings—laughter and sympathy. It was the clandestine tragic-comedy of a helpless old man trying to protect his world with his pale, trembling hands . . .

Sokolov, the young editor, made an entirely different impression upon me. Before me was a European man of aristocratic traits; his conduct polite, his conversation calm and full of tact, his gestures resembling those of a European writer, "a son of Jepheth," but upon the mere mention of a Jewish literary or communal question, there suddenly was revealed the authentic Jewish scholar, the sharp and learned man of the old *Beth Midrash*. When you were in Sokolov's company you were struck with amazement, as if you were standing before one of the wonders of the world, before a phenomenon, and you did not know what to admire more, whether his detailed knowledge of Jewish and world literature, his sharpness of mind—"uprooting mountains and grinding them against each other"—or his Jewish humor compounded of shrewdness and naiveté at the same time. He would open his mouth and pearls would come forth. He would take a saying of our sages and combine with it a word of one of the great philosophers; he would join a historical event with a memory of his youth. You would just sit and listen, sit and absorb. Unconsciously you would say very little so as not to waste the precious minutes, you would want to sit for hours on end to catch the jewels which came from the mouth, linked to each other by an artist's hand. [. . .]

CHAPTER 18

Of all the cities that I visited in Bessarabia, Volynhia, Poland and Lithuania during my many trips the city of Kovna [Kovno; Kaunas—eds.] made the most distinct impression upon me. Immediately upon reaching this city you felt that you had come to a different district, a different environment even though the Russian language and Russian law were still dominant here. You saw before you different Jews, new faces, lacking the ugly poverty of Lithuania, the gross materialism of

Bessarabia and the extreme orthodoxy of Poland. A certain grace and aristocracy of the spirit are present on the faces and in the manners of the Jews of Kovna. Even the most Orthodox among them, who are mindful of the slightest commandment, do not wear long garments, comb their hair and beards and strictly mind their collars. It is possible that this is due to the influence of the Prussian border which is close to Kovna, but it is a fact that the Jews of Kovna do excel in the neatness of their apparel and the civility of their manners.

The city itself impresses you with its beauty and the splendor of the surrounding country. Mountains encircle the city. The most beautiful is Mount Peter and it is a great experience to stand at its peak and to look down on the city with all its streets and squares, with its walls and towers. It is a tradition of the Kovna Jews that [the Hebrew novelist] Abraham Mapu loved to be alone in the mountains and to write his books there. The pure and pleasant air, the soft fresh grass, the complete and delightful stillness would lift him on the wings of his imagination and he would see before his eyes the splendor of Lebanon and Carmel, the Valley of Sharon and Mount Hermon and Jerusalem, built-up in all its glory.

The city is further adorned by the two rivers, the Nieman and the Vilija (Neris) that flow on both its sides till "they become one" to the west of the city.

Among the mountains that encircle the city is a valley called the "Valley of Mitzkevitch [Mickiewicz—eds.]." In this valley the great Polish poet composed his poems and saw his splendid visions. Mapu and Mitzkevitch both sang their songs on the soil of Kovna, on foreign soil. They were both poets of nations in exile, but even so how great was the difference! The place where Mitzckevitch lived and worked is a historical place to the Poles and is called by the name of their poet, while no one knows exactly where Mapu lived and wrote.

There is exile and exile within exile!

When I came to Kovna I considered it my first duty to visit its Rabbi, the elderly sage, Rabbi Yitchak Elchanan [Spektor—eds.]. I had heard much of this great man, of his aristocratic personality, of his great heart aware of every communal problem and I had a great desire to see him and to enjoy his company. He was staying then at a summer home outside of the city. I went with his son, Rabbi Zvi Hirsch the Rabbi of Vilna to meet him. I found him lying in the shade of a large tree, sleeping. A cool breeze blew and caressed his full white face and the white hair of his beard. There was a mystic silence all around. At the Rabbi's hand there lay a small book

which he was obviously reading before he fell asleep; the wind played with the book and turned its pages. It was interesting to see what book served as light reading for this scholar before he napped. As I came one step closer I was able to make out the title, *Chosen Mishpat* [volume of the *Shulchan Aruch* compilation of Jewish law] . . .

We waited a few minutes until the Rabbi awoke. When he saw us he immediately stood up, rubbed his hands on the grass and greeted us. When his son introduced me his face lit up and he invited me to come into his cottage. He said to his son. "All strength to thee [*yeshar ko'ah*] Herschele, for bringing me so distinguished a guest!"

As we walked, I wanted to take the pillow on which he had been lying from him and carry it. But he refused to give it to me, saying: "Let my son fulfill the commandment of honoring his father," and handed it to Rabbi Zvi Hirsh.

When we reached the cottage he called out happily: "Wife *(Rabbanit [Rebbitzin—eds.])!* Set the table. We have distinguished visitors today."

We sat at the table a long time and talked. In the course of his conversation, whose main theme was the condition of our people, I got to know this remarkable man. His great learning and his continuous preoccupation in replying to religious queries from far and wide did not confine him to the narrow world of religious law, to "the four cubits of Halacha" so to speak. Everything that was happening in Jewish circles was known to him and close to his heart. A forthcoming edict that would expel Jews from yet another region of the Russian empire, the question of ritual slaughter, improving the conditions of Jewish soldiers in the Russian army— these and similar problems occupied his heart and mind and he dedicated his energy and time to them. When he would speak of the trials and tribulations of Israel a cloud of sadness would come over his face and his words would come from the innermost chambers of his heart. It seemed as if he were personally experiencing all the sufferings of Israel in his body and soul. He was very gracious to everyone and would receive all people, even the non-Orthodox, most cordially. All these fine qualities placed him at the head of Russian Jewry and in effect he was not the Rabbi of Kovna, but of that entire Diaspora.

When I looked at his splendid face, as I listened to his words, when I saw the graciousness with which he received callers, I imagined that Hillel the Elder [the great sage from the days of the Second Temple] was standing before me.

At this time the controversy over the *Musar* (Ethical) Movement was raging in the Hebrew press (*Ha-Melitz* and *Ha-Tsefirah*). The Kovna writer, S. Rosenfeld, had started this controversy. In bitter articles he opposed the leaders of the Musar movement who were all established in Kovna. He showed by citing facts "and portents" that they were deniers of the world and misleaders of the *Yeshivah* students. When I was on the spot in Kovna, I decided to visit the strongholds of the *Musar* adherents to see whether "the outcry that had come to me" was true. In the company of that eminent Talmudist, the writer, Aharon Michal Borochov, I visited the *Musar Yeshivah*. I must confess that I shuddered when I saw how the *Musar* disciples comported themselves. The way of *Musar*, as it existed in Kovna, was not the way of life, but the way of death. The *Musarites* went about like shadows and the melancholy sadness of men condemned to death could be seen in their eyes. My heart bled to see these young boys, the pride of the *Yeshivah*, who had not yet tasted life, and were already looking at the whole world through a gloss of sadness and melancholy. The *Musar* movement killed all feeling of joy in them and choked off all desire for life, so that they seemed like flowers that had withered before their time. Not for nothing did Rabbi Yitchak Elchanan and his son, Rabbi Hirsch, oppose the *Musar* movement and the antics of its leaders, such as [Rabbi Yozel] *Ba'al Ha-horim* ["Master of the Holes"]. . . .[1]

Before I departed from Kovna, I delivered a eulogy on the great Rabbi [Naftali Zvi Yehuda—eds.] Berlin, the NaTSIV of Volozhin. Great multitudes of people came to pay their last respects to the departed Sage, among them many of his pupils. I described to them the extent of the loss we suffered by the death of this great Sage and the worth of the *Yeshivah* of Volozhin, to which he had consecrated his life, and the great assemblage wept with me.

The trustees of the German Synagogue invited me to preach in that Synagogue where a *Maggid* [preacher] had never before appeared on the platform. The government-appointed rabbi, Rabbi Schnittkind, and two university students, the Bramsohn brothers, headed the synagogue committee. I spoke to a huge audience, which included ultra Orthodox, for two hours. The makeup of my audience was considered a miracle in the Kovna of those days.

I went to take my leave of Rabbi Yitzchak Elchanan together with the writer Aaronsohn, the translator of S. R. Hirsch's books. We spent several hours conversing with him. I could not take my eyes away from his shining face, his fine build, his fair white hands and above all from his eyes that were so full of love and compassion.

Suddenly he broke off his conversation, asked my leave and went into his room.

After ten minutes he reappeared and handed me a letter saying:

"Please take these few words which describe the peculiar gift which God has bestowed upon you. They may be of help to you in the future. I am old and grey, but you are young and have the strength to work for our people, our faith and our Torah. As I see it, you are destined to cross the Ocean to America. Everyone goes there. May you come to them and strengthen them. Tell them in my name to strive to maintain our Holy Torah, which has been 'our life and length of our days' these last two thousand years!"

We parted with a kiss and a tear. [. . .]

Chapter 28

London made an unfavorable impression upon me. The great city with its multitude of inhabitants, with its tall buildings blackened by soot and gray of smoke, with its befouled atmosphere, its constant humidity and cover of dark clouds—all this was very depressing. You feel as though you have arrived in a different world, a world beneath "the Mountain of Darkness," and you are walking slowly, feeling your way cautiously, involuntarily bending over as you go along. The tall buildings crush you, as it were, by their height and mass, and their dull gray color cast a mysterious dread over you . . . But when you behold the Englishmen standing erect with their blue eyes and smooth faces, when you consider their "gentlemanly" walk, their fine manners, their nobility of spirit and their calm glance—you have the feeling that an ancient and noble people is standing before you, a free people, to whom political and individual freedom are of their very essence and spirit.

The east side of London, East End, is a special world in itself, inhabited mostly by Jews. When you enter this section it is as if you had come to Vilna or Minsk. At every step you come across stores owned by Jews. At their doors stand the storekeepers, with their bearded faces, of the type of the mild young scholars of Russia, or their energetic wives with their black hair and eyes like the "women of valor" of the Lithuanian towns. In the market there are haggling tradeswomen dressed in blouses and covered with kerchiefs, selling bagels and fruit. Heads covered with skullcaps, faces heavily bearded with side locks peep forth from the cellars as their owners are bent over a shoemaker's bench or sewing machine. The children of Israel earn their livelihood with difficulty and not with ease, a bare sustenance with no luxuries.

Ugly poverty prevails among the Gentile inhabitants of this quarter. Almost all of them are habitual drunkards, who drink in solitude and in company, young and old, women and children. Drink wreaks havoc among them and ruins them completely. It is not a rare sight on Saturday night or early Sunday morning to see men and women, the latter with infants in their arms, standing in line in front of the saloon waiting for their turn to buy a glass of whiskey. The women give it to their infants, inoculating them with the poison of drink from their earliest childhood. Drunkenness produces such poverty among them that they literally have no bread to eat, no clothes to wear and no place to live. They loiter aimlessly in the streets, on the ledges of the houses, half naked and hungry, drenched with rain, frozen with cold and even this "rest" is controlled by the police.

I preached my first sermon in East End in the neighborhood of the Lithuanian and Polish Jews who understood me and my language. "I saw a topsy-turvy world" among them: "the upper [class] underneath and the lower on top"—both in the material and spiritual realms. Those who have been rich in Continental Europe were now poor, and the former poor were now wealthy. Religious and God-fearing men had thrown off all restraints and had become free thinkers and anarchists. Radicals and free thinkers returned to the fold as penitents and become Orthodox fanatics in whose eyes truly God-fearing men had no standing whatsoever. As our sages expressed it: "In the place where penitents stand even the wholly righteous cannot stand."

One morning a committee from the Anarchist Club of London came to challenge me to a public debate on religions. I was astounded to recognize among the members of the committee two students of a well-known *Yeshiva* in Lithuania. At home they had been *Musar* [Ethics] students, ascetics, studying day and night, but when they came to London they freed themselves from all restraints, passed through the Mission stage and entered the camp of the anarchists and now they were spreading the gospel of Kropotkin among the Jews of Whitechapel and the East End. They were

pouring fire and brimstone upon the people of Israel, their Torah and their faith. Their hatred for things Jewish was as thorough as that of full-fledged anti-Semites.

I refused to have anything to do with this delegation.

As they left a second deputation arrived in the name of the society of Observers of the Sabbath and Strengtheners of the Faith. They invited me to speak for the society, to increase the membership and activities. I was shocked to recognize in the chief spokesman, the notorious anarchist from the city of N. in Russia, who had inspired many Jewish youths to leave the paths of Judaism, and had been pursued by the Czarist authorities. He fled to London, and here he repented and became an Orthodox fanatic. He embittered the life of his wife, who did not wear a wig, while in Russia he would try to prevent her from kindling the Sabbath candles. More times than one he had thrown out the candlesticks with the candles.

When I saw the two extremes—utterly confounded—pious students of *Musar* become anarchists, and an anarchist become a pillar of the faith, I said in my heart: "How great is your power O London! You are as the Red Heifer. You render the impure pure and the pure impure. . . ."

With great reverence I went to visit the Chief Rabbi, "The Great Eagle," who controlled all the congregations in Great Britain and its dependencies. All the Rabbis, "Reverends," ritual slaughterers and cantors were dependent upon him and without his consent could not function in the communal field. The name Rabbi Naphtali Adler is well known throughout the world. While he was still in the house of his father, Rabbi Nathan Adler, author of *Netina la-Ger* on the Onkelos translation of the Bible, certain Rabbis entitled him "Exilarch" [Leader of the Diaspora] and praised him and his works. I, who especially in the course of my travels, had come to know the great Rabbis of Russia and Poland, thought that I would find here the greatest sage and scholar. I was bitterly disappointed when, after I had discussed various topics with him, I found him to be like one of the government-appointed Rabbis of Russia and not the best of them. He excelled only in diplomacy. He knew life and he knew how to act with different classes of people. When he stood upon the platform in the Synagogue he was a God-fearing Jew; in the company of Englishmen he was an English gentlemen and aristocrat. In his rabbinical court in the East End he was a bitter fanatic; he persecuted the non-Orthodox as ruthlessly as the Hasidic leaders did in Galicia and

Poland. But how "enlightened" was this "High Priest" in the society of the British aristocracy in the West End! He conducted his rabbinate with a high hand and those who were dependent upon his good will, stood before him as slaves before their master. This is a brief sketch of the Chief Rabbi's character. He was especially known as one who showed little love for the Jews of Russia and their Rabbis. When the Jewish community of Manchester summoned the Great Rabbi Isaac Jacob Reines, founder of the *Mizrahi* [religious Zionist] movement, to serve as its Rabbi, Adler demonstrated, in his diplomatic way, his true attitude towards the immigrants and their Rabbis. It was then that I coined the phrase, which was accepted by all English Jews: Rabbi Nathan Adler, I said, was author of *Netina la-Ger* [extending one's hand to the convert or sojourner—eds.] and his son, Rabbi Naphtali Adler, is author of *Sin'ah la-Ger* [i.e., hatred of the convert or sojourner—eds.].

Our Hebrew writers spill gallons of ink when they describe the poor and chaotic state of education in Russia. If they came to London, they would soon see that education in London is seventy-seven times worse. It is horrible to see the old established Jews leaving their Judaism, with only the singing of *Yigdal* in the synagogue and the eating of the fish surviving on Friday nights. Their children are educated in the public schools. Those who mourn read the *Kaddish* in English letters in the back of the *Siddur*. What about the Jews newly arrived from across the channel? These latter are more faithful to the tradition and don't leave out anything they did in their little hamlets. They see to it that their sons are taught mechanical reading in Hebrew and the cantillation of the Bible by teachers of a former generation who really do not know the Hebrew language and history, not to speak of English. The majority of these "educators" cannot write an address correctly.

I had no satisfaction from the Zionists in London either. They are divided into scattered groups all building up themselves and heaping slanders on the others. [. . .]

The two parts of the city of London, the West and the East, symbolize the extreme contrasts—the "Lord" uptown and the "Yokel" downtown.

In the West End one never grows tired of gazing upon the beauty and glory of the squares, parks and houses in which live millionaires who are supported by their ancestral holdings that pass from father to son, tilled by enslaved workers, and by their wealth piled up in the Bank of England.

But when you come to the East End, a walk of just ten minutes, you are shocked by the poverty and degrada-

tion you meet. Poverty lurks in the narrow alleys, over the coffin-like houses, on the faces of the naked and barefoot beings in the guise of men and women. The lot of these living grave dwellers is better than that of thousands of their brothers and sisters in the lower part of the city. These latter ones walk about in the shadows of Whitechapel at night until they fall exhausted in the filth of the saloons. The watchmen who make their rounds in the city take them to collection centers which are too small to take them all in. The plague of drunkenness is widespread; even the women, the mothers of the future generation, drink the national drink, whiskey, brandy or gin, to use its proper name, until they fall upon the sidewalks. The human likeness has departed from those women and the last vestige of self-respect has disappeared from their countenances. Every morning you can see hundreds of these poor unfortunates being led away by the police. They are used to insults, rebukes and even blows despite the English law which accents respect toward women, a law observed all over the Empire. But this law only warns against abuse of the healthy and satisfied women of the upper classes. But who cares if it is breached in the case of these poor unfortunates who have nothing but their tattered bodies and souls . . . ? [. . .]

It was a pleasant experience for me to visit the Synagogue of the Sephardic Jews. It is a very old structure and the glory of age hovers over it. It has no electric or gas lights, but is illuminated solely by large candles in ancient copper candlesticks. All this gives the impression of antiquity and you are carried hundreds of years back in time. As I considered the Synagogue and listened to the monotonous oriental tunes of the Sephardic Jews, I seemed to be in an ancient prayer house in Cordova or Granada. But when I approached the Cantor and the community leader after the services and greeted them in Hebrew they did not understand my words and looked upon me as a speaker in a Barbarian tongue.

To such a sad state have the descendants of Judah Halevi and Ibn Gabirol sunk! [. . .]

America

Chapter 34

The papers announced that I was to deliver my first speech on the Saturday noon, July 11, at the *Beth Ha-Midrash Ha-Gadol* [The Great Synagogue]. Subject: Peace Overseas.

On Friday night I went to the abovementioned synagogue for Sabbath prayers. The cantor and choir conducted a very pleasant service. And yet I was astonished by the announcement made by the *Shamash*, of a type I have not heard in my entire life. Before the concluding prayer of *Aleinu* he stroked a leather pad with a small leather hammer and proclaimed in a strange voice: "Let no man say *Kaddish*. It is *Jahrzeit*."

I was astonished by this strange announcement and could not understand its nature. Why should no man say *Kaddish*? And what does it have to do with the marking of a *Jahrzeit* and who is doing so? And if a man is marking a *Jahrzeit* why should he not say the mourners prayer—the *Kaddish*?

All these queries were answered for me by a respectable elderly man from my hometown:

"This is the custom in America, and nowhere else, for it starts with 'business' and with 'business' it ends, and the spirit of 'business' prevails in all the institutions, the synagogues, the hospitals and even the cemeteries. When you have spent more time in America you will understand the nature of things."

"But explain to me, please, what the *Shamash*'s announcement means? What has 'business' to do with non-recited *Kaddish*?"

"Yes, my friend," the elderly man answered with a smile, "non-recited *Kaddish* prayers are a 'business' for the synagogue and especially for the *Shamash*. In America the Jews do not go to synagogue morning and evening, and only a small number, a limited quorum, come for *Schacharit* and *Arvit* [morning and evening prayers]. And who are those who do come? They are the mourners, and those who have a *Jahrzeit*; they come since they have to say *Kaddish*. *Kaddish* and *Jahrzeit* are the pillars of the synagogues of America, even of the Reform temples. The customs pertaining to the dead cast fear on the living and they fulfill them with greater care than they do the entire Torah. Every mourner is, during his twelve-month period, a source of income for the synagogue and the *Shamash*. But the main source comes from the people marking a *Jahrzeit* who come to synagogue once or twice a year. They pay the synagogues handsomely for an *Aliyah* [for being called up to the Torah], and reward the *Shamash* for a memorial prayer. When a *Jahrzeit* observer comes to the synagogue the Shamash shuts up all the mourners so that the right to say *Kaddish* is reserved for the man marking a *Jahrzeit* alone. And now you, my townsmen the greenhorn, tell me what do the sexton's announcement and the non-recited *Kaddish* prayer have to do with 'business.' When you spend more time in America, you will become wiser and understand to what extent death revives and sustains all of American Jewry. You must have heard of the large 'orders' and their 'lodges' that count their members by the hundreds and thousands. These are useful institutions that would have harbored much good for the entire people of Israel had they possessed the living spirit of Judaism. Unfortunately they are great only in quantity and nil in quality as they too live on death and its customs, on things such as land, cemeteries, tombstones, fences, fees for the mourners during the *shivah* and these issues fill their lives completely."

Leaving the *Beth Ha-Midrash Ha-Gadol* with my good and clever townsman, I was shocked by what my eyes saw. Outside, at the entrance to the synagogue, stood a group of Jewish youngsters and sold Jewish newspapers. The boys half naked, bare footed, rushed around the people leaving the synagogue crying out in joyous youthful voices: "Two papers for a cent!"

Passersby and some people who just emerged from the synagogue bought papers in public while the cantor's voice was still echoing from inside the synagogue, "The Israelite people shall keep the Sabbath. . . ."

On Saturday afternoon at the scheduled time I went to deliver my first speech in the *Beth Ha-Midrash Ha-Gadol* [Great Synagogue]. When I reached the corner of Grand and Norfolk Streets, where the synagogue was situated, a great crowd was standing ahead of me, and I could not take one step forward. A multitude of people, old and young, men and women, were standing packed closely together and making their way toward the entrance of the synagogue. The crowd reminded me of the Sabbath of the *Hanukah* festival in London when I spoke at the New Synagogue. Here too, in New York, like in London, policemen helped me enter the synagogue.

A feeling of love and gratitude to America and its institutions overwhelmed me at the touch of the policemen. At that moment I recalled my contact with the Russian policemen who interrupted my sermons and pulled me out of the synagogues in Odessa, Kishinev, Lodz etc. with savage cruelty. Tears of joy streamed from my eyes as I sensed the difference between the policemen of New York and those of Kishinev. The latter, full of revengeful fury like ferocious animals, pulled me out of the synagogue, the former, respectful and courteous, escorted me into the synagogue. Light and darkness, bondage and freedom—how great the difference! And my lips whispered: "Blessed are you, America, and blessed is your freedom."

I ascended the platform with great effort. As I looked at the dense crowd that filled the *Beth Midrash*, including the women's gallery, completely, I felt inspired. On their faces I could see the expectation to hear something new, something extraordinary. The synagogue was packed and yet quiet and still. Four thousand pairs of eyes were fixed upon me. All this ran through me like an electric current and elevated me higher than my usual state of mind when ascending the pulpit. How amazing. I have been accustomed to address crowds of people in synagogues and great halls in different cities and different countries, but I have never been in so exalted a mood as when I delivered my first sermon in America at the *Beth Ha-Midrash Ha-Gadol*.

At that time I felt that a new period in my life had begun. I sensed that this land of America, refuge to a quarter of a million of the children of Israel, was to become a safe haven and a desirable, good and broad land for millions of our brethren wandering in their masses from the poverty-stricken lands of Europe. I sensed that my first speech would enable me to put an end to my own exile. My heart prophesied that I could establish my own home here in New York, a city destined for greatness, as I had found here a new sphere for my work, a new field to till. It was a deserted and abandoned field, lacking order and focus, with no spirit, no knowledge and no will. The Jewish immigrants coming from different lands, speaking different languages and practicing different customs were like the dead in prophet Ezekiel's vision of the dry bones.

With a loud and powerful voice that caused all my limbs to tremble, I started my first sermon by quoting our sages of blessed memory (tractate *Brachot* 58a [of the Babylonian Talmud]): "If one sees a crowd of Israelites, he should say: 'Blessed is He who discerneth secrets.' If he sees a crowd of heathens, he should say: 'Your mother shall be ashamed,' etc." This profound saying served as the foundation upon which wove various images of the life of the Jewish people in exile. I spoke for two straight hours during which I led my audience through different states of mind, causing them to weep and to laugh, to be sad and be happy.

After the sermon the audience expressed its appreciation with heartfelt blessings of *Yeshar Koah*, many embraced and kissed me and shook my hand with much love.

At that time I felt my fate was cast, I am to stay in America. I am a free citizen; fear of the policemen shall no longer terrify me. From now on I shall no longer

speak in allegorical terms, my tongue shall know no fetters, it shall be free to speak according to its own will, not to follow that of others.

The next day articles in praise of my talent were published in the Jewish and foreign press, including even the *Deutsche Staats Zeitung* and the *New York World*. Soon I was asked to come to various cities to address their audiences. The first city to invite me was Baltimore, at the initiative of the group of veterans of *Hovevei Zion* who were living there at the time.

I was in no hurry to leave New York. I wanted to learn more about the nature and character of the new life in this new land. I delivered dozens of sermons in various synagogues some of them large like the synagogue on Eldridge Street, the synagogue of the Kalwarie community and the like.

Wherever I went the large signs of *Kosher* on all establishments dealing with foodstuffs, and the title of "The Workingman's Friend" on all saloons, upset me. It seems that of the ten *kabs* [measures] of *Kashruth* and friendship to the workingman that descended to the world, nine were taken by New York and one by the rest of the world . . .

CHAPTER 35

When I was still in Russia I read a description in the Hebrew papers *Ha-Tzfira* and *Ha-Melitz* of the grand reception the New York Jewish Community gave in honor of its first Rabbi, the Rabbi of Vilna, the Great Rabbi Ya'acov Yoseph who was appointed Chief Rabbi of New York. This great Rabbi was well known all over Lithuania as a brilliant student of *Halacha* and an extremely talented interpreter of *Aggadah*. In his praise the people gave him the name of Rabbi Yankale the Sharp Minded. Bringing Rabbi Ya'acov Yoseph over was no easy task for the community of New York as it meant removing him from his seat of honor in Vilna, "The Jerusalem of Lithuania," to the newly established community of New York. He received a grand regal reception when he disembarked. The representatives of synagogues and congregations came to greet him. Hundreds of carriages (there were no motor cars at the time), and tens of thousands of people escorted him to the living quarters prepared for him and his family. Many kissed his coat tails. They carried him from the carriage to the house with tears in their eyes. Not all were fortunate enough to see him and greet him personally. Legends of his greatness in Torah and wisdom started to spread. The reception for the Chief Rabbi was carried out in American style, with great pomp, loud announcements and such tumult that the Christians started to take interest in the "Chief Rabbi" since the English press published articles in his praise.

Yet, like all sensational movements that start with fire and tumult and end in cold and freezing, so has been the tragic fate of the great Rabbi. His aura and glory soon faded. The papers started to mock and ridicule him. Suddenly it turned out that all "The Holy Beasts" that rose in his honor with "great tumult" did so only for their own honor and benefit. They were not concerned with the Rabbi but with the business of *Kashruth* [dietary laws]; they did not need his knowledge of Torah and his wisdom but rather his signature of authorizations—*hechsher*—guaranteeing the ritual cleanliness of meat and foodstuffs. The pernicious cry of the Israelites in the desert "if only we had meat to eat" burst out with vehemence, and seals of authorization, *hechshers*, butcher shops and slaughter houses bearing the sign "authorized by the chief Rabbi," sprung all over the Jewish neighborhoods in the East Side of New York. Even today, twenty years after the death of the Chief Rabbi one can still find these authorizations—*Hechsher*—on the windows of a number of commercial establishments dealing in *Kosher* commodities.

The Chief Rabbi was shocked at the outrages preformed around him and in his name. He realized he had made a mistake when he decided to trade Vilna for New York. In his heart he sensed the disgraceful acts carried out by his entourage. He started to feel and understand, but it took some time. He could no longer save the situation. His great heart burst inside him and he lost the feeling of his limbs one by one.

It is in this deplorable state that I found him lying in bed, lonely and neglected. When I introduced myself he sat up on the bed, embraced and kissed me as he looked at me with eyes full of tears. Using no words his gloomy look said: "Woe to me that you have seen me in such a state!"

At that very moment I recalled the saying of our sages: "How is a scholar regarded by the ignorant?—At first like a golden ladle; if he converses with him, like a silver ladle; if he [the scholar] derives benefit from him, like an earthen ladle, which once broken cannot be mended." So was the fate of the great Rabbi. The communal workers of New York and their patrons made him into a "fragile potsherd." The Rabbi lay in his bed ill and despondent and the members of his household lived in deprivation and poverty.

I had no quiet, no rest. I did all I could. In my sermons I alerted public opinion to the terrible state of the sick Rabbi. I also attended a number of meetings of the communal workers on the East Side and something was indeed done to alleviate the suffering and pain of the great man.

"How dull-witted are those people," I exclaimed in one of my sermons, quoting the saying of our sages, "'who stand up [in deference] to the Scroll of Torah, but do not stand up [in deference] to a great personage.' You respect the Torah scroll, pour a lot of money out of your pockets for synagogues, and do not concern yourself with the plight of this great man of Israel!"

The last days of the Chief Rabbi were terrible and tragic indeed, and his death and funeral were even worse. The funeral turned into a national disaster, an insult to the people, and an anti-Semitic riot in the land of freedom, in America.

"The chief Rabbi is gone," "The great Rabbi has departed," "Rabbi Ya'acov Yoseph is no longer with us"— so announced large headlines in all the newspapers of New York on Wednesday, the 24th day of the month of *Av* [Aug. 15], 1902. The distressing information spread rapidly all over the city. Thousands and tens of thousands of people from New York and the nearby towns streamed to the East Side, to the home of the Chief Rabbi, to pay their last respects to the great deceased and fulfill the ancient dictum [based on the names of three sequential portions in the book of Leviticus]: "After a man's death of his holiness do speak." All the streets were full of people, a live wall of human beings stood upright, no one could leave or enter.

"People, children of Israel" my heart cried inside me, "where were you yesterday and the day before, where were you a month ago and a year ago, when the Rabbi needed help and companionship? Had but one percent among you come at that time, you would have had no need to crowd together for a funeral now. . . . "

It was with great effort that the police managed to maintain order among the mourners, and to make way for the coffin and hundreds of carriages. A large group of pupils from *Talmud Torah* schools walked in front of the coffin reciting Psalms. The procession followed by thousands of mourners flowed through East Broadway to Grand Street, all walked in silence, their backs bent, their faces darkened with grief.

When the procession arrived at Hoe's Factory where hundreds of German workers were employed, suddenly as though an earthquake started, an avalanche of stones, wood planks, mud and mire poured down on the coffin and on the heads of the mourners from the windows of the factory. The crowds became as agitated as a stormy sea, and within a minute hundreds of glass panes in the windows of the factory were smashed. The crowd stormed the factory, broke its doors and a bloody fight ensued between the Jewish multitude and the factory workers. There were many wounded on both sides till the policemen pushed their way in, arrested the culprits and calmed the agitated masses. The mourners then went on their way to the Grand Ferry towards Brooklyn.

Thousands and myriads filled the cemetery. The coffin was lowered into the ground with great respect and in total silence. The entire crowd wept out loud upon hearing the words of the speakers, who overwhelmed them with their eulogies. I was one of the speakers.

Just this did my heart cry out within me: "Where had all of you been when the great Rabbi was still with us, alive and tormented . . . ?"

[. . .] Where then did the tens of thousands of Jewish children in New York study? Who were the educators of the new generation? There were only two *Talmud Torah* schools, no Hebrew Schools whatsoever, only few old style *Hadorim* and yet the children of Israel did study Torah, but under a reversed system. It was not the children who went to the Torah, it was rather the Torah that came to them. It came to their homes. Decrepit old men, weaklings recently arrived from overseas, who lacked the strength to go from door to door with merchandise, peddled Torah instead. Equipped with a prayer book and Pentateuch under their arm they would go from street to street, knock on doors, spend fifteen to twenty minutes in each place teaching one or two children. They would read a bit of Hebrew or translate a verse from the *chumash* [Pentateuch], and then proceed to other homes to teach other children Torah and the wage thereof was a quarter or a half of a dollar a week.

It is not difficult to imagine how beneficial this learning is for a child who just came back from public school and is suddenly placed in the hands of an old feeble Jew, speaking to him in a mixture of Hebrew and Yiddish, neither of which he understands. The child, naturally confused, regards his teacher with fear and his mind does not apprehend what this strange Jew is talking about and what he wants from him. Once he gets used to this instructor he mocks him and his teaching.

A story is told about a teacher-peddler of this type who sat in an apartment on Henry Street in the middle of the day as the children were leaving school. He was instructing a pupil in a separate room, when suddenly the child's father heard the *melamed* cry out "*Gewald*, Help!" The master of the house opened the door of the room and was shocked to see his son, his beloved child, holding his teacher's beard and pulling at it with his two strong hands.

"My son," the father scolded, "what are you doing? Stop that!"

The sobbing child answered:

"Believe me, Papa, he started. . ."

While every man of Israel who still has a spark of religion and national feeling in his heart would bemoan the notoriously chaotic Hebrew education, he would also be totally shocked when seeing and hearing what takes place in the public meetings for the youngsters held in various halls. This was the notorious period of destruction when balls took place on *Yom Kippur* [the Day of Atonement], when blasphemy and curses were directed at the Heavens and a furious war against religion and tradition was waged. Ardent speakers "set their mouths against heaven" and desecrated everything holy with words of contempt and vituperation, both orally and in writing. One of the newspapers, of extreme liberal inclinations, would publish a series of articles on Saturdays, exposing the lack of modesty of our Mothers—Sarah, Rebecca, Rachel and Leah. The articles were full of venom, written with hair-splitting left-wing folly and nonsense. [. . .]

CHAPTER 39

I had no personal acquaintance with the Reform Movement. I had heard about it but not seen it, so to speak. I read a lot about the Reform Movement in the nineteenth century including the biographies of its founders: Holdheim, Geiger, Einhorn etc. I strived to understand the struggle in the camp of Israel during the initial stage of the movement's growth, the arguments that were raised for and against it. I was aware of the struggle Rabbi [Shimshon—eds.] Rephael Hirsch waged against it with all his might and soul. In the 1880's the great author Peretz Smolenskin came out against these "masters of prayer" as he named them, in his periodical *Ha-Shachar* with all his national fervor. I knew all this full well. But reading and hearing are as far from seeing, as theory is from practice. And we are not to judge a matter by hearsay alone.

In Chicago I had the opportunity to see Reform Judaism as it really was. I got to know its rabbis, saw them at work and behind the pulpit, studied their "Prayer Books," and listened to the music of the organ accompanied by a women's choir. I must truthfully admit that all these phenomena, complete with their external glamour, made a terrible impression on me. Grey temples with no devotees to pray in them; learned rabbis with no true sense of the Torah; "Prayer Books" without prayers; music without a Jewish tone—Jews devoid of Judaism. Zion and Jerusalem were eradicated from the prayers that were recited almost completely in English, while the 1% that miraculously survived in Hebrew within the skimpy prayer book seemed weird and strange to the congregants, since most of them had no knowledge of Hebrew whatsoever, and Hebrew letters seemed to them like Chinese or Japanese characters. The original verse of the *Shema* or *Kedushah* prayers was not recited by the congregation but came trilled from the mouths of the Christian singers accompanied by the organ. As though the skimpy size of the translated prayer book was not enough, the rabbi had to announce before each and every prayer: turn to page so and so. A chill of 40 degrees below zero, a true Siberian chill, prevailed in the Temple during services. There was no warm feeling, no pouring out of the soul, no eye shining with a spark of prayer to a living God, no indication of spiritual elevation, not even in the prayers of the cantor. The service was quiet, cold, monotonous and moribund from beginning to end, frozen, cold, dead.

The reader can easily imagine my mood as I went, for the first time in my life to pray the *Sabbath prayers on Sunday*; the synagogue bore the name "Sinai," the name of the Holy Mount, the mountain God had chosen to dwell upon, and from which peak to bestow the Sabbath on the world. And the Sinai Synagogue is closed on the Sabbath Day. . . .

How great the disgrace and immense the pain to see a faith four thousand years old committing suicide and selling its soul to endear itself to its wayward daughter so that she say "how fair you are"; that very daughter who suckled from her breasts and finally bit her nipples to bloodshed, and the blood is still flowing . . .

Good Heavens! How distorted must a heart be to substitute the Sabbath for Sunday; only a fool would not understand that work precedes rest, a man tired of his labor is in need of rest. And so have we been commanded: "Six days you shall labor and do all your work, but the seventh day is a Sabbath." Placing rest before work is madness indeed!

It is self-evident that the change was but a spiteful action brought about by the wayward daughter: "You, mother, were commanded to rest on the Seventh Day, and so I, to bring about your fierce anger, shall rest on Sunday. . . ." Till this day there are hundreds of thousands of Christians who cannot accept the strange idea of placing rest before labor and therefore observe the Sabbath day. And here, in Chicago, the Temple of "Sinai" has replaced the Sabbath with Sunday! [. . .]

After the service at the Temple I had the honor of being asked to report to the Reform Rabbi, the great scholar Emil G. Hirsch. He was a young man at the time, handsome and strong, a great scholar and an excellent speaker. He was extremely knowledgeable in Judaic studies, proficient in Bible, a connoisseur of the Talmud and spoke fine and fluent Hebrew, which was the language we spoke to each other. The man had a sense of humor and appreciated a good joke. Yet all these fine qualities of his increased my feeling of animosity towards the Reform movement and its supporters even more. "How does he find the service in the Temple and its order, Sir," Hirsch asked me, "it seems to me that this is the first time he has visited a Reform Temple. Tell me the truth, the entire truth: what impression has all this made on you?"

"My dear Doctor," I answered, "you have asked a difficult question. To tell the truth is my duty as a human being. And yet I cannot do so from a moral point of view. I am your guest Sir, and *derech erets* [proper behavior—eds.] preceded the Torah. My impressions are still fresh, so I have not yet clarified them to myself fully. I am seeing this type of Judaism for the first time and cannot pass judgment on it. There is only one thing. I shall allow myself to say to you, Sir, esteemed Dr., and hope for your forgiveness."

"Say whatever is on your mind, speak and I shall listen," was the serious answer the Reform rabbi gave me.

"Today, as I visited his Temple, I learned that I am a complete desecrator of the Sabbath while you, Sir, are a lawful observer. I work on the Sabbath, furthermore I work on the Sabbath more than I do on weekdays, while, you, Sir, close your Temple 'Sinai' on the Sabbath and open it only on Sunday."

A smile appeared on his lips; he understood my message . . .

I met him several times in the years to come; we addressed the same meetings and shared the same platform, so that I got to know him. He was a wonderful speaker, and as good a writer in his articles written for his English weekly *Reform Advocate*. And yet he had one drawback both orally and in writing: he was inconsistent, disloyal to himself and his views. He never produced two articles or made two speeches that resembled each other in their spirit and principal ideas. You could not recognize his different speeches as products of the same orator or his articles as products of one writer. One day he would deliver a stormy speech from the pulpit against the adherents of the Jewish national idea and the Zionists, pouring burning fire on them out of his very mouth; a week later he would praise the Zionist ideal and express his great enthusiasm at the beauty of the national sentiment as though he were a comrade of Herzl and Nordau.

There was a diligent journalist in Chicago whose goal it was to point out the contradictions between one Hirsch and another. He would attack Hirsch almost weekly by demonstrating his contradictions. It was the old-time Zionist and fine journalist Mr. Leon Zolotkoff who did this. I used to enjoy reading his argumentative articles against Dr. Hirsch very much. [. . .]

CHAPTER 40

From Chicago I went to Cleveland. The Jews of Cleveland gave me a cordial reception. Among them were Mr. Berman, the *shochet* [religious slaughterer], a clever and fine-looking Jew, father-in-law of the famous physicians Burstein and Biskind; the affluent Mr. Brudno; Mr. Joshua Rocker, editor of the *Yidishe Velt*, a clever and accomplished man of Hungarian descent who was closely associated with the Lithuanian Jews; Mr. Laufman, the *Maskil* and several others greeted me when I arrived and kept me company constantly during the two months I spent in Cleveland.

On the first evening of my stay the Presidents of the different synagogues came to see me and asked that I speak to their congregations. Each one introduced himself to me as follows: Mr. So and So, President of the Russian Synagogue; Mr. So and So, President of the Lithuanian Synagogue, the Polish Synagogue, the Hungarian, the Dissenting Hungarian etc.

"Sirs!" I addressed them with a question I had also asked in London, England, "which one of you is President of the Jewish Synagogue? I am indeed surprised, your synagogues in Cleveland belong to various nationalities, but where are the synagogues of the Jews? The names of the synagogues reflect our sorry state, the separation and weakness, legacy of our long, dark exile. Scattered in different countries and amidst different peoples for hundreds of years, we were asphyxiated with their languages, customs and names, to the extent that even when we left those dark and ignoble lands and came to America, the Land of Liberty, where we build our synagogues unhindered yet still give them the names of the Lands of Darkness whence we have fled. Why should we give our temples foreign names? What have we, here in the Land of Liberty, to do with Lithuania, that small, poor and primitive land? What have we to do with Russia, the Land of pitch darkness? What have the minor Polish noblemen to do with our synagogues? Even the Magyars, to the best of my judgment, have not merited a remembrance and name in our synagogues. Have you ever heard, gentlemen, Presidents of Synagogues, of names such as Russian-Turks, Turkish-Russians, Italian-French, French-Italians, English-Germans and German-English? Yet we, the ancient People of Israel, are crumbling to bits: Russian Jews, Polish Jews, Lithuanian, Hungarian, Turkish, Persian and Greek. And where are the Jews, the Children of Israel? Already in New York and Chicago I was disgusted to hear of large synagogues serving affluent communities that bore the name of small towns in Russia, like: 'The Kalwarie Synagogue,' 'The Marijampole Synagogue.' Do you know what these names mean? Kalwarie is the name of the mountain [Calvary], upon which that man delivered his sermons, in which we have no share. What have we to do with this Mount that we should have a large synagogue named for it? 'Marijampole' means 'City of Mary,' and this does not refer to the prophetess, sister of Moses and Aharon, but to the mother of that man, who is not to be counted among the People of Israel. Why should we, the Jews of America, name a large synagogue in Chicago 'The Marijampole Synagogue'?"

My guests, the Presidents of the Synagogues, listened to me. Some did not know what I was talking about, others looked at each other with surprise: "What does this strange Jew want of us? Why doesn't he like the names of our synagogues?" But my friend Joshua Rocker, the Hungarian with the soul of a Lithuanian Jew, was my interpreter that night and explained my intention to them very well, so that even the President of the Dissenting Hungarian Synagogue started to grasp my ideas and national feelings.

They arranged the order of my sermons among themselves—in what synagogue I am to speak first and in which last. And so I spent two months in Cleveland and delivered twenty sermons in the different congregations. [...]

NOTES

Unless indicated by the editors, words in brackets appear in the original translations.

1. This rabbi was receiving food through two holes, one for meat and the other for dairy products, as he was completely sequestered in his home (translator's note).

Translated by Isaac Schwartz and Zviah Nardi.

Other works by Masliansky: *Kitvei Masliansky*, 3 vols. (1929); *The Sermons of Rabbi Zvi Hirsh Masliansky* (2009).

Alfred Döblin

1878–1957

The German novelist Alfred Döblin grew up in poverty in Berlin, where he trained and practiced as a physician. With little Jewish education and no contact with Jewish religious life, he took an interest in Jewish matters for a short period in the 1920s. He made a two-month tour of Poland in 1924, recording his impressions of Polish Jewry, on which he based his *Journey to Poland* (1925). A central figure in German modernism, Döblin's most famous novel is *Berlin-Alexanderplatz* (1929). He spent the Nazi years in exile in Paris and then in Los Angeles, where he converted to Roman Catholicism in 1940. After the war, he returned to Germany and continued to write.

The Jewish District of Warsaw

1925

[...] The eve of the Jewish Day of Atonement. In the morning, I wander down Gesia Street, a long thoroughfare. A few stores are still open, the majority are already closing. A tremendous human surging fills the street, the trolley is mobbed. I walk past an old, long building, a military prison; red iron crates are attached to the windows; the light enters the cells only from above. One shop is called Kirschensaft, a barber's name is Nordwind. Many men coming my way—only Jews—have a slip of paper on their lapel. I don't understand; is this a demonstration? The side streets teem incredibly. A graveyard announces itself with stonecutters' yards. This is the eve of the Day of Atonement; the Jewish Day of Judgment is imminent, people have to repent, cleanse themselves. But first they have to appease their dead.

Now they are going to the cemetery, to their dead, begging them for forgiveness, pleading with them to plead with God on their behalf. A human torrent is surging toward Okopawa Street. That's where the big cemetery is located; it's surrounded by a low red wall; the iron gate is open. Inside, a forecourt with benches occupied by men, mostly in caftans and skullcaps or vizored caps; a few are smoking cigarettes. Along the wall, at the tree trunks, between the trees, men stand, alone or in groups, each man holding a book, murmuring, humming, rocking, shifting from foot to foot. Here, I already notice the grumbling noise that comes from my right, from the cemetery: individual cries, very loud, disjointed talking, also chanting. There must be a large crowd, a very large crowd here; I don't see it as yet. It's like being near a large assembly. Sometimes the singing, calling, the general confused din are so intense that the place sounds like a county fair. The human torrent veers right along the wall. The main current flows between the graves, a broad triumphal avenue. Rich monuments, marble plaques, black and white, loom up here, Hebrew and Polish inscriptions, many only Hebrew, long texts. One high plaque is covered with a scaffolding; the visitors surround the grave, reading, pointing: "Peretz, Peretz." I see another strange monument: a serpent twisting round a tree trunk, plus a broken wheel, a broken wagon shaft. Another gigantic plaque with a long Hebrew text; above it, the gold image of a crowned stag and a hand holding a knife.

I am startled by a woman's fierce, piercing shriek. It begins and ends, often renewed, with a long painful chant. No one pays it any heed. And as I thread my way through the rows of graves, I find a headstone; but on the ground—everything in the cemetery is covered with green grass, with lovely, leveling grass, with rampant meadow flowers, white, red, blue—on the ground lies an elegantly dressed young woman next to an elderly one. The older woman, curled, clinging tight to the bottom of the headstone (I can't see her face, her head and shoulders are covered by a large black shawl), she screams, calls, calls, moans. She calls, in Yiddish:

"Father, our beloved father, you were such a good man, you sat next to me in the room, all these years, in the shop. I've stayed here. I'm here. Help me to get the children to study so that they'll be well off. Life is hard. Life is so hard, Sarah is here. We're not well off. Why did you die, for us. I didn't do anything bad to you."

Now and then, the younger woman sits up, blows her nose, wipes her eyes, lies down again.

And when I follow the bend of the wall, when I leave the row of marble graves, the boulevard of the notables, I can no longer see anything of the burial mounds. I find a large agitated meadow, with small rocks, sunken into the earth and edged with larger ones. It looks wild, churned up. Men with prayer books stand here and there, behind the gravestones. And from all over the meadow, even from where I see no people, I hear chanting, shrieking, wailing, moaning. Like single plumes of smoke rising up and turning into a dense cloud. Now and again, something emerges from the green, a back, a head, a face. Always women, girls, in shawls, plumed hats, under the old flowery wigs. They lie on the graves, weeping, lamenting, accusing themselves, calling, appeasing the dead. Many call in a simple tone of pain and lament. Many women use a liturgical singsong, similar to the chanting in temple. This is the place where they pray aloud; the divine service of the women is over the graves. The men with the prayer books stand upright, murmuring, bowing earnestly and solemnly; at their feet, the women and the girls huddle in the grass, lamenting, moaning, emitting the shrill singsong.

More have now arrived, in hired carriages; automobiles, private vehicles, the elegant men, the women. The women walk next to the men. With reddened eyes, twitching lips, they stand at the graves, staring at the plaques. A dreadful staccato moaning comes from one side. At a column, a broken one, stands a woman in modern dress. She clutches the smooth column with hands gloved in fine yellow leather. The moans emerge from her, staccato, helpless. Sometimes, gasping for air, she removes the handkerchief from her face; her face is all puffed up. She can't hold back her moans. Now, her hands slide away, down the column, she drops to the grass, over the grave, her face down, wailing. From elsewhere comes a female voice, virtually scolding at intervals. An old wrinkled woman kneels and lies there; she screams loud, barking, always with brief pauses. She embraces the headstone with both arms. A group of men in a circle around a grave; rocking with their books; one man reads aloud, resonant. The graves are all set up in one direction, overgrown, overrun with thick grass. Raw broken bricks, sometimes heavy pebbles, lie on many headstones, sometimes even on the marble monuments; they hem in sheaves of grass that have been placed there as tokens. White tissue paper has been put around one grave; the paper bears black letters, carrying its plea across the grave. Many people walk about, seeking, pushing apart the grass that already completely shrouds the graves.

By the time I pull myself out of the sea of murmuring, moaning, female shrieking, and push my way toward the exit—it is almost eleven A.M.—all the beggars in town have gathered along the main cemetery road, and so have the adolescent representatives of the Jewish welfare organizations. Today, people give, as if hoping to redeem themselves from punishments for the wicked things they once did to the people who are now dead and for all their sinning of the past year. The day of the dead and the poor. Scores of beggars, blind people, deaf people now lie in front of the rows of graves. They stand in the center of the thoroughfare, dividing the human torrent. They push their way in between the people. Calling, lamenting, grabbing, seizing the hands of passersby; they are relentless—like the self-reproaches of these people. There are mutes, who babble as they stretch out their hands. One of them babbles a powerful litany. From everywhere, you hear: "Jews, *rakhmones* [pity]! Jewish children, give!" Dreadfully, dreadfully ragged women carry children swathed in shawls; yellow crones stand in their hard wigs. A large circle of people has formed around a marble grave: a young man lies in front of it, blowing foam. His arms and legs jerk rhythmically, his hands follow slackly. His cap lies next to him. I glanced at him on the way in; he is still lying there. His cap is filled with banknotes; money keeps flying down to him amid words of pity. His thick foam moves with his breathing; it's soapsuds, the man is a professional, a swindler.

Wallets and breast pockets are opened everywhere, bills and coins fall, some beggars have whole piles of paper. The male and female helpers of Jewish organizations stand under the trees, holding cans. They have pins and blue, red, white slips of paper in readiness; the slips that I saw out on the street. The helpers call, head toward the passersby, plunge the pins into coat collars.

At the exit, the mob of people is dreadful. A hazardous thronging. The shrieks are tremendous; the young helpers follow the passersby into the street. A car park has accumulated outside. The trolleys run more often, but without reducing the huge crowd.

Cold shivers run up and down my spine when I see and hear these things. I ride back on the trolley, climb the hotel stairs, sit in my room; it takes me awhile to collect my thoughts. This is something horrible. It is something primordial, atavistic. Does this have anything to do with Judaism? These are living vestiges of ancient notions! These are vestiges of the fear of the dead, the fear of wandering souls. A feeling handed down to the members of this nation with their religion. It is the remnant of a different religion, animism, a cult of the dead.

In the evening, I go to a *shul*. Across the courtyard of an apartment house into a long narrow room with electric lighting. It is crowded with people. The women's gallery runs upstairs. At the entrance, there are posters by a Palestinian rabbi and his portrait: an appeal for donations to a fund; this *shul* belongs to a Zionist congregation. My guide and I have a hard time pushing our way through the wall of men, squeezing past the *bimah*, the enclosed platform in the front third of the room, where they read aloud, from the Torah; until I arrive at the front wall next to the cantor and his small choir.

Amid the utter hush of the assembly, the cantor intones the ancient Kol Nidre prayer. He is squat, has a white beard, a white coat, a prayer shawl over it. He wears a skullcap, it is made of velvet, embroidered with gold threads. The prayer shawls of the other men are simple and plain. A few wear elaborate ones with silver embroidery. The cantor has begun very softly. He chants the same prayer once again, louder. And now, for a third time, in a full lamenting voice.

This chant ushers in the evening, intensely and powerfully. The people do not seem consistently anxious and agitated. Here and there, I see them chatting. The small choir gets into gear; the teenagers and young men sing from memory. The cantor conducts them himself; during the singing, he caresses this boy or that, nodding to them. Then comes a passage that forms the climax of the evening. The white-bearded man, as a preparation, has drawn his prayer shawl all the way over his head. Others in the room do likewise. The cloth drops down over his forehead; he squeezes the cloth together under his chin. And what I then hear, what he then sings is an echo of the wailing and yammering that I heard at the cemetery this morning. But now it's in the chant. In this ardor, the man sucks himself in just as he has drawn himself into his shawl, in an ardor that moves everyone. He truly weeps, he truly sobs. Sobbing has become singing. Singing borne by sobbing. The song sinks into its primal element. He trills; his voice drawls down level by level. Then, desperate and pleading, he throws it high again, it sinks back, woeful. And again he throws it high. The weeping overflows into the women's gallery. Like the man, who never yields in his yammering and urging, who intensifies them, the women, overhead, give in completely. Their weeping

grows louder, stronger, drowning out his weeping. Ultimately, a truly anxious universal weeping has spread out, reverberating through the room. The men rocking in their prayer shawls sing, deep and dismal. The head of the bearded old man is still bent back, his eyes are shut. His tears flow visibly down his cheeks. Then he grows stiller. Solemn chants come, also strange and joyous songs. And in the end, when everything is over and they are leaving, someone launches into a song. And old and young, male and female join in: the proud, hopeful "Hatikvah," the Zionist anthem.

In the courtyard, I see bright windows; lights burning in them. I look through a window; men in prayer shawls are sitting there on a bench: a Hasidic *shtibl* [prayer room]. They sit there praying all night long. The next morning, I reenter the Zionist prayer room. Here too, many have remained overnight. Horribly stuffy air; some lie with their heads on the benches; the white-bearded man leads the prayers. On Nalewki Street, I walk through a house lobby. The vast courtyards are lifeless. A boy jumps around, wearing a round black skullcap, a long black belted coat. He's pale, scrofulous, dirty. With my companion, I walk across the second empty gigantic courtyard; an elegant young Jewish woman shows us the way. The rear wing contains a large prayer room of the Gura people, followers of the great, the mightiest rebbe, the one from Gura Kalwarja. A couple of boys run in front of a door, dressed like the scrofulous one, but in nice white woolen stockings, and they wear slippers.

And, as we begin to climb up the dark stairs, along worn steps between crumbling masonry, this is a very special place. Loud, indeed shrill singing, no, not singing, already resonated across the courtyard. It resonated from here. Now, down the steps, comes a wild confused shouting, then a murmuring with individual cries, a sonorous tangle that sometimes fuses into a single noise and roar. The men stand and sit on the stairs; we have to step gingerly across legs. The entrance is two flights up. There is an awful thronging and almost no possibility of penetrating it. But my companion is bold; I'm embarrassed because our clothes stand out, West European; here, everyone wears a skullcap and a caftan. Then, when I stand among them in a large room, which opens into an even larger one, I recognize how festively earnest, profoundly earnest—no, agitated—these people are. Now, I also realize what their beards mean. You understand the beard when you see these men standing there in their big wide prayer shawls, which they have drawn over their heads. These are Arabian heads, these are men of the great sandy desert. I can picture the huge mounted camels next to them. Their sharp richly expressive overly lively faces. Something mighty, lordly, heroic lies upon them. I can see them as warriors; these are not men on Nalewki Street in Warsaw. So many old men, dour men loom here, facing the large adjacent room, which sometimes emits an especially loud lone voice, the cantor's, no doubt. Innumerable boys read next to the adults; everyone is tensely, intensely concentrated. The men all read the same passage, but each on his own, a priest to himself; you can tell by how tremendously serious they are. The worshippers here rock in a peculiarly sharp and expansive way. At one point in the prayers, one man suddenly kneels, then, tumultuously, all the others; they get back on their feet, slowly and chaotically. The simple brown-bearded man next to me prays strong and loud. Now his voice changes: I can't follow what he reads: he weeps. The others also have broken voices. Now their voices rise in a chorus, an ecstatic tangle begins, a shrill chaos. Mute rocking, then sudden shrieks. And now, what's this; a singing, in unison, a joyous song. The place livens up, it's like a dance, an exuberant rejoicing. It starts with words, then, like laughter, ends as "lalala."

The people surge and billow. Men keep pushing from front to back, from the neighboring room into this one. They push all the way back to the back wall. A faucet is running there; they return with dripping hands, which they hold aloft, shaking them dry. They have to wash after every contamination of their hands, even if they have only touched their head. They all wear white coats, with prayer shawls over them; I see their caps and coats hanging on the wall in the large room. How dignified they stand. The black glow in the eyes of these simple men. How proud and self-assured the boy next to them prays with his full round beardless face.

The terrible stairs going down. In the courtyard, through a ground-floor window, I see absorbed men sitting in prayer shawls. They are followers of a different, not so powerful rebbe. Down the streets to a different rear wing, as woeful and decrepit as the first. And how densely beleaguered the stone stairs are here. The whole Jewish nation is praying, they all lie down before their god. They pray on the stairs. We climb up between them. In the corridor upstairs, older boys punch and fight one another, trying to push into the *shtibl*. An old man intervenes with terse words and ominous glares. At the doorway to this apartment, the men sit on the floor. In the wide vestibule, they huddle along the wall, their heads wrapped up in their prayer shawls. Inside, in the small room, they stand cheek by jowl, holding their books. No one prevents us from entering; but every so often we receive an astonished, unfriendly scowl. And now an old man sitting on the floor gapes at me for a long time, especially at my feet: "Shoes are not worn here." We quietly push our way downstairs.

On this eve of the Day of Atonement, the Polish air force scheduled a recruitment concert at the Philharmonic. I'm told that only eleven people showed up; this is told not without pleasure. In the morning, a communist scandal: outside the prayer rooms, Jewish communists hawk gazettes with caricatures attacking "clericalism." The news vendors are driven away; they yell, "Religion is the opium of the people," fistfights break out. At a workers' kitchen, Jews have eaten and smoked on this high holiday; a brawl here too. Jews emerging from pastry shops were harassed by pious Jews. [. . .]

Translated by Joachim Neugroschel.

Other works by Döblin: *Wallenstein* (1920); *November 1918: A German Revolution*, 4 vols. (1983–1987); *The Three Leaps of Wang Lun* (1991).

Osip Mandelstam

1891–1938

Osip Mandelstam grew up in St. Petersburg and studied at the Sorbonne and Heidelberg University. In 1911, he was baptized, and thus was able to attend St. Petersburg University. Mandelstam was a founder of the Acmeist school of poetry, in response to the Futurist movement. While not fully supportive of the Bolshevik takeover, he nonetheless remained in Soviet Russia, settled in Moscow in 1922, and began to explore Jewish themes in his prose. His poetry, however, was dominated by Helleno-Christian mythology. As a result of the patronage of Nikolai Bukharin, Mandelstam's poetry and literary criticism were read by a niche of the Soviet intelligentsia, and he made a living from translation. Mandelstam's contribution to anti-Stalinist rhetoric precipitated his arrest and exile in 1934. During his exile in Voronezh and thereafter, under unbearable mental stress, Mandelstam attempted to find favor in the eyes of the Stalinist regime and present himself as a rehabilitated Soviet man. In 1938, he was denounced by his colleagues in the Writers' Union and sentenced to five years of labor. Mandelstam died in a transit camp that same year. His widow, Nadezhda Mandelstam, memorized his work and preserved it through decades of repression until eventual publication beginning in the 1960s.

The Noise of Time
1925

VI. The Judaic Chaos

There once arrived at our house a person completely unknown to us, an unmarried lady of about forty, in a little red hat and with a sharp chin and angry dark eyes. On the strength of her having come from the small town of Shavli, she demanded that we find her a husband in Petersburg. She spent a week in the house before we managed to send her packing. From time to time wandering authors would turn up—bearded and long-skirted people, Talmudic philosophers, peddlers of their own printed aphorisms and dicta. They would leave us autographed copies and complain of being tormented by their evil wives. Once or twice in my life I was taken to a synagogue as if to a concert. There was a long wait to get in—one practically had to buy tickets from scalpers—and all that I saw and heard there caused me to return home in a heavy stupor. There is a Jewish quarter in Petersburg: it begins just behind the Mariinskij Theater, where the ticket-scalpers freeze, beyond the prison angel of the Litovskij Castle, which was burned down in the Revolution. There on Torgovaja Street one sees Jewish shop-signs with pictures of a bull and a cow, women with an abundance of false hair showing under their kerchiefs, and, mincing along in overcoats reaching down to the ground, old men full of experience and philoprogeneity. The synagogue with its conical caps and onion domes loses itself like some elegant exotic fig tree amongst the shabby buildings. Velveteen berets with pompoms, attendants and choristers on the point of physical exhaustion, clusters of seven-branched candelabra, tall velvet headdresses. The Jewish ship, with its sonorous alto choirs and the astonishing voices of its children, lays on all sail, split as it is by some ancient storm into male and female halves. Having blundered into the women's balcony, I edged along stealthily as a thief, hiding behind rafters. The Cantor, like Samson, collapsed the leonine building, he was answered by the velvet headdress, and the awesome equilibrium of vowels and consonants in the impecca-

bly enunciated words imparted to the chants an invincible power. But how offensive was the crude speech of the rabbi—though it was not ungrammatical; how vulgar when he uttered the words "His Imperial Highness," how utterly vulgar all that he said! And all of a sudden two top-hatted gentlemen, splendidly dressed and glossy with wealth, with the refined movements of men of the world, touch the heavy book, step out of the circle and on behalf of everyone, with the authorization and commission of everyone, perform some honorary ritual, the principal thing in the ceremony. Who is that? Baron Ginzburg. And that? Varshavskij.

In my childhood I absolutely never heard Yiddish; only later did I hear an abundance of that melodious, always surprised and disappointed, interrogative language with its sharp accents on the weakly stressed syllables. The speech of the father and the speech of the mother—does not our language feed throughout all its long life on the confluence of these two, do they not compose its character? The speech of my mother was clear and sonorous without the least foreign admixture, with rather wide and too open vowels—the literary Great Russian language. Her vocabulary was poor and restricted, the locutions were trite, but it was a language, it had roots and confidence. Mother loved to speak and took joy in the roots and sounds of her Great Russian speech, impoverished by intellectual clichés. Was she not the first of her whole family to achieve pure and clear Russian sounds? My father had absolutely no language; his speech was tongue-tie and languagelessness. The Russian speech of a Polish Jew? No. The speech of a German Jew? No again. Perhaps a special Courland accent? I never heard such. A completely abstract, counterfeit language, the ornate and twisted speech of an autodidact, where normal words are intertwined with the ancient philosophical terms of Herder, Leibnitz, and Spinoza, the capricious syntax of a Talmudist, the artificial, not always finished sentence: it was anything in the world, but not a language, neither Russian nor German.

In essence, my father transferred me to a totally alien century and distant, although completely un-Jewish, atmosphere. These were, if you will, the purest eighteenth or even seventeenth century of an enlightened ghetto somewhere in Hamburg. Religious interests had been eliminated completely. The philosophy of the Enlightenment was transformed into intricate Talmudist pantheism. Somewhere in the vicinity Spinoza is breeding his spiders in a jar. One has a presentiment of

Rousseau and his natural man. Everything fantastically abstract, intricate, and schematic. A fourteen-year-old boy, whom they had been training as a rabbi and had forbidden to read worldly books, runs off to Berlin and ends up in a higher Talmudic school, where there had gathered a number of such stubborn, rational youths, who had aspired in Godforsaken backwaters to be geniuses. Instead of the Talmud, he reads Schiller—and mark you, he reads it as a new book. Having held out here for a while, he falls out of this strange university back into the seething world of the seventies in order to remember the conspiratorial dairy shop on Karavannaja whence a bomb was tossed under Alexander, and in a glove-making shop and in a leather factory he expounds to the paunchy and astonished customers the philosophical ideals of the eighteenth century.

When I was taken to Riga, to my Riga grandparents, I resisted and nearly cried. It seemed to me that I was being taken to the native country of my father's incomprehensible philosophy. The artillery of band-boxes, baskets with padlocks, and all the chubby, awkward family baggage started upon its journey. The winter things were salted with coarse grains of naphthalene. The armchairs stood about like white horses in their stable blankets of slip covers. The preparations for the trip to the Riga coast seemed to me no fun. I used to collect nails at that time—the absurdest of collecting whimsies. I would run my hands through piles of nails like the Covetous Knight and rejoice at the growth of my spiky wealth. Then they would take my nails away.

The trip was alarming. At night in Dorpat some sort of *Vereins* returning from a large songfest would storm the dimly lit carriage with their loud Estonian songs. The Estonians would stamp their feet and throw themselves through the door. It was very frightening.

My grandfather, a blue-eyed old man in a skull cap which covered half his forehead and with the serious and rather dignified features to be seen in very respected Jews, would smile, rejoice, and try to be affectionate—but did not know how. Then his dense eyebrows would draw together. When he wanted to take me in his arms I almost burst into tears. My kindly grandmother, wearing a black wig over her gray hair and a house coat with little yellow flowers, walked with tiny little steps over the creaking floorboards and was forever wanting people to eat something.

She kept asking, "Pokushali? Pokushali?" (Have you eaten?)—the only Russian word that she knew. But I did not like the old people's spicy dainties, with their bitter almond taste. My parents left to go to the city. My sombre grandfather and sad, bustling grandmother made an effort to distract me with conversation and ruffled their feathers like offended old birds. I tried to explain to them that I wanted to go to mama—they didn't understand. Then I represented my desire to leave by putting my index and middle figures through the motions of walking on the table.

Suddenly my grandfather drew from a drawer of a chest a black and yellow silk cloth, put it around my shoulders, and made me repeat after him words composed of unknown sounds; but, dissatisfied with my babble, he grew angry and shook his head in disapproval. I felt stifled and afraid. How my mother arrived just in time to save me I don't remember.

My father often spoke of my grandfather's honesty as of some lofty spiritual quality. For a Jew, honesty is wisdom and almost holiness. The farther one went back amongst the generations of these stern, blue-eyed old men, the more honesty and sternness one found. Great grandfather Veniamin once said, "I am closing down the business—I need no more money." He must have had just exactly enough to last him till the day of his death, since he did not leave a kopeck behind.

The Riga seaside is an entire country in itself. It is famed for its oozy, pure yellow, and astonishingly fine sand (even in an hour-glass one could hardly find such sand!) and also for the little boardwalks consisting of one or two hole-riddled planks that had been thrown down across the twenty versts of the villa-dotted Sahara.

There are no watering places anywhere that can compare with the swing and scope of the *dacha* life along the Riga coast. The boardwalks, flower beds, enclosed front gardens, and decorative glass balls stretch out in a huge, endless city, all on a yellow, finely milled, canary sand, such as children play with.

In the backyards Latvians dry and cure flounder, a one-eyed, bony fish, flat as a broad palm. The wailing of children, piano scales, the groans of patients from the innumerable dentists' offices, the clatter of crockery in the little resort pensions, the roulades of singers and the shouts of the peddlers—these noises are never silenced in the labyrinth of kitchen gardens, bakeries and barbed wire, and as far as the eye can see along the sand embankment run little toy trains, shod with rails and filled to overflowing with "hares" who leap about during the trip from prim German Bilderlingshof to congested Jewish Dubbeln, which smelled of swaddling clothes. Wandering musicians strolled about among the sparse pine groves: two convoluted trumpets, a clarinet and a trombone. Forever being chased away, they blow out their mercilessly false brass note and now here, now there, strike up the equestrian march of the splendid Karolina.

The whole region was controlled by a monocled baron named Firks. He divided his land into two parts: that which had been cleansed of Jews and that which had not. In the clean half, German students sat scraping their beer steins about on small tables. In the Jewish section babies' diapers hung from lines, and piano scales would gasp for breath. In the Germans' Majorenhof there were concerts: Strauss's *Death and Transfiguration* played by a symphony orchestra in the shell in the park. Elderly German women, their cheeks glowing and their mourning freshly donned, found it consoling.

In Jewish Dubbeln the orchestra strained at Tchaikovsky's *Symphonic Pathétique*, and one could hear the two nests of strings calling back and forth to each other. [. . .]

What conviction sounded in those violin voices, softened by Italian docility but still Russian, in the dirty Jewish sewer! What a thread it is that runs from these first wretched concerts to the silk flame of the Nobility Hall and frail Scriabin, whom one expected to see crushed at any moment by the still mute semicircle of singers about him and the string forest of *Prometheus*, above which there hung like a shield a sound recording device, a strange glass apparatus.

Translated by Clarence Brown.

Other works by Mandelstam: *Utro akmeizma* (1913, 1919); *Tristiia* (1922); *Feodosiia* (1923); *Egipetskaya marka* (1928); *O poezii* (1928); *Chetvertaia proza* (1930); *Puteshestvie v Armeniiu* (1932); *Rozgovor o Dante* (1932); *Moskovskie tetradi* (1934); *Voronezhskie tetradi* (1935–1937).

Abraham J. Zhitnik

1890–1964

Abraham J. (Avrom-Yankev) Zhitnik grew up in a Hasidic family near Zhitomir, Ukraine. A rabbi, orator, and Zionist, he wrote and edited in Kiev, supporting Jewish laborers. After the Russian Revolution, Zhitnik settled in the United States, where he served as a rabbi (known as Z. Abrams) in Chicago.

The Jews of Soviet Russia
1925

Chaim the Coachman Becomes a Farmer

4

[. . .] [T]here was a lecture in the big union hall on the topic of Soviet food policy. The wife of our protagonist also wanted to go and listen. You didn't need an admission ticket, after all. In Russia such things don't cost any money. So why should she stay at home and wait for her husband to come back and tell her? It's better for her to go as well.

And so they listened to someone lecturing on why the Soviet regime must now regulate the food question for the general population, and why it did not allow private commerce. This is how the speaker explained it:

"Due to the bloody imperialist war, the country is impoverished. Its natural resources cannot be processed in adequate numbers. Then, the civil war came and markedly devastated the country's possessions. We are not able to operate all our factories and plants. The machines are ruined and we are unable to fix them. In places where machinery works, there is a lack of sufficient fuel, and so even the healthy factories cannot be fully utilized. We lack the amount of products that the country must have. Take, as an example, such an essential item as sugar. With great effort, our sugar industry can now produce an eighth of a pound a week per person, at most. Supplying the sugar factories with fuel demands great sacrifice. The wagons that we use for transporting the necessary materials to the factories and from the factories, fall victim to criminal and counterrevolutionary fronts. Workers in the sugar factories remain hungry and, while greatly exhausted, they strive to produce the maximum product.

"Further, when the sugar goes out on the market, it falls, first of all, into the hands of individuals who always want to use the people's misfortune for their own profit. They buy out the sugar and store it somewhere, so as to drive the price up to absurd heights, and helpless citizens cannot get even a small lump of sugar. When speculators decide that it is profitable to take their sugar out of storage, poor citizens cannot afford it due to the high price set by the blood-sucking speculators. Wealthy exploiters fear scarcity and can pay the price, so they buy not an eighth of a pound per person, but five pounds and often even more, and they stock up not for a week, but for a few months.

"It is a common occurrence that a sugar factory worker, the same worker who manufactures sugar with such devotion, himself cannot afford even a small lump of sugar, due to the depraved speculator's unbridled lust for money.

"And this is the case not only with sugar. It is the same with oil. And the same with flour, and salt, and all other essentials. Well, can the workers' government see this and remain silent? Can we, at this time, stand aside and witness how a handful of overfed, satisfied bloodsuckers hold in their paws the fate of millions of productive, honest citizens? Millions of little children are starving because of criminal speculation, and the new generation's physical growth is hindered. This new generation is meant to take over our revolutionary legacy. Their blood, their innocent young blood, impels us to put an end to this devilish debauchery, and we, ourselves, must distribute life's necessities to all citizens, according to the principles of our revolutionary directive." [...]

5

Instruction, accompanied by daily experience with unbridled speculation, was bound to convince the honest citizens of the second element of the Jewish population—the so-called middle class—that in their adaptation to the Soviet way of life, they gained equal rights, as well as the "understanding" of why they suffered. This, in and of itself, alleviated some of the difficulties of transition, after which everything was to begin getting better.

This "understanding" had another, simultaneous, effect: such a Jew, in his adaptation to the Soviet way of life, not only gave his compliance as a citizen, but also began to fully comprehend that he himself must become a productive citizen. He had to ask himself about his own value to society. And he had to think long and hard about this question, since we are talking here, primarily, about the kind of Jew who until now didn't have specific work. His livelihood was impalpable, like air: buying and selling, brokering, and the like. After everything he saw, heard, and experienced since the establishment of the Soviet regime, he could no longer fool himself into thinking that his occupation was productive, leastwise within the current order of things.

When they came home from the lecture, his wife asked him:

"Nu, what do you think?"

They looked at each other for a while, as if in despair. They had nothing to say. Others did all the talking for them already. . . . Their silence was soon interrupted by the husband's self-important response:

"They are," he said, "right. But I am also right. Until now, in Nikolai's time, I could not be anyone other than what I am. Now that another time has come, I also have to try to 'become another.'"

And at this point (becoming another), the above-mentioned second element was put aside and, as if facing a mountain of fire, with burned bridges at one's back, there was no return.

The Jews of the first element were doing well. They found their way, and have been working with the Soviet regime for a long time. They were now immersed in the heat of struggle, and endured all misery with love. Everything was worth it, they said.

The third element of the Jewish population, the outspoken opposition to the Soviets, was also doing well. They also knew the cause of their suffering. They only needed to wait for the Soviet regime to end. They didn't doubt, not even for a minute, that if not today, then tomorrow, its end was assured. "What, is Denikin sleeping? Is Petliura dead? And where are the Poles? And France, also? I think—what's the point of even saying it, everyone can see it—that the Bolsheviks are holding on by no more than a thread." That is how this element talked and that's how it hoped. Therefore, nothing was left for them to do than wait a while until the thread was torn and the Soviet regime broke its neck. Eh, it dragged on a bit too long, but never mind. It's fine to wait a little longer, as long as they got rid of this affliction—Bolshevism—that they hated like poison, like venom. [...]

But the second element, the middle class, was doing terribly. They were torn away from the old way of life, already made peace with the Soviet regime somehow, but did not arrive at the new way of life, as demanded by the current regime, and didn't even know how they might reach it.

The new regime thought that "getting to work" means becoming a worker. The second element accepted that a father of grown children in his middle age would now have to make a living in a way that he always considered to be contemptible. It's no small thing—to take on a trade, to become a craftsman! He forgave this dishonor. But how does one go about getting a job? How does one become a craftsman, and also make a living at it? A living!?

6

For Chaim the coachman the problem was even more acute. When another Jew couldn't make a living, he had to worry about himself and about his wife and children. When he, Chaim the coachman, lost his livelihood, it wasn't enough that he went crazy over how to get a piece of bread for his wife and children, but he also had to rack his brain over how to afford a bit of fodder for his two horses.

These days, he didn't know what to do with the horses at all. When Smolensk was still a commercial center for the surrounding towns, Chaim the coachman had work driving the Mstsislav storekeepers to Smolensk. A year ago, when Smolensk no longer had enough goods even for itself and stopped playing the role of a commercial center, Chaim felt the change quite quickly. He lost one client after another, and at the end of five weeks was barely able to cover the expense of the horses. Then he decided: instead of driving the Mstsislav storekeepers "for free," it was better for him to pack up his little bit of hardship and move to Smolensk. Here, in Mstsislav, he had nothing to do anyway, and there, in the big city, would God abandon him?

For the first six months, he managed his miserable trade somehow. A big city, after all. When he didn't have passengers, he made deliveries. One way or another, he was able to get a piece of bread for his wife and children, and a bit of fodder for his mute souls.

But his fortune, such as it was, did not last long. Winter days passed by, then the pre-Passover muck. Then, when the weather was nice and dry, there weren't many who were willing to part with a couple of nickels for delivery, not even in the large city of Smolensk. What, didn't they have their own pair of shoulders? They could lift their bookshelves, their bags, and anything else and deliver them on their own, and they held on to their ten to fifteen kopecks this way.

Then, after Passover, the days grew longer, and Chaim was stuck in the heat all day, watching his animals suffering. Their mouths kept chewing the bridle-bits and their tails kept chasing flies away from their desiccated backs. The ravenous flies flew off whenever they felt the tails' lash, only to resume their work on the horses' front legs; the mute souls stomped their feet and shook their entire bodies. The poor things were at war with the mean hungry flies as well as their own hunger, and Chaim felt that the suffering of these innocent mute creatures was completely his fault. [. . .]

The bells of the big church by the market square were already ringing in four o'clock, and Chaim hadn't even had his first "sale of the day." He felt cold sweat covering his body. His knees buckled, and his head was spinning. He couldn't stand straight. He felt his powers leaving him. A man in a patched-up robe passed him by, carrying a dresser on his shoulders. Chaim saw the man buckling under the weight; it seemed as if he would fall at any moment. He wanted to offer him his horse and wagon, and his tongue started to move—but no words came out.

He collected his last bit of energy and flung his body into the empty wagon, and the hard boards were piping hot from the scorching sun.

7

The horses threw a glance back at their "provider," who only just now flung himself into the wagon and was already stretched out, as if he hasn't slept for ten nights straight. Their greedy eyes also examined the man in the patched-up robe, who was buckling under the heavy dresser. It was as if they were saying in their mute language:

"What a loser! A job opens up, and he runs to sleep all of a sudden!"

And so they stood, these mute creatures, and in their horse brains there was a tangled hodge-podge of green meadows and sweet-scented hay. Their village equals were leisurely pulling a plow and had a supply of green, fresh grass, and they also had fodder, mixed in with oats. [. . .] They loathed the market square with its scorching sun above and glowing stones underneath. The horses' blood was boiling at the parasites, the bloodsuckers, the revolting flies that kept gnawing at them. And there, stretched out, was their loser bread-winner, who didn't even begin to care.

They knew the road from Smolensk to Mstsislav quite well. Even in a pitch-dark night, with their eyes shut, they wouldn't stray from the dirt road. On both sides, there was only forest and meadows with sweet-scented grass. Did they really have to stand here in the terrible heat, their mouths watering from hunger? And so the horses started moving. Noticing that no one was stopping them, they started going lively and quickly, and in twenty minutes, they were already outside of town, passing a forest clearing, a sweet May aroma filling their nostrils. The hunger that was tormenting them the entire time became even more relentless. Skipping over the narrow trench that separated the green meadow from the road, they were already bowing their heads to the green grass, paying no mind to their provider.

Translated by Alexandra Hoffman.

Other works by Zhitnik: *Dos harts fun folk* (1928); *Sefer ha-zikaron* (*The Book of Memories*) (1932–1934).

Abraham Cahan
1860–1951

Born near Vilna, Abraham Cahan received a traditional Jewish education, but while studying at a teacher-training institute, he lost his religious faith and embraced socialism. He immigrated to New York City in 1882 to avoid arrest for radical political activities. He became a journalist, contributing to Russian-, Yiddish-, and English-language newspapers. From 1903 to 1946, he edited *Forverts*. During his years in America, his socialism lost its radical edge, and he became an opponent of communist influence in the labor movement and a supporter of Franklin Delano Roosevelt. He was also an accomplished novelist and short-story writer in English.

Pages from My Life
1926

Two

[. . .] In time, I lost my shyness. I became a "big shot" in one of the Am Olam groups. In our debates it became clear to me that it was still a beautiful idea to start colonies in which we would not live egotistically but only for the best interest of mankind. (Others spoke of the best interest of the Jewish people, I only of mankind.)

I had no practical understanding of socialism. I knew it was necessary to destroy the power of private property, kings and religion. As Marx pointed out, the capitalist system was heading toward self-destruction. I read *Vperiod*, *Chorny Perediel*, and *The Will of the People* and was familiar with the debates between the anarchists and the socialists. But all this was just theory.

I joined the Balta Am Olam even though it was not a socialist group. I resolved to propagandize them. Carried away with the excitement of debate, I once said to one of the group, "You're a conservative! You don't care that those who toil and produce are robbed and oppressed."

"Then why are you traveling with us?" he demanded.

"I'll propagandize among you!" was my proud reply. "I'll work in the fields and in my free time I will teach you."

"Who's asking you to? Who needs you?"

I had been tactless; it made a bad impression. But I soon smoothed everything out. When I received about a hundred dollars from home I put two-thirds of it into the treasury of the Balta group to pay for the trip to New York. Then I continued the impatient wait for the day we would board the train.

During the period of waiting in Brody many of the refugees married. Most of them took girls from Brody. We considered the Galician women to be beautiful and virtually every home in Brody had a young refugee boarding in it. Romances blossomed. For the poor parents it was a good opportunity to marry off their daughters; they would be off to America and perhaps, soon after, would send for the older folks.

The young man, at the same time, considered the advantages of coming to his colony in America with a young wife to set up his household. There was an epidemic of weddings.

I remember a Saturday night scene I witnessed about two weeks after my arrival in Brody. I had turned a corner into a desolate street where each structure was a burned-out ruin. But this night musicians were playing among the ruins in the street, and the street rocked with dancing and revelry.

I stopped someone and asked, "What are they celebrating?"

"They're getting married."

"On the street? A wedding?"

"Yes, on the street."

The fiddlers stood in the middle of the street, simultaneously servicing three weddings: one on each side of the street and one in a nearby ruin. They played furiously. Far down, in the distance, there was more music, more weddings.

I walked through the dancing crowd. Someone recognized me and pulled me toward his beautiful bride for an introduction. He swept me into the dancing.

So they had banished the loneliness and the longing that gnawed at their hearts. Away from home for the first time, torn from friends and family, free from the restraints of home, they had shed the canons of behavior and discipline. The hunger was for a comrade to whom one could pour out one's heart. Was it really love or only an illusion? It mattered not. One married.

Three

Some of the refugees waited in Brody for months; I waited only three weeks until the Saturday night on which our Balta group set out. As our train began to move slowly out of the station, the air rang with the cheers of well-wishers.

"Long live the Balta Am Olam! Long live freedom and the American republic!"

These were magic words—freedom, republic—that refreshed our souls. In the moment of departure even the young dandy who had mocked me for being a Litvak peered into the carriage and shouted in Russian, "Good luck to you and your colony!" Deeply touched, I shook his hand.

We traveled third class—slowly, all night—loaded with honeymooners and arrived next morning in Lemberg. We were received by the committee who brought tea and rolls and later provided meat and soup. We spent an entire day in Lemberg. I went with some of the others to see the center of the city—a beautiful small park.

We went to the Jewish part of the city. "It looks just like Vilna," I remarked to one of my companions.

"Every place looks like Vilna to him, as if there were no other city in the world," was his comment.

We returned to our train by horsecar. The conductor used a small whistle to communicate with the driver. It was a bright new streetcar.

We arrived in Cracow the next morning and were again met by a committee with tea and rolls. The Kiev Am Olam had come the same route a week earlier. Now we caught echoes of the stir they had made. They had spent a week in Lemberg during which the local committee had found quarters for the travelers in the best homes.

In Cracow, the group was welcomed by a gentile Pole named Onufrovitch, who had a fine reputation as correspondent for the Russian-Jewish weekly, *Russky Yevrey*. He presented a gift to the Kiev group, a lavishly bound copy of Marx's *Capital*, in French translation.

The Kiev Am Olam carried with it a Torah scroll, which it displayed wherever it made a stopover. It was handled and shown not as an object of religious holiness but as if it were a flag of national purpose.

Our next stopping place was Breslau, Germany, where the welcoming committee consisted of well-dressed German Jews. I ran to see the city during the short stopover. For the first time I could see the marks of a highly civilized nation.

On the best streets of Petersburg I had seen people in heavy boots and without collars and neckties. In Breslau, it seemed to me, everyone dressed like a nobleman. And I marveled at the cleanliness.

Our stop in Berlin was short and I was not able to see the city. One of the welcoming committee, a banker named Magnus, gave Mashbir some gold coins with instructions to purchase books for self-instruction in English.

All I saw of the beautiful city of Hamburg were some of the narrow dirty portside streets. We arrived at night and in the dark went directly to the ship that was to take us to England.

I had anticipated an ocean that would be wondrously beautiful. But aboard ship everyone around me was sick. I was not affected. The sky was a heavy gray fog and the roll of the ship produced scenes of agony. I looked over the side and the waves seemed to be angry, evil spirits.

Hull, on the eastern coast of England, is vaguely remembered by me as the place where a Jewish storekeeper said to some of us, "Soon, in a few years, you'll be fine American merchants."

Each of the cities through which we had passed had left its own peculiar impressions. But only Brody and Liverpool made my eyes widen with wonder. Wherever I turned I beheld in Liverpool something new, something wonderful.

Bicycles, with the rider atop the high, large wheel, looking from a distance as if he were walking on air. Or the two-wheeled hansom cabs, still to be seen in England and for a time in New York, with the coachman sitting high in the rear, lashing his whip over the roof of the cab.

I was shocked at the sight of the bootblacks, poor boys who lined the sidewalks to shine shoes. I had read about them in Vodovozova's *The Life of European Peoples*. But it is one thing to read about such poverty and another thing to see it with one's own eyes.

We marveled at the Liverpool railroad station. Almost silently, long trains arrived and departed without tumult, without fuss. In Russia, these are occasions for running, kissing, crying.

Because of these things, and my trouble with the language, I felt that there was more freedom here than in Austria. I concluded that a free country had to look different from Russia or Germany and that the peculiarities of Liverpool, being a reflection of freedom, were indications of what lay ahead in America.

With Magnus' gift we bought books that would help us learn English. I went off in search of a bookstore where I could buy an English-Russian, Russian-English dictionary. I asked persons on the street for directions. Even though I gesticulated, rolled my eyes, shouted, sighed and came up with my German and French words, I could not make myself understood. But from the way in which these English listened to me I perceived that they were a very patient and friendly people. No doubt, so are Americans, I thought.

Guided by a sailor who knew some Russian words, I found my bookstore and my dictionary.

English seemed as unnatural to me as the bicycles, bootblacks and hansom cabs. Perhaps the mouths of Englishmen were formed differently from ours. At the Liverpool immigrant committee headquarters, Mashbir and I were interviewed with the aid of an interpreter. I watched especially the lips and tongue of the committee member who spoke to us. He wore gold-rimmed glasses and was shaped like a dumpling.

When he spoke his jaws seemed to be chopping his words into tiny bits which then spurted from his mouth like sparks from a blacksmith's anvil. And this was the crazy language I would have to learn!

The English were good people. But at times I grew impatient with their restraint and deliberateness. Such cold fish!

Once our housekeeper's daughter came into the sitting room while holding her baby in her arms. She spoke politely to us but we couldn't understand a word. Nevertheless, it was fun to answer, even in Russian. We joked and laughed. But she neither laughed nor was offended. To all of our quips and warm compliments she answered only with a polite, "Yes, yes." That was all we could get out of her.

I met a friend from Vilna. From him I learned great news. A band of Jewish revolutionaries from my Vilna group had set out for America, led by Boris Caspe. The group included my comrades, Saul Badanes and Solomon Menaker. Caspe's younger brother was also to follow soon after.

Now I felt fully justified in choosing America. I would not be the only one of our group going to that land. I would find friends from home. I would not be lonely.

Finally, our Balta Am Olam group, together with a large number of others waiting with us in Liverpool, was escorted to the *British Queen*, the ship that was to take us to America. We traveled in the steerage.

We had been warned to take along plenty of lemons. I bought two dozen. But because I never suffered from seasickness I made no use of them myself. One day I saw a slight young man named Heimovitch moving among the passengers, pleading for a lemon for his suffering wife. I gave him all my lemons. In the days that followed, the Heimovitches kept thanking me, the young wife insisting that I had saved her life with my lemons. To this day, when we meet, it is the lemons we remember first.

For us, in steerage, the captain was a remote, mysterious and majestic power whom we perceived, even at a distance, only rarely. But there was no mystery about the steerage steward. He was a real power. We were serviced, fed and lorded over by him.

Fortunately, he was not an angry lord. We were heavily dependent on him and we felt that our fate, especially the fate of the sick, lay directly in his hands.

My simple, uneducated fellow passengers heard him called "Mister" and immediately concluded that this was his name. I explained that "mister" was the equivalent of "herr" in German or "gospodin" in Russian. But it was to no avail so that even in his absence they continued to refer to him as "Mister," saying, "Let's ask 'Mister'" or "Who can figure out what 'Mister' wants from us."

"Mister" was my first English-language teacher. I would come to him with my bilingual dictionary or "self-teacher" book and ask him to pronounce the word or phrase to which I was pointing. It was never easy for me to repeat the sounds he made.

The English vowels seemed to have indefinite sounds which were not natural to human speech. The effect of the cometz and pasach signs under the Yiddish vowels seemed not to be reflected in the English translations. And "Mister's" pronunciation never corresponded to that indicated in my book. In my frustration I would jokingly say that when I write "Benjamin" he reads "Jacob."

Nevertheless, "Mister" was a most useful teacher. Our crossing took thirteen days and each day I learned something from him. In turn, I was also useful to him. Whenever he had to speak with one of my fellow travelers, he would take me with him. He would write the words on a sheet of paper in English; I would find their meaning in my dictionary and transmit the spoken message. Then, if there was an answer, I would reverse the process and "Mister" would receive the reply. This shipboard experience with language was the subject of my short story "Dumitru and Sigrid," which appeared in *Cosmopolitan Magazine* in March 1901.

Shavuoth, the holiday marking the giving of the Torah, occurred during our crossing. We had among us a blond young man from Odessa. For days he had kept us on our toes with his pranks and his obscene talk. On the day of Shavuoth I spotted him dressed in his best clothes, rocking on his feet in a corner of the room. He had a prayer book in his hand and although he saw me approach he continued his prayers.

Only after he had finished did he turn full face to me. Now it was not the face of a jokester.

"Good yom tov! After all, it's Shavuoth. . . . We're on the water, after all. Anything can happen. . . ."

When we were well under way, we became accustomed to the vibrations of the ship and to the choking, salty odor that rose from the cellar hole called the steerage. In time, the sick recovered and began to crawl up out of the shallow wooden boxes that passed for beds onto the decks where they sat out the remaining days of the trip.

Hours on end, I stood at the rail of the ship like one cast into a dream by a sorcerer. I remember neither the ship's captain nor his officers. I remember only that whenever I looked up there was always an old sailor high on the bridge, studying the weather. He would touch his forehead with the outside of his hand, his eyes fixed on some distant point. I was completely spellbound by him so that sometimes I stared at him for as much as fifteen minutes as he stared at the heavens.

I was enchanted by the great ocean. I came to believe that there was no end to the expanse of waves. Back home I had made two trips by boat. Once I had traveled for three days on the Dnieper River, the greatest river I had ever seen. Another time I had traveled with Sokolov's brother by steamboat from Petersburg to Kronstadt on a body of water that was part of the sea and I had been deeply impressed.

But both times the shore remained within sight and always I could see villages, houses, people. Now the hours added up into days, and then it was a week and more, and still there was only water as far as one could see, no shoreline, and it seemed after awhile that there would never be one and that even the place called America was only a figment of the imagination.

Evenings were filled with the magic hues of sunsets. But as the wonderful colors sank with the sun, our hearts would fill with a terrible longing for home. Then we would draw together and sing our Russian folk songs filled with nostalgia and yearning.

The others, the Norwegians, the Swedes and the few Englishmen, would listen to our singing. Then the English would sing and we would listen. Or the Norwegian would dance and we would watch. I can still see as in a dream one of their couples turning and turning.

Holding his young lady in his arms, our slim, blond, Norwegian cavalier stomps to the vigorous rhythms of the dance. And during a pounding rhythm, his pince-nez slips from his nose, he catches it, returns it to his nose where he holds it for a moment to make certain it is firmly in place. Then he lets go of it, whirls around, and down it comes again while all the time he breaks neither rhythm nor posture.

How can one describe the emotions with which an immigrant, after thirteen days on the ocean, beholds in the distance for the first time the thin line of land that means America? As the *British Queen* approached the shore, the green foliage stood bright in blazing sunshine and the water and the sky were blue with the blueness of paradise and all around us the sea gulls hailed us with their cries. The endless ocean had enchanted me; this magic land overwhelmed me.

Coming to America has changed from what it was when I arrived. The newcomer today is greeted by countrymen and relatives who preceded him in the crossing and who welcome him to the new land with love and friendship. The new homeland is no longer a land of mystery. Millions of letters to the old homeland have spelled out its wonders and its opportune ties.

But in my time a letter from America was a rarity in Europe and a returning visitor was unknown. In our minds, we were coming to a country of wonder and mystery. I had imagined that all Americans were tall and slender and that all the men wore yellow trousers and high hats. Perhaps I had derived this picture from a novel which I had read in Russian translation. As the ship moved up the bay to Philadelphia, I stood at the rail and strained to behold my first American.

Translated by Leon Stein, Abraham P. Vonan, and Lynn Davison.

Other works by Cahan: *Yekl: A Tale of the New York Ghetto* (1896); *The Imported Bridegroom and Other Stories* (1898); *The Rise of David Levinsky* (1917).

Barukh Ha-Levi Epstein

1860–1941

Barukh Ha-Levi Epstein was raised in Novarodik (Nowogrodek [Polish]; today, Navahrudak, Belarus), the son of the rabbi and scholar Yekhiel Mikhl Epstein (1830–1908). He studied in the Volozhyn yeshiva, wrote on Hebrew grammar, and is best known for his biblical and Talmudic commentaries, as well as his memoir, *Mekor Barukh*. The memoir provides one of the only sources for the life and thought of Rayna Batya Berlin, his aunt and the granddaughter of the founder of the Volozhyn yeshiva.

Mekor Barukh—My Memoirs
1926

Chapter 23: New and Old

1

In general, the power of the influence exerted by the Master, R. Mendele, on my revered father over many years since his return from (studying with) him, was very great. [. . .]

The Master was very great and exceedingly distinguished in all areas of the Torah, and in virtually all Talmudic and halakhic matters, whether of a practical or an academic nature. [. . .]

And his knowledge was similarly great in branches of secular wisdom and the sciences, such as in astronomy, higher mathematics, and so forth. [. . .]

"Learn and pray!" he would say—and he would accord Torah study priority over prayer.

This formula bore fruit, for, truth to tell, there were to be found among the Hasidim of Habad (or, as they used to call them in Lithuania, Hasidim of Lubavitch) numerous great Torah scholars, and not merely among the rabbis and rebbes, but also among the ranks of laymen—merchants, middlemen, and such as were familiar with the ways of the world. [. . .]

At that time, the echo of the enlightenment [Haskalah] could already be heard in the camp of Israel, and its roots had begun to shoot forth as blossoms and to release sprouts in greater or in lesser measure, affecting every home and family in Israel; and slowly but surely it began to emerge with strength in many cities in general and the city of Vilna in particular. [. . .]

This Rebbe, Mendele, was well known as a determined campaigner against the enlightenment, with a mighty soul and vehement spirit. Later, the fortitude of his spirit was seen in his refusal to sign the document containing the proposals of the minister of education in regard to the expansion of enlightenment among the Jews, at the time when he was invited to the committee of rabbis that convened in the office of the minister of education in the year 5608 [1848] [. . .]

Thus, our ancestors, the inhabitants of Liteh, saw fit to forget "old scores" with the Hasidim [. . .] and to make peace with it, in order to perform the sacred task in unison, and fight this mandatory battle [against the enlightenment] together. [. . .]

2

One of the most visible aspects of the influence of the Master on my father was this: he discouraged him from accepting any novel idea in the religion and in the Talmud if that idea ran counter to that which had been accepted by the early interpreters and decisors, or even if it merely contradicted accepted tradition—and this was applicable even where this novel idea was very easy to accept, and also pleasing to the ear and in line with reason: "Because (these were the words of the Master) in general the introduction of innovations, of whatsoever kind they may be, reflects the lustful desire of the soul and the delight of the eye, and they have the slickness of speech wherewith to attract the heart and draw the soul toward them; and if not we ourselves and our children, then the later generations will be able to proceed further along the paths of these 'innovations,' slowly but surely, step by step, up to a point from which they will not wish, nor indeed will they even be able, to return. And therefore it is best to erect fences and boundaries in relation to them right from the outset . . . and an additional fence of steel, capable of withstanding every broad breach, and also every narrow crack that, in the future, has the potential to become wider and eventually to burst with peals of thunder and commotion, and bring about breaches and cause shattering in all aspects of the life of the spirit—up to a point where neither fortresses nor enclosures, nor mighty rocks nor fortified walls will be of any avail."

[. . .] "And now"—the Master ended his words with the following admonition—"now it is up to you and to us to guard with the utmost care the laws of and fences around our Torah, the traditions of our faith, and the acceptance of our religion, so that no cracks and no plain fissures, which are liable to appear as a result of the existence of 'innovations' such as these, will occur within the edifice of Judaism." [. . .]

3

Now I recollect that when I was in the royal city of Vienna some thirty years ago, and was there acquainted with the great rabbi, a venerable old man, Rabbi Zalman Spitzer, the rabbi of the ultra-Orthodox community there, who was one of the disciples, and from the family, of the most brilliant sage, the Hatam Sofer [. . .]

Rabbi Zalman Spitzer related that he was well acquainted with several of the great sages who were grieved about the matter, that on account of fear of "innovations," which they sensed as being a type of infectious disease, they were unable, or did not wish, to introduce any new thing—even of the type that they would have desired to create because they found it to be in conformity with the truth of Torah—but were frightened to go ahead on account of the limited grasp of the masses of the people, who could not distinguish between one matter and another, and would think that since one innovatory matter was permitted, so was another; "and the strap would be untied" [i.e., every restriction would be removed]. [. . .]

And likewise there were great men, who, in their hearts, were inclined to permit the baking of matzot by machine (as I have mentioned above in connection with the book *Divre ḥayim*), because they considered that, with a machine, there is a greater degree of active care and a superior measure of protection against the fear of their becoming leaven than there is in the case of matzot baked manually by masses of men and women who are occupied with this task for many hours, by day and by night, and they are frequently so tired and exhausted, wearied and oppressed by their involvement with the enforced and haste-driven toil up to the point where, in the very course of their work, they were overtaken by drowsiness and light sleep, and they felt themselves diffused and dejected in body, in soul and in spirit, up to a point where they could keep control over their bodies only with difficulty, so as to prevent their tottering and falling, and their labor was carried out when they were half awake and half asleep; and all these factors would not be applicable and equally prevalent where matzot were manufactured by machine. [. . .]

Now in the year 5623 [1863], a certain *dayan* from Minsk, R. Israel Ozdaner, brought a machine of this kind to Jerusalem; and there were present there the giants of halakhah R. Meir Auerbach and R. Moses Leib of Kutna, and they made no protest on this score; and in the year 5625, the aforementioned *dayan* died, and the process of baking matzot by machine ceased until the year 5666, in which year they brought it to Jerusalem, and it was then that several rabbis bestirred themselves to prohibit it; but R. Samuel Salant stood by his permissive stance, and in the year 5668, as people were relying strongly upon his permission, he personally ate from the machine-baked matzot.

But, as against this, there was a band of rabbis prohibiting the practice. [. . .]

4

And who could properly evaluate and describe the thunder and the commotion and the rumbling sounds emitted by the shepherds of Israel, its rabbis, its sages, its financial providers, and its leaders in the previous generation, at the time when "the innovations" dared to break through the wall of our faith, albeit by means of a crack the size of a needle-point, or even though it were nothing more than partially to dislodge one of the customs of Israel and of the ancestral tradition? [. . .]

At the beginning of the final quarter of the last century [according to our system of counting, the year 5575 (1815)], after devastation and destruction had finally come upon the monstrous tyranny represented by the empire of Napoleon the First, and in that very manner in which he had initially caused countries to quake and agitated kingdoms, attacking peoples and weakening nations, he kindled a bitterly cold fire from numerous battles in various countries and regions, and stirred up sparks of strife among nations and kingdoms, and brought about much calamitous evil upon the entire world, and misfortune resulting in despair upon the whole of humanity;—

At that time the heavens, as it were, called for freedom, and the earth—for relief, and people began to long for a spirit of freedom in a mood of love and brotherhood; and they went about in the open places in a spirit of ease and tranquility. [. . .]

And the Jewish people too did not separate themselves in this regard from the international community, and likewise chimed in with the spirit of the new life, which was good and free; the bounty of the world was also given over into their hands, and, in common with all the rest of humanity, they knew how to utilize it for their happiness, and for the happiness of their rest and tranquility, the covenant of love and brotherhood, of life and of peace which the Almighty had decreed for the world!

And there was an additional consideration for the Jewish nation at that time and in that battle, for they were not satisfied with merely obtaining freedom insofar as the life of this world was concerned, but also dug deeper, to ascend the steps of the House of God and to find ease likewise [. . .] in regard to faith and tradition, in the precepts and the pathways of the Torah, and to fit the spirit of the religion into the ways of secular life; that is to say, freedom and liberty, freedom from the burdens of life and liberty from the Kingdom of Heaven!

And the first to feature in this crisis were the inhabitants of the city of Hamburg, in Germany; the first of their acts was that a small group of young men assembled together, [. . .] and now they believed they were perceiving a fresh world before them, "a world of license," in which it was within the power of everyone to do whatever his heart desired and what was right in his sight; no one would disturb him, and no one would raise a protest against it!

And . . . they perceived a straight path in front of them. [. . .] to create a special House of Prayer for themselves, and they called it "The Holy Temple" and referred to themselves as "the Congregation of the Temple."

They proceeded further with their work, which consisted in chopping and trimming, in altering and changing the prayer rituals, and deleting from them matters and themes that had been established by ancient tradition and were directed toward reestablishing the Jewish nation; and they prepared and established a new order of prayer, neither full nor overflowing in content but cut by half, a third, or a quarter of its standard length.

A further step forward taken by them was to explore ways of weakening our adherence to our mother-tongue, and they directed that the Order of Prayer compiled by them be translated into pure German, and they made it obligatory to pray from this liturgy and in its new language.

At the beginning of this "new creation," virtually no one paid any attention to it, as they regarded it as an act of folly by young men of an unstable and unruly nature, who barely constituted even a worthy topic of conversation. People thought it best to leave it alone and it would dissolve of itself, melting continuously until such time as its roots and trunk would simply wither away, and that in the same sudden manner as it had appeared, it would vanish without a trace.

However, this calculation did not prove correct because all of a sudden, a savior was discovered for this group of men, a mighty redeemer, from the ranks of the rabbis themselves, who possessed a firm grasp of Talmud, was conversant with rabbinic literature, and acquainted with and well known to many of the great rabbis of that generation. This rabbi compiled a book containing everything he could find to shield and shelter this group, and to justify its actions; and in this work, he investigated and proved that, judging by the fundamentals of the religion, nothing perverse or sinful was to be found in these actions of theirs. On the contrary, such activities were, as a whole, in conformity with the spirit of the Torah and with the ways of the Talmud and the mode of life of the Jewish nation during those times when it was established upon its own land and had its kingdom [. . .] with each man enjoying life under his vine and under his fig tree! [. . .]

This was the rabbi in the city of Arad, in Hungary [today, Romanian Transylvania], Aharon Chorin. [. . .]

And it was then that the great sages of Israel and its shepherds were proved right—this was not a time to remain silent, and that if they were not now to make a stand to close up the breach before it burst in a mighty thunderstorm, and before the "innovations" sent their fall-out [lit., side-locks of hair] over the surface of the world, the survival of the faith would be endangered throughout the land. It was virtually certain that it would also spread, like an infectious disease, to other countries too; and then, slowly but surely, and step by step, broken fragments and breaches, both broad and deep, would increase in the wall of the faith, from one side and another, from the front and rear, until it would all burst open and explode, thus bringing about the ruin of Judaism as a whole.

[. . .] The quarrel spread with mighty force, and even reached the houses of officialdom in the country; everyone became involved in it—from officials and governors to deputies and ministers—right up to the very heads of government. The vast majority supported those who were endeavoring to fence in the breaches, and they resolved that "it is not religion that has to bow to the times, but the times that have to bow to religion, because times are transitory, whereas religion endures forever!" [...]

[Rabbi Epstein cites several instances where even the most stringent Orthodox decisors accepted innovations. They include: "in the year 5596 [1836] in the royal city of Vienna, when many young children died as a result of circumcision, and the doctors recognized that the cause of this was the practice of sucking out the blood of the circumcision with the circumciser's mouth, since often the circumciser was not physically in perfect health and in that way the symptoms of this disease became attached to the blood of the tender baby who had undergone circumcision, and he was unable to tolerate it—and died. [...] At that time, the rabbi who was head of the *bet din* in Vienna, R. Eleazar Horowitz, a disciple of the yeshiva of Rabbi Moses Sofer in Pressburg, advised his teacher to permit the sucking out of the blood through a utensil which had been specially manufactured for this purpose; and the Master responded to him—and in the manner of a Talmudic genius, he proceeded to give a most satisfactory explanation of the reason for his permitting it—that apart from the mandatory obligation to save life, which would in itself have been a sufficient basis for granting permission, the very practice of sucking out the blood—as explained by our sages of blessed memory—was neither an obligatory matter nor a precept in its own right; that is to say, it did not constitute a part, or a detail, of the commandment to be circumcised. [...] Nowadays, the majority of circumcisers in the Western world employ a utensil for sucking out the blood, namely the mechanical device of a glass tube with a soft, spongy material inside to absorb the blood sucked out] [...]

5

[...] Furthermore, there were in the previous generation men of distinction who went further "in hatred of novelties," even [...] in practical affairs and the ways of the world! And with every new invention that appeared in the world, they would explore and seek the origin of its existence [and find] "in reality, the basis of this or that 'novelty' was already in existence within the world, and now it is only a matter of the thing attaining perfection or being completely developed and emerging into reality" and therefore—they would assure us—and therefore, at the end of the day, there is no such thing as a novelty!

Thus [...] when the telegraph came into practical use [...] these people attempted to show that the

fundamental principle underlying it had already been known in ancient times, and they demonstrated that it appeared in a certain work, entitled *Ma'arekhet elohut* [The Divine Order], by R. Peretz Ha-Kohen, one of the Tosafists, with the commentary known as *Minhat Yehudah* [The Offering of Judah] by R. Judah Hayyat, a Spanish sage, in the third century of the current millennium (printed in Ferrara in the year 5318 [1558])—where, in the chapter entitled "The Gate of the Divine Chariot," while in the course of clarifying a certain obscure matter, the commentator writes as follows:

"The lower world has a force which it is capable of exerting upon the upper worlds, etc., and there is a strong allusion to this force within nature in the magnetic lodestone that attracts iron, for, when you hold it firmly and extract its dross, and then break it into two pieces, and you place one segment in one corner, and the other segment in another corner, even though they are a thousand miles distant from one another, and you place the iron close to one of these segments, you will find that corresponding to every movement made by that segment, the other one makes the same movement simultaneously."

[...] Now it is well known that the entire concept and design of the telegraph is built upon the fundamental basis of the force of magnetism, and accordingly—so the "enemies of novelties" used to say—the basic principle of the telegraph was already known to the world, and it is simply that the idea has now come to full fruition—and it is nothing more than that. [...]

And when the invention of the telephone came out (in the year 5637: 1877), they discovered within it a most awesome thing ... contained in the work *Shevut Yaakov*, where an enquiry was made in the month of Shevat 5482 [1722], in connection with speaking to another person at a distance on the Sabbath, in view of the prohibition of exceeding the Sabbath boundaries; and the author of the aforementioned work permitted this, and in the course of his discussion he writes as follows:

"And in particular, by means of instruments specially designed for the purpose, which can cause sound to be heard at a distance of many, many miles, a person is able to speak with his friend; and should such a thing be prohibited on the Sabbath? We have never heard anyone opening his mouth to cast the slightest doubt upon this!"

[...] Since these words were written roughly two hundred years have elapsed (and I am writing these words in the winter of the year 5683 [1923]), and he goes on to write that: "We have never heard anyone opening his mouth to cast any doubt upon the matter . . . is this not a plain and explicit allusion to the existence of "instruments for speaking at a distance" about three hundred years ago? Now this is truly a most amazing thing; and so far as I am aware, no reference to this matter occurs in any of the ancient works, nor have we ever heard, even by way of the faintest allusion, that in former generations, they made use of a type of "instrument for speaking at a distance"—how astonishing this matter then is!

[. . .] And there is similarly, in the case of our telephones, a factor militating against their use on the Sabbath, in that at the moment when one is preparing to speak, an electric current is released in the nozzle inside the receiver of the person being spoken to, and this comes under the category of the prohibition of creating a fire; however, there are many issues that one can raise concerning this point; and it would have been appropriate for the great halakhic authorities to clarify this matter. [. . .]

In our generation, many people have explored the question of whether it is permissible to use the telephone for legal matters, such as for bills of divorce—is it permitted for the husband who is divorcing his wife to request the *dayanim*, and the scribe, and the witnesses, by telephone, to write out and sign a bill of divorce for his wife? Likewise are the *dayanim* allowed to accept relevant testimony by way of telephone, and matters of a similar nature? They investigated, and found no halakhic impediment to this; and if the concern is that the parties do not see one another, surely, as a result of the telephone conversation, they can recognize the identity of the speaker by his voice; and it is an established Talmudic principle that "the perceptive sense created by the sound of the voice is valid" (Gittin 23a). [. . .]

There is, nonetheless, on the face of it, a factor militating in favor of a prohibition—for at the place where they receive the message by telegraphic means, they copy the fused letters and arrange in proper order on a sheet in plain script, and they then deliver the sheet to the person to whom the message has been sent; and that being the case, there exists here the prohibition of instructing a non-Jew to perform work on the Sabbath.

[. . .] And in our generation and in our own days, the power concealed within the radio, which can transmit sound over several thousand miles, has been discovered, and a strong allusion to this is to be found in the Talmud, in tractate Yoma (21a), where the radio is reck-

oned as among those things the sound of which travels from one end of the world to the other—though Rashi ad loc. interprets this expression in another way. [. . .]

And at the time when it became customary (halfway through the last century, according to the secular system of counting) to hold contests in bodily wrestling with strength and might, and in alertness and speed in respect of hand and leg movements (which is called in the vernacular tongues *athletics*), and likewise in (the area) of swift racing on foot and on horseback (sport), and of attempting to toss a ball into the goal—there were some who demonstrated that this too is no novelty, and that it existed from ancient times, and they accounted for each of these activities as I shall detail here below:

1. Concerning Bodily Wrestling and Physical Combat

They pointed to the Midrash Rabbah on Genesis, Section 21 and Section 77: "This may be compared to two athletes (even the term itself refers to what it is nowadays) who were standing and wrestling in the presence of the king," etc.; "And Abner said to Joab: 'Let the young lads arise and disport themselves in combat in our presence!' And twelve men of the tribe of Benjamin and belonging to Ish-bosheth, and twelve of the servants of David arose, and each man seized the head of his companion, and they fell down dead together" [II Samuel 2:14–16].

It is explained in the words of the ancient chronicles that the Romans constructed gymnasiums and stadiums for athletic wrestling in the city of Lod, and that the slaves wrestled with one another or with wild animals unto the point of death, for the delight of the spectators who derived pleasure from witnessing those who had been slain struggling convulsively in a state halfway between life and death, with rivers and streams of blood gushing forth before their eyes (it would have to be seen to be believed!); and likewise they erected training-houses in this city especially devoted to this purpose; and they did not prevent the trainees from having every manner of healthy nourishment entering their bodies, so as to prepare them for the slaughter (as [the work] "Erets Kedumim," Part 2, informs us).

[. . .] However, according to what has been explained, one may state with virtual certainty that this is with reference to the residents of the city of Lod, who were regularly accustomed to be trained in wrestling and physical combat, and who would attempt to feed the trainees with the best and healthiest foodstuffs . . . and one of the good aspects of this was the feeding of them at a very early hour of the day, as this contributes toward the improvement of bodily health as does consumption of a piece of bread in the early morning;

[...] As to the reason why a type of entertainment as undisciplined as this—witnessing wrestling and physical combat to the death—was more prevalent in the city of Lod than in other cities, one has to say that it was because this city was generally laden with great wealth, and enjoyed a surfeit of sustenance and of good-quality and happy living, due to the fact that business boomed in it in extraordinarily large measure, since within it there were to be found all the conditions suitable for the development of commerce: the soil was fruitful and gold was extracted from its surrounding mountains. [...] Moreover, it constituted the center for unloading and loading of merchandise arriving from the distant lands of Asia and proceeding on to Europe; and in the Talmud too, its merchants are referred to by the distinguished epithet of "the merchants of Lod" (Bava Metzia 49b, in the Mishnah). As a result of the abundance of good things and of their merriness of heart, they did not refrain from treating themselves to all the delights life could offer, and, as is explained in the Talmudic Tractate "Shabbat" (119a), they were accustomed to use golden tables; and as a result of the abundance of the good life they enjoyed, they became stout-hearted and brazen of spirit to such a point where they could not control themselves from deriving entertainment out of seeing men wrestling with wild beasts to the death, and obtaining pleasure from witnessing them struggling convulsively in a state halfway between life and death, and sinking in rivers and streams of blood, as we have written above.

And a form of this wild entertainment is still in vogue in our own times in Spain; indeed it is well-known that its inhabitants are stout-hearted and of violent temperament, shedders of blood and tears, from times of old. [...]

Insofar as the enthusiasm for wrestling and physical combat is concerned [...] in recent generations, Jews play only a very small role in contests such as these and the like; and the reason for this is almost certainly that, quite apart from the fact that its fundamental basis—involving all its wrestling and violence—is not at all in accord with the spirit of the Jewish people, there is also the additional factor that the lengthy and bitter exile, and the harsh and bitter persecutions, and its enforced peregrinations, following closely one upon another, and the numerous and oppressive wanderings, and all the waves of its vicissitudes and the hardships, and the

abundance of troubles and evils that have passed in anger over its head from the time it left its own land and inheritance, and went about from one nation to another and from kingdom to another without finding a resting-place for its feet or quietude for its soul. [...] All these have weakened its physical prowess and caused its strength to fail, and destroyed its might, and have also diminished its bodily development, by comparison to the nations around them who always dwelt on their own soil and rested in tranquility, for indeed "even birds living on their own territory are healthier and fatter than those who go into exile" (Tractate "Shabbat" 145b).

And therefore there are some who advocate and supervise schools of the kind where the matter of "bodily vigor" is treated as one of the parts of the curriculum, who take particular care over Jewish pupils that they should perform well in this sphere, and that they should renew their days through display of physical fortitude and strength as in former times, those days when the Jewish nation was dwelling and established upon its own land and had its own kingdom, in the days of its tranquility [each man dwelling] under his vine and under his fig tree.

And so far as can be determined, the theme of bodily vigor was generally regarded as a worthwhile and desirable pursuit for our people from ancient times, as it has the effect of energizing the flow of blood within the body and of keeping it flowing so that it does not congeal, and it also develops the limbs of the body, broadens the spirit, and effects the efficiency of life in general.

Accordingly, among the other requests and prayers for goodly aspects of life that the sages fixed for recitation prior to the Blessing for the Coming Month—we ask also for "a life of bodily vigor!" [...]

Translated by David E. Cohen.

Other works by Epstein: *Safa le-neemanim* (1893); *Ḥamisha ḥumshe tora im ḥamesh megilot: Torah temimah* (1901–1902); *Sefer-Makor Barukh: yakhil korot khaye avotai vekhayay ani* (1928).

Edmond Fleg

1874–1963

The French writer and poet Edmond Fleg grew up in an observant Jewish home in Geneva. He moved to Paris at age eighteen to pursue a university education, soon abandoning religious practice. Stunned by his encounter with the Dreyfus affair and stirred by his reading of Israel Zangwill's haunting short story "Chad Gadya!" in 1904, he worked his way back to Judaism. *The Boy Prophet* (1926) and *Why I Am Jewish* (1927) evoke his journey of return. Although he wrote on secular subjects, Jewish themes dominate his writing. In 1948, he and Jules Isaac founded the Amitié judéo-chrétienne de France.

The Boy Prophet
1926

I

Mariette was preparing for her first communion. This was serious:

"The most beautiful day of my life, you understand!"

I didn't understand.

"There'll be bells ringing and music and lights: celebrating me, like a queen!" . . . When I make my way up to the altar and reach the last step . . . Jesus, my God, I'll be scared to death. . . . And when I have to speak, just me, out loud, with everyone there in the church . . . I'll never have the nerve!"

"Do you have to speak?"

"Of course, to make my vow."

"What vow?"

"The vow my godfather said in my name when I was little, at my christening. Now I'll be the one saying it."

"What vow?"

"To renounce Satan and all his works and pomps."

"Pomps?" I didn't understand.

"If my first communion goes badly, I'll be forever damned, you see; I'll go straight to Hell. Whereas if my first communion goes well, I'll be with the angels. So I'm making sure to prepare."

"How are you preparing?"

"I have a confessor who helps me. . . . I examine my conscience. When I go to bed, for example, before I go to sleep I ask myself, 'What have you done wrong today? What have you done right?' And I write everything down in my notebook, my victories and my failures."

"What victories?"

"Victories over my capital sin."

"You have a capital sin?"

"All my sins are capital! Pride, above all: I always have to be the one in charge. And then gluttony: I'll eat

rotten apples. And then my impurity: I love my bath too much, especially when it's hot. . . . And you know, I've read forbidden books!"

"Forbidden books?"

"The Gospel, in French! Papa had it in his library. . . . Children aren't allowed to read it. Well! I've read it!"

That night I was thinking, as I lay in bed:

A confessor! Someone who talks to her about herself! . . . How lucky she is! . . . Me, they say to me, "Hold onto your fork. . . ." "Don't throw your bread away. Remember, some children go hungry. . . ." "Never lie; a man doesn't tell lies. . . ." But who helps me reflect on things?

Her capital sin . . . and what about me? What is my capital sin? Oh, I know! But what to call it? I don't know. . . .

I'm always afraid someone near me will say the word "Jew": that's my capital sin. No one says it, that word, when I'm around, but I'm still afraid they will. . . . My classmates, during recess . . . and in the hotels during the holidays, when I play with kids who don't know me—I'm always sure they're thinking of it! . . . How can I rid myself of this failing? I've tried: I can't!

"Jew," what is that? I know no more now than when I was five years old.

It seems Hebrews and Jews, they're the same thing. . . . When I was just starting out at the lycée, there was a chapter on the Hebrews in my history book, but it was much shorter than the ones about the Egyptians or the Assyrians. . . .

The Hebrews were a small tribe. They were nomads, wandering around with their animals and living in tents. They were slaves in Egypt. Moses led them across the Red Sea. And then, they had patriarchs who made a covenant with God. . . . A covenant with God! . . . They thought they were the chosen people! . . .

They also had kings: Solomon succeeded David around 973 BC and built the Temple where they made burnt offerings. In the Temple there were candlesticks with seven branches. Nebuchadnezzar lay siege to Jerusalem, burned down the Temple, and led the Hebrews in captivity to Babylon. . . .

And they had prophets, also, who said that other gods were false gods, and that their god was the only God, creator of heaven and earth. And they prophesied that one day a Messiah would come to deliver them and bring justice to the world. . . .

Where are they, these Hebrews? What have I to do with Them?

Israel, God's people! . . .

Coming back from school, I stop in front of the newspaper stand at the corner of the bridge. There's always a newspaper spread open in the window, and I read: "The Jews and Bolshevism" . . . "America Delivered Over to the Jews" . . . "France Betrayed by the Jews." . . .

So Papa, who enlisted, who returned to the front in spite of the medical officers, with a bullet in his lung and his ribs shattered . . . he betrayed France?

What are these Hebrews? What are these Jews?

II

I was leaning on the bridge railing, looking at the water. I continued to think about my Jews and my Hebrews. And suddenly I heard someone whistling behind me, a very happy tune I hadn't heard before. I turned around. It was Marnier, who said to me:

"What are you doing there, daydreaming? You're always daydreaming. Oh! I see you all right, all alone in your corner during recess. You should come with us."

"You, who?"

"The Scouts, that's who. We have fun. We become stronger. We walk, we run, we jump. We cook for ourselves. We sew on our buttons. We live in tents like explorers."

"Oh! Well I ride horseback sometimes, I swim a little, that's good enough for me!"

"Because you're at the head of the class? That's very nice, being first. But you also need to know how to get along in life, old boy. Look, for example. . . . You live in this neighborhood?"

"Yes, that house over there next to the quay."

"OK, then! Tell me where there are some nearby pharmacies."

"There's one on the Rue Saint-Louis-en-l'Île."

"And then?"

"And then. . . ."

"You only know of one? That's not a lot. And the fire stations? You don't know? If you were a Scout, you'd know. . . . We learn to be useful. We help those in need. We're the Knights of Modern Times. You should come

one Sunday to see. I'd be proud to have you in our troop. You'll come? Don't say no. Don't answer. Think about it. We'll talk more about it later, right?

And he shook my hand. And he laughed, showing his dimples. And he took off, whistling. . . .

Be a Scout? No thank you: I'm thinking about the Hebrews!

III

Every afternoon around four thirty, Mariette would go to Notre Dame for her "visit to the Blessed Sacrament." And I, on my way home from the lycée, would wait for her in front of the church door. We'd walk a bit in the garden, then I'd walk with her to her house, which was nearby on the Rue Chanoinesse. . . . It didn't last long!

Mariette would look so worried, coming out of the church! She'd say, "I prayed badly today."

Or else, "I was distracted. I didn't feel He was there. . . . Because He is there, you know, in the tabernacle on the altar. . . . He is there, just as He was among the apostles, as He was with the Blessed Virgin and with Mary Magdalene. . . . Oh! if only I could feel, just once, that He was there, without thinking of anything else at all: I would enter the kingdom of heaven, you understand?"

I didn't understand.

I'm waiting at the door one day when Mariette comes out: I run to her. . . . What? She doesn't see me? She's looking away? She doesn't want to know me anymore? She's leaving? Why? What have I done to her?

Oh! The long needle that sank right into my heart! And my whole body turning to stone, just like Saint Denis up there above the porch with his head cut off! . . .

And I remembered that Christmas long ago: "little Jews are punished . . . little Jews are unhappy. . . ."

For two days I didn't go to wait for her. The third day, I couldn't bear it any longer . . . I went back.

I'm looking for her, trembling. . . . Is she here? Will she come out? . . .

There she is! . . . She saw me! . . . What will she do? . . .

The old blind woman stretches out her hand. Mariette puts a sou in the begging bowl. . . .

I too would like to stretch out my hand! . . .

Not a glance. . . . She passes on. . . . She's gone. . . .

What bad work I did, that whole week! . . . For the first time in my life, I flunked recitation. Mama couldn't understand it at all. I wasn't sleeping.

Oh! I was careful not to pass in front of Notre Dame on my way back from the lycée. I just cut through the garden in the back, taking little steps, so slowly, so slowly! . . .

Who knows! Maybe I'll run into her without intending to! . . .

And one day, at the very end of the week . . . I had sat down on one of the benches, my Greek grammar book open on my lap. I told myself I was studying the first declension . . . . Someone is there! . . . I raise my eyes: Mariette! . . .

"I hurt you, didn't I, my dear Claude? What could I do? I was thinking about you too much in the presence of the Blessed Sacrament: I had to punish myself!"

On another occasion she said to me, very mysteriously, "Wait for me tomorrow at the tip of the island, you know. . . ."

That was our favorite spot, the end facing the Pont-Neuf and the Louvre, where the trees hang over the water.

I was waiting. The sky was red. . . .

. . . What does she have to tell me?

And I thought about later, when we would be married. . . . Her silver ring, I still had it, but now it was too small for my finger. . . . I pulled it out of my pocket to look at it.

And seated on the low wall at the edge of the water, I looked at it and thought:

. . . I'll write books. I'll dictate, like Uncle Jacques; and instead of a typist, she'll be the one taking it down. . . . We'll travel; just like Chateaubriand, we'll go to see the Great Sachem by the Mississippi River. . . . And then we'll have a house near the sea where poor children will come during the holidays.

I was dreaming of these things when all at once there was a hand on mine.

How Mariette cried that day!

"My poor Claude! My poor Claude! What's happening to us! . . . My confessor. . . . My confessor told me. . . ."

She could hardly breathe. Her cheeks were aquiver.

"It seems a Christian girl and a . . . a . . . "

"A Jewish boy?"

"Yes . . . a Jewish boy and a Christian girl are not allowed to marry!"

And her arms stretched out to hold me. And she cried, how she cried!

IV

I said to myself, I want to know what they'll have to say about it. Papa will have that little smile of his, but so what. I'll ask the question at lunch.

But Papa had invited a government official to lunch: and I ate alone in my room.

. . . Well, then, tonight, after the soup!

After the soup Papa was explaining his wireless telephone to Mama. How could I interrupt?

. . . Well, when Justin serves the asparagus, then!

Justin serves the asparagus. Mama tells Papa about her Stravinsky quartet. . . . Stravinsky, that's sacred! What can I do?

Fortunately, at dessert I had more luck. The word "marriage" came up by itself!

"She's a young Kahn," Mama said.

"You mean there are more?" Papa said.

"Jacques met her this summer in Vittel," Mama said.

"I thought the cure was harmless!" Papa said.

"But you're not going to like this, my dear: they're getting married in the synagogue. Grandfather Kahn insists on it."

"The eternal grandfather!"

"My brother gave in, you see. . . ."

"That's just like him!"

"And Claude, dear, you'll be a groomsman . . . ."

And Mama looked at me so sweetly.

"You'll have to look your best!"

And suddenly I'm the one talking. I'm astonished to hear myself; my voice sounds strange.

"Mama, is it true that Jews can't marry Christians?"

"Who told you that?" said Papa.

"A friend."

"So! Well, do me the pleasure of telling your friend: first of all, you don't say 'Jews,' you say 'Israelites'; second, we're not living in the Middle Ages anymore."

"Really? They couldn't do it in the Middle Ages? And now they can?"

"They can, my boy; they can, and in fact they must. Remember this for the rest of your life, young fellow: there are no more Jews, there are no more Christians: there are human beings."

And lying in bed I said to myself:

"She could! We could! She's the one who doesn't want to! . . . Because I'm a little Jew, yes, I know! . . . I'll never see her again, never! . . . If I even think of her, I'll punish myself!"

How hard I worked that whole week! Three compositions: first in History, first in French, first in Latin! . . . I no longer went past the church. I no longer cut across the garden. . . . I hurried home as fast as I could without looking up.

No, I don't want to see her again! No, I don't want to see her again! . . . I've thought of her: a punishment!

My punishment was to work a problem. . . . I was often at a loss in math class. . . . Ah! what progress I made in math during that time!

. . . I will not see her again! I will not see her again!

V

Marnier had another go at me.

"What are you thinking about there in your little corner?"

"And what about you, what do you think about when you're alone?"

"Depends. Out on the street, I look at people passing by, the expression on their faces, the way they walk; or else I look down to see if there are any orange peels or watches or coin-purses: you never know. . . . Then I count the turns, I calculate the width of the sidewalks, the height of the houses, I pick out landmarks. . . . In my room, it's different: I try to remember which stores I passed by, what was in the windows. Or else I ask myself what I'd do if the neighbor's place caught fire, or if a thief was on the roof. Or else I get ready for our next outing: this Sunday I'll need to know how to send a message in Morse code, sixteen letters a minute, how to

pluck a bird and cook it, and know which way is north without using a compass. Ah! It's hard work being a first-class Scout, old boy!"

Marnier's an odd duck, it's as if his thoughts turn outward, while mine turn inward. He doesn't even know if he's feeling anything or not. But I know what I'm feeling even before I feel it.

Is it because I'm Jewish?

VI

One day the slow-talking concierge says to me, in a formal manner meant to be funny, "A package for Monsieur Claude."

A package? For me? . . . Immediately I think: It's from her!

"I was told to give it to Monsieur Claude in person."

. . . It's from her! It's from her! I won't open it!

"I'm therefore presenting it to Monsieur Claude in person."

Quickly, the package in my book bag! I climb the stairs two at a time without waiting for the elevator. I ring the bell. I'm in my room. The package is on my table. I touch the string. . . .

. . . I won't open it! I won't open it! . . .

And I open it.

First, a letter falls out:
My Dear Claude,
I told you it's forbidden. But I've learned something new: if one isn't a Christian, one can apparently still become a Christian. And then it is all right.
Love,
Mariette

And along with the letter, a very small book.
I read the title:
The Gospel of Our Lord Jesus Christ, according to Saint Matthew.
Always Jesus!

Translated by Michele McKay Aynesworth

Other works by Fleg: *Anthologie juive* (1923); *Le chant nouveau* (1946); *Écoute Israël* (1954).

Louis Golding

1895–1958

The prolific novelist, poet, and travel writer Louis Golding was born in Manchester and educated at Manchester Grammar School and Queen's College, Oxford. His best-known novels, including *Magnolia Street* (1932), which won him international recognition, drew on his intimate knowledge of immigrant Jewish life in his birthplace, which he called Doomington in his fiction. Although sometimes hailed as the successor to Israel Zangwill in Anglo-Jewish literature, his work lacked the latter's staying power and was rarely read after his death.

Those Ancient Lands, Being a Journey to Palestine
1928

Chapter V. Dawn in Palestine

I cannot linger in Egypt. They that came before me tarried too long. I have had the taste on my tongue and the dead air in my nostrils. Enough. That will serve.

Zagazig, the swarthy faces. Ismalieh, the British faces, the cascading flowers, the trim hedges. The desert again. Sand sifting remorselessly through the chinks in the sealed train. The dark canal and the dark desert. A liner from Suez ramming the darkness with a pole of light. The ferry-boat at El Kantara. Catholic pilgrims fingering their rosaries; Russian priests stroking their beards; tall Arabs standing for'ard, hitting the stars with their heads. A gentle English lady, so well-connected, so ineffably descended. And Jews. They do not talk horse-racing or Shechita (which is Ritual Slaughter), as they did in my native city. Not stocks and shares, as they do in Throgmorton Street, in London. What is this they are saying? So many more dunams bought, so many more might be put under cultivation this year! This cistern might be taken as containing so much water. So much more water must be brought in from the well down the valley. They are talking English, the Jews nearest me, others German. They are talking another language, too, but I cannot yet make it out, in the scuffle and confusion. It takes not many minutes to heave to against the shelf of Asia.

Yes, it is Hebrew, of course. The porters speak it at El Kantara, the agents. Nobody does not, excepting I, and the gentle English lady. And the pilgrims, of course,

and the priests. But the Arabs speak a Semitic ghost of it. And when I ask the young man in the train in one language and another whether the corner is occupied, he does not understand. English is foreign to him and French and German, Yiddish even. No, he does not understand Italian. A tall Briton in khaki with whom I have passed a few words of impeccable English is standing near us. He wears the astrakhan tarbouche on his head, which is the distinctive feature of British uniform in Palestine. The tall Briton in khaki translates my question into Hebrew, and the young gentleman bows and makes it evident that the corner is not occupied. I blush with humiliation and strike my rucksack fiercely.

Hebrew lulls me to sleep. Hebrew awakes me. My eyes open on a long, green lowland of orange-groves. Sinai that was the evil dream of forty years, is the swift dream of a night. It is early morning. An exquisite air floods all cool space. We are at Lydda. The gentle lady from the shires in England goes on with the train to Haifa. I am for Jerusalem. The train lingers. We embark upon her favourite topic of genealogy, this thin, refined lady and I, in the crescent sonorous dawn. No, she belongs to the Warwickshire branch of the family, not to the Yorkshire. I congratulate her on her choice. The Warwickshire branch goes back not merely to the Crusaders; they go back to Charlemagne.

Am I drunk with the air of this land? "Madame," I protest," in Warwickshire I should have been astounded. But I confess that in the Vale of Sharon my stupefaction is less serious. I have a more redoubtable ancestry. I go back to the Kings of Judah. I go back to the Patriarchs of Israel!"

She looks away a little uneasily. She is not certain, after all, despite our common interest in Giovanni Bellini, that I am quite a nice person to know. The train separates us.

Another lady from England is in the train for Jerusalem. But England was only a stage on her journey. She is a Palestinian. It is on her lips I first hear the word "Jew" as if it were not a thing to qualify, to temporise over, but to proclaim with not less pride than an Anglo-Indian colonel proclaims the word "Englishman." Oh, but the pride she has in the groves of orchards and olive that the train passes! How her eyes shine as she points them out, planted and grafted and pruned by her own sisters and brothers. We halt at a small station, duly announced in English and Hebrew and Arabic. A band of young men and women from an adjacent colony get into the train. Had you allowed your mind—dazzled by the light, stupid with happiness—to go wandering for a moment, it might have seemed to you that you were transported to Bavaria of the Hackenkreuzlers, or the *gemütlich* plains of Sachsen, where the pretty maidens *wachsen*. For here are young men in black or khaki jerkins, open at the neck, and shorts half-way down an expanse of bronze thigh. And here are girls with lustrous hair unbound or cut firm to the head. They have a strong head. You might deem them *Wandervögel*. But they are not. Kurt and Gretl are twanging litanies on their guitars to Wodin and Thor in the far Norse forests. These are Jewish lads and maidens, pioneering. These are the *chalutzim*. They find their places in the train, and suddenly the whole train shakes with the song they break into— a Hebrew folk-song, arisen as spontaneously among their own wheat as the poppies that still blaze scarlet there. And the Palestinian lady beside me suspends her English and joins in the tune, marking time with her head and fingers. Then the song ceases, and she resumes the thread of her fervent exposition.

The train has left the green valley now. We have entered the defiles of the mountains of Judea. Higher and higher we ascend towards the city on the hills. It is evident that these slopes—steeper than I had thought to find in Palestine—were terraced with vines once. The platforms are still apparent, despite the ignorant centuries which have sought to obliterate them with rubble. But be very sure, says the Palestinian lady, that the purple clusters will hang down, terrace upon terrace, to the green tops. Now and again we pass near enough to a settlement for the small children to run out to the sound of the train and shout to us and wave their hands. What red cheeks, what sturdy limbs, what lively eyes! A man must enter into closer acquaintance with them. Are these kindred to the sallow little creatures we were and knew in Sheffield, in Pittsburgh? Of all the flowers and fruit that grow in this land, are there any of more promise?

We have ascended so high into a stony world that the houses, even of the Arabs (whose deficiencies the Palestinian lady points out with just a shade too much asperity), are of stone, not of sun-baked mud. Of a sudden, stone houses, buildings, warehouses, collect and jostle against each other. The engine shrieks. The brakes grind. We are in Jerusalem.

Now if you enter Jerusalem in a romantic spirit, like Ivanhoe, or ivy, or the Moonlight Sonata, you will be disappointed. You will find no assembly of *Chassidim* (those joyous mystics) at the station engaged upon a round of ritual dancing, nor a company of Muslims upon their prayer-rugs facing towards Mecca and crying upon the Prophet with their hands at the lobe of the ears. You will not even find a synod of Greek bishops sharpening their knives against the throats of a conclave of heretics from Abyssinia. You will plunge at once into an atmosphere even more thrilling than this—an atmosphere of things at once older than the hills upon which Jerusalem stands and of things newer than the latest shack in a new oilfield in Texas. The earlocks of a pious scholar from Galicia sway in the wind of onset caused by a furious Buick. An immaculate curate from a theological college in Oxfordshire gazes sentimentally upon a Bedouin shepherd bringing in his flocks, without a ghost of a suspicion that the same harmless and picturesque gentleman held up the car in which his own Bishop was driving to Shechem, shot the Bishop's chauffeur dead and landed a bullet under the collarbone of the Bishop's lady. And swiftly, efficiently, with decision at the corners of their mouths, the pioneers go about to perform those duties which have brought them up to the city, and must not keep them too long from the acre which must be cleared of stones and the saplings which must be cherished.

But even these, despite the amount of work to be got through, cannot quite conceal their excitement. The whole air thrills with it. You might expect the ladies in the polite suburb of Telpioth to react to it visibly and audibly. But the excitement of Palestine communicates itself far beyond the Jewish fringes, into congregations with blonde skins and ebony skins, into the hearts of serious young gentlemen bristling with fountain-pens and obscure bandits armed with rifles. Curates fumble their service at tennis. Muslim guardians of the tombs of prophets forget to ask for baksheesh. The Jews are in Palestine. Even about the flat grave-stones that ascend the Mount of Olives from the depths of Kidron, there is a shimmer of light, a movement of air. The fellaheen, the Arab labourers on the land, add unto themselves gramophones. The effendis, the Arab gentry, add unto themselves motorcars. The Jews are in Palestine.

Not only the living Jews are in Palestine, the dead are there. But it was not of those countless dead of long ago I was reminded, the day of my arrival in Jerusalem— the countless dead who heaped themselves up to be the walls of her cities and sanctuaries, when the stone walls were breached. I was reminded of those who died a decade ago, among their British companions, when Palestine was wrested from the Turk. It was the day of the unveiling by Lord Allenby of the great cemetery upon Mount Scopus, on the flank of the hill away from the Hebrew University. I could not help thinking it a significant juxtaposition—the monument to the men who had died that wisdom and beauty might live safely in this land which was once their fountain-head. I do not use the word "cemetery" happily of a monument which subdues itself so admirably to the landscape it is set in. And I divorce from my mind a consideration which somewhat rankled in the minds of the Jews of Jerusalem. For the day was the Jewish Sabbath, and it was felt that it was inelegant, to put it no more strongly, that the authorities should not have chosen the day for the unveiling more carefully. It meant that the Muslim sheikhs, who had been the enemies of the lads who lay under these simple stones, were represented there, and the negroid clerics from Abyssinia; but that the Rabbis of the Sephardim and the Ashkenazim were absent from the graveside of the Jewish lads.

But in that radiant air, and looking down upon that supernal landscape, we had it in our hearts to forgive, perhaps too swiftly, this sad breach of decorum. Turning away towards the city, whither the graves also face, spread out before us was such a pageant of domes and spires and towers as the world does not offer elsewhere. And upon one hand was the great trench of Jordan that falls into the Dead Sea, and upon the other the stony plateau of Judea that breaks into the plain and the Mediterranean. And beyond the Jordan the alabaster wall of Moab, translucent in the strong sun. And we turned towards the graves again and included in the vast compound were nearly two score Jewish youths, and not the most rigorous there could but feel that both the cross on the Christian stones and David's Shield on the Jewish stones were both glorified by their unprecedented contiguity. The flowers of their home places bloomed before them equally, marigold and geranium and stock, and small hedges of rosemary were everywhere odorous in the hot late noon. And those of the Jews who were London "Schneiders," tailors from London, as some certainly were, would not be less grateful for these flowers in the cool of the evening than Rifleman Hargreaves, who came from a small town in Lancashire, and the boy named Sneath who drove a straight plough over the rich tilth of Lincolnshire. For you, O Private Mittelman, and you, O Private Goliansky, are in truth successful where the Maccabees, your progenitors, failed.

You wrought well with your fierce weapons. But in the smithies of the University not far from your graves,

they are forging gentler weapons to achieve the work you began with grenade and bayonet. The test-tubes seethe in the laboratories. And in edges of the horizon beyond stony Judea, the whet-stone is sharp upon the scythes and upon the pruning hooks. O my London tailors, you will not rest unhappily among the low hedges of rosemary.

Other works by Golding: *Forward from Babylon* (1920); *Give Up Your Lovers* (1930); *The Doomington Wanderer* (1934); *Tales of the Silver Sisters*, 4 vols. (1934–1951); *The Jewish Problem* (1938).

Israel Joshua Singer

1893–1944

Israel Joshua Singer was born in Lublin province, and was the brother of Esther Singer Kreitman and Isaac Bashevis Singer. He traveled to Moscow in 1918 but returned to Warsaw in 1921, where he became—along with Peretz Markish, Melekh Ravitch, Uri Zvi Greenberg, and others—a member of the expressionist group Di Khalyastre. Singer worked as a European correspondent for *Forverts* from 1924 and settled in the United States in 1934. The last of his European novels, *Yoshe Kalb,* was successfully adapted for the stage in New York. His novel *The Brothers Ashkenazi*, published in 1936 in Yiddish and in English translation, became representative of the pessimistic view of Jewish culture (traditional, socialist, or Zionist) in a hostile East European environment, whether tsarist or Soviet.

The New Russia: Pictures from a Journey
1928

Across Borders

The compartment of the Berlin–Warsaw–Moscow train is warm and pleasant. The dining car is fully packed. One can hear various languages—French, German, English, Russian, Chinese, and some Polish, too. At one little table sit several heavy-built, blond people; they speak English in a loud voice. Their loud and free talk and the fact that—ignoring etiquette—they sit in the dining car in sweaters [without a jacket], is an instant giveaway that they are Americans. They must be traveling to Russia to get concessions, business.

At another table sit several short, lean, brownskinned French people; they speak quietly and wear dark suits and white shirts. One often hears the word *Moscou*. All three Chinese passengers, two men and one woman, wear huge, American glasses and are dressed according to the latest fashion. The fat Chinese woman wears a pink jumper and looks rather funny in it. She serves the two gentlemen soup from a jar, which is not a simple task for her. Her hands are probably more used to operating Chinese chopsticks for eating rice.

The Russians, most of them employees of Soviet consulates and embassies, have the demeanors of diplomats: they are elegant, quiet, somewhat conceited, and somewhat ironic. Dressed in fine lace, the diplomats' daughters are modest and alluring at the same time. They smoke long, thin cigarettes and read large newspapers in various languages with a certain degree of skepticism.

In my compartment there is a mixed company of travelers. There is a young Russian engineer who had been sent abroad by the Soviets to study modern technology. He is quite straightforward, like most Russians, and openly expresses his joy about coming closer and closer to Russia.

"It has been very interesting everywhere," he says, "but I am homesick. Here it is still raining, but back home in Moscow everything must be white by now, covered with snow. *Ekh, dayosh Moskve*" [Oh, to get to Moscow], he finishes his speech like a soldier. [. . .]

I call attention to the fact that Russians have developed a strong sense of patriotism lately, something that was foreign to most Russians before, with very few exceptions. Russians have always considered that which was theirs crude. The Russians admit to it:

"It's true, we have become patriots. . . ."

Soon the actor Kareniev begins to talk to me. It turns out that he knows the artist Vofsi [Solomon Mikhoels] from the Yiddish Chamber Theater as well as other Yiddish artists, and that he is a Jew himself.

I start to talk to him in Yiddish. He understands, but answering is too difficult for him.

"Unfortunately," he explains himself in Russian, "I am used to speaking only Russian."

In a situation like this a Polish Jew would not find it necessary to justify why he doesn't know any Yiddish. But here even his wife felt a little embarrassed. The husband tried to console her:

"But you don't have to know Yiddish. After all, you are Russian."

"Yes," she says, "I am Russian, but my husband is a Jew."

This was so natural and simple that even the Polish diplomat wasn't surprised. [. . .]

Minsk

Four languages—Belorussian, Russian, Polish, and Yiddish—are posted at the train station. [. . .] I come across them wherever I go. Signs are displayed in these four languages in every commissariat and every office, everywhere.

When in 1919 the Bolsheviks hung up, for the first time in Kiev on Great Vasilkov Street, a sheet of paper that said "Y. L. Peretz Street" in Yiddish, Jews themselves laughed in their fists:

"Ha-ha-ha, it's written in Yiddish . . . they are crazy!"

By now this has become routine. I am probably the only one who is puzzled.

A Jewish wagoner drives me to the Europa Hotel. They have no meter, and no matter how much money you give them they will bargain anyway.

The hotel is clean and neat. For five rubles a day I get a large room.

The porter, a young man takes me to the first floor by elevator. Some fellow, wearing nothing but a shirt, pulls up his pants and asks me in a drunken voice:

"Are you with a woman, or without one?"

For a while I think that I am back in the Russia of 1918–1920, but then the porter apologizes:

"Sorry, he is drunk," and he takes me to my room, a nice large room with electric lighting and soft furniture, and I realize I was wrong; it turns out that my fellow travelers in the train were right when they said that "war communism" has vanished without a trace. [. . .]

I enter an optician's shop—I want to buy frames for my new glasses. An elderly Jew with a tormented face and a patched caftan looks at me with an anxious look in his eyes.

"Lenses? We can't get those anymore."

Finally he manages to dig up a pair of green frames for me. He wants to charge two rubles. "In Warsaw, these cost one zloty and fifty grosz," I say to him. "All right, bring me a couple of frames and I will pay you a ruble fifty for each." We continue to talk. Until the revolution he was the best optician in town. Now he only has a few broken frames left. . . . He warms himself by the brazier.

"Things are better now," he says, "I work independently, I am a *kustar* [craftsman], people envy me. But what good is it if you have no merchandise? There is one factory in Russia that produces bad eyeglass frames, so you don't sell anything privately." And I heard the same thing from almost every merchant and store owner.

"Look at them," they point out the cooperatives. "Every day they push us further out of business, and we can't find anything else do. There is nothing left for us but to throw ourselves into the river.

In spite of all this everyone agrees that Minsk is still a joyful, lively city. To this day it has retained the charm of Litvish Jewish cities situated not far from the border, where great ideas and smuggling, fearfulness and lawlessness, religious devotion and heresy, modesty and dissoluteness, antiquity and modernity are compressed together in the narrow, grubby alleys and houses, and fill the city with life, restlessness, and hope.

Here people are still more provincial and old-fashioned, more sluggish and thus have more faith. Here, unlike in Moscow, the eyes of the youth still sparkle with enthusiasm, just as in the early days of the revolution. Young people attend lectures and courses more frequently than in Moscow. Almost everyone has a pack of *dokladn* in their briefcase, reports on how to save the country, how to revolutionize the world.

Jewish life is more meaningful, has more significance here than in Moscow. Of course, Moscow has a much larger Jewish population than Minsk. In Moscow there is the Yiddish Chamber Theater, there are publishing houses, clubs, a Jewish Department, courses. Important Jewish leaders and writers live in Moscow, too, but on the flag of the great, genuinely Russian Moscow built of hard stones and churches Jewish life is nothing but a strange stain, an absurd mark.

Kalinin had good reason to say at the convention of the GEZERD[1] that if he were a rabbi he would curse all the Jews who abandoned Jewish culture and the Jewish masses and moved to Moscow.

In fact, this is why antisemitism is stronger in Moscow than anywhere else; why Jewish leaders who have lived in Moscow for a while are angrier, more embittered, and more russified than Jewish leaders elsewhere; why Yiddish writers in Moscow are so abstract; why the [newspaper] *Emes* [Truth] is so dry, rigid, and easily translatable. This is why the great, genuinely Russian Moscow built of hard stones and churches can't stand the little Jewish nuisance that has latched onto it.

In Minsk having Yiddish signs, schools, courses, a theater, a newspaper, a court of law, and a scholarly institution is the natural way of things. What is unnatural is that they did not exist before the revolution; and this

is why people feel so good in Minsk; this is why Jewish leaders in Minsk are more humane and have more integrity; and why the youth here is more "heimish" and warm.

AT THE JEWISH COURT

[. . .] Dozens of Jewish men and women have gathered in the run-down courtroom. The table is covered with a red tablecloth. Lenin's portrait hangs on the main wall. The court convenes late. There is too much work. Almost all Jews turn to the Jewish court with their legal issues, so the judges constantly have to work overtime. The women who have appeared are restless.

"Mariaske," says one Jewish woman to another, "I won't wait any longer. I am going home." "Go on," says her neighbor, "Yisroelke the militiaman will come to 'call' you." Mariaske stays. She knows that Yisroelke the militiaman takes his job seriously. If you don't appear in court you will be punished. She continues to wait and complain:

"I left the little ones at home alone—it's a sin against God!"

A Jew with a trimmed beard jokes with her:

"God doesn't exist anymore. Can't you see that Lenin is on the wall, not God?"

"In Kamarovke we still have a god," says the woman.

Kamarovke is a neighborhood in Minsk. Finally a dark-skinned young man enters the court room, rings the bell, and says:

"All rise—the court is here."

Everyone stands up and my acquaintance whispers to me:

"The secretary of the court is a young poet, very talented."

The poet, a young man wearing glasses, sits down at the table. On the two sides of the table sit a man and a woman, both of them workers wearing poor clothes—they are co-judges who are selected from the residents of the city, the way they used to select the jury.

"The case of Kahan-Shtieglitz," calls out the judge.

An elderly Jew walks up to the table.

The charge against him is that he is not providing support to his wife whom he had left some time ago, even though the court had ordered him to pay a certain amount of alimony. Goldberg the militiaman went to seize Kahan's lace ware but Kahan took the goods and put them into the room of his landlady, Mrs. Shtieglitz, and then claimed that they weren't his, that they belonged to his landlady.

"I am a poor man; where would I get the money to pay alimony when I myself don't have any? Those goods belong to my landlady, Comrade Judge. . . ."

The abandoned wife screams from the bench:

"You should live as long as this is true, you old sinner! Shtieglitz is not your landlady but your lover! You live with her!"

The judge rings the bell.

"Citizen Kahan! You will have a chance to speak, too; do not interrupt the proceedings!"

But citizen Kahan can't hold back:

"What an old scoundrel, what a good-for-nothing!"

The judge threatens Mrs. Shtieglitz with a fine. Her lawyer barely manages to contain her and calm her down.

Goldberg the militiaman speaks in a newspaper-style Yiddish:

"I know the street where Kahan lives like my ten fingers. I can confirm that the goods that I came to take possession of belong to him. His explanation does not correspond to the truth."

The witnesses are interrogated for another hour. Then it's the lawyers' turn to speak.

Lawyers in Russia are not in an enviable position. Whereas lawyers in other countries sit in front and wear tailcoats and waistcoats, lawyers in Russia sit on the bench together with the audience; the judge hears them out but doesn't argue with them, doesn't make much fuss over them.

In fact, here comes an older lawyer who defends the former husband, citizen Kahan. He is the type of an old provincial *prisiazhniy paviereny* who knows the entire legal code by heart, just as well as a religious Jew knows *Ashrei* [a prayer recited several times a day]. Now, however, he has to speak in Yiddish, and that is not at all easy for him.

"Comrade Judge," he begins his speech.

The judge corrects him:

"Citizen Judge!"

"Forgive me, Judge Citizen," he continues.

But he quickly realizes that he made a mistake again and, wanting to correct himself, gets even more mixed up:

"Comrade Citizen . . . ah . . . I mean Citizen Comrade. . . ."

Everyone in the room laughs. The old man becomes even more confused. He speaks half-Yiddish half-Russian, and paragraphs pour from his mouth like from a sack full of holes.

The wife's lawyer is young; he is a good orator, a modern man. He speaks a pure Yiddish in a style that is actually too lofty, and instead of quoting paragraph after paragraph he uses "psychology."

"What a delightful young man," the girls whisper to each other secretly.

"All rise," commands the secretary.

The judge consults with the co-judges and passes the verdict. For a while the two parties and the witnesses make a commotion. The next case is already being called, this time a criminal case. A Jewish woman, a butcher who works in a cooperative in the meat department, has been accused of theft. The court is filled with butchers, agents. The mood is tense; a prison sentence is likely.

I pay a visit to the judge in his chambers. He was once a worker, then he fought at the front for a while, and finally he was appointed the judge of Minsk. He has no legal training, of course, but learned the code of law by heart.

Even though he is very busy he is delighted to devote a few minutes to talking to me.

"There is a lot of work," he says. "Eighty percent of all Jews turn to the Jewish court, even from other districts, and especially in criminal cases."

"Why is that?"

"First of all because of the language—people can present their arguments in Yiddish; secondly, because of the environment. There are many court cases that require the judge to know the [social, religious, and cultural] environment. The judge needs to understand the circumstances, the conflicts, the customs, and even the tone of voice. That's why people turn to the Yiddish court. In fact, they come to us too often—they turn to the court even with the most insignificant issues."

"And how do Jews relate to the court?"

"By now things have improved. At the beginning people talked and argued too much, they behaved as if they were talking to their rabbi. By now they have become used to discipline, but they still take offense that they can't pour their hearts out. [. . .]

I am at the Institute for Belorussian Culture, the *Inbielkult*.

In the corridor a servant takes my coat. Bright, beautiful apartments. Many young men and women work here, all light-haired and light-eyed. This is the first time that I hear Belorussian spoken in the Belorussian Republic.

In the Jewish Department people sit. Here no one knows anything about politics—they just work and work. Folklore, history, philology, bibliography. They collect everything that has been created by Jews in various languages. They are preparing a Yiddish academic dictionary. Students sit and enumerate the words of the Yiddish classics, in order to collect all the words used in Yiddish literature. People collect material for the [description of] Yiddish dialects. They send out little cards in order to collect Yiddish expressions. They go on expeditions to towns where Yiddish writers were born and wrote their works. There are commissions working in the fields of local studies [gegnt-kentenish], the Jewish way of life [lebns-shteyger], economics, statistics, and demography.

These people take their work very seriously and are deeply committed to it. If only we had such scholars like Dubnov, they tell me, so that the world would have the greatest trust in the scholarly academy into which our department should be transformed. We will forgive them all of their sins just so they come and work with us. [...]

I have met several Belorussian writers, the most prestigious of them Yanka Kupala. He has accumulated many political sins against the Soviets but was excused anyway, and he didn't even have to repent, like us Jews. I think he is on a state stipend. Among the Belorussian writers there is also a Lithuanian Jew with a head of curly hair—the Belorussian poet Biadula [pseudonym of Shmuel Efimovich Plavnik]. His portrait hangs in many Belorussian schools.

He tells me, in a village Yiddish with a strong rolled r-sound, about the Belorussian literary journal for which he works.

The place of knowledge is just as pure, clean, and clear as knowledge itself.

[...] In the besmedresh [chapel, small study hall] Jews pray heartily. They say Kaddish. But there are not many young people among them.

They look me up and down. I am the only one wearing a hat. They all wear bicycle-hats, caps, fur hats—but no one wears a regular hat.

"Do you need to say Kaddish?" a skinny Lithuanian Jew turns to me. Based on his appearance he must be the beadle.

"No, I just came to see how Jews pray."

"You came from abroad?"

They all surround me. An older man tells me his story:

"I used to be, as you see me here, a great forest merchant; today I sell wood by the pood, sometimes by the pound, but I am not complaining—as long as things are calm and safe and Jews can live with a raised head."

"If there is nothing to eat," says a little Jew, "you will lower your head automatically." "Jews shouldn't complain about Soviet power," interjects another Jew with a trimmed beard. "Jews have never had the kind of rights they have now. . . ." "You have it good, you are a kustar [private artisan, craftsman]," a tall young man reproaches him. "Kustars have a good life. I'd like to see how content you would be working in a store. . . ."

Kustars are held in high esteem these days, and they are strong supporters of the Soviet regime. Jews in Russia used to abstain from handwork that was considered improper; today, however, they embrace it as a respected profession.

"I am a kustar!" a handworker announces proudly in the prayer house. Thus, he will be given the honor of reading the sixth passage [aliyah] from the Torah.

I am visiting one of Minsk's several Yiddish schools.

The discipline there is weak. They teach according to the Dalton system—I don't know much about pedagogy, unfortunately. I talk to the children. The sharp-eyed and sharp-tongued Litvak Jewish boys and girls are at ease; they talk freely. There is no trace left of their one-time bashfulness.

"I am about to graduate from school," says one girl.

"What are you planning to do afterwards?"

"I want to study tailoring."

"Are your parents tailors?"

"No, they are storekeepers. But I want to work."

I learn from the teacher that the girl's parents are not poor. For this girl working is not a necessity but an ideal, the result of the school's apotheosis of work.

"And I want to be a mechanic," says a fifteen-year-old boy.

"Is that what you have an inclination for?"

"Not at all. But we have to build up industry, so we need mechanics."

"And I am going to the Ped-Technikum," says a skinny girl who wears boots. "I want to be a teacher."

A little boy, pale and lean, his head like an old man's, comes forward and asks me:

"You are from Warsaw—do you happen to know my brother?"

He says the name of a well-known activist of the Tse'ire Tsiyon in Warsaw.

I tell him about his brother who happens to be an acquaintance of mine.

"Will you also join the Tse'ire Tsiyon?" I ask the boy.

"Oh, no, not me!" says the little boy and his face turns red from shame.

He is already a Komsomolets [member of the communist youth league], he can recite all the teachings of the Komsomol by heart, just like a talented yeshiva *bokher* [student] who knows the Talmud. He leads meetings, writes theses, and gives lectures. And suddenly such a shame! [...]

PIGS

Even after I grew up and became somewhat of a heretic I still could not fathom how non-Jews could eat pork.

Oh, how disgusted I used to feel when, during market days, the pig slaughterers would stand right by our window holding sides and topsides of pigs! I remember how I pitied those poor non-Jews who would come, ask for a piece of white, greasy pork fat and eat it right there, and they even paid money for it!

I remember that Jews in the *besmedresh* used to say that only peasants eat pork; noblemen and other aristocrats won't touch it, just like Jews.

I had believed this completely, and it gave me solace. But when I saw for the first time in my life that the nobleman of our town ate pork, and that on top of that he ate an entire pig in one sitting, a roasted pig, one that stands on four feet, and with parsley in his mouth, I felt very offended. I imagine that all Jewish boys must have felt like this once.

Nowadays there are pigs in almost every Jewish colony—big, fat, English pigs that are covered in mud, rubbing themselves on every wall, shrieking, sighing, followed by entire herds of small pigs sniffing with their snouts and supporting the oink choir.

"Oink-oink," a peasant woman imitates their sounds and looks at them lovingly. Initially I was sure that she was a non-Jewish peasant woman but very soon she started speaking in a genuine Podolian Yiddish, pronouncing o-sounds instead of a.

"I raised her myself," she says proudly, "and now she is going to have little piglets. And when they grow up, *God willing*, we will make a few rubles off of them."

"Who else keeps pigs in your village?" I was interested to find out.

"Who doesn't keep pigs?" her husband answers my question with another question.

It turns out that Jews in the Poltava District were raising pigs already before the war, and they even slaughtered them themselves and prepared the meat for the winter.

"Of course we raise pigs," says an older Jewish peasant in a red fur coat who doesn't even look like a Jew. "Here is mine! Oink, oink, oink."

And I thought I knew what Jews were like!

[...] The small town of Smolevitsh that counts five hundred Jewish families has a seven-grade Yiddish school with two hundred and fifty students and nine teachers; almost all the teachers come from the Yiddish technikums and "Pedfaks" [pedagogical faculties].

The school is bustling. The older boys and girls are making banners that are to be hung in honor of the ninth anniversary of the revolution. I noticed that on every banner they wrote *Zol lebn der altveltlekher proletariat.*[2]

I call their attention to the spelling mistake; I tell them that they probably meant to write *Zol lebn der alveltlekher proletariat.*[3] They don't understand the difference the letter "t" makes. Finally the teacher explains it to them.

"And who are you?" the older students ask me.

"A Yiddish writer from Poland."

"What is your name?"

I tell them my name.

The students scrutinize me suspiciously. They have never heard my name; the teachers don't know who I am, either. They probably think that I am a show-off. But I am not an exception—they have never heard about other writers, either, writers who are older and more famous than I. True, students in the seventh grade and Yiddish teachers should be familiar with Yiddish writers, but the fact that this is not the case doesn't diminish by a hair the importance of the fact that in remote, God-forsaken Smolevitsh all Jewish children study in a Yiddish school at the state's expense.

On the Sabbath there is no instruction. The parents don't want it. The parents—at their own initiative—collect money every year and contribute to the renovation costs of the school. [...]

In Bobruisk

In the train Jews often tried to guess my profession. As I was traveling around between various cities and towns in Poland I received various business propositions. Some people assumed that I was a salesman, others that I was a butter merchant, or a leather merchant. In Bobruisk everyone thought that I was in the timber business.

"A *liesnik*?" asked the wagoner as he drove me to the hotel.

I got the same skeptical question in the tiny private hotel on Hirsh Lekert Street: "A *liesnik*?"

"Will you rent me a room?"

"I'll rent you two, if you'd like," answers the owner, an impoverished-looking Jew dressed in proletarian clothes—boots and a cap.

"You have no guests?"

"From where would I get any?" he asks back. "Once upon a time people often traveled to Bobruisk. Timber was exported from here to other countries in large quantities. Many foreigners came, noblemen used to come here to the court, as well as high-ranking officials. Today there are no noblemen, no one goes to court anymore, and if a Soviet official does turn up here, he is poor, barely has enough money to cover his expenses, so we don't make any money."

On the broad main street which is generally called either Karl Marx Street or Revolutionary Street or Soviet Street or Lenin Street, unemployed Jews walk around idly, sniffing around for a way to earn some money. But they wouldn't approach anyone to ask. These days you cannot just go up to any Jew with a business proposal. Once upon a time you could; it was safe to talk to Jews. As we say in Yiddish, "*Az men heyst Mendl, meg men esn fun zayn fendl.*" If he is called Mendl it is safe to eat from his pot.

Today you can no longer be sure whether Mendl is a kosher Jew. Mendl might be an ardent communist, an inspector, or an agent; one must be very careful.

A Russian-looking Jew who is my neighbor at the hotel strikes up a conversation with me: "Things are not good for those of us who are not 'working-class citizens,'" he says. "We have no rights, and our children face difficulties at school." Everyone complains—all the merchants, store owners, and others with nonproductive occupations—that their children have great difficulties getting accepted to schools, especially to institutions of higher education.

"And if that's not enough," adds my acquaintance, "they don't teach them [in] Russian."

"What do they teach them?"

"Yiddish. Have you heard of such a thing?"

"But they teach [in] Russian, too."

"Yes, but mostly they teach *zhargon* [Yiddish]."

"And what's the problem with that?"

"What do you mean? What kind of practical purpose does that have?"

Children from Yiddish schools are accepted everywhere. In addition, there are Yiddish technical schools, pedagogical faculties, and departments at general universities. With Yiddish you can become a technician or a clerk, but Jews still live according to their old values and purposes in life.

"And what is the new purpose?"

"What will you do with the children?"

"They study in Belorussian."

"And does learning in Belorussian have more of a practical purpose?"

"No, not really."

"Then why do you send your children to Belorussian schools instead of Yiddish schools?"

"You are right, that's also bad, but still better than having them learn in Yiddish."

"Why?"

"What do I know? Belorussian at least they don't understand."

"And why is that good?"

"At least they have to learn it. Yiddish everyone understands—why teach it?"

Just a few steps further I encounter an entirely different world.

I arrive at the building of the trade unions. They take me to see the president of all the trade unions of Bobruisk and the whole district.

His office is big and spacious. A typist is tapping away at the machine; administrators come and go, deliver documents. The telephone rings.

The president is a well-built, full-blooded young man, one of those black-haired, black-eyed Jewish boys who are bursting with energy from every part of their body—their eyes, their hair, and their tall, straight legs; their every motion and move is energetic.

"You must be from a Menshevik newspaper, right?" he asks me with a benevolent smile. "Well, that is quite all right. You want to hear about the workers' situation—please."

He takes out various bundles of papers, statistical figures, and lists, and reads them to me:

"In the Bobruisk district there are 20,000 workers; in Bobruisk itself there are 8,000 workers. Of all workers in the entire Bobruisk district, 36 percent are Jews. In our factories work is always conducted in the language spoken by the majority of the workers in any given factory: tailors, tobacco workers, veneer makers, leather workers, and box makers all conduct their professional activities in Yiddish. Wherever the majority speaks Russian, they work in Russian; but everyone, even the minority, is allowed to speak their language everywhere."

He makes a call, orders someone to bring him certain files and shows me how the Council of Professional Unions carries out its official work in several languages—in Russian, Belorussian, Yiddish, and Polish.

"In some places," he says, "we actually have to fight for Yiddish among Jewish workers. They don't speak Russian well but don't want to speak Yiddish—what buffoons! We, however, carry out what the majority wants."

He conveys the information with great accuracy and precision, as if he were giving a report. "We have attracted many Jews to the factory—masses of girls and women who used to carry around heavy baskets selling things are now working happily at our factories."

After the official conversation we continue to chat a bit, and I realize that this energetic Jewish boy is quite an interesting person.

It turns out that only seven years ago, in 1920, this bureaucrat who holds such a highly responsible position and has to conduct his work in several languages—Russian, Belorussian and Yiddish—was just a simple blacksmith who couldn't even sign his name.

"Nothing to boast about," says the healthy, good-looking man. "My father could not write, either, so he didn't teach me."

But he got lucky, by coincidence. One time a foreign army was stationed in Minsk where he lived. A soldier hit him in the face for no reason whatsoever, just because he was a Jew. The blacksmith decided to take revenge. As soon as the Bolsheviks came back to Minsk he joined the Bolshevik army in order to beat those who had hit him in the face for no good reason whatsoever.

He served in the army for two full years, fought at the front. It was during his army service that he held a pen in his hand for the first time, and he threw himself into studying with the great enthusiasm of an ignorant man.

Now he is president of the professional unions and is excellent at his job. He has a whole array of people working under him, including intellectuals, and everyone respects, honors, and fears him.

The way this blacksmith works is truly admirable. He remembers everything, knows everything and everyone well; he learned Belorussian, the official language, very quickly and speaks it fluently.

"You speak like a born Belorussian," I say to him.

"If you have to, you do," he says. "After all, this is Belorussia. . . ."

Among the various professional unions there is also one for white-collar workers such as doctors, engineers, and the like. Here is one of the educated people sitting with the president having a conversation. The black-smith from Minsk can orient himself well in high intellectual matters and can talk to doctors and engineers in a smart and tactful way.

"It is not good," he lectures the educated representative. "You have to hold more consultations."

He knows that it is much easier to work with shoemakers and tailors. The intelligentsia doesn't like to come to consultations. But he also knows that they must have the intelligentsia under their control.

"Now," he says to me, "I will try to get a leave from work. I want to go to VUZ.[4] But I doubt they would give me a leave of absence."

I have another meeting—this time not with a heroic young man but with an ordinary young woman.

The young woman they have me meet is tiny, unremarkable and doesn't come from a prominent family background; her father is not a shoemaker, a tailor, nor a peasant, just a poor little merchant, unfortunately. Nevertheless, she has a government position and works as an agronomist.

God only knows how the daughter of a Jewish merchant from Bobruisk came up with the idea of becoming an agronomist.

But, however it happened, she went to study agriculture, excelled in her studies, and then got a job with the government in the Department of Agriculture.

This Jewish girl from Bobruisk goes around the villages and hamlets of Belorussia and teaches the Belorussian peasants how to plow, how to sow wheat, plant a garden and fruit trees, and keep animals.

She has a meager salary of 70–80 rubles a month, even though she works day and night. A horse and a buggy are not always available for her to travel around the villages, so she puts on her boots, ties her head with a kerchief, and walks tens of kilometers from one remote village to the other.

"Good morning, Comrade!" she greets the peasants. "How is your cow doing? What does the orchard look like? What's new in the fields?"

And the peasants follow the instructions of this nice little Jewish girl from Bobruisk, because who would know better than her how to fertilize the land, eradicate worms from an orchard, sow, plough, and harvest?

At noon a peasant woman brings out a large bowl of potatoes and pork cracklings for the whole family, puts it on the bench and gives everyone a wooden spoonful of it, and one portion for the guest, too. The whole family sits together, everyone takes from the large communal bowl, and so does the Jewish girl from Bobruisk.

Then she wraps herself in a canvas raincoat and continues her way from one village to the next, slowly moving on roads and passing through valleys, swamps and mud, rain and snow. And when night falls, she goes into a peasant house and spends the night in a barn of hay, on the large oven, or sometimes on the hard bench, her boots under her head. [. . .]

No, not everyone is a worker in Bobruisk, and not everyone is well settled.

The Jewish woman at whose house I ate lunch is in distress. Her son is at home studying, he can't get accepted to any institute of higher education on account of his bourgeois family background, and his mother is in despair:

"What will happen to him? How will he be able to find work?"

The highest aim they can strive for is for him to be accepted as a member of a trade union and become a worker. But how can this be achieved?

This is the greatest problem. A generation grows up, a new generation that strives to study and work, a generation that sympathizes with the Bolsheviks, hates the bourgeoisie, is entirely proletarian, and still can't get any work. The fathers' greatest worry is what to do with their children. How can they make them workers?

Many are drawn into industry, but the industry is small. For now the largest industry in Russia is having children. Cities are growing, children are growing, but what do you do with them?

"Things are bad," I hear fathers of the non-working-class element complain. "Life is bitter. Our children are not accepted to schools, not employed by factories or the army—all that's left is to throw them into the river.

One Jew actually wanted me to get England and America to make order here. When I told him that England and America are not interested in this, he became my blood enemy.

"What do you mean?" he screamed at me. "Do they intend to allow such chaos in the world?"

A Jew explained to me in utter despair that the old world must die out, just like the generation of the wilderness that could not be brought into the Land of Israel.

"You understand," he told me in a Talmudic sing-song, "these people hate the old, they want to get rid of us old folks. Young people like them and they like the young people."

There is much truth in what this man said. Young people are, in fact, mostly content. Just like in America, being old does not bring you respect in Russia, either. For young people there is the social club, there are performances, lectures, newspapers, courses—they have it good. They can enjoy this world for a few pennies. The cafeteria at the social club is cheap. And even non-working-class people—as long as they are young—are not as depressed as the older generation. They are trying to adjust to the situation, to proletarize themselves. But older people are miserable. They cannot conduct business. They don't get honored in the synagogue anymore. No one respects their knowledge or their beard, not even their own children. So what is left for them? [. . .]

Jewish Vagrant Children

Among these *bezprizorny*, vagrant children, there are few Jews. Rarely do you see a Jewish child among them.

When it comes to compassion, Jews are still different from non-Jews. Jews help their orphans; they support them and don't let them sink so low.

Nevertheless, I did encounter a couple of Jewish vagrant children, or rather formerly vagrant children who are now once again living in a home and are on their best behavior.

I met one such child in Minsk. When I visited the director of the Minsk Yiddish Theater, M. Rafalski, a twelve-year-old boy with black eyes and curly hair came in—only his side locks were missing, otherwise he would have looked like some Hasidic boy.

Suddenly I heard the young boy speak Russian with a Russian man. I was very surprised—Jewish children in Minsk usually don't speak Russian so well.

I tried to talk to the boy in Yiddish but he didn't understand a word. I couldn't believe my ears—how is it possible that a Jewish child in Minsk doesn't understand a word of Yiddish?

It turned out that not long ago this beautiful dark-complexioned Jewish boy with the Hasidic-looking face was still a vagrant child in Moscow, a *bezprizorny*. Together with other vagrant children he was digging in garbage cans and went around begging, half-naked.

One day a couple of young Jewish actors walked along the streets of Moscow eating ice cream. Suddenly a vagrant child ran up to them and said,

"*Dyadya, day marozhenoye!*"[5]

The actors were very surprised. Never before had a *bezprizorny* asked for something. They usually don't ask but grab things from people's hands.

The actors started to talk to the boy and found out that he was Jewish. They managed to convince him to live a decent life. He followed their advice.

It happens very rarely that such a child would want to leave the street behind. But this child had a hard time with the other kids. First off, he suffered on account of being Jewish. Apparently, the fight against antisemitism has not been very strong in *bezprizorny* circles. . . . Secondly, this boy was a very gentle, tender child, and among vagrant children a strong fist is very important.

The boy was happy to exchange the street for a home. Now he is in Minsk with the actors. He runs errands, works, and gets food and clothing. He is a theater child. The theater is his home, his mother and his father, and he will probably be an actor himself.

Looking at this dark, curly-haired boy who is delicate like a flower, it is hard to believe that he was once a member of the terrible legion of the *bezprizorny*.

I met the second such child in Kharkov. He is a bit older, sixteen years old, lean and gloomy, and wears light summer clothes even during the winter.

He is a fiery *komsomoliets*, a *rabkor* (workers' correspondent) for three newspapers at the same time— a Yiddish, a Russian, and a Ukrainian one. He is the pride and joy of the Kharkov *komsomoltses*, taking an active part in every meeting, giving speeches, engaging in polemics, and, in addition, writing poems and short stories in Yiddish and Russian.

He, too, was once a vagrant child roaming the streets who preferred to live a decent life. But this boy is not as delicate as the other one in Minsk.

He is morose but not a bad person, and he likes to argue.

As soon as we met he immediately wanted to pick a fight with me.

I was introduced to him as a Yiddish writer.

"I have never heard of him," he said angrily.

Apparently he wanted to have a "reciprocal fight" with me. When he realized that I had no intention of fighting back he changed his tone a little bit but was still very stiff.

"So you are a revolutionary writer?" he asked me.

"Only a writer, I think. . . ."

"And where do you work?"

"I write for the *Forverts*."

The boy almost ate me up alive.

A few weeks earlier he had attended a meeting where in a harsh tone he criticized a young Yiddish poet who had come to Russia:

"And where were you," he screamed at the poet, "when we were spilling blood?"

I tried to joke with him:

"How old are you?"

"Sixteen," he answered.

"And when did you have the opportunity to spill blood?" I asked him.

The boy was beside himself:

"You are hung up on words," he said. "When I say 'we' I don't mean specifically myself; I mean all of Russia."

He scrutinizes me and adds resentfully:

"You will describe me and make fun of me. We don't need that. . . ."

He was right; I am describing the boy, but I am not making fun of him. He is a very good, smart, and talented young man. If only the other vagrant children could achieve a tenth of what he accomplished!

By the way, he writes short stories. He is a colleague, actually! What a pity that I had so little time and didn't have the chance to listen to his stories. [. . .]

About Literature, Theater, Art, Education, and Yiddishism

During the revolution in Soviet Russia, literature and art were misconstrued in an awkward way. In every other field the revolution brought forth a certain simplicity and clarity, offering the broad masses the best opportunity to enjoy all cultural values. But in the arts exactly the opposite happened: artists made every effort to reduce everything to the level of the abstract. They used unintelligible words and allusions as if they were not addressing the people but the antiquated aristocracy, degenerates who don't like anything natural, only the perverted. This is what happened to literature, theater, and painting. The less comprehensible, the more revolutionary. Realism was considered reactionary. Jews, of course, followed the general course, as always. With their typical Jewish stubbornness they actually went overboard in terms of "artistic leftiness."

Now things are taking a turn back to the right in Russia. Together with the disappearance of war communism and all its consequences, the so called revolutionary art is also on the ebb.

One can see this first and foremost in the street: gone are the once widespread but now outmoded posters, pictures, and plaster statues depicting all kinds of triangles, rectangles, and phantasmagorical figures.

Paintings, drawings, and sculptures are now realistic, almost naturalistic.

Revolutionarism is disappearing in the theater, too. I had the opportunity to see one of Meyerhold's performances called *Richie Kitai*, a piece that has absolutely no literary value, a work of pure propaganda that shows how England torments China; what's interesting is that even Meyerhold, the rebbe of revolutionary theater, for whom reducing everything to such a level of abstraction that not even a trace of the depicted subject would remain identifiable was a basic artistic premise—this same Meyerhold staged *Richie Kitai* in a very simple and ordinary style. People walk on their feet, touch with their hands, talk (a little bit still like marionettes) with their mouths, and he even put a body of water on stage, a pool with boats and Chinese ships, so that we get the image of a seaport harbor. [. . .]

Pushkin, whose statue in Moscow was ordered by Mayakovsky to be removed back in the good old days, who was evicted so that Mayakovsky could requisition the pedestal for himself, was now given back the crown of Russian literature and people bow and scrape to him once again. Prose is dominated by realism on every front. Babel, Seyfulina, Ivanov, Romanov, Glodkov, etc. Revolutionary poetry disappeared, only Yesenin's good pieces are left, nothing else. Poets like Mariengof, Kamienski, and their like who were screaming so loud during the revolution rarely let their voices be heard these days. [. . .]

Even Trotsky was among those who stepped up to fight against all Proletkult theories and demanded good literature, even if it was old school.

The Yiddish proverb says, *azoy vi es kristlt zikh, azoy yidlt zikh.*[6] And so it was this time, too, but not quite.

The Jewish public no longer appreciates acrobatic numbers as they did in 1917–1920. And just as Pushkin got back the Russian literary crown, so did Jews, too, crown their own Pushkin: Avrom Reisen. The very same Avrom Reisen who for years was taboo, old-fashioned, and reactionary, and "Reisenism"—a label put upon all the realist writers in Kiev, like a blemish in the family—this very same Reisen is now considered the cream of the crop. They praise [Izi] Charik so much because he takes his inspiration from Avrom Reisen.

Soviet Yiddish prose hasn't yet produced such great writers as Russian literature or Yiddish literature "in foreign countries." But at least they started to write prose works, and this means that they are beginning to stand with both feet on the ground. [. . .]

Literature for the sake of literature, however, still doesn't have the same right to exists as music for the sake of music or singing for the sake of singing. It is not justifiable, not kosher. Everything must educate the masses, must have educational goals. Books, theater performances, and paintings—everything must educate.

In fact, this new trend is no different than the Proletkult from which Russian artists and political leaders already distanced themselves a long time ago. Proletkult continues to flourish on the Jewish street, but since the old-fashioned name is passé, they call it by a new name: "Educationalism."

Jewish artists must always, whether they like it or not, keep one eye on society and politics so that they know how to "educate" because education is a relative concept. Today politics says one thing, and you need to educate accordingly. Tomorrow it might say something else, and you need to follow the new educational direction.

During the war on the village and the small town, Izi Charik ended his poem with the words, "Shtetl, disappear!" But when things turned around and the new slogan became "face to the village," which Jews turned into "face to the shtetl," then what do you do with the line "Shtetl, disappear?"

Here is an idea: delete it! And what will happen if tomorrow there is another twist and people turn away from the village and the small town? Maybe you will need to be prepared for any eventuality, like that Russian theater hero who was caught up between two armies that kept moving in and out of his town, so he made a double portrait for himself: on one side Nikolai the Second, and on the other side Karl Marx; when the Denikinists come in the picture of Marx is turned toward the wall and Nikolai is showing; when the Bolsheviks come in, Nikolai is hidden and Marx faces the viewer. [. . .]

The situation of Yiddish theater is even worse.

At a time when on the Russian stage Meyerhold remains the only revolutionary in Moscow (and even he is slowly but consistently returning to the old style), Yiddish theater is still revolutionary all over the Soviet

Union, just as in the beginning. There is no other kind of theater.

The Moscow Chamber Theater still performs old-style. They move like marionettes, their voices sound as if they were speaking in an empty barrel, and they play ceremoniously. They work hard at the theater, there is great discipline and thorough professional training; the actors know how to move and dance well, they employ good painters and musicians, but everyone completely misunderstands the essence of theater. They are stuck, they can't crawl out of it and they are treading in the same place.

Starting from the grotesque, with a tendency to make fun of the old Jewish way of life, to show its deformity and hunchedness, they slowly sank into an upside-down art, into mimicking and caricature. Once submerged in caricature it is difficult to move on to positive things, to human voice, human movements, human joy and suffering. The actors themselves became marinated marionettes. And, as always, constant revolutionarism turned the theater banal.

Instead of dramatic theater, opera, and comedy, they performed some sorts of operettas with revolutionary demands; these were initially somewhat interesting and would have been acceptable had they served only as a step toward further development, but by now they are utterly boring.

If only there was at least a bit of humor! But they take Sholem Aleichem's works and give them to Dobrushin to adapt them. . . .

And if someone dares say a word he is in mortal danger!

"Education!"

And the same story in Minsk and in Kharkov.

I went to the Minsk Jewish State Theater that is under the directorship of M. Raphalski. At the age of forty he spent several years in Moscow studying, working at the state's expense. They gave him everything—food, an apartment, clothes, studies, and he finally began to work at the theater in Minsk. Now they are performing Peretz's *Polish oyf der keyt* [Chained in the Synagogue Anteroom]. The furnishing is gorgeous—it would be considered classy even in Berlin, not just in Minsk. The stage decoration is done by the painter Ryback. The actors are all well trained—excellent rhythm, plasticity, diction. But there are no more than maybe one hundred people in the audience, everyone yawning, bored. [. . .]

At the Kharkov Jewish State Theater they play in the old style. They have a number of good actors, older ones. There I saw a performance of *The Two Kuni-Lemls*; the audience laughed hard and enjoyed themselves. It is not great theater, but good to watch. However, in order not to be old-fashioned and to satisfy the requirement of "education" they slapped on some modernism that doesn't belong there at all.

I also had a chance to see an agitational show that is supposed to depict Kiev during the struggle between the Reds and Whites. The play is badly made, boring, and one feels sorry for the poor actors.

The curse of "education" lies on every Jewish theater. They are supposed to have their own plays, and it somehow just doesn't work out. At Stanislavski's theater I saw a performance of Gorky's *Tsar Fyodor Ioannovich*. The tsar is presented as characterless but saintly. We see churches and crosses on stage. At the Jewish theater these are not the only things that are *treyf*. It is also forbidden to show on stage even the tiniest thing that may have a reference to old-style Jewish life. Other than a few pieces by Peretz, Sholem Aleichem, Goldfadn, and some others that have been performed, people must make do with not too good productions and sad couplets about [Ramsay] MacDonald and [Aristide] Briand. Jewish theater has been hidden in a dead corner.

The Yiddish book market in Russia has changed radically. Everywhere outside of Russia, belletristic works constitute the bulk of the Yiddish book market. In Russia, belletristic works have disappeared, and instead you have school textbooks, pedagogical, technical, professional, and party literature. This is a positive phenomenon, the result of the fact that there are large numbers of Yiddish schools, teacher training schools, workers' faculties, peasant schools, courts, Soviet militia, etc. Textbooks are very popular; they are often sold in 20,000–25,000 copies. Two hundred thousand pupils at the Yiddish schools need textbooks—those have to be supplied.

And belletristic works that usually sell much better than any other field of literature are actually sold much less in Russian than one would expect. With the immense growth of the Yiddish school system there is little demand for belletristic literature. The two literary and cultural journals, *Di royte velt* [The Red World] in Kharkov and *Shtern* [Star] in Minsk publish 2,000 copies, no more. The government funds them. Belletristic works sell 1,000 to 2,000 copies; the reason for this is that they only publish "their own" literature and no Yiddish works written abroad. Readers want novels and short stories, and instead they are fed poems and experimental skits. There are no great works of art, and therefore people choose to read Russian fiction. They study in Yiddish and read in Russian.

The leadership claims that, quite naturally, people don't want to "take in" anything "foreign," anything nonrevolutionary, but librarians tell us that the most read authors are Mendele, Sholem Aleichem, Peretz, and Asch, and the few remaining copies of [Yosef Opatoshu's] *In poylishe velder* [In Polish Woods] have been read to pieces. [. . .]

Writers in Soviet Russia live better than almost anyone else. Most leaders of Soviet Russia must take to writing at some point in order to cover their living expenses. Literature, however, is paid well. Mayakovsky gets paid three rubles for a line. At the time when teachers earn 40, 50, or maybe 80 rubles for slaving away for a whole month, a respected poet gets this sum for writing twenty short lines.

Artists are the most privileged people in Soviet Russia. They are allowed to travel abroad purportedly for literary purposes but in reality to buy clothing.

I went to the Iskustvo in Moscow one night. People were dancing, partying, drinking wine, and spending heedlessly, very much unlike in a proletarian country. The artists at the Parisian Café Rotundo who sit there all day with half a cup of espresso would be happy if they could afford to spend a tenth of what Soviet writers spend.

Of course, the most prominent writers earn nowhere near as much as they used to earn before the war, but in general artists and writers live well. [. . .]

Yiddish writers live quite well, too, although the circulation figures of Yiddish books no way compare to those of Russian books.

Yiddish writers have the opportunity to come into contact with the non-Jewish literary world, too. Yiddish and Russian writers appear together, and the works of Yiddish writers are read in institutes of higher learning. The tenth anniversary of Sholem Aleichem's death was commemorated all over the country by the government and by non-Jews, too—it was a demonstration of great significance. Several Yiddish writers get stipends from the government.

Many people were present at the literary evening in honor of the convention of GEZERD that took place in the gorgeous Hall of Columns in Moscow. The participants were, alongside the Yiddish poets, Commissar of Education [Anatoly] Lunacharsky, writers [Vsevolod] Ivanov, [Vladimir] Mayakovsky, [Boris] Pilniak, Romanov, and others, the cream of Russian literature. I even saw the secretary of the Polish embassy among the guests.

Never before has the Yiddish word enjoyed such a high status as currently in Russia, and still one can detect a strange phenomenon among many Jewish communists: they are scared stiff of Yiddishism, which basically means Yiddish.

Yiddishism is a curse word; any time Yiddish is mentioned people add, "of course, this is not important," and things along these lines. People are very much afraid of making a fetish out of Yiddish, but at the same time they do fetishize Russian. Jews speak Russian among themselves, even though they all know Yiddish well. Thus, for instance, [Abram] Merezhin, a former Yiddish teacher, chaired the first few days of the GEZERD convention in Russian.

Russian is spoken in numerous Jewish institutions. In Minsk, a conversation about Peretz's *Polish oyf der keyt* that is performed at the Yiddish theater took place in Russian; lectures at the Odessa Yiddish club are held in Russian; Jewish leaders almost always speak Russian among themselves, and this has an effect on the people who see Russian as a fetish. [. . .]

And, as always in this and every other respect, the half-communists are more pious than the pope. With a communist you can still talk and argue, but with a half-communist who doesn't want to and cannot become a party member it is entirely impossible to discuss things. They won't listen, just scream their slogans of hurrah communism. These are the most repulsive people, toady bootlickers.

I had the opportunity to raise the question of Yiddish with a group of such people. They all hushed me down. But once I left, a Bundist came up to me in the street and, after carefully looking around to make sure no one was nearby, he quietly told me that he agreed with what I had said.

He acted just like a Jew in the olden days who wanted to say something bad about the emperor.

And this man used to be a fighter! He had sat in every prison in the tsar's times. I sensed the same panic among some of the Yiddish writers when [Moyshe] Litvakov was present. Once two young Yiddish writers actually abandoned me in the middle of a conversation when they caught sight of Litvakov; they weren't sure if it was permissible to talk to me. . . .

Compared to this, the full communists are much more independent and free.

NOTES

1. [Society for the Settlement of Jews on the Land (OZET in Russian).—Eds.]

2. [Long live the old proletariat.—Eds.]

3. [Long live the international proletariat.—Eds.]

4. [Institute of higher education (Russian abbreviation). —Eds.]

5. [Uncle, give me ice cream! (Russian)—Eds.]

6. [As the Christians do, so do the Jews.—Eds.]

Translated by Vera Szabó.

Other works by Singer: *Shtol un Ayzn* (1927); *Yoshe Kalb* (1932); *Blood Harvest* (1935); *Khaver Nakhmen* (1938); *East of Eden* (1939); *Di mishpokhe Karnovski* (1943; *The Family Carnovsky*, 1969); *Of a World That Is No More*, 1970).

A. Beilin

Unknown

A. Beilin was in the revolutionary movement in the Russian Empire and likely remained within the Soviet Union. His memoir appeared in the work *Royte bleter, Zamelbukh far der geshichte fun der revolutzionerer bavegung ba Yidn* (Red Pages: Collection of the Revolutionary Movement of the Jews).

Memories
1929

I. Childhood [. . .]

I must revive the experiences of the revolutionary path traversed in order to share memories and knowledge with workers and the younger generation. They want and need to have an understanding of the work done underground twenty years ago, and not only in major factory cities such as Petrograd, Moscow, and Ivanovo-Voznesensk where there was a large concentrated mass of workers and big factories. They also need to know how workers organized, labored, and struggled in remote cities, shtetls, and villages of the so-called "Pale," where they were dispersed among small

workshops. The revolutionary workers' movement—which seized factory centers on a larger scale and with stronger organization—also reached remote small cities and shtetls on a smaller scale and with weaker organization, but also with great enthusiasm. Wherever there was an exploited worker, the revolutionary wave would find him. [. . .]

All that I am writing about happened more than twenty years ago in the *uyezd*-city [administrative center] of Mstsislav (in the former Mogilev *gubernia*) and in its surrounding villages and towns. [. . .]

I was five years old when "Yoshe the Redhead" became my heder teacher. I remember how Yoshe the Redhead came to our house. He patted my cheek and gave me a candy. He then haggled with my mother over his salary. They settled, I think, at 11 roubles a semester, and I became a heder student. The first time my mother took me to heder, I found myself in a low-ceilinged, dark little house in a courtyard adjacent to a boulevard. The courtyard was extraordinarily dirty and always smelled horrible. When I was brought to the heder, I was seated at the table among the other children. I counted exactly nineteen boys. The rebbe began showing me the "aleph-beyz" [alphabet] in the siddur. Suddenly, from the ceiling above, candies started falling down.

"An angel is throwing them down from the sky for you," the rebbe explained. "If you are a good boy, good and religious, if you study with enthusiasm, obey the rabbi, pray, and go to *besmedresh* [small chapel, study hall], then the angel will always throw candies to you from heaven." The children didn't get along. There was perceptible friction between the poorer and wealthier children. Children of rich parents—Moyshe Frumkin's sons Dovid and Leizer, Bransburg, and others—studied in the same heder with me and other poor children.

One cannot say that Yoshe the Redhead was a very bad teacher. In my opinion, he was the best of all the teachers with whom I studied. In the evenings, he would take us to pray in the synagogue, in "Sorke's *besmedresh*," and on the Sabbath he would come to my house to quiz me in front of my parents in order to prove to them how much he had taught his student. My father was very satisfied with my studies and used to treat the rebbe by pouring him some Sabbath tea.

Every Friday the heder boys used to play "firemen" in Moshe Frumkin's courtyard. Moshe Frumkin donated red armbands as well as red hatbands from his store. All this was supposed to mean that we were true firemen: climbers and hose men. With this gift, Moshe Frumkin wanted to bribe us poor children so that we should not, God forbid, bother his wealthy kids. We hated the rich kids with all our hearts and fought our first childhood "class wars" with them. [. . .]

The rebbe forced me more than once to take off my trousers and lay down on two chairs. Two boys would hold me down, one at the head and the other by my feet, and Yoshe the Redhead would flog quite skillfully. I don't remember the precise number of times I got it from him, but I remember that it was many and with vigor. I suffered primarily not so much from the pain as from the indignity and anger. The question burned in us like fire: how come he whips only us and doesn't even come close to the few wealthy children in heder, who sometimes studied worse than us? [. . .]

One time the following happened. We had been studying Torah and really didn't understand what we were reading. The rebbe leaned forward in order to slap me, but he missed and hit my nose. It began bleeding profusely. Yoshe the Redhead was startled and immediately put cold water on my nose and warned me not to talk about this episode at home. I respected his request and kept it secret. However, things got even worse when I left this heder and entered a new one. The story went this way: One time my uncle, the teacher Kalman, came over to our house. He started cursing at the top of his voice and making a "scandal," at which he was very good. [. . .]

How can it be, why is this acceptable, that his own relatives took their heder-aged boy to another teacher, when his own uncle is a teacher and a certified rabbi, and is much better than the other teachers, who are all heretical and ignorant? My mother didn't like Uncle Kalman at all and under no circumstances did she want him to be my teacher. She always considered him to be a bad, base person. However, Uncle Kalman was not silent. He created real chaos for my father in *besmedresh*, so I was sent to his school, willy-nilly. This was the beginning of my true living hell. All of my schooling was based on beatings and curses. Kalman fought and cursed everyone: all the students and even with the rebbe's wife. We had to witness quarreling the whole day and cursing too, between our rebbe and his wife.

Uncle Kalman was very stingy and always tried to save money, so aside from teaching he would also occupy himself with usury. In addition, he would charge a high percentage. Truly, he would skin you alive. Uncle Kalman would not care for his own children. As soon as they were weaned, he would send them to yeshivas in order to save household money. [. . .]

The entire day he would be praying, and forced us to do the same. He didn't know how to speak even one word of Russian, and couldn't write either. He was very sly and wicked. He didn't have any respect for anything aside from his money, which he would count and recount ten times a day. Before Passover, he would make raisin wine and we, the students, had to help him. He forced us to work in the cellar so that the police wouldn't find out. He intimidated so badly that we didn't tell anyone about this, not even our parents. The work was very difficult, and we didn't even get paid with a piece of bread. [. . .]

We heder boys had to work a lot. We had to squash raisins, bake *matzo-shmura* [matza of the highest religious standard], go to funerals, recite Psalms for the dead, and other such important jobs. It was no wonder that there was no time left for learning. The few hours that we did sometimes learn were wasted on beatings, whippings, tears, curses, and yelling.

This is how our childhood passed. In such an environment, I and thousands of other poor Jewish boys received our first "education," ages five to thirteen. I graduated from this excellent "school" after eight years. I was almost a full-blown boor. [. . .]

II. Mstislavl and Its Surroundings

Mstsislav, where I spent my early years, is an old historic city. They say that it was established and built up in the twelfth century. [. . .] Nature in Mstislavl is beautiful and rich. The hills and dales, which were artificially created at the time of the Napoleonic wars, add to the town's charm. [. . .]

What one can note is that the social division was very substantial. On the one hand, a relatively large (relative to an *uyezd* town in the Pale) stratum of wage workers and poor *kustars* [craftsmen]; on the other hand, the influential *kustars* with their many workers, wealthy grocers, merchants, and religious functionaries.

The Belorussian "bourgeoisie" element lived in the suburbs. Their basic livelihood came from working the land. Besides this, they would trade on the side. Although their origins were Belorussian, many of them had become russified. The more influential of them married into the Russian functionary class and strove to become city people, occupying official positions in the magistrate's court, the city Duma, and the like. [...]

Due to a series of proclamations, most *shtetls* were allotted to wealthy landowners, which added a new concern to all the troubles of the shtetl. On land where there was a house or a hut, one now had to pay a tax. If a poor man could not come up with the tax money on time, he would be thrown out of his house and out of the town. Often the *porets* [landowner] would pick on a renter and literally ruin him by denouncing him, or claiming that he did not honor the landowner enough, or the like. The *porets* also would occupy himself with "administrative activities" and would give out various commands. I remember how the fat-bellied *porets* Halinsky gave an order that no more goats were allowed in the town. Apparently, the *porets* did not appreciate the fact that the goats would wander the streets. [...]

Three large monasteries were in this district, the Tupichiner, the Mazolover, and the Pustinker. [...] There were many times when the monks of Pustinker monastery would rape the religious girls who made the several-hundred-*verst* pilgrimage to the "holy place" in order to pray and bring gifts for the monastery. And so we know the trial of the monks and the son of *porets* Filiman over the rape of a seventeen-year-old peasant girl who had come all the way from Chernigov *gubernia* to offer prayers in the monastery Swiato Pustinok. After the rape, the girl was choked and drowned in a pond. The whole episode was then uncovered. These "good deeds" of the monks and nuns opened the eyes of the peasantry, who previously had great faith in the monasteries and brought them gifts of linen, wax, and money. Consequently, the monasteries lost their authority. [...]

The Jewish religious functionaries were no better. After the death of the old Mstislavl Rabbi Hillel, the Jewish community sent a delegation to the Lubavitcher rebbe to request that he send someone to take on the holy rabbinical seat in the town. The town's small storeowners—led by the tailors Yude the Hunchback, Bere Pesin, and Dovid Bachrach-Stolyer, who had large workshops—invited another rabbi to come to the town.

In this way, Mstislavl acquired two rabbis. The "elite" of the town received the "yellow," and the masses got the "black." They were known as such because one had a long yellow beard and the other had an equally long, tangled, black one. These two rabbis were forever arguing. A sort of class struggle went on between them,

into which large groups of Jewish people were drawn. The struggle was very ardent, and each side boycotted the other. The *besmedresh* was a site of endless quarrels and fights, and the police often had to wade in. The police would usually defend the aristocratic rabbi, but not persecute the "black one" too strictly, of course. However, the masses did not give in. The city and surrounding villages were split into two enemy sides. They would go from house to house agitating people to a protest and to collect money. Secret conferences and meetings were organized. Conspiracies were organized until, at last, the "black-bearded" rabbi won. The struggle lasted five years.

III. At Work

I was fourteen years old when I was apprenticed to Ayzik the carpenter. The workshop employed ten or twelve workers. [...]

You would never hear a good word from Ayzik. Turning to him was a last resort, and even then he wouldn't answer right away, as if he didn't hear anything. And when he did finally answer, he would shower you with insults: "May a dark year [*shvartzyor*] be upon you; what do you want?"

He was always sulking, walking around the workshop grumbling and yelling that everyone was wishing him into poverty. I do not remember a time that he talked to a person respectfully. Often, he would come up to a worker, stare at him with a surprised look, and begin ranting:

"Look me straight in the eyes, you, I want to know, are you a 'democrat' or not?"

His glasses would always be perched at the end of his nose, bound around his head by some thread. In the workshop, he walked around without a *kapote* [caftan], with long *tsitses* [ritual fringes], an old greasy yarmulke on his head, and a greasy vest. His moustache was stained green from sniffing too much tobacco. He would yell at the worker who could not hold his stare: "Are you a 'democrat'? You cannot look an honest person in the eye . . . you belong in hell, and not in my workshop, you are bloodsuckers, all of you. . . ."

On the Sabbath, he liked to pray at the pulpit, and always boasted that no one led the services as well as he did. He also was always very enthusiastic about reading the third and sixth portions of the Torah reading, and it would spell trouble not only for us workers, but also for his wife and daughters, whenever anyone else managed to snatch up the pulpit or haggle the invitation to read the third and sixth portions. At those times, we were in for real hell.

The situation was especially strained in the workshop if time passed and no one in the town passed away. It was as if someone were doing this on purpose. Since he was a big shot member in the *ḥevra kadisha* [burial society], he was a pallbearer and delighted in funerals. If there were no funerals for a short time, he would completely abandon human form. He would long for a funeral and fidget, unable to eat, drink, or sleep. . . .

When a funeral took place, especially in a place with some food, Ayzik would become a completely different person; he would guzzle down wine and make us drink as well. Out of a sense of great joy, he would order us to join him in a little dance. Drunkenly, he would maintain: "You should thank God for Ayzik. Such a boss, you have to search for far and wide." [. . .]

If we, the apprenticed boys, had trouble from the boss, we had even more trouble from the boss's wife. Ayzik had two apprentices, and we were bidden to go with the boss's wife to the market to carry her baskets. She had a way of buying more than needed and was always looking for bargains. She wasn't a regular at any store, but would frequent all the butcher shops and grocers to see who had the cheapest produce. The storekeepers would put aside the old, stale products for her, since she didn't care if the meat was fresh, as long as it was a good deal.

She'd curse and complain—she was a specialist in cursing, using a wide range of phrases. She'd wander through the rooms, stalking like a witch, cursing the workers, saying that they were stealing produce from her: "I can't hide a thing. They devour everything. May a bolt of fire enter their cold innards. May the great, strong God never help them. May they catch cholera in their stomachs. May their gizzards burst. May stones and snakes grow in their stomachs from my bloody foodstuffs." [. . .]

The situation was difficult in every way. There was a great deal of undermining of us students with humiliations and curses. But I had to learn a trade, and life was no better in the other workshops. [. . .]

IV. In the Movement

Thus life continued until 1905. Ayzik the carpenter became more "personable" when the first strike oc-

curred, involving Dovid Bachrach, Yuda the Hump-Back, and the tailor Bere Lessin. The strikes were very well organized and all the demands of the workers were satisfied. This strike action somewhat undermined the bosses. Our Ayzik also became more subdued. People started saying that the bosses got together and went to the black-haired rabbi to seek advice on how to influence the workers.

And indeed, after this talk, every Saturday the rabbi started to deliver sermons in which he would articulate that the behavior of the "democrats" is shameful and criminal, and that the good and the bad, wealth and poverty, are all the result of God's work, and the "democrats" cannot alter the order of the universe.

One time on the Sabbath during the Days of Awe, the black-haired rabbi gave a sermon. By the way, he was a good speaker. He was able to really hypnotize the masses, which were comprised of old men, women, tradesmen, and artisans. This time he chastised the people as to why faith in God was becoming weaker. [. . .] The youth, the "democrats," have completely turned away from Almighty God. They desecrate the Sabbath by smoking and forgetting God's commandment that wealth and poverty all come from the Almighty.

The synagogue was packed with people. The rabbi stood in his white robe and *tallis* by the Holy Ark of the Covenant that had been opened wide. On both sides of him stood the *shamosim* with Torah scrolls in their hands. He himself, a fat man with ample girth, dressed in a long white robe with a *tallis* draped over his shoulder, with rolled up sleeves, was cursing with deadly curses the heretics and libertines, who did not believe in God and desecrated the Sabbath. [. . .]

We were also in the synagogue at that time. "Khatshe-Puze," Mote-Andrey, and Yankl Pesin were there also. "Khatshe-Puze" couldn't control himself any longer. He went up to the *bimah* and cried out that "all the curses with which the rabbi has cursed out the masses should fall upon his fat rabbinical stomach. All of it was make-believe, a lie. Don't believe the fat rabbi."

Then a terrible tumult arose. Those who were in the synagogue behaved as if they had been done in.

"Throw him down, the bandit, the heretic, the filth!!" they yelled.

"Throw him out, that cobbler, beat him up"!!

Khatshe came off the *bimah* and approached us, but the sermon could no longer continue.

And when the rabbi's followers wanted to jump on him, the carriage-drivers defended him: Ayzik,

Leyvik, Shoyel the coachman, and "Gdalye Goy" the handcart-driver.

"He is right. He is telling the truth. Don't be afraid, Khatshe, let them dare put a finger on you."

We all left the synagogue very shortly afterwards.

The year 1905, the year of turmoil, was such that the rabbi's sermons couldn't help much. In Mstsislav, a revolutionary organization was being created and the bosses became softer, but they didn't lose hope that all this would pass. [...]

I remember that I would give anything to become "an *eygener*," one of the crowd. Even though I was ignorant at the time . . . instinctively I felt that I was doing a great and good thing. I was joining the ranks of my people by dedicating myself to the revolutionary struggle—the struggle for workers' rights. I didn't think about anything else at the time; that one could suffer all kinds of repressions, be sent to prison, to a work camp, be hanged, be harmed by gendarmes and policemen, be hunted like an animal, not spend even one day and one night in one place, be kicked out by the boss onto the street—all these things were not on my mind at the time. I was ready for anything. I only thought about one thing: how to get into the revolutionary organization faster. Which organization? In this, I had little discernment. Instinctively, I only hated the Zionists, though not because I knew their program, or their work. Most of what bothered me about them was that their party was a legal one, and the police did not persecute them. This took away their charm for me. [...]

Translated by Ruth Bryl Shochat and Alexandra Hoffman.

N. Chanin
1885-1965

Nokhum Chanin was born near Minsk. He received a traditional Jewish education and delved into secular studies independently. Chanin was an active Bundist in tsarist Russia and was imprisoned for seven years. He escaped to the United States in 1912 and continued his involvement with the Jewish workers' movement as a leader in Jewish socialist associations and in the Arbeter Ring. He contributed to various Yiddish periodicals, including *Forverts*.

Soviet Russia as I Saw It
1929

Culture on the Jewish Street

[...] We have heard so much about the achievements of the Evsektsiia [Jewish sections of the Communist Party] in the field of Jewish culture that for this alone many of us forgave them for destroying the Jewish economy. Their great cultural achievements were described not only by writers who served as professional communist propagandists but also by quite a few non-party Yiddish writers who had the honor of receiving an entry visa to the Soviet Union and visited the country. And when a chorus of communist and non-party-aligned writers all sing in one voice, they will surely overwhelm the world, and no one will be able to out-sing them.

The life of a cultural nation and its cultural development is usually reflected in four main features: [...] the daily newspaper, the book, the school, and the theater.

In Russia there are more than two and a half million Jews. Three Yiddish newspapers are published: *Oktyabr* [October] in Minsk, *Shtern* [Star] in Kharkov, and *Emes* [Truth] in Moscow. To my great surprise I found out that the circulation of all three newspapers together is 19,000 copies. A distant observer may assume that the Jewish masses must read the Russian press. That is, however, not the case. The Jewish masses live in cities and towns, mostly in towns. To the extent that I had contact with cities and towns, I saw that the Jews read nothing. There is no such cultural force in Jewish life that would be concerned about ensuring that people read. The only "culture-carrier" in Jewish life in Russia is the Evsektsiia, the Jewish communists. However, the broad Jewish masses detest the Evsektsiia.

The primary reason the Jewish masses detest the agents of Evsektsiia is that they have been waging a vicious war against the Jewish school, the heder, and the Jewish religion. The fight of the communists in the Jewish street took a rather ugly form. Secondly, Russian Jews blamed the Evsektsiia for the destruction of their economy, because the Evsektsiia were the official representatives of Russian communism in the Jewish street. Therefore, even when they tried to do something to raise the Jewish masses to a more cultured life, they could not achieve anything because people detested everything coming from them. [...]

In Russia there is no other newspaper than the communist one. There is no other source of culture in the country. All social and cultural activity that is not communist has been banned, especially in the Jewish street. [. . .]

In the past, the Zionist movement played a great role in the Jewish cultural life of the Jewish petty bourgeoisie in Russia, just as the Bund and other socialist parties did for the working class. In the course of a few decades Zionism and Bundism raised the Jewish masses to a high cultural plane. The new movements shook up the uncultured Jewish masses; they brought the worker out of the factory and the yeshiva student out of the yeshiva. They brought the atmosphere of secular culture to the Jewish street.

The Evsektsiia attempted to eradicate religion from the Jewish street. But the result was exactly the opposite. Religion among Jews is much stronger today than it was earlier. It is true that in public life religion does not occupy such a prominent position as before, but at home Jews are more religious today than they were twenty-five years ago. [. . .]

As I visited Jewish houses, I seldom saw books. I was very surprised. [. . .]

In Minsk I went to several Yiddish bookstores; I wanted to buy Yiddish books, talk to the people who manage their sales, and find out from them the situation of the Yiddish book. To my great surprise I was told everywhere that Yiddish books did not sell well, and people did not read them. [. . .]

Other than the Chamber Theater there are no other Yiddish theaters in Russia. If you see an announcement in the newspaper that a Yiddish theater is going to play in Kiev, Minsk, or Vitebsk, you should know that this means an amateur theater-troupe, theater-lovers, not professional actors, and they are very far from the true theatrical art. In America no one would go see such a performance. No cultured person in Russia takes the buffoonery of these amateur troupes seriously.

Even in Moscow, where there are close to 200,000 Jews, I was unable to get hold of a Yiddish newspaper. In order to obtain a copy of *Emes* in Moscow I had to go either to the editorial offices of the newspaper or to the Commissariat of Jewish Affairs. Other than these two places I was unable to find a Yiddish newspaper. [. . .]

Yiddish cultural life in Russia, except for elementary schools, is of little value. It is nothing to be proud of. [. . .]

Looking into the catalogues, one cannot help noticing that the publishers put out many of the works of Moyshe Taytsh, who had the ability to become a communist in time, and a "faithful communist" at that. Moyshe Taytsh, who did not occupy any place in Yiddish literature, became a Yiddish classic in Soviet Russia. Is this any wonder? In a country where every cultural treasure created before the October Revolution has been destroyed—in such a country it is no wonder that the most prominent places will be occupied by people who lack any talent, provided they are loyal to communism and willing to cross themselves in front of Lenin's picture three times a day. [. . .]

Opatoshu visited Minsk, Moscow, Kiev, Kharkov, and Odessa. Has he not noticed the valley of tears there, in which the Jewish masses live? Has he not seen the rags people wear? Has he not seen the terrible apartments they live in? I do not know if he saw them or not, but he certainly did not write about them. He saw a gypsy dancer on Pushkin Boulevard. He even noticed that the peasants were afraid of *natchalstvo* (officialdom) and they hid their homemade brandy when they were warned that an official was coming. But Jewish life—not a word about it! I am afraid to say this, but I thought to myself: "Could it be possible that the reason they kept quiet about the terrible situation of Jews, about their impoverishment and the destruction of the Jewish people, is that they managed to sell their own books in Russia?"

There are other Yiddish writers, too, who have traveled around in Soviet Russia and are grateful for being permitted to visit Moscow. For this alone they are willing to sell out one and a half million Jews in Russia who live in terrible conditions. Here is Peretz Hirshbein, for example. He considers it a great achievement of the Soviet government that they let Jews into Moscow. I understand why many Jews are awestruck by this and feel obliged. But the gates of Moscow were opened to Jews by the first revolution that was spearheaded by Russian socialists, democrats, and liberals. Would it occur to anyone to be grateful to the French government for letting Jews into Paris, or to the German government for letting us into Berlin, or to the Polish government for letting us into Warsaw? [. . .]

When you set foot in Russia, you can feel the terrible dictatorship that reigns over there; you can see that people are afraid to express even the smallest critique of the Soviet government. The prisons are filled with political enemies. Thousands of workers, some Trotskyists and some not, who have a different idea about how the government should be run, are sent to Siberia. And here comes Peretz Hirshbein and asks naively, innocent as a lamb: Who says that there is no political freedom in Russia? Are workers not allowed to protest against global capitalism on the First of May? Are they not allowed to sing revolutionary songs? Of course they are, but they can only protest the way Stalin orders them to protest, they can only sing songs the Soviet rulers permit them to sing, and they can only think what the Cheka [secret police] wants them to think. If you think differently, you will rot in prison or be exiled to Siberia.

I condemn Yiddish writers who, with few exceptions, consciously avoided talking about Jewish cultural and economic poverty that they had seen with their own eyes in Soviet Russia, and did so only because they traveled to Russia as salesmen. After all, a salesman will keep quiet about anything for the sake of selling his goods. [. . .] I did not go to Russia to sell my goods. I went there to see how the people live. I saw their struggle and despair, and I am telling all about it as loudly as possible. Maybe it will help. [. . .]

Currently there are 110,000 children who study in Yiddish schools in all of [the Soviet Union]. All subjects are taught in Yiddish. In the Yiddish schools in Ukraine children also study Ukrainian and the Russian language. In the Yiddish schools in Belorussia they study Belorussian and the Russian language. The fact that 110,000 children study in Yiddish schools in Russia is itself, no doubt, greatly beneficial for Yiddish culture and for the Yiddish language.

But what does this mean for the future? If a Jewish child who graduated from a Yiddish elementary school wants to go to university to study medicine, law, or engineering, he has to pass exams in every subject in Russian. What he had learned in the Yiddish school has very little significance. He has to relearn everything in Russian, anyway.

The result is that children do not want to go to the Yiddish school, and their parents do not want to send them there, either, but they have no choice; they must attend the Yiddish school, because that is what the law says. They cannot go to any other school, unless they have "connections" that help them circumvent the law. [. . .]

I had the opportunity to sit in a literature and a history class; the teaching of both subjects seemed very strange to me. In the literature class I heard how the teacher spoke about Sholem Aleichem. But the focus was not Sholem Aleichem the artist, the humorist, or the classical writer. Instead, the teacher used one of Sholem Aleichem's characters, Menachem Mendl, to show that Jews had never wanted to work, that they have always lived on air, at the expense of the peasants, at the expense of the Russian population.

Had this not been a Yiddish school and a Jewish teacher I would have walked away thinking that the teacher was an antisemite, an enemy of the Jews, and that is why he spoke in such a hostile tone about the Jewish characters whom Sholem Aleichem depicted with warmth and compassion. The teacher did not even consider it important to point out the political and social circumstances of which Sholem Aleichem's Menachem Mendl was a victim. He did not even mention the terrible role that tsarism played in crippling Jewish life in Russia.

[. . .] Even though Jews enjoy cultural autonomy in Soviet Russia and there are 110,000 children studying in Yiddish schools, the children have very little spiritual connection to Jewish life. And if the Jewish folk spirit is missing from the entire educational system, then probably neither the parents nor the children feel connected to the Yiddish school, and are attracted to the Russian school. Because even though the Russian school is governed by the same spirit, at least it has some practical results.

Translated by Vera Szabó.

Other works by Chanin: *Marksizm in undzer tsayt* (1933); *Berele* (1938); *A rayze iber tsentral un dorem amerike* (1942).

Khanke Kopeliovitch

b. 1876

Details of her life are unknown.

The Beginning of the Battle (Memories)
1929

In the year 1885—when I was nine years old—I started working. My first job was in a little candy factory, where a few girls worked. I used to work a lot: 14–15 hours per day. My pay was 25 kopecks per week. After a few years this rose to 40 kopecks per week. My hatred of the owners increased day by day. I used to see how their children, who were the same age as I, lived in luxury, how they were taken to school and brought home. And I would take from my home a bit of black bread and cheese for a groshen and live on that the entire day. I used to have to go home very late at night on my own in Komarówka, where we lived then. I worked in this way for a few years. Around that time my parents moved from Komarówka to the city. There I became friends with a girl from our courtyard, who worked in a match factory. My friend took to persuading me that in the match factory the wage was 1 rouble per week. The factory was in the brickyards, two versts from the city. I could not understand how people went there every day in the winter in the frost, in the snow. I was 11 years old. But the need in our home was great. My father, a melamed [teacher of small children] made very little money. There were seven children at home. Therefore my parents agreed to let me go to work in the match factory, under the factory owner Kalman Lampert. We had to start going to work at 6 in the morning. My friend and I would take a lantern and pieces of bread and go on our way up to our necks in snow. Frozen, we would fall into the factory at 8 A.M. The walk would take two hours— we had to start work at 8. I was a packer; in those days the matches had paper coverings. In the work room there also stood the pot in which the sulfur was cooked and into which the matches were dipped. All day long we went about our work in the poisonous, sulfurous air. The sulfur poisoned the gums and our teeth began to fall out. We worked by the little box, toiling very hard because we wanted to make more money. The wage was between 80 kopecks and 1 rouble per week. We worked in this way for three months and they did not pay us. We were 20 girls working there and a few men. I was the smallest. As Passover approached, instead of paying each of us what we deserved, the factory owner gave us each a couple of roubles, and that's it. All the girls were very upset, for why did they not give us any money, especially before the holiday? We all agreed that when the factory owner would come we would tell him that he should pay us and if he would not give us any money, we would not work anymore, because at any rate we had nothing. The factory owner came and the girls started poking each other, which one should go tell the owner that we want money. No one dared to go into the office, until I went and said that all the girls want to be paid. Lampert became murderously angry. He sacked me straight away, without even paying me what he owed. Later, when I came with my father to ask for money, he said that we could go home, he would not pay and if I were to make a lot of trouble, he would send his workers to punish me for making the false accusation that they were asking for money. In this way the money was lost and I was left without a job. But I was not empty-handed long. Right away I came to a wrapper factory in which 20 girls worked. We worked with thousands [of wrappers], gluing the cases, corking and packing them in boxes. For this they paid us, I think, 5 kopecks per thousand. I would do 2,000 per day, working from 8 in the morning until evening without a break for lunch. The wages were very low. The girls never thought of asking for more. A girl named Golde worked alongside me, a miller's daughter; her sisters were seamstresses. They used to say that they were socialists. I very much wanted to become acquainted with them. As I got to know her better, Golde invited me to visit on Shabbes, and in her home I met her two seamstress sisters—with their hair cut short, and a lot of young men and women, I remember a number of names: Temkin, a teacher, Kerstein—a wallpaper hanger. On the table were Russian books. One would read and all the others would listen. I became a frequent visitor and they took me into their circle, but I understood very poorly. The books were old fashioned and wordy ["banned books"]. The first poem I heard there in Yiddish was Vintshevshky's:

I beg you, explain my poor brothers,
Who toil so hard in today's world,
They work out the marrow from their bones
And offer themselves up on the altar of money.
Those who saw and sand and cut every day
Who pull the wire and knead the lime
Nevertheless they live poor and miserable
And have no house and have no home, etc.

I liked this poem very much. I learned it by heart and later sang it to the girls in the paper factory. So they crowned me "the socialist." [. . .]

There was no mass movement yet at the beginning of 1893. Then they advised me to get closer to the girls. Our girls used to love going to enjoy themselves; among us we called this—"balls." Girls would lay out 20 kopecks to buy some nosh and arrange a "dinner" at the home of one of the girls from the factory. On those evenings they would invite young men they knew, and we used to dance, sing, and play. I started going to the "balls" together with all the girls, in order to get closer to them and influence them. I took a few of the younger ones under my wing and became their teacher. I started to teach them to read and write in Yiddish and the Russian alphabet. I held one such "ball" at my home. All the factory girls came. From among my acquaintances I brought along Kalmen Fertshiken, Avrom-Chaim Koiler—a painter, Dvoyrke—a seamstress, Khiene—a baker. Later they were the top leaders of the mass movement. They used the ball for the purposes of agitation. We talked about the economic situation of the workers and about the need for us to take action in order to improve conditions in the factory. We also talked about the ignorance that reigned among the workers, we agitated that they must learn. Instead of enjoying themselves it would be better to learn to read and write. This had a positive effect on a few, but the majority laughed at me and my young men—"the ones who go barefoot," that's what they called the socialists.

Our factory was often visited by the factory inspector who would come, ostensibly, to inquire as to how we were treated and about our working conditions. We could never tell him the truth, since with him came the owner, the accountant, and the master craftsman, and not one of us dared to speak. We knew that if we were to speak out, we would be thrown out of the factory. I nevertheless took to looking for ways to improve the workers' conditions in the factory. During this time I became acquainted with Lyube Yozefovitch. She was the director of the women's craft school. I chose a few of the better girls from the factory and she read agitation books with us: The "Work-Day," the "Four Brothers," and other books which I do not remember anymore. Another girl and I were given a "literacy" teacher—Frume Frumkin (she belonged to the S. R. Party. Afterwards she attempted to assassinate the chief of the gendarmes, for which she was arrested and later hanged.). Later I became acquainted with Moyshe Neifeld—a watchmaker—and Bentshe Levin—another watchmaker. Moyshe Neifeld began helping me operate among the factory workers. After a consultation with Neifeld it was decided that we would go to the factory inspector and tell him that they paid us no money, keeping it secret from the girls. At that time there were still factory books, in which the work from every day was written and it was noted how much money and for what month we had been paid. The two of us, Neifeld and I, went to the inspector and told him everything and overall that we had to work for three months before we got any money for one month. The inspector suddenly appeared at the factory the next morning alone, without his retinue, and directly picked up a book from a girl.

From the book it was apparent that she was owed money for four months. The inspector right away ordered the owner to pay each girl the amount she was owed, and if the girls were not paid immediately he would close the factory and the owner would be severely punished. Immediately there was a great racket in the administration. All of them became infuriated, like evil dogs, the master, the bookkeeper, the factory owner. They all ran one to the other crying that this thing is finished.

The next day everyone was given money for two months and the factory was closed. Then they announced: "One of you went and informed on us; now all will suffer. There is no more work for you here. The factory stays closed." When the girls began to beg for the rest of their money, the owner proposed that he would pay everyone and start the factory up if they would tell him who went to the inspector. The girls were very pleased that the owner would reopen the factory. The need was very great. Parents, whoever had some means, would not send their children to a factory. It would be better to make a child a seamstress, an underwear-maker, a sock-knitter, just not a factory worker. In a factory the real paupers worked.

The older girls said that they thought that Khane Kopeliovitch did it. Charlip called all the girls into the storeroom and Bentshe Charlip, the owner's son, called upon all the girls to arrest me for this, since on my account they had all been left without work. He boasted about how good he was to keep the factory open for the good of the girls, so that they could earn money.

I didn't confess, but only said with pride that I didn't know who should be arrested, me or him. Then he called upon the girls again and said that they must arrest me, that I am a socialist and I answered him back. At the end of it they started working again and took down 5 kopecks per thousand. I was dismissed. [. . .]

We often used to organize evenings. We would look far outside the city to rent an apartment from its owner for a few roubles and there congregate the better people from the masses. There we would gather more than 300 people whom we could trust. Security was very strict. We would organize the evening with patrols and passwords. Lads were stationed along the entire way and they sent people onward from one to another until they arrived at the place. In the evening we would take a young man and woman, make them "bride and groom," meaning that the entire crowd had come to their engagement party; under this cover people would give speeches, economic and political.

We also used to have meetings of all the agitators, male and female, every week. These were called agitator gatherings. At these meetings everyone would give a report of his work and each would be given directions as to how to operate. Once every two weeks a meeting known as a *razborke* was held. The intelligentsia would also attend the *razborkes* and whoever wanted would write notes without a signature and throw them in a little box, and after that people would figure them out. The *razborkes* interested everyone very much and were indeed extremely fascinating. [. . .]

Over time our movement grew very large. It embraced almost the entire Yiddish working public of Minsk. Dissatisfaction increased among some of the workers, and they created an opposition under the leadership of Avrohom Valt (the poet Liesin). Around him congregated many dissatisfied members of the intelligentsia: Levin—from Smorgon, a teacher Khane Shlisel—a seamstress, known throughout Minsk as a socialist although she never did anything, and many others. The slogan of the opposition was the need to oppose agitation. Agitation gives nothing. It only angers the workers and they remain ignorant. First the masses must be prepared, education circles are needed to teach everyone "literacy" and develop, and only then, when the workers would be knowledgeable, would they be ready to join the battle.

The so-called "opposition" would arrange meetings and organize circles. They would come to our meetings and make statements against the organization and throw dirt at it. But the opposition did not last long. Some of them quickly returned to the organization and the rest were weakened.

Translated by Rebecca Wolpe.

Joseph Roth

1894–1939

The German-language novelist and journalist Joseph Roth was born in Galicia and attended university in Lvov and Vienna. He served in World War I and witnessed the dissolution of the Habsburg Empire, experiences that were the focus of much of his fiction. In the interwar years, he lived and worked in Berlin and later Paris as a well-respected and highly paid journalist. His masterpiece was *The Radetzky March* (1924). He died of alcoholism just before the outbreak of World War II.

Wailing Wall
1929

In these days when Jews are being killed in Palestine, I chose to go to Grenadierstrasse—not to Jerusalem. I had the feeling it was better to be with the bereaved than the dead. I paid a condolence call on Grenadierstrasse. It was a hot day. All the doors were open, as were many windows. There was a reek of onions, fish, fat, and fruit, of infants, mead, wash, and sewers. The Jews were milling or walking around in Grenadierstrasse, showing a clear preference for the middle of the road over the sidewalk, and most of all for the edge of the pavement. They formed a kind of running commentary to the pavement. A kind of traffic fixture on Grenadierstrasse, cause unknown, and purpose mysterious; as if, for instance, they had been taken on by the Jewish faith to demonstrate some particular ritual. Women and children clustered in front of fruit and vegetable stands. Hebrew letters on shop signs, nameplates over doors, and in shop windows, put an end to the comely roundness of European Antiqua type with its stiff, frozen, jagged seriousness. Even though they were only doing commercial duty, they called to mind funeral inscriptions, worship, rituals, divine invocations. It was by means of these same signs that here offer herrings for sale, phonograph records, and collections of Jewish anecdotes, that Jehovah once showed himself on Mount Sinai. With the help of these terrible jagged letters he gave the Jews the first terrible moral law, for them to spread among the cheerful, blithe peoples of the world. It takes, I thought, a truly divine love to choose this people. There were so many others that were nice, malleable, and well trained: happy, balanced Greeks, adventurous Phoenicians, artful Egyptians, Assyrians with strange imaginations, northern tribes with beautiful, blond-haired, as it were, ethical primitiveness and refreshing forest smells. But none of the above! The weakest and far from loveliest of peoples was given the most dreadful curse and most dreadful blessing, the hardest law and the most difficult mission: to sow love on earth, and to reap hatred.

No! If Jews are being beaten up in Palestine, there is no need to go to Jerusalem and study the question of the British Mandate to understand why. It's not only in Jerusalem that there is a Wailing Wall. Grenadierstrasse is one Wailing Wall after another. The punishing hand of God is clearly visible over the bent backs of the people. Of all the thousand ways that they have gone, and go, and will go, not one is a way out, not one leads to a concrete, earthly goal. No "fatherland," no "Jewish homeland," no "place of refuge," no "place of liberty." There are various opportunities to discern the so-called will of history. And nowhere does it show itself as plainly as in all the many Grenadierstrassen in which Jews don't so much live as drift up and down. (Theirs is no pathological-degenerative unrest so much as a historically conditioned one.) Clearly it is the secret "will of history" for this people to have no country to live in but to wander the roads. And that daunting will corresponds to the daunting constitution of the Jews. In seeking a "homeland" of their own, they are rebelling against their deeper nature.

They are no nation, they are a kind of supranation, perhaps the anticipation of some future form of nation. The Jews have already lived through all the others: a state, wars, conquests, defeats. They have converted infidels with fire and sword, and many of them also have been converted to other religions, by fire and sword. They have lived through, and emerged from, their primitive periods of "national history" and "civic culture." The only thing that was left to them is to suffer as strangers among strange peoples, because they are "different." Their "nationalism" is of no material kind. There is not even an absolute physical identity in common; not even a fixed form of belief. The religion of their forefathers has softened into the common daily life of the descendants; it has become a way of life, of eating, of sleeping and sexual conjunction, of trading, or of working and studying. Only, the conditions of their external surroundings were more tempting and more binding than the laws that were left of their religion. It is impossible to adhere to these laws and live. And, above all the commandments of the Jewish faith, there is the supremely implacable commandment: to live. Every day demands a further concession. It's not that they fall away from the faith of their fathers—their faith falls away from them. Or: It becomes sublimated in their descendants. It determines the way they think, act, and behave. Religiosity becomes an organic function of the individual Jew. A Jew fulfills his "religious duties," even if he doesn't fulfill them. Merely by being, he is religious. He *is* a Jew. Any other people would be required to affirm their "faith" or their "nationality." The Jew's affirmation is involuntary, automatic. He is marked, to the tenth generation. Wherever a Jew stops, a Wailing Wall goes up. Wherever a Jew settles down, a pogrom goes up. . . .

It should be understood, at long last, that Zionism can only be a bitter experiment, a temporary, opportune degradation of Judaism, or perhaps merely the reversion to a primal, long since outmoded, form of national existence. Maybe it has succeeded in arresting or delaying the "assimilation" of Jewish individuals or groups. But in return it seeks to assimilate an entire people. If it appeals to the warlike traditions of Judaism, then one should counter that the conquest of Canaan is less of an achievement than the Bible, the Psalms, and the Song of Songs; also, that the present of the Jews is greater, possibly, than their past: being more tragic. . . .

It might even be more "practical" in a "political" sense, if the young Jews who are "going back" to Palestine today, did so as the grandchildren not of the Maccabees, but of the priests and prophets. In the course of my wanderings through the Jewish ghetto in Berlin, I bought some Jewish nationalist newspapers from Eastern Europe. Their reporting of the fighting in Palestine was indistinguishable from the war reports we read in our German newspapers. In the same dreadful Borgis bold type, in comparison to which spilled human blood seems a pretty thin and inconsequential fluid, those Jewish nationalist newspapers report on the Jewish "victories over the Arabs." And in the war correspondents' familiar gobbledygook you could read, in appalling black on white, that these were, thank God, not pogroms, but honest-to-goodness "battles." Here you could finally understand that the view of the Jews as cleverer than other peoples is erroneous. Not only are they not cleverer, they are even sometimes more stupid. They aren't ahead of the times, but if anything lagging behind. They are aping the recently failed European ideologies. Now, of all times, they are setting about their original Jewish steel baths. Of course it's only natural that they should put up a fight in Palestine. It's too bad that they were attacked. But to have their heroism confirmed to them in the newspapers—having been uncommonly heroic over thousands of years without journalistic clichés—that furnishes final proof that there are no seven wise men of Zion directing the destiny of the Jewish people. No, there are several hundred thousand idiots of Zion, who have failed to understand the destiny of their people.

Translated by Michael Hofmann.

Other works by Roth: *Job* (1931); *Hotel Savoy* (1986); *The Legend of the Holy Drinker* (1989).

Leon Trotsky

1879–1940

Leon Trotsky was born Lev Davidovich Bronshteyn in Kherson province, Ukraine. He became a member of the Social Democratic movement when he was eighteen and spent several years in prison and exile before escaping abroad in 1902, where he wrote for *Iskra*. Trotsky leaned to the Menshevik faction of the Russian Social Democratic Workers' Party, which led to a conflict with Lenin in 1903; that same year, Trotsky condemned the Bund for their nationalism. He slipped into Russia after the 1905 Revolution and was arrested that same year, but he escaped. In 1917 he again returned to Russia, joining the Bolsheviks and becoming central to military and foreign relations during the October Revolution and its aftermath. He founded the Red Army and advocated worldwide revolution. With Lenin's death, Trotsky competed with Stalin for power for several years and lost, being expelled from the party in 1927. He was exiled in 1929, his citizenship was revoked in 1932, and so was accused of an attempt on Stalin's life in 1936. He was assassinated by the NKVD in Mexico.

My Life
1929

[. . .] In the country as well as in the town, I lived in a petty-bourgeois environment where the principal effort was directed toward acquisition. In this respect, I cut myself off both from the country of my early childhood and from the town of my youth. The instinct of acquisition, the petty-bourgeois outlook and habits of life—from these I sailed away with a mighty push, and I did so never to return.

In the spheres of religion and nationality, there was no opposition between the country and the town; on the contrary, they complemented one another in various respects. In my father's family there was no strict observance of religion. At first, appearances were kept up through sheer inertia: on holy days my parents journeyed to the synagogue in the colony; Mother abstained from sewing on Saturdays, at least within the sight of others. But all this ceremonial observance of religion lessened as years went on—as the children grew up and the prosperity of the family increased. Father did not believe in God from his youth, and in later years spoke openly about it in front of Mother and the children.

Mother preferred to avoid the subject, but when occasion required would raise her eyes in prayer.

When I was about seven or eight years old, belief in God was still regarded in the family as something officially recognized. On one occasion a visiting guest before whom my parents, as was their wont, were boasting about their son, making me show my sketches and recite poetry, asked me the question:

"What do you know of God?"

"God is a sort of man," I answered without hesitation.

But the guest shook his head: "No, God is not a man."

"What is God?" I asked him in my turn, for besides man I knew only animals and plants. The guest, my father, and my mother exchanged glances with an embarrassed smile, as always happens among grown-ups when children begin to shake the most firmly established conventions.

"God is spirit," said the guest. Now it was I who looked with a smile of confusion at my seniors, trying to read in their faces whether they were serious or joking. But no, it was not a joke. I bowed my head before their knowledge. Soon I got used to the idea that God was spirit. As became a little savage, I connected God with my own "spirit," calling it "soul," and already knowing that "soul," that is, "breath," ends when death comes. I did not yet know, however, that this doctrine bore the name of "animism."

On my first vacation at home, when I was getting ready to go to sleep on the sofa in the dining-room, I got into a discussion about God with the student Z., who was a visiting guest at Yanovka and slept on the divan. At that time I was not quite sure whether God did exist or not, and did not worry much about it, though I did not mind finding a definite answer.

"Where does the soul go after death?" I asked Z., bending over the pillow.

"Where does it go when a man is asleep?" came the answer.

"Well, it is then still . . ." I argued, trying to keep awake.

"And where does the soul of the horse go when he drops dead?" Z. persisted in his attack.

This answer satisfied me completely, and I fell into a contented sleep.

In the Schpentzer family, religion was not observed at all, not counting the old aunt, who did not matter. My father, however, wanted me to know the Bible in the original, this being one of the marks of his parental vanity, and therefore I took private lessons in the Bible from a very learned old man in Odessa. My studies lasted only a few months and did little to confirm me in the ancestral faith. A suggestion of a double meaning in the words of my teacher, concerning some text in the Bible which we were studying, prompted me to ask a question which I worded very cautiously and diplomatically: "If we accept, as some do, that God does not exist, how did the world come to be?"

"Hm," muttered the teacher, "but you can turn this question against him as well." In this ingenious way did the old man express himself. I realized that the instructor in religion did not believe in God, and this set my mind completely at rest.

The racial and religious composition of my *realschule* was very heterogeneous. Religion was taught respectively by a Russian orthodox priest, a Protestant parson, a Catholic priest, and a Jewish instructor. The Russian priest, a nephew of the archbishop, with the reputation of being a favorite with ladies, was a young and strikingly good-looking man, resembling the portraits of Christ—only of the drawing-room type; he had gold spectacles and abundant golden hair, and was, in brief, impossibly handsome. Before the lesson in religion was to begin, boys of different persuasions would divide into separate groups, and those not of the orthodox Russian faith would leave the classroom, sometimes under the very nose of the Russian priest. On such occasions he put on a special expression, in which contempt was only slightly softened by true Christian forbearance, as he watched the boys walk out.

"Where are you going?" he would ask some boy.

"We are Catholics," came the answer.

"Oh, Catholics!" he repeated, nodding his head, "I see, I see. . . . And you?"

"We are Jews."

"Oh, Jews, I see, Jews! Just so, just so!"

The Catholic priest came like a black shadow, always appearing right against the wall and disappearing so inconspicuously that throughout all my years there I could never get a look at his shaven face. A good-natured man by the name of Ziegelman instructed the Jewish boys in the Bible and the history of the Jewish people. These lessons, conducted in Russian, were never taken seriously by the boys.

In my mental equipment, nationality never occupied an independent place, as it was felt but little in every-day life. It is true that after the laws of 1881, which restricted the rights of Jews in Russia, my father was unable to buy more land, as he was so anxious to do, but could only lease it under cover. This, however, scarcely affected my own position. As son of a prosperous landowner, I belonged to the privileged class rather than to the oppressed. The language in my family and household was Russian-Ukrainian. True enough, the number of Jewish boys allowed to join the schools was limited to a fixed percentage, on account of which I lost one year. But in the school I was always at the top of the grade and was not personally affected by the restrictions.

In my school there was no open baiting of nationalities. To some extent the variety of national elements, not only among the boys but among the masters as well, acted as an important check on such policies. One could sense, however, the existence of a suppressed chauvinism which now and again broke through to the surface. The teacher of history, Lyubimov, showed marked partisanship when questioning a Polish boy about the Catholic persecution of orthodox Russians in White Russia and Lithuania. Mizkevic, a lanky, dark-skinned boy, turned green and stood with his teeth set, without uttering a word. "Well, why don't you speak?" Lyubimov encouraged him, with an expression of sadistic pleasure. One of the boys burst out: "Mizkevic is a Pole and a Catholic." Feigning surprise, Lyubimov drawled: "Is that so? We don't differentiate between nationalities here."

It hurt me quite as much to see the concealed cad in Lyubimov's attitude toward Poles, as to see the spiteful captiousness of Burnande with Germans, or the Russian priest's nodding of his head at the sight of Jews. This national inequality probably was one of the underlying causes of my dissatisfaction with the existing order, but it was lost among all the other phases of social injustice. It never played a leading part—not even a recognized one—in the lists of my grievances.

The feeling of the supremacy of general over particular, of law over fact, of theory over personal experience, took root in my mind at an early age and gained increasing strength as the years advanced. [. . .]

Translator unknown.

Other works by Trotsky: *Iz rabochago dvizheniia v odesse i nikolaeve* (1900); *Do deviatogo ianvaria* (1905); *Terrorizm i kommunizm* (1920); *1905* (1922); *Voyna i revolyutsiya* (1923); *Kak vooruzhalas' revolyutsiya* (1923-1925); *Literatura i revolyutsiya* (1924); *Moia zhizn'* (1930); *Permanentnaia revoliutsiia* (1931);

Istoriia russkoi revoliutsii (1932–1933). Many of these have been translated into English.

Boris D. Bogen
1869–1929

Boris D. Bogen was born in Moscow and graduated from the University of Moscow in 1888. He left for the United States in 1892 and worked as a school administrator for more than a decade. Beginning in 1916, he worked for the American Joint Distribution Committee, traveling to Europe under its auspices and the American Relief Administration. Bogen organized a postwar relief operation in Eastern Europe staffed by American-trained social workers. He returned to the United States in 1924. His autobiography was published a year after his death.

Born a Jew
1930

Chapter XVI. The Pinsk Tragedy

A letter from Zuckerman, the commissioner, evidently written by an agitated hand. It had come from Brest Litovsk bringing the news of horror. He had been in Pinsk and had organized there a committee to distribute food for the Passover in order that the Jews might celebrate properly one of those occasions when the hand of God reached out to deliver their forefathers.

And after his departure the committee had assembled with no little rejoicing. The Passover was to be observed in the old way in Pinsk, and there was to be enough of food for everyone. It was to be again as in the good times when even the poorest was not lacking. The committeemen were conscious of a holy joy at having been designated for the service of the distribution, for a mizvah (the privilege of a good deed) had been conferred.

Their deliberations were disturbed by an imperative knocking at the door which was suddenly flung open to admit soldiers; the committee was herded like cattle in the corrals of our ranches; and whoever protested was seized by rough hands.

So away with them through the city's streets, and in an hour not one of the thirty-four was alive. The soldiers were digging their graves where they fell; all had been shot without trial and without accusation of crime.

The next day an official notice in a Pinsk newspaper reported the tragedy coldly, briefly, and falsely: A Bolshevik Jewish organization had been discovered in Pinsk and a few of the ringleaders had been shot.

There was no sleep for me this night and the next morning I was returning to Warsaw, stopping at Brest Litovsk, where trains were changed and where Mr. Zuckerman was waiting, disheveled, distraught, and weeping for his brethren.

"Would that they had taken me with those innocent victims," he cried. "Why did I leave them? At least, I would not be here just to tell the story."

There was no use for Mr. Zuckerman to remain longer in Brest Litovsk where the Polish authorities were following his every step and had searched his rooms and even his person. He left with me for Warsaw on the next train.

In Warsaw we found an eyewitness, a boy of fifteen, Zalman Lichevski, though by reason of privation he looked no more than ten, a pogrom orphan from the Ukraine. He had been a wanderer in the world with four brothers and sisters, living by begging and bartering. He had been in Pinsk that dreadful night.

"We lived in Pinsk, you know, on the grand street just a few houses from the Zionist Center," he began. "They had a meeting there that night and everybody knew about it because the American delegate had been in the city. He had come a few days before. Everybody was on the streets to see him because he was not like any of the Jews in the city.

"So they had a meeting and it was about Pesach. Everybody knew that. I was home taking care of the little ones, for Dweirke, my sister, had gone to visit our sick aunt. All at once I heard a noise of shouting and crying and the firing of guns.

"I knew what the sound of guns meant. The Bolsheviks had been in the city and there had been much shooting on the streets. I guessed the Bolsheviks were coming back, and I got the children up and was already beginning to think 'Where should we run?' when Dweirke came back wringing her hands and crying.

"'What happened?'" I asked.

"'Terrible! Terrible! The people in the Zionist Center are taken to the tlea' (to death), and then she cried and cried and couldn't talk any more. I asked her questions but she could not say a word.

"So I left her with the little ones and ran into the street. The houses were all dark and few people were on the streets except soldiers, and there were some shadows of people hurrying home under the dark houses. I, too, went the same way in the shadows.

"All at once I heard shots again and again, and there were thousands of echoes, as if from all the walls.

"Soon automobiles were coming toward me, maybe three or four, and I hid in the doorway of a house, and when they had passed I ran. At last I came to the big wall, and a few soldiers were there who were burying dead men, and some officers were watching them.

"I did not wait any longer but ran back toward home, but on the way I went into the house of one of the men who I knew had been to the meeting. He was an old man and I wanted to know if anything had happened to him. I knocked at the door and when they had found out who I was they let me in. There were candles on the floor and I knew somebody had died. The old man had escaped, but they had killed the one who was to be his son-in-law.

"I asked how it happened, and the old man said, 'We were sitting in the room making out a list of the people who were to receive flour for matzo which the Americans were bringing. But black was the hour that we learned that we should have matzo this year, for at once shooting started. We wanted to run, but where could we run?

"'The house was surrounded by soldiers and we were beaten into line and told to go with the soldiers. We did not know where we were to go, but we thought to the prison, for who should think they were leading us to the tlea?

"'I escaped on the road in the darkness.'

"'And the old man and his family cried and wrung their hands and tore their clothing. And the kahle, the one that was to have been married to the man who was killed, sat over the candle and was like crazy.

"I thought, 'What should I do?' And I said, 'Home I should not go, for what could I do there? I shall do better if I go to Warsaw and tell everybody what is happening in Pinsk. Maybe we can get help before all the Jews are killed.'

"So I left Pinsk without telling anybody and went on the road to Warsaw. I walked all night and in the morning I came to a little Jewish place and told the people what had happened. These Jews were afraid themselves for their lives and they gave me a little food and money, and I stole a ride on a train and so I got to another place, and then here."

The child spoke with the mature intelligence of one far beyond his years; his truthfulness was not to be doubted. I hastened to Colonel Grove of the American Mission, who had already heard about this catastrophe. He was perturbed and at first could not believe that the victims were entirely innocent. They must have been guilty of some flagrant crime against the government. Such wanton slaughter was beyond the comprehension of a civilized man. . . . Surely, there must have been a good cause. . . . To destroy men wholesale. . . .

I told him of the boy. He must himself hear the story from the boy at once, he said, and without adding or subtracting a detail the lad repeated to the colonel the story he had told me. The next day the colonel had him for luncheon and for this occasion we removed his rags and gave him new shoes and clothing.

The colonel had managed a dramatic setting, for when I arrived with the boy we found ourselves in a glittering group of Polish officials and noblemen who were likewise the colonel's guests that day.

Here sat this and that proud noble and there this and that pompous official, and among them the Jewish boy Zalman Lichevski, who had just come out of his rags. And one and another inquired who he was and soon it was known about the table that he had come from the slaughter at Pinsk to tell the world. And though no word was spoken of that tragic event it brooded at the table, as if the haunting ghosts of the thirty-four dead were themselves in attendance. Zalman Lichevski was the silent accuser.

But justice was only in heaven with the dead, for the smell of Jewish blood had whetted the thirst of newspapers and stimulated the appetite of the multitudes. Whoever spoke other than compliments of Poland was denounced by the newspapers as an agent of American Jews. Such was a former member of the Red Cross who had left Poland and had spoken with no flattering words of the Poles; such was an American correspondent who had failed to burn sweet-smelling incense for them. In all Poland there was no voice of the press lifted to cry down the murders at Pinsk, and if it were mentioned at all it was only for justification.

These dead were Bolsheviks, it was said. There was no room on the earth for Bolsheviks. Bolsheviks must die. Was the killing without semblance of trial even? For Bolsheviks there must be no processes of justice.

Even our own Americans were not to be persuaded otherwise than that these dead had been Bolsheviks, plotting against the government. One of them had gone to Pinsk to find the truth; but truth, the immortal bird of legend, was not to be found in the fog of prejudice and fear which lay heavy on Pinsk and all Poland, and all the world, for that matter. Even in America we were pursuing phantoms of Bolshevism, and whoever could not feel the current hates, and whoever spoke for constitutional liberties, and whoever forgot to lift his hat for a patriotic hymn, were Bolsheviks.

But there was an ounce of satisfaction later on, though sad enough it was. A Parliament commission had investigated the killing of the thirty-four at Pinsk, and had reported that the slaughter of these Jews was not justified for any reason. A terrible mistake had been made, it was confessed.

It had been alleged that a shot had been fired from within the building in which the Jewish committee was assembled. And, to be sure, there was a hole in the door. But Mr. Gruenebaum, a member of the commission, found the bullet imbedded in a wall within the house and directly opposite the door. This was the proof that the shot had been fired from without.

The thirty-four dead, shot without trial, were vindicated and justice came to weep at their graves. But there was justice only for the dead, and the persecution of Jews continued with increasing fury and Jews lived in fear of to-morrow.

When in the tragic circumstances of the time courageous voices were needed, only the Zionists were to be heard. The Assimilationists spoke in deprecating whispers. "Ah, gentlemen, we must be quiet. We must not embarrass the government." . . . The Orthodox raised their voices only for flattery of the authorities.

A few months later I myself visited Pinsk, which was then still an island surrounded by bayonets. I called a meeting of the Jews of Pinsk, but few came, for the fate of the thirty-four was still a horror in the hearts of the people. They had died because they had gone to a meeting—a Jewish meeting that had to do with the hunger of Jews. Another such meeting I had now called, for the hunger of the Jews of Pinsk was no less; but only the boldest dared answer the summons.

They sat under a loaded machine gun in the hands of a soldier standing on the platform of the hall. With one sweep of its barrel he could have wiped out the pitiful handful that sat before him; and little would they have cared, for death had become the least of afflictions in Pinsk.

What mattered death for Miss S——who had seen worse than death? She was in the meager audience and I observed her particularly because she seemed a fig-ure of tragedy. She was one of four women who had attended the meeting the night the thirty-four men were shot. The women had been spared for tortures that caused them to envy the swift death of the men as a happy end.

Imprisoned, they suffered degradations until the day of their release. Daily the officers amused themselves by threatening them with death; daily they were undressed and flogged until they lost consciousness; two of them became insane, one had disappeared, and only this one was left in the community.

Her friends said: "She thinks only of death."

And I replied: "We will give her something to live for."

I made her a member of the local committee and I saw the aspect of tragedy fall from her face. Life had been an evil, haunting past; suddenly there had been set before her a hopeful future with work to be done, with the promise of relief for the suffering that was on Pinsk.

"I thank you," she smiled. She entered the discussion, full of plans. This must be done and that, she suggested. . . . Then, suddenly, the soldier spoke. Curfew time had come. The meeting must disband.

The girl came to my side with a young man. Would I remain in the city a while? I must depart early the next morning, I answered. But could I not find time to stay at least until the evening? Very well!

And early the next morning they were at my door, and a lovely speech the girl had.

"Our good friend," she began, "you came to us when there seemed no more hope of good on the earth. Since that terrible time the Jews had not been permitted to meet, until last night. And we had passed each other on the streets like strangers, not daring to meet two together. And each of us must suffer alone. You see, suffering is less when many suffer and each can share his suffering with his neighbor. But it is dreadful to suffer alone.

"But last night you made it possible for us to meet for the first time since the murder, and merely in touching each other's elbows was comfort. We felt there was goodness again in the world and hope had come again. Various visitors have been here to ask about the murder, but these only opened up the old wounds and only despair was left after they departed.

"You have made us forget the past and think of the future. We wanted to present you with some gift, but you were in a hurry and our stores were closed and there was nothing we could get here. So we went to a Jewish farmer, a distance from the city, who we knew had something hidden away, and here it is."

Before me they placed a package in a rag which upon being unfolded revealed an inkwell, a pencil, and a penholder. It was not a thing of value nor of great beauty; but now, ten years later, the little glass inkwell stands as the loveliest ornament in my house, a precious belonging.

One day about this time the walls of Warsaw became gay with gaudy placards summoning the people to a pogrom. The Poles had liberated themselves from the hands of their Russian masters but had saved their masters' worst habits. It was Passover week and the Warsaw Jews sat at their meager Seder feasts thanking the Lord, with choking voices, for delivering them from the Egyptian hands.

For the Jew there is always something to be thankful for in the past.

The walls call for the slaughter of Jews, but once upon a time the Red Sea parted for the passage of the Jews while the Egyptians were destroyed after they had suffered nine plagues. The blood of the thirty-four cries from the earth at Pinsk, but once upon a time the hand of the wicked Haman was diverted from its purposes by the grace of God, and Haman himself was hanged. The enemies assembled on the streets muttering against Jews, but once upon a time it was given to the hands of Judas Maccabaeus to defeat with a feeble army the great power of the Syrians.

The Warsaw Jews, awaiting pogroms, were not without faith in the Most High who had destroyed the Egyptians and caused Haman to be hanged and had made the Maccabean strong enough to defeat the Syrian hosts with a handful; but they were afraid. There were ominous assemblies on the streets, and though the government, at the request of Colonel Grove, had removed the incendiary placards, the welcome summons to a pogrom had remained in the heart of the mob.

The fear of violent death haunted every Jewish house, made bitter the bread that the generosity of America had provided, and drove sleep from the night.

It was early in the morning after the night of the first Seder that I was awakened by the screams of a woman in the Jewish house in which I lived; and I heard a loud knocking at the front door with the sound of clubs, and a voice crying, "Open, or it will be the worse for you."

In the street I saw a clutter of shadows.

"Open! Open!"

"This is the end," the father of the household said with the calm courage becoming to one who was the heir of a history of unhappy ends.

"This is the tlea," the mother cried, gathering her children about her.

I ran to the telephone which, since I became a member of the household, had been installed as a special privilege by the government; I called the police.

"Oh," they said, "it is only some of our men who are hunting a fellow who has evaded military service."

So it came to pass in that unhappy time that the noise of a window rattling, the cry of a child in the street, a shout made the hearts of Jews cold. And one day a deafening noise in the street brought me to the window before which all the rabble of Warsaw—beggars, loafers, soldiers—was running and shouting and throwing stones in a pursuit of Jews. It was like a mad wind of hate suddenly let loose, before which Jews were driven like straws.

A Jew in a long coat running and now and then turning his blood-streaked face to his enemies to cry for their mercy; a woman with an infant, now felled by a stone, now rising again to run; a whole family, now holding one to the other, now scattered and trampled.

The mistress of the house cried to me: "Go away from the window, for God's sake!"

But other members said: "No, let him stay. His uniform may save us. They will not dare to come in here when they see him."

I opened the window and shouted to the crowd. I spoke with that stentorian authority that military men like to affect.

"Stop! What does this mean?"

They stopped and regarded most respectfully my uniform, for the world had not yet come out of the nightmare in which uniforms were respected even more than life; and the while they lifted their eyes in adoration of my uniform, the Jews ran to grateful shelter.

I scarcely knew what to say or do next, but the police themselves relieved my anxiety, for down the street there was heard the rattling of a police wagon and the sound of shots fired in the air, and the mob dispersed.

But if a fear stays long enough it ceases to hurt any more, like any pain that in time becomes a familiar experience. And soon Jewish life in Warsaw was moving again in its rather sluggish course, although the talk of pogroms was still whispered and although Easter came, when to the glory of the risen Christ it was the custom in old Russia to make a sacrifice of Jews.

Chapter XXX. *The New Freedom*

Now our work proceeded under the favor of one of the noblest women of Russia—Mme. Olga Kamenev, the wife of the Acting President of the Republic. She was the chairman of that commission through which the government dealt with foreign-relief organizations; a woman of unusual ability and intelligence, a daughter of Jews. Her noble presence was like an admonition and the graft and the favor-seeking disappeared from the affairs of Russian relief administration, and men were ashamed to ask aught for themselves. [. . .]

The Kamenevs lived in three rooms on the second floor of a building in which were the living quarters of other officials as well. This space must suffice not only for the President of the Republic, his wife, and two children, but also for his secretary and two servants.

The rooms were modestly furnished, but in good taste. There was a select library in the study room, and the name of the aristocratic personage who once had owned them was still in the books. But this aristocrat, had he known, would have felt assurance that his beloved books had fallen into gentle hands, for the Kamenevs were people to the manor born.

Mme. Kamenev thought of herself as one of the family of mankind and to be a Jew was therefore to seclude one's self from the common life. She cared for Jews as people and not as brethren exclusively hers; they were brethren, to be sure, but as the Tartars were brethren, as the Bashkirs were brethren. But in unguarded moments hidden recesses of her heart opened to reveal a deep affection for the people of whom she was born. She was concerned with their good name in the world.

"You see," she said, "it is impossible to have you do everything for the Jews and nothing for the others. After all, to do for others does good to the Jews, for it promotes better understanding."

Mme. Kamenev labored furiously at her tasks, crowding every hour with service, for blindness was falling upon her and she must fill the days with work before darkness came.

Mr. Kamenev seemed even more distant from the Jews than his wife. It was said of him that he was the son of a converted Jew. He was the most respected of the Communist leaders, though not loved as Trotsky was. Among his political enemies I heard no ill spoken of him; these loud fellows said only that he was too mild and too modest. He was a prodigious worker, and though there was a multitude of detail to be served in the presidency of the Republic, he still found time to lecture on technical subjects and scarcely a month passed without a new book of his appearing in print.

Not that Kamenev was indifferent or hostile to Jews; they were brethren, but not special brethren, who must be treated justly. His beloved friend was the Jew, Professor David Shor, the musician, who was often with him in friendly discourse and who was the voice of the Jews speaking to the ears of the president. Shor found friendly ears in Kamenev, and often it was Kamenev himself who pointed ways out of Jewish difficulties that Shor brought to him. One day Shor brought to him a delegation of rabbis pleading for recognition of their calling and for the rights of the Hebrew language which had been declassed as something counter-revolutionary. Though the objects of their visit came to no success, still it was brought home to fanatical Jewish Communists that the Acting President himself had given gracious audience to rabbis, and it was as if Kamenev had said to his comrades, "We may despise the teachers of religion, but may we not be gentlemen?"

But Kamenev's gentle tolerance was quite wasted as an example for his truculent Jewish comrades, who demanded that Hebrew must be stricken from the tongues of men, since it was called a holy language and since nothing holy must be tolerated, and to whom synagogues were useful only for confiscation and conversion into Communist clubs.

When the kindly Kamenev proposed to the rabbis that they draft a petition asking the government's indulgence for Hebrew, it was the Jewish Communists who protested against any favor that would give any legal sanction to Hebrew. And the pious portion of Jewry cried, "Oh, that our brethren should do this to us! Oh, that the feet of our own children should now be on our necks!"

So Hebrew had become a secret language, a sort of Marrano, and was taught behind closed doors and the little boys no longer raised their voices in the well-known singsong of the Hebrew schools. But in unguarded moments the boys quite forgot themselves and chanted their lessons in the traditional way. One day I visited a Jewish shelter home with Mme. Kamenev and even before we came to the door Mme. Kamenev's Communist ears were assailed by the singsong that told us little boys were studying Hebrew there. And what a hurrying there was to hide the Hebrew books as we entered and what a blushing as the pupils put away their hats which must be worn when the holy language is on the tongue! And what a stammering by the teacher making explanations to Mme. Kamenev, who smiled a sweet tolerance that, alas! was not common in this new Russia, furious and unbending in the pursuit of the new ideals.

The teacher opened his coat and displayed a badge to her.

"You see," he said, "I am the commandant here."

In every house the government had a "commandant" who was a faithful Communist and whose duty was to make report to the authorities on the comings and goings of all the inhabitants. A commandant was also in every school and his functions included janitor service.

This one was a faithless commandant, perpetrating treason against Communism in order to be faithful to Israel! Placed in the school to keep his eyes open against Judaism, he himself was teaching it; on guard to keep it out, he was stealthily imparting it to the hearts of the children. Faithless Communist! Faithful Jew!

Like all things that are prohibited, Hebrew came to be greatly desired by the Jews and in the Ukraine and White Russia it was bootlegged, as we would say in the United States, by hundreds of teachers. These imparted the language to furtive groups of five and ten, meeting in the basements of synagogues, with lookouts at the doors to give warning of the approach of intruders.

And time and again there were raids on these classes by Jewish Communists, bringing the secret police of the Cheka which was the most feared and the most hated of the institutions of the new order. The Cheka was the instrument of *Schrecklichkeit* by which Communism maintained itself in the beginning, an all-seeing eye seeking enemies, an iron fist that crushed them. But after Russia had become safer for Communism the remorseless Cheka became more mellow and made concessions to gentleness; now the Cheka no longer was permitted to execute people offhand and formality of trial was required. It even changed its evil name and became the GPU. [. . .]

In this new Russia, at that time, Jews predominated in the high places of the government, but not consciously as Jews, for they had set themselves apart from Judaism as they had from capitalism, and there was none among them to say, "I am a Jew"; they knew only the proletarian unity.

Nor was there any in Russia, at that time, to point scorn publicly at these new rulers and say, "They are Jews." And I who had been born in the old Russia and had lived in it until my young manhood, felt myself in a topsy-turvy world in which the despised had come to sit on the throne, and they who had been the least were now the mightiest, and I was like one waking up from a dream, uncertain between fantasy and reality.

There was that May Day in Moscow, a grand parade. The Red Army marches. The workers march with banners and floats, singing. The procession, miles long, snakes through the winding streets and comes, at length, to the Kremlin where the puissance of Communism is assembled.

Where homage was once for Tsars, the heavens are rent with hoarse, exultant tributes for the Jew, Trotsky, the idol of the people—then.

Where the soldiery did obeisance to emperors, the battalions now stand before the Jew, Kamenev, Acting President of the Republic, to recite after him the oath of allegiance.

He is flanked by generals who were of the old régime and now are of the new. At his right Budiani, the dashing cavalry-man, whom the Tsar loved.

One sees these things and says, "But, after all, this is not Trotsky the Jew or Kamenev the Jew. They have repudiated Judaism and feel no unity with Israel. Are they of us, then?"

Then one argues: "But they are Jews. Is the Jewish quality something that can be renounced with a word? Can our spiritual inheritance be cast off by a man as some garment? These are Jews."

Trotsky the Jew receives the salute of the army. . . . Budiani, the favorite of the Tsar, stands at attention as the Jew [Budyenni] Kamenev speaks.

This is not to say that there was no anti-Semitism in Russia then. Oh, there was enough of it and, perhaps, the more dangerous because it was suppressed. The government sat on the lid, and when Jews met to discuss the comparative happiness of their new state, there was always the terrifying question, "But what would happen if the government fell?"

And men feared to venture the answer, being seized with unspeakable dread; for every Jew knew that the fall of the government would release such an explosion of hate as would fade St. Bartholomew's eve to a brawl. And the prayer was that there might be no change even though Jewish Communists were most obnoxious and persecuted Judaism, even while the Jew himself was safe.

The Jewish Communists knew how to rationalize the persecution of Judaism. This persecution, they said, was really good for the Jews in the long run. They must take this attitude of opposition to Judaism in order that it might appear that even among the Jewish Communists there was no special favor for Judaism in this new Russia in which all religions had been declassed. Seeing Jews barking at Jews, the dogs of anti-Semitism might be content and seek other objects at which to snap.

But, in reality, the Jewish Communists were moved by inspirations less complicated, and these partly had to do with their own prestige in the party and partly with the nature of the Jew who is forever afraid of what the neighbors may say about him. If in America it is a time for hysterical patriotism he must seem more hysterical than others, lest it be said that he is not patriotic enough, as we saw in an earlier chapter of this book. If in Russia religion had come to be despised, the Jew must be seen tearing down synagogues. [. . .]

In a pamphlet of which hundreds of thousands were printed, under the title "What We Are Doing to the Rabbis," Esther Froomkin enumerated the hundred and one indignities that rabbis had suffered. And if the mediaeval church burned Jews to save their souls, no less did Esther Froomkin persecute Judaism to save Jews.

One day I reproached her.

"Why do you go out of your way to violate the most sacred feelings of your people? It is bad enough that you are making life miserable for the rabbis. But why do you take the trouble to stir up the Jews against rabbis, to lead the young against institutions their fathers respect?"

"I am right!" she exclaimed. "You do not understand the danger that the Jews are facing. If the Russian people should once get it into their minds that we are partial to the Jews, it would go hard with Jews. It is for the sake of the Jews that we are absolutely objective in our dealings with the clergy—Jewish and non-Jewish alike. The danger is that the masses may think that Judaism is exempt from anti-religious propaganda and, therefore, it rests with the Jewish Communists to be even more ruthless with rabbis than non-Jewish Communists are with priests. So we must popularize prejudice against rabbis; the Russians who have lost the poor consolation of their priests must be persuaded that there is no special favor for rabbis."

But a few weeks later the god Trotsky spoke and peace fell upon the turbulent spirit of Esther Froomkin; for Trotsky in his new book, "The Problems of Life," counseled moderation in the methods of anti-religious propaganda. It was quite a mistake, he said, to antagonize believers too much and advised "a milder and even respectful attitude toward those who, because of their background, cannot lift their minds to an understanding of modern ideas."

Thereupon Esther Froomkin who had been flaunting fiery banners lifted a pure white one of pity, and thereafter rabbis were not fellows to be thrown to the wolves but poor, benighted creatures who deserved the sympathy of all who perceived the new light that issued from the Kremlin. [. . .]

We were free of the partnership of the anti-Judaistic Evsectzia, for under the terms of our contract with the government we functioned as a nonsectarian organization.

We had to appear less Jewish in order that we might serve Jews more. As a nonsectarian organization we were enabled to serve Jews who had no favor in the eyes of Communist Jews. To be sure, we had to pay for being free of the Evsectzia, for we were obliged to use about one-third of our funds for purposes designated by the government in places where there were almost no Jews. So we granted a loan once for combating wolves in Northern Russia, for they had become a serious menace to life, and in Hartaria our money helped to rehabilitate institutions for the care of children that were not of Jewish birth. And who could have it in his heart to find fault that Jewish money saved Christians from the depredations of wolves or that Jewish money nurtured Tartarian children?

Indeed, we came to be regarded as the lords bountiful in Russia, the generous and magical Americans who had balm for every ill, and missions from the far-flung Soviet Republic were sent to us with pleadings for the construction of canals and roads and what not. [. . .]

But when Passover came our nonsectarian rôle failed us and, in response to pleas for matzoth, we were obliged to insert notices in the press announcing we could not help make a Jewish holiday, because, under the terms of our contract with the government, we were not permitted to assist in any enterprise that had to do with religious observance.

The good Mme. Kamenev, whose heart had rejected Judaism but was still Jewish, intervened the next day. Since matzoth were bread, she argued, and none other could be eaten during the seven days, it was quite unjust to say that people might not have them. And straightway she called a meeting of her cabinet and shortly we were permitted to distribute funds for matzoth and quickly we sent couriers to distribute our money.

And when this became known that zealous Evsectzia, Jewish but not Judaistic, raised a protesting voice.

"Under the auspices of the government," it said, "a religious observance is fostered. This enlightened Communistic government gives aid and comfort to a holiday by which Jews remember that they were slaves once. This must not be permitted."

And they shouted so long and with such violence and with such effect that the permission was withdrawn; but too late. Already the couriers had reached their destination and distributed our funds.

It is difficult for the Jew to play nonsectarian, for Jewish problems are always stepping on his toes. One day when they put into our hands a non-Jewish orphan asylum we insisted that a just proportion of Jewish children must be placed in it, in order that there might be no doubt of its nonsectarian character. And so to start with, five children of Israel were transferred from a Jewish orphan asylum to this one. The Jewish institution was crowded and lacked the comforts that made the other one a model of its kind.

But one morning when the bell rang summoning the orphans to arise, the beds of the five Jewish children were vacant.

"Esther, Moishe, Yankele, Sarah, Abba," the attendants called through the halls, and a while afterward they were found—in the Jewish orphan asylum whence they had come.

"And why," we asked, "did you run away? Were you mistreated?"

And they answered: "Could we be treated any better? But it was no place for Jewish children. There were no Jews there but we, and no Yiddish and everything Goish. Was that a proper place to put Jewish children?"

They embarrassed us with reproachful eyes.

"There is even no chance to get a Yiddish book or to be Jewish. What sort of a life is it for Jewish children? It is good for Goim, but for Jewish children it is better here, even if here we do not eat so much."

And only upon our promise to send a larger number of Jewish children to the better asylum would they go back. So even in a proletarian society in which all beings had been reduced to a common level and in which all racial and religious barriers were cut down, the Jew still was a fellow apart, saying, "I am a Jew. I am different." And his children said it, as if it were born with them in their hearts.

And when one hundred illiterate Jewish children were found in Moscow and it was proposed to send them to various non-Jewish institutions for learning, there was heard a swelling protest arising from Moscow Jewry.

"This is impossible. Jewish children must be kept together. They will be lost to us if distributed among the Goim. Only when Jews stand together do they live as Jews; in separation is death. Our children must live together that they may be Jews; otherwise we destroy them as Jews." [. . .]

Our all-embracing charity that took in a non-Jewish orphan asylum and fed starving workingmen students without distinction of race or creed was not applauded at home where, it was asked, "Did we give our money to feed the Goim?" And it was idle to explain the necessity of this. And hot was the blast of reproach that enveloped us when it became known in America that we were helping to feed these students.

Even if we were not obliged to do this, our consciences would have driven us to the succor of these noblest of young men who had come from distant places of the Republic in quest of knowledge. Hunger and privation was their portion, and they slept in the railroad stations, lacking other shelter, and some froze to death in the bitter winters, but few abandoned their ideal. The good life was in knowledge, they said; the good life was worth any sacrifice, for their cloud-capped heads were too high above the stomach to feel its pangs.

Among them were many Jews. The position of the Jew in university life had vastly changed, and it is worth while to offer the comparison as described by Professor Minor, a renowned neurologist.

"My father was the chief rabbi in Moscow," he began, "and when it came time for me to enter the gymnasium I was not admitted. There was a numerous clausus that limited the number of Jews to one-tenth of the non-Jewish student enrollment. Since there were in the gymnasium 175 non-Jews, the number of Jews was fixed that year at 17½. A half a Jew being physically impossible save, perhaps, in the butchery of pogroms, the number of Jews actually admitted was 17. But when an appeal was made to the Governor of Moscow, he made a concession: I might be the half a Jew left over in the quota, and so I was admitted.

"At length, I entered the university and for twenty odd years I was a privatdozent (a sort of tutor), for, being a Jew, I could never hope to be a professor. I was approached again and again with suggestions that I accept Christianity for the sake of promotion.

"Oh, our world has been turned upside down and much evil we have suffered, and all that I possessed has been taken from me, and I have endured privation and even now lack meager comforts, and for old age there is no promise, but I am conscious of a certain happiness. The Jew has come at length to his rights as a man. What the Jew has suffered in this new Russia is the common suffering, but he shares also the common rights and privileges. For that reason I am happy even amid discomfort, for in time one may adjust himself to physical pain, but the oppression of the spirit is not to be endured.

"Though in the old Russia I could get no promotion for twenty years by reason of being a Jew, to-day I am not only professor but also dean of the medical school. I am not a radical, but I must acknowledge the debt of the Jews to the new rulers." [. . .]

Chapter XXXI. A New Way, a New Life

[. . .] It was springtime when Dr. Rosen and I proceeded on an inspection trip which took us to the Jewish agricultural colonies in the Ukraine, where we were fascinated beyond measure by the spectacle of new life being born out of the soil.

Bereft of all their possessions, having torn themselves out by the roots from age-old habitations, and having been torn out of their occupations, hundreds of Jewish families had come here to plant a new life in this rich earth. And, lo! Israel was again at his ancient occupation. More than seed he sowed here; his spirit also.

There were old Jewish colonists here as well, families that had been tilling the soil long before the war, and had suffered the raids of the bandits afterward, and had lost relatives and friends in pogroms which were no less in these bucolic scenes than in the towns.

"My son, my daughter, and her two children were killed," said an old colonist with whom we stopped.

The years had served to heal the wounds, and he told us of his sorrows with the detachment of one reciting the history of a distant past. The dead were of the earth, but the ruin of his former good estate was still visible and for this he wept.

He took us to the orchard where his ruined fruit trees stood, gaunt stumps, and his eyes filled with tears.

"I remember when my father, blessed be his name, and I planted these trees."

It was double toil for the old colonists—to rebuild on the ruins of their former prosperity and to plant anew for the next harvest. They asked for tools, seed, and horses.

If we gave them tools we must, under our agreement with the government, give tools also to their non-Jewish neighbors. But what would these Jews say about this? These neighbors had robbed them and burned their houses in the pogroms. They had fallen eagerly upon them when the bandits came through. What would these Jews say to see us comforting them? We asked them and discovered they held no grievance.

"Our peasants are good goim," they answered. "They were misled by a few. And, besides, is it not better to show them kindness? Can we make friends of them if we hold ourselves as enemies against them? We need their friendship and we can make friends only by being friends. It is good that you give to them as well as to us."

"So peace and friendship were upon these acres, and the Jews were quickly rebuilding their ruined fortunes, and, with the aid of our loan fund, were going into new enterprises, such as cooperative cheese factories. Seeing these things, Dr. Rosen rejoiced, for his work was already good; the workers were not content to be helped, but were helping themselves as well.

Now the pioneers were pouring into the land from the wretchedness of the cities and towns, applying their hands to unaccustomed toil, bending to plows their backs that had carried the peddler's pack, giving to the soil a portion of the spiritual devotion that was once only for synagogues.

Among these were the chalutzim, young men and women, who had come here to prepare for Palestine, the distant goal. Here they would prepare and become strong for the greater labor in the Holy Land where the desert waited for their hands, and they worked with religious fervor.

This was only an interlude, and next year or the next the Holy Land, and this soil was only a little less holy since from it would come the strength and the knowledge for their work in the desert. Their housing was poor and their clothing was rags, but they felt the elevations of rapt priests. A little success, the sight of new-sown seed sprouting, the completion of a habitation wretched enough, was celebrated as a triumph. They sang, as they worked through long, hard hours, those songs that spring from the anguish and the hopes of Jewish hearts. And when night fell they read or played games or sat spinning their dreams; and we saw among them the loveliness of the friendship that is between people held together by a common ideal and sweating for it.

Their dreams ran ahead of their means, and in one place these chalutzim had established an agricultural school even before their first crop was gathered, and shortly the school was filled with young pilgrims who had come from the cities in pursuit of the chalutz ideal. And what if there was want and misery, and what if they must eat sparingly to-day in order that there may be food enough for the morrow, and what if they were in tatters? Their hearts were light with the dream, and happiness was in toil. And when we offered to supply clothing for the rags they wore, they answered quickly, "Send us, rather, implements." [. . .]

On this journey it fell to us to rescue a confiscated synagogue and restore it to the devotion of the Jews, and it was the privilege of our hands to set free imprisoned Jews who had offended the Communist Jews by being too zealous in their piety.

It was in a Jewish colony near Sympheropol I met a wife weeping for her husband. And what had happened? Oh, he had been arrested and put in jail for praying in the synagogue of the Caraites whose religious practices were generally Jewish and yet who were not considered Jewish enough to suffer the limitations that were put on Judaism by the Jewish Communists. When their synagogue was confiscated, the Jews went to pray with the Caraites, and when they were caught bootlegging Judaism in this way, they were imprisoned or fined; and for that reason the husband of the weeping wife was in jail.

But shortly he was out by our intercession, and so freedom came also for a number of others who were in jail for the same offense, and thus, too, the synagogue was taken from the impious hands of the Communist Jews and restored to the hands of the righteous who cleansed it first, considering it to have been defiled.

And happy was the reunion of the husband and the wife whose weeping had brought about this good con-clusion. Life would be pleasant enough to live in this Russia were it not for the devilish Communist Jews, he sighed. He had been a wealthy landowner who had lost everything, but what mattered that, he asked, in a country in which no one was rich? Wealth was only a relative state.

Now he was permitted to have no more land than he needed for his living, and what more needed a man ask for in the world? Now, being an expert in cattle, he worked for the Jewish coöperative, buying stock, and this increased his living. And where once his family had far more than enough to eat, to-day they had no more than enough, and why should the stomach have more than enough? he asked. Was it good for the stomach?

"But, my friend, the best is that we have the right to live. It was a daily fear in the old times. To-day I might offend one of the nobility and to-morrow I might be without a home and without my land and a wanderer in the world; for we lived here by sufferance. And wherever I went I was unwanted, being a Jew.

"The other week I was the convoy for a shipment of cattle to the Caucasus and when I came to the boundary line of the Crimea I was stopped, as is the custom. I showed them my credentials from the coöperative—the Jewish coöperative, mind you—and they read it, and the officer said, 'This is a herd of the Jewish coöperative,' and they let me through without delay and with great respect.

"This is worth something: To be a man, the equal of all others. To be respected and to have enough for life— is there more to be asked for? It is only the Communist Jews who make life miserable; of the government we have no complaint."

Rosen and I had gone to the Crimea to spy out the land and its opportunities for Jewish colonization by the aid of the Joint Distribution Committee. And we saw immense tracts of rich land lying idle for whatever hands would apply themselves. The natives were friendly and the government of the Crimea was willing, but it rested with Moscow to say whether land should be bestowed for the colonization of Jews. Indeed, already large numbers of Jews had come to the soil of the Crimea on their own account, and were already planting on rented ground, living in the open until the harvest when there would be time to build shelter. We returned to Moscow, thrilled with the idea of making these beautiful acres available to Jewish farmers.

In Moscow we found the enthusiasm for this project no less than our own, and Citizen Bragin—the one who had created the universal exposition—became a burning prophet for it. He lifted it as a new banner and proclaimed it as the solution of the Jewish problem. He elaborated it.

"Why not establish a Jewish republic or some kind of autonomous unit in the Crimea?" he asked. "A republic in which the Jew will be self-governing and live his own life!"

This Utopian had plans and specifications, for Bragin was not of those dreamers who shoot aimless arrows. Nor was he one who fashions dreams for his own contemplation; he demanded an audience and the government patiently and seriously inspected his plans and felt the substance of reality in them.

"In Russia we have three million Jews," he said, "the inhabitants, in the main, of cities and small towns, formerly small merchants, to-day without occupation, declassed, a social problem.

"If you teach them trades, do you improve the situation? You add so many more to the working classes and so increase unemployment.

"Already official life is overflowing with Jews, and soon the young Jews will come like a flood from the universities seeking employment in the government, and where will you place them?

"Whichever way he turns the Jew finds himself superfluous in our overcrowded world. If he is a worker with his hands, he finds many hands already at work and no employment for his own; if he is a worker with his mind he is embarrassed because there are too many Jewish minds already working for the government. Already people are seeing the Jews are too prominent and it is only right that in Russia the government should be largely of real Russians.

"Where, then, is escape for the Jew? In the old Russia the Jewish problem was 'solved' by repression; in this new Russia the problem must be solved by providing the Jew with the widest opportunity for self-development. If he is permitted to develop in the midst of the general population he soon causes irritation, for he is an amazingly precocious individual; then we have anti-Semitism again.

"No! He must be permitted to exercise and increase his great talents apart from the mass—in a separate republic of, for, and by Jews. Then his hands will not come to compete with non-Jewish hands, causing strife; then his mind will not come to overcrowd a government already filled with Jews whose presence is already the cause of envious comment.

"For his educated mind there would be a government of his own to serve and for his hands there would be work of his own to do. In the Crimea are vast tracts of idle lands for hands. A Jewish republic!" [. . .]

In the United States the Zionists said "No!" being jealous for their own nationalistic and political project. Bragin's republic would be a competitor.

The Reform wing of American Judaism said "No!" because it always had been opposed to any separate political and nationalistic identity. Jews must be Jews by reason of religion only, they said.

The Orthodox said "No!" because they were sure that a Jewish republic under Communist auspices would be a godless republic and Judaism would perish at its source.

The majority of radical Jews said "No!" for long ago they had ceased to have any use for the Communists and they were sure that a Jewish republic would strengthen the Communist hands.

And so Bragin's republic perished, but not the plan to colonize the Crimean lands with Jews, and eventually a limited sum was appropriated by the Joint Distribution Committee for this purpose, and colonization of the Crimea was established as the important item of the future program. As for the rest, we would begin to liquidate our interest in the Jewish institutions we had been supporting.

Other works by Bogen: *The Psychology of Acquiring a Foreign Language* (1899); *Jewish Philanthropy* (1917); *Through the Ukraine with Bogen* (1922).

Moshe Goldstein

d. 1944

Moshe Goldstein, a follower of the Munkacs rebbe, Chaim Elazar Shapiro, accompanied the latter on his journey from Czechoslovakia to Jerusalem, keeping a journal of the voyage.

The Book of Jerusalem Journeys
1930

In 1930, Chaim Elazar Shapiro (Spira), the Hasidic rebbe of Munkacs, Czechoslovakia (today, Mukachevo, Ukraine), traveled by rail to Vienna and Trieste and by ship to Alexandria, where he and his retinue spent the Sabbath. They then went to Palestine. The trip lasted thirteen days. In Palestine, Rabbi Shapiro met with the kabbalist Shlomo Eliezer Alfandri.

We put on Sabbath clothes and blessed the candles. The ship's officials gave us the large auditorium for prayer and the meal (because there is no one from the nations of the earth [non-Jews] on this ship aside from our group). Our rebbe came from his stateroom wrapped in a *talis* [. . .] and recited the prayer in his strong voice. All of us were stirred and when we said the prayer for sea travelers each of us was moved profoundly with the fear of God and his majesty, that of the creator of the sea and who disposes of all souls, and we prayed that He would lead us in peace to our country. [. . .]

From Alexandria we traveled by railroad via Benha–Kantara–Lod [. . .] to the Holy City but, due to our many sins, when we arrived in the Holy Land it seemed to us like an alien country because we saw the Jewish officials approach and we distanced ourselves from their ways, these innovators, that is, the freethinking Zionists who spoke to us in Hebrew which is spoken in all stations of steam conveyances [railroads?], they having made the language a vernacular, despised by all those who fear God because this is but the holy tongue of our Torah. [. . .] (except for the Sefardim who speak the holy tongue since ancient times and they do it in holiness). [. . .]

We arrived in Jerusalem on Thursday, the tenth of Iyar [. . .] and when a person comes close to holiness his heart opens up and his mouth is filled with praise for having merited this. [. . .] [When the rebbe arrived] he tore his clothes [a sign of mourning] in a way that cannot be repaired. With a broken heart and tears running down our faces, we tore our clothes, made the blessing when a person dies (without saying the name of God), said the prayer upon death . [. . .]

Because of our sins, [on the Temple Mount] the Arabs ["Ishmaelites"] built a castle of impurity . . . to the shame of the Shekhina [God], as if it were, and to the shame of Israel his closest people. [. . .][1]

[. . .] We arrived at the Munkacs Kollel[2] in the new part of Jerusalem [. . .] so the rebbe could find a place to rest, and the courtyard was full of men, women, and children. The streets we passed by on foot were full of people, and [. . .] we were amazed to hear even from the pious women who were whispering that a holy man was passing by [. . .] and "may his arrival bring our salvation," their lips trembling in a feeling of holiness. That impressed us greatly and we realized that they were not living off the fat of the land but, like most residents of the Holy Land, had difficult, sorrowful lives and nevertheless they anticipated the deliverance [. . .]

who is like your people Israel [. . .] because of the merit of righteous women they merit to be liberated.

The land is very, very good. We journeyed [to Safed] among the hills of Jerusalem, seeing the undulating hills and valleys. The fruits, grains, and vineyards were a delight to the eyes and the rebbe, may he have a good and long life, enjoyed seeing this. It revived him and he breathed the breath of life and remarked, how lovely and pleasant this land is that God gave us and promised us as our heritage.

But in contrast, we were agitated and depressed when we passed by the ugly encampments [. . .] some colonies of the Zionists or religious Zionists [*mizrahim*— the name of the religious Zionist party was Mizraḥi][3] and their like [. . .] who had come and defiled our holy land, they and their wives, sons, and daughters. They resemble evil, filthy things inwardly and outwardly. They know not of God, do not observe the Torah, and anger God with their deeds. [. . .]

[In Safed-Meron, on Lag ba-Omer, they witnessed the first haircut of a three-year old boy, as is the custom among some *Haredim*.]

A child of three was brought into the House of Study [. . .] dressed in nice clothes, with beautiful eyes, very good looking, reflecting the visage of God, and with his side-curls arranged very nicely. They shaved him in the House of Study, distributed baked goods and drinks and, with warm feelings, they danced. The father hoisted the boy on his shoulders and his relatives did likewise, and they danced around. It was a pleasure to see this holy picture, which gladdened the heart and brightened the eyes. It's worthwhile to have sons on whose faces the fear of God is seen, and to rejoice with them in a mitzvah and with love because they are our lives and the span of our days.

Around midnight, from our windows in Safed we could see the bonfires in Meron [. . .] the rejoicing of thousands of Jews went on through the morning. [. . .] But on the advice of the *Haredim* of Jerusalem and Safed, our rebbe, may he have a long and good life, did not go to Meron, since because of our many sins, there was a mixture there of the good and the worst. At night, a mob of men and women pioneers of the Zionists, Satan lurking among them, danced—boys and girls together. They made merry and joked around in the holy of holies. [. . .] On the morning of Lag ba-Omer when we traveled from Safed to Meron, we met these evil people as they were returning, boys and girls together, and they sang together, even though the voice of a women is seductive [*kol isha ervah*]. And the holy Tanna [rabbi of the Mishnah], Rabbi Shimon Bar Yohai[4] [. . .] will certainly take revenge upon them.

We passed the devastated holy places in Safed which, last year [1929] the Arab Ishmaelites destroyed. They had no mercy and slaughtered the innocent holy lambs, Jewish souls and those who fear God. They showed us the house that had been the residence of a great rabbi who was the first victim when the evil ones suddenly burst into his house as he was studying Torah and spilled his blood as if it were water—may God take revenge for his blood. These sights shattered our bones; the ears shall ring of everyone who hears these things, and now God shall arise and will take revenge on his enemies.

The rebbe decided to eat the third Sabbath meal in his residence, but the Hasidim of Sanz [Nowy Sacz, Poland] begged him to eat with them [and they agreed to yield their customary songs and words of Torah to the rebbe's way of doing these things].

The rebbe girded his loins and spoke pure words in a fired-up way, reproving his listeners, all of whom trembled, for having permitted the breach of allowing the thugs (the Zionists and their ilk) to desecrate the holy city of Safed with their schools [. . .] which leads their students into *sheol* [hell]. He said with bitter tears, "have pity my beloved brothers on your male and female children and on the public and rise up against the rebels and raise the flag of Torah on the old way of teaching, which is pure and holy. [. . .] My brethren, do not fear and guard your souls so that their terrible fires not burn among you. Adhere to the Torah of Moses given to us at Sinai and that will hasten the complete redemption. [. . .]

We deviated a bit from our route in order to pass through the city of Tel Aviv. We saw there a solidly built city with beautiful palaces but at the lowest possible spiritual depths because most of the residents are Zionists and *mizrahim*, farmers who violate the Sabbath openly and in secret and eat nonkosher food and are not careful regarding the laws of family purity, just as in the agricultural colonies. [. . .]

[Rabbi Shlomo Eliezer Alfandari] was very sorry about the establishment of the chief rabbinate, created in Palestine by the freethinking Zionists. He related that when the English monarchy conquered Palestine [1917], because of our sins the freethinkers gathered together all of the rabbis of Jerusalem to establish a chief rabbinate (which he called a rabbinate of heretics). Another rabbi wrote to him (we know his name) asking, in the name of all Sefardic rabbis, that he should be made the Sefardic chief rabbi and he would restore the glory of the Torah." [Rabbi Alfandari rejected this request and wrote] [. . .] "You believe those Zionists! [. . .] I can tell you that now the Zionists are choosing the elderly, but later they will despise them and replace them with black-bearded rabbis [. . .] and later with rabbis who have no beards at all. Therefore, you should know that the destruction of Torah and Judaism in the Holy Land begins with you, and you will have to render an account in heaven for all the sins of the coming generations, etc."

They asked him [Alfandari] about the Agudah.[5] He replied that there is no difference between the Zionists and *mizrahim*, and the Agudah, only in name do they differ. [. . .] And he was very pleased to hear from the rebbe that he knelt before none of the political parties and sects, but protests against all of them.

When the rebbe was in Jerusalem the greats of the *Haredi* rabbis asked him what to do about the Slobodka Yeshiva [founded in Kovno/Kaunas, Lithuania] which used to be in Hebron and after the riots came to Jerusalem. Most of them (though they are learned) and their students have short side-locks and trimmed beards. They do not shave their heads and that's the way they were in their country. [. . .] [The rabbis were fearful] that the Jerusalemites would be influenced by them. The rebbe [. . .] replied very wisely that one should treat them kindly because of all they had suffered when some students from their yeshiva were killed [in the Arab riots] . . . and if you bother them they will drift toward "that man,"[6] Kook and the Zionist rabbinate. [. . .] And he explained that their rabbi, Moshe Mordechai (Epstein), is learned, but he loves money very much. And Kook is like that [. . .] but if the rebbe comes out against them, that they, the Slobodniks would join Kook and his faction, and that's not worth it.

NOTES

1. [The Mosque of Omar.—Eds.]

2. [An institution where mostly married men study Torah and are supported by their wives' work and by fundraising.—Eds.]

3. [In recent years, *mizrahim* has come to be the adjective used to describe Jews of North African and Middle Eastern origins (the earlier term was *sefardim*). In this context, the rebbe is probably referring to supporters of the Mizrachi, the religious-Zionist party.—Eds.]

4. [This second century CE rabbi is buried in Meron. He is said to have died on the 33rd day of the counting of the Omer (between Passover and Shavuot), or Lag ba-Omer.—Eds.]

5. [Agudas Yisroel, anti-Zionist organization of the *Haredim*, or "ultra-Orthodox."—Eds.]

6. [Among *Haredim*, this is a euphemism for Jesus. Rabbi Abraham Isaac Ha-Kohen Kook (1865–1935) was the first chief rabbi of Palestine under the British Mandate. He was an Orthodox rabbi but reached out to the nonreligious.—Eds.]

Translated by Zvi Gitelman.

Other works by Goldstein: *Tiḳun 'olam: yakhil kitve kodesh mi-maranan ye-rabanan . . . neged shitat ha-mitḥadshim she-hem Tsiyonim, Mizraḥim, Agudim, yishuvisṭen ye-khol ha-mista'ef me-hem be-Erets Yisra'el uve-ḥu.l / nitḥaber u-mesudar 'al yede Mosheh Goldshṭain b[en] . . . Yehuda (1936).*

Khane

b. 1912; presumably perished in the Holocaust

Details of Khane's life are unknown.

Autobiography
1932

Seven versts from Kaunas stood the oldest fortress in Lithuania. After the war, it was all battered and shot up. Bricks and scraps of iron lay strewn about the place, which had once stored weapons and gunpowder. Nothing remained but the walled-in underground barracks, tunnels, canals, and other secret, subterranean chambers, cisterns, and stairways that linked the entire fortress. When we arrived, there were already twenty-five refugee families living in the four large barracks. The walls in these rooms were always shiny from the water that ran down them. All the available space was already taken. People lived everywhere. Peasants even lived in huts they had built on top of the barracks.

There was a big field over the underground barracks, where people could live and even have a well and a cow grazing by the door. At the entrance to the part of the fortress occupied by Jews there was a small room where no one lived, because it was said to have once been a latrine. In fact, the walls were covered with pitch, and it had an odor that never went away. The floor was made of cement. There were two windows: one was narrow and bright and looked out onto the street; the other was big and dark—like the walls, from which dripped big,

black drops of water—and looked out on a dark tunnel that seemed to be endless. It was frightening to look through this window, even during the day. Not having any alternative, we moved into these quarters, together with another family, and made this our home.

Each day, everyone left the house to look for work in the city. I stayed behind to take care of my little sister, who was still in diapers. I was ten years old at the time. I lived in this place for four years. During this time I changed from a child into a young woman, and my emotions and my reason matured. Those four years of underground life were filled with dismal, lonely, painful, despairing days.

It was winter when we first set foot in the place. There was no oven in our little room. I made food for the baby and myself on a small burner. The baby was very irritable under my care. If she was wet, she screamed. If I didn't diaper her well, she screamed again. I used to run all over the house with her, not knowing what she wanted from me. During the long winter nights, when everyone else who lived with us was still in town, I would sit in a corner with the child in my arms and tremble with fear. It seemed to me that demons were dancing in the tunnel, and whenever I accidentally looked through the dark window, an icy chill ran through my body. I was even afraid to move my own hand. I was afraid of my own shadow. Many times I wanted to cry but was afraid to make a sound.

I wasn't allowed inside the big, decaying barracks, because the people who lived there considered me a spy. Our neighbors had a son who fell in love with a girl who lived in the big barracks. His parents were against the relationship, so they sent me to spy on their son and report back to them. I also reported on other couples whom I encountered at unseemly moments. When the people who lived in the barracks found out about this, they cast me out and never let me back.

Among the twenty-five families who lived there was a quiet, forlorn couple with a small child. The three of them had a very difficult life. They had no trade, and it was hard for them to get work so far away from town, so they were always hungry. Life in the fortress didn't suit them well, either. In this cauldron, seething with more than a hundred lives, people oppressed one another. The strong dominated the weak. This family lived in constant hunger and fear. They couldn't go off to look for work, because they had nowhere to leave their child. Mother took pity on them and told them to leave the child with me. This is how I came to care for two children.

It was hard for me during those long, cheerless winter nights, when I was alone with the children. To my despair, they'd both cry at the same time. Their voices frightened me. It seemed to me that between their screams I could hear another voice. Many times I was scared even to move about the room to get something to quiet the children. I was so afraid that one cold night I took both children in my arms (one of them still asleep) and stood in the entryway. Although the darkness and the iron gates of the tunnel scared me even more, I felt better being closer to other people.

After we had lived in our little room for a year, a place opened up in the main barracks. We moved in with our few rags, boxes, and the boards that we used as beds. We had barely arranged our "furniture" in a corner near the door when our neighbor, whose space was next to ours, came in drunk and wrecked everything. He pounced on us and beat us. He needed this corner, he said, to keep his kitchen things. It was a terrible night. Everything we owned lay in pieces near the door. Our uneaten dinner had been spilled along with our belongings. It looked like a true catastrophe. We had nowhere to sleep, and we stayed up all night out of fear, sitting among our broken, scattered possessions. The next day, when the drunk sobered up, we talked him into letting us stay.

My life passed like a long, overcast day. I didn't know that there was a world with better people. I only knew that I had to care for children. Later, I also became a cook. When my mother came home from town she found dinner ready, and on Friday everything was ready for the Sabbath. At first, I had no girlfriends. I was always busy, and besides, no one interested me. And when I did occasionally feel like standing at the side and watching people play cards or jacks, they would shoo me away. I spoke little. I was always apart, always by myself. That life underground, far from the hustle and bustle, is amazing. You live simply because you aren't dead, and that is all. You know nothing else. You will do tomorrow what you did today; there is no difference between today and tomorrow. And yet time doesn't stand still. Days, months, and years fly by, just as they do in the mansions of the rich. Only there, it is more noticeable. Here, there's nothing but trouble, hunger, cold, and suffering, and it seems like one big, long day.

I became a wage earner. I carried water and took care of children, for which I was paid. Carrying water was no easy job! I had to climb up onto the roof, where there was a cistern, covered by a kind of hut with no door. The water was drawn through a wide, deep window. I had to lie down on the window ledge to pull up a pail full of water. I always had to bring a small can to fetch the water, because the pail was heavier than I was at twelve years of age.

Thursdays were especially hard for me, because then the women would go to town to shop for the Sabbath and would leave their children with me, for which I was paid. I would be surrounded by four or five children; they all had to be diapered, and I had to prepare each one a different meal. They were so much trouble! I would run from one crib to the next. As soon as one child fell asleep, another one woke up. It was really awful when they all started screaming at once. Also, sometimes a child would fall and get a scrape or a bump. Then his mother would yell at me and not want to pay me.

Summer days, when the warm sun shone, were very hard for me. From the fields and woods came the smell of raspberries, and the air was like perfume. The barracks emptied, and everyone went off into the woods: mothers with little children, boys and girls, boyfriends and girlfriends. Smaller children who were my age used to play hopscotch and other games near the fortress. But I remained shut behind the fortress's earthen walls, overgrown with mushrooms, breathing the poisonous air and looking after the children. There were moments when I sat by the window with a sleeping child in my arms and the others playing quietly on the floor around me. I would look out the window at the children playing outdoors and cry. My heart filled with childlike longing and sadness. The beauty of nature beckoned and tugged at my heart. But those cursed earthen walls kept me from everything. I loved to gather berries in the woods. When I heard that a whole group was getting ready to go out, it upset me so much that I couldn't go along; I'd accompany them as far as the door and then watch with tears in my eyes as they disappeared into the hills. It was hard to tear myself away from the door; I wanted to leap up, escape into the woods, and never return. The cries of the children called me back into the house. I could only go into the woods during the winter, when I tried to avoid the watchman as I stole branches to burn for heat. Many times, I was scared by the sight of the watchman with his rifle. I would scramble up the high hills until I collapsed, breathless and bloody, inside the fortress. But I never complained about my fate. I never told anyone about the longing in my soul. My heart trembled for only one thing, for my mother. My love for her continued to smolder and never cooled, despite the fact that she had grown a little cooler toward me since my sister was born.

There were all sorts of people in the fortress: drunkards, gamblers, and common loafers who lived from hand to mouth. Not a night went by without fighting, quarreling, and cursing. It was especially bad for the weak, who didn't have anyone to protect them. In addition to receiving frequent beatings, they never had a moment's peace. Even as they lay in bed, they were surrounded by people dancing, shouting, singing, and playing cards until early in the morning.

Mother couldn't ignore these injustices, and she often got into fights that came to blows. Nothing in the world was worse for me. Whenever I saw that this was about to happen, I would run like a madwoman, first to my mother, then to the person with whom she was fighting, and beg them to stop. But this had little effect. They didn't pay any attention to me. When they did start fighting, I'd run through the barracks looking for Mother's good friends and tearfully beg them to help her. Sometimes, as I tried to protect her, I would get beaten or trampled in the confusion myself.

Eventually, I adopted a new approach. When crying and pleading didn't prevent a fight, I threw myself on the ground and started to bang my head against the cement floor. There would be a big commotion, Mother would try to calm me down, and the fight would end. I thought little about myself, because my heart was always full of fear that my mother would be beaten. Whenever I heard a row, I would run to make sure that she wasn't in the middle of it.

On lonely Sabbaths, when I would lie in the grass and rest or wander in the woods looking for berries, I often thought about my sisters and was overcome with longing for them. Every time I thought of them, I'd see before my eyes the time I hit my younger sister. This thought gave me no rest. What wouldn't I have given to see them and beg her forgiveness? I always imagined them thin and pale like me, and I pitied them.

One evening in the fall, it was raining outside and gloomy within my heart; supper had been burned, and I stood there, full of worries. Some girls ran in and told me that one of my sisters was on her way. (Mother wasn't at home.) I couldn't believe it. I thought they were fooling me. When they convinced me it was true, I ran to meet my sister. As I ran, I imagined I would find her thin, pale, and bent like me. I imagined how we would embrace and kiss each other and cry, and tears started to flow from my eyes. But when I saw her, I stopped short, frozen to the spot. I didn't even have the courage to get close to her. There before me stood a girl with a fat, flushed face, her cheeks ruddy. She was four times as wide as I was, so fat that she even had trouble walking. She stood there and she looked at me with a cold and contemptuous gaze. An apathetic kiss reminded me that we were sisters.

From that first day, there was a distance between us. She looked down on me; I disgusted and embarrassed her. She called me nicknames like "Bent Tree" and "Skeleton."

Why did she come to visit us? This is what happened: a few weeks after Mother and I had left home following the divorce, my sister had stolen some flour from Father, sold it, and left to look for us with a family that was going to Lithuania. When she didn't find us, a teacher brought her to a small town, where she was taken care of as if she were the teacher's own child. Recently she had found out about us, and now she was here.

Coming from a better, more refined life, where children studied and didn't have to work, she always acted conceited and capricious. My sister made friends. She went to the movies and the theater and Mother was delighted with her. Mother treated me worse and worse every day; she often hit me and looked at me coldly. I would sit in a corner, alone and in rags. I saw how much Mother liked her other daughter, and I began to hate my sister.

No one could notice my hatred, because I was always quiet, gloomy, preoccupied, and grim. But suddenly it exploded over a trivial matter. Mother never made me any new clothing, nor did I make anything for myself. Whatever I earned I gave to her. She often told me that I should use the money to make some new clothes for myself, but whenever I saw that someone needed money, I gave it away. All I owned were a shawl and a colorful hat that I hardly ever wore, guarding it like a treasure. One time my sister felt like dressing up in my hat and going to the movies. This bothered me a great deal—not so much because she put it on, perhaps, as because she was going to the movies and not I. (I didn't even know what movies were then.)

I followed her, and on the way I snatched the hat from her head. But she was stronger and grabbed it back. In my agitated state, this infuriated me. All of a sudden, something erupted from me—an outcry against my silent suffering, against all the hard work I did and the way I was oppressed by everyone, culminating in my rage against my sister. But I wouldn't fight with her. With one move she could have torn me to pieces. Besides, I didn't want to fight with her at all. She was nothing more than the spark that ignited my frozen anger, which had been so patient and silent. I no longer saw my sister in front of me, but all of my futile suffering. I wanted to run off into the wide world, to wander the streets and never return to the cursed fortress. I ran off in no particular direction. Meanwhile, word of what had happened spread inside the fortress, and a crowd had gathered. The road was thick with people chasing me. I ran as if driven by some external force. No one could catch me.

When she saw that I was running away in earnest, my sister shouted, "Mother fainted and fell into a ditch." As soon as I heard this, I completely forgot where I was, what had happened to me, or what was going to happen. Immediately, I ran back, shouting, "Where's Mama?" Then they caught me, tied me up, and brought me back to the fortress. Mother hadn't fainted. They just said that to trap me. She was standing there, waiting for me with a big, heavy club. It was soft, made out of some sort of animal hide. The local toughs spent their days off trying to break it, without success. That was the club my mother was holding. They laid me out on a bench on the middle of the barracks. Everyone from the fortress gathered around, pushing and climbing on each other's shoulders. They all wanted to get a better view, as if it were a circus arena. My mother beat me, without stopping even to take a breath—now I believe she didn't realize what she was doing, and that it's possible the crowd had whipped her into a frenzy—until the club broke in two. There was an uproar, as people yelled about the destruction of the club and expressed pity for my thin, bony body and bloody mouth. I don't remember what happened after that. When I came to, I was lying in bed and Mother was sitting next to me.

The scene left no impression on me. When I saw Mother beside me, looking at me perhaps with regret and fear, I immediately forgot what had happened and felt happy that she was there. Later, I became so used to these blows that they no longer bothered me. The more Mother beat me, the more I loved her. So the days continued to pass.

My stepfather had a son who was serving in the military. Mother used to send him packages with money. At about this time he came home from the army along with a friend. Mother treated them both as if they were her own. When they came home from work, their food had to be ready. Meanwhile, my sister went to work in a coffee plant. My situation became worse day by day. I had to care for an entire household and, in addition, Mother brought home feathers for us to trim. In the morning, before she went to town, she would fill a pot with feathers and order that they be done by nightfall. In the evening, Mother wouldn't let my sisters and me leave the table. We sat and trimmed feathers until late at night.

I hated the people in the fortress very much. They were always fighting, quarreling, cursing, and insulting one another. They were frivolous and careless, always singing, dancing, engaging in lewd talk, and splitting open each other's heads. Every girl of thirteen or fourteen already had a "fiancé." Wise parents concerned about their children's future put them in a children's home, where they were taught to write and raised to be responsible people. The children's home only accepted children at an early age. When they reached thirteen or fourteen, they were sent back to their parents at the fortress. I simply idolized these children. Their refined speech, their writing skills, and their good nature enchanted me. I couldn't take my eyes off them. These were my first girlfriends. (Later they became like all the other girls there and had "fiancés" at an early age.)

I saw the city for the first time when I was twelve years old. I went with Mother to help her wash floors. The people in one house liked me and hired me as a servant. From then on I worked for others.

At the first place where I worked the people had a dry-goods store and also made tea bags at home. Once I settled in, I had three jobs: working in the store, making tea bags, and trimming feathers at night in the fortress with my mother. I felt no peace of mind at work. I could barely wait until the hour when I could go home to see what was happening there.

Two years passed like this. I was fourteen years old and my sister was seventeen. We began to realize where we were. The lewdness of life there disgusted us. We were ashamed even to say that we lived in the fortress. My sister had made some friends in town, and she nagged Mother to find an apartment somewhere and leave the fortress. When we moved out with our few boxes of belongings, I was overcome with longing for the fortress. I forgot about all the suffering I had experienced there. It suddenly became precious to me, and I didn't want to leave. I followed behind the wagon with a heavy heart.

A new life began. I found a new job in a bindery. As soon as I started to work there, I excelled at a job that no one else could do as well. I did the work of two people: at the bindery during the day, and at home until one o'clock at night. At first, my life didn't change much. I still had no girlfriends. I still worked day and night. I was always lonely; no one took an interest in me. My sister and I still had a distant relationship. She was ashamed even to admit that I was her sister. This bothered me very much. When I met her in town with her friends, she would turn away, as if she didn't even know me. I would come home crying and complain to Mother.

At fourteen, I was tall but very thin, and because of that I developed a stoop. People thought that I would remain hunchbacked for life. I was like a child who had been raised in the wild. The world seemed strange to me. Ordinary objects were foreign to me. I didn't even know the names of many things. When I learned that there were places called schools, where children were taught how to write and had books to read, it made me sad, because I had no one to teach me. If I saw someone reading, I was so resentful that I would cry. Once, when I saw a woman reading a Russian book, I went up to her and asked her to teach me to read. She laughed at me. But when I insisted, she taught me several letters. From then on, whenever I saw a piece of paper with writing on it, I looked for the familiar letters. I was happy if I found them.

The bindery had a union. I used to go with the other workers to meetings. Although I was not very worldly, they said I was smart. I began to take an interest in things that were unfamiliar to me. People gradually got closer to me. A general strike broke out in my line of work, and I became involved in a political party.

The very first lecture that I heard opened up a new world for me. I learned that humanity was divided into two classes: the hungry and the full, those who labor and those who do nothing. It was hard for me to understand everything all at once, but since I had experienced some of this in my own life, I didn't even give a thought to my lack of understanding. Passionately I

plunged into the waves of my new life. With an ardent flame in my yearning heart, I devoted myself to party work. Every task I was assigned made me happy. The only thing that disturbed my happiness was the fact that I couldn't write. Late into the evening I sat with my stepfather, and he taught me the *alef-beys*, which I learned quickly. I began to write entire words. My stepfather told me what letter to write, and I would do it. For example, if I had to write *tish*, he would tell to me to write *tes*, *yud*, *shin*.

That's how our lessons went. I couldn't write a word on my own, and I was afraid that I would never be able to do so. So I started to do some studying on my own. I stayed up nights racking my brain, thinking. I no longer turned to my stepfather for help. It was difficult for me to figure out the correct method for writing a word on my own. But once I understood the right way, it became very easy. That's how I learned how to write. When I read over the first postcard that I wrote, I was the happiest person in the world. I started to take books out of the library, even though I couldn't read quickly yet and I didn't understand everything that I read. But I got a great deal out of this; it opened up the world for me a little, so that I could look inside it. When I got used to reading and could read quickly, I couldn't go anywhere without a book. Wherever I went I brought a book with me, so that I could read it in a free moment. My regular time for reading was from midnight until two o'clock in the morning.

Later on I found another new job, working in a large coffee plant along with my sister. My life was regulated like a machine. After work, I was busy in the city with party work from five until ten o'clock at night, from ten I knitted socks at home, from twelve until two I read. I got up at six to go to work. I slept for four hours a day; the other twenty I worked, either physically or intellectually.

My love for my mother cooled. What love I had belonged now to the party, to my ideals. Mother began to interfere with my work in the party. We began to quarrel, at first mildly; later, the battle between us raged. It wouldn't be accurate for me to say that my mother didn't love me. She did. But being a simple, overworked woman, and living in such surroundings, she couldn't have raised me differently. Moreover, she had been abandoned by my father and had no education. She couldn't display her love tenderly, like other mothers, but kept it hidden within her heart. And that is why she didn't want me to devote my life to the party.

My external appearance changed. I gained weight, I stood up straighter and held my head higher. My gait became more certain. People even said that I didn't look any worse than my sister. The way that people related to me changed completely. In the party they had complete confidence in me. My sister also behaved differently toward me. She would now walk with me in the street. She asked me for advice and about the meaning of words she didn't know. (She had learned to write a little from a teacher before she came to live with us.)

My mother had three children, all girls, with my stepfather. Her life grew worse from day to day. She had to be both a mother to her children and a breadwinner. Her energy was exhausted at a young age, and she became weak, thin, and old. By the time she was thirty-five, she was as bent over as a woman of sixty. Her children caused her great anguish. Our political activities tormented her, but we paid her no mind. Our ideals were the most important things in the world for us, and when she got in our way we turned our backs on her.

The political organization I belonged to was the most sacred thing in my life. It made me forget what was happening around me. I devoted three quarters of my life to this inspirational work, and it even made the hard physical labor that I did seem easy. My life was like a stream of water overflowing its banks after the winter thaw, growing higher and faster by the minute. I climbed higher and higher. I occupied a respected position in the party. I was also very proficient in the factory where I worked. I could take the place of an accomplished artisan who had been working there for fifteen years, even though as I sat at work, my mind was occupied with getting ready for lectures, reading, and so forth. After work, my life was completely scheduled; every hour had its task. This lasted until twelve or one o'clock at night. When I came home, tired and hungry, Mother would greet me with a scolding and curses for coming home so late. Her screaming unnerved me so much that I would go to bed without dinner. So the days passed, one day the same as the next.

In the turmoil of my life I often thought about my other sister, who had remained with our father. I also reminded Mother about her, and eventually we wrote to her. I donated my entire savings to bring her to live with us. When she arrived she was thin, starved, and wild. I made it my task to "civilize" her. I taught her how to behave among other people, brought her books to read, and introduced her to other young people. It was hard for me to devote myself to her because I had so

little time. But no one had an effect on her as I did. She would often hug and kiss me and say that she would do whatever I told her.

About three years passed like this, years about which I could say much. These were the most interesting years of my life. But I can't talk about them openly, because I don't want to reveal anything about my party activity. I was healthy, enduring the hardest work and the most difficult experiences. I walked through mud and snow up to my knees. I washed my muddy socks in the river, put them on still wet, and continued onward without even feeling how my feet were freezing. There were even times during the worst, coldest weather when Mother would hide my socks and coat, so that I wouldn't go into town. I would go anyway, wearing only my dress, and nothing bothered me. I never lacked energy and never complained. Without eating, without sleeping, I did everything calmly and with determination.

Translated by Daniel Soyer.

Meir Berlin
1880–1949

Meir Berlin, whose name was later Hebraized to Bar-Ilan, was born in Volozhin (Belarus) in 1880, and studied in yeshivas and at the University of Berlin. He joined the Mizrahi movement in 1905. He served as the president of U.S. Mizrahi, and then as the president of the World Mizrahi Center. Berlin settled in Jerusalem in the 1920s, where he founded the daily newspaper *Hatzofeh* in 1937 and the *Entsiklopediya talmudit* (Talmudic Encyclopedia) in 1942.

From Volozhin to Jerusalem
1933

Where the Fires of Hell Burn

Even in the past, some thirty to forty years ago, when Jewish life in Russia was still very conservative, there was a difference between those cities and towns located deep inside the country—far from the railway and from any waters, that is—and those places that were connected to the world. It is not that in the "outlying" places people were less "enlightened" and in places with a train or ship connection people were more "progressive." Quite often the situation was exactly the opposite. In those towns—regardless of whether they were large or small—where [. . .] people had to take lengthy and drudging trips to reach a large city (with a horse and buggy through the mud in summer, and with a horse and sleigh through the snow in winter), in these places life was quieter and more calm, business was slower, and therefore people devoted themselves more to learning: older people to traditional Jewish study and younger people to modern, secular education that the Enlightenment promoted. In places with direct rail or ship connections people were comparatively more involved in conducting business on a larger scale. As a result, people generally studied less, but at the same time were also less preoccupied with the ideas of the Enlightenment. Thus, there was a difference between towns far away from the railway and towns on the railway line. This difference had less to do with people's *thinking* than with their *practices*. It is an old rule: nothing reinforces the evil inclination as much as sin itself. It is not just the evil inclination that brings about sin; very often it is sin that induces the evil inclination. [. . .]

My grandfather, the *Arukh ha-shulḥan* [Yehiel Mikhl Epstein], told me that for a few years after the train started running, every time people saw it pass by they would say, "here comes the *apikoyres* [freethinker, heretic]." [. . .] They felt instinctively that if people were going to travel around, they would be less bound by the place where they lived; many people would start to become more lenient in various issues, and leniency would then become widespread. [. . .] Two things happened at around the same time: the Russians began to conscript Jews into the army the standard way, not by catching young children, and railway lines were established in those parts of Russia where Jews resided. [. . .] As a result Jews began to leave their homes the normal way; consequently, they were alienated from the traditional way of life, from their parents' house, from the customs with which they were born and raised, and this had an effect on reshaping life even when people later returned to their original environment. In some places the rail connection had not only such an indirect effect but also a very direct one. When the train passed through on Saturday, some taverns could not resist opening their doors to the transit passengers. [. . .] The owner of the tavern was seemingly passive, but the *khilel-shabes* [desecration of the Sabbath] in his house and in the surrounding streets was serious. There were also some merchants—not the most distinguished people, of course—who went to the station to find out from the transit passengers where the price of wheat stood, or simply to hear news from the world, and, without any bad intentions, slowly got used to seeing that some Jews desecrated the sanctity of the Sabbath; and the distance from being used to seeing something to being used to doing something is not too great. [. . .] Some respectable people, especially salesmen, began to practice "double bookkeeping:" they behaved one way at home and in a different way on the road. [. . .]

As much as the appearance of the railway led to the desecration of the Sabbath, ship traffic did so even more. Namely, what the trains did *be-isur* [under prohibition], ships did *be-heter* [with rabbinical permission]. In harbor cities and towns where ships departed and arrived daily, the Sabbath was not completely holy. The sanctity of the Sabbath may not have been desecrated according to the letter of the law, but it was *khilel-shabes* because the Sabbath itself became like a weekday. In cities like Berezin or Bobruisk, where ships would depart and arrive Friday night and Saturday during the day, there was a strange feeling: people prayed like on the Sabbath, they ate like on the Sabbath, but while they prayed and ate their festive meals they could hear the steamship come and go; thus, their *shabesdik* mood vanished, and they were surrounded by a weekday atmosphere. [. . .]

Therefore, it is no wonder that if you could sense the decline of religious observance in some of the smaller towns with heavy traffic, the effect could be felt even more strongly in a big city such as Odessa. Odessa, one of the largest and most important port cities in Russia, was known as a very liberal city. People used to say that "the fires of hell burn seven miles around Odessa." [. . .] In Warsaw and Vilna there were no fewer *maskilim*, and maybe even more. In fact, some of them were quite famous, and yet their impact was not so palpable. We should also note that in Odessa the wide Jewish masses barely knew who the local *maskilim* were. The Jews of Odessa were too preoccupied with business and, to some extent, worldly pleasures. Additionally, most people were far more under the influence of the Russian daily press than the best article or lecture of a Jewish *maskil*. Odessa was religiously liberal because it was an "open" city with trains and ships coming and going constantly, with busy trade and traffic, both domestic and international. All this must have led to the fact that the Sabbath in Odessa became just like any weekday; and when the Sabbath is not *shabesdik*, then all the other six days are no longer Jewish either. [. . .]

Whatever the reason—whether the influence of certain people or the lifestyle of a city with massive traffic, or maybe the fact that Odessa had an immigrant Jewish population with no tradition of its own (a factor much more important in Odessa than in other cities or countries), or because Odessa was one of the youngest and newest cities in Russia—the fact is, that when a Lithuanian or Polish Jew came to Odessa from Lithuania or Poland, [. . .] the *khilel-shabes* was very strongly visible because it was not something rare and considered over the line, but rather an almost normal phenomenon. Synagogues were well attended in Odessa on Friday night and Saturday morning. There were some famous cantors there, such as Minkowski, Razumni, and others, and they attracted a large audience. [. . .] At the same time, however, not far from the synagogues some Jewish stores were open on Saturday, and even those who went to synagogue would stop off afterwards to buy the local Russian newspaper. Every couple of years, when a new rabbi came to town, the older rabbis and their followers started to persecute him [. . .] their most commonly used weapon was the accusation that the new rabbi was not pious enough. [. . .] One such new rabbi [. . .] who had just been appointed to a full, salaried position, was attacked by Rabbi Chaim Soloveichik in a sharp letter. He wrote that this rabbi should not be accepted, his decisions should not be trusted, and the like. Here is how someone responded:

"Odessa was looking for a nonobservant rabbi, but they could not find one. Their searched 'failed,' they kept getting solid, honest, observant Jews. Now that they received Rabbi Chaim Soloveichik's *haskomeh* [approbation, endorsement] confirming that the rabbi they chose was, indeed, not observant, people can rely on this ruling and welcome the new rabbi properly. [. . .]"

The development of Hebrew literature and the presence of famous writers such as Mendele Moykher Sforim, Lilienblum, Ahad Ha-Am, and others also contributed to the high stature of Jewish life in Odessa. The general Russian press was under the influence of Jews, too, since many of its staff members were Jews. Zionism was very popular in Odessa. . . . In the Yavneh synagogue Zionist sermons were delivered every Sabbath. The best local speakers gave talks there, and also guest speakers from out of town. It was very interesting and pleasant to speak there in front of a large audience; the synagogue was always fully packed, and in the audience one could always find some of the most important and most respected Lovers of Zion.

Jerusalem of Lithuania

It is the historians' and geographers' job to find out when people started calling Vilna *Yerushalayim d'Lite* [Jerusalem of Lithuania] and what other cities in various countries are called *Yerushalayim*. [. . .] It is possible that there were more Talmudic scholars, more *maskilim*, more pious Jews, and more philanthropists in Vilna than in other communities, but it is not the numbers that mattered. The point is that the Talmudic scholars of Vilna were different from the Talmudic scholars of other places, the *maskilim* of Vilna were different from the *maskilim* of other places, and the pious Jews and philanthropists of Vilna had something different about them, too. Every Jew in Vilna showed some sign of spiritual aristocracy, some noble humility, a gentleness of the soul. [. . .]

Torah scholars in Vilna [. . .] were successful merchants occupied with business and finance all day long, who owned houses, and ran other undertakings, and at the same time had the ability and talent to write *sforim* [Torah commentaries/holy books]. They were not the type called *a balebatisher lamdn*—a great scholar among businessmen and a great businessman among scholars. In Vilna, there were dozens of Jews, if not more, who were both great businessmen and true scholars at the same time. In any other place such people would have been rabbis or authorities well respected for their extensive knowledge. [. . .] Where else did Jews pray as much as they prayed in Vilna? In the Vilna *shulhoyf* [synagogue courtyard] people never stopped praying. Until noon there were various quorums reciting *shakhres* [morning prayers], one after the other, in one synagogue; then, right after noon, they started reciting *minkhe* [afternoon prayers] in another synagogue, again one quorum after the other, and as soon as evening fell, the same thing continued with regards to *mayrev* [evening prayers], one quorum after the other, until midnight. Then came *khtsos*, the prayer recited at midnight in memory of the destruction of Jerusalem, and after that Jews would just sit around in one *kloyz* [house of study] or another studying or reciting psalms; they were in a spiritually elevated religious state continuously. [. . .]

Social Activism

[. . .] Jewish Vilna was a center of Jewish issues, one could even say for all Jewish issues. The life of Russian Jews in those days was concentrated in Vilna. These were years when social issues were boiling over in Russia, and the same process was taking place in Jewish society. The failure of the revolution did not lead to despair. On the contrary, it strengthened people's will to fight. What had happened in 1905 was considered only one phase of the revolutionary movement, a phase that had been overestimated, but one that was not completely without effect nonetheless. The Duma existed, political parties had been formed, and the press had—for better or worse—a social-political character. The same sentiment was prevalent among Jews—a feeling that one should not withdraw from political activities. All kinds of assemblies, conferences, and discussions took place, political groups were formed, and there was a strong press in three languages: Hebrew, Yiddish, and Russian. [. . .] There were three main groupings in Jewish life in Russia in those days: the *national* group, led by the Zionists; the *general political* group whose aim was to achieve equal rights for Jews, led by a group of activists in St. Petersburg with the famous Vinaver at their head; and the *socialist* group, in which the Bund played the main role. The first and the third group, the Zionists and the Bundists, fought bitterly and constantly. [. . .]

Therefore, it was natural that when some religious Jews began to sense that it was necessary to start organizing observant Jewry politically—this happened in Vilna, too. People started to realize that it was not normal that religious Jewry, which was large in numbers and strong in spirit—and in any case, religious feeling was still the strongest force, stronger than any other sentiment in Jewish life—should keep quiet when all other parties and groupings were talking and screaming, demanding and proclaiming. [. . .] And then, as a result of the activities of one of the most respected local rabbis, a man, who, in addition to being a great Torah scholar, had a strongly developed sense of social activism, the will emerged to create an organization called Kneses-Yisroel [The Congregation of Israel].

An incident of greater significance for religious Jewry was at the great rabbinical assembly that took place in Vilna to which all the great rabbis and [Hasidic] rebbes of Russia and Russian Poland were invited. Approxi-mately thirty people attended the assembly, among them the most renowned Lithuanian rabbis and the most popular Hasidic rebbes. [. . .] The two main leaders, Rabbi Chaim Soloveichik and the Lubavitcher Rebbe, Rabbi Shalom Ber Shneerson, remained behind the scenes. These two people were very different from each other both in character and in intellectuality, but there was one common issue that united them: the danger of introducing new things in Jewish life. They both shared the will to keep everything the way it had always been, without any changes. [. . .] In the rabbinical and yeshiva world Rabbi Chaim Soloveichik's word and opinion were authoritative. He was considered a great *gaon* [genius] with a sharp mind and fearless spirit. The Lubavitcher Rebbe was the greatest Hasidic rebbe. He involved himself in communal issues more than anyone else in the Hasidic world. Thus, his words were heard far and wide. The difference between the two men was obvious. The Lubavitcher Rebbe's strength was organized power. He came accompanied by a large group of rabbis, his followers, and wherever he went, one of his Hasidim followed him and served as secretary, carrying around a nice portfolio and taking notes, writing down the Rebbe's every word, etc. Rabbi Chaim Soloveichik, on the other hand, came to attend the assembly in Vilna all by himself, as usual; he was quiet and kept to himself, always made sure that there was no one around him. It was very interesting to see that any time the Lubavitcher Rebbe was going to say something at the assembly, and, according to the rules of parliamentary procedure, he stood up to speak, most people in the assembly stood up, too—everyone close to him, all the rabbis, his followers, etc. Intentionally or unintentionally, this made quite an impression. Some Misnagdim became envious of the honor Hasidim gave their rebbe. Misnagdim could not do this even if they wanted to. [. . .] Rabbi Chaim never gave long speeches. He said what he thought was necessary briefly and then took one of his confidants by the arm and went outside to "chat a little." The difference was clear. Here are two leaders—one of them a commander who gives orders, the other a spirit who commands respect. [. . .] Some issues on the assembly's agenda had to do with the government, such as the issues of divorce. [. . .] and there were many internal issues. They discussed questions of education, the rabbinate, and also talked about establishing a religious-oriented newspaper. Naturally, those who espoused the viewpoint that everything new was dangerous were opposed to the idea of publishing a newspaper, too. One Hasidic rebbe from Poland argued against the proposed newspaper on the grounds that although a religious newspaper would certainly have some benefits, how can one publish a religious newspaper without knowing what the nonreligious newspapers write about? Thus, the editor would be forced to read "those other" newspapers. But the editor must be an observant Jew, so how can we, argued the rebbe, ask a pious Jew to read *treif* newspapers?

Most interestingly, several participants of the assembly mentioned (only very quietly, of course) that for this reason, the rebbe himself could be the editor, because he reads "other" newspapers anyway. [. . .] When some participants who took the question of the newspaper more seriously asked who would edit the newspaper, Rabbi Eliezer Gordon from Telz suggested with his usual bluntness that if there was enough money, one could get even the best editor of another newspaper, and he named a popular editor who would, for good money, write whatever *we* want him to write, and it would be a good religious newspaper.

Another question discussed at the assembly was that of the *yeshivah ketanah*, a yeshiva for boys in their early teens. One of the oldest participants argued with great excitement that every rabbi in every town must set up a heder where he studies Talmud with the boys. And the respectable speaker said, "This is the finest and the most essential thing a rabbi must do. It is better to be a *melamed* than a rabbi, and every rabbi should be happy if he can also be a *melamed*."

The assembly [. . .] made a favorable impression, but only on a very limited number of people, because it was—and it had to be, on account of the government—closed to the public. The public received only small news items about it, and this could not make the appropriate impression. But in terms of real effect—the assembly was almost completely ineffective. A few issues regarding legal questions related to Jewish law were then transmitted to St. Petersburg, but all other resolutions remained on paper. If there is no organized power to carry out its decisions, even the best assembly remains no more than a demonstration at best. [. . .]

The Lida Yeshiva

[. . .] A new yeshiva was founded, one that was to become one of the greatest centers of Jewish learning. This yeshiva was founded in the town of Lida, where the famous *gaon* and leader Rabbi Reines had already been the rabbi for many years. [. . .]

Rabbi Reines [. . .] was subjected to constant persecution even just for intending to set up a yeshiva with a curriculum different from that of all other yeshivas. [. . .] When he was already the rabbi of Lida and much more renowned than before, and Rabbi Reines decided to realize his dream and set up the planned yeshiva, and the curriculum was already printed and sent out— which in itself was an extraordinary phenomenon for a yeshiva—it still did not happen exactly as he had expected. Only later, when there was a strong upsurge of social life, when anyone who had the will and energy to create something could take advantage of the right time and mood—only then was Rabbi Reines's long-harbored wish fully realized. [. . .]

Rabbi Reines [. . .] emphasized that there must be a yeshiva where general subjects were taught. Due to his thorough knowledge of Torah Rabbi Reines could be considered one of the most brilliant *gaonim* of his time. As far as his piety is concerned—people who knew the greatest rabbis of his generation could not find even one point on which Rabbi Reines would have been more lenient or less stringent than they. Additionally, his perseverance was great. There were only two things that may have prompted people to think differently of him. One is that he adopted a new style of writing Torah commentaries, and the second is that he was very ambitious; he was always looking for something, and because of this constant quest everyone, even he himself, had the impression that he wanted something different, that he wanted to create something new.

The expectations—both hopeful and fearful—of many regarding general subjects that would be taught in the Lida yeshiva also proved to be exaggerated. Students learned Tanakh, grammar, and a little bit of Russian, but this did not leave a special mark on the yeshiva. Some said jokingly that the printed curriculum of the Lida yeshiva contained two parts: the first part was traditional Jewish studies, the second part was general studies, and the general studies began with Tanakh. [. . .]

The nature of Rabbi Reines's "secularism" is comparable to the Tanakh being a general subject. He did not know any foreign languages; he read almost everything in Hebrew, but he did not go any farther. Of course, his inborn intellectual abilities manifested themselves clearly. He was familiar with various secular problems, he was interested in political questions, but this was not his strong side. He was more of a genius than an expert, more pious than modern, and more practical than theoretical. As a practical person he strongly empathized with the sad situation of the Jewish people. He had a very strong sense of *ahavas yisroel* [love of Israel]. His attitude to Zionism and his leadership of the *Mizrachi* stemmed from his *ahavas yisrol*, just as his *hibas tsiyen*. Of course, like every good Jew, he knew that the Land of Israel had absolute value, and he emphatically conveyed this, as we have mentioned before. But his priority was always trying to find help for the Jewish people and redeem them from their great sufferings. This explains why he agreed to Uganda, which many people did not understand. [. . .]

The Yeshiva of Volozhin

Because the Volozhin yeshiva stood at an intellectually and spiritually higher level than any other yeshiva of its time, the ways of life there were also different from other yeshivas, even the big ones. For a start, designations were different. The term *yeshiva bocher* was not in use; instead, students were referred to as a "yeshiva man," or "yeshiva men" in the plural. If the concept of *yeshiva bocher* was associated with poverty and pity, the name "yeshiva man" expressed independence and pride. Even the poorest student who came to Volozhin depressed and downcast by the situation in his impoverished home or by the intellectually meager environment in some small-town *bes medresh*—as soon as he came to Volozhin, he recovered his cheerfulness and self-esteem. [. . .]

The yeshiva men enjoyed intellectual independence, too. The usual method of determining who knows more and who knows less by way of *farhern* [oral examination] was not used in Volozhin, except with the very young students. The supervisor [*mashgiekh*] would examine the youngest students in certain topics, but the majority of the yeshiva men were exempt from this. Upon arrival students reported to the *rosh yeshivah* [head of the yeshiva] and presented him with a letter introducing the newcomer written by a well-known rabbi. This letter already indicated the student's talent and learning. Every rabbi knew how to hint at the skills and knowledge of the boy or young man. Nevertheless, a few days after his arrival every new yeshiva man considered it his duty to look up either my father, of blessed memory [Naftali Zvi Yehuda Berlin, "the Netziv"], or Rav Chaim Soloveichik, and sometimes both of them

in order to "converse in learning" with them. [. . .] This "conversing in learning" revealed the student's degree of achievement in [Torah and Talmudic] learning. As we mentioned before, there was no official student evaluation and there were no classes. All students were supposed to be considered equal. Nonetheless, everyone in the yeshiva knew "who was who." Everyone was appreciated according to his talent and erudition [*bekies*]. [. . .]

In Volozhin [. . .] the lecture was [. . .] a perpetual daily offering.[1] It was held at exactly 12:30 P.M. every day, except for the Sabbath, holidays, and the Ninth of Av. [. . .] My father, blessed be his memory, had a brother in Pinsk, Reb Aharon Meyer Berlin. He had not heard from his brother for quite a while, and he was very worried because he knew that his brother was ill. One day a visitor arrived from Pinsk, and he came to our house just when my father was getting ready to go and give his lecture. After greeting the guest my father asked the visitor if he knew how his brother was doing. The guest did not give a straightforward answer. My father let him go and he himself went to give the lecture. After the lecture he sent for the visitor and asked him about his brother's condition. He found out that his brother had died. Then my father sat *shiva*, of course.

The independence and dignity of yeshiva students in Volozhin was notable in terms of their material life, too. Most students received financial support from the yeshiva. This was called *vokher* [weekly], because the amount of the aid was determined by the week: a *bocher* [unmarried young man] was allocated between sixty kopecks to one rouble and twenty-five kopecks a week, and a *yunger man* [married young man] received one to two roubles. Money distribution (it was called the *khalukeh*) took place once every other week, and it was not done automatically. Although at the beginning of each semester it was determined how much money each student would get, yet twice a month, *motsey shabes* [Saturday evening] every other week, a meeting was held in order to prepare the distribution list. Attending these meetings were the heads of the yeshiva, the supervisor, one of the "directors"—Lipa the Director, a great Talmudic scholar and a God-fearing man, and Hershele Yeshaye the Beadle—a famous man at the time, a simple but very smart, astute, and perceptive man—stood by. [. . .] Yeshiva students were not disturbed while they were learning. Instead, their [. . .] hostesses—received the money they were allocated. Thus, a *bocher* or a *yunger man* did not have to endure the embarrassment that some people feel when they receive support. [. . .]

Women played a great role in the life of the "Rabbi's Family." We must also add that in the direct line of the "Rabbi's Family" the daughters distinguished themselves more than the sons. Reb Itchele's daughters as well as his granddaughters were all very smart women. They were very knowledgeable both in Jewish and in secular topics, they were of fine appearance, equipped with a sharp mind and powerful speaking ability. The women of the "Rabbi's Family" occupied important places not on account of the men but on their own merit. For many years after the passing of Reb Eliezer-Yitzhok, Reb Itchele's first son-in-law, his wife played an important role. She ran a "salon" in her house, where all kinds of people came to visit: people from the city, from the yeshiva, and sometimes foreign visitors, too. She was called "the old *rebetsn*," and when she died, everyone acknowledged that they had lost a great intellectual power.

The New Yeshiva

After the old building of the yeshiva burned down it did not take long until the new one was ready. The new yeshiva building was much nicer both externally and internally. It was designed with the idea that the entire yeshiva is one unit. There were no separate rooms, like before; every one of the hundreds of students studied together, in one large and beautiful space that had good lighting; the tables were set up comfortably so that it was not only possible to study but also pleasant. At that time and place people did not know that there were technical and optical rules influencing pedagogy, but common sense dictated some technical details in the new yeshiva that did not exist until then and even later in other yeshivas. Not all study tables were the same. Some were higher and others lower, so that every student could choose the table most comfortable for him according to his height, vision, and custom of standing upright or with a somewhat bent back, etc. [. . .]

Everyone found the new building of the yeshiva appealing. It looked best on winter evenings when everything around was quiet and still, like in a small town. The courtyards and the ground everywhere were covered with clear white snow, and in the middle stood the yeshiva with lights shining and sparkling from its dozens of windows. From the distance one could hear hundreds of sweet, hearty voices, permeated with infinite love and indescribable enthusiasm, of hundreds of young men, full of life and energy, both in the physical and spiritual sense.

[. . .] The yeshiva was an entirely separate state, the exclusive realm of the yeshiva students. When they invited a local Jew to lead the High Holiday prayers in the yeshiva, it was a great honor. And Volozhin Jews could recite Musaf, Kol Nidre, and Neilah like no one today! There was no one who could chant a *hineni ani* or an *unesane tokef*[2] like Noyekh-Avrom the Messenger, or Mendl the Postman, a simple Jew who knew almost the entire Mishna by heart. These were prayer leaders who not only prayed for the congregation but also for themselves and for the Almighty.

The heads of the yeshiva had nothing to do with local Jews, except in individual cases, even though officially the *rosh yeshivah* was also the rabbi of the city. This has been the custom since Chaim of Volozhin. The city paid him a fee, although it was only nominal. My father, of blessed memory, received five roubles a week and everyone knew to whom he passed on this money. But all important city affairs were conducted only with his approval, of course. As far as praying is concerned, my father, of blessed memory, prayed only in the yeshiva, not in the *besmedresh* of the city. Only on Yom Kippur, after Kol Nidre did he leave the yeshiva and go to the *besmedresh* to give a sermon on ethics and, naturally, the majority of the yeshiva students followed him.

Life in the Yeshiva

One characteristic feature of the Volozhin yeshiva was *khumesh zogn*, studying the Five Books of Moses. The Five Books of Moses were not taught in any yeshiva, as far as we know. Why would grownups, great scholars, study the Five Books of Moses? That is for little boys! What adult, especially if he is a *talmid ḥokhem* [learned man] does not know the Five Books of Moses? But in Volozhin a different spirit ruled. My father, of blessed memory, used to say, "These days, yeshiva students are not familiar with the Torah—not the Five Books of Moses, not the Prophets, and not the Writings. How could they be, when it is never taught in a serious way? Later, when these yeshiva students graduate and become rabbis and they have to give a sermon, they will have to familiarize themselves with the Prophets and the Writings, but the Five Books of Moses they will never learn." [. . .]

An example of the Volozhin-style *khumesh* study can be seen in the commentary *Haemek davar* with the side comments *Harachar davar*. However, this is no more than an example, because even the best printed source cannot reproduce the great joy felt while listening to my father, of blessed memory, teaching *khumesh*. It is hard to imagine the enormous enthusiasm for every word of the written Torah and the immense love for the oral Torah, in the interpretation of the commentators that the students felt. [. . .]

This was the order of study in Volozhin. Everything was done in its time. Students were expected not to waste even a minute of valuable study time, but also not to drain their physical strength by depriving themselves of food and sleep. Nevertheless, there were a few over-zealous students [*masmidim*] in the yeshiva who did not eat or sleep, who studied eighteen, twenty hours a day, and had no sense of what was happening around them. They were constantly sleep-deprived, befuddled. These *masmidim* were admired for their spiritual strength and strong will, but they were not considered the best students. [. . .]

The true spirit of learning, steady, continuous enthusiasm, ruled in Volozhin like nowhere else. The yeshiva was never empty. The sounds of Torah were heard twenty-four hours a day. The regular time of study was from 9:00 A.M. until 12:30 P.M., then there was the lecture and study continued from approximately 2:00 P.M. until 9:00 or 9:30 P.M. But there were always some yeshiva students who studied outside of these times, too. Many were awake during the first half of the night, studied until 2:00 or 3:00 in the morning, and then went to sleep; others did exactly the opposite—slept until 2:00 or 3:00 in the morning and then studied until it was time to say the morning prayers. The yearning to study was so great that there were always people who had already studied some Gemara or looked at one of the commentaries before morning prayers. On Friday night there were generally even more yeshiva students who stayed up and studied all night long. The same was true on the holidays, including Rosh Hashanah, Yom Kippur, and Simchas Torah—there were always a select few of the best students who studied all night. The yeshiva was never empty. [. . .]

And yet all this did not get in the way of the overwhelming merriment during the holidays at the Volozhin yeshiva. [. . .] Whoever has not seen the merriment in Volozhin, especially at the Water-Drawing Celebration on Sukkot, has not seen merriment at all.

This is very true. All the youthful energy, all the fire and fervor that prevailed among the four to five hundred yeshiva students revealed itself during the holidays. But all the holidays with their great merriment were not as meaningful and impressive as the Passover seders. The seders always took place at our house, and every single yeshiva students was invited, no exceptions. Knowing what a "Volozhin seder" was, meant all the yeshiva students wanted to stay in Volozhin for Passover. They would forego going home to their parents just so they could attend my father's seder. Just imagine a seder with hundreds of people around the table, and my father at its head. The seder lasted for six to seven hours. After the second seder, which usually began later, we went straight to say the morning prayer exactly at sunrise. [. . .]

During the first part of the seder, until the second cup of wine, there was a solemn mood, an atmosphere of inner discipline; everyone sat still and listened to every word of the Haggadah and the explanations with the utmost attention. Between the second and the third cup of wine, after the meal, when everyone was already a bit tipsy, youthful merriment took the upper hand. No matter how many bottles of wine were served it was never enough; people asked for more and more, claiming they needed their third cup filled.

My father, of blessed memory, also enjoyed this prank and the *tish* went on for several hours in extraordinarily joyful mood. People told jokes about great learned scholars, and between the various courses of the meal they drank and sang, sang and drank. Nonetheless, no one ever got drunk. As soon as they started to recite the grace after meals, with the third cup of wine in hand, the mood changed back to "students sitting around a great rabbi." Only after the seder was finished—at around 2:00 or 3:00 A.M. on the first night and at around 4:00 or 5:00 A.M. on the second night—did they begin to dance and celebrate.

NOTES

1. [A play on the daily sacrifice offered in the Temple in Jerusalem.—Eds.]

2. [Important prayers of the High Holiday services.—Eds.]

Translated by Vera Szabó.

Other works by Berlin: *Vos tut der mizrakhi in erets-yisroel?* (1925); *Ha-matsav ha-dati ba-yishuv u-va-tsiyonut* (1935); *Beshviley ha-Techiah* (1940); *Erets-yisroel in der milkhome un nokh der milkhome* (1943); *Yesod ha-yesodot shel ha-tsiyonut ha-medinit* (1944).

M. Osherovich

1888–1949

Mendel Osherovich was born in Trostinets-Podolsk, Ukraine, and settled in New York City in 1910. There he wrote for Yiddish periodicals and joined the staff of *Forverts* in 1914. He worked there until his death. He was a prolific writer and translator and held leadership positions with the Federation of Ukrainian Jews, the Committee to Protect the Jews in Ukraine, and the Yiddish PEN club.

How People Live in the Soviet Union
1933

Signs of the New Life in the Decline of the Old Life

Signs of the new life and of the new "construction" in Trostinets can be discerned, strange as it may sound, in the destruction of the synagogues and study houses that had once functioned there. Their demise can be seen as a sign of the emergence of the new way of life.

[. . .] Trostinets has never been an especially pious town. Its youth—Jewish and Christian alike—pursued education, and the town has always had a radical intelligentsia. The local factory—a hub that attracted a fair number of enlightened people with a decent education—has always had a great influence on the town. Even the poor families, both Jewish and non-Jewish, did everything they could to send their children to study in a big city, and in the summer one encountered a fair number of high school students, university students, and students in professional schools in the streets and around the railway station of Trostinets who spoke Russian without an accent, and no one was surprised or outraged when they saw a young Jewish man walk around with a walking stick on the Sabbath, and with a cigarette in his mouth. [. . .]

No one was surprised or outraged when they saw Jewish workers from the factory ride in a carriage, a phaeton, or just on a horse on the Sabbath. The town was quite liberal; freethinkers, nonobservant Jews were nothing out of the ordinary.

Nonetheless, Trostinets had quite a few synagogues. In the old days there used to be a synagogue (*shul*), a study house (*besmedresh*), a *kloyz* and a *klayzl* (small prayer houses) too. [. . .] And since the Jews of Trostinets were great lovers of music, every house of worship had its own cantor with a choir; in fact, they did not just have one cantor but two: a separate *bal-shakhris* and a *bal-musef* to recite Shaḥrit and Musaf, and, occasionally, when they really wanted to live it up, they would bring in a third one, a great cantor from a big city for the Sabbath or for a holiday. I still remember that once, many years ago, when I was a little boy, they brought to Trostinets for one Sabbath the world-famous Nisi Belzer. [. . .] On this occasion the whole town got excited—not only Jews but Christians, too, came to the synagogue to hear the famous cantor. After that for a long time people tried to reproduce his melodies in various ways, and Simon the Tailor, who was very knowledgeable in music but did not have a good voice, was so carried away by Nisi's *Ono bechoyekh* that he just had to sing it while he was working; and he did not even sing it by himself but together with all the apprentices who worked with him. As soon as Simon picked up his scissors he automatically started to sing Nisi's song; [. . .]

The prayer houses of the town were not so much centers of religious piety but rather of festiveness. People came dressed in their best clothes. People not only prayed but also discussed matters of the world, and then they went home absolutely certain that today they would have a much nicer and better meal with their wife and children than yesterday or the day before yesterday.

Now, however, everything changed, everything looked different. The *besmedresh* has been turned into an elementary school, where they teach Yiddish, Ukrainian, as well as Russian. One of the Ukrainian teachers is my youngest sister who was six months old when I left home twenty-three years ago. She has a teaching position there—she gives lessons on Ukrainian literature and history in Ukrainian. I do not know whether her desk and chair are in the same place where my father had his seat in the *besmedresh*, where he prayed with *talis* over his head, swaying back and forth in front of his lectern with great fervor. I tried to determine this during my visit, but the school is so different from the former *besmedresh;* it has changed so much, that is was impossible to find the seat where my father once prayed. [. . .]

My sister the Ukrainian teacher introduced me to the other, [mostly female] teachers, and they were all eager to hear something new about America. I, however, was even more curious to hear something new about the *besmedresh* that is now the school, so I steered our conversation in such a way that I would talk less and listen more. And this is what I was told:

"The study of Yiddish at our school consists of acquainting pupils with the works of our Yiddish writers."

At that point they listed the names of a couple of Soviet Yiddish writers. When I noted that Yiddish literature was written not only in Soviet Russia but also in America and Europe, I got the following answer: "Bourgeois Yiddish literature is none of our concern. We believe that literature must serve the revolutionary proletariat. We do not recognize any other Yiddish literature."

Trying to argue was completely pointless. Just as there was no sign left of the old *besmedresh* in the school, so one could not detect even a trace of doubt in any of the teachers. They spoke with the certainty of people who had convinced themselves that they already know everything and there is nothing else they need to know. [. . .]

I also visited the *kloyz*, but the *kloyz* is no longer a *kloyz* either, but a factory where they manufacture covers for wine bottles. [. . .]

In the *kloyz* that is now a factory of wine-bottle covers works a man who used to be the gabbai there. He is a man of venerable age, with a gray beard and gray side-locks. But he is still full of life, and he is not the type of man who would let himself be carried along by others; he is always in the front line—a true *gabbai* by nature. But in the factory of straw wine-bottle covers he could not be a *gabbai*, so he became an *udarnik* [shock worker]—one of the best and most diligent workers. He produces more wine-bottle covers than any other worker, and he has a booklet in which it is clearly stated in writing that he is an *udarnik*—and this is no trifle! The booklet substantiates that he is among those with great socialist *yikhes*, and he certainly takes great pride in it, just as he used to be proud of being the gabbai of the *kloyz*. This became obvious right away, because as soon as he was introduced to me, he immediately showed me the booklet stating that he was an *udarnik*. [. . .]

But then one Sabbath the former *gabbai* now *udarnik* suddenly developed a desire to pray, and not just by himself but in a minyan, standing by the pulpit. He was convinced that he had a good voice and could lead the prayer. In the morning he went to the synagogue where some Jews still pray regularly. There he stood at the pulpit and prayed, singing in a highly ornamented style, his voice quavering, just like back in the olden days when he was *gabbai* and in charge of everything. And after that he went to work to the *kloyz* where he was once *gabbai* and is now *udarnik* of the wine-bottle covers. [. . .]

On Rosh Hashanah and Yom Kippur the single remaining old synagogue is fully packed. Older Jews come to pray, pour out their hearts, and have a good cry—and they cry even harder than in the old days. The women's section is jam-packed, too; there are enough older women to fill the room with heart-rending laments. They get very small portions of bread because they are not part of the working force. They do not contribute to building the country. They are "superfluous people," and no one owes them anything. Thus, their situation is terrible. Their troubles are great and they have plenty of reasons to wail and cry. [. . .]

An additional source of grief for pious Jewish mothers in their old age is the fact that their children have completely abandoned Judaism. People told me how last year on Yom Kippur an elderly mother was beside herself because her son, a Soviet official, a communist, was working that day. Swaying back and forth with her prayer book and beating her chest saying *al khet* [penitential prayer] she cried hard and begged God to forgive her son, the communist, who was working on Yom Kippur. "Dear God," she pleaded, "you must know that he does it only for the meager livelihood. [. . .]

Some religious Jews in Trostinets do not go to synagogue, even on Rosh Hashanah and Yom Kippur, because they are afraid that this might endanger their children who are Party members or occupy a government position. It is true that no one keeps pious Jews from going to synagogue and praying as much as they wish. But going to synagogue is linked with thousands of important or not so important other things that can cause difficulties—things that are connected with the new way of life so closely that they cannot be detached under any circumstance. [. . .] And even at home you suffer because your grandchildren will attack you. Your grandchildren are very good children, actually, but they study in Soviet schools; they are indoctrinated and repeat automatically everything they are taught. They make fun of their grandfather and grandmother:

"There is no such thing as God! . . . There is no such thing as God!" [. . .]

I was looking for signs of the emerging new way of life in my town, but I did not anticipate finding that the rise of the new would be manifested in the decline of the old. I did, indeed, find a few new things that were good, such as the Jewish population's sense of security that under Soviet rule pogroms could no longer be carried out; knowing that after having no rights whatsoever in Russia Jews now enjoy equal rights to the fullest extent, that they can learn and study and occupy even the most important state offices. It was also good to find that in several government institutions and even in the GPU State political administration [security organ], where I spent quite some time and had a very interesting conversation, there was a significant number of truly intelligent people, all from poor families, children of workers and peasants; it was also nice to learn that a Ukrainian newspaper is now published in my town, and its editor is a Jewish young man who is very devoted to his work; it was also good to see the cordial relations between Jews and gentiles; and there were several other things that warmed my heart.

At the same time I saw great destruction everywhere. People live under such difficult and sad circumstances that I simply could not understand how they could suffer so much, nor where they get the strength to endure so much pain! And while signs of the emerging new way of life are hard to find, signs of decline and destruction are so great in number and so obvious that they immediately hit you in the eye. And it's not just in the eye—if you expect to see a more joyous and easier life in Soviet Russia, you will feel stabbed in the heart. [. . .]

Market Day and the Sabbath in Town

The new regime has left its mark on almost everything in town—the destruction, the poverty, and the many hardships of life—but there are still a few things untouched by it, things that are still exactly as they were in the olden days.

In the town of Trostinets, Thursday has been market day for many generations, and this has not changed to this very day. Although God only knows why they need a market and what purpose it serves. [. . .]

At the market peasants sell almost exclusively food items: stale bread for ten, twelve, or fifteen roubles a piece; radishes, dried pears, eggs, onions, garlic, and other things. Everything is extremely expensive, like gold. When a woman can afford to buy a whole chicken for ten or twelve roubles, she has to keep looking over her shoulder on the way home to make sure no one grabs it from her hands. [. . .]

Although there was still snow on the ground, I saw people walking outside without shoes, completely barefoot. Next to one house stood an emaciated, barefooted peasant; he was obviously very cold, freezing, so he kept "changing" his feet—he rested one foot on the wall while he stood on the other in the snow. [. . .]

It was a pitiful sight.

But it seemed to me that I was the only one to look at him with pity—no one else did. They were already used to seeing people barefoot on a cold winter day. [. . .]

As I walked through the market I met several acquaintances. I had to stop to talk to all of them, and each time a whole circle of people gathered around me.

"How are you?" I asked each one of them. And the answer was always the same:

"How can I be? We are all rotting away." [. . .]

But in the street you cannot feel that it is the Sabbath. Very rarely do Jews dress differently than on the other days of the week. They simply have nothing to wear. And in the homes there is not even a trace of any festive food for a Sabbath meal, not even a piece of white challah. People have long forgotten what challah tastes like.

The synagogue, the old synagogue that is locked up all week long, is opened on that day. It is the sexton, an old, dejected Jew who opens the building, who has lost all hope. People told me that every time he takes off the lock of the synagogue his tears are pouring. [. . .]

And he cries even harder when he locks up the synagogue again. [. . .]

Jews come to the synagogue, quickly recite the prayers, and then go home quietly. At home they eat whatever they have, and they rest up a bit from the hard work. Everyone in the town works very hard. If someone does not work at the kolkhoz [collective farm], he works at the Artel [cooperative], and if he does not work at the Artel he just works hard to put bread on the table. Resting a bit from the hard work—that is the extent of keeping the Sabbath. [. . .]

I saw such terrible poverty, such utter darkness, such despair in every home that my heart sank. The only bright ray of hope for these people was the future of their children. Their children are studying, striving hard for a better future, and surely they will achieve something; they will not stay in the town, they all want to move to Moscow. And you have to know that today's Jewish children in the provinces are not like Chekhov's provincial *barishnyes* [young ladies] who would wake up in the middle of the night and cry "To Moscow!" expressing their deep yearning, but then never leave their homes in the stale provinces. [. . .] When a Jewish young man or young woman today decides to move to Moscow, they will find a way. They will take a deep breath and go. [. . .]

Fathers and mothers were afraid of their own children. [. . .]

And this changed the mood immediately.

One old Jew said with a deep sigh, "Oh, what times we lived to see! You cannot say a word any more. And with whom do you have to be careful? With your own children!" [. . .]

The "High Priests" in the Family

The more you travel around Soviet Russia and the more you listen to what people are telling you about their lives, the stronger your impression that with the exception of the faithful and committed communists who truly believe that this is the road to socialism, the majority of the population considers the current regime a form of state serfdom, the likes of which has never existed before.

In Odessa I talked to people from a variety of professions and trades; I met workers, engineers, doctors, pharmacists, teachers, and various kinds of Soviet employees, and from what they told me about their lives it became clear that *most* of them feel that they are under intense pressure, and cannot even imagine having control over their own lives. They are constantly in distress and feel as if they were harnessed and trying to pull a heavy wagon out of a ditch, but its wheels were stuck, and the driver of the wagon kept beating them with his huge whip and cutting stripes into their backs until they were bleeding. [. . .]

Although it is also true that in some factories and industrial plants you encounter people who can hardly be torn away from their work when it is time to go home because they are faithful and committed communists and truly believe that with every bit of extra energy that they put into their work they help build the country. [. . .]

Mothers

One of the people who came to see me in Tulchyn was an elderly Jewish woman whose children were in America. She wore ragged clothes and looked like a beggar, devastated and distressed; she stood there with a grimace on her face and told me that her children wanted her to follow them to America.

"My children keep nudging me to come, but here they don't want to let me out [of the country]. . . ."

She told me the same thing several times, and then made the following remark:

"And why do they not let me out of here, you will ask me? They need me here desperately. So may I know evil, the way I know why they are not letting me out of here!"

This poor mother whose children live in New York while she wallows in Tulchyn cannot understand why. Other mothers cannot understand it, either. They sit at home hungry or walk around in the streets like they are lost, and when they receive a letter from America they run to ask someone to read it for them once, and twice, and three times, and then they send their blessings back to their children on the other side of the ocean: May they have a long life over there! May they never know of any troubles!

They themselves are already resigned to the fact their own lives will pass without joy and happiness, because they are not allowed to leave the Soviet Union. They only wish that at least their children should be happy in that faraway land and should not know any troubles. But they are worried, because they heard that right now things are not the best in America, either. Thus, when a visitor comes from America, they are eager to get fresh news.

Tell us, they ask, is it true that in America people are dying of starvation in the street, just like here? Is it true that things are much worse there than here? If they cannot send us money, at least they could send a letter! They should write to us! May they never know of any troubles!

But in Tulchyn there are not only mothers whose children live in America but also children whose mothers are in America. One evening a couple came to see me—the husband wanted to ask me a favor. He begged me to go see his mother in Brooklyn and do everything I could to convince his mother to "forget about that crazy idea of hers."

"What kind of crazy idea?" I asked the man.

"You see," he began to tell me the story, "my mother has lived in America for many years now. She has other children there, and grandchildren, too, and she has a fairly good life. Here, take a look at the card she sent us. She is dressed very elegantly, and she looks so nice and healthy that it's a pleasure just to look at her.

But she took it into her head that she must come back here. Do you understand how crazy that is—to come back here? She thinks that she is much needed here. She writes that in America she does not feel at home. She thinks that here she will feel at home . . . I am begging you—you can see everything with your own eyes here, you see how much we suffer here, tell her the truth, and make sure that she does not come back here." [. . .]

While the man spoke there were several elderly women at my house, too—they brought me the addresses of their children in America. Having overheard what the man said to me they shook their heads and one of them said:

"What a world! Mothers here are dying to go there, and mothers there are dying to come here. " [. . .]

The only difference is that when mothers in America want to go back to their children in Soviet Russia, no one in is holding them back; they can go wherever they want. But the mothers in Soviet Russia are not allowed to leave the country and travel to their children in America—there are too many difficulties and obstacles.

It is impossible to forget the naïveté of that poor mother who said, "They need me here desperately." [. . .]

A Truth One Grasps Only Later

While visiting Tulchyn I spent one evening in the company of some very interesting young people. There were several communists among them, and they all listened attentively as I told them what a dreadful impression I had traveling around Soviet Russia. They admitted that embarrassing, characteristically Russian wrongdoings were committed quite often, and they even admitted that the current situation was very bad.

"All this is true," said one of them, a very honest and serious-looking fellow. "This is the truth of our reality, our life. But we also have *another truth, the truth of our theory*, and this one will be beheld only later. Guests from abroad can grasp this truth only after they leave and no longer see the sad truth they encountered here; but we, the truly faithful and committed communists, we can grasp it because we are already used to the sad truth of our reality. We do not live today, in the *present*; we live in the *future*."

The way the man spoke was a little too abstract, and he even went on to elaborate on his theory:

"This may explain," he continued, "why many people who left Russia escaped from the revolution to other countries, and later became our strong supporters; they grasped *the truth, the truth of our theory* from far away, and *this truth, our truth is socialism. It is your truth, too*. You just do not agree with our methods, with the way we are building socialism. Well, history will be our judge!"

Translated by Vera Szabó.

Other works by Osherovich: *Without Obligations* (1910); *Crown Prince Fyodor* (1926); *The Plight of Judaism in Soviet Russia, What Americans Don't See in Russia* (1932); *Moshe Montefyore* (1941); *Geshikhtes fun mayn lebn* (1945).

Sholem Schwartzbard

1886–1938

Sholem Schwartzbard was born in Izmail, Ukraine, and grew up in Balta, where he learned to be a watchmaker. As a youth, Schwartzbard was active in the Russian radical socialist movement and in Jewish self-defense units. In 1910, he settled in Paris and fought in the French army during World War I. In 1917, he joined the Red Guard in Odessa. During the civil war of 1918–1920, pogroms were rampant. Symon Petliura, a Ukrainian nationalist and the minister of war, was perceived to be responsible for the violence. Schwartzbard returned to Paris in 1920 and wrote widely about atrocities committed against Ukrainian Jews. On May 25, 1926, he assassinated Petliura in Paris. The long and sensational murder trial that followed did much to complicate Jewish–Ukrainian relations. Elye Tsherikover and his archive of the Ukrainian pogroms of 1918–1921 played an important role in Schwartzbard's eventual acquittal. In the last ten years of his life, Schwartzbard traveled and lectured widely. He died in Cape Town.

Memoirs of an Assassin

1933

Paris, Tuesday, May 25, 1926, half past three in the afternoon. The car in which I had suddenly found myself honked and barely managed to drive through the dense throng, with people screaming on all sides: "Kill him, kill him!"

"Murderer!"

"Lynch him!"

"He's not a Frenchman, but a foreigner!"

"He should be torn limb from limb!"

Out of the tumult comes the weak voice of my escort, the policeman, trying with all his might to ward off the crowd: "Let him alone. We have laws to take care of this. Let him go." The car moves very slowly, the mob surges forward with sticks and fists.

"Drag him out!"

"Let's lynch him. Kill! Kill!" Finally the car breaks through, as out of a fire. Rescued! Just barely saved! The chauffeur drives at full speed; the screaming grows fainter until it dies away altogether.

"The devil," says the policeman, as if to himself, "that was a wild mob. They would not have given me kid-glove treatment either." He wipes the sweat from his face and brow and straightens up his torn uniform.

"Out of danger at last," he says, again as if to himself. "That was some wild mob. That was some job." Then, turning to me, "Well, you got beaten up, eh?"

"Nonsense."

"Some nonsense," he says ironically. "That mob could have torn you apart right there. You really got off well."

"I've been through worse."

The car came to a halt. We were at the Odeon police station. We went into a room where two clerks sat, their heads buried in books. My escort greeted them and reported, "Murder."

No one answered, no one stirred, the clerks continued doing what they were doing, as if nothing had happened. They were not astonished; for them that was no news. My escort pondered a while, then took me into another room, where a man sat at a table, his back to me. Probably a stenographer, I thought. The policeman greeted him and reported, "Murder." The man did not even turn his head; the same indifference as in the other room.

The policeman did not know how to begin; in a little while he told me to sit in a corner. He himself wiped the sweat from his brow, talking, as to himself. "Oh, that was some job." And then grew silent.

The silence lasted a few minutes. All at once he said to me, "Empty your pockets—everything. The suspenders, the shoe laces, the garters, the belt, everything."

A door opened and a man entered—in his forties, medium height, with a large shiny forehead and a bald pate, a friendly face, and two black searching eyes surveying the room. My escort jumped to attention, taut as a string, greeted him, and reported: "Inspector, murder at the corner of Racine and Boulevard Saint-Michel."

But the inspector was not interested and went out. Several policemen came in, changing duty. My escort told them what a tough job he had just had.

"What about?" one of them asked, pointing at me.

"Murder," my escort replied indifferently, belittlingly.

"Whom?"

"I don't know, and I didn't ask. Some old bean pole. It just happened right in the street. Imagine, I'm standing at my station, all of a sudden I hear shots. I run in the direction of the shooting and I see this body stretched out on the sidewalk and this fellow standing over him with a revolver. The revolver was all discharged except for the last bullet, which jammed."

"Great!" the others beamed. One turned to me.

"Would you not have spared him even that last bullet?"

"Lucky for you the revolver didn't jam at the first bullet," commented another.

"Ah," remarked my escort, "he would have come off worse. The shot fellow had a cane. He surely wouldn't have spared him any blows."

"When you arrested him, did he resist?" someone asked.

"No. He stood there quite calmly and gave me the revolver."

"And the crowd attacked him?"

"And how. As soon as they saw I had taken his revolver, they attacked him like hornets and would have torn him to pieces. I got some of it too, but he got the better part. Lucky someone from the department came in a car. Even then, the crowd began to fight with sticks."

"Oh, people are like wild animals," someone commented. "If they see danger, they scatter like flies. Don't we know the mob?"

"That's just what it was like," assented my escort. "When they heard the shooting, they dispersed in all directions. Afterward, they wanted to lynch him. Oh, that mob!"

All at once they stopped the conversation and began to inspect me from head to foot. All the time they had been talking, I sat in a corner, resting from the blows to which the mob had treated me. My head ached badly and my face was inflamed. My eyes were burning and swollen. But my heart did not fail me. It beat calmly and quietly as usual. I felt as if I had been liberated from an enormous oppressive burden; instantly I felt good and relaxed. I followed their conversation without particular interest, as if it were not about me, and became aware of them only when they began to inspect me.

"Who is that someone you killed?" one of the police asked me.

"He was a Ukrainian general. Petlura was his name," I replied.

"What kind of bird is he?"

"A general, the leader of a barbarous army."

"That's good," a policeman responded.

"Once in a while they ought also to know the taste of death," another policeman commented, "instead of only sending others to break their heads. So it was a political act. That's not so terrible."

"He probably was a real bastard," said a second.

"Not worse than most of that rank," philosophized a third.

"Are you sure that he was the right one? You didn't accidentally shoot someone else by mistake?" one of the police asked me.

"I think not."

The last question, so innocently put, upset me. I felt disturbed. Perhaps? Who knows? I had to pull myself together. I tried to remember various details, but my head was not working. Had I made a mistake? Was it possible I had been wrong all along? What a calamity! What a crime! Suppose I had killed an innocent person? My breath grew short. My heart, which a few moments before had been relaxed, began pounding violently. Fear and despair seized me. I wiped off the sweat and tried to calm myself and banish the frightful thoughts. The harder I tried, the more impossible it became. How terrible! Now I would die like a common criminal undeserving of any sympathy.

The inspector came in, scrutinized me a while, and then told me to follow him into his office. He sat at his desk, and showing me a chair facing him, said, "Now we have time to talk."

"I am ready." I felt feverish, as if intoxicated, my eyes blurry, but I tried to control myself.

"Now, tell me, why did you do this deed?"

For a while I was silent. I felt everything I had to say was concentrated in one word and I blurted it out: "I am a Jew!"

"An Israelite," the inspector corrected me. "Proceed."

Slowly, with a beating heart I began to tell about the Jewish calamity, the horrible tragedy that had befallen us in the Ukraine, the massacres and pogroms, beginning with the bloody days of Chmielnitsky down to Petlura.

The inspector sat with his head bowed and kept writing, recording.

"All right," he said, "But I want to know who this Petlura is. All that stuff about the seventeenth and eighteenth centuries is pretty old. We are now living in the twentieth century. Tell me about the murdered man. Who was he?"

"In short, he was the second Haman. The first wanted to destroy the Jewish people and this one most brutally destroyed a great part."

The inspector smiled.

"Yes, yes. Put it in your report, do it at my request," I urge him, but inside, the painful question comes up again: Did I make a fatal mistake"? Just then my arresting policeman entered.

"Inspector, I have come from the hospital. The wounded man died. His identity papers were found. He is called Semyon Petlura."

Then I was right! I had shot not an innocent man, but the murderer Petlura. To tell the truth, my original certainty that the man I had shot was Petlura was not very soundly based. After all, I had never seen the beast; I had no idea what he looked like. Despite all my investigations, it was impossible to find out anything about him. My numerous acquaintances in Jewish and non-Jewish circles could not satisfy my curiosity. When I first learned in a Russian newspaper that Petlura was in Paris, I could not rest. I began chasing around, searching, investigating. Many people thought my inquiries about Petlura peculiar, and some even mocked me, inquiring whether perhaps I planned to kill him. The futile searches and the ironic comments often brought me to tears. Sometimes I just became sick at the petty comments of friends who suspected something, who tried to dissuade me, saying that I should leave his punishment to other hands, not ruin the livelihood that I had. But the knowledge that this murderer was alive and well, and so near, would not let me rest. Ceaselessly I looked for his traces; at the end of each unsuccessful day I gnashed my teeth in sorrow. Often I wanted to express my anger against those whose irony exacerbated my hurt. Most of all, I suffered in the quiet night hours, lying on my bed and thinking about the further pursuit. It was impossible to conceal my sufferings from my wife, who began to notice my nervousness and even my tears.

"Why are you crying?" she used to ask.

I would pull myself together and put on an innocent mien. "What gives you such a notion? My eyes are tearing from my work." But my excuses were not always convincing. My wife kept noticing ever more that change that was coming over me.

Several months passed in dreadful suffering. In this time all I could find out was that Petlura went about incognito, had a younger brother, and was a frequent visitor in certain Jewish homes. But thereafter, all threads of information snapped.

My only photograph of Petlura I had cut out of my Larousse. But it could hardly do. It was absurd to hope to meet Petlura on a Paris street and expect to recognize him from this small, bad picture.

Then the lucky chance came. A Ukrainian paper which had just begun to appear in Paris came to my rescue by printing a photograph of Petlura with Pilsudski. If not for this chance, who knows how long my suffering would have lasted. For a time I was not yet quite certain that the person whom I had seen several times and heard speaking Ukrainian was Petlura. When finally I decided it was he, I found him several times in the company of a woman and a little girl. The fear of hurting an innocent victim restrained me. When chance once again brought me together with him when he was all alone, I was so struck with my luck that I abandoned any opportunity to check my information, and I raised my arm to punish. . . .

On hearing that he was in truth Petlura I felt a heavy burden had rolled off my heart. At that moment everything seemed to me radiant and beautiful. I felt happy, jubilant, satisfied, and like one born anew—like a young man in love who loves the whole world. Even though I had never felt any liking for the police, I wanted to embrace the policeman who brought me the news, to kiss him and press him to my heart.

The Speech I Did Not Make

My judges:

Whenever I read the chronicles of world history, my heart bleeds each time I encounter human injustice. As long as there have been people on this earth, the most pitiless enemy of any human being is another human being.

The classical world knew tyrants like Herod, Caligula, Nero, Diocletian, who drowned whole generations in blood. Those fine spirits Tacitus, Pliny the Younger, Marcus Aurelius in their writings mocked the unfortunate Jews and the martyred Christians. The Middle Ages witnessed Attila, the Crusaders, the religious wars, the Mongol Tamerlane, St. Bartholomew's Night, Torquemada, and Ivan the Terrible. Accusations about the use of blood were directed first against Christians, then by Christians against Jews, from the Middle Ages until today.

If we put the past on trial, is not history one long bill of accusation against humanity? Yet the old stories of brutal deeds and persecutions appear as child's play when compared to the horrible massacres which were enacted before our eyes. Our learned generation, with its diverse sciences, our fine philosophers, and gentle moralists have not succeeded in extirpating the bestial instinct in man.

I cannot contain my tears when I recall the great sufferings which our people endured the last centuries in the Ukraine, that vale of tears. For three hundred years Jewish blood flowed without halt on Ukrainian soil. In 1648, Herman Bogdan Chmielnitsky and his Cossacks drenched the Ukraine with our blood. They slaughtered old people, tore little children limb from limb, raped women and strangled them afterward. This massacre lasted until 1654, and 500,000 Jews met their death in the severest agonies.

The Jewish people was destroyed with fire and sword in the Ukraine. A Polish memoirist describes this epoch:

When Kievan Ataman Charchevsky entered Kanev, the Cossacks massacred all its Jews. It was their custom thus to entertain themselves. In Nemirov an Ataman and his Cossacks lashed hundreds of Jews together and drowned them. Little children were ingeniously severed in half. Six thousand Jews were murdered in Nemirov.

That was how the advance units operated. Then came the great Cossack hordes, headed by Bogdan Chmielnitsky and his aide Krivonos.

In Tulchin all the Jews were assembled and ordered to be baptized. With one voice they cried out: "Hear, O Israel: the Lord our God, the Lord is One."

The same Polish memoirist tells us, the Cossacks assaulted the Jews, cut off their hands and feet, raped women in the sight of their husbands, smashed children against walls to crush their skull, carved open the bellies of pregnant women and forced cats in. . . .

They desecrated synagogues, ripped apart Torah scrolls, and sent entire towns up in flame and smoke. The Jewish communities of Pereyaslav, Borisovka, Piryatin, Boryslaw, Dubno, Lachowicze, and many others were destroyed. Streams of blood flowed over the Ukrainian roads.

That was the first time these wild Ukrainian creatures emerged in the arena of world history.

In 1768, one hundred twenty years after the first grim massacre by the Zaporogian Cossacks, Chmielnitsky's descendants, Ivan Gonta and Maxim Zheleznyak duplicated the atrocities committed by their ancestors. The heartless and soulless Haidamaks began their orgies and demons' dances in Lisyanka. Archimandrite Melchizedek Yavorsky gave them the blessing of the sword and promised them complete absolution if they would slaughter the unfortunate Jews. The hordes charged out and destroyed the Jewish communities in Uman, Zabotin, Chihirin, Smela, Kanev and Cherkassy.

In his poem "Haidamacks," Shevchenko described the following episode: A new Bartholomew's massacre was brutally enacted in 1768 by the Haidamacks and Cossacks in Uman. The chief actors were Gonta and Zheleznyak. Cooling their hatred of Jews and Catholics in streams of blood, the Haidamacks found, in a Jesuit monastery that they plundered, two children their chief Gonta had had by a Polish Catholic woman. They brought the children to their father, saying:

"You have sworn to destroy all Jews and Catholics, regardless of age or sex. Before you stand your own two children reared by the Jesuits!"

Gonta did not waver; with his own hand he stabbed his children.

Under the light of the conflagration which they had set, the Haidamacks feasted and celebrated their victory. Amid the ruins and heaped-up corpses they abandoned themselves to fiendish orgies. The horrifying spectacle lacked none of the usual ingredients: vats of wine, wild dancing, and virtuous Jewish daughters abducted to be violated. Gonta and Zheleznyak puffed their pipes, as the river ran red with blood.

Our tragedy is intensified when poets and historians glorify these grisly deeds. The barbarous epic of savage sadism committed by animals in the guise of men evokes no pity for our martyrs, no sympathy, no regret. For these poets and historians, too, the Jews are creatures without legal protection, scapegoats, animals to be driven and slaughtered with gratification. Historian Kostomarov, novelist Nikolai Gogol, and poet Shevchenko depicted these scenes of horror in tranquil tones and lauded the heroes who did these deeds. The victims appear to them as comical creatures. The Haidamacks boasted that they were heroes because they were cruel. They were thought vigorous because they were not deterred from butchering infants in their cradles.

The gruesome massacres, the ghastly acts committed by the Haidamacks of Ataman Petlura in 1918, 1919, and 1920, in their cruelty and evil surpassed the earlier deeds of the Ukrainian heroes.

I need only recall that dreadful time for a shudder to pass over my body. The hideous visions pursue me always, though I strive to ward them off. Though I seek to expunge them from my memory, they remain always fresh and fearful. Pogrom scenes I witnessed float before my eyes and at night keep me awake. I jump up from sleep and cannot shake off the bloody nightmares.

All the remembrances of my life are gruesome, as is our whole history of martyrdom. My anguish grows greater when I cannot aid my suffering brothers and sisters. There are times when private sorrows disappear in public woe, like a drop of water in the sea. But as for him who suffers for humanity, his sorrows continue and are vast as the world. These sensitive souls suffer every injustice done on earth, on their bodies they feel the whiplash, they cannot endure the oppressor's arrogance and the slow pace of justice. They must act.

The blood of the innocent and of the martyrs demands justice and vengeance.

My life was the theater of all misfortunes and afflictions. Sometimes actor, always witness and spectator, I was ever engaged in the struggle against tyranny and could never escape from it.

At the end of July, 1919 I arrived in Zhidowska-Grebla, two days after the Haidamack pogrom. The first Jewish home I entered looked as if it had suffered an earthquake. Two old women sat on the ground and lying next to them an old man, his face bloodied, his eyes bloodshot, blood still running from his bandaged head, and from him issued one lament, "My God, my God, why hast Thou forsaken me?"

In that town, eight of fifteen families were completely annihilated. A widow with six children, whose husband had fallen at the front, was violated and then strangled.

In Cherkassy on the Dnieper, the first Jew I encountered told me: "We have just buried a thousand victims of the last pogrom. All lie in one mass grave. One gets accustomed to calamity. It is Providence."

At the end of August, when I was in Kiev, Petlura's advance guard entered. They murdered all the Jews they met on their way. In the center of Bolshaya Vasilkovskaya Street, I saw the corpse of a young man stretched out on the pavement, and, her head on his dead body, a woman lamenting for her one and only son. Hoodlums shouted obscenities, mocking her despair. One sermonized: "This is good. We'll show you, damned Jews, we'll slaughter you all."

Kozyr-Zyrko, Petlura's aide, the hero of the massacre in Ovruch, selected thirty old Jewish men for his amusement. Haidamacks encircled them and ordered them to sing and dance. The Haidamacks were free with their whips and revolvers, mocking, deriding, goading the dancers. When one Jew or another broke out in a lament, the torturers beat them, ordering them to continue dancing and singing, and they shouted "Long live our Father Kozyr-Zyrko." Then they shot all the old men and piled the bodies in a heap.

Palenko, another of Petlura's aides, told a Jewish delegation in Kiev: "I will not listen to you. Do you think that for a few damned Jews I would disrupt my boys' amusements?"

And the great Petlura himself stated: "Do not make a quarrel between me and my army."

In all the cities they posted placards with insults, hatred, and threats against the Jewish population: "You, cursed people, whom all nations despise." . . .

They forced unfortunates to eat their excrement. They shoveled earth over them and buried them alive. Nor did they spare the dead. They desecrated the cemeteries and refused permission to bury the martyrs.

In Tripole on the Dnieper, Petlura's birthplace, after the fifth pogrom, forty-seven corpses of the old, the sick, and the children were left lying in the street, and no living soul remained after them. Dogs began to pick at the bodies and pigs to nibble. Finally, a Gentile who used to work for Jews, out of pity dug a grave and buried them. The Haidamacks learned of it and for that they murdered him.

In Ladyzhin only two Jewish girls remained alive. They were raped, their noses bitten by sadists, and in-fected with venereal disease. They came for help to a hospital in Kiev.

Intoxicated with blood and uncontrolled hatred, the twentieth-century descendants of Bogdan Chmielnitsky, Gonta, and Zheleznyak completed the mission of their ancestors. Are these the flag-bearers of the New Testament, of civilization and of hope for a nobler mankind?

Judge me, my judges.

Translator unknown.

Other works by Schwartzbard: *Troymen un verlekh-kayt* (1920); *Sefer khayay* (1930); *In krig mit zikh aleyn* (1933); *In'm loyf fun yorn* (1934).

Leon Dennen

1907–1974

Leon Dennen was born in the United States, was educated there and in Russia, and worked as a foreign correspondent for the Newspaper Enterprise Association. In the early 1930s, Dennen was associated with the Friends of the Soviet Union publishing house. After the Moscow trials, however, he denounced Stalinism, "the imperialist Soviet regime," and its allies. In the 1940s, he became an editor of *The New Leader*. Dennen also wrote literary criticism and translated works by David Dallin and Vladimir Mayakovsky. He died in New York.

Where the Ghetto Ends: Jews in Soviet Russia
1934

PIONEERS

I

Much has already been written about the Jewish colonies in the Crimea. Unfortunately, most of the information is buried under a mountain of statistics, historical data, and political arguments. And yet, for one who has seen the death of the Russian ghetto, it is easy to wax lyrical—yes, even grow sentimental over the new life that is being forged by Jews on soil.

The Crimea is a sunny and flowering peninsula, washed by the Black and Azov seas. It is a country, I was told by the colonists, "blessed with the best of climates and the most fertile of soils." About the size of Holland, it has vast, hitherto uncultivated and uninhabited steppes.

In these steppes, in 1924, small groups of Jewish pioneers decided to recommence life as tillers of the soil. They were assisted in this task by the Soviet Government as well as by the Agro-Joint (American Society for the promotion of agriculture among Russian Jews), headed by one of the most remarkable men I have ever known, Dr. Joseph Rosen.

It was a difficult task. The land was virgin; it had to be cultivated. The land was arid; it needed irrigation. The process was slow and painful. Ten years have passed—years of hard toil. Not in vain. The collective farm, Horepashnik, for instance, has already become one of the most prosperous farms in the Crimea. A small group of pioneers pointed the way out. Thousands of Jews who would have slowly perished in the ghettos, followed them.

Today more than 29,000 Jews have settled on land in the Crimea. They are organized in 83 collective farms. The Freidorf district, the Jewish autonomous region in the Crimea, has 33 village Soviets composed primarily of Jews. The entire district is under Jewish administration. The colonists have more than 3,000 houses, 200 buildings for collective and agricultural purposes, several factories in which they manufacture various commodities out of their own raw materials, a number of hospitals, clubs, theatres, movies and various other social and cultural institutions, including 73 elementary schools, 14 high schools and two agricultural technical schools of which I shall speak later. Unlike the work of other farming nationalities in the Crimea, or even throughout Russia, the agricultural work of the Jews is more than 75% mechanized.

Some interesting incidents are related about the beginning of the Jewish colonization in the Crimea. When the first group of settlers arrived, they were met by strong opposition on the part of the local peasantry. This was, of course, attributed to the peasants' inherent anti-Semitism. Undoubtedly, the anti-Semitic element was there. More important, however, I believe, was the peasants' extraordinary love and reverence for the land. They feared that the "holy land" was being desecrated.

"To whom are they giving land?" they asked in amazement. "What will they do with it?"

Indeed, the typical ghetto Jew, destroyed and demoralized, inspired very little confidence in his ability to work on the soil. It was necessary to have the daring inspiration of a revolution to transform these Jews into peasants. It was an experiment. It is now a reality. The ghetto Jew is gradually being transformed into a new man.

I say gradually, for it must not be imagined that the settling of the Jews on land in Soviet Russia has already been accomplished. It is only beginning. While there is nothing in the make-up of the East European Jew to prevent him from ultimately becoming a sturdy farmer, it will take perhaps more than one generation before he is freed finally from the destructive claws of the ghetto psychology. The Soviet Government, it is commonly assumed, is capable of accomplishing in a decade what it took other governments to accomplish in a century. That, in a sense, is true. That is the power of revolution. One, however, cannot rid himself so quickly of a heritage in which he has been rooted for centuries and centuries. Also, the fleshpot plays its historic rôle here, too. It will take many more years before the ghetto Jew will learn to become a free and productive member of society. For one thing, the Jew is traditionally a city man. And for a city man to become a peasant, means that he has to free himself from his old habits and traditions. This process of transformation is usually slow and tortuous. Secondly, there is that "class conflict" within the Jewish race itself, which, even as among the Russian peasantry, is an obstacle in the path of Jewish colonization in Russia.

In its broader aspect, Jewish colonization is organically linked up with the agricultural revolution that has been taking place in Soviet Russia—the movement to collectivize Russian land. It is this movement which is undoubtedly the outstanding factor in the Soviet program.

From the very outset of the Bolshevik revolution, it was Lenin's dream to collectivize all Russian land. For it was in the private holdings of the peasants that he foresaw the future enemy of socialism. This, however, could not be done at once. In order to assure the success of the first stage of the Revolution—the conquest of power—the Bolsheviks needed the vast Russian peasantry as an ally. To the peasants, on the other hand, rich or poor, the Revolution meant that they would be given free land which they had so long coveted. Having achieved their dream, having gotten the land that was confiscated from the landowners, they were satisfied. Their age-old peasant yearning was realized and as far as they were concerned, the Revolution was completed. Not so the Bolsheviks. To them the distribution of the land among the individual peasants was merely a tactical move. The final aim of the Revolution, they said, is the creation of socialist society. Real socialism can only be established in a society where private property no longer exists. As long as the peasants own the land privately and not collectively where everything is produced and shared in common, so long will the final aim of the Revolution not be achieved.

Thus, on the second year of the Five-Year Plan in 1930, referred to by the Soviet leaders as the year of the "great break," the Soviet Government set out "to liquidate" private property. The movement to collectivize Russian land commenced. Superficially, the aim of this movement was to industrialize agriculture, to get control of the food supply of the entire nation and increase it by scientific methods. Fundamentally, as I have already pointed out, the issue was much deeper than that. It was the historic struggle between individualism and collectivism, between private enterprise and collective ownership. Because the Russian peasantry was the most individualistic and property-conscious element in Russia, this movement presents the most dramatic aspect of the Five-Year Plan.

As it was to be expected, the peasants did not give in without a battle to the Government's program of collectivization. They replied with a stubborn resistance. At first they stopped sowing. Much of the country's arable land became wasteland. The country was plunged into a period of hunger and starvation. But such forms of passive resistance were not the only methods they adopted in their fight against the Government. The kulaks—rich peasants—instituted a reign of terror. Because of their tremendous authority in the village, they succeeded in inducing the poorer peasants who could only benefit through collectivization, to set fire to villages, to kill out their livestock and destroy all property that they could lay their hands on. Many Soviet officials were killed during this reign of terror.

The Government answered terror with terror. Rebellious peasants, particularly kulaks, were forcibly exiled to distant places in Siberia. During 1931 and even 1932, one could see whole carloads of such peasants all over Russia. They were a pitiful sight. Many of them lived under the most miserable conditions. A great number were killed in the fight or died of disease. It was a fierce and ruthless struggle. Cruel and unforgivable acts were committed on both sides. Whether they were justified or not, one thing is certain: private property no longer exists in Russia. At least 95% of its land is completely collectivized.

The instinct for private property, however, is still alive. That is what the Bolsheviks call "the class struggle in the village." Many of the peasants, particularly kulaks, have realized the futility of fighting the Soviet Government in the open. They have joined the collective farms and carry on sabotage activities secretly. Sometimes these acts of sabotage result in serious damage to Soviet agriculture and industry. How long the fight will go on I do not know, but it is a problem which, it seems to me, the Soviet Government will have to face for many years to come.

Strange as it may seem, particularly since the vast majority of the Russian Jews were never permitted to own any land, this "class struggle" is also a problem in the Jewish colonies, although in a less violent and somewhat different form. This was related to me by Chaskin, the agronomist for the Agro-Joint, with whom I was traveling through the Jewish colonies in the Crimea.

2

The sun had already set beyond the Crimean mountains, when we approached Horepashnik. Night was slowly descending upon the steppe. Suddenly, it was lit by numerous glittering lights.

"Look!" exclaimed Chaskin. "The steppe is being electrified." Indeed, the steppe was being electrified. Every few moments new lights would appear in the distance. They belonged to various collective farms. Chaskin, who knew the region well, could recognize each of them. The collectives Icor, Horepashnik, Molotov, all were casting their light upon the steppe.

"And if you look hard enough," remarked Chaskin smiling, "you may get a glimpse of Freidorf, the 'Jewish Kingdom,' where even the G.P.U. speaks Yiddish."

Yes, that was the steppe which I had longed to see. Only the day before I left Kiev, my host showed me, in the Yiddish newspaper *Emes*, a dispatch which read:

"The Jewish collective farms Horepashnik, Molotov, The Jewish Peasant and the commune Voyenovo, have been electrified for the celebration of the Fifteenth Anniversary of the Bolshevik Revolution.

"In Horepashnik the water power, too, has been electrified and the results are excellent."

An outsider could not realize why this dispatch should be cause for rejoicing. To an American, electricity is no longer a wonder. Neither, as a matter of fact, is it anything new to the Russian in the big city. But to the Jewish colonists its significance cannot even be measured. For them, this accomplishment signified that their survival was beyond doubt.

"It is an assurance of new life," said Chaskin, "for you must remember that only two years ago this was wilderness and wasteland. Ordinarily, to cultivate land like this would take many decades. You know the story of your own American pioneers. With the aid of electricity, however, we have taken a jump on history. The sooner we develop our colonies, the speedier will be the solution of the Jewish problem in Russia and perhaps over all the world." [. . .]

The original task of the agronomists was primarily technical in nature, to teach and train new farmers. But Jewish colonization in Russia is as much social in nature as technical. Thus, the agronomist soon became to the colonists not only an instructor in agriculture but also a counsellor, referee and friend.

Fortunately for the colonists, the majority of the agronomists, at least those whom I met, are of the stuff from which real leaders are made. Unknown to the outside world, it is they who carry the burden of Jewish colonization upon their shoulders.

Here is Chaskin, for instance: He was a medical student before the Revolution. Because of his revolutionary activities, he was expelled from the university and from the age of nineteen had led the precarious existence of a hunted animal. The Tsarist secret police were always on his trail.

After the Revolution he fought in the Red Army and when the civil war came to an end he began to attend agricultural school.

Tall, broadshouldered and dark, with naïve blue eyes and a face radiating confidence and sincerity, at the age of 37 Chaskin is as alert and alive as a man in his early twenties. He is still animated by the same ideal—the creation of a better and richer life for all who are exploited and persecuted—that inspired him and gave meaning to his existence when he was nineteen. During our trip through the Crimean steppes, I had long and intimate conversations with Chaskin. I discovered that he was not only an excellent agronomist but also an expert diplomat.

"You could qualify in America as a soul healer," I once remarked to him after I had seen the effect of his presence upon the colonists.

"What can I do?" he replied. "Sometimes I must even assume the duties of a worshipper when I am among religious colonists on a Saturday and there aren't ten men for prayer. I am everything around here. I also settle disputes between husbands and wives and between children and parents. You've got to understand the psychology of every person with whom you are dealing. There are former merchants here, village tailors, shoemakers and marriage brokers. Now conditions are becoming somewhat normal, but at the beginning it was real hell around here. Many Jews came from the villages expecting to find everything ready for them. Others came to seek a new field for business. When they discovered that they must build their new life by the sweat of their brows, they fled back to the ghettos or to the large cities. But not for long. In the town they faced a miserable existence. In the cities, without the knowledge of any trade, they were doomed to starvation. Of course, those who were experts in their fields—such as former grain and flour merchants, horse dealers, and so on, were given Government jobs. The others went back. They came and went, came and went. There was a continuous traffic around here. Now the majority are settled and satisfied."

"How about the former Jewish bourgeoisie?" I asked. "Is it true, as the *Emes* and other Yiddish newspapers report, that they carry on sabotage activities in the collective farms?"

"Not quite. In order to emphasize that the Jews are no different than the rest of the national minorities in the Soviet Union, the *Emes* sometimes uncovers cases of sabotage where there was merely incompetence. Besides, there cannot be any kulaks among the Jews if by kulaks we mean rich peasants. On the other hand, the Jews are blessed with their own type of 'class enemies'—the typical village *gesheftsmen* who came here to continue their old professions."

"But one cannot indulge in private trading in the Soviet Union?"

"Theoretically, no, but actually, yes. That is we call the transition stage. The collectives still retain a form of private property. Each worker, for instance, gets paid by the number of days he works. He is paid not in money but in products. The surplus of his products he is permitted to sell in the 'open' unofficial market where the prices are ten times as high as those in the official government stores. That is how speculation asserts itself all over again. Many of the *gesheftsmen*, instead of working, go about buying up the surplus products from the other colonists and sell it in the 'open' market. One evasion of the law leads to another. Thus, there are many instances where these speculators steal grain, flour, cattle and equipment. In some collective farms it became a real organized business. Through counter-revolutionary propaganda—and here is where they are like the kulaks—they influence the discontented elements in the farms. They get themselves elected as managers and naturally under such management the farms usually go to pieces. But that is becoming less and less of a problem because once we uncover a person like that there is no mercy for him. By far the vast majority of the colonists are hardworking people who are eager to make a new start in life."

Chaskin also explained to me the advantage the Jewish colonists have over the rest of the farming population in the Soviet Union. The Jews have no agricultural tradition. Thus, while the Government is still trying to wean the peasant away from his primitive agricultural methods, the Jewish colonists at the start learned to use the most modern agricultural implements. The Freidorf district, as an instance, has six "M.T.S." (tractor stations) with 475 tractors. Some of the ablest men are in charge of these "M.T.S." whose function, incidentally, is as much educational and political, as technical. Moreover, the Jewish farms from the very outset were organized as collectives. [. . .]

Leah Botnik and the Other Women

I

[. . .] According to her bosom friend, Dinah, Leah Botnik came from a very rich family. Her house in the town where she lived before the Revolution was nicknamed the "House of Romanoffs." Naturally, the Revolution did not spare this House of Romanoffs either. After the Bolshevik seizure of power, Leah's husband, a rich flour merchant, deserted her. He escaped to Germany where he died in misery and poverty. Leah, to escape starvation in the town, was forced to join the collective farm.

"At the beginning," related Dinah, "it was difficult for Leah to get used to the new life. After all, she was used to rolling in milk and honey, and here she had to work. Leah was a snob. She would not associate with us who had scrubbed her floors, sold vinegar to her or repaired her shoes. . . ."

Time conquered pride. Today, although no longer young, Leah, with a healthy tan on her cheeks, is an excellent worker. She is also the cultural leader of the kolhoz. In her spare time she organizes lectures, the-atre performances and teaches those who are illiterate to read and write.

I met Leah for the first time at the collective's millinery shop. It is one of those shops organized and subsidized by the American organization, Ort (society for the promotion of trades among Jews), which are particularly useful in the winter months when there is little work in the fields. Such shops, I was told, are part of a scheme to develop the handicraft industry among the colonists and will eventually add to their material welfare.

I entered the shop late in the evening. Work had already ceased and the workers—old women and young girls—were sitting in a circle around Leah, debating heatedly. My appearance caused some excitement. But not for long. Soon I, too, was sitting in the circle and participating in the discussion.

The interrupted debate continued. Dinah, a short plump woman of about forty, with coarse peasant features, was speaking.

"As I was saying, comrades, I neither approve nor disapprove of intermarriage. That is a purely personal problem. On the other hand, in accordance with the national policy laid down by the Party, it is the duty of every nationality to perpetuate and develop its culture. From this angle the problem of intermarriage should be discussed."

Leah smiled.

"Dinah is practicing upon us the speech that she is going to deliver at the forthcoming regional congress of women shock-brigaders," she explained to me. "She has been thus honored because she had done the best work in our truck gardens. Besides, Dinah is a clever woman. Even in the old days, when she worked for me there was a rebellious streak in her. With a little polish I have no doubt that she will go far. Do you hear her quoting: 'As comrade Stalin said. . . .'"

"As comrade Stalin said," Dinah continued, gesticulating with her calloused hands, "we should develop a culture that is national in form and proletarian in content. . . ."

"Wait a minute," a young girl of about nineteen interrupted her, "we are speaking about intermarriage and you have already drifted into culture. Why, comrade Dinah, don't you learn to stick to one subject?"

"She is speaking to the point," an elderly woman protested, "you think that because you are a member of the Komsomol you can teach everybody around here. Dinah is right."

"I insist that this is a bad case of opportunism," retorted the Komsomolka.

Immediately the circle divided into two camps—the youth who were on the side of the Komsomolka, and the older women who agreed with Dinah. A heated verbal fight commenced. It seemed to me that it would eventually end in a fist fight, but Leah's clever diplomacy saved the situation.

"Comrades," she said in her quiet voice, "I think we are unfair to the guest. We have not told him what the argument is about. Let us first explain to him the nature of our discussion and then proceed."

These words of the tall, full-breasted woman, with dark hair and soft gray eyes, produced the desired effect. The shouting ceased. One could see that Leah's words, even though some were suspicious of her because of her bourgeois past, as I later found out, carried weight with the women of the kolhoz. After all, she was the most cultured woman among them, and culture was what they were yearning for.

"Well then," continued Leah, "that is how the argument started. Do you see our Feygele over there in the corner? She is already blushing. . . ."

In the corner pointed out to me by Leah, a young girl of about seventeen was sitting, sewing. She wore a man's blouse opened at the neck and top boots out of which extended two husky calves. Conscious that we were speaking about her, she pretended to be deeply engrossed in her work.

". . . so Feygele in Yiddish means bird. But look at her red cheeks and powerful physique; does she strike you as being a bird? Of course not. She is as strong as a mule. You ought to see her at work."

We all laughed. Leah lowered her voice:

"You see, she is an orphan. A few years ago I found her in our town, a little girl. Now she is twice as big as I am. She does the hardest work in the kolhoz. In the summer she manages to work in the fields and attend to our cows. If you have the opportunity, look into our 'maternity ward' where Feygele's cows give birth to calves. That is her domain. She is the undisputed ruler there.

"But," Leah winked mischievously, "that is only half of the story. The best is yet to come. . . ."

All eyes turned upon Feygele. The younger girls giggled. The older women smiled condescendingly. Feygele, it was obvious, was annoyed.

"To make a long story short, she has decided to get married. She found herself a young Tartar at Saki and in a few weeks we will dance at her wedding."

"That is how the discussion about the problem of intermarriage began," commented the Komsomolka who had nearly precipitated a fight.

"A problem?" Leah interrupted her. "Was there a problem when you went with Joseph the tractor driver? Or is your Joseph, the Jew, better than Akhmed, the Tartar? Where is there a problem, I ask? She fell in love with a Tartar and is going to be married. That is all."

The Komsomolka was not satisfied with Leah's explanation:

"You are evading the question, comrade Leah. Pretty soon you will accuse me of being an anti-*Goy* or a Jewish chauvinist. We are discussing here intermarriage as a matter of principle and I think that you have not gone to the root of the problem. Suppose there will be children, what are they going to be: Tartars or Jews?"

"If there will be children—and I am sure there will be—" replied Leah, "they will be simply Soviet citizens, like the rest of the children in the Soviet Union."

"That doesn't answer the question. . . ."

I agreed with the Komsomolka. Leah's solution seemed to me too simple. In America I had heard many discussions about the degeneration of the Jewish race in the Soviet Union. Only too often have I heard American students of Soviet affairs report that the Jew in Soviet Russia is rapidly assimilating. "It looks," one of them remarked, "as if the Jew might in time be absorbed."

Superficially these statements may be right. At least twenty per cent of the marriages in Soviet Russia today are mixed. As years go by and race differences are entirely wiped out, there will undoubtedly be more of them. That, however, is as much true of the Tartars, Uzbeks, Ukrainians and other nationalities that populate Russia as it is of the Jews. Does that mean that all these nationalities will eventually be absorbed and assimilated, or is it true only of the Jews?

I asked Leah this question. Her reply was typical of the attitude of many intelligent Jews who have given this question any thought at all:

"You see," she said, "when we speak of assimilation we mean assimilation as it was practiced in the Tsarist days, or as it is still practiced among a certain strata of the Jews in Poland and Germany. In those countries Jews assimilate for two reasons. The first one is psychological; they are ashamed of being Jews. Secondly, through assimilation they hope to profit materially, as for instance, in Poland. In Soviet Russia such causes for assimilation do not exist. Whether you are a Jew or a Tartar all doors are open to you."

"But will not intermarriage," I asked, "eventually play havoc with your Jewish culture?"

"Decidedly not. If you ever visit our collective schools you will see that children of mixed marriages are not only studying Jewish history and literature, but also Yiddish as a language. Jews in Russia are gradually disappearing as a religious unit, but they are getting stronger and stronger as a cultural unit. By culture we don't mean, of course, that sort of wisdom that was dispensed to the children of the ghetto in the elementary religious schools by ignorant and incompetent Bible teachers. For samples of this culture, you don't have to look far. Here is Dinah, she has been taught for years to pray in Hebrew, a tongue which she does not understand, and what does she know? Nothing. She has to begin her education all over.

"But enough of problems . . . Let us talk about life. What I can't understand is where Feygele got the time for love-making. She works in the field and takes care of the cows during the day and attends my classes in the evening. Incidentally, my classes are for adults only, and they are conducted in Yiddish. And as that isn't enough, she is also a member of the Komsomol and tries to run us all by the nose."

"You are getting as sentimental as an old cow," Feygele at last replied mockingly.

"You are right," said Leah, "I am getting sentimental, perhaps a little jealous, too. When I think about you girls, I can't help reminding myself of the old days. It was quite different then. A girl like you, Feygele, would have had to give some good-for-nothing a dowry. And if you had no dowry, you couldn't get married. You'd have to wait for some idealist to make you his wife for nothing. In the meantime, your plaits would turn gray, your face wrinkle and your body bend in two."

A young man who had evidently just returned from a journey rushed into the shop and whispered something into Leah's ear.

"Fine," said Leah, "fine . . . Comrades, I wish to announce that Dinah's candidacy as a delegate to the regional conference of women shock-brigadiers has been approved by the district committee of the Party. . . ."

"Bravo," cried out the girl who had hitherto been Dinah's opponent, "hurrah for our delegate!"

Dinah's face broadened into a smile. Her eyes began to glisten. I could visualize her at the moment on the platform addressing the conference: "Comrades, as comrade Stalin said . . ."

Other works by Dennen: *White Guard Terrorists in the USA* (1935); *Trouble Zone: Brewing Point of World War III?* (1945); *The Soviet Peace Myth* (1951).

Simon Dubnov

1860–1941

Simon Dubnov (Dubnow) was born in Mstislavl, Belorussia. Inspired by the Haskalah, he began writing for the Russian Jewish press in St. Petersburg, where he resided illegally and briefly. The work of Heinrich Graetz, whom he met in the late 1880s, was the inspiration for Dubnov's magnum opus, *World History of the Jewish People*, published in German, Hebrew, and Russian in the 1920s and 1930s. Upon moving to Odessa in 1890, he became part of the Jewish intellectual circle that included Ahad Ha-Am and Bialik, and he continued his research into Jewish social history. He promoted diaspora nationalism or "autonomism," helping to found the Folkspartey and influencing Bundist ideology. Dubnov returned to St. Petersburg in 1905, founding the Jewish Historical-Ethnographic Society and the journal *Everiskaia starina*. Dissatisfied with the Bolshevik takeover, he left for Berlin in 1922 and helped to establish the YIVO in Vilna. When Hitler was elected, Dubnov moved to Riga and was later murdered by the Nazis.

Book of My Life

1934–1935

Chapter 63

THE DAYS OF RED TERROR (SEPTEMBER–DECEMBER 1918)

[. . .] In the early autumn of 1918 we entered a new circle of Bolshevik hell, the period of mass Red Terror. The murder of Uritskii and the attempted assassination of Lenin enraged the Bolsheviks, and they resolved to implement their dictatorship in all its cruelty. From this point onward, the real government of the Soviet Republic was the Cheka, the Extraordinary Commission for the Struggle against Counterrevolution.[1] Beginning in September 1918 it called for mass Red Terror, arresting people by the hundreds and packing them off to be executed. They shot people not only for actions directed against Soviet power, but even for words and thoughts.

As in war-time, they seized hostages from opposing parties, and at the first setback killed them. From that moment the Red Army, Trotsky's creation, also grew stronger. Tens of thousands of the hungry joined the Red Army in order to "have something to eat," and the military authorities tore the last morsel of bread from the mouths of the civilian population to maintain these mercenaries, who rescued Lenin's throne. Life in Petersburg became even more nightmarish than previously. The only bright spot in the darkness was the series of great events in the West: the cessation of war, the utter defeat of monarchist Germany, and the expected intervention of the Entente in Russian affairs. At the end of 1918, Petersburg awaited the arrival of English saviors, but the Allies were too busy healing the wounds of war at home and the intervention was delayed. And we in the "Northern Commune" were dying of hunger and cold, for not just bread but firewood had disappeared.² [. . .]

September 3

[. . .] For the time being, the reply to individual terror is fierce mass terror on the part of the Bolsheviks. In speeches at Uritskii's grave they were already calling for complete "extermination of the bourgeoisie and White Guard"; in newspapers there are hundreds of bloodthirsty resolutions calling for vengeance, for mass hangings and shootings without trial. Monstrous arrests are taking place here and in Moscow; they are seizing all the leading figures from the opposition parties. Here and in Moscow the English consulates were destroyed; during a search here, agents of the English government were killed, others were arrested. . . .

The intensified editorial work of *Jewish Antiquities* stretches on. . . . The uncertainty of the near future is terrifying. The noose of hunger is pressing against us. . . . With its plundering civil war the Bolshevik army has cut Petersburg off from all sources of food, and the vast city is dying. . . . In Samara a new government is being organized,³ a Constituent Assembly is being prepared . . .

September 4

Horrors. Mass executions. There is talk of several hundred executed "bourgeois" and anti-Bolsheviks, of piles of corpses outside the city. [. . .] There is alarm in the city. There have been searches and arrests at the homes of acquaintances. Everyone involved in political activity is afraid: during the night people may burst in and seize him. [. . .]

September 6

Something monstrous has occurred. It has been officially announced that a few days ago, in accordance with a resolution by worker-Bolsheviks concerning "merciless Red Terror," 512 "counterrevolutionaries and members of the White Guard," including ten Right SRs, were executed. The names of the executed, as is customary with Bolshevism's inquisitors, have not been published, and we do not even know who these martyrs are. On the other hand, a list was published of arrested hostages, who will be executed at the first assassination attempt on a Bolshevik. A motley list comprising surviving members of the House of Romanov, bankers, merchants, officers and little-known Right SRs (including a young man I know, the son of the late V. Berman, orphaned after the death of his father). The Commission for the Struggle against Counterrevolution declares "to be continued"; the list will grow. . . . Trotsky speaks of "blood and iron," like Bismarck. . . . It is strange that I do not experience personal terror in the face of this. After all, they may take me too, as a hostage from among the "White Guard" (although I never was one) and declare me guilty of hatred toward the new absolutism on the basis of this diary. I sometimes hide my precious diary among the books in my library as I did during the days of tsarist fury, in expectation of being searched. In those days I would have been threatened with exile to Siberia; now—with execution.

September 8, New Style (the second day of Rosh Ha-Shanah, when I became fifty-eight years old)

In view of the transition from the old calendar to the new, my old September 10 has lost its previous significance, and I have decided from now on to time the anniversary of my birth to coincide with the original Jewish date—the second day of Rosh Hashanah, when, according to my late mother, I appeared in the world. I spent this day as follows. In the morning: correcting proofs of the Pinkas (from Lithuania, for publication as a supplement to *Starina*). Then reading *Pravda,* with bloodthirsty speeches by Zinoviev and other Marats, who arouse the bestial instincts of the masses, along with resolutions by the Bolsheviks declaring all the White Guards, Mensheviks, and Right SRs to be "outside the law." . . . The murdered executioner Uritskii has been declared a saint, and the Tauride Palace, where he broke up the Constituent Assembly, will be called the Palace of Uritskii. As for Lenin—now well on the road to recovery—he has been elevated to nothing less than a deity: in his name people swear to destroy, to execute, to gun down. The Commission for the Struggle against Counterrevolution (that is, counter-Bolshevism) has been declared an institution dear to the people ("The people love this commission," Zinoviev arrogantly declared in his speech).

Having poisoned my soul with this reading, I went with Ida to dinner at Rosa Emanuil's in order to reminisce about the old days. But here too the horrifying sounds of the day burst in: a certain youthful ensign from our circle of acquaintances has been taken hostage in Moscow. . . . After dinner I went to see a staff writer from *Jewish Antiquities* who lives nearby (Dr. I. Tuvim) with a corrected proof, and purposely turned at the corner of Troitskaia Street and Izmailovskii Prospect, where I glanced at our former abode from the years 1883–1884. . . .

September 11

[. . .] A decree on replacing current apartment building committees with "committees of the poor" (*kombedy*) composed of Bolshevik tenants, who are supposed to be settled in "bourgeois" apartments for purposes of "observation"—that is, spying. They are not supposed to permit gatherings or meetings in these apartments or even the purchase of essential items from "bag men." And because in the absence of a bread ration card we all buy from these peddlers—flour at 12 roubles a pound and other items—this means dooming tens of thousands of families to death by starvation.

Visitors during the afternoon. . . . From all directions, a single moan: we must flee from the Petersburg slaughterhouse, from hunger and bullets, arrest and robbery. . . . But where to? How on earth can I tear myself away from that which keeps me alive: writing, thoughts, books? The minute I abandon my apartment they will install hooligans who will destroy my entire life's work. . . . Should one save one's life at the cost of that life's meaning?

September 15 (eve of Yom Kippur)

I have just finished writing the "Bibliography" for the volume of *Jewish Antiquities* and now I am composing a wordless prayer: "Who from the sword and who from hunger?"[4] How close are the alternatives: death by hunger or by the bullet of a Red Army soldier! [. . .]

September 16 (Yom Kippur, evening)

Since morning the sky has been casting its gloom over this criminal land. I got dressed after noon, for the first time in autumn clothes, and went to the Botanical Garden. I sat down on a bench, looked at the fallen leaves. . . . I thought: amidst hunger, cold, and Red Terror I am still managing to live somehow, as long as the link with the past, the integrity of my soul, is not severed. But if they burst into my abode and take away the fruit of many years of labor—the manuscript of *History* [*of the Jewish People*]—if they seize my diaries of thirty-three years, they will take away a part of my soul; they will destroy both the meaning and the integrity of my life . . . I made my way back through the lime-tree alleys on the bank of the Neva and thought: Should I leave or stay? Should I tear myself away from the altar and save my life or remain at my post and save my soul, preserving the thread of the past?

I listened to a visitor who had arrived from Ukraine, the Don, Belorussia; he told me how people are living there under the Germans, Hetmen, and Cossack chieftains. It is sad everywhere. . . .

September 22

[. . .] The arrival of Lur'e, the secretary of our committee (of the Historical Society) interrupted my work. In his capacity as a "bourgeois" (he receives a salary from us, which currently is not enough to buy bread) he was recently dragged off to "labor conscription," to load ammunition onto railway cars. Along with a whole group of intellectuals he worked for half a day without food or even a sip of tea and returned home ill.

The food problem is more and more threatening. . . . Sometimes there is not enough bread, sometimes potatoes, milk, butter, sugar, firewood. Ida goes to the market and often returns empty-handed. I chop wood chips for the small portable hearth and help as best I can. The bag man comes with flour, potatoes, milk—we buy at an unbelievable price, spend several hundred roubles each time, and in a few days we will again be without provisions. Soon our savings (monetary) will be exhausted, and then. [. . .]

October 8

Something immense is approaching. After its withdrawal from the war, the defeat of the Turks in Palestine, and the victorious march of the Allies on the French front, Germany has sued for peace. Both it and Austria already agree to Wilson's entire program. . . .

The world, holding its breath, awaits the response of the Allies. . . . Is it possible that the end of the world war is approaching, a war that overturned our entire life? Is it possible that a peaceful culture will be reborn, that militarism will be crushed, that a League of Nations will arise—everything that we have been dreaming of? Is it possible that after the reconciliation of peoples the savage civil war in Russia will also come to an end, and the crusaders of the revived civilization will come to pacify the beasts who have donned socialist masks? Is it possible that soon we will regain elementary civil rights, security of the individual, inviolability of homes, freedom of speech and of assembly? Is it possible that soon we will stop going hungry? [. . .]

October 16

In order that I be transferred from the third category of bread ration cards to the first, which now gives the right to three-eighths of a pound instead of one-sixteenth (owing to a new decree on teachers at institutions of higher education), Ida and I for several days now have been making the rounds of offices to get certifications, signatures, seals. In order to receive, by doctor's prescription, a pound of dry crusts and half a pound of cooking fat, poor Ida has to stand in dozens of lines in the cold, and then an entire day in the kitchen at the small hearth (there is no wood for the stove) to concoct something from the meager provisions to satisfy our hunger. We chop old furniture into wood chips for the hearths, for there is no firewood, and besides, it is so expensive that it is cheaper to chop up a bookcase and use the wood chips for heating (200–250 roubles for a *sazhen*[5] of firewood). [. . .]

Just now I was reading issues of the Jerusalem newspaper *Khadashot me-ha-Arets*[6] from August of the current year, which made their way here by way of Stockholm. In Palestine, under English occupation, things are joyful and calm. The foundation for the Jewish University on Mount Scopus[7] was laid with great ceremony. The organizer of the ceremonies was my old friend Mordechai ben Hillel Ha-Kohen[8] from Gomel' and Rechitsa. . . . I recalled distant times, before our present prison conditions. I had visions of a journey to Palestine in two or three years, when I will have finished the chief labor of my life, in fulfillment of the vow I made long ago. And who knows whether the historical homeland will not captivate me, whether the new university will not enthrall me, whether the song of Judea will not be a lullaby for the exhausted son of the dias-

pora? Perhaps I am fated to die there, in the place where I would like to begin to live if I could have a second life. . . . These visions give so much warmth under the vaults of a cold prison. [. . .]

November 11 (noon, in the middle of work)

Finally: revolution in Germany. The abdication of Wilhelm II. The pillar of monarchism and militarism has collapsed. In Bavaria there is a republic. In several places there are councils of workers and soldiers according to the Russian model, if one can believe the telegrams of the Bolshevik newspapers. A new world is being created in torments. The greatest war should have called forth the greatest revolution. But will it proceed by a normal path from monarchy to democratic republic, and not to an anarchic-communist regime or to a class-based dictatorship as in Russia? One does not want to believe that Europe has grown savage and imitated the dark mass of its eastern half. We are waiting for something else: democratic Western Europe will set out to liberate Russia from the grip of anarchy. . . .

December 13 (evening)

The story of one day. I got up early in the morning, got dressed, covered myself in a coat, galoshes and hat (in our rooms it is 7 degrees above zero)[9] and sat down at my desk. I wrote with numb fingers about the Dominicans and the French inquisition of the thirteenth century. At ten o'clock I had a bite to eat, took a look at the newspaper, and went to the firewood department of the regional council for a coupon for firewood. I found myself in line with hundreds of people, stretching along the steps of the back staircase of a huge apartment building (on Kamennoostrovskii Prospect), from the ground floor to the fourth. For two hours I stood in this thicket of unhappy, distressed people and along with hundreds of others I left with nothing: we did not get our turn, and an employee announced from an upper landing that they would not be giving out any more coupons today. He told us to come tomorrow, but many people have already been coming for several days. If only the "authorities" had heard the curses directed at them! The occasion could not pass, of course, without some hissing directed at "Jews, who have taken over everything." . . . I arrived home defeated, after buying a pound and a half of bread along the way with the recovered bread card that had been lost recently. In the courtyard of our building there was both happiness and grief: an acquaintance had done us a good turn and sent a cart with a *sazhen'* and a half of firewood, which he had bought for us for 450 roubles, but there was no one to carry it to the shed and pile it up. It was dangerous to leave it in the courtyard: people will pilfer in an instant, given the hunger for firewood. The building attendants came to the rescue: for 20 roubles they carried it to the shed. Ida and I took turns guarding it in the freezing weather, having quickly eaten supper in the meanwhile. The day drew to a close. Weary, I set about my work, which had been interrupted in mid-word. I finished writing the paragraph and now I am sitting and thinking. We are "fortunate": there will be something with which to heat the kitchen (I myself carried up several heavy loads of wood), and poor Ida will not freeze or run around to other people's kitchens to ask permission to place a pot on the stove or to bake something. The kitchen is secured for two months, but not the building's central heating: we are freezing and exhausted from cold more than from hunger. [. . .]

NOTES

1. [*Cheka* (Russ., *Chrezvychainaia komissiia*, Extraordinary Commission), first of a number of Soviet state security organizations, established in December 1917 and succeeded by the NKVD, OGPU, and KGB.—Trans.]

2. [The Northern Commune (short for Union of Communes of the Northern Region) was a Soviet administrative unit established in April 1918 and abolished in February 1919.—Trans.]

3. [On June 8, 1918 the city of Samara, in the southeastern part of European Russia, was taken by the Committee of Members of the Constituent Assembly (Komuch) with armed support of the Czechoslovak Legion. They aimed for a democratic counter-revolution during the Russian Civil War and fought against the Bolsheviks. The city fell to the Red Army in October 1918.—Trans.]

4. [A reference to the "Unetaneh tokef" prayer recited on Rosh Hashanah and Yom Kippur, which includes the lines "who will die at his predestined time and who before his time; who by water and who by fire, who by sword, who by beast, who by famine, who by thirst, who by upheaval, who by plague, who by strangling, and who by stoning."—Trans.]

5. [The *Sazhen'*, an old Russian unit of length, is equivalent to roughly seven feet.—Trans.]

6. [*Khadashot me-ha-Arets* (News from the Land [of Israel]), a Hebrew daily newspaper published in Jerusalem since 1919 as successor to a weekly of the same name produced by the British military government. Since December 1919 it has been published under the name *Ha-Arets*, and is currently one of Israel's main newspapers.—Trans.]

7. [The cornerstone for the Hebrew University on Mount Scopus (Har ha-Tsofim) was laid on July 24, 1918. It was opened seven years later on April 1, 1925.—Trans.]

8. [Markus G. Kagan.—Trans.]

9. [7 degrees Celsius corresponds to 44.6 degrees Fahrenheit.—Trans.]

Translated by Benjamin Nathans.

Other works by Dubnov: *Jewish History: An Essay in the Philosophy of History* (1903); *History of the Jews in Russia and Poland: From the Earliest Times to the Present Day*, 3 vols. (1916–1920); *History of the Jews*, 5 vols. (1967–1973).

Jacob Mazeh
1859–1924

Jacob Mazeh was born in Mogilev, Belorussia, to an observant family and studied at Moscow University. He wrote for *Ha-Melits* and founded the Bene Tsiyon society in Moscow, and also visited Palestine. Mazeh was appointed state rabbi of Moscow in 1893. He publicly defended Mendel Beilis during the 1913 blood-libel trial. Following the Bolshevik Revolution, Mazeh remained dedicated to Zionism and the Hebrew language.

A Conversation with Gorky
1936 (posthumous)

On Sunday, 6 Tammuz, 5681 [July 12, 1921], I visited the author Maxim Gorky [. . .] and I told him the alarming news that had come to me from various cities about the horrible pogroms that had occurred in recent days, and when I described the cruelty of the persecutors of Israel to him, his eyes ran with tears. [. . .]

The beginning of our conversation was about the terrible famine in Samara and other cities, and Gorky told me that the Patriarch Tikhon had written an appeal to America, England, and other countries, to be merciful to those dying of hunger and send food and clothing, and he asked me to write such an appeal. I said to him:

[. . .] I fear that the act might be thought of as a sin in the eyes of the Soviet government, and that I might bring upon myself and my nation a curse and not a blessing, since any kind of relation at all with the Entente arouses suspicion. And there is proof because the Zionist Committee, whose eyes and heart are for the Land of Israel alone, was banned about three months ago because of suspicions of good relations with the Entente. Not only that, how could I sign such a petition, at a time when Jewish blood is being spilled in Russia, and all the orphans and widows who remain need great support, and it is entirely impossible to obtain it from abroad, as happened in 1903 after the pogrom in Kishinev and the pogroms that followed it? Now that assistance, too, has ceased, because even the support that was received from America for the victims of the pogroms was not delivered to the Jewish public. [. . .] In such a time, can a person sign a petition regarding the general disaster and need of the Russian people, since everyone knows in advance that this help will not reach the Jewish people? After all, the Patriarch is asking for mercy for his brethren, the sons of his nation and religion, and for whom should I ask mercy? [. . .]

My interlocutor was very moved and said to me with a great sigh:

I confess, that the Russian nation is a matter of hell and destruction, and no person can contemplate it, its history, and its acts of cruelty, without despair. And the people of our generation, who strove for the freedom of the Russian people and its liberation from servitude and poverty, those who shed their blood and gave up their lives for it, appear to me like a young man who in all the ardor of his youth strives to find a way to the heart of a beloved maiden, and after he has succeeded in attracting her heart to him, he finds her damaged and polluted from head to foot. Woe to us and to our generation! And with an open heart I tell you, that the situation of your nation is also a situation of "beyond despair" in my eyes because the persecutions against it have reached their greatest height, and, since you mentioned the Crusades, I must comment to you that in our day there is a campaign of the writers of all the nations in the world in all the languages to sow hatred in the hearts of the multitude and to arouse them to join together in order to remove the Jewish people from the world. [. . .]

People always call the pogroms by some other name, and they cover up the concept of pogrom with various words. [. . .] In these days they also call the pogroms by an essentially counterfeit name: *Banditism.* What is this "banditism"? Murder for the sake of robbery? Does a robber distinguish between nation and nation or between religion and religion? Was it the custom of pirates to fall upon a ship and differentiate among the passengers: Jews, to the right; non-Jews, to the left—and to kill only the Jews and to plunder only their property even if they are rags, and to leave golden treasures in the hands of non-Jews? Should this be called banditism? Is it not a pogrom! Riots particularly against the Jews. And when the Jewish people demands of the government that it save them from their murderers, their

robbers, their rapists, they are answered: "What do you want? We are fighting vigorously against banditism." True, any bandit is likely to make a pogrom, but not everyone who takes part in pogroms is a bandit. And in any case, it is clear as day that the bandits do not mix the pogroms with their robbery. This truly leads to despair. Self-defense is forbidden. To flee is forbidden. Emigration from the land that sheds their blood leads to punishments, "according to law," and when they need to use the signature of some Jew to help the hungry in some places in the country, they speak to him in the name of "general decency" and say to him: "Come and sign." They silence his appeal regarding the torture of his people, and they say to him: Raise your voice about the distress of others. [. . .]

I heard your words with attention said Gorky, and I no longer dare to ask you to sign the petition, because you are absolutely right. We are living in amoral times, the destruction of an entire people is thought of as a trivial matter, which cannot be dealt with. And nothing can stand before politics. [. . .]

After he promised to speak to Lenin himself and to ask him to give me an interview, and he promised me to report his answer to me, I rose from my seat and bid him goodbye.

Ten days passed, and I received no answer. Be that as it may, a deep impression remained in my heart that Gorky was full of despair about the future of my people, and even more about the future of his people; he usually did not express his political attitude explicitly, but his tears, when he remembered the victims of famine of the good people of Russia and the victims of the pogroms of the Jewish people these were "tears of opposition." [. . .]

When he saw me out, he said to me that if I had any problem I could turn to him at any time and any hour. And thereupon we parted. [. . .]

Translated by Jeffrey M. Green.

Other works by Mazeh: *Zikhronot,* 4 vols. (1936).

Jacob Mazeh

Lunacharsky and Hebrew
1936 (posthumous)

During the summer of 5679 [1919] the government suddenly stopped supporting Tarbut and its schools, and after regaining our composure, we decided to address [Anatoly] Lunacharsky regarding this question. [. . .] I received a telegram from Yaroslavl addressed to me, saying: "Comrade Dolgorukov reported to me about your desire to meet with me, and I would be very pleased to meet you if you come to Yaroslavl." It was signed with his name in full: Commissar for Matters of Public Instruction [Enlightenment], Lunacharsky. Naturally I showed the telegram to Rodnitsky, and accordingly we immediately received a permit and also tickets to travel to Yaroslavl. [. . .] Since I was ill at that time, I also took my secretary with me, A. A. Zusmanovitz, and the three of us set out. On Thursday evening we left Moscow and on Friday morning we arrived in Yaroslavl. [. . .]

We looked for a hotel but couldn't find one. We wanted a place to drink tea, and we couldn't find that either. And when we got into the center of the city, we found a house, which once was, it seems, openly, a tavern, and now it had become a secret tavern, pretending to be a place where one drinks tea. We went in and found the proprietor, a man with a big belly, a "true" Russian, with murder in his eyes, sitting at a table, and when he saw the faces covered with the veil of Jewishness—he became very furious. But his commercial instincts wouldn't let him insult me, because he realized at last that in any case I wasn't asking him for money, but he would receive money from me. He asked me: What do you want? And when Rodnitsky and Zusmanovich told him that we wanted tea, he said: Go into the other room.

We went into that room, and it was full of smoke. I went back to the corridor and said to him, "Maybe there's a room without smoke?" And he answered me: "There is, but in Berdichev [a "classic" Jewish city in Ukraine]."

We wanted to leave the place immediately, but fatigue overcame us, and we stayed sitting there for a while, and already without asking us, they served us tea. Of course, that tea had neither taste nor smell. We rested for a while and paid whatever they asked, and I said to myself: This time I paid for pain, healing, and humiliation (that is: I thought of the repose as healing). [. . .]

To avoid wasting time, I went into a barber shop, which I had seen in a street, and the barber was a Jew, an exile from Brisk [Brest-Litovsk] in Liteh [today, Belarus], one of the exiles banished by Nikolai Nikolayevich, the chief general from the days of the old regime,

and he immediately called me by name, and I asked him, "Where do you know my name from, sir?"

He said to me: "According to your photograph.

"Are you not Jacob Isayevich Mazeh, and certainly you wish to have your hair cut in honor of the Sabbath and because of his honor the Minister Lunacharsky, to whom you have come."

Hearing those words, I was astonished, and at the same time I remembered what I had read in Sholem Aleichem's books, and even more what I had heard from his mouth, that the Jews have a well-developed sense of smell, and from a thousand miles away they sniff out every new person who enters their domain. I had my hair cut and went outside to walk to Lunacharsky through alleys and twisting paths, so that the people with "a sense of smell" wouldn't know where I was headed. And I almost managed the whole way. But at the entrance to the hotel I saw a lot of Jews standing in a line, and when I went in, they called out "Shalom" to me. [. . .] I understood that all my efforts had been in vain, and that these people had a "sense of smell," and they had acted cagily by not following my steps as I walked on my way, except to greet me upon my entry to the hotel. [. . .]

[When the hour came for the reception] I went into the "lord's" room—for that is what Jews are used to calling anyone in power. It was a splendid room, full of beds, with a desk at one end, and around it girls writing on machines [typewriters]. One of them, a very beautiful Armenian, with eyes burning like fire, met me with a smile floating on her lips, and asked:

"Have you come to see Anatoli Vasilievich? He's a little busy, and he'll come in half an hour."

She asked me to be seated and also gave me a local newspaper. In that newspaper I read the speech that Lunacharsky had given at a large assembly the day before. There he quoted the prophet Amos, whom he called a "communist," and in a general way he said: "All the prophets were communists in their day because it is impossible for any honest man not to be a communist," and with the clarity of his tongue he explained the justice of that system and its principles in a popular manner. Just as I finished the article, its author himself entered. He greeted me and sat opposite me. [. . .]

Then he asked me a question: "What is this about?" [. . .]

From my pocket I withdrew the telegram, which I had received from my friend, the activist H. Gissin of Mogilev, who was then in Gomel. It was a long telegram, in which he complained that they had closed the model Hebrew school in Gomel without any cause, only because the Hebrew language prevailed there. He concluded the telegram with this language: "The parents, the teachers, and the pupils appoint you to intercede with the Commissariat for Education to revoke the decree." Lunacharsky read the telegram and returned it to me, and he began to speak, and the Armenian girl was already tapping the machine: "Moscow." [. . .] "Telegraph urgently: By whom and when and according to what principles did they use repressive measures against the Hebrew school in Gomel?"

He immediately signed and said: "Send this telegram right away."

Then I began to speak to Lunacharsky about the whole matter at length. [. . .]

"You certainly know, sir, as the man who heads all the institutions of learning for the people in Russia, the great value of the Hebrew language in the world of science in general, and that there is no university in enlightened countries which does not support scholars in the discipline of the philology of this language, in the subjects of the poetry of its most ancient literature, which everyone admits is one of the most beautiful languages that the ancient world created, and that its literature is full of treasures of scholarly investigations in philosophy, theology, linguistics, and that all the greatest sages in the world from time immemorial have dealt with it no less than with the languages of Rome and Greece, and the sages of the nations of the world have written marvelous books about its language, its lexicons, and historical investigations. Is it possible that the Jewish people, which bears this language, would not make an effort to have its sons know it? [. . .]

"In this language all the Jews in the world pray, in this language they exchange letters with one another, in this language, I assure you, sir, our ancestors even kept their accounts, in this language they write all sorts of business documents, and many of them were used to speaking this language, and now has begun a time when this language is spoken about secular matters, and the aspiration is the inner aspiration of the nation, not a party matter, as they say, of the Zionists alone, *this is the aspiration of the entire nation.* And since the new law says explicitly that any group of no less than twenty-five people can start a school for all sorts of studies that they choose, and the state will support them—why should the lot of this language be worse than that of all the other languages? [. . .]"

Lunacharsky: "I don't know anyone who denies the value of the Hebrew language except Jewish communists, who share our opinions, and we cannot refrain from believing what they say, that the Hebrew language is a language of the bourgeoisie, and not the language of the people, and this is only a bourgeois or clerical ornament, and the schools for the people should be in the language of the people and not in the language of the people's history, and it seems to me, that this is the bone of contention. You think that this is the language of the people, and they come in the name of the people and deny it."

I: "I can promise your honor, that I am familiar in all its details with everything that is done in the inner life of my people, and I never heard any Jew when he was talking, say, 'The time has come to teach my son,' that he was not referring to the language I am speaking of, because he does not teach the dialect [*zhargon*, that is, Yiddish] at all, since he knows it anyway, and it is not regarded by him as something worth studying. And as for the bourgeoisie, let me say, and I can testify, that any bourgeois, or anyone who regards himself as worthy of being bourgeois in the future, does not teach his children the Hebrew language. He teaches them all the languages in the world except Hebrew, and only the children of the poor, the children of the masses, raised up all the Hebrew authors for the Jewish people, everyone who knows the Torah, all the scholars of Hebrew literature, and also all the great poets of our time, all of them are the sons of the streets of the poor and not the rich: And what will be the end of the matter? The dialect [Yiddish] will be forgotten from the mouths of their children, and they will not know the Hebrew language, and thus the Jewish people will be left without its national language."

Lunacharsky: "It's not such a great catastrophe if the Jewish people remains without a special language, but what you assert, that the Hebrew language is the language of the poor, this is entirely new in my eyes, though I now remember, that you have a poet named Bialik. Was he also from a poor home?"

I: "Not only poor, but the poorest of the poor. His ancestors' ancestors were poor, and not only Bialik but also all the other Hebrew authors, aside from a few exceptions that a boy could name, all of them came from the poor of the Hebrew nation."

Lunacharsky: "And was Sholem Aleichem also one of the poor?"

I: "He, at any rate was from the people who were called wealthy in their village, but it seems to me that any bourgeois would faint if he heard that his friends were wealthy like that. All the wealth of wealthy people like that lay in that they had a bit of bread every week and a slice of white bread, that is, on the Sabbath. It seems to me that the author Maxim Gorky, who is well versed in the life of 'rich' Jews of that kind, will testify to your honor that they were proletarians from birth to death."

Translated by Jeffrey M. Green.

Dov Ber Slutsky

1877-1955

Dov Ber Slutsky was a philologist, novelist and short-story writer, and publicist from Ukraine who wrote for *Der fraynd*. In Kiev he worked at the Institute for Yiddish Culture. After World War II, Slutsky moved to Birobidzhan. He was arrested by the Soviets in 1949 and died in Siberia.

Jewish Badkhonim-Actors
1936

Some decades ago Jewish *badkhonim*-actors [jesters] were still a very common phenomenon. Most of the time the *badkhn* was not only an entertainer improvising rhymes and funny sayings, but also an actor performing for an audience with all the actors' paraphernalia, makeup, costumes, etc.

Badkhonim-actors were not a local phenomenon. They were active in Kiev province, in Mogilev province, as well as other regions. Of course, the word *actor* was not used back then; these performers were called *marshelikes* or *badkhonim*.

Here I would like to cite examples of two types of *badkhonim*: a Litvak *badkhn* from Mogilev province, and a Polish *badkhn* from Kiev province. The words *Litvak* and *Polish* are not used as geographical terms here; it would be more precise to call them Polish or Belorussian and Volhynian.

I. Dovid Badkhn from Bober, Mogilev Province

[. . .] Bober was very tiny—it consisted of a few dozen houses, it was poor and limited to its *daled ames*, four cubits of space, like all other Polish small towns. But this town had all the religious functionaries nec-

essary to maintain Jewish religious life, including a *badkhn*.

Dovid the *badkhn* of Bober was forty-five years old. He looked no different from all the other Jews of Bober, except maybe for the fire in his eyes. Like every Jew, he wore a long caftan, had a long beard and side-locks. He was not much of a scholar but was a gentle, very pious man.

He lived with his family in Bober, but would travel around with a band of musicians, going to weddings. His task was that of all *badkhonim*: to perform the *kale bazetsn* and *zogn gramen*—compose and recite rhymes for the ceremony in which the bride is escorted to the bridal chair where she is veiled. But that was not the main attraction. Dovid *badkhn*'s main task was to entertain the wedding guests during the festive meal that took place after the wedding ceremony.

And on these occasions Dovid *badkhn* appeared quite differently—he would perform in disguise. At first he performed some hocus pocus such as pulling ribbons from his mouth, etc.; then, when the audience was already warmed up, together with them, he, Dovid *badkhn*, started to perform plays. Dovid *badkhn* did not improvise. He had several pieces—some his own, some written for him—that he presented everywhere. He went about this very seriously and with great enthusiasm.

The following pieces were the best-known and most beloved numbers in our neighborhood:

1. *A goy bay yidn af peysekh* [A Non-Jewish Guest for Passover]
2. *Der polyak* [The Pole]
3. *Der yerushalmi* [The Jew from Jerusalem]
4. *A tants mit Malanien* [A Dance with Malania]
5. *Biografye* [Biography]

His most popular show was *The Goy*.

Dovid *badkhn* would dress up as a Belorussian peasant: he would pull his shirt out from his trousers, roll up his beard, put a *manerke* [a Polish hat] on his head, *lapti* [bast shoes] on his feet, and he wrapped his legs all the way up to his knees, as was the custom of Belorussian peasants. Then he recounted how he, a Belorussian peasant, was a guest in a Jewish home for the Passover Seder and what he saw there.

If someone didn't know Dovid *badkhn* he would have thought he was a real ruffian. He looked very much like a real peasant—his gait, his movements, and his Belorussian pronunciation. That's how he told his stories, and the audience would explode with laughter. This was a humorous, artistic monologue that reflected with true realism and artifice the naïveté, crudeness, primitiveness, and ignorance of the peasant. [. . .]

One time Dovid *badkhn* almost suffered a mishap because of this act.

He attended a wedding that took place in the tavern of a *yishuvnik*, a village Jew. As is usual in villages, the tavern was full of peasants. When Dovid *badkhn* got onto a wagon in front of the tavern and started to perform *The Goy*, at first the peasants thought that he was really a peasant. But when they heard the monologue they realized that somebody was making fun of "one of them," a non-Jewish peasant. At that point they got up and approached the wagon—they wanted to beat up the performer. It was quite a job to save him from the beating. After that Dovid did not finish his performance as usual. [. . .]

About this the wagon driver said, *haynt hot er mekatser geven inem orl.*[1]

The second number was "A yunger sheygets tantst mit Malanien der shikse" [A Young Brat Dances with Malania, a non-Jewish Girl—*sheygets* and *shikse* are pejoratives.]

He would dress up as a peasant, cross his hands and stretch them out in front of him as if he were embracing Malania, and dance. He would start slowly and then dance more and more passionately, feverishly, until he was dancing like a fire, like a storm; at the same time he was singing ecstatically, with passionate love, like a real *sheygets.*

Hey, hey tukatshiki
Hey, hey buraviki
Hey, hey Malania, hey, hey Malania!

His face would turn red and he would start drooling, and then dance even more feverishly, like a whirlwind.

In general he was a good dancer, dancing with momentum.

"DER POLYAK—A YOYRED" [THE POLE—AN IMPOVERISHED MAGNATE]

In this piece Dovid would dress up as a Polish nobleman, a little down at the heels but still with honor, like an impoverished Polish magnate; he would take two whiskers from his wide beard and twist them so that they didn't fall back again and become a thick broom; he would hold the two tips with his two hands; under his nose he would attach a large Polish moustache and would recite verse and sing in Polish about the miserable situation of an impoverished nobleman. This was a satire of the rich nobility and the impoverished noblemen. After each verse he would let out a Mephistophelian "ha-ha-ha":

Kto pieniadze ma(je)
W karecie jezdzi
Kto pieniadze nie ma(je)
Ten pieszko chodzi—

He who has money
Travels by carriage
He who does not
Goes on foot

"BIOGRAFYE" [BIOGRAPHY]

Dovid *badkhn* would tell the story of his life in a nonsensical style.

In a very funny way he would tell how his father gave birth to him, how he was raised, went to heder, etc. As he told the story he would move into a singing voice, a *recitativo*, the tone of Purim players. He would demonstrate how he learned *gemore*, Talmud, in a singsong:

"Eeboiee lehu ["they asked"—Aramaic]," the yeshiva students asked a question, and Dovid would ask questions, talk nonsense and make fun of *pilpul* [casuistry]; the audience was generally rolling with laughter; even the Hasidim laughed.

He had a show imitating a Jew from Jerusalem, a pious Hasid. He would make fun of everyone, and the wedding guests enjoyed his performance very much. True, these numbers were not so popular among the *kleykoydesh* [clergy], religious. [. . .]

He also used to imitate how non-Jews accompany the dead:

Akh, tatutshka, ti moy [Russian, "O, my father"].

Surely, he must have had other numbers, too, but those did not survive. There must still be some old Jews in Bober who still remember something about Dovid *badkhn.* [. . .]

III. Court Jesters of the [Hasidic] Rebbes

Some rebbes had their own merrymakers-jesters [*badkhonim-leytsonim*], court jesters [*hoyfletsn*]. One of them was Peysekh-Eli with the nickname Pudele at the Lubavitcher court. Pudele was from Bobruisk, he was a learned man and a *badkhn*; he was invited to perform at wealthy people's weddings, he was a distinguished *badkhn*. He would tell jokes at the rebbe's court, at the rebbe's *tish*.[2]

Sender *badkhn* was a court jester, too, but of a somewhat lower grade, even though he was also a very famous *badkhn* and he, too, was often invited to perform at wealthy people's weddings. Sender was a large man with a considerable belly and a thick neck; he had rich clothes, and a gold watch chain hung on his chest.

At the weddings of Hasidic rebbes their *badkhonim* would come together and have a contest in front of the rebbes.

At one such wedding the two famous rival *badkhonim*, Pudele and Sender, got into a duel. This is what happened:

The Lubavitcher rebbe sat at the head of the table. When the guests began to beg him to "say something," he answered:

"Let Pudele say something today."

Pudele replied:

"You think, rebbe, that you know much more than I, so I will surely be ashamed to speak in front of you. But you are wrong, I am not ashamed. I will speak as I can.

"The following question arises: as is well known, Hasidic Jews used to live very simply in the olden days. They themselves were simple people, and everything in their homes was simple. They had simple tables, simple chairs. Today's Hasidim behave like lords and live like noblemen, with all their worldly pleasures. The question arises, rebbe, why is that?"

The rebbe answered:

"What do I know? You answer the question."

"I will tell you. You probably saw people bring a rooster to the market. May it be the biggest and most beautiful rooster in the world, how much will people pay for it? Twenty kopecks, maybe twenty-five. But then a painter comes and brings the picture of a rooster to the market, a painted, imitation-rooster that is painted so well that it looks like a real rooster, not an imitation; he is about to spread his wings and crow, he is made so artistically. How much do you think people will pay for this artificial rooster? They will pay 25 or 50 [roubles], and maybe even more. It is the same with Hasidic Jews. Once upon a time they were real, true Hasidim, and they lived a simple life. Today's Hasidic Jews are imitations, and therefore they put themselves higher, value themselves more."

The Lubavitcher rebbe laughed out loud. Upon this, Peysekh-Eli said:

"It is very interesting—whoever I tell this parable thinks that it is not about him."

"Eh, you have quite a sharp tongue," responded the Lubavitcher rebbe.

After that Sender got up onto a bench and started to rhyme about Peysekh-Eli, twisting his words and making fun of his *pilpul*. (Peysekh-Eli would engage in *pilpul* and always made things so complicated that one had to have a really sharp mind to understand it. This was a kind of *badkhones* for learned people.) Peysekh-Eli didn't say a word; he pretended that he hadn't heard anything, that it was not even worth listening to such ignorant talk. But when Sender finished, Pudele began to answer him. His answer was built on the letters of his name—it was an acrostic of "Sender badkhn." His entire *droshe* was carefully built; every word began with one of the eight letters of "Sender badkhn." He mocked and taunted the conceited, rich *badkhn*.

Peysekh-Eli *badkhn* published poems, too. One of his poems was *Der telegraf* (this is the poem that Moyshe Moreḥovski would later often perform). Shimen Dobin and his father Yankev both remember these published poems. This is how "The Telegraph" began,

Zog nor mir gotr
Makh mir klor,
Vos batayt es far a vor,
Stolbes shteyn gor, uav.

Tell me please,
Explain to me,
What does it really mean [that],
Poles are standing straight, etc.
(They could not guarantee complete accuracy.)

NOTES

1. [Pun that can mean both, "today he shortened the Non-Jew," referring to the monologue, as well as "today he made the life of non-Jews miserable." Another possibility is "today he circumcised the uncircumcised."—Eds.]

2. [Festive meal presided over by a Hasidic leader, attended by his followers.—Eds.]

Translated by Vera Szabó.

Other works by Slutsky: *Far erd, far frayhayt* (on the Bar Kokhba rebellion; 1991).

Jiří Langer

1894–1943

Born into an acculturated Prague merchant family and educated in Czech schools, Jiří Langer shocked his friends and family when, in the summer of 1913, he settled in Belz (eastern Galicia) at the court of the Belzer rebbe to immerse himself fully in the life of what he considered authentic Judaism. In 1918, he left the Belz court and, after studying at the Hebrew Pedagogical Institute in Vienna for several months, returned to Prague. He was part of the circle of Jewish intellectuals around Franz Kafka and Max Brod. In 1919, he began to publish articles in Hebrew, German, and Czech that combined his unique synthesis of Talmud, Kabbalah, Hasidism, Freudian theory, and European literature. His Hebrew poetry, which drew on medieval liturgical poetry, was daring in its blatantly homosexual references. In 1939, he escaped from Nazi-occupied Prague to the Land of Israel, after which he wrote almost exclusively in Hebrew. He was the brother of the well-known Czech writer František Langer.

A Youth from Prague among the Chassidim
1937

Scenes from everyday life are scarcely to be found in these pages. Rather you will feel that you have been transported for a while to some far-off, exotic country where different flowers grow and different stars shine, to some primeval age in which reality was a dream and a dream was reality. [. . .]

It is an impassable road to the empire of the Chassidim. The traveller who pushes his way through the thick undergrowth of virgin forests, inexperienced and inadequately armed, is not more daring than the man who resolves to penetrate the world of the Chassidim, mean in appearance, even repellent in its eccentricity.

Only a few children of the West have accomplished this journey, hardly as many—when I come to think of it—as there are fingers on the hand that writes these lines.

One summer's day in 1913, a nineteen-year-old youth, brought up like all the youth of his time in the dying traditions of the pre-war generation, left Prague inspired by a secret longing which even now after the passage of so many years he still cannot explain to himself, and set out for the east, for strange countries.

Had he a foreboding of what he was losing on that day?

European civilization with its comforts and achievements, its living successes called careers? Had he a foreboding that his soul would no longer be capable of feeling poetry which up to that time he had been so fond of quoting, that, from the first moment when he heard the rhythms of the Chassidic songs, all the magic charms of music would be swamped once and for all, and all beautiful things which his eye had ever conceived would in the future be half hidden by the mystic veil of the knowledge of good and evil?

He hardly suspected that, at the very moment when he believed he had reached his goal, the most impassable part of his journey was only beginning. For the gate to the empire of the Chassidim never opens suddenly for anyone. It is closed by a long chain of physical and spiritual suffering. But he who has once looked inside will never forget the riches he has seen.

The rulers of this empire are hidden from the eyes of the world. Their miraculous deeds and all-powerful words are only, as it were, of secondary importance—they are merely the hem of the veil in which their being is wrapped, while their faces are turned away from us towards the distant calm of the Absolute. Only a faint reflection of their souls falls on our too material shadows. Yet, even today, years afterwards, these shapes haunt me one after the other. Not only those I knew personally but also those I have heard so much about and read about in the old Hebrew books; they rise again before me in all their greatness and strength. I feel overcome. Something compels me to take up my pen and faithfully write down everything as best I can.

It is a Friday afternoon. The small town of Belz, the Jewish Rome, is preparing to welcome the Sabbath.

Small towns in eastern Galicia have all had the same character for centuries. Misery and dirt are their characteristic outward signs. Poorly clad Ukrainian peasant men and women, Jews wearing side-whiskers, in torn caftans, rows of cattle and horses, geese and large pigs grazing undisturbed on the square. Belz is distinguished from other places only by its famous synagogue, its no less famous House of Study and the large house belonging to the town rabbi. These three buildings enclose the square on three sides. They are simply constructed. But in this poor, out-of-the-way region of the world they are truly memorable. Belz has somewhat more than three thousand inhabitants, half of whom are Jews.

It is a long summer afternoon. There are still six or seven hours before dusk, when the Sabbath begins and even the lightest work is strictly forbidden. In spite of this, the shops are already shut, the tailors are putting away their needles, and the casual labourers—wearing side-whiskers like the rest—their hoes and spades. The housewives in the cottages are adding the last touches to their preparations for the festival.

The men hasten to the baths. After a steam bath we dive—always several of us at the same time—into a small muddy swimming-pool, a *mikve*, or special ritual bath. As though in mockery of all the rules of hygiene, a hundred bodies are "purged" from the spirit of the working day. The water, like all the water in Belz, smells of sulphur and petroleum. . . .

Although everybody is in a tearing hurry on this day, the whole community already knows that a *bocher*, or young lad, has come to Belz all the way from Prague. A hundred questions are fired at me from every side. I am embarrassed because I do not understand a single word. I have never heard "Yiddish" spoken before, that bizarre mixture of mediaeval German and Hebrew, Polish and Russian. It was only later that I gradually began to learn it.

The Sabbath candles are already lit in the rabbi's house. I enter with the other guests—there is a long queue of them—to greet the saint for the first time. He has been told that I am the lad from Prague; indeed they have told him a very wonderful thing—that I have succeeded in plaiting (in the prescribed fashion, of course) four fringes to my *Leib-zidakl*, or vest, with my own hands. For this work of art he calls me to him once again. Once again he shakes my hand, this time lingeringly, and regards me kindly. He looks at me with only one eye. The other eye is blind. It seems to me that a ray of light shines from his seeing eye and pierces me to the heart.

He is a sturdy, tall, old man, with broad shoulders and an unusual, patriarchal appearance, dressed in a caftan of fine silk, wearing, like all the other men, a *shtreimel*, a round fur hat worn on the Sabbath, on his head, round which hang thirteen short sable tails of dark brown colour. (On weekdays, he wears a *spodek* which is a tall, heavy velvet cap, worn by rabbis, similar to a grenadier's cap.)

Such is the welcome the youth from Prague receives from Rabbi Yissochor Ber Rokach—may his memory be blessed—the grandson of the holy Rabbi Sholem and perhaps the only person still living who can remember the old man. He addresses me in a kindly voice. I realize that he is asking me about Prague. Many years ago he

was there with his father, to pray in the Old-New Synagogue and to visit the grave of his famous ancestor, the Great Rabbi Loev.

The spacious Belz synagogue has meanwhile filled with people. There are a hundred lighted candles. In a way the interior reminds me of the Old-New Synagogue in Prague. The men, for the most part tall and well-built, old and young, await the arrival of the rabbi, talking quietly among themselves. In contrast to their weekday appearance, they are all absolutely clean. Their festive caftans of black silk reach down to the ground. On their heads the older ones wear *shtreimels*, which smell of the perfumed tobacco they carry in their tobacco pouches. Some are from Hungary, others from far away—from Russia. Owing to the bad state of the roads they have journeyed for weeks on end to get to Belz, and it may be that they will not be staying there more than a single day. The next day, Sunday, they will set out again on the wearisome journey home. Next Sabbath others will come in their place.

Dusk is already well advanced when the rabbi enters the synagogue. The crowd quickly divides, to let him pass. Perhaps the waters of the Red Sea once divided in the same way before Moses.

With long, rapid strides he makes straight for the *bimah*, or reading desk, and the strange Chassidic service begins.

"*O give thanks unto the Lord, for He is good; for His mercy endureth for ever.*"

These words from Psalm 107 are used every Friday by the Chassidim when they greet the coming Sabbath. So it was ordained by the holy Baal-Shem when he was delivered out of the hands of pirates on his abortive journey to the Holy Land.

"*O give thanks unto the Lord, for He is good; for His mercy endureth for ever.*"

It is as though an electric spark has suddenly entered those present. The crowd, which till now has been completely quiet, almost cowed, suddenly bursts forth in a wild shout. None stays in his place. The tall black figures run hither and thither round the synagogue, flashing past the lights of the Sabbath candles. Gesticulating wildly, and throwing their whole bodies about, they shout out the words of the Psalm. They knock into each other unconcernedly, for all their cares have been cast aside; everything has ceased to exist for them. They are seized by an indescribable ecstasy.

Do I dream?—I have never seen anything like this before! Or maybe I have? . . . Have I perhaps been here before? . . Everything is so peculiar, so incomprehensible!

"O give thanks unto the Lord! . . . whom He hath redeemed from the hand of the enemy; and gathered them out of the lands, from the east, and from the west, from the north, and from the south."

The voice of the old man at the *bimah* is heard clearly above all the rest. It expresses *everything*—in immense, joyous humility, and at the same time in infinitely sad longing, as though it would flow into the Infinite, as though the king's son, after being cast out for six days, were returning to face his royal Father. With deep sobs he does penance for our sins.

"They wandered in the wilderness in a solitary way; they found no city to dwell in. Hungry and thirsty, their soul fainted in them."

At this moment the power of the saint's prayers brings deliverance to the souls of those who for their great sins have found no peace after death, and been condemned to wander through the world. The *sparks* of the holy Wisdom of God, which fell into Nothingness when God destroyed the mysterious worlds that preceded the creation of our world, these sparks are now raised from the abyss of matter and returned to the spiritual Source from which they originally came. [. . .]

The old man at the *bimah* raises his right hand as though to bless an unseen stranger. It is as though healing balsam flows from his quivering fingers.

"They that go down to the sea in ships, that do business in great waters. He raiseth the stormy wind which lifteth up the waves thereof. They mount up to the heaven, they go down again to the depths. They stagger like a drunken man, and are at their wits' end. Then they cry unto the Lord in their trouble, and He bringeth them out of their distresses. Then they are glad because they be quiet; so He bringeth them unto a haven of hope. Oh that men would praise the Lord for His goodness and for His wonderful works to the children of men! . . . Come then, Beloved, come to meet thy Bride, let us hasten to greet the Sabbath! . . ."

The old man throws himself about as though seized by convulsions. Each shudder of his powerful body, each contraction of his muscles is permeated with the glory of the Most High. Every so often he claps the palms of his hands together symbolically.

The crowd of the devout swirls and streams, hums and seethes like molten lava. Suddenly, as though at a word of command, all remain with their faces towards the west, towards the entrance of the synagogue, bow-ing their heads in expectation. It is at this moment that the invisible Queen of the Sabbath comes in, and brings to each of us a priceless heavenly gift: a second, new, festive *soul.*

"Come in peace, oh crown of the Lord, in the joy and exultation within the true ones of the chosen people! Come, oh Bride, come, oh Bride, come, oh Bride, Sabbath Queen!"

Once again we raise our heads.

"Come, Beloved, come to meet thy Bride. . . ."

The service ends. The ecstasy is over, the mystic vision has melted. Gone is the ecstasy. Now we are again in this world. But the whole world has been made sublime. Joy sparkles in the people's eyes. There is a festive, carefree atmosphere—the peace of the Queen Sabbath.

We walk past the saint in single file and wish him "good Sabbath!"

How hungry we all are!—That is because of the "second soul" that comes on the Sabbath. . . . We hasten to the inns to have a quick meal, so as to be in time at the saint's table. The stars have long since come out in the deep sky above the Ukrainian steppe. They are large like oranges.

The women are not in the synagogue. Their duty is to light the sacred Sabbath candles at home and wait for the return of their husbands and sons. They do not come out till the Saturday morning. We run into groups of them on the square—wearing traditional costumes in which the predominant colours are green, yellow and white.

Let us not look at them too closely—neither the old women in their aprons and hoods, nor the girls, fair and dark, bare-headed! They might wrongly interpret our attention, and that would cause no small scandal!

. . . On weekdays I spend most of my time at the *Bes Hamidrash,* or House of Study. It is open day and night for all who thirst after knowledge. The high shelves round the walls are stuffed full of books from the floor to the ceiling. The tables are littered with a jumbled mass of folios. Anyone may take out any book he likes and study in the *Bes Hamidrash* whenever he wishes. Here of course there are only holy, theological Hebrew books. A devout man would not touch any other. Even to know a single Latin or Russian letter is an indelible stain upon the soul. I sit and study the books from morning till evening, leaving them only for a short while to go to evening prayers or meals. Yet even the nights are not made for rest but—as the Talmud says—for the study of the Law of God. Spiteful insects remind me of this impressively enough as soon as I lie down. It is forbidden to kill insects. I already know that it would be a sin, so I prefer to go to the House of Study. I either study or listen to someone else, in another corner, reading aloud to himself in a drawling, plaintive chant. The *Shames*, or caretaker, hands us round candles. We hold the lighted candles in our hands so as not to fall asleep over our studies.

One afternoon I dive into the ritual bath in the same way as before prayer, for on this day I am going to the saint with my *kvitel*. A *kvitel* is a small piece of paper on which one of the saint's clerks writes the name of the supplicant and the name of his mother—not his father!—the supplicant's place of origin and, in a few concise words, the substance of what he is coming to ask of God. The Chassidim, it must be explained, do not bring their petitions to the saint by word of mouth but in writing. On my *kvitel* are written the words: "Mordecai ben Rikel mi-Prag, hasmodoh be-limud ve-yiras shomayim," which means that I am asking God "that I may persevere in my studies and in the fear of God." Not one word more. That was how the Chassidim advised me to write it. The saint's entrance hall and room are already crowded—in Belz it is always crowded—with scores of supplicants, mostly women. Some come to ask the saint to intercede with God for success in their business, others for recovery from an illness, others for advice for or against a marriage. The needs of the Chassidim are many and varied, and only *he*, the saint, can satisfy them through his intercession with the Most High. After reading some of the petitions, the saint asks for details before beginning to pray or give advice. He reads some petitions with obvious displeasure, especially those asking for cures. He scolds the supplicant and tells him to go to a doctor. But he wishes him a speedy recovery. Some bring a *matbeya*, that is, a coin which the saint will endow with secret power and which can then be used as a *kameo*, or amulet. The saint places the coin on the table and draws three circles round it. He does so with obvious reluctance. But once the coin has been consecrated by the saint's hand, the supplicant receives it back with an expression of radiant joy on his face. Besides the *kvitel*, we place a *pidyen* on the saint's table; this is a small sum of money according to one's means. The saint is *in duty bound* to ac-

cept gifts. This custom was instituted by the holy Baal-Shem, and it has a metaphysical background. When the saint intercedes with God on behalf of us unworthy people, the Lord asks him: "Of what importance is this sinner to you? Have you any obligation towards him, dearly beloved son?" And the saint can reply to God: "Yes, I have an obligation towards him. He has assisted me and my family." Our money offering is thus the only link, mean as it is, between us and the saint; it is the necessary prerequisite for our prayers to be heard. Hence the saint accepts gifts. But he returns the gifts of poor people immediately. From declared unbelievers he will not take any gifts at all. The devout who live outside Belz send their petitions and contributions to the saint's office by post, or if the matter is urgent, by telegram. The supplicant obtains relief as soon as the clerk unsticks the telegram even though the saint has not yet received the remittance. Those who come to Belz from Hungary kiss the saint's hand. The Poles do not. I am last in the queue. The saint reads my *kvitel* with undisguised delight. When I come out of his room, the Chassidim are waiting for me outside, to wish me luck: "Git gepoilt!"—"Well done!"

When the moon is full, the saint cures mental maladies. The people stand in a sad queue in his room while the saint pores over the Talmud by the light of large candles. I once knew a girl who was completely cured of melancholia in this way.

The saint never looks on the face of a woman. If he must speak to women—as, when he receives a *kvitel*—he looks out of the window while he speaks. He does not even look at his own wife, a somewhat corpulent woman, but still beautiful. On a later occasion, when the holy man was alone with his wife, it was only natural that the lad from Prague should seize this rare opportunity of peeping through the keyhole when no one was watching. She had come to ask her husband's advice about their domestic worries, of which they had their full share. Even on this occasion the saint looked out of the window, with his face turned away from her, as though he were talking to a strange woman, not his wife. The Talmud tells of one devout man who did not notice that his wife had a wooden stump instead of a leg, until her funeral. . . . That man was a teacher. Thus far the Talmud.

From the window of the entrance hall to the saint's apartment one can see far out across the Ukrainian steppe. For miles round there is nothing but a flat plain, without a single tree or hill to be seen. It is a fen with a narrow path made of boards running across it. In the distance a small bridge leads into a barren little field; then the path leads on across the bog into the unknown. When I am weary of the House of Study, I cross this bridge and lie down in the little field. This is the only bit of nature where one can find spiritual refreshment in all this wilderness!

I can endure it no longer. This life of isolation from the rest of the world is intolerable. I feel disgusted with this puritanism, this ignorance, this backwardness and dirt. I escape. I travel back to my parents in Prague. But not for long. I must perforce return to my Chassidim.

One night I cannot sleep. I am lying down, facing the kitchen door, which looks towards the East. I have left the door ajar. I have just been reading some holy Hebrew book in the kitchen. The kitchen windows are open, open towards the East, the East where Belz lies at the end of a train journey of a few hours more than a day and a night. . . . It is useless for me to close my eyes to induce sleep. Suddenly I am dazzled by a bright light penetrating into my dark bedroom through the half-open door. What is it?—I know that I have put out the lamp, and there is no one in the kitchen. I stare at the light, and in the middle of it, a few steps in front of me, I can see quite clearly through the half-open door—*the saint of Belz!* He is sitting in his room at Belz looking fixedly at me. On his expressive countenance shines that barely recognizable, sublime smile of his, full of wisdom. I have no idea how long the apparition lasts, but it is long enough to shake me.

So I travel to Belz a second time, this time firmly resolved. I am no longer alone as on my first pilgrimage. This time I have a companion, a Prague lad like myself, who has also decided for Chassidism.

My vision of the saint of Belz that night was a great favour. So the Chassidim said when I told them about it. To behold a living saint from far away and, moreover, while still awake, is not indeed an absolutely isolated phenomenon among the Chassidim, but it is a greater expression of God's favour than, for instance, a conversation with someone who is dead or with the prophet Elijah.

Translated by Stephen Jolly.

Other works by Langer: *Die Erotic der Kabbala* (1923); *Piyyutim ve-shirei yedidut* (1929); *Talmud: ukázky a dějiny* (1938); *Meat tsori: shirim* (1943).

Elkhonen Zeitlin

1902–1942

Elkhonen Zeitlin was born in Rogachev (Russian Empire, today Belarus), the son of Hillel Zeitlin and younger brother of Aaron Zeitlin. Zeitlin settled in Warsaw in 1921 and was active in cultural, theatrical, and literary Jewish organizations. He was the coeditor of *Undzer ekspres* (Our Express), and contributed to Yiddish periodicals. His memoirs are an important testament to Jewish intellectual life in Warsaw. Like his father, Elkhonen died in the Warsaw ghetto.

With Spektor

1937

Mordkhe Spektor [1858–1925] was the "honorary chair" of the "Society of Gluttons and Drunkards." Though he had not been elected to this "post," everyone felt that Spektor was the singular candidate for this honorable mission. He, by his very nature and experience, was the uncrowned monarch of the "kingdom of the gluttons." And indeed, he ruled with an iron fist. Not only was he *king*, but also *ruler*. He was the leader in practice, but also its theoretical founder. His word was decisive for both those who worked in the kitchen and for those who ate from the kitchen. He, and no one else, would be questioned about the menu. He advised housewives about what delicacies to serve their guests. He also made the final decisions for the "tea" calendar: where, when, and at whose home [the meetings would take place]. Everyone relied on his expertise. If he said that a dish was tasty, you could eat it "with your eyes closed," without worrying about its freshness, no need to call for a doctor. With compassion, Spektor looked at those who ate reluctantly, without a full appetite, without using all their senses, as though they were half-human, as though they were ailing. He would shake his great, round, bald head and commiserate. Because my father [Hillel Zeitlin] was a light eater, Spektor especially wanted to teach him how to find pleasure at the "teas." He would seat himself next to my father and watch over him, all the while giving him something else to sample: "Eat! Taste it, Reb Hillel. It's good, it's succulent. . . ."

And when my father did not obey, smiling instead above Spektor's white head which was respectfully bent over a wide plate, Spector would encourage him: "Enough gazing at the heavens above, Reb Hillel. Look into your plate."

Spektor was a lover of life, through and through. He did not ask complicated questions, did not contemplate too much, would not afflict himself with the complex problems of life. He was an observer. He looked at life the way it existed. He took things as they came and enjoyed them. Even with life's challenges—and he did experience some family difficulties—he overcame them with strength and serenity. In any case, the difficulties did not have a lasting effect on the solid, robust Spektor. With his small, beer-colored eyes, he observed things tenderly and optimistically, appreciating the value of every little thing as though each event contained a deep, important meaning. He drank the juices of life with a full, vigorous mouth. And he couldn't comprehend how it could be any different. He had inside himself many qualities of a villager, of the Jewish peasant whose life he portrayed with such broad colors in his novels and stories. Behind his outward serenity and unrefined quality, a primitive, sound intelligence was hidden.

In the literary circle, there was no end to the jokes about Spektor's great love of eating—and his outrageous appetite. It was told that, after finishing his midday dinner at home, he would go to a restaurant for a second dinner. In all his stories and feuilletons, you could find an aggrandizement of the act of eating, such as in his description of a dinner party. In his stories, Spektor seldom portrayed a hero who left on an empty stomach without eating some food. And if you were to read Spektor's Shavuos story without having eaten beforehand, the saliva would run from your mouth, when [in the story] they fried the wide blintzes in sour cream. . . .

When Spektor would eat, the broad nape of his neck would swell and redden, and his thick, drooping, yellowish-gray whiskers would always rise up, wet and greasy, from deep in his plate. Not only was Spektor engrossed in eating, but he also participated in the housekeeping. Nothing in the household was accomplished without his involvement. He found pleasure in being helpful with things in the kitchen, with cooking, cleaning, laundry, chopping wood, bringing in a few of pails from the well. Spektor did not leave the house while there was laundry to be done. He might be hot and sweaty, yet no one could say a word to discourage him. One time, he was called into the city to the publishing house for an important reason. It was supposed to be an urgent meeting. All members of the editorial staff who lived in their country cottages came back into the city. Only Spektor didn't attend. Later they asked him: "Spektor, why didn't you show up? We waited for you!"

He slowly shrugged his broad shoulders: "I couldn't come. I had a major laundry to deal with."

Spektor didn't like skinny, emaciated people. He preferred full-bodied personalities, "whole" people. He didn't appreciate contemplative, dreamy folks and dismissed them as "not my kind of people." Toward me, however, he was very friendly. Delighted by my chubbiness, my healthy appetite, and my pranks, he very much enjoyed pinching my full, pudgy, red cheeks.

At the same time, he kept his distance from [my brother] Aaron.

He couldn't understand Aaron's contemplative, quiet nature. He couldn't grasp that such a young boy was so often lost in his own thoughts. He was somewhat afraid of Aaron, of his melancholy eyes, of his education.

When Spektor would meet with my father and the discussion would come down to Aaron's writings—the things that had already been published (in Shmul Niger's journal *Yiddishe velt* and a larger piece, "Metatron"). Then Spektor would grumble between his wide whiskers: "He is something of a genius, your Aaron." [. . .]

Every morning, when the first pale beams of sunlight appeared through the spaces between the shutters of our little summer house [in Yusefov], there was a soft knock on the shutters. It was Spektor who knocked. Every day, in the early hours when the fields smelled of dew and the trees from the nearby woods had just awakened, he would walk barefoot to Shvider to bathe in the nearby river. On his way, he would stop by to take me swimming with him. For such a long distance, he didn't like to walk alone. He found it depressing to walk across the wide, uninhabited field by himself.

He had more enjoyment from this morning ritual "immersion" in the little Shvider River when I joined him for the swim. I would wait for Spektor's knock on the shutters. When I heard the first rustle at the window, quietly so as not to wake anyone else in the house, I would steal out of bed, throw on my pants. I would take with me the little bag with a towel and a sheet that always lay ready under my pillow and sneak outside on my tiptoes through the kitchen door. Spektor would wait for me, barefooted and "white": The "whiteness" came from his underwear peaking out from his rolled up pants—mixed in with the whiteness of his round head, his whiskers, and his early morning face. During the entire walk, Spektor would ramble on about the importance of an early morning swim in a river, how this would lengthen your life. And those who didn't bathe in flowing water were fools.

He would jump into the river, agile as a little boy. And if I hesitated and did not immediately jump into the water, he would get angry with me. Once, I got bogged down in the river under the bridge, where the water was quite deep. Not wanting to leave me on my own, Spektor followed me. And he was truly wise: I suddenly found myself in a deep spot and started to choke. Water ran from my ears, from my throat, from my nose. I couldn't catch my breath. Unexpectedly, someone lifted me up out of the water and I found myself stretched out on the sand, breathing shallowly. It was Spektor who had noticed I was in trouble and, in a twinkling of an eye, he lifted me up over his head with his strong arms and threw me onto the shore. On the way back, we decided not to tell anyone at my house about what had occurred. First, we didn't want to worry my parents. Second, we might endanger our daily swims in the Shvider River. After hearing such a story, my parents might be afraid to let me go "by myself." You never know what could happen. . . .

On the way home from Shvider, we would always stop in Yaroslav, at a remote peasant hut where there stood a crooked, forgotten tree. From the hut came the smell of hay and horse manure. An elderly peasant woman, with a light gray scarf on her head and dirty bare feet, would wait for us there. When she saw us in the distance, she would lead her cow out of the stall and would quickly milk it.

After our swim each morning, it was Spektor's habit to drink a cup of warm milk straight from the cow, along with a piece of fresh black bread with butter—so that he would not faint from hunger. Of course, Spektor would invite me, his constant swimming companion, to join him with milk and bread. And then he would carefully watch to make sure that I should, God-forbid, not leave any milk or bread untouched. Meanwhile, Spektor would launch into his entire theory of the importance of eating black bread for one's health and the unhealthiness of white bread. As an example, he gave the state of the peasants, so healthy and strong because they nourish themselves with black bread. They did not care for the overly refined white rolls of the city.

As we dragged ourselves over the narrow sandy field during our daily sojourns on the way home to Yusefov, Spektor would also not forget to explain the profound

reason for going barefoot. Here, too, he would use the example of the peasants who are "strong as iron" and live long.

"You shouldn't squeeze your feet into tight, narrow shoes or boots. Shoes should be worn only in the rain, or when you go to the city—you can't walk around barefoot in Warsaw! But here in the country, you can forget about city shoes, just as you can forget about tight, restrictive collars. Both feet and neck," he explained to me, "need to be free. They need to breathe, just like we need to eat." . . .

Spektor didn't talk much about literary topics. From time to time, he would pass me a newspaper and show me a feuilleton signed with his pseudonym "Pinye Tintler."

"So, here, read this!" [he would say]. [. . .]

It turned out that during that very same summer I would meet Sholem Aleichem in person, and even in Yusefov. Sholem Aleichem had been brought to Warsaw and Łódź for several readings. In Warsaw, he read from his pieces in the Nowości Theater. When Sholem Aleichem arrived on Bielańska Street at the theater, it caused an uproar. Though it was summertime, when public events were generally not well attended, the auditorium was packed with people standing shoulder to shoulder. After Sholem Aleichem's recitation, the enthusiastic crowd asked for more, not wanting him to leave the stage.

Wiping his sweat and catching his breath, Sholem Aleichem was exhausted, but he was also delighted by his Warsaw audience. He enjoyed their appreciation and the great adoration that was showered upon him.

He came to Yusefov to visit Spektor, his close, beloved friend, for a *shabbes* tea with the Society of Gluttons and Drunkards. When Spektor secretly told me this elevated guest had been invited to tea, I couldn't believe it—that Sholem Aleichem would actually go out of his way to come to Yusefov. He did however arrive, and not alone but with his wife.

It was a sultry, sweltering day. Sholem Aleichem wore a light-weight bright-green suit, white linen slippers tied with thin leather straps, and a small round Panama hat. The first thing that struck me with surprise were his spectacles. Such spectacles I had never seen before in my life. The lenses were half-sized, cut in the shape of a boat. I wondered why the lenses were cut in half, hardly visible, rather than whole lenses which covered the entire eye. It had to be the fancy of a humorist! Along with this, behind the half-sized spectacles, Sholem Aleichem squinted his small gray eyes—it appeared as though his eyes were half-sized as well.

Somehow, as soon as Sholem Aleichem climbed up on Spektor's veranda, the property began to fill with curious strangers. Mostly it was young people dressed in Hasidic garb, skinny, tall, pale, sickly, caught in the act. They hung around, timidly, between the sparse pine trees, fearful of getting closer to the veranda. Occasionally, one of the braver ones would stealthily climb the walls of the veranda, to steal a peak through the slats—then jump down, like a "hero." Afterwards, the hero would be embraced by his group, as he told of the "wonders" that he had seen "on the other side."

With much envy, these young people looked at the more fortunate ones who did not need to steal onto the veranda for a peak—those who, with confidence and familiarity, approached Sholem Aleichem, greeted him and had discussions with him.

Sholem Aleichem was on kissing terms with Spektor. He also enjoyed seeing my father. He shook his hand for a long time and began to ask my father questions about matters of the Warsaw press and, more to the point, whether he liked his novel, which was currently being serialized in a Warsaw newspaper. [. . .]

Sholem Aleichem spoke Yiddish with everyone, but with his wife and with me he constantly spoke Russian. He started pinching my full pink cheeks and asked me about the subjects that I was studying in gymnasium. After every question, he rested a while, looked keenly at me through his weird glasses, and questioned me in Russian, as though at an examination:

"Nu, do you know geography?"

"I do.". . .

"What about arithmetic?" he continued in a sing-song lilt.

I blinked and answered, "I know it well."

"Nu and are you also studying Hebrew?"

[Meanwhile] Spektor panted from too much sweating and exuberant joy. With great respect, he listened to the "learned" discussion that Sholem Aleichem was carrying on with me. Sholem Aleichem wrinkled his brow and slapped me with pleasure on my wide shoulders, saying, "*Ladno, ladno* (good, good)."

I couldn't understand why Sholem Aleichem spoke with me in Russian. He must know that any son of Hillel Zeitlin knows Yiddish. Later my mother explained it to me:

"It is more appropriate to speak in Russian to a gymnasium student who wears a uniform with brass buttons, do you understand me?"

"And as for his wife, why did he constantly speak in Russian to her?" I asked.

"It is no doubt also more appropriate to speak to her—a midwife, a trained woman, an educated woman—in Russian, don't you understand?"

By the time that Sholem Aleichem began to get ready for his return to the city, the sun had long set. The young people were still loitering about the property, beneath the veranda, waiting for Sholem Aleichem to descend so they could get another glimpse of him. We all accompanied the guest for some distance. Far behind us, there was a black blotch: following our group were the young people, who were also accompanying Sholem Aleichem to the train.

On the way, Sholem Aleichem complained to my father about his health, explaining that he needed to travel abroad for a rest, to take a cure. But as for money, he had none—my father shouldn't know from it. That is why Sholem Aleichem had to come to Warsaw for the readings. He also complained about his editors, who would not let him rest, constantly demanding more material for the newspaper. Though he, Sholem Aleichem, wrote quickly and with ease, he felt that if he didn't have to write on demand, his writings would probably turn out differently.

After Sholem Aleichem's departure, Spektor wouldn't stop talking about his guest. He kept asking me how I liked Sholem Aleichem, how did I like the food that he had prepared for him, and what did I think of Sholem Aleichem's discussion with me, of his "excellent" Russian?

I was envious of Spektor that he was so intimate with Sholem Aleichem, that Sholem Aleichem had kissed him. And from that time on, I formed a greater respect for Spektor.

Of course, one thing had nothing to do with the other: Respect is respect. But swimming in the early morning in the Shvider River was still necessary. And after the swim, eating a piece of fresh black bread with butter and washing it down with warm milk is still a pleasure. Following Sholem Aleichem's visit, Spektor kept up his custom, and every morning we continued to trudge over the quiet, untouched sands and silent fields to Yaroslav to the yellowish-green water. And so we continued our sojourns until that dark Tishe be-av

[Jewish fast day that commemorates the destruction of the First and Second Temples in Jerusalem] of that year when that insane "fire" enveloped the world, which could only be quenched with entire oceans of blood, not with the shallow water of a secluded river. . . . [outbreak of World War I, August 1914].

So we all went back to the city, everyone into his own corner. And only when the Russian army left Warsaw did Spektor turn up in the literary house on Shlikse Street [our home]. He came to say goodbye before leaving for Russia, for Odessa. No one was at home at the time. My father and mother had gone somewhere, taking along Aaron and Rivkele, my sister. I was alone in the house, listening to the dull, distant echo of canon fire. I had felt depressed, melancholy, but when I saw Spektor's round, gray-shiny head, and his silent, drooping whiskers, I suddenly felt warmth and familiarity.

Spektor, however, was unhappy and worried. A large crooked wrinkle appeared on his wide red forehead. I could see his head had sunk more deeply between his shoulders. He was upset, bit his whiskers, and remained silent, looking pensively through the windows. After a while, he got up hastily and wandered around the room with quick steps. He noticed, hanging on the wall, a photograph of a group of writers. Spektor was one of the group. He stood there for a long time, staring at the picture.

I couldn't tell whether he was looking at himself or at someone else. But when he turned away, I noticed a tear in the corner of his greenish-gray eye. I imagined he felt sorry for himself. In his old age, childless and alone, he was about to trudge across a faraway, dangerous road, in these bloody dark times. Who knew if we would see each other again, or if he would return. . . .

Probably, Spektor suspected that I had noticed something unusual in his demeanor. So, he suddenly straightened up and, as in the good old days, he pinched my cheeks:

"Remember, you brat, write to me in Russia, you understand? And I will answer you. But you must write like a *mentsh*. On the envelope, don't simply write 'M. Spektor,' but 'To Mr. M. Spektor,' in proper Russian. Like a *mentsh*, you hear?"

When the door closed behind the short, stout, good-hearted little man and I heard the sound of his dainty steps shuffling slowly down the steps, I didn't realize that this would be the last time that I heard Spektor's voice,

that this would be the last time he closed our door. But a strange grief came over me and, slowly, I took a hand-kerchief to my eyes.

Translated by Sarah Silberstein Swartz.

Other works by Zeitlin: *A bikhele lider* (1931); *In a literarisher shtub* (1937); *Bukh un bine* (1939).

David Pinski

1872–1959

The novelist and fiction writer David Pinski was born in Mogilev, Belorussia. He moved at age thirteen to Moscow, where as a teenager he wrote fiction in Russian, Hebrew, and Yiddish. At first attracted to Zionism, he became a socialist, and came under the influence of I. L. Peretz in Warsaw. He moved to Berlin in 1896 where he attended university, tutored Hebrew, and married Hodel Kaufman, the sister-in-law of his Warsaw publisher, Mordkhe Spektor. Pinski then immigrated to the United States, and was a pioneer in Yiddish socialist literature. His themes dealt with workers' struggles, relations between the sexes, biblical legends, and folklore. From 1916 he became active in the Zionist-socialist movement (Po'ale Tsiyon), was a founder of the Central Yiddish Cultural Organization (CYCO), and was active politically. Pinski wrote over two hundred works, including more than seventy plays. Among his most popular were *Der oytser* (The Treasure) and *Yankl der shmid* (Yankl the Blacksmith), which was made into a movie. Pinski immigrated to Haifa in 1949, fulfilling his dream of making aliyah. He was active in Israeli literary circles and continued to write for Yiddish newspapers in New York.

Book of Travels

1938

Jews in the Soviet Union

The situation of Jews in the Soviet Union may well be the greatest of all the great wonders of the world. The history of Jews in tsarist Russia has been centuries of darkness and hardships. When the light of day began to shine upon Jews almost everywhere else, in tsarist Russia things became even darker and more oppressive. Horrible persecutions, inhuman insults during the war years, gruesome pogroms after the war—and then suddenly the long-awaited, painfully desired dream came true: equal rights, and with a wonderful addition: equal worth. Jews in the Soviet Union have not only been granted equal rights, just like all the other peoples in the socialist fatherland, but they are now considered to be of equal worth, too. They are no longer considered to be of lesser value. They are no longer second-class citizens. They are no longer the targets of random stone-throwing, no longer the spittoon of those who degrade and besmirch others. The centuries-old, deeply rooted Jew-hatred has been dug up by its roots, or buried so deep underground that it can no longer be seen, heard, or felt. Insulting Jews has become a criminal offense, a counterrevolutionary act. If someone does not like the Jewish nose he is not allowed to even make faces.

In my youth I had lived in Moscow. To be sure, I have not forgotten the nightly *obloves* [raids] on Jews! Jews were stopped in the street, dragged out of their beds, interrupted in the middle of a peaceful meal with the menacing words: passport and residential permit! I have not forgotten the grimaces, the swear words, the cursing and name-calling, being called a *zhid*, a dirty Jew, which Jews were constantly subject to in Moscow wherever they went. Now I walked around there with my wife and evoked for her the evil, shameful insults of the past, the onetime Jewish rightlessness and worth-lessness. Where did all this go, how could it disappear so fast? Will I really not hear the word *zhid* ever again? Will I really not see the grimaces ever again? Will I really not be stopped in the street, and will no one demand to see my residential permit?

I already told the story of a former merchant from Moscow who once, when he was drunk, started to talk about "citizens of Jerusalem" in a bus and was immediately arrested for this. [...]

In the course of solving the question of nationalities, the Soviet government also determined the status of the 2.5 million Russian Jews. They are a people, a nationality, one of the 150-something nationalities that make up the Soviet Union. Dispersed all over the republics of the Soviet Union, a minority everywhere, they, too, just like all minorities that live among other nationalities, have their cultural autonomy: the right to live and develop as a cultural unit in their own language, having their own schools, literature, theater, courts, etc. A people equal with all the other peoples of the Soviet Union.

But these Jews do not want to be a people. Of all the peoples of the Soviet Union, Jews are the only ones who *want* to disappear, to be swallowed, to melt in. They have been liberated politically, and now they want to be redeemed from themselves.

Throughout the history of exile, religion has been a separating force. As long as Jews were religious, their religion was a fence that surrounded them. When they were not religious, the Christian religion was the separating wall. In the Soviet Union all the fences and walls of religion have been removed. Judaism and Christianity are both living out their last days; they have ceased to be a factor in the lives of the peoples.

What can now divide Jews from their non-Jewish neighbors? National history is a divider. Consciously relating to one's past creates separation. Using one's own language is a fence. The will to live life in one's own language is a manifestation of the will of independence. Cultural autonomy is a base, it is self-determination, it is the will to be a people and remain a people.

I have not found evidence of any of this among the Jews of the Soviet Union. The date of the Bolshevik Revolution is the date when the Jews' thousand-year-old history came to an end, when the past was cut off and the connecting bridge eliminated. The designation *Jewish people* calls forth protest, *Jewish nation* means backwardness, bourgeois Zionism, counterrevolution. And it was leading Jewish spokesmen who declared this, not understanding or not wanting to understand what this meant for the national future of Jews: disappearing, ceasing to exist, being dissolved. Why should we continue to hang around as a separate unit among the nations? Our economy is the same as the economy of the peoples among whom we live, and the culture of others has always been more attractive to us than our own. That's it! The end!

The Soviet government gives Jews every opportunity to live as a separate people. Government funds are available to support schools, the publication of newspapers, periodicals, books and the [Yiddish] theater. And yet the schools are half empty, no one reads the periodicals, barely anyone goes to the theater, and books are published in small quantities because no one buys them.

The city library of Minsk has a large section of Yiddish books. We found one single reader there, no more—an eighty-year-old man reading Masliansky's[1] sermons.

In the city park of Minsk a young couple sat next to us on the bench. They spoke Yiddish among themselves, a good, literary Yiddish. They must have studied at the

Yiddish school. But with their four-year-old child they spoke Russian.

"Explain to us, dear people, why do you speak Russian to your child?"

"It is very simple. Soviet law prescribes that children must go to school in the same language that they spoke before they were enrolled in school so as not to confuse them. If we speak to him in Yiddish, he will have to go to the Yiddish school. We want him to go to the Russian school; that is why we speak to him in Russian. This way he will have to go to the Russian school. . . ."

"Why do you want him to go to the Russian school?"

"It is more useful."

We brought greetings to a man in Minsk from his brother who is a teacher in a Yiddish-language elementary school in Poland—a martyr of his profession. The man refused to even try to understand his brother. How can he sacrifice himself for such a thing like a Yiddish elementary school? He is a reactionary!

"Don't you have Yiddish elementary schools here, too?"

"We do not want them! We do not need them! They are half empty. They will soon be completely empty. They will be closed. Those schools are counterrevolutionary, too, even if they teach nothing else but class struggle. Their goal is to create separation. We do not want to be separated."

"Should Jews disappear, then?"

"Why not?"

Once upon a time he was just as crazy [about Yiddish] as his brother. He was a Yiddishist, hailed the Czernowitz Conference, and studied the works of Dr. Chaim Zhitlowsky. Now he can explain away exactly what had happened: people were forced. It was the brutal tsarist government that forced people. They forced Jews into the ghetto—so Jews ghettoized themselves. They had something valuable—their own language, their own literature and creativity. But what is the use of all that now? No Yiddish word is heard in his house, and he does not remember the last time he read a Yiddish book. There is a Yiddish newspaper in Minsk, it is called *Oktyabr*. By coincidence he just happens to know that it still exists.

"You should see that newspaper! It is worthless! Minsk has a population of 15,000 Jews, and the newspaper is printed in no more than 3,000 copies—but I might be exaggerating. And who reads it? Who takes even a glance at it? And who needs it? We have here

in Minsk a Yiddish theater, too. I can assure you that I have never set foot there. . . ."

And the situation in Odessa and Kiev is just like in Minsk: the Yiddish elementary school is half empty; the newspaper, printed on bad-quality paper, is not even published every day, it is not read by anyone, and barely anyone goes to the theater.

The actors of the Yiddish theater speak Russian among themselves. For them, Yiddish is not a cultural language that should be maintained and developed but an instrument to make a living. Done with the performance, off the stage, time to put away the instrument . . .

"Yiddish is in bad shape here," I said to the director of a Yiddish theater.

"In bad shape? What do you mean?" he wondered.

"It is going to disappear." [. . .]

Yiddish Literature and Theater in the Soviet Union

[. . .] The situation of Yiddish literature and theater is endlessly sad. They have become caricatures of themselves; they have been distorted to a caricature, degraded. In the Yiddish literary world even the dictatorship of fear is more boorish, its enslaving effect stronger. If Jewish writers are afraid that their words may be misinterpreted, the fear of Yiddish writers is twice as great and is much more justified. Their words will most definitely find an ill-willed interpreter—on account of the Jewish tradition of *pilpul*.[2] What kind of beasts are those Yiddish critics that they twist every word and sentence? And it is a vicious circle. Today you are the judge, tomorrow you are convicted. Today you ban someone, tomorrow they ban you. Today you are a big shot, tomorrow you are nobody. Today you get to interpret and punish others, tomorrow you will have to acknowledge your sins and apologize publicly. The path of Yiddish literature in the Soviet Union has been paved with such rejected and outcast judges. Dunets, Nusinov, B. Orshanski and more, and more. . . . In the case of most of them we can let out a jolly sigh of relief and say *borukh sheptorani*, blessed be the One who relieved us from him—good riddance! But in some cases the loss is regrettable.

Der Nister put down his pen; Leyb Kvitko gave up the struggle. A young, talented writer, A. Abtshuk, wrote a fine short story called "Hersh Shammai." The story was very well received; Abtshuk gained respect. But then suddenly someone discovered a "dangerous expression" in his story, and now Abtshuk's name may not be mentioned. When I asked about him, people lowered their heads in fear.

A talented young Yiddish poet experienced a personal tragedy. His beloved wife died in childbirth. He expressed his dark mood in a number of poems, but the poems were not published the way they were written because the editor ruled that in the Soviet Union one may not be sad. This young Yiddish poet will cease to be a Yiddish poet.

Something happened in Yiddish literature that, as far as I know, has not happened in the literature of any other nationality in the Soviet Union. Immediately following the Bolshevik Revolution there was a tendency for everyone to want to break with the past. Even the great Russian classics were doomed to be hidden as they were called class enemies. [Then] Stalin and Stalinism liberated them and returned them to the Russian public. Pushkin is now the most celebrated poet, Tolstoy's works are printed in millions of copies, Ostrovsky is once again the most popular playwright, competing with Shakespeare for first place in the Russian theater. Taras Shevchenko, who sang his songs in the 1850s, is now the spiritual light of Soviet Socialist Ukraine. There is barely a city in Ukraine that would not have a Shevchenko memorial. The medieval poet Rustaveli has been crowned the king of Georgian literature in the Soviet Socialist Republic of Georgia. Generally, the creative powers of the past occupy a prominent place in the Stalinist cultural autonomy. There is great respect for every nation's artistic creations and their creators.

Yiddish literature was the only one to excommunicate its authors. Only those works and writers are admitted who can be sealed with the kosher stamp of class struggle.

Sholem Aleichem was too popular among the Jewish masses and respected by Gorky, on top of it. They would not dare ban him, so they tagged him with the "class" stamp. In an emergency Sholem Aleichem becomes the writer of the Jewish proletariat; they stop short of calling him a revolutionary and a socialist. And poor Mendele Moykher Sforim had the same fate. . . .

Peretz, however, is banned. Not the Peretz of the weak social [realist] stories, but the great Peretz of the Hasidic tales and his adaptation of folktales. [. . .]

Yes, the greatest works of Peretz became the unfortunate victims of the misreading and twisted interpretation of a bunch of scribblers who lost their minds from fear, of petty cowards who butter up to the rulers and extol the revolution which they do not even begin to understand. [. . .]

Yiddish theater in the Soviet Union has bountiful resources and means, but lacks a good repertoire. There is not even one play that would reflect on the current state of Jewish life and its meaning. Not one that would show the way to the future. No Jewish people—no Jewish drama.

Their repertoire consists of a number of dramatizations of works by Sholem Aleichem and Mendele enhanced with the idea of class struggle, several weak, trifling dramatic pieces by emerging Soviet Yiddish writers, and finally Shakespeare.

When I was in Minsk they were preparing for the performance of Moyshe Kulbak's *Boitre*, the drama of a Jewish criminal that was later also staged by the Moscow Yiddish Theater and will likely be performed by every Yiddish theater. The story line of *Boitre* is typical.

Chaim Boitre becomes a criminal [. . .] in the course of fighting against injustice in the world. The injustices in Boitre's world are *yikhes* that block his way to the girl he loves; a wildly fanatic, hypocritical and greedy rabbi; a head of the Jewish community who is a spy intermingled with the police, etc. There is hypocrisy—talking of God while picking people's pockets, and moralizing—trying to tie down Samson, the proletarian. . . .

But not all of this emerged from the pen of the very talented Moyshe Kulbak; he does not see the Jewish past in exclusively ugly colors. Many things were added by the theater people who are specialists in class struggle. The same ones who infused Goldfaden's play *Shulamis* with class struggle.

I was wondering why the [Yiddish] theater in Kiev would want to perform *Shulamis*, such a primitive play that takes place in the Land of Israel, to top it off. But what I saw on stage was not the good old *Shulamis* at all! It was a funny burlesque, *Shulamis* with class struggle. In this performance Avshalom is a rich young man with all the meanness of a bourgeois. Shulamis is in love with a poor shepherd but her father is against the match. The High Priest and all the other religious functionaries are repulsive and unworthy people. The High Priest's daughter is an outcast, and the finest character in this class struggle burlesque is the African slave Tsingitang. . . .

The Kiev Yiddish Theater's troupe has fifty-six members and it is one of the largest Yiddish troupes in the world. Every actor gets a regular salary. They do not need to worry whether the theater director will pay their salary or not, they do not need to be concerned that the theater might close in the middle of the season. A new theater building is being built for them. Comfortable apartments are being built for them. Yet none of them believes in the future.

Yiddish theater and Yiddish literature are conscious of and responsive to the fact that they have lost their audience, the people. Authors know that they have no readers, playwrights know that there are no theatergoers. Many of them do not take this to heart—they have a backup, the Russian language. Those, however, who dream of a future as a Yiddish writer or actor are looking to Birobidzhan. A Jewish autonomous region, possibly a Jewish republic, a Jewish land of our own, Jewish culture, Jewish future, and all this in Yiddish. Birobidzhan is our deliverance.

But they also know that Russian Jews do not wish to move so far away to Asia; they do not want to go to Birobidzhan. The economic whip does not force them to go, and the desire to be and to remain a people has been ridiculed and annihilated by none other than the Yiddish writers and spokesmen themselves.

Thus, Yiddish writers are looking to Birobidzhan with longing hearts; they sing songs of praise about it and express their admiration in stories, but they do not know from where Jews will go to Birobidzhan, unless its borders are opened to the large Jewish masses in Poland and Romania who are looking for a place of refuge. Only then will Birobidzhan become a place of refuge for Yiddish literature and for the Yiddish theater.

My Encounters with Yiddish Writers in the Soviet Union

Forget, thou, Yiddish writer, what you have contributed to Yiddish literature, forget your place in it, forget your name and fame! Remember nothing but which party you belong to and which one you do not; remember only your political faith, because you will be judged based on this only and nothing else! You are going to visit Jews in the Soviet Union!

Remember that you are a member of the Po'ale Tsiyon [socialist Zionist party], and that is the end of you. Ever since you took it into your head that the Land of Israel should and could become a Jewish socialist country, your writing has quickly deteriorated and became subpar; you have reached complete artistic and spiri-

tual bankruptcy. You forgot how to write entirely. Even if you once had some talent, you wiped it out with the gangrene of the rotten Po'ale Tsiyonist counterrevolution. . . .

In case you don't know yet, just read what the critics and spokesmen of Yiddish literature in Soviet Russia write about you. It does not matter that during the years before the revolution they delighted in everything you wrote. Back then, they themselves did not know to which world they belong. Back then, they themselves were the Po'ale Tsiyon, Tseire Tsiyon, Zionist Socialist Workers and Socialist Territorialists. But now they found themselves, and found you out! You are a sociofascist who spreads fanaticism, an airhead, a pogromist, a betrayer of the working class; you sold your soul and became a slave of the bourgeoisie, a common usurping imperialist—every possible evil!

You are no longer alive. You are dead like all the other dead, and thus deserve utter contempt, just like the souls wandering around in the world of chaos.

Carry your shame with yourself, and better not show up around here. And if, while in the Soviet Union, you accidentally run into those through whom the revolution sings and reveals its sanctity, do not disclose your name! Keep it secret, so they shouldn't have to humiliate you! [. . .]

We are in Minsk. How could I not look up Izi Charik? I know his writings, and want to get to know the writer himself. I will knock on his door, and look at him in an American-uncle way. I knocked. He is not at home. He will be at home at exactly one o'clock in the afternoon. For sure? For sure.

At exactly one o'clock I telephoned.

"Is Comrade Charik there?"

"Yes."

"Can I talk to him?"

"Who are you?"

I forget about the masquerade and say my name. There is silence on the other end of the line. Hello! Hello! Silence. I hang up the receiver and call again.

"Can I talk to Comrade Charik, please?"

"Comrade Charik is not at home. He left."

"When will he be back?"

"He is going on vacation."

That's how it began. A good start, my dear wife, isn't it?

There is a Yiddish theater in Minsk, its director is Mark Rafalskii. I heard he was a good artist and a good person. I should meet him. I called him up. His wife answered the telephone. She was not scared by my name. In fact, she was quite friendly. Rafalskii is not at home right now. He will be back in the evening. He will surely be glad. He will call me back. . . .

He did not call me back. No hard feelings, I will call him again. His wife answers again: "I am very sorry, Rafalskii had to leave town. . . ."

I ran into Moyshe Kulbak in the street accidentally. He was pleased to see me. He accompanied me some of the way, even though he was in a hurry to the train station to pick up his wife. As soon as he takes her home, he will get in touch with colleagues, with Charik and others. He will arrange a meeting in the evening at the Writers Club. He will come pick me up at my hotel at 8:00 P.M., I should wait for him. I waited at 8, I waited at 9. He did not show up, and he did not even call me on the phone.

Oh, what a confusion I caused at the editorial office of the Yiddish daily newspaper *Oktyabr*! Had I called them ahead of my visit, they would all have fled town, probably. So I surprised them: I arrived unannounced. The person who sat in the editor's chair, a certain Comrade Kazakov, turned completely red in the face, and in his excitement threw away the heavy key he was holding in his hand. Another person who was sitting at the table turned pale as a corpse. Neither of them was able to look at me; in their great embarrassment they both stared down at the table, as if their death sentence had been laid out there.

I was so cruel that I began to tell them, in cold blood, about the wonderful achievements of the Jewish workers in the Land of Israel. Just a bit more and someone's death would be on my conscience. . . . That's all I need! Adieu, Yiddish writers of Minsk! I am going to Moscow. There lives Dovid Bergelson, who will surely not hide from me, and Alexander Khashin, with whom I have a strong friendship that cannot be broken by some party lines, and Lipman Levine, who wrote in his biography for Zalmen Reyzen's *Leksikon* that he started writing in Yiddish "under the influence of Dovid Pinski"—he will, surely, not deny me. . . .

The first two did not cause me disappointment. Khashin and Bergelson were truly glad to see me; Lipman Levine, however, got lost somewhere on the other end of the telephone line. He is not feeling well right now. He will call me back. And I never heard from him again.

But in Moscow there is also Peretz Markish, a pillar of our Yiddish literature, and [Moyshe] Litvakov, the "Torquemada" [Grand Inquisitor] of Yiddish literature. I have to meet them.

I called the editorial office of *Emes*. "When can I meet with Comrade Litvakov?"—"Who is this?"—"Dovid Pinski."—"Comrade Litvakov is ill." That was it! No, there was more. . . .

In the afternoon, an acquaintance of mine visited me. It occurred to me that he should call *Emes* and find out when Litvakov is available. And that is what happened. When asked "Who is this?" he gave some random, ordinary name; he was told that today was already too late, tomorrow is a day off for the editors of *Emes*, but the day after tomorrow at one o'clock he can meet with Litvakov.

It was very not nice of us, but the day after tomorrow at one o'clock we surprised Litvakov, even though we had been warned that he was ailing. Thank God, the surprise did no harm to his well-being. How were we received? Well, what kind of reception can you expect from someone who thought he had already gotten rid of you? A regretful one, naturally. . . .

The next day there was a two-line announcement on page four of *Emes* stating the news that the American Yiddish writer Dovid Pinski was in town. That evening, when we met Litvakov at the Vakhtangov Theater, he said to me deceitfully:

"Have you seen the announcement about you in *Emes*? I completely forgot! I only realized it when I got home. Then I called in those two lines. I should have written more. I will probably amend it later." . . .

Bergelson connected me with Peretz Markish by telephone, and it was decided that on September 4th, Friday evening, we will gather in the home of Peretz Markish. A reception! Aha! Moscow is not Minsk! We had tickets to see the opera *Yevgeny Onegin* at the Bolshoi that Friday evening. "We will sacrifice the tickets, right, my dear wife? Friends are more important! We will go to see them, and give away the tickets!" But not so fast! Hold on to the tickets. And can you imagine what happened? Friday afternoon at four o'clock Markish comes with the news that the gathering must be postponed because of an important party meeting. There is nothing to be done. How fortunate that we have not given away our opera tickets! At the opera, however, I ran into several of those who were supposed to be at the important party meeting. . . .

"Aren't you supposed to be at a meeting?"

"What meeting?" they asked back surprised. [. . .]

My visit [in Odessa] to the local Yiddish newspaper was a very pleasant surprise. They were so excited to see me, and so disappointed to hear that I was staying in Odessa only for a few hours. I am insulting Odessa, I am insulting them! Oh well, they probably did not know that I had been declared *treyf*, that I have been dead for quite some time now, that I have been wandering around in the world of chaos! What an ignorant bunch they must be!

We arrived in Kiev and on the same evening went to the Yiddish theater. The news that I was at the theater spread quickly, and writers and actors started to come up to me and introduce themselves one after the other. How come? Do they not know that I have been cast off? Is this not a counterrevolutionary act? Among those who came up to me were Itsik Feffer and Dovid Hofshteyn. My encounter with Dovid Hofshteyn turned into an intimate friendship, and during the few days I spent in Kiev we were inseparable. He very much wanted to organize a meeting with other colleagues, but this did not work out. Individually you can applaud Pinski as much as you want, but publicly? May the good God of the Revolution protect you! And yet, something happened in Kiev against the will of the good God of the Revolution.

On the second day of Rosh Hashanah an antireligion gathering took place. Dovid Hofshteyn suggested that they invite me to the gathering and ask me to read something from my writings. It was decided that this was impossible, but that Hofshteyn could bring me as a guest to the gathering.

When we entered the hall, Mishkovski was in the middle of his talk about the Jewish holidays. The chairman interrupted him and announced to the audience that the long-lived Yiddish writer Dovid Pinski, who first introduced the character of the Jewish proletarian into Yiddish literature forty-four years ago, was here. An ovation broke out, and I was invited to step up to the podium. When I got up to the podium the ovation resumed, and when I sat down to the presidium table people starting collecting pieces of paper and gave them to the chairman. One of these pieces was right in front of my eyes. It said, "We ask that you finish the program as soon as possible and give the floor to the writer Dovid Pinski."

"Will you take the floor?" whispered to me the chairman.

"If you give it to me, I will take it," I whispered back.

He asked me twice, and I gave him the same answer twice. I sensed panic and fear around me. How could we ask him to speak, when we did not even want to allow him to read from his writings?

"Read something from your work," said my good friend Hofshteyn.

People from the audience started calling my name, and I was given the floor. When I got up to talk, everyone in the audience stood up, too. Behind me, however, I heard someone whisper horrified: "What will you say? What will you say?" And when I looked at the enthusiastically applauding audience, who believed that I remained faithful to the interests of the Jewish working class even in my later work, written after my proletarian short stories, I thought to myself: the Soviet Yiddish writers who were fooled by the dictatorship of fear and lost their integrity wanted to destroy me, but I am still alive in the hearts of the people.

I could think this not only about myself but about every Yiddish writer and artist, everyone who writes and creates beyond the borders of the Soviet Union. [. . .]

The wonderful Dr. Yisroel Tsinberg in Leningrad was interested in everything and everyone. A chemist by profession and employed at the famous Putilov Factory since 1899, Dr. Tsinberg devoted every single evening and all of his free time to Yiddish research, and produced the monumental ten-volume *Di geshikhte fun literatur bay yidn* [A History of Jewish Literature] on which he had been working since 1915.

Jewish opinion leaders in the Soviet Union refused to accept this work. They declared it nationalistic and chauvinistic, reactionary and murky, erroneous and unscientific—a work that one should disregard and scorn. The work had to leave the Soviet Union, where it was born, and had to be published by the Tomor Publishing House in Vilna. The first seven volumes had already appeared when non-Jewish opinion leaders realized what had happened and became very angry. Such a colossal work that was created in Leningrad and would have been a pride to the Soviet Union, should be published abroad? How could this happen? Where were people's brains, minds, and intelligence? The Jewish opinion leaders of Moscow, who were always afraid and never sure about anything, came to Dr. Tsinberg in Leningrad to ask if they could possibly get his work.

No, it is no longer possible. The work has already been published abroad.

Dr. Tsinberg lived to see his revenge served, and he is sure that he will see more. He is the only one among the Soviet Yiddish writers who has not denied the wholeness of Jewish literature, who continues to see the Jewish people behind the creative work, and he hopes that the traitors and those who deny this wholeness will have regrets. [. . .]

NOTES

1. [Zvi Hirsh Masliansky (1856–1943) was a popular Yiddish orator in pre-revolutionary Russia, Europe, and the United States.—Eds.]

2. [Casuistry, dialectical argument.—Eds.]

Translated by Vera Szabó.

Other works by Pinski: *Der eybiker yid* (1906); *Altinke* (1910); *Arbeter-lebn* (1910); *Libe* (1910); *Der oytser* (1911).

Edna Ferber

1885–1968

The novelist, short-story writer, and playwright Edna Ferber grew up in small Midwestern towns, the daughter of a Hungarian-born shopkeeper. Growing up in the American Protestant heartland, she faced antisemitism on a daily basis. This is reflected in her work, which frequently includes characters who are victims of discrimination because of their ethnicity or for other reasons. Her heroines are almost always strong, assertive women. In New York, where she lived as an adult, she was a member of the Algonquin Round Table, a group of writers, wits, critics, and actors who met daily for lunch at the Algonquin Hotel on West 44th Street. Several of her novels, including *So Big* (1924), *Cimarron* (1929), and *Giant* (1952), were turned into successful Hollywood films.

A Peculiar Treasure

1939

On Saturdays, and on unusually busy days when my father could not take the time to come home to the noon dinner, it became my duty to take his midday meal down to him, very carefully packed in a large basket; soup, meat, vegetables, dessert. This must be carried with the utmost care so as not to spill or slop. No one

thought of having a sandwich and a cup of coffee in the middle of the day, with a hot dinner to be eaten at leisure in the peace of the evening.

This little trip from the house on Wapello Street to the store on Main Street amounted to running the gantlet. I didn't so much mind the Morey girl. She sat in front of her house perched on the white gatepost, waiting, a child about my age, with long red curls, a freckled face, very light green eyes. She swung her long legs, idly. At sight of me her listlessness fled.

"Hello, sheeny!" Then variations on this. This, one learned to receive equally. Besides, the natural retort to her baiting was to shout, airily, "Red Head! Wets the bed!"

But as I approached the Main Street corner there sat a row of vultures perched on the iron railing at the side of Sargent's drugstore. These were not children, they were men. Perhaps to me, a small child, they seemed older than they were, but their ages must have ranged from eighteen to thirty. There they sat, perched on the black iron rail, their heels hooked behind the lower rung. They talked almost not at all. The semicircle of spit rings grew richer and richer on the sidewalk in front of them. Vacant-eyed, they stared and spat and sat humped and round-shouldered, doing nothing, thinking nothing, being nothing. Suddenly their lackluster eyes brightened, they shifted, they licked their lips a little and spat with more relish. From afar they had glimpsed their victim, a plump little girl in a clean starched gingham frock, her black curls confined by a ribbon bow.

Every fiber of me shrieked to run the other way. My eyes felt hot and wide. My face became scarlet. I must walk carefully so as not to spill the good hot dinner. Now then. Now.

"Sheeny! Has du gesak de Isaac! De Moses! De Levi! Heh, sheeny, what you got!" Good Old Testament names. They doubtless heard them in their Sunday worship, but did not make the connection, quite. They then brought their hands, palms up, above the level of their shoulders and wagged them back and forth, "Oy-yoy, sheeny! Run! Go on, run!"

I didn't run. I glared. I walked by with as much elegance and aloofness as was compatible with a necessity to balance a basket of noodle soup, pot roast, potatoes, vegetable and pudding.

Of course it was nothing more than a couple of thousand years of bigotry raising its hideous head again to spit on a defenseless and shrinking morsel of humanity. Yet it all must have left a deep scar on a sensitive child. It was unreasoning and widespread in the town. My parents were subject to it. The four or five respectable Jewish families of the town knew it well. They were intelligent men and women, American born and bred, for the most part. It probably gave me a ghastly inferiority, and out of that inferiority doubtless was born inside me a fierce resolution, absurd and childish, such as, "You wait! I'll show you! I'll be rich and famous and you'll wish you could speak to me."

Well, I did become rich and famous, and have lived to see entire nations behaving precisely like the idle frustrated bums perched on the drugstore railing. Of course Ottumwa wasn't a benighted town because it was cruel to its Jewish citizens. It was cruel to its Jewish citizens because it was a benighted town. Business was bad, the town was poor, its people were frightened, resentful and stupid. There was, for a place of its size and locality, an unusually large rough element. As naturally as could be these searched for a minority on whom to vent their dissatisfaction with the world. And there we were, and there I was, the scapegoat of the ages. Yet, though I had a tough time of it in Ottumwa and a fine time of it in New York, I am certain that those Ottumwa years were more enriching, more valuable than all the fun and luxury of the New York years.

New England awoke, horrified and ashamed, after its orgy of witch-burning. Ottumwa must feel some embarrassment at the recollection of its earlier ignorance and brutality. A Nazi-infested world may one day hide its face at the sight of what it has wrought in its inhuman frenzy.

There was no Jewish place of worship in Ottumwa. The five or six Jewish families certainly could not afford the upkeep of a temple. I knew practically nothing of the Jewish people, their history, religion. On the two important holy days of the year—Rosh Hashana, the Jewish New Year; and Yom Kippur, the Day of Atonement—they hired a public hall for services. Sometimes they were able to bring to town a student rabbi who had, as yet, no regular congregation. Usually one of the substantial older men who knew something of the Hebrew language of the Bible, having been taught it in his youth, conducted the service. On Yom Kippur, a long day of fasting and prayer, it was an exhausting thing to stand from morning to sunset in the improvised pulpit. The amateur rabbi would be relieved for an hour by another member of the little improvised congregation. Mr. Emanuel Adler, a familiar figure to me as he sat in his comfortable home talking with my parents, a quaint long-stemmed pipe between his lips, a little black skullcap atop his baldish head as protection against drafts, now would don the rabbinical skullcap, a good deal like that of a Catholic priest. He would open on the high reading stand the Bible and the Book of Prayers containing the service for the Day of Yom Kippur; and suddenly he was transformed from a plump middle-aged German-born Jew with sad kindly eyes and a snuffy gray-brown mustache to a holy man from whose lips came words of wisdom and of comfort and of hope.

The store always was closed on Rosh Hashana and Yom Kippur. Mother put on her best dress. If there were any Jewish visitors in the town at that time they were invited to the services and to dinner at some hospitable house afterward. In our household the guests were likely to be a couple of traveling salesmen caught in the town on that holy day. Jewish families came from smaller near-by towns—Marshalltown, Albia, Keokuk.

I can't account for the fact that I didn't resent being a Jew. Perhaps it was because I liked the way my own family lived, talked, conducted its household and its business better than I did the lives of my friends. I admired immensely my grandparents, my parents, my uncles and aunt. Perhaps it was a vague something handed down to me from no one knows where. Perhaps it was something not very admirable—the actress in me. I think, truthfully, that I rather liked dramatizing myself, feeling myself different and set apart. I probably liked to think of myself as persecuted by enemies who were (in my opinion) my inferiors. This is a protective philosophy often employed. Mine never had been a religious family. The Chicago Neumann family sometimes went to the temple at Thirty-third and Indiana, but I don't remember that my parents ever went there while in Chicago. In our own household there was no celebration of the informal home ceremonies so often observed in Jewish families. The Passover, with its Sedar [sic] service, was marked in our house only by the appearance of the matzos or unleavened bread, symbolic of the hardships of the Jews in the wilderness. I devoured pounds of the crisp crumbling matzos with hunks of fresh butter and streams of honey, leaving a trail of crumbs all over the house, and thought very little, I am afraid, of the tragic significance of the food I was eating or of that weary heartsick band led by Moses out of Egypt to escape the Hitler of that day, one Pharaoh; or of how they baked and ate their unsalted unleavened bread because it was all they had, there in the wilderness. I still have matzoth (matzos, we always called them) in my house during the Passover, and just as thoughtlessly. Now they come as delicate crisp circlets, but they seem to me much less delicious than the harder, tougher squares of my childhood munching. Ours were not Jewish ways. My father and mother and sister Fan and I exchanged many friendly little calls with the pleasant Jewish families of the town—the Almeyers, the Adlers, Feists, Silvers, Lyons, living in comfortable well-furnished houses, conducting their affairs with intelligence and decorum, educating their children. They saw a little too much of one another. There was a good deal of visiting back and forth, evenings. At nine there would be served wine or lemonade and cake, a moment which I eagerly awaited. The Ferber specialty was a hickory-nut cake, very rich, baked in a loaf, for which I was permitted to crack the nuts and extract the meats. This was accomplished with a flat-iron between my knees and a hammer in my hand. The nuts went into the cake and into me fifty-fifty. Once baked, it was prudently kept under lock and key in the cupboard of the sitting-room desk, rather than in the free territory of the pantry.

My mother, more modern than most in thought and conduct, had numbers of staunch friends among the non-Jewish townspeople, and these enormously enjoyed her high spirits, her vitality, her shrewd and often caustic comment. She, too, was an omnivorous reader, so that when life proved too much for her she was able to escape into the reader's Nirvana. Certainly she was the real head of the family, its born leader; unconsciously she was undergoing a preliminary training which was to stand her in good stead when she needed it. [. . .]

There never was such a town for sociability. At the least provocation Japanese lanterns burst into bloom on a hundred lawns, and lemonade-punch bowls were encircled by organdie-clad girls, and boys in white duck pants (peg-top) and blue serge coats (with silk revers). The dour days—the seven lean years through which we had just passed—were dispelled like fog before the sun of Appleton's warm-generous friendliness. If Ottumwa had seemed like some foreign provincial town in its narrowness and bigotry, Appleton represented the American small town at its best. A sense of well-being pervaded it. It was curiously modern and free in the best sense of the words. Cliques, malice, gossip, snobbishness—all the insular meannesses—were strangely lacking in this thriving community. Trouble, illness and death were to come upon us there in the next few years, but sympathy and friendship leavened them and made them bearable.

The mayor of Appleton that year, and for many years thereafter, was old David Hammel, a Jew. A handsome patriarch with a high-bridged nose, a bearded leonine head, ruddy color, a superb physique. He and his handsome white-haired wife and their sons and daughters lived in a big Victorian frame house on North and Durkee streets. Later, when we moved to North Street, just across the way from the Hammel house, I saw much of their family life as I read and rocked and munched cookies and played on our own front porch. It was a lesson in loyalty and family devotion.

There were about forty Jewish families living in the town. Of these perhaps thirty families were German-born or of German ancestry. The rest were Russian or Polish. At that time the German-born Jew practised the most absurd snobbery toward the Russian or the Polish Jew. Much of this still persists in America, even in these days when the Jews of the world are combating a fresh outburst of medieval persecution. To the average Gentile a Jew is a Jew. In the mind of the Jew himself there exist gradations based on ridiculous standards. The Polish Jew is looked down upon by the Russian Jew; the German and Hungarian Jew feels himself superior to the Russian; and the Spanish and Portuguese Jew feels himself above all the tribe. It may be that this was not, in the past, quite so ridiculous as it appears, since it was based on hundreds of years of difference in the freedom, economic condition, customs, occupations, habits, health and education of the various nationalities.

In Appleton most of the Jewish families were interrelated and even intermarried. With the exception of ourselves and two or three other families they hailed from the little German town of Gemünden. There was a snarl of brothers, sisters, uncles, cousins, very puzzling to the outsider. The children and grandchildren had been born in Appleton. The men were, for the most part, in the business of buying and selling Wisconsin farm lands and horses—all sorts of horses from beautiful spirited carriage chestnuts or blacks to mammoth pudding-footed draught animals. They were a full-blooded open-handed sort, these husbands and fathers. They smelled too pungently of the horse barns even when dressed in their Sabbath blacks. Their wives were placid, home-loving; their sons and daughters well educated and intelligent. The children did not stand spectacularly high in their studies, in the athletic field, or in any of the arts, probably because they never had experienced racial or religious oppression. It is usually the persecuted Jew who naturally tries to compensate for oppression. It always has been my contention that the Jew, left in peace for two hundred years throughout the world, would lose his aggressiveness, his tenacity and neurotic ambition; would be completely absorbed and would vanish, as a type, from the face of the earth. The Jew, like the Protestant or the Catholic, fights the battles of his own country, be it America, Germany, Italy, France, England; he works for his living, educates his children, travels, lives the normal life of his country as richly as his condition permits. Suddenly, from the headlines of every newspaper in the so-called civilized world, blaring out of the radio, screaming from a thousand platforms, he sees and hears quoted, to his amazement and heartsick despair, "Jew! Jew! Jew! Down! Down!" If these fools really want to destroy us they need only leave us alone. Incredibly adaptable, gregarious, imitative, we soon would be absorbed by the world about us. Yet invariably, just as we are slipping into the world mass, our identity to be forever lost, along comes a despot who singles us out as an object on which to vent his hate or to satisfy his own or his country's psychological perversion. So then, outnumbered but terribly persistent, we again muster what defense we can, draw close together for protection, the stronger helping the weak as we stumble along. Thus for centuries we have been saved from complete absorption or utter oblivion by such fanatics, megalomaniacs or perverts as Pharaoh, Hitler, Ivan of Russia, Philip of France or Edward I of England. If one must build bricks without straw or die, one contrives, somehow, to build bricks without straw. So, through the centuries, the weakest of us have perished; the strong, the courageous, the cunning, the tenacious have survived the repeated blasts of hatred and prejudice. Any biologist or horticulturalist will tell you that that is not the way to weaken or destroy a strain; that is the way to strengthen it. If, in past centuries, the Jew has grown pale of skin, undersized, rather badly articulated, overeager, oversensitive, it is because the ghetto to which he was condemned was the tenement of the Middle and Dark Ages—crowded, airless, mean, dark. Tenements then and now do not make for stature, beauty, health or self-confidence. The German Jew, following these past few years of torture, will need a century to recuperate, if ever he is given the opportunity at all.

So, then, again and again deprived of property, of liberty, of land, of human rights, we have turned to the one thing of which only death can rob us: creative self-expression. An old Chassidic book says:

> There are three ways in which a man expresses his deep sorrow: the man on the lowest level cries; the man on the second level is silent, but the man on the highest level knows how to turn his sorrow into song.

So then, because of a Hitler, the Jew of Europe (and of the world) has perforce become more intensely racial. In the mercantile class and in the professions he has clung to the last to his rights; he will emerge more tenacious, more aggressive unless he is completely destroyed. But before that happens let us hope that, seeking in self-expression some relief for our pain, we may again, as in the past, produce for the delight of the whole world another Mozart, another Mendelssohn, another Bernhardt, golden-voiced; another Heifetz, another Rachmaninoff, another Menuhin, another Zimbalist, another Gershwin, turning centuries of sorrow into song. And by that legacy of beauty justify our living and our dying; justify even those who, by torturing us, have produced our poignantly beautiful death cry. For, paradoxical though it may seem, in spite of the degradation of the body, the humiliation of the spirit, the agony of mind, the torture of the soul which has been visited upon the Jews of the so-called civilized world in the past five years, the gorgeous irony of it is this: Adolf Hitler has done more to strengthen, to unite, to solidify and to spiritualize the Jews of the world than any other man since Moses.

I never have heard a satisfactory answer to the riddle of the world's attitude toward the Jew. I remember my shock of horror when, having been taken to an early-morning Mass by the hired girl Sarah, in Ottumwa, I looked upon my first sight of agony and bloodshed—a church statue of the crucifixion. I have wondered many times since just how deep and widespread an effect in later life this same experience has had upon hundreds of millions of children.

It is generally accepted among intelligent people that very early impressions, deeply implanted, influence us for the remainder of our lives. Certainly the psychiatrist is interested in fishing up, not the events and people and thoughts that occupied us at fifteen, twenty, twenty-five, but when we were three years old, four, five, six.

Small children are ordinarily shielded from sights and sounds of horror. Even the rhymes and the pictures in Mother Goose are sometimes seriously debated.

There was a man in our town,
And he was wondrous wise.
He jumped into a bramble bush,
And scratched out both his eyes.

Dear me! says the child-psychologist. No good can come of that. The child will grow up suspecting hidden horrors in every bush it encounters, and probably will develop eye trouble at fifteen. But at the age of four or five this child is deliberately confronted with its first vision of sanguine tragedy. In a picture or a statue he sees a man's nude figure drawn and distorted in agony. Nails through the hands and feet pin him to a cross of wood. On his head is a crown of thorns. From head, hands and feet the scarlet blood streams over the tortured body.

The child's face is a mask of fascinated revulsion. "What is that?"

"That is Our Lord Jesus Christ."

"What is the matter with him? Why is he like that?"

"He is nailed to the cross. He died for you and me."

"Who nailed him?"

"The Jews."

This has gone on for hundreds of years. The fact that Jesus was tried by Pontius Pilate, the Roman governor, and sentenced by law according to the court proceedings of that day, and that he was then crucified by Roman soldiers is universally ignored. He was one of thousands of that period who died on the cross. The life and death of this Jew, distorted through the centuries, has deeply affected the life and death of millions of Jews, and will until the historical truth is generally accepted.

These Appleton townspeople of Jewish faith—first-, second- and third-generation Americans—owned big comfortable houses, richly furnished; they lived well, had carriages and horses. The horses were well matched high-stepping beauties, the carriages beige- or plum-cushioned victorias with silver-trimmed harness, the whole topped by a coachman on the box. The wives used these for afternoon shopping, for paying calls, for rather aimless drives east to the end of College Avenue, then west to where the Chute ended in the state road.

Appleton boasted its millionaires, but none of these was a Jew. The McNaughtons, the Van Nortwicks, the Pattens, the Peabodys—of Dutch, Scotch or New England descent—these were the really moneyed people of the town.

During the first year or two of our coming to Appleton my mother rather grandly established Friday afternoons At Home. Our hired girl of that day was of German descent: Tillie Schultz, a treasure of purest ray serene. Tillie was a naturally gifted cook. On Friday mornings the house was fragrant with the scent of baking dough; of sugar and spice, of fruits bubbling on the bosom of plum, apricot and apple kuchen. The cheese kuchen, made from a recipe in which cottage cheese was smartened by lemon juice and grated lemon peel, was a specialty of the house. At about four o'clock the tantalizing fragrance of coffee would be added to the rest. These Friday afternoons became something of a stampede.

My mother was rather a bombshell in this placid society. American-born, alert, original, she found she had little in common with these somewhat slow-thinking and sheltered wives. She gravitated toward two families in the Jewish community: one named Lyons who had come up to Wisconsin from the South; the other named Spitz. Mrs. Spitz, tiny, quick-witted, top-heavy with a magnificent crown of braided red hair, was, like my mother, married to a Hungarian.

Other works by Ferber: *Show Boat* (1926); *The Royal Family* (1927), with George S. Kaufman; *Dinner at Eight* (1932), with George S. Kaufman; *Saratoga Trunk* (1941).

Maurice Sachs
1906–1945

Born Maurice Ettinghausen in Paris, the decadent writer Maurice Sachs grew up in a wildly dysfunctional family of well-to-do unobservant Jews. Louche, dissolute, and untrustworthy, he associated with the leading homosexual writers of the interwar period, including Jean Cocteau, Max Jacob, and André Gide. He was converted to Catholicism by Jacques and Raïssa Maritain in 1925 and even studied for the priesthood for a while, but he did not remain a practicing Catholic for long. During the German occupation of Paris, he engaged in various dubious business activities and possibly acted as a Gestapo informer. He was deported to Germany and died there in 1945. His autobiography, *Witches' Sabbath*, was written in 1939 but published only in 1946.

Witches' Sabbath
1939

Thus there began to form, or to show itself within me that heart so proud and yet so tender, that effeminate and yet indomitable character which, constantly vacillating between weakness and courage, between flabbiness and virtue, has endlessly brought me into contradiction with myself.

—Rousseau

It was at the Collège de Luza, to which I had been sent as a boarding student, that I began to lose my innocence.

I had a habit of leaving under my pillow, before I went to bed, a doeskin wallet that was my dearest possession. I don't know how it happened that I began rubbing my body with it, but gradually the wallet shifted its position until it was between my thighs. I went on rubbing, and soon an intense pain contracted my whole being, a vague froth moistened the sheet, and the enthralled, stupefied, and released body suddenly went limp. The first sexual pleasure deserves to remain fixed forever in our memory, for accidental and naïve as it is, it is also the promise of human continuity and of its wildest excesses. I should prefer not to have experienced it alone, and I envy those men—if they exist—who have enjoyed such pleasures in beloved arms.

From that moment, the scales fell from my eyes, and I was truly born to life. For it is no exaggeration to say that my body had hitherto moved through life without my soul's being aware of anything. Had I been a mineral or a vegetable instead of a man, I would not have felt the difference. After that first bout of pleasure, I looked around me, and finally perceived the restricted but quite original universe in which I was growing up without virtue.

The object of this new perception was a pretty eighteenth-century chateau, in front of which lay a broad meadow divided by a little stream, with a thin woods on the other side. But this calm landscape is not enough to make a school: the chateau was inhabited by some hundred students from all over the world, who were quite a lot like the little lovers of Larbaud's *Fermina Marquez*. Here were children from the best families of Europe, future diplomats, Portuguese Jews, virtuous Protestants, a few industrialists' sons from the North, and even one or two children of kept women. Some looked a little as if they had been stranded here by their families that were traveling somewhere; others received beautiful letters blossoming with escutcheons. This world of children spoke every language imaginable, and French received many new contributions. There was a great deal of snobbery about great names, and almost as much about

great wealth in the Collège de Luza, which prided itself on importing into France, before the Collège de Normandie and the Ecole des Roches, all the advantages of British education. (That is, we already practiced that Anglo-Saxon hygiene which has made such progress on the Continent: we washed, we were exposed to fresh air, and we were prepared for the examinations without being crammed with information learned by rote.)

It might have seemed that this was the ideal spot in which to grow up. And if I hadn't been myself, I would doubtless have been perfectly happy here. But no sooner had I opened eyes that understood a little more about the world than I was horrified by all that separated me from it.

For a name, I had only my father's, Ettinghausen, to offer, and no one in my mother's house had taught me to be proud of that, besides which, in the middle of the war it had the dubious advantage of being a German one.

For fortune, none at all. I knew we were poor. I knew I had been sent to the school only by my grandfather's generosity, which was too much like charity.

In the sports that were one of my schoolmates' great sources of pride, I was an absolute nullity. My body found no resources within itself for games, or for track events. I lost my wind, my nerve, my coordination, and could not manage to get interested in either hockey or cricket or soccer. And less still in gymnastics. I scorned all these efforts, but I scorned myself even more for being incapable of showing to good advantage in them.

And now I *discovered*, as if all these defects had not already sufficed, that I was Jewish. (I call them defects because for a child everything is a defect that makes him different from the rest.)

The school accepted only a ten per cent quota of Jewish students. This already seemed alarming to me, as if a healthy body consciously allowed itself a few microbes, but not too many, so as not to die of them. The Jews, moreover, were accepted along with others in the Collège, for these sons of great families all had a drop of Jewish blood in their veins, and a great deal of Jewish money in the family banks. But I did not even feel in close communion with my co-religionists, for coming as they did from good Portuguese families or the great French bankers' families, they prided themselves on being Jews, and if they felt separate they felt superior as well. Their parents had told them they belonged to the chosen people. I had been told nothing of the kind. My family was free-thinking and fanatically republican.

No one ever mentioned religion. I had never even been informed that there were different beliefs to be found throughout the world. Mad as it may seem, I did not know that Christ had come and that the Synagogue of my race had produced a New Church, the majority of whose disciples were entitled to hate me in the name of their gentility.

I learned this all at once, while there echoed in the free and empty Sunday air the tender hymns sung by those sweet, breaking voices. When we studied music, we were all obliged to sing, whatever faith we professed, the words of Handel's *Hallelujah*:

Lift up your heads
O people of Is-ra-el.

But I lowered mine again on Sunday morning when we were not privileged to sing the *Hallelujah* with the rest, when ten little Jews strolled, arms dangling and souls vacant, around the forbidden chapel, myself the gloomiest among them, for I didn't even believe I was entitled to lift up my head with the people of Israel, and knew I was not even a faithful member of that people. I belonged nowhere; I was what in those days counted most in the Chamber of Deputies and least in the Collège de Luza: a free-thinker, but one panic-stricken by his own solitude.

An accursed child of the accursed daughter of the accursed branch of a family over whom hung the double malediction of divorce and ruin, I thirsted for new curses.

Here is how I discovered that one can be ashamed of loving.

We were supervised, according to the British method, by the older students, and each of them had his favorite, called his "chou-chou" in the school jargon. I had the misfortune to please their *capitaine général*, and responded with a chaste but violent passion. There developed between us a true attachment which I never suspected could afford me any other pleasure than that of the heart, much less that such a pleasure was a culpable one. Jean Bersa wrote me every day; I answered with the same regularity, and I soon arrived at a remarkable state of exaltation. The moments of freedom no longer seemed adequate for correspondence. I began writing during study hours. Entrenched behind a dictionary, I pieced together the most excessive endearments, taken at random from my vacation reading, and did not hear the monitor creeping up behind me one afternoon, until

he snatched away the page over which I was bent, and exclaimed in a tone more amused than severe: "What's this, writing to a sweetheart?"

An extraordinary shame filled my heart. My face turned deep red and I cried out, supposing I was justifying myself:

"Oh, no, Monsieur, not to a sweetheart, that's to Bersa!"

A thunderous burst of laughter shook the room.

"Get out!" shrieked the supervisor, who didn't know what else to say.

That evening when Jean Bersa appeared at dinner, his eyes were still swollen with tears. I was crying helplessly, and in my grief dropped the little farewell note he slipped into the palm of my hand as we left the dining hall; it was found on the stairs and whisked, by magic, assuredly, to the principal's office. The latter called me in and tried to explain my crime to me. But I failed to understand it, for I had up till then done nothing but love.

This unsolved problem left me hesitant, apprehensive, and more self-conscious, more withdrawn than before.

Which is why the distractions provided by the little wallet were of great help. On the night's threshold, this moment of pleasure made me malleable to sleep, and what better refuge than sleep, from the day's miseries? It is undeniable that I suffered dreadfully from being at school.

It was rare that I fell asleep other than in tears. I had not been very happy at home, but in comparison with school, what a paradise! This was because it was the custom to make martyrs of the *new boys*. I did not escape the rule: secret punches, refined tortures, all kinds of tasks and errands for which you were thanked by being thrown into the brook or whipped by nettles—such was my daily bread for a whole year. I conceived enormous longings for vengeance, on which my ambition fed.

A certain Bara *rinsed me off*, as we said at school. He had anticipated and coordinated my incomplete and scattered suspicions. He boasted of the pleasures of the flesh, exhibited all the advantages of his body, and gradually persuaded me to accept a secret rendezvous, where he promised to initiate me into certain pleasures of which I was still ignorant.

The exercise he described to me in detail seemed quite wicked.

"Listen, it's not good to do that," I told him.

"It's not bad," he said, "my parents do it."

"How do you know?"

"I saw them through the keyhole!"

This convinced me, for I did not believe that Monsieur and Madame Bara, who were respectability itself, could do anything wrong. But Bara did not show up at our meeting-place and was suddenly expelled from the school without any of us learning the reason.

The diversions Bara had suggested seemed to me quite unconnected with the affection I had felt for Bersa, and I was sure they had nothing to do with love. But a few months later, I experienced what must, despite my youth, be called true love. Though I was only twelve or thirteen, this profound and terrible love made me suffer no less than certain unhappy loves I experienced later.

The object of this passion was a delicate, pale boy my own age with long, straight, fine blond hair. He had a rather angelic expression. I was so troubled by his presence, I scarcely dared speak to him, and I forget how we managed to be walking together in the woods one day. A bower of fallen leaves suddenly appeared: we lay down in it at the same time and flung our arms around each other without a word. And soon, without knowing how, an extraordinary fever inflamed my whole body, and without even offering a helping hand, we were flooded by pleasure.

This unique incident made me understand the profound links that existed between love and pleasure; nothing seemed higher to me. But I learned on the same occasion what venality is, for this boy with his angelic face did not conceal from me that he longed for a fine tennis racket I had. I gave it to him, but the minute he received it, he withdrew from me quite openly.

This episode at least instructed me that there are better things in the world than a wallet, and I suddenly realized that what I had just done with Aser was a habitual practice throughout the school.

A great wave of sensuality swept through this institution. Lustful practices were rife, affected every grade, and it is no exaggeration to say that out of a hundred students, over fifty were making love together. Only the youngest and a few boys of a sturdy virtue who deliberately excluded themselves were exempt from our excesses. The older boys pursued the younger. In certain recreation periods, we would go in troups of eight or ten, sometimes, to roll together in the hay that filled a barn; we could come back exhausted, happy, covered with wisps of hay.

It was surprising that the authorities suspected nothing for so long; ultimately, of course, something gave us away and a major purge was instituted. As might be expected, I was high on the list of the students expelled so politely that our parents, luckily, had no idea of what had really happened.

I think the reason for this indulgence was the fact that more than one teacher, especially our British masters, was among the guilty.

Thus, ingloriously, ended my time at boarding-school. I had spent four years at the Collège de Luza. But all I had gained during that time was a number of bad habits. And today it seems to me that I might have drawn up the balance-sheet for that year of 1919 thus:

I had developed a great love of literature, and gave evidence of an undeniable talent for writing. I loved English (thanks to what Suze had taught me in the nursery), and recited quite well. Lastly, I had made several of those discoveries by which one realizes that one is gradually assuming a human form.

First of all, the discovery of friendship: I was especially attached to a tall, dark, solemn, affectionate boy, as intellectual as it was possible to be at that age, whose name was Vidal; then to a schoolmate no less fond of reading, chaste, reserved, good-natured and very pale, whose name was Hervé. We were no longer too young to read Racine and to talk through whole recess periods about the writers we were getting to know. At first these were our schoolbook authors. Since I was so lazy, studying only *French* because anything else discouraged me, I soon knew all the texts of the great authors to be found in the standard textbooks. And since these are the best, I owe a great deal to these readings, especially the realization—quite early—that only badly written books could be boring. It was thanks to this bit of solitary education that I never had a rival for first place in French composition.

Hervé and I spent almost every spring night talking about poetry, for we slept in the same dormitory. We drew the beds in front of the window, and by fixing our eyes on the moon ("It's supposed to drive you crazy to stare at the moon," he said), we forced ourselves to stay awake; deep in those long discussions a grown-up mind finds incomprehensible, we waited for daybreak with the delicious feeling of being heroes who never hesitated to suffer *nuits blanches* for art's sake.

It was as a result of our readings and in these endless conversations that art finally seemed to me an entity, a kind of sacred figure that could play a role in my life.

From this to trying to play a role in the life of art was only a step, and a step I took. At those moments when all children ask each other: "What do you want to be when you grow up?" I invariably answered: "I'm going to be a writer." I saw nothing else that was worth living for. Moreover, I see nothing else even today that could make me live a happy life. But alas, a thousand times alas, if only I had kept to the splendid longings of my childhood! How many worries, how many misfortunes and how much remorse I would have avoided! What a delightful life I might have had, if I had not supposed myself, later on, to be a talented businessman. At fifteen, I saw myself clearly. O cursed blindness that sealed my eyes for the next fifteen years and let me wander through so many disastrous or futile undertakings, when I might have written so much (for I do not think much of the wretched little books I produced between 1932 and 1940, written as one steals a pleasure, my mind filled with a swarm of worries).

I see only one way to explain this deviation from my fate: since art seemed to me the holiest, the highest, the most sublime of human possibilities, I considered myself unworthy of approaching it too closely. Yes, that was it. That is why, while dreaming of the joy of writing, I already forbade myself its exercise, out of timidity, out of humility, out of a sense of guilt. ("Unhappy only," Stephen Spender says, "because he believed that some doom had made everything good in the world *outside* himself.")

With the years, I sank deeper into this error, and I who imagined no other joy than that of becoming, as Chateaubriand calls it, "a machine for making books," forbade myself to do so with an obstinacy about which I am deeply grateful to psychoanalysis for having enlightened me.

Translated by Richard Howard.

Other works by Sachs: *André Gide* (1936); *Chronique joyeuse et scandaleuse* (1948); *The Hunt* (1965).

Mark Vishniak

1883–1977

Mark Vishniak was born in Moscow and graduated from Moscow University. Inspired by the political events of 1905, he was a socialist revolutionary, and wrote in Russian radical periodicals. In 1918 he was secretary of the Constituent Assembly, but the assembly was disbanded but hours after its creation. After the Bolshevik takeover in Crimea, Vishniak left for Paris, living there from 1919 to 1940. He became active in Russian-speaking intellectual and political life, writing political analyses that focused on the problem of democracy under Bolshevik rule. He also co-founded the political-literary journal *Sovremennye zapiski*. He then moved to New York, where he remained until his death, contributing to social and political periodicals.

Doktor Veitsman

1939

The people were hardworking, sprightly, and seasoned. They sailed all the way to Danzig and Memel and back, and knew the worth of merchandise as well as of people. The Jewish population made a living primarily in the lumber industry: they hired workers for merchants, transported wood, served as brokers for the buying and selling of forest dachas. Human civilization spreads along the rivers, and human resourcefulness and intelligence depend on rivers, and so along the rivers of Polesie, a unique human character formed and evolved. "Motolyanets" [Motol-dweller] or, more broadly, "Pinchuk" [Pinsk-dweller] was not just a geographical designation; it was a certain psychological type: they were unperturbed, husky, sturdy and arrogant people, who liked to eat their fill and drink well, self-assured and lacking in any particular respect or reverence for anyone.

The family of Mikhoel Chemerinskii has been living in Motol for a long time, renting land from a Polish landowner. The family was prosperous, and his youngest daughter Rokhl-Leye was brought up in a way appropriate for a pious shtetl family at that time. She was taught to be a good housewife, to manage the home, to cook and sew. It so happened, however, that Chemerinskii was renting out a room to a Polish military paramedic, a high-school dropout, who had a French wife and the last name Semashko. Later on, this name was made famous by his grandson, a national commissar of health under the Soviet regime; in Motol, Semashko the grandfather was drinking himself away, and his wife, for lack of any other company, befriended the nine-year-old Rokhl-Leye and became attached to her. The French woman brought a radical transformation to the Jewish child's upbringing. The girl not only took up French words and expressions, but also adopted manners and tastes that were unfamiliar in Motol; she learned how to do needlework, appreciate elegance, and love beauty.

When the girl turned eleven, the pale and melancholic thirteen-year-old Eyzer (Yevzor) Veitsman appeared on her horizon. He was sent to be educated with relatives in Motol by his parents who were struggling with abject poverty in a neighboring shtetl. This education consisted of the child's spending his entire days in the synagogue praying and studying Talmud, only to return to his relatives' house in the evening, for a meager meal and brief rest.

Rokhl-Leye and Eyzer met, and the lively, decisive Rokhl-Leye, who, as the family's favorite, had never been denied anything, declared that she found her husband to be. Her father was agreeable: "If you want Eyzer, let it be Eyzer!" . . . Objectively as well, a Talmud scholar and a potential rabbi appeared, in the eyes of the wealthy yet simple Chemerinskiis, an entirely suitable groom for their daughter. The future son-in-law was allotted a little room at Chemerinskiis' home, and he continued his Talmud study with his former diligence.

And then came the day when Rokhl-Leye's long black braids fell victim to the old Jewish ritual. Her girlfriends observed the tradition by weeping, and the fourteen-year-old bride, in a wig and a puffy new dress, accompanied by relatives and guests gathered from the surrounding shtetls, walked to the chuppah. The musicians from Pinsk broke into a melody, and so began the wedding and the week-long feast. People danced in the old manner, as well as the new.

The wedding did not transform the young couple's daily life. They continued to live at the Chemerinkiis' house. The sixteen-year-old husband continued to study the subtleties of the Talmud, but they no longer satisfied his inquisitiveness and curiosity. Eyzer tasted the fruit of secular literature—first in Hebrew, and then in Russian—and became addicted to it. From the father of Jewish Haskalah (Enlightenment), Isaac-Ber Levinson, he learned that religion does not at all preclude the study of grammar of the holy text, and that a pious Jew is not prohibited from studying even non-Jewish grammar and science. Eyzer secretly started learning Russian and became more interested in the non-Talmudic world.

During this time, his wife Rokhl-Leye took care of the home. She also discovered an aptitude for business. Life went on in this way until it was time for her to become a mother. Eyzer was faced with the question of how to stop relying on his father-in-law's tutelage and live independently. The selfless study of holy and other texts had to be abandoned so that he could look for work. He started working like everyone else in Polesie: first he looked for and hired workers for the forest industry and sugar factories, and then started conducting rafts with wood across the Dnieper–Bug Canal on the Vistula, to Danzig. For weeks at a time, he traveled on the rivers, between heaven and earth, getting lost in abstract thinking and coming into contact with the local population—lumberjacks and raftsmen, foresters and foremen, constantly surrounded by dirt and dampness, columns of tobacco smoke and alcohol vapors.

Rokhl-Leye managed the house, and nursed and educated the children, who were being born almost annually. Over the course of twenty-two years, she bore, with the help of the same midwife, a total of fifteen children for Eyzer. She was trying to make the home comfortable and neat, in spite of their poverty. She planted flowers in the garden and was teaching her children how to take care of them. In Motol, this type of Jewish life was unusual, and provoked jealousy and objections. The neighbors would gossip: "They eat unpeeled potatoes in Rokhl's house, but they do it on a white tablecloth and with silver spoons" . . . "Rokhl-Leye has flowers in her garden, like a priest. Now I ask you, is that appropriate for a daughter of Israel?"

Rokhl-Leye was thick, tall, cheerful, and talkative. Eyzer was her opposite—short and puny: nothing but skin and bones, if you don't count his invisible and weightless soul. She had a natural sense of humor. She wielded a rare and unique assortment of words and expressions, and so personified the entirety of Jewish folklore. Eyzer, silent by nature, preferred to smile pensively and quietly into his unruly and disheveled beard. Whenever he spoke, he did so intelligently and wittily: his wit spread throughout Motol and even Pinsk. Since he was bookish by upbringing as well as inclination, Rokhl-Leye's healthy, spontaneous, down-to-earth joy was foreign to him. She was religious, old-fashioned. Eyzer was well-versed in the holy texts and the Talmud, but still maintained a healthy dose of skepticism; he was in a sense an "apikoyres"—a heretic. He had a pleasant voice and, when he led the prayers on Rosh Hashanah, the "highs" and "lows" of his praying melody were appreciated by the congregants for a long time after. Eyzer was good-natured, interested in social issues from a young age, and enjoyed certain authority in his circle. He was the first Jew in Motol to officially represent the shtetl.

Eyzer was busily self-educating all his life. In Motol he was reputed to be a mathematician as well as a lawyer. Having acquired and studied a corpus of Russian civil law, he composed a plethora of appeals to legal and administrative institutions in Kobrin and Petersburg. Eyzer Veitsman belonged to a generation of Jewish enlighteners ("maskilim"), who believed in enlightenment not only as a value in and of itself, but also as a necessary and adequate means of overcoming the obduracy of the masses who were inclined toward fanaticism. Like others of his generation, Eyzer Veitsman had to go through a spiritual crisis, but that happened later. In the seventies of the nineteenth century, the elite of Jewish intelligentsia observed with ecstasy and anticipation the reforming activity of Alexander II. Almost every Jewish home displayed a portrait of the liberating tsar. With the passion of neophytes who were granted the freedom to breathe for the first time, enlightened Jews believed in the beginning of a new and permanent era.

The allure of freedom affected a yearning to reject national insularity and a pull toward Russification, in the name of broader and deeper questions of man and humanity. There were other roads leading toward assimilation: the Jewish "public" schools, gymnasia, universities, which were now open to Jewish youth. The pupils of stuffy heders and yeshivas were eager to revel in the free air, shaking off the dust of their extreme and obscurantist fathers and forefathers, and exchanging rabbinical scholasticism and Hasidic mysticism for a new revelation—positivism and evolutionism. "Fathers and Sons" has become the leitmotif not only of Russian life and literature, but Jewish as well; not only for Turgenev, but for Mendele Moykher Sforim as well. Chernyshevskii, Dobrolyubov, Gertsen, and Pirogov were the demigods of Jewish youth, along with Darwin, Buckle, Mill, Spencer.

Progressive Jews, just like progressive layers of Russian society, rejected with equal force the dilapidated forms of the age-old Jewish way of life, the intellectual slumber of Hasidic circles, and the fossilized forms of rabbinical obscurantism. There was even a warm feeling between new Jewish intelligentsia and the autocratic regime. The "Society for the Promotion of Culture among the Jews of Russia" was not only one of the most useful cultural institutions, but also a symbol and a program of a complete resolution of the Jewish question.

Even the pogrom on Passover 1871 in Odessa did not disrupt Russian–Jewish relations. The pogrom was explained away as an unfortunate coincidence; it was considered a bitter exception, especially since its main perpetrators were Greeks, who competed with Jews in trade and the export of Russian bread. True, the Greeks—the instigators and initiators of the pogrom—were joined by local Russian thugs, who, for three days, destroyed Jewish property, desecrated synagogues, and beat Jews under the gaze of apathetic armies and police. The central government was interested in the pogrom only to the extent that they were concerned about the blossoming of a revolutionary movement, and worried that it would, beginning with Jews, also direct itself against landowning lords and the regime.

Russian schools and literature rapidly assimilated the Jewish student youth into Russian cultural streams and movements. And the former students of heders and yeshivas were imbued with the sense of an unpayable debt to the masses. And so they moved closer to the people and the revolution, so as to push the quick absorption of the benefits of civilization by the masses and, above all, for the light of knowledge. This movement captured the most self-sacrificing forces of Jewish youth, for whom the question didn't even arise at the time: *which* or *whose* people should they approach? It seemed clear that the realization of the Russian populist ideal would fully resolve all specific problems, including the Jewish one. The Jewish people—a religious group that now lived beyond its time, along with other analogous groups, was doomed to disappear. In the consciousness of progressive Jewish circles of the seventies and eighties, the 1807 formula of Napoleon's Sanhedrin kept its force and persuasiveness: "the Jewish people does not constitute a nation."

Translated by Alexandra Hoffman.

Other works by Vishniak: *The Legal Status of Stateless Persons* (1945); *An International Convention against Antisemitism* (1946); *The October Revolution: Promise and Realization* (1967).

Daniel Charney

1888–1959

Daniel Charney (Tsharni) was born in Dukor, Belorussia. In 1902, he followed his older brothers Shmuel Niger and Borekh Tsharni to Minsk and Vilna, where he began publishing poetry and short stories. After 1914, Charney lived in Petrograd and Moscow. After the Bolshevik Revolution, he had a leadership role within the Moscow Circle of Yiddish Writers and Artists and was the editor of a number of Soviet Yiddish periodicals. In the 1920s, he lived in Moscow and Berlin, and continued to contribute to both Soviet and international Yiddish literature and culture. Charney left Germany in 1934 and, after wandering through Europe, arrived in the United States in 1941, where he continued his organizational and creative work.

What a Decade! 1914–1924
Late 1930s

My Conversation with Kalinin

Nineteen nineteen was one of the most difficult years for the Bolsheviks. The civil war flared up in every corner of Russia. In Ukraine, Petliura, Grigoriev, Denikin, Makhno, and other titled and untitled rebels and bandits rampaged across the country. Jews were robbed and murdered left and right under the slogan *Bey Zhidov—spasay Rosiyu* (Beat the Jews—and save Russia).

Trotsky ran from one front of the civil war to the other, trying to pump new courage and faith into the barefoot, hungry soldiers of the Red Army. Trotsky's courage and heroism were really quite remarkable.

Russian Jews were proud of the fact that he led the heroic fight against the *pogromnik*s, but, at the same time, they were also terrified that if, God forbid, the Bolsheviks lost, Jews would have to pay dearly for Trotsky-Bronstein.

There were some critical moments when everyone thought this would be the end of the entire October Revolution. Kolchak was approaching Moscow from Siberia. General Yudenich was threatening Petrograd. In Belorussia, in addition to the Poles, Bułak-Bałachowicz and Savinkov, the former Socialist Revolutionary terrorists, were raging.

Thus, even pious Jews in Moscow prayed to God that the enemies of the Soviet power should not, God forbid, "bite off the *pitum*"[1] (Petrograd, Tula, Moscow)—prayed to God three times a day that the enemies of the Soviet power should not, God forbid, that is, lay their hands on *P*etrograd, *T*ula, and *M*oscow.

Those few Jewish Bolsheviks who gathered around the Jewish Commissariat in Moscow just remained idle. Once again, they were separated from the Jewish working class. Once again, they lost the broad Jewish masses of Lithuania, Belorussia, and Ukraine. At first, the commissar of Jewish affairs, Dimanshteyn, wanted to renew publication of the newspaper *Der emes* [The Truth], but because the transportation system was in ruins, it made no sense to publish a daily newspaper for Jewish refugee settlements far out in the Volga region. Thus, the Jewish commissar settled for the monthly journal *Di komunistishe velt* [The Communist World]. The first issue of the journal was published on May 1, 1919, by Sh. [Shmuel] Agurskii, formerly an anarchist in America, whose long-held dream has been to publish his own journal. Let both his friends and his enemies in America see what an important personality he was for the Bolsheviks!

The boorish Agurskii, with his anarchist hairstyle and wide, watery eyes, did, in fact, work his way up and landed the most important position of manager and leader of the Jewish division of the State Academy of Science of Belorussia—he was almost a professor! Thanks to his friendship with Kalinin, with whom Agurskii traveled around the Jewish areas of Belorussia in 1918 as the Jewish propagandist of Bolshevism, he (Agurskii) managed to persuade the *starosta* [elder, leader] of the entire Soviet Russia to address the second conference of Jewish communists in the name of VTsIK (All-Russian Central Executive Committee), which took place in Moscow at the beginning of 1919.

This conference was attended by a total of twenty-plus-something "delegates," who represented no more than eight hundred Jewish workers altogether. This conference laid the groundwork for the Evsektsiia.

Kalinin came to address the Jewish communists toward the end of the conference. The *starosta* of Soviet Russia was actually a simple man of the people, a rather sentimental Russian. When he began to talk about the terrible pogroms carried out in Ukraine, Kalinin began to cry. He had to interrupt his speech until he gathered himself. At the end of his speech, Kalinin turned to the Jewish communists with a request—he asked them to let the Jewish bourgeoisie know that these recent pogroms were all the work of the counterrevolution, and as soon as the counterrevolution was choked off, the pogroms would stop immediately.

The Jewish communists felt deeply insulted by Kalinin's request. His words implied that they, the Jewish communists, were in some kind of contact with the Jewish bourgeoisie. This suggested that the Evsektsiia and the Jewish bourgeoisie were somehow one family, and it was simply a matter of the Jewish bourgeoisie not yet understanding that only Soviet power could save Jews from pogroms. The Jewish communists were so upset by this that one of them, a certain Al'ski, had to respond to Kalinin's speech and call the all-Russian *starosta*'s attention to the fact that this was not a conference of Jewish nationalist communists but of communist Jews who had no connection whatsoever to the Jewish bourgeoisie. The Evsektsiia considered the Jewish bourgeoisie an organic part of the general counterrevolution that carried out pogroms on Jewish laborers.

Apparently, Kalinin was not pleased with the awkward "anti-Jewish" response he received from the Evsektsiia to his heartfelt, sentimental speech and left the conference hall right away. As a result, the Jewish communists became even more upset. Dimanshteyn winked at me, signaling that I should leave the room. After all, I was the only non-party-aligned "comrade" present, and Dimanshteyn did not want me to hear the huge fight that was about to follow Kalinin's address.

Thus, I left the conference hall right after Kalinin, and that is when I had the great opportunity to have an intimate conversation with Mikhail Ivanovich (Kalinin) in the lobby of the Hotel Metropol, where the conference took place, and to ask him about the years of his youth, which were of special interest to me.

I wanted to know how this simple man of the Russian people was able to work his way up to such a high position,[2] one that was officially even higher than Lenin's and Trotsky's posts. The jovial and sentimental Kalinin began to tell me that when he was young, he was constantly tortured by the problem of the twig branches. At the time, people began to cut down the forests in the vicinity of Tver. (The city of Tver is called Kalinin today.) The young Misha (that's what he was called in his village) was greatly alarmed by this; he was afraid that there would not be enough branches for people to thrash themselves in the bathhouse. After all, how else could people beat off the village dirt from their bodies if there were no good, leafy branches? He was haunted by the horrible possibility of a branch shortage all the time, until years later when he started working at the Putilov factory in St. Petersburg. It was only there, at the factory, that Kalinin once noticed how one of the engineers was washing himself after work with some kind of a rubbery sponge that released a foaming soap.

It was at that time, at the young age of seventeen, that he decided his goal was to ensure that every Russian peasant and worker had such a rubbery sponge. This way, they could stop using branches, which sometimes left bloody wounds when they beat themselves to clean their bodies.

I have to admit that I had a strong urge to tell Comrade Kalinin that I actually owned such a rubbery sponge—I'd brought it with me from Germany—but that my "piece of civilization" (the sponge, that is) had been withering for a few years now, that it was shrunken and dried out because there was no hot water and no soap. . . .

But I decided not to brag to Comrade Kalinin unnecessarily about my "bourgeois" past, so I just said to him, en passant, that in order to use the rubbery sponges, you first needed hot water and soap. . . . "Of course," Comrade Kalinin consoled me cordially. "We are just about to introduce the 'bathing week' [in Russian, it was called *nedellia banii*] all over Russia." This gave me a great idea for an article headline: "Jews, to the bathhouse!"

After that, I returned to the conference hall, where the debate about Kalinin's address had already concluded.

The Evsektsiia members sat there all heated and sweaty, as in a bathhouse. Comrade Sh. Agurskii seemed to have been "thrashed with the branch" more than anyone else because he was the one who had not informed Kalinin properly that he would be addressing not a conference of *Jewish communists* but a conference of *communist Jews*. They punished Agurskii by depriving him of his post as editor of the journal *Di komunistishe velt*, and he was "banished" to Vitebsk where he was a commissar. The incident with Kalinin's speech was, of course, not recorded in the official protocols of the conference. . . .

The "Cheka" and Poetry

The monthly journal *Di komunistishe velt* was the organ of the Jewish section of the Russian Communist Party, known by the popular name Evsektsiia. The official and de facto editor of the journal was still Sh. Dimanshteyn. In fact, Dimanshteyn could not always separate his own offices in the Jewish Commissariat and in the "Jewish section" of the Communist Party. The Jewish Commissariat was an official organ of the Soviet government, and the Evsektsiia was the official organ of the Communist Party. But, in fact, the Soviet government itself was nothing but the official organ of the Communist Party. For the outside world, the Communist Party had its own higher authority—this was the Comintern (Communist International), but within Soviet Russia, the Bolshevik government could not pass a single decree without the consent of the communist leadership, the Politburo. This was what confused Dimanshteyn, too, because he was responsible to both the Sovnarkom [government agency responsible for post-revolution legislation] and the Politburo at the same time.

When Dimanshteyn appointed me editor of the literary section of *Di komunistishe velt*, he did not know for a long time from which budget he should pay my salary: from the funds of the Evsektsiia or the Jewish Commissariat. He had the money of both organizations at his disposal, and he paid me sometimes from one and sometimes from the other, depending on which account had more money.

But salary did not matter so much at that time. What mattered was the *paiok* [the ration], and the free lunch that we got at the *stolovka* [cafeteria] of the Communist Party. This was a special cafeteria for the responsible coworkers of the Central Committee of the Russian Communist Party, an eatery with a more refined ambiance—tables covered with tablecloths. Occasionally, even some people's commissars set foot in this cafeteria, whenever they were too lazy to go to the Kremlin for lunch. Educational commissar Lunacharsky and Kamenev, the chairman of the Moscow Soviet (Trotsky's brother-in-law), often came to have lunch at the party cafeteria. Whenever foreign visitors came from the Comintern, they were brought to eat here, at the party cafeteria, where they had a chance to meet the responsible functionaries of the Communist Party personally. Of course, the known and "unknown" representatives of the Cheka were frequent guests here, too. I must admit that I often felt rather uneasy at the party cafeteria, just like a yeshiva *bocher* who eats at a decent house. Yes, indeed, in those days, I "ate days" at the Central Committee of the Russian Communist Party. Very rarely did I hear Yiddish spoken there because those few Jewish communists who had the privilege to eat at the party cafeteria spoke Russian among themselves.

There was only one occasion when I met a Jewish communist at the party cafeteria who addressed me in Yiddish because, as he said, he recognized me after Vladek. Back in the Bundist years, he was a close friend of Vladek, and now, when he saw me, he thought I was Vladek. . . . When I told him my name, he was very pleased to tell me that our works had been published together in Avrom Reyzen's journal *Dos naye land* [The New Land]. His literary name was Bere Henye Khashes, and he also wrote poetry. He lived in Germany for years, was there during the revolution of November 1918; he was a member of the Spartakus-bund [Spartacus League] and held an important position at Centrotextil. He lived at the Hotel Metropol, where all the important guests of the Soviet Republic and key communist functionaries stay. He invited me to visit him—he would give me a gift, a shaving instrument with good German blades. In those days, this was a truly valuable gift, especially for me, since—having lived abroad—I was used to shaving every day.

When I visited my colleague Bere Henye Khashes at the Hotel Metropol, he bragged to me that he had brought six suits from Germany, all different colors and cuts; he also had six pairs of shoes and lots of shirts and neckties, like a real gentleman. In Germany, he worked at a large herring company, and that is why in Moscow he was immediately appointed the director of Centrotextil.

But the truth is that he was not the director of Centrotextil but the political commissar, whose job was to make sure that its employees were all "kosher" Bolsheviks. At the same time, this Spartacist fighter was also longing to become a poet again, a Jewish Soviet poet in the style of Demian Bedny. Demian Bedny was one of the most popular and beloved Communist "court poets" at the time. He wrote his poems in the style of the Russian *chastushka* and *bylina*, with lots of humor and lightness. Bere Henye Khashes decided that he wanted to become the Yiddish Demian Bedny, and he flooded me with Soviet *badkhones* [entertaining poetry] and gibberish that had no literary value whatsoever. Naturally, I did not publish his poems in the only journal there was at the time, *Di komunistishe velt*. He then reported to the Cheka, which he frequented, that the Jewish commissar Dimanshteyn employed a nonparty-aligned individual who oppressed Communist poets as the literary editor of *Di komunistishe velt*. . . . When Dimanshteyn was questioned by the Cheka whether it was true that I oppressed Communist poets, I suggested that he invite Comrade Moroz, the Cheka's specialist on Jewish affairs, to the Commissariat—let him rule whether the poems of the ambitious Spartacist fighter were publishable or not. Comrade Moroz did, in fact, come to the Jewish Commissariat, and

I showed him all the poems of the "Jewish Demian Bedny." He read the poems carefully and immediately ruled that in times like these, when there was a shortage of paper, it would be a sin to waste some on such nonsense. . . .

After that, anytime a graphomaniac tried to bombard me with his poems or short stories, I would send them straight to the Cheka to get Comrade Moroz's stamp of approval. Dimanshteyn was so impressed with my idea that he immediately gave me a month's vacation—he told me to go somewhere in the Volga region to improve my health.

Thus, I traveled to Samara—today called Kuibyshev. [. . .]

Social Struggle in Yiddish Literature

In the years between 1918 and 1922, Moscow—by now socialist Moscow—became the capital of Yiddish Soviet literature, too. There was not a single Yiddish writer from the former Russia who would not have passed through Moscow, just like one passes through a quarantine in times of an epidemic. Some Yiddish writers came to the "quarantine" of Moscow so that they could quietly escape from Soviet Russia to Kovno [Kaunas, Lithuania], Warsaw, Berlin, New York, and even further. Others came to Moscow in order to absorb the enthusiasm of the October Revolution and make themselves at home in the newly emerging proletarian literature written in Yiddish.

Upon arriving in Moscow, all communist-minded Yiddish writers would first report to the Evsektsiia and then come to Malaia Dimitrovka Street 29, Apartment 3, where the office of the Moscow Association of Yiddish Writers and Artists was located, whereas the writer-émigrés and would-be émigrés reported first to the chairmen of the Moscow Literary Circle and only after that to the Evsektsiia.

Since between 1918 and 1922 the chairman of the Moscow Association of Yiddish Writers and Artists was none other than the author of these lines, I can confirm that literally the entire Yiddish literary establishment—from its greatest "stars" to absolute beginners—passed through my apartment on Malaia Dimitrovka Street. [. . .]

I could write a separate chapter about each and every one of these writers because they all brought with them the horror stories from the pogrom years in Ukraine and Belorussia, all their terrible experiences during the civil war, the hunger and great misery. Only the capital of the "world revolution," Moscow, could possibly set them free. In any case, all of them were famished and destitute when they arrived, so the Yiddish writers first had to be supplied with clothes, shoes, and the allocated ration.

The Evsektsiia found it sufficient to give them a free lunch at the party *stolovka* and once a month the meager ration, which was not enough for more than a few days.

At the same time, the Evsektsiia kept making strong demands of the Yiddish writers, and on January 12, 1922, Moyshe Litvakov published an article in *Der emes* attacking the entire literary family of which he himself had been one of its main leaders in Kiev.

It is worth taking this opportunity to quote from that article, which produced so much bad blood at the time even among those Yiddish writers who were quite sincerely looking to find their way to proletarian Yiddish literature in Soviet Russia. [. . .]

> All those publicist-comrades and sympathizer writers who are not helping us with their works during these difficult years of our emergence should consider themselves warned that once *Der emes* takes root and has more time for collecting old, unpaid bills, we will definitely be most eager to do so!

Moyshe Litvakov did, in fact, keep his word. He used *Der emes* as his whip to thrash people near and far until one day he himself fell victim to his own "truth."

Moyshe Litvakov's life ended quite tragically—he died in a Moscow prison as a "counterrevolutionary" and an "enemy of the people"—but the last twenty years of his life as an editor were no less tragic. He had always been surrounded by writers and aspiring writers whose communist *yikhes* [pedigree] was much greater than his, and therefore he could never finish them off.

Shmuel Agurskii, who was appointed Jewish commissar in Vitebsk, where he edited newspapers and journals all by himself, was full of rage because the Evsektsiia sidelined him from the entire publishing apparatus, and he never stopped inciting against Litvakov.

Chaim Gildin, who had been a proletarian poet in Warsaw already in Peretz's times, started hammering the nails in Litvakov's coffin already in his first book, *Homers klangen* [Homer's Sounds]. He accused Litvakov, saying that in Moscow he continued to conduct the old "Kiev politics"—meaning that Litvakov promoted

Hofshteyn, Markish, and Der Nister rather than him, the first proletarian poet in Yiddish.

Berl Orshanski, who had literary and communist experience as an underground activist in the occupied territories, could not forgive Litvakov because he [Litvakov] had once advised him on the pages of *Der emes* that he should start writing his memoirs, like Yekhezkel Kotik, rather than dramas about the October Revolution that were neither dramatic nor revolutionary. [. . .]

Moyshe Taytsh, who used to be a Folkist and then suddenly became a communist, also had a stack of proletarian poems and short stories written especially for *Der emes* that Litvakov refused even to read. So Moyshe Taytsh went and complained to the Central Committee of the Communist Party that Litvakov, the former such and such, oppressed communist Yiddish writers who came directly from Jewish poverty. [. . .]

Litvakov was afraid to launch an attack on me, though, because he knew that all Yiddish writers in Moscow would stand by me through thick and thin because the famished and destitute Yiddish writers of Moscow knew full well that the easiest way to get in touch with the Joint [Distribution Committee] was through me. . . .

This is why, throughout all the years I spent in Moscow, I had to remain the president of the Moscow Association of Yiddish Writers and Artists—which, incidentally, I founded in 1918, when the entire family of Yiddish writers consisted of only Moyshe Broderzon, Z[almen] Vendrof, Menashe Halperin, and myself. [. . .]

All the great social struggles for the new Yiddish Soviet literature at the time were about these small packages handed out by the Joint. Receiving one herring more or one herring less was enough of a reason for people to switch from one group to another, but all the herring groups strongly opposed the recently emerged Evsektsiia, which—according to the Yiddish Soviet "classics" such as Moyshe Taytsh, Chaim Gildin, and Berl Orshanski—was captured by people like Moyshe Litvakov and [Aron] Tshemerinski, who became communists only recently. [. . .]

On the other hand, Yiddish writers in Moscow were in a much more privileged situation than their non-Jewish colleagues because they enjoyed the support of the Joint.

The Joint distributed not only food packages and clothes but often cash, too. Some Russian Jewish writers such as Andrey Sobol (a brother-in-law of the Yiddish poet Elisha Rodin) and the literary critic

Yuri Eichenvald found out about our privileges, so I added their names to the list of Yiddish writers and artists who could and should receive aid from the Joint. [. . .]

But even the great "social struggle" around the Joint ration was carried out in the name of the October Revolution, of course. On one occasion, for instance, the Joint gave an entire barrel of herring to the Moscow Association of Yiddish Writers and Artists. The board of directors then held two stormy meetings in my apartment discussing how to distribute the herring.

Should we adopt the principle of "each according to his needs," and everyone should receive from the herring according to the number of people in his family (Moyshe Taytsh strongly supported adopting this principle since he had a family of eight),[3] or should we distribute it according to people's literary and communist seniority—a principle advocated by Chaim Gildin, who did not have a family. A writer like Dovid Bergelson or an artist like Marc Chagall, Gildin argued, should receive one herring more than Sh. Godiner or Yisakhar Ber Rybak, and Chaim Gildin should also receive one herring more than Moyshe Taytsh, because he became a communist a few years earlier than Moyshe Taytsh.

In the end, we adopted the family principle, but how could we determine in advance how many pieces of herring everyone should receive when we did not know how many herrings there were in the barrel?!

Finally, two members of the Moscow Writers' Circle, the pedagogue Dovid Hochberg and Menashe Halperin, agreed to count all the herring and then distribute them according to the agreed scheme. This difficult task had to be carried out at night in the unheated premises of the Kultur-Lige on Kuznetsky Most Street at a temperature of twenty below zero Celsius. As compensation for this work, Dovid Hochberg wanted to get the barrel because, he explained to us, a herring barrel is very useful since you can keep cabbage in it. Menashe Halperin only wanted the herring broth, because his wife was running a private cafeteria where, incidentally, many Yiddish writers dined.

The distribution of the barrel of schmaltz herring we received from the Joint was one of the most magnificent moments in the history of the Moscow Writers' Association. Neither the Evsektsiia nor the "academic ration" had ever seen a schmaltz herring like ours!

But the real struggle for the *bkhore* [right of primogeniture] in Yiddish Soviet literature began only after the just distribution of the herring. This struggle was set off by Z. Vendrof, who had been excluded from the distribution of the herring because he used to send correspondence to the *Forverts*. In Moscow, people used to call him the *dolkor*, the dollar correspondent. [. . .]

NOTES

1. [The *pitum* is the end of the *etrog* (citron) used on the Sukkot holiday. If it is bitten or cut off from the *etrog*, the latter is rendered unfit for use (*pasul*).—Eds.]

2. [Kalinin was chairman of the Presidium of the Supreme Soviet, the largely honorific national legislature.—Eds.]

3. ["A Family of Eight" is the title of a famous poem by Avrom Reisen about poverty.—Eds.]

Translated by Vera Szabó.

Other works by Charney: *Mishpokhe-khronik* (1927); *Untervegs: lider* (1929); *Barg aroyf* (1935); *Afn shvel fun yener velt* (1947); *Lider* (1950); *Dukor* (1951); *Vilne* (1953); *A litvak in poyln* (1955); *Di velt iz kaylekhdik* (1963).

SCHOLARSHIP

Traditional Jewish scholarship continued to flourish in the interwar period, especially in Eastern Europe. At the same time, university-educated Jewish scholars, following in the footsteps of the pioneers of Wissenschaft des Judentums, continued to explore Jewish history, sociology, linguistics, and philosophy from a Western, critical perspective. Most of them held academic or research positions, in comparison to earlier periods, when Jewish studies flourished outside the academy. On the whole, their work was neither disinterested nor dispassionate. In many cases, it was motivated by and embedded with deeply held ideological concerns. Nonetheless, even if dated and ideologically driven, these texts continue to merit serious attention—for their contribution to the chain of Jewish scholarship, for their revelation of the cultural temper of the time, for their exploration of enduring ideas of Judaism and Jewishness, and for their accentuation of issues that have remained relevant long after the period covered by this volume.

Louis Ginzberg

1873–1953

Born in Kovno (today, Kaunas), Lithuania, the rabbinics scholar Louis Ginzberg studied Talmud at the yeshivas of Kovno and Telz, and history, philosophy, and Near Eastern languages at Berlin, Strasbourg, and Heidelberg. He immigrated to the United States in 1899 and found work as the rabbinics editor at the *Jewish Encyclopedia* in 1900. From 1903 until his death, he taught Talmud at the Jewish Theological Seminary in New York, where he influenced two generations of rabbis and shaped the development of the Conservative movement, not only through his teaching but also through his responsa. His best-known work is his seven-volume *Legends of the Jews* (1909–1938), a compendium of stories, anecdotes, and tales from midrashic texts that he forged into a continuous narrative of ancient Israel's history from the patriarchs to Queen Esther. He was a founder of the American Academy for Jewish Research and served as its president.

Jewish Thought as Reflected in the Halakah
1920

It was not without hesitation that I accepted the kind invitation extended to me to deliver the Zunz Lecture of this year. Greatly as I appreciated the honor conferred upon me, I did not find it an easy task to free myself from a deep-rooted conviction that, to speak in the words of the great Frenchman, Pascal, most of the mischief of this world would never happen if men were contented to sit in their parlors and refrain from talking. As a compromise with this strong conviction, I have chosen as my subject, "Jewish Thought as Reflected in the Halakah." On a subject of this sort one would talk only when one has something to say, or at least thinks so,—otherwise one would be prompted to keep silence.

To be candid, keeping silence strongly commends itself to one who has spent the greater part of his life in the study of the Halakah and, believing himself to have a good deal to say about it, is at a loss how to do so within the limited space of a single paper. It would be impossible within the compass of anything less than a substantial volume to present an analysis of the ideas comprised or implied in the term Halakah, or even to set forth the various senses in which the term has been employed. It has often been observed that the more claim an idea has to be considered living, the more various will be its aspects; and the more social and political is its nature, the more complicated and subtle will be its issues and the longer and more eventful its course. The attempt to express the "leading idea" of the Halakah I must perforce leave to those whose forte is omniscience and whose foible is knowledge. What I propose to do is something less ambitious than to sketch the nature and scope of the Halakah. It is more closely connected with the problem of the nature of Jewish history.

The Talmud remarks: "He who studies the Halakah daily may rest assured that he shall be a son of the world to come." The study of the Halakah may not commend itself to everyone as a means of salvation. Some may desire an easier road thereto; but we may well say that he who studies the Halakah may be assured that he is a son of the world—the Jewish world—that has been. Not that the Halakah is a matter of the past; but the understanding of the Jewish past, of Jewish life and thought, is impossible without a knowledge of the Halakah. One might as well hope to comprehend the history of Rome without taking notice of its wars and conquests or that of Hellas without giving attention to its philosophy and art. To state such a truism would be superfluous were it not for the fact that the most fundamental laws of nature are often disregarded in dealing with the Jews, and their history has undergone strange treatment at the hands of friend and foe alike.

If we further remember that Jewish historiography in modern times dates from the days when the Hegelian conception of history reigned supreme, the "peculiar" treatment of the history of the "peculiar people" is not in the least surprising. Historians who believed with Hegel that "history is the science of man in his political character," and consequently were of the opinion that there could be no history of a people without a state, could not but ignore the Halakah, a way of life that was rarely sustained by the power of the state but was frequently antagonized by it. What was the result of this conception of history applied to the Jews? The three main subjects dealt with in works on Jewish history in post-biblical times are: religion, literature, martyrology, to which a little philosophy with a sprinkling of cultural history is added; but of actual history in the modern sense of the word we find very little indeed. History as now generally understood is the science establishing the causal nexus in the development of man as a social being. The Jew may well say: *homo sum, nihil humani a me alienum puto.* State or no state, even the Jew of the diaspora lived for almost two thousand years a life of his own and has developed accordingly a character of his own.

Modern students of man teach us that three elements contribute to the formation of his character—heritage, environment, and training. What is true of individual character holds good also of national character. We hear a good deal of the importance of heritage or race, to use the favored phrase of the day, in appraising the character of the Jew and in the interpretation of his history. Dealers in generalities especially are prone to call in the racial features and characteristics to save the trouble of a more careful analysis which would show that these racial qualities themselves are largely due to historical causes, though causes often too far back in the past to admit of full investigation. The explanation of history from the narrow point of view of race is tantamount to affirming, as Hegel did, that the whole wealth of historic development is potential in the beginnings of mind, a view which it would be impossible to justify historically. The lessons of history indicate rather that at certain times men of genius initiate new movements which though related to the past are not explained by it, and that there are various possibilities contained in a given historic situation. Which of the possibilities is to become real would depend solely upon the training of the people confronted with the historic situation. Nothing is easier and nothing more dangerous than definitions. I shall not define what Halakah is; yet one is safe in asserting that its chief feature is education of oneself or training. Accordingly, the Halakah is a true mirror reflecting the work of the Jew in shaping his character.

No man who is badly informed can avoid reasoning badly. We can hardly expect to understand the causal nexus of our history if we disregard the most valuable source of information we seek. Here is a plain example in arithmetic to prove it. The literary output of the eighteen centuries from the beginning of the common era to the year 1795, the date of the emancipation of the Jews in France and Holland when the modern history of the Jew begins, contains seventy-eight percent of halakic material. We may easily convince ourselves of the exactness of this statement by looking at the classification of the Hebrew books in the British Museum, the largest collection of its kind in the world, prepared by such an eminent and careful bibliographer as Zedner. Yet it is not the quantity of the halakic Literature that makes it so valuable a source of Jewish history; by far more important is its quality.

Historians divide historical sources into two main groups: (a) historical remains and (b) tradition. By the first group we understand all that remains of an historical event. For instance, we find in certain parts of Germany ruins of Roman castles, places with Roman names, burial-grounds containing the bodies of Romans, their armor, pottery and so on. Let us suppose for a moment that the writings of Caesar, Tacitus and other Roman historians treating of the relations between Rome and Germania had disappeared; these remains of the actual life of the Romans in Germany would suffice to establish beyond any doubt the fact that at a certain time in history the Romans lived in Germany and were its masters. The second group of historical sources, tradition, is much less reliable, since it is only a subjective reflection in the human mind of historical events and can therefore be made use of only after a critical analysis has separated the subjective element of reflection from the objective facts reflected. We often hear of the lamentable dearth of sources of Jewish history. As far as historical tradition is concerned, the correctness of this statement is beyond dispute; but of historical remains we have in the Halakah a veritable treasure of material. The Halakah, as its meaning "conduct" indicates, comprises life in all its manifestations,—religion, worship, law, economics, political, ethics and so forth. It gives us a picture of life in its totality and not of some of its fragments.

You will ask how it could happen that all the historians and scholars who devoted their lives and great abilities to the study of Jewish history ignored its most important source, the Halakah? The answer to this question is not a difficult one. The importance of the Halakah as an historical source is equalled by the difficulty of its utilization. Its faults lie not in its substance but in the form which the conditions of its growth have given to it. It is a system extremely hard to expound and hard to master. So vast is it and so complicated, so much are its leading principles obscured by the way in which they have been stated, scattered here and there through the vast expanse of the "sea of the Talmud," in an order peculiar to the latter, which is the perfection of disorder, that it presents itself to the learner as a most arduous study, a study indeed which only a few carry so far as to make themselves masters of the whole. Hence the favorite phrase that a general impression of the Halakah suffices without the study of its details. Of course this is a cover for incapacity. To understand the whole, the knowledge of the parts is as indispensable in the study of the Halakah as in any other branch of human thought.

I do not wish to be misunderstood. Not everything that happens is history, and, consequently, the first requirement of the historian is to distinguish between essentials and non-essentials, between historical and non-historical happenings. The individual performs countless acts daily which the most conscientious and careful Boswell would pass over in silence as irrelevant. So also in the lives of nations and peoples, many things happen daily that are of no historical value. Not all the minutiae of the Halakah are historical material, but to quote the saying of an old Jewish sage: "If there be no knowledge, how could there be discernment?" To distinguish the essential from the non-essential in the Halakah one must master it entirely if one is not to become a prey to his subjective likes and dislikes,—and we all know how Jewish history is marred by bias and prejudice.

The problem of subjectivity in the presentation of Jewish history leads me to remark on another aspect of the Halakah,—its authoritative character. Writers on the phase of Judaism that comprises Jewish theology and ethics in post-biblical times have based their studies exclusively on the Haggadah, which means that they erected their structures upon shifting sand. Whatever else the Haggadah may be, it certainly is either individual, consisting of opinions and views uttered by Jewish sages for the most part on the spur of the moment, or creations of popular fancy. The haggadic sayings of the rabbis belong to the first division; the apocryphal-apocalyptic writings belong to the second.

All work, it is true, is done by individuals. We have nothing beyond the dicta of definite—known or unknown—persons. Yet the great men of a people give the impulses only, and all depends upon what the mass of the people make thereof. It is doubtless as important for the history of Judaism to know what Hillel said, what R. Akiba thought and what R. Meir taught as it is important for Christianity to study the writing of Augustine, Luther and Calvin. But not all Christians are Augustines or Luthers, nor all Jews Hillels and Akibas. The great moulders of Christians thought did indeed succeed in making the masses of Christianity accept their doctrines at solemn council and representative covenants, but that was not true of the spiritual leaders of the Jews. Even if we admit that whatever is alive in the nation finds expression in the works and words of individuals and that many individual contributions are products of the national spirit, there still remains a vast array of intellectual products that are temporary, accidental and individual, in which the national soul has but a small share. The devil, according to Shakespeare, quotes Scripture. But if he is really as clever as he is reputed to be, he ought to quote the Talmud, as there is hardly any view of life for and against which one could not quote the Talmud.

No less uncritical is the attempt made by many theologians to give us a system of the religious thought of the Jew based upon the apocalyptic literature, the fantastic fabric of popular imagination. As the author of a large work on Jewish legends, I believe myself to be above suspicion of lacking sympathy for the creations of popular fancy. Theology, however, is a rational system of religious values and cannot be built up of material furnished by fancy and imagination. As often as I read books on Jewish theology, and I may say with Faust: *Ich habe leider auch Theologie studiert*, the diametrically opposing views expressed in them remind me of the following story so popular in my native country, Lithuania. A rabbi, trying a case—for the rabbi of olden times was more of a judge than a theologian—after listening to the plaintiff, exclaimed: "You are right, my son"; and then made the same remark to the defendant, after the latter had pleaded in his own behalf. The rabbi's wife, who was present at the trail, could not refrain from remarking to her husband: "How can both litigants be right?" To which the rabbi in genuine meekness, as becoming a husband and rabbi, replied: "You, too, are right, my dear." I frequently feel like saying to the diametrically opposed theologians: What you say is so profoundly true and so utterly false! You are profoundly right in what you tell us about the beliefs and doctrines of this rabbi or that apocalyptic author, but you are utterly wrong in your attempts to stamp as an expression of the Jewish soul what is only an individual opinion or transitory fancy.

It is only in the Halakah that we find the mind and character of the Jewish people exactly and adequately expressed. Laws which govern the daily life of man must be such as suit and express his wishes, being in harmony with his feelings and fitted to satisfy his religious ideals and ethical aspirations. A few illustrations will often explain better than long abstract statements, and I shall therefore present a few concrete examples of the Halakah applied to the study of Jewish thought.

At the risk of causing Homeric laughter I shall begin *ab ovo*, not as the poet did, with the egg of Leda, but rather with that no less famous one that, to speak with Heine, was unfortunate enough to be laid on a holiday. He who does not appreciate Heine lacks the ability to appreciate something genuinely Jewish, and I, for one, greatly enjoy his merry remarks on that unfortunate egg. But grave historians, or rather theologians, the majority of whom are not usually distinguished by a sense of humor, do not show deep historical insight in ridiculing the great schools headed by Shammai and Hillel for discussing the question whether an egg laid on a holiday is permitted for use or not. We hear a great deal of Judaism being a view of life for which religion is law. I am at present not interested in showing the fallacy of this dictum nor in inquiring why we hear so little about the second part of this equation, to wit: for the Jew law is religion. But if it be true that religion is law for the Jews, the conception underlying Jewish law must necessarily be expressive of Jewish religious thought. The discussion of the old schools about the egg is tantamount to the question of the extent to which the principle of intent is to be applied. *Actus non est reus nisi mens sit rea*, say the Roman jurists, and similarity the Rabbis: Actions must be judged by their intent. Since, according to biblical law, food for the holy days must be prepared the day before, the progressive school of Hillel maintained that an egg laid on a holy day must not be used because, though prepared by nature, it was without the intent of man and hence can not be considered prepared in the legal sense. As strong men exult in their agility, so tendencies that are strong and full of life will sometimes be betrayed into extravagancies. It may be extravagant to prohibit an egg laid on a holy day on account of not having been intentionally prepared for food. But of what paramount importance must intention have been to the religious conscience of the Jew if it could assume such an exaggerated form as in the case before us! And could there be a better criterion of the development of a religion than the importance it attaches to intent, the outcome of thought and emotion, in opposition to merely physical action?

Now let us assume another Halakah that might throw light on the question as to the relation of thought and emotion to acts and deeds in Jewish theology. Sin, we are told by leading theologians, consists, according to the Jewish conception, in acting wrongly, and hence forgiveness, or, to use the more technical term, atonement, is of a purely mechanical nature. Originally there were different kinds of sacrifices, the sin offerings, the guilt offerings, and so forth, by means of which the sinner could right himself with God. Later the Rabbis substituted prayer, fasting and almsgiving for the sacrifices which, after the destruction of the Temple, could no longer be brought. So far our theologians. And now let us hear what the Halakah has to say about it. In a large collection of laws treating of marriage with conditions attached, which is to be found in the Talmud, we read: If one says to a woman, I marry thee under the condition that I am an entirely righteous man, the marriage is valid, even if it is found that he was a very wicked man, because we apprehend that at the time of the contraction of marriage he repented in his heart. If one says to a woman, I marry thee under the condition that I am a completely wicked man—sin is homely but also attractive—the marriage is valid. For even if it is found that he was very pious, we apprehend that at the time of the contract he had thoughts of idolatry. Sin as well as forgiveness are thus understood by Jewish law to be entirely independent of acts and deeds; the evil thought in the heart turns the perfectly just into the completely wicked, and vice versa, the change of heart changes the completely wicked into the perfectly just.

The ethical principles and ideals that shaped and formed the Halakah have been made a subject of study by many; however, as we are still in need of a thorough investigation of Jewish ethics, a few remarks on the Halakah as a source of Jewish ethics may prove to be profitable. I shall, however, content myself with touching upon those parts of the Halakah that treat either of ceremonial law or of the forms of civil law; my purpose in doing so being to show to what use the knowledge of these minutiae may be put.

Whether Jewish ethics are of a positive or a negative nature is a question often propounded, and of course answered according to the nature of the quotations one is able to gather from Jewish writings. A favorite argument for the negative character of Jewish ethics is drawn from the number of the commandments, which is said to consist of two hundred and forty-eight positive and three hundred and sixty-five negative. I doubt whether the good Rabbi who first computed these numbers was aware of the consequence of his statistics. There can, however, be no doubt in my mind that modern theologians are not aware of the fact that statistics are as fatal to theology as theology to statistics. A prompt and decisive answer to the question concerning Jewish ethics is given by the Halakah in its ruling: that in all conflicts of laws the positive takes precedence of the negative. This legal maxim applies of course to conflicts of ceremonial laws, but it is the outcome of the legal mind or, to use the more adequate term of the Germans, *das Rechtsbewusstsein*, of a people which conceived ethics as something very positive.

Many of us are undoubtedly acquainted with the favorite diversion of many popular writers who deny to the Jew any claim to creative genius; his religion and his ethics are said by them to be merely different manifestations of his commercial spirit; *do ut des* being the guiding power of his life. Hence the insistence upon the dogma of reward and punishment in his religion and the utilitarian character of his ethics. We have had enough of theology for the present and I shall not enter upon a discussion of the dogma of reward and punishment. Yet I cannot help quoting to you the wise words of one of the finest minds among contemporary thinkers. The world, says Mr. Balfour, suffers not because it has too much of it—the belief in reward and punishment— but because it has too little; not because it displaces higher motives, but because it is habitually displaced by lower ones. To those who maintain the utilitarian character of Jewish ethics my advice is: study the part of civil law in Jewish jurisprudence which treats of gifts. While the ancient Roman law, as has been pointed out by the great jurist and legal philosopher Ihering, does not recognize gratuitous transfer of ownership, but only for value, the promise of a gift attained an independence of form in the very earliest stages of the Halakah. For the Roman law gift is a sort of exchange; one makes a gift in order to receive a gift in return, or, in the words of the Roman jurists: *ad remunerandum sibi aliquem naturaliter obligaverunt, velut genus quoddam hoc esse permutationis.* The Halakah, on the other hand, had overcome the egoism of man, and beneficence and love dictated by altruism had come to full right in legislation as well as in life. The importance of this phenomenon only he can fail to recognize who sees in the form of the laws mere forms and not the expression of ideas.

The only point where liberality comes to the surface in the Roman law is in regard to wills, and it is highly interesting for the appraisal of the Jewish character to notice that Jewish law is rather inclined to limit the power of the testator to the extent that it prohibits the disin-

heritance of an ungrateful and wicked son in favor of a good and dutiful son. It has been noticed by others that bequests have psychologically not the value of gift—the gift of the cold hand is compatible with an icy cold heart; it is not a gift of one's own, but from the purse of the legal heir. In the long course of the development of the Jewish people the underlying bond was the family; the ties of blood were of absolute and undisputed strength. Consequently, the Halakah is not in favor of any measure that might disrupt this bond of union. In this connection I may call attention to the fact that the Halakah failed to develop the law of adoption, notwithstanding the fact that the Bible offers some precedents in certain forms of adoption. The idea of blood relationship forming the basis of the family was too strong with the Jew to permit the development of a law that would undermine it.

This leads us to the burning Jewish question of the day: Are the Jews a nation or merely a religious community? Of course I am not going to discuss it from the point of view of the Jew of today, but justice to my subject requires that we discuss this question from the point of view of the Halakah. And the answer to this question is given unmistakably in the following two laws of inheritance. A Jew, converted to paganism, inherits his father's estate, whether the father also becomes a convert or not. The idea underlying these Halakot is that the ties of blood binding the Jew to the Jewish people can never be loosened, and that, on the other hand, by becoming a Jew, a pagan severs his national connections with those to whom he previously belonged. There is a logical contradiction in these two laws of inheritance as formulated by the Halakah. But what is life but a conglomerate of logical contradictions? The Halakah would not be a true mirror of Jewish life, if it were free from all logical inconsistencies. The Jew is bound forever to his people, and yet anybody who enters Judaism becomes a true son of Israel.

A little reflection will, however, convince anyone who comes to the question with an open mind that both these theories concerning Judaism, the purely nationalistic as well as the purely religious, are alike incomplete and, being incomplete, are misleading. They err, as all theories are apt to err, not by pointing to a wholly false cause but by extending the efficiency of a true cause far beyond its real scope. Considered from an historical point of view there is no such thing as nationalism in general. History knows only a particular form of nationalism. It is not the military or economic organization of a state which makes it a national body but the spiritual idea represented by its people. When we speak of the Greek nation we primarily think of the form in which the genius of the nation expressed itself. And is not Jewish nationalism an empty phrase if we do not connect with it Jewish religion and Jewish ethics, Jewish culture and the Jewish mode of life which gave it its individuality?

Other works by Ginzberg: *Geonica* (1909); *Perushim ve-ḥidushim la-yerushalmi*, 4 vols. (1941–1961); *On Jewish Law and Lore* (1955).

N. M. Nikolskii

1877–1957

Nikolai Mikhailovich Nikolskii was born in Moscow and graduated from Moscow University. In the 1920s, he lectured in Jewish studies at the Belorussian State University. As a historian of religion, his approach was anthropological, and he explored polytheistic elements within Judaism, pre-Christian Slavic mythology, Belorussian wedding rites, and ancient Babylonian history.

The Ancient People of Israel
1920

I. Why Do We Need to Know the History of the People of Israel?

This book will discuss the people of Israel (the name by which the Jewish people were known), showing the history of their joys and sorrows. They were a small people, who even in their prime years were sparse in number. The population in our larger provinces as well as in the main city, Jerusalem, numbered no more than 60,000. This was also true of our central provincial city. Many places with larger populations could envy those with these smaller populations. In ancient times, the Jewish people had mighty neighbors, including Egypt, the wonderful kingdom of the Pharaohs. Who could comprehend the power of the Assyrian and Babylonian kingdoms when they conquered the ancient cultural world by the sword? Yet the Assyrian and Babylonian empires died out; their cities and entire culture decayed. Today their little burial hillocks are unearthed and the treasures of Assyro-Babylonian cultures are shoved aside and hidden.

The dark earth is once again revealed to the bright world. It teases, it is understood, it provokes the curiosity of learned and educated people. People study and show great interest. However, one still finds them cold; it is as if these artifacts were the stones of rocky seashells or the bones of ancient animals. The memorials of Babylonian culture are intriguing; however, they do not have emotional appeal; they do not awaken our feelings. Many people have never heard of them. Egypt inspired the same attitude. We marvel at their colossal pyramids and sphinxes, which stand even today as mighty and as motionless as they once were at the shores of the Nile River. We can still see the bodies of the pharaohs in museums, observing mummies that are thousands of thousands of years old. Chemists have tried to figure out how the Egyptians embalmed their dead. We wonder at all this. However, emotionally, this fascinating system does nothing for us in terms of moving our hearts.

The Egyptians and the Babylonians are interesting objects for studying impressive works of the ancient world. Their literature existed not only in their lands but also became well known in Greece and Rome. Their religious practices are somewhat recalled in names and customs. But though these are interesting representations, they do not have living or practical significance.

The fate of ancient Israel was very different. In contrast to the Babylonians and Egyptians, the ancient Hebrews were like Pygmies. But from ancient Thebes as well as ancient Babylonia, the only ruins that remain today are those of Nineveh. By contrast, Jerusalem still exists. Only a small portion of Babylonian and Egyptian literature has come down to us, just fragments. That which was written down has been preserved for scholars to peruse: specialists study these early forms of literature. The best-preserved fragments of ancient literature of the Jewish people were largely protected throughout the generations and are well known throughout the world.

With regard to Babylonian history, under the theme of prophets, Pushkin wrote his famous poem, "The Prophet." And Lermontov wrote his "Yiddish Melodies" that are pervaded with the deep sorrow of the children of Israel in the diaspora. Other Russian and foreign poets have depicted various dramatic moments of Jewish history. The great poets wrote about many biblical subjects: an example is *Paradise Lost*, the immortal poem by the English poet Milton. Another is Byron's *Cain*. French playwrights, too, created dramas using Jewish historical subjects. A people that had such a substantial effect on the cultural life of European people;

a people who demonstrated cultural longevity through many generations: these people have earned our close observation of their history. They have earned the right for us to examine their history with our own eyes. [. . .]

When one talks about the origins of the people of Israel and their lives in ancient Israel, we understand their habitations from the Bible. However, perusing the Bible does not provide enough for us to acquire sufficient background knowledge; it is also not easy to relate to the information found in the Bible. The people of Israel lived independent lives in their own kingdom for more than five hundred years. Within this approximate eon, the religious sects in Judah lived after their exile from Babylonia, spending almost the entire time under foreign rule. Over these thousand years, the Bible was created. This work was a creation of generations, many of whom competed over their achievements and merits. A Jew from the days of King David had limited success, as did a Jew from the time of Christ. This would be like taking, for instance, a person from Kiev at the time of Prince Vladimir, comparing him to a contemporary citizen of Kiev. This is why biblical stories are told differently in various parts of the Tanakh. [. . .]

This is the Bible—a holy book for Jews and Christians alike. But only lifeless pictures of Egyptian and Babylonian gods remain. And the singular God of Israel has also become God to Christians. Yeshua, born a Jew—the one who became the basis of Christianity— lived and preached in the ancient world. Afterwards, his followers spread Christian beliefs abroad. They also dispersed many Jewish beliefs, customs, and laws. The Jewish people themselves live on in the present, even though their independent kingdom is now long gone. The Jews themselves destroyed it at first. Thereafter, the Babylonians demolished it, and from that time, the people of Israel could barely revive to remain an independent nation. Nevertheless, not all Jews assimilated in captivity. Part of the population, the Bnei Yehudah, refused to assimilate and thus protected their national independence and their beliefs from annihilation. Generation after generation passed. Rules came and went. After the Babylonians, Persians ruled. Next came the Greeks and Romans. Finally, the Arabs destroyed the entire ancient Jewish culture, imposing an entirely new system of living upon the old demolished places.

The new world (America) was discovered. European culture along with European colonization spread out over the earth. However, the Jewish people still persevered, still not giving in to the influences of new peo-

ples. The Jews still maintain their own language and religion.

One cannot be indifferent to such people. Too many threads binds us to their past. Today, as ever, one is unconsciously reminded of every move that the grandchildren of the patriarch Abraham made. At churches, we hear readings and incantations from the book of Psalms—holy songs that were written with the poetic spirit of the Jewish people in mind. In synagogues, one can learn the holy history and tales of the Jewish people. If one visits an art gallery or an exhibition, one can see paintings depicting the actions of heroes from Jewish history. There is practically no great writer who was not inspired by them. [. . .]

In the same period, each biblical book was written in a different way. This is because the writers of the two books lived in different times, separated by several hundred years. Scholars, particularly from Germany, worked hard to gather information from these books. They researched ways in which the Bible could be employed to help us understand the history of Ancient Israel.

I will do more than simply relate biblical tales. I am choosing from among them and will attempt to explain them. Thus, my historical research does more than the usual common religious studies that simply tell the tales one after the other.

2. Palestine and Its Ancient Peoples

The land in which the ancient Children of Israel settled is known as Palestine. The Children of Israel were not the first settlers in this land. They took over the land and subjugated its residents.

The Pentateuch tells us that the Children of Israel who wandered through the desert had earlier, before entering into Palestine, sent spies ahead of them. These spies were instructed to check out the land to see if it was good. They were to observe its inhabitants, to see if they were a strong and mighty people or a weak and small one. They were to seek out the trees and fruits. The spies returned with so large a bunch of grapes that it had to be transported on a pole. They had also brought olives and pomegranates. They reported that the land was very good, running over with milk and honey. It was filled with fruit. The people who live there were very strong and lived in fortified cities.

Translated from Yiddish by Ruth Bryl Shochet, from A. Rozental's translation from Russian to Yiddish.

Other works by Nikolskii: *Yidishe yonteyvim* (1925); *History, Pre-Class Society, the Ancient East and the Ancient World* (1935); *Communism Means Peace* (1962).

Lev Deutsch (Deich)

1855-1941

Lev Grigoryevich Deutch (Deich; Leo Daytsh) was born in Tulchin, Ukraine, to a russified family and studied in Kiev. He initially followed maskilic ideology, funding Jewish schools that would promote assimilation. After repeated frustrations, Deutsch became a *narodnik* (populist) and revolutionary socialist. He left Russia in 1880; three years later in Geneva, he, with Georgi Plekhanov and Pavel Axelrod, formed the Group for the Liberation of Labor, to disseminate Marxist ideas in Russian. He was soon arrested and returned to Russia, where he was sentenced to deportation. He escaped in 1901 and joined the Russian Social Democratic Labor Party, and later belonged to the Menshevik faction. After multiple imprisonments and escapes (including to the United States), he returned to Russia following the February 1917 revolution.

Jews in the Russian Revolution
1924

Chapter Six

JEWISH YOUTH AND THE EMERGENCE OF THE REVOLUTIONARY MOVEMENT

[. . .] Not only did Jews not have anything to do, even remotely, with oppositional circles expressing discontent with the controversial politics of the "reformer" tsar, but they were actually enraged by the revolutionary attempts of leftists in general and Karakazov's assassination attempt specifically. "Murdering such a good emperor is a great sin," I remember Jews voicing their fury, and I, a young child at the time, would repeat what I had heard from the grown-ups. The Jews' gratitude toward the tsar for making their lives a tiny bit easier was so vast that it did not diminish even in the late 1860s, and progressive and even leftist Jews continued to feel obliged to him up until his tragic death. I must admit that I had belonged to these leftists myself: despite all the crimes Alexander II had committed I did not think he deserved such an end. [. . .]

Thus, I think, the facts fully confirm my opinion that not only were Jews not the initiators of the Russian rev-

olutionary movement but that they didn't even join the struggle undertaken by the progressive Christian youth right away. That for a long time there were no Jewish students among the first Russian revolutionaries can be explained, of course, primarily by the fact that the number of Jewish students studying in high schools and universities was relatively low at the time. Additionally [. . .] we were very grateful to the tsar and therefore very loyal. But our feelings were also a consequence of our despondency and the oppressed situation of Jews in the country in general. Of course, our parents' admonition that one should never provoke the "goyim" and especially the police in any way probably had some effect on our psyche, too.

Jewish youth studying in the upper classes of high school and in institutions of higher education knew full well, of course, that expressing even the tiniest dissatisfaction with the Russian order would lead to the most severe punishment and to making the acquaintance of the terrible "Third Division" [secret police], about which horrible stories had been told. From this inquisition-prison the culprit would go straight to the no less horrible Petropavlovsk Fortress, where he would either be doomed for good, walled up in the "stone sack," or go on, barely alive and wearing heavy chains, to the Vladimir "Road." [. . .]

With a few exceptions, all the progressive people who joined the lines of revolutionaries began their social activities in the legal, cultural-enlightenment field, and only gradually—some earlier, some later—were they forced to withdraw into illegal activities due to government persecution. [. . .]

At the end of the 1860s in St. Petersburg, a small, tight-knit circle of intellectuals [. . .] set as their goal to distribute good books [. . .] among the students. In order to do this, members of the circle began to buy up large quantities of copies of already published books from the publisher, or suggested the publication of other similar works, guaranteeing to buy a certain number of copies. After buying the books at a discount, they sold them to students for a cheap price.

Mark Natanson, a very energetic twenty-year-old young man, was one of those who took great initiative in this essentially peaceful educational undertaking. This, of course, did not go unnoticed by the all-seeing eyes of the *spies* of the "Third Division," and he was soon arrested for this "criminal activity" and exiled, without trial, by an administrative order, to a faraway corner of the northern edge of European Russia.

Thus, this Jewish student became if not the first then certainly one of the first Jews who paid with prison and forced labor for an activity that was not forbidden by Russian law: for buying and selling legally published books in large numbers. [...]

Chapter Twelve

THE JEWISH WOMEN'S MOVEMENT

[...] I only want to point out that, as is well known, many of the participants of the "Trial of the 50" were women. Additionally, the defendants did not carry out their propaganda activities among village peasants but among factory workers. Furthermore, there was not one Jewish woman among those accused in the "Trial of the 193," whereas the "Trial of the 50" had no Jewish male participants at all. Among the participants of the "Trial of the Propaganda in 36 Districts" there were some young Jewish girls, too. [...]

1. Betty Kaminskaya

Betty, the daughter of a wealthy merchant from the city of Melitopol, who lost her mother when still a child, enjoyed unlimited freedom in her family. She first encountered the widespread deprivation and poverty of the time as a little girl, playing with other children in the street. It made a deep impression on the sensitive girl. Betty learned to read Russian very quickly and after that she could not be torn away from books. In addition to simple novels she also read Russian classics and this brought about a profound change in her. The playful, lively, and carefree Betty was still too young when she became serious, introverted, and always immersed in thought. [...]

Having seen widespread deprivation and poverty around her—her knowledge only enhanced and broadened by reading the works of the great Russian writers—Betty was still very young when she began to contemplate how to help and ease the burden of the miserable, poor masses. In order to find the answer to the question that occupied her every thought Betty decided to travel to Zurich and enroll at the university there. Betty Kaminskaya, only eighteen years old then, had to put up a considerable fight with her father, who did not want to let his beloved daughter travel to such a faraway, foreign country, but she prevailed.

At that time most girls who traveled to Zurich from Russia in order to study quickly abandoned the university or polytechnic and devoted themselves to studying social problems. Betty Kaminskaya became one of the most devoted activists in this movement, and soon (in late 1874) she returned to Russia, with some of her new friends and comrades, to work and fight for the welfare of the poor masses.

The tender Betty Kaminskaya arrived in Russia on a false passport under the name of the soldier Maria Krasnova and started to work at a textile factory in a Moscow suburb. [...] Kaminskaya and the other women worked in the factory until late at night under terrible conditions. As they stood on the wet and filthy floor, their job was to sew pieces of cloth together. The dust from the fabric filled the air and clogged their ears and noses and burned their eyes. There was no ventilation in the building except for the door. For this work, which the women performed for up to sixteen hours a day, they got paid 4 roubles and 50 kopecks a month, from which they had to pay rent and buy food and other necessities.

The girls lived in barracks, in a stone-floored cellar, wet and filthy from sewage water. Its small windows were covered by snow in the winter. Along the walls were two-story plank beds—this is where twenty women slept, body to body. As bedding they used their dirty overcoats to cover themselves. The stench and the stifling air in these "bedrooms" were unbearable. All kinds of insects proliferated in great numbers. There was no place for these working women to cook, but they had nothing to cook anyway. They had to make do with black bread, kvass, and pickled cucumbers.

The tender Betty voluntarily took it upon herself to live under this horrible forced-labor regime. The young Jewish girl decided to share the difficult fate of Russian working women so that she could explain to her unfortunate comrades why they were forced to work under such conditions and to show them a way out of this situation.

To get closer to the working women Betty even moved to the barracks after a short while. Here, however, no matter how tired she was at the end of the day, the insects, the stifling air, and the snoring of her comrades kept her from falling asleep until very late. And when she finally did fall asleep, someone shortly came to wake them all up: they had to get up and go to work. Betty would rush to the factory exhausted, unwashed, and without having a cup of tea or warm food, just like everyone else. Her work became even harder when she, like many others, had to carry heavy bundles of two and a half pood [40 kg] of fabric up and down the stairs and across the courtyard. Betty, who was small and skinny like a child, stooped under the weight of these heavy bundles and could barely stand on her feet without falling on the slippery stairs. She often felt so bitter about her own weakness that her caring, pensive eyes filled with tears. This heroine-martyr often cursed her own weakness that kept her from carrying out this tremendously difficult work, unlike the healthy Christian working women.

One would think that after enduring such immeasurably difficult conditions nothing worse could happen. But the poor girl was transferred to a larger textile factory of thousands of workers, where men and women of various ages all worked together and the conditions were even worse. Betty had to carry out the most strenuous and intensive labor continuously for fourteen hours a day. [. . .]

Betty Kaminskaya conducted her work of propaganda for socialism under such conditions. It is not hard to imagine how difficult this task was for her. [. . .] But it was not only the impossible work conditions at the factory that made carrying out her mission hard. To some extent it was the working women themselves, among whom this eccentric girl lived, that presented an obstacle to achieving her goal. The coarse and illiterate working women who were emaciated from hard labor could dream of nothing but resting and, to the extent possible, spending their days off work enjoying the company of men. Getting them interested in the ideals of socialism was an extremely difficult task. But Kaminskaya did everything she could to influence these working women, and if she saw that the results of her work were insignificant, she blamed only herself for the failure, her poor preparedness, and lack of strength.

Working with women was not enough for Betty—she tried to have an impact on men too. But in doing so she encountered, in addition to the above mentioned difficulties, even more problems.

In the Russian factories male and female workers used to be strictly separated; they would live in separate barracks and work in separate workshops, and thus men and women saw each other only in passing, and exchanged only a few, mostly coarse words. The unmarried working women took lovers, and the married ones trailed after their husbands to make sure they didn't fall in love with another woman. [. . .]

Whenever she had a chance she enthusiastically and passionately started to explain to the workers, teaching them about their life and work conditions, telling them about the lives of other workers in other countries. [. . .] She was so caught up in propaganda work, and she spoke with such enthusiasm, that her audience listened to her with undivided attention and interest. When the factory whistle calling workers to return to the job forced Betty to end her speech, the workers would ask her to continue the conversation with them after work. [. . .]

And yet it was not easy for the young propagandist to recruit followers from among her attentive audience. She often noticed that even though people had listened to her speeches with great sympathy, they remained completely apathetic to the content of her words. She knew this could be explained by their exhaustion and desire to rest, and so Betty came close to despair; she used to cry hard, become depressed, and take her failure very much to heart. But in the end she did succeed in establishing a small circle of enlightened workers. [. . .]

In the spring of 1875 she and her friends who worked in Moscow were arrested. They were turned into the defendants of the court case that later became known as the "Trial of the 50." The arrested were all young, enthusiastic girls, just like Betty Kaminskaya. [. . .]

Being arrested and imprisoned together with her dear friends, whom Betty liked more than her own family, made such an impression on Kaminskaya's sensitive soul that she thought it was all over, that the cause so dear to them was completely doomed. During the second month of her solitary confinement in prison this exceptional girl lost her mind. She was overcome with deep melancholy, refused to eat, and lay all day long on the floor. Despite these clear signs of madness the poor girl was kept in solitary confinement for many months before she was transferred to the prison hospital. The circumstances there were horrible—suffice it to say that the guards would beat the poor patients.

After lengthy efforts Betty's father finally managed to convince the cruel gendarmes to release his beloved daughter to his care on bail. Once out of prison, Betty began to recover. She even began to do propaganda work among the people, and for this purpose she moved to St. Petersburg and started to work in a shoemaker's workshop in order to learn the trade. [. . .]

After she found out from the files of allegations that she was not going to be charged—the reason for which, of course, was her psychological state—she decided to travel to St. Petersburg to report to the prosecutor that she had completely recovered, that she was healthy now to stand trial together with all the other defendants. Her father opposed this plan unequivocally. She, on the other hand, wanted to be sentenced together with her friends no matter what. Afraid that she would take a dangerous step, her relatives decided to keep her under strict supervision. Despite their efforts the plan failed: not seeing a way out of her situation and thinking everything was lost, Betty poisoned herself. After three days of agony, during which Betty kept calling the names of her friends who were accused in the trial, this wonderful and deeply miserable girl passed away. [. . .]

Jewish Women's Demonstrations

[. . .] The progressive youth had been waiting for a chance to express their rage for quite some time. This opportunity arose, as is well known, before the "Trial of the 50" in St. Petersburg; with the death of the student Tshernishov, who was almost tortured to death in prison. His relatives managed to get him pardoned, which gave this unfortunate young man the opportunity to die at home rather than in prison. The revolutionary youth turned his funeral into a huge demonstration. The procession with the coffin, without any religious ceremonies, stopped at the jail and at the famous "building by the chain bridge." [. . .] Speeches were given here condemning the government system that murders the best people in the country. The novelty of this demonstration confused the police. Only later did they realize what was happening and intervened too late. It took great effort until they managed to have this unusual funeral performed at the appropriate cemetery.

This demonstration roused strong reactions among the people. The progressive elements in society were mostly pleased: their resentment of the horrible government in power gained expression openly at least in this way. The government, on the other hand, was infuriated with the police for their negligence. An order was passed requiring that innocent victims of cruel treatment be buried secretly. This, of course, did not keep the progressive youth from wanting to bring their protest to the streets because in those days there was no other way to express protest. The group of students was soon joined by some enlightened workers who also wanted to express their sympathy for the people who had sacrificed so much for propagating their ideas as well as for directing their own rage against the cruelty of the government. [. . .]

The Novakovsky Couple

At the beginning of the 1870s I met a young Jewish man in Kiev, a yeshiva *bocher* type, whom I mentioned before. He looked about twenty or twenty-one years old; he spoke Russian with mistakes but seemed fairly well read and was preparing to study at the university as an extern. [. . .]

He was tall and lanky, had an elongated face with a little, black, sparse beard growing on the sides. Already at our first meeting Novakovsky impressed me as unworldly. [. . .]

Only a few weeks had passed since his arrival in St. Petersburg when Novakovsky and his wife, along with other participants in the demonstration, were arrested on Kazan Square. [. . .] From the account of people of his generation, we know that the participants in this demonstration did not foresee that the government would respond as cruelly as it did in the end. Additionally, this was the first time that the retribution for such political action was a trial. The participants in this demonstration were, for the most part, very little or not at all connected to each other. And in the end the police could not come up with any legal proof against the majority of the arrested.

This was one reason why the majority of the defendants in this trial, as opposed to the defendants in other political trials at the time, did not admit clearly and immediately that they had, indeed, been present at Kazan Square, and that they had heard and agreed with the speech that had been delivered there. On the contrary, in spite of the available evidence they claimed that they had been on the square "accidentally," or that they were not among the demonstrators at all, that they just happened to be passing by. Novakovsky was one of these people. [. . .]

He was sentenced to exile in Siberia nonetheless, and was deprived of his civil rights. [. . .]

To Novakovsky's great fortune his young, loving wife, who had somehow been cleared of the accusation of visiting Kazan Square together with her husband, went with him to Siberia voluntarily. [. . .]

In the town where Novakovsky and his wife had been sent after the amnesty [. . .] the living conditions were better there than where they had been in eastern Siberia. After seven or eight years of languishing in various prisons, marching with different groups of prisoners under escort, and living in remote corners of Siberia, the Novakovskys could finally breathe a sigh of relief.

But, unfortunately, even this relative "happiness" did not last very long.

One day, one of their comrades, a fellow-deportee, went to see the Ispravnik [district chief of police] at the administrative office about some issue. But as soon as he started to explain why he had come, the Ispravnik began to yell at him and called him a *zhid* [kike].

"I am not Jewish at all. I am Christian," said the man, and gave his last name. If I am not mistaken it was Leonid Bulanov, who is no longer alive today.

"Forgive me," said the Ispravnik. "I thought you were Novakovsky."

When Bulanov returned to his comrades and told them about the incident, there was a great uproar among the deportees. People vehemently argued that they should not let such an insult pass without a word, even if the Ispravnik said it behind their backs. [. . .]

Day after day, meeting after meeting passed, but Novakovsky's comrades could not decide what to do. People calmed down and the incident would probably have been forgotten. The Novakovsky couple was rather bitter and resentful about this. It was especially Mrs. Novakovsky who took the Ispravnik's insult to heart. Having seen that the comrades' debates led nowhere, she decided to do something herself, without telling anyone, not even her husband.

During work hours, when the Ispravnik and his assistants and clerks were all at the office, Mrs. Novakovsky went to see him. The Ispravnik had already heard rumors about the widespread dissatisfaction among the deportees, so when he saw her, he politely offered her a seat. But Mrs. Novakovsky went up to him and slapped him in the face with full force, saying:

"This is for calling us *zhids*." [. . .]

Of course, Mrs. Novakovsky was arrested right away. She was handed over to the court and charged with offending "an officer while carrying out his official duty." For this crime she was sentenced to exile in eastern Siberia and deprived of all her civil rights. [. . .]

News of her "slap" subsequently reached even the remotest corners of Siberia, and, even though in the European part of Russia a period of horrible antisemitism was to ensue, over in Siberia, in the lawless region of forced labor and exile where every petty official behaved like an absolute monarch, as far as I can remember none of the numerous Jewish political deportees was insulted ever again. [. . .]

Translated by Vera Szabó.

Other works by Deutsch: *Kak my v narod khodili* (1910); *Russkaia revolyutsionnaia emigratsiia 70-kh godov* (1920); *Pochemu ia stal revolyutsionerom* (1921); *Za polveka* (1923).

Simon Dubnov

World History of the Jewish People
1925–1929

General Introduction

1. THE SOCIOLOGICAL METHOD OF JEWISH HISTORIOGRAPHY

This is a universal history of the Jewish people in that it fully corresponds to the contents and the scope of this extraordinary part of the history of mankind. The term "universal" is applicable to the history of civilization throughout the world, as distinguished from the histories of individual peoples and countries. But the destiny of the Jewish people has manifested itself—through almost the entire extent of the civilized world (with the exception of India and China) and throughout the entire duration of the recorded history of mankind—in such a way as to have its own universal history in the literal sense.

Within this great world, the macrocosm of mankind, Jewry represents a microcosm, subject to the general laws of history, yet also having its own idiosyncrasies. If there is to be a scientific formulation of the general and particular laws, there must be a correct understanding of the processes of Jewish history, which up to now have been obscured by old conceptions of the role of the mere "historical" nation. In the historiography of the antique or biblical period, the *theological method* dealing with the tradition of "sacred history" and its religious pragmatism has hitherto prevailed. Even the partisans of the "free Biblical criticism"—for the most part Christian theologians—cannot renounce the theological method and have merely replaced this Old Testament pragmatism with that of the New. The same method has prevailed in the historiography of later epochs, which, in keeping with the old terminology, are known as talmudic or rabbinical, or by some similar term borrowed from religious or literary history. Here, even the works of free-thinking historians, the *spiritualistic* method, based on the proposition that a people which has been deprived of its statehood and its territory can be the active subject of history only so far as its spiritual life is concerned, whereas in its social life it represents no more than a minor aspect of the history of the nations among which it lives. That is why the historiography of such schools as those of Zunz and Graetz has adopted the theory to two primary motifs in the history of the Diaspora; namely, intellectual creativity and heroic martyrdom (*Geistesgeschichte und Leidensgeschichte*). The chief content of the life of a people in such studies has been reduced to a history of literature on the one hand, and to a martyrology on the other; the historical horizon is confined within these limits.

Only of late can one detect the shift to a broader scientific conception of Jewish history, to a *sociological* method. Underlying this method is the idea, originating out of the whole range of the phenomena of our history, that the Jewish people at all times and in all countries has had a history of its own, not only spiritually but socially as well. During the periods both of its own statehood and of the Diaspora, the history of Jewry is a vivid expression of nationalism, not merely of a religious group among other nations. This continuously living nation has always and everywhere defended the autonomous existence not only of its social life but also of all the areas of its culture. The Diaspora, which was widespread even during the Judean sovereignty, had everywhere its autonomous communities; in many places it had even central organs of self-government, including both legislative and judicial institutions (the Sanhedrin, the academies, and the Patriarchate in Roman-Byzantine Palestine; the Exilarchate, the Gaonim, and legislative academies in Babylon; the "alchemy" and congresses of communal delegates in Spain; the Kahals and Vaadim or Kahal Sejms in Poland and Lithuania; and many others). Pre-eminently bound up with this historical process, the latest national movements in Jewry, combining the immemorial heritage of *autonomism* with the modern principle of the "rights of national minorities," testifies to the ineradicability of this eternal prime mover of Jewish history, which has survived even in an age of assimilation and of great changes in the life of the nation.

The reasons for the unilateral concept of Jewish history in the recent past are now clear. Our scientific historiography was engendered in western Europe in the middle of the 19th century, when the dogma of assimilation reigned: "Jewry is not a nation, but merely a religious group." Historiography, submitting to the general tendency, busied itself for the most part with Judaism rather than with its living creator, the Jewish people. Even such an apostate from the generally accepted dogma as our best historian, Graetz, could not withstand the current. A profound overturn in our national self-consciousness, signalizing the present epoch, was needed to bring about a corresponding change in the conception of the historical process. The secularization of historiography, its liberation from the trammels of theology, and likewise of "spiritualism" and scholasticism, was bound to follow the secularization of the Jewish national idea.

A new understanding of Jewish history is maturing which corresponds more to its actual content and scope. It is becoming clear that the Jewish people during the millennia have not only "thought and suffered," but have in all possible circumstances proceeded to build their life as a separate social unit; and, accordingly, that to reveal this process of the building of its life as a separate social unit is the primary task of historiography. The object of scientific historiography must be the people, the *national entity, its origin, growth, and struggle for existence.* Through a succession of ages, the embryonic nation emerged from the tribal milieu of the ancient East which surrounded it, took on a definite national form, achieved and then lost its statehood, reconstructed in its own fashion the elements of general culture which it had received, and finally rose in spiritual creativity to the summits of prophecy. The formation of the national type coincides with the moment of the first political debacle, the Babylonian captivity; and the succeeding epochs—Persian, Greek, Hasmonean, and Roman—are characterized by the rivalry of theocracy and secular government. The second political debacle, under the scourge of Rome, called forth new forms of the scattered people's struggle for national unity; it was not in governmental but in other forms that Jewry's indomitable aspiration for *autonomic* existence, social and cultural originality in the midst of alien nations, was manifested. Toward this end the entire spiritual activity of the nation has been directed: *Judaism's view of the universe is founded upon an image of the social existence of the nation and not otherwise.*

The practical sociological method in Jewish historiography leads to the reappraisal of many important phenomena which have been wrongly interpreted from the theological and scholastic points of view. We will cite several striking examples of the new and the old methods in the illumination of the important facts of Jewish history.

The fundamental question of ancient history is precisely this: Why were Israel and Judah the creators of the highest spiritual culture, the culminating socio-ethical ideals of the prophets, while Assyria, Babylon, and Egypt, so strong in their material culture, failed to attain the humanitarian and pacific ideal which the Jews had proclaimed to mankind? Theologians and metaphysicians explain this by divine or supernatural predestination of a "chosen people," but a sociologist offers a more simple explanation: a small, peaceful nation situated between political giants, its territory forming a corridor between Mesopotamia and Egypt, could not dream of expansion through conquest; rather, it had to think in terms of safeguarding its cultural independence from the invasion of alien elements, of preserving an inner autonomy such as was possible only under the reign of peace and justice upon earth that would permit the peaceful co-existence of wolves and sheep in the arena of universal history. All the energy of the entire nation was concentrated not on conquest but on defense—a defense which was primarily spiritual rather than physical. Hence, the spiritual character of the Jewish national life, and the subsequent inner conflicts between this spiritual beginning and the later secular tendencies expressed in the slogan, "Let us be like unto all the nations!"

The old historiography became hopelessly entangled in the question of the Pharisee and Sadducee parties, whose interaction dominated the national life during the Hasmonean and Roman epochs. Even those historians who are unhampered by theology have traced the genesis of those parties to religion-ritualistic and dogmatic dissensions. Basing their analysis upon the Hellenic-philosophical additions of Flavius Josephus, on the one hand, and on the other upon late talmudic legends whence the political element issued, these historians have transformed into a struggle between "sects" or "schools," a dispute which actually was concerned with the very form of the Jewish nation: whether it was to be a secular or a spiritual, an ordinary or a distinctive member of the international family. The dispute of the two parties also had a social background: the aristocratic Sadducees, hankering after the right to exercise authority in the government, and the democratic Pharisees, who set great value upon their spiritual power over the mass, were here at odds.

This sociological view of the genesis and activities of two parties, which will be set forth in the second volume of the present work, is derived from all the accounts of the collision of the Pharisees and the Sadducees in the political and social arena and of their various activities from the epoch of the Hasmoneans to the fall of the Judaean regime. Religious and ritualistic dissensions were only an outgrowth of the underlying national and social antagonism between these parties; the differing attitudes toward the Oral Law stemmed from dissension over the expediency of assimilation and over the uniqueness of Judaea in the Greco-Roman world.

Another example of the same kind of distortion of historical perspective can be seen in the usual evaluation of the role of the Sanhedrin in Jabneh. At the moment of greatest disruption in Jewish history, following the destruction of the Jewish commonwealth by the Romans, Jabneh was a self-governing center in a city close to the devastated Jerusalem. Relying upon the naïve though very beautiful legends about how Rabbi Jochanan ben Zakkai, with the permission of the Romans, fled from besieged Judaea to open in Jabneh a school for the study of the Torah, historians have variously evaluated the significance of this school for the future destiny of Jewry: some glorify the exploit of erecting a rampart of learning upon the ruins of a state, while others have seen in it the beginning of the end for Jewry as a nation and of the petrifaction of Judaism into the letter of the law. Both are mistaken, since the supposition concerning the academic center at Jabneh is a radical error.

In reality, what was consummated there was one of the most significant acts of national and social reorganization. It was not a theoretical school that was established in Jabneh but a center of nomocracy, of rule through the discipline of law. Here the organ of jurisprudence was fused with that of legislation, namely the Sanhedrin—which, after the collapse of the state, was called upon to weld together a scattered people by means of homogeneous laws, to begin regulating its internal life into a new kind of autonomy. Here was sounded the rallying cry for the reorganization of the shattered national army, and for the beginning of a new social discipline in the place of the governmental discipline that had been lost. It was above all a chapter in the building of a national life, and only secondarily a chapter in the history of religion, scholarship, and literature.

In the light of the sociological method, other tangled historical problems also become intelligible. The antinomy of nationalism and universalism that underlies the struggle between Judaism and primitive Christianity thus becomes understandable. While of necessity Judaism developed as a national religion, adapted to serve as a spiritual bulwark for its people against the hostile milieu around them, evangelical Christianity was an individualistic religion and hence potentially a universal one. The apostles of Christianity preached that the separate individual was valuable in his own right, but not the collective historical entity that had become part of a nation; thus these new prophets were urging the Judaean nation toward the abyss of non-being at the very moment when it was desperately struggling for its life against that world predator, Rome—and the wholesome instinct of self-preservation compelled the Jewish people to recoil from the bellmen of national suicide.

Hence, the entire subsequent historical meaning of talmudism, with its iron national discipline within an integument of religion, likewise becomes clear. The Talmud is first and foremost a written monument to the national integrity of Jewish autonomous centers in Roman Palestine and in Persian Babylon, a monument to the age-long exertions of the leaders of the people to forge an armor of laws about the shattered core of their nation.

The foregoing are a few examples of the important developments of the history of the Jews as seen in the light of the sociological method. This method leads us out of the labyrinth of theological and metaphysical opinion and places our historiography on a bio-sociological basis. The subject of our investigation proves to be not an abstraction but a living organism, developed from the embryo of the tribe into a complex cultural-historical entity—into a nation. The method of investigation here is strictly based upon the principle of evolution. First, the period of the formation of the collective entity will be investigated and thereafter the period of struggle for an independent existence, for the preservation and development of characteristic national traits and of a culture accumulated through the ages. In dealing with this double process of individualization and the defense of individuality, we take as our point of departure the axiom that a stable and vividly expressed national personality, as a product of history, is in itself not only a natural phenomenon but also a thing of definite cultural value. This does not mean, however, that a historian is bound to see value in every means, whether straight or devious, that has led to the preservation of this collective personality. For example, while considering a certain degree of insulation a necessary condition of a national life, the historian is in duty bound to indicate also those moments when cultural insulation was increased—frequently out of necessity, for the sake

of self-defense—to sorry extremes, bringing about the complete disassociation of a given nation from the best cultural achievements of humanity as a whole. The historian is in duty bound to depict the struggle, unavoidable in every national organism, between centripetal and centrifugal forces and the tragic collisions engendered thereby in the depths of national life. It goes without saying that in upholding the subjective cultural value of national character, the historian will tend to give greater value to the results of the nationally constructive, centripetal forces than to the results of destructive, centrifugal forces.

The sociological method obligates one, of course, to assign an appropriate place in historiography to those social-economic factors which the old school of historians disdained. But this does not at all mean an inclination toward "historical materialism," which subordinates all the phenomena of history to the evolution of an economic order of things. We do not have to forego an antiquated historical spiritualism only to fall into the hands of its opposite—the doctrine of historical materialism—which is no less one-sided, no less prone to distort the perspective of the past. Bossuet was mistaken when he saw in universal history nothing but the struggle of religious or ecclesiastical tendencies; equally mistaken were Buckle and Draper, who saw in history only the struggle of intellectual tendencies, an alternating succession of ages of faith and reason; but Marx also was mistaken in reducing all historical processes to the struggle of economic interests, the struggle between capital and labor. It is high time to recognize that the life of any people is governed by a mixture of material, psychic, and spiritual factors, interests, ideas, beliefs, emotions, and passions—religious, political, national, and economic—which through the millennia have determined the life of mankind in varying combinations. It is true that quite often material interests, individual or collective, have worn the mask of religious or ideological forms, and in such instances the historian must bring them to light, but it cannot be said that material interests lie at the basis of *all* historical movements, just as it cannot be maintained that in the life of an individual man who has emerged from a primitive condition the struggle for daily bread plays the only role.

The total significance of the new conception of Jewish history can be particularly appreciated by those who, like the author of this book, have themselves wandered far away from the winding path of Jewish historiography. In my time I also paid tribute to generally accepted axioms. In the quest for a synthesis of Jewish history that has absorbed me from the first day of my activity as a scholar, I went through all the aforementioned phases of historical thought. My debut as a youth whose views were colored by a strong religio-reformistic tendency, represented the application of the theological method turned inside out. In a succession of further works, in which my inclination toward a secularization of Jewish historiography was already beginning to appear, I still could not free myself from the ideological domination of the school of Graetz; my innovation consisted solely in an attempt to squeeze a national-social program into the old frame of the history of ideas. Only when, after many years of working out the details of Jewish history from their sources, I myself was compelled to write it as the history of a people and not a literature, did the shortcomings of the old methods become evident; the horizon of investigation and generalization widened, and what had hitherto been hidden in a fog of scholastic obscurity stood revealed. What had been arrived at by the inductive method was then checked by the opposite method, that of deduction, and the conclusions which had become my premises were confirmed when I applied them to historical material.

2. Periodicity and System of Hegemonies

In the universal history of the Jews, the method of synthesis must predominate, just as it must in the universal history of mankind. To disclose general trends in historicity over the ages and throughout the world to determine the organic link between different divisions of time and space during the 3,000-year evolution of a nation—such is the chief problem of the historian of the present day. While dealing with material already gathered and to some degree put in order, the historian-synthesist is, of course, not exempt from searching for fresh materials or from independent analysis—criticism of the sources and examination of the facts which during so long a passage of time could not but suffer so far as exactitude and completeness are concerned. But the historian's chief aim should be to bring out the general processes which are hidden in the mass of facts, to work out an exact architectural plan and to construct a lofty historical edifice in keeping with that plan.

Thus, the new method of Jewish historiography entails a new architectural plan for it and a new classification, or periodicity. The division into periods and epochs must be based upon social dynamics, upon changes in the destiny of a nation as a whole, and not merely in this or that area of its life and development. This periodicity is determined by the historical milieu in which the nation finds itself at a given period, and by the hegemony exercised by a particular part of the nation from one of the changing geographical centers. During the period of statehood—which to this day is often divided, in keeping with the religious significance, into the epochs of the First Temple and the Second Temple—history should be treated politically in accordance with the status of Palestine among the worldwide empires of the ancient East: Egypt, Assyria, Babylonia, Persia, the Hellenic sovereignties of the Ptolemies and Seleucids, and finally the Roman Empire. During its stateless period, when the Jewish nation was without any one center, the division must of necessity be geographical, in accordance with the shifting of hegemony of the various centers of Judaism. At every epoch the scattered people had a major center of some sort, and at times even two such centers, which according to the extent of their national autonomy and the level of their culture, acquired hegemony over other parts of the Diaspora.

In the universal history of the Jewish people two great primary periods emerge: the Eastern period, when the main centers of the nation were to be found in Asia Minor and North Africa—in Palestine, Syria, Mesopotamia, and Egypt—and the Western period, when these centers shifted to Europe, to the colonies of the Jewish Diaspora which had arisen there.

Within the limits of the Eastern period three epochs are to be distinguished, according to the political and cultural milieu: (1) the epoch of the strictly Eastern milieu, the time of the conquest of Canaan, of the Israelite-Judaean kings and the subsequent rule of three universal monarchies—Assyria, Babylonia, and Persia (approximately 1200-332 B.C.; (2) the epoch of the mixed Eastern-Western milieu, or the Graeco-Roman rule in the East, with intervals of the Judaean independence under the Hasmoneans, until the fall of the Judaean state (332 B.C. to 70 A.D.); (3) the epoch of the two hegemonies—the Roman-Byzantine and the Persian-Arabian in Babylonia—that culminated in the division between the Christian and the Moslem worlds. During this epoch, which embraced the first millennium of the Christian era, the old hegemonies gave way to new: the Palestinian hegemony of the time of pagan Rome (2nd and 3rd centuries A.D. was replaced by the double Palestinian-Babylonian hegemony during the isochronal sovereignty of Byzantium and Novo-Persia in the East (4th to 7th centuries of the Christian era) and finally by a single Babylonian hegemony during the great Arab Caliphate (7th to 9th centuries A.D.). It is by just such historical upheavals that the alternation of the epochs during the course of the second millennium of Jewish history are determined—an era which in the earlier historiography was generally designated as the Talmudic period, with a scholastic subdivision into the epochs of the Mishna and the Gamara, of the Tannaim, Amoraim, Saboriaim, and Gaonim.

The 2nd millennium of the Eastern period of Jewish history (which represents the 1st millennium of the Christian era) was the colonizing period for the Jewish Diaspora in Europe, preparing for the transition of the national hegemony from the East to West. The 11th century of the Christian era represents a line of demarcation between two broad periods of Jewish history—the Eastern and the Western. The national hegemony was beginning to shift to the centers of the large Jewish settlements in Europe. During the Middle Ages, Moorish and Christian Spain in the 11th–15th centuries, the south and north of France (12th–13th centuries), and Germany (13th–15th centuries) were dividing this hegemony among themselves. During the Renaissance (16th–17th centuries) the hegemony was being divided between Germano-Austria and the Jewish center in Poland. Toward the end of the 18th century, under the influence of the Enlightenment, it underwent a cultural division: German Jewry took its place at the head of the Western progressive movement, while Polish-Russian Jewry still remained the citadel of the traditional culture down to the middle of the 19th century, when it began to be drawn into the dynamics of Western Europe.

The whole of the "recent history" (1789–1914) has run its course amid profound social and cultural crises, produced by the rapid alternation of brief epochs of emancipation and reaction in civic life and a parallel struggle between conflicting tendencies of assimilation and nationalism in the inner life of Jewry in Western and Eastern Europe. Along with the growth of anti-Semitism on one hand and the Jewish national movement on the other (1881–1914), a profound change began in the destiny of the Jewish nation: the exodus of great masses from Europe. During the course of three decades one group of emigrants created a great center of the Diaspora in America, while another, considerably smaller, group laid the foundations for a renewed national center in Palestine, its ancient homeland. The devastation of the First World War and the Russian Revolution (1914–1920) dealt a blow to the larger of the former Jewish centers, namely the one in Russia; and the monstrous backward surge of racism, Nazism, and Fascism in recent years destroyed the ancient cultural centers of the Diaspora in the West, those of Germany, Austria, and Italy. Now, while Europe is being threatened by a new barbarism, the double-visaged sphinx of Jewry stands with one face toward the western Hemisphere, toward North and South America, and with the other toward the east, toward Palestine. After two succeeding periods of Jewish history, the Eastern and the Western, the Asiatic and the European, the dualism of the European-American west and of the Palestinian East now becomes possible. The division of the hegemony between West and East may be expected to follow.

Great difficulties surround the disposition of the materials covering the many centuries of an omnipresent people's history. These difficulties are not so great in the early stages of that history, where we have to deal only with the synchronism of the Israelite and Judaean kingdoms at the time of their dual reign, and with a minor Diaspora during the epoch of the Persian domination; but with the growth of the Diaspora, at first in the East and subsequently in the West, the difficulties continually increase. Even during the Graeco-Roman period the attention of the historian is divided between Judaea and the Great Diaspora, whereas during the Roman-Byzantine and the Persian-Arabic periods it is divided between two dominating centers, Palestine and Babylonia and the growing colonies in Europe.

In the history of the later Western period, moreover, one is obliged to cope with a multiplicity of countries where the fate of the Jewish population is bound up with a diversity of political and cultural conditions. Here the historian is presented with a choice between two equally inadequate means of exposition: either of expounding the history into a mechanically combined series of monographs, or of telling concurrently the history of the Jews in all countries and thus turning historiography into a chronological listing of events which coincide in time yet differ utterly in local conditions.

Graetz, the prime architect in our historiography, usually preferred the synchronism of the latter method. In his extended work one is frequently brought up short by an unexpected lead from one country to another, within the confines of a single chapter. Such artificial conjoining of heterogeneous events has the obviousness of synoptic tables, but lacks the indispensable element of a scientific synthesis; the interweaving of events with local conditions is lost sight of in a chronological exposition. In the case of Graetz, the confusion is increased by the mixing of political, social-existential, and literary data.

In order to avoid all these shortcomings the material must be trisected—as to time, place and subject. It is necessary to expound the history of each epoch in each of the various countries and to account for both the outward and inward life of the people in each, as well as for the interrelations between one and another. The history of the different groups within a given epoch must deal first with its chief hegemonic center, and next with other countries, in the order of their importance for the history of the people as a whole. Occasionally the exposition should begin with an account of a pivotal event—a predominant political or social movement which takes in a number of countries and puts its impress upon the whole epoch. Such an event would be the First Crusade in France and Germany, the resettlement of the Sephardim after their expulsion from Spain, the Messianic movement of the Sabbatians which spread from Turkey, the first French Revolution, the beginning of the emancipation of the Jews, or German anti-Semitism in the last decades of the 19th century.

In the present work, each epoch is preceded by a General Survey, for the purpose of noting briefly some of its central and peripheral characteristics. Insofar as is possible, external-political, internal-social, and literary phenomena, are treated separately throughout. A chapter dealing with any separate state will ordinarily be arranged in the following sequence: the political and economic situation, self-government in the communities, their spiritual life, and their literature. The history of literature enters our history of the Jewish people only to the extent that this or that literary phenomenon influenced social dynamics, or was itself the product of a social movement. We are interested not so much in individual literary works as in literary currents indicating the direction of social thought.

Translated by Moshe Spiegel.

Tuvia Heilikman

1873–1948

Tuvia Heilikman was born in Mogilev, Belorussia, and studied in Kiev. He helped found the Bundist party

in Kiev and coedited the Vilna Bundist weekly *Nashe slovo* in 1906. Settling in Moscow after the February revolution, he continued his Bundist activities. Heilikman worked in the Central Jewish Education Office. His *Geshikhte fun der gezeshaftlekher bavegung fun di yidn in poyln un rusland* competed with Dubnov's history by focusing on internal Jewish class conflict and emphasizing the role of communal organizations in perpetuating oppression. Heilikman worked at the Department of Yiddish Language and Literature at Moscow State Pedagogical Institute until its close in 1938, taught briefly at the Belorussian State University, and helped to reestablish the Bureau of Proletarian Jewish Culture in Kiev after World War II.

History of the Social Movement of Jews in Poland and Russia
1926

Chapter I

Our point of departure in historical research is the basic tenet that the development of social life depends on the development of the means of production that are ultimately determined by the development of forces of production.

The same historical materialism must be applied to the history of the Jews. We are going to discuss the applicability of this statement here because some historians have found it necessary to emphasize that Jewish history is an *ato bekhartonu* [chosen people] history, that Jewish history is unique because we are God's chosen people and historical materialism cannot be applied to it.

Thus, for instance, in his *Letters on Old and New Judaism* Sh. Dubnov claims that historical materialism is "an effort to place the economic factor at the head of the historical process and subordinate to it all of social and spiritual-intellectual [*gaystik*] development." He points out that "in its absolute form" (!) the doctrine of historical materialism is flawed, and finds it necessary to add that "it attracted especially many followers from among the offspring of a people whose entire history is a sharp challenge to this doctrine." Elsewhere in his work Sh. Dubnov discusses Karl Marx and repeats the same idea. He points out that the founder of historical materialism "could not rise to understand the spirit of the nation whose entire history contradicts this narrow doctrine."

Setting aside the not too successful formulation of the doctrine criticized by Dubnov and his appeal to the fairly shady concept of "national spirit" [natsyonaler gayst], we will see that Dubnov's main idea is the following: the doctrine of historical materialism is flawed as it is, but its flaw becomes most apparent when we apply it to Jewish history. Unfortunately, he does not even attempt to substantiate the correctness of his own idea: why is the history of Jews different from the histories of all other nations, and in what way does it most clearly contradict this "narrow idea?"

To answer this question it is necessary to explain what exactly constitutes the uniqueness of Jewish history, and whether this uniqueness contradicts the principles of historical materialism.

The historian P. Marek tried to address the question of this uniqueness.

"If no nation can claim"—he writes—"that it was steering the course of its own affairs independently, that its historical path has never intersected with the historical paths of other nations, then the Jewish people can make such a claim even less justifiably. The lifelines of a people that lives dispersed among other peoples of a different faith and in a foreign national environment must, one way or another, be interwoven and interconnected with the lifelines of those other nations. In accordance with this standpoint, the basic method of researching the history of Jews in Russia as well as in other countries must consist of exploring two processes. On one hand, the small cogwheels of Jewish life became entwined in the giant cogwheels of the Russian government; on the other hand, forces generated outside the Jewish population were constantly transformed into a carefully planned effort toward the spiritual-intellectual and economic adjustment to the circumstances and atmosphere of the surrounding non-Jewish environment. Indeed, Jewish history draws its subject matter and topics from following the lines and combines these two processes. The first process relates to the second as the circumstances relate to the deed, as an algebraic sign relates to a mathematical expression enclosed in brackets. Both the positive and negative aspects of Russian life are unavoidably reflected in the fate of the Jews."

If we abstract ourselves from the numerous metaphors (lines, cogwheels, algebraic signs, etc.) we will find that the above mentioned idea is partially correct. The uniqueness of Jewish history lies in the fact that the life of Jews was more dependent on other nations at a time when those other nations were already relatively "independently steering the course of their own affairs."

But P. Marek did not discuss this characteristic any further, and he did not even touch upon the question of drawing any conclusions from this special "idiosyncrasy of Jewish history with regard to historical materialism."

In claiming that the course of Jewish history is determined by that of the history of other nations do we also acknowledge that the *political factor*—the dependence of Jews on other nations—is the one that determines Jewish history exclusively? In other words, does Jewish history constitute an exception in that the political factor is more dominant in determining its course than the economic factor, and does this really sharply contradict the principles of historical materialism?

History knows not only the kind of dependence where a national minority is integrated into a foreign body but also a dependence created as a result of conquest. Are we then going to say that the political factor, i.e., the conquest, came before the economic factor?

Thus, Professor Kliuchevski finds that the main characteristic of the historical development of Western Europe, as opposed to Russia, was that there the political moment came before the economic one because the changes were direct consequences of a political factor—the attacks of a new class that rules over society by way of conquest.

In his work *The History of Russian Social Thought*, G. V. Plekhanov splendidly illuminated the flawed nature of Kliuchevski's opinion that in this case the political moment could come before the economic one.

"The changes that take place in the economy of a country under the influence of the political factor of conquest"—writes Plekhanov—"represent the consequences of a political factor, but this is just a simple tautology. The question is not whether we can consider changes that were caused by the political factor the consequences of this factor. Of course, we can, and we should. The question is what determines the character of changes caused by a political factor. What is their character dependent on? In other words, why is it that a given political factor—the same conqueror, for instance— causes one change in the national economy in one case, and a completely different change in another case? There is only one answer to this question: because in the different cases the *defeated* are at different stages of economic development, and because the victors are also at different stages of economic development. This, however, means that the possible consequences of a political factor are previously determined by the economic factor."

Plekhanov's argument can be justifiably applied to the history of the Jewish people. Although it is true that the relationship of ruling classes and Jews in Western Europe, Poland, and Russia was not that of victor and defeated, this does not change things essentially. It does not matter whether the political factor appears as the rule of a national majority over a minority or the conquest of one people by another. The political moment could yield different consequences in both cases, regardless of whether it is conquest or simple rule, depending on how the economic development of both the victor or ruler, and the defeated or oppressed, had unfolded. Therefore, the very same factor, subordination, yielded one result for the Jews of Western Europe and a different one for the Jews of Russia.

In Western Europe the development of large-scale industry brought on the assimilation of Jews, whereas in Russia not only did Jews not assimilate but they actually developed a foreign dialect into their own national language. The reason for this must be sought in the social-political circumstances in which Jews had once lived in Poland. Under the influence of these social-political circumstances Jews were organized into a national organization which to some extent constituted a state within a state. Within certain boundaries they had political rights—legislative, judicial, and taxation. Why did this happen in Poland and not in other countries? To answer this question we need to examine carefully the special circumstances of the Polish state. Only in Poland, where the state apparatus was poorly developed, power was decentralized, cities with a German majority were politically weak, and feudal relations lasted very long, delaying the development of Poland, could the ruling classes of Jews transform the *kahal* from an instrument of collecting taxes into a complex autonomous organization that consolidated their rule over the Jewish masses. But these special circumstances of the Polish political order were themselves the consequences of the country's economy. On the other hand, the autonomous Jewish *kahal* system also grew out of Jews' earlier economic activities.

Therefore, in researching Jewish history we must direct our attention to a twofold sequence of phenomena: the historical process of the ruling nation, and the changes it caused in Jewish social life. Additionally, both sequences must be interpreted not in isolation but in connection with economics. This makes understanding Jewish history more difficult and more complicated, but historical materialism never offered a uniform and rigid template. Only by properly applying this scientific method can one understand the historical processes that will leave idealists helpless and confused.

By applying the method of historical materialism not only do we confirm that social change depends on economic factors, but this dependence will be the basis of our analysis of social relations that develop through class struggle. The history of social development is the history of social struggle, and when talking about the history of Jewish social development, our task is, of course, to explore the social contradictions that propelled Jewish social relations forward.

And at this point the idealist will step forward and argue that his protest against historical materialism is the protest of Jewish history against this "narrow doctrine." After all, the dependence of the Jewish people upon others and the persecutions they suffered had to unite all classes for the purpose of self-defense. In the face of national danger, all class contradictions had to be blurred.

There is no doubt that Jewish lack of rights had a powerful influence on the development of Jewish chauvinism; it is equally certain that the ruling classes exploited this lack of rights to further their own goals, to blunt class contradictions. Least of all do we need to convince Jewish Marxists who had, no doubt, often encountered exquisite examples of this Jewish "uniqueness" in their own practice. One could say that this was one of the causes that held back the development of Jewish social relations and at the same time contributed to the deep-rooted mistaken belief that the method of historical materialism can apparently not be applied to Jewish history under any circumstance.

However, the fact that national persecutions were once used as a tool to preach national peace and unity and to blunt class conflict does not justify concluding that Jewish history represents a "permanent civil peace" and embodies the apotheosis of national idealism.

On the contrary, social contradictions within Jewish society actually developed most clearly when protecting ourselves from the "common danger." Thus, for example, the activities of the Jewish representative body in Poland—the Council of Four Lands—whose task was to protect the Jewish community from external persecutions and restrictions, always led to the exact same result: the persecutions and restrictions the Jewish community suffered affected the poor the most. The social stratum of the rich exploited the absence of rights in order to consolidate its own social position and make the situation of the masses worse.

The lower social classes were handicapped as Jews by the ruling classes of the national majority, as well as by their own oppressors. Moreover, in the latter case they were doubly handicapped because the well-to-do transferred the weight of almost all the entire burden that fell on the community.

Thus, the statutes and regulations [takones] of the Council of Four Lands, their entire tax policy, and all kinds of monopolies simply reflected the obvious fact that when Jews were persecuted, the masses suffered more than anyone else.

This singularity of the Jewish historical process not only did not preclude class struggle but actually made class struggle appear especially clearly. Social conflicts developed precisely because of this uniqueness. The entire history of the *kahal* and the later history of Jews reveals the struggle for these material interests. Despite historians' extensive efforts to cover up every friction and conflict in Jewish politics [klal-yisroel-politik] that emerged during the history of the *kahal* as a result of this struggle, following the further development of their own contradictions the Jewish masses themselves destroyed the foundations of the Council of Four Lands before outside forces could dissolve it. [. . .]

The fall of the Council of Four Lands was a step forward on the road to liberating Jewish society from the chains of the *kahal*'s oligarchy. But the social force that rose against the *kahal*—the small tavern keepers, innkeepers, leaseholders, and artisans—who suffered from the *kahal*'s orders were unable to formulate common demands that would have united them into a broader social movement. On the contrary, since their social status was too close to what we call petty bourgeois today, they themselves were permeated by hatred for radical social reforms.

Now let us say a few words about the limitations of the above-mentioned singularity. To avoid some misunderstandings, we must not fetishize this uniqueness; we must not draw any conclusions about "special paths" of the Jewish historical process based on this originality. Since we already explained that Jews were affected by the circumstances—especially the economic conditions—of the ruling national majority, it is unnecessary to detail how this uniqueness differed from the surrounding environment only *in its form* but not *in its content*. Not only did the social life of Jews reflect the social life of the nations among whom they lived, but it was itself a part of the general social life, sort of a national sector of the very same circle, only painted in a special color.

If we examine closely the measures introduced by Jewish legislators we shall see that they differ from the laws passed by the state concerning the general population only in their form. From this standpoint, the *khazoke*, for instance, is different from other forms of monopoly only in that has a Hebrew label. In its essence it reflects the monopolistic character of pre-capitalistic commerce, the difference being that in Jewish society the monopolistic character of commerce was especially sharp because of the above-mentioned effect of external circumstances. The same thing can be said about the reform of the *heter iska,* which allowed Jewish lenders to take interest from Jewish borrowers. Regardless of their Talmudic clothing, at a certain stage of usury capital, all the Hebrew terminology, all the responsa of the rabbis, the whole *pinkes* [book of records of a Jewish community] and all of its regulations, do not mention the distinct features of Jewish life such as Jewish forms of punishment—*kheyrem* [excommunication], *kune* [site at entrance of synagogue where a person condemned by the community tribunal would suffer an insulting punishment, or cell where the community could lock up one of its members for a brief punishment] and *malkes* [lashes]. They do not talk about the "national spirit" of the Jewish criminal code. On the contrary, for research on typical forms of pre-capitalistic commerce and usury capital the forms of Jewish economic life are just as applicable as the other nations'. What Marx wrote in volume III of *Capital* about pre-capitalistic relations can very well be illustrated by the economic processes of Jews in Poland.

But history is not limited to researching material economic and political changes. These are accompanied by the transformation of spiritual-intellectual life which reflects the material changes. Every class rules over other classes not only because it exploits them, not only because in order to ensure their rule the state apparatus helps the ruling class with its army, police, and bureaucracy, but also because it strives to consolidate its rule by way of spiritual-intellectual influence. Every ruling class strives to spread ideas and opinions that justify in the people's minds the social order that serves its interests. The system of ideas and opinions that reflect the interests of a class constitute its ideology. When we talk about Jewish ideological movements—about the top of the Marxist edifice, the area farthest away from society's foundation, the economy—can we also say that Jewish ideology is an exception to other ideologies and the laws of historical materialism do not apply to it?

We must answer this question with a categorical no: Jewish ideology is not an exception; it, too, reflects the struggle of material interests. In the case of *kahal*, for instance, Jewish potentates held the Jewish masses in their hands, but in order to consolidate their power they needed a certain ideology to help them keep the masses in spiritual-intellectual slavery. The rabbinism of those times was suitable for carrying out the goal dictated by the class interest of the *kahal* oligarchy. rabbinism with its scholasticism and petty customs enchained Jews' lives; it required absolute submission to the order, protecting the aspirations of the potentates, and punished any disobedience with *kheyrem*.

When the *kahal* began to fall apart due to internal contradictions, Hasidism stepped up against Rabbinism. Hasidism was the ideology of the masses who opposed the *kahal* and were dissatisfied with its orders. Hasidism preached religious opinions and ideas that were contrary to the interests of the *kahal* oligarchy. It was the ideology of the petty bourgeois masses who suffered gravely from the order imposed upon them by the *kahal* or could not find a way out of their difficult situation and needed consolation and some hope for a miracle. Hasidism fulfilled this need. [...]

Let us now summarize what we said above.

We must give a positive answer to the main question whether the principles of historical materialism can be applied to Jewish history, not only because a negative answer regarding the life of one nation would mean that the entire doctrine is flawed, but also because the validity of the fundamental law of historical materialism, namely social relations depend on the development of productive forces, can be splendidly corroborated even for such a complicated and entangled social phenomenon as Jewish history.

A fight for material interests took place among Jews, but it had its own nuances. Social groupings were created, but these had a special character. They had their political institutions and establishments, but with special characteristics. Jewish ideological movements reflected social relations, but they carried a unique mark. The framework of this uniqueness has been discussed above.

Translated by Vera Szabó.

Felix Theilhaber

1884–1956

A physician by training, Felix Theilhaber was a pioneering sexologist and early sociologist and demographer of German Jewry. In books, pamphlets, and

papers, he campaigned for sexual reform, especially the liberalization of abortion and the legalization of contraception. A Zionist and "race scientist," in 1911 he published *Der Untergang der deutschen Juden*, a provocative demographic study of the decline and degeneration of German Jewry that pointed to a falling birth rate and rising rates of conversion and intermarriage to bolster its case. In his view, German Jewry had no future. In 1935, he left Germany for Palestine, where he founded a health insurance company and acted as its medical director.

Social Hygiene of the Jews
1927–1930

For Jews, social hygiene embraces the entire domain of religious laws and customs of Judaism on maintaining the purity and health of the body. These traditions partially, and certainly at their core, go back to very ancient times in the life of the people. To the extent that compliance with health-promoting codes of conduct was not left to an individual's own discretion but was firmly established according to persons, dates, and occasions, Jewish social hygiene differs fundamentally from that of other peoples of classical antiquity. This compulsory character brings the biblical and Talmudic hygienic body of laws into the realm of social hygiene— for Europe, incidentally, still a very new concept—even though many of the relevant rules did not originally have a hygienic but a purely religious reason and purpose, or were later casuistically overstated. The points of departure and the final goals of biblical-rabbinic social hygiene are to preserve the strength of the Jewish collectivity—and with bodily purity also come mental and spiritual purity, individual, national, and religious-ethical integrity. The fact that Jewish social hygiene has not only a purely religious character but also a national one is illustrated, on the one hand, by the contrasting example of the solely religious Christianity, which knows virtually no dietetics of the body, which is certainly not as generally binding, and the charity of which—at times highly developed—applies only to the sick, poor, and feeble. On the other hand, there is the example of Islam, which in accordance with its national quality converges with Judaism in various social hygienic prescriptions. It was to a fundamental extent their social hygienic laws that kept Jews in the diaspora strictly segregated from the people around them and protected them from intermixture; the preservation of the Jewish people, despite expulsion from their homeland and their later countries of residence, despite continuous wanderings and the bloodiest persecutions, is thus due not least of all to the faithful observance of these laws. This social hygiene of the Jews is relevant, in particular, to the following areas of application (see also their purity laws):

1. Diet: Proper foods. [. . .] Modern meat inspection is an ancient Jewish institution, observed with utmost scrupulousness [. . .]; there is also moderation in drinking.

2. Dwelling, clothing, and care of the body: Separation of the sexes; "disinfection" [. . .]; the Talmud contains numerous suggestions for building suitable houses, bathhouses, and for cleansing the body.

3. Illness: Isolation of the contagious, "disinfection" of touched objects (through burning, etc.); circumcision (*brit milah*); burial of corpses.

4. Sexual life: Prescriptions about menstruation, mikveh, chastity; sexual hygiene.

5. Care of the young: Protection of the newborn, infant welfare, child-rearing in relation to the body, sleep and rest, etc. [. . .]

6. Work: Recommendations about physical work, and of handicrafts and agricultural activity in the Talmud.

7. Rest from work: Observance of the holy Sabbath and protection from exploitations of physical strength are of decisive significance for social hygiene. This concept is only now gradually becoming established in the cultured world; Germany, for example, has had mandatory Sunday rest only since 1891.

The barbaric cramming-together of Jews in the ghettos of the Middle Ages had very diverse effects with respect to social hygienic rules: cramped and constant proximity facilitated, for example, the observance of Sabbath rest and created appropriate conditions for the ritual procurement of meat, but also naturally led to disastrous consequences with respect to housing; the Middle Ages was already suffering from unsanitary urban construction. However, the advantages afforded the Jewish masses by their better hygiene turned out to be a calamity for them at the time of the Black Death: when Jews were stricken much less frequently with the plague than the people around them because they were bound by stricter segregation laws, the rabble invented the myth that the Jews had poisoned the wells and knew how to protect themselves from the deadly water.

In the nineteenth and twentieth centuries, Jewish social hygiene, depending on the outlook of individuals and groups regarding issues of the Jewish past, present, and future, underwent the following developments:

Orthodoxy still adheres to biblical-rabbinic law as it was codified in the Middle Ages, in particular by Maimonides and Joseph Karo (in the *Shulḥan arukh*), also with respect to hygienic prescriptions; in the aforementioned as well as in almost all compendia of religious law, rules about hygiene occupy extensive space. But the wretched living conditions of Jews in Eastern countries in many cases do not permit the full enforcement of hygienic rules as prescribed by religious law.

Liberalism (as in Reform Judaism), which considerably narrows the binding nature of ceremonial law, at first was content to omit the social hygienic parts of religious law largely from observance, without providing a positive replacement in Jewish terms. Only in the second half of the nineteenth century did people in liberal circles begin—under the influence of modern social hygienic ideas, under the pressure of Eastern Jewish adversity, and with growing awareness of the inadequacy of mere ethical postulates with respect to concrete wrongs—to replace isolated aid measures with constructive overall solutions. In Germany, this was reflected particularly in the establishment of the Independent Order of B'nai B'rith; in Eastern Europe and in the Middle East with the Alliance Israélite Universelle. The Hilfsverein der deutschen Juden [Aid Society for German Jews], OSE [Society for Protection of Jewish Health], and ORT [Society for Handicraft and Agricultural Work among the Jews of Russia], as well as the American Joint Distribution Committee, have made lasting contributions to the revival of Jewish social hygiene by creating a wide range of social institutions.

Zionism, which from the beginning strove not only for the political and cultural rebirth of the Jewish people, but also for their physical recovery, sought in various ways to do justice to the historical and national-religious peculiarities of Jewish life and to cast the old goals of Jewish collective hygiene in modern forms. In Western Europe, Max Nordau was probably the first to broach the problem of the physical fitness of the Jews ("Muscle Jews"). As early as the end of the 1890s, the gymnastics movement emerged in Jewish nationalist circles. The social hygiene program of Zionism, closely linked to the goal of occupational retraining, has culminated in the constantly increasing settlement since the end of the World War of independent farmers who work in agriculture, gardening, cattle breeding, and so on, and in the promotion of homegrown handicrafts in Palestine.

The concept of social hygiene has also strongly influenced Jewish social welfare work. Under the influence of the work of the Americans in Eastern Europe as well as the efforts of ORT and OSE, Jewish welfare work in Germany today is in harmony with social hygiene. The whole sphere of welfare work, education of orphans, support of the poor and beggars (migrant welfare), occupational guidance, and so on, is aimed at sociopolitics and has abandoned the system of individual support through monetary donations. Education and prevention seek to avert social disease; welfare aims to guide people before they become sick and poor. Youth welfare and care of the handicapped and the infirm are increasingly guided by broad social hygienic perspectives. At meetings of the Zentralwolfahrtsstelle der deutschen Juden [German Central Welfare Office], of ORT and OSE, it has become increasingly apparent that the anomalies of economic life are the main sources of adversity and misery and that such problems must be addressed with large-scale, social-demographic measures (occupational guidance, occupational retraining, housing assistance, productive welfare for the poor and unemployed, hygienic education, support for sports and gymnastics organizations, marriage counseling agencies, propaganda for early marriage, for nursing by mothers, etc.). Throughout the East, large-scale efforts aim to make the Jewish economy productive. Projects include the agricultural settlement of the Jewish masses in Ukraine and Crimea. In Germany, however, the Society for the Promotion of Agriculture among the Jews, for example, has not achieved importance. In Poland, with its acute, horrific economic adversity, these efforts have particularly great significance. The economic misery of the Jewish masses, the epidemic rise in the numbers of suicides, and the decline in the birth rate are ominous symptoms of a descent that can no longer be stopped through use of the old means of treating individual symptoms but only through large-scale social hygiene and systematic population policy.

Translated from the German, edited by the volume editors.

Other works by Theilhaber: *Das sterile Berlin* (1913); *Die Juden in Weltkriege* (1916); *Goethe, Sexus, und Eros* (1929).

Hillel Alexandrov

1850–1935

Hillel Alexandrov graduated from St. Petersburg University. Best known as a regional historian of Jewish Minsk and other Belorussian towns and shtetls, he published *Research Your Shtetl* in 1928 as a guide to Jewish regional ethnography and a justification of shtetl ethnography as instrumental for Sovietization. After 1933, the Stalinist regime restricted Alexandrov's scholarship. He taught in Minsk and Leningrad.

The Jewish Population of the Cities and Towns of Belorussia
1928

Preliminary Remarks

Our study examines the changes that took place in the size of the Jewish population of Belorussia over the last three decades, based on data provided by two censuses: the general Russian census of 1897 and the city census of 1923. We are looking at only changes concerning the characteristics of Belorussia's economic development, specifically the composition of the population in cities and towns, and are not addressing other questions that should actually be part of every demographic study, such as the composition of the population according to age, gender, etc. Such an undertaking would broaden the framework of this study considerably; however, the general city census of 1923 does not give us the necessary data, as it did not include nationality. Thus, our task is narrower: we will try to analyze the changes that took place in the Jewish population of Belorussia 1) in its size; and 2) in terms of the regrouping of the Jewish population in cities and towns. [. . .]

The Jewish Population of the Cities of the BSSR

The BSSR [. . .] is an agrarian country where the rural population is many times larger than the urban population. [. . .]

As we can see, Belorussia has not been urbanizing very quickly. While in Russia we are witnessing a steady growth of the urban population, the urban population of Belorussia is not developing at the same pace. [. . .]

The average for all urban areas in Belorussia is as follows: while the overall population growth in the twenty-five cities was 19.4 percent since 1897, the Jewish population decreased by 5.6 percent and the non-Jewish population increased by 50.5 percent. The relative proportion of the Jewish population in the urban areas in Belorussia decreased from 55.3 percent (in 1897) to 43.6 percent (in 1923).

It would be a mistake to assume that the relative decrease of the Jewish population in the urban areas in Belorussia was caused exclusively by the war and revolution.

The unsteady numbers and ratio of the urban population in Belorussia, which we pointed out earlier, were, of course, reflected in the size of the Jewish population in the cities of Belorussia, too. The information we have from various years during the second half of the nineteenth century and the beginning of the twentieth century from various districts in Belorussia gives us the following picture: [. . .]

The ratio of the Jewish population in the cities of Belorussia was constantly decreasing in some districts (Minsk and Vilna), and increasing in the Vitebsk and Mogilev districts. The unsteady numbers and dissimilar tendencies give us reason to believe that the decrease of the Jewish population in the cities of Belorussia—as we will later see—was connected to the development of Belorussian cities themselves. [. . .]

During the period between 1897 and 1914, the pace of the relative decrease of the Jewish population was faster in the larger cities (55.1 percent in 1897 and 50.1 percent in 1913–1914) and slower in the smaller ones (53.8 percent in 1897 and 52.7 percent in 1913–1914); during the period between 1914 and 1923 we see the opposite phenomenon: a faster relative decrease in the smaller cities (52.7 percent in 1913–1914 and 42.3 percent in 1923), and a slower pace in the larger cities (50.1 percent in 1913–1914 and 44.6 percent in 1923).

This is very characteristic of Belorussia, where the development of cities before the second half of the nineteenth century did not happen in linear upward fashion but in a zigzag, sometimes up and sometimes down. Only select cities were similar in the pace of their population growth to the general pattern of urban development (Białystok, Gomel, Minsk, to some extent Vitebsk, and Vilna in the nineteenth century); the majority of Belorussian cities grew only at the expense of natural population growth.

The two social-economic factors that affect the growth of cities and represent [. . .] two sides of the very same phenomenon—the growth of industry in the city and agrarian overpopulation in the village—are expressed in a unique way in Belorussia. Belorussian industry, which does not have very powerful resources, relies mainly on agricultural raw materials, and due to the low level of agricultural technology could not develop very strongly. For the same reasons—weak industrial development and low-level agricultural technology—the agrarian overpopulation of Belorussia had to take another direction: the peasantry did not move to the cities, where the factories and plants could not give them work, but migrated to the colonized areas of Russia—mainly Siberia and the Ural region, as well as the mines of the Don Basin. It is enough to point out that between 1896 and 1915, 560,000 peasants migrated to Siberia from the Minsk, Mogilev, and Vitebsk provinces; in 1908, migrants from Mogilev province constituted 7.6 percent of all migrants from all of the Russian Empire. This was the situation in the prewar period.

The situation changed completely during the war and the revolution. During the civil war migration stopped, naturally, and it remains limited even today because the state has limited means. During the last years of the war and in the years immediately afterward, the redundant rural population had to look for work within the territory of Belorussia. Obviously, the population of the villages went primarily to the smaller urban settlements which are more closely connected to the villages and where it was easier to find employment in agricultural professions. This explains why the non-Jewish population grew at a faster rate in the smaller urban settlements than in the larger ones. This also explains the unsteadiness of the aspect we pointed out before and the "zig-zaggy" line of the development of urban population that we discussed earlier.

The situation of the Jewish population in Belorussia developed exactly the opposite way. The causes that hindered urban development in Belorussia had an objective economic character and as such affected the Jewish and non-Jewish population alike. But the former was confined to the Pale of Settlement. Then the Pale of Settlement was eliminated, and the Jewish masses of the Belorussian cities and small towns—who before the war emigrated primarily to America—now quickly started to move to the internal districts in Russia—first to the large centers, where they had built up significant settlements during the past ten years. This internal migration of the Jewish population was happening at a much faster pace than emigration to America. This absorbed the entire natural growth and, additionally, absolutely decreased the size of the Jewish population in the cities and, as we will see later, in the small towns.

Translated by Vera Szabó.

Other works by Alexandrov: *Der veg tsum ershtn may* (1926); *Forsht ayer shtetl* (1928); *Undzer kant* (1929); *Sotsyalistisher boy* (1930); *Yidn in v.s.s.r.* (1930).

Salo W. Baron
1895-1989

Salo W. Baron was the most important Jewish historian in the United States in the middle decades of the twentieth century and one of the key figures in the integration of Jewish studies into the American liberal arts curriculum. Born in Tarnów, Galicia, into a wealthy banking family, he received rabbinical ordination at Vienna's modern rabbinical seminary in 1920 and three doctorates from the University of Vienna—in philosophy (1917), political science (1922), and law (1923). He was teaching at the Jewish Teachers College in Vienna when Stephen Wise offered him a position at the newly established Jewish Institute of Religion in 1926. In 1929, he was appointed to an endowed chair in Jewish history at Columbia University, where he taught until his retirement in 1963. A master of twenty languages, he was the last Jewish historian to attempt to write a comprehensive history of the Jewish people from antiquity to the modern age.

Ghetto and Emancipation
1928

The history of the Jews in the last century and a half has turned about one central fact: that of Emancipation. But what has Emancipation really meant to the Jew? The generally accepted view has it that before the French Revolution the Jews of Europe lived in a state of extreme wretchedness under medieval conditions, subject to incessant persecution and violence, but that after the Revolution a new era of enlightenment came to the nations, which forthwith struck off the bonds that fettered the Jew and opened up the gates that shut him off from civilized life. Prisoner in the Ghetto, denied access to the resources and activities of Western society, distorted intellectually, morally, spiritually by centuries of isolation and torture, the Jew was set free by the Emancipation. In the words of Graetz: "The Revolution was a judgment which in one day atoned for the sins of a thousand years, and which hurled into the dust all who, at the expense of justice and religion, had created new grades of society. A new day of the Lord had come 'to humiliate all the proud and high, and to raise up the lowly.' For the Jews, too, the most abject and despised people in European society, the day of redemption and liberty was to dawn after their long slavery among the nations of Europe. It is noteworthy that England and France, the two European countries which first expelled the Jews, were the first to reinstate them in the rights of humanity. What Mendelssohn had thought possible at some distant time, and what had been the devout wish of Dohm and Diez, those defenders of the Jews, was realized in France with almost magical rapidity."

Emancipation, in the judgment of Graetz, Philippson, Dubnow and other historians, was the dawn of a new day after a nightmare of the deepest horror, and this view has been accepted as completely true by Jews, rabbis, scholars and laymen, throughout the Western world. It is in terms of this complete contrast between the black of the Jewish Middle Ages and the white of the post-Emancipation period that most generalizations about the progress of the Jews in modern times are made. Prophecies as to the future of the Jew are also of necessity colored by an optimism engendered by this view. If in so short a time the Jew has risen from such great depths, is it not logical to hope that a few more years will bring him perfect freedom?

Unfortunately, in the light of present historical knowledge, the contrast on which these hopes are built is open to great qualification. A more critical examination of the supposed gains after the Revolution and fuller information concerning the Jewish Middle Ages both indicate that we may have to revaluate radically our notions of Jewish progress under Western liberty. A wider, less prejudiced knowledge of the actual conditions of the Jew in the period of their deepest decline—during the sixteenth, seventeenth and eighteenth centuries—seems to necessitate such a revision. If the status of the Jew (his privileges, opportunities, and actual life) in those centuries was in fact not as low as we are in the habit of thinking, then the miracle of Emancipation was not so great as we supposed.

In the Jewish "Middle Ages," it is said, the Jew did not have "equal rights." But to say that pre-Emancipation Jewry did not have "equal rights" with the rest of the population does not mean that Jewry was the subject of special unfavorable discrimination. The simple fact is that there was no such thing then as "equal rights." In this period the absolute State, like the medieval State, was still largely built on the corporations. The corporations were legally recognized groups of people belonging to different corporate organizations, each with distinct rights and duties. The corporation of the nobility had its rights and duties, among them that of administration and defense of the country. The clergy was entrusted with spiritual and cultural affairs. While mercenaries and standing armies had to some extent replaced feudal military, and the Church had begun to give way to secular agencies of culture, the traditional powers of both were still recognized down to the very opening of the Revolution. The urban citizenry (not the peasant or proletarian mass) formed the real third estate, and its chief function was the maintenance of economic life and the replenishment of the State treasury. Below these corporations in large was the peasant body, the vast majority of the population, in many countries held in complete serfdom, and everywhere with few rights and many duties.

It is, then, not surprising and certainly no evidence of discrimination that the Jews did not have "equal rights"—no one had them. Moreover, it may be said that if the Jews had fewer rights than nobles and clergy, their duties were hardly ever greater. Their legal status was comparable to that of the third estate, and, indeed, they were largely an urban group. In some periods they had equal, in some, fewer, in some, more rights than other town inhabitants. At the very opening of the modern period, Jewish rights after a long decline happened to be on the average lower than those of their urban Christian neighbors, yet even then they belonged to the privileged minority which included nobles, clergy and urban citizenry.

Certainly the Jews had fewer duties and more rights than the great bulk of the population—the enormous mass of peasants, the great majority of whom were little more than appurtenances of the soil on which they were born. When the land was sold they were included in the sale. None could move away without the master's consent. Like cattle they were *glebae adscripti*, but less free than cattle to mate. The larger part of their produce went to landlords or to the State. On every important occasion—at a birth, marriage or death—the landlord had rights to be considered. In every legal contest his was the only competent court. Seen by La Bruyère, the peasants in 1689 even in comparatively happy France

were "savage-looking beings . . . black, livid, and sunburnt . . . they seem capable of articulation and, when they stand erect, they display human lineaments. They are in fact men. They retire at night into their dens where they live on black bread, water, and roots."

In contrast to this class, the Jews were well off. They could move freely from place to place with few exceptions, they could marry whomever they wanted, they had their own courts, and were judged according to their own laws. Even in mixed cases with non-Jews, not the local tribunal but usually a special judge appointed by the king or some high official had competence. Sometimes, as in Poland, the Jews even exercised influence in the nomination of such a *judex judaeorum* for mixed cases.

The disabilities under which medieval Jewry suffered have been made much of. Jews could not own land, or join most of the guilds, and were thereby effectively barred from certain branches of craft and commerce. But these were, in legal theory, restrictions made on the privileges granted them, and not limitations on any general rule of equal rights. Every corporation had similar restrictions, and in this respect the Jews' case was no different in principle from that of other privileged groups.

True, the Jews were *servi camerae* (servants of the Treasury), but this status can neither in theory nor in practice be compared with that of the peasants, who were serfs of their local masters. If one may introduce a modern legal distinction not thoroughly applicable to medieval conditions, this difference becomes clear. The peasants were really serfs in civil law, that is, they belonged to a private owner as a kind of private property. The Jews were, so to speak, serfs in public law, and as such belonged to the ruler as representative or embodiment of the State, and they were inherited by his successor in office through public law. The man elected to the Imperial throne was their master, and not the private heir of the former Emperor's private estates, or the heir even of those German countries which, like Austria, he could claim on dynastic grounds. Now we ought not to forget that even today we are, in effect, serfs of the State in public law, notwithstanding all theories of personal rights, natural rights of citizens, and the sovereignty of the people. In fact, even more so today than formerly. The State can levy taxes little short of confiscatory; it can send us to war; in democratic countries, and even more so in Fascist Italy or Soviet Russia, it is complete master of all lives and property. This situation, expressed in medieval terminology, is a serf relationship applying to all citizens. The Jew then, insofar as he was *servus camerae*, was in substantially the same position all modern free citizens are in. In a word, the difference in the legal status between Jew and peasant was what David Hume, writing in that period on the condition of ancient slaves, called the difference between "domestic slavery" and "civil subjection." The first, he recognized, is "more cruel and oppressive than any civil subjection whatsoever."

The Jews' status as servant of the Emperor only, which had been opposed in vain by Thomas Aquinas and Pope Innocent III (these had it that he was the property of the different kings and princes in Christendom), was based on the erroneous theory that the Holy Roman Emperors of the German nation were direct successors of the ancient Roman Emperors and thus inherited the authority exercised over Jewish prisoners by Vespasian and Titus after Jerusalem's fall. Vespasian had levied the *fiscus Judaicus*, and the medieval rulers levied a similar tax—*Schutzgeld* (protection money). In practice, the theory of Imperial overlordship of Jewry was occasionally a disadvantage, as when the argument was made in fourteenth-century France that these subjects of a foreign monarch be expelled from the country. But in general it was a profitable theory, for the Emperor often did provide the protection for which Jewry paid, as when he used his considerable power on their behalf in several of the German free cities.

Indeed, the status of the Jew in the Middle Ages implied certain privileges which they no longer have under the modern State. Like the other corporations, the Jewish community enjoyed full internal autonomy. Complex, isolated, in a sense foreign, it was left more severely alone by the State than most other corporations. Thus the Jewish community of pre-Revolutionary days had more competence over its members than the modern Federal, State, and Municipal governments combined. Education, administration of justice between Jew and Jew, taxation for communal and State purposes, health, markets, public order, were all within the jurisdiction of the community-corporation, and, in addition, the Jewish community was the fountain-head of social work of a quality generally superior to that outside Jewry. The Jewish self-governing bodies issued special regulations and saw to their execution through their own officials. Statute was reinforced by religious, supernatural sanctions as well as by coercive public opinion within the group. For example, a Jew put in *Cherem* by a Jewish court was practically a lost man, and the *Cherem* was a fairly common means of imposing the will of the community on the individual. All this self-governing apparatus disappeared, of course, when the Revolution brought "equal rights" to European Jewry.

A phase of this corporate existence generally regarded by emancipated Jewry as an unmitigated evil was the Ghetto. But it must not be forgotten that the Ghetto grew up voluntarily, as a result of Jewish self-government, and it was only in a later development that public law interfered and made it a legal compulsion for *all* Jews to live in a secluded district in which no Christian was allowed to dwell. To a certain extent the Ghetto in this technical sense was a fruit of the counter-Reformation, having its origin in Pope Paul IV's Bull, *Cum nimis absurdum*, issued against the Jews in 1555, and in its extreme application it was, of course, obnoxious. In origin, however, the Ghetto was an institution that the Jews had found it to their interest to create themselves. Various corporations in the State had separate streets of their own; the shoemakers, for example, or the bakers, would live each in one neighborhood. In addition to their growing mutual interest as a corporation of money dealers, the Jews wished to be near the Synagogue, then a social as well as a religious center. Furthermore, they saw in the Ghetto a means of defense. Thus, it was the Jews themselves who secured from Bishop Rudiger in Spires in 1084 the right to settle in a separate district and to erect a wall around it. There were locks inside the Ghetto gates in most cases before there were locks outside. The Ghetto, in the non-technical sense, was then a district in which most Jews and few gentiles lived long before the legal compulsion which came when Christian authority found it necessary to mark the Jews off by residence district, in order to prevent complete social intercourse between them and Christians.

In this Ghetto, before compulsion came and after, Jewry was enabled to live a full, rounded life, apart from the rest of the population, under a corporate governing organization. The Jew, indeed, had in effect a kind of territory and State of his own throughout the Middle Ages and early modern period. The advantages of this autonomy, lost through the Emancipation, were certainly considerable; they must have contributed in large part toward the preservation of Jewry as a distinct nationality.

Again, the terrors of the Inquisition play a large part in all descriptions of the state of medieval Jewry. Its horrors have been fully portrayed, and many assume that whatever normal Jewish life might have been potentially, the constant incursions of the Inquisitor made it abnormal. It should be remembered, however, that the Inquisition was legally instituted only in a few European countries, and even there had no jurisdiction over professing Jews, beyond censoring Hebrew books. Therefore, far from being a special prey of the Inquisition, Jews belonged to a small, privileged group which had virtual immunity from its operations.

In the eyes of a contemporary European, the Inquisition was no more than an ordinary court of justice, proceeding along the ordinary lines of criminal prosecution in cases of capital crime. Apostasy from Christianity, by an old law of Church and State, was punishable by death. To the religious conscience of the Western man it seemed to be a holy task to burn the body of such a criminal in order to save his soul. According to the interpretation of Canon Law prevailing throughout the Renaissance, Marranos (secret Jews) were regarded as apostates. True, the highest Church authorities taught that enforced baptism was criminal, but most of them understood by force real physical compulsion, the *vis absoluta* of the old Romans, and in this sense the baptism of few Marranos could be viewed as enforced, even though a strong *vis compulsiva* existed in the menace of deprivation of fortune and expulsion. Furthermore, many authorities contended that once baptism occurred, even by compulsion, for the neophyte to return to his former faith would be apostasy. (If the sixteenth-century Popes permitted Marranos to return to Judaism in Rome itself, theirs was certainly a laxer attitude than that of earlier and later church teachers and jurists.) At least in pure legal theory, then, the Marranos were apostates. They were, therefore, subject to the jurisdiction of the Inquisition, and the governments of Spain and Portugal were acting with strict legality in applying to them the strict interpretation of laws concerning apostasy.

As to the horrible means of procedure depicted with such vividness in the classic histories of Jewry, we must say again, with no effort to justify but in an effort to understand, that they were not extraordinary for their times. The "Inquisition" was a characteristic form of legal procedure, prevailing in civil as well as ecclesiastical courts, in which the judge was at the same time prosecutor and attorney for the defendant. The use of torture was based upon the belief that circumstantial evidence is insufficient, and that a confession

must therefore be extorted. Many also believed that such bodily sufferings were salutary for the soul. Such principles are shocking to the modern mind, but in a period of such draconic secular law as the *Constitutio Criminalis Carolina*, issued by the enlightened ruler of Germany, Spain, the Netherlands and all the New World, they are hardly extraordinary. Nor is it surprising that Jews were tortured and killed in an age when not less than 40,000 Christian "witches" were burned because they confessed to relations with demons. Regarded by itself or measured by absolute standards, the position of the Jews under the Inquisition was certainly unenviable. But by comparative standards they were, if anything, in a preferred position. For if as apostates or heretics they ran afoul of the Inquisition, they were no worse off than Gentile apostates or heretics, while as professing Jews they were beyond its jurisdiction.

Legally and in theory, we have seen, the status of the Jew was by no means an inferior one. But did actual events—persecutions, riots, pogroms, monetary extortions—reduce their theoretical legal privileges to fictions in practice? Even here the traditional answer of Jewish historians does not square with the facts.

First of all, it is certainly significant that despite minor attacks, periodic pogroms, and organized campaigns of conversion, the numbers of Jewry during the last centuries preceding Emancipation increased much more rapidly than the Gentile population. The Jewish population in the middle of the seventeenth century probably did not exceed 650,000 out of the more than 100,000,000 inhabitants in Europe. In 1900 the Jewish population of Europe exceeded 8,500,000 while the general population was about 400,000,000. That is, the Jewish rate of increase from 1650 down to the beginning of the twentieth century (when the mass of Jewry was still unemancipated) was three times the rate of Gentile increase. Furthermore, in the same period European Jewry built the great American center.

It may be worthwhile to analyze in some detail the population increase previous to the Emancipation. From 1650 to 1789, when no Jews were yet emancipated, the Jewish population increased from 650,000 to 1,700,000, or more than 160 percent, while the European general population rose from 100,000,000 to 177,000,000, an increase of only 77 percent. During the period 1789–1848, when only the Jews of France and Holland (less than 5 percent of all European Jewry) were emancipated, the Jewish population increased from 1,700,000 to 3,700,000, or about 120 percent. In the same period the general population increased only 40 percent. Even more amazing are the figures for France and Holland themselves. The chief Jewish settlement in France (Alsace) increased from 3,300 in 1700 (pre-Emancipation) to 26,000 in 1791 (year of the Emancipation), or about 700 percent, while in the six decades following 1791 their number rose only to about 40,000, an increase of less than 50 percent. In Holland the Jewish settlement started in the sixteenth century, developed rapidly during the next 200 years, and when Emancipation came there were about 50,000 Jews in the country. During the first decades of the Emancipation the general population of Holland rose from 1,882,000 (1805) to 2,640,000 (1830), while the Jewish population decreased about 20 percent. Only about 1840 did it again touch the previous high figure of 50,000. As for Russia, Rumania, Austria and Turkey, to which Emancipation came late, there was a great increase in the Jewish populations century after century. Is it not clear then that, despite the fact that pre-Revolutionary Jewry suffered massacres and other sanguinary persecutions, the population increase went on at least as rapidly before Emancipation as after?

As a matter of fact, a comparison between the loss of life by violence in the two eras—pre- and post-Emancipation—would probably show little improvement since the French Revolution. Between Chmielnicki and Human [Uman, Ukraine, where there was a major pogrom in 1763—Eds.], the two great pogrom movements of earlier East European Jewish history, more than a century intervened, whereas three major pogrom waves have swept Eastern Europe between 1880 and 1920, despite the coming of Emancipation. And if the Emancipation era did not relieve the Jew of pogroms, it did burden him in addition with the obligation of military service, from which (except in rare and temporary situations of abnormal character) he had always been free. During the continuous wars of the sixteenth, seventeenth, and eighteenth centuries, when even the non-combatant Christian felt the curse of religious conflict, the Jews were neutral and suffered few losses. If they had been combatants they might have lost more than in all the pogroms.

What of the economic situation of the Jew? Despite all the restrictions placed on his activities, it is no exaggeration to say that the average Jewish income much surpassed the average Christian income in pre-Revolutionary times. This is hard to prove, and certainly excessive wealth was rare except among high nobles and clergy. But is it not remarkable that the most typical ghetto in the world, the Frankfort Judengasse, produced in the pre-Emancipation period the greatest banking house of history? And even before Rothschild's day, such Central European *Hofjuden* as the Oppenheimers and Wertheimers, and such West European bankers as the Pintos, Modonas and others, were not far behind rich Christians in their financial power.

Paradoxical as it may seem, the very restrictive legislation proved in the long run highly beneficial to Jewish economic development. It forced them into the money trade, and throughout the Middle Ages trained them in individual enterprise without guild backing, compelled them to set up wide international contacts (the banking house of Lopez was established by five brothers in Lisbon, Toulouse, Bordeaux, Antwerp and London), and equipped them with vast sums of ready cash. With the dawn of early capitalism, and the need for ready money for the new manufactures and international trading ventures, the Jew fitted readily into the new economic structure. One need not accept Sombart's exaggerations to see that the Jew had an extraordinarily large share in the development of early capitalism, and received corresponding benefits. For several hundred years before the Emancipation many individual Jews were to profit from the old restriction which had trained them in money economy, and some of those profits were to seep down to the Jewish mass.

There were, of course, many impoverished Jews, particularly in Eastern Europe. But there were not so many of them, even relatively, as there were poor peasants. Their standard of life was everywhere higher than that of the majority of the populace. Particularly in Western and Central Europe the frequent complaints about the extravagance of some Jews, and the luxury laws of certain large Jewish communities, indicate a degree of well-being which is surprising. Furthermore, there existed in the Jewish corporations numerous relief agencies, a whole system of social insurance against need, in startling contrast to the often exposed and defenseless situation of the mass of the population.

Compared with these advantages, social exclusion from the gentile world was hardly a calamity. Indeed, to most Jews it was welcome, and the ghetto found warm champions in every age. There the Jews might live in comparative peace, interrupted less by pogroms than were peasants by wars, engaged in finance and trade at least as profitable as most urban occupations, free to worship, and subject to the Inquisition only in extreme situations (as after the enforced baptisms in Spain and Portugal). They had no political rights, of course, but except for nobles and clergy no one did.

When the modern State came into being and set out to destroy the medieval corporations and estates and to build a new citizenship, it could no longer suffer the existence of an autonomous Jewish corporation. Sooner or later it had to give to the Jews equal rights in civil and public law and to impose upon them equal duties in turn. After the French Revolution one state after the other abrogated their economic disabilities, and granted them full freedom of activity. Finally they opened public offices, elective and appointive, to Jews, and made them citizens with "equal rights."

Emancipation was a necessity even more for the modern State than for Jewry; the Jew's medieval status was anachronistic and had to go. Left to themselves, the Jews might for long have clung to their corporate existence. For Emancipation meant losses as well as gains for Jewry.

Equal rights meant equal duties, and the Jew now found himself subject to military service. Political equality also meant the dissolution of the autonomous communal organization: the Jews were no longer to be a nation within a nation; they were to be thought of and to think of themselves as individuals connected only by ties of creed—Frenchmen, Germans, Englishmen of the Jewish "Confession." This meant that politically, culturally and socially the Jew was to be absorbed into the dominant national group. Eventually, it was hoped, his assimilation would be complete.

In the face of Emancipation traditional Jewish ideology underwent great revision. The concept of the inseparability of nationality and religion—which had been increasingly abandoned in Europe after the bloody Wars of Religion—had persisted in Judaism down to the Revolution, and after. Now the theory was put forth that the Jewish religion—which the Jew was permitted to keep—must be stripped of all Jewish national elements. For national elements were called secular, and in secular matters the Jew was to avow allegiance to the national ambitions and culture of the land in which he lived. Jewish Reform may be seen as a gigantic effort, partly unconscious, by many of the best minds of Western Jewry to reduce differences between Jew and gentile to a slight matter of creed, at the same time adopting the gentile's definition of what was properly a matter of

creed. The reality of the living Jewish ethnic organism was to be pared down to the fiction of the Jewish "Confession." Jewish nationality was to be declared dead and buried. Assimilation via Reform was the Jewish destiny, as the nineteenth-century European, Jew and non-Jew, saw it.

There emerged at this point the new *Wissenschaft des Judentums*, intrinsically connected with Reformation and Emancipation, a movement of scholars anxious to assist the completion of the process of emancipation with their learning. Confronted by the general suspicion in which Germany and the modern world in general held the Jew, and convinced of the desirability of complete emancipation, they consciously or unconsciously sought a tool in history and evolved this argument: "The Jews may be bad, but if they are it is because of your persecution; change your attitude, welcome the Jews into the modern State on terms of perfect equality, and they will become good." Ardent advocates of liberalism and democracy, visioning a reformed society guided by beneficent rationalism, believing religiously that the world in general and the Jews particularly could be improved by an extension of rights, it is easy to see how they found it useful to take as black a view as possible of the pre-Revolutionary treatment of the Jews. The exaggerated historical picture of the horrors of the "Dark Ages" which we have been examining was the result.

This view of the Jewish past, outlined by the earliest advocates of political and social equality, was seized on and elaborated by advocates of Jewish Reform in the nineteenth century. Eager to widen the breach with the past, to demonstrate a causal relation between the treatment given the Jew and his general acceptability and usefulness to society, Reform advocates proclaimed in unmeasured terms the wretchedness of the age that preceded them. They explained Jewish "peculiarities" as results of oppression. The more radical expounded the idea that to achieve a new, free Jewish religion based on the Bible, the entire literature of the Diaspora must be abandoned. The Talmud, which grew up in the Diaspora, did not reflect Judaism's innermost spirit, they maintained, but was a mirror of the "abnormal conditions" in which Jews had lived.

At the end of the nineteenth and in the twentieth century, this view, originated by the anti-nationalist leaders of Reform, was to find reinforcement, paradoxically, from Zionism. Zionism wished to reject the Diaspora in toto, on the grounds that a "normal life" could not be led by Jewry elsewhere than on its own soil. So, notwith-standing their profound differences, Zionism and Reform both found that their positions were best supported by that view of history which held that before the Revolution European Jewry had lived in extreme wretchedness. They differed only in that the Zionists denounced the post-Revolutionary period as equally bad.

It should be pointed out at once that this conception of modern Jewish history is indispensable neither to Reform nor to Zionism. Indeed, each has begun to shift its ground. Particularly among the younger intellectual leaders of national Judaism one discovers a note of romantic longing towards the Jewish ghetto, its life, and its culture. In literature, the revival of Chassidism, at least as a cultural force, in the writings of Martin Buber, Peretz, Berditchevsky and others, represents the new tendency. The establishment of national Jewish minorities in Eastern Europe has done much to reverse former animosity to ghetto ideas of Jewish self-government. As for Reform, strong wings of the movement in America and Germany endeavor to reconcile it with Zionism. Even those who do not fully adopt Zionist ideology have become far less antagonistic to Hebrew culture than were their forerunners in the *Sturm und Drang* period of Reform. Thus medieval Jewish life takes on new values for Reform, and the old need for rejection of all that preceded the Emancipation disappears.

Such revaluations of the Middle Ages are part, perhaps, of a general modern tendency in historical studies, reflecting changes in our modern outlook. Liberal laissez faire is being more and more supplanted by a system of great trusts, protectionism, Fascism, Sovietism. Growing dissatisfaction with democracy and parliamentarianism has brought about a movement back to a modified medievalism. This is a medievalism on a higher plane, perhaps, but a medievalism just the same, of organization, standardization, and regulation.

That Reform and Zionism have both begun, though timidly and slowly, to reconsider the Jewish Middle Ages is encouraging. The future will certainly not see a reversal toward an obsolete and impossible corporational system. With other national minorities the Jews claimed and are claiming, not without success, the equilibrium between their full rights as citizens and the special minority rights they think necessary to protect their living national organism from destruction and absorption by the majority, a process that has often proved to be harmful both for the absorber and the absorbed.

At any rate, it is clear that Emancipation has not brought the Golden Age. While Emancipation has meant a reduction of ancient evils, and while its balance sheet for the world at large as well as for the Jews is favorable, it is not completely clear of debits. Certainly its belief in the efficacy of a process of complete assimilation has been proved untenable. Autonomy as well as equality must be given its place in the modern State, and much time must pass before these two principles will be fully harmonized and balanced. Perhaps the chief task of this and future generations is to attain that harmony and balance. Surely it is time to break with the lachrymose theory of pre-Revolutionary woe, and to adopt a view more in accord with historic truth.

Other works by Baron: *The Jewish Community*, 3 vols. (1942); *A Social and Religious History of the Jews*, 18 vols. (1952–1983); *History and Jewish Historians: Essays and Addresses* (1964).

Saul Borovoi

1903–1989

Saul Borovoi, from Odessa, defended his dissertation on the history of Ukraine in 1940. Writing in Yiddish and Russian, he also studied and translated Hebrew. Borovoi wrote about Jews in the Khmelnytsky uprising and about the Nazi occupation of Odessa. His memoirs were published posthumously.

Jewish Agricultural Colonization in Old Russia
1928

Preface

Now, when the attention of broad circles of society has been drawn to issues of the Jewish land system, it is especially tempting to recall the distant past of the first Jewish agricultural settlements in our country. Having arisen more than a hundred years ago on the steppes of Ukraine, they exist to this day. Behind them lies an interesting, and in many respects instructive, history that has been insufficiently studied. [...]

Tsarist Russia approached the very complex problem of the Jewish land system with the simplistic methods of police reformers. In colonization they saw the surest means of adapting the "useless and harmful Jewish element" to the social order of their serfdom-based country. Therefore, their "concerns" about the

Jewish colonies arose not independently but in connection with the latest "campaigns" in Jewish policy: their expulsion from the villages, the law on cantonists, the "sorting," and so on.

In the "new way of life," the Jewish masses, which had been knocked out of their economic positions by the historical process and squeezed by the fiercest legislation, sought salvation from need and hunger and protection from the "reforms of Jewish daily life." Colonies were created. Human material was selected randomly and often poorly. Local authorities saw the colonies primarily as a source of personal enrichment. All the colonies grew; through agonizing difficulties they proved their right to exist and awaited better times. [. . .]

[. . .] Due to the peculiarities of *kahal* organization, the harsh legal and fiscal system acquired unforeseen and burdensome features, and the bulk of the burden weighed on the lower classes. The spheres for labor were restricted to an extreme, and as before, human reproduction had a drastic effect on all spheres of Jewish labor and business. Keen internal competition, combined with legal restrictions, made the struggle for survival impossibly difficult. The law on cantonists completely demoralized the *kahal*. The cantonist era, which stretched into the second quarter of the century, had a grave effect on the Jewish population's economic situation as well, creating an atmosphere in which, according to contemporaries, there was no interest in business, and Jewish affairs remained mostly as before: commerce, trades, and leases. The village, the main basis of the Jewish economy, grew poorer, brought down by excessive requisitions by the debt-issuing landowner. Agricultural technology remained almost entirely at the old level, but the landowner's demands increased, and he mortgaged and remortgaged his lands. He strove to squeeze more and more money out of the Jewish lessor, while peasant solvency remained at its old level. Often, in trying to "rationalize" his affairs, the landowner began cutting out the Jewish middleman. The alignment of social figures in the village (peasant–Jew–landowner) remained as before, and this led to inevitable consequences: expulsion and the tendency to expel Jews from rural locations.

As a result of resettlement and expulsion, the already sizable Jewish population increased in towns and small towns. Proclaiming a prohibition against Jews living in the villages of a given province, of course, could not alone restructure the country's economic life on new principles. Government decrees only made advancement through economic channels more difficult and complicated. [. . .]

At the very start of the century, the government attempted to use encouraging words to attract Jews to factory activity. At the time, this was connected with the larger schemes of the "Statute." Nothing came of that, though. Now, early in the second quarter of the century, Jews in certain places were playing quite a notable role in the country's burgeoning industry. This had come about imperceptibly. What a government declaration had not been able to do, the economic situation accomplished without a word being said. We learn that in 1832, 93 percent of all factories in Volhynia and 32 percent in Podolia were in Jewish hands. In the Kiev region, Jews also had notable influence in industry. [. . .]

Becoming even more noticeable was the role of Jews in large-scale, primarily foreign trade. The south's export and import trade was concentrated to a significant degree in the hands of Jewish merchants. [. . .] It should also be pointed out in that same 1827, when cantonist duty was introduced for Jews, there was one other reform that played a very large role in the economic position of the empire's Jews: the government vodka monopoly was reorganized as a lease monopoly. This "reform" created a fairly significant group of Jewish "excise" lessees. Materially independent, often rich, detached from Jewish daily life, culturally they comprised a new group of the russified quasi-intelligentsia, marked by a few unique features.

It was these Russian Jews who welcomed the government's major new plans to transform daily life and to bring about decisive and definitive "reform."

Russia's rulers believed that there was no place in the country's nation-state organism for Jews, such as they were. [. . .]

They had to be bent to the existing order and shown their precise place in the serfdom-based state. From the fiscal standpoint, the Jews were in an extremely bad way. Huge arrears were piling up for them, and their indebtedness was mounting steadily. [. . .] Jews were highly restricted in their labor opportunities and so faced the most difficult obstacles in all spheres of economic activity. [. . .]

But the uniqueness of Jewish policy of this period manifested itself primarily elsewhere, in the sovereign and "merciful" imposition of "reforms" and "enlightenment." [. . .] The whole secret was that by "enlightenment" the government meant turning them onto "the path to truth" and "the destruction of foolish Talmudic superstitions." This plan, precisely formulated in certain secret documents, explains many of the government's measures. A definite and precise task was set: the Jewish question had to be eliminated by destroying, if not the Jews, then that entire set of national, everyday, and social characteristics that have characterized the Jews as a noticeable and distinct group of the population. The Jews were seen to have violated the style and harmony of the country-barracks. They were to be arrayed in European dress and distributed among the existing class categories. Hence the laws about yarmulkes and the famous distribution into "useful" and "useless" occupations [. . .]

Chapter XVI

We are already familiar from the preceding discussion with the figures of Jews "who became agriculturalists." We know approximately the milieu from which the future colonists were recruited for the first resettlements and what the primary stimulus for resettlement was at the time. For the first resettlements, it was the disarray provoked by the Statute of 1804 and its implementation. For the second resettlement, it was the Belorussian famine and the *kahal*'s aspiration to be rid of its insolvent members. Now, the cantonist levy played an especially sinister role in Jewish life. Release from it, which was promised to the settlers, constituted the colonies' main attraction. But added to this now was one more circumstance that proved extremely "fruitful" for Jewish agriculture. During these years an event occurred that might seem incredible even to someone familiar with the experiments of the Nikolaevan government on Erets Yisrael. A short while after the promulgation of the new statute, Finance Minister Kankrin proposed settling the vacant lands of Siberia with Jews. [. . .] Very quickly groups of Jews responded to the invitation. Jewish society at the time was ready for anything. Volunteers were enlisted in Belorussia, where a permanent expulsion of the Jews was under way, and in Lifliandia [Latvia], where, as has been noted, "measures to decrease the number of Jews" were being taken at the time. [. . .]

Later, when the "invitation" to resettle in Siberia became widely known in the Jewish world, even more were found who wished to go there, to a region heretofore totally unknown to Jews. Petitions filtered in from hundreds of family groups. [. . .]

In the western territory there is not a town left, according to Nikitin, from which Jews have not asked to go to Siberia. [. . .] Many set out. Individual parties of Jews penetrated quite far into the depths of Russia. They would turn up in Tambov, where their tormented look and impoverished situation aroused sympathy among local benefactors. A group of twenty family groups from Mitava [present-day Jelgava, in Latvia; also Mitau] would follow a route to Siberia through Kazan. Late in 1837, seventeen family groups would get stranded in Simbirsk, twenty in Vladimir, and four each in Novgorod-Seversk and Glukhov. Individual families were encountered in Kamyshev, Penza, and other places.

Translated by Marian Schwartz.

Other works by Borovoi: *Evreiskaia zemledel'cheskaia kolonizatsiia v staroi Rossii: Politika, ideologiia, khoziaistvo, byt* (1928); *Arkhivni metody v bibliotechnii raboti* (1929); *Kredit i banki v Rossii* (1958).

Nahum Gergel

1887–1931

Born in Ukraine, the historian Nahum Gergel studied in Kiev, and witnessed the pogroms in Ukraine in 1918–1921. He moved to Berlin in 1921 and explored the topic of pogroms. Gergel was a founder of Obshchestvo Zdravookhraneniia Evreev (the Society for the Protection of Jewish Health) in Berlin. In the 1920s, he criticized the role of the Yevsektsiya (Jewish Section of the Communist Party) in opposing the emigration of victims of pogroms.

The Pogroms in the Ukraine in 1918–21
1928

Much has been written concerning the pogroms of Jews in the Ukraine in 1918–21. Countless reports of the atrocities perpetrated by the bandits in various cities and towns were published in the Jewish press, but no comprehensive study of these events has yet appeared. Nor has there appeared as yet a general statistical survey of the scope of the pogroms.[1] The purpose of this article is to fill this gap and, on the basis of materials gathered by the East-European Historical Archives in Berlin, to shed light on several problems related to these pogroms.

The East-European Historical Archives has a record of 688 places in the Ukraine in which pogroms occurred. Detailed and reliable information is available only concerning 524 such places; with reference to the other 164 places, mostly small townships and villages, the information is meager. Even the number of pogroms that occurred there has not been exactly determined. The data on the aforementioned 524 places are not complete either, particularly those bearing on places on the left bank of the Dnieper, where the number of pogroms was undoubtedly larger than that on our record. [. . .]

In addition to the data regarding the 524 places in the Ukraine, we have added statistical material for 7 cities in Great Russia, in which pogroms were made by the volunteer army, in this manner completing the picture of the pogroms carried out by the Denikin troops. The following tables thus comprise 531 places. In these places 1,236 pogroms and excesses occurred. If we assume that in each of the other 164 places only one pogrom occurred (actually the number was larger in many of the places), the total number of pogroms and excesses that occurred in the Ukraine and in the seven places outside of the Ukraine would reach 1,400.

It is very difficult to define clearly what is meant by "excesses." Frequently the Jewish population was exposed during "excesses" to the same suffering and tortures as in pogroms and hence these excesses may qualify as pogroms. The usual characteristics of the pogrom—massacre, arson, pillage and destruction of Jewish property, derision of the Jewish population, desecration of its sacred places, and the like—may also be applied to excesses. To be sure the number of persons killed was as a rule smaller, although there were also cases in which this number was quite high (in Kiev, in August 1919, over 100 killed). On the other hand, there were also quite a number of pogroms in which there were no fatalities. The distinction between excesses and pogroms cannot, therefore, be made on the basis of the number killed. We have designated as excesses those instances in which the violence did not assume a mass character.

Of the total number of 1,236 instances, 349, or 28 percent, were excesses. This means that nearly three-fourths of the other disorders took on a mass character and affected the entire Jewish population.

Table I shows the geographical distribution of the pogroms and excesses, according to provinces. At the head of the list is the province of Kiev, in which 516 (41.7 percent) pogroms and excesses occurred. Then follows the province of Podolia, with 293 (23.7 percent) and the province of Volhynia with 202 (16.3 percent) pogroms and excesses. The other provinces suffered less, and the provinces of Kharkov, Ekaterinoslav and Tver had less than ten pogroms and excesses each.

The main center of the pogroms was on the right bank of the Dnieper, where civil war and nationalist passions raged in full fury. The Petlura movement, which accounted for the largest number of Jewish victims in the Ukraine, had its roots here. Here too a number of atamans and partisan leaders stirred up the peasants that were dissatisfied with the Communist experiment against the Jewish population. Denikin's army raged on the left bank of the Dnieper, in the province of Kiev and partly also in the province of Podolia.

TABLE I

Distribution of Affected Places, Pogroms and Excesses by Provinces

District	Number of Affected Places	Number of Pogroms	Number of Excesses	Absolute Total	Average per Place
Kiev	175	384	132	516	2.9
Podolia	121	213	80	293	2.4
Volhynia	90	122	80	202	2.2
Kherson	54	66	15	81	1.5
Poltava	36	41	22	63	1.8
Chernigov	29	32	14	46	1.6
Kharkov	11	9	4	13	1.2
Ekaterinoslav	4	9	–	9	2.3
Tver	4	4	–	4	1.0
Central Russia	7	7	2	9	1.3
TOTAL	531	887	349	1,236	2.3

TABLE II
Pogroms in the Ukraine, 1918–21, by Month

Month and Year	Pogroms	Excesses	Total
To Dec. 12, 1918	21	25	46
Dec. 12, 1918–Dec. 31, 1918	9	25	34
January 1919	24	27	51
February 1919	30	25	55
March 1919	36	25	61
April 1919	39	23	62
May 1919	120	28	148
June 1919	71	24	95
July 1919	109	29	138
August 1919	127	32	159
September 1919	68	17	85
October 1919	20	7	27
November 1919	8	2	10
December 1919	33	10	43
January 1920	8	4	12
February 1920	15	–	15
March 1920	11	2	13
April 1920	16	4	20
May 1920	12	4	16
June 1920	11	9	20
July 1920	1	2	3
August 1920	9	–	9
September 1920	23	5	28
October 1920	25	3	28
November 1920	6	1	7
December 1920	5	2	7
Jan. 1, 1921–April 1, 1921	15	1	16
Date undetermined	15	13	28
TOTAL	887	349	1,236

The close relationship between political developments and the pogroms is clearly reflected in Table II, showing the chronological distribution of pogroms and excesses in the years 1918–21. This table is a kind of calendar of political events in the Ukraine in so far as they were reflected in pogroms against the Jews.

From the fall of 1917 to December 1918, there were twenty-five excesses and twenty-one pogroms. Some of these were made by starved deserters from the front; others by the Petlura and Haidamak armies.

In November 1918, the Ukrainian National Council, under the leadership of Petlura and Vinichenko, proclaimed an insurrection against Hetman Skoropadski. The Hetman was soon ousted from the Ukraine by the victorious nationalist armies which gathered around the Council and its leadership. Simultaneously, an active Bolshevik agitation was initiated among the people, followed by the war between the Ukrainian and Soviet governments. To combat Bolshevism the atamans began to organize pogroms on the Jews which soon increased in violence and assumed the character of frightful massacres. The process began in December 1918, with the terrorization of the Jewish population by Ukrainian detachments in several places. Towards the end of December, pogroms occurred in Ovruch and other villages. In January 1919, pogroms occurred in the large Jewish centers of Berdichev and Zhitomir, and in February 1919, Petlura's ataman, Semosenko, organized the ghastly massacres of Proskurov [today, Kmel'nytski, Ukraine] and Felshtin. From January to April 1919, the rate of pogroms was steady, averaging about 50–60 per month.

In May 1919, there was a sudden rise in the rate of pogroms. The Soviet military commander, Grigoriev, rebelled against the Soviet government. This uprising was accompanied by terrible pogroms against Jews and it also encouraged other hordes to similar atrocities. One hundred and twenty pogroms and twenty-eight excesses were organized by Grigoriev and other atamans in that month. Toward the end of May, the Bolshevik army defeated Grigoriev's armies and began the liquidation of their remnants. Henceforth the pogroms, which in June numbered 95, were made almost exclusively by the atamans and leaders of the Petlura armies.

In July came the march of Denikin's army on the Ukraine. From July to September, Denikin occupied practically all of the Ukraine, devastating the Jewish communities in his path. Simultaneously, Petlura and the regular divisions of the atamans began a march on Kiev from the right bank of the Dnieper, continuing their pogrom activities during the months of July and August. These were the most critical months for the Jewish population in the Ukraine. In July 1919 there were 138 pogroms and in August, the highest number for any month, 159.

In September, the pogrom activities of the Ukrainian detachments came practically to a stand-still, but the Denikin officers and soldiers raged unchecked. Eighty-five pogroms occurred during that month. November was comparatively quiet. Following the intervention of foreign governments, Denikin's generals decreased their pogrom activities. In that month only ten pogroms occurred.

In December 1919, the Denikin army began to evacuate the Ukraine and it renewed its pogrom activities in the half-ruined Jewish settlements. The number of pogroms rose to 43.

The first three months in 1920 were comparatively quiet. The Soviet army occupied all of the Ukraine and the Jewish population breathed freely. In several isolated spots, mainly on the border of Podolia, the remnants of Denikin's army were still active. In April 1920, the Poles together with Petlura began their march on the Ukraine. The Petlura hordes perpetrated frightful pogroms in Tetiev, Khodorkov, Zhashkov and other towns. In the beginning of May, Petlura and the Poles captured Kiev, the capital of the Ukraine. Their victory, however, was shortlived. In June they were driven out by the Soviet forces. This episode cost the Jewish population 50 pogroms.

In July all of the Ukraine was under Soviet rule. Only three pogroms were recorded in that month. But in August the Soviet army suffered reverses near Warsaw and began its retreat. The Poles again crossed the Ukrainian border and the pogrom activities of the atamans were revived. Part of Budeny's Soviet cavalry, former Denikin regiments, became totally demoralized and carried out 27 pogroms in the provinces of Volhynia and Kiev. A wave of pogroms was set in motion again. In September and October, the number of pogroms was 28 per month. [. . .]

The pogroms on Jews were thus closely linked with political events. They were a kind of political barometer, indicating the course of the battle of the various political tendencies in the Ukraine. The darkest period were the months from May to September 1919, when the civil war reached its climax. These five months saw 625 pogroms and excesses, that is more than one-half of all the recorded cases. Complete order was restored only after the conclusion of the civil war.

As stated above, 1,236 pogroms and excesses occurred in 531 places, i.e. 2.3 pogroms and excesses for each place (see Table I). In the province of Kiev the average number of pogroms and excesses per place was 2.9. In the provinces of Podolia and Volhynia the average number was about 2.3, and on the regions on the left bank of the Dnieper the number of pogroms per place was considerably lower.

The number of pogroms per place is illustrated in Table III.

More than half of the victimized places (273) experienced more than one pogrom; a third of the places more than two pogroms. At the head of the list were the provinces on the right bank of the Dnieper, with 10 and more pogroms in some towns. The provinces of Chernigov, Poltava and Kherson registered a maximum number of 5 pogroms per place, and the other provinces on the left bank of the Dnieper had a smaller rate. The greatest number was in Stavich, in the province of Kiev, which had 14 pogroms, and Khastchevata, in the province of Podolia, which had 12 pogroms.

It should be noted that the number of pogroms in this or that place is not necessarily the same as the number experienced by the Jewish population of that point. In an investigation of 7,876 homeless families it was found that over 60 percent had experienced 3 or more pogroms, several families had gone through more than 20 pogroms and for only 20 percent of these was the average 1.3 pogroms.[2] The apparent discrepancy between

TABLE III
Distribution of Affected Places According to Number of Pogroms Suffered

Pogroms per Place	Kiev	Podolia	Volhynia	Others	Total Number	Percentage
1	75	46	40	97	258	48.6
2	27	35	22	27	111	21.0
3	20	15	12	13	60	11.3
4	13	12	8	5	38	7.1
5	10	5	3	3	21	4.0
6	10	3	4	–	17	3.2
7	8	3	–	–	11	2.0
8	5	–	–	–	5	0.9
9	5	1	–	–	6	1.1
10	1	–	1	–	2	0.4
11	1	1	–	–	2	0.4
TOTAL	175	121	90	145	531	100.0

these figures and data in Table III is due to the fact that during the pogrom period the Jewish population fled from place to place. The victimized population in the villages and smaller towns sought safety in the district and provincial capitals but these too did not escape the pogrom wave and the homeless refugees, therefore, experienced additional pogroms in these larger centers. The average number of pogroms experienced by the population is, therefore, considerably higher than the average number of pogroms per geographical place.

We now come to the question of the participation of the various armies and groups in the pogroms.

Forty percent of all the pogroms, i.e., 493 pogroms in 293 places, were made by the followers of Petlura. We have considered as such all the pogroms carried out by the armies of general Petlura and those atamans who were directly linked with Petlura's military or political organization, namely, Voliniets, Shepel, Sokolovsky, Mordalevich, etc. This group ranked first in the number of pogroms organized. Second came the insurgents and hordes with 307 pogroms in 210 places; third place is that of Denikin's army with 213 pogroms in 164 places.

Petlura's and Denikin's armies along with the insurgents formed the central pogrom groups, and they were responsible for 1,013 pogroms, or more than four-fifths of the total number. Included in this category was also the Grigoriev army, which in the course of only a few weeks perpetrated 52 pogroms, characterized by exceptional brutality. The other groups played a lesser role in the pogroms. The Polish army was responsible for 12 pogroms and 20 excesses. The "miscellaneous" group comprises minor pogroms made by unidentifiable parts of the army and several pogroms made by the disorganized parts of the Russian army in their flight from the front at the end of 1917. This group includes also 8 pogroms and one excess made by the army of General Bulak-Balakhovich in the Ukraine. The other pogrom activities of Bulak-Balakhovich were centered mainly in White Russia [Belorussia, today Belarus], especially in the vicinity of Mozir [Mozyr], and are not within the scope of this study.

The pogroms carried out by the Soviet army occupy a special place. Although the total number of 106 pogroms and excesses is an impressive one, the Soviet army can by no means be classified with the other pogrom-making groups. Quite the contrary, the Soviet army took all means at its disposal to protect the Jews from pogroms. Even in the places where such pogroms occurred the Jewish inhabitants in these places remained, nevertheless, sympathetic to the Soviet army, knowing that these pogroms were carried out against the will of the authorities and that the guilty ones were being severely punished. The pogroms made by Soviet soldiers were exceptions and accidental. They were made, in the main, by detachments of other armies that had gone over to the side of the Soviets. These troops, under the stress of civil war, broke the military discipline and started making pogroms in the same way they had carried on under anti-Soviet leadership. [. . .]

Considering the number of pogroms and excesses among the various groups, we note that among the in-

TABLE VII
Distribution of Killed According to Provinces

Province	Number of Killed	Percentage of Total Killed	Percentage of Total Pogroms	Percentage of Total of Affected Places
Kiev	16,569	53.3	41.7	33.0
Podolia	8,111	26.1	23.7	22.8
Volhynia	1,952	6.2	16.3	17.0
Kherson	2,693	8.7	6.5	10.2
Chernigov	523	1.7	3.7	5.5
Poltava	366	1.2	5.1	6.8
Ekaterinoslav	564	1.8	0.8	0.7
Tver	20	0.1	0.3	0.7
Kharkov	24	0.1	1.1	2.0
Central Russia	249	0.8	0.8	1.3
TOTAL	31,071	100.0	100.0	100.0

surgents the excesses comprised one-third of all the instances, among the Petlura followers one-fourth and among Denikin's followers only one-seventh. The pogroms made by Denikin's army assumed a mass character. They were exceeded in this respect, only by those of the Grigoriev army, whose ratio was fifty pogroms to two excesses. [...]

Taking these aspects into consideration, the number of killed in the Ukraine, even conservatively estimated, may be put at between 50,000 and 60,000.

Table VII shows the number and percentage killed in ratio to the number and percentage of pogroms made by each group. It will be seen that in the case of the followers of Petlura the percentage of those killed was considerably higher than the percentage of pogroms (53.7 and 40.0 respectively), in the case of Denikin's army the percentages were about the same (17.2 and 17.0), and in the case of Grigoriev's army the percentage of killed was 11.2 and that of pogroms 4.2. With the other group the percentage of killed was lower than the percentage of pogroms. Among the insurgents the respective figures were 14.8 and 24.8, and among the Soviet troops 2.3 and 8.6.

It should be noted, generally, that the number of killed in the pogroms made by the Soviet troops was comparatively small. In the 106 pogroms made by these troops, 725 were killed; in the 52 pogroms made by Grigoriev's army 3,471 were killed. In 50 pogroms made by Soviet troops there were no persons killed at all. Similarly, in the 32 pogroms made by the Polish army the number of killed was insignificant. In 19 of

TABLE IX
Age of Persons Killed

Age	Number	Percentage of Total Killed
0–1	45	0.4
1–7	288	2.9
8–16	764	7.7
17–20	1,130	11.4
21–30	2,124	21.4
31–40	1,493	15.1
41–50	1,501	15.1
51–	2,571	26.0
TOTAL	9,916	100.0

these pogroms, that is in a majority, there were none killed at all. [...]

Special interest attaches to the age and sex of the persons killed. The East-European Historical Archives contain a list of names of 16,262 persons killed. In the case of 9,916 the age of the victims is established. Table IX shows these figures.

It will be seen from Table IX that even infants are not spared by the perpetrators of pogroms. At the same time, a tendency to exterminate certain groups of the Jewish population is clearly discernible. Nearly two-thirds (63 percent) of all the persons killed were between the ages of 17 and 50. Of the 15,026 whose sex was established, 11,395 or 76 percent were men and 3,631 or 24 percent women. Over three-fourth of the killed were men.

There is, unfortunately, very little material regarding the wounded. [. . .]

The extent of property damage caused by the pogroms on Ukrainian Jews cannot be gauged even approximately. The investigation conducted by Jacob Lestchinsky among the refugees in Kiev in 1920 indicated that this damage was colossal and that the great majority of the affected population was completely ruined.

NOTES

Notes appear in the original translation.

1. Since the writing of this article there has appeared Rosenthal, E. D., *Megilat hatebab*, vols. i–iii (Jerusalem 1927–30). See also Tcherikower, E., *Antisemitizm un pogromen in ukrayne 1917–1918* (Berlin 1923); Kheyfets, Ilya, *Pogrom-geshikhte* (New York 1921), also available in English translation (New York 1921); Khazanovich, L., *Der Yidisher khurbn in ukrayne, Materyalm un dokumenin* (Berlin 1920); Latzki-Bertoldi, V., *Gzeyras Denikin* (Berlin 1922); Revutsky, A., *In di shvere teg oyf ukrayne* (Berlin 1924); Shtif, N. *Pogromen in ukrayne. Di tsayt fun der frayviliker armey* (Berlin 1923); Schechtman, J., *Ver is farantvortlekh far di pogromen in ukrayne* (Paris 1927); Lestchinsky, J., "Der shrek far tsifern," in *Tsukunft*, vol. xxvii (1922) 528–32 and vol. xxviii (1923) 546–50, and "Pogrom-korbones in podolyer gubernye 1918–1921," in *Bleter far yidisher demografye, statistik un ekonomik*, vol. ii (1924) 290–91; Koralnik, J., "Pogrommateryaln," in *Bleter far yidisher demografye, statistik un ekonomik*, vol. i (1923) 24–27.—*Ed.*

2. Cf. Lestchinsky, *op. cit.*

Translated by YIVO Institute for Jewish Research.

Other works by Gergel: *Di lage fun di yidn in rusland* (1929); *Yidn un der ruslendisher komunistisher partey un in komunistishn yugnt farband* (1931); *Pogromy dobrovolcheskoi armii na Ukraine: k istorii antisemitizma na Ukraine v 1919–1920 gg* (1932).

Israel Koralnik

1901–1953

Israel Koralnik was born in 1901 in Uman, Ukraine and studied economics and statistics in Berlin. In 1919 he became director of ORT's Department of Statistics, for which he compiled a report in Yiddish on Jewish refugees and victims of pogroms in Ukraine, based on data from the 1917 census. In 1921 he cofounded the first Yiddish statistics magazine, and then became director of the Information Department of the Central Organization for Jewish Immigration, known as Hicem, and later of the Statistics Department of the Central Organization for the Protection of Jewish Health. He served as assistant to the Jewish statistician Jakob Lestchinsky, and in 1929 he became editor of a journal on Jewish demography and statistics. He moved to Paris in 1933, serving as secretary-general of the ORT union. During World War II, Koralnik and his family crossed into Switzerland, where they were placed in refugee camps. He settled in Geneva in 1945.

On the Issue of Causes of Death among Jews
1928

We are limiting ourselves here to reworking the materials about causes of death and illnesses among Jews. The causes have in recent years been shown to the public in the official statistics of various countries.

Biology and pathology about Jews remain by today's standards a dark domain, as in the past. Science still searches to no avail for an answer to cardinal questions and becomes entangled in race theories and assumptions. Research into illness and the causes of death in the Jewish population lags far behind. Here we lack not only rational explanations for the distinctive features of the Jewish population, in comparison to the surrounding population, but also exact descriptions and characteristics of the distinctions themselves. Here the dominance of race theories is especially strong. [. . .]

When we look through the accumulated material on these specific problems, we must conclude that they are still far from thoroughly researched. It is far from certain that one can build upon unproven theories about racial distinctions in Jewish mortality.

The conclusion regarding racial distinction in Jewish mortality can be justified when all other social and cultural explanations seem bankrupt. No researcher, however, would undertake to prove that scholarship in this specific question was really brought to bear on all the methods available. In addition, it is hard to show that they have truly penetrated the depths of the problem. The opposite is true. [. . .]

At blame are really a series of objective factors that will not be able to be removed and will for many years hide the path to the real reasons behind those remarkable realities. These draw out pathologies of the Jewish population in many different countries and differing times. It will take some time to be able to work with data that has many disadvantages. These data do not enable us to distinguish the causes of death among Jews, as compared to others, and social structures.

All that has been gathered thus far is no more than small fragments put together and gathered by random communities. For a number of years the information was adapted according to varied methods and not according to the terminology used in this particular science. Researchers of Jewish pathology must start almost from the beginning. The time for generalities and suppositions has not yet arrived. To build a solid foundation, one must first collectively find fresh and conclusive material. One must research typical Jewish communities, large Jewish collectives for longer periods of time, delving deeper into the analysis and refine the research methodology.

In the last ten to fifteen years, much interest has been shown about the pathology of the Jewish population. In addition, economic characteristics have engendered a wave of the worst epidemics that have spilled over into East European countries, particularly to the compact Jewish populations. Endemic diseases break out into epidemics. The population experiences an everlasting hail of shocking occurrences.

Capturing this picture and researching the distinctiveness of Jewish pathology in such a situation, especially for those who study the mortality of the Jewish population in the hub of such epidemics, can in very distinct measure enrich the quality of research and allow for sound data to control and revise previous experiments and theories.

The materials presented here are relevant to a large number of Jewish communities, most significantly to Warsaw, Łódź, Lemberg [today, Lviv, Ukraine], Kraków, and Budapest. However, the latest information can also be used to approach questions about Vienna, Berlin, Riga, and individual Russian and American oblasts and states. The materials from Warsaw cover a period of approximately eleven years, starting in 1916. Statistics for Warsaw cite both causes of death and religious affiliation through 1926. Łódź is represented for nine years, starting in 1918 to 1926. Kraków is followed over a ten-year period, 1915–1924. The list for Lemberg comprises eleven years, 1912–1922. Budapest is represented only minimally, for a twelve-year span from 1914 to 1925. Vienna and Riga, which before the war had excelled in widely recording elaborate statistics on causes of death according to religion, have in the last years only provided brief information. Riga includes the years 1922–1925 and Vienna 1924–1925.

We have reviewed official statistical yearbooks from the above places. We have not yet used the archival materials from the statistic offices for Kraków and Budapest for the years 1914 to 1925. [. . .]

Because of the many disadvantages discussed above, our materials are not final. [. . .] However, we can already cite data that were not available previously. These are as follows:

1. The causes of death are cited according to uniform nomenclature for international illness (Bertilion nomenclature, established in 1910, and used again in 1920). Thus, comparisons can be made between various towns and various years.
2. The diagnoses of the causes of death are more certain than they were during the World War.
3. In a number of cases, the data allow for a combination of causes of death due to old age. Sexually transmitted illnesses are also observed as causes of death in rare cases, as in employment.
4. For some cities, we succeeded in correlating the data, in similar periods, on deaths from whatever disease with the number of people who had suffered from that particular disease. [sic]

We were convinced from all over to introduce research materials embracing 150,000 Jewish deaths, concentrated in a short time period and in the typical Jewish communities of Eastern and Western Europe.

General Section

Before we venture into the data themselves, we will attempt to provide a general picture of the distribution of the dead, within both Jewish and non-Jewish populations, arranged according to distinct causes of death and by the mortality coefficient of all specific group illnesses. One cannot use the materials for all the years for this purpose. It is clear that including the epidemic years would produce a distorted picture, especially as these epidemics had such tremendous strength in the majority of cities. We therefore take every city to account even when an epidemic had already been so powerful and the mortality rate of the population had returned to its normal state.

Table 1 [not included in this selection] gives the causes of death for Jews and non-Jews in Warsaw over the six-year period of 1921 to 1926, according to the succinct international terminology with thirty-eight types of illnesses. Absolute numbers for distinct years remain stable almost all the time in the majority groups; therefore, we will not err greatly when considering the relative numbers for the sum of all six years at once.

Among all groups of illnesses, three stand out in the Jewish community; 55.2 percent of all Jewish deceased fall into these three categories. Group V cites Lung Diseases (including all forms of tuberculosis). Group I deals with Contagious Diseases (also including tuberculosis). Group IV covers the narrow area of heart failure. Of a total of 20,674 deaths, Group V cites 4,648 or 22.5 percent of deaths. In Group I, a total of 3,760 or 18.2 percent and in Group IV, 2,989 or 14.5 percent constitute the number of deaths. Group VI follows in fourth place, illnesses of the Digestive Organs, with 7.7 percent, after which Group II follows with Cancer and Other Abnormal Growths in which more than one-fifteenth of all deaths were placed (6.7 percent). Following these are Urinary and Sexual Diseases (Not Venereal), as well as diseases of the nervous system, old age, feebleness at birth, and accidental deaths and murder. An insignificant percentage of cases of death from suicide (1.0 percent), pregnancy, and confinement (0.6 percent) are noted as well.

The picture changes in different ways for the non-Jewish population. The absolute majority of the deceased, 53.9 percent, fall into the same three categories as those cited for Jews. However, the order and proportion are truly different. Epidemic illnesses (Group 1) take first place, affecting one-third smaller numbers than those mentioned for Jews (15.6 percent). Heart failure, which for Jews marks third place, here moves to 9.7 percent. The number of deaths for the Christian group was 1.5 times larger in the remaining groups, at 11.0 percent, in contrast to statistics for Jews.

Cancer, nervous-system illnesses, and old age in both groups were the same, taking fifth, seventh, and eighth place with very similar percentages. Last standings were also reflected by the non-Jewish population in Group XI, which dealt with accidental deaths and murders, and Group VIII, which included Illnesses of Pregnancy and Confinement. Urinary and Sexual (Not Venereal) Illness play a very much smaller role for non-Jews than for the Jews. A larger role was detected in death by "feebleness" at birth in the non-Jewish groups. [. . .]

From these specific distributions of the deceased, it cannot yet be surmised which of the two groups die more frequently from one disease or another. This is because even though patients show similar resistances to specific illnesses, their representation in the general total of death numbers turns out to be similar to the scale of the groups for old age and sexual illnesses. The latter groups suffer the most from the illnesses and the comparison of the two populations varies. This specific comparison is not superfluous as some have suggested. It shows causes of death straight from the characteristics and distinctions of causes of death for Jews. A coefficient comparison can first be attained when one configures the absolute number of deaths from one or the other illness groups, regarding the general number of people in each of the two populations to the given points in time. The results achieved in this method give us a picture of the proportion of each illness group in both the Jewish and the general populations.

The above-mentioned ratios in the case of Warsaw are now changing to some degree.

The colossal difference in deaths from heart failure disappears. Among 10,000 Jews, 15.5 die of this specific illness. Among 10,000 non-Jewish citizens, 15.9 people die. The difference is also less pronounced in the group of lung diseases. In this category we find the highest proportion among Jews. Among every 10,000 Jews, 24.1 die of lung diseases. Among non-Jews of the same number (10,000), 25.6 die. Also, 4.7 out of 10,000 Jewish people die of old age. For every 10,000 non-Jews, 15.2 die.

The Jewish population exceeds the non-Jewish population in deaths from urinary and sexual diseases (not venereal), numbering 5.1 as opposed to 4.0. However, in all other disease groups, we find that the Jewish population has fewer incidents compared to the non-Jewish group. Interestingly, dealing with mortality as a result of cancer and other abnormal growths, the Jewish community of Warsaw has a lower proportion of deaths (7.2) as opposed to the non-Jewish group (8.5). The same findings appear in neurological illnesses, where Jewish mortality is expressed through 4.8 of 10,000 by a not much higher coefficient of 6.2 in the non-Jewish population.

Another distinct difference between Jews and non-Jews is very apparent and can be seen in three of the groupings.

1. One difference can be detected in epidemic diseases, and of endemic character where various forms of tuberculosis are figured in. Here Jewish mortality appears in 19.5 out of 10,000 citizens, whereas in non-Jews it appears in 47.0 out of 10,000.

Table II
Causes of Death in the Jewish and Non-Jewish Population ins Warsaw

Per 10000		1921–25		1925		1924		1923		1922		1921		Causes of Death
Christians	Jews	Christians	Jews	Christians	Jews	Christians	Jews	Christians	Jews	Christians	Jews	Christians	Jews	
10.5	9.1	336	1467	801	312	722	289	632	294	642	275	566	297	II. General Noninfectious Diseases
10.8	8.3	3467	1333	703	256	732	256	639	278	680	261	713	282	III. Neuro and Sense-Organ Diseases
17.6	15.8	5640	2548	1133	566	1205	569	1095	466	1136	502	1071	445	IV. Circulation Diseases
20.2	9.8	6485	1578	1394	281	1297	295	1292	350	1399	298	1103	354	VI. Digestive Diseases
4.8	5.9	1530	951	274	122	264	164	304	191	329	242	359	232	VII. Urinary and Sexual Organ Diseases
0.7	0.8	271	111	70	32	64	23	50	21	51	16	36	19	IX. Epidermal and Other Skin Diseases
0.4	0.2	116	35	24	3	22	10	22	4	19	7	29	11	X. Bone Diseases [. . .]

TABLE XXXVII

Mortality as a Result of Tuberculosis in Jews and Non-Jews, Male and Female, of the Same Ages in Lemberg [then in Poland as Lwow, now in Ukraine as Lviv]—1922

Non-Jewish Population						Jewish Population						
Women			Men			Women			Men			
Death due to Tuberculosis			Death due to Tuberculosis			Death due to Tuberculosis			Death due to Tuberculosis			
Per 10000	Absolute	All	Per 10000	Absolute	All	Per 10000	Absolute	All	Per 10000	Absolute	All	Age
42.6	109	25598	40.1	95	23678	16.4	24	14591	20.5	29	14153	0–20
32.9	102	31001	64.1	138	21529	14.4	22	15261	27.1	34	12554	20–40
36.6	64	17450	66.1	92	13926	13.0	10	7701	35.8	27	7547	40–60
77.3	45	5863	78.3	27	8489	19.0	5	2657	39.2	9	2390	60+
40.0	**320**	**79912**	**56.2**	**352**	**62622**	**15.2**	**61**	**40210**	**27.0**	**99**	**36644**	**Total**

2. Another difference occurs with diseases of "twisted" organs. There is higher than twice the coefficient seen in non-Jews, 18.0 as opposed to 8.3.

3. There are differences apparent in the cases of feebleness at birth, a disease of newborn babies. These occur in 7.5 of every 10,000 non-Jews as opposed to 3.4 out of 10,000 Jewish babies.

From the two specific examples of Warsaw and Łódź, it is clear that even for the straightforward illness of tuberculosis, in terms of Jews and non-Jews the total for groups regarding tuberculosis mortality is greater among the "proletarians," that is, among the non-Jews. This is apparent when we examine the data from both Jews and non-Jews within distinct professional and social groups.

A second important fact, which points to the lowering of the general mortality numbers of tuberculosis in the Jewish population, is the lower rate of tuberculosis mortality among Jewish women. It is a well-known fact that we observe in different countries: the data show that it is much less common for Jewish women than for non-Jewish women to be drawn into active economic life. They are hardly to be found in industry. The natural result is that disease and mortality among urban Jewish women are less prominent than among urban non-Jewish women.

We can illustrate this specific conclusion with statistics acquired from Lemberg, for which we compare the number of deaths by tuberculosis in 1922 with the general number of deaths as mentioned above from 1921.

Table XXXVII clearly indicates that the difference between the death rates of Jewish men and women is greater than those of non-Jews. The differences in mortality between Jewish and non-Jewish women are greater than the difference shown when comparing the mortality figures for Jewish and non-Jewish men. We can see the same results in statistics for the people of Amsterdam.

Table XXXVIII deals with the years 1901–1913. We have taken these data from the monograph of Jews in Amsterdam, which was composed by the urban statistician H. van Zanten. The death rate among women is, in general, everywhere less than in the non-Jewish population. For the years 1918–1926, the average in Łódź was 48.8 percent by non-Jews as opposed to 45.0 percent by

TABLE XXXVIII

Mortality of Tuberculosis by Jews in Amsterdam—1901 to 1913

| Non-Jews | | Jews | | |
Women	Men	Women	Men	Age
9.2	13.7	2.8	4.1	0–1
7.2	9.3	2.6	3.1	1–4
3.8	2.8	1.6	1.3	5–13
14.7	10.2	6.0	5.9	14–19
17.3	20.5	5.8	14.0	20–29
17.6	18.9	8.5	12.2	30–39
16.9	24.5	10.4	14.0	40–49
17.8	31.1	9.1	17.8	50–64
18.6	24.3	8.6	17.1	65–79
13.2	8.5	—	23.7	80+

TABLE XXXIX
Mortality of Tuberculosis by Jews and Non-Jews in Warsaw According to Distinct Vocational Groups in the Years 1924–1925

Non-Jewish Population			Jewish Population			
Death due to Tuberculosis		Total in the Year 1921	Death due to Tuberculosis		Total in the Year 1921	Professions
Per 10000	Absolute		Per 10000	Absolute		
6.7	59	86360	8.7	112	129251	Business and Insurance
32.8	680	206731	9.4	108	115707	Industry and Trade
45.6	208	45551	8.1	6	7413	Metal Industry
33.8	174	51459	12.0	66	54808	Clothing Trade
17.2	35	20394	5.4	8	13942	Alimentation
21.8	239	109740	13.4	19	14189	Liberal Professions and Job Positions
8.6	11	12692	14.3	8	5597	Cultural
23.5	228	97048	12.8	11	8592	Other
54.9	201	36621	12.5	13	10003	House and Personal Service
14.0	40	28512	10.6	8	7034	House Service
33.5	**2097**	**626379**	**12.1**	**375**	**310334**	**Total Population**

Jews. It must logically follow that the totals in tuberculosis mortality have to fall more favorably on the Jewish side than on the non-Jewish population.

It is clear that the mortality rate for tuberculosis is lower among Jews. Tuberculosis touches only 8.6 of every 10,000 citizens, at a time when mortality due to tuberculosis in the Jewish sub-group "Cultural" presents a coefficient of 14.8 for 10,000.

"Other" comprises the group in which social, cultural, and material aspects within the population take a higher standing. This area refers more to lawyers, doctors, and so on, whereas within the non-Jewish population it reflects groups such as official and civic workers with high status. Here there is a cultural "fall-off" and material positions take top place, enabling us to see the low mortality rate on the Jewish side. There appear to be contrasts between the Jewish and non-Jewish tuberculosis mortality rates in the groups of "industrial populations." On average, the difference here is almost 250 percent. Here we can see interesting gradations.

The greatest discrepancies between Jewish and non-Jewish death rates turn out to be for metal workers. Non-Jewish workers' levels are more than 450 percent higher than those of Jewish workers. It suffices to look at the social structure in the metallurgy industry regarding Jews and non-Jews in Warsaw to understand this distinct, strong difference. Jewish workers are mainly self-sufficient business people. In large industry, Christians are most often workers rather than bosses who run the business.

Work conditions also play a role in differentiating between Jews and non-Jews. Working conditions for Jewish metal workers are better than those of non-Jewish metallurgists. Jews are more often employed in workshops and are less affected by dangerous lung ailments. Non-Jews, by contrast, are concentrated more within factories and in areas of metal trades that could cause perilous conditions for lungs.

In the food industry, the non-Jewish mortality rate is more than 200 percent higher than the Jewish rate. This is a consequence of different types of working conditions. Non-Jewish food employees work in factories and mills, whereas Jews chiefly work at home in such trades as butchers or bakers. The result is that both the place and the work are less likely to affect their lungs.

Translated by Ruth Bryl Shochat and Alexandra Hoffman.

M. Veinger

1890–1929

Mordkhe Veinger (Veynger) was born in Poltava and studied in Prague and at Warsaw University. While still a student, Veinger published studies of Yiddish syntax. From 1914 to 1916, Veinger served in the army and after 1918 worked for the Soviet government. Then he lived in Central Asia, including in Tashkent (where he was a member of the Bund and then the Soviet Communist Party, and a lecturer and administrator at the Central Asian Communist University). In 1923, he settled in Minsk, teaching Yiddish and Germanic philology at the Belorussian State University, and playing a leading role in the Jewish studies section of the Institute for Belorussian Culture. He published widely, and initiated a Yiddish dictionary and an atlas of the Yiddish language in the Soviet Union.

On Yiddish Dialects
1928

The following descriptions of Yiddish dialects have the same goal as the work published in Volume I of the *Tsaytshrift* [journal]. For the most part, the material has been collected the same way, namely from individual representatives of each dialect whom I was able to find in Minsk. As secretary of the Language Commission this year I was finally given the opportunity to travel to the shtetls themselves and collect the necessary material there, from among the masses of inhabitants. I had the opportunity to spend three days in Slutsk County—in Kapulye—half a day in Lenine (formerly Domanove), and one day in Slutsk itself. [...]

Lithuanian–Belorussian Dialects

Slutsk County
Kapulye—Kopyl

ABOUT THE CONCEPT OF DIALECT

If the saying "as many heads, so many opinions" is true only under certain circumstances, the parallel to this saying, "as many mouths, so many dialects," is true theoretically, at least with regard to the pronunciation in a given settlement.

In reality, the population of every larger settlement develops over a long period of time as a result of immigration. It may be that the basic constitution of the population came to the given place as a more or less unified group. But even if we disregard the fact that Jewish settlements have not emerged this way very frequently, we still have new immigrants from various places continuously joining the original population group.

In Kapulye, for instance, there are people who migrated from several surrounding settlements. [. . .]

And even if a family that came to Kapulye did assimilate to the local population and adopted its pronunciation, the researcher will always find in the pronunciation of such families smaller or larger traces of their home-pronunciation.

It can also not be ruled out that new immigrants had a linguistic influence on the already settled population.

Not only the entire population as an entity, but even individual families, very often include people born in different areas.

Eighty-year-old M. Lotvin—the first subject of my research—was born in Kapulye; his wife is from Kletsk (thirty verst from Kapulye on the other side of the [Polish] border), but even after many years of living together their dialects did not merge. In Kletsk "s" is pronounced much more often as the "sh" sound of literary Yiddish than in Kapulye. As the old man points out, where Jews in Kapulye say "s" instead of "sh," his wife points out that "in Kletsk we speak differently."

In addition to immigration, the changing of generations needs to be considered.

There is a view in linguistics according to which if newly born children grew up isolated from the educational influence of adults, they would develop their own language that would possibly be completely different from the language of their parents. We do know that children create their own words, their own sounds, because a child's speech is not yet able to produce many of the sounds that an adult's speech apparatus can produce freely. Young generations are an important factor in the changes that occur in languages.

That is why the language of children and the young generation is different from the language of adults everywhere.

School plays a great role in differentiating the language of the young and the old. Children in the sixth and seventh grade of the Kapulye Soviet Yiddish school usually no longer change the "sh" sound to "s" and the "tsh" sound to "ts."

Analogous changes occur in the children's vocabulary, morphology, etc. Depending on their age, children are either more exposed to the influence of their mothers and other female members of the family and the community, or to their fathers and the broader society of the settlement.

Until the age of 7–8 the child's pronunciation is closer to the mother's dialect; after that, they are more influenced by broader social circles that are mostly male.

Seven-year-old Kopl in the family of my subject no. 3 speaks a dialect closer to his mother's. The sixteen-year-old communist "Yitzl" (Hirshl) speaks like his father and surpasses him in speaking a dialect closer to the literary language.

The mother's and father's influence in the development of the child's dialect is important also because the two genders do not speak the same way, not even if they are of the same origin and the same age. This has social and physiological reasons. The physical organization, the gender functions, and the economic role of the woman created a difference between men and women in the home and in public life. This is why a woman's speech produces sounds that are completely different from what we hear from men.

The extent to which they are involved in social life increases the difference in the language of men and women. Today's intensive social life—conventions, lectures, press, and literature—evens out the men's dialects faster than those of the women, who are, generally speaking, still stuck in the kitchen and tied to the cradle.

That is why we see that women are more inclined to preserve their pronunciation of "s" (*fisl* [rather than] *fishl*), "ts" (*ments* [rather than *mentsh*]), "z" (*vize*), etc.

The Nisenzons, husband and wife, were both born in Kapulye. Nevertheless, the husband says *shnayder*, *shuster*, *shikn*, while the wife says *snayder*, *suster*, *sikn*.

Travel related to work, spending shorter or longer periods of time outside of one's birthplace, also lead to changes in a person's dialect. Many of Kapulye's residents spent time in America, Minsk, Slutsk, or other places.

All these reasons validate our saying, "so many mouths, so many dialects." And only typification, as disregarding individual details, creating a general formula for the particular dialect, makes it possible for us to talk about "a pronunciation" as a unique unit.

My Subjects

[. . .] One cannot research a dialect just by listening to how people talk in the street, at the market place, at meetings, etc., because this way one will also hear things that have nothing to do with the given. Research must be based on the speech of individual residents. For this, one must select representatives whose dialect is least exposed to the negative influence of the above-mentioned factors, and who will reflect those factors necessary for the comprehensive and accurate understanding of the given dialect.

The subjects from whom we draw our information must illustrate the following dimensions: 1) generation; 2) gender; 3) possible isolation from the linguistic influence of other dialects; 4) the presence of secondary linguistic influences. That is why we selected these subjects.

1. M. Lotvin, 80 years old. His speech apparatus, especially his teeth, are preserved to the extent that they don't disturb proper articulation. He and his parents were born in Kapulye.

2. M. Peker, 70 years old. Horse merchant, still active in his profession. He as well as his parents were born in Kapulye.

3. Y. Shkliar, 60 years old. Bricklayer by profession. He and his parents were born in Kapulye. Nearly illiterate. Never left Kapulye.

4. Grozak, 56 years old. Shoemaker by profession. He can read and write, and reads the press. He participates in social life.

5. E. Nisenzon, 42 years old. He is a tinsmith, a *kustar* [craftsman]. He and his parents were born in Kapulye. He lived in Oriol for three and a half years. His wife Henye, 38 years old, is also from Kapulye, as are her parents. Both of them can barely read and write Yiddish.

6. B. Bliakher, 30 years old. Hairdresser by profession. Barely literate. He and his parents were born in Kapulye. Lived in Minsk for three years (1914–1917).

In addition to these representatives of the adult population I also include two female pupils from the seventh grade of the Kapulye Soviet school.

Hinde Kaplan, 14 years old. Her father is a shopkeeper. Her parents are 50 years old and both were born in Kapulye.

M. Lotvin, 15 years old. Her father is a blacksmith. Both her parents were born in Kapulye.

In the following description [not included] we will point out those basic characteristics of the Kapulye pronunciation that usually show the special features of the Belorussian dialect, at the same time pointing out deviations according to our subjects.

Translated by Vera Szabó.

Other works by Veinger: *Forsht yidishe dyalektn!* (1925); *Yidishe dialektologye* (1929); *Yidisher shprakhatlas fun Sovetn-farband* (1931).

Meir Viner

1893-1941

Meir Viner (Weiner) was born in Kraków, lived in Vienna, and studied in Basel and Zurich. In his younger adult years, Viner was committed to Jewish mysticism and Zionism. In 1925, he joined the Austrian Communist Party and settled in the Soviet Union a year later. There he worked in Kharkov, Kiev (as the head of literature and folklore studies in the Institute of Jewish Proletarian Culture), and Moscow (as the head of the Department of Yiddish Language and Literature at the Moscow State Pedagogical Institute). Viner was killed in action in World War II while serving in the Moscow Writers Battalion. In addition to his works of literary criticism, he wrote poetry and novels.

The Role of Linguistic Folklore in Yiddish Literature
1928

Introduction: Formulation of the Problem

Linguistic folklore in literature is a component of realistic style. At first, new or renewed literature is usually realistic. The same reasons that introduce common language into book-literature—the subversive urge to elevate a certain social or political stratum and make it independent of the prevailing social orders—and to make it independent from the ruling social layers—these reasons lead, as a matter of course, to primitive realism: it is an instrument used to criticize the social or state-political order. On the other hand, the same reasons lead, initially, to a populist, romantic relationship to linguistic "ethnography" with all its decorative elements. Not only because in order to be able to write at all in a literarily not yet or only slightly stabilized language you must at first write the way people speak, the way it rolls off the tongue, but also because there is an explicit sentimental attraction to this folkloristic national treasure. This is common to every literature.

However, as soon as primitive realism has developed [. . .] into an artistic realistic style, it turns its educational-critical aim not only against the "external"

social-political order, but also against the "internal" defects in the way of life of the social stratum it wants to serve. And at that point, the attitude to linguistic folklore will also become differentiated. [. . .] This becomes ever more apparent in Yiddish literature with time, until after Mendele and Sholem Aleichem. And, since the folksy language element in itself has a character-defining meaning in Yiddish literature, it would be useful to take as an example a work from one of the most interesting writers of the renewal period, Shloyme Etinger's *Serkele*, and by analyzing it find out: 1) why is it that the anecdotes of the negative figures use abundant linguistic folklore; 2) as for a general and [. . .] normative evaluation—to what extent is the use of folkloric language and idiom in literature good and useful?

Origins and Degeneration of the Idiom

[. . .] When a primitive or culturally backward person has to express a chain of thoughts or verbally react to events that are too complicated for existing adjectives and other ways of expression, he will help himself out with borrowed descriptions or the imagery of affective expressions. If such a sequence of words that was improvised for the first time is used again and again and in various situations, its meaning is obvious, and it becomes consistent. This sequence of words will gain emphatic effect, and if it is agreeable, it will become part of general usage. [. . .] It will then frequently be used even in such situations when it does not fit the concrete meaning and content in every detail. It will be used more and more often, whether because of part of its meaning (the dominant one) or because of one of its connotations, or even just part of a connotation that aims to clarify certain characteristics of concrete phenomena or emphasize a certain meaning. By being used repeatedly in situations where it is only partially appropriate, the idiom will become polished, and so it will have a chance to overcome several difficulties. In order for an idiom's meaning and connotation that are most of the time only partially appropriate to become comprehensible, one has to arrive at a number of interpretative thought processes: the idiom absorbs a whole range of associations. This makes the idiom a suitable tool for expressing concrete cases. Born out of inaptness, the idiom becomes a sharp and multidimensional instrument of expression. [. . .]

In addition, we need to consider the consciousness of the speaker. His manner of speech is not objective, he is not saying what his main point is. He talks with a grin, somewhat indisposed. [. . .] An apologetic smile meddles in the conversation constantly. The tone of language becomes more and more parodic, defensive, and filled with bitter self-irony. The language becomes ironic, parodic; it ferments like potatoes grown in a basement that sprout again and again unhealthily, pulling moisture not from the earth but from the humidity of the basement and from itself.

And that is how it happens that at a certain point in time, language—especially if it is still in a pre-literary state, i.e., it is still an idiom or a regional dialect that has barely been touched by literary language—consists of nothing but rubbed out, thick, and swollen idioms, flowery expressions, sayings, proverbs, folk-song lines, meaningless words, expression of emotions (curses, blessings, swear words, praise words, etc.), and other types of linguistic folklore. The language no longer expresses what the speaker wants to say, but rather what the language itself wants and can express. [. . .]

Now the original essence of linguistic folklore surfaces and becomes clear. Linguistic folklore was, from the very beginning, a form of emergency help: instead of calling things by their name, instead of characterizing them with a precise adjective, they imperfectly described or circumscribed concepts and images. Now this inadequacy appears to its fullest extent. [. . .] The inexactness of the idiom will now be exploited by all those who, by using flowery expressions, stereotypical phrases, and meaningless language signs, actually want to conceal their ideas rather than express them, those who speak loquaciously and do not actually "get to the point." In this phase, this "funny" proverbialism and forced [use of] phraseology no longer has any connection whatsoever to "healthy primitivity," "freshness," and "naïveté," which people usually mistake for the nature of all linguistic folklore. [. . .]

This kind of speech is not "naïve" at all; on the contrary, it is highly guileful, although essentially limited and defective. Crafty and thoroughly tested in usage during long periods of backwardness, this overgrown manner of speech is an instrument of trade, of bargaining; it is the common language of commerce. The poor small-merchant and the *luftmentsh*—in other words, the lumpen petty-bourgeoisie—of remote and politically and economically crippled Tuneyadevke, Glupsk, and Kabtsansk is trying hard [. . .] to arrive at some favorable position, whatever that might be. [. . .]

Book Phraseology in Manner of Speech

At the beginning of its renewal (early nineteenth century), the Yiddish language was loaded not only with its own linguistic tradition but also with lots of linguistic material, phraseology, and syntactic forms that did not grow from its own linguistic soil. What we mean here are those elements that came from the inherited Hebrew religious and cultural tradition. [. . .]

However, as much as the Yiddish language has been bound to written Hebrew and its influences for centuries, Yiddish also played a role in fossilizing Hebrew. The influence was double: 1) direct influence through the constant flow of religious, secular, and especially abstract terms, words, entire phrases, quotations, idioms, proverbs, curses, blessings, etc. in their original, not at all or only slightly adapted ("Yiddishized") forms; and 2) direct influence through the significant translation literature that always remained slavishly faithful to the original text, took over its archaic forms, sentence structures, and used every possible means to preserve the character of the original.

A struggle became necessary, which was not unlike the struggle of the Russian literary language against the hindering effects of Church Slavonic in the eighteenth century, or the struggle of the European national languages against Church Latin. Yiddish literature had the task of freeing Yiddish, both the spoken and written language, of its own linguistic folklore and the linguistic folklore imposed by Hebrew [. . .], and to do it very carefully, without causing harm to its important parts. [. . .]

Summary

Returning to the problem we formulated above, the following conclusions can be drawn:

The hypertrophic, exaggerated linguistic folklore of a certain period is the linguistic expression of social and societal paralysis. In life, the actual function of this manner of speech is to cunningly hide the speaker's real intention. In this manner of speech we can feel a playful flippancy and self-irony; the density of the folkloristic elements sometimes sounds like one big farce, mockery of their own social and societal situation. Thus, in its literary reproduction, this manner of speech serves as an instrument of satire, critique (in the works of writers from Wolfsohn and Levinson until Sholem Aleichem). To some extent this manner of speech, which at times has been treated sentimentally, itself becomes the object of criticism. [...]

Thus, we cannot say that the use of linguistic folklore, linguistic folksiness, regional dialects, and sociolects always indicates "healthy freshness," "originality, and creative naïveté."

However, those parts of the old and regularly blossoming new linguistic folklore, book language, regional idioms, etc. that can serve—if they are applied with discipline and reformulated—to express hitherto unexpressed phenomena need to be evaluated positively in an artistic sense. Everything else is doomed to fall apart and disappear, and is only relevant for philological documentation.

This must be emphasized especially today, because new language sources are gushing to the surface from the masses and from the hitherto silent provinces, and with their overflowing abundance they produce a stream of verbiage, misuse, and seemingly new discoveries that are actually often recurrences; they reformulate concepts that had already been successfully fixed in the language a long time ago. New language material must be curbed by strict and merciless critical discipline that rejects superfluous loquaciousness and sets itself a goal: achieving maximum understandability with the utmost frugality in using linguistic devices; achieving maximum clarity, plasticity, flexibility, and ability to express nuances with the minimum use of linguistic shifts.

Translated by Vera Szabó.

Other works by Viner: *Die Lyrik der Kabala* (1920); *Messias: Drei Dichtungen* (1920); *Anthologia Hebraica* (1922); *Von den Symbolen. Zehn Kapitel über den Ausdruck des Geistes* (1924); *Ele Faleks untergang* (1929); *Kolev Ashkenazi* (1934); *Tsu der geshikhte fun der yidisher literatur in 19tn yorhundert* (1945).

Pinchas Kon

d. 1941

Historian Pinchas Kon lived and studied in Vilna from the year 1919. He ran a law firm and published essays in the Polish, Yiddish, Hebrew, German, and Russian presses, writing primarily about the Jewish community in nineteenth-century Vilna. Kon worked with YIVO and was a member of the Association of Jewish Writers and Journalists in Poland. He was arrested by the Nazis in 1941.

Jewish Women in the Midwifery School of Vilna University
1929

At the beginning of the nineteenth century, women did not participate in the free professions regularly because at that time institutes of higher education had not yet opened their doors to them. The only professional field in which women could involve themselves was in assisting births. Since the number of doctors was very limited in Lithuania in those days, midwives played a great role in providing hygienic care to people in general. Thus, the government made sure that midwives received appropriate training, and for that purpose established special schools for them. During the second half of the eighteenth century professional midwives were trained first at the medical school established by Mizenhoyz in Grodno, and later at Vilna University, where a special midwifery school was opened at the beginning of the nineteenth century.

The Vilna Midwifery School was part of Vilna University; it was associated with the Faculty of Medicine and was run by its professors. Thus, there were two separate midwifery courses at the university at the same time: one for university students, and one for students of the Midwifery School. Some of the well-known professors who headed the Vilna Midwifery School at one time or another were professors Renie, Andrzej Matusewicz, Mikolai Mianowski, and others.

Although the Vilna Midwifery School had only a fairly limited number of students, Jewish women were among them almost from the day the school was founded.

In 1811, a certain Meir ben Rav Meir from Vilna, whose two daughters Golde and Reyze had just finished their studies at the Vilna Midwifery School, turned to the Jewish community with a request that they issue a "certificate of orderly conduct" for his two daughters. This certificate had to be presented to the authorities of Vilna University so that the two girls would be permitted to take the final examination. This is what the father wrote in his request to the Jewish community:

> To the leaders of the Vilna Jewish Community
> From me, the undersigned Meir ben Rav Meir

A REQUEST

My two daughters, one of them Golde and the other one called Reyze, have studied the medical profession called midwifery at the academy in Vilna and now the time has come for them to complete their studies and take the general examination. Therefore, according to the order of the university, they are required to submit a letter from the Jewish community providing evidence that their name and reputation in the community is immaculate and unblemished. That is why I ask the highly esteemed leaders to fulfill my request and issue a certificate for them, thereby confirming that my request has found favor in the Almighty's eyes.

Meir ben Rav Meir

The second day of Cheshvan or 26 of October in the year 5572 (1811)

In the papers of the Vilna Jewish community this is the only such request submitted in 1811.

The archival material of the Jewish community of Vilna from subsequent years also contains information regarding Jewish girls who attended the Vilna Midwifery School; this time, however, the university approached the Jewish community directly in order to obtain the oath [shvue] from the Jewish girls that was necessary in order for them to graduate from the school as midwives. Thus, for instance, we find in 1819 a note in which the dean of the Vilna University's Faculty of Medicine turns to the Jewish community and asks them to "obtain an oath" from the midwives Helena Heyman and Maria Pinias. A remark accompanying this note mentions that the oath was taken on the same day and they received their letters of attestation [from the Jewish community]. [. . .]

Maria Pinias received the exact same attestation, and both were signed by the heads of the Jewish community: Snifiski, Yofe, and Klatshko.

Helena Heyman was the daughter of the famous Vilna doctor Yakov Leyboshits and the wife of the banker Solomon Heyman. [. . .]

The first decades of the nineteenth century saw a struggle between the Jews and the magistrate regarding the prohibition that had existed in town from ancient times forbidding Jews to live in the streets leading from Ostrobros [Ostrobrama?] to Cathedral Square (i.e., today's Ostrobros, Wide Street, and Castle Street), and from Troker Gate to the Jan Cloister (today's Troker, Dominikaner, and Jan Street). During the years of upheaval in the eighteenth century, Jews managed to move into the forbidden main streets and the magistrate was adamant about banishing them from there. On behalf of the magistrate the case was conducted by the lawyer Zdankiewicz. This Zdankiewicz led the fight against the Jewish ghetto-breakers with great perseverance, utilizing any available means. He even made the effort to provide the general governor of Vilna with a detailed list of all the Jews who lived outside the ghetto, with precise instructions regarding each and every one of them.

Thus, a special investigative commission was formed whose task was to check on-site the veracity of the information provided by Zdankiewicz. In fact, on December 29, 1827, the investigators paid a visit to every designated house and compiled a list of all the "guilty" Jews and noted their suggestions in each individual case. On this list we find that in house number 429, Mrs. Meyerova's house, located on the corner of Dominikaner and Glezer [today, Stikliu] Street, lived no fewer than six Jewish families, among them "the Jews Yoachim Pines whose occupation was making varnish, feathers, and other things." The commission voiced its opinion according to which even though this was a corner house and Glezer Street was part of the Jewish ghetto, the six Jewish families were not permitted to live there because their apartments were on the side of Dominikaner Street. As a matter of fact, five Jewish families had to leave their apartments, but the sixth one, the Pines family, did not want to give in, so they went from one office to the other trying to negotiate. In one of his letters submitted to the civil governor of Vilna in 1828, in which he requested permission to stay in the apartment where he had lived until then, he declares that he was born in Königsberg and came to Vilna in 1794. He settled here and earns a living from making varnish and feathers. He has lived in Mrs. Meyerova's house for the past twenty-eight years continuously. He has two daughters who are employed as midwives in the district, one in Ladoga and the other in Yakobshtat; his third daughter has already received permission to take the examination to become a *teacher*. (This is the first piece of information we have regarding a female Jewish teacher in Lithuania!) He also has a son who is in his fifth year of high school. Pines then mentions that he "does not wear clothes dictated by Jewish custom at all" and asks that he be permitted to continue to live in his current apartment due to his old age. The civil governor sent all materials over to the general governor ("military governor"), Rimsky-Korsakov, and suggested that Pines be granted the requested permission. We have no information about what happened to Pines in the end.

Translated by Vera Szabó.

Other works by Kon: *Dawny Uniwersytet Wileński a żydzi* (1926); *Z doby Berka na Litwie* (1934); *Di haschole fun jidiszn druk-vezn di erszte jidisze zecer in Grodne un Vilne* (1936); *Di gefunene tajln fun vilner khileszn archiw (1808–1845)* (1937).

Yisroel Sosis
1878–ca. 1967

Historian Yisroel Sosis was a member of the Bund until 1920 and then of the Soviet Communist Party. He was affiliated with the Institute of Belorussian Culture in Minsk but was severely criticized as being too favorable to the Bund and insufficiently "Party-minded."

The History of Jewish Social Aspirations in Russia in the Nineteenth Century
1929

From the Publisher

This book was submitted for publication two years ago.

Considering that within the realm of Jewish history in nineteenth-century Russia there is no systematically consolidated material—material essential for students who undertake a course on the history of the Jews in Russia—the publisher found it necessary to bring this book to light.

However, the publisher wants to inform the reader that the book contains a series of fundamental flaws; this is especially necessary now, in this time of intensified class struggle.

Our purpose here is not to point out all the discernible flaws. That will be the task of specialized reviews. We only wish to indicate, as mentioned above, some basic errors.

First, the terminology is far from strictly consistent. One example is the section about finance-capital in the seventeenth century and the struggle between different social strata during the Haskalah. [Avraham

Uri] Kovner's stance against the wealthy and exploitation, as well as [Alexander] Tsederboim's defense of the wealthy, are presented by the author as a conflict between idealism and realism. Instead of *bourgeoisie*, the author inappropriately uses the neutral term *third estate*.

In various instances we find it essential to note:

1. The role of the *kahal* [autonomous Jewish government] is depicted in an unclear and indistinct way. While demonstrating that the *kahal* defended the interests of the ruling elite of the Jewish community, the author simultaneously creates the illusion that the *kahal* was initially the protector of the entire Jewish community and only later became a tool of the oppressor.

2. The author compares every stratum of the Jewish community with its corresponding Polish stratum, and concludes that the wealthy *arendar* [Jewish lessor (steward)] was of a lower standing than the wealthy *porets* [Polish landowner]. The Jewish dealer and merchant were classified at a lower standing than the Polish merchant. The Jewish artisan was at a lower standing than the Polish artisan, and so on. The author thereby creates a Jewish martyrology; that is, the Jew, no matter who he is, is always oppressed. At the same time, the comparison between the Jewish landowner and the Polish peasant is completely forgotten. The role of the Jewish exploiter is diminished.

3. The author overestimates the role of antisemitism in many instances. Even though he does not formulate it explicitly, it appears as if Jewish nationalism has always been a direct reflection of antisemitism and inequality. The author even transposes this model to the workers' movement.

4. The author was in a real conundrum when speaking of the Haskalah in the period of Nicholas I. To the extent that those *maskilim* called for Jews to abandon their national constraints and engage with Russian culture [. . .] they were a progressive phenomenon at that time. However, these same *maskilim* accepted tsarist administration and saw it as the conveyor of culture and knowledge. They idealized the tsarist government and its apparatus. They thus supported Nicholas I's reactionary program. However, this second point is not emphasized by the author and, in certain instances, the author justifies the *maskilim*.

5. The author errs in his assessment of [Lev Osipovich] Levanda and Levanda's attitude to the uprising of 1863. Levanda, while in Vilna, spoke out sharply

against the uprising and even carried out propaganda against it, defending "Russian interests." This was a clear indication that Levanda was a "learned Jew" ["uchennyi evrei"] working for the Vilna Governor General [Mikhail Nikolayevich] Muravyov, and so was explicitly carrying out a mission servile to the Russian monarchy. Still, the author maintains that "Great Russian political nationalism was foreign" to Levanda. In this way, the author attempts to defend Levanda. He also fails to explicate the Jewish-nationalistic character of Levanda's argumentation. Furthermore, he does not emphasize who Muravyov the Hangman really was.

6. The author's assessment of the Bund is also unsatisfying. He pays very little attention to this subject, but even in the small space allotted to it he makes several errors. He explains the opportunism of the Bund exclusively as a result of objective circumstances and does not thoroughly assess the role of the Bund itself as a *factor* for opportunistic perspectives. The author does not speak about the part played by Jewish workers in the general Bolshevik revolutionary movement. In this way, he equates the Jewish worker with the Bund. In addition, there are terminological blunders, when the words "revolutionary perspective" are bound up with cultural-nationalist autonomy.

Regarding the author's silence on the participation of Jewish workers in the Bolshevik movement, he was led astray by the book's basic claim that is "the history of *Jewish* sociological currents" as opposed to the "history of social currents among Jews."

We see the necessity of pointing out these major errors so that readers can orient themselves properly and make correct conclusions when using the factual material.

Introduction

1

At the very end of the eighteenth century, after the second and third partition of Poland, a significant number of Jews who were previously subjects of the Polish government were transferred to Russia, along with the new territory and the Lithuanian-Belorussian population.

The history of the Jews in Russia begins at this point. Before the end of the eighteenth century, there were small groups of Jewish merchants on the borderlands of the Russian Empire. In this part of Ukraine (on the left bank of the Dnieper), which was transferred to Russian rule much earlier (in 1677), there were small Jewish communities. They were bound, historically as well as culturally, to Polish Lithuanian Jewry. [. . .]

Only in the fourteenth and fifteenth centuries, and especially at the end of the fifteenth and the beginning of the sixteenth century, did eastward Jewish immigration from German lands to Poland, Lithuania, and Belorussia begin to assume a more massive character. Entire Jewish communities were migrating to these new countries, bringing along capital that was concentrated in the hands of a small but powerful group of Jewish financiers. They also brought along their old business customs, communal organization, Judaized-Germanic language, religious traditions, and system of Talmudic education. Under the new conditions of economic and political life in Poland, Lithuania, and Belorussia, the above-mentioned domains of economic and cultural life continued to evolve. Along with all this, internal social differentiations inside the Jewish ghetto became even stronger.

In the second half of the eighteenth century when the partitions of Poland took place one after the other, the economic and cultural way of life of Polish, Lithuanian, Belorussian, and Ukrainian Jews had long been formed. To understand the later evolution of Jewish life in the so-called "Pale" under tsarist rule, one must begin not with the history of Russian law regarding Jews, which had been the case until now, but with the history of the socioeconomic order, community organization, and spiritual culture of the Jews in Poland, Lithuania, Belorussia, and Ukraine.

Poland had opened its doors to the Jews who had been exiled from Western Europe in the Middle Ages (especially after the Crusades) and in the beginning of the modern era. The older Polish historians relied upon this fact to indicate the friendly, humanistic, and tolerant ways of the Polish royal regime. In fact, however, the determining factors were the prosaic interests of the Polish public treasury and of Poland's general economic development. [. . .]

The Polish monarchy was interested exclusively in the capital of wealthy Jews, as well as their business connections in international markets, their financial organizational capabilities, and their energy and entrepreneurship. The Jews were brought into Poland (later also into Lithuanian Belorussia) above all as major creditors of the national treasury and as initiators and organizers of such areas of the treasury as the mint and the collection of various taxes (tariffs, the excise tax on liquor, and the like).

For many centuries, the monarchy and the *szlachta* [Polish nobility] came into contact exclusively with these representatives of Jewish finance-capital: bankers, minters, concessionaires of tax payments, lessees of estates, and so on. These Jews were the first recipients of privileges and royal allowances, which gave them the opportunity to move and conduct their business freely, the right to personal and property inviolability, and independence from the local administration and the local court (from the onset, Jews were subject to the king's courts in Poland).

At the end of the fifteenth and the beginning of the sixteenth centuries, there was a change in the character and social composition of Jewish emigration to Poland, Lithuania, and Belorussia. Increasingly, the immigrants (mostly from Germanic lands) were not only wealthy Jews searching for a way to administer their capital, but also middle-class Jews and poor Jewish masses who had been expelled from their established homes through competition and through the resulting national and religious hatred and persecution. [...]

In spite of its economic strength, the Jewish financial aristocracy could not play a sociopolitical role. Jews had no direct access to municipal administration, *sejmiks* [regional assemblies], or the Sejm [Polish parliament]. However, Jewish lessors, concessionaires, and wealthy merchants appointed themselves as leaders of the community through the organization of the *kahal* and the unification of smaller communities into a strong and very effective territorial organ, the *va'ad* [general council] (for Poland as a whole and later, from the 1620s on, also separate ones for Lithuania and Belorussia). As *kahal* representatives, they also received a certain degree of power in the magistrature, the *sejmiks*, and even in the Sejm in Warsaw. Behind the scenes of different institutions, they continued to pursue their politics, not only as a way to defend the interests of the *kahal*, but also to increase their own privileges. They played the role of community *shtadlonim* [intercessors] while also pursuing their own personal interests with both religious and royal authorities. [...]

At the end of the sixteenth century and especially in the seventeenth century, along with the big Jewish les-

sors, who were a very effective social group, we encounter another category, the village Jew: the small-time lessee, the tavern-keeper, and the innkeeper. The economic crisis in the city kept pushing the Jewish masses toward the countryside, where they transferred from city to village the same principles of goods-management and economic mediation. This mass with no capital fell completely under the power of the *porets,* who strove to become wealthier by exploiting its commercial and entrepreneurial abilities. In this way, the village Jew, burdened with high rent and many duties, became the landowner's weapon for extracting assets from the peasantry. [...]

The Cossack rebellion and the war between Russia and Poland intensified the crisis in the city and brought ruination to the Jewish population. The process of the proletarization of the Jewish masses was growing progressively and expressed itself in pauperization— against which the community struggled—and, most importantly, in the transition to home-craftsmanship. This craftsmanship had been highly despised among Jews, but unbearable adversity was increasingly forcing significant numbers of Jews to turn to trades at which they were unskilled by comparison to Christian guild-artisans. [...]

2

The Jewish population did not fit into any of the ways of life that existed within the Polish feudal system. Having been isolated within the Jewish ghetto, the Jewish population further developed and strengthened their old form of autonomous governance, the *kahal.* [...]

Economic relations, leases of all kinds, home-ownership, house-building, residence rights (foreign Jews would receive such a right only with the permission of the *kahal*), trade prices of brand-new items, weights and measures—all was regulated by the *kahal.* [...]

Jewish spiritual leaders were also materially dependent on the *kahal*'s management: rabbis, cantors, ritual slaughterers, and preachers, as well as scribes, printers and publishers of religious books, heads of *yeshivot*, and others.

In carrying out their affairs, the *kahal* was also responsible for the synagogues and houses of learning. Other responsibilities of the kahal were education of youth, sumptuary laws (so as to ensure punctual payment of taxes), health care, care for the poor and the sick, the redemption of prisoners (by paying ransom), support for poor brides, and the like.

Kahal representatives acted in the outside world: in court, before administration, behind the scenes of the Sejm, before the government, and as *shtadlans* and defenders of their people. [. . .]

It is therefore natural that for quite a long time the *kahal* had a strong moral authority over the Jewish masses. However, *kahal* power did not depend on this alone. It also had at its disposal an array of tools of repression and fines for those who were insubordinate to it. There were monetary fines, as well as corporal punishments, arrests, and excommunication, the latter of which was the most terrifying punishment for a Jew. [. . .] The mere threat of excommunication already terrorized the masses, since excommunication meant not only exclusion from synagogues, but a complete boycott by the Jewish community. No one could have any relationship with one who had been excommunicated; one was forbidden to marry them, socialize with them, conduct business with them, and the like.

At the service of the *kahal* was the authority of the rabbis and both the local and higher religious courts. However, in the seventeenth and eighteenth centuries, opposition toward the *kahal* grew more pronounced. [. . .]

At the same time, the *kahal* functioned as a national representative of the Jewish people for the government. During the periods of pogroms, the Jewish community came together firmly under the auspices of *kahal* institutions. [. . .] However, deep within this same *kahal* order there were intrinsic elements of breakdown, disorder, and demoralization. These elements were linked to the stubborn battle over personal material interests that were concentrated around the *kahal*. The leaders of the *kahal* itself were drawn into this battle. [. . .]

3

[. . .] In the period of Babylonian exile, there developed among Jews a business class that was already estranged from both biblical social motifs and the primitive simplicity of biblical stories and legends. For example, the Bible strictly condemns taking interest from a Jewish borrower. However, commerce cannot function without credit transactions. The protests of the prophets against the wealthy and the speculators became incomprehensible to the mercantile class,

which adapted its social morals to the monetary system: *tsedakah* [charity] exempts the wealthy from their obligations to the poor. [. . .]

The Talmud, which developed among the Jewish mercantile class in the large trade centers of Babylon and Jerusalem, reflects the interests of the marketplace, of buying and selling, and of all the legalistic aspects of commerce and credit transactions. However, the expression of economic and spiritual life of the entire nation found a voice in the Talmud. This explains the diversity of Talmudic literature itself. There are pieces of sharp casuistry, the wit of which was accessible only to the intelligentsia of the mercantile class, which sharpened its logic through complicated mercantile and credit transactions. There are also pieces of purely folk literature and legends, the so-called *aggadot,* which stand on their own against halakhah, the purely juridical literature. One can also find within it democratic traditions that speak of the importance of work, of workers, and so on. Hostility toward the simple masses, however, is clearly visible in the Talmud, and became characteristic of Jewish financial and spiritual aristocracy in all later periods of Jewish history. The simple *amorets* [plain folk, later understood as ignoramus] in biblical times was the chief creator and carrier of the culture. In Talmudic times, the opposite became true; the upper classes now viewed him as the embodiment of ignorance and uncouthness. [. . .]

The Talmud—especially its legal side, halakhah—became the basic source of spiritual culture for the Jewish merchant class. While the complicated nature of mercantile relations helped widen the horizons of this class, it remained locked within its spiritual ghetto due to a range of economic conditions and various persecutions that beset the Jews. For this reason, the Talmud continued to be the only realm for spiritual activity. The inquiring mind found more and more "problems" within it and tried to solve them through complicated commentaries. Talmudic tractates were learned not only for the sake of religious commandments, but also as a "spiritual sport," which often brought in elements of excitement and competition in the economic life of the mercantile class.

The legal sections of the Talmud were obscure and inaccessible to the working Jewish masses. They sought their spiritual nourishment in legends detailed in other parts of the Talmud, specifically in the *aggadah,* full of biblical motifs, folk morals, stories about miracles, and so on.

The Talmud itself points to the fact that the halakhah finds its audience among the wealthy classes of the Jewish population, and the Bible and the *aggadah* among the poor Jewish masses. The particular diversity of spiritual needs that emerged from differing basic social positions prevailed from the Middle Ages into the modern period. This was especially true in Poland, where significant social differentiations among the Jewish people had crystallized. [...]

The pogroms and persecutions that the Jews lived through in the seventeenth and eighteenth centuries left significant traces on the spiritual life of the Jewish masses. [...] As rabbinical authority declined, the strength of superstition and belief in the power of miracles became stronger. These were favorable conditions for the development of messianism, which was linked specifically to the name Shabbetai Tsevi. He preached the belief that the Jewish people would very soon be redeemed of all their sorrows and would return from the diaspora to the Land of Israel. This belief found masses of Jewish supporters in Poland, Lithuania, Belorussia, and Ukraine. [...]

Similar conditions in Jewish life—a period of economic crisis in combination with decay of the *kahal*'s rabbinical authority—prepared the soil for the rise and spread of the new spiritual movement Hasidism.

Hasidism opposed rabbinism on the grounds of the latter's dry style of learning and stance of superiority and hatred toward the "simple man." It appealed to the masses with a simple, approachable way of learning. [...]

It tried to show that a Hasid—that is, a "pious" Jew—was not the one who had a wealth of Torah knowledge and wisdom, but the one who had a pure heart. It was therefore enough to pray with deep conviction and "ecstasy" and do good deeds in order to win God's favor. Thus, thanks to Hasidic teaching, the *amorets* could also achieve self-dignity and believe in the possibility of his own spiritual perfection without the help of Talmudic erudition.

Hasidism, which arose in the second half of the eighteenth century, preserved its democratic character until the beginning of the nineteenth century. Its supporters were the poor, the stepchildren of the *kahal*. The *tsadikim* [Hasidic leaders] were not distinguished from the masses in erudition, nor in their way of life. They cir-

culated in the villages. They healed the sick, comforted the unhappy, and obtained very little remuneration for their efforts. Along with their followers, the Hasidim, they were despised and persecuted by the rabbis and the *kahal*. Nonetheless, the effects of Hasidism grew. Even more, its propaganda began to attract a few representatives of the rabbis and some wealthy Jews. And so, as early as the end of the eighteenth century, there were some educated Talmudists among the *tsadikim*, and their Hasidic followers included more wealthy people. [...]

Aside from this, one notices a great interest taken by women of the educated and wealthy classes in the practical activity of the rabbi, that is, his miracles. The Jewish woman was always very distant from learned teachings. She nourished herself with stories and legends about all kinds of miracles. She would read the women's prayer book as well as ethical literature. The Hasidic practice of bringing legends and miracles into daily life must have attracted the attention of women, including the wealthy, especially during hard and tragic periods in their personal or family life. She, the woman, often played the role of an instigator in this sense, influencing her husband, who may have been a *misnaged* [opponent of Hasidism], to go seek the rebbe's help. ...

All this, together with the generally uncertain economic situation—which often affected the wealthier Jewish middle class as well, making them into *yordim* [rendering them déclassés]—assisted the spread of Hasidism within the learned and wealthy world.

Translated by Ruth Bryl Shochat and Alexandra Hoffman.

Other works by Sosis: *Di sotsyal-eknomishe lage fun di ruslendishe yuden: in der ershter helft fun nayntsenten yorhundert* (1919); *Tsu der antviklung fun der yidisher historyografye* (1929).

Shmuel Veisenberg

1867-1928

Shmuel Veisenberg was born in Yelisavetgrad (later Kirovohrad, now Kropyvnytskyi, Ukraine) and studied medicine at Heidelberg University. He lived in Constantinople (Istanbul) for six years before coming back to practice medicine in his hometown. His interest in Jewish anthropology and ethnography led him to travel in 1908 and 1911 to the Middle East, Central

Asia, and Crimea. He published his findings in German and Russian-Jewish studies periodicals, focusing on themes such as wedding and funerary rites, klezmer argot, folk art, cuisine, and festivals.

Jewish Family Names in Ukraine
1929

The question of family names in general and of Jewish family names in particular is interesting in many ways. Unfortunately, Jewish scholarship has thus far devoted very little attention to this question. My works in this field are almost the first. In Western Europe, however, and especially in Germany, extensive monographs have been devoted to the topic of family names, their origins and character, as well as to their historical and philological significance. [. . .]

Family names in general are a product of the most modern times exclusively. Of course, the more civilized a country, the earlier its inhabitants began to use family names, even before it was required by law. We have to assume—and the facts emerging from research in this direction confirm our assumption—that it was not just the higher classes, the nobility, who held nicknames [*tsunemen*] they had once received in high esteem and made every effort to pass them on as their heritage, but the bourgeoisie and the wealthy peasantry, too. So, for instance, German intellectuals contend that in Germany family names were in common use already around the sixteenth century. [. . .]

In Russia, Jews who had settled there earlier used personal names only, and when the occasion required they added the russified version of their father's name. The 1804 "Decree Regarding Jews" was the first to order Jews to take a permanent family name, but it granted Jews freedom to choose a name of their liking. The law of 1835 repeated this order, but, as a matter of fact, only in 1844 did the regulation regarding Jewish family names come into full legal force, and, due to the dissolution of the communities, oversight of this issue was placed in the hands of the local governments.

In Poland, Jews were first obligated to obtain permanent family names following the decision of March 27, 1821, with the threat of expulsion from the country. However, since many people were not alarmed by this severe measure, the magistrates were granted the authority to give family names to those who had neglected to obtain one.

One would think that since the institution of family names among Jews emerged relatively late, they would have been preserved in a clear form, and their literal meaning should be easy to understand and interpret—this is, after all, what makes family names interesting as a scholarly research topic. Unfortunately, this is not the case, and many Jewish family names are no longer decipherable today. [. . .]

Turning now to the explanation of the meaning of the 3,020 family names that I have collected. [. . .] I have to note first that the holders of these family names are all more or less permanent residents of Ukraine in that they were born there. The family names presented here are from my note-taking of many years, from reports of various philanthropic societies from Elizavetgrad and Odessa, as well as from the Duma's lists of eligible voters in Elizavetgrad and the surrounding districts. All these materials are from before the [First World] war; thus immigrants do not appear in them at all. [. . .]

When family names were not yet obligatory for Jews, there was no doubt about their literal meaning because they were written in Yiddish letters; however, it is possible that already by then many names had lost their meaning due to their having been misspelled in the past or because they were taken from foreign languages, etc., as we see in the case of Jewish personal names. In any case, it is certain that the mishmash we see today emerged when the registration of Jewish family names was put into the hands of non-Jewish authorities. Although the law of 1844 specifies that "councils and city halls are responsible to make sure that the name and family name of every Jew is written completely correctly," this was easier said than done. A language is not something that is set once and for all. [. . .]

Due to folk etymology, it is possible that many family names with the ending -*in* were changed to -*ind*, for example: Ziskin–Ziskind, Zalkin–Zalkind, and the other way round, Shulkind and the Old Yiddish Gutkind sound to the Russian ear as Shulkin and Gutkin; analogically, Elboym can turn into Albom.

The absence of the "h" sound in the Russian language, and the corresponding letter in the Russian alphabet, brought about lots of awkward results when rendering Jewish family names, often completely obscuring the meaning of the name. The German "h" is rendered in Russian as "г" and sometimes as "x." Interestingly, in Yiddish family names the "ה" is often completely left out. In this case we have instead of Hartsman–Artsman, Helfman–Elfman, Hendel–Endel,

Hokhman–Okhman. In those cases where the family name is rendered using the [Cyrillic] letter "г" (g), it is difficult to distinguish words starting with a "ה" from those that really start with a "ג." For example, the Russian "гут" can be the rendition of either "gut" or "hut"; "гейбер" can be "geiber" or "heiber"; "гарбер" can be "garber" or "harber." In these instances, Russian renders words of different origins in one graphic form. The "H" sound is rendered as "x" (ch) in the family name Khonikblum–Honikblum. [. . .]

Here is a summary of this type of classification:

Family names that consist of Russian words with a certain meaning, such as Apteker [pharmacist], Baran [sheep], Vishnya [cherry], Zayats [rabbit], Kosoglyad [squint-eyed], Tkatch [weaver], etc. total (except for the Ukrainian ones) 145

With the endings "-yevsky," "-ovsky," "-sky," and "-tsky" 779
With the endings "-yev" and "-ov" 266
With the endings "-in" 185
With the endings "-itsh," "-yevitsh," and "-ovitsh" 108
With the ending "-ik" (occupation, profession: botvinik, kamenshtshik) 33
With the endings "-ik" and "-ek" (diminutives, etc.: Zaytshik, Zubak, Korolek) 45
With the endings "-ak," "-yak," "-uk," and "-yuk" 32
With the ending "-ko" 31
With the endings "-ats" and "-yets" 14
Total number of Russian and Russian-like family names . . . . . 1,638, that is more than half of all registered names.

Even if we deduct from this number those 224 family names that have a Hebrew or Yiddish root, such as Abovsky, Beylin, Veynerov, Gabayev, Zilberov, Figerovitsh, etc., we are still left with 1,414 Russian family names. In other words: Russian family names make up almost half of all family names of Jews in southern Russia [today's Ukraine].

The second-largest group is Yiddish family names. I classified them in the following categories that might be of interest for further research. We have to note that Yiddish family names, just like German family names, with which they generally have some connection, most of the time do not have specific suffixes. Therefore, I selected from the large quantity of simple and compound words those whose last segment is relatively frequent. Of the rare German family name endings we can find

among our family names "-s" and "-er." The first one is the possessive ending (genitive)—which corresponds to the Russian "-in" or "-ov" (Beylin–Beylis). The second refers to the origins and corresponds to the Russian "-sky" (Voliner–Volinsky).

Jewish family names that are Yiddish words with a meaning, such as Aynbinder [bookbinder], Bak [cheek], Ber [bear], Blayvays [white lead], Zilbergeld [silver money], Ruf [call], and others 296

Family names that end in "-man" [man] 208
Family names that end in "-shteyn" [stone] 65
Family names that end in "-berg" [mountain] 61
Family names that end in "-burg" [castle, city] . . . 9
Family names that end in "-baum," "-boym" [tree] 16
Family names that end in "-holts" [wood] 5
Family names that end in "-hund" [dog] 8
Family names that end in "-land" [land] 9
Family names that end in "-feld" [field] 5
Family names that end in "-zon," "-son" [son] . . . 32
Family names that end in "-is," "-es," "-s" 45
Family names that end in "-er" 23

Total number of Yiddish family names . . . . . 792, that is one-quarter of all registered names, and less than half the Russian names. If we add to this number those Yiddish family names that have a Russian suffix, among which we can also find names of Hebrew origin, it will still reach only one-third of all registered names. Thus, Yiddish family names take second place after Russian family names.

In addition to family names with pure Yiddish origins, there are also a good number of family names with Hebrew roots. Some of these can be considered Yiddish because the words have become part of the Yiddish language. Since they are interesting from a lexical and onomatological [how something is expressed] point of view, I will list them here in the order of the Hebrew alphabet.

Hebrew family names:

Avidan, Avidor, Ivry, Eydes, Inklos, Ufa, Yishaye, Aloyts, Ashkenazi, Asher/Osher, Apiryon, Bogod, Bagrash, Bazyan, Balegul, Bamze, Batsme, Barez, Bardekh, Barkan, Badarakh, Benham, Benikhem, Beryak. [. . .]

This still does not exhaust the linguistic makeup of our family names. It is very interesting to look at a group of Ukrainian family names, some of which have not been included in the general Russian list. Just by looking at the large number of family names with endings that are specific to Ukrainian, such as "-ak," "-yak," "-uk,"

"-yuk," and "-ko," we can assume that there must also be Jewish family names with Ukrainian roots. But since Russian and Ukrainian are so closely related, it is not always possible to determine the origin of a certain word. Therefore, in the following text we only bring those family names that are almost undoubtedly Ukrainian.

Ukrainian family names:

Otsheretyaney [from Otsheret [. . .]? [. . .], Arkush [. . .]? [. . .], Borovik [a kind of mushroom], Barkhan [. . .]? [. . .], Borshtsh, Budnik [worker in a potash factory], Buhayev [from Buhay], Bidrat [. . . ? . . .], Bisnovatey [. . . ? . . . terrible?], Beyer [a crumb?], Bevzen [a fool], Garman? [a barn], Gots (Hots?) [a jump], Gorelik [from . . . ? . . . , brandy], Gubenko [from . . . ? . . . lip], Nuzik, Gulish [from Kulish?, a kind of food], Gusak [gander], Guralnik [brandy distiller], Grabadnik [miner], Granatur [. . . private? . . .], Gretshanik [a pastry made of grits]. [. . .]

These are the main linguistic elements that entered the stream of Jewish family names in southern Russia. In addition to the main stream, some smaller rivers flowed into the pool, and those should be mentioned for the sake of comprehensiveness.

It is quite conspicuous that the number of purely Polish family names is negligible. These include Adamowsky, Bazilewsky, Wiltshur, Zholti, Stanislawsky, Kazimirow, Kwiat, and others. This, however, is only seemingly true, because we can assume that many family names ending in "-sky" are actually from Polish and not from Russian; after all, Jews had lived in Poland for a long time, and Russia acquired Jews only with its annexation of Poland. But, unfortunately, the difference in spelling is so minimal—if there is one at all—that it makes distinguishing categories according to these two languages very problematic. [. . .]

At the beginning of our work, we pointed out the significance of nicknames with regard to the creation of family names. Nicknames emerged right after personal names; they constituted the second phase of identifying a person. Therefore, it is no surprise that later, when the need arose to create family names, many nicknames were turned into permanent family names. In fact, there are a large number of family names that cannot be considered anything but former nicknames; many of them have been preserved in their original form, without any grammatical modification. [. . .]

Family names—nicknames (*tsunemenishn*):

Oystatsher, Imber, Altin, Antik, Ostry, Okun, Oks, Armut, Bober, Bodian, Bas, Basoy, Bak, Bokser, Boroda, Baran, Bulgatsh, Bik, Blat, Blayvays, Blinder, Benun, Beloausov, Bren. [. . .]

It is also interesting that other family names have their equivalents in every language used by Jews, for example: Krimer [Krumer]—Hink—Khiger [Hager]—Khromoy; Kleyner—Kuts (Ukrainian)—Maley; Yofe [Yafe]—Prigozhi—Sheyn. [. . .]

One would imagine that patronymic family names, created from the name of the father or some paternal ancestor, would be the most widespread. But, as we have seen, this is not the case. It turns out that nicknames got the upper hand, and even the patronymic family names emerged from personal surnames that, for one reason or another, gained permanent character. [. . .]

An ethnographically unique feature of Jewish family names is that they are often formed from women's names. Usually, women take on their husbands' family name. In southern Germany, in Switzerland, as well as in Spain, however, the wife's maiden name will be added to the husband's name. This phenomenon is not exactly the same as the corresponding feature of our Jewish family names, though, because for us the point is not the continuity of the family name, but the femininity of the family itself. [. . .] All duties such as providing food and raising the children fell on the woman, and so it is no wonder that people talked about the woman, this *eshes khayil* [woman of valor], and the children were also called after her. If her name was Grune or Sosye, the children—and sometimes the husband, the *talmidkhokhem* [religious scholar], too—were called Grunes or Sosyes or Soshkes. The list below shows that family names in this category usually end in the Russian suffix "-in" or the Yiddish suffix "-s." Among the family names we will also find names with all the other patronymic endings, but only seldom; by contrast, there are many family names with a masculine name as root and the "-s" ending. Thus, among the patronymic ending there is only one name with the ending "-ov," Perlov, if we assume that this is from the female name "Perl," and one with the ending "-ovitsh," Libovitsh. Names ending in "-sky" are Pansky, Khinsky, Esterovsky, and Persky; names ending in "-zon"/"-son" are Khaynson, Khinson, Perelson, Feygenzon; names ending in "-kind" are Itkind, Elkind, Rokhkind; names ending in "-man" are Gitelman, Libman, Perelman, Rozelman. There are also female names without any etymological endings—Yekhvid, Sobol, Sheyndl. Family names ending in "-man" are more understandable here because "man" can also mean "husband." Thus, Gitelman means "Gitel's husband."[1] In order to characterize matronymic family names I will present an almost complete list here.[2]

Matronymic family names:

[. . .] Merims, Minkin, Mintsis, Mikhlin, Motkin, Nekhamkin, Perlin, Pesis, Raskin, Reyzin, Reynis, Rivkin, Rodkin, Ronis, Rokhlin, Sifrin, Slavkin, Sosis, Soskin, Toybin, Toybis, Temkin, Tublin, Feygin, Fradkin, Fridkin, Frumkin, Khaykin, Khaytshin, Khasin, Khesin, Khinis, Khinkin, Tseytlin, Tsipis, Tsipkin, Tshernis, Sheynis, Shifrin, Eydis, Eldin?, Estin, Esterkin, Yudis, Yudashkin, Yudashkis, Yakhnes.

In my humble opinion, the large number of matronymic family names used by Jews can be considered evidence of the respect Jewish women enjoyed in their environment. In any case, if nothing else, it is important that it was not shameful for Jewish men and children to be called after their wife or mother; among Russians this almost never happens; Russian people usually call the wife by the husband's name. [. . .]

Due to the multilingual character of our family names each profession appears in polyglot names. For example: Glezer–Skliar; Sapozhnik–Shevts–Shuster–Sandler (Sandlar); Kravets–Portnoy–Shneyder–Khayet.

The following list of the pertinent family names [. . .] gives us an idea of the kind of occupations that were common among Jews around the time when family names were established. Hebrew and Ukrainian family names of this kind are also cited in the pertinent lists.

Professions as family names:

Anbinder/Aynbinder [bookbinder], Apteker/Apteyker [pharmacist], Arkhitektor [architect], Utshitel (Lerer) [teacher], Bankhalter, Bankir [banker], Banshtshikov (Beder) [bath-house attendant], Basist [bass player], Beygel-treyger/Beygl-treger [bagel deliveryman], Beyder (Beder) [bath-house attendant], Beytelman [purse-maker or miller?], Beker, Bekerman [baker], Blekhman, Blekhshmid, Bliakher [tinsmith], Bonder [cooper], Botvinik [?], Brantvaynbrener [brandy distiller], Bulotshnik (Zemlbeker) [roll baker], Bukhbinder [bookbinder], Bukhhalter [bookkeeper], Galantirnik [haberdasher], Gerber (Garber) [tanner], Gleyzer/Glezer [glazier], Goldshmid [goldsmith], Gontsharov (Teper) [potter], Degtyarov [?], Desiatnikov [supervisor of the ten], Doktor, Dukhovny [religious functionary], Handel [?], Heytsman [stoker], Hendelman [merchant], Vekselman, Veksler [money changer], Vinokur (Bronfntrayber) [liquor distiller], Vodovoz (Vaserfirer) [water deliverer], Vodonom [wa-

ter carrier], Voskoboynik (Vaksmakher) [wax/candle maker], Zeygermakher (watchmaker), Zinger [singer], Tendler [dealer in second-hand goods], Teper, Teperman [potter], [. . .] Tkatsh (Veber) [weaver], Tolmatski (Dolmetsher) [Interpreter], Treyger/Treger [deliveryman], Magaziner [warehouse-keeper], Maler/Moler [painter], Mantelmakher [coatmaker]. [. . .] Sapozhnik (Shuster) [shoemaker], Slesar (Shloser) [locksmith], Solodovnik (Maltsmakher) [maltster], Solomianik (Shtroymakher) [straw maker], Stoliar/Stolier [carpenter], Piekar (Beker) [baker], Pereplyotshik (Aynbinder) [bookbinder], Pivover (Birbroyer/Bierbreuer) [beer brewer], Pletner [collector of lottery tickets], Povar (Kukher) [cook], Portnoy (Shnayder) [tailor] [. . .] Kreymer/Kremer [shopkeeper], Kreytshmer [innkeeper?], Krupnik [?], Kravits/Kravets (Shnayder) [tailor], Kuznyetsov (Shmid) [smith], Kutsher [coachman], Kaler/Keyler [butcher], Kamenshtshik (Shteynhaker) [stone cutter]. [. . .] Koyfman [merchant], Kirzhner [furrier], Kloyzner [student of religion], Rabotnikov [worker], Rukhvarger/Roykhverger [fur trader], Ribak (Fisher) [fisherman], Reznik (Shoykhet) [slaughterer] [. . .]

We have to keep in mind that the underworld used to consist not just of thieves in the narrow sense of the word; certain classes of manual laborers were considered part of it, too, and especially all itinerant elements such as poor people and musicians. Jewish musicians have retained a special language of their own to this day, a lingo that shows many similarities with the thieves' languages. It is hard to determine now who brought the pertinent family names into Jewish circles. They could have been musicians or pickpockets or petty thieves.

Such thieves' family names are possibly:

Baran [bribe], Blat [crime], [. . .] Benegun [bedbug], Gratsh [pickpocket], [. . .] Volover [a thief who likes to boast], [. . .] Talyansky [homeless], [. . .] Khamut [a robber who suffocates his victim so he can rob him], [. . .] Malina [thieves' home], [. . .] Kryepki [a loser who had fallen victim to cheaters many times already], [. . .] Shpeyer [revolver], [. . .]

Geographical names as family names (from Russia): [. . .]

It is also interesting to note that the absolute majority of geographical names as family names are those with the Russian ending "-sky"; occasionally we find some with the Yiddish ending "-er" and even less frequently the name of a town without a suffix, such as Kalish, Yarmolinyets. Some names feature the Yiddish version of the geographical name, e.g., Amtshislavsky instead of Mstislavsky, Skverski instead of Skvirski.

The group of geographical family names consists not only of Russian ones. A number of Jewish family names refer, no doubt, to foreign origins. But in this case sometimes it is even harder to say whether we have the right to connect the family name to the corresponding geographical name, even if we manage to find them. What does the family name "Goldberg" represent, for instance? Is this a reminder of a great-grandfather who had emigrated from the Prussian town of that name, or is this just a well-sounding euphemistic byname of the kind that Jews adopted with special pleasure when they received family names? To this last category belong most family names ending in "-boym" ("-baum"), "-berg," "-tal," "-feld," "-shteyn," etc. that appear to be geographical names. Nevertheless, from this chaos of family names we can separate a group that indicates with a great degree of probability that their owners emigrated from Germany or Austria. [. . .]

Abbreviations as family names:

Ash–Altshuler or Ayzenshtat, Bak–Bney-kedoyshim, Bardakh–Ben Rabbi Dovid Kharif, Baron–Ben Rabbi Nakhman, Beril–Ben Rabbi Yehuda-Leyb (Halevi), Gots–Ger Tsedek, Zak–zera kodesh [holy seed], Zakheym–zera kodesh hem [they are of holy seed], Ma-zye-me-zera Israel Isserlin [from the seed of Israel Isserlin], Mazya-me-zera Aharon ha-Kohen Mats [from the seed of Aharon ha-Kohen Mats]. [. . .]

Finally, let me point out one more reason why studying family names in a national context is important. If we look at family names as a national characteristic, then preserving them, even if the owner of the name left the tribe for a different camp for whatever reason, carries, doubtless, not only historical interest but also a racial interest, in as much as others want to see in race an unchangeable spiritual and cultural factor. Thus, in today's Germany we can recognize according to their family names the Germanized Huguenots who had been expelled from France. In the very same Germany, antisemites, in order to fight Jews on a racial basis, introduced exact lists of Jewish family names. These lists, however, are of interest to the Jews themselves, as they can now identify their former "co-religionists." In tsarist Russia Jews who converted had the right— until the middle of the nineteenth century—to change their family names at the time of conversion and thus conceal their great sin. Mandatory baptism of forcibly conscripted Jewish child soldiers (*kantonistn*) was always followed by giving them a new family name, often a euphemistic one, such as Dobrovolsky, for instance. This right was later eliminated and changing your family name required a permit from the highest authorities. The revolution gave everyone complete freedom in this regard; people were free to change their names as they pleased, and many people took advantage of this and changed their ugly-sounding family names to something appropriate, often not for ideological reasons at all. Because of this, there is often no trace left of people's racial origins, and this is actually not always convenient.

NOTES

1. [This is not always the case. *Gitelman* is also the Russian transcription of *Hitelman*, which indicates a male cap maker—Eds.]

2. [The list has been truncated here—Eds.]

Translated by Vera Szabó.

Other works by Veisenberg: *Die sudrussischen Juden* (1895); *Das Volkstum der Meschen* (1911).

Osher Margolis

1891–1976

Osher Margolis (also Margulis), born in Rivne, Ukraine, was a Soviet historian who applied Marxist-Leninist theories to Jewish issues in the Russian Empire. Margolis taught at the Jewish Pedagogical Institute in Kiev and served as head of the historical section of Kiev's Institute of Jewish Proletarian Culture. During World War II he was active in the Jewish Anti-Fascist Committee.

History of the Jews in Russia: Studies and Documents
1930

> Osher Margolis was one of a handful of Soviet professional historians of Jewry. Like the others, he brought a Marxist perspective to his work. The work below, though focused on the nineteenth century, is included because it brings to light rarely seen and interesting documents and because it illustrates the class focus of Soviet Jewish scholarship in the interwar period.

91. The Artisans' Struggle against the Communal Leadership (Petitions of the Dubno Jewish Artisans to the Minister of Internal Affairs)

According to the inquest [census] of the year 1834, the list of guild Jews in the city of Dubno was compiled separately from the bourgeoisie through various statistics. Yet the Bourgeoisie Association, which despises our artisans (despite the fact that the former earn their daily bread through the labor of the latter, and despite the fact that their social position grants them some legal privileges), after the eighth inquest of the lists, has built three recruiting stations in the Jewish community of Dubno, scattering our artisans among all three stations with the intention that primarily guild Jews would be taken as recruits. And they were successful in this. For example: when it was ordered that six recruits be taken for every thousand members of the entire Jewish community (which would mean no more than four recruits should be taken from the artisans, who numbered 656 souls), instead, the number of recruits from the guild has been consistently six, and eight, and more, and so on. [...]

In order to halt such oppression of the artisans by the bourgeoisie, and in particular, to reduce the recruits' obligations in future times [...] we want to establish a separate recruiting station for the artisans. Following the eighth inquest, many of the bourgeoisie have become artisans (and have therefore been transferred into the guild book by the government) and they must [...] for the sake of following the statute, complete the ninth census and be registered separately from the bourgeoisie. Thus, a recruiting station for a full thousand could be built, but the Bourgeoisie Association [...] is hindering this process. More specifically, those who compile the lists of the bourgeoisie also include within these lists Jews who are artisans and who have been written into the guild book. We complained to the Dubno city council regarding this matter, and to the chief of Volyn Province, but have not received any satisfactory reply. [...] We humbly request a decree, addressed to whoever necessary, that the Bourgeoisie Jewish Association should, at this current ninth inquest, also assign us the Jews who were still registered as bourgeois in the eighth inquest, but who, at this point, have been transferred into the guild books because they are artisans, and thereby bring them into the guild recruit list [...] (from the petition on 16 June 1850).

II

Our petition [see the previous petition] was forwarded to the Dubno city council, so that its opinion could be heard. When we found out about this, we submitted a petition to the council in which we calculated that, since the recruit-selections of Jews have started, up to a half of the recruits were taken from our artisans, at a time when, according to the total number of artisans, one should have taken from them no more than a fifth. We requested that higher authorities be informed about this, and since the ninth census-lists were due already, we requested a decree ordering the list compilers for the bourgeoisie to no longer register any artisans who, according to the eighth inquest, had been registered in the list of the bourgeoisie, and who are dispersed among all three recruitment stations. Instead, those compilers should allow for a group specially elected from our guild to register such persons in a separate guild list. But the Dubno city council, since it doesn't include any specially elected member of our guild, has—while delaying for three months the decrees from the higher authority, which resulted from our petitions [...] in other words, stalling until the lists were already due—expressed its opinion about our petitions in favor of the bourgeoisie and forwarded this opinion to the authorities back in October (as we learned from an indirect source) [...] (from the petition of 13 December 1850).

III

According to the decree of the Volyn provincial government about holding citywide elections in Dubno on the 12th of December, the Jewish community of the city of Dubno—that is, merchants, bourgeois, and our guild members—gathered, according to the decree of the city manager [chief], to elect city councilmen from the Jewish community. And when the attending officials asked us to put forward six candidates for city council, the heads of our guild did so; they came to the elections because according to articles 312, 313, and passim of the third volume of the statute about elections, city residents have the right to take part and vote in elections. Since our guild amounts to a third of the entire Jewish community, in accordance with article 371 of the indicated statute, we put forward for election one of our guild members, whose competence and confidence distinguish him to occupy the post of councilman, in hopes that he would be a loyal member and a defender of our guild. The merchants and the bourgeoisie, however, without any legal reason (and with the exclusive goal of depriving us of the right to be represented and to vote in the elections), didn't allow us to put forth our candidate, and all six candidates were chosen according to their will. Even though our entire guild begged the officials present at the meeting to include the candidate put forth by us, all our pleading was for naught, and the elections proceeded without our candidate, according to the will of the merchants and the bourgeoisie. [...]

We take upon ourselves the boldness to ask most humbly and obligingly [...] to allow our guild, which constitutes a third of the entire Dubno Jewish community, to elect, according to our allowance and independently from the merchants and bourgeoisie, one councilman to serve in the city government [...] so as to comply with your [own] transparent decree [...] without forwarding this request for a vote or opinion by the provincial or local authorities [...] (from another petition of 13 December 1850).

IV

[...] As we learned from a third party, our petition [see petition III] required a clarification from the officials who were present at the elections. The officials claimed "that the candidate put forth by the artisans wasn't put up to a vote because he doesn't have a permanent residence, and that the artisans participated in electing other persons to the city council." The candidate we put forth was one of us, Hersh Hendler; he has already served as a councilman from July 1846 to July 1849, and has a permanent residence here in Dubno, as can be seen from the attached certificate from the Dubno apartment-commission. Still, a few of the merchants and bourgeoisie hold personal resentment toward Hendler because of the memorandum that he submitted to the governor general of Kiev uncovering the mismanagement of a secret society that existed here and to which the aforementioned merchants and bourgeoisie belonged. It was exclusively for this reason that they wouldn't allow Hendler to come forth as a candidate for councilman. And even though the artisans intended, because of this, to boycott the elections entirely, when the governor of the town explained that he would consider our actions civil disobedience, we were forced to vote for the candidates that were put forth by the above-mentioned merchants and bourgeoisie. And even though all these candidates received black check marks from the artisans, since the number of merchants and bourgeoisie at the elections was larger than the number of the artisans, their candidates were elected even without the approval of the artisans [...] (from the petition of 2 July 1851).

(The Archive of Internal Affairs, Agricultural Department, 1 page, 2 City Department, 1851, File 25.)

Translated by Vera Szabó and Alexandra Hoffman.

Other Works by Margolis: *Viazoy lebn yidn in Sovetfarband* (1940); *Yidishe folksmasn in kamf kegn zeyere unterdriker, XVIII–XIX yh* (1940).

Yitshak (Ignacy) Schiper

1884–1943

Yitshak (Ignacy) Schiper (Schipper) was born in Tarnów and received both a traditional and a secular education, studying at universities in Kraków and Vienna. From 1919 to 1927, he represented the Po'ale Tsiyon and then the General Zionists in the Sejm. He served on the YIVO Historical Section and coedited the multivolume *Żydzi w Polsce Odrodzonej* (Jews in Reborn Poland; 1932–1935). Schiper continued his work as an archivist in the Warsaw ghetto, both officially and underground, through the Oyneg Shabes ghetto archive. After the Warsaw ghetto uprising, he was murdered in Majdanek.

Jewish History
1930

Volume I. Foreword

This work, which I here make public, answers a scholarly need that became evident to me twenty-five years ago, when I was still a young student writing my first book, *The Beginning of Capitalism among Western European Jewry*. Without any guide, without any paradigm, I attempted then to unravel the problems of Jewish economic history as an independent scholarly discipline. [...] I began with studies of the economic history of Polish Jewry. As a result, as early as 1908 I completed a book about Jewish–Polish economic history, encompassing the entire Middle Ages. Since then I have conducted further research in Polish archives and have collected materials for an economic history of the Jews in Poland and Lithuania during the modern period. In the midst of this, the world war broke out. [...] Before events transformed me into a soldier, I had the opportunity to spend two whole years in Vienna and use the free time available to a "refugee" to become acquainted with the rich collections of Jewish historical literature found in the Vienna community library. [...] Sadly, the war drew me into its clutches and I managed to publish only fragments of the work.

I continued collecting materials [...] when I once again became a civilian. [...] I could not do this with the same intensity as before. I felt that other problems were more important. It was difficult to write history while "history was being made," while the foundations for a new life and different circumstances were being laid—and I had the occasion to experience such a lofty and difficult time along with my brothers in Poland. [...] Only during breaks from my political and public work could I turn to my scholarly workshop and seek a rest from the current history that was being woven before my eyes. [...] The subject kept me occupied— with longer and shorter breaks—for about twenty-five years, but I would not have begun to work on the great deal of material that I had managed to accumulate were it not for a timely, completely accidental stimulus. Two years ago the Central Publishing House approached me with a proposal to work on additions to Graetz's Jewish history. I liked the proposal and took on the project. However, I immediately became convinced that this task was almost interminable, as no general Jewish economic history exists which would constitute a basis for such additions. I therefore changed the original plan and began working on materials I had collected as an independent work. It became clear that my preparations were far from complete and that it would be worthwhile to investigate many more details thoroughly before moving on to the writing. However, I refused to do this, since the preparatory work nonetheless had to come to an end. [...]

Thus, this book, which I now present here to the reader, developed. It is a complete work in its own right and at the same time serves as a call for further volumes about Jewish economic history in the modern period. [...] In my preparatory work I often questioned whether I was not wrestling with problems that ignore the "necessities of the present time." These doubts, however, dissipated when in the framework of my public work I met with Jewish youth and Jewish workers. In these circles—which are our hope and our future—I continually noticed how little the old way of understanding Jewish historical questions satisfied them. Moreover, in the course of the last two decades I have also noticed a characteristic trend in the Jewish scholarly world. It is a sign of the times that Jewish researchers and schol-

ars, who would previously approach problems of Jewish economic history in the best case as a contribution to Jewish cultural history (compare, for example, Moritz Güdermann's works), recently have been occupied with economic historical materials as an independent research subject. [...] Reality has confirmed the idea, which I already declared in 1908 when writing the introduction to my economic history of the Jews in Poland, that the portrait of the "Shabbesdik Jew with his Yomtovdik soul" given to us by the old generation of Jewish historical scholars is no longer sufficient for our modern consciousness; rather, we yearn "to become acquainted with the history of everyday Jews," the history of those mostly anonymous "hundreds of thousands who wove a memory for the future . . . of their toil and hard labor." [...] Certainly in light of this book people will single me out as an advocate of the materialist historical approach. This was already done in connection with my previous economic historical monographs. If one understands "historical materialism" as a view that negates Jewish themes in history, I must emphasize that I have no link whatsoever to such a raw and primitive historical approach. I mean "materialist" in the sense that I see economic forces as an enormous stimulus for historical development and I will prove this scientifically. The materialist historical approach is one of the surest research methods—I agree with this. I do not agree, however, that a method should be transformed into ideology. [...]

Volume II. Jewish Settlements in Poland and Russia and Their Economic Profile in the Period 1241–1350

Using the material presented here, we have demonstrated that both the center of Jewish life and the main route of the Jewish eastern trade route moved from Rus (the Kiev and Ludmir region) to Poland and Silesia from the year 1241. Now we will see what kind of elements made up the Jewish settlements that blossomed in the period under discussion in the territories of the Piasts. We have already highlighted one of the migration flows—the stream that was linked to eastern Jewish trade from Asia and Greece and due to which Asian and Greek Jews established themselves in the Polish-Silesian territories in the period under discussion. The second migration stream came from the west and it, too, played a decisive role in molding Jewish life in Poland. For this period we possess two kinds of sources that provide us with evidence of contemporary migration from the west: 1) one is the names of Polish Jews found in the

Polish Acts from the first half of the fourteenth century. Most are German or Hebrew names with German diminutive endings. Thus, for example, Jews in Kraków at the time were called Merklin, Koslin, Mushin (from Moshe), Yakola, etc. We encounter these names in the same period among the Jews of Nuremberg and Vienna, as well as among the Jews of Styria (Steiermark) and of Czech and Silesian towns; 2) the second source is the oldest privileges granted to the Polish Jews. These are the privileges given by Duke Bolesław of Kalish to the Jews in the year 1264 and the privileges that Casimir the Great granted to the Jews in 1334. Both sets of privileges were based on the well-known Austrian privileges granted in the year 1244 and include a characteristic remark, that they are given "ad peticiones Judaeorum" [through the petitioning of the Jews]. Indeed, the initiative originated with the Jews. The Jews themselves searched for a model for the privileges, and the fact that they adopted as their model the famous Austrian privileges of the year 1244 is proof that they were in constant contact with German Jewry, as they formed an eastern branch of the latter. [. . .]

Following the Western model, Polish Jews in this period were organized into communities, which were ruled through the so-called *episcope iudaeorum*. In matters concerning themselves (with the exception of capital cases), Jews were judged by autonomous Jewish courts, which gave rulings according to Jewish law.

The documents that shed light on the economic life of Polish Jewry reveal the first information about Jewish credit operations during the century under discussion. [. . .]

Life in Poland then reached such a level that the rope with which one wanted to fetter the Jewish credit-business no longer had any substance. So too, limiting the Jewish credit business was not in the interest of the Jewish patron, and the latter was then strong enough to defeat all efforts to damage the profits that he received from the credit business of his Jewish serfs.

Our period ends with a catastrophe, the so-called "Black Death," which together with all its tragic accompanying phenomena sent shockwaves through Jewish society in Poland. As the Polish chronicler, Jan Długosz, reports (1348), one-third of the Polish population was killed by the plague [. . .] in the year 1349, noting that the Jews then "poisoned springs and wells and therefore were slaughtered in almost all of Poland: some were killed by the sword, others were burned at the stake." [. . .] Likewise, Hebrew sources mention

that Jewish blood was spilled in Kraków and Kalish at the time. However, the reports do not suffice to create a clear picture of the events—in particular the socioeconomic factors—that worked together in the terrible events.

Translated by Rebecca Wolpe.

Other works by Schiper: *Studya nad stosunkami gospodarczymi żydów w Polsce podczas średniowiecza* (1911); *Kultur-geshikhte fun yidn in poyln beysn mitlalter* (1926); *Geshikhte fun der yidisher teater-kunst un drameh* (1927–1928); *Dzieje handlu żydowskiego na ziemiach polskich* (1937).

Shalom Spiegel

1899–1984

The scholar of medieval Hebrew Shalom Spiegel was born in Romania and received his higher education in Vienna. He taught in Mandatory Palestine from 1923 to 1929, and then settled in New York City. He taught initially at Stephen Wise's Jewish Institute of Religion and then, until his death, at the Jewish Theological Seminary. He published work on both biblical and medieval Hebrew literature. His much-praised *The Last Trial* (1950) is a study of the reworking of the story of the sacrifice of Isaac in medieval Hebrew texts. Sam Spiegel, the Hollywood film producer, was his brother.

The Miracle of Hebrew Reborn
1930

I

Hebrew reborn—but, was it ever dead? Or, if it was, how can a dead language be born again?

The millions of Jews all over the world who say their daily prayers in Hebrew, not only understanding but fervently feeling their sense, will reject the notion of a rebirth of Hebrew as impudent sacrilege. And the educated Jew, having for hundreds of years without a break used Hebrew for all his cultural needs, reading and writing the language and even at times employing it in purely commercial correspondence, will be able to see no sense in talk about a Hebrew revival. It would make him indignant to be told that Hebrew had ever been dead. Much more so even than the classical philologist who, when it was pointed out to him that Greek and Latin are dead because they are no longer heard in life, replied with feeling: then there are many other dead languages, correct English for example.

Such a jest evades, it does not solve the problem. Taken in all its gravity, the problem reaches down to the very roots of renascent Hebrew. For it questions nothing less than its genuineness, its very existence. It asks: Can a forgotten language actually be revived, made really alive again? Is the rebirth of such a language authentic?

No one doubts that it is possible to learn a language, any language at all, in such a way that its use will convey an impression of life. This can be done not only by single individuals, but by large groups, whole classes of society. However, expansion in numbers is still no proof that a language is actually alive.

A ready example of this is, of course, the Latin language, despite the annoyance of our philologist. True, it had an important history in antiquity, and was for centuries the medium of expression of all the cultivated classes of western Europe. It had important scientific achievements: not only works like the *Summa theologia* of Aquinas, but tremendous secular creations like the *De revolutionibus orbium coelestium* of Copernicus, the *Meditationes de prima philosophia* of Descartes, Spinoza's *Ethica more geometrico demonstrata*, and even Newton's work of genius on the mechanics of the universe—to mention only a few titles—were written in Latin. And yet the language was dead; despite all possible scientific precision, it was irresurrectably dead. The living forces that had once impelled it, from Plautus and Aennius down to Caesar and Cicero, had spent themselves. No longer was there the ring of verses of such unimpeachable authenticity as those of Propertius, as even the love lyrics of the learned Horace, not to mention the folk-accents, so full of life and vitality, of Ovid: take, for example, his magnificent cry of horror, which could have resounded only in a living language and escaped only from a born poet, that his words unconsciously shape themselves into songs: *Sponte sua carmen numero veniebat ad aptos.*

In later centuries, despite its wide currency, the Latin language was a subject of scholarly education only. No longer was its unspoken law, its mystery of natural growth, carried in the bloodstream. Its inner life was extinguished, dead.

Is it otherwise the renaissance of Hebrew?

Before attempting a reply to this question, let us make it even more difficult. It seems to me that when a man of our time with some knowledge of history hears of the renaissance of the Hebrew language, he is bound to associate with it the notions he entertains concerning its namesake in general history: The Renaissance and Humanism in Italy of the fifteenth century, which later spread over the whole of western Europe. It must at once be said that Hebrew does not gain by this association of ideas. For modern historic science seems to have liberated itself from the judgment of the humanists, finding their evaluation of that period warped and exaggerated. The Renaissance was picturesque, alluring—but an illusion. Classical antiquity could not be conjured back to life. It was, as stated, irrevocably dead. The humanistic interest in antiquity was not the driving force of that age, as the classical philologists would like us to believe. This interest was and remained the affair of a small circle of "intelligentsia" (scholars, artists, humanists), but it had no real depths. We may be critical of Oswald Spengler, the poet of history, but he did sum up the yields of the historic science of our day when comparing the Renaissance with the volume and power of a true movement such as the Gothic, which pervaded the remotest recesses of life. From the knightly tournament to village architecture, from the cathedral to the peasant's hut, from language-structure to the bridal ornament of the village maiden, from the oil painting to the song of the minstrel—everything bore the stamp of a unified symbolism. Compared with so true and forceful an outburst of life, it is seen how extrinsic, unsubstantial and unreal was this so-called Renaissance, this conscious reaching-back to the obsolescent forms of antiquity. It was a drawing room affair for world-shunning dreamers; at best, a matter of good taste in the castles of the princes and Maecenases of those days. It was only because the science of history itself was for long dominated by the humanists that it was not recognized how superficial and immaterial had been the hold of the classical upon that age; how, at most, it had manifested itself in costume and gesture, but had never penetrated down to the roots of existence.

The true power of that age was not galvanized antiquity, but the renaissance, or better, the *naissance* of the Italian folk which had concealed itself behind the external classicizing forms. And even though Petrarch himself was particularly proud of his Latin imitations of the Horatian odes, not only his fame, but his real significance, lie in his work in the language of the vulgus, *volgare*, which he esteemed very lightly, but which to-day is the Italian tongue. The Horatian world lay buried deep, it could never again be roused to life. "The larger part of me will escape Death," wrote Horace. Yes, as a memory in the minds of scholars; never again in the hearts of a living people. No longer did any mother croon to her baby Latin lullabies whose rhythm would later influence the thinking and writing of the grown man. No longer did any peasant drive his plow singing Latin songs of village life and labor, whose folk accents still echo in the courtly, pruned verses of the bucolics and georgics of Virgil. No longer did anyone sing erotic songs of allurement in Latin, roguish and merry as those that delight us even in the consciously creative Horace. No longer did anyone curse so roundly, so powerfully, or so vividly as in the comedies of Plautus. The life of the Latin language was gone, irredeemably gone. One might learn its petrified forms, but no life of its own could be awakened within it.

Now, perhaps, the whole scope and weight of the problem will become clearer: Has there really been a rebirth of the Hebrew language? Has Hebrew really awakened to a freely creative life, to a natural, organic growth. At this point it no longer suffices to say that Hebrew lived on in the synagogue, in learned discussion, in correspondence, in books. For medieval Latin also lived on in the same way. And it still lives in the church. Just as with the Latin of the scholars, the whole life of Hebrew grew out of books, its roots were always in the book, in the Holy Book primarily.

That is not so in Palestine to-day.

II

Jabniel, a tranquil nook in Lower Galilee. A flock of geese trail down the hill, two sturdy, sunburnt girls following. They speak enchanting Hebrew. Their father, a farmer devoted to his farming—and a *Maskil,* voices his doubts. "Every morning I face a dilemma: Whether to send them to the pasture, or to school. Which is more important, that they do lessons or tend the geese? Who can say?"

The girls lead the geese into the poultry yard. You join them. One of them, evidently assigned to the care of the fledglings, explains how the incubator works. "Our poultry is multiplying," she says, and her eyes flash with pleasure. She turns the eggs twice a day. In order not to interchange them, she marks each egg, before placing it in the incubator, with the word "evening" or "morning." Then she knows when they are due to be turned, and toward which side of the incubator. "And there was evening, and there was morning, one day!"

She smiles coquettishly, picks up a booklet which had fallen to the floor and wipes it off on her apron. It is a Hebrew booklet on poultry-raising.

I was reminded of the psychological tests we used to have at the university, when we would give a "stimulus word" to a subject, and he had to respond with the first word that came into his mind through association of ideas. Were this girl to be such a subject she would undoubtedly react to the word *'erebh* (evening) with—"incubator." And, if she happened to be of the eye-minded type, she would visualize the top of an egg in an incubator bescrawled with a blunt pencil.

Try to imagine how a *Talmid chakham,* a learned Jew of former generations, would have reacted to such a "stimulus word." He would doubtless have called up words from books, especially from sacred books. And were he, also, of the eye-minded type, he would have visualized an old book such as Bialik somewhere describes, of crude, crumpled parchment, spotted with tallow and wax dripped from candles in lonely midnights, between its pages faded white hairs plucked from beards in meditative speculation, and silk threads from prayer-shawl fringes, now ritually void, and yellowed with age and wear.

What wonder then that the Holy Tongue of the *Talmid chakham* has a totally different ring from the secular Hebrew, so rustic and dewy fresh, of the goose girl of Jabniel. Hers is not a bookish language, and far less is it a language of sacred books. If there be any traces of books in her speech, it comes from the booklet on poultry-raising which slipped out of the incubator on to the floor.

How important is such a booklet for a language! Here names are given to things, *direct* names, much more difficult than learned palaver or even poetic embellishment, which talk *around* things. This latter cannot be indulged in a booklet on poultry-raising written for village use: Here one must give each thing its correct, living, only name.

Therefore, were I asked to name books which testify to the resurrection of Hebrew, I would refer the inquirer not to belles-lettres, but to a few other booklets similarly concrete in topic, for instance to the recent publications of the agricultural experiment station in Palestine on "Diseases of the Eggplant," "Sterility in Cows," "On Manure," etc. These are the new *Seder Zera'im* in the *Mishnah* of our renewed life.

Moreover, some of these booklets, though written for practical uses, already show certain literary values. Were I asked to name the best book of modern Hebrew prose, I should choose, not a resounding name from among famous contemporaries, but Eliezer Joffe's book on "Vegetable-Growing." And if surprise were expressed at my choice, I should insist: May such works be multiplied in Israel! For its sake I would gladly forego the toy lyrics of our ultra-modernists. The Hebrew language has always been strong in poetry, it is the old domain of the "jubilee horn of the sanctuary." Its conquest of the secular, however, is a new distinction. In the book of vegetable-growing are found the three virtues of all plain prose: precision, brevity, and clearness. These qualities, combined with inimitable rustic simplicity, make its prose classic. Every piece of a farming implement, every part of a plant, every agricultural task, the chemical processes of fermentation—each has a distinct name of its own. A language of this kind is adapted, not only to express "scientific results" with an exactness possible only in languages with a long culture, but—what is far more difficult of achievement—it is fit to be the medium of secular daily life, to convey the spontaneous outcry, to express the crudest and most primitive needs, to afford speech for life in its most contradictory manifestations.

Hebrew in Palestine no longer has the remoteness of a "holy language." It has been forced from the narrow confines of exalted utterance, from the Sabbath limits of choice usage, from the atmosphere of rigid solemnity, from the resounding notes of a "trumpet of brass." No longer is it a cathedral of unearthly height, but a homelike cottage for daily use.

Hebrew in Palestine is no longer a language of abstractions, anaemic, unimpressionable, unresponsive to current needs and experiences. It has recovered its faculties—its sight and its hearing, its senses of touch and smell, its capacity for motion. Again it pulsates, and plays up and down the whole color-scale of life.

In Palestine, the reign of the *Melitzah*, of the stereotyped Biblical manner, is a thing of the past. Formerly, spoken Hebrew used to be a series of quotations. (It still is so in the Galuth.) Anger was expressed in wrathful words from Amos. Distress in the terms of the Psalms. Doubt via Ecclesiastes. The innovators and revolutionaries of those days went to the length of quoting the later Hebrew of the Midrashim, the Talmud, the Prayer-book. The current language was a fixed coinage which might be exchanged, but never melted down and reminted. The Bible verse either tapped the way before them like a blind man's stick, or trailed after them. The

thought was born of the form which forced itself into the hand, and not the reverse. Hebrew speech or writing consisted of scattered fragments from the Bible in varying mechanical combinations. Bible verses were simply dismembered and joined together again in new unions. The language was used like inorganic matter; even when knowledge and command of Hebrew were adequate, shells of language were gathered without any feeling that a living mollusc dwelt within.

In Palestine of to-day the mollusc has awakened within the shell, the creative potencies of the language have been renewed. Hebrew is completely freed from its enslavement to the Biblical text. Its metal has been smelted down in the furnace of a revived language-sense, and minted anew. Word origins have been forgotten. Exactly as in other living languages, the paternity of words has ceased to be remembered by those in whose mouths they are current. Conquests and discoveries in which individuals take pride have been absorbed into the language and become the possession of the general public, freely enjoyed by every one. Even the old language forms are known chiefly in their new incarnations. A Palestinian teacher relates that once, as he was explaining to his class some peculiar usages of the Hebrew of the *Mishnah* and its deviation from the Biblical standard, they came upon the phrase *Me'emathai mathchilin* ("When does one begin?"). He asked whether anyone knew the source of the quotation, referring, of course, to the passage in the *Mishnah* which reads, "When does one begin the morning (or the evening) prayer?" A young girl slipped a note to her friend which the teacher indiscreetly captured as usual and read: "I know the source. Isn't it, 'When does one begin to love'" (alluding to the opening sentence in Moshe Smilansky's popular Hebrew novel *Toledoth Ahavah Achath*). The girl was joking, of course, but she had doubtless seen the words for the first time not in the *Mishnah*, but when secretly devouring the captivating love story, hidden from the eyes of her father.

The young Palestinian generation, born and bred in Hebrew, inhale the language from the air, from the street, from their whole environment. The heritage of the entire lingual past is in their speech, yet they are not aware of it. They have not the memory of an epigonus, the oppressive sense of carrying a barren inheritance. Past and present coalesce in their language, one enriching the other. Both elements have fused so thoroughly that they are no longer to be distinguished.

I recall the wonder of some Palestinian children when questioned by a newly arrived young teacher on whose diploma the ink had hardly dried. Like a philological pedant, he asked them how many times the word "already" occurs in the Bible. "Too many to count," replied a pupil, "you can't help using it in almost every sentence." The surprise of the class was intense when they heard that it occurs only in Ecclesiastes. The question itself was alien to them, although (or perhaps because) their understanding of the Bible is far truer than that of the graduate who comes with a headful of wisdom from Marti, Duhm, Ehrlich and the others. For the children of Palestine, no work is more intimate, more vivid or impressive than the Bible. It is for them a contemporary book, while Bialik is one of the elder writers who needs commentaries and tiresome explanations that chill the warmth of immediate impression.

Hebrew in Palestine has to-day the force of an accomplished fact, a fact in the soul and in the blood—the force of nature. The old virtues that Hebrew retained even in books have continued with it in Palestine: unique conciseness, allusiveness, concomitant by-values of meaning possessed only by a language heavy with ancient memories. To all this Palestine has added unexpected resiliency, mercurial adaptiveness, the naturalness and freshness of the instinctive, the pungent simplicity of village talk, of the gossip of women, the chirping of babies. There is in the language an untranslated genuineness of thought and feeling.

Let me prove this with an anecdote. There is often much historic value in anecdotes even when they are fictitious. Novalis was right when he called them historical molecules. Life has a way of symbolizing itself in the form of a simple, unrepeated and yet typical moment, which is to say, in the anecdote.

Though I do not vouch for its authenticity, a story is current in Tel Aviv to the effect that Ahad Ha'am and Bialik once stood together in the street talking Russian, either absent-mindedly or from force of habit. A small boy who happened to be passing reproached them with the slogan of the *Gedud Maginne Hassafah* (Legion of the Defenders of the Language), shouting" "Jew! Speak Hebrew!" They were amused, of course, and decided to find out whether a little Yiddish or Russian had not stuck to the boy in his parents' home, whether Hebrew was really his primary tongue. Bialik began to talk to him, and Ahad Ha'am pinched his ear. The youngster immediately yelled out the Hebrew equivalent of "Leggo!" And, not knowing who his interlocutors

were, he called back as he ran away, "*Chamor Zaken!*" ("You Old Donkey!"). We may assume that the old philosopher was less hurt at the boy's insult than overjoyed at the genuineness of his Hebrew reflex.

Other works by Spiegel: *Amos versus Amaziah* (1957); *Avot ha-piyyut* (1996).

Meir Bałaban

1877–1942

A major Polish historian, archivist, and educator, Meir Bałaban was born in Lwów to a Misnagdic family. He studied law without graduating, only to return to study history, and wrote a dissertation about Jews living in sixteenth- and seventeenth-century Lwów. He taught high school, served in the Austrian army during World War I, and taught at the University of Warsaw from 1928. The same year he founded the Institute for Jewish Studies. Bałaban was director of the Judenrat archive in the Warsaw ghetto. He died in the ghetto.

History of Jews in Kraków and Kazimierz, 1304–1868
1931

In 1867, starting in Austria, the idea of equality made its way into normal constitutional life in Galicia. This wasn't an easy thing to accomplish, due to prejudices that had been cultivated over long centuries and that had been upheld both by groups and individuals. It was immediately decided that total assimilation of the Jews would dissolve these prejudices and that the Jewish question would be resolved. In fact, assimilation in Galicia had two angles: Polish and German. One had to work for many years before being able to scrape off one's Germanic patina, which had been applied by Joseph II. The road to assimilation was education, which the youth eagerly embraced and the older generation strongly supported. Already within the years 1869 to 1879, Dr. Samelsohn, together with Prince Sapieha, financed a democratic newspaper entitled *Nation*, wishing to fill it with tools to fight the clerical times. The editor of *Nation* was a young Jewish scholar, Dr. Ludwik Gumplowicz, who in 1867 published one of the first scholarly works in Poland based on a kabbalistic archival source, and a work in the field of the history of Jews in Poland entitled *Polish Legislation Regarding Jews*. On the basis of this work and others, Dr. Gumplowicz believed that these young scholars should receive habilitation [post-doctoral degrees] at the Jagiellonian University; however, the university's *veniam legendi* did not acknowledge his wishes. He himself also had trouble achieving a habilitation in the department of medicine. Another Jewish activist, Dr. Jozef Oettinger, also had difficulty receiving habilitation; however, he managed to overcome this difficulty and became the first Jew to present lectures at Jagiellonian University.

Jewish intellectuals didn't understand that with the total assimilation of the Jews certain valuable aspects of Jewish culture would be lost, aspects that had been cultivated over hundreds and thousands of years. Instead, they believed that these values had been acquired in the ghetto, therefore, and with their destruction a new Jewishness that would be clear as crystal and free of all ethnic and nationalistic inclusions would remain. Krakovian Orthodoxy, which was brought in by [Rabbi Shimon] Schreiber, had another opinion, as did Galician Orthodoxy, which had been divided into Hasidim and Misnagdim. Hasidim themselves were divided, as they followed various courts (Sacz [Sanz], Sadagora, Belz, etc.). In fact, in the year 1868 they even fought among themselves (Sacz vs. Sadagora). Soon, however, the intellectuals became organized and the Hasidim reconciled among themselves, even reconciling with the Misnagdim (anti-Hasidim). From 1880 to 1890, two organizations of opposing camps were formed: the intellectuals and the "enlightened" Orthodox in political association with *Shomer Israel* in Lwów, and Orthodoxy of all kinds in association with Maḥzikei Hadas, who had their offices in Belz and their headquarters in Kraków. Rabbi Schreiber was the head of all Galician Orthodoxy. The power struggle was, as it had been previously, about dominance in Jewish communities, and therefore was also concerned with the upbringing and education of youth, and the preservation of traditional forms of Jewishness. At first it appeared that Orthodoxy would dominate, and that the government would acknowledge the "model statute" of the Jewish communities, established by the Congress of Lwów (1882). However, with the death of Schreiber (1883), the progressives took the lead, forming around the Shomer in 1890. The government decided on a literal statute for the Jewish communities, which was in effect in Galicia until 1927. The introduction of democratic electoral regulations by the Polish authorities put the community back into the hands of the strengthened Orthodoxy.

Simultaneously with the dispute between the progressives and the Orthodox, another dispute was being played out among the intellectuals, likely in 1848. After a period of dominance of centralism and Germanization, a period of Polonization took hold. This period saw the art of fraternization between Jews and Poles peak. Jews had equal rights throughout this time. With pogroms in southern Russia after the death of Alexander II, ideological antisemitism came into being in Germany. [...] The excessively slow progress in acquiring equal rights for the Jews of Galicia, as well as slow progress on all economic fronts (the salt monopoly, the union of farmers, etc.) undermined the belief that assimilation was the solution to the Jewish Question while also creating an environment that alienated and discouraged young Jewish intellectuals. As a result, at the end of the nineteenth century the majority of Jews opposed assimilation and strove with all their might to realize their own agenda. The workers' sector broke off from the national movement, and with time adopted a socialist agenda and began to dispute authority figures from the overall socialist movement in the Jewish streets, as though the Polish Socialist Party were fighting their Jewish combatants.

This was the situation of Galician Jews and therefore also in Kraków in the post-constitution period.

Translated by Lizy Mostowski.

Other works by Bałaban: *Żydzi lwowscy na przełomie XVIgo i XVIIgo wieku* (1906); *Z historji Żydów w Polsce; szkice i studja* (1920); *Toldot 'am Yisrael ve-sifruto* (1930); *Yidn in Poyln* (1930); *Le-toldot ha-tenuah ha-frankit* (1934).

Naum Abramovich Bukhbinder

1895–1940s

Naum Abramovich Bukhbinder was born in Odessa and studied in St. Petersburg at Lesgaft University, the Herzen Pedagogical Institute, and the Institute for Higher Jewish Studies. After the October Revolution he helped to found Bolshevik Yiddish periodicals, and wrote in both Yiddish and Russian about Jewish working-class history and the Jewish revolutionary movement. He was killed during the Stalinist purges.

A History of the Jewish Labor Movement in Russia
1931

Chapter I

During the nineteenth century the lives of Jews in Russia underwent enormous changes. In pre-reform times most Jews lived in villages and small towns. Most were engaged in trade and wholesale commerce: they would buy landowners' and peasants' grain and sell it to wholesale merchants, and deliver handicrafts to them. The wholesalers (there were not too many of them), in turn, would trade with foreign countries: they would transport grain and lumber to Danzig and Königsberg, and travel to Leipzig to attend fairs. Another sector of the Jewish population would obtain various state leases, work contracts, and supply contracts, the lease of taverns, inns, the postal service, etc. Internal commerce took place at fairs that were held at specific times in various cities. Peasants would bring their products to the fair and exchange them: sell them and purchase tools and other products they needed. The class of manufacturers among Jews was fairly small. Jews considered manual labor a lowly occupation that befit only the masses. They looked upon manual labor with contempt and loathing. In Jewish community life the bourgeoisie held power over the community, and they limited the rights of artisans and, in some cases, levied special high taxes upon them. They also handed them over to the authorities for military service and their children to serve as cantonists in a much higher ratio than the children of other segments of the Jewish population. In those days the number of Jewish religious functionaries—rabbis, ritual slaughterers, preachers, etc.—was quite high. Up until pre-reform times Jews lived under terrible conditions. Almost everyone lived in deep poverty.

The 1860s and the following years that brought about the rise and enormous growth of industrial capitalism also shook the old traditional Jewish way of life. With the abolition of serfdom and the intensive building of the railway system the Jewish population was pushed out of its previous way of life. Their earlier occupations were not compatible with the changes. The landowners, for whom the Jewish population of the small towns worked as middlemen and deliverers, no longer needed the services of Jews; they eliminated the intermediary and started selling and exporting their grains directly. The Jewish population of the villages and small towns began to migrate to the large cities. In a relatively short time quite a few large urban Jewish centers emerged. Having been expelled from their accustomed position, the Jewish population forgot about its previously held prejudices and took to manual labor in large numbers. Soon, a Jewish artisan class of considerable size came into being. By the end of the nineteenth century this class was already so large that it was doomed to face great competition. At the same time, a class of Jewish wage laborers also emerged, and thus a sizable Jewish manual-labor proletariat was created, and they were soon engaged in an organized economic and political struggle. [. . .]

On May 3, 1882, during the reign of Alexander III, the famous May Laws were passed, forbidding Jews to live in the villages of the Pale of Settlement and to buy land, lease farms, and manage real estate. In 1881, at the beginning of his reign, a number of pogroms took place, and in 1891 Jews were expelled from Moscow.

According to the data of the *Algemeyner Folks-tsaytung*, the occupational distribution of the Jewish population in Russia was as follows:

Communication 3.98%
Trade/Commerce 38.65%
Day laborers, servants, etc. 6.61%
Free professions, state and social positions 5.22%
Unspecified occupations 5.49%
Military 1.07%
Agriculture 3.55%
Industry 35.43%

The participation of Jews in agricultural work in Russia was not extensive. At the beginning of the nineteenth century, in the eras of Alexander I and Nicholas I, the government wanted to attract Jews to farming. Jews were assigned specific plots of land and received various privileges. Above all, they were exempted from mandatory twenty-five-year military service. Thanks to these measures, a number of Jews took to farming. But in the second half of the nineteenth century the attitude of the Russian government toward Jewish farmers changed completely. Whereas earlier they had leaned toward supporting and encouraging agriculture among Jews, now they suddenly changed, and as a result of the so-called May Laws, as we mentioned earlier, Jews were forbidden to live in the villages of the Pale of Settlement, to buy land, lease farms, and manage real estate. Due to this law further growth of the Jewish peasantry stalled. [. . .]

[. . .] Artisanry was widespread among Jews. The correspondents of IK"A¹ registered 500,986 Jewish artisans, constituting 13.2 percent of the entire Jewish population. In twenty-five provinces in western Russia, Jewish artisans constituted approximately 10 to 20 percent of the total Jewish population.

Jewish workshops were generally small; they had only one or just a few workers. The owner and his children used to work together, too.

Due to the strong competition and the low level of technology, the situation of the Jewish artisan was lamentable. Artisans opened their own workshops and strived to become independent even before they had a chance to learn the trade properly.

As a result of the capitalization of artisanal work, the simple and primitive way of manufacturing and selling products had to be replaced by a more complicated method. Alongside artisans who worked directly for the consumer, there began to appear artisans who produced goods for fairs. As a consequence, one began to notice mass-production for stores and for transporting to faraway corners of the country. In this case the artisan was already completely removed from any direct contact with the consumer, and most of the time he worked from raw material delivered to him by an entrepreneur. Now his situation was such that even though he was a small business owner, he was not very different from the wage-workers. [. . .]

Women and children were often employed in artisanry. [. . .] Regarding the participation of women in artisanal work we can read in *Zamlbukh vegn der ekonomisher lage fun di yidn in Rusland* [Collection about the Economic Situation of Jews in Russia] the following: "Not long ago there were few women among Jewish artisans. Jewish women worked mostly in commerce, at inns and taverns, guesthouses, and the like. Artisanal work was considered a lowly occupation that diminished the honor of 'women of a fine lineage.' Now, however, circumstances have changed radically: the demand for women's work has been growing fast, and Jewish women are forgetting their prejudices and, pressured by necessity, are joining the lines of working women." [. . .] In twenty-five provinces, 76,548 female workers were registered, which makes 15.3 percent of all Jewish artisans. Most were milliners, seamstresses, undergarment makers, hosiery makers, glove makers, tobacco workers, etc.

The number of Jewish workers in factories and plants was very low. According to reports of the IK"A correspondents, 33,933 people were employed in such work places, 20,081 of them men, 6,586 women, and, of the children, 2,407 boys and 2,841 girls.

Jews generally worked in Jewish-owned factories. In Poland, the number of Jews working in non-Jewish factories was minimal. [. . .]

Finally, we must talk about the circumstances of the Jewish proletariat. [. . .] We have to note that the situation of the Jewish worker was much worse than the situation of the Russian worker. The latter had at least a factory inspector whose task it was to ensure that the factory complied with labor laws. These inspectors were able to limit exploitation to some degree. The working conditions of Jewish workers, most of whom were employed as small artisans, were unsupervised, and the boss could exploit them as his heart desired: they had to work as much as the boss demanded. [. . .] In Gomel, for instance, in the 1890s, the workday began at 8:00 A.M. and lasted until midnight, and on Thursday until dawn. Thus, the workday was sixteen to seventeen hours long. [. . .]

Wages were very low. [. . .]

Jewish workers lived in overcrowded, dirty apartments with no air or light. Tuberculosis and other diseases often struck, killing or debilitating people quickly. [. . .] The famous Jewish economist Jacob Lestchinsky described the situation of the Jewish proletariat very accurately: "Pauperism—poverty and misery, hunger and destitution in the full sense of the word, sweatshop system, sunken chests, dried-out eyes, pale faces, hollow cheeks, sick, tubercular lungs—this is the image of the Jewish street, these are the circumstances of the Jewish factory-proletariat from which he is to fight for social reforms, for the ideal of the future. Whoever can escapes the Jewish street; whoever has the physical ability and the material means leaves the Jewish street, looks for a better life in any corner of the world."

Chapter II

The revolutionary movement of Jews in Russia began in the 1870s. The powerful stream of "going to the people" swept away sensitive Jewish youth. The center of revolutionary propaganda in those days was the rabbinical seminary in Vilna. It was not a mere coincidence that the seminary became the source whence revolutionary ideas were spread: the students here were all children of poor parents or were orphans. In the atmosphere of the seminary students broke with old traditions; to some extent they stood on the margins of Jewish society, the masses who lived with the old, stale prejudices; they were an excellent audience for revolutionary propaganda: they absorbed new ideas quickly and easily.

The first to start spreading revolutionary propaganda was a student at the rabbinical seminary in Vilna, Yankl-Aba Finkelstein. Unfortunately, very little material is available concerning this person who, no doubt, deserves our attention.

He was born in 1851 and was a resident of the city of Vladislavov, Suvalk [Suwalki, today in Poland] province.

At the rabbinical seminary Finkelstein distinguished himself with his independent character. The director disliked him because Finkelstein caused him much anguish: he was impertinent, stubbornly refused to attend morning prayers, and often went into the city by himself without permission. [...]

In 1872 Finkelstein created a library of illegal socialist books at the rabbinical seminary. He would lend the books to students of the rabbinical seminary and some other private persons for a fee of fifty kopecks to a rouble, but, more often than not, for free. He maintained the library partially at the rabbinical seminary and partially at the apartment of his uncle. [...]

In 1872 Finkelstein's activities came to the school director's attention—he was denounced, as it turned out. The Ministry of Education expelled him from the rabbinical seminary and denied him the right to study at any military or civil educational institution. Then the governor general of Vilna banished him from Vilna province and sent him home to Suvalk province under police observation. [...]

II

After Finkelstein was expelled, revolutionary activity among students of the rabbinical seminary of Vilna ceased temporarily, but was soon renewed.

It was now led by a student of the seminary, Aron Zundelevitsh, who later became a respected populist.

In 1872, he gathered a group of fifteen people, mostly students at the rabbinical seminary and some students at the gymnasium and the *Realgymnasium*. [...] Members of the circle were A. Lieberman, who later became the editor of the first Hebrew socialist paper, *Ha-Emet* [The Truth], A. Zundelevitsh, Lev Semen, Veyner, Yokhelson, Leyb Davidovitsh, and others. The membership changed constantly. [...]

The circle would usually meet in the home of A. Zundelevitsh; they would read and discuss illegal literature which they received from St. Petersburg. Thanks to Anna Mikhailovna Epstein they were able to connect with revolutionary activists in St. Petersburg. [...]

Members of the circle dreamt of working with the broad Jewish masses. "Back then we thought"—recounted A. Zundelevitsh—"that it would be easiest to infiltrate the masses of working people if we ourselves become workers. Thus, we thought it was very important to learn a trade. We hired a Jewish shoemaker who would come to my house or to the house of V. I. Yokhelson every day for two to three hours and teach us and two or three other friends." [...]

The circle failed because of the following circumstances: someone informed the director of the Vilna Teachers' Seminary that his students were distributing illegal literature. On the night of June 30, 1875, members of the pedagogical council of the Vilna Teachers' Seminary [...] conducted an investigation among the students. They checked students' belongings, looked through their books and notebooks. [...]

Everyone in whose possession illegal literature was found was punished. [...]

According to A. Zundelevitsh "the task of the circle was to go to the people," meaning to work among Russian peasants. As for working with the Jewish people— this was not considered a special task of the circle, and none of the members had plans to expand work among Jews. The only exception was Lieberman, whose viewpoint, in the words of Zundelevitsh, "did not resonate with any member of the circle at the time." Lieberman regarded working among Jews not just as a way of recruiting additional forces to the Russian revolutionary army, but also as a means to raise the national consciousness of Jewry, whose national cultural characteristics he appreciated highly as a program and factor in the development of humanity in general.

III

[...] Two police agents—the Jews Mordechai Globus and Avrom Disler—managed to get close to some members of the Vilna circle and even joined it. Consequently, the police knew exactly who the circle's members were and the kind of activities they carried out. [...]

V

One of the pioneers of the revolutionary movement among Jews in Russia was Aron Lieberman. As we mentioned before, he was a member of the Vilna circle. In opposition to his friends in the circle, Lieberman introduced the idea of working among the Jewish population. Later, when he was abroad, he tried to realize this idea among the broad masses. In 1876, Lieberman organized Jewish workers in London in a "Hebrew Socialist Union." It held several large meetings, lectures, and discussions, and had a professional union. It did not become very popular among the Jewish immigrants and a year later it fell apart completely. Shortly before that, due to intrigues and discord with other members, Lieberman bolted the union and left London for Vienna.

In his memoirs V. Tsherkezov describes one of Lieberman's very interesting character traits. "I met Lieberman"—he writes—"in 1876 in London, in the editorial office of *Vpered* [Forward]. [. . .] But his whole self was permeated with one idea and one aim. The idea was the fraternity and solidarity of the nations based on social justice; and the aim was to propagate this idea among the Jewish people in their own language." [. . .]

In May 1877 Lieberman published the first issue of the Jewish socialist journal *Ha-Emet*:

"It was not the love of our nation"—says the prospectus—"that motivated us to publish this journal. We cannot place our nation above other nations. No nation should be considered more prominent than any other nation, just as no individual should be considered more prominent than any other. It is universal human love, the love of our nation's children as *human beings*, as well as their endless suffering that compels us to tell them, in their own language, the 'truth.' Because if we, who know how they live and how they suffer, are not for them, who, then, is?"

Only three issues of *Ha-Emet* were published. [. . .] After the third issue, the publication was stopped because the Russian censor prohibited its circulation within Russia. Soon after that Lieberman was arrested by the Austrian authorities. He was accused of having ties with foreign revolutionaries and conducting anti-state propaganda. [. . .]

There were no more attempts to publish revolutionary literature in Hebrew. In 1880, a group of Jewish socialists issued a call to the Jewish intelligentsia, voicing their disapproval of "the Jewish socialists' distancing themselves from the Jewish masses" and calling upon them to work among "the masses of Jewish workers" in "jargon," that is, in Yiddish. They concluded by announcing that they had decided to establish "a free Yiddish printing press" in Geneva.

It turns out that this call had been published at the initiative of M. P. Dragomanov. This highly respected Ukrainian intellectual, political activist, and publicist treated the question of socialist propaganda among Jews with utter seriousness. [. . .] Having thoroughly considered the situation of Jews in Ukraine in the late 1870s, Dragomanov stopped thinking of Jews "as a people of only exploiters and parasites, as a people of solely unproductive social elements." [. . .] Dragomanov organized a small group of Jewish socialists to conduct socialist propaganda among the Jewish population of Ukraine and Galicia.

The group realized that in order to carry out their work successfully, they first needed to set up a Yiddish printing press abroad. The rest of the *émigrés*, however, were strongly opposed to this idea. At an *émigré* gathering where the group of Jewish socialists tried to present arguments in favor of their program, "the reaction was such that even the most energetic people had to throw up their hands." [. . .] The activities of Jewish socialists did not extend beyond publishing the above-mentioned call. They were unable to establish a Yiddish printing press. They could not find either the means or the people to carry out such a "narrow nationalist" undertaking. [. . .]

In 1881 the Populists tried to implement Dragomanov's idea of conducting socialist propaganda among the Jewish population of Russia in Yiddish. Someone—it is not clear who—published the first issue of the hectographed organ *Arbeter-tsaytung* [Workers' Newspaper], which reprinted two articles from the [Russian] *Rabochaia Gazeta* [Workers' Newspaper], edited by Zheliabov, in almost literal [Yiddish] translation. Apparently, the Yiddish *Arbeter-tsaytung* did not become widely popular. [. . .]

NOTE

1. [Idisher Kolonizatsie; Jewish Colonization Association.—Eds.]

Translated by Vera Szabó.

Other works by Bukhbinder: *Di oktyabr-revolutsiye un di yidishe arbets-masn* (1918); *Materialy dlya istorii evreyskogo rabochego dvizheniya v Rossii* (1922).

Y. Osherovich

1879–ca. 1937

Born in Ponevezh (Panevezys), Lithuania, into a working-class family, Y. (most likely Elieh) Osherovich became active in the Jewish labor movement, initially among Zionist socialist groups and then in the Bund, where he worked until 1918. In 1919 he joined the Communist Party. He worked as a Yiddish journalist and editor of Communist newspapers. Osherovich was elected to the Central Committee of the Communist Party of Belorussia. He was also one of the first organizers of Soviet Yiddish writers in Belorussia. He was arrested in 1937, and may have perished in the Gulag. The editors believe that Y. Osherovich is the author of the work included in this volume.

The Shtetls of the Belorussian Soviet Socialist Republic in the Period of Reconstruction
1932

6

The Age Composition of the Population in the Researched Shtetlekh

The problem of organizing the work resources correctly and rationally is closely connected to the age composition of the population, the way it is divided into employable, partially employable, and unemployable age groups. What does the population of the researched *shtetlekh* look like from this point of view? Table Six provides the answer to this question.

[. . .] If we look at these figures we will see that the most employable age group is represented by a relatively smaller percentage among Jews than among Belorussians. As we get closer to the older, less employable age groups, their percentage becomes higher among Jews than among Belorussians. It is obvious that this is the typical result of emigration. [. . .]

Inasmuch as the distribution of age groups is closely connected to the process of emigration, it is clear that the characteristics we outlined here are much more blatant in those places where emigration has taken faster forms. Young people move to larger centers where they are absorbed into the industry—this is a phenomenon that anyone can see with their bare eyes.

7. *Self-Sufficient and Dependent Population: Social and Professional Composition*

[. . .] We have already noted the distribution of the self-sufficient and dependent population in both

TABLE SIX
The Distribution of the Population of the Researched Twelve *Shtetlekh* According to Age and National Composition

Nationality	Age Groups						
	Up to 18	18–24	25–29	30–39	40–49	50–59	60 and above
Belorussian							
Absolute	4,520	1,337	931	1,338	940	715	950
Percentage	42.1	12.4	8.7	12.5	8.7	6.7	8.9
Jews							
Absolute	4,683	1,091	804	1,374	1,118	1,030	1,622
Percentage	39.8	9.3	6.9	11.7	9.6	8.9	13.8
Russians							
Absolute	66	27	35	52	10	11	14
Percentage	30.7	12.6	16.3	24.2	4.6	5.1	6.5
Poles							
Absolute	128	48	35	35	42	27	37
Percentage	36.4	13.7	9.9	9.9	11.9	7.7	10.5
Ukrainians							
Absolute	26	7	17	7	8	2	4
Percentage	36.6	9.9	23.9	9.9	11.3	2.8	5.6
Others							
Absolute	255	62	45	68	46	50	51
Percentage	44.2	10.7	7.9	11.8	7.9	8.7	8.8
Total							
Absolute	9,678	2,672	1,867	2,874	2,164	1,835	2,678
Percentage	40.9	11.0	8.0	12.2	9.1	7.6	11.2

genders, among both Jews and Belorussians. We have seen that self-sufficiency is different among Jewish and Belorussian men. In general, self-sufficiency is lower among women than men, and it is a lot lower among Jewish women than Belorussian women.

From the information we have about 22,627 people, we can conclude that there are 9,348 self-sufficient and 13,279 dependent individuals, i.e., the ratio of self-sufficient and dependent is about 100:142. Among the Belorussian population this ratio is about 100:107, and among the Jewish population it is 100:173. This difference is quite significant; it is, as we determined earlier, the result of the disproportionate distribution of self-sufficient and dependent people among Jewish and Belorussian women.

When we compare the ratio (of the self-sufficient and dependent) in the Jewish population to the corresponding ratio before the revolution, we can see that an enormous change has taken place. According to the census of 1897, the ratio of the self-sufficient and dependent among the Jewish population was 100:231.

The change and increase of the number of self-sufficient people shows us best in what direction the October Revolution had led social changes amongst Jews. Socialist building increased the number of the self-sufficient in general, and Jewish workers of the *shtetlekh* were also part of this process. [...]

Speaking about the changes in the social composition of the Jewish population since the October Revolution and especially in the period of reconstruction, we cannot fail to mention the new quality of the working population at the time of our research.

Changes in the social composition of the population happened according to the program of socialist building. Thus, the working man we have here is not the kind who works in his own workshop inside his cold, dark, and damp apartment where the shoemaker or tailor workshop is located right next to his bed, table, and kitchen. The working man we have here is not the kind who is "self-employed," his own boss, who depends on the caprices of the private buyer or merchant.

Today's working men in the *shtetlekh* are mostly organized in the pre-socialist sector of crafts and agriculture. The more than 13 percent of workers that we have in the *shtetlekh* work in communal institutions, in state factories and enterprises. The 20.3 percent of employees work in state-, cooperative-, and economic institutions and factory-plant enterprises. In some *shtetlekh* more than 60 percent of the population has been drawn into the pre-socialist sector of the national economy. [...]

It is clear, however, that this kind of employment is insufficient. Further strengthening of our socialist economy will require an increasingly skilled workforce, of which there seems to be a great shortage currently all over the Union and BSSR. The *shtetlekh* must be prepared for this. [...]

We must set up networks of professional technical schools and run short-term courses to prepare the working population of the *shtetlekh* for the new tasks that are and will continue to be created in the new specialized *raion*. We envision that in the new system of specialized *raions* if there is an agricultural *raion*, the shtetl—being in the geographical center of the *raion*—will be transformed into a kind of agrarian-industrial settlement; the *shtetlekh* must be prepared for this role. [...]

8. Political and Cultural Situation

The changes in the social composition of the *shtetlekh* as a result of the expansion of state and cooperative industrial enterprises, the liquidation of unemployment, and the increase of the cultural and material level of the working people changed the political profile of the *shtetlekh* a great deal. All these achievements are a result of the success of the socialist attack on the capitalistic, parasitical elements in the *shtetlekh* who have exploited the difficulties of socialist building in order to spread nationalism and Zionism among certain strata of the population. With the help of right-wing opportunists they infiltrated some Soviet institutions and cooperatives, where they attempted to poison the atmosphere with Zionist tones. This proves that the class enemy won't surrender its position without a struggle, and the fight against them must be strengthened. [...]

These changes in the social face of the *shtetlekh* led to changes in their cultural character and lifestyle as well. There has been a break with the religious and folk customs of the *shtetlekh* with their old-fashioned traditions. Shabbat rest has been liquidated in almost every industrial *artel*, with a few insignificant exceptions. In some *shtetlekh* when the local rabbi left, they did not hire a new one for the "vacant" position. The new lifestyle is becoming more and more natural among the working population of the *shtetlekh*.

The authority of the Soviet school has grown very strong. The heder has been almost completely eliminated, *melamdim* are disappearing from the scene.

Newspapers are widely read in the *shtetlekh*. In some of the researched *shtetlekh* local newspapers are published. [. . .] The central newspapers, published in Minsk and Moscow, are circulated in hundreds of copies. The circulation of Yiddish and Polish language newspapers is much more modest. [. . .]

[. . .] The lack of systematic political enlightenment work can be felt very strongly. Political enlightenment work is the weakest link in the cultural work of the *shtetlekh*. The people's cultural centers do not carry out systematic work; there is no mass work at the libraries; you can still find ideologically foreign books on the shelves, antiquated trashy novels, and these are lent out to readers. Cultural work among the *kustars* is practically nonexistent. There is no doubt that if systematic political enlightenment work were to be carried out, our achievements in the field of planting communist culture and fighting the old lifestyle would be much greater and more profound. [. . .] We must take measures to make sure that the pertinent organs take the necessary steps to strengthen the political enlightenment work in the national languages in the *shtetlekh*. [. . .]

Translated by Vera Szabó.

Julius Guttmann
1880–1950

The German-born scholar of Jewish philosophy Julius Guttmann was a graduate of the University of Breslau and the Breslau Rabbinical Seminary. From 1911, he was a *Privatdozent* in philosophy at the University of Breslau, and from 1919, as Hermann Cohen's successor, he taught at the Hochschule für Wissenschaft des Judentums (the Reform rabbinical seminary) in Berlin. In 1934, he fled Germany and settled in Jerusalem, where he became professor of Jewish philosophy at the Hebrew University. He is often described as one of the last representatives of the German school of modern critical scholarship, Wissenschaft des Judentums. His best-known work is his monumental *History of Jewish Philosophy from Biblical Times to Franz Rosenzweig*, which has been translated into many languages.

The Basic Ideas of Biblical Religion
1933

The Jewish people did not begin to philosophize because of an irresistible urge to do so. They received phi-

losophy from outside sources, and the history of Jewish philosophy is a history of the successive absorptions of foreign ideas which were then transformed and adapted according to specific Jewish points of view.

Such a process first took place during the Hellenistic period. Judaeo-Hellenistic philosophy is so thoroughly imbued with the Greek spirit, however, that it may be regarded, historically speaking, as merely a chapter in the development of Greek thought as a whole. It disappeared quickly without leaving behind any permanent impact upon Judaism.

Philosophy penetrated Jewish intellectual life a second time in the Middle Ages. It was Greek philosophy at second hand, for the philosophic revival took place within the orbit of Islamic culture and was heavily indebted to Islamic philosophy, which, in its turn, derived from Greek systems of thought. This time, however, the vitality of Jewish philosophy proved stronger than during the Hellenistic period. It persisted from the ninth century to the end of the Middle Ages, and some traces of it are still discernible as late as the middle of the seventeenth century. Nonetheless, it is true to say that throughout this time, Jewish philosophy remained closely bound to the non-Jewish sources from which it originated.

After Judaism had entered the intellectual world of modern Europe, modern Jewish thought remained indebted to contemporary trends of European philosophy. This applies not only to the contribution of Jewish thinkers to the philosophic labors of the European nations, but also to those systems of thought specifically concerned with the interpretation and justification of the Jewish religion. The former has its place in the general history of modern philosophy; its dependence on contemporary thought is consequently a truism. But even Jewish philosophy in the specific and narrow sense of the term, like its Christian counterpart, operated within the framework, the methods, and the conceptual apparatus of modern European philosophy.

The peculiar character of Jewish existence in the Diaspora prevented the emergence of a Jewish philosophy in the sense in which we can speak of Greek, Roman, or German philosophy. Since the days of antiquity, Jewish philosophy was essentially a philosophy of Judaism. Even during the Middle Ages—which knew something like a total, all-embracing culture based on religion—philosophy rarely transcended its religious center. This religious orientation constitutes the distinctive character of Jewish philosophy, whether it was concerned with using philosophic ideas to establish or justify Jewish doctrines, or with reconciling the contradictions between religious truth and scientific truth. It is religious philosophy in a sense peculiar to the monotheistic revealed religions which, because of their claim to truth and by virtue of their spiritual depth, could confront philosophy as an autonomous spiritual power.

Armed with the authority of a supernatural revelation, religion lays claim to an unconditioned truth of its own, and thereby becomes a problem for philosophy. In order to determine the relationships between these two types of truth, philosophers have tried to clarify, from a methodological point of view, the distinctiveness of religion. This is a modern development; earlier periods did not attempt to differentiate between the methods of philosophy and religion, but sought to reconcile the contents of their teachings. Philosophy was thus made subservient to religion; and philosophical material borrowed from the outside was treated accordingly. In this respect the philosophy of Judaism, whatever the differences in content deriving from the specific doctrines and the concepts of authority of the religions concerned, is formally similar to that of Christianity and of Islam. Appearing for the first time in Jewish Hellenism, this type of philosophy, though not productive of original ideas, nevertheless proved of far-reaching significance and influence. From Jewish Hellenism it passed to Christianity, was transmitted to Islam, from whence it returned, in the Middle Ages, to Judaism.

This special character of Jewish philosophy may justify a short introductory description of its underlying assumptions, implicit in the Bible and the Talmud. We are not concerned here with a full evaluation of the religious motives of the Bible and Talmud, but rather with those of their conceptual elements that are relevant to an understanding of Jewish philosophy. In connection with this, and for the reasons already given, only the barest indications will be given concerning the place of Jewish-Hellenistic philosophy in the total context of the history of Judaism.

The distinctiveness of biblical religion is due to its ethical conception of the personality of God. The God of the prophets is exemplified by his moral will; he is demanding and commanding, promising and threatening, the absolutely free ruler of man and nature. This conception of God developed only slowly in the history of Israelite religion. Neither God's uniqueness nor superiority over the forces of nature nor his character

as pure will were to be found in its beginning. Only after a long process of evolution did the God of Israel become the God of the world. It also took a long time before he could shed his primitive attributes as a nature God, making it possible to think of him in purely personal terms. Even in the primitive understanding God, of course, we could point out those traits which anticipated later developments, but the final result was a completely novel and original creation whose substance was unpredictable on the basis of the earlier conception. This "prehistory" of the Jewish idea of God is beyond the scope of our present enquiry. We shall be concerned with the idea of God as it is already present in the earliest literary prophets of Israel, and which, in its essential characteristics, remained substantially the same despite obvious and inevitable variations in detail.

This idea of God, not the fruit of philosophic speculation but the product of the immediacy of the religious consciousness, was stamped with its definitive character during the crisis which saw the destruction of the kingdoms of Israel and Judah. The destruction of Jerusalem and the exile of the nation were looked upon by the people as visitations of their own God, who became thereby a universal God: the kingdoms of the world were his tools, and he established the course of world history according to his will. Jewish monotheism grew out of this fundamental experience, and through it were established all those religious characteristics that were, in turn, transmitted to Christianity and Islam. The decisive feature of monotheism is that it is not grounded in an abstract idea of God, but in an intensely powerful divine will which rules history. This ethical voluntarism implies a thoroughly personalistic conception of God, and determines the specific character of the relationship between God and man. This relationship is an ethical-voluntaristic one between two moral personalities, between an "I" and a "Thou." As God imposes his will upon that of man, so man becomes aware of the nature of his relationship to God.

Communion with God is essentially a communion of moral wills. The meaning of "nearness" to God or "estrangement" from him is determined by this perspective. This purely formal determination still allows of great variety in the relations between God and man. For Amos, the relationship seems to have been determined by an acute sense of the "numinous" majesty and grandeur of God, whereas his immediate successor, Hosea, appears to have experienced the divine will primarily as a loving communion between God and his people. Whereas for Isaiah, the essential stance of man before God is humility before his awesome majesty, the Psalms testify to the feeling of closeness between God and man. Despite variations in its material forms of expression, the personalist character of this relationship remains the same throughout.

God's relationship to the world is conceived along the same lines. He is the Lord of the world, he directs it according to his will, and he realizes his purposes within it. His relationship to the world is not grounded in a natural force, but in the unconditioned freedom of his will. This conception empties all the ancient accounts of creation of their mythological content, and permeates them with its own spirit. The omnipotence of the divine will appears most clearly when the world itself is looked upon as nothing but the work of this will. The creator-God is not a part of, or link in, the world; but God and world face each other as creator and creature. This trait emerges with increasing distinctness in the course of the evolution of the biblical idea of creation. At first, creation was conceived of as a kind of "making," or "fashioning," by God; in the end, it is the Creator's word that calls the world into existence. The divine act of will is sufficient for bringing everything into being. The biblical idea of creation does not pretend to provide a theoretical explanation of the origin of the universe; it is the form in which the religious consciousness of the nature of the relationship between God and the world has become articulate.

The personalist character of biblical religion stands in the most radical contrast to another, basically impersonal, form of spiritual and universal religion, which underlies all mysticism and pantheism. Whatever the significant differences between mysticism and pantheism, their general divergence from biblical religion becomes more evident as its radically different conception of the relationship between God and the world becomes apparent. God is not conceived by them as a sovereign will ruling the universe, but as the hidden source from which all being emanates, or as the inner life-force which pulsates throughout the cosmos. This difference is not a matter of choosing either a theoretical or an imaginative representation of the idea of God, but is a matter of fundamental religious attitudes, as is convincingly demonstrated by the completely different relationship between God and man which mysticism and pantheism affirm.

Neither pantheism nor mysticism knows a personal, moral communion between God and man; in its place, there is union with the Godhead. It does not matter, for our present purpose, whether this union is experienced by man as an accomplished fact, or as the ultimate goal of his religious aspirations; whether it is envisaged as an essential identity of the self with the divine life of the universe, or as a merging of the soul in the mysterious divine ground of Being. The living relationship between persons is replaced by the extinction of personal individuality, which is felt to be the main barrier separating us from God.

Disregarding, for the moment, all mixed or transitional forms, our distinction between the two types of religion remains valid, even when they apparently use the same language. The *amor dei* of pantheism and the love of God of the mystic are as different in essence from the personalistic love of God (however enthusiastically the latter may experience the raptures of the divine presence) as is the mystic shudder before the hidden abyss of the divine being from the experience of the sublime majesty of the personal God.

The same distinction is again seen when we compare the respective relationships between God and the world in the various types of religion. Here, too, it is not just a matter of conflicting ideas, but of fundamentally contrasting religious attitudes. The transcendence of God as personal Creator is foreign to the doctrine of pantheism and mysticism because, according to the latter, the world is not subject to a sovereign divine will. This is too obvious to require further elaboration, particularly with regard to those views that conceive of God as the "inner life of things." Of greater interest is a comparison of the acosmism of the mystical notion of a divine "ground" of the world, with the transcendence predicated of God the Creator. In theoretical terms the difference is usually formulated by saying that for mysticism, the divine "ground," or source, does not create the world, but rather expels it from its own substance. In religious terms, this means that God is not conceived as the will which determines the world, but rather as a transcendent self-subsistent Being, completely withdrawn into itself. To elevate oneself to God, therefore, would mean separation from the world, that is, detaching the soul from the confusing multiplicity of the world and breaking through the barriers which the world places between the soul and God. In a way, the transcendence of God to the world is even more extreme here than in the notion of the personal Creator-God, who, despite his transcendence to the world, is still related to it, and, thereby, also confers upon it a measure of religious significance. Nonetheless, the relationship between God and the world, as envisaged by mysticism, is essentially characterized by a peculiar dialectic; however much the difference between God and the world may pervade the religious consciousness, the world is at the same time seen as the manifestation of God.

The radical distinction between God and the world is blurred even more by all those systems that consider the transition from one to the other as continuous and gradual, and posit an intermediary, suprasensual world between the Godhead and the world of the senses. Whereas the Creator-God stands over and against the world, his creation, the God of mysticism becomes the principle underlying the suprasensual world. Even the ascent of the soul to God is nothing more than the final completion of its way to the suprasensual or "intelligible" world. Such an interpretation helps us to account for one of the most significant phenomena in the history of religions: the differing attitudes of biblical religion and pantheistic-mystic religion toward polytheism. The latter could easily admit that alongside the oneness of the divine ground of all being, the multiplicity and variety of its manifestations should also be regarded as divine. There was no difficulty, therefore, in patiently tolerating the many gods of polytheistic religion. Personalist monotheism, however, can make no such concession. Even where it pictures a kind of celestial world inhabited by angels, neither the basic difference between God and his creation, nor the uniqueness of God himself is compromised.

Mysticism and pantheism did not cross the path of Jewish religion until after the close of the biblical period; we have compared the two only in order to better grasp the essential quality of biblical religion. Of more immediate historical significance is the battle which biblical religion waged against magic and myth.

The purging of magical and mythical elements which were embedded within biblical religion in its beginnings marks one of the most important achievements of biblical monotheism. This development was, from the nature of things, inevitable, because mythology and magic are possible only where the gods, in their actions and passions, are conceived as natural forces. The well-known observation that the characteristic quality of thinking lies in its personification of natural forces is only half of the truth; the other half is the fact that even anthropomorphic personification is conceived completely in natural categories. As is well illustrated by the many creation myths and their mixture of natural processes and divine actions, the personal and the natural are commingled and undifferentiated. The same may be said also of the basis of magic, for magic, too, assumes that gods and demons are subject to some mysterious natural necessity.

In the voluntaristic religion of biblical monotheism, the personal was radically dissociated from its natural and material elements. It is true that the struggle against magic in the preprophetic age did not proceed on the assumption that magic was ineffectual, but rather that it was sinful to attempt by magic to coerce God. In spite of granting to magic a modicum of efficacy, this attitude bespeaks a religious consciousness for which magic and a genuine relationship between God and man had become incompatible. By its very nature this kind of religious consciousness ends by so exalting the notion of God that any thought of magical influence is completely excluded. To the extent that man realizes his relationship to God in its utmost purity, by complete submission to the divine will, he also realizes a spiritual conception of the divine personality which transcends all "natural" forms of existence. This specific conception of the nature of the divine will also give a new significance to all other parts of the religious system. Thus, a miracle is essentially distinct from magic not only in that it is a completely free divine act, but more particularly in that it subserves the intelligible purposes of the divine will. In the same way, revelation is different from oracle and augury, for the secrets of the future are not unlocked by a mysterious causality, but are revealed by God himself for a specific purpose.

All the external similarities between prophetic and magical ecstasy notwithstanding, prophecy differs essentially from soothsaying. An analogous transformation was accomplished in the sphere of cult and ritual. No doubt a great many of the cultic practices recorded in Scripture originally had magical significance. Although biblical monotheism retained these practices, it invested them with completely new meaning. Many old practices were supplied with an ethical content and even those which were not formally converted into commandments of the divine will, were at least deprived of the last trace of magic. Reality as a whole becomes related to the ethical content of the divine will and thereby susceptible to rational comprehension. True, Judaism was unable to withstand forever the periodic eruptions and invasions of magic. During the Hellenistic period as well as in the Middle Ages, magical practices and, in particular, astrology found their way into Jewish life, but were never able to penetrate the inner sanctum of the religious relationship to God. The struggle against magic was continuously renewed during the peaks of the religious history of Israel.

The above considerations apply equally to the relationship of monotheism and mythology. The myths of creation and of the flood are among the better-known examples of how biblical monotheism stamped with its own characteristic spirit the mythological legacy which it had received from its surroundings. At times mythological themes are used partly for purposes of poetic imagery. We are not now concerned with the question of whether traces of mythical thought have survived in the Bible. The point at issue here is this: religion is as different from myth as it is from magic, and the same force underlies its separation from them both. The idea of creation marks the point of cleavage between myth and religion, since it excludes any evolution or emanation by which the world proceeds naturally, as it were, from God, and posits the free will of God as sole cause of the world. Here too, the voluntaristic and personalist character of God forms a barrier against mythological intrusions, for over and against the voluntary and half-natural causality of the cosmogonic myths, it posits the absolute freedom of God in the act of creation. Nature has lost its divine quality; from the dwelling place of the divine it has itself become the work of God's hands.

This conception of nature dominates the story of creation found in the first chapter of the book of Genesis. Nature here has a substantial life of its own, but is conceived as inanimate and subordinate to the purposes of God, which, as such, are foreign to it. Man himself, the end and purpose of creation, is not conceived solely as part of nature, but as standing over and against nature, as the image of God. This anthropocentric conception grants man the right to conquer the earth, and relegates astral "divinities" to the role of mere luminaries for the earth; it redirects all religious feeling from nature towards the transmundane God. Henceforth man sees himself as a being superior to the forces of nature, which in a natural religion would be considered as divine. The nature poetry of the Bible expresses the same attitude; nature is looked upon as a manifestation of the majesty of God; any kind of pantheistic feeling is quite alien to it. Nature remains the work of God's hands, and above the rest of creation there is always present the thought of man's superiority. This opposition between man and nature has, as yet, no metaphysical connotation. There is certainly no hint of an opposition between the world of the senses and a suprasensual world. Man is a creature of this world, and it is only his character as a person that raises him above things natural. This also explains why, in the later history of monotheism, periods of intense "personalistic" piety tended toward a mechanistic conception of nature; both a mechanistic science and a rejection of all metaphysics are in accord with a religiosity which promotes man's mastery over nature.

From its very beginnings Israelite religion viewed God as the Lord of history. Israel saw its history as rooted in a covenant between YHWH and his people Israel; the covenant was upheld by Israel through its observance of the divine commandments, and by God through the providence he extended to his people. The history of the people thus became the locus wherein God might be known. This historical conception was raised by the later prophets to the level of world history. The impending destruction of the Israelite state by the Near Eastern kingdoms was interpreted, as has already been noted, as an act of judgment of the God of Israel who uses great nations as tools for the accomplishment of his own ends. As God was transformed into the God of history, he likewise became the God of the universe. The divine perspective now embraced both past and future.

The consciousness of the prophets was primarily directed to the future. The destruction of the nation which they predicted would not seal the end of Israel but would be followed by renewal, a new communication between God and Israel, and a new salvation. This future blessing, not the property of Israel alone, would be consummated in the kingdom of heaven in which all the nations would share. From this religious eschatology there emerges a unity of purpose which joins together the varied elements of the traditional past, embraces all nations, and turns them toward a common point to which all history is directed. The early history of the Israelites and the tribal legends of the patriarchs are combined with myths about the creation of the world and the first men, forming an historical picture which unfolds according to a divine plan. The resulting view of history, predicated as it is upon the uniqueness of the historical process, unites past and future in one great vision. It is in the unique historical process and not in the unchanging being of nature that the revelation of God's will and the satisfaction of all religious aspirations are to be found. There, more than anywhere else, the contradiction between the biblical God and the God of mysticism dwelling within himself, beyond all time, becomes apparent. For biblical religion the world of time does not dissolve into empty nothingness; on the contrary, the moral activism of the Bible envisages the world as the scene of the realization of a divine order, which is an order of moral will and moral life.

Biblical religion is essentially historical in yet another sense. It sees its origin in an historical revelation, through which Israel became the people of God. Every subsequent revelation refers back to this parent revelation and bases itself upon it. The prophets do not claim to reveal something radically new, but merely seek to restore the ancient pristine faith of Israel. In the days of living prophecy this reference to an ancient faith certainly did not imply an explicit belief in a definite body of teaching communicated from outside, but rather expressed the faith that the truth given by God to the prophets was the same as that revealed to the patriarchs. Gradually, however, the reliance upon a definite historical event became stronger. Moses came to be thought of as the greatest of prophets "like unto whom there arose none in Israel." The revelation granted to him—which is the source of Israelite faith—is greater than any succeeding revelation. The decisive step in this direction was taken with the growth of a sacred literature ascribed to Mosaic authorship. Finally the whole Pentateuch was considered Mosaic writing. The text of the original revelation, as it was considered, was placed as a norm of the religious history of Israel; subsequent revelations could merely bear witness to it and confirm it. When prophecy itself ceased and became an inheritance from the past, the notion of historical revelation ruled supreme in religious life.

Religious truth was thought of as something historically "given"; development was possible only by reading new ideas back into the traditional faith. The importance of this type of religion (that is, the religion of historical revelation) lies in the fact that it created the supreme expression of religious truth. Biblical monotheism, denying the very existence of all the gods of

polytheism, claimed for itself final and exclusive religious truth as given in the divine revelation. The combination of profundity of content with rigidity in conception made it possible for all religious life and thought to be subordinated to the law of this "given" religious truth. In this way Judaism became an example for Christianity and Islam. By developing the notion of "revealed truth" it also created what was to become later the main issue dividing religion and philosophy.

During the biblical period the fundamental notions of biblical faith, which we have described, received an additional development. The religious thought of the prophets, nourished by their awareness of a crisis within the life of Israel, was centered upon the relationship of God to the people; the sin of the people had brought down God's punishment upon the nation; but it was to the same nation or to its remnant that God had promised a future redemption. The subject of religion was thus the nation. Even the historical universalism of the prophets adhered to this national, "political" view. Humanity, a concept created by the prophets, was a community of nations. The individual, for the moment, was secondary to the people.

The relationship of God to the individual, already found in preprophetic popular religion, was never denied by the prophets, though their religious pathos was mainly focused upon their concern with history. The problem of the individual, however, appears with the later prophets. Individual religiosity, too, was subjected to the prophetic view of the divine. The problem of individual moral responsibility, though it can hardly be considered to have been discovered by Jeremiah, was clarified by him, and even more by Ezekiel. Every man was responsible before God for his own deeds, and according to those deeds—not according to the merit or demerit of his ancestors—he would be judged. This notion of individual responsibility evolved together with that of individual retribution. Divine justice manifests itself in the individual too, and not only in the collectivity of the people, though, of course, the relation of individual destiny with that of the nation is never obliterated.

In post-exilic literature the individual aspect of religion gains in importance and outstrips the limited ambit of rewards and punishments. The idea of a loving relationship with God is extended to the individual, especially in the Psalms; the greatest happiness of the pious becomes the nearness of God. At the same time, the notion of divine retribution loses none of its significance, but becomes the starting point for the problem of theodicy.

Jeremiah asks the perennial question concerning the prosperity of the wicked and the adversity of the righteous, and post-exilic literature amply illustrates to what extent this problem exercised the minds of the post-exilic prophets and psalmists. It is this problem, too, which has made the Book of Job the earliest poetic expression of religious reflection in the Bible. We need not detail here the many and varied answers to this problem. Some held the opinion, despite all external evidence to the contrary, that suffering came as a result of sin; others considered the suffering of the righteous a means of purification for the soul. Deutero-Isaiah introduces the figure of the Servant of the Lord who suffers for the sake of the collective sin of the people. Finally, the Book of Job concludes with faith in the majestic and sublime God, who is above and beyond all human questioning.

It is noteworthy that the idea of a heavenly reward is never proposed as a possible solution to the problem. Apparently the belief in reward in the hereafter did not yet exist at the time; existence after death was thought of in terms of the popular ideas about a shadow life in *Sheol*—a Hades-like underworld. Nevertheless, there is little doubt that the problem of theodicy was the point at which beliefs appeared in two forms: the resurrection of the dead and the immortality of the soul. It is a matter of some doubt whether they were borrowed from others, and more particularly, whether belief in resurrection was taken over from Persian religion. Even if there was borrowing, it could only have taken place because the inner development of Judaism rendered it susceptible to influences of this kind. The emergence of these eschatological beliefs brought a change in religious perspective that was to prove of great consequence for future developments. The religious meaning of the world is no longer fulfilled within it, but in another sphere of existence. Alongside of the historical future towards which the prophets had directed their hopes, there exists a transcendent world of ultimate fulfilment. This certainly holds true of the belief in the immortality of the soul, whereas the notion of a resurrection of the body inserts itself into the historical perspective of prophetic religion.

The problem of theodicy is important not only for its contribution to the content of Jewish religion. Its significance, from a formal point of view, resides in the fact that it represents the first fruition of religious reflection in Judaism. Whereas prophecy had been the product of the immediacy of religious consciousness, we find here, for the first time, an intellectual wrestling with religious truth. Traces of this change are present in the later prophets. Ezekiel is something of the schoolmaster when he expounds his notion of individual responsibility by means of the parable of the evil son born to a righteous man, and of the righteous son born to an evil man.

Reflection in its full sense, however, comes to the fore in the Book of Job. The dialogue form of Job is essential to its content. With the play of opinion being expressed through question and answer, the problem of divine justice becomes one that can be solved by thought. Thought pits the differing possibilities one against the other, and through the clash of opinion seeks for truth. However, this thought is not yet reflection concerning religion; it is the religious consciousness itself, which in its anguish calls to thought, which tries to solve it in a mighty struggle. Various forms of faith are arrayed against each other. It is characteristic of the book that the final answer is given in the form of a divine revelation. The struggle of faith comes to rest in the immediate certitude of divine majesty. The very fact that it is at this juncture that religious reflection reappears, emphasizes the distinctiveness of biblical religion.

Jewish thought is not oriented towards metaphysical questions. The sloughing off of mythological cosmogonies eliminated all potential starting points for the growth of metaphysics. The notion of a Creator provides no occasion for a theoretical interpretation of the world. This may well be part of the answer to the question: Why did Judaism not develop its own philosophic system? The first attempt at reflective thought was directed toward an understanding of those of God's acts which appeared dubious. For the monotheism of the prophets, the belief in the moral quality and purposive nature of the divine will was an absolute certainty which informed all aspects of religious life. It was the basis of their understanding of history. To interpret reality in terms of the purposiveness of the divine will, and to uphold this purposiveness in the face of the facts of experience—this was the task that necessarily followed from the basic assumptions of Jewish religion.

The form in which the problem of theodicy posed itself corresponded precisely to this context. It was not a reason for "suffering in general" that was sought. The question underlying the ancient story of the Garden of

Eden—how suffering and death came into the world— was never taken up again. Not suffering in general, but rather the suffering of the righteous, causes us to doubt the justice of God and becomes a stumbling block. The Book of Job especially reveals to what extent everything revolves about this one question. Job does not revolt against the magnitude of his suffering. He would resign himself to it, if only he knew its reason. He is driven to rebellion because he suffers without cause, and because he feels himself the victim of God's despotism. He finds peace once again when he regains his belief in the meaningfulness of God's acts.

It may be said, therefore, that the first movements of reflection within Judaism took place within the sphere of religious meaning, and emerged from the immanent problems of biblical religion. Jewish religious speculation was to continue along the path. The premise underlying such thought is the notion that God's moral will is accessible to human comprehension. The theoretical question, whether ethics as such was independent of God or dependent upon him, was completely beyond the intellectual horizon of the prophets. They were all the more conscious of the inner evidence of the moral claim as something proceeding from God. Every man apprehends intuitively what is good or evil. The intelligibility of moral obligation implied the rationality of the divine will. Hence God, too, in his actions conformed to moral standards and could be measured by them. At the same time there existed also the opposite recognition that God was incomprehensible, and that his ways were higher than the ways of man, even as the heavens were higher than the earth. All this, however, did not detract from the belief in the moral reasonableness of the divine will. Only the Book of Job seems to question this principle when, as its sole answer to the doubts raised by humanity, it points to the impenetrable majesty of God. In spite of some signs apparently pointing to Moslem and Calvinist doctrines of the absolute and sovereign superiority of the divine over all ethical criteria, this is hardly the real intent of the Book of Job. The problem of theodicy is not settled for Job by saying that God is above all ethical criteria, but rather by the recognition of God's utter incomprehensibility paradoxically becoming a ground for trust in the meaningfulness of his providence, a providence of love and justice which is no less meaningful for remaining impenetrable to human understanding. Thus, even where biblical religion seems to verge most on an irrational conception of the divine will, it never relinquishes the basic conviction of an essential meaningfulness. Even the intelligibility of the divine will is merely limited, not nullified, by our deficient human understanding.

Translated by David W. Silverman.

Other works by Guttmann: *Kants Begriff der objektiven Erkenntnis* (1911); *Dat u-madda* (1955).

Umberto Cassuto

1883-1951

The historian and biblical scholar Umberto Cassuto was educated at the University of Florence and the Collegio Rabbinico. He taught at both institutions and, from 1914 to 1925, served as chief rabbi of Florence. In 1933, he was appointed to the chair in Hebrew and comparative Semitic languages at the University of Rome, where he taught until 1939. When the Fascist racial laws forced him from his position, he continued his academic career at the Hebrew University of Jerusalem. Early in his career he concentrated on the history of Jews in Renaissance Italy. Later he focused on biblical exegesis and the question of the redaction of the Hebrew Bible, especially the validity of Julius Wellhausen's documentary theory of the formation of the Pentateuch. Toward the end of his career he made important contributions to the field of Ugaritic studies.

The Documentary Hypothesis and the Composition of the Pentateuch
1934

Lecture VIII. Conclusions

The tour of inspection on which I invited you to accompany me during this course has come to an end. We must now retrace our steps and review the results achieved by our tour. To this review I propose to devote today's lecture—the concluding lecture of this series.

There stood before us an imposing edifice, accounted one of the most important and durable of contemporary scholarship, the structure of the Documentary Hypothesis. Those who built and perfected it, and are still busy decorating its halls and completing its turrets, were proud of it. But latterly there have arisen a few among them who have criticized one or other de-

442 SCHOLARSHIP

tail of its plan. They have argued, for example, that the design of this hall or that tower should be altered; or that a certain window should be closed or a new one opened in its place, and so on. Yet they have not dared to touch the main lineaments of its pattern. It seemed as though this structure could still endure for generations. *Wisdom has built her house*, as the Biblical poet sang, *she has hewn her seven pillars* [Prov. 9.1]. Although in the present instance the house rested on five pillars and not on seven, as did Wisdom of old, yet the five pillars upheld the building in all its strength and glory.

So it seemed. But we did not permit the splendour of the edifice to blind us, nor did we allow the profound impression it apparently made on those who gazed upon it to mislead us; we decided to enter it with open eyes in order to test its stability and to probe the nature and value of the five pillars on which it rested.

We started with the first pillar, the variations in the use of the Divine Names, and a detailed study of the subject showed us that these changes depended on the primary signification of the Names and on the rules governing their use in life and literature, rules that applied to the entire body of Biblical literature and even to post-Biblical Hebrew writings, and are rooted in the literary traditions common to the peoples of the ancient East. Since we saw that these factors fully solved the problem of the changing of the Divine Names—leaving nothing unexplained—on the basis of principles that are radically different from those of the documentary theory, we came to the conclusion that the first pillar is void of substance.

We then approached the second pillar, the inequalities of language and style, of which we examined the most important examples. As a result of this investigation we found that these linguistic disparities, in so far as they really existed, could be explained with the utmost simplicity by reference to the general rules of the language, its grammatical structure, its lexical usages, and its literary conventions—general rules that applied equally to every Hebrew writer and every Hebrew book. We thus saw that in this respect, too, there was no question of different documents, and that the second pillar was only an empty delusion.

Thereafter, we probed the third pillar, the differences in the subject-matter of the sections. We made a study of some of the most significant and typical instances of these divergences, and we learnt that where there were actual discrepancies between the sections, they were not of a kind that could not be found in a homogeneous

work. On the contrary, such incongruities were inevitable in the multi-faceted book like the one before us, which contains materials of varied origin and character, and consequently presents its themes from different viewpoints. Hence we concluded that the third pillar was also incapable of withstanding criticism.

After this, we proceeded to the fourth pillar, the duplications and repetitions. We considered classical illustrations of each of these categories, and we clearly saw, as a result of our study, that underlying both of them was a specific intention, which was reflected not only in the final redaction of the sections but was evident even in their original composition. We consequently decided that the fourth pillar was not stronger than the preceding three.

Finally, we turned our attention to the fifth pillar, the composite sections. For the purpose of investigating the conventional theory regarding the division of these sections, we examined in detail one of the most characteristic examples of this analysis, and we realized that this hypothesis relied on evidence that in truth did not point to a composite text; on the contrary, exact study revealed unmistakable and conclusive indications of a close connection between the parts of the section that were considered to belong to different sources. From all this, we judged the last pillar to be likewise without foundation.

I also added that apart from what we observed together in the course of this tour, a more comprehensive and detailed inspection of all the relevant material could be made in my company by those who would study my Italian work *La Questione della Genesi* on this subject. But I believe that the main conclusions that we have stated have been amply demonstrated and made clear to you.

But now what is the principle that emerges from these conclusions?

Since we saw in the first lecture that the whole structure of the documentary hypothesis rested on the five pillars enumerated, and subsequently we found that all these pillars were without substance, it follows that this imposing and beautiful edifice has, in reality, nothing to support it and is founded on air.

However, one of the critics of my book argued that my contentions were not conclusive because the structure of the hypothesis was not upheld by each pillar separately but by their combined strength, and that the views of the exponents of the documentary theory were based on the total effect created by all the evidence taken together. But this stricture is easily answered. If I had only shown that the pillars were weak and that not one of them was a decisive support, then the argument would have been valid; and in the past it was rightly used by the adherents of the dominant theory in rebuttal of the partial criticisms levelled by other scholars against their hypothesis. Although each pillar by itself was unable to carry the weight of the entire building, possibly they could do so unitedly. However, the evidence that I adduced went much further. I did not demonstrate that it was *possible* to solve the problems in a different way from that of the documentary theory, but that they *must* be resolved differently, and that it was *impossible* to find a solution on the basis of this doctrine. I did not prove that the pillars were weak or that each one failed to give decisive support, but I established that they were not pillars at all, that they did not exist, that they were purely imaginary. In view of this, my final conclusion that the documentary hypothesis is null and void is justified. If you wish to draw a heavy cart by means of a rope, and the rope you have is too frail for the task, it is certainly of help to twine two or three similar cords together, so that jointly they may be strong enough to draw the wagon; but if you have no real ropes but only figments of the imagination, even a thousand of them will not avail you to move the cart from its place. The sum of nought plus nought plus nought *ad infinitum* is only nought.

But should you ask what kind of structure in Biblical scholarship would be capable of taking the place of the documentary theory, which has not stood the test of our criticism, I must tell you, friends, that to answer this question requires an entire series of lectures, and the answer cannot therefore be given at the end of this lecture. Furthermore, the new edifice has not yet been completed, and it is not possible to describe something that is non-existent. Nevertheless what I have stated so far already points to certain features in the design of the new building that I visualize.

I have, on several occasions, referred to the fact that there were undoubtedly current among the Israelites, before the Torah was written, numerous traditions relating to the beginning of the world's history and the earliest generations, to the fathers of the Hebrew nation and to what befell them. Without doubt these traditions were far more extensive than those that were actually incorporated in the Torah. In Scripture itself we find a number of passing allusions to matters that are not specifically dealt with. We are told for instance at the

end of the story of the Garden of Eden: *and at the east of the Garden of Eden He placed the cherubim, and the sword-flame which turned every way, to guard the way to the tree of life* (Gen. iii 24). Since "the cherubim" and "the sword-flame which turned every way" have the definite article, it is clear that the forefathers of Israel were familiar with them. So, too, the statement with regard to Enoch, *And Enoch walked with God, and he was not; for God took him* (Gen. v 24), refers to miraculous events which are not detailed in the passage. Haran is described as *the father of Milcah and the father of Iscah* (Gen. xi 29), indicating that Milcah and Iscah were well-known, although Iscah is mentioned nowhere else in the Bible, and concerning Milcah we have only a few genealogical notices. The following allusion brings out the point even more clearly: *he is Anah who found the hot springs in the wilderness, as he pastured the asses of Zibeon his father* (xxxvi 24). It would be easy to enlarge still further on the matter and to cite many more verses that testify to the existence of numerous sagas among the Israelites before the Torah came to be written; but those we have mentioned will suffice for the present. We would only add that the rabbinic sages were of the same opinion, for they tell us that, when the children of Israel were in bondage under Pharaoh, they possessed many scrolls in which they found pleasure Sabbath by Sabbath (Shemoth Rabba v 22).

It is no daring conjecture, therefore, to suppose that a whole world of traditions was known to the Israelites in olden times, traditions that apparently differed in their origin, nature and characteristics. Some of them preserved memories of ancient events, and some belonged to the category of folk-lore; some were the product of the Israelite spirit and some contained elements that emanated from pagan culture; a number of them was handed down by the general populace and others were subjected to the close study of the exponents of the Wisdom literature; there were stories that were given a poetic and consequently a more fixed form, and others that were narrated in prose that was liable to suffer changes in the course of time; there were simple tales and complex, succinct and detailed, lucid and obscure, unpretentious and most sublime. From all this treasure, the Torah selected those traditions that appeared suited to its aims, and then proceeded to purify and refine them, to arrange and integrate them, to recast their style and phrasing, and generally to give them a new aspect of its own design, until they were welded into a unified whole.

Of the elements that were not accepted, some sank slowly into oblivion and were completely lost. But others continued to exist for generations, and although in the course of time their form changed considerably—they were elaborated or emasculated, and much new material was grafted on them—nevertheless they were preserved in the Jewish national tradition till a late date. The stream of this tradition may be compared to a great and wide-spreading river that traverses vast distances; although in the course of its journey the river loses part of its water, which is absorbed by the ground or evaporates in the air because of the heat of the sun, and it is also increasingly augmented by the waters of the tributaries that pour into it, yet it carries with it, even after it has covered hundreds of miles, some of the waters that it held at the beginning when it first started to flow from its original source. In its upper course, among the high mountains, its waters formed themselves into a Divine pool, wondrous and enchanting, in which the blue heavens are reflected: this is our Book of Genesis. In its lower reaches in the plain, it created other delightful pools, like the Book of Jubilees or Bereshith Zuṭa, and still lower down—Bereshith Rabba.

With the help of this theory we can find a solution to the problems connected with the *narratives of the Torah*. It also opens for us the way to the solution of the questions appertaining to its *statutes*. Obviously it is impossible for us now, at the last moment, to touch upon this type of problem, with which we have not dealt at all throughout our lectures. But this at least may be stated: the results of the new hypothesis relative to the Pentateuchal stories will serve, in the same way as did the conclusions of the documentary theory concerning these narratives, as a basis and guide for research in the legal sphere.

To this we may add something else at this stage—be it only by way of the cursory reference, since we are nearing the end of this, the final, lecture and there is no time to elaborate—something with regard to the general character of the new edifice that is to be built in place of the old, collapsed structure, to wit, that in two principal aspects, in particular, the second building will differ from the first.

The first will be the tendency to recognize the unity of the Torah—a unity, in truth, that does not exclude, as you have heard, a multiplicity and variety of source materials, nor even their reflections in the text before us; but a unity, none the less. The Jewish people is one throughout the world, despite the many differences be-tween its members, who belong to various communities, places of abode and groupings; the same applies to books. Suffice it to mention, if I may revert again to the illustration I cited from Italian literature, the *Divina Commedia* of Dante Alighieri. Dante derived his material from the Christian tradition and Greek and Roman culture, from the Hebrew Bible and the New Testament and the works of the classical poets and thinkers, from contemporary science and popular folklore, from philosophical speculation and the concepts of the populace, from historical records and the living trends of his environment, from the antagonisms between the states and the strife among the factions, from the contemplation of the nature and reflection on the mystery of God's existence. The multi-faceted character of the sources from which he drew his material is reflected in his poetry, which contains the dramatic and very graphic descriptions of the "Inferno" and the doctrinal discourses of the "Paradiso," and varies its style and phraseology from passage to passage with the change of subject, using, as occasion requires, harsh words or dulcet tones, sentences sharp as a double-edged sword and others that are sweeter than honey. Despite all this, the poet left on the whole of this variegated material the unmistakable impress of his wonderful spirit, and succeeded in transforming the chaos of the conglomeration of sources into a perfect, unique harmony, and in fusing all the separate elements into a homogeneous work of art. This is the peculiar attribute of great books: that what they take from their sources receives in them a new form; it is integrated, knit together and unified as the author deems fit. It is impossible for the scholar to solve the problem of their sources without paying heed to the added element, since apart from the material deriving from the sources, and transcending it, there exists something that no investigator can probe, the enigma of the soul of the writer and the mystery of the burgeoning of his literary work.

The second characteristic—in this respect, too, a few words will suffice, since I discussed the subject at length in an essay that I wrote in Hebrew seven years ago—will be the determination of the relative chronology of the Pentateuch and the Prophetic writings. The latter did not precede the Torah, as the generally accepted view of our day maintains, but *vice versa*. The precedence is not chronological only, as Yeḥezkel Kaufman supposes, taking the view that although the

Pentateuch was written before the prophetical works, they "are two polarically different domains." In my view they constitute rather a single sequence. The divergences between them are explicable on the basis of the difference in their content, aim and orientation. The laws and regulations of any association differ in character from the propaganda addresses of its leaders and the critical speeches that are delivered at the meetings of its members; nevertheless both are the product of the same spirit. So, too, one spirit moves the Torah and prophecy. Prophetic literature has its roots in the Pentateuchal literature, from which it draws its sustenance. Even the oldest of the "literary prophets," Amos and Hosea—the prophets of righteousness and love respectively—at no time proclaim new ideals or concepts or beliefs, and this is true *a fortiori* of those who came after them. The prophets speak of their ideals and concepts and beliefs as of principles with which their listeners are already quite familiar. They rebuke their brethren for not acting according to these tenets, or for not understanding them properly, or for drawing wrong conclusions from them; and they teach them how to conduct themselves in accordance with these ideals, how to understand them, how to draw the necessary inferences from them; but they never claim to have created new doctrines or laws. Moreover, it is manifest from their prophecies that no such thought occurred to them, nor was it possible for their audiences to have entertained such an idea. When we examine their speeches without any preconceived ideas, we see clearly that their words can be explained only on the premise that prophecy developed on the foundation of the Torah writings.

These, if I do not err, will be the principal features of the new edifice that the Biblical scholars of our generation are called upon to erect.

Translated by Israel Abrahams.

Other works by Cassuto: *Gli ebrei a Firenze nell'eta del Rinascimenta* (1918); *The Goddess Anat* (1951).

Elias Bickerman
1897-1981

The Ukrainian-born historian of the Greco-Roman world Elias Bickerman was educated at the University of St. Petersburg and the University of Berlin, where he served as *Privatdozent* until 1933. He fled to Paris

and then, in 1942, to New York City. He taught ancient history at Columbia University from 1952 to 1967 while also holding a research position at the Jewish Theological Seminary. He published widely on the Seleucid Empire and the Second Temple period. Bickerman was the first scholar to argue that the Maccabees were not anti-Hellenistic and were willing to absorb Greek values and customs.

The Maccabees
1935

Genesis and Character of Maccabean Hellenism

Today it is possible for us to observe the process of Hellenization in individual features only. But these features are sufficiently significant to enable those who wish and are able to do so, to grasp the unity of the historical reality.

A first indication of "assimilation" is the accommodation of proper names to the taste of the surrounding world. The leaders of the reform party called themselves Jason instead of Jeshu, Menelaus instead of Onias; the real name of the High Priest Alcimus was Jakim. The Maccabees, on the other hand, bore purely Hebrew names. Mattathias, son of Yohanan, son of Simon, called his children Yohanan (John), Simon, Judah, Eleazar, Jonathan. His companions in the struggle were called Joseph, Azariah, Mattathias, Judah. When emissaries were to be sent to Rome, to be sure, they had to be persons fluent in Greek, and they bore such names as Jason and Eupolemus. But already Simon's son-in-law was called Ptolemaeus, and the sons of John Hyrcanus, Simon's grandson, had double names, Aristobulus-Judah, Alexander Jannaeus (*Yannay*, a short form of Jonathan). John Hyrcanus and Aristobulus struck their coins only in Hebrew; Jannaeus' coins are bilingual, bearing "King Jonathan" in Hebrew and "King Alexander" in Greek.

These coins were struck about 100 BCE. But forty years earlier, when the struggle with the Seleucids was still being waged, the Maccabees, who are customarily regarded as the bitter enemies and destroyers of Hellenistic culture, proclaimed the adherence of the Jewish people to the Hellenistic world. This took place in 143, under the High Priest Jonathan.

From the time of Alexander the Great, Greeks had been masters of the East. It was natural that the peoples and tribes of the East endeavored, by means of more or less skilfully contrived genealogical constructions, to attach themselves to the Greek people and to profess a kinship with them. Such a connection constituted, as it were, a ticket of admission to European culture. Thus, for example, the Pisidian city of Selge and the Lydian settlement of Cibyra in Caria, both mixed "barbarian" settlements in southwest Asia Minor, declared themselves to be Spartan colonies. In the year 126–125 Phoenician Tyre officially informed the Delphians of their kinship with them. Such derivations were promoted and facilitated by the tendencies of Greek science to link all new peoples, more or less naively, with those already known. The medieval practice of fitting newly discovered races into the framework of the biblical roll of nations (Gen. 10) is analogous. On the basis of an ingenious combination Greek scholarship had contrived a connection between the Jews and the Spartans. This was known as early as about 170 BCE. When Jason, the leader of the reform party, was ousted by Menelaus, he fled to Sparta and there claimed hospitality on the grounds of tribal kinship.

But as soon as the Maccabee Jonathan, who had so unexpectedly risen to the High Priest and chief of Jewry, was firmly in the saddle, he sent an embassy to Sparta (about 143) to renew the ancestral bond of brotherhood. His missive to "his brother Spartans" is extant. In it Jonathan refers to a letter of a Spartan king to "Onias the High Priest," and he subjoins a copy of this letter. The Spartan letter is a patent forgery, fabricated by some writer in Jonathan's service. In the spirit of the cosmopolitan philosophy of the period the Spartans are represented as saying to the Jews: "Your cattle and your possessions are ours, and ours are yours." But most important, the alleged Spartan declares that "in a writing concerning the Spartans and the Jews, the statement is made that they are brothers and, indeed, of the race of Abraham."

The forgery is not very skilful, but it is perfectly consonant with the spirit of the time. Men were eager to "discover" ancient evidence as a basis for the most recent friendships. But in all the forgeries and fictions of this class it is always the barbarians who claim a Hellenic descent: Romulus, the founder of Rome, is descended from Aeneas, a hero of the Iliad. It is significant of the Jewish forgery that the relationship is reversed: the Spartans are connected with the biblical patriarch.

Here the character and significance of Maccabean Hellenism is plainly revealed. The reform party wished to assimilate the Torah to Hellenism; the Maccabees wished to incorporate Hellenic culture in the Torah. The process was like that of the Europeanization of Japan: Japan possessed scholars who wrote about Botticelli and scientists who made bacteriological discoveries, but at the same time it could proclaim the Mikado's divine right of sovereignty on the ground of his direct descent from the goddess of the sun.

This accommodation of new elements to the Bible, this consideration for native tradition, characterizes the Hellenization carried through under the Maccabees, and differentiates it from the rationalistic assimilation which had been the aim of the reform party. Let us consider, for example, the decree of 140 BCE by which the people invested Simon with the rulership. The document is thoroughly Hellenistic in character. It must have been drafted in Greek. In any case, the form is altogether that of a Greek honorary decree, utterly impossible in Hebrew. A long-winded and awkward period sets forth the reasons for the decree, and the decree itself is then expressed in an appended sentence. The very notion of drawing up a document to establish a constitution is purely Greek; the Bible provides no pattern for this. According to Hebrew models one would expect a general obligation of the people to Simon by means of an oath. But in this very document, which prohibits the wearing of purple or of the gold brooch which are the insignia of Hellenistic royalty, which offers Simon the rule out of gratitude for his deeds and in which he accepts it, a sharp distinction is nevertheless drawn between the privileged priesthood and the people; and the rule is secured to Simon with the limitation, "until a faithful prophet shall arise." Only a divine revelation, not an assembly of the people, could proclaim eternal law for Israel.

Let us glance for a moment at Jonathan's letter to the Spartans. It is his desire to make known the kinship of the Jews with this Greek people. But at the same time he emphasizes that "the holy Scriptures we possess bring comfort to the Jews, and the help of Heaven delivers the Jews out of the hand of their enemies." Naively, he informs the Spartans that the Jews will remember them in their prayers, "as proper duty requires that brothers be remembered." We may imagine that the Spartans were somewhat puzzled by this missive. Their reply contains only a diplomatically courteous acknowledgement.

A third example. In antiquity as today, a proper legal title was sought for every conquest. Greek opinion held that the original legitimate owners of a territory might maintain a permanent claim upon it if it had been wrested from them by force. Thus the opponents of the Maccabees in the Greek cities of Phoenicia and Palestine maintained at the time of the Maccabean conquest that the Jews could have no claim upon Palestine because they were immigrants who had destroyed the Canaanites: "Are ye not a people of robbers?" It is of the highest significance for the Hellenization of Judaism under the Maccabees that the Jews engaged in this dispute without objection, that is to say, they recognized Greek opinion as arbiter in the case. Thus, it is important to note, they accepted the legal principle of their opponents. Whereas the Bible eschews any secular legal basis for the claim upon the land and derives the Jews' right to Canaan from the divine promise, under the Maccabees the Jews sought a historical basis for their claim to the Holy Land. But, and this is characteristic of the manner of their Hellenization, they applied this new principle to the Bible. They declared, for example, that Palestine originally belonged to the heritage of Shem and had then been occupied by Canaan in robber-fashion; or they identified Shem with Melchizedek, the priest-king of Jerusalem, thus seeking to prove that Palestine was Shem's heritage; or they employed some similar device. But it did not occur to them, for instance, to follow the Greek historian Hecataeus and dismiss all the charges of their opponents with the claim that Palestine was completely uninhabited at the time of the Jewish immigration. In territorial disputes of this nature the Greeks always cited the writings of the historians, ancient documents, and similar sources, or even Homer; if one party to a quarrel found that some passage in the document to which it was appealing did not suit its argument, it declared that the offending passage had been interpolated. The Jews took over the Greek manner of argumentation, but for them the only source of knowledge remained the sacred Scripture, even when its evidence was against them.

The accommodation of Hellenistic civilization to the Torah, begun by the Maccabees and carried forward under their rule, gave Judaism the form that it was to have for centuries and that, in part, prevailed until the Emancipation. Judaism of the post-Maccabean period is Pharisaic. But Pharisaism, which is first mentioned in the period of John Hyrcanus, who was a disciple of the Pharisees, is in part characterized precisely by the introduction of certain leading ideas of the Hellenistic period into the world of the Torah.

The Pharisees or *perushim*, as they are designated in Hebrew, are the "Separated" who stand apart from the pagans and also from other Jews in order to gain sanctity. For them *parush* becomes a synonym for *kadosh*, "holy." They are not the only ones who separated themselves. The Essenes, another sect, who seem to have introduced something of the ideas and the forms of life of Greek Pythagoreanism into Judaism, desired to be "holy" no less than the Pharisees, and their striving in this direction was even more pronounced than the Pharisees'. But the Essenes sought to realize their goal for themselves alone, for the members of their own order; the Pharisees, on the other hand, wished to embrace the whole people, and in particular through education. It was their desire and intention that everyone in Israel achieve holiness through the study of the Torah, and their guiding principle was: "Raise up many disciples."

All of this is alien to biblical Israel. The prophets looked forward to repentance as issuing from the pressure of events and as a result of prophetic admonitions and divine chastisement, not as the fruit of study. Even for Jesus, Sirach, who wrote his Book of Wisdom on the eve of the persecutions of Epiphanes, the scholar is a distinguished man and a rich one. An artisan or peasant, in his view, could not attain learning. "He that hath little business," he says, "can become wise. How can he become wise that holdeth the goad?" But the Pharisees wished to bring everyone to the Torah. "The crown of the Torah is set before every man." For Sirach, as for biblical Judaism, as indeed for all the East, it is assumed that only the pious can be wise: "All wisdom cometh from the Lord." The Pharisees adopted this principle entirely, adding to it, however, that piety was teachable and to be attained only through teaching. Consequently the entire people must study the Torah.

But this is a Hellenic, one might say, a Platonic notion, that education could so transform the individual and the entire people that the nation would be capable of fulfilling the divine task set it. Hellenism introduces the first epoch of general popular education in the Occident. The Hellenes and the Grecized Orientals assembled in the gymnasia that were everywhere to be found and that served at once as athletic fields, schools, and clubs. In late Hellenistic Alexandria, as in the Greek community of the reform party in Jerusalem, the rights of citizenship were granted only after a sort of "proficiency test" was passed.

The Pharisees adopted these ideas and tendencies of the Hellenistic world, in that they associated the public sermons that had been customary since the time of Ezra with the teaching of the Torah. But it was not their ideal to fashion a Greek *kalos kai agathos*, or "gentleman," but to fulfil the precept which introduces the revelation on Sinai: "Ye shall be unto Me a kingdom of priests, and a holy nation."

To become a holy nation, indeed, was a goal common to all the Jews. But the Pharisees differed from the others by seeking its achievement through education and by not limiting this education to the Torah of Moses; they added many precepts wanting in the Torah, as, for example, the rule of washing the hands before meat. Any law written down naturally needs to be added to, and affords room for interpretation. One sect of Judaism in the Maccabean period, the Sadducees, wished to limit the laws to those expressly contained in the Torah. If something was neither prescribed nor forbidden in the Torah, they did not wish to make it so. Their principle was: "Only what is written is authoritative." But the Pharisaic idea of education promoted the tendency to develop the Torah as time and circumstance demanded. As the source for such development, the Pharisees looked to tradition, or, as they later termed it, the "oral" law, which they set on a footing with the written Torah. This singular notion of setting traditional usage or *halakhah* alongside the written law is again Greek. It is the concept of the "un-written law" (*agraphos nomos*), which is preserved not on stone or paper but lives and moves in the actions of the people. But whereas in the Greek world this notion often served to negate the written law, Pharisaism used the oral law to "make a fence for the Torah."

In this way Maccabean Hellenism succeeded in parrying spiritual movements which might otherwise have destroyed traditional Judaism. For example, the Hellenistic world surrounding Judaism was caught up by a new revelation that solved the problem of evil on earth: retribution would come after death, when the wicked would be punished and the righteous rewarded and awakened to new life. Such notions are alien to the Bible, indeed in contradiction to it, for the Torah promises reward and punishment in this life. Hence the Sadducees rejected the new doctrine and ridiculed the Pharisaic teaching of resurrection. If they had been the only authoritative representatives of Judaism, Judaism would either have lagged behind the times and grown rigid, as was the case with the Samaritans, who also rejected the new belief, or the course of history would have submerged Judaism and undermined the Torah. The Pharisees, on the other hand, adopted the Hellenistic doctrine of resurrection, but subsumed it under the principles of the Torah. What to the pagans was an event dictated more or less by necessity, appears among the Jews as the working of the free will of God. According to the account of Flavius Josephus, the Pharisaic doctrine of the future life derives from the Greek teaching of the Pythagoreans. But among the Pythagoreans each soul must automatically return to new life after death, each according to its merit. For this fateful and continually operative necessity, the Pharisees substituted the single event of the Last Judgment, whose day and scope God would determine, and so dovetailed the new Hellenistic idea into the structure of biblical ideas. In its new form the adopted doctrine of resurrection developed into a characteristic element of Jewish belief; it became, with biblical monotheism, its central doctrine. The Jewish prayer book still reads: "Praised be Thou, Lord our God and God of our fathers, God of Abraham, God of Isaac, and God of Jacob. . . . Thou art mighty for eternity, O Lord, Thou quickenest the dead."

Translated by Moses Hadas.

Other works by Bickerman: *Institutions des Séleucides* (1938); *From Ezra to the Last of the Maccabees* (1962); *Studies in Jewish and Christian History*, 3 vols. (1976–1986); *The God of the Maccabees* (1979).

Leo Strauss

1899–1973

The German-born political philosopher Leo Strauss came to the United States in 1937 after failing to find an academic position in England, to which he had fled to escape Nazism. He taught at the New School for Social Research in New York City from 1938 to 1948 and then at the University of Chicago, where his impact on the development of political philosophy in the United States was enormous. He was particularly influential in shaping the study of medieval Islamic and Jewish philosophy. In his *Persecution and the Art of Writing* (1952), he argued that there was a tradition of philosophers not stating their views openly but wrapping them instead in ostensibly orthodox language. This approach resonated in particular with Maimonidean scholars, who searched *The Guide of the Perplexed* for heterodox ideas that might be hidden in conventional terms.

Philosophy and Law: Contributions to the Understanding of Maimonides and His Predecessors

1935

Introduction

In a phrase of Hermann Cohen, Maimonides is the "classic of rationalism" in Judaism. This phrase appears to us to be correct in a stricter sense than Cohen may have intended: Maimonides' rationalism is the true natural model, the standard to be carefully protected from any distortion and thus the stumbling-block on which modern rationalism falls. To awaken a prejudice in favor of this view of Maimonides and, even more, to arouse suspicion against the powerful opposing prejudice, is the aim of the present work.

Even if one is free of all natural inclination towards the past, even if one believes that the present, as the age in which man has attained the highest rung yet of his self-consciousness, can really learn nothing from the past, one still encounters Maimonides's teaching as soon as one seriously attempts to make up one's mind about the present so assessed. For such an attempt can succeed only if one continually confronts modern rationalism as the source of the present, with medieval rationalism. But if one undertakes a confrontation of this kind seriously, and thus in the freedom of the question which of the two opposed rationalisms is the true rationalism, then medieval rationalism, whose "classic" for us is Maimonides, changes in the course of the investigation from a mere means of discerning more sharply the specific character of modern rationalism into the standard measured against which the latter proves to be only a semblance of rationalism. And thus the self-evident starting-point, that self-knowledge is a necessary and a meaningful undertaking for the present, acquires an unself-evident justification: the critique of the present, the critique of modern rationalism as the critique of modern sophistry, is the necessary beginning, the constant companion, and the unerring sign of that search for truth which is possible in our time.

The present situation of Judaism—leaving aside, therefore, the fundamental constitution of Judaism, which is not affected in or by this situation—is determined by the Enlightenment. For all phenomena peculiar to the present—if one does not let oneself be deceived by their foregrounds and pretenses—refer back to the Enlightenment, that is, to the movement of the seventeenth and eighteenth centuries initiated by Descartes' *Meditations* and Hobbes' *Leviathan*, as their source. This fact is hard to contest; only its bearing and significance are, certainly, contestable. The premises about which the present is at one with the Age of Enlightenment have now become so self-evident that it is only or chiefly the opposition between the Enlightenment and the present that tends to be remarked and taken seriously: the Enlightenment appears long since to have been "overcome"; its legitimate concerns, which have now become "trivial," appear to have been taken into account; its "shallowness," on the other hand, appears to have fallen into deserved contempt. How remote from our age is the quarrel about the verbal inspiration vs. the merely human origin of Scripture: about the reality vs. the impossibility of the biblical miracles; about the eternity and thus the immutability vs. the historical variability of the Law; about the creation of the world vs. the eternity of the world: all discussions are now conducted on a level on which the great controversial questions debated by the Enlightenment and orthodoxy no longer even needed to be posed, and must ultimately even be rejected as "falsely posed." If the matter could be left at that, the influence of the Enlightenment on Judaism would be in fact as unworthy of serious reflection and care as it is taken to be not, indeed, by all contemporary men, but certainly by all contemporary "movements." But are the premises of the Enlightenment really trivial? Is the Enlightenment really a contemptible adversary?

If, however, the foundation of the Jewish tradition is belief in the creation of the world, in the reality of the Biblical miracles, in the absolutely binding character and essential immutability of the Law, resting on the revelation at Sinai, then one must say that the Enlightenment has undermined the foundation of the Jewish tradition. Indeed from the very beginning it was with complete consciousness and complete purposefulness that the radical Enlightenment—think of Spinoza—did this. And as far as the moderate Enlightenment is concerned, it had to pay for its attempt to mediate between orthodoxy and radical enlightenment, between belief in revelation and belief in the self-sufficiency of reason, with the contempt from which it cannot now be rescued even by the greatest fairness of historical judgment. Later thinkers, who saw that the attack of Hobbes, Spinoza, Bayle, Voltaire, Reimarus could not be warded off with the defenses of a Moses Mendelssohn, began by giving their support to the Enlightenment as opposed to orthodoxy; thus they began by accepting all real or supposed conclusions and all explicit or implicit premises of the critique of miracles and the critique of the Bible; but in their own view they then re-established the foundation of the tradition through the counter-attack they raised against the (radical) Enlightenment. In other words, the later thinkers, who recognized that any compromise between orthodoxy and the Enlightenment is untenable, accomplished the move from the level on which the Enlightenment and orthodoxy had done battle, and on which the moderate Enlightenment had striven for a compromise, to another, a "higher" level, which as such made possible a synthesis of Enlightenment and orthodoxy. Thus it was on this newly won level that the later thinkers re-established the foundation of the tradition—of course, as cannot be otherwise in a synthesis, in a modified, "internalized" form. But it is not at all difficult to see that the "internalizing" of concepts like creation, miracles, and revelation robs these concepts of their whole meaning. The "internalizing" of these concepts differs from the disavowal of their meaning only in the well-intentioned, if not good, purpose of its authors. If God did not create the world in the "external" sense, if He did not really create it, if the creation therefore cannot be affirmed theoretically—as simply true, as the fact of creation—then one must in all probity disavow the creation, or, at the very least, avoid any talk of creation. But all "internalizations" of the basic tenets of the tradition rest at bottom on this: from the "reflexive" premise, from the "higher" level of the post-Enlightenment synthesis, the relation of God to nature is no longer intelligible and thus is no longer even interesting.

That the "internalizations" which are so common today are in truth disavowals—this fact, manifest to the impartial view, is obscured only by the circumstance that at the outset—that is, so long as we do not purposely struggle against our own prejudices through historical reflection—we find ourselves fully in the power of the mode of thought produced by the Enlightenment and consolidated by its proponents or opponents. This partiality comes to light especially in the way in which the "internalization" of the basic tenets of the Jewish tradition has been justified. There is no "internalization" of this kind for whose innocence one cannot discover and bring forward as witness some statement or other of some traditional authority or other. But—even ignoring completely the unprincipled way in which statements torn from their context are often brought forward as conclusive testimony—such really after-the-fact defenses depend upon one of the two following errors, or upon both at once. First, one appeals against the orthodox, "external" view to such witnesses as belong to an undeveloped stage of the formulation of belief. In this way one can protect oneself, for example, against the doctrines of verbal inspiration, the creation as creation *ex nihilo*, and the immortality of the individual. But whenever these doctrines first emerged historically, they stand in a connection of such manifest necessity with the doctrines about whose Biblical origin there is no quarrel that one can hardly doubt them if one intends to remain in harmony with the "religion of the prophets." By appealing against the completed expression of the Jewish tradition to those very elements that stand in the foreground in the Bible, and especially in the latter prophets, one is following the method of the Enlightenment, which has been acknowledged especially by "religious liberalism" as authoritative. This fact is generally recognized, and insofar as liberalism has latterly fallen into disrepute, partly on very good and partly on very bad grounds, the biblicist or historical-critical method of "overcoming" orthodoxy is less and less in use. Second, one appeals against orthodoxy to extreme statements that have been ventured within the Jewish tradition. In this way one can protect oneself, for example, against the doctrine of the absolute immutability of the law and the doctrine of miracles. But—however well attested and however often repeated an extreme statement may be—it is one thing to have a very "bold," very "free" statement which, being meant as a daring venture, has a solid basis in the beliefs in creation, miracles, and revelation that permit it in the first place, and which therefore, according to its own meaning, is erroneous and even preposterous when separated from this basis; it is quite another thing to use a statement grounded in this way as a foundation. Now, insofar as one makes an extreme statement—like the peak of a pyramid—into the foundation of the Jewish tradition, one again shows that one is altogether partial to the Enlightenment's mode of thought. For precisely this is characteristic of the Enlightenment: that, in its supposedly or only ostensibly "immanent" criticism and development of the tradition, it makes extremes of the tradition into the foundation of a position that is actually completely incompatible with the tradition.

If therefore it must be insisted that the "internalizing" of the basic tenets of the tradition robs these tenets of their meaning; if therefore it turns out that not only every compromise between orthodoxy and Enlightenment, but also every synthesis of these opposed positions, is finally untenable; if therefore the alternative "orthodoxy or Enlightenment" may today no longer, or rather, may today not yet be evaded; then one must first of all, and at the very least, climb back down onto the level of the classical between the Enlightenment and orthodoxy, as onto a level on which battle was done and could be done about the one, eternal truth, since the natural desire for truth had not yet been stifled by the newer dogma that "religion" and "science" each has in view the "truth" belonging to it. In order to reach this level, one need not even withdraw very far from the magic circle of the present: the radical Enlightenment still lives today, and it is in a certain way, viz. as regards its last and furthest consequences, far more radical today than in the seventeenth and eighteenth centuries; and orthodoxy too still lives today. The quarrel between orthodoxy and the Enlightenment that is thus possible without further ado must be resumed—or rather, as one recognizes if one does not intentionally shut one's eyes, the quarrel between the Enlightenment and orthodoxy, already longstanding and still ever-continuing, must be understood anew.

But has not the demand for a resumption or a reunderstanding of this quarrel long since been tacitly fulfilled? Why then stir up yet again what at long, long last has become calm? Is not the critique of the "internalizations," to which that demand is chiefly due, a forcing of an open door? Did not the movement whose goal is to return to the tradition, the movement whose exemplary and unforgotten expression was the development, if not the teaching, of Hermann Cohen—did not that movement have as its actual, though often hidden, impulse precisely the insight into the questionableness of the "internalizations" with which the nineteenth century generally contented itself? Has not the situation of Judaism, thanks to that movement, changed from the ground up in the course of the last generation?—

That the situation of Judaism has changed as a result of the return movement must be admitted; that it has changed from the ground up must be contested. It has not changed from the ground up precisely because, in the entire course of the return movement, there has not ensued a fundamental reflection on the quarrel between the Enlightenment and orthodoxy, a fundamental review of the results of this quarrel. And yet nothing would have been more urgent, within the meaning of that very movement, than such reflection and review. It was not without reservation that the return to the tradition was carried out by precisely the most important advocates of this movement. To the end, Cohen raised explicit reservations against the tradition in the name of freedom, of man's autonomy. And Franz Rosenzweig, who, in a sense at least, went even further on the road of Cohen than Cohen himself, left no doubt that he could adopt neither the traditional belief in immortality nor the view of the Law allegedly peculiar to contemporary German orthodoxy. These or related reservations—which, as one immediately recognizes on a closer view, and as Cohen and Rosenzweig did not hesitate to admit, are of Enlightenment origin—would require, precisely because the return to the tradition claims to stand in relationship with a "new thinking," a coherent and fundamental justification from the new basis. And one dare not assert that they have received such a justification—which would be, in the nature of the case, also a partial justification of the Enlightenment—in such a way as to satisfy reasonable demands. Rather, the return to the tradition was carried out in discussion only with the post-Enlightenment synthesis, especially with Hegel. It was believed that one could dismiss any direct and thematic discussion with the Enlightenment, since it was assumed—logically, in the sense of the "overcome" Hegelianism—that with the "overcoming" of Hegelianism one had simultaneously "overcome" the Enlightenment which Hegelianism had "transcended." In truth, however, the critique of Hegelianism had actually led, in the nature of the case, to a rehabilitation of the Enlightenment. For what, if not a rehabilitation of the Enlightenment, was the critique of the "internalizations" carried out in the nineteenth century, especially among the successors of Lessing—the critique on which the return to the tradition depended? If the tenets of the tradition have also and especially an "external" sense, then the attack of the Enlightenment, which had aimed only at the "externally" understood tenets of the tradition—against their "inner" sense Hobbes, Spinoza, Voltaire wrote and would have written not a single line—was not based on a fundamental misunderstanding of the tradition. This fact should have been admitted and emphasized, and, since part of the Enlightenment's critique of the tradition was being accepted in a way that was not fundamentally clear, it should also have been admitted and emphasized that the quarrel between the Enlightenment and orthodoxy was not only not meaningless but had not even been dealt with. But all those who have attentively observed the movement under discussion can testify that neither the one fact nor the other has been admitted and emphasized. Thus precisely in case the motive of this movement is justified, it is most important that the classic quarrel between the Enlightenment and orthodoxy be resumed and re-understood.

For this quarrel has by no means been made groundless by the so-called "victory" of the Enlightenment over orthodoxy. One would have to be of the opinion that world history, that just the history of two or three hundred years, is the final judgment; whereas in truth, as the Enlightenment itself still knew, victories are "very ambiguous evidences of the just cause, or rather . . . none at all," and thus "he who wins and he who should have won" are "very seldom one and the same person." So if the object is to discriminate between the party that has won—the Enlightenment—and the party that should have won—presumably, according to Lessing's rule, orthodoxy; if, in other words, the object is to carry out a critique of the victory of the Enlightenment over orthodoxy, then one must, as things stand, drag out the dusty books that are to be considered the classical documents of the quarrel between the Enlightenment and orthodoxy. And yes, one must hear the arguments of both parties. Only by doing this, or more precisely, only by having the full course of that quarrel before one's eyes, may one hope to be able to attain a view of the hidden premises of both parties that is not corrupted by prejudices, and thus a principled judgment of right and wrong in their quarrel.

The critical examination of the arguments and counterarguments brought forward in this quarrel leads to the conclusion that there can be no question of a refutation of the "externally" understood basic tenets of the tradition. For all these tenets rest on the irrefutable premise that God is omnipotent and His will unfathomable. If God is omnipotent, then miracles and revelations in general, and in particular the Biblical miracles and revelations, are possible. Of course for orthodoxy, and therefore also for the Enlightenment, it is a question not so much of the possibility or impossibility as of the reality or unreality of the Biblical miracles and revelations; but in fact almost all of the Enlightenment's attempts to demonstrate the unreality of the Biblical miracles and revelations depend on the express or tacit premise that the impossibility of miracles and revelations in general is established or demonstrable. Yet in carrying out their critique, precisely the most radical Enlighteners learned—if not as something clearly known, then at least as something vividly felt—that as a consequence of the irrefutability of orthodoxy's ultimate premise, all individual assertions resting on this premise are unshakable. Nothing shows more clearly that this is the case than the main weapon which they employed, and which they handled so adeptly, so masterfully, that it—it alone, one might say—decided the victory of the Enlightenment over orthodoxy. This weapon is mockery. As Lessing, who was in a position to know, put it, they attempted by means of mockery to "laugh" orthodoxy out of a position from which it could not be dislodged by any proofs supplied by Scripture or even by reason. Thus the Enlightenment's mockery of the teachings of the tradition is not the successor of a prior refutation of these teachings; it does not bring to expression the amazement of unprejudiced men at the power of manifestly absurd prejudices; but it is the refutation: it is in mockery that the liberation from "prejudices" that had supposedly been already cast off is actually first accomplished; at the very least, the mockery is the admittedly supplementary but still decisive legitimation of a liberty acquired by whatsoever means. Thus the importance of mockery for the Enlightenment's critique of religion is an indirect proof of the irrefutability of orthodoxy. As a result, orthodoxy was able to survive the attacks of the Enlightenment, and all later attacks and retreats, unchanged in its essence.

But, although the Enlightenment's attack on orthodoxy failed, the battle of the two hostile powers has still had a highly consequential positive result for the Enlightenment: the Enlightenment has succeeded, one may say provisionally, in defending itself, for its part, against the attack of orthodoxy. Even if—to cite an example that is more than an example—it could not prove the impossibility or the unreality of miracles, it could demonstrate the unknowability of miracles as such, and thus protect itself against the claims of orthodoxy. Thus, what is true of the Enlightenment's offensive criticism is not true of its defensive criticism. Through the quarrel between the Enlightenment and orthodoxy it became more clearly and easily recognized than it had been before that the premises of orthodoxy—the reality of creation, miracles, and revelation—are not known (philosophically or historically) but only believed, and that they therefore do not have the binding character peculiar to the known. And not only that: whereas pre-Enlightenment science was in a certain harmony with the doctrines of belief, the new science, which proved itself in the battle against orthodoxy, if it did not indeed have its very raison d'être in the battle, stood in often concealed but, at bottom, always active and thus always re-emerging opposition to belief. Thus the emergence of the new science brought it about that fundamental teachings of the tradition, deemed knowable by the older science, were now considered more and more to be merely believed. The undermining of natural theology and of natural right, which was prepared, to say the least, in the Age of Enlightenment, is the most important example, indeed the specific sign, of this development. The final result is that unbelieving science and belief no longer have, as in the Middle Ages, the common ground of natural knowledge, on which a meaningful quarrel between belief and unbelief is possible, but rather any understanding of even the possibility of an opposition between them was on the verge of being lost. Orthodoxy actually had no share in the world created by the Enlightenment and its heirs, the world of "modern culture"; if it remained true to itself, it did not even have access to this world; it survived the nineteenth century as a misunderstood relic of a forgotten past, more despised than wondered at.

Thus the Enlightenment was not distracted from the construction of its world by the failure of its attack on orthodoxy. One must rather say that it was forced into constructing a world by this very failure. For it would not rest content with dismissing the tenets of orthodoxy as not known but merely believed; having been impressed by the claim of these tenets, it wanted to refute them. But the tenets that the world is the creation of the omnipotent God, that miracles are therefore possible in it, that man is in need of revelation for the guidance of his life, cannot be refuted by experience or by the principle of contradiction; for neither does experience speak against the guidance of the world and of man by an unfathomable God, nor does the concept of an unfathomable God contain a contradiction within itself. Thus if one wished to refute orthodoxy, there re-

mained no other way but to prove that the world and life are perfectly intelligible without the assumption of an unfathomable God. That is, the refutation of orthodoxy required the success of a system. Man had to establish himself theoretically and practically as master of the world and master of his life; the world created by him had to erase the world merely "given" to him; then orthodoxy would be more then refuted—it would be "outlived." Animated by the hope of being able to "overcome" orthodoxy through the perfection of a system, and hence hardly noticing the failure of its actual attack on orthodoxy, the Enlightenment, striving for victory with truly Napoleonic strategy, left the impregnable fortress of orthodoxy in the rear, telling itself that the enemy would not and could not venture any sally. Renouncing the impossible direct refutation of orthodoxy, it devoted itself to its own proper work, the civilization of the world and of man. And if this work had prospered, then perhaps there would have been no need for further proof of the justice of the Enlightenment's victory over orthodoxy; indeed as long as it did seem to prosper, it was believed that no further proof was needed. But doubts about the success of civilization soon became doubts about the possibility of civilization. Finally the belief is perishing that man can, by pushing back the "limits of Nature" further and further, advance to ever greater "freedom," that he can "subjugate" nature, "prescribe his own laws" for her, "generate" her by dint of pure thought. What is left, in the end, of the success of the Enlightenment? What finally proves to be the foundation and the vindication of this success?

The Enlightenment's critique of orthodoxy, in spite of its opposite appearance, is in truth purely defensive; it rests upon the radical renunciation of a refutation of orthodoxy; not the impossibility but only the unknowability of miracles on the premises of the new natural science. Thus the new natural science appears to be the proper vindication of the Enlightenment. In fact it cannot be disputed that the decisive thing for the Enlightenment's success was in the first place the belief that the science of Galileo, Descartes and Newton had refuted the science of Aristotle and the "natural world-view" explicated by it, which is also the "world-view" of the Bible. This success was only delayed, not called into question, by the harmonizations between the "modern world-view" and the Bible which proliferated especially in the seventeenth and eighteenth centuries and which are often enough attempted even today; for ultimately these harmonizations always function as vehicles of Enlightenment, not as dams against it: the moderate Enlightenment is the best preparation of the soil for the radical Enlightenment. The new natural science, made acceptable by the moderate Enlightenment, entered upon its triumphant progress as the confederate and scout of the radical Enlightenment. But the new science itself could not long maintain the claim to have brought to light the truth about the world "in itself"; the "idealistic" interpretation of it was already latent in it from its beginning. Modern "idealism"—perfected on the one hand in the discovery of the "aesthetic" as the purest insight into the creativity of man and, on the other hand, in the discovery of the radical "historicity" of man and his world as the definitive overcoming of the idea of an eternal nature, an eternal truth—finally understands modern natural science as one historically contingent form of "world-construction" among others; thus it makes possible the rehabilitation of the "natural world-view" on which the Bible depends. As soon as modern "idealism" has fully won out, the victory of the Enlightenment over orthodoxy thereby forfeits its originally decisive justification: the proof of the unknowability of miracles as such becomes invalid. For it is only under the premise of modern natural science that miracles are unknowable as such. So long as this science stood firm as the single way to the one truth, one could lull oneself with the view, certified by historical research, that the assertion of miracles is relative to the pre-scientific stage of mankind and thus has no dignity. But in the end it turns out that the facts certifying this view allow of the opposite interpretation: Is it not, ultimately, the very intention of defending oneself radically against miracles which is the basis of the concept of science that guides modern natural science? Was not the "unique" "world-construction" of modern natural science, according to which miracles are of course unknowable, devised expressly for the very purpose that miracles be unknowable, and that thus man be defended against the grip of the omnipotent God?

Thus modern natural science could be the basis or the instrument of the Enlightenment's victory over orthodoxy only so long as the old concept of truth, which it itself had already shaken, still ruled men's minds and, in particular, determined their conception of modern natural science. There was only one reason why it was temporarily possible to attempt to ground the modern ideal, the ideal of civilization, by means of natural science: it was believed that the new concept of nature was the adequate foundation of the new ideal precisely because the old concept of nature had been the adequate foundation of the old ideal. But this was a delusion. It had yet to be ascertained that the "end-free" and "value-free" nature of modern natural science can say nothing to man about "ends and values," that the "Is," understood in the sense of modern natural science, involves no reference at all to the "Ought," and that therefore the traditional view that the right life is a life according to nature becomes meaningless under the modern premise. Hence, if modern natural science cannot justify the modern ideal, and if there is nonetheless unmistakably a relation between the modern ideal and modern natural science, one sees oneself compelled to ask whether it is not, on the contrary, the modern ideal that is in truth the basis of modern natural science, and thus whether it is not precisely a new belief rather than the new knowledge that justifies the Enlightenment.

If the question is posed in this latter form, it loses the disreputability that understandably clings to the question of the moral source of modern natural science. For even the most devout adherents of this science concede that the arrival of a new ideal, a new conception of the right life for man—even if only secondary to the success of natural science—was decisive for the victory of the Enlightenment over orthodoxy. And in fact, in their view, the meaning of this ideal amounts to the ideal of freedom as the autonomy of man and his culture. But this view can be maintained only if one confuses "freedom" understood as autonomy with the "freedom" of conscience, the "freedom," or the philosophic tradition's ideal of autarky. Freedom as the autonomy of man and his culture is neither the original nor the final justification of the Enlightenment. This ideal was viable, rather, only during a peaceful interlude: in the interlude when the battle against orthodoxy seemed to have been fought out, while the revolt of the forces unchained by the Enlightenment had not yet broken out against their liberator; when, living in a comfortable house, one could no longer see the foundation on which the house had been erected,—in this epoch, after the decisive entry into the state of civilization as the self-assertion of man against overpowering nature, one could set up the "higher" ideal of culture as the sovereign creation of the spirit. The Jewish tradition gives a more adequate answer than the philosophy of culture to the question of the original ideal of the Enlightenment. The Jewish tradition characterized defection from the Law, rebellion against the Law, in most, if not all, cases as Epicureanism. Whatever facts, impressions or suspicions led the rabbis to this characterization, this description of defection, it is corroborated by historical investigation of the original Epicureanism. Epicurus is truly the classic of the critique of religion. Like no other, his whole philosophy presupposes the fear of superhuman forces and of death as the danger threatening the happiness and repose of man; indeed, this philosophy is hardly anything but the classical means of allaying the fear of divinity and death by showing them to be "empty of content." The influence of the Epicurean critique on the Enlightenment comes to light if one follows the tracks of the Enlightenment step by step from its beginnings down to Anatole France: the Epicurean critique is the foundation, or more exactly the foreground, of the Enlightenment critique. The Epicurean critique thus undergoes an essential change in the age of the Enlightenment. Of course for the Enlightenment too, and just precisely for the Enlightenment, it is a question of man's happiness, his peace of mind, which is threatened preeminently or exclusively by religious ideas. But the Enlightenment understands this happy peace, this tranquillity, in a fundamentally different way from the original Epicureanism—it understands "tranquillity" in such a way that the civilization, the subjection, the improvement of nature, and particularly of human nature, becomes indispensable for its sake. While the battle of the Epicureans against the terrifying delusion of religion was aimed preeminently at the terror of this delusion, the Enlightenment aimed preeminently at the delusoriness itself: regardless of whether the religious ideas are terrifying or comforting—qua delusions, they cheat men of the real goods, of the enjoyment of the real goods; they steer men away from the real "this world" to an imaginary "other world," and thus seduce them into letting themselves be cheated of the possession and enjoyment of the real, "this-worldly" goods by the greedy clergy, who "live" from those delusions. Liberated from the religious delusion, awakened to sober awareness of his real situation, taught by bad experiences that he is threatened by a stingy, hostile nature, man recognizes as his sole salvation and duty not so much "to cultivate his garden" as in the first place to plant himself a "garden" by making himself the master and owner of nature. This "crude" conception has long since been "overcome," of course, by a conception which completely ex-

poses the self-proclaiming and self-betraying tendency in the transformation of Epicureanism into the Enlightenment. The latest and purest expression of this is that the religious ideas are rejected not because they are terrifying but because they are desirable, because they are comforting: religion is not a tool which man has forged for dark reasons in order to torment himself, to make life unnecessarily difficult, but rather a way out chosen for very obvious reasons, in order to escape the terror and the hopelessness of life, which cannot be eradicated by any progress of civilization, in order to make his life easier. A new kind of fortitude, which forbids itself every flight from the horror of life into comforting delusion, which accepts the eloquent descriptions of the misery of man without God as a proof of the goodness of its cause, reveals itself eventually as the ultimate and the purest ground for the rebellion against the tradition of the revelation. This new fortitude being the willingness to look forsakenness in its face, being the courage to welcome the terrible truth, being toughness against the inclination of man to deceive himself about his situation, is probity. It is this probity, "intellectual probity," that bids us reject all attempts to "mediate" between the Enlightenment and orthodoxy—both those of the moderate Enlightenment and especially those of the post-Enlightenment synthesis—not only as inadequate, but also and especially as without probity; it forces the alternative "Enlightenment or orthodoxy" and since it believes it finds the deepest unprobity in the principles of the tradition itself, it bids us to renounce the very word "God." This atheism with a good conscience, or even with a bad conscience, differs precisely by its conscientiousness, its mortality, from the conscienceless atheism at which the past shuddered; the "Epicurean," who became an "idealist" in the persecutions of the sixteenth and seventeenth centuries, who, instead of being willing to "live in hiding" safely, learned to fight and die for honor and truth, finally becomes the "atheist" who rejects for reasons of conscience the belief in God. Thus it becomes clear that this atheism, compared not only with the original Epicureanism but also with the generally "radical" atheism of the age of Enlightenment, is a descendant of the tradition grounded in the Bible: it accepts the thesis, the negation of the Enlightenment, on the basis of the way of thinking which became possible only through the Bible. Although it refuses, since it is unwilling to disguise its unbelief in any way, to represent itself as a "synthesis" of the Enlightenment and orthodoxy, yet it itself is the latest, most radical, most unassailable harmonization of these opposed positions. This atheism, the heir and judge of the belief in revelation, of the centuries-old, millennia-old struggle between belief and unbelief, and finally of the short-lived but by no means therefore inconsequential romantic longing for the lost belief, confronting orthodoxy in complex sophistication formed out of gratitude, rebellion, longing and indifference, and also in simple probity, is according to its own claim as capable of an original understanding of the human roots of the belief in God as no earlier, no less complex-simple philosophy ever was. The last word and the ultimate justification of the Enlightenment is the atheism stemming from probity, which overcomes orthodoxy radically by understanding it radically, free of both the polemical bitterness of the Enlightenment and the equivocal reverence of romanticism.

Thus at last the "truth" of the alternative "orthodoxy or Enlightenment" is revealed as the alternative "orthodoxy or atheism." Orthodoxy, with its hostile eye, recognized from early on, from the beginning, that this is the case. Now it is no longer contested even by the enemies of orthodoxy. The situation thus formed, the present situation, appears to be insoluble for the Jew who cannot be orthodox and who must consider purely political Zionism, the only "solution of the Jewish problem" possible on the basis of atheism, as a resolution that is indeed highly honorable but not, in earnest and in the long run, adequate. This situation not only appears insoluble but actually is so, as long as one clings to the modern premises. If finally there is in the modern world only the alternative "orthodoxy or atheism," and if on the other hand the need for an enlightened Judaism is urgent, then one sees oneself compelled to ask whether enlightenment is necessarily modern enlightenment. Thus one sees oneself induced—provided one does not know from the outset, as one cannot know from the outset, that only new, unheard-of, ultramodern thoughts can resolve our perplexity—to apply for aid to the medieval Enlightenment, the Enlightenment of Maimonides.

But has not the Enlightenment of Maimonides long since been overcome? Is it not the precursor and model of just that moderate Enlightenment of the seventeenth and eighteenth centuries that was least able to stand its ground? Is it not even altogether more "radical" in many respects, more dangerous to the spirit of Judaism, than the modern Enlightenment? Is it not based on the irretrievable Aristotelian cosmology? Does it not stand or fall with the dubious allegorical method of interpretation? Is not the modern Enlightenment therefore, with all its questionableness, still preferable to the medieval?

It would be unpardonable to ignore these or similar doubts. Rather than discuss them thoroughly point by point, which would be possible only in the framework of an interpretation of Maimonides's *Guide of the Perplexed*, we shall attempt in what follows to point out the leading idea of the medieval Enlightenment that has become lost to the modern Enlightenment and its heirs, and through an understanding of which many modern certainties and doubts lose their force: the idea of Law.

Translated by Eve Adler.

Other works by Strauss: *What Is Political Philosophy?* (1959); *The City and Man* (1964); *Natural Right and History* (1965); *Liberalism: Ancient and Modern* (1968); *Leo Strauss on Moses Mendelssohn* (2012).

Yitshak Baer

1888–1980

The historian Yitshak Baer was born and educated in Germany in a modern Orthodox milieu. He was teaching at the Akademie für die Wissenschaft des Judentums in Berlin when, in 1930, he was appointed to teach medieval Jewish history at the Hebrew University in Jerusalem. Although he specialized in the history of medieval Spanish Jewry, he also wrote wide-ranging historiosophical essays, imbued with his conviction that the history of the Jews was not the history of a religion or an ethnic group but of a single, unified nation whose origins were in the Land of Israel. A theme running through both his archive-based monographs and his sweeping programmatic essays was the corrosive impact of diaspora life on Jewish religious faith and national pride.

Galut
1936

Chapter I. The Jewish Concept of History during Late Antiquity

The word "Galut" embraces a whole world of facts and ideas that have appeared with varying strength and clarity in every age of Jewish history. Political servitude and dispersion, the longing for liberation and reunion, sin and repentance and atonement: these are the larger elements that must go to make up the concept of Galut if the word is to retain any real meaning.

The picture begins to take shape at the time of the Second Temple. A national state still exists in Palestine, and the holy place embodying a power sufficient to redeem all humanity still stands. The goal is to bring the whole world under the leadership of the Jews and to the salvation of their religion; the Diaspora is not simply a consequence of political enslavement—it serves also to spread the knowledge of the true Teaching throughout the world. True, the political situation of the Jews does not permit the attainment of this ideal. Enslaved, contemned, and rejected, all over the world the Jews pray that they may be politically reunited on their own soil—only then will it be possible to fulfil the whole Law. For *politeia* (the order of law and doctrine), nation and soil belong together.

Thus in the Hellenistic-Roman Diaspora we can already distinguish all the essential elements of the medieval Galut. And antisemitism, too, makes its appearance. Antisemitism is the inevitable consequence of the Jews' exalted consciousness of religious superiority and of their mission among the nations, a consciousness all the more infuriating because it exists in a nation totally without power. The problem of being a Jew is inseparably bound up with the Galut. Already it is a distinguishing mark of Galut that there is persecution, outrage, and injustice from which specious privileges give no relief.

The nation suffers because of its faith. "For Thy sake are we killed all the day; we are accounted as sheep for the slaughter" (Ps. 44:23). The nation is so proud of its martyrs because, in effect, the whole nation has consecrated its life to martyrdom and taken upon itself the yoke of the kingdom of God. But suffering for the sake of the unity and the freedom of the people is also part of this martyrdom. Even in Philo the messianic hope of reunion is as strong as it was in the later prophets and will be in every medieval Jew, and it expresses itself in the same terms—by divine force shall the Jews be brought to Palestine, simultaneously and from every corner of the earth.

The destruction of the Second Temple widens the breach in the nation's historical continuity and augments the treasury of national-religious jewels whose loss is to be mourned: the Temple and its cult, the mutilated theocracy, the national autonomy, the holy soil

ever further from reclamation. "The righteous are in their graves and the prophets sleep, but we are driven from our land, Zion is taken from us and we have nothing now but God and his Torah" (Syr. Apoc. of Baruch). Because of this the growing tradition of Torah interpretation becomes a crucial factor in the life of the people—but the Torah is still but one surviving part of the holy structure of nation, law, and land that an imminent redemption is to bring together again in all its completeness. This certainty of speedy redemption is grounded upon the promises of the prophets and upon a concept of history that lives in the heart of the nation and has been pondered and broadened, in close connection with the Bible, from generation to generation.

The Bible had told of the slow process of selection and ripening that took place among God's people; it confirmed their claim to the promised land of Palestine and showed them their special place in the history of the nations. The Midrash completed the concept of history that developed during the time of the Second Temple, and lovingly depicted the nation's character and the process of redemption that was the meaning of its history and of the history of all humanity. For the creators of the Midrash, the only true history has been set down once and for all in the Holy Scriptures. The Scriptures are the master pattern of all later history; what has happened once must happen over and over again in ever-widening circles, and thus the individual event of later times loses even its individual value.

Certainly the history of the nations was not ignored; the Jews made learned parallel complications of sacred and profane history, which were later carried forward by the Christians. But the history of the Jewish people remains distinct from the astrologically determined history of the nations (i.e., a history determined by causes operating within the finished framework of nature), for the Jewish people in its special relationship to God is removed from the context of natural law.

The gradual descent of the *Shekhinah* (the Divine Indwelling) on Israel and the holy places is described again and again in the Midrash, most profoundly in the commentary on the Song of Songs. From this description, world history is revealed as a universal process of redemption fulfilling itself in fixed stages foreseen by God. As there were six days for the Creation, so there are six ages of world history: the first four days of the holy history, during which the Temple still stands, are followed by the fifth and sixth days bringing the ascendancy of the wild beasts—i.e., the empires of this world—until the Sabbath of the world will restore the disturbed harmony on earth and in heaven. The surviving Jewish literature from this period frequently classifies history in terms of the rise and fall of empires. The process of atonement consists in Israel's enslavement by the empires and expiatory pilgrimage among the nations; the meaning of this process is immeasurably deepened by the idea that the *Shekhinah* itself takes part in the Galut and also waits for deliverance. And the picture of the suffering servant of God in the fifty-third chapter of Isaiah is already accepted in the Diaspora at this time as the permanent symbol of the sufferings of the Jews in the Galut—which is the meaning given this passage by the Jews of the Middle Ages. Even the deaths of the martyrs of Bar Kokhba's rebellion are regarded as atonement for the sins of all mankind. Like the blissful Golden Age, so also the martyrdom of later ages is symbolized in the Song of Songs, "for it is all fear of God and assumption of the yoke of the kingdom of heaven." The more terrible the suffering of the Diaspora, the more it operates as seed thrown forth in the world for the dissemination of the true faith. Abraham, the primal ancestor of Israel, is the prototype of the pilgrim who wanders through the world to usher *gerim* (proselytes) under the wing of the *Shekhinah.*

Thus the Galut acquires its place in history, but only in order that its abolition may be the more surely guaranteed. Martyrdom is at the same time a fight for national autonomy, for a home soil, for a base of rebellion against the supremacy of Edom (Rome), the last empire. The struggles of the Zealots for political freedom and the firm establishment of God's supremacy continued from the time of Bar Kokhba's revolt up to the conquest of Palestine by the Arabs. Only after stubborn resistance was the lesson learned: that love cannot be prematurely aroused, that the kingdom of God cannot be set up by force, that one cannot rise in rebellion against the overlordship of the nations.

Chapter II. The Idea of Galut in the Teachings of the Church Fathers

The Jews gave to Europe the laws that govern its religious experience, insofar as these laws are derived from the concept of man's responsibility before God and the attainment of his inner freedom through love of God. But the Jews gave more than this: until the age of romanticism, the best that Europe had to say on the subject of nation and history stemmed also from Jewish sources.

The historical thinking of the Middle Ages is Jewish doctrine; Christianity took the historical-religious ideas of the Jews out of their original context and transposed them into the idiom of Western peoples. To the extent that modern scholarship has failed to seek a true understanding of Jewish historical thought, to that extent has it failed until now to recognize the Jewish foundation on which rest the ideology of history and the moral precepts taught by the Church Fathers.

In the teaching of the Fathers, the historic role of God's people is taken over in the concept of the *Civitas Dei,* which consists of the secretly chosen ones who wander on a pilgrimage through the world. The meaning of the word "Galut," in its dual aspect of religious propaganda and of suffering for the sake of humanity's redemption, is given to the idea of the *Civitas Dei,* while the true Galut of the Jewish people, stripped of its meaning as sacred history, of the drama of salvation, becomes an object of contempt and ridicule. But in practice the Church allied itself with the heathen empire, and the clear boundaries separating enslaved Israel from ruling Edom were blurred and lost in the changing relations between Church and state.

In Paul's view, the political bondage of the Jews was the visible manifestation of an inner bondage, and this in turn provided justification for tightening the political bondage. The prophets of ancient Israel had prophesied the Galut to their own people in order to bring about an internal conversion. But the declarations of the Christian theologians, damning the Jews to eternal servitude, were aimed at strangers outside the group to which the authors of these declarations belonged—and they made sure that the servitude they prophesied should come to pass.

The history of antisemitism here reaches its high point. No earlier enemy had looked with so strong a hatred at the historical-religious positions of the Jewish people, into whose inheritance these new persecutors believed themselves to have entered. On the other hand, a certain timidity kept them from completely exterminating the people from whom they had consciously taken the best of their own teachings. Out of these ambivalent feelings there grew the artificial doctrine of the necessary preservation of the Jews until the end of days. According to this doctrine, the Jews are scattered through the world in order that they may serve, through their books and miserable condition, as a testimony to the truth of Christianity. The Jews wander through the world like Cain—who is for Jew and Christian alike the archetype of the penitent pilgrim—and the sign of the Covenant, which was for the Jews a guarantee of survival, is now, like the sign of Cain, a mark of evil—"lest any finding him should smite him" (Gen. 4:15). Thus the Jews are condemned to perpetual political servitude, and handed over to the kings and princes of the nations. [. . .]

Chapter XVI. From the Ancient Faith to a New Historical Consciousness

In the second half of the seventeenth century, the foundations of the old Jewish faith were already undermined from two sides by rationalism and by the self-contradictions of the Messiah doctrine. Nevertheless, the Judaism recognized as legitimate continued to exist until the middle of the eighteenth century, still unshaken in its ancient constitution and spiritual character. Essentially, this Judaism remained as it had been two thousand years before, or at least, if it had developed, it had developed only in nuances. It still upheld the same eschatological concepts of history, with the chosen people as center—except that the framework of this concept had been enlarged in the course of the centuries to include the historical and philosophical materials that had gradually accumulated around it.

Inner attitudes to history changed very slowly. Out of the compact and somewhat pugnacious doctrine of election had grown a naive mythology of history full of wonderful light and an involved and metaphysical system of historical speculation, half magical in its atmosphere. A rational philosophical trend that prepared the way for later skepticism split off from this system. But it all still remained within an identical historical framework, secured by tradition and by the naive faith of the people against essential changes. The most exalted speculations, the soberest rationalism, the grayest tones of everyday life—all remained bound to the firm realities of people, land, and Torah, past and future greatness and the inexplicable sufferings of the Galut. The people are kept together by a national consciousness unique in the world. The land is the *real* land of Palestine, however veiled by religious imagination and mystery, however bereft by political circumstances of its beauty and productivity. And the much criticized Talmudic dialectic still leads always back to the miracle of the Torah. The religion renews itself in every gen-

eration through a strength that comes from the people and is at the same time mythos and purest intellect. The day-to-day fate of the people is still completely comprehended—as it was in the days of the Bible—through a firm faith in the direct influence of God upon every historical event. This is no timid spinning out of old dreams, nor is it mere inertia under the burden of an incomprehensible destiny; rather, it is a system of religious concepts—complete in itself, if overloaded—of which every representative of the tradition can give a clear account.

This old system of thought is by no means unhistorical, for it has history as its foundation; the decisive historical events of ancient and recent times retained their fixed place in Jewish thought, more than in other religious systems, becoming milestones in the story of the testing of God's people. No complex historiography could develop out of this system, for at bottom it is always a repetition of the same ideas applied to the changing materials of history. Precisely the last epochs before the emancipation yield very numerous accounts dealing with individual historical events, which are always treated as new examples for the trial, proving, and delivery of the people of God; the apocalyptic visions, which continue almost to this time, are the constantly repeated expression of an unshaken spirit that sees in history the signs of the coming end.

The greatness and unity of this religious world are not essentially disturbed by the frequently abstruse forms of its expression or the unpleasant external circumstances of social and economical life. The community life of the Jews of this time displays no weaknesses that are not to be found also in the Christian bourgeois society. The much criticized Jewish factors and agents in the courts of the German nobles did their good and their evil acts, just like the Christian courtiers of the time. The economic behavior of the Jews of the time displays the general virtues and vices of early capitalism—to the extent, at least, that the business affairs of Jews developed sufficiently to warrant the use of such a term. There never were any specific, religiously determined, Jewish economic traits. The exigencies of the Galut forced the Jews to do the best they could with the few means of livelihood that were open to them. Commerce with its drudgery and constant risk is regarded as a burden imposed by heaven, as a form of asceticism in a dismal world, but never as a value in itself, and economic success is no subject for religious contemplation. All of the above is not noted to extenuate the faults of this generation; but it must be understood that these faults were observed and criticized by the Jews themselves as abuses and signs of worldliness.

In the last decade of the seventeenth century, however, rationalism began its victorious progress through the world. In Holland and England, the principle of religious toleration was first proclaimed, and was applied, in part, to the Jews. The Jews were given no equality in terms of politics and citizenship, but they were permitted to practice their religion freely and were guaranteed a degree of human consideration that had never before been accorded to Jews anywhere in the world. This was at a time when in the Catholic countries of Southern and Eastern Europe, especially in Poland, the treatment of the Jews was determined by the blackest bigotry or the most senseless superstition, and when in Protestant Germany the Jews were hemmed in by a frustrating system of restrictions that was about to lose its religious trappings and turn into an instrument of race hatred and racist politics.

In the more favorable intellectual atmosphere of the western countries, which gradually spread also to Germany, there arose a new approach to the basic questions of Jewish life. The Jews who partook of the new rationalism were not, like da Costa and Spinoza, rebels against an established way of life; they were simply skeptics and men of pleasure, or even men who, with no thought of undermining the tradition that had been handed down to them, gave up their political ties and their responsibility to the Jewish nation as a whole, and tried to make themselves as comfortable as possible in their "homes" in the *Golah* ("Exile"). Such types had always existed, but from the end of the seventeenth century on they became steadily more numerous until they finally stood in the foreground of Jewish life.

The first clear evidence of this new attitude may be found in the book *Sefat Emet* ("Language of Truth"), by Moshe Chagis (published in Amsterdam, 1707). Chagis came to Western Europe as an envoy from Jerusalem in order to collect money for Palestine, if possible to improve the methods of collecting money, and, as was customary with the *sheluhim* ("envoys"), to preach to the Jews and turn their hearts toward the Holy Land. In passionate words taken from the tradition, he preached to the Jews of the real and religious significance of Palestine. But the lukewarm and the skeptical among the Sephardic Jews greeted him with doubt and indifference. Their arguments were old, but at this moment

they had a special importance, for they represented the starting point of the theories of two centuries. The value of the Holy Land is called into question with the usual arguments about the desolation of the country and the unfortunate conditions prevailing there in respect to political affairs and within the Jewish community. The assertion is made that, until redemption, every country is as good as Palestine; God hears men's prayers everywhere; that indeed it is contrary to God's command to live in Palestine, for Palestine must lie waste until the end of days. This is Marrano theology in a modernized and more comfortable form.

Chagis can classify these arguments as coming from skeptics who throw off the yoke of the commandments and think only of enjoying their wealth and their new political freedom. They consider their present home their Jerusalem, and do not concern themselves with the needs of the Holy Land or the needs of the Jews in Turkey, Germany, Poland, or Africa. These frivolous persons declare that they would be delighted if the Messiah came for the poor Jews, so that they might be left in peace; but if the Messiah is going to equalize the rich and the poor, why do they need him? And they do not fail to cite authority in the support of these arguments. These comfortable Marranos were accustomed to interpret the words of Jeremiah—"and seek the peace of the city whither I have caused you to be carried away captive, and pray unto the Lord for it; for in the peace thereof shall ye have peace" (29:7)—as meaning that it is a Jew's duty to remain in the Diaspora, whereas this passage had earlier been interpreted only as prescribing the obligations to pray for the peace of the world and its rulers. These skeptics even dared to quote the words of the Talmud (Ketuvot 111a): that "love must not be awakened too soon." Earlier, these words had been advanced against the false prophets who sought to force the redemption by an exaggeration of religious exaltation. No pious Jew would ever have thought of employing the passage in any way that could weaken religious ardor or shake that Jewish faith which rested on real values.

In Sephardic circles of this period we find for the first time an optimistic consciousness of progress. They feel themselves to have had a hand in the libertarian development of Holland. From the Sephardim of England and Holland, rationalism spread to the Jewish skeptics in France and even to the Jews of Germany. Moses Mendelssohn (1729-1786) merely gathers together the thought of his time and gives it an authoritative form, raised above mere libertinism. The tendencies of modern Jewish history that were set in motion in Mendelssohn's time have been exhaustively analyzed and criticized in recent times; we can only examine here some of the consequences of these tendencies in the history of the concept and conditions of the Galut.

Recent Jewish history has carried to its conclusion a long process of disintegration. The gap between religious promises and the debased body of the Jewish people, of which Jewish rationalists had before been aware, led to a complete or partial abandonment of the nation. Loss of faith in the national future and in the folk strength of the religion led to a denationalization of the religion. The nation's specific political constitution in the Diaspora and the consciousness of Jewish unity were destroyed. At first it was believed that this was only to reorganize Judaism legally and socially on a higher, more objective, and more reasonable plane. In reality, it quickly became clear that the result of this effort was to replace the historically determined individuality of the Jew with a different individuality, no less determined by history. Such a transformation, however, proved impossible. The medieval difficulties in the way of the relations of Jews and non-Jews simply continued, though in a more humanized form; and, in addition, the tensions that first developed out of the emergence of the Marrano problem, unique in the late Middle Ages, became characteristic of the modern Jewish question. This was less a problem for the baptized Jews than those Jews who, though they might remain in the Jewish camp, had nevertheless undergone a change of faith. For in reality what they had done was not to take over elements of European culture and incorporate them into their own religious-national organism; rather, they had given up essential elements of that organism in favor of different ways and views of life.

This change had come about through no visible external force, but through a conscious or unconscious moral pressure. Now the historical forces that in the course of centuries had formed the Jewish character were deflected from their path—a path that might have led to the rise of full, conscious, and responsible community life. The historical forces forsook the nation. The vision of Ezekiel, as Judah ha-Levi had interpreted it, was now fulfilled. Of the living body of the nation, there were left only scattered and dry bones, and no one could foresee that these, in the words of the

prophet, would unite again into a living whole. The scattered segments of the nation either entered, in the process of assimilation, into new and fruitful human and historical amalgamations, or they retained the stamp of the history of the Galut upon their inert and hardened flesh. Out of such conditions during a very brief period in Jewish history, a comprehensive historical construction was built up in the age of historical awareness that was accepted as true by both friends and enemies of the Jews and was yet, in a historical sense, more erroneous than any previous generation's view of Judaism.

The historical thought of modern Judaism still suffers from the effects of an improperly understood religious-political heritage. The old concept of history was abandoned, but it continued to have some hold on historical thinking; no one attempted a real and thorough analysis of the factors that determined Jewish history. Not only the national character of the Jews was misunderstood, but also—following medieval rationalism in this respect—the character of the Jewish faith, which flows from the people and is bound up with the destiny of the people, and can also be renewed only by the people. Attempts were made not to clarify the situation historically, but to defend it from a fixed standpoint. The Jewish apologetics of antiquity and the Middle Ages developed out of the need to defend certain conditions of which no one was in a position to know the causes and which no human effort could change. But in the modern world there is no place for apologetics; failings and difficulties are recognized and, so far as possible, traced to their origins and overcome. Only the human tendencies of Jewish apologetics remain valid. It is the privilege of the oppressed people to arouse the conscience of the victors and to draw the moral from a millennia-long history in which not human power but God was recognized as the determining historical factor.

The plan of this book now requires that I say one more word concerning the nature of the Galut in our times. All modern views of the Galut, from whatever orientation they arise, are inadequate: they are unhistorical; they confuse cause and effect; they project the patterns of the nineteenth century into the past. There really does not exist any serious and systematic effort to analyze the material of history, or any conscientious desire to understand and appreciate the ideas of earlier generations of Jews. This is true equally of the antisemitic conception of the Galut as a symbol of political decay and general disintegration and exploitation, of the assimilationist idea that the Galut serves as an instrument for progress and the spread of culture, and of the religious theories of later Jewish theology.

Jewish theology is wrong in appealing to ancient Judaism's concept of a historical missions. The old idea of a Jewish mission was tied up with a particular conception of history and with the reality of political servitude that was to be done away with by the Messiah. The idea of the mission could be put forward only in time of suffering and need. It presented—together with the ideas of purification and atonement—only one of several interpretations of the Galut. Even for the Hellenistic Jews, the Galut did not have the particular and special significance that the early Christians ascribed to their own Diaspora. And the carrying on of the missionary task in the Galut must surely involve religious propaganda, which the Jews have given up precisely because of the pressures of the Galut, and probably for all time. In recent times, it has been often said that the old faith in the Messiah cannot be absorbed in the ideas of religious progress.

All modern interpretations of the Galut fail to do justice to the enormous tragedy of the Galut situation and to the religious power of the old ideas that centered around it. No man of the present day, of no matter what religious orientation, dare claim that he is equipped to carry the burden of the centuries as did his forefathers, or that the modern world still presents the internal and external conditions necessary to realize a Jewish destiny in the older sense.

The Galut has returned to its starting point. It remains what it always was: political servitude, which must be abolished completely. The attempt which has been considered from time to time, to return to an idea of the Galut as it existed in the days of the Second Temple—the grouping of the Diaspora around a strong center in Palestine—is today out of the question. There was a short period when the Zionist could feel himself a citizen of two countries, and indeed in a more deeply moral sense than Philo; for the Zionist was prepared to give up his life for the home in which he had his residence. Now that the Jews have been denied the right to feel at home in Europe, it is the duty of the European nations to redeem the injustice committed by their spiritual and physical ancestors by assisting the Jews in the task of reclaiming Palestine and by recognizing the right of the Jews to the land of their fathers.

Rabbi Judah Liwa Ben Bezalel of Prague, a sixteenth-century writer who was completely rooted in ancient Judaism, opens his book on the messianic redemption with the statement that the nature of the redemption can only be rightly understood through its absolute opposite, the Galut. The fact of the Galut itself is for him the decisive proof of the expected redemption. For the Galut is the abolition of God's order. God gave to every nation its place, and to the Jew he gave Palestine. The Galut means that the Jews have left their natural place. But everything that leaves its natural place loses thereby its natural support until it returns. The description of Israel among the nations is unnatural. Since the Jews manifest a national unity, even in a higher sense than the other nations, it is necessary that they return to a state of actual unity. Nor is it in accord with the order of nature that one nation should be enslaved by the others, for God made each nation for itself. Thus, by natural law, the Galut cannot last forever.

We may appeal to such ideas today with the consciousness that it is up to us to give the old faith a new meaning. If we seek to end the Galut, let us not attribute our desires to earlier generations; rather, we must draw from the ideas of earlier generations those consequences which follow from a changed spiritual approach to an unchanged political situation. The Jewish revival of the present day is in its essence not determined by the national consciousness of the Jews, which existed before the history of Europe and is the original sacred model for all the national ideas of Europe. However, it is undeniable that this turning home must involve a coming to grips with the ancient Jewish consciousness of history, on whose foundation European culture constantly and repeatedly reared itself in the decisive epochs of its history, without wishing to acknowledge its debt in a serious and conclusive manner. The question is how we ourselves stand in a relation to a belief whose foundations have held unshaken for more than two thousand years. For us, perhaps, the final consequence of modern causal historical thinking coincides with the final consequence of the old Jewish conception of history, which comes to us from no alien tradition but has grown out of our own essential being: "*Our* eyes saw it, and no stranger's; *our* ears heard it, and no others." If we today can read each coming day's events in ancient and dusty chronological tables, as though history were the ceaseless unrolling of a process proclaimed once and for all in the Bible, then every Jew in every part of the Diaspora may recognize that there is a power that lifts the Jewish people out of the realm of all history.

Translated by Robert Warshow.

Other works by Baer: *Yisrael ba-'amim* (1955); *A History of the Jews in Christian Spain*, 2 vols. (1961, 1966); *Mehkarim u-masot be-toldot am yisrael*, 2 vols. (1985).

Simon Rawidowicz
1896–1957

The Polish-born Hebraist and historian of Jewish thought Simon Rawidowicz moved to Berlin when he was in his twenties to pursue a university education. When the Nazis seized power in 1933, he took refuge in England, where he taught in London and Leeds, before leaving for the United States in 1947. He taught at the College of Jewish Studies in Chicago and later headed the Department of Near Eastern and Judaic Studies at Brandeis University. His crowning work, *Bavel vi-Yrushalayim* (1957), which was published posthumously, set forth his conception of Jewish history and analyzed the impact of the creation of the State of Israel on modern Jewish life. He was known particularly for rejecting the Zionist doctrine of *shelilat ha-golah* (negation of the diaspora) and arguing that the Land of Israel and the diaspora were mutually supportive, vibrant centers of Jewish creativity.

Moses Mendelssohn, the German and Jewish Philosopher
1936

2

Moses Mendelssohn's German Philosophy did not survive him and his generation of the German *Aufklärer*. As the leading German philosopher, apart from some psychological and aesthetical theories, he was soon overtaken by two powerful philosophical movements: the one was that philosophical system of criticism created by Immanuel Kant, further developed by Solomon Maimon, Fichte, and others; the second was the romantic movement, both in literature and metaphysics, advocated by Jacobi, Goethe, Herder and the *Sturm und Drang*. All the philosophers of the *Aufklärung* were thrown on the scrap-heap in the eighties of the 18th century. This would have been the fate of

Mendelssohn had he not been at the same time Rabbi Moshe Mi-Dessau, the *first* representative of the Jewish-German problem, or more than this, of the Judaism-world problem in modern history.

Judaism and the world outside was and is one of the most burning and actual problems of Jewish thought and life since the days of the development of the first Jewish center outside Palestine. From Philo of Alexandria to Mendelssohn and to our own days, the best Jewish thinkers were always faced with the problem of the system of relationships between Judaism and the world. This problem has many aspects: religious, metaphysical, philosophical, national, sociological, at which we cannot even hint here. Almost every Jewish thinker since Philo considered it to be his most imperative duty to build a bridge between Judaism and what we may call generally non-Judaism. Some of them spent all their lives in collecting the material for this bridge which they never succeeded in building.

In modern Jewish history and thought, Mendelssohn was the first bridge-builder between Judaism and non-Judaism. The pillars were taken both from the world and from Judaism. The basis was the European *Aufklärung* and a special conception of Judaism.

Mendelssohn based his ideal of *Aufklärung* on the principle of harmony: metaphysical harmony, well-established harmony in the cosmos; religious-political harmony: harmony between state and religion, between society and church; even physio-psychological harmony: harmony in man, harmony of mind and body, and so on. Both the conditions of Jewish life in his time and his philosophical conception helped him in coming to the conviction on which he based all his life and thought, that there is a natural, elementary, everlasting harmony between Judaism and non-Judaism. It exists, according to him, in religious and general thought, and needs but an extension in the social and political sphere.

Mendelssohn did not see any difference between Judaism and non-Judaism as he conceived them both. Practically, his being a Jew and German was not any problem to him. There was not to him any dualism in serving both masters. He was a traditional, strictly orthodox Jew, on most intimate terms with the representatives of orthodox Jewry, with Rabbi Jacob Emden, Rabbi Hirschel Levin, and others. He was even entrusted to compile together with Rabbi Hirschel Levin a kind of *Kitzur Hoshen Mishpat* for the Prussian Government. At the same time he was the pioneer of German philosophy and literature, representative of the German mentality—*das deutsche Wesen*—of his time. Imagine a Ghetto-Jew, about 1760, a *Schutzjude* in Berlin of that day criticizing Frederick the Great for his French assimilationist tendencies and corresponding with Rabbi Jacob Emden on halakhic problems, living the same life with Rabbi Jacob Emden and Rabbi Hirschel Levin and sharing the same interests with Lessing, Nicolai, and the other Christian *Aufklärer*; imagine this *Schutzjude* in 1760 stressing at every opportunity his being a Jew and teaching Germany what Europe and culture mean, what good taste in aesthetics and sound judgment in metaphysics is, what Germany of to-morrow will be—imagine all this and you see what a complex of perplexing and exciting problems is connected with Mendelssohn's personality and historical milieu. It should also be taken into consideration—here I must be very short—that Mendelssohn in 1760 was, as regards German culture, no less a German than, for instance, Walter Rathenau 150 years afterwards, and at same time no less a strict Jew than any member of the *Breuer-Gemeinde* of Frankfurt am Main—take this short hint into consideration, and you see what a difficult problem Mendelssohn set to the generations which came after him. It shows us also that we must forget much of what we have been told about Mendelssohn, so as to find our way to the real Mendelssohn, to Mendelssohn as he lived and thought in the middle of the 18th century.

Since Mendelssohn's Jewish philosophy was so often misunderstood both by the right and left wing in Jewry, we have to dwell a little upon it. A new examination of Mendelssohn's philosophy and historical positions is a very urgent need. Mendelssohn's philosophy, which started with the ideal of individual and social perfection and happiness and culminated in the immortality of the soul, was in no way antagonistic to Judaism. Then came the preparatory work of the English and French enlightenment, the rationalism of Leibniz and Wolf, the cosmo-political tendencies of the 18th century, the tendencies to level down as much as possible the differences between all religions and cultures, the great interest which was then aroused in the Orient and Oriental cultures, the ardently propagated postulate by all the *Aufklärer* of the one universal religion, the religion of the best Jews, best Christians, and best Mohammedans, this which should become the religion of the

international *Aufklärer* the world over—all this made it possible for Mendelssohn to be most deeply convinced of the harmony, nay, much more, of the identity in principles between Judaism and this new non-Judaism. He had no need of a painfully elaborated synthesis between these two worlds—they were one to him.

What is Judaism, according to Mendelssohn? Briefly: the elementary *Naturreligion* or *Vernunftreligion* (religion of nature or reason) plus the Sinaitic revelation, that is plus the Law, the *Torah u-mitzvot*. The fundamental principles of the Jewish religion—which are to Mendelssohn the same as to Joseph Albo, the author of the *Ikkarim*—are the fundamental principles of religion as such, of the *Natur- und Vernunftreligion*, as far as God, providence, etc., are concerned. Religion generally is imaginable without revelation. Men can reach the ideal of perfection and happiness through the *Naturreligion* without any special revelation. The eternal truths, *vérités de raison*, which are the fundamental principles of the *Naturreligion* are a kind of *ideae innatae*, inborn ideas, and do not need a special revelation. This revelation did not intend to repeat the elementary fundamentals of religion, but to give them Law, *Torah u-mitzvot*, *Zeremonialgesetz*, without which no Jew can reach the ideal of perfection and happiness. No non-Jew needs this Torah, no Jew can exist without it. This *Torah* can never be eliminated from Jewry, nor can it be changed. The *mitzvot, Zeremonialgesetz*, are obligatory on Jewry and on Jewry only, both for national and metaphysical reasons. We have according to Mendelssohn only to add *Torah* and *mitzvot* to the religion of reason and nature and we get as a result this very Jewish religion. In this conformity and compatibility with reason and nature Mendelssohn sees the greatest power and truth of Judaism as the possibility of a new harmony between Judaism and non-Judaism.

The relation between these two is never that of thesis and antithesis. Mendelssohn's Jewish philosophy is based on the often overlooked theory that there are three planes in Judaism:

(a) the fundamental plane, the eternal ideas concerning God, providence and the soul, which are the fundamentals of the ideal universal religion; on this plane there is no need of compromise.

(b) the second plane consists of historical verities, the information about the Jewish past since Abraham which is well established by sufficient historical evidence.

(c) the third plane: the *Torah* and *mitzvot* given by revelation. [. . .]

3

I must confess, there are still some problematical points in Mendelssohn's philosophy of religion and Judaism. Parts of it have more the character of a personal than of a general solution. But this criticism cannot be made by arguments coming from outside and not from his own philosophy, methods of "immanent criticism" alone being here admissible.

As to Christian criticism of his own time, this was chiefly levelled both against Mendelssohn's religious ideal and Judaism. [. . .]

Why are you a Jew? Mendelssohn was not spared this challenge. The challenger was a Christian priest of Basel, Johann Caspar Lavater, an enthusiastic priest with strong missionary tendencies who wanted to convert Mendelssohn, which would have been the greatest sensation in Europe of those days. Here we see Mendelssohn in an extremely difficult position and in quite a peculiar rôle: Mendelssohn as the defender, the *sanegor*.

One of his best Jewish features was his being a defender of Israel. The mute Jewry of Prussia and other countries of the 18th century found in Mendelssohn their voice. He never asked for mere mercy. Mendelssohn defended Jewry by accusing Europe of its cruelty towards Jewry. The first powerful *J'accuse* in modern Europe was not that of the French Zola, but of the German Jew Mendelssohn. In the footsteps of Manasse Ben Israel who negotiated with Cromwell for the admission of Jews into England, he started a campaign for justice and tolerance towards the Jews in the German countries. Mendelssohn's introduction to the translation of *Vindiciae Judaeorum* by Manasse Ben Israel is one of the most powerful indictments against the ill-treatment of the Jews by the majority of European states in the 18th century. Much of it could have been said yesterday and, I am afraid, may be said tomorrow.

"It is curious to observe how prejudice assumes the forms of all ages, on purpose to oppress us, and puts obstacles in the way of our civil admission. In former superstitious days it was wantonly defiling sacred things; stabbing crucifixes and setting them bleeding; secretly circumcizing Christian babes and then feasting our eyes with mangling them; using Christian blood at our Passover, poisoning wells, etc. Now times are altered; those calumnies have no longer the desired effect. Now

it is even superstition and ineptitude, want of moral feelings, taste and good manners, unfitness for the arts, sciences and useful trades, and particularly for the military and civil services, an unconquerable proneness to cheating, usury, and all nefarious practices which have come in the place of those grosser vituperations, for the sake of excluding us from the mass of efficient citizens, and casting us out of the maternal bosom of the state. Formerly, all imaginable pains were taken with us, and several establishments provided for the purpose of making us 'useful citizens.' Oh, no, Christians. . . . Now the zeal for converting has abated, and we are utterly neglected. We are still kept far removed from arts, sciences, useful trades, and the professions of mankind, every avenue to improvement is still blocked against us, and the want of refinement made a pretence for our oppression. They tie our hands, and scold us for not making use of them!" And later on: "Generally speaking: Men superfluous to the state, men of whom a country can make no use at all—seem to me terms of which no statesman should make use. Men are all more or less useful. . . . But no country can, without serious injury to itself, dispense with the humblest, the seemingly most useless of its inhabitants, and to a wise government, not even a pauper is one too many, not even a cripple altogether useless. . . ." (From the introduction to the German translation of *Vindiciae Judaeorum* by Manasse ben Israel, 1782, translated by M. Samuels.)

Mendelssohn's *J'accuse* brought to shame and repentance the best men in that Europe, the elite of the enlightened in and outside Germany. Governments and masses of course took little or no notice of Mendelssohn's *J'accuse*. More than this: Mendelssohn did not only defend his suffering brethren, he himself was the best defense for them. His personality, his position did more to defend Jewry of that time than his *shtadlanut*. It was his position in the cultural life of Germany too, which compelled Europe to re-examine their prejudices against Jewry and Judaism. It was Mendelssohn who forced many of them to see the Jew in a new light.

But Mendelssohn was still greater and more original as a defender of Judaism. Defenders of suffering Jews were before and after him, among Jews and non-Jews. But it was the defense of Judaism in which Mendelssohn paved a new way.

Why are you a Jew? The priest Lavater challenged him, who could not understand either Mendelssohn's *shaharit* or his *musaf*, either his *Aufklärung* or his Jewishness. How can a Jew be the leader of German philosophy, German cultural life? Is not German culture a Christian concern? How can a Ghetto-Jew be its spiritual guide? Lavater challenged Mendelssohn publicly: either become a Christian or give a criticism of Christianity and explain why you are not a Christian! So arose the famous dispute between Mendelssohn and Lavater which lasted about two years, from 1769 till 1771. Apart from this, Lavater's challenge was a great shock to Mendelssohn who had hoped to arrive at a peaceful understanding and to tolerable relations even with the Christian theologians in Germany—how could he dare to criticize Christianity in Prussia of 1769! The King, Frederick the Great, was said to be an atheist, a pupil of Voltaire. But what was allowed to the Christian King of Prussia, was *streng verboten* to the *Schutzjude* Mendelssohn.

And here we see Mendelssohn from a new angle. Should he give an apology for Judaism, or for his Jewishness? Never! It was Mendelssohn's deepest conviction that Judaism has no need of any defense or of any apology.

Not only Lavater, but also many leading Christians looked eagerly for Mendelssohn's explanation of why he was a Jew—but Mendelssohn is not to be forced to this self-defense. He does not fall into the trap. In 1769 he has not yet published his *Jerusalem* where he shows how *he* and just he can be the philosopher of the *Aufklärung*, still he refuses to accept Lavater's challenge and to write an apology like so many of the apologists of the 19th century. His only answer to Lavater was that he, Lavater, had no right whatever to ask him why he was a Jew. He owed no explanation to any man for being a Jew. Judaism is his formula of existence— and no apology.

One of the greatest offenses to an *Aufklärer* was to have any prejudice (*Vorurteil*). That rationalistic age considered any prejudice as something immoral, as a mistake in logic. Now when Lavater came for a second time and said publicly to Mendelssohn: "Perhaps you are not able to discuss the question 'Christianity or Judaism' because you have prejudices in favor of the belief of your fathers"—how offended and angry became the *Aufklärer* in Mendelssohn. But even this challenge did not work. Mendelssohn answers so unlike an *Aufklärer*, so absolutely non-apologetically: "Whether I am prejudiced in favor of my religion I myself am unable to decide, as little as I can know whether my breath smells badly."

Mendelssohn's Judaism is his breath, something primary, beyond any apology and justification, elementary, natural, whether it pleases his Christian challengers or not. Mendelssohn never cared whether his Judaism pleased the non-Jews or not. He never looked for their approval or approbation. I have looked again and again in the apologetic literature of the 19th and 20th centuries, and failed to find any Jewish apologist of the time of the emancipation, after Mendelssohn's generation, who dared to say what the *Schutzjude* of 1769 said: Judaism is my breath, whether it smells sweetly or badly.

Much more than this: Mendelssohn's system of defense is far removed from the Jewish apologetics in the 19th and 20th centuries. While Jewish apologists usually follow an *a priori* method, Mendelssohn starts a new method, *a posteriori*, if I may say so. While they used to demonstrate the truthfulness, beauty, divinity, and usefulness of Judaism in order to find an apology or justification for a right of existence of Jewry— Mendelssohn followed the opposite way: the very fact of our being Jews should demonstrate the truth of Judaism. Not Judaism qua religion or philosophy justifies the existence of Israel qua nation, people or community, but on the contrary: it is the very existence of Israel which demonstrates the eternal values of Judaism. If we, Israelites—this is the deeper meaning of Mendelssohn's attitude—preserve so eagerly our Judaism under such terrible persecutions, without enjoying the most elementary rights of human beings, if we have gone on for so many generations suffering and existing as Jews, ergo, Judaism is true, is good. Does Judaism need a more powerful proof? Cannot the non-Jewish world be satisfied with it? Why should they always repeat the same: Why are you a Jew?

This kind of non-defending Judaism, this method of stating the very fact of Jewish existence as sufficient— was one of the finest and proudest defenses modern Judaism has ever known. [. . .]

5

Far be it from me to look for any apology for that tragic development of Judaism which took place in Germany after the death of Mendelssohn. But historical justice and scientific truth urge us to draw a dividing line between Mendelssohn and the generation which came after him; they forbid the usual attribution of that decay to Mendelssohn's account.

On the other hand, they are also mistaken who think that the emancipation was responsible for that decay. Emancipation as such can never be blamed—but rather a certain negative destructive ideology which was connected with this emancipation. In commemorating Mendelssohn we must say: Emancipation can never be a kind of a present for which we have to pay, to give up anything that is essential to us, for which we feel obliged to please our "benefactors." Emancipation, political and cultural freedom, are a necessity both for the emancipators and for the emancipated. It is the most elementary duty in national and international life. A society which cannot afford it, which deprives its members or minorities of this elementary right, does not deserve the name of a human society. But we Jews must understand correctly the post-Mendelssohnian development which says: Emancipation alone is not enough! Emancipation must be always backed and supplemented by the maximum of Jewishness, of Jewish life and thought. It must be not only emancipation of the individual, but of the Jewish community as a whole, and this emancipation must be free from any destructive ideology and political illusion.

When we now commemorate Mendelssohn we pay our tribute to one of the leading Jews of the 18th century who was very keen to cultivate this maximum, according to the conditions of his time, the Jew who never stooped to water down his Jewishness, the Jewish philosopher who did not give up anything of this Judaism in order to make it easier to get an *Einlasskarte* (admission ticket), a permit to stay in the world outside. It was this Mendelssohn whose bi-centenary was celebrated on such a great scale in 1929. [. . .]

In 1929 we all thought Mendelssohn belonged to ancient history. Then came the year 1933 and showed us that the political fight of Mendelssohn was to be taken up anew and from a new Jewish position, from a world Jewish reality which is *toto genere* different from that of 1729, the year of his birth, or 1786, the year of his death.

In 1933 ancient history became the burning problem of the day.

In 1933 Mendelssohn was defeated. But not Mendelssohn alone! With him were defeated John Locke, the father of European enlightenment, he and his pupils in France and all over the world, he and all who stood for those human ideals to which Mendelssohn had devoted all his life.

In the fight for scientific truth and human freedom, which can never be separated one from the other, there will never be forgotten the German and Jewish philosopher Mendelssohn who believed with all his heart and soul in a new, free humanity, in freedom and peace for the world and for Jewry.

Other works by Rawidowicz: *Studies in Jewish Thought* (1957); *Iyunim be-mahashevet yisrael*, 2 vols. (1969, 1971); *Israel: The Ever-Dying People and Other Essays* (1986).

YIVO

Established in 1925

Founded in Wilno, Poland, the Yidisher Visenshaftlicher Institut (YIVO) gathered and analyzed a wide range of materials relating to East European Jewry. Some of its material was destroyed by the Nazis, some went to its branch in New York before World War II, and some was recovered in the 1990s.

The World Convention of YIVO (Yiddish Scientific Institute) upon the Tenth Anniversary of Its Founding
1936

Held in Vilna between 14 and 19 August 1935

SEVENTH MEETING, SECOND SCHOLARLY SESSION (SUNDAY, 18 AUGUST, 5:00 P.M.) [1935] [. . .]

Professor Fishl Shneerson (Warsaw): Out of great respect for YIVO I do not want to give the lecture I have prepared on "The Emancipation of Yiddish Scholarship" now; although it is purely academic, it may not be suitable for the contentious atmosphere of this convention. After all, we have gathered to celebrate YIVO, which has had the luck to work in a fiery milieu that reacts strongly to every statement. Even purely academic lectures arouse heated discussions. Gogol's story "Taras Bulba" depicts how Taras tries to fight with his two sons, the Cossacks. But the two sons give their father a good beating, and the more they beat him, the more the father rejoices and cries out, "good Cossacks!"

The activists of YIVO should be pleased that people are not indifferent toward them and they receive beating after beating. This room is filled with good Cossacks!

But let us not forget the most important thing, that YIVO's main task is the emancipation of Yiddish scholarship; this burning question of Jewish world culture is now on the historical agenda.

The process of emancipation, the struggle for national independence, first began in Yiddish literature and then immediately spread to Yiddish pedagogy and public health, and to a variety of research branches. In these fields emancipation has successfully awakened and allowed the expression of the creative powers of the people. Yiddish literature has emerged rapidly and is often translated into other languages; the enormous achievements of Yiddish pedagogy and public health arouse much admiration. Thus, the time has come for the general emancipation of Yiddish scholarship, which is, after all, the basic foundation of the steadily growing Yiddish culture.

But here we are facing an unanticipated difficulty. It turns out that scholarship, which creates methods for all its fields, skipped itself, forgot about itself as a whole. It has not yet given an answer—in fact, it has not even posed the question: how do we instill an appreciation of scholarship in a collective? What are the methods and the principles? And in the case of a newly emerging culture such as ours there is an additional question: does Yiddish scholarship as such already exist? So far there have been individual research projects in some fields—are these nothing more than the work of individuals, or do they constitute the beginnings and part of an organic collective creation?

In the history of scholarship there have been only a few endeavors in this direction. As is well known, the creator of sociology Auguste Comte established the law of the three periods in the development of scholarship (teleological, metaphysical, and empirical). It appears that scholarship has its own, immanent developmental tendencies that one has to take into consideration in the construction of scholarship. We will go a step further. Regardless of how you relate to Comte's much contested division, it is clear that he failed to see the fourth period of the history of scholarship, the current one that can be called the political period. The pull of historical events in the modern period is so strong that scholarship, just like art, must adapt itself, even if only in a very correct, "kosher" way. Not, God forbid, through deceit, as it is done only by the outcasts of scholarship in every regime, but by bringing to the foreground from the numerous equally accepted fields and methods those that are more suited to the given social conditions and by putting better (but not exclusive) emphasis on them.

A second endeavor in this direction was undertaken before the war in Germany by [Hans] Schmidkunz, who established academic pedagogy [*Hochschulpädagogik*] as a separate discipline and gave it the special name *andragogy* (the science of educating adults as opposed to pedagogy, the science of educating children). What Schmidkunz created was only the beginning. We also need to separate the field of popular education [*folksbildung*] or folk andragogy (popular universities, evening courses, etc.), and the most complicated and valuable field, the national pedagogy of scholarship (or, allow me to use such a difficult expression, the natiogogy [*natsyogogik*] of scholarship). This refers to the methods for instilling an appreciation of scholarship in a national collective.

If we look at how scholarship developed among various nations we can inductively establish some principles and tendencies that have practical significance for us, too.

The first principle is the primacy of philology and history within scholarship. It is a fact that language and history are the first weapons of a national culture's emancipation. Philologists and historians are its natural vanguards and spokesmen. Together with all their tremendous accomplishments the latter bring with themselves a dangerous inclination to hypertrophy or one-sided overemphasis on philology and history at the expense of other branches of scholarship. Still in the previous century in Germany, the famous natural scientist Wilhelm Ostwald struggled with the all-powerful philologists who pushed natural science to the sidelines. But in the case of nations that have a state, social conditions are favorable for the development of natural sciences—they are brought to their proper place by real life itself. Minority nations, however, such as Jews and Ukrainians, direct their attention to natural sciences in the ruling culture, whereas in their own culture they let themselves be unilaterally dominated by historical-philological scholarship. This happened at the Ukrainian Society, and the same thing is happening at YIVO, where after ten years of existence there is still no section for public health, whereas pedagogy and psychology are sandwiched together in one of YIVO's four sections.

It is worth recalling a characteristic episode. The first founding meeting of YIVO took place in Berlin, hosted by Shteynberg and attended by Shtif, Lestschinsky, Tsherikover, and myself. When Shtif read out the program, I objected and asked him why he philologized Yiddish scholarship. Lestschinsky's response was: What do you mean? Would you rather that it be psychologized?

But let us inductively highlight the tasks and principles of scholarly emancipation.

The first task is to make scholarship accessible to the people. Equally important is the second task, to make the creative powers of the people fertile for scholarship. The first task is not purely utilitarian, i.e., [the goal is not only] to enlighten the folk masses and arm them with the heavy weaponry of scholarship in their difficult existential struggle. It is no less important that popular education will bring spiritual-intellectual nourishment to the people, awaken and satisfy the higher interests of the folk masses. [. . .] If the natural desire of the soul cannot be satisfied by higher intellectual-spiritual interests, individual and social life will both suffer from neurosis and degeneration. Therefore, *scholarship for the people is not just an ideal to strive for but a requirement of the psychological health of the people.*

The second task, making the creative powers of the people fertile for scholarship, is closely connected to this. It can best be illustrated by the following fact in the history of scholarship: when the English scientist [Humphry] Davy gave popular lectures on science, one of his listeners, a certain [Michael] Faraday, who was a bookbinder by profession, got very interested in his lectures and became an assistant in Davy's laboratory. He learned and developed there, and later became the creator of modern physics. Who knows how many Faradays are in the midst of our folk masses who could be awakened and drawn to scholarship by its emancipation. In short: scholarship for the people will bring the people to scholarship.

We will briefly mention the principles that are in agreement with the above-mentioned tasks. The first step of emancipation pertains to the *vernacular* [*folksshprakh*]. Scholarship must be written in the vernacular of the people, as this will allow scholarship to put down roots into the national ground. [. . .] Not works of Jewish scholars written in various languages, but scholarly works written in Yiddish will further the emancipation of our scholarship. The second principle is *being realistic*. This means that the emerging scholarship should concentrate primarily on those fields that are connected to the life of the people [*folkslebn*], be-

cause only in this way will scholarship take root in the life of the people. That is why we argue that the current issues of Yiddish *schooling (pedagogy), public health, sociological, psychological, and psycho-pathological problems must have their respective sections in YIVO* if the institute wants to be in touch with the totality of the people's life. In connection with this comes the *principle of creativity*, i.e., the stimulus to original creation. On the one hand, an enormous amount of material has been gathered in every field and still awaits scholarly treatment. (There is a well-known saying about the overzealous student who studies so much that he has no time to know anything. The same way, our institutions are so deeply involved in their daily work that they have no time left to process their own findings in a scholarly fashion.) On the other hand, there are enough talented and able-bodied people in every field who should be given access to original scholarly work.

And now we have come to the last important point: the *principle of creativity* cannot, in fact, be realized in a national culture without the decisive step of overcoming "external" authority. Here the national pedagogy (natiogogy) of scholarship encounters the general problems of education. It is natural that every educator inspires authority. Reactionary, compulsory education forces authority upon the people, whereas with free education the authority of the beloved teacher is internally recognized. But every authority restrains creative initiatives—this is the dialectical obverse of education. Shatzky's free educational movement is Russia is actually directed against this suppressive authority, which, according to the law of dialectics, is the essence of education. Thus, he demands "education without an educator." This problem is even more acute with regard to the emerging national scholarship, which initially must adopt and learn a lot from the more advanced nations whose authority will unnoticeably become ingrained and will oppress the creative initiative of the people. Thus, we must set up our own national authority [*folksoytoritet*] against it early on, and we must immediately claim the right to "ordain" our scholars. Prizes should be given not for good translations but for daring original works. From this point of view it is harmful that there are so many external authorities on YIVO's board of directors. Only faith in our own national strength will bring us the glory of national creativity [*folksshafung*] and the true emancipation of Yiddish scholarship. [. . .]

Eighth Meeting

SESSION OF THE CONVENTION (MONDAY, 19 AUGUST, 10:00 A.M.)

Max Weinreich opens the meeting, apologizes for the delay—some of the delegates were busy working in the commissions until 6:00 A.M.; he reads the greetings of several people, among others Professor Korododzhini, Professor Marian Dzięchowski, Sholem Asch, Borukh Glazman, Sh. Niger, Mane Katz, and from Jewish immigrants on their way to South America. *(Applause)* [. . .]

Gershon Pludermakher (Vilna): He begins with the analogy that Yiddish schools are the first floor [of the building] and YIVO is the second floor. The comparison does not hold well. It is more appropriate to say that Yiddish schools and YIVO are children of the same mother. At one time people had planned to create a general cultural center. This mother left behind two children: YIVO and the school system. Until 1925 it was YISHO [the Yiddish school system] that determined Yiddish orthography, represented Yiddishism in the world, and carried out enlightenment work. Ten years ago YIVO took over these functions. It is clear that the two should have established some contact [with each other]. This did not happen, though, and the lack of contact was very harmful. YIVO has not satisfied our cultural needs. For example, YIVO did not create and publish a Yiddish grammar for the Yiddish schools. YIVO activists maintained that this was the task of the teachers, and the teachers thought it was YIVO's job. The result is that children in the Yiddish schools know Polish grammar better than Yiddish grammar. There is a new subject, demography; the textbook for this subject had to be compiled by the teachers themselves. It is necessary to publish an academic edition of the Yiddish classics with explanations for the teachers and the intelligent reader. Due to the lack of such an edition, some teachers have actually suggested taking Mendele out of the curriculum because his works were outdated. But YIVO is not thinking about how to combat such contemptuous attitudes toward our classics because there is no connection between the institutions, for which they are both to blame: YISHO is not active enough to fight for its needs and YIVO is dominated by an aristocratic attitude. YIVO argues that no cheap popular literature should be published—they need to think about publishing good material. This abnormal relationship between YIVO and YISHO must come to an end. The result of this relationship is that the weakest section of YIVO is the Pedagogical-Psychological Section. The secretary of this section, Leibush Lehrer, is in America and does not come here; he has been alienated from us. Every article had to be sent to the other side of the ocean and then back, and then the proofs had to be sent back again. [. . .] At this point Dr. Max Weinreich said that YIVO must be willing to face problems of real life, and it has not been facing the part of life called the Yiddish School Organization.

I suggest that we do not adopt a general resolution such as "we must conduct enlightenment work among the masses" or something similar; instead, we should accept specific proposals. I propose that we establish a section for schooling and education within YIVO. This section's task should be to deliver scholarly services to the schools. YISHO is not in a position to do this even with the best of its intentions. We cannot maintain two separate centers. This new section will have to carry out the suggested work. YIVO must help write the necessary textbooks, publish popular scholarly literature, and publish educational material for the masses about the value of Yiddish. YIVO's work coordinated with YISHO should create the Yiddish cultural center, the [Yiddish] Cultural League [Kultur-lige].

Sh. Bastomski (Vilna): The activists of YIVO are afraid of any kind of criticism. YIVO has grown into an enormous authority in our life, a powerful stronghold. [. . .] You are producing scholarship, but for whom? Take for example the standardized rules of Yiddish spelling that you have adopted. They are very good rules, but Noyekh Prilutski's journal is published in the most outdated orthography. Spelling rules must be enforced. The naturalization of Hebrew words in Yiddish has been introduced sporadically; it has been done in Argentina, for instance, but you are lagging behind, and you are not even trying to explain why you are not carrying out the decision of the spelling conference that took place in 1931. YIVO must be willing to address the real-life needs of the Yiddish-speaking masses and the Yiddish schools. [. . .]

Dr. Yaakov Shatzky: I have heard many complaints against YIVO, but once YIVO's task is clarified, there will be no more complaints. It seems like YIVO has become an institute for remedying social problems. The moment YIVO loses its academic character it loses everything. YIVO is declining, especially in America—both financially and morally. What happened to

YIVO's theological spirit? Where is it now? YIVO's job is not to publish popular literature but to prepare material and research it in a scholarly fashion. No one will launch the kind of complaints against the Ukrainian Academy of Sciences that they have against YIVO. YIVO should be addressing the people's real-life needs! But when this issue was raised by some speakers, the majority of the audience left the lecture hall. (*Interruption: Not true!*) It is true, I saw it myself.

I am in favor of the naturalization of Hebrew, but if it were carried out by YIVO, which does not have state power, it would be a disgraceful failure because such a thing can only be carried out by a state, as it was done in the Soviet Union. Making compromises is a sign of life. When I heard how delegates of YISHO spoke in America I thought I was listening to preachers raising funds for an orphanage.

Yaakov Pat: This is malicious gossip! But I understood them because one often needs to enter into compromises for the sake of the goal. We are not so sensitive, we can listen to criticism, but it should be objective criticism, not demagogic and semi-demagogic assaults.

Y. Shargel (Haifa): I ask that my words not be interpreted as hatred of the country where I come from. I have come on a pilgrimage from Jerusalem to the Jerusalem of Lithuania in order to be rejuvenated, to gain strength, to absorb the atmosphere of this illustrious gathering of Yiddish scholars, writers, and cultural activists about which I have been dreaming for so long. I come from a land where one can be beaten bloody just for speaking Yiddish in public. I come from a land where the bosom buddies of our American friends such as Comrade Shmidt, the Histadrut, passed a law saying that two years after their arrival to the country workers are forbidden to utter a single word in Yiddish, not even if they come to ask for a day of work. I come from a land where one of the most important workers' leaders, Y[itzhak] Ben-Zvi, justified a pogrom carried out at a movie theater just because some Yiddish songs had been sung there. This is how Hebrew writers write about our language in serious Hebrew-language publications over there. (*He reads excerpts from one of R. Zeligman's articles published in* Gilyonot, *in Sivan 5685.*) [. . .]

Yr. Shapiro (Vilna): The demands made on YIVO remind me of the demands made by out-of-town in-laws at a wedding where they did not receive the appropriate honor. Compromises must be made; even Botoshanski agrees with that. YIVO must research the impact of

Hebrew-language education on the Jewish child, and compare the physical development of Jews in the diaspora and in the Land of Israel. When Jews in the diaspora achieve records in sports it is worth researching that topic, too.

Trembovelski (Chortkov [Chortkov/Czortkow, then in Poland, now Ukraine]): You have to live in Galicia in order to understand in what kind of mood we came here to Vilna to this celebration of Yiddish culture. Close to three decades have passed since the Yiddish Language Conference in Chernovitz [today, Chernivtsi, Ukraine], but, just like back then, participants are still divided in their opinions and have an unclear attitude about the struggle for Yiddish and secular Yiddish culture. Those of us who do practical cultural work know full well that without compromises no work can be accomplished. But the compromises should not affect the fundamental essence. The fact that YIVO did not take a stance on the persecution of Yiddish in the Land of Israel and the fight for the secular Yiddish schools in Poland is more than a compromise. YIVO must not be just an institute of Jewish studies in Yiddish. We live in completely different cultural circumstances than other peoples. For us Yiddish is the national attribute and YIVO is the world Yiddish cultural center; as such, YIVO must be the final judge in all questions and problems that have to do with Yiddish creativity and Jewish life in Yiddish. [. . .]

Dr. E. Ringelblum (Warsaw): A. Tsherikover criticized Dr. R. Mahler because the Marxist line was missing from his work *Der tsol-register fun 16tn yorhundert* [The Customs Register of the Sixteenth Century]. And yet Dr. Mahler does have a Marxist influence on young historians. It is due only to Mahler that we have today in Poland a whole array of Marxist intellectuals. At the International Congress of Historians in Warsaw, Mahler's lecture was the center of interest. The difference between Marxists and non-Marxists is not what topics they work on. A study of the customs register can utilize the Marxist approach, too. We are not against working together with intellectuals whose approach is different; we need to stay in touch even with Western European Jewish historians. It is regrettable that we are not in contact with historians in the Soviet Union. It is impossible to research the history of Jews in Poland without being familiar with the archives over there. Now some closer relations are becoming possible. There is a commission whose task is researching social movements during the nineteenth and twentieth centuries. This Polish commission is part of an international commission active within the International Historians' Commission, the initiator of the Congress of Historians. [. . .]

The Polish commission is currently working on two [*sic*] areas:

1) Registering archival materials of social content from the second half of the nineteenth century; 2) collecting materials regarding the strikes in Poland starting in the 1880s; 3) collecting materials from workers' correspondence that have been published in the workers' press.

Thus, cooperation with the Soviet Union will be very fruitful.

Popularization work does have to be carried out, and in an organized fashion. In this regard I do not agree with Shatzky. Popularization will stimulate research. [. . .]

Yaakov Pat: [. . .] During the discussion there has been criticism of the delegates of YIVO and the elements they represent. Mr. Reisen rebuked us for not doing enough for YIVO and therefore we have no right to criticize. In fact, we are doing the same work but in two different cultural sectors. Since we represent the secular Yiddish school system in Poland, we do have a right to voice our concerns here. The existing popular libraries [*folks-biblyotekn*], popular universities [*folks-universitetn*], thousands of cultural events (throughout the year), lectures—these are all the achievement of the same sector. Thus, Mr. Reisen's reproach was inappropriate. Here you have heard the statements of a whole array of old cultural activists—you should listen to what they are saying. If they have complaints, it is a sign that the complaints are justified. The question is: What is YIVO's character? When our ancestors created Wissenschaft des Judentums, Jewish culture—they were directed by the *shekhinah*, a divine light. Ahad Ha'am followed a divine light, too—the survival of the Jewish people. But what is your guiding principle? What inspires you? YIVO's guiding principle should be none other than the *shekhinah* of socialism . [. . .]

G. Urinski (Pruzhene [today, Pruzhany, Brest region, Belarus]): [. . .] The persecution of Yiddish in the Land of Israel has been much talked about here. But YIVO has not protested against the pogrom on Yiddish in Poland, either. You should know that children in the Tarbut schools are raised not only with the hatred of Yiddish but of culture in general (*Interjection: Not true! Applause.*) We are going to survive these difficult times

because we are working with faith, but we have to plan and set objectives for our work. The Yiddish school system is in a disastrous situation because of the dire shortage of Yiddish studies teachers.

Engineer M. Shrayber (Vilna) delivers greetings from the Association of Jewish Engineers in Vilna and the Yiddish Technical School of ORT. During its short fifteen years of existence the technical school was possibly the first to produce technical literature in Yiddish, and YIVO played an extraordinary role in this. The speaker describes this one-and-only Jewish technical school in Poland where the language of instruction is Yiddish. It is modeled on the most famous technical schools in Germany; nevertheless, it is not a copy but an original, completely Jewish learning institution, adjusted to the conditions of Jewish life and the situation of Jewish youth in those countries where graduates of the school may be placed to make use of the knowledge they had acquired. A special, broad program had to be designed, both theoretical and practical; they had to produce the necessary textbooks in Yiddish, and build a whole array of mechanical and electro-technical workshops. All this has been achieved with fifteen years of hard work . [. . .]

Sh. Mendelson: [. . .] It is impossible to build culture in Poland without a cultural struggle. More than sixty schools have been closed, and more than half a million subsidies cut. If you give this some thought, you will understand why we are so nervous. We, the entire delegation of YISHO, did not come here to cause bad blood, but because we noticed that the feelings of the workers toward YIVO were cooling and we are afraid that YIVO might lose its attractiveness to the entire Jewish population. We are one organism, and if one part is sick, it poses a danger for the entire organism. We have been accused of coming here to stick a rod into the wheel of the wagon, but when the wagon is going downhill, it is a good thing to do that.

Dr. M. Sudarsky (Kovno): YIVO is facing too many demands. People want YIVO to be everything: an academy, an educational institute, a pedagogical seminar. All these institutions are necessary, but the possibilities are limited. I can understand the feelings of the teachers and cultural activists who work under such unbearable conditions. But YIVO must limit itself to scholarly work. Professor Fishl Shneerson made a good joke: the caretaker of the synagogue flogs every member of the community with whom he is angry once a year. Here it

is the other way round: every member of the community gathered here in order to beat the caretaker. Everybody sinned against YIVO. Scholars were compelled to
tear themselves away from their work in order to raise
funds—this should not have been allowed to happen.
People should have sent in their contributions voluntarily. And the same applies to the Yiddish schools.
Very few people are concerned with and provide for
Yiddish culture; thus, everyone bears responsibility for
our cultural downfall. When everyone comes together
to support the institute, the difficulties will be eliminated and there will be no more complaints. [. . .]

Yoysef Aronovitsh (Vilna): [. . .] I am in favor of
Mr. Virgili-Kahan's position according to which the
institute must stand on a broad foundation, but the
coalition must be supported by friends of the working
class, and the interests of the working class must be of
primary concern. We do not require any partisan allegiances, but we must always keep the working class in
mind. [. . .]

Noyekh Prilutski: If YIVO weren't an independent
organization but a state academy, only scholars and
guests would be attending this meeting. But we also
have delegates here. From a certain point of view this
is a democratic phenomenon. But this brought about a
situation where our nonscholarly friends keep demanding various things from YIVO. People come to YIVO
like they go to the rebbe. They launch their criticism
uncritically. Are the activists of YIVO magicians? Is
YIVO in a position to do anything when schools are
closed? The activists of YIVO understand that what
they do must produce tangible benefits. A cultural
struggle [kultur-kamf] is taking place, and YIVO is the
staff headquarters. If the headquarters is hit, all is ruined. As our highest cultural position, YIVO must be
taboo, armed, and must not mix directly into the political struggle.

Translated by Vera Szabó.

Ben-Zion Dinur

1884-1973

Born Ben-Zion Dinaburg into a traditional home in
a small Ukrainian town, the yeshiva-educated future
historian was an autodidact in secular subjects. He
received advanced training as a historian in Berlin
and Bern and sailed to Mandate Palestine in 1921.

He found employment teaching Jewish history at the
Hebrew Teachers Seminary in Jerusalem, where he
remained for almost thirty years, producing a stream
of books, articles, and reviews. In 1932, he also began
teaching modern Jewish history at the Hebrew University, but on a part-time basis. He was not appointed
to a professorship until 1948. He is best known for his
multivolume series, *Yisrael ba-golah*, a collection of
primary sources for the study of Jewish history over
the centuries. More than other Jerusalem-based historians of his generation, he emphasized the centrality
of the Land of Israel in every period of Jewish history,
arguing that the urge to return to the Land was always
the driving force of its history.

The Modern Period in Jewish History: Its Distinctiveness, Essence, and Shape
1937

1

The terms "recent generations" or "modern times"
are commonly employed to denote the period of history which is close to us not only in time, but also in
character—in its material circumstances, philosophical
outlook, and general view of life. The problems which
exercised the people of that period, the goals which
they set themselves and the methods by which they
sought to attain them, are all readily intelligible to us,
precisely because they are so similar to our own views,
aspirations, and ways of action. That is why the history
of these recent generations can truly be called modern
history, since in them the past imperceptibly merges
with the present by the very nature of the historical
circumstances. However, when it comes to determining the beginning of modern Jewish history, we find
that scholarly opinion is divided. Until very recently,
the generally accepted theories of Jewish historiogra-
phers on "modern times" in Jewish history were based
on the views of Graetz and Dubnow, both as explicitly
expressed in the remarks of these historians on these
times and as evident in the general historiographical
structure of their works, and also as implied by the
whole tenor of their writing about this period. Some
scholars adopted Graetz's method and began the modern period of Jewish history from the second half of the
eighteenth century (1750), while others followed Dubnow in dating the beginning of this period to the time

of the French Revolution at the end of the eighteenth century (1789). The difference between these two views stems from two different estimates of the character of "the new type of Jew." Was he the Europeanized Jewish intellectual with the new modern outlook or the recently emancipated citizen whose equal status was officially recognized by the state? The year 1750 is the date of one of the first public manifestations of the *Haskalah*, the Enlightenment movement associated with the name of Moses Mendelssohn: in this year Mendelssohn started to publish, in Berlin, the Hebrew journal *Kehillat Musar*, in which he proclaimed the need for the cultural enlightenment of the Jewish masses. To Graetz's way of thinking, the character of modern Jewish life has been determined, in the main, by the *Haskalah* movement, which, in the lifetime of its most important representative, also became a kind of symbol of the whole course of Jewish history in recent times as a steady, continuous ascent from humiliation and degradation to that self-recognition and self-respect the growth of which characterizes the fourth and latest phase in Jewish history (the preceding three being the time of the First Temple, the time of the Second Temple, and the period from the destruction of the Second Temple down to 1750). This "self-recognition" found expression in two great movements which have together determined the character of "modern" Jewish history: "Enlightenment" and "Emancipation."

Of these two, the Enlightenment was first in time and importance. *Haskalah* was not only a matter of the Jews adopting the languages of the states under whose rule they happened to be living and of the peoples in whose midst they dwelt, nor yet of their acquiring the modern culture which enabled them to meet their antagonists on equal terms. Historically speaking, *Haskalah* was essentially a process of inner liberation and spiritual purification from which resulted all the achievements of Jewry in the fields of education and teaching, science and literature, social organization and religious reform. All the changes that occurred in the inner life of the Jews were inseparably bound up with the various aspects of the growth of Jewish self-recognition and self-respect—in the emergence of free thought and the awakening of scientific criticism, the widening of general knowledge and the development of Jewish studies, the aesthetic quest to improve taste and style and the attempts made by a rationalistic theology to modernize the forms of divine worship. Emancipation itself was also an outcome

of a form of recognition—the gentiles' legal and social recognition of Jewish equality. This recognition enabled the Jews to develop their potential powers and to enter fully into the economic, cultural, social, and political life of the gentile nations. The phase of growing Jewish self-knowledge thus begins with Mendelssohn's first public activities.

In the opinion of other scholars, however, Emancipation is the decisive fact in modern Jewish history. It was the new social status of the Jews that determined both the content and scope of modern Jewish life and the mutual relations, based on joint participation in the cultural and civic fields, which now developed between Jews and non-Jews; and it was this status that also changed the direction of the individual Jew's way of thinking and the content of his intellectual awareness, by releasing him from the confines of his own narrow world and making him a citizen of modern European culture. On this view, too, the character of modern Jewry has been determined by two movements: the one for emancipation, including all the efforts made by the Jews in modern times to obtain full civic and social equality in the modern state; and the other for assimilation, as manifested in all the great activity, both individual and communal, in this period that was aimed at reducing the specifically Jewish content of Jewish life, and at bringing about the greatest possible merging of the Jews with the peoples in whose midst they dwelt and deepening their sense of national, social, and spiritual identity with them. But the first in time and importance of these two movements was the one for emancipation, which determined the whole spiritual development of Jewry in these years. Assimilation was only, so to speak, a social and cultural reflection of emancipation; and the nationalist awakening came in a period of political reaction, when the Jews banded together in self-defense. The struggle between emancipation and reaction is thus paralleled by the struggle between assimilation and nationalism; and these two conflicts in fact constitute the whole content of modern Jewish history. It is therefore the historical course of the movement for emancipation that determines the different phases of Jewish history in modern times.

2

However, the prevailing view of more recent scholarship is that the beginning of the "modern period" in

Jewish history should be pushed back much further. The arguments for this earlier dating are clear enough. For, even if it is agreed that Enlightenment and Emancipation were the two most important and significant phenomena in the life of modern Jewry, it will still not be correct to identify the beginning of the *Haskalah* with the work of Mendelssohn, and the beginning of the Emancipation with the French Revolution. It is true, of course, that the *Haskalah* movement aimed at making the Jews of the day aware of the need for a purely rationalistic reappraisal of historical realities, and even attempted such a reappraisal of its own, on the basis of which it advocated that Jewish life and education should be brought into line with the requirements of reason and the demands of the time. It is also true that the *Haskalah* sought to reform educational methods and to improve public and domestic conduct, challenged the absolute spiritual authority of religious tradition, and even went so far as to pour scorn on time-honored customs and to repudiate accepted beliefs. Nevertheless, from the historical standpoint, it is not true that these revolutionary changes in Jewish life were brought about by the searching criticism of the *Haskalah*. Indeed, the exact opposite is the case: it was only after the foundations of traditional Jewish life had already been shaken that they also began to be subjected to rationalistic criticism. It was the collapse of the whole structure of Jewish beliefs and values that led to the individual Jew's self-effacement vis-à-vis the gentile world, thus leaving that whole generation of Jews all too ready to be influenced by the cultures of the nations amongst whom they lived, to steep themselves in their opinions and outlooks, and to adopt their manners and ways of life. It was only after this new feeling of life had penetrated into certain circles of the upper strata of Jewish society, and only after the elements of this different outlook on the world had taken root in their hearts, that another attitude to the religious tradition and the accepted Jewish way of life made itself felt. Then it was that the *Haskalah* also appeared on the scene as a social movement whose watchword was rationalistic criticism. The aim of this criticism was thus to rebuild a world that was already in the process of being destroyed. It is therefore historically correct to date the beginnings of the *Haskalah* movement back to the processes that led to the collapse of the inner world of Judaism. The origins of these processes are rooted in the failure of the Sabbatai Zevi movement, and their most striking symptoms had,

by the first half of the eighteenth century, become part of the normal phenomena of Jewish life.

The same is true of Jewish Emancipation. This is not to be regarded merely as a matter of political proclamation, or juridical principle, or civil courtesy. Like the movement for Jewish Enlightenment, Emancipation also comprises the whole complex of the processes by which the Jews became an organic part of the economic, civic, cultural, and political fabric of the nations among whom they lived and the states in which they dwelt. And the origins of these processes, as has been conclusively proved by the most recent historical research, go back ultimately to the vital functions performed by the Jews in organizing the economies of the modern nation-states, functions which in fact had already become part of the normal features of Jewish life by the first half of the eighteenth century. Not a few able and enterprising Jews rose to positions of power and amassed great wealth. The secular rulers needed them for their experience and advice, their practical efficiency and organizational talent. Whether these Jews were purveyors of military supplies or procurers of loans, minters of coins or financial agents, jewel merchants or "court" speculators, traders or industrialists—or practised all these occupations simultaneously—they were in every case always firmly entrenched in the secular life of the State. The great majority of them, it is true, contented themselves with the economic power and royal favor that they enjoyed, and frequently sought to demonstrate their aloofness from political affairs. But, even so, the economic position occupied in the state by this upper stratum of the Jewish community was an augury for the future, the first step in the full integration of the Jews into the life of their host nations. Moreover, the fate of these few "great Jews" was itself of very great general historical significance. Take, for example, the well-known case of Süss Oppenheimer, the financial agent of the Duke of Würtemberg, who rose from being a subordinate taxfarmer to the position of chief political advisor, and even tried to draw conclusions from this meteoric rise with regard to his own way of life and his conduct in non-Jewish society, only to end his days on the gallows. His life-story not only illustrates the actual nature of the "integration" of this stratum of "great Jews" into the fabric of the secular state, but also brings out the tension of the struggle which, already in those early days, was inseparable from this process. Much the same lesson may also be learned from the story, a few decades earlier, of the checkered career of Samuel Oppenheimer in Vienna.

This rise of the upper stratum of the Jewish community marks the beginning of "modern times" in Jewish history, since it provided the social framework both for the growth of the *Haskalah* movement and for the first stirrings in Jewry of the struggle for emancipation.

3

There are also other reasons for putting back the beginning of the modern period in Jewish history to the first part of the eighteenth century. "Enlightenment" and "emancipation" are far from exhausting the whole content of the historical reality of Jewish life in modern times, even if we use these terms in their widest possible sense and attribute to the power and influence of these two movements both the radical change in the professional composition of Jewry that occurred in these generations, and also the social, cultural, and political awakening of the Jewish masses and their emergence as an active new factor in determining the nation's destiny in this period. A historiographical approach that regards the enlightenment and the emancipation as the central features of modern Jewish history entirely fails to take account of, or at least relegates into the background, some of the most important aspects of Jewish life in modern times, those very aspects in which the "historical activity" of Jewry in those times was in fact most intensely displayed. The rise of the great new centers of Jewish population that came into being in this period in Russia, North America, and Palestine, where, in a short span of years, masses of Jews were concentrated in unprecedented numbers; the origin, growth, and spread of Hassidism which, in the mass appeal of its religious revivalism, the persistence of its influence and the effectiveness of its organization, had for generations had no parallel in Jewish history; the movement of "revolt against the *Galut* (Exile)" which, during the last sixty years, has gradually and steadily spread to all sections of the Jewish people, renewing its political and cultural unity, and rousing it to acts and achievements such as had not been performed by Jews since the beginning of the Dispersion, and which changed the whole character of the nation—all these vital developments do not, according to the accepted historiographical viewpoint, constitute the framework of modern Jewish history; indeed, they are not even in the mainstream, so to speak, of this period and can only be brought into it by the *Haskalah* and Emancipation movements.

Such a historical point of view is obviously untenable. The beginning of the modern period in Jewish history cannot be fixed without due attention being paid to the first halting-places in the mass migration of Jews, which had already started from the centers of Jewish population in eastern Europe and the countries of Islam in the early part of the eighteenth century, with the first clear indications of the approaching decline and extinction of those centers. Nor can the limits of this period be determined without proper note being taken of the beginnings of Hassidism, which developed out of the inner disintegration of the communal structure of Polish Jewry as a result of the crisis through which the latter passed in the first part of the same century. And account must also be taken of the appearance at this time of the first proponents of the revolt against the *Galut*, orthodox Messianists who, undaunted by the failure of messianic mysticism, persevered determinedly in their search for new ways of bringing nearer the redemption and finding an outlet for their pent-up messianic energies. [...]

5

Modern Jewish history begins with the immigration to Palestine of one thousand Jews led by Rabbi Judah the Pious [He-Ḥasid] in the year 1700. The great significance of this act for the vital content of Jewish history in those times does not lie only in the symbolical value of this organized mass immigration to the Holy Land under the leadership of a prophet of redemption, himself a religious rebel against the *Galut*, as a portent for the future, a pointer to generations whose historical experience was largely one of mass revolts and mass migrations in search of national salvation. Of no less importance were the causes of this immigration, the way in which it was organized, and the nature and consequences of its failure, all of them signs of the twilight of the Middle Ages and the dawn of the modern era.

Following as it did on the decline of the Sabbatai Zevi movement, this immigration not only demonstrated the persistence of the messianic ferment and the continuity of "the boundless yearning" to hasten the redemption in every possible way; it also marked the beginning of a more realistic course of messianic activity, which made it possible to keep alive the eagerness for redemption in the common people's hearts by finding for it forms of expression that could be unquestionably accepted into the fabric of Jewish life. The immigration of pious, God-fearing and observant Jews, and the resettlement of the Land of Israel by their labors, now came to be regarded as a necessary preliminary to the redemption of the whole nation. The immigration of this first organized group prepared the way for all the waves of immigration that followed during the next hundred and seventy years. Immigration to Palestine, by separate individuals and whole groups, henceforward became a very common phenomenon. Particularly numerous amongst the immigrants were great Sages of the Law and famed Kabbalists, many from the important congregations of the Western Diaspora but some also from the remote and isolated Oriental communities. Their total number ran into hundreds. From their ranks subsequently came those emissaries from the Land of Israel who worked to spread a greater awareness of the importance of the *Yishuv* for the whole of Jewry and its vital role in hastening the redemption, and thereby to increase the influence of the *Yishuv* and strengthen its spiritual authority over the communities of the Diaspora.

Every one of these groups of immigrants had to pass through a period of great hardship in establishing itself in the country; and at the same time, the resulting growth in the population of the Yishuv still further increased its economic difficulties and made it urgently necessary to organize the financial assistance provided by the Diaspora communities on an efficient and permanent basis (the *Halukah*). The result of this dual effort was the steady growth of the old *Yishuv*—the Jewish population dwelling within the walls of the "four towns" (Jerusalem, Hebron, Safed, and Tiberias)—which in modern times exercised a kind of magnetic attraction over all those men of vision who refused to bow to the prevailing trends and could not come to terms with the new spirit of nihilism and atheism which was sweeping through the whole world, and from which Judaism too was not exempt. By its devoted preservation of this special character, the old *Yishuv* became a new and very influential factor in the strengthening of the physical bonds between the nation and its land, to an extent unequalled for many generations. However, this extreme conservatism of the old *Yishuv* was not the sole characteristic of the early groups of religious immigrants, any more than asceticism was the only dominant trend amongst them. There were also other elements and other sects, including even "the Sabbatians," heretical followers of Sabbatai Zevi who regarded the

abolition of all religious prohibitions and restrictions as the first step towards bringing about the nation's redemption. These other circles also had no small influence at first, even in Jerusalem, though they were not able to maintain themselves there for long and most of them eventually left the country, while some even adopted Islam. Nevertheless, when these emigrants returned to Europe they created a considerable stir there. Only a few of them abandoned Judaism and cut themselves off from their people completely. Of the remaining majority, some joined the underground followers of Sabbatai Zevi and helped to direct their propaganda, thus reinforcing the active opposition in the various congregations to the established religious and social leadership; while others, by encouraging the spread of a laxer approach to the observance of the practical commandments, still further increased the disregard of the rabbinical authorities already prevalent in wide circles of Jewry. Both these developments formed an integral and important part of the whole spiritual environment that gave rise to the *Haskalah* movement as the dominant force in Jewish life in the Diaspora. The symbolic significance of the immigration to Palestine of Rabbi Judah the Pious and his group of followers as marking the beginning of modern Jewish history is thus not merely historical and ideological, but must be considered, both in conception and execution, in its social and physical aspects too. Seen from this standpoint, it was an ideological and social expression of the *Wanderlust* that had already gripped considerable sections of East European Jewry who, feeling their whole existence as Jews threatened, especially in Poland, by a growing sense of territorial and physical insecurity and fear of the morrow, began a mass migration to the countries of central and western Europe, entering these lands and filtering into their Jewish communities, despite all the legal and physical obstacles placed in their way. Hence, Rabbi Judah's immigration to Palestine also symbolically marks the beginning of the migratory movement of Jews that is to be regarded as one of the most distinctive characteristics of Jewish history in modern times.

There was also something entirely new in the fact that this was an *organized* immigration; and both the nature and the purpose of its organization also mark the opening of the modern era in Jewish history. Neither the existing Jewish congregation nor the authorized institutions of Jewry played any part in the planning and execution of the whole enterprise, which was carried out entirely by a new grouping of social elements brought into being by a common ideology. This is the first full-scale instance of the unifying, dynamic force of "ideology," which was to play such an important part in the whole course of modern Jewish history, from the first bands of *Hassidim* down to the organized political parties of our own day. This first organized group of immigrants did not fall apart on its arrival in Palestine, but remained knit together and formed a new community or congregation, a new social unit, which was headed not by rabbis or communal leaders, but by *Hassidim*, men whose authority was derived from the power of their own personality and was never a matter for dispute. The immigration of the group was made possible by the help that it received from various Diaspora communities and from wealthy and influential individuals in them, and also by the great moral support given it by the Jewish masses. This popular sympathy was due both to the personal influence of the "leader" (Rabbi Judah the Pious) and to the opposition to official Jewry implicit in the whole enterprise. Here is the prototype of the hassidic "congregation of the pious" and "community of the righteous," which Rabbi Judah's group closely resembled not only in name, but also in form of organization. A further feature of this *aliyah*, which is of symbolic significance for the modern era in Jewish history, is its "pan-Jewishness." The original members of the group, who came from Poland, were joined by immigrants from Germany, Hungary, and Moravia, and assistance was provided by many congregations in Germany, Austria, Holland, and Turkey.

No other event of that time was destined to have such a deep and lasting effect on all the different paths subsequently followed by Jewish history in modern times as this immigration, the starting-point of the many and varied highways and byways that have led to the heights and depths, the glories and tragedies of this decisive, turbulent and tortured period.

Translated by Merton B. Degut.

Other works by Dinur: *Yisrael be-artso* (1938); *Be-mifneh ha-dorot* (1955); *Be 'olam she-shaka* (1958); *Dorot u-reshumot* (1978).

Yehezkel Kaufmann

1889–1963

The Ukrainian-born historian of ancient Israel Yehezkel Kaufmann immigrated to the Land of Israel in

1928. He taught at the Reali School in Haifa for more than twenty years and then, in 1949, was appointed professor of biblical studies at the Hebrew University, where he trained a generation of biblical scholars. While he was a master of modern biblical criticism, he was critical of its Christian biases, especially its tendency to downplay the originality of Israelite religion. This is one of the central motifs in his eight-volume history of Judaism from biblical antiquity to the Second Temple (1937–1957), of which there is only a one-volume condensed translation (1960).

The Religion of Israel: From Its Beginnings to the Babylonian Exile
1937

Chapter 1. The Basic Problem

If one examines the biblical account of the origins of Israelite monotheism and the story of its battle with and eventual triumph over paganism, he will discover a strange fact: the Bible is utterly unaware of the nature and meaning of pagan religion.

The pre-exilic age was, according to the witness of the Bible, the age of Israelite "idolatry." The people repeatedly backslid and worshiped the "other gods" of the nations round about. Biblical literature is dedicated to fight "idolatry," and biblical law, prophecy, and poetry have all left an abundant record of this generations-long battle. Biblical scholars of all shades of opinion have therefore assumed, as a matter of course, that the biblical age was intimately acquainted with paganism. No one, apparently, has ever doubted this assumption or criticized it in the light of the date. It is taken for granted that the biblical age knew the god-beliefs of the pagans and their myths, for were these not part and parcel of the idolatry of Israel? The war upon idolatry is presumed to have struck at the myths as well: monotheism prevailed as Israel's evolving religious consciousness triumphed over pagan mythological beliefs. The time and manner of this victory are the subject of debate among scholars. But it is agreed on every hand that during the biblical period mythological polytheism was prevalent in Israel as elsewhere and that biblical religion proper came into being only gradually as the product of the great struggle against it.

There is, of course, no question that Israelite religion and paganism are historically related; both are stages in the religious evolution of man. Israelite religion arose at a certain period in history, and it goes without saying that its rise did not take place in a vacuum. The Israelite tribes were heirs to a religious tradition which can only have been polytheistic. The religion of YHWH could take hold of the people only after overcoming the ancient faith, and the fossil remains of pagan notions that have been preserved in the Bible testify that it was never wholly eradicated. But what was the nature of this upheaval and what do we know of its history? The study of biblical religion hinges on the answer to this question.

Studies of the origin of biblical religion inquire after the extent to which the popular religion, and even the votaries of YHWH at first, recognized the existence of other gods. It is commonly assumed that the religion of YHWH began as henotheism or monolatry, recognizing him as sole legitimate god in Israel, but acknowledging the existence of other national gods. This stage is said to be attested to in the biblical record. The problem is then posed: when did the idea arise that not only was Israel's worship of other gods illegal, but that those gods had no reality whatsoever; i.e., when did henotheism or monolatry become monotheism?

This view is founded on the tacit assumption that the pagan gods were conceived of identically by both Israelite and pagan. The passage from the earlier to the later stage is taken as the repudiation of the pagan idea of the reality of the gods. But what does the Bible itself tell us concerning the Israelite conception of the nature of these gods and the nature of their worship?

The pagan conceives of the gods as powers embodied in nature, or as separate beings connected with nature in some fashion. Deification of cosmic forces provides the soil for the growth of mythology. Popular religion conceives of the gods as persons who inhabit the entire universe and are related in specific ways to each other and to men. They are the heroes of popular myths, the subjects of epic poets; to them temples are built, monuments and images erected. In the cult, material objects usually play an important part, the natural or manufactured object being taken as the bearer of divine power, the dwelling place of deity, or its symbol. While worship of material objects is not an essential feature of paganism, it is its natural outgrowth. Homage is done to the god through the care given to his image. The cult of images is thus intimately bound up with the belief in personal gods, who have specific forms, who inhere in natural phenomena or control them.

The polytheism of the ancient Near East during biblical times was highly developed. Its gods and goddesses appear in literature, art, and culture in fairly standardized forms, which were presumably familiar not only to the clergy but to the laity as well. There are gods of sky and earth, of life, love, and fertility, of death and destruction. The gods have specific roles. There are gods of light and darkness, of thunder and lightning, of wind and rain, of fire and water. Mountains, springs, rivers, and forests have their gods also. The gods have sexual qualities, the existence of male and female deities being essential to pagan thought. These characteristics serve as the material for elaborate myths in which the histories and adventures of the gods are related. Theogonies tell of their birth and lineage. Myths tell of their wars, loves, hatreds, and dealings with men. The cult is closely connected with these myths, which are the vital core of priestly and, in a measure, of popular religion.

What would we know of this had we no other source than the Bible?

The Bible knows that the pagans worship national gods, certain of whom are mentioned by name: Baal, Ashtoreth, Chemosh, Milcom, Bel, Nebo, Amon, etc. But it is remarkable that not a single biblical passage hints at the natural or mythological qualities of any of these named gods. Had we only the Bible, we should know nothing of the real nature of the "gods of the nations." In a few isolated passages the pagans are said to worship spirits and demons, but these are anonymous, whereas what we know to have been mythological gods are, in the Bible, mere names. Not a trace remains of the rich store of popular myths associated with these names.

The Bible has a great deal to say about the image cult that was associated with the named gods. But if the god is not understood to be a living, natural power, or a mythological person who dwells in, or is symbolized by, the image, it is evident that the image worship is conceived to be nothing but fetishism.

A few passages permit the inference that the nations worship living gods. Thus in the ancient poem of Numbers 21:29 (cf. Jer. 48:46), Chemosh may be represented as active. Jephthah too speaks of Chemosh as if he gave the land to the Ammonites (Judg. 11:24). Belief in a living god Baal may be alluded to in the story of Judges 6:25-32, telling of Gideon's destruction of his altar. Elijah's taunts also represent Baal, if only mockingly, as a living god (I Kings 18:27). Similarly I Kings 20:28 has the pagans speak of gods of the valleys and of the mountains, if indeed only with reference to the God of Israel. Apart from this we find the notion that later became widespread among Hellenistic Jews (and passed from them to the Christians) that the gods of the nations are spirits or demons (Deut. 32:16 f.; Ps. 106:37). It must be stressed, however, that this is a vaguely generalized conception; no named god of the Bible is so represented. In the above-cited passages the gods of the nations are alluded to not merely as cult objects, but as active beings, whether so in reality or only in the minds of the heathen. Although it is possible that in some a mere personification of idols is intended, there can be no doubt that in a few there is the suggestion that the pagans worship not only idols but gods and spirits as well.

Biblical writers are also aware of the pagans' belief that their idols have the power to act. The pagans worship and sacrifice to idols hoping to receive benefit and aid from them.

We have now arrived at the limit of the Bible's knowledge of the nature of pagan belief. We find no clear conception of the roles the gods play in nature and in the life of man. No cognizance is taken of their mythological features. The named gods are characterized only by the nations that worship them: "Ashtoreth, god of the Sidonians," "Milcom, the abomination of the Ammonites," "Chemosh, the abomination of Moab," and so forth. No god is ever styled according to his function or place in the pantheon, as so often occurs in the literatures of Egypt, Mesopotamia, and Canaan. Nor is the sexual differentiation of the gods ever alluded to; gods and goddesses are both comprised under the masculine rubric *'elōhīm* (e.g., "Ashtoreth, the god of [*'elōhē*] the Sidonians"), there being, in fact, no word in biblical Hebrew for "goddess."

Observe now what is said regarding the worship of the "host of heaven." Several of the named gods—Ashtoreth (Ishtar), Bel, Marduk, Nebo, etc.—are known from pagan sources to have been astral deities, yet not once does the Bible connect them with the worship of the "host of heaven." The "host" and the idols (i.e., the name-bearing images) are always treated as two distinct classes of pagan deities. Thus Deuteronomy 4:16–18 first forbids worshipping images of any animal, winged or earthbound, following this (vs. 19) with a separate prohibition of the worship of sun, moon, and host of heaven. Again the sun, moon, and host of heaven are repeatedly listed alongside of—not as identical with— "other gods" (17:3; Jer. 19:13). Thus, too, the "queen of heaven" (Jer. 44:17 f.; apparently, the moon) is never identified in the Bible with Ashtoreth or any other de-

ity that the Bible knows by name. And although Ezekiel sees the elders bowing down "eastward to the sun," he fails to link this solar cult with that of the "idols of Israel" which he saw just before (Ezek. 8:16). Nor does he give any hint that this deified sun bears any of the personal mythological traits of the Assyro-Babylonian Shamash. What the Bible calls the "worship of the host of heaven" it apparently understands to be the cult of the heavenly bodies as such. It knows of no connection between the "host of heaven" and the named gods whose idol-worship it condemns.

The mythological motifs that are found in the Bible are considered evidence of pagan influence on Israelite religion during biblical times. The question here is this: Did Israel, after the rise of the religion of YHWH, take over the myths of the pagans along with their idols? The fact is that the Bible recognizes no mythological motifs as foreign, pagan. In all the legends and allusions with such motifs YHWH is the only active divine being. There are no active foreign gods. There are allusions to battles that YHWH fought with primeval creatures such as Rahab and his "helpers," the dragon, Leviathan, and the fleeing serpent (Isa. 51:9; Pss. 74:14; 89:11; Job 9:13; 25:12 f.), but these are not considered by biblical writers as pagan concepts (whatever be their true historical derivation). They belong to Israel's stock of legends, and may well be a legacy of pre-Israelite times. Such creatures appear in Israelite legends—but never Tiamat, Marduk, Hadad, or the like. The myths of the pagans are not even derided as idle tales, as fabrications, nor are they utilized in poetic figures. No foreign god is counted among the enemies of YHWH. Quite remarkable is the fact that precisely in the creation legends (Gen. 1–11), where the bulk of mythological matter is imbedded, paganism is entirely absent; primeval man knows only the god YHWH. In sum, then, there is no evidence that the writers were conscious of any connection between the mythological motifs imbedded in their narratives and the pagan gods.

These phenomena go too deep and are too pervasive to be explained merely as monotheistic reworking. Moreover, while monotheism could not acknowledge the divinity of the pagan gods, it need not have denied them legendary roles. We have seen that occasionally the Bible does allow them the status of demons; these might have been permitted to play the part of evil spirits or enemies of YHWH. A battle with Bel and Nebo as demons is no more damaging to the unity of God than a battle with Rahab or the dragon. Later

Judaism saw no harm in stories of God's battles with rebellious angels.

This is not to say that the Bible knows of no battles of YHWH with the "gods of the nations." Indeed, YHWH does battle with them and "works judgments" upon them. But in every case the objects of his fury are the idols, as we shall see. These complementary phenomena can only be explained on the assumption that the biblical age no longer knew pagan mythology.

The Gods of the Nations in the Narratives

Just as no foreign god is active in the creation stories, so no god other than YHWH ever appears at work in Israel's early history or in the battles between Israel and its neighbors. YHWH fights Israel's enemies, but no god ever appears as his living antagonist; when the Bible tells us of YHWH's battles with foreign gods, it is always idols that are meant.

Thus YHWH "works judgments" on the "gods of Egypt" (Exod. 12:12; Num. 33:4), and similar expressions are to be found elsewhere (e.g., Isa. 46:1, with regard to Bel and Nebo). In several cases it is not clear whether the reference is to gods or idols, but we may interpret these in the light of unequivocal passages. Jeremiah follows, "I shall punish Bel in Babylon" with, "I shall punish the graven images of Babylon" (Jer. 51:44, 47, 52). Nahum warns Assyria, "I shall cut off idol and molten image from your temple" (1:14). And so does Ezekiel prophesy, "I shall destroy idols and put an end to images in Memphis" (30:13). Jeremiah 50:2, "Bel is shamed, Merodach dismayed," is interpreted by the prophet in the very next clause, "her images are shamed, her idols dismayed." From the total absence of any reference to activity (such as, say, flight, which would be appropriate in these cases), we may conclude that such expressions as "trembling" (Isa. 19:1), or "kneeling" (Isa. 46:1) refer to the movement of idols being cut down and removed from their sites. It is characteristic that instead of fleeing, the pagan gods must be borne away on pack animals, or are carried off into exile with their priests (Isa. 46:1 f.; Jer. 48:7; Dan. 11:8).

The account of the humiliation of the Philistine god Dagon (I Sam. 5), the only detailed story of the "judgments" that YHWH wreaked on a "god of the nations" may serve as a model for all such "judgments." The Philistines captured the ark and set it in the temple of Dagon, "beside Dagon." YHWH's revenge strikes at the people of Ashdod through a vile disease, and Dagon is discovered one morning "fallen on his face before the

ark of YHWH." On the morrow, not only is he again fallen, but "Dagon's head and his two hands were cut off and lying on the threshold." The Ashdodites decide to get rid of the ark of the God of Israel "because his hand has lain heavily upon us and our god Dagon." We hear nothing of Dagon proper, Dagon the living god; not even the Philistines are said to suggest that the fall of the image portends evil for the god. They, too, see in their idol's fall and mutilation the "judgment" of YHWH on their god. This is how Israel told of the victories of YHWH over the "gods of the nation."

We should not wonder that the Bible speaks of YHWH's "judging" these idol-gods. The idols are "vanities," it is true, but they are more; they are not religiously neutral, but a source of impurity. Even though it is emphasized over and over again that they are "no-gods," as objects of a magical cult the biblical writers hold them in a measure of awe. The Bible does believe in magic and sorcery, and considers the idols as bearers of occult powers. It is as such that YHWH the God wreaks his judgments upon them.

Two stories illustrate vividly the nature of Israel's battle with idolatry: the story of the golden calf, in which Israelite idolatry is typified (Exod. 32), and the late story of the image set up by Nebuchadnezzar (Dan. 3), in which the worship of the pagans is portrayed.

When Moses delays his descent from the mountain, the people demand that Aaron "make them a god who will go before them"; the priest makes them a "molten calf." The people make a feast in honor of their manufactured god in which they cry before it, "This is your god, O Israel, who brought you up out of the land of Egypt" (Exod. 32:1–6). In this portrayal of Israel's prototypal sin we have a classic representation of the biblical view of idolatry. The sin is not that the people represent YHWH in the figure of an ox. The people, having despaired of Moses and the God who brought them out of Egypt, demand that the priest make them a god in place of YHWH (Exod. 32:1, 4, 8; cf. Ps. 106:20 "They exchanged their glory for the image of a grass-eating ox"; Neh. 9:18; cf. also I Kings 12:28; 14:9). They do not give their allegiance to a living god, one of the gods of the nations or of their own ancient pantheon, but to an anonymous image, just now fashioned out of their own trinkets. In this calf, this idol that was not the image of a god, but a god itself, the Bible embodies its conception of Israelite idolatry as fetishism.

In the later story Nebuchadnezzar sets up a huge image in the plain of Dura and orders all his subjects to worship it under penalty of death in a fiery furnace. Hananiah, Mishael, and Azariah refuse to obey the king's order; they are thrown into the furnace but are miraculously saved by an angel of God. Nebuchadnezzar, beholding this miracle, does homage to the God of the three youths. Here, again, idolatry is the worship of an anonymous idol, an idol that represents no god at all, but is itself to be worshiped. Thus we see that even as late as Persian and Hellenistic times the Jewish attitude toward paganism was determined by the belief that the pagans worshiped idol-fetishes.

The Polemic against Idolatry

A large part of biblical literature is dedicated to the battle against idolatry, striving to expose its absurdity and discredit it in the eyes of its believers. When this material is examined it appears (a) that the gods, whom the pagans believe to inhabit heaven and earth, are never said to be non-existent; (b) that nowhere is the belief in myths or their telling prohibited; (c) that no biblical writer utilizes mythological motifs in his polemic; (d) that the sole argument advanced against pagan religion is that it is a fetishistic worship of "wood and stone."

The Bible conceives of idolatry as the belief that divine and magical powers inhere in certain natural or man-made objects and that man can activate these powers through fixed rituals. These objects, upon which magical rituals are performed, are "the gods of the nation." The Bible does not conceive the powers as personal beings who dwell in the idols; the idol is not a habitation of the god, it is the god himself. Hence the oft-repeated biblical stigmatization of the pagan gods as "wood and stone," "silver and gold." Hence also its sole polemical argument that idolatry is the senseless deification of wood and stone images. We may, perhaps, say that the Bible sees in paganism only its lowest level, the level of mana-beliefs.

This view finds clear expression in the prophetic polemics against idolatry.

Literary prophecy brought the religion of YHWH to its climax. Chapter upon chapter records denunciations hurled at apostate Israel for their straying after the gods of the nations. If ever there were a struggle with pagan myths and mythological conceptions of deity, we should expect to find its traces here. But we search in vain: not one word have the prophets for mythological beliefs, not once do they repudiate them. Not only do they fail to brand the pagan gods as demons or satyrs, they fail even clearly to deny their existence. In short, the prophets ignore what we know to be authentic paganism. Their whole condemnation revolves around the taunt of fetishism.

Amos, the first known literary prophet, hardly mentions the belief in gods. In 8:14, he speaks of Ashimah of Samaria; in 5:26, he names gods that the Israelites "made" for themselves. Thus the prophet, who is considered by many to have been the first to arrive at pure monotheism, fails entirely to express himself on the nature of the polytheism which he allegedly leaves behind.

In the first three chapters of Hosea the Baal worship of Jezebel's age is reflected, when court circles in Samaria were influenced by the Sidonian queen's imported cult. [. . .] Chapter 2 poetically portrays Baal as an illegitimate lover who has displaced YHWH in the affections of "harlot" Israel. But even here none of the distinctive mythological features of the Canaanite Baal are mentioned. Prosperity is a gift of YHWH which Israel has falsely ascribed to Baal (vss. 7–11). In the later chapters 4–14, Baal worship (9:10; 13:1) is but one among several sins of the past, and the manner in which the prophet conceives of Baal is seen clearly enough in 11:2 where "Baals" are parallel with "graven images." Israel is "joined to idols" (4:17), has made a molten calf of silver, "the work of craftsmen" (13:2), not understanding that "the craftsman made it, it is no god!" (8:6). When will Israel be reconciled with its God? When it says, "Assyria will not save us . . . neither will we say any more 'Our God' to the work of our hands" (14:4). Idolatry is nothing more than the worship of "the work of hands."

It is the same view that we meet with in Isaiah, who speaks of idolatry as the sin of humanity at large. Idolatry entered Israel together with the advent of silver and gold, horses and chariots. As the latter increase, "their land is also full of idols; every one worships the work of his hands, that which his own fingers have made" (2:7 f.). When the Lord humbles man's pride in his final great theophany, "man shall cast away his idols of silver, and his idols of gold, which they made for themselves to worship . . ." (2:20). Isaiah's *Götterdämmerung* is thus the twilight of silver and gold images; he makes no allusion to polytheistic beliefs.

Similarly Micah: On the day of doom all Samaria's "graven images shall be beaten to pieces . . . and all her idols will I lay desolate" (1:7); "And I will cut off your graven images and your pillars out of your midst; and you shall no more worship the work of your hands . . ." (5:12).

Jeremiah speaks of idolatry more than all his predecessors. He mentions anonymous "other gods" (11:10) who are impotent (11:12), whom Israel knew not (19:4); these he represents as the gods of foreign lands (16:13). It has been asserted that Jeremiah acknowledged the existence of other gods, objecting only to their worship in Israel. But Jeremiah amply sets forth his conception of pagan religion: it is the worship of wood and stone (2:27) or the host of heaven (8:2). The "other gods" are not the mythological beings of authentic paganism, nor even demons, but the handiwork of men (1:16), "stone and wood" (3:9), "graven images and strange vanities" (8:19), "no-gods" (2:11; 5:7), and so forth. On the day when the nations repent of the sin of idolatry they will say, "Our fathers inherited naught but lies, vanity and things wherein there is no profit. Shall a man make for himself gods, they being no gods?" (16:19 f.). When men stop worshiping fetishistic "no-gods" idolatry shall come to an end. This conception of pagan religion is expressed most clearly and emphatically in 10:1–16 (cf. 51:15–19). Owing to their resemblance to the viewpoint of the Second Isaiah, these verses have been dated to exilic times. For our purpose, however, the dating is immaterial, inasmuch as all of prophetic literature is unanimous in its conception of idolatry.

In Ezekiel we do find what appears to be an allusion to a foreign pagan myth: the lamenting of Tammuz (8:14; cf. also Zech. 12:11, "the mourning of Hadadrimmon"). Did Ezekiel or his contemporaries know the myth of the death of youthful Tammuz, the beloved of Ishtar? Or did they know only the pagan rites that Ezekiel mentions? The mass of worshipers, even among the pagan nations, had at times only very dim notions of the mythological basis of their rites. Did those "Weeping women" know the Tammuz myth? Is it certain that they were Israelites, and not rather pagan priestesses of the royal cult (like the imported pagan priests of Jezebel in an earlier age)? It is certain only that Ezekiel (whom Gunkel believes "filled with mythological material") never once argues against pagan mythology. Despite the fact that he polemizes often and heatedly against idolatry, he has not a word to say about the myths of Tammuz or any other god, nor does he ever employ an argument based on a mythological motif. He, too, characterizes pagan religion as fetishism. His favorite epithet for the gods is *gillūlīm* (dung-pellets); Israel's silver and gold, out of which they "made themselves their abominable images and loathsome things," were their stumbling blocks (7:19 f.). In chapters 16, 20, and 23, the prophet describes Israel's apostasy in detailed visions and allegories; Israel have made "male images" of gold and silver, made offerings to them, even sacrificed to them their sons and daughters. They have adopted the idol-worship of their neighbors throughout their history, from the Egyptian sojourn onward. The imagery is sensual and erotic; the dominant motif is the idol-images, those illegitimate partners of Israel's harlotry, from which the prophet readily passes to the lusty men of the foreign nations—the panoplied soldiery—after whom Israel went a-whoring also. Plastic imagery dominates; in fact the prophet is so involved with the idols that he ignores the gods entirely. It is most remarkable that Ezekiel, fascinated as he is by erotic symbolism, never once utilizes the sexual themes of mythology. He is silent concerning the strong erotic motif of the Tammuz myths. He uses the awkward image of Israel playing the harlot with stocks and stones, with gold and silver images. But he neglects the mythological store of themes that could have furnished rich material for his imagination. Can it be that Ezekiel knew the myths of the pagans in spite of his failure to employ even one of their motifs in his visions? We are not left to inferences. Ezekiel has himself supplied an epitome of his view of the pagan gods: to the elders of Israel he says, "You say, let us be like the nation, like the families of the countries to serve wood and stone" (20: 32). What the pagans worship, then, is nothing but deified wood and stone.

The classic polemics against idolatry found in the Second Isaiah express the biblical conception of pagan worship in its most vivid form. No previous prophet ever arraigned idolatry, ever heaped abuse upon it with such zeal and persistence. And yet, this unremitting attack, this stream of taunts and mockery, plays on one theme only: the monstrous folly of believing that idols can be gods. How much energy and poetic artistry are devoted to prove this single point!

> The makers of idols are all of them a mockery, their beloved images are good for nothing. . . .
>
> The workman in wood draws a measuring-line over it, shapes it with a pencil, works it with planes, shapes it with compasses, and makes it into the likeness of a man, with a beauty like that of the human form—to sit in a house!

A man cuts him down a cedar, or takes a plane or an oak, or lays hold of some other tree of the forest. . . . He takes part of it and warms himself, he kindles a fire and bakes bread; then he makes a god and worships it, he molds an image and prostrates himself before it. Half of it he burns in the fire, and on its embers he roasts flesh. . . . And the rest of it he makes into a god—his idol!—prostrates himself before it, worships it, and prays to it, saying, "Save me, for thou art my god!"

They have no knowledge and no intelligence; for their eyes are besmeared so that they cannot see, and their minds are dulled so that they cannot understand. . . . [44:9–18]

Over and over again the prophet ridicules the belief that inanimate objects are gods. Only when the nations perceive that a "block of wood" (vs.19) is not good will idolatry vanish. This from a man who, so it is alleged, was thoroughly acquainted with the polytheistic religion of his environment and even employed mythological motifs in his writing (51:9). And yet he has not a word about the gods or their myths. It never occurred to him to contrast the sublime God of Israel with the contentious, lustful deities of the pagans and to argue from this contrast that the gods are vanity. If our author had but dipped into the treasury of Babylonian myths, what a mine of material he would have found for his satires: gods who are born and die, who procreate, who eat, drink, and sleep, who make war on their mother, and crowd like flies around the sacrifice. Here was an arsenal which might have armed him to strike at the very heart of paganism: the faith in mythological gods and goddesses and in their dominion over the universe. And yet, in asserting his God's claim, he can say only, "I am YHWH, that is my name, and my glory I shall not give to another, nor my praise to idols" (42:8)—"to idols," not to "a born god," "a dying god," "a lustful god." YHWH evidently has no other rivals beside the idols and the graven images.

IDOLATRY IN THE LAWS

The Pentateuch also represents pagan religion as mere fetishism, and again there is no difference between sources; all agree in their view of idolatry.

There is no law in the Pentateuch interdicting the belief in pagan gods, or the telling of their myths; in Exodus 23:13, the use of their names in oaths is forbidden (cf. Josh. 23:7). The standing Pentateuchal prohibition concerns the "making" (i.e., the manufacture) of "other gods" and their worship (e.g., Exod. 20:4 f.).

Twice we meet with prohibitions against the worship of beings other than YHWH: the satyrs (Lev. 17:7) and "divine beings" (ʾelōhīm, Exod. 22:19). In both cases, however, foreign gods are not involved, but Israelite demons and divine beings. Whenever foreign gods are mentioned explicitly, it is clear that nothing but idols are meant.

In the Pentateuch, as throughout the Bible, "other gods" include all kinds of images, whether belonging to the cult of YHWH or to pagan cults. Images of the YHWH cult are assumed to be the product of foreign influence, and a cult involving them is regarded as no worship of YHWH at all, but of "other gods" (Exod. 20:3 ff.; Deut. 5:7 ff.). The fetishistic conception is predominant; after banning the worship of Canaanite gods, Exodus 23:24 commands to "demolish them utterly"; Leviticus 19:4 complements "Turn not to the idols" with "nor make for yourselves any molten god." Deuteronomy is particularly illuminating. The two categories of pagan cult objects are the idols and the host of heaven, which God himself has apportioned to the heathen for their worship (4:19; 29:25). The gods of the nations, the "other gods" (6:14 and elsewhere), are unknown to Israel before they learned to worship them from the pagans (11:28; 13:3, 7, 14; 28:64; 29:25). They are "the handiwork of man," "wood and stone" (4:28; 28:36, 64), "silver and gold" (29:16), and the like. The sum total of idolatry is the worship of these fetishes plus the worship of the host of heaven (17:3). Nowhere in all its diatribes does Deuteronomy allude to a belief in living gods and goddesses. What is the folly of idolatry? That its gods "see not, and hear not, and eat not, and smell not" (4:28). It is the same pattern of mockery that we find elsewhere in the Bible (e.g., Pss. 115:4 ff.; 135:15 ff.; Dan. 5:23; Jer. 10:5). Not that they are gluttonous and drunkards—but that they "eat not"! Can we suppose that the biblical authors knew the stories of the banquets of the gods and yet were content with this harmless jeering at the idols alone?

This verdict of the Bible upon pagan religion is too pervasive to be explained as the product of artifice or later editing. Nothing can make plausible the suppression of a polemic against polytheistic beliefs, had such a polemic been in existence.

Does the Bible portray pagan religion as mere fetishism because the writers themselves disbelieved in the gods? If this were so, the writers must have failed in their primary objective, which was to undermine the faith of those who did believe in them. To this end, there was no point in belaboring the fetish-argument to the entire exclusion of the main claim, that the gods were nonexistent. As a matter of fact, it is abundantly clear that the writers naïvely attribute their own viewpoint to the idolaters. The prophets look for the end of idolatry at the time when the idolaters will come to understand that man cannot "make" him gods, and that wood and stone cannot save. When Sennacherib boasts of how he defeated the gods of the nations (II Kings 18:33 ff.; 19:11 f. [Isa. 36:18 ff.; 37:12]), the writer explains, "he cast them into the fire" (II Kings 19:18 [Isa. 37:19]). And Isaiah, too, ascribes this thinking to the Assyrian: "As I did to Samaria and its idols, so shall I do to Jerusalem and its image." The pagan fails to realize that while the gods of the nations are "the handiwork of man, wood and stone," Israel's God is a "living God" (II Kings 19:16, 18 [Isa. 37:17, 19]). There is, of course, no hint that Sennacherib ascribes his triumphs to the god Ashur who triumphed over the gods of these nations.

It may be suggested that the biblical polemic takes this form because, in fact, the mass of people did have this fetishistic concept of the idols, and it was urgently necessary to combat it. Now there was, to be sure, a fetishistic side to paganism: the cult was bound up with an image; the image was, in a sense, the god. This consideration can explain why the fetishistic argument plays an important part in the biblical polemic; it cannot explain, however, the total absence of polemic against the belief in living gods, which was, after all, the root and heart of pagan religion. Greek thinkers in their attacks upon the popular religion gave due attention to its fetishistic aspect, but they did not permit this to distract them from combating the popular myths. Nor did the later Jewish and Christian polemics rest content with the fetishistic argument only. And yet we find that the Bible fails entirely to come to grips with the essence of polytheism—the belief in gods.

Those who have recognized this remarkable peculiarity are too enthralled by the assumption that the biblical writers knew the pagan myths to recognize its significance. The fetishistic argument is said to imply that the biblical writers repudiate the existence of the pagan gods. But where do they? If they meant to say that idols are vain because the gods they represent are nonexistent, why do they persist in arguing that idols are things of naught because wood and stone are of no avail? Why do they conceal the denial of the gods behind the façade of mockery and abuse of images? But the attitude toward the idols is only one aspect of the puzzle. How is the silence of the entire Bible—prophets, narrative, and laws alike—concerning the pagan mythology to be explained? Not only does the Bible fail to deny the existence of the gods, it nowhere repudiates the pagan myths.

In point of fact, as we shall see later, everything in the biblical view of paganism is strangely distorted. It is entirely ignorant of the close relationship between magic and the gods; it knows nothing of the cosmic-mythological basis of the pagan cult; it has no appreciation of the symbolic value of images.

The Basic Problem

It seems incredible that Israel should have been totally unaware of the nature of pagan beliefs. For Israel was always in contact with its pagan neighbors and, moreover, had believing pagans in its midst. Certainly there were circles who knew about paganism more than is reflected in the Bible. What is shown by the fact that the Bible bases its whole polemic on the argument of fetishism is that the chief influence of foreign beliefs on Israelite religion did not involve mythological materials and that the age-long battle of the Bible with idolatry did not involve mythological polytheism. This compels us to examine anew the conventional views regarding foreign influences on Israelite religion during biblical times. Moreover, we shall have to re-examine fundamentally the nature of Israelite "idolatry" during this period.

It is clear now that the question as to the origin of Israelite monotheism has been erroneously formulated. We cannot ask whether it was during the preprophetic or prophetic age that the religion of YHWH came to deny the reality of the foreign gods. The Bible nowhere denies the existence of the gods; it ignores them. In contrast to the philosophic attack on Greek popular religion, and in contrast to the later Jewish and Christian polemics, biblical religion shows no trace of having undertaken deliberately to suppress and repudiate mythology. There is no evidence that the gods and their myths were ever a central issue in the religion of YHWH. And yet this religion is non-mythological. Fossil-remains of ancient myths cannot obscure the basic difference between the Israelite religion and paganism. It is precisely this non-mythological aspect that makes it unique in world history; this was the source of its universal appeal.

The Bible's ignorance of the meaning of paganism is at once the basic problem and the most important clue to the understanding of biblical religion. It underscores as nothing else can the gulf that separates biblical religion from paganism. A recognition of this gulf is crucial to the understanding of the faith of the Bible. Not only does it underlie the peculiar biblical misrepresentation of paganism, it is the essential fact of the history of Israelite religion.

Translated by Moshe Greenberg.

Other works by Kaufmann: *Golah ve-nekhar*, 4 vols. (1929–1930).

Gershom Scholem

1897–1982

The Berlin-born historian of Jewish mysticism Gershom Scholem was one of the towering intellects of Jewish scholarship in the twentieth century. Born into a highly acculturated family with weak Jewish attachments, he embraced Jewish nationalism (more cultural and spiritual than political in content) in his youth and immersed himself in the study of Judaism in the face of parental opposition. In 1923, he settled in Jerusalem and began working as a librarian at the Hebrew University. In 1925, he was appointed lecturer in Jewish mysticism and several years later promoted to professor. Scholem pioneered the study of the much-maligned Jewish mystical tradition, insisting that it was often the major current in Jewish history. When his massive study of Shabbetai Tsevi was translated into English and other European languages, his work became known in intellectual circles outside the world of Jewish studies.

Redemption through Sin

1937

1

No chapter in the history of the Jewish people during the last several hundred years has been as shrouded in mystery as that of the Sabbatian movement. On one point, at least, there is no longer any disagreement: the dramatic events and widespread religious revival that preceded the apostasy of Sabbatai Zevi in 1666 form an important and integral part of Jewish history and deserve to be studied objectively, to the exclusion of moralistic condemnations of the historical figures involved. It has come increasingly to be realized that a true understanding of the rise of Sabbatianism will never be possible as long as scholars continue to appraise it by inappropriate standards, whether these be the conventional beliefs of their own age or the values of traditional Judaism itself. Today indeed one rarely encounters the baseless assumptions of "charlatanry" and "imposture," which occupy so prominent a place in earlier historical literature on the subject. On the contrary: in these times of Jewish national rebirth it is only natural that the deep though ultimately tragic yearning for national redemption to which the initial stages of Sabbatianism gave expression should meet with greater comprehension than in the past.

In turning to consider the Sabbatian movement after Sabbatai Zevi's conversion to Islam, however, we are faced with an entirely different situation. Here we find ourselves still standing before a blank wall, not only of misunderstanding, but often of an actual refusal to understand. Even in recent times there has been a definite tendency among scholars to minimize at all costs the significance of this "heretical" Sabbatianism, with the result that no adequate investigation yet exists of its spiritual foundations, its over-all impact on eighteenth-century Jewry, or its ultimate fate. It is impossible, in fact, to read any of the studies that have been done in these areas without being astounded by the amount of invective directed against the leaders and adherents of the various Sabbatian sects. Typical of this approach is David Kahana's *A History of the Kabbalists, Sabbatians, and Hasidim* (in Hebrew), but the angry moralizing that characterizes this volume has not been confined to any one historical school; rather, it has been shared by writers of widely differing points of view, secular as well as religious. The problem itself, meanwhile, remains as recondite as ever.

Two enormous difficulties, therefore, confront the student of the Sabbatian "heresies": on the one hand, there are the obstacles posed by the sources themselves, and on the other, those created by the attitude generally taken toward them. To a great extent, moreover, these two sets of difficulties have always been related.

Why should this be so?

The Sabbatian movement in its various shadings and configurations persisted with remarkable obstinacy among certain sectors of the Jewish people for approximately 150 years after Sabbatai Zevi's conversion. In a number of countries it grew to be powerful, but for various reasons, internal as well as external, its affairs were deliberately hidden from the public eye. In particular, its spokesmen refrained from committing their beliefs to print, and the few books that they actually published concealed twice what they revealed. They did, however, produce a rich literature, which circulated only among groups of "believers" (ma'aminim)—the term by which Sabbatian sectarians generally chose to refer to themselves, down to the last of the Dönmeh in Salonika and the last Frankists in the Austro-Hungarian Empire. As long as Sabbatianism remained a vital force within the Jewish ghetto, threatening to undermine the very existence of rabbinic Judaism, its opponents labored ceaselessly to root it out and systematically destroyed whatever of its writings came into their possession, "including [even] the sacred names of God [azkarot] which they contain," as the bans upon them read. As a result many of their writings were lost without a trace, and had it been left solely up to the rabbinical authorities nothing would have come down to us at all except for certain tendentiously chosen fragments quoted in anti-Sabbatian polemics. In addition, although an extensive religious literature was still to be found in the hands of Frankists in Moravia and Bohemia at the beginning of the nineteenth century, the children and grandchildren of these "believers" in Prague and other Jewish centers themselves attempted to obliterate every shred of evidence bearing on their ancestors' beliefs and practices. The well-known philosopher and historian of atheism Fritz Mauthner has preserved the following interesting story in his memoirs: in the declining days of the movement in Bohemia, Frankist "emissaries" came to his grandfather (and undoubtedly to other members of the sect as well) and requested that he surrender to them a picture of "the Lady" and "all kinds of writings" that he had in his possession. The emissaries took them and left. The incident took place sometime during the 1820s or 1830s. In spite of all this, at least two large manuscripts from these circles have survived.

One must therefore bear in mind that in dealing with the history of Sabbatianism powerful interests and emotions have often been at stake. Each for reasons of his own, all those who have written on the subject in the past shared one belief: the less importance attributed to it, the better.

Authors and historians of the orthodox camp, for their part, have been anxious to belittle and even dis-

tort the over-all role of Sabbatianism in order to safeguard the reputations, as they have conceived of them, of certain honored religious figures of the past. Such apologetics have had their inevitable effect upon the writing of history, as has the fundamental outlook of their proponents, tending as it does to idealize religious life in the ghetto at the expense of completely ignoring the deep inner conflicts and divisions to which not even the rabbis were necessarily immune. To acknowledge the Sabbatianism of eminent rabbis in Jerusalem, Adrianople, Constantinople, or Izmir, Prague, Hamburg, or Berlin, has been in the eyes of such authors to openly impeach the integrity of an entire body of men who were never supposed to be other than learned and virtuous defenders of Jewish tradition. Given such an attitude, it is hardly to be wondered at that one should instinctively avoid the kinds of inquiry that might lead to the discovery of heretical opinion, to say nothing of actual licentiousness, in the most unlikely places. One might cite endless examples of this kind of mentality in historical literature dealing with rabbinical and congregational life in the eighteenth century, and in at least one case, A. L. Frumkin's *A Historical Account of the Scholars of Jerusalem* (in Hebrew), the author goes so far as to "acquit" some of the most dedicated Sabbatians we know of the "scandal" of heterodoxy! Secularist historians, on the other hand, have been at pains to de-emphasize the role of Sabbatianism for a different reason. Not only did most of the families once associated with the Sabbatian movement in Western and Central Europe continue to remain afterwards within the Jewish fold, but many of their descendants, particularly in Austria, rose to positions of importance during the nineteenth century as prominent intellectuals, great financiers, and men of high political connections. Such persons, needless to say, could scarcely have been expected to approve of attempts to "expose" their "tainted" lineage, and in view of their stature in the Jewish community it is not surprising that their wishes should have carried weight. Furthermore, in an age when Jewish scholarship itself was considered to be in part an extension of the struggle for political emancipation, the climate for research in so sensitive an area was by no means generally favorable. In consequence, those Jewish scholars who had access to the wealth of Sabbatian documents and eyewitness reports that were still to be found early in the century failed to take advantage of the opportunity, while by the time a later generation arrived on the scene the sources had been destroyed and were no longer available even to anyone who might have desired to make use of them.

The survivors of the Frankists in Poland and of the Dönmeh, or "Apostates," in Salonika formed yet a third group having a direct interest in disguising the historical acts. These two Sabbatian sects, both of which formally renounced the Jewish religion (the Dönmeh converting to Islam in 1683, the Frankists to Catholicism in 1759), continued to adhere to their secret identities long after their defection from their mother faith; the Dönmeh, in fact, did not disappear until the present generation, while in the case of the Frankists, whose history in the course of the nineteenth century is obscure, it is impossible to determine at exactly what point in time they were finally swallowed up by the rest of Polish society. There is reason to suspect that until the eve of World War II many original manuscripts and documents were preserved by both these groups, particularly by a number of Frankist families in Warsaw; but how much of this material may yet be uncovered, and how much has been purposely destroyed by its owners in order to conceal forever the secret of their descent, is in no way ascertainable.

Nevertheless, the total picture is not as dark as it may seem to have been painted: despite the many efforts at suppression, which supplemented, as it were, the inevitable "selective" process of time itself, a considerable amount of valuable material has been saved. Many of the accusations made against the "believers" by their opponents can now be weighed (and more often than not confirmed!) on the basis of a number of the "believers'" own books, which were not allowed to perish. Little by little our knowledge has grown, and although many of the historical details we would like to know will undoubtedly never come to light at all, there is reason to hope that this important chapter in Jewish history will yet be fully written. In any event, it is clear that a correct understanding of the Sabbatian movement after the apostasy of Sabbatai Zevi will provide a new clue toward understanding the history of the Jews in the eighteenth century as a whole, and in particular, the beginnings of the Haskalah [Enlightenment] movement in a number of countries.

I do not propose in this article to trace the outward history of Sabbatianism in its several manifestations over the century and a half in which it retained its vitality, nor (although I can hardly conceal my opinion that the entire movement was far more widespread than is

generally conceded even today) do I mean to debate the question of whether this or that particular individual was or was not a Sabbatian himself. Suffice it to say that the sources in our possession, meager as they are, make it perfectly clear that the number of Sabbatian rabbis was far greater than has been commonly estimated, greater even than was believed by that anti-Sabbatian zealot Rabbi Jacob Emden, who has almost always been accused of exaggeration. In the present essay, however, I shall put such questions aside and limit myself to the area that has been the most sadly neglected in the entire field, namely, the origins and development of Sabbatian thought per se.

If one accepts what Heinrich Graetz and David Kahana have to say on the subject of Sabbatian theology, it is impossible to understand what its essential attraction ever was; indeed, if it is true, as both these writers claim, that the entire movement was a colossal hoax perpetrated by degenerates and frauds, one might well ask why a serious historian should bother to waste his time on it in the first place. And if this is the case with Sabbatianism in general, how much more so when one ventures to consider what is undoubtedly the most tragic episode in the entire drama, that of the Frankists, the psychological barriers to the understanding of which are incomparably greater. How, for instance, can one get around the historical fact that in the course of their public disputation with Jewish rabbis in Lvov in 1759 the members of this sect did not even shrink from resorting to the notorious blood libel, an accusation far more painful to Jewish sensitivities than any of their actual beliefs? A great deal has been written about this incident, particularly by the eminent historian Meir Balaban, in whose book, *On the History of the Frankist Movement* (in Hebrew), it is exhaustively dealt with. Balaban, who makes the Lvov libel a starting point for his over-all inquiry, reaches the significant conclusion that there was no organic connection between it and the Frankist "articles of faith" presented at the disputation. The members of the sect, in fact, were reluctant to make the accusation at all, and did so only at the instigation of the Catholic clergy, which was interested in using them for purposes of its own, having nothing to do with their Sabbatian background. That they finally agreed to collaborate in the scheme can be explained by their desire to wreak vengeance on their rabbinical persecutors.

Thus, though the behavior of the Frankists at Lvov must certainly be judged harshly from both a universal-ethical and a Jewish-national point of view, it is important to keep in mind that the blood libels against the Jews (the indications are that there was more than one) do not in themselves tell us anything about the inner spiritual world of the sect, in all of whose literature (written one and two generations after the Lvov disputation) not a single allusion to such a belief is to be found. The truly astonishing thing is that although several important texts of Frankist teachings actually do exist, not a single serious attempt has so far been made to analyze their contents. The reason for this is simple. Graetz and A. Kraushar, two reputable scholars, one of whom wrote a full-length study of Jacob Frank and his Polish followers, were both of the opinion that there was no such thing as a Frankist "creed," and that *The Sayings of the Lord* (*Slowa Pańskie*) which has come down to us in a Polish version alone, was incoherent nonsense. According to Kraushar, Frank's sayings are "grotesque, comical, and incomprehensible," while Graetz, whose attitude toward all forms of mysticism is well known, could hardly have been expected to show much insight into the religious motivations of the sect. Balaban, on the other hand, is mainly concerned with the outward history of the Frankists up to the time of their mass conversion, and his reconstruction of their theology is based solely on the positions publicly taken by them in their disputations with the rabbis. It is his reliance on these "articles of faith," in fact, which were actually far from accurate reflections of the Frankists' true beliefs, that leads him to conclude that after 1759 the history of the sect was "determined more by the personalities of Jacob Frank and his disciples than by any intrinsic religious relationship to Judaism."

I myself cannot agree with Balaban on this point, and in the following pages I shall attempt to show, at least summarily, that Sabbatianism must be regarded not only as a single continuous development, which retained its identity in the eyes of its adherents regardless of whether they themselves remained Jews or not, but also, paradoxical though it may seem, as a specifically *Jewish* phenomenon to the end. I shall endeavor to show that the nihilism of the Sabbatian and Frankist movements, with its doctrine so profoundly shocking to the Jewish conception of things that the violation of the Torah could become its true fulfillment (*bittulah shel torah zehu kiyyumah*), was a dialectical outgrowth of the belief in the Messiahship of Sabbatai Zevi, and that this nihilism, in turn, helped pave the way for the Haska-

lah and the reform movement of the nineteenth century, once its original religious impulse was exhausted. Beyond this, I hope to make the reader see how within the spiritual world of the Sabbatian sects, within the very sanctum sanctorum of Kabbalistic mysticism, as it were, the crisis of faith that overtook the Jewish people as a whole upon its emergence from its medieval isolation was first anticipated, and how groups of Jews within the walls of the ghetto, while still outwardly adhering to the practices of their forefathers, had begun to embark on a radically new inner life of their own. Prior to the French Revolution the historical conditions were lacking that might have caused this upheaval to break forth in the form of an open struggle for social change, with the result that it turned further inward upon itself to act upon the hidden recesses of the Jewish psyche; but it would be mistaken to conclude from this that Sabbatianism did not permanently affect the outward course of Jewish history. The desire for total liberation, which played so tragic a role in the development of Sabbatian nihilism, was by no means a purely self-destructive force; on the contrary, beneath the surface of lawlessness, antinomianism, and catastrophic negation, powerful constructive impulses were at work, and these, I maintain, it is the duty of the historian to uncover.

Undeniably, the difficulties in the face of this are great, and it is not to be wondered at that Jewish historians until now have not had the inner freedom to attempt the task. In our own times we owe much to the experience of Zionism for enabling us to detect in Sabbatianism's throes those gropings toward a healthier national existence that must have seemed like an undiluted nightmare to the peaceable Jewish bourgeois of the nineteenth century. Even today, however, the writing of Jewish history suffers unduly from the influence of nineteenth-century Jewish historiography. To be sure, as Jewish historians we have clearly advanced beyond the vantage point of our predecessors, having learned to insist, and rightly so, that Jewish history is a process that can only be understood when viewed from *within*; but in spite of all this, our progress in applying this truth to concrete historical situations, as opposed to general historiosophical theories, has been slow. Up to the present only two men, Siegmund Hurwitz in his *From Whither to Where* (in Hebrew) and Zalman Rubashov [Shazar] in his essay "Upon the Ruins of Frankism" (in Hebrew), have shown any true appreciation of the complexities of Sabbatian psychology, and their work has by and large failed to attract the attention it deserves.

And now, one last introductory comment. In dismissing the need for objective research on the Sabbatian and Frankist movements, it has often been asserted that since the phenomena in question are essentially pathological, they belong more properly to the study of medicine than to the study of history. Indeed, an article on "Frank and His Sect in the Light of Psychiatry" (Bychowski, *Ha-Tekufah*, Vol. XIV) has actually been published, but it only succeeds in demonstrating how incapable such an approach is of dealing satisfactorily with the problem. From the standpoint of sexual pathology it can hardly be doubted that Frank himself was a diseased individual, just as there can be no question that at the center and among the ranks of the Sabbatian movement (as in all radical movements that spring from certain particular tensions, some of which are not so far removed from those of "ordinary" life) it would be possible to find cases of marked mental aberrance. But what is the significance of all this? We are not, after all, so much concerned with this or that prominent Sabbatian personality as with the question of why such people were able to attract the following that they did. The diagnosis of a neurologist would be of little value in determining why thousands of human beings were able to find a spiritual home in the labyrinth of Sabbatian theology. We must refuse to be deluded by such convenient tags as "hysteria" or "mass psychosis," which only confuse the issue at the same time that they provide an excuse for avoiding it and comfortably reassure one of one's own comparative "normality." It is undoubtedly true that Jacob Frank was every bit the depraved and unscrupulous person he is supposed to have been, and yet the moment we seriously ponder his "teachings," or attempt to understand why masses of men should have regarded him as their leader and prophet, this same individual becomes highly problematic. Even more than the psychology of the leader, however, it is the psychology of the led that demands to be understood, and in the case of Sabbatianism, a movement built entirely upon paradoxes, this question is crucial indeed. Whatever we may think of Sabbatai Zevi and Jacob Frank, the fact is: their followers, while they were certainly not "innocents"—if there was one thing lacking in the paradoxical religion of the Sabbatians it was innocence!—were sincere in their faith, and it is the nature of this faith, which penetrated to the hidden depths and abysses of the human spirit, that we wish to understand.

2

As a mystical heterodoxy Sabbatianism assumed different and changing forms: it splintered into many sects, so that even from the polemical writings against it we learn that the "heretics" quarreled among themselves over practically everything. The word "practically," however, must be stressed, for on one essential, the underlying ground of their "holy faith," as they called it, the "believers" all agreed. Let us proceed then to examine this common ground of faith as it manifested itself both psychologically and dogmatically.

By all accounts, the Messianic revival of 1665–66 spread to every sector of the Jewish people throughout the Diaspora. Among the believers and penitents a new emotion, which was not restricted to the traditional expectation of a political deliverance of Israel alone, began to make itself felt. This is not to say that hope for a divine liberation from the bondage and degradation of exile was not an important element in the general contagion, but rather that various psychological reactions that accompanied it soon took on an independent existence of their own. Prior to Sabbatai Zevi's apostasy, great masses of people were able to believe in perfect simplicity that a new era of history was being ushered in and that they themselves had already begun to inhabit a new and redeemed world. Such a belief could not but have a profound effect on those who held it: their innermost feelings, which assured them of the presence of a Messianic reality, seemed entirely in harmony with the outward course of events, those climactic developments in a historico-political realm that Sabbatai Zevi was soon to overthrow by means of his miraculous journey to the Turkish sultan, whom he would depose from his throne and strip of all his powers.

In the generation preceding Sabbatai Zevi's advent the rapid spread of the teachings of Rabbi Isaac Luria and his school had resulted in a grafting of the theories of the Kabbalists, the *de facto* theologians of the Jewish people in the seventeenth century, onto the traditional Jewish view of the role and personality of the Messiah. Mystical Lurianic speculations about the nature of the redemption and "the restored world" (*olam ha-tikkun*), which was to follow upon its heels, added new contents and dimensions to the popular Messianic folk-myth of a conquering national hero, raising it to the level of a supreme cosmic drama: the redemptive process was now no longer conceived of as simply a working-out of Israel's temporal emancipation from the yoke of the gentiles, but rather as a fundamental transformation of the entire Creation, affecting material and spiritual worlds alike and leading to a rectification of the primordial catastrophe of the "breaking of the vessels" (*shevirat ha-kelim*), in the course of which the divine worlds would be returned to their original unity and perfection. By stressing the spiritual side of the redemption far more than its outward aspect the Kabbalists of the Lurianic school, though by no means overlooking the latter, gradually converted it into a symbol of purely spiritual processes and ends. As long as the Messianic expectancies they encouraged were not put to the test in the actual crucible of history, the dangers inherent in this shift of emphasis went unnoticed, for the Kabbalists themselves never once imagined that a conflict might arise between the symbol and the reality it was intended to represent. To be sure, Lurianic Kabbalah had openly educated its followers to prepare themselves more for an inner than for an outer renewal; but inasmuch as it was commonly assumed that the one could not take place without the other, the procedure seemed in no way questionable. On the contrary: the spread of Lurianic teachings, so it was thought, was in itself bound to hasten the coming of the historical Redeemer.

The appearance of Sabbatai Zevi and the growth of popular faith in his mission caused this inner sense of freedom, of "a world made pure again," to become an immediate reality for thousands. This did not of course mean that Sabbatai Zevi himself was no longer expected to fulfill the various Messianic tasks assigned him by Jewish tradition, but in the meantime an irreversible change had taken place in the souls of the faithful. Who could deny that the Shekhinah, the earthly presence of God, had risen from the dust?

"Heretical" Sabbatianism was born at the moment of Sabbatai Zevi's totally unexpected conversion, when for the first time a contradiction appeared between the two levels of the drama of redemption, that of the subjective experience of the individual on the one hand, and that of the objective historical facts on the other. The conflict was no less intense than unforeseen. One had to choose: either one heard the voice of God in the decree of history, or else one heard it in the newly revealed reality within. "Heretical" Sabbatianism was the result of the refusal of large sections of the Jewish people to submit to the sentence of history by admitting that their own personal experience had been false and untrustworthy.

Thus, the various attempts to construct a Sabbatian theology were all motivated by a similar purpose, namely, to rationalize the abyss that had suddenly opened between the objective order of things and that inward certainty that it could no longer serve to symbolize, and to render the tension between the two more endurable for those who continued to live with it. The sense of contradiction from which Sabbatianism sprung became a lasting characteristic of the movement: following upon the initial paradox of an apostate Messiah, paradox engendered paradox. Above all, the "believers," those who remained loyal to their inward experience, were compelled to find an answer to the simple question: what could be the value of a historical reality that had proved to be so bitterly disappointing, and how might it be related to the hopes it had betrayed?

The essence of the Sabbatian's conviction, in other words, can be summarized in a sentence: it is inconceivable that all of God's people should inwardly err, and so, if their vital experience is contradicted by the facts, it is the facts that stand in need of explanation. In the words of a Sabbatian "moderate" writing thirty years after Sabbatai Zevi's apostasy: "The Holy One, blessed be He, does not ensnare even the animals of the righteous, much less the righteous themselves, to say nothing of so terribly deceiving an entire people. [. . .] And how is it possible that all of Israel be deceived unless this be part of some great divine plan?" This line of argument, which was adopted by many persons from the very beginning of the Sabbatian movement, is known to have impressed even the movement's opponents, who were equally disinclined to find fault with the entire Jewish people and sought instead some other explanation for what had happened.

During the century and a half of its existence Sabbatianism was embraced by those Jewish circles who desired to prolong the novel sensation of living in a "restored world" by developing attitudes and institutions that seemed commensurate with a new divine order. Inasmuch as this deliberately maintained state of consciousness was directly opposed to the outlook of ghetto Jewry as a whole, of which the "believers" themselves formed a part, the latter of necessity tended to become innovators and rebels, particularly the radicals among them. Herein lay the psychological basis of that spirit of revolt that so infuriated the champions of orthodoxy, who, though they may at first have had no inkling of the lengths to which it would be ultimately carried, rightly suspected it from the outset of striving to subvert the authority of rabbinic Judaism. Herein, too, lay the basis of all future efforts to construct a Sabbatian theology, to the consideration of which we must now turn our attention.

In the history of religion we frequently encounter types of individuals known as "pneumatics" (*pneumatikoi*) or "spiritualists" (*spirituales*). Such persons, who played a major role in the development of Sabbatianism, were known in Jewish tradition as "spiritual" or "extra-spirited" men or, in the language of the Zohar, as "masters of a holy soul." These terms did not refer to just anyone who may have had occasion in the course of his life to be "moved by the spirit"; rather, they applied only to those few who abode in the "palace of the king" (*hekhal ha-melekh*), that is, who lived in continual communion with a spiritual realm through whose gates they had passed, whether by actually dwelling within it to the point of abandoning their previous existence, or by appropriating from it a "spark" or "holy soul," as only the elect were privileged to do. One so favored was in certain respects no longer considered to be subject to the laws of everyday reality, having realized within himself the hidden world of divine light. Naturally, spiritualistic types of this sort have always regarded themselves as forming a group apart, and hence the special sense of their own "superiority" by which they are characterized: from their lofty perspective the world of material affairs tends to look lowly indeed. Here, then, we have all the prerequisites for the sectarian disposition, for the sect serves the *illuminati* as both a rallying point for their own kind and a refuge from the incomprehension of the carnal and unenlightened masses. The sectarians regard themselves as the vanguard of a new world, but they do not therefore need to renounce the parent religion that inspired them, for they can always reinterpret it in the light of the supreme reality to which they owe their newly discovered allegiance.

For a number of reasons, which cannot be gone into here, such spiritualists were rarely allowed to develop within the Jewish community after the period of the Second Temple. In part this was a consequence of Christianity, to which many of them ultimately passed; but even when they continued to exist within Judaism itself, it was always as isolated and unorganized individuals. It is a well-known fact, for instance, that spiritualism particularly abounds in the domain of religious mysticism; and yet, as the history of Kabbalism amply demonstrates, despite the opposition between conventional religion and the ecstasy, at times even abandon, of the pneumatic, medieval Judaism was capable of absorbing the latter into its orbit. Such was not the case, however, with either Christianity or Islam: here the conflict broke out openly and fiercely on numerous occasions, and the spiritualist sects it produced went on to play important roles in the development of new social and religious institutions, often giving birth, albeit in religious guise, to the most revolutionary ideas. To take but one example, historical research during the last several decades has clearly shown the direct connection between Christian sectarianism in Europe and the growth of the Enlightenment and the ideal of toleration in the seventeenth and eighteenth centuries.

The existence of similar forces in Jewish history, on the other hand, has been all but neglected by the historians, an oversight facilitated by the fact that Jewish spiritualism has either long been outwardly dormant or else, as in the case of Kabbalism, has always preferred to work invisibly and unsystematically beneath the surface. Indeed, as long as Jewish historiography was dominated by a spirit of assimilation, no one so much as suspected that positivism and religious reform were the progeny not only of the rational mind, but of an entirely different sort of psychology as well, that of the Kabbalah and the Sabbatian crisis—in other words, of that very "lawless heresy" that was so soundly excoriated in their name!

In the Sabbatian movement, which was the first clear manifestation (one might better say *explosion*) of spiritualistic sectarianism in Judaism since the days of the Second Temple, the type of the radical spiritualist found its perfect expression. To be sure, *illuminati* of the same class were later prevalent in Hasidism too, particularly during the golden age of the movement; but Hasidism, rather than allow itself to be taken over by such types, forced them after a period of initial equivocation to curb their unruly spirituality, and did so with such success that it was able to overcome the most difficult and hazardous challenge of all, that of safely incorporating them into its own collective body. Unlike Sabbatianism, whose followers were determined to carry their doctrine to its ultimate conclusion, it was the genius of Hasidism that it knew where to set itself limits. But the Sabbatians pressed on to the end, into the abyss of the mythical "gates of impurity" (*sha'are tum'ah*), where the pure spiritual awareness of a world made new became a pitfall fraught with peril for the moral life.

Here, then, were all the materials necessary to cause a true conflagration in the heart of Jewry. A new type of Jew had appeared for whom the world of exile and Diaspora Judaism was partly or wholly abolished and who uncompromisingly believed that a "restored world," whose laws and practices he was commanded to obey, was in the process of coming into being. The great historical disappointment experienced by the Sabbatian had instilled in him the paradoxical conviction that he and his like were privy to a secret whose time had not yet come to be generally revealed, and it was this certainty, which, in Hebrew literature of the period, imparted a special meaning to his use of the terms "believer" and "holy faith," the peculiar shadings of which immediately inform us that we are dealing with a Sabbatian document even when there is not the slightest allusion therein to Sabbatai Zevi himself: by virtue of his "holy faith" in the mysterious realignment of the divine worlds and in the special relationship to them of the Creator during the transitional period of cosmic restitution (*tikkun*), the "believer," he who trusted in the mission of Sabbatai Zevi, was exalted above all other men. Hidden in the "believer's" soul was a precious jewel, the pearl of Messianic freedom, which shone forth from its chamber of chambers to pierce the opaqueness of evil and materiality; he who possessed it was a free man by power of his own personal experience, and to this inner sense of freedom, whether gotten during the mass revival that preceded Sabbatai Zevi's apostasy, or afterwards, in the ranks of the "holy faith," he would continue to cling no matter how much he knew it to be contradicted by the outward facts.

The Sabbatian doctrine had as its aim the resolution of this contradiction. The conflict was bitterly clear. Those who were disillusioned by Sabbatai Zevi's apostasy were able to claim that nothing had really changed: the world was the same as ever; the exile was no different than before; therefore the Torah was the same Torah and the familiar Kabbalistic teachings about the nature of the Godhead and the divine worlds remained in force. A great opportunity had perhaps existed, but it had been missed; henceforth the one recourse was a return to Israel's traditional faith in its God. The "believers," on the other hand, could say in paraphrase of Job, "our eyes have beheld and not another's": the redemp-

tion had indeed begun; only its ways were mysterious and its outward aspect was still incomplete. Externals might seem the same, but inwardly all was in the process of renewal. Both the Torah and the exile had been fundamentally altered, as had the nature of the Godhead, but for the time being all these transformations bore "inward faces" alone.

The Sabbatian movement soon developed all the psychological characteristics of a spiritualist sect, and before long many of its followers proceeded to organize themselves along such lines. The persecutions against them on the part of various rabbinical and congregational authorities, their own special feeling of apartness and of the need to preserve their secret, and the novel practices that their beliefs eventually compelled them to pursue, were all factors in bringing this about. I do not propose to dwell at length on the history of any of these groups, but I do wish to emphasize briefly at this point that large numbers of Jews, especially among the Sephardim, continued to remain faithful to Sabbatai Zevi after his conversion. Even such opponents of Sabbatianism as Jacob Sasportas, who claimed that the followers of the movement were now an "insubstantial minority," was forced to admit on other occasions that the minority in question was considerable indeed, particularly in Morocco, Palestine, Egypt, and most of Turkey and the Balkans. Most of the Sabbatian groups in these areas maintained constant contact with each other and kept up a running battle over the correct interpretation of their "holy faith." From these regions came the first theoreticians of the movement, men such as Nathan of Gaza, Samuel Primo, Abraham Miguel Cardozo, and Nehemiah Hayon, as well as the believers in "voluntary Marranism," who went on to form the sect of the Dönmeh in Salonika. In Italy the number of Sabbatians was smaller, though it included some of the country's most important Kabbalists; within a generation after its appearance there, Sabbatianism had dwindled into the concern of a few rabbis and scholars (chief among them Rabbi Benjamin Cohen of Reggio and Rabbi Abraham Rovigo of Modena), in whose hands it remained for a century without ever penetrating into wider circles. In Northern Europe Sabbatianism was also restricted at first to small groups of adherents, devotees of such "prophets" as Heshel Zoref of Vilna and Mordecai of Eisenstadt in Hungary, but after 1700, following the commencement of a "Palestinian period" during which organized Sabbatian emigrations to the Holy Land took place from several countries, the movement spread rapidly through Germany and the Austro-Hungarian Empire. In Lithuania it failed to take root, but in Podolia and Moravia it became so entrenched that it was soon able to claim the allegiance of many ordinary Jewish burghers and small businessmen (according to Jacob Emden, the numerical value of the Hebrew letters in the verse in Psalms 14, "There is none that doeth good, not even one," was equivalent to the numerical value of the letters in the Hebrew word for Moravia!). In Prague and Mannheim Sabbatian-oriented centers of learning came into being. The influence of the "graduates" of these institutions was great; one of them, in fact, was the author of the heretical treatise *Va-Avo ha-Yom El ha-Ayin* ("And I Came This Day Unto the Fountain") which provoked so much furor at the time of the controversy surrounding Jonathan Eibeschütz (1751) and led to a polemical "battle of the books" that has enabled us to trace the identities of many Sabbatians of whom otherwise we would have known nothing at all. In the middle of the eighteenth century many of the Sabbatians in Podolia converted to Christianity after the example of their leader Jacob Frank, but still others remained within the Jewish fold. Finally, a Sabbatian stronghold sprang up again in Prague, where Frankism was propagated in a Jewish form. After 1815, however, the movement fell apart and its members were absorbed into secular Jewish society, like the Frankist ancestors of Louis Brandeis.

Translated by Hillel Halkin.

Other works by Scholem: *Major Trends in Jewish Mysticism* (1941); *The Messianic Idea in Judaism and Other Essays in Jewish Spirituality* (1971); *From Berlin to Jerusalem* (1980).

Louis Finkelstein

1895–1991

Born in Cincinnati, Louis Finkelstein received his Jewish education from his father, an Orthodox rabbi. He attended both Columbia University and the Jewish Theological Seminary, where he taught for more than half a century, serving as its head from 1940 to 1972. Under his direction, the seminary grew tremendously, emerging as the chief institution in Conservative Judaism. Finkelstein himself was the dominant figure in the movement before his retirement and took an active role in American public life, especially in interfaith dialogue.

The Pharisees: The Sociological Background of Their Faith
1938

VIII. The Doctrine of the Resurrection and Immortality

The fiercest of all the conflicts between Pharisee and Sadducee concerned the doctrine of the resurrection, for in it the class conflict was most explicitly formulated.

Crushed under the heel of the oppressor and exploiter, the artisan and trader of Jerusalem in the fourth century BCE sought compensation in an ideal world beyond the grave, where all human inequalities would be levelled down before the overwhelming power of God. The bitterer his lot in this world, the more passionately he clung to his hopes of the next. An abstract immortality might satisfy the philosopher; the hungry slumdweller of Jerusalem could be comforted by nothing less than the Egyptian and Persian doctrine of physical resurrection and restitution.

The expectation that the struggles of the world would culminate in a glorious Messianic Age, ushering in peace and tranquillity reminiscent of Adam's Paradise, had long been prominent in Israel's thought; and this offered an excellent background for the new faith. Several passages in the Second Isaiah seem to indicate that already he had been thinking in terms of the resurrection; but it remained for a later prophet, the author of Isaiah, chapters 24–27, to avow the belief clearly and explicitly.

> "Thy dead shall live, my dead bodies shall arise—
> Awake and sing, ye that dwell in the dust—
> For Thy dew is as the dew of light,
> And the earth shall bring to life the shades" (26.19)

But this doctrine had been so long and so pointedly ignored among the Jews that the introduction of it might well have appeared to be defection to foreign worship. Moreover, appealing as a future life might seem, the belief in it was derived from animism, ancestor worship, and other primitive errors which were hated and despised by the Jewish religious teachers. Throughout the duration of the First Commonwealth they had struggled against its infiltration from Egypt and had on the whole succeeded in keeping Jewish faith free from the taint both of the resurrection and of the superstitions associated with it. But by the fifth century BCE the peril of idolatry had almost disappeared in Jerusalem, and there was less reason for objection to a doctrine which in itself had so much that was pure, inspiring and morally helpful. It was inertia rather than religious policy which opposed the new article of faith; even after such "radicals" as the author of Isaiah 26 had spoken, official Judaism still regarded the belief in the resurrection with strong suspicion.

We may, however, see a possible concession in the Torah itself, where the Egyptian practice of embalming is accepted with approval for both Jacob and Joseph. True, the resurrection is not even mentioned in this connection. But in Egyptian thought the preservation of the body was a necessary preparation for its ultimate quickening. Conscious opposition to the doctrine of the resurrection would surely not be compatible with the ascription of this practice to the revered patriarchs.

But while we have these scattered and indirect allusions to the resurrection in the earlier writers, the first picture of a revivified world is given by the inaugurators of the Enoch literature, who are supposed to have lived about the year 200 BCE, shortly before Antiochus Epiphanes initiated his unsuccessful effort forcibly to Hellenize the Jews.

> And no mortal is permitted to touch this tree of delicious fragrance till the great day of judgment, when He shall avenge and bring everything to its consummation forever; this tree, I say, will [then] be given to the righteous and humble. By its fruit, life will be given to the elect; it will be transplanted to the north, to the holy place, to the temple of the Lord, the Eternal King. Then will they rejoice with joy and be glad: they will enter Thy holy habitation: the fragrance thereof will be in their limb, and they will live a long life on earth, such as their fathers have lived: and in their days no sorrow or pain or trouble or calamity will affect them (Enoch 25.5-7, R. H. Charles' translation).

The apocalyptist was himself doubtless one of the "humble" of whom he speaks so affectionately. But he uses that term not as we do, to indicate the affectation of the mighty who put on "meekness" as a social amenity. The humility which he has in mind is not a virtue but a condition. The word "'anavim,'" which was certainly the original rendered by the English "humble," came like its English equivalent, to mean "pious," "saintly," and "meek," because it signified the unprotesting, non-

resisting, unambitious, lowly, the social opposites of the wealthy, who find it so difficult to enter the kingdom of heaven.

It was this aspect of the Jewish doctrine of the resurrection—its democracy—which gives it more than theological importance; and which indeed prepared the way for its spread throughout the world. Egyptian immortality was to be attained through power. The Pharaoh, the princes and the nobility, not only possessed this world, but by costly burial arrangements they could ensure their return from death itself. Such a perpetuation of the wrongs of the mundane world would have aroused little enthusiasm in Jerusalem's market place; and, indeed, it is altogether probable that the resistance to it explains in large part the failure of the earlier Israelite and Judaite teachers to recognize the larger spiritual potentialities of the teaching of the resurrection. Only when the doctrine was presented as one of salvation for the righteous, be they rich or poor, Jew or Gentile, noble or plebeian, did the masses of Jerusalem become converted to it.

While, however, the poor of the fourth century BCE and later times sought solace in the new faith, the patricians felt no impulse to abandon the traditional negation of future life. The patricians were not content with monopolizing this life; they even begrudged the poor another and better life beyond the grave. To assert the truth of the resurrection was to them nothing less than heresy, a recession from a standpoint to which prophetic Judaism had steadfastly adhered through almost a millennium, and an acceptance of the foreign influence of Egypt and of Zoroaster.

It is not among those who have enjoyed the triumphs of this world that we should look for preoccupation with the consolations of the next. It is an almost universal feature of religious history that the longing for another and better life to come was confined, in its strongest forms, to those who had been the victims of life as it is here. This was not less true among the Jews than among others.

The cleavage between the plebeian artisans and traders of Jerusalem and their wealthy neighbors was sharpened by the mature concept of personality and the individual which was becoming current in the market place. The rural and aristocratic families and clans were held together as units by well remembered traditions, and above all by the property, nominally held by the father but actually the means of support to the whole group—wives, children, slaves and retainers. The members of the family lived, worked, prospered and suffered together. Their interests were inextricably interwoven, and, as everywhere, mutual interdependence gave rise to a sense of solidarity unknown in other circles. The family of Bathyra, for instance, acted as a unit in its interpretation of the Law; the high-priestly families were powerful clans, the individuals of which were merely organs of their general group. Such clan-consciousness was altogether lacking among the poorer classes, where there was no common property or traditions to unite the members of the family. On the contrary, the city was full of divisive forces tending to disrupt the family unit. Wife and children could earn their livelihood without the assistance of husband and father; they made friendships of their own, and tended to become independent in their judgments, thoughts and desires. Sociologists have long noted this disruptive effect of city life on the primitive family, but it is important to remember that the centrifugal force was especially strong among the laborers and tradesmen, and rather weak among the patricians, who in ancient times, as today, laid great stress on genealogy and family associations.

True, the tendency toward the cult of the individual had shown itself early in Israel, but it was limited to the property-less groups, and was continually opposed by the land-owning patricians. The story of the argument between Abraham and God concerning the fate of Sodom is a case in point. "That be far from Thee," says Abraham, "to do after this manner, to slay the righteous with the wicked, that so the righteous shall be as the wicked, that be far from Thee; shall not the Judge of all the earth do justly?" (Gen. 18.25) The point of the story is lost, and the vehemence of Abraham remains inexplicable, unless we bear in mind that Abraham is here inveighing against a definite moral and theological conception—the tribal feud, or the vendetta. The principle was even more clearly expressed in Deuteronomy, where the slaying of children for the sins of their father was explicitly forbidden (24.16) and where we are told that God's wrath descends from father to son only *for His enemies* (7.10), that is, as the Talmud correctly understands, when the sons imitate their fathers' wickedness. In another passage of the Torah, the defense of individual responsibility is attributed to Moses. When God threatens to destroy Israel for the sins of Korah, Moses asks Him in accents which ring through the ages, "Shall one man sin, and wilt Thou be wroth with all the congregation?" (Num. 16.22). A special notation is made, in that connection, of the fact that the sons of Korah were *not* punished when their father was destroyed (ibid. 26.12). Nevertheless when Amaziah put this rule into practice by sparing the children of the murderers of his father, he made an indelible impression on the memory of the people (II Kings 14.6). Men's thoughts had to be completely revolutionized before they became conscious of their own ego. Even Jeremiah, prophet as he was, but coming from the fields of Anathoth, assimilated the new doctrine only by steps; it was not until Ezekiel's maturity that the principle received its full and final formulation.

No sooner, however, had this been done, than the question of individual reward and punishment, hardly mentioned before Ezekiel's day, became a burning issue. If the individual rather than a group is the unit of moral responsibility, why do the wicked prosper and the righteous suffer? Isaiah had not asked the question, for individual prosperity or adversity were irrelevant in the social scheme as a whole. Jeremiah in his later years had struggled with it and had come to no definite conclusion. The writers of Job could not escape the problem, which flowed inescapably from Ezekiel's theology.

The doctrine of the resurrection offered a full solution to the difficulty and was altogether in the spirit of the individualism which prompted it. The individual is not an indistinguishable part of the community; he is an immortal being, for whom, if he has merited it, there waits another and happier life when God shall say the word.

The plebeian artisan and trader was thus doubly prepared for the doctrine of the resurrection, by his tendency to respect the individual and by his overpowering impulse to believe in some place where the world was in moral balance. To these factors was added the continual contact with Persian and Egyptian traders and travelers. The rural farmers naturally escaped this influence, and even the city patricians were partly immune to it.

We must not overlook, of course, the powerful effect of the natural piety of the plebeians on their willingness to accept the belief in the resurrection. It seemed to the religious teachers patent common sense that God would not forsake the righteous even after death. The idea that all mankind would find its permanent and ultimate home in a shadowy Sheol must have horrified the intelligent thinkers of this group, once they had rid themselves of the inherited prejudice in its favor. But this piety and intellectual outlook were both, as we shall see, far more fully developed among the city plebeians than among the aristocrats. They strengthened the influences which were making for the spread of the new doctrine; they could not bring it to any new section of the populace.

Yet such was the opposition to the new faith that it could hardly have won acceptance without the special assistance of other circumstances. The plebeian writers of Enoch who preached it were more than matched by the great patrician teachers who denied it. Foremost among these opponents of the doctrine of the resurrection was Ben Sira (ca. 200 BCE), himself a scion of aristocracy, who had, like many others in different ages, chosen to associate himself with the suppressed classes rather than with his own peers. He became a scholar and teacher, opposed to the Hellenism of his day, and generally sympathetic to the Hasideans. But as frequently occurs with patrician leaders of plebeian groups, he could not altogether enter into the soul of the oppressed whom he wished to lead. He sympathized with them, and like his great master, the High Priest, Simeon the Righteous, gave wider currency to some of their pronouncements. But in fundamental matters his early breeding, with its ingrained bias, inevitably asserted itself. The teaching of the resurrection must have been particularly repugnant to him. The prophets, most of the psalmists, the writers of the main body of Job, had denied it; yet it was making its way into Judaism. The plebeian acceptance of it seemed to him as assimilationist as the Hellenistic pastimes and affectations of the aristocrats.

So we find him saying with explicitness not found elsewhere:

"For when a man dieth, he inheriteth
Worm and maggot, lice and creeping things" (Ecclus. 10.11).
"For what pleasure hath God in all that perish in Hades,
in place of those who live and give Him praise?
Thanksgiving perisheth from the dead as from one that is not" (17.27)
"Fear not death, it is thy destiny;
Remember that the former and the latter share it with thee" (41.3).

Another Hasidean teacher, Antigonus of Socho, whose Hellenized name gives evidence that he, like

Ben Sira, was one of those who had renounced the privileges of their aristocratic heritage and thrown in their lot with the despised plebeians, tried to remove the burning issue from theological discussion. He appealed to the principle of virtue for virtue's sake, enunciating it with a vigor and dignity which, as Toy remarks, is quite without parallel "in the Old Testament or the New Testament."[1] "Be not," he taught, "like servants who obey their master in the hope of receiving reward" [m.Avot 1:1]. In the cautious ambiguity of the words, we still can see, as did the later sages, the denial of the doctrine of resurrection. The sage does not denounce it as heresy. He simply holds that its spread would interfere with the highest morality of "virtue for virtue's sake."

Whatever this politic evasion may have done to dull the edge of the controversy in the time of Antigonus and immediately after, its effect was completely wiped out in the turmoil of the Jewish resistance to the armed tyranny of Antiochus Epiphanes, distinguished as the first of a long line of religious persecutors of Judaism. The assimilationist movement among the Jews was too slow for him; in his efforts to hasten the consummation, he actually became the unconscious and unwilling instrument of their salvation. The listless and passive opposition to Hellenism, which had been initiated by Simeon the Righteous, Antigonus of Socho, Ben Sira and others, would in all probability have failed to catch up with the natural influence of environment; it was suddenly stimulated into furious zeal. Jewish piety had, until this point, been contemptuously ignored by the conqueror; it now became punishable with death. The bodies of the "criminals" remained unburned; synagogues were burned. The scrolls of the Law were desecrated and destroyed. Thousands of Jews, forbidden to practice their ancient customs and observances, fled to the paleolithic caves which abound in the land. The rage of the tyrant sought them out even there.

As they were faced with extinction and did not dare to anticipate the incredible victory which ultimately came, the vague and incipient suspicion of the Hasideans that their kingdom was not of this world, crystallized into rigid belief. It was now clear to them that all must perish before better times would come. The doctrine of the resurrection which had been held by a few eccentrics and progressives spread to ever wider circles. The writer of the Book of Daniel asserts it proudly and assures the dying martyrs that they will be called back to life eternal, while their oppressors also would be revived, but for everlasting derision and contempt.

That the writer of Daniel was an inhabitant of Jerusalem, hailing from plebeian rather than patrician circles, is implicit in the text. The sin which fills up the measure of Nebuchadnezzar's wickedness and brings about his expulsion from among men was not of the kind which could ever have awakened either the astonishment or resentment of an oriental noble. Arrogance was so proper to an aristocrat as actually to escape his attention. And the man who denounced it in the great king could be addressing himself only to the lowly. "The king spoke and said: 'Is not this great Babylon, which I have built for a royal dwelling-place by the might of my power, and for the glory of my majesty?' While the word was in the king's mouth, there fell a voice from heaven: 'O king Nebuchadnezzar, to thee it is spoken: the kingdom is departed from thee'" (Dan. 4.27). In his prayers Daniel speaks continuously of Jerusalem rather than of the whole land. "O Lord, according to all Thy righteousness, let Thine anger and Thy fury, I pray Thee, be turned away from Thy city, Jerusalem, . . . and Thy people are become a reproach to all that are round about us" (9.16). And then again, "O Lord, hear, O Lord, forgive, O Lord, attend and do, defer not for Thine own sake, O my God, because Thy name is called upon Thy city and Thy people" (ibid. 19). He advises Nebuchadnezzar to save himself from impending doom, not by ritual and prayer such as a patrician might recommend, but by almsgiving, the virtue peculiarly dear to the plebeian (4.24).

All remaining doubt that the plebeians were the first adherents in Israel to the doctrine of resurrection must be set at rest by a study of the actual events of the war. The Hasideans were joined in their resistance to Antiochus by the distinguished priestly family of Mattathias of Modin. In slaying the Jew who was about to offer an idolatrous sacrifice and the Syrian officer who was superintending the ceremony, the aged Mattathias raised the standard of revolt. These priests combined in themselves religious zeal with great ability and a hypnotic power of leadership. They were not the men to endure present oppression and persecution in the prospect of other-worldly restitution. Such was the contagious effect of their example that for a time they overcame even the passivity of the Hasideans, rousing them out of their dreams of consolation to an active assertion of their rights. The assassination of the apostate and of the royal agent was the first blow in a bitter war, which was not to end before the Syrian power in Judea had been destroyed. Certain Hasideans who, having fled to the wilderness, were attacked on the Sabbath by Syrian soldiers, permitted themselves to be cut down in cold blood, rather than violate the sacred day. "And Mattathias and his friends knew it, and they mourned over them exceedingly. And one said to another, If we all do as our brethren have done, and fight not against the Gentiles for our lives and our ordinances, they will now quickly destroy us from off the earth. And they took counsel on that day saying, Whosoever shall come against us to battle on the Sabbath day, let us fight against him, and we shall in no wise die as our brethren died in the secret places" (I Macc. 1.39–41). To the modern mind this decision seems to be the simplest common sense; to the Hasidean it meant a moral revolution. The thousand pietists who yielded themselves up to Syrian attackers were under no delusion as to the fate which awaited them. They had fled to the mountains in order to practice what was forbidden in the cities; their offense was punishable with death. But, filled with the conviction of individual resurrection and regarding this world as nothing more than a prelude to a greater and finer life, they faced their executioners calmly and perhaps even cheerfully. The Hasmoneans who, under pressure of necessity, were prepared to make a radical alteration in the interpretation of the Sabbath law, were men of a different stamp. They were warriors and diplomats, planning victory in this world, instead of dreaming of compensation in the next.

Two mutually opposing ideals were momentarily united in the rush of victory. But the forces of life continued, year in, year out, to recreate those mutually hostile social and religious forms which could never find ultimate reconciliation. The Hasidean saints, overwhelmed by the boldness of the Hasmonean priests, were ready to forget for a time what their class and experience represented. But life does not forget. Gradually the cleavage between the plebeian followers and the patrician leaders reasserted itself. Some Hasideans broke away when Jonathan continued the war after autonomy had been won. Others still remained loyal; but their descendants were ultimately forced to withdraw when King John Hyrkan openly broke with them.

The divergence was the same; it expressed itself in new names. The Sadducees who rallied about the Hasmonean House vehemently denied the resurrection, while the Pharisees, drawn essentially from among the descendants of the earlier plebeians, as vehemently continued to affirm it. The victory lay with the Pharisees. By their faith in the life beyond death they won adherents throughout the Jewish world. The Jews of the diaspora were almost altogether Pharisaic; and in Palestine the Sadducees were reduced to a few noble families.

The rural farmers, among whom urban individualism had made no inroads, were yet won to the soothing belief in human immortality. No matter how much the peasant might be lost in his family and his clan, he was easily brought to an understanding of his own ego by the plebeian teacher who came from Jerusalem. The doctrine of salvation, through which Christianity was destined ultimately to conquer the whole Roman Empire, was the means whereby the Pharisee won the plebeians, at least of Judea, to himself. But the Sadducee could not yield. His negation of the doctrine was not merely agnostic; it was religious, based, as we have seen, on prophetic tradition. On the other hand, with each war and each martyrdom, the pharisaic devotion to the new belief became more passionate, so that the Mishna regards it as a cardinal teaching of Judaism and condemns the dissenter to loss of future life.

The Pharisees would not permit anyone denying it to recite public prayers in their synagogues, and to make certain of correct belief, they inserted at the beginning of their main service an avowal of it.

"Thou art mighty, feeding the quick, quickening the dead. Blessed art thou, O Lord, who dost quicken the dead."

With the passing of years, the Pharisees, now more sophisticated, accepted the Greek philosophic doctrine of immortal souls, which renders belief in bodily resurrection superfluous and unnecessary. Yet such had been the struggle for the teaching of resurrection that it could no longer be forgotten. They continued to profess the older faith in a renewed world peopled with the revived dead, and at the same time denied that man can truly be said to die. The logical contradiction involved remained a puzzling and disturbing factor in rabbinic theology, and also in Christianity which is—in this respect—derived from it.

NOTE

1. Crawford Howell Toy, *Judaism and Christianity: A Sketch of the Progress of Thought from Old Testament to New Testament* (Boston: Little Brown, 1892), 260.

Other works by Finkelstein: *Jewish Self-Government in the Middle Ages* (1924); *Akiba: Scholar, Saint, and Martyr* (1936); *New Light from the Prophets* (1969).

Bernard D. Weinryb

1900–1982

Bernard Dov Weinryb was a prolific social and economic historian of East European Jewry. Born in Poland, he studied in Breslau at the Jewish Theological Seminary and at the university. In 1934 he moved to Palestine and in 1939 to the United States, where he taught at various universities and Jewish colleges.

The Jewish Economy
1938

1

When we speak about the economy of a given nation, about the German, French, or Polish economies, we don't mean the economic lives of all the people belonging, according to their race, language, nationality, to the German, French, and Polish people scattered throughout the world, but to the economic life of that part of the people located in a specific territorial unit governed by a given regime—in the German, French, or Polish state.

The economy, as a public activity, is formed within such a land area that constitutes the organic environment for all the varied and differing economic activities wherein they combine into a complete entity, whether the one complements the other or is derived from it. Also in its attitude to other units—other countries—the world economy proceeds via the channels of this national-political unit that impresses on the actions of the individuals and the groups its own characteristic features and makes them dependent on one another.

All of this is true for normal countries and nations, but in the case of the Jews as a people not concentrated in a given territory, the individuals and groups belonging to it and active in it economically do not constitute a complete unit: they exist within a foreign public where they perform certain functions. However, these functions of the Jews themselves do not constitute a complete unit but are absorbed within the other functions of the nations among whom they dwell. Therefore, should we, under such circumstances, speak about a "Jewish economy," about the economic activity of the Jewish public, or about "economy of the Jews," about the activity of Jewish individuals? And if we speak about Jewish economy, what are the characteristic features whereby we distinguish Jews from non-Jews, and what is the background against which the economic life of the Jews takes place?

Such questions must arise in anyone who observes the economic life of the Jews, who sees the Jews not as single atoms but as a more or less united public. But no real effort has so far been made to find a satisfactory answer to this.

Economic theory constitutes a much-neglected area of Jewish studies; *Chokhmat Yisrael* (or Jewish studies) in the West was born and developed in the wake of the Romantic movement, which saw the forces active in the world as "historical ideas." The nation, about which they speak so much, more than it being a human group whose life is influenced by its own specific economic needs and interests, is an abstract idea of "the spirit of the people" [*Volksgeist*], a unique spirit possessed collectively by each people or nation. To know the "spirit of the people," it was therefore unnecessary to refer again to the real details of the national life, but they believed that it could be revealed through spiritual things. In Judaism alone, in that same direction of reducing the world to matters of the spirit, it also led to the struggle for equal rights, against the theory of the "Christian state" that served as the basis for denying the rights of the Jews in the period after the Napoleonic wars—and which found support in the scholarship of that period—the Jews created other scholarly methods and sought to prove that Judaism was not in opposition to the general policy. This apologetic tendency led Jewish scholarship to face outward, whereas, on the other hand, the scholars, instead of considering matters of substance or close to reality where the Jews were sometimes separated from the peoples among whom they dwelt, preferred to deal with morality, ethics, and spiritual issues, whose traces they strove to discover in the past. And just as the proponents of *Chokhmat Yisrael* did not see, or did not wish to see, the true reality of life in their day, the powers and the interests of the nations among whom the Jews lived and who were opposed to equal rights for the Jews, and despised them and their sources of income that were considered unfair and not capable of standing up to the "progress" and "spirit of the time"—so, too, the Jews themselves failed to see the forces at play outside the spiritual life and that also influenced the spiritual life.

Non-Jewish economists, in the course of their research, also came across the role of the Jews in the general economy, and sometimes also touched on this issue in their general research, or at times devoted a small part of a larger study to it. But this investigation was no more than an addition to their main researches, a sort of by-product, which left its imprint on the whole process of the research both from the standpoint of content and method. They were interested mainly not in the economic life of the Jews as such, but in their role in the general economic life. They saw, therefore, only a part of the Jewish economy in relation to their own or of others to them. Where methodology is concerned, they transferred to the specific Jewish economic reality the method and laws applying to the general reality, which did not always correspond to the economic life of the Jews.

This one-sidedness, which was manifested at times also with an added antisemitic tendency, on more than one occasion left its mark on investigations of this type, and, as a result, also elicited a reaction on the part of the Jews. But from the very nature of the reaction, which was also one-sided, such studies were perforce mainly apologetic in nature. At times they tried to show the nations the benefit which the Jews had brought to the development of the economy and the culture, as well as the economic benefit that the rulers and the nations had derived from the Jews. And sometimes they were influenced by some non-Jewish scholars who pleaded the cause of the Jews [. . .] who sought to prove that certain negative traits in the character of the Jews and certain negative facts in their lives were related to socioeconomic factors. From here they came to the conclusion that a tragic inner contradiction governed almost all of *Chokhmat Yisrael*—that, on the one hand, its point of departure was idealism, and, on the other hand, it tried to explain certain phenomena with arguments based on materialist and Marxist theories. The prohibition of interest in the Torah, for example, is not, in their view, mainly the result of the primitive economy, but the fruit of a sublime idea that prevailed among the ancient Jews; on the other hand, they regard the excessive interest which the Jews took in the Middle Ages and in more modern times as only an economic necessity since they had no other source of livelihood. Furthermore, they also saw in the community regulations concerning charity for the poor the "compassionate heart" of the Jew. But that part of the regulations granting a monopoly to the wealthy members of the community, or forbidding poor Jews to come to the city to live there, was in their view only the result of the politics of the rulers toward the Jews. And they even reached the following "consistent" conclusion that the development of trade and commerce in various countries showed the great enterprise of the Jews who labored in it, fostered and increased it by their strength and energy, while admitting, at the same time, that commerce itself was inferior to other professions, but since other sources of livelihood were closed to them, the Jews were compelled to engage in it.

The Jewish-economy theory failed in Western Europe with the process of the segregation and atomization of the Jews who, due to their relatively small numbers, were absorbed for the most part into the economic life, and to a large extent also into the cultural life, of their country. Because of this, they only saw the individual Jew without seeking to find the common elements among these individuals that made them into a separate community.

With the Jews of Eastern Europe, we encounter a totally opposite process: they have been coalesced into a national bloc (or blocs) due to their large numbers and their economic and cultural isolation. The existence of a large and crowded Jewish collective necessitated the perception of a complete unit, hence also the aspiration for synthesis. Although in Jewish studies in Eastern Europe a greater interest in reality and in the economic lives of the Jews can be discerned, here too the methodological and systematic connection is lacking. They either consider the Jews from their economic standpoint as merely part of the environment (in Russia)—or wrestle with the contradiction between their collective as a public and their role in the economy of the general environment. Jacob Lestschinsky, in his study "The Development of the Jewish People in the Last 100 Years" (1928) says: "The Jews are everywhere an organic part of their social environment—and only the participation of the Jews in specific branches of the economy of the various countries highlights their role in the economic life of those countries"—that is to say, not Jewish economy but economy of the Jews. A few years later, at the opening of Volume 2 of *Ekonomishe shriften*, Lestschinsky again emphasized that "from the scientific point of view one cannot speak of a Jewish economy even in

the relative sense." Nevertheless, he immediately added that this does not mean to say "that the Jewish public is comprised of individuals who are socially disconnected, and yet is entirely integrated into the economy of the different national environments." But the Jewish public is dependent on two factors: it is influenced both by the environment and by the relations between Jews themselves. Finally, he left in his file the question of "Jewish economy or economy of the Jews," and raises the question regarding the nature of the economic basis on which the Jewish public has developed.

2

It is not easy to resolve such questions. As long as we approach them according to the criteria of economics in general, and use concepts borrowed from the economy of a normal nation, there is no hope of emerging from this tangle. Just as they failed to resolve the question of whether the Jews are a nation or a people, a cult or a religious community, as long as they sought to find among the Jews all the characteristics of a normal nation—country, territory, state, language, etc., with regard to a people whose destiny is different from that of other peoples—one must also adopt different criteria, which nevertheless are also applicable to other ethnic groups whose fate is comparable to that of the Jews.

It is certainly not necessary always to create new concepts for the economy of the Jews, and a great number of economic laws and processes are common to both Jews and non-Jews. The basic concepts of economics—production, distribution, consumption—are applicable to each and every public body, although sometimes a specifically Jewish nuance is liable to affect their content and undermine their legality. Economics is not simply a mechanical process that always comes and goes in the same scope, measure, and form. Here one must take into account mental processes, assumptions, and considerations that change the essence of things among the Jews. Furthermore, also from the legal standpoint, the Jews are by and large separated from the peoples among whom they live. Nevertheless, there are basic concepts common to each public, or that differ slightly in tone for the Jews. It will therefore be necessary first of all to distinguish the background and its varied nuances and combine them into a single unit from which the results of these changes can be adduced without our having to delve beneath the very structure of economic science.

If we attempt to define several concepts with greater clarity, it will be possible, in our opinion, to highlight the basic differences between the Jewish people and a normal people, to see them as one unit and thereby also to insert them into a framework of the uniform economic theory.

It seems to us to be a good idea to be assisted here by a concept that has yet to become generally accepted in economic science and which may make our task easier—the concept of *habitat*. The concept of *habitat* ("Lebensraum" or "living space") is taken from the natural sciences, where it is used to define the land and conditions of a uniform environment in which there are certain animals or plants. In recent decades, in German literature they have used the term *Lebensraum*—"living space, habitat" (the living space of the German nation)—to express the external conditions within which the nation is situated. If we transfer this concept to the economic field, it can adequately define the background of economic life.

[. . .] The people and the place are tightly bound together. For the people's life and work, land is required upon which they can lead their lives. For a nation sitting secure on its own land, the territory and its borders represent its wealth, its position among the neighboring countries, its political power both externally and internally, that same "living space" within which are interwoven all of its life in general, and its economic life in particular. Among the possibilities connected with and dependent on this "habitat" are its produce, its quality and its quantity, its distribution, means of production and distribution, the occupations of the populations, their low or profitable livelihood—in short, all its economic life.

The economic life of the Jews in the diaspora is also conditioned by their "habitat" and economic state. Their means of livelihood, their occupations and the changes they undergo correspond to the possibilities that their "habitat" affords them. However, that same "living space-habitat" of the Jews in the diaspora, in a specific country, is not identical to the habitat of the nation living there, even though it is dependent on it.

The Jews, as an extraterritorial people, cannot exploit all the possibilities offered in all parts of the territory in which they dwell, but only those which the "masters of the country" have not yet taken over, or have allotted them (willingly or forcibly). If the economic life of each and every nation can develop only according to

the extent of the possibilities which the state of their country—by definition, their "habitat"—offers them, so, too, the economic life of the Jews is the result of their condition and of the possibilities available to them in their "habitat" when they dwell among the nations. And just as a normal people, when its "living space" becomes too restricted, or when it wishes to go out of it and encounters the neighbors and their interests, has to go to war (a bloody war or a competitive war in industry, commerce, etc.) in order to expand the "living space-habitat," similarly, the Jewish collective, when it goes beyond the bounds of its habitat, encounters "the neighbors"—the peoples among whom it dwells—and their interests, and must wage its struggle (with various means) for the possibility of expanding the area of the habitat. This "habitat" of the Jews, which is generally smaller than that of the nations—more correctly, is only a part of it—constitutes the background and basis on which their economic life unfolds.

3

A

[. . .] In the case of the Jewish people (or a part of it) in its habitat, the difference between the general economy and the Jewish one starts not with the basic question and the point of departure, which are more or less constant, but at the secondary levels. Not in the approach to the subject, but rather in the manner of the approach, while distinguishing the absolute and fixed possibilities. The researcher must take into account the relative restrictions arising from the situation of the peoples among whom they dwell and which change and alternate frequently. And yet—if he takes into account both the varying and the permanent features in the Jewish habitat, and discovers the connection between them, he must take care that the need to take the general environment into account will not lead him into making that very usual error with regard to the economic history of the Jews, which is to equate its role with a description of the part of the Jews in the general economic life.

B

[. . .] The national majority, which also wields political and social power, strives to occupy the best economic positions, and leaves to the minorities the occupations that it has not yet occupied or is not able to do so for the present—mainly those of the second and third degree. And this causes the Jew, as a result, to fulfill in the economy functions other than those of the nations among whom they live.

[. . .] We may accept as a recognized fact that almost nowhere in the diaspora was the distribution of occupations among Jews equal to that of the peoples among whom they dwelt. There were always occupations—even productive ones—that were considered to be specifically "Jewish," and others that the Jews did not have any foothold in whatsoever or only minimally. This phenomenon we find, incidentally, in almost every nation or ethnic or even religious group, which in its wanderings arrived in a foreign country—not as a victor—and settled among another people—namely, among every minority group. In modern times we find such economic isolation among the Baptists who settled in sixteenth-century Moravia, and among the Dutch and Huguenots who settled in Germany from the end of the seventeenth century on, whether they engaged there in their old occupations or undertook new occupations. In any event, they, too, were unable, at least for a certain time—seeing that all the time they were foreigners—to penetrate into all branches of the economic life of the country. [. . .]

If these occupations do not provide sufficient income, or the settlement of the minority expands, or the value of their occupations increasingly declines, as a result of the changes in the overall economy, the members of the minority must go beyond the bounds of their habitat to expand it and take up new positions. In this process they encounter their "neighbors," the members of the majority population, and there erupts an economic war between them that also encompasses other areas (for example, an economic war between the nations of two countries that sometimes spills over from an economic to a bloody war). Only when the sources of livelihood in the habitat of the country have expanded, or for various reasons they took over positions that previously had been held by the majority nation, the members of the minority are able—as a rule, here too not without a struggle—to expand their habitat and take over new positions. And if they do not, then they are pushed backward and sometimes lose also a part or even all of their old positions. Sometimes this clash also leads to expulsion. [. . .] Such a struggle broke out also against the Protestants and the Baptists in Germany and Moravia. In Berlin and other places, the townspeople fought against these Protestants (sometimes against them and

the Jews together) with complaints to the authorities and with other means, at times bringing about the reduction in the size of their habitats. In Frankfurt-am-Main, a part of the Dutch who had settled there in the seventeenth century were forced to leave the city. The same happened also to the Baptists in Moravia. Some twenty years after their arrival, there were complaints about them, which increased in the second half of the sixteenth century, accompanied also by increased legal restrictions against them. This struggle intensified in the seventeenth century, and in 1622 they were expelled from the country.

This phenomenon is almost constant in the history of the Jews: on the one hand, exception to the habitat and the desire to expand it and to acquire new positions, and on the part of the national majority the wish to limit their habitat and drive them out. And between the two sides the war does not cease. It weakens or even ceases when the sources of livelihood in general increase, and intensifies at a time when the sources of livelihood are increasingly blocked or reduced.

C

At the time when the members of the national majority were supported in this struggle by their political power, the Jews were compelled (like members of other minorities who lacked this same power) to compensate for this lack with additional action and by various means—by investing hard work, energy, and additional forces. [. . .] The extra energy that they are required to invest will also enable them to penetrate into occupied sources of livelihood and to turn occupations of little importance into important sources of livelihood, and will act also as an alternative to the ruling power that only on very rare occasions supported the economic activity of the Jews.

In contrast to non-Jewish artisans, those with rights, who, by virtue of the law and the accepted customs, were able to sit at their ease in their stores and wait for customers to come and pay the fixed price, Jews revealed a greater adaptation to the needs of the purchaser; they brought his goods to his home, supplied him on credit, changed one item for another, reduced the price, and so on. In contrast to the non-Jewish producer and large merchant backed by the local state political power, the Jews who lacked this power were forced to use other stratagems: personal contacts, better-quality goods, [. . .] flexibility in response to the market demands—

incidentally, something which the members of other subjected peoples, who were also lacking in political power, also did. Just as every individual who, from a social or legal standpoint, etc., was in a worse position than his comrades, and had to work more intensively in order to subsist—to invest greater energy and work than they, the same applied to entire peoples, subject peoples, whose land was conquered by another people. They always required additional energy, additional action, in order to survive. In this way they created a sort of alternative that was equal at times to the power of the ruling nation that put obstacles in the way of the subject nation. The continued existence of the subject nations was always dependent on whether and to what extent they were able to achieve this "additional action." And not infrequently, it happened that this alternative of the subject nation, which was created as a counterweight to the political power of the ruling nation, in the course of time outweighed the importance of the political power; the decline of the conquering nations who were wiped off the face of the earth, and the rise of other nations on the stage of history are things that happened more than once. However, sometimes this additional intensiveness does not encompass all the areas but is necessarily limited to certain aspects of life, particularly when the subjected and persecuted people is not bigger or when smaller groups are involved (such as religious and ideological cults). In such cases they attain a one-sided "expertise" so that in one or more fields the persecuted group—as a result of its additional efforts—becomes a leading force at a time when in other areas it lags behind and its power and importance are much inferior to those of the ruling nation, or else it has been totally excluded from those areas altogether (the sociologists Weber and Zimmer and others have already dealt with such phenomena). The same thing happened to the Jews in their lands of exile. Their lack of political power, and the reality of another people ruling in the territory where they dwelt, led to the reduction of their habitat and, as a result, to the adoption of additional power through "additional action."

D

What is the "outcome" of our definition of a solution to the question regarding the nature of the Jewish economy, and of a common Jewish economic basis? The introduction of the concept of "habitat" to describe an organic environment in which a minority people dwells in the territory of another people, the majority people, gives us the possibility of perceiving the common background of all the members of this minority, thereby creating a uniform concept, combining details into a single whole, and revealing the connections between them. This makes it possible, on the one hand, to give general expression to the differences between majority peoples and minority peoples, and, on the other hand, the uniform background against which the economic life of the minority people takes place. It also helps us to explain the economic contrasts between the minority peoples and the majority nations, as well as the stratagems of the minority people in its economic struggle. It also helps to explain the specific professional distribution of the minority people, or their penetration into all the functions, as well as their economic isolation. All this makes it possible to include the Jewish economy in the field of study of economics as a whole, without our being required in each case to use special definitions, which contradict the very existence of a uniform theory. The different organic environment within the aforesaid "habitat" already includes all deviations from the general line. Jewish economic theory is no longer satisfied with an external approach accentuating only the relationships intermingled with the non-Jewish economy without any connection between each other except that their connections and their affiliations are dual in nature, both with regard to the non-Jewish environment and for their own environment as well.

To a certain extent this gives us the opportunity also to discover the connection between the Jews in different countries. The lines which we have highlighted, the existence of a special "habitat" that also has repercussions on the different distribution of occupations, the struggle over sources of livelihood between the majority nations and the Jews, the "additional action" as an alternative to duress, and the government assistance of the majority nations—incidentally, phenomena that are found also among other national minorities—are common to the Jews of the various countries. In this way it is possible to find, to a certain extent, a connection between the Jews in different countries with regard to their economic basis.

Incidentally, also in the economy of the Jews in Erets Yisrael one can discover several elements that were previously enumerated, due to their lack of political power and the presence of another people in the same area that puts obstacles in their path. However, that is a matter for special research.

Of course, one must not consider our interpretation as being a sole and absolute solution to the question of the Jewish economy, its nature and role. We have made an effort here to find such a solution and to provide a uniform and full explanation, and for this reason it was necessary to make abstractions from some concrete things. Certainly, the definition of *habitat* is an abstract construction, but this is the way of all theory and of every method, to forego many details and individual signs in order to produce a uniform and complete platform containing the main points, and to create a rational construction in order to explain fully and uniformly the isolated and individual phenomena.

Translated by David Herman.

Other works by Weinryb: *Neueste Wirtschaftsgeschichte der Juden in Russland und Polen . . . 1772–1881* (1972); *The Jews of Poland: A Social and Economic History of the Jewish Community in Poland from 1100 to 1800* (1973).

Religious Thought

The texts in this section span the spectrum of Jewish belief and practice in the interwar years—from traditionalist Orthodoxy in Eastern Europe and the Land of Israel; to modern Orthodoxy in Western Europe and the United States; to Conservative, Reform, and Reconstructionist Judaism in the United States. Included in this section as well are philosophers, like Martin Buber, Franz Rosenzweig, and Hermann Cohen, whose influence extended beyond denominational borders. Many of the texts in this section show how religious leaders responded to political events, such as the rise of Nazism in Germany or the emergence of a quasi-autonomous Jewish community in the Land of Israel, and how they drew on religious traditions for inspiration or adapted religious traditions to fit new circumstances.

Martin Buber

1878–1965

Martin Buber was one of the best-known Jewish thinkers in the Western world in the twentieth century. His neoromanticism and use of *völkisch* terms of analysis in his early writings exerted an enormous influence on Jewish youth in Central Europe, as did his popular (and frequently unreliable) accounts of Hasidic teachings. Perhaps more than any individual he was responsible for introducing Hasidism to Western-educated Jewish audiences. In 1923, he published his best-known philosophical work, *I and Thou*. In 1938, he moved to Jerusalem, where he was given a chair at the Hebrew University. Before 1948, he was among those in the Yishuv (mainly German-speaking, Central European intellectuals) who advocated a binational state in which Jews and Arabs would cooperate. After World War II, he was much lauded, both in Europe and America, as a great humanitarian.

Herut: On Youth and Religion
1919

> "God's writing engraved on the
> tablets"—read not *harut* (engraved)
> but *herut* (freedom).
> —Sayings of the Fathers VI, 2

Among all the problems of present-day Jewish life, that of youth's attitude toward religion is probably most in need of elucidation. But, one may ask, does youth really have a special religious problem? Is youth, as such, concerned with religion at all?

Is youth concerned with religion? This means: individually, young people may be religious or irreligious, depending on their personal disposition, upbringing, or environmental influences; but in what way does youth, as youth, have a definite attitude toward religion? Are we justified in demanding that it have one? Youth is the time of total openness. With totally open senses, it absorbs the world's variegated abundance; with a totally open will, it gives itself to life's boundlessness. It has not yet sworn allegiance to any one truth for whose sake it would have to close its eyes to all other perspectives, has not yet obligated itself to abide by any one norm

that would silence all its other aspirations. Its quest for knowledge knows no limits other than those set by its own experience, its vitality no responsibility other than the one to the totality of its own life. Sooner or later it will have to subordinate its own power of perception and volition to the restrictive power of natural and moral laws, thus losing its boundlessness. The decision of whether to submit to religious or other theorems, to religious or other rules, should therefore be left to youth itself. Whoever imposes religion upon it closes all but one of the thousand windows of the circular building in which youth dwells, all but one of the thousand roads leading into the world.

This admonition would be justified if religion were really, by nature, the dispenser of fixed orientations and norms, or a sum of dogmas and rules. By nature, however, it is neither. Dogmas and rules are merely the result, subject to change, of the human mind's endeavor to make comprehensible, by a symbolic order of the knowable and doable, the working of the unconditional it experiences within itself. Primary reality is constituted by the unconditional's effect upon the human mind, which, sustained by the force of its own vision, unflinchingly faces the Supreme Power. Man's mind thus experiences the unconditional as that great something that is counterposed against it, as the Thou as such. By creating symbols, the mind comprehends what is in itself incomprehensible; thus, in symbol and adage, the illimitable God reveals Himself to the human mind, which gathers the flowing universal currents into the receptacle of an affirmation that declares the Lord reigns in this and in no other way. Or man's mind captures a flash of the original source of light in the mirror of some rule that declares the Lord must be served in this and in no other way. But neither symbol nor adage makes man unworthy or untrue; they are rather forms the unconditional itself creates within man's mind, which, at this particular time, has not yet developed into a more effective tool. In mankind's great ages, the Divine, in invisible becoming, outgrows old symbolisms and blossoms forth in new ones. The symbol becomes ever more internalized, moves ever closer to the heart, and is ever more deeply submerged in life itself. [. . .] It is not God who changes, only theophany—the manifestation of the Divine in man's symbol-creating mind—until no symbol is adequate any longer, and none is needed; and life itself, in the miracle of man's being with man, becomes a symbol—until God is truly present when one man clasps the hand of another.

But such is the mysterious interconnection of the mind that, in this most essential of all human concerns, every human being comprises, potentially, all of mankind, and every human destiny, all of history. At some time or other, be it ever so fleeting and dim, every man is affected by the power of the unconditional. The time of life when this happens to all, we call youth. At that time, every man experiences the hour in which the infinite beckons him, testing whether, sustained by the power of his vision and the creation of symbols, by his dedication and response, he can unflinchingly confront it. In this most inward sense, every man is destined to be religious. Indeed, what the total openness of youth signifies is that its mind is open not merely to all, but to the All. But most men fail to fulfill their destiny. Whether they remain close to their ancestral religion or become alienated from it, whether they continue to believe in and to practice this religion and its symbolism or refuse to adhere to its command, they are unable to withstand the impact of the unconditional and therefore evade it. They do not approach it with the power of their vision and their work, with their dedicated and responsive deed; they turn away from it, and toward the conditional.

It should not, however, be assumed that by the conditional we mean secular things, not at all. We mean rather the things that have been stripped of their consecration and robbed of their bond with the unconditional. For the man who wholly gives himself to the unconditional—whatever he may call it—consecration resides in all things; in his dealing with them the divine Presence becomes manifest, and all is immortal. But the man who denies himself to the unconditional lives out his life amidst unholy conditionalities; he is ever surrounded by turmoil, and fulfillment comes apart in his hands.

We are not concerned, then, with imposing religion upon youth, or with forcing it into a system of the knowable and doable, but with awakening youth's own latent religion; that means: its willingness to confront, unwaveringly, the impact of the unconditional. We must not preach to youth that God's revelation becomes manifest in only one, and in no other, way; rather, we must show it that nothing is capable of becoming a receptacle of revelation. We must not proclaim to youth that God

can be served by only one, and by no other, act, but we must make it clear that every deed is hallowed if it radiates the spirit of unity. We must not ask young people to avow as exclusively binding in their lives only that which emanated at some hour of the past, but we must affirm for them that "every man has his hour" when the gate opens for him and the word becomes audible to him. We who stand in awe of that which is unknowable do not want to transmit to youth a knowledge of God's nature and work. We who consider life as more divine than laws and rules do not want to regulate the life of youth by laws and rules attributed to God. We want to help youth not to bypass its destiny, not to miss its metaphysical self-discovery by being asleep, and to respond when it senses within itself the power of the unconditional. By so doing, we do not diminish the openness of youth but promote and affirm it; do not curtain any of its windows, but let it absorb the all-encompassing view; do not shut off any road, but make it easier for youth to see that all roads, if walked in truth and consecration, lead to the threshold of the Divine.

But one may ask: "If religion's basic significance lies not in the mores or institutions of a community united by precept and cult but rather in acts derived from an innate awareness common to all men, that is in 'universally human' acts, how then is it possible to speak of a specific kinship between Jewish youth and religion? Or, to put it more generally, how is it possible to speak of a specific kinship between the youth of any people and religion?"

For an answer, we must first look at the general aspect of this question, and then investigate whether some special elements, nonexistent in any other people, are not at work in Judaism and its youth.

I have pointed out the error that threatens all young people and to which many fall prey: unable to withstand the impact of the unconditional, they evade it. But there exists still another, and more serious, error: the *pretense* of withstanding—a deception not only of others but of oneself. The unconditional affects a person when he lets his whole being be gripped by it, be utterly shaken and transformed by it, and when he responds to it with his whole being: with his mind, by perceiving the symbols of the Divine; with his soul, by his love of the All; with his will, by his standing the test of active life.

But it may happen, by some odd perversity, that an individual entertains the illusion that he has surrendered himself to the unconditional whereas in fact he has evaded it: he interprets the fact of having been affected by the unconditional as having had an "experience" (*Erlebnis*). His being remains wholly unperturbed and unchanged, but he has savored his hour of exaltation. He does not know the response; he knows only a "mood" (*Stimmung*). He has psychologized God.

The first of these errors, evasion, was especially characteristic of an earlier generation, which inclined toward superficial rationalism; the second, a quasi-acceptance, is common to the new generation, which is given to no less superficial emotionalism. This latter error is by far the more serious one, for a quasi-affirmation is always more questionable than a negation. In some way, religiosity may possibly penetrate the evaders but never the pretenders. One can be a rationalist, a free-thinker, or an atheist in a religious sense, but one cannot, in a religious sense, be a collector of "experiences," a boaster of moods, or a prattler about God. When the teeming swarms of the marketplace have scattered into the night, the stars shine over the new stillness as over a mountain silence; but no eternal light can penetrate the fumes of the chatter-filled public house.

But how can youth be saved from this error? Or rather, how can youth save itself from it? It has a great helper by its side: the living community of the people. Only the disengaged man, incapable of drawing upon any source deeper than that of his private existence, will degrade the unconditional's impact to an "experience" and respond with literary effusions to the music of the spheres. The man who is truly bound to his people cannot go wrong, not because he has at his disposal the symbols and forms that millennia of his people's existence have created for envisioning as well as for serving the unconditional, but because the faculty to create images and forms flows into him from this bond to his people. Right here it must be pointed out that a declaration of solidarity with one's people does not yet mean that one is truly bound to it. It means, at best, only the desire for such a bond.

When bound to his people, man is aware that the living community of this people is composed of three elements. Preceding him, there is the people's sacred work, expressed in literature and history, the scroll of words and deeds whose letters tell the chronicle of this people's relation to its God. Around him, there is the present national body in which, no matter how degenerate it may be, the divine Presence continues to live, immured in the tragic darkness of the everyday, yet shedding upon it the radiance of its primordial fire. And within him, in his soul's innermost recesses, there is a silent, age-old memory from which, if he can but unlock it, truer knowledge pours forth for him than that from the shallow wavelets of his private experiences. But this deep wellspring can be unlocked only by him who has made his wholehearted decision for such a bond.

Three elements that compose his people's living community, a threshold source of strength for the young, a threefold anchorage for his relation to the unconditional!

It should be remembered that the unconditional's effect upon individual man represents, as it were, a fore-shortening of its effect upon mankind's mind in general. How could an adequate response develop in individual man, how could he even conceive of an appropriate symbol, were he not part of the continuity of mankind's spiritual process? Response and symbol, however, are given to individual man directly only in the absolute, that is, the religiously creative, life of his people. Here mankind's wordless dialogue with God is condensed for him into the language of the soul, which he is not merely able to understand, but to which he himself can add new expressions, as yet unspoken. Without this language, he could do no more than stammer and falter. For even the founders of new religions, however new their words and deeds may seem to be, stand in fact within the continuity of their people's creation of symbols and images; and when they strike water out of the rock, this water was already flowing, invisibly and inaudibly, deep within the stone before their staff ever struck it. All religious founding, all genuine personal religion is merely the discovery and raising of an ancient treasure, the unveiling and freeing of a folk-religion that has grown beneath the surface. Without a bond to his people, man remains amorphous and adrift when God calls him; it is only from this bond that he derives contour and substance, so that he can dare to confront his Caller.

What I said about the young person's relation to the religious life of his people is especially relevant to Judaism, for two reasons. The first is the autonomy of Judaism's religious development, an autonomy not experienced by Western peoples. Among them, the natural growth of religious tendencies and forms was circumscribed and transformed by a spiritual principle imposed from the outside, Christianity; and despite all the artful attempts of the church to incorporate into its doctrine and its service the primal forces that had been at work in pagan myth and magic and had stirred the peoples' emotions, no perfect unity was achieved. Hence, in Christianity, the young person who wishes to derive sustenance and support for his personal relation to the unconditional from his association with his people must turn not so much to religion proper as to the primal forces that live on, covertly, in the faithful images of a people's life: its customs and tales, songs and sayings. In Judaism, however, other influences notwithstanding, all religious development sprang exclusively from forces inherent in the people's own soul, and foreign elements had no part in the conflicts that accompanied this development. Here, therefore, the young person faces a unified realm and when the official outward forms of his religion do not provide him with the help he needs, he need not turn away from them to another sphere of his people's existence; he has only to descend into their own depths, to those ramifications of Jewish religiosity that, not having become dominant, still continue to live beneath the surface.

But an even more essential reason is the fact that he *cannot* turn to any other sphere of his people's existence, for in the life of the Jewish people no sphere is unconnected with the religious one. Not only is Judaism's specific productivity bound up with its relation to the unconditional, but so too is its specific vitality. Any distinction between different fields of endeavor, characteristic of most other peoples, is alien to the nature of Judaism; its extrareligious elements are either so peripheral as to have no part in its creative expression, or they are, in one way or another, determined by and dependent upon religious factors. It is characteristic that even the people's original defection from the God of biblical religion assumed a religious form: the defecting masses were not content with surrendering themselves to their newly freed instincts; they expressed their driving passion by gathering together their valuables for the casting of an idol. The case of the modern Hebrew poet who, not content with forswearing allegiance to the old God, worshipped instead Apollo's statue, exemplifies the same characteristic. No matter what form religious creativity may assume in Judaism, it never loses its basic character. The greatest philosophical genius Judaism has given to the world, Spinoza, is the only one of the greatest philosophers for whom, in reality, God is the sole subject of thought; and ancient Messianic dreams live on in the ideologies of Jewish socialists.

I am well aware that ever since the demand for Jewish regeneration in our time became more insistent there have been men who deplore the predominance of the religious element in Judaism, though they are far from holding any shallow enlightenment theories. They see in this predominance a narrowing of the people's life, a weakening of its vitality, and a divergence of its energies from their natural tasks. These men demand a secularization of Judaism, and, given the vegetating *galut* life in which religious demands in their narrowest sense have so frequently stifled the people's vitality, I recognize that there is justification for such a view. Nevertheless, it is based on a fundamental error that mistakes the historical outward forms of its religion for Judaism's great religious creativity. Religion is detrimental to an unfolding of the people's energies only where it concentrates—as it has indeed done to an ever-increasing degree in the Diaspora—on the enlargement of *thou shalt not*, on the minute differentiation between the permitted and the forbidden. When this is the case, it neglects its true task, which is and remains: man's response to the Divine, the response of the total human being; hence, the unity of the spiritual and the worldly, the realization of the spirit, and the spiritualization of the worldly; the sanctification of the relationship to all things; that is, freedom in God. But Hasidism, though still closely tied to the tradition of the *thou shalt not*, already presents a great, though unsuccessful, attempt at a synthesis between the spiritual and the worldly order, a fusion of fundamental religious consciousness with the unaffectedness and fullness of natural life. And the future of creative Judaism lies not in a weeding out of religiosity but in the direction of this synthesis. The growing striving for this synthesis is youth's guarantee that it will not find decomposing rocks but the waters of genuine life when it descends into the depths of Jewish religion in search of help for its soul.

Intellectualization, in the making for centuries and accomplished within recent generations, has brought a depressing loneliness to the youth of present-day Europe. By intellectualization I mean the hypertrophy of intellect that has broken out of the context of organic life and become parasitic, in contradistinction to organic spirituality, into which life's totality is translated. Because the bridge of immediate community, whether its name be love, friendship, companionship, or fellowship, connects only man with man, and hence spirit with spirit, but not thinking apparatus with thinking apparatus, this intellectualization begets loneliness. Not the exultant loneliness of the summit experienced by the first climbers who are waiting, with silent hearts, for their companions who have fallen behind, but the negative loneliness of the abyss experienced by the lost and the forlorn. Out of the anxiety and depression of such a state of mind, modern Europe's youth longs for community, longs for it so powerfully that it is ready to surrender to any phantom of community, as we have so abundantly experienced. But, owing to the anomaly of *galut* life, intellectualization has progressed still further, and the loneliness of Jewish youth has been intensified. In addition, a large segment of Jewish youth, especially in the Western world, is cut off from its natural national existence and gradually loses the illusion that it has organic ties to another one. And this too intensifies its longing for community.

Only a genuine bond with the religiously creative life of its people can still this longing of Jewish youth, and overcome the loneliness of its intellectualization.

I have already indicated why youth needs this bond for the building of its inner religious life: to enable it to confront the unconditional not with the arbitrary mood of the dreamer who has had an "experience" but with the readiness of the fighter and worker who, despite all personal freedom, binds himself to his people's creativity and pursues it in his own life. But youth needs this bond no less for its inner national life. It must no longer permit itself the illusion that it can establish a decisive link to its people merely by reading Bialik's poems or by singing Yiddish folksongs; nor by the addition of a few quasi-religious sentiments and lyricisms. It must realize that something bigger is at stake: that one must join, earnestly and ready for much struggle and work, in Judaism's intense creative process, with all its conflicts and subsequent reconciliations; that one must recreate this process from within, with reverence of soul and awareness of mind; that one must participate in it not only with his inwardness but with his total life, by affirming and translating into reality all one finds along the way; that what needs to be done is to get ready for renewal. For the idea of renewal must not—as so happens to ideas in the short-winded Jewish movement of our days—degenerate into a comfortable slogan that would exempt us from the effort of struggling, studying, and building, a slogan in which emotions may luxuriate and the mind go slack. The idea of renewal must be the banner carried at the head of the procession by those who put their beliefs into practice. Renewal is in

the making when Judaism's spiritual process, which is a process of religious struggle and religious creativity, is restored to life, in word and deed, by a generation earnestly resolved to translate its ideas into reality.

But restoration demands something more creative than mere joining-in, though it cannot be achieved without it. And here the basic question comes to the fore: what should the nature and the object of this joining-in be?

Depending on whether the essence of Jewish religion is viewed as lying in its teaching or in its law, two ways are advocated for today's youth to follow: to commit itself either to Jewish teaching or to Jewish law.

I shall begin with the first of these views. Its leading proponents sublimate the many-faceted and vital fullness of religion into a system of abstract concepts. But in the process the nurturing, creative, inexplicable element of religion, the awareness of its suprarationality, is lost. Dogmas, primarily the dogma of God's oneness, and moral commandments, primarily the commandment to love one's neighbor, are singled out and summarized in formulations that as a rule are shaped to fit one or another dominant philosophical school. Consequently, to anyone unfamiliar with the suprarational wealth of Jewish religiosity, Judaism appears to be a curious, awkward detour to some modern philosophical theorems—as, for instance, the idea of God as a postulate of practical reasons, or the categorical imperative—a detour that historically was probably unavoidable, but that has now become wholly superfluous.

The originators of such theories overlook the fact that religious truth is not a conceptual abstraction but has existential relevance; that is, that words can only point the way, and that religious truth can be made adequately manifest only in the individual's or the community's life of religious actualization (*Bewährung*). Indeed, they overlook the fact that a master's teachings lose their religious character as soon as they are taken out of the context of his own life and the life of his followers and transformed into a wholly non-personal, autonomous maxim, recognizable and acknowledgeable as such. Frozen into a declaration of what is or into a precept of what ought to be, the words of religious teaching represent a more in-spirited, but also a more primitive, variation of a metaphysical or ethical ideology. But viewed as part of the utterances of a great life to which conceptualization cannot do justice, they are beyond the sphere of all ideologies and not subject to their criteria; they are truth *sui generis*, contingent upon no other: religious truth. Here, not the words themselves are truth, but life as it has been, and will be, lived; and the words are truth only by virtue of this life. In Judaism, therefore, the truth of God's oneness encompasses not only the "I shall be there" but also all of Moses' life; not only the "Hear, O Israel" but also the death of the martyrs.

Furthermore, the authors of the aforementioned theories overlook the fact that religious truth is not static but dynamic; that is, it neither belongs to nor is finished with any single historical moment in time. Nor can it be taken out of the context of such a single moment. Instead, every moment of the past, no matter how rich in revelation, is one phase of this truth, as is in fact every religiously creative period. Thus, in Judaism, conjoined to the truth of God's oneness is its entire development and all its transformations: the multiplicity of God's biblical names in their gradation from a natural plurality to a spiritual singularity; and equally the separation of the *shekhinah*, in correspondence with the growing awareness of the empirical world's imperfection. The heavenly hosts who are asked to create man are part of it, and so are the *sephirot* through which the Divine emanates into the world—all of which, instead of diminishing oneness, intensify it. Some subsequent developments are also part of it, and, I daresay, some that are yet to come.

Religious truth, in contradistinction to philosophical truth, is not a maxim but a way, not a thesis but a process. That God is merciful is an abstract statement; to penetrate the religious truth that lies beyond it, we must not shrink from opening the Bible to one of its most awful passages, the one where God rejects Saul, His anointed (upon whom, at election, He bestowed a new spirit), because he spared the life of Agag, the conquered king of the Amalekites. Let us not resist the shudder that seizes us, but let us follow where it leads as the soul of the people struggled for an understanding of God. We shall then come to that wondrous passage in the Talmud where, according to an old biblical interpretation, God rejoices in Goliath's soul and answers the angels who remind Him of David: "It is incumbent upon Me to turn them into friends." Here we see a religious truth.

Purity of soul is an ethical concept. Nevertheless, let us not recoil from reading, in the third Book of Moses, the paragraphs that describe purification by the blood of sheep and doves as well as the great purification through the scapegoat. And when our hearts tremble under the impact of the great, ancient, but also alien, symbol, let us follow the way the people's soul took as it struggled for its purity, a way leading beyond prophets and psalmists to Akiba's liberating cry: "God is the purifying bath of Israel!" Only then will we become fully aware of the religious element in this concept of purity.

A bond between virtue and reward has become unacceptable to our own sensibility toward life and the world. But we must not read this attitude into the records of the ancient Jewish religion where, from God's covenant with the patriarchs, through Moses' blessing and curse, to the promises and threats of the prophets, the belief in reward and punishment constitutes a self-evident basis for the moral postulate, a belief perpetuated even in the abstraction of the Maimonidean articles of faith. At the same time we must not close our eyes to the struggle in which men of sacred will turned, with ever increasing determination, away from this belief. We can follow the progression of this from the lofty talmudic phrase "for the sake of the Torah itself" to that hasidic tale in which the Baal Shem (who, owing to a transgression, is to be denied life in the world to come) gratefully rejoices, for only now will he be able to serve God wholly for His own sake. Here, a religious truth unfolds for us.

We must therefore reject commitment to a claim that Jewish teaching is something finished and unequivocal. For us, it is neither. It is, rather, a gigantic process, still uncompleted, of spiritual creativity and creative response to the unconditional. It is in this process that we want to participate with our conscious, active life, in the hope that we, too, may not be denied a creative spark. But to achieve this participation, we must fully discern this process—discern not merely some of its isolated aspects or effects, not only maxims or theses, but, in earnest awareness, its whole development up to the present, recreating it in its entirety from within. Yet this is not enough. We must truly *will* this process, all of it, from its beginnings, through all its ups and downs, conflicts and reconciliations, up to ourselves—the lowly but God-inspired sons of a transitional generation, doing their share to the best of their abilities—and beyond our time.

The second of the two views I spoke of renders the word Torah not as "teaching" but as "law"; its proponents bid Jewish youth to commit itself to Jewish law. By the term "law" they mean the sum of all the statutes, preserved at first in unwritten form but later committed to writing, that God, according to tradition, gave to Moses on Mount Sinai, within the hearing of the assembled people of Israel. The tradition of this giving of the law, reinforced by the life and death of a long chain of generations, is so powerful and venerable that some of its power and venerability is imparted to every man who truly dwells within it; that is, to the man who with his total being adheres to its commandments and prohibitions, not because he was taught and conditioned to do so by his parents and teachers, but because he feels certain in his soul that these 613 commandments and prohibitions are the core and substance of God's word to Israel. Samson Raphael Hirsch is fully justified in assigning a central position to this principle used by his antipode, Mendelssohn, in his dispute with Lavater, as the main argument for the validity of Judaism. Having pointed out the fact that all of Israel had heard the Lord's voice without any intermediary, Hirsch continues: "By this fact, which excludes any possibility of error, the Torah has been established, immutably, for all generations and for all times."

Genuine affirmation of the law must be anchored in this certitude of the fact of revelation and that its content has been faithfully preserved in the 613 *mitzvot* and their framework. Indeed, such affirmation has religious value only insofar as it is supported by this certitude. The legitimacy of the life of the man whose observance of the law is grounded on this basis is unassailable, the legitimacy of what, to him, is truth, irrefutable. He deserves our esteem and approbation, especially when, for the sake of observing the law, he gladly assumes the burden of overcoming the countless difficulties and temptations presented by our society. But if he lacks this certitude, his sacrificial spirit, whether a result of piety or of habit, loses its religious import and hence its special sanctity.

Observance of commandments because one knows or feels that this is the only way in which to live in the name of God has a legitimacy all its own, essentially inaccessible to all outside criticism, whose criteria it can reject. But observance without this basic attitude means exposure of oneself as well as the commandments to a test by criteria of a wholly different ethos. For relationship to the unconditional is a commitment of the total man, whose mind and soul are undivided; to divorce the actions indicative of this commitment from the yea-saying of man's undivided soul, to sever them from their accord with man's undivided mind, is to pro-

fane them. But it is such profanation that is perpetrated by those blind followers of the law who demand that it be accepted not out of certitude of its divine origin but out of obedience to the authority of the collective Jewish will. They declare that, first and foremost, the law must be observed; everything else will then follow. The law, they say, restrains the will but leaves the personality free.

We reject this dialectic completely. In the image of man to which we aspire, conviction and volition, personality and performance, are one and indivisible. And though it may yet take lengthy, indescribably difficult battles against the enormous resistance of external and internal forces before this unity is realized in all other areas, there is one particular area in which there must be no further delay: the area of religiosity. For this is the true realm of unity, the realm where man, in every other respect still divided, split apart, and torn by conflict, may at any moment become whole and one. [. . .]

For those who have not been granted the certitude I spoke of, this insight charts a course that is incompatible with the acceptance of traditional law. And no one familiar with the new religious consciousness of a new youth—this planet, still aglow and uncongealed, that is as yet aware only of revolving around its own axis, with barely a first inkling of an orbit around the unknown sun—no one who has ever been close to the secret of this becoming will think it could contain the belief in a one-time revelation, transmitted in its entirety and binding for all time.

It would seem, however, that the passionate will for community that I spoke of is motivating Jewish youth to commit itself to traditional teaching and law after all. It feels an ever-growing urge to truly find its way back to its people—not merely to this people's recorded past and dreamed-about future but also to its actual present—and to become an organic part of the people, to merge with it. And it seems to some of them that such a merging can be achieved only by acceptance of the special teachings and customs of the Jewish people, which constitute the teachings and customs of Jewish tradition. They are supported in this view by exhorters and zealots who, dissatisfied with their experience of Jewish nationalism—dissatisfied because, in their opinion, it is not Jewish enough; dissatisfied, in truth, because it is not human enough—now proclaim as the last and redeeming word a commitment to the law of their common tradition. But those who clutch at this belief are blind to the signs appearing, at this hour, on the firmament of our destiny and the destiny of the world. There is greatness in the national body, and its faithful adherence to the law is awe inspiring. Yet greater still is the working of the national spirit, and he who, in sensitive awareness, has opened his soul to it knows that something new will rise out of it.

But neither will this new element rise out of nothingness. It, too, will develop and transform already existing material; it, too, will be a discovery and raising of an ancient treasure, an unveiling and freeing of something that has grown beneath the surface. It behooves us, therefore, to grasp the old, with our hearts and minds, but not lose our hearts and minds to it. We want to remain faithful to the intent of that great spiritual movement which we call the Jewish movement, a movement that is not romanticism but a renascence. For even though the admonishers and zealots may not concede it, it is always romanticism when the spirit, in its search for a people, submits and surrenders to the forms developed in that people's past and transmitted, in word and custom, from that past. And it is always a renascence when the spirit brings to life the primal forces encapsuled in those forms, calling them forth to new creation—when it encounters a people and makes it creative.

In the light of this perception we shall try to find an answer to the question occupying our mind. But first I must explain to whom I refer by this "we," and to whom I am united in question and answer. They are the people for whom this address is intended. There are only a few of them. They are those members of Jewish youth who genuinely participate in the evolving religious awareness of an evolving generation. By this I mean those young men and women who are concerned not with acquiring security in the chaos of our time by conforming to the tested order of the knowable and doable but solely with confronting, unwaveringly, the impact of the unconditional at this hour of twilight, an hour of death and birth. A detached, ego-centered life cannot provide youth with the contour and substance required for such a confrontation. To acquire such contour and substance, man must commit himself totally to all the forces that have shaped the human spirit up to now, and which are given to individual man directly only in the absolute, that is, the religiously creative, life of his people, whose spiritual process he must restore to life

in word and deed. To be sure, such restoration requires something more creative than mere commitment, but it cannot be achieved without it. We asked ourselves what manner of commitment this should be. We shall now try to find an answer to our question.

As we have seen, we cannot commit ourselves to an acceptance of Jewish teaching if this teaching is conceived as something finished and unequivocal; nor can we commit ourselves to Jewish law if this law is taken to mean something closed and immutable. We can commit ourselves only to the primal forces, to the living religious forces which, though active and manifest in all of Jewish religion, in its teaching and its law, have not been fully expressed by either. [. . .] They are the eternal forces that do not permit one's relationship to the unconditional ever to wholly congeal into something merely accepted and executed on faith, the forces that, out of the total of doctrines and regulations, consistently appeal for freedom in God. Though religious teaching may assign to the Divine a Beyond from where our world is enjoined, rewarded, and punished, the primal forces point beyond this division (apparently without violating religious teaching) by permitting the birth of unity in the free deed of the complete human being. And though the law may proclaim a differentiation between the holy and the profane, these primal forces overcome this differentiation (apparently without violating the law) by permitting the hollowing of the profane in the free deed of the complete human being. Their task is to call forth man's response to the Divine, the response of the complete human being, and, hence, the unification of the spiritual and the worldly: the realization of the spirit and the hallowing of the worldly, the sanctification of the relationship to all things, that is freedom in God. God's writing on the tablets constitutes freedom; the religious forces persistently strive to rediscover those symbols of divine freedom again. God's original tablets are broken. The religious forces of eternal renewal persistently strive to restore the blurred outlines of divine freedom on the second tablets, the tablets of the teaching and the law. The eternally renewed effort of these forces denotes the endeavor to fuse, once again, fundamental religious consciousness with the unbiasedness and fullness of natural life, as they had been fused on God's original tablets. There are intimations of a new endeavor. We believe it will succeed; we have faith in the new element trying to emerge from the people's spirit. To help prepare this emergence of the new, a generation willing to put its ideals into practice and to restore Judaism's spiritual process to life, in word and deed, must commit itself to the primal forces. They are the treasure that must be uncovered and raised, the subterranean growth that must be brought to light and freed. We need their help in order to withstand the impact of the unconditional in this hour of death and birth.

Mankind's religious longing, awakening at this hour, is akin to Judaism's primal forces. Today, thinking men can at last no longer tolerate the dualism of spirit and "world," the antithesis between the soul's hypothetical independence from the world's deadening hustle and bustle and life's dependence on it. They no longer want to bear the yoke of this conflict sanctioned by the churches; they want to grasp the unity of spirit and world, realize it, and thus bring about true freedom, that is, freedom in God. Divided man is, of necessity, unfree; only unified man becomes free. Divided man can never effect anything but division; only unified man can establish unity. Unified, unifying, total man, free in God, is the goal of mankind's longing that is awakening at this hour, just as he is the meaning of Judaism's religious forces. Herein resides the power that alone can raise Judaism above degeneracy and torpidity, and by so doing enable it to once again write its message into the history of the world.

But comprehension of their fundamental tendencies hardly constitutes sufficient commitment to these forces. Such comprehension is only the gateway to full awareness of their entire course. We must, I repeat, participate from within in the mighty spiritual process with reverence and awareness of mind. Having thus joined in this process, we must, by our active participation in it, begin affirming and realizing all we have found there with the totality of our life.

But we cannot participate in this spiritual process, nor walk inwardly along the path of the primal forces, solely with our emotions. It must be done in reverent and unbiased knowledge, a knowledge that, though it will always owe to intuition its access to the heart of things, cannot dispense with the reliable tools of assembling, sifting, and examining the facts before it can find this access. Only the fusing of all that has been found will be the business of our freely creative emotions.

I say reverent and unbiased knowledge, for it is a painful failing of our youth to approach matters of Jewish religion partly without reverence and partly without freedom from bias. This lack of reverence is by no means characteristic only of those who have no religious inclinations; it is characteristic also of those who do have religious inclinations but, content with these inclinations, treat the great historical religious systems either as obsolete or irrelevant to their own religious emotions. If, instead of simply luxuriating in them, these young people would ask themselves whether their emotions are actually anything more than a mood, they would recognize their lack of substance. They would also perceive that, no matter how lofty they may appear to be, these emotions will remain sterile if they fail to derive nurture from the records and forms in which the effect of the unconditional upon the spirit of the people has become manifest during the four millennia of its path. Others, on the other hand, easily fall prey to the bias that views these records and forms, so long as they are sanctioned by official tradition, as an undivided whole in which no distinction may be made between living and dead forces, or between symbols of vital or of negligible import. But, though it is indeed possible to accept them without an unbiased, discerning view, it is not possible to choose from them—and it is this that is of decisive importance here.

Our religious literature must become the object of reverent and unbiased knowledge. The reader of the Bible must attempt to understand the spirit of its original language, the Hebrew—an understanding that is service (*dienendes Wissen*); he will approach it not as a work of literature but as the basic documentation of the unconditional's effect on the spirit of the Jewish people; whatever his knowledge of old as well as new exegesis, he will search beyond it for the original meaning of each passage. No matter how familiar he is with modern biblical criticism's distinction between sources, he will penetrate beyond this criticism to more profound distinctions and connections. Though unafraid of bringing to light the mythical element, no matter how initially alien it may be to him, he will not advance a mythical interpretation where there exists an adequate historical one. He will read the Bible with an appreciation of its poetic form, but also with an intuitive grasp of the suprapoetic element which transcends all form. To such a reader the Bible will reveal a hidden treasure and the operation of primal forces from which the seed of new religiosity can derive sustenance and substance. Such reading of the Bible should be followed by earnest study of later literature, without omitting the unwieldy and seemingly unpromising material.

Similarly, the Jewish masses and all their beliefs and customs must also become an object of reverent and unbiased understanding. We must come close to their inner life, submerging ourselves in its inwardness and ardor, which have not been diminished, and indeed cannot be diminished, by any misery; must perceive how the Jewish people's old religious fervor still endures among them, though in distorted and occasionally degraded form, and how there burns within it the desire, as yet unstilled, to hallow the earthly and to affirm the covenant with God in everyday life. We must discern, simultaneously, two things: that this people is in need of regeneration and that it is capable of achieving it, for, along with those of decadence, it carries within it the elements of purification and of redemption.

Together, these two undertakings, exploring the people's literature and probing the depths of its life, will enable a generation that possesses reverent and unbiased understanding to go step by step along the course of the primal forces as it leads up to its own time.

For us, even more distinctly than for other men, this is a time of doom as well as of liberation, of going astray as well as of returning. Whether the presently unfolding religious consciousness of a new generation will grow to full maturity, and whether this generation will then assume leadership, will be decisive for mankind's fate. As for Judaism's fate in particular, it will be decisive whether a generation at the turning will be capable of resuming the course of the primal forces; that is, whether it will be able to find once again within its own soul the readiness for struggle and the creativity of the forces whose original struggles and creativity they have discerned and experienced. Both fates, mankind's general and our particular one, are connected at their core. For mankind's religious longing, awakening at this hour, is akin to the primal forces of Judaism.

Walking along the pathway of the primal forces, the generation at the turning encounters its own self; it can encounter it solely along this pathway. But only when it finds that the forces it has discerned dwell also within its own self can it make a choice and give direction to its own innermost powers.

When the primal forces become truly alive within a new Jewish generation, and desirous of being reactivated, then, in close linkage to them, this generation must resume their work; must begin to prepare a new work site for them within its own community, on the soil where, under cinders and ashes, still glimmer sparks of the old forge.

We must create a community, cemented by joint labor and joint sacrifice, a community of men who, in the name of the nameless God, will journey to the Zion of His realization. The mystery within their hearts is swelling, beyond all confines of teaching and law, toward the still inexpressible, the still formless. Discernment of the primal forces has disclosed to them the power whereby the inexpressible and formless can undergo a new incarnation: the human response to the Divine, the unification of spirit and world. There is only one road that will deliver us from the doom of our time: the road leading to freedom in God. If we know this, not through concepts or "moods" but through genuine awareness of a life of decision, then, no matter how far removed from all tradition we may seem to an insensible glance, we will have committed ourselves to the great course of Judaism.

NOTE
Brackets appear in the original translation.

Translated by Eva Jospe.

Other works by Buber: *Tales of the Hasidim* (1947); *Two Types of Faith* (1951); *Eclipse of God* (1952); *The Legend of the Baal Shem* (1955); *The Tales of Rabbi Nachman* (1956); *For the Sake of Heaven* (1969).

Hermann Cohen

1842–1918

Hermann Cohen was the most important Jewish philosopher in Europe in the late nineteenth and early twentieth centuries. Cohen, who spent his entire career at the University of Marburg, was one of the leading figures in the movement calling for a revival of Kantian thought to counter the decline of German idealism in the second half of the nineteenth century. Although Cohen eventually became the leader of this neo-Kantian movement, known as the Marburg School, and published extensively on Kant, he broke with him in his approach to Judaism. Whereas Kant considered Judaism to be an obsolete religion, Cohen presented it as the source of the religion of reason, especially in his posthumously published, last great work, *Religion of Reason: Out of the Sources of Judaism* (1919). Cohen was a fervent German patriot and outspoken opponent of Zionism. He considered Judaism to be an inherently ahistorical religion whose spiritual mission transcended the narrowly nationalist aims of Zionism.

Religion of Reason: Out of the Sources of Judaism
1919

The Sources of Judaism

1. We have now obtained a preliminary articulation of reason and religion; we turn now to the *sources of Judaism,* out of which the religion of reason should be derived. We ought not to begin with the concept of Judaism, for the latter should be demonstrated as the religion of reason. Through this demonstration, which this book has to give, the concept of Judaism will come to be determined. If we wished to begin with the concept of Judaism, we would still have to anticipate its sources. Rather, we have to start with the general methodological meaning of these sources.

Basically, even in the sources the whole concept of Judaism is anticipated. For from the sources emerges everything that comes to light as Judaism. There is, however, good methodological reason for separating institutions and monuments, on the one hand, from literary sources, on the other. Only the latter bring to light the content of monuments, so that they come to be properly understood only through the written sources.

The literary sources are the immediate manifestation of the spirit, which in other monuments works through more remote means. The literary sources are the true sources for the workings of the spirit, of a national spirit, which in turn becomes the prime ground for the individual.

2. The literature of the Jews, as primary in its origin as it is, is a national literature. This characteristic of a primary origin has been and remains the common feature of Jewish literature; to the extent to which the primary origin is preserved, to that extent the national character of Jewish literature is preserved. Its primary origin, however, consists in, and is rooted in, the idea of the unique God. The words "Hear, O Israel" and "the Eternal is Unique" complement each other. The spirit of Israel is determined by the idea of the unique God. Everything that comes forth from the spirit of Israel comes forth just as much from the unique God as it does from the national spirit in its primary origin and peculiarity.

However, the productions of this basic idea are manifold; they traverse a long history. Even the first beginnings do not lack a great and seemingly contradictory variety.

It is characteristic that Deuteronomy refers to the "statutes and ordinances" for the value of its new teaching. Moral forms of legality are spoken of as products of the new religion. Thus, there arises *a connection between religion and social politics.* For the "statutes and ordinances" through which the "wisdom" of this people, as well as God's guidance, are to be proven are forms of legality in which social and individual morality are to be established and strengthened. Deuteronomy assumes a reciprocal action between religious theory and ethical practice. Through this the religious sources extend over the institutions of the state. This connection between theory and practice remains decisive for Judaism and therefore for its literary sources as well.

The entire Pentateuch uniformly has this twofold characteristic. It teaches not only the knowledge of God and man but also the care and encouragement of this knowledge. It is therefore a source both for the productions of the mind, which the national spirit creates, as well as for its practical creations. The "teachings" (תורות) appear in Deuteronomy later than the "statutes and ordinances" (חקים משפטים).

3. The scope of the sources, however, is even broader in the whole Old Testament. The national literature begins with the national *history* and with the myths and sagas that surround it. This history gradually changes into *politics.* This process of change is accomplished through the ideas of the prophets and for this change, also, Deuteronomy is an instructive document. In it Moses, in his speech, traces the early history, in order to expound its application to future politics. Politics seems *to be properly native* to the ideas of the prophets. Solon, too, has been called a prophet, but even he lacks the degree of primary origin that distinguishes prophetic naiveté. Prophecy is the spiritual focus of Jewish creativity. Its root lies buried in history, in national history, with its native ethics, and this root still gives to the stem, the higher it grows, its life-giving sap. What is the distinguishing characteristic of the prophetic idea? It is the notion that religion and politics are inseparable. Politics is for religion a lifeline that has to die when politics ceases. And what becomes of it then?

4. Other powers of a genuine national spirit are also alive in Judaism. The *lyric*, which is the root of poetry, is also a Jewish national source. *Thus the psalms grow out of prophecy.* Again, another peculiarity of the Jewish spirit is the unity of the spirit of the people with its creation, namely, with religion. The psalms have been

compared with the *Babylonian* psalms. The comparison holds true for the external form of the triumphal song and for the hymn to gods and heroes. However, the kinship of the psalms to prophecy is lacking there, and no loftiness of poetic soaring is able to replace the lack of this unity; otherwise, it would be possible to call the songs of Pindar psalms. It is no accident that parts of the prophetical writings could have wandered over into the psalms, and vice versa.

Though the psalm becomes *epigrammatic* poetry, it does not contract and ossify into prose; Koheleth soars up to the Song of Songs, and the Proverbs deepen into Job. Thus, with the exception of the drama, the whole range of poetic forms is here the literary source, and the reason for the omission of drama now becomes intelligible. Prophecy exhausted and surpassed all tragedy, albeit not its specific form. The practical aspect of prophecy absorbed the form of this art.

Perhaps the greatest riddle in these religious sources is their duality. In all other traditions there is only one origin, only one kind of source. Israel is an exception even in this, and this exception continues without interruption to bring forth new exceptions. The prophets already are independent bearers of the tradition, next to Moses, who lived long before them, in deep obscurity, so that they have to lift the veil of myth from him. And after the prophets, the writers of the Hagiographa become an independent source. How singular, how instructive is this characteristic, which the national literature stamped upon its holy writings. However, the marvel becomes even greater.

5. The Canon had not yet been established, when already new carriers of the old world appeared. Their name, "scribes" (סופרים), is the more peculiar as it carries in it a historical contradiction. For these "scribes" were much rather speakers, as of old only the prophets and the singers were. When the Canon fixed and closed the written teaching, there had long since existed an "oral teaching," which grew out of the national spirit and which was held in no less regard. It was not the caste spirit of those learned in the writings who wished to measure themselves against the authority of the Bible, but it was the original force of the national spirit, which was aware of its own naturalness, which recognized its right even with regard to the original written teaching. It was this national spirit, which intended to, and had to, carry through the homogeneous development of the original teaching. The Torah would have had only temporal value if this continuation had not

been recognized as the continuous development of the fundamental national spirit.

Thus, the *Talmud* and the *Midrash* become sources of Judaism as valid as the Bible in its manifold parts. One should not take offense at the manifold content of the Talmud; the "statutes and ordinances" are the original documents of the Torah.

The natural strength that brought forth the Talmud shows itself in the fact that the Talmud originated in Babylon as well as in the motherland. The people were not content with the lively communication that was continuously maintained between the scholars of Babylon and those of Palestine; thus originated the *Babylonian Talmud* and the *Palestinian Talmud*, though the latter was less voluminous. Hence, the two great creations grew up as "oral teaching," and even with the loss of the ancestral home the national spirit did not feel itself paralyzed; on foreign soil, too, there bloomed, with the same national strength, the ancient spirit of the "statutes and ordinances," in which the oral teachings were rooted.

6. The duality of this undivided national spirit also presented itself in another way. Already in Deuteronomy it is generally not understood how the prophetic spirit could cling to national customs. Particularly in the case of sacrifice, this ambiguity seems offensive. Although one can usually understand national and political adaptation to local conditions, one is inclined, on the contrary, to demand of the prophets that they be pure angels of their doctrine. Even Jeremiah, radical as he is, is not entirely free from the one-sidedness of patriotism, Ezekiel, however, was a great master of political practice. After the state had been irretrievably lost, Ezekiel wanted to save the people in the *congregation* (קהל), and in order to rally the congregation he needed the sanctuary and therefore also the sacrificial cult. He anticipates the future politics of Ezra and Nehemiah.

Therefore, one should not be surprised that Deuteronomy does not abolish sacrifice, though it urges the inmost purity of intention. One should think that henceforth the main emphasis was firmly placed on the religion of the heart, since through Ezekiel, particularly, repentance became the inward substitute for sacrifice.

7. Just as, however, piety for sacred institutions created no schism in the prophetic teaching, so also were poetry and prose preserved in all the sources and through the whole history of Judaism in harmony with religious fertility. This duality is established by the

unity of *Halachah* and *Haggadah* in both Talmuds and in all forms of Midrash.

The Halachah is the "law" as it is called in Deuteronomy. The law originally was civil law and state law. The law, however, included sacrificial law, and the latter in turn included the whole sphere of the ceremonial law, in which the dietary laws are prominent. The Halachah is concerned in the first place with the civil code, as it grew out of the Pentateuch; and, in connection with Roman and Byzantine law, the Talmud established a legal system for the protection of property.

Law is directly connected with logic, and, therefore, it was jurisprudence especially which discovered and developed the *rules* that guide and control the deduction of legal cases from legal principles. Practical application, therefore, also introduced *logical theory* into the sources of Judaism.

However, already in Deuteronomy the statutes and ordinances have a definitely moral character. Just as the prophets begin with the statutes and ordinances, and as poetry arises out of prophetic teaching, so does this fusion continue its development in the oral teaching. The Midrash is not only halachic Midrash but preeminently Haggadah. Moreover, the Talmud does not only discuss Halachah; rather, sermons with an edifying devotion suddenly intrude themselves into the midst of legal discussions. It is characteristic of this duality that it does not put two separated styles side by side, but that these grow as two branches of the same tree. The Halachah is hardly thought of as a special subject next to the Haggadah, and in no way can the Haggadah be considered separate or of less value than the Halachah. The logic which the Halachah employed for jurisprudence became the sole source of legitimation, covering all interpretations of the Haggadah, including the play of wit. In this unity the "oral tradition" had to prove itself. It is spontaneous, as the "fruit of the lips," whereas the written tradition is stamped on brazen tablets.

8. There is another characteristic of the "oral teaching"; it is not an immediately finished product, but an open one, one that always continues to be produced. The book is closed; the mouth, however, remains open; for the sake of the national spirit it may not become silent. The "oral teaching" bears the stamp of lasting national productivity.

Out of this national feeling arose a term that otherwise would seem paradoxical: revelation took place not only in the Torah on Sinai, but also in the Halachah which was revealed to "Moses from Sinai" (הלכה למשה מסיני).

This continuation of revelation seems perfectly natural. There is no arrogance in this assertion of the scribes (such an opinion is based on a lack of historical information); it is rather the outflow of a critical self-consciousness with regard to the written law. The original critical feeling of Deuteronomy, that "the Torah is not in heaven but in your heart," remains alive in this thought and in the courage and clearness of this assertion. The national spirit is not dead, and it is not localized in Palestine. The testament of Rabbi Jochanan ben Zaccai became the journeyman's book of the Jewish people: where the Talmud is taught, there the Torah is alive. It should not remain merely the written Torah: it is in your heart, in your mouth; hence it had to become the oral teaching.

This oral teaching had to become as fully valued a source of Judaism as the Bible, and in all its stylistic forms, the oral teaching had to retain its full value as a source. Both are supported by the *one* logic, by the same methodological deduction.

9. One misunderstands the talmudic exegesis of the Bible if one wishes to understand it merely on the basis of this formal logical deduction. The opposite is the case. First, the thought is thought, whether it occurs in the Haggadah as a moral thought in the imaginative style of poetry or in the Halachah as a law for which, as for all other thoughts, one will subsequently find the sanction in the Bible.

Through this psychological form of thought, the claim of the oral teaching becomes all the more understandable. Otherwise, it would be almost inconceivable that the memory of the talmudic scholar could find in the great treasure of biblical words and its sentence structure the analogy exactly appropriate to the case at hand. The opposite case makes it conceivable. As much as the problem is alive, so is the word. The written teaching itself becomes an oral one. Logic confers seriousness upon the imagination, because the imagination is sustained and supported by the stern objectivity of a problem.

10. However, the sources are in no way exhausted by the two Talmuds and the many collections of the Midrashim. At all points at which Judaism came in contact with other peoples it absorbed influences from them, even in religion itself. It was this way in Persia, it repeated itself in Alexandria, and it occurred with particular fruitfulness in the Arabic Middle Ages. In Alexandria the relation of Judaism to Greek philosophy was already established; the latter was also received by

Islam, and thus the relation between the Jewish religion and Greek philosophy was strengthened.

The dialogue with philosophy bore fruit in two directions. First, the Jews participated, by right, in philosophy itself, and books originated that made philosophy most important even in their titles. Besides, philosophy grew into religious inquiry itself. Already the Mishnah, in the "Sayings of the Fathers," and also the Midrash have recognizable traces of this. Now, however, the independent science of the exegesis of the Bible and the Talmud establishes itself. Often the same authors are devoted to independent philosophy and to Bible exegetics. Thus philosophy is unintentionally brought into religious literature, *and the whole wide sphere of Bible exegetics becomes a source of Judaism.*

11. The claim to be a source is now all the more befitting to independent philosophic work, since the latter is the native soil of exegetics. As in all monotheistic religions, in Jewish thought, also, a vehement conflict is kindled on the border of religion and philosophy, a conflict that can never be entirely extinguished. Maimonides is the focal point of these unceasing agitations. However, his predecessors as well as his successors are no less genuine and productive sources of living Judaism. They produced the popular devotional and educational literature. The title *"Books of Discipline,"* under which these moral teachings are collected, stresses the practical character of these writings and makes their value as sources of religion indubitable.

12. The area of the sources becomes ever greater, and it is not yet exhausted. For a large sphere of religious poetry enlarges the old liturgy with constantly new additions of poetry, which are received by the yearning prayer into its own cycle. These new poetic compositions even became historical sources, for they depict in lamentations the persecutions that marked the Jewish Middle Ages up to modern times. The name which is attached to them, "prayers for forgiveness" (סליחות), bears witness to their religious character. The history of the Jews grows more and more into the history of Judaism. "Sufferance is the badge of all our tribe." With this sentence Shakespeare uttered a historical judgment.

However, we may also use this sentence for the history of religion. In the liturgical poetry of the Middle Ages, which is a continuation of the psalms, some seed for a new fertilization of religious thoughts and feelings may be contained. Again, the greatest of these poets, Yehudah Halevi, was perhaps an independent philosopher, and perhaps even greater as a religious thinker

as well as philosopher was Solomon Ibn Gabirol, who since the thirteenth century was temporarily veiled as an Arab, under the mutilated name of Avicebron. In this case, also, religious practice merges in a living way with religious and philosophic speculation.

13. Thus, we now come to a more precise comprehension of the concept of *Judaism*, which the title of this book contains. Judaism means religion. Yet, as much as this religion, as messianic religion, from its very outset intends to be the world religion, it has nonetheless been, and remains everywhere, and during the whole time of its development, the uniform expression of the Jewish *national spirit*, and this, in spite of all the influences of which it partook. This religious productivity bears witness to the national spirit. The concept of this national spirit is therefore not based on a racial unity, but, objectively, on the uniformity of this religious literature. The religious literature is the most significant source of the Jewish national spirit.

Whatever the Jews have accomplished in the course of history in trade and commerce, in all the branches of earning a livelihood, in the sciences and arts, surely the religious spirit has stamped upon all this, upon all their cultural achievements, its characteristic, but this characteristic is not unambiguous. In all these achievements, culture in general has as great a share as the Jewish religion itself. The meaning of Jewish nationality is determined by religious sources the only life sources of Judaism.

This idea establishes also the *uniformity* of the history of Judaism. Deep inner struggles, to be sure, mark the history of Jewish religion, making its unity questionable. We have already encountered the conflict between the prophets and the priestly religion. In present-day biblical studies, the opposition between prophetic religion and law is considered unbridgeable. We now disregard the question already touched upon, whether the opposition of principles must also be opposition in the consciousness of the persons. The opposition of the principles of intellectualism and mysticism offers at this point an analogy, which shows that in the most profound representatives of mysticism this opposition came to a most fruitful solution. We would like at this point, however, to profit from the ambiguity, which usually affects a *national* religion, in order to clarify the religion of Judaism with regard to its uniformity.

Among our own contemporaries the problem of a unified Judaism is the main difficulty in respect to practical politics also. The uniformity seems to be almost as much a miracle (*Wunder*) as the continuance of the Jews and their religion. How can this miracle be explained?

14. The magic word, which contains the watchword, also contains the solution of this riddle. What the "Hear, O Israel: the Eternal our God, the Eternal is unique" means for the inner life and continuance of the Jews, this, one may say, is entirely misunderstood outside of Judaism. Biblical studies therefore try to change the translation. Out of "unique" they want to make "only one," in order to explain away the historic-systematic strength of the passage and to deprive it of the weighty character which it indubitably carries in the context of Scripture as an introduction to the idea of the love of God. The emphatic expression "Hear, O Israel" also has the meaning of a historical formula. This formula is the rallying idea, the unifying concept of Judaism. One may believe as much as one wishes in the letter of the sacrificial and ceremonial law; the unity of God elevates belief to such a speculative height that by comparison all other problems become secondary, even if one treats them as questions of main importance by bestowing upon them objectives and historical motives. Moreover, on the other hand, he who takes offense at the many accessories that surround the core of the Jewish religion will find that as soon as the call "Hear, O Israel" comes alive in him, all skepticism is silenced, and the unity of God strengthens the unity of religious consciousness.

Judaism is a unifying concept not only for the unity of the people but also for the unity of religion. This unity proves itself in the same way in the concept of the unique God as in the concept of man who himself is unique among all the beings of nature. Thus, we arrive at another consequence, which is to be derived from the concepts united in the title of this book.

15. Usually a distinction is made between religion and morality, not only between religion and ethics. Ethics originated in Greek philosophy and has been preserved in systematic philosophy. Only by analogy can this concept be used outside philosophy. Therefore, in this book we have already anticipated our method, according to which the religion of reason attains and preserves its own peculiar task, insofar as it acknowledges and verifies for its own method the autonomy of ethics.

With regard to religion the autonomy of ethics consists in the laying down of first principles for its own concepts. These first principles, however, separate themselves into a system, and have no effect beyond it. Thus, we have recognized humanity and the individual as the limits of ethics, at which point religion establishes its own foundations. In the concept of the individual, the ethical concept of man is incorporated into religion.

If, however, this incorporation of man into the religion of reason is a consequence of the sources of Judaism, then the religions of reason cannot recognize a distinction in content between religion and morals, between Jewish religion and Jewish morals, with the exception of the methodological distinction between ethics and religion. The concept of man belongs to the Jewish religion, and for the content of this concept it does not concede any supremacy to ethics, except for recognizing its systematic method.

In the same way, the concept of the unique God belongs to Jewish moral teaching. Jewish sources make it unmistakably clear that it was in teaching about man, not only about man as an individual but also about nations and mankind, that the idea of the unique God came to be discovered. All the particulars in the wide variety of "statutes and ordinances," every moral regulation, every moral precept, every moral institution, all are rooted in the "Hear, O Israel." *There is no distinction in the Jewish consciousness between religion and morals.* Only where pantheism undermines the modern subconsciousness is skepticism with regard to the so-called existence of God entertained, and one then tries to recover at least moral teachings from an insolvent Judaism. This recovery is not even sufficient for the popular mind; for the latter also is affected by the pantheistic sickness through monism and the poetry of nature. Only pantheism is responsible for the fact that religion has crept into hiding behind moral teaching.

Religion itself is moral teaching or it is not religion, and moral teaching is autonomous only as philosophical ethics. This autonomy, however, is not impaired by the borrowing from history, which ethics has to make from religion for its concepts of God and man, as it has had to borrow from all other factors of history and science. Only *one* condition is attached to this assimilation of religious insights to ethics: the original communion, which is designated as reason, by virtue of which religion is characterized as the religion of reason.

How could religion be the religion of reason, if at the same time it were not moral teaching? In this identity of religion and morality, the religion of reason also proves itself subjectively to be Judaism, the uniform production of the Jewish people, the people who attest themselves as one people through this uniformity of religious production. From the unique God, the view of Judaism is directed to one mankind, and in the same way to each individual man in his own uniqueness. This point of view determines the originality and peculiarity of the Jewish spirit.

It is claimed that for this Jewish spirit only God exists and not the world. This saying might at most be valid with regard to the indifferent world of nature, but never for man. Only an alien pattern, innocently taken into Judaism from malicious polemics, can erect an opposition between God and man, between religion and morality in Judaism. The well-known saying of the prophet speaks against it: "It has been told thee, O man, what is good" (Micah 6:8). Thus, with regard to the problem of the good, God and man come into a necessary community. God has to proclaim the good and proclaim it to man. Does he have anything else to say at all? And is there any other being to whom he has anything to say? Reason with its principle of the good unites God and man, religion and mortality.

16. Thus, the principle of reason has led us to the unity of religion and morality, and if the sources of Judaism unveil the religion of reason, then, in addition, this concept of reason will also grant to the Jewish religion its true unity. All considerations of a material character, however much one tries to transfigure them, remain material, so long as they are tied up with consanguinity. They not only make it difficult to understand spiritual analogies, which are found *among other* blood lineages, but also make them suspect. If, however, reason is the guiding principle, then a safe standard is achieved, which not only delineates the peculiarity of a certain religion but also rallies and secures the community of the spirit at large. In this community the peculiarity of a certain religion does not become a barrier which excludes the possibility of other religions. Insofar as they attest themselves as religions of reason on the basis of their sources, they prove their religious legitimacy. The sovereign concept of reason opens the possibility that many religions may be collected under it.

The *philosophy of religion* has scientific truthfulness only when it strives objectively and impartially to refer to its sources, excavate them through its own research, and to illuminate them through its own criticism. I know myself to be free from the prejudice of all shades of Christian theology and Christian philosophy of religion, insofar as they proclaim the *absoluteness* of Christianity; I do not assert that Judaism alone is the religion of reason. I try to understand how other monotheistic religions also have their fruitful share in the religion of reason, although in regard to *primary origin* this share cannot be compared with that of Judaism. This primary origin constitutes the priority of Judaism, and

this priority also holds for its share in the religion of reason. For the primary origin is the distinctive mark of creative reason, which makes itself independent of all other charms of consciousness, and which produces a pure pattern. Primary origin bears the marks of purity. And *purity* in creativity is the characteristic of reason.

Translated by Simon Kaplan.

Other works by Cohen: *Reason and Hope: Selections from the Jewish Writings of Hermann Cohen* (1971).

Abraham Isaac Kook
1865–1935

Abraham Isaac Kook was the first Ashkenazi chief rabbi of Palestine, a post in which he served from 1921 to his death, and a mystical thinker. He was born in Latvia and first settled in the Land of Israel in 1904. He spent part of World War I in London but returned to Palestine. Kook forged a religious Zionism that emphasized the role of human activity in bringing the messianic age and, unusually, argued that secular pioneers, who were conventionally the targets of Orthodox wrath, were unwittingly doing God's work by settling the land and thus creating the necessary material substratum for the Messiah's coming. Long after his death his thinking was a major influence on the messianic Zionist movement Gush Emunim.

On the Election of Women
1919

An Open Letter to the Committee of the "Mizrahi" Association

I was honored to receive your request to express my opinion on the current question of electing women to the Jewish representative assembly of the Land of Israel. Though I am not worthy of being approached, circumstances require that I expound my opinion, and I will do so with the greatest possible brevity.

In my opinion the issue divides into three headings:

a. Regarding the law: Is it permitted or prohibited?
b. Regarding the common good: Which of the options will promote the common good for Israel?
c. Regarding the ideal: Which of the opinions does our moral consciousness support?

The exposition must take all these values into account, for I must relate to all ranks [of the public]: the completely faithful of Israel for whom the halakhic ruling is central, those for whom the nation's good is decisive, and those whose main concern is the moral ideal in itself.

Regarding the law I have nothing to add to the words of the preceding rabbis. In the Torah, in the Prophets, and in the Writings, in the *halakhah* and the *aggadah*, we hear one voice—namely, that the duty of fixed public service falls upon men, for "It is man's manner to dominate and not woman's manner to dominate" (BT Yevamot 65b). Roles of authority, judgment, and testimony are not for her, as all her glory is within. Striving to prevent the mixing of the sexes in public gatherings is a theme that runs through the entire Torah. Thus, any innovation in public government that leads to a routine mixing . . . is certainly against the law.

What remains for us to discuss is the aspect of the common good. I believe . . . [that the Balfour Declaration was given on the basis of the] view that the best of the gentiles generally, and in particular the best of the British people, rightly have of our divinely sanctioned connection to the Land of Israel. They are thus influenced by the holy light of the Bible, which is regarded as sacred by the greater part of civilized nations today. The spirit of the Bible is understood even now by the weightiest part of the world to require modesty and to avoid the social depravity that might result from human weakness with respect to the sexual inclination. The special feeling of respect toward woman in the Bible is based and centered on domestic life and the improvement of inner life and of all the delicate human works branching out therefrom.

Both the internal and the external enemies of Israel make much use nowadays of the libel that young Israel has lost its link to the holy book and therefore has no right to the biblical land. Our duty is to stand guard and demonstrate to the whole world that the soul of Israel is alive in its true character and that the biblical land is deserved by the biblical people, for with all its soul it lives in the spirit of the holy land and this holy book. . . .

Hence it is our holy duty to ensure that the initial steps toward a political-social character of our own be clearly marked by the sign of biblical integrity and purity with which our life has been imbued from time immemorial. This will be obvious only if we avoid the European innovation—alien to the biblical spirit and to the national tradition deriving from it—of woman's entanglement in the tumultuous and multitudinous activities of elections and public life.

It should be emphasized that we are not treading the path of our redemption in order to be mere followers of European culture. According to all the profound critics who are not overawed by its imposing stature, this culture—at least in regard to morality and the purity of virtues—is bankrupt. We aim, instead, to bring to the entire world our message, drawing from our internal source, vigorous, holy, and clear. In any event, we ought to walk upright now in this great hour of need, emphasizing our national character in our social life in our land. We may rest assured that this assertiveness will confer honor upon us in the world far beyond that which we might attain through any external imitation, which usually follows from inner weakness.

Now as to the ideal: Indeed, the ideal of being unblemished by any sin is deeply imprinted in our soul. When this ideal is realized, the world will be purified, and then proper and secure ways will be found for the pure, delicate, and holy activity and influence of woman, the mother in Israel . . . according to her special inner worth, in the fulfillment of the vision: "A capable wife is a crown unto her husband" (Prov. 12:4). But this future vision is as yet not glimpsed in temporal cultural life, which though outwardly adorned is inwardly rotten. Any careless step taken in the course of our public life, without regard for our deeply held view of Woman's present and future value, merely impedes this ideal course. Only Israel's return to its footing in the land, to its kingdom, its holy spirit, its prophecy and its temple, will eventually bring the world that sublime light which all the noble souls of humanity yearn for.

NOTE
Words in brackets appear in the original translation.

Translator unknown.

Other works by Kook: *The Lights of Penitence, The Moral Principles, Lights of Holiness, Essays, Letters, and Poems* (1978); *The Essential Writings of Abraham Isaac Kook* (1988).

Abraham Isaac Kook

On Women's Voting
1920

. . . We believe that our outlook on social life in general is more refined and purer than that of contemporary civilized nations. Our family is sacred to us in a manner more profound than [is the case in] the rest of the modern world, and this is the basis of the happiness and dignity of the Woman of Israel. Among the other nations, the family is not the foundation of the nation and is not as firmly established and deeply rooted as it is among us. Therefore they are not as dismayed by fissures in family life, the consequences of which will not cause much harm to national life. The psychological cause of the call for women's right to participate in public elections comes fundamentally from the unhappy position of the masses of women in these nations. If the family's situation had been as peaceful and dignified as it generally is in Israel, women themselves, as well as men of science, morality, and high ideals, would not demand what they term "rights" to vote for women in a manner that might ruin domestic peace. Ruining peace at home necessarily leads to a great degeneration of political and national life in general. But out of desperation and bitterness consequential to male crassness in the family, they [gentile women] hoped to use public empowerment to ameliorate their devastated situation at home, regardless of the additional fissures that might be added thereby, since the breaches are already so many. We have not descended, nor will we descend, to such a state, and we will not want to see our sisters in such a low state. The home is to us a dwelling place of holiness. We dare not obliterate the splendor of our sisters' lives, and embitter them through the din of opinions and disputations of elections and political questions. . . .

Our family is the foundation of the nation. The house of Jacob [bet ya'akov] will build the people of Israel. We prepare the building of the nation according to the nature of our psyche. We are always prepared to recognize the moral obligation within every household of Israel of listening to women's opinions concerning general social and political questions. But the agreed-upon opinions must come specifically from the home, from the family in its wholeness, and it is the burden of the man, the father of the family, to bring it into the public domain. The obligation of making known the family opinion is placed on him.

When we demand of the woman to go out into the public political domain and become entangled in expressing her opinion in weighty and political questions in general, we do one of two things: Either she learns through this to flatter the man and cast her vote according to his vote and not according to her conscience, by which we spoil her morality and inner freedom; or,

through the tempest of divergent opinions, the status of domestic peace is destroyed. And the fissures in the family must result in a great breach in the nation. . . .

Do not touch the foundation of foundations: the rights of our mothers, sisters, and daughters, the original rights, which are founded on the beautification of the special internal moral and natural power and on the sacred, refined, and noble value of the woman in Israel. For [these original rights] create deep roots in life, bringing a lasting happiness. Do not exchange them for trivial written rights . . . and a superficial external freedom, the consequences of which will embitter their lives inside the home.

NOTE
Words in brackets appear in the original translation.

Translator unknown.

Abraham Isaac Kook

Excerpts from His Sacred Writings
ca. 1920

54. There are two paths toward faith; one is the absolutely true one, and the other is the rational one. The latter changes in accordance with the times. There are occasions when, if there is some well-publicized and established scientific theory in vogue, it will harm the foundation of the apparent elements of faith from the perspective of absolute truth; and since the world of science has taken on a different form in the course of time, that rational type of faith will have lost its value, yet publicizing that theory per se will cause no harm to any absolute idea based on faith, which did in the past cause harm by being publicized. And what we are saying can be taken further still, insofar as it can happen that one specific form of logic would be incontrovertible at one particular point in time, to the extent that that scientific belief, based on reason, then shaped its configuration in a specific format, and subsequently that particular format alone would harm absolute faith; and then there arises an obligation to publicize the annulment of the prevalent rational theory. The basis of the distinction between the two parts of faith was already alluded to by Maimonides, but it requires a unique strength of mind to withstand the challenges posed in an era of darkness such as ours.

55. To achieve internal spiritual strengthening, a man—in particular one attuned to spiritual reflection

and ethical influences—must battle the wickedness and folly of illusory pride, which brings in its wake an unbalancing of the intellect and subdues all the splendor of the soul, to become lowly and perpetual slaves to the vain and crude imaginings that dwell in the heart of the masses. In the first instance, pride removes the ability to adapt itself to any noble and refined idea on account of its inherent haughtiness and loftiness. The love of praise and acquiescence to the mores of society continually injures morality and knowledge and engenders a terrifying weakness within the progress of the soul in its entirety. The man who wishes to save his soul, so as to bring about some genuine benefit related to his particular talents in the world, is forced to empty his heart of all the despicable dust of this ugly character trait; and even if, against his will, he becomes entitled to some honor, large or small, he should not harbor any thoughts of grandeur on account of this apparent good fortune. His permanent mindset must have clarity of understanding, so as to increase the fine influence that is liable to emanate from each individual from whatever internal place it was previously prepared. The task needs to be dearer to him than everything else. [He has to be, in the words of scripture]: "One who delights in His commandments"—and not one who merely desires the reward for obedience to His commandments.

56. It is necessary to uncover, from the depths of the soul, the light of the attachment to the divine in the fullness of its illumination, to the point where it has the potential to flow over into the mightiest and purest love, into all the deeds and teachings of the practical aspect of the Torah, and all the requisite desire to illumine every hidden detail—to bring it out into the open, using the full force of the skill and diligence of the intellect, in order that engagement in the Torah and the divine commandments for their own sake may grow progressively greater in a manner commensurate with the measure whereby the soul becomes elevated through its lofty perspectives. However, that love branches out into the broad expanses of the world of action only once it has become sated with the beneficence and delight of the divine within its own borders, and does not lack the "moisturizing liquid" required for its spiritual demands; after the soul will have derived pleasure from the excellence of the feeling that becomes elevated and ever mightier through the power of prayer—the divine song and melody—at the most appropriate seasons, and from the radiance of the intellect purified by noble and majestic ideas, beautified by the perfection of their expansion, the light will increase and shine forth beyond the boundaries of the spirit.

57. Love of Israel is engendered by faith in the divine light of the community of Israel, which is its personal treasure that will never depart from it. This supreme love, and its cause, the inner faith in its divine roots, need urgently to be stirred up within men of understanding and spirit at a time of deterioration in the nation's spiritual state, at a time when the trampling of sanctity and contempt for religion comes to the fore with full power and strength, in order to discern that, notwithstanding all this, the power of Israel is great and mighty vis-à-vis its God, and to gaze at the inner light penetrating the spirit of the community, and whose abode is located within each individual soul in Israel, either openly or privately, and also within the backsliding soul that has strayed far from the way of the Almighty. The revelation that the righteous man who loves the essence of the nation with all the strength he possesses, the divine goodness concealed within it, helps the person who is engaged in this authentic defense of his people, to elevate him above those who live a coarse and constrained life, who go around mournfully in their depressed state of anger. And the effect reverberates in an especially valuable way upon the nation in general and upon its individual members, imbuing them with a strength that arouses the grace and kindness of God, that He may pave a path for them to repent, motivated by love of the Almighty.

58. Regarding repentance, how vital and glorious it is to illuminate all of life! The conduits of the spirit are shut up on account of human sin. The thirst for the divine and all its appurtenances, which constitute the enlightenment provided by practical and content-filled ethics to the essence of the soul—it struggles, it starts to jerk and to move around with lively movements, and it falls down again, because the filth of transgressions weighs it down; and not only to the sin of the individual, but more so to the sin of the community. Those special individuals who are hoping to receive the light of the Almighty suffer from the sin of the entire community. Their love for the community is infinitely strong. The force of the goodness within their souls yearns exclusively for the general good, but the community defiles them on account of the sins clinging to it. However, these truly righteous men voluntarily suffer all the things blocking progress, all the material and spiritual wounds, so long as they may attain their goal, to become wise and to do good, to increase goodness and

light, to pave a path toward the light of the Almighty and His pleasantness, so that it may enter directly into every heart and spirit, so that all may delight in the beneficence of the Almighty; so that the Lord may rejoice in His works! [. . .]

62. An individual needs to be perpetually attached to the beneficent divine essence connected to the root of the soul of the entire community of Israel. And it is by this means that he obtains the merit of being capable of repentance, since his shortcomings and sins will be constantly apparent to him, stemming, as they do, from the source of his alienation from the godly nation, which is the rock from which he was hewn and the origin of all the goodness he possesses. He should not be dismayed by being attached to the root of the soul of the entire nation, even though [. . .] evil and coarse individuals are also to be found. This does not diminish in the slightest the beneficent divine illumination of the nation as a whole; and the spark of the souls of these people rests likewise within all the individual souls that have fallen to the lowest level. And because the community of Israel embraces the divine beneficence within it, not only for itself but for the entire world—for the totality of existence—it proceeds, from the powerful attachment lying inherently within the midst of the national soul, to an attachment to the Living God, through the medium of divine knowledge, which is all-encompassing, and the light of divine presence rests upon it in all its glory and strength. [. . .]

64. The sciences that are progressively becoming ever clearer in relation to the senses and their reality are continually driving out disturbing belief, blind faith, which is constructed upon a lowly and gloomy image of the divine. And, inevitably, they simultaneously perform two mutually opposed tasks: they destroy and they build. They destroy foolish faith, and inevitably pure faith now comes in its wake and prepares to reign on earth in its stead. The concept of faith itself becomes ever purer. It is not constructed on the basis of the weakness of life, but rather upon its strength and power. Before the pure knowledge of the divine illuminated the dark places of the world, the practical aspect of faith, and its emotional element, leaned heavily upon foundations of ignorance, which is intermingled with wickedness. And it grieves the heart to perceive the sensation of faith continually dwindling away, and the practice of faith continually dissolving. But beneath this destruction is hidden a noble edifice. For: "The Lord is our judge, the Lord is our lawgiver, the Lord is our king— He shall save us!"

65. All the sciences are soundly based upon two principal conditions; first, upon their specialized definitions—that it may become perfectly clear to those researching in them what their fundamental basis is, into which may be incorporated the unique format of the particular branch of science they wish to acquire and the full depths of which they wish to plumb; and secondly upon their general association with, and relationship to the sciences that lie beyond their fields. Then, when each science stands well fortified in its own right, and with this captures for itself all the capital required for it from the entire gamut of sciences, it blossoms and becomes elevated. The science of faith and knowledge of God, in all its branches, is similarly obliged to travel on that path, upon which have traveled all the great personalities of the world, who have done this successfully. It is imperative to protect most carefully the image of sanctity, the defining feature, through its sacred splendor, of this noble and exalted science, that embraces within it all happiness, both present and eternal; and alongside this, it is vital to be fully aware of the points where the branches of all the sciences make contact with it to receive from it and to flow over onto it. True faith will then accrue to us, replete with strength, knowledge, and wisdom. [. . .]

Additional Sections

[. . .] 3. There are two ways of attaining spiritual purity. One is by being very particular with the finer points of character traits, to make them straight and direct them in such manner that they will become purified, and as a result of the influence they project, life as a whole becomes pure. The second way is to view things from an intellectual perspective, and to elevate the soul to the highest level in the light of the Almighty, and by this means one's fine character traits will inevitably become elevated in a general form, because their source becomes blessed, and they become automatically blessed from the source of their growth. [. . .]

4. Every human being has his own route to attain his happiness—the real purpose of his existence—through which he becomes attached to his Creator. He cannot attain the object of his desire by any other route, notwithstanding that it is the correct route for others. Accordingly, each individual has to value his own unique path immensely. And this applies to an individual, and a fortiori in the case of the nation as a whole; for in the measure commensurate with the elevation and the

numerical superiority of the community over the individual, in like measure increases the obligation and intense precision required to protect that unique pathway through which the entire community finds abundant happiness. [. . .]

7. Our objective, always, is aimed not merely at being released from dire straits, not simply at being healed of our wounds, and to be spared from illnesses, not just to escape from the imprisonment of poverty and the darkness of blindness. [. . .] No! We seek incomparably more than this; the uncovering of the full light, the outpouring of the streams of eternal life from the source of the Holy of Holies, from the source of Israel, from the source of its supreme soul, from the source of love of the delight of the Everlasting Rock, which illumines the way for us with the splendid rays of the desirable Land, the Holy Land, the Land of Life, and the Land of Light. [. . .]

8. Every thought has many strata and layers, one on top of the other. Only one layer is openly apparent—that is the retention of memory, by which means we know what we are thinking, but there are numerous layers lying concealed within that thought itself, beneath the power of mental recall, and our entire essence is deeply enveloped in them; and it both operates by means of them, and operates upon them. The closer we approach the light of the intellect—the purity of the soul—the greater the number of layers, both higher and more secret, contained within every thought, that will become revealed before us—greater in worth and more glorious in influence. Happy therefore is he who walks on an upright path, who sanctifies his ways and directs aright the course of his life, both in the practical and spiritual spheres; for he becomes elevated to such a high level that every thought that he takes hold of will be revealed to him in the abundant wealth of its many layers, and they will thereby illumine all the compartments of his soul with precious light, and with the revelation of the secrets of the Almighty to those who fear Him. [. . .]

20. The basis of fear of all sin is putting aside intellectual understanding, for sin causes the divine light to become far removed from the soul of a human being, and in line with this, from the world as a whole. [. . .] Accordingly, our eyes and our hearts should constantly be directed toward the task of filling up the links of the chain of life, and keeping at bay anything causing a separation of links in the sacred chain, in order that the light of divine knowledge may flow perpetually onto us and give us light in the full flow of its illuminations, which are all-encompassing in their joy, saturated with pure delights. [. . .]

21. In the realm of opinions too, the rule of absence taking priority over existence applies. And when we see the spirits of human beings in fermentation, and when well-established and strongly held views seem shaky, we must be on the lookout for innovations within the formation of the spirit. And there can be no doubt that the innovations are aimed at amelioration, for the power of the work of Creation lay in the fact that the Holy One, blessed be He, repeatedly created worlds and then destroyed them, until such time as He declared, in connection with a world that was well suited to attainment of the goal of enduring goodness: "*This* gives Me satisfaction!" In precisely the same fashion does the quality of creativity progress. Also, throughout the course of the previous epochs and passing generations, a period during which much dross has accumulated within the battle lines of the spiritual sphere, even though it may be of a holy and exalted nature, the thunder claps hailing destruction are necessarily bound to burst. This is, however, a sign heralding the birth of a fresh spirit, which will establish many new edifices of a more highly perfected nature than those that preceded them.

Therefore, let not our spirit be downcast when we witness crises in the ways of the spirit that trample down much of the good now in existence, for it is not a program of destruction that the crisis heralds, but rather a program of innovations of form, and good tidings of a novel perfection, which, when completed, will constitute a mighty force for removal of all the dross and for the production of a wholly pure refined vessel. [. . .]

Translated by David E. Cohen.

Ben-Zion Hai Uziel

1880-1953

Jerusalem-born Ben-Zion Hai Uziel was Sephardic chief rabbi of Tel Aviv from 1923 to 1939, of Mandate Palestine from 1939 to 1948, and of Israel from 1948 to 1954. He was active in the political life of the Yishuv and was a prolific writer, publishing many volumes of rabbinic responsa and homiletics, as well as essays on contemporary Jewish life. He was particularly concerned with the question of the conversion of non-Jews to Judaism and issued rulings that were markedly compassionate and inclusive.

Women's Rights in Elections to Public Institutions
ca. 1920

A. Women's Rights in the House of Representatives and in Institutions of Public and Yishuv Leadership

This issue was the focus of controversy in *eretz yisrael*, and the whole land . . . quaked with the debate. Posters and warnings, pamphlets and newspaper articles, appeared anew every morning, absolutely prohibiting women's participation in the elections. Some based their argument on "Torah Law," some on the need to ensure domestic peace. All relied upon the saying "Anything new is forbidden by the Torah." . . .

The issue subdivides into two headings: (1) The active right to vote; (2) The passive right to be elected.

Regarding the first we find no clear ground to prohibit this, and it is inconceivable that women be denied this personal right. For in these elections we raise up leaders over us and empower our representatives to speak in our name, to organize the matters of our *yishuv*, and to levy taxes on our property. Women, whether directly or indirectly, accept the authority of these representatives and obey their public and national directives and laws. How, then, can one simultaneously "pull the rope from both ends": lay upon them the duty to obey those elected by the people, yet deny them the right to vote in the elections?

If it is argued that women should be excluded from the voting public because "their character is weak" [*da'atan kalot*, BT Shabbat 33b] and they do not know how to choose who is worthy of leading the people, we reply: Well, then, let us also exclude from the electorate those men who are "of weak character" (and such are never lacking). However, reality confronts us clearly with the fact that both in the past and in our times, women are equal to men in knowledge and wisdom; they deal in commerce and trade and conduct all personal matters in the best possible manner. Has it ever been heard that a guardian is appointed to conduct the affairs of an adult woman against her will?

The meaning of our Rabbis' statement *da'atan kalot* is entirely different. Also, the statement "Women have no wisdom except in the spindle" (BT Yoma 66b) is only a flowery phrase intended to circumvent the question of [woman's capacity]. And indeed, the Talmud itself states that the woman who asked the question was wise: "A wise woman posed a question to Rabbi Eli'ezer." And our Rabbis expressly stated: "'And the Lord fashioned [*banah*] the rib' (Gen. 2:22)—this teaches us that more insight [*binah*] was granted to Woman" (BT Niddah 45b).

But perhaps [voting] should be prohibited because of licentiousness? Why? What licentiousness can there be in each person going to the poll and entering a voting slip? If we start considering such activities as licentious, no creature would be able to survive! Women and men would be prohibited from walking in the street or from entering a shop together; it would be forbidden to negotiate in commerce with a woman, lest this lead to intimacy and hence to licentiousness. Such ideas have never been suggested by anyone.

Or perhaps it should be prohibited for the sake of preserving domestic peace? . . . If so, we must also deny the right of voting to adult sons and daughters still living in their father's home. For in all cases where our rabbis concerned themselves with ensuring tranquility, they gave equal treatment to the wife and to adult sons living at home (see BT Bava Metzia 12a). It might still be objected that denying this right to adult children should indeed have been proposed. Since it wasn't, let us at least not increase friction even more by allowing women to vote! But the truth is that differences of opinion will surface in some form or other, for no one can suppress completely his opinions and attitudes. But familial love grounded in the shared enterprise [of the members] is strong enough to withstand differences of opinion.

"A great innovation" was advanced by Rabbi Dr. Ritter, who advocates denying suffrage to women because they are not [part of the] *kahal* or *edah* and were not counted in the census of the people of Israel nor subsumed into the genealogical account of the families of Israel. . . . Well, let us assume that they are neither *kahal* nor *edah* and were counted neither in the census nor in the family [genealogies], nor anywhere [else]. But are they not creatures created in the divine image and endowed with intelligence? Do they not share common interests that the representative assembly, or the committees it will choose, will be dealing with? Will they not be called upon to obey these bodies regarding their property and the education of their sons and daughters?

B. Elected Women

The second issue is, Can a woman be elected to public office? Prima facie this involves an explicit prohibition. For, in the *Sifre* it is written: "You shall set a king over you—and not a queen" (Deuteronomy 157). From this source Maimonides derived the following: "A woman may not be appointed to the throne. . . . And likewise, all public appointments in Israel are to be male, not female. Therefore a woman should not be appointed as head of a community" (Laws of Kings 1:5).

But I myself am in doubt whether this rule stems from (1) women being basically ineligible to function as judges or from (2) the principle of the dignity of the community. This would make a difference when it is not the *bet din* that appoints her but, rather, some of the public who choose her as their representative and proxy. According to alternative 1, such a public choice would be invalid, exactly like a woman's evidence in matters of marriage and divorce, which no individual can decide to acknowledge, since the Torah has deemed her ineligible; whereas according to alternative 2, we would say that their choice is valid and that only the whole public or the judges are barred from electing her to public office, but a part of the public may choose her as their representative and proxy.

Now, the explanation provided by the Tosafot that Deborah was a judge by virtue of having been accepted by the public implies that such acceptance is valid even on the part of the whole public. And even according to their explanation that she was chosen by special prophetic authority, one may argue that the acceptance [of the public] is valid in principle, though for reasons of public dignity it should be avoided. . . . Thus, there is no prohibition against appointing women to public office; indeed, they may be appointed when necessary. It is, however, [on this view,] an insult to the community that they could find no one but some female to judge them.

Clearly, the *Sifre* is to be explained accordingly: A queen may not be appointed over Israel by a *bet din*, on account of public dignity. However, an individual—or several individuals—may with full right elect a woman, and by their right she may join the representative body.

Similarly, a woman may rule as queen if she is the only heiress of the royal house, or in light of her achievements and the need of the hour, like Deborah in her time. . . .

C. Appointing Women to Positions of Political Power

Although we have established that the Talmud provides no source whatever for denying women appoint-

ments to positions of authority, an adversary could still claim: "Absence of proof is no proof." Therefore, I shall now indicate a positive proof for my position. [When discussing the problem of Deborah], the Tosafot (BT Niddah 50a, s.v. *kol ha-kasher*) provide two solutions. According to one, a woman is legally fit to serve as a judge, because the verse "These are the [legal] norms that you shall set before *them*" (Exod. 21:1), which equates women to men regarding all civil matters under the law, refers to judges too [cf. §6]. Clearly, the Tosafot reject the *Sifre*. Otherwise, how can a woman be appointed judge, obligating the public to appear before her? Is this not a position of authority?

The Tosafists' alternative answer is that although women are basically unfit to judge, Deborah simply served as a public teacher and mentor. . . . Thus, a woman's ineligibility relates only to hearing pleas or taking evidence, but she is eligible to decide law and to legislate. Now, is this not a publicly dignified office? Both opinions presented by the Tosafot prove, then, that the position advocated by the *Sifre* should not be considered an undisputed rule.

Still, if we hesitate—and rightly so—to reject the view of the *Sifre* and Maimonides without explicit proof to the contrary, women's eligibility to be elected [to office] can be justified on other grounds. This prohibition relates only to an appointment made by the Sanhedrin, whereas here the issue is not one of appointment but rather one of acceptance. For by the process of election, the majority of the public express their acceptance of, and confidence in, certain persons as their representatives and designate them as agents in supervising all their public affairs. Now, regarding such a case even Maimonides acknowledges that there is not the slightest prohibition.

[Uziel here cites Adret, §20, and other similar views.]

In conclusion, it is clear that even according to the *Sifre* a woman may be accepted as judge in the sense of leader, and she may render legal decisions—just as one can accept a relative. Therefore . . . the law allows the election of women, even according to the positions of the *Sifre* and Maimonides. No dissenting opinion is found among the medieval authorities.

D. Halakhah and Morality

Nevertheless, there is still room for the following concern: Even though the acceptance [of an elected woman] is legally valid, it still might be forbidden from the standpoint of morality and the conventions of modesty. Yet [Rabbi Hayyim Hirschensohn] correctly wrote that ethics and Torah are one. Therefore, since the Torah prohibited only the appointment of a woman [by the *bet din*], there is no basis for a [general] prohibition on grounds of licentiousness; otherwise, the Torah would never have permitted it [in other cases]. Still, to be cautious in matters of law, let us investigate along these lines as well and see if there are any grounds for concern over licentiousness.

Reason [*sevara*] dictates that serious assemblies or profitable discussions do not give rise to licentiousness. Every day men meet and negotiate with women in commercial transactions, and yet all is peace and quiet. Even those inclined to sexual licentiousness will not contemplate the forbidden while seriously transacting business. Our Rabbis' injunction "Do not engage in much conversation with a woman" (Mishnah Avot 1:5) refers only to idle, needless chatter. This sort of conversation leads to sin, but not that of debate over important, communal issues. Meeting in the same enclosed area for the sake of public service—which is tantamount to divine service—does not habituate people to sin or cause levity; for all Israel, men and women alike, are holy, and they are not suspected of violating conventions of modesty or morality. Nor is there room for objection on the basis of the sages' teaching that "originally the women were within [the women's section of the temple courtyard] and the men without, but as this caused levity, it was instituted that the women should sit above and the men below" (BT Sukkah 51b). This refers only to a mass assembly of upright and immodest people together, and in such circumstances there is room for concern over the licentious minority, particularly when they are engaged in celebration and prone to the evil inclination. But it does not refer to a gathering of elected officials; to deem those elected by the people sexually licentious is unheard of in Israel! . . .

Conclusion: (1) A woman has a perfect right to participate in elections, which is a condition for her inclusion in the collective obligation to obey those elected to lead the people. (2) A woman may also be elected by the consent and ordinance of the public.

NOTE
Words in brackets appear in the original translation.

Translator unknown.

Other works by Uziel: *Mishpetei Uziel*, 1st ed., 3 vols. (1935–1960); 2nd ed., 4 vols. (1947–1964).

Leo Baeck

1873–1956

The German Reform rabbi Leo Baeck was trained at the Breslau Rabbinical Seminary and the Hochschule für die Wissenschaft des Judentums in Berlin, as well as the Universities of Breslau and Berlin. He served as a rabbi in Germany and, from 1933, as head of the representative body of German Jewry. Despite entreaties to leave, he remained in the country, believing it was his duty to offer spiritual support to his fellow Jews during the horrors of the Nazi years. In 1943, he was deported to the Theresienstadt concentration camp. He survived and settled in London after the war. He originally wrote *The Essence of Judaism* as a response to the Christian theologian Adolf von Harnack's *The Essence of Christianity*.

The Essence of Judaism
1922

Unity and Development

During the thousands of years of its history, Judaism has learned and experienced a good deal. In its people the commanding urge to think further, to struggle with ideas, has persisted through the centuries. Whether by choice or compulsion, Jews have taken many and diverse roads in this world, and their experiences have become part of the total experience of Judaism. Through its people scattered over the world, Judaism has been able to receive the impact of the spiritual experiences of human civilization.

With its wandering, Judaism has also undergone changes; its very destiny has been shaped by the fluctuations of its history. A rich variety of phenomena is found in that history. Not all of these are of equal value or scope; for life, unable to maintain a constant level, has its rises and falls. What is most characteristic of a people is best found in the highest levels of its history, so long as these levels are reached again and again. In this undulating movement from historical peak to peak, the essence of a people's consciousness—what is achieved and preserved—is manifested. Such constancy, such essence, Judaism does possess despite the shifting phases of its long history. Because of the persistence of that essence, all phases have something in common. The consciousness of possessing a world of their own, a binding spiritual kinship, has always remained alive in the Jews. They all live in one religious home.

This unity already had a firm historical foundation in the people out of whom Judaism first grew, and in that people it still has strong roots. The Jew realized that he was not merely of this day, but that his life derived from the men who in the ancient past had given birth to his faith. For the fathers of his race were also the fathers of his religion. He was aware that he spoke the words telling of the God of his forefathers—the God of Abraham, Isaac and Jacob—as though his were the voice of a child to whom the heritage had been given. Simultaneously, when he thought of the future, he felt that the days to come would live through him, that his own existence and future pointed to the existence of the ancient God on earth.

These, then, were the voices emanating from every Jew. But the surrounding world spoke with a different voice. Soon the children of the great fathers became dispersed, a fate which brought not only separation, but sometimes actual dissolution. The Jewish community, moreover, dispensed with those means to which other peoples resorted to maintain their ties. It neither strove to turn away from surrounding peoples and ideas by rejecting alien cultures, nor did it set up such rigid and binding limitations around its own culture as to live assured and assuaged. If Judaism did preserve its unity, it was by reason neither of a world-renouncing solitude nor of self-imposed walls of dogma and ecclesiasticism.

Admittedly there were times, especially those within memory, when the Jewish community seemed completely walled in. But this seclusion was only spatial; it was, moreover, a compulsory barrier to which Judaism never acquiesced. Only at very rare periods did the Jewish world, and even then only sections of it, exist in a spiritual ghetto. The inhabitants of the ghetto examined with curiosity and eagerness the intellectual movements which stirred the centuries. It is sufficient to point to the influence of Jewish thinkers and scientific investigators on the thought of the Middle Ages, and to the way in which that thought in turn influenced them.

Still another factor prevented the Jews from living in a spiritual ghetto. In no other religion is such a high value placed on the learned man of faith. Among the countless men who remained faithful to Judaism in the martyrdom of life and the martyrdom of death, there have probably been few so immersed in their own tradition as to know nothing about the ideas developing outside of it.

It could scarcely have been otherwise. The actuality by which the Jews were surrounded seemed to speak with convincing and logical evidence—established by hard facts and underlined by each new persecution and oppression—of conclusions which appeared as contrary to the claim of Judaism. The contradiction between what was promised by the old prophecies and what each generation actually experienced, produced too sharp a tension to make it possible for the Jew simply to retire into himself. The downtrodden, the underdog, will always be able to believe in himself and in fact must believe in himself if he is not to perish. But so long as he lives in the midst of the world, it is impossible to surround himself merely with the closed circle of his own conceptions, to know of and look upon himself alone. That is the exclusive privilege of the fortunate few who wield inherited authority.

The Jews have always been a minority. But a minority is compelled to think; that is the blessing of its fate. It must always persist in a mental struggle for that consciousness of truth which success and power comfortingly assure to rulers and their supporting multitudes. The conviction of the many is based on the weight of possession; the conviction of the few is expressed through the energy of constant searching and finding. This inner activity becomes central to Judaism; the serenity of the world accepted and complete was beyond its reach. To believe in itself was not possible for it as a matter of course, but remained the ever renewed requirement on which its very existence depended. And the more confined its outward life, the more insistently did this inner conviction of life's duty have to be fought for and won.

Whether developed along the casual lines of ancient times or the systematic basis of the Middle Ages, Jewish religious doctrine was, above all, the product of this struggle for self-perpetuation. It was thus neither a scholastic philosophy, providing routine proofs for routine questions, nor one of those transient philosophies which serve but to justify the powers that be. Since it was wrought in the continuous struggle for spiritual existence, it lived as a philosophy of religion. The ideal existence of the entire community, the desires of all those who consciously wished to belong to the community and be educated in it, were expressed through this philosophy of religion. Through it the never ending meditation and speculation of Jewish life were developed. In hardly any other way did the Jewish community express itself so characteristically as in this sort of philosophizing; it gave the Jew his uniqueness, the revealing profile of his spiritual personality.

In the course of this philosophizing various ideas achieved dominance, according to the influences of time and place. No matter how firmly were established the fundamental principles of the religion, there were still significant shifts in the emphasis given to one or another of its constituent values. And thus a certain wavering seemed to characterize Jewish thought. The price Judaism paid for the possession of a philosophy was the sacrifice of certainty, of a formula or creed.

If we view the word "dogma" in its restricted sense, it might indeed be said that Judaism has no dogmas and therefore no orthodoxy, as religious orthodoxy is usually understood. Of course, in any positive religion, classical phrases will pass from generation to generation, each of which will view these phrases as the ancient and holy vessels of religious truth. Wherever there exists a treasury of faith, a *depositum fidei*, it is expressed in sacred words which ring with the tones of revelation and tradition. But that does not yet constitute a dogma in the precise sense of the word. A dogma is present only when a definite formula of conceptions has been crystallized, and only when this formula is declared binding, with salvation made dependent on it, by established authority.

None of these presuppositions is found in Judaism. In it there was no need for a constant, inviolable formula; this is necessary only in those religions at the heart of which lies a mystical, consecrating act of faith—an act which alone can open the door to salvation and which therefore requires a definite conceptual image to be handed down from age to age. Such acts of salvation and gifts of grace are alien to Judaism; it does not pretend to be able to bring heaven to earth. It has always maintained a certain sobriety and severity, demanding even more than it gives. That is why it adopted so many commandments, and refused sacraments and mysteries; if it had any tendencies in the latter direction, they were overcome at an early stage.

Nor did the urge toward complete knowledge result in the attempt to define once and for all the entire sphere of belief. Such attempts are required only in those religions where divine enlightenment and salvation are deemed to be equivalent, where complete knowledge alone—gnosis—leads to salvation. In such religions each shortcoming or error bars the way; the slightest false move may be fatal. Where the true faith is considered as a gift of grace, upon which everything depends, then it indeed requires a precise definition and an ultimate finality. But in Judaism articles of faith never attained such significance; they were never the condition of salvation, implying the choice between all and nothing.

In Christianity, the sense of mystery is made visible and tangible through the sacrament. But in Judaism the idea of mystery has a different significance; it remains in the sphere of the ideal, signifying the unfathomable that belongs to God but not to man—the unfathomable that man can approach only through his feelings. Veiled in a dark remoteness which no mortal eye can penetrate, the being of God can be approached by man only through pious behavior and silent meditation. Man's function is described by the commandments: to do what is good; that is the beginning of wisdom. In the Jewish view, God makes certain demands upon man, but these demands are in relation to the life in which he has placed man. The "principles of the Torah" are therefore, as the Talmud remarks, the principles of pious conduct. These principles are embodied in definite religious forms. On the other hand, the religious doctrine itself remains in many aspects free, without final and binding conclusions.

The high value which Judaism places upon the pious and good *deed* is one of the strongest possible checks against dogmatism. A precise, conceptual determination of creed arises in the Church, where the creed is regarded as knowledge which, on the other hand, is presented to the people as creed. Many of the authors of Church dogma were men who had come to religion through philosophy and then rediscovered philosophy in religion. The truth which they had found in philosophy was to be presented to the multitude in finished form as a religious creed—as the truth for those whom Origen called the "poor in spirit"—a view of the religious creed of the church also shared by Hegel. The religion of the learned and the religion of the ignorant were thereby to be unified in dogma. But in Judaism this unity was achieved by insistence on principles of conduct, a demand imposed on, and the same for, all; through it was to be created the "kingdom of priests and a holy nation" (Exod. 19:6). With such attitudes there was little room in Judaism for dogmatism.

Moreover, the Jewish religious community lacks an authoritative head who can create dogmas, especially since the disappearance of the powers vested first in the

Sanhedrin and later to a more limited degree in the so-called "Geonim." Only an ecclesiastical authority is entitled to lay down binding formulas of creed; to speak in the name of the community; to demand obedience; and to enforce it against those reluctant to obey. Whoever has power can decide what shall be regarded officially as truth. This manner of creating dogma was established in the early centuries of the Church when the dominant sect could enforce the acceptance of a dogma by decree or by the sword; and later, after the Reformation, when the lord of the land was also the lord of its religion. With ecclesiastical authority—whether pope, bishop, council, or secular church body—lies the power of decision. But for Judaism such authorities never existed. True, there was an assured tradition in the succession of teachers; but no ecclesiastical or secular hierarchy of any kind. When, occasionally, established authorities did appear—though always soon disappearing again—they never had powers to decide matters of faith. So even if a need had been felt for dogmas, there were no bodies with authority to establish them. The will to belong and the conviction of adherence were the decisive criteria for Judaism.

From time to time attempts have been made to codify rigid formulas. In an important passage of the Talmud there is a sentence which declares that those who deny certain doctrines are refused eternal life; but it is significant that it confines itself to the negative. During the Middle Ages, Karaite teachers under Islamic influence did set up articles of faith. It seems probable that this same influence was responsible for the attempt of certain other religious thinkers of the same period, including one held in high and lasting esteem, to embrace all of Jewish doctrine in a number of articles. Yet these articles did not become dogmas. The dominant form of Judaism always remained that of a religious philosophy of inquiry, a philosophy which produced method rather than system. Principles always remained of greater importance than results. There was always tolerance and even indifference toward modes of expression; it was the idea which was held to be central. Judaism, and the Jew as well, retained an unorthodox air; they neither could nor would rest in the easy comfort of dogma.

Many felt that something was lacking precisely because of the absence of dogma. The opinion was expressed that Judaism, because it had no definitely worded creed, was everything but a religion. And even within the Jewish community this opinion was frequently echoed, especially in times of transition: men missed the precisely formulated sentences of a creed to which they could cling. Without dogma, the faith seemed to lack that definitive and safeguarding form by which it could be perpetuated. No doubt there is some truth in this opinion. But this absence of the supporting crutch of dogma is in the very nature of Judaism, an essential result of its historical development. Jewish religious philosophy had as its purpose the constant renewal of the content of religion, by means of which it was best preserved and protected from the deadening rigidity of formula. It was a religion which constantly imposed upon its adherents new labors of thought. [. . .]

The ability of Jewish genius to absorb within itself varied elements of civilizations with which it has contact, bears witness to its creative power; for it has proved itself capable of digesting and completely assimilating them. Only seldom did it lose itself in the alien influences, but even then its own free and peculiar nature eventually triumphed. The influences were subsumed into the Jewish tradition and given a uniquely Jewish character. Thus in early times certain foreign terms were borrowed, but they were soon given an entirely new connotation. Two persons saying the same thing do not necessarily convey the same idea. For instance, the word which the Bible uses to designate a prophet betrays its foreign derivation. But how much has been added to this word by Israel! With what a personal ring, with what depth of thought, has this name become invested! The value the word has acquired is exclusively an Israelite contribution. For purposes of religious etymology or of tracing the course of human civilization, the origin of this or some other heatedly debated word may be important, but for the meaning of the Jewish religion it is not.

Occasionally a foreign conception slipped in with a foreign word; yet in the long run nothing was conceded to it. If it was permitted to enter, it was sooner or later overcome. Not until it had been recast in specifically Jewish terms did it find a permanent place in Jewish thought. That which was inferior was cast aside or rendered innocuous. Only that which could be made genuinely Jewish became part of the permanent heritage. However much the Jewish religion exposed itself to alien influences, it never changed its essential character, nor abandoned itself to those influences. For this contention there is no better evidence than the fact that Judaism has preserved its monotheism stern and pure.

When we compare this preservation of individuality with the history of other religions, we gain a real appreciation of the achievement of the Jewish religion. Religions which have been transported to new lands have come upon a set of customs, habits, and ideas with which they have often merged but without having arrived at a clear understanding of the relationship between the two. Such religions either put up with the traditions they happened to encounter or made unessential surface adaptations. It was easy for them to win victories at the cost of their own individuality. That Buddhism, for example, should concede everything to its adherents and guarantee an undisturbed existence even to the lowest forms of religion, is implied in its very nature and has in fact been a cause of its expansion. The greatest experts on Islamic history agree that Mohammedanism is a cloak under which pagan ideas and activities can find warm shelter. In like manner it has been said of the Greek Church that it wears the garb of the old Greek religion interwoven with strands of Christianity. And could not these examples be increased in number? Mass success of a religion has always resulted in a loss of its distinctiveness; speedy external victories entail internal impoverishment.

The Jewish religion, however, established a limit beyond which foreign influences could not be admitted. To defend this barrier a lengthy contest was often necessary—a contest which was not always immediately crowned with success! But the decisive battles for the retention of distinctiveness were always won. Especially in times of the greatest temptation and danger was the uniqueness of Judaism preserved with the greatest certainty. Precisely when it had to associate with old and new civilizations, whose dissolvent influences other religions had not been strong enough to resist, did Judaism remain most true to itself. This conflict with external influences which expressed itself also as a self-conflict within Judaism was a freely accepted challenge; it arose from no mere accident of circumstances and was no mere natural process. It was rather created by and stamped with the spiritual seal of those historical personalities—prophets, reformers, religious thinkers—who pointed the way for Judaism.

These observations are sufficient to show the nature of Israel's independence. Its originality consists neither in an innovation of spiritual elements nor in a complete lack of connection with any past. Its unique originality lies in its powers to struggle for that individuality of spirit by which it brings to life the given material. Independence manifests itself not so much in the germination of an idea as in the power to take an already existent idea and make it productive. This is what Goethe, who at times had doubts even about his own independence, believed. "The finest sign of originality," he says, "consists in one's ability to develop a received idea in so fruitful a manner that no one else would easily have discovered how much lay hidden therein." This originality in molding and shaping—leaving aside for the moment the religious discoveries of the prophets—is a considerable factor in establishing Israel's independence. [...]

The conception of development, and particularly of development conditioned by personalities, is essential to an understanding of the growth of the Jewish religion. For everything in the Bible points to the path which the Jewish religion had to follow—from Abraham to Moses to Jeremiah, from Jeremiah to the author of the Book of Job. The abiding continuity of its different epochs gives to Jewish history its homogeneous character. Only in its totality can Judaism really be understood. Even in the two religious creeds which to a certain extent derived from Judaism this principle also applies. Christianity has been especially praised for being the "most changing" of religions. But one of the fathers of the modern science of comparative religion has justly pointed out that Christianity possesses this emphasis only because of its connection with Judaism.

In all processes of evolution there are both stationary elements which assure equilibrium amid change, and dynamic forces which provide the impetus to change. This distinction may also be seen as that between the authoritative and the developing factors of a religion. Often the dynamic factors become in the course of time an element of conservatism. What at first was a bold question becomes later an obvious truth. An antithesis to one generation becomes a thesis to another. Here we see the regular movement of evolution; the road of progress runs from the paradox to the commonplace.

In the Bible Judaism has its secure and immovable foundation, the permanent element amid changing phenomena. With the old Israelite tradition of the patriarchs coming to an end in Moses, some historical foundation had already been laid. But with the Bible—*the* book which binds together as testimony of God the legends of the forefathers, the words of the men of God, and the preachings of the prophets—this historical foundation was solidified for all generations.

Not only was the Bible's historical and religious content preserved; it became as well the established authority for the changing eras. Prophecy and teaching were not mere transient periods of ancient history. That vision which the prophets strove to perpetuate remained the ideal of Judaism. It is a frequent claim that Israelite prophecy was replaced by so-called legalistic Judaism. Such claims regard the two as contrasting epochs. But in reality the contrast between them is merely that between an epoch in which a truth is fought for and one in which the truth is accepted. The scribes saw the prophets not as obsolete predecessors, but rather as proclaimers of eternal truth. Men so exalted that their words became Holy Writ can never be replaced

The Bible is the most authoritative element of Judaism. But it is not the only one. Just as it had been preceded by tradition, so was it soon followed by tradition, the "Oral Law," which strives to penetrate into the essence of the Bible's written word. The Oral Law strives to apply the teachings of the Bible to all the events of existence; to provide religious and moral standards for all of life's activities; and to realize the Bible's teachings in the whole Jewish community. This tradition which was ultimately established in the Talmud had at first to fight for recognition; subsequently, it too became a conservative factor in Jewish religious life. It need scarcely be pointed out that as regards religious influence, inner power and effectiveness, the Talmud takes second place to the Bible. But the Talmud often proved to be an even more conservative factor. Its role was to put up a protective fence around Judaism. And as such it was particularly honored and cherished during the long ages of oppression. The Jews felt guarded by the Talmud, and so they in turn guarded it. For side by side with and second only to the Scriptures, the Talmud prevented the religion of Israel from going astray. The historical continuity and continued equilibrium of Judaism were largely the result of the canonical character acquired by the Bible and the decisive authority imparted to the Talmud.

Yet had not both the Bible and the Talmud had in them driving and dynamic forces which made possible further development, they would have declined into static texts. The dynamic element of the Bible lies in its significance for the Jewish *faith*. To the faithful it offers the word of God which persists for all the ages; each age must search in it for what is most relevant and peculiar to itself. Each generation heard in the Bible's words its own wishes, hopes, and thoughts; each individual his heart's desire. The Bible lay so near to the heart that it could not be viewed from the historical standpoint. Never in Judaism did it become an ancient book to be read during later ages; it remained the book of life, of each new day. Divine revelation is intended for all men and not only for those who lived at the time it was delivered; it speaks to all of us about ourselves. "Thou art the man" (II Sam. 12:7) is the motto which stands at its head. And with it go the sayings: "For thee also God has performed these miracles"; "Thou too art come out of Egypt"; "Thou too standest before Sinai to receive the word of revelation."

The Bible was able to satisfy the new problems of each new day: the new cares and new demands with their moral and religious implications. For the cares the Bible was to offer consolation, for the demands it could grant satisfaction. And not least of all, each day taught new truths, and to these too the Bible was relevant. With the dominating idea of each age it had to come to some understanding; and with every important thought it had to compare and if possible unite itself. With each conquest of human thought the Bible took on a different meaning; but still the ancient word proved its power and wealth of significance. So the Bible itself moved forward with the times, and each age won its own Bible. What characteristic differences there are between what a Philo, an Akiba, a Maimonides, a Mendelssohn have found in the Bible! They read the same book, and yet in many ways it was a different book to each of them. As the Talmud often remarks, each epoch has its own biblical interpreters. And it is most happily expressed in that wonderful legend of Moses who hears Rabbi Akiba expound the Torah and does not even recognize it as . . . his Torah!

In the Jewish tradition the Bible was ever created anew, for it is in the nature of every true idea to struggle forward to greater precision; it contains within itself the power of generating persistent mental activity. Unfinished and unbounded, every creative idea of the human spirit constantly reveals itself anew to men and is thus always able to attract new thought to itself. To each generation it poses the problem of its meaning; one cannot be close to the Bible without feeling this as a spiritual necessity.

When men realized that the teaching of God was no heritage that one accepts passively but rather a heritage that has to be won, they began to see this relationship to the Bible as a religious obligation. It became a supreme commandment to "study," to explore the Scriptures.

To explore—that means to consider the Bible as a challenge rather than a gift. With such a fluid concept one cannot reconcile rigidity, compulsion, restraint and immutability of tradition. Faith based on mere authority therefore became impossible. The duty to "explore" requires further thinking; each end becomes a new beginning and each solution a new problem. As a result the traditionally received doctrine was not accepted as something final but rather as a force constantly renewing itself in the consciousness of the community. Hence Judaism's desire to comprehend the ancient word ever afresh; to take another, even a contradictory attitude toward it; and finally, the feeling of never having finished with it but ever pursuing it in the search for its true meaning.

This quest was favored in Judaism, particularly in later times, by the fact that the author usually remained in the background of his work and was often even left wholly out of account. If the individual stands in the center, he naturally becomes a dominating and restraining influence with regard to its own words. But if the idea is considered of greater importance than its originator, one can discuss it with less restraint.

Of even greater importance in this regard is the form of the Bible, the very way in which it is written. The Holy Scripture is, as a whole, roughhewn, unfinished, and unsystematic; it presents but the "fragments of a great confession." It leaves many things open, it is full of questions; what is merely suggested has to be followed to the end; passages which appear to be contradictory have to be reconciled; and what has been left open has to be filled in. The Holy Scripture is the most stable element of Judaism and at the same time its most dynamic force. Much the same can be said of the Oral Law, which is a development of the presuppositions implicit in the Bible. The very notion of an Oral Law implies, as has been correctly pointed out, that it can never be brought to a conclusion; it is a permanent quest. Even if it were recorded in writing, no definite limits could be set to it. The Oral Law has served as an important stimulant to the development and freedom of the Judaic tradition. [. . .]

Since the ancient Scriptures carried with them the command for constant study, they could not become a dead weight; they implied the adaptation of the materials of the past to the present. Even the forces of authority in Jewish religious life had to acknowledge and accept the tendency of constant reinterpretation. Thus authority did not lead to dogmatism. The mental struggle to discover the true idea, the true command, the true law (a hundred-sided question without a final answer) always began anew. The Bible remained the Bible, the Talmud came after it, and after the Talmud came religious philosophy, and after that came mysticism, and so it went on and on. Judaism never became a completed entity; no period of its development could become its totality. The old revelation ever becomes a new revelation: Judaism experiences a continuous renaissance.

And from this recurring renaissance, with its powers of spiritual regeneration, there arises the unique historical character of Judaism. Again and again it awakened and opened its eyes. Each of its epochs was shaped by a particular experience from which Judaism discovered new meanings with which to shape its spiritual life. The urge to realize thought and commandment in practice caused the Jews restlessly to dig deeper down into the traditional, but eventually this very same urge led them simultaneously to look into their own spirit. The prophetic word of the "new heaven and new earth" (Isa. 66:22) has come true in the history of Judaism.

Only rarely, and that during periods of tradition, did Judaism find its religious past a heavy burden. The Jews were always conscious of their unique history, with all its blessings; they felt elevated by the consciousness of the divine rule throughout the centuries of Jewish existence. Seldom did they feel their religious past to be an impediment to the present. In each period those Jewish thinkers who trod new paths of thought always felt certain that they were standing on the firm ground of traditional Judaism. Few things in the religious literature of Judaism are so prominent as this feeling of harmony with the past. True, there were often tensions between old and new conceptions, but these were for the most part products of the attempt of Judaism to broaden the horizons of its life. Judaism preserved its living actuality; it felt itself always to be part of the present.

There were periods of course—and sometimes they were rather prolonged—when Judaism showed signs of weariness, when life appeared to stand still and when ideas seemed to falter. Nothing could be easier than to find in one Jewish document or another passages which fall short of the highest religious ideal. But this proves nothing against Judaism; for it was always able to rise again and rediscover itself. And thus its true history is a process of renaissance. Of many peoples and communities it has been said that they had too great a past to expect a future. Even if this judgment be applicable to a religion, it can certainly not be legitimately applied to the Jewish religion, because in it there arose a constant renewal of the central religious self—quite apart from the great idea of the future as it was propounded by Judaism. Like living genius reawakening from generation to generation, the ancient prophets are ever in the world of Judaism.

Translated by Irving Howe, Victor Grubenwieser, and Leonard Pearl.

Other works by Baeck: *The Pharisees and Other Essays* (1947); *Judaism and Christianity* (1958); *This People Israel* (1965).

Dante A. Lattes

1876–1965

Dante Lattes was a well-known Jewish journalist and educator—and rabbi, although he hardly ever acted in that capacity—in twentieth-century Italy. He edited the Trieste-based *Il corriere israelitico* from 1904 to 1916. In 1925, he published the first volume of *La rassegna mensile di Israel*, which became a widely circulated literary periodical. He was an active Zionist from his youth—indeed, among the first to champion Zionism in Italy. He delivered hundreds of speeches in different communities and translated the works of major Zionist thinkers into Italian. He took refuge in Palestine from Italy's Fascist racial laws from 1938 to 1946, when he returned to Italy to continue his work as an educator and a writer.

Apology for Judaism
1923

The Messiah of Israel does not come to redeem men from some original sin they never committed, nor from sins which they can liberate themselves of every day, through divine mercy and their own powers, but to crown humanity's suffering, to celebrate the ascension that men have achieved. In this sense we already have redemption within us: it is an act of the human spirit, which has attained perfect good through its own efforts.

The path of life has already been drawn, and it is one of justice and goodness: men can and must follow it. The far-off days of peace, serenity, and happiness are the destination toward which men must tend with their work. The prophetic message is the announcement of this moral impulse to possess the goodness that is found in men and peoples. The Kingdom of God comes to the extent that we make it come; and every day the Jew announces its coming to himself, he accepts and proclaims it when he proclaims the unity of and love for God. Yet the Kingdom of God must converge not merely in individuals but in humanity. The individual always has the Kingdom of God within him, whenever he wishes it. But it must take hold in the world and in history—not through some exterior influence descended from on high, nor through a theoretical proclamation, but as a reality acquired from within. There is nothing otherworldly or supernatural about the Kingdom of God; rather, it is the reign here below of the divine will and spirit that has been truly realized among men; it is the above descended to earth; it is the union of the real and the ideal that has come into being through the deeds of men. "When Israel said: We will do all that the Eternal has spoken, that was a Kingdom of God." The word of the Kingdom of God, according to the Pharisees as well as in the gospel, is: Listen, Israel, the Eternal is our God, the Eternal One (Rosh Hashanah 16a).

Human history thus takes on religious worth and moral unity. The spirit makes itself known in humanity. History moves forward through man's sufferings toward the sanctification of the name of God. Man's destiny is fulfilled not with armies or with force, but in the spirit of God. And from men's renewed heart, from the earth, and from the new skies bursts forth that new universal hymn to God, a hymn of salvation, which finally reigns over regenerated men (Psalm 96).

It is the realization of the unity of men in the world, and thus of the unity of God and of the perfect unity of God in men.

"Then all men will invoke the name of God with pure lips, they will adore him in perfect unity."

Jewish messianism, symbolized at first in the person of a *man*, in whom justice makes itself known and is carried out, becomes and is an idea: the idea of That Which is to Come, of man's yearning, both individual and collective, for justice and religion to make themselves known in history. The Jewish collective conscience is gathered and centered on the belief that human suffering must flow together toward that dawn of redemption, in which evil will no longer reign on earth. It is no longer the person but the time and the *fact* that matter. It is reality. And humanity moves toward this reality through hard work. The Messiah is continually coming.

All peoples contribute to the coming, and every man is the messiah of himself and other men. The Messiah—man of the age of heroes, the ideal man of the future, the Son of David, who is the actualization of the idea, the man on whom the spirit of God rests—the spirit of wisdom and worth, the spirit of the knowledge and fear of God—the man who is the judge of the wretched and who girds himself with faith and charity, becomes the people-messiah. Israel is the "servant of God" who suffers for the salvation of the world, for the conversion of the world: a people of suffering, experts in martyrdom, whom men believed had been abandoned by God while instead it was the holocaust of wickedness and the world's incomprehension.

But the most vivid and essential element of Jewish Messianism is the belief in people, the belief that a new life that must arise on earth: the wait for the "days of the Messiah." Days that have not yet come but that will come for all of humanity. The Jewish messianic idea is truly an interior palingenesis [rebirth] not only of the individual but of all of humanity, in whose complex form the One is revived and realized. Daniel's "son of man" (7:13) is not just one man but humanity lifted up to the throne of God; and the "holy spirit" is the force of good, the impulse of honest action in which the divine is revealed. The "holy spirit" can descend on everyone. "I call as witness heaven and earth"—says the Tanna debei Eliyahu—"that the holy spirit descends on all, pagan or Hebrew, man or woman, male or female slave, according to their works."

The essential thing, then, is the renewal of the spirit: the rest is a marvelous fantasy, a poetic dream that Jewish writers' lively imaginations have woven from the day the first prophet announcer of the ideal rose up in Israel until the times of Jewish apocalypses and the *agadah*. Jewish fantasy has always embraced the marvelous idea, embroidering its substance with endless fancies that are not the ultimate cause of the forms the Christian message assumed. Around the time of the gospels, in the Jewish world apocryphal and pseudo-epigraphic literature flowers. On the one hand, it heralds the Talmudic *agadah* and, on the other, it becomes the transitional bridge to primitive Christianity in its Judaic form: apocalyptic, messianologic, eschatological literature, all color and fantasy, all fervor and hope. The gospel is inspired by these popular fantasies, which enveloped the messianic idea around the person of the Messiah. In its moral preaching, evangelical messianism, for all its interiority, profundity, and energy, is pure Judaism; the Christian story/event is an episode of Jewish history up until its syncretism with Western values, up until it forgets the beginning of the action and creates the dogma to which Judaism could not and cannot subscribe.

For Judaism, the Messiah is coming, but he has not come yet. "Time has run out," says Rav in the Talmud (b. Sanhedrin 97). "Now everything depends on conversion and good works."

Messianic times will be fulfilled when "the new skies and the new earth," which were prophesized, become a reality. When Rabbi Menachem of Vitebsk—so says the Hasidic legend—lived in Palestine, it happened that a fool climbed up the Mount of Olives and sounded the horn. A rumor spread among the frightened people that it was the trumpet announcing redemption. When the rumor reached the rabbi's ears, he opened the window, looked out onto the world and declared: "There is no renewal."

Judaism is awaiting this renewal through the works of men.

Translated by Virginia Jewiss.

Other works by Lattes: *Leggendi orientale* (1927); *Nuovo commento alla Torah* (1976).

Franz Rosenzweig
1886-1929

Franz Rosenzweig was one of the most important Jewish philosophers of the twentieth century. Born into an unobservant Jewish family in Cassel, Germany, he considered converting to Christianity in 1913 but reversed himself and began leading the life of an observant Jew and studying Hebrew texts. While serving in the German army in 1918, he completed a systematic philosophy of religion, *The Star of Redemption* (1921). After the war, he was instrumental in establishing the Freies Jüdisches Lehrhaus in Frankfurt, an experimental adult education project. Aside from Rosenzweig, the faculty included Martin Buber, Erich Fromm, Leo Strauss, Nathan Birnbaum, Gershom Scholem, Ernst Simon, and Leo Baeck. Rosenzweig suffered from progressive paralysis from 1921 but continued to write. He completed a translation of the poems of Yehudah Ha-Levi into German, and, with Buber, he began to translate the Hebrew Bible into German.

Apologetic Thinking
1923

I

It has often been said, and even more often repeated, that Judaism has no dogmas. As little as that may be correct—a superficial glance at Jewish history or into the Jewish prayer book already teaches the opposite—something very correct is nevertheless meant by it. Namely, Judaism indeed has dogmas, but no dogmatics. Already noteworthy in this respect is the point at which the Talmudic literature enters the discussions, to which later attempts at ascertaining Jewish dogmas had to revert. In the context of the regulations concerning criminal procedure and criminal law appears also the problem of punishment in the hereafter; and here the things are listed whose denial causes the Jew to lose his "portion of the world to come." It was here that Maimonides and others were able to find a starting point. It is thus a legal context in which the problems of religious metaphysics appear. This is surely noteworthy if one thinks of the often-cited metaphysical inclination of our stock [unser Stammes], which can be established for the present with certainty.

The matter becomes even more noteworthy if one considers the content of these dogmas. They deal with God, with the revealed law, with Messianic redemption, and with that which is connected with it: missing is the thought that wholly permeates Judaism, which alone can make the law comprehensible and which alone can explain the preservation of the Jewish people, the thought of the chosenness of Israel. This truly central thought of Judaism, which, say, a Christian scholar, coming from Christology, would expect to find perhaps in first or, at least, immediately after the doctrine of God, in second place, in Jewish dogmatics, does not occur at all in, for example, Maimonides's "Thirteen Articles of Faith" or in his philosophical work, which after all was supposed to be a guide to those perplexed about the basic truths of Judaism. Here, too, as everywhere, the thought of chosenness of the Jewish people is a prerequisite for thought as well as life; yet it is never articulated; it is self-evident. Never do prayer and poetry tire of clothing it again and again in new words; the exegetical legends mirror it in myriad facets; mysticism sinks deep into it to the point of mythological hypostasis: it becomes word, meaning, form, but never a dogmatic formula, never—with the one great exception, nourished, to be sure, by all those forces, of Yehuda Halevi's *Kuzari*—a philosophical topic. Existence is filled with it and borne by it, all immediate utterance of existence is moved by it—however, when consciousness seeks to soar beyond mere existence, it denies it.

That has deep reasons and far-reaching consequences. A spiritual community withdraws its innermost essence here from spiritual exposure. This means that the community does not wish to be only a spiritual community, but wants rather to be what it actually is in contrast to other communities connected by spirit/intellect alone: a natural community, a people. The monstrous actuality of Jewish being has created for itself a self-protection. But what here has a protective and actuality-preserving effect, the deflection of consciousness from the secret source of life, would have had to have a paralyzing effect on life in a community which in its essence is purely spiritual, such as, for example, the Christian church. In the latter, the continually renewed lifting into consciousness of the foundation of existence, in this case the constant reformulating of Christological dogma, again and again, becomes the inner condition for the external continuation of the community. Inaccessible mystery stands opposed to inexhaustible mystery, substantiality to spirituality.

But this has an effect also on the direction and the reach of scholarly thought in general. Not only has Jewish patristics never produced an Augustine, a thinker who, in almost corporeal vision, set the stage for the history of the coming millennium, producing instead of him the powerful swimmers through the "sea of the Talmud," but Jewish scholasticism also never brought forth a Thomas. The *Summa* of Aquinas, that mighty system of a comprehensive Christian science, whose great and truly systematic intention could not, however, overcome the historical birth defect of scholasticism's apologetic-dialectical method and was therefore not able to realize itself, has on our side no counterpart in Maimonides's philosophical work, the *Guide of the Perplexed*, but rather in *his* "Great Ḥibbur," as he himself calls *his* giant halakhic opus, which actually snaps up the entire universe as well, but in the sieve of Jewish law. Here, in a different way, is the same immediate totality as was intended there, the same will to make the heart of one's own religious life the center of a spiritual cosmos; one was justified—starting out from considerations different from those developed here—in interpreting "my great Ḥibbur" in Maimonides's mouth as meaning "my summa." *The Guide of the Perplexed*, however, would disappoint one who approaches it in the expectation of finding a system. Just as it starts with a lengthy treatise, which unfolds all the material on the problem of biblical anthropomorphism, so it is thereafter the apologetic thread on which the individual treatises making up the work are strung. The defense is directed against the attacks of philosophy, not or only peripherally against other religions, by which the defense could therefore have been taken over. The apologetic nature of the fundamental attitude yields the completely unpedantic character, which still today is a fresh breeze for the reader and strikes him as in no way "scholastic"; this thinking has what systematic thinking cannot have so easily: the fascination—and the truthfulness—of thought reacting to the occasion; but therefore a limit is also set for it which only systematic thinking removes: exactly the limit of the occasional; only systematic thinking determines the circle of its objects itself; apologetic thinking remains dependent on the cause, the adversary.

And in this sense Jewish thinking remains apologetic thinking. It is characteristic that here it does not arrive at the phenomenon in which the self-sufficiency of thinking usually manifests itself within a culture, the struggle of schools within the common thinking. With us, the conflict between nominalism and realism has its counterpart in the Maimonidean controversy, with its labor pains and after-pains and its own two phases, separated by a century—thus not the struggle within thinking, but rather the cultural struggle over thinking itself, the struggle between those who heeded the call of the occasion and those who themselves denied it. Neither did it become different in the 19th century, when after a fallow period of nearly four hundred years once again—in Germany since the [18]20s—a Jewish philosophy developed, which until today has not been appreciated in a way commensurate with the quality of the achievements. All reservation about apologetics has not been able to prevent the fact that the legitimate method of thinking itself remained apologetic. One did not become a Jewish thinker in the undisturbed circle of Judaism. Here, thinking did not become a thinking about Judaism, which was simply the most self-evident thing of all, more being than an "ism," but rather it became a thinking within Judaism, a learning; thus ultimately not a fundamental but rather an ornamental thinking. Anyone who was supposed to reflect on Judaism had somehow, if not psychologically then at least spiritually, to be torn at the border of Judaism. Therefore, however, his thinking was then determined by the power which had led him to the border, and the depth horizon of his gaze was determined by the degree to which he had been carried to, on, or across the border.

The apologetic is the legitimate force of this thinking but also its danger. Two significant works of the recent time are to be considered from this perspective in what follows.

II

Gustav Landauer reacted to the publication of the nucleus of [Max] Brod's confessional book [*Anschauung und Begriff* (1913)?] with a reply that was moved by an injured sense of justice: he saw it as yet another attempt to comprehend one's own domain in its ideality and the foreign one in the entire breadth of its historical and historically tainted actuality. I would think that this danger belongs among those that, just because they are so obvious, can be easily avoided. Quite on the contrary, it seems to me that the danger of all apologetics lies much more in the fact that one takes one's own, which, after all, one knows oneself, in its full breadth and depth of actuality, while the foreign, of which one has only "taken notice," for the most part only as it occurs in a book, i.e., therefore precisely as an—ideal. For every actual observer of human nature knows that personal statements can be used as sources only with much caution. And this is by no means because, on account of natural bias, they create in general too favorable a picture, but rather on the contrary, because they tend to come out too theoretical, too absolute, too bony, and to lack the correction of theory by practice, the flesh covering the bones. The well-known utterance by a man who ought to know—"Give me two written words by anyone, and I'll bring him to the gallows"—is valid also for spiritual movements. We all know what a tragicomic caricature of Judaism results if, apparently with complete objectivity, one strings a series of quotations together; and in doing so, it hardly matters whether the assembling is done by the Jewish or antisemitic side; on the contrary, the things that [Johann Andreas] Eisenmenger and his predecessors produce as "fiery Satanic bullets" from the arsenal of the Talmud could more truly lure one to this book than many a recent collection of carefully filtered "rays of light." This is certainly connected with a peculiar lack of self-consciousness in Judaism, which is discussed in the first part of these remarks; it is indeed impossible to make a Talmudic passage comprehensible to someone who does not already understand it; for this purpose one would have to be able to open, so to speak, each time a whole complete pictorial atlas of Jewish history, Jewish faces, Jewish life, which of course cannot exist. Yet, one could not do a greater injustice even to Christianity, which points to self-consciousness so intensely, one could not do a greater injustice than to present it in terms of its own catechism. It is the first duty of theoretical neighborly love (which among us creatures committed to mutual peeping and judging is no less important than the practical one—because being perceived wrongly hurts no less than being treated wrongly) that we never forget to ask ourselves about each opinion that we form about another person: can the other, if he is as I here depict him, still—live? For that is what he wishes and ought to do—"like myself." These legalistic machines, lacking humor and soul, whom the Christian so gladly represents under the [name] "Pharisees," would be incapable of living; just as little as those pale lilies of heaven, whom the Jew, on the basis of a reading of the Sermon on the Mount, would recognize as the only "true Christians." If one wants to understand a spirit, then one must not abstract it from the body that belongs to it. As little as the body is a decayed manifestation of the spirit, as little is that in the historical image of a community which does not fit its classical records to be judged without further ado as decay, as an "amalgam"; perhaps it is, quite on the contrary, the necessary and, in a certain sense, even the originally "intended" correction of those origins. An adult may long all his life for the purity of childhood, but he is by no means merely a decayed manifestation of the child because of this. Quite on the contrary, one may perhaps even recognize the traits of the child in their whole significance, only if one tries to fathom them in retrospect from the known face of the man.

And just here lies the weakness of Brod's book. An actual weakness, because an unnecessary one, not one of those that are only the shadow of the strength. That he also improperly schematizes "paganism" matters little in comparison, because paganism, despite the three-tiered title and the basic thought constructed in three parts, does not fall within the book's core, through which the bloodstream of experience pulses. But the depiction of Christianity, precisely because it lies near the heart of the book, suffers greatly from that method of "unfair idealizing," whereby he lends more credence to schoolmasters and theology professors than to saints and knights. It is very characteristic that the two vital Christians who have not sprung from the catechism and who have been admitted into his book because they were too close to the author to be able to remain outside—Dante and Kierkegaard—are not treated as Christians, but rather, comical as it may sound, as—Jews dispersed within Christianity. If only, even here, he had also trusted his experience more than theory, even if it was his own theory.

For his strength is that he does so in the core of the book. The book is, in a good sense of the word, what its subtitle states: a confessional book. It does not burden the reader with the private affairs of the author, as one might well fear because of the title; rather it narrates the life's journey of a way of knowing; and because this life's journey was, at the same time, the life's journey of a generation, the goal he achieves is of more than private significance. Brod, in his own manner, has worked his way through the fog of theories to the actuality of historical Judaism. He succeeded in this because he did not allow himself to be led on this journey by the theoretical question about which is the correct Judaism, but rather was propelled by the practical question about which is the right life. This book answers the question of the essence of war with the essence of Judaism. It became a good theological book because it is—oh, strangest, easiest and most difficult of all sciences!—not a theological book, but rather in its origin and its organization a war book. And it became a bad theological book when in the end it still wanted to be a theological book and to the degree that it wanted to become that.

With magnificent verve, the book's thought is refracted from the concepts of "noble" and "ignoble misfortune," which were discovered wholly personally and wholly unscholastically in war (and probably also already in prewar), across the elevated viewpoints of the "incompatibility of things belonging together" and the "earthly miracle," on a path into the middle of the aggadah. The concepts with which the wisdom of religion teachers of the past century had dragged this matter down to its own level remain unused by the side; this is self-explanatory; the internal apologetics of the book take to task just those concepts, which had desiccated Judaism to a mummy in the foolish belief that this would make it more "adequate to the times." Yet the intensity with which the aggadic is thoroughly investigated here is completely new. Only very few Talmudic passage are dealt with by Brod; but these passages are examined in respect to their content with a methodical seriousness that to the Talmud reader of the old school is totally alien, even incomprehensible, when applied to the "merely aggadic." In all modesty, the *am ha-aretz* [ignoramus] Brod becomes here a pioneer of a new method in the ancient domain of Talmudic studies. Issues that hitherto only the preacher, and in more recent times at best the historian, had considered worthy of detailed attention are now taken completely seriously with regard to their content, one is almost tempted to say: with halakhic seriousness. Before the eyes of a generation returning home to the old book with a new attitude, there now lies not simply the old book, but also a renewed, rejuvenated one.

Manifest here is the strength of apologetic thinking, which brings about what naïve thinking never could. Yet, here also the danger takes effect. As Brod discovers in Judaism the things that lift him beyond the living needs of his thinking, he is similarly, all-too-similarly prepared to discover in them the "specifically Jewish," and he does not pose to himself the question whether the remedy that he discovers for his human need is not just—as human as the need, and whether Judaism has a part in it only by virtue of its participation in—the human. Should not the restriction of the human to that which is specific to us, which is certainly necessary and blessed, and the restriction of the universal to that which is proper to us, not have more easily led to a coloration, which is certainly likewise necessary and also likewise blessed, of that light which, dazzlingly encompassing all colors, has risen for the human species? In Christianity, Brod himself sees very clearly where the point of this restriction is located: in the narrowing of divine grace's unlimited possibility of finding its way to the human, by means of the one dogmatically correct way of the experience of Christ. This is indeed correct; and in the fact that Judaism does not know, is not allowed to know such a binding of divine grace— even if it is, as for the Christian, a binding to its own great deed—lies the greatest strength of Judaism; here it was permitted to preserve for its children the heavenly wine it pressed, unadulterated in the most primordial fire. Yet Brod misses the point which he could already have noticed in his story of Simeon ben Yoḥai and the remarkable "institution" which he finally establishes: where this point of restriction lies for Judaism. In faith, we may be unconditioned; God does not prescribe the way of miracles for Judaism; but He does prescribe the way of His action to the human being; here, Judaism is not unconditioned but rather restricted to the one condition of the law. That the circle of this condition is cast so enormously wide that it hardly intersects with any conceivable circles of the world and its actions, changes the fact that it is a restriction of action as little as the enormous bearing of the Christian experience of Christ, which potentially can touch all human experiences, changes the fact that it is a narrowing of faith. And actually what Brod has to say about the law remains completely at the nationalistically agitated surface of the problem, although his attitude toward it is well-meaning and receptive, because of the general an-

tiliberal atmosphere of today's generation of intellectuals. And thus it is that exactly where his book descends into the depths, it reaches a central point to which the title question with its oppositions can no longer follow and where what he pronounces in the name of his and our Judaism is true only in an ultimate sense, but not in a penultimate sense.

III

In one passage of his book, Brod sweeps "the humane mediocrities of a Baeck and a Lazarus" from his table with one of those broad gestures for which a confessional book may allow. One senses that, under the pressure of his own thinking, he has not found the quiet to read what has been thought before him. Even of Lazarus the harsh judgment—or may I speak for once for our, my own as well as Brod's generation: the harsh prejudice?—does not hold true; his book is, as by the way was already shown by the vigorous attack that Hermann Cohen had directed against it when his Kantianism was in full bloom, better than its reputation, which is perpetuated here by Brod, too. But with respect to what concerns Baeck completely, I might apply to Brod—and again, in memory of a former prejudice, to myself—here the Goethean sarcastic aphorism: "*Pereant, qui ante nos nostra dixerunt.*" For, on the one hand, in outer as well as inner form, a greater contrast can hardly be imagined than between Brod's confessional book and Baeck's *The Essence of Judaism*. While in the former one sees throughout the path that has led to the goal, and the attractiveness of the book depends not least on the way it obliges its reader to accompany it on this road, in the latter the scaffolds have been dismantled without a trace, and only the completed building offers itself to the gaze.

So much for the form. In content, on the other hand, the two books are as similar as two books of such different form can possibly be. Baeck's book too is, after all, apologetically occasioned. The part that Christian speech and communication in his social circle and his circle of friends have obviously played for Brod was assumed for Baeck, in a significant way, by a literary event: Harnack's *What is Christianity?* This book, which with the usual learned lack of misgivings depicts a Judaism whose only possibility of existence is that it forms the dark background of the Christian light, and which without this function would have to crumble with a rattle because of the inherent improbability of its life, has caused Baeck, not, however, against Harnack, but for itself and for us, to depict Judaism, as it is, not as a foil for something else but rather in itself, in its own roundedness and fullness. And what he depicts, not with the passion of the discoverer and confessor but rather—especially in the second edition, in which the book has first grown to its full inner and outer weight—with the deep calm love of the intimate servant at home in the whole wide mansion of Judaism, is exactly what has shaken Brod: freedom's origination from grace, or put in Baeck-like terms: the origination of the commandment from mystery, the earthly miracle, or, again put in Baeck-like terms, the great paradox. Brod depicts the paradox in the strong spare dramatics of his book confession and life; Baeck depicts this in the tireless and never tiring dialectics of his book of knowing and essence, which collects manifold material within a narrow space. It will remain a matter of taste whether one prefers the content to be mediated to oneself in the purely ecstatic form of the former or in the purely classical form of the latter—perhaps even a matter of the maturity of one's own way of knowing; in the life of knowing, after all, the time of blossoming is certainly no more worthless than the time of fruition.

As the two books are similar in what they deliver, they are also remarkably similar in their weaknesses. What has been said above about Brod's treatment of Christianity could be repeated almost verbatim for Baeck, too. If this does not come to the fore in *The Essence of Judaism*, with its only incidental treatment of Christianity, as clearly as in Brod, then it does so all the more in the more recent publication *Romantic Religion*, where at best it is mitigated by a certain methodological awareness which deliberately poses the problem as a definite abstraction, whereby the danger for the reader does not, of course, become smaller.

It follows likewise from the related fundamental constellation of both books that both must break down before the problem of the Law. Again it seems to me, however, that the superior consciousness of the problem is under Baeck's control. Yet Baeck sees, as little as Brod, that the critical point lies here, where the essence of Judaism recognized by him is more *essence* of Judaism than essence of *Judaism*. And it will perhaps happen to him, as happened to Brod at this point where the acting emerges from the believing, that the Christian reader follows him here completely without hesitation, while the Jewish reader comes to a standstill. The fact that nearby, although by the way and not with

central weight, very fine things are said by Baeck about the Law, is just as much to be noted as the fact that the liberal rabbi, especially in the second edition, has said things about the Jewish people and Jewish history of a profundity hardly ever reached by what the Zionist poet says about it. Perhaps the Jewish present shows no symptom richer in hope than this exchange of roles.

IV

Why is the word "apologetics" particularly afflicted with such a bad odor? In this regard, it is probably similar to the apologetic profession *par excellence*, that of the lawyer. Against him, too, exists widely the prejudice that considers lying, as it were, his legitimate task. It may be that a certain professional routine appears to justify this prejudice. And yet, defending can be one of the noblest human occupations. Namely, if it goes to the very ground of things and souls and, renouncing the petty devices of a lie, ex-culpates with the truth, nothing but the truth. In this broad sense, literary apologetics can also defend. It would then embellish nothing, still less evade a vulnerable point, but would rather make precisely the most endangered points the basis of the defense. In a word: it would defend the whole, not this or that particular. It would not at all be a defense in the usual sense, but rather a candid exposition, yet not of some cause, but rather of one's own [self]. To what degree the two reviewed books approximate this lofty concept of apologetics may well be gathered from what has been said.

They are both answers to attacks. They have let their theme be determined by the attack. The theme is the very essence. One could think that it would now come to its highest awareness. But precisely the apologetic character of the thinking prevents that. Insofar as the thinker looks into his innermost [being], he indeed sees this innermost, but for this reason he is still far from seeing—himself. For he himself is not his innermost but is to the same extent also his outermost, and above all the bond that binds his innermost to his outermost, the street on which both associate reciprocally with each other. Yet, without further circumspection, he equates his innermost with his self and does not sense that his innermost, the more it is innermost, is the innermost of every human being. Thus, although he means himself, he speaks of the human being, of all [human beings]. And thus his self, the binding of the elements of humankind into the bundle that he himself is, remains a mystery to him. Apologetic thinking does not cross this barrier. He is denied the ultimate strength of knowing as he is spared the ultimate suffering of knowing. For ultimate knowing no longer defends, ultimate knowing adjudicates.

NOTE
Words in brackets appear in the original translation.

Translated by Paul W. Franks and Michael L. Morgan.

Other works by Rosenzweig: *God, Man, and the World: Lectures and Essays* (1998); *Cultural Writings of Franz Rosenzweig* (2000); *Philosophical and Theological Writings* (2000); *The Star of Redemption* (2005).

Samuel Chaim Landau
1892–1928

Born into a Polish Hasidic environment, Samuel Chaim Landau became a religious Zionist after World War I (when he was taken hostage by the Germans) while maintaining Hasidic observance. He had a leadership role with the Mizrachi organization in Poland and later in Palestine, and he organized Zionist youth movements. Writing in Hebrew, he published articles on the interrelationship of the Torah, labor, and nationalism. He moved to the Land of Israel in 1926, where he died at age thirty-six.

Toward an Explanation of Our Ideology
1924

Jewry, and religious Jewry in particular, has always attached prime importance to the rebuilding of Eretz Israel. The Hovevei Zion regarded it as a national duty; for the religious it was a divine commandment as well, one equal in importance to all the other precepts of the Torah. In the religious view it was, therefore, an ultimate value, and the sense of obligation to this task was unconditioned even by national loyalty. "To dwell in the Holy Land is a *mitzvah*"—the commandment might be interpreted as either national or religious, but it was essentially abstract and mystical. The role of the nation in the process of rebuilding the land was realized solely through the obedience of its individuals to this commandment; it bore no relationship to the national existence and character of the Jewish people. Such a viewpoint could not inspire our people to labor for the rebuilding of the land. Its effect was largely negative, because the commandment to dwell in the land, under-

stood only as a *mitzvah* incumbent upon each individual Jew, could be obeyed in many ways that were totally unrelated to a true rebuilding.

Zionism came into the world to announce a fundamental change. This movement emphasized that the concept of nationhood is the primal value of our people. The entire program of Zionism, therefore, revolves around this idea, and all other national values are significant only to the degree that they serve as instruments of the absolute—the nation. Even the rebuilding of the land is secondary, for the land was created for the nation and not the nation for the land.

This approach is shared by the religious wing of the Jewish national movement as well; even though it may derive its reason for rebuilding Eretz Israel from the divine commandment mentioned above, this *mitzvah* itself is understood as rooted in the idea of the national renaissance. Did not the Talmud teach that "the Torah was created for the sake of Israel?" It is therefore self-evident that our approach to the rebuilding of the land must be governed by the ultimate goal, the national renaissance. We can admit only such guidelines as indispensable to our labors as are logically implied by the one absolute value. Even the idea of "Torah Va-Avodah" (Torah and Labor), which we have made our fundamental blueprint for the regeneration of Eretz Israel, must be measured by this yardstick.

What do we mean by Torah?

This "Torah," the heritage of Israel, has two basic meanings: The first refers to the Torah as a code of law which is incumbent upon the individual, which every single Jew must obey; the second connotes the Torah as a totality, as the national spirit, the source of its culture and life—i.e., the national and collective aspects of the Torah. (These ideas are, of course, not new.) In its individual aspect the Torah is unrelated to the nation as nation; it relates only to the children of Israel as individuals. In this sense it is an obligation that rests on every Jew in the Diaspora, and all the more so in the Land of Israel. This, however, implies no specific and essential connection between the Torah and the process of rebirth in Eretz Israel. The second meaning of Torah, as the collective spirit of the people, implies a totally different relationship. The Torah, interpreted in this sense, permeates completely the process of the national renaissance, appearing as both cause and effect, and it is therefore as related to the essence of the renaissance as the flame is to the glowing ember. A national renaissance is inconceivable without the national spirit, "for our people is not a people except through its Torah," and the spirit of our people cannot express itself unless there be a national revival in our own Land, for "the divine spark can influence our people only in its own Land."

In this sense—but only in this sense—the Torah is more than the command which individual Jews, the national vanguard in the Holy Land included, must obey; it is the *primum mobile*, the essential element, and the efficient cause of the national revival. It is more than the signpost and mold of individual and collective life; it denotes the ultimate spiritual source of the movement.

II

What we have said about "Torah" applies also to "Avodah" (Labor).

Seemingly, there is now general agreement that labor is an important factor in the colonization of Eretz Israel, and all who come or intend to come must work, and indeed that only those have a right to *aliyah* who are trained and prepared to work. Nonetheless we cannot deduce from this that labor as *ideal*, as a basic and essential component of the general idea of the national renaissance, has prevailed within our national movement. To subscribe to the necessity and usefulness of labor is not necessarily to accept the concept which was born in the mind of the founders and vanguard of the labor movement in Eretz Israel, that labor as idea and value possesses the power to effect our national regeneration. Labor out of intellectual commitment, informed by the right intent and attitude of the worker, can rise to the level of an act not merely of obligation and individual compulsion but of national rebirth.

This concept requires much elucidation. What does "Avodah" mean?

If "Avodah" is intended only as solution of the economic problem, it bears no more than a temporal relation, one of day-to-day existence, to the national movement. It affects the individual members of the nation, be they few or many, and involves the community only in the quantitative sense, through the individuals that comprise it, and not the "eternal life," the quality of the people. "Avodah" determined by such "practical" considerations is bereft of any basic positive value as the premise of a movement engaged in creating a new life. To serve such a function "Avodah" must be elevated

to a higher level related to the very essence of national ideology.

What is this higher level? Some identity it with the moral aspect of labor. Commerce, so they assert, is shot through with swindle and deceit; only the life of labor contains objective possibilities for ordering society on foundations of justice and righteousness. This idea can, however, be contradicted. To be sure, it supplies labor with moral significance by ascribing to it a purpose nobler than the mere filling of the stomach, but even so lofty a purpose does not make for a movement of national renaissance. Its intent is not to deal with the forms of social life but to create a basis for national existence. It is concerned with the fundamental problem, the creation of life, and all questions of economic, social, and moral order are subsidiary in rank. The desire to make "Avodah" a basic premise of the renaissance is actually an organic expression of the essence of the movement of national rebirth—this is the new word of the labor movement in Eretz Israel. Labor is important not for economic reasons, or even for the sake of social morality and righteousness (lofty though these values be), but for the sake of the renaissance. All the rest is commentary on this basic idea, that "Avodah" is identical with the national renaissance and the return of its children to a forsaken people.

III

[...] A nation which has no land, which—whether willingly or perforce—has severed itself from natural life, and which is subject to the will and whims of others—such a folk, despite all its unique spiritual qualities, genius, and abilities, is, by definition, not a nation. Conscious and unconscious parasitism, both individual and collective, has become its second nature. It knows that it is always sustained by others, and dependent upon them for its daily bread; it therefore regards itself as an adjunct of other nations and not as something existing in its own right—hence, the negative attitude toward labor and productivity, the lack of respect for the worker as a partner in the divine process of creation, and the feeling of pity tinged with contempt for anyone who "must," alas, be a workingman. In short: "When a people falls into ruin . . ."

This is the area in which the work of revival must begin.

Its object and purpose is to imbue a scattered and disintegrated conglomerate with new life, with a collective personality, and to make this conglomerate into a "nation" by restoring to it the conditions which are necessary—nay, imperative—to national being. This is the source of the desire for the return to Zion, and it is also the *mystique* of the labor movement.

Labor—this is the beginning of rebuilding the ruins of our nation. National life means total creative independence, activism, and separate existence and sovereignty. It necessitates war against all forms of parasitism—a war the weapons of which are labor and creativity. Labor is therefore the beginning and foundation of the renaissance.

There is a basic difference between a labor movement in this sense and the proletarian movements in general. The latter are concerned with the question of the economic order or, at their highest, with social justice. A precondition of such movements is an already existing life which they propose to reform. This is the obvious and natural situation among nations which are really enjoying a national life, of whatever moral stature, in their native lands. The labor movement in Eretz Israel faces a radically different problem, for its basic task is to create the very beginnings of national life.

This fundamental distinction between seemingly similar labor movements necessitates many other differences in the scope of activity and the tactics to be used to attain their respective goals. Moreover, it is beyond doubt that the more the labor movement in Eretz Israel approximates the program and tone of the general proletarian movement, to that degree it is estranging itself from its own proper form, denying the idea which gave it birth, emptying itself of national spiritual content and substituting for it values which are foreign and antithetical to the spirit which molded it at its origin. But our present subject is the idea, the spiritual essence, of the labor movement and not the aberrations of those who make it act in the real world in a way alien to its real self. What I am defining is the doctrine of "Avodah" and the way of life that properly follows from it.

IV

[. . .] "Torah and Avodah" are united by their spiritual origin and their ultimate goal. They cannot be severed from each other without mortally wounding both, because a half-form and a half-renaissance are inconceivable.

Torah cannot be reborn without labor, and labor, as a creative and nation-building force, cannot be reborn without Torah—Torah which is the essence of the *Renaissance*.

This is the whole of our ideology.

Translator unknown.

Abraham Isaac Kook

Speech on the Opening of the Hebrew University, 1925
1925

The prophet of consolation prophesied (Isaiah 60: 4-5): "Lift up your eyes and look about; they have all gathered and come to you. Your sons shall be brought from afar, your daughters like babes on shoulders. As you behold, you will glow. Your heart will fear and rejoice—for the wealth of the sea shall pass on to you; the riches of the nations shall come to you."

Today's great event, the opening of the Hebrew University in Jerusalem on Mount Scopus, in such glorious ceremony and splendorous festivity, amidst a gathering of tens of thousands of our sons and daughters from all parts of the land Israel and from all the lands in the Diaspora, is—on a reduced scale—the living fulfillment of the holy vision of this prophecy. True, not all have gathered together, and the beginning of the ingathering of the exiles is on a small scale, yet this very ingathering is a sure sign that the set time has come, and that the gates of redemption are opening before us. Our hopes are strengthened that the great day is near when all the exiles will gather together and join us, the redeemed ones joyously going up to Zion.

We note in this first step today the fulfillment of the prophet's words: "As you behold." With our own eyes we behold the wonders of the Redeemer of Israel, who has performed this great deed on our behalf. He has raised up the glory of His people among the nations of the world. He has given us a portion in Judah, and girded us with strength and spirit so that we can begin to rebuild the life of our nation, as before, in the Holy Land. We also note the fulfillment of the prophet's words: "You will glow." The glowing joy on the faces of the thousands gathered here is an expression of gratitude and esteem to such distinguished guests as Lord Balfour, the representative of the great nation that issued the Declaration; His Excellency the High Commissioner, Sir Herbert Samuel; His Excellency Lord Allenby; and the distinguished rabbis and sages whose presence graces this festive gathering. Their presence causes the souls of all those gathered here, as well as the souls of tens of thousands of our brethren from afar who will hear about the great glory of our nation on this day, to glow.

But why "fear"? Why did the prophet preface the phrase "Your heart will rejoice" with the notion of fear? When, however, we look back in retrospect at past generations, and at the spiritual and intellectual movements that have influenced us. We readily understand that the notion of fear, in conjunction with rejoicing, is appropriate.

Two tendencies characterize Jewish spirituality. One tendency is internal and entirely sacred; it serves to deepen the spirit and to strengthen the light of Torah within. Such has been the purpose of all Torah institutions from earliest times, especially the fortress of Israel's soul—the yeshivot. This includes all the yeshivot that ever existed, presently exist, and will exist in order to glorify Torah in its fullest sense. This spiritual tendency is fully confident and assured. "Those who love Your Torah enjoy well-being; they encounter no adversity" (Psalm 119:165). Despite such confidence, Rabbi Nehunyah ben Haqanah, upon entering the house of study, used to pray that nothing go awry with his presentation and that it not lead to error.

The second tendency characterizing Jewish spirituality served not only to deepen the sacredness of Torah within, but also as a means for the propagation and absorption of ideas. It served to propagate Jewish ideas and values from the private domain of Judaism into the public arena of the universe at large. For this purpose we have been established as a light unto the nations. It also served to absorb the general knowledge derived by the collective effort of all of humanity, by adapting the good and useful aspects of general knowledge to our storehouse of a purified way of living. Ultimately, this absorption too serves as a means of a moderated propagation to the world at large. Toward the attainment of this end, the Hebrew University can serve as a great and worthy instrument.

Here, dear friends, there is room for fear. From earliest times, we have experienced the transfer of the most sublime and holy concepts from the Jewish domain to the general arena. An example of propagation was the translation of the Torah into Greek. Two very different Jewish responses to this event emerged. In the land of Israel, Jews were frightened—their world darkened. In contrast, Greek Jewry rejoiced. There were also instances of absorption. Various cultural influences,

such as Greek culture and other foreign cultures that Jews confronted throughout their history, penetrated into our inner being. Here too, many Jewish circles responded to absorption with fear, while other Jews rejoiced.

When we look back on the previous generations, and reckon with hindsight, we realize that neither the fear nor the rejoicing was in vain. We gained in some areas and lost in others in our confrontation with foreign cultures. This much is clear: Regarding those circles that welcomed absorption and propagation joyously, with unmitigated optimism and with no trepidation, very few of their descendants remain with us today, participating in our difficult and holy task of rebuilding our land and resuscitating our people. For the vast majority of them have assimilated among the nations; they found themselves caught up in the waves of the "wealth of the sea" and the "riches of the nations" that have come to us.

Only from those who resided securely in our innermost fortresses, in the tents of Torah, enmeshed in the sanctity of the law, did emerge the truly creative Jews—that great portion of our nation who are loyal to its flag—who work tirelessly to build our great edifice. Among these were many who propagated and absorbed. They exported and imported ideas and values on the spiritual highway that mediates between Israel and the nations. Their attitude, however, toward this undertaking was never one of rejoicing only. Fear accompanied their joy as they confronted the vision of the "wealth of the sea" belonging to the "riches of the nations."

Quite rightly did the prophet say: "As you behold, you will glow. Your heart will fear and rejoice—for the wealth of the sea shall pass on to you; the riches of the nations shall come to you."

But how does one overcome the fear? How do we assure the safety of the nation against the mighty stream engulfing it?

As a representative of the Jewish community, standing on this honored platform, I submit to you the reflections of many distinguished segments of the community of traditional Judaism. It must be understood that the Hebrew University by itself cannot fulfill all the educational requirements necessary for the success of our national life. We must realize that, first and foremost, it is the great Torah yeshivot, those that now exist and those to be constructed that are worthy of the name—including the Central Yeshivah which we are establishing in Jerusalem, which shall be a light onto Israel in all areas of Torah, whether halakhah, aggadah,

Jewish action, or Jewish thought—that uphold the spirit of the nation and provide for its security. Moreover, the Hebrew University must maintain standards so that the name of Heaven, Israel, and the land of Israel are sanctified, and never desecrated, by it. This applies to administration, academic staff, and students alike. In particular, it is essential that academicians teaching Jewish studies, ranging from biblical study—the light of our life—to talmudic study, to Jewish history and thought, aside from their academic excellence, be personally loyal emotionally and intellectually to traditional Judaism. Only then will the fear we experience, together with the magnificent vision we behold this day, lead us to glow and rejoice in blessing.

These are our aspirations regarding the institution crowned today with the glory of Israel by the "wealth of the sea" and the "riches of the nations" that have come to us. May the prayer of rabbi Nehunyah ben Haqanah be fulfilled in us: May my presentation not lead to error.

"Then my people shall dwell in peaceful homes, in secure dwellings, in untroubled places of rest" (Isaiah 32:18). May we witness the joy of our nation, the rebuilding of our Temple and our glory, to which the nations shall stream in order to receive Torah from Zion and the word of the Lord from Jerusalem, Amen.

Translated by Shnayer Z. Leiman.

Abba Hillel Silver

1893–1963

Born in Lithuania and raised in a traditional home, Abba Hillel Silver came to the United States with his parents when he was nine years old. He was ordained at the Hebrew Union College in 1915, and after a short period at a small congregation in Wheeling, West Virginia, he spent the rest of his life as rabbi of The Temple in Cleveland, Ohio. A Zionist from his youth, Silver was a leading proponent of the movement in the United States and an outstanding orator on its behalf. He served as president of the Zionist Organization of America during the critical period 1945–1947.

Why Do the Heathen Rage?
1926

I

The latest attempt to salvage poor shipwrecked Judaism in America is on. The *Menorah Journal* summoned

the doughtiest intellectuals to this heroic task. These came highly equipped with trenchant pen, with Jovian thunder and unmistakable boldness. They labored valiantly; they plumbed the very depths and brought to the surface—a bucket of water.

There is an element of the Purim-spiel in this most recent drama of national salvation. Dr. Kallen, whose distaste for the "Judaistic religion," except as a soporific for the unenlightened, is notorious, sets himself the task of reviewing the curricula of the Jewish theological schools of America. He even suggests a new type of rabbi—a cross between a Freudian clinic intern and a graduate of the New School for Social Research. Mr. Cohen, who to this day has successfully hid his scholarly achievements under a bushel, becomes the valorous champion of Jewish scholarship, and fairly devastates with the breath of his scorn the unlettered rabbis of our age. Lastly, comes Mr. Hurwitz, mediatory and reassuring, and joyously announces that as a result of the Menorah Organization's activities, its summer school and its lecture bureau and its proposed Foundation for Jewish Research, the terrible night which had descended upon American Israel, and which was so graphically described by the above-mentioned writers, is about to end. "Our day dawns," he exclaims, in sanguine anticipation of an "adequately financed and endowed" Menorah movement.

A periodic inventory of a people's cultural assets and liabilities is a necessary and commendable service. But clearly, if it is to have any value, it must be undertaken in a dispassionate and scientific spirit, and by men qualified through knowledge and experience to pass judgment. Prejudices are obstructions to inventories. Broad denunciation and cynical flouting of what one does not happen to relish cannot be regarded as adequate stocktaking. One is entertained or outraged by them according to one's prejudices, but one is not enlightened. Above all, whoever presumes to approach the sanctities of a people's life must do so in a spirit of reverence. Thoughtful men do not employ a cheap and easy cleverness in discussing spiritual values which might be the very lifeblood of men.

From the essay of Mr. Cohen I cull the following few specimens to indicate the quality of the newer criticism to which American Judaism is being subjected:

> The Elders of Zion myth is a by no means distant cousin of the "Jewish mission" myth (p. 439).
>
> The little respect our culture receives is that paid to a people who stumbled [*sic*] on some spiritual

ideas capable of being incorporated, in a greatly improved form of course, in the culture of the West (p. 448).

Lacking wisdom, our leaders take refuge in speech. Good Watsonian behaviorists, they discover the springs of thought in the voice box (p. 427).

Speeches and sermons are born of the air and destined to vanish with the breath that gave them birth (p. 430).

But they [the rabbis] are guilty certainly of a too weak acquiescence in the degradation of the rabbinical function to that of a spokesman—i.e., mouthpiece—of the ignorance, ambitions, and fears of the influential Jewish laity (p. 44).

We submit that for sheer "brass" in this sad Age of Brass one need not look elsewhere . . .

III

Mr. Cohen is rendered furious by the fact that some Jewish writers and public men have praised the Jew and Judaism excessively. This seems to be the sum and substance of his twenty-five-page indictment. Seemingly it is good taste, and altogether proper, to proclaim to the world that the *Menorah Journal* is "the best-printed, best-edited, and best-written periodical" and that its advent marks a turning point in American Jewish history, but it is nothing short of "bluster, braggadocio," etc., to assert that Israel has been the monitor of monotheism in the world, the pathfinder in moral idealism, or that the Jews may be justifiably proud of their history and of their contribution to mankind. [. . .]

A phrase of the rabbis comes to mind to which we are sure Mr. Cohen would not subscribe: "God said to Moses, 'Praise and extol Israel as much as thou possibly canst, for I shall in the days to come be extolled because of them, as it is written; and He said: "Thou art my servant, Israel, in whom I shall be praised"'" (Lev. R. II: 4).

If in recent years spokesmen of our people have found it necessary to stress anew the moral excellencies of their faith and to remind men of the decisive contributions which Israel has made to the cultural assets of mankind, should not these facts in all fairness be attributed to the desperate emergencies with which Israel was suddenly confronted in the recrudescence of anti-Semitic propaganda, rather than to conceit and vainglory? In the face of the numerous traducers of our race who suddenly appeared here and elsewhere, bent upon maligning the Jew and Judaism, depreciating our

worth and defaming our name, should it be accounted a sin in these spokesmen if they sought to counteract this propaganda by calling attention to the services which the Jew has rendered the world, and by dwelling upon the true inner worth of their faith?

IV

Had this vocation of counter propaganda been the only interest of American Israel during the last decade, the critic's indictment would have had validity, but the latter knows quite well that this was not the case. The last ten years have witnessed a remarkable renaissance in Jewish life and an intensification of Jewish activities in nigh every field. The World War, the desperate plight of our brothers abroad, the challenging opportunity of our National Homeland, the threat of organized anti-Semitism, and, by no means least, the inner urge toward self-expression combined to stir American Israel to a remarkable pitch of alertness and enterprise. One need not dwell upon the truly herculean efforts made by the American Jew for the relief of his war-stricken fellow Jews abroad—an effort which is even now being renewed. But one ought not to miss the vital implications of this albeit purely humanitarian enterprise. In the hour of crisis, Israel was not found wanting, either in loyalty or generosity. This is evidence of an inner soundness which ought not to be disregarded. Again, this major philanthropic effort, in which all elements of Jewry participated, tended to draw the disparate groups of our people closer together and to establish numerous contacts which, fortunately, have increased rather than decreased with the years.

In the field of Jewish education marked progress has been made. Countless schools, Talmud-Torahs, yeshivas, and religious schools, have been established, in many instances with splendid buildings erected to house them. A growing sense of community responsibility in the matter of the religious and cultural training of our youth has been manifested in the organization in some of the larger cities of bureaus of Jewish education, headed by competent educators. Side by side with the increase in facilities has gone an improvement in curriculum and in standards of instruction. Teachers' training schools have sprung up, and the serious lack of textbooks has been partially met. The vast problems of Jewish education in America have by no means been solved, but American Israel has during recent years wrestled with them earnestly, and, to a degree, successfully. [. . .]

And, lastly, American Jews have built and are building synagogues and temples at an astounding rate. Judging from the jeremiads of our critics, this is to be taken as positive proof of Jewish decadence and disintegration. We beg to differ. Not so long ago one heard the justifiable complaint that our synagogues were physically unattractive, and that they were repellent to the esthetically minded young American Jew. It was said, and rightly said, that these shabby structures were uncomplimentary to a people as prosperous as the American Jew. The plaint of David was repeated: "Shall we dwell in houses of cedar, but the Ark of God dwell within curtains?" Now that American Israel is erecting sanctuaries which in their outer form seek to body forth the beauty of the faith which they enshrine, now that we are bringing a bit of the charm of Japheth into the tents of Shem, the cry is raised. "The Stone Age!" In building spacious and beautiful synagogues American Israel is following an authentic Jewish tradition. For wherever Jews found peace, security, and prosperity, they raised noble religious edifices and attempted to express their religious life esthetically. [. . .]

So that American Israel has been engaged in many other activities in recent years besides blowing the loud bassoon of self-praise.

V

And American rabbis, too, have done much more than preach, although preaching the word of God is still, by some, regarded as an honorable profession. And, if done in consecration and sincerity, one of life's supreme privileges. The organization of the religious life of American Jewry, the establishment of schools, synagogues, theological academies, and the training of teachers has been almost entirely the work of American rabbis. [. . .]

It should be borne in mind that the most pressing tasks which confronted the Jewish ministry heretofore have been those of organization and upbuilding. Millions of Jews in the brief period of a generation or two were transplanted from the four corners of the earth to these shores. Communities, some small, some enormously large, sprang up, as it were overnight. They were structureless and disjoined. They possessed neither philanthropic agencies, nor schools, nor synagogues—in fact none of the facilities which go to make up a community life. All these had to be built and it fell largely to the share of the American rabbis to build them. Ac-

cordingly most of the thought and energy of these men went perforce into this indispensable groundwork of organization—a tiring and exacting employment which is not yet completed.

If, therefore, the American rabbi has not been more of the scholar, if in many instances his preaching has not measured up in intellectual quality to that of his European confrere, it is due not to his inherent mediocrity but to the high endless time- and energy-consuming community responsibilities which the conditions of Jewish life forced upon him. [. . .]

When the press of community work eases up, when Jewish laymen in larger numbers take over the administrative tasks which are rightfully theirs, and when congregational life becomes more departmentalized, American rabbis will be able, as they are eager, to devote themselves more definitely to their essential prerogatives—"to learn and to teach."

In passing, we wish to remark that when we speak of American rabbis we do not refer to the vaudevillians in the pulpit. Unfortunately there are some rabbis who have cheapened and vulgarized the Jewish pulpit, by sacrificing the timeless for the "timely" in their discourse, by pandering to Jewish morbidities in the choice of their themes, by weekly recourse to struts, antics, and noise. On the bulletins of some of the large synagogues of America it has become increasingly rare to find a subject which does not have a distinctly "Christian" angle, a savor of the even palatable "prejudice" theme, or the "kick" of the latest play. Fortunately such pulpits are not typical, and some day, when a few conscientious laymen in the pews will bestir themselves sufficiently to express their disgust, the heroic occupants of these pulpits will beat a hasty retreat.

VI

In the catalogue of Jewish self-laudations, Mr. Cohen places the idea the idea of the "mission of Israel."

> The claim of Israel to a prima donna role among the nations is totally presumptuous and is, as a matter of fact, ignored by the world. To a mind with the least regard for truth it is obvious that Israel is not the primal moral force to which all the peoples look for guidance, the spring of all modern philosophy, science and letters, the intellectual aristocrat in a heathen world, the exclusive repository of the spiritual resources of mankind. There are only the slimmest evidences of fact to support these hifalutin pretenses.

To maintain these notions is to be guilty of the most preposterous nonsense; to believe them is to cherish the most palpable delusions (p. 434).

Per contra one would like to give the conclusions of a *non-Jewish* intellectual—Matthew Arnold: "As long as the world lasts, all who want to make progress in righteousness will come to Israel for inspiration, as to the people who have had the sense for righteousness most glowing and strongest." And of still another *non-Jewish* writer—Leo Tolstoi: "The Jew is that sacred being who has brought down from heaven the everlasting fire and has illuminated with it the entire world. He is the religious source, spring and fountain, out of which all the rest of the peoples have drawn their beliefs and their religions." [. . .]

Mr. Cohen errs when he assumes that the ideal of the mission of Israel is a recent discovery. He suspects that he is in error, and he seeks refuge in a footnote, hoping to prove by means of dexterous *drush* that the ancient ideal of the mission and the modern are the same but different. The shibboleths of the newer psychology are all mustered: inferiority complex, defense mechanism, etc., etc. But the rooted and disconcerting fact nevertheless remains, that consistently through the ages for more than twenty-five centuries the Jew has stressed and underscored his mission to the gentiles. There is a certain sacred objectivity to a fact which even clever intellectuals ought not to tamper with. It was not Geiger or Holdheim or Einhorn who invented the phrases:

"And ye shall be unto Me a kingdom of priests and a holy nation" (Exod. 19:6).

Or, "The remnant of Jacob shall be in the midst of many peoples as dew from the Lord, as showers upon the grass" (Mic. 5:7).

[. . .] Our apocryphal and apocalyptic literature fairly rings with this theme. The great missionary activity carried on by the Jews in the centuries immediately preceding and following the beginning of the Christian era was inspired by this idealism, and the whole Messianic saga of our race is surcharged with this imperial faith.

The leaders of modern Reform Judaism simply reemphasized this ancient Jewish ideal. Their error was in assuming that this ideal was opposed to Jewish nationalism, whereas in reality it is inextricably intertwined with it. Deutero-Isaiah, who of all Jews most eloquently vocalized this missionary aspiration, was of all Jews the most nationalistic and "Palestinian." A people need not expatriate itself in order to be apostolic, and universalism and nationalism rightly conceived are, of course, never antithetical. [. . .]

[. . .] Only the religious Jew who will continue steadfast to his faith will conserve and carry on the culture and the traditions of Israel. The rest will disappear, as they always have, as they inevitably must. In other words, Judaism, far from being "a small part of the total fullness of the life of the Jewish people which I [Horace M. Kallen] am accustomed to call Hebraism" (p. 557), is in reality its very heart and lifeblood. [. . .]

The mission ideal of Israel is neither apology nor vainglory. It concerns the non-Jew only as the object; it concerns the Jew as the subject of the service. The *Jew* is to serve. The Jew is called upon to undertake the burdens, the self-discipline, and the crucifixions of moral leadership. Leadership is a crown, to be sure, but a crown of thorns. It is not by strutting and declaiming that a people leads, but by the forceful example of sacrificial loyalty to great ideals, by holy lives and consecrated purposes. Is there a worthier ideal to hold up before our people? [. . .]

X

In conclusion, a word about Jewish unity and Jewish leadership in America, the lack of which is so sadly lamented by many.

Throughout the writings of Cohen, Kallen, and Hurwitz, one finds a pathetic hankering after organic unity in American Israel. Each one blandly assumes that the differences which exist are slight, and could be easily composed if the rabbis were not such bunglers, or if the seminaries were not such morgues, or if some great leader would arise who by the wave of some magic wand would reintegrate the scattered life of our people. Thus Mr. Hurwitz writes: "Third, and this is the basic evil—there is no real leadership in American Jewry; no leadership that, transcending all the various prevailing sects, parties and propagandas, possesses the intelligence to see Jewish life steadily and as a whole, with all its genuine needs and stirring potentialities; religion and culture and philanthropy and industry, Diaspora and Zion; or possessing the intelligence, has the courage and energy to bring American Jews to serve all of these needs integrally together." [. . .]

But all this is frightfully naïve. There is no Jewish community in the world, unless it be in the small backwater centers, untouched by modern life, where such a unity exists. There is much less unity in the great centers of Jewish life, in Poland and in Russia, than there is in the United States. The Jewish communities there are split most decisively along numerous nationalistic, economic, and religious lines. At times the political emergencies of a minority group will weld them together into a temporary truce, but they possess neither a central authority, an acknowledged leadership, a common purpose, nor a common program. This is true also of the countries in western Europe. Everywhere Jewry has its nationalists and its assimilationists, its Yiddishists and its Hebraists, its modernists and its fundamentalists, its pietists and its atheists, its radicals and its bourgeoisie, its Bolshevists and its bankers; and as the process of secularization on the one hand and religious individualization on the other continues, there will be still greater differentiation among the groups in Jewry. This is true of all peoples. It is also true of the Jewish people. [...]

The plain duty of the thoughtful American Jew today is to discover for himself the particular interpretation of Jewish life which appeals to him, and affirmatively to follow it through, joining with others of like mind in an effort to make that view and that tendency as dominant in Jewish life as possible. There will never be a "comprehensive vision and compelling leadership in American Jewry," any more than there is in American life in general or in the life of any civilized people.

There will take place from time to time a pooling of resources when common interests, chiefly political and economic, are at stake, when anti-Semitic propaganda or unfavorable legislation threaten the security of all the groups, or when humanitarian sentiments make a common appeal. At times the various religious groups in Jewry will meet in conference to foster educational agencies whose programs are acceptable to them all. But beyond this commendable "opportunism," it is folly to expect solidarity and unity in American Israel.

NOTES
Words in brackets appear in the original source document.
This article is based on the papers of Elliot E. Cohen, "The Ages of Brass," *Menorah Journal*, October 1925; Dr. Horace M. Kallen, "Can Judaism Survive in the United States?" April and December, 1925; and Henry Hurwitz, "Watchman, What of the Day?" February, 1926.

Other works by Silver: *A History of Messianic Speculation in Israel* (1927); *Religion in the Changing World* (1930); *Where Judaism Differed: An Inquiry into the Distinctiveness of Judaism* (1956).

Mordecai M. Kaplan
1881–1983

Mordecai M. Kaplan, founder of the Reconstructionist branch of Judaism in the United States, was born in Lithuania and brought to America when he was nine years old. He studied at the Jewish Theological Seminary but was ordained privately in 1908 by Rabbi Isaac Jacob Reines and initially served Orthodox congregations in New York City. His radical views led him to break with Orthodoxy, and he created what became Reconstructionist Judaism, whose ideological foundation was the idea that Judaism was an all-embracing civilization and not just a religion in the conventional sense of the term. His conception of God was starkly naturalistic, rejecting the notion of a supernatural Being. Despite his views, he taught at the Jewish Theological Seminary from 1909 until his retirement in 1963.

Toward a Reconstruction of Judaism
1927

For the first time in its career, Judaism is challenged by the Jew more vigorously even than by the Gentile. However anxious the modern Jew may be to remain a Jew, he finds himself today in a quandary. Western civilization has become as necessary to him as breathing. But as he acquires that civilization and becomes imbued with its spirit, he finds much of his Jewish heritage crowded out or rendered irrelevant. He feels about Judaism as Matthew Arnold felt about Christianity when he said, "We cannot do without it, we cannot do with it as it is."

Yet what is being done to help those who take this attitude toward Judaism? Jewish life is governed by a short-sighted empiricism without plan or program. The hectic activity of campaigns and drives passes as the highest expression of Jewish idealism and achievement. When we turn our attention, however, to the inwardness of Jewish life, we are terrified at the appalling poverty of spirit. Those who manifest an interest in Judaism may be divided into two classes: those who live in the past, and those who live on the momentum of the past. Outside of the neo-Hebraic literary output of recent years and a few readable works by Jewish-German scholars, there is nothing to occupy the mind of the average intellectual Jew who is not given to research work. Much is done to advertise or "sell" Jewish education, but there is very little to give those who answer the advertisement. Jewish education is poorer in content than it is in students. The supply of information and inspiration being always more limited than the demand causes the demand itself to wane. It is this poverty of spirit which explains why the molders of opinion, the makers of the new age, and the creators in the arts, find nothing in Judaism to employ their powers.

Not only are the men of great intellectual and artistic gifts leaving us, but even the number of publicly spirited Jews is menacingly small. The handful of Jews who shoulder the responsibility for relief work, congregational endeavors, and the upbuilding of Palestine, is like a stage army that keeps going back and forth, in and out the wings, giving the onlookers the illusion of an entire regiment.

The blame for this condition rests with those who exercise leadership in Jewish life and who ought to use their influence to put first things first. Unfortunately, there are many among them who are at heart assimilationists. They would prefer to see Judaism ended rather than mended. They believe in killing Judaism with charity. But those of our leaders who are really interested in the conservation of Judaism ought to be made to realize that they should give priority to the problem of readjusting the spiritual life of the Jew, so that his inheritance may cease to be a liability and come to be recognized as an indispensable asset in the socializing, humanizing forces of the present world.

Nothing worse can happen to Judaism than to underestimate the seriousness of the crisis in which it finds itself at the present time. For fear that too careful a diagnosis of the ills that afflict Jewish life might throw the patient into a panic and weaken his power of resistance, many a good physician is willing to turn quack and give the impression that the problem of Judaism is merely a recurrence of a chronic ailment. This method of treating the spiritual ills of the Jew has been in vogue for over a century, with the result that while the malady has been progressing, the possibility of finding a cure is as remote as ever.

The time has come when nothing can be lost and much might be gained by facing the truth. A thorough and detailed study should be made of each of the factors that enter into the situation which confronts the Jew, in order to determine the specific character of the challenge. It is not enough merely to state in a general way that the traditional values of Jewish life are jeopardized. Those who can speak with authority on the educational, religious, and social problems of Jewish life should cease giving us general impressions and devote themselves to the careful gathering of the details that constitute the maladjustment of Jewish life. All that we can attempt here is to suggest the lines of investigation that are still waiting to be undertaken.

One line of investigation should deal with the changes in the social framework of Jewish life necessitated by the new political status of Jewry created by the Emancipation. The Emancipation has deprived the Jews of that social autonomy which they retained until the present era. While that autonomy entailed the usual price of segregation and narrowing of cultural horizon, it afforded atmosphere, solidarity, and the stuff of social existence out of which patterns of conduct, thought, religion, ethics and the creative arts are woven. Citizenship in a modern nation carries with it political implications that could not even have been anticipated in a medieval state. Throughout the Middle Ages the Jews, whether tolerated or persecuted, formed a state within a state, and carried on a communal life in which there was enough of social and civic autonomy to give rise to a network of organizations and of social, cultural and educational institutions that marked out the Jews as a distinct nationality.

On the other hand, a modern nation expects its citizens to become completely integrated with it, to share not only its life and its risks, but also its culture and its spirit. What that integration really implies has seldom been thought out. Those who called the modern state into being found themselves constrained by the logic of their position to grant the Jew freedom from all civic and political disabilities. Yet neither they who were most instrumental in bringing about the Emancipation of the Jews, nor the Jews who greeted the Emancipation as the arrival of the millennium, were fully aware of what was involved in the change of the political status of the Jews. Only a few instances are known of refusal to accept the rights and responsibilities of emancipation. Otherwise, both parties assumed without further question that the modern state was based on the principle of religious tolerance. The theory that religion was a matter between each individual and his God, or that everyone had a right to worship God as he chose, seemed not only axiomatic in itself but capable of ending all controversies as to the relation of state to religion.

In reality, however, the solution proved illusory. It will be a long time before men will come to a clear understanding of the functions of state, of church, and of religion and of their relations to each other. It devolves mostly upon us Jews to ascertain precisely what those functions are because we are more seriously affected in our spiritual life by the maladjustment of these functions than any other class of citizens.

Another element in the present-day situation brought on by the Emancipation, which menaces Jewish life and which cannot be dealt with without careful study, is the economic. If the Jewish masses have become indifferent to Judaism, it is because as city dwellers they are more exposed to the effects of the industrial revolution than any other element of the population. It is well known that machine industry has a larger share than any other single factor in undermining the medieval religious outlook both in Judaism and in Christianity. According to that outlook, man's chief task in this world was to prepare himself to be worthy of a share in the world to come. This notion grows irrelevant as production increases and the livelihood of the individual worker becomes all-important. Economic problems begin to eclipse all others. The philosophy which usually furnishes the background of these problems assumes that religion has been employed by the exploiting classes as a means of holding their victims under control. All religious ideals come to be regarded by the working classes as little more than a means of diverting the minds of the disinherited masses from their interests. The so-called philosophy of economic determination is coined into catch-phrases that develop an antipathy for tradition.

The disintegrating influence of the economic factor in the present-day situation extends into the ranks of the middle classes. Politically, the modern state does not hinder or interfere with Jewish ceremonial or worship. But even this last vestige of Judaism has to give way before the economic element in contemporary life. Those who might otherwise have kept the ritual practices are forced to abandon them one by one because they prove to be a handicap in the economic struggle against non-Jewish competitors. Relatively few Jews find it economically possible to observe the Jewish Sabbaths and Festivals. With the breaking down of these institutions, the home is denuded of all distinctive Jewish influence. The very motive for being affiliated with a congregation is destroyed. For a while, the habit of observing the dietary laws hangs on in the home, but with all the rest of Jewish thought and emotion absent, that too is soon bound to give way, and so we have the complete elimination of traditional practices from the life of the Jew.

A second line of investigation should concern itself with the effect upon Judaism of what is usually termed the Enlightenment. If the destruction of the social organism that the Jews possessed before the Emancipation had the effect of an earthquake, the effect of our new knowledge of nature and human life may be compared to that of a tidal wave sweeping before it all that is left of the earthquake. It is not so much any specific conclusion reached by science or philosophy that threatens the traditional values of Judaism, as the entire spirit of modernism. Under modernism we understand three things: (1) scientific method of approach to all traditions; (2) accepting human welfare, in a socialized sense, as a criterion of the good; and (3) the cultivation of esthetic values as essential to the life of the spirit.

(1) Enlightenment has shaken the foundations of the traditional Jewish ideology. That ideology—being entirely pre-scientific, and most of it even non-intellectual, that is, not based upon individual attempts to grapple with reality at first hand—cannot constitute a functioning part of the mental complex of the Jew of today. The traditional outlook upon life is based upon divine revelation as a physical experience, upon the historicity of the miracles narrated in the Bible, and upon the attainment of life in the world to come as the goal of salvation. This outlook upon life is challenged by sciences like comparative religion and psychology, which prove that the interpretation of certain experiences as revelation of deity and as the communication of His will is current among all peoples at a certain stage of development. From the standpoint of modern thought, most of the traditions concerning God's intervention in human life must be regarded as the interpretation given by men of limited experience and knowledge to natural occurrences, and not as a reliable record of supernatural events. Add to that the devastating effect of Biblical scholarship upon the doctrine of the infallibility of tradition, and you can understand why the traditional ideology cannot flourish in the modern intellectual climate.

(2) In keeping with the theocentric conception of life, which characterizes the traditional point of view, God's will is the determinant of what is right. A thing

is right because God wills it. The modern view, which was occasionally anticipated even in the Middle Ages by philosophizing believers, is that because a thing is right God wills it. Metaphysically, one view may be as correct as the other. The problem is altogether too involved to be capable of an immediate solution; but from a social and psychological standpoint, the tradition that whatever God wills is right deprives the human being of any initiative in the determination of what is right and leaves him entirely at the mercy of tradition. The very notion that laws which govern man's relation to God and man's relation to man are eternal and fixed is repellent to the modern mind. The tendency to regard the law as existing for man and not man for the law is becoming ever more pronounced. As man's circumstances keep on changing and shifting, any law that remains fixed is bound to work harm rather than good, and the law that does harm to human life cannot be a just law. This is the merest suggestion of the dissolvent effect which the modern ethical outlook has upon traditional Judaism.

(3) Moreover, the general assumption that the cultivation of esthetic values is essential to the life of the spirit has made decided inroads into traditional Judaism. With the awakening of esthetic yearnings which are stimulated by the opportunities presented for their cultivation by the various Occidental civilizations, the Jew looks to his people not only for religious and moral inspiration and education, but also for esthetic experience. There are, to be sure, many phases to present-day Jewish life which have an esthetic appeal, but it is not the appeal which comes from a healthy and vigorous life of a people seeking expression in work and play. So far as traditional Judaism is concerned, the element of beauty which it possesses is due to the tragic realization that the life which it consecrated and gave meaning to is passing away, and that its place is being taken by new ideas and ideals, new fashions in thought and action. There is a sunset beauty to dying civilizations and lost causes, but the beauty which we want Israel to furnish us, if we are to identify ourselves with its life, is that belonging to a people in the heyday of its career.

The recognition that Judaism is confronted with a difficult problem is not only of today. It is to be expected therefore that attempts should have been made to solve it. The main movements in Jewish life during the last century and a quarter which have been attempting to meet the challenge of the modern environment have been the Reformist and the Orthodox.

Orthodox Judaism boldly accepts the challenge of the modern world. The term Orthodoxy is here applied to the retention of the beliefs and practices which have been handed down by tradition, when that retention is willed and deliberate in the face of challenge. Of course, I refer to the attitude of mind which is Orthodox by persuasion. There has of late sprung up an attitude of mind which may be described as Orthodox by evasion. It finds expression in the policy of playing safe by evading all mooted questions and confining itself to the conservation of a few externals in Jewish life. It therefore cannot be taken seriously. The only type of Orthodoxy which has any program is that of men like S. D. Luzzatto, Samson Raphael Hirsch, David Hoffman, Z'ev Yavetz, and Isaac Halevi Herzog. These are the only champions of Orthodoxy whose opinions are worth considering. Of them the only one who made an effort to restate the whole of traditional Judaism in terms that reckon with the challenge of modern thought and life was Samson Raphael Hirsch.

Orthodoxy's answer to the question, "What shall the Jew do with his social heritage?" may be summed up in the following statement. The humanistic assumption underlying the present-day ideology, that the purpose of human existence is to be found in happiness and perfection, should be repudiated. Of what good is it to accept such an aim if it does not help us in any way to decide what to do and how to live? What higher destiny can man have than to obey the will of God? But how is one to know the will of God except through the Torah in which God made his will known? The crux of the entire apologia for traditional Judaism is the question whether or not the Torah is divinely revealed. It is upon the supernatural origin of the Torah that the modernist ideology has concentrated its attack. If the claims of modernism can be disproved, we need not be in the least concerned about the possible disintegrating influence of the political and economic forces. Surely the word of God can withstand all the contrivings of man. How then shall the claims of modernism be disproved? David Hoffman adopted the slow and scientific method of patient research. He resorted to a detailed analysis of the hypotheses advanced by Higher Criticism, and to some extent proved them to be unfounded. But Hirsch was by temperament too little of the historian and the scholar to enter into a plodding refutation of Higher Criticism. To him the entire matter reduced itself to the question: "Is the statement, 'And the Lord spoke unto Moses saying,' which introduces all the laws of the Jewish Bible, a lie?" If it is not, then we must keep those commandments, fulfil them in their original and unabbreviated form. We must observe them under all circumstances and at all times. This word of God must be accepted by us as an eternal standard, transcending all human judgment, as the standard according to which we must fashion all our doing; and instead of complaining that it is no longer in conformity with the times, we should rather complain that the times are no longer in conformity with it.

If Judaism is a divine institution, he argues, then it has been appointed to influence the times and not to allow itself to be influenced by the times. From the very beginning, God appointed Judaism and its devotees as a protest against the spirit of the times. Judaism cannot and should not be measured by the yardstick of ordinary experience. The Jew who abandons his heritage forfeits the salvation of his soul. No matter how difficult from a social standpoint, or how incompatible with the canons of science and history that heritage may appear, its supernatural origin is guarantee of its validity and permanence. The only cure for all the ills of Judaism is a return to the *status quo ante*.

There will always be found people who are impatient with the limitations of the mind and with its hesitations and doubts whenever it has to declare itself on matters of vital import. We may count upon them to take delight in the very irrationality of the proposition, so long as it makes for positive and determined action, especially if it holds out the reward of salvation. Tertullian had that type of mind. "I believe because it is absurd," is a psychological phenomenon with which all who want to understand the spirit of orthodoxy should never fail to reckon. Very few, however, possess such minds. The position of a good many of those who call themselves Orthodox may well be described in terms of the suggested formula: "I believe in believing all that I say I believe." But the majority of Jews are temperamentally and intellectually averse to basing their lives upon a premise which they find difficult to reconcile with the rest of their experience. However energetically the works of Orthodox Judaism may be set in motion, they cannot be geared into the wheels of the working and thinking world of today.

According to the Reformists, the intellectual enlightenment has made the Orthodox version of Judaism as a supernatural revelation altogether untenable. What is indisputable is the fact that the Jewish people evolved a truer and better religion than all other peoples in ancient times. That religion was as much the expression of the spiritual genius of the Jewish people as art was of the esthetic genius of the ancient Greeks. Genius is but another name for divine revelation. Now that the Jews are expected to become an integral part of the various nations of the world, they should give up their nationality and all other elements of their former civilization, and retain only the religion which they have evolved. Traditional Judaism was a civilization, but henceforth it is to continue merely as a religion based upon a religious philosophy of life. The literary material of ancient Judaism should form the basis of that philosophy and the religious community which traces its descent from the ancient Jewish people should constitute the social group which is dedicated to its promulgation.

It would take us far afield to enter into a detailed criticism of the Reformist Movement. We shall merely point out two or three outstanding fallacies which make it unworkable as a method of reconstruction.

For the last three thousand years all Jews have regarded themselves and have been regarded by the rest of the world as a nationality. To change their status, they might elect representatives with full power to alter it at their discretion. Even then, it is a question whether a fact that is too patent to be denied can be legally ruled out of existence. Assuming Jewish nationality to be a fact, no legislature could vote it out of existence, any more than it could vote that grass is red. To illustrate how nationality may be such a fact, suppose there were an immigration law restricting the number of members in a family who may be admitted into the country. Let us assume that a whole family by the name of Cohen is anxious to come into the country. What is to be done? One of them hits upon a capital idea. From now on they shall no longer regard themselves as a family. Their status shall henceforth be that of a society. But a society must have a purpose. Hence, their purpose shall be to practice Cohanism, that is, to come together periodically to perform the ritual of blessing the world. Somewhat similar has been the procedure of the Reformists with regard to the question of Jewish nationality. Assuming (falsely) that the Emancipation precludes the granting of civic rights to those who declare themselves members of the Jewish nationality, that supposed prohibition is circumvented by voting that the Jews are no longer a nation.

It seems as if the only creditable thing for the Jew to do when he finds Jewish nationality irksome is to read himself out of it. That is quite different from reading the Jewish nationality out of existence. Whether Judaism has gained by the action of the Reformists is questionable, but that the Jews throughout the world who have refused to accept Reform have been embarrassed by their action is certain. The inevitable effect of declaring that Judaism has nothing to do with Jewish nationality is to impugn the civic patriotism and loyalty of those who insist upon retaining their Jewish nationality.

Certain it is that transforming Judaism from a civilization into a religious philosophy so alters the character of Judaism as to make of it a new spiritual entity. To reduce a civilization to a philosophy is like changing a rosebush into a bottle of perfume. But if the transformation were at least logical and worthwhile, we could forego the loss of the original entity. Unfortunately, Judaism as transformed by the Reformist Movement is neither. Logical consistency demands that if Judaism is to be a religious philosophy, adherence to it should be entirely a matter of choice and not of birth. Judaism ought to be based entirely upon consensus of belief and should have nothing to do with blood relationship. The spokesmen of Reform grudgingly admit that Judaism is more than a religion; yet failing to note just wherein it is more than that, they naturally fall into the fallacy of treating that plus or differentia as a product of physiological heredity. Thus says Kohler in his *Jewish Theology*: "It is very difficult to give an exact definition of Judaism because of its peculiarly complex character. It combines two widely differing elements, and when they are brought out separately the aspect of the whole is not taken sufficiently into account. Religion and race form an inseparable whole in Judaism. A Jew is born into Judaism and cannot extricate himself from it even by the renunciation of his faith." But why should any philosophy confine itself to the experiences of one people, even if that people be one's own? Why should a philosophy refuse to be eclectic in its content, and why should its acceptance be in any way determined by birth?

But the most fatal weakness in the Reformist Movement is that it only *speaks* about a religious philosophy. So far, it has had nothing to offer except an abbreviated edition of Kant, or of some other modern thinker with a penchant for ethics. When we think of a religious philosophy, we naturally call to mind a system of life like that proposed by Stoicism. What has Reform Judaism to offer that can in any way measure up to stoicism in originality, content and force of appeal? What in its theology can compare with the novelty of the idea that Stoicism advanced concerning God, that God is to the world what the soul is to the body; or with its teaching that the function of reason is to learn the will of God as expressed in nature? Of what great work on the conception of God or on ethics can the Reformist Movement boast in the course of a century and a quarter of its existence? To reduce Judaism to the last degree of intangibility is quite different from transforming it into a religious philosophy.

In view of the unworkable character of the program of either Orthodoxy or Reform, we venture to bring forward a program of Jewish life that has been in the process of crystallization within the last fifty years. Krochmal, Zunz, Frankel and Graetz, and others of the Historical School established the thesis beyond a doubt that Judaism of the past was not merely a religion but the life of a nation, with a national literature and national institutions. Hess, Smolenskin, Pinsker, Achad Ha-Am and Dubnow, and others of the Nationalist School advanced various lines of reasoning why Judaism must continue to function as a civilization.

The program which is the outcome of both these schools of thought is based upon the proposition that Judaism can be nothing less than the *tout ensemble* of all the elements that enter into what is usually termed the cultural life of a people, such as language, folkways, patterns of social organization, social habits and standards, spiritual ideals, which give individuality to a people and differentiate it from other peoples.

Judaism is the funded cultural activity which the Jewish people has transmitted from generation to generation. It is the living, dynamic process of intellectual, social and spiritual give-and-take of Jews in the course of their relationship to one another as individuals and as members of various groups.

In a word, a civilization.

If the problem "What shall be done with our social heritage to render it creative and soul-satisfying?" is to find a solution, we have to reckon with a number of conditions which are indispensable to any civilization.

A civilization must be lived, not by a purposive group held together by voluntary association, but by a living and continuing people. If it is to continue as the product of common social interests, it can flourish only among those who live in physical propinquity. A civilization cannot arise out of social cooperation which is based merely upon some temporary aim. Only actual living together, working together, and being animated by the same group ideals can keep a civilization alive. Its vehicle must be a particular language which serves as a medium for writings that incorporate group memories and aspirations. Its content must consist of law codes, mores, expectations and sanctions that are calculated to produce a sense of continuity in successive generations, and a sense of unity among the contemporaries of each generation. It has to be transmitted from generation to generation by the method of education, suggestion, imitation, public opinion and authority. A civilization does not wait for the child to mature so that he may adopt it as a matter of choice. It insists upon shaping the very character and personality of the child. That is its main prerogative.

The elements in a civilization which we usually designate as language, literature, law and religion are related to each other organically, so that the functioning of each is bound up with and conditioned by every other. To try to preserve any of these elements without the others is like trying to cultivate roses in a vase. It is this organic character of the various elements in Judaism that makes it a civilization and that must determine all our attempts to live it and to transmit it to our children.

What then is to be Judaism's answer to the challenge of Enlightenment and Emancipation? How does it mean to reckon with the changes which have taken place in the social and intellectual life of mankind? Enlightenment and Emancipation do not make it necessary for Judaism to give up its character as a civilization. They only make it necessary for Judaism to transform itself into a new type of civilization.

To be sure, no civilization has been known to survive a radical change in its religious outlook. Judaism is the sole exception. Its history records three different stages of development corresponding with the changes in its religious outlook. The first stage lasted about six centuries, roughly speaking till about 600 BC. During that earliest period it cannot even be called Judaism. It was then a henotheistic type of civilization, almost indistinguishable to the outward observer from the civilizations of such neighboring peoples as Ammon and Moab. When David, referring to his persecutors, said, "They have driven me out this day that I should not cleave unto the inheritance of the Lord, saying 'Go serve other gods,'" he thought in terms of a cultural life that centered about YHWH as a national deity,

to whom were ascribed Israel's escape from Egyptian bondage and the conquest of the land of Canaan.

About two centuries after David, we note the beginning of a new development. Prophecy arises and enlarges the conception of the national deity to such an extent that He alone comes to be regarded as God, the Creator of the world. Thus was prepared the way for the second stage of Judaism, the theocratic. During that stage the Torah—which was regarded as having been given by God and which was extended to include all customs and laws, both those recorded in the Pentateuch and those which for a long time remained unwritten—was made coextensive with every phase of human life. It was then that Jewish civilization attained a high degree of self-consciousness.

During the latter part of that second epoch in Judaism, circumstances arose which led to the belief that the present world order would be supplanted by new heavens and a new earth. To be qualified for a share in the world to come or, as it is termed in theology, to be saved, constituted the governing principle of Jewish life during the eighteen centuries preceding the era of Emancipation. Thus in its third stage Judaism has been an other-worldly civilization.

That Judaism was able to maintain its identity through two such radical metamorphoses encourages us to believe that it will pass into the new stage now awaiting it without a break in its continuity. If the Jewish consciousness is to survive, it will no doubt be a transformed consciousness. If Judaism is to have a future, it will have to evolve into a modern spiritual civilization. It will have to remain a civilization, insofar as it must consist of a tangible social life which will find expression in a maximum of Jewishness. It will have to become modern insofar as the content of that civilization must be recognized through the assimilation of what is best in all other cultures. And it will be spiritual insofar as the central place in that content will be given to religion, not of the thaumaturgic or credal type which flourished in the past, but of the humanist type which is based upon vital needs and aspirations, both personal and social.

There are already certain concrete changes in Jewish life that are actually beginning to appear as a result of this conception of Judaism. Instead of being left to chance and whim, they should be intelligently directed. Those changes have to do, first, with the social structure of Jewish life, and, second, with its content.

In its social structure Jewish life will no doubt have to undergo readjustment. Its continuance is, therefore, to a large extent a problem in social engineering. If it is to be lived as a civilization, it will have to insist upon retaining enough of social structure and milieu to render possible the functioning and growth of the various elements of cultural life. If Judaism is to survive, the Jews must be permitted to constitute an international people, with Palestine as its homeland. That involves, first, the establishment of Palestine as a Jewish homeland where Jews can constitute a commonwealth; secondly, the insistence upon minority national rights in those countries where the political structure permits it and where the Jews can live as cultural groups; thirdly, the organization of Kehillahs, or what might be termed "Kulturgemeinden"—in contrast with the "Kultusgemeinden" that exist in Germany—in countries where no minority peoples are recognized.

Only in an Erez Yisrael is it possible to achieve those environmental conditions which are essential to Judaism becoming once again creative. Judaism has proved an exception to other civilizations only in being able to survive changes in type of religion. But it has proved the rule that no civilization can survive loss of habitat. Though Jews did not live physically in Palestine for over fifteen centuries, their civilization survived, but only because their life continued to be bound up with it.

The main obstacle to Palestine being restored to the Jews is the claim that both the Christian and Mohammedan civilizations have upon it. But they lay claim to a different kind of Palestine from the one which we should demand and are prepared to upbuild. They need the Palestine of the holy places. We need the Palestine of agriculture and industry, of schools and synagogues and University. It is our duty to respect and leave undisturbed the Palestine of Christendom and Mohammedanism; but it is their duty to restore to us the Palestine that is ours. A far nobler crusade than any which Christendom undertook in the Middle Ages to rescue its holy places from the rule of the infidel, would be a crusade on its part to make amends for the historic wrongs it has inflicted upon the people to whom it owes its Christ, whose life and death are associated with these Holy places. Instead of confining ourselves, as we have done hitherto, to ineffectual assertions in our worship and through our customs that we have never relinquished our claim upon Palestine, we should henceforth voice that claim before the nations as part of our rights as human beings.

In having granted us civil and political rights, the nations have given us the freedom not to be Christians, but they have withheld from us the means essential to our living as Jews. It is poor restitution to a prisoner who has been unjustly deprived of his freedom for many years, merely to open doors of the prison to him, without giving him a chance to reinstate himself in the world outside of prison.

The recognition of the rights of minority nations in Eastern Europe will no doubt affect the future of Judaism in ways hitherto unsuspected. It is unfortunate that the new possibilities for cultural development opened up by the legally recognized status of the Jews as minority groups have found us totally unprepared. That status constitutes a problem by itself which cannot be dealt with on this occasion. We shall confine ourselves to the consideration of Jewish life in America. Our task here is to devise some kind of social framework which is compatible with the most progressive interpretation of Americanism.

There are social institutions which are indispensable to Jewish life in those countries where our political status is of the American type—the Synagogue and the Kehillah. The first has to be organized; the second is still to be established. The Synagogue must become a Beth-Am, a neighborhood center where Jews may foster their social and cultural as well as religious interests. The Synagogue must be transformed into a communal center to which Jews should be able to resort with a goodly number of their workaday problems. It should provide them with opportunities for utilizing their leisure to best intellectual and spiritual advantage. It should strengthen the bonds of friendship among them and endeavor to prevent by means of arbitration committees their litigating in the courts. A Synagogue in the sense of a Beth-Am would lead to a more fruitful division of labor among those who hold the position of leadership in Jewish life. The rabbi, the scholar, the social worker, and the lay leader would each have his well-defined function and would serve in a capacity that would make him a potent factor for the enhancement both of the outer and inner life of Jewry, so that men of high talent would be attracted to the exercise of Jewish leadership. As an instance of how the Synagogue as at present constituted does little to enrich Jewish spiritual life, we may cite the fact that the American rabbi has been prevented, by the manifold duties imposed upon him that lie outside of his proper field, from making any worthwhile contribution to Jewish scholarship that can in any way compare with those made by rabbis in Germany. Nor can the American rabbi boast of having made much headway in the field of Jewish education. Whatever Jewish scholarship we possess in this country is practically all imported. The mental energy that should have been used for the creation of permanent forms of religious expression such as is embodied in liturgical hymns and prayers and music, is dissipated in endless sermonizing, the value of which at best can never be more than transient.

The second social institution which is essential to Jewish life in America is the Kehillah. The Kehillah should be an organization of individual Jews who, differ as they may in religious belief and practice, are agreed that Jewish group life in the Diaspora should be continued and developed. In view of the intellectual and religious diversity of those constituting such a Kehillah, it would have to be organized on party lines. But all parties would have to agree on the following aims:

1. To make it possible for all Jews, regardless of financial status, to share the benefits of a Beth-Am or Synagogue.
2. To promote a fully developed system of Jewish education comprising kindergartens, weekday afternoon schools, evening courses (both elementary and advanced) for adults, training schools for rabbis, teachers and social workers.
3. To maintain philanthropic institutions.
4. To further the upbuilding of Palestine.

Without a serious effort in social engineering along the lines suggested, it is futile to look forward to any kind of Jewish unity other than that which is forced on us by pogroms and the economic ruin of some part of Jewry. The Jewish people is bound to figure as the Humpty Dumpty of the nations. It has had a tremendous fall and has shattered into fragments. Without a program of social reorganization, all the king's horses and all the king's men will not be able to put it together again.

What of the reconstruction which should take place in the content of Judaism? As a civilization, the content of Judaism presents problems which may be classified as those dealing with (1) the reinterpretation of its ideology, (2) the reorganization of its laws, (3) the expansion of its language, (4) the utilization of the creative arts, and (5) the humanization of its religion.

1. The traditional ideology by means of which we have maintained a sense of historic continuity, and

which has hitherto served as a means of giving articulate expression to our common aspirations, is entirely thaumaturgic in its outlook. All that idea material must be reinterpreted. We are no less dependent as a people upon the memories of the past than were our ancestors. But national memories, to be an incentive to national life, must be believed in as historical. The thaumaturgic version of the early history of Israel no longer being acceptable, we are like a person who has suddenly been stricken with aphasia. The average layman who has acquired a modern education, finding himself in a different universe of discourse from that of our ancient literature, experiences great difficulty in orienting the Jewish people in the history of mankind. Such orientation will not be possible so long as we refuse to face the issues raised by Biblical scholarship.

Furthermore, if the Torah is no longer to be viewed as communicated by God to Moses, but is to be treated together with the other books of the Bible as reflecting the spiritual development of Israel, it becomes necessary to revise all notions as to the authoritative character of the past. Supernatural origin can no longer serve as a sanction for the functioning of the Jewish literary heritage. That heritage will have to undergo a very elaborate process of reinterpretation at the hands of scholars and thinkers before it can become sufficiently assimilated to the thought life of the modern man, and acquire that relevance which can make of it a means to mental and moral growth.

2. Judaism as a civilization must be anything but antinomian. No permanent social structure is conceivable without law. It is because at the beginning of the Christian era the Jewish people refused to give up its nationality that it also refused to give up its Torah. Despite all attempts to prove that Torah is coextensive with the whole of life, it is essentially a system of law. In the Reformist transformation of Judaism into a religious philosophy, there is as little room for law as in Pauline Christianity. It is that which renders the Reformist movement a belated admission that Paul was right, and that eighteen centuries of national suffering was a tragic mistake. But the only kind of law which can henceforth survive in Judaism is what is usually termed positive law—the kind of law that comes under the heading of jurisprudence. Since in any modern civilization no rule of conduct is enforceable which does not directly affect one's neighbor, it is a misnomer to apply the term "law" to ceremonies and religious practices, and it is incongruous to reckon with them in a spirit of legalism. So

long, of course, as they were regarded as of supernatural origin, they might in a sense be called "laws." But since we assume a reinterpretation of the Jewish ideology, an entirely different rationale from that which is based upon law will have to be supplied for such customs and practices as help to give Jewish life character and individuality. If they will be presented to us as folkways, as national or religious customs, we are more likely to observe them than when we are asked to believe that they are divinely ordained. Of course, that implies a greater freedom in the details of practice and an entirely different attitude of mind from that which was brought to bear upon them in the Judaism of tradition. Not only is such freedom the only chance for their survival but it is also the indispensable condition to their enrichment and spiritual potency.

The scope of positive law will necessarily have to vary with the three different types of social organism that we have found to be feasible for Jewry in the modern world. In Palestine, Jewish positive law will deal with all phases of jurisprudence pertaining to every type of human relationship. In Eastern Europe, the scope of Jewish law will depend upon the extent to which the dominant nationality permits minority groups to have courts of their own. In America, domestic relations afford the only field within which a Jewish code of laws can function. While the scope is narrow, it is of momentous social consequence. In all other social relationships, Jewish life in America cannot possibly be in a position to enforce laws. It can only promulgate principles as to what constitutes desirable action. It will have to evolve formularies of ethical principles and standards of ethical conduct which can look for their sanction only to public opinion. Jews will have to develop among themselves standards of honesty and devotion to the cause of peace similar to those means whereby these standards can be made effective, if Judaism is to function as an ethical influence in their lives.

3. A particular language is preeminently the distinctive mark of a civilization. In the words of Zangwill: "Language is the chief index of life. As no man is dead so long as the mirror to his lips reveals a breath, so no race is extinct so long as there comes from its lips the breath of speech. A people that speaks is not dead; a people that is not dead, speaks." Although Judaism during the greater part of its history has been a bilingual civilization, the Hebrew language has always enjoyed the advantage of being able to supply the elements of historical continuity and of present solidar-

ity. The modern renascence of the Hebrew language is typical of the power of self-adjustment which the Jewish people still possesses. It is incontrovertible evidence of the vitality of the Jewish spirit. Modern Hebrew has succeeded where Jewish law and ritual have failed. Out of the ancient threads modern Hebrew has woven new patterns of thought and idealism adapted to the intellectual and spiritual needs of the present day.

It is unnecessary to urge the revival of the Hebrew language in Palestine where it is flourishing as a vigorous vernacular. But if Judaism is to be lived as a civilization also outside of Palestine, some knowledge of Hebrew will henceforth have to constitute a requisite to being a Jew. For conveying a sense of the reality, the unity and the creativity of the Jewish people, there are few elements in the Jewish civilization that can compare with a knowledge of Hebrew. But in order that its acquisition become general, it will have to be expanded and developed to a degree that will make it teachable and usable with ease, which is by no means the case at the present time.

4. If Judaism is to function as a modern civilization, it will have to draw upon the creative arts to enrich its content. With all the cultural content which Judaism inherited from the past, it is bound to be swamped by the great civilizations of the day unless it is enriched by a new output of cultural material. Creations in literature, music, drama, painting, sculpture and architecture will have to be much more than a by-product of Jewish life. They will have to become a very integral part of Judaism. We have learned to demand from a civilization much more than people did formerly. We expect it to do much more for us than to help us adjust our relations to our neighbors and to God. We expect it to introduce us into a world of esthetic values. A civilization should either offer us opportunities to be creative in the world of art, if we have the ability, or at least, to hold out to us opportunities for enjoying what others have created under the stimulus of its spirit. It is the synthesis of the universal with a particular, which takes place to a higher degree in art than in any other phase of human activity, that renders art so essentially human. An art-producing civilization is therefore its own *raison d'être*.

The arts which purpose to be more than ornamental must come out of an abundance of life. Life abounds only where people, in addition to living together and being held together by everyday interests, have noble traditions and great aspirations. It is mainly in Palestine, and in the countries where Jews will be permitted to live as a minority nation, that Judaism will become an art-producing civilization. In America, we shall probably have to depend upon the Jewish art of those countries. But if we are to have any kind of Jewish life in America, a serious attempt must be made to have our homes, our Synagogues, and our public institutions become a field for Jewish creativity. There is no reason why Jewish homes should be designed after the Chinese or the Japanese style, or in the style of some remote French or English period, when it is possible to have them designed in a style that is distinctively Jewish. The various Jewish social institutions and centers where young people engage in all kinds of artistic efforts, where music, drama and literature are encouraged, where often even painting and sculpture are taught, should regard it as their duty to infuse a Jewish soul into those activities. Above all is it important that the Synagogue should come to be regarded as affording the Jew the chief opportunity for the highest form of self-expression in literature, music and architecture.

We might indeed be skeptical as to the feasibility of realizing this need in Judaism if it were not for the vast amount of Jewish talent that is waiting eagerly for the call to be of service. What untold artistic possibilities lie dormant at the present time may be appreciated when we consider the prolific creativity of the Jew in all fields of art outside of Jewish life, and when we realize how, even in works inspired by non-Jewish civilizations, something of the Jewish differentia is always discernible.

5. The one cultural element in the Jewish civilization which will have to constitute the object of outstanding interest in the future, as it did in the past, is religion. In saying this we do not mean to imply that we should like to see the now extinct theological volcanoes become active again. But there is a sense in which religions is no less essential to civilization than literature and the fine arts. The modern attempt to secularize civilizations is really an attempt to substitute new religions for old. By banishing the religion which it designated as an opiate, Sovietism is trying to create a religion which is to act as a tonic. It has already furnished Russian civilization with new saints.

It is generally admitted that the kind of religion which will thrive in the future will not be based on tradition and authority. Its source and its point of reference will have to be personal experience. It will represent an original grasp upon life, and not adherence to tradition for tradition's sake only. However, the mistake generally made about this kind of religion is in the belief that it will be purely cosmopolitan and will have nothing to do with any civilization in particular. The truth, however, is that religion must have a degree of particularity, as much as literature or any of the arts. That does not prevent it from possessing universal significance. The end of clericalism does not mean an end to public concern in the fostering of religion. No work of art that fails to be an expression of personal reaction to reality can have any value. We can, nevertheless, conceive a whole nation deeply interested in encouraging works of art. Likewise, the Jews, by reason of their past contribution to the religious life, should feel a stronger urge to encourage creativity in the field of religion than any other people. The Jewish civilization henceforth should demand not belief in religious dogmas or the observance of religious practices in a spirit of obedience to authority, but an active interest in religion and in its possibilities for the enlargement of human horizons and the socialization of the human being.

The question whether living Judaism as a civilization would impair the Jew's loyalty to his country cannot be answered intelligently unless we note carefully what the actual inner life of any citizen in a modern state must be. As a result of a peculiar conjuncture of historic forces, the citizen of a modern state is not only permitted but encouraged to give allegiance to two civilizations: one, the secular civilization of the country in which he lives, and the other, the Christian civilization which he has inherited from the past. He turns to the civilization of his country for his political concepts and institutions and for his literary and esthetic values. From his national life arise those duties of political allegiance which the political experience of the nation have evolved. He turns to the Christian civilization for his moral and spiritual sanctions. It has been said that only when a church has taken its place along with his earthly fatherland in the deepest recesses of his heart, is a man saved from becoming a mere reasoning machine. The very separation of church from state has put into the class of hyphenates all who adhere to both institutions. The hyphenism which justifies the Christian in hyphenating his Christianity with Americanism, justifies also the Jew in hyphenating his Jewishness with Americanism.

In sum, those who look to Judaism, in its present state, to provide them with a ready-made scheme of salvation in this world, or in the next, are bound to be disappointed. The Jew will have to save Judaism before Judaism will be in a position to save the Jew. The Jew is so circumstanced now that the only way he can achieve salvation is by replenishing the "wells of salvation" which have run dry. He must restate, rethink and reorganize the civilization of his people. To do that he must be willing to live up to a program that spells nothing less than a maximum of Jewishness. This is by no means a task for those who love comfort and regularity. It calls for a degree of honesty that abhors all forms of self-delusion, for a temper that reaches out to new consummations, for the type of courage that is not deterred by uncharted regions. If this be the spirit in which we shall accept from the past the mandate to be Jews, and allow the present to inform us how to be Jews, the contemporary crisis in Jewish life will prove to be the birth-throes of a new era in the civilization of the Jewish people.

Other works by Kaplan: *Judaism as a Civilization* (1934); *The Future of the American Jew* (1948); *Judaism without Supernaturalism* (1958).

Isaac Herzog
1888–1959

Isaac Ha-Levi Herzog was the Ashkenazic chief rabbi of Mandate Palestine from 1937 to 1948, succeeding Abraham Isaac Kook, and of Israel from 1948 until his death. Born in Łomża, Poland, he was brought to England at the age of nine when his father was appointed communal rabbi in Leeds. Although he never attended a yeshiva, he became a major figure in rabbinic scholarship. He studied at the Sorbonne and at the University of London, where he received a doctorate for a thesis on the type of blue dye used in ancient Israel for *tsitsit*, knowledge of which was subsequently lost. From 1916 to 1936, he held rabbinic posts in Ireland, where he established close ties with leading Irish nationalists and earned the sobriquet "the Sinn Féin rabbi."

The Ban Pronounced against Greek Wisdom
1929

Maimonides, the greatest Jewish philosopher of the Middle Ages, was of the opinion that the principles and methods of metaphysics formed part of the traditional lore of the sages of the Mishnah and the Talmud, the mental heirs of the prophets. According to him philoso-

phy had been originally a specifically Jewish science, but owing to certain historic factors and developments, internal and external, it found its way into Greece and eventually became lost to our own people, until it was taken up again by Jews in the later Gaonic period under the influence of the Arabian school of the *Mutakallamin*.

Needless to say, this view is not shared by any modern historian of philosophy. And yet it is not impossible that the Maimonistic hypothesis, however fanciful, contains just a grain of historic truth. The Alexandrian school of Jewish philosophers headed by Philo had maintained a like theory. It might be urged of course that this, too, was sheer projection into the past. But can we be really sure that Plato, the prince of Greek philosophers, was not in some measure influenced by the teaching of the Torah, the Prophets and the Psalmists?

It is known that he travelled extensively in the East, and spent a considerable time in Egypt studying the various systems of theology and theosophy then in vogue in that melting-pot of ancient religions and cultures. We also know, on the other hand, that already at that time there existed in Egypt a large Jewish colony. A close perusal of Plato's works would, I think, reveal a number of passages dealing with religion, metaphysics, ethics, law and politics, suggestive of Mosaic and prophetic influence. The translation of the Torah into Greek took place, it is true, long after Plato. But the existence at that time of literature imparting some knowledge of Judaism in a language accessible to Plato, is not beyond the realm of possibility. [. . .]

Aristotle, the second pillar of Greek philosophy, is also of interest in this connection. Already about 200 BCE the Alexandrian Jewish philosopher Aristobulus expressed the opinion that Jewish revelation and Aristotelian philosophy were substantially identical. Flavius Josephus, the celebrated historian, virtually asserts that Aristotle was greatly indebted to Judaism. "I do not now explain how these notions of God are the sentiments of the wisest among the Greeks, and how they were reared upon the principles that Moses afforded them." And he supports his statements by a highly interesting quotation from the writings of Clearchus, a disciple of Aristotle. [. . .]

The Talmudim and Midrashim here and there make mention of "philosophers," invariably referring to gentile thinkers, *pilisufim*. But, so far as I can remember, "philosophy"—*pilisufiah*—is nowhere distinctly named in these ancient sources. The general term by which they designate philosophy, would seem to be "Greek Wisdom," or "Greek science"—*ḥakhmat yevanit*. But in all probability this designation is much more comprehensive.

The term *ḥakhmat yevanit*—"Greek wisdom"—probably comprises a variety of subjects—literature, poetry, rhetoric, history, logic, etc., and also philosophy as defined by Aristotle, viz., "the science which deals with the universal characteristics of the system of knowable reality as such, and the principles of its structure in their complete universality, and also inquires into the nature of those causative factors in the system which have neither body nor shape and one not subject to any mutability."

Philosophy as understood, taught and developed by the Greek genius, although not known in Judaea, would hardly seem ever to have become an integral part of the specifically Hebraic world of thought. Unlike the Judeo-Alexandrian thinkers who confounded the philosophy of Plato and Aristotle with Judaism, the Palestinian teachers would seem to have regarded it as an exotic plant.

As already intimated *ḥakhmat yevanit*—Greek Wisdom—while not improbably including philosophy, is a term of very wide signification, denoting, I think, Greek learning in a general sense.

Now in the Babylonian Talmud a tradition has been preserved to the effect that a ban was pronounced against "Greek Wisdom"—*ḥakhmat yevanit*—about the year 66 BCE, at the time of the civil war between the two claimants to the Jewish throne, the brothers Hyrcanus and Aristobulus. The war between these two Hasmonean princes marks one of the saddest chapters in our tragic history. It led to the direct interference in our internal affairs of the far-flung power of mighty and covetous Rome, and eventually brought about the loss of our political independence. In the course of the siege which Hyrcanus laid to Jerusalem, so the Talmud relates, a lamentable incident occurred which caused "the whole land of Israel from end to end to tremble and quake."

As it was necessary to offer the daily sacrifices in the Temple, the besieged came to an understanding with the besieging army whereby the latter were to convey each day across the city-walls the lambs required for the *Korban-tamid* in return for a considerable amount of gold coin. This proceeded for some time. One day, however, the basket delivered by Hyrcanus' men was found to contain a pig instead of a lamb. At that

moment, the Talmud states, the very land of Israel, throughout its length and breadth, experienced horrible sacrilege.

The Talmud names a certain old man who had managed, "through Greek wisdom," to place himself in communication with the beleaguering army, advising them to stop the supply for the daily sacrifices, for by these means alone the city would be compelled to surrender. At that time, tradition further records, the authorities enacted a prohibition against Greek wisdom. "Accursed be the man who will teach his son Greek wisdom." Josephus relates something similar, but with very appreciable variations. He also omits any reference to Greek science or culture in this connection. This omission on his part does not, however, by itself prove much, as it may have been due to a desire to avoid giving offence to his Greek readers, for whom he had great solicitude.

The Talmudic statement: רמז להם בחכמת יונית *ramaz lahem baḥokhmat yevanit*—he gave them a hint through the medium of Greek wisdom—is rather obscure. It cannot possibly be that he simply sent communications in Greek, for Greek must have been known to more than one Jew in Jerusalem. Nor would the military sentinels allow correspondence to pass in a language unintelligible to them. The Greek language as such would, moreover, hardly be described as "Greek wisdom."

Maimonides explains that the old man in question wrote his treacherous communiqués in an allegoric or enigmatical style very much in vogue at that time among cultured Greeks, but scarcely understood by the average Jew. Similar styles and forms of speech in Hebrew were sometimes used by the Talmudic sages, and were known as *leshon ḥakhmah*—the speech of wisdom. Convinced that already the prophets and after them the sages cultivated philosophy, Maimonides could not of course think of a ban ever having been pronounced against Greek philosophy, which the term "Greek wisdom" would naturally comprise. Yet the references to Greek wisdom in all other connections scarcely warrant the delimitation of this term by the narrow sense assigned to it in Maimonides' comment. It obviously covers a far wider range.

The Tosafists point out a difficulty presented by the text under consideration; for if, say they, a prohibition against Greek wisdom had already been promulgated in the year 66 BCE, how is it that the Mishnah at the end of Tractate Sotah records placing Greek under the ban at a much later date, during the war of Titus (67–70

CE)? The difficulty would, however, admit of an easy solution, if we would take the term "Greek"—*yevanit*—in the Mishnah, as referring to the Greek language rather than to Greek culture. The Talmud, however, in Sotah 49b, evidently understands *"Yevanit"* in the Mishnah as applying to Greek wisdom or learning, being of the opinion that the teaching and study of the Greek language were never prohibited. Though not distinctly stated, this is clearly implied by the Tosafists. In this connection the Talmud, furthermore, calls attention to the fact that Rabbi Judah HaNasi (189 CE), the redactor of the Mishnah, himself advocated the adoption of Greek by the Palestinian Jews as their ordinary medium of speech. "Of what good to us is the Syrian language in Palestine?" he said. "We ought to speak either Hebrew or Greek."

It would carry us far beyond the limits of the present article to attempt to analyse this point somewhat thoroughly. A few general remarks will have to suffice. Difficulties really abound in relation to this matter. Thus, for instance, Ben Dama, a nephew of R. Yishmael, is reported to have asked the latter whether having mastered the whole of the Torah it was permissible for him to engage in the study of Greek wisdom. The answer given was, "Is it not written, 'This book of the Torah shall not depart from thy mouth, and thou shalt study it day and night?' Find a time which is neither day nor night and during that time thou mayest pursue the study of Greek wisdom!" Why did not R. Yishmael rather remind Ben Dama of the ban pronounced against Greek wisdom during the war between Hyrcanus and Aristobulus? The point is already referred to by the Tosafists. A similar problem is presented by another ancient source, the *Tosefta* in connection with R. Joshuah ben Hananiah.

We have so far dealt with this question only on the basis of the tradition recorded in the Babylonian Talmud. The Palestinian Talmud, however, puts a somewhat different complexion upon the matter. The Palestinian authorities relate with considerable variations the sad incident which, according to the Babylonian Talmud, occasioned the prohibition of Greek wisdom; but they omit all mention of Greek, or Greek learning in reference thereto. Evidently this is a case of conflicting traditions. It is not improbable, I think, that strong feelings against Hellenic culture arose about 66BCE in Palestine, though they need not have materialized into actual legislation. This would account for the existence of the tradition which the Palestine Talmud obviously ignores.

No one with the slightest knowledge of the history and literature of the period of the second Temple will suppose that the Maccabean triumph had the effect of completely eradicating Hellenism. Hellenism in Palestine was certainly subdued, but just as certainly it did not altogether vanish from the land of Israel. The Greek language and Greek culture undoubtedly continued to maintain their hold upon certain sections of Jewish society. The retention of Greek culture would be fostered by relations with the outside world when Hellenic civilization reigned supreme. No active opposition would probably be offered to the study of the Greek language and of Greek literature so long as it constituted no menace to Jewish religious and national life.

It is, however, within the realm of probability that in the course of time Hellenic culture began to reassert itself to such an extent as to arouse violent hostility on the part of the faithful watchmen of Zion, the custodians of the Torah and tradition, though by no means assuming such alarming dimensions, in depth and extent, as during the Hellenic period. Grecian influence would nevertheless tend to act as a disintegrating, denationalising force, impairing Jewish sentiment, both religious and patriotic. The authorities would come to regard with particular apprehension the ever-growing practice of teaching Greek wisdom—*ḥakhmat yevanit*—or, in other words, Greek literature and philosophy, to the young. In many cases the youth who had thus assimilated the alluring culture of Greece before they imbibed sufficient Jewish knowledge and attained Jewish self-consciousness, would grow up to be very indifferent Jews.

It may, therefore, very well be that a movement had sprung up against Grecian culture already about the time of the civil war between Hyrcanus and Aristobulus, though it was only during the war with Titus that the climax was reached. The bitter experiences at the hands of Hellenising Jews, perhaps including Josephus himself, in the course of that supreme national crisis, were calculated to raise anti-Hellenic feeling to the highest pitch. [. . .]

The reference to Greek in the Mishnah, end of Tractate Sotah now calls for elucidation. "In the war of Titus— בפלמוס של טיטס *bipolemus shel Titus*—they decreed that one may not teach Greek to his son."

Unlike the Babylonian, the Palestinian Talmud clearly understands "Greek" in the text as the Greek language, which is, of course, the more natural sense of the term.

The Mishnah offers a problem of its own. As already mentioned, this is partly treated in the Babylonian Talmud. But the solution therein given, that the Mishnah refers to Greek wisdom and not to the language, cannot of course hold good from the standpoint of the Palestinian Talmud.

The suggestion made by one of the principal commentators in the *Yerushalmi* [Palestinian Talmud], appears to me to afford a satisfactory solution. He holds that the prohibition against Greek which the Mishnah records, was confined to the teaching of that language to young children, but was not meant to apply to adults already well-grounded in Jewish knowledge. Thus it would be quite in order for R. Judah HaNasi to plead for the adoption of Greek by the Jews in Palestine as their vernacular, for once the adults made it an invariable practice to converse in Greek, the children would acquire it in the natural course without there being any necessity for them to be instructed in Greek letters in their tender age.

And even if the ban proclaimed against Greek learning dated from the year 66 BCE, and provided that it concerned the imparting of such knowledge only to the youth, the question addressed by Ben Dama to Rabbi Yishmael regarding the permissibility of his engaging in Greek studies, as well as the latter's answer, would become perfectly intelligible, But, as already remarked, according to the Palestinian Talmud the ban belongs to a much later period.

The motive which gave rise to this anti-Grecian enactment subsequently fell into oblivion, and we find the Palestine authorities of the third century endeavouring to discover the ground for the prohibition against teaching Greek to one's son. A suggestion that this was simply based upon the Scriptural injunction to study the Torah day and night is refuted by the objection that if this be so, then one would be precluded from teaching one's son a trade or a profession—which is in reality a religious duty devolving upon the father. [. . .]

It is questionable, in fact, whether the prohibition against Greek was ever intended to be operative beyond the limits of the Holy Land. In the highly Hellenised provinces of the Roman Empire such a restriction would be hardly practicable. In the Eastern portion of the empire, Greek exercised supreme sway as the language of science and literary and cultured intercourse, and it was largely used by Jews as their natural medium of speech. Particularly in overwhelmingly gentile centers, the study of literary Greek by boys would almost be a part of their necessary equipment for the battle of

life. Nor do we know the exact age-limit fixed in this connection for the Palestinian youth.

Even within the confines of the Holy Land itself the prohibition was by no means of universal application. Exceptions were made to meet the exigencies of certain families whose station in life and official position brought them into frequent contact with the governmental spheres. Thus the house of the *Nasi*, or hereditary spiritual chief of Palestinian Jewry, were expressly exempted on account of their necessarily close relations with the governing classes.

In order to carry out with efficiency and impressiveness their manifold and important functions as the representatives of Jewry before the secular rulers, and to be able to uphold the dignity of Judaism in their intercourse with cultured gentile society, thorough proficiency in Greek, the language of the learned and official non-Jewish circles, and in Greek literature and philosophy, was an absolute necessity for these princes in Israel. As the descendants of the House of David, they exercised great influence and authority both within and without the community. There would appear, in fact, to have existed a sort of college attached to the court of the *Nasi*, and presumably under his direct control and supervision, at which instruction in Greek letters and culture was imparted to young men or youths of promise, not necessarily of his own family, who were likely to be of service to the community in a representative and mediatory capacity.

On the whole the allusions to Greek wisdom, or to the "wisdom of the nations"—*hakhmat yevanit*—or *hakhmat umot haolam*—give the impression that the aversion felt by the ancient teachers for these non-Jewish branches of knowledge was chiefly grounded upon the fact that the pursuit of such studies constituted a serious rival to the intensive study of Torah.

It would be, however, entirely unjust to charge the old masters of the Torah with a hostile attitude towards secular knowledge in general. Although in the interests of national self-protection and preservation our ancient sages at times had to erect barriers for the purpose of keeping away Greek influence from the rising generation, they yet displayed a breadth of view and a fairness of judgment sufficient to obviate any ground for suspecting them of a tendency towards narrowness and exclusiveness.

The abhorrent idolatry, crass superstition and appalling social and moral corruption characteristic of the contemporary heathen world, coupled with its

Jew-baiting policy, were calculated to insulate the teachers of Israel with an utter contempt for, and an absolute horror of, all that was distinctively non-Jewish. And yet despite all this, the Jewish sages declared that the just and righteous of the gentiles would have a share in the world to come, and they enjoined the dispensing of charity and benevolence without discrimination of race or creed. The ancient authorities of the synagogue entertained the highest regard for knowledge and learning irrespective of nationality. "Should someone tell you that there is no wisdom—ḥakhmah—in Edom (i.e., the gentile world) believe him not." On seeing a gentile eminent in science and learning, so the sages ordain, one should pronounce a thanksgiving unto God for having imparted of His wisdom to His creatures. [. . .]

The reaction against Greek literary and philosophical culture, or against Greek—ḥakhmat Yevanit or leshon Yevanit—now and again set up by the exponents of the Torah, should on no account be misconstrued as a reaction against secular knowledge in general. In the first place, even in its acutest form the opposition to Greek learning, as already indicated, never exceeded certain limits. Nor would the aversion to such studies on the ground of the menace they offered to the assiduous study of the Torah, seem to have represented the majority view. The general tendency was hardly to take the Scriptural injunction, "Thou shalt study it (the Torah) day and night" in its absolutely literal sense. And thus we find masters of the Torah, even outside the family circle of the *Nasi*, proficient in Greek learning.

That the movement against Greek culture was in no way directed against secular knowledge as such, must be obvious to anyone who has the slightest acquaintance with Talmudic literature. Medicine, astronomy and mathematics were favorite studies of the sages of Israel, and formed, in a certain measure, auxiliary and ancillary branches of the Torah itself.

NOTE

That the anti-Greek campaign discussed in my article must have been of a qualified and considerably restricted nature, is likewise evidenced by the fact that long after the Greek language was placed under a ban the sages of the Mishnah and the Talmud still permitted the Torah to be written in Greek and in Greek only (Meg. 9a–b). The ancient rabbis, in fact, despite the ban, long retained a great admiration for the beauty and music of the Greek language. They counted Greek among the four most beautiful languages of the world, emphasizing its phonetic harmony and melodiousness, and they regarded it as the only suitable medium for the translation of the Torah. "The beauty of Japhet (Greek language) shall dwell in the tents of Shem."

Other works by Herzog: *The Main Institutions of Jewish Law*, 2 vols. (1936, 1939); *Heikhal Yitsḥak*, 3 vols. (1959/1960–1971/1972).

Abraham Isaac Kook

The Light of the Messiah
1929

[. . .] That sacred foundation, which constitutes the main theme of all this great vision, contains within it a hidden ray of the light of the Messiah, the redeemer who is revealed and concealed, and then revealed once more. Because of this, we perceive numerous changes during the course of the ongoing process of the revival of the nation and the expansion of settlement in the Land of Israel—ascents, descents, and further ascents. Each descent in our fortunes along the route of the undertaking constitutes proof of the concealment of the redeemer, and each ascent in our fortunes that occurs subsequently constitutes proof of his revelation to us ("Ha-Har": Elul 5689).

The redemption is an ongoing process. The redemption from Egypt and the complete redemption in the future is a single operation that never ceases—the workings of the mighty hand and the outstretched arm of the Almighty, which commenced in Egypt and effects its operations in all environments. Moses and Elijah are redeemers within a single, ongoing redemption. He who commences, and he who completes the process—both the one inaugurating it and the one setting the final seal upon it—together fill the same unit, and the spirit of Israel pays attention to the sound of the movements of the deeds of redemption, which travels on through all environments until such time as the flowering of the might of salvation is complete, in its fullness and beneficence (Orot).

The fundamental principle of the unity between the written Torah and the oral Torah is like the brotherly relationship that exists between the plain meaning and the esoteric meaning of scripture. Just as internal reflections march along in tandem with external reflections on the world, on life, on reality, on causes, and on symbols, in mankind and in existence, so too is the unity between the miraculous and the natural, both in practice and in faith. Penetrating, profound contemplation unites the separated parts that the mediating intellect originally separated. The light of the Messiah, the foundation of which is high and exalted and exceedingly elevated, is an illumination from the most sublime essence where the miraculous and the natural are united—and all the workings of nature, from the smallest to the greatest, operate on its behalf and in conjunction with it, literally through it and by virtue of its influence, like miraculous occurrences.

[. . .] Prophecy effected no miracle without its having been connected, in some measure, to a natural phenomenon, even if this was weak and insignificant, bound together with the requisite clip which will be from the upper world, from the shining forth of the dominion of the spirit upon the lower world, which is, by its very nature, limited and restricted. Both here and there, beings that are deeply rooted and highly organized in the spheres of wisdom, of liberty, and of total sanctity are on the move—and everything is becoming progressively brighter.

The light of the Messiah is bound up with the salvation of Israel, with the might of this eternal nation, a single unity within the world, in whom the Creator of all worlds is praised through its glory: "And who is like your people Israel, a unique nation upon earth?" For this supernal light, which is comparable to the crown on the top of the scroll of the Torah, which, on account of its great strength and glory, is not allowed to be touched by hand, there will, at the end of days, be found broad paths and thoroughfares, fresh routes to be traversed, to attain its ultimate practical and great objective. At the end of days, there will arise a silent movement, filled with strength and desire, with contrasts and contradictions, with lights and dark places, and intending to row to the shore for the salvation of Israel. The weak light of the Messiah is concealed therein. Many of those holding firmly onto this little torch of light have, on the face of it, betrayed that great light that is held by the lengthy cord belonging to the everlasting light. But the salvation of Israel is always the salvation wrought by the Almighty—"I and He, save us, we pray!" And just as "You redeemed the nation and its God from Egypt," so too will be the nature of every salvation, be it the greatest of the great or the smallest of the small! In the midst of the humble tangible strip of land, bereft of any vigorous sap from above, broad rivers will be opened for the light of the Messiah, for the amelioration of the world, filled with notions of eternity, guaranteed by the Head of Faith, the divine assurance inscribed in iron and in

blood, with the covenant of the flesh and the covenant of the sacred language, with the covenant of the Holy Land and the covenant of the nation, with the everlasting covenant and the covenant of the life of all worlds (Orot).

That holy spark from the basis of the redemption, emanating from the holiness of the name of the Messiah, which was created prior to the creation of the world, which was hidden away and concealed in thousands of fetters from the time when our kingdom was destroyed, when our Temple was laid in ruins and we were exiled from our land, began to get enflamed once more from beneath the successive piles of ashes of the bitter exile that had been lying upon it for hundreds of years. Slowly, slowly did this sacred spark start to awaken through the institutions of the Old Yishuv, and in the most recent period it began to gain strength in respect of its practical aspects, through the movement Ḥibbat Tsiyon, which predated Zionism; and the spirit of the Almighty, and his promise, which remains true forever, to recall the kind deeds of the patriarchs and to bring redemption to their descendants, shone forth over this sacred task in all its elements, both the material and the spiritual, up to the point of the great spiritual arousal, which is extending continuously within the Assembly of Israel, in all its sections, with the assistance of the Zionist movement through its diverse currents. And this was the Almighty's doing, for the world war brought about great changes in the established order of kingdoms and states, until such time as the British conquest became a reality and the mandate of the Holy Land came under its jurisdiction, and the Balfour Declaration put the political seal upon the odyssey of the return of the children [of Israel] to their borders. And lo and behold! These great signs of the times constitute sure testimony to the workings of the One who is perfect in knowledge, the Redeemer of Israel and his Holy One, who, like a shepherd tending his flock, guards them to raise them up as a people for himself upon the heritage of their ancestors, as in days of yore ("Ha-Har": Elul, 5689).

Translated by David E. Cohen.

Chaim Ozer Grodzensky
1863-1940

Chaim Ozer (Khayim Oyzer) Grodzensky studied at the Eishishok and Volozhin yeshivas. In 1887, he was appointed as a *dayan* (religious judge) in Vilna and was offered the title of chief rabbi. A revered halakhic authority, scholar, and a leader of Orthodox Jewry, Grodzensky was one of the founders of Agudas Yisroel (Agudat Israel) in 1912. During and immediately following World War I, he worked in Russia to establish Orthodox organizations; he later continued to advocate on behalf of rabbis persecuted in the Soviet Union. In 1919, he returned to Vilna and helped establish the Va'ad ha-Yeshivot (Council of Yeshivot) in 1924.

A Call for the Assistance of the Refugees from Germany
1933

The situation of our brethren in Germany is so frightful that it is unparalleled since the Middle Ages and the time of the decrees of 1648 and 1649. [. . .] In "cultured" Germany an enemy has arisen who robs our brethren of their human rights, and deprives hundreds of thousands of Jews of all possible means of survival and sustenance. Their blood and their possessions have become a free-for-all, and they are given over to all manner of afflictions, extortions, and reproach. [. . .]

The situation of our brethren in Germany is awful and tragic. They had always been in the vanguard in the establishment of general charitable organizations—and invariably obtained generous responses, given the high standards of organization unique to them, for relief of the burdens of their coreligionists throughout the world. But now they have reached the lowest depths, to the point where they themselves now need assistance.

In every country, Jews have been stirred to come to the aid of our coreligionists in Germany who are sinking fast; our very best communal lay leaders have taken the necessary work upon themselves; committees have been established and huge sums collected for the benefit of refugees so as to ensure their continued survival. [. . .]

However, in order to combine the different organized forces, and to introduce proper order and a planned program for the relief work, a large committee was recently set up in London, with the participation of representatives from all countries and from all the central relief organizations; in this committee, various groups and organizations of the Jewish people have united together, so as to come, with complementary strengths, to the assistance of our brethren in Germany

with all forms of aid—a timely support for the tens of thousands of needy refugees and victims of famine—to involve ourselves with them with a view to the possibility of their obtaining employment and sources of livelihood—to lend support to committees and institutions within Germany to prevent their destruction, and, in particular, to find a safe haven for our afflicted and persecuted coreligionists in new lands where they will be able to find guaranteed survival for themselves.

The task of settling of some of the refugees in the Land of Israel is of special importance. [. . .] Besides the saving of the refugees themselves, there also exists a great opportunity for building up our holy land [. . .]—though let it be understood that all the aid operations in general, and in the Land of Israel in particular, should be carried out in an entirely nonpartisan manner.

It is an obligation of the community as a whole, just as much as it applies to specific individuals. [. . .]

Now may the Almighty have mercy upon an impoverished and needy nation, and hasten to our relief and our salvation, in accordance with the desires of the one who hopes for salvation, who now writes and signs herewith, this third day of Kislev 5694 [November 21, 1933] , in Vilna.

Translated by David E. Cohen.

Other works by Grodzensky: *Aḥi'ezer* (1922–1939).

Chaim Ozer Grodzensky

On the Issues of the Economic Boycott of Germany
1933

[. . .] In regard to the boycott [of German goods], in my view, the rabbis ought to have stood aloof, at a distance, and not to have involved themselves with this at all, as this is an issue exclusively concerning our brethren in Germany, who may be harmed as a result of this, for they envisage this as leading to bloodshed; and as for the pretext put forward that the boycott is a good thing, so that other countries should become aware of the true situation—surely it is a question of Torah law whether it is permissible to act in this way. [. . .] Moreover, this matter is connected with the fury of the masses, who have everywhere become enraged against the wicked government and its head [Adolf Hitler], may his name be obliterated; and the masses act without thinking;

but it is for the teachers, who are of settled and patient temperament, to consider the matter carefully, as to whether they are permitted to act in this way by the law of the Torah; and I have indeed drawn this to the attention of the association of rabbis in Poland also, though it appears that they too stood under the influence of the businessmen and the national newspapers—for it was uncomfortable for them that people should say that the rabbis have no feeling for the distress of our nation, heaven forbid!

Translated by David E. Cohen.

Chaim Ozer Grodzensky

On the Transfer of the Rabbinical Seminary from Berlin to Erets Yisrael
1934

[. . .] I wrote yesterday to my friend, the illustrious rabbi, our teacher, Rabbi S. Ahronson, and to Rabbi Meir Hildesheimer himself, may his light shine, in a sharp tone, making it clear that I would not maintain silence or cease agitating about this issue. [. . .]

His illustrious and righteous father of blessed memory [Esriel Hildesheimer] founded the seminary to combat the reformers. [. . .] His son, may he enjoy long life, is now proposing to come to the Holy Land, a place where there are Torah academies and rabbis outstanding in Torah learning and in fear of God, to introduce German culture there, which has destroyed the world—and we have already witnessed what has befallen us there [in Germany]. So it is the duty of the rabbis and Talmudic scholars in the Holy Land to cry out bitterly in protest against this, in order not to allow "plague-infested stones" to remain there. [. . .]

I am very perturbed over this and since I and Rabbi Hildesheimer are dear friends, I wrote to him yesterday administering an open rebuke out of love!

Translated by David E. Cohen.

Chaim Ozer Grodzensky

When You Suffer, They Shall Find You
1934

The time (in which we live) is truly "a time to work for the Almighty," and great is the responsibility now falling upon every Jew with the ability to do so. [. . .] All the lands of the diaspora are aflame with fire—synagogues and houses of study, together with scrolls of the Torah, are being publicly burned to ashes; bitter decrees against us are increasing daily; our enemies have determined to uproot us together with our holy faith. [. . .] Tens of thousands of Jewish families are living between the borders of foes and murderers. [. . .] Now, to our misfortune, when faith in Israel is weakened to such an extent in the lands of the West, the Reform movement has struck powerful roots that have brought in their wake assimilation in the worst degree [. . .] and from there evil has emanated [. . .] the first signs of the powerful hatred of Jews have manifested themselves, and from there the poison and the abominations have spread to other countries; and in the lands of the east there are an increasing number of important people who have rejected the Almighty who exert force and pressure over our brethren, the children of Israel, to seduce them and lead them astray from the Torah and the faith.

But we are not allowed to be swept along by this stream. We are compelled to repent wholeheartedly in a spirit of perfect repentance, as the Torah tells us that "When you are in dire straits, and all these things befall you, at the end of days, you shall return to the Almighty, your God." [. . .]

Translated by David E. Cohen.

Leo Jung
1892–1987

Born in Moravia, Leo Jung was raised in the Torah im Derekh Erets [Judaism along with secular culture] tradition of Samson Raphael Hirsch. He studied at the universities of London, Cambridge, Berlin, and Vienna and at the Hildesheimer rabbinical seminary in Berlin and at *yeshivot* in Hungary. In 1920, Jung came to the United States to occupy the pulpit at Congregation Knesseth Israel in Cleveland. In 1922, he became rabbi at the Jewish Center on West Eighty-Sixth Street in Manhattan, where he served for sixty-five years. Jung was a major force in shaping an English-speaking, modern Orthodox Judaism and an unusual figure on the American scene at the time—a bearded English-speaking Orthodox rabbi with a Ph.D. Unlike the leading ultra-Orthodox rabbis of the period, he was a strong Zionist, affiliating with Po'ale Agudat Yisrael.

The Rambam in True Perspective
1935

In our national gallery—the *gibbore ha-umah*—there are three great Moseses: the law-giver of Mt. Sinai, Moses Ben Maimon of Cordova, and Moses Isserles of Cracow. Twice was the winged word coined: "From Moses to Moses there was none like Moses." The second Moses, our Rambam, had been attacked for his philosophy no less than on account of his code. The judgment of Jewish history has embraced the *Mishneh Torah* as a work of imperishable importance and has admired the "Guide of the Perplexed" as a *horaath shaah*—matchless effort to meet a situation, and the definitive answer, not of historical Judaism, but of Judaism in the reign of Aristotle.

It is significant beyond cavil of misinterpretation that the third Moses, whose work is based on the Rambam's code and which has assumed in Jewish life the place the Rambam had hoped to attain for his own work, that this third Moses placed at the head of the Shulhan Aruch as its motto, a passage from the "Guide" containing Rambam's interpretation of God-consciousness. Maimonides borrowed technique, syllogisms, method, from the Greeks. He Judaized Greek thought even as Philo had done. But where Greek view differed from Jewish creed, Maimonides asserted his loyalty to the Torah in unmistakable terms. To search for truth was his ideal, but the Torah was his way of reaching it. Not only the goal was the Torah to him, but the way. His *imitatio dei* found form and substance, beginning and end, in the laws and statutes of the first Moses.

These points must be emphasized to prevent a distortion, in the popular mind, of Rambam's personality. For, it has become fashionable in some quarters to call the Rambam a liberal, such description not being uninfluenced, perhaps, by the hope that Rambam's "liberalism" may be considered precedence and justification for one's own attitude toward the theory and practice of the Torah. This description is also reasonably connectable with the effort to explain an embarrassing failure of general acceptance of iconoclastic views by the modest suggestion that Maimonides, too, had been misunderstood by his own generation.

In one respect, the term "liberal" may be justly applied to Maimonides. But in that aspect it is not only the Rambam who is "liberal," but Judaism. In Judaism, interpretation has been not only a privilege, but a duty. Where Jewish *halakhah*—religious practice—is

not affected, such exegesis is obligatory. Through interpretation and re-interpretation of the divine Torah, progressive revelation of the will of God and His guidance of man has been maintained. The text of the Bible has been subjected to ever new interpretations, each of which has been hailed as the fruit of the faith and welcomed as an additional source of mental and spiritual enrichment.

In his "Guide of the Perplexed," Rambam makes full use of this freedom of interpretation and yet he only follows similar expressions on the subject by the Talmud and the Geonim. But whilst endorsing freedom of exegesis, Rambam would unhesitatingly condemn any liberties taken with the Law! By no stretch of imagination may his liberalism be carried into the sphere of the *Din Torah*—Jewish practice. The Rambam of the "Guide" insists on calling Jewish laws "*mitzvoth hashem*," the commandments of the Lord, to indicate our abiding obligation of conformity with His revealed will. The Rambam, as a liberal in interpretation, just as in his insistence on undivided loyalty to the *mitzvah*, continues the tradition of rabbinic literature.

Those aspects of Rambam's teaching which are most attractive to the modern temper—his freedom from *odium theologicum*, his insistence on *interdenominational* respect and friendship, his passionate love of *enlightenment*—are not due to any infusion of outside lore; they are for him *paragraphs* of the *Jewish law*. He was not a philosophizing Jew—to use the words of Ludwig Stein—the usual source of much annoyance to Jewry and little profit to non-Jews; nor another, not unusual type of philosopher of Judaism, forcing upon our unwilling creed the garb of an ill-fitting synthesis. Rambam was a Jewish philosopher who recognized the centrality of the *Halakhah* not only in Jewish life but in Jewish thought.

Interpretation of metaphysical passages is a *mitzvah*, a "commandment," a good deed. Such variety helps to keep the Torah a book of life. But a true Jewish philosopher will not rest his system on the ingenious individualisms of *Hagadah*, the Jewish religious folk lore, but on the *Halakhah*, the legal portions of the Torah.

We may agree with Theodore Gompertz that no new idea has been uttered since the last Greek philosopher was laid to rest. We know that there may be many "guides for the perplexed," patterned after Rambam's great work, each interpreting in its own categories the problems of the time; but Maimonides insists there is only one immutable Jewish law developing through application of precedent to new conditions.

If Rambam were today to convey to our generation the implications of God's Torah, he might offer us some ingenious new interpretation, a combination of the solid elements of Kant, Whitehead, and Dewey. But for the Jewish life, he would insist on the *din Torah* as the unfailing guide for the perplexed in Israel.

The message of Rambam for today would be in accord with the verse he chose as the motto of his life: "Seek the Lord in all thy ways." You will find Him in the ecstasy of the Psalmist, in the moral indignation of the Prophet, in the loyalty to principle of the *mitzvoth*, in the common sense of the Book of Proverbs, as in the awesome solemnity of Sinai.

God-consciousness teaches the middle way between arrogant nationalism and flabby cosmopolitanism, between the reduction of Judaism to ethical commonplace and its sterilization by unintelligent intellectualism or undisciplined emotionalism! None has ever rightly proclaimed that Jerusalem was too narrow for him to find spiritual lodgment therein. The Rambam would insist: "Look upon life as God-given; upon the Torah as divine guidance to peace and happiness. Make reason your *favorite servant* so that you may attain such spasmodic glimpses into the sphere of ultimate verities as are vouchsafed to our comprehension." The knowledge of God, he said, "has been the first and foremost passion of my life. In my early boyhood, the Torah was betrothed to me as the wife of my youth. It is true that I have taken strange women to my house, *even astronomy, logic, medicine,* and *the like,* but I employ them merely as hand-maidens of the Torah." This is Rambam's own confession of faith endorsed again and again in the second and third book of his "Guide." Maimonides emphasizes that, whereas it is our duty as Jews to occupy ourselves with the Torah and to seek to discover the motives underlying its laws, such quest must be clearly understood to justify neither the assumption that loyalty to the Torah could ever depend on our discovery of satisfactory motives, nor that any interpretation which we essay may be assumed to be *definitive*. The definitive interpretation of the non-legal part of the Torah has not yet been achieved.

Hence, whilst admiring Maimonides, while extolling him as a giant of the intellect, as a genius of saintliness, whilst proud of him as a man of science and conscious of his great import in the scheme of human culture, let us not forget that in theory and practice he emphasized loyalty to Jewish law as a paramount duty of the Jew and that for the attainment of truth and ethi-cal perfection, he knew no other guide for the Jew but the Torah, the *direction* revealed to Moses, transmitted by the sages and brought up to date by the Responsa of the rabbinic authorities of every age. He is enshrined in the hearts of the Jewish people as one of its greatest sons, who revered the Lord, obeyed His Torah, hence loved His people and His land, and called every man his brother.

Other works by Jung: *Fallen Angels in Jewish, Christian, and Mohammedan Literature* (1926); *Business Ethics in Jewish Law* (1987).

Abraham Joshua Heschel

1907–1972

Abraham Joshua Heschel was born into a family of Hasidic rabbis in Warsaw, but at age twenty he moved to Berlin, where he studied philosophy at the university and enrolled at the Reform rabbinical seminary. He remained in Germany until 1938, when he was expelled to Poland. In 1939 he found refuge in England and in 1941, through the intervention of the Hebrew Union College, obtained a visa to the United States. He taught for five years at the Hebrew Union College and then spent the remainder of his career at the Jewish Theological Seminary. He was one of the most widely read philosophers of religion in the United States, his work known in both Jewish and Christian circles. He also played a prominent role in the civil rights movement in the United States in the 1960s.

The Meaning of Repentance
1936

The mystery of prayer on the days of Rosh Hashanah presents itself with characteristic familiarity: it reveals itself to those who want to fulfill it, and eludes those who want only to know it.

Prayer on these days is a priestly service. When we pray we fulfill a sacred function. At stake is the sovereignty and the judgment of God.

The world has fallen away from God. The decision of each individual person and of the many stands in opposition to God. Through our dullness and obstinacy we, too, are antagonists. But still, sometimes we ache when we see God betrayed and abandoned.

Godliness is an absolute reality which exists through itself. It existed prior to the creation of the world and will survive the world in eternity. Sovereignty can exist only in a relationship. Without subordinates this honor is abstract. God desired kingship and from that will creation emerged. But now the kingly dignity of God depends on us.

At issue is not an eschatological vision, a utopia at the end of time, or a kingdom in the beyond. Rather, we are talking about the present, the world that has been bequeathed to us, a kingdom of everyday life. We have to choose God as king; we have "to take the yoke of the kingdom of God upon ourselves."

Does this demand—the essence of Jewish law—signify an esoteric symbol, a mystical act? It signifies a close, this-worldly and everyday act. The establishment or destruction of the kingly dignity of God occurs now and in the present, through and in us. In all that happens in the world, in thought, conversation, actions, the kingdom of God is at stake. Do we think of Him when we are anxious about ourselves or when, driven by apparent zeal for general concerns, we engage in life, whether deliberately or in a carefree way?

These days are dedicated to establishing God as king within us. The whole year long we call him "Holy God!"; on this day "Holy King!"

"God took on kingship over the peoples. God placed himself on the throne of his sacredness. The princes of the peoples are assembled. For the shields of the earth are God's."

The deepest human longing is to be a thought in God's mind, to be the object of His attention. He may punish and discipline me, only let Him not forget me, not abandon me. This single desire which links our life and our death will be fulfilled on the Days of Awe. The "Holy King" is a "King of Judgment." The season of Rosh Hashanah is the "Day of Memory," the "Day of Judgment."

Before the judgment and memory of God we stand. How can we prove ourselves? How can we persist? How can we be steadfast?

Through repentance.

The most unnoticed of all miracles is the miracle of repentance. It is not the same thing as rebirth; it is transformation, creation. In the dimension of time there is no going back. But the power of repentance causes time to be created backward and allows re-creation of the past to take place. Through the forgiving hand of God, harm and blemish which we have committed against the world and against ourselves will be extinguished, transformed into salvation.

God brings about this creation for the sake of humanity when a human being repents for the sake of God.

For many years we have experienced history as a judgment. What is the state of our repentance, of our "return to Judaism"?

Repentance is an absolute, spiritual decision made in truthfulness. Its motivations are remorse for the past and responsibility for the future. Only in this manner is it possible and valid.

Some people, in moments of enlightenment, believed they saw in the year 1933 an awakening to God and of the community, and hoped Jews would be heralds of repentance. Yet we have failed, those who stayed here just as much as those who emigrated. The enforced Jewishness still sits so uneasily in many of us that a new wave of desertions could occur at any moment. The apostasy of the past is matched by the superficiality of today. Is this disappointment surprising? Repentance is a decision made in truthfulness, remorse, and responsibility. If, to be sure—as is often the case among us—instead of deliberate decision we have a coerced conversion; instead of a conscious truthfulness, a self-conscious conformity; instead of remorse over the lost past, a longing for it; then this so-called return is but a retreat, a phase.

Decay through return!—that is the apocalyptic *mene-tekel* inscription on the walls of our houses.

Marranos of a new metamorphosis: Jewish on the outside, Marranos of different degrees multiply within our ranks. Such victims of insincerity—as historical experience teaches—can become tragic.

It is also deplorable when a spiritual movement deteriorates into bustling and pretense. It is unclean when a holy desire is misused by the selfishness of the clever. When one wants to become a Jew because of the "situation," not out of honesty, the result is conflict and misery. Jewishness cannot be feigned!

There is no return to Judaism without repentance before God. Faithfulness to Him and to the community to the point of utmost readiness remains the fundamental idea of Jewish education.

We must recognize that repentance has yet to begin! Each person must examine whether one is part of a movement forced upon us by the environment or whether one is personally motivated, whether one is responding to pressure from outside or to an internal sense of urgency. At stake is not the sincerity of the motivation but the earnestness and honesty of its expression. This considered reflection has to become a permanent part of our conscience.

Not everyone is capable of maintaining self-examination. It is up to the teachers among us to explain the meaning and content of repentance. Enlightenment about repentance is the central task of our time.

It is a great good fortune that God thinks of us. We stand before the judgment and the memory of God. We know the reality of human judgment and we pray: God, you judge us! We must stand firm before the judgment. The possibility to do so is given to us. Woe to us if we cease; woe to us if God should forget us.

Other works by Heschel: *Man Is Not Alone* (1951); *The Sabbath* (1951); *God in Search of Man* (1955); *The Prophets* (1962).

Joseph Isaac Schneersohn

1880–1950

Joseph Isaac (Yosef Yitzchak) Schneersohn was the son of the Chabad rabbi Sholom Dovber and became the head of the Lubavitch yeshiva Tomchei Tmimim in 1898. After his father's death in 1920, he took on the position of rebbe, struggling to maintain a network of Chabad institutions, ranging from schools to kosher food banks. He was arrested by Stalin's regime in 1927 and was tortured and exiled. In 1940, following the Nazi invasion of Poland, Schneersohn arrived in New York, where he continued his work of organizational growth through religious and social networks and institutions. Schneersohn's son-in-law, Menachem Mendel, became his successor as the Lubavitcher Rabbi.

Some Aspects of Chabad Chassidism
1936

III

As in the case of Israel and the Torah, so in the case of G-d there are the apparent or conceivable attributes, and the hidden or inconceivable attributes.

What is *conceivable* of the Divine Being is that He Creates and forms the Universe and the creatures, and, creating them from nothing, constantly vitalizes them, as it is written: המחדש בטובו בכל יום תמיד מעשה בראשית—He who in His goodness each day, constantly, renews the work of the creation. This means that G-d renews the existence of the world and all creatures constantly, creating

and forming them from nothing every moment; in other words, the work of the Creation is *continuous*, repeating itself in the same way as in the beginning of Creation.

King David, King of Israel, recognizes "Him that spake and there was the world" by observing Nature, as he frequently exclaimed, מה גדלו מעשיך ה' "How great are Thy deeds!" or מה רבו מעשיך ה' "How many are Thy deeds!" In the Psalms he teaches us wisdom, understanding and insight to recognize in nature and its beauty—its Creator, our Father and King, blessed be His name. [. . .] And this is the secret of our prayers, which are in part composed of Psalms—the soul's expression of yearning and desire to cleave to the Lord of all the Universe, the source of all life.

What is *inconceivable* about the Divine Being is the essence and entity of the supreme Creator, and what lies beyond the point of "Life creating life," as it has been said, "Not that is the essence of the Divine Being that He creates worlds and creatures and sustains them."

It is written: מבשרי אחזה אלקה—"From my flesh I visualize G-d." Man consists of body and soul. Just as the soul fills the whole body and vitalize it, so does G-d fill the whole world and vitalize it. But can we say, the *entire* essence and function of the soul is that it sustains the body? Similarly, we cannot say that it is the entire essence of G-d that He creates and sustains the worlds and all creatures. Here lies a great deal that is inconceivable to the human mind. However, the realization of the greatness of the Creator must move us to a longing and yearning to cleave to the Lord of all things. [. . .]

IV

[. . .] Israel, the Torah and G-d are joined together into complete union, as it is said: "The Holy One blessed be He, the Torah and Israel are all one," and their union comes about through the revealed and hidden qualities of each of them, mentioned above.

However, the manner of their uniting is two-fold:

a) The revealed qualities of Israel unite with the revealed attributes of G-d by means of the revealed part of the Torah; and the latent qualities of Israel unite with the latent attributes of G-d by means of the latent part of Torah;

b) The revealed qualities of Israel are connected with the hidden qualities of Israel, and the hidden qualities of Israel in turn unite with the revealed part of the Torah; the revealed part of the Torah is connected with its hidden part, and this in turn unites with the revealed attributes of G-d; finally, the revealed attributes of G-d are connected with His hidden attributes and thus the union is completed.

The common feature of these two manners of uniting is that both tend to reveal the concealed, which in itself creates nothing new, as the three rings mentioned above are essentially interlocked even when they do not come to be revealed.

V

It follows therefore that this union with G-d is extant in every one of Israel, man or woman, young or old, whether learned in the Torah or ignorant of it. At the same time, however, there are various factors which influence the *feeling* of the said union, either strengthening it or weakening it.

This will be understood by an example: Two men are walking in a busy street, one of them deaf and the other sound. The deaf person does not hear the sound of hooting or the exclamations of the drivers, but the healthy person does. However, when the noise of the traffic becomes exceedingly great, the healthy person, too, is deafened by the noise and hears no better than the deaf one. On the other hand, the deaf person can also notice signs and feel the actual touch.

The tumult of worldly material life deafens the ears of reason and dulls the senses of the brain and heart. This is particularly true of youth born amid wealth and brought up into a life devoid of Torah and religion. In them and their like the bonds of spiritual attachment are broken, their ears become deaf to the word of G-d, to observing the practical precepts, and their eyes, likewise, are closed to behold the charm of G-d's Torah.

Two causes may account for an impulse to "Teshuvah" (repentance and return to G-d): a) abundant good, and b) exceeding poverty. Although nowadays the cause of religious reawakening is, to our regret and misfortune, very bitter, the effect—the return to G-d, to His religion and Torah—is sweet, showing that the Jewish heart is alive, and the soul of Old Israel is perfect.

VI

One of the spiritual diseases of our generation is the habitual neglect of simplicity, and the preference for so-called "enlightenment" and outer brilliance.

The sons and daughters of Israel, of the enlightened and educated classes are now, to be sure, eager to return to our religion and Torah, but they long for dewy brilliance of the wisdom, discernment and insight of religion, which alone, in their opinion, could satisfy their souls and bring about their spiritual revival.

But the real truth is that true revival lies in the fulfilling of the practical precepts, such as observing the Sabbath, Family Purity, Kashruth, putting on Tefillin, etc., and in stirring up one's consciousness, lying dormant at the bottom of one's heart, to the love of G-d, love of the Torah and love of Israel. [. . .]

Thus the main task of the Jewish scholars and Rabbis everywhere is to make the Jews realize that the essential aspect of Judaism is—keeping the practical precepts.

One of the things that offer spiritual pleasure and delight is the sight of a beautiful painting. We all know that the most talented artist is the one who can ably express a simple, natural scene such as a corn-field playing in the breeze, or the sight of sea-waves, or the setting of the sun and rising of the moon upon a wide landscape crossed by a stream, in all of which the Creator implanted a simple, natural beauty and a wonderful splendor.

So it is also with regard to the worship of the Creator, blessed be He. Sincere worship, by the practice of the ritual precepts with simplicity, is worthier than all the cultures and conceptions which have nothing but an outer brilliance. [. . .]

VIII

The saintly Rabbenu Hazaken, founder of Chabad Chassidism [Shneur Zalman of Liady, Belarus, 1745–1813], says in one of his teachings that the main object of Chassidism is to mould one's character, i.e., that the essence of man's service must be concentrated on himself—to mould his own character. [. . .]

Translated by Nissan Mindel.

Other works by Schneersohn: *An Anthology of Talks* (2012); *Lubavitcher Rabbi's Memoirs: The Memoirs of Joseph I. Schneersohn* (2016).

Elhanan Wasserman

1875-1941

Elhanan Bunim Wasserman, born in Birz, Lithuania, was a disciple of the Hafetz Chaim (Israel Meir Kagan). Wasserman served as head of the yeshiva in Brisk [today, Brest-Litovsk, Belarus] from 1910 to 1914, and he was one of the Lithuanian Misnagdic rabbis who promoted the Brisker method of Talmud study in his yeshiva Ohel Torah in Baranovitsh [today, Brest-Litovsk, Belarus]. He was active in Agudas Yisroel (Agudat Israel), strongly opposing Zionism in particular and nationalism in general. He was murdered by Lithuanian Nazi collaborators.

The Opinion of the Torah: Illuminating the Present Jewish Condition According to the Light of the Torah
1936

Written on the Occasion of the Ritual Slaughter Decree in Poland, 1936 [Parliament considered a bill to have animals killed by electricity, rather than by a knife, as required by Jewish law. The bill was never adopted.]

1. It is customary that when things go well a person finds the reason for this in himself. His wisdom, his energy—"My power and the might of my hand" [Deuteronomy 8:17]. Or even his merits—in my righteousness and the uprightness of my heart [based on Deuteronomy 9:5]. When a man finds himself in a difficult time, he puts the blame on this or on that, on everyone but himself. But the Torah advises the opposite. [. . .] No one is guilty for a man's sorrows but himself. The Rambam writes: "A man has no part in the Torah of Moses until he believes that everything that comes to pass in the world, both en masse and for individuals, is a miracle, only if he keeps the *mitzvot* will he merit his reward, and if he transgresses them his punishment will come from above." The foundation is made clear by a verse with three [Hebrew] words: "His judgments are in all the earth" [Psalm 105:7]. In all, without any exceptions. He who does not believe in this foundation of all foundations, he is no Jew.

2. [. . .] To correctly illuminate the entire world history and its details from beginning to end, one must be knowledgeable in the wisdom of the Most High [Numbers 24:16]. There is no one like this now. One must search for this in the Torah, which reveals every hidden thing. [. . .]

5. Regarding special, Jewish events, it is very dangerous if we forget that the hand of God was among us. [. . .] And as in the case of a fire in which one cannot extinguish the structure, which is already consumed by the fire, one can at least succeed in localizing the fire so that it should not spread further; so we must be careful not to reach the level of "and I also will chastise you

seven times for your sins." The advice therefore is this: we should clearly understand—"For it is not a coincidence for us," but rather "God's hand was among us."

6. [. . .] We know that the punishment is always lesser than the sin. "And you punished us less than our iniquities deserve" [Ezra 9:13]. And here we find the opposite. But we should know that when the Jews must be punished, it is God's will that this not be known by the nations of the world. [. . .] When a calamity comes it is clothed in a general form. When the Jews must lose their livelihood, a world crisis begins. If we immediately understand that this is intended for us, we will break out of it. But when one says "it's just a coincidence," this is a world crisis, misfortunes happen—especially to the Jews: then there will remain no room for error. We must clearly see that this is intended for us. Therefore it comes about that Jews are punished twice over: 1) in the general forms of punishment and 2) with special Jewish troubles.

7. If we acknowledge this, it is clear that no one is guilty for our sufferings. "We are verily guilty!" [. . .] "And that nation, whom they shall serve, will I judge" [Genesis 15:14]. This does not apply to us. We must look for counsel for ourselves. Just as we know who beats us, we must know why. "What is this that God hath done unto us?" [. . .]

8. "And thou shalt consider that, as a man chastens his son, so the Lord thy God chastens thee" [Deuteronomy 8:5]. A father does not punish his son with the aim of revenge, but rather to improve him. [. . .]

9. We are struck threefold: economically, physically, and spiritually, that is, decrees against religion; this goes in order. First, to all: economic, [. . .] if one does not learn from economic troubles, then comes the physical blow. The physical blows are at first light and later become harsher and harsher, until we are completely abandoned. Until anyone can hit a Jew over the head with an iron rod, without receiving punishment. Economically in two ways: on the one hand, one cannot make a living, all sources of income are taken away, and on the other hand, everything that the Jews previously owned is taken away. "Therefore they did set over them taskmasters to afflict them" [Exodus 1:11]. Taskmasters—a totally normal thing. In every country there must be taskmasters. [. . .] All that happened in Egypt now repeats itself in the footsteps of the Messiah.

10. What is the reason for the punishment? "He that gets riches, and not by right; in the midst of his days he shall leave them" [Jeremiah 17:11].

12. Acts of violence: one should remember our own inner acts of violence, carried out among different parties.

[...] The war of the "comrades" [socialists] against the *shtreimel* [fur-trimmed hat worn by Hasidim and some other religious Jews]? How many provocations and how many acts of violence have been committed? The miracle is that we are under foreign rule. Were that not the case, [Jewish] man would have raised up a sword against his brother.

13. We are now in a situation of anarchy. Whoever wishes to do so can strike the Jews. How did this come about? The Hafetz Chaim of blessed memory used to say: The Holy One, blessed be He, guard of the nation of Israel, is He a paid guard? No! We pay Him no wages for His protection. He guards for free. But a free guard, when he does not want to, does not guard. When does He not want to guard? It says in the Torah, "Lest he see anything unseemly in these and turn away from you." [Deuteronomy 23:15]. No unseemly thing means corruption; that is, the violation of modesty. Once there was a rule, Daughters of Israel are modest, today the rule is the opposite. Therefore we were warned "and He will turn away from thee"; that is the Holy One blessed be He will take away His protection from us. This is the level to which we have sunk and we are abandoned; without protection. [...]

14. We have a press which sees its task as mocking and discrediting the Torah and its flag bearers. It completely ignores the Torah, as though it does not exist at all. [...] Among us were parties which sought to anger religious Jews. There arose much stronger parties among non-Jews, with the aim of angering all the Jews. [...]

We needed to establish schools to instill in the Jewish youth love of Torah and piety; instead, people founded among us national and international schools that instilled in our children hatred of the Torah and anarchy. Now there have arisen non-Jewish schools on a much greater scale, which instill among their children deathly hatred of all Jews. We have an intelligentsia which hates Jews who wear *tsitsis*. Now their [non-Jewish] intelligentsia makes terrible suffering for all Jews. We needed to stick together. [...] Today who is like Israel, a nation divided? Today all enemies of Israel are friends. Midian and Moab are making peace among themselves in order to make a war against the Jews. In short: as it is with the Jews, so it is with the Christians, and not the opposite. [...]

16. Of all the decrees against religion, the most dangerous is removing children from the rabbi's education through compulsory schooling. "Thy sons and thy daughters shall be given unto another people, and thine eyes shall look, and fail with longing for them all the day; and there shall be naught in the power of thy hand to save them" [Deuteronomy 28:32]. This places the entire existence of the nation and faith in danger. The destruction of religion in Western Europe resulted from this decree. Today it is known that in the course of one hundred years a million apostates have gathered in Germany and of the remaining half million Jews there, a great proportion are candidates for apostasy. However, removing the children from learning with the rabbi was not initiated from outside but from within. Among us in Poland this began on the one hand with the "Ḥaverim" [comrades] and on the other hand with the nationalists, both of whom strive for one goal: that the house of Israel will be like the other nations; they just use different methods. While the "Ḥaverim" want to give a death blow to the soul of the Jewish people, that is the Torah, [...] the nationalists want to bring about the same aim through the kiss of death. [...] But our modern-day leaders say [...] we must be "like all the nations," with equal rights. All that is found among the nations, so we must do the same. Among them are different parties and factions, etc. Each faction must be divided into right and left and so on and so forth. [...] It has become so logical: that we must not be different from the nations in any way. We must even have enemies of Israel among us. The nations laugh at the Jewish beards and side curls, so we must also do the same, with more enthusiasm. Now has come the time to cry, the time for laughing has passed. [...]

18. The Sunday Decree. As long as Jews observed the Sabbath, no one knew about Sunday. When Jews began to break the observance of the Sabbath, we should have made every effort not to allow desecration of the Sabbath—we should have placed guards—but we did not do this, or people mocked the guards. Now there are guards to enforce the observance of Sunday. [...]

19. The Ritual Slaughter Decree. The project is approximately fifty years old. At this point people began to break the laws of eating kosher food. At the same time, the project of forbidding ritual slaughter was born. As long as eating kosher food was strong among us, such a project could not arise. As eating kosher became weaker among us, the project had more chances of realization. [...]

23. [. . .] Jews cannot exist without a Torah. The nations of the world exist in a natural way. However, Jews have no way of existing in natural ways. The situation of the Jews is such that they shall always be "one sheep among seventy wolves." These wolves can tear the sheep apart, and also have the will to do so, they truly tear apart; yet the sheep is not torn apart. [. . .]

25. [. . .] When one sees that the decrees come without any pause, we will know that these are already the birth pangs of the redemption. Usually with birth pangs, one cannot know in advance how things will end. But with the birth pangs of the Jewish people as a whole one can be assured that it will end in a birth. "Shall I bring to the birth, and not cause to bring forth? says the LORD" [Isaiah 66:9]. We must understand that we are now in the period of the footsteps of the Messiah. [. . .] How long the pangs will last, none can know. This is hidden from every living thing. "The heart does not reveal to the mouth." But it is clear that the time is already here and we are not far from the birth. The Torah tells us in advance that before the redemption the Jews will have enemies and foes. [. . .]

NB. No one should suspect that the author of this article sets himself up in the role of preacher of this generation. He makes no such great mistake to think that he is worthy of this. Here he only gives a brief *da'as Torah*, based on the words of the sages and from holy books.

All the ideas expressed herein are taken from the Torah. [. . .]

Maintaining the Torah

[. . .] We see that in the countries in which the Torah expires, many segments of Jews die out. What remains of the Jews of Italy, France, where there were once large Jewish communities? Nothing is left of them apart from a remnant of the destruction.

We see a terrible fact in Russia, that in the course of twenty years a group of three million Jews have died. Why? Because they remained without Torah. Because of the decrees of the Jewish apostate members of the Communist Party. Those that say that the Jewish people can exist without the Torah, but only with the national idea: they are false prophets. Those who preach to the Jews "we will be like the nations" are mortal enemies of the Jewish people.

The way for the Jews is laid out in the Torah: "Lo, it is a people that shall dwell alone, and shall not be reckoned among the nations" [Numbers 23:9]. [. . .] The

parts of Jews who have broken from the Torah are dead limbs in the body of the Jewish people.

But how do the yeshivas exist and in what conditions do they live? One cannot imagine this. The material need and sorrows of yeshiva students are indescribable. They are willing to be tortured, yet they learn Torah with exceptional commitment and toil. From where do they draw these superhuman powers? It is impossible to understand. But just as the existence of Israel among the nations is a miracle, so is the existence of the Torah in Israel a miracle within a miracle. We have no concept of what powers the Torah gives a Jew who studies it. And in reality, the yeshivas only exist on the basis of spirituality—this is the self-sacrifice of the students and their rabbis. It is evident that maintaining the Torah falls on the Torah students themselves; they shall uphold the yeshivas by being prepared to suffer hunger and cold. [. . .]

Translated by Rebecca Wolpe

Other works by Wasserman: *Ohel torah* (1923–1932); *Da'as toyre: a balaykhterung fun yetstikn yidishn matsev al pi da'as toyre* (1936).

Central Conference of American Rabbis

The Central Conference of American Rabbis is the professional association of Reform rabbis in North America. It was founded in 1858 by Rabbi Isaac Mayer Wise of Cincinnati. The platforms that it approved at annual meetings in Pittsburgh (1885) and Columbus (1937) represent respectively the principles of classical Reform Judaism in the United States and the modification and softening that those principles subsequently underwent.

The Columbus Platform
1937

In view of the changes that have taken place in the modern world and the consequent need of stating anew the teachings of Reform Judaism, the Central Conference of American Rabbis makes the following declaration of principles. It presents them not as a fixed creed but as a guide for the progressive elements of Jewry.

A. Judaism and Its Foundation

1. *Nature of Judaism.* Judaism is the historical religious experience of the Jewish people. Though

growing out of Jewish life, its message is universal, aiming at the union and perfection of mankind under the sovereignty of God. Reform Judaism recognizes the principle of progressive development in religion and consciously applies this principle to spiritual as well as to cultural and social life. Judaism welcomes all truth, whether written in the pages of scripture or deciphered from the records of nature. The new discoveries of science, while replacing the older scientific views underlying our sacred literature, do not conflict with the essential spirit of religion as manifested in the consecration of man's will, heart and mind to the service of God and of humanity.

2. *God.* The heart of Judaism and its chief contribution to religion is the doctrine of the One, living God, who rules the world through law or love. In Him all existence has its creative source and mankind its ideal of conduct. Though transcending time and space, He is the indwelling Presence of the world. We worship Him as the Lord of the universe and as our merciful Father.

3. *Man.* Judaism affirms that man is created in the Divine image. His spirit is immortal. He is an active co-worker with God. As a child of God, he is endowed with moral freedom and is charged with the responsibility of overcoming evil and striving after ideal ends.

4. *Torah.* God reveals Himself not only in the majesty, beauty and orderliness of nature, but also in the vision and moral striving of the human spirit. Revelation is a continuous process, confined to no one group and to no age. Yet the people of Israel, through its prophets and sages, achieved unique insight in the realm of religious truth. The Torah, both written and oral, enshrines Israel's ever-growing consciousness of God and of the moral law. It preserves the historical precedents, sanctions and norms of Jewish life, and seeks to mould it in the patterns of goodness and of holiness. Being products of historical processes, certain of its laws have lost binding force with the passing of the conditions that called them forth. But as a depository of permanent spiritual ideals, the Torah remains the dynamic source of the life of Israel. Each age has the obligation to adapt the teachings of the Torah to its basic needs in consonance with the genius of Judaism.

5. *Israel.* Judaism is the soul of which Israel is the body. Living in all parts of the world, Israel has been held together by the ties of a common history, and above all, by the heritage of faith. Though we recognize in the group loyalty of Jews who have become estranged from our religious tradition, a bond which still unites them with us, we maintain that it is by its religion and for its religion that the Jewish people has lived. The non-Jew who accepts our faith is welcomed as a full member of the Jewish community. In all lands where our people live, they assume and seek to share loyally the full duties and responsibilities of citizenship and to create seats of Jewish knowledge and religion. In the rehabilitation of Palestine, the land hallowed by memories and hopes, we behold the promise of renewed life for many of our brethren. We affirm the obligation of all Jewry to aid in its upbuilding as a Jewish homeland by endeavoring to make it not only a haven of refuge for the oppressed but also a center of Jewish culture and spiritual life. Throughout the ages it has been Israel's mission to witness to the Divine in the face of every form of paganism and materialism. We regard it as our historic task to cooperate with all men in the establishment of the kingdom of God, of universal brotherhood, Justice, truth and peace on earth. This is our Messianic goal.

B. Ethics

6. *Ethics and Religion.* In Judaism religion and morality blend into an indissoluble unity. Seeking God means to strive after holiness, righteousness and goodness. The love of God is incomplete without the love of one's fellowmen. Judaism emphasizes the kinship of the human race, the sanctity and worth of human life and personality and the right of the individual to freedom and to the pursuit of his chosen vocation. Justice to all, irrespective of race, sect or class, is the inalienable right and the inescapable obligation of all. The state and organized government exist in order to further these ends.

7. *Social Justice.* Judaism seeks the attainment of a just society by the application of its teachings to the economic order, to industry and commerce, and to national and international affairs. It aims at the elimination of man-made misery and suffering, of poverty and degradation, of tyranny and slavery, of social inequality and prejudice, of ill-will and strife. It advocates the promotion of harmonious relations between warring classes on the basis of equity and justice, and the creation of conditions under which human personality may flourish. It pleads for the safeguarding of childhood against exploitation. It champions the cause of all who work and of their right to an adequate standard of living, as prior to the rights of property. Judaism emphasizes the duty of charity, and strives for a social order which will

protect men against the material disabilities of old age, sickness and unemployment.

8. *Peace.* Judaism, from the days of the prophets, has proclaimed to mankind the ideal of universal peace. The spiritual and physical disarmament of all nations has been one of its essential teachings. It abhors all violence and relies upon moral education, love and sympathy to secure human progress. It regards justice as the foundation of the well-being of nations and the condition of enduring peace. It urges organized international action for disarmament, collective security and world peace.

C. Religious Practice

9. *The Religious Life.* Jewish life is marked by consecration to these ideals of Judaism. It calls for faithful participation in the life of the Jewish community as it finds expression in home, synagogue and school and in all other agencies that enrich Jewish life and promote its welfare. The Home has been and must continue to be a stronghold of Jewish life, hallowed by the spirit of love and reverence, by moral discipline and religious observance and worship. The Synagogue is the oldest and most democratic institution in Jewish life. It is the prime communal agency by which Judaism is fostered and preserved. It links the Jews of each community and unites them with all Israel. The perpetuation of Judaism as a living force depends upon religious knowledge and upon the Education of each new generation in our rich cultural and spiritual heritage.

Prayer is the voice of religion, the language of faith and aspiration. It directs man's heart and mind Godward, voices the needs and hopes of the community and reaches out after goals which invest life with supreme value. To deepen the spiritual life of our people, we must cultivate the traditional habit of communion with God through prayer in both home and synagogue.

Judaism as a way of life requires in addition to its moral and spiritual demands, the preservation of the Sabbath, festivals and Holy Days, the retention and development of such customs, symbols and ceremonies as possess inspirational value, the cultivation of distinctive forms of religious art and music and the use of Hebrew, together with the vernacular, in our worship and instruction.

These timeless aims and ideals of our faith we present anew to a confused and troubled world. We call upon our fellows Jews to rededicate themselves to them, and in harmony with all men, hopefully and courageously to continue Israel's eternal quest after God and His kingdom.

Yehiel Yaakov Weinberg
1884–1966

An influential thinker and *posek* (decisor) in the world of modern Orthodoxy, Yehiel Yaakov Weinberg was trained in a Lithuanian yeshiva but moved to Germany before World War I and received a university education. He identified with the Berlin school of modern Orthodoxy (Torah im Derekh Erets) and headed the Hildesheimer Rabbinical Seminary in Berlin until 1939, when he fled to Warsaw. During the Nazi years he became modern Orthodoxy's most prominent halakhic authority in the face of mounting persecution. The core of his approach during that difficult period and after the war was that insisting on increasing stringency in matters of halakhah would drive Jews away rather than keep them within the traditional fold. He survived the war and settled in Switzerland, where he continued to issue important responsa.

Rosh Hashanah Sermon for the Jewish Father
1937

Assimilation in our day has spoiled and distorted the essence of our festivals. It has turned Rosh Hashanah into a day of festivity filled with the sound of music and song. However, the first day of the Jewish year possesses another kind of purpose: it is a day of contemplation, a day of soul-searching, the Day of Judgment that calls for repentance and return, a day whose penetrating sound ends in *Shuva* [return] *Yisrael*. Its gaze harks back to the past, but only in order to shape the future. And thus it is possible and incumbent upon us to determine on it how we should look upon our life's role.

In the forefront of the obligations on whose fulfillment the future depends, there stands the question of the education of our children, which is in reality a question of survival for our people.

Undoubtedly, the impressions of youth, which are the most intense in life, are those which shape a person's future development and his religious outlook. At an early stage, while still in the parental home, the fates decree whether one belongs to the community of Israel as the people of Hashem, or alternatively to be estranged from it. And we are grateful to the father and mother if Judaism lives within us. We, however, see the yawning abyss between us and between the youth, and ask the question: how much can we influence our children so that they follow the path of belief in God? Why do we lack the power to do what our forefathers achieved?

And we immediately hear a great number of excuses that will also serve as an explanation for today's perplexity—and at the same time will serve to defend those who have failed in the educational enterprise. First of all: times have changed, and too great were the sacrifices of all kinds that youth had to bring had they been told to live according to the commandments of the Torah. Thus maintain the "good ones," those who seek the welfare of the future generations. However, most are slaves to materialism and subject to lives of pleasures and luxury not bound by strictures of the law. Nonetheless, to these we answer: so what is the poverty of a religious Jew today as compared with the suffering of our people in the course of thousands of years? Yes, and how easy would it be even for the youth of today who grow up for the most part pleasurably by comparison with the asceticism and the abstemiousness of our youth when we were sent to yeshivas with very minimal sums to learn Torah, and notwithstanding that even the Torah had ceased being a "career."

And there are also those who see the purpose for a more spiritual reason. They believe that knowledge has distanced our youth from the font of belief, its power weakened in the face of the progress of the younger generation. However, this view is also without foundation. First, this assumption contradicts a not insignificant group among German Jewry who combine piety and secular knowledge and make them into a single unit. Apart from this—is it not disgrace and abuse of our fathers and ourselves to maintain that Judaism has existed only through ignorance and lack of understanding? Does this not mean that now it has no right to exist, and that the hour of its death is coming after we have gained knowledge, and Haskalah is increasingly penetrating into everything?

And also to maintain that our youth are less inclined to make sacrifices than the previous generations is unjustified. [...]

It is therefore worthwhile to reflect on the relations between fathers and sons, on the misunderstanding and incompatibility between generations, since the future depends on this. In particular Rosh Hashanah requires this outlook. The shofar's alerting call contains moral lessons which our sages expressed in a wide range of articles: "Blow the shofar of the ram and I shall raise you up as if you had bound yourselves in sacrifice" and again, "Why do we blow? In order to frighten Satan!" So what then is the power of Satan and what is the power residing in the shofar that has the capacity to prevent the dangers that the former secretes within him?

[...] The eyes of Satan roam over everything; his hand is everywhere where it is possible to disturb growth and development and to implant there instead canker and degeneration. He sows strife and schism everywhere. Furthermore, with extreme delight he penetrates into that same circle that is highly qualified to guard and preserve the good and noble front and foster the fear of God: he tears the family circle limb by limb, separating fathers and sons and planting seeds of estrangement.

One thing is certain: we must recognize the right of youth to its independent character; absolute equality between parents and children cannot be demanded. [...] However, something altogether different is occurring before our eyes. A very tragic and terrible event is taking place in the family. It is that the father has stopped intervening decisively in the development of the child. The parental generation did not surrender to the situation without a fight. The war between fathers and sons lasted for several decades, and from the outset the fathers fought for what was most holy to them. And now they have already become reconciled for some time to the estrangement and see in this a process required by nature. They don't feel the humiliation involved in being solely the breadwinner and provider of the children, and to stand before the youth deprived of any right and full of debts, and also without any right whatsoever to take an interest in the affairs of the sons.

On no account must we continue with this situation in the future because it leads to great tragedies. And today on Rosh Hashanah we must especially stress with due seriousness, and from this place, how great is the contrast between this situation and Judaism which demands agreement between the fathers and those who come after them. [...] The educational traits of the parents protected the people of Israel from every storm that came upon it, and the Jewish father was the guarantor of Israel's eternity.

The Jews of our day have lost this educational aptitude. However, if we cast a look backward and study the teachings of the Sages and their sayings, we shall surely discover the secrets of the art of education.

The Torah portion of the Akedah [near-sacrifice of Isaac] that is read on Rosh Hashanah is a manual of education. According to the explanation which the sages gave, it became a sublime educational instruction, and my advice to sermonizers is: instead of your tasteful and well-made addresses you would do well on this day to let our ancient sages, who saw into the very depths of the human soul, speak in their irreplaceable wisdom.

Let us now turn to the matter of the Akedah. In the sayings of the sages it is preceded by the story of Mesha, king of Moab, who also sacrificed his son. However, precisely the intention of this act reveals the contrast. He sacrificed him through cruelty and lack of understanding, and because he thought to bring in this way a gift to his god and thereby win his favor, so that his act was devoid of all moral worth.

In descriptions of great power the sages of the midrash show us the true value of the Akedah. The greatness does not lie in the sacrifice itself—that was brought also by others, from Mesha, king of Moab, until the lovers of the homeland of our day—the intention is the decisive factor. That same marvelous combination of courage, daring, and humility, of strength and pleasure, is what enchants.

The father obeys each and every order, ties up the son and sheds tears that mingle with those of the son, a deep pain and, nonetheless, also joy: in fulfilling the will of his creator.

And the son? Willingly he lays down his life in order to prove his love of God. And only about his father's pain is he anxious, and his heart feels sorrow for the father's sorrow. This scene also affects the hearts of the angels. They had often already seen blood and tears in the days of the flood and in the days of the generation of the tower of Babel, but the sorrow of this innocent youth moves them deeply. Such is true heroism and suffering.

After the Akedah, so the midrash relates, Abraham at once sends his son to the *bet midrash*, correctly recognizing that it is the birthplace of the spirit of Israel. And here is the place of the young man, not at the front but in front of the Gemara. The diligent yeshiva student is the Jewish hero and not the soldier.

And here we realize the magical power of the heroism of Israel: *bet ha-midrash*. However, the boy must also find there his father, happy and joyful.

And this is the lesson of Rosh Hashanah—that the father has the ability to make his son into an Isaac.

However, he must teach him that Judaism is not something commonplace but is a deep heartfelt feeling. [. . .]

It is not the will to bring sacrifice that our sons lack—but the shining example.

"In order to alarm the Satan." Satan has created an abyss between fathers and sons—however, it is possible to build a bridge over it, announces the shofar, if only the father will set his heart for his role.

"And these are the generations of Isaac, Abraham's son—Abraham begot Isaac."

Give me a father according to the model of Abraham and I will give you sons like Isaac.

Translated by David Herman.

Other works by Weinberg: *Mehkarim be-Talmud* (1938); *Seridei esh*, 4 vols. (1961–1969).

Max Kadushin

1895–1980

Born in Minsk, the rabbinics scholar Max Kadushin immigrated to Seattle in 1897. He received his undergraduate education at New York University and rabbinic ordination from the Jewish Theological Seminary in 1920. He held pulpits in New York City and Chicago, served as director of the Hillel organization at the University of Wisconsin from 1931 to 1942, and taught at Jewish schools. In 1960 he began teaching rabbinics and ethics at the Jewish Theological Seminary. While a student there he had come under the influence of Mordecai Kaplan, but he later moved away from Reconstructionism and argued for the enduring significance of the *agadah*. Where other scholars characterized rabbinic thought as random and unsystematic, Kadushin believed that a small number of concepts informed and integrated the writings of the ancient rabbis.

Organic Thinking: A Study in Rabbinic Thought
1938

Chapter I. Introductory

I. The Problem of Coherence

"There is (thus) a zone of insecurity in human affairs," remarks William James in his essay on The

Importance of Individuals, "in which all the dramatic interest lies; the rest belongs to the dead machinery of things. This is the formative zone, the part not yet ingrained in the race's average, not yet a typical, hereditary and constant factor of the social community in which it occurs."[1] While stressing the importance of individuals, James does not mean to deny, of course, that "the race's average" is the matrix of such individuals. A few sentences back, he qualifies his assertion that any man's virtues and vices might be just the opposite of what they are by adding "compatibly with the current range of variation in our tribe." But James does pass over here the essential problem of how the "zone of insecurity in human affairs" relates to the "typical, hereditary and constant factor of the social community in which it occurs." In the realm of values, the problem is to discover the principle of coherence which renders them a typical and constant factor of the social community and at the same time makes possible for them a degree of inconstancy or indeterminacy in the lives of individuals. The coherence or order inherent in such values cannot be that of logic for that would leave no room for indeterminacy. Perhaps the "zone of security" will be less shrouded in mystery when we begin to perceive that "the race's average" cannot be dismissed as "dead machinery."

The problem of the coherence of rabbinic theology appears to be precisely that which we have just raised with regard to values in general. Any representation of rabbinic theology as a logical system, such as Weber's *System der Altsynagogalen Palästinensichen Theologie*, is bound to be a distortion. Careful scholars agree with Schechter who says "that any attempt at an orderly and complete system of Rabbinic theology is an impossible task."[2] Instead they aim at "letting Judaism speak for itself in its own way,"[3] to use Moore's words, and therefore, for the most part, merely offer collected data on rabbinic concepts or attitudes in the form of centos of rabbinic passages on these themes drawn from various sources. The very fact, however, that disparate passages drawn from rabbinic sources that were composed at different periods and under divergent circumstances can yet be brought together so as to elucidate a rabbinic concept—that fact is proof positive that rabbinic theology possessed some kind of unity, some sort of coherence. And this is, indeed, the conclusion of the great masters in the field. Schechter insists that "Rabbinic literature is, as far as doctrine and dogma are concerned, more distinguished by the consensus of opin-

ion than by its dissensions," and points out that there is remarkable agreement in doctrine not alone among Rabbis of the same generation but even between Palestinian teachers of the first and second centuries and Babylonian authorities of the fifth and tenth, "though the emphasis put on the one or the other doctrine may have differed widely as a result of changed conditions or surroundings."[4] Bacher states that in both method and content haggadic literature was already well developed at a very early period, and that, therefore, it is more correct to speak of the *enlargement* rather than of the *development* of the Haggadah.[5] If, during the later centuries of rabbinic religious thought there was enlargement rather than development, the pattern of rabbinic theology must have remained the same. Yet, as Bacher goes on to say and as Schechter also recognizes, there was no complete submergence of differences among the individual teachers. On the contrary, the individual Tana or Amora expressed to the full, in the haggadic statements he uttered, his personality and the tendencies peculiar to himself.[6] The principle of coherence of rabbinic theology, then must have been such as made for unity of thought over great stretches of time and still gave room for differences due to changed circumstances and to the divergent proclivities of individuals.

Since rabbinic theology and social values in general present the identical problem as regards coherence, the former would seem to be but a special case of the latter. Now once we penetrate to the principle of coherence, avenues will be opened up for the investigation of other problems of rabbinic theology; the relation of rabbinic theology to the Bible and of rabbinic theology to rabbinic ethics; and the rabbinic experience of God. If rabbinic theology is but a special case of social values in general, the more we shall learn concerning the coherence of rabbinic theology and cognate matters the greater will also be our knowledge of the valuational life in general.

II. On Method and Text

Despite the conviction of the modern authorities that rabbinic theology does possess some kind of coherence or unity, a conviction not only expressed but implicit in their treatment of any aspect of rabbinic theology, they have made no attempt to describe this coherence. It may be that the method employed in the analysis proved an insurmountable handicap. In culling rabbinic literature for the purpose of explaining rabbinic concepts, attention is centered upon the particular concept under discussion and diverted from other concepts which may be involved. Furthermore, when the passages culled are juxtaposed in the presentation, the original settings of the separate statements may often be ignored. What is not taken account of then is the connective tissue between the concepts or, more accurately, the inherent relationship between the concepts.

In the present study we avoided this difficulty by sifting, examining and endeavoring to classify every statement contained in one rabbinic work. We were forced, therefore, to reckon with *all* the concepts involved in any single statement and with *all* the passages mentioning any given concept. Under these circumstances the endeavor to classify the concepts at length revealed the inherent relationship between them. It will not be necessary, however, to present here an analysis of all the concepts in the book. The description of a fairly large number of them will be sufficient to establish and illustrate the principle of coherence, and will also afford material for the discussion of problems on which that principle sheds light. Moreover, when once we are aware of the principle of coherence we may even use the method of culling various rabbinic sources for the exposition of any concept to advantage. Such an exposition is certain to be richer in detail than one based on a single rabbinic source.

The rabbinic text we have analyzed is Seder Eliahu Rabba and Seder Eliahu Zuṭa. The only critical edition of this text is that of M. Friedmann; and when Seder Eliahu is here referred to by page it is always to that edition.[7] Various difficulties present themselves in any attempt to establish the date and provenance of our text. Seder Eliahu is mentioned in the Talmud and described by the ʿAruk, a talmudical dictionary of the twelfth century.[8] But according to the ʿAruk's description, the Rabba should contain three large divisions and thirty chapters and the Zuṭa twelve chapters. Our text, however, has no large divisions at all, and the Rabba contains thirty-one chapters while the Zuṭa has twenty-five. Further, even granting that the dates mentioned in the text are later interpolations, on the basis of internal evidence some parts seem to have been written before and some parts after the close of the Talmud, some passages refer to an author in Palestine and other passages certainly imply a land outside of Palestine. These considerations have led to a number of contradictory theories. Some scholars, insisting that our Seder Eliahu is not the one mentioned in the Talmud, say that it was written in Babylon; others take it to be a product of the gaonic, post-talmudic period; and still another scholar declares the author or compiler to have been a man named Eliahu who lived in Palestine in the sixth or seventh century. Friedmann, basing himself on the talmudical story, advances the view that Seder Eliahu is the result of direct religious experience on the part of rabbi ʿAnan and others, and that, in the main, it must have been written before the close of the Talmud and after the composition of the Mishnah. In attempting to adjust the text to the description of the ʿAruk, he characterizes large sections similar in style and content to the rest of the book as later interpolations, and further excises the last ten chapters of the Zuṭa, without doubt written at a late period, from Seder Eliahu proper and dubs them "Additions to Seder Eliahu Zuṭa."

New evidence adduced from Genizah fragments enables Louis Ginzberg to state that Seder Eliahu was at one time composed of a Mishnah, or rather Baraita, which was composed early and a Talmud, or commentary, which was added later, certainly after Talmud Babli. We should not be surprised, therefore, if some passages reveal an earlier and some a later origin. Our text not only confuses Baraita with "Talmud" but is very much shorter than the original Seder which the ʿAruk apparently describes. In the course of our discussion, we shall point out instances where traces of Mishnah and commentary can still be discerned, corroborating Ginzberg's theory.

III. The Organic Character of Rabbinic Theology

The coherence we find in Seder Eliahu consists of an inherent relationship between the concepts and is therefore a mental coherence. All the concepts employed bear an organic relationship to one another, interweaving with each other so as to produce a definite, though an extremely flexible, pattern. In using the term "organic," be it recognized, we do not mean to surround it with that aura which it assumes in fascist vocabulary where the term is vague, unbuttressed by demonstration, as well as honorific. We propose to depict in some detail the order which the rabbinic concepts exhibit, *to demonstrate*, that is, the existence of this order, and then to indicate why it can be characterized as organic.

There are four fundamental concepts in rabbinic theology—God's loving-kindness, His justice, Torah, and Israel. We wish to emphasize that these four are fundamental not because they are the most important. Other concepts—the sanctification of the Name and the World to Come, for example—are certainly as important as those we have called fundamental, if importance here implies being essential to the rabbinic world-outlook. The fact is that rabbinic concepts are not like articles of a creed, some of which have a position of primary importance while others are relegated to secondary rank. All rabbinic concepts are of equal importance, for the pattern would not have the same character were a single concept missing. We have, however, called God's loving-kindness, His justice, Torah, and Israel fundamental concepts because all the rabbinic concepts are built, woven rather, out of these four. To demonstrate this we must be permitted what is in effect a brief résumé of our earlier study, *The Theology of Seder Eliahu*.

Every rabbinic concept is constituted of the four fundamental concepts. For instance, the sanctification of the Name occurs, that is, God is recognized by the world as the one true God, when Israel demonstrate their readiness to die as martyrs for this truth, when Torah is exalted before men, when God's absolute justice or His love is vindicated. Likewise, *Malkut Shamayim*, the sovereignty of God (not the *kingdom* of God), is accepted by Israel upon themselves by declaration, and by the recognition of His love and justice. Though the two concepts are very much akin, both having to do with the recognition of God, sanctification of the Name, *Kiddush Hashem*, refers to the effect upon others whereas *Malkut Shamayim* refers to the subjective acceptance or acknowledgement of God by individual or nation. The kinship in idea, however, brings with it similarity in other things. *Malkut Shamayim* is affirmed by declaration; *Kiddush Hashem* is achieved by declaration, as well. *Kiddush Hashem* possesses an obverse in *Hillul Hashem*, the profanation of the Name; *Malkut Shamayim* possesses an obverse in "strange worship," the acceptance of strange or false gods, a perverse worship that will disappear *le'atid labo* when mankind at large will perforce recognize the sovereignty of God. Since the two concepts are so greatly similar, they naturally blend into one another occasionally. The destruction of idols is sanctification of the Name, and martyrdom is crowned with an affirmation of God's sovereignty. We shall find in rabbinic theology other examples of kindred concepts which also blend into one another at times yet which are distinguished, again like the two concepts just described, each by its own individual features. The inherent relationship between all the concepts, to anticipate a later discussion, is of such a nature that every concept must possess its own distinctive features, no matter how closely related it may be to another concept.

The Rabbis' conception of nature and their use of angelology conform to the four fundamental concepts. Notions of a fixed physical order and natural law are absent in rabbinic theology. Everything in nature—heaven and earth, the sun and the moon and the stars, insects and beasts—serves as a vehicle for the fundamental concepts. Rain falls and grass grows because of God's love for man; noxious animals performing their mission are agents of God's justice; Israel's twelve tribes are mirrored in the twelve stars and constellations in the firmament; and when God created the world "He consulted only the Torah." As to angelology, there is no rabbinic theology when angels appear otherwise than in the service of a fundamental concept. The angels, with their complaints against man, serve to bring God's loving-kindness toward him into stronger relief; they are the instruments of God's justice, both in reward and punishment; they help to emphasize the transcendence of Torah; and they accentuate that God's special concern is with Israel. Though names of angels are found, and other details that lend concreteness to the angelology, neither the constitution nor the number of angels is a fixed and dogmatic affair. Angelology, then, is employed but as background for the fundamental concepts.

The "independent attributes" and the anthropomorphisms are also incidental to the four fundamental concepts. By "independent attributes" of God we mean the attributes of eternity, omniscience, humility, omnipresence, creativity and the like, "independent" in the sense that they are additional to the fundamental concepts. Additional they may be but dissociated they are not. God employs His omniscience to aid His mercy and loving-kindness; His humility is associated with Torah; His ways of truth apply to His just recompense; and His universality is joined with His election of Israel. Anthropomorphisms are confined to the fundamental concepts and to the independent attributes associated with the latter. God's "hands are stretched forth to receive those that repent," an expression of His loving-kindness; He will consent to walk with the righteous in Paradise, an anticipated reward; He devotes one-third of the day to the study of Torah; he weeps over the tragedies of Israel. Out of reverence, the Rabbis refrain from employing the biblical terms for God, and instead have many terms of their own. A number of these names or terms derive from the fundamental concepts, and the multiplicity of the rabbinic names for God is thus no mere idiosyncracy of rabbinic theology.

Besides entering into the constitution of all the other concepts, the four fundamental concepts are constitutive of each other, inextricably intertwining with one another. The concept of God's loving-kindness, for example, possesses several aspects or sub-concepts: Providence, or the loving care for the welfare of every individual, mercy or forgiveness in the moral sphere; repentance and atonement; and prayer. We shall indicate the organic interpretation of the fundamental concepts in the case of repentance and in that of prayer. Repentance refers to the complete change of heart not only on the part of the sinner weighed down by the consciousness of specific wrong-doing but on the part of every individual who determines to live the good life. The ability to repent is given man because of God's love; if he repents, he is rewarded, if not, he is punished—in either case there is the infallible operation of God's justice. The means of his reconciliation with God—atonement—are to be found in the study and practice of Torah and association with Israel and the Patriarchs. A sub-concept of atonement is vicarious atonement, the doctrine that an individual Israelite atones through the sufferings visited upon his person for the sins of all Israel; and this doctrine, incidentally, intertwines with the concept of God's justice, for the ideas of corporate personality and corporate responsibility which underlie vicarious atonement also underlie, as we shall soon see, the concept of corporate or collective justice. Prayer is effective because of God's love: God "hears prayer immediately" since He is "merciful and gracious, full of great compassion." Israel, Torah, and God's justice and love are frequently combined into one theme in prayer; Torah is the authority for the prescribed prayers, and sets down their order; Israel is saved by prayer; God's justice, besides being invoked or extolled in prayer is counted on when reward is expected for reciting prescribed prayers. The rabbis fully realize the danger of mere ritualism lurking in prescribed prayer and seek to overcome it in various ways, one of which consists in the rule to engage in Torah before one "stands in prayer."

The concept of God's justice, sometimes personified, also has its various aspects or sub-concepts, each of which depicts God's justice as universal in scope. One such concept is the justice due the individual, the belief that whatever befalls anyone, for good or evil, comes as recompense for his own acts, with the moral temper of the individual taken into account. An elaboration of this kind of distributive justice is the concept of "measure for measure," poetic justice, frequently employed by the Rabbis to supply ethical causes for afflictions mentioned in the Bible. Corporate or collective justice is another aspect of the concept of God's justice, an aspect which permits the Rabbis to regard reward or punishment for the deeds of an individual as visited by God not only upon him alone but upon others as well. The Rabbis resort to this concept of corporate justice in their resolution of the problem of evil; and when employed in their accounts of how the fathers' good deeds affect the children's welfare and vice versa, the concept appears in its special forms of Merit of the Fathers and Merit of the Children. The contradiction between the concept of corporate justice and that of the justice due the individual as well as the ethical evaluation of both by the Rabbis will be dealt with in this study later on. At present we need only recognize that the two concepts imply two different apprehensions of individuality. As several rabbinic passages reveal, corporate justice implies that the individual is not merely a person but that he is merged into a kind of corporate personality of which he is only one link, as it were. All the individual persons composing the corporate personality participate in, and must share in the consequences of, any action by any component member—in other words, there is corporate or collective responsibility. With the remaining aspect of the concept of God's justice—chastisement, or corrective justice—we shall demonstrate the interweaving of the concept of God's justice with the other fundamental concepts. According to the Rabbis, chastisements are sent by God in order to correct and purify men, and hence there are also "chastisings of love," an interpretation the Rabbis are particularly apt to place upon the afflictions of the righteous. By the same token, God chastises Israel because of His love for them, "For whom the Lord loveth He correcteth, even as a father the son in whom he delighteth" (Prov. 3:12). He that is engaged in Torah knows how to accept chastisement properly, and, indeed, Torah may be efficacious in enabling him to avoid chastisement altogether. The aspects of the concept of God's justice touched on above combine with the other fundamental concepts in a similar manner.

The concepts of rabbinic theology thus exhibit a definite pattern. The four fundamental concepts interlace with each other and with the rest of the rabbinic concepts. This is again demonstrated, and perhaps in even stronger fashion, in our discussion in the present volume of the various aspects of the concept of Torah. We shall notice that not only do the fundamental concepts intertwine with one another but that a full description of any fundamental concept actually involves all the concepts of rabbinic theology.

The pattern inherent in the concepts of Seder Eliahu is not confined to that Midrash but is characteristic of rabbinic theology in general. The theology of the Mekilta possesses the same pattern, as we hope to show soon in a forthcoming study, and the Mekilta, an early, halakic Midrash, is indubitably representative of rabbinic thought. The conclusion that the pattern of concepts we have traced here is typical of rabbinic theology in general does not really stand in need, however, of such verification. As is illustrated by the relation of Seder Eliahu to other rabbinic works, there are numerous parallel passages in various rabbinic sources. How could these passages have been placed in different haggadic literature generally? And if the concepts are the same, the pattern most likely is the same. This consideration is supported by two more. According to Ginzberg, whose theory is substantiated here in a number of instances, our text was written or compiled during the entire rabbinic period; and it can be taken, therefore, to be representative of that period. Finally, the kind of unity which both Schechter and Bacher saw in rabbinic theology, a unity presupposed in any modern treatment of the subject, can be accounted for only by the principle of coherence informing the pattern we have described.

IV. The Coherence of Organic Thinking

The coherence of rabbinic theology can only be characterized as organic. Rabbinic theology is a unitary pattern or complex of concepts wherein the four fundamental concepts are interrelated with each other and with all the rest of the rabbinic concepts. Without coherence, or relation to other concepts, no concept can possibly possess meaning. But the coherence between the rabbinic concepts is not such that one concept proceeds from another in inferential fashion. Instead, here the integrated pattern or complex as a whole supplies coherence, relationship with the other concepts, meaning, to each of its individual constituent concepts. The relationship of the rabbinic concepts to one another consists, therefore, in the relationship of each to the whole integrated complex—an organic relationship. Our conclusion, then, is that the rabbinic concepts are organic concepts and their pattern or complex an organic complex. Being thus a mental organism, a thought-organism, this organic complex provides us with an example of organic thinking.

The coherence of organic thinking renders the "zone of insecurity" or indeterminacy a characteristic alike of rabbinic theology and of social values in general. Since no rabbinic concept inevitably follows from any other concept, any given situation is not necessarily interpreted by a single combination of concepts. The same concept, as we have learned, can be combined with any of the four fundamental concepts; hence it happens not infrequently that the same or a similar situation may be given several interpretations "contradictory" to each other. Thus, at one time the Rabbis declare that because God loves the scholar's devotion to Torah He deliberately withholds from him wealth which would distract him from study, and at another time they affirm that wealth is the reward of those who study Torah. The first statement combines Torah with the concept of God's love; the second, Torah with the concept of God's justice. Furthermore, a situation may be interpreted differently by the various sub-concepts of the same concept, and so again different interpretations may be based on a common ground. The organic complex, therefore, is flexible, allowing for divergencies in interpretation either wide or subtle without losing thereby its essential unity. Fluid yet unified, the organic complex gives room for differences in temperament among individuals, even for different moods in the same individual, for the stressing of different concepts in different historical periods—in brief, for all those differences which may distinguish one midrashic compilation from another. We shall take up these matters at greater length under the caption, "The Fluid Character of the Complex."

Organic thinking and logical thinking are not mutually exclusive. Two distinct orders of thought, two distinct types of coherence, they are at one in that both make for the integration of man's mental life. We shall learn later on of the tremendous rôle which logical thinking plays within the framework of the organic complex. The only occasion for conflict between organic and logical thinking occurs when an attempt is made to supply logical coherence to the organic concepts, and the organic complex, we shall also learn, brooks even this attempt to a limited degree. An out-and-out attempt, however, to erect a logical, hence dogmatic, structure of values or beliefs is utterly out of keeping, as we can see even now, with the organic complex. It is organic coherence, not hard-and-fast logical consistency, that permits the development and expression of individuality.

A striking feature of organic thinking is its concreteness. Though often mentioned by name, the rabbinic concepts are very seldom found without an exemplify-

RELIGIOUS THOUGHT 1938   589

ing situation. Indeed, since the concepts interpret for the Rabbis the concrete situations of every-day life, the concepts are usually imbedded, as it were, in those situations. Our theory of organic thinking bears the same relation to the concrete complex of rabbinic theology as grammar does to a language, and, like grammar, can best be grasped through the actual analysis of a good sample of the literature. The analogy—it is probably much more than that—goes even further. Just as the rules of grammar always have reference to a specific language, so the implications of the theory of organic thinking have reference to a particular organic complex. Before turning to the consideration of these implications, let us then, by means of the detailed analysis of a concept, first become more familiar with the theory and with the organic complex itself. The fundamental concept of Torah as exhibited primarily by the text of Seder Eliahu will be our theme for the next two chapters.

NOTES

1. William James, essay on "The Importance of Individuals," in *The Will to Believe* (New York, 1919), pp. 257-258.

2. See Kadushin, *The Theology of Seder Eliahu* (New York, 1932), p. 17. This book is hereafter designated as TE.

3. See ibid., p. 19.

4. See ibid., p. 20. Note 11 there should be corrected to read: "Schechter, opus cit., Preface, pp. xi–xii."

5. W. Bacher, *Die Agada der palästinensischen Amoräer* I (Strassburg, 1892), Introd., p. ix.

6. Ibid., Introd., pp. xi–xii.

7. M. Friedmann, *Seder Eliahu Rabba und Seder Eliahu Zuṭa* (Wien, 1902) and *Pseudo-Seder Eliahu Zuṭa* (Wien, 1904), published by Achiassaf, Warsaw, and bound in one volume.

8. It has recently been proved that the 'Aruk copied from an earlier source, and that the date of Seder Eliahu must be fixed at no later than the eighth century—see Appendix, below, p. 262.

Other works by Kadushin: *The Theology of Seder Eliahu* (1932); *The Rabbinic Mind* (1952); *Worship and Ethics* (1964).

Elhanan Wasserman

Tractate: The Onset of the Messiah
1938

Deeds of the Fathers

4. [. . .] The Gaon of Vilna writes [in his *Even Shelemah*] that the second chapter of *Vayishlaḥ* is the chapter of the "footsteps of the Messiah." When Jacob returned from his exile, it says: "And he put the handmaids and their children foremost" [Genesis 33:2]. The Gaon says: This shows that in the [era of the] "footsteps of the Messiah" the "mixed multitude" will lead the Jews. Maimonides writes in his *Letter [to Yemen]*: A promise exists, that: "And may also believe thee forever" [Exodus 19:9], meaning that Jews will always be believers in the Torah. However, we see that there are unbelievers among us. It is known that "Their ancestors did not stand at Mount Sinai" [B. T. *Nedarim* 20a], that they are descendants of the "mixed multitude" and not of the seed of Israel. When we see that unbelievers are now our leaders, it confirms the words of the Gaon that they are of the "mixed multitude." "And Leah and her children after" [Genesis 33:2]. This shows that the majority of ordinary Jews [the pious ones] will be under the "mixed multitude"; that is, the "mixed multitude" will rule over them. We see this now in the red land [i.e., Soviet Russia] and another place [Germany?] where the "mixed multitude" are in power and oppress pious Jews. "And Rachel and Joseph hindermost" [Genesis 33:2]. These are the Torah scholars, the lowest of all. Everywhere there still remains a remnant of Torah scholars, one sees how they are demeaned and debased.

5. It is written further: "And there wrestled a man with him" [Genesis 32:25]. Jacob is the pillar of Torah. The "man" is Samuel (satan). This means that in the [era of the] "footsteps of the Messiah" impurity will wage war against the study of Torah (ignorance is alive and well). "And the hollow of Jacob's thigh was wrenched" [Genesis 32:26]. Jacob's thigh alludes to the small children, the young schoolchildren, who were the foundation of the existence of the nation for thousands of years. They will be fractured during the [era of] "footsteps of the Messiah" by all kinds of agents, both internal and external. This has taken place throughout the Jewish diaspora. The great majority of Jewish children are being raised as complete gentiles.

6. A second meaning of "Jacob's thigh" is: Support of the Torah. This is the strengthening of Torah, the support of those who study Torah, and making provisions for studying Torah in peace. This is something that existed among Jews since they became a nation (the tribes of Yissakhar and Zevulun). It becomes fractured during [the era] of "footsteps of the Messiah." One sees this everywhere now, even in those lands where at present Jews are still able to give money. They give for anything, but leave only pennies for Torah. In the best

case they are indifferent to Torah. This is quite natural, because the new generation is completely estranged from the Torah and does not understand at all why Torah is needed. The result is disrespect for the [religious] schoolchildren and disrespect for the strengthening of Torah, and one leads to the other. How does Heaven respond to this? For the sin of disrespect for Torah, with sword and destruction. As it is written, "And I will bring a sword upon you, that shall execute the vengeance of the covenant" [Leviticus 26:25]. The covenant is the Torah, as it is written, "If My covenant be not with day and night, if I have not appointed the ordinances of heaven and earth" [Jeremiah 33:25], therefore, annulling Torah will be punished with sword and plunder, for it states, "I will bring a sword of vengeance over you, the vengeance for My covenant." Covenant means the Torah. As it says, "Were it not for My covenant, I would not have made day and night, or established heaven and earth in nature" [*Mishnah Shabbat, Perek 2, Bameh madlikin*]. In one city—Vienna—Jews have been robbed of almost forty million dollars. "Woe to those people who have contempt for the Torah" [*Mishnah Avot 6:2*].

"We Will Be as the Nations"

7. Ezekiel prophesies that in the [era of] "footsteps of the Messiah" a solution will be proposed among Jews: "We will be as the nations" [Ezekiel 20:32]. The actualization of the prophecy began with the Berlin Enlightenment (*Haskalah*), almost 150 years ago. Its proponents masked what they were doing with the words, "Be a Jew in your home and a person in public." The fruits of this approach quickly ripened. Their children apostasized. Their slogan amounted to an undermining of the foundations of the Torah. The Torah had warned that Jews should be separated from the nations in their whole lifestyle. "And have set you apart from other peoples, that ye should be Mine" [Leviticus 20:26; see Maimonides, *Mishneh Torah, Hilkhot Avodah Zarah*, ch. 11]. The *Maskilim* came and said exactly the opposite: "Be only like the nations." God said about this: "In that ye say: We will be as the nations . . . shall not be at all." "Surely with a mighty hand, and with an outstretched arm and with fury poured out" [Ezekiel 20:32-33]. It will begin with "a mighty hand." If that does not help, the "outstretched arm" will come. If this also does not help, then there will be a "fury poured out." We cannot know in which of the three processes we now are. The near future will show us. In any event,

it is clear that the prophecy of "shall not be at all" will be realized. The nations are driving us away from them in a murderous way. It is said, that it is difficult to be a Jew. A wonder has occurred in recent times. It is increasingly difficult to become a gentile. The gentiles are driving us back.

It is said in the name of the *Gaon* [dean of scholars Yosef Dov Ber Soloveichik], the author of *Beit Halevi*, of blessed memory: It is written, "He who separates between light and darkness and between Israel and the gentiles" [*Havdalah* service at end of Sabbath]. There is a specific distance between light and darkness [twilight]. One cannot change the distance, lengthen or shorten it. It is the same between Israel and the gentiles. There is a specific distance as to how far they should be one from the other. If the Jews approach too closely, the gentiles push them back. From this one can understand why the more the Jews have approached the gentiles, the more severely the Jews have been repelled. We see this now in the lands where Jews have completely assimilated, how horribly the gentiles push back. It was also this way in Egypt when the servitude became difficult. The Jews began to emulate the Egyptians, thinking that through this their situation would become easier. What did God do? "He turned their heart to hate His people" [Psalms 105:25]. The more they wanted to assimilate with the Egyptians, the greater the animosity of the gentiles toward them. When the Jews realized their mistake, the redemption came. The same will be with us. [. . .]

The Shepherds

8. In Ezekiel [ch. 34] there is a clear picture of the generation of the "footsteps of the Messiah" and its shepherds. The generation is divided into five classes [regarding spirituality]: (1) weak ones, (2) sick ones, (3) ones with broken limbs, (4) those led astray, (5) lost ones. This is all in relation to Judaism. The last three categories refer to various sorts of heretics—those who separate themselves from the community of Israel by not yielding to the discipline of one or more commandments of Torah. The Gaon of Vilna says: A heretic with regard to one commandment is one who lacks a limb in his soul [he is crippled]. There are two sorts of heretics to all of Torah: the denier is the same as an apostate, but the denier is still together with Jews. These are the ones led astray. A second kind is one who has mixed with gentiles. These are the lost ones. Nobody knows any more that they are from the seed of Israel. [. . .] Those whose grandfathers and grandmothers converted 120-130 years ago will be

sought out. It will be discovered that they are not Aryans. They will be beaten over the head: Know that you are Jews and that is what you must remain. In a country where there are thousands of gentiles for every Jew, the lost Jews will be sought and found. At the moment we are at that point. The process is not at an end. It is still going on and spreading quickly from one land to other lands. When this will end, all the lost ones will be found. Then the second events will come: "And will bring back that which was driven away." The formerly lost ones will also be incorporated into those gone astray. Then the third: "And I will bind up that which was broken," etc.

. . . 9. There is more to note concerning the expression in the prophecy "My sheep wandered" [Ezekiel 34:6]. This prophecy indicates that those of the generation in general—excluding the shepherds—are thought of in heaven as unintentional sinners. For whenever the people sinned unintentionally, it turns out that it would not have been difficult to bring the Jews back to the Torah had the shepherds not acted as a steel wall between Israel and their Heavenly Father. The teachers, the leaders, the writers, the party leaders, let no ray of light from the Torah penetrate among Jews. They have *their* Torah, *their* Torah sages, *their* leaders of the generation. They darken Jewish minds and hearts with a new Torah and new commandments. It is noteworthy that on that rare occasion when Jews do have the opportunity to hear true Torah thoughts, they swallow them like people parched with thirst. However, the shepherds give them stones instead of diamonds. Instead of Torah thoughts, the readers and listeners are given heretical thoughts. In the most fashionable circles one reads and hears jokes and idle gossip mixed with profanity. These are the shepherds that the prophet prophesied about for our times.

10. The prophecy mentions a category of sheep, "The fat and the strong" [Ezekiel 34:16]. Such are many of our modern wealthy people. They meet to give money to all those things to which we should not donate. Where they should give, where the Torah tells us to give, they are nowhere to be found. They are surrounded by guards who do not let them be approached. [. . .]

13. [. . .] The nature of a dog is that if one throws a stone at it, the dog runs to bite the stone. When a Haman arises against Jews, we need to know that it is only a stick with which Jews are being punished from Heaven. "O Asshur, the rod of Mine anger" [Isaiah 10:5]. There is no sense in waging war with the stick, since there is no shortage of sticks in Heaven. There are "many messengers to the one God" [*Midrash Bamidbar Rabbah*,

Parashah 18, *Siman* 18]. We need rather to employ measures so that Heaven will not cast the stick. However, in the [era of] "footsteps of the Messiah" there will be no knowledge. We will run like the dog to bite the stick. We see this now, when our modern [Jewish] leaders have declared war on the mightiest nations in the world. What is our strength and what is our power? We take shots with articles in Jewish newspapers? With what result? It only incites the snakes further against the Jews. The leaders only see the sick. "Yet the people turneth not unto Him that smiteth them" [Isaiah 9:12].

14. "In the [era of] footsteps of the Messiah, arrogance will increase (*yisge*)" [*Mishnah Sota* 9:15]. Another meaning of *yisge* is greatness (*gedulah*). To be one of the generation in earlier times demanded learning, piety, and wisdom. In the [era of] "footsteps of the Messiah" a "leader" will be one who possesses arrogance. The more arrogant he is, the greater the leader he is. We see it now among the political leaders whose only qualification for leadership is arrogance. [. . .]

Who are these speakers? Hired party agitators with the job of putting the audience to sleep with sweet dreams about the "redemption" that their party will bring for Jews—the nationalists—or for the whole world—the internationalists. Even though everyone sees that the dreams will melt away. All the idols that people had hoped for are being unmercifully broken and smashed. However, the false prophets are not being silenced. When the biblical spies uttered lies they threw in a bit of truth, because something that is completely false is not fulfilled [Rashi *ad* Numbers 13:27]. However, the current liars are not concerned about their lies being fulfilled. If one lie is invalidated they already have thirty other lies ready under different names. [. . .]

21. There are two primary false gods whom Jews serve and to whom they offer sacrifices: socialism and nationalism. The "torah" of modern nationalism consists of [the] words: "We will be as the nations" [Ezekiel 20:32]. To be a Jew, it is enough to be nationally [Zionist] minded. One needs no more. Just pay a *shekel* [as dues] and sing [the national anthem] *Hatikvah*. This absolves one from all the commandments of the Torah. It is quite clear that such a system, according to the Torah, is idolatry. The hearts and minds of the whole Jewish youth are darkened by these two false religions. Each false religion has an entire headquarters of false prophets in the form of writers and speakers who are committed to their work. A miracle has occurred: In Heaven these two false religions have been combined into one. A terrible stick of wrath to punish Jews

murderously in all corners of the land, national-socialism, has been created from the mix. The same impurities that we worshipped are now punishing us. "And thy backsliding shall reprove you" [Jeremiah 2:19].

22. The prophets prophesied that there will be a time of troubles for [the people of] Israel, such as they never had since becoming a nation. The Gaon of Vilna writes [in *Even Shelemah*]: In the passages of Scripture, the travails of the entire exile are similar to the pregnancy of a woman. The birth pangs of the Messiah (*hevlei mashiaḥ*); [see B. T. *Sanhedrin* 97–98 and Rashi *ad* Isaiah 26:17] are like the throes of birth. Just as the anguish of pregnancy cannot be compared to the anguish of giving birth, so too, the troubles of exile cannot be compared to the troubles of the birth pangs of the Messiah. There is a specific order as to how the troubles of exile are to [unfold]. The order was established in the "chapter of the exile" [the beginning of *Parashat Vayishlaḥ*]. It is written there: "The camp which is left shall escape" [Genesis 32:9]. When Jews were being persecuted in one country there was always a second place to which to escape. During the Spanish expulsion, Turkey and Poland were open to Jews and later Holland. During the birth pangs of the Messiah, it will not be this way. Jews will be persecuted and they will have nowhere to escape. They will be pursued everywhere and admitted nowhere.

NOTE
Words in brackets appear in the original translation.

Translated by Gershon Greenberg.

Chaim Ozer Grodzensky

Responsa of Achiezer
1938–1939

With the Help of the Almighty

[. . .] During the Middle Ages and the decrees of the year 5408 [1648], when our brethren the children of Israel believed with real faith in the Almighty and in His Torah, and that the God of Israel would not cast off or abandon His people, their faith gave them strength and fortitude to endure the terror of the tyrants, and they still built great centers of Torah. [. . .] But now, because of our many sins, faith has weakened, and in the countries of the West, the Reform movement has already struck roots for several generations, and many have arrived at a state of real assimilation and inter-

mingling with gentiles as a result. And from there have emanated the current evil decrees—to persecute them with wrath, to destroy them, and to drive them out of the land. [. . .]

It is our duty to repent wholeheartedly, as it is written [in the Torah]: "When you are in distress, and all these things befall you . . . etc., you shall return unto the Lord your God." We are obliged to exert ourselves, to encourage ourselves and strengthen ourselves, and to fortify our brethren with actions and deeds, appeal to the emotions of those who are crushed, who are exiled and who are persecuted, and strengthen them with words of comfort, and give encouragement to their afflicted spirit. [. . .] The root of the disease lies in the disgraceful education that the younger generation receives in secular schools lacking in Torah and faith, and it is as a result of this that boorishness and ignorance, mockery and licentiousness have become prevalent.

In particular, it is our duty to take care to strengthen the Torah academies—both large and small—the fortress of Judaism, the ancient institutions throughout every generation, from where Torah and light issued forth throughout the Jewish diaspora and illuminated the darkness of the exile.

Translated by David E. Cohen.

Shlomo Zalman Ehrenreich
1863–1944

Shlomo Zalman Ehrenreich was born in Beregszász [today, Berehovo, Ukraine]. After gaining a reputation as a scholar and strict legalist, he was appointed as the rabbi of Shamloy, Hungary, in 1899. He was a strong conservative leader, exerting influence in city politics, and wrote multiple commentaries on the Tanakh and the Talmud. He was bitterly opposed to Zionism. He remained with his congregation and was murdered in Auschwitz.

What I Preached on Sunday [of the Week of] the Torah Portion Tetsaveh, *26 February 1939*
1939

On a Day When Communal Fast Was Declared Because of Israel's Troubles

Gentlemen, today is the seventh of *Adar*, the anniversary of the death of Moses our teacher, of blessed memory. We have gathered in the synagogue to pray and to recite Psalms because the troubles of Israel have increased greatly. A communal fast day has been declared today for the whole country. It is elucidated in the holy books concerning the words of King David, of blessed memory, in Psalms 106:2. "Who can express the mighty acts of the Lord, or make all His praise to be heard?" that whoever wants to annul and smash them so that they do no damage should "make all His praise to be heard." That is, recite the whole book of Psalms and thereby destroy the evil decrees. We also remember the rabbis and sages who died since the last seventh of Adar: Rabbi Menaḥem Brody, of blessed memory, rabbi of Kalov (Nagykallo); Rabbi Naftali Teitelbaum, of blessed memory, of Nyirbator; Rabbi Benyamin Ze'ev of Monostor; Rabbi Benyamin Shenfeld, *Av Beit Din* [head of the religious court] of Mihaifalav (Ermihalyfalva) [all of Hungary]. I had loving friendships with them. We should shed tears for them and cry ceaselessly for this group of holy sages who have left us to our wretched plight.

The rabbinic Sages said that when a scholar dies, he has no replacement [*Midrash Bereshit Rabbah, Parashah* 91, *Siman* 11]. We need to clarify. When it says "He has no," should it not say, "We have no" substitute? We should explain this according to what our teacher, the Ḥatam Sofer [Mosheh Schreiber], may his merit protect us, explained in his introduction to [the talmudic] tractate *Ḥullin*. We [Jews] follow the rule that the day follows the night. For the nations of the world the night follows the day. But when it comes to sacrifices, we follow the rule that the night follows the day, as do the nations of the world. This should be explained. It seems that for us, this world is called night. What is essential is the world to come. One hour of contentment in the world to come is more pleasant than all of life of this world. Therefore the rule is that the night is first and the day follows. However, among the nations of the world this world is primary. As long as they live in this world, this world is day for them and the world to come is night for them. For the nations, the day precedes the night. Now when it comes to sacrifice, the important thing for the rabbinic sages is to serve God. This is not so in the world to come, where the dead are free of the commandments. In this respect the primary category becomes this world. For one hour of repentance and good deeds in this world is better than all the life in the world to come. If so, this world is the day and the world to come belongs to the category of night and is second-

ary. Accordingly, when it comes to sacrifices the night follows the day. Up to here, the holy words of the Ḥatam Sofer.

I have discussed this at length elsewhere. As such, the primary aspect of the life of the sage is to occupy himself with the Torah, to investigate, innovate, argue, and enjoy Torah in this world. This world is more precious in his eyes than the world to come. Even though the sage would enjoy the spiritual pleasures in the world to come, the pleasure of repentance and good deeds [here] are more important to him than all the life in the world to come. When he dies and enjoys the pleasures of the world to come, they are no substitute. This is because the pleasure of his worship in this world is more precious to him. Let this be understood. As such, how much is there to mourn over the loss of the great sages who were taken from us?

But at this time the words of Jeremiah the prophet are being fulfilled, "Weep ye not for the dead, neither bemoan him; but weep sore for him that goeth away, for he shall return no more, nor see his native country" [Jeremiah 22:10]. So it is at this time. Thousands of Jews have been expelled from Germany and Austria. Everything has been taken from them and they suffer immeasurable troubles. They have nowhere to turn. They are not allowed to enter the Land of Israel or America. They are betwixt heaven and earth. There is more to mourn over this than over the loss of pious ones who have gone to their eternal rest. Thousands of Jews are sighing. They have been expelled from their homeland and their home to become wanderers. The Holy One will not do anything unjust. It is forbidden for us to question the Holy One, heaven forbid. As the tribes [i.e., Joseph's brothers] said, "We are verily guilty concerning our brother, in that we saw the distress of his soul, when he besought us, and would not hear; therefore is this distress come upon us" [Genesis 42:21]. They did not pin it on accident, but said [the distress] was of the hand of God. We can only do penitent return (*teshuvah*). Every person should become embittered in his heart and say, "Woe, what have I done? I have sinned, I have transgressed, I have done wrong, I have not behaved as a Jew. I wanted to be Mr. Herrschaft. That is why these troubles have come upon us. It was [the resultant] jealousy toward us which caused it." [Yitsḥak] Abravanel writes that this is what caused the exile from Spain and Portugal. Every person should say, "I will go and repent" [source uncertain]. The purpose of the troubles is that we do penitent return. [. . .]

At this time there are unheard-of troubles for Israel. The people who passed in a transport through Grosswardein (Oradea) had swastikas [branded into] their faces and their flesh. Some had no fingers; the evil ones bit them off. There were those whose fingernails were torn out and other such things. Things which wild animals do. Some think this is an accident. In Germany the people are educated. How could such cruelty be found among people? Expelling people and taking their wealth to the last penny? With such great troubles? [No.] It is the hand of God, on account of the greatness of the sins that were done in Germany. [The Jews in Germany] assimilated among the gentiles. For several generations they married non-Jewish wives. A certain rabbi expelled from Germany was told that God was right in His judgment against them. The rabbi told about hundreds of divorce decrees which he wrote for people who came from Russia and Poland to live in Germany. They sent the divorce decrees to their wives and they all married gentile women. Similarly, in Vienna there was no end to the sins committed by Jewish daughters who came from Poland, including daughters and granddaughters of rabbis and Hasidic *Rebbes*. They sat in their houses on the third floor while their daughters, wives, and granddaughters went to the theater, and on and on.

There were still Jews in Vienna who were pious and God fearing, but as the rabbinic Sages said in B. T. *Baba Kamma* 92a, "They are also taken out to be punished." It says in the Torah portion *Beshallaḥ* [Exodus 13:17–17:16] that there were evildoers who went out to collect manna on the Sabbath, and God said to Moses, "How long refuse ye to keep My commandments and My laws [Torah]?" [Exodus 16:28]. It is difficult to understand why He would punish the innocent. But one cannot question this. It is God's judgment. When God will help us and redeem us, we will understand all this. In the meantime, heaven forbid that we should open our mouths to speak evil or to question Him. We should repent as our ancestors did in Egypt. Most certainly the Holy One will save us and the salvation will be very soon. But everything depends on the gravity of our transgressions. Moreover, the sins and inequities should pain us more than the troubles.

We find in the midrash for the Torah portion *Toldot* [Genesis 25:19–28:9], that Isaac our patriarch says, "The voice is the voice of Jacob, but the hands are the hands of Esau" [Genesis 27:22]. Eunomos of Gedera was a great sage among the nations of the world. The people of the nations came and asked him if they could mate with Israel, heaven forbid, in order to cause Israel evil and troubles. He said to them:

> Go and look at the synagogues and study houses. If the children are raising their voices [studying Torah] then you can do nothing against them. If not, then you can prevail against them. For their patriarch assured them saying, "The voice is the voice of Jacob. As long as the voice of Jacob is in the synagogue and study house, the hands of Esau will not prevail." [*Midrash Bereshit Rabbah*, *Parashah* 65, *Siman* 20]

[. . .] That is, when the voice is the voice of Jacob and the written Torah and the oral Torah are being studied, the hands of Esau have no power over us. This is excellent, blessed be God.

As over against this we need to understand the statement, "But the hands are the hands of Esau" [Genesis 27:22]. Does it mean, heaven forbid, the contrary? [. . .] In my humble opinion, we need to see what is written in Isaiah 10:5, "O Asshur, the rod of mine anger. In whose hand as a staff is My fury." Rashi writes, "I have made Assyria the rod of My anger to subdue My people with it and the staff is My anger in the hands of the Assyrians." David Altschuler, the author of *Metsudot Dovid*, comments that the anger present when God is angry over Israel, is [materialized] in the hands of the Assyrians as the staff. Through it, God punishes Israel according to His will. If so, when the nations of the world rise up against us, it is the staff of the Holy One that is rising up. It is not their [own] hands. From their hands we have nothing to fear. As King David said in Psalms 119:161, "Princes have persecuted me without cause. But my heart standeth in awe of Thy words." Holy texts have commented on this: "When princes persecute me without reason, it is in vain and does nothing for them. But my heart fears Your word. That is, my fear is that You command them to do this and that it comes from Your word" [source uncertain]. If so, there is nothing for us to fear except if the hands of Esau are the hands of the Holy One, the rod of His wrath. Surely, if Israel observes the Torah and the voice of Jacob is heard in the synagogue and the study house, then the hands will remain the hands of Esau and not those of the Holy One. Obviously they will not be able to have power over us. Let this be understood.

Therefore, we need to do penitent return. This is the essence of the fast: to repair and to remove the obstacles, as the rabbinic Sages said. It is the same in the *Shulḥan Arukh, Oraḥ Ḥayim, Siman* 576:15. If we take it upon ourselves to observe the holy Sabbath, the laws of family purity, and not to eat nonkosher meat or other forbidden foods and to strengthen the holy Torah, then God will certainly hear our voices and will have mercy. He will relate to us mercifully and redeem us from our troubles. Our enemies will wither away and His holy name will be sanctified in the world.

The rabbinic Sages said in B. T. *Ḥagigah* 9b, "The Holy One did not find an attribute for Israel as good as poverty." The reason is contained in the explanation of Rabbi Ḥananel: In order that we should have a broken heart, He sends us troubles and poverty." If we already have a heart broken into pieces as we do today, it is appropriate for the Holy One not to conduct Himself with us with this good attribute any longer [. . .] Because in our day we [already] have a broken and depressed heart. God should [rather] have mercy on us. He should bring down and destroy our enemies before our eyes and before those of the whole world. He should sanctify His great name in the world, and send us our righteous Messiah, speedily in our days, amen.

Concerning that which I wrote above, it would seem that we can interpret what King David, of blessed memory, said in Psalms 51:19, "The sacrifices of God are a broken spirit; a broken and a contrite heart, O God, Thou wilt not despise." We have to understand that King David said first that a contrite spirit is a sacrifice to God, like an offering. Do not turn around and despise it, saying that it is much less than a sacrifice. Do not despise it. It would seem that David's enemies despised him and said despicable things about him and shamed him. King David, of blessed memory, asked: "Is not the reason for the troubles, that I should have a contrite heart and a broken heart, which is as precious in Your eyes as a sacrifice? My heart is certainly [already] broken within me." Concerning this, King David said, "The sacrifices of God are a broken spirit" [Psalms 51:19]. That is, "Whoever has a broken heart is as precious in Your eyes as a sacrifice. Therefore, I ask out of a broken and contrite heart: 'Master of the universe, Do not allow the one who has a broken heart to be despised and do not allow me to be despised.'" Let this be understood.

NOTE
Words in brackets appear in the original translation.

Translated by Gershon Greenberg.

Other works by Ehrenreich: *Even shlemah, Lekhem Shelomo* (1924); *Tiyul be-fardes* (1939–1942).

Moshe Kroneh

1913–1993

Moshe Kroneh was an Israeli educator affiliated with the religious Zionist movement. In 1945, he was the first Bnai Akiva *shaliaḥ* (envoy) to the United States. He later headed the Department of Torah and Culture of the World Zionist Organization and the religious education department of the Jewish Agency.

On Our Movement in These Days
1939

Letter 11, December 1939 (Delivered at the Kibbutz Council in Ramat Hashomron)

Despair before loss. The first reaction in relation to our world movement and its status in wartime was among many: despair and loss of faith. The first reports from the movement front in embattled Europe had not yet arrived and there were not yet reports on the results of the war in Poland in its initial stage, and there were already many among us, and perhaps the vast majority, who hastened to issue a verdict of extinction on the movement. Forgotten in a moment were the mighty efforts invested in this movement, in its education and development over many years. [. . .] This strange phenomenon was not only peculiar to us. Even in the leadership of the major Zionist institutions they hurried to evince despair and mock those who ventured to say in those alarming days of the beginning of the war that the more the Zionist educational and party activity intensified—in the end the more it would exist and grow anew despite the harsh blows of the hour. [. . .]

Decrees of destruction and martyrdom. It is quite unnecessary to explain what would be our lot in the near future if there were truth in all the dark predictions that were forecast beforehand. The aim is to design the spiritual character of our movement in Israel without the wellspring of forces of the movement in Poland and the two Galicias. It seems that this was, God forbid, an irreparable loss. However, this description is at the moment superfluous. The facts and events whose echoes reach us from across borders testify that if indeed the foundation has been shaken and if indeed Polish Jewry, and with it our movement, have been dealt a harsh blow—then in the ideological and movement sense we have not been defeated or dealt a blow. The movement mechanism has been shattered and the organizational instruments broken, but the ideological spirit, the faith in the God of Israel and in the destiny of the Jewish people, the devotion to our values, have intensified and become firmly established in these very days. [. . .]

However, concerning Nazified Poland it would seem that our calculation was nonetheless overly optimistic. We knew in advance what this barbaric regime was liable to inflict on Polish Jewry devoted to tradition and the values of the Jewish people. We surmised beforehand that the body of Israel would suffer here together with its civilian and economic status, but we did not conceive that the axe would be raised over the soul of the nation here too and in such a terrible manner. The reports arriving from afar tell of horrifying decrees—of spiritual destruction, the prohibition of Sabbath observance and Torah study, the burning of holy books and the destruction of synagogues, and that today it is difficult to distinguish one Jew from another—the bitter truth is that the contaminated Nazi axe is mainly raised over the head of faithful observant Jewry and the youth who remain faithful to the tradition of the fathers. The Nazis have apparently succeeded in seeing in this part of the Jewish people (how terrible are the attacks on the "Talmudists") the essence and leaven, the backbone of the people.

Let us console ourselves therefore again by the revelation of the light on the surface of this dark and depressing report. It seems that a mass *kiddush hashem* of Torah ve-Avoda and the Ha-Shomer ha-Dati youth appears in all its power and glory in Nazi Poland and on the borders in the north of the country. In these very days of siege and bloodshed they do not desecrate the Sabbath or indulge in forbidden foods; they observe the mitzvot behind closed doors. Letters tell us that precisely at this time religious faith among the great masses is increasing, even among those who have of late grown distant from it—suffering leading to full repentance. [. . .]

Translated by David Herman.

Other works by Kroneh: *Yavneh* (1946); *Ha-rav Meir Bar-Ilan* (1953); *Morai ve-rabotai, aḥai ve-reai* (1987).

Moshe Zvi Neriah
1913–1995

Moshe Zvi Neriah was an Israeli educator and politician. Born in Łódź, he was educated at yeshivas in Minsk and Shklov. He came to Palestine in 1930 and studied with Abraham Isaac Kook. Neriah was one of the founders of the Orthodox Bnai Akiva youth movement and for many years its spiritual leader. In 1940 he established the first Bnai Akiva yeshiva. He served in the Knesset from 1969 to 1974, representing the National Religious Party.

Issues of the Hour
1939

Lecture at the National Council of Bnei Akiva, Sukkot, 1939

This period of time is marked by four phenomena. Three of them concern everyone, and one concerns religious youth specifically.

1. Despair and powerlessness; 2. Loss of faith in the value of the modest enterprise; 3. Extreme egotistical aspirations; 4. Wayward religious thinking and disregard for the practice of the *mitsvot*.

We must direct our educational work to these. Not only in order to preserve what exists, but also to exploit the high spiritual tension of the current issues in order to deepen the appreciation of our own special content. [. . .]

3. Extreme Egotistical Aspirations

These days people have become more self-centered. Each wants to save his soul. The moment he might be in danger he discards the remnant of his morality. He wants to preserve and to fortify himself at all costs at the expense of others and on the ruin of others. This is the meaning of the profiteering phenomenon.

And yet, on the other hand, it is precisely these days which instill in us the understanding of the need for public discipline and public organization. The individual begins to appreciate more the importance of strengthening collective power, and he puts himself at the service of the public—the volunteering phenomenon.

The two phenomena together act alternately in a person's heart, and one must ensure that the second becomes increasingly dominant to the eventual exclusion of the first.

We must immediately adopt the slogan: From boy and girl friends to brothers and sisters! The club must turn into a big family home. Everyone will take a greater interest in the condition of his fellow.

We must urgently establish in branches "a mutual assistance fund," whose revenues will come not only from additions to the monthly membership fee but also from varied voluntary enterprises. Such activities, together with the information forthcoming in communal discussions, will make the youth aware of the issues of the hour and of its current obligations.

However, the group collective orientation in the organization as a whole must now receive additional reinforcement. We have to remember and reiterate: only our united collective strength will guarantee the existence and expansion of the Yishuv presence.

And from reinforcing help and shouldering the burden of the situation in the organization, in the movement, and in the Yishuv—to sympathizing with the troubles of "our brethren of the House of Israel as a whole, subject to misfortune and captivity."

The youth of Erets Yisrael have committed a sin. It did not know the diaspora nor did it suffer its tribulations. It was not sick for it, nor was it concerned for it. And will it now, too, seeing the destruction of the most important sector in the diaspora, remain nonchalant and indifferent?

The destruction of a Jewish community places additional obligations on existing groups. Two things will now be demanded of the youth in Erets Yisrael, and principally the religious youth: 1. To increase the spiritual and moral content of the Yishuv, in order to fill the vacuum; 2. To be prepared to act and rebuild ruins in the diaspora, as soon as it will be possible to do so.

3. Errors of Thinking on the Part of the Religious Person and Disregard for the Practice of the Mitzvot

The loss of hundreds of thousands of people—men, women, and children—arouses thoughts and questions concerning the divine order of the world and the leadership and providence of the Almighty. It is very difficult to justify the judgment. And one of the great Hasidim has already said, "You shall not do thus to the Lord your God—don't say yes to all the deeds of Hashem." However, if among the firm believers all the amazement and difficult questions end in one simple answer, "because His thoughts are not our thoughts and our ways

are not His ways," so among the tender youth the questions are liable to undermine belief in the heart and to make their souls fall victim to the war before they have reached the front.

Obviously, it is difficult to supply satisfactory answers to these questions, and, as stated, such things are beyond a person's understanding, but this does not exempt us from attempting to understand, to explain, and to clarify.

The best way is: broaden the historical view. The sting of events is removed by seeing them in their broad historic context, what preceded them and what is going to come after them.

Knowledge of what preceded explains to a large extent the "death by human hand" in the terrible war which is coming upon us, the death toll [. . .] and the subsequent hope which encourages and heralds a better future for humanity, for which it is worthwhile perhaps to make so many sacrifices.

As for laxity in the practice of *mitsvot*, this phenomenon is not associated particularly with weakness of thought. In most cases it is due to practical factors. Municipal military training has a markedly adverse effect on the Shabbat, as does camp life, both in terms of kashrut and prayer. And above all these: the excessive association with those who throw off the restraints of the Torah has a disastrous impact on the soul of the religious adult, to say nothing of that of the young person.

Of course, the main part of the struggle with these phenomena should be direct, by establishing religious units, etc. However, much can be achieved indirectly by immunizing the soul of the youth and its public religious consciousness, as well as by meticulous observance of the *mitsvot* in public, such as praying and learning together in public.

And finally: "If you see kingdoms making war—expect the footstep of the Messiah." The discovery of the depth of the evil necessarily drags after it the revelation of the depth of the good. Turn then, please, the horrors of the war into tremendous forces which will sever the chains of the Messiah and bring redemption to the world, redemption to the entire nation and the entire world.

Translated by David Herman.

Other works by Neriah: *Kuntres ha-vikuah: hilkhot ha-shabbat va-halikhot ha-medinah* (1951); *Ha-yahadut ha-datit ba-medinah* (1952).

Elimelech Neufeld

1892–1956

Elimelech Neufeld was a leader of Mizrahi, the religious Zionist party, and a member of the presidium of the World Zionist Organization. He attended every World Zionist Congress from the twelfth in 1921 until his death.

From Lack of Concern and from Lack of Feeling
1939

Well done! *Hatsofeh* was the first newspaper in Erets Yisrael to react to the indifference of the public in the Yishuv in general and the administration of the Jewish Agency in particular with regard to the tragedy and destruction of Polish Jewry. None of the newspapers in Israel has dealt at length until now with the lukewarm attitude of the Yishuv and the Sokhnut [Jewish Agency] administration toward what is now happening to the Jews in Poland. *Hatsofeh* did react to this. But this is not sufficient; we must protest incessantly concerning the destruction of Polish Jewry until a change of attitude takes place—the attitude of the Yishuv in Israel and that of the Jewish Agency.

If it were only possible to imagine or comprehend what the evil masters of wickedness have done to us over the past few months, with a degree of cruelty far in excess of what the Vandals achieved in their day. No feeling of compassion exists even toward the elderly and suckling babes. All are subject to abuse.

It is beyond the power of the pen of even the greatest poet in the world to put on paper the new elegy of the history of the Jewish people in Poland during the last four months.

Nevertheless, the people whose own flesh and blood are suffering this terrible ruin and destruction are not ashamed to raise their legs, not to kick at the wicked ones, but [. . .] to dance at parties.

Nevertheless, the leading elements in the Yishuv remain immersed in their daily concerns and fail to see a large and important part of Jewry plunged in torment and death throes.

The Nazis have talked of a "lightning war" against the great powers and have failed to achieve it. But they inflict on our brother Jews in Poland lightning annihilation and there is none to save or deliver them.

While it is true that there is war in the world and the sufferings of war are harsh, what is being done to our brothers and sisters in Poland is not war but extermination, extinction, and destruction.

And against such a process of extermination one must move heaven and earth. One must set in motion all the powers of influence of American Jewry and expedite real assistance and not simply make do with lamentation and eulogies.

The Yishuv has to play a very prominent part in the assistance work, for who else must feel the tremendous suffering and sorrow of the greater part of the Hebrew nation in Poland? What is our portion and what is our future without the source of Jewry in Poland? The Yishuv in Erets Yisrael should have taken the lead in initiating and promoting every act of assistance and rescue of the Jews of Poland. And not simply because the origin of more than half of the Yishuv is Poland, but in order to stress the importance of the center of the nation here, and to highlight the power of its feeling, the power of its involvement, and the power of its reaction to what is taking place in the Jewish world.

Translated by David Herman.

Elhanan Wasserman

Periodization of the Eras and the Evolution of the Generations
ca. 1939

Rabbi Elhanan related:

"I once asked the Hafetz Chaim:

"Granted that we are accustomed to a division of eras in Jewish religious history—the Tannaitic era separately, and the Amoraic era separately, the era of our rabbis the Savora'im separately, the era of the Geonim separately and the era of the Rishonim separately—one may concede that this division applies in the time of our sages of blessed memory, who possessed the power to distinguish the different eras, as they were aware of what was written in 'the *Sifra* of Primeval Adam,' i.e., 'Rabbi [Judah the Prince] represented the conclusion of the Mishnah; Rav Ashi and Ravina the conclusion of halakhic teaching' (b.Bava Metzia 85b). However, from then onward, where are the boundary lines to enable us to determine when a certain era ended and a fresh era commenced?"

The Hafetz Chaim replied to me:

"The successive generations are continually diminishing in focused learning, each generation being of lower standard than its predecessor, but the pace of the decrease within each era in itself varies in degree. A succeeding generation still retains some connection in its basic essence to a section of the previous generation; but when an era changes, an immense chasm is created at one stroke; the spiritual descent of the generation is then, insofar as its type of fall is concerned, like 'from a high rampart into a deep well'; and wherever one sees that the generation in general is not in the same category as the preceding one, one realizes that a new era has begun.

"There is this too: we possess a tradition that at the end of each era, there lives and flourishes a great man who is greater than virtually all the great ones of his era, and who, in his essential nature, is comparable to the previous generations; that is to say, that in accordance with his measure of greatness, he would have fitted in more appropriately with early periods. For instance, Rav Hai Gaon, the last scion of the Gaonic age, is considered the greatest among the Geonim, and solely on account of his greatness did one instinctively sense, when he departed this life, that his era had really and truly ended. There is generally nothing at all to which to compare it; and so it is upon every occasion when an era ends."

And Rabbi Elhanan added:

"He too—the Hafetz Chaim—marked the end of his age. As to when this era commenced, I do not know. Perhaps it was from the days of the Gaon R. Elijah [of Vilna], and possibly even before his time; but I do know when it ended. We feel that, after he was taken from us, a new era commenced in Israel. There is nothing at all with which to compare it. And since he was the last scion of his era, he was the greatest within it. His greatness did not bear any relationship to that of the sages of his generation, but was like a remnant of preceding generations."

Rabbi Elhanan similarly asked:

"For what purpose is the soul of an outstandingly great individual, belonging in its essence to a previous era, brought down into a later generation?"

And the response was:

"The generations are diminishing, progressing ever downward on the spiritual slope. It is the function of the greatest man of his generation to slow down the pace of the descent. But there are occasions where the descent is proceeding at such a high rate that no one can arrest its progress except for the soul of one of the genuine ancients!"

Translated by David E. Cohen.

Abraham Isaac Kook

On the Division between Zionism and Religion
Date Unknown

[. . .] I find myself obliged to commence with a general preface, which I bring to the fore on each occasion that I have occasion to speak about the way of "the Mizrachi" [movement] and its value: that there is one "statute" that it is obliged, in my view, to engrave on its banner, by means of which alone the light of its inner soul can shine forth upon it, freed from the shackles of self-contradiction weighing heavily upon it. This "statute" is: that "the Mizrachi" should express openly that despite the faithfulness that it always shows to general Zionism, from the aspect of its joining together with it in regard to the philosophy of nationalism and its realization in practice, it nonetheless battles against it in regard to that particular branch which is still solidly engraved within Zionism by reason of its First Congress, which declared that "Zionism has nothing in common with religion." This decree, in reality, makes all the "Mizrachist" propaganda fraudulent, since "Mizrachi" stands firmly upon the plain of Torah, and the word of the Almighty is a lamp to its feet; and we, all those of perfect faith within Israel, are clearly aware that it is only upon the quality of the faithful connection of the nation, in its entirety, to our Torah way of life—that Torah of the Almighty which is perfect—that the success of Zionism, and the instant prevalence of its force for succeeding generations, depends, and there is no expectation or hope to be entertained by virtue of the abandonment of Torah, and every blossom is bound to be as rottenness and every root as stone—and how will "the Mizrachi" be able silently to transgress this statute, which uproots the entire burden of its soul? In my humble opinion, there is no hope for "the Mizrachi" unless it states in plain terms that for all its love for Zionism in general, and for all that the alien and far-removed deeds and views of many within Zionism cannot cause it any reverse or any waning of strength, thereby allowing it to abandon its diligent work on the plain of national revival in the ancestral land in particular—notwithstanding all this, it battles with all its might against this shameful declaration; and it will neither remain tranquil nor at rest until such time as it has toppled it from the high altar of Zionism, and in its stead will be engraved the statute for Israel as it is in reality: "Remember His covenant forever, the word which He commanded to a thousand generations; the covenant which He made with Abraham, and His oath to Isaac, and established it to Jacob for a statute, to Israel for an everlasting covenant, saying: 'Unto you will I give the land of Canaan, as the lot of your inheritance.'" The vehement opposition to the aforementioned elevated statute must of necessity project forth through all the corners of the Mizrahi. It needs to be reiterated many thousands of times over, at every assembly, whether a freshly convened one or a preexisting one. [. . .]

[. . .] Broad general Zionism, by dint of its program, is incapable of speaking in the name of the people as a whole in any manner whatsoever. The clause that "Zionism has nothing in common with religion" represents, in the first place, a complete reversal of what the whole nation has been thinking, imagining, hoping, and believing throughout its generations, and the complete reversal of the noble aspiration that the *bien-pensants* within Jewry and among the gentile nations have been thinking in relation to the future Jewish destiny in the world. The nation as a whole, for all its greatness and spiritual power, for all the pride of its soul, cannot be limited, in any way whatsoever, exclusively to the narrow circle of the vision of Dr. Herzl of blessed memory, despite all its beauty and strength, in accordance with its worth. Zionism, practical and theoretical, political and diplomatic, and all its various branches together, in the form that they have emerged from potential to material realization to this day, contain within them exalted and superior elements, which we are called upon, from the very depths of our Jewish existence, to support with all the material and spiritual forces at our disposal; but all these in conjunction are no more than the Zionist body. However, we are imminently called upon to inject a spiritual element onto this carved-up corpse, so that it should really become worthy of its name, in such manner that it will acquire for itself, both instantly and for succeeding generations, that great magnetic force that will enable it to draw the entire nation toward it, from their greatest to their smallest, from all the various parties, ranks of men, groups, and scattered, unattached elements, and that it may give the wider world the same concept as the source of Zionism—namely, the sacred, divine source, the Bible—gives to it, along with the full profundity and splendor of tradition. It is not solely the echoed sound of a voice, contending that if the nation that is hated by the world is now in the process of seeking a secure haven of refuge from its persecutors. It is is only right that this eternal movement should have its life restored to it, but it is rather that the holy nation, the special treasure among the peoples, Judah, the lion's whelp, has awoken from its long, deep slumber, and is now returning to its heritage, to "the pride of Jacob, whom He loves—Selah!" And it is impossible for this spiritual notion to be injected into the movement for so long as the mark of Cain is engraved upon its forehead, declaring that "Zionism has nothing in common with religion."

[. . .] The riots, the delay in further progress, and the cheapening of the value of the revival—all these factors—the results of this fearsome agreed statement, that Zionism has nothing in common with religion, we can see all too abundantly in every corner of the world where the movement exists, and in particular, "Zionism has nothing in common with religion"—can instantly be interpreted to express the idea: "Zionism destroys religion" or "Zionism is a new living entity, which hopes to be constructed upon the ruins of the ancient tradition." This is already a familiar maxim in the mouths of not just a few upstarts, and the practical results of this are: severing the yoke of heaven, and public denigration of the sacred values of the nation, through the existence of nationalism, in literature, in educational institutions and in numerous corners of the fields of the revival. What do all of these achieve?—An emptiness in the spirit of the nation, despair and enmity and the fury of deadly venom, which is ready to be transmitted as an inheritance to future generations, this being applicable to the entire movement.

[. . .] It is not by virtue of the spirit of modern European literature that we yearn to arise and to become a nation—despite the fact that we imbibe all the general humanistic values common among men possessed of high culture—but by virtue of the spirit of our Torah, by virtue of the spirit of our prophets, by virtue of the spirit of the Lord God of Israel resting upon His people, in such manner that it cannot be severed from the Torah and its revival, insofar as it is the heritage of the congregation of Jacob. The divine ideals, which constitute the life of the Torah and of prophecy—these are, by dint of our spirit, the future destiny of the world, for it is our revival that leads towards their realization in life. We aspire to stand at the center of humanity but only with our ancient and exalted standard, which is for us the source of everlasting pride. In the name of our God will we set up our banners, and, as in days of yore, we will not alter or exchange it for another banner, even for the most modern kind. [. . .]

[. . .] Zionism cannot find its full justification in the fact that it is a "modern" movement, as not everything that is "modern" is correct. Even cruel warfare is "a modern movement," and in any event look at how much wickedness there is involved in it. And "modernity" per se is still unable to travel entirely along this path without inquiring as to the views of every individual. On the contrary, in a "modern movement," which is based upon some firm principle, anyone who explicitly destroys that principle, through his disclosed views, by his utterances, and in practical terms, in a decisive manner, cannot be accepted as a befitting force within that movement. The eternal strength of the people of Israel is its spiritual life, through which it fortifies itself with a stronger measure of confidence than all the high walls of all the kingdoms of the gentile nations, and it is inconceivable that this protective wall should become ownerless property, free for anyone who so desires to sling stones at it, to make breaches in it, in a definite and permanent form.

[. . .] The question, regarded from the perspective of "statehood" and "religion," is a complete side issue. The evaluation of the Jewish people in the Land of Israel is inherently manifest, that it stands above any normal measurement of "statehood" and "religion," and when the spirit of the nation within it becomes fortified as a result of its return to its land and its realm, its valued ancient treasures will begin to emerge into the light of the world, and the spirit of prophecy in its divine majesty will come forth from its hiding place, and will be elevated above all those notions of "freedom of speech," which are merely apparent and transient, that are operative in countries that are civilized, by the standards of the ethos of our era. And is it not inevitable that, in the course of a certain period of time, a revolutionary reli-

gious movement will emerge out of the might of Israel, to purify and to refine all the forms of dross of idol worship and of crass materialism that are circulating within the ethos of the nations and of the various religions, in order to refine all the arrangements of the spirit of mankind, in such manner that it will be adequately prepared for acceptance of the virtues of peace and of absolute liberty, [as scripture declares]: "And I shall remove his blood from his mouth, and his abominations from between his teeth, and he too will remain a devotee of our God" and [as the rabbis state]: "The theaters and circuses in places outside the Land are destined to become locations in which the princes of Judah will teach Torah in public" (b.Megillah 6)—whether this be a political type of Torah, bringing good tidings of forthcoming peace and liberty, in accordance with the view of the Tosafists that within [these theaters and circuses] are the ordinary houses of popular associations, or whether it be a spiritual type of Torah, illumined by the purity of the light of knowledge of the divine truth and the love of the ways of the Almighty within the life of both the individual and society at large, in accordance with the view of Rashi in [tractate] Megillah, and it will then become elevated beyond the parameters of this specific question. To summarize the matter: The state will be called "the Land of Israel," and the valued treasure of Israel, in its purified form, will exercise dominion there; and even if, at the outset, it occasionally suffers from some turbulent winds, all things will ultimately attain a state of tranquility by virtue of the light of life emanating from the soul of the life of worlds, which is about to effect the revival of His especially treasured nation upon its desirable land. [. . .]

Translated by David E. Cohen.

VISUAL CULTURE

In the interwar years, Jews were prominent in movements that changed the face of the visual and plastic arts. While historically few Jews took up painting or sculpture, this began to change in the early twentieth century, and by the 1920s and 1930s Jewish artists were in the thick of modernist trends. Not all artists of Jewish descent, of course, pursued Jewish themes and subjects in their work. Some, like Amedeo Modigliani, were indifferent to their origins. Those whose work is reproduced in this section identified themselves in one way or another as Jewish and frequently introduced visual markers of this into their work. Some saw their work in the context of the cultural revival of the Jewish nation, especially those who settled in the Land of Israel. Given the large number of Jews who made their mark as artists in the interwar period, we have included, from necessity, only one work of art for each artist, with a few exceptions.

The maps in this section show how the outcomes of World War I dissolved four empires and created new states (Estonia, Czechoslovakia, Latvia, Lithuania, and Yugoslavia) and reestablished Poland as an independent state.

Solomon Yudovin

1892–1954

Born in Beshenkovichi, a village near Vitebsk (today in Belarus), Solomon Yudovin was a Russian graphic artist and book illustrator. Unlike his contemporaries Marc Chagall and El Lissitzky, he was not a modernist and worked within a figurative, realist tradition throughout his life. He is known especially for his woodcuts and linocuts of Jewish life in the Pale of Settlement and for his series of Jewish folk ornaments.

Yidishe Folkspartei Election Poster
ca. 1918

The Moldovan Family Collection.

געזעלשאפט משה בראדצערזאן.

חנוך באָרצינסקי   „יוחנן המטביל"

Henryk (Hanokh) Barcinski

1896–ca. 1941

Henryk Barcinski was a Polish-born painter and graphic illustrator who worked in the expressionist manner. He studied in Łódź, Warsaw, and Dresden and lived in Berlin from 1927 to 1934, when he returned to Łódź. He was associated with the Yung-yidish group from 1919 to 1921. His linocut of John the Baptist is representative of the group's rebellion against the conventions of Jewish piety and respect-ability. He died in the Tomaszów Mazowiecki ghetto during World War II.

John the Baptist
1919

Yaacov Ben-Dov

1882–1968

Born in a Ukrainian shtetl near Kiev, Yaacov Ben-Dov (b. Lasutra) was a pioneer of both still photography and motion pictures in the Land of Israel. He moved to Palestine in 1907 and continued his studies at the Bezalel Academy of Arts and Design, where he later taught photography. He began filming key historical events in 1917 and made nine films between 1918 and 1932, which the Zionist movement used worldwide to garner support. He retired from filmmaking in the early 1930s as a result of his inability to adjust to the introduction of sound.

Bezalel Student as Ruth the Moabite
1919

Israel Museum Collection. Purchased with the help of Rena (Fisch) and Robert Lewin, London. B01.0119/n308.

Joseph (Iosif) Chaikov

1888–1979

The Kiev-born graphic designer and sculptor Joseph Chaikov belonged to the group of young Jewish artists who studied and worked in Paris before and after World War I. He returned to Kiev in 1914 and was a cofounder of the Kultur Lige in 1918. He illustrated children's books and produced billboards and other forms of propaganda. He moved to Moscow in 1923 and concentrated on sculpture, at first in the style of cubo-futurism, and later, after the crackdown on artistic freedom, in the style of socialist realism. His work figured prominently in the Soviet pavilions at the Paris (1937) and New York (1939) world's fairs.

Front cover illustration for Hans Christian Andersen's Finf arbeslakh *(Five Peas)*
1919

General Modern Collection, Beinecke Rare Book & Manuscript Library, Yale University.

Marcel Janco

1895–1984

The avant-garde artist, architect, and art theorist Marcel Janco was born into an upper-middle-class home in Bucharest. He lived in Zurich from 1914 to 1921, where he took a leading role in the city's bohemian cultural scene, cofounding the Dadaist movement, along with his fellow Romanian Tristan Tzara (né Samy Rosenstock). He broke with Dadaism in 1919 and became a leading proponent of East European constructivism. In January 1941, he and his family fled Bucharest and settled in Mandate Palestine. In 1953, he founded the artists' colony Ein Hod, southeast of Haifa.

Portrait of Tzara (Mask)
1919

Photo: Philippe Migeat, Musée National d'Art Moderne, © CNAC / MNAM / Dist. RMN-Grand Palais / Art Resource, NY, © 2015 Artists Rights Society (ARS), New York / ADAGP, Paris.

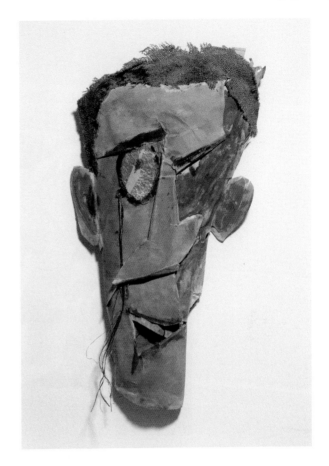

Jacob Kramer

1892–1962

The painter Jacob Kramer was born in Ukraine and moved with his family to Leeds in 1900. He studied at the Leeds School of Art from 1907 to 1913 and at the Slade School of Art in London from 1913 to 1914. His paintings were included in the Jewish section of the landmark 1914 Whitechapel exhibition of modern art. His early works, including his later masterpiece *Day of Atonement*, were strikingly original examples of English expressionism. In the 1920s he returned to Leeds and his career took a downturn. He lived in alcohol-soaked poverty, producing second-rate portraits of local figures.

The Day of Atonement
1919

Leeds Museums and Galleries (Leeds Art Gallery) U.K. / The Bridgeman Art Library. The Estate of John David Roberts. By Permission of the William Roberts Society.

El Lissitzky

1890–1941

El Lissitzky, a native of Pochinok, Russia, was an active participant in the creation of a new Jewish art in Russia in the years before and after the revolution. He studied drawing with Yehudah Pen in Vitebsk, pursued architectural engineering in Darmstadt, and traveled extensively in Europe, visiting galleries and sketching buildings and landscapes. He returned to Russia in 1914 and participated in the Jewish Historical and Ethnographic Society's expeditions in the summers of 1915 and 1916. He published drawings of synagogue frescoes, illustrated Yiddish and Hebrew books, and participated in 1917 in the first exhibition of Jewish artists in Moscow. Beginning in 1919, he

began to relinquish the idea of creating a Jewish national style and increasingly adopted the nonrepresentational supremacist style. In the 1920s and 1930s, he was an innovative presence in the world of Soviet art as an abstract painter, graphic designer, architect, pavilion designer, typographer, and photographer.

The Fire Came and Burnt the Stick
1919

From *Had Gadya Suite* (Tale of a Goat), 1919. © 2015 Artists Rights Society (ARS), New York. Image courtesy of the YIVO Institute for Jewish Research.

Abraham Manievich

1881–1942

The Russian-born painter Abraham Manievich studied painting in Kiev and Munich and enjoyed early success. After the Russian Revolution, he returned to Kiev, where he taught until immigrating to the United States in 1921. His most striking work is in the cubo-futurist style. The mislabeled *Destruction of the Ghetto, Kiev* (there was no ghetto in Kiev), with its harsh angularity, refers to the Kiev pogrom of 1919, in which one of his sons was killed. The stray goat in the foreground is a symbol of the once-vibrant Jewish community of the city.

Destruction of the Ghetto
1919

The Jewish Museum, New York / Art Resource, NY. Gift of Deana Bezark in memory of her husband Leslie Bezark. Accession number 1991–30. Photo by John Parnell.

Ludwig Meidner
1884–1966

The expressionist painter and printmaker Ludwig Meidner was born in Silesia and studied art in Breslau (Wrocław, now in Poland) and Paris. He was a radical exponent of expressionism and a champion of pacifism and socialism. From 1912, he produced a series of "apocalyptic landscapes" envisioning the catastrophic collapse of the German city that eerily presaged later events, and after World War I a series of portraits of prophets. In 1939, he and his artist wife, Else, fled to England, where he was interned for a time on the Isle of Man as an enemy alien. Unrecognized in Britain, he returned to Germany in 1953, while his wife remained in London.

The Prophet
1919

Photo: © Stiftung Museum Kunstpalast—Horst Kolberg—ARTOTHEK. © Ludwig Meidner-Archiv, Jüdisches Museum Frankfurt.

Lasar Segall
1891–1957

The son of a Torah scribe in Vilna, Lasar Segall traveled alone at age fifteen to Berlin to study art. He became involved with the expressionist school, and his work, like that of many German expressionists, dealt with the themes of poverty, powerlessness, and social deprivation. In 1923, he settled in Brazil, where three of his siblings were already living. Though geographically distant from the horrors that engulfed Europe in the late 1930s and 1940s, in his work he powerfully addressed the upheaval, dislocation, and brutality unfolding there.

Eternal Wanderers
1919

Lasar Segall Museum. IBRAM/MinC. Photo by Jorge Bastos.

Max Weber

1881–1961

The Polish-born artist Max Weber was one of the pioneers of modernism in the United States. His family settled in Brooklyn when he was ten. From 1898 to 1900, he was a student at the Pratt Institute in Brooklyn, where he studied under Arthur Wesley Dow, who introduced him to new approaches to creating art. After teaching at public schools in Virginia and Minnesota, he moved to Paris in 1905 and immersed himself in modernist art circles. He returned to New York in 1909 and introduced cubism to America. Although the initial critical response to his paintings was hostile, a more positive appreciation emerged over time. In 1930, the Museum of Modern Art honored him with a retrospective of his work, the first solo exhibition of an American artist at the museum. After World War I, his style became less avant-garde and more representational and expressionist.

Sabbath
1919

The Jewish Museum, New York / Art Resource, NY. Gift of Joy S. Weber, 2005-51. Photo by John Parnell. Estate of Max Weber.

Avraham Soskin
1881–1963

The Russian-born photographer Avraham Soskin came to Palestine in 1905, settling in the German Colony in Jerusalem. His photographs of the birth, construction, and growth of early Tel Aviv are a valuable source for the city's history. One in particular has become iconic: his photograph of the lottery of housing parcels on the sand dunes three kilometers north of Jaffa, the future site of Tel Aviv, on April 11, 1909.

Tents of New Immigrants in the Vicinity of Allenby Street, Tel Aviv
Early 1920s

Soskin Collection, Eretz Israel Museum, Tel Aviv.

Boris Aronson

1898–1980

The well-known American set designer Boris Aronson was born in Kiev and came of age during the Russian Revolution. Initially, he worked in various media: painting, sculpture, and costume design, as well as scenic design. While in Moscow, he embraced the constructivist style. He left the Soviet Union and, after a short time in Berlin, settled on the Lower East Side of New York City in 1923. He began designing sets and costumes for the more experimental Yiddish theaters and then, in the early 1930s, began to work on Broadway. He was responsible for the design of major Broadway productions, including *The Crucible*, *The Diary of Anne Frank*, *Fiddler on the Roof*, *Cabaret*, *Follies*, and *A Little Night Music*. He won the Tony Award for set design six times.

Shtetl

1920

In Boris Aronson, *Sovremyennaya evreiskaya grafika* (Berlin: Petropolis, 1924), 44. The Dorot Jewish Division, The New York Public Library, Astor, Lenox, and Tilden Foundations. The Russian publisher reproduced this woodcut backwards, hence the reversal of Hebrew letters spelling *kosher* on the storefront at the left side of the image.

Menachem Birnbaum

1893–1944?

Born in Vienna, the book illustrator and portrait painter Menachem Birnbaum was the son of the ideologically peripatetic activist Nathan Birnbaum. He lived in Berlin from 1911 to 1914 and then from 1919 to 1933, when he moved to the Netherlands. He was arrested by the Germans in 1943. The violence and horror of his expressionist illustrations of the song "Had Gadya" (from the Passover seder) are a commentary on the tumult of World War I and its aftermath.

"The Shohet" (illustration in Chad Gadjo*)*

1920

Illustration in *Chad Gadjo* (Berlin: Welt Verlag, 1920). Courtesy of The Library of The Jewish Theological Seminary.

David Bomberg

1890–1957

The painter David Bomberg was one of the "White-chapel Boys," the cohort of Jewish writers and painters who emerged from the immigrant quarter of East London in the early twentieth century. He studied at the Slade School of Fine Art from 1911 to 1913 but was expelled for the radicalism of his style, which was influenced by Italian futurism and cubism. After the war, his style changed and he began to focus on landscapes. From 1923 to 1927, he painted and sketched in Mandate Palestine with the financial support of the Zionist movement. He is considered one of the greatest painters of twentieth-century Britain.

Ghetto Theatre

1920

© 2015 Artists Rights Society (ARS), New York / DACS, London. Courtesy of Ben Uri, the London Jewish Museum of Art.

Vincent Brauner (Yitskhok Broyner)

1887–1944

The son of a wealthy industrialist from Łódź, Vincent Brauner studied painting in Warsaw, Kraków, and Berlin. Taking the name Vincent in tribute to Van Gogh, he was a member of the avant-garde artistic and literary circle Yung-yidish in Łódź (1918–1921). He continued to paint in the Łódź ghetto after the German conquest of Poland.

Woodcut No. 1

1920

In Moyshe Broderzon, *Tkhiyes-hameysim* (Lodz: Yung-yidish, 1920). JT1 PJ5129.A4 B75 T4. Courtesy of The Library of The Jewish Theological Seminary.

Yitshak Frenkel (Alexandre Frenkel-Frenel)

1899–1981

The painter Yitshak Frenkel was born in Odessa, where he first studied painting. He came to Mandate Palestine in 1919, but then studied and painted in Paris from 1920 to 1925. When he returned to Palestine in 1925, he opened the Histadrut Art School in Tel Aviv. His work was closer to abstractionism than to the orientalism that was popular in interwar Palestine. Some consider him the first abstract Israeli artist.

Man with Torah

1920

Ben Uri Gallery, The London Jewish Museum of Art. © Estate of Yitshak Frenkel-Frenel.

Max Liebermann

1847–1935

The son of a wealthy Berlin textile manufacturer, the painter Max Liebermann was a dominant figure in the German art world in the late-Imperial and Weimar periods. He was a leading proponent of impressionism and led the then avant-garde Berlin Sezession from 1899 to 1911. He was famous for his portraits (more than two hundred commissions) and his scenes of bourgeois life. He was elected president of the Prussian Academy of Art in 1920 and served until 1933.

Self-Portrait
1920

The Israel Museum, Jerusalem. Gift of Jean Weinblatt, Milan. B52.2156. Photo © The Israel Museum, Jerusalem, by Elie Posner.

Bruno Schulz

1892–1942

The Polish short-story writer Bruno Schulz was also a gifted painter and graphic artist. While little of his work survived World War II, the pen-and-ink drawings that did are remarkable, especially the erotic ones that were drawn to illustrate Leopold von Sacher-Masoch's novella *Venus in Furs* (1870) and that were published posthumously. *The Meeting* is his only surviving oil painting.

The Meeting: A Jewish Youth and Two Women in an Urban Alley
1920

Adam Mickiewicz Museum of Literature in Warsaw.

משה בראדערזאן

די מלכה שבא.

Moyshe Broderzon

1890–1956

Moyshe Broderzon was born into a wealthy merchant family in Moscow. He lived in Łódź from 1918 to 1939 and was a founder of the Yung-yidish group. When the Germans invaded Poland, he fled to Moscow. In Stalin's crackdown on Jewish cultural activity, he was sent to a Siberian labor camp in 1948. Released in 1955 and repatriated to Poland, he died soon after his return. He was a man of many talents: he wrote poetry,

journalism, drama, songs for children, and libretti for opera. He founded little theaters, produced plays and puppet shows, and even turned his hand to prints and drawings.

Cover, Di malke Shvo: dramatishe poeme
1921

Cover, *Di malke Shvo: dramatishe poeme* (Łódź: Yung-yidish, 1921). Courtesy of the YIVO Institute for Jewish Research.

Jacob Epstein

1889–1959

The pioneering modernist sculptor Jacob Epstein was born on the Lower East Side of New York. He studied art in New York and Paris and settled in London in 1905. Much of his early work, with its explicit sexuality, rough-hewn composition, and indebtedness to non-European sculptural traditions, challenged taboos on what was appropriate for public art and aroused intense controversy. Later he became known for his bronze sculptures of the heads of public figures. Jacob Kramer (1892–1962) was an expressionist artist living in Leeds.

Jacob Kramer

1921

©The estate of Sir Jacob Epstein. ©Tate, London 2013. Photo credit: Tate, London / Art Resource, NY.

Isidor Kaufmann

1853–1921

The painter Isidor Kaufmann was born in Arad (now in Romania), where his father commanded a Hungarian army regiment in the imperial army. He studied art in Budapest and in Vienna, where he spent the remainder of his life. He was known for his romantic, exquisitely detailed portraits of traditional Jews and genre scenes of Jewish life in East Central Europe. Painted with great sensitivity and emotion, they take no note of the poverty, persecution, and forces of modernity that were transforming traditional Jewish society.

Of the High Priest's Tribe

1921

The Jewish Museum, New York. Bequest of Helen Kaufmann, 2010-4. Photo by Richard Goodbody, Inc. Image courtesy of The Jewish Museum, New York / Art Resource, NY.

Gyula Pap

1899–1983

Born in Hungary, Gyula Pap moved with his family at age fourteen to Vienna. He studied art in Vienna and Budapest and metalwork at the Bauhaus school of art and architecture in Weimar from 1920 to 1923. He taught in Berlin from 1926 to 1933. With the rise of the Nazis, he moved to Budapest, where he lived until his death. He worked in several mediums: oil painting, typography, photography, textile design, graphic art, and industrial design.

Seven-Branched Candelabrum
1922

The Jewish Museum. Purchase: Hubert J. Brandt Gift in honor of his wife, Frances Brandt; Judaica Acquisitions Fund; Mrs. J. J. Wyle, by exchange; Peter Cats Foundation, Helen and Jack Cytryn, and Isaac Pollack Gifts, 1991-106. Photo by Richard Goodbody, Inc. © 2015 Artists Rights Society (ARS), New York / HUNGART, Budapest. Image courtesy of The Jewish Museum, New York / Art Resource, NY.

Henryk Berlewi

1894–1967

The painter, graphic designer, and typographer Henryk Berlewi was born into a polonized Warsaw Jewish family. He trained in Warsaw, Antwerp, and Paris and became known for his theater posters, book jackets, and page designs in Hebrew and Yiddish. In the 1920s, he took up constructivist abstraction, creating paintings employing simple geometric forms. In 1928, after moving from Warsaw to Paris, he abandoned the avant-garde and began painting portraits and nudes in a figurative style. He survived the war in Nice, serving in the Resistance, and in 1957 returned to painting abstract works, which are often considered precursors of op art.

Cover of Albatros, *no. 3*
1923

Courtesy of the YIVO Institute for Jewish Research.

Leonid Pasternak

1862–1945

The impressionist painter Leonid Pasternak was born in Odessa and trained there and in Munich. In 1889, he settled in Moscow, where he taught from 1894 to 1918. Although not a nationalist painter, he often painted Jewish subject matter and was close to Jewish intellectual circles. He moved to Berlin in 1921, leaving behind in Moscow his son, the poet and novelist Boris Pasternak, a convert to Russian Ortho-doxy who shared none of his father's Jewish interests. Leonid Pasternak lived in Berlin until 1938, when he fled to Great Britain, living first in London and then Oxford.

Portrait of Saul Tchernichovski
1923

Collection Tel Aviv Museum of Art. Gift of the artist, Berlin, 1935.

Reuven Rubin

1893–1974

The Israeli painter Reuven Rubin was born in an
isolated village in Romania. He studied at the newly
founded Bezalel School in Jerusalem for a year and
then for several years in Paris. After World War I, he
lived in Italy, the United States, and Romania. He
settled permanently in the Land of Israel in 1922 and
became one of its best-known painters. He is most
known for his figurative paintings of the life and
landscape of the Jewish homeland, which he rendered
in an orientalized, idealized manner.

First Fruits
1923

Rubin Museum, Tel Aviv.

Issachar Ber Ryback

1897–1935

Born in Elizavetgrad (today, Kropyvnytskyi, Ukraine), Issachar Ber Ryback studied at the Kiev School of Art. Believing that a modern Jewish art could be created on the basis of Jewish folk art, he employed expressionist and cubist devices to render folk themes and symbols in a modernist vein. He lived in Berlin from 1921 to 1925, where he illustrated Yiddish children's books and published two graphic albums on prewar Jewish shtetl life. He returned briefly to the Soviet Union to design sets for the Yiddish theater and then moved to Paris in 1926, where he remained until his death.

Der Shokhet

1923

In *Shtetl, mayn khorever heym: a gedenkenknish* (Berlin: Farlag Shveln, 1923). Courtesy of the YIVO Institute for Jewish Research.

Abraham Walkowitz

1878-1965

Born in Siberia, the painter Abraham Walkowitz immigrated to the United States as a young child with his widowed mother, settling on the Lower East Side of New York. He studied art in New York and Paris and was attracted to modernism. Between 1912 and 1917, he was part of the avant-garde circle of artists associated with Alfred Stieglitz's gallery 291. His best work—cubist paintings and drawings of New York cityscapes capturing the dynamism of modern urban life—was done early in his career. He is also known for his five thousand drawings of the dancer Isadora Duncan, whom he first met in Paris before World War I.

Metropolis No. 2

1923

Hirshhorn Museum and Sculpture Garden, Smithsonian Institution. Gift of Joseph H. Hirshhorn, 1966. Acc. no. 66.5542. Photography by Lee Stalsworth.

Alfred S. Alschuler

1876–1940

Chicago-born architect Alfred S. Alschuler was a prominent figure in the city's flourishing architecture scene in the first half of the twentieth century. He designed warehouses, department stores, industrial and office buildings, and synagogues. His design for the synagogue now known as KAM Isaiah Israel in the Kenwood neighborhood, across the street from President Barack Obama's family home, is in the Byzantine style and was inspired by photographs of the second-century Severus synagogue that was excavated in Tiberias.

KAM Isaiah Israel Congregation, Chicago, Detail of Decoration at the Balcony Level

1924

Photograph © Paul Rocheleau.

Barukh Shlomo Griegst

1889–1958

The silversmith Barukh Shlomo Griegst was born in Lithuania and settled in Copenhagen in 1902. He worked mainly in the style of Central European art nouveau (Jugendstil). In this silver Hanukkah lamp from 1924, the influence of the Jugendstil can be seen in the organic movement of the many elements in the backdrop, including the sinuous plant form of the Magen David.

Hanukkah Lamp
1924

The Jewish Museum, New York. Purchase: Judaica Acquisitions Fund and Bjorn Bamberger Gift, 1994-6. Photo by John Parnell. Image courtesy of The Jewish Museum, New York/ Art Resource, NY.

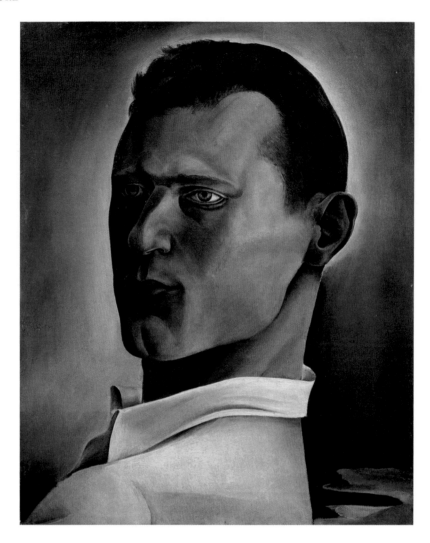

Arieh Lubin

1897–1980

The modernist Israeli painter Arieh Lubin was born in Chicago. In 1913, his Zionist parents sent him to Tel Aviv to study at the Herzliya Gymnasium. When World War I broke out, he returned to Chicago and enrolled at the Art Institute of Chicago. In 1917, he volunteered to serve in the British-sponsored Jewish Brigade, which fought against the Ottomans in Palestine. After the war, he returned to Chicago to complete his studies. In 1922, after a short period of travel in Europe, he returned to the Land of Israel. His work shows the influence of cubism.

Self-Portrait
1924

The Israel Museum, Jerusalem, bequest of the artist. Photo © The Israel Museum, Jerusalem.

Chana Orloff

1888–1968

The Ukrainian-born sculptor Chana Orloff settled in
Ottoman Palestine with her parents in 1905. She
moved to Paris in 1910 to study and soon became an
important member of the avant-garde École de Paris,
many of whom were also East European Jewish artists.
She remained in Paris the rest of her life, with the
exception of the war years, when she found refuge in
Switzerland, but she remained emotionally attached to
Israel, which she visited frequently. Her work, mostly
in wood, stone, bronze, and marble, was influenced by
both cubism and the vogue for "the primitive."

Portrait of Madame Peretz Hirshbein
1924

The Jewish Museum, New York. Gift of Erich Cohn, JM
91-64. Photo by John Parnell.
© 2015 Artists Rights Society (ARS), New York / ADAGP,
Paris. Image courtesy of The Jewish Museum, New York / Art
Resource, NY.

Chana Orloff

Portrait of Peretz Hirshbein
1924

The Jewish Museum, New York. Purchase: Sol and Ethel
Poler Gift, 2003-12. Photo by John Parnell. © 2015 Artists
Rights Society (ARS), New York / ADAGP, Paris. Image
courtesy of The Jewish Museum, New York / Art Resource,
NY.

זוסקין   ראגאלער ·   שאפירא   "געט„

Isaac Rabichev

1896–1957

The painter and stage designer Isaac Rabichev was born in and studied in Kiev. Along with Issachar Ber Ryback, Abraham Manievich, Marc Chagall, and Robert Falk, he was a central figure in the artists' division of the Kultur Lige that was established in Kiev in 1918. Their work sought to fuse traditional Jewish motifs with avant-garde techniques. He moved to Moscow in 1922 with several others in the group and turned to costume and set design for the Yiddish theater.

Set Design for Sholem Aleichem's Get *(Divorce)*
1924

Moscow State Yiddish Theater. Photograph from the collection of Hillel Kazovsky.

Yosef Zaritsky

1891–1985

The painter Yosef Zaritsky was born in Ukraine and studied art in Kiev. In 1923, he settled in Mandate Palestine, where he became a prominent figure in the development of Israeli art. He associated with the younger generation of artists who were rebelling against the academic style of the Bezalel School of Art. During his long life he worked in a number of styles. In the 1920s, his watercolors of Safed, Tiberias, and Jerusalem combined an intense focus on the Israeli landscape with a commitment to quasi-abstractionism. His later work was more rigorously abstract in style.

Safed
ca. 1924

The Israel Museum, Jerusalem. Purchase, Riklis Fund. B69.0313. Photo © The Israel Museum, Jerusalem.

Robert Falk

1886–1958

The painter and set designer Robert Falk was born in Moscow and received a secular Russian education. Although he converted to Christianity in 1907, prior to his marriage, critics identified him as a Jewish painter. During World War I, he became closer to the Jewish art world, and in the interwar years he frequently designed scenery and costumes for the Soviet Yiddish theater. In the 1940s, the Soviet regime banned him from exhibiting publicly because of the "formalism" and "political indifference" of his work.

Costume Design (Bearded Male) for Peretz's **A Night in the Old Marketplace**
1925

© Federal State Budget Institution of Culture "A. A. Bakhrushin State Central Theatre Museum," Moscow. © Estate of Robert Falk.

Ze'ev Raban

1890-1970

The painter and decorative artist Ze'ev Raban
(originally Wolf Rawicki) was born in Łódź, and
studied art there and in Munich and Brussels, where
the influence of art nouveau was then at its zenith. He
settled in Jerusalem in 1912 and joined the faculty of
the Bezalel Academy of Art. (Most of the objects
produced in its workshops between 1914 and 1929
were of his design.) His style combined elements of art
nouveau with motifs from traditional Syrian and
Persian art. He created the decorative elements for
such well-known Jerusalem buildings as the King
David Hotel and the YMCA and also designed a wide
variety of everyday objects, including playing cards,
banknotes, tourism posters, jewelry, commercial
packaging, and Zionist insignia.

Elijah's Chair
1925 (completed)

The Israel Museum, Jerusalem. Gift of Yossi Benyaminoff,
New York. 363.82. Photo © The Israel Museum, Jerusalem
by Peter Lanyi. Courtesy of Doron Vinter families, Jerusalem.

William Rothenstein

1872-1945

The son of a prosperous German Jewish wool merchant who had settled in Bradford, England, the
painter William Rothenstein studied in London and
Paris. He was known especially for his portraits of
famous men, over two hundred of which are in the
collection of the National Portrait Gallery in London,
and for his work as an official war artist in both world
wars. At the turn of the century, he produced an
important group of paintings of East End immigrant
synagogue life, but, aside from his portraits of contemporary Jews (such as that of the graphic designer and
lithographer Barnett Freedman), he never returned to
Jewish subjects in later decades.

Barnett Freedman
1925

Tate Gallery, London, Great Britain. Presented by the
Trustees of the Chantrey Bequest 1943. Photo Credit: Tate,
London / Art Resource, NY.

Jakob Steinhardt

1889–1968

The German-born painter and woodcut artist Jakob Steinhardt studied in Berlin before World War I and was much influenced by the expressionist movement. As a soldier in the German army during the war, he served in Lithuania and Poland, where his encounter with traditional East European Jewish society left a lasting impression on him and his work. In 1933, he and his wife fled Berlin and settled in Jerusalem. He is best known for his woodcuts of biblical and Jewish figures.

Entering to House of Prayer
1925

The Israel Museum, Jerusalem. B37.04.0355. Photo © The Israel Museum, Jerusalem, by Elie Posner.

Ziona Tagger

1900–1988

Born in Jaffa, the daughter of immigrants from Bulgaria, Ziona Tagger was the first Israeli-born woman artist. She studied at the Bezalel Academy of Arts in Jerusalem but found its aesthetic traditionalism (for example, its adherence to strictly representational art) too restrictive and moved to Paris to continue her training. When she returned to Mandate Palestine, she took part in exhibitions of the young modernist artists. She was known for her portraits and landscapes, whose style drew on cubism and naïve art.

Poet Avraham Shlonsky
1925

Collection of the Tel Aviv Museum of Art. Courtesy of http://www.tagger-siona.co.il.

Louis Lozowick

1892–1973

The painter and graphic artist Louis Lozowick was born in a small village in Ukraine. He studied art in Kiev and then, in 1906, he moved to the United States, where he continued his training. He received a BA from the Ohio State University in 1918 and then spent several years after the war traveling in Europe, where he was exposed to modernist currents in painting. In the 1920s, he contributed a series of articles about Jewish artists working in Europe and America to the *Menorah Journal*, and in 1947 published the first

survey of American Jewish art, *100 Contemporary American Jewish Painters and Sculptors*. His hard-edged, linear style exalted the urban landscape, especially skyscrapers and machines.

New York
1925–1926

Walker Art Center, Minneapolis. Gift of Hudson D. Walker, 1961. © Louis Lozowick Estate, courtesy Mary Ryan Gallery, New York.

Moshe Castel

1909–1991

The Israeli painter Moshe Castel was born into a Sephardic family in Jerusalem that had lived in the Land of Israel for centuries. He studied at the Bezalel Academy of Arts from 1922 to 1925 and then in Paris, where he lived from 1927 to 1940. With the Nazi conquest of France, he returned home. After the war he divided his time between Paris and Safed. Although the style in which he worked changed dramatically over his career, he continued to paint Jewish and Israeli subjects.

Two Jews
1926

Ben Uri Gallery, The London Jewish Museum of Art. All rights reserved to Moshe Castel Museum of Art, www. castelmuseum.com.

Nahum Gutman

1898–1980

The Bessarabian-born painter Nahum Gutman moved to Tel Aviv with his family when he was seven. He studied at the Bezalel Academy and, in the 1920s, in Vienna, Berlin, and Paris. He returned to Mandate Palestine in 1926. His oils and watercolors often feature massive, exuberantly painted, highly stylized individuals. Although influenced by French expressionism, he saw himself as a rebel, turning his back on European traditions of painting and championing a style in harmony with the light and landscapes of the Land of Israel.

Resting at Noon
1926

Collection of the Tel Aviv Museum of Art, Acquisition, 1983. By permission of the Nahum Gutman Museum of Art.

David Petrovich Shterenberg
1881–1948

The Russian painter David Petrovich Shterenberg was born in Zhitomir, Ukraine, and studied art in Odessa and then in Paris, where he lived from 1906 to 1912 and was a member of the East European Jewish artistic colony. He did not return to Russia permanently until 1917. In the 1930s, his avant-garde individualism, shaped during his Paris years, fell out of favor with the regime and he was forced to work in a more realistic style. This did not spare him, however, from being marginalized by the Soviet art world.

Aniska
1926

Tretyakov Gallery, Moscow, Russia / RIA Novosti / The Bridgeman Art Library
Art © Estate of David Petrovich Shterenberg/ RAO, Moscow / VAGA, New York.

Raphael Soyer
1899–1987

Born in Borisoglebsk, Russia, the painter and graphic artist Raphael Soyer moved to the United States with his parents and brothers in 1913. He studied painting in New York and lived there for the rest of his life. He was a staunch social realist, painting genre scenes of immigrant and city life, as well as portraits of family, friends, and fellow artists. In addition to working in a representational style, he defended it in print against the rising fashion of abstractionism. His brothers Moses and Isaac were also painters.

Dancing Lesson
1926

The Jewish Museum. Gift of the Renee and Chaim Gross Foundation, 2008-225. Photo by Richard Goodbody. Image courtesy of The Jewish Museum, New York / Art Resource, NY. ©Estate of Raphael Soyer, courtesy of Forum Gallery, New York, NY.

Léon Weissberg

1895–1943

Born into a wealthy Galician family, the painter Léon Weissberg studied in Vienna. After serving in the Austrian army in World War I, he continued his studies in Berlin and Munich. He traveled in Italy and the Netherlands before settling in Paris in 1923. With the German advance on Paris, he took refuge in the Unoccupied Zone. French police arrested him in 1943, and after a short time in the internment camps in Gurs and Drancy, he was deported to Maidanek, where he was killed on arrival.

Jewish Bride
1926

Collection of the Tel Aviv Museum of Art.

Natan Altman

1889–1970

The Russian painter, theatrical designer, and sculptor Natan Altman was born in Vinnitsa (Vinnytsya), Ukraine. He studied in Odessa from 1903 to 1907 and moved to Paris in 1910 before returning to Russia. In the 1920s he produced abstract constructivist set designs for the Yiddish theater. During this period, he painted the portrait of the Yiddish actor Solomon Mikhoels, later the director of the Moscow State Yiddish Theater. Altman lived abroad from 1928 to 1935, and when he returned to the Soviet Union agreed to work in the then-required style of socialist realism.

Portrait of Mikhoels
1927

© Federal State Budget Institution of Culture "A. A. Bakhrushin State Central Theatre Museum," Moscow. Art © Estate of Natan Altman / RAO, Moscow / VAGA, New York.

Luciano Morpurgo

1886–1971

Luciano Morpurgo was one of the most important Italian photographers of the twentieth century. Born in Split, Dalmatia (then part of the Austro-Hungarian Empire), into a prosperous commercial family, he was educated in Venice. While studying there, he became interested in photography. In 1915, he moved permanently to Rome, where he eventually founded a graphic arts company that produced postcards of Italy. Photographs from his 1927 journey to Palestine and Trans-Jordan captured the lives of ordinary Jews, "simple folk" from communities that often attracted little attention.

Jewish Woman of Safed Whitewashing Her Home in Preparation for Pessah
1927

Courtesy of Istituto Centrale per il Catalogo e la Documentazione, Rome.

Zvi Orushkes (Oron)

1888–1980

Born in Białystok, the photographer Zvi Orushkes (Oron after 1948) settled
in the United States in 1914. Once a socialist-territorialist, he became a
Zionist at the outbreak of World War I and fought with the Jewish Legion in
Palestine in 1918. On demobilization, he remained in the country and
established a photography studio. For commercial reasons, he courted the
British and in 1929 became official photographer to the government. Although he worked for Jews and Arabs as well, some Zionist officials resented
his British contacts and ostracized him.

Billboards for Municipal Elections, Tel Aviv

1927

Courtesy of Central Zionist Archive, NZO626750.

Ossip Zadkine
1890–1967

The sculptor Ossip Zadkine was born in Vitebsk, the
son of a Jewish father and a Scottish mother, and
received his early training at Yehuda Pen's art school
there. From 1905 to 1909, he lived in England. He
then went to Paris, where he remained for most of his
life (except for the war years, when he found refuge in
the United States). Until the mid-1920s, he worked in
the cubist idiom; afterward, he developed a style of his
own, one that drew on African and Greek influences.

Rebecca, or The Large Woman Carrying Water
1927

Jacob S. Baars

1886–1956

The Dutch architect Jacob S. Baars designed several Jewish buildings in Amsterdam. A follower of the father of modernist Dutch architecture Hendrik Berlage, he built the synagogue in Linnaeusstraat, Amsterdam (demolished in 1962), in the style of the Amsterdam school, the Dutch version of international expressionism.

Synagogue, Linnaeusstraat, Amsterdam
1927–1928

Photograph by J. van Dijk. Courtesy of Gemeente Amsterdam Staadtsarchief and Fotobureau J. van Dijk.

Harry Elte

1880–1944

The Dutch architect Harry Elte was born in Amsterdam and studied with Hendrik Berlage. Elte built several synagogues and Jewish hospitals in the Netherlands. His synagogue in Jacob Obrechtplein in Amsterdam (known as the Rav Aron Schuster Synagogue) was built in the style of the Amsterdam school and influenced by the work of Frank Lloyd Wright. It was his most important building. During World War II, he was deported to Westerbork and then to Theresienstadt, where he died.

Aron Schuster Synagogue, Obrechtplein, Amsterdam
1928

Photo by Klaas Vermaas.

Todros Geller

1889-1949

The artist Todros Geller was born in Vinnitsa (Vinnytsya), Ukraine, and studied art in Odessa, Montreal, and Chicago, his home from 1918 until his death. He worked in several mediums, including oil paintings, woodcuts, wood carvings, and etchings, often with Jewish themes. A left-wing Yiddishist and admirer of the Soviet Union, he believed that art could be a tool for social reform. Despite his radicalism, he also designed stained glass windows for synagogues and took part in the communal life of Chicago Jewry.

Strange Worlds
1928

Gift of Leon Garland Foundation, 1949.27, The Art Institute of Chicago. Art courtesy of David I. Silverman. Photography © The Art Institute of Chicago.

Chaim Gross

1904-1991

The sculptor Chaim Gross was born in the Carpathian mountains in Austrian Galicia, the son of a lumber merchant. Uprooted by the mayhem of World War I and its aftermath, he settled in New York City in 1921 and pursued the study of sculpting. He became known for direct carving in wood and did not turn to modeling and casting in bronze until the 1950s. He worked in a figurative style. From the 1950s, biblical and Jewish themes dominated his work.

East Side Girl
1928

The Metropolitan Museum of Art, New York. Gift of Mimi Gross, 1982. © 2015 Artists Rights Society (ARS), New York. Image copyright © The Metropolitan Museum of Art. Image source: Art Resource, NY.

Israel Paldi

1892–1979

The Israeli painter Israel Paldi (b. Feldman) was born in Radynsk, Ukraine. He moved to Palestine in 1909 and enrolled at the Bezalel Academy. From 1911 to 1914, he studied in Munich. At the outbreak of war, he tried to return to Palestine but was unable to and was forced to spend the war years in Turkey. On returning in 1918, he joined the modernist revolt against the more conventional style taught at Bezalel. His paintings of the 1920s featured folkloric motifs and exotic "oriental" figures. In later years he experimented with other techniques—abstraction, collage, and assemblage.

Pastoral (Ein Karem Landscape)
1928

Collection of the Tel Aviv Museum of Art. Acquisition through a contribution from the Discount Bank Fund, 1979.

Ignaz Reiser

1863–1940

The architect Ignaz Reiser was born in Slovakia, the son of a wholesale wine merchant, and grew up in Pressburg (today, Bratislava) and Vienna, where he practiced until his death. He built residential and commercial buildings and synagogues and communal buildings for the Viennese community. His earliest buildings were in the neo-Baroque style, whereas his later ones, such as the ceremonial hall at the New Jewish Cemetery in Vienna, were more modern, showing the influence of expressionism.

Ceremonial Hall, New Jewish Cemetery, Vienna
1928

From *Der neue israelitische Friedhof in Wien und seine Bauten* (1928). Courtesy of the YIVO Institute for Jewish Research.

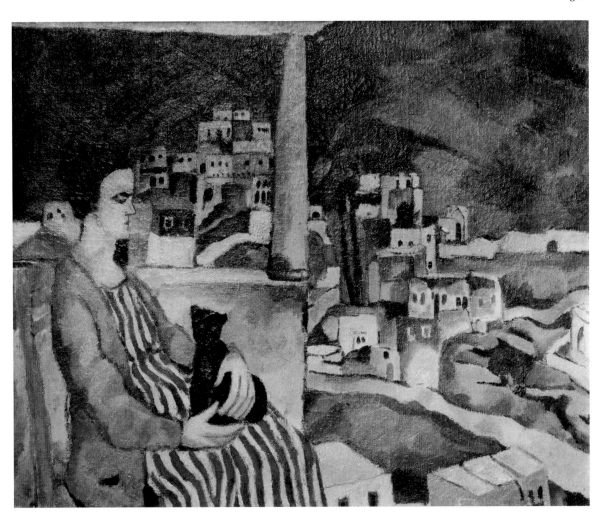

Menahem Shemi

1897–1951

The painter Menahem Shemi was born in Bobruisk (now Belarus) and studied art in Odessa before coming to Palestine in 1913 and enrolling at the Bezalel Academy. During World War I, he was drafted into the Ottoman army, but he deserted and eventually fought with the Jewish Legion. His paintings reflect a desire to create a distinctive Land of Israel style while remaining true to the modernism of the school of Paris.

The Artist's Wife with Cat
1928

Haifa Museum of Modern Art. Courtesy the Haifa Museum of Art, Israel. Photo by Shahar Amit.

Aleksandr Tyshler
1898–1980

Born in Melitopol, Ukraine, the son of a carpenter, the artist Aleksandr Tyshler studied in Kiev and, after serving in a propaganda unit of the Red Army, continued his education in Moscow. He worked in various mediums: painting, sculpture, graphic design, and theatrical design. Beginning in the late 1920s and continuing through the 1940s, he designed sets for both the Yiddish- and Russian-language theaters.

Costume Design for Dovid Bergelson's **The Deaf One**
1928

© Federal State Budget Institution of Culture "A. A. Bakhrushin State Central Theatre Museum," Moscow.
© Tyshler Foundation, Brussels, Belgium.

Unknown Artist

Since "religion is the opiate of the masses," diverting the attention of the exploited toiling masses, in the early 1920s Soviet authorities launched a nationwide campaign against all religions, using art, literature, movies, school curricula, public "trials," demonstrations, and lectures to "enlighten the masses." This poster, designed by an unknown artist, tries to convince Jews that religion impedes economic, particularly industrial, progress.

Religion Is an Obstacle to the Five-Year Plan
ca. 1928

The Moldovan Family Collection.

Fritz Landauer

1883–1968

The modernist architect Fritz Landauer was born in Augsburg, Bavaria, and practiced in Munich until forced into exile. One of the few architects working in the international style in southern Germany, he designed important synagogues in Augsburg and Plauen. After settling in London in 1937, he designed the North Western Reform Synagogue, Alyth Gardens, Golders Green, and the Willesden Synagogue, the latter a rare example of a British synagogue influenced by a modernist aesthetic.

Reform Synagogue, Plauen
1928–1930

Virtual reconstruction. Courtesy Technische Universität Darmstadt, Digital Design Unit.

Ze'ev Raban

Come to Palestine
1929

Photo © The Israel Museum, Jerusalem, by Elie Posner. Courtesy Doron Vinter
families, Jerusalem. The biblical verse is from the Song of Songs.

Jennings Tofel

1891–1959

The Polish-born painter Jennings Tofel (b. Idel Talflewicz) immigrated in 1905 to New York City, where he first began to study art. From 1925 to 1930, he lived mostly in Europe, studying and exhibiting. He returned permanently to New York in 1930. He contributed essays on art, language, and philosophy to the Yiddish- and English-language press. Jewish themes occupy a prominent place in his work.

Family Reunion
1929

Hirshhorn Museum and Sculpture Garden, Smithsonian Institution. Gift of Joseph H. Hirshhorn, 1966. Photography by Cathy Carver.

Tsadok Bassan

1882–1956

The pioneer Jerusalem photographer Tsadok Bassan was born in the Old City into a religious Zionist family. He received a yeshiva education and acquired informally a hands-on knowledge of photography. At age eighteen, with the aid of his family, he purchased a photography studio in the Old City. He became, in effect, the "court photographer" of the Old Yishuv, photographing their institutions and daily life. He worked for many of the city's Jewish charities, photographing their work, often for fund-raising purposes in the diaspora.

Diskin Orphanage, Jerusalem
1920s

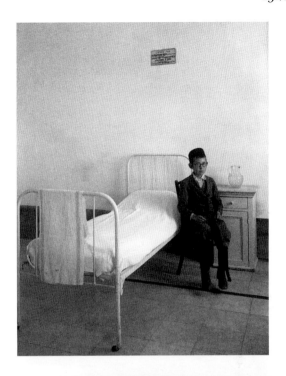

Diskin Orphanage, Jerusalem, 1920s. Courtesy Central Zionist Archive, GNZB401481.

Bezalel School of Arts and Crafts

The Bezalel School of Arts and Crafts was established in Jerusalem in 1906 by the artist Boris Schatz with the support of the Zionist movement. It promoted the creation of a Jewish national art, one that would blend European and Middle Eastern artistic traditions. Its distinctive style drew on the contemporary arts and crafts movement in Europe and the United States and the Jugendstil movement in Central Europe.

Carpet Depicting Rachel's Tomb
1920s

Courtesy of Spertus Institute, Chicago.

Alter-Sholem Kacyzne

1885–1941

In addition to writing Yiddish fiction, poetry, drama, and criticism, Alter-Sholem Kacyzne was also a photographer of East European Jewish life in the interwar period. Born into a working-class family in Vilna, he opened a photography studio in Warsaw in 1910. In 1921, the Hebrew Immigrant Aid Society of New York commissioned him to photograph the misery of Polish Jews who were seeking to immigrate to the United States. Soon after Abraham Cahan hired him to contribute photographs on a regular basis to the *Forverts*. Most of his photographic archive was lost during the Holocaust. Kacyzne was murdered by Ukrainians in July 1941.

Teacher and Students in a Heder, Lublin
1920s

Courtesy of the YIVO Institute for Jewish Research and the Forward Association.

Shimon Korbman

1887–1978

The Russian-born photographer Shimon Korbman was active in Tel Aviv in the interwar years. His photographs convey the nascent urbanity of Jewish life in Tel Aviv and the importance of beach life—swimming, strolling, sunbathing, and bicycling—in the daily life of its residents.

Self-Portrait on Tel Aviv Beach
1920s

Korbman Collection, by special permission of the Administrator General, The State of Israel, as the executor of S. Korbman Estate & Eretz Israel Museum, Tel Aviv.

Yehudah Pen

1854-1937

The painter and graphic artist Yehudah Pen was born into a traditional Jewish home in a Lithuanian shtetl. He initially earned his living as a house painter. He studied at the Academy of Arts in St. Petersburg from 1880 to 1886. In 1897, he opened a school of drawing and painting in Vitebsk, where he trained several hundred Jewish youth, including Marc Chagall, Ossip Zadkine, and El Lissitzky. The orientation of the school was nationalist, and Pen's own work focused on the everyday life of common Jews, especially artisans. Even in the Soviet period, Pen was able to continue focusing on traditional Jewish subject matter.

The House with a Goat
1920s

The National Art Museum of the Republic of Belarus, Minsk.

David Heinz Gumbel
1896?–1992

Born in Sinsheim, Germany, to a secular family of silverware manufacturers, David Heinz Gumbel studied silversmithing in Berlin in the late 1920s. While working at the family factory in Heilbronn, he began producing handmade Jewish ritual objects of silver and other materials. While he never studied at the Bauhaus, the school's avant-garde aesthetic greatly influenced his work, which is distinguished by its sleek elegance and unadorned surfaces. In 1934, Gumbel fled Nazi Germany and settled in Jerusalem, where he began teaching silversmithing, hammered work, and jewelry design at the Bezalel Academy.

Hanukkah Lamp, Heilbronn, Germany
Early 1930s

The Jewish Museum, New York. Gift of Hannah and Walter Flegenheimer, 2002-9a-d. Photo by Richard Goodbody, Inc. Image courtesy of The Jewish Museum, New York/Art Resource, NY. Malka Cohavi & Studio. D. H. Gumbel is the sole owner of the exclusive copyrights of the design.

Mané-Katz (Emanuel Katz)

1894–1962

The painter Mané-Katz was born in Kremenchug, Ukraine, and was destined for the rabbinate. At age seventeen, he left home to study art in Vilna and then Kiev, and in 1913 went to Paris. He was in Russia during World War I but then returned in 1921 to Paris, which remained his home, except during World War II, when he lived in the United States. Like Marc Chagall, he favored overtly Jewish themes drawn from his childhood in Eastern Europe.

Homage to Paris

1930

Courtesy of Mané-Katz Museum. Photo by Shahar Amit. © 2015 Artists Rights Society (ARS), New York / ADAGP, Paris.

Hermann Struck

1876–1944

The master etcher Hermann Struck was born into an Orthodox family in Berlin and remained an observant Jew throughout his life. An active Zionist from an early age, he moved to Palestine in 1922 and spent the rest of his life in the Land of Israel. He was known for his portraits of European cultural figures and for his landscapes and character studies of traditional Jews, both Ashkenazi and Mizrahi.

Yemenite Jew
1930

Harvard Art Museums / Busch-Reisinger Museum, Gift of Pearl K. and Daniel Bell. 1998.141.
Photo: Imaging Department © President and Fellows of Harvard College.

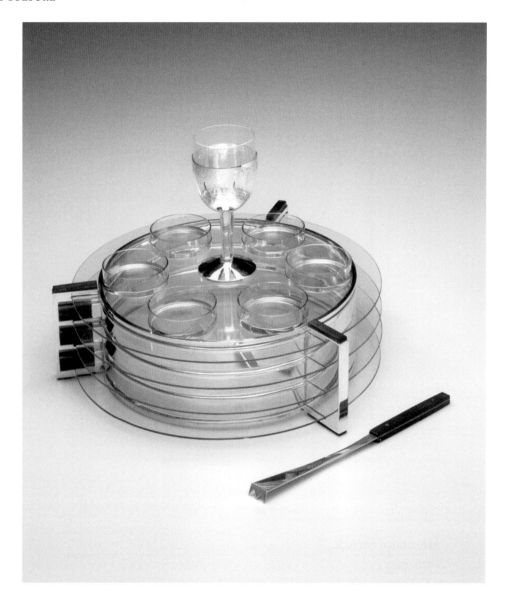

Ludwig Yehuda Wolpert

1900–1981

The son of an Orthodox rabbi, Ludwig Yehuda Wolpert was born in Hildesheim, Germany. He studied sculpture and then metalworking in Frankfurt and began creating modern Jewish ceremonial art. His Passover set of 1930 shows the strong influence of the Bauhaus school. In 1933, he settled in Jerusalem and in 1935 began teaching metalwork at the Bezalel Academy. In 1956, he went to New York City to direct a workshop for Jewish ceremonial art at the Jewish Museum. His work and teaching influenced generations of artisans and craftsmen of Jewish ceremonial objects.

Passover Set
1930

© Copyright Passover Set. New York, United States, 1930 Frankfurt, produced 1978. The Jewish Museum, New York. Gift of Sylvia Zenia Rosen Wiener. Photo by Richard Goodbody, Inc. Image courtesy of The Jewish Museum, New York / Art Resource, NY.

Hyman Bloom

1913–2009

The painter Hyman Bloom was born in Latvia and immigrated to Boston with his parents when he was seven. His talent was recognized early, and he entered Harvard on a scholarship, along with his friend Jack Levine. He painted in a highly emotional, figurative style, and his later work was permeated with occult and mystical concerns. After World War II and the Holocaust, he turned to explicitly Jewish themes.

Portrait of a Boy in a White Shirt (Self-Portrait)
ca. 1930

Harvard Art Museums / Fogg Museum, Bequest of Denman W. Ross, Class of 1875, 1936.76
Photo: Imaging Department. © President and Fellows of Harvard College. © Stella Bloom, Estate of Hyman Bloom.

Isaac Dobrinsky

1891–1973

The painter Isaac Dobrinsky was born in Makarov, Ukraine, into a traditional Jewish home and received a yeshiva education. When his father died suddenly, Dobrinsky moved to Kiev to study sculpture. In 1912, he left for Paris, where he remained until his death. Within a year of his arrival, he abandoned sculpture for painting. He and his family spent the first two years of World War II in Paris and then fled to the Dordogne. In the 1950s, he painted a memorable series of about forty portraits of Jewish boys and girls from an orphanage whose parents had been murdered in the Holocaust.

Léon Weissberg
ca. 1930

Photo Niels Forg © Musée d'art et d'histoire du Judaïsme © 2015 Artists Rights Society (ARS), New York / ADAGP, Paris.

Boris Schatz

1866–1932

The Lithuanian-born artist Boris Schatz is often described as "the father of Israeli art." Schatz was working in Sofia, Bulgaria, when he met Theodor Herzl in 1903. Two years later, having moved to Berlin, he was introduced to the Zionist leaders Franz Oppenheimer and Otto Warburg, to whom he proposed establishing a Jewish art school in Jerusalem. The Bezalel School of Arts and Crafts opened in 1906, with Schatz as its head. The aesthetic aim of the school was to forge a visual expression of Jewish yearning for national and spiritual independence and to synthesize the artistic traditions of Europe and the Jewish craft traditions of the East and West. The school closed in 1929 for financial reasons. Schatz died in Denver, Colorado, while on a trip to raise funds to reopen the school—which it did in 1935.

Self-Portrait

ca. 1930

The Jewish Museum, New York. Gift of Dr. Harry G. Friedman. Photo by Richard Goodbody, Inc. Image courtesy of The Jewish Museum, New York / Art Resource, NY.

Chaim Soutine

1893–1943

The expressionist painter Chaim Soutine was born in Similovitchi, Belarus, into an impoverished traditional family. He fled his family and hometown in 1909 and studied painting, first in Minsk and then later in Vilna. In 1913, he left for Paris, where he lived the remainder of his life, except for the years 1940–1943, which he spent in the French countryside, hiding from the Nazis. Although his work was never explicitly Jewish in terms of its subject matter, critics always viewed him as a representative Jewish artist, in part because of the emotional intensity of his style and in part because he associated with other East European Jewish artists who settled in Paris.

Portrait of Moïse Kisling

ca. 1930

Philadelphia Museum of Art, Gift of Arthur Wiesenberger, 1943. © 2015 Artists Rights Society (ARS), New York.

Jankel Adler

1895–1949

The painter Jankel Adler was born in Tuszyn, Poland, into a Hasidic family. He studied engraving in Łódź in 1913 and received further training in Germany. He later moved back to Łódź and helped to launch the Yung-yidish cultural movement, championing the themes and stylistic features of German expressionism. In 1920, he moved back to Germany, aligning himself with the left-wing avant-garde. His pictures from the Weimar period include no Jewish references. He lived in France from 1933 to 1940, and then fought with the Polish Free Army before being evacuated to Scotland in 1941. He eventually moved to London. He returned to painting Jewish themes in the 1940s, and his work frequently registered the suffering of European Jewry in the Nazi years.

Purim Spiel (Purim Play)
1931

Collection of the Tel Aviv Museum of Art. Gift of Jacob Sonnenberg and Aaron Mazur, Danzig, 1938. © 2015 Artists Rights Society (ARS), New York / VG Bild-Kunst, Bonn.

Helmar (Helmut) Lerski

1871–1956

Among the most important innovators in twentieth-century photography, Helmar Lerski was born in Strasbourg as Israel Schmuklerski, the son of immigrants from Poland. He grew up in Zurich but in 1893 sailed to the United States, where he joined a German-speaking theater troupe (and changed his name). He did not take up photography until 1910, when he was thirty-nine. In 1915, he moved to Berlin, where he worked as a cameraman and a lighting technician on expressionist films. In the late 1920s he returned to portrait photography in the expressionist style, which he continued to pursue after settling in Tel Aviv in 1931. In 1948, he returned to Zurich.

Jew from Poland
1931–1935

Copyright Estate, Helmar Lerski, Museum Folkwang, Essen.

Joseph Mendes da Costa

1863–1939

The sculptor and ceramicist Joseph Mendes da Costa was born in Amsterdam, the son of the sculptor Moses Mendes da Costa. He was taught by his father initially and later enrolled in art school. He was known for his sculpted ornaments and reliefs for buildings, many of which featured owls and monkeys (they were also prominent in his smaller sculptures and bronze work). His small statuettes were often inspired by the Bible or by the daily life of Jews in Amsterdam.

Moses' Death
ca. 1933

Collection Jewish Historical Museum, Amsterdam.

Isaac Lazarus Israëls

1865–1934

The Dutch impressionist Isaac Lazarus Israëls was the son of the much-respected and better-known painter Josef Israëls. Displaying precocious talent, he studied in The Hague and Amsterdam. In the course of his life he traveled widely, spending extended periods in Belgium's mining districts, Paris, London, the French Rivera, India, and the Dutch East Indies, everywhere finding subjects for his work.

The Collector

1934

Collection Jewish Historical Museum, Amsterdam.

Avraham Melnikov

1892–1960

The sculptor and painter Avraham Melnikov was born in Bessarabia. While studying medicine, he decided to become an artist. When his parents refused to support him, he moved to Chicago, where a brother lived. He fought with the Jewish Legion in Palestine during World War I and remained there after being demobilized. His monumental statute at Tel Hai, with its notable evocation of Mesopotamian art, is his most famous work. After its completion, he left for England, where he remained for the next twenty-five years, returning to Israel only a few months before he died. In England, he made a reputation for himself as a portrait painter.

Roaring Lion
1934

National Photo Collection. Amos Ben Gershom, photographer, Government Press Office, Israel.

Arthur Szyk

1894-1951

Arthur Szyk was born in Łódź and studied art in Paris and Kraków. He worked primarily as an illustrator, illuminator, and caricaturist. In the interwar period, he divided his time between Poland and Western Europe, and from 1940 he lived in the United States. His unique style was influenced by medieval illuminated manuscripts and Persian miniatures. Much of his work addressed the themes of antisemitism and Jewish resistance. During World War II, he produced a series of powerful anti-Axis caricatures, grotesquely portraying the Germans and their allies.

The Four Sons
1934

The Four Sons, 1934, full-color illustration from *The Haggadah* (London: Beaconsfield Press, 1940). Reproduced with the cooperation of The Arthur Szyk Society, www.szyk.org.

Jacob Benor-Kalter

1897–1969

Jacob Benor-Kalter was a man of many talents: photographer, graphic artist, architect, publisher, and cinema-house entrepreneur. Born in Poland, he trained as an engineer there and made aliyah in 1921. In 1926, the Pro-Jerusalem Society, a project of Sir Ronald Storrs, published an album of his Jerusalem photogravures that was widely distributed in London. In the early 1930s, he published an album of Tel Aviv photographs that included, unusually for the time, a number of photomontages, such as this one of a policeman towering over the traffic of a Tel Aviv street.

A Jewish Policeman
ca. 1934

Courtesy Silver Print Collection, Ein Hod. © Estate of Jacob Benor-Kalter.

Ben-Zion
1897–1987

The Galician-born painter Ben-Zion came to the United States in 1920. Dedicated to the revival of the Hebrew language, he published poems and fairy tales in Hebrew under his full name, Ben-Zion Weinman. (He later shortened it, remarking that artists needed only one name.) In the 1930s, depressed by the limited audience in the United States for Hebrew literature, he devoted himself exclusively to painting. He was a member of the avant-garde expressionist group called "The Ten," which included Mark Rothko and Adolph Gottlieb, but he did not follow their path to abstract expressionism and remained loyal to figurative art.

Jacob Wrestling with the Angel
1935

The Jewish Museum, New York. Purchase: Jula Isenburger Bequest; gifts of Mrs. Ethel L. Elkind and Mr. and Mrs. Jacob Shullman, by exchange, 2003-1. Photo by Richard Goodbody, Inc. Image courtesy of The Jewish Museum, New York / Art Resource, NY.

Tim Gidal

1909–1996

Tim Gidal (né Nahum Ignaz Gidalewitsch) was one of the founders of modern photojournalism. Born in Munich, the son of East European Jews, Gidal was a Zionist from an early age. When he received his degree from the University of Basel in 1935, he moved to Mandate Palestine. Struggling to make a living as a photojournalist there, he left for Britain. After two years there, he returned and joined the British army as a photographer in 1942. After the war, he moved to the United States, where he worked for *Life* and taught at the New School for Social Research in New York. In 1968, he moved to Zurich, and in 1970 he returned to Jerusalem, where he lived until his death.

Night of Meron
1935

The Israel Museum, Jerusalem. Gift of Gary B. Sokol, San Francisco, The Pritzker Foundation, San Francisco, Larry Zicklin, New Jersey, Dr. John Sumers, New York. Photo by Nahum Tim Gidal, © The Israel Museum, Jerusalem.

Martin Monnickendam

1874–1943

The artist Martin Monnickendam was born in Amsterdam, where he was educated and lived his entire life. He was prolific, with more than four thousand known works, and a master of many genres, including oil, watercolor, pastel, drawing, etching, and poster. He also produced illustrations for newspapers and magazines. He is best known for his theater paintings, which focus on the patrons in their seats rather than the actors on the stage. He died a natural death in Nazi-occupied Amsterdam.

Service in the Great Synagogue to Mark the Tercentenary of the Ashkenazi Community on 14 November 1935
1935

Service in the Great Synagogue to Mark the Tercentenary of the Ashkenazi Community on 14 November 1935. Collection Jewish Historical Museum, Amsterdam.

Roman Vishniac

1897–1990

Born into a wealthy, Russian-speaking family that settled in Berlin after the Bolshevik Revolution, the photographer Roman Vishniac traveled extensively in Poland, Romania, and Czechoslovakia in the late 1930s, photographing pious and impoverished Jews. The images he created, which were widely distributed in the postwar period, shaped popular perceptions of Jewish life in Eastern Europe before the Holocaust. He came to America in 1940 and after the war worked extensively in photomicroscopy, building on his earlier training in biology, zoology, and endocrinology.

Porter Nat Gutman, Warsaw
ca. 1935–1938

© Mara Vishniac Kohn, courtesy International Center of Photography.

Moisei Solomonovich Nappelbaum

1869–1958

Born in Minsk, Moisei Solomonovich Nappelbaum (Nappelboim) was one of the most important portrait photographers of prerevolutionary Russia and the early Soviet Union. He elevated studio portraiture into a form of art photography, using light to give psychological characterization to the sitter's face. In the Soviet period, he photographed the most prominent revolutionaries, commissars, cultural figures, and scientists, many of whom were Jews. However, he considered himself a Russian photographer and did not pursue Jewish subjects.

Isaac Babel
ca. 1935

© Estate of Moisei Solomonovich Nappelbaum / FTM Agency Ltd., Moscow.

Eric Mendelsohn

1887–1953

The architect Eric Mendelsohn was born in Allenstein, Germany. His earliest buildings were influenced by expressionism, but his style soon turned in a more linear direction. In Germany, he built strikingly modern department stores for Salman Schocken. When the Nazis came to power, he fled to England, where he was one of a handful of architects building in the internationalist style. In 1935, he opened an office in Jerusalem, and in 1939 he moved there. In Mandate Palestine, he did some of his best work; among the iconic buildings he designed were the Hadassah Hospital on Mount Scopus, Chaim Weizmann's home in Rehovot, Salman Schocken's home and library in Jerusalem, and the Anglo-Palestine Bank in Jerusalem. In 1941, he moved to San Francisco. While the synagogues he designed in his American years were modernist in style, they were less remarkable than his work in Germany and Palestine.

Schocken Library, Jerusalem
1936

Photo © Judith Turner, 1984.

Ben Shahn

1898–1969

The painter and graphic artist Ben Shahn was born in
Kovno (Kaunas, Lithuania) and in 1909 came to New
York City, where he received formal art training. From
the late 1920s until about 1950, he worked mainly in a
social realist tradition, attacking injustice, prejudice,
and brutality. During the Great Depression, he was
employed as a photographer by the Farm Security
Administration to document the unemployed and the
poor, government homestead projects, and rural,
small-town life. After 1950, his work became more
allegorical and symbolic and he turned increasingly to
producing illustrated Hebrew texts.

East Side Soap Box
1936

The Jewish Museum, New York. Purchase: Deana Bezark
Fund in memory of Leslie Bezark; Mrs. Jack N. Berkman,
Susan and Arthur Fleischer, Dr. Jack Allen and Shirley
Kapland, Hanni and Peter Kaufmann, Hyman L. and Joan C.
Sall Funds, and Margaret Goldstein Bequest, 1995-61. Photo
by John Parnell. Image courtesy of The Jewish Museum, New
York / Art Resource, NY. Art © Estate of Ben Shahn/
Licensed by VAGA, New York, NY.

Liselotte Grschebina

1908–1994

The photographer Liselotte Grschebina was born in
Karlsruhe, Germany. She and her husband settled in
Tel Aviv in 1934. From the 1930s to the 1950s, she
took photographs for WIZO, the Palestine Railways,
the dairy cooperative Tnuva, kibbutzim, and various
businesses. Her work was innovative and startling,
portraying subjects through surprising vantage points,
strong diagonals, and the play of light and shadow,
techniques she had learned from the revolution in
photographic art in Weimar Germany.

Sports in Israel: Discus Thrower
1937

The Israel Museum, Jerusalem. Gift of Beni and Rina Gjebin,
Shoham, Israel, with the assistance of Rachel and Dov
Gottesman, Tel Aviv and London. Photo by Liselotte
Grschebina. © The Israel Museum Jerusalem. Accession
number: B01.0244(1823).

Ze'ev Ben-Zvi

1904–1952

The sculptor Ze'ev Ben-Zvi (b. Kujawski) was born in Ryki, Poland, and studied in Warsaw before settling in Mandate Palestine in 1923. There he continued his studies at the Bezalel Academy of Arts. He is best known for his cubist-inspired portrait heads in beaten copper and mounded plaster, which influenced a generation of Israeli sculptors. In the 1940s his work became more abstract, and in 1946 he completed one of the first Holocaust memorials in the world at Kibbutz Mishmar Ha-Emek. (Aharon Meskin was an Israeli actor.)

Portrait of Aharon Meskin
1938

From the collection of Museum of Art, Ein Harod, Israel.

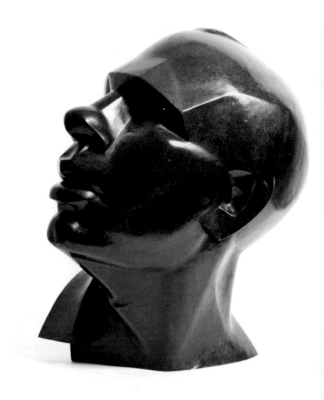

Marc Chagall

1887–1985

Marc Chagall is perhaps the best-known Jewish artist of the modern period. Born into an impoverished Hasidic family in Vitebsk, he attended art schools in Vitebsk, St. Petersburg, and Paris, where he lived from 1910 to 1914. He was swept up by revolutionary fervor following the overthrow of the tsarist regime but soon became disillusioned and left the Soviet Union for good in 1922. He lived the rest of his life in France, except for the years between 1941 and 1948, when he lived in the United States. His work creates an imaginary world, saturated with color, drawing on his childhood in Vitebsk. His use, beginning in the 1930s, of the crucifixion of Jesus as a symbol of Jewish suffering was and remains controversial.

White Crucifixion
1938

Jacques Lipchitz
1891–1973

Born in Druskininkai, Lithuania, into a prosperous family, the sculptor Jacques Lipchitz went to Paris to study in 1909. He remained there until 1941, when he left for the United States. His earliest work shows the influence of cubism, but in the mid-1920s his style began to loosen, becoming more fluid, curvilinear, and dynamic. The growing political violence of the late 1930s led him to sculpt many variations on the theme of violent struggle against mythical monsters, as in *Rape of Europa*, featuring knotted, writhing forms.

Rape of Europa
1938

Anonymous gift, The Art Institute of Chicago. © The Estate of Jacques Lipchitz, courtesy Marlborough Gallery, New York. Photography © The Art Institute of Chicago.

Walter Rosenblum
1919–2006

The photographer Walter Rosenblum was born in New York City, the child of East European immigrants. In 1937 he joined the Photo League, a group of socially concerned documentary photographers. During World War II, he served as a combat photographer with the U.S. Army Signal Corps and photographed the D-Day landings on the Normandy beaches in June 1944. He was the first Allied photographer to enter the liberated Dachau concentration camp.

Synagogue, Pitt Street
1938

© Rosenblum Family.

Sol Libsohn

1914-2001

The early documentary photographer Sol Libsohn was born in Harlem, the son of East European immigrants. Self-taught, he went to work for the Works Progress Administration in the 1930s, recording the lives of New Yorkers struggling during the Great Depression. In 1936, he was one of the cofounders of the Photo League, a group of left-wing photographers, most of whom were Jewish, who were committed to documenting everyday urban subjects and ordinary American lives.

Hester Street

ca. 1938

Copyright The Estate of Sol Libsohn, courtesy Howard Greenberg Gallery, NY.

William Gropper

1897–1977

The painter and political cartoonist William Gropper was born in New York City, the son of East European immigrants who worked in the garment industry. A political radical who was sympathetic to communism (but was never a party member), Gropper contributed political cartoons in the interwar years to both radical and liberal newspapers and magazines. He painted in a representational style that employed cubism's pronounced angularity. In the 1930s, he received government and business commissions for murals. In the wake of the Holocaust, he turned frequently to explicitly Jewish themes.

Minorities
1938 or 1939

Acquired 1940. The Phillips Collection, Washington, DC. Courtesy of the Gropper Family. Photo by Edward Owen.

Hans Feibusch

1898–1998

The painter Hans Feibusch was born into a nonobservant Jewish home in Frankfurt am Main. After studying in Munich, Berlin, and Paris, he settled in Frankfurt. When the Nazis came to power, he fled to England. The experience of exile strongly influenced his work, as, for example, in his painting *1939*. Beginning in the 1940s, he won wide acclaim for his murals in Anglican churches, executing projects in thirty churches in all. In 1965, he was baptized into the Church of England but in his nineties he abandoned Christianity and on his death was buried in a Jewish cemetery.

1939

1939

Leopold Krakauer

1890–1954

Leopold Krakauer was born in Vienna, where he trained as an architect. He made aliyah in 1924. While he earned his living as an architect, building several prominent buildings in the internationalist style, he was also a gifted draftsman and produced a body of sober drawings of the Jerusalem landscape, especially thistles and olive trees, with gnarled trunks often suggesting human bodies in torment.

Landscape
1939

The Israel Museum, Jerusalem. Purchase Ms. Trude Dothan (the artist's daughter), Jerusalem. B71.0166. Photo © The Israel Museum, Jerusalem.

Jack Levine

1915–2000

The son of immigrants from Lithuania, the painter Jack Levine was born in Boston's South End and grew up in Roxbury. He attended Harvard, where his painting first attracted attention. He was a figurative painter, but his bold use of color and distortion of forms stamped him as a modernist. Much of his painting was overtly political, skewering politicians, capitalists, military men, and racists. After World War II and the Holocaust, he began to paint works with specifically Jewish content. Notable among them was a series of miniature portraits of biblical kings and postbiblical scholars.

The Neighborhood Physician
1939

Collection of the T. B. Walker Foundation, Gilbert M. Walker Fund, 1943. Art © Susanna Levine Fisher / Licensed by VAGA, New York, NY.

Felix Nussbaum

1904–1944

The painter Felix Nussbaum was born in Osnabrück, Germany. He was studying in Rome when the Nazis seized power, and he spent the next ten years in exile and eventually in hiding, mainly in Belgium. The Germans arrested him in 1944 and deported him to Auschwitz, where he was murdered. Like much of his work from the Nazi years, *The Refugee* is suffused with fear and despair. The man slumped in the chair, his walking stick and bundle on the floor, is trapped in a jail-like room, unable to find refuge anywhere.

The Refugee (European Vision)
1939

Collection of the Yad Vashem Art Museum, Jerusalem. © 2015 Artists Rights Society (ARS), New York.

Moshe Rynecki

1881–1943

The painter Moshe Rynecki was born into a traditional Jewish home in a small town near Siedlice, Poland. He received a yeshiva education before studying art in Warsaw in 1906–1907. He painted familiar scenes from Warsaw Jewish life, both everyday activities and religious holidays and rituals. After the German conquest of Poland, he was forced into the Warsaw ghetto, where he painted this scene of refugees from elsewhere in Poland arriving in the ghetto. He was deported to Maidanek in 1943.

Refugees, Warsaw Ghetto
1939

Collection of the Yad Vashem Art Museum, Jerusalem. Gift of Alex Rynecki, California. Courtesy of www.rynecki.org.

Shmuel Yosef Schweig

1905–1984

The Austrian-born photographer Shmuel Yosef Schweig settled in Jerusalem in 1923. From 1925 to 1927, he worked for the Jewish National Fund, following which he established his own studio in Jerusalem. He also served as curator of the photography department at the Rockefeller Museum. His work, which circulated widely, helped to shape the world's perception of Zionist activity in the Land of Israel. He was the first artistic photographer of landscape and archaeology and the first local photographer to employ color film.

At the Foot of Mt. Gerizim
1930s–1940s

Copyright Chanoch Ido, Courtesy Silver Print Collection, Ein Hod.

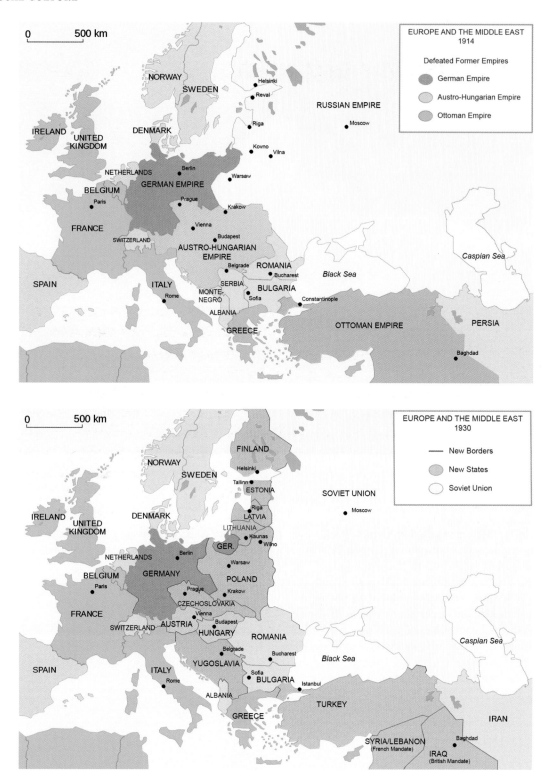

The two maps show the differences in state boundaries before and after World War I. The striking alterations resulted from the dissolution of four empires, the emergence of new states and the shrinking or expansion of others.
Original map by Historicair. Creative Commons Attribution-Share Alike 3.0 Unported, https://creativecommons .org/licenses/by-sa/3.0/deed.en. Redrawn and adapted by Deborah Nicholls.

FICTION AND DRAMA

The category of Jewish fiction and drama raises the hoary questions of who is a *Jewish* writer and what is a *Jewish* novel, short story, or play. Those Jews who wrote in Hebrew and Yiddish, whose readers were mostly Jewish, and whose subjects (their characters and their milieus) were also Jewish are not problematic in this regard. The question arises, however, in considering the work of writers who wrote in European languages and whose work attracted a more diverse readership. Rather than deciding a priori what are distinctively Jewish tropes, concerns, and values and whether their presence in a work stamps it as Jewish, we have opted to use more prosaic, nonessentialist criteria. The writers in this section were Jewish writers by virtue of their descent and their decision to focus on or include characters who are Jewish and whose experiences were familiar to Jews at the time. They were also Jewish by virtue of their often-explicit choice to fictionalize issues that occupied Jewish intellectuals and communal leaders in other arenas. By these standards, Isaac Babel was a Jewish writer, whereas André Maurois (né Émile Salomon Wilhelm Herzog) was not.

Sholem Asch

1880–1957

Sholem Asch was born in Kutno (Poland) into a Hasidic family. Self-educated in European literature, Asch moved to Warsaw and began to write under I. L. Peretz's patronage. He joined Peretz in championing Yiddish at the Czernowitz Conference. In 1914, Asch settled in New York, worked for the *Forverts*, and was among the co-founders of the American Jewish Joint Distribution Committee. Returning to Europe after the war, Asch settled in Warsaw in 1923 and was a leader of the Yiddish PEN club in 1932. He returned to the United States in 1938. During his long and prolific literary career, Asch was the center of multiple controversies. He spent the end of his life in Bat Yam, Israel.

Kiddush Ha-Shem
1919

Chapter Eight. The Captive

[. . .] From the other side of the fence was heard a murmur of Jewish voices as of people praying aloud. On a carpet before the door of the courtyard sat Murad Khan, and near him burned a vessel filled with pitch. Before him on the carpet lay little heaps of copper and silver coins, various Turkish articles, carpets, objects of barter. Murad Khan, a sickly man, with a long drooping mustache and calm, lack-luster eyes, sat silent; near him stood two Tatars with covered heads and called out in Cossack language:

"Little brother Cossacks, bring your captives to Murad Khan. Murad Khan, the great merchant, is buying up slaves."

"Cossacks, Cossacks, Murad Khan pays for slaves with good Turkish money."

A small Tatar approached the group of Cossacks, looked Shlomo over, felt him, and pointed with his hand at two small coins.

"With a pot of Tatar beer," the Cossack haggled.

The Tatar shook his head.

"Then I'll kill him,—as God lives, I'll kill him. If you give me a pot of Tatar beer to treat the Cossacks with, then well. If not, I kill him."

The Tatar approached Murad Khan who sat squatting on his feet, sorrowful and mute like one who is being consumed by some disease. His face was listless and his sad almond-shaped eyes were without expression.

Murad Khan shook his head.

"In that case, let us kill him and not sell him to the Tatars."

"Wait, dear little Cossacks, wait," says the old lyre-player, and coming close to the Tatar, he whispered in his ear and gesticulated:

"That captive, there, is a very important Jew. I know him, he is a rabbi. The Jews of Smyrna will pay a big ransom for him. A rabbi, that's what he is."

Again the Tatar approached Murad Khan and repeated to him what the old man had said.

Murad Khan nodded. The Tatar took a pitcher of beer, which stood near Murad Khan, and carried him to the courtyard among the captives.

From the other side of the fence was heard the singing of Psalms:

"The Lord is my light and my salvation; whom shall I fear?"

"Come, dear little comrades, let us drink," said the Cossacks, and sat down on the meadow to drink the Tatar beer.

"And you, lyre-player, play us something jolly, and sad also," some of them begged.

The Cossacks sat in a circle around the player. He took up his instrument, plucked at the strings, and sang to them the following in a strange medley of Hebrew and Polish:

Oh Thou, *Ribbono shel olom*,
Why dost Thou not notice,
Why dost Thou not witness
Our bitter *golus*, our bitter *golus*?
Our bitter *golus* we shall vanquish,
To our land we shall return! [. . .]

Chapter Nine. The Dice

A little fire of twigs was burning in the steppe. Near the fire sat three Cossacks, haggling among themselves:

"I saw her first, therefore she belongs to me," one of them, an old man, said. His shriveled face was illumined by the blazing twigs, and his small eyes, which were imbedded in his big broad face like two raisins in a lump of dough, glistened in the dark. He bent down towards the girl, who lay a little distance away from them on the bare field, covered with a long, white, Cossack cloak. He tried to stroke her with his old hairy hand, but it was forced back by the hand of an old woman, who was kneeling near him in a crouching posture, watching over the girl.

"It means nothing that you saw her first when she was hiding in the jungle," said the second. "What you saw was an old donkey, and it turned out to be a pretty little filly. An old grandmother is what you saw, a little old Cossack woman, before we scared her out of the bushes. And then it was I who recognized in her the young Jew girl. I pulled the cloth from her head and washed from her face the mud with which the old witch had disguised her. You saw an old blind plug, a lame old donkey, that is what you saw, and I found a young eaglet, a little dove. Well, now, to whom, does she belong, to me or to you?" Thus did a young Cossack blood argue with the old man. The fire lighted up his full round face, which looked out from his high fur cap. He had a pair of black, childlike eyes, which looked out good-naturedly, even in anger.

"And I say, all three of us found her, so she belongs to all three. That would be comradely and in true Cossack fashion," said the third Cossack, who sat near the fire. He did not excite himself, nor shout, as did the other two, but spoke firmly and with assurance. His two mustaches hung down over his mouth like the two feelers of a lobster. He was half naked, and the fire played on the copper color of his skin. He was holding a lump of pork on a spit over the flame. Drops of molten fat dripped into the fire, and made it crackle noisily. The fire cast a red glow on his copper-colored face, which now assumed an ashen hue. His elongated black eyes were buried deep in the sockets. His face also was elongated, his cheek bones protruded sharply, and on his chin stiff black bristles were scattered. His head was shaven, and a long wisp of hair, which was left on his forehead, came down across his cheek, and this lent to his face a tense and mute expression, as though it had never been visited by a smile.

"Belong to all three? Oh no, comrade, either to one of us or to none," replied the young one.

"Ho there, little suckling, don't talk back to an old Cossack. The times we live in!" the first old man groaned.

"Otherwise, let us kill her," remarked the squatting Cossack.

"It would be a pity to kill her, dear little comrade," the first Cossack replied. "It would be better to bring her to the Tatars; the Khan hasn't such a one in his harem. He will give us a little bag of gold for her, and the gold we will divide up."

"And what else will you take to the Khan? Your own wife and daughters? Ah, the times that have come upon us! Cossacks have become the servants of the Khan. Chmelnik has sold us completely to the Tatars. A Cossack can no longer afford himself a pretty Jew girl. Everything must be taken to the Khan. No, dear little comrade, either she will belong to one of us or else let us kill her," rejoined the half naked Cossack, and saying this, he took out from his girdle a little bag and shook out of it some bone dice.

"Comrades, let us act like Cossacks, let us throw dice, and whomever the dice will indicate, to him she will belong. It will be his good fortune, and let there be no jealousy among Cossacks on account of a pretty Jew girl."

"Right! Spoken like a comrade and a Cossack! Whomever the dice will indicate, for him God intended her, and let there be no jealousy among Cossacks on account of a Jew girl."

The young Cossack stood in silent thought, and with his velvet eyes gazed at the white coat under which lay the victim.

"Give way, little brother; shall Cossacks fall out on account of a Jew girl? Whomever God will designate, to him she will belong; and if not to you, then you will be able to get other Jew girls, enough to fill up your mother's stables. Krivonos will lead us to Tulchin, where Jewish women from all of Ukraine have gathered, and you will be able to pick to your heart's content."

The young Cossack bent suddenly down toward the fire, took the dice and threw them.

"Three, eight, five," they began to count.

"Six, three, ten."

"Good throw!"

"Five, eight, twelve," someone called out and laughed, and his laughter re-echoed in the night from the edge of the field.

Under the white Cossack cloak lay Deborah, and her shining eyes watched the game of dice by the light of the fire. She knew that the game was for her. She was the stakes. But not for a minute did she despair. An inner assurance that God would help her overflowed her heart. She believed in all Shlomo had said to her before their parting, that God would bring them together and that they would live together again. In her extremity, she remembered and longed for the happiness of the days when she was together with her husband. In that remembrance she found calm, and believed firmly that the time would come when God would deliver her from all her troubles and restore her to her husband. And this faith gave her strength to live.

Again cries arose near the fire.

"Three, six, five."

"Seven, three, eight."

"Ha, Ha, Ha!"

"Four, eight, twelve," a hollow voice laughed heavily in the night.

At this moment there suddenly rose up from the grass the black spot which was kneeling near Deborah, and which they believed had been silenced forever by the blow she had received from the Tatar Cossack.

"For your souls may you throw dice, for your mothers, but not for my eaglet, my little one, not for her whom I brought up with so much suffering, not for my precious own one," old Marusha cried to the Cossacks, and bending down to the young woman, she embraced her and comforted her.

"Precious soul mine, God will help us, you will see, God will send a fire down upon them. Ah, the Cossacks have become wild, forgotten their God, forgotten their own fathers and mothers, there is no fear of the king in them and they obey no law. Ah, God's anger will destroy you with thunder and with lightning! He will burn down the bridges beneath you. He will cause the earth to split open. You will sink down into Hell, you sons of dogs."

"Be silent, old witch, be silent, you, who have sold yourself to the devil."

"Let us cut her tongue out."

"No, rather the head, then you will not have to cut the tongue separately."

From beneath the white cloak the shining black eyes now looked up into the sky and into the stars. They were full of the faith that there among the stars sat He who knows and sees all.

Of one thing she was certain, that she did not wish to die. She would live and fight for her life as long as she would be able to, even as she had promised Shlomo. Not for her own sake but for her husband's, that she might be privileged to be the mother of his children.

The Cossacks were throwing dice for the last time:

"Three, six, five."

There now came to her mind the morning of that Shovuos festival before the great disaster, when the green trees and meadows looked in through the windows of their little room. She sees him again sitting over the Talmud, swaying over it, and studying aloud. She hears his voice, and it rings in her ears like a song. And she stands near the chest and decks herself out for his sake, no, for the sake of God, in order to go to synagogue—in the holiday jewels which he had brought her from Lublin, and she approaches him in her pretty head-dress, and he lays his hand upon her head and looks deep into her eyes.

From near the fire there now sprang up a tumult, clapping of hands, a wild, bestial laughter. She did not understand what it meant, but she knew that the crucial moment was at hand, and that now God would help her.

From near the fire someone rose up. The silent naked Cossack approached the white spot with shuffling steps, and tore away the Cossack cloak. In the starry night there was revealed a girlish body, half wrapped in torn rags, which curled up and shrank into itself like a worm.

"You will not come near, you will not do my child evil, I will scratch your eyes out," old Marusha cried, and sprang up like a maddened cat between the Cossack and the young woman, and stretched out towards him her two bony hands.

She wanted to say something more, to utter some prayer and entreaty, but suddenly a blow rang out, and old Marusha crumbled to the ground like a bag of broken bones and groaned: "Have mercy, Father."

The Cossack stretched out his hand and tried to seize Deborah, but with the agility of a cat, she sprang aside. Her eyes sought for help, and there flashed before her the soft form of the young Cossack, lighted up by the fire where he stood. His sad, velvet glance seemed to caress her, and a sudden hope of salvation flashed up in her mind.

"Save me from him, I don't want to belong to him," she said, and clung to the young Cossack, seeking shelter near him, as does a child under a tree when it rains.

The young Cossack quivered. Her girlish voice, which he heard for the first time, since he had captured her, made his heart leap, and when she looked into his face with her moist prayerful eyes, he was unable to bear her glance, and avoided it. He remained standing firm as a tree, and did not stir. His face became pale and his heart began to beat strangely.

For a minute the second Cossack looked to see what the young man would do, then with heavy steps he approached the girl and stretched out his hand towards her.

"He cheated in the game, I will not go to him," Deborah cried, when the Cossack began to approach her.

The young man was still standing mute and motionless as a tree. But in his eyes a little fire had lighted up.

"Be silent, accursed one, and come to your master." He tried to seize Deborah by the hand and drag her to himself.

The young Cossack moved swiftly to one side and placed himself directly opposite the other.

Two knife-blades flashed up in the light of the fire.

"Cossacks, what are you doing? Will you slaughter one another for a Jew girl? Are there not enough Jew girls in Ukraine? Cossacks, reflect what you are doing," the third one shouted.

But he was afraid to approach. Both Cossacks stood facing each other, looking into each other's eyes, and the curved Turkish knives glistened in the light.

And suddenly, like a wild animal, the young one leaped upon the other with his knife, and the next moment the older man lay on the ground and rattled heavily in the night.

"Curses on you, you sinful soul! For the sake of a Jew girl you have murdered a Cossack, may the sin lie upon you like a heavy burden wherever you turn and wherever you go," the second old man cursed. Then he spat out and walked off by himself into the night.

For a moment the young man stood and seemed lost in thought. Then he appeared to remember something and called after the retreating Cossack into the night.

"Ho there old man, where are you going?"

"I will not have anything to do with you, you have sold your soul to the devil," a voice replied to him from the blackness of the night.

For a minute he stood still, not knowing what to do. He looked about him, seeking the girl with his eyes. He found her lying on the grass unconscious.

He stooped, lifted her up and brought her to the fire. Then he took his cloak and covered her. He sat down near her alone. The light of the fire illumined her face. He saw how white her face was, and the lids which were drawn over her eyes as in a dove, and a tender feeling took possession of him for the frail creature that lay near him.

Translated by Rufus Learsi.

Other works by Asch: *A shtetl* (1904); *Got fun nekome* (1907); *Motke ganef* (1916); *Onkl Mozes* (1918); *Farn mabul* (1921–1931); *Der tilim-yid* (1934); *The Nazarine* (1939); *Three Cities* (1943); *East River* (1946).

Peretz Hirshbein

1880–1948

Peretz Hirshbein (Hirshbeyn) was a prolific Yiddish writer, remembered chiefly for his travelogues, his memoirs, and his dramatic works. His legacy includes a range of plays, from naturalist dramas rich in political symbolism to his beloved, understated plays concerning the lives of rural Jews. Hirshbein lived an itinerant life, traveling constantly around the world together with his wife, the Yiddish poet Esther Shumiatsher-Hirshbein, and producing dozens of travelogues about locales both exotic and mundane. He eventually settled in Los Angeles.

Two Cities
1919

Dramatis Personae

REBBE LEVI YITSKHOK
TSINE, his wife
KHAYIM, their son
GNENDL, their daughter
TAYBELE, their daughter
HENEKH YOEL, gabbai
OYZER, butcher
ZAVL, butcher
ITSHE
MORDKHE
MOYSHE
KHVEDER, shabes-goy
PAVETINE, town madman
A CROWD, MEN, WOMEN, OLD, YOUNG [. . .]

Act I

[REBBE LEVI YITSKHOK's *large rabbinical house. Bookshelves with holy books on the walls, the ark and the pulpit at the eastern wall. One door leads outside, the others lead to the inner rooms. It is around Shavuos. Warm and sunny. The windows are open, and through them the noise from the market can be heard.*] [. . .]

[REBBE LEVI YITSKHOK *enters.*]

HENEKH YOEL: Hello, Rabbi.

REBBE LEVI YITSKHOK: And hello to you.

HENEKH YOEL: How are you, Rabbi?

TSINE: Bless the Eternal, all's well. [. . .] I heard that guests are coming today, Levi Yitskhok.

REBBE LEVI YITSKHOK: Guests? What a surprise!

HENEKH YOEL: I see that some of you know about it!

REBBE LEVI YITSKHOK: What happened?

KHAYIM: If two cities will fight, it will be . . .

REBBE LEVI YITSKHOK: There is a fight behind my back?

HENEKH YOEL: In shul, they say that Khayim must have a hand in it and that's why he abandoned the shul.

REBBE LEVI YITSKHOK: What's the big deal? I also liked solitude when I was his age.

HENEKH YOEL: True, Rabbi. Solitude is a great thing; but, when one causes the whole city grief—an entire city, Rabbi.

REBBE LEVI YITSKHOK: I really don't understand what you're talking about at all. Am I, God forbid, causing some aggravation?

[GNENDL *and* TAYBELE *enter.*]

TAYBELE: I'm so happy we're leaving.

GNENDL: Really?

TSINE: You know about this, children?

TAYBELE: Khveder told us.

REBBE LEVI YITSKHOK: Really now, Khveder knows what is going with Levi Yitskhok? Ha-ha-ha.

HENEKH YOEL: The shul is in turmoil over it.

REBBE LEVI YITSKHOK: This must be some kind of a trick. Well then, is there a shortage of rabbis, or of respectable Jews?

TAYBELE: I'm so happy we're going to another town.

REBBE LEVI YITSKHOK: What is this, does everyone know and I am like a child, who doesn't know what's going on? What do you say, Reb Henekh Yoel?

KHAYIM: If you change your place, you change your luck.

REBBE LEVI YITSKHOK: You also know, then? I am thoroughly shocked. And how would you like it if Levi Yitskhok doesn't let this happen? He-he-he.

HENEKH YOEL: A town is a town. Perhaps the salary is too low, but we can call a meeting and see what we can do. If the rabbi's house is too small—there is talk that the town may build a bigger one.

TSINE: I am by no means dissatisfied here.

REBBE LEVI YITSKHOK: Sure, and a fight also; and grief, of course. . . . So no one asks me anything. Come with me, Reb Henekh Yoel, I am thoroughly shocked. [*He exits with* HENEKH YOEL.] [. . .]

[OYZER *and* ZAVL *enter.*]

OYZER: The rabbi isn't here?

GNENDL: He should come any minute now.

[GNENDL *and* TAYBELE *both exit.*]

ZAVL: What do you think?

OYZER: If anything happens, I won't be holding my tongue.

ZAVL: If a town sneaks up the road. . . . Do you think an entire city can do that? A city can be taught a lesson as well . . .

REBBE LEVI YITSKHOK [*enters*]: Hello, Oyzer. Hello, Zavl.

OYZER: Hello, Rebbe.

ZAVL: How are you, Rebbe?

REBBE LEVI YITSKHOK: Well, then, how was your week? Something wasn't kosher, most likely.

ZAVL: What does it matter? Even if twenty of my oxen would have become *treyf*, I wouldn't be as upset as I am about the news I just heard.

OYZER: How could this happen in our town?

ZAVL: We are talking about the fact that another city wants to take you away from us.

REBBE LEVI YITSKHOK: Is that it? So what? Greater rabbis than me are sitting around waiting for a job.

OYZER: You are being humble, but I understand what's going on.

ZAVL: Our town is famous, and it isn't because of me or because of Oyzer. I'm referring to you, Rabbi.

REBBE LEVI YITSKHOK: Every Jew merits that for his sake the world should continue to exist; I am no more than a Jew among Jews.

OYZER: This means that the Rebbe already knows about everything? . . .

REBBE LEVI YITSKHOK: Yes, I know.

ZAVL: What does the Rebbe intend to do?

REBBE LEVI YITSKHOK: I will do according to the will of the One who is in heaven.

[HENEKH YOEL *enters.*]

OYZER: The Rebbe knows already.

HENEKH YOEL: It is still in God's hands.

REBBE LEVI YITSKHOK: So, two towns are fighting over Levi Yitskhok. Interesting.

OYZER: Their heads are not shrunken.

[*Three Jews enter excitedly, with a "Hello!"*]

REBBE LEVI YITSKHOK: How are you, Itshe? How are you Reb Mordkhe and Moyshe?

ITSHE: Is it really true, Rabbi, what they say?

REBBE LEVI YITSKHOK: What, is the world coming to an end, God forbid? What's all the fuss about?

HENEKH YOEL: True, true.

MORDKHE: You are abandoning us.

REBBE LEVI YITSKHOK: What, are you little children?

MOYSHE: It is unimaginable.

ITSHE: There will be blood. [. . .]

MORDKHE: When a town has no leader, it is a city with no head.

REBBE LEVI YITSKHOK: I examined my own heart closely; I weighed my deeds against the deeds of the community . . .

MORDKHE: What is there to talk about, Rabbi. . . . The town was terribly shaken. In some houses, there is weeping. My father was planning to come here himself, but couldn't take a step from the house, the poor thing.

MOYSHE: The people were wondering why Khayim left the shul and locked himself up in the rabbi's house. They couldn't make sense of it.

REBBE LEVI YITSKHOK: Don't magnify me so. Don't elevate me. I know nothing about this at this point. There is probably a city though I know nothing about it. There is probably a rabbi there and they want a feud. . . . But Levi Yitskhok will not consent to this. . . . Ha-ha-ha, it's amazing [. . .]

ITSHE: Why are we just standing around? We should call a meeting, and decide what to do.

A JEW [barges in]: That's wrong, you criminals. A city full of criminals. Goyim act like this, but not Jews, especially Jews that have such a righteous rabbi!

REBBE LEVI YITSKHOK: What's the matter? The earth itself started its shaking because of you. Who are you? Somehow unfamiliar. . . . Hello.

JEW: I am Binem from Horotshin, I came here with another Jew, and they blocked my way. It's been close to two hours, since I am trying to get in here.

OYZER: You're lucky that I wasn't there. I would have shown you how to get in here, alright.

JEW: It's a disgrace to hear such talk in a rabbi's house.

REBBE LEVI YITSKHOK: I'm begging you, Reb Oyzer, and you, Reb Zavl, don't start any trouble.

JEW: I came here with a partner of mine only to hear your legal judgment, and nothing more; and they attacked me as if I was planning to rob the town.

ITSHE: We know very well why you came here, but I say we should give the rabbi a higher salary and build a new rabbi's house. I'm going to inform the town.

JEW: Rabbi, I came here to have your legal judgment. Let them allow my partner to enter. They took my horse and wagon, and the horse will starve.

REBBE LEVI YITSKHOK: That has to be a joke! Jews wouldn't do such a thing!

BINEM: That's what I'm saying, this is a disgrace.

ZAVL: I will see to it that they release the horse and wagon to you, but only on the condition that you and your partner will mount it and go home in peace.

[REBBE LEVI YITSKHOK says nothing and exits.]

BINEM: It's a disgrace to say such things in the rabbi's private chambers. In Horotshin such a thing could never have happened.

ITSHE: You'll get your bones broken. Go home, and say that Horotshin will perish in fire if they try to fight with Khotshover Jews.

BINEM: It's a dishonor to the Torah, that Rebbe Levi Yitskhok is your rabbi.

OYZER: I will do anything to stop you from making it happen.

BINEM: It's a dishonor to have him stay in your little town.

ITSHE: Come to shul, Jews; come, Jews, let's see what we can do. [Exits along with MORDKHE and MOYSHE]

[KHAYIM enters.]

HENEKH YOEL: Here's Khayim. What's going on out there?

KHAYIM: Jews are fighting over the Torah and the Torah is in the holy ark. [. . .]

HENEKH YOEL: This is terrible!

[REBBE LEVI YITSKHOK enters, many Jews appear at the door. Outside even more of them. The crowd is silent, as if waiting for REBBE LEVI YITSKHOK's words. He is walking around, up and away, his yarmulke moved up to the top of his head.]

HENEKH YOEL: What do you plan to do, Rabbi? Will we be left like a flock without a shepherd?

REBBE LEVI YITSKHOK: Jews, merciful people, why would you, with all your greatness, place your faith in one person, and now, when I may move, it is as if I diminished your greatness. If I do move away, it will not be my will. It is the will of the One who sits among angels. I will not stand in His way.

A MAN [from the crowd, with tears in his voice]: The community will not be able to get through this.

ANOTHER MAN: There is justice yet: we will take justice into our own hands.

REBBE LEVI YITSKHOK: Such justice I do not approve of, and you, my son, will you approve of such justice?

KHAYIM: I stand before you as a student before his rabbi.

HENEKH YOEL: I also feel that the community will not be able to bear it.

A MAN: A dark cloud is spreading over our heads.

[More Jews appear at the door. It seems as if they want to insist on being let into the house, but are not allowed.]

VOICES:

—They are not worthy of crossing the threshold.

—Don't let them in.

—It's bloodshed.

—They are spilling our blood . . .

—Jews, don't lose your minds.

—Jews, don't humiliate a fellow Jew.

—A shame, a disgrace.

—Sodom!

REBBE LEVI YITSKHOK [*who has been standing with his face buried in religious books on the shelf, turns to the crowd at the door with a shaky voice*]: Jews, be hospitable, don't disgrace our city, let them through, let me welcome the Jews from another town. . . . Please!

[*The crowd at the door silently makes way and a few unfamiliar wealthy Jews come in, go silently to* REBBE LEVI YITSKHOK *and greet him. The crowd looks on in silent sorrow.*]

Translated by Alexandra Hoffman.

Other works by Hirshbein: *A farvorfn vinkl* (1912); *Di puste kretshme* (1913); *Dem shmids tekhter* (1918); *Grine felder* (1918); *Mayne kinder-yorn* (1932).

Lamed Shapiro
1878–1948

The Yiddish writer Lamed Shapiro was born in a Ukrainian shtetl forty miles south of Kiev. Much of his life was peripatetic, as he struggled to earn a living, first in Poland and Ukraine, and later in the United States—in New York, Chicago, and Los Angeles, where he died a penniless alcoholic in 1948. Depressed and at times suicidal, he tried his hand at writing for the Yiddish press, running restaurants, and inventing a method for producing color film. His dark and troubling short stories and novellas were groundbreaking in Yiddish literature. Psychologically complex, they are riven with violence and extremes of human behavior, including murder, rape, and sadism.

White Challah
1919

1

One day a neighbor broke the leg of a stray dog with a heavy stone, and when Vasil saw the sharp edge of the bone piercing the skin he cried. The tears streamed from his eyes, his mouth, and his nose; the towhead on his short neck shrank deeper between his shoulders; his entire face became distorted and shriveled, and he did not utter a sound. He was then about seven years old.

Soon he learned not to cry. His family drank, fought with neighbors, with one another, beat the women, the horse, the cow, and sometimes, in special rages, their own heads against the wall. They were a large family with a tiny piece of land, they toiled hard and clumsily, and all of them lived in one hut—men, women, and children slept pell-mell on the floor. The village was small and poor, at some distance from a town; and the town to which they occasionally went for the fair seemed big and rich to Vasil.

In the town there were Jews—people who wore strange clothes, sat in stores, ate white *challah*, and had sold Christ. The last point was not quite clear: who was Christ, why did the Jews sell him, who bought him, and for what purpose?—it was all as though in a fog. White *challah*, that was something else again: Vasil saw it a few times with his own eyes, and more than that—he once stole a piece and ate it, whereupon he stood for a time in a daze, an expression of wonder on his face. He did not understand it all, but respect for white *challah* stayed with him.

He was half an inch too short, but he was drafted, owing to his broad, slightly hunched shoulders and thick short neck. Here in the army beatings were again the order of the day: the corporal, the sergeant, and the officers beat the privates, and the privates beat one another, all of them. He could not learn the service regulations: he did not understand and did not think. Nor was he a good talker; when hard pressed he usually could not utter a sound, but his face grew tense, and his low forehead was covered with wrinkles. *Kasha* and borscht, however, were plentiful. There were a few Jews in his regiment—Jews who had sold Christ—but in their army uniforms and without white *challah* they looked almost like everybody else.

2

They traveled in trains, they marched, they rode again, and then again moved on foot; they camped in the open or were quartered in houses; and this went on so long that Vasil became completely confused. He no longer remembered when it had begun, where he had been before, or who he had been; it was as though all his life had been spent moving from town to town, with tens or hundreds of thousands of other soldiers, through foreign places inhabited by strange people who spoke an incomprehensible language and looked frightened or angry. Nothing particularly new had happened, but fighting had become the very essence of life; everyone was fighting now, and this time it was no longer just beating, but fighting in earnest: they fired at people, cut them to pieces, bayoneted them, and sometimes even bit them with their teeth. He too fought, more and more savagely, and with greater relish. Now food did not come regularly, they slept little, they marched and fought a great deal, and all this made him restless. He kept missing something, longing for something, and at moments of great strain he howled like a tormented dog because he could not say what he wanted.

They advanced over steadily higher ground; chains of giant mountains seamed the country in all directions, and winter ruled over them harshly and without respite. They inched their way through valleys, knee-deep in dry powdery snow, and icy winds raked their faces and hands like grating irons, but the officers were cheerful and kindlier than before, and spoke of victory; and food, though not always served on time, was plentiful. At night they were sometimes permitted to build fires on the snow; then monstrous shadows moved noiselessly between the mountains, and the soldiers sang. Vasil too tried to sing, but he could only howl. They slept like the dead, without dreams or nightmares, and time and again during the day the mountains reverberated with the thunder of cannon, and men again climbed up and down the slopes.

3

A mounted messenger galloped madly through the camp; an advance cavalry unit returned suddenly and occupied positions on the flank; two batteries were moved from the left to the right. The surrounding mountains split open like freshly erupting volcanoes, and a deluge of fire, lead, and iron came down upon the world.

The barrage kept up for a long time. Piotr Kudlo was torn to pieces; the handsome Kruvenko, the best singer of the company, lay with his face in a puddle of blood; Lieutenant Somov, the one with girlish features, lost a leg, and the giant Neumann, the blond Estonian, had his whole face torn off. The pockmarked Gavrilov was dead; a single shell killed the two Bulgach brothers; killed, too, were Chaim Ostrovsky, Jan Zatyka, Staszek Pieprz, and the little Latvian whose name Vasil could

not pronounce. Now whole ranks were mowed down, and it was impossible to hold on. Then Nahum Rachek, a tall slender young man who had always been silent, jumped up and without any order ran forward. This gave new spirit to the dazed men, who rushed the jagged hill to the left and practically with their bare hands conquered the batteries that led the enemy artillery, strangling the defenders like cats, down to the last man. Later it was found that of the entire company only Vasil and Nahum Rachek remained. After the battle Rachek lay on the ground vomiting green gall, and next to him lay his rifle with its butt smeared with blood and brains. He was not wounded, and when Vasil asked what was the matter he did not answer.

After sunset the conquered position was abandoned, and the army fell back. How and why this happened Vasil did not know; but from that moment the army began to roll down the mountains like an avalanche of stones. The farther they went, the hastier and less orderly was the retreat, and in the end they ran—ran without stopping, day and night. Vasil did not recognize the country, each place was new to him, and he knew only from hearsay that they were moving back. Mountains and winter had long been left behind; around them stretched a broad, endless plain; spring was in full bloom; but the army ran and ran. The officers became savage, they beat the soldiers without reason and without pity. A few times they stopped for a while; the cannon roared, a rain of fire whipped the earth, and men fell like flies—and then they ran again.

4

Someone said that all this was the fault of the Jews. Again the Jews! They sold Christ, they eat white *challah*, and on top of it all they are to blame for everything. What was "everything"? Vasil wrinkled his forehead and was angry at the Jews and at someone else. Leaflets appeared, printed leaflets that a man distributed among the troops, and in the camps groups gathered around those who could read. They stood listening in silence— they were silent in a strange way, unlike people who just do not talk. Someone handed a leaflet to Vasil too; he examined it, fingered it, put it in his pocket, and joined a group to hear what was being read. He did not understand a word, except that it was about Jews. So the Jews must know, he thought, and he turned to Nahum Rachek.

"Here, read it," he said.

Rachek cast a glance at the leaflet, then another curious glance at Vasil; but he said nothing and seemed about to throw the leaflet away.

"Don't! It's not yours!" Vasil said. He took back the leaflet, stuck it in his pocket, and paced back and forth in agitation. Then he turned to Rachek. "What does it say? It's about you, isn't it?"

At this point Nahum flared up. "Yes, about me. It says I'm a traitor, see? That I've betrayed us—that I'm a spy. Like that German who was caught and shot. See?"

Vasil was scared. His forehead began to sweat. He left Nahum, fingering his leaflet in bewilderment. This Nahum, he thought, must be a wicked man—so angry, and a spy besides, he said so himself, but something doesn't fit here, it's puzzling, it doesn't fit, my head is splitting.

After a long forced march they stopped somewhere. They had not seen the enemy for several days and had not heard any firing. They dug trenches and made ready. A week later it all began anew. It turned out that the enemy was somewhere nearby; he too was in trenches, and these trenches were moving closer and closer each day, and occasionally one could see a head showing above the parapet. They ate very little, they slept even less, they fired in the direction the bullets came from, bullets that kept hitting the earth wall, humming overhead, and occasionally boring into human bodies. Next to Vasil, at his left, always lay Nahum Rachek. He never spoke, only kept loading his rifle and firing, mechanically, unhurriedly. Vasil could not bear the sight of him and occasionally was seized with a desire to stab him with his bayonet.

One day, when the firing was particularly violent, Vasil suddenly felt strangely restless. He cast a glance sidewise at Rachek and saw him lying in the same posture as before, on his stomach, with his rifle in his hand; but there was a hole in his head. Something broke in Vasil; in blind anger he kicked the dead body, pushing it aside, and then began to fire wildly, exposing his head to the dense shower of lead that was pouring all around him.

That night he could not sleep for a long time; he tossed and turned, muttering curses. At one point he jumped up angrily and began to run straight ahead, but then he recalled that Rachek was dead and dejectedly returned to his pallet. The Jews . . . traitors . . . sold Christ . . . traded him away for a song!

He ground his teeth and clawed at himself in his sleep.

5

At daybreak Vasil suddenly sat up on his hard pallet. His body was covered with cold sweat, his teeth were chattering, and his eyes, round and wide open, tried greedily to pierce the darkness. Who has been here? Who has been here?

It was pitch-dark and fearfully quiet, but he still could hear the rustle of the giant wings and feel the cold hem of the black cloak that had grazed his face. Someone had passed over the camp like an icy wind, and the camp was silent and frozen—an open grave with thousands of bodies, struck while asleep, and pierced in the heart. Who has been here? Who has been here? During the day Lieutenant Muratov of the fourth battalion of the Yeniesey regiment was found dead—Muratov, a violent, cruel man with a face the color of parchment. The bullet that pierced him between the eyes had been fired by someone from his own battalion. When the men were questioned no one betrayed the culprit. Threatened with punishment, they still refused to answer, and they remained silent when they were ordered to surrender their arms. The other regimental units were drawn up against the battalion, but when they were ordered to fire, all of them to a man lowered their rifles to the ground. Another regiment was summoned, and in ten minutes not a man of the mutinous battalion remained alive.

Next day two officers were hacked to pieces. Three days later, following a dispute between two cavalrymen, the entire regiment split into two camps. They fought each other until only a few were left unscathed.

Then men in mufti appeared and, encouraged by the officers, began to distribute leaflets among the troops. This time they did not make long speeches, but kept repeating one thing: the Jews have betrayed us, everything is their fault.

Once again someone handed a leaflet to Vasil, but he did not take it. He drew out of his pocket, with love and respect, as though it were a precious medallion, a crumpled piece of paper frayed at the edges and stained with blood, and showed it—he had it, and remembered it. The man with the leaflets, a slim little fellow with a sand-colored beard, half closed one of his little eyes and took stock of the squat broad-shouldered private with the short thick neck and bulging gray watery eyes. He gave Vasil a friendly pat on the back and left with a strange smile on his lips.

The Jewish privates had vanished: they had been quietly gathered together and sent away, no one knew where. Everyone felt freer and more comfortable, and although there were several nationalities represented among them, they were all of one mind about it: the alien was no longer in their midst.

And then someone launched a new slogan—"The Jewish government."

6

This was their last stand, and when they were again defeated they no longer stopped anywhere but ran like stampeding animals fleeing a steppe fire, in groups or individually, without commanders and without order, in deadly fear, rushing through every passage left open by the enemy. Not all of them had weapons, no one had his full outfit of clothing, and their shirts were like second skins on their unwashed bodies. The summer sun beat down on them mercilessly, and they ate only what they could forage. Now their native tongue was spoken in the towns, and their native fields lay around them, but the fields were unrecognizable, for last year's crops were rotting, trampled into the earth, and the land lay dry and gray and riddled, like the carcass of an ox disemboweled by wolves.

And while the armies crawled over the earth like swarms of gray worms, flocks of ravens soared overhead, calling with a dry rattling sound—the sound of tearing canvas—and swooped and slanted in intricate spirals, waiting for what would be theirs.

Between Kolov and Zhaditsa the starved and crazed legions caught up with large groups of Jews who had been ordered out of border towns, with their women, children, invalids, and bundles. A voice said, "Get them!" The words sounded like the distant boom of a gun. At first Vasil held back, but the loud screams of the women and children and the repulsive, terrified faces of the men with their long earlocks and caftans blowing in the wind drove him to a frenzy, and he cut into the Jews like a maddened bull. They were destroyed with merciful speed: the army trampled over them like a herd of galloping horses.

Then, once again, someone said in a shrill little voice, "The Jewish government!"

The words suddenly soared high and like a peal of thunder rolled over the wild legions, spreading to villages and cities and reaching the remotest corners of the land. The retreating troops struck out at the region with fire and sword. By night burning cities lighted their path, and by day the smoke obscured the sun and

the sky and rolled in cottony masses over the earth, and suffocated ravens occasionally fell to the ground. They burned the towns of Zykov, Potapno, Kholodno, Stary Yug, Sheliuba; Ostrogorie, Sava, Rika, Beloye Krilo, and Stupnik were wiped from the face of the earth; the Jewish weaving town of Belopriazha went up in smoke, and the Vinokur Forest, where thirty thousand Jews had sought refuge, blazed like a bonfire, and for three days in succession agonized cries, like poisonous gases, rose from the woods and spread over the land. The swift, narrow Sinevodka River was entirely choked with human bodies a little below Lutsin and overflowed into the fields.

The hosts grew larger. The peasant left his village and the city dweller his city; priests with icons and crosses in their hands led processions through villages, devoutly and enthusiastically blessing the people, and the slogan was, "The Jewish government." The Jews themselves realized that their last hour had struck—the very last; and those who remained alive set out to die among Jews in Maliassy, the oldest and largest Jewish center in the land, a seat of learning since the fourteenth century, a city of ancient synagogues and great yeshivas, with rabbis and modern scholars, with an aristocracy of learning and of trade. Here, in Maliassy, the Jews fasted and prayed, confessing their sins to God, begging forgiveness of friend and enemy. Aged men recited Psalms and Lamentations, younger men burned stocks of grain and clothing, demolished furniture, broke and destroyed everything that might be of use to the approaching army. And this army came, it came from all directions, and set fire to the city from all sides, and poured into the streets. Young men tried to resist and went out with revolvers in their hands. The revolvers sounded like pop guns. The soldiers answered with thundering laughter, and drew out the young men's veins one by one, and broke their bones into little pieces. Then they went from house to house, slaying the men wherever they were found and dragging the women to the market place.

7

One short blow with his fist smashed the lock, and the door opened.

For two days now Vasil had not eaten or slept. His skin smarted in the dry heat, his bones seemed disjointed, his eyes were bloodshot, and his face and neck were covered with blond stubble.

"Food!" he said hoarsely.

No one answered him. At the table stood a tall Jew in a black caftan, with a black beard and earlocks and gloomy eyes. He tightened his lips and remained stubbornly silent. Vasil stepped forward angrily and said again, "Food!"

But this time he spoke less harshly. Near the window he had caught sight of another figure—a young woman in white, with a head of black hair. Two large eyes—he had never before seen such large eyes—were looking at him and through him, and the look of these eyes was such that Vasil lifted his arm to cover his own eyes. His knees were trembling, he felt as if he were melting. What kind of woman is that? What kind of people? God! Why, why, did they have to sell Christ? And on top of it all, responsible for everything! Even Rachek admitted it. And they just kept quiet, looking through you. Goddam it, what are they after? He took his head in his hands.

He felt something and looked about him. The Jew stood there, deathly pale, hatred in his eyes. For a moment Vasil stared dully. Suddenly he grabbed the black beard and pulled at it savagely.

A white figure stepped between them. Rage made Vasil dizzy and scalded his throat. He tugged at the white figure with one hand. A long strip tore from the dress and hung at the hem. His eyes were dazzled, almost blinded. Half a breast, a beautiful shoulder, a full, rounded hip—everything dazzling white and soft, like white *challah*. Damn it—these Jews are *made* of white *challah*! A searing flame leaped through his body, his arm flew up like a spring and shot into the gaping dress.

A hand gripped his neck. He turned his head slowly and looked at the Jew for a moment with narrowed eyes and bared teeth, without shaking free of the weak fingers that were clutching at his flesh. Then he raised his shoulders, bent forward, took the Jew by the ankles, lifted him in the air, and smashed him against the table. He flung him down like a broken stick.

The man groaned weakly; the woman screamed. But he was already on top of her. He pressed her to the floor and tore her dress together with her flesh. Now she was repulsive, her face blotchy, the tip of her nose red, her hair disheveled and falling over her eyes. "Witch," he said through his teeth. He twisted her nose like a screw. She uttered a shrill cry—short, mechanical, unnaturally high, like the whistle of an engine. The cry penetrating his brain maddened him completely. He seized her neck and strangled her.

A white shoulder was quivering before his eyes; a full, round drop of fresh blood lay glistening on it. His nostrils fluttered like wings. His teeth were grinding; suddenly they opened and bit into the white flesh.

White *challah* has the taste of a firm juicy orange. Warm and hot, and the more one sucks it the more burning the thirst. Sharp and thick, and strangely spiced.

Like rushing down a steep hill in a sled. Like drowning in sharp, burning spirits.

In a circle, in a circle, the juices of life went from body to body, from the first to the second, from the second to the first—in a circle.

Pillars of smoke and pillars of flame rose to the sky from the entire city. Beautiful was the fire on the great altar. The cries of the victims—long-drawn-out, endless cries—were sweet in the ears of a god as eternal as the Eternal God. And the tender parts, the thighs and the breasts, were the portion of the priest.

Translated by Lawrence Rosenwald.

Other works by Shapiro: *The Jewish Government and Other Stories* (1971); *The Cross and Other Jewish Stories* (2007).

Fradl Shtok

1890–after 1942

Few biographical details are known about the Yiddish writer Fradl Shtok. She was born in Galicia, orphaned at age ten, and subsequently raised by an aunt. She immigrated to New York City in 1907 and probably found employment in the garment industry. Beginning in 1910, she published poems and short stories in Yiddish anthologies and miscellanies, especially those associated with the literary movement Di Yunge. In 1918, she published a collection of thirty-eight short stories in which female eroticism and repressed sexuality are prominent themes. The collection received mixed reviews, some quite negative, and scholars hypothesize that this led her to cease writing in Yiddish. She published a novel in English, *Musicians Only*, in 1927, but it received no critical attention. By the early 1930s, she had disappeared from the Yiddish literary scene. The place and date of her death are unknown.

The Archbishop
1919

While the townsfolk knew that an archbishop was coming, no one in Skalle [Skala, today Ukraine] made a big fuss about the news. It was only when pine gates were set up at the entrance that people began talking about it in the street.

Mótkele the Redhead, whose brother was a big cheese at the town hall, explained: "Do they really have a clue? They think archbishops are a dime a dozen! Imagine how long it takes to climb that high! First you gotta study for the priesthood—you're not born a priest. Then you become a canon, then a supreme canon, then an elder, which he knows and which he's already forgotten—Ah, a blessed man. And then you become a bishop. And it's not till a long, long time later that you become an archbishop."

Why was an archbishop coming to Skalle? Nobody knew for certain. One person said that an archbishop visited Skalle only once every fifty years. Another person said that an archbishop came by only when the Christians were about to build a church. Henekh the Marriage Broker, who was standing nearby, glanced at the old Catholic church. He figured it wouldn't be such a bad idea: the town really needed a new church. He spit superstitiously, but he secretly mused: "A new church. The town'll become more genteel, more civilized." For Henekh knew how many matches had been nipped in the bud purely because Skalle was uncivilized.

In short, the idea kept growing on Henekh, and so he tried to convince everyone that it was a fact, that it couldn't be truer. And the Jews started believing him, because if Henekh wanted to talk you into something, he did so hands down.

Alter asked: "Well, so what's gonna happen with the town clock? What's the town gonna look at?"

The fact of the matter was that Alter wanted to get rid of the town clock. His home was next to the Polish church, and being a usurer, he had nothing to do. So he spent all day looking at the town clock, but by now he was totally sick of looking at it. He felt that if it hadn't been for the clock, he could have eaten one meal after another—only the clock didn't allow it. For instance, when he drank his cup of cocoa in the morning and the dial face said eight, it seemed to him that the hands would be approaching twelve, which was the reason he wasn't hungry and couldn't finish his lunch so soon.

Meanwhile a few other people were worried, because their own timepieces kept pace with the town clock, and if it were removed, their own timepieces would have nothing to keep pace with. And if all the clocks in town stopped working, how would they know? Without a clock, you can kick the bucket and not know when.

Now Shloyme the Deaf Man pointed out that it would bring good luck and prosperity for Skalle if a new church was "construcked."

"Prosperity from a church, Shloyme? Please explain." Avrom the Chatterbox was delighted that he had tripped up Shloyme.

The deaf man didn't like getting tripped up, especially by Avrom. So he snapped: "Goo aargue with yourseelf!" (Shloyme drawled because he came from a different region). He looked at Henekh and addressed him, but he actually meant Avrom. Whyy in the world didn't hee geet it? A goyish miind! "Wheen you construck a chuurch, you doo need engineers—aarchitecks, that is. Plus woorkers. They'll bring in the woorkers from other towns, peasants from the four corners of the world'll come to our fairs. Doo youu geet it noow—goyish mind?"

He meant Avrom, but he said all that stuff to Henekh, who caught the drift and held his tongue.

In short, the Jews looked forward to the arrival of the archbishop as they did to the coming of the Messiah (if you'll forgive my mentioning them in the same breath). Bórekh promised Sluk the dowry after the archbishop's visit. And when Henekh had to pay tuition for his son, he begged Shloyme to wait until after the visit—God bless us!

A bit later it was rumored that the town rabbi would welcome the archbishop with a Torah scroll. A few curious men pounced on the beadle, Shloyme Perets, in the street and asked him whether it was true. Shloyme winked his blind eye (which could spot a bad coin faster than a seeing eye) and he snuffled: "How should I know?"

"They're putting up a gate at the beginning of the street and another gate right by the pharmacy, and Dvoyre is standing there."

Alter's daughter Godel asked him: "What's Dvoyre doing by the pharmacy? Tell her to come home for lunch."

Godel explained that Dvoyre was standing there with her friend Shayndl, they were watching the construction of the gate.

"If she's with Shayndl, that's fine. Shayndl is a decent girl." And he went home.

By now, though, Dvoyre was standing without Shayndl, as she was watching the construction. And she didn't even give Lutsuk a second thought. Well, when Lutsuk came out alone, he came out alone—was it her fault? Was it her fault that the gate was being constructed by the pharmacy? And if he greeted her and doffed his hat, shouldn't she respond?

"It's too bad," said Lutsuk. "So many young pine trees shattered!"

"Yes, too bad." Shouldn't she have responded?

When Lutsuk looked at her, she looked away.

She stood there for a minute, then fled. She felt as if the entire marketplace could see that she yearned for the Christian.

She then had an urge to go to the wineshops. There she counted the young trees, one, two, three, four, five. "So many young pine trees shattered!"

A Gentile was walking home in a new straw hat with a peacock feather. He was strumming a mandolin and singing a Ukrainian folksong: "Hey there under the mountain." And the feather's greenish-blue eye sang along.

Dvoyre felt alien among the trees, with the Gentile who was walking home all alone to his village, but she wasn't afraid. She had an urge to go back to the marketplace, to the shops, with their Jewish merchandise.

The days wore by and the weeks wore by, and Dvoyre lived through her days and nights with the words: "So many young pine trees shattered!"

She felt it was sinful to think about the Gentile. In her depression she helped her mother, Brayne, darn socks. Her mother didn't have a clue, but she wouldn't let Godel do anything spiteful to Dvoyre.

Alter, as usual, stood at the window, gazing at the town clock, intent on what he wanted from life. At eleven, for instance, the roast wasn't ready as yet, but it *was* ready by twelve noon. He argued that with God's help couldn't he live to see the roast done a bit earlier today?

His wife Brayne replied that everything required a little effort, otherwise . . .

Alter caught the hint and he broke in: You couldn't see any steam on her, the fat wasn't oozing from her double chin. And as corpses ate, that's what they looked like—was she listening or not?

Of course she was listening, and she replied that he ought to set his mind on more important things, there was a marriageable girl in the house—the mother groaned that her world was so dark and wretched.

Alter was at a loss to reply, but he didn't want to be tripped up. So he exclaimed: "What can I do? She's turned down Mayer Zisi. How come, girl, how come? Who can we talk to, who?"

Dvoyre was used to all this, she was used to hearing Mayer Zisi's name no matter where she happened to be.

He was a good man, a fine man, Mayer Zisi with his big Adam's apple and his hammered shoulders.

She was used to seeing her mother shake her head:

She didn't want to? Didn't want to? She had something to boast about—a girl was a precious thing. Mayer Zisi had a problem, a boy had a problem—oh, sure! It was a reasonable thing, it couldn't be more reasonable! . . . A reasonable dowry there, a reasonable dowry there, a reasonable legacy at death—God forbid! Our own cousins—what could be more reasonable?

But Dvoyre was already used to it.

It was harvest time. The reaped wheat and rye lay in stacks in the fields, and people walked across the hayfields to go swimming in the river, and the swimming and the summer sunsets gave Dvoyre a tan. Lutsuk's voice haunted her everywhere—on the paths, among the stacks of wheat and rye, far, far, reaching all the way to the mill. And she was ashamed to undress in front of his voice, which followed her, burning her back, echoing her footsteps—wasn't her gait beautiful, wasn't it graceful! Peered into her eyes, from all mirrors, beautiful eyes, Dvoyre? Undo her braid, long hair, Dvoyre? No, short hair, a short braid wasn't beautiful, smear salves in her hair, soak it in the juice of yellow flowers, then the braid will grow, grow, grow. And can you sing, Dvoyre? Sing, softer, softer, don't squeal, it's not appropriate for a Jewish girl. Just a sigh, very soft, shh, keep it to yourself.

So many young pine trees shattered! . . .

The Gentile was walking home all alone to his village, strumming his mandolin so beautifully and singing: "Hey there under the mountain."

Become a Christian and die!

Next Tuesday morning Moyshe-Yoyne beat the drum, telling the merchants to close their shops. Anyone who failed to do so would be fined. The Jews realized that *he* was coming today.

That morning, Alter had yelled at Godye, warning him not to go and look, for it was rumored that military personnel would be present, and he might get crushed. Later on, during the big commotion, Alter ran into him and he shouted: "Go home! A Jew mustn't look at him! I'm going to synagogue."

But later on, they bumped into one another where a Jew mustn't look.

The marketplace was mobbed. Well, now everyone had seen that it was no simple matter. Yugan, the school principal, hadn't gone to spend the day getting drunk in Móyshele's tavern. At the crack of dawn, when the rooster had crowed, Yugan had sneaked in for no more than one drink.

The peasants, who had driven in from the surrounding countryside, were all in their Sunday best, and you could have said that their heads had swelled because of the great honor done to their town.

Dvoyre was standing near Hanzel's shop, gazing at the ring of spectators formed by the policemen. They were under the command of Commissioner Prakavitsh, who was riding his horse, with his fearful police mustache flying apart and with a pine sprig in his lapel. And Moyshe-Yoyne the Drunkard, who had hung up his drum, reeled after him, shouting: "Keep back! Keep back!"

Dvoyre, upon seeing the throng of Christian strangers in her Jewish marketplace, felt like a householder visited by unknown guests, who turn everything upside down, who bring along alien things and linger for a while.

She was looking forward to their returning to their lairs, their cottages, their fields. This was not their place.

Nobody knew why the police had formed the spectators into a ring. A jokester swore that the ring was meant to keep the pigs from going through.

It was getting late, and Yugan the school principal was still hurrying around, drenched in sweat.

Everyone was now looking at the priests, fat and skinny, tall and short, their bodies indicating the kinds of brains they had, fat or skinny.

But noisiest of all was the canon, who was the local priest and who had the face of a yearling heifer. His own cook said that he was an honest priest.

Suddenly the crowd began to stir and mill, to hustle and bustle. Someone announced that he was arriving.

Who was arriving? Apparently the archbishop—no, it was the town rabbi. They were going out to receive the archbishop right there, there. "Cut it out, stop shoving, you—I mean, Alter."

"Who is it, who is it, Mottye, can you see him? The archbishop—I mean the rabbi?"

"Ah, ah, if you'll forgive my mentioning them in the same breath. What crap! An ox has a long tongue, but he can't blow a ram's horn!"

"What business is it of yours?"

"Shush! There you have it! Jews have found a time to fight. Shush, quiet, they're singing. Who's singing, what's singing? Are you deaf or something? The beadle's singing. There's the rabbi, he's walking with

a minyan and he's got a Torah scroll. Itsik and Velvel are holding him by his arms. The beadle is singing. Shloyme Perets with his blind eye? What is the beadle singing? The imperial anthem, he's singing the imperial anthem."

"Alter, now then! Lemme have a look!"

Alter didn't retreat from the box he was standing on. He stayed there, and even though he recognized Shloyme's voice, he pretended not to hear, then he answered deliberately, harried, dazed by the noise: "What's the big deal? Huh? An archbishop? Ain't you never seen no archbishop before?"

A minute later, however, Alter himself was so dumbfounded that he gave Shloyme a tiny space on the box. "Stand there, slowly, don't tread on my foot. Wow! Wow! The rabbi's coming!"

Dvoyre came running over. "Papa, let me stand on your box!"

He let her climb up, and she watched.

The rabbi with the beautiful beard was walking under a canopy, escorted by two fine congregants. He was carrying a Torah scroll. Four young men in silk caftans bore the four poles of the canopy over the Torah.

The archbishop stood facing them—an old, gray priest sporting a high, square hat and escorted by priests who were holding crosses and wearing lace robes with expensive silver embroidery. Two priests in strange high, angular hats and white stoles were carrying the statue of Jesus.

As the rabbi approached the archbishop, both groups halted.

The Torah versus Jesus.

The marketplace grew so still you could have heard a fly soaring past. There were as many people as grains of sand on the earth, and they all suddenly hushed up.

Shh.

The archbishop bowed his head to the Torah.

"Oh, Jews! I can't stand it! The Messiah is coming!"

"Did you get a load of that? He bowed his head!"

"Of course, how could he not? The Torah is older, we're older."

Dvoyre stood there as if in a dream.

If they walk across an iron bridge, they'll fall in, and if we walk across a cobweb, we won't fall in.

She peered at the old, bent rabbi holding the Torah. Its old velvet mantle was embroidered with gold, and both the velvet and the gold had faded long since. But noble and respectable like an old, rich woman, with a silk cloth, her genteel and aristocratic nature lying in the creases in her face, lying in the dust of the velvet folds.

"Dvoyre, why don't you want Mayer Zisi, why don't you?"

The glad tidings spread throughout the town: He had bowed his head, he had bowed his head.

And, as she hurried home, those words hurried after her: "Of course, how could he not? The Torah is older, we're older."

Translated by Joachim Neugroschel.

Other works by Shtok: *Gezamlte ertsylungen* (1919).

Sh. An-ski

The Dybbuk
1920

[. . .] REB AZRIELKE: God's world is great and holy. The holiest land in the world is the Land of Israel. In the Land of Israel the holiest city is Jerusalem. In Jerusalem the holiest place was the Temple, and in the Temple the holiest spot was the Holy of Holies. [*Brief pause.*] There are seventy peoples in the world. The holiest among these is the People of Israel. The holiest of the People of Israel is the tribe of Levi. In the tribe of Levi the holiest are the priests. Among the priests the holiest was the High Priest. [*Brief pause.*] There are 354 days in the year. Among these the holidays are holy. Higher than these is the holiness of the Sabbath. Among Sabbaths, the holiest is the Day of Atonement, the Sabbath of Sabbaths. [*Brief pause.*] There are seventy languages in the world. The holiest is Hebrew. Holier than all else in this language is the holy Torah, and in the Torah the holiest part is the Ten Commandments. In the Ten Commandments the holiest of all words is the name of God. [*Brief pause.*] And once during the year, at a certain hour, these four supreme sanctities of the world were joined with one another. That was on the Day of Atonement, when the High Priest would enter the Holy of Holies and there utter the name of God. And because this hour was beyond measure holy and awesome, it was the time of utmost peril not only for the High Priest but for the whole of Israel. For if in this hour there had, God forbid, entered the mind of the High Priest a false or sinful thought, the entire world would have been destroyed. [*Pause.*] Every spot where a man raises his eyes to heaven, is a Holy of Holies. Every man, having been created by God in His own image and likeness, is a High Priest. Every day of a man's life is a Day of Atonement, and every word that a man speaks with sincerity is the name of the Lord. Therefore it is that every sin and every wrong that a man commits brings the destruction of the world. [*In a trembling voice.*] Human souls, through great anguish and pain, through many an incarnation, strive, like a child reaching for its mother's breast, to reach their source, the Throne of Glory on high. But it sometimes happens, even after a soul has reached exalted heights, that evil suddenly overwhelms it, God forbid, and the soul stumbles and falls. And the more exalted it was, the deeper is the abyss into which it falls. And when such a soul falls, a world is destroyed, and darkness descends on all the holy places, and the ten Sephiroth[1] mourn. [*Pause, as though awakening.*] My children! Today we will cut short our repast of farewell to the Sabbath.

[*All except* MIKHOL *leave silently, deeply impressed by what they have heard. Brief pause.*]

MIKHOL [*approaches the table with uncertainty*]: Rebbe!

[REB AZRIELKE *looks up at him wearily and sadly.*] Rebbe, Sender of Brinnits has come.

REB AZRIELKE [*as if repeating*]: Sender of Brinnits. I know.

MIKHOL: A great misfortune has befallen him. His daughter is possessed by a dybbuk, God have mercy on us.

REB AZRIELKE: Possessed by a dybbuk. I know.

MIKHOL: He has brought her to you.

REB AZRIELKE [*as if to himself*]: To me? To me? How could he have come to me if the "me" in me is not here.

MIKHOL: Rebbe, all the world comes to you.

REB AZRIELKE: All the world. A blind world. Blind sheep following a blind shepherd. If they were not blind they would come not to me but to Him who say "I," to the only "I" in the world.

MIKHOL: Rebbe, you are His messenger.

REB AZRIELKE: So says the world, but I do not know that. For forty years I have occupied a rebbe's seat, and I am not sure to this very day whether I am a messenger of God, blessed be He. There are times when I feel my closeness to the All. Then I have no doubts. Then I am firm and I have influence in the worlds above. But there are times when I do not feel sure within. And then I am small and weak as a child. Then I need help myself.

MIKHOL: Rebbe, I remember, once you came at midnight and asked me to recite the Psalms with you. And then we recited them and wept together the whole night through.

REB AZRIELKE: That was once. Now it is even worse. [*With a trembling voice.*] What do they want of me? I am old and weak. My body needs rest; my spirit thirsts for solitude. Yet the misery and the anguish of the world reach out to me. Every plea pierces me as a needle does the flesh. And I have no more strength. I cannot!

MIKHOL [*frightened*]: Rebbe! Rebbe!

REB AZRIELKE [*sobbing*]: I can go no further! I cannot go on!

MIKHOL: Rebbe! You must not forget that behind you stand long generations of tsaddikim and holy men. Your father, Reb Itchele of blessed memory, your grandfather the renowned scholar Reb Velvele the Great, who was a pupil of the Baal Shem. . . .

REB AZRIELKE [*recovers*]: My forebears. . . . My saintly father, who three times had a revelation from Elijah; my uncle Reb Meyer Ber, who used to ascend to heaven in his prayers; my grandfather, the great Reb Velvele, who resurrected the dead.

[*Turns to* MIKHOL, *his spirits restored.*] Do you know, Mikhol, that my grandfather, the great Reb Velvele, used to exorcise a dybbuk without either holy names or incantations, with merely a command. With a single command! In my times of need I turn to him and he sustains me. He will not forsake me now. Call in Sender.

[MIKHOL *leaves and returns with* SENDER.]

SENDER [*stretching out his arms imploringly*]: Rebbe, have pity! Help me! Save my only child!

REB AZRIELKE: How did the misfortune occur?

SENDER: In the midst of veiling the bride, just as. . . .

REB AZRIELKE [*interrupts him*]: That's not what I'm asking. What could have caused the misfortune? A worm can penetrate a fruit only when it begins to rot.

SENDER: Rebbe! My child is a God-fearing Jewish daughter. She is modest and obedient.

REB AZRIELKE: Children are sometimes punished for the sins of their parents.

SENDER: If I knew of any sin of mine, I would do penance.

REB AZRIELKE: Has the dybbuk been asked who he is and why he has taken possession of your daughter?

SENDER: He does not answer. But by his voice he was recognized as a student of our yeshiva who some months ago died quite suddenly in the synagogue. He was meddling with Cabala and came to grief.

REB AZRIELKE: By what powers?

SENDER: They say, by evil spirits. Some hours before his death he told a fellow student that one should not wage war against sin and that in evil, heaven protect us, there is a spark of holiness. He even wanted to use magic to get two barrels of gold.

REB AZRIELKE: You knew him?

SENDER: Yes, he ate regularly at my house.

REB AZRIELKE [*looks attentively at* SENDER.]: Did you perhaps in any way cause him grief or shame? Try to remember.

SENDER: I don't know. I don't remember. [*In despair.*] Rebbe, I'm only human, after all. [*Pause.*]

REB AZRIELKE: Bring in the girl.

[SENDER *leaves and returns immediately with* FRADE, *both leading* LEYE *by the hand. She stops stubbornly at the threshold and refuses to enter.*]

SENDER [*tearfully*]: Leye dearest, have pity. Don't shame me before the Rebbe. Go in.

FRADE: Go in, Leyele. Go in, my dove.

LEYE: I want to enter but I cannot!

REB AZRIELKE: Maiden! I command you to enter. [LEYE *crosses the threshold and goes to the table.*] Sit down.

LEYE [*sits down obediently. Suddenly she springs up and begins to shout in a voice not hers*]: Let me go! I refuse! [*She tries to run.* SENDER *and* FRADE *restrain her.*]

REB AZRIELKE: Dybbuk, I command you to say who you are.

LEYE [DYBBUK]: Rebbe of Miropolye! You know who I am, but I do not wish to reveal my name before others.

REB AZRIELKE: I do not ask your name. I ask, who are you?

LEYE [DYBBUK] [*softly*]: I am one of those who sought new roads.

REB AZRIELKE: Only he seeks new roads who has lost the right one.

LEYE [DYBBUK]: That road is too narrow.

REB AZRIELKE: That was said by one who did not return. [*Pause.*] Why did you enter into this maiden?

LEYE [DYBBUK]: I am her destined bridegroom.

REB AZRIELKE: Our holy Torah forbids the dead to abide among the living.

LEYE [DYBBUK]: I am not dead.

REB AZRIELKE: You departed from our world and you are forbidden to return to it until the great ram's horn is sounded. Therefore, I command you to leave the body of this girl so that a living branch of the eternal tree of Israel may not wither and die.

LEYE [DYBBUK] [shouting]: Rebbe of Miropolye, I know how powerful, how invincible you are. I know that you can command the angels and the seraphim, but you cannot sway me. I have nowhere to go! For me every road is blocked, every gate is shut, and everywhere evil spirits lie in wait to consume me. [With a trembling voice.] There are heaven and earth, there are worlds without number, but not in a single one is there a place for me. And now that my anguished and harried soul has found a haven, you wish to drive me forth. Have pity. Do not conjure or compel me.

REB AZRIELKE: Wandering soul, I feel great pity for you, and I will try to release you from the destroying angels. But you must leave the body of this girl.

LEYE [DYBBUK] [with firmness]: I will not leave.

REB AZRIELKE: Mikhol, summon a minyan from the synagogue. [MIKHOL leaves and soon returns followed by ten Jews, who take their places at one side of the room.] Sacred congregation, do you give me the authority in your name and with your power to expel from the body of a Jewish maiden a spirit who refuses to leave of his own free will?

ALL TEN MEN: Rebbe, we give you the authority in our name and with our power to expel from the body of a Jewish maiden a spirit who refuses to leave of his own free will.

REB AZRIELKE [rising]: Dybbuk! Soul of one who left our world, in the name and with the authority of a holy congregation of Jews, I, Azrielke ben Hadas, command you to leave the body of the maiden Leye bas Khanne and in leaving not to harm her nor any other living creature. If you do not obey my command, I will proceed against you with anathema and excommunication, with all the powers of exorcism and with the whole might of my outstretched arm. If, however, you obey my command, I will do all in my power to reclaim your soul and drive off the spirits of evil and destruction that surround you.

LEYE [DYBBUK] [shouting]: I do not fear your anathemas and excommunications and I do not believe in your assurances! There is no power in the world that can help me! There is no more exalted height than my present refuge and there is no darker abyss than that which awaits me. I will not leave!

REB AZRIELKE: In the name of Almighty God I charge you for the last time and command you to leave. If you do not, I excommunicate you and give you over into the hands of the destroying angels.

[A fearful pause.]

LEYE [DYBBUK]: In the name of Almighty God, I am joined with my destined bride and I will not part from her forever.

REB AZRIELKE: Mikhol, have white robes brought in for all those present. Bring seven ram's horns and seven black candles. Then take from the Holy Ark seven Sacred Scrolls. [Awesome pause while MIKHOL goes out and returns with the ram's horns and black candles. He is followed by THE MESSENGER carrying the white robes.]

MESSENGER [counts the robes]: There is one extra robe. [Looks around.] Perhaps someone is missing here?

REB AZRIELKE [worried as though reminding himself]: In order to excommunicate a Jewish soul, permission must be obtained from the rabbi of the city. Mikhol, for the present put away the horns, the candles, and the robes. Take my staff, go to Rabbi Shimshon and ask him to come here as quickly as possible. [MIKHOL gathers up the horns and candles and leaves with THE MESSENGER, who is carrying the robes. To the ten men.] You may go, for the present. [They leave. Pause. REB AZRIELKE raises his head.] Sender! Where are the groom and his party staying?

SENDER: They remained at my house in Brinnits for the Sabbath.

REB AZRIELKE: Send a rider to inform them in my name that they are to stay there and await my command.

SENDER: I'll send a rider at once.

REB AZRIELKE: In the meantime you may go out and take the girl into the next room.

LEYE [awakens, in her own voice, trembling]: Granny! I am afraid. What will they do to him? What will they do to me?

FRADE: Don't be afraid, my child. The Rebbe knows what he is doing. He won't harm anyone. The Rebbe cannot do any harm. [She and SENDER lead LEYE into the next room.]

REB AZRIELKE [sits sunk deep in meditation. As though awakening]: And even if it has been otherwise decided in the worlds above, I will reverse that decision. [. . .]

NOTE

1. According to Cabalistic doctrine, the emanations of God.

Translated by Joseph C. Landis.

Joseph Chaim Brenner

1881–1921

The Hebrew novelist, editor, and literary critic Joseph Chaim Brenner was born into a pious but impoverished family in Ukraine. He became alienated from religious tradition while still in his youth and turned to Bundism and then Zionism. He was drafted into the tsar's army, and in 1904, at the outbreak of the Russo-Japanese War, he fled to England and lived in London's East End until 1908, working as a typesetter. He emigrated to Ottoman Palestine in 1909 and remained there until he was brutally murdered by Arab rioters in 1921. His novels and short stories mirror the deprivations and travails of his own life and of the primitive conditions he encountered in early twentieth-century Palestine. The protagonists in his fiction are uprooted, self-conscious intellectual antiheroes, unable to make their way in the world, battered and besieged, tossed to and fro by powerful historical forces and events.

Breakdown and Bereavement
1920

I

It was an afternoon in the middle of April when the accident occurred. The year was a leap year, rainy and warm, and on that summery spring day in the commune he had already been given the job of getting in the hay. He and Menahem, the hired hand, were at work in the field; Menahem up above, on top of the wagon, and he, Hefetz, down below; Menahem at a leisurely pace, without visible exertion, like all the migrant help who were one day in Dan and the next in Beersheba, and he, Hefetz, the regular member of the commune, zealously straining every muscle, as had always been his way, particularly since his last return from abroad. Rivulets of sweat streamed down his face and his eyes shone triumphantly with the effort, as if to say, "See, I too can hold my own!" He worked without letup, tiring his partner and driving himself ever closer to exhaustion with each bale of hay he pitched upward. Before Menahem, quick as he was, had finished setting one load in place, an even bigger one would come flying at him like a mad bull.

The wagon filled bale by bale; the distance between the two men grew gradually greater and with it, Hefetz's exertions. His Arab *kaffiyeh* slipped unnoticed from his head. The sun beat down with its usual fierceness. Sud-denly the man below uttered a soft groan and staggered slightly with the load on his pitchfork. Menahem looked down to see a large bale of hay, the heaviest yet, overturned on the ground, and Hefetz squirming beside it. "The devil!" he cried, slipping down from above. What could be the matter? Sunstroke? Malaria? Chills?—No, a sharp pain . . . a pain below the waist . . . ach, what an ass!

That evening the members of the commune assembled in the kitchen and decided to send Hefetz to Jerusalem at the expense of the sick fund. True, it was nearer to Jaffa, but in Jerusalem, it had meanwhile been discovered, the injured man had some distant relatives. The elected head of the commune even recalled how several years previously there had been some other trouble with Hefetz, on account of which (Hefetz himself had not been consulted) it was decided to send him to Jerusalem too, only then (how times had changed!) there was no choice but Jerusalem, either Jerusalem or Beirut, because . . . because in Jaffa they didn't have the right sort of place for him . . . only meanwhile Hefetz had decided to leave the country, which put an end to the affair. It seemed, though, that a man couldn't escape his proper destiny. No, indeed. . . .

Indeed, so it seemed. In the course of the evening two or three other old settlers also recalled Hefetz's journey abroad and the events that led up to it. These were described most vividly by "the Master-of-intrigue," a scarecrow of a man with two left thumbs whose favorite tactic was to boast and threaten at once that he was imminently about to receive a ticket for passage from his brother in Brazil; in the meantime—for this had been going on for five years—he did his best to turn one friend against the other, and particularly, to complain about the cook, who wasn't fulfilling her duty, the duty of a cook in an agricultural commune in the Land of Israel. Ah yes, Hefetz' madness. "I tell you, we should all have the luck to be as mad as he was!" (If only his brother in Brazil would come to his rescue already . . .) The business with Hefetz had happened several years before. The commune was not then in existence; in fact, there were no communes at all; in other words, the new form of life developed by the pioneers in Palestine, the agricultural collective, had not yet appeared on the scene. In those days they all worked in the "colony," or more precisely, passed the time there, Hefetz as well. Several days before the first night of Passover ("Hasn't anyone noticed? This time it's almost Passover too!") he had fallen ill. "Still, his illness then, gentlemen, was of a different sort." It was a nervous, a . . . what was the word? . . . a *psychic* disturbance. In fact, he seemed to have gone slightly mad. On the other hand, there was no need to exaggerate: he was far from completely deranged. In any case, there was nothing dangerous about his condition. What was it someone had said? Yes, someone had hit the nail on the head: it was the sort of illness that concerned the patient alone. It was an attack of . . . what was the word? . . . of *anxiety*.

"But it wasn't just that," added some of the other old-timers. Anxiety . . . of course . . . but in general . . . morale at the time was terribly low. It was a critical period, a time of transition, for the Jewish workers in the settlements . . . and Hefetz, who had a bad case of malaria, had been on a diet of quinine and was very weak. To be sure, there was nothing out of the ordinary about this; but because of his weakness and his inability to work during the day, he had decided to become a night watchman. The dangers of being a watchman, of course, were not then what they were now, but since his nerves were on edge and the work was new to him ("After all, he was no great hero to begin with," observed a voice from the side to the general approval of all) . . . on account of all this, it was said, he panicked one night while on duty and imagined he was being attacked. It was this fright that undoubtedly brought on his illness.

"In any case, you can't but feel sorry for him," remarked the Master-of-intrigue in an unusually mild tone. "It wasn't wise of him to go abroad. Others could have left at the time and didn't—and he could have stayed and he left. It all goes to prove that he was already out of his mind. After all, we all know that you have to be mad to want to leave this country, don't we, my friends? Still, looking back . . . abroad, you know, the cooks are better than ours, ha ha . . . say what you will, he came back with his belly full. He must have feasted like a king over there. What a character, that Hefetz! The man runs away, so it seems, because he's gone quite berserk, shows up again, I won't say recovered, but anyway, with some . . . what's the word? . . . *flesh* on his bones, and then goes and loses that too. And all in a few months. Our commune simply has no luck, my friends."

"But who's going to take him to Jerusalem?" asked the head of the commune deliberately interrupting the talk; his heavy eyes stared down at the ground, as they always did when it was a question of general concern.

The posing of a practical question led to discussion, dissent, innuendo. Those who were disinclined to make the trip to Jerusalem with the injured man were quick to put forth their candidacy, offering to sacrifice themselves for the common good, while taking care at the same time to present their case in such a way as to make their going clearly out of the question; while those who would have been only too happy to take a few days off from work and see Jerusalem at no cost to themselves did their best to seem reluctant—though if duty called, of course, they would have no choice but to comply. . . .

"Gentlemen, it's one o'clock in the morning," tired voices called out. "We've got to put an end to this." They had just resolved to cast lots when Menahem, the hired hand, volunteered his services.

This young man of twenty-two had already been "everywhere"; indeed, he had even met Hefetz once before somewhere in Western Europe, before coming to Palestine, and had taken a liking to him. Menahem's knowledge of geography—he could all but tell you the exact distance in kilometers between any two cities in Austria, England, Germany, France, even Belgium and Holland—did not come from books. He had a weakness for stations and train tickets and his favorite saying was: "The devil take it! Fish look for deep waters, men for sweet!" His eyes, though round as an owl's, were not owlish at all; they were merry, open, honey-colored, but not too sweet or cloying; they were rather like the honey that is fresh from the hive and still dripping bright with pure brilliance. Menahem took to new surroundings as no one else, plunging straight into them as into a clear mountain pond, lazily greeting each stranger with a fond hello, as though inviting him to partake of his honeyed essence. He liked to go barefoot and even took pride in the fact; yet somehow this failed to annoy Hefetz the way the exhibitionalistically barefoot types generally did. The simple, childish way he enjoyed things made up for everything. He liked to swear—"the devil take it!"—to stake all on an oath—"upon my life!"—to break into laughter, to gossip about the girls in the nearby settlement, to tell an occasional indecent joke (at times such as these Hefetz would become strangely pliant and laugh submissively); none of this, however, offended a soul, for it was done without the slightest malice, in a comical, almost piping voice. "I don't like to talk about my troubles," he would say to Hefetz. "If talking about them could drive them away, why not? Then I'd talk about them all day long, I'd do nothing else, just like you. But as it is—I leave it to you. . . ."

The debate over Menahem's proposal gathered strength. Those who were averse to going and feared to draw the unwelcome lot threw caution to the winds and declared (it was really too late to keep up pretenses) that it was only right for the hired hand, who had come with Hefetz from abroad, to go with him too; the opposing party, however, had persuasive arguments of its own, the most powerful among them being that a nonmember of the commune should be made to travel at his own expense. Menahem's acceptance of this last condition hastened the final decision in his favor.

And so Menahem went with Hefetz to Jerusalem.

On the way, as they approached Jerusalem, Hefetz thought he felt better and began to regret having come. The whole thing now seemed to have been something he'd imagined. Why must he blow up everything out of proportion? He had collapsed while at work—was that any reason to go running to the doctor? What an amateur he was at suffering! It was really just like him.

Menahem spit through his teeth in his fashion and tried to console him. If the condition wasn't serious, so much the better. The pain was real enough. Since he would be unable to work for a few days anyhow, what did he stand to lose?

Hefetz listened and felt reassured; still, he announced in advance that he had no intention of seeing a doctor in Jerusalem. The latter would only laugh at him, that much was certain, and he was not going to make a fool of himself. In fact, it had already once happened to him that he had thought he was ill and had actually been in great pain; by the time he'd arrived at the doctor's, however, the pain had disappeared and he hadn't known what to say! He wouldn't say anything to his relatives, either, simply that he had come to Jerusalem for the holiday. If he should have to stay a while longer, he could always tell them the "truth": he was malarial, the quinine no longer helped; he needed a change of air, and so he had decided to stay in Jerusalem and not go back to the farm. . . .

And yet, when all was said and done, he needn't have come. It was really just like him. Always on the run. . . .

His trip abroad, for example—what made him take it? He had been about twenty years old when he first came to Palestine, strong, healthy, undemanding, a little bit odd perhaps, but still—popular enough. Elsewhere, abroad (in Hamilin's circle of students, for example), he had been a dull-witted, clumsy, solemn young man, at a loss to get on with the weaker sex and in general having no luck with it, in short: the very opposite of well-liked. No, elsewhere someone like him had no chance at all. In

the workers' inn in the colony, on the other hand, surrounded by bearded, bookish, ascetic votaries of labor; there where everyone was an eccentric of sorts, a bit of an "original"; there and only there could he too, Hefetz, be a good companion, even if he wasn't contentious like the rest of them and didn't argue at the drop of a hat or take sides in every quarrel or play politics out of sheer boredom and the need to pick a fight. . . .

And yet he went abroad. It was just like him. Even before that, all the time he was in the colony—a period of several years, all together—he had gone about with a strange feeling. He had felt as though he were trapped in a long corridor, but only for the moment; somewhere ahead was a room that was still to come, that had to come. He was incapable of saying or describing what this room was like; yet there was no end of fantasies about it, bizarre, impalpable, but sweet nonetheless. At any rate, it was clearly intolerable for things to go on forever without these dreams coming true . . . and not only because life as it was wasn't good and deserved to be better. Of course, he wanted this too, and at times the desire would actually get the best of him, but deep down it was not the main thing. The main, the overriding thing was . . . if only everything weren't so dry and bitter and hard: the burning, sweat-sucking air, the filthy inn, the sickening, poisonous food, the alien cold surroundings; it was impossible not to dream of a comfortable place to live, a good meal, shade, a cool stream, tangled woods, tree-lined streets . . . but in any case, it wasn't this that mattered most . . . on the contrary: sometimes he would deliberately resist the slightest improvement in his life, refuse to escape the desolation, the apathy, the packed quarters, the filth, even for a moment. No, what never failed to crush him was the utter pointlessness of it all: it seemed monstrous to him to have to go on living like this, for no reason, as a Jewish "farm hand" always looking for work; monstrous when he found it to have to go out every morning and compete with a horde of strange Arabs; monstrous to have to fight all day long with the ill-mannered foreman; and then to return to the inn at evening and gulp down a sour, gassy gruel that boded ill for the stomach; and afterward to drop by the workers' club to yawn once or twice and read an old newspaper; and then back to the inn again, to a bachelor's sleep bitten into by all kinds of bugs; and once more to rise with the ringing of the clock and work all day long until evening. And the work had no meaning, and the end was far, unclear, invisible, non-existent . . . to go a year like that, two years, ten years, forever . . . and never any change; no relief, no progress, no hope. . . . *What? Everyone lived that way*, Menahem said? Yes, of course, everyone did; his spleen and his ennui had been banal, of course, but he had suffered from them all the same. A kind of apathy had come over him, a total indifference to what he ate, the way he dressed, where he slept. He could have gone for months without changing his clothes or lain in an unmade bed from one week to the next and let his mind wander or not wander as it pleased. He loathed it when his roommates took the trouble to tidy up. It was a strange thing, his illness . . . the word "melancholia" did not exactly fit it . . . it was as though some horror of life had taken hold of him, a revulsion toward everything around him. Food disgusted him; he grew thinner every day, and the less he ate, the more he dreamed and talked, as if to escape his inner fears. He had never been much of a talker before.

What did he talk about? About everything except his unspeakable fantasies. . . . *The darling little girl whom he had seen in the school in the colony would grow up to be a young beauty. A woman's grace, a man's strength, would join in her soul. One day she would be seventeen . . . and he would be thirty-five, twice her age, a weary castaway . . . but she would say: "It doesn't matter . . . I've seen all your suffering and I want to share it with you. . . . Father is the richest man in the colony, and I'm the most beautiful woman, I know. . . . But I'm leaving it all for you because it's you that I want. . . ." No, she would not say it that way; she would not speak so commonly. . . . She would put her hand in his without a word—everything would be understood, transformed into infinite bliss. . . .*

Hefetz talked about practically everything during those terrible, garrulous days, but he did not talk about things like these, not about his wild, insane imaginings. As though by itself, with no effort on his part, his conversation turned to matters of the general interest—matters, that is, which might have pained him, even moved him deeply in ordinary times, but which at bottom, and especially now, meant nothing to him at all. The more remote a problem was, the less he or anyone else could do anything about it, the greater his concern. He talked a great deal, for example, about the Arabs; he spoke of their national awakening and of their hatred for the Jew; he was obsessed by the possibility of a pogrom, over which he wracked his brain, soliciting advice and making endless plans for rescue and relief. Once an Arab woman from one of the families in the village had stopped by the inn, which was near her house, to inquire of those seated on the bench outside whether they

had seen her little brother, who had gone off somewhere unannounced. He, Hefetz, who had been sitting in the doorway, turned as white as a shroud. He didn't attack her or lay hands on her—it hadn't yet come to that—but when he heard the word *zrir*, meaning child, he jumped to his feet like a shot and leaped backward over the threshold as though looking for a place to hide, from where he began to stamp his feet and to shout: "*Zrir, zrir*, I know what she's after! We're not cannibals here! We don't drink human blood! But just try to convince her that we don't have her brother when the Arabs are awaking and the germs of hatred have infected them too. . . . See where it gets you!"

Under the circumstances, as long as Hefetz carried on this way his companions were understandably not upset; they saw that he had changed, of course, but while his preoccupation with the common good lasted, they did not give it much thought. They were all, after all, neurasthenics, cosmic worriers, who bore the world's burdens on their shoulders and judged everything in terms of the group. If one of them traveled abroad, for example, he had not simply gone someplace else, but had "given up" and "betrayed the ideal"; if someone stood guard in a vineyard he was not just a lookout, but "a watchman in the fatherland"; if the cook burned the food in the inn—and when did she not burn it? and who really cared, anyway, except that it was something to talk about?—she was an execrable cook, of course, but she was also "an irresponsible woman with no sense of duty to her comrades."

Soon, however, a reaction set in and everyone realized that Hefetz was not just another victim of general conditions. His final metamorphosis made this apparent. He looked as unwell and distracted as before; but now not only his mind, but his tongue too, seemed to have gone out of order. It was all very well for him not to talk, but there was silence and there was silence! For days on end he refused to say a word. It then became obvious that his previous chatter had been one thing, his illness another, and that the latter derived not from the common predicament, but had private origins, underlying irritations, which were purely personal in nature and had nothing to do with anyone else. Only what was to be done? During several meetings held in the sick man's absence, though not without his knowledge, much was said about the need for treatment, namely, for "bandaging up the old wounds" that had come open and begun to bleed again, etc., though at the same time, of course, a "permanent cure" was perhaps "out of the question," "but as a temporary measure" . . . Jerusalem or Beirut. . . .

But when Hefetz, overcome by inner desire, sheepishly announced that he was about "to take a trip," in other words, to go abroad completely, respect for him reached a new low. As always, it was a time when the number of settlers who came and went far exceeded the number of those who stayed; still, the custom persisted, and not always as a mere matter of form, to grumble aloud about all those who "fled the field of battle" and betrayed the national cause. . . .

Hefetz was ill . . . but with what? Hefetz was going . . . but where? To others he murmured that he wished to see the world a bit, but to himself he would add: *I want to live, to live.* In spite of the privileges conferred on him by his illness, he didn't, he couldn't, tell this to anyone else; he himself, however, was perfectly aware of the drives that impelled him—primitive, ugly drives, if you will, which in any case, would never, could never, be fulfilled. Yes, he was tired of this monotonous, unbearable life, without a spark of pleasure, without a woman; he had to free himself of it, somehow cast its yoke from off his neck. Even his distant, feckless dreams had come to disgust him. He knew them only too well. . . . *There in Europe there were great cities with all the good things of life. . . . There was no end of possibilities. . . . He would get a job, he would work hard, harder even than here. . . . But the pay would not be bad. . . . And at night, after work, his time would be his own, to do with as he pleased. . . . He would enjoy himself, he would live like a human being and forget all this. . . . He would walk the streets in the evenings, visit the music halls, the theaters, whatever he desired. . . . There would be piquant, fantastic encounters. . . . And other houses, too, which he would not shy away from. . . . Perhaps he might even meet a gentle, attractive young girl. . . .*

Hefetz wandered for some three years in Western Europe, from city to city, from place to place, without rest. Penniless and hungry, he lifted eager, curious eyes to the twentieth century's civilized glitter: to the busy, magnificent streets with their modern traffic, the giant department stores crammed with riches, the brightly lit marquees, the sparkling restaurant windows, the exhibitions of art and trade. Languages he had never heard before rang sharply in his ears; elegant strange men and proudly-mincing women passed before him. In Paris he worked for three months in a Jewish philanthropy for "our unfortunate brothers from the East"; then his time

was up, and again out of work he wandered somewhere else, and from there to French Switzerland . . . by which time he realized that the change he desired was not to be had by changing place. Wherever he stayed he slept in the same foul bed in the house of the same immigrant peddler in the same foul Jewish quarter; only the speech of the men and women who lived in these streets (their children already went to school and spoke the local tongue) no longer seemed Jewish, was not the Yiddish he knew, but another patois, new, queer, and unfamiliar. . . . The cities changed name, the bed was the same. . . . And when work was not to be found he passed the same tediously slow time in the same "Jewish Workers' Club" in the ghetto, which was the same gathering place as always for the same bored, down-and-out, unwanted, discontented drifters like himself. . . .

Life in newer pastures had proved no greener. No, not only no greener; he was worse off now than he had been before, much worse. Whereas in Palestine, at least, he had been a person like everyone else, here he was of a distinctly lower standing, something that was impressed on him in various ways. There, for example, he had spoken the native language of a Jew from Eastern Europe, and this had seemed perfectly natural, certainly nothing to be ashamed of; and if now and then he had actually conversed in Hebrew with a teacher, or a student, or an aspiring young girl, they had all felt a bit superior. But here, if he turned in Yiddish to some immigrant from Russia, to say nothing of the immigrant's children, he was made to feel that he was speaking some pitiful jargon, while his partner in conversation addressed him condescendingly in Russian or the language of the country. How differently one expressed oneself then! Here the question of language was no longer a "Jewish Problem," but something that life took care of quite casually, cruelly, on its own.

After Hefetz had been abroad for nearly two years, however, his racial instinct for adjustment got the upper hand, and objectively, his situation began to improve. He obtained a job as a clerk in a Jewish old-clothes store and gradually set about to transform himself into another person. The spiritual caprices of the past, his "oriental whimsies," seemed, as it were, to disappear by themselves, and at the time that Menahem first met him his name was not even Ezekiel, Yehezkel Hefetz, but something entirely different and not in the least prophetic or oriental or Palestinian.

Menahem met Hefetz in the city in French Switzerland, in the home of a Jewish *emigrée* from Russia who

had wandered with her family to England only to be refused entry there, and had finally made her way to one
of the Swiss provinces, where she had hoped to find a
certain rich relative. The relative, however, could not
be located, and meanwhile the woman's husband went
off on some business in search of a commission and
never returned. It was said that he died on the way of
the same illness that had barred him from England, but
there was no way of knowing for sure.

This abandoned woman was something of an eccentric. Despite her poor health, which kept her from
working and supporting her large family, and the in-
firmity of her children, "the poor little orphans," she
obstinately insisted that each single one of them, from
the youngest on up, should continue his education
through high school—grammar school, mind you,
was not enough—and that none of them, if she could
help it, should have to work, but should study, study
all the time. What little strength she had left she devoted to seeing that her brood was respectably dressed.
(Whether or not they had enough to eat concerned her
less, and here her standards were lower.) To accomplish this she was ready to sacrifice her eldest daughter,
who had never been consecrated to learning, but who
was in her opinion an extraordinary beauty whom she
was determined to marry off to the first good earner to
come along, despite the fact that the girl was still very
young, perhaps not even sixteen; however, as she was
developed for her age, her mother pretended that she
was two years older than she was, a daughter, thank
God, of whom there was no need to be ashamed. In
fact, the girl was not pretty at all and had a sickly nature; yet there was something attractive, pleasingly
frail, about her pinched face, her high breasts, her
straight but slender neck, and the tiny, almost invisible
freckles on either side of her turned-up nose which she
had acquired in the Swiss city, to whose climate she
had never adjusted. She liked to dress in bright colors:
in her flaming blouse and darkly hued skirt with its un-
fashionably long blue hem she made one think of some
magical, tropical bird. And yet unconsciously, without
knowing quite what she was doing, she adjusted her
style to suit whoever was staying in the house at the
moment. Once, when the boarders were several young
men who had some connection with the military, she
developed a sudden interest in dancing and even in
women's athletics. Later, when these were replaced by
a group of college students, she took up calligraphy,
geography, and grammar. One of the students, in fact,

managed to teach her world history as far as Alexander
the Great.

Hefetz alone, though he too became a permanent
lodger in time, inspired no change in her. But he did
have a decent job, and the girl's mother, who took to
calling him "our commissioner," did all that she could
to persuade her daughter that he would provide her
with everything and mustn't be refused (the woman
was actually mad enough to believe that Hefetz had laid
away a small fortune of which no one but herself was
aware), especially since he loved her to distraction and
would devote his whole life to making her happy.

To begin with, Hefetz's "love" and its symptoms
amounted to nothing more than the overcourteous,
slightly cynical manners of a weak single man toward
a delicate girl. When he first discovered the house—he
had been looking for a "Russian" home to eat in—he
felt sorry for the abandoned family and did everything in his power to help out, perhaps even more than
was in his power; the girl, however, he ignored completely, because she wasn't to his taste. As though on
orders from the doctor he deliberately sought someone
healthy, healthy and strong, though at bottom this too
was a sham. Of course, he thought about marriage; orders were orders; it was impossible not to think of it,
after all, impossible for his heart not to quicken when
he did; there were even times (most often when he was
made to remember some revolting thought or scene
that none but a bachelor's four walls ever witness) when
he resolved to make up his mind, to have done with it
no matter what; only he was so unsure of himself and
had so little self-respect, that he didn't take, didn't dare
try to take, the first practical step. All his dreams of
"encounters" and "affairs" had come to less than nothing. He would be drawn to someone, he would tremble
with emotion—and he would get cold feet. In the end
he developed perfect contempt for both his feelings
and his fears. The one thing he couldn't decide was
which derived more from his weakness, his outward
correctness or his cynicism in private, and this made
him more bitter yet. And yet he was genuinely pleased
when the forsaken mother scolded him affectionately in
front of her daughter for his "spendthrift ways" . . . on
himself he spent nothing, only on them . . . what did he
see in them? Why did he do it? He would blush with
pleasure and stammer that it was nothing . . . nothing at
all . . . he earned well . . . he had more than enough . . . it
was only a loan . . . they could always pay it back. Then
the mother would look significantly at her daughter,

who would go to the window and stare at the people outside. . . .

And then all of a sudden, one overcast day, Hefetz noticed the girl and was smitten by her special frailty. The next morning he declared to himself: "I love her and I'm going to marry her." His doubts as to whether they were truly meant for each other were short-lived: he was poor, after all, and she was spoiled, unused to hard work (the boardinghouse, which was always untidy, was cared for by a chambermaid); besides which, he felt sincerely guilty for a while for "having realized"— a realization which he knew was in all probability untrue, but which he was disinclined to disbelieve—that all his kindness to the family had been on account of the girl alone. Once this brief period of uncertainty was over with, however, his love grew even stronger and he began to actively woo her. The doubts, of course, did not vanish completely; as always in these matters, in all matters, really, there remained a subtle residue of intangible, ephemeral, indefinable emotion.

And yet even in the period that followed, when her heart was officially his and he considered himself, both with her mother and in public, to be her "fiancé," there were times when all the tedium, the insanity, of his life in Palestine would come back to him as in an echo, overpower him, call upon him to return; then his interest in the girl would flag; his feelings would cool; and he would suffer immensely both because of the unnecessary relationship in which he was trapped and because of its weakening hold on him. He had already begun to regret the loss of his frightful, voluptuous dreams, the unwilling surrender of his bachelorhood, to which he had grown comfortably accustomed. And yet at the same time, he was struck with horror when he contemplated the collapse of the entire venture, horror for the girl, of course, for the way he was making her suffer, but also for the evanescence of his own infecund feelings, which weighed on him like an unpaid debt. *So this too has gone up in smoke*, said a terrible voice inside him. *How do you like it now, your "eternal love"?*

And still he pulled himself together and persisted. He forced himself to overlook many things and resolved to drain the cup come what may. There were fine, clear days on which he went with her for long walks, drank the fresh air by her side, dismissed each uncharitable thought, fondled her, cried in her lap, thought himself the happiest of men, marveled at his good fortune—yet all along he was haunted by a vague sense of dread that he did not believe in his happiness, that he was pretend-

ing to be someone else, that it was all a delusion. And the trouble was not only with her—though it was obvious to him that she did not deserve to have him cry in her lap or to make him happy—but above all, with himself . . . in spite of which he now spent all his time in his future mother-in-law's house and gave her every penny that he earned, even borrowing from his salary in advance. He was not yet convinced that the girl was right for him; he was still gnawed by doubts that robbed him of what peace he had left; yet his other self, the clerk in the old-clothes store—and perhaps not only the clerk— was content, sure that he had found bliss at last in this faraway city. He would sacrifice everything if he had to, but he would keep things from falling apart. *Then they could, then they might fall apart?* No, he mustn't think of it. It was too frightful a prospect.

Among his acquaintances at the time was a student named Hamilin, who hailed from the woman's home town. Though Russian by birth, in manner and appearance he was more like a Levantine who had somewhere acquired a smattering of European education. Yehezkel Hefetz had met many like him in Palestine and en route there among the Greeks and Armenians who had married and mixed with the Christian Arabs of Syria, or among the enterprising Arab guides in the cities who catered to the tourists. Hamilin's voice was hoarse and husky, like a syphilitic's, but his complexion, though swarthy, was clear and smooth. Yet despite its youthful good looks, his face was far from good-natured; a kind of sullen, bullish obstinacy leaped out at you even from his smile, which was thick and greasy, and in any case, infrequent. Among his student friends he was careful to make a point of his bourgeois, well-to-do, nonplebeian origins by eating and dressing especially well. Unlike others of his type, however, he did not particularly pride himself on his immunity to spiritual distress, or feel the need to express contempt for all "idealists"; poses such as these were foreign to his nature and he couldn't have cared about them less. If anything troubled him at all, rather, it was his desire to play a more brilliant role in life than either his talents or powers permitted, so that he worried over every new wrinkle in his face or clothes, though professing to pay it no attention. Among the careerist Swiss students there were many who were just as vulgar and complacent and no more concerned about hiding it, though all this was generally concealed by a thin, two-century-old veneer of culture, something that Hamilin, the middle-class Jew, was totally without; in the pell-mell, helter-skelter world of the immigrant Jewish students, on the other hand, he was absolutely unique, and he treated them without exception, as he put it, "like a pack of grinning beggars." More exactly, he simply ignored them, as though they were so many more wrinkles to disregard. He went his own way and looked for better company.

And yet from time to time, Hamilin dropped by the Russian woman's boardinghouse.

And then a little episode took place which Hefetz was still retelling to Menahem with much self-mockery several weeks after his return to Palestine. In fact, he even had a name for it, to wit, "A Tale of Two Houses, or, 'The Making of a Skeptic.'"

Across the street from the boardinghouse, far in the Jewish quarter, there was another house, a "house" in quotation marks. Though he occasionally paid his countrywoman a visit, Hamilin, it must be said, would have nothing to do with her cooking, a gentleman like him being used to other fare. Naturally, the woman held this against him even more than she did his having abandoned his wife and children in her home town (Hamilin, she knew, had married a woman with whom he had never gotten along, though he continued to let her support him along with his parents); to her daughter she broadly hinted that while the young student came only rarely to see them, this was not at all the case with the house across the street. *There* he was indefatigable, he didn't miss a night. More than once she had gone out to do her shopping in the morning and spied him on his way home. . . .

Of course, she exaggerated. The "indefatigable" Hamilin, particularly in recent years, was a lover of moderation and not at all the *roué* she made out. The young bride, however, believed every word of it and was duly impressed. She was also impressed by Hefetz's imprudent warning, coming on top of her mother's, that she must never be seen any more in Hamilin's company. The debauched scoundrel, it seemed, had already taken to boasting about town of his "little affair with the innkeeper's daughter." . . .

One evening Hefetz and Hamilin met in the street. Without a word of greeting they walked together as far as the two houses and parted ways. "He to his house and I to mine—which is the better off?" thought Hefetz, not without a flicker of pride. A feeling of warmth stirred within him, fed by the certain knowledge of the future that lay ahead, the family and home on which he would securely build his life. He was then at the very height of his epithalamial mood and had even begun to

buy a few gifts for the wedding, which was only a few weeks away. But when he stepped inside the house, the girl wasn't there. Where had she gone? Her mother, who didn't know, insisted crossly that she must have waited for him and left when he hadn't come.

"But how could she have waited?" This was the usual hour he returned from work. He always came home at this time.

"Ah, what does it matter? She must have gone for a walk with some friend."

But when an hour went by and Hefetz had finished his meal and she still wasn't back, he went to look for her in the public park. She was nowhere to be seen. He started back in a foul mood. And then, as he walked toward a bench on a small arbored lane that adjoined the street of the two houses, he saw the young couple: she was lying in Hamilin's lap.

Hamilin didn't remain in the city much longer, because meanwhile he had been discovered cheating on some kind of examination and was permanently expelled from school. But despite the favorable prospects created by his departure, Hefetz too was soon on his way. It was no consolation to tell himself that while he, Hefetz, had acted all along in perfect good faith, without the least deception, Hamilin had taken advantage of the girl's inexperience to seduce her with his wiles—no, none at all. He was hurt to the quick, more hurt than in love. It did not even matter that he could now "have her all" to himself, in the words of her mother, who did everything in her power to patch things up between them and simply could not understand the ravings of the wretched groom.

"Suppose you're right . . . suppose I'll be the reality, since he's no longer here. But what kind of reality will I be? The heart is also real . . . and he still has a place in her heart. . . ."

"Heart?" The woman argued. "What heart? What does a girl like her know about hearts? She's a child, she doesn't feel she's done wrong . . . if she did, she'd never be able to look you in the face. See for yourself. . . ."

Yes, Hefetz saw everything, knew everything too, even . . . even that now that it was over he was glad it had turned out this way, glad that nothing had come of it. Was not this the inevitable fate of all "loves" like his? But he still could not settle down. More and more he felt a single urge: to get away . . . away, no matter what. . . . It was then that he began to regret having ever left Palestine. How could he have made such a mistake? There the people were different, completely different, and relations between them were different too. Ah! If only he had been able to appreciate life in the colony. Now he was being made to suffer. There such an episode could never have taken place. There was simply no way for it to happen—that much, at least, was certain. He would go back. . . .

Translated by Hillel Halkin.

Other works by Brenner: *Ba-ḥoref* (1904); *Mi-kan u-mi-kan* (1911); *Collected Works*, 4 vols. (1978–1985).

Gershom Shofman

1880-1972

The East European Hebrew short-story writer Gershom Shofman received a traditional Jewish education but also immersed himself in Russian and Hebrew literature. In 1913 he moved to Vienna, where he lived until 1938, when he settled in Tel Aviv, then later in Haifa. His short stories are known for their brevity, frugality, and succinctness, and they leave much to the reader's imagination. Charged with eroticism and often focused on cruelty, they were considered daring at the time. His characters tend to be weak, sickly, and apathetic—unheroic, in short.

The Voice of Blood
1920

I

Most of the way by tram till outside the city. Endless streets and alleys. But now the last stops come. Here's the *remise*, the resting place of these tram cars, where they look like animals in repose after work, like horses in their stables. Just a bit more and the city is behind you.

But the fresh meadows, the most splendid grass, are fenced with iron wires, and at every step a sign: "No Entry"—and the policemen on their horses keep watch vigilantly. Of necessity you fall upon a trampled patch of grass, fetid and parched by the sun, cheek by jowl with wild and impudent boys playing football, with goats grazing on the remaining weeds under your elbow, and little girls rolling around with their privates exposed. . . . As you look from here, heat-struck, at the forbidden gardens and fields, you begin to grasp with all your being the value of land: especially when you

know that at this very time battles are raging for the borders all around, blood flows in stream after stream, and masses of people are killed for a small piece of land, for a clod of earth. The sweet globe of the earth isn't so large after all—so don't neglect your two or three flowerbeds!

Now it's pleasant to let your imagination dwell on the two or three flowerbeds of the distant days of your youth, but thoughts about the actual home of your birth are driven back. It was the only Jewish house in a gentile neighborhood, which even in those good days existed by a miracle there—and certainly no saving remnant of those days remains!

But all that is distant, blurry, in a fog. Distance in place and time has done its work, the stones of cities, the cities abroad, where he has walked alone for fifteen years, have begun to harden his heart too. How good it is for a person to be alone!

Alone, alone—in this mysterious, bereaved city, full of possibilities, that now flickers from afar with its towers, churches, and orchards. Between all of them, like a flow of molten lead, the Danube sparkles. What, does it flow here?! Dreaming women wander on the sidewalks and look long at display windows. They sit on the corners of benches: some of their legs don't even reach the ground. . . .

He hurriedly rises, shakes off the dust, the ants, and the worms, and returns to the city.

II

The emperor's army has dispersed and been disbanded, and in its place the People's Defense force was established, mainly composed of young lads, as delicate and fair as their sisters. In order, as it were, to shake off the shameful defeat and start everything from the beginning, they changed the old uniform and in place of the former, narrow army hat, they've installed a broad-brimmed one for themselves, the "plate hat." In the evening twilight sometimes a single soldier can be seen among the red barracks, walking from the storeroom in the new hat, which he has just received, as noted, and in his hand is the old hat—and never was my mercy for the defeated nation so stirred as at that moment.

He walked arm in arm with Grettel, the darling orphan, thin and tall (her father fell on the Italian front), and she said:

"Our Rudi also wants to join the People's Defense."

"You have that brother and also a younger sister, I believe."

"Yes, Bertha."

"How wonderful. I'm the same: a brother and a sister."

"How I'd love to know them," the Viennese girl of tender years spoke enthusiastically.

They were crossing the Brigitta Bridge, and she asked:

"Do you get letters from them?"

"There's no postal connection with Russia yet," he answered distractedly and followed the Danube into the distance, in the direction of Kahlenberg.

"When will you come to visit us?!" Grettel started to simper like a baby. "Mother wants to meet you, no matter what! She says, 'You've been going out with him for about half a year, and I still haven't met him. That isn't done!'"

This time things had gone too far. He was enmeshed. Against his will he had received an official character. Until now he had been used to seeing only other men's brides, and now, recently, he was seeing his own. "Is this my bride?" He looked at her from the side, as though at the reflection of his fate, and his feeling was like that of someone who sees a photograph of himself for the first time in his life.

He found her mother's house, to his surprise, very similar to the house he was born in, despite the whole worlds that seemingly separated between them. Like that one, this house stood in a suburb, and the mother was short and wore a kerchief on her head, coughed like his own mother, and, like her, wore spectacles on her nose when she was patching a dress. Everything like in his home! The torments of the war had rubbed and worn down, as it were, everything inessential and everything random that stood between nations and races, and only the pure human remained. Her brother Rudi was like his brother Shlomo: bashful and quiet, and ready for every self-dedication. Now he was smelling his new shoes, which he had obtained with great difficulty, in these calamitous times, and looking at them with love. That was how Shlomo had looked at his new boots, after suffering for many days in torn boots. He turned them over and felt them and smelled them, until one Friday afternoon they were stolen from him in the bathhouse, and he, Shlomo, whose nature it was to stifle his sorrow, could not contain himself this time, and he wept out loud: "But I didn't even want to go to the bathhouse; my heart foretold it!!" And here was Bertha, too. Like his sister Batya in the past, when she came home from school in her black apron, and because of the poverty in the house she didn't feel her hunger, but turned directly to her schoolbooks. The same purity, the same intelligence, the same patience.

Because of the housing shortage that the war brought, the young couple had to live here, too. An old clock chimed the hours with a familiar melody, close to the heart. There was no trace of sacred pictures on the walls. Nothing of Christianity was felt here at all, except for the tree on the holy night. It imbued the house with the scent of the woods, but the smell of the branches that covered the sukkah of his childhood was more pleasant.

III

At midnight, a night of strong frost, with large stars, he went in Bertha's company to call the midwife who lived not far away. The distant, distant sound of a clacking train could be heard. The snow made the fifteen-year-old girl glow, and she walked, light and hovering, with her suppressed pride, as if she, Bertha, were an entirely different creature, and she would never be in the condition of her older sister. She looked around with curiosity and called out happily:

"I've never been outdoors at such a late hour!"

When they brought the midwife, with her box of instruments, there was relief.

"Such a harsh winter!" she greeted the people of the house cordially, with the encouraging smile peculiar to the women of her profession. Exactly like "Granny" Mereh in the past. The world midwife, who is everywhere the same, is that precious woman who, in a moment, dispels the dark mood and frightened expectancy within the house, in the middle of the night.

Energetically, confident in her strength, she put on her white apron and turned to Grettel, who was lying in bed, writhing in labor.

His mother-in-law said to him:

"You, go to my bedroom. I'll call you later. You can lie down in my bed, too."

"Yes, yes. We have no need for men now," the midwife confirmed.

That bedroom—to reach it you had to go through the living room—wasn't heated, and, with his hair standing from the cold, he walked back and forth in it. Frost on the windows. Above the bed hung two big portraits, yellow with age, one beside the other: a pair of householders on their wedding day. Apparently ordinary faces, but their great beauty was in them, the beauty that was later revealed in the image of their daughters.

Heavy fatigue was felt in his whole body, after all the various tribulations of the recent days, while life demanded great strength of him for the new burden. And that numbness! The strange numbness that enveloped him particularly in the moments of the great event.

When the windows started turning blue, he threw himself on the open bed in his clothing and fell asleep for a while. Immediately the sound of crying came to his ears, distant and thin. . . . In a very sad daylight, like that of a solar eclipse, his home city lay, and he ran along the street by the low wooden houses with their shutters drawn. A girl ran in front of him, and he saw the knot of her hair on the nape of her neck, as it rocked back and forth and was about to scatter at any moment, since no hairpin was stuck in it. It was clear that in her great fear she hadn't managed to do that. And here was the garden of his childhood. Among the beds of poppies, the poppies in their blossoming, three large goyim popped up, one of whom had an army hat on his head. They gave him a hoe and ordered:

"Here dig a grave for yourself!!"

And the distant screaming grew louder. Now he was awake, and his mother-in-law entered with the news:

"A boy!"

Translated by Jeffrey M. Green.

Other works by Shofman: *Kol kitvei G. Shofman* (1960).

I. M. Veisenberg

1881–1938

I. M. (Isaac Meyer) Veisenberg was born in Żelechów, Poland, to a working-class family. He worked as an artisan in his youth, and started his literary career in his twenties. I. L. Peretz and other Warsaw intellectuals encouraged and mentored him, and his first short stories were published in Peretz's *Di yudishe bibliotek* in 1904. Veisenberg's naturalist novella, *A shtetl*, published two years later, was reprinted several times. After Peretz's death, Veisenberg himself became a mentor to the new generation of Yiddish writers as an editor of *Yudishe zamlbikher* in 1918–1920. Positioning himself against Sholem Asch and other sentimentalists, he also published other literary journals.

A Hot Shabbat Day

1920

It was Shabbat morning. I was still lying in bed. My mother was already up and awake, wearing her clean white headdress. The other bed opposite mine, where my mother would sleep, was already made, piled up high and covered with a clean white sheet. The brass candlesticks stood on the little table. The room was quiet, my father had already gone to the synagogue. It must have been fairly late. The golden face of the sun was well into the sky, right above our opposite neighbor's roof, staring into our house through the window, filling the entire room with light, shining cheerful brightness into every corner. I jumped out of bed and right into my pants, and then went straight to the window [. . .] where the greenish shadow of the vast fields peered into the room, adding some late-spring dark green shade. I stood by that window and looked outside. I saw that our goy, a stout peasant, was already standing behind the wall of the straw-roofed barn hitching up the horse to the buggy with the removable sides that can be used as ladders, ready to go out to the field. He hadn't even touched the reins yet when the black, jumpy dog with shiny fur and glittering eyes had already lined himself up by the horse, stood there wagging his tail restlessly, waiting for the horse to get going. [. . .] I was overcome with a quiet sadness. I went behind the wall of the barn and started picking maidenstears that grew there.

In those days, two months ago, my mother used to take me every day early in the morning, before the sun rose, to the stream trickling in the field to wash my mouth in the flowing water. People said that I had scurvy, that my teeth and gums would soon decay. The fact that my mother took me through the white, dewy fields every morning, that we were sneaking through the grasses quietly at a time when there was no one else there, only my mother and I, when everyone else was still quietly asleep, wrapped in the darkness of night, made me think bad thoughts. I thought that they were seeking out some magic spell for my sake, that they were trying to cast a magic spell on me; even the heavens fell silent, I thought, as they watched the two of us going out to the fields every morning before dawn. This left me sad, and the sadness has remained with me ever since—I can feel it even now as I stand behind the wall. [. . .]

Also, one of my little sisters died not long ago. I can still see her all the time: she had been so still, deeply brokenhearted because she was torn from the world at such a young age, torn from her parents, brothers, and sisters with whom she had been so close, and now she is no longer in our family. God ordered her to go up to a distant, unknown world, to heaven, and her face in the grave is still constantly thinking about us and longing to return to us, who are alive. [. . .]

By the time I got back to our house from the field the sun was already above our porch—only then did I realize how long I had been lost in my thoughts. The whole area in front of our house was gilded with brightness. Thousands of tiny, radiant spears of glass and stones sparkled and flashed in the pale, glowing sand. At the end of the street, where the Blendever *shtibl* stood, Jews had already poured out to the street and were standing around in front of the *shtibl* in their silk Sabbath *kapotes*; they had already put away their *taleysim*. [. . .]

My father must have gotten home a long time ago, I thought.

Sure enough, he was home already. To my great fortune, however, his good friend Zelig was also there. My father was content, and my mother was also busy with something; thus, I was a little happy too.

They just asked me where I had been running around, and that was it. I don't remember if I was able to give them an answer or if I just stood there still, but I do remember that I had grateful thoughts about Zelig. I loved him secretly and quietly. He was pale and handsome, had strong, broad shoulders, a small black beard and an intelligent, calm look in his eyes. Furthermore, he wore a nice short overcoat and shined boots that I liked to use as a mirror to look at myself.

I figured that after lunch we would go for a walk, and that is exactly what happened.

Right after lunch—Zelig ate with us, too—I was all ready to go, my heart trembling with joy. I was dressed in my new cloth pants, green calico overcoat and calico hat with a golden star in the front. I took my father and Zelig by the hand and we set out, me walking in the middle.

The yellow sand shot off thousands of radiant arrows. Butterflies fluttered among the tiny tree branches, occasionally landing on a green, glittering leaf, and then moving on to another one. The white fluff of the dandelions that grew in the meadow blew around in the air. Everything, every blade of grass and every single tree, glittered so brightly that it blinded the eyes. I felt like a little boy, completely overwhelmed with the surrounding glare, and I couldn't open my eyes because of the fiery spears hanging over my head.

But soon we turned into a narrow side street behind the cooper's house.

I was very happy when we started to climb up the high mountain: white, smooth stones rolled around under my feet and rasped under my father's and Zelig's tread . . . and the peak of the mountain spread its brightness all over the mountain back. The crevices in the earth glittered with yellow sand. It cracked under our feet as we climbed higher and higher, to the very top, where I caught sight of the green fields spread out at the feet of the mountain.

And up there it was so still, so spacious. . . .

The blue sky encircled the vast fields and forests . . . still and quiet . . . tranquility flooded my whole body. [. . .]

And God only knows what is going on in the old castle. . . . It has been enchanted since the days of Creation, and maybe there is a captive princess in there, too! A princess with a pale, royal face and golden locks, chained to a wall. I am suddenly overcome with great pity for her. [. . .] What can I do, how can I rescue her now? If I at least had a long sword, like the ones princes have, and a horse with a golden bridle so I could tie him up behind the castle . . . but I don't have such things. . . . And on top of it I am on a faraway, deserted island . . . and the sun is blazing overhead with a hellish fire that almost burns my eyes out. Zelig is fanning his burning face with his white handkerchief, he is so hot, and my father has unbuttoned his *kapote*; he, too, is dying of the heat. He bends down to me and asks if I am hot, too. . . . I tell him that I am thirsty. Then we come to a place where the mountain takes a sheer drop above a wide, sandy path that cuts across the middle of the mountain. We descend through a side path on the left. Now we are between two mountains, between two identical walls. The walls are blocking the sunshine; they cast some shade over the sandy path where we walk. Here it was cool, finally. Here the sun was not burning so much, and we saw only a streak of blue sky overhead. We walked and walked until we heard the rushing sound of a stream. . . .

The stream ran in a green valley, flowing and bubbling with millions of glittering eyes; it poured under a fence and flowed with a silver-sounding murmur into a wooden carriage, overgrown with moss, that had sunk into the ground behind the fence.

My father, Zelig, and I were all faint from the heat by then. We knelt down and bent over the stream, stretching our mouths toward the cool water and drank.

But it was very hard to drink like this. The walls had sunk into the wet grass. So my father came up with an idea. He took off his hat, filled it with water and drank from it. Zelig and I did the same thing. I took off my hat, filled it with water up to the star, and drank. This is how one drinks on the road, in a faraway, deserted place where there are no people. . . .

This is how, my father told us, he had drunk once when they went on a maneuver in the Caucasus Mountains. . . . It was very hot, 50 degrees C, the piercing sun was burning our eyes and peeled the skin off our neck. Soldiers fell one after the other like flies from the heat and from thirst. We came up to a pool of green standing water covered with white worms. Our unit commander, a tall man with a moustache of a knight, was the first to go. He took off his hat, filled it with water, and drank. . . .

And that is exactly what we did—my father, Zelig, and I drank just like people in the Caucasus Mountains drink. . . .Then we started to look for some shade where we could cool off. The sun just burned and burned, and we could not find any shade. The fields and the trees are wilting, yearning for some cool wind—just a breeze! Every blade of grass and every leaf is faint and weary from fatigue and thirst. [. . .]

Until we passed through and came to a bright big open square where we caught sight of the small houses at the edge of the town. The square was so bright and the sand was glowing so much that we could not keep our eyes open. Here people were building a house, and they worked so quietly as if they were doing something secretly while the town was asleep. The wide street in the middle of the town lay sunken in stillness. The street is asleep, all shutters closed; only the scorching stones glitter. In the square where we stand some walls are already halfway up. They are building a brewery, my father said. Some workers stand upright relaying the bricks while others are bending over the walls and laying the bricks; and all this is happening very quietly . . . above them the heat is burning, and they are doing their job quietly, attentively. But they are so tired and so sleepy that you would think they may fall asleep any minute, like the town, and continue to work in their sleep. . . . One hand raises a brick, another hand swivels the trowel—and then quiet again, stillness. . . . The workers who stand upright in a line hold their heads toward the sky; they pass the bricks from hand to hand with such devotion as if they were passing on the world's greatest secrets, or as if the world had made them into a secret and exhibited them here in order to enchant the entire square and cast it into a sunken stillness. . . . And the low blue sky is stretched out over the entire square.

The town is asleep, the sky is silent, the sun is silent, quietly observing the silence of the workers grow ever deeper. [. . .]

Translated by Vera Szabó.

Other works by Veisenberg: *A shtetl* (1906); *A shlekhte froy un andere dertseylungen* (1921); *Virklekhkeyt* (1925); *Goyroles vos lakhn* (1931); *Shtarker fun toyt* (1931).

Ojzer Warszawski

1898-1944

Ojzer Warszawski was born in Sochaczew, Poland. He received a traditional Jewish education and settled in Warsaw in 1912. His first novel, *Shmuglars* (1920), was published in multiple editions. Warszawski moved to Paris in 1924, joined the Montparnasse artistic community, and published avant-garde periodicals. In addition to his painting and literature, Warszawski published art and literary criticism. After the German occupation of Paris, he fled to different parts of France and was eventually evacuated to Rome, where he was captured and sent to Auschwitz.

Smugglers
1920

Chapter I

Pantel the wagon driver stretches out under the covers and sits up, yawning. The house is dark but a faint light is just beginning to penetrate through the peepholes in the shutter.

"It's early," he stammers, rubbing his eyes and looking around the cold, dark room. When he sees the icicles hanging outside the window a feeling of gloom overcomes him.

"Glicke . . . Glicke," he calls over to the other bed.

"Eh, what," moans his wife, turning to him. Her eyes are glued together and her mouth is open wide in a yawn.

"See, another frost," says Pantel, pointing to the window. Then he puts both hands inside the warm vest he sleeps in all winter and scratches his chest with one hand and his shoulder with the other.

"What did you say?" she asks again, sighing as she moistens her fingers and pulls her sticky eyelids apart.

"There's no money," he answers.

"We have to buy some coal and a rye bread at least," she says, more alert now.

"There's a frost," he blurts out again.

He takes his hand out from under his vest and pulls the cover up to his nose as he watches the steam rising from his wife's mouth.

"Oh, what will happen to us?" she cries, knowing full well that he has no answer for her.

A child's angry voice is heard coming from the kitchen at the front of the house, "Move over! Who do you think you are, spreading out like that?"

"Shut up," answers a deeper voice.

"I hope the cholera gets into their bones," shouts Pantel. "A tired man can't even get a little rest around here."

"What will happen to us? Oh, what will happen to us?" Glicke moans. "The baker won't give us another crust of bread. At least if we had a little coal burning in the kitchen." And she begins to scratch her head, pushing her nightcap back and forth as if she were grating horseradish.

Pantel, warmer now, lifts a corner of the cover and enjoys the cold, refreshing air on his strong body. But when he sees the frozen windowpane he covers himself again. Soon he begins to perspire, first just his arms and then his entire body. The stiff, dark hairs on his head and face are shiny with perspiration—they look like they're covered with dew. He draws his short, muscular legs up and then stretches them out, repeating the movement over and over again like a horse running across a field.

"Thief," his wife shouts. "Go ahead, tear up what's left of the cover!"

Pantel pays no attention to her and continues to kick the cover. He seems to be absorbed in something, an idea, maybe something concerning a livelihood.

"You could use a new brocade dress," he says suddenly, in a voice as soft as Pantel's voice can get. The cover is torn to shreds by now and he becomes silent again, trying to figure out what he can do to provide her with a better life.

She is silent, too, thinking about their plight. They can't go on like this. The wagon trips to and from the railroad bring in nothing—water for kasha. Everything in the house is falling apart, everything is torn. They need linens, shoes, coal, wood. There's no end to what they need.

Suddenly Pantel jumps out of bed, oblivious to the cold. "I have a plan," he says. "Don't worry. God is good." Then he wraps long rags around his legs, pulls on his boots and goes into the stable to water the horses.

The sun is just coming up.

Chapter II

Pantel's sons are still lying on the wooden bench in the kitchen when Kopel comes in, stamping up and down in his heavy boots and rubbing his hands together. Pots and pans are strewn everywhere and a large pot filled with water stands near the sleeping bench. The house is freezing cold and the windowpanes are covered with frost.

"Good morning," bellows Pantel, blowing into his fists. His deep voice resounds through the whole house. "Ooh—ah, is it ever cold!"

He walks over to the table near the window and pushing his hat back behind his ears sits down on a bench.

"Why didn't you drive to the train?" asks Pantel before reciting his morning prayers in his large, yellowing prayer shawl, which completely engulfs his strong, compact body.

"No one is going to the train," complains Kopel and starts to cough, probably from the schnapps he drank at home. "Who travels in a frost like this?"

At the end of his prayers Pantel takes three steps backward, bows to the left and spits, bows to the right and spits, takes off his prayer shawl and phylacteries, rolls down his sleeve, pulls his sheepskin hat up to his eyebrows and finally turns to Kopel.

"Last night I thought of a scheme," says Pantel, smiling from ear to ear as he grabs the lapel of Kopel's thick fur coat. "Come, let's get Yankel and go over to blonde Elye's house. Then we'll talk."

"Everything is covered with frost today," says Kopel, pointing to a row of sparkling trees that light up the street with their shimmering beauty.

"You'll see, there'll be blight on the fruit trees this summer because of this frost," Pantel murmurs. [. . .]

Blonde Elye has set out brandy glasses and a flowered dish filled with his own special cakes. They are the best—no one can make them better. The men raise their glasses in unison, place their hands behind their necks, toss their heads back and drain their glasses in one gulp. Then they put the empty glasses on the table and sit down to eat the cakes.

"I'll make it short," says Pantel as Kopel and Yankel listen with open mouths. "What's the point of driving people to the train? What do we earn? The gall creeps out of our bodies till we find the passengers, especially at night, knocking on shutters and waiting for them to wake up: 'Who's there? Who's there?' As far as I'm concerned the devil can eat their mothers' insides. There's no profit in it. Let's become partners and start smuggling in Warsaw. I know as sure as I live that we'll do well. One good month and we'll be on our feet again. Eh?"

Pantel sits quietly for a while, observing his companions and waiting anxiously for their reactions to his proposal. Kopel, whose opinion he is most interested in, jumps up and gives Pantel such a blow on his shoulders that the floor shakes. "On my soul," he thunders, "you're right!"

"It makes good sense," says Yankel, a taciturn man by nature though never too shy to get into a fight.

"We could still drive people to and from the train," Pantel adds, heartened by Kopel's response. Pantel needs his sanction because Kopel is the one who has enough money to buy flour and bread. "We can share the work," he continues. "Two of us will stay here and two will travel to Warsaw—when they come back we'll trade places."

"It makes good sense," says Yankel again, taking another brandy. Kopel joins him.

"*L'chayim, l'chayim!* Good luck to us all." [. . .]

Chapter IV

That first smuggling trip from the shtetl causes a great stir—everyone has something to say about it and it soon becomes the major subject of conversation at home, in the synagogue and in the marketplace. In the wealthier homes the subject is treated more casually, but in the poorer homes they discuss every detail: who went, what merchandise they took, and most important of all, how much money they made.

The shtetl people are as impatient for the wagon to return as they are for the coming of the Messiah. Some even wait on the highway and whenever they see a wagon coming they walk over to it in a long procession, their heads bent against the cold—first the women in their long shawls, then the men and children. It looks like a funeral procession.

The little boys amuse themselves by throwing snowballs at each other. Sometimes they extend the honor to the grownups, too, and get roundly cursed for their efforts. Gimpel's Chana, walking one step ahead of the men and women, disgraces her family by blowing her nose into her apron and shouting out in her high-pitched voice, "Now tell me—am I smart or am I smart? Didn't I tell you the day before yesterday that the wagon drivers were up to something? What do you think they were doing at Yankel the flour dealer's?"

Shayke, a stooped, weak man of seventy-four, sounds like a goose gasping for air as he walks on the footpath alongside the ditch. "Did you say they were at Yankel the flour dealer's?"

"Yes," answers Gimpel's Chana, "they bought a whole sack of flour and then they went to Itchele the baker."

"Did you say Itchele the baker?"

"Yes, they bought a hundred and twenty pounds of bread from Itchele," she says, and blows her nose. [. . .]

Even old Shayke hardly feels the cold air blowing into every hole in his coat and into his tattered slippers that look like whales opening their mouths with every step he takes. He is thinking of all the good meals and the good bread he has eaten in his life, and all the coffee and beer he has drunk. He can smell the food. "Ai-yai-yai, the things I have lived through," he says to no one in particular, "things were different once, everything was different." And recalling those bygone days brings a spark of light back into his fading eyes.

He thinks of his daughter-in-law, her infant sucking at her emaciated breasts and drawing out her last bit of strength without getting anything to swallow. But this picture soon disappears and in its place he sees a huge rye bread surrounded by smaller round breads flying at him from all sides.

They think that I'll never do anything useful again, he thinks. Well, I'll show them. There's still a God who lives and old Shayke isn't dead yet either. I'll buy a little merchandise and take it to sell in Warsaw. I'll make a ruble yet, even a half a ruble is money! Better than nothing.

The only one who stayed at home is Zilpe. Gimpel's Chana stops by to tell her that she is going to meet the wagons. Zilpe desperately wants to go along. She would give anything to get out of bed, but she can barely lift her head off the pillow. Her only son, Dovidl, sits by her side, his black eyes filling with tears. Silently he questions God. "Why do You punish us so? Are we more sinful than others?"

Zilpe's eyes are closed but she isn't sleeping. She knows that her only child is crying—a mother can see through closed eyes. And she knows that the tears in her son's eyes are for her and that he is entreating God to restore her health. For a moment she feels a slight improvement—her weak, pain-racked body seems lighter. Maybe she is getting better, she thinks. But almost immediately the pain returns in her left side and in her back and legs. "Lord, God of the Universe, dear God in Heaven, help me, please help me!" she cries weakly, writhing in pain.

But to her son she says, "Why are you crying, foolish child? Never mind. I feel better than I did yesterday. I think that by the middle of the week, maybe by Thursday, I'll be able to get out of bed."

Her prematurely aged face shines with motherly love and tenderness. Woe is me, she thinks, he's so pale, there's not a drop of blood in his face. He hasn't eaten a thing since yesterday. "Dovidl, please, take a slice of bread."

"I will."

She waits. "Bring me the bread from the table," she finally says, and as soon as she sees it she knows that he hasn't touched it.

"You haven't eaten one bite, not one single bite! Is it right to deceive a mother? Well, is it?"

"No, it is not permitted, but Mama, you're weak and I'm not hungry."

"Now eat, you wicked child. Do you hear?" She tries to sit up and break off a piece of bread, but the strain has made her dizzy and she has to brace herself to keep from fainting. "Oh oh," she moans, but quickly restrains herself. The boy looks like an old man and she wants to tell him something positive, something to cheer him up.

"Listen, Dovidl—Gimpel's Chana told me that the wagon drivers have gone off to smuggle. So I thought that as soon as I can get out of bed, right after *Shabbes*, God willing, I'll do the same. I'll ask Yankel to give me flour on credit and I'll start earning money, too. Things will be different then, you'll see."

The son is sunk in despair. He knows how sick his mother is. She won't get out of bed this *Shabbes*, or next *Shabbes*, or any *Shabbes*, he thinks. And then his face suddenly lights up.

"Mama, do you know what I've been thinking? I want to go to Warsaw to smuggle."

She is shocked. The expression on her face unsettles him, but he cannot contain his excitement.

"Don't you believe that I can do it? It's not hard. I'll buy some flour and take it to Warsaw by wagon. I'll keep the basket with me during the whole trip and when I get to the big city I'll sell the flour and return to the shtetl with the money. Listen to me, Mama, I promise as I live that everything will be fine. I'll be very careful, I swear I will, and I'll earn money."

Dovid's eyes shine like stars. He imagines himself returning from the smuggling trip, entering the warm house, placing his earnings on the table and counting the money while his mother serves him a hot dinner. And there is so much money to count that his food gets cold.

He gets up, takes the bread from his mother and cuts off a slice. "*Nu*," he begs, "eat a little, Mama."

She feels her heart bursting with pride, and with bitterness, too, as she silently takes the bread, moistens it with spit, bites off little pieces and tries to swallow.

The first rays of the sun sparkle on the lacy, filamented windowpanes and the frost flowers slowly melt, dripping like tears on the windowsill. [. . .]

Chapter XI

Pantel's head is swirling. Ever since the guards confiscated his flour he behaves like a grumpy, silent bear, ignoring his pregnant wife and starting every sentence with a curse—a cholera on you—even when speaking to his sons. And he beats the younger one with anything that comes to hand, though he doesn't dare try it with Mendel, his oldest. Mendel takes after his mother. He is tall and broad—a giant, easily two Pantels.

The guards never let Pantel get away with anything and constantly confiscate the goods from his wagon. Kopel is back on the road again and takes Fayfke and the loose woman with him on every trip. They buy their goods together and whenever a guard stops them she tells him that the goods are hers. They never confiscate her goods. Old Shayke jokes about it. He calls the woman Fayfke's "bride." Fayfke doesn't care what he says or what anyone else says either. It all rolls off him like water off a duck's back.

If I had a "bride" like that with me, Pantel thinks, they wouldn't confiscate my goods, either. And a "bride" is a big help in other ways, too. It isn't easy to cope on one's own in Warsaw. Food is hard to get, and being alone is no fun.

Not that it's so great at home! His wife slouches around the house all day with her big belly, sure that she is carrying another boy. Ugh, he can't bear to look at her.

These thoughts don't give him any rest. Even when he returns from the road at dawn, exhausted and frozen through and through, he thinks about it as he drops off to sleep. Then he wakes up angry, curses his wife and storms off to Yizchak Yona's where he drinks one glass of brandy after another.

Occasionally he is free of these thoughts, but only rarely and then always on *Shabbes* when friends come to visit—people like Chaim Kaiser's father, Leyzer, who likes to tell stories about the days when Pantel and the others were boys. The things they would do! They would burn down a shop in the blink of an eye!

"Eh, my good brothers! I tell you one thing. The good old days will come back, I promise you," says Leyzer. This helps to restore a little of their old optimism.

Pantel changes on the Sabbath. He becomes a different person, more spiritual. And after *Shabbes*, when the stars come out, he helps Shayke climb up into his wagon and repeats the stories he heard from old Kaiser. Shayke almost splits with laughter. Little Orke, who has begun to accompany them to Warsaw occasionally, is all ears. He is very proud of the nasty tricks his father used to play back then.

One *Shabbes* at Pantel's house Leyzer Kaiser regales them with a story they have heard many times before: "One Friday evening a group of Russian railroad workers came to the shtetl to make trouble," he begins, stroking his white beard. "They started to beat up Jews who were walking to the synagogue. And what do you think old Kaiser did? He jumped into a courtyard, ripped a plank off a wagon, and began swinging it left and right. The Russians fell like flies. Then a tall Russian appeared with an iron crowbar in his hand. He was a hairbreadth away from breaking Kaiser's head when Pantel jumped on him and pummeled him so hard with his bare fist that the Russian fell to the ground."

Little Orke is fascinated by this story and in his excitement he punches his father on the back. This annoys Pantel and without thinking he strikes the child and gives him such a blow that he turns somersaults and ends up stretched out on the floor.

"What did you do?" cries Glicke. "What do you have against the boy? You could have killed him, you murderer. I hope your hands rot off your body."

Angry and guilt-ridden, Pantel gets up to leave. His face is flushed and his eyes are wild, and he is conscious only of the deep loathing he feels for his wife. It takes all his self-control to keep from hitting her, too. Instead he spits in her direction and storms out of the house, banging the door behind him.

In the stall he strokes the stallion and begins to calm down. Thinking about his troubles, he decides that his wife is to blame for everything, even for the confiscated goods. Remember, Pantel, he says to himself, if they confiscate your goods one more time you're left with nothing. You won't even deserve to live. I wish her father would croak, too. Then he gives the stallion a kick and yanks his long tail.

Crawling up into the loft, he covers himself with hay and lies there for a long, long time, alone with his thoughts. Finally he makes a decision: he doesn't know how exactly, but he knows for sure that he's going into partnership with a *shikse*. Obviously he doesn't intend to approach any *shikse* he happens to meet and say, "Hey, you, come with me!" But the sooner he begins to look, the better it will be for him.

And not long after his decision he has a stroke of good luck. He meets a woman who is clearly destined for him. And it doesn't lead to a scuffle with the younger men, either. [. . .]

Chapter XXII

When they return to the shtetl everyone goes his own way, leaving Pantel and his sons in the wagon with Natasha. By now everyone has a "bride" of his own. Blind Grunem, who travels with Yankel Tshap, actually brought his "bride" home right from the start. He told his wife to get out of bed and his *shikse* lay down and went to sleep in her place.

At first there was a great brouhaha in the shtetl about the "brides." They were willing to forgive the younger men—after all, boys will be boys. But grown men! Husbands with wives and children at home—*feh*.

Grunem's wife screamed and wailed and clawed at him and at herself and humiliated him in public, all to no avail. One day he said, "Enough! If you don't like it, you can leave."

"I only pray that you are torn limb from limb," she answered. "What about the children?"

"If you're so worried about them, swallow the pain and stop making trouble!"

They say he beats her, that her whole body is covered with black and blue marks. People try to help her, but all he has to do is look at them with his sick eye and the blood in their veins turns to ice. Nobody wants to start up with Grunem, the murderer!

Once his wife's brother, a shoemaker, grabbed him by the throat. "Dead or bread," he threatened, "throw the *shikse* out of the house, or else!" And would you believe it? Grunem stabbed him in the hand with a knife! The man is still walking around with a bandage.

That's just the way things are, and since even husbands have "brides" the young men feel there's nothing for them to be ashamed of.

Pantel is not ashamed either, and he warned his wife not to make a fuss. "Don't you dare say a word!"

So she went him one better. As soon as she hears them coming into the house, she gets up and gives the *shikse* her bed to sleep in.

Glicke has gotten used to jumping out of bed, putting on her slippers and her short velvet robe and going into the kitchen the minute she hears the clatter of horses' hooves, or at the latest when she hears the horses snorting in the stall. She is prepared to do anything, so long as she doesn't have to deal with the *shikse*. This way the two lie down, Pantel in one bed and the *shikse* in the other, and they sleep soundly under separate covers.

But every once in a while, when she recalls an earlier time before they began to smuggle, a sense of melancholy seizes hold of Glicke and she is overcome with shame. Already in the last stage of pregnancy, she cries bitter tears and bemoans her fate to her father. He is not sympathetic.

"*Feh*, you should be ashamed of yourself talking like that about your own husband. What do you want from him? Doesn't he support you? Don't you have bread to eat? And potatoes aren't lacking in the house either. What is it you want? A lot of women would be happy to be in your place. And you'll be making a *bris* soon, too, eh? Think of that."

But she sobs so bitterly that finally the old man is moved by his daughter's pain. He takes his wooden stick and goes to his son-in-law to talk things over with him.

When he enters the kitchen he sits down at the table and looks around the house. "Thank God," he says, "you have everything you need." But she doesn't let up, tugging at his sleeve and winking toward the bedroom. Finally he limps over to the door, opens it slowly and walks in.

No one knows what he saw there—he never talks about it. But he ran out of the room as fast as he could and hobbled back into the kitchen mumbling, "Sh, sh, sh, sha, sha," over and over again. Then he put on his hat and left.

"Oh my, oh my, what man is capable of," he cried when he was out of earshot, "and in his own house, with his wife there—oh my, oh my."

In time Glicke becomes used to having the *shikse* around. Sometimes when Pantel is not at home and she needs money, the *shikse* gives her some of hers. And when she returns from a smuggling trip they often sit together and Glicke listens to the stories of her adventures on the road. The *shikse* goes into great detail and Glicke is fascinated. They have come to a modus vivendi of sorts, and life has become easier. [. . .]

Book II. Chapter VIII

Do you remember when the mobilization began? There was trouble everywhere, but things got really bad when the Germans came. The Gentiles informed on us. Remember when Matshizshak told the Russians that I was a spy. Think of it—Ahrele a spy! But they paid no attention to him. Later, just after they received the order to drive out the Jews, an evening patrol heard a shot coming from Yankel Felcher's house and ran in to investigate. The police made everyone stand outside— Yizchak Yona, Zangvil Melamed, Hote, Yankel Felcher and all their wives and children. They were ready to shoot each and every one of them."

"Yes, yes, we remember," say the women in unison.

Old Shayke stops singing and playing with the children. He sits very quietly, as if the words coming out of Ahrele's mouth are alive and have triggered a fear of the Russians.

"At the time the commandant happened to tear his overcoat so he asked the soldiers if they knew a good tailor in the shtetl, someone who could sew a neat patch. Naturally they told him about me, and the commandant came into my house with two soldiers at his side.

"'Can you fix this coat?' he asked in Polish.

"My wife looked as if she would faint when I told him, in Polish, without a sign of fear, that I could do it. After that the commandant's voice became softer. He pointed to the tear in his greatcoat and asked, 'Can you fix it so that the patch won't be seen?'

"'Of course I can, Sir,' I said.

"He took off his coat and I sat down at the table to work. My boys threaded the needles and I told my wife to bring me the iron, and to make sure that it was sizzling hot! She added a full load of coals to the fire and blew on it, and when the iron was good and hot she set it down on a brick next to me. The commandant stretched out his hand toward the iron and smiled. The weather was cold already. I saw that he wasn't a bad sort, so I told my wife Hannake to give him a glass of tea.

"He smiled and sat down on the table next to me to watch me repair the coat.

"Meanwhile Hannake took a glass and saucer from the Passover set and one of her good spoons and polished it until it glistened. Then she put tea and sugar and four cookies in front of him. It was a beautiful sight! The officer didn't wait to be asked twice. Remember, it was very cold. He drank his tea and asked for a second glass. Then he watched me again. 'Why are you looking at my hands?' I asked him. 'It makes me nervous and I won't do a good job.' He laughed, but he continued to watch me work. 'Why are you fumbling with the coat instead of sewing on the patch?' he asked. 'I'm almost finished putting on the patch,' I answered. 'I can't believe it,' he said, 'I can't see the patch at all.' [. . .]

"I showed him the place where I sewed on his patch and he looked and looked but he couldn't find it. It wasn't until I took his finger and rubbed it over the exact spot that he began to appreciate what I did.

"'Ahrol, you're a splendid fellow! How much do you want for your work?'

"I told him that I wasn't finished yet. The buttons hadn't been sewn on firmly enough by his tailor and I wanted to do them again. And I wanted to press the coat, too. He didn't argue with me. And when I brought him the finished garment and he put it on and looked at himself in the mirror, he was so happy that he put his arm around my shoulder. 'Tell me how much I owe you. I'll pay you whatever you want,' he said, taking his wallet out of his pants pocket.

"'I don't want a single kopec, not one groschen!' I shouted, but he interrupted me. 'Tell me what you want. Don't be embarrassed! I'll give you whatever you want.'

"And then I said it. I don't know how I had the presence of mind to think of it and where I got the nerve to say it, but I did. 'Sir Commandant, the lives of seventeen people have been ruined, and all because of a false accusation. They weren't involved in the shooting, they're not guilty. There's Yizchak Yona, a simple tailor who patches second-hand clothes. He can't even bring himself to give his child a little slap. And there's Chezkel, a teacher—imagine, a teacher!'

"My boys stood frozen in place and Hannake, who was about to faint, winked at me to stop talking. But I ignored her and continued to make my point, willing to be a martyr for the sanctification of God's name! I only stopped when I saw that he wanted to say something. 'Ahrol,' he said, 'did you serve in the army?' I told him that I served in the Siberian regiment, seventh brigade, in the sewing workroom. 'I like you,' he said. 'There aren't many Jews like you. I'll ask about you and if what you say is true and the imprisoned men are innocent, they will not be shot—they'll be freed.'

"We all surrounded him—I, Hannake and my boys. We wanted to kiss his hands, but he held them above his head."

At this point Ahrele stops to catch his breath and drink a glass of beer. He swallows it in one gulp and then looks at his audience silently—his expression is worth a thousand words. He drinks another glass of beer, but he doesn't continue with his story. Everyone knows what happened next, how the rabbi with the long white beard and the big fur hat and satin coat, may his memory be for a blessing, came to Ahrele's house with the most respected members of the congregation. And how they set the table with a white tablecloth and the rabbi drank a *l'chayim* to Ahrele. And how he shook his hand and blessed him and told him that he hoped Ahrele would live to see the Messiah because he had done such a great deed in saving seventeen people from death. [. . .]

This story about Ahrele spread throughout the shtetl. Yizchak Yona still can't forget that Ahrele rescued him from certain death. Every week, as sure as there's a Friday, he sends him money. Ahrele is reluctant to take it. "It's a lot of money for him!"

When Ahrele finishes the story it is almost dark. Jews are rushing to the synagogue after their third *Shabbes* meal to say the evening prayers. The men in the room get up to go, too, all except Grunem who has fallen asleep in his chair.

"You should get cholera in your nose," says Kopel, waking him. "What do you mean, falling asleep?"

Grunem wakes with a start and seeing how dark it is outside he almost leaps to the door. "*Nu*, let's go to the wagons."

"No," says Pantel, "you're not going today. I don't know exactly when you are going—maybe tomorrow."

Old Shayke gets up, holding the sleepy child who is now wrapped in his *tallis*. His ritual prayer shawl keeps her warm in the cool night air as he walks home to his daughter. [. . .]

Book III. Chapter V

In the dark he suddenly feels weak again and at that moment the image of Berek, Yankel Latitutnik's son, comes to him.

How is it that of all people he is reminded of Berek now? Berek became a Christian. Mendel remembers the days when he and his friends used to chase him and throw stones at him. But when he saw the look in Berek's eyes he would run away as fast as he could.

Despite everything Berek remains Yankel Latitutnik's son. When he was still called by his Yiddish name, Berel, he used to go to the priest's house to bring him his new pair of low-cut boots or a pair of shoes he had repaired. And sometimes, for no special reason, the priest stopped to talk to him in the street, quite an honor for a shoemaker's son. Berel found more and more reasons to visit the priest and their discussions about the shoemaker's craft and his mother and father's poverty often ended in a question: had the young man ever thought about being rich? Berel answered that he had often thought about it.

"Berek," said the priest, "I have a solution for you. But don't talk to anyone about it. Not a word, not even to your father. I will see that something is done for you."

He introduced him to a wealthy village maid who had inherited several large fields, a house of her own, two horses and a cow. Berel was deceived—he walked around town with a tormented expression on his face and was as pale as a ghost.

"Do you see, the shoemaker's son is growing up a fool," said people who saw the way he looked.

But he wasn't bothered by what people said. What does it have to do with anything? The priest continued to talk to him in the most pleasant way and one Sunday, when the peasant maid came to church, he brought them both upstairs and left them there alone while the congregation was at prayer. She put her hand on his chin and smiled at him. Then she put his hand inside her bosom and sat on his lap. The long and short of it is that he went to the priest.

"Sir, I want to become a Christian," he said.

The wedding took place in the same town. They rang all the bells and the priest, wearing his white robe, sprinkled him with holy water. He had an enigmatic smile on his face.

They led the bride and groom across the marketplace and into the church. Wedding guests came from all the surrounding villages. Noblemen sent gifts—horses, harnesses, grain, watches—and Berek became a rich man.

After the wedding Berel seldom came into town—he was too embarrassed. As time passed, however, he began to come more often. His wife had children to take care of and couldn't work the fields the way she used to, and Berel neglected the estate. The truth is that Berel wasn't suited to that kind of work. Give him a boot or a shoe to repair and he would do it with pleasure. But he had no idea of what to do with a pitchfork and a spade. He started to drink and every time he came to town he visited his father and stayed with him for hours at a time. They say that he used to speak to him in Yiddish. Once, when he was very drunk, he swore in the name of Jesus that he would convert back to Judaism.

This is the Berek who came to mind after all these years. Why? What does Berek have to do with him? When Natasha sits down on the quilt, he asks her about her parents and where she came from. She tells him all about her previous life—her childhood and her father's work in the factory, everything up to the time that Stepka took her to live with her. That part of her life she can't talk about. She mustn't.

Mendel tells her about various incidents in his life. It's hard for him to tell her a whole story in Polish, but she understands what he's saying. They sit for a long time talking about themselves.

It's still warm in the room, and the light from other houses and from the moon and the stars shine through the window and bring Mendel back to his former good spirits. His speech becomes more animated and they begin to jostle one another. She tweaks his ear and he pulls her arm toward him under the quilt and squeezes it so that she is forced to lie with her face close to his. He kisses her, she kisses him and then he pulls her other arm toward him. She pulls away from him and lifts her head, turning and twisting it like a snake.

Mendel feels the way he did in the Illusion Theater. The same waves of heat overcome him and the same odors assail his nostrils. Suddenly even the few clothes he is wearing make him feel constricted and he wants to tear them off his body.

Natasha feels amorous, more amorous than ever before. She takes great delight in enticing him and then backing off. She wants to tease him, to induce the handsome young man to fondle her, so she throws her head back and moves her legs from side to side. Then, overheated from all the activity, she wants to strip her clothes off, too. She presses her lips to his cheek, takes a bit of his skin in her small, sharp teeth and bites him. It's only a little bite and doesn't hurt much but it torments him more than the most piercing pain. Throbbing with excitement, he lifts her up with the greatest ease, moved by a force so strong that it finally leaves him weak. She cries out in pain, frightened that he might break her arm, but only for a moment. Now she feels nothing, only his body next to her. She is a child again, a little bashful village girl who knows only the garden and the cow. They look at each other and begin to shiver.

"Are you cold?" he asks in a quiet voice.

"No," she answers, "I'm not cold."

Silence again. In her mind the tension that was between them after they washed has returned. In Mendel's mind Berek the apostate has come back to haunt him.

What if I would convert, too? he asks himself.

He believes it would be dreadful, much more dreadful than the illness he has just overcome. And remembering his illness he feels a headache coming on, a stronger headache than he had before. He lies down with his head on the pillow and closes his eyes.

The entire scene comes back to him now: driving into Zayazd, being beaten, falling down. And afterwards, when he woke up from his long and troubled sleep, seeing her bending over him. He can still feel her tender caresses and this makes him feel better. The pain is gone. He feels as good as he did before his illness—better. Nothing hurts him and he is lighter than air.

"Won't you go to bed?" he asks her, and he wants her to say yes—and no. He doesn't know what's gotten into him these last few days. If Fayfke were here he would laugh at him. What is he, a Chasid? A yeshiva boy?

"Why aren't you sleeping?"

"Because I'm not tired. I'm so used to waiting for you to fall asleep before me that I can't close my eyes while you're awake."

"How long have you been waiting for me to fall asleep first?"

"What do you mean, how long? During the first two weeks I didn't even think about sleeping."

She says this in the most natural way, without boasting about what she did for him, simply stating a fact. And he accepts it in the spirit in which it was said. Still, he is filled with enormous gratitude to her, a gratitude he felt from the first moment he woke up from his feverish sleep.

"Natasha," he says, "I was sick and you nursed me. I . . . I love you," he suddenly bursts out.

These last three words bring everything back to her. She used to hear those words ten times a day back "then"—everyone said those words to her. And she can actually smell the foul odor of tobacco mixed with sweat, and see the squalor and filth. It all flashes by her slowly, as if lit by Mendel's words. She feels guilty, very

guilty. Oh, if only he would beat her, beat her black and blue!

"Mendel, you know that my aunt Stepka and I lived together in the apartment. I came here right after my mother died. I was hungry, so hungry. All along the way I looked into people's windows to see what they were eating. When I arrived there were a couple of young men and an older army officer in the apartment. There was brandy and beer on the table, and rolls and ham. And it was so warm and comfortable. Oh, oh," she suddenly screams. She sees red rings and circles flashing from all sides. Jumping up from the bed she looks at him with her blue eyes. They are open so wide that even in the semi-darkness they frighten him. Again she screams out and points to something across the room.

"Do you see? In that bed . . . there, with the old officer!"

Her stinging words have the effect of softening his heart even more. A great tenderness flows through his whole body and he is filled with pity for her. Taking her hands, he is on the verge of tears, but he doesn't know for whom—for her, or for himself.

"I love you, I love you," he repeats over and over again as he strokes her hair.

His loving acceptance puts her into a peculiar situation. She doesn't believe that he really loves her. If he did he would surely beat her black and blue. But she continues to cling to him. She's lost anyway. She wants him to take her the way "they" did, to talk to her crudely, to reek of tobacco and sweat.

He is also confused. The effect of her movements on him is hard for him to understand. He's never felt like this before, he's never been so responsive to her young, soft body, to his own sweet Natasha who watched over him for two whole weeks, never sleeping, never eating. He is almost in tears yet his mind is as clear as a crystalline stream. He is beginning to understand a great deal that puzzled him in the past. Without being aware of having moved his arms, he finds himself embracing Natasha and kissing her face passionately. They remain in bed, silent.

The softness Mendel feels is so pure that if he plucked the most delicate lily, it would become even whiter in his hand, refined through his tenderness.

Translated by Golda Werman.

Other works by Warszawski: *Di literarishe revi* (1926); *Shnit-tsayt* (1926); *Rezidentsn* (1955).

Morris Hoffman

1885–1940

Born in Latvia, the Yiddish and Hebrew writer Morris Hoffman settled in South Africa in 1906. He spent most of his life earning a living as a shopkeeper in the arid, sparsely populated Little Karoo, an intermontane plateau basin in the Western Cape. He published prose and poetry in South African Yiddish and Hebrew periodicals. His fiction takes a realistic, unsentimental view of Jewish life in the Little Karoo. It portrays the burdens of living as a Jew in rural districts where Afrikaners, who became increasingly anti-Jewish during the 1930s and 1940s, were the majority white population.

Adoons's Jealousy

ca. 1920

His strong, coal-black hands crumpling and twisting his faded old hat, the thirty-year-old Adoons said in a quiet but firm voice to his employer, Mr. Waldman, the produce dealer,

"*Baas*, I'm finishing off at the end of this month."

The tall, slim, forty-five-year-old bachelor Waldman opened his brown eyes wide in amazement.

"And then, Adoons?"

"Then I'll go and look for work somewhere else."

"Why do you want to leave so suddenly? Don't you get enough to eat? Or don't you earn enough money?"

The fingers of Adoons's right hand fiddled nervously with the copper earrings of his elongated right ear, and the whites of his large eyes flashed as he lowered his pitch-black, crinkly-haired head.

"No, *baas*, you pay me well and I get enough to eat. You clothe me well and you treat me better than other bosses, but I want to leave . . ."

"You're mad, Adoons!" Waldman murmured with a forced smile.

"Maybe I am mad," Adoons's thick lips mumbled, "but I want to go, *baas*."

The affair distressed Waldman and niggled at his heart but he could find no explanation.

Waldman remembered well that it had been almost twenty years that Adoons had worked for him. Adoons had come to him during the flu epidemic which had raged in the city and surroundings and carried off great numbers of people. Many medical people had lost their lives. In the black townships people had dropped like flies, and the survivors lay sick in their shanties. The whites had been rendered helpless without their workers, who had become unobtainable at any price. Waldman was at that time also lying sick in his room—lonely, neglected, with no one to bring him even a glass of water. Suddenly through half-closed eyes Waldman discerned standing in front of him, like a miracle, a tall black youth, as if a magician had conjured him into the room and placed him next to his bed.

The weakened Waldman had burst into tears at this unexpected gift. "Who are you? Who brought you here?" Waldman asked in a choking voice.

"I am Adoons. I ran away from the location. All the black people are dying there . . . In our shack ten sick people were lying on straw bags, covered with old rags. My mother and father have died. Two tall whites came with a big wagon to our shack to collect the dead, and at the same time they also started to pull at the sick. Two of these cried out, 'Why are you pulling us by our feet?' 'We have to bury the dead,' the whites answered. 'But we are still alive!' 'Then hurry up, we have no time,' the white gravediggers told them. I got a terrible fright and ran away. Running past your house I remembered that I once tanned a few skins at your place and you gave me half a loaf of bread and a piece of meat . . . and now I am very hungry . . . two days without food."

From that day Adoons entered Waldman's world. During all the years that he worked for him, not one angry word ever passed between them. Waldman knew that, of the few people who worked in his business, Adoons was the most trustworthy and devoted. Adoons made Waldman aware of it in the following manner.

For several years Waldman had in his employ a business supervisor who won his trust with cunning and flattery. The affairs of the entire business, its accounts and secrets, passed through his hands. But Adoons hated him, and he warned Waldman:

"*Baas*, beware of this man, he is a *skelm*."

"How is it possible? What are you saying, Adoons?"

"Yes, he is not faithful to the *baas*. I saw how he sent several bags of mealies to a shopkeeper and he didn't record it in the book . . ."

"You are making a mistake, Adoons."

"*Baas*, I am sure . . . When that shopkeeper comes, they whisper to each other and discuss secrets like thieves. Watch them, you'll see . . ."

Waldman took his advice. And watching, he discovered that if not for Adoons he would have been ruined.

All Waldman's employees knew how honest and faithful Adoons was to his employer, and they all hated him for it.

"A black dog that he is! . . . Is he rewarded for his blind devotion?"

And indeed Waldman gave Adoons very little for serving him with all his soul and body. Although he often thought that there was no limit to the value of such devotion, it did not occur to him that Adoons might have more extensive needs. What? Did he also have to worry about a future, a purpose?

Adoons, on the other hand, demanded very little in return for his hard work and his faithfulness. A few appreciative words from his *baas* were more precious to him than gold; he was ready to kiss his feet and carry him on his broad, strong shoulders for it.

Adoons knew, too, that his *baas* liked him; he knew that his employer was also lonely and forlorn, that he had no parents, no wife, sister or brother . . . the lonesome *baas* would feel very sad in this house without Adoons and Prince, the big yellow dog whom the *baas* loved so much . . .

For many years Adoons had been tortured by the question of whom the master loved more—him or the dog? He knew well that Prince played an important role in the life of his *baas*. Prince was a handsome and clever dog that performed intricate tricks which he and the *baas* had taught him. He jumped through a hoop and could stand for several minutes on his hind legs. When the master said "Good morning," "Good night," "Hello, Prince," the dog lifted his right foreleg and pushed it into the master's right hand. "Go to bed, Prince!"—and the dog grabbed a cushion from a chair with his mouth, placed it next to Waldman's bed, stretched himself, put his jowl on his paws and fell asleep. Adoons noticed how the boss swelled with pride when Prince stood up on his hind legs and tilted his yellowish-brown head sideways; how Waldman was fascinated when Prince shut one eye and with the open one expectantly watched his master's pocket where—he knew—there was always a piece of chocolate for him.

Adoons believed that Prince had as much claim on his master's love as he had because, like himself, the dog also entered his boss's life forlorn, lonely, hungry and starved, and had been living ever since in luxury. Yet he had always wanted to know who stood in greater favour with the master.

And just recently it had become clear to him.

For many years Waldman had never left the town. He had worked and toiled for so long that he started suffering an acute pain in his chest and the doctor gave him strict instructions to take a rest at the coast for a few months. Adoons felt very upset by his boss's departure. While he was packing his master's bags, Prince rushed around him, excitedly wagging his tail, nervously rubbing his body against Adoons and sniffing the luggage with a strange curiosity.

Adoons mumbled with deep concern, "*Hai*, are we both going to feel lonely without our master!"

Just before his departure, Waldman, half upset, looked round the house in all directions and said in a detached manner to Adoons from a distance, "Good bye, Adoons. Look after the house, after the business, and after Prince . . ." And to Prince he stretched out his hand, took the dog's right foreleg and pressed it a long time with warm affection.

At that moment, Adoons's heart almost burst from gnawing jealousy.

While Waldman was gone and Adoons remained alone with Prince in the yard under the pepper tree, he looked with anger at the dejected dog and muttered bitterly, "You damn mute creature! The *baas* loves you more than me, he greets you with his hand, but not me . . . Your four thin legs with your stupid tail are dearer to him . . . May you die!" Adoons made his firm resolve when his master returned. A happy and healthy Waldman exclaimed from a distance to his black servant, "How are you, Adoons?" But Prince he embraced with great affection and could not stop shaking his paw with effusive joy. Then Adoons could no longer bear the biting envy, and silently said to himself, "Now I can see the *baas* loves the dog more than me . . . I am leaving . . ."

All Waldman's efforts to change Adoons's decision were to no avail. Dumb, silent and indifferent, Adoons listened to Waldman's promises to raise his pay and to buy him new clothes. A faint smile, mingled with a dim sorrow, hovered over his thick lips and a cloudy moisture appeared in his eyes. He maintained a stony silence and just shook his head to say no . . .

A wave of impotent anger surged through Waldman: "An evil madness has possessed him!"

Translated by Woolf Levick and Joseph Sherman.

Other works by Hoffman: *Woglungsklangen* (1935); *Unter afrikaner zun* (1951).

Ernő Ballagi and Jenő Nádor

Ballagi, 1890–1964

Ernő Ballagi was a liberal lawyer and journalist. He was active in Hungarian Jewish communal life and cultural activities, frequently acting as a lawyer for Jews who sued newspapers for defamation.

Nádor, 1892–1970; biography unknown

The Story of a Nose
1921

Lajos Kelemen was an upright and honest man throughout his life. He arrived in this world in June, thereby sparing his mother the ever-present concern whether or not he would catch a cold while being bathed or whether it would be windy when he was put out in the open air. He started school at the age of six. He did not cry when he was left on his own in the classroom among the many children, and he became a fairly good student. He was revaccinated at the proper time and it took effect. When he was thirteen he had his Bar Mitzvoh and recited the prayers in a firm voice in the synagogue. He graduated from high school on time and was judged acceptable by the draft board. By all standards, he was a "good boy." He always handed over his pay to his parents without holding anything back for himself, and he had no harmful habits. He was not tempted by the devil of vanity, and he was not interested in playing cards or horse racing. He avoided women like a wolf that, having satisfied its hunger, would leave the lonely wanderer in peace deep in the forest. With respect to morals and mental ability, Lajos Kelemen was an irreproachable person. His appearance? Well, his appearance was not at all objectionable.

He was fairly tall, his legs were straight, and he walked with an erect posture. His face was inconspicuously regular and his well-shaped mouth revealed good teeth. His hair was thick without being curly, and his eyes sparkled with humor and intelligence. His nose—well, there was a little problem with the nose. Its incline began too close to the forehead and stuck out more conspicuously and was longer downward than the average nose. Yes, the nose was somewhat hooked, like the course of a stone thrown into the air, which the professor in a physics class would demonstrate by drawing a curve. Of course, there was nothing especially wrong with the nose. As far as size, it was quite big and its incline somewhat courageous, but on the whole it was as regular as the man himself. It was not disfigured by small mounds and bridges and its color was not unlike that of the noses of average people. Yet, Lajos Kelemen often had to endure malicious remarks on account of his nose. He would stand, not infrequently, in front of the mirror, blaming fate for having given him, an average person, such an undesirable, big facial feature. He did not miss a chance to counteract that overgenerous miscalculation of nature. He experimented with growing moustaches of various shapes and anxiously stood in front of the mirror examining if the short, then gradually growing moustache, curving upward or stretching far apart, had already cast a protective shadow on that unfortunate branching out of his face.

Nothing went right. The nose stuck out even more triumphantly above the thick, dark moustache. After that he shaved off his moustache, hoping that the whiteness of his face would absorb the undesirable contour. There were also times when he did not even find his nose unpleasantly large. He almost forgot about it. He could divert attention from it quite successfully by wearing colorful neckties. He had his tailor raise and broaden the shoulders of his jackets. The broad shoulders gave his nose yet another perspective. Lajos Kelemen became a pleasant, considerate young man, and his acquaintances gradually forgot about his nose. Their remarks about it were fewer and fewer and when they did say something, they said it in a good-natured, friendly manner. Lajos Kelemen was quite happy. He succeeded, it seemed, in correcting nature's mistake. As time went on, he realized that his nose was not even large. The mistake was in the past. The nose, he thought, had developed sooner than the other parts of his body. Gradually the rest of his body caught up with the nose. He believed that some early deficiencies would correct themselves in time. Lajos Kelemen became an irreproachable man physically as well as intellectually and spiritually. At least, that is what he thought of himself.

The old problems came up again in the army. It was not only that army life had instantly eliminated the artificial counter measures that he had been using so successfully to divert attention from his nose. He could not wear colorful neckties with his army shirt. No tailor could raise or broaden the shoulders of his army coat. Worse yet, the narrow collar of his army shirt, which buttoned tightly under his chin, made his figure look slenderer and lighter than it actually was. According to army regulations, all volunteers had to grow a moustache; a thick, short-trimmed English moustache. That little brushlike phenomenon above the mouth looked as if it had been made to accentuate the nose. Anyway, nothing could have worked for him. Army life went by the book, exactly, to the last detail. No one could deny or conceal anything. Everything looked as it actually was.

Lajos Kelemen's nose caused him no less trouble in the performance of his duties. His troubles began early in the morning. At seven-thirty, the regiment lined up in the courtyard, forming rows of seven as straight as arrows for a tour of inspection by Captain Nemeskövy. The captain arrived and accepted the sergeant's report. Then Corporal Tompor issued the command, "Fall-in! Line-up!" As all the heads stiffened into a forward gaze, Corporal Tompor stepped to the right end of the line. He made a left turn, closed his left eye, and looked at the straight line of profiles. That straight line, however, came to an unexpected obstacle—Lajos Kelemen's nose.

"Kelemen!" the corporal roared. "Backward, one step!"

As the line straightened out, Corporal Tompor stepped to the left, crouched down, and reviewed the heels of the volunteers from that perspective. Again it was Lajos Kelemen. His heels stuck out, breaking the straight line. Poor Kelemen had to be adjusted and re-adjusted, yet they could not make him fit the line. And all that was on account of his nose, that unfortunate nose.

In the war, Lajos Kelemen's nose created fewer problems. The gray uniform made it less conspicuous and on the front few people paid attention to such triviality. At times, when Kelemen peered through the spy-hole, Captain Nemeskövy would warn him, "Kelemen, watch out for the nose. It presents a target to the enemy."

On the whole, however, that most troublesome nose was overlooked in the front line. As a matter of fact, it went quite well with the small and large medals for bravery.

"It makes a nose look small," quipped the colonel, as he personally stuck the second decoration on Kelemen's chest at Komarov. And what's more, that merciless spoiler of Lajos Kelemen's life actually brought him good luck in the war.

In the spring of 1916, the regiment truly distinguished itself in the fighting at Zborow. The men approached the enemy trenches and created panic in the enemy's rank by successfully exploding subterranean mines. Then, with a brave charge, they broke through the steel wall of defense along a wide section that they had been staring at hopelessly throughout the winter. The general praised the regiment and asked the colonel to submit the names of those heroes who had especially distinguished themselves. When the time came for the presentation of the gold medals, the highest decoration in the infantry, the adjutant handed the colonel a list of names.

"We can't give so many gold medals all at once," the colonel said. "We must leave some for the battles to come."

The adjutant started reading the list, "Klein, Schwarz, Schlesinger, Kelemen."

"Only one of the four can get the gold medal," the colonel said. "The rest will get silver."

"Schlesinger," the adjutant recommended. "He has distinguished himself before, too."

"Kelemen," the colonel decided. "If there are so many Jewish heroes in the regiment, let's decorate one who looks like a Jew even from afar. That Kelemen fellow—he's got a good nose on. Let those people in Budapest see that religion makes no difference in the 895th Regiment. Let Kelemen's nose make them see that we recognize bravery even in a Jewish soldier, if he has done his duty."

And that's how Lajos Kelemen got the gold medal for bravery and, aside from bravery, on account of his nose—that unfortunate nose which had caused him so much bitterness in life.

Lajos Kelemen proudly wore the shiny medal. On the street, in the theater, everyone gazed at it reverently. The large nose disappeared again. The gold medal replaced the necktie in diverting attention from his nose. People seemed to notice only the shiny medal about Lajos Kelemen. And it was the medal that the beautiful and rich Margit Fenyvesi, the spoiled society girl, noticed. She immediately fell in love with him and uttered the joyous "I will" when, after a brief courtship, Lieutenant Lajos Kelemen asked her to marry him. Margit was deeply in love with the gold medal. She kept stroking it fondly and bragged about it to her friends. That medal made her fiancé a legendary hero in her eyes. Its brilliance blinded Margit, who did not even notice his nose, although she was very critical and had rejected many a suitor on account of something about his appearance that she did not fancy and would have liked to erase from the past of her family. Margit was a Jewess, but did her best to keep it secret. She had been looking for a man whose physical features would not betray her secret. She failed to notice the dangerously conspicuous nose on Lajos Kelemen. She saw Kelemen only as a hero, a brave soldier, a strong man who had returned with a gold medal from where death was a frequent visitor and where only the greatest among the heroes received the king's image in gold.

Lajos Kelemen could thank his nose for his happiness. He had every reason to forget the troubles it had caused. As a matter of fact, it was his nose that saved his life. He was vacationing in Budapest when the king's humane order was issued, according to which those heroes who had received the highest decoration for bravery should not be sent back to the front. Lajos Kelemen was transferred to a small town in the Alföld, where he became the commandant of a military hospital. His happiness was complete. He and Margit made plans for the wedding and talked of moving to the small town as husband and wife. All signs seemed to indicate that they were headed for an unusually happy and pleasant honeymoon. The wedding, however, had to be postponed. A devoutly religious girl, Margit wanted their wedding to be performed in a religious ceremony, but in a non-Jewish religious ceremony. After all, why would she, Margit Fenyvesi, walk down the aisle in the Dohány Street synagogue? She thought a church would be much more appropriate. But first, of course, she had to choose another religion. Margit was not only religious, she was intelligent as well. She was convinced that if someone happened to be in the enviable position of becoming the member of a religious community without having been born into the fold, that person should choose the religion that is the most suitable for his convictions. So Margit and Lajos started studying various religions with great zeal. They bought many books and became absorbed in various ethical and religious tenets. They excluded the teachings of only one religion—Judaism. They showed no interest in them. Yet, if only they had considered Judaism, they might have become—Jews. There were many problems with the other religions. They objected to the metaphysical concepts of one, disagreed with the ethical system of another, and found fault with the ceremonies of the third. Finally, they agreed on a religion that did not belong to any of the accepted religions and was usually classified in statistical reports as "other." Margit liked the tenets of that religion the most. It was a difficult choice, indeed. After all, it is easy to belong to a religion by virtue of birth, but how much more difficult it is to choose a religion as a mature person who is not guided by self-interest but by conviction!

Finally, they came to terms with their conviction. Everything was going to work out well. Suddenly that unfortunate doubt emerged again: would Lajos Kelemen's nose be accepted by the new religion? After all, a Jew with a nose like that would hardly be objectionable. It could even be overlooked on a hero decorated with a gold medal. But how would that nose go with someone who was classified as "other"? Would the people not laugh at hearing Lajos—with that nose—respond "other" to a question about his religion?

Margit and Lajos agreed to investigate what the noses of those belonging to other members of the "other" religion were like. However, there were very few members of that "other" religion in Budapest. They had no place of worship, and most of them frequented the churches of those religions whose ceremonies resembled theirs, despite slight differences in metaphysical concepts.

Having thus studied religious doctrines, the young pair devoted much time to the study of noses. They examined the noses of classical statues, carefully examined the portraits of medieval churchmen, read medical reports about the nose, and even visited synagogues to take a closer look at the Jewish noses. They left the synagogues with the reassuring conclusion that no nose among the Jews looked like Lajos's nose. The Jewish nose was not so evenly curved, nor did it have such a definite outline as his nose. They were also reassured by some classical statues. In a contemporary painting, they discovered a certain similarity between Lajos's nose and the nose of Gábor Bethlen, Prince of Transylvania. However, they learned in the lexicon that Cyrano was not a Jew. Furthermore, Rostand's detailed description did not entirely fit Lajos. His observations might have been made in the interest of rhyme and rhythm. Therefore, they agreed that the nose of Lajos Kelemen was not a Jewish nose. And with that the theoretical objection to changing religions was overcome.

They were married according to the ceremonies of the "other" religion and traveled happily to Lajos's new station. And they lived there—happily ever after? No, not until then. Only until the end of the war. Then they returned to Budapest. It brought no changes in their lives. They lived like a happily married couple, good citizens, and devout members of the "other" religion. The man worked, the woman busied herself at home keeping the cupboard in order and, as Schiller wrote in "The Song of the Bell," when the bell tolled she hurried to church and prayed fervently according to the tenets of the "other" religion among people of a different faith.

That is how the first year passed. Such a decent life could not go unrewarded. A little over a year after the war, the woman happily whispered to her husband the secret that women since Eve have been happily whispering to their husbands. There was great rejoicing and preparations were made. The woman prayed even more fervently and sewed baby clothes diligently for the little newcomer. She was preoccupied by one thought: whom would she select as godfather for the youngest Kelemen?

At last the day arrived. The event filled the young and old of the Kelemen family with indescribable excitement and happiness. The youngest Kelemen arrived. A boy. He was born with thick hair, crying loudly, which attested to healthy lungs, and weighing four and a half kilos. Everything seemed to be in order. Only—only his nose. An enormous nose stuck out of the child's small, pleasant face. It curved menacingly, unexpectedly, and disconsolately. It was as big as his father's but not so even. Its curve did not start at the forehead and its outline was irregular. It formed a hump at the middle. His parents' knowledge of noses offered no mitigating explanations. That nose did not resemble the classical statues, was unlike the nose of Gábor Bethlen, Prince of Transylvania, and did not even remotely fit Rostand's description. The nose of little Gergely Kelemen was typically Jewish. All efforts by the nurse and the guests, who offered explanations by showing picture books in attempts to convince the anxious mother that the features of infants tended to change in the course of time, were futile in light of the fact. Little Gergely's nose became more and more definite and expressive. The christening ceremony was performed with the godfather smiling kindly at the little fellow. The mother kept going to church hoping that her prayers would correct her son's physical defect. Little Gergely's nose, however, did not want to assume more pleasing proportions.

The father looked at his son's face. That nose really hurt. He felt guilty about it. He remembered his youth, the suffering, the sarcastic poems of schoolboys, the army, Corporal Tompor, his studies in theology, the classical statues, the medieval paintings, and his wife, who neglected her household because of her frequent visits to the church, by which she hoped that little Gergely would be helped. He realized that nothing would change that nose. Other things must be changed, he concluded. One day, he started talking to his friends about changing his faith. He converted to a religion in

which Gergely's nose was accepted without classical statues and scientific studies and that had not prevented his father from becoming an honest man and a soldier decorated with a gold medal.

Translated by Andrew Handler.

Fishl Bimko
1890-1965

The dramatist, journalist, and fiction writer Fishl Bimko was born into a Hasidic family in Kielce, Poland. As a teenager he spent time in prison for his revolutionary sympathies. Bimko's works are characterized by realism and dialogue that depicted shtetls, military life for Jewish soldiers, and the world of poverty and crime, as particularly exhibited in his play *Ganovim* (Thieves), staged by the Vilna Troupe in 1919. Bimko moved to New York in 1921, where he continued to compose dramatic works and wrote for the Yiddish press.

Before Conscription
1921

Right after Passover, with the first rays of the gentle summer sun, a new worry erupted for the Jewish inhabitants of all the small towns—the call-up for military service. The "young toughs" began to erase and strike out certain names from the list of recruits, who would need to present themselves to the draft board this year. The names included Gemara students, sallow youths, and ordinary, more refined craftsmen eager for good marriages (once, God-willing, the call-up was finished).

They, the young toughs, the Jewish hooligans who flitted about all year long sponging off the community, would make deals with the goyim of the town: the butchers, thieves, pick-pockets. They needed the gentiles to do them a favor, to threaten all the refined little people who were the pride and joy of the town. Firstly, they intended to milk them dry. And, more so, they needed the gentiles to protect the town, so that nothing bad should, God-forbid, happen when the peasants, those destructive louts, came to town in the autumn. The young Jewish toughs did this, not so much out of love for their fellow Jews, but out of hatred for the *goyim*.

Nor did the young toughs care that a Jewish shop might get damaged. They wanted to give the peasants, those louts, a punch in the face that they would remember for the rest of their lives. Once upon a time, they, too, had to report for the draft.

And right after Passover, when the deformed gentile from the town magistrate distributed the slips to all the youths who must report to the draft board this year, a new worry transpired in the households of those soft, sallow little people. The fathers of the household developed more wrinkles on their foreheads. So worried were they that when they went on a trip, they stopped by the rebbe's for advice. The mothers began to whine in the sing-song lilt of the high holiday *tekhines* [women's prayers]. With every few words, they invoked the merits of their ancestors in order to save their children from the hands of the gentiles.

Berl the Ruffian, one of the young toughs, received a draft deferral, a lucky slip that he couldn't even read properly. He wondered what they wanted from him? Then, suddenly he understood what it was and tapped his forehead: "Aha!" Feeling celebratory, he went to Laizer Yankel's tavern.

"Oh, Reb Laizer! What did I tell you? Did you already forget?"

After he had become inebriated, downed a few pitchers of beer, he was extraordinarily jubilant. As was his wont when he was drunk, he began to talk to himself:

"Ever heard of such a story? Every year I think this must be the time. But they seem to forget and deliberately overlook me . . . hee, hee, hee. . . ."

In the late afternoon, he went to see the other draftees on the list, those whose time had come to serve, and began to cheer them up. He reminded them what they might need to do in the coming year. They must take over the administration of the town and become the true bosses.

"Oh, those boors!" he cried with tearful eyes, and pressed his fists together. "We will show them what destruction means. We will terrorize the town." They were at his beck and call.

At dusk, Berl dropped by the study house during evening prayers and went up to Laizer Makhels, an affluent person in the town, who apart from his properties and mills, also had a good heart. More to the point, he had a son who was about to be married. [Berl told him that he would go to serve in the military in place of Laizer's son.]

With a whining voice, he said: "If I, Berl the Ruffian, go to serve in the military, I will remain Berl the Ruffian. And, if I am a good soldier, I won't lose my life in battle. I might even get a medal or two. As for the liquor,

that will never be a problem." But the main thing was that he didn't have the cash to outfit himself as a soldier.

Berl swore that he would report to the military, finish his service, and come home safely. And he was equally certain that Laizer Makhels's son would remain at home.

Apparently, Laizer Makhels understood the meaning behind Berl's rant and silenced him with a rouble, which he secretly pushed into Berl's paw while no one was looking. As an aside, Laizer assured him that, when the time came and the deal was complete, Berl would have all his needs met for the trip—shirts, pants, buttons, brushes—whatever a soldier required to fill his trunk. Even some cash.

Berl left the *besmedresh* [study house], grabbed a few mugs of beer at the first, best tavern he came across, paid for his drinks, then staggered out onto the street, dead drunk, hardly able to stand up.

Coincidently, he happened upon a recruit—one of the "soft" people, the son of a father and the son of a father-in-law, a refined young man, skin-and-bones, a slender soul. And he, Berl the Ruffian, gave him a whack on his back and exploded with laughter:

"Here is a soldier, a good guy . . . hee-hee-hee . . . tsk, tsk . . . and what a soldier he is . . . hee-hee-hee."

Berl began to order him around: "Now to the left, now march. . . ."

The young man stood confused. With the first blow, his glasses had fallen off the bridge of his nose. When he turned around, he saw the bully who had beaten him up [. . .] and his terror dissipated. But he was embarrassed in front of the circle of people that had soon gathered around them. His cheeks reddened like those of a young girl receiving a first kiss. In order to free himself from Berl, he agreed with Berl's rant:

"Without a doubt, a soldier is not a bear! If you must, you obey and serve your country. . . ."

Berl the Ruffian was delighted with the "brave" soldier and began to kiss him. The youth tried to escape. But Berl, with his tottering, broad-boned body, hindered his way and waved his hands so close to his face that the young man had to cover his head so that he wouldn't be hit in the nose. For this audacity, Berl became very angry and shouted:

"What? You want Berl the Ruffian to be the scapegoat for you and all your piggish, arrogant ones, you who wear galoshes on your princely little shoes even in summertime, and eat meat at your evening meal on an ordinary Wednesday?"

At the same time, Berl grabbed him by his lapels and shook him so hard that the youth realized he was in trouble. He managed to pull himself out of Berl's hands and made a quick getaway through a gate, disappearing. Berl stood alone and swore.

Slowly, his anger dissolved, but he continued to gesture with his hands to all those who passed by. With tears in his eyes, he talked his heart out to them:

"I, Berl the Ruffian, am leaving to serve the country and this will be the end of Berl. The town can already forget that there even was such a Berl. From this town, he will leave for the military, shooting, stabbing, murdering."

And he cried as though it were a certainty that he would be leaving for war, maybe even tomorrow, and would never come home again.

The summer ended, almost unnoticed. Berl had stopped working and idly wandered about town. And the townsfolk were correct in thinking it was a miracle that he didn't go crazy. How does such a fellow feed himself? But looking at his face, there was no noticeable hardship, God forbid.

The excuse for his idleness was: a recruit lives on community charity. Laizer Makhels, Sholem Yankels, Boruch Moshes—such Jews with property, flour and saw mills—there are many of these in the town. But should they not have so much money, with their bulging full bellies, they do all have sons who face the draft. To remedy this there would be a "pay back."

He, Berl, knew well the list of all the recruits. He knew which of them had departed, where they had departed to, for what reason they had departed, and what they did there. . . .

In the beginning, Berl was alone. With time, he attracted followers. One was the tall Shmuel, who began to "walk" [away from military service]. Actually he could always walk, especially on his feet. In fact, standing on his feet, he was very tall, tall as King Og. But this current "walking" was due to something else. It was because of the varicose veins that were said to be visible on his meaty legs. And for this reason, apparently the doctors told him to wear elastic stockings.

But the tall one was no fool, and he wouldn't allow himself to be talked into this stupidity.

A dispute erupted between him and his father. The father kept saying, "Remember, Shmuel, do what you are told!" And Shmuel responded, "Nonsense!"

Recently, just before he had to report for the draft, the foolish lad had sobered up and took the situation to heart. His hope was that he would come out with a blue slip.

Shmuel took Berl as his partner. Both had to go to the military. But Berl had no idea why Shmuel led Berl on all those empty roads and pathways. Until he finally caught him in the act [of injuring himself]. With a friendly smile, Berl slapped him on the back, as was his wont:

"You're a rascal of a boy. You, too, want to stay at home? And who will take your place? Ruven, the widow's only son, the loser? Should they take him to the military, crush him like a worm under the feet of the soldiers?"

In time, another person came to Berl, the diminutive Baruch. Everyone knew he would receive a white slip. But everyone forgave him for this, because he considered himself the child of the group. Once Berl took him on his lap and, with the thoughtful tenderness of a father, made fun of him:

"Nu, Baruchl, you have a hernia on your right side. God should grant you another one on the left side. Then you will be worthy to wear a girdle on both sides, and you will come out with two white slips."

In the month of Elul, it could be noticed that conscription hung in the air. Along with the atmosphere of the high holy days, you could feel a special "draft." The cold wind blew. Yellow leaves fell from the trees.

Chestnuts fell, cracking open. Crowds of recruits roamed the streets. They had already stopped working and ambled around with walking sticks in hand. Like students on holiday, but without joy in their hearts.

And from time to time, they were asked: "What will you accomplish with this ambling around?" They shrugged their shoulders, sadly wrinkled their brows, as if to say: What can you expect from us, since we don't know what tomorrow will bring?

In the prayer and study halls, you could see more young folks, those who remained in the fold, reciting evening prayers deep into the Elul night—relatively longer than a normal summer night. Many sat and studied with zeal, absorbed in pious thoughts, humming a *nigun*, swaying back and forth, over an open *Gemara*. It seemed as if they were voicing their own bitter feelings:

"These are meaningful days, oh Lord, my Father. On what other occasion can one pray to stay at home?"

After a while, a youth with dark fiery eyes stopped studying aloud, but continued to sway with a sallow, God-fearing little face. His curly sidelocks bounced on his cheeks, and a deep sigh escaped from his skinny, hollow chest:

"Oh, Lord, let me not be thrown amongst the gentiles. Torn away from Jewishness, from Torah study. Help me, Father, send salvation. . . ."

By the stove sat simple craftsmen who prayed from the siddur, embarrassed. They had stopped shaving and grew unkempt little beards. In imitation, they wrinkled their brows and mumbled the melodies. One of them spoke to God in silence, like a Jewess from a women's prayer book.

"Though we don't know how to study, we are still your people. We keep the Sabbath, we keep the High Holy Days. See merit in this, so that we are not sent to wander far away from home. So that we shouldn't, God forbid, have to eat nonkosher food or desecrate the Sabbath and the holidays."

This was how the Jews of the town were divided. Half of them were the "soft" people, those who could mold themselves like figurines of clay; they were the ones who went to the prayer house. The other half, the young toughs led by Berl the Ruffian, went to Laizer Yankel's tavern. This group was made up of robust tailor apprentices, journeymen, who hadn't learned to read Hebrew language texts. They never took "military service" seriously. To them, it was rubbish.

In the military, they would soon find themselves in workshops, sewing smocks, making boots, baking bread. Where was the problem? The few years would pass by, like nothing. Three years was not that long. And they would receive a few hundred roubles for service to bring home. In the meantime, they would get to see the world—after which they might even manage to make a decent marriage match. . . .

Becoming a recruit was part of life in the real world. You only live once, and only once are you eligible for conscription. And therefore, live it up to the hilt, Jew, with all your strength!

A military guardsman walked by. The young toughs led him to Laizer's tavern where they got him completely drunk. After which, Berl the Ruffian put him on the tabletop and told him to dance a "kamarinska." The eyes of the guardsman began to close. The aquavit began to boil up inside him. When the glassy-eyed crowd began to whistle with their fingers in their mouths, the inebriated policeman thought to himself:

"It must be Easter in the barracks. . . . Boys! Strike up the drums!"

He pulled up his coattails and did a dance, threw a foot upward and gave a punch into the air nearby. He continued to dance, a river of sweat pouring down his face. Red as a lobster, his hair glued to his forehead, he danced for so long and so wildly that he forgot that he was among Jewish recruits. He even forgot that he was in Laizer Yankel's tavern. He drew his sparkling sword from its sheath and waved it over everyone's head. And from his hoarse, drunken throat, he shouted:

"Eh, Jew-boys, we should slaughter you all."

The group became furious. Only Berl the Ruffian didn't lose control. He pulled the sword from the soldier's hand, quickly and gracefully, and gave him a punch in the solar plexus, so that his body reverberated like a bell. . . .

"If you are a pig, you shouldn't come together with humans. You should lie in the earth. . . ."

Doubled up from the punch, the guardsman fell to the ground, like a children's ball. His face looked as though he had indulged in an entire glass of liquor all at once. He begged tearfully: "No, I swear, it's not what you think. . . . No, I meant nothing by it. . . ."

In unison, the crowd shouted wildly and demanded revenge:

"Tear up his epaulets. Break his sword!"

Only Berl the Ruffian stuck up for him: "Leave him alone, guys, we shouldn't harm him."

He helped the soldier back on his feet, wiped the sweat off his face with his handkerchief, and defended him.

"What do you want from him? It's the drink in him that's talking. By nature, he is good guy for an uncircumcised fellow. Let him go. He has an old lady and seven small fry at home."

The crowd soon took pity on the goy. They even gave him a couple of kopeks for the insult. They tied the coins into his shirt, so that he wouldn't lose them. The tall Shmuel and the diminutive Baruch took it upon themselves to lead him out. With "great honor," they led him onto the street. The whole crowd followed.

Outside, they all stood and wondered what to do with this military guardsman.

The crowd shouted, "Throw him out!"

"Release him on the street!"

Berl the Ruffian said, "Have pity on him!"

Someone in the crowd argued, "Throw his head underground!"

And Berl repeated, "He has an old lady and seven small fry at home!"

Someone else responded, "Take him home!"

Little Baruch made a crack. In his female voice, he screamed into his ear: "Where do you live?"

The guardsman shook his head, tried to stand up on his feet. The crowd howled. At last, with much singing and whistling, everyone moved into the road. The guardsman flew up in the air, soaring.

When they came to the corner, everyone stopped, looked around and gaped. "Where is the soldier?"

The guardsman was gone.

The attendants began to shrug their shoulders. "The devil took him!"

"What have you done with him?" shouted Berl in anger.

Someone answered, "He has likely slipped away." The crowd snickered.

"Find him!" shouted Berl.

The crowd made a racket. "A plague on him . . . the devil!"

"Find him!" shouted Berl, irate, above their voices. No one listened to him.

They all ran back to the town, knocking on the windows of the rich young people.

"Are you asleep?" they shouted.

"A demon in your father's bones!"

"Wake up to say the psalms!"

"Wake up to penitential prayers!"

It was a sleepless night in the town.

For the High Holy Days, all the recruits had already come home. For the most part, they did not come home at any set time—but they did come for the Jewish holidays. For Rosh Hashanah, they made an effort to travel back to their town.

Of course, they must come home Rosh Hashanah! And they must do their military service, as well! And as it happened, they had to find out about something. . . .

For Rosh Hashanah and Yom Kippur, all the recruits appeared in the prayer house. Everyone held a *maḥzor* [holiday prayer book] in hand, although it was rather doubtful whether they actually prayed.

Only the elderly pious Jews questioned it:

"For these people, there is conscription every year. You would think, they are Jews and thus should know how to pray. . . ."

And Berl the Ruffian, with a modicum of self respect, exerted himself and stood up for the entire Yom Kippur in the anteroom, delirious with hunger—for he had

fasted. During the prayers, when he saw everyone else beat their breast, so did he.

The morning after Yom Kippur, as soon as the deadline for divine judgment had passed, the young toughs all returned to their same old routine, getting really drunk and making chaos in the streets all night long. Berl the Ruffian again became Berl the Ruffian. Whenever there was a trial, he was the judge. Whenever there was a celebration or a funeral, he was the director. And if he said it was day, it was day.

He was angry with some of the wealthy sons because they had refused to pay him a bribe. He swore to himself that they must go to serve in the same regiment as he. Even though they had bandaged their heads and their ears, stuffed their shoes with cotton, and knocked out all their teeth, it wouldn't release them until the day they died.

On Simkhes Torah, he and his whole gang went to the prayer house again—dead drunk. Berl could hardly stumble onto the prayer platform. He climbed up on all fours, struck the reading desk with his paw, and gave a long speech. Because he and his whole gang of young toughs were about to go into military service, and this was already a well-known fact, the *gabbai* was obligated to give them the honor of carrying the Torah.

So be it, this was what they deserved! They were all given the honor of holding the Torah scrolls. The cantor stood with them around the Torah-reading platform. And the cantor in his high-pitched voice said a prayer to help the poor. The entire congregation was doubled over with laughter from this scene.

The young toughs became red and agitated. Such a disgrace! They were almost ready to throw down the Torah scrolls. What else would you expect from such ruffians? And they beat up both the *gabbai* and the cantor.

In the evening, they made the town pay for the insult. They wrecked all the householders' sukkahs. They broke the scaffolding and, with the walls and branches, dragged it all away across the four corners of the earth. . . .

Translated by Sarah Silberstein Swartz.

Other works by Bimko: *Rekrutn* (1916); *Fun krig un fun fridn* (1920); *Afn breg vaysl, drame in 3 aktn* (1921); *Tunkele geshtaltn* (1925); *Hele blikn* (1926); *Ist-sayd* (1929).

Else Lasker-Schüler

1869–1945

The highly original German poet Else Lasker-Schüler
was born into a well-to-do, nonobservant Jewish family in Ebersfeld. By 1910, she had been married and
divorced twice. Following the failure of her second
marriage, she lived an unsettled bohemian life in
Berlin and Munich. She associated with leading expressionist writers and artists, wore exotic "oriental"
costumes, and exhibited eccentric behavior. She fled
to Switzerland in 1933 and settled in Palestine in 1939,
where she continued to live hand to mouth. Her Jewish
interests are most explicit in her *Hebräische Balladen*
(1913), which focus on the Patriarchs, and in her story
about a wonder-working rabbi in medieval Barcelona.

The Wonder-Working Rabbi of Barcelona
1921

During the weeks that Eleazar spent in pious contemplation in old Asia, the people of Barcelona took pains
to persecute the Jews. It was they, once again, who
made it hard for Spanish merchants to charge excessive
prices, but, at the same time, spread their redemptive
ambitions among the poor of the city. Apostolic figures
among them preached equality and fraternity, and they
broke their hearts in their bosoms and gave them to
the poor, as Jesus of Nazareth shared the bread of his
blue heart with them. But no matter how the Jews behaved, they aroused resentment, which in truth originated with a single disappointed Spaniard who had
once clashed with a Hebrew, and was transferred to the
people. This year, as before, Eleazar, the wonder-working rabbi, returned to Barcelona at the stated time. His
dignified head, mysteriously enlarged and made more
real as though seen through a magnifying-glass, and
framed by the arched window of the palace, nodded
kindly to everyone who passed, whether Jew or Christian. Rumours about Eleazar were whispered throughout the Spanish town. He was said to be Gabriel, the
great archangel, who never died; the unmelting snow
of his beard enveloped the Ark of the Covenant. The
Jews, however, were more familiar with Gabriel; they
often saw the wonder-working rabbi smiling; once he
jubilantly clapped his slender, delicate hands, even in
prayer before the altar, for he had seen Jehovah . . . and
he became—a child. The old Jews, heirs of their fathers,
had inscribed on the calendar of the hearts the day on
which their supreme rabbi had been born to them. On

the seventh of the month of Gam children and grandchildren made a pilgrimage up the hill to the Jews'
palace, to bring their wonder-working priest branches
from the woods, hung with sweet and bitter berries, for
Eleazar loved the wild corals and liked to inhale their
scent, whereupon he would satiate his hunger and re-
fresh himself with the pure flesh of the humblest fruit,
and have all the other foodstuffs distributed to the
needy of Barcelona. This year, however, the Jews intended no longer to conceal from their sacred jewel the
sufferings that awaited them annually in his absence.
On that same wet and misty evening, the hard-pressed
Jewish nobility, assembled in a cellar, resolved to leave
this world. Scattered everywhere, planted, a flavour-
ing to the dough, tired of sweetening it for the sake of
a slight, bitter aftertaste, a whole people, tired of being humiliated for millennia. Thus the tormented Jews
were dimly conscious of their destiny. The yearning for
their lost country, which they had possessed only on
sufferance, rose higher in them all, and each of them
solemnly watered the bed of his recollection; even their
wonder-working rabbi could not tell them where they
would land; for some young Jews had taken roots in the
soil of Spain, in the enchanting perfume of roses, and
their sisters with Jerusalem eyes had given Christians a
painful awakening. But Eleazar replied to the worried
community: "Anyone who does not bear the promised
land in his heart will never get there." And this God, he
said, revealed Himself to all men as their noblest and
most ancient quality. And when asked how this could
be, since most creatures were so godless, the highest
priest said with heartfelt sorrow that only a few were
able to be gardeners for their God, to honour and tend
their most precious seeds. And there was no greater impoverishment on earth than to allow the heavenly blossom of the heart to wither.

Whenever Eleazar, the wonder-working rabbi, called
out the awe-inspiring name of Jehovah, the Jews heard
it devoutly, down to the grain of their pulses, and all
their good deeds awoke and they repented of their bad
actions. The Spaniards, however, shut their ears to
the redeeming sound, which scratched the temples of
the Jews to let them drink divine lymph, and exacted
a drop of blood as payment from many a one whom the
sound shook to the core. Among the Jewish people of
Barcelona there lived a poetess, the daughter of a distinguished man who had the task of building the watch-
towers of Spain's great cities. Wishing for an heir to his

building skills, Arion Elevantos brought up Amram, his daughter, like a son. Early each morning Amram and her father ascended the incomplete buildings, the highest skeletons of the town, so that she often thought she had been paying a visit to God. And her eyes had gazed up into the domes of wood from Lebanon and pure gold which Arion extended over the roof of the splendid house, a present from the wealthy Jews, to shield their wonder-working rabbi from mischance. Descending the ladder that led from the still unattached crest, little Amram in her haste fell from the sacred building on to a sandy hillock where Pablo, the little son of the mayor, was playing. And the boy thought pale Amram was an angel that had tumbled out of a cloud in the kingdom of heaven, and looked at her in astonishment. After that Amram smiled in her dreams whenever Pablo thought about her.

Pablo, at night I hear the palm leaves
Rustle beneath your feet.

Sometimes I have to cry a lot
From happiness about you.

Then a smile grows
On your hooded eyelids.

Or a rare joy opens for you:
Your heart's black aster.

Whenever past the gardens
You see the end of your pathway, Pablo,

—It's my eternal thought of love
Desiring to join you.

And often a glow will fall from heaven,
For in the evening my golden sigh goes searching for
   you.

Soon the languishing month arrives
Over your dear city;

Under the garden tree there hang
Flocks of birds like gaily coloured grapes.

And I too wait enchanted
Hung about by dream.

You proud native, Pablo,
I breathe from your countenance strange sounds of
   love;

But on your brow I want to plant my fortunate star,
Rob myself of my luminous blossom.

As the Señor grew up, signs appeared to him unexpectedly in ancient harp-writing. The officials, his father's subordinates, interpreted them scornfully as the writing of dogged, obdurate Jews who pestered his father, the supreme councillor, with rebellious writings. The mayor's son would have liked to knock at the palace of the wonder-working rabbi, to assure him of the unshakeable respect he felt for his people, but he feared the gossip of the townsfolk and, above all, his father's anger. Once, however, he disguised himself to follow a Jewish caravan that was making its way up the hill into the Jew's palace, and he felt in his heart the benefit of the blessing. The Spaniards only reluctantly allowed the synagogue among the houses of their city and felt it to be an alien member, this timid building on their roads. The Jews' mysterious prayer-house lay concealed behind an inn where Spanish students danced and shouted in the upper rooms or practised fencing within the walls. Sometimes the riotous crew, inflamed by hot wine, would kick the door of the synagogue on Friday evening. The women behind the railings quaked gently, and Amram felt a foreign continent growing between her and Señor Pablo, the mayor's son. The commandments in the Jews' prayer-books were read from the outside to the inside, and so, ever since their birth, their Jewish eyes had to be pointed in a different direction from those of all other nations. Eyes that dared not remain fixed on their object, eyes that hid in the book's stitching, always fled back to the column. "Eyes that steal"—declared the mayor firmly to his blenching son. For the latter was recalling the secrecy of the time when they were still children and Amram his "bride," when this she-angel of the heavenly hosts had girded herself, with light in her eye, and told him that she had murdered the tailor with her little dagger and buried him in the sand, as the prophet did the Egyptian who maltreated the Jews under his yoke of slavery. "Tailor" was the children's name for the bony, skinny-legged sweet-seller, who kept his little shop behind the school and was notorious for often having attacked Jewish children. He accused the innocent creatures of theft, after he had magically put sweets in their pockets like a wizard. Threatening to tell their parents about his crimes, the young, wailing victims, whom he dragged into a dark subterranean hole in his house, let him satisfy his filthy lust on them.

One day a big ship was standing in the market-place. Human effort, horses, and ox-power could not remove the mysterious vessel from the city, though it damaged trade and the market. But the excited Spaniards advised their mayor to consult old Gabriel, the wise magician, and they pointed out the Jews' glittering house, with pure sunshine bleeding from its windows. And the Spanish patricians, the citizens and workers, along with many Jews, and Pablo's worthy father, the mayor of Barcelona, at their head, stood outside the gate of the golden palace; they were so busy that they had overcome their inexplicable shyness. Since the previous evening, however, the small, decent company of the Jewish elders had been with Eleazar, for they had resolved to tell their wonder-working rabbi gently about their fears, and to ask him not to leave the town this year. From the blessed hilltop Barcelona could be seen, empty and starved, lying in its valley. Only the mayor's big, long-haired dog, Abraham, was hurrying through the town, through the streets of Barcelona, constantly sniffing at the ship that had given ear to two people's yearning overnight. At the helm, Señor Pablo and Amram, the Jewish poetess, were playing unconcernedly in the sun, just as after the little accident on the sacred hill outside Eleazar's palace they had so often delighted in their notions when they were children. Transfigured by immense love, they remained invisible behind the wing of the sail. And only the dog witnessed how the seas' enormous messenger, moved by love, passed lightly across the market-place, through the streets of the town that stretched out devout arms, then vanished through the gate as carefully as a solemn bridal carriage. Eleazar refused to receive the mayor with his mass following, for what was the use of talking to sleepers! And the small number of Jews who did not behave in a restrained and timid way, as is proper for heirs of an ancient people, cared for him, strengthened by the stories of the Jewish elders who had surreptitiously left the garden door of the supreme palace. During the night, spurred on by the wonder-working rabbi's refusal, the Christians now felt justified, the pogrom began. Raising their fists to form a hill, the Spaniards cried that Gabriel, the false archangel, the wicked magician, had drawn the great ship from the sea and in this trickery he had had the assistance of none other than Arion Elevantos, who, having built the Jews' palace, knew all its archways, secrets, and passageways, and the evil powers of its denizen, which could petrify the breath of the people of Barcelona. Even in the Bible the devil hid behind the score of his sins, and kill him, "Kill him, the old procurer!!!" The bewildered Christians superstitiously

confined themselves to breaking the windows of their good, cheerful master builder; forgot that he gave shelter in his buildings to many thousands of the poor of Barcelona, taking nothing in return. They gagged him; but he laughed in his dismay, as he used to rejoice in his boyhood, when a playmate grabbed him in a game of cops and robbers; till the mayor's wife approached and stirred up the people, alarmed though they were, to kill the father of the Jewish girl who had abducted her son. She herself tore the heart from the innocent victim's bosom to be a red foundation stone where masterless dogs should do their business. And the Jews, who had kept waking anew on hearing the name of Jehovah, all lay mutilated, savaged, their faces separated from their bodies, children's hands and tiny feet, tender human foliage, here and there in the alleys, into which these poor souls had been driven like cattle. But the evening breezes, the sweet liars who sang outside the palace of the great wonder-working rabbi, told tales that were dreamlike and false. "Your sons are sitting by the hedges, Eleazar, suspecting nothing, counting the days and the hours that separate them from Palestine, and the delicate daughters of David are embroidering cushions with silk and pearls for the blessings of your hands. The feast of Passover is approaching, and the bakers are baking pious unleavened bread for your table, great wonder-working rabbi." He leafed through the atlas of creation and read how at the beginning of things the Father made the world of earth and water and squeezed it into a ball, his "wedding manna-cake," with all the golden ingredients of His heavenly blood, and how He took man from the great shape of the world and from him in turn He powerfully drew the nations and the nations' nations and the nations' nations' nations and invited them all to eat together. By His heart, however, He placed the Jews, for though they were few, of all the nations it was they who had turned out most in accordance with His orders and hence they were more obedient to him and more tender. "And the all-loving Father," praised Eleazar singing, "plucked a star from His robe, and lifted up the child among the nations and placed the light on his brown forehead. With this little light on the divine body of the world's guardian, the Lord made the enlightened Jews into the people of the prophets, to serve Him in every land, in every nation, on every road. Amen. For the great sibling nations, however, instead of the glorious ray, He made a home for them amid the green foliage of the august earth, in the rocking, refreshing rest of the water and beneath the pure winter snow of the breezes, to maintain a loving order, and every man, amid the men of all nations, should point to men above the nations." The great hermit closed the faded book, whose commandments had fallen asleep in the hearts of most creatures, even in the blood of Judah. He loved his people and he constantly evaded their questions about home. Forced to leave the cities where they had been primordially destined to sow God, the Jewish thoughts that were still awake took refuge in the lap of the High Priest. But that Palestine was only the observatory to watch the stars of their home, that was something of which the wonder-working rabbi dared not remind the weary chosen people.

Now Eleazar's eyes, fixed on Barcelona—in the lightning of terror—split . . . wept. "Lord, in truth, the boat on the waves of the sea awakened the awe of Your name."

In immense yearning for the third time in his life the prophet cried out the awe-inspiring name of his Lord. And at the redeeming sound of Jehovah's name the dead of the dead awoke. They were the Christians and through them all the Christian nations of Christendom. Yet he mistrusted the penitent brother nations and their reawakening! The omnipotence of his great Lord made him angry.

אין תקר לדרכי אדני

Unfathomable are the ways of the Eternal. . . . "You let your dearly beloved son be slaughtered ever and again and again, that the trumpet of Your holy name may awaken the nations of the Christians, and You reward their atrocities with enlightenment." And Eleazar waited in the forecourt of his palace for God, the yearned-for guest. At last the Invisible One offered the impatient one His fatherly hand. But in the midst of the interior of the solemn chamber the priest's trembling, kneeling servant saw his great and holy maestro reaching out to the air's cool semblance, seizing it as the brave torero seizes the bull's horn in the arena—and then— on the stone arabesques lay the wonder-working rabbi bleeding. All night he went out wrestling in riddles with God; darkened and broke away from Him. The priest shook the pillars of his house till they broke like arms. The roof rolled down in heavy blocks and shattered the houses in the street. An enormous quarry, He, the great wonder-working rabbi, a nation plunged from the sacred hill, which was transfigured by the golden fragments of the dome's mosaic, upon the Christians of Barcelona, who were penitently laying the last tortured Jew

to rest, and extinguished their enlightenment, crushed their bodies.

> The angels spread a cloud-white tablecloth for the
>   heavenly meal,
> God took the heart of the high homecomer from its
>   dish
> To test the stubborn consecrated ore,
> O Eleazar's heart was rubbed on heart,
> Setting his stone ablaze!
> Into his jug, Jerusalem, pour your wine
> And let it ferment, stored up in the vale.

Translated by Ritchie Robertson; the poem "Pablo" translated by Robert Newton.

Other works by Lasker-Schüler: *Mein blaues Klavier* (1943); *Hebrew Ballads and Other Poems* (1980); *Your Diamond Dreams Cut Open My Arteries: Poems by Else Lasker-Schüler* (1982); *Three Plays* (2005).

H. Leivick

1888–1962

Born Leivick Halpern in Belorussia, the Yiddish poet and dramatist H. Leivick was active in the Bund as a young man and later exiled to Siberia for life in 1912. He escaped and fled to the United States in 1913. His commitment to the left found expression in his poetry and plays, especially in his descriptions of suffering— in the pogroms in Ukraine, in the sweatshops of New York, and in the death camps of the Holocaust—and in his concern with the struggle for justice and redemption. He broke his ties to the New York communist newspaper *Der frayhayt* in 1929, however, when it defended the Arab attacks on Jews in Mandatory Palestine. His most celebrated work, the verse drama *The Golem*, is still performed.

The Golem
1921

SCENE I. CLAY

[*A deserted place on the bank of the river outside of Prague. Daybreak. All is dark and silent. Reb Levi Bar Bezalel, or* THE MAHARAL, *an old man of seventy, stands over an outlined mound of clay, kneading the figure of a man. He finishes.* ABRAHAM THE SHAMMES *stands near him, helping with the work.*

THE MAHARAL *straightens up from his work and addresses* THE SHAMMES.]

MAHARAL: It's done. All done. Now hurry to the synagogue,
  To Isaac and to Jacob and bid them come.

SHAMMES: And should I stay there, Rabbi?

MAHARAL: Stay in the synagogue. But Abraham,
  Remember, lock forever in your heart
  The secret you were privileged to know.
  Let no one ever hear of it from you.

SHAMMES: Forever, Rabbi.

MAHARAL: And do not tell them yet that all is done.
  They must see it for themselves.
  The day begins to dawn. Hurry.
  [*Exit* SHAMMES.]

MAHARAL [*bends over the figure*]: Yes, all is done and
  darkness covers all.
  The hour of wonder comes with the day,
  And as I look upon this great frame
  That has been shaped and kneaded by my hands,
  I can descry his shadow striding here,
  The shadow of a being breathing life.
  [*Raises his head to the sky.*]
  But who am I to say: "My hands have shaped?"
  Blind was I until You gave me sight—
  A puff from heaven's height upon my brows—
  And showed me where the slumbering body lay.
  How many generations has he slept
  While somewhere else his soul in longing wanders?
  Or has the soul forgot, in age-long wandering,
  The road's return to where the body sleeps?
  Or does it, too, somewhere lonely slumber,
  Waiting like its frame for You again
  To free my eyes, reveal again . . .
  I hear the rush of wings about my head.
  The night around is filled with flutter.
  Expectantly the figure lies outstretched.
  His head, uncovered, looks aloft to heaven,
  And from within his lips a prayer seeks release.
  [*He covers his face with his hands. Remains in this
  position a long while. Steps back in fright.*]
  Who was it flew across my eyes?
  Who touched my brow with something sharp?
  Who pierced my ear with screeching shriek?
  Whence comes the blunted echo that I hear?
  [*Looks around and listens.*]
  I see no one. Silence. The river flows.
  The stars go out, each after the other.
  The eastern sky should have grown light,

And yet it darkens. O give me strength, Creator.
  In the midst of joy and pride I saw
  A second shadow of this great frame.
  [*A distant rustle is suddenly heard and something
  completely black strides across the river, sways and
  revolves.*]
  Who walks upon the surface of the river?
  Approaches me yet comes no nearer;
  Withdraws from me yet is no further?
  [*A* FIGURE *appears before* THE MAHARAL.]

MAHARAL: Who are you, dark presence?

FIGURE: You do not know me?

MAHARAL: I cannot see your face.

FIGURE: You do not recognize my voice?

MAHARAL: Your voice is like a cold wind
  That blows in a deep pit
  Without entrance, without exit.

FIGURE: I have a voice that is not yet a voice.
  I have a heart that is not yet a heart.

MAHARAL: Who are you? Speak. What is your name?

FIGURE: Not till later will I be known by name.
  I am not yet among mankind.
  I am as yet a shadow's shadow.

MAHARAL: Whence do you come?

FIGURE: I have come to warn you: create me not.
  Do not dislodge me from my rest.

MAHARAL: Vanish. I order you.

FIGURE: I tell you once again; again I warn:
  Create me not!
  You see: the stars go out, each one.
  So will the light go out
  In every eye that looks on me;
  And where my foot will tread,
  A blight will grow upon that place;
  And what my hand will touch,
  To dust and ashes will it crumble.
  Do not exchange my darkness and my stillness
  For the tumult of the streets and for the noise of men.

MAHARAL: O, help me in this heaviest hour, God.

FIGURE: I know you will not hear my plea.
  Therefore I come to give you warning—
  And let my warning be a plea.
  The whole night through you kneaded me;
  With coldness and with cruelty you shaped me.
  How good it was to be mere clay,
  To lie, lifeless and calm,
  Among the sands and stones of earth
  Between eternities.

MAHARAL: Now vanish to your refuge, Figure,

And take your fear of life,
Your sorrow, with you to your lair.
When the hour of wonders comes
As soon as night retreats before the eastern sun,
Then, too, will your despair retreat.
For I was sent by God to knead you,
Disjoin you from the stony earth
And with the first ray that lights the sky
Breathe into you the breath of life.

FIGURE: I do not want it.

MAHARAL: Your days and nights and all your deeds
Have been decreed.
You are created for more than merely life.
In silence and concealment you will do
Great wonders, but your deeds will be in secret.
No one will know the hero. You will seem
A hewer of water, a cutter of wood.

FIGURE: A Golem, a thing of clay.

MAHARAL: A people's champion, a man of might.

FIGURE: A servant—to be ruled, commanded.

MAHARAL: A living man.

FIGURE: A living man? Why do you stand and wait?
Where is the soul that will be breathed in me?
Why do you leave my eyes still shut?
Why is a heart not given me?
Where is the tongue, the teeth, where is the blood
That must be poured to flow in me?
How would you have me? Blind or mute?
Or lame? Or deaf, perhaps?
Or all at once? Speak. The night departs;
The day arrives. O darkness, darkness!
One moment more conceal me in your depths!
One moment more what I have been till now:
A lifeless mound of arid clay.
[*The figure dissolves into the darkness.*]

MAHARAL: A darkness has invaded the desire
I strove so hard to render holy, pure.
With words of fear I have myself
Produced a flaw within the heart to be.
O, I did not surmount temptation
Nor did I guard my heart from sorrow,
From anguish and from pity. Great and greater
Grows the weight of every frightening word.
My own hands have turned his fate
Into the road of pain, confusion, and dismay.
How many weeks, how many days and nights
I strove to purify my heart and mind,
To shed entirely self and world
And be transformed into a single thought—Yours!

I saw but one within my mind, but one.
I saw him come and open wide his eyes,
A covert smile upon his lips,
And iron strength within his arms.
He sees, yet no one knows he sees;
He walks, yet no one knows his ways.
His life, his death—one silent breath,
One act of secret faith serene.
He comes to none; he speaks to none.
A corner somewhere is his waiting place
Until the moment that his summons comes.
What is there now to do? Doubt and fear,
The bitter and the angry loneliness
Have placed their taint upon the living word.
I see I am unworthy in Your eyes;
Perhaps I was ambitious, proud,
Too eager to descry what no man yet
Has seen before. I see, I see—
Before You what am I? A crawling worm,
A lump of earth, a grain of dust.
[*A long silence.* THE FIGURE OF THADDEUS *the priest
appears. It approaches* THE MAHARAL *at once.*]

MAHARAL: Thaddeus. Yes, it's he. He comes this way.
My mind just spoke his name—
Is this a second sign from God?

FIGURE [*collides with* THE MAHARAL. *Steps back*]: What
brings you here this middle of the night?

MAHARAL: It is not night but break of day.

FIGURE: What brings you here at break of day?

MAHARAL: I do at break of day what God commands.

FIGURE: And what did God command you do
That I should have to be there too?

MAHARAL: You need not stay. Go freely on your way.

FIGURE: That I can go my way is widely known.
Thaddeus can manage well.
But what causes that strange look within your eyes?
They flare with murder and black strength.
Murder in a rabbi's eyes? I have seen
In dungeons, at the stakes of holy courts
So many faces of so many Jews,
So many eyes of every sort, but I
Have never chanced to see two Jewish eyes
That looked upon me with true fury,
With murderous rage and hate, as yours do now.
They seem the eyes of some Golem run wild.
[THE MAHARAL *covers his face with his hands. His
shoulders heave.*]

FIGURE: Why have you suddenly concealed your face?
Grown silent? What is this? Who lies upon the ground?

A corpse? Or what? I've stood here all this while
And did not see it.
[*Bends down and looks at the clay figure.*]
What do my eyes discern?
What is this? A figure fashioned out of clay
Lies full length upon the ground!
[*Steps back and crosses himself.*]
O holy Jesus!

MAHARAL: Until the time that he is fit for life,
  To raise his arm, to stand upon his feet,
  I bear the look that lives within his eyes.

FIGURE: Protect me from the Evil One, from all
  Who are unbaptised, cursed, and damned, O Christ.
  [*Disappears*]

MAHARAL [*is silent a long while. Awakens as from a
  trance. Looks around.*]: Is this a second sign that has
  been sent?
  I see that it must be. The hand of God
  Has ringed us round within a single ring
  And paired me with this little mound of clay.
  And all that I conceive, I see;
  And everything I see, will be.
  It will; it must!
  And now my heart is light and glad. For I—
  What am I? Your portents speak the truth.
  It must be! And it will!
  [*From the road leading to the city,* THE MAHARAL'S
  two students arrive, ISAAC *the Kohen and* JACOB *the
  Levite.* JACOB *carries a bundle of clothes in his hands.
  They come quietly and seem scarcely to touch the
  ground.*]

MAHARAL [*going to meet them*]: You come in time. [. . .]

MAHARAL: Were you in synagogue till now?

ISAAC: Yes, Rabbi. Apart from one another
  We stood in prayer, and loud we prayed and lit
  No candle till the night was half-way gone.
  The dark surrounded us like a thick wall
  And cut off each from each. So far we seemed,
  We could not hear each other's prayer or speech.
  At first the distance frightened me, as though
  I sought a path in some dark wood
  And finding none, into its dark recesses
  I ran more swiftly. But suddenly I grew
  Quite calm, and felt the distance growing greater.

JACOB: And Rabbi, hear what happened after that:
  We stood, we thought, far from one another.
  It was so dark, and neither of us moved,
  As though we each were fastened to the floor,
  And each one thought that in the synagogue

He stood alone. And then at midnight, as you
Bid us, we lit the candles we had each
Prepared, and when we did, behold the wonder:
We stood together, side by side,
And each one's candle lit the other's face.

ISAAC: A great marvel, Rabbi.

MAHARAL: A favorable sign. Your hearts
  Have cleansed themselves in prayer
  And grown worthy to speak the blessing
  Which your lips must soon recite.

ISAAC: Rabbi, may one look at him?

MAHARAL: You may. Go close and look. [*Both bend over
  the figure and look at it.*]

JACOB: As yet there is not much to see. Clay.

ISAAC: The clay is moving now; its eyes open.

JACOB: It moves its legs.

ISAAC: Its face contorts. It laughs. [*He recoils in fright.*]

MAHARAL: What ails you, Isaac?

ISAAC: I looked at him and then was seized by fright,
  Reminded of a dream that I once had.

MAHARAL: A dream? When?

ISAAC: Forgive me, Rabbi, I have sinned.
  At midnight, when we lit the candles and took
  A Torah scroll out from the Ark as you
  Instructed, and when to Genesis we rolled
  It open, and each one called the other up
  To read the Book, and seven times we each
  Had read its early verses, no one disturbed
  The reading.
  We returned the Torah to the Ark,
  And silently we each began the Psalms.
  And as I stood there, face to wall, reciting,
  Suddenly my lids began to stick.
  I struggled hard to keep from dozing, raised
  My voice to chant aloud. All at once
  I heard a clamor. Despairing cries came near
  And nearer. Doors and windows then flew open.
  The synagogue was filled with Jews in panic,
  Who threw themselves in every corner, fell
  And, breathless, crawled to hide beneath the tables.
  And as they lay in silence, a man rushed in.
  His face was strange, his head was large, his body
  Tall, arms long, and eyes of piercing green.
  He held a sword and thrust it everywhere.
  Up and down he slashed and right and left.
  And soon they all lay, gashed and slaughtered;
  The darkness covering their bloody dying.
  And then he raised his arm to me and would
  Have brought it down upon my head—when you

Arrived, Rabbi.

MAHARAL: I?

ISAAC: As soon as he perceived you, he appeared
  Discouraged. He dropped his sword and to the door
  He rushed. But you were there to bar his way.
  You seized the sword from him and aimed a blow
  Across his face, but woe!
  You failed.

MAHARAL [*beside himself*]: I failed?

ISAAC: You struck the air.

MAHARAL: He ran away?

ISAAC: Like a shadow he dissolved and vanished.
  That shape of clay reminded me of him.

MAHARAL [*to himself*]: So many signs! So many adverse
    omens!
  Will not a single ray of hope shine through?
  Lead me, O God, along whatever roads You choose,
  But let your brightness gleam through all
  That is concealed from me.

JACOB: In synagogue they spoke of evil times
  Of old and of the rumors that now thrive
  In Prague about a savage tyrant who
  Has slaughtered multitudes of Jewish folk—
  And so he dreamt this dream, Rabbi.

MAHARAL: Yes, my students, evil times will come,
  And with evil times come great ones too.
  We must be ready to receive those days.
  As you see, God has brought us now
  To the dawn of great and trying times.

ISAAC: My hands are trembling with fear, Rabbi,
  Shall I lay the bundle down?

MAHARAL: Is everything contained in it?

ISAAC: Everything, Rabbi.

JACOB: Where will he stay? In the synagogue?

MAHARAL: An end to questions now. Contain your
    fears.
  Secrete them in your hearts, and with your fears
  Hide all that you will see and hear.
  And now come to the water. We wash our hands.
  [*They go to the river.*] [. . .]

[THE MAHARAL *returns followed by* THE GOLEM *carrying his axe. He stands in the middle of the room, curiously rigid, his hands hanging at his sides.* THE MAHARAL *studies him a while, takes the axe from his hand.* THE GOLEM *does not move. He looks as though he is asleep standing.*]

MAHARAL: You stand like stone
  And do not see me come towards you.

[THE GOLEM *stands rigid.*]
  Lift up your head and raise your eyes.
  Let me look into them.
  The cries you wakened still re-echo. Fear
  Still lurks behind you, staring
  Over your shoulder, ready to attack.

[THE GOLEM *does not move.*]
  For you, I prayed to God for wonders—
  My prayers of tears and pain were answered:
  That you might see where no one saw,
  And hear all things that no one heard;
  That you might feel beneath your step
  The doings nine ells in the deep;
  That fire might not consume your flesh;
  That in water you might not drown;
  Aromas borne by farthest winds
  Your nostrils might perceive and know;
  And if need be, your body might
  Become transparent as the air
  Or to another be transformed;
  That you might see and not be seen.
  I give you glory for your life,
  And for your hands, a blessed strength.
  And you—you stand as stiff as wood;
  Your eyes are dull, your mouth, distorted.
  Upon your shoulders, massive walls,
  Still lies the lifeless woe of clay;
  Primordial, dust-encrusted worms
  Upon your arms are crawling still,
  And from your breath, for miles around,
  Erupts the stench of rotting rock.
  Your life is old a single day,
  And yet how soon the man in you
  Has hurried to reveal himself
  In hatred, passion, and misfortune.
  Did I convey you here among us
  That you might be like other men?
  Well, let us say there fell upon you
  The heavy weight of fear and darkness,
  Despair and dread that each one feels,
  But where is there upon your face
  The gleaming light, the radiant glow
  Of our common trust and faith?
  Why are you dumb? Reply, reply!
  Before I raise my staff against you!

[THE GOLEM *comes to, stretches out his hand in joy to* THE MAHARAL.]

GOLEM: Where am I? Rabbi, where am I?
  And where did everybody go?

Everyone was shouting so
And crying, milling round about me;
I could not understand the reason.
When suddenly it grew so still;
My eyelids to each other stuck.
Rabbi, I was asleep.

MAHARAL: You were asleep?

GOLEM: I am uncertain, Rabbi. Under me
The earth began to move and sway.
A hand reached out and drew me off,
And flung me high into the air
And then it hurled me down again.
I fell. Whereupon the earth
Was in an instant split apart
And broken into separate halves.
I flew into the deep abyss
But had no place to fall upon,
And as I flew I noticed: You
Were riding on my back and urging,
Driving me deep into the void.

MAHARAL: Speak on.

GOLEM: Your face I saw in double image:
One half was large—as large as mine,
The other—smaller still than yours;
Your eyes were four—and all were dead.
In one alone a spark of red,
And from it burning blood was dripping.
Then suddenly I saw your head
Begin to bob and toss about,
To beat itself against my own,
And with the eye that dripped hot blood,
It burnt its way into my brow,
And bit by bit into my brain
It sank until it reached your neck;
And as you sank, I saw,
Your neck was long and white and lithe.
I threw my hands around your throat
And fiercely I began to choke you.

MAHARAL: Let words your hatred dissipate.

GOLEM: Am I asleep? I can see nothing more;
I cannot see your face or eyes.
It was *my* throat that someone's hands were choking.
I thought at first that it was yours.
Oh, stay with me and do not leave me.
[*He stretches full length upon the floor at the* RABBI's *feet.*]
Oh, stay with me, or else—drive me away.

MAHARAL: Get up. I see your grief,
And I forgive you.

GOLEM: Do not leave me.

MAHARAL: Stand up.

GOLEM: A little longer, Rabbi,
Let me lie here at your feet.

MAHARAL: Stand up.

GOLEM: One moment longer, Rabbi.
I feel so good, so much at ease.
It grows so bright.

MAHARAL [*overjoyed*]: Did you say bright? What do you see?

GOLEM: You.

MAHARAL: And now?

GOLEM: You touch me with your hands.

MAHARAL: I bless you. Now what do you see?

GOLEM: Fire! Fire!
A great flame spins and churns.
It tries to set me blazing but it cannot.

MAHARAL: And now?

GOLEM: A mass of water streams and whirls.
I sink and yet I do not drown,
And stones hail down upon my head
And bound away.

MAHARAL: What else?

GOLEM: And vicious dogs attack me
But my flesh remains unharmed.

MAHARAL: What do you hear?

GOLEM: Deep beneath the ground,
I hear muffled voices;
I hear the talk of stones and roots;
I hear the steps of feet that hurry;
I hear a wind. It whirls about.
It calls me by my name,
And I am not afraid of it.
And, Rabbi, see the face that stares at me,
A face entirely made of light,
A body huge, like mine;
He flutters over me
And soars as though on wings.
He grows out of my shoulders
And spreads out of my arms.

MAHARAL: Stand up.
[THE GOLEM *stands up.*]
And now what do you see?

GOLEM: I see a man attired in black;
He comes this way with silent steps,
With steps that lurk for theft.

MAHARAL: Now open wide your eyes again.
Again behold the light,
The wings of one invisible

That grow from you.
Go forth unto the Fifth Tower,
And there you stay, and there you sleep.
[THE GOLEM *bounds out of the room with a leap.* THE
MARAHAL, *himself astounded, leans his face against
the wall. His shoulders heave.*]

Translated by Joseph C. Landis.

Other works by Leivick: *Di keytn fun meshiakh*
(1907–1908); *Der volf* (1920); *Shmates* (1921); *Ikh bin
nisht geven in treblinka* (1945).

David Bergelson

1884–1952

David Bergelson was a pioneering Yiddish novelist and
dramatist. Born in Ukraine in 1884, he established a
model for modernist aesthetics and literary impressionism in Yiddish from early in his career. An influential
member of the Kiev grupe and Kultur-lige before and
during the Russian Revolution, Bergelson spent much
of the 1920s in Berlin, solidifying that city's reputation
as a nexus of Yiddish culture in the interwar period.
Much to the shock of the Yiddish reading public, Bergelson expressed strong support for the Soviet Union
as the only place with a secure future for Yiddish
letters in his widely read 1926 essay "Dray tsenters."
Although Bergelson's writing took on an increasingly
ideological bent after he moved to the Soviet Union
in the early 1930s, his novels were still well regarded
by critics and readers alike. A leading member of the
Jewish Anti-Fascist Committee, Bergelson was a victim
of the postwar repression of Soviet Yiddish culture and
was murdered by the state alongside other members of
the Soviet Yiddish intelligentsia on August 12, 1952.

The Beginning of December 1918
1922

In came the beginning of the month of December
1918.

Like the cheerless, cold drizzle, dirty frozen air hovers over the fields. Everywhere fragments of sky seem
to be scattered over mounds of earth—darkened, torn,
as though trampled underfoot, but the trampling feet
have moved on: they are no longer here—they have disappeared, vanished into hiding.

From the large Jewish shopkeepers' quarter right
across the entire area around this locality an acrid old

world lingers, a God-forsaken world, exposed to the
chill of winter, to the wind that might gust down from
the north, and to the trouble that had yet to erupt and
sweep down from very far away, from a God-forsaken
town in the furthest distance where it had already
erupted and come to pass: a massive slaughter had
taken place there.

And the dirt of the sky knows of it, and the winter
day, and the sleepy village that lingers on in nerve-
racked silence and suspense . . . and appears mute when
Jews travel through it.

As in every country, days here were once full of life.
Now those days are still-born, they are instantly frozen
and fade away in the mist. And protracted weeks of
grey days from which the sun has been eclipsed drag
out endlessly. Jewish communities from nearby towns
correspond secretly about self-protection, and in the
blank, bare vicinity here the first Jewish murder victim had already been found. On a winter's day, not so
much frozen as stretched out like cold sour-dough, he
was discovered next to the narrow-gauge railway line
between the ice-bound river Sob and Lik, the almost
snowed-under village in the valley. He lay there face upwards, abandoned, murdered and frozen, his arms outstretched to the wide world, his chilled eyes open, his
head split from his left eyebrow to the crown of his furrowed forehead and his lips pursed and fixed, as though
in their silent anguish they had not wished to cry out,
but to smack together in astonishment:

—Oo . . . Va! . . . Oo . . . Va!

And that was all. A tall corpse flung from the train; a
lump of grieving pity in the shape of an unknown Jew—
a passing traveller whose journey had been eternally
interrupted.

And he lay like that for a whole day, and a second,
and a third, until a God-fearing old peasant loaded him
on to his wagon and as an act of compassion transported
him to the nearby *shtetl* in the valley.

All this took place while it was still the beginning of
December in that acrid time when an unseeing day, biting and sluggish, hung over the long river Sob. Ravens
flew up and down, and idle telegraph-wires moaned in
the wind. Ravens rested on them before bearing their
black shrieks further down where they invested a single, solitary poplar tree standing there. Opposite the
poplar, old and tired, lay the valley of the *shtetl*. There
row upon row of tiled roofs dozed, nestling guiltily one
next to the other, slipping down, ever downwards, towards the very brink of the river.

A pale speck gleamed where the misty marketplace began: for hours on end a white goat stood there with a feeble-minded old man in tatters at her side. He stroked the animal, and both simpleton and goat stood immobile, chewing the cud.

As on a fast-day, all was silent and sombre and cold.

And next to the crooked old community-house, the wagon bearing the unknown murder victim still waited, and the windows of the houses opposite were crowded, and staring as, one by one, people approached the conveyance. Unemotionally and in silence they came up to it over there, like dogs or wolves to one of their own; there each one silently sniffed at the dead one, and went away.

A back door slammed in a place where there was weeping, emitting nothing more than the sound of a father yelling at his child:

—Stay in the house!

And once again the world outside was mute and dead. For a long time now, no one had left the *shtetl*, and the fields were empty and the Jews forsaken. A chimney on a roof barely sent up a wisp of smoke.

And opposite, in the marketplace not too far away, there was still the dark outline of a little group—no more than four long patriarchal beards stood there, all looking in this direction in bewilderment. One gave off the stench of an old billy goat, another, the odour of an empty milk-jug, a third the juice of winter apples stored in a cellar. And the fourth was a fool. He stank of the tannery, continually stared across at the wagon in astonishment, and asked:

What does this all mean? . . . Are there really no more fairs?

During the second half of the month of December, savagely and wildly, the region once again attempted to discharge the pus from itself, and here and there in the great expanse of the south-western region, as though on the fevered flush of an oedema, glared the fresh wounds of towns.

Now snow fell on them—

It snowed and snowed on the red wounds of towns.

And here at that long river the Sob, days still turned to mud, wrenched the molars from the mouths of shopkeepers, paid rent for the *shtetl's* valley with ruined homes, with raped women . . .

Then there was vacancy all around: cold, dirty frozenness—desolate emptiness. Dead, deaf telegraph-wires moaned through the valley, stretched far away into icy blankness as though into distant desert-steppes, and no longer reached the great mother city. The *shtetl's* valley had long anticipated some comfort from there, but, overtaken by darkness, was left dumb, fainting and waiting. . . .

For a long while now, no one went out into the main street. Only from time to time, in one of the windows of a large house over there, the last of the virgins tires her eyes with watching—sorrowful, age-old eyes suffused with the nightmares of two thousand years watch the way the black-garbed hangman rides by on horseback, tricked out each day in white puttees, with Gonta's smile on his lips, with a single long lock of hair on his otherwise shaven head; day after day, age-old eyes, filled with the nightmares of two thousand years, stare out on him there.

And in the sour cold and winter filth, one day lost consciousness here, and one night—a night of the holy Sabbath.

In the grey morning dawn, from the distant misty village an old church bell spoke to God, nagging and complaining. For observant Jews the long, desolate street here in the valley remained tense and alert, gaping in disbelief, yet listening, listening with questioning envy:

—Has someone actually concealed a furtive bit of God?

Somewhere an old sayer of Psalms remained quietly in his home, felt a throbbing in his heart, and no longer knew what God was, or whose he was.

The alien bell pealed once again. And in the valley of the *shtetl*, a black cock went on crowing from yesterday on; a sluggish wind blew alarmingly, accompanied by the creak of fast-closed shutters, crossing and re-crossing all that Sabbath day. At night a door was slammed shut somewhere. A shot like disjointed laughter could be heard not far away. But now the hoarse old wall-clock stared unblinkingly at the Sabbath candlesticks on the covered table and suddenly croaked out in drawn-out death-agony: "Nine." An old grandfatherly nose was suddenly filled with the odour of a *minyan* robed in prayer-shawls, with the tallow of the candles on the prayer-stand, and with the sound of Sabbath psalm-singing. An old ear heard an unexpected sound—an entire congregation was reciting in the distance:

—May Thy mercy rest upon us even as our hope rests on Thee . . .

And he waited a while in this way, listening intently with pounding heart, and suddenly, as though in a dream, heard once more:

—For a thousand years in Thy sight are like a day that passes . . .

And quickly, quickly, he flung round his neck the grubby, half-yellowed prayer-shawl, threw his Sabbath coat over it without thrusting his arms into the sleeves, and swiftly, swiftly, with trembling feverish hands unlatched a side-door, poked his white beard out into the freezing cold, and rushed out, but soon stopped stock-still—he heard a shot close by, sniffed at the air in the direction of the empty synagogue, desecrated weeks past, and hurried back, back, latching the door behind him.

Now it was already late—it was broad day . . .

In the valley of the *shtetl*, from yesterday, a black cock was still crowing. A sluggish wind blew alarmingly, accompanied by the scrape of a shutter being closed, crossing and re-crossing all that Sabbath day.

And the murdered Sabbath outdoors froze over. No one passed by; a page torn from a prayer-book drifted past—a yellowed page bearing the words "Bless, my soul," the first words of the psalm recited before enfolding oneself in a prayer-shawl, a page harried by the wind, driven over frozen mud, over clods of earth, and everything stood without any restoration—eternally, ever lastingly, without any restoration.

Translated by Joseph Sherman.

Other works by Bergelson: *Arum vokzal* (1909); *Nokh alemen* (1913); *Opgang* (1920); *Mides hadin* (1929); *Bam Dnyeper* (1932).

Rokhl Brokhes

1880–1942

Born in Minsk (in present-day Belarus) and educated in the tradition of the Haskalah, Rokhl Brokhes was a prolific writer of novels, short stories, plays, and children's literature in Yiddish. Her work was known for its rich depictions of women's lives and the poverty of the Jewish working class writ large in a style blending realism with a certain lyricism. The bulk of her work appeared in periodicals, including *Der fraynd*, *Di tsukunft*, *Der shtern*, and *Oktyabr*. An eight-volume comprehensive edition of her collected works was slated for publication in the Soviet Union, but the plans were never fulfilled due to the Nazi invasion. She died in the Minsk ghetto.

The Zogerin

1922

"No I say; ENOUGH is enough! On their behalf I prayed, for their benefit I cried my eyes out. Enough! I say, no! May I be struck dumb if I will say one more word, not even my name, Gnesye." She had a strong chin. She was a *zogerin*. A very good one and she argued:

"*Reboyne-sheloylem*, kind Father, You alone know how I have prayed both summer and winter, never missed a *Shabes*, never stinted on a *tkhine*. On their behalf what have I not prayed for? Wealth, length of days, pleasure from the children. . . . Comes *Reshkhoydesh*, my heart simply melts, my soul leaps. It's no small thing, *Reshkhoydesh*! I pray for everything, everything! Weep for everything! My heart, my heart . . . not to even mention the *Yomim noroim*. Every year I leave the synagogue absolutely sick, hoarse, distraught, worn out. Had I been chopping wood or digging ditches I couldn't have worked so hard. It's no small thing to be a *zogerin*!

"So many women around me, maybe more than twenty . . . the air, stifling, . . . the din . . . the bickering and complaining among them—this one doesn't hear, she's sitting too far away, she wants to be closer. Another one is leaning too close to the one beside her. Yet another one thinks that I'm ignoring her, that I failed to remember her grandmother during the *yisker* service. This one, that I forgot about her Khatskele; that one, that I didn't pray for her Iserl."

She complained and fumed, standing in her little room, peering out strangely from under her brow as if searching for something. On the edge of a bench her grandson sat restless. He was some eleven years old. Perplexed and afraid. What was the matter with his grandmother? She was so angry today, bad-tempered and swearing . . . he wanted to say something to her, ask her not to scream or cry so much. He felt today her crying was not like other times. This time her tears were different. He lifted up his thin little hand silently and then let it drop again.

Her heart was pounding. "Better to fall ill, better to be struck dumb than to have wasted my life praying for fat Teme that she might have such a grand house and so many stores; for Faytl's daughter Shtishe, a rabbi for a son-in-law and such good grandchildren; for that scabrous Tsipore a legacy of ten thousand. For whom have I not prayed and for whose sake have I not pleaded? And what have I gotten from it all? They paid me only a fiver a week and that's *enough*! All they paid me was a pittance to keep my mouth shut. 'Here, choke on it and shut up, for you that's enough.' Can you believe it?"

Her wig askew, eyes blazing, lips foaming in anger, her thin hands fanned herself, here, there and everywhere. Her whole body shook.

"Did I not find a spot for them? They came to the *besmedresh*, that precious Dina, so high and mighty, all puffed up. Pshaw! Came in silk and velvet, a neck thick with pearls. No small thing! And me, Gnesye the *zogerin*, I don't know where to seat her . . . and I sob and I pray on her behalf, for wealth, for all that's good and what does she give me? A sixer, a copper, from her munificence! One sixer, for all that I pleaded, for all that I sobbed . . . She gave me only one sixer and nothing more. She, the rich one, while I, Gnesye the *zogerin*, Gnesye the pauper. . . ."

The little boy became even more frightened. His grandmother paced the tiny room, screaming. What was the matter with her? He wanted to come up to her saying, "*Bobinke sha, Bobinke* don't cry, be quiet *Bobinke*," but he was afraid. The entire night she had sat up on her cot; leaning over his bed, waking him, speaking to him and to herself, not budging even an inch to eat the evening meal, that's how angry she was.

"It happened one *Shabes*," she complained. "It was a winter day, my bones were aching. My throat was so swollen I couldn't swallow and all my limbs were aching. It seemed to me, maybe a person could have stayed in bed resting herself, but no, to that I didn't pay any attention. Off I hurried to the *besmedresh*. I moaned, I pleaded. When I came to the *tkhines*, I absolutely melted away, so intense was my prayer."

"*Bobinke sha*, *Bobinke* be quiet," the child spoke out. Women were standing in the doorway.

"Don't you know?" she screamed, grabbing his hand with her burning one, her eyes crazy clear.

"*Bobinke*, stop," the child begged.

"Be quiet; you don't know, you can't know. All this is not your concern. It's mine. I lamented, I pleaded before the *Reboyne-sheloylem*. All He gave me were my bloody tears. This is all me and my prayers, you hear, Shmertsik? Me and my prayers. Do you hear, Shmertsik, all mine and they repay me with a penny, a fig, like a beggar at the door. My whole life, twenty years, I pleaded for them, on their behalf I fasted. About myself I forgot altogether. I am poor. You see how I wear an old worn-out shirt. . . . You see how I eat only a dried out crust of bread. . . . *They* live in palaces and sleep on soft beds, silken dresses *they* wear. All that is *mine, my* hard-working prayers for more than twenty years."

Actually, the little boy wanted to plug his ears to keep from hearing his grandmother's tirade, wanted to hide himself to elude her gaze.

"Listen, Shmertsik, do you hear? My tears, my widow's tears pierced the very heavens, and all for them. Shmertsik, my child, my bitter little orphan, you are the only one left to me from my seven children. Did *they* want to hear what was in my heart? I knocked on all their doors. No, *that* doesn't belong to them! Everything they own is mine, mine! You hear, Shmertsik? Mine! That Faytl's daughter Shtishe, she wouldn't even give me a scrap of food to feed you with and Hertse's daughter Zlate, she wouldn't give me an interest-free loan from *gmiles khesed*. Teme's daughter Zundl didn't even want to enroll you in the new *Talmud Toyre*. I went to that scabrous Tsipore. In front of her I wept, told her all that was in my bitter heart, 'have pity, help me with something for my little one, my poor orphan' but she had no time for me. She was too busy. In the middle of the week, she won't even acknowledge that she knows me.

"'Mama, some kind of poor old woman wants to see you, probably needs a hand-out,' her daughter says to her. 'A strange woman.'

"'Mother is not at home, we tell you.' So angry, this daughter.

"Naturally, on *Shabes*, she is entirely different, she has an entirely different hide *then*, she becomes so gentle. Then she needs me, Gnesye the *zogerin*.

"'Cry, plead on my behalf,' she says. 'I am a wealthy woman. My tears are so precious, they're worth silver. *My* eye, *my* heart, I need to save them for the good things in life.'

"No! I say, do you hear, Shmertsik? Enough!"

Right away the little boy began to cry, sobbing; that's how frightened he was. "*Bobinke sha, Bobinke* be quiet," he stammered. "Look, *Bobinke*, how all the women are staring at us from the window, from the doorway, see?"

She became quiet, pensive. Her eyes bored deeply into herself. She bowed her head low and her old wrinkled face lost its angry red colour. All at once she became deathly yellow. The women at the door and the window went off slowly, whispering and telling secrets quietly among themselves. The little boy practically fell apart from pity. They were talking about his grandmother, but he didn't know what to do, how to calm her.

"Ha," she said, and her gaze fell on the child, an angry, hard look and her voice became entirely different, strong now and full of venom. "No," she said again and stomped her foot. "No, I'll show them. Do you hear, Shmertsik? I'll go on praying, I'll go on weeping but now I'll pray for me, just for me. I'll pray for a disaster to fall on them, on all my enemies . . . they are my worst enemies. They took away my prayers, my tears, my years. . . . Do you hear, Shmertsik? All that they have is mine. I'll pray for it back. I'll take it back, you hear, Shmertsik. I'll take it all back. I'll be avenged on them. My prayer will be a prayer of revenge, do you hear, Shmertsik . . . ?"

"Be quiet, *Bobinke*," the child whimpered. "Look how they are watching, wondering, the women are shaking their heads."

"Shmertsik, are you listening? I'll ask for it all back. I'll pour out my heart in tears. I'll plead for my own sake and with an outstretched hand. I'll pray for myself. Do you hear, you women, you can plead for yourselves." With outstretched hand, wild voice and flashing eyes, she lunged towards the door. The women moved away.

"Look out," whispered one of the women, "look out. Gnesye the *zogerin* is out of her mind." "God help us! The Lord's miracles!" "It's dangerous to let her out on the streets. She could hurt someone," said a third. "The poor little grandson." "Sh, sh, she's coming."

But she stayed in the tiny room. Only her voice, angry and vengeful, could be heard echoing far, far, all the way into the third courtyard.

Translated by Shirley Kumove.

Other works by Brokhes: *A zamlung dertseylungen* (1922); *Gelkeh: dertseylungen* (1937); *Avremelekh/Little Abrahams* (1998).

Lev Lunts

1901–1924

Lev Lunts was a playwright, essayist, prose writer, and literary translator of Jewish origin who wrote in Russian. A native of St. Petersburg, he was a leader of the Serapion Brothers literary school, a group dedicated to humanistic ideals, fantasy, narrative, and "radical apoliticism." Scorned by the Marxist establishment, Lunts was nevertheless acclaimed by writers across Europe, including Maxim Gorky and Luigi Pirandello, who applauded his imaginative work for the stage and his essays on the printed page. He died in

Hamburg, shortly after his emigration from Soviet Russia. Written out of official literary histories in the Soviet Union, Lunts's work circulated in the postwar period in samizdat and was published in Russian in book form for the first time in 1994.

The Homeland
1922

for V. Kaverin [Veniamin Kaverin, born Zilber, Soviet writer]

I

"You do not know yourself, Venya," I said. "Just take a look at yourself."

A mirror. And in the mirror: a tall man with a powerful face. Black hair lashes about his stern forehead, and savage, deep, desertic eyes shine passionately under his calm, clear brows.

"Venya, you do not see yourself. You looked like this when you came out of Egypt to Canaan, remember? That was you lapping water from the Kidron, like this, with your belly to the ground, quickly and thirstily. And remember how you overtook him, the detested one, when he caught his hair in the branches and hung over the ground? You killed him, and you screamed, and he screamed, and the cedar screamed."

"You're nuts," answered Venya. "What's got into you? I don't like Jews. They're dirty."

"Sure, Venya. But in every Jew, even in you, there's—how can I put it?—an ancient prophet. Have you read the Bible? Look, I know what I'm like. I have a high forehead, but that's about it. I'm small and puny, my nose turns down and peers at my lip. Lev they call me—like Judah—but where is the lion in me? I want to, but can't force it out of myself. I can't master up what is serious and beautiful . . . That's pathos, Venya. But you can. You have the face of a prophet."

"Leave me alone, Lyova, would you? I don't want to be a Jew."

On a summer evening in Petersburg my friend and I are sharing home brew. In the next room, my father, an old Polish Jew, bald, with grey beard and ringlets, prays to the east, and his soul mourns that his only son, the last scion of the ancient race, drinks home brew on the holy eve of the Sabbath. And the old Jew sees the blue sky of Palestine, where he has never been, but which he *has seen, now sees and will see*. And I, not believing in God, I also mourn. For I want to, but cannot see the distant Jordan and the blue sky, because I love the city in which I was born, and the language I speak is a foreign one.

"Venya," I say, "do you hear my father? Six days a week he trades, deceives and grumbles. But on the seventh day he sees Saul, who threw himself on his own sword. You too can see, you should see, in you there is rapture, and frenzy, and cruelty, Venya."

"I'm all dried up and don't care," he answers. "I don't like Jews. Why was I born a Jew? Still, you're right. I'm foreign to myself. I can't find myself."

II

"Well, I'm going to help you," I said. "Let's go."

Behind the wall, my father stopped praying. They sat down at the table: father, mother, sister. They didn't call me; for three years they had not called me. I lived like a Philistine in their home. Their home stood under an eternally blue sky, surrounded by vineyards, on a hill in Bethlehem. But my home faced Zabalkansky Prospekt—straight, foreign, but beautiful. And my sky was dirty, dusty and cold.

The Revolution: empty streets. A white evening. The street swims along like a railway track receding in the distance. Streetcar posts fly by like a flock of birds.

"Venya, when I look at this city, it seems to me that I've seen it sometime before it was hot, straight and monstrous. And it was there that we met. You were the same, only wearing different clothing, strange clothing. You're laughing at me."

But he's not laughing. On Obulkhovsky Bridge he is black and wild. He stands up taller, stretching his hands out over the river. His grey cloak flies out behind his shoulders, and his desertic, passionate eyes see.

"Yes!" he shouts, his voice singing like a violin string, long and powerfully. "I remember. We sailed on a boat together. It was round as a ball. And we poled it with boat hooks. It was hot . . ."

"It was hot!" I shout in answer.

We exchange frenzied looks, standing taller, feverish, and we recognize each other. Then, suddenly, we shrink back down and laugh.

"What an oddball you are," says Venya. "Even I couldn't hold out. Such nonsense."

A white summer evening. The choral synagogue stands surrounded by dry stone houses. We go up the broad steps, and the vile custodian, an old shamesh, comes out toward us.

He says: "Ach, sho it's you again? Not today. Today is Shaturday."

This is directed at me. It's not the first time I have come to him. And it's not the first time I have turned away from him in disgust.

Looking aside, I thrust some money into his hand, and he slips away like a mouse, leading us noiselessly through the vestibule and into a gigantic sleeping hall.

Venya, bored, walks along and looks lazily about. But I take careful, deliberate steps, lowering my eyes.

"Thish way," says the shamesh.

A barely noticeable door screeches open, and a bitter cold grips us. Slippery stairs lead down. The lamp flickers. And the door closes behind us. [. . .]

The descent is long and stifling. And the farther down we go, the louder the rumbling. The lamp keeps flickering.

The stairs end. A wall. Behind the wall sounds a heavy rumble, the roar of wheels and the cracking of whips. And there goes the lamp.

"Lev," he says, "come on!"

"There's a wall here, Venyamin. I've been here many times. There's no way through."

And again in the dark his voice sings out like a violin string, long and powerfully.

"Judah! Here! I know the way!"

The stone door heaved open, and the blazing gold of the sun struck me furiously in the face.

1

The first thing Judah remembered:

The street, straight as the royal way. The heavy, sleepy sun dazzles the great city, and a translucent white dust floats over Judah. Judah—a boy in a dirty flaxen mantle and a dirty tunic—sits on the roadway and breathes in the dust. A chariot flies by. The powerful horses, spread out like a fan, run snorting and tossing their stupid snouts in the sky. Toward them speeds another chariot and, with a dusty rattle, the two chariots cross in the narrow street, maintaining their steady pace. Judah sits between them, and the sonorous Lydian whips whistle over his head.

The first thing Judah loved:

The great city, the straight and precipitous streets, the straight, precise angles and the huge, quiet houses. In Babylon was Judah born. He was short and fast, and his spirit was weak, like that of a senseless but cunning bird. He had no father, no mother, no grandfather, no friend, and no one knew his family or tribe, but he was a Judean.

Judah knew:

Far to the west, beyond the desert, lay a beautiful land, from which came his mother, whom he did not know, and his father, whom he did not remember. Judah saw his tribesmen praying to the west, praying to the mysterious and terrifying Yahweh to return them to the land of their ancestors. But Judah did not pray. For he lived in the street, and he loved the translucent white dust of the city in which he was born, Babylon.

2

But when the wind blew from the west, the translucent dust turned yellow and stung the eyes. Then Judah arose and ran until the wind abated. Like a wild Nisaean horse, he flew along the straight streets. Babylonians lay on the ground, basking in the sun and breathing in the dust. Judah jumped over them, outstripping the chariots, and his red Judean hair rippled in the wind like the mane of a lion. The wind blew from the west, across the desert, from the land whence came his father, whom he did not know, and his mother, whom he did not remember. And the yellow wind of the desert lifted Judah and swept him through Babylon like a grain of sand.

Babylon spread out on the Euphrates with straight streets and straight intersections. Straight as sunbeams at noon, the streets dropped to the river, proceeding under the high embankments, tearing through the brass gates and descending in steps to the river. Like a stone from a sling, Judah ran beneath the gates, plunged into the rapid river and swam. The river was mottled with boats and more than once boat hooks struck the Judean, and more than once they called to him coarsely and painfully. But Judah neither heard nor saw. Crossing the river, he ran up the steps and flew on, not stopping to shake the cold bright drops from his mantle, pursued by the western wind.

He was weak and sickly, but when the wind blew from the desert, he ran from sunrise to sunset and sunset to sunrise—faster than the hangars, runners of the king. He ran past the old palace on the right bank and under the bright new palace on the mountain. Eight times he circled the temple of Bel Marduk and eight times the towers standing one to eight on top of each other. Four times he circled the mound of Babil, where the mysterious gardens hung in four storeys high over the city. The guards beat him with the blunt ends of their lances, and

the archers drew a thick bowstring to see if an arrow would pass him. The arrow did pass him. But Judah, tireless as the yellow wind blowing from the desert, ran on and on through the city.

Around the city crept Nimitti-Bel, the great wall. It looked out on all four sides of the Earth, and all four sides were equal in handsbreadths. A hundred gates cut through the wall, and at the hundred gates the Bactrian trumpets trumpeted at sunset. The rampart was as wide as a street, and indeed there was a street on the rampart. Toward evening, Judah climbed the western wall and ran along its edge, looking out into the desert from whence the wind blew. And when the wind abated and the dust again became translucent and white, the Judean lay down on the wall and looked to the west where there lay a mysterious, beautiful, foreign land.

3

And when the wind blew from the swamps, a damp stench crept into Babylon. Then the people went inside, and the horses lowered their heads and slowed their gait. And then a yearning floated into Judah's soul. He got up and walked solemnly across the bridge to the right bank where the Judeans lived in low, gloomy houses. He walked along heavily, swaying like a youth returning for the first time from a woman's bed. And, coming up to his fellow tribesmen, he listened avidly to the ringing and cruel words of a prophet telling of a marvelous distant land. But Judah did not believe the prophet, and the yearning grew in his soul.

And it came to pass that once, as he listened to the prophet, his gaze fell on a young man standing off to the side. He was a tall fellow with a powerful face. Black hair lashed about his stern forehead, and savage, deep, desertic eyes shone passionately under his calm, clear brows. Judah recognized him but couldn't recall where he had seen him. And incomprehensible words spoke in his soul. He saw a grey, unfamiliar, cold sky, and a cold wind whistled in his ears.

And the young man looked at Judah and recognized him. His stern forehead knotted painfully, his eyes looked deeply: they saw a grey, unfamiliar, cold sky.

Judah went up to him and asked: "Who are you, lad?"

And the young man answered: "I am Benjamin, but my father's name I do not know. And who are you, lad?"

And Judah answered: "I am Judah, a Judean, but my father's name I do not know."

Then Benjamin said: "I have a strange yearning, Judah. As if I came to Babylon from somewhere else. Where is my homeland?"

And Judah repeated: "Where is my homeland?"

And they both fell silent. Their breathing quickened, became shallow, and incomprehensible words rose up from their souls. Suddenly Judah noticed that on the young man's left arm, just below the shoulder, was a triangle formed by three white spots, like the marks of a sore. And the two youngsters cried out in a strange, foreign tongue.

And Benjamin said: "I know you."

And Judah said: "I know you."

They stood a long while looking in confusion. But then the prophet shouted that deliverance was at hand, that Yahweh was coming with his forces of Kouresh, King of Persia, to return the Judeans to the promised land. [. . .]

5

And the years flowed like the waters of the Euphrates plunging into the Erythraean Sea. New days rolled behind the old. Judah grew, a beard grew on his face and love grew in his heart for Remat, a Babylonian girl, daughter of Ramut the engraver. Remat was small and dark and not very pretty, but she had blue eyes like the slave girls from the north. Judah himself was needy and naked. He had the soul of a bird and he lived like a bird: senselessly and clearly. But when a beard grew on his face and love grew in his heart, he got up and went through the city seeking work. But found none.

Every day Judah met Benjamin and shivered with fear and joy, seeing the cold grey sky of his home, though he did not recognize it. The two youngsters looked a long time at each other and parted without a word.

But once, Benjamin came up to Judah and said: "Judah, you are hungry."

And Judah said: "I am hungry."

And Benjamin said: "Come with me. I know a boat which has no boatmen."

And Judah asked: "Where shall we take it?"

And Benjamin answered: "To Ur."

And Judah said: "So be it."

6

From Babylon to Ur they floated fabrics from Malta, copper from Cyprus, bronze articles from Chalcedon and skins of wine from Chios. Thus it was done: the vessel was made of Armenian willows joined together and covered by skin. It was round and deep and filled with straw. Judah and Benjamin poled it downstream with long boat hooks. Their goods lay on the straw, and an ass stood on the goods. And when they came to Ur, they sold the goods, the vessel and the straw, but the skin they removed and packed on the ass. Then they returned along the bank to Babylon, for the Euphrates was rapid, and no man could master its current.

Not once and not twice, the young men coursed the Euphrates from Babylon to Ur, and more than once they measured the road from Ur to Babylon. Their old master, Abiel, had already died, and now they bought and sold the wares and the boats by themselves. Judah now had three changes of clothes and a pair of low Boeotian shoes. The girls began to look at him. And once, when returning from Ur, he and Benjamin were met on the road by some women. And Judah said: "I love you, girl." And she answered: "All right." And she lay down in the sand. Benjamin stood off by himself and looked to the west. There in the west were sesame fields cut through with canals, fig orchards and the yellow desert beyond. But beyond the desert lay a beautiful and unknown land, from whence came his father, and where once lived the father of his father.

And Judah began to love Benjamin, and Benjamin began to love Judah. But they loved each other in silence. Not once and not twice, they made the journey without saying a word to each other. Then one day, as they neared the brass gates of Babylon, the western wind arose from the desert and stirred up Judah's heart. And Judah exclaimed, his hand pointing west: "Isn't that where my homeland is?" And Benjamin shouted: "No!" And he shouted again: "No! I hate you. Yahweh, cruel and malicious god. Our sins lie upon your head, and your crimes lay upon your heart." And Benjamin fell to the ground in convulsions, foaming at the mouth. And he exclaimed:

> "Thus says Yahweh, who created you, O Jacob! Fear not: For I have redeemed you; you are mine. When you pass through the waters, I will be with you; and through the rivers, they shall not overflow you. For I am Yahweh, your God, the Holy One of Israel!
>
> I will bring your seed from the east, and gather you from the west. I will say to the north, Give up; and to the south, Keep not back: Bring my sons from afar, and my daughters from the end of the Earth. I am

Yahweh, your Holy One, the creator of Israel, your King."

And Judah understood that the spirit of Yahweh had descended upon Benjamin, and he prostrated himself. But off in the distance, through the dust, he could make out the great wall, the eighth tower of the temple of Bel Marduk and the hanging gardens on the mound of Babil, and he recalled the straight streets and the translucent white dust, and said: "I do not believe!"

And on the following day Benjamin the prophet got up, took his knife and stripped the skin from his left arm beneath the shoulder. But when the wound healed and the skin grew back, once again there showed the three white spots in the shape of a triangle.

7

And it came to pass, that Yahweh took Kouresh, King of Persia, by the hand to subdue the nations before him, and he loosed the loins of kings to open the gates before him. He went before Kouresh and made the crooked places straight, broke the gates of brass and cut in sunder the bars of iron.

Then Kouresh, King of Persia, diverted the waters of the Euphrates into a lake; and when the star Tishtrya arose, he set out for Babylon along the dry bed. There he slew the king of Babylon and all those close to him. The king's treasures he took for himself, but the wives he distributed among his soldiers.

And that very night, when the star Tishtrya arose, Bai-Biul, the bird of love, sang in Judah's heart. For Ramut the engraver was on the wall defending the city from its enemies, and Remat his daughter let down a thick cord from her window. Judah climbed up the cord, and on that great night he knew Remat and he knew happiness.

But in the morning Habiz, a Persian, came to tell Remat that he had killed her father and that henceforth she would be his slave.

8

Thus says Yahweh through the lips of Benjamin the prophet:

Fear not, O Jacob, my servant, whom I have chosen, for I will pour water upon him that is thirsty, and floods upon the dry ground. I will pour my spirit upon your seed and my blessing upon your offspring, and they shall spring up as among the grass, as wil-

lows by the water courses. Remember these things, O Jacob and Israel, for you are my servant. I will blot out, as a thick cloud, your transgressions and, as a cloud, your sins. Rejoice, O ye heavens, for Yahweh says this. Shout for joy, ye depths of the Earth. Break forth into singing, ye mountains and forests. Thus says Yahweh, your redeemer and he that formed you from the womb. I am Yahweh, who made all things, who stretched forth the heavens alone, who spread abroad the earth by myself, who frustrated the tokens of liars and made diviners mad, who turned wise men backwards and made their knowledge foolish, who says to Jerusalem, You shall be inhabited, and to the gates of Judah, You shall be rebuilt, who says to the deep, Be dry, and who says of Kouresh, He is my slave.

And Judah, alone from all the crowd of the Judeans, spoke up: "I do not believe!"

And Benjamin the prophet said; "Be damned!"

9

Along Aibur-Shabu, the processional way, across the canal Libil-Khegalla, across the bridge to the western gates crept the Judeans. The neighing of horses and the lowing of mules, the screaming of singers and the crashing of Judean cymbals, all these and the plucking of Judean harps glorified Yahweh and Kouresh, King of Persia. Horsemen in high hats contained the crowd with whips. And they were in number forty-three thousand six hundred people. From Bethlehem, Netophah, Azmaveth, Kirjath, Shaaraim and other places. All were going to the land from whence came their fathers and where once lived the fathers of their fathers. They went in tribes, in families, with wives, with children, with chattel, with utensils. And Sheshbazzar, the son of Jehoiakim, led them.

And so they went out of Babylon.

Babylon spread out on the Euphrates with straight streets and straight intersections. Straight as sunbeams at noon, the streets went flying, and under the cruel, sleepy sun, the huge, quiet houses kept burning. A translucent white dust arose over Babylon.

Around Babylon crept Nimitti-Bel, the great wall. On its western side, by the large gates, lay Judah. And after the sons of all the tribes walked by, a band of men who did not know the names of their fathers came out on the road. Benjamin the prophet was at the head. He was straight and tall, and he looked to the west. And

Judah shouted at him: "Benjamin!" And Benjamin answered: "Be damned! One day you will come to me and tear off your clothes and sprinkle your head with ashes and say, 'Take me with you!' But you shall be repaid for your deeds, and for a traitor there is no forgiveness. Be damned!"

And when evening came, the wind blew from the swamps. Then Judah got up and went to Habiz, the Persian, saying, "Give me your slave Remat for wife." And Habiz asked him: "What will you give me in return?" And Judah said: "Myself!" And they shaved off his beard and he bowed down to Ormuzd, and so he became a slave of the Persian and married the slave girl Remat.

10

On the fourth day, Judah the slave went out into the street and lay down in the middle, as once he had lain as a boy. And he inhaled the translucent white dust of his hometown, breathing quickly, deeply and joyfully. Passersby stepped over him, chariots flew past him, cracking Lydian whips over his head.

But it came to pass, when the sun stood in the west, that a yellow wind arose from the desert. And the wind lifted up Judah. And Remat the Babylonian girl asked him: "Where are you going?" But he did not answer.

And the wind bore Judah to the western gates, to the road that ran through Circesium and Riblah to Jerusalem. It was hot, and Judah ran, snorting like a horse, tireless as a horse, or a hangar, runner of the king. The road was hard and resounding, and Judah ran. His body was torn and bleeding, his head hung heavily on his shoulders, and he ran. Huffing and wheezing, yet barely making a sound as his heels struck the hard road, he ran all day and he ran all night. Blood flooded his eyes, foam coated his body, strength took leave of his soul, but the western wind blew as before, and he ran.

On the third day, toward evening, he saw the Judeans away in the distance. He shouted and stretched out his arms to them, and kept on shouting and stretching out his arms, but he could not overtake them. Then he fell on the ground and crawled on the road like a snake. His body was torn and bleeding, his soul was dripping with blood, and he crawled. The sun went down and came up again, and came up again. Dust rose up in the distance; the Judeans were walking to their homeland, and Judah crawled. Behind Judah, a bloody track crawled on the road. The wind kept blowing from the west.

On the sixth day he reached the Judeans. Behind all the others walked the men who did not know the names of their fathers, and Benjamin the prophet was leading them. And when they stopped to rest beside a broken-down wayside house, Judah crawled up to them.

And Benjamin said: "He has betrayed his people and shaved off his beard. Kill him, Judeans!"

And Judah said: "Brother!"

But Benjamin answered: "You are no brother to me."

Then Judah stood up. His knees were bent, his body was dripping with blood, his arms were covered with blood, but there on his left arm three white spots formed a triangle beneath his shoulder. Blood spurted from his mouth and together with the blood he spat out unfamiliar words, foreign and cold. And the slave grabbed Benjamin by the left arm, and the Judeans saw three white spots beneath his shoulder forming a triangle. And the prophet trembled and screamed in a foreign, sonorous tongue, pulling his arm away from Judah and thrusting his left arm out to Zaccai, a soldier, saying, "Cut it off!" And Zaccai the solder severed his left arm from the collarbone, and the arm fell onto the ground. And the Judeans saw the three white spots on the arm, just like the marks of a sore.

With his right hand, Benjamin lifted it up and threw it at Judah. Judah fell, and the Judeans stoned him. The stones landed loudly and steadily, collecting into a great heap.

Without a sound the door heaved closed and a grey gloom peered at me. But the gold of a desertic, sleepy sun still lingered in my eyes.

"Venyamin!" I cried. "Take me with you, Venyamin!"

A steady rumble answered me from behind the wall, like stones falling on stones. And suddenly a voice rang out, long and powerfully, like a violin string: "Be damned!"

And the clatter of numberless feet. I pressed against the damp wall, brushing it frantically. My wounded body, covered with blood, cried out in pain. The clatter died out in the distance. Then silence.

"Venyamin!" I cried. "Brother! Why have you left me?" And again silence.

Minutes, perhaps days passed. I do not know how long I remained standing there, without moving, without thinking, in pain. And I do not know why I suddenly hunched over and went up the stairs. The ascent was difficult and stifling. My torn feet slipped, my knees touched the stairs and suddenly I stumbled. At that moment the lamp flickered, and I saw on the step before me my clothes, Venyamin's clothes and Venyamin's left arm. Warm blood was oozing from the shoulder, and standing out whitely and triumphantly, forming a triangle, were three *pock marks*, the eternal stamp of sapient Europe.

III

I went out in the street. My beloved old pea jacket, my beloved old pants covered a ragged tunic and ragged body. I was no longer in pain; the clothing stopped up my wounds like a plaster. Yet a golden, hot sun still roamed in my eyes.

A store. In the window, a mirror, and in the mirror: a little man, bald, with a narrow forehead and moist, cunning eyes. It is I: dirty and abominable. I recognized myself. And I understood. Everything beautiful and ancient in me, my high forehead and enraptured eyes, everything remained there on the road which runs through Circesium and Riblah to Jerusalem. The Judeans are walking along that road to their homeland. Sheshbazzar, the son of Jehoiakim, leads them, and behind them comes Benjamin, the one-armed prophet.

Petersburg, with its straight streets and straight intersections, spread out on the Neva. Precipitous as sunbeams were the streets and the huge, quiet houses. And over Petersburg lay a cold, grey sky—the sky of my homeland, but foreign.

Translated by Gary Kern.

Other works by Lunts: *Vne zakona* (1921); *Na zapad* (1923); *Obez'iany idut!* (1923); *Patriot* (1923); *City of Truth* (1929).

Israel Joshua Singer

Repentance
1922

I

Rabbi Ezekiel of Kozmir and his followers were great believers in the divine principle of joyousness.

Reb Ezekiel himself was a giant of a man, standing a full head above his Chasidic followers, and broader in the shoulders than any two of them placed side by side. On Holy Days the court of Reb Ezekiel was jammed with visiting Chasidim, and in their synagogue the mighty head of Reb Ezekiel, swathed in the silver-worked headpiece of his prayer-shawl, swam above all others, a banner and a crown, an adornment to the gathering and the symbol of its glory.

Reb Ezekiel is no more than a memory today, but there are still extant two of his possessions: an ivory walking-stick and a white satin gaberdine which fastens at the front not with buttons but with silver hooks and eyes. The grip of the stick is so high that no man is able to use it for walking-purposes. A certain grandson of Reb Ezekiel, inheritor of the dynastic rights of this rabbinic line, puts on Reb Ezekiel's gaberdine once a year, on the New Year, when the ram's horn is to be blown for the opening of the heavenly gates; but if he tries to take a step in this mantle of his grandfather, he stumbles over the ends, which trail along the floor. To protect him not less than the illustrious garment, the followers of the grandson put down a carpet of straw on the floor of the synagogue for the two days of the New Year.

Rabbi Ezekiel and his followers believed not only in joyousness, but in the virtue of good food.

Of the fast-days which are sprinkled throughout the sacred calendar, Reb Ezekiel and his followers observed only the Day of Atonement. Even on the Ninth Day of Ab, the Black Fast which commemorates the tremendous calamity of the storming of the Temple, Reb Ezekiel and his followers ate. If it came to pass once in a while that a fool of a Chasid, having had a bad dream, insisted on fasting, he had to leave the court and go across the Vistula to the village opposite Kozmir.

At the court of Rabbi Ezekiel there were always dancing and singing; there was perpetual drinking of wine and mead. It was a common saying with the Rabbi, his children, the Chasidic followers and visitors:

"It is not the study of the Law that matters, but the melody which goes with the studying; it is not the praying that matters, but the sweet chanting of the prayer."

One day a strange thing happened. Rabbi Naphthali Aphter, the greatest opponent and critic of Reb Ezekiel, actually came on a visit to the town of Kozmir, for the Sabbath of Repentance.

Rabbi Naphthali Aphter was the exact opposite of Reb Ezekiel of Kozmir. He was a weakling, a pygmy of a Jew, skin and bones, something that a moderate wind could carry away. He fasted every day of the week, from Sabbath to Sabbath, that is. He broke his fast evenings with a plate of soup, nothing more; and lest he should derive from the soup anything more than the barest sustenance, lest he should take pleasure in the taste of food, he would throw into the plate of soup a fistful of salt. On Saturdays he permitted himself meat and fish, in honour of the sanctity of the Sabbath; he ate the eye of a fish and a sinew of flesh. When he ate, every swallow of food could be traced in its passage down his slender, stringy throat. Further to mortify his body, Rabbi Naphthali slept no more than two hours a night; the rest of the time he sat before the sacred books. And when he studied he did not follow the traditional custom, which bids the student set his repetitions to a sweet chant; this he considered a sinful concession to the lust of his ears. He muttered the words dryly under his breath. [. . .]

He repeated for the thousandth time, in the harsh mutter of his study: "*Shivoh medurei gehinom*, there are seven chambers in the courts of hell. The fire of the first chamber is sixty times as hot as the fire we know on earth; the fire of the second chamber is sixty times as hot as the fire of the first chamber; the fire of the third chamber is sixty times as hot . . . and thus it follows that the fire of the seventh chamber is hotter by sixty times sixty to the seventh time than the fire which we know on earth."

He continued: "Therefore happy are those who are only transformed into fish and animals, into trees and grasses. And there are also human souls which wander in the wildness of space, and there are others which are flung about as with slings, and their plight is bitterest of all."

Rabbi Naphthali had sundered himself completely from the things of this world. He had even separated himself from his wife and knew her no more. But wicked thoughts, evil visitations, tormented him, especially in the nights, and gave him no peace.

And this was not only when he lay down for the two hours of slumber which he permitted himself. Even while he sat at his sacred books shapes and phantoms in the likeness of females surrounded him. It was useless to close his eyes on them, for with closed eyes he only saw them better. They penetrated his ears, also. They shook down great masses of black hair, they sang with voices of piercing sweetness, they danced immodestly, and they flung their arms round him. They caressed his sparse little beard, they played with his stiff, flat earlocks, twining these round their fingers.

He fled from these visions and voices to the ritual bath, which lay in a corner of the yard of his house. He tore off his clothes, stumbled down the cold, slippery stone steps, and flung his weak body into the black, icy water. But even then it seemed to him that he struck with his head not against the harsh water, but against soft, silky cushions; and his body lay on down, tempting and exciting.

A naked woman, irresistibly beautiful, held him close in the hot bands of her arms. . . . He fled from the water and took vows to be harsher with his rebellious and pampered body. He halved his allowance of soup at the end of the day and doubled the salt with which he spoiled its taste. He wept day and night, and his eyes were never dry. But the Evil Inclination, the Wicked One, whispered mockingly in his ear:

"Fool that you are! You have separated yourself from your wife, who is a pure and good woman, to sin in secret with abominations of the night; you have left your simple couch of straw and feathers to loll on divans of silk and down. . . ." [. . .]

Then, in the end, Rabbi Naphthali decided to visit the rabbinic court of Kozmir.

"If fasting and mortification of the flesh will not help, perhaps Reb Ezekiel has better counsel," he thought.

He slung a sack over his shoulders, took his prayershawl and phylacteries under his arm, and set out for Kozmir, planning to arrive there for the Sabbath of Repentance.

When they learned in the court of the Kozmir Rabbi that Naphthali himself, the bitterest opponent and critic of Rabbi Ezekiel, had arrived on a visit, there was great rejoicing. Reb Mottye Godel, the chief beadle and grand vizier of the Kozmir Rabbi, stroked his beard proudly and said to all the Chasidim:

"This is a great victory. If Reb Naphthali himself comes here, the others will follow, and soon all the Jews will acknowledge our Rabbi. I tell you, we will live to see that day."

Rabbi Naphthali arrived, of course, not on the Sabbath itself, but on the preceding day; and he asked at once to be admitted to the presence of Reb Ezekiel. But the Kozmir Rabbi could not receive him. He was going, he declared, to the baths, to purify himself for the Sabbath. He remained in the baths longer than was his wont. In the steam-room he climbed up to the highest and hottest level of the stairs and shouted joyously to the attendants to pour more water on the heated stones and to fill the room with more steam. His followers, who would accompany him to the highest steps, fled from him this time, unable to endure the heat. The Rabbi laughed loudly at them.

"Fools," he cried, "how will you learn to endure the flames of hell?"

When he returned from the baths, Reb Ezekiel lay down on the well-stuffed, leather-covered couch on which he rested in the day-time, and he seemed to have forgotten entirely about Reb Naphthali. After he had taken a nap he commanded that the Sabbath fish be brought in to him to taste, and then he remembered Reb Naphthali.

"Mottye," he said, "bring in the fish prepared for the Sabbath—and Reb Naphthali too." [. . .]

When Rabbi Naphthali entered, conducted by the chief beadle, Reb Ezekiel greeted him joyously:

"Welcome, and blessed be thy coming," he exclaimed in a thundering voice which sent tremors through Reb Naphthali. He put out his hand, seized Reb Naphthali's, and squeezed it so hard that Reb Naphthali doubled up.

"What good tidings have you for me, Reb Naphthali?" he asked happily.

"I have come to ask your counsel on the matter of repentance," answered Reb Naphthali, trembling.

"Repentance?" shouted Reb Ezekiel, and his voice was as gay as if he had heard the sweetest tidings. "Repentance? Assuredly! Take a glass of whisky. What is the meaning of the word 'repentance'? It is: to turn! And when a Jew takes a glass of whisky he turns it upside down, which is to say that he performs an act of repentance."

And without waiting, Reb Ezekiel filled two silver beakers with brandy in which floated spices and little leaves.

"Good health and life, Reb Naphthali," he said, and pushed one beaker forward.

Reb Ezekiel emptied his own beaker at a gulp. Reb Naphthali broke into a stuttering cough with the mere smell of the drink, but Reb Ezekiel would not let him put it down.

"Reb Naphthali, you have come for my counsel. The first thing, then, which I will teach you will be the mystery of eating and drinking."

He forced Reb Naphthali to swallow the brandy and then pushed toward him a huge piece of stuffed carp, highly seasoned.

"This," he said with a smile, "comes from the hand of my wife. She is a valiant woman, a pearl of price, and her stuffed fish have in them not less than one sixtieth of the virtue and taste of Leviathan himself."

The first piece Reb Naphthali tried to swallow stuck in his throat. But Reb Ezekiel would not be put off, and he compelled Reb Naphthali to eat.

"Rabbi Naphthali, the road of repentance is not an easy one, as you see. But there is no turning back on it."

When it was impossible to make Rabbi Naphthali eat another bite, Reb Ezekiel took him by the hand, led him into the other room, and bade him stretch himself out on the well-stuffed leather-covered couch.

Rabbi Naphthali refused to lie down.

"What?" he said; "lie down and sleep in the middle of the day? And with the Sabbath approaching?"

"It is better to sleep two days than to entertain one thought," said Reb Ezekiel, and closed the door on him.

During the Ten Penitential Days which stretch from the New Year to the Day of Atonement Reb Ezekiel taught Reb Naphthali the mystery of food and the inner significance of joyousness. Every day there was another banquet in the rabbinic court, and wine and mead were consumed in barrelfuls. The singing in the court was heard throughout the whole townlet of Kozmir; it echoed in the surrounding hills and carried across the Vistula.

"Well, Reb Naphthali, are you visited by thoughts, by fantasies?" Reb Ezekiel asked him every day.

"Less now," answered Reb Naphthali.

"In that case here's another glass of mead," said Reb Ezekiel, and took care that Reb Naphthali drank it all down.

And every day, when the banquet was over, he led his guest into his own room and made him sleep on his leather-covered couch.

"Sleep!" he said. "Ordinary, unknowing Jews are permitted to sleep in the day-time only on Sabbaths. But good and pious Jews who are followers of a Chasidic rabbi are enjoined to sleep by daylight every day in the week."

When they all sat at the dinner which precedes the eve of the Day of Atonement, Reb Ezekiel kept closer watch than ever on the visitor. Not a minute passed but what he pressed on him another tidbit.

"Reb Naphthali, eat, I say. Every mouthful you swallow is written down in your heavenly account as a meritorious deed. Eat heartily and swell the account."

In the court of Kozmir the Day of Atonement was the merriest day of the year. [. . .]

All prayers were set to a happy chant in Kozmir, even the most doleful, even the martyrologies. The House of Prayer was jammed with Jews in prayer-shawls and white robes. Above them all towered the Rabbi, his head adorned with a skull-cap wrought with gold embroidery, the crown and glory of the congregation. His voice rang as loudly in the closing prayer of the Day of Atonement as it had done in the opening prayer of the evening before, though he had not tasted food or drink for twenty-four hours. Around him stood his dynasty, his sons and grandsons, all in silk and white satin, and their voices sustained him throughout the whole service. The melodious tumult of this choir was heard in town, in the hills, and in the village across the river; the congregation helped to swell it, and the day was observed with dancing as well as singing. Round the door of the House of Prayer stood the feminine half of the dynasty, the Rabbi's wife, his daughters, his daughters-in-law, his grand-daughters. They, too, were dressed in silk and satin; on their bosoms shone gold-embroidered coverings; on their heads wimples glittered with precious stones; and their lips moved piously in whispered prayer.

Reb Naphthali bent down to the earth in the fervour of his devotions. He longed to squeeze at least one tear from his sinful eyes, but all his efforts availed him nothing. The riot of song all about him deafened him, and he could not concentrate on one miserable thought.

When the Day of Atonement was over, the congregants took the stubs of the burning candles from the boxes of sand and went out into the synagogue yard to the Benediction of the Moon. The moon swam luminously in a clear sky, and the congregants rejoiced in her light.

"Welcome," they cried to her, dancing joyously. "Be thou a good sign and a bringer of good luck."

Reb Ezekiel stood in the midst of his Chasidim, radiant as the moon in the midst of the stars.

"Welcome!" he cried thunderously to Reb Naphthali, and took him by the hand as if he were about to draw him into a dance. But in that instant Reb Naphthali was seized with a violent trembling, and before anyone could take hold of him he had slipped to the ground.

The Chasidim dropped on the ground beside him, but when they felt his hands and face, these were as cold as the damp grass on which he lay. There was no sign of breath in the frail body.

Panic descended on the assembly. Hundreds of congregants tried to touch the body where it lay, wrapped in prayer-shawl and white robe. But those that were at the centre lifted up the body of Reb Naphthali, carried it into the House of Prayer, and laid it down on the pulpit, where the Scroll is laid for the reading of the Law.

Those that could not get into the House did not go to their homes, but remained standing, petrified, and some of them began to weep audibly.

The panic lasted only a minute or two.

The door of the Rabbi's room opened, and the Rabbi, his face as radiant as when he had stretched out his hand to Reb Naphthali and the latter had fallen to the ground, looked out above the congregation. He had withdrawn for a moment and he was back with the congregation. His voice rang out:

"If anyone wants to weep, let him take a row-boat and pass to the other side of the Vistula. There is no weeping in Kozmir."

Amazed, silent, the Chasidim followed the gesture of the Rabbi and filed into his room.

The table sparkled with gold and silver in the light of a hundred candles. Ranged along its centre were dusty bottles of wine and mead, each surrounded by a heap of grapes and pears and pomegranates.

The Chasidim seated themselves. The Rabbi drank, sang happily, and distributed morsels to his favourites. This night he was more generous than ever before. Children and grandchildren sat at the head of the table, snatched his gifts, and followed him in song.

The feasting lasted through the night, and only when the morning star was peeping in through the window did Mottye, the chief beadle, give the signal that the Rabbi was now prepared to make an utterance. The Chasidim crowded close to him, their hands upon one another's shoulders.

Many minutes passed before the Rabbi came to his utterance. He sat playing with the silver watch which lay in front of him on the table. He picked up a heavy bunch of grapes and moved it up and down as if he were estimating its weight. And throughout all this he chanted a Chasidic melody to himself.

When he had finished the melody and had let all the echoes die down about him, he opened his mouth and spoke:

"I wanted to teach him the great mystery of joyousness, but he was unable to grasp it."

He looked out of the window toward the House of Prayer, where the little body of Reb Naphthali, wrapped in prayer-shawl and white robe, lay on the pulpit, and he ended his utterance:

"He had sunk too far into habits of gloom, and there was no saving him."

Translated by Maurice Samuel.

Jacob Steinberg

1887–1947

The Hebrew and Yiddish writer Jacob Steinberg was born in Ukraine and at age fourteen moved to Odessa and then later to Warsaw, both centers for Hebrew literature at the turn of the century. He published stories and poems in Hebrew initially but from 1909 began writing extensively in Yiddish. However, when he settled in Tel Aviv in 1914, he stopped writing in Yiddish. He translated (and revised) many of his earlier Yiddish stories into Hebrew, including "The Blind Woman." The style of the Hebrew poetry he wrote in Palestine was unique: he was the only Hebrew poet living there who employed Ashkenazi pronunciation and stress. He also was known for his landmark essays on Yiddish and Hebrew writers.

The Blind Woman

1922

Hannah the blind woman was told before her wedding that her future husband was a widower in the tobacco business; at first they also assured her that this widower had been left with no children from his first wife. However, when that assurance was made, Hannah's mother remembered that the blind woman used to get angry at every lie that was told her—so the old woman began to speak copiously about the roomy house and the two children "who won't even take up any space in the house," and who were "quiet and easy like two doves."

"So help me God," the mother swore and rushed to distract her daughter with the matter of the house: "It's really a mansion, with the addition of a large plot of land; there's a courtyard, a large courtyard, because the house stands at the edge of the city; and this, too, my daughter: in the first days after your arrival there, don't walk far away from the house by yourself, because the place is at the edge of the town. The man is a tobacco merchant, and he lives among goyim—you'd be better off sitting at home."

The blind woman listened silently to her mother's many words. Her eyes were open, and her eyelashes didn't quiver, although the blind woman's heart raged within her: and after keeping silent the blind woman groped at the table with her hand once or twice and asked with repressed anger:

"How old is he?"

"So help me God, my daughter, the man is only thirty years old," the mother rushed to swear. "The marriage-broker swore to me about that. A year more or less. That has no importance, my daughter. Only so help me God."

The mother stopped talking. The blind woman stood without moving, and only her hand groped the edge of the table from time to time. It was clear that the blind woman's heart was raging within her, and she didn't believe her mother's words. The old woman didn't say any more. She only removed the blind woman's hand, which was still trembling, with great caution from the edge of the table, and her pursed lips whispered something—the dim whisper of a miserable mother.

On the first night after the wedding ceremony the blind woman waited until her husband fell into a slumber and began quietly to finger the hair of her husband's beard; and after doing that once or twice she already knew clearly that they had seduced her with a lie before the wedding: he was not thirty. The man they had given her for a husband was advanced in years. Her heart was full of fierce fury. She lay awake for a long time, and with every one of her husband's coughs, the blind woman's thoughts became clearer: "What is his occupation: is he a water-carrier, a rag-merchant, or a wood-cutter?" It was clear that a tobacco merchant wouldn't cough that way. . . . She turned from side to side in her anger, and her new nightgown, which had not yet been in water, rustled softly. Suddenly the blind woman slipped out of bed, and for a few minutes she crawled along the floor of the room, until her hand touched a pair of her husband's boots; for a moment the woman felt the rumpled, coarse boots, and then she threw them aside in fury. Judging by the boots, the blind woman described her husband's appearance to herself: a tall, gaunt Jew, who walked bent over, with a geriatric yarmulke, and heavily tromping legs beneath a long, patched gabardine.

She passed a long, sleepless night, and in the morning the blind woman didn't cease listening to her husband's steps, and after he left the house, she also went out after him, and with the silent steps of a blind person she sneaked after him over a long way. How he banged his staff on the hard earth of the courtyard, knock after knock. The blind woman knew that only a man advanced in years pounds so evenly with his thick staff. Who, then, was her husband, and what was his work? Now it was very clear to her, that they had told her a lie before her wedding: his trade was not in tobacco.

II

Only after the Sukkot holiday, when the rainy season began, and the members of the household clearly demonstrated to the blind woman that in a little while, as she was about to give birth, the jouncing of travel would be hard for her—only then did Hannah rise and go to her husband. The wagon entered the village at night, passed through the Jewish alleys, which were sunk in great silence, and then, step after step, the wagon passed through the marsh of the market. Here, too, there was silence. Not a dog barked. Only the watchman sounded measured knocking with two wooden staves, and the blind woman immediately guessed that here was the marketplace with the stores. In a little while the wagon began to go faster without turning right or left. On all sides the barking of dogs was heard, and the blind woman understood that now they were traveling through the long streets of the goyim. While thinking about that, Hannah remembered her mother's telling her that her husband's house was at the edge of the village settlement. But why was the trip so long? Now the wind had arisen, and the wagon was rolling heavily up the mountain—and this was a clear sign to her that the wagon had now left the boundary of the settlement. But finally the horses stopped walking, the driver got off and told her to sit and wait until he knocked on the window and woke up the people of the house. Hannah remained seated in the wagon, listening to the sound of the driver's steps, moving away from her. Then she closed her eyelids in fatigue, and suddenly she was shaken—the horses were standing in place, and a storm wind blew on her from all sides. Where was the wagon standing? In a field? But now from a distance she heard the driver knock on a window of the house. For a moment, the blind woman leaned her head into the hollow of the night, and immediately it became clear to her: that was how you knocked on a small window of a goy's house. The sound of a man knocking on the window of a Jewish house was entirely different. . . . So her husband lived like a goy, and they had told her he was a tobacco merchant! Suddenly the blind woman heard the voice of the driver shouting: "Mr. Israel! Mr. Israel!"—What was her husband like, if they called him "Mr. Israel! Mr. Israel"?

Finally that Mr. Israel came out, helped his wife climb down from the wagon, took her hand, and led her to his house. As they went down the corridor, the blind woman realized, as she walked, that it was a kind of broad passageway, common in the houses of goyim, and when the door was opened, and great warmth wrapped her face all at once—the blind woman thought once again that everything here was unlike among the Jews: apparently a cooking stove stood in the living room! In a moment the woman bent her head toward the crying of a child. "That's the little one"—her husband answered her, even though she hadn't uttered a questioning word. The man went out to prepare the samovar, and the blind woman began to walk to and fro in the room.

On her way the blind woman felt with her hands and met with two beds: one was unmade and cold, and in the other, while groping with her hands, she woke a child who started to cry loudly. The father rushed into the room, quieted the child, and sat his wife down at the table. When everyone was quiet in the house, the blind woman began to listen to the trees thrashing in the raging autumn wind. "Did a large garden really grow in front of our house?" As was her way, when it was hard for her to imagine something to herself, the blind woman closed her eyelids and wrinkled her forehead in thought.

Meanwhile her husband brought in the samovar and started to cut the sugar into small pieces with his knife. While he was doing that, a little piece of sugar fell on the floor—the man leaned over and picked it up with the groan of an old man. At that moment the blind woman groped on the table, found the knife, and examined it with her fingers, to see what it was like: was its handle thick, and made of bone, like the knives in Jewish homes? Some time passed, and her husband served Hannah a cup of tea, poured it into a bowl, and asked his wife:

"Shall I put it in your hand?"

Hannah blushed and answered: "I can drink without help."

The blind woman took a first sip, and her heart pounded, and the teacup trembled in her hand. She knew that her husband was fixing his eyes on her now and watching her drink. At last the tea spilled from the cup trembling in her hand and scorched the blind woman's knees. She gave in and agreed to drink the cup of tea from her husband's hand.

Suddenly, when her husband began to make the bed, the sound of loud knocking was heard at the window, and a voice shouted, "Mr. Israel! Mr. Israel!" Hannah, who had already begun taking off her clothes, stood pale and silent and couldn't understand why her husband walked so calmly and with such great moderation to open the door—but certainly something had happened, if they were knocking on the door at night! Hannah listened to the unclear conversation between her husband and the stranger. In the end she heard a sigh come from her husband's mouth—and the door closed.

"What happened?"—the blind woman asked, and her body, with only a nightgown on it, trembled all over.

Her husband told her that his aunt had fallen sick that night and they had come to call him. The blind woman was silent, and only her big eyes were wide open, and her face expressed astonishment—that was the emotion that filled her heart so often. Hannah went to bed right away, covered herself with the warm bedclothes, but she wasn't warm, and she trembled, trembled.

III

The oldest of the children knocked on the window-panes with his small hands. The blind woman, who was busy at that moment, hurried to the child and put her hand on his shoulder. But this time she didn't heed the boy's happiness as she felt with her hand or his knocking on the little window. For minute after minute the blind woman stood next to the boy and didn't try to speak with him, because he was slow of speech, even though he was already four years old. While standing there, the blind woman thought for a moment, that maybe an illness had befallen the child, and he was swaying and knocking the window in pain—but, as she thought, she passed her hand over his head and cheeks, and she realized right away that the child was healthy, not ill. But why hadn't the child learned to talk? Suddenly it occurred to her that her husband also spoke very little, and that it was his way to utter the few words that he spoke with a sigh. Certainly he dealt only with goyim. The boy was also slow of speech because nobody talked to him.—This was because their house stood alone outside the settlement. But while she was thinking those thoughts, the blind woman didn't forget her astonishment at the child's knocking. "Why was he standing near the window? Did he see something outside?"

She went to the window and stuck her ear against the glass. Silence. The silence was so great that the blind woman could hear the cawing of a crow that flapped its wings as it flew by. Minutes passed, and Hannah didn't move as she listened to the silence. It seemed to her that something had changed outside, that everything had become quieter, and a tranquil wind was floating outside, as in her mother's house on the eve of the Sabbath, when she sprinkled sand on the floor. The longer the blind woman stood, the more her mind pictured the change taking place outside: the first snow was falling without a sound. That the boy had knocked on the window—that was also a sign that snow was falling. Hannah wanted to ask her husband, but he wasn't in the house then. In general he stayed in the house a lot, but sometimes someone would knock on the window and a voice would call from outside, "Mr. Israel! Mr. Israel!" Then her husband would go outside for many hours, and when he returned he would always wash his hands in water. . . . Where did he go? She didn't ask him about that, because she spoke very little with her husband. He brought all the things needed for the house from the city by himself, and she didn't meet with people at all— so what would she talk about with her husband?

The blind woman moved away and headed toward the stove, to taste the food. Suddenly a noise was heard outside. She remained standing where she was and listened to the sound of steps. Was it her husband coming? But many steps came mixed together, and that was a sign to the blind woman that a group of people was passing close to their house, but where had a crowd of people come from suddenly, walking together? Were they goyim returning to the village from the city? But Hannah could recognize the steps of goyim: they were measured and heavy. True, it was easy for her to swear that now she was hearing the sound of Jews' steps. The blind woman kept listening, and she remembered that this was not the first time she had heard the sound of many steps from outside. What was the meaning of this? Hannah picked the boy up toward the window and said to him: "Yossele, look and see, who is walking outside?" The boy became merry from pleasure and knocked on the window. The blind woman listened to the boy's laughter, and it seemed to her that she should heed the boy's movements and the sound of his laughter, and then she would be able to understand what was happening outside. It would be good if she herself went outside—she had been yearning for the sound of a Jew's steps for many days—but walking was hard for her now: she was already in advanced pregnancy, and because of that she had stopped going in and out.

Hannah kept standing at the window and yearning for a human voice; she greatly desired to hear a person's steps up close . . . and now the door opened, and her husband entered the house. Before saying anything to his wife, he removed a handful of bronze coins from his pocket, scattered them on the table, and counted them one by one, growling his usual growls. By the sound of the coins, the blind woman knew that her husband was counting pennies. Hannah waited until her husband finished counting his money, and then she asked him a question:

"Israel, maybe you know, who were the people who ran by the house?"

The husband answered with a growl: "What do you care?"

The blind woman kept inquiring: "There was a lot of noise. Maybe a fire broke out?"

This time the husband replied with an angry growl: "You don't have to know. Sit at home—that's enough!"

Hannah lowered her eyebrows, as she always did when she was angry but didn't want to say anything. But now she heard that her husband was walking toward the door, and she asked:

"When will you eat lunch?"

From the door Hannah heard her husband's growl: "I have more important things to do than lunch," and the man went out right away and closed the door behind him. Groping her way, Hannah went to the corner where her husband usually left his staff, and after a moment of searching her hand touched the staff, which was standing in its regular place. This was a sign to the blind woman that her husband had not gone on a long walk, but rather that he had gone to visit a Jew who lived in the neighborhood. Hannah felt the length and thickness of the staff, with her head lowered and her brow furrowed: Where did her husband get such a long, thick staff?

IV

At the beginning of winter, with the arrival of cold days, the blind woman bore a daughter. Night after night the midwife would take the baby out of Hannah's bed and lay it in a different place, and a few days passed before the blind woman realized that the old woman was afraid that the blind mother might smother the infant in her sleep. But Hannah laughed in her heart when she realized that. Didn't she know everything that happened in the house, although her eyes did not see? On the third day after the birth something happened, because the old midwife served her soup in a bowl, and in a moment Hannah picked up the infant and lay her far from herself, so that her hand or foot wouldn't

touch her—and then the old lady, who was watching the blind woman's actions and movements, thought that the mother wasn't completely blind, and that her eyes could see some light of day.

Hannah's face had a new look when she rose from giving birth; the repose that had always infused her face grew sevenfold. Until then the blind woman had spoken little, but after the day she rose from the birth bed she almost stopped speaking at all, except for tunes she hummed at the baby's cradle. As soon as she sat by her daughter's cradle, the two boys, her husband's children, would rush over to her and stand at her side, one boy on either side. Hannah placed one hand on one boy's shoulder and her other hand on the other boy's head, and her mouth sang the songs she knew. Sometimes a long time passed that way, until the blind woman's husband would return home and, as he entered, growl his usual growl. Hearing that growl, Hannah would always knit her brow slightly, because she couldn't tell from a distance whether her husband was angry or not.

Before the Purim holiday, the cold increased greatly. Once Hannah went out to the hallway in the morning to bring in some firewood, and the wind, which was very strong outside, blew the door open, and assailed the woman with fierce cold, as she continued to gather pieces of wood with hands riddled with cold. But when the cold riddled her flesh, the blind woman thought in her heart that the wind was so fierce because nothing could stop it, because their house stood in a field. For a moment Hannah stopped picking up the wood, took a few steps toward the open door, and stood with the bundle of wood in her arms, listening to the whoosh of the wind in the field. The snow hit her in the face, and Hannah listened with attention to the swish of the snow falling at her feet and the whir of the wind bearing the snow and throwing it far away. It was clear to Hannah that an empty place extended all around the house, and with every puff of the wind, the blind woman inclined her head and listened: it seemed to her that something stood before their house and blocked the blowing of the wind. What was that thing? Now the winter was coming to an end, and with the warm days, the blind woman thought in her heart, she would walk all the way around the house.

Now the ice began to melt, and all day long the sound of icicles falling from the roof was heard in the house. On that first day of the melting of the snow, at lunchtime, Mr. Israel opened his mouth to his wife and said, with his regular growl:

"Diphtheria is spreading in town."

A few days later Hannah heard a new pronouncement from his mouth:

"Babies are dying every day."

Hearing those words a piece of bread stuck in the blind woman's throat, and great astonishment suffused her face: Why was he saying those things and arousing fear and panic in her heart? From that day on the blind woman began to do less housework. She sat next to the baby's cradle all the time, and every minute she would pass her hand over the baby's face, to see whether she was well. From time to time the blind woman would lean over the back of the cradle and listen to the sound of the baby girl's breathing. It was clear to Hannah that it would be easy for her to tell whether even a slight illness affected the child. Every day, when her husband came home from the city, she began a conversation with him and asked about the disease that was spreading in the city among the babies. The man, Mr. Israel, growled and answered:

"Like flies they're gathered up, the infants."

The blind woman, hearing her husband's words, spoke in a groan, with impatience, lowered her eyebrows, and cold gripped her flesh. Why was he growling that way about the dead children? Did he get any benefit from it?

Meanwhile the warm days came. Puddles of water began to accumulate outdoors; the man, when he returned from the city, was covered with mud up to his knees—the blind woman knew that by his heavy steps. Every morning the birds chirped outside the window, and the bigger boy suddenly became a dancer, and he also babbled in front of the window all day. Only the blind woman's mood was dark as she sat next to the girl's crib, though she had not told her husband that her heart felt something bad. Suddenly the words that had been hidden in her heart for several days burst out of Hannah's mouth: "Look, please Israel, at the baby." The woman spoke to her husband when he returned home once and was cleaning the mud off his boots. "It seems to me that her breathing is heavy."

While the blind woman was speaking, great fear fell upon her: At that moment it became clear to her that the girl was sick. She remained frozen where she was standing. Her eyebrows were lowered, and her fingers gripped each other like a vise. But her husband didn't say a thing. He placed his staff in the corner reserved for it and began to wash his hands, taking too much time. At that moment Hannah knew that her daughter's illness didn't arouse any fear in her husband's heart.

For a few days the baby lay sick, and Mr. Israel would come and go as usual, and even when he was present in the house, he busied himself with all sorts of things and sometimes would stand for a long time, cutting the sugar into many little pieces. The blind woman was sunk in her sorrow. She didn't light the stove, and no food entered her mouth. From day to day her heart came to hate her husband: Why was he at ease as always, and why were his steps as measured and heavy as ever? Once it happened that the blind woman was unable to bear her rage, and she stormed upon her husband with screaming and howling:

"Murderer! You have eyes! Tell me what's the matter with the baby!"

With a growl the man fled from the blind woman's hands. She was silent, listening to her husband's steps: she wanted to know whether he had approached the girl's cradle, because the baby's heavy wheezing could be heard in the whole room. But that didn't happen. The man took his staff from the corner and went out of the house.

At night, when the man's snoring could be heard all over the house, and from outside the knocking of icicles falling from the roof could be heard, the woman sat for long hours next to the cradle and listened to the baby's breathing. The blind woman already knew that the child would die, but she didn't have the strength to cry anymore. Only her lips moved all the time, and she whispered softly: "May the gravedigger come. I won't give him the baby. May he come." While the blind woman sat with her head down and her lips moving, it seemed to her that she had passed many years next to the baby's cradle, and that she would sit in that place until the end of her days. From outside the banging of the icicles could still be heard, but the man's heavy snoring suddenly stopped. The blind woman lowered her head even more, her brain empty of any thought, her heart as though turned to stone, and slowly, slowly she sank into sleep. Now she shook herself and leaned over the back of the cradle. Silence, and the baby's breathing couldn't be heard. For a few moments the blind woman kept listening, and suddenly she leaped up and shouted out loud.

The blind woman howled all night long, but she sat next to the cradle alone, because her husband came and went by turns, and Hannah, who was immersed in weeping, didn't notice him coming or going. At dawn the blind woman stopped weeping, because she was very weary, but she didn't move away from the cradle. Her hair was disheveled, her head shook constantly, and her lips also moved, whispering from time to time, "May the gravedigger come, may he come, please." Suddenly she put her hand in the cradle, wishing to touch the dead baby's body once more. But the baby was no longer in the cradle. A dreadful shriek left the blind woman's throat: "Israel, where is the baby?" But no answer came. Something like the pangs of death attacked Hannah as she made her way to the door, shouting time after time: "Israel, where is the baby?" Outside, in front of the house, she stopped walking and stood in silence. It was morning. No wind blew. A drop of water from the roof fell on her face, and she shook herself. The blind woman bent her head and pricked her ear toward the field. It seemed to her that from far away, from the field, the sound of her husband's steps was coming. She moved from her place and dragged herself toward the sound of those steps. For a moment she moved forward at a run, but she immediately tripped on something and fell to the earth. She picked herself up and started taking step after step, but her feet kept bumping into stones. Suddenly her whole body struck a large stone, and her fingers groped. A dreadful shriek burst from the blind woman's throat: she realized that her feet stood in the cemetery.

Translated by Jeffrey M. Green.

Other works by Steinberg: *Kol kitvei Yaakov Shteinberg* (1957).

Kurt Tucholsky

1890–1935

The left-wing Berlin-born journalist, satirist, critic, and poet Kurt Tucholsky studied law but turned to journalism even before completing his degree. His service in the German army turned him into a pacifist and a bitter critic of nationalism, militarism, authoritarianism, and human stupidity. After 1924, he spent most of his time abroad, mostly in France, Switzerland, and Sweden, where he killed himself in 1935, overwhelmed and depressed by events in Germany. Although he left the Jewish community in 1911, he remained unable to marginalize his Jewishness and wrote sixteen caustic monologues about the fictional Herr Wendriner, whom he cast as the archetypal materialistic, ultra-assimilationist, spiritually empty bourgeois Jew of the Weimar period.

Herr Wendriner Makes a Phone Call
1922

On the day of Walter Rathenau's funeral in 1922, all mail and telephone service in Germany was suspended between 2:00 and 2:10 pm

"If he won't honor our invoice, I'll simply give him a buzz. Put the envelopes on the chair for now. What's Skalitzer's exchange? Königstadt? Just wait, boy, till I. . . . What's that? Huh? What's the matter? Operator! Why don't you answer? How do you like that—she doesn't say why she doesn't answer. Operator! Doesn't the phone work? Miss Tinschmann, whatsamatter with this phone? Is it out of order? How often have I told you . . . ? What? What is it? Service suspended? What's the meaning of this? Why. . . ? Oh, on account of Rathenau. Thanks, you can go now. . . . On account of Rathenau. Very well. That's only fair. The man was a merchant prince, our greatest statesman. Can't deny that. A disgrace they shot him. A real decent person. Knew his old man well—that's what I call merchants! Well, they had quite a memorial program for him in the Reichstag. Most impressive. A terrific editorial this morning—first-rate. Yes, the government is going to take some pretty strong measures—it has already issued an order. Shooting him from a car—outrageous! The police ought to. . . . Operator! Guess the ten minutes aren't up yet. Must have been dead shots, those fellows. Officers, maybe. . . . Can't really imagine that, though. . . . Had all the boys from Walter's regiment over for dinner that time, didn't I? Such nice, high-class people. Terrific personalities, some of them. I got a big kick out of it when the boy became a reserve officer. Operator! The longest ten minutes I ever saw. Operator! If they're on strike one minute more than ten, I've got a good mind to send in a complaint. Operator! I've got to talk to old Skalitzer. A hell of an idea to shut off the phone because of that. That won't bring him back. Let 'em spread out the taxes more fairly, that would be more in the spirit of the deceased. Operator! Who's going to shut off the phone when *I'm* gone? Nobody! Crazy idea, to shut off the phone! How'm I supposed to get through to Skalitzer now? By the time I do, the old boy will be out to lunch. Scan'alous! Those people want more pay, that's all. What kind of trick is that, to shut off the phone right in front of your nose, in broad daylight. All sorts of things happened under the Kaiser, God knows—but I've never seen anything like this! It's an outrage! This is a public nuisance! Let 'em kill each other or not—but they've got to keep it out of our business! And another thing, a Jew shouldn't make such a spectacle of himself. That only stirs up anti-Semitism. Since the ninth of November we haven't had law and order in this country. Is it necessary to shut off the phones? Who's going to pay me damages if I don't reach Skalitzer? Operator! Just listen—they're making a demonstration outside. Look—red flags yet—just what I like! What are they singing? Operator! They'll carry on like this until there's another revolution! Operator! They can take the whole Republic and. . . . Operator! Operator! My political principles are. . . . Operator! It's about time! Operator! Give me Königstadt . . . !"

Translated by Harry Zohn and Karl F. Ross.

Other works by Tucholsky: *Deutschland, Deutschland über Alles: A Picturebook* (1972); *Berlin! Berlin! Dispatches from the Weimar Republic* (2013).

Semyon Yushkevich

1868–1927

Born in Odessa, Semyon Yushkevich (Iushkevich) was a prolific and popular author and playwright of Jewish literature in the Russian language. Writing in a neorealist style, Yushkevich was known for his stark and gritty and often controversial depictions of Jewish urban life, poverty, violence, and sexuality. Widely published in a range of journals and in book form, Yushkevich is credited with bringing the Jewish Question into the mainstream of Russian literature as well as beginning a new era of Jewish literature in Russian, and was invited early on in his literary career to join the prestigious Moscow-based group known as Sreda (Wednesday). After the Bolshevik Revolution, he briefly immigrated to the United States in 1921, where a number of his plays were translated into Yiddish and staged to popular acclaim. He eventually settled in Paris.

Dudka

1922

He married Sonechka early, out of love. He loved her passionately only for the first two years. Then he lost interest but didn't even notice it. He wasn't thinking about love and women as a rule. He didn't have time for it! But when he "made" a hundred thousand, his heart was jolted. Women started to materialize out of thin air. Here, a fresh, pink cheek with a dimple was emerging, there, a lavish feminine arm was looming, exposed up to the shoulder, or a bare neck was sparkling with its whiteness. . . . These and other seductive images disturbed his imagination.

And so it happened. . . . He was drinking his midday coffee at Leybakh's. A diamond was shining like morning dew on his simple but expensive tie. Close to his heart, a Patek Philippe watch was ticking. An elegant gold chain was resting on his vest.

She came in and gracefully took a seat by a table. Dudka felt a heavy blow to his heart.

He immediately reminded himself, however, that there are twenty thousand in his pocket for coffee and kerosene, and felt encouraged.

"Most importantly, is she Jewish or Russian?" he was asking himself. "I prefer and desire a Russian one . . . I know what a Jewish woman is, but I've never had an affair with a Russian. Dudka, you deserve an affair with a Russian woman at this point. Remember that you have twenty thousand and don't be an idiot. But she's so pretty! Russian eyes, not like my Sonechka's, but really, purely Russian. Jewish eyes, after all, always express suffering! Yes, most definitely, these are Russian eyes," he decided, "the eyes of the Russians of the steppes, grey and devilishly beautiful. . . . I want a Russian kiss," he said to himself with passion. . . . "Dudka! But what will Sonechka say if she finds out? It would be a nightmare! A nightmare!"

"Ah, I'm so tired of Sonechka all the time," he dismissed the tiresome thought, "and actually, I have never cheated on her! When I do cheat, that's when I will pay the price. There it is again, Jewish suffering. This has to be done cheerfully, Dudka!"

"Very well, cheerfully, I agree," Dudka thought, "but how would I get to know her? How do I begin? Should I smile? Just smile for no reason? This Russian woman will think I'm too bold. She may even yell at me. Oh my God, such a mouth she has! Such wonderful Russian teeth! These are your teeth, Dudka, in her mouth!"

He jumped up abruptly, as if he were stabbed in his side; he made a step toward her and, as aristocratically as he could, picked up the kerchief that she had dropped . . .

"My lady," said he, passing her the kerchief in such a way that she would notice his three-carat diamond,

"My lady, may I have the pleasure of handing you your kerchief?"

"Thank you," said the stranger in a silvery voice, bowing graciously to Dudka.

"I would like," Dudka said gallantly, straightening the diamond on his tie, so as to draw her attention to it, "to pick up your fallen kerchief for all eternity."

"You would tire of it very quickly," the stranger replied, smiling indulgently at such a strange desire.

"You may be wrong, my lady," said Dudka, and was terribly happy and truly prepared in that moment to pick up the kerchief innumerable times. . . . "Test me. . . ."

"No, I am not as cruel as that," she replied harmoniously, as her fork pierced the steak, which the server brought her . . .

"Oh, I don't doubt that," Dudka said gallantly, stealthily approaching her in his mind, as if he were approaching a dose of painkillers that also promised him a profit of five thousand.

"A Russian woman," he was passionately thinking at the same time, falling all the deeper in love with the stranger. "A true Russian—not a hot face, as it is with Jewish women. It is cold, frozen, and yet it warms you up from head to toe."

The conversation was taking off. Dudka, using purely Russian expressions, asked for permission to sit by her table, and when he was granted permission, he took out, as if casually, the Patek from his vest pocket, innocently looked at the watch and said:

"Out of all watches, my lady, my favorite are Patek watches. Perhaps you've heard of it, a business in Geneva. It's terribly difficult to get one of them these days, but I managed to. . . . And reasonably . . . for fifteen hundred. Stylish, wouldn't you say? Very compact. You can hardly tell it's a watch."

He let her hold the watch, leaned in closer as she was looking at it, and he fell even deeper in love with her, having smelled her hair. Then, having lost his head for a moment, he invited her for a cup of Turkish coffee. And after the coffee, some ice cream. All this was favorably accepted. He seemed preoccupied while eating the ice cream. How best to share his feelings? If he were sitting with a Jewish woman, everything would be settled in a couple of minutes. He knows his own people. But a Russian? Damned if he knows what he can talk to her about. Surely, she doesn't understand the Jewish soul, raised on misery. Russians cannot stand this misery! And precisely in this must lie the Russian woman's charm. She is easy in other ways as well. Just try to get

with a Jewish woman! Dudka tried once and had to get married! But with a Russian woman, one can say "I have kissed you, I no longer wish to kiss you, and so farewell!" But a Jewish woman will call her father, her mother, and all her relatives after just one kiss. All this is fine, but how can I interest her, how can I attract her? Here I must play on the chords of a Russian heart!

"What are you thinking about?" the stranger asked harmoniously.

In reply, Dudka quietly laughed and said:

"I will never tell you. It is unthinkable for me to confide my thoughts to you!"

"Are these thoughts so terrible?" the stranger was smiling in turn.

"Yes," Dudka said with sudden sharpness and determination. "I was thinking that ice cream, for example, is a definitely Russian dessert. Jews could not have invented ice cream. Jews eat plum or raisin compote and k . . . k . . . pudding. In any case," he added, looking at her, "I have to say that I prefer the Russian to the Jewish, even though I am a Jew myself."

"Well played!" he praised himself.

"Why is that?" the stranger was surprised.

"Such is our character," he said humbly, burning with love. "Let's take Jewish behavior as an example. Have you ever heard two Jews talking? You may think, *gevald*, they're being murdered! And what about ten Russians? You can't even hear them. And so much more! Who is always conspicuous? A Jew! You can't even hear a Russian! Among the speculators, for instance! Russians are the most desperate speculators and everybody knows that they cashed in hundreds of millions, but have you ever heard of a Russian speculator? Jews also cashed in, though a thousand times less, but everyone is talking about them! And why is that? Because these fools are too conspicuous; they yell, scream, holler; on the streets, they don't walk but leap about! I have to admit, I love Russians."

"I am talking like a scoundrel," Dudka thought, "but how can I not be a scoundrel with her? And no one can hear anyway, and she may like me. All Russians are antisemites, right? My God, such eyes she has! Such lips!"

"Excuse me," she said, "but you are an antisemite!"

"I'll tell her that I'm an antisemite," thought Dudka, "What do I care? Nobody will sue me for it!"

"Yes, I am an antisemite," he said with nobility. "We Jews are not tolerant of our people's flaws. You, Russians, are much more forgiving toward your people than we are."

"It seems that you took me for a Russian," the stranger broke into laughter. "But you are mistaken. I am from a shtetl . . . near Bender!"

"Really," Dudka exclaimed with amazement, "What do you know? I would never have guessed! Really?" he said again, having already lost interest in her and looking into her face.

And all of a sudden, it was as if a screen was lifted from his eyes. Real Jewish eyes, expressing eternal suffering! How did he not recognize them immediately? And her face is hot, Jewish.

"An affair with a Jewish woman!" he thought with horror. "Even if she was as beautiful as Venus, I wouldn't want to! She will pour sulfuric acid on my Sonechka if she lets me kiss her even once. She probably has dozens of aunts and uncles, two grandmothers, cousins. . . . She may demand my hundred thousand too. I have to get out of here!"

He rose, disappointed, sadly paid for the coffee and ice cream, and said goodbye quite unceremoniously. Does he have to be ceremonious with a Jew?

"Ah, you, Dudka," he was cursing himself on the street. "You didn't recognize a Jewish woman! Idiot!"

Translated by Alexandra Hoffman.

Other works by Yushkevich: *Raspad* (1895); *Evrei* (1904); *Leon Drei*, 3 vols. (1908–1919).

Isaac Babel

How Things Were Done in Odessa
1923

I was the one who began.

"Reb Arye-Leib," I said to the old man. "Let's talk about Benya Krik. Let's talk about his lightning-quick beginning and his terrible end. Three shadows block the path of my thoughts. There is Froim Grach. The steel of his actions—doesn't it bear comparison to the power of the King? There is Kolka Pakovsky. The rage of that man had everything it takes to rule. And could not Chaim Drong tell when a star was on the rise? So why was Benya Krik the only one to climb to the top of the ladder while everyone else was clinging to the shaky rungs below?"

Reb Arye-Leib remained silent as he sat on the cemetery wall. Before us stretched the green calm of the graves. A man thirsting for an answer must stock up

with patience. A man in possession of facts can afford to carry himself with aplomb. That is why Arye-Leib remained silent as he sat on the cemetery wall. Finally he began his tale:

"Why him? Why not the others, you want to know? Well then, forget for a while that you have glasses on your nose and autumn in your heart. Forget that you pick fights from behind your desk and stutter when you are out in the world! Imagine for a moment that you pick fights in town squares and stutter only among papers. You are a tiger, you are a lion, you are a cat. You can spend the night with a Russian woman, and the Russian woman will be satisfied by you. You are twenty-five years old. If the sky and the earth had rings attached to them, you would grab these rings and pull the sky down to the earth. And your papa is the carter Mendel Krik. What does a papa like him think about? All he thinks about is downing a nice shot of vodka, slugging someone in their ugly mug, and about his horses—nothing else. You want to live, but he makes you die twenty times a day. What would you have done if you were in Benya Krik's shoes? You wouldn't have done a thing! But he did. Because he is the King, while you only thumb your nose at people when their back is turned!

"He, Benchik, went to Froim Grach, who even back then peered at the world with only one eye and was just what he is now. And Benya told Froim, 'Take me on. I want to come on board your ship. The ship I end up on will do well by me.'

"Grach asked him, 'Who're you, where d'you come from, what's your bread and butter?'

"'Try me, Froim,' Benya answered, 'and let's stop wasting time spreading kasha on the table.'

"'Fine, we won't waste time spreading kasha on the table,' Grach said. 'I'll try you.'

"And the gangsters called a council together to decide about Benya Krik. I wasn't at that council, but word has it that they did call together a council. The elder back then was the late Lyovka Bik.

"'Anyone know what's going on under Benchik's hat?' the late Bik asked.

"And one-eyed Grach gave his opinion.

"'Benya talks little, but he talks with zest. He talks little, but you want that he'll say more.'

"'If that's so, we'll try him out on Tartakovsky,' the late Bik pronounced.

"'We'll try him out on Tartakovsky,' the council decided, and those who still housed a trace of conscience turned red when they heard this decision. Why did they turn red? If you listen, you'll find out.

"Tartakovsky was known as 'Yid-and-a-Half' or 'Nine-Raids.' They called him 'Yid-and-a-Half' because there wasn't a single Jew who had as much chutzpah or money as Tartakovsky had. He was taller than the tallest Odessa policeman, and heavier than the fattest Jewess. And they called Tartakovsky 'Nine-Raids' because the firm of Lyovka Bik and Company had launched not eight raids and not ten, but exactly nine raids against his business. To Benya, who was not yet King, fell the honor of carrying out the tenth raid on Yid-and-a-Half. When Froim informed Benya of this, Benya said yes, and left, slamming the door behind him. Why did he slam the door? If you listen, you'll find out.

"Tartakovsky has the soul of a murderer, but he's one of us. He sprang forth from us. He is our blood. He is our flesh, as if one mama had given birth to us. Half of Odessa works in his stores. Not to mention, his own Moldavankans have given him quite a bit of grief. They abducted him twice and held him for ransom, and once, during a pogrom, they buried him with chanters. The Slobodka thugs were beating up Jews on Bolshaya Arnautskaya. Tartakovsky ran away from them and came across the funeral march with chanters on Sofiyskaya Street.

"'Who are they burying with chanters?' he asked.

"The passersby told him that Tartakovsky was being buried. The procession marched to the Slobodka Cemetery. Then our boys yanked a machine gun out of the coffin and started shooting at the Slobodka thugs. But Yid-and-a-Half had not foreseen this. Yid-and-a-Half got the fright of his life. What boss in his place would not have been frightened?

"A tenth raid on a man who had already been buried once was a crass deed. Benya, who back then wasn't yet the King, knew this better than anyone else. But he said yes to Grach and on that very same day wrote Tartakovsky a letter, typical of those letters:

Most esteemed Rubin Osipovich,

I would be grateful if by the Sabbath you could place by the rainwater barrel a . . . , and so on. Should you choose to refuse, which you have opted to do lately, a great disappointment in your family life awaits you.

Respectfully yours,

Ben Zion Krik

"Tartakovsky, not one to dither, was quick to answer:

Benya,

If you were an idiot, I would write you as to an idiot. But from what I know of you, you aren't one, and may the Lord prevent me from changing my mind. You, as is plain to see, are acting like a boy. Is it possible that you are not aware that this year the crop in Argentina has been so good that we can stand on our heads but we still can't unload our wheat? And I swear to you on a stack of Bibles that I'm sick and tired of having to eat such a bitter crust of bread and witness such trouble after having worked all my life like the lowliest carter. And what do I have to show for my life sentence of hard labor? Ulcers, sores, worries, and no sleep! Drop your foolish thoughts, Benya.

Your friend, a far better one than you realize,

Rubin Tartakovsky

"Yid-and-a-Half had done his part. He had written a letter. But the mail didn't deliver it to the right address. Getting no answer, Benya became angry. The following day he turned up at Tartakovsky's office with four friends. Four masked youths with revolvers burst into the room.

"'Hands up!' they shouted, waving their pistols.

"'Not so loud, Solomon!' Benya told one of the youths, who was yelling louder than the rest. 'Don't get so jumpy on the job!' and he turned to the shop assistant, who was white as death and yellow as clay, and asked him:

"'Is Yid-and-a-Half in the factory?'

"'He's not in the factory,' said the shop assistant, whose family name was Muginshtein, his first name Josif, and who was the unmarried son of Aunt Pesya, the chicken seller on Seredinskaya Square.

"'So who's in charge when the boss is out?' they asked poor Muginshtein.

"'I'm in charge when the boss is out,' the shop assistant said, green as green grass.

"'In that case, with God's help, please open the safe!' Benya ordered, and a three-act opera began.

"Nervous Solomon stuffed money, papers, watches, and jewelry into a suitcase—the late Josif Muginshtein stood in front of him with his hands in the air, while Benya told stories from the life of the Jewish people.

"'Well, ha! If he likes playing Rothschild,' Benya said about Tartakovsky, 'then let him roast in hell! I ask you, Muginshtein, as one asks a friend: he gets my business letter—so how come he can't take a five-kopeck tram to come visit me at home, drink a shot of vodka with my family, and eat what God has seen fit to send us? What stopped him from baring his soul to me? Couldn't he have said—Benya, you know, such and such, but here's my balance sheet, just give me a couple of days to catch my breath, to get things rolling—don't you think I'd have understood? Pigs at a trough might not see eye to eye, but there is no reason why two grown men can't! Do you see what I'm saying, Muginshtein?'

"'I see what you're saying,' Muginshtein answered, lying, because he was at a loss as to why Yid-and-a-Half, a respected, wealthy man, one of the foremost men in town, should want to take a tram so he could have a bite to eat with the family of Mendel Krik, a carter.

"But all the time misfortune was loitering beneath the windows, like a beggar at dawn. Misfortune burst loudly into the office. And though this time it came in the guise of the Jew Savka Butsis, it was as drunk as a water carrier.

"'Ooh, ooh, ah!' Savka the Jew shouted. 'I'm sorry I'm so late, Benchik!' And he stamped his feet and waved his hands. Then he fired, and the bullet hit Muginshtein in the stomach.

"Are words necessary here? There was a man, and now there's none. An innocent bachelor, living his life like a little bird on a branch, and now he's dead from sheer idiocy. In comes a Jew looking like a sailor and doesn't shoot at a bottle in a fairground booth to win a prize—he shoots at a living man! Are words necessary here?

"'Everyone out!' Benya shouted, and as he ran out last, managed to tell Butsis, 'On my mother's grave, Savka, you'll be lying next to him!'

"So tell me, a young gentleman like you who cuts coupons on other people's bonds, how would you have acted in Benya Krik's position? You wouldn't know what to do? Well, he did! That's why he was King, while you and I are sitting here on the wall of the Second Jewish Cemetery, holding up our hands to keep the sun out of our eyes.

"Aunt Pesya's unfortunate son didn't die right away. An hour after they got him to the hospital, Benya turned up. He had the senior doctor called in and the nurse, and, without taking his hands out of the pockets of his cream-colored pants, told them. 'I have a whole lot of interest that your patient, Josif Muginshtein, recovers. Just in case, let me introduce myself—Ben Zion Krik. Give him camphor, air cushions, a private room, from the depths of your heart! If you don't, then every doc-

tor here, even if they're doctors of philosophy, will be doled out six feet of earth!'

"And yet, Muginshtein died that same night. It was only then that Yid-and-a-Half raised hell in all Odessa. 'Where do the police begin and Benya end?' he wailed.

"'The police end where Benya begins,' levelheaded people answered, but Tartakovsky wouldn't calm down, and to his amazement saw a red automobile with a music box for a horn playing the first march from the opera *I Pagliacci* on Seredinskaya Square. In broad daylight the car raced over to the little house in which Aunt Pesya lived. Its wheels thundered, it spat smoke, gleamed brassily, reeked of gasoline, and honked arias on its horn. A man jumped out of the automobile and went into the kitchen where little Aunt Pesya was writhing on the earthen floor. Yid-and-a-Half was sitting on a chair waving his arms. 'You ugly hooligan!' he shouted, when he saw the man. 'You damn bandit, may the earth spit you out! A nice style you've picked for yourself, going around murdering live people!'

"'Monsieur Tartakovsky,' Benya Krik said to him quietly. 'For two days and nights I have been crying for the dear deceased as if he were my own brother. I know that you spit on my young tears. Shame on you, Monsieur Tartakovsky! What fireproof safe have you hidden your shame in? You had the heart to send a paltry hundred rubles to the mother of our dear deceased Josif. My hair, not to mention my brain, stood on end when I got word of this!'

"Here Benya paused. He was wearing a chocolate jacket, cream pants, and raspberry-red half boots.

"'Ten thousand down!' he bellowed. 'Ten thousand down, and a pension till she dies—may she live to be a hundred and twenty! If it's 'no,' then we leave this house together, Monsieur Tartakovsky, and go straight to my car!'

"Then they started arguing. Yid-and-a-Half swore at Benya. Not that I was present at this quarrel, but those who were, remember it well. They finally agreed on five thousand cash in hand, and fifty rubles a month.

"'Aunt Pesya!' Benya then said to the disheveled old woman rolling on the floor. 'If you want my life, you can have it, but everyone makes mistakes, even God! This was a giant mistake, Aunt Pesya! But didn't God Himself make a mistake when he settled the Jews in Russia so they could be tormented as if they were in hell? Wouldn't it have been better to have the Jews living in Switzerland, where they would've been surrounded by first-class lakes, mountain air, and Frenchmen galore?

Everyone makes mistakes, even God. Listen to me with your ears, Aunt Pesya! You're getting five thousand in hand and fifty rubles a month till you die—may you live to be a hundred and twenty! Josif's funeral will be first-class. Six horses like lions, two hearses with garlands, chanters from the Brodsky Synagogue, and Minkovsky himself will come to chant the burial service for your departed son!'

"And the funeral took place the next morning. Ask the cemetery beggars about this funeral! Ask the synagogue *shamases*, the kosher poultry sellers, or the old women from the Second Poorhouse! Such a funeral Odessa had never seen, nor will the world ever see the like of it. On that day the policemen wore cotton gloves. In the synagogues, draped with greenery, their doors wide open, the electricity was on. Black plumes swayed on the white horses pulling the hearse. Sixty chanters walked in front of the procession. The chanters were boys, but they sang with women's voices. The elders of the Kosher Poultry Sellers Synagogue led Aunt Pesya by the hand. Behind the elders marched the members of the Society of Jewish Shop Assistants, and behind the Jewish shop assistants marched the barristers, the doctors, and the certified midwives. On one side of Aunt Pesya were the chicken sellers from the Stary Bazaar, and on the other the esteemed dairymaids from the Bugayevka, wrapped in orange shawls. They stamped their feet like gendarmes on parade. From their broad hips came the scent of sea and milk. And behind them plodded Rubin Tartakovsky's workers. There were a hundred of them, or two hundred, or two thousand. They wore black frock coats with silk lapels, and new boots that squeaked like piglets in a sack.

"And now I will speak as God spoke on Mount Sinai from the burning bush! Take my words into your ears. Everything I saw, I saw with my own eyes, sitting right here on the wall of the Second Cemetery, next to lisping Moiseika and Shimshon from the funeral home. I, Arye-Leib, a proud Jew living among the dead, saw it with my own eyes.

"The hearse rolled up to the synagogue in the cemetery. The coffin was placed on the steps. Aunt Pesya was shaking like a little bird. The cantor climbed out of the carriage and began the funeral service. Sixty chanters supported him. And at that very moment the red automobile came flying around the corner. It was honking *I Pagliacci* and came to a stop. The people stood, silent as corpses. The trees, the chanters, the beggars stood silent. Four men got out from under the red roof, and with quiet steps carried to the hearse a wreath of

roses of a beauty never before seen. And when the funeral ended, the four men lifted the coffin onto their steel shoulders, and with burning eyes and protruding chests, marched with the members of the Society of Jewish Shop Assistants.

"In front walked Benya Krik, who back then nobody was yet calling the King. He was the first to approach the grave. He climbed onto the mound, and stretched out his arm.

"'What are you doing, young man?' Kofman from the Burial Brotherhood shouted, running up to him.

"'I want to give a speech,' Benya Krik answered.

"And he gave a speech. All who wanted to hear it heard it. I, Arye-Leib, heard it, as did lisping Moiseika, who was sitting next to me on the wall.

"'Ladies and gentlemen,' Benya Krik said. 'Ladies and gentlemen,' he said, and the sun stood above his head, like a guard with a rifle. 'You have come to pay your last respects to an honest toiler, who died for a copper half-kopeck. In my own name, and in the name of all those who are not present, I thank you. Ladies and gentlemen! What did our dear Josif see in his life? One big nothing! What did he do for a living? He counted someone else's money. What did he die for? He died for the whole working class. There are men who are already doomed to die, and there are men who still have not begun to live. And suddenly a bullet, flying toward the doomed heart, tears into Josif, when all he has seen of life is one big nothing. There are men who can drink vodka, and there are men who can't drink vodka but still drink it. The former get pleasure from the agony and joy, and the latter suffer for all those who drink vodka without being able to drink it. Therefore, ladies and gentlemen, after we have prayed for our poor Josif, I ask you to accompany Saveli Butsis, a man unknown to you but already deceased, to *his* grave.'

"Having finished his speech, Benya Krik came down from the mound. The people, the trees, and the cemetery beggars stood silent. Two gravediggers carried an unpainted coffin to an adjacent grave. The cantor, stuttering, ended the prayer. Benya threw the first spadeful of earth and walked over to Savka. All the barristers and ladies with brooches followed him like sheep. He had the cantor chant the full funeral rites for Savka, and sixty chanters sang with him. Savka had never dreamt of such a funeral—you can trust the word of Arye-Leib, an aged old man.

"Word has it that it was on that day that Yid-and-a-Half decided to close shop. Not that I myself was there. But I saw with my own eyes, the eyes of Arye-

Leib—which is my name—that neither the cantor, nor the choir, nor the Burial Brotherhood asked to get paid for the funeral. More I couldn't see, because the people quietly slipped away from Savka's grave and started running, as if from a fire. They flew off in carriages, in carts, and on foot. And the four men who had arrived in the red automobile left in it. The musical horn played its march, the car lurched and hurtled off.

"'The King!' lisping Moiseika, who always grabs the best seat on the wall, said, following the car with his eyes.

"Now you know everything. You know who was the first to pronounce the word 'King.' It was Moiseika. Now you know why he didn't call one-eyed Grach that, nor raging Kolka. You know everything. But what use is it if you still have glasses on your nose and autumn in your heart? . . ."

Translated by Peter Constantine.

Elisheva Bikhovsky
1888-1949

Elisheva Bikhovsky (or "Elisheva") was an ethnic Russian, non-Jewish Hebrew poet, and novelist born Elizaveta Zhirkov. Encountering Hebrew at first through chance glimpses at newspaper ads in the Jewish press, she began her writing career as a translator of Yiddish and Hebrew fiction into Russian and was a Russian-language poet in her own right on Jewish themes. In 1925, she moved to Palestine to take part in the nascent modern Hebrew–language cultural scene in Tel Aviv, and she met with significant acclaim as the "Ruth of the Volga" (although she never actually converted to Judaism) by fellow literati and the general populace alike. Her positive reception was short lived, however, and she lived in poverty for most of her final years. Later critics, on the contrary, have praised Elisheva for enriching Hebrew literature of the era with the starkly cosmopolitan themes of her writing, the stylistic innovation carried over from futurist and acmeist Russian poetry, and, perhaps most important, the feminist perspective she brought into all of her work.

An Unimportant Incident
1923

1

A shady incident took place in Moscow a few days before Easter. At noon, in the center of town, they seized an old Jew, poor and wretched, who was carrying a burlap sack on his back and in it the body of a child. A large crowd gathered around him, clamoring and arguing, voicing their opinion about the matter. And the matter, indeed, is very old and well known to all since time immemorial: every year, Jews kidnap and slaughter Christian children to use their blood for the baking of the Passover matzot. Nothing unusual. Still, the outcome of this incident was quite different from other such cases in the past. After all, this was the fifth year of the "New Order." The police dispersed the crowd, arresting a few of the loudest, and took the old Jew with them in order to investigate the matter. It turned out that the dead child was a Jewish boy, whose poor parents could not afford a proper funeral; the old man had agreed, for a few coins, to take the body to the Jewish cemetery; he put the body in a burlap sack and was on his way. [. . .]

A few days later, the case was brought before a judge, and a very interesting and amusing spectacle ensued: against the solemn backdrop of the court stood the ignoble and farcical accusers, who tried, in broad daylight, to resurrect and raise from the grave the long dead—the blood libel. The matter was resolved, the city was calm, and all were satisfied with the outcome. [. . .]

But she, Manya Libin, a "Soviet girl," one of many like her, now walking to her place of work, as she does every morning, is downcast and somber. Even the spring sun has dimmed in the sky, and the sky itself is devoid of color and luster; stifling dust permeates the air, and the wheels of the carts clank louder than ever. The passersby, as always, are lowly and nasty, and if one of them happens to brush against her, she shrinks away with disgust.

And it seems to her that this is how it will always be, for all eternity! [. . .]

Indeed, something happened to her last night, very small and insignificant, and it happened precisely during those cherished evening hours, while visiting her friend Vera. [. . .]

4

The shady insignificant incident—about the Jew being caught with a dead child in his burlap sack—brought about another incident, just as shady and insignificant. It occurred in Vera's room, and it embittered Manya's life and dimmed the spring sun in the sky.

It happened the night before, a few days after the old Jew had been brought before the judge. The spectacle, still in the news, was a favorite topic of conversation, and those who had gathered at Vera's were no different. After they told and retold the story, enjoying the tragi-comic "drama" of the old "accused" and his preposterous "accusers," the conversation casually turned to a broader and more precarious subject. They began discussing the matter of the blood libel in general terms. They wondered whence this belief that had taken hold among the nations of the world—what were its sources? A relation of Vera's, a young scholar who specialized in the history of faiths, began by giving a lengthy talk about the strange customs, the many cults and amazing beliefs one encountered when studying ancient civilizations. It was evident that he was trying to impress on the listeners the depths of his scholarship and his scientific approach. He provided precise details and soared to the heights of religious philosophy. . . . Everyone listened attentively and, seemingly, with great interest, even if they understood only half of what he was saying.

Manya, sitting a little to the side near an open window, also listened, but she did not feel quite right, and could not wait for the scholar to end his lecture, which seemed to go on forever. . . . Throughout the evening, she mostly kept to herself. She watched the pure spring sky outside the window and listened to the sounds that came from the street below. In the distance, young voices were heard, laughing and playing the piano, and a strong passion stirred in her heart, wishing the company around her to discuss other, more pleasant subjects, more spring-like: theater, poetry, summer excursions, youthful love. [. . .]

At long last, the young scholar had exhausted his material. He went back and repeated a few things several times—and finally was quiet. For a moment, everyone sat still. Meanwhile, the sun had set, and evening shadows began to spread in the room; Manya, in her unsettled state, imagined that together with the evening shadows, other shadows, dark, formless, and ominous, had gathered around them, the shadows of very old things, now resurrected. . . . And she was therefore glad when one of the guests broke the silence and began to speak.

Manya had never met this woman before, an acquaintance of Vera's. She taught school in one of the provincial towns and had come to Moscow for the Easter holiday. She was about forty-five years old, a bit chubby, and seemed placid and good-natured. And then she spoke:

"This is all very well and excellent, and there is no doubt that in this particular case we are confronted with the stupidity of the ignorant masses. . . . But, please tell me: Why is it that this belief has persisted in the minds of people everywhere, and for many generations? We have just heard from the distinguished Vasili Nikolaevich, whose scholarship is above reproach. . . . And, as we know, there are many strange customs, some of them despicable, when we study faiths and the practice of religious traditions. And if you say: How does it happen that an entire nation, or even a cult within that nation, would allow such a terrible act?—Well, how would you explain the famous lynch trials? Only the other day, I read in the newspaper that last year three thousand people were executed in lynch-trials! Imagine—three thousand people are killed in such a brutal and disgusting manner! And yet Americans are considered to be, and undoubtedly are, a cultured and civilized people—one of the great nations in the world. . . . And I say to myself: if, for instance, I were asked . . . I would not take it upon myself to offer a definitive answer, be it in favor or against! After all . . . On the one hand, these Jews, who have been living in our midst for years and generations, have remained a distinct nation unto itself, foreign and insular, practically unknown to us. . . . On the other hand, considering the hodgepodge of religious beliefs, all the cults and trends and the many superstitions. . . . What if our own divine Christian symbol of 'the holy blood' had been appropriated by the Jews, and in the primitive form of their faith had become. . . . Who knows? Who, once and for all, can tell us the truth?"

She spoke sincerely, calmly, with no acrimony, as one whose only wish was to voice her doubts, seeking a solution.

When she was done speaking, a brief confusion followed, with the rise of many, if unclear, voices at once. Some had begun speaking, but instantly stopped, as if they had something to say but were not quite sure what it was exactly. Then one recalled the Last Supper, celebrated by Jesus and the Apostles, which, indeed, had taken place on the Passover of the Hebrews, and the mystifying words: "This is my blood. . . ." Another mumbled something about "the lasting alienation between Jews and Christians," while expressing regret that no effort had been made to get closer to and be better acquainted with this people. . . . All that was said was delivered in weak, uncertain voices, and the formless shadows continued to hang over the assembled friends.

And Manya, who had been sitting all this time by the window, suddenly felt herself redden, as if a rush of warm water had washed over her. As soon as she heard the innocuous question: "Who, once and for all, can tell us the truth?" she thought she would rise and hurl in their faces a sharp and conclusive retort that would reprove them all. . . . But soon, her resolve weakened, and she remained seated in her corner, suspended in silence and a peculiar numbness. At that moment she experienced, in all its intensity, the awful alienation the others had just talked about. These people could sit and calmly discuss this subject as they discussed any other subject. And they—only they—could evade the obvious answer and simply say: "Oh, we don't know, and we don't really care. . . ." But she—did she know?

As if through a fog, fragments of images, shards of hazy memories from her childhood, rose before her eyes. She saw her late father seated at the head of the table, the white tablecloth, the new and polished glass and silver tableware, the red wine sparkling in the glasses, and the two candles burning in the tall silver candlesticks. She knew that this image was a memory remnant of a Passover seder from long ago, before her parents stopped celebrating the seder, and she was a young child of three or four years old. She still had the taste of the matzot in her mouth—those thin matzot they, the children, loved to crack between their teeth, thinking the matzot, because they were so different, were some kind of special treat. And so she too had partaken, if briefly, of the "strange customs" and the "shameful acts" these people just discussed in her presence. Still, the real meaning and substance of the issue were a mystery to her, and she had no ready reply. . . . And even if she did find something to say to them, she would not be able to speak up because of the heavy feeling—the dark and humiliating fear gnawing at her—would they truly believe and trust her?

Manya looked at Vera, who was sitting at the edge of the table and wiping the glasses. She knew that in past years Vera had had occasion to work in many places in Russia, coming in contact with different people, including Jews. Manya also remembered stories Vera had told her about her past: her family had Jewish friends, they were neighbors, and when Vera was in high school, she was a regular visitor in their homes. She had also celebrated the Passover seder with them, eating the holiday meal with them. Vera, at the very least, must know; she must have a clear opinion about the matter: when she sat in that home, partaking of their meal, was she in the home of evil-doers? And another small detail: during one of the difficult winters, when bread was scarce, the two of them—she and Vera—baked matzah crackers in the small iron oven, and Vera joked and said that the "real" matzot she used to eat in her neighbors' house were much better. . . . And so, the taste of matzot was not foreign to her—the very same matzot made with Christian blood. [. . .]

Indeed, Vera had taken her time joining the discussion. Wiping the glasses dry with a towel, then deliberately placing them, one by one, on the table, she seemed to be entirely absorbed in her work. Only a trace of displeasure marred her radiant face and her usually clear forehead. She had not had occasion to forewarn her teacher friend that a Jewish girl would be in their company, and therefore was now discomfited by the too overt tenor of the discussion.

After a few minutes of silence, when Vera realized that all present had nothing more to say, she said, as if reluctantly, and in a subdued voice:

"In my opinion, since there are always things we have no answers for, matters we will never have a definite answer for, I think it is best not to discuss them, and this way avoid hurting someone's feelings, however unwittingly. . . . For instance: our lovely Klavdia Mikhailovna was unaware that a Jewish girl is sitting among us—Manya, who is also lovely, and is loved and admired by all of us. . . . On the one hand, it is clear that Klavdia meant no harm when she spoke; and, on the other hand, Manya is not such a fanatic who would interpret every word said about Jews in general as directed at her personally. . . . And yet, all in all"—Vera concluded with a light chuckle, waving her hand as if dismissing the entire matter—"is there no topic we can discuss other than the blood libel?"

And the good-hearted schoolteacher, who, indeed, had not looked at Manya closely and had not recognized her as Jewish, was embarrassed and did not know what to say. And the young scholar, who despite his great erudition was not very smart, reinforced Vera's reasoning, saying with a laugh:

"Do not discuss ropes in the house of the hanged. —Very well said, Vera Ivanovna!"

This concluded the discussion, and the guests turned to other matters.

Translated by Tsipi Keller.

Other works by Bikhovsky: *Minuty* (1919); *Tainye pesni* (1919); *Kos ketanah* (1926); *Simta'ot* (1929).

Efraim Kaganovsky

1893–1958

One of the first Yiddish writers to set his work in the city rather than the shtetl, Efraim (Froyim) Kaganovsky was a prolific writer of short stories about Jewish life in Warsaw. With a focus on the everyday drama of the Jewish street, Kaganovsky was widely read, his work serialized in multiple newspapers and printed in books in several editions. After spending World War II as a refugee in the Soviet Union, Kaganovsky participated in the rebuilding of Jewish culture in postwar Poland and eventually settled in Paris.

Tenant Number 88

1923

Some sort of strange, humid day. . . . Some sort of day with a ragged sun and low, dark clouds, like threads of smoke, already happened once before in the past: in distant years long ago, when our present-day Marcus Krul was still a boy.

Now he stands in the middle of the yard before the dark, gray house with its three wings, which he inherited from his father. Near him stands old Volf Blacharz with his green, crumpled beard and people are talking about repairing the roof.

The tenant from the garret comes every day with the same complaint: the roof is leaking. There is no other solution; the roof needs to be covered with new sheet metal. Old Blacharz spits out tin-plated words about sheet metal and breathes with salty, sour breath. But the landlord, Marcus Krul, is thinking about something else. He's thinking about the tenant from garret number 88, the young wife with her large, playful eyes, who comes about getting the roof repaired and who speaks with a spent voice, a slightly hoarse voice, as if she had a cough drop in her mouth.

Marcus Krul knows that a landlord needs to be hard-hearted and stern and not dare give in. He remembers what his "dearly departed father," Mr. Asher Krul, the former landlord, said in his last words before dying: A tenant is a bandit, an enemy, and one must chase them away, like the dogs. . . .

But the young wife from the garret comes on foot every day, speaks in her spent voice and looks at him with her squint-eyed gaze.

Mr. Landlord. . . . My roof is leaking. . . . The other day it rained, dripped into my baby's cradle. . . .

She has hands that are white and full, her lips are pale and full, and her teeth sparkle on her face like little white flames. She bolsters herself with her hands on her hips and her blouse suddenly tightens around her.

She goes on talking about the roof and the ceiling, where the rain is leaking in. Marcus Krul does not want to hear of it.

Right away, all of the tenants will come. . . . And in the bargain the paupers from the garrets and the cellars. . . . And they will all be ordering "repairs." For this one, repair the oven. For that one, the floor. . . .

But the young wife doesn't grow angry, doesn't yell. When he refuses her wish, she smiles and the little white flames of her teeth sparkle.

She doesn't push and all of a sudden he begins to fear that she is going to leave.

Yes. It appears from the books—that she already owes three months' rent. . . .

His "dearly departed father," Mr. Asher Krul, would not have waited, he would have evicted her.

What sort of a young wife is this. . . .

Marcus Krul is stern, as always. Just now he has buried his heavy, greenish eyes in the pipe grown rusty from the leak.

Some sort of strange, humid day. The sky is smoking. The house, the old house with its three wings, is lit up on one side with a white light, like limelight. On the second side it is dark, as at evening. A dense, humid darkness is visible around the house, as if it were sweating. This old house cannot be helped by any plaster or whitewash; it is rusting, full of lichens and mold. The sheet metal on the windows and on the roof is bluish black, like the roof of a hearse.

On just such a day as this, his "dearly-departed father" was standing here in the yard, leaning on his cane, with this same Volf Blacharz. It was long ago. Marcus was still a boy. He had friends; all of them were sons of landlords. He didn't dare befriend any others. And his father continually told him to listen attentively to every one of his words.

A person must thoroughly calculate everything that he does beforehand. . . .

A person must remember. . . . A person must know. . . . And suddenly Marcus Krul senses that he is, indeed, his father, Mr. Asher, and that time has stopped moving on this strange, humid day. And from all the little corners of the old house memories and repetitions swim up and reveal themselves to him. Just there in the corner, in the dark house, on the old worn steps, which lead to the humble attic number 88, his father used so often to disappear; he held his head up somewhat stiffly and with a sanctimonious air; leaning heavily on his cane, he climbed the tortuous steps.

It has been twenty-three years since the landlord was carried out of the house. The great doctors couldn't help, nor the carriages, which came every day. It was a large funeral and the street turned black with people. Quite a man, Mr. Asher, the landlord. . . . And, now, there is the young wife from the garret apartment number 88 in a corner of the house, standing still.

The pretty, darkly charming young wife, because of whom his mother, the great, ample landlordess, Dorote Krul, wept, and his older sisters spoke in whispers in the back room. . . .

A strange, humid day.

Old Volf Blacharz, with his green beard, is still nimble as a cat. He already has his tools prepared along with the soldering iron and the brand new sheet metal. His feet long ago acquired their feline softness, evoking sad and lonely roofs.

The young wife from number 88 let her shoulders relax out of joy; three clasps burst from her blouse.

She has disappeared into the dark corner of the house, raising her skirt too high.

And here's Marcus Krul walking with his head held up in a slightly twisted, sanctimonious position, over to the dark corner, leaning on his cane. He has still never been there and it seems to him that he is his father. How dimly worn the steps are here. Poor children wrapped in rags, with green little faces and red little noses, sit spread out on the steps. They don't know that he is the landlord and don't get out of his way. His "dearly-departed father" would have shouted because of that and struck with his cane.

Marcus Krul is not harsh at this moment. He just wants to go up to the garret, to tell her that she is the only one for whom he repairs a roof. . . . The only one. . . .

You listen. . . . Mrs. . . . I will repair the roof there. . . . Just there. . . . Because I don't do repairs for anyone. . . . Yes. . . .

She is standing close to him. He detects the scent of a small child, of milk and moisture. And somewhere, from her full hands, such warmth gushes out. The warmth gets under his skin, into his head, and intoxicates him.

With his cane he pushes the door open into her home. She becomes embarrassed. But he sees: a cradle—a brown, wooden and heavy, old-fashioned cradle on two rockers. Such a cradle strikes in poor rooms at night like a clock: *tick-tock.* . . .

In the green, crudely painted little house there is a shimmer of purity. On the table lies a pink doily. It is set as if someone were due to come.

Did she know, then, that the landlord would come up here, to garret number 88?

A wooden, dark bed, carefully made up with a red blanket. She sleeps in that bed. . . .

Just you listen, Mrs. . . . Your husband . . . What does he do? . . . What does he look like? . . .

The landlord doesn't know him at all. A tenant from the garret.

Snicker, snicker . . . He owes rent. He could be evicted . . .

The young wife doesn't grow upset. She doesn't beg. She sticks out a leg, fixes her skirt on her hips. Her leg is unusually long. And she has a child in the cradle. A child . . . With round little cheeks.

You listen, Mrs.

His cane falls with a hard clap . . . Yes, she understands now . . . Of course, such an impressive visitor. The landlord himself . . . Wants to come up, *snicker, snicker* . . .

Her blouse splits open. And she has become huge. The whole garret is full of her . . . No, this is not Marcus. This is his "dearly departed father . . ." Mr. Asher, Mr. Asher Krul. . . .

Translated by Maia Evrona

Other works by Kaganovsky: *Tirn-fenster* (1921); *Noveln* (1928); *Figurn* (1937).

Viktor Shklovsky

1893–1984

A native of St. Petersburg, Viktor Shklovsky was a leading literary theorist and critic, the founder of the Opoiaz (Obshchestvo Izucheniia Poeticheskogo Iazyka, or Society for the Study of Poetic Language), and one of the intellectual architects of Russian formalism. Within the framework of this latter school of thought, he developed the influential and daring concept of *ostranenie* ("to make strange"), whereby the familiar is made novel through literature and arts. While

Shklovsky defended freedom for the arts from ideology in the early Soviet period, he largely succumbed to the pressures of the Stalinist era toward methodological conformity and gave up literary criticism in favor of other genres of writing for several decades. Shklovsky returned to his earlier and bolder style later in life, producing complex works that combined fiction, memoir, documentary, and criticism all within a single given work.

Zoo, or Letters Not about Love
1923

Letter Seven

About Grzhebin on canvas, about Grzhebin in the flesh.[1] Since the letter is written in a penitent mood, the trademark of the Grzhebin Publishing House is affixed. Here too are several fleeting remarks about Jewry and about the attitude of the Jews toward Russia.

What to write about! My whole life is a letter to you.

We meet less and less often. I've come to understand so many simple words: yearn, perish, burn, but "yearn" (with the pronoun "I") is the most comprehensible word.

Writing about love is forbidden, so I'll write about Zinovy Grzhebin, the publisher. That ought to be sufficiently remote.

In Yury Annenkov's portrait of Zinovy Isaevich Grzhebin, the face is a soft pink color and looks downright delectable.[2]

In real life, Grzhebin is pastier.

In the portrait, the face is very fleshy; to be more precise, it resembles intestines bulging with food. In real life, Grzhebin is more tight and firm; he might well be compared to a blimp of the semirigid type. When I was not yet thirty and did not yet know loneliness and did not know that the Spree is narrower than the Neva and did not sit in the Pension Marzahn, whose landlady did not permit me to sing at night while I worked, and did not tremble at the sound of a telephone—when life had not yet slammed the door to Russia shut on my fingers, when I thought that I could break history on my knee, when I loved to run after streetcars . . .

"When a poem was best of all
Better even than a well-aimed ball"—[3]
(something like that)

. . . I disliked Grzhebin immensely. I was then twenty-seven and twenty-eight and twenty-nine.

I thought Grzhebin cruel for having gulped down so much Russian literature.

Now, when I know that the Spree is thirty times narrower than the Neva, when I too am thirty, when I wait for the telephone to ring—though I've been told not to expect a call—when life has slammed the door on my fingers and history is too busy even to write letters, when I ride on streetcars without wanting to capsize them, when my feet lack the unseeing boots they once wore and I no longer know how to launch an offensive . . .

. . . now I know that Grzhebin is a valuable product. I don't want to ruin Grzhebin's credit rating, but I fervently believe that my book won't be read in a single bank.

Therefore I declare that Grzhebin is no businessman, nor is he stuffed either with the Russian literature gulped down by him or with dollars.

But, Alya, don't you know who Grzhebin is? Grzhebin's a publisher; he published the almanac *Sweetbriar*, he published *Pantheon* and now he seems to have the most important publishing house in Berlin.

In Russia, between 1918 and 1920, Grzhebin was buying manuscripts hysterically. It was a disease—like nymphomania.

He was not publishing books then. And I frequently called on him in my unseeing boots and I shouted in a voice thirty times louder than any other voice in Berlin. And in the evening I drank tea at his place.

Don't think that I've grown thirty times narrower.

It's just that everything has changed.

I hereby give the following testimony: Grzhebin is no businessman.

Grzhebin is a Soviet-type bourgeois, complete with delirium and frenzy.

Now he publishes, publishes, publishes! The books come running, one after another; they want to run away to Russia, but are denied entry.

They all bear the trademark: ZINOVY GRZHEBIN.

Two hundred, three hundred, four hundred—soon there may be a thousand titles. The books pile on top of each other; pyramids are created and torrents, but they flow into Russia drop by drop.

Yet here in the middle of nowhere, in Berlin, this Soviet bourgeois raves on an international scale and continues to publish new books.

Books as such. Books for their own sake. Books to assert the name of his publishing house.

This is a passion for property, a passion for collecting around his name the greatest possible quantity of things. This incredible Soviet bourgeois responds to Soviet ration cards and numbers by throwing all his energy into the creation of a multitude of things that bear his name.

"Let them deny my books entry into Russia," says he—like a rejected suitor who ruins himself buying flowers to turn the room of his unresponsive beloved into a flower shop and who admires this absurdity.

An absurdity quite beautiful and persuasive. So Grzhebin, spurned by his beloved Russia and feeling that he has a right to live, keeps publishing, publishing, publishing.

Don't be surprised, Alya. We are all capable of raving—those of us who really live.

When you sell Grzhebin manuscripts, he drives a hard bargain, but more out of propriety than greed.

He wants to demonstrate to himself that he and his business are real.

Grzhebin's contracts are pseudo-real and, in that sense, relevant to the sphere of electrification in Russia.

Russia dislikes Jews.

All the same, though, Jews like Grzhebin are a good remedy for low blood pressure.

It's nice to see Grzhebin, with his appetite for the creation of things, in idle, skeptical Russian Berlin. [...]

Letter Twelve

Written, it would seem, in response to a comment apparently made by telephone, since the dossier contains nothing in writing along these lines; the comment had to do with table manners.
Also contained in the letter is a denial of the assertion that pants absolutely must be creased. The letter is liberally garnished with Biblical parallels.

So help me, Alya, pants don't have to be creased!
Pants are worn to thwart the cold.
Ask the Serapions.[1]
As for hunching over one's food, maybe that ought to be avoided.
You complain about our table manners.
We hunch down over our plates to minimize the transportation problem.
We will no doubt continue to surprise you—and you us.

A great deal surprises me about this country, where pants have to be creased in front. Poor people put their pants under the mattress overnight.

In Russian literature, this method is well known; it's used—in Kuprin—by professional beggars of noble origin.[2]

This whole European way of life provokes me!

Just as Levin was provoked (*Anna Karenina*) when he noticed how fruit was being canned in his house—not his way, but the way it had always been done in Kitty's family.[3]

When Judge Gideon was gathering a guerrilla band for an attack on the Philistines, he first of all sent home all the family men.

Then the Angel of the Lord commanded him to lead all the remaining warriors to the river and to take into battle only those who drank water from the palm of their hands, and not those who hunched over the water and lapped it like dogs.[4]

Are we, by any chance, bad warriors?

Well, when everything collapses—and that will be soon—we will leave two by two, with our rifles on our shoulders, with cartridges in the pockets of our pants (not creased); we will leave, firing at the cavalry from behind fences; we will head back to Russia, perhaps to the Urals, there to build a New Troy.[5]

But it is preferable not to hunch over one's plate.

Terrible is the judgment of Gideon the judge! What if he refuses to take us into his army!

The Bible repeats itself in curious ways.

Once the Jews defeated the Philistines, who fled, fleeing two by two, to seek safety on the other side of the river.

The Jews set out patrols at the crossing.

On that occasion, it was difficult to distinguish a Philistine from a Jew: both were, in all likelihood, naked.

The patrol would ask those coming across, "Say the word 'shibboleth.'"

But the Philistines couldn't say "sh"; they said "sibboleth."

Then they were killed.[6]

In the Ukraine, I once ran across a Jewish boy. He couldn't look at corn without trembling.

He told me this:

When the killing was going on in the Ukraine, it was frequently necessary to check whether the person being killed was a Jew.

They would tell him, "Say 'kukuruza.'"

The Jew would say "kukuruzha."

He was killed.[7] [...]

Letter Twenty-five

About spring, the Prager Diele, Ehrenburg and pipes.[1] *About time, which passes, and lips, which renew themselves—about a certain heart that is being worn to a frazzle while the lips in question are merely losing their paint. About my heart.*

It's already forty-five degrees outside. My fall coat has become a spring coat. Winter is passing and, come what may, I won't be forced to endure a winter like this again.

Let's believe in our return home. Spring is coming, Alya. You told me once that spring makes you feel as if you've lost or forgotten something and you can't remember what.

When it was spring in Petersburg, I used to walk along the quays in a black cape. There the nights are white and the sun rises while the bridges are still drawn. I used to find many things on the quays. But you will find nothing; all you know is that something has been lost. The quays in Berlin are different. They're nice, too. It's nice to follow the canals to the workers' districts.

There, in some places, the canals widen into quiet harbors and cranes hover over the water. Like trees.

There, at the Hallesches Tor, out beyond the place where you live, stands the round tower of the gasworks, just like those at home on the Obvodny Canal. When I was eighteen, I used to walk my girl friend to those towers every day. Very beautiful are the canals—even when the high platform of the elevated runs along their bank.

I am already beginning to remember what I've lost.

Thank God it's spring!

The little tables in the Prager Diele will be carried outdoors and Ilya Ehrenburg will see the sky.

Ilya Ehrenburg promenades in Berlin as he promenaded in Paris and in other cities full of émigrés—always bent over, as if looking on the ground for something he's lost.

However, that's an incorrect simile. His body is not bent at the waist: only his head is bent, his back curved. Gray coat, leather cap. Head quite young. He has three professions: 1) smoking a pipe, 2) being a skeptic, sitting in a cafe and publishing *Object*,[2] 3) writing *Julio Jurenito*.[3]

Later in time than *Julio Jurenito* is the book called *Trust D. E.*[4] Rays emanate from Ehrenburg; these rays bear various names; their distinctive feature is that they all smoke a pipe.

These rays fill the Prager Diele.

In one corner of the Prager Diele sits the master himself, demonstrating the art of smoking a pipe, of writing novels and of taking the world and his ice cream with a dose of skepticism.

Nature has endowed Ehrenburg lavishly—he has a passport.

He lives abroad with this passport. And thousands of visas.

I have no idea how good a writer Ilya Ehrenburg is.

His old stuff isn't any good.

But *Julio Jurenito* gives one pause. It is an extremely journalistic affair—a feuilleton with a plot, stylized character types and the old Ehrenburg himself, garnished with a prayer; the old poetry functions as a stylized character.

The novel develops along the lines of Voltaire's *Candide*—though with a less variegated plot.

Candide has a nice circular plot: while people look for Cunégonde, she is sleeping with everybody and aging. The hero winds up with an old woman, who reminisces about the tender skin of her Bulgarian captain.[5]

This plot—more accurately, this critical orientation on the idea that "time passes" and betrayals take place—was already being processed by Boccaccio. There the betrothed woman passes from hand to hand and finally winds up with her husband, assuring him of her virginity.

The discoveries she made during her travels were not limited to hands. This novella ends with the famous phrase about how lips are not diminished but only renewed by kisses.[6]

But never mind, I will soon remember what I've forgotten. Ehrenburg has his own brand of irony; there is nothing Elizabethan about his short stories and novels. The good thing about him is that he chooses not to continue the traditions of "great" Russian Literature; he prefers to write "bad stuff."

I used to be angry with Ehrenburg because, in transforming himself from a Jewish Catholic or Slavophile into a European constructivist, he failed to forget the past. Saul failed to become Paul. He remains Paul, son of Saul, and he publishes *Animal Warmth*.

He is more, though, than just a journalist adept at organizing other people's ideas into a novel: he comes close to being an artist—one who feels the contradiction between the old humanistic culture and the new world now being built by the machine.

Of all these contradictions, the most painful to me is that while the lips in question are busy renewing themselves, the heart is being worn to a frazzle; and with it go the forgotten things, undetected.

NOTES

Letter Seven

1. Zinovy Isaevich Grzhebin (1869–1929), an artist who became editor of the journals *Parus* [Sail] and *Shipovnik* [Sweetbriar] and then owner of a publishing house connected with Gorky's project to publish all the classics of world literature in Russian translation. Grzhebin emigrated at the end of 1920, spent a few months in Stockholm, then settled in Berlin, where he founded the most important émigré publishing house.

2. Yury Pavlovich Annenkov (b. 1889), artist, director, and writer. A color reproduction of the portrait may be found in Annenkov's book *Portrety* (Petrograd, 1922), p. 67.

3. This couplet may be a paraphrase of the first three lines in Pushkin's poem "Domik v Kolomne" [The Cottage in Kolomna].

Letter Twelve

1. The Serapion Brothers, a group of young people who organized in February 1921 to learn how to write under the collective aegis of [Maxim] Gorky, Shklovsky, and Evgeny Zamyatin. Their brilliant prose and poetry contributed in a decisive way to the regeneration of Russian literature after the revolution.

2. Aleksandr Ivanovich Kuprin (1870–1938), a short story writer who began his career as a member of Gorky's Znanie (Knowledge) group, and who specialized in sensational stories braced with strong plots. Kuprin was living in Gatchina when it was occupied by the White army of General Yudenich in the fall of 1919. When the Whites withdrew in October, he accompanied them. After spending a few months in Finland he moved to Paris, where he resided until his return to the Soviet Union in 1937.

3. Part VI, chap. ii.

4. Judges 7:4–8, where Gideon, gathering an army to lead against the Midianites, reduced his forces from 32,000 to a more workable 300 by the criterion discussed in the letter.

5. A reference to the Trojan émigré Aeneas, who, according to legend, gathered the survivors of ruined Troy and led them, after many adventures, to Italy, where they founded Rome.

6. Judges 12:1–6, where the Gileadite clan, led by Jephthah, defeated the Ephraimite clan. "Shibboleth" means "corn."

7. "Kukuruza" means "corn."

Letter Twenty-five

1. Ilya Grigorievich Ehrenburg (1891–1967), prolific novelist and journalist. During the civil-war period, Ehrenburg sympathized with the Whites and seriously contemplated emigration, but after the defeat of Wrangel's White army in the fall of 1920, he returned to Moscow. In the spring of 1921, he was sent abroad as a foreign correspondent for Soviet publications. Expelled from France after being denounced to the police as a dangerous Bolshevik (by Aleksei Tolstoy, according to Nina Berberova), he spent the summer in Belgium, where he wrote *Julio Jurenito*, then moved to Berlin, where he remained until 1923.

2. Ehrenburg and the painter El Lissitzky (1890–1941) published three issues of *Veshch'* [Object] during 1922 in Russian, French, and German. It was the first international publication of the seminal constructivist movement. As an organ of the movement's radical faction, it stressed the irrelevance of pure art to the modern world and advocated the cultivation of utilitarian art forms—industrial design, architecture, films, posters.

3. *Neobyknovennye prikliucheniia Khulio Khurenito i ego uchenikov* [The Unusual Adventures of Julio Jurenito and His Disciples] (Berlin, 1922), which most critics consider Ehrenburg's best book.

4. *Trest D. E.: Istoriia gibeli Evropy* [Trust D. E.: A History of the Demise of Europe] (Berlin, 1923).

5. Cunégonde's fond memory of the Bulgarian captain actually occurs during her first reunion with Candide—in chapter eight, where she is still young and beautiful, though slightly frayed.

6. From the Decameron: seventh story of the second day.

Translated by Richard Sheldon.

Other works by Shklovsky: *O teorii prozy* (1925); *Zametki o proze russkikh klassikov* (1953); *Za i protiv* (1957); *Tetiva* (1970).

Andrei Sobol

1888–1926

Andrei Sobol was a writer, literary translator, poet, and essayist. Born in Saratov, Russia, he lived a turbulent life, arrested for the first time in 1904 for illegal Zionist activities, before escaping Siberia four years later and living in Western Europe. Returning to Russia illegally in 1914, Sobol fell repeatedly in and out of favor with communist authorities, spending several years in prison while later holding a position in the All-Russian Writers Union. His essays, poetry, and prose work often centered on Zionist themes, in addition to sharp critiques of Russian antisemitism, what he saw as Jewish passivity, and other social ills. He translated Sholem Aleichem's works from Yiddish into Russian. He committed suicide in Moscow.

Man Overboard
1923

Cellar

[. . .] And the Lieutenant-Captain was seriously tired of other people's passports, of never-ending family names, from Ivanov to Chavchavadze, and of registration.

The barrister has been spinning like a top with every knock at the door, concealing under a floorboard rings, gold watches, and letters written by Milyukov during his presidency at the Kadet Provincial Committee, and he was longing for Paris: either to hear the truth from Milyukov, or to have a break from the constant searches.

David Potbelly, on the other hand, didn't correspond with Milyukov, didn't admit nor expel Tsaritsyn, and yet he had three crosses to carry, a triple struggle: he was a Jew, he had a wart of catastrophic proportions, its tail hanging down to his lip, and he had his last name. The first of these got him regular beatings; the second one made him the object of mockery; and the third made life completely unbearable.

From spring until fall, Potbelly was scurrying among different cities. When the sun rose, Potbelly rose as well and departed from Golta. Green was spreading everywhere; in the forest, lilies of the valley were blossoming. Meanwhile, in Golta, shutters were being nailed down, mothers were clutching their children, and old people were wandering around aimlessly. When the sun was at its fiery zenith, Potbelly would go through yards and fields to the train station, and the Chieftain Marusia would sneak toward the pillows, the synagogue candlesticks. As the sun was setting, Potbelly was escaping Voznesensk, and Angel's gang was tumbling in on their carts with uproar and boom.

How many nights can a person go without sleeping? Fields sleep; the sky sleeps above; even stars take naps; but Potbelly doesn't sleep. Every minute he has to look around him; every moment he has to listen guardedly to catch the beating of hooves, or drunken singing, he has to, he has to . . .

And it is clear to Potbelly that what he needs is Palestine, that he needs a Lebanese cedar to lean against, to stretch out his stiff legs and, having glanced at the Jewish sky, to fall into blessed, childish sleep at the tomb of Rachel the Matriarch—"Blessed be God, our Master, who grants sleep to weary eyes."

And the wart also: it seems that while there are Black Army soldiers, chieftain women, county-clerk chieftains, fugitive ensigns crawling out of the dense forest—head hunters—one should really forget about the wart, that same wart that, many years ago, Yakov Milkhiker the pharmacist, wordsmith, and correspondent for the business paper *Birzhevka*, used to call: "A comet among luminaries." *Birzhevka* is long gone. Milkhiker is somewhere in the East, either in Afghanistan or in India, doing diplomatic work, but the comet remains, and its tail remains. Potbelly has no diplomatic skills; Potbelly needs a Jewish colony next to Arabic huts.

And the last name also: at the police station, as they were renewing his passport, they asked: "What's the last name? Paunch?"

And again, it seems that all Jews are being attacked, Mendeleviches are being attacked, as well as Goldbergs, and it doesn't matter to Ol' Danilchik who to pierce with his bayonet—be it Diamond, a person with such a loud last name, or Yankelevich, who himself doesn't care about anything anymore. And yet: Potbelly, Potbelly, Potbelly—always uproarious laughter.

There must be a land, after all, where simplicity and pride may be found: David son of Simon—an ancient, pleasant name under one's own ancient and pleasant sky.

Translated by Alexandra Hoffman.

Other works by Sobol: *Rostom ne vyshel* (1914); *Pesn' Pesnei* (1915); *Pyl'* (1915); *Tikhoe techenie* (1918).

Anzia Yezierska
1885–1970

The American novelist and short-story writer Anzia Yezierska was born in Poland and came to New York in 1898. Her stories reflect the dislocations of immigration, the grinding poverty of teeming immigrant quarters, and the clash of values and aspirations between parents and children. Her talent was recognized early in her career with the publication of her book of short stories, *Hungry Hearts* (1920). Samuel Goldwyn offered her a contract as a screenwriter, but the Hollywood scene depressed her. Finding it sterile and superficial, she returned to New York. Feminist critics rediscovered Yezierska's work in the 1970s and celebrated her for her portrayal of young women struggling to escape immigrant poverty, oppressive social norms, and restrictive religious practices.

Children of Loneliness
1923

I

"Oh, Mother, can't you use a fork?" exclaimed Rachel as Mrs. Ravinsky took the shell of the baked potato in her fingers and raised it to her watering mouth.

"Here, *Teacherin* mine, you want to learn me in my old age how to put the bite in my mouth?" The mother dropped the potato back into her plate, too wounded to eat. Wiping her hands on her blue-checked apron, she turned her glance to her husband, at the opposite side of the table.

"Yankev," she said bitterly, "stick your bone on a fork. Our *teacherin* said you dassn't touch no eatings with the hands."

"All my teachers died already in the old country," retorted the old man. "I ain't going to learn nothing new no more from my American daughter." He continued to suck the marrow out of the bone with that noisy relish that was so exasperating to Rachel.

"It's no use," stormed the girl, jumping up from the table in disgust; I'll never be able to stand it here with you people."

"'You people?' What do you mean by 'you people'?" shouted the old man, lashed into fury by his daughter's words. "You think you got a different skin from us because you went to college?"

"It drives me wild to hear you crunching bones like savages. If you people won't change, I shall have to move and live by myself."

Yankev Ravinsky threw the half-gnawed bone upon the table with such vehemence that a plate broke into fragments.

"You witch you!" he cried in a hoarse voice tense with rage. "Move by yourself! We lived without you while you was away in college, and we can get on without you further. God ain't going to turn his nose on us because we ain't got table manners from America. A hell she made from this house since she got home."

"*Shah*! Yankev *leben*," pleaded the mother, "the neighbors are opening the windows to listen to our hollering. Let us have a little quiet for a while till the eating is over."

But the accumulated hurts and insults that the old man had borne in the one week since his daughter's return from college had reached the breaking-point. His face was convulsed, his eyes flashed, and his lips were flecked with froth as he burst out in a volley of scorn:

"You think you can put our necks in a chain and learn us new tricks? You think you can make us over for Americans? We got through till fifty years of our lives eating in our own old way—"

"Woe is me, Yankev *leben*!" entreated his wife. "Why can't we choke ourselves with our troubles? Why must the whole world know how we are tearing ourselves by the heads? In all Essex Street, in all New York, there ain't such fights like by us."

Her pleadings were in vain. There was no stopping Yankev Ravinsky once his wrath was roused. His daughter's insistence upon the use of a knife and fork spelled apostasy, anti-Semitism, and the aping of the Gentiles.

Like a prophet of old condemning unrighteousness, he ran the gamut of denunciation, rising to heights of fury that were sublime and godlike, and sinking from sheer exhaustion to abusive bitterness.

"*Pfui* on all your American colleges! *Pfui* on the morals of America! No respect for old age. No fear for God. Stepping with your feet on all the laws of the holy Torah. A fire should burn out the whole new generation. They should sink into the earth, like Korah."

"Look at him cursing and burning! Just because *I* insist on their changing their terrible table manners. One would think I was killing them."

"Do you got to use a gun to kill?" cried the old man, little red threads darting out of the whites of his eyes.

"Who is doing the killing? Aren't you choking the life out of me? Aren't you dragging me by the hair to the darkness of past ages every minute of the day? I'd die of shame if one of my college friends should open the door while you people are eating."

"You—you—"

The old man was on the point of striking his daughter when his wife seized the hand he raised.

"*Mincha*! Yankev, you forgot *Mincha*!"

This reminder was a flash of inspiration on Mrs. Ravinsky's part, the only thing that could have ended the quarreling instantly. *Mincha* was the prayer just before sunset of the orthodox Jews. This religious rite was so automatic with the old man that at his wife's mention of *Mincha* everything was immediately shut out, and

Yankev Ravinsky rushed off to a corner of the room to pray.

"*Ashrai Yoishwai Waisahuh!*"

"Happy are they who dwell in Thy house. Ever shall I praise Thee. *Selah!* Great is the Lord, and exceedingly to be praised; and His greatness is unsearchable. On the majesty and glory of Thy splendor, and on Thy marvelous deeds, will I mediate."

The shelter from the storms of life that the artist finds in his art, Yankev Ravinsky found in his prescribed communion with God. All the despair caused by his daughter's apostasy, the insults and disappointments he suffered, were in his sobbing voice. But as he entered into the spirit of his prayer, he felt the man of flesh drop away in the outflow of God around him. His voice mellowed, the rigid wrinkles of his face softened, the hard glitter of anger and condemnation in his eyes was transmuted into the light of love as he went on:

"The Lord is gracious and merciful; slow to anger and of great loving-kindness. To all that call upon Him in truth He will hear their cry and save them."

Oblivious to the passing and repassing of his wife as she warmed anew the unfinished dinner, he continued:

"Put not your trust in princes, in the son of man in whom there is no help." Here Reb Ravinsky paused long enough to make a silent confession for the sin of having placed his hope on his daughter instead of on God. His whole body bowed with the sense of guilt. Then in a moment his humility was transfigured into exaltation. Sorrow for sin dissolved in joy as he became more deeply aware of God's unfailing protection.

"Happy is he who hath the God of Jacob for his help, whose hope is in the Lord his God. He healeth the broken in heart, and bindeth up their wounds."

A healing balm filled his soul as he returned to the table, where the steaming hot food awaited him. Rachel sat near the window pretending to read a book. Her mother did not urge her to join them at the table, fearing another outbreak, and the meal continued in silence.

The girl's thoughts surged hotly as she glanced from her father to her mother. A chasm of four centuries could not have separated her more completely from them than her four years at Cornell.

"To think that I was born of these creatures! It's an insult to my soul. What kinship have I with these two lumps of ignorance and superstition? They're ugly and gross and stupid. I'm all sensitive nerves. They want to wallow in dirt."

She closed her eyes to shut out the sight of her parents as they silently ate together, unmindful of the dirt and confusion.

"How is it possible that I lived with them and like them only four years ago? What is it in me that so quickly gets accustomed to the best? Beauty and cleanliness are as natural to me as if I'd been born on Fifth Avenue instead of the dirt of Essex Street."

A vision of Frank Baker passed before her. Her last long talk with him out under the trees in college still lingered in her heart. She felt that she had only to be with him again to carry forward the beautiful friendship that had sprung up between them. He had promised to come shortly to New York. How could she possibly introduce such a born and bred American to her low, ignorant, dirty parents?

"I might as well tear the thought of Frank Baker out of my heart," she told herself. "If he just once sees the pigsty of a home I come from, if he just sees the table manners of my father and mother, he'll fly through the ceiling."

Timidly, Mrs. Ravinsky turned to her daughter.

"Ain't you going to give a taste the eating?"

No answer.

"I fried the *lotkes* special' for you—"

"I can't stand your fried, greasy stuff."

"Ain't even my cooking good no more either?" Her gnarled, hard-worked hands clutched at her breast. "God from the world, for what do I need yet any more my life? Nothing I do for my child is no use no more."

Her head sank; her whole body seemed to shrivel and grow old with the sense of her own futility.

"How I was hurrying to run by the butcher before everybody else, so as to pick out the grandest, fattest piece of *brust*!" she wailed, tears streaming down her face. "And I put my hand away from my heart and put a whole fresh egg into the *lotkes*, and I stuffed the stove full of coal like a millionaire so as to get the *lotkes* fried so nice and brown; and now you give a kick on everything I done—"

"Fool woman," shouted her husband, "stop laying yourself on the ground for your daughter to step on you! What more can you expect from a child raised up in America? What more can you expect but that she should spit in your face and make dirt from you?" His eyes, hot and dry under their lids, flashed from his wife to his daughter. "The old Jewish eating is poison to her; she must have *trefa* ham—only forbidden food."

Bitter laughter shook him.

"Woman, how you patted yourself with pride before all the neighbors, boasting of our great American daughter coming home from college! This is our daughter, our pride, our hope, our pillow for our old age that we were dreaming about! This is our American *teacherin*! A Jew-hater, an anti-Semite we brought into the world, a betrayer of our race who hates her own father and mother like the Russian Czar once hated a Jew. She makes herself so refined, she can't stand it when we use the knife or fork the wrong way; but her heart is that of a brutal Cossack, and she spills her own father's and mother's blood like water."

Every word he uttered seared Rachel's soul like burning acid. She felt herself becoming a witch, a she-devil, under the spell of his accusations.

"You want me to love you yet?" She turned upon her father like an avenging fury. "If there's any evil hatred in my soul, you have roused it with your cursed preaching."

"*Oi-i-i*! Highest One! pity Yourself on us!" Mrs. Ravinsky wrung her hands. "Rachel, Yankev, let there be an end to this knife-stabbing! *Gottuniu*! my flesh is torn to pieces!"

Unheeding her mother's pleading, Rachel rushed to the closet where she kept her things.

"I was a crazy idiot to think that I could live with you people under one roof." She flung on her hat and coat and bolted for the door.

Mrs. Ravinsky seized Rachel's arm in passionate entreaty.

"My child, my heart, my life, what do you mean? Where are you going?"

"I mean to get out of this hell of a home this very minute," she said, tearing loose from her mother's clutching hands.

"Woe is me! My child! We'll be to shame and to laughter by the whole world. What will people say?"

"Let them say! My life is my own; I'll live as I please." She slammed the door in her mother's face.

"They want me to love them yet," ran the mad thoughts in Rachel's brain as she hurried through the streets, not knowing where she was going, not caring. "Vampires, bloodsuckers fastened on my flesh! Black shadow blighting every ray of light that ever came my way! Other parents scheme and plan and wear themselves out to give their child a chance, but they put dead stones in front of every chance I made for myself."

With the cruelty of youth to everything not youth, Rachel reasoned:

"They have no rights, no claims over me like other parents who do things for their children. It was my own brains, my own courage, my own iron will that forced my way out of the sweatshop to my present position in the public schools. I owe them nothing, nothing, nothing."

II

Two weeks already away from home. Rachel looked about her room. It was spotlessly clean. She had often said to herself while at home with her parents: "All I want is an empty room, with a bed, a table, and a chair. As long as it is clean and away from them, I'll be happy." But was she happy?

A distant door closed, followed by the retreating sound of descending footsteps. Then all was still, the stifling stillness of a rooming-house. The white empty walls pressed in upon her, suffocated her. She listened acutely for any stir of life, but the continued silence was unbroken save for the insistent ticking of her watch.

"I ran away from home burning for life," she mused, "and all I've found is the loneliness that's death." A wave of self-pity weakened her almost to the point of tears. "I'm alone! I'm alone!" she moaned, crumpling into a heap.

"Must it always be with me like this," her soul cried in terror, "either to live among those who drag me down or in the awful isolation of a hall bedroom? Oh, I'll die of loneliness among these frozen, each-shut-in-himself Americans! It's one thing to break away, but, oh, the strength to go on alone. How can I ever do it? The love instinct is so strong in me; I can not live without love, without people."

The thought of a letter from Frank Baker suddenly lightened her spirits. That very evening she was to meet him for dinner. Here was hope—more than hope. Just seeing him again would surely bring the certainty.

This new rush of light upon her dark horizon so softened her heart that she could almost tolerate her superfluous parents.

"If I could only have love and my own life, I could almost forgive them for bringing me into the world. I don't really hate them; I only hate them when they stand between me and the new America that I'm to conquer."

Answering her impulse, her feet led her to the familiar Ghetto streets. On the corner of the block where her parents lived she paused, torn between the desire to see her people and the fear of their nagging reproaches.

The old Jewish proverb came to her mind: "The wolf is not afraid of the dog, but he hates his bark." "I'm not afraid of their black curses for sin. It's nothing to me if they accuse me of being an anti-Semite or a murderer, and yet why does it hurt me so?"

Rachel had prepared herself to face the usual hailstorm of reproaches and accusations, but as she entered the dark hallway of the tenement, she heard her father's voice chanting the old familiar Hebrew psalm of "The Race of Sorrows":

"Hear my prayer, O Lord, and let my cry come unto Thee.

For my days are consumed like smoke, and my bones are burned as an hearth.

I am like a pelican of the wilderness.

I am like an owl of the desert.

I have eaten ashes like bread and mingled my drink with weeping."

A faintness came over her. The sobbing strains of the lyric song melted into her veins like a magic sap, making her warm and human again. All her strength seemed to flow out of her in pity for her people. She longed to throw herself on the dirty, ill-smelling tenement stairs and weep: "Nothing is real but love—love. Nothing so false as ambition."

Since her early childhood she remembered often waking up in the middle of the night and hearing her father chant this age-old song of woe. There flashed before her a vivid picture of him, huddled in the corner beside the table piled high with Hebrew books, swaying to the rhythm of his Jeremiad, the sputtering light of the candle stuck in a bottle throwing uncanny shadows over his gaunt face. The skull-cap, the side-locks, and the long gray beard made him seem like some mystic stranger from a far-off world and not a father. The father of the daylight who ate with a knife, spat on the floor, and who was forever denouncing America and Americans was different from this mystic spirit stranger who could thrill with such impassioned rapture.

Thousands of years of exile, thousands of years of hunger, loneliness, and want swept over her as she listened to her father's voice. Something seemed to be crying out to her to run in and seize her father and mother in her arms and hold them close.

"Love, love—nothing is true between us but love," she thought.

But why couldn't she do what she longed to do? Why, with all her passionate sympathy for them, should any actual contact with her people seem so impossible? No,

she couldn't go in just yet. Instead, she ran up on the roof, where she could be alone. She stationed herself at the air-shaft opposite their kitchen window, where for the first time since she had left in a rage she could see her old home.

Ach! what sickening disorder! In the sink were the dirty dishes stacked high, untouched, it looked, for days. The table still held the remains of the last meal. Clothes were strewn about the chairs. The bureau drawers were open, and their contents brimmed over in mad confusion.

"I couldn't endure it, this terrible dirt!" Her nails dug into her palms, shaking with the futility of her visit. "It would be worse than death to go back to them. It would mean giving up order, cleanliness, sanity, everything that I've striven all these years to attain. It would mean giving up the hope of my new world—the hope of Frank Baker."

The sound of the creaking door reached her where she crouched against the air-shaft. She looked again into the murky depths of the room. Her mother had entered. With arms full of paper bags of provisions, the old woman paused on the threshold, her eyes dwelling on the dim figure of her husband. A look of pathetic tenderness illumined her wrinkled features.

"I'll make something good to eat for you, yes?"

Reb Ravinsky only dropped his head on his breast. His eyes were red and dry, sandy with sorrow that could find no release in tears. Good God! Never had Rachel seen such profound despair. For the first time she noticed the grooved tracings of withering age knotted on his face and the growing hump on her mother's back.

"Already the shadow of death hangs over them," she thought as she watched them. "They're already with one foot in the grave. Why can't I be human to them before they're dead? Why can't I?"

Rachel blotted away the picture of the sordid room with both hands over her eyes.

"To death with my soul! I wish I were a plain human being with a heart instead of a monster of selfishness with a soul."

But the pity she felt for her parents began now to be swept away in a wave of pity for herself.

"How every step in advance costs me my heart's blood! My greatest tragedy in life is that I always see the two opposite sides at the same time. What seems to me right one day seems all wrong the next. Not only that, but many things seem right and wrong at the same time. I feel I have a right to my own life, and yet I feel just as strongly that I owe my father and mother something. Even if I don't love them, I have no right to step over them. I'm drawn to them by something more compelling than love. It is the cry of their dumb, wasted lives."

Again Rachel looked into the dimly lighted room below. Her mother placed food upon the table. With a self-effacing stoop of humility, she entreated, "Eat only while it is hot yet."

With his eyes fixed almost unknowingly, Reb Ravinsky sat down. Her mother took the chair opposite him, but she only pretended to eat the slender portion of the food she had given herself.

Rachel's heart swelled. Yes, it had always been like that. Her mother had taken the smallest portion of everything for herself. Complaints, reproaches, upbraidings, abuse, yes, all these had been heaped by her upon her mother; but always the juiciest piece of meat was placed on her plate, the thickest slice of bread; the warmest covering was given to her, while her mother shivered through the night.

"Ah, I don't want to abandon them!" she thought; "I only want to get to the place where I belong. I only want to get to the mountaintops and view the world from the heights, and then I'll give them everything I've achieved."

Her thoughts were sharply broken in upon by the loud sound of her father's eating. Bent over the table, he chewed with noisy gulps a piece of herring, his temples working to the motion of his jaws. With each audible swallow and smacking of the lips, Rachel's heart tightened with loathing.

"Their dirty ways turn all my pity into hate." She felt her toes and her fingers curl inward with disgust. "I'll never amount to anything if I'm not strong enough to break away from them once and for all." Hypnotizing herself into her line of self-defense, her thoughts raced on: "I'm only cruel to be kind. If I went back to them now, it would not be out of love, but because of weakness—because of doubt and unfaith in myself."

Rachel bluntly turned her back. Her head lifted. There was iron will in her jaws.

"If I haven't the strength to tear free from the old, I can never conquer the new. Every new step a man makes is a tearing away from those clinging to him. I must get tight and hard as rock inside of me if I'm ever to do the things I set out to do. I must learn to suffer and suffer, walk through blood and fire, and not bend from my course."

For the last time she looked at her parents. The terrible loneliness of their abandoned old age, their sor-rowful eyes, the wrung-dry weariness on their faces, the whole black picture of her ruined, desolate home, burned into her flesh. She knew all the pain of one unjustly condemned, and the guilt of one with the spilt blood of helpless lives upon his hands. Then came tears, blinding, wrenching tears that tore at her heart until it seemed that they would rend her body into shreds.

"God! God!" she sobbed as she turned her head away from them, "if all this suffering were at least for something worth while, for something outside myself. But to have to break them and crush them merely because I have a fastidious soul that can't stomach their table manners, merely because I can't strangle my aching ambitions to rise in the world!"

She could no longer sustain the conflict which raged within her higher and higher at every moment. With a sudden tension of all her nerves she pulled herself together and stumbled blindly downstairs and out of the house. And she felt as if she had torn away from the flesh and blood of her own body.

III

Out in the street she struggled to get hold of herself again. Despite the tumult and upheaval that racked her soul, an intoxicating lure still held her up—the hope of seeing Frank Baker that evening. She was indeed a storm-racked ship, but within sight of shore. She need but throw out the signal, and help was nigh. She need but confide to Frank Baker of her break with her people, and all the dormant sympathy between them would surge up. His understanding would widen and deepen because of her great need for his understanding. He would love her the more because of her great need for his love.

Forcing back her tears, stepping over her heartbreak, she hurried to the hotel where she was to meet him. Her father's impassioned rapture when he chanted the Psalms of David lit up the visionary face of the young Jewess.

"After all, love is the beginning of the real life," she thought as Frank Baker's dark, handsome face flashed before her. "With him to hold on to, I'll begin my new world."

Borne higher and higher by the intoxicating illusion of her great destiny, she cried:

"A person all alone is but a futile cry in an unheeding wilderness. One alone is but a shadow, an echo of reality. It takes two together to create reality. Two together can pioneer a new world."

With a vision of herself and Frank Baker marching side by side to the conquest of her heart's desire, she added:

"No wonder a man's love means so little to the American woman. They belong to the world in which they are born. They belong to their fathers and mothers; they belong to their relatives and friends. They are human even without a man's love. I don't belong; I'm not human. Only a man's love can save me and make me human again."

It was the busy dinner-hour at the fashionable restaurant. Pausing at the doorway with searching eyes and lips eagerly parted, Rachel's swift glance circled the lobby. Those seated in the dining-room beyond who were not too absorbed in one another, noticed a slim, vivid figure of ardent youth, but with dark, age-old eyes that told of the restless seeking of her homeless race.

With nervous little movements of anxiety, Rachel sat down, got up, then started across the lobby. Halfway, she stopped, and her breath caught.

"Mr. Baker," she murmured, her hands fluttering toward him with famished eagerness. His smooth, athletic figure had a cock-sureness that to the girl's worshipping gaze seemed the perfection of male strength.

"You must be doing wonderful things," came from her admiringly, "you look so happy, so shining with life."

"Yes,"—he shook her hand vigorously,—"I've been living for the first time since I was a kid. I'm full of such interesting experiences. I'm actually working in an East Side settlement."

Dazed by his glamorous success, Rachel stammered soft phrases of congratulations as he led her to a table. But seated opposite him, the face of this untried youth, flushed with the health and happiness of another world than that of the poverty-crushed Ghetto, struck her almost as an insincerity.

"You in an East Side settlement?" she interrupted sharply. "What reality can there be in that work for you?"

"Oh," he cried, his shoulders squaring with the assurance of his master's degree in sociology, "it's great to get under the surface and see how the other half lives. It's so picturesque! My conception of these people has greatly changed since I've been visiting their homes." He launched into a glowing account of the East Side as seen by a twenty-five-year-old college graduate.

"I thought them mostly immersed in hard labor, digging subways or slaving in sweatshops," he went on.

"But think of the poetry which the immigrant is daily living!"

"But they're so sunk in the dirt of poverty, what poetry do you see there?"

"It's their beautiful home life, the poetic devotion between parents and children, the sacrifices they make for one another—"

"Beautiful home life? Sacrifices? Why, all I know of is the battle to the knife between parents and children. It's black tragedy that boils there, not the pretty sentiments that you imagine."

"My dear child,"—he waved aside her objection,—"you're too close to judge dispassionately. This very afternoon, on one of my friendly visits, I came upon a dear old man who peered up at me through horn-rimmed glasses behind his pile of Hebrew books. He was hardly able to speak English, but I found him a great scholar."

"Yes, a lazy old do-nothing, a bloodsucker on his wife and children."

Too shocked for remonstrance, Frank Baker stared at her.

"How else could he have time in the middle of the afternoon to pore over his books?" Rachel's voice was hard with bitterness. "Did you see his wife? I'll bet she was slaving for him in the kitchen. And his children slaving for him in the sweat-shop."

"Even so, think of the fine devotion that the women and children show in making the lives of your Hebrew scholars possible. It's a fine contribution to America, where our tendency is to forget idealism."

"Give me better a plain American man who supports his wife and children and I'll give you all those dreamers of the Talmud."

He smiled tolerantly at her vehemence.

"Nevertheless," he insisted, "I've found wonderful material for my new book in all this. I think I've got a new angle on the social types of your East Side."

An icy band tightened about her heart. "Social types," her lips formed. How could she possibly confide to this man of the terrible tragedy that she had been through that very day? Instead of the understanding and sympathy that she had hoped to find, there were only smooth platitudes, the sightseer's surface interest in curious "social types."

Frank Baker talked on. Rachel seemed to be listening, but her eyes had a far-off, abstracted look. She was quiet as a spinning-top is quiet, her thoughts and emotions revolving within her at high speed.

"That man in love with me? Why, he doesn't see me or feel me. I don't exist to him. He's only stuck on himself, blowing his own horn. Will he never stop with his 'I,' 'I,' 'I'? Why, I was a crazy lunatic to think that just because we took the same courses in college, he would understand me out in the real world."

All the fire suddenly went out of her eyes. She looked a thousand years old as she sank back wearily in her chair.

"Oh, but I'm boring you with all my heavy talk on sociology." Frank Baker's words seemed to come to her from afar. "I have tickets for a fine musical comedy that will cheer you up, Miss Ravinsky—"

"Thanks, thanks," she cut in hurriedly. Spend a whole evening sitting beside him in a theater when her heart was breaking? No. All she wanted was to get away—away where she could be alone. "I have work to do," she heard herself say. "I've got to get home."

Frank Baker murmured words of polite disappointment and escorted her back to her door. She watched the sure swing of his athletic figure as he strode away down the street, then she rushed upstairs.

Back in her little room, stunned, bewildered, blinded with her disillusion, she sat staring at her four empty walls.

Hours passed, but she made no move, she uttered no sound. Doubled fists thrust between her knees, she sat there, staring blindly at her empty walls.

"I can't live with the old world, and I'm yet too green for the new. I don't belong to those who gave me birth or to those with whom I was educated."

Was this to be the end of all her struggles to rise in America, she asked herself, this crushing daze of loneliness? Her driving thirst for an education, her desperate battle for a little cleanliness, for a breath of beauty, the tearing away from her own flesh and blood to free herself from the yoke of her parents—what was it all worth now? Where did it lead to? Was loneliness to be the fruit of it all?

Night was melting away like a fog; through the open window the first lights of dawn were appearing. Rachel felt the sudden touch of the sun upon her face, which was bathed in tears. Overcome by her sorrow, she shuddered and put her hand over her eyes as though to shut out the unwelcome contact. But the light shone through her fingers.

Despite her weariness, the renewing breath of the fresh morning entered her heart like a sunbeam. A mad longing for life filled her veins.

"I want to live," her youth cried. "I want to live, even at the worst."

Live how? Live for what? She did not know. She only felt she must struggle against her loneliness and weariness as she had once struggled against dirt, against the squalor and ugliness of her Ghetto home.

Turning from the window, she concentrated her mind, her poor tired mind, on one idea.

"I have broken away from the old world; I'm through with it. It's already behind me. I must face this loneliness till I get to the new world. Frank Baker can't help me; I must hope for no help from the outside. I'm alone; I'm alone till I get there.

"But am I really alone in my seeking? I'm one of the millions of immigrant children, children of loneliness, wandering between worlds that are at once too old and too new to live in."

Other works by Yezierska: *Salome of the Tenements* (1923); *Bread Givers* (1925); *Red Ribbon on a White Horse* (1950).

Isaac Babel

Gedali
1924

On the eve of the Sabbath I am always tormented by the dense sorrow of memory. In the past on these evenings, my grandfather's yellow beard caressed the volumes of Ibn Ezra. My old grandmother, in her lace bonnet, waved spells over the Sabbath candle with her gnarled fingers, and sobbed sweetly. On those evenings my child's heart was gently rocked, like a little boat on enchanted waves.

I wander through Zhitomir looking for the timid star. Beside the ancient synagogue, beside its indifferent yellow walls, old Jews, Jews with the beards of prophets, passionate rags hanging from their sunken chests, are selling chalk, bluing, and candle wicks.

Here before me lies the bazaar, and the death of the bazaar. Slaughtered is the fat soul of abundance. Mute padlocks hang on the stores, and the granite of the streets is as clean as a corpse's bald head. The timid star blinks and expires.

Success came to me later, I found the star just before the setting of the sun. Gedali's store lay hidden among the tightly shut market stalls. Dickens, where was your shadow that evening? In this old junk store you would have found gilded slippers and ship's ropes, an antique compass and a stuffed eagle, a Winchester hunting rifle with the date "1810" engraved on it, and a broken stewpot.

Old Gedali is circling around his treasures in the rosy emptiness of the evening, a small shopkeeper with smoky spectacles and a green coat that reaches all the way to the ground. He rubs his small white hands, tugs at his gray beard, lowers his head, and listens to invisible voices that come wafting to him.

This store is like the box of an intent and inquisitive little boy who will one day become a professor of botany. This store has everything from buttons to dead butterflies, and its little owner is called Gedali. Everyone has left the bazaar, but Gedali has remained. He roams through his labyrinth of globes, skulls, and dead flowers, waving his cockerel-feather duster, swishing away the dust from the dead flowers.

We sit down on some empty beer barrels. Gedali winds and unwinds his narrow beard. His top hat rocks above us like a little black tower. Warm air flows past us. The sky changes color—tender blood pouring from an overturned bottle—and a gentle aroma of decay envelops me.

"So let's say we say 'yes' to the Revolution. But does that mean that we're supposed to say 'no' to the Sabbath?" Gedali begins, enmeshing me in the silken cords of his smoky eyes. "Yes to the Revolution! Yes! But the Revolution keeps hiding from Gedali and sending gunfire ahead of itself."

"The sun cannot enter eyes that are squeezed shut," I say to the old man, "but we shall rip open those closed eyes!"

"The Pole has closed my eyes," the old man whispers almost inaudibly. "The Pole, that evil dog! He grabs the Jew and rips out his beard, *oy*, the hound! But now they are beating him, the evil dog! This is marvelous, this is the Revolution! But then the same man who beat the Pole says to me, 'Gedali, we are requisitioning your gramophone!' 'But gentlemen,' I tell the Revolution, 'I love music!' And what does the Revolution answer me? 'You don't know what you love, Gedali! I am going to shoot you, and then you'll know, and I cannot *not* shoot, because I am the Revolution!'"

"The Revolution cannot *not* shoot, Gedali," I tell the old man, "because it is the Revolution."

"But my dear *Pan*! The Pole did shoot, because he is the counter-revolution. And you shoot because you are the Revolution. But Revolution is happiness. And happiness does not like orphans in its house. A good man does good deeds. The Revolution is the good deed done by good men. But good men do not kill. Hence the Revolution is done by bad men. But the Poles are also bad men. Who is going to tell Gedali which is the Revolution and which the counterrevolution? I have studied the Talmud. I love the commentaries of Rashi and the books of Maimonides. And there are also other people in Zhitomir who understand. And so all of us learned men fall to the floor and shout with a single voice, 'Woe unto us, where is the sweet Revolution?'"

The old man fell silent. And we saw the first star breaking through and meandering along the Milky Way.

"The Sabbath is beginning," Gedali pronounced solemnly. "Jews must go to the synagogue."

"*Pan* Comrade," he said, getting up, his top hat swaying on his head like a little black tower. "Bring a few good men to Zhitomir. *Oy*, they are lacking in our town, *oy*, how they are lacking! Bring good men and we shall give them all our gramophones. We are not simpletons. The International, we know what the International is. And I want the International of good people, I want every soul to be accounted for and given first-class rations. Here, soul, eat, go ahead, go and find happiness in your life. The International, *Pan* Comrade, you have no idea how to swallow it!"

"With gunpowder," I tell the old man, "and seasoned with the best blood."

And then from the blue darkness young Sabbath climbed onto her throne.

"Gedali," I say to him, "today is Friday, and night has already fallen. Where can I find some Jewish biscuits, a Jewish glass of tea, and a piece of that retired God in the glass of tea?"

"You can't," Gedali answers, hanging a lock on his box, "you can't find any. There's a tavern next door, and good people used to run it, but people don't eat there anymore, they weep."

He fastened the three bone buttons of his green coat. He dusted himself with the cockerel feathers, sprinkled a little water on the soft palms of his hands, and walked off, tiny, lonely, dreamy, with his black top hat, and a large prayer book under his arm.

The Sabbath begins. Gedali, the founder of an unattainable International, went to the synagogue to pray.

Translated by Peter Constantine.

Isaac Babel

My First Goose
1924

Savitsky, the commander of the Sixth Division, rose when he saw me, and I was taken aback by the beauty of his gigantic body. He rose—his breeches purple, his crimson cap cocked to the side, his medals pinned to his chest—splitting the hut in two like a banner splitting the sky. He smelled of perfume and the nauseating coolness of soap. His long legs looked like two girls wedged to their shoulders in riding boots.

He smiled at me, smacked the table with his whip, and picked up the order which the chief of staff had just dictated. It was an order for Ivan Chesnokov to advance to Chugunov-Dobryvodka with the regiment he had been entrusted with, and, on encountering the enemy, to proceed immediately with its destruction.

". . . the destruction of which," Savitsky began writing, filling the whole sheet, "I hold the selfsame Chesnokov completely responsible for. Noncompliance will incur the severest punitive measures, in other words I will gun him down on the spot, a fact that I am sure that you, Comrade Chesnokov, will not doubt, as it's been quite a while now that you have worked with me on the front. . . ."

The commander of the Sixth Division signed the order with a flourish, threw it at the orderlies, and turned his gray eyes, dancing with merriment, toward me.

I handed him the document concerning my assignment to the divisional staff.

"See to the paperwork!" the division commander said. "See to the paperwork, and have this man sign up for all the amusements except for those of the frontal kind. Can you read and write?"

"Yes, I can," I answered, bristling with envy at the steel and bloom of his youth. "I graduated in law from the University of Petersburg."

"So you're one of those little powder puffs!" he yelled, laughing. "With spectacles on your nose! Ha, you lousy little fellow, you! They send you to us, no one even asks us if we want you here! Here you get hacked to pieces just for wearing glasses! So, you think you can live with us, huh?"

"Yes, I do," I answered, and went to the village with the quartermaster to look for a place to stay.

The quartermaster carried my little suitcase on his shoulder. The village street lay before us, and the dy-ing sun in the sky, round and yellow as a pumpkin, breathed its last rosy breath.

We came to a hut with garlands painted on it. The quartermaster stopped, and suddenly, smiling guiltily, said, "You see we have a thing about spectacles here, there ain't nothing you can do! A man of high distinguishings they'll chew up and spit out—but ruin a lady, yes, the most cleanest lady, and you're the darling of the fighters!"

He hesitated for a moment, my suitcase still on his shoulder, came up very close to me, but suddenly lunged away in despair, rushing into the nearest courtyard. Cossacks were sitting there on bundles of hay, shaving each other.

"Fighters!" the quartermaster began, putting my suitcase on the ground. "According to an order issued by Comrade Savitsky, you are required to accept this man to lodge among you. And no funny business, please, because this man has suffered on the fields of learning!"

The quartermaster flushed and marched off without looking back. I lifted my hand to my cap and saluted the Cossacks. A young fellow with long, flaxen hair and a wonderful Ryazan face walked up to my suitcase and threw it out into the street. Then he turned his backside toward me, and with uncommon dexterity began emitting shameless sounds.

"That was a zero-zero caliber!" an older Cossack yelled, laughing out loud. "Rapid-fire!"

The young man walked off, having exhausted the limited resources of his artistry. I went down on my hands and knees and gathered up the manuscripts and the old, tattered clothes that had fallen out of my suitcase. I took them and carried them to the other end of the yard. A large pot of boiling pork stood on some bricks in front of the hut. Smoke rose from it as distant smoke rises from the village hut of one's childhood, mixing hunger with intense loneliness inside me. I covered my broken little suitcase with hay, turning it into a pillow, and lay down on the ground to read Lenin's speech at the Second Congress of the Comintern, which *Pravda* had printed. The sun fell on me through the jagged hills, the Cossacks kept stepping over my legs, the young fellow incessantly made fun of me, the beloved sentences struggled toward me over thorny paths, but could not reach me. I put away the newspaper and went to the mistress of the house, who was spinning yarn on the porch.

"Mistress," I said, "I need some grub!"

The old woman raised the dripping whites of her half-blind eyes to me and lowered them again.

"Comrade," she said, after a short silence. "All of this makes me want to hang myself!"

"Goddammit!" I muttered in frustration, shoving her back with my hand. "I'm in no mood to start debating with you!"

And, turning around, I saw someone's saber lying nearby. A haughty goose was waddling through the yard, placidly grooming its feathers. I caught the goose and forced it to the ground, its head cracking beneath my boot, cracking and bleeding. Its white neck lay stretched out in the dung, and the wings folded down over the slaughtered bird.

"Goddammit!" I said, poking at the goose with the saber. "Roast it for me, mistress!"

The old woman, her blindness and her spectacles flashing, picked up the bird, wrapped it in her apron, and hauled it to the kitchen.

"Comrade," she said after a short silence. "This makes me want to hang myself." And she pulled the door shut behind her.

In the yard the Cossacks were already sitting around their pot. They sat motionless, straight-backed like heathen priests, not once having looked at the goose.

"This fellow'll fit in here well enough," one of them said, winked, and scooped up some cabbage soup with his spoon.

The Cossacks began eating with the restrained grace of muzhiks who respect one another. I cleaned the saber with sand, went out of the courtyard, and came back again, feeling anguished. The moon hung over the yard like a cheap earring.

"Hey, brother!" Surovkov, the oldest of the Cossacks, suddenly said to me. "Sit with us and have some of this till your goose is ready!"

He fished an extra spoon out of his boot and handed it to me. We slurped the cabbage soup and ate the pork.

"So, what are they writing in the newspaper?" the young fellow with the flaxen hair asked me, and moved aside to make room for me.

"In the newspaper, Lenin writes," I said, picking up my *Pravda*, "Lenin writes that right now there is a shortage of everything."

And in a loud voice, like a triumphant deaf man, I read Lenin's speech to the Cossacks.

The evening wrapped me in the soothing dampness of her twilight sheets, the evening placed her motherly palms on my burning brow.

I read, and rejoiced, waiting for the effect, rejoicing in the mysterious curve of Lenin's straight line.

"Truth tickles all and sundry in the nose," Surovkov said when I had finished. "It isn't all that easy to wheedle it out of the pile of rubbish, but Lenin picks it up right away, like a hen pecks up a grain of corn."

That is what Surovkov, the squadron commander, said about Lenin, and then we went to sleep in the hayloft. Six of us slept there warming each other, our legs tangled, under the holes in the roof which let in the stars.

I dreamed and saw women in my dreams, and only my heart, crimson with murder, screeched and bled.

Translated by Peter Constantine.

Isaac Babel

The Rabbi's Son
1924

Do you remember Zhitomir, Vasily? Do you remember the River Teterev, Vasily, and that night in which the Sabbath, the young Sabbath, crept along the sunset crushing the stars with the heel of her red slipper?

The thin horn of the moon dipped its arrows in the black waters of the Teterev. Little, funny Gedali, the founder of the Fourth International, who took us to Rabbi Motale Bratslavsky for evening prayer. Little, funny Gedali, shaking the cockerel feathers of his top hat in the red smoke of the evening. The candles' predatory pupils twinkled in the rabbi's room. Broad-shouldered Jews crouched moaning over prayer books, and the old jester of the Chernobyl line of *tsaddiks* jingled copper coins in his frayed pocket.

You remember that night, Vasily? Outside the window horses neighed and Cossacks shouted. The wasteland of war yawned outside and Rabbi Motale Bratslavsky, clutching his tallith with his withered fingers, prayed at the eastern wall. Then the curtains of the cabinet fell open, and in the funerary shine of the candles we saw the Torah scrolls wrapped in coverings of purple velvet and blue silk, and above the Torah scrolls hovered the humble, beautiful, lifeless face of Ilya, the rabbi's son, the last prince of the dynasty.

And then, Vasily, two days ago the regiments of the Twelfth Army opened the front at Kovel. The victors' haughty cannonade thundered through the town. Our troops were shaken and thrown into disarray. The Politotdel train crept along the dead spine of the fields. The typhoid-ridden muzhik horde rolled the gigantic ball of rampant soldier death before it. The horde scampered onto the steps of our train and fell off again, beaten back by rifle butts. It panted, scrambled, ran, was silent. And after twelve versts, when I no longer had any potatoes to throw to them, I threw a bundle of Trotsky leaflets at them. But only one of them stretched out a dirty, dead hand to grab a leaflet. And I recognized Ilya, the son of the Zhitomir rabbi. I recognized him straightaway, Vasily! It was so painful to see the prince, who had lost his trousers, his back snapped in two by the weight of his soldier's rucksack, that we broke the rules and dragged him up into the railroad car. His naked knees, clumsy like the knees of an old woman, knocked against the rusty iron of the steps. Two fat-breasted typists in sailor blouses dragged the dying man's timid, lanky body along the floor. We laid him out in the corner of the train's editorial compartment. Cossacks in red Tatar trousers fixed his slipped clothing. The girls, their bandy bovine legs firmly planted on the floor, stared coolly at his sexual organs, the withered, curly manhood of the emaciated Semite. And I, who had met him during one of my nights of wandering, packed the scattered belongings of Red Army soldier Ilya Bratslavsky into my suitcase.

I threw everything together in a jumble, the mandates of the political agitator and the mementos of a Jewish poet. Portraits of Lenin and Maimonides lay side by side—the gnarled steel of Lenin's skull and the listless silk of the Maimonides portrait. A lock of woman's hair lay in a book of the resolutions of the Sixth Party Congress, and crooked lines of Ancient Hebrew verse huddled in the margins of Communist pamphlets. Pages of *The Song of Songs* and revolver cartridges drizzled on me in a sad, sparse rain. The sad rain of the sunset washed the dust from my hair, and I said to the young man, who was dying on a ripped mattress in the corner, "Four months ago, on a Friday evening, Gedali the junk dealer took me to your father, Rabbi Motale, but back then, Bratslavsky, you were not in the Party."

"I was in the Party back then," the young man answered, scratching his chest and twisting in his fever. "But I couldn't leave my mother behind."

"What about now, Ilya?"

"My mother is just an episode of the Revolution," he whispered, his voice becoming fainter. "Then my letter came up, the letter 'B,' and the organization sent me off to the front. . . ."

"So you ended up in Kovel?"

"I ended up in Kovel!" he shouted in despair. "The damn kulaks opened the front. I took over a mixed regiment, but it was too late. I didn't have enough artillery."

He died before we reached Rovno. He died, the last prince, amid poems, phylacteries, and foot bindings. We buried him at a desolate train station. And I, who can barely harness the storms of fantasy raging through my ancient body, I received my brother's last breath.

Translated by Peter Constantine.

Enrique Espinoza
1898–1988

Enrique Espinoza was the pen name of Samuel Glusberg, a Ukrainian-born writer and editor who became a major figure on the Argentine literary scene. He edited the monthly literary review *Babel*, which appeared between 1921 and 1951; helped found the Argentine Writers' Association; and published many works by major Argentine writers. Although well integrated into Latin American society, he wrote frequently on the difficulties of creating a national identity from the various collective groups that made up the population of multiethnic states like Argentina. His 1953 essay on Heinrich Heine, "El ángel y el león," discussed the predicament of Jewish writers who lived on the margins of two cultural worlds.

The Cross
1924

"Sonia! . . . Sonia! . . . Where the devil have you gone, child? Sonia!"

A Jewish woman calls her little girl in from the patio of her apartment.

It's five in the afternoon, and as it's midwinter, night is falling.

The woman—Sara is her name—has just finished blessing the Friday evening candles and she and the household are already entering the Sabbath.

"Sonia . . . Sonia . . ." Sara continues calling.

No one answers.

Finally irritated, tired of the cold, she enters the room.

"Have you seen your little sister? What a shameless girl!" she says in Spanish to Ruben—a nine-year-old who'd arrived a bit earlier from Hebrew school and was just having tea with his sailor cap pulled down to his ears.

And she adds in Yiddish: "It seems the devil's taken her; that child is always wandering around."

Ruben, busy having tea, doesn't answer her. But finally, when he finishes with a loud and noisy slurp, he raises his head—the name "General Belgrano" on his cap in gold letters. Then he answers:

"Sonia's probably with the Castro girls." And he shakes some crumbs off of his windbreaker.

"No, what a thought! She'd have heard me. I've been calling her for half an hour!"

But Ruben, realizing that his mother is exaggerating, opens the door and goes out in search of Sonia.

The boy returns after five minutes.

"I have gone," he says, "to all six apartments and haven't found her anywhere." Then he adds: "Doña Teresa told me she thought she'd seen her going off to school with her daughters."

"What!" Sara exclaims, surprised, "in school at this hour? Washing the seats with lemon oil again! That can't be!"

"Do you want me to go look for her, Mama?" Ruben proposes.

"No, I'll go," the woman says, and asks, "Where's my shawl?"

"Ah, in the other room," she answers herself, and goes to look for it.

She's back in an instant, covering her head and shoulders with a thick, checkered shawl, like the ones Jewish women bring from Russia.

"Take care of the baby, he's sleeping," she tells Ruben before going out. And at the door, she turns back to remind him to be careful with the candles.

A few minutes after doña Sara's exit, Reb Sujer, her husband, enters the house. He is small with a pointy chickpea-colored beard, black cap, blue overcoat and a bill collector's satchel under his arm.

"Good afternoon, Papa," Ruben greets him as he hides his pen knife and takes off his cap.

"Good Sabbath, son," the man answers as he enters and asks, "Where's mama?"

"She went to look for Sonia; she'll be right back."

In fact, Sara arrives shortly dragging Sonia behind her, a little eight-year-old redhead who is pouting and rubbing her eyes with her free hand.

"*Oi, vei is mir! Vei is mir!* A misfortune has befallen us; a disgrace!" doña Sara clamors, seating her round body in a chair and taking off her shawl.

"What's wrong, woman?" Reb Sujer turns to her frightened while Ruben opens his big eyes in surprise.

"*Oi Vei is mir! Vei is mir!*" clamors doña Sara even louder. "They've made us lose our child—my God what a misfortune!"

Because of her yelling, the baby in the next room wakes up and begins to cry.

"Ruben," his mother says, twisting her fingers and sighing, "go check on the baby."

Ruben obeys.

"*Oi vei is mir!* What a misfortune!" the woman wails again.

"But what is it, Sara, what is it?" Reb Sujer asks impatiently.

"They have converted our Sonia . . . *Vei is mir!* What a misfortune! My God, if you only knew!"

And while Sara loudly explains, without her husband understanding a word about the misfortune that has happened, the baby continues crying and wailing in the next room.

Finally, in answer to Ruben's insistent calls, the woman goes in to the next room.

"Straighten things out with your daughter," she says to her husband before leaving the room. "Teach her about becoming Christian with a good beating!"

Sonia, who was leaning on the edge of her seat, starts sobbing even more at this threat. Reb Sujer, a bit angry, his gray eyes moist and shining, looks at the menorah with its ritual candles and thinks about the sacred calm of the Sabbath. This thought makes him turn gently to his daughter.

"Where were you, little Sonia? What happened? Tell me about it," he says tenderly, drawing her to him.

Calmed by her father's voice, the child answers:

"Nothing, Daddy, nothing," still weeping.

"But where were you, little one? Where did Mama find you?"

"In school, Daddy. I went with Magda and Angelica, to religion class, and Mama came to get me out."

Having said this, Sonia breaks into tears again.

"Come now, that's enough tears. Tell me, what class? Where?"

"In school, Daddy, when the afternoon session is over, a priest comes to teach us catechism. All the girls go and I do too."

Reb Sujer buries his face in his hands.

"But don't you know," he shouts, "that a child of Israel cannot have anything to do with priests or the church? Who gave you permission to go?"

At this sudden change in her father, the little girl again bursts into tears. Then overcome by this paternal anger, she pleads in a tremulous little voice:

"Forgive me, Daddy, forgive me . . . I won't ever go again."

"The thing is you never should have gone! This is all we need! Your father is an Israelite, your mother is an Israelite, you and your brother are Israelites, all the family are Israelites and you are going to be a Catholic! Whoever heard of such a thing?"

"I'm sorry," Sonia says, "I won't ever go again; but I get so bored at home. Doña Teresa's girls go there and leave me all alone. Doña Teresa lets them go."

"Of course, because she's Catholic! But you have nothing to do with Jesus. Do you hear? I forbid you to go and that's the end of it . . ."

Because the little girl continues to cry, Reb Sujer softens his voice and promises to let her learn to play the piano so that she won't get bored.

At that, Sonia's little face lights up.

"And you'll send me to the conservatory, Daddy?"

"Yes, little one."

"To Saint Cecilia's?"

"Yes, my child."

"How wonderful, Daddy! How wonderful! I swear, I'll never go to religion class again!"

And to confirm her oath, Sonia pulls a small chain out from under her blouse and kisses the cross hanging there.

"Oh woe is me! Woe is me!"

Translated by Rita Gardiol.

Other works by Espinoza: *La levita gris* (1924); *Ruth y Noemí* (1934); *El castellano y Babel* (1974).

Chaim Hazaz

1898-1973

The Hebrew novelist and short-story writer Chaim Hazaz was born in a village in the province of Kiev and received a traditional Jewish education. He left home at age sixteen and lived a peripatetic life until 1921 in Russian cities. During these years of turbulence and upheaval, he witnessed events that became the foundation of his works. From 1921 to 1931, he lived in

Istanbul, Paris, and Berlin. He settled in Jerusalem in 1931 and remained there the rest of his life. Central to most of his work is the tension between the old Jewish world and the wish for redemption through political movements such as Zionism. He was one of the most popular Hebrew writers of his time.

Revolutionary Chapters
1924

I

The war went on and would not be stopped. On the contrary. It proved futile to hold it to any schedule or limit. At no prearranged time would the land be quiet, not at harvest time, not near winter, and not in the spring.

At harvest time, and near winter, and also in the spring it was as if the war had just begun setting to work in earnest.

Like a pot left on the fire: the water starts simmering and is about to come to a boil.

In short, all the filth and noxious scum rose to the surface. Rasputin, secret spies, a wireless hidden in a Holy Ark in the House of Study, alas, a windmill somehow waving its sails and transmitting signals to the Germans, Jews driven out, old Jews hanged on trees as spies . . .

And the whole country, from one end to the other, full of war, darkness, poverty and the fear of sudden death.

Man and all his generations perished!

Sons called to the army shortened their years as much as possible, violating their faces and shaving their whiskers very, very close every day, to remain boys, absolute youngsters, while the fathers added on years and grew older and older—

But to no avail!

The war visited fathers and sons together, old man and youth—no one was exempt.

Old and young, fathers and sons, all together joined the army! Everyone in the world took up a gun, shaking arms and legs, walking from the barracks to the bathhouse, humming tunes.

"No end to her, damn her!" men shouted to themselves and to their comrades. "What's to be done about the bitch?"

Eventually, but not necessarily at the appointed time, when the Revolution occurred, the dream came true at last. Then everyone was like a dreamer: joyful, surprised, a bit apprehensive, as one is sometimes surprised and apprehensive after a dream.

Even the heavens and earth seemed to have been created only to assist the dream: blue skies, sparkling and fresh. . . . The snow melted outside, and the heavens were planted in their waters, the roofs were scoured and dripped bright drops of water. A cool breeze blew. And people were drawn outside, walking in crowds, bright, glowing, like throngs of blind men, singing, raising their voices, shouting, and yelling—they truly withdrew their souls from their bodies! Weeping, they hugged and kissed each other, red flags fluttered in the breeze above their heads and the wheel of the sun shone and rolled above them, and it seemed as though the throngs led the wheel of the sun wherever their spirit happened to take them. . . .

War had not yet fallen silent in the land. But now it was of another degree, another degree and a different flag.

"War with no annexation or confiscation," the formula passed from mouth to mouth.

"War to the final victory!" some said.

School children learned how to deliver those proclamations and spread them throughout the world.

The deserters, who had hidden in corners all during the war, became human again and emerged into daylight.

A huge mass of people marched through the streets toward the railroad station, all of them bearing rifles with a song on their lips:

"Arise, ye workers of the people! . . ."

The deserters made a great name for themselves in town. . . .

Nevertheless, the benefit proved to be flawed. How is that?

The reason is, to borrow from Torah cantillation, that *darga*, the rising note, precedes *tevir*, the falling one.

Thus said Reb Simcha Horowitz.

Reb Simcha was an expert Torah reader, a true connoisseur of notes and signs.

Then the word got out: the soldiers have mutinied. . . . They've had their fill of war. . . . Impossible to keep them in the trenches . . .

"Of course! They aren't laying hens, and who could get them to hatch these?"

Conspirators pressed and insinuated themselves into the crowds, grumbling:

"An end to the war! True liberty!"

Also Henya Horowitz, Reb Simcha's daughter, had plenty of demands:

"An end to the war! Enough!"

"Everyone will immediately stop what he's doing and listen to you," Reb Simcha chided his daughter. "Don't mix into other people's business!"

"Let them put an end to the imperialist war!" Henya spoke in denunciation.

That is just the phrase she used: "the imperialist war!"

Henya had an infernal spirit, a rotten pest, not a maiden, an agent of destruction! Since the confusion of tongues, no tongue was ever found like Henya's.

"Do you really think," Reb Simcha asks her, "that since I never studied geography and Sherlock Holmes, I lack all understanding?"

Why, she couldn't see the strength of his position at all! . . .

Round and round revolved the wheel. Events took a bad turn and sprouted up like weeds in the land. The front collapsed and soldiers flowed up out of all the fields and the paths over the mountain crests, they and all their hordes—horror! The whole land rumbled before them.

As though through an open door, they passed through the town.

Generally speaking: the war was abandoned.

"It must be because the town is situated in the center of the earth," says Reb Simcha, "right in the middle, and that's why those passing through here are so numerous they cannot be reckoned up in real numbers, with no end to them. . . . And perhaps the soldiers have lost their course, and they go back and forth, back and forth, because the earth is round, and since those marchers have no set and determined longitude, they come back again and again."

Yes, that brigade had already been through once, like a rat trapped in a maze, without officers or military equipment, with only a large cooking pot, on their way to their home country somewhere. . . . Then, the first time around, they had stood, perishing with empty bellies. They broke into all the ovens and removed the *cholent* and all the Sabbath food, without the tiniest leftover, cleaning everything out spotlessly, and they sat in the center of the marketplace and ate away their hunger and pain, even dancing and celebrating. Now the brigade came back, the very same one with the same quality—as borne out by their looks: without officers and without military equipment, only a large cooking pot. . . .

"What's this?" the townsmen explain to them. "We are of the opinion that you have already gone through here once."

"No, no, not us," the answer. "That is, we have not yet gone through. We are considered another brigade, so to speak."

As it seemed, they spoke the truth. Since they left without breaking into the ovens.

Such righteousness!

"Happy are we and happy our lot," says Reb Simcha, "that surveyors are not commonly found amongst us. For if that were not so, those splendid orators and all the public speakers who have risen up over us would propose and demand miles and long miles and plots of land. . . . Now, since we have only storekeepers, those speakers will offer up their deceitful arguments and claims and all their imaginary assurances according to the length of their own yardstick.

"They have one title—Bolshevik! Such a sect. Jewish sinners. Blast their souls for having studied the Revolution with Rashi's commentary! Not the literal meaning, but the homiletic meaning: what's mine is yours, and what's yours is mine. . . . And their ulterior evil intention is visible to everyone who is at all knowledgeable about them."

In one swoop like the tail of a comet, in the wink of a single eye, the plague spread through the world: bolshevism.

"The world is holding a memorial service," says Reb Simcha, "and so all the minors with parents still living have been set loose!"

All the young people and boors have usurped the birthright and begun ruling, even Henya has been made a commissar. A regular commissar.

The worms in the earth would wreak less destruction than they!

"Absolute redemption!" Henya girded her loins against Reb Simcha and mixed things up. "Now redemption has come to the proletariat! . . . The rule of workers and peasants . . . Wars will cease, poverty and slavery will be no more, no oppressors and no oppressed."

In short, the whole world is grace, mercy and peace. And the wolf shall dwell with the lamb. . . .

A rotten pest, not a maiden! The spirit of redemption throbs in her breast! . . . Just get a load of her theories and doctrines! Try and plead a case against her!

Bad, bitter, helpless. There is no restoration in the world, no one setting things right. What has come to pass! . . .

"Where are you going, comrades?" Reb Simcha shouts, confused and distraught. "What are you doing for the bitter sorrows of our soul?"

The comrades, armed to the teeth, reply:

"Remember this, old age, and pay heed: the whole land is in the hands of the aroused people. Don't you wish to go along with the people in their uprising?"

"Have pity and mercy, comrades, for you are murderers, armed robbers, oh Lord of the universe."

"Spare us your poetry, comrade Reb Simcha, your Lord of the universe has created a new spirit within us—to raise the edifice, to give it an upper story."

Those are the words of Henikh the carpenter to Reb Simcha, and as he speaks, he raises his hand high and calls out:

"True, comrade! . . . We agree!"

"The Holy One blessed be He created a will in us, to submit our will to His blessed will!" Reb Simcha shouts to Henikh.

"Look, look!" Henikh thrusts his callused, soiled hands in Reb Simcha's face. "Did you see? We don't know how to study the Mishnah! Since the start of this imperialist war, I haven't set eyes on a book. Understand?"

Another "sinner" like that went up to Reb Simcha, stared at him with murderous, robber's eyes, as though to slay him:

"You old dog's nose, where are you sticking yourself, eh? If I step on your foot, you'll be lame. If I crush you in my closed fist, you'll no longer exist. Old louse!"

A second sinner walked up to Reb Simcha, yawned in his face as if he were a dog, took his hand and pushed him to the side, saying:

"Get out of here."

To be sure, Reb Simcha left. By the skin of his teeth, you could say, he slipped away from the murderers and hid in a cellar beneath his house.

Nothing restrains those heretics! All who are compassionate have compassion for Israel. All dwellers in the dust will beg for mercy.

The next Sabbath Reb Simcha was called to the Torah and made the benediction for escaping death.

II

The world is mad, the world is satanical, torn to shreds. Band after band, piled up and confused, quarrel with each other, speaking in floods of words. Life is enveloped with hunger and blood, dread and darkness. And the mainstay, scattering hunger and blood and dread and darkness from one end to the other, is comrade Polishuk.

The winds snatched up that fine comrade and brought him to the town!

"Authorization," people reported. "He has one in his pocket from Petrograd itself, to put things right."

And people even found it amazing: a young man of short stature, skin and bones, tattered and worn, and he sets out to conquer towns and cities—what a man! People tried to avoid direct encounters with him. They knew that he had an authorization from Petrograd itself and that he came swooping down in a train bearing a sign in red letters: "Death to the Bourgeoisie!"

Comrade Polishuk took up residence in the home of Reb Simcha. Henya herself brought him.

Reb Simcha was secretly fuming, grumbling to himself about the comrades, men and women, and their evil seed. Finally he became reconciled: "Very well, let him stay. What can we do? Eventually he'll probably go away. Perhaps a spirit from on high will be aroused in him, and he'll go. Perhaps the blessed Lord will grant that his days be short."

So he stayed. He stayed in the large *zal*. He slept on the old sofa. He folded his coat beneath his head and slept. At his head, on the wall, hung his rifle, and on the table the pistol and several deadly pellets scattered about.

"I wouldn't make room for anyone else in the *zal*," says Reb Simcha. "Only for you."

Comrade Polishuk smiled as if to say: "As though it depended only upon you and your wishes."

It was evident right away: fine fruit! . . . A vicious foe, inside and out!

"What is the main reason for your coming here?" asks Reb Simcha.

Reb Simcha wants clear and straightforward information.

"To put things in order," Polishuk answers vaguely.

"Well," Reb Simcha offers advice, "put things in order so those bastards won't be bastards!"

"That's not my job," Polishuk says with a sneer, the words trickling drop by drop, even freezing.

It looks as though he himself is quite a bastard. If only the house would vomit him forth forever.

Thus thought Reb Simcha, putting his hand over his mouth.

But what comrade Polishuk left obscure during the day, he clarified at night. His sleep told the story. Night, darkness and silence—suddenly he was hauled from his bed as though a fire had broken out in the house, perish the thought!, and he paced irregularly back and forth in the room looking for some kind of bomb.

"It's me . . . me," Henya takes him by the hand every now and then. "It's me, comrade Polishuk!"

"Happiness at last!" Reb Simcha was annoyed at his daughter. "It's me, it's me! . . . Leave him alone, please."

In short, that was the only telltale sign of who that person really was.

Day by day the town declined, oppressed in low spirits and heavy with melancholy and mute silence, like a deserter.

"No doubt," says Reb Simcha, "Like a deserter, like a number of deserters all in the same place.

"Now these are the three categories essential to a person's needs: children, life and food. None is quite in the shape it ought to be; quite to the contrary.

"The children are bastards, criminals, sinners, Amalekites, not children. Life is nothingness, absolute zero, inimical to the heart and soul. And as for food, it's extremely dear when it's to be found at all!

"But it is known to those who know, and the truth is, as it is written: behold the eye of the Lord is upon those who fear him. . . .

"Only the problem is known too: where did those Jewish sinners come from, who at first were neither seen nor known at all?

"Since the souls of all the Jews come from the same place, and things taken from the same place are a single entity through and through, it follows that every Jew is implicated in his fellow Jew's sin, for they are a single building. Like the body, for example, if the feet rush off to do evil, isn't the evil in the whole bodily frame?

"The difficulty: where were all those cruel, evil bastards and sinners taken from? And Thy whole nation is righteous?

"*Gevald!*" Reb Simcha shouts to himself. "Robbers, murderers! Yet all of Israel are responsible for one another, so what are you going to do?"

Daily they came to the town. Some in sheepskins and others in greatcoats and still others in leather jackets. What they all had in common was that they were all bastards. . . .

Daily they came to the big stores owned by Brilliant and by Margolin and that of Hayyim Zelig the blacksmith, and they loaded wagons full of goods. Then they went their way.

"Anarchy! The world is lawless! Liberty is abroad in the world," grumbled Reb Simcha. "Only there's no freedom from robbery and theft, only there's no freedom from the enemies of the Jews, from 'thou shalt murder,' and from 'thou shalt steal,' and from 'bear false witness against thy neighbor.'"

"Are things good this way?" Reb Simcha challenged Polishuk. "How does it seem to you, comrade Polishuk, is it good this way?"

"Thank God," answered Polishuk. "Nothing's wrong. One could even say it's good . . . a Bolshevik doesn't know how to complain."

Reb Simcha cannot bear it any longer. His heart is hot within him. He cannot simply stand there because of his anger and the coursing blood.

"Good? Good? Get out of my house! . . . Right away! Get out! This is my house! Mine! M-i-n-e."

Polishuk measured Reb Simcha with his eyes, at his own pace, slowly, with his eyelids and eyebrows, slowly, as though wishing to root him out of his sight and remove him seven cubits from the face of the earth. Then he looked at Henya and gave another glance at Reb Simcha, turned his back, and left.

"You get out too, you hussy!" Reb Simcha was boiling with angry rage. "Bolshevik! . . . I won't stand for it! . . . Not for a single minute! . . . Get out! . . . May your names and memories be blotted out, sinners, boors, carpenters' and shoe-makers' apprentices!"

That very day Polishuk returned, took up his rifle and went to live in the bathhouse.

Fear then seized Reb Simcha to hear about such a person—a madman like that, God in heaven!—going to live in the bathhouse! Then Reb Simcha even regretted the whole affair. But regret is not the stuff of a merchant. "Let him break his skull and neck! To the bathhouse—the bathhouse, the devil take him! And may everyone else 'from his abode' be equally blessed!"

A good man is comrade Polishuk, and a better one is comrade Soroka—so similar looking!

With the town like a wide open door, if you please! Some leave, some enter: disturbers of the peace, ruffians, their unsavory faces skinned, their eyes mad and evil. . . .

On foot came comrade Soroka on the road leading up from the woods. Walking, sheepskins on his head, a military coat hanging on his back and dragging a small machine-gun behind him by a rope held in his hand. . . .

That very night, in the stillness of the dark, came a shriek from the steam power station in the village of Svirodovka, and on all sides the sky turned fiery red.

Dread and fearful silence spread through the whole town.

From mouth to mouth: "What happened? What happened? What happened?"

From mouth to mouth:

"Fire in Czupowski's manor."

"Fire in Kowalewski's manor."

"Fire in Count Branicki's manor."

The whole town was surrounded by fire on all sides and stood hiding with its face covered as though by a crow's wings.

The steam power station shrieks. The church bells strike with a great din. Dogs howl at their masters' heads, and a storm rolls through the air, raising itself ever higher and piling up like a huge mountain, flying and passing by with a howl, pulling the treetops after it. . . . And suddenly, in the meanwhile, an oppressive silence, the peace of death . . .

Now the sky was bright and clouds of smoke and flames wander and roam. Comrade Polishuk went down on his knees before the snowy plain, stretched his arms before him and cried out:

"Revolution, behold, Ha-ha-ha!"

"Revolution, ha-ha-ha!" Henya repeated after him.

They looked at each other and leapt into each other's arms. . . .

Night after night the sky burned around the town. Night after night the sky was red, flaming and smoky, without stars or constellations.

It was as though comrade Soroka wished to uproot not only the stars and constellations, but also all the angels, as it were, the seraphim and heavenly host.

For nights and weeks the sky was wrapped in flame.

All those weeks Soroka was never seen in town. Until once he came and went through the street: sheepskins on his head, a military coat hanging on his back, and his fingers were reddish blue as though uprooted, pulling behind him a small machine-gun on a rope, and so he walked, clanging with an iron key:

"Arise, ye workers of the people!"

Of all the huge quantity of booty stolen by the peasants from the noblemen's estates, Soroka took for himself only an iron key that had fallen from a smashed door.

Soroka's voice was heard from the street. Immediately all the comrades, men and women, leaped up and went out, shouting, "Hoorah!" "Long live the rule of the workers and peasants!" With a waving of hats and hands in the air, they raised their voices in the "Internationale."

At the sound of the song, comrade Soroka stood at attention, stretching his whole body upwards, turned his stern face to the side and raised his hand in a salute. . . .

The crowd took hold of comrade Soroka by his arms and legs, picked him up in the air, carried him in their hands, bearing him to the council building.

A mass of men pressed at the entrance, and Jews from everywhere were drawn after them as though to a circumcision or bar mitzvah.

Soroka stood in the middle of the room, extended his hands to all present and spoke:

"Ha, shake my hand, but hard! . . . Even though you're no Bolshevik, as I can see, and not at all different from a bourgeois, nevertheless, shake, as I am a Jew."

That evening, in comrade Polishuk's residence, in the bathhouse, festivities and celebration.

The whole band of comrades from the town, men and women, gathered at the bathhouse.

Polishuk kept the commandment of offering hospitality in proper fashion. Nothing necessary for a celebration was lacking, neither food nor drink.

By candlelight all the comrades, men and women, sat in a circle on logs and inverted tubs, indulging themselves with lard, pickles, brandy and tea. They drank tea in famous fashion: wrapped in towels till the seventh degree of sweat—one slurping from a cup, another from a soldier's mess tin and yet another from a plate with Hebrew writing in red letters on a white background: "Bread and salt shalt thou eat, and reap the truth."

At midnight, when their hearts were gladdened with eating and drinking, they shook the benches and beams of the bathhouse with their mighty dancing, as much as their legs could dance.

From the hole in the oven, flames reached out and licked the sooty bricks. The stones heaped up around the boiler turned black, and splinters of flame flickered. Above the boiler a thick column of steam rose to the beams of the black ceiling and veiled the benches. Heels pounded. The bodies were linked in a single chain, spinning, rocking, a chain of whirling skirts, red shirts and gun-belts, boots, wild hair, shouted song, whistles, sudden outcries and guttural, throaty sounds. . . . Everything in the bathhouse danced dizzily: the boiler and the stones, the ritual bath and the regular bathtub, old bundles of twigs, piles of full sacks and even comrade Gedalia hopped on his crutch.

Then the poor bathhouse, torn in roof and ribs, saw joy, one joy for all the days to come! The homes of rich landlords and officials in their glory were never honored with even a sixtieth of that honor from the time that the temple—the temple of the bathhouse—was a bathhouse. Truly that was a happy occasion!

But what was even more marvelous was the end, the end of the celebration!

The festivities, the singing and dancing were like the air all around, invisibly filling up space, like something not properly understood.

At the end of the night, when everyone was acting in his own way and dancing according to his own nature: one prancing on an upper bench and another hopping inside the empty, steaming bathtub, someone shouting: "Help! Help!" and someone else had made himself into a wagon and rolled along the floor on his belly—comrade Polishuk fled outside as though mad with worry and anger. He ran to the river and plunged in through a crack in the ice.

The other comrades noticed immediately and raised a panicked outcry. The women wept and wailed, the men ran with iron tools, laboring to crack the ice, some hastily smashing it, others peering into the black water. . . . Shouts all around, then suddenly a dreadful silence, the howl of the snowstorm, fear and dread and the sound of breaking ice. Suddenly Polishuk's head gleamed on the rushing water. . . . Hubbub, racing about, shouting, shoving . . . Polishuk was stuck between chunks of ice. Looking about him, supported by the arms reaching to him, he jumped up out of the river, healthy and strong, running to the bathhouse on his own feet with the whole crowd behind him—in a noisy, rushing tangle.

In the bathhouse all the comrades pressed around the one standing there, trembling in all his limbs, everyone astonished and enjoying the sight.

Soroka stood above him, gave him brandy to drink, hugged him and kissed him on his blue lips, asking how he felt:

"Is your soul restored? Is your soul restored, tell me, hey!"

Henya cried and laughed, wrung her hands, cried and laughed, and all the others hastened to do something, making loud noises to each other.

"*Mazel tov! Mazel tov!*" cried out Polishuk and enthusiastically animating his blue face and leaping into the steam room, with Henya after him. Henya was nearly crushed between the door and the frame.

The whole crowd wandered around the room in little groups, everyone by himself, but all together in a single mass, dark, moving, singing in joy and enthusiasm:

"*Mazel tov! Mazel tov! Mazel tov!*"

Nothing like it had ever been heard.

Only Soroka stood at the door of the steam room and shook his head from side to side, clapping to the sound of the singing and shouting:

"To kill the lion in the well on a snowy day!"

Such a high level of devotion.

V

It was a bright morning, rough, bristling with frost and snow.

The trees stood drawn like Sukkot palm branches—decorated and veiled with marvelous playthings and ornaments—of pure silver.

The houses were sunk in snow and the bright glow.

With joy and song like sharpened knives the snow creaked underfoot.

The frost burned with flames and searing.

On an upturned tub, without raising his head from the ground, sat Soroka before the flaming hole in the furnace.

He had returned to his seclusion with his little machine-gun.

He passed several days just in thought and cogitation.

That day Polishuk transferred his residence from the bathhouse to a room he rented for himself. It was a fine room in every respect. A room that was a house in itself, sitting in a large courtyard, peaceful and quiet.

"Join me," Polishuk spoke to Soroka. "The room's big, and there's only Henya who'll come and live with us."

Soroka delayed his answer, as though weighing his words very very carefully before speaking.

Hardly was the crunch of the snow under Polishuk's feet heard as he went away from the bathhouse, before Soroka sat down and repeated his motto:

"In this world every dog is attached to his own tail."

Soroka hadn't managed to repeat that saying a hundred times before going out and heading for the staff courtyard.

In the staff courtyard Soroka reviewed his men, went out before them, strutted and paced back and forth,

stood, and with his second in command, comrade Gedalia at his side, he called out:

"Comrades! At this moment I still have the power to give you orders! Therefore, first: drum major! . . . Second—always remember this: the force of the union of Jewish soldiers has no right not to be hanged, not to be shot, not to be burned and not to be buried alive! . . . Now, friends, as you have heeded me, so shall you heed the head of the union, comrade Gedalia."

The troops were bewildered. A secret voice of complaint passed from one end to the other.

"Comrades!" Soroka made a circle in the air with his arm, "Obey the order! Now your chief will be comrade Gedalia, and I leave you to go to my work and my activities, and the like. . . . I thank you, comrades, for your work and your assistance, may you be well."

"*Kru-gom mursh!*" comrade Gedalia spoke out after Soroka.

Soroka turned his back and left.

Soroka disappeared, he and his machine-gun together, as though the wind had taken him away, a silent wind, and no one knew where he went.

VI

In Reb Simcha's house, silence and barrenness—enough to make you burst!

Reb Simcha angrily paces about his house, wandering here and there like a colt blasted with rain and wind. Conversation between him and Henya has ceased. He but sees her and turns his head away so as not to look at her impure face.

Sometimes Motl Privisker comes and has a heart-to-heart talk with Reb Simcha:

"If the blessed Lord can sit and see the troubles of the world and keep silent, then we, Reb Simcha, can suffer in silence. Anyway . . ."

He also spoke to Henya:

"Tell me, Henya, wouldn't you ever think: 'What's happening to me?' You're stuck far away, absolutely distant!"

As for Henya, nothing touches her soul, and today passes like yesterday: beautiful as though drafted with a compass, her mouth reddish and her cheeks white. Beauty and splendor.

Grief, grief. Reb Simcha restrains himself. He sits with his feet up in front of the oven, burning logs, and sighing to the oven:

"Oy-oy-oy."

If only Motl Privisker could stifle that grief of his! If he could but be silent or pour his heart out like water in a humble voice and spirit submissive to the very center of his heart! Tears flow from both his eyes without cease.

"You're stuck far away, absolutely distant!"

"Henya, tell me what in the world you're doing? . . . Do you know what in the world you're doing!"

Motl Privisker spoke, giving Henya a look, a look of Reb Motl Privisker's sort, till Henya became completely ill at ease and didn't know where to turn or what to say.

"I ask you, what are you actually doing?"

Motl took large steps and walked across the room, sitting in his chair, putting his head on the table, then raising his head and putting it down again.

"The world is destroyed. . . . The world is destroyed. . . . Oh Lord, Oh Lord . . . The world has gone mad, mad . . . What can we do? What can we d-o-o?"

He stood up and shouted:

"Henya! Henya!"

Then he went back and resumed where he had stopped:

"The world has gone mad, mad. . . . And I'm mad . . . completely. . . ."

"Motl, I am very surprised at you," Reb Simcha broke in. "I'm astonished! What idea have you fixed in your mind?"

"That I shall cut them to pieces!" Motl put a hand over his mouth and turned away from Reb Simcha.

"Motl," Reb Simcha spoke sternly. "I don't understand. What do you expect? Why won't you return to your home and your wife?"

"Not me, not me, teach your *daughter!*" shouted Motl, and his eyes glowed like fire. "There you have someone to instruct!"

Reb Simcha fell silent. He gave up. Motl's eyes almost turned white, but Reb Simcha would not say what should be said at such a moment.

The logs didn't burn. Reb Simcha sighed. He mumbled the first words of the afternoon prayers and dealt with the furnace. He pulled himself together and dealt with the furnace.

A bluish light surrounded the room.

Motl Privisker stood in the corner, swaying and moaning a weepy chant, saying his afternoon prayers. During the central portion of the prayers, when he reached, "Forgive us, our father, for we have sinned," he secretly wept, and tears flowed ceaselessly from both his eyes. [. . .]

IX

Like a green wave, pushed back and leaning into the distance, lay greenish the layers of snow, and the crimson of the sunset was on and around them.

Among the columns of smoke rising from the chimneys of the houses the wind hung as though among the masts and shrouds of ships in the heart of foamy seas.

Suddenly a rumor was heard, noise, a tangle of voices, massive and fearful:

"They're coming."

"The murderers."

"Murderers."

Polishuk flashes through the street garbed in the flames of the sunset and, with his right hand, drawing the pistol at his side:

"Toward the enemy! . . . Toward the enemy!"

Like a spirit he went by the House of Study, contemplated the three old men who had come to say their afternoon and evening prayers:

"And even to defend," he shouted from his throat, "this House of Study!"

Outside, flight and hubbub.

They ran away from Polishuk to the right and left, hopping and running and limping and groaning.

Not two were left together.

Silence blanketed the street and houses.

Sky blue and white.

As though no human soul had been there for many days.

The snowy wasteland, an abandoned salt mine . . .

Red the sun sets. The snow soaks up its dark blood.

Leaving the courtyard in front of the Union of Jewish Soldiers' headquarters, at an hour when the eye can no longer distinguish between one thing and another, on his horse, bound to the saddle by ropes in pride and glory, was comrade Gedalia, and behind him, like a river, flowed the files of armed men.

The snow gleamed.

Chill and darkness floated up into one's eyes.

The footsteps whistled in the dark blue of the snow.

Row upon row, two by two, in good order, the armed and silent men went up.

They all passed under Polishuk's critical eye, as he stood at the side, supporting and fortifying them with his voice:

"One two, one two!"

"Who brought you here?" Polishuk raised his voice against a few of the men coming up. "Wh-who took you out? I order you to stay behind and guard the town!"

"Comrade Polishuk, are we one-armed or one-legged cripples, that we must sit in the rear?"

"Wh-what? . . . Are you still arguing with me? . . . Follow my orders! . . . On the double, march!"

"Ah, may his guts collapse!" the ones left behind muttered, wrinkling their noses and turning to the side like whipped dogs.

In a moment they lifted their feet and raced after the camp.

The files moved over the snow like black stains.

From a distance they were visible, near the old cemetery, which they passed with loud singing, the new and carefree life disturbing the ancient dream of those lying in the earth.

Then they were swallowed up in the darkness.

In the town life stopped.

The silence of death.

Darkness.

All night the dead town was silent.

In the morning the soldiers returned, with the sound of singing and joy they returned.

"It's a brigade of soldiers on their way back from the front, not murderers!" the returnees announced.

The town came back to life.

In the afternoon the soldiers entered the town. They went to the council building and began speaking:

"Comrades, regarding the Jewish brigade with you in the town, let them lay down their arms, comrades."

"What's this? Comrades, you . . ."

"Now, do as we said: lay down your arms, no more!"

"How can you say that, comrades?" Polishuk negotiated with them out loud. "They are in favor of the rule of soldiers and workers."

"Don't argue with us, shorty! See this?" They waved grenades in the air.

As ashamed as a jilted bride removing her jewels, the members of the Jewish brigade were humiliated, walking with their heads down, quietly cursing and swearing, each man to himself, with filthy and vile curses, returning their weapons to the armory.

Actually only a few returned them. Most hid them in the bathhouse, in the poor-house and in potato pits.

They returned their weapons, and they were all summoned, all the members of the union, to the courtyard of the council building and ordered to stand against the wall.

Their faces turned black, their eyes went dark, as when the stars come out.

"Low, low," they whispered quietly.

"We have failed."

Ten soldiers with angry faces, silent, stony, looking and waiting, stood in the middle of the courtyard. Every one of their movements, every blink evoked the fear of death.

The courtyard was barren, full of snow piled up, pink and blue.

Silence fell. Then Polishuk appeared at the gate, with his hair and eyes wild, running into the courtyard with a single breath and stood at the wall among the rest.

The soldiers went up to each of the men standing at the wall, searching him.

No weapons were found.

The men standing there moved away from the walls.

To the sound of laughter and cries of contempt the fighters were dismissed and sent away.

Near the fence stood one of them, all dressed in black, weeping.

That was a day of utter defeat, of humiliation. Every heart burned like fire. Every heart cried out against the injustice.

That night the soldiers left the town.

X

Every house is heavy with melancholy and worry.

Every eye expects enmity. All the lips are bluish—you mustn't speak out, only curse and cry out against injustice silently.

Driven from the house is every favorable sign, all cheerful expressions and grace.

Oblivion and expiration whisper, fasting and cold rustle about. . . .

No more is the woman of valor who nurtured and raised her children as commanded by the blessed Lord.

No more is the active householder with his sharp eye and quick pace, searching here and pecking there, dragging a grain and bearing a bundle, urgently rushing, reading the cantillation marks vigorously and gloriously like a rooster, disagreeing with God. . . .

No more are the maidens, preparing dowries with skillful hands and waiting for bridegrooms.

The women of valor lie still, exhausted, like sick goats, mourning, with dried dugs.

The sons die untimely.

The solid citizens race about like roosters with their throats extended, slaughtered, dripping blood. . . .

And the maidens—

"May you know a good year!"

The world has gone mad. Heartbreak! . . . Heartbreak . . . And the blessed Lord knows! There is nothing left to do but "get up and lie in the street and laugh!"

In the month of Shevat, the name of which is related to the word for severe judgment according to Motl Privisker, Henya left her father's house and went to live in Polishuk's room.

That made no impression in the town. The town had seen so much lawlessness and wild living that it had become used to it.

The town was silent. It saw and was silent.

Not her alone, but another one too:

For comrade Polishuk also opened his room to Nechama, the daughter of Reb Meyer the slaughterer, and Leyzer Potashnik's Shprintsa, also to comrade Gedalia and comrade Henikh the carpenter, and they all lived there together:

"A commune!"

"They strung up a rope," it was whispered in town, "from one wall to another across the room: dividing the women's beds from the men's!"

The town looks for similarities between Sodom before it was destroyed and Polishuk's "commune." The deeds of the former are like those of the latter. . . .

"The daughters of such righteous men, ah? Will you split their bellies, Lord of the universe!"

"Reb Simcha," people whispered about him, "has gone completely mad!"

That seemed quite likely. . . . True, one could go mad.

"Reb Simcha," they whispered, "is sitting in mourning, nodding his head ceaselessly and whispering, 'I have no daughter. . . . I have no daughter. . . . I have no daughter!'—nothing more."

On Friday Motl Privisker visited Reb Simcha and told him an interpretation of the verse: "Because thou hast forgotten me and cast me behind thy back." "How is it possible that a daughter of Israel could be cast away? . . ."

"I have no daughter. . . . I have no daughter. . . ." Reb Simcha sat on the floor and nodded his head.

Motl Privisker turned his face away from him and remained standing there.

"Reb Simcha, Reb Simcha! . . . You are a father, are you not?" . . . shouted Motl in a tearful voice. "Are you not a father? . . . Are you not a Jew, and the Lord is in heaven? . . . Why are you silent?! . . . Why are you silent and doing nothing?"

"I have no daughter. . . . I have no daughter. . . ."

"Why are you silent!" cried Motl in tears. "Lord, Lord of the world, why are you silent, oy, oy! . . . Why don't you watch over your children, for they are in great misery."

"I have no daughter. . . . I have no daughter. . . ."

"Simcha!" Motl Privisker jumped, raising his head and hands in the air. "I want to break the law! . . . I want to curse. . . . To violate the Sabbath in public! . . . I want to be an adulterer! . . . I will transcend my nature! . . . Master of the whole world, master of the whole world." He grasped both his earlocks, "May I not be given a Jewish burial! . . . I'm a Bolshevik!" He pounded the table with his hand till the windows rattled. "Now, now the time has come. . . . Enough! I want to be a Bolshevik!"

"I have no daughter. . . . I have no daughter. . . ." Reb Simcha's desolate voice was heard.

Motl leaped up onto his long legs. The hem of his jacket fluttered in Reb Simcha's face, as he sat and whispered, "I have no daughter. . . . I have no daughter. . . ." And as though stones were being split, the door slammed against the doorpost, and the corners of the room shuddered—Motl was gone!

XI

Lying in the snow, shoved and pressed together, the humiliated houses crouched. The winds wept bitterly over them. The barren, red sun set over them.

On the surface of the snow runs a purplish shadow.

Silence outside.

No one is to be seen. No one greets his friend, no one wishes anyone well. Silence and snow. As though the snow had covered the towns and settlements forever. Neither good nor evil will ever find that place.

Just one man, who appeared drunken in the full, pure whiteness of the snows, was Motl Privisker. He too was like a soul that had already died, whirling and wandering in the world of chaos.

Nightfall in the silence and snow. An encrusted city preserved in the sinking red sun . . .

The snow whistles and whistles beneath one's feet, making a sound like a radish being sliced.

Spread before one's eyes is snow, near and far, sparkling on the ground like a bridegroom's prayer shawl.

Is this a dream or reality? Is it Motl Privisker there in the snow or some lone, forgotten, derelict out after the curfew? Who is it? Is it a poor teacher who lost his way, or some crazy man whose brains have been addled? Is that silence only apparent? Or are they voices, calling loudly, and after them the silence came? He is not clever enough to understand. . . .

The snow sparkles and sparkles like crates and crates of candles lit all at once to make a great light! . . .

No matter, for he is weary unto death! No matter, for he has been beaten into silence! No matter, for he is bereft of kindness or joy, of motive or interest. . . .

He walked slowly and heard a kind of silence, voices calling. Slowly he walked and looked at the moonlit snow, glowing under his feet.

Motl Privisker walked slowly by himself, until the voices of nearby people overtook him, real voices. They were Polishuk and his bunch, who appeared in the street. As if they had come outside just to rule over the silent snows. Motl Privisker was alarmed. He looked at Henya walking, dressed in a leather coat, a pistol belted around her waist, booted, and his heart wept within him. In a moment his heart returned and was joyous. Motl spoke to himself:

"I was meant to suffer, and I have suffered already."

He looked again at her reddish mouth, her cheeks and forehead, and he said again: "I was meant to receive suffering, and I have received it already."

"Ah, comrade Reb Motl," Polishuk greeted him. "Where are you going?"

The people crowded around him, standing there and stamping their feet.

"Comrade Motl," Polishuk continued. "Come with us! Be a Bolshevik, ha-ha. . . ."

Motl Privisker raised his eyes toward Henya, who was standing at the side, and he said:

"If I am destined to go to hell, I wish to do so as a kosher Jew!"

"Ha-ha-ha! . . . Ha-ha!" the people raised their voices in laughter.

The silence returned to what it was. No one was visible. No one greeted his friend.

Silence. A silvery round moon overhead. A long shadow on the snow below.

"I was meant to suffer, and I have suffered already."

And sometimes:

"For it is forbidden to look her in the face, forbidden, forbidden!"

XII

Time passed, bringing other skies to rise over the town. A young sun with lovely rays melted the snow and opened spots of light outside. The winds chewed up the snow by the mouthful, and with every bite they wandered on, full of thoughts and melodies of spring.

The houses shed the white piecrusts from their shoulders and stood warming themselves in the sun, dark, old and a little distant from each other.

The roofs wept before the glowing sun like little children.

Bit by bit the snow yellowed and fell into its water.

Puddles spread in the street like big clouds spread in the heavens.

Before the gates calves jumped, wild-eyed with tails erect.

Crows moved in the boughs of the trees, calling "krak-rak."

Motl Privisker was covered with his prayer shawl and phylacteries—and lo: no oppression or injustice in the world, no evil and malicious joy, but everything was as in earlier times:

"The Lord is one. . . ."

Then, during prayer, while he was standing and acknowledging the Creator as King, proclaiming "The Lord is one!" in came two soldiers and shouted:

"Citizen Mordukh Karasyk, in the name of the Soviet Socialist Republic of Russia, you are under arrest!"

As though preparing himself to study it very thoroughly, Motl Privisker took the paper that was handed to him, and all his eyes saw on the paper was the signature: Henya Horowitz.

Afterwards Motl Privisker turned to face the soldiers and said,

"That's how it is."

"That's the way it is. Come with us!"

They didn't offer to content him by allowing him to finish his prayer.

Motl Privisker removed his phylacteries, took off his prayer shawl, draped himself in his balding catskin coat and went. All the time he was walking in the street between the two armed soldiers, the image of Reb Simcha, the floorboards ripped up, and Henya never left his eyes. . . . His throat was warm with the heat of sated thirst, and his heart beat within him as at a time of arousal and desire.

Many days passed, days and weeks.

But, could it be that many days passed, and yet comrade Soroka is walking down the street!

The days that passed were not many—many were the deeds done by comrade Soroka! Many are the nests he burned and many the fires he lit in the country he went through!

From the end of the street, which was darkened with gunpowder, went forth Soroka.

It was a debilitating spring evening.

Saturated silence, thick and dark, as it is sometimes in the depths of one's heart.

Swallowed in a gullet, the berry of a blue night is seen.

The town crouched in its mud like a sick, mourning goat with dried dugs.

Following footsteps stamped in the mud, large and small footprints of men and women, Soroka walked till he reached Polishuk's house.

When he opened the door and went in, his eyes saw a rope before him, stretched from wall to wall, and two beds on either side of the walls, full of bodies, bodies like cadavers.

Soroka placed himself in the center of the room and shouted:

"Are you asleep, you devils! . . . Get up: the Germans are coming!"

Translated by Jeffrey M. Green.

Other works by Hazaz: *The End of Days* (1933) ; *The Gates of Bronze* (1956); *Mori Sa'id* (1956).

Sh. An-ski

Two Martyrs
1925

For four hours I sat engrossed while old Gershon Falk told his story, feeling all the while as though I were listening to a fantastic saga—as though I were in the presence of one from another time, not of my own generation.

Though he was over ninety, he had all his faculties: not only was he in good health but he had the vigor of a much younger man. He was tall and sturdy, with distinctive features: a broad fleshy nose, a thick moustache and a long luxuriant beard, streaked with gray and parted in the middle. His voice was clear, and so deep and rich that it almost boomed. He was not in the least tired after talking for four hours. He wore a black frock coat and a top hat—put on for my benefit, as a visitor from Petersburg.

And not only was Falk's appearance imposing; everything he did was on a grand scale. He had twenty-three children, close to a hundred grandchildren, and scores of great-grandchildren. He lived in the city of Vyatka, where I met him, and where he was the proprietor of eight large buildings and two department stores. He was said to be worth half a million rubles.

He spoke a colorful Russian, full of idiomatic expressions and turns of phrase. His facial features were typically Slavic: that broad nose, along with prominent cheekbones and an open look, without the slightest sign of Jewishness. All the same he was a Jew—and what a Jew!

He came from a small town near the city of Shklov. At the age of nine, though small and scrawny, he was already studying the Talmud, along with Tosafot and Ma-Harsha. Under ordinary circumstances, the boy would have grown up frail and wizened, a poor teacher in the elementary school like his father. But he was destined instead for an eventful and varied career—Nicolai Pavlovitch having intervened . . . Yes, Czar Nicolai intervened in that career. Oh, not directly: it was a Jewish *khapper*, a kidnapper, who, with a few henchmen, broke into the house at midnight and seized the boy from the top of the stove where he slept, pushing aside his mother. During the struggle his father called out, "Gershon, swear by God, you will always remain a Jew!" And the boy replied, "I swear, father!"

The boy was taken to the nearest city and placed with others like himself, Jewish boys kidnapped for future military service. His own clothes were thrown away and he was given a military uniform, with an overcoat that hung all the way to the floor. Old soldiers, known as *dyadkas*, were their custodians, and treated them cruelly.

The unfortunate youngsters were transported, alternately by wagon or on foot, to the far-off Tula region, where they were conducted to the steambaths and told they would meet a famous general. Lined up several ranks deep in a large assembly hall, they faced an old general, his chest covered with medals. He told them: "Little ones, until now each of you had a father and a mother. From now on you are to forget them, since you now have a new father—Czar Nicolai Petrovitch." And he led them in shouting "Hurrah!"

There was among the boys one named Avremel, who understood Russian, and who interpreted what the general said. So the youngsters called out a "Hurrah!" for their new father. The general then went on to say that their new "father" was kind to those who obeyed him, but ruthless to those who did not. And so they had to understand that he called on them to renounce their Jewish faith, and to accept the glorious gospel of Jesus Christ. And once again he commanded a shout of "Hurrah!"

This time Avremel transmitted what the general decreed in a tremulous wail—and the children said "Hurrah!" with a wail of their own.

Suddenly, a priest carrying a large silver crucifix appeared. He made the sign of the cross over the assembly, holding out the crucifix for each of the boys to kiss. Each recoiled in fright—but one complied. Hysterical whimpering erupted. Some fainted, others began the *Shema Yisroel* ("Hear, O Israel, the Lord our God, the Lord is One!").

The blood vessels in the general's eyes reddened; he brought down his feet in his wrath with the children and their guards. "Confounded little Yids," he screamed, "I'll have you flogged to death!"—and ordered them back to the barracks.

The *dyadkas* pummeled and flogged their wards. But that night at bedtime, when they were alone, the boys would huddle together and swear not to submit to conversion, whatever happened.

On the day following they were given no food, and on the day after that they were taken back to the assembly hall, where a table on which loaves of bread, cakes, butter, honey and other sweets were visible. Several hours went by; then an officer spoke to the by now famished as well as frightened children, telling them in Yiddish that as a Jew he, too, had held back for a long time from converting, until he realized that there was no alternative and became a Christian; and now he was happy. He declared that God would not punish them, that they were simply carrying out the orders of the Czar. And he ended by saying that any boy who promised to convert—who merely promised—could come to the table and eat all he wanted.

The twelve-year-old Avremel was the first to break down and help himself to the alluring fare. He was followed by a few others. But the majority did not give way. So that the Evil One should not get the upper hand, they tried to avert their eyes from the table; but their guards forced them to watch the few who were indulging their hunger. All the same, none of the rest yielded to the temptation, and before long they were allowed to leave the hall.

Only those who had refused to convert were returned to the barracks; the others were isolated for as long a time as it took for them to give in and be christened. Meanwhile the starving youngsters in the barracks were given slices of bread.

Among the children was a lanky ten-year-old with glowing eyes, whose name was Mendel. Though he was the son of a common tailor, he stood out because of his Talmudic learning and his piety. From the first day he took charge of the rest of the group. He exhorted them to risk their lives *al Kiddush ha-Shem*—for the Sanctification of the Divine Name—after the example of Daniel, Hananiah and Mishal and Azaria, reminding them of the glory that would be theirs in the world to come. Within a relatively short time he had such influence among them that the rest were ready to follow him through anything. He got them to make a vow to stay together. He started getting them up early enough to say their morning prayers without arousing the suspicion of their wardens. Now and then he would wake up the little ones in the middle of the night and by heart teach them the *Mishnah*.

There was no limit to the measures used by the guards to induce the children to submit to baptism: beating, starvation, or forcing them to stand barefoot for hours in freezing weather. Once they were lined up and told that those prepared to convert were to remain where they were, while those still unwilling to do so were to step back three paces. As they backed up, these latter ran into bayonets held at the ready. A number were injured. The same trick was repeated; and with just two exceptions, the boys again stepped back. Another time, they were lined up on the bank of a river in a suburb, while soldiers sat in rowboats. An order was given: those ready to convert were to get into the boats, while those who persisted in remaining confounded little Yids were to cross the river on foot, in their clothes. The river was both wide and deep, and the boys could not swim. A crying few in panic headed for the boats; the rest stayed where they were. The soldiers repeated their command for the boys either to get into the boats or to wade into the river. As they began to moan, Mendel stepped forward and exclaimed, "Children, to *Kiddush ha-Shem!*" And with the cry "*Shema Yisroel!*" he became the first to step into the water. Others followed and started to go under. The soldiers, who had not expected the youngsters to make this plunge into the river, became alarmed and rushed to save them. Two were drowned, and several others were dragged out half dead. The group endured still other ordeals. And they endured.

Before long the twelve-year-old Avremel reappeared in the barracks. Having become an apostate, he had been delegated to convert the rest of them. He managed to convert only one sickly seven-year-old boy. Then he began a conversation with Mendel, talking with him in a whisper for a very long time. Finally he went away, leaving the other children baffled.

A month passed. Then, one night, two soldiers brought an object in a military overcoat into the barracks and put it on the floor saying, "Take it—it's yours!" And they left. When the children opened the overcoat they found Avremel, unconscious, his body bloody and mangled, his back lacerated, the bones sticking out. When he came to, he asked his friends to recite with him the *Viddui*, the deathbed confession. But no one remembered the words, so instead of that, they recited the *Al Het* prayer. But he passed out again before finishing the prayer. He died at dawn. The children were given permission to bury him in accordance with the Mosaic Law. Later on, they learned that at Mendel's urging, Avremel had decided to do penance and to sacrifice his life, *al Kiddush ha-Shem*. Once, as a group of the young converts were being led to the church, he tore off the tiny cross he was wearing and began to trample it and curse it. Taken into custody, he was tried and sentenced to being flogged five hundred times, *skvoz stroy*, to run the gauntlet.

Though the children stuck together, there were fewer and fewer of them; some died from the beatings and from malnutrition; others committed suicide. Twenty or so of them were assigned to peasants in the villages, where they endured privation. Separated from their friends, they became countryfied, coarse, and submitted to baptism, by and large. While farmed out, Mendel escaped, was captured, flogged, and then returned to his peasant master in the village. Captured after his second escape, Mendel was held for trial. He jumped from a third story to his death.

It was the second year. The Cantonists were sent to Vyatka. Of the original two hundred children, only twelve remained Jews. After Mendel's death, Gershon Falk became their leader. His influence over them was strong, and they persevered as Jews. With respect to keeping the faith, they introduced discipline similar to the one they'd had in the barracks. They kept a ledger, listing the punishments for the different transgressions. Thus, for neglecting to pray on weekdays—five lashes; for neglecting to pray on the Sabbath—twenty lashes; for desecrating the Sabbath—thirty lashes; for eating non-Kosher food—fifty lashes. Punishment was meted out strictly, kept secret from the camp authorities.

The hardships and the struggle for survival lingered on for four years. The barbarians gradually got tired of their tasks and gave in. Some of them showed a certain respect for the children's courageous affirmation of their religion. One time, an old general summoned them and asked, "Are you Jews?"

"We are, Your Excellency," they answered together in chorus.

"And you don't want to convert under any circumstances?"

"Under no circumstances, Your Excellency."

"I compliment you. Continue to be faithful to your God. Whoever is faithful to his God is faithful to the Czar," the general declared.

That statement made a tremendous impression upon the youngsters. A legend arose among them that the general was Elijah the Prophet in disguise.

After that, their situation improved. During the fifth year they were freed for Yom Kippur so that they could pray in a *minyan* (a quorum). There being no other Jews in town, they arranged a *minyan* among themselves. From their piddling allowance they had saved up thirty kopecks—enough to buy a prayer book for fifteen kopecks from wandering exiled Jews; for three kopecks, they rented a room for the services; and they bought candles for ten kopecks. Gershon officiated at the service. When he started to chant the *Kol Nidre* prayer, a wailing that grew in intensity echoed from the outside. Stepping outside, the worshippers beheld about fifty of the baptized children, who did not dare to enter, but who repeated the words of the prayer, weeping all the while.

On reaching their eighteenth birthdays, the Cantonists were regarded as soldiers and were permitted to marry. But where was one to find a Jewish bride? So it occurred to them to keep an eye on the groups of Jewish exiles passing through there occasionally, on their way to Siberia. Some of the groups included entire families from whom the Cantonists used to buy girls—to become their wives. Gershon bought a wife for twelve rubles. And he lived with her for sixty years, and she bore him twenty-three children.

Gershon served the required military service of twenty-five years in Vyatka, where he stayed on, engaged in business and became wealthy.

The elderly Gershon told me his life story in the exhilarated tone of a conqueror. And a conqueror he was, indeed: after all, he had triumphed over Czar Nicolai I and his brutal regime. The horrible tortures he had been subjected to had not weakened his resistance. On the contrary, living out of doors, the disciplined regime, and the coarse but nourishing food had strengthened his body just as the ordeals had strengthened his soul. He spoke with pride about his grandchildren who included physicians, lawyers, engineers. He showed me a photograph he had received of his oldest great-grandson. His family name is Melnikov—"my daughter's grandson," he reminisced. "He is a student in Petersburg. If you meet him there, give him regards from his great-grandfather. Tell him that I too went through a university—Nicolai Petrovitch's university, and although I am not a doctor, he need not be ashamed."

I looked at the photograph. There was no resemblance to him: a gaunt, bespectacled, intellectual face.

A year passed. Once, while visiting a prominent Russian lawyer and political activist whom I knew well, I was introduced to a young man who wore glasses, a student with a typical Jewish look, by the name of Melnikov. The face and name flashed through my mind. But I paid no more attention to it: one meets so many people in a lifetime.

My famous host was a well-known friend of Jews, and on several occasions had stood up in the Duma— of which he was a member—to champion the Jewish cause, in no uncertain terms, against the anti-Semitic policy of the government. Among other things, we discussed that issue: Jews were discriminated against in many ways.

"Let me relate an incident that transcends all the government's evil acts against the Jews," my host stated. "That young man," he pointed to Melnikov, "my son's friend, had the misfortune of being born a Jew. First he endured all sorts of hardships in being admitted and finishing high school. And when he got to the university he came up against the quota system as well as the

crooked business associated with it. To make a long story short, the young man was barred from the university. He lost one year and there was a likelihood of his forfeiting a second and a third year. Suddenly, an alternative appeared. In Vibarg [Viborg], Finland, there was a clergyman by the name of Peer, who for a fee, would register a Jew as a convert, without insisting on any religious rites. You didn't even have to see the clergyman personally. A simple formality. So a number of Jewish young men, including Melnikov, took this opportunity, and when they'd received a document testifying to their conversion, were admitted to the university right away. But the Holy Synod issued an edict to the effect that all those who had been baptized by the Pastor Peer were not considered authentic converts—and reverted to their restricted Jewish status. Following that decree, Melnikov and his classmates were dismissed from the university. Moreover, they are about to be deprived of their privilege to live in Petersburg. What do you think of such an outrage?"

I looked again at Melnikov and recalled having seen his photograph during a visit with old Falk.

"Tell me, do you have a great-grandfather by the name of Gershon Falk in Vyatka?" I asked the young man.

"Yes, of course. How do you know? Do you know him?"

"I met him a year ago. He showed me your photograph."

"Is that so? So you two met. How did he impress you? A genuine grand old man. Am I right?"

"Yes, indeed. Very much so," I agreed with him. And then I proceeded to tell my host about Melnikov's great-grandfather—and the ordeals he had endured.

Melnikov followed my narrative with delight, nodding approval from time to time. When I concluded, he said to the lawyer:

"As you can see, it is hereditary in our family. My great-grandfather also suffered a great deal from his Jewishness . . ."

"Not from his Jewishness but rather *for* his Jewishness," I corrected him.

Melnikov failed to grasp the difference between the two words. So did my host.

Translated by Moshe Spiegel.

Asher Barash

1889–1952

The Hebrew writer Asher Barash was born in Lopatin, Galicia, and received both a secular and a religious education. He began writing at an early age and published poetry, stories, and plays in Hebrew, Yiddish, German, and Polish. In 1914, he moved to Ottoman Palestine, where he taught Hebrew language and literature, first in Tel Aviv and then, after World War I, in Haifa. While much of his fiction drew on memories of his childhood in Galicia, his later writing portrayed the struggles of the pioneering generation in the Land of Israel. Although best known for his short stories, he also wrote essays on literature and culture and children's literature.

At Heaven's Gate
1925

When "Papa" Gonta bore down on Tetayev at the head of his Cossack army in the summer of 1768, the little town had a strange look about it: the houses large and small stood desolate, their shutters drawn, no smoke wreathing up from their chimneys to the clear skies. Only from one low-roofed house that stood awry could voices—hoarse, drunken voices—be heard. From the countryside that fringed the township a few stray farmers, wearing their Sunday best and their well-waxed top-boots, lumbered at a leisurely pace in the direction of this house, the only one that was *alive*. Like heavy moths they were drawn, slowly and irresistibly, to the flame of the pothouse.

Nailed to the large wooden crucifix that drowsed in the heavy summer's heat, the frail figure of the Christ exposed the nakedness of its twisted body to the empty desolation of the central square. Facing one another above the rooftops of the Jewish houses and shops, the tall synagogue with the mildewed old walls of stone looked across at the timbered church, blackened with age, with its tiers of little toylike turrets and spires. The two seemed to be locked in a mute trial of strength.

It was now three days since the townspeople had got word that "Papa" Gonta was marching on Tetayev. The Polish army had entrenched itself at Uman, and Gonta, joining forces with Zheleznik, commander of the Haidamek revolt, directed his campaign against the Polish stronghold, leaving a wide swath of blood and fire in his wake. The news that came through told of the merciless butchery of masses of Jews and the firing of all their property. There was no hope of deliverance, all will or ability to resist crumbled. The strongest weakened at the approach of the ravaging human beasts, erupting like a volcanic tide to engulf all that stood in their path. The only course left open was headlong flight. The entire Jewish community of Tetayev fled in good order, salvaging such chattels as they could carry with them (while the farmers, their wagons hitched, stood at the gates of their farmyards with their hands in their pockets, watching the flight of the refugees). They made for the provincial capital, a town with thousands of Jewish inhabitants, three days' journey away. The score of Poles who lived in the town joined them in their flight, blindly hoping that this road led to safety and little realizing that in a week's time they, too, would be slaughtered.

Even before the town had emptied of its Jewish inhabitants the gentiles, who lived on the outskirts, were deliberating whether to set about plundering the Jewish property right away, or wait for "Papa" to arrive. Those in the know said that "Papa" did not like anything to be done without his being present, and at the local council meeting, therefore, it was decided to wait. The tavern presented a problem, however: how could they allow the tavern to remain closed with all those hogsheads of liquor full to the brim inside? A way out of this difficulty was suggested by one of the shrewder villagers: as soon as the Jewish exodus started, a score of fearless village lads, armed with axes, would lie in wait for "Chamka" (Nehemiah), the Jewish inn-keeper, at the edge of the wood. They were to seize him and bring him back to the inn, where he would be forced to serve them drinks willy-nilly—and all this quite legal as far as "Papa" was concerned.

This plan was indeed carried out. Rudely hustled back to his deserted inn, Nehemiah was at first stunned at having been torn away from his family and people, crazed with terror at being surrounded by hostile, jeering gentiles. His yellow beard and earlocks seemed to go ashen grey and limp, and his frightened eyes stared with uncomprehending sorrow like those of a chained beast. The next day, however, he was able to take stock of the situation; he served generous drinks to his tormentors—old friends of his—and acknowledged their coarse jests. He even jotted down the figures in his notebook out of some obscure hope: "Cast your bread upon the waters . . . you can never know," he thought. "Don't despair of doing a stroke of business, even at the gates of hell!"

There was a Jewish beadle living in Tetayev at the time, Israel Michal, a thick-bearded, taciturn man in his prime, who had officiated at the synagogue for more than twenty years—an office that had been in his family for generations. He had never been known to do or say anything unseemly for a man who held this post, having humbly served even the meanest of the congregants. When the community, at a meeting held in the synagogue, decided on flight, Israel Michal slipped away unobserved and hid in a large barrel that stood in the garret where dilapidated leaves from holy books were stored. Only when the community had departed, leaving behind an empty silence, did he come out of hiding and noiselessly descend to the courtyard, where stood a heap of heavy, rough-hewn stones that were to have been used for renovating the old synagogue building. With strong, trembling hands he carried the stones singly into the vestibule and there arranged them in a pile. He knew only too well that before long the unclean gentile hordes would storm in to defile the House of the Lord, bemire the large tomes of the Talmud and other sacred books (the refugees had taken the Scrolls of the Law with them, but had been unable to carry the other holy books in addition to their vital provisions), and scatter the torn leaves that were so zealously stored away. But he would not allow them to enter the House of Prayer! He would keep them at bay, hurl stones at the heads of any who dared approach!

He locked the heavy door on the inside. Then he placed a table against it, set a chair on the table and clambered up. He smashed the stained glass fanlight—shaped like a Star of David in six colours—making an aperture large enough to fling the stones through when the moment arrived. This done, he again tried the door to make sure that it was locked, then lay down on the cold floor next to the table. He lay like that for two days, without food or drink, waiting for the destroyers to arrive. Unremembered were his wife and five children, who had fled with the others, forgotten was the whole community, dispersed and shattered. His mind was filled with but one thought: the inviolate sanctity of the House of Worship, and his visions of the shattered heads of those that would defile it gave him strength and vitality.

It was thus that only two Jews remained in the whole of Tetayev: the one that served liquor to the drunken gentiles, and the other, who crouched like a lion at the entrance to the Lord's House to preserve its sanctity.

Part Two

"Papa" Gonta sat firmly astride his mount, a squat but fiery Cossack horse, thick of shank, small-headed and somewhat shaggy. Gonta wore his large Cossack *kalpak* at a jaunty angle over one ear. His long sword almost trailed on the ground. His little, cunning eyes were deep-set in his fat, glistening face. His long brown mustache coiled down like snakes' tails on either side of his full, red lips. After him walked a motley crowd of minstrels playing a variety of instruments, followed by a large troop of horsemen, their drawn swords laid across the pommels of their saddles. Behind them came, on foot, a ragged mob of rebels, armed with picks, axes, scythes and other farmyard implements. A train of carts, loaded with provisions and plunder, brought up the rear. The procession was marshalled by mounted officers, who rode up and down the line on either side.

All the villagers, men, women and children, had turned out in their holiday attire and lined the road on either side. They cheered boisterously, waved scarves and flags, and some even threw flowers at the marchers. The skies were distant, clear and serene—as they were in the Sinai Desert before the Giving of the Law; the Feast of Pentecost was a week away.

The procession came to a halt in the center of the town, filling the circular market-place around the large cross and the Christ in the last throes of agony. The jostling crowd poured into the square, were pressed back against the walls of the shuttered houses. Without dismounting from his horse, "Papa" Gonta made a short speech; the enthusiastic mob cheered wildly and flung their caps into the air. Then his aides briskly set up his tent in the shadow of the cross, and laid out a carpet of coarse red wool at the entrance. The Cossack chief then sat down to conduct the business of the day.

To begin with, he ordered the leading members of the *Haromada*, the local council, to be brought before him. The next instant, a dozen village notables stood around him in a half-circle, fur caps in hand, bowing obsequiously.

"I want every Zhyd and Liach brought here at once," Gonta roared.

"They have run away, Papa, all of them," the farmers answered in abject apology.

"What, are none of them left?"

"Not a single one of the Liachs."

"And the Zhyds?"

"All gone, Papa. There's only Chamka the inn-keeper, whom we kept behind to wet our thirsty souls. If Papa will give orders to let him live . . . for the good of the town . . ."

"Very well, we'll keep him alive for the time being. Now I want two of you to go and fetch me some of that liquor, the best there is. The rest of you go and see to it that your people get armed. At sunrise tomorrow we march on Uman."

After the farmers had left, two Cossack officers wearing Polish kalpaks came over and stood respectfully before him.

"Well?"

"What shall we do about the horses, Excellency?"

"Put half of them in the Polish church and the other half in the Zhyd synagogue," their commander told them.

The officers having left to carry out his orders, Gonta settled down to the two large, pot-bellied bottles of vodka that had been brought from the inn. Ever since he had launched the insurrection against the Poles, allying himself with his fellow-Haidamaks, he had progressively doubled, then trebled, his daily dose of liquor.

There were more than a hundred horses to be stabled in the synagogue. The Cossacks led them there by their bridles at a slow walk. The horses had been washed and were dripping wet, their shaggy coats had been combed down, their saddles and trappings hung from them loosely, and their long, swishing tails almost reached their small ears. The Cossacks carried pails of oats in their hands, and some bore sacks of fodder on their shoulders. They went about their business calmly, ingenuously, looking to all the world like the serfs that served the rich farmers or Polish noblemen. Little did they suspect what trouble lay in store.

From afar they saw that the doors of the synagogue were barred.

"The dogs shut the place up!" said one of them, shaking his head in annoyance.

"Pity they ran away," another joked. "We could have rammed the door open with their mangy heads."

"Let's get something to use as a battering-ram."

"Nah! You can break that door down with an ordinary club!"

"Just let Tarras put his behind to it, and it'll fly open."

"Ho ho, that's a good one! When Tarras lets wind, it can bring a castle down!"

They continued exchanging their coarse jests till they came to the doors of the House of God.

Hearing the noise of the approaching crowd of men and horses, Israel Michal was buoyed by a wave of vigorous excitement, which turned his arms to tempered steel and set his heart afire. He leapt up from where he lay and crouched to peer through the keyhole. Then he raised his arms towards the Holy Ark and offered up a silent prayer to the Lord for having brought his enemies within his reach, that he might wreak havoc among them. Taking a stone from the pile, he sprang lightly onto the table, like a boy, mounted the chair, and then, without taking aim, hurled the stone through the broken fanlight onto the massed crowd below. The stone tore the ear of one of the Cossacks and dislocated his arm. At his agonized yell, his bewildered comrades pressed forward against the front of the building to see what had happened. Men and horses were bombarded by the heavy stones which came down in a steady stream, one by one. Before they had time to draw back and see what was happening, a number of dead and wounded lay on the ground. The frightened horses neighed wildly, rearing up on their legs.

"By god! Their God's fighting back at us!" cried one.

"Jesu and Maria! Did you see those stones! Straight down from the sky!"

"By the life of Papa! No man could lift such a stone!"

"They're magicians, they are! F— their mothers!"

"We've got to bring up the battering-rams!"

"Don't be a ninny! We've got to get Papa. He'll tell us what's to be done."

The stones kept falling, one by one, at regular intervals, but now they landed with a dull thud on the soft earth, or on the body of one of the slain.

Before long "Papa" Gonta arrived in person, his squat, blubbery body waddling in rhythm with the song of the liquor that swilled about inside him. After surveying the field of battle, he ordered his men to shoot at the door with their muskets. The door was soon riddled like a sieve, but still the stream of stones did not cease.

"The place must be full of devils!" the commander roared in fury. "My children, lay logs all round this stable and set it on fire."

That same moment, a solitary shot having been fired at the door, the hail of stones let up.

After a few minutes of amazed silence, the Cossacks were ordered to break down the door with their hatchets. Great was their astonishment, however, when, bursting in, they found the vestibule deserted save for an elderly Jew who sat on the floor next to a pile of stones, nursing a wounded leg and biting his lips in agony; his hair was dishevelled, blood and sweat streamed down his face, and his eyes gleamed with a mad light. They leapt over his crouching form and erupted into the synagogue with drawn swords to look for any others that might have barricaded themselves inside. They found not a soul; the whole synagogue—the dais, the curtainless Holy Ark that stood wide open, the lecterns, the candelabra—all were as silent as death. Rushing back to the vestibule, they dragged the wounded beadle outside and flung him at the feet of their commander.

"Here he is, Papa, the devil that's been killing off our brothers. It's all we found."

"Papa" Gonta regarded him speculatively for a moment, kicked him, turned him over with his foot, spat on him, then ordered him to be dragged out of the way while the horses were taken into the "stable." With much heaving and tugging the frightened horses—strangely reluctant to enter—were finally stabled in the synagogue.

This done, the Cossack chief turned to the business of passing sentence on the beadle, who had caused the death of three soldiers and one horse and had injured four soldiers and five horses more. Flanked by his officers he faced the crowd, his head slightly canted under the weight of his Tartar fur-cap. For moment he toyed with the silver hilt of his long, curved sabre, and then, clearing his throat loudly two or three times, he pronounced judgment slowly, deliberately as though counting over money:

"Strip him naked and tie him down, with his head against that door," he waved his head in the direction of the synagogue. "Four guards will stand over him, two at his head and two at his feet, and Ivan Zorbilo," a burly giant of a Cossack pushed his way through the crowd and stood before his chief, "will flog him with his knout. Flog him slowly. D'you hear, you whoreson? Give it to him slowly, easy, easy, like this, one after the other. Don't lay it on too hard, d'you hear? And take your time over it, easy, easy. But don't stop, d'you hear? Don't stop for a moment. Just keep at it till that black-bitched soul of his packs up and clears off. Easy now, carefully, lovingly, gently, with all your heart, till his devil's soul flies off, haw, haw, haw!"

The Cossacks guffawed boisterously in wild appreciation of their chief's wit.

"Easy now, d'you hear?" Gonta sternly reminded Ivan, then a smile flitted across his mustaches. "And now, my little ones, let's have some dancing at the tav-

ern. My daughters back home in Rosschov are probably dancing too right now—on the red-hot stoves of the mother-f---ing Polacks." Tears glistened in his eyes, and the admiring mob was moved to compassion. "Come children, let's go."

"The whoresons! No matter, Papa, we'll kill them off, cut their throats to the last mother's son!" Roaring these and other words of comfort at their chief, the crowd surged in a mighty wave towards the pothouse.

Part Three

The yard in front of the synagogue emptied, save for the four guards, the giant Ivan Zorbilo who was to administer the flogging (the dead and wounded had been evacuated to the main square), a few idle spectators who had been too lazy to go to the pothouse, and the condemned man. Israel Michal lay spreadeagled on the ground, stark naked, his head on the threshold of the Lord's House, his hands and feet bound, his wounded leg dripping blood. Tears welled up in his eyes, but the strange light there quickly dried them.

The giant Cossack set about his task. To begin with, he unplaited the leather thongs of his knout, and they became four sharp, flicking tongues. Then he stared appreciatively at the butt, patted it once or twice and balanced it in his palm. The guards smoothed their mustaches in anticipation, gazing down at the victim.

Zorbilo began to administer the flogging.

The fiery-tongued thongs enlaced the giant frame lovingly, endearingly, as though seized with a passionate desire to cling to the holy body. Silently, with barely a swish, but with a restrained violence as with an ardent kiss, they came to rest on the chest, curled round and embraced the ribs, leaving four red weals when the knout was raised. At the first touch of the lash the body quivered and writhed slightly, the face contorted and the beginnings of a moan escaped through the lips, but was immediately stilled. The tortured man shut his eyes, bit his lips and was henceforth silent.

The giant performed his task dutifully, with painstaking deliberation. He was careful not to strike the same spot twice, enjoying the pattern of bloody weals he was raising on the naked body. He directed the lashing downward from the chest to the thighs, but carefully avoided striking the genitals. In his childhood—he remembered—his father had once hit him there with a whip, and he had never forgotten the dull, gnawing agony of it. No, he wouldn't lay it on there! But there were still other places! The lashes curled round the thighs, the knees, the shinbones, adorning the legs with a series of crimson bangles and anklets. The rope that pinioned the legs snapped, but the legs remained together, motionless and taut. The lash flicked up again from the toes to the chest, and thence up to the head, but stopped at the neck. No, he wouldn't disfigure the face! He began all over again from the place where he had started.

The guards and onlookers, tired of standing, squatted down on the ground and watched tensely. The tortured man's face was contorted. The pain, lacerating at first, had made way for an agonizing dullness that crept through his whole body and which, reaching his heart, seemed to rend it as with fiery pincers. His bound arms and legs felt numb, especially his wounded leg; the dripping blood had formed a little pool on the ground, which had coagulated and glistened in the sun for a brief moment, soon to be joined by further drops of fresh, warm blood.

From the tavern in the town square came the beating of drums and blowing of fifes and the sounds of drunken carousing. Seared with pain and hunger, Israel Michal's mind succumbed to strange visions. His eyes tightly closed, he saw in his tortured imagination how his brethren, the whole Jewish community of Tetayev, were being hounded and butchered in the streets of the town. He saw the Haidamaks riding them down with drawn swords and whistling knouts, trampling them under their horses' hooves, impaling babies on their lances. He saw his wife sprawled across the threshold of their house, her skull smashed in in her attempt to bar the way to the ravaging Cossacks. He saw his sons and daughters lying on the floor in pools of blood. But he was undisturbed by these visions. On the contrary, the bloody scenes filled him with a pleasurable sensation. The lashes that kept descending in a regular rhythm, too, had begun to mean for him an orderliness, an established scheme of things, quite understandable and justified. He was now possessed by a single fear—that the flogging would stop and upset this order.

The noonday sun beat down mercilessly. From the tops of the tall trees that fringed the synagogue the birds twittered in reply to the sounds that came from the tavern. In some deserted farmyard, a lone cock crowed his protests with stubborn persistence. Zorbilo flogged on, his pillar-like legs planted firmly apart on the ground, his back slightly bent forward, his face red-

dening with the exertion. He whipped off his fur cap and flung it into the lap of one of the guards, baring a close-cropped fair head which gleamed in the sunlight. Rivulets of sweat streamed down his boorish face onto his corded neck. The guards sat cross-legged, waiting for the two boys they had sent off to the tavern to fetch them something to drink. On the boys' return with a massive flagon of spirits, the guards took swigs at it in turn, their heads thrown well back. They offered the bottle to Zorbilo, but he refused it with a shake of his head. No, he mustn't stop. "Papa" had ordered him not to. He must keep at his flogging.

Israel Michal's mood underwent a change. A sweet sensation of utter weariness crept over his body and spirit. There was still that gnawing at his heart, his sinews seemed stretched to breaking-point, his whole body was a swollen, bluish-red mass, but he felt no pain, and was at ease. Gone also were the nightmarish, bloody pictures of the Haidamaks' butchery, having made way for pleasant visions: festival services of the synagogue, wedding celebrations, circumcision rites. He heard the cantor and his choir chant the merry, lilting tune of a New Year prayer; he saw himself spreading out the large *tallith* (prayer shawl) on the Feast of the Rejoicing of the Law; he was walking in the pleasant, dewy coolness of daybreak to wake up the worshippers for the Prayers of Intercession. The scenes came through to him, through his closed eyelids, with such sharp clarity, with such radiance and glory. He had never felt a happiness such as this before.

His eyes remained closed, and Zorbilo flogged on.

A few reeling drunks came out of the tavern. They lurched over to see what was going on, spat on the prostrate figure and went their way. Zorbilo did not stop.

Israel Michal had plunged into the dreamworld of childhood, into that Eden where the trees are ever in blossom and cherubs walk about in human form. His heart pounded in furious ecstasy, his soul smiled. Zorbilo swayed as if in prayer.

The sun had swung down from its zenith, plunging the synagogue in shadow—long shadows which swallowed in darkness the head of the tortured beadle, then slanted across to the church that looked on from afar. The sounds that came from the tavern rose to a menacing pitch, soon followed by the noises of windows being smashed and doors battered down. The Jewish houses were being ransacked and looted, now permitted by "Papa" Gonta in his expansive drunken benignity. Horses whinnied, wagons creaked under the loads of spoils that were being carted to the surrounding villages. Here and there flames leapt up from among thick coils of smoke.

Doggedly, Zorbilo flogged on. His knees wavered from long standing, his heart was fit to burst with hunger and thirst and exertion. But he must not stop. So long as the chest of the prostrate figure heaved—though ever so faintly—there was no stopping. A few times already, the guards had run their hands over the lacerated body, but it was still warm, and Zorbilo went on flogging.

Suddenly Israel Michal opened his eyes, looked up with a clear, untroubled gaze that shone with the purity of the Eternal Light. He saw the gigantic Gentile looming over him, and the thongs that descended to cut into his flesh in a ceaseless rhythm, yet he did not move an eyelid. He saw the two guards squatting at his feet, the cluster of idle onlookers, the synagogue yard, the wooden palings of the fence, the branches of the solitary tree that stood next to the church opposite—and all appeared so clear, so lucid and sharply-defined. What might have been a smile hovered on the bloodless blue lips, but it was swallowed up in the deep shadow that had now crept half down the neck, seemingly cutting it in two.

Zorbilo swayed wearily. His giant's strength was failing, becoming spent. Countlessly he had changed hands, but this no longer relieved the numbness in his arms, which moved mechanically as though of their own accord. He was *afraid* of stopping. He feared—not "Papa" Gonta, whom he had completely forgotten—that if he stopped now he would never again be able to move an arm. He had put his entire spirit, his very heart and soul, into the whipping. His whole attention was now focussed on the face of the tortured man, had been riveted there ever since the eyes had opened. The calm gaze seemed to flow into his soul, merge with his inner being, thawing and softening the hardness there; the purity and holy innocence it gave out made him oblivious of all, of yesterday's butchery and tomorrow's battles, of his commanders, of the march on Uman and the fort that was to be stormed—all was forgotten. There was only himself communing with the soul of the tortured man. He lashed on, and his heart went out in prayer to the Jew who lay before him.

The guards had untied his hands, but not a limb stirred. He lay inert on his back, his face waxen, only his eyes alive, gazing into the depths of Zorbilo's soul as he stood over him, lashing him with palsied arms.

Israel Michal felt himself being taken up and borne aloft, higher and higher, to the Gate of Heaven, to the eternal serenity and the Hidden Light beyond. But before his eyes stood a tormented man, gasping painfully as he labored futilely in the last stages of exhaustion; and he felt the need to speak to the sufferer, comfort him.

The shadows had crept down to the lifeless waist, when Zorbilo suddenly noticed a faint movement of the blue lips and the saintly eyes beckoning to him to bend down. He answered this mute call, the whip in his deadened arm still flailing at the outstretched legs, the sweat streaming down his ashen face onto his sodden shirt. And as he stooped, his ears strained to listen, the lips parted slightly to whisper to him, distinctly, in his own language:

"You are tired, my son. Rest, rest a while, rest . . ."

A strangled cry, like the raucous rasp of a dying man, burst forth from the giant's heaving chest, the knout slipped from his hand, and he sank to his knees at the feet of the martyred man.

The guards and onlookers leapt up in alarm. On the martyr's lips his last smile remained affixed for all time, alight with the radiance of the Lord of Mercy and Forgiveness.

Translated by Yosef Schachter.

Other works by Barash: *Kol ketavav*, 3 vols. (1952–1957); *Collected Stories* (1963); *Pictures from a Brewery* (1972).

Lion Feuchtwanger
1884–1958

The German novelist Lion Feuchtwanger was widely read, but his literary reputation plummeted after midcentury. Feuchtwanger came from a prosperous Orthodox family in Munich and considered an academic career but, knowing he would have to convert to succeed, abandoned the idea. Before World War I, he worked as a theater critic and wrote a number of one-act plays on Jewish themes. His novel *Jud Süss*, about the eighteenth-century southern German court Jew Joseph Süss Oppenheimer, brought him international recognition. His historical novels, many of which were on Jewish themes, were his most successful works. He also wrote essays on contemporary Jewish topics. He took refuge in southern France in 1933 and, after the

German invasion, escaped to the United States, where he lived in Los Angeles and was a central figure in the German exile community there.

Power/Jew Süss
1925

[. . .] After the intractable insolence shown by Süss when his sentence was pronounced, he was fettered cross-wise in the Chamber of Nobles, where he was to be confined until execution, and kept without food all day in a bleak and completely bare room. He had quieted down immediately after his outburst before the judges, and with a smile and a shake of the head regarded the blood and dirt with which he was smeared. He squatted, cramped by his fetters, on the floor by the wall of the brilliant and empty room. Haman, the Minister of Ahasuerus, came to visit him; he had Herr von Pflug's hook-nose and hard, arrogant voice. Goliath came, and with Herr von Gaisberg's hand smote him bluntly, jovially and heavily on the shoulder, so that it hurt. Others came who were more friendly, speaking half in Swabian and half in Hebrew. Eliezer, the faithful Pfäffle, was there; and Abraham in the guise of Johann Daniel Harpprecht disputed with God about justice. And the men came who had appeared to Naemi; Isaiah the prophet grumbled and consoled him in the ill-tempered voice of his uncle; and by his rich hair Absalom hung in the branches; but the hair was white and the face under it was his own.

But a sudden yelping and baying and bellowing broke in upon him. Oh, that was Hoffmann again, the Town Vicar, extolling the blessings of the Augsburg Confession. Yes, the zealous saver of souls was once more on the spot; he believed the fruit was now ripe enough to pluck. But Süss was not at all disposed to argue with him. That coarse voice overwhelmed the softer ones around him. Quietly and without sarcasm he asked him to refrain; if he could only be left alone he would gladly leave ten thousand dollars in his will to the Evangelical Church for its attentions. The clergyman gave up all hope and departed in chagrin.

Another unexpected visitor appeared. A fine, elderly gentleman with a head like a greyhound's and expanded nostrils, inconspicuously and very elegantly clad. The Duchess Dowager's father, the old Prince Thurn and Taxis. This affair had given him no rest, had driven him hither from the Netherlands. It would not do, one could not allow Süss to die like that. A man

whom his daughter had visited, and with whom he himself had shaken hands. A man whose services the Catholic Church had accepted, not officially, but yet in such a way that all the Courts were aware of it. No, no, that did not accord with his notions of courtesy, he had been too well brought up to suffer such a thing to happen. A man with whom one had gone so far was a gentleman. Tact, decorum and good manners required one not to allow such a man to come in contact with the gallows. The old Prince came himself to Stuttgart, incognito, as Baron Neuhoff. He had never been able to stand the Jew; he had never forgotten how Süss had killed his yellow coat with the yellow salon at Monbijou, and his wine-red suit with the wine-red livery of his footmen. It would be in bad taste to feel gratified now at the man's misfortunes, but, still, he did not need to be afraid that the Jew's surroundings would throw him out of focus this time.

He came with a sound plan. He would help Süss to escape as he had helped Remchingen. In the Jew's case that would not be so simple; but he was determined to spare neither effort nor money. Perhaps after all the uncongenial old boor and booby of a Regent would be glad to get rid of the Jew in such a way. At any rate, he would manage. He would lay down only one condition. It would not do to take so much trouble for a Jew. He would have to stop being a Jew. Yes, the Jew would have to become a convert, and situated as he was he would be unlikely to make any fuss about it. It would be a gain, a triumph, for the Catholic Church to receive into its bosom such a wily financier and shrewd politician, one who was besides much more of a cavalier than most of the so-called gentlemen of Swabia.

The elegant Prince, after crossing the threshold with a smile, relishing the surprise he was to bring, recoiled in horror. What was this? It was a crooked old Jew from the Ghetto crouching there. Was this the Finance Director? Was this the great Celadon? An uneasy feeling crept over him as if he himself were dirty. Süss saw his visitor's face. "Yes," he said, with an imperceptible smile; "yes, your Highness, it is I."

A bench, a stool and a table had now been put into the room. The Prince sat down carefully and ill at ease. He absolutely could not reconcile the man crouching before him with the elegant gentleman he remembered. Was the Jew trying to bluff the world again? Was it all a trick? He had the same unpleasant feeling as he had had in the yellow salon and on being confronted with the wine-red liveries. Had the Jew achieved the impossible and beaten him again in these circumstances, in this cell? Well, others might be imposed on, but not he. He had no mind to be limed by the Jew. He, a prince and a gentleman with his knowledge of the world and his scepticism, was not to be bluffed.

"There is no need to keep up pretences before me, your Excellency," he ventured smoothly and politely, as if he were in a drawing-room. "You cannot suppose that I believe in this mummery. It is a trick. Under the gallows you will suddenly whisk off your disfiguring beard and appear again as the clever, well-bred and accomplished cavalier of old days. It is a manoeuvre," he asserted triumphantly. "Of course it is a manoeuvre. But, my dear erstwhile Director of Finance, it is a comedy which may delude the gentlemen from Parliament, but it does not delude me. You cannot take me in."

Süss said nothing. "Apparently you still have a trump in your hand," ventured the Prince again, "which you mean to produce at the last moment. I imagine that you are playing the suffering saint now so as to have a more glorious resurrection. But be careful! They are in a dangerous mood here. Perhaps they will not give you the chance. Perhaps they will hang you—excuse my mentioning it—with all your trumps still in your hand."

Since Süss was still silent he became impatient. "Your Excellency! Man! Show some understanding! Speak, at least! I have come to help you. It can scarcely have been predicted for you that a ruling German prince would give himself so much trouble on your account. Listen to me! Say something!" Paralysed by the other's attitude he explained boldly his plan and its condition. When he had finished, Süss made no movement, nor did he open his mouth. The fine Prince felt himself more completely routed than ever. He had made this journey, and now the Jew sat there without even a pathetic refusal, simply saying nothing. The Prince felt suddenly old and weary, he could not endure the silence any longer, and he said with forced sarcasm: "You have forgotten your good manners in captivity. When anyone takes so much trouble about you, you might at least say '*Mille merci!*'"

"*Mille merci!*" said Süss.

The Prince stood up. He felt it as a personal insult that this Jew would not let himself be rescued, but preferred to hang on the gallows in broad daylight. "You are a large-sized fool, my dear fellow," he said, and his courteous voice became surprisingly sharp. "Your stoicism is completely out of date. One no longer dies to get a better showing in the school history books. Better

a living dog than a dead lion, was very justly remarked by your King Solomon." He dusted his coat, and concluded, already at the door: "Have your beard shaved off, at least, and put on a good suit of clothes if you"—and he wrinkled up his nose—"*partout* insist on swinging. One may ask that much of a man whom one has received as a friend in one's circle. You have a numerous and prominent public. You have cut a good figure all your life. Don't undo your own reputation as a cavalier when you make your exit from this world-theatre."

And with that he went.

The gallows on which Süss was to be hanged had been constructed a hundred and forty years previously. It was expensive, having cost three thousand South German gulden in those good old days of cheapness; it was altogether unusual, very different from the ordinary wooden gallows. It towered up for five and thirty feet. It was entirely made of iron, constructed from thirty-six hundredweight and eighteen pounds of iron procured by the alchemist Georg Honauer to make into gold for Duke Friedrich, a transaction in which the Duke was done out of two tons of gold. This gallows had been erected in honour of the same Georg Honauer, painted a pretty red ornamented with gold, and employed to hang him on.

Various alchemists accused of swindling Duke Friedrich had followed him in rapid succession. The first was an Italian called Petrus Montanus. A year afterwards it was Hans Heinrich Neuscheler from Zürich, known as the Blind Goldmaker. Still a year later came another Hans Heinrich, whose name was Von Müllenfels. His luck had lasted for a longer time; he had often made merry over his three colleagues swinging in the air; but now he swung as they did. Then for a long time the gallows was unused, until a smith from the county of Oettingen had the idea of taking it down and stealing it piecemeal. He had already pried off three shafts and made away by night with more than seven hundredweight of iron, when he was caught and hoisted on the instrument of his crime.

For more than a century since then the iron gallows had stood empty. Now Herr von Pflug, who had undertaken the arrangements for the execution, designed to make the Jew the sixth to suffer death on this extraordinary contrivance. From the beginning of the prosecution the lean, hard man had been waiting to prepare the banquet of his hate. Now he intended to celebrate it in such a way that Europe would never forget it.

He planned the execution with every refinement of opprobrium. The Jew's lewdness and carnal sins, the circumcised dog's violation of Christian German women, had unfortunately and sore against his will found no place in the charge-sheet. But for the execution he had a free hand. He would show up the Jew's lust and shameless depravity. He would not have him hanged simply on the gallows, no, he would hang him in a bird-cage, as a vulgar pun on Süss's dissolute nightly activities.

The Commission spent a lot of money on the solemn fulfilment of its verdict. Comfortable boxes for the ladies and gentlemen were erected on the place of execution, the Tunzenhofer Hill, also called the Gallows Hill, on the road to Prague. The soldiers who were to escort the delinquent and regulate the crowd rehearsed their parts. The iron gallows was thoroughly repaired, the tumbril was fitted with larger wheels, the malefactor's bell was given a new rope, and the hangmen put into new uniforms.

The greatest importance was attached to the proper execution of Herr von Pflug's witty idea. The Jew had jeered, saying that they could not hang him higher than the gallows. They would show him what they could do. They would simply hoist the iron bird-cage high up over the gallows.

The construction of the cage, all its complicated apparatus, was entrusted to the master-smiths Johann Christoph Faust and Veit Ludwig Rigler. The cage was detachable into two pieces; it was eight feet high and four feet wide; it had fourteen hoops round it and seventeen upright bars. Ingenious machinery enabled it to be swung easily above the gallows. Its construction was extraordinarily costly. In the end every smith in town had to ply his hammer on it. Two days before the execution the monstrous thing was dragged up the steep Tunzenhofer Hill by six horses. The school-children of the Capital ran alongside. Wine and beer were on sale in hastily-erected booths, and hawkers offered broadsides with satiric verses and the Jew's picture. In the cold weather people thronged noisily to the place of execution, watched with interest the construction of the boxes, and admired the polish on the gallows and the ingenuity of the cage.

The bird-cage had an even greater success with the populace than Herr von Pflug had anticipated. An enormous grin ran through the town and over the whole country. Countless verses about birds were made, and sung by the children in the streets. Only, people refused to believe that Herr von Pflug had been the author of this excellent jest; they preferred to ascribe the ingenious idea of the bird-cage to their favourite, the widely popular Major von Röder. So that the verses about the birds were usually followed by the song containing the lines:

"Then shouted Herr von Röder,
'Halt, or you're a deader!'"

Rabbi Gabriel and Rabbi Jonathan Eybeschütz sat in Süss's cell. The grand pass of the Netherland States had opened the prison gates without further ceremony to Mynheer Gabriel Oppenheimer van Straaten. Now the three men sat together and shared a meal. Rabbi Gabriel had brought in fruit, dates, figs and oranges, as well as pastry and strong wine of the South. Süss wore his scarlet-coloured coat with a skull-cap on his white hair, and his brow like those of the two Rabbis was cleft above the nose by three furrows making the letter Shin, the first letter in Shaddai, the name of God. He dipped figs into the wine. This was his last meal. Rabbi Gabriel divided an orange with his thick fingers. The three men sat and ate the fruits, silently and with great seriousness. But their thoughts flowed in a heavy tide from one to the other. Rabbi Gabriel and Süss were one, and for the first time Rabbi Gabriel felt his bond not as a compulsion and an evil fate, but as a privilege. The third man, however, Jonathan Eybeschütz, felt the same influence as they did, but was excluded from it; he stood on the shore and the wave did not carry him away. He sat with them, he drank with them, like them he bore the mark of the Shin, like them he was an initiate and a seer; but the wave did not carry him away. Rabbi Gabriel carefully sprinkled the orange sections with sugar and shared them out. He poured out the black Southern wine. The cell was full of the unspoken word, full of thought, of vision, of God. But Rabbi Jonathan was consumed with bitterness and envy. He carried it off with a sardonic jest; it was easy to be exalted when one was going to be hanged. But this cold comfort was of no avail, and he, the rich and learned man, felt himself poor and envious, and half a traitor. And as he intoned in his turn the grace after meat, fine in his silken caftan and his flowing milky beard, reverend, wise, and highly honoured, he was a poor, troubled, lost man.

While upstairs the sentence was being once more pronounced on Süss and the staff broken over his head in the lobby of the Town Hall, the mild and faded Rabbi of Frankfurt, the burly and sanguine Rabbi of Fürth, and Isaac Landauer, excited and shivering, all waited for him. Large melting flakes of snow were falling and a pale sun fitfully pierced the murky clouds. Outside before the doorway there was a countless swarm of curious sightseers, Herr von Röder on his old chestnut at the head of a military escort, and around the gallows-cart, which towered bleakly on its high wheels, the hangman and his assistants in their crude colours.

At last Süss was led down the steps. The Jews had received permission to speak to him here for the last time. He bent his head, and the small Rabbi Jaakob Joshua Falk laid his mild and withered hands on it, and said: "The Lord bless thee and keep thee. The Lord let the light of His face shine upon thee, and be gracious unto thee. The Lord lift up His countenance upon thee, and give thee peace." "Amen. Selah," responded the other two.

The Jew was formally placed in the high gallows-cart and bound. In spite of the frost and the damp the whole marketplace was thronged with people. All the windows of the Chamber of Nobles, the Town Hall, the chemist's shop and the Sun Inn were white with faces. Boys were clustered on the fountain and even on the wine merchant's crane and trestles. The people stared in silence. Herr von Röder in his rasping voice gave his riders the word of command. The escort moved forward, first the Town Riders, then two drummers, and then a company of grenadiers on foot. One of the hangmen's assistants swung himself on to the tumbril horse and clicked his tongue, and the beast started. The little Rabbi Jaakob Joshua Falk repeated with blenched lips: "And give thee peace." The headstrong Rabbi of Fürth could not restrain himself and flung wild curses after the cart against Edom and Amalek, enemies and unbelievers. But Isaac Landauer broke into loud and uncontrolled howling like an animal. It was strange to see the great financier beating his head against the door-posts of the Town Hall and howling unrestrainedly. And now the malefactor's bell began to toll. Thin, sharp and resonant, it mingled with the howls of the Jew, piercing to the marrow as it rang through the wet and snowy air.

It echoed into Magdalen Sibylle's chamber. She had born the birth well, but she was still confined to bed. She looked at her child, a normal child, neither big nor small, neither beautiful nor ugly. She heard the sharp tinkle of the bell and she crumpled up nervously; she looked at the child which was hers and Immanuel Rieger's, and she did not love it.

The bell echoed into the Castle, too, where the old Regent was sitting with Bilfinger and Harpprecht. The three men were silent. At last Harpprecht said: "That tolling is not pleasant to my ear." Karl Rudolf said: "I had to do it. I am ashamed of myself, gentlemen."

Meanwhile Süss was conducted through the town towards the Gallows Hill. He sat on the tumbril uplifted like a heathen image, in his scarlet coat, and with the solitaire gleaming on his finger; the Duke Regent had forbidden him to be deprived of the ring. The streets were packed with people; snowflakes were falling; the procession's advance was strangely soundless, and strangely soundless was the mass of spectators. Once the delinquent was past, the thousands of onlookers fell in behind and around the escort on foot, on horseback and in carriages. In the pale and misty air, among the dirty melting snowflakes, everything moved twice as heavily and silently. Instead of taking the shortest way, they conducted the Jew slowly and formally by a circuitous route, for many spectators had come from afar, the whole country wanted to look on—there were even some from beyond the frontiers—and everybody had to see the show. Süss was throned aloft on the cart, bound and rigid, with snow falling on his clothes and on his white beard.

Mögling the advocate stood by the wayside. He was troubled and oppressed, because his defence had been of no avail. He could certainly assure himself that he had done all he could, and, besides, the *vox populi* was loud and unanimous against the condemned man. But still it was bitter and depressing to know that the accused, who had been entrusted to him, was to be hanged without sufficient legal warrant. He felt shivery and uncomfortable. He caused one of the assistant hangmen to reach a beaker of wine up to Süss. Süss did not take it, he did not even say: "Thank you," but remained completely motionless; still, the advocate felt warmer and more relieved.

Schertlin's wife, the Waldensian, also stood waiting by the roadside. She saw Süss pinioned and remarkably still, as motionless as a holy image escorted in a procession through the town, with snow in his beard and on his coat. She alone of all the spectators had an inkling of the fact that this martyrdom was a voluntary one. She gazed greedily at the man, with scornful but despairing triumph, her small red lips half open, and her long eyes burning. A woman beside her muttered in broad Swabian: "He always wanted to be high up. Now he'll be high enough." "*Sale bête!*" said the Waldensian to the falling snowflakes.

At another turn of the road stood Johann Jaakob Moser, the publicist. When the procession came in sight he began to deliver a short, pithy and patriotic address. But his fiery words kindled nobody; the snow blotted them out and the people were unmoved, so that he closed his mouth again before he had finished. Shortly before the procession reached its end it passed Nicklas Pfäffle, the pale, phlegmatic secretary. As his master went by for the last time, he saluted him profoundly. Süss saw him, and nodded twice. When the cart was past Nicklas Pfäffle did not follow it to the end, but turned aside and sobbed.

Snow and clouds had cleared away by the time the procession reached the gallows. The vineyards were clear and frosty under the pale bright sky. The Jew looked up to the terraces and saw the little watch-tower,—the baths. He turned round and looked at Stuttgart, at the cathedral of Saint Leonard's, at the old Castle and at the new palace for which he had promised the money. On his left the high wooden gallows raised its bleak head. But it was insignificant beside the daring, ingenious, gigantic iron structure designed for him. A double ladder with innumerable rings and many supports soared into the air, and there was an involved network of wheels, pulleys and chains to hoist up the cage. The wide space was filled with people. They swarmed in eager expectation on every projection, on fence and tree. Those who were a long way off gazed through large round telescopes. The snow on Süss's coat was frozen and in the frosty brightness tiny crystals glittered on his cap and in his white beard.

On two grand-stands, each accommodating six hundred people, sat the ladies and gentlemen, the senior civil servants and officers, the foreign ambassadors, the members of the Commission and of Parliament. Privy Councillor von Pflug was well to the fore. He had been afraid up to the very last that the Hebrew beast would escape after all through some crafty Jewish trick. But now the hour had come, now the aim of his life had been achieved. Now, now this very minute, his hated enemy would swing aloft and be strangled. The Privy Councillor's hard eyes greedily spied out under the coat collar the Jew's neck, the place for the halter. It is glorious to look on at the death of an enemy, it is as balm to the eyes; pleasant and lovely is the sound of the death-drums, and the clang of the bell. Among the ladies were many who had known Süss intimately and yet escaped the inquisition for some reason or other. They now gazed at the man with whom they had been involved,

alienated and shuddering. For he had passed as very young, and he had possessed a young man's strength, as they knew, and he could not be more than forty at the very most; but now he had white hair and looked like an old Rabbi. One should really feel ashamed of having been in bed with him. But it was remarkable that they did not feel ashamed. They gazed at this extraordinary man with eager fascination. In a minute he would be dead, in a minute he would be dumb for ever, and all danger would be over and they would be disentangled from him by a forcible and gruesome deed. They sat waiting for that, eager and trembling, yearning for it, and shrinking from it in terror. Most of them would rather have lived all their lives in fear of discovery if he could have been kept alive.

Young Michael Koppenhöfer was also on the grand-stand. At last the millstone would be ground to powder which had for so long hung round the country's neck; at last the corrupter of the land would die a disgraceful death. But—this man had not been dismissed by Elisabeth Salomea, casually and hastily among bundles of books and underclothing, this man had taken her, without even having to exert himself particularly. The old and broken Jew, what was it he possessed? What was his secret? With bitter envy he stared at the man in the gallows-cart. But the young Privy Councillor Götz, sitting among the Commissioners, looked on with silent and gloomy satisfaction. Now his mother's and sister's disgrace would be wiped out. Let everybody dare to look askance at him after this! How he would blast them! How well he would know what to do!

Weissensee, old and worn, sat, elegant and feeble, on the tribune. Thou hast conquered, O Judaean! Thou hast conquered, O Judaean! Ah, the Jew had triumphed over him again. The Jew had tasted of every dish—had relished with his eyes, his sense and his brain all the daintiest pleasures of the world, had emptied to the dregs every cup of triumph and despair, had been filled with the tragic end of his child and then had prepared and accomplished a conspicuous, over-subtle, hellishly diabolical revenge; and now he died this death with the eyes of the whole world upon him, this romantic and apparently voluntary death, much more heroic than death on the field of battle. Surrounded by raucous hate and cherishing love, ambiguous and great. What would be left of himself, Weissensee? A couple of lamentable verses by his poor bourgeoise daughter. But the other was sure of immortality. What he was, his life, his observations, his thoughts and his death, would be of perpetual interest to later ages; his ideas, his life, his feelings and his death would be appreciatively re-enacted.

Süss was unbound from the gallows-cart. He stood blinking, his limbs numb. He saw the people in the boxes, the periwigs, the painted faces of the ladies. He saw the troops, who made a cordon round the gallows place. Aha, they had exerted themselves! There were at least five companies round the gallows alone. Of course Major von Röder was in command, and conspicuously at his post. Yes, it needed a lot of strategy to get him completely out of the world. Süss saw the tens of thousands of faces, curious women, with their mouths ready to bawl, men ready to smack their lips and growl with satisfaction, children's faces, chubby and large-eyed, destined to become as empty and malicious as the ugly visages of their parents. He saw the breath of the mob, rising in a white vapour, very solid in the clear frost, the ravening eyes, the stretched necks, which had formerly bowed before him so devotedly. He saw the bird-cage, the complicated and dishonourable devices for his execution. And while he was looking at all this something lowed and bleated in his ear. It was the Town Vicar Hoffmann who had insisted on waiting for him by the gallows and was now speaking to him once more of heaven and earth, forgiveness of sin, of God, faith and atonement. Süss gazed around him while he listened to the other, and then slowly looked the Town Vicar up and down, and turned away and spat. Eyes opened wide, and a low hiss of indignation arose from the crowd and as quickly died away.

Now the assistant hangmen in their gaudy new uniforms seized him and opened his coat. At the touch of their coarse, clumsy hands he recoiled with disgust, his numbness disappeared and he hit out desperately to defend himself. All necks were stretched still further. It was curious to see how the man in the white beard and the fine clothes, with the diamond blazing on his hand, fought and struggled with the assistants. The children laughed with glee and clapped their hands; on one of the stands a rouged lady began to scream shrilly and continuously, and had to be removed. The Jew's cap fell on the damp ground and was trodden into the slush. The hangmen seized him firmly, tore off his coat, pushed him into the cage and put the halter round his neck.

There he stood. He heard a little breeze, the breathing of the mob, the clattering hoofs of horses, the curses of the clergymen. Were these the last things he was to hear on earth? He thirsted to hear something else, he

opened wide his heart and his ears, yearning to hear something else. But he heard nothing else, save his own breathing and the pulse of his own blood. The cage was already rocking and rising. And then, through the empty and cruel hubbub there soared another sound, the sound of loud and guttural voices crying: "One and Eternal is the God of Israel, Jehovah, Adonai, the Everlasting, the Infinite!" It is the Jews, the small Jaakob Joshua Falk, the burly Rabbi of Fürth, the shabby Isaac Landauer. They are standing wrapped in their praying-cloaks, they and seven others, making ten as is prescribed; they pay no heed to the crowd, which turns its eyes away from the gallows towards them; they sway their bodies wildly, and they stand crying, shrilling, wailing the prayer for the dying, clear over the broad square. "Hear, O Israel. One and Eternal is Jehovah Adonai!" The words mount from their lips as white vapour in the strong frost, up to the ears of the man in the cage, and the son of Marshal Heydersdorff opens his mouth and cries in answer: "One and Eternal is Jehovah Adonai."

Nimbly the gaudy hangmen swarm and clamber up the ladders. The cage rises, the halter tightens. Underneath, the Town Vicar execrates the dying man: "Depart into hell, accursed Jew and villain!" But the shrill Adonai of the Jews is in the air and in the ears of everyone. It is returned from the cage, until the voice is strangled by the halter.

Right in front of the stand, Privy Councillor Dom Bartelemi Pancorbo has stood up, and propping his lean bony hands on the railing he stretches his fleshless, purple head out of his enormous ruff. His eyes behind their wrinkled lids greedily follow the cage as it sways aloft, and in it the man with the fine scarlet coat on whose finger the solitaire blazes like a rainbow in the clear wintry air.

After the cordon of troops was removed the mob thronged to a closer view of the gallows, and one or two boys climbed halfway up the ladders; they examined the scaffolding and saw above on the bars of the cage black birds sitting in dense flocks.

The crowd wound slowly back to the town. The day was held as a holiday, there was good eating and drinking, carousing and dancing and brawling in the beerhouses. The young citizen Langefass had looted Süss's trodden cap out of the mire; he was a jolly fellow and a famous wag; he cocked the cap on his head, and set it on the heads of girls and waiting-maids, who screamed in affright at the touch of the cap of the hanged Jew. But all the same the right holiday mood did not come. One did not quite know why but the day did not come up to expectations; it should have been freer and merrier. People sang: "The Jew must hang!" and they sang: "Then shouted Herr von Röder, Halt, or you're a deader.'" But they could not get the Adonai of the Jews out of their ears. The children played at hanging, and the game went like this: one child stood aloft and cried "Adonai," and the others stood below and cried and screamed and hallooed "Adonai."

Translated by Willa Muir and Edwin Muir.

Other works by Feuchtwanger: *Success* (1930); *Josephus*, 3 vols. (1932–1942); *The Oppermanns* (1934); *Raquel, the Jewess of Toledo* (1956); *Jephtha and His Daughter* (1958).

Alter-Sholem Kacyzne

1885–1941

Hailing from Vilna, Alter-Sholem Kacyzne was a Yiddish writer, playwright, and photographer. A close associate of Sh. An-ski and a devoted student of I. L. Peretz, Kacyzne wrote numerous novellas, short-story collections, and plays, and served for many years as a literary editor at *Literarishe bleter* and at other journals. His novel *Shtarke un shvakhe* (Strong and Weak) tells the story of Warsaw Jewry in epic fashion. He is best remembered for his photographs of Jewish life across Poland, Western Europe, North Africa, and the Holy Land taken for the Hebrew Immigrant Aid Society, the *Forverts* newspaper, and other outlets. He was murdered by the Nazis in Tarnopol (in present-day Ukraine) in 1941.

The Duke

1925

Act I

A porch stage left, a little window. A tree at right. Under the tree a table on a wooden beam. Two solid old benches. In the background, a fence with an entrance in the middle. Behind the fence, an uphill slope.

SCENE 1

[MOYSHE THE INNKEEPER *sits at the table, partially dressed in his Sabbath clothes. He is reading a holy book.* PESSIE *sits nearer to the porch, hands on her hips. She looks right.*]

PESSIE: [*Yells offstage.*]: Kazik! Hey, Kazik! Get that saloonkeeper's horse out of those oats! What a pain! Every Friday I have her as my guest!

MOYSHE: She's just passing through . . . Don't make a scene, woman . . .

PESSIE: Sure, husband—as if people like that embarrass easily. Drive them out of the door, they'll come in through the window . . . what was I going to say, Moyshele? Maybe a little glass of milk, hm? Since Friday is a short day and you don't get to really eat.

MOYSHE: And have you already sent some milk to the old man in the woods? He sits there from morning prayers on, fainting away.

PESSIE: As if I could possibly forget! Once that man picks up his fiddle and heads off to the woods to welcome the holy Sabbath, it's like the world doesn't exist! No eating, no drinking—ridiculous!

MOYSHE: Aha! That's grandpa for you! We'll have to send Nekhamele to him . . .

PESSIE: Speaking of Nekhamele, Moyshele, we really need to talk about her . . . But near the bar, with the drunken peasants, is that the place to talk about this, Moyshe?

MOYSHE: [*Impatiently.*] What's been eating you this past week, woman? Coming, going . . . Nekhamele, Nekhamele . . . our child isn't tainted goods, God forbid. And her hair hasn't gone gray yet, either.

PESSIE [*Noting* DVOYRE *approaching from the porch.*]: Shh . . . here she is, our uninvited guest. Don't say a word . . . God damn it! My daughter's beautiful work in those grubby hands of hers!

MOYSHE: Hush, woman!

SCENE 2

[DVOYRE *the saloonkeeper descends from the porch. A young widow with pretensions to coquettishness.*]

DVOYRE: Pessele, my little jewel, you are the most blessed of mothers! Golden hands that Nekhamele of yours has, no evil eye! I'll tell you the truth: you go into the finest houses these days, you see all the beautiful things they've got there—of course, they should all rot in hell for what they do to the Jews—you go to embroider all sorts of curtains, tapestries, all sorts of embroidered crinolines . . . you know, Pessele, everyone's wearing crinoline these days—it's a pleasure to see, I'm telling you . . . the flowers start here, in the front, and fall in row after row. Like real flower beds! Don't take it the wrong way, Reb Moyshe, all this silly women's talk . . . [MOYSHE *waves his hand dismissively, picks up his book, and goes inside.*]

DVOYRE: Look here, Pessele, it's a whole world of its own. Just look at the peacocks, the little beads, the golden flower! [*She is delighted with the embroidery that she's holding.* PESSIE *takes it out of her hands.*]

PESSIE: My daughter showed this to you herself?

DVOYRE: Who? Like she'd show it! I stumbled across it by chance. I was looking around for my cap—oh, it's so late! I'll never get home by the Sabbath! . . . So I'm looking around, and I see in the corner, on the table, a pretty little something. Really pretty! "Nekhamele, is this your work?" "Mine," she says. I liked it right off, and now I can't let it out of my hands . . .

PESSIE: She said that? I'm going to . . .

DVOYRE: You've got yourself a business, Pessele! A golden goose! But tell me, Pessele, my little jewel, I'm just a sinful woman, and, you know what they say: the truth will out. Are congratulations in order? Hm? Do I hear wedding bells?

PESSIE: Dvoyrele! If there's any news, God willing, you'll be the first to know.

DVOYRE: But I thought . . . well. May God send joyful tidings in good time, Pessele! I'll have my horses harnessed . . . may we all have a good Sabbath.

PESSIE: And a good Sabbath to all the Jewish people.

DVOYRE: And don't take my dropping in like this the wrong way. "Friday guest, host's oven don't rest." But what can you do, Pessele, when my livelihood demands it? I need to run to settle up accounts with the bishop . . . since my scholar has begun to get so ill, poor man . . .

PESSIE: Ay, Dvoyrele, don't mention it . . . we're thankful that you don't forget us. Go in good health. [DVOYRE *exits right.*] Go . . . to that bishop of yours. What are you doing bringing that brazen face of yours into a Jewish house? Have you ever heard such a thing? "Her scholar" . . . don't make me laugh! . . . Arele the drunk . . .

SCENE 3

[NEKHAMELE *descends from the porch, holding a small pitcher of milk.*]

PESSIE: You're going to the woods to see Grandpa? Good girl.

NEKHAMELE: Daddy told me to.

PESSIE: And you didn't have the sense to do it yourself, child?

NEKHAMELE: When you don't see him around, you forget about him, like a shadow.

PESSIE: What sort of talk is that, child? And that Dvoyrele, may she never darken our door again—ripping that beautiful work right out of your hands!

NEKHAMELE: No, mama, it really wasn't work.

PESSIE: Why not, my child? Mind your mother. Take a needle and silk thread, and go to your grandfather in the woods. He'll be giving a concert there for the birds, and you'll sew them into the velvet with golden thread. It's holy work, child. You need to finish by the High Holidays.

NEKHAMELE: God knows if I'll be able to. . . .

PESSIE: Oy, *vey iz mir*! Tfu, tfu! Daughter! I don't want to hear that kind of talk from you! Drive that nonsense right out of your head!

NEKHAMELE: Mama, take the ark covering into the house. Maybe I'll get to it after the Sabbath.

PESSIE: Well, go, child. I'm not going to press you. But have mercy on your poor mother! [*Goes to the porch.*] Oy, *vey iz mir*!

NEKHAMELE: Nonsense . . . how do you know I'm talking nonsense, Mama? Have you been seeing my dreams?

SCENE 4

[DVOYRE, *with a cap in her hand, enters from right.*]

DVOYRE: I looked for this all over the house—it was lying in the wagon . . .

NEKHAMELE: What?

DVOYRE: This cap. Nu, Nekhamele, my dear! The coach is ready. I have to go into the city before candle lighting. Everyone's going to be pointing at me: "Look at the sinner!" May they see as much bread in their houses as actual sins of mine. But Nekhamele, my dear, I can't move an inch from here. I have to know the whole story, from beginning to end, with all the details. Because if I don't, you're going to find me passed out in a ditch somewhere. [*She guides* NEKHAMELE *to a bench and sits her down, almost against her will.*] Nu, quickly, the Sabbath waits for no one and someone might still come by.

NEKHAMELE: Just look, your eyes have perked up like two squirrels: what are you making such a secret about all of this for? So he was here, the young duke, so what?

DVOYRE: Oy vey, I can't stand it. So what?!—The young duke? Do you have any idea who the young duke is?

NEKHAMELE: He's a goy, like all the other goyim.

DVOYRE: Oy, they're going to find me dead in a ditch! It's the duke, the greatest of the princes, a monarch!

NEKHAMELE: Good for him. What are you so excited about?

DVOYRE: My God, girl! Do you have any idea what you're saying? They have all the luck, those nobles! He must have come into the inn when your parents were away at the fair.

NEKHAMELE: Even Zlate the maid ran off somewhere in the heat of the moment. I thought I was going to die of shame. I even ran outside in my shift.

DVOYRE: Oh, wonderful, what a stroke of luck for the nobleman!

NEKHAMELE: And what was so lucky about it?

DVOYRE: Sometimes I'm not sure if you're a child or a mooncalf! If your parents had been here—you would have been locked up behind seven doors, hidden under seven curtains . . . in your shift!

NEKHAMELE: It was so embarrassing! It was so flimsy. I was even barefoot!

DVOYRE: Tell me, Nekhamele, my dear, how did he look at you, the duke?

NEKHAMELE: Stared at me, like this. He smiled and twirled his mustache.

DVOYRE: Twirled his mustache?! And what does he look like? Is he handsome?

NEKHAMELE: Yes, very handsome.

DVOYRE: Really, truly?

NEKHAMELE: How should I know? You'd know better.

DVOYRE: Ay, I would know better, but who's ever gotten a look at him? He's just arrived from abroad, traveling through all the foreign lands. They say he knows every language under the sun. They even say that he learned Hebrew from the rabbis.

NEKHAMELE: Hebrew? A goy—Hebrew?

DVOYRE: And that's not all! They tell all sorts of incredible stories about him. Some people even think he converted.

NEKHAMELE: [*Still thinking.*]: Yes, he's handsome. He's very handsome.

DVOYRE: Did you like him?

NEKHAMELE: Yes.

DVOYRE: Just take a look at the poor little thing! . . . And what sort of eyes did he have for you?

NEKHAMELE [*Remembering.*]: Naked.

DVOYRE: What sort?

NEKHAMELE: Naked.

DVOYRE: Shame on you! Where did you pick up that kind of talk? Naked eyes!

NEKHAMELE: What? It can't be? Look—a naked hand, a naked foot. Why can't you have naked eyes too?

DVOYRE [*Shrugging.*]: And how did the two of you meet?

NEKHAMELE: I was sitting by the trough, washing my feet. I heard some sort of commotion from the highway, horses riding, someone pulling up at the inn. Happens all the time, right? But then there was a shout: "Moshek!" And so scornful. I ran out.

DVOYRE: Did you see him?

NEKHAMELE: I saw a coach. Three horses in tandem. In the coach were two young nobles. [. . .]

DVOYRE: What happened next? [. . .]

NEKHAMELE: I wanted to cry. And then it hit me: I was in my shift. How embarrassing! I wanted to run away. The young duke jumped down off the coach, tripped, and almost fell on his face. *I* burst out laughing.

DVOYRE: You're killing me!

NEKHAMELE: He grabbed me by the hand and asked my name. I told him. "Nekhamele"—he said—"you're a beautiful girl." He took a good look at me—such bright, naked eyes . . . like he had spread a blanket over me . . . what are you trembling for?

DVOYRE: A breeze must have blown through me. Nu, nu, nu?

NEKHAMELE: They went into the inn . . . ordered ale.

DVOYRE: Tell me, sweetheart, tell me all your secrets . . .

NEKHAMELE: What secrets? So he said, "I drink to your health."

DVOYRE: Really? And what did you answer?

NEKHAMELE: What do you think? That I don't know how to talk to people? I thanked him nicely and drank to his health. It was such strong ale. The old stuff, Castilian. Buried somewhere in the cellar. It went straight to my head . . .

DVOYRE: Why have you gotten so quiet?

NEKHAMELE: Ay, Dvoyre, this is just a joke to you. But something about it bothers me. The young duke grabbed me and gave me a kiss. Oy, I wanted . . . I don't know what I wanted: to cry or to laugh. God would have spat on me. I wanted to get out of there, to escape [. . .]

DVOYRE: Nu, nu?

NEKHAMELE: He kissed my eyes, my lips, my cheeks. Maybe five, ten times. They left such fiery traces. Maybe more than ten times.

DVOYRE: So who's counting?

NEKHAMELE: And he went away. [DVOYRE *disappointed*, NEKHAMELE—*thoughtful*.]

DVOYRE: Now I understand why the ark covering isn't the first thing on your mind.

NEKHAMELE: Dvoyre? You must have some idea of what sort of people these are, these nobles? What sort of a world it is, of huntsmen and monkeys and pointed mustaches? What sort of a world it is, where people stare at you while getting drunk on old Castilian ale? Where you sit on a duke's lap?

DVOYRE: Oy, vey, it's late! I have to run already!

NEKHAMELE [*Starts.*]: Sit! I almost forgot the pitcher of milk for my grandfather!

DVOYRE: So come, Nekhamele, I'll take you in my coach, it's right on the way. What sort of people, you ask? What sort of world? A different world. Nekhamele, different people, a whole different way of life. Sometimes it seems strange. But once you get used to it, you can't live without it. By the way—about luck. My child, noblemen need luck too. Ay, luck, luck! A good thing, luck! [*Both exit right.*]

Translated by Joel Berkowitz and Jeremy Dauber.

Other works by Kacyzne: *Arabeskn* (1922); *Shtarke un shvakhe* (1929).

Gustave Kahn

1859–1936

The symbolist poet and literary critic Gustave Kahn was born in Metz, but when Germany annexed Lorraine in 1870, his parents moved to Paris. Kahn was a contributor to many literary reviews and in the interwar years wrote weekly columns for daily newspapers. From 1932 until his death, he edited the French Zionist journal *Menorah*. One of the first French poets to write free verse, he was also an avid advocate and defender of the new literary style. The Dreyfus affair made him more conscious of his Jewish background, as did the mounting antisemitism of the 1930s, and although he was distant from communal affairs, he was a supporter of Zionism.

One Yom Kippur
1925

For a long time, Slimsohn had been saving considerable time and money on food. He had started by lim-iting himself to just one meal a day, towards evening, then delaying it until that undefinable moment when a snack of coffee and a croissant can take the place of dinner, if at that solemn moment when soup is normally served one is careful to think about something else. Thus for several months, the content and duration of Slimsohn's dinner and his breakfast were exactly alike. That balance was upset when it suddenly dawned on Slimsohn that he couldn't pay the rent on his garret at the end of the month. He was fond of his garret, although not because of its furnishings, which consisted of the thin seaweed-stuffed mattress and bolster he used to separate his dreams from the tile floor of his lodgings. His rented recess spread out oddly under one corner of a roof where the architect had daringly married a cupola with a pagoda. When this headgear was placed atop the tenement building, the architect, together with the owner, gazed from across the street and decided it didn't look so bad after all. They might have to make a few monetary concessions, though, in renting some of the garrets, since these were lopsided, low at the door, higher under the gutters, with no more than a small oval window. The walls sloped. Near the door a square chimney-shaft rose, but ironically, the unbroken wall left no opening for a fireplace or grate. On certain wintry days, however, Slimsohn would receive a few gusts of tepid air in his hovel, in much the same way he might have heard the faint echo of a confidential conversation whispered on the ground floor. In this horn of poverty, Slimsohn had a few books he wouldn't have parted with even under the worst of circumstances. But that would have been utopian, so great was the weariness they exhaled from their broken bindings.

Slimsohn's poverty was not the fruit of his indolence. He was a hard worker, but he had chosen his career without giving any thought to material considerations. Just as a ten-centime coin dropped into the slot of a vending machine brings forth a token or candy, a question about an erudite trifle placed into Slimsohn's ear would yield a long, precise, detailed answer from his mouth. But who needs erudition in this world? Every morning the newspapers furnish factual errors so contradictory on all subjects and in such numbers that they seem like mere nuances of opinion to be chosen at will. Slimsohn had no market for his products. So he did without his roll for breakfast, and the balance between his two little meals was broken.

Newspapers couldn't have recourse to his superior knowledge. The alphabetically arranged errors in encyclopedias supplied enough background for their reporters. As far as magazines were concerned, Slimsohn had wisely snubbed them. In magazine offices they're more sympathetic towards shiny hats or multicolored jackets, less exacting when a question required handling a book or two. The editors there preferred a footnote or a little article for which the wage was equivalent to that paid to a fashion-house apprentice.

But at the precise moment when Slimsohn had succeeded in publishing a long article on Cossack messianism during the Middle Ages in the scholarly review, *Danube et Volga*, Duger, the editor, stopped paying cash and started paying by draft. The banks hadn't yet equated these two instruments. With every effort to cash Duger's note, which Slimsohn kept inside the moleskin holes he used for a wallet, it bore a greater resemblance to a wrinkled railroad ticket to La Châtre.

As ill-suited as Slimsohn was for any financial considerations except those having to do with historical deeds, he realized the weakness of this claim to universal exchange. But hunger calls for bold moves. At one point in Slimsohn's quest, the owner of the local café referred him to a wine merchant, who sent him to a liquor dealer, each one eager not to endorse the note, but careful to conclude their discussion with this polite petitioner by giving him some more or less chimerical information or superfluous recommendation. Which is what led Slimsohn to Charley Dicky, maker of bicycle bearings.

Slimsohn found Charley Dicky in his office, two meters square set off from the store by a glass partition. Dicky was alone. He had already read the morning newspapers. It was eleven-thirty.

His correspondence was finished because, having only received demands from creditors, he found it pointless to respond. His mood was composed, even cordial, since he hadn't yet exhausted a small profit gleaned at the races the previous Sunday. No clients had come to see him, so Slimsohn's arrival made it seem as though he had a visit. As soon as he saw Slimsohn's frizzy hair and noble, aquiline nose, he remembered that he, Charley Dicky, had originally received the name Isidore Lehmann from his people. After Slimsohn had produced his letter of introduction and as he was disclosing the reasons for his visit, Charley thought back, somewhat joyously, to some love poems

he had penned in his youth. He had Slimsohn explain the matter over and over, appeared to be looking for a solution, then abruptly changed the subject and asked Slimsohn to tell him about himself. Slimsohn became so engrossed in telling his story that he forgot all about his request, going so far as to confide in Dicky his plan for the future Jerusalem, immediately achievable, just as in the Golden Age, including the reconstruction of the Temple, merely an easily solvable problem of financing. Dicky went back to his newspaper, consulted a calendar, then interrupted a splendid disquisition on the industrial capacity of the Jews during the Middle Ages, simply saying, "I'm not sure what to advise you. Let me think about it. Perhaps you could leave me your draft."

"Here it is," said Slimsohn, with a trusting flourish.

"No, I'll think about it, we'll see, but hold on, why don't we discuss it over lunch?"

Slimsohn suddenly felt dizzy. Lunch! How could he possibly pay? Had Dicky invited him?

"I'm inviting you for lunch," continued Dicky. "I find what you say most interesting. One rarely comes across anyone as interesting as you in the business world."

"Not really, I'm just . . ."

"It's clear to me that you have an educated and inquisitive mind."

"No, just a bit well informed, actually. All of that is its own reward, I mean, it's not very rewarding financially," muttered Slimsohn with melancholy. "No, I'll come back. I can't accept such a kind offer."

Dicky realized that Slimsohn was proud and wouldn't want to appear to be cadging a meal for anything in the world. He felt esteem for this poor fellow, who was certainly as awkward as he was unlucky. He began to look for a scheme.

"Listen, Monsieur Slimsohn, please have lunch with me. Maybe over dessert I can ask you to help me correct this brochure I'd like to send out for my business."

"We'll do it right away. You don't need to invite me to lunch for that!"

"Now you're making me uncomfortable."

All the same, for the past several minutes Slimsohn had been listening to the chiming of two differently pitched bells in his head. One, deep and sad, rang in his ears like a knell, resonating through his entire body! It was the knell of hunger! In contrast, a whole set of small emphatic chimes, like stacks of dinner bells in palaces and castles and doorbells in apartments, babbled, "Eat! Eat!"

"I accept," he said, with simple straightforwardness, like someone resolving to act inhabitually.

Dicky was concerned about calming his guest's lingering sensibilities. He understood their sincerity.

"Nothing fancy, you know, just the corner bistro."

Slimsohn bowed with serious nobility.

"I am especially touched by your kindness."

Slimsohn was happy. In the evening at his café (when he could afford to go), even at night when the lateness of the hour makes numb ears more indulgent, as he tried to outline to his companions his plan for the future Jerusalem, immediately achievable, they would reach for their hats and overcoats, making up excuses about waiting wives or an urgent business meeting at dawn. So it was neither the cutlet nor the Beaujolais that had put Slimsohn in a mood of fond candor and winged enthusiasm as he confessed to Dicky his adherence to the faith of his fathers.

After the coffee and the cognac, offered with graceful insistence and accepted after an intricate defense, Dicky said off-handedly, "Yes, I'll bring up your matter to my friend Blum, the tire manufacturer. Perhaps you have heard his name mentioned?"

"I'm afraid I don't know who he is."

"You might have met him. He associates with Jewish circles, although he hasn't practiced the religion since he was young. Back then, on Yom Kippur, when he couldn't get a bite to eat at home, he would get me to treat him at my little restaurant. On this day twenty years ago, it would have been easy for me to introduce you to him. True, he wouldn't have been very useful to you. Twenty years ago he would have been asking me for a cutlet today."

"Today?" asked Slimsohn, horrified.

"Yes, today is Yom Kippur. Didn't you know? I read it in the newspaper."

He handed the folded page to Slimsohn, who sputtered, "Yom Kippur! Lunch!"

He was very upset.

"By the way, Monsieur Slimsohn, tell me, did you eat lunch yesterday?"

"No," Slimsohn said weakly.

"Or dinner?"

"No. I didn't."

"And the day before yesterday?"

"Well, no . . . yes . . . a little lunch, no dinner."

"Then you were early, that's all!" murmured Dicky, savoring the double pleasure of having treated a coreli-gionist to lunch and made him miss Yom Kippur. . . . "A cigar, Monsieur Slimsohn?"

"Well, yes," answered Slimsohn, crushed, his voice fallen.

Translated by Glenn Swiadon.

Other works by Kahn: *Contes juifs* (1926); *Images bibliques* (1929); *Terre d'Israël* (1936).

Hersh Dovid Nomberg

1876–1927

The poet, novelist, editor, and politician Hersh Dovid Nomberg grew up in a Hasidic family in Mszczonów (Amshinov, in Yiddish), Poland, but was drawn to Haskalah philosophy and abandoned his wife and child to settle in Warsaw. There he came under the influence of I. L. Peretz and lived with the writers Avrom Reisen and Sholem Asch. Nomberg embraced both modern Yiddish and Hebrew writing (at the Czernowitz Yiddish-language conference in 1908, he advocated Yiddish as a national language). He was active in the Folkspartay, which advocated cultural autonomy, and also supported Yiddish secular schools and organizations, promoting their expansion in visits to Argentina, Palestine, and the United States. He was a frequent contributor to the Warsaw newspaper *Moment*.

The Rebbe's Grandson

1925–1926

1

The terrace of the large coffee house in Berlin was almost empty, save for the occasional occupied table. The season had already turned autumnal. The weather was unpredictable, and the air carried a certain unexpected chill. At one such table, in the midst of many empty little chairs and other tables, deserted and neglected, sat a man, probably in his forties: Doctor of Philosophy Berelson, by name. He never liked to sit in the midst of an unfamiliar crowd. He always felt lost in a fully packed cafe. Also, today's weather excited him, ignited his imagination, and tore him from the ennui and heaviness that had most recently oppressed him.

While he wiped his hand across his dense forehead, then slowly rubbed his eyes, his mind carried scraps of memories, torn and floating like the thin clouds above, which rapidly flew over the gloomy sky: memories of the blowing of the shofar, of Yom Kippur prayers, of the white satin rabbinic vestments, and of oppressed hearts that cry to heaven with grief.

He sat with his wife, who was hidden from sight behind his more obvious presence. He was a formidable looking man: a full-blooded, dark-haired Jewish type—with a black, neatly respectable beard and a long, well-chiseled nose. He had inherited his stately appearance from his grandfather and great-grandfathers. His dark eyes crinkled strangely with a kind of sadness, like that of a coddled first-born child. She, on the other hand, was a diminutive person, her face quite delicate looking. After much contemplation, one could read only one predisposition from her face: a strong, female stubbornness was deeply creased around her small mouth with its tight, thin, pale lips.

Thoughts pulsed feverishly in the head of the bearded man. In such moments, everything around him acquired a heightened weight and meaning. The faces of the people told him so much; even their clothing and their movements had something to say. The little bird skipping on the street and pecking something from the pavement became heavy with meaning. Across the way, the golden cross over the large church seemed to sway in prayer, as though it were a living limb in an animated world. A sense of unease wafted from the shadows of the houses that appeared along the street and disappeared with the fleeing clouds above.

Everything became more animated; everything breathed eternal air. And he, the living human being with his watchful eye and mind, felt himself closer, more harmonized with the world—almost a step away from reaching the world's ultimate secret, its hidden meaning.

"Why is it not our fate to be like the clouds that come and go, which blend with dust from the earth and transform themselves into diverse shapes, then disappear again and become nothingness again, only to be reborn?"

He spoke his thoughts quietly, as if to himself, but he knew that the small feminine creature next to him took careful note of his words. He felt her concentrated gaze upon him, even though he did not glance at her. He knew his words would not disappear into emptiness. They were grasped, pressed together by the sustained will that he, himself, was lacking.

This was because, in his solitary state, his wife was his only admirer. He had her to thank that he could oc-casionally raise himself above his own sense of worthlessness. For who is he, Dr. Berelson, to all the other people—other than a beard? Is he more than the clothing that covers his body?

As he spoke his words and thought his thoughts, he held one of his hands—the one wearing the wedding ring—on the table. It was a respectable, solid hand, a bit hairy. And the sparkling, sharp eyes of his diminutive wife concentrated on that hand; she couldn't tear her eyes away. Her desire to touch his hand was stronger than all her other deliberations. She was in love with her husband, in love as if she were a young maiden. With each passing day, her love grew, in line with her rapid aging. When she caressed his hairy hand with her own soft one, she could not help but blush.

Under her own, his hand gave a twitch. With an insecure, lost look, he glanced at her with a certain estrangement. It passed in a second. She sighed and, embarrassed, pulled her hand away. Since she had no mirror in front of her, she could only observe a portion of her outward appearance: the line of her withered breasts. But this was enough for her. Through her own cold calculation, she imagined that the erotic moment had been destroyed. She looked at him again with both rapture and sorrow: he was, after all, a virile man in his best years!

As luck would have it, just then young female figures moved in from all sides: slim, elastic bodies, each holding a promise. They came with their men or they walked by, coquettishly on their own. Not one of them dared to look directly at the bearded gentleman. The diminutive wife lost heart and pulled her lips more tightly together. And, with an even greater stubbornness, her eyes gazed and twinkled like green, polished steel.

2

There had been another reason for Dr. Berelson's withdrawal. Just today he had received a letter from Reb Isaḥar Ber, a landowner in eastern Galicia, who had been his secret friend and patron since he had left the home of his grandfather, the Rebbe. (Dr. Berelson's father had died young and he had been brought up in his grandfather's house.) The letter had shaken him—not so much with its content, as with its tangible signs of aging and the foreshadowing of death, so sharply evident in the handwriting. The once shapely, upright little letters with their elegant, refined ornamentation were now hurled about by a shaking hand, and in some places a letter or a whole word was missing. When forceful, authoritative people like Reb Isaḥar Ber are debilitated to such a level of deterioration, they will not last long and their days are numbered. This is what the handwriting and the tone of the letter implied.

The letter was written in old Hebrew, but it was noteworthy that the traditional expression, *be'ezras hashem* (with God's help), was missing. Reb Ber wrote about his circumstances after the horrible incidents of recent times. Some of his children had been killed in the war; others were scattered throughout the world. Only one daughter lived with him now, and she was half-crazy. All his wealth had also been destroyed. He could hardly maintain himself on his estate.

"I feel I am losing my strength and I wait for you, the light of my eyes, that you should come to illuminate the darkness. When will your book appear? My soul begins to fade, while waiting for it."

"A life is extinguished and passes away without a scrap of consolation," Dr. Berelson thought as he repeated the last words of the letter. Something had become ominous, and he felt guilty about the broken state of his old friend. And why was it that in this letter—perhaps the man's last one—the name of "God" seemed to be deliberately missing? This was especially odd, considering that Reb Isaḥar Ber had never before allowed disturbing thoughts to interrupt his life. He believed in the Rebbe, but also he also had faith in his heretic grandson, Elimelekh, who would undoubtedly enlighten the world. It had made good sense to him that the professors in Bern were impressed by Elimelekh Berelson and worshiped him.

"One can always trust Elimelekh," Reb Ber thought. Throughout all of Berelson's years of studies, Reb Ber had supported him with money. For he believed that Elimelekh was preparing an important book that would revolutionize the field of philosophy. From his letter, it was clear that he feared leaving this world without experiencing that great event when Elimelekh's name would become famous throughout the whole world. And when all nations, Jews and gentiles alike, would observe a great illumination of thought.

In recent years, Dr. Berelson had been waiting for a revelation. The war, which had passed by like a dismal dream and had squandered away his best years, wasn't a time for concentrated creativity. But now the war was over. Now the work could no longer be put off, so he prepared himself and waited for a spark of motivation to fire him up; he must get to work on completing his opus, "Man and the Cosmos," which was to be his life's work.

Lost in his own thoughts, Dr. Berelson was reminded of Reb Ber, a tall, healthy Jew with a bit of a paunch. That is how he had looked twenty years ago, when he, Berelson, had been a guest at Reb Ber's estate.

They went for a walk together, uphill in the Carpathian landscape on the way to a waterfall that cascaded like foam over a precipice. Joy and love flowed from Reb Ber, who constantly consoled Berelson and, gesturing with his strong broad hand, gave him to understand that it didn't matter; all must be good and all will be good. And God is a righteous father who does not let anyone sink.

"As long as you are serious about your work," said Reb Ber, shouting over the noise of the falling water. "Elimelekh does not need to tell me who he is: I already know him. There are few others like Elimelekh, and the merits of your ancestors stand behind you!"

At the time, Berelson became silent and stared into the abyss. Only when he lifted his gaze did his eyes meet those of Reb Isaḥar Ber, who observed him with much love and delight.

"Elimelekh actually wants to depart from here? Your grandfather, may he live a long life, will be heartbroken."

"It can't be avoided. It must be this way," he answered succinctly.

Reb Isaḥar Ber continued to stand over him in his yellow boots, and with great pleasure looked at the grandson of the Rebbe and his eyes seemed to say it all. "We are simple people," he uttered with humility, a helpless smile playing on his face. Meanwhile, he began to rock his huge frame, back and forth, as though he were studying Talmud. "What can *we* comprehend? I want Elimelekh to say something. . . ."

Reb Isaḥar Ber longed for some wisdom, a piece of Torah, from Elimelekh. He couldn't stand the dryness of Elimelekh's pronouncement that "It must be this way."

Suddenly, the instinct of his forebears were awakened in the grandson, an instinct that had taught his Hasidic forebears how to deal with thirsty human souls.

He said with the ceremoniousness of reading from the Torah, as though he himself were a Hasidic rabbi interpreting scripture for his followers: "The water flows into the abyss, whether it wants to or not. And from the rivulets emerge rivers, and the rivers flow into the sea. And the sea never overflows."

"And the sea never gets full," Reb Isaḥar Ber hummed along in Hebrew and nodded his head in grave seriousness.

Afterward, Reb Isaḥar Ber took him to his home and they drank some strong spirits together. Hasidim came to the door to get a glimpse of Elimelekh, the grandson of the Rebbe. But Reb Ber did not let them in. There was a secret understanding between them—Reb Ber and Elimelekh—and the Hasidim didn't belong there. Reb Isaḥar Ber was very moved that he alone, and no one else, was with Elimelekh.

And now this very friend was moving toward the shadows, dying. The world was now becoming full of holes and worms. Unless a great illumination were to refill it. . . .

Two ladies arrived at the café and took a table beside them. Both glanced at him. One unabashedly smiled at him. Once again, he felt a certain temptation—which consistently befell him of late—running through his blood.

And his diminutive wife continued to make her demands: "We're going home. . . . It's getting late. . . ."

Translated by Sarah Silberstein Swartz.

Other works by Nomberg: *Fun a poylisher yeshive* (1901); *Di kursistke* (1908); *Dos bukh felyetonen* (1924); *Erets-Yisroel ayndrikn un bilder* (1925); *Gezamlte verk* (1928).

Itsik Kipnis

1896–1974

Born in Sloveshne, Ukraine, Itsik Kipnis was a writer of Yiddish literature for children and adults. He is best known for his popular prose work *Khadoshim un teg* (Months and Days), a first-person narrative of shtetl life in a period of violence and revolution. Moved by the Holocaust and the unique experience of Jews in the Soviet Union during World War II, Kipnis began to write in a vein considered too "nationalist" for Soviet authorities and was subsequently exiled to a labor camp until 1956. He is remembered today in large part for his children's stories, many of which were translated into Russian during his lifetime.

Months and Days
1926

[. . .] And we get out of their way; we move in the opposite direction, toward where they've come from, toward Petroshi.

And you see, they do not forbid it. And it may be that in Petroshi, where they live, we will be permitted to spend the night somewhere. After all, we are "Sloveshne Jews." Isn't it true that they have a high regard for "Sloveshne Jews"? Haven't we often heard them say so? And indeed, my father is going to one of his clients there, a fellow who brings hides in to be cured.

"That fellow," my father says, "will welcome us. Arkhip is his name. He'll give us the best food that he has."

And my hope is that all of these Jews may have a client like him in Petroshi who will welcome them; who will give them the best food that he has.

My father brags about his clients. And his one-horse trap is already rolling into Petroshi.

Ah, were we ever stared at in Petroshi!

The whole family sat together in the wagon and a crowd of Jews who arrived earlier is already there. Now we are a considerable group. And we move on.

There are swaggerers among them who bum cigarettes, who light them and smoke unconcernedly, the way they would on a fast day.

And there are already a number of Jews at Avrom's house in Petroshi. (I'd seen Avrom's house filled with Jewish men and women once before. But that was when he was marrying off his older son and the whole town gathered to celebrate.)

Perhaps there was no guard at Avrom's now.

The priest was talking with Avrom at a fence facing the house. He was talking about Jews and Sloveshne.

A fine priest in Petroshi. A man in his thirties, good looking. He made clucking sounds with his lips and wondered why the Jews were suddenly suffering so much in Sloveshne. "A pity, a pity, a pity."

And perhaps he was not being hypocritical. It's possible that there is one priest in a hundred who doesn't meddle.

The brim of Avrom's hat was pulled down on one side. "So many guests, God save us." And, "May God keep everything calm."

A fine Jew, that Avrom. Tall and stocky, bearded, with a gentle, freckled face and large expressive eyes. He wore an alpaca jacket and was friendly to everyone. He could be a pal even with the children, though he was himself already the father of five grown sons. Furthermore, he was by no means shy when he talked; he spoke loudly, giving his words a village pronunciation. That was Avrom of Petroshi.

Father got down from the wagon, and whispering into Avrom's ear, he asked where a certain Arkhip lived. And Avrom told him what he knew and we drove to Arkhip's house. We were followed by two other families, who carried with them children, a cat and small pitchers of milk. "The milk is to shut the mouths of the little ones in case they wake at night."

But since there was no law that guaranteed that Arkhip had always to be at home—he could, after all, be away in the woods or on a trip somewhere—it was just our luck that he turned out not to be at home and one of his younger sons talked with us—a boy some fourteen years old. A shepherd.

"I won't allow it without my father."

"Don't be a child. Your father brings me hides to be tanned every year. . . . Your father is an old pal of ours. If you try to keep us out, he'll very angry with you."

"I can't do anything by myself. Without my father."

"Well, when will your father be back?"

"I don't know. Perhaps tonight."

"Well, that's fine. Let us into the barn until he gets here."

Willingly or unwillingly, the shepherd boy brought out a large wooden key and unlocked the barn. We unharnessed the horse (the others had rented wagons and sent them back to their owners), and we spread out sackcloth and carpets and lay down.

We were three families in the barn, and each family had some additional people.

And if a child whined, it was given milk. There was a sick child, not a member of a family, who lay there and wanted nothing. And older children, because they had nothing to say, just sat there and were silent.

As I went out to cover the horse and to give him a bit of fresh hay, an old neighbor woman, barefoot and wearing a linen blouse and a dress made of two aprons, one in front and one behind, came up to the wagon. She was weeping.

She wept because she had lived to see what she was seeing. "Think of it. Just think of it. What a desolate and bitter generation has grown up. Is it likely that they'll live to enjoy the property of strangers? No, such things were once unheard of. Maybe it's the damned war that has so spoiled the people."

A while later, she wiped her eyes, pulled a wisp of straw from the wagon and tried chewing it with her rotten teeth and mused, "There is one thing in which you are a little bit at fault, my dears. You shouldn't have hidden the salt. You ought to have known how the people lacked salt. Well, I won't ask you why you had to do such a thing. There's nothing worse than food without salt. We even add salt to a cow's drinking water. What else needs to be said? Even a cow. Ah, my dears, how bitter it is for us without our bit of salt. It may be that that's the reason the people are angry. It's searching for salt."

"Yes," I said to her. "The people are angry. They're looking for salt."

"God preserve us and those we love from such behavior. Just wait a bit, dearie, I'll be right back." And in the space of two minutes, she went a few doors down and returned with a bowl of eight or ten roasted potatoes. "Give it to the children. Give it to them, my dear." And she wiped her old eyes with an apron. [. . .]

The floor in the barn where we were was dry and smooth. There was room for all three families. Buzi was already dozing, and I was anxious to take off her shoes before she fell asleep, but I did not want to wake her. Mother was also dozing and the children as well. Father, apparently, was not yet able to get to sleep. He wanted just to lie still without disturbing anyone. There was silence all around him. All that one heard was the steady, monotonic sound of the horse's chewing. I had already removed one sweaty, sticky sock from one foot and was removing the other. Someone opened the door. In barns, the doors are very wide. And the moon over the village was full and low in the sky so that the entire barn was filled with moonlight. But who was coming into the barn at such a late hour? After all, it was bedtime. It was the shepherd once again.

"Jews . . . Jews . . . go away. I don't want you here. I'm scared."

"Who are you afraid of?"

The boy didn't know and couldn't say. He was still a kid. "I'm scared they'll burn the barn." And he wept.

Evidently there was nothing to discuss. The matter was simple. We had to go. The question, however, was, Where?

Little by little, the people in the barn came awake. They looked into each other's faces. Questions were asked. Everyone said what everyone else was saying. That they had just settled down and were getting cozy—and now, this. There was no rest for the weary. But slowly, the situation became clear, though no one offered any suggestions. It was not really their business. A couple of men discussed what to do, as if it was up to them. They would decide what to do, and whatever they decided the others would do.

And that, if you like, is where the trouble lay. Because the men had no idea what to do either. Perhaps one ought to leave and then later sneak back in. Perhaps they ought to harness the horse and ride off—but now that would be hard—and spend the night somewhere in a field, in the open. (But that might be dangerous, eh?)

Maybe this. Maybe that. Return to Sloveshne (we all know the way). But that won't do either.

Father went to the village. It turned out that the Jews in Avrom's house also didn't know where they would spend the night. Perhaps they would hang around the house. We, for our parts, had little children with us. Well, what to do?

And Father had a discussion with Esther of Petroshi. "She's already placed two families with little children among the peasants. She'll advise us, too. Come on."

Esther led us into a garden that was wet with dew. "Sit here for a while." And she went off somewhere. [. . .]

And there was no Esther.

She's been gone for so many hours. And she's left us here among the cultivated rows. Perhaps she won't come back at all. That's it. She's not coming back. The peasants talked her out of it.

Mother tore off a blade of grass and studied it. She was thinking something over. She would gladly have told us what she was thinking, but now was not the right moment to talk aloud.

"Well, people, come on."

It was Esther who had returned and was calling us. Esther was a coarse speaker. When she said "Come," one could hear every letter in the word as she pronounced it. But it didn't matter. "May she live long, that Esther . . . ah, what a service she's doing for us—at a time like this."

Mother thanked her, then everyone, adults and children, as best as they could, climbed over a strange fence. And she was surprised that we hadn't stolen anything.

"Sleep well," she said. The place belonged to good peasants. They had set out a bed where, usually, a young couple slept. A clean, well-carpentered little stable.

Mother thanked Esther and wished for her all the good fortune she deserved, and we entered into a well-prepared haven whose owners we had not yet seen, and whom we might not see for several days.

How close are we to dawn? (It was, after all, a summer's night.) And we parceled out and divided the space, as well as the bed belonging to the young cou-ple. But several of us were beyond falling asleep. And there was someone knocking on the other side of the wall. Not knocking, exactly, but more as if someone was climbing on the walls.

Who could it be? What if it was young peasants with knives. Oughtn't we to have sticks nearby? [. . .]

Buzi was lying down with the girls. Perhaps she had fallen asleep, too. And my mother has to be shunted from pillar to post, from one stable to another. And Hershele . . . What wouldn't I give to keep Buzi and my mother and Hershele from being shoved about like this? And my father . . . and my sisters. The other mother and her children were far away. Where were they spending the night? In a stable or in a house? And in Radomishl, how are they spending the night? And in Proskurov?

It can't be possible that they could massacre three thousand Jews in Poskurov? Three thousand is an exaggeration. Meanwhile, the knocking on the other side of the wall continued. If it's a lone peasant youth, I'll kill him. Even if there are two or three. But if there are many, I won't budge from my place.

Young peasants are on their way to some celebration. They talk loudly and laugh.

. . . Better let them pass. Good. They're gone. . . .

Now, I would really like for it to be dawn, or to fall asleep.

Does the passage of every night take up so much time before dawn comes? And perhaps it wasn't peasant youths banging on the other side of the wall. Perhaps it's just a pen for sheep.

"Sheep," I whispered so softly I could hardly be heard. "It's a pen for sheep. And they're making the noise on the other side of the wall."

If anyone had chanced to be awake, they would have heard me and would certainly have been relieved by what I said.

And, evidently, I too fell asleep. Because I did not get to see the arrival of the dawn.

It was a lovely morning in Petroshi, and we were safe and sound. What did we lack?

"Let Ayzik drive into town and find out what's happening there." And if Ayzik goes, you must know that Buzi is going too. She feels uncomfortable without him. [. . .]

Father's horse was a good one. We would be in Sloveshne in less than twenty minutes.

The wagon rolled downhill. The horse moved along amiably. The world was alive. What a pleasure. On the outskirts of town we met a herdsman with all kinds and colors of cattle.

"Cattle, you spent the night in Sloveshne. Maybe you have something to tell us. Maybe you can give us some news about the home we left behind in strange hands on a dismal night——"

Hush. There goes Naum and his oxen. He's on his way to the forest for wood. You see him there, a short little peasant. His face is shaven, and he has a pair of long Ukrainian mustaches. An unhurried fellow. Whatever you may be thinking, he has thoughts of his own. He's not interested in any one's else's business.

"Naum, what's going on in town?"

"Phoo! In town? What's going on? Nothing. There were beatings last night. Banging and breaking."

"And in general, what's happening in town?" And the sun, meanwhile, dapples the red-colored backs of his oxen and makes a different design on my horse's ash-colored hide. We're riding *into* town, he's riding *out* of town. "In general, what's going on in town, Naum?"

"In general—nothing. They brought four dead Jews from Gorodishche. All but Khitrik's son-in-law were strangers."

"Khitrik's son-in-law? The tall one?"

"Yes."

And Khitrik's son-in-law was a tall, well-built fellow, like a pine tree. Mordkhe-Leyzer Gershteyn! If they could overcome a fellow like Gershteyn and kill him, things must be pretty bad. "Wait a minute, Naum. When did it happen? When were they brought in?"

"When were they brought in? Yesterday. It seems to me they were put away yesterday. It's too bad—Khitrik's son-in-law. He was a good Jew."

"And now, what's happening in town?"

"Now it's quiet. I think. Gee up!"

"Giddap."

It's a lovely sun. The window panes gleam in the school on the outskirts of town. And the morning looks just as it would if it were cheerful.

Buzi holds on to my hand. She's very unhappy because they killed Mordkhe-Leyzer, Khitrik's son-in-law. She lived with them in the same apartment for a year. In a room in Mordkhe-Leyzer's house and with his lovely children. The two older ones were now grown up.

Buzi looks into my eyes and asks, "Ayzik, is it that simple to cut someone's throat with a knife? Like a cow or an ox at the slaughter?"

"I've never seen anything slaughtered."

"And a cow? You've seen a cow slaughtered?"

"No."

It was a calf that Buzi saw being slaughtered in her garden. Its legs were bound, and it made a terrible death rattle. She didn't want to say any more. She felt nauseated, remembering. For more than a week she had been unable to look at their neighbor, the ritual slaughterer. It had seemed to her that he was a very ugly creature. Ugh . . .

Our streets were crisscrossed with threads of fear. But as we moved along them, they became familiar again, our streets. And dear to us. It was hard to turn off into another street or lane. Until you passed over the threshold of gloom, after which it was easier once more. And our streets had a look that was neither like Purim nor like the Interval Days of Passover and Sukkot. The shops were neither closed nor open. The shopkeepers were not doing business. The shoemakers were not hammering. Everyone sat scattered about on earthen mounds as if drying in the sun. Or perhaps taking the air. Or perhaps neither the one nor the other, and they were merely keeping warm.

It was quiet in town. Whatever had happened at night had happened. Now, the town was quiet. Buzi will walk about. It may be she'll hear news of her mother and the children. Meanwhile, I'll get our people.

We moved spiritedly. It was bright, sunny. Easy.

Thursday is Thursday, and people are people. Our situation was not what anyone would call good, but by now that was nothing new for us. It had been a long time since we had slept in our own beds. And a long time since we ended our days where we began them. It should be no surprise to us that our local peasant boys teased us. They teased us and we were silent. Because for each five of us there were thirty of them.

"Go, children. Go to Sokhvye's Hane and drink your fill of milk." It was Mother sending us to Hane, Shmayle's wife. Our milk was there.

So we went to Sokhvye's Hane. She spoke to my sister as to a friend. Talked about household matters; housewifely things. Her stove was hot, and she gave us milk to drink. If we liked, we could drink right out of the jugs. Hane had a square face, a square jaw and white teeth and intelligent eyes. When she laughed, it was with her whole face, including her intelligent eyes and her white teeth. And, it may be, that this was not the first time that we had been beggars. And so we drank half sour milk at Hane's. The upper part of the milk was buttery and smeared one's lips and nose. Then all of a sudden there was a gush of the thinner sour milk that spattered one's clothes. Nothing to worry about. The clothes were not made of silk, though perhaps it was unpleasant for Hane. We could take our own jugs home with us; to our tumbled, our abused home. And there we would . . .

"Hane, may we?"

"All right, then. Take them. But bring the jugs back so that I'll have something in which to put your cow's milk." (We still had a cow.)

"Hane, how come you have the little red chair and the two stools?"

Hane crimsoned. Was there any reason for her to be embarrassed before us? She would have liked to make a different answer, but she would say what she could. Enough said.

"I thought I would carry something away. If you came back, it would be yours again. And if not—well why should strangers have it? Here are your forms, too. Your forms and your baking tins."

Hane is red-faced, embarrassed. She is a bit confused. But she is right. What she did is good. We carried the jug with the half sour milk home with us.

"And bread. Just see how we've forgotten. We don't have any bread."

Tonight, we made more intelligent preparations. Tonight, we even scraped the starter dough out of the kneading trough. There was not a bit of breadstuff left in the house.

Khvedosia, who lives near Yisroel-Dovid's house, was carrying buckets from the well on a yoke over her shoulder. She wanted to pass us by as if she did not see us, but Mother stood in her way.

"Khvedosia, you're on your way home. Lend me a bit of bread, for the children's sake."

"Bread?"

She hadn't baked bread for our sakes, Khvedosia. Bread. She is Adamke's sister. Adamke who lives right next door to Zeydl. And she's really wicked. But she can't be an utter pig. After all, she lives right next door to us.

"Mama, Khvedosia gave us a cake."

"May God punish her. The cake is moldy."

We break the old cake apart. It's true. Its innards are all mold. How did Mother know it would be? But it had to be eaten, moldy or not.

What puzzles me is why we didn't lock the door yesterday when we went away.

"So that they wouldn't break the windows," says Father. And Motl, Feygl's son, wonders why I'm wearing such tattered trousers.

"So that I won't be left wearing only underpants," I explain. And Buzi and I go into town. There it is being said that the furrier Yeshue had hidden himself and his family and that people broke into his barn—it was early in the evening—and killed his wife and two sons.

One of them, the older one, Dovid, is also a tailor. A man about my age.

Dovid Frenk.

Yeshue's family was considered one of the best in town. And it was said that Dovid was survived by a wife and child.

Buzi was very anxious. Her mother and the children had gone off in the same direction. Buzi wept, but there was nothing to cry about. If, God forbid, something had happened, we would have heard about it. There were some thirty people in their group.

"Buzi dear, don't cry. And let's think a bit about Dovid Frenk. Of his mother and his brother Khayim-Leyb. It was not long ago that he wanted to buy himself a violin—Khayim-Leyb. He wanted to learn how to play it."

And it was neither Purim nor the Interval Days on the street. Jews sat on hummocks or on their porches. And various of their peasant neighbors sat around, doing nothing too. Some of them talked to Jews; some of them sat before their doorways. All at once, we heard a woman's musical voice. Everyone flushed, and one's hair stood on end. Some woman was wandering about, singing. Her hands hung at her sides. Her scarf was flung negligently across her shoulders. And its fringed ends hung down on both sides. That's how her hands dangled. That's how she wore her scarf. So that her movements would be freer; so that she would not be put to trouble on its account. And the way she walked was also like that. Not near the walls nor along the sidewalk but out in the middle of the street, where the wagons drive. That's how she walked, her figure loose, unbound. She came from Dolnye, past the marketplace. Now she was walking in the dead middle of Listvene Street. Singing.

What a fool I am. What a downright idiot. Who's singing? She's not singing. That's Dovid's wife. Dovid Frenk. Who was murdered last night in Behun. Together with his mother and his younger brother. This is Dovid's wife. And she's not singing. She's preaching like a priest. No. She's declaiming in a hoarse, careless fashion as if she were in a theater. And indeed she does sing a little bit, too. In a moderate tone, as if she were talking to someone. And she walks slowly, with her hands at her sides, as if she had nothing at all to make her hurry. As if by walking she would disappear. And she sings.

Of course you all know Dovid,
Dovid Frenk of Dolnye,
Yeshue the furrier's son.

He was a furrier, too.
But he was dearer to me than a prince.
Dovid . . . that Dovid . . . was my husband.

Of course you all know Dovid,
There was no reason to look into his face.
Murderers killed him in Behun.

He was vibrant and lively
When they tore him from my arms.
I begged them:
Murderers, kill me too.

Murderers, have you no human heart?
You must also have wives and children.
Murderers, kill me too.

I kissed their feet. . . .

I humbled myself before them,
And I begged:
Murderers, kill me too.

Dovid, you can't go. . . .
You can't go without me.
And what shall I do with your child?

Ah, Jews—if you only knew. . . .

She goes, meandering like water, and she sings; and we can feel our blood curdling. Buzi and I stand near a wall. The two of us are still whole. And she will come and demand her share.

And what will I do if she sees me and comes up to me.

"Ayzik, you knew Dovid Frenk. Ayzik, have you any idea why they killed Dovid Frenk yesterday? He was so good looking; so warm; and now he lies there, rigid. Come now and look."

And my blood chills. And Buzi turns as pale as a wall, and my impulse is to go up to Dobe and ask, "Dobe, do you happen to know whether they are going to kill Jews tomorrow, too? No doubt you know what's going on. If

they're going to kill again, then tell me, so we can figure out ways to escape."

It was with great difficulty that I got Buzi home. She was nearing her time, and she wasn't supposed to cry.

We already knew who the most important celebrants were at our grim little festival. They were Kosenko (Klim's son), the captain of the guard and Maritshko Lukhtans—our neighbor, the poor Gypsy, the liar who loves Jews.

Maritshko is unbelievable. There he was on Thursday, standing at the fence beside his grapevines, popping grapes into his mouth, actually shouting at a couple of peasant women, "Ah, what sort of idiot business have you gotten yourselves into? Do you expect to have Jewish bodies and to wear Jewish clothes?"

The peasant women replied that they hadn't meant any harm. They had simply come to look around in Sloveshne. But he had jumped down from the fence and, unbuttoning their swollen jackets, he removed several children's sleeveless shirts, an old waistcoat and a pair of children's shoes. He looked them over quickly, gauging their value.

"Here," he said to Yisroel-Dovid's Feygele. "Give these back to poor Jewish children so they can wear them."

"Bravo Marko, bravo! That's how to pay the bloodsuckers." And the two peasant women, one young and pretty and the other a mother-in-law, crimsoned and beat a retreat to the accompaniment of his jibes, "Go on. Go home, you foolish donkeys. There's nothing here for you. If we should need you, we'll send for you." [. . .]

Meanwhile, crowds of young peasants from Levkovich, Mozharia and Verpia kept crossing our fields. Young peasants who wore their shirts over their belts, who were barefooted and had beady eyes. Ugly, filthy young peasants. The hems of their shirts were wet as if bepissed. They looked uglier than carrion birds. And now they were here. In Mikita's lane, it had already been clear that they were drifting this way. Ugly folk. And by no means bold. One loud shout would scatter them all. But I was not about to do it. There were many of them. Like locusts. And it's said that even mice, if they attack in their numbers, can kill a man.

The peasant boys crept about our attic, searching. In our attic; in my aunt's. Searching. Whatever they found would be pure profit.

The young peasants teased us. Behaved boorishly toward us. They were angry with us because we had taken many things of ours back from them. We had called our neighbors together and instigated them to scold the ugly young fellows.

And, of course, our neighbors had to do what we told them; they had driven them away and taken things away from them. And, as a joke, they had even locked a couple of the young men into a locker in my aunt's house.

A flock of peasant women as well as boys and girls found their way into the lower courtyard of the tannery. It was a group that had come to town carrying various vessels in their hands on the chance that they might find some gasoline or grease. In short, they were ready for anything that might come their way.

Evidently they had asked directions to the tannery and started off, some fifty of them. They moved with slow deliberation. They were women, after all, and who knew what might happen?

"I'm going to drive them away."

"No need," said Mother.

"I won't let you," said Buzi.

"Let them choke on the grease," said my sisters and our neighbors.

But I very much wanted to scare those peasant women. Not just because I was angry, but for the sheer fun of it.

"I won't let you," said Buzi.

"There's no need to do it," said Mother. I searched for and found a splintered log—there was no stick available, and I started toward the "Philistines."

"Hey, the devil take you all." And the women, poor things, like frightened hens fluttering their wings, leaped first to one side, then to the other. "God help us," and they ran. But a couple of them managed to find their way to the Holy of Holies.

"I only meant to find a little grease," one of them said, climbing down from a window.

"Damn it to hell, what you meant can get you killed," I said. "You didn't find any grease." And I swung at her with the bit of log. The second woman fell into a tub, while a third made her way out of the window and ran off.

"Damned mares! The devil take you and your filthy faces." Then, like a gander after a fray with a cat, I turned to my women, glowing with the joy of victory.

And Buzi said, "I didn't tell you to do it. They'll call their men and tell them that you beat them. It'll be worse for us, then."

Buzi, as if she were talking to Yosele or to Meylekh, talked to me like a teacher and proved, with examples, that I would have done better to follow her advice.

But I noticed that my family had laughed when the peasant women and girls ran off like wet hens. And Buzi had also laughed. And so I bragged a little about my exploits against the women who, I said, would be afraid to show their faces here again. And I was very pleased with myself.

Meanwhile, we had news from town that eight families were getting ready to go to Turov.

"Smart, very smart. Because who knows where it will all end?"

"Maybe we ought to harness up and drive to Turov, too?"

Mother would not agree to that. Well, we didn't go.

The news from town was that the families had decided not to drive to Turov. Why not?

Because all at once the wagon drivers made excuses and said they could not go. They had, evidently been threatened by the pogrom committee. One way or another, they would not be permitted to drive out of town.

The news from town was that the pogromists wanted a meeting. They wanted to try the Jews. The priest would make a speech. The rabbi would be there too.

The men went off to the gathering. My older sister and Buzi wanted to come too.

It was a strange trial. It was a day that was neither a working day nor a holiday. A little like a fair in the center of the marketplace, and yet no business was conducted. The priest and the rabbi stood at the center of the crowd. The rabbi was bloodstained, but he neither wept nor groaned. He did not wince, but it was clear from the way that he sweated that his strength had been sapped. There was no trial here of equal strengths where, at some point, one could call a halt and an authority would say, "Right. That's right. Right. That's right."

The priest spoke first. "We will have to persuade the people to restrain themselves. To stop its turbulence; or the Jews will have to be careful (about what?). The Jews will have to (what?) . . ." The priest spoke guardedly, ambiguously. He was still in his right mind and knew that power was not with the church now. In church he could speak quite differently. Here, he had to be a bit careful.

Now it was Stodot's turn to talk. The name Stodot may not mean anything to those who are not acquainted with that bumpy-featured murderous bastard with the gray, protruding eyes. A huge man in his forties. Perhaps because he had neither children nor prosperity, he devoted himself to finding ways to bathe in Jewish tears. Jews, he said, were foreigners; they were harmful. Jewish cattle devoured the pastures. Jews cut down whole forests in order to make brooms. Jewish geese spoiled the wheat fields, so that the community was put to the trouble of rounding up Jewish livestock every year. And, if Stodot was in charge of the roundup, any Jewish woman who owned a cow had a hard time of it. Now it was Stodot Popak who spoke. And, as far as Jews were concerned, there were things that he loved to say loud and clear. And he was saying them.

"And Jews have always been like this. They even sent noodles to the Germans during the war. Now, we don't want them to be communists."

"What? Communists? Who?"

But hold on a minute. Stodot is right, after all. During the night, when Velvl, the senile shoemaker's windows were being broken, people shouted, "Communist. You're a Jew and a communist. Just wait. We'll kill you. If not today, then tomorrow."

Ugh. Ugly words.

And Marko, our neighbor, was there and said, "Jews, give money. Our brothers need money. And let that be the end of the matter."

And so the Jews met in the synagogue and collected money.

And later, Marko advised the Jews, "Since the people are rebellious, let the Jews gather in one place at the center of town and we'll put an armed guard around them. But I can't guarantee the safety of those who don't come to the center. The populace is restless."

Have you got the picture of Marko? He counts the money. He issues commands.

"What do you think, Marko? Ought we, perhaps, to go to Motl, the commissioner?"

"A good idea. All of you go to Motl, the commissioner's house." [...]

Father brought good news: "It will be quiet tonight. One can even spend the night at home. But if we don't want to do that, we can go to Motl Rattner's."

Yes. Father had paid not only for himself but for others as well.

For such news, Father no doubt deserved well of us. It was no trivial matter. But it was hard to believe that the pogrom's black maw would be shut so mechanically.

"Choose your rooms, people. Lower the shutters; shut your doors and sleep well."

Mother did not want to go to Motl Rattner's. She had no faith in such good luck.

"Well, then, where shall we spend the night?"

Opposite our house and opposite our door there stood Yisroel-Dovid's stable. Shoulder to shoulder with our house, as it were. There were oak logs piled before the stable. Some were already squared off, and from the beginning of the pogrom, it was among these logs that we spent our time. We lay there, taking the sun; it was there that we received news from town. That's where we had our quarrel with the peasant youths. That's where we argued about the peasants. Nor did we feel like going inside the house. It felt eerie, and it smelled musty there. The rear legs of the table had been twisted off because one of our neighbors (we knew who it was) had suspected that there was money hidden in the table's locked drawer.

What if that's where his wallet is—the one he keeps large sums of money in? What then? The table drawer is locked with a lock. Well there's a remedy for that. Twist the table legs around. And if necessary, lose your temper a little.

And indeed, the slob lost his temper and twisted the table's hind legs about.

And left satisfied.

Not that there was any money in the drawer. Only Father's packet of cheap tobacco, cigarette papers and his passport.

Well, too bad. And the table lay sprawled in the house, like a pig that spreads its hind legs out when it's being beaten on its back. Perhaps you've seen how it does. Though mother was constantly after us not to beat the pigs. A pig's back is its most tender part.

Well, where are we going to spend the night?

Mother and the children to Avdei's barn and father to Rattner's house?

When will my father be smarter in such matters instead of always choosing what is not good for him? This is not a time for families to part. In money matters perhaps it's alright to hide things in various places. If it's dug up in one place, there's still some hidden someplace else. But money is not to the point in this case. Money is something altogether different. [...]

"Where shall we spend the night?—"

"Yevrosi of Listve. My father is working on a hide for him." He came by and sat next to my father and talked with him. A peasant who only recently returned from military service. A large young fellow and, it would seem, an intelligent one. With a twisted and sporty blond mustache.

I might as well overhear what he is saying to my father.

"When will you be finished with my hide?"

"On such and such a date, perhaps. The disturbances are dying down."

"They are? I haven't heard that they're dying down."

My father explained to him that it was certain. As certain as could be.

What was his reason for coming to us? "Maybe you'd like to hide your horse and wagon with me? The stables are certain to be robbed at night."

I was mistaken to think he was intelligent. He thought that we would keep the horse in the stable so that he, Yevrosi, could come to steal it at night. But the horse has been in a stable since yesterday, and perhaps Yevrosi knows in whose.

"No," said Father. "Nobody will take the horse. I don't have to hide it, not even with a fellow like you."

"And the cow?"

"No one will take the cow either."

How do you like that? However cleverly starched Yevrosi's mustaches may be, he was still far from intelligent. Because he was truly a fool if he thought he could deceive us with quiet flatteries and with favors.

He hemmed and hawed for another quarter of an hour and left with what he had come with. But he was very, very unhappy.

"See to it, Panye Leyb . . . see to it that my hide is whole. Because . . ."

"As for your hide, for the time being no one will touch it. You may be certain of that. Go home and eat supper."

And he left, hardly bothering to say good night. [. . .]

And the wooded clearing suddenly had visitors. Unexpected and suspiciously silent.

Little wood, I'll tell you what. Don't bother us, and we won't bother you. Just leave us alone, and we'll get through the night quietly.

How fine it will be . . . how fine if the night passes like a quiet yawn. And may the night pass as quietly as a yawn at Motl Rattner's house as well.

At sunset, Pugatshov (he's a Lederman), his wife, who is better looking than he, and their children crept in among us in the wood. The older boys, seven and nine, were all girt up in their overcoats. They were eager and willing whenever an older person needed their help. "Come, adjust that thing on my shoulders," and the small-fry were always ready to help. "Here, let me do it." "No, let me."

It's good that you're here. But more quietly, please. More quietly.

And the evening approached. A lovely Tammuz evening. And when little birds ready themselves for sleep, they must first sing their little bit of song.

Well, why not? Sing, little birds. Sing and enfold us in the web of your song as with thin strands of distant violin strings. Enfold us and protect us here in our cool and unfamiliar beds.

Certainly all will be well when this night is done. But I feel that I have not done well by my mother or Buzi or Hershele or my sisters. I should have provided them with a better and a safer place to rest. Yes, it all devolves on me.

The smaller children are already asleep, but the adults are still whispering among each other. They assure each other that it will be a peaceful night. My father and Pugatshov are the ones who are most convinced of it. They are merchants, and they know how much was paid to whom and for what.

"We were foolish not to have gone to Motl Rattner's instead of lying about here." [. . .]

Motl's was a wooden two-story house. And now it was packed with Jews, with their wives and children. All sorts of people, including, perhaps Dobbe Frenk and Mordkhe-Leyzer's wife. I was very anxious to know how they were all getting on in such crowded conditions. All jammed together as on Atonement night. And what was Motl Rattner's big-city daughter-in-law doing? Is she perhaps saying *Pardon* and "I'm sorry?" Eh? And I'd like to see how many people were in Motl's house for the first time. And most of all, I'd like to know what was happening above in the painted houses. I hope they're not feeling out of place. It's clear, too, that the Ovrutshev families made a big mistake—those who live in two towns.

What? The Ovrutshev pogroms weren't enough for them.

And I'd like to see how the women at Rattner's give their children suck. It's a crowded house, God bless it, with men in it. And many young mothers who have to suckle their babies. And it must be so hot at Motl Rattner's that the closeness will put the lamps out. Just think of it—how crowded it is. And how do they pass the time there in Motl Rattner's house? The house has many rooms. Perhaps there's a different group in each of the rooms.

Have the workingmen gathered together in the kitchen because they're embarrassed to be with the middle-class young people?

And, if I had a pair of binoculars, I would be able to see how they blessed the wine at the head post office. . . . There were Jews who had asked to be let in and were gathered in the director's cellar. And they could hear the sounds of merriment, of drinking, singing and dancing going on above them. Who was the object of the toasts of those drinkers: of the director, the military commandant, various clerks and four or five other young people? Marko drinks toasts to the noblemen and is on intimate terms with them. He makes them in Russian, and he sings lovely songs in unison with them. The Jews in the cellar are not calm. They are by no means calm. [. . .]

And do you know what, Klimko? It doesn't even occur to you that I'll live to see you dead. Your death and your son's. Though now you stand all alone looking out at the dark Antonovitch Street. Lonely and with a sense of expectation in your filthy heart that something will happen.

"Klimko, damn your ugly mug. You're waiting for something, aren't you?"

And if I had binoculars, there are many things I would have seen. How mother and the children were spending the night, and groups of village Jews who are wandering about from pillar to post. But they are the most likely to be safe from all danger. Though Dovid Frenk was killed in one of those villages. Dovid Frenk with his mother and brother as well as Osher Gershteyn's father. No, mother and the children must by now be far away. And there are Jews spending the night in the priest's attic. So that if there should be a reckoning he can say, "On the contrary, I hid Jews."

And Jews are spending the night in various peasants' stables. Though who knows whether the owners of those stables will spend the night in their homes?

What's being said? There ought to be a radio antenna on Motl Rattner's house because Motl Rattner's house is now like a train station and the house is the very nerve center of a number of worlds.

But I don't have binoculars with me. I sit in the dark, hidden among trees, and it is dark all around me. And there is grass growing near me. Yes, grass.

What's that noise beside me. What?

Maybe it's a beetle, or perhaps a young bird in its nest stirring in its sleep, shifting from one place to another.

Almost all of my people are asleep.

"And Ayzik, you sleep too. When you wake up all the evil will have disappeared, evaporated into the empty fields and the dry woods. It'll all enter into stones and logs." I desperately wanted someone to whisper that to me. And I wished to be a child again, even younger than Hershele and Yosele. As young as the child sleeping in my aunt's daughter-in-law's lap. And Buzi is sleeping not far from me. I can feel her shoe with my hand and I think, "Buzi dear. Your hands and feet are cold because of the freshness of the evening. Your thin dress isn't much of a blanket for you. But I can feel—ah how I feel it—how your young blood courses back and forth endeavoring to keep you warm."

It's well, my dear, that I can feel your blood moving about. Because, from that point of view, it's all over for Dovid Frenk.

And I have an impulse to wake Buzi. To let her know, even more urgently, that she is here. That she is mine. [. . .]

Then I dream of a bright courtyard filled with glowing people. Transformed people, not from here. And they are not really people. Rather, they are heavy sheep and cattle on a green pasture. So heavy the earth can hardly hold them. So heavy . . . And the wealth of it all makes one swell with pride and the lightfooted evening sun wearing a veil of grace is strolling about. Suddenly, the cattle begin stamping their feet, and there is a dense cloud and then thunder and lightning. I woke up. There was no rain. It was dry. There was a strange feeling in the air. Dogs were howling. Countless dogs. A multitude of them howling in all parts of the town. I tried to open my eyes; to test whether I was dreaming or whether what I was hearing was real. . .

Vrrroooom. A grenade exploded somewhere; and the thunder continued to rumble, exploding over the earth. You could hear its echo for perhaps half an hour.

Yes, it was happening in town.

Our families—half of them wake up. They wring their hands; they turn pale. And those who are still asleep—would that they would stay asleep.

Vrrroooom. Thunder again.

There are explosions on all sides. Our hair stands on end. And dogs!! Where did so many dogs come from?

We are on a hillock. The town is below us, and we can hear screams and cries.

They're not drunken cries. They are the cries people make at the point of death.

There is a banging of crowbars and the rattling of tin. Maybe there's a fire. Maybe the town is burning. And again we hear cries and shouts. Who can be screaming like that? Jewish children? I've never heard them cry like that.

Then someone comes to us from out of the trees.

Don't be frightened. Don't be frightened. It's Shmuel-Yankl, the shoemaker's son and his family. They've spent the night near us. And none of us knew the others were there.

Who else is coming out from among the trees? Ah, it's Mikhl the baker and his wife. They didn't want to stay in the peasant's stable, and they crept here. Good. Good. But quieter, please. As quiet as possible. The children are waking up. Then let their mothers do what must be done. And again, the outcries from the town. Girls are being dragged by the hair. Girls and young mothers being dragged from their beds.

"Down with communists and Jews. Hurrah!"

And Sloveshne shrieks and chokes itself on blood.

What's going on in town? Streams of blood are flowing. Ah. Blood is pouring. It's pouring. And in Motl Rattner's house the blood is flowing perhaps from the upper-story windows. Red streams. Oh Lord, why are they shrieking like that in town? And we stand there, a silenced cluster, with wives and children and people staying with us.

"Yankl," I say to my former boss, "we've no weapons in our hands. Let's at least go and find some axes. It's not far."

"Be still," Yankl replies. "Be quiet. We won't go."

"But what if Kosenko comes here? Kosenko or Marko? Let's at least have a stick of some kind."

"Be still," Yankl begs. "We won't go."

And Buzi kneels before me, and her eyes are lifted to me, she whispers so low she can hardly be heard, "Ayzik, you won't go anywhere. I won't let you."

Now where did Buzi suddenly acquire the look of a madonna? And why does her voice tremble as she pleads? Is it because she loves me; is it because she's scared?

"Both, Ayzik. Both," I make my own reply.

Why didn't we take an axe with us yesterday? A couple of axes? We could have carried them under our clothes. We believed what Marko and Kosenko said. We trusted them. And I look at Shmuel-Yankl's wife—at Sarah, Shmuel-Yankl's. There she is in our crowd, with daughters, sons-in-law and grandchildren. She says nothing to anyone. She is simply pale. Waiting. Listening very attentively.

No, I'll not turn her over to Kosenko—to that wormy Kosenko. He'll not get any of these sleepers. I'll crush him like a bedbug. I don't care if he's got a gun, I'll crush him like a bedbug. A couple of weeks ago he announced

that he was a watchmaker. Aha! He wanted to deceive his own brothers. What a peasant can think up. That all the Jewish watches in town would find their way to him. To him at his father's house. Some watchmaker he is.

Well, what about his partners? What will they steal? Kosenko, you're too smart.

And it's two weeks now since he's been driving about among the villages on Jewish business. And now he's running about the town with a gun in his hand. All infected. No, he's too young to be so exalted. To have priests and headmen and whole villages consulting him on Jewish matters. He is too young to be riding around on a horse maligning me in the villages. I'll stomp him!!

Is it daylight yet? Yes, it's daylight. And there's no sound of shouts coming from town. No shrieking. Only dogs bark one after the other. Evidently a great deal happened while we were asleep. While we slept, our town was convulsed.

Yisroel-Dovid is here, bringing us the news from town.

"There was a great slaughter at Motl Rattner's house. The rabbi is at his last gasp, he's been stabbed in the heart. The daughter-in-law was killed. Many people were killed in Motl Rattner's house, though it's not yet clear who they were. There's a great bloody pile of them."

"Is it likely they'll come here?" some women asked uncertainly.

"When there's more light, we'll leave this place. All of us . . . all of us will leave," someone says with determination.

We put our faith in daylight as if it were a powerful guardian. It might reveal us, but it would not turn us over to our enemies.

We hear the cries of Jews running across the fields. And someone is chasing them, crying, "Stinking Jews, don't crush my oats; I'll cut you down like dogs."

"It's Shmayle," says my sister. "That's his voice." Well, if Shmayle is in the game, then everyone is in it. So that's how it is. Jews run, but they have short feet. And Shmayle pursues them, his features contorted with rage. But perhaps he won't do anything. It's daylight already.

Baran's Yisroel is here.

"People, let's go. Nisl the Beech has been killed. He's lying near Yekhiel Dorfman's house."

"What do you mean, killed?"

"Killed with a scythe. One of his neighbors from below the river."

"Yontl's Hershke also killed. By the same peasant."

Yontl's Hershke, my boss? He recently came back from the war and was just gathering his family together. He had curly hair, like a young ram's. Curly and very black. That curly hair must have been smeared with blood. He didn't know where to run to and, seeing a ladder next to the widow's house, he started to climb it when the peasant pulled him down and killed him with a scythe across his throat. The same thing happened to Nisl the Beech.

A tall, dark fellow, that Nisl. In middle age. A furrier.

Dovid the grocer, also killed. Mikhoel stabbed. Naftoli-Yoshke's daughter killed. Zisha Guretske's wife . . . the old market woman . . .

"Naftoli-Yoshke's daughter? The one who lived beside the river. The seamstress?"

"Yes. She was engaged to be married. She's lying not far from the church."

(It all happened so quickly, I wasn't even able to ask, "When will we kill peasant girls? And young peasant women? Women as simple as Naftoli-Yoshke's daughter, the seamstress who lived beside the river—or any others who may come to hand and whom no one ever expected to kill.")

Rokhl, Baran's daughter, lost a two-year-old child as she was running. The child's marrow spilled on a stone not far from her house. Rokhl, with her other children, kept running. Now you could hear her calling her husband, "Shloyme, my dearest love. Where are you? Shloyme, my dear. My darling, where are you?"

A quiet woman, that Rokhl, and now she is confused, calling as loudly as she can. She's no longer in town, but calling aloud in the fields. Hoping that her husband will respond to her. She now has only one thing on her mind, and she keeps on calling.

All of us in our hiding place among the trees can hear her. We recognize her voice, and we don't know whether we ought to call out to her or not.

"People, come."

And mother says, "Come, let's get away from here."

And we do what she says. We go.

See, now we are out in the bright sunlight.

Kosenko, here we are.

We scramble over the most distant of the fences and we go. There are many Jews near us. And we go.

And the Jews! Just look at them. There's hardly any difference between the living and the dead.

Just look at them. Zisl has been killed. Zisl who was talking to you is now dead. I'll believe it. Because the very least thing separates those of us who live from the others.

I cannot believe that the tormented ones are dead. And those who speak—I cannot believe that they are alive.

And on whom does the mark of the scythe show? Can you tell? Because a single nighttime hour or an expelled daytime breath can achieve that which an entire century will not erase. Look, then, at our living and at our dead. [. . .]

What was it like for Yontl's Hershke under the scythe? For the rabbi under the point of the spear? I don't know. I've never in all my days felt the blade of a knife at my throat or had anyone want to kill me or been at the point of death. I'd like to know what that's like. Giddap. You won't get there until tomorrow. And the old market woman—all of her children are in America. And she lies murdered all by herself in her little house. And I owe her some money, the old market woman. I owe her some money. [. . .]

Translated by Leonard Wolf.

Other works by Kipnis: *Die shtub* (1926); *Mayn shtetl Sloveshne* (1971).

Armand Lunel
1892-1977

The novelist and librettist Armand Lunel was born in Aix-en-Provence into a family of Provençal Jews who had lived in southern France for centuries. His knowledge of Provençal Jewish legends informs his literary work, much of which is centered on Carpentras and its ancient Jewish quarter. He was the longtime librettist of his childhood friend Darius Milhaud. His first libretto—for *Esther de Carpentras* (1926), which was based on a Provençal Purim play—became the opéra bouffe *Barbra Garibo* (1950). He survived the German occupation of France in Monaco, where he had been teaching at the lycée since 1920.

Nicolo-Peccavi, or The Dreyfus Affair at Carpentras
1926

It was, in fact, our aunt who had commissioned the bus. Madame Léa Josué Chanaan was our aunt and we called her Aunt Chanaan, just as we called her husband, Monsieur Josué Chanaan, our uncle, although none of

us in the Jewish community of Carpentras was really their niece or nephew. They must have had real nieces and nephews somewhere—but who knows where?—just as they were reputed to have sons and daughters even farther away. But a certain Chanaan, a French diplomat in China; his brother, a correspondent in New York for the great Paris newspapers; their youngest brother, the director of an emigration agency in Palermo; and their sisters, married to rich bankers from Amsterdam, Berlin, or Constantinople—these were the kind of people who could not admit that they were born in Carpentras or in Landerneau, as if these small towns existed only in the legends of *Pêle-Mêle* or *Charivari*. (For you see that while Carpentras has given birth to personalities eminent both in Paris and throughout the world, no one is aware of this, and no one will pay her homage.) It should be noted that the elderly Chanaans, after having enjoyed a considerable fortune amassed in the madder-dye industry under Napoleon III, were almost ruined by the advent of artificial colors. But all the Jewry of Carpentras, admiring the philosophical attitude with which they had withstood the vicissitudes of fortune, showed them a concern and kindness which gave them almost complete consolation. There was hardly a family in which they were not treated as if they were members.

Judging from what could be learned at the Agricultural and Musical Union from the pictures in *L'Illustration*, Chanaan looked exactly like Francisque Sarcey—which at that time and in our city, brought a kind of glory. That handsome old man, blunt, rustic, and full of aphorisms, was noteworthy as well for the birthmark on his right hand, to which he owed his nickname of Red Hand. It was a broad stain, startling, bright in color and awe-inspiring, at which we gazed with a religious dread, for it reminded us that we had before us not only the greatest retired dye-maker of France, but also the man who had performed the *milah* on all the young male Jews of the Comtat region, and still did so. People say that for many generations before our own, Red Hand (like Abraham, when he inaugurated this practice on his son) operated with a sharpened flint—taken from a flintlock, the old man used to say, without noticing the anachronism, as he showed his cannibal-like teeth. This Judeo-Comtadine joke, far from provoking laughter, brought forth a shiver along the spine, especially among those who heard it for the first time. It is understandable, in any case, why so many of us called Monsieur Chanaan Uncle, and had such respect for him, after our eighth day of life.

If we had the greatest respect for Uncle Chanaan, what we felt for Aunt Chanaan was love, admiration, adoration, and veneration, because it had always been common knowledge that she was as much lovable, admirable, and adorable as she was venerable. This elderly lady, to whom growing old was something foreign, had more youth and life in her than many young girls, who would have paid dearly to obtain her charm and sprightliness. There were still men younger than forty who practically courted her, not that she had maintained the slightest physical seductiveness (it would appear that she had never had any), but she still had lightheartedness, insouciance, and mischievous naïveté of another age, in all their freshness. Wherever Aunt Chanaan appeared, her charm bracelet jingling, there was of course wit, excited talking, plays on words, good humor, and surprising stories. If in those days we laughed at everyone, she was the first to laugh at herself, her past grandeur, the servants she no longer had, and especially her carriage, put up for auction; it was after this that, for lack of anything better, she hired the city bus for her afternoon visits.

This time, however, it was not for her own purposes that Aunt Chanaan had ordered the bus. Just as she used it for herself, for lack of anything better (that is to say, a carriage), she had requisitioned this humble and plebeian vehicle for the use of the oldest Jewish women of Carpentras. But you would have sought her in vain among the passengers: because of her rheumatism, she had felt it sufficient to be represented by Léonide, her old cook. Léonide had been given the duty of knocking on doors and introducing in turn each invited guest, in accordance with the list (a duplicate of which had been given to Jean-Hilaire).[1]

Beginning on the day that the pardoned Dreyfus—instead of seeking refuge in England or Alsace, as was believed at first—came in search of peace and quiet to the outskirts of Carpentras, where part of his family lived (our neighbors, the Valabrègues), all we Dreyfusards and anti-Dreyfusards, through the amazing effect of local patriotism, were reconciled little by little, with the same feeling of restlessness and pride. All of France, and the world with her, were going to have—indeed, already did have—their eyes fixed on the Captain's place of refuge, and might even discover a noble and peaceful town, beneath the slander of humorists. As the *Comtat Sentinel* wrote so elegantly: "Our dear town, taking its turn after Rennes and Devil's Island, found itself at the forefront of current events. Mr. and Mrs. English Tourist, coming and going from La Fontaine de Vaucluse, will soon see a side-trip to our small, ancient town as a must." But a certain caution was necessary! We had to remain calm, maintain our dignity, and under no circumstances give a handle to the malicious curiosity of journalists or the satirical indiscretion of photographers—all people from the North, whose disagreeable manners hid under apparently harmless exteriors, and who could not register or even eat a steak at the Grand Hôtel de l'Univers et d'Orient without everyone's finding out about it and being secretly titillated.

The shock was particularly strong in the rue Vitrée, also known as the Passage Boyer, which constitutes the barometer of public opinion, since the Carpentras character is particularly strong there. Strangers who ventured into this famous street during that time carried away with them the memory of those dark and often angry glances they received from its residents—"the same terrible look," they would say upon returning home, "as if we had unknowingly entered their bedrooms and trampled on their bedside rugs." For you see, the shopkeepers—and their wives even more so—regarded the Passage as their private property, and kept watch from morning to night on the thresholds of their shops, in order to prevent violations of their homesteads; only their neighbors and well-known customers, whom they could name and tell stories about, had the right to go by without raising an alarm. These impertinent people, however, these indiscreet strangers, who were they? Where were they from? How long would they keep up their little game? It was the custom for everyone to remain at home. Would we have moved in on their territory? The invaders were seen as unlikely reporters, agents of the secret police, maybe even spies—in any case, they were certainly obtrusive. Was all this wrong? Certainly, the presence of a good Sardinian Republican (who, it was decided, bore a resemblance to Garibaldi) was very curious, as was that of a rather ridiculous delegation of Danish socialists. All these odd types came to greet Dreyfus, and took an interest in his case or feigned to do so. It is true that the sale of *berlingots* did not suffer one bit.

We were not at all mistaken in thinking, that evening so long ago, that the Dreyfus Affair would put forth a new branch in our Carpentras. We were not, however, the only ones to realize this, and the unexpected cutting produced foliage and fruit of very amusing kind.

My grandfather had been asked by an old and very dear friend of his, an editor at *Le Figaro*, to keep him apprised every day of the comings and goings of the Captain, as well as of the reactions of the natives. My grandfather thought that his friend was making fun of him, but after receiving no word, the editor repeated his request by telegram. Abranet then responded with a week's worth of telegrams of this sort: "Dreyfus has taken a bath." "Dreyfus has smoked a pipe." "Dreyfus has drunk a bottle of beer." The joke—which, of course, had not really been one, since this was all that could be reported to the Parisians—was considered to be exceedingly funny in the provinces.

The Jewish bus (as it came to be called) was precisely the last of those events of local history which, tied more or less closely to the Affair, saw Carpentras in turmoil just before 1900. It was much ado about nothing. No one today thinks about it at all. As I attempt, after a period of twenty-five years, to clarify my childhood memories by comparing them to authentic evidence, when I interview survivors of that grand time, I find nothing—nothing but shrugs and a feigned or real indifference, I am not sure which. Was there in fact no Dreyfus Affair in Carpentras? Was there also no Peccavi scandal, grafted onto the Dreyfus Affair? What about the bus?

If you go to Tarascon, you will at last be shown, after much reluctance, Tartarin's house. If you go to Rouen, you might still find some very old people whose parents witnessed the hurried passage of Emma Bovary's hackney, with its silver lanterns—and they will describe it with guarded words. But you will find no one in Carpentras who can speak of the Jewish bus, in which Aunt Chanaan gathered the matrons of the Jewish quarter in order to make it possible for them, as for the Parisians (and these women deserved it just as much), to go see Captain Dreyfus. It was, to be sure, a collective demonstration of Israelitic solidarity, but also a simple visit, motivated by courtesy and sympathy, with a good dose of curiosity. If one of those accursed journalists still prowled our avenues on that Wednesday, he suspected nothing, and even today the citizens of Carpentras continue to deny the existence of that bus. How can this conspiracy of silence be explained? Could it be fear of ridicule? Just wait for what comes next.

It is for these reasons that, though I believe I am faithfully reconstructing my memories, as carefully as one arranges a jigsaw puzzle, I am afraid lest I put in inauthentic pieces and create a veritable novel, a work of pure imagination—because I am absolutely alone before the truth. I fear not being believed. I'm sure that no one will believe me. But that's life. Beside, I've gone too far. I can't stop. . . .

Now comes the time to recall without error the identities of all our travelers; then—as if I had before me the roll given to Léonide by Aunt Chanaan—to put each one in her proper place in the bus.

What were they called? Like the names of most Jews, theirs derived from the places their families had first settled in.

There are Israelites who bear the names of great cities and even capitals, proudly, as if this were an unquestionable sign of their importance and social position. "Yes, I am nothing but a pauper, and it is my fault," said a Monsieur Amsterdam, "but you can tell just from my name that my ancestors were diamond kings in Holland."

At least in Carpentras, especially in the bus (and with few exceptions), names differed only in degree of unpretentiousness. There were names most often of small southern towns (many in France, some on the Iberian Peninsula and in Italy) or of almost unknown villages or hamlets in the area nearby. Perhaps we should also recall Biblical names; nevertheless, I know that by examining a gazetteer of Provence and Lower Languedoc I could pick out the names of a good third of my ancestors.

I have already recognized the wives of Samuel Orange, David Perpignan, and Joseph Caylar, seated to the right of Léonide. Even if their ancestors, thank God, neither figured in the records of the stock exchange nor traded in precious stones, some of the most distant were surely among the philosophers and poets who composed the glorious school at Lunel during the Middle Ages. Renan has certainly referred to them in his *Histoire littéraire de la France*, although their great granddaughters knew nothing about all this. Yet with their thin faces and fine, immobile wrinkles, these women gave an impression of ingenious patience, and behind their huge metal-rimmed glasses their eyes shone with a light so penetrating that popular wisdom (which is never mistaken without knowing, however, why it is right) had called them for some time "the sages." Yet Madame Orange traded in sewing notions; Madame Perpignan was only a linen dealer; and Madame Caylar sold nothing but candles, wax, and small brooms. But all three ladies brought unconsciously to their humble dealings the same subtle ardor shown by their ancestors in disputes regarding the views of Maimonides.

Immediately after them came the cousins, Vonvoune and Franquette Carpentras, still formidable despite their unpretentious names; formerly attendants at the ritual bath, these two shrews, with their dragon voices and Amazonian bearing, continued to inspire awe of a kind reserved most often for religion and the army.

I can see them all, sitting on the bus seats in small intimate groups, just like at a public meeting. There were eternally inseparable couples, former students at the Muscat Boarding School, who visited each other every day and always left with a ceremonious "Let's get together one of these days." There too were the bonneted Esther Beaucaire and Bellette Tarascon, and a solid block of grandmothers: the two sisters and two brothers of the Roquemartine family had married the two brothers and two sisters of the Sisterons. Next, alone in a corner—wishing to be with all the others, however, but not daring to offend anyone through an unwarranted preference—was the discreet and obliging Madame Sinigaglia, smiling and nodding almost imperceptibly right and left, unceasingly.

All were dressed soberly in black, some hatless with a plain kerchief over their bangs, others wearing aprons like the two bathhouse attendants, all proper, often elegant, and almost uniformly small and of slight means, talkative, restless. Showing here and there remnants of gracefulness despite their age, there they sat, the old Israelitic women of the town; some among them, those who had been the most beautiful, were reminiscent of ancient Oriental Mireilles. Lyonette, the widow from Lyons (small as a comma); Miette David (the little *e*, or the ant); Méliton Milhaud (called Milhaudette); Fénella Mossé (called Mosséchonne); Précile Narbonne. . . . ; and Bengude, Blanquette, Astruguette, Isaquette, Belle-Bottine. . . . Last names, first names, nicknames collided in the rocking of the bus. "Is it believable, is it possible, that so many Jewish women were there?" you might ask. Am I mixing them up? Am I adding some? Am I mentioning some who had not been out for twenty years, centenarians, who might have even been dead? Could the bus not even have been that big? How could it have held them all? Of course, three or four small Jewish women can sit in the space occupied by a fat commercial traveler. No, that remarkable magic bus is not yet full, and it still rolls on, meandering through Carpentras.

I know full well that today in Carpentras there are hardly a dozen Jews and that the temple has been closed for lack of members. But 1899 was still a different century; everyone flocked to temple on the sabbath and the decline of the great Jewish community had scarcely begun.

"Let us be counted, and re-counted," said our elderly ladies.

Each in turn spoke tirelessly of another era, even further removed, in which they had been more numerous, another century in which "the Jewish quarter" had not been an empty phrase, when the temple was kept in its full splendor. That time of the Popes, so longed for by Jean-Hilaire in his driver's seat, was almost longed for as well by the Jewish ladies in the bus.

Have patience, poor Jean-Hilaire! A few more turns, a few stops, some sips of local wine at the more hospitable houses, and your task, with the receipt of the hard-won coins, will come to an end.

"Two seats for the Azulaï sisters!" cried Léonide, and there arose an entire Jewish chorus calling, "Azulaï! Azulaï!"

What a beautiful name! How exquisite! Before seeing them, merely upon hearing their name, one thought of something very poetic, very sweet, such as *azure*, of course, but infinitely more rare; then, of the beauty of pearls and a distant sky, exotic and perhaps still showing the blue, shaded freshness of Spanish gardens.

"Please take your seats, I beg you, ladies."

And in the presence of these Jewish women, imported to Carpentras from Gibraltar, one could admire the loveliness of Hispano-Arabic pottery, but their beauty was in truth too unusual, showing too frequent mending and a glaze marred by flakes.

NOTE

1. Jean-Hilaire: the driver of the bus.

Translated by Michael T. Ward.

Other works by Lunel: *L'imagerie du cordier* (1924); *Jérusalem à Carpentras* (1937).

Dovid Mitzmacher

1904-1941

Dovid Mitzmacher was a Yiddish journalist and prose writer active in interwar Poland. Educated in both a traditional heder and at a Russian-language gymnasium, he was part of a circle of proletarian writers in Warsaw and wrote for journals and newspapers including *Di ilustrirte vokh*, where he debuted as a writer in 1924; the leftist *Literarishe tribune* (Łódź), where he

served on the editorial staff; and *Der fraynd* (Warsaw), where he also served on staff. At the beginning of World War II, he fled to Białystok, where he published stories and other writings in the *Bialistoker shtern*.

Rag Pickers
1926

Always, by the time the humid, breathless, summer night lifted its veil and a quiet, rosy dawn emerged, when some glimmers of soft, opaque light began to filter through the dried muddy, dusty window into Nekhemye's "commercial" cellar abode—Gele, Nekhemye's wife was always up by that time, doing the housework, busy as a bee. The pail with its unclean contents that stood all night long in its place by the door was long gone by then. The floor, damaged by constantly leaking water, had already been swept clean, and whatever little furniture they had—the small cupboard with its broken doors, the table and the bench—Gele was wiping them hard with a rag until small pieces of the remaining paint chipped off of the wood. The clay oven had already been heated and a pot of black coffee was boiling on it. On the table lay a small loaf of freshly baked bread with a golden brown, shiny face, waiting to be blessed by Nekhemye.

At the same time Nekhemye would be sliding off the thin, dirty bedcover and getting up from the wobbly, wooden bed that squeaks angrily at the smallest movement; he would pour *neglvaser* on his hands, go to the window, and there, with eyes closed, facing the sky, say the *moyde ani* with fervor, just like his father used to do every morning.

Once he is dressed, he goes to a niche of the room to wake up his oldest son, Vigdor, who is stilling snoring heartily on a heap of rags, his bronze-color face covered in sweat.

Vigdor, who helps his father earn a living, digging all day long in village- and city-garbage cans, opens his eyes with a shudder, as if awakened in the middle of a nightmare. He slightly raises his head with its tangled, strange-colored hair, looks at his father for a while, then glances around with a bewildered look in his eyes and dozes off again, snoring, his sweaty face buried in the pile of rags.

But Nekhemye won't give up. He wakes his son again and again, until Vigdor opens his rheumy eyes once again; he turns his head toward the window, thus breaking the thread of saliva that is flowing from his mouth onto the rags; he swallows the greasy saliva and then asks sleepily:

"How late is it?"

Nekhemye does not answer. He puts the bucket next to Vigdor and gives him a scoop of water. He says:

"Pour the *neglvaser* and get up."

Vigdor struggles to untangle himself from the mound of rags; he notices the freshly baked, fragrant bread on the table and starts to throw on his clothes quickly.

Meanwhile, Nekhemye's wife, the tall Gele, who has to walk around with her head bent all day long on account of the low ceiling, makes the beds, fixes the mound of rags Vigdor just got up from, goes outside and shakes out the two sacks father and son are taking on the road, and then starts to look for more housework. [. . .]

Nekhemye already said the Morning Prayer, put down the yellow, patched tallis, washed his hands, and recited the blessing over the bread with great fervor, just like his father used to do. Now Vigdor is saying the Morning Prayer, wearing his father's tefillin, making mistakes as he reads; he watches with envy how his father eats, so he speeds up, skipping some words.

His mother notices it. She puts a cup of hot coffee on the table for Vigdor and cuts him a few slices of bread.

"At least let him finish the prayer," says Nekhemye in a tone of mild disapproval.

"You can see how hungry he is," she is gesturing to her husband so that Vigdor doesn't notice, as if she were saying, "just let it go this time."

A little while later father and son are both ready to go. Vigdor is already standing behind the door in the dark entranceway to the cellar, calling his father impatiently in a strange, drawn-out tone:

"Fah-ther! Nu, come on! Fah-ther, yu comin'?"

Nekhemye is still inside, holding his fleshy hand on the naked *mezuzah*; something is not letting him cross the threshold, as if he had forgotten to take something with him.

Vigdor runs back inside. He throws down the empty sack from his shoulder and shouts angrily:

"Why have you stopped here? Pinkhesl and Abe must have gone out to the village a long time ago. They will take everything before we get there."

Deep wrinkles appear on Nekhemye's forehead, which he presses with one hand. His wife, the tall Gele, looks around, helps him search with her eyes, then hesitantly stretches out her long hand, pointing to the window sill where there are a couple of books.

Nekhemye's dark blue eyes suddenly begin to smile and the wrinkles on his forehead smooth out. He goes to the window, takes a small book that tells the stories of great *tsadikim* and pious Jews, and hides it in his bosom.

"Nu, Fah-ther, come on!" hearkens him Vigdor.

Then, father and son throw the empty sacks over their shoulders once again.

Nekhemye gives his wife some money so she can cook a soup, takes his muddy walking stick from the corner, and they leave, saying "good day."

"A good day, a successful day to you, too," the tall Gele shouts after them.

And now, after their departure, comes Gele's most difficult task: to wake up the two younger boys and send them on their way—the tall Sroel, whose back is slightly hunched, and the very young, sunbrowned Hershl with his round, brown face like a bread-roll. They spend all day standing around the train station, carrying suitcases and packages for the businessmen who arrive to town, or, in the summer, they ride the wagon drivers' horses to the river to bathe them.

Now both of them are still asleep in a niche of the room, their heads covered with feathers, under a thin, dirty bedcover which they constantly kick off of them.

Gele leans over the boys, wringing her hands, covers them from time to time, sticks her wrinkled finger under her faded wig; she is treading in one place impatiently, waking the boys:

"Nu, get up already, it is well into the day already."

The tall Sroel opens one eye, lets out a sleepy "Ha?" and dozes off again.

Gele knows how tired they are. She thinks, "Let them sleep a bit more. They already missed one train anyway." And she continues to look for work that needs to be done. Wiping the cupboard, swishing the bench, sweeping the floor. Meanwhile she remembers that today is wash day at the rich Goldberg family's house. She, Gele, will go there, as always, to help her daughter Genendl who has served at their house for a few years now. She wants to get there early, before they start, together with the robust peasant laundrywoman. If she gets there on time, when rich Madame Goldberg is still in bed, and her maid brings out from her bedroom a silver tray with an empty fine porcelain cup and a piece of sweet-smelling pastry. . . . And she—Gele thinks—will breathe in the aroma of the delicious food, and, of course, Madame Goldberg will say to Genendl, pointing at Gele with a half-raised hand:

"Don't forget, Genendl, that today you need to cook lunch for one extra person."

And Gele suddenly realizes that she might get there late; she leans over the boys' bed, touches Sroel's head and repeats a few times, louder and louder:

"Sroel, get up! People are already rushing to the seven-o'clock train!"

Sroel jumps up from the bed petrified and asks:

"Ha? What? The seven-o'clock train?"

"Yes, yes," Gele nods her head.

The seven-o'clock train is the most important one for Sroel because it comes directly from Warsaw and brings rich merchants with huge, heavy suitcases. There you can earn good money, and sometimes they even treat you to a drink.

That is why Sroel jumps up so fast and stands the young Hershl on his feet, too, who, with eyes still closed, starts to curse his brother:

"May you be struck by epilepsy!"

It takes only a few minutes for them to put on their black-dyed sackcloth clothes; stuffing some bread into their pockets they are running fast, barefoot, their feet muddy, toward the old train station.

"Today I will not bring you lunch!" shouts Gele after them.

Doing the laundry takes several days at the rich Goldberg family, sometimes a full week.

On these days Gele would leave the cellar very early and get home late, tired to the bone, carrying home from the rich people's house a package of food that she saved from her own meals for her husband and sons.

Nekhemye and the boys would first feast their eyes, just look at the food, and only then would they start to eat slowly, with restraint, the way one enjoys fine food.

Standing all day long by the washtub, Gele saw this scene in front of her eyes in the soapy bubbly water. Recalling how Nekhemye sucks on a goose bone for half an hour before he chews it with a shining face, she says to her daughter Genendl:

"You know what? I just can't eat now. Pack up my lunch.

Genendl understands what her mother means by this. She packs up her lunch and makes sure that her mother, too, eats something, separately.

After that Gele carries on with the wash with a calmer mind. She knows every piece of clothing well, remembers whom they each belong to: this blouse with the silk lace belongs to the youngest daughter, the one with

the round pink cheeks who plays the piano for hours in the third room. And under this bedcover sleeps Madame Goldberg herself. Gele remembers every piece she washes, and she wishes ten times a day: if only she could give her Nekhemye a clean white shirt like the one she is washing to wear every Friday afternoon.

From time to time thoughts come up in her mind as she leans on the washtub with both hands: she did not sweep the floor well today, everything must be covered in dust; her two sons, Sroel and Hershl, must be sitting in the gutter by the train station now, watching with envy the porters who are gulping down large spoonfuls of soup that their mothers brought them, while they are eating bread and onions that they bought at Avromtshe's tavern.

But this will only last for a few days, until the Goldbergs' wash is done and Gele returns to the cellar to her usual household duties.

The room has been swept. Everything is in order. Sroel and Hershl are eating soup from a pot just like the other porters, and Gele is standing on the side, surrounded by the other women, telling them about the wonders she saw at the Goldbergs.

"Don't worry, Gele. I already have a match for Genendl"; that's what Madame Goldberg told her.

And all the women, mothers of grown girls, envy her.

Translated by Vera Szabó.

Other works by Mitzmacher: *Afn bruk* (1931); *Di kapelye* (1936).

Karel Poláček

1892–1945

Karel Poláček was one of the wittiest writers in interwar Czechoslovakia. Born into a Czech-speaking home in a small Bohemian town, he became a journalist after serving in the Habsburg army in World War I. He wrote plays, film scripts, short stories, novels, and short humorous essays. They targeted political extremism, stereotyped political thinking, bourgeois narrow-mindedness, and the clichés of everyday life. Although he formally withdrew from the Jewish community in 1919, he published his *Stories of the Israelite Faith* in 1926 and a collection of Jewish humor. He was deported to Terezín in 1943 and then to Auschwitz in 1944 and probably died on a death march in 1945.

A Discussion of Religious Questions
1926

So, Mr. Blum?

So, Mr. Blau?

What's with you, Mr. Blum?

What should be with me, Mr. Blau?

How should I know what's with you, Mr. Blum? I'm asking you. May I not ask? Why are you staring so?

I'm staring? I'm not staring.

You are staring. You will not tell me anything. I see into you, Mr. Blum. You are sad, Mr. Blum. You are angry, Mr. Blum.

I'm not sad, Mr. Blau. I'm not angry, Mr. Blau. I'm happy, Mr. Blau. I have reason to be happy, Mr. Blau.

Why are you happy, Mr. Blum?

Am I happy Mr. Blau? Cer-tain-ly! I am happy. Let my worries be upon my enemies. So may it be that they should be as happy as I, Mr. Blau.

What I wish for you, Mr. Blum, may the Lord also apportion to me. Quit staring at me!

I am not staring at you, Mr. Blau. What I wish for you, may the Lord also apportion to me. I am happy— yes, I tell you, Mr. Blau.

So, Mr. Blum?

What do you want from me? Do you want to strip off my overcoat? Do you want to tear pieces from me? Am I some sort of baron? Am I the owner of silver mines in Arizona?

Oh please, Mr. Blum. I do not want to tear pieces from you.

You do not, Mr. Blau, but those ones! I ask you, is there now so much business that a man can spend money every which way? Overhead, is it nothing? Does a household cost nothing? Where's the food, Mr. Blau? Where's the income tax, sales tax, luxury tax, municipal surcharges, Mr. Blau? Where is the lighting, gas, and heating, Mr. Blau? Where is the clothing, Mr. Blau? Where are schoolbooks for the children, Mr. Blau? Tear a piece from me. I can give. I'm a millionaire. Am I a Guttmann? Am I a Rothschild? Am I an . . . an . . . an oil . . . um . . . king? Do I have mines?

Shhhhh—Don't yell, Mr. Blum. *They* do not need to hear everything.

Let them hear. I am not afraid, Mr. Blau. I paid just as they did. For this, they won't throw in money on my behalf.

So speak, Mr. Blum. What has happened to you?

What has happened to me, Mr. Blau? Yes, what has happened to me? Yesterday, Mr. Kopperl visited me . . .

Ah, Mr. Kopperl.

Mr. Kopperl, the shammes [sexton]. He arrives: "An honor," supposedly. "I bow to you, Mr. Kopperl." I say, "What have you brought me, Mr. Kopperl?" "What should I bring, Mr. Blum?" says Mr. Kopperl. "Here, I bring you a slip regarding the religious tax, Mr. Blum." "You, Mr. Kopperl," I say, "are so gallant with me. You always only bring me these little slips." "Gallant how, Mr. Blum?" says that Mr. Kopperl, with his squinty eyes—and he looks at me so—you know, how should I say——so maliziös—(these people have chutzpah)—and he says, "Not gallant, Mr. Blum. What I am commanded to deliver, I deliver." "If," he says, "they order me to bring a grandfather clock, I would bring you a grandfather clock. As I purchase, so I sell." I say, "You, Mr. Kopperl, will not appear again before my eyes with that crooked mouth. I do not want to see you with my eyes." To that he responds, "I bow to you, Mr. Blum," and he left. And do you know, Mr. Blau, what was on that slip?

Nu, what was on the slip?

They raised my church tax to 75 crowns. "You are obliged," was written there—a wickedness! And I told my wife of that blow, "Molly," I said, "Gird yourself. We are going to withdraw from the faith. This would make religion expensive for us. One does not know where to spend his money first."

You want to withdraw from the faith, Mr. Blum?

I am withdrawing, Mr. Blau, so that I can remain in good health.

What will you do? You won't do it!

What wouldn't I do? I'm doing it!

I will lead away you from this path, Mr. Blum.

Nothing is going to lead away me from this path, Mr. Blau. I have spoken!

So, good, Mr. Blum. You, so to speak, will withdraw from the faith. So, you will no longer go to temple?

I won't go.

Not even on Yom Kippur?

No.

Not even on Rosh Hashanah?

No.

Will you not celebrate Pesach?

I won't.

Will you not carry [the Torah] right behind Mr. factory-owner Schnabel, the financial councilor, on Simchat Torah?

I'll donate that kovod [honor] to you.

Will you not go to temple when Mr. Štědrý has *yahrzeit*?

Let them find a minyan *without me.*

And when your departed father has *yahrzeit?*

I will say kaddish *at home.*

Mr. Blum, Mr. Blum. How you make one's head spin! But tell me one thing: How do you like *beilik* [steamed goose breast with garlic and ginger]?

Beilik? *I love beilik with* cholent. *When it is properly prepared, as my departed mother made it, oh!*

And as my wife makes it, oh!

A bit of pepper on it, properly grease it. That's for me, ah!

I prefer Yom Kippur, Mr. Blum.

Yom Kippur? That's the most tedious holiday. The whole time a man should only beat his breast: Avinu Malkeinu!

No, I don't mean that, Mr. Blum. I mean the evening beforehand. To the table first must arrive the soup . . .

With dumplings, Mr. Blau. It must be like oil and hot, Mr. Blau. Otherwise, it isn't soup. Then comes the veal roast.

That must be served with compote, Mr. Blum.

Stewed plums and apples. Then one rests and then . . .

Then the chickens are carried to the table.

By you there are chickens? By me there must be goose!

Oh, come now, Mr. Blum. Chickens, young chickens that crisp up so well, ah!

But goose, young goose—and baked potatoes, that's something. That's what I call a holiday. That's deliziös, Mr. Blau.

Let it be—but on the holiday of *matzot* one also eats well, Mr. Blum!

Young goat with spinach, mmm! Mr. Blau!

Matzo cake! Mr. Blum!

Ay, yay, yay! My Molly knows how to make that!

Aunt Lucy makes the best *matzo* cakes. And what about *kugel*, Mr. Blum?

Oy, yoy, yoy! But that's a little heavy on the stomach, Mr. Blau.

You cannot eat everything at once. You rest—and then you eat on. One mustn't be like that old Ignác Wasservogel, who on the High Holidays ate so much that he said, "Nothing tastes good to me anymore. I'm an old man" and died.

There is nothing better than Jewish cuisine, Mr. Blau. You will not find anything like it in the whole world.

They are incapable of cooking so, far from it. Jewish cuisine! And all this you would like to cast aside, Mr. Blum?

Me, Mr. Blau? Who said anything about that, Mr. Blau?

You want to be expunged from the faith, Mr. Blum.

Me? Who told you so? What are you talking about, Mr. Blau? What one is born into, in that he must stay, just as my departed mother said.

You were speaking of those taxes . . .

Who spoke? I spoke? It never even dawned on me. You spoke, Mr. Blau. I am no penny pincher, Mr. Blau. I am Adolf Blum, Mr. Blau. Always gallant, Mr. Blau. Remember that, Mr. Blau. I'm not just anyone, Mr. Blau. I still hold fast to religion, Mr. Blau. I am Adolf Blum, old school. You can ask anyone about me.

Translated by Jacob Ari Labendz.

Other works by Poláček: *What Ownership's All About* (1928); *We Were a Handful* (1946).

Dvora Baron
1887–1956

The short-story writer Dvora Baron was the first woman to make a literary career in Hebrew. Born in a shtetl near Minsk, she received a Hebrew education in her father's heder, unusual for a girl at that time, and later traveled to Minsk, Kovno, and other large cities in the Pale of Settlement, where she received a secular education and established a reputation as a writer, first in Yiddish and then in Hebrew. In 1910, she settled in Ottoman Palestine but was deported to Alexandria by the Turks during World War I and did not return until 1919. In 1922, she became a recluse in her own house and in the last twenty years of her life rarely left her bed. During the period of her self-chosen seclusion, she wrote her most widely admired stories. Unlike other writers in the Yishuv, she did not make the state-building activities of the pioneers the focus of her fiction and wrote instead about the world of her childhood in a Belorussian shtetl.

In the Beginning
1927

On the beginning of the new rebbetzin's life in Zhuzhikovka, the locals say:

She, the rebbetzin, was brought here a few years ago from some distant city in Poland.

There, in that city, the Polish one, her parents had a house made of polished stone, which was built like a kind of palace, with balconies and columns, and it was tall—ten Polish cubits high. They also had a garden to stroll in beside their house, and among the trees of this garden were flower beds and fountains, in which water rose up and spurted on its own, like the waters that flowed from the rock Moses smote. Was it any wonder, then, that when the rebbetzin arrived in Zhuzhikovka and took one look at the ruin of the community house and its desolate yard, she stopped in front of the door and decided that she wasn't going in?

She did go into the house, though, later on. She took off her hat, revealing a golden wig, a tumble of curls—and entered. But after that, at night, when the welcoming reception had come to an end and the guests had gone off to their own houses, she sank in her city clothes onto the naked bench in the community hall and cried bitterly, while he, her young husband in his silk caftan, his rabbinic sash wound around his hips, stood beside her—at a loss.

This whole story should begin differently, in a more appropriate version—and here it is:

When the new rabbi was about to arrive and ascend to the rabbinic seat, the community president ordered that the streets be swept and the synagogue whitewashed just as if it were Passover or the High Holy Days. And since the guest was due to arrive at the station on Friday afternoon, the shtetl folk changed their usual practice and made sure to heat the bath-house on Thursday before sundown.

That night every stove and oven in every house was stoked. And the women cooked and baked and shampooed their children's hair and made sure to darn their tattered clothing, so that no shame would come upon the community as they waited at the station to greet the newcomer.

Early the next morning, just as the sun emerged from behind the synagogue roof, the entire community set out with its women and children, fanning out along the paths that led to the train station.

It certainly was a sight, this crowd of Jews in their colorful rags, threading their way across the wide fields at such an early hour. The farmer women, crouching over their vegetable beds, straightened up in amazement, shielding their eyes with their hands to stare long and hard after this motley crew.

When the crowd arrived at the village of Kaminka, not without some trepidation they skirted the pasture, where the dogs roamed as freely as the cattle. There was still a stubble field to cross after that, with the over-grown thorns scratching their legs, especially those who were barefoot.

But here, at last, appeared the station, a garish clapboard building with its windows sealed shut and its dusty copper basin by the entrance, the corroded dipper hanging from a chain over it. A bell rang, wheels clattered and roared, and two men, pillars of the community, came pushing through the crowd toward the rumbling train that had come to a halt, the new woolen sleeves glinting with strange innocence on their old Sabbath caftans—and they presented the young rabbi with his writ of appointment.

Yes, it's true, all those men had new sleeves sewn into their caftans, but these new sleeves only made the drabness of their threadbare outfits stand out more starkly, and the young rebbetzin, leaning with charming urbanity on her parasol, rubbed her eyes as if in shock, scarcely able to believe what she was seeing.

But now a trumpet blast shook the air. And then a drumbeat and a fife were heard, and the procession moved: the young rabbi in his silk caftan at its center, with the congregation leaders at his right and left, and around them the rabble, merry shouts, and a cloud of dust, and inside the carriage that lumbered behind—the rebbetzin, suede gloves on her hands, the ostrich feather in her hat nodding to the rhythm of the swaying carriage.

Along the roadside: groves of trees, haystacks at the edges of fields, flocks of sheep with their dogs herding them, and before the rebbetzin's eyes finally appeared the shtetl, with its poor huddled houses propped up on their poles, the forsaken wooden hoist suspended over the mouth of the well, and the windmill with its sluggish arms sagging listlessly by the mountainous garbage dump.

From here, atop the straw seat inside the carriage, it was also impossible not to notice the narrow wooden racks attached to the cornices and suspended from the beams of every house, and the blocks of cheese drying on them were so perfectly triangular that it was hard to believe that they had been made by hand and not some sort of machine.

And soon enough the "community house" itself came into view, a small building propped up, like the others, on poles, and on the heap of garbage in the yard—would you believe?—stood a milk goat, a white goat with innocent eyes, who, noticing the carriage stop beside the house, approached and grabbed a mouthful of straw from the underside of the rebbetzin's seat, and then stood and chewed it with goatish seriousness.

And now is when the story they tell about the rebbetzin refusing to enter the community house took place.

The old woman, Sarah Riva, who had been hired as a housekeeper even before the new owners arrived, afterward described in detail how she, the rebbetzin, threw herself down in all her finery on the community bench and sobbed, while he, her rabbi husband, dressed in silk, paced the room—in consternation.

When it came to the point where she, the rebbetzin, raising her head and looking at him through a flood of tears, mentioned that strange creature, the goat—he could no longer hold back his laughter, pausing for a minute at the bench to stand beside her.

"Well, the truth is that you're just an inexperienced little goat yourself," he said.

Long and perplexing days followed, late-summer days in a remote Lithuanian shtetl. The silk-embroidered tablecloths, which were taken out of the bridal chest every once in a while, only heightened the poverty of the room when they were spread out over the tables. The curtains turned out to be much too wide and long for the windows, and the rebbetzin, after unsuccessfully trying a few times to make them fit, was forced to return them to the chest.

Nevertheless, these were bright summer days, and in the morning, when she opened the shutters, the radiant sunshine that flooded everything amazed her. And if on one side it illuminated only the dusty, gloomy alley, with its unpainted houses, on the other side the eye was transfixed by the meadow, a wide green meadow, over which stretched a sky at least as deep and blue as the city sky back in Poland.

This was a bustling hour in the alley and around it. At the well, the water carriers came and went with their buckets. Women gave the goats their morning milking by their front doors and little boys, with fringed garments over their short pants, streamed with their books to the cheders.

Very soon, from the end of the alley, their voices rang out and continued throughout the day, voices sweeter and clearer than any she, the rebbetzin, had ever heard.

The young rabbi, noticing how she stood listening to those voices, once asked her whether she had seen the charity boxes in these poor houses yet. And, indeed, in the very same spot where the racks for the cheese were attached to the outside of the houses could be found, on the other side of the wall inside nearly every house, a whole shelf full of tin cans, with the acronyms of all the yeshivas in the world inscribed on their rounded sides. Precisely how coins were deposited into these cans was captured, to the consternation of the locals, by a roving photographer who came through here once on a Friday afternoon.

He, the stranger, standing at the threshold of his inn as the sun was setting, was fascinated to see the landlady take some copper coins out of a special pouch and arrange them on the tabletop, from which she had folded the tablecloth back for that purpose. The house had been straightened up and scrubbed. At the head of the table, under a satin Sabbath cloth, lay two loaves of challah while across from them, at the other end of the table, the candles stood ready in their candlesticks for lighting, and she, the woman, sweeping the coins into her hand and raising her youngest child in her arms toward the charity boxes, was handing him the coins to toss into the slots, when now, suddenly, turning her head, she caught sight of the "case" in the visitor's hands and saw what he was doing to her and to her son, and she collapsed onto the bench before her and burst into tears.

Yes, these Zhuzhikovkans were a strange bunch—the rebbetzin shook her head as she listened to the stories people told her, though her face no longer darkened to hear these things as in the beginning.

She was peaceful and content even after that, when the autumn came, and the mud closed in on the shtetl from every side.

Now the meadow lay yellowish and withering on the other side of the windows, while the goats wandered up and down the alley with sagging bellies and sparse coats, bleating pitifully. How terrifying was the sight of the shadowy shops, with their flimsy signs hanging by a thread, and the barrels of annihilated and frozen Dutch herring, from whose round, wide-open eyes, despair itself now peered out.

Beside the well in the market square, in the middle of the day, the carriage drivers could be seen trudging along, sodden, behind their unharnessed horses, and limply pulling the slippery water hoist.

Desolate lay the roads of the town, desolate.

In the early mornings, the women no longer went outside to lay out wedges of cheese to dry, and if a woman appeared on the expanse of mud, it was some courageous mother slogging along, in men's boots, carrying her children to their cheder.

These were hard, hard days in the remote shtetl.

The young rebbetzin, if she heard the goat bleating, would go out in her plush coat and tenderly offer her a little straw from the dilapidated roof.

At night the wind blew, wrestling with the roof and ripping off the new patches of thatched straw. Far away, somewhere outside the town, dogs barked and their brethren on the gentile street responded with long wails. And the young rebbetzin, waking from sleep with fragments of dreams still caught between her eyelids—distant dreams with the afterimage of city lights—would gaze out into the darkness of her poor home, frightened and amazed at what she would see when she awoke, though she was no longer as despondent as in the early days. For together with the howl of the wind outside the windows she could also hear the voice of the rabbi, who sat at the table by lamplight, reading, chanting, and singing. And if sometimes a tear rolled down her face, it was only a consoling tear, brought forth by the sound of the mournful singing.

Once, on a night like this, the rabbi sat at the head of the table, rehearsing aloud the sermon he would be giving on the weekly Torah portion, the chapter "And Jacob left." He spun and wove together the various themes with ease, illuminating each of them in the refined light of his mind, pronouncing every word, as usual, as clearly and distinctly as if he were counting coins. This happened at the beginning of the month of Kislev, perhaps the most forbidding season of the year. The rain, which poured all day and all night, had flooded even the last of the dry footpaths alongside the roads and fields. There was no more bread to be had in the shtetl—and the young rabbi, sitting at his desk, delved ever more deeply into Jacob's leave-taking of Beersheba, how the sun had set upon him as he made his way through a field, and how, as he lay lonesome and lost, a stone for his pillow, on that very first night of exile God showed him the marvelous ladder, the one whose feet stood on the ground and whose head reached to the very heavens.

"Behold, I am with you, and shall keep you," the rabbi sang God's promise, weaving together more and more strands of the tapestry of his sermon, strengthening it from time to time with further prooftexts from various places.

For while the verses of the Torah portion served him as the foundation and building blocks, the words of the Prophets and later Writings were the mortar and ornamental detail.

Thus, for example, when he reached the place where it was recounted how Jacob met our Mother Rachel and how he rolled the heavy boulder from the well, he brought in the verse from the Song of Songs, that "Many waters cannot quench love, neither can the floods drown it."

By and by he came, also, to the passage of Rachel's longing for children, and from that to how the Lord remembered her, listening to her and granting her a son:

"Enlarge the place of your tent, for you shall break forth out on the right hand and on the left," the rabbi rose from his seat and paced the length of the room, trilling his words in a mournful and tender tone—so mournful and tender that the rebbetzin on the other side of the partition couldn't stop herself from standing up and holding her arms out toward the room.

Is there any need to describe the things that passed between those two in the still of the night, in the raging heart of autumn? In any case there's no way of knowing all the details, since the old housekeeper had set up her bed that night in the kitchen, at the far end of the other room. What is clear is that the rabbi, who was now standing beside his wife, no longer called her "little fool" or referred to her as an inexperienced young goat, as he once had. He just soothed her with kind words, hinting to her about the child that she too would soon embrace, like the matriarch Rachel in her day, and he stayed with her until she had calmed down.

Autumn in the shtetl was meanwhile coming to an end and in its place came winter, white, aggressive, and brilliant, and changed everything all at once.

In the weekly Torah portions, though, the story continued to be as parched, summery, and wearisome as before.

Pharaoh still saw in his dream the cows on the banks of the Nile. In the Land of Canaan there was famine, bread could not be found anywhere and starvation lay heavy and oppressive, while here in Zhuzhikovka the snow fell and covered the fields and roads, and the rebbetzin, when she found a windowpane free of frost, gazed serenely at the winter sleighs that slid along toward the shtetl, laden with an abundance of food.

Birch wood, brought straight from the forest, caught fire at the entrance to the stove as soon as it was lit, without any kindling or additional help. At daybreak, the smoke rose from the chimneys toward the sky in a straight line, unwavering. American potatoes, substantial and heavy, were peeled, breaking into floury, appetizing fissures as soon as they came to a boil, and over the well at the end of the alley the hoist with its bucket squeaked powerfully and diligently.

Days of plenty had come to the town and among those who came to the market square were Jews from the far reaches of the surrounding country, able-bodied villagers wearing farmers' hoods, and when they swung their heavy fur coats with their thick collars, they gave off an aroma foreign to the town air, the smoky scent of resin ovens and the pine forests that stretched to the Polesian marshes and beyond.

One of these villagers, who came for his first visit to the new rabbi, brought, in addition to a bag of chickpeas, a large fatted goose with white feathers, who, as soon as the housekeeper loosened the rope around his legs, immediately stuck his neck into the chicken coop and gobbled up the hen's feed with the calm self-assurance common only among those fat creatures who have no concern for anyone else's property.

"Serve him up with those," the man gestured with the tip of his whip toward the sack of chickpeas.

Although old Sarah Riva had decided that these peas should be set aside for some other time—a time of celebration and "Mazel tov"—she nodded good-naturedly. And later that evening the rebbetzin, as she sat by the lamp and passed her hand over those chickpeas, cool and smooth, felt a shiver run through her, sweeter than any she had ever felt.

Within the next few weeks lambs, tender and newly weaned, also began to arrive from the surrounding farms, and the first of the dairy products.

The cheese, which was brought in capacious earthen farm jugs, was sometimes covered with a fine layer of frost that crackled lightly when it was removed. In order to knead it into rounds, first the cheese had to be brought close to the oven to soften and thaw, and then a special fragrance would suffuse the house, signaling the approach of spring.

Early, as on a winter's sleigh, the days now slid by. Among those who arrived at the railroad station, finally, were the emissaries from the yeshivas, men with noble beards dressed in rabbinic caftans, who, with their special hammers, without a speck of rust, pulled the charity boxes off the wall with amazing efficiency, and as they arranged the coins in rows on the table, the narrow rectangle where the cans had been nailed stood pale and waiting, as if ashamed of its nakedness.

And in the weekly Torah portion, meanwhile, Pharaoh's stubbornness and his refusal to let the Israelites go out of Egypt ended. The plagues came—incessant, harsh, and surprisingly inventive.

After the three days of darkness came the final blow, the decisive one—the plague of the firstborn. And the rout was complete:

Moses and Aaron were called to Pharaoh in the middle of the night, and the Israelites were compelled to leave in a frenzy, even before their dough had risen.

As they camped for a moment on the verge of freedom, before Baal-Zephone, another unpleasant little incident intervened:

The Israelites lifted their eyes and behold—Egypt was riding in pursuit. But salvation came in the blink of an eye: the waters were split and the sea became dry ground before those being pursued, and the finest of Pharaoh's horsemen were hurled into the deep, and the Israelites walked out with their heads held high.

It was the Sabbath when the Song of the Sea was read in the shtetl. On the windowpanes of the synagogue the ice had melted in the course of the service, and the rays of sunlight streaming through them fell across the wooden lions that crouched like two kindly steers at the top of the Holy Ark, beside the velvet curtain.

The Song of Deborah was also read:

They that are delivered from the noise of archers in the places of drawing water, there shall they rehearse the righteous acts of the Lord. They fought from heaven, the stars in their courses fought against Sisera, and during lunch, when the door was opened so that crumbs could be thrown to the birds, the sound of their chirping burst into the house and spread a new spirit all around, the breath of spring, which although it tarried, speedily would come.

The approach of spring was also soon prophesied by the new wooden vessels that were brought from the villages to be sold.

The beets were brought up from the cellar. The women, in their clean cotton aprons, came with the first of their questions about the laws of Passover and, while the rabbi sat at the head of the table, looking into his book, the women couldn't take their eyes off the rebbetzin, who now—she had slimmed down after the birth and looked even taller—had become so beautiful. Once, on a day like this, the rebbetzin went out to the front yard, a thin sanded board in her hand.

Outside the roofs dripped merrily. Behind the garden gates the newborn chicks clucked musically, with clear, abrupt cries—like spring, and the rebbetzin, lifting the board high, marked the place on the wall for the rack where the cheese wedges would dry in the summer, and she hammered in the nails with her own hand.

The sound of the hammer woke the newborn, who was lying in her cradle, and she let out a kind of coo, which sounded very much like the murmur of the spring waters rushing down the foot of the nearby slope. The rebbetzin, when the sound reached her, hurried back to the community room, went over to the cradle and looked down at the baby, and a smile appeared on her lips that slowly illuminated her entire face—that smile was the very first thing that each of us children of the rabbi of Zhuzhikovka saw the moment we emerged into the light of day.

Translated by Naomi Seidman and Chana Kronfeld.

Other works by Baron: *Stories* (1942); *The Thorny Path and Other Stories* (1969); *Parshiyot mukdamot* (1988).

Lajos Hatvany
1880–1961

Born into an ennobled industrial and banking family in Budapest, Lajos Hatvany was a novelist, poet, playwright, and patron of literary modernism. A liberal, he supported the unsuccessful bourgeois revolution that followed World War I and then went into exile in Germany and Austria. He was jailed for nine months after he returned in 1927. In 1938, he left Hungary again and lived first in Paris and then in Oxford. He returned to Hungary in 1947 and taught at the University of Budapest. He was a radical assimilationist, openly promoting conversion and intermarriage, and was himself baptized. In the 1920s, however, as integration into Hungarian society became ever more difficult, he modified his views. His most important novel, the semiautobiographical *Urak és emberek* (1927), the first part of which was translated into English as *Bondy Jr.* (1931), describes the pitfalls and failures of the Jewish entry into Hungarian society.

Bondy Jr.
1927

III

At the *Realschule* fathers and mothers were lined up in single file in the director's room. Parents who took the occasion very seriously appeared in couples with their young hopefuls. The director, who performed his task of entering the names with the maximum of fuss and pomposity, was perspiring freely in the heat of the crowded room. Bending over his table in the window, he entered each boy in turn in the big so-called classbook, took his papers, and called up the next candidate over the heads of the waiting crowd. He had already dealt with Ludányi Gáspár, Purt Iván, Naschitz Elemér, Samelik Géza, Pártosi Kornél, Kovács Béla, Szende János, Brestyan Tódor, Kohn Károly, Timár Bogdan, Hevesi Richard, Purébly Antal, Marschall Kornél, Ferenczy Árpád, Hajós László, Mandello Bertalan.

And every five minutes, when a new name was called, Sigi was able to move up a step with his father, hopefully expectant of the moment when the director would ask for Bondy Zsigmond. He trembled at the thought of that great moment, but felt its secret fascination. How nice it would be when so many strange people heard for the first time that there existed a pale curly-haired boy with obtruding ears, called Bondy Zsigmond! He prepared himself to face this transformation of Sigi into Zsigmond under the eyes of so many critical observers as if it had been his first appearance before the footlights, and in his nervousness he mopped his forehead and moist hands incessantly with his handkerchief.

On the wall there hung a spotty mirror over which the autumn flies crawled dully. The boy looked at himself. "I'm not really so ugly," he decided, remembering also the words of his pretty Aunt Betty: "The little mite has clever eyes." To make them appear still cleverer Sigi stretched them to their widest before the mirror, forming line upon line of folds on his forehead.

There was only one woman, with golden-yellow hair, with her canary-haired boy, in front of the Bondys now. Sigi followed each movement of the director, the blonde mamma, and the blond boy with intense interest so that he in his turn might commit no blunders and be informed as to every detail in the ceremony of registration. He wished to make a good impression, do it all properly, for he felt that his whole school career depended upon a successful début.

"Platschek Ödön," called the director, summoning the fair-haired boy. Then, turning to the powdered mamma with the unnaturally red lips, he said: "May I ask for the baptismal certificate?"

An odd thing now happened. The golden-haired lady, who a moment before had been looking about her so gaily, stole a glance at the Bondys behind her, became suddenly embarrassed, and sank with a white face on to the cane chair before the desk.

"The certificate, please," repeated the director, politely but dryly.

"Here it is," said the mother in a low voice, handing him the document.

The director glanced at the paper, then back at the mother of the boy Platschek. A mild and serious man was the director, a kindly clever man, bald, with reddish side-whiskers forming a thin stripe past one ear and down to below the chin, where, though cut short, they became bushier, while on the other cheek they climbed sparsely upward to the bald head.

"Come here, my little fellow," he said to the boy, drawing him with his right hand between his black-trousered legs, which were like two large air-filled bolsters, up to the watch-chain which dangled over his prominent stomach. From under his bushy eyebrows he looked into the child's gentle nut-brown eyes with kindliness, though with all the dignity of his office, and his left hand gently stroked the fluffy locks. "You poor child!" Then, holding out his right hand to the mother, he added: "We'll make a respectable citizen of him all the same."

"Oh, thank you, thank you, director," lisped the lady, wiping a tear from her eye.

What did it all mean, Sigi wondered, squinting past mother and son into the class-book, in which the director had just written something most extraordinary and mysterious under the heading: "Name of Father." The word was "Un—known!"

What could it mean? Unknown! Sigi looked up at his own father, the mighty Hermann. Was it conceivable that a father should be unknown, that anyone should not know his father? Before Sigi had recovered from his astonishment, the director had written under another heading: "Illegitimate." Sigi did not know what it meant, but he began to feel like choking. A tender affectionate leaning towards the fair boy with the nut-brown eyes he already felt, but also—he could not help himself—something akin to contempt. Instinctively he knew that this boy was not as other boys. He was different. He did not know his father and was therefore not legitimate, but illegitimate. Yet he was a Catholic, a Roman Catholic. And had a certificate of baptism. That was a thing Sigi did not possess. And that again raised him in Sigi's eyes.

So short a time had gone since the floods of his father's wrath had passed over his head, yet the effect was already fading; Sigi intended that it should. All day long he had been repeating to himself Herr von Szalkay's saying that a good Jew could also be a good Hungarian. But now, in the eyes of the public, in the terrible moment of his first contact with an official paper, he was conscious of a growing certainty with regard to a fact as to which he had had misgivings since his earliest childhood: the fact that something about him was not quite in order. It could be nothing within him, for he lived, breathed, thrived, and grew just as other boys did. The fault must be something outside him, something which could somehow be read from the document certifying his birth. What could it be? An expression of his father's flashed across him: a Jew, a swine of a Jew, he had said. And the safe spot in his heart in which was stored his happy pride in his Magyarism now became filled with doubt and uncertainty. The more he felt this inner wavering, the deeper became the folds on his forehead, the wider did he open his eyes. He even stood on tiptoe in order to impress the crowd at the decisive moment.

"May I have the leaving-certificate from the elementary school?" asked the director, turning again to Platschek's mother, who was drying her eyes. But in her agitation she failed to understand this demand, suspecting a further attack on her private life behind the polite but solemn official tones.

"You have seen everything in the papers. I am a singer. I look after the boy myself. Oh, please, is there anything else?"

The words gushed out as if she were defending herself against all attacks. Then, as if to justify herself, she kissed the child, who stood there like a suffering angel, with passionate emotion.

"I only asked for the last elementary-school-report," explained the director soothingly. Greatly relieved, the mother handed up the report. But at this moment one side of the window beside the table flew open, setting all the reports and documents dancing.

"Shut the door!" shouted the director to the newcomers, who, however, did nothing of the sort. They merely pushed their way unconcernedly through the ranks of waiting parents who were crowded round the table, displacing Hermann, Sigi, and even the blonde Frau Platschek and her son by an unknown father, in order to plant themselves immediately in front of the director.

Then the father said, simply: "Deputy Thomas von Zelnicky of the Reichstag."

"Your humble servant, sir. Forgive me for not recognizing you on the spot."

The director's colourless face had turned red with excitement. His pen fell from his hand, making blots not only on the class-book but on all the papers concerning the boy Edmund, which had narrowly escaped being blown out through the window.

Being very long-waisted, the director looked tall when sitting, but on rising stood revealed as a tubby little man with grey coat-tails flapping over his slovenly trousers. Yet he managed to impose himself upon all who were present when, full of directorial dignity, he gave the order:

"Shut the door."

No sooner had an old woman in black tremblingly closed it than the director turned to the deputy with a face that had lost its fiercely tyrannical expression and changed to one of lackey-like gentleness.

"What can I do for you, sir?" he asked.

The deputy explained that he had come, like any other parents, to enter his son's name.

"Please wait," cried the director to Frau Platschek, pushing Edmund's papers back to her for the moment. Bending over the class-book, but keeping one eye on the deputy, he then said:

"I do not need to ask the father's name. That is known throughout the land. So now, my son, what is yours?"

The smiling question was addressed to the deputy's little boy, who replied in a raised voice, full of self-confidence:

"Thomas von Zelnicky junior."

Meanwhile Hermann was moving about in the crowd, muttering curses, and fanning the general indignation of this unheard-of procedure.

"I have been waiting an hour in this crush," said a pock-marked man angrily.

"The fellow seems to think I have nothing better to do than kick my heels here," remarked Hermann.

"Our deputies apparently forget that time is money for one of our sort," said another man, at the same time introducing himself to Hermann: "Dr. Vida, attorney. You know my brother, I think: Wottitz, wholesale wool, in the Adlergasse."

"Do I know him indeed! Artur, David Blau's son-in-law. Well, I never! Then your wife must have been a Schwarz?"

"Quite right. Elise, daughter of Gustl Schwarz. And this is my boy here, my Schimi. (Make a nice bow to the gentleman.) And this is your youngster, I suppose.

Servus, young man. How old is he? Nine? Mine is ten. Come, children, shake hands."

Little Vida, whose face was almost bloodless, held out his skeleton hand to Sigi, the five fingers spread out like a spider's legs.

"A dear little lad," said Hermann politely.

"Yours is a dear little fellow, too," returned Vida, adding in the same breath: "And how much longer is this to last? Do these people think we have stolen our time?"

"I ought to have been at the Bourse long before this. Who will make good my losses?"

The attorney replied to this outburst with a shrug.

"You see, we live in a country that is under patronage."

It was now the turn of the woman in the black shawl. The deputy had left the door open and she had had to shut it. And she had done so. But not a word of thanks from the director.

"Ha ha!" laughed pretty Frau Platschek mockingly, sending out pungent whiffs of patchouli wherever she went, "he is quite demented over his deputy. If he knew what I know!"

What Frau Platschek knew they were soon all to learn. It was that the deputy ran a flourishing solicitor's office and had a terribly rich wife who had brought him a thousand jochs as her dowry; but that he also had a lady friend, a certain Tertcski Kállay, whom Frau Platschek knew very well.

But the gossiping, dissatisfied tongues were suddenly silenced, for the deputy, who had the vigour of a peasant and the face of a country court judge, had begun to speak so loudly that his private talk with the director resolved itself into a form of address:

"Yes, you see I intend to set an example. The Hungarian ruling class must be reconstituted from the roots. The State is not there to support drones. Not every Hungarian noble can become a deputy or a cabinet minister. I have therefore resolved to send my son to the *Realschule* and subsequently to the Academy of Commerce. I am going to make a merchant or an industrialist of him."

"This fellow talks differently from our moonstruck friend," was Hermann's approving comment, and he proceeded to relieve his mind on the subject of Herr von Szalkay to Vida. But Dr. Vida was of opinion that that sort of people, Junkers and aristocrats, would always do best in the service of the State and the country, "for of what use is study to them when they are born just to order people about and not for business."

The director, meanwhile, lauded the deputy's good example and the new race of practical-minded Magyars. The nasal, dragging speech of the director sounded doubly slow after the crisp accents of the deputy. When the whole edifying ceremony of registering the deputy's son had come to an end, accompanied by mutual compliments, formalities, and bowing, the father and son hurried out, passing down the path made for them by the crowd of men, women, and children as they passed. Sigi looked after them enviously. Of course they again left the door wide open.

"Shut the door," ordered the director again.

This time Dr. Vida obeyed the command. And as, this time also, no thanks were forthcoming, he drew the director's attention to the fact that the door was now closed.

"It is shut. I have closed it."

But the director had neither eyes nor ears for Dr. Vida's services as door-keeper. Still under the impression of the recent scene with the deputy—to him a historical and epochal event—he had the feeling that the *Realschule* and its director had acquired an extraordinary added distinction. He made short work of the blond Platschek, whom he dismissed almost without looking. Hermann and his son now walked up to him. The fatal hour for Sigi, the decisive moment in his life, had come at last, and it was small wonder if the boy felt his heart throbbing in his throat.

The director did not honour them with a glance.

"The baptismal certificate, please."

"What may that be?" laughed Hermann, and pointed to his son. "Does he look the kind of boy to have a baptismal certificate?"

The people in the hall laughed. But the director either did not understand the joke or wished it to appear that he did not.

"May I have the birth certificate, please?"

While the director was inscribing, with fine upstrokes and thick down-strokes, the names of Bondy Zsigmond's father and mother and noting that he belonged to the Mosaic confession, the boy quite forgot to strain open his eyes and look clever or to arrange his forehead in wrinkles. He forgot to stand on tiptoe too. His little face looked upset and intimidated. There he stood with his back bent, dissolved into nothing before the director. The droning of men's women's, and children's voices sounded painfully like derisive laughter in his ears. Oh, the best would be to dash out of the room, out of the country, out of a world in which a little blond

Edmund could have an unknown father, and himself, little angel, be illegitimate, while he, Sigi—his mother's "dear sweet little one" and "sweet precious child," her favourite son, in fact—had nevertheless no baptismal certificate and was different from all the others, according to his birth certificate: for he was of the Mosaic confession.

When the business of registration was complete and Hermann turned towards the door, the people did not make way for him or form an avenue. Quiet sniggers accompanied him and his son as they passed out.

"Let us be honest," said Dr. Vida, who as a baptized Jew felt embarrassed at having the Jewish question brought so brazenly before the public: "this performance was as tactless as it was unnecessary."

"What you call bad taste is perhaps what I call good taste. And what is superfluous for you may be essential for me," said Hermann, with his defiant shrug.

"Usurer!" Vida shouted after him.

"Pettifogger!" replied Hermann from the door.

"Silence!" ordered the director.

Thus ended this duel of chivalry, but the hearty laughter of those in the room rang out into the street.

Sigi trotted behind his father, who strode angrily ahead, with short tripping steps. "Jew, usurer, usurer, Jew": the insulting words hammered painfully at the transparent temples. "It's all over," said the boy to himself, "all spoilt." He bit his lips until they bled. Despair and anger were blended in a last defiance. To spite these people one would have to show them—yes, what could one show them? Why, this new youth who had just been born, at the moment of this first public appearance, though not in very favourable circumstances. This youth was no longer the little Sigi of the Bondy family, but the very famous Siegmund Bondy, destined to play a great role in public affairs. Yes, he must indeed show these people a superb Bondy Zsigmond, a real genuine Magyar boy, whose beauty one only did not see from outside because he kept it hidden within him. Sigi therefore—that is, Zsigmond—Zsigmond, therefore—that is, Sigi—resolved that—he did not know himself what he had resolved. He only murmured again and again between his teeth: "Anyway I'll be first in class."

Translated by Hannah Waller.

Other works by Hatvany: *Ady* (1959); *Urak és emberek*, 3 vols. (1963).

David Bergelson

On a Soviet Sabbath
1928

Citizen Voli Brener[1]

A Moscow snowy morning, sun-streaked and dry. When it falls on a Sunday, the morning shines with a thousand Moscow sparkles—rejuvenating white lights that charm and shimmer, as if there is no more suffering in the world—myriad myriads of diamond sparks.

From inside the precious warmth of his room, Voli Brener looks through the rickety windows—the white cotton insulation and double panes make them look like girls recovering from an illness, their throats neatly covered—and he sees quite clearly and distinctly:

The white-sparkling outdoors are everyone's equally, a warm bosom friend, as if there are no more counter-revolutionaries in the world, as if all the passersby are constantly sneezing, and the outdoors keeps wishing each one of them cheerfully:

"Gesundheit . . . Bless you. . . ."

Brener is in a good mood. His eyes smile through all the wrinkles surrounding his young blue eyes. He feels like sticking his tongue out to the world outdoors:

"Well, well, well. . . . A bit too much salt. . . ."

From afar, from the kitchen at the end of the corridor, the screaming of about six of his neighbors' kerosene stoves is heard, one of them is hoarse and gets exhausted very quickly. It is as if the stoves are saying their Sabbath prayers and are already deep into them—they are even past the *borkhu.*

Voli Brener is still standing by the window and looking outside:

"Counter-revolutionaries," he thinks, "in the thousands, even here, but anyway, never mind them . . . truly . . . it's enough that I have to deal with them during the week. . . . Do I need to worry about it on Sunday too?"

He hears the screaming of the ovens in the kitchen and thinks further:

"Oh, there it is . . . it's almost an entire verse: 'if he had given us Sunday but hadn't given us Sabbath—*dayenu,* it would be enough.'"

Leisurely, just like on Sabbath back in the day, he walks in his slippers to the cupboard by the door, and gets the issues of *Pravda* that his three daughters habitually stack up for him in order—seven every week. He always reads the stacked *Pravda*s for a few hours—not

so much "from cover to cover," but with a sharp eye and "focused mind." Reading the newspapers, he often says no more than:

"Oh well! It's time to read the weekly portion."

As soon as he sits down to read, before doing anything else, he scans the papers for workers' strikes around the world, and he does this with grave solemnity. All hell could break loose around him; he wouldn't pay it any mind or even cast a glance. A week of multiple strikes in capitalist countries was, for him, a week promising good fortune to the Soviet regime and, therefore, to the great business in which he and his three girls have a share. He really feels like the exchange rate isn't rising so much as leaping.

After the strikes around the world, he becomes engrossed in an article that doesn't have an author, strokes his beard, half to the right, half to the left, bites his lips, squints his eyes, thinks and thinks, until he understands, from the topic, who the author is and returns to the beginning of the article with new-found interest. Then, he forgets himself and starts swaying and even singing out loud, just like he used to when he still read the Talmud:

"Ay, ah! . . ."

"So if it's like this? . . ."

"I have to start reading again from the beginning, then. . . ."

"Alright, then . . . Rabbi Yaroslavski[2] said. . . ." [. . .]

As he sits like this at the table and reading, old man Berish Kahan—a formerly wealthy swindler in the forest industry—enters his room. Berish is a strangely big Jew with tired, discolored eyes and with many large pockmarks, which have long riddled his sagging cheeks and his fleshy, fat nose. He has been living the past couple of years here, in Moscow, with his sons, who are NEPmen to this very day. Sitting here at the table, he breathes very loudly through his nose as if he had to ascend countless series of steps to come here, to Brener's room. He is sitting and not saying anything. It seems as if he may fall asleep at any moment now. Suddenly, he begins to talk about his children whose lives may take a turn for the better any minute now.

"Nu? . . . We see now. . . . Before, when they were told: 'Get Soviet jobs,' they didn't want to. . . . Now they would have wanted, but well, well. . . . Who could've guessed?"

The old man is telling exactly the same story he already told last week and two weeks ago, but to him, probably, it seems as if he is saying something new:

"Bad times," he complains, "It's difficult, Reb Voli Brener; it's difficult to make a living. . . ."

"Sure . . . it's not easy."

Voli Brener looks at the old man with young blue eyes and with a deliberate nose. On his left cheek, around the small mole, his hovering charm begins to smile. This charm always helps him get along with complete strangers:

"Tell me, Reb Berish, where is it written, that it may be difficult to be a Jew but that it has to be easy to be a Soviet citizen?"

He is yelling this very loudly, as if to a deaf person.

"I can hear you, I hear you," the old man nods his head and yet puts a palm to his ear, "you can speak quieter."

Voli Brener looks at the old man for a while with squinted eyes:

"I'll tell you the truth," he justifies himself, "it appears as if all my old acquaintances have become gravely deaf in the past few years. . . ." [. . .]

When Sunday brightness arrived in the morning, the girls washed up and put the beds behind the partition.

With lightning speed, immediately after getting up, they took the cot into the corridor and, nimbly, all three of them together, cleaned the room. Always, whenever they had anything that needed to be done, they did it together, even moving a heavy cupboard, and they made it seem as if they were cheerfully dancing, smiling, and playing. In the process, the middle one, Lote, the dark one, gave the orders; she was a Party woman and always had more work on Sunday than the other two; she wouldn't even let them catch a breath:

"Well?"

"Faster!"

"Just look at you, standing there and day-dreaming!"

"Move a bit!"

Agile, slim legs in well-fitting, neat stockings suitable for shop windows, ran around the room clapping in their old, hole-filled shoes that the girls wore at home for the sake of thrift. The beat-up shoes had high, deformed heels, but the girls made them look good. Voli Brener threw glances at them from the side with one eye and saw that he had provided for them:

"Even if you don't have anything to wear, you still have nothing to worry about. . . . May I live as good as you look! . . .You could wear a hole and still be all dressed up, looking fancy. . . ."

They were already moving the heavy sofa and wouldn't let him, the father, touch anything:

"Come on now, we'll manage without you."

"When we need you, we'll send someone to call for you."

"Oh, again he's here! No need, we're telling you!"

With a bent arm, Lote was already buttoning the blouse on her back.

"Done?" she asked, "either way . . . I don't have any more time . . . not even a moment . . . I have to run."

But when the sofa was moved, it turned out that the youngest—the seventeen-and-a-half-year-old, Polye—had torn one of her stockings quite badly.

"Polye," the eldest, the fair Guste, smiled with all her blondness and bent down to see whether the hole was still mendable, "You are so reckless! . . . Aren't you ashamed? You have become quite deft at tearing stockings. . . . Hey, take a look at this, Lote. . . ."

Lote only had time to help with a glance from afar—she grabbed her short winter coat and ran off.

Polye was feeling intensely guilty and immediately pulled the torn stocking off. Her full young, tender leg—it still had to grow and surpass her older sisters' legs in its slimness—was shimmering in its nakedness and remained standing, helplessly, on the bare floor. Her shoulders were lifted in guilt, as she moved her head to shake the shortened hair from falling into her eyes. Her mouth was pouting with a childish charm, which had lingered to this day—the charm of a baby that was weaned too soon. Her eyes were filled with guilt for her older sisters' having to help her out. She couldn't tear them away from the hole in the only pair of stockings that she, the seventeen-and-a-half-year-old reckless girl, possessed.

"I will mend it," she said without looking up and with a strange stubbornness in her voice, "it's ok. . . ."

"You little fool. . . ."

Voli Brener was still looking at Polye, who couldn't take her eyes off the stocking; he couldn't restrain himself any longer:

"Why are you such a little fool . . . ," he said. "How are you guilty? . . . Your leg is young—it grows, and so it tears the stocking. . . . The state-economy today, the state-economy tomorrow—what does it understand? It's no more than a leg, after all. . . ."

"Right, right," Guste mocks him, "When did you ever see a leg going around tearing stockings for no reason? . . . Becoming a counter-revolutionary for no reason. . . . Here you go, the table is ready; you can sit down to your *Pravdas*. I am also late already."

Guste left, just like Lote with no time to put her coat on straight.

So there you have it:

Just as Guste is leaving, Polye has to quickly run behind the partition with her naked leg and the torn stocking in her hand, since, with the appearance of a trustworthy person, who could sometimes arrive late but would never cancel a visit, old Berish Kahan comes into the room. He coughs heavily as he enters, not so much coughing as croaking. Sixty-nine years are leaning on him, screeching.

This time he was sticking around longer than usual, blowing his fleshy, pockmarked nose very loudly, like a languishing in-law who was enjoying his sighing and groaning after a bath:

"Ooh . . . ooh . . . Ah . . . ah . . ." [. . .]

Old Berish was old and crooked like Terah even back in the day when he was still a big shot in the forest business, and when Brener was still his half forest-keeper, half forest-broker. Berish used to walk only with aides, never taking even one step for free. Now he comes here deliberately to say that his children are not doing well and that they can no longer be moguls . . . quite the opposite. . . . And, truth be told, he, Brener . . . his former forest-man, was enjoying this quite a bit. . . .

"Ay," the old man is complaining, "Ay, one toils and toils until one becomes a pauper! . . ."

"And why not?" thinks Voli Brener, looking into *Pravda*, "Why not, really? . . . It's actually fair for wealthy men to work a little for a change. . . ."

"Nevertheless," the old man carries on, "My eldest, Peysi, still has a few roubles left. . . . You could say, more than a few. . . . But it's still the same story when one is just sitting and eating away at those roubles. . . . I mean, really eating them as if they were one's own flesh. . . . He has, knock on wood, a big family. . . . His eldest son, Solomonchik, is gorgeous . . . and he's no lazybones; he found a way out; you understand? He graduated as a doctor under the Soviet regime, no less. . . . Nu? And then what? . . . They won't let him into the union. . . . They say no, and there is nothing you can do about it—bourgeois heritage, they say. . . . He can't have a practice, can't accept a position—no one will accept him. And he's a fine young man, Solomonchik, but he has nothing to do, the poor thing. Gets up every day at around eleven o'clock . . . with—with—with combed and parted hair, sits at the table, picks at a piece of bread and reads the news in *Izvestia*. . . . Reads the *Izvestia*. . . . And so I was thinking, I beg your for-giveness . . . what kind of a situation is this? There is Voli Brener . . . a good Jew. . . . He used to be a servant in a forest that I owned with partners . . . was one of the best forest-men . . . and he has three beautiful girls. Fine girls. He managed to arrange a job for each of them . . . with connections. . . . Couldn't they also find a place for Solomonchik, by recommendation. . . . And, when one thinks about it, there's nothing dishonest about it. . . . Why shouldn't there be a match . . . I mean specifically with uh. . . ."

"With what?"

Before proceeding, Voli Brener must, first of all, put his pince-nez on his nose (he uses it only on festive occasions, as for example on the October holiday, when one goes out to watch the parade on the Red Square). [. . .]

"Now," he says, "it's clear why you've been coming to visit me so often lately. . . . You're looking for a reward for your efforts, I understand. . . ."

He takes his beard in his hand and leans closer to the old man:

"Listen," he says, "to what I am telling you: you've got some nerve!"

Having warmed up, he lets his mouth go:

"This is some nerve and audacity and ugly baseness! Did you ever hear of such a thing! . . . Tell me, I beg you: you used to be a magnate, my boss, and I was a pauper, your man. . . . Fine! . . . You had had a marriageable son, Peysi, and I was responsible for marrying off my sister—a poor girl, Khaye. I am now citizen Voli Brener and have good Soviet children. So? . . . So how dare you come to me and say: take my Solomonchik for one of your girls? . . . How do you get the nerve? . . . Did I dare come to you and say: take my Khaye for your Peysi? Wouldn't you have thrown me out if I had? . . . I'm irritated by your nerve, most of all! Since I've never had the mannerisms and 'virtues' of a mogul, I won't be throwing you out, but I will tell you one thing, so listen well: anything that has to do with my daughters, you should ask them yourself what they think of your Solomonchik. . . . But as for me, then look . . . look, one of them is sitting behind the partition with no stockings on. . . . She was also planning to go to a meeting somewhere and couldn't. . . . She is without stockings. . . . She's my youngest—Polye . . . Polye! Polye! . . . Come here, Polye! Come here, I'm telling you. . . . Come out from behind the partition! . . ." [. . .]

"Polye, come on!"

"Polye, come here, I'm begging you. . . ."

Polye finally makes up her mind and comes out with a naked leg from behind the partition.

"What do you want?" she asks sullenly.

But Voli Brener doesn't want anything aside from her presence.

"You see?" he is showing her to the confused, terrified old man, "Her leg is naked, without stockings. . . . But I swear to you: may I be afflicted before I give her to you. . . . You hear me? Even without stocking . . . even without stockings. . . ."

Berish Kahan is already standing up from the table. He is still confused, his cheeks hanging, his eyes frightened, his shoulders shrugging:

"As you wish. . . . May a misfortune befall me," he says, "May I be damned if I know what just happened here. . . . What did I ever do to offend you? You used to be my man, after all. . . ."

"What?!" Voli Brener is losing his temper now.

He jumps up from his chair, throws both his fists back and begins advancing toward the old man:

"If you don't know," he screams, "that's even worse! I am no longer your 'man'! You don't have any more 'men.' 'And he will be his servant forever' it is written, but even Rashi interprets it: only until the jubilee, until the Soviet regime. . . . And I am telling you, really: if you are still coming to me as if I were your 'man,' then, then . . . get the hell out! . . ."

NOTES

1. The first chapter of the story "Citizen Voli Brener" (Birger voli brener) can be found in *Velt-oys velt-ayn* (B. Kletskin publishing house, vol. 6).

2. Emelian Yaroslavsky, pseudonym of Minei Izrailovich Gubelman, head of the League of the Militant Godless, founded in 1925.

Translated by Alexandra Hoffman.

David Bergelson

A Ten-Rouble Man
1928

A foreign crawling black stain, that's what he was—the kosher butcher—in the new, not yet completed, but sparkling white Jewish settlement. Leading up to the High Holidays, he chastised impiety at every barrack in the steppe and even at the few remote houses, from which the mountains could be seen. At the colonist Gershon Yaroshever's place, where there wasn't any-

thing to slaughter, he prayed at great length and very piously—out of spite, like an angry in-law. After praying, he washed his hands in preparation for food in an angry muteness, very devoutly and very slowly (he brought his own bread, baked long-ago, wrapped like holy manna in a red kerchief in the uppermost pocket, in the vent of his black *kapote*). Then he said the blessings, as if out of spite, at great length, very piously with a sobbing melody, as one does on the High Holidays. He exited the house without saying goodbye. As he was leaving, he seemed to throw something into his mouth with his free hand. He was chewing curses as if they were chewing gum. Without turning around, he left the following words behind him:

"God won't be silent . . . God will not put up with this. . . ."

And a few days later, precisely on the eve of the Jewish New Year, as if conspiring with the butcher, Frume Pritse, Gershon Yaroshever's two-and-a-half-year-old heifer wandered away from home into the steppe. She, along with the white spots on her neck, on her forehead and next to her hard black lips, wandered off for the first time ever and didn't even offer a measly "goodbye," just like an animal would. One could interpret this as:

"The butcher is right . . . I don't want to stay with you." [. . .]

Next to the barrack was a small, firmly trampled, piece of plaza.

On the plaza, around a heap of sunflowers, some fifteen young men and women sat crammed in a circle, as if in a barn. Using sticks, they were threshing out the kernels from the strong, dry sunflower heads. The entire gang was disheveled, bare-footed, more or less undressed, and extremely dusty. All this seemed deliberate, and even if their current appearance was worse than the one they had at home, at least it was different.

Their hands worked quickly and diligently. The threshing sticks didn't ask anyone: "Should we stop or not?" Only glances, many glances, were fixated on the approaching Yaroshever. The closer he drew, the more bewildered their eyes became, piercing through his plain, dusty face, and cutting through his beard.

This went on for a while. No one was in a rush, and so Gershon kept pacing.

Then one of them, a barefooted little guy in patched-up clothing, fourteen or so, suddenly stopped threshing and pointed at Gershon with his stick. His eyebrows shot up. He turned his head on his thin neck and started speaking in a very thin but very sonorous tone, like a heder-boy:

"Oh! Oh! Oh! . . ."

"A Jew! . . . A Jew! . . ."

"On New Year's!!!"

At that point, many sticks started pointing at Gershon. The circle welcomed him with some kind of a strange, wonderfully cheerful and wonderfully noisy "Hurrah!"—the way that a man who used to be king would be greeted if he walked by. The "Hurrah" continued for a couple of minutes or more, periodically becoming fainter, as if coming to an end, and then renewing with a fresh, energetic vigor. The thin, loud voice of the youngest boy, the fourteen year old, was the last to still hang in the air:

"Hurrah! Hurrah!"

Gershon sensed a cheerful reception, a readiness to welcome him as one of their own. And in spite of the sadness in his empty, gnawing, and weepy heart, he managed to squeeze out a smile—not with his mouth, but with a contorted, hairy, tanned, and sweaty cheek. One of his eyes was completely shut while the other one studied the circle, the entire gang, with embarrassment and, along with his mouth, quietly asked everyone, both collectively and individually:

"Komsomol. . . . Ah?"

Someone in the circle couldn't resist answering:

"What you see is what you get."

Gershon couldn't believe it:

"All of you?"

He stood a while, kept looking "askance," and then extended his hairy arm in its torn sleeve. He was pointing at the badly cut beard on one of the middle-aged guys:

"And that one there?"

The fourteen year old, seemingly overcome with joy, couldn't speak except by stretching the highest tones of his thin throat:

"That one? He's a long-standing apostate. He swears that even at home he smoked a cigarette every Sabbath."

Someone added very quietly:

"In the outhouse . . ."

Everyone aside from the girls burst into laughter. The middle-aged fellow with the badly cut beard didn't want them to talk about him, and so he was the first one to resume threshing with his stick.

"Nu, nu," he said, "the day doesn't stand still!" And, he started to sing in a Bible-melody, as if he was a heder-boy again:

"*Veosafto*—and you should harvest, *es tvuosekha*—your grain, *veosafto*—and you should harvest. . . ."

A black-haired girl not far from Gershon's feet—a girl in a red hat and with extremely round, black eyes—wrinkled her forehead. She also indulged in turning to her nearby girlfriend:

"Oy . . . Oy. . . . Again he's singing . . . I can't stand it . . ."

The work with the sticks resumed. In the middle of the circle, with the voice of an elder, a large-boned, energetic young man with an unpleasantly small nose, gave a delayed command:

"Enough! We've been yawning long enough . . ."

And without turning around, he yelled over the clapping clamor to Gershon, who sat down exhausted behind his back:

"Where from?"

Gershon called out the name of his settlement. Lying on his stomach behind the young man's back, he was looking into the steppe's expanses, tired and absent-minded.

"My heifer is done for," he sighed.

He chewed on the words too quietly for the surrounding noise, but the young man half-heard him:

"A heifer?"

Gershon began to enumerate her identifying features:

"Red, with white spots. . . . Out of nowhere, on the eve of the New Year, she decides to wander off from home."

And he began to tell his story from the very beginning, about the departed European, about his brother Kopl, and about the butcher:

"Such a pest, disgusting. . . . Just *had* to open the door with his head . . ."

Gradually, the young man with the unpleasantly short nose began to thresh less and listen more. The urgently wrinkled muscles around his eyes didn't want to waste any time:

"Tell me: do you think that the butcher stole the heifer or enchanted her?"

"What? No! He's such a wimp. . . . He's a cantor also! Right there in the settlement. When the heifer left the house, he was probably already trilling. . . . But maybe. . . . Who knows? Today is New Year's, and I was thinking. . . ."

But the young man was no longer listening.

"Khane!" He yelled out. "Here you go! Yesterday you were craving some antireligious company, like in the good old days. Here's a comrade just for you. . . . Go ahead, give him some 'Agitprop' . . ."

"No, wait, I like this story. Give him here. . . . Here, uncle, take a seat next to me for a while, right here on the grass."

Later, as the sun was setting, close to where the sunflowers were being threshed, they boiled water in old copper pots. They were skillfully hopping under the wagon holding a large barrel, washing their faces, yawning, and rubbing their dusty cheeks. Somewhere far away—in distant shtetls—people were hastily finishing the New Year Psalms, or going to perform *tashlikh*.

Seated with her profile to Gershon, like a woman riding sidesaddle, the girl with the red hat was picking at the surrounding weeds, as if she wanted to punish the earth with pinches for some reason. Her black, extremely round eyes threw frequent glances up at Gershon and swallowed hurriedly with every breath, to save time. Words were falling from her lips with great ease and such skill that not even one of them got stuck in her sharp, white teeth:

"Now, now, come over here. Tell me, you are a ten-rouble-man,[1] right? I ask you, what kind of god conspires to take a heifer away from a ten-rouble-man? And why? Because you haven't prayed on New Year's? Who is he, this sod? What is his name? Bring him over here to us! . . . Do you know where New Year comes from? Listen with your head. . . ."

The girl talked to Gershon's head, but even Gershon's head was now occupied by his heart, and the heart was longing for Frume Pritse. The more the girl talked, the more he felt at home, and the more his heart ached:

"She was red with white spots on her neck and next to her hard black lips, and she had a rare veil, an invisible veil. . . ."

"And the man from Kremenchug said: 'That's no heifer, that's a real lady.' And later he said: 'Do you even know what you have? . . . A well! . . . She will cover you with milk' . . ."

He, Gershon, was very grateful to the girl for speaking. If he hadn't been so embarrassed, he would have told her:

"I beg your pardon for interrupting, but perhaps you know? . . . How much does a cow cost these days? . . ."

NOTE

1. [Ten-rouble-men (*tsenrublike*) was a Soviet-Russian term for migrants who, when they settled the land as agricultural colonists, had no more than ten roubles.—Trans.]

Translated by Alexandra Hoffman.

Ilya Ehrenburg

1891–1967

Ilya Ehrenburg is widely considered one of the most prominent and prolific Soviet writers of the postwar period. Known in the interwar period for his many novels and war reportage, Ehrenburg was a popular literary figure in leftist circles in Europe. Throughout his career as a journalist, he often reported on issues of antisemitism and anti-Jewish violence in Eastern Europe and elsewhere. A member of the Soviet Jewish Anti-Fascist Committee during World War II, Ehrenburg spearheaded a project to document Nazi atrocities against the Jews, in the so-called *Chernaia kniga* (The Black Book), a publication that was not released in its entirety in the Soviet Union until 1980. Ehrenburg's short novel *Ottepel'* (The Thaw), which broke with socialist realist conventions of creativity, was to give its name to an entire political era, the age of post-Stalinist liberalization under Nikita Khrushchev.

The Stormy Life of Lasik Roitschwantz
1928

2

Lasik's downfall did not come because of his name. It was only because of that sigh. Perhaps it was not even the sigh, but rather the economic situation, or the hot weather, or perhaps even certain other lofty problems. After all, who knows, why tailors from Homel must be annihilated? . . .

It was indeed unbearably hot that certain day. The river Sosch dried up before the very eyes of the inhabitants of Homel. On the other hand, Comrade Kugel, the examining magistrate, was soaking wet, as though he had just been dragged out of the water.

It was around seven o'clock in the evening when Lasik decided to pay a visit to Fenitchka Hershanowitch, the cantor's daughter.

Fenitchka sang international songs in the club "Red Awakening." Quite frankly, she became a member of the club in a very sneaky way. For indeed, what kind of small businessman was this fellow Hershanowitch? What did he manufacture? He circumcised innocent little boys for three rubles apiece. The "cell" could have easily found out that Fenitchka lived on the shameful income of her father. The old Hershanowitch had said to his daughter:

"This fellow Schatzman stares at me for ten minutes without batting an eyelash. There are two possibilities—either he wants to marry you, or he wants to send me away to the Northern Narym. I beg of you, sing them a hundred international songs. Perhaps you can make them forget that I sing, too. If Daniel knew how to tame real lions, why should you not know how to calm those Jews? You will see, they will kill me yet, and I am only sorry that I ever circumcised them." I do not know whether Fenitchka's trills softened the hearts of the government committee members, but anyway Lasik heard her and he fell in love, passionately and silently. His name did not disturb Fenitchka—she was modern and broadminded. But the one thing she could not get used to was Lasik's shortness. And anyway what else is there for a cantor's daughter to do nowadays? To dream of a career like Mary Pickford and to dance foxtrots with people who did not belong to the party? With Lasik? . . . I must admit, Lasik's head just about reached Fenitchka's armpit. To be sure, he tried to walk on tiptoe, but that merely gave him more corns. How could he express his ardent feelings under such circumstances? How could he kiss Fenitchka's cheek stealthily on a quiet lover's lane? Even with a leap, he could not have reached her.

If Homel was broiling hot that day Lasik was doubly so: his heart was on fire, too. He had just finished pressing Pfeifer's pants. He got ready to leave the house and in order not to arouse any suspicious thoughts, he said to his neighbors:

"I am going to attend the course of political studies. If you only knew what the Chinese Question is! It is even more difficult to understand than the Kabbala. If I were Schatzman, I would forbid the small business people to occupy their minds with such weighty problems. This should be a matter of consideration and thought for some very high committees, but not for tailors in Homel. . . ." He sighed, but it was not that sigh that ruined him, nor even the next one which came from the thought of Fenitchka's being so unattainable. Today he would tell her everything. He would tell her that David was small and Goliath, on the other hand, a boorish strong fellow, just like Schatzman. He would say that the nightingale was much smaller than an Indian turkey. He would tell her that, keeping in mind present history, a small organized minority can become victorious. He would tell her . . .

He might have surely come up with something to convince even the frivolous Fenitchka, but suddenly his attention was drawn toward the one-eyed Natik, who was busy pasting an enormous poster on the garden fence of the former Episcopalian School.

Whatever could have happened in this big world? Perhaps an Operetta Theater from Moscow had arrived for guest performances in Homel? In that case, one could not help but spend all his money for the best seats: Fenitchka was a very musical person. Or, it could be that they have come up with some new editions in favor of that Chinese manslaughter? Or perhaps that rascal Dishkin wanted to get rid of his stupid, nineteenth century guide for writing love letters, under the pretext of a campaign for enlightenment?

The poster was intended for citizens of average height, and Lasik had to stand on his toes, just as though Fenitchka Hershanowitch would be right in front of him. As soon as he had read the first sentence, he started with a jolt and quickly looked around. Next to him stood a woman citizen unknown to him. A member of the Moscow Operetta? Or was she an income-tax collector? The more Lasik read, the more he became agitated. His polka-dotted necktie fluttered, his diminutive head sitting on top of the indestructible celluloid collar bobbed up and down, the marvelous American atomizer with its miraculous scent of orchids that Lasik intended to present to Fenitchka, danced in his trouser pocket. Even his trousers shook, these exceptional pants made of English cloth (a spendthrift had to leave them behind when he was arrested in a raid after the second fitting). The giant letters on the poster swayed back and forth. The garden fence reeled. The sky shook.

"The proven leader of the Proletarians of Homel, Comrade Shmurigin, is dead. For six long and glorious years, the Red sword in his calloused hands made all international bandits tremble. And even though great men pass away, their ideas remain with us forever. Instead of the one, ten new fighters will appear who will punish all the hidden enemies of the revolution, relentlessly. . . ."

And here it happened that Lasik heaved a deep sigh, loud and doleful, let us say freely, from the bottom of his heart. Was it pity he felt for Comrade Shmurigin, who had died of a twisting of the bowels? Or was he seized by panic because of the ten new fighters that were to follow? Where should he get hold of their portraits? And furthermore, what would their position be toward all these half class-conscious minor tradespeople like him? And the trousers he had failed to declare to the Inspector of Finance, Pfeifer's trousers . . .

After that sigh, Lasik proceeded on his way. But he was not to tell Fenitchka anything of Goliath's infamous demise, nor was he to spray her with orchid perfume from the American atomizer.

Comrade Kugel, the examining magistrate, said to him in a foreboding voice:

"You have reviled the shining memory of Comrade Shmurigin, in public."

"I only sighed," Lasik sighed humbly. "I sighed because it was very hot and also because his sword has fallen from his calloused hands. I always sigh like that. If you do not believe me, you may ask the Citizen, Miss Hershanowitch, and should the Citizen Hershanowitch not be the proper witness because she is the daughter of a synagogue employee, you can ask the messenger boy of the Inspectorate of Finance. He knows very well how loud I always sigh. I might even tell you that last year they were going to force me to quit the union because my sighs were so unbearable to everybody. At night I am preoccupied with the political course and naturally I sigh for myself, but the Pfeifer family insist that I disturb their hard-earned sleep."

Comrade Kugel interrupted him:

"First of all, you talk too much. The bourgeoisie has invented not only the Taylor system but at the same time also the notorious aphorism: '*Time is money.*' With this they express the admiration of the dying class for the miserable increase of material values. We, however, say just the opposite: 'Time is *not* money.' 'Time is more than money.' You have just robbed me, and consequently the entire Workers' state of five most valuable minutes. Therefore, let us get to the point! The Citizen Matilda Pukke stated that you, after reading the poster in question, broke out into triumphant laughter, using an expression that cannot even be repeated here."

Lasik smiled politely. "I do not know who this Citizen Pukke is. Perhaps she is deaf-and-dumb or completely out of her mind. I can tell you only one thing: I am not even capable of triumphant laughter. When I had to laugh triumphantly in the Comrade Lunatcharsky's comedy, I was completely dumbfounded at the sight of the duchess, even though Lewka, the prompter called out at me: 'Laugh, you idiot.' I assure you, Comrade Kugel that if I could use certain expressions and laugh triumphantly in bright daylight on Main Street, I would certainly not be an unhappy, insignificant tailor. I would either lie in some unknown grave or else,

I would sit in Moscow on the most important peoples' committee . . ."

"You are pretending that you have just fallen down from heaven into our classless society. But it will hardly help you. I am accusing you under paragraph 87 of the penal code, which provides for punishment for offense of the Flag and Coat of Arms." When he heard this, Lasik wanted to sigh, but he controlled himself in time.

Translated by Leonid Borochowicz.

Other works by Ehrenburg: *Chernaia kniga* (1943); *The Extraordinary Adventures of Julio Jurenito* (1958).

Shmuel Godiner

1893–1942

A native of Belarus, Yiddish writer Shmuel Godiner spent much of his early literary career in Warsaw, under the tutelage of I. L. Peretz and other leading cultural figures. Godiner supported the Bolshevik Revolution and was associated with the Moscow journal *Der shtrom.* He shifted stylistically from his earlier symbolist work toward the so-called proletarian aesthetic of early Soviet literature. Godiner's novels and short stories, on themes such as the Russian Civil War, the Sovietization of Jews, collectivization, and the purges, were well received and widely translated into Russian before and after World War II. Godiner volunteered for the Red Army during the war and was killed at the front.

A Shklov Moon on Arbat Street
1928

The other day I met a Jew from Shklov on Arbat Street, directly opposite the entrance to the Vakhtangov Theater, and he told me about the moon he knew in Shklov, which urged him to Moscow. The Jew was sitting at a Moscow Rural Cooperative Administration drawer with cigarettes and held a holy book in his hands. All Moscow Rural Cooperative Administration sellers hold books in their hands and read. It passes the long hours during which they must sit by their drawers, and for short periods it brings happiness and sadness, distant and pale light, which shine out from the pages. [. . .]

I was interested to see what book he was reading. I got closer to him and saw—he was looking at his book— that the Jew was holding a copy of *Ḥok le-Yisra'el* in his hands [. . .] and I had the impression that my own father was sitting there, and I wanted to cry out, "Father, how did you come to be here?"

My father was an honest fisherman, a hardened laborer who would sail out on the lake to catch fish in the evening with his net. My father was a pious Jew and would often sit on Shabbat afternoons with *Ḥok le-Yisra'el* in his hands on the bench outside his village home. However this was another life, in another world, a world which has already disappeared. [. . .]

As I child I loved my father. I barely imagined who my creator was, but for me it was enough that he showed me the most beautiful moon in the world. Once he took me out onto the lake with him in the evening. He showed me how the moon rose up from one coast, pale and weak, and along the way grew and became clearer, and the lake shone in its light and bright beauty. [. . .] The same every night. Therefore I loved my father. But if it would now seem that my father had returned from the lake and settled himself here at work with selling cigarettes, I would feel hatred and would not want to know him. I moved closer to the Jew, asked him for a packet of "Extra" and meanwhile took a good look at him, the Jew, to see if it is my father or not.

No, this is not my father. This is indeed a Jew. A fine Jew. A Jew from Shklov. He could also be on the lake, but he sits here, at work. I neither loved nor hated him. But I found it difficult to leave him: in his breast pocket he kept his moon from Shklov and he was selling cigarettes. [. . .]

It's a whole story, how he came to Moscow. It begins with a wife and prison. He lay in the prison, his wife had sent him an invitation from ZAGS [an organization that registers marriages, births, and deaths in Russia], he crept out of the prison. And now he is looking for a bride.

"Yes. Did you imagine that you have met a man of seventy years? It happened a total of forty years ago. We walked about. We talked about the *Der shvartser yungermanshtik* [a novel by Dinezon] and *Yevgeny Oniegin*. We went together to *Shulamis* and *Bar Kochba* [plays by An-sky]. We sang Eliokim Zunzer's songs together. And the moon, my beloved friend, was always the same. [. . .]

He becomes a bookkeeper and she watches him closely and gives him a son. It didn't all happen so quickly—my dear friend—Life too defends itself, it does not submit and a decade went by until it changed. And then another seven years went by. When we had lived together for seventeen years we became a bit cooler to each other, and one starts feeling unsatisfied in a cer-

tain place, considering a Jewess of thirty-five years who doesn't want any more children. [. . .]

"It was all completely normal, my dear friend. A person's life—either it is made up of material trivialities with a God in heaven or it is made up of material foolishness with a demon in the soul. A demon settled in her soul [. . .] she wanted to be a midwife. [. . .]

"A war broke out. There are always wars and—so be it! But when there was a revolution and then a second he became a bourgeois, and was left without a stitch to his name. And she became the provider and she brought new people into the home and new arrangements, and people said: he is sick, an idler. [. . .] People told him to go to work—he did not want to do so. Raissa Samoilovne—one must not write on Shabbat. It's not good for the house . . . we lived together, but terrible cracks appeared in our lives, like a wedge in a log of wood. The children were in the city and we went about like two strangers and angry people, as though in a hostel. [. . .]

"She wanted to go to war. To which war? The Polish war. She wanted to go to Warsaw with Budionny. A Jewess from Shklov conquering Warsaw. [. . .] She was bored and from boredom she could do God knows what. She—a Jewess of around forty—took courses and became a doctor, but not a doctor—a doctor's helper.

"Yes, how she went to war, when the Poles reached Kiev—I don't know. But she came home with a green soldier's jacket, with her hair sheared off. [. . .] And I walk around my own home, like an unwanted guest. I was a Jew, like all Jews, not very pious. I kept Shabbes, but that Erev Yom Kippur, after she came back from the Polish war, it was very happy in my home, like at the home of a fervent Hasid on Simches Torah: people gathered and she became a spokesperson—sitting above and commanding, holding a meeting there during Yom Kippur. And she laughed at me with her green laugh: [. . .]—and you—she said—are you going to shul or to the club? She was always free thinking—her father—a dried-out old *maskil*, a kinsman, a heretic—but before it wasn't like this—to Kol Nidre in the club! What could I answer her? Why are you laughing? I ask her. —It's funny—she answers—my soul was always constrained, but now it has become free. I feel younger, don't you see? And you have completely lost it! You are finished! People told me—that you went to the rebbe, I found it funny—after thirty-five years of living together our relationship is over? . . . and the children are on my side. And I don't even know what kind of doctor to call for you. But I won't stop you. Go to shul and I will go to the club. [. . .]

"I took pity on her and sent a psychiatrist to her, as an old friend, ostensibly. He sat with her for half an hour and then left the room bright red, with his forehead beaded with sweat. She is healthy—he said—there is a lot of it about lately—mass psychosis.

"So may it be; I left the reins. I went alone to the bank of the river. The moon was out then. Alone, I recited the blessing for the new moon. I stretched out a hand and waved hello—hello. It was a clear sign: I had become an empty pot—everything had been taken from me and I accepted this with love.

"I went to the Lubavitcher Rebbe. I told him—Rebbe, what should I do?—Silence—he said—and unite your soul with God, it will be easier for you. And it became easier. I come home—and I find a note—an invitation to go to prison. I go. [. . .] In general there sat young people. With my Shklover luck this time a really handsome man was sitting there.

"What happened to you?—he asked and moved me under an original [painting]—Nothing—I answered him—Where do I sign? Here?—and signed my signature.

"Wait—he said—don't be in such a hurry. You have three months to consider, perhaps you don't want to. Perhaps you want something from the children, the house or the things in your home.

"I have already considered—I answer him and put a period after my signature. And above I catch sight of a little line: And the furniture, and the belongings, in the home of Citizen Beni Hurwitz . . . I add to it: 'everything belongs to the citizen Raissa Samoilovne Hurwitz.' She didn't change the family name—either she liked the family name, or for the children. She got a certificate from the prison: 'Beni Hurwitz is divorced.' And now I am looking for a wife. How can a Jew live without a wife? And the Lubavitcher Rebbe ordered it also. But it's not so easy to find one suitable for me with my ideologies." [. . .]

"Yes, good. But how did you get to Moscow? And why are you selling cigarettes?"

"My good friend"—the Jew spoke softly to me—"I left her for Leningrad; there I had an old friend with a great knowledge of history and languages; I met there the Lubavitcher Rebbe. I asked him:

'Rebbe, where to? Kharkov or Odessa? Or perhaps here with you?'

"He answers me:

'To Moscow.'

"One doesn't ask the meaning. I came to Moscow." [. . .]

So my Jew finished. [. . .] The Jew started packing up to go home, tying a veneer casket to the painted Moscow Rural Cooperative Administration drawer. But something bad happened to my Jew. While he stood bent over his boxes and went to tie them tighter, and I wanted to help him, a passerby caught him with his foot and he fell, his armpit catching the corner of the box, and he remained lying in a faint.

The end was not sad. I had some more dealings with the Jew: something started acting up in him and he couldn't get up from the spot, and he looked at me with the poor, sick eyes of a sleeping man. I sat him on a wagon and ordered it to take him home. He also agreed with me and even thanked me:

"Yes, it happens to him sometimes. It will pass. Thank you, young man."

Very good.

But the Moscow moon hung over the high roofs of the city . . . and the moon from Shklov? and certainly quickly in a corner there lay down to sleep.

In this way the moon from Shklov was a guest on Arbat Street.

Translated by Rebecca Wolpe.

Other works by Godiner: *Der mentsh mit der biks* (1928).

David Khait

1899–1979

A prolific, if minor, Soviet Jewish writer in the Russian language, David Khait wrote about Jewish identity and other issues, strictly following the guidelines of 1930s socialist realism. His writing was marked by frequent praise of Stalin, the successes of Birobidzhan, and the wonders of the Soviet project writ large.

Blood
1928

The train pulls up to the platform, steaming and boiling like a samovar.

Lazar is standing on the platform—short, glowing, joyful—waving his dirty handkerchief at the cars.

The train is on its way to Moscow. On the platform is the usual train station commotion, the ringing, pushing, and smell of coal and sand. Lazar and Ruth are running past the windows—bewildered, smiling, happy. They're looking in the windows as if it were a movie screen, afraid to miss a single movement in a window.

All of a sudden, Lazar stops by a car's steps, his cloudy eyes stare, and he shouts, "Oy! It's them!"

Ruth runs up behind him and then they both—short, old, and bent—scramble onto the top step and reach for the baby with their greedy hands. Eva is standing with the baby on the step.

Lazar looks at the baby's shaggy, birdlike head, sees his plump white body, gazes at his chin and lips, kisses the baby, and shouts to him, "Leonidinka!"

The strangers frighten the baby and he cries, furrowing his father's bluish lips. He puts his arms around his mother's neck and clings to her, his legs slipping in the folds of her dress as if he were climbing out of a bog.

"It's me, your grandfather, your grandpa, grandpa, grandpa," Lazar says, and he tickles the baby with his big, spring-pricked finger. "Ooh you, ooh you, what a big little man. Ooh, little boy, eat, little boy, eat the candy I brought you."

"He can't have sweets," Eva says, wrapping the baby in a blue blanket.

"He can't?" Lazar stares at her perplexedly. "What can he have? What does he need? What can I give him? And what is his name?"

"Vitya."

Lazar looks at Vitya and says with emotion, "Leonidinka!"

Ruth takes a pinwheel out of her pocket, and spinning it over the baby's head, says, shaping her lips into a smile, "Gragra.[1] Oh, what a pretty gragra!"

The baby is silent, entranced by the swiftly turning red and green spokes. His big black eyes look at it whirring, and he reaches for it and smiles.

"Oy! He's laughing," Lazar exclaims, and he kisses the baby on the chin.

Lazar makes kissing noises, as if he were calling a dog, wags his glowing head, and intones, "Ay yay ay yay. . . ."

He picks up the baby, firmly grasps his resilient body, puts the baby on his shoulders, gives a tug, and the blanket falls down, baring the baby's legs, immobile and bent at the knees, like a puppet's. Lazar looks at the baby's legs, looks at the place below his tummy, and shudders.

Lazar's face turns pale, his eyes cloud up, and he becomes smaller all over. His head sinks completely into his shoulders.

"What's this?" Lazar murmurs, looking at the place below his tummy. Fear quivers in his voice. He's holding the baby like a log and repeats uncomprehendingly, "What's this?"

He sees Leah, Eva's mother, as in a fog. She's come out of the train car onto the top step. She's standing by the door, her head bowed, and all he can see is her large, red, tear-stained nose. She, too, is looking at the place below his tummy, and shaking her head, she wipes away her tears and says in unison with Lazar, "Oy vey iz mir!"

Ruth freezes with the pinwheel in her hand, looks at the baby's legs, and falls silent. The baby is looking at the pinwheel and smiling.

Leah crosses her arms like a corpse, inhales through her nose, which makes her yellow cheeks sink in even more, and says to Lazar, "Oh Lazar, oh it's not too late, is it?"

She speaks in a muffled, sepulchral voice, leaning on the "oh," which makes it sound like oh-lazar and oh-its.

"No, no," Lazar replies, recovering a little from unexpected hope. "No, of course not. It's not too late. Can't he be circumcised in a year? That's possible, too. The Turks get circumcised when they turn thirteen."

Leah looks at Eva, at Lazar, and at the people running down the platform as if she were looking at lost luggage. The straying noonday sun breaks over the station roof, floods her with light and warmth, and slides down her drawn temples. Leah looks down at her kerchief, for some reason covers her mouth, and stands on the step stock-still, her head shaking slightly.

The bell rings on the platform. Lazar puts the baby in Eva's arms and climbs down the tall steps, pale and bent, leading Ruth behind him.

"Let's go, old woman," he tells her. "There's nothing for us here."

The train lurches forward. Lazar is standing on the platform, totally at a loss. The train pulls away in a fog, though the day is clear and golden. Lazar rushes after the receding train, gesturing as if trying to catch it.

"Stop and don't tremble," Ruth tells him, holding him back.

"What's this?" Lazar murmurs. "What's this that's happened?"

"He didn't circumcise him," Ruth says.

Lazar listens to these words, as if only now understanding their meaning. In his mind, like the train moving down the tracks, he hears these words: "it's not too late." But it doesn't matter. Stones weigh on his chest and there is a wall in front of him. A tall, steep wall. It shuts Lazar off from his son, Leonid. And now his son and grandson are complete strangers. Lazar feels that something huge, difficult, and irreparable has happened. So huge that Lazar is crushed, knocked off his feet as if by a whirlwind, and this huge thing—new and incomprehensible—has killed Lazar.

"Goy!"[2] Lazar shouts, looking into the distance, toward Moscow. "Goy!"

"I have no son!" Lazar shouts. "And I have no son of my son!"

Only now does Lazar realize that here, at the train station, just now, his son has been lost forever. As has everyone that will ever issue from his son.

"What was it that happened?" Lazar murmurs. "He fired a bullet into our family. And I sired the kind of son who has destroyed our whole life, the life started by our ancestors. How are we going to live now, Ruth? Something has happened the likes of which the world has never seen!"

NOTES
1. [Pinwheel.—Trans.]
2. [Russian.—Trans.]

Translated by Marian Schwartz.

Other works by Khait: *Alagarnaia ulitsa* (1930).

Ludwig Lewisohn

1882–1955

The novelist and critic Ludwig Lewisohn was born in Berlin but came to the United States in 1890. He was raised and educated in Charleston, South Carolina, where he adapted to Southern ways and became a Christian. While doing graduate work in English literature at Columbia University, he was told that he would never teach in an English department in the United States because he was a Jew. His bitter disappointment, as well as the anti-German prejudice he faced during World War I, led him to embrace his Jewishness and become a harsh critic of American Jewish assimilation, a central theme in his memoirs and his best-selling novel *The Island Within* (1928). In Europe in the mid-1920s, to which he had fled with a young woman half his age, leaving his wife behind, he became a Zionist and was analyzed by Sigmund Freud. He was appointed professor of comparative literature at Brandeis University at its founding in 1948.

The Island Within
1928

Book Four

V

They became steady friends and lovers. Better friends than lovers. She adored kissing and touching him; she adored his physical nearness. Her ultimate inhibitions were never quite broken down.

"I suppose I can't get out of being a parson's daughter and granddaughter," she said, wistfully. "The repudiation of the body and its instincts is rooted deep."

He put the entire distance of a room between them and asked her if she felt any strangeness in him because he was a Jew.

"Silly," she said. "Look at Joanna, look at most of my best and kindest friends. I love your Jewish darkness and ardor. I wouldn't have you different on any account."

They were spending a brief week-end in a little inn near Peekskill. They walked along the hill roads under the fresh green trees. He begged her to stay over until Tuesday. She said she couldn't; she might lose her job.

"And haven't you a patient coming?"

"I'd put her off. I think I'll send her packing, anyhow. She's a faded elderly woman who can't get over her loss of sexual importance."

"Did Prout send her, too?"

"Prout has sent no one directly. He's only gone about saying that, to judge from the experience of a friend of his, I'm next door to a miracle-worker. I'd be doing well if I had the cheek to charge what some of my colleagues do."

"Why don't you?"

"I don't believe I'm worth it. I haven't been to Vienna; I haven't yet been analyzed myself. I ought to be, you know. I can't see myself charging twenty-five dollars the half-hour."

It was marvelous to talk oneself out to some one. Elizabeth was a delightful listener; she was a delightful talker, too. That unconscious lyrical touch brightened and softened all that she said, especially her favorite stories of her childhood. Arthur came, through her anecdotes, to know that penurious Protestant life with its hardships and repressions and its faint cool breath of poetry. All summer her father would take an axe and cut the wood for the coming winter. He believed that a preacher should not be divided from his parishioners by any avoidance of hardship or any cloistered ease. He set little store by such slender learning as he had. He was great in brotherly love; great in humility. His pay was pitifully small and the farmers knew it. Their wives gave the parson pound-parties; they brought a pound of coffee and one of tea and three pounds of sugar and a peck of potatoes and sometimes a chicken. Elizabeth thought that the humiliation of these parties had helped to kill her mother. She remembered one fat tall farmer's wife who would seem to fill the little parlor. The woman had bitter lines about her mouth and great red rough hands and a booming voice. She would say: "I think there ought to be a prayer of thanks here for what the good neighbors has brought." And Elizabeth's father would kneel down and pray. Afterward her mother would be almost hysterical. But her father would say: "No, Sister Tompkins has no humility. But that is no reason why we should forsake our Lord by not having any." Little Elizabeth used to lie awake at nights inventing strange and grotesque tortures for Sister Tompkins. . . . Elizabeth would ask Arthur to tell her about his childhood and adolescence. He tried. He stopped. He had so little to tell. He was inhibited from telling her about Georgie Fleming and about the rough boys at the corner whom he feared so and about the scene in the gymnasium in High School. He found that he couldn't break down the inner resistance that kept him from telling her these things, and that resistance evidently communicated itself to much else, so that his words came slowly and conventionally. He tried to communicate to Elizabeth something of the quality of his mother and father and sister and the atmosphere of his home. She shook her head. "I don't get the feeling. I don't seem to see clear." He groped his way as along a psychical wall of glass. He saw that, somehow, there was very little that was salient about his home or his people, that there was something curiously flat about his past. Yet he could have sworn that essentially his father and mother were very much more salient, emphatic, peculiar personalities than Elizabeth's were or could have been. He shied at the thought that his family lived at the cost of constant suppressions and exclusions: the suppressions and exclusions had become habitual, had become, in that expressive phrase, a second nature, at all events. Of that he was sure for a moment. And then again unsure as he suddenly remembered his father at certain moments of high excitement, in that hour, for instance, now far in the past, when the question of Hazel's marrying Henry Fleming had arisen. He found that that scene had burned itself for all time into his mind, and that, in retrospect at least, the figure of his father in that scene assumed something of nobility, something almost of grandeur. An elemental or, at least, an historic instinct had burned in his father on that evening and Arthur suddenly thought of that instinct as venerable and even beautiful. He started to try to communicate a sense of that hour and scene to Elizabeth, and then, remembering that she was a Gentile and might be estranged or even hurt by the story, closed his lips. . . . Her father evidently had not come in contact with Jews; none of her anecdotes concerned a Jew. It was amusing and contrary to common experience that one of his anecdotes should touch on race prejudice and none of hers, that he should be in danger of wounding her with his past and not she him with hers. . . . And that simply showed how intricate and subtle and infinitely vexing the whole problem was. . . . He tried once to imitate his father's English and phraseology for Elizabeth. She laughed a kindly, tolerant, amused laugh. Her laugh appealed to him for comradeship, took it for granted that his attitude to his father—like her attitude to hers—was, despite an element of true admiration, kindly, tolerant, and amused. He found, a little to his own astonishment, that what she took for granted violated a strong primitive feeling within himself. He saw his father clearly enough as a human being with very definite limitations. Yet he discovered now that somehow he revered him. In his character as procreator merely? Absurd. And equally surely not as an intellectual being. As what then? Under what guise? He meditated long upon this point. He went over the past. He discovered that, upon the whole, all the Jews he knew had something of that same reverence for their parents coupled with a perfectly sane and objective view of them as human beings. It seemed to him, too, that Charles Dawson's attitude toward his father was not as wholly unlike the Jewish attitude as Elizabeth's was. Dawson felt his father to be the representative of his people and his family and the historic tradition of his race and house—the Scottish Dawsons of Inverness. . . . Jews, even Jews who had wholly lost their traditions and their pride, evidently still had that instinctive feeling for their parents as mothers and elders in Israel. . . . Funny, Arthur thought, almost fantastic. . . . He must be mistaken in his analysis. . . . Yet he knew that he could never share Elizabeth's affectionate but wholly detached attitude to her father as to a lovable, muddle-headed, funny little man with a brown beard with whom her connection was more or less accidental—a biological accident, say—but to whom she was allied by no deep-rooted and subconscious instincts. . . . He said one day that she had better meet his people and she said that she would love to, of course. But somehow the time and opportunity didn't come and wasn't sought. She failed to seek it, however, not because she was in the least unwilling, but because it did not seem important to her. Not in the least. He, on the other hand, did not press the point because he had a secret dread of the meeting, though he hadn't the least definite idea of what discomforts it might involve. And he was so happy with Elizabeth and felt so much at home in the world whenever he was with her and listened to her talk, which was clear and lyrical and blithe despite her undertones of sadness, and saw the free lifting of her head and kissed her hair, that he was tempted to pray that time might stand still and leave him and her forever in their sweet and secret isolation. [. . .]

VII

Elizabeth was already at home when he returned. She seemed rested and softened. She clung to him for a moment when they met and he blamed himself for feeling even in that clinging the presage of farewell. The child was still in Far Rockaway and so Arthur and Elizabeth were alone together as they had been during the early days of their union. The memories of those early days were here to haunt them with their pathos in the bright, tense, perishing autumnal days. . . . They had dinners out and Elizabeth told Arthur of the renewed impressions she had received of the countryside and the people of her childhood. She thought she would like to spend a rather quiet winter and try to do a novel, a slightly new kind of novel for a contemporary American of their set. Not a book of implicit and explicit criticism and protest, but a sort of idyll, recounting those simple lives of the Protestant farmers from within, from their own point of view. The centre and pivot of the story would be a full-length portrait of a man like her father. She lifted her head in that proud, sweet, girlish way which had never lost its magic for Arthur and said:

"Dad was too dear and pathetic for words. He asked me whether you and I were quite happy. I told him that I was afraid that I wasn't altogether the right kind of a wife for you. Do you know what he answered?" Arthur shook his head. "'You must try to obey and please your husband in every way—especially in this case.' I

was curious and asked: 'Why especially in this case?' 'Because,' Dad said—and you should have seen the utter innocence and conviction in his eyes—'because you might bring him to Christ.'" She played with a spoon in front of her and looked down at the table. "Does that seem very ridiculous to you?"

"Not at all. It was beautifully in character, of course."

She looked up. "Isn't life funny? Father is quite Christ-like. So, in the sense of patience and kindness and not judging, are you. Oh yes, you are! It came all over me—I hadn't seen Dad in three years, you know—how alike you and he are. It's conviction with him and instinct with you. I'm the rebel and the pagan. But I can't help it."

They were silent for a while. He put his hand over hers.

"What are we going to do, Elizabeth?"

"Don't know yet, darling. Do you mind this uncertainty terribly? Of course, it depends a little or, rather, more than a little, on you."

He withdrew his hand. "It's not for me to be impatient or intolerant, Elizabeth. I only know that I seem to be living in a void. And it seems to me more and more as though many Jews are living in a void. Now what they do is to settle down and establish a real home in the quite old-fashioned sense and cling to that and so shut out the sense of emptiness and of not belonging anywhere. I have the same impulse, but it seems that this complete settling down is repugnant to your instincts. You don't need it. You're not living in a void. You belong somewhere and in fact everywhere. Even if you forced yourself to do outwardly as I wish, I doubt whether that would solve the problem. I'm on the edge of perceptions that I dare not admit even to myself. They are so extreme that you would laugh at them. They are so extreme that my father and mother would think that I'd lost my mind; my Jewish colleagues would be quite sure of it. So, you see, I have no more certitude than you have. I have less, in fact, far less. Who am I to be impatient?"

She looked at him earnestly. "I'm a fairly intelligent human being, Arthur. Why don't you tell me what's really in your mind?"

"I will as soon as it is clear and so articulate. Today it isn't. I don't know enough. I'd like to spend a quiet winter, too, and take up some studies that have nothing to do with either medicine or psychiatry. But I want to raise a practical problem that cuts into the root of the matter: How are we going to bring up John?"

She nodded. "Dad raised the same question. But I put him off. He is afraid, of course, that John's soul won't be saved. Well, we're not."

"I am." He saw her utterly astonished look. "You're saved, Elizabeth, because you live in a stream of tradition that is native to you. The stream changes. You don't believe what your father believes. The intellectual processes and assents are different. But the stream is the same. You are an American Protestant. Your divergences from your ancestors are normal divergences within the native tradition of your race and blood and historic experience. But I and many like me have tried to live as though we were American Protestants or, at least, the next best thing to that. And we're not. And the real American Protestants know we're not. And so we live in a void, in a spiritual vacuum. The devil of it is we don't know exactly what we are. Now, to come back to John. I'd be perfectly willing to have him brought up as a partaker in your tradition and have him feel at home in his country and its life as a Protestant American. But I can't help to bring him up that way. And, what's worse, his name *is* Levy and the more of a Protestant American he were in his heart and soul the more disastrous to him would be the things which in a Protestant American civilization are bound to happen to some one named Levy. I don't see all that clearly enough yet. But I see it."

Her eyes were wide. "I think I see what you mean, Arthur. But don't you think you overestimate the prejudice?"

"No, I'm afraid not. Your international literary crowd in New York is no criterion."

A look of fear, instinctive and unavertable, came into Elizabeth's eyes. "You don't mean to say, Arthur, that you would think of having John brought up as a religious Jew?"

He did not answer at once.

"Tell me, Arthur," she repeated. "Is that what you mean?"

"I'm not prepared to go as far as that. I told you that I was only on the edge of perceptions. But your instinctive terror at the very thought is enormously instructive."

She drew herself up. "It's all a nightmare. Can't we all just be human?"

Arthur smiled. "What is it to be human? Nothing abstract. Show me a human being who isn't outwardly and inwardly some *kind* of a human being, dependent, though he were the most austere philosopher, in his human life on others of more or less the same *kind*. There

is no place of *kindless* people in the world. And if you established a colony of extra-religious and supra-national philosophers and sages, male and female, their extra-religiousness and supranationalism would establish their kind and their inner kinship, and, far from having broken up the families of mankind, we would have added but another family—a magnificent one, I grant you—to those that already exist. In a word, this vague cry, let us be human—it's a favorite cry among Jews—means nothing and gets you nowhere."

Elizabeth smiled. "How brilliant you are, Arthur. You ought to write something about that. It would make a gorgeous article."

They laughed together.

"You know I don't write. And, anyhow, what good would that do John?"

"Poor little John," she teased. "Don't let's be so solemn and intellectual about it all. I have a notion that it will all take care of itself in some natural way. As Dad always says, God is good." ...

A few days later the elder Levys returned to the city and the child with its nurse came home. The summer had done the little fellow good. He was sturdier and more vivid. He looked more and more like Hazel. His nose was almost as straight as Elizabeth's. But he was, in coloring and expression, a Jewish child. He had never been continuously with his grandparents before. He had taken a tremendous fancy to them. He wanted his grandpa and his grandma. Elizabeth said with a tang of bitterness:

"Of course he's spoiled. Your mother bettied around after him all day long. I can't quite do that." John was on Arthur's lap. Elizabeth looked at them. "I suppose you think that's what I ought to do."

"No, I don't think *you* ought to do it."

"Which is to say that you wish John had a mother who would and could and wanted to."

Arthur put the child down. "It isn't like you, Elizabeth, to try to pick that sort of a female quarrel."

"I suppose not. But don't be so terribly superior. I must say, Arthur, I do think that that is a Jewish characteristic. It's probably an excellent thing for John that the world doesn't rotate about him when he's at home. Run along to nurse, John. No, you must obey mother. Run along. You see, Arthur, he's very nearly unmanageable." Her face was slightly red.

"What's irritated you so, Elizabeth?" Arthur asked, quietly.

"I don't know. I'm sorry."

"Is it that John struck you as looking particularly Jewish today?"

She tugged at a little handkerchief which she was holding. "I think you're trying to goad and nag today, Arthur. That isn't like you, either. The best thing for me to do will be to go out. Don't wait dinner for me. I'll be late."

He sat beside the child's crib until late that night. He sent the nurse to bed and watched the sleeping child hour after hour.

He did not think; he did not reason. Neither can it be said that he indulged in vivid emotion. He brooded over the child, over himself. He recalled his own childhood and boyhood and its difficulties and he wondered how this boy of his would adjust himself, by what inner means of adaptation or resistance he would adjust himself to a hostile and complicated world. . . . He remembered his own clinging to his father's house, later to streets and squares. John did not even have a house to cling to, only an apartment, an office, a passageway. . . . But perhaps he would not need that sense of protection and refuge; perhaps, like his mother, he would be at home in the world. . . . At home in the world . . . at home in the world. . . . How did one achieve that? His father and mother had it upon some terms that Arthur could not quite make clear to himself. His generation had lost it—he and Hazel and Joe; and even Eugene and Joanna only persuaded themselves and feigned to themselves to have it by a specific kind of refuge in a small and unique society. . . . Where would be the spiritual dwelling-place of his boy? . . . He heard the latch click. Elizabeth was coming. He was glad that she had a little trouble with the key. It gave him time to slip unobserved into his own bedroom. . . .

Book Eight

I

The winter of 1921–22 was the quietest that Arthur and Elizabeth had spent together. Elizabeth was working on her novel. She worked in the evenings and often late into the night. Eugene Adams, whose publishing-house had become one of the most notable in America, encouraged her, begged her to drop all other work, and told her jestingly to draw on him for money if Arthur was stingy. Arthur, closely examining his conscience, discovered that he would be genuinely pleased if Elizabeth were to be as successful as Eugene hoped and be-

lieved. What was it, then, that irritated and chilled him during those long evenings on which his wife was working? Had he not asked for quietude? Had he not wanted time to contemplate himself and his world? It would not be the result of Elizabeth's labor that would annoy him; no, it was the process, it was the labor itself. First his home had been a gate and a roadway. Now it was a workshop. But was it not his workshop, too? That is what Elizabeth would immediately and crushingly have replied. Very true. Had the thing anything to do with marriage or with the fact that Elizabeth was a woman and he a man? Perhaps not. Perhaps no two people could comfortably work so closely side by side, the weather and tempo and aims of whose minds and tempers were so different. Two friends, wholly independent of each other, might leave such a situation still tolerable. But married people were not independent of each other and could not be. Even in the loosest and most modern union, if there had ever been any deep feeling, an emotional interdependence had been established. Fine psychical threads led from one to the other. Fine but firm. One or the other could tug at these threads. Arthur came to the conclusion that for his home and for his work he needed either a wife in the traditional sense or no one. A working colleague in the house, and a working colleague, above all, on whom his emotions and his nerves were dependent—ah, that was another matter. He sat there and the door between the rooms was open and the slight scribble of Elizabeth's pen or the rustle of her movements or her sigh constituted a continuous small rumor that brought him a sense of her absorption and detachment. Was he not, when engaged in his scientific work, equally absorbed and detached? No, not equally detached. His heart was more vigilant. It might not always be speaking; it was never asleep. He worked for the sake, first of science, secondly of his wife and child, thirdly to satisfy the pride of his parents. He never worked for the sake of what Elizabeth called ambition. Not that she was not a conscientious and deeply feeling craftswoman. But what impelled her ultimately, impelled her even to perfect herself in her craft, was neither the craft itself nor any human love or kinship, but something which it would be harsh to call mere self-assertion, but which had in it an element of mere vanity in the sense that it was utterly unaware of the vanity of things. What ailed Elizabeth, as it ailed many women of her type and precise period, was not wholly unlike the thing that ailed so many Jews. She had an inferiority complex as a woman. She needed to compensate. She must vote, write, succeed, be active—never permit herself to lapse for a moment into the immemorial moods and occupations of her sex. She was not racially or historically used to this feeling. It made her hard. Jews were so used to it that the hardness it induced was tempered. They might be ruthless to competitors; they did not forget father and mother and wife and child. Because beneath their hardness was an old, old knowledge of the ultimate vanity of all things except a few fundamental and very simple human things. No, Arthur was quite sure that he was not jealous of Elizabeth's work as work. He was simply aware of the fact that her work shut him out—him and the child—and that his work never shut her out. Thence arose an unnatural inequality, a fatal disturbance of the necessary equilibrium of life. . . . He sat there with his nerves ever so slightly on edge. But when, her evening's work done, she came in to see him for a while, he gave no sign of the exact character of his thoughts and feelings, because he knew that to do so would change nothing and only irritate her and perhaps impede her work. . . . There is no use in demanding what is not given one freely. Pressure never produces a gift, only a tribute. . . .

He himself had ordered for the evenings of this winter some books on Jewish subjects. He had done so with a curious touch of inner shame. It was shame partly of his own ignorance. He had looked over book catalogues and ordered almost at random. He wanted to know, and yet felt, deeply ingrained in him by all the forces of his environment, a doubt whether there was anything profoundly worth knowing. He passed over the few books he saw that dealt with Talmudic lore. That, of course, was mere unhistorical and unscientific trash. Worse that mediaeval. It never occurred to him to reëxamine the Old Testament. It was hopelessly connected in his mind with—*kosher* cooking, not a bad thing hygienically, perhaps, but unimportant. He finally selected the English translation of Graetz's *History of the Jews*. He found the heavy red volumes—physically heavy and unmanageable—hard reading. A German professorial style of the worst type, he thought, graceless and unctuous at the same time. The book also seemed to him confused in narrative structure. So little, it seemed to him, was known of the earlier periods and Graetz tried to make that little big and important with mountains of words. Gleams came to him from the later volumes, gleams of a dim grandeur. But nothing took on life or meaning. Old, unhappy, far-off things. . . . He hadn't even read Zangwill hitherto. He now read the amusing Ghetto stories, but he was afraid that his amusement

had in it an element of condescension. Then he read the same writer's book *Dreamers of the Ghetto* and, though he perceived that it was romantic and had touches of both rhetoric and pretentiousness, yet he got at last the sense of something greatly and richly alive. So there had been Jewish heroes and philosophers and saints in the more recent centuries? So that was the countenance of Uriel Acosta and such the legend of the founder of the despised *Chassidim*? . . . He remembered how once, many years ago, his father had told a story of his early days and had said contemptuously: "Dere vas a little town dere, full of *Chassidim* . . ." Arthur, who was then a child had taken it for granted that these were poor and degraded people of some outlandish locality. . . . He now saw that, faintly enough, his father was the bearer of a great tradition, the tradition of a long and profound battle over what did in truth constitute the spiritual life of mankind—a battle with its martyrs and saints and legends and gospels. And all that had happened no longer ago than the middle of the eighteenth century. . . . And Arthur wondered whether any of his own ancestors had met the Master of the Name. . . . An ancestor of Elizabeth's father had fled and preached and been wounded by the stones of villagers in the early days of John and Charles Wesley. . . . Was it sentimental to feel, as he had felt more and more, the ache of kinlessness and kindlessness? But he had seen the security and, yes, the human dignity, that a tradition lent to the freest minds. There had been Dawson with his Scotch tradition; there was Elizabeth with hers. She wasn't a Methodist, of course. Her immediate ancestors had even left that particular communion. But she was rooted; she continued something alive; she had something to rebel against. To rebel with pain. The rebellion still cost her something; it still had a touch of the heroic, for what she rebelled against was her father's faith and the tradition in her blood. . . . Jews of his generation had nothing even left to rebel against. Oh, it was easy enough for them to join the Christian rebels. And no doubt they thus fulfilled a very useful function. But what they rebelled against was not their own and hence there was no true virtue in their acts. . . . They were terribly poverty-stricken, the Jewish men and women of thirty. . . . Unconsciously they clung and allied themselves to anything Jewish in the world or anything that seemed of Jewish origin: the new psychotherapeutics, like himself, the doctrine of salvation through economic reorganization like Joe Goldmann. . . . Neither he nor Joe had been conscious of the fact that his choice of a profession and a philosophy had been a Jewish choice or, rather, a profoundly human choice in that it is human to share the vision and the appetences of one's own kind. . . . Of course. And the mentalities. . . . Following this strain of thought one got into deep waters. . . . The ultimate conclusion was that Jews like himself who denied any tradition or character of their own were really trying to do a thing that was unhuman, that no one else was trying to do. . . . No one. . . . Not the freest minds. Not the most exalted. . . . Men like Bertrand Russell and Henri Barbusse were pacifists and internationalists and revolutionaries, political and moral, and on a merely conceptual basis one might express their fundamental thoughts in the same formulae. But those formulae would be mathematical, unpersuasive, stripped and dead. What made these men splendid and prophetic was the flesh, blood, substance of their work and vision and these were everlastingly English in the one case, indescribably French in the other. And just as the artist must express himself through some medium—words, sounds, paint, marble—even so in the larger sense human expression is effected through the medium of some national culture. . . . There is no expression in a void. . . . But was not the assumption of his friends, Arthur reflected, that they were Americans? . . . Elizabeth came in, as usual, after her work, as he had been passionately struggling with these thoughts. He took her unawares:

"Elizabeth, am I an American?"

She was still warm and preoccupied with her work. She wiped an inky finger on her hair. "What did you say? Are you an American? No, of course not." She wandered about the room. Suddenly she stopped. "What were we talking about, Arthur? I really was not thinking. I was full of my story. It's going fine. Did you ask me whether you were an American?"

"Yes."

"What a quaint question! And did I say you weren't?"

"You did."

"Oh well, I wasn't thinking. Certainly you are. Oh, but I'm tired. I'll drop right to sleep. Good night."

Other works by Lewisohn: *Israel* (1925); *The Case of Mr. Crump* (1926); *Mid-Channel* (1929); *The Last Days of Shylock* (1931).

Peretz Markish

1895-1952

The Yiddish poet, playwright, and essayist Peretz Markish was born in poverty in the town of Polonnye (in present-day Ukraine). From early on, his poetry was marked by a fiery, chaotic tone and a quasi-apocalyptic cosmology. He spent much of the interwar period in Warsaw, where he was a member of Di Khalyastre (The Gang), a prominent group of Yiddish literati, and cofounded the journal *Literarishe bleter*. During this period, he wrote a great deal of poetry about the pogroms that accompanied the Russian Revolution and Civil War, including his haunting cycle "The Mound" in which a heap of murdered Jewish corpses speaks in gruesome detail. Markish later became one of the most decorated and significant members of the Soviet Yiddish intelligentsia, only to be murdered on August 12, 1952, by the very state he supported alongside other Soviet Yiddish writer. His poetry was widely translated into Russian after his official, posthumous rehabilitation in 1955.

The Workers' Club
1928

Every now and then a different door in the long corridor of the IsPolKom [Executive Committee] would yawn open, partly exposing the profiles of the office workers, emit a hum of muffled chatter and the clatter of typewriters, draw a breath, and shut again.

A young man in a greatcoat, with a canvas portfolio under his arm, emerged from behind one of those doors. An ash-grey beard drooped from his face like a small feed-bag from a horse's neck. It seemed as if this young man, canvas portfolio, ash-grey beard and all, had emerged not merely from a room but from a trench, some sort of rearguard dugout where the Revolution had rallied reinforcements against its enemies, a dugout lacking rifles and bayonets, without cannons in distant, smoky fields, but filled with papers and decrees, orders and typewriters, and a perpetual buzzing that droned up through the windows to the upper levels of the stone walls outside which continued to glare down with hostility and mistrust at the IsPolKom.

And it seemed as if this young man, who'd only just burst out of one room, saw no one and nothing in the crowded corridor apart from the second doorway through which he was about to enter. His face grew feverish and anxious; his eyes gleamed with nervous excitement. He'd evidently been talking a great deal on the other side of the door from behind which he'd just emerged, and though he'd been annoyed and affronted, he'd nevertheless restrained himself. Noticing no one in the corridor, with a resigned expression he now flung open a huge door bearing an enamel sign reading PartKom [Party Committee].

Entering quickly, he approached a red-covered table, set down the canvas portfolio on one side of the table, and said to the secretary:

—Here you are, Comrade Andrei, take back this rag! Give me back my army rucksack!

Andrei, the secretary, turned to the young man with a smile on his face and responded:

—Kopelman! Bored already? So soon!

Kopelman barely heard him. Shoving the portfolio across the table with disgust, he went on:

—You continually carry it from one place to another, and the devil only knows what you're carrying about with you! An order, a piece of paper! Such a tiny thing, yet a whole portfolio's needed for it! What kind of work is that?

The secretary Andrei smiled. Though he was a little embarrassed by Kopelman, he was pleased all the same; he also felt a pang of guilt about this young man from the front line who'd so unceremoniously shoved the canvas portfolio back at him and was now pleading:

—Andrei, give me back my army rucksack! I like a simple soldier's rucksack stuffed with a few underclothes, some foot wrapping, a piece of bread, and ammunition to use against the counter-revolution. That's what I understand! Then I know what I'm carrying about with me!

Suddenly discomfited, the secretary started needlessly shuffling the papers on his desk. Hearing Kopelman mutter the word "workers," he smiled and glanced through the window at both sides of the street below, where it seemed as if one row of walls was toiling uphill while the other slid downhill. Lighting a cigarette, he offered one to Kopelman.

After Kopelman had taken his first drag, he turned to the secretary and said calmly:

—Send me back to the front, Comrade Andrei, do you hear? Back to my division. I'm unhappy here.

He removed the cavalry cap from his head, and wiped his forehead and neck with its lining. Turning his head this way and that as the cap soaked up his warm sweat, he repeated his entreaty:

—Send me away, Comrade Andrei, send me away! I can't stop sweating here. Can't you see?

The corridor was as crowded with people as a railway station. Strangers, bustling beards with bulging briefcases under their arms who'd come from small towns and villages, cooperatives and other institutions; people with suspicious, darting eyes and lips tightly compressed to ensure that no word of the talk, plans,

or news that each had brought from his home to the Party committee inadvertently fell from their mouths; people with broken hearts, closed stores and manifest complaints—all of them moved along the corridor of the IsPolKom. They jerked back the hems of their overcoats when these were periodically sucked in among the backs and legs of new arrivals in the crowd, wiped their perspiring faces, and impatiently scanned the notices and numbers on the rooms, as though these were carriages in an express train they had to board in order to hurry somewhere on business and were afraid of arriving late. [. . .]

Through this crowd, three panting, frightened Jews elbowed their way.

They were Jews like every other; bearded, with winter wadding poking out of their shabby sleeves, with boots and upturned fur collars that looked like mangy cats around their necks. Peering intently about with frightened, feverish eyes, they pushed their way through, until finally one of them stopped a young woman trapped in the crowd to ask her:

—*Tovarishch*, where is the *Yevsek* here? [. . .]

All through the previous week, Jews had held meetings at Berl the carpenter's place to explore different stratagems. A fast had even been called for. They were evidently quite convinced that the blow was imminent, that at any moment the axe would fall upon the neck of the big synagogue across town which looked up towards heaven through its little coloured windows. Soon the knife would caress its brick throat, and there would be no more synagogue, no more Holy Place.

—You'll see, people!—argued Hershl the butcher—You mark my words! One of these days the accursed ones will order the keys to be handed over, you'll see. I wish I were telling lies!

—What do you mean, they'll order?—the others flared up—What does that mean—they'll order?

—And what's become of freedom? Does this mean a Jew can't go into a synagogue any longer?

—And what do the Other Ones do about such things?

—Who?

—Them, the gentiles, pardon the comparison.

—It's the same with them!

—Really?

Berl the carpenter was pale, his beard quivering like a sheet of plywood. Stooped over a plane on a pine board, he was staring through the window into the distance. He saw himself twenty years earlier when, still a young man, he'd been webbed into a network of a high scaffolding right under the ceiling of the big synagogue, installing the new Holy Ark that he himself had carved. He'd spent a long time adorning it with lions, leopards and stags, and the whole town was agog:

—That little carpenter can certainly make a Holy Ark, can't he? Just like for the Temple in Jerusalem. He has golden hands, that little carpenter; may they serve him well . . .

And Berl himself, smartly dressed with a paper dickey, would go into the synagogue on the Sabbath and tap the gilded wood, the glue and the paint with his work-worn fingers and ask himself:

—Eh? It's not cracking, is it?

And later, when the Holy Ark was ready, he came to regard the synagogue as his own personal property. He would enter it like a complete stranger only for the sake of gazing from the threshold with hidden pride at his excellent workmanship. He would also call over the schoolboys in their caps and say:

—Come here, you ruffians! You ignoramuses! You're not supposed to stand right next to the Holy Ark. Look from over here! From a distance, that's where you should be looking from. Just like me, you see!

But the boys, on the contrary, wanted to look at it from close up, and Berl would smile and follow them with his eyes and click his tongue:

—Ignoramuses! Ruffians!

Twenty years had passed since then. The synagogue wardens, the wealthy householders, the state power itself—all had changed utterly. He himself had ceased to be a master craftsman and had become simply some kind of commonplace woodworker. There were no Holy Arks to be carved any longer. Things that had been carved long before were now being broken up. And the Holy Ark, his Holy Ark, was being smashed up as well.

Overwhelmed, he now stood among his fellow Jews and demanded:

—What do you mean—with them? Is it the same with the gentiles?

And he added:

—So where's the fine liberation for the Jews? So where's the fine freedom?

—I'm telling you—Hershl the butcher sounded off—I'm telling you, blood will be spilled! Blood will be spilled!

Every now and then, he wiped his nose with the palm of his hand. After every such wipe he glanced through the window and rasped with resentment:

—If that louse Kutsikl, their special mate, is hanging around here and snooping about, I'll cripple him, that bastard!

It was then, into the very middle of this gathering, that a young man in a greatcoat with a canvas portfolio under his arm made his way. Instantly, silence descended. Berl the carpenter gestured for quiet with the plane to his mouth:

—*Sha*! I think he's here again.

Those assembled immediately broke off what they were saying:

—The boss of the town!

—The governor!

—The fine Jew!

—The *tovarishch*!

The man who'd just entered glanced around briefly, passed through the carpenter's workshop and asked:

—Which of you comrade workers here is the warden of the synagogue?

The Jews immediately exchanged glances. Some nodded at Berl the carpenter while others shook their heads.

But Berl, pretending not to understand, tried to interrupt:

—*Sha*! Of what synagogue?

—Of this one, of the big synagogue here—answered the newcomer in the greatcoat, glancing at the contents of his canvas portfolio, and then repeated:

—Yes, yes, of the big synagogue!

Berl the carpenter cast a resolute glance at all the Jews around him and, as though he'd been stripped naked, he stammered in embarrassment:

—Well, well! I'm the warden, if you can call it that! A fine warden, indeed! A warden's shadow! Nowadays . . .

Silence intensified in the warden-carpenter's workshop, the same sort of silence that always precedes a storm. Each of the assembled Jews instinctively turned away, looked in a different direction, and waited. It seemed as though they'd all tensed their backs in preparation for this announcement to fall. But the young man in the greatcoat was in no hurry. He sat down, pushed his cap a little higher up on his head, laid the portfolio on his knee, took from it a piece of paper, and, having first read it through, as though to reassure himself that it was indeed the same order and that everything in it was as it should be, he slowly began:

—Therefore, according to the decision of IsPolKom . . . yes, IsPolKom—he glared around the gathering before scanning his piece of paper in search of the place at which he'd paused—yes, IsPolKom, the big synagogue, on Broda Street, is to be requisitioned for a workers' club.

He took a deep breath, inhaling, together with the air, the numb distress of all those assembled, and continued:

—The warden, Comrade Berl the carpenter, is directed by IsPolKom to hand over the keys.

For a while longer, he skimmed through the printed page as though in his opinion something was missing from it, and then, extending the paper towards those gathered round, he concluded, with his head half raised:

—Here is the order!

In the workshop, the pieces of unfinished furniture seemed suddenly to bond together of their own volition. The glue groaned. Sawdust rose into the air. The sweet shavings from the pine planks tickled Comrade Kopelman's nostrils, and he was the first to break the strained silence with a sneeze that echoed round the room.

—May he burst!—thought Hershl the butcher, leaping to his feet shouting:—What? What did he say he wanted to do with a Holy Place?

And then loud cries broke against the walls:

—Panhandlers! Plunderers! It's not a club they want to make, it's a grave!

Berl the carpenter put his hand to his mouth as a signal for silence, and turned amicably to the young man in the greatcoat:

—You're *Tovarishch* Kopelman, aren't you?

—So?

—Listen here, *Tovarishch* Kopelman, we're artisans. Simple artisans. As you can see.

Every now and then he took a breath and pleaded:

—Don't interrupt me! Only don't interrupt me! Talking's hard for me. I don't like talking. As you can see.

And he stumbled on:

—And we've been in this synagogue for a long time. And we're no strangers here. We've carved that Holy Ark there. D'you hear that?—The Holy Ark! Twenty years ago now. Even before the last tsar's time. And now there's freedom, Comrade Kopelman—you yourself are part of that freedom. So you tell me now, where was it ever heard that one Jew tells another Jew . . .

He glanced at the men all around him, keen to see how they were reacting to his words, but finding each with his head turned in a different direction, he suddenly lost the thread of what he was saying, which he thought he'd begun so well, and overcome with guilt,

was now ashamed to look either at his audience or at Kopelman.

Comrade Kopelman was aware of the intense hatred towards him emanating from those assembled. From the start, he'd known that this requisition wouldn't be easy. He'd expected it. He expected anything from this element. And he was prepared for it. He, Comrade Kopelman, never accepted an assignment unprepared. Only for a moment did he feel again the weight of insult that had oppressed him ever since he'd returned from the front, ever since he'd been forced to drag himself about here in the rear with this canvas rag under his arm.

—Well, what was he supposed to do?—he wondered sadly—Was he supposed to stand up and tell these benighted petits-bourgeoises, these backward artisans, something along these lines:

—Now listen here, you! Do you know what a Revolution is? Do you know what the class struggle is? Do you know what mass consciousness is? Do you know what four years of civil war signify? Do you know what it means to lay foundations under the cause of freedom? Do you know . . . do you know . . . do you know . . .— and was he supposed to ask them a few other, similar questions so that they'd recognize how he, Comrade Kopelman—he who'd gone through the Revolution and the civil war in the front line of various battles—how he was demeaned because he had now to haggle with them over so trivial a matter, one that was necessary for the Revolution in general and for mass consciousness in particular—eh? Was he supposed to tell them all this?

Yet instead of challenging them with a list like that, he regarded them all with pity, and, holding back his sadness, asked very calmly:

—Well, well, comrade workers, do you recognize Soviet authority?

Berl the carpenter sensed that all this had something to do with state power, and in the name of all the people assembled in the house he stammered:

—What do you think, Comrade Kopelman? Do you think we're not in favour of freedom? That we're not workers?

Hershl the butcher kept pinching him in the side and glaring at him with his butcher's eyes, but Berl pretended not to notice and went on:

—What do you mean, Comrade Kopelman, what do you mean? What else?

—Well, well,—said Kopelman, closing the canvas portfolio quite calmly, as though the keys were already in his pocket—well, well, if that's the case, read the order and hand over the keys to the synagogue. If you refuse, tomorrow you'll have to bring them to the IsPolKom, to the *Yevsektsiia*, to Comrade Rosen.

With these words Comrade Kopelman departed, leaving behind him in the workshop a heated, dusty hubbub, great agitation, and frightened, exasperated people.

The men were outraged, their fists clenched in their pockets. Hershel the butcher's beard and eyes seemed to kindle into fire. He rushed into the workshop shouting:

—There won't be any keys! There won't! Blood will be spilled! We'll all lie down beside the *shul* with our wives and children and scream "Unjust"! We have freedom, don't we? A fine freedom this is! Let it all burn down together with Kopelman!

—*Sha*!—Berl the carpenter was already angry at the butcher—Don't yell! You're not being murdered! *Sha*! We'd better handle matters calmly! People—he turned to the assembly—people, listen. Let's go as a deputation to the *Yevsek*. A deputation of workers. Workers have influence on today's authority. We'll give him to understand in plain Yiddish. He's a Jew, that *Yevsek*, isn't he? He has some kind of Jewish heart. And we have freedom, don't we? It'll save the *shul*. And the High Holy Days are drawing closer now. We'll handle everything calmly. You'll see, we'll manage everything. We're workers!

The men reflected, considered the matter thoroughly, and saw the sense of this. At the same time they felt somewhat disheartened and therefore less inclined to shout. Only their mouths kept opening and shutting and words scattered like the last shavings from under a plane:

—Keys! Hand over the keys! Nothing less will do! Bosses over us! Go and make clubs!

It was already Friday afternoon. They rushed through all the Sabbath services as though they were about to charge off somewhere. They swallowed Sunday like prescription medicine, and barely endured until Monday.

And that Monday morning, all three of them went as a deputation to the *Yevsek*. [...]

Behind the door of Room Number 24, which bore the enamel sign NatsMen, Comrade Rosen was seated at a desk piled high with mounds of papers.

Keeping one eye fixed on the documents, he used his other eye to deal with his visitors.

Among these heaps of papers was a plan for a workers' club to be created by converting the big synagogue on Broda Street. Rosen was pushing for the official opening to take place on the first of May.

He instinctively glanced at the calendar and mentally started counting off the days that still remained until then.

From under dozens of calendar pages, the red numeral "one," denoting the first day of May, flashed before his eyes like a flame. He pictured to himself the former reading desk in the big synagogue on Broda Street transformed into a platform draped with red flags. On each flag there were golden slogans, each letter mounting higher and higher, and on the eastern wall itself hung a semicircular sign:

"Workers of the world, unite!"

And he, Rosen, would turn to the workers with an opening speech:

"Comrade workers! Hmm . . . Our town, one can say . . . yes . . . the former bastion of nationalism and chauvinism . . . well, yes . . . is not lagging behind in its revolutionary *Kulturkampf*, so to speak, and . . . well, yes . . ."

Just at that moment he found it difficult to patch together the whole speech he'd be obliged to give at the opening, but he'd more or less understood and memorised its principal theme. His forehead was glistening, and a dry cough made him avert his head from the calendar where the flaming red, festive numeral "one" denoting the first day of May flared under several pages. He lit a thin cigarette and turned to the adjacent desk.

—Comrade Bella! Comrade Bella!—he called to the typist a second time—Ring Comrade Kopelman. Ask him about the keys. Yes, hmm . . . and when's the work going to begin? Give me the receiver; I want to speak to him myself.

Comrade Rosen took the receiver, transferred it from one ear to the other, and blew into it:

—Is that you, Kopelman? . . . Well? . . . Yes . . . Well, well . . . Indeed? . . . Refused? . . . Well, well? . . . Good . . . They'll be here? . . . Good . . . Very well, then . . . Yes! But you hire the workers. Yes, we've only got a few days left until the first . . . All right, good, yes, Kopelman, I'm leaving today. It's all up to you now. Well then, good! . . .

Only after Rosen had replaced the receiver did he remember that he'd wanted to tell him something else. Yes. That Kopelman should keep him informed. He even wanted to tell the typist Bella to ring Kopelman again, but his head was drawn from the telephone by six frightened, feverish eyes piercing him like hot forks. All three Jews were standing next to his desk, and all three began speaking at once:

—Comrade *Yevsek*! Comrade *Yevsek* . . .—and then they immediately stopped as though overwhelmed by the heavy burden of their presentation.

Instinctively, Comrade Rosen tapped the plan of the club he'd been studying all morning and began helping the Jews out of their embarrassment:

—You're from . . . hmm . . .—he waited for them to answer for themselves, making a strenuous effort to prevent even the slightest smile from crossing his face, which was growing ever more grand and serious.

Berl the carpenter coughed, wiped the sweat from his wrinkled neck and placed two red, blood-swollen stubby fingers on the edge of Rosen's desk. Hershl the butcher and the shopkeeper Kurman nodded agreement behind him, despite not yet knowing what the carpenter was about to say.

—You understand, Comrade *Yevsek*, we few Jews have come . . .—with his eyes Berl indicated the butcher and the shopkeeper, the two deputies who'd accompanied him, and saw them nodding their head and repeating:

—Jews, Jews . . .

—And Jews—Berl the carpenter continued—have Jewish hearts . . .

—Good!—said Hershl the butcher, poking the shopkeeper—Quiet, he's speaking well.

—And the slaughtering knife is at our throats, Comrade *Yevsek*, and . . .

Rosen reached out, needlessly dipped his pen into the ink, and scribbling various ciphers on the red blotting paper covering his desk, interrupted in his low baritone:

—Hmm . . . what exactly do you want to say?

In company with two other women, the housewife from whom the three deputies had earlier enquired about the *Yevsek* was by now also standing in the room behind Hershl the butcher, blowing her nose on her sleeve and tearfully shaking her head at Berl the carpenter's speech:

—May God only be as merciful as he's speaking well, that Berl!

—May God only annul this evil decree in the same way,—the other women wailed.

—I don't know what you want.—Comrade Rosen finally stood up, but then abruptly sat down again.

—Stop swaying backwards and forwards! You're not praying in a *shul* here! Say what you want to say!

The men glanced round at one other. Their cheeks were as red as though they'd only just emerged from the bathhouse.

—We've come—Berl the carpenter began, again dragging out his words as though pulling a heavy cart—a whole deputation of Jews, to beg you, Comrade *Yevsek*, to have mercy and revoke the evil decree . . .

And Hershl the butcher rounded off his speech for him:

—Such an evil decree upon Jews! Upon a Holy Place, poor thing!

Comrade Rosen stared at them in utter bewilderment; in more bewilderment than was appropriate considering the menace of the issue, and interrupted:

—What? About the club?

Silence instantly fell. The men moved slightly away from the desk and shuffled closer to one another. Hershl the butcher pinched Berl the carpenter from behind:

—Go on, Berl, or let me do it. You hear, he's already said "club." Speak, Berl, speak!

But the carpenter trod on the butcher's foot to silence him.

Comrade Rosen bustled round to the other side of his desk, picked up the plan of the club, and waving it in the air, called out:

—Listen, comrades, I don't have much time to talk with you, and anyway, there's nothing to talk about. It's a decision of the IsPolKom. And what does it matter to you people, that there's going to be a club? Is anyone taking the *shul* away from you? It's only being converted! And for whom, if not for you? It's being done for your benefit. And you? . . .

—That's supposed to be a benefit?—all the Jews interrupted at once—You call desecrating a Holy Place a benefit?

This tête-à-tête made Rosen catch his breath. His cheeks flushed a little. From the pack in his trouser pocket he took out a thin little cigarette and having filled his lungs with some sweetish, choking smoke, he coughed out:

—Quiet! Don't speak all at once. One at a time.

An idea suddenly struck him. And this idea—it occurred to Rosen—would be the perfect bait with which to catch them.

—Listen—he asked them once again—answer me. — He glanced at each of them in turn as he put the question: —You, and you, what's your occupation?

—What d'you mean, me? I've been a carpenter all my life—answered Berl, not knowing whether he was supposed to answer this way or not.

The men sensed that the *Yevsek* was setting a trap for them but they couldn't work out what it was.

—And you?—Rosen turned to the next one.

—What, who? Me? Don't you know? A butcher!

—For whom do you work?

—What do you mean, for whom? —they pondered in embarrassment, clearly feeling the *Yevsek*'s hook already firm and jerking in their gullets. —What do you mean, for whom? For the sake of the work!

—Does that mean—Rosen made it easier for them—does that mean, for yourselves?

—Hmm?

—What's "hmm"?

—Hmm?

—Don't you dare hum here!—Comrade Rosen started growing angry. —Does that mean you're . . . hmm . . . Wait a moment . . . Do you employ people to work for you?

—Who? We work on our own.

They stretched out their hands and yelled at him:

—We work by ourselves with our own hands!

Rosen sensed that his scheme had failed but, unwilling to abandon it, he tried starting all over again:

—If that's the case, does that mean you're workers? Eh?

All suddenly murmured like rushes ruffled by a breeze:

—Workers?!

—Does this mean that you workers refuse to carry out the order of the IsPolKom!

—Who?

—Does that mean you're—Rosen was already bearing down on them—counter-revolutionaries? Does that mean you're on the side of the rabbis hand in glove with all the exploiters and clericalists that Soviet power is fighting? . . .

He hastily shuffled the papers on his desk as though he needed quickly to document his words and a hullabaloo broke out among the Jews.

The wanted to retreat as though from cannon fire under the pressure of Rosen's every word; but their retreat was blocked by the cluster of women standing behind them, women in shawls and men's boots who turned every now and then to ask:

—What did Reb Berl say?

—What did he say, can you see, eh?

—*See-shmee*! Don't get in our way, women. Is this your business? Go!

But the women would not give way and kept on asking:

—So what's happening? Will he give the *shul* back, eh? Reb Berl, why are you so angry? We're not to blame.

And Comrade Rosen's words, loud and commanding, echoed through the whole room:

—Workers, clericalists, rabbis, exploiters . . .

The whole deputation was impressed by the *Yevsek* with the Jewish heart. They didn't understand what it all meant, and they didn't know how to answer. Only Hershl the butcher, with his face half turned towards the door, furiously demanded of the other two men:

—Deputies! Deputies! And Berl, their great leader! Well, have you got the *shul* back yet? You can say *Kaddish* for the *shul* already!

All this time, Comrade Rosen pretended to be occupied with other matters, yet he nevertheless found time to remark to the deputation:

—So, you should go and hand over the keys to Comrade Kopelman right away. Hm . . . yes . . .—and he added hastily:

—Comrade Bella, ring up Kopelman straight away. [. . .]

Comrade Kopelman and Comrade Bella the typist wandered around the tall stone building of the big synagogue on Broda Street contemplating the soon-to-be workers' club.

A melancholy darkness from empty nests under high roofs and windows and the damp reek of mouldering, worn old leather bindings floated out of every crack in the huge old building.

The synagogue stood gazing across the roofs through its diamond-shaped coloured Venetian glass windows and mused, as though it had been given time to ponder and review the event that was to occur within it, and would soon have to give an answer to that young man in the greatcoat, to Comrade Kopelman.

But still it went on pondering, this old synagogue building, and could come to no decision. Today, the diamond-shaped coloured panes of its aristocratic Venetian glass windows glimmered a little more sadly than usual in the setting sun. Today they more closely resembled inflamed eyelids over the eyes of a sick old man or the lenses of tinted spectacles that turned the world green, red, and multicoloured.

Shaded in the depths of the distressed old eastern wall was the Holy Ark, concealed behind an ancient velvet curtain as though a mourner's black veil had been cast over its face.

The doors of the Holy Ark had been masked behind this black velvet curtain for several years, from the time insurrectionists and followers of Petlyura had burst into the synagogue and burned the Torah scrolls. For a long time after the burial of what fragments remained of these scrolls, people maintained that their letters had flown up into heaven with the flames, just like living souls. And from that day on, the curtain behind which the Holy Ark was shielded from view had never been replaced with a coloured one. From that time on, no decoration could possibly conceal the grief of the eastern wall.

Soughing like autumn leaves within the deep folds of the black mourning velvet that shrouded the face of this eastern wall were the petrified screams of Jews, old Jews who'd been slaughtered on the same day on which the Torah scrolls had been set alight.

Never had the Holy Ark been so illuminated as on that day when the flames rose from the ancient, wrinkled parchments. In the blink of an eye, the gilded lions and stags had turned flaming red, and their rubescence had flowed over the entire melancholy hollowness of the old synagogue and up over the murderous faces of the bandits.

Then in terror the bandits noticed the finely fashioned antlers of the stag that Berl the carpenter had carved for the Holy Ark, and as they took to their heels they yelled out:

—Brothers, smash the horns of the Jewish God! Smash them!

From that time on, the stag on Berl the carpenter's Holy Ark in the old synagogue had been deprived of its antlers. Afraid to break anything more, the bandits had fled from the synagogue.

That was the last time the Holy Ark had been illuminated in flaming red.

When Berl the carpenter entered the synagogue a few days later, he glued back the wing of the eagle that now hung from the Holy Ark as though it had been shot down, and he caressed the head of the stag, murmuring:

—It's hopeless . . .

—It's difficult to get hold of a piece of wood like this nowadays. Very difficult . . .

—Hopeless . . .

Thenceforth the velvet mourning cloth had shrouded the Holy Ark, and its creases enfolded the petrified cries of slaughtered old men. So it hung, waiting to be torn down, for the Holy Ark to be broken up, for many lights to be lit and much fire to be kindled, so that it might grow drunk from light and throw off its sorrow and melancholy.

Comrade Kopelman wandered around with the typist, Comrade Bella, examining the old synagogue building from the outside, every now and then enquiring of his companion:

—Do you see?

The old nocturnal birds that kept their nests in the eaves above the windowsills repeatedly circled the synagogue like the dark, winged thoughts of this old Holy Place and had no desire to rest. The night spread itself over the synagogue like a shabby black prayer shawl over the head of a worshipper, enfolding it completely. And only then did the synagogue seem as though it had finally abandoned hope:

—It's all the same! Do as you wish with me! [. . .]

Stretched out and motionless, the synagogue allowed itself to be examined, measured, examined like an old reserve soldier at a military medical, waiting for the young man in the greatcoat to say:

—Fit for service!

And Comrade Kopelman went on giving the typist, Comrade Bella, the benefit of his great architectural expertise:

—The Holy Ark will be handed over to the local drama circle. But you appreciate . . .—Kopelman continued as though to himself, falling into a reverie.

Fresh, bathed in cool moonlight, the evening settled round the town, and the bare, winter branches of the municipal trees creaked loudly and joyously, sensing the coming of spring.

Kopelman and Bella strolled on unhurriedly. Every now and then Kopelman would transfer his canvas portfolio from under one arm to under the other and ponder.

—What are you thinking about now, Comrade Kopelman?—enquired Bella. —Tell me!

Kopelman gazed deep into the blue vastness of the pre-spring night, and remarked into those depths:

—I'm thinking about solutions, Comrade Bella. Solutions that have to be implemented in this club.

Bella lowered her head a little. She certainly hadn't expected an answer like that. She wanted to snap back at Kopelman, to make him ashamed of his constant preoccupation with the devil only knew what. She suddenly felt a strange hatred towards the synagogue, towards the club, and towards everything that wrenched Kopelman away from her. She wanted to tell him:

—Always solutions. Solutions day and night. Why didn't he think up a solution for himself, for her, for . . . well, just for . . .

But Kopelman interrupted her brooding:

—I've been thinking about solutions ever since I've been fighting this battle. I've already considered some, but they seem too military to me.

He smiled shyly at Bella:

—I still think like a military man, Comrade Bella. And here one needs different solutions, building solutions . . .—and he fell into a reverie once again.

In this way they wandered all over the synagogue. Bella kept both hands in the pockets of her overcoat. The man's hat covered the evident insult that flooded her hot, angry face. In several places Kopelman tested the walls with the heels of his boots; beating his foot against the old stones of the synagogue wall, he tapped out his speech:

—It might be, Comrade Bella, that we'll have to take it by storm!

Bella smiled bitterly:

—Oh, stop talking about your storms and your synagogues, Comrade Kopelman. I'm already a little bored with them.

Kopelman, however, paid no attention to what she said and went on calmly:

—This is quite obviously a stubborn element, Comrade Bella. One might describe it as a *kulak*, a closed fist! And now the whole thing's become a matter of political strategy.

Bella's blood boiled. She felt that any moment she would turn round to him and say:

—Good night, Kopelman, good night! You can stay with your synagogues, your storms and your political strategies! I don't need them! Keep them for whomever you wish!

But Kopelman's composure, and his concentration on this big old stone building which he'd been circling all this time like a cunning and ravenous animal, this deep-rooted composure spoilt her desire to tell him anything. On the contrary, she remembered the calm, determined look on his face during meetings, and felt a strength in him that she was unable to resist. Her eyes shone, and a warmth spread over her whole face; suddenly, and unexpectedly even to herself, she said in a vaguely apologetic voice:

—You know, Comrade Kopelman, you have this thing . . . well . . . how can I express this?—You have a nature that one might call masterful . . .

—Proletarian!—Kopelman wanted to correct her.

Instead he simply transferred the canvas portfolio from under his right arm to under his left, and with the restrained, sceptical smile of one who despises praise, he remarked indifferently:

—Well, Comrade Bella, what is it you don't understand?

—Dictatorship of the proletariat!

They walked on. Fortified by Bella's confession, Kopelman suddenly felt that the night tasted like spring and found the breeze warm and rousing. He noticed that clusters of Bella's blonde hair poked out from under the man's hat she wore; that Bella's delicate hands had elongated fingers; and that everything was good, quite simply good. And the whole starry sky, it seemed, was itself a sparklingly comprehensible solution. Quite suddenly the whole synagogue together with the executive order, the Jews and the workers all disappeared. He wanted to shout out loudly into the night, to howl out of himself, like an animal, the four long years of war, the railway cars, the trenches, and the long, hard nights of marching across fields and swamps. He felt like lifting his foot and kicking the old stone synagogue with his boot:

—Take that! No more, Kopelman! No more! Kopelman's no longer at the front! Kopelman's a human being! An ordinary, living human being!

He felt the urge to take his ragged portfolio, sling it into the windows of the old synagogue, and scream:

—Here you go! Choke on the order!

Overwhelmed with emotion, angry and heated, he leaned towards Bella and said:

—Do you understand, Comrade Bella, do you understand, today is . . . such a night . . . today, it's so pleasantly warm . . . and today I must . . . I must have the keys to the synagogue in my hands! Yes. Do you understand?

He found it difficult to disrupt his mood, that wild, sweet, drunken excitement which had already enmeshed him in the intoxicating web of the fresh, spring night. But now he was already talking more firmly, peremptorily, like one in command:

—Today, Comrade Bella, absolutely! And tomorrow I'll begin the renovation. I still have to telegraph Comrade Rosen about this today, and start preparing myself for the opening. The first of May is very soon, Comrade Bella.

—Very soon! [. . .]

Twice that evening Comrade Kopelman, the PartKom club-commission's inspector, had bidden goodnight to

Comrade Bella, the typist from the *Yevsektsiia*, and he evidently felt that he'd have to say goodnight to her several times more before he could finally depart.

He found it difficult to clarify even to himself what was actually confusing him. What could it be?

Was it the fresh, mild warmth that streamed from Bella's moon-pale face or the solution to the problem of the workers' club that he hadn't yet shared with her, or was it the heavy greatcoat that enveloped his former Red Army legs right down to the awakening, damp early spring earth?

He'd still not taken off this old greatcoat, which had been with him since his days in the army. On the contrary, he'd gone on wearing it with the particular proud grief of a zealous revolutionary who, with that heavy greatcoat on his shoulders and an even heavier rifle in his hands, had defended the Revolution on various fronts. He'd worn that greatcoat as a symbol of the combat readiness which a true Communist should always be prepared to show when struggling against capitalism and the counter-revolution.

—It's already quite warm, Comrade Kopelman, —Comrade Bella remarked, half smiling and with respect. —Since it's already so warm, Comrade Kopelman, why are you still wearing this greatcoat?

Kopelman sighed mildly and distantly, and casting a feverish glance at the starry heights, replied:

—You have to understand, Comrade Bella—had you been a Communist, a Party member, had you been among our ranks . . . our *proletarian* ranks—he immediately corrected himself—you wouldn't have asked such a question.

Kopelman deeply regretted that Comrade Bella, this typist from the *Yevsektsiia* at the PartKom, did not feel the special, unique, revolutionary beauty embodied in the simple greatcoat of a frontline revolutionary; the commonplace charm that lay in the simple, unadorned clothes of people who couldn't and didn't care about such matters as dressing up. He regretted this and even felt slightly insulted and hurt.

On the other hand, however, he was pleased that he could discuss the subject more generally with her:

—You have to understand—he said, gazing into the limpid blue of the early spring evening sky—you have to understand, Comrade Bella, that we Communists haven't yet finished with imperialism . . . [. . .]

After those last words he felt relieved, as though he'd wormed his way out of a difficulty, as though he'd crossed heavy, clinging ground, and with a gleam of sorrow in his eyes he began speaking more freely and warmly:

—We still have so many fronts, so many fronts and so many battles and so many . . .

Comrade Bella summoned up all her powers of attention:

—Well?

And Comrade Kopelman went on talking exactly as if he hadn't heard her interruption. Every word he now said to her seemed to him so sweet. He wanted to go on speaking at length, pouring out that simple, commonplace charm, that deep revolutionary grief that lay beneath his austere army clothing, utterly unconscious of the fact that he'd already transferred the canvas portfolio from under one arm to under the other six times; he pursued his theme, stressing every word: [. . .]

Quite often now the thought had occurred to him that Comrade Bella, she with the thick, blonde ringlets and the man's hat that hid three quarters of her face, kept him on a leash like a shambling, silent, faithful dog in a greatcoat, and that wasn't at all seemly for a true Communist. This thought had occurred to him several times by now, and he'd decided to share it with her. But every time she looked at him, he didn't know what to say, so with his heart racing he lost himself in abstract discussions with her.

—He felt no possessive jealousy in regard to her—a thought crossed his mind. True, he wasn't overly pleased at the way Comrade Rosen bossed her about. But to be jealous of Rosen? It didn't even occur to him. Nevertheless, a vague, distant feeling of unspoken and restrained anger at Rosen gnawed at him, although he quickly regained his composure and told himself through clenched teeth:

—So what! Rosen? His forehead always sweats. And the cigarettes he smokes! Those stinking cigarettes . . .

And right away, feeling reassured that Rosen's sweating forehead and stinking cigarettes would unfailingly protect Bella, he again brooded inwardly:

—So that's that! . . . But what if . . .—with incomprehensible resentment the thought again occurred to him—. . . what if he simply finds her attractive?

—Blind?

Kopelman suddenly perceived her as distant, alien, someone who was hiding something from him, someone who hid three quarters of her face with a man's hat, and of whom he could never make sense—who and what was she? . . .

She was half a head taller than he, slim, with firm hips tightly encased in her light winter overcoat, as though in a corset. He constantly imagined, even when he was standing right next to her, that he saw her walking with someone else, with someone tall, smartly dressed in a light, loose-flowing *paletot*, and that every now and then she would turn round and cast a glance at him, Kopelman, standing in his grey greatcoat with his canvas portfolio under his arm, unable to utter a single word from the depths of his being that would convince her of her unfairness. And he grew even sadder because of the imagined distance he suddenly sensed in Bella.

—But a Communist . . .—he tried to retrieve his thoughts—. . . can't just bestow his affections indiscriminately!

—If you're not with me, you're against me!—One of his revolutionary slogans floated into his head.

Comrade Kopelman had pondered and puzzled over all this more than once and, as was fitting, had prepared himself for it—yet now, like a knife, her every glance sliced off pieces of his heart. And before they parted, he himself had willingly given her those pieces to take with her, like titbits one gives a capricious child when it goes off on a trip.

But with half-turned head and piercing eyes, Comrade Bella kept on repeating the same thing again and again:

—You're still so strange, Comrade Kopelman; you ought to take off your greatcoat! It's already so warm! And it smells of carbolic acid, Comrade Kopelman.

Suddenly Kopelman felt unsteady on his feet. He felt hot, strangely hot, and he started sweating. He turned his head away and, transferring the canvas portfolio from under his left arm to under his right, reflected with determination and anger at himself that he'd been a fool and an idiot, and that he actually didn't think highly of women at all.

—Women! The wiles of women!

—There are no interesting women,—he began, suppressing his feelings and consoling himself with this thought,—none at all!

He came to this conclusion rapidly, as though he had only a little time and was therefore obliged completely and immediately to think through everything that had hitherto occupied his mind. And his thoughts crowded one another, all of them suddenly and simultaneously, and he wanted to think them through all at once and be rid of them.

—There had been one woman in the whole world—a lightning thought flashed through his mind—only one.

—Comrade Rosa. Rosa Luxemburg.

—That was a woman! . . .

The scent of the early spring evening floated down from the hills that protectively encircled the town from all sides and laid itself, so blue and mild, with silent grace upon the very heart.

They kept silent a little longer.

Bella was thinking about this young man, Kopelman, with his grey-blond beard and a greatcoat that smelled of carbolic acid, and Kopelman was thinking that no proper women existed; that there had been only one, Comrade Rosa Luxemburg. Bearing this thought in mind, he once again took his leave and marched off to the workers to resume his campaign for the club. [. . .]

Berl the carpenter's home, reeking of glue, wood shavings and furniture polish, was loud with the grating rasp of boards being sawn and workers blustering.

Hanging on the wall were saws, chisels, planes, the Vilna Gaon, Moses Montefiore, Trotsky, and the blank cardboard of a used calendar displaying a landscape of fly droppings.

Part of an unmade bed and a suspended child's cradle that looked like a hanging lamp were both visible through the half open door to the alcove.

Before the gathering of workers assembled in Berl the carpenter's home and awaiting the Party instructor, Hershl the butcher was hacking words like a forequarter of beef:

—People, I want to know, tell me—what are "workers"?

—What sort of mysterious language is that—"workers"? [. . .]

Someone had opened the door and come in. From the fact that the person entering had almost tripped over a piece of furniture, they concluded that it was probably "he" who'd arrived. Silence fell and Berl called out commandingly:

—*Sha*! Who's there?

Comrade Kopelman entered the carpenter's workshop like a goat falling from the attic. Tapping his canvas portfolio to check that it was in its proper place, and well before he'd said "good evening," he remarked, with an attempt at military humour, to those assembled:

—Comrade workers, your workshop is like a barricade!

—*Kade-shmade*—the men grumbled under their breaths.

—Is that so? That's something new! Workers with barricades!—Hershl the butcher barked.—As though what we had before wasn't enough!

They all moved close to the walls as though, in response to some unspoken signal, they were making room for him. As they exchanged sidelong glances, Kopelman, peering into his canvas portfolio, asked a business-like question:

—Do you have a quorum assembled, comrade workers?

—War room?—Hershl the butcher shot out.—What war room? Has he come here to work out ways to kill us?

Shrugging his shoulders, he grumbled:

—So now it's suddenly the End of Days—war room, all of a sudden! What do you need a war room for?

The assembly fell uneasily silent and Comrade Kopelman sought to set their minds at rest with a serious smile:

—It's not a war room, comrade workers—listen to what's said. A *quorum*! What it means is, are you here in sufficient numbers to start the dialectic?

—Electric? The electric starts by itself! There you have it, people—war room, electric, workers! Make a start, and let's get the massacre over and done with,—Hershl the butcher muttered under his breath.

—What do war rooms and electric have to do with this? Surely he can see quite clearly that this is a carpenter's workshop. And he . . .

Little by little, silence descended. Tension heightened.

Comrade Kopelman sat down at the table, as though taking up a strategic position on a battlefield, briefly rummaged about in the portfolio, and lifting his pale face—its grey-blond beard like an extension of the shabby grey-blond greatcoat that now dragged on the floor—he counted them all with his eyes and began, a little hoarsely:

—Comrade workers!

A female head suddenly poked out of the alcove, and a little girl emerged on tiptoe, catching Comrade Kopelman's eyes with a sideways glance. A dusty oil lamp with a metal cap at its side drooped from the workshop's ceiling. One side of the room was in total darkness; the barely illuminated bits of furniture lay scattered about, one on top of the other, as though in the aftermath of a pogrom. Their shadows darkened the walls like muffled, strangled screams. The odour of babies' nappies wafted in from the alcove. Forcing himself to turn his glance, unexpectedly suffused with sweet tenderness, away from the little girl, Kopelman began once more:

—So, comrade workers!

He instantly forgot the opening words he'd prepared for his speech. In his agitation, he again rummaged about in his canvas portfolio, as though elegant thoughts lay scattered within, and little by little he began dragging his speech out of it:

—So, the question of opening your club is a question of organizing the entire body of workers and incorporating it into the ranks of the revolutionary proletariat.

He felt that he was not speaking as he, Kopelman, ought to speak. Even his voice had altered slightly. Something was tickling his palate, as though he had a hair in his throat. But slowly he began regaining his confidence.

—Comrade workers, your politically enlightened education must be organized. Your club must be created so you can derive the fullest benefit from political life. You must be drawn into industry, and not lag behind all other liberated citizens of our revolutionary country . . .

As Kopelman steadily unwound, his words started flowing more smoothly. Berl the carpenter glanced at Kopelman, and then flicked a meaningful glance at Hershl the butcher, indicating that he should stop shaking his head and calling out "Well, well!" all the time in response to what Kopelman was saying.

Gradually the carpenter's shop filled with workers. And after every sentence that Kopelman completed, Kutsik the tailor nodded vigorously at Berl the carpenter:

—Do you hear, Berl? That's a speech!

And indicating Hershl the butcher with his eyes, he mimicked the way he was wiping his nose with the palm of his hand. Every time he glanced at the butcher, he'd put a finger to his forehead and mutter:

—A brilliant intellect! He understands a lot, that side of beef!

He stood with his back to the butcher, unwilling to look in his direction, but after he'd heard Hershl yell out, "Kutsik louse!" for the third time, he responded, looking steadily at Berl the carpenter:

—All things considered, you ought to go and pull a bull by its tail and not take part in formal meetings! Such an intellectual! You side of beef!

Berl the carpenter made silencing gestures with his beard in the direction of both the butcher and the tailor, but without turning round, Kopelman continued:

—So, I propose, comrade workers, according to the resolution passed by IsPolKom . . . I propose that you hand over to the jurisdiction of the club committee the keys to the synagogue, so that it can be converted into a club of proletarian enlightenment, workers, and can in this way place itself firmly within the massed ranks of the proletariat and of the Revolution, which combats all forms of clericalism together with rabbis and all religious functionaries, in order to build a new, bright proletarian future. I have finished.

From the crowd assembled before him, a furious rush of hands rose as though from a seething vat. It was impossible to tell what those hands meant. A dusty commotion of beards and sawdust shook the whole workshop. All were trying to outshout one another. Kutsik the tailor ran from one man to another, screeching in a shrill voice, forcing his way towards Kopelman. Some hands were clenched into fists. Berl the carpenter moved aside to shut the alcove door, and Hershl the butcher cried out:

—What does it mean? A *shul*? A Holy Place? Because Kutsikl the louse says so? And what about us? We don't want a club! You want a club? Make a club for yourselves! Make yourselves workers, make yourselves war rooms and electric, make yourselves whatever you want!

He had gathered a circle of butchers around him, spraying them with foaming spittle as he yelled:

—Never mind! Blood will flow in the streets! Freedom? Fine freedom indeed! You think the town will keep quiet? We'll go to Moscow! We'll appeal! This isn't a world without order! And Kutsik the louse won't get his way with this conversion!

Hershl felt that he was losing Berl's support. With every passing minute there were fewer men gathered around him, even from among the butchers. He crossed the workshop to Berl's wife who was peering out of the alcove, and confided to her in an embarrassed whine:

—Do I care about a club? Do I care about the *shul*? Eh? The only thing that bothers me is why Kutsik the louse should have his way? That's what bothers me!

No one in the workshop knew exactly what was going on. Kutsik the tailor darted about like a weasel. In those places where he was unable to pass, he skipped over pieces of furniture like a waiter. But all the time this great tumult raged in the workshop, Comrade Kopelman calmly regarded the little girl, the only one looking at him sympathetically and with evident pity. From under the tight confines of her young breast, her girlish

heart yearned to protect him from these wild men, and he very much wanted to go up to her and say:

—Just look at those for whom we made a Revolution! Just look at those for whom we lay in trenches on the front for four years! Just look for whom we spilled blood! Look, look, for whose benefit we don't take off our greatcoats!

But he patiently listened to the yelling until it stopped. When he raised his hand to the gathering, Berl the carpenter shouted:

—*Sha*! Jews, quiet! Let him speak! He wants to speak! Speak! Let's hear!

Again Kopelman waited until the clamour subsided, and fanning himself with the top cover of his canvas portfolio, he finally ordered authoritatively:

—Listen, comrade workers! I'm giving you twenty-four hours for deliberation. Either you hand over the keys at this time tomorrow, or we'll take them from you ourselves. The Socialist Soviet Republic will find the appropriate methods for this!

His last words sounded like an ultimatum to a besieged fortress.

Amidst the howls and outcries that sprang out like wood shavings from under planes, Kopelman strode out, leaving behind in the workshop his authoritative voice:

—In twenty-four hours!
—Exactly at this time tomorrow!
—That's all!

The next day, with his butcher's apron around his waist, Hershl the butcher popped in to see Berl the carpenter and in the subdued voice of a Talmud scholar remarked to the plane that was gliding up and down on a board:

—I want to tell you the whole truth, Berl: I don't know myself what to say any longer. Go start an argument with the authorities! What a thing! Go mess around with the state power! Are these authorities at all? They're Bolsheviks! Muscovites!

Dribbling like a steaming samovar, he twisted the corner of his stained butcher's apron:

—Why should we stick up for the whole community council by ourselves? Eh? What do you say, Berl?

Without lifting his head, Berl planed on, waiting to see whether Hershl had anything more to say. Then he blurted out:

—It's quite clear—there's no Brodsky any longer! Brodsky's gone! The sugar factory's gone! The *shul*'s gone! Brodsky isn't the head of the community any longer! Let things happen as they will. The local workers won't take God's part against the Bolsheviks.

Deep in thought, he went on planing for some time, every now and then checking the tool's blade with his hand and murmuring morosely:

—And she, my old woman, look at her, in the alcove there—she's nagging me to death. Clubs, she says, let there be clubs! If, she says, you want to pray, Berl, you can pray at home. Who's going to forbid it? Will they be able to spy on what you're saying in the privacy of your own house?

—So, what's it going to be, Berl, eh?—In growing irritation, Hershl grabbed Berl's plane.—Stop working for a minute, will you! You can plane later. It won't run away. I'm asking you!

—How should I know?

—What do you mean, how should you know? Who else should know? Berl, all this has to end! The time's up soon! Just think of that one with his little Bolshevik beard—he's quite capable of coming over here with the Cheka! Would you mess around with them? He can bring a machine gun! He can turn your house upside down as soon as look at you with his fancy little beard! Who knows what else might happen . . . So?

—What do you mean, "so"?

—I mean about the keys, Berl?

—So what do you want?

—What do *I* want? I don't want to hand them over to him with my own hands.

—So what do you want to do instead? Do you want to hire someone especially to hand over the keys to him?

They went on bickering and wrangling for some time over which of them should give Kopelman the keys until with a shriek, dishevelled, with one breast bare, having forgotten to cover it after nursing the baby, the carpenter's wife burst out of the alcove:

—Stop this! Stop! Stop! "I won't, he won't!" Put them down somewhere. He'll take them himself when he comes, and good riddance! And let there be an end!

Glaring angrily at the carpenter's wife, Hershl the butcher snatched the plane from Berl's hand and, waving it in the air in the direction of the door, hissed angrily:

—I'd certainly much rather shove this plane in his belly!

That evening, Comrade Kopelman, armed with the keys to the big synagogue on Broda Street, was walking to the post office with Bella the typist, and explaining to her:

—Do you understand? *This* is called the dictatorship of the proletariat, Comrade Bella!

Translated by Joseph Sherman, with the assistance of Aleksandra Geller.

Other works by Markish: *Shveln* (1919); *Di kupe* (1922); *Eyns af eyns* (1934); *Der fertsikyeriker man* (1978).

Rodion Markovits
1888–1948

The left-wing writer Rodion Markovits belonged to the Hungarian-speaking Jewish community of Transylvania. He trained as a lawyer but devoted most of his career to journalism. While serving with a Hungarian army infantry unit in 1916, he was captured by the Russians and spent the next seven years of his life in Siberia and the Russian Far East, first in a prisoner-of-war camp and then with the Red Army. He described his experiences in *Siberian Garrison*, a hybrid of reportage, autobiography, and fiction, which became an international bestseller and was his one great book. While he regarded himself as ethnically Hungarian, he nonetheless maintained links with secular Jewish culture. The publication of his collection of rural Jewish tales in 1939 alienated the Hungarian-reading public in Romania.

Siberian Garrison
1928

Chapter LV

The pride of the Germans was Kinderlyn. He was taller even than Leona Lakner, and he carried a very small head on a huge body. He was a real actor; he was said to be a member of the Dresden National Theater. The Germans also organized a company but for one performance only: They planned to present a drama— of course with Kinderlyn in the leading role—and two or three small bits by Schnitzler. This performance also took place, and the Germans raved with bated breath during the first play in which Kinderlyn acted the part of a half-naked, leopard-skinned, helmeted individual who was bellowing inarticulately throughout the play. The rest of the actors were merely supers around him. The play was a German classic, but only Kinderlyn got a rôle in it. He recited throughout the play and the Germans enjoyed it immensely. Goldegg played in "Literature," one of the Schnitzler playlets; it had been expected that he would. He portrayed the authoress who married the aristocrat at the end. He was very good, he brought out the varied sentiments of the play very well, he was passionate with the count and a foolish little Bohemian girl with the author. Old captains were beside themselves with enthusiasm, the Germans yelled proudly and triumphantly. The Hungarians did not like it very much, some of them remarked: Our plays are different, there is life in our plays and temperament. But there were others who said that, on the other hand, there was literature in Germany, and taste and culture.

But from then on, the cultures of the nations united and they helped each other mutually. They even decided that they would present a bilingual vaudeville performance on New Year's Eve. That is to say, the performance would be given in the two leading languages, in Hungarian and in German, because every one understood at least one of these two, even the Imperial Ottoman officers spoke a little German.

The command, of course, made the best of the pro-theatrical sentiment. It gave all the help possible to the theater because it sensed, and very correctly, too, that this form of amusement, and its various side branches, drained off many things. Until now, the mob had had only bread, now they had circuses, too, and they looked at events through a pleasant mist. One could not touch the theater, it was the apple of their eye, and as far as the other camps were concerned, an object of envy.

One day the [prisoner-of-war] camp began to receive relief packages, and from that day cases were arriving every day. Chinese quilts and Chinese boots arrived and, before they were distributed, the theater was asked what it needed. It asked for everything: the boots it needed for the theatrical employees, who often worked in the yard in bitter-cold weather in the interests of the community, and the quilts partly because of their cotton stuffings, which were used up in the property furniture, and partly because of the cloth-coverings, which served as canvas on the settings. The command governed the camp through the theater, and since so many things were constantly arriving, the command was no longer a negligible factor. It was strengthened by various hangers-on. The major was no longer independent; now that there were things to be distributed, more and

more officers asked for a share in the government. The major was not exactly forced to surrender his power, but he had his weak point and this was completely taken advantage of by those who demanded to be admitted to the government. The major, as a matter of plain fact, was not a major, only a captain, and the climbers used this bit of information to exert pressure on him. As long as there had been no reason for doing so, nobody had cared to bring up this matter, but now one could often hear a senior officer remark, as if it had been merely a slip of the tongue: "The captain, oh, I am sorry, I should have said, the major—"

The captain-major did not object. Willingly or not, he had to acquiesce in the fact that a sort of council attached itself to him. And within a very short time, this council was in command of everything. These men were not as tolerant as the major had been. As soon as the camp acquired a Cabinet, discipline became more severe. As soon as a Treasury came into existence, the social classes were definitely segregated. There were some who suddenly turned up their noses and no one knew why. Exclusive societies were organized on the most fantastic grounds. Thus, for instance, a fox-hunters' society came into being. Only captains, *Kammerherren*, and gentile cavalry officers were admitted to it. They met every Friday evening for a few glasses of wine and they planned a banquet for next year's St. Hubertus' Day.

To be sure, they did not discriminate against artists and newspaper men, and especially not against actresses. They often invited the artists as their guests. But religious controversies arose and these disturbed even the peace of the arts. The first clash occurred at a vaudeville performance shortly before New Year's Eve, on account of Monis Neumann. He played because he was the one who best remembered the humorous little skit they wanted to present and he would not let them have the script unless he was permitted to play in it. Monis portrayed a Hungarian soldier. The other character, a German soldier, was played by him. The two of them got together in a *café*, one of them did not speak Hungarian, the other one knew nothing but German, but they became quite good friends. In the course of the play Monis Neumann ejaculated:

"God damn it—"

Whereupon Lieutenant Czernin, brother, or nephew, of our Bucharest ambassador, leapt to his feet and yelled out:

"*Schweinerei—*"

And he walked out of the room. The performance continued in a depressed spirit. Lieutenant Czernin was a very influential man at home, some of them said that, after the return, he would report, about the camp, directly to the Court and that he would be in a position to drop a few words in favor of some of his comrades and also a few words of damnation against others.

Lieutenant Czernin immediately submitted a written report to the command in which he complained that the Christian religion had been insulted at the performance, he had heard distinctly that Lieutenant Monis Neumann had cursed the Holy Mary. The height of infamy! Several of them suddenly began to remember that Monis had really said the incriminated phrase. Some of them even went so far as to declare most definitely that they themselves had not left the auditorium merely because they had not wanted to create a scandal. Monis defended himself, he said he had submitted the rôle to the censor and he had not intended to insult anybody. The Hungarian soldier, alas, used the phrase in question quite often, nevertheless, he had not said it. At this point, the situation was this: the Jews did not remember anything, not even the phrase Monis admitted, and the anti-Semites remembered everything, including the phrase Czernin submitted in his report.

Storm was brewing in the camp. The prospects were that either the order of the camp would be completely overturned or the Jews would have to be moved to a separate camp. Practically all of them cursed the Jews, but if, by accident, there was a Jew among them, they invariably added: "Of course we don't mean you, you are an exception." There was one exception in practically every box. The actors tried to bring about peace, but their efforts were unsuccessful.

Disorder reigned in the camp now, and bitterness against the Jews, especially when some one brought the news that Monis Neumann complained to the Russians about the persecution of the Jews, and that even that lousy Waletzky, the greatest anti-Semite on the Eastern Hemisphere between Warsaw and Vladivostok, greatly disapproved of the friction. He said it was unheard of and he would have to intervene himself.

The news arrived at two in the afternoon, and within an hour they were already forced to call together an officers' meeting. The excitement had reached its climax. Neumann was asked whether he had really complained to the Polish captain, and whether he knew what the consequences of such a dastardly move were. By this time, the roommates in the various boxes were no longer on speaking terms.

At the meeting it was disclosed that Waletzky had learned of the incident quite by accident. It was Monis's great luck that First Lieutenant Körös, one of the "reliable" men, had been present when Waletzky had asked Neumann. He testified that Waletzky had already known of the affair, that he had merely asked Monis whether there had been any affairs, and that Monis had answered: "I have had no affair with anybody, not a word of it is true, the Captain has been misinformed."

But this did not put the excitement to sleep. The anti-Semites merely remarked: "They have escaped this time—"

A similar incident occurred in the *"Baubezirk."* Some of the senior officers in that camp organized a society: the Society of Those Who Will Not Return the Salute of a Jew. First Lieutenant Almoslino, the postmaster, did not know who the members of this society were and, one day, he quite accidentally saluted one of them. The club-member, of course, did not return the greeting.

Almoslino was a rich Spanish Jew who had moved to Budapest from Bosnia. He did not create an affair of honor out of this incident, he merely went to the commander of the *"Baubezirk"* and demanded an officers' meeting. The commander did not deem it necessary to call together the meeting, for, after all, it was a private affair, but since the excitement had reached quite a high point, the officers' meeting was called together. First Lieutenant Almoslino rose and, taking a small cross out of his wallet, said:

"As a reward for my work done in behalf of Catholic churches destroyed by Mohammedans in Bosnia-Herzegovina, His Holiness, the Pope, gave me the cross of *Pro Ecclesia et Pontifice.* Here it is. For these very same activities, the Hungarian Cardinal-Primate sent me his paternal blessings and I treasure the postal-card on which he sent them after me to prison in gratitude and reverence—"

First Lieutenant Almoslino then pinned the cross on his chest and handed over the card to the commander of the camp.

The case of First Lieutenant Almoslino put an end to the persecution of Jews once and for all.

Chapter LVI

But there were also definite achievements to which the command and its councilors could point with pride. First of all, the material prosperity of the camp was beyond dispute. The Red Cross visits and the consuls and the various things sold on the installment plan created luxury. Science and the arts were generously succored and, at last, peace reigned among the various sects. It spoke highly of the commander's wisdom and tact that he placed a Jewish cornet on the Christmas Eve program. Indeed, the Jewish cornet's Christmas tale was the high point of the festivities. The first number on the program was a sermon delivered by the camp chaplain, then Captain Benkö said the Lord's Prayer, and this was followed by the Christmas tale. It was said that the cornet warned the commander that the anti-Semitic feelings had not yet completely disappeared, and that, although he was not afraid, it would be perhaps wise not to place a Jew on the Christmas Eve program, especially not after the chaplain and the Lord's Prayer, because it might hurt certain persons.

"Army Regulations never discriminate against any religion. What matters is that I have confidence in your talents. It is, however, important that the tale should be solemn and touching—"

So the Jewish cornet stepped on the platform, and at the foot of the glistening Christmas tree, at the foot of the green tree of peace surrounded by symbolical barbed-wire fences, he began his tale:

"This is the tale of a little Hungarian cow.

"The tale of an ordinary country cow which grazed peacefully on the fields until the very end of its life.

"Until the day the fate of all aged cows overtook it.

"For when it grew old, and weak, it became sick— perhaps because of an indiscretion in its youth—and then the charming, good, old cow was no longer of any service. There was nothing to do now but to slaughter it, and they slaughtered it and skinned it, my friends. Its flesh—the war had broken out in the meantime—was taken to the packer's.

"Its flesh was cut to small pieces and put into a big iron kettle, Makó onion was added to it, and Szeged paprika and Mármaros salt and it was cooked, and then it was put in small tin cans, and the tin cans were sent to replacement troops, the tin cans containing our little cow.

"The cow was now in haversacks, and it traveled into all the four directions of the compass, it went to war with beflowered soldiers. The cow's heart went to the Italian front, its liver went south, and a piece of its leg found its way to the Russian front.

"The tale will now concern itself exclusively with that part of the cow which went to the Russian front.

"The tin was now in the haversack of an old aspirant and the good tin waited patiently until it would be con-sumed. But it was a tin to be reserved for emergency purposes only; therefore it was not permitted to be eaten, unless specially commanded. The special command, however, did not arrive. There came many commands but never this one.

"The tin began to think now that they had forgotten all about it. But it was mistaken. Once the battalion orders of the day asked whether it was still there.

"Of course it was there, although it was quite tired of trench warfare, but, alas, the weather was not advantageous for an advance. The weather was fine for patrolling, however, and it went patrolling every day. Every day it went for a walk with the aspirant toward the Russian trenches.

"There were times when the aspirant had to crawl, at other times he had to run, sometimes he jumped and sometimes he was creeping forward on his belly. The poet tin was very much afraid. It was so afraid that it often hung on to something. Once the aspirant remarked.

"'Why, this tin in my haversack is quite heavy—'

"But once the lying down was of no avail. Lying down was of avail only against bullets, anyway, it did not protect one against bayonets.

"It did not protect him now either, but the aspirant was not killed because the bayonet did not touch any of the important organs. It went through his tongue only and pierced his right cheek, but that was all.

"Then the enemy soldier pulled the bayonet out of the aspirant, because he needed the rifle. The enemy made a stretcher out of this rifle, with the help of another one, because he was taught to do so on the drillground. With another Russian, the aspirant was taken to Russia, on this stretcher.

"The enemy put the haversack under the aspirant's head in order that he should lie more comfortably. If they had not done this, the aspirant could not have breathed, he had lost a lot of blood, and it would have been very unpleasant for him if he had not been able to breathe.

"The aspirant was slowly cured in the Russian hospital. His recovery was slow, but not on account of the tongue. It was delayed on account of his belly, because later they discovered that that too had been shot through.

"At last he was completely cured. He lost some weight, to be sure, but they sent him off to a camp of prisoners of war just the same.

"These prisoners lived in infinite Siberia, far away, on the shores of the Yellow Sea. They lived there in sorrow, but they managed to make room for the aspirant.

"And he began, too, just like the others, he began, too: to wait for peace.

"He built a tent, too, just like the other prisoners, he built a box out of colored cardboard and planks. He procured for himself a table and some small chairs. He put his treasures in order: he hung the Japanese and Lake Baikal picture cards on the cardboard walls, put his summer and winter underwear in a cigar box, in short, he tidied up the house.

"And he gazed at his rescued belongings, which he had been carrying ever since he had left home: three camp postal cards, two little notebooks and the tin can with the cow's flesh. The tin can he had not yet opened because it had not been commanded.

"The command had not arrived.

"'And now—it will never arrive,' the orphaned aspirant reflected.

"The old aspirant only gazed and gazed at the tin can and one day Christmas came.

"Christmas came again, the Siberian Christmas came again, although all the cabbalas, and all the magic formulas, and even the great Napoleon's own solitaire said that there would be no more Siberian Christmas.

"Nevertheless, the Siberian Christmas was here again.

"The Siberian Christmas Eve was here again and one could not see the prisoners in the low-walled boxes because they all buried their heads in their hands.

"Their sighs came sadly; the invisible telegraph machines of times and distances, and the tearful wagon of memories raced with them to far-away snow-covered yards, to faraway Christmas trees—

"There was a huge Christmas tree in the heart of every prisoner, a great, big, brilliant, crying, glistening Christmas tree.

"There were little lamps with paper shades on the little tables in the boxes, and great silence, solemn, churchly silence hung in the rooms. The prisoners prayed and their hands trembled and their hearts fluttered. And the aspirant's hands trembled too and his heart was also full of reverence and he took his knife out of his pocket, and he took the battered, worn, battle-scarred tin can off the shelf. He stuck his knife in the can, and now all the prisoners, hearing the noise, turned and looked at him. He opened the tin can and rose in the dimly lighted room, the bearded aspirant rose, and it seemed as if he had been a priest, and his voice sounded as if it had come from a pulpit.

"He raised high the battered, worn, battle-scarred tin can and, in a colorless, ghastly voice, he spoke:

"'There are peace-meat and peace-blood, peace-skies and peace-earth—there are peace-grass and peace-meadows, peace-water and peace-air in it—and peace-flowers and peace-sun-rays—'

"And all the miserable and unfortunate prisoners gathered around him and they ate out of the tin can, of the cow's flesh.

"They ate of it and cried.

"It was like a ceremony addressed to the hearts, like an inspiring prophecy, like a magic message, like a cheerful and peaceful holiday.

"It was like all these, and peace and patient hopes settled in their hearts for the night. . . ."

The tale had a great effect on the prisoners, some of them even cried, they were so touched. The editor of the *Siberian Gazette* asked the cornet for the tale, he said he wanted to publish it in his paper. Then everybody might copy it out of the paper and keep it as a souvenir.

The prisoners stayed together until very late on Christmas Eve and, silently lost in thoughts, they sipped tea in the study. Many went up to the Jewish cornet to congratulate him, even the extremists were pacified and they all shook hands with him. They said, this was different, this was something. One wouldn't have thought that there were people who so thoroughly felt the spirit of the holiday of Brotherly Love.

Lieutenant Gotthilf [a Zionist] also went up to the cornet and sat down next to him. He was silent for a while, then said:

"Why doesn't a man like you show himself in a museum?"

"What's that? What did you say, please?"

The poor cornet stuttered in his amazement.

"What did you say, please?"

"I said, why don't you show yourself in a museum? No, not in a museum! I should have said, in a freak show!"

"What do you want of me? Why should I show myself in a museum?"

"Because you ought to be stuffed. Because you are the greatest conformer on earth. Because you're a model for assimilation and adaptation. Why can't you write such brilliant tales for your own holidays—"

"Of course, I can—I can—"

Dr. Gotthilf smiled sarcastically: "Don't wait another minute. Go over to their side right away."

German officers came to his table and stared at him in admiration. They had already been told of the story and they looked at the cornet as if he had been a magician.

"*Braver Kerl—Braver Kerl,*" they said.

A captain was enthusiastically explaining to a Tyrolese yager lieutenant that there had not been so clever a tactical move in the entire war. The command has done this beautifully. All the aspirants and cornets in the camp had now been placed under an obligation. For hadn't it been a cornet who had shone so brilliantly? And the anti-Semites were also disarmed, and the Jews, too. To put this Jewish cornet on the program was a superb move on the part of the command. To be sure, he was a talented chap, one had to admit that the whole thing wouldn't have been worth a damn without him. But just the same, it had been a clever move on the part of the command.

"Well, tell me," Dr. Gotthilf's sharp voice yelled at one of the tables, "tell me, what if Almoslino has no Papal cross? Then do they have to kill all the Jews? Suppose this cornet is untalented. Does that necessarily mean that you have to stage a pogrom? Because, don't forget, there almost was a pogrom here—"

First Lieutenant Haertl approached the cornet with a sly grin on his lips. He blinked from behind his glistening pince-nez at the story-teller and discreetly gave him a piece of paper under the table. The story-teller put the folded paper on the table. What did Haertl want of him in secret?

It was an order for a black overcoat, free of charge, from the warehouse of the Welfare Committee.

The poor story-teller went pale and ambled out of the room with trembling knees.

As he was approaching the door he heard two half-baked aspirants arguing in the anteroom:

"You didn't understand the whole story. I tell you, it was a revolutionary story. The Jews are always thinking of the revolution. He wanted to say that the seed of the revolution is there in every man's haversack. But they don't open it, not until the Great Holiday. Then the one who has most faithfully preserved it, will open it and then everybody will eat of the cow's flesh, people from all over the world will go in pilgrimage to him and everybody will feast on the tin can of the haversack—"

"Perhaps he didn't mean any symbols? Perhaps he merely wanted to tell us a tale, a Christmas tale—"

"Ah, don't be crazy—"

Translated by George Halasz.

Other works by Markovits: *Aranyvonat* (1929); *Reb Ancsli és más avasi zsidókról szóló széphistóriák* (1940).

Joseph Opatoshu

Brothers
1928

At three in the morning, Rabbi Sholem Tuvim returned home from visiting his sick father. His father was in great need of comfort, and he, Reb Sholem, would have stayed by him the entire night if the sick man had not abruptly insisted that his younger son be sent for—Fishl, who years ago had gone crazy.

For the rabbi, it was a shock. Ten years earlier, his father had driven Fishl off. He had not been able to bear to hear his name mentioned, and now, when Fishl was so distant that nothing bound him to the Jews, now, at this very moment, when their father was in need of comfort, he decided to summon Fishl.

Not wanting to encounter his brother, the rabbi went home.

Night filled the house. From the open rooms, sleep drifted, bringing with it words from another world.

Quietly the rabbi entered the room where he held court and sat down near the open window. The moon, stuck somewhere behind the houses, left a residue of congealed flames. In the grayness, stars flickered and went out, covering the world with shadows.

Two milk wagons drove by, stopped before a house. The milkmen traded talk from wagon to wagon, and in the gray light, it sounded like a husband and wife conversing before dawn.

The synagogue with its marble hearth-plates, with its iron gate graying opposite the rabbi's window, stood there, locked up, dead.

The rabbi looked at the building and thought about how Judaism was declining in America. Weeks went by without anyone coming to him with a question of Jewish law.

Leah, the rabbi's wife, came downstairs, barefoot, in her nightgown. She snuggled up to her husband, rubbed her sleepy eyes, and asked him anxiously, "How's your father, Sholem? Better? Go lie down. You didn't sleep last night, either."

"I can't sleep, Leah. See how the synagogue across the way stands vacant?"

"What are you thinking of? It's night! What do you want? For people to come sit in the synagogue at night? It's enough that the dead are there!"

"And who comes to synagogue during the day? The dead, too. God's house stands vacant, and I, the high priest, guard an empty Holy Ark. Don't you know I can barely pull together a minyan of old men, and not even every day? And that when my brother, Fishl, the offender against Israel, speaks in Madison Square, twenty thousand workers come to hear him? Let all the rabbis in New York try to call together even ten thousand Jews. . . I think that Jews should hear Torah, it's Torah that they should hear. . . No one will come, Leah!"

"Judaism isn't dying yet, not even in America," Leah put her face against her husband's beard, "and who is obligated to solve all the world's problems? Believe me, Sholem, somehow we'll manage to get through our remaining few years honorably."

At the first ring of the telephone, the rabbi grabbed the receiver in his hand and held it for a while. He was afraid to bring it to his ear. When he placed it there, his hands began to shake.

"What, Sholem?"

"It's all over."

Leah's shoulders writhed under the thick nightgown. She began to weep quietly and keenly. Tears fell on the rabbi's beard, on his hands. He did not comfort his wife, did not soothe her, but lightly unwound himself from her arms, took up his stick with the silver head, and walked slowly out of the house.

Behind the window, the crying grew quieter, keener, jabbing at the night like a needle and thread mending a cut body.

The rabbi walked through the dark, empty streets, step by step. He did not think about the fact that his father was dead. He could not free himself from his brother, who now must be sitting by the corpse, and whom he, Sholem, had not seen for the past ten years. Recently, Fishl had gone completely mad. It was rumored that he had not circumcised his youngest child, and instead of naming him Israel, after his grandfather, he named the child Lenin. All this gossip didn't make sense to him—he had doubts. In the end, in spite of it all, Fishl had not been baptized.

For the rabbi, Lenin was as *treyf* as Titus. Titus had obliterated the land of Israel, and the Great Russian Lenin wanted to destroy the entire world. Life around the rabbi divided in two. He, Rabbi Sholem, represented one half, and his brother, Fishl the other. After today he would tell this to Fishl, he would swear on the bones of their father, that as long as Fishl refused to repent, there could be no peace between them. Fishl was not the first villain the Jews had encountered. They would survive him, too.

These thoughts gave the rabbi courage. He began to walk faster, set the stick down before him, and heard the iron knob of the stick resound across the sidewalk, repeating his words.

He absolutely could not make peace as long as his brother, Fishl, was such a . . . was entirely outside, outside . . . he, Sholem, never attempted to say even a word to Fishl . . . If . . . what does the Gemara say: Even a sinful Jew is not equal to a Gentile prophet. Who was it who wanted to convert to Judaism? Yes, Onkeles, Titus's cousin, wanted to convert to Judaism. With magic, he summoned Titus, asked his uncle for advice. His uncle not only dissuaded him, he ordered him to persecute the Jews. Balaam, the same thing. So when Onkeles summoned Jesus, Jesus said that there was no better "nation and tongue" than the Jews.

The rabbi entered the corridor. A nauseating smell wiped across his face, reminding him that his father was dead. He grew softer, yielding. Now there was pressure on his heart. His eyes overflowed with the heat. He couldn't see where he was going.

In the house, strangers were wandering about. Two candles in holders covered with drippings burned at the head of the corpse. The flames drew toward the open window. Fishl sat on an overturned box, holding his face in his hands and barely moving. As the rabbi entered, he did not take his hands from his face.

The rabbi set his stick aside. He took a volume of *Mishnayes* from the shelf of holy books, shuffled, leafed through it, set it back on the shelf, and reasoned with his brother wordlessly.

His hands, his face, above all, his eyes, spoke, complained, could not untangle themselves from Titus, who had destroyed the Temple, Jerusalem, a nation, but left a people. Now that this people has been destroyed, a corpse lay on the earth, listen, Fishl, on the ground lies a corpse over which we must weep, over which we must recite Lamentations. Is this not also a destruction?

Fishl raised his head. His weeping eyes recognized his brother, and he stood up: "Sholem."

The rabbi blinked rapidly, took his beard into his mouth, stuffed it in like a handful of straw to keep his shout from bursting forth, and through clenched lips began to recite the Psalms.

He leaned his hands against the wall, his head on his arms, and roared. His shoulders curved, sharpened, grew. His hands dropped down of their own accord. His nose became pale, longer, and the rabbi began to shake, squinting in one eye.

Fishl caught him, set him down on the bed, rubbed his hands, his temples, and when the rabbi came to, he wept.

Through the window, the morning intruded, playing with the little flames, pleating the black bedsheet around the corpse's stiff feet. The brothers noticed how the sheet stirred and then ripped itself off the bed. Immediately they realized it was the wind, and remained sitting across from each other, forgetting their hatred. Fear was written in their eyes: Maybe Father is still alive, maybe he is still alive.

Translated by Kathryn Hellerstein.

Yisroel Rabon

1900–1941

The Yiddish novelist and poet Yisroel Rabon grew up in Bałuty, an impoverished quarter near Łódź that he described in his novel *Balut: roman fun a forshtot* (1934). Rabon spent most of his life in Łódź but escaped to Vilna after the German invasion of Poland; there he was shot to death. Rabon's realistic fiction and poetry show marginalized youths and soldiers in urban settings; his writings explore homelessness, sex, and violence. Rabon was also an editor, translator, and writer of pulp fiction.

The Street: A Novel
1928

13

For two months, enfolded from head to foot in crusted, freezing snow, we lay in the trenches on the Polish–Bolshevik front in White Russia. We lay about sleepily, suffering from fatigue, immobility, lassitude, and inertia. Looking up at the sky, we saw the sun rise day after day; and day after day it went down on the cheerless white snow-and-ice-gripped fields and steppes.

Bored out of our minds with nothing to do, we peered over our trenches at the thin-legged, black-beaked crows that stood on the ground above us, pecking, tapping away at the food we had thrown out of the trenches. They aimed their sly, sharp glances at us and waited. Waited for something. Always waiting, never leaving us.

Each of the soldiers had his own crow, his personal guardian. Strange. Occasionally it would flap its black wings, rise into the cold air, and caw something to the snowbound fields. Then it flew off for a moment, only to return at once to its former place, where it resumed its waiting.

No one can imagine the horror of such a guardian. Day in and day out, sunrise after sunrise, always the crow with its black, pointed beak and its sly, small, treacherous black eyes. A crow as guardian—a secret, bizarre, false guardian of death.

I had lived for many years in a village, but I had never heard, not even from the wisest old peasants, that a crow could attach itself to someone whom it would refuse to leave.

I am a pale, anemic, fearful sort of person. Until I was fourteen I believed in ghosts and devils. My mother used to dress me in white as a talisman to keep me from dying young, the way my departed brothers and sisters had. My father had warned me to avoid churches, crosses, and crows, and a hostility toward churches, crosses, and crows had seeped into my blood. When, as a child, I saw a boy draw a cross in the sand with a stick, I avoided him and did not speak to him for years.

The waiting of the nearby crows intensified a secret, incomprehensible dark terror in our souls. We were not afraid of death, but the crows terrified us.

The cold was sharp, searing. The air stabbed at us as if with the points of knives. If anyone spilled a bit of water, it turned instantly into ice. The sullen skies seemed armor-plated, and our voices rising in the air gave off a sharp metallic echo, as if they had struck walls of steel and concrete.

We prayed for action: attack, movement, struggle. Man-to-man combat. The blood in our veins turned leaden. The sounds of rifle fire poured like buckshot into our ears.

At last, one evening when darkness slid across the pale fields, a voice, drunk with blood lust, was heard in the trenches: "Attack, brothers. Hey! Hey! Attack!"

We climbed out of our holes. We ran and ran. Ran into the dark and saw nothing. There was a cannonade, and, from the sky, a flaming rain of artillery shells and exploding shrapnel poured into the night. The earth and air shuddered. We saw nothing. We ran.

Suddenly there danced before us some dark, squirming little men. Dolls which moment by moment grew taller. Then wild creatures with madness in their eyes and contorted, inflamed faces arrived. They carried gleaming bayonets between their clenched teeth. There were deafening cries. Daggers glittered. Artillery thundered and spat out gouts of fiery lava.

Then silence. Not a breath of air. Not a soul. No fire.

I can't remember what happened. I know only that when I woke I was lying on the ground. It was cold and dark. Blue snow and black night everywhere on field and steppe.

A dull pain tore at my left foot. As I looked around I saw several corpses with glazed eyes, but I was in pain and ignored them. I stumbled about, moving unsteadily, drunkenly over the frozen earth like a man who has been felled.

When I bent to take a good look at my foot, I saw that a plug of bloody, hardened flesh dangled from it, as if a great nail had been driven through the foot.

It was dark. Silent. I walked on for an hour. Two. Then I felt my strength leaving me. Any minute now I would fall to the ground. It was still searing cold, even colder than it had been by day. I went on, not knowing where. I bit my lips against the cold. I felt myself trembling. My teeth chattered. I tucked my numbed hands between my thighs and tried to warm them.

My voice sad, subdued, desperate, I called, "Hello. Who . . . Who . . . Hello. Who . . . Who?"

On that vast silent steppe neither man nor dog replied. Nobody stirred. Nothing breathed. Not a gleam, not a light from a settlement or a village or a hut anywhere that my eye fell. I dragged on, exhausted, fainting. My lips were dry, my mouth leathery.

If only I could warm myself. Oh, for a glowing coal, for a bit of warmth to melt my frozen blood. That's all I asked.

Another step or two and I would fall to the ground. My knees buckled; my body swayed.

Dear God, is there a city somewhere? A town?

But only the hard wintry darkness caressed my gaze, and the cold seared and burned as if it meant to penetrate my clothing, to lick my naked body with its cold steel tongues.

"A bit of warm water . . . The cold will drop me to the ground like a frozen bird from a tree. I'm falling . . ."

Then my feet tripped on something heavy and huge. I fell.

As a hungry infant senses the smell of its mother's breast in the dark, so now I sensed warmth. My groping fingers touched something silken, soft, and warm.

"Ah!" It was a cry of joy torn from my mouth, and I fell clumsily, like a beast, upon whatever the thing was as onto a soft warm lap. When I looked more closely, I saw that I lay on a large, exhausted Belgian draft horse. A mass of black-and-red congealed blood hung from the horse's half-open mouth. At its base the mass was a jagged lump of tangled hair, but at its tip it came to a sharp point, like a goatee. The thing looked like the three-cornered hat of an Assyrian king.

The horse was still alive, gasping for breath with its last strength. I pressed myself against it. Like a madman, I flung myself from one side of the horse to the other, sucking in its warmth, breathing it in through my mouth, through my nostrils.

The horse, feeling the weight of my body, uttered a weak, pathetic groan. I put my bloody, wounded foot under one of its limbs and pressed my frozen face against its warm belly and nestled against its hide.

But I was still cold. I thought I would die of the cold. Suddenly I had a wild thought that made me shudder. I shouted aloud with the mad joy of someone rescued from death. Leaping to my feet, I stepped a pace away from the horse. In the space of a single breath I had my carbine knife out and *whack*! Gritting my teeth, I plunged the knife into the horse's belly with all my strength.

"Ahhhhhhh." There was an abrupt whistling sound in the air. It was the choked, profoundly human cry of a life being cut short.

No. I cannot believe that a dying horse could scream with a voice as profoundly human as that. No. I don't believe it.

Perhaps it was I who cried out for the horse I had murdered. Perhaps it was I who uttered that scream for a dying creature that no longer had enough strength of its own to scream.

A spurt of thick warm blood gushed over me. A caressing warmth, soft and heavy, flowed over my fists—which still grasped the carbine knife. The warmth flowed over my chest, my face, my neck. With the relentless tenacity of a predatory beast, with my last strength, with my hands, with my whole body I tore at the horse's belly till I had ripped its entrails out.

A red darkness blinded me. The horse's blood turned the night red. But then, I had no idea what sort of stuff blood can be. I cut and tore and plucked at the horse's entrails, flinging them aside.

Time passed.

I was covered with a cold sweat and soaked with blood. Finally the body was empty. I jumped for joy; then, squeezing myself together on the ground beside the horse, I crawled into its belly.

I was warm. Wonderfully warm. I was comfortable in the horse's huge roomy belly. I turned wearily over on my side and fell instantly into a deep sleep.

When I woke, the sun, like an alert soldier standing watch over a newly conquered land, stood in the eastern portion of the cold sky.

As I tried to climb out of the horse's belly, I sensed a certain heaviness—as if I were stuck to the inner walls of the creature's body. I made a convulsive movement and broke free.

A cold, sharp, biting wind together with a strange searing cold embraced me as in arms of steel. The cold immobilized me. I could not take a step. I spread my arms out only to see the most horrid thing imaginable. I was frozen to the earth. From head to foot I was enclosed in a Bordeaux-colored armor. I could not drop my arms. They stayed outstretched. My feet were stuck fast to the ground. I looked like a cross.

My God, I was rooted to the earth like a bloody red cross.

I was a bloody cross on the White Russian steppe.

It was frightful. Terrifying. Uncanny. I stood in an empty field where there was no sign of human life, no trace of a habitation. I stood, a frozen, human-shaped red cross.

I tried to shout and could not; to weep, but I could not. I felt how the bloody cross that imprisoned me, that rooted me like a tree to the earth, gnawed slowly at my life.

Near me, to one side, lay the dead horse with its ripped-up belly from which protruded my hat, covered with frozen blood. On the other side lay the creature's ripped-out heart, lungs, and intestines, all of them covered with silvery frost as by a winding sheet. Between the hat and the entrails I stood—a living bloody cross.

How was it that I, who as a child could never stand to watch my friends torturing a cat—how could I have cut open the belly of a living horse with my own hands?

The horse's blood shrieked accusations at my body. It tortured me. It choked me. It sucked my breath.

I tried to move and could not. I stood welded in place.

"Ohhhh," I wailed like a child who tries to walk but cannot. I stood in the empty waste like a frozen tombstone with the cross of myself upon it.

All at once the glazed eyes of the murdered horse acquired life and laughed at me. "Ah, humanity."

My head throbbed. I could no longer hear, and then before my eyes the day's brightness turned into a mixture of darkness, dizzying pallor, and blood.

I dozed off. It grew dark. Night became the entire world—enormous, profound, velvety night. My eyes grew heavy. My doze began to rock me to sleep.

With the last strength of a dying man, I shook my arms—and I achieved my desire: the cross broke. My arms were free. Then, with the remnant of my waning strength, I began to beat my body everywhere. I slapped my cheeks, beat my chest, my head. And the bloody ice broke everywhere on me, like shards.

Finally I was entirely free. I was no longer a cross.

The horse, with its sardonic congealed eyes, watched me beat at my body, punishing myself. Driven by some interior force, I dropped to my knees beside it and prayed for forgiveness. I wept. I yelled. I tore the hair, the bloody hair from my head.

Translated by Leonard Wolf.

Other works by Rabon: *Untern ployt fun der velt* (1928); *Groer friling* (1933); *Balut: roman fun a forshtot* (1934); *Lider* (1937).

Isak Samokovlija

1889–1955

Born in the eastern Bosnian town of Goražde, Isak Samokovlija is considered one of the first modern writers of Jewish literature in the Serbo-Croatian language. By profession a physician, Samokovlija was known for his expressionistic style, his detailed portrayals of the life of Jews and other minorities in Yugoslavia, and his overall mastery of the short-story form. He was considered a prominent member of the Yugoslav literary establishment in the immediate postwar period, serving for a brief time as the editor of the journal *Brazda* and at the state publishing house Svjetlost. Many of his stories and plays were later adapted for television and film, including *Hanka* (1955), the Yugoslav entry for the 1956 Cannes Film Festival.

The Kaddish
1928

I

They buried her into the darkness itself. As Miko was leaving the cemetery an old Jew took him by the hand. The man called out to his wife from the door: "I've brought him home . . . I couldn't leave him out there in the road . . . an orphan . . ."

It took the woman a moment to absorb his words and then a glow appeared in her eyes!

"Good, Señor Judah!"

She made the boy a bed next to the children and gave him dinner. Miko fell fast asleep as though nothing had changed in his life. He simply fell silent, his head bowed.

Later they discovered that he had epilepsy and, not wishing him to frighten the children, they removed Miko. And so he was passed on from house to house. Children ran away from him, and he would hide in the flower and vegetable gardens, and behind the tombstones in the cemetery.

When even Biño the tinsmith would not take him in, not even for money, they sent him away from their little town. Thus it was that he found himself here in the city, and got to know its streets. He passed from hand to hand like a tarnished coin, turning as dark as a gypsy. He would go out early, be it winter or summer, to make the rounds of the *mahalas* and city centre, stocky in his blue chintz outfit which buttoned up at the back, prompting the children to pluck at the patterned shirt underneath. He peered out of his small eyes like a blind man groping his way through a sunny day. He went barefoot and always carried pieces of coloured glass and scraps of cloth in his hand, crying out in a drawl (when the children teased him): "Nooo, I don't waaant to . . . I don't waaant to!" His voice was like a screeching bird's. He would hold up his hands, fingers splayed, as if defending himself against attack from the air.

That is how he was when Sarucha found him.

"So you are Tia Bea's grandchild, are you? May God be good to her in that other world! And he's got epilepsy, you say. Well, what can one do? The trials sent by God . . . blessed be His name! . . . just have to be borne. I will take him in for the sake of my own soul, and for the sake of his grandmother—may God be good to her in that other world!"

Sarucha took him home with her. They entered the courtyard and sat down at the bottom of the wooden stairs.

"Sit down, Miko mine, sit down. I am old and asthmatic, I have to rest . . . these wretched stairs will be the end of me . . . and I will die before my time. . . . Sit down, my child, sit down . . . I knew your grandma . . . I knew her well . . . she was a midwife, a good woman, may they be good to her in that other world! She was my midwife, for my one child, I never had any more . . . yes, son, it was God's will . . . His will. . . . And she nursed me back to health. I came down with a fever after the baby was born. I was bed-ridden from the third day after *Sukkoth* till just before *Purim* . . . Had it not been for her, for your grandma, I don't think I would have lived to praise the Lord. With God's help she put me back on my feet again. She gave me herbal brandy to drink and I recovered, my boy, I recovered. . . . Later both the child and Señor Liacho died. . . ."

Sarucha burst into tears, and Miko drew his legs together, pulled up his knees, crossed his arms on top of them and rested his head. When they reached the top of the stairs, Sarucha took him into the kitchen. There she cut his hair with scissors, bathed him with hot water over the copper basin and took him, swathed in a sheet, to a little room where she lay him down on the mattress. She brought him bread and cheese to eat.

When Miko had fallen asleep, Sarucha kneeled down beside him and gazed at his face.

"He has sent you to me . . . He, Lord of the Universe . . . for you to say the *kaddish* when my time comes. He who rules the world, our Lord, has sent you, for there to be someone to say the *kaddish* for me and for Señor Liacho, and in return I will take care of you and save you from poverty."

Sarucha burst into tears right there next to the child, who was sleeping so sweetly and peacefully, perhaps for the first time since his mother died. The blank face and thick lips were brushed by the shadow of a smile.

"Smile, my child, smile, God gave everyone a Sabbath—His day of joy, which He created and graced with the holy *Torah*." Again Sarucha sobbed, like all old women who thus express the sorrow and the warmth which sometimes touch their hearts.

After a while she rose to her feet, lifted the arched lid of her treasure chest and took out a small bundle. The soft jingling of the Turkish gold coins echoed in the silence.

"Sarucha will use one of these to buy you clothes, my child," she said solemnly and, chanting, placed a gold *rushpa* on Miko's brow, sliding it down over his cheek.

She remembered that Miko had not kissed the *mezuzah* upon entering the house. She went to the door, placed two fingers on the small rectangular glass, then raised them to her lips and kissed them. She stared at the letters inside, but as the *mezuzah* hung in the shadow she went back to fetch a candle. She stood there gazing at it for a long time, with candle in hand, and then again she placed two fingers on the *mezuzah*, carried the fingers across the room and, kneeling down next to the child, pressed them against his lips. Startled, Miko cried out in that drawling way of his: "I don't waaant to . . ." and began to pull his hands out from under the covers.

"*Los malachim que lo guarden*," whispered Sarucha as if in prayer, and prepared for bed.

Sarucha had suffered great hardship. When she was widowed she had had to accept charity. Later some good people had helped her and she eventually became known as "la tradeswoman." She went from house to house selling chintz, fine silk, kerchiefs and shawls, earning enough to eat, and even to put aside a little something for her old age. She had not abandoned her occupation even now. Having devoted herself to trade, it was as if she had committed herself to a life of passing from one courtyard to another, one street to another, squeezing her heavy, lumbering frame through the side gates, offering her wares to Muslim and Spanish homes at a cheap price, but only for ready cash. Death was always on her mind and whenever she felt her chest tighten and started to wheeze, she would be scared. That was why Miko had so gladdened her heart. Now she would have someone to be by her side, she would not be alone at night, she would have someone to read the *kaddish* . . . the *kaddish* . . . to read the prayer.

When Liacho died, her greatest sorrow had been that there was no one to read the *kaddish* for him: "I did everything I could for him, but God did not let me do the most important thing," she would say. Her first child had died, and she never bore either male or female again. She went to the *khoja* and to the rabbi, she jotted down everything they said, she drank all the herbs they recommended, she even went to the spa in Priboj, but all to no avail. She remained barren. And as she did not conceal her defect, no one wanted her after Señor Liacho died, although she was not yet forty.

In the morning she got up and, not wanting to disturb Miko, tiptoed into the kitchen where she opened the window and looked down into the gardens below. She wanted to see a face, to say hello, to say a word, to anybody, to the first person who appeared at a window or on one of the rickety wooden verandas. It was still early. The arrogant, defiant crow of the roosters had only just pierced the air, and a white thin mist was threading its way through the plums and quinces, their leaves still wet with dew. The blush of morning rose above the Yellow Fortress. Sarucha inhaled the fresh air. It smelled of something, a herb, a flower, wallflowers, pumpkins . . . she tried to remember what it was. She thought of a time which had long since passed. She sighed deeply. Suddenly something soft and warm brushed her bare leg. She bent down, her face red, and the purring olive cat leaped into her arms.

Sarucha held it and pressed it against her cheek.

II

Miko grew into a quiet, doleful boy.

At first everything in Sarucha's house came to life. The cobwebs disappeared from the corners. Two pots of redolent young rue stood on the window sill. The little meat-pie pans came back from the tinsmith looking like new, and on Fridays Sarucha rose early and spent all day preparing for the holy Sabbath. She only just managed to finish everything by nightfall. She washed Miko with a cheap bar of scented soap, dressed him in his clean underwear, Saturday suit and smartly blocked fez, and then changed her own clothes, wrapped a silk scarf around her cap, lit the lamp and descended with Miko to wait at the bottom of the stairs for Rebbe Yako.

Old Yako came every Friday evening straight from temple to recite the *kiddush* in the widow's house. In his faded green cloth *jubbah*, he looked taller and thinner than he was. He climbed the steps slowly, humming a Sabbath hymn. When Sarucha kissed his hand he blessed her in the manner of the great rabbis and famous *shaliahs*. He placed his hand slowly on her cap, closed his blue eyes, furrowed his brow, tossed back his head and recited the Hebrew blessing in a ringing voice.

After completing the *kiddush* he would leave, solemn and mysterious, and for Sarucha it was as if a saint or the legendary Elijah the Prophet himself had visited her house. She would watch his departing figure disappear, but those blue eyes with their white lashes, that wrinkled face framed by the white beard and side curls under the fez would float before her eyes long after he had gone.

"Miko mine, Rebbe Yako will easily teach you how to read, easily, my boy," she would say and then add: "Shabbat Shalom, Miko!"

Miko would walk over, kiss her hand, sit down next to her on the wooden bench, and eat his dinner in silence, while Sarucha talked about how wonderful it would be once Miko learned how to read the prayers, recite the *kiddush* and sing the songs of David.

"Will you work hard, Miko?"

"Yes," Miko replied, shyly dipping crusts of bread into his fish chowder.

After dinner Sarucha would spread out the mattresses and Miko would take the pieces of glass from his pockets and hold them up to the light of the lamp:

"Oh, oh, Tia, red, red! Look! Look! Oh, oh, green, green . . . yellow, yellow . . . oh, oh. . . ."

And Rebbe Yako started coming every day. He brought with him a thin little book and Miko started learning the alphabet. They would sit at the bottom of the stairs—Sarucha returned early from her rounds—the rebbe would rock back and forth and repeat with Miko: "*Aleph*—wing, *beth*—mouth, *gimel*—tooth, *daleth*—hammer," and so on down to the last letter, to *tav*—crippled leg, and then go back and do it all over again, and again, until they heard Sarucha rattling the cups and coffee-pot upstairs, preparing to come down.

Rebbe Yako would take out his handkerchief, wipe his mouth, moustache and beard, and say:

"That's enough for today, my child. Kiss the book and say amen!"

Miko would close the book, put it aside and lift the olive cat onto his lap. His head was spinning. All the bold angular Hebrew letters and their symbols seemed to fly out at him from the darkness, and he lost consciousness in a bedlam of wings, mouths, hammers, thick lines and thin, points and corners. His head jogged rhythmically up and down, his ears ringing with: "*Aleph, beth, gimel, daleth*. . . ." And so he would doze off.

"What do I think? Well, good woman, first of all ours is a difficult law. It is not easy to learn to read our sacred letters. And Miko? God is great. God has given an abundance of brains to some and He has given at least some to everyone, including Miko. Today, tomorrow, Miko too will learn something. Something; we don't really know very much ourselves. What do the rest of us know, good woman? Barely enough to fathom the depth and greatness of our holy *Torah*," Rebbe Yako would say.

But Miko made poor progress and was wasting away.

He lost weight and looked wan. All day long he would amble around the courtyard, climb the fence and look into the next-door gardens, and when he heard Sarucha's footsteps around the hour of *ikindia*, the Muslim afternoon prayer, he would run sluggishly to the closed courtyard gate and start hopping from one foot to the other: "The street, I want to go out, Tia, dear Tia, out into the street . . ."

Sarucha would take him by the hand and lead him to the bottom of the stairs.

"Wait a minute, boy, wait Miko mine, I've brought you something. . . ."

And she would take out a cube of Turkish delight or a lollipop or some fruit, and Miko would stop to eat it, to lick it, his tongue darting out at the candied stick, now and then repeating wildly, as if in a dream:

"Into the street . . . the street. . . ."

Then one day he disappeared. The olive cat searched the house for him, and when it noticed the broken window, it jumped onto the sill, miaowed several times and then returned downstairs to lie in the sun and wait for Sarucha. When she did not find Miko at home Sarucha went out of her mind. She flailed her arms, checked with the neighbours and finally, exhausted and gasping, sat down and wept.

Just before nightfall Miko entered the courtyard as incorporeal as a shadow. The cat leaped down from Sarucha's lap. Startled, she said:

"Miko . . . oh . . . my poor Miko. . . . Sinner that I am . . . where have you been? . . ."

Miko quietly and very slowly crossed the courtyard, carrying a fez full of glass fragments as if it were a cup full of water, saying:

"Red, red . . . oh, oh . . . yellow, yellow . . . oh, oh . . . Tia . . . Tia . . . red. . . ."

That winter Sarucha fell ill. There was a wheezing in her chest. She wailed: "I'm going to die and you're not paying attention, you're not studying, you don't even know the *kaddish* yet . . . oh, sinner that I am. . . . And you're back to your old ways, you're big. All summer I paid Rebbe Yako . . . and all you do is loll around. . . . God Almighty, I'm going to die, die. . . ."

Sarucha was convulsed with coughing. Miko sat contritely by her side, resting his head on his knees, slowly drawing out the words and saying softly to himself: "*Aaaleph . . . beeeth . . . giiimel . . . daaaleth . . .*," thinking that he was saying the greatest of prayers for Tia Sarucha's recovery. All through her illness, he would go down to the bottom of the stairs, take the little book from inside his shirt, sit down and recite the Hebrew letters. Every so often he would look up at the sky and heave a great sigh. In the evening, when Sarucha started to moan and groan again, and to cough, he would snuggle up to her and, after long hesitation, say: "Tia, don't be afraid. . . . Don't be afraid, Tia . . . you won't die. . . .," and then he would resume his prayer: "*Aleph, beth, gimel, daleth*. . . ."

Sarucha recovered time and again.

And so their life continued until the second summer, when Miko took to traipsing around town. He stayed out all day; Sarucha combed the area, asking around for him, and only just managed to find him. And where was he? He was sitting by the road, watching the children swim in the Miljacka River. Coated in dust and sweat, he was tapping a stone on the ground, gazing at the water. The other children squealed, screamed, splashed in the water, jumped off the rocks, swam, went diving, and those who did not know how to keep afloat puffed up their wet trunks and then carefully lowered themselves into the water, floating like big colourful bubbles.

"My, oh my, sinner that I am, what on earth will become of you?! Why did I ever take you in? Good God! Why, you're no longer a child . . . no you're not. . . ." Sarucha scolded him, gasping, wet under her shawl.

She took him home; on the way she got him some Turkish hazelnuts and when they reached the stairs she sat him down on the bottom step, stroking his face, and said to him fondly:

"Well, Miko, it's time for you to mend your ways, make a poor sad woman happy and open your eyes; I'll adopt you as my very own, so that you are not orphaned a second time, without knowing your mother. . . . Miko, open your eyes and look into mine. All this will be yours; God gave it, all I ask of Him is an easy death. . . . Do you hear me, Miko? All of it, everything will be yours, the house, the courtyard, the chest and everything inside it, and there is a lot inside it, Miko, yes there is; you'll be able to open a shop of your own. . . . Do you hear me, Miko?"

Miko was sitting beside her, stroking the cat with one hand, and turning over a piece of glass with the other.

"It's me who will die first, me!"

"God forbid," cried Sarucha getting up. "God forbid! Look, Miko, you are getting your life back, you are!" She took his hand in hers and stroked it: 'You won't die, no you won't, God willing you will recover completely, yes you will, you'll grow up to be a man . . . and Zimbula has a girl in Sterluca, Miko mine; never mind that she is cross-eyed, she will be a girl like her mother and you can get married and have children, born right here; may the first one be a boy, and when you promise him to our Lord may this house and this courtyard burst into song and the sound of music and may you live long, Miko, and be here to say the *kaddish* for me . . . the *kaddish* . . . for me and for Señor Liacho. . . ."

Sarucha clasped his head in her hands to kiss him on the brow, and choked with elation, he laughed, opened his mouth, drew two or three breaths, then twitched, turned his foot, clenched his fists, rolled back his eyes until only the whites showed and toppled over in a faint,

jerking and twitching in pain. He had an epileptic fit whenever he felt joy.

For a while Miko was better. He did not leave the house, until one morning he disappeared again. He went into the city's back streets, and even down to the Turkish cemetery. At nightfall he crept back into the house and slept under the stairs, only to disappear again at daybreak. Sometimes the Muslim children would chase him away with stones and he would come home all bloody and go to Tia Sarucha with head bowed, repentant. Sarucha lost hope, she saw that nothing would come of him and she scolded and berated him, and when he had had enough he would leave the house again.

III

They were picking plums and making jam when word spread among the Jews that Miko the epileptic was in the new hospital, the one built by the Austrians behind Mustai-Bey's plum orchard. They immediately ran to tell Sarucha, but she was in bed herself. Her legs were as swollen as pillars.

"Oh my," she wailed, "oh my, sinner that I am, for this to happen to me just now!"

She offered the woman taking care of her a whole *sechser* to go and see how he was, but the young woman refused, frightened and offended that Sarucha could even think of such a thing.

"You surprise me, Tia Sarucha, you of all people! How can you even think of a woman going there, for God's sake, to a hospital on the outskirts of town? . . . God forbid!"

For the first time the town started taking an interest in what would happen to Miko. He was the first Spanish Jew to be in hospital. The eldest member of the *hevra kaddisha* decided that the sexton should go there daily and inquire whether the Spaniard, Miko Pardo—the epileptic—had died. He needed to be buried according to Jewish law and what did those Krauts up there know about that? According to Jewish law he had to be buried immediately, as soon as the soul departed from the body. But those people up there might leave him for two or three days. God forbid such a thing should happen to a Jew, even if it was just Miko the epileptic! And so the decision was taken and every morning the sexton walked around the iron railings of the hospital gate. People walked in and out, but he just bided his time until the gate-keeper asked him what he wanted.

"Has that fellow . . . Pardo . . . Miko . . . the Spaniard . . . the epileptic . . . died?"

And every time the sexton came back with fresh news. They had shut Miko up in that building where they amputate legs, cut open stomachs and take out eyes. The guess was that they must have sliced off a piece of his intestine, or opened up his head to see where the epilepsy came from. Some said he had been bitten by an adder in the Turkish cemetery at the foot of Sedrenik and that they had amputated his leg just below the knee.

Months went by.

Summer drew to a close and Sarucha's olive cat amused itself alone at the bottom of the stairs. Upstairs Sarucha was moaning, but down below the sun was still warm and the cat could stretch out contentedly in the noon-day heat. Reclining on its side, stretching out its paws, it squinted with golden-green eyes, the black pupils barely visible thin lines. Its sprawling stomach rose and fell, its little nipples pink among the fine grey fur. The courtyard gate squeaked, the cat lazily turned its head and suddenly it leaped to its feet bristling, as if a dog was coming its way. It was Miko. Tall, his eyes bright, a strange smile on his face. When he knocked at the door and stepped into the room, Sarucha almost fainted. He walked over to her bed, all tall and thin now, and kissed her hand. Sarucha looked at him. He had changed so much. His skin had become white, there was an openness about him, his lips had thinned out. He was wearing a thin yellow suit and red-laced canvas shoes.

When she got over the shock she burst into tears. Stroking his face and head she said:

"Miko mine, dear . . . Miko. . . . See what you've reduced me to? . . . See? . . ." Sarucha uncovered her legs.

There lay two strangely deformed legs, swollen, chalk-white, bloated with water, cold, with a cadaverous sheen.

"Everything will be all right, Tia Sarucha, everything, don't you worry! Look, feel here . . . that's where they hit me with the rock . . . the Turks . . . up by the wooden mosque. . . . Whack, the rock hit me and . . . when I woke up I was lying in bed. My head was wrapped in cotton . . . I'm fine now, I feel lighter, as if something fell out of my head . . . yes, Tia Sarucha, everything will be all right now . . . everything. . . ."

Miko lay his head on her breast and burst into tears. Sarucha stroked his hair and when he stopped sobbing, she asked him:

"Miko, will you recite the *kaddish* for me when I die, will you know how now . . . will you?"

"Yes, I will," said Miko, his tears muffling the words. Sarucha pulled herself up.

"Come now, son, get up, open the old chest; here are the keys. There is a book at the bottom . . . take it out, son. . . ."

Miko held the book out to her and she took it with both hands, lifted it to her lips and kissed it. For a long while she stroked the silver-studded crimson velvet binding, and then she held it out to him.

"Here, Miko, take it, it's from Señor Liacho . . . for you to be a good Jew and to pray to our Lord, to live in His glory . . ."

Miko kissed her hand and Sarucha started to cry.

From that day on Miko never strayed far from the house again. He nursed the patient, roasted coffee for her, made her swollen legs comfortable, changed the compresses on her head, fed her soup made by the neighbours, brewed herbs for her, sat by her side all night reading from the prayer book, speaking the Hebrew words, singing to himself, drawing out the word endings and rolling his eyes.

When old Tia Sarucha began to turn blue, the women had to practically drag him out of the room so that he would not see her dead. Sad, pale, sleepless and hungry, he stood hunched by the door, the book under his arm. From inside came the choking, strangling sound of her death rattle. Miko began to shake and, pulling himself away, he staggered down the stairs. At the bottom of the steps he stopped. The evening sun bathed him in its warm red glow. Miko shivered as if he had a fever. He listened for any sound from the room upstairs, then he turned around and gazed at the sky. Its beautiful russet redness filled his eyes, pouring into him as if he were a bottomless pit, and within two or three seconds, as if saturated, big red stains appeared on his cheeks. Miko then opened the velvet prayer book, found his place, and began to read the *kaddish*, the prayer for the dead.

He read it aloud, word by drawn-out word, in a strange kind of chant, entranced. He opened and closed his eyes, swaying back and forth on his toes. His cheeks went red, and a white foam gathered in the corners of his mouth. His entire body shook.

Entering the courtyard gate, passers-by, Jews and Muslims, looked at Miko in wonder. His sad, solemn voice rose and fell into the silence of the flushed evening.

"*. . . Amen . . . ye . . . e . . . sheme . . . rabba. . . .*"

Thus he sang until he had completed the prayer. Then silence descended. A furry butterfly flapped its orange wings against the white wall. Miko closed the book, kissed it, stood on his toes, lifted his arms up in the air and stood there like that for a minute; then, as if broken into four, his body collapsed at the bottom of the stairs. People ran over to him. Some offered their keys. Avdaga the baker, who made soft white bread rolls at the corner in Pehlivanusha St., crouched down beside Miko, picked up his wrist and felt it.

"No, *djanum*, it's not epilepsy. There's no need for the key! It's over, he's burst an artery. It's *damla*, a stroke, a bad stroke," he said lowering the arm. "*Allah rahmetile*! May God rest his soul."

They covered him with a white sheet; upstairs a door opened and in a subdued voice a woman told the people in the courtyard:

"Tell them to pour out the water. Sarucha has left the living. May God have mercy on her soul!"

In the spring they dragged everything away from Sarucha's house. They put a new lock on the courtyard gate and peace descended. Rays of sunshine broke through the cracks in the roof and little rings of light glittered like gold coins on the rafters in the dark attic. The door stood wide open. Every so often one of the old oak columns would groan. At the bottom of the stairs the olive cat was basking in the sun. It had carried its litter down from the attic, one by one. Lying on its side, it squinted, a fluffy little kitten hanging from each of its nipples.

It was noon.

To the sound of an accordion being played in one of the white blossom gardens, the new cathedral in town down below struck the hour:

Dong . . . dong . . . dong. . . .

Ong . . . ong . . . ong . . . came the mysterious echo from Sarucha's house.

Gently sprouting from the dried-up stalk of rue in the cracked flowerpot on the window sill was a new serrated leaf. Passing by Sarucha's big house, people with a discerning sense of smell knew from its scent that spring had arrived.

Translated by Christina Pribićević-Zorić.

Other works by Samokovlija: *Od proljeća do proljeća* (1929); *Nosač Samuel* (1946); *Solomunovo slovo* (1949).

Yitshak Shami
1888–1949

Yitshak Shami was an unusual contributor to the world of Hebrew literature in the interwar years: his background was Mizrahi rather than Ashkenazi, and his fiction featured Palestinian Arabs. Born in Hebron to a Syrian Jewish family, he moved to Jerusalem at age seventeen, adopted Western dress, and attended a teachers' seminary, where he received a certificate in 1909 and began publishing short stories. He taught in Jewish schools in Damascus and Bulgaria and then returned to the Land of Israel in 1919, where he made his home first in Tiberias and then in Hebron. His literary output was slim: a book of short stories and two novellas, written largely in the 1920s.

The Vengeance of the Fathers
1928

Chapter Five

From here to the shrine of Nabi Moussa was some twenty-five miles. Allah, wanting to placate his favorite, and mitigate the punishment which He had imposed on him in His anger, had promised Moses before he died that He would not leave him alone in the distant desert, to be visited only by heat and dust. He had therefore instructed the faithful, through the mouth of the Prophet Muhammad—peace and prayers be with him!—to attend at his grave every year, during the month he had died in, for seven successive days of feasting and dancing, and had commanded the three most important *sanjaqs* to visit him at his shrine with much splendor and ceremony. To make the pilgrimage less of a burden, He had moved the grave several parasangs closer to the places of habitation, and had made the road leading to it pleasant and easy, so that even old people and children could make the journey without difficulty. Half of it He had set between mountain ridges in a long continuous descent, so that your feet moved forward of their own accord without any effort, and the remainder on the flat and level plain. Marvelous sights greeted the pilgrims at every step. He had gathered pools of cold water from the rains and preserved them in crevices among the rocks, not allowing them to evaporate, to quench the thirst of birds and pilgrims alike. With carpets of grasses and fragrant flowers He had decorated the desolate desert for this brief period, for the sake of those who performed His will, giving them refreshing sights to restore their souls and dissipate their fatigue, inspiring them with renewed vigor.

In the normal course of events, the flag-masters lead their camps on without any unnecessary delays. They complete the journey in less than six hours, hoping to bring their followers to the tall white wall surrounding the great square shrine with its towers and wings and domes by the time the *muezzin* on the minaret chants the call for the sunset prayer.

Experienced leaders, who know their people and care for them as a father for his children, have always tried to conclude this part of the pilgrimage in daylight. This way they have time to find resting places inside the buildings for the women, the children and the sick, and to see that the distribution of meat and rice is conducted properly according to the established quota. Above all, they have time to spend what remains of the day resting, so that their charges may regain strength before the lighting of the torches which will illuminate the desert with dancing flames, while celebrants prance around them to the sound of hundreds of drums and other instruments, at the beginning of the noisy and enthusiastic dances which will continue all night long.

As storks train their young to fly, now taking to the heights, screeching and encouraging the fledglings to join them, now returning, to flutter around, support them by their wings, and push them forward, so do the leaders circle around their groups and urge them to walk faster. Now they pass them at a gallop, with gleeful cries; now they mingle among them or drive from behind, occasionally lending a hand with an animal that has collapsed under its load, or coaxing stragglers on with all kinds of tricks and proverbs. As they give themselves over completely to joy and fun, the road leaps out to greet them and they arrive with the speed of a dream at their destination.

Since the imaginations of the participants are very active all this time, in years to come they will generally recall only the most prominent or impressive event of the pilgrimage, forgetting all the other trivial details. But the incidents which precede or cause such an event are so powerful that they too become engraved in the memory for ever. Such was the case this time too. The strange occurrences and amazing sights which attended this pilgrimage determined the atmosphere and created the framework for the awful spectacle that followed, all the parts and links of which were flooded with the red glow of a single flame.

As told by extremely reliable eyewitnesses from among the *ḥajjs* and dervishes, seers of things present and future, it appears that while the flag-masters were standing calmly and peacefully side by side with their flags held high, and the Mufti was reciting the *fatiḥah*, the holy and venerated opening prayer of the Qur'an, far down in the valley two crows rose from among the tops of the olive trees. Screeching bitterly, they fell upon each other, gouging and scratching one another with their beaks until large quantities of feathers fell around the flags like autumn leaves. After weaving circles in the air several times, forming a covenant with the agents of hell, they drew tight the ring of enchantment and disaster above the pilgrims' heads and flew off swiftly and silently, to vanish eastward beyond the mountains.

And from that moment onward the pilgrims' leaders were caught in a snare from which there was no escape. The Devil had driven his nose-ring through their nostrils and now led them as he willed, using them as tools for the perpetration of his schemes to profane the pilgrimage and the pilgrims. His chief agents, disastrously for themselves, were Abu Faris and Abu al-Shawarib.

After the Mufti and his entourage had left these two, they lost all their self-control, revealing to all present their true faces, which were full of hatred and cold calculation. The passion for honor and revenge burning inside them darkened the light of their reason, dragging and driving them from error to error, to insane and inconsistent actions.

Just as fish, darting about around an open net, instinctively follow one of their group who swims into it—so did the throngs of pilgrims become entangled in the hellish fabric woven by their leaders, with their whispered and muttered barbs, their contemptuous treatment of each other, the venom that pervaded their movements and comments whenever they passed one another, the fractiousness and contradictions in the commands they gave, and the perversity in their hearts which spread like an epidemic, infecting the thousands of sunstruck heads of men who followed them with eyes closed as if smitten with blindness, and inflaming the lust for blood latent in their souls.

Very soon they all lost their way and forgot their objective. The desire to destroy, to injure, to raise riot, became the only driving force in all the camps.

The invisible Devil, who had been working all that day with all the means at his disposal, had now also taken the sun as an ally, using it to close the circle of disaster around the pilgrims by bringing to ripeness all the notions of hatred that had not yet fully taken shape.

That terrible day was a day of stifling heat. Even before completing half its journey the sun had lost its luster and taken on that dull silver hue that presages the *ḥamsin*. At the fringes of the mountains there were still a few patches of shade here and there where the pilgrims could find some relief, but as soon as they descended into the Jordan Valley they walked into an east wind that blew from the desert as if from the mouth of a white-hot furnace. The wind swept before it gusts of sand and dust, whirling them around as in a devil's dance. The blazing and charged waves of air stretched the pilgrims' nerves taut, poured fire into their arteries, and worked up a storm in their hearts.

As beasts of burden plodding along lethargically may suddenly run amok for no reason at all, tearing off their harness, flinging off their loads, kicking and biting at each other—so did the pilgrims clash at every step. Trivial incidents, which during any other pilgrimage would have been passed over or laughed away, developed into unending series of quarrels, which often flared up into a large-scale brawl.

When the shouting and screaming brought the leaders of the two opposing camps running to the scene of the incident, they made no effort to soothe the vexed spirits. Instead, fuming with anger themselves, they either stood there with folded arms like impartial observers or, pretending to be separating the antagonists, misused their status in order to favor their own side. Thus they would grab the arms of someone on the opposing side only if he seemed to have the upper hand, allowing the weaker antagonist, of their own side, to hit him freely.

Prominent among these ugly waves of hatred, bobbing up everywhere, was the *suss* vendor. On this day there was almost no one who did not become aware of his presence and his strength. His name was an abomination in the Hebronite camp. In every cluster that formed around a brawl or a dispute he could be recognized from afar, by his mop of hair that bristled on his head like a hawk's comb, and by the dark paint around his eyes which had spread with his sweat to smear his cheeks and neck. As long as all he did was to push spectators about or place himself in the middle, shouting abuse at the Hebronites and giving indirect assistance to the Nablusite hotheads, the Hebronites tolerated him and treated him cautiously, careful not to provoke him further. But when his cries of derision grew more numerous than their blows, some of the more daring Hebronites ganged together and cunningly inveigled him into a spot concealed from the sight of his fellows, where they surrounded him and began to rain blows upon him. He, however, did not call out for help. Skillfully swinging his staff—a split pomegranate branch with a rounded head—he drove back his attackers, breaking their ring and making them flee. By the time some

Nablusites saw him and rushed to his aid he had completely extricated himself and came striding proudly toward them. Still cursing his attackers violently and calling them by all the known names of abuse, he tore a long strip from the lining of his caftan and bandaged his bleeding forehead with it. Then, straightening his *abayah* and waistband, like a triumphant cock preening his feathers after a hard battle, he stepped forth with head held high into the midst of his townsmen, who stood staring at him in amazement and awe at the bravery he had just displayed.

And so he became the leader of all the Nablusite hotheads who wanted to revenge themselves on the world at large and to terrify everyone they met. As their chief, he devised numerous tricks. He conducted attacks, aroused brawls, and infected all his followers with his own blazing temper anti rebellious anger, the result being that the malice and impudence of this wild gang soon broke down all barriers of order and discipline.

In this chaos of quarrels and brawls which burst out time and again with ever greater frequency, the flag-masters found that they no longer had any control over the conduct of the procession, and could not have stopped the rioters even if they had really and truly wanted to. Almost without realizing what was happening, even the more moderate people suddenly seemed to have lost the ground under their feet, and all of them rolled down into a deep abyss of savage strife among brothers, conducted with bared teeth and clenched fists and immeasurable cruelty.

Things went so far that at the well of Maaleh Adumim a fierce struggle took place between Hebronite donkey-drivers who were drawing water for their animals and a group of Nablusites who had come hurrying rowdily after them to try to capture the place for themselves. Yelling fierce battle cries, calling on the name of Allah, the new arrivals snatched up the reins of the drinking animals, beat them, and scattered them in all directions. The Hebronites were not tardy in retaliating, and fell upon their attackers with hoarse cries. Men fought and kicked each other, many of them rolling on the ground, screaming and striking until the water in the troughs was red with their blood. This shameful incident aroused many hearts against the Nablusites, and drew in its train other acts of revenge and infamy.

This year, as in previous years, the proprietors of the al-Akhmar *khan* welcomed the flag-masters, and then brought them to a shelter behind the building where they could rest, serving them the banquet that had been waiting for them here since morning.

Abu al-Shawarib and his officers sat down on the mats around the steaming, fragrant dishes. A little later Abu Faris arrived with his party. They too allowed the *khan* owner to lead them to the shelter. But when they saw who was seated inside their expressions changed visibly and they quivered with hatred. Without discussing this among themselves, they all turned about at once and strode off, loudly and angrily, the spurs on their boots jangling as they walked. In vain did the bewildered and insulted proprietor plead with them. They denied him the benefit of their presence, and refused to eat or taste anything in his establishment. Glowering, they shook their heads coldly at him, mounted their horses, and commanded their followers to continue on their way and bypass the *khan*.

When they had traveled far enough so as to no longer hear the din of the Nablus camp, they stopped to rest on the slopes of a reddish hill that was covered with adonis and poppies which bent on their stems with the east wind that blew against them from the desert around Jericho. Here the tired Hebronites lay down to rest, some simply sprawling where they dropped, without moving a limb, while others crawled into the elongated shadows of their camels to find shelter from the blazing sun.

If they were angry when they lay down, they were doubly angered when they were suddenly brought to their feet to see groups of Nablusites who had deliberately left the road and were now rapidly leading their heavily laden animals with shouts through the field where they lay, maliciously disturbing their brief rest. A general pandemonium spread everywhere with nothing to inhibit it, like water pouring down a slope. From all sides came curses, oaths, frightened cries of women and children, and angry voices yelling "Hit them!" "Without mercy!"

Abu Faris and Abu al-Shawarib did not lift a finger to try to stop the uproar. They circled around the hill-slope like wolves seeking prey, in reply to the desperate pleas addressed to them, and to the just demands of the Jerusalemites that they put an end to the dispute, they only shrugged their shoulders and flung back in response "Let's see if you can stop this!"

The few policemen accompanying the procession were also powerless to quell the riot. In their attempts to restore order they did not have the courage to burst in among the combatants and use firm measures against them: they contented themselves with spoken appeals,

and most of the time ran about helplessly in all directions. Finally their Turkish officer lost patience with the effort, and with a furious expression on his face blew a long blast on his whistle, assembled his policemen, whispered something to them, and then they all galloped off on the road to Jerusalem to request reinforcements.

This simple and daring tactic, together with the untiring efforts of the Jerusalemites, had some effect on the milling crowd, bringing back a modicum of reason. The brawling petered out, and gradually the circles of angry men, which had been whirling about like lakes into which a rain of stones has been hurled, dispersed and quieted down.

All this wrangling had cost them a lot of time. Instead of reaching the mount at the customary time of the evening offering, to pray the third prayer of the day in public assembly, they now arrived at its foot, exhausted and scattered, just before evening, when the setting sun was at the height of a camel and his rider above the horizon. And when they reached the top of the mount, it seemed as if the shrine of Nabi Moussa, with its precariously tall tower, its rounded domes and arched windows, was enveloped in flames from the setting sun, and that the bare hills around it were alight in a bluish-orange hue, like burning sulfur, their long shadows spreading across the plain.

While waiting for the stragglers, the first arrivals moved about wearily, busying themselves with gathering stones and piling them up in little hillocks for markers, and with repairing the many piles that had become scattered since the previous year. Old men and young, fearful of being late for the sunset prayer, hurriedly formed circles and moved aside, while the red glow of before-dusk rested on their faces, which were contorted with exhaustion and sorrow. Silently they took off their *abayahs*, spread them out on the ground, and stood on them barefooted, with folded arms, in long rows, erect and frozen, like the cliffs and hills beneath them, then bowed and prayed fervently, all bending in unison, like ripe corn when the wind blows through it. When they had completed their whisperings and prostrations they stood up again with a sigh, shaking their heads with concern as they rejoined the many gangs who, forgetting the customs and ignoring the reverence due to their elders, now passed by them, without pausing to wait for them until they had finished their prayer.

For another half hour people kept coming from among the hill-slopes. The camels, sensing that they were soon to arrive and receive their fodder, held their heads erect and joyfully shook the bells hanging around their necks. With no prodding from their owners they moved forward and clambered with broad strides to the top of the last hill that bounds the plain where the mosque stands. Their owners hurried to catch up with them, and everyone advanced more quickly. Going down the hill on the other side, the owners finally caught up with their camels, grabbed their reins, and, pouring out their wrath upon the animals with blows and curses, held them back and forced them to a halt.

According to custom, they were supposed to wait here for the final rite during which the flags were brought into the mosque of Nabi Moussa by the flag-masters at the heads of their parties. So an increasing crowd of people continued to gather here, and one could discern among them many whose faces were filled with the savage anger that had burst out earlier. Their fury and excitement were manifest in their very postures and movements. Of their own accord they divided up into two camps with a large space between them, and a great bustle of movement, marking the final preparations, swept over them like a stormy wave. Now their leaders passed among them with officious speed, moving them excitedly backward and forward, hitting them to get them to form into columns, the bounds of which each leader determined as he wished. The din increased with the bleating of sheep and goats and the snorting of camels that were also being pushed about. The hundreds of drums and other instruments which pounded out their sounds in total disorder made the earth tremble and startled the horses and the mules, increasing the clamor and filling the hearts of the pilgrims with rage and resentment at the conflicting commands which could in no way be carried out.

And suddenly, like a wind blowing among the trees of a forest, a whisper traveled from mouth to mouth: "There they go! There they go!" Fear and anxiety appeared on every face. Now all the screaming stopped and each man easily found his proper place. The pilgrims divided their camps into three sections: those on foot first, behind them the riders, and last of all those in carriages. All eyes turned in a single direction, all hearts pounded fiercely, and with bated breath they drew themselves erect and gazed disbelievingly at the spectacle unfolding before them.

From the opposite hilltop the flag-masters descended slowly on their noble steeds bedecked in checkered trappings. The flags they bore did not budge, and de-scended in folds around their poles, which were as long as masts. In the center, a step ahead of the others, rode Abu al-Shawarib, cantering proudly and freely, his face beaming with the joy and pride of victory. On his right and a little too far back rode Abu Faris, courageously bent over his steed, like a tiger about to pounce. His legs were drawn back, his stomach drawn in, and he and his horse looked as if they had been glued together. His thick eyebrows arched over his flashing cat's eyes, which stared unmovingly ahead and clearly expressed his dark decision of intrigue.

They reached the very heart of the camps which still stood, immobile as walls, waiting for the flag-masters to ride past them so that they could turn and follow them. The *suss* vendor was standing at the head of a column of Nablusites, beside the sacrificial camel. Girding his loins and thrusting the ends of his *kaftan* into his belt, he somersaulted onto the beast's neck and from there climbed up, nimble as a squirrel, to stand erect on its back. When the flag-masters were some twenty meters from him he bent his head backward a little, pressed his hand to his temple, and declaimed in a loud voice:

> Nimmer, Nimmer, on his white stallion proud,
> His sword a lightning bolt, his flag—a cloud,
> Eagles chose him to lead their ring
> Roaring lions have crowned him their king,
> Those who love him rest in his shade
> His enemies fall before him and fade!

"Ai! . . . Ai! . . . Ai! . . . Support him! Praise him! Follow him!" came the cries from the Nablusite camp. In wild enthusiasm they roared and cheered, greeting their leader and their flag with a triumphant song. Then again they cried: "Ai! Ai!" and "Support him! Praise him!" with increasing fervor and deafening roars.

Abu Faris started laughing—strange, contemptuous short bursts of laughter. His left leg began to tremble, knocking with his spur on his horse's thigh. The well-trained horse looked from side to side and did not move from the spot, and soon his master calmed down. He had understood that the time had not yet come to act, and looked about stealthily to see if his secret intrigue had not been discovered. On seeing in Abu al-Shawarib's face the expression of one who is confident of his own power and high degree, he restrained himself, disguised the fury and contempt in his eyes, and again put on an air of unconcern and scorn, as if what had happened did not affect him in the slightest.

In the Hebronite camp, tears of indignation and shame could be seen on many faces. The *suss* vendor had aimed his pointed barbs well, and they lodged deep in their hearts.

But their downfall did not last long. Soon enough a redeemer was found among them, who removed the disgrace and returned it sevenfold upon their foes. A man arose from among their rear ranks, tall as a giant. As he walked forward he threw the flap of his *abayah* over his shoulder with pretended casualness, freed a hand, and motioned to one of his companions to kneel down. Taking off his shoes, he climbed up on the other's shoulders. Then, taking his *kaffiyeh*, which he had rolled up like a snake, and waving it around his head in all directions to draw the attention of all present and to tell them to be silent, he too declaimed, in a lion's voice:

> Soon will come the day of redress
> With wrath overturning distress
> Then the faces of the oppressed will all shine
> And the faces of the robbers be shamed!

"Raise him! Raise him! . . . Again! Again! . . ." roared the Hebronites. Hundreds of arms reached toward him, grasped him, lifted him into the air like a feather and held him high, cheering all the while. They did not cease calling out even when their leaders urged them to move off. Only when their limbs grew weary and their throats hoarse did they respond to their leader's commands, and moved off with much noise and clamor.

Then the dervishes enthusiastically began singing a sacred song:

> To you, the Prophet Moussa,
> We will pour out our hearts,
> Our bodies—your redemption,
> Our souls—your compensation.
> *Moussa kalim Allah*
>
> Like a father who watches our growth
> Like a craftsman who suckles our art,
> Bless us to seek your shrine
> Pour on us your spirit so fine,
> *Moussa kalim Allah*
>
> In your flame we are consumed
> To your tomb we are attuned
> Shade us in your shelter,
> Bathe us in your splendor,
> *Moussa kalim Allah!*

Their intoxication spread to all the pilgrims, and thousands of wild voices responded to the song, which merged into a single fierce and prolonged shout, savage and sad as the desert. Heads swayed to the rhythm of the singing, and it seemed as if the entire plain was singing and swaying with the people and the animals and the flags and the swords.

Twilight deepened, the last gleams of day began to fade and slip away from the wide enclosure, which steamed with the evening, emitting its heat in thin, pale, mistlike clouds. In the midst of these moved the flag-masters, their shapes already blurred. Some had already completely vanished from sight and only their flags could be seen, stretched like moving sails in the misty air.

Darkness had descended on the walls and the wide-open gate of the shrine. When the flag-masters were some three hundred lance-lengths from it, Abu al-Shawarib, excitedly sensing the importance of the event he was about to take part in, drew in his reins, stood up on his stirrups, and looked back to see if everything was in order among his followers. At that moment he heard the sound of a stick whistling through the air a little to his right, followed by a pounding of hoofs: the red horse of Abu Faris, who had been riding behind him, shot past him like a flash of fire; the unfurled Hebronite flag swelled out in front of him, fanning him with wind as it flew on, like the flapping of a mighty wing.

Astonished at first, Abu al-Shawarib stared at the flag as if unable to believe the terrible sight he had just seen. But his sharp eyes had recognized Abu Faris, and now a sudden clarity flashed through his brain and set all his limbs aquiver. At one glance he took everything in, and understood the whole of Abu Faris's cunning and perfidy. His blood boiled and hummed in his temples, his eyes darkened, and he struck himself hard on the head. He let out a mighty roar: "Perfidy!" dug his spurs deep into his white stallion until the blood flowed, and, bending slightly forward over his saddle, slashed down with his reins.

The stallion, sensing his master's agitation, burst into the speedy gallop for which he was famed. Neck down, tail flying, he seemed to glide through the air without touching the ground. Very soon he had caught up with the horse ahead of him, and ran so close to him that the legs of the riders were touching. Several paces away from the gate he succeeded in passing him by a whole step, and then Abu al-Shawarib thrust his drawn sword in front of the eyes of his opponent's horse, without touching him. The red horse reared and drew back. Before he could start riding forward again Abu al-Shawarib had blocked his path and forced him to stand still on the spot.

The two animals of different breeds stood there staring at each other in hatred, and a dreadful and ominous silence ensued. Then Abu Faris shrugged his shoulders impatiently, beat upon his horse's neck with all his might, changed his position, and struck his horse again with the intention of evading Abu al-Shawarib and passing around him.

Abu al-Shawarib grasped his intention and moved his own horse around to block his path again. Coming close enough to his rival to touch him, he stammered in a hoarse, strangled voice:

"Get back, traitor! . . . And if you don't . . ."

"Your mother's cunt!" hissed Abu Faris, and gave him a hard shove in the ribs with the end of his flagpole. Abu al-Shawarib swayed and groaned in pain, but quickly recovered. Trembling with rage, his mouth ajar and his eyes dilated, now totally in the grip of one of those frenzies that bring a man to sin, he rose up on his stirrups and bent toward his enemy. He grabbed the flag in an attempt to wrench it from Abu Faris's hands, and the flag tore. Abu Faris reached for his belt, to draw his revolver, but Abu al-Shawarib was quicker, and thrust his sword into the other's breast with all his might.

"To me, my men! The son of a whore has killed me! . . ." Abu Faris gurgled, and spoke no more. He fell on his face, his head landing on the neck of his killer's horse. A stream of blood poured from his mouth onto the saddle, and sprayed onto his face and clothes. The stallion gave a start and moved away, and the lifeless body turned over and fell to the earth, landing with a dull thud.

Abu al-Shawarib stood rooted to the spot, bewildered and astounded, staring at the dark form lying in the sand in the growing pool of blood which now divided into two streams advancing toward him like snakes. Suddenly a huge mounted figure rose up beside the dead man, large as an elephant, and began wailing in bitter, heart-rending tones: "The Muslims are finished: the end has come! My brothers! . . . Help! . . . Help! . . ." And from further away, in the other direction, came a loud cry: "Flee, Abu Nimmer! The dogs are after you!" Abu al-Shawarib shrank in fear. Without knowing what he was doing he brandished the flag he was holding and sent his horse galloping toward the gate of the shrine before the shadows, now advancing upon him like wolves could reach him. By their flash-

ing swords and their angry cries he knew the danger he was in, and understood that he would be hopelessly lost if he did not get away from them quickly. Casting a quick glance to the side, he placed the flag by the gatepost and galloped on to the right, in the direction that was clear of people. The wails, the cries for help, and the shots cutting through the air behind him increased his fear and the speed of his flight, and his horse flew along the treacherous paths among the hills as if borne on the wings of mysterious forces. To Abu al-Shawarib it felt as if he were flying down into some deep abyss. Only when the noise of pursuit was far behind him and he found himself surrounded by darkness did he stop his horse for a moment. He leapt to the ground, put his ear to the earth, and listened attentively for its secret pulses. When he was sure that no pursuers were coming after him he got up again, his knees shaking. Still breathing heavily and sweating profusely from every pore, he pressed his trembling hand to his chest to calm the dreadful pounding of his heart. Concentrating all his senses in his ears, he laid his head sorrowfully on his horse's neck and hugged the animal the way a terrified child presses close to his mother's breast.

"Ḥikmat Allah!" he muttered over and over between compressed lips, in an attempt to overcome his weakness and distress, and to grasp the torturing thought which kept fluttering through all the other dark visions of chaos that flew about in his brain like withered leaves on a stormy day. The words, however, neither penetrated to his heart nor restored his strength. He struggled to exercise the thought and free himself of it, but he could sense it roaming through his soul, hovering above him and bunting his forehead. He closed his eyes and tried to catch it, and sank into a kind of idea for which there is no concept.

Several minutes passed. They were like hours to him. His consciousness returned and he shuddered like a man falling from a great height in a dream. Something like a giant flame lit up in front of him, illuminating all the dark and secret places of his soul. Hitting himself on the head with both hands, he roared like a madman:

"Coward that I am! What have I done to myself and to my people? . . . Why did I flee? . . . O the glory! . . . O the shame and disgrace! . . ."

The more he thought about it, the more his blood streamed to his temples, and he was filled with self-contempt. His entire being sobbed silently, and a great remorse consumed him. But now a new idea seized him and filled him with enthusiasm, and being by nature very changeable, he decided that he must return immediately to the field of conflict, even at the cost of his life.

The natural instinct which guides creatures that are in danger spurred Abu al-Shawarib to be cautious. With trembling hands he took off his *abayah*, cut it into long strips with his sword, and bound his horse's hoofs so that its galloping might be silent. The darkness which encompassed him on all sides encouraged him in the hope that he might succeed in stealing back into his own camp, even if his pursuers were still roaming about and lying in wait for him to return.

He tried to mount his horse again, but the horse's chest was rising and falling like a bellows from having run so much; its breath came in snorts and the sweat poured from it, moistening Abu al-Shawarib's hand, which slid gently along the horse's neck. He could not mount. Knowing that there were still many obstacles ahead of him for which he had to conserve the horse's strength, he grasped the reins and began walking, leading the horse. He advanced silently and with great caution, his eyes darting around him as if trying to rip apart the mists now rising across the plain like dense white steam from the Dead Sea that glinted like steel on his left and from the Jordan slumbering on his right in its gray *abayah*.

After walking in the sand for about an hour, his legs now weak and unsteady, he finally caught sight of the white rows of hills. He stopped beside the steep path which gleamed in the darkness, and considered whether to continue along it or to change direction. He decided to make the rest of his way directly through the huge rocks which rose above each other like a camel caravan that has stopped to rest by the wayside. These rocks, he hoped, would give him cover. He crawled forward among them, crouching, with feeble steps. Slowly, very carefully, feeling his way forward with his hands, he climbed to the ridge of the hill whose peak rose to the clouds.

Although his hands and knees were soon scratched and bruised all over by the thorns and clumps of rock he kept bumping into, he ignored the pain and kept on going. But whenever his horse's hoofs dislodged some stones his heart went tearing after them, trembling in his chest as he listened to the noise they made rolling down the hillside. Then he would take a deep breath and bend forward again to continue crawling forward.

With great effort he reached the peak and climbed onto its humptop alone. There he lay down and blinked, molded his body to the shape of the hilltop, and scanned the surroundings. Strain his eyes as he might, all he could see was a deep chasm descending into invisible depths, and behind it a dark wall, terrifying in its stillness. And more than he could see he sensed that the descent on this side was steep, and that more peaks, higher than this one, rose ahead of him.

"It's a bad way I've chosen," he thought to himself, and his spirits fell. "My horse will never get down this cursed slope."

Nevertheless he continued to crawl on. With the stubbornness of an ant he circled around trying to find a path. He stopped being careful, and stepped out with broad steps, until he stumbled and fell into a pit.

Through the darkness he saw the ravine he had almost fallen into, next to the pit. Although the sweat was pouring from him, he suddenly felt terribly cold all along his spine. Gritting his teeth he dropped heavily to his knees, and, leaning with both arms over the brink of the ravine, he mumbled in a tone of self-derision:

"Serves you right. . . . Maybe now you'll learn. . . . Why be stubborn?"

The despair mounting in him, he retraced his steps and reached his horse. He wound the reins around the horse's head and placed his hand on its back, to let the horse lead him. The horse understood him and began to descend. Now digging its hoofs into the ground and slowly dragging its body forward, now twisting itself around rocks, the horse made its way painfully down the slope.

When they were finally on the plain again, Abu al-Shawarib hurried the horse on and turned it toward the path he had left earlier. No sooner had he entered the fissure that was like a tunnel than the horse shuddered, stepped backward, and jerked its ears up: only a few steps away a figure seemed to have risen out of the bowels of the earth, clearly visible since it was darker than the darkness of the night. The figure moved, and then spoke in an urgent whisper:

"Nimmer! Is that you? . . ."

Abu al-Shawarib recognized the voice, and his fear vanished. Like a drowning man who has been offered a lifebelt he ran straight to the other man, fell upon his neck, embraced him, kissed him, and held him tight, not letting him go while he pelted him with questions.

The *suss* vendor stood there bewildered and unmoving. He was stunned by this fierce outburst of love from a man so much higher and more exalted in rank than himself. The flag-master's frightened voice, and his tone of suppressed sobbing, made the hard heart of the *suss* vendor tremble, as air in a dark room trembles when pierced by a large beam of light. An inner joy such as he had never known flooded through every corner of his soul and overflowed its banks. Placing his hand under Abu al-Shawarib's arm he held the flag-master firmly and led him back to the horse. Grasping the bridle, he led the two of them quickly onto the plain, mumbling fragmented and disordered pieces of information:

"Pray to the Prophet! The disaster is great. All the blame is being placed on you. The riot was enormous. There are many killed and wounded. I knew you'd be lying in wait so I escaped to try to find you and tell you. Flight is one half of bravery. That dog's head who leads the Jerusalemites, the *hajj*, cursed be his father!—he wails and laments over the corpse of Abu Faris, as if he were his own brother. He goes among the groups and the camps carrying the torn flag of al-Khalil, and crying for vengeance. You have been shamed in the eyes of all the camps. Even the Nablusites will not shelter you. The soldiers who came from Jerusalem have arrested all our leaders. They're searching for you along all the paths. Allah has hidden you. It is your duty to escape. If you don't get away in time, you'll rot in the bloody prison at Acre, or you'll hang in the streets in Stamboul."

On hearing all this Abu al-Shawarib drew his arm out of the other's grip, made a gesture as if defending his soul, swayed like a drunken man, and fell helplessly to the ground.

His head dropped to his knees and continued falling toward the ground. He buried his face in his hands. A despairing groan burst from his throat, the savage moan of a man who has been defeated by a mighty power from which there is no escape. Then he fell silent, and a terrible stillness filled the air.

Shocked and confused, the *suss* vendor gazed around him with eyes peeled. He heard no suspicious sound, and calmed down a little. Then he turned to Abu al-Shawarib, bent over him, touched him pityingly on his trembling shoulders, and tried to lift him.

"Enough, my brother," he whispered. "Listen to me, what is past is past! Everything comes from Allah, praise Him and exalt Him! What is done was written and what is thought was decreed!" Seeing that his words were having no effect on Abu al-Shawarib, he went on in a more energetic tone:

"There's very little time left. Rise, and cross the Jordan before the moon comes up and reveals your tracks. With Allah's help, in a week or ten days you'll get to

Wadi el-Arish. There nothing can harm you, and the blood-avengers and the authorities won't be able to touch you. In a year or two things will settle down, Abu Faris's family will be reconciled to their loss and will agree to accept a ransom. That's my advice to you. Let's make an effort now. I'll arrange everything. I promise to watch out and let you know everything that happens. Get on your horse. I'll accompany you to the Jordan crossing. From there I'll head left to Nablus. It'd be best if I disappeared too. Those dogs, may Allah not have mercy on their fathers' bones! They're surely planning to do me harm."

He grasped Abu al-Shawarib around the waist and raised him from the ground. Noticing that Abu al-Shawarib's *abayah* was not over his shoulders, he took off his own and wrapped it around his leader, and then held the horse's stirrup to help him mount.

For a long time they traveled in their hasty flight, like animals fleeing before the hunters. To conceal their tracks they left the paths and wended their way among the pools and waterholes, over crystals of salt that crackled under their feet and twinkled and faded like stars in the dark sky. They passed beside the swamps and the mouth of the Jordan, pushing their way through reeds and bullrushes and many other marsh plants that fastened around their legs and waists and impeded their progress.

When they drew near to the crossing, the *suss* vendor turned his sheepskin inside out and began crawling forward on all fours. He cautiously inspected the entire area, looking, as he moved, like a jackal stealing through the fields. While he was doing this, Abu al-Shawarib remained hidden among the bushes, waiting fearfully for his return.

The *suss* vendor came back, walking erect, and Abu al-Shawarib took courage, left his hiding place, and mounted his horse. Straining to overcome the trembling of his voice, he spoke to the *suss* vendor, instructing him of the messages he was to bear to his family and household. When he had finished speaking, he continued standing on the spot, gazing blankly into space.

"Hurry now," the *suss* vendor urged him, offering him his hand in farewell. Abu al-Shawarib felt a flush of joy, and kissed the other man on the head, wept on his neck a little, and then spurred his horse on.

Several times he turned his head back as he rode, to gaze at the immobile figure of the *suss* vendor. When the figure had completely merged into darkness, he sighed deeply and continued riding forward, sorrowing and bent under the desperate suffering and agony of men exiled from the land of their birth. . . .

Translated by Richard Flantz.

Other works by Shami: *Hebron Stories* (2000).

Avigdor Hameiri
1890-1970

Born Avigdor Feuerstein in a small village in Carpathian Ruthenia in the Habsburg Empire, the Hebrew writer Hameiri received both a traditional religious education and a secular education. While still in his teens he became a Zionist and began writing Hebrew poetry. He was drafted at the start of World War I and served for two years in Galicia fighting the Russians before he was captured, at the end of 1916. He suffered torture and imprisonment in Asiatic Russia and was freed only as a result of the Russian Revolution. His experiences in the trenches and in prisoner-of-war camps shaped his early literary output. He settled in Odessa after being liberated and then, in 1921, left for the Land of Israel with a group of writers. He was a prolific writer; his work included novels, poetry, stories, memoirs, feuilletons, satires, and children's books. In 1927, he established in Tel Aviv the first Central European-style, Hebrew-language satirical cabaret.

The Great Madness
1929

2. Madness

For the past four years I had not seen the morning sun. The newspaper work generally ended about three o'clock in the morning and who can go to sleep right after work? After work one socializes. Social life goes on till dawn. Social life—it means music, art, philosophy, women, dancing and science. In the morning one goes to sleep before the sun comes up, so as not to run into people. People are strange creatures. They are creatures of money-worries and anxieties, preoccupied, dried up, foolish. Perfectly good citizens but sickening to talk to. "How are you?" "Fine, thank you. And you?" "Thanks. All right, still alive. A thousand sovereigns would save me." That's humour. "What's the news?" "The news?" You tell him the news. The theory of relativity. In the final analysis, he, the citizen, the gentle reader, really despises you in his heart of hearts. After all, it's for him that you sweat and scribble. And then, what are you?—an idler, who spends his nights with dancing girls.

Fear of the citizen surmounts all other fears. You rush home at dawn, turn on the light and read a book until about eight o'clock, then fall asleep.

You get up about four in the afternoon. Once again to the café, to work for a couple of hours or more. Poems, stories, articles. Then, a visit to the editorial office. Then you go and cover the theatre, or a concert, until about ten, or later. And after all this, hard labour creating a newspaper, until three o'clock in the morning.

Then the same thing, all over again.

Four years of this. The life of a night owl.

The red slip hardly sobered me up. Should I go to the Town Hall? Very well. But when?—Ten o'clock in the morning is bad. One is sure to meet people. Perhaps it can be managed by telephone. I go to the editorial office and ask for the Town Hall on the telephone.

—The Town Hall, please, miss.

—Town Hall!

—Hello! Is that the Town Hall? This is the editorial office of "The People's Voice." This morning I received a red slip. What is it for?

—A red slip?—It means you have to present yourself for conscription.

—Conscription? What do you mean? I have to be a soldier?

—So it would seem.

—Can't it be managed without me? I am terribly busy. Especially in the mornings. In the mornings I sleep. Surely you know what newspaper work is like.

Laughter on the telephone. Then:

—We are very sorry. But it would seem that one cannot die heroically through the telephone.—And that was it.

They laughed. So it had to be a serious matter.

A few colleagues come in.

Now I am laughing:

—One can't die heroically through the telephone. One must join mankind.

—Have you been in town? The city's gone mad.

My lodgings are two minutes away from the office. Just around the corner. No, I hadn't been in town.

—Let's go downtown. I tell you—people have all gone mad. Really! We go downtown, and find it buzzing. There's a parade down the street. A soldier carries a flag, followed by a mob of urchins all shouting deafeningly:

—Long live the war! Long live the Homeland! Long live Emperor Franz Josef the First! Long live Kaiser Wilhelm, our noble friend! Long live King Emanuel of beautiful Italy!—And the anthem:

"To thine Homeland, O Magyar,
Be thou faithful as a rock!"

Odd. It's a long time since we last heard this naïve chant. Where did it hide, before suddenly bursting out of this rag-tag and bob-tail?

"Homeland"—what is the meaning of this word?

—The song of our apish ancestor, the Australopithecus, that's what this song is, somebody says behind me.

I look back: there is the pale and delicate Dr. Garay.

—Well, what do you think? I ask him.

—You know what I think.

—Do drop your paradoxes, my friend. Oh yes, have you received a red slip?

—Yes. I arranged it by messenger.

There was only one among us who was not hugely amused by Dr. Garay's "arrangement," and that was me. I saw something in that jubilant crowd which the others missed. I could not believe my eyes. I looked again and rubbed them—

—What is this? Can't you see? Look!

Beside the flag-bearer, to his left, bursting with national pride, marched our dear friend, the famous Italian anarchist Signor Grappolini.

—But he's been in prison for the past six months?

—What do you mean, in prison?—Haven't we been raising hell for months, bringing every pressure to bear to improve his conditions and even get him released?

—They must have forced him to go free, somebody said. But it was evident that he himself did not believe it.

We all stared at the speaker: what nonsense! Compel someone to fight against all his own ideals? Why, even in Russia they don't do such things!

The mob reaches the "Meteor" café and stops. Signor Grappolini is still in the vanguard.

—This is madness. Grappolini and war?

But facts are facts. Signor Grappolini enters the café and orders all the customers—Out! This is an order which brooks no disobedience. He is accompanied by several policemen and a young officer who pulls out his sword and waves it about—Out! Out!

The customers come out and Signor Grappolini gathers the mob around him, places the flag-bearer on a table in the terrace, and then he himself stands on a table and begins to make a speech.

He speaks and speaks enthusiastically, with a flushed face, with his blood and heart and full lungs—in the name of the great ally Italy—in the name of the nation of Michelangelo, of Machiavelli, of the sainted Garibaldi. . . .

We pushed our way in. This is a delightful business. Grappolini talking in the name of the ally Italy, enthusiastically calling for war. In the name of Garibaldi. He's quite a lad, that one. He's making fun of the whole business. After all, we know him. He's a humorous sort of chap. Soon everybody will be laughing. . . . Some naïve person in the crowd, obviously humourless, called to the vehement speaker:

—Well, what's stopping you from dying a heroic death?—Go, and good luck to you!

We had hardly turned around to see who it was when a cry, a yell of pain, was heard, and then we saw the naïve person's face all bloodied, and immediately he was arrested and taken away. The crowd raved and the entire street seethed and bubbled:

—Long live the war! Long live our ally Italy! Long live the gracious and all-powerful Kaiser Wilhelm!

Somebody laughed. And after the laughter—ouch! His face is bloodied, too. . . .

—Let's get out of here. It's dangerous.

—Why? We can stand by and listen in silence.

Dr. Garay bends and whispers in my ear: I want to see if there really is not a single man or woman who is opposed to it in this whole crowd.

—But you see there are, and they get beaten up.

The speaker grows ecstatic. The Homeland is in danger. We must pull out the teeth of the Serbian dog, tear out the French serpent's tongue, cut off the British lion's head, shatter the skull of the Russian bear!

—Hurrah! Hurrah!

We look at the crowd: the faces are all exulting, they are all in accord!

Finally: the anthem.

"To thine Homeland, O Magyar,
Be thou faithful as a rock!"

By now there is not a mouth in the whole street which is not gaping and singing.

—What's the meaning of all this enthusiasm?

—These are all mercenaries. Can't you see—it's a rabble.

Dr. Garay gazes at the frenzied crowd, listens to the speaker and then turns to me with his eyes shut and says very deliberately:

—We are all mistaken, my dear. We are much too clever. Did you hear what he said?—the Serbians have crossed the Danube. They are coming closer and closer.

—But that's a lie.

—And what if it's all true?

Then we would all know it.

—You know everything, my dear fellow. But did you know this—that the masses are ready to march singing to their death?

—I don't see it yet. I do see them yelling aloud.

Dr. Garay grew angry:

—Why are you quibbling? They're all willing to go, all of them! I fell silent, and he went on solemnly:

—Do you know what it means to march towards death?

—I don't know.

—To march towards death means searching for a new meaning in life.

Opium. A sacred madness. We are rotten. . . .

He said that and left us quickly. Simply vanished.

We laughed.

The enthusiasm of the crowd killed the laughter on our lips.

—The People. The Heaven-blessed People.

The anthem came to an end, followed by a dramatic declaration:

—Whoever wants to volunteer to join the sacred war for the defence of the Homeland—let him come here!

And the mob began to push and crowd against the table until it became positively dangerous. Everybody volunteered.

—Put me down, too.

I could not believe my eyes: our pale and delicate Dr. Garay. . . .

I blinked and laughed: what a wonderful joke.

Dr. Garay pierces me almost angrily with his feeble eyes:

—What are you laughing about?!

I burst out laughing, take his hand and press it: You're a great fellow, a war hero. Well then, go. The Homeland's in danger. . . . Dr. Garay throws me one last look, pulls his hand out of mine and rushes to the table. I follow him, still convinced that he's only fooling.

But no—he really registered.

—What's all this?

—We'll see how it'll turn out.

Dr. Garay, looking like someone who has done his duty faithfully, returns from the table, his face beaming, his fragile frame erect.

I went up to him: Congratulations! I wanted to shake his hand, but he avoided me. He stared at me piercingly, his expression full of suppressed hatred and anger mixed with contempt. He turns to go. I grin and he walks away, then turns back and hisses at me, only one word:

—Jew!

I was thunderstruck.

It's ages since this word has been uttered in such a manner among us. I cannot restrain myself from answering him, but my throat is dry and the tongue paralyzed.

—Garay! I finally called out, almost in tears.

It must have reached him. Dr. Garay heard. He turned back, came up to me and whispered very deliberately:

—How can you know what a homeland means?

My head began to spin. I closed my eyes and leaned against a lamp post.

Somebody pushed me. I roused myself and went to the office.

The editorial office is empty. I sit down and wipe my sweating face.

How fearful is this emptiness.

On my desk lie last night's cables: the Einstein observatory, the international university, Esperanto.

And in the streets—a storm.

I can't go on sitting here. I must go out.

An artillery regiment passes. On either side of the street a multitude of women give the marching soldiers money and cigarettes.

Some of the women fall on the soldiers' necks and kiss them.

"To thine Homeland, O Magyar—"

Translated by Yael Lotan.

Other works by Hameiri: *Be-gehenom shel mata* (1932); *Mivḥar sipurei Avigdor Hameiri* (1954); *Yalkut shirim* (1976).

Alter-Sholem Kacyzne

Shayke
1929

Once this was the heart of Warsaw—this labyrinth of sad narrow streets between tall tenement houses. Now this is a remote place, an ancient tumor on the body of the modern city, where its blood flows differently, and differently, too, throbs its pulse.

The Mokem—as Jews call the Old-City—has its own breath, its own light, which does not flow with the light of the rest of Warsaw. Likewise, the residents of Mokem have a different appearance, both Jews and Christians. They are withered, the residents of Mokem, as if the dust of past generations were stuck to them, were pressed into the folds of their clothes, into the wrinkles of their faces. And they are gray.

They carry with themselves the shadow of the cramped streets between tall tenements. Presently they shuffle along the wall, over the narrow sidewalks, like children, brushing against their mother's knee. And the mothers—the tenements—are narrow and tall and, it seems, they stand, those tenements, on swollen knees: they are broader below than above, and the gray wall slides down onto the sidewalk in a slope, so as not to collapse. There are no gates here. Narrow arched doors with ancient grease lead from the street into dark arched corridors. And by day with their darkness, in evening—with the only lantern, which hangs down from the arched ceiling—the narrow archways exhale a fright and a warning into the cramped street: *Watch out, people! There are witches in the world!* And devils lurk in every corner. And evil people, even worse than devils, have concealed themselves within their darkness.

Not for nothing are alcoves present in the thick walls above the first floor. And there stand, nailed in their eternal watch, madonnas and saints. And however old and however neglected the walls—the madonnas with their holy lusters, with the sky-blue oil paint of their freshly painted clothes, wear fresh little garlands on their heads. [...]

If the Old-City is the ancient heart of Warsaw, then the old marketplace is the heart of the heart.

The old marketplace is a large quadrangular box. Its walls are the four rows of narrow, tall tenements—tall as five or six stories, narrowing down to three or four windows. And all the tenements here are gray and all, it seems, all so alike. And clearly—they are distinct. Every tenement with its face, with its air of an impoverished aristocrat. Great individualists they are, the tenements of the old marketplace. What holds them together here, shoulder to shoulder, squeezed together in crampedness? They have been staring intently with their browless eyes at the Water-Dame who sits on her pedestal in the middle of the cobblestoned square. A witch she is, the Warsaw Water-Dame, with wanton

breasts and a perverse tail of scales. With her shield and with her sword, which she holds in her hands, she has bewitched the old tall tenements with their madonnas, with their saints, and the old stone individualists have lined themselves up in four rows and locked the square into a box.

It is no longer a square, but a giant room without a roof, a community-room to be used by the hands of the local residents.

Little children play in haste around the Water-Dame. They cannot run far away. She has also bewitched them. Older women sit on the stone steps of the pedestal, count their stocking-stitches and complain about their bitter lots. One about this—that her old man doesn't make a living; the second—that her old man drinks and beats her; the third is jealous of them both: her man has long been resting in peace.

On summer evenings workers strike out in blue vests with cigarettes in their mouths to catch some conversation at the Water-Dame.

One people, one house, but without a roof. Therefore one can at least breathe freely.

Jews feel closer and more at home here with Christians than they would somewhere else. The tenements have packed them together here in crampedness. Heavy want oppresses everyone equally. No rich men live in the Old-City. And the shadows of past generations weave them together with a common secret.

On the square, near the Water-Dame, toward evening, two workers stopped. They had met, walking from work, and paused to talk a bit.

"Well, you've got some work?" the taller, blond one asked—he asked for no reason, only so as to talk. It really did interest him, whether his friend had work or not—chiefly, whether he wanted to work.

His friend responded after a brief hesitation.

"I want to tell you, Yisroel, you know very well that I am not fond of work. What's the purpose, Shayke, I ask you, of painting flowers on the houses in Franciscan Street? I've got a good design for them, those potbellies! Oh yes, you see, it was truly worthwhile to come to Warsaw. . . ."

The blond man good-naturedly clapped him on the shoulder:

"Take it easy! Kraków was not built all of a sudden." [...]

"Shush, Yisroel," Shayke grew earnest and shoved his hat down on the hair over his forehead. "What's the story with my poems? When will I see a published word?"

Yisroel promised him that in the party's forthcoming review he would find his poems published. But Shayke would not relent. "When?"

"Obviously one cannot fill a political review with poems, you yourself know that well. It's still missing material. Today I'll be going to Shmuel for the editorial."

Shayke had no patience. His muse was not waiting. Just then he already had another poem in the pocket of his painting pants. But to go show Yisroel, when the man has still not published the first poem. No, he will not show it.

He again gazed upward in wonder. In his little Chinese eyes there glowed a little flame, and his lips opened in a childlike smile. High on a roof there stood a little street urchin and he waved in the wind with a stick, five times longer than he was himself. To the stick a rag was tied. It waved in the wind, as if bewitched. Perhaps he wanted to paint over the whole sky above the old marketplace. And perhaps he waved this to the setting sun, so that it would return. No, with this the dark little silhouette on the roof was conducting a flock of silver doves. High, high ringed their number in airy wantonness. Silver little flowerbuds poured from a rose-colored cloud. And with a drop downwards—a pile of dark little rags. And with a scale upwards—once more silver flowers. Just then they flared up rose.

"You know, Yisroel, for us in the shtetl the turkey hens are already going to sleep. They nestle into one another and before sleep they recount their nightly dreams:

Too—loo! Loo—loo—loo! Tool, lool! Loo—loo—loo!"

Like so, Shayke performed such an ingenious whistle, as the turkey hens recount their dreams, that Yisroel burst into laughter.

"Get lost, you singular poet! Shayke the Piper, good night!"

Translated by Maia Evrona.

Irène Némirovsky

1903–1943

Born into a wealthy Russian family that settled in Paris after the Bolshevik Revolution, Irène Némirovsky burst onto the Paris literary scene with her novel *David Golder* in 1929. Although Némirovsky was unaf-

filiated and nonobservant, she was obsessed with her Jewishness and incorporated conventional antisemitic tropes into her debut novel as well as others that followed it. In later years she regretted the harshness with which she had drawn Jewish financiers and their wives in her work. In desperation, she converted to Catholicism during World War II, but neither her new faith nor her ties to right-wing literary figures were able to save her from arrest and deportation in 1942. The discovery and posthumous publication of her masterpiece, *Suite Française*, in 2004, as well as its subsequent translation into many languages, kindled new interest in her work.

David Golder
1929

Chapter I

"No," said Golder.

He moved the shade with a brusque gesture, so that the lamp light fell full on the features of Simon Marcus, who sat opposite him, at the other side of the table. For a moment he looked at the lines and wrinkles that seamed Marcus's dark face, that rippled over it, whenever he moved his lips or his eyelids, so that it looked like a dark sea, stirred by the wind. But the heavy, sleepy, Oriental eyes, remained calm, bored, indifferent. It was a face as blank as a wall. Carefully Golder lowered the flexible metal stand from which the light hung.

"At a hundred, Golder? Have you reflected? It's a price," said Marcus.

"No," Golder muttered again. And he added: "I don't want to sell."

Marcus laughed. His long, shiny teeth, filled with gold, gleamed fantastically in the dim light.

"What were these famous oil shares of yours worth, in 1920, when you bought them?" asked Marcus, with a laugh. His voice was nasal and ironic; it drawled his words.

"I bought at four hundred. If those pigs of Soviets had returned the nationalized lands to the oil drillers it would have been a fine deal. I had Lang and his crowd behind me. Even in 1913 the daily production at Teisk was ten thousand tons. That was no bluff. After the Genoa conference my shares fell first from four hundred to one hundred and two, and then . . ." He made a vague gesture. "But I kept them. In those days I still had money."

"Yes. Now, do you realize that oil-bearing lands in Russia in 1926 are worthless—to you? Good Lord—I don't suppose you've either the money or the inclination to exploit them yourself, have you? The best you can hope to do is to make a few points by manipulating the stock on the Exchange. A hundred is a good price."

Golder rubbed his swollen eyelids, burned by the smoke that filled the room. When he spoke again it was in a still lower tone.

"No," he said, "I don't want to sell. At least, not until—well, when Tubingen Petroleum has completed its negotiations for the Teisk concession—you know all about that—then I shall sell."

Marcus muttered a sort of "Ah, yes," that was smothered in his throat, and that was all. Golder said, slowly:

"I mean the deal you have been carrying on behind my back since last year, Marcus—that's the very one. They'd give you a good price for my shares, I suppose, once the concession was granted?"

He was silent, for his heart was beating painfully, as it always did when he won a victory. Marcus slowly crushed out his cigar in the overflowing ash-tray.

"If he proposes a fifty-fifty split he's done," Golder thought, curtly. He leaned forward, the better to hear Marcus, who said, after a short silence: "How about going halves, Golder?"

"What?" Golder raised his eyebrows. "No!"

"Ah, you're wrong to make another enemy, Golder," said Marcus, lowering his eyes. "You have enough already."

Marcus's hands were pressed against the polished wood of the table; they moved feebly, with a faint crackling of the nails, nervous and feverish in its implication. Lighted by the lamp, his long, white, thin fingers, laden with heavy rings, shone on the mahogany; they were trembling. Golder smiled.

"You're no longer very dangerous, my lad. . . ."

Marcus was still for a moment, staring fixedly at his polished nails.

"David—let's go halves! Come—we've been partners for twenty-six years. Let's wipe the slate clean and make a new start. If you'd been here in December, when Tubingen spoke to me . . ."

Nervously Golder fumbled with the cord of the telephone, twisting it about his fingers.

"In December," he repeated. "Yes—you're very good—only—"

He fell silent. Marcus knew as well as he that in December he had been in America, seeking capital for the

"Golmar," that enterprise that had held them together for so many years as a ball and chain holds two galley slaves linked. But he said nothing.

"David, there is still time," Marcus went on. "Oh, it will be better so, believe me! We'll deal with the Soviets together—shall we? It's no easy matter. As to commissions and profits—fifty-fifty in everything—eh? That's fair, I hope—that's being loyal? David? Won't you? Or else . . ."

He waited a moment for some reply—acquiescence, even an insult, but Golder was breathing with difficulty and remained mute.

"Look here—it isn't as if there were only the Tubingen—"

He touched Golder's inert arm as if he wanted to wake him.

"There are other, newer companies—newer and—and—more inclined to speculate," he said, choosing his words carefully. "Companies that didn't sign the oil agreement of 1922 and that, as a result, can disregard your former rights. They could . . ."

"Amrum Oil, for instance?" said Golder.

"Oh—!" Marcus's face showed his dismay. "So—you know about that, too? Well, then, listen, old man, I'm sorry, but the Russians are going to close with Amrum. And now, since you won't trade, you can keep your Teisk shares till the Day of Judgment, you can be buried with your shares in your grave. . . ."

"The Russians aren't going to close with Amrum."

"They have signed!" cried Marcus.

Golder swept his words away with his hand.

"Yes, I know. A provisional agreement, which must be ratified by Moscow within forty-five days. That was yesterday. But, as there was, once again, nothing definite, you are worried—you have come to try me again. . . ."

Coughing, he finished what he had to say, quickly.

"I'll explain to you. Amrum has been poaching on Tubingen in the Persian oil fields for two years—you know that? Well, this time, I think, Tubingen would rather crush a rival than give in. Up to now that sort of thing has been all right—they've made good offers to the little Jew who was dealing with you in behalf of the Soviets. Go ahead and telephone now—you'll see."

Marcus cried out, suddenly, in a strange, sharp voice, like that of an hysterical woman.

"You lie, you swine!"

"Telephone—you'll see!"

"And the old man—Tubingen—he knows?"

"Of course!"

"That's your doing—you mutt—you scoundrel—!"

"Yes. What do you expect? Do you remember the Mexican oil business last year, the Mazout deal three years ago, and all the millions that passed from my pocket into yours? What did I say then? Nothing. And then . . ."

He seemed to be seeking more arguments, to be assembling them in his mind. Then he rejected them, with a shrug of his shoulders.

"Business," he said, with great simplicity, as if he had named some all powerful deity.

Marcus was silenced at once. He took a package of cigarettes from the table, opened it, applied himself to striking a match.

"Why do you smoke these filthy Gauloises, Golder, when you are so rich?" he asked. His fingers trembled violently. Golder looked at them, saying nothing, as if he were seeing the death struggle of some wounded beast.

"I had to have money, David," Marcus said, all at once, in an altered voice. A sudden grimace twisted the corner of his mouth. "I—I am in terrible need of money right now, David. Won't you—won't you let me make a little? Don't you believe that—"

Golder struck the empty air before him with his fist, savagely.

"No!" he said.

He saw the pale hands on the table clasp one another, lie one upon the other, the curled fingers interlaced, the nails biting into the flesh.

"You are ruining me," said Marcus, in a strange, dull voice.

Golder, his eyes obstinately cast down, did not answer. Marcus hesitated; then he got up, pushed his chair back, gently.

"Good-bye, David," he said. "What did you say?"

"Nothing. Good-bye," said Golder.

Chapter II

Golder lit a cigarette, but it began to choke him with the first puff, and he threw it away. A nervous, asthmatic cough, harsh and stifling, shook his shoulders and brought up a bitter rheum that nearly suffocated him. A sudden rush of blood colored his cheeks, which ordinarily were white, of a deathlike, flat pallor, lined, and with the blue shadows under his eyes. He was a man past his sixtieth year, enormous in bulk, with large, soft, fat limbs, eyes of a watery color, though vivid in their paleness; thick white hair crowned a ravaged face, that was as hard as if it had been carved from stone by a rude and heavy hand.

The room was redolent with smoke, and with that odor of cooled perspiration that is peculiar, in summer, to Parisian rooms that have been occupied for a long time.

Golder, swinging about in his chair, opened the window a little. For a long minute he looked at the Eiffel Tower, which was illuminated. The red liquid fire ran like blood across the fresh twilight sky. He thought of the "Golmar." Six golden letters, luminous, startling, which also revolved, like suns, to-night, in four of the great cities of the world. The "Golmar," those two names, his and Marcus's, combined into one. His lips were tight.

"Golmar—David Golder, alone, now."

He picked up some pads beside his hand, and read the heading:

GOLDER & MARCUS
All Petroleum Products Bought and Sold
Aviation Gas, Light, Heavy and Medium Gas.
White Spirit.
Gasoline. Lubricating Oils.
NEW YORK, LONDON, PARIS, BERLIN

Lightly he erased the first line, and wrote "David Golder," in his thick script, which indented the paper. For he was alone at last. He thought, with relief: "It's over, thank Heaven—he'll get out, now." And later, the concession at Teisk finally granted to Tubingen, when he himself would be a participant in the greatest oil enterprise in the world, he could easily rebuild the "Golmar."

In the meantime . . . He set down figures, quickly. The last two years had been terrible ones. Lang's failure, the 1922 agreement . . . Well, at least, he wouldn't have to pay for Marcus's women any longer, his rings, his debts. He had plenty of expenses of his own. Heavens, how costly was this idiotic life he lived! His wife, his daughter, the Biarritz house, the Paris house. In Paris alone rent and taxes came to sixty thousand francs; the furniture alone, when it was bought, had cost more than a million. For whom? No one lived there. The blinds were drawn, dust was over everything. He stared, with a sort of hatred, at certain objects he especially detested: four Winged Victories, in bronze and black marble, that served to support a lamp; an enormous, empty square inkstand, decorated with golden bees. All must be paid for—and where was the money coming from?

"Imbecile, you're ruining me—and then?" he grumbled, angrily. "I'm sixty-eight years old. I suppose it will start all over again. That's what's happened to me often enough in the past."

He turned abruptly toward the great mirror over the empty fireplace, and looked with distaste at his drawn features, scarred, marred by bluish spots, with two lines about his mouth, deeply creased in his thick skin, like the hanging jowls of an old dog.

"I'm growing old," he grumbled, bitterly. "Yes—I'm growing old." In the last two or three years he had grown tired more quickly. "I must get away to-morrow," he thought. "That's vital. Then a week or ten days of rest at Biarritz. If they don't let me have some peace I'll break down."

He took the calendar, and put it on the table, against the gold frame of the picture of a young girl, and turned the leaves. It was marked with figures and names; one date, September 14, was underlined in ink. Tubingen would be expecting him, that day, in London. That meant a week, at the most, in Biarritz. Then London, Moscow, London again, New York. He gave vent to an irritated little groan, stared fixedly at his daughter's picture, sighed, and then turned away and gently rubbed his sore eyes, heavy with weariness. He had come from Berlin that day, and for a long time he had been unable to sleep in a sleeping car, as, of old, he had always done.

Nevertheless he got up, mechanically, to go to the club, according to his habit. But he saw that it was after three o'clock.

"I'd better go to bed," he thought. "To-morrow it'll be the train again."

He saw a sheaf of letters on the corner of his desk, awaiting his signature, and sat down again. Every night he read over the outgoing mail the secretaries had prepared; they were a race of donkeys. But he preferred them to be such. He smiled as he thought of Marcus's secretary, a little Jew with fiery eyes, who had sold him the secret of the Amrum deal. He began to read, and his thick white hair, that had once been red, hung low under the light, so that over his temples and on his neck there lingered still a little of the old, flaming color, as fire lingers under the cooling ashes of a half-extinguished fire.

Chapter III

The telephone beside the head of Golder's bed broke out suddenly into a long peal, strident, interminable. But Golder slept on; his sleep, in the mornings, was as deep and still as death. Finally he opened his eyes, groaning, and reached for the receiver.

"Hello—hello—"

For a minute he kept on saying "Hello," not recognizing his secretary's voice. Then he heard:

"Mr. Golder—he's dead—Mr. Marcus is dead." Silence. The voice again. "Hello—don't you understand, sir? Mr. Marcus is dead."

"Dead?" Golder repeated, slowly, while strange little shivers crawled between his shoulders. "Dead? Impossible. . . ."

"It was this very night, sir. In the Rue Chabanais. Yes, in a house. . . . He shot himself in the breast with a revolver. They say—"

Very gently Golder thrust the receiver down among the bedclothes and drew up the covers over it, as if he would stifle the voice, which he could hear, still droning on, like some great imprisoned fly. Finally it was still. Golder rang.

"Draw my bath," he said to the servant who came in with his mail and his breakfast tray. "A cold bath."

"Shall I pack your dinner jacket, sir?"

Golder's eyebrows twitched, nervously.

"Pack? Pack—? Oh, yes—for Biarritz. I don't know—I'll be going tomorrow, perhaps—maybe later—I don't know."

He murmured an oath. Then:

"I must call tomorrow. I suppose the funeral will be on Tuesday—yes, of course. Damn—"

In the next room his man was letting the water run in the tub. Golder swallowed a mouthful of hot tea, opened a few letters at random, then threw them all on the floor and got up. In the bathroom he sat down, crossed the skirts of his dressing gown on his knees and watched the water running with a gloomy and absorbed regard, the while he mechanically rubbed the silk tassels at his belt.

"Dead . . . dead. . . ."

Little by little anger took possession of him. He shrugged his shoulders, and growled, full of hatred:

"Dead. . . . But does one die? Suppose I—I—"

"Your bath is ready, sir," said his man.

Golder, left alone, approached the tub, dipped his hand into the water, left it there. All his movements were extraordinarily slow, uncertain, incomplete. The cold water chilled his fingers, his arms, his shoulders, but he did not move. He remained, his head bowed, looking stupidly at the reflection of the electric light that hung from the ceiling, which shone in the water.

"Suppose I—" he repeated.

Old, forgotten memories rose from the depths of his being, strange, obscure thoughts. The whole of a hard life, full of struggle and difficulty. Today wealth, tomorrow—nothing left. Then—start over. And do that again and again. Yes, truly, if he had been going to kill himself it would have been long ago! He straightened up, dried his wet hand mechanically, and went to lean on the window sill, holding up first one and then the other of his cold hands to the warmth of the sun. He shook his head, and spoke aloud.

"Yes—I should say so—in Moscow, say, or it might have been in Chicago, that time, perfectly well."

His mind, unaccustomed to dreaming, pictured the past in broken scenes. Moscow, when he had been nothing but a little, thin Jew, with red hair and piercing, pale eyes, with worn-out shoes and empty pockets. He had slept on benches in the parks, in those dismally cold nights at the beginning of autumn. It seemed to him that after fifty years his bones could still feel the penetrating dampness of those first thick, white fogs which clung to one's body and left on one's clothes a sort of stiff, frozen rime. The snowstorms, later, and the winds of March. . . .

And Chicago . . . the little saloon, the phonograph that squeakily ground out an old European waltz, that sensation of a devouring hunger when the warm smells of the kitchen blew across his face. He closed his eyes and saw again, with an extraordinary precision, the black, shining face of a Negro, drunk or sick, who lay in a corner, on a bench, and wailed mournfully, like an owl. And again . . . His hands were burning now. He laid them, carefully, against the pane, wriggled his fingers, rubbed the palms, gently, one against the other.

"You fool," he murmured, as if the dead man could hear. "You fool—why did you do that?"

Translated by Sylvia Stuart.

Other works by Némirovsky: *The Ball* (2007); *The Dogs and the Wolves* (2009); *The Wine of Solitude* (2012); *The Fires of Autumn* (2014).

Zalman Shneour

1886–1959

Zalman Shneour was a prolific, popular, and influential writer in both Yiddish and Hebrew. Born in the town of Shklov (in present-day Belarus), Shneour was praised while still a teenager as a burgeoning poet by Bialik, cementing his status as an increasingly prominent figure in Jewish letters. Schneour moved to Odessa, Vilna, and then to Western Europe. His poetic style matured and evolved over the first few decades of the twentieth century, shifting from short lyric musings to epic explorations of philosophy and Jewish fate in quasi-prophetic tones. After publishing several multivolume poetry collections in the early 1920s, Shneour tried to settle in Palestine but, unimpressed by the lukewarm reception he received in Tel Aviv, eventually settled in Paris. The late 1920s were marked by a shift in his literary production to focus more on Yiddish prose rather than Hebrew poetry. Working in this genre, he gained a large and enthusiastic American readership and was able to sustain a comfortable lifestyle. Escaping Europe in 1941, he split his final years between the United States and Israel.

Making Jam
1929

Aunt Feiga is making jam today. She has to hurry. The raspberry season will soon be over. So Aunt Feiga is all in a swivet; she has bought a huge bowl of raspberries and fifteen pounds of sugar and is cooking away.

She has tied the ends of her kerchief at the nape of her neck: a sign of a great domestic project! Today she is at the height of her housewifely calling. Today marks the creation of a housewifely chef-d'oeuvre for the whole year.

Aunt Feiga's cheeks are flaming; the blood of the raspberries had made not only her finger tips but the tip of her nose sticky as well. Her eyes have regained their youth, and today all of her is as sweet, sticky, dexterous, and touchy as a bee at honey-gathering time.

The band of youngsters, from the youngest sprout to the eleven-year-old Talmudist, is behaving well, keeping off to one side; they instinctively sense that it is dangerous to start anything with Aunt Feiga today. Mustn't grab anything off the plates, mustn't go sniffing around, mustn't ask questions, mustn't even think of snatching a few raspberries—the way they ordinarily can when Mother returns from market with the shopping bag bulging. Want to remain alive in the world today? Then sit still and keep quiet! And so they sit and peep out of their nooks, like lesser imps in an infernal kitchen. All you can see of them is the sparkle of their eyes.

The ripe raspberries have been picked out and placed on a large platter like a red, aromatic pyramid of rubies. It has permeated the whole house with the scent of the wild forest where at dawn, amid the dew, the berries were gathered by the peasant woman. Each berry is, by itself, a tiny pyramid of minuscule garnets set close together—a fit gem for the ruby ring of a marquise.

Not far from the raspberries, on a sheet of white paper, rises another pyramid, of sifted granulated sugar. And the whiteness of this sugar is like that of freshly fallen snow, drifted by the wind against a fence in the heart of winter. The white mound of sugar sets off the red pyramid of fresh raspberries. And both structures are enthroned so regally, imposingly, and festally on the freshly scraped wood of the kitchen table. Seems a sin to take them and start cooking them together in the same huge copper basin and make of them a single red porridge—the jam.

However, Aunt Feiga knows no mercy. Even so a sculptor will show no mercy for the white block of marble which he hacks, chips, and trims in the full play of his creative power.

Aunt Feiga measures off water into the basin with a clear polygonal tumbler. Half a tumblerful for every pound of sugar lying ready on the table. Her face while she is engaged in this task is strained; her lips move, whispering something: Is it an incantation or a prayer? Who knows? Her face is every bit as imbued with mysticism when she measures off the wicks for the candles to be used on the Day of Atonement.

Next she lights the dry kindling, lying in wait on the hearth under a tripod. Like a thaumaturgic signal the first small blue flame appears in the heart of the kindling. Then the crackling commences, and the fire waxes greater, more intense. The poor, dingy, sooty hearth is inundated by a red, quivering reflection. Oh, but it is in a beatific state this day, is that hearth! It has waited all through the cold of winter and through part of the summer—and at last the anticipated day has come!

The polished copper of the basin laughs, grimaces, gleams. A patch of sultry blue sky, such a sky as comes toward the end of Tammuz, peeps in at the window. Aunt Feiga's tucked-in headkerchief, the mound of raspberries, the whiteness of the sugar, the blueness of the sky, the aureate glint of the basin, the fire on the hearth, the crackling of the resinous kindling—all these blend into a single lilting symphony of summer.

The jam is cooking.

Uncle Uri, too, is somehow different from his everyday self. He's in something of a holiday mood. Following his after-dinner nap he paces the kitchen in his ritual fringed vest; his shirt sleeves are snowy and his skullcap is of silk. His cross eyes glance now at Aunt Feiga, now at the ragamuffin crew—but there's not a word out of him. Not a peep! Contrary to his wont he isn't driving the youngsters off to Hebrew school. For a moment or so he seems to become intoxicated from the aroma of the raspberries, from their scarlet succulence, from the whiteness of the sugar, the flaming cheeks of Aunt Feiga. He thrusts his hands in his pockets and traverses all the rooms a couple of times with the air of a paterfamilias, while some sort of amiable musical phrase escapes in a trill through his nose and half-open mouth.

Then he seats himself on the sofa and picks up some book or other of a pious nature. But when it comes to concentrating on it—well, that's something else. The mixture of raspberries and sugar he has just glimpsed in the kitchen blushes between the lines, the flames on the hearth flicker between them also. Mundane matters thrust themselves in full force into things pertaining to heaven. He keeps turning the pages of his book and pondering something; he toys with one of the ritual fringes lying on his lap. He is yearning for tea. But on this occasion he is restrained, yielding, and half in love with Aunt Feiga's flushed cheeks, and he makes believe that he is not in the least concerned because the samovar has not yet been brought to the table, even though it is so late.

"O-ho-ho, Father in Heaven!" A sigh, by no means sad, escapes him. "Pretty soon Tammuz will be over—summer is passing. . . ." And he indulges in another musical phrase.

But Aunt Feiga keeps right on with the jam.

At first she boils the dazzling white sugar. She demolishes the beautiful white pyramid and pours it into the seething basin. And when the sugar has been thoroughly boiled she tests it—molten amber pours from her large wooden ladle. She pours out a little on a small plate, blows on it and tips it, to check the consistency of the syrup. By now the sugar has the appearance of pale honey.

Next she begins to trickle the culled raspberries into the seething syrup. Lord, how is it that a Jewish woman can show no pity for such juicy, tender, soft, little raspberries? Lord, why does she condemn them to such an inferno?

At first all you hear issuing from the basin is hissing, burbling groans. It is the raspberries, pleading—

"Police! Save us, fellow Jews! Oh, we're dying—we'll never live through this!" Then, for a moment, the basin quiets down. The gentle raspberries have evidently swooned away. Then, suddenly, the burbling resumes, and it keeps up until the cooking assumes an even pace.

And that's just when the most hazardous moment in jam making comes. At this point you must keep both your eyes peeled. A leonine crease forms on Aunt Feiga's brow. She stands by the fire like an apothecary and stirs, and tastes, and skims off the froth and the tiny seeds loosened by the steaming. A treat for the children, this scum. The sticky redness with its aromatic foam flows like honeyed blood against the whiteness of the small plate tilted to test it.

The eyes of the little ruffians light up and their nostrils twitch. If the froth is being skimmed off it means the jam will be ready soon. With all the freshness of their childish senses they scent in it the embalmed taste and fragrance of summer, of the field and the far-off green forest where only the peasants and their women may gather raspberries, but where Jewish children must not go, where only tailors and their apprentices may go strolling on a Sabbath. As for decent children, they must sit in their religious schools, perspiring, and reading certain edifying texts. But their mother is cooking, is preserving all the tang of summer and will capture it and seal it away in a glass jar. On wintry Sabbaths, when it is dismal outside, she will serve it with tea. You have to try but a teaspoonful, and your whole mouth fills with an aromatic tang: the tang of summer itself. Thanks unto her for that!

"There, that'll do, I think!"

That's what Aunt Feiga declares from behind the pall of fire and steam; whereupon she grabs the huge copper basin from the incandescent tripod, carries it out to the entry and places it on some sticks of wood laid out in a triangle. The sweet, fragrant steam from the basin pervades the whole entry. You could go and just sniff the air with both lips, and give them a treat. The basin is all sooty underneath, covered with a beautiful velvety blackness. But inside—inside the copper glints just as before. And glowing crimsonly within is a honeyed mass of embalmed raspberries.

The fire on the hearth is put out. And once more the hearth stands there, dismal, despondent, enigmatic, its sooty blackness stretching somewhere, ever so far upward, to a point where no eye may penetrate. The house reverts to its weekday atmosphere, as after the saying of farewell to the Princess Sabbath. Aunt Feiga washes herself with cold water and reties her headkerchief with the ends under her chin. This signifies that she is again the mother and the mistress of the household. She has demonstrated her art—and that's that.

Uncle Uri starts driving the small fry off to school:

"Whoever heard of schoolboys hanging around the house so late? Eh?"

He orders the samovar to be brought. His throat, he declares, is all parched by now. By this time—may this be said only of the foes of Israel—by this time his heartburn has started. . . .

The schoolboys become downcast, somehow, and fretful. They are reluctant to leave the fragrant kitchen, where the air is so delectable, so pleasant. Each of them gets two slices of a stale Sabbath loaf smeared with the fresh skimmings from the jam. This consoles them to some extent and unwillingly they trudge off to school.

And toward evening, when they're reading the Prophets in the stuffy schoolroom, there still lives in their childish imaginations the great copper basin, filled with the thick, fresh essence of summer and the blood of raspberries. Underneath it is dully black, but within the copper gleams. It is standing somewhere in a corner of the entry on three sticks of birchwood, cooling and cooling—that great, sweet copper basin.

The children recall this, and their lessons become somewhat more agreeable to them.

Translated by Moshe Spiegel.

Other works by Shneour: *Im sheki'at ha-chamah* (1906); *Gesharim* (1914); *Feter Zhome* (1930); *Restless Spirit: Selected Writings of Zalman Shneour* (1963).

Zalman Shneour

Shklover Jews
1929

I know a town in White Russia [Belarus] on the River Dnieper. Its name is Shklov. I was born there, went to heder there, which is why I know it so well.

The flame of life burns calmly there. Nobody turns it up too high; people are as sparing with it as with kerosene. It does not flare up, it does not smoke, like the perpetual flame in the *kalte shul* [big, hence unheated "cold" synagogue].

Not everyone has a clock there. In the morning, when the steamboat on the Dnieper sounds its horn, people know it's ten o'clock. In the evening, when the boat hoarsely asks "who-oo?" they know it's half past seven, time for supper.

There, two Russian constables, in their caps with worn bands, stand around. Nobody knows why they are there. It is after all a pious Jewish community, so who asked for them and who needs them here? And if nevertheless they make trouble, they are given a tumbler of brandy and a piece of challah and are seen no more.

The Jewish girls, with warm shawls on their thin shoulders, do not wear perfume there. Nevertheless, they give off healthy odors—of hay, of freshly baked bread, of red berries. In the evening they sit on the green porches and sing quietly, longing for their intended husbands. And when they marry, there are other girls sitting in their places, humming longingly like bees that have gone astray. [. . .]

There is a kind of frog that lives in the reeds of the millpond. When the sun sets, it begins to sigh like a lost soul: "u-hu, u-hu!" People say that it is the lament of the "water-ox." Fishermen, they say, have caught him more than once in their nets and let him go. He must not be touched, otherwise. . . . Otherwise what? And what does he look like? No one knows.

On the other side of the pond, which sparkles amid the gray huts and the fields, you can see the cows returning from pasture. If a red cow comes forward, the next day will be hot. If it's a black cow, that's a sign that tomorrow will be a rainy day. That is a proven fact.

If someone cuts his finger there, cobwebs are placed on the cut. The dustier it is, the better the remedy. Sometimes the finger heals, sometimes it becomes swollen, but no one dares question this excellent, free-of-charge remedy.

No one drinks sweet tea there—only sick people and deadbeats. Pieces of sugar were made to be bitten off while drinking tea one tiny bit at a time, sparingly and sensibly. To this day, coachmen drink tea with hard sugar. It's more economical and doesn't get dirty in their quilted trousers. Voveh the miller once got tangled up in debts and they confiscated his furniture. To this day people explain this unhappy event very simply: "Those skinflints gulped down lots of cups of sweet tea!" [. . .]

One year, at the beginning of winter, a new charitable society was founded—Soymekh Noflim—"Support for the Fallen." It was established by well-off young men to help failed shopkeepers, out-of-work artisans, and respectable widows, the kind of people who would be ashamed to resort to pawnshops or go to the out-dated Gmiles Chasodim—Free Loan Society—with its bearded old members with their old-fashioned ways who put you through an ordeal before you got your "voucher." . . . Soymekh Noflim, on the other hand, began to give out loans on the strength of one's word alone, in secret, seldom asking for a signature. Without interest, to be repaid in small amount over the course of a year, out of one's receipts or wages. . . . And everything was done pleasantly, with a smile, without fuss. The young fellows soon became celebrated. They were praised in the marketplace as well as in the prayer houses. But the old Gmiles Chasodim society did not care for this development. Its trustees began to grumble, to intrigue, to whisper that it is forbidden to give money into the hands of "the shaven," that is, to young men without forelocks. . . . But that didn't do them much good. Almost all the respectable members of the community signed on to make monthly contributions to the Soymekh Noflim society.

It was now the turn of Leybeh-"Horb" (the "Hunchback"), in his brick house. The hunchback hid himself as long as possible, but to no avail. The trustees of Soymekh Noflim were young fellows, after all. They spared no effort. They were Khoneh the son of the *dayen* [religious judge] and Itsheyzhe the son of Zhameh. Both have long and energetic legs and if they don't catch him today, it'll be tomorrow, and if not tomorrow, then the day after tomorrow. Both had taken into their heads: once and for all, Leybeh-Horb the usurer must sign up for monthly contributions to Soymekh Noflim.

They happened to catch him as he was eating dinner while Hershkeh-*Kop* (the "Brain"), the Russian teacher, was giving lessons to Zeldeleh and to Uri's schoolboy son. Naturally, they didn't manage without Fayvkeh's help. It was from Fayvkeh that they found out when Leybeh-Horb is at home and can be confronted face to face. Itsheyzhe, Uncle Zhameh's only son, did the questioning and then dropped in on Leybeh-Horb's dinner like a cold rain into a sukkah.

Leybeh-Horb still tried to worm out of it. Not finishing his roasted meat, he launched into the blessing after meals, drawing out the *Noyde lekho* ("We thank You") as if it were a tale from the Arabian Nights. He tried to take care of the trustees, as he had taken care of Gitkeh the Widow, with "nu-nu," and with mock-prayers ending in "-nu" and garbled Bible quotes: "*pirnasnu* [sustain us], *harvichnu* [grant us prosperity], oh, oh," that is to say: "We'll see, can't you tell we're busy" and "nu, nu, *lihday matnes boser-ve-dom, ve-loy liday halvoes on, oh*" ["let us not be dependent on the alms of flesh and blood and not on their loans"], which is to say: "What do I have to do with providing loans? God will take care of you even without me."

But Leybeh-Horb had made a terrible mistake. These were not turkeys and dowdy old ladies like Git-keh. The deputation from Soymekh Noflim consisted of wily individuals. Both Itsheyzhe and Khoneh the Dayen's Son pretended that they understood not a word of Hebrew, stared at Leybeh-Horb and his Hebraic gestures with incomprehending eyes and then . . . as if by prearrangement:

"Keep blessing, Reb Leybeh," says Itsheyzhe and winks at his cousin, Fayvkeh.

And Khoneh the Dayen's Son stares at the ceiling and adds:

"Don't worry, Reb Leybeh, we have time. We'll wait."

Leybeh-Horb sees that he won't be able to worm his way out and makes it short, with all his pious theatrics. He starts to swallow his blessings, like hot noodles—slurp-slurp into his mouth and mmm-mmm out of his mouth . . . he wipes his moustache with the edge of the tablecloth and invites the trustees into another room, behind the chintz curtain, as far as possible from the teacher's eyes and Fayvkeh's ears.

What happened there and what kind of conversation was carried on behind the curtain, Fayvkeh doesn't know. He only knows, that in the half-dark little room, where the big chest with pawned goods stands, there was for a quarter of an hour the muffled hum of three excited voices. Then the trustees of Soymekh Noflim came running out from behind the curtain looking humiliated. Sweat was pouring from the brow of Itsheyzhe, Fayvkeh's cousin. Taking hold of the doorknob, he shouted to his friend Khoneh the Dayen's Son: "What an ugly hunchback!" slammed the door and went out.

Since then the talk in Shklov was that they would get even with Leybeh-Horb. Meanwhile the young trustees vented their anger by speaking ill of the usurer and dragging his name through the mud. Never had there been so much ridicule and so many ugly stories about Leybeh-Horb, his house, his wife. . . . Doesn't everyone know that Bas-Sheva hates him like poison? Doesn't everyone know that she often goes to see Alter the watch-maker, the pimply old bachelor whose workshop stands close to Leybeh-Horb's grocery? True, they were once supposed to get engaged and the usurer pushed his way

in. . . . But what business does she have with him now to run to his shop? Does Leybeh-Horb have so many watches that need fixing? But it's "well known." [. . .]

While drinking tea at Itsheyzhe's house Khoneh the Dayen's Son told the following story:

"Have you heard? One evening a guest arrives at Ley-beh-Horb's house, an older relative of his. The hunch-back says to him: 'Well, you've probably already eaten and certainly had tea, so why don't you hear out my boy [on his religious knowledge] and give him a kopeck?'"

Itsheyzhe's wife, with her green eyes, was rolling on the floor laughing and Fayvkeh laughed so hard his sides were splitting. But that wasn't all. Khoneh the Dayen's Son imitated Leybeh-Horb teaching his children how to walk in the street:

"When you see sweets in the shop," Khoneh says, "don't look. What's the use of looking? It's all just in order to get your money. For example, at Alter the Watchmaker's shop there's a silver watch hanging in the window. It's just to get hold of your two *groshn* [two kopecks]. You think he wants to do you a favor? The two *groshn*!"

"Ah, the two *groshn*!"

"Nothing but the two *groshn*!"

"Where does he put his interest payments?"

"In his hump."

"A hump full of five-kopeck coins."

"With ten-kopeck coins."

"I tell you, it's gold pieces."

"We ought to let him have a 'hump' of a come-uppance!"

"So he'll remember Soymekh Noflim all too well."

"Well, then!"

"*Nu*, let's go. . . ."

And the hour of vengeance came. It arrived in the middle of winter. [. . .]

The Magid "Rubs His Chin"

In the middle of winter the *Magid* [itinerant preacher] Sholem-Meyer Piskun ["Big Mouth"] arrived in Shklov—a gray-haired elderly Jew, with a flattened nose and a nasal twang.

At one time, they say, in the days of [Hebrew novelist and journalist Peretz] Smolenskin he was a *maskil* [a proponent of the Haskalah, the Jewish Enlightenment], and a Hebrew grammarian. But later he became devout and began delivering God-fearing sermons in the synagogues.

But he nevertheless couldn't completely renounce his "Enlightenment" and used to mix all sorts of miscellaneous stuff into his sermons. Simply amazing things! "Geagraphy" and "philasuphy" and "geametry" and how animals and birds live, and how in Warsaw a man was born with the head of a bird and how the earth rotates and how the blood circulates in the veins and what kind of "technical science" was once possessed by Bezalel, who built the Ark of the Covenant, and about "the immortality of the soul," which the most learned of the philosophers of all the nations now believe in—because even a burned piece of paper does not get lost—there's your proof. . . . In short, all the secular knowledge that Zelig Slonimski had crammed into his Warsaw [Hebrew-language newspaper] *Ha-Tsefirah,* in place of the forbidden subject of politics back in the days of Tsar Alexander III. Among older Jews Sholem-Meyer was not quite "kosher," but in return the young people thought highly of him.

No sooner had this *magid* Piskun with his nasal twang appeared in town, than the trustees of Soymekh Noflim paid him a visit at his inn and treated him to good cigarettes. And Itsheyzhe invited him to dinner at his home and invited Khoneh the Dayen's Son as well.

What the three of them talked about during dinner—and after dinner—nobody knows. But from the notes pasted on the copper washstands at the entrances to the synagogues, it was learned that

with the help of God, may he be blessed, on Tuesday—a doubly good day—after *minḥah* [the afternoon prayer] the Preacher of righteousness, the Chastiser at the Gates, Reb Sholem-Meyer Piskun, renowned *magid* of the holy community of Mohilev, will preach a sermon in the Old Besmedresh [Prayer House] in the holy community of Shklov. . . .

It was an ordinary announcement of the arrival of a *magid*, but at Uncle Uri's house they knew that the Old Besmedresh had deliberately been chosen because Leybeh-Horb prays there and that the "Preacher of Righteousness," Reb Sholem-Meyer Piskun of Mohilev, will "rub his chin" [give him a dressing-down?]. Shh, be quiet! Don't talk about it." . . .

Fayvkeh was beside himself with joy that Reb Leybeh would "get his chin rubbed in it." He imagined the thing as follows: the Magid from Mohilev with his snub nose will climb up on Leybeh-Horb and will rub his chin with scouring sand, like Paskeh the maid does with the brass samovar just before the holidays. He was

eager to see such a remarkable scene, finally to see vengeance taken on that ugly hunchback. So he asked Aunt Feygeh to let him go hear the *magid*. It wasn't hard to get her permission, because Aunt Feygeh herself dearly loved hearing a *magid* preach and was pleased that her schoolboy son took after her.

Tuesday after *minḥah*, when Fayvkeh ran from heder to the Old Besmedresh, he encountered a wall of people. The *besmedresh* was already full. People were standing on the pulpit and around the Ark. From the black wooden grating across the women's balcony bits of noses, foreheads, eager eyes, curls of wigs, shawls, kerchiefs, girls' braids, and women's lips were visible.

First of all Fayvkeh takes a look to see if Leybeh-Horb is sitting at his accustomed place near the stove. Yes! Leybeh-Horb is there. He slowly edges himself closer and warms his hump on the hot, smooth tiles. His sheepskin coat with the high collar was half off his shoulders, half under him, since he was always worried that someone might steal such a valuable garment. So he sits there in his brown goat's wool caftan on top of his fur coat like a crooked small nut on its shell, listens, puts his palm to his ear, and keeps one eye shut because Piskun the Magid of Mohilev is already preaching. That means that Reb Leybeh doesn't know that something is up, has no idea what others are planning to do to him. . . .

Fayvkeh was barely able to push his way forward to where he could see both the *magid* and the hunchback at the same time. He sees that at the platform of the Ark, at a red lectern, wearing a prayer shawl and skullcap, Sholem-Meyer Piskun is already standing and talking through his nose. On both sides of the Ark, the trustees of Soymekh Noflim are standing guard: Itsheyzhe, Uncle Zhameh's only son and Khoneh the Dayen's Son. Both are keeping an eye on the *magid* to make sure he keeps his word and "rubs the nose" of the person in question. [. . .]

But before [the *magid*] took pity and patched back together the biblical verse he had torn to pieces, he jumped over to a bit of midrash [biblical commentary] and from there to Gemara [part of the Talmud], and from Gemara he went back to King Solomon. The midrash, according to the *magid*, "takes a stand," the Gemara "stubbornly maintains," and King Solomon "arrives." For example, the Gemara "stubbornly maintains" the following: "For three transgressions," women die in childbirth—because they do not separate *challah* [the piece of dough burned as a sacrifice before baking bread], because they do not bless the Sabbath candles, and because they do not observe ritual cleanliness during menstruation. The *magid* talks through his nose, draws out and stresses the harsh words, resoundingly and melodiously, slowly and terrifyingly, like a bell announcing bad news—"ding-dong, ding-dong." At the same time he looks up at the women's section, where the women are confined behind the black wooden grating, like goats sold at a loss.

The sonorous, drawn out 'N's in the *magid*'s nasal drawl give his voice even greater similarity to a mourning bell:

"Oh, for three-n transgre-nssions . . . the wo-nmen die."

When such undoing—may all Jews be spared—is heard in the women's section, the old ladies burst into a flood of tears and the young matrons open their eyes wide and turn pale as chalk. From time to time a woman's stifled sigh or fearful shriek emerges. When Sholem-Meyer, the nasal twanger, hears that he has deeply affected the "weaker sex," he decides that he has tormented them long enough and turns his flat nose to the male audience, and his protruding eyes blink and sparkle like those of a billy-goat after it has grabbed a mouthful of cabbage from a fenced garden: "But the *midrash* takes a stand and says thus. . . ." He peppers his speech with hair-splitting arguments, spices it with interpretations, and shakes over the whole thing the salt of deep knowledge he has brought from Mohilev and from old copies of *Ha-Tsefirah*. He goes on and on until he comes up with "geagraphy."

The word *geagraphy* by itself stuns all ears, but before people can catch their breath from such erudition, Sholem-Meyer Piskun has already made a remarkable discovery, that "ha-aretz agulah ke-beitzah," in other words, that the world is as round as an egg—period. That's it exactly! He has been able to discover nothing rounder than an egg. That wouldn't be so bad, but it comes out of his flat nose, with its bladder-like nostrils, threaded with 'N's: "ha-a-nretz a-ngulah ke-be-ntsah—the ear-nth is nround like an e-ngg." [. . .]

But the trustees of Soymekh Noflim have run out of patience. Both Itsheyzhe and Khoneh the Dayen's Son have pushed their way to the Ark and made wry faces at the *magid*. Khoneh the Dayen's Son couldn't even restrain himself and started to cough. And when Piskun the Magid looked at him, he pointed very clearly with his finger to the stove. . . . Only then did Sholem-Meyer realize that he had strayed too far afield and began to

turn the sermon around and come out against those Jews who . . . who . . . that . . . which is to say . . . what was the reason that he reminded the Jews of Shklov about the *kaareh* [the collection plate placed outside the synagogue on Yom Kippur] and *mezoynes* [*mezonot*, the food a husband must provide for his wife]? Doesn't he, Sholem-Meyer, know full well that the Jews of Shklov are famous for their charity, their hospitality, their support of learned scholars, for giving away their last two kopecks for a *magid*? But on the other hand, there are among them those who sit all day and study and pray, but when it comes to subscribing to a society like Soymekh Noflim, a society that makes great sacrifices in order to help the poor and middle-class people who have fallen on hard times or to make a contribution to a *magid* that has a daughter to marry off. [. . .]

Then suddenly Sholem-Meyer Piskun's voice bursts forth with such force and such nasal twang as if it were issued by a brass trumpet. From the height of the Ark, he points with his finger toward the stove, and his nasal voice trumpets over the whole *besmedresh*:

"Where is the e-nvidence, gentlemen, in the Tor-nah for such Jews? Here it is: *ha-ngamal* [*ha-gamal*], that camel, that hump, that crooked back! *He cheweth the cud*. He sits and 'chews the cud' all day. He moves his lips, and prays and studies. . . . But: *he divideth not the hoof* . . . his paw is not open. *He is unclean to you!*"

Here Reb Sholem-Meyer Piskun finished like a trumpeter: "Let such a Jew be *trey-nf* to you!"

And now what Fayvkeh and the trustees of Soymekh Noflim had been awaiting all evening with palpitating hearts has finally happened. Leybeh-Horb kneaded his brows under his quilted cap, took his hands off the warm stove, and stood up suddenly as if he had been stuck with a red-hot needle. The men sitting next to him on the same bench jumped away from him as if from a monster that had just appeared—half-camel, half-human. Leybeh-Horb turned pale, sat down, and then got up again. Around him men laughed into their beards with lowered eyes. The further people were from him, around the pulpit and near the Ark, the louder and more biting the laughter became. Fingers, like spears, pointed at the hunchback from all sides. From the women's cage, between the black grates, small white fingers were also sticking out like crooked candles: "There he is. . . ." And Piskun the Magid, inspired by the support of the community, repeated yet again his ingenious biblical interpretation:

"He is unclean to you! Let such a Jew be trey-nf to you!"

Now Fayvkeh clearly understood what is meant by "rubbing his chin." He realized that the effect of that kind of "rubbing" is a lot stronger than rubbing the samovar with scouring sand, because Leybeh-Horb's face began to turn all kinds of colors—from red to yellow and from white to green. With trembling hands Reb Leybeh was barely able to pull on his half-undone sheepskin coat, turn up the high, hairy collar and like a drunkard began moving toward the door. The congregation, laughing in their beards, made a "gangway" for him. People moved apart into two giggling walls and let the hunchback pass through to the exit. In that manner Reb Leybeh disappeared into the night, without saying *mayrev*, the evening prayer. After him came running a couple of boys, a pair of misbehaving impudent chums.

Meanwhile, there was a bit of commotion in the Old Besmedresh. Older men now began to complain that a [pious] Jew with a long beard had been humiliated. Those who had been mocking him now looked at each other shamefacedly. But the young men, especially the trustees of Soymekh Noflim, and all those who sided with them, continued to laugh out of spite even after Leybeh-Horb had run away. The women's gallery cackled like a henhouse. Piskun the Magid realized that no one was listening to him anymore, so he made it short. He mentioned the collection plate again and closed with the traditional: "*u-va le-tsiyon goel . . . ve-noimar amen*" ["And a redeemer shall come to Israel, and let us say Amen"]. [. . .]

Translated by Solon Beinfeld.

David Vogel
1891-1944

The peripatetic Hebrew novelist, short-story writer, and poet David Vogel was born in Satanov, Russia [today, Sataniv, Ukraine]; lived in Vilna and Lvov in his youth; and settled in Vienna in 1916. He moved to Paris in 1925 and sailed to Palestine in 1929, but left a year later. He returned to Paris in 1932 after stays in Warsaw, Vienna, and Berlin. The Germans arrested and deported him in 1944. His introspective, restrained poems attracted much critical attention from the 1950s on. His psychological novel *Married Life*, written between 1929 and 1939 and republished from manuscripts in 1986, recounts the pathological love affair between a Jew and a well-born non-Jew in post–World War I Vienna.

Married Life
1929

5

On his way home Gurdweill tried without success to find the reason for Lotte's strange behaviour. He went over everything he had said in her house in his mind: there was nothing that could have given her the least offence. In the end he came to the conclusion that there was nothing behind it but her own nervousness, and he felt a little sorry for her, for this Lotte, who was actually a very sweet girl, a dear soul, and for whom he had long felt sentiments of the warmest friendship.

In the meantime the sky had partially cleared. Between the murky clouds patches of deep blue appeared, fresh and clean. Gurdweill remembered happily that there were only three hours left until the meeting, and unconsciously he quickened his pace, as if to reach the appointed hour sooner.

At home he found a letter from his sister in America waiting for him, with a ten-dollar bill folded inside it. It's come at just the right time, thought Gurdweill. He would be able to pay a few debts, and re-open old sources of loans. And most important of all: he would not go to the meeting empty-handed. Apart from the concrete benefits involved, Gurdweill saw the fact that the unexpected letter had arrived today of all days as a favourable omen. Without a doubt, this was the beginning of a new, happy time.

The money-changers in the vicinity were already shut, but Gurdweill remembered in time that it was possible to change money at the railway station too. Then he bought himself a new collar and a bite to eat and went home again.

Soon afterwards Ulrich returned. He too had brought food, bread, butter and sausage, and they sat down to eat. Ulrich told him that he had seen Lotte at the café half an hour before, and that she had asked him to give Gurdweill her regards and to ask him to drop into the café that evening if he was free. She was sitting with Dr. Astel and seemed in high spirits.

"She's a pretty girl," added Ulrich. "Especially her eyes, they're quite extraordinary."

"Yes, very pretty," agreed Gurdweill absent-mindedly.

"I hear that she's already officially engaged to Dr. Astel," remarked Ulrich, and after a moment he added: "It doesn't seem like a good match to me."

"In these matters you can never tell in advance. There are always surprises. Anyway, why shouldn't it be a good match? Dr. Astel seems very much in love with her. And presumably she loves him too."

"I wouldn't be so sure."

"Why on earth not?" Gurdweill became unreasonably excited. "Tell me why not? She's maybe a little eccentric, perhaps. But in that respect she's no different from a lot of other people in our generation."

"That's not what I'm talking about. In my opinion, she's too good for him. And besides, I don't think she loves him."

"How on earth do you know? On the contrary!"

But in his heart of hearts he knew that Ulrich was right and he was wrong.

After eating Gurdweill stood up and began putting on his coat. Ulrich asked if he would come to the Café Herrenhof later.

"No, I'm meeting someone." (He was too shy to say her name.)

"The girl from yesterday?" asked Ulrich simply. And in order to give pleasure to his friend, for whom he felt true affection, he added: "She's very nice. There's a hidden charm about her, which you don't notice right away."

Gurdweill arrived at the café fifteen minutes early. He selected an empty table in the corner opposite the door, and ordered coffee. The few customers scattered around the square, smallish room, all seemed like old acquaintances and well-wishers to him, although he was seeing them for the first time in his life. He would have been delighted to shake them all by the hand and ask after the health of their families. He could not understand his former bitterness towards people like them. Weren't they all—all of them without exception—simple and good and deserving of love?

When the waiter brought his coffee Gurdweill asked him if the Baroness had not already been there this evening. He described her in detail—her face, figure and clothes. It gave him a peculiar pleasure to talk about her to this stranger.

"She's my fiancée, you see . . ." he concluded.

"No young woman of that description has been here. She's not one of our regulars."

"And could you tell me what the exact time is now?"

"Eight o'clock."

"In that case she'll be here directly. She's supposed to come after eight . . . she's very punctual. . ."

Gurdweill sipped the coffee and watched the door vigilantly. He smoked a cigarette, and then another one, and the Baroness did not come. It was already a quarter past eight. Perhaps it was the wrong café?—the doubt flashed through his mind. No, impossible! They had definitely arranged to meet in the Café Alserbach! He could not possibly be mistaken!

At that moment the Baroness entered the café. She walked straight up to him, as if she had known in advance that he would be sitting in precisely that corner. Gurdweill leapt up and went forward to meet her, his face radiant.

"I'm not late am I?" smiled the Baroness and held out her hand.

"Yes, you are late. Because I've been waiting since yesterday . . ."

"But not all the time here, I hope. That would have been rather boring."

She sat on the upholstered seat against the wall, took a packet of cigarettes out of her bag, lit one for herself and offered one to Gurdweill. She inhaled the smoke avidly, like an addict who had denied herself too long, and ordered black coffee.

Gurdweill was full of various things he wanted to say to her, but his tongue seemed stuck to the roof of his mouth. He sat opposite her and gazed at her tenderly, smiling weakly with pleasure and embarrassment. The Baroness finished her coffee and asked him what his first name was.

"Ah, Rudolf," she said. "Rudolfus, Rudolfinus! My cousin's name is Rudolf too. He's taller than you by two heads—but he's an ass."

"I—I'm very glad that he's an a-ass . . ." stammered Gurdweill with an idiotic smile.

"What? You're glad that my cousin's an ass?" The Baroness burst out laughing.

"I only meant," Gurdweill recovered and tried to correct himself, "What I meant was . . . That's not what I'm glad about, of course . . . I didn't express myself properly . . . I imagine him tall and skinny, with straight, oiled hair parted in the middle, his shoes always polished until they shine. Patent-leather shoes. And when he looks at anyone he inclines his head slightly to one side, like a chicken, and puts on a very dignified expression—because, of course, he's really nothing but an ass . . ."

"You've described him very well—but never patent-leather shoes. Brown ones. And you forgot the gold-knobbed cane . . . 'Dorothea'—he always calls me 'Dorothea' because it sounds more dignified and traditional—'Dorothea'—he says, ridiculous and pompous as an old man, 'you are the scion of an ancient race. Your ancestors were Crusaders, don't forget! You must be on your guard against the Jews. The city of Vienna has become Judaized from one end to the other. Blood doesn't matter any more. They're poisoning the air. But for them, we would never have lost the war.' And all the time he himself is running after a little Jewess who's turned his head completely."

"And do you obey him, Baroness?"

"In what respect?"

"Preserving the purity of the race?"

To this the Baroness responded with a loud burst of hard, unruly laughter.

"You know what," she said suddenly and irrelevantly, "Why don't you just call me Thea? Titles bore me."

Gurdweill gave her a grateful look. For some reason he suggested having a brandy. A spirit of recklessness entered him: his pale, slender, feminine hands sought some object to hold, to absorb the energy coursing through them, and underneath the table they found one of the Baroness's unresisting hands. The waiter brought two little glasses of brandy, and Gurdweill emptied his in a single gulp. The Baroness announced that the next day, Saturday, she did not have to go to work because her "General" (which was what she called the lawyer for whom she worked) had gone away for the week-end, and she could stay out a little later tonight.

"Good, wonderful!" enthused Gurdweill.

They talked and fell silent and began talking again—talk which was apparently trivial, but was nevertheless full of a kind of hidden significance—and the time flew by as imperceptibly as an open plain by the side of an express train.

It was already eleven o'clock. Both of them at once suddenly felt the need to leave the café. Gurdweill called the waiter and paid him.

Outside the Baroness linked her arm in his, and they walked silently down Alserbachstrasse and turned into Sechsschimmelgasse. Suddenly she said, half seriously and half jokingly:

"You'll marry me, won't you, Rudolfus? I fancy you and I don't mind saying so."

Gurdweill was astonished. Such a possibility had not even crossed his mind. She was certainly an interesting girl! The way she said it—so simply! He had never heard anything like it before . . . He made haste to reply: "Of course! Of course! I'm ready! I've got no objections!"

And after a moment: "But what about your family? They won't give their consent will they?"

"My family?" she exclaimed scornfully. "Who? My cousin Rudolf? And what about me—where do I come in? I'm used to doing as I see fit! And by the way, my father is a very nice man. You'll meet him and see for yourself. I know he'll like you."

They walked down the slumbering streets, discussing the matter at length. The Baroness wanted a "real" wedding, in other words, a religious ceremony "according to the Jewish tradition." In order to do this, she would have to convert to Judaism, which did not seem to present any problems as far as she was concerned. She did not want any unnecessary delays, and they agreed to "take the necessary steps" and get married as soon as she was converted. To tell the truth, Gurdweill felt a certain flicker of uneasiness at the changes which were about to take place in his way of life, but he immediately suppressed it as groundless. Now, he thought with boundless happiness, now the dream he had been cherishing in his heart for so long would come true! Within a year! Or even two! And from who? From her! A son from her! Two ancient races! (For Rudolf Gurdweill came from an ancient Jewish family. He could trace his descent to a great and famous rabbi from Prague.)

So great was his joy that he stood still and embraced the Baroness in the middle of the street.

"A son," he whispered ardently, "you'll give me a son, won't you?"

The Baroness gave him a strange look and smiled without saying anything. It seemed ridiculous to her that this little man wanted a son . . .

They were in an ill-lit side street. It must have been about half past midnight. In the desolate silence their footsteps echoed with a hollow sound. Not far off the signboard of a hotel sticking out into the lane twinkled with orange bulbs. From the open door of the hotel a tongue of light protruded on to the paving stones and climbed halfway up the opposite wall. Gurdweill felt his companion's footsteps slowing down without understanding why. When they reached the hotel entrance she stopped. She bent down to Gurdweill as if he were a child and whispered:

"Why don't we celebrate our wedding night now, my little fiancé . . ."

It was only now that he noticed the brightly-lit hotel, which had previously escaped his attention. He felt as if the ground was slipping from under his feet. A dull flicker of rebellion stirred inside him and died down immediately. Before he knew what was happening they were already in front of the receptionist's desk. Gurdweill signed the register mechanically: Rudolf Gurdweill, born on such and such a date, in such and such a town, and his wife . . .

With an expression of total indifference on his tired, sleepy face the bellboy led them up the shabbily carpeted stairs and showed them into a square, sparsely furnished room on the second floor.

"If you need anything, just ring here!" He pointed to an ivory button next to the door, and pocketed the tip which Gurdweill offered him.

The Baroness made herself at home, glancing at the water jug to see if it was full and lifting the blankets to look at the sheets. Gurdweill was suddenly assailed by an alien, hostile spirit, reeking of sordid affairs and unexpected accidents—the spirit of all such squalid hotel rooms, and for a moment he came to his senses. The whole business, you had to admit, was rather strange. Before he could turn around, he found himself in a new, ambiguous situation, no longer in control of his actions or capable of directing them at his will. What was he doing here in this strange and disagreeable room? For a moment he regretted the whole thing and wanted to run away. He felt a kind of shame. This was not the way to begin the new stage in his life! He stood in the middle of the room with his coat on, his hat in his hand, as if he were on the point of leaving. Then he turned to face his companion, who had removed her hat in the meantime and loosened her long flaxen hair. He felt very embarrassed. He looked for somewhere to put his hat and in the end he put it back on his head. He went up to the window and drew the curtain and looked outside without seeing anything. Then he returned to Thea, who was already sitting on the bed and undoing her shoes. Her long, jutting chin twitched spasmodically and her bosom heaved. Gurdweill sat down beside her on the bed. She immediately left her shoes alone and turned to face him. There was a cruel, bloodthirsty expression on her face. She fixed him with eyes flashing like spears, as if to subdue him completely, and with one swift movement she threw herself back and stuck her teeth in his elbow, like a beast of prey. Gurdweill let out a strangled groan. He felt as if he were about to faint with pain and desire at once. He sensed his strength draining out of his body. Flaming red daggers danced before his eyes and sweat burst from his brow. At the same time he wished that it would go on forever, that

the pain would increase a thousandfold, that it would annihilate him entirely. No woman had ever made him feel like this before.

Thea suddenly jumped up.

"Get undressed, Rudy!" she commanded in a slightly husky voice, and she herself began tearing off her clothes and throwing them on a chair. Then she seized hold of Gurdweill, lifting him like a doll, and laid him on the bed.

At half past five in the morning, after seeing Thea home, Gurdweill dragged himself through the dead streets. Taking small, slow steps he tottered down the middle of the street, his head heavy and at the same time absolutely empty. Fresh morning breezes whipped across his face, suddenly changing direction and buffeting him from the side and the back, trying to rob him of his hat. He took it off with a mechanical movement and abandoned his rumpled hair to the wind. A row of big carts, piled high with vegetables, trundled slowly towards the market; the heavy wheels creaked and scraped on the street, vanquishing the stubborn silence. High up on their perches the drivers slumbered, huddled in sacks against a possible rainfall and the morning chill, withdrawn into themselves like lifeless bundles. It seemed as if they had been driving thus for years on end, driving on and on without a pause. The lamplighters bobbed up in their filthy cloaks, zigzagging from one side of the street to the other, and putting out the gas lights with the long bamboo poles they carried on their shoulders like tremendous spears. From time to time a solitary milk cart emerged from a side street, the big tin containers lined up one on top of the other, or a closed bread van from the "Hammer" or "Anker" bakery. Here and there people were already waiting for the first trams: prostitutes with wilted, tired faces, their unmade-up eyes naked and wrinkled. How depressing they looked in their garish, crumpled dresses, their gay hats awry. Women from the poorest of the poor, one with a bundle of morning papers wrapped up in a bottle-green shawl, one with a huge basket of vegetables. A few workers. The newborn morning invaded the street with a pale, milky light and everything seemed strange and dreamlike to Gurdweill. The night had left him with a feeling of measureless oppression, strangely combined with a kind of reckless hilarity. He was already on the quay, and suddenly he stopped dead and laughed to himself with a lopsided grin on his face. Anyone who saw him would surely have thought him drunk. He set off again, crossed the Ferdinand Bridge, and stopped to wait for a tram. With lustreless eyes he looked at the two prostitutes waiting there, and the picture of the hotel room in which he had spent the night rose up before him. The memory gave him such a disagreeable feeling that he was forced to avert his eyes. But at the same time he was filled with a great longing for Thea. For a moment he imagined that he would never see her again, that he had parted from her forever, and he felt utterly abandoned, fatally ill, and completely useless. At that moment he could have burst out crying. Gurdweill now knew, without the shadow of a doubt, that he was enslaved to her, to this strapping, blonde girl, forever, and that without her he was a broken vessel, fit for nothing. He moved away from the tram stop and walked down Praterstrasse on shaky legs.

When he entered his room it was already morning. And from the next-door room he could already hear the yells of "Aalbert," the old landlady's grandson, and his Auntie Siedl, fighting as they always did when the boy spent the night in their house.

Translated by Dalya Bilu.

Other works by Vogel: *Kol ha-shirim* (1966); *Takhanot kavot: novelot, roman, sipur, yoman* (1990); *In the Sanatorium* (2013).

Stefan Zweig
1881–1942

The Viennese biographer, dramatist, poet, essayist, and novelist Stefan Zweig grew up in luxury and security in a wealthy, nonobservant family in the last days of the Habsburg Empire. With the rise of Hitler, he moved to England in 1934 and then to the United States in 1940, but before the year was up, he left for Brazil, where, depressed by the collapse of European civilization, he committed suicide in 1942. His work was translated into many languages, and in the interwar years he was one of the most famous writers in the world. He was known particularly for his biographies of historical and literary figures (e.g., Marie Antoinette, Amerigo Vespucci, Honoré de Balzac) and for his novellas. His much-read autobiography *The World of Yesterday* (1943) is both praised (as elegiac) and damned (as naïve).

Mendel the Bibliophile
1929

Back in Vienna again, on my way home from a visit to the outer districts of the city, I was unexpectedly caught in a heavy shower of rain that sent people running from its wet whiplash to take refuge in such shelter as the entrances of buildings, and I myself quickly looked round for a place where I could keep dry. Luckily Vienna has a coffee house on every street corner, so with my hat dripping and my shoulders drenched, I hurried into one that stood directly opposite. Inside, it proved to be a suburban café of the traditional kind, almost a stereotype of a Viennese café, with none of the newfangled features that imitate the inner-city music halls of Germany. It was in the old Viennese bourgeois style, full of ordinary people partaking more lavishly of the free newspapers than the pastries on sale. At this evening hour the air in the café, which would always be stuffy anyway, was thick with ornate blue smoke rings, yet the place looked clean, with velour sofas that were obviously new and a shiny aluminium till. In my haste I hadn't even taken the trouble to read its name outside, and indeed, what would have been the point? Now I was sitting in the warm, looking impatiently through window panes veiled by blue smoke, and wondering when it would suit the vexatious shower to move a few kilometres further on.

So there I sat, with nothing to do, and began to fall under the spell of the passive lethargy that invisibly emanates, with narcotic effect, from every true Viennese coffee house. In that empty, idle mood I looked individually at the customers, to whom the artificial light of the smoke-filled room lent an unhealthy touch of grey shadow round the eyes, and studied the young woman at the till mechanically setting out sugar and a spoon for every cup of coffee served by the waiter; drowsily and without really noticing them I read the posters on the walls, to which I was wholly indifferent, and found myself almost enjoying this kind of apathy. But suddenly, and in a curious way, I was brought out of my drowsy state as a vague impulse began to stir within me. It was like the beginning of a slight toothache, when you don't know yet if it is on the right or the left, if it is starting in the upper or the lower jaw; there was just a certain tension, a mental uneasiness. For all at once—I couldn't have said how—I was aware that I must have been here once before, years ago, and that a memory of some kind was connected with these walls, these chairs, these tables, this smoky room, apparently strange to me. [. . .]

I reached out into the room, straining all my senses, and at the same time I searched myself—yet damn it all, I couldn't place that lost memory, drowned in the recesses of my mind. [. . .]

But here was a strange thing: I had hardly taken a couple of steps across the room before the first phosphorescent glimmers of light began to dawn in my mind, swirling and sparkling. To the right of the cash desk, I remembered, there would be a way into a windowless room illuminated only by artificial light. And sure enough, I was right. There it was, not with the wallpaper I had known before, but the proportions of that rectangular back room, its contours still indistinct in my memory, were exactly the same. This was the card room. I instinctively looked for individual details, my nerves already joyfully vibrating (soon, I felt, I would remember it all). Two billiard tables stood idle, like silent ponds of green mud; in the corners of the room there were card tables, with two men who looked like civil servants or professors playing chess at one of them. And in the corner, close to the iron stove, where you went to use the telephone, stood a small, square table. Suddenly the realization flashed right through my entire mind. I knew at once, instantly, with a single, warm impulse jogging my memory: my God, that was where Mendel used to sit, Jakob Mendel, Mendel the bibliophile, and after twenty years here I was again in the Café Gluck at the upper end of Alserstrasse, to which he habitually resorted. Jakob Mendel—how could I have forgotten him for such an incredibly long time? That strangest of characters, a legendary man, that esoteric wonder of the world, famous at the university and in a small, eminent circle—how could I have lost my memory of him, the magician who traded in books and sat here from morning to evening every day, a symbol of the knowledge, fame and honour of the Café Gluck?

I had only to turn my vision inwards for that one second, and already his unmistakable figure, in three dimensions, was conjured up by my creatively enlightened blood. I saw him at once as he had been, always sitting at that rectangular table, its dingy grey marble top heaped high at all times with books and other writings. I saw the way he persistently sat there, imperturbable, his eyes behind his glasses hypnotically fixed on a book, humming and muttering as he read, rocking his body and his inadequately polished, freckled bald patch back and forth, a habit acquired in the *cheder*, his Jewish primary school in eastern Europe. He pored over his catalogues and books here, at that table, never sitting anywhere else, singing and swaying quietly, a dark, rocking cradle. For just as a child falls into sleep and is lost to the world by that rhythmically hypnotic rocking movement, in the opinion of pious Jews the spirit passes more easily into the grace of contemplation if one's own idle body rocks and sways at the same

time. And indeed, Jakob Mendel saw and heard none of what went on around him. [. . .] As a young man, I had seen the great mystery of total concentration for the first time in this little Galician book dealer, Jakob Mendel, a kind of concentration in which the artist resembles the scholar, the truly wise resembles the totally deranged. It is the tragic happiness and unhappiness of total obsession.

An older colleague of mine from the university had taken me to see him. At the time I was engaged on research into Mesmer, the Paracelsian doctor and practitioner of magnetism, still too little known today, but I was not having much luck. [. . .]

So the two of us went to the Café Gluck, and lo and behold there sat Mendel the bibliophile, bespectacled, sporting a beard that needed trimming, clad in black, and rocking back and forth as he read like a dark bush blown in the wind. We went up to him, and he didn't even notice. He just sat there reading, his torso swaying over the table like a mandarin, and hanging on a hook behind him was his decrepit black overcoat, its pockets stuffed with notes and journals. [. . .]

My friend introduced me, and I explained my business, first—a trick expressly recommended by my friend—complaining with pretended anger of the librarian who, I said, wouldn't give me any information. Mendel leant back and spat carefully. Then he just laughed, and said with a strong eastern European accent, "Wouldn't, eh? Not him—couldn't is more like it! He's an ignoramus, a poor old grey-haired ass. I've known him, heaven help me, these twenty years, and in all that time he still hasn't learnt anything. He can pocket his salary, yes, that's all he and his like can do! Those learned doctors—they'd do better to carry bricks than sit over their books."

This forceful venting of his grievances broke the ice, and with a good-natured wave of his hand he invited me, for the first time, to sit at the square marble-topped table covered with notes, that altar of bibliophilic revelations as yet unknown to me. I quickly explained what I wanted: works contemporary with Mesmer himself on magnetism, as well as all later books and polemics for and against his theories. As soon as I had finished, Mendel closed his left eye for a second, just like a marksman before he fires his gun. It was truly for no more than a second that this moment of concentrated attention lasted, and then, as if reading from an invisible catalogue, he fluently enumerated two or three dozen books, each with its place and date of publication and an estimate of its price. I was astonished. Although prepared for it in advance, this was more than I had expected. But my bafflement seemed to please him, for on the keyboard of his memory he immediately played the most wonderful variations on my theme that any librarian could imagine. Did I also want to know about the somnambulists and the first experiments with hypnosis? And about Gassner's exorcisms, and Christian Science, and Madame Blavatsky? Once again names came tumbling out of him, titles and descriptions; only now did I realize what a unique marvel of memory I had found in Jakob Mendel, in truth an encyclopaedia, a universal catalogue on two legs. Absolutely dazed, I stared at this bibliographical phenomenon, washed up here in the shape of an unprepossessing, even slightly grubby little Galician second-hand book dealer who, after reciting some eighty names to me full pelt, apparently without taking much thought, but inwardly pleased to have played his trump card, polished his glasses on what might once have been a white handkerchief. To hide my astonishment a little, I hesitantly asked which of those books he could, if need be, get hold of for me.

"Well, we'll see what can be done," he growled. "You come back here tomorrow, by then old Mendel will have found you a little something, and what can't be found here will turn up elsewhere. A man who knows his way around will have luck." [. . .]

He knew more in every field than the experts in that field, he was more knowledgeable about libraries than the librarians themselves, he knew the stocks of most firms by heart better than their owners, for all their lists and their card indexes, although he had nothing at his command but the magic of memory, nothing but his incomparable faculty of recollection, which could only be truly explained and analysed by citing a hundred separate examples. It was clear that his memory could have been trained and formed to show such demonic infallibility only by the eternal mystery of all perfection: by concentration. This remarkable man knew nothing about the world outside books, for to his mind all the phenomena of existence began to seem truly real to him only when they were cast as letters and assembled as print in a book, a process that, so to speak, had sterilized them. But he read even the books themselves not for their meaning, but their intellectual and narrative content: his sole passion was for their names, prices, forms of publication and original title pages. [. . .]

By trade, to be sure, Jakob Mendel was known to the ignorant only as a little dealer in second-hand books.

Every Sunday the same standard advertisement appeared in the *Neue Freie Presse* and the *Neues Wiener Tagblatt*: "Old books bought, best prices paid, apply to Mendel, Obere Alserstrasse," and then a telephone number which in fact was the number of the Café Gluck. He would search through stockrooms, and every week, with an old servant bearded like the Emperor Joseph, brought back new booty to his headquarters and conveyed it on from there, since he had no licence for a proper bookshop. So he remained a dealer in a small way, not a very lucrative occupation. Students sold him their textbooks, and his hands passed them on from one academic year to the next, while in addition he sought out and acquired any particular work that was wanted, asking a small extra charge. He was free with good advice. But money had no place within his world, for he had never been seen in anything but the same shabby coat, consuming milk and two rolls in the morning, the afternoon and the evening, and at midday eating some small dish that they fetched him from the restaurant. [. . .]

Holding a precious book meant to Mendel what an assignment with a woman might to another man. These moments were his platonic nights of love. Books had power over him; money never did. Great collectors, including the founder of a collection in Princeton University Library, tried in vain to recruit him as an adviser and buyer for their libraries—Jakob Mendel declined; no one could imagine him anywhere but in the Café Gluck. Thirty-three years ago, when his beard was still soft and black and he had ringlets over his forehead, he had come from the east to Vienna, a crook-backed lad, to study for the rabbinate, but he had soon abandoned Jehovah the harsh One God to give himself up to idolatry in the form of the brilliant, thousand-fold polytheism of books. That was when he had first found his way to the Café Gluck, and gradually it became his workplace, his headquarters, his post office, his world. Like an astronomer alone in his observatory, studying myriads of stars every night through the tiny round lens of the telescope, observing their mysterious courses, their wandering multitude as they are extinguished and then appear again, so Jakob Mendel looked through his glasses out from that rectangular table into the other universe of books, also eternally circling and being reborn in that world above our own. [. . .]

Only through the twin circles of his glasses, only through those two sparkling lenses that sucked everything in, did the billions of tiny organisms formed by the letters filter into his brain; everything else streamed over him as meaningless noise. In fact he had spent over thirty years, the entire waking part of his life, here at his rectangular table reading, comparing and calculating, in a continual daydream interrupted only by sleep.

So I was overcome by a kind of horror when I saw that the marble-topped table where Jakob Mendel made his oracular utterances now stood in this room as empty as a gravestone. Only now that I was older did I understand how much dies with such a man, first because anything unique is more and more valuable in a world now becoming hopelessly uniform. And then because, out of a deep sense of premonition, the young, inexperienced man I once was had been very fond of Jakob Mendel. In him, I had come close for the first time to the great mystery of the way what is special and overwhelming in our existence is achieved only by an inner concentration of powers, a sublime monomania akin to madness. And I had seen that a pure life of the mind, total abstraction in a single idea, can still be found even today, an immersion no less than that of an Indian yogi or a medieval monk in his cell, and indeed can be found in a café illuminated by electric light and next to a telephone—as a young man, I had sensed it far more in that entirely anonymous little book dealer than in any of our contemporary writers. Yet I had been able to forget him—admittedly in the war years, and in an absorption in my own work not unlike his. Now, however, looking at that empty table, I felt a kind of shame, and at the same time a renewed curiosity.

For where had he gone, what had happened to him? I called the waiter over and asked. No, he was sorry. [. . .] No, there was no one from the old staff here now . . . or yes! Yes, there was—Frau Sporschil was still here, the toilet lady (known in vulgar parlance as the chocolate lady). But he was sure she wouldn't be able to remember individual customers now. I thought at once, you don't forget a man like Jakob Mendel, and I asked her to come and see me.

She came, Frau Sporschil with her untidy white hair, her dropsical feet taking the few steps from her area of responsibility in the background to the front of the café and still hastily rubbing her red hands on a cloth; obviously she had just been sweeping or cleaning the windows of her dismal domain. From her uncertain manner I noticed at once that she felt uneasy to be summoned so suddenly into the smarter part of the café, under the large electric lights—in Vienna ordinary people suspect

detectives and the police everywhere, as soon as anyone wants to ask them questions. So she looked at me suspiciously at first, glancing at me from under her brows, a very cautious, surreptitious glance. What good could I want of her? But as soon as I asked about Jakob Mendel she stared at me with full, positively streaming eyes, and her shoulders began to shake. [. . .]

So I suggested that we might go into the card room, to Mendel's old table, and she could tell me all about it there. Moved, she nodded to me, grateful for my understanding, and the old lady, already a little unsteady on her feet, went ahead while I followed her. The two waiters stared after us in surprise, sensing some connection, and some of the customers also seemed to be wondering about the unlikely couple we made.

Over at Mendel's table, she told me (another account, at a later date, filled in some of the details for me) about the downfall of Jakob Mendel, Mendel the bibliophile.

Well then, she said, he had gone on coming here even after the beginning of the war, day after day, arriving at seven-thirty in the morning, and he sat there just the same and studied all day, as usual; the fact was they'd all felt, and often said so, that he wasn't even aware there was a war going on. I'd remember, she said, that he never looked at a newspaper and never talked to anyone else, but even when the newsboys were making their murderous racket, announcing special editions, and all the others ran to buy, he never got to his feet or even listened. He didn't so much as notice that Franz the waiter was missing (Franz had fallen at Gorlice), and he didn't know that Herr Standhartner's son had been taken prisoner at Przemyśl, he never said a word when the bread got worse and worse, and they had to serve him fig coffee instead of his usual milk, nasty stuff it was. Just once he did seem surprised because so few students came in now, that was all. "My God, the poor man, nothing gave him pleasure or grief except those books of his."

But then, one day, the worst happened. At eleven in the morning, in broad daylight, a policeman had come in with an officer of the secret police, who had shown the rosette badge in his buttonhole and asked if a man called Jakob Mendel came in here. Then they went straight over to Mendel's table, and he thought, suspecting nothing, they wanted to sell him books or ask for information. But they told him to his face to go with them, and they took him away. It had brought shame on the café; everyone gathered round poor Herr Mendel as he stood there between the two police officers, his glasses pushed up on his forehead, looking back and forth from one to the other of them, not knowing what they really wanted. [...]

This was what had happened. One day the military censorship office, where it was the duty of the officials to supervise all correspondence sent abroad, had intercepted a postcard written and signed by one Jakob Mendel, properly stamped with sufficient postage for a country outside Austria, but—incredible to relate—sent to an enemy nation. The postcard was addressed to Jean Labourdaire, Bookseller, Paris, Quai de Grenelle, and on it the sender, Jakob Mendel, complained that he had not received the last eight numbers of the monthly *Bulletin bibliographique de la France,* in spite of having paid a year's subscription in advance. The junior censorship official who found it, in civil life a high-school teacher by profession and a scholar of Romance languages and literature by private inclination, who now wore the blue uniform of the territorial reserves, was astonished to have such a document in his hands. He thought it must be a silly joke. Among the 2,000 letters that he scanned every week, searching them for dubious comments and turns of phrase that might indicate espionage, he had never come across anything so absurd as someone in Austria addressing a letter to France without another thought, simply posting a card to the enemy country as if the borders had not been fortified by barbed wire since 1914, and as if, on every new day created by God, France, Germany, Austria and Russia were not killing a few thousand of each other's male populations. So at first he put the postcard in his desk drawer as a curio, and did not mention the absurdity to anyone else.

However, a few weeks later another card from the same Jakob Mendel was sent to a bookseller called John Aldridge, at Holborn Square in London, asking if he could procure the latest numbers of *The Antiquarian* for him; and once again it was signed by the same strange individual, Jakob Mendel, who with touching naiveté gave his full address. [...] [A]n hour later Jakob Mendel was under arrest and, still stunned with surprise, was brought before the major. [...]

First the man was asked his name: Jakob, originally Jainkeff Mendel. Profession: pedlar (for he had no bookseller's licence, only a certificate allowing him to trade from door to door). The third question was the catastrophe: his place of birth. Jakob Mendel named a small village in Petrikau. The major raised his eyebrows. Petrikau, wasn't that in the Russian part of Po-

land, near the border? Suspicious! Very suspicious! So he asked more sternly when Mendel had acquired Austrian citizenship. Mendel's glasses stared at him darkly and in surprise: he didn't understand the question. For heaven's sake, asked the major, did he have his papers, his documents, and if so where were they? The only document he had was his permit to trade from door to door. The major's eyebrows rose ever higher. Then would he kindly explain how he came to be an Austrian citizen? What had his father been, Austrian or Russian? Jakob Mendel calmly replied: Russian, of course. And he himself? Oh, to avoid having to serve in the army, he had smuggled himself over the Russian border thirty-three years ago, and he had been living in Vienna ever since. The major was getting increasingly impatient. When, he repeated, had he acquired Austrian citizenship? Why would he bother with that, asked Mendel, he'd never troubled about such things. So he was still a Russian citizen? And Mendel, who was finding all this pointless questioning tedious, replied with indifference, "Yes, I suppose so." [...]

Why hadn't he immediately reported to the authorities as a foreigner? Mendel, still unsuspecting, replied in his sing-song Jewish tones, "Why would I want to go and report all of a sudden?" The major saw this reversal of his question as a challenge and asked, menacingly, whether he hadn't read the announcements? No! And didn't he read the newspapers either? Again, no.

The two of them stared at Mendel, who was sweating slightly in his uncertainty, as if the moon had fallen to earth in their office. Then the telephone rang, typewriters tapped busily, orderlies ran back and forth and Jakob Mendel was consigned to the garrison cells, to be moved on to a concentration camp. When he was told to follow two soldiers he stared uncertainly. He didn't understand what they wanted from him, but really he had no great anxiety. What ill, after all, could the man with the gold braid on his collar and the rough voice have in store for him? In his elevated world of books there was no war, no misunderstanding, only eternal knowledge and the desire to know more about numbers and words, titles and names. So he good-naturedly went down the steps with the two soldiers. Only when all the books in his coat pockets were confiscated at the police station, and he had to hand over his briefcase, where he had put a hundred important notes and customers' addresses, did he begin to strike out angrily around him. They had to overcome him, but in the process unfortunately his glasses fell to the floor, and that magic spyglass of his that looked into the intellectual world broke into a thousand pieces. Two days later he was sent, in his thin summer coat, to a concentration camp for civilian Russian prisoners at Komorn.

As for Jakob Mendel's experience of mental horror in those two years in a concentration camp, living without books—his beloved books—without money, with indifferent, coarse and mostly illiterate companions in the midst of this gigantic human dunghill, as for all he suffered there, cut off from his sublime and unique world of books as an eagle with its wings clipped is separated from its ethereal element—there is no testimony to any of it. But the world, waking soberly from its folly, has gradually come to know that of all the cruelties and criminal encroachments of that war, none was more senseless, unnecessary and therefore more morally inexcusable than capturing and imprisoning behind barbed wire unsuspecting civilians long past the age for military service, who had become used to living in a foreign land as if it were their own, and in their belief in the laws of hospitality, which are sacred even to Tungus and Araucanian tribesmen, had neglected to flee in time. It was a crime committed equally unthinkingly in France, Germany and England, in every part of a Europe run mad. And perhaps Jakob Mendel, like hundreds of other innocents penned up in a camp, would have succumbed miserably to madness or dysentery, debility or a mental breakdown, had not a coincidence of a truly Austrian nature brought him back to his own world just in time. [. . .]

Good Frau Sporschil was able to give me a first-hand account of Mendel's return to the café from an infernal underworld. "One day—Jesus, Mary and Joseph, thinks I, I can't believe my eyes!—one day the door's pushed open, you know what it's like, just a little way, he always came in like that, and there he is stumbling into the café, poor Herr Mendel. He was wearing a much-mended military coat, and something on his head that might once have been a hat someone had thrown away. He didn't have a collar, and he looked like death, grey in the face, grey-haired and pitifully thin. But in he comes, like nothing had happened, he doesn't ask no questions, he doesn't say nothing, he goes to the table over there and takes off his coat, but not so quickly and easily as before, it takes him an effort. And no books with him now, like he always brought—he just sits down there and don't say nothing, he just stares ahead of him with empty, worn-out eyes. It was only little by little, when we'd brought him all the written stuff that had come

from Germany for him, he went back to reading. But he was never the same again." [. . .]

No, Mendel was not the old Mendel, no longer a wonder of the world but a useless collection of beard and clothes, breathing wearily, pointlessly sitting in his once-oracular chair, he was no longer the glory of the Café Gluck but a disgrace, a dirty mark, ill-smelling, a revolting sight, an uncomfortable and unnecessary parasite.

That was how the new owner of the café saw him. This man, Florian Gurtner by name, came from Retz, had made a fortune from shady deals in flour and butter during the starvation year of 1919, and had talked the unsuspecting Herr Standhartner into selling him the Café Gluck for 80,000 crowns in paper money, which swiftly depreciated in value. He set about the place with his firm rustic hands, renovating the old-established café to smarten it up, buying new armchairs for bad money at the right time, installing a marble porch, and he was already negotiating to buy the bar next door and turn it into a dance hall. Naturally enough, the odd little Galician parasite who kept a table occupied all day, and in that time consumed nothing but two cups of coffee and five rolls, was very much in the way of his hastily undertaken project to smarten up the café. [. . .]

Jakob Mendel was in a bad way. The last banknotes he had saved had been pulverized in the paper mill of inflation, and his customers had disappeared. These days he was so exhausted that he lacked the strength to start climbing steps and going from door to door selling books again. There were a hundred little signs of his poverty. He seldom had something for lunch brought in from the restaurant now, and he was behind with paying the small sums he owed for coffee and rolls, once as much as three weeks behind. At that point the head waiter wanted to turn him out into the street. But good Frau Sporschil, the toilet lady, was sorry for Mendel and said she would pay his debt.

Next month, however, a great misfortune happened. The new head waiter had already noticed, several times, that when he was settling up accounts the money for the baked goods never worked out quite right. More rolls proved to be missing than had been ordered and paid for. His suspicions, naturally, went straight to Mendel, for the decrepit old servant at the café had come to complain, several times, that Mendel had owed him money for six months, and he couldn't get it out of him. So the head waiter kept his eyes open, and two days later, hiding behind the fire screen, he succeeded in catching

Jakob Mendel secretly getting up from his table, going into the other front room, quickly taking two rolls from a bread basket and devouring them greedily. When it came to paying for what he had had that day, he denied eating any rolls at all. So that explained the disappearance of the baked goods. The waiter reported the incident at once to Herr Gurtner who, glad of the excuse he had been seeking for so long, shouted at Mendel in front of everyone, accused him of theft and made a great show of magnanimity in not calling the police at once. But he told Mendel to get out of his café immediately and never come back. Jakob Mendel only trembled and said nothing; he got up from where he sat, tottering, and went away.

"Oh, it was a real shame," said Frau Sporschil, describing this departure. "I'll never forget it, the way he stood there, his glasses pushed up on his forehead, white as a sheet. He didn't even take the time to put on his coat, although it was January, and you know what a cold year it was. And in his fright he left his book lying on the table. [. . .]

The good woman was greatly agitated, and with the passionate volubility of old age she repeated again and again that it was a real shame, and nothing like it would have happened in Herr Standhartner's day. So finally I had to ask her what had become of our friend Mendel, and whether she had seen him again. At that she pulled herself together, and then went on in even more distress.

"Every day when I passed his table, every time, believe you me, I felt a pang. I always wondered where he might be now, poor Herr Mendel, and if I'd known where he lived I'd have gone there, brought him something hot to eat, because where would he get the money to heat his room and feed himself? And so far as I know he didn't have any family, not a soul in the world. But in the end, when I still never heard a thing, I thought to myself it must all be over, and I'd never see him again. And I was wondering whether I wouldn't get a Mass read for him, because he was a good man, Herr Mendel, and we'd known each other more than twenty-five years.

"But then one day early, half past seven in the morning in February, I'm just polishing up the brass rails at the windows, and suddenly—I mean suddenly, believe you me—the door opens and in comes Herr Mendel. You know the way he always came in, kind of crooked and confused-looking, but this time he was somehow different. I can see it at once, he's torn this way and that,

his eyes all glazed, and my God, the way he looked, all beard and bones! I think right away, he don't remember nothing, here he is sleepwalking in broad daylight, he's forgot it all, all about the rolls and Herr Gurtner and how shamefully they threw him out, he don't know nothing about himself. Thank God for it, Herr Gurtner wasn't there yet, and the head waiter had just had his own coffee. So I put my oar in quickly, I tell him he'd better not stay here and get thrown out again by that nasty fellow" (and here she looked timidly around and quickly corrected herself) "I mean by Herr Gurtner. So I call out to him. 'Herr Mendel,' I say. He stares at me. And at that moment, oh my God, terrible it was, at that moment it must all have come back to him, because he gives a start at once and he begins to tremble, but not just his fingers, no, he's trembling all over, you can see it, shoulders and all, and he's stumbling back to the door, he's hurrying, and then he collapsed. We telephoned for the emergency service and they took him away, all feverish like he was. He died that evening. Pneumonia, a bad case, the doctor said, and he said he hadn't really known anything about it, not how he came back to us. It just kind of drove him on, it was like he was sleepwalking. My God, when a man has sat at a table like that every day for thirty-six years, the table is kind of his home."

We talked about him for some time longer; we were the last two to have known that strange man—I, to whom in my youth, despite the minute scope of his own existence, little more than that of a microbe, he had conveyed my first inklings of a perfectly enclosed life of the mind, and she, the poor worn-out toilet lady who had never read a book, and felt bound to this comrade of her poverty stricken world only because she had brushed his coat and sewn on his buttons for twenty-five years. And yet we understood one another wonderfully well as we sat at his old table, now abandoned, in the company of the shades we had conjured up between us, for memory is always a bond, and every loving memory is a bond twice over. Suddenly, in the midst of her talk, she thought of something. "Jesus, how forgetful I am—I still have that book, the one he left lying on the table here. Where was I to go to take it back to him? And afterwards, when nobody came for it, afterwards I thought I could keep it as a memento. There wasn't anything wrong in that, was there?"

She hastily produced it from her cubby hole at the back of the café. And I had difficulty in suppressing a small smile, for the spirit of comedy, always playful and sometimes ironic, likes to mingle maliciously in the most shattering of events. The book was the second volume of Hayn's *Bibliotheca Germanorum Erotica et Curiosa*, the well-known compendium of gallant literature known to every book collector. And this scabrous catalogue—*habent sua fata libelli*—had fallen as the dead magician's last legacy into those work-worn, red and cracked, ignorant hands that had probably never held any other book but her prayer book. As I say, I had difficulty in keeping my lips firmly closed to the smile involuntarily trying to make its way out, and my moment of hesitation confused the good woman. Was it valuable after all, or did I think she could keep it?

I shook her hand with heartfelt goodwill. "Keep it and welcome. Our old friend Mendel would be glad to think that at least one of the many thousands who had him to thank for a book still remembers him." And then I went, feeling ashamed in front of this good old woman, who had remained faithful to the dead man in her simple and yet very human way. For she, unschooled as she was, had at least kept a book so that she could remember him better, whereas I had forgotten Mendel the bibliophile years ago, and I was the one who ought to know that you create books solely to forge links with others even after your own death, thus defending yourself against the inexorable adversary of all life, transience and oblivion.

Translated by Anthea Bell.

Other works by Zweig: *The Collected Stories of Stefan Zweig* (2013); *The Collected Novellas of Stefan Zweig* (2016).

Albert Cohen

1895–1981

The French novelist Albert Cohen was born and spent his early years in Corfu, the inspiration for much of his fiction. His family moved to Marseilles in 1900, and after his baccalaureate, he moved to Geneva, where he trained as a lawyer and spent much of his life. A Zionist, he founded the short-lived journal *Revue juive* in 1925. During World War II, he worked in London for the Jewish Agency maintaining contacts with governments-in-exile. His major novels constitute one extended autobiographical fiction. Their protagonist, Solal, is a handsome League of Nations civil servant (as Cohen was for many years) who is torn between his Jewish loyalties and the beauty and sensuality of non-Jewish society.

Solal

1930

XXVI

In the swirling ballroom, chandeliers poured a corrosive milk over diamond-laced shoulders, and perfumes spun coils of desire between men and languid women swept round by the orchestra. Solal, the new Minister of Labor, looked upon his personnel with satisfaction. Hirsute members of parliament, waxed diplomats, generals, bankers, and the hastily acquired footmen, towering and flamboyant. His wife Aude pushed aside a window curtain and recognized Uncle Saltiel, prowling the livid street in the company of another old man.

Solal was thinking: "No more letters or phone calls from my uncle. Those two must have left for Cephalonia. Too bad. Me first. Me alive. Long live me."

He took in the new spectacle with immense pride. The mighty, all those decorated black hobgoblins, seemed to find it perfectly natural to be hosted by the vagabond who walked with Rehoboam. Aude, exquisite in her glittering gown, bestowed her grace equitably, knowing how to deploy an assortment of nuanced smiles as she greeted the new arrivals. And, in just an hour, this spectacular creature would be his naked slave, marvelously maltreated.

A servant came to tell him that someone in the parlor, having doubtless used the backstairs to sneak in, said it was urgent that he see Monsieur le Ministre.

"Your livery is in bad taste, wouldn't you agree, Sir George? A parvenu's livery."

He lit a cigarette and entered the parlor. There he saw Saltiel, who rose and began speaking.

"Two weeks ago I came to see you with joy in my heart. You had promised to come, then nothing! Your father's joy the next day. He waited for you from eight in the morning, poor old man, wearing his holiday best. And you didn't come. We waited and waited. That evening, he had an attack. For two weeks I've cared for him. When he was asleep, I'd write to you. No reply. Your servants have denied me entrance, I, I who've been a second father to you, who held you in my arms, our Monday outings to the fort, my hopes in you, everything, everything. Those gentiles, your servants, drove me from your house! In my old age! Your father has insisted on leaving his room and wants to see you now. Sol, it's sinful to make two old men suffer, lost in this great city. Oh Sol, be a true son, do not be sinful. Receive your father. Old men have little time left. Oh Sol, may God inspire me! Last night he and I, two old men, took each other's hands in the dark room and wept. Oh Sol, return to yourself, to your blessed nation, to the chosen people, oh my son!"

"Enough of the chosen people. I'm fed up with the chosen people. I have no time for that. Chosen people, really! How can that little bunch of scared rats be chosen? No one wants them, so these rats put on airs and say they won't stoop to mix with anyone else! What a farce. An animal would see the humor in it. Tell this story about a chosen people to a cat and it will bark delightedly, and the dogs will stand on their heads and spin around! Sons of the prophets, these brokers who fast once a year to be pardoned for their sins? Ah, the fine people of the Spirit! Yes, like hunted rats you've clung together. You haven't been allowed to mix with other people, and like swaggering clowns, these braggarts glory in their persistence and their purity! As for your prophets, what have they done that's so extraordinary?" (He yawned.) "The Greeks gave the world an hour of greatness, of smiling courage. And you, with overwhelming presumption, ten measly, ten elementary rules of bourgeois conduct!" (Each sentence seemed to be the single most essential one he'd ever spoken.) "You still haven't got over that grandiose invention! The Law of Moses!" (He rubbed his nose.) "How noble not to covet thy neighbor's ox! How heroic! And, in any case, you take his ox as collateral! And if you could devour his whole herd, you'd be ecstatic!" (He strode energetically about the room, reveling in the easy exercise of his wit. Like a child, he delighted in his intelligence and took Talmudic pleasure in proving the opposite of the truth.) "And as for those ten miserable precepts, all that biblical display of Oriental ferocity! Death sentences are rife in your Deuteronomy. Epictetus did better, and with more modesty. And who are your great men?" (He tapped his chest.) "A Spinoza, who put the universe in an icebox, or that German socialist? Or some physicist who postponed the difficulty? Race of frogs who imagine they're the chosen because, when showered with blows, they croak: 'Justice! Justice!' Or perhaps a Heine, that tubercular ape with his clever witticisms? Enough." (His eyebrows rose at an angle.) "You have made good Christians believe you're an extraordinary people, and naïvely, in good faith, they've taken you at your word! The very name of Israel tires me." (Saltiel covered his ears with his hands to keep from hearing.) "And even admitting that this story of the chosen were

true—degenerates need to know their reason for being— so what? In a few million years, won't this cold pumpkin go spinning through space without its mushrooming humans? So what's the use? Will the Messiah's reign be temporary? There, again, what foolishness! When the Messiah comes, all will be sweet little children. Bored stiff. None but the just. And that's all. Why so much enthusiasm for this meager repose? I'm a renegade, thank God; tell that to the Jewish rabbi and leave me in peace. I'm not asking you for anything. Don't ask anything of me. I shall not receive the rabbi. You can go."

Solal rummaged around in a cabinet, drew out the Hebrew prayer shawl, showed it to his uncle, and threw it out the window. A draft blew open the door to the ballroom. Applause broke out for the female singer. Saltiel shuddered and walked out.

Solal told the servants not to allow that man, or another "of the same type," into the house. A few minutes later, at the very moment when he was bowing before a bishop who was thanking his amiable host, exclamations were heard, sounds of a struggle and of broken glass. A door opened with a loud crash and old Gamaliel walked in.

His hands, slashed by the glass of the door, which the servants had tried to keep shut, bloodied the strip of Jewish cloth that Solal had thrown in the mud. On the rabbi's robes, bits of snow. Breathing heavily, looking dazed, he leaned against the doorframe. The musicians smiled and the couples separated.

Aude went up to Gamaliel, but he pushed her away. Dazzled by the lights, he looked for his son and didn't see him. He called to him. The crowd began to move, instinctively leaving a space around Solal as he advanced. The luxuriant vegetation quivered imperceptibly and passed into the animal kingdom. Lady Normand thought of King Lear. Her brother-in-law, caressing his humanitarian locks and his positive mustache, seized his monocle. The Greek minister pushed his small hands into the pockets of an obese jacket and left, followed by two Poles who were blowing their noses with satisfaction.

Gamaliel spotted his son and looked at him tenderly, a big, sickly smile on his face. He made a sign for him to approach and not to fear, for he was his beloved son, unjustly accused. One after the other, the guests departed. He held out his hands and the cloth he was holding fell to the floor.

Solal threw him a venomous glance. This man, having made him an object of ridicule and shattered his painfully constructed life, had the stupid audacity to smile. Crazed with shame, he moved closer, ready to strike. But a sudden inspiration made him stop. His eyes burned with malice. Slowly, exultantly, he crossed himself. On an order discreetly given by M. de Maussane, a tall footman put his hand on the arm of the rabbi, who shook himself loose. Without a glance, he pushed away the servant, whose head hit the wall. Then Gamaliel looked at his dead son, hooked the collar of his black robe with one hand, pulled on the fabric until it ripped, raised his arms as if to praise the God of retribution, and walked out.

Translated by Michele McKay Aynesworth.

Other works by Cohen: *Paroles juives* (1921); *Mangeclous* (1940); *Belle du seigneur* (1995); *Book of My Mother* (1997).

Mike Gold

1893–1967

Mike Gold was the pseudonym of the New York–born, communist journalist Irwin Granich. His writing was impassioned, scathing, and often sentimental. An advocate of proletarian literature, he was a caustic critic of bourgeois writers who were far more skilled at their craft than he. He was editor in chief of *The New Masses* from 1928 to 1934 and a columnist at the *Daily Worker* until his death. A champion of the Soviet Union throughout his life, he consistently hewed to the party line. His one work of lasting importance was his autobiographical novel *Jews without Money* (1930), which brilliantly evoked the squalor, insecurity, and violence of immigrant life on the Lower East Side. It was a bestseller, was translated into many languages, and became a prototype for the American proletarian novel.

Jews without Money
1930

Chapter 3. A Gang of Little Yids

1

I first admired Nigger in school, when I was new there. He banged the teacher on the nose.

School is a jail for children. One's crime is youth, and the jailers punish one for it. I hated school at first;

I missed the street. It made me nervous to sit stiffly in a room while New York blazed with autumn.

I was always in hot water. The fat old maid teacher (weight about 250 pounds), with a sniffle, and eyeglasses, and the waddle of a ruptured person, was my enemy.

She was shocked by the dirty word I, a six-year-old villain, once used. She washed my mouth with yellow lye soap. I submitted. She stood me in the corner for the day to serve as an example of anarchy to a class of fifty scared kids.

Soap eating is nasty. But my parents objected because soap is made of Christian fat, is not kosher. I was being forced into pork-eating, a crime against the Mosaic law. They complained to the Principal.

O irritable, starched old maid teacher, O stupid, proper, unimaginative despot, O cow with no milk or calf or bull, it was torture to you, Ku Kluxer before your time, to teach in a Jewish neighborhood.

I knew no English when handed to you. I was a little savage and lover of the street. I used no toothbrush. I slept in my underwear, I was lousy, maybe. To sit on a bench made me restless, my body hated coffins. But Teacher! O Teacher for little slaves, O ruptured American virgin of fifty-five, you should not have called me "LITTLE KIKE."

Nigger banged you on the nose for that. I should have been as brave. It was Justice.

2

Ku Klux moralizers say the gangster system is not American. They say it was brought here by "low-class" European immigrants. What nonsense! There never were any Jewish gangsters in Europe. The Jews there were a timid bookish lot. The Jews have done no killing since Jerusalem fell. That's why the murder-loving Christians have called us the "peculiar people." But it is America that has taught the sons of tubercular Jewish tailors how to kill.

Nigger was a virile boy, the best pitcher, fighter and crapshooter in my gang. He was George Washington when our army annihilated the redcoats. He rode the mustangs, and shot the most buffalo among the tenements. He scalped Indians, and was our stern General in war.

Some of the gang have become famous. Al Levy was known to us simply as "Stinker"; now he writes wealthy musical comedies.

Abe Sugarman is a proud movie director. He also has become a Spanish nobleman. His Hollywood name is Arturo De Sagaar, no less.

Lew Moses shoots craps with high stakes, with skyscrapers; he is a big real estate speculator.

Others of the boys are humbler comedians. Jake Gottlieb is a taxi driver, and feeds his three kids every day. Harry Weintraub is a clothing cutter. Some of the boys are dead.

There was always something for boys to see in the free enormous circus of the East Side. Always a funeral, a riot, a quarrel between two fat mommas, or an accident, or wedding. Day after day we explored the streets, we wandered in this remarkable dream of a million Jews.

Our gang played the universal games, tag, prisoner's base, duck on a rock. Like boys in Africa and Peru, we followed the seasons religiously for kites, tops and marbles.

One of the most exciting games was invented by Nigger. It was the stealing game. Nigger ran the fastest, so he would march up to a pushcart and boldly steal a piece of fruit. The outraged peddler chased him, of course, which was the signal for us to grab fruit and run the other way.

With a penny one could buy much; a hot dog, or a cup of cocoa, or one of thirty varieties of poisoned candies. Watermelon, apples, and old world delicacies like Turkish *halvah* and *lakoom; liver knishes;* Russian sunflower seeds; Roumanian pastry; pickled tomatoes. For a nickel a mixture of five of these street luxuries produced amazing Jewish nightmares.

We turned on the fire hydrant in summer, and splashed in the street, shoes, clothes and all. Or went swimming from the docks. Our East River is a sun-spangled open sewer running with oily scum and garbage. It should be underground, like a sewer. It stinks with the many deaths of New York. Often while swimming I had to push dead swollen dogs and vegetables from my face. In our set it was considered humor to slyly paddle ordure at another boy when he was swimming.

What a dirty way of getting clean. But the sun was shining, the tugboats passed, puffing like bulldogs, the freight boats passed, their pale stokers hanging over the rails, looking at us, the river flowed and glittered, the sky was blue, it was all good.

Nigger taught us how to swim. His method was to throw a boy from the steep pier. If the boy swam, well and good. If he sank and screamed for help, Nigger laughed and rescued him.

Jack Korbin died that way, I almost drowned, too.

But it was good. We were naked, free and coocoo with youngness. Anything done in the sun is good. The sun, the jolly old sun who is every one's poppa, looked down as affectionately on his little riffraff Yids as he did on his syphilitic millionaires at Palm Beach, I am sure.

3

Let me tell of a trait we boys showed: the hunger for country things.

New York is a devil's dream, the most urbanized city in the world. It is all geometry angles and stone. It is mythical, a city buried by a volcano. No grass is found in this petrified city, no big living trees, no flowers, no bird but the drab little lecherous sparrow, no soil, loam, earth; fresh earth to smell, earth to walk on, to roll on, and love like a woman.

Just stone. It is the ruins of Pompeii, except that seven million animals full of earth-love must dwell in the dead lava streets.

Each week at public school there was an hour called Nature Study. The old maid teacher fetched from a dark closet a collection of banal objects: birdnests, cornstalks, minerals, autumn leaves and other poor withered corpses. On these she lectured tediously, and bade us admire Nature.

What an insult. We twisted on our benches, and ached for the outdoors. It was as if a starving bum were offered snapshots of food, and expected to feel grateful. It was like lecturing a cage of young monkeys on the jungle joys.

"Lady, gimme a flower! Gimme a flower! Me, me, me!"

In summer, if a slummer or settlement house lady walked on our street with flowers in her hand, we attacked her, begging for the flowers. We rioted and yelled, yanked at her skirt, and frightened her to the point of hysteria.

Once Jake Gottlieb and I discovered grass struggling between the sidewalk cracks near the livery stable. We were amazed by this miracle. We guarded this treasure, allowed no one to step on it. Every hour the gang studied "our" grass, to try to catch it growing. It died, of course, after a few days; only children are hardy enough to grow on the East Side.

The Italians raised red and pink geraniums in tomato cans. The Jews could have, too, but hadn't the desire. When an excavation was being dug for a new tenement, the Italians swarmed there with pots, hungry for the new earth. Some of them grew bean vines and morning glories.

America is so rich and fat, because it has eaten the tragedy of millions of immigrants.

To understand this, you should have seen at twilight, after the day's work, one of our pick and shovel wops watering his can of beloved flowers. Brown peasant, son of thirty generations of peasants, in a sweaty undershirt by a tenement window, feeling the lost poetry. Uprooted! Lost! Betrayed!

A white butterfly once blundered into our street. We chased it, and Joey Cohen caught it under his cap. But when he lifted the cap, the butterfly was dead. Joey felt bad about this for days.

4

To come back to Nigger.

He was built for power like a tugboat, squat and solid. His eyes, even then, had the contemptuous glare of the criminal and genius. His nose had been squashed at birth, and with his black hair and murky face, made inevitable the East Side nickname: "Nigger."

He was bold, tameless, untouchable, like a little gypsy. He was always in motion, planning mischief. He was suspicious like a cat, quick to sidestep every sudden kick from his enemy, the world. The East Side breeds this wariness. East Side prize fighters have always been of the lightning type; they learn to move fast dodging cops and street cars.

The East Side, for children, was a world plunged in eternal war. It was suicide to walk into the next block. Each block was a separate nation, and when a strange boy appeared, the patriots swarmed.

"What streeter?" was demanded, furiously.

"Chrystie Street," was the trembling reply.

Bang! This was the signal for a mass assault on the unlucky foreigner, with sticks, stones, fists and feet. The beating was cruel and bloody as that of grown-ups, no mercy was shown. I have had three holes in my head, and many black eyes and puffed lips from our street wars. We did it to others, they did it to us. It was patriotism, though what difference there was between one East Side block and another is now hard to see. Each was the same theosophist's fantasy of tenements, demons, old hats, Jews, pushcarts, angels, urine smells, shadows, featherbeds and bananas. The same gray lava streets.

One had to join a gang in self-protection, and be loyal. And one had to be brave. Even I was brave, an odd child cursed with introspection.

Joey Cohen, a dreamy boy with spectacles, was brave. Stinker claimed to be brave, and Jake Gottlieb was brave, and Abie, Izzy, Fat, Maxie, Pishteppel, Harry, all were indubitably brave. We often boasted about our remarkable bravery to each other. But Nigger was bravest of the brave, the chieftain of our brave savage tribe.

Nigger would fight boys twice his age, he would fight men and cops. He put his head down and tore in with flying arms, face bloody, eyes puffed by punching, lips curled back from the teeth, a snarling iron machine, an animal bred for centuries to fighting, yet his father was a meek sick little tailor.

Nigger began to hate cops at an early age. The cops on our street were no worse than most cops, and no better. They loafed around the saloon backdoors, guzzling free beer. They were intimate with the prostitutes, and with all the thieves, cokefiends, pimps and gamblers of the neighborhood. They took graft everywhere, even from the humblest shoelace peddler.

Everyone knew what cops were like. Why, then, did they adopt such an attitude of stern virtue toward the small boys? It was as if we were the biggest criminals of the region. They broke up our baseball games, confiscated our bats. They beat us for splashing under the fire hydrant. They cursed us, growled and chased us for any reason. They hated to see us having fun.

We were absorbed in a crap game one day. Suddenly Fat yelled: "Cheese it, the cop!" Every one scattered like rabbits, leaving around 15 pennies on the sidewalk. The cops usually pocketed this small change. It was one of our grievances. We often suspected them of being moralists for the sake of this petty graft.

Nigger didn't run. He bent down calmly and picked up the pennies. He was defying the cop. The cop swelled up like a turkey with purple rage. He slammed Nigger with his club across the spine. Nigger was knocked to the sidewalk. The cop forced the pennies out of Nigger's hand.

"Yuh little bastard," said the cop, "I'll ship yuh to the reformatory yet!"

Nigger stood up quietly, and walked away. His face was hard. Five minutes later a brick dropped from the sky and just missed the cop's skull.

It was Nigger's grim reply. The cop rushed up to the roof, and chased Nigger. But Nigger was too daring to be caught. He leaped gaps between the tenements like a mountain goat. He was ready to die for justice. The cop was not as brave.

For months Nigger remembered to drop bricks, bundles of garbage and paper bags filled with water on this cop's head. It drove the man crazy. But he could never catch the somber little ghost. But he spread the word that Nigger was a bad egg, due for the reformatory. This cop's name was Murph. It was he who later tipped the balances that swung Nigger into his career of gangster.

5

Delancey Street was being torn up to be converted into Schiff Parkway, and there were acres of empty lots there.

On our East Side, suffocated with miles of tenements, an open space was a fairy-tale gift to children.

Air, space, weeds, elbow room, one sickened for space on the East Side, any kind of marsh or wasteland to testify that the world was still young, and wild and free.

My gang seized upon one of these Delancey Street lots, and turned it, with the power of imagination, into a vast western plain.

We buried pirate treasure there, and built snow forts. We played football and baseball through the long beautiful days. We dug caves, and with Peary explored the North Pole. We camped there at night under the stars, roasting sweet potatoes that were sweeter because stolen.

It was there I vomited over my first tobacco, and first marveled at the profundities of sex. It was there I first came to look at the sky.

The elevated train anger was not heard there. The shouting of peddlers like an idiot asylum, the East Side danger and traffic rumble and pain, all were shut by a magic fence out of this boy's Nirvana.

Shabby old ground, ripped like a battlefield by workers' picks and shovels, little garbage dump lying forgotten in the midst of tall tenements, O home of all the twisted junk, rusty baby carriages, lumber, bottles, boxes, moldy pants and dead cats of the neighborhood—every one spat and held the nostrils when passing you. But in my mind you still blaze in a halo of childish romance. No place will ever seem as wonderful again.

We had to defend our playground by force of arms. This made it even more romantic.

One April day, Abie, Jakie, Stinker and I were playing tipcat under the blue sky. The air was warm. Yellow mutts moved dreamily on the garbage. The sun covered the tenements with gold. Pools of melted snow shone in the mud. An old man smoked his pipe and watched us.

Boys feel the moments of beauty, but can't express them except through a crazy exuberance. We were happy. Suddenly a bomb shattered the peace.

The Forsythe Street boys, our enemies, whooped down like a band of Indians. They were led by Butch, that dark fearless boy whose "rep" was formidable as Nigger's.

They proceeded to massacre us. There were about fifteen of them. Abie and Jake were buried under a football pyramid of arms and legs. Stinker, who had earned his nickname because he would whine, beg, weep and stool-pigeon his way out of any bad mess, howled for mercy. Butch worked on me. It was a duel between a cockroach and a subway train.

At last they permitted us to get to our feet.

"Listen, you guys," said Butch, sneering as he wiped his hands on his seat, "this dump belongs to us Forsythe streeters, see? Get the hell out."

We ran off, glad to escape alive. Our shirts were torn, our stockings chewed off, we were muddy and wounded and in disgrace. We found Nigger. He was loaded with an immense bundle of men's coats which he was bringing to his family from the factory. His family worked at home, this was his daily chore.

He turned pale with rage when he heard of the massacre. All that afternoon strategy was discussed. We spied on the Forsythe streeters, we visited the Eldridge streeters and formed an alliance against the common enemy.

The very next day the historic battle was fought. Some of our boys stole tops of washboilers at home, and used them as shields. Others had tin swords, sticks, blackjacks. The two armies slaughtered each other in the street. Bottles were thrown, heads cut open. Nigger was bravest of the brave.

We won back our playground. And after that we posted sentries, and enjoyed passwords, drills and other military ritual. The old maid teachers would have been horrified to see us practice their principal teaching: War. War.

6

But the Schiff Parkway was an opponent we could not defeat. It robbed us of our playground at last.

A long concrete patch was laid out, with anemic trees and lines of benches where jobless workers sit in summer.

We went back to our crowded street. Joey Cohen was killed by the horse car not long afterward.

He had stolen a ride, and in jumping, fell under the wheels. The people around saw the flash of his body, and then heard a last scream of pain.

The car rolled on. The people rushed to the tracks and picked up the broken body of my playmate.

O what a horrible joke happened. The head was missing. Policemen arrived, Joey's father and mother screamed and moaned, every one searched, but the head could not be found.

Later it was discovered under the car, hanging from the bloody axle.

Our gang was depressed by this accident. Jake Gottlieb said he would never steal another ride on a horse car. But Nigger, to show how brave he was, stole a ride that very afternoon.

Joey was the dreamy boy in spectacles who was so sorry when he killed the butterfly. He was always reading books, and had many queer ideas. It was he who put the notion in my head of becoming a doctor. I had always imagined I wanted to be a fireman.

Other works by Gold: *Change the World!* (1935); *The Hollow Men* (1941).

Sarah Lévy

Dates unknown

Sarah Lévy was the pseudonym of a novelist and poet who was active in Paris in the 1920s and 1930s. Her sensationalist novel *O mon goye!* (1929), with its harsh portrayal of Jews, was much discussed in Jewish and non-Jewish circles.

My Beloved France
1930

Have I made it clear how much I indulge my husband? Seven years of love had been simply one long series of concessions, joyfully made in a whirl of happiness. I adjusted to everything, all the Christian customs, so long as they didn't compromise my loyalty to Judaism. I even came out here to find out more. The consequences were just now dawning on me. Upon arriving home with Ghislaine, I collapsed on the sofa, confessing, "I can't go on like this anymore. . . ."

That night, Ghislaine returned to Paris. The next day, my mirror, reflecting a tense, pale, and older face, certainly older, kept repeating, "Hussy, hussy. . . ."

Then, the days went by. My daily routine covered up what had happened. I didn't speak about it. Better to avoid mentioning it. Until one morning, in a stack of brochures and unimportant letters, I recognized Rosen's handwriting on a long, heavy envelope.

Poor friend! It had been days since I had called him. What could have caused him to write? The envelope contained ten or fifteen sheets, covered with Ghislaine's hieroglyphic scrawl. Notes written with a blue pencil, in large, despotic letters, were sprinkled throughout the margins. The last one, at the end of the final page, especially caught my eye: "We must get you out of there. DO YOU NEED MONEY?" This was underlined three times.

Here is what Ghislaine had written:

Dear Monsieur Rosenlafeuille,

Since last week I have been staying at our friend Sarah's house. The visit has been enjoyable. The countryside is charming, so is the house. You know my hosts better than I do, and you have been friends with Sarah longer. I feel that the close friendship you and she have shared for so long obliges me to call upon your help.

I must inform you that Sarah is unhappy. Much to our surprise and in spite of our warnings, she married a Christian. That was her business. Then, she dazzled us with her happiness, her entrance into a new world, her marvelous social life. No one was happier for her than I. Seeing her now in her present situation, nobody feels worse for her. I'm not the type of person to lord it over her by saying, "I told you so." But she had it coming, all the same.

Why should she come here, of all places, three hundred kilometers from Paris, the end of the world as you will soon see? When I ask her, she answers languorously, "I did it for him!"

It was something else, though, that caused her downfall. I am too accustomed to unraveling the motives of others to be wrong about this.

You know how she is, haughty at times, like a man who makes a successful business deal, sometimes humble like a woman who has succeeded in love. She is too proud to confide in either of us. She certainly won't ask her lord and master for help; that's not how the game is played. Like all men, he is completely selfish, all the more since—given their respective origins—he imagines he is doing her a favor by shutting her up in his horrid little village shanty. Does she still love him? Yes, her love for him endures. You know how our women use their submission to buy affection. That is how our Sarah, so bright and refined, has ended up in the muck heap, the endlessly boring routine of a village whose five hundred inhabitants—devious and sullen by nature—are all she has for company. It is a radical change; from the heights of Parisian civilization she has fallen upon the bleakest soil. When I think that it will be months before the poor dear will set foot in a theater!

Well, I am sure Sarah has fancied herself the lady of the manor. She loves flowers, trees, creatures of all kinds! You can't possibly imagine, my dear Monsieur Rosenlafeuille, how she has pledged herself to living out the absurd drama she has created. Before she arrived, the peasants had already declared all-out war on her. They torture her with stories about an old woman who always goes to mass and never eats meat on Friday. The whole village has united against the Jewess, the vague and faraway symbol of money, worldliness, cosmopolitan pleasures.

Oh, my dear Monsieur Rosenlafeuille, we control the press, the Parliament. You have banking in the palm of your hand, and I literature. We enjoy the right to vote and run for office, and yet we are denied entry into the sweet garden of France.

If a fortuitous combination of events had not brought me here, I never would have imagined the scandal of Sarah's mustering up, after a miserable day, a welcoming smile for her master, who, as you well know, simply hides his villainy behind a benevolent appearance.

(In the margin: DO I KNOW YOUR HUSBAND? AND HOW! BETTER THAN YOU DO!)

Yes, I openly admit it! In the interest of her happiness, I eavesdropped on them. I wanted to plumb the depths of their souls. I hoped, nay felt sure, that behind their bedroom door, Sarah would be the same energetic Jewess, passionate and strong in her fight against injustice, delighting in uncovering her heart.

Really, Ghislaine had listened in on our conversations! What a dangerous little snake!

And so, what do you think I heard? No screams, no tears, no stamping feet. I swear to you, Monsieur Rosenlafeuille, they were hardly alone for two minutes before she threw her arms around his neck! It broke my heart.

(In the margin: MEN, JEWS OR NOT, ALWAYS NEED TO BE RULED WITH AN IRON HAND.)

I believe, Monsieur Rosenlafeuille, that we are witnessing an unacceptable deterioration. I find it inadmissible that a Jewess be scoffed at, as in the worst moments of our history, and happily accept it.

I bring the matter before you, as one of the most powerful representatives of our race in the City of Lights: Paris! Paris, where the highest honors at school were rightfully awarded to a handful of Jewish students, to nobody's surprise! Paris, where teachers and schoolmates silenced their prejudices, in deference to true merit! Paris, where one is treated fairly at all levels of society! Parisians would burst out laughing, then cry out indignantly at the news that a place mired in medieval ways still exists in France. I cannot imagine what form your intervention could take, but I know that you will act as befits your strong character. Those bumpkins need a lesson, as does the husband. Blinded by her female submission, Sarah needs to be shaken up. But while it is true you must save a coreligionist, your first responsibility is to uphold the banner of civilization.

(In the margin: INDEED.)

Here is a task all the more worthy of your efforts. You know our friend so well. She cannot be left in such a dazed stated. Deep down, she is intact. Even when she was young, we were struck by her sense of pride. Someday soon, instinctively, she will rise up full of spirit against the unfortunate fellow who was playing for high stakes when he married her. I would feel sorry for him if I did not know how unpleasant your dealings with him have occasionally been.

I think that, rather than concerning yourself with their happiness, you should let your friendship for Sarah inflame your sense of indignation in these unprecedented circumstances. I know Sarah has not always reacted favorably to your attentions. In the future, a man of your character shall certainly enjoy more consideration. The Jewish gentleman in you, as well as the generous-hearted man, will soon find an opportunity to collect on a debt that has been deferred for too long.

And, no less, she finishes with protestations of friendship for me! I paled with rage as I read her scribbling through to the postscript.

p.s. I think I can work passages of this letter into a book I am writing. Please hold on to it for me!

Here, I burst out laughing. Rosen's note claiming to know Henri better than I do would have done much to relieve the bad taste left by such racial intransigence and female jealousy, to use the authoress's expression, if some remorseful feeling for my old friend hadn't troubled me. In his eyes, my love for a goy makes me more beautiful, especially since this particular goy has shown himself to be quite clever in the business dealings Monsieur Rosen arranged for him. Monsieur Rosen never thought I would marry Henri, and once I did, never imagined I would stick it out. His admiration of these exploits has intensified feelings on his part that were not strong enough to be voiced at the appropriate time. He stirs within me indulgence of the kind one has for an old friend who has underestimated one's character. I imagine him trying to seek sweet revenge from this turn of events, as a financial wizard profits from overly optimistic prognostications.

I can just see him. His beard must have become even redder, his jaw harder at each page, his eyes glazed over, and at the last line, who knows, a smile may even have lit up his features. I'm genuinely fond of him, this dear friend, especially for not rushing to see me. He didn't want to gloat over my troubles. His triumph was modest, and yet it would have done me good to talk to this former apprentice of my father's, who used to accompany me to temple every Friday night. I could have told him of the confusion in my mind, of my loneliness and chagrin, of my humiliating error. He could have understood how deeply they cut.

The image of Ghislaine, writing cholerically, sweeps aside that of Rosen sighing for my, or rather his lost happiness. What a liar she is! If this is how she writes her novels, they must make for fine reading.

I could have disregarded all of this, but as Henri says, life is a question of ebb and flow. According to him, knowing how to live means figuring out the right moment to jump in the surf so as to be carried along without a struggle. An irresistible wave is taking my life further and further out. Now I know it for sure. The movement has strengthened with the arrival of another letter corroborating Ghislaine's.

It took weeks for my aunt and uncle Alphonse from La Chaux-de-Fonds to digest the news of my arrival at Saint-Félicien. They were sure I would finally benefit from their experience:

> We cannot understand why you foolishly insist on living in that backwater. You must realize that such places are not meant for us. I, who understand life, intend to take advantage of my next visit to my clients in Paris to warn you once again. . . .

They too disapprove. This compilation of various opinions has finally made things clear to me. The peasants' sly gestures towards my house as they pass on their way to market ("That's where the Jewess lives . . . how could Monsieur Henri . . ."): *rishes*![1] The mailman's refusal when, imitating my husband, I offer him a glass of wine in the kitchen (this civil servant is in the church choir): *rishes*! The shop-girl's indignation when I, insisting on paying cash, flout the traditional trust extended to my husband's family; the refusal to repair my car or my roof, to sell me the best cuts of meat; the disdain for my hygienic recommendations; that Planchenault woman and her insults; the disobedience of the servants; a thousand veiled threats, and a thousand insolently precise replies: *rishes*, all of it! I knew this, and it made me laugh. It's not as easy as I thought it would be to put up with. Indeed, it's quite impossible to endure this latent anti-Semitism, this unanimous disapproval in my daily dealings with others which, while I was growing up, we denounced with the Hebrew word *rishes*.[2]

NOTES

1. *Rishes*: a Yiddish word of Hebrew origin, meaning "ill will," used to denote anti-Semitism before that term gained currency in Yiddish. [. . .]

2. I'm not even mentioning here the disparaging allusions to my relationship with the country doctor, unfortunately neither old nor unattractive, whom I had made a point of meeting in case I took ill. Coming from eastern France, he had brought a spirit of social progress to the region. He was the only person kind enough to let me know what everyone was saying behind my back. He told me all so that I might have the strength to resist. Given his combative spirit, his ardent soul and fiery pronouncements, he too ended up leaving the area. He had no choice. He couldn't take them all on.

Translated by Glenn Swiadon.

Moshe Stavi

1884–1964

Born Moshe Stavsky in Antopol, Russia, Stavi originally wrote in Yiddish. In 1907, he moved to Warsaw and gradually started writing in Hebrew. There he married the Yiddish poet Anna Margolin, but they later divorced. In 1911, he moved to Palestine and worked variously as a clerk, a dairy herder, a guard, a farmer, and a labor union official. He was one of the few Hebrew writers of the period whose stories featured Arab characters.

The Year of Abundance

1930

God relented. And the whispered prayers of the toiler returned not empty, and the tears of the sower reached to heaven.

With great, with manifold mercy the windows of heaven were flung open, flung wide by a generous hand to abundance and rich blessing.

At the beginning of Cheshvan the rains began to fall, beautiful in their order and pleasant in their seasons. Week in and week out, Sabbath to Sabbath, Sabbath to Wednesday, and Wednesday to Sabbath alternately, with slight pauses until the plowing and sowing were done, and again from week to week, Sabbath to Sabbath, Sabbath to Wednesday, and Wednesday to Sabbath, as in the generations of complete purity and God-fearing men.

And when Tebet came, the fields were all plowed, plowed and sown, pregnant with fruit, rich in blessing, and drunken with rain.

To the farthest horizon, as far as the eye encompassed, it fed on verdure, bright green and yellow green. Soft and gentle and pale were the first sprigs of wheat which cracked the crust of the earth and shot forth their heads into air, delicate, languid and tender.

Light green and dark green, sun bright—beans and barley, vetch and barley, vetch and oats—light green and dark green. Sun and rain—deep-rooting, high-stretching, black-spreading—sated and oversated, filled to overflowing. Like a well-favored child who rests on the knees of a mother blessed with abundant milk and sucks his fill, and being replete pushes away the breast without sucking to the end—not half—not a third—and falls with his head thrown back, weary of fullness, and foam dribbles from his mouth and about his neck, foam and saliva, sweet foam, sweet and white.

Joy, satiate joy arises from the earth, fills the spaces of the air, rises and pours itself over the face of the earth like the savor of good ointments—joy and blessing.

To the village abundance reached and to the colony, to the large colony and to the small colony, to the *moshav* and to the *kvutzah*; it knocked at the doors of the Arab *husha*, at the doors of mansions and huts, at the tent flap and the wooden barracks. It knocked exultingly, with exceeding joy. It shouted, "Here am I. I have come to you with blessing. Once in seventy years. Few are the graybeards that remember me.

"Behold your prayers are answered; the tears of your babes have reached me. I have come to you—and with me grass for the cow and the goat, milk for the suckling and the calf, seeds for the hen and pigeon, grain for the millstone, grain for sowing, grain for the granary."

At once worry fell away, strife ended, and hate was torn up by its roots—complete strangers with careworn faces looked at one another joyfully—delight and gladness were companions—exultation met with rejoicing.

People heavy with age and full of trouble sought out the tenderest words and the pleasantest names to call their happiness. In ringing voices like the clinking of gold against silver—

The most blessed year, the greenest year—
Year of milk, year of corn!
The whitest year, the greenest year,
Year of the lamb, year of the calf—
The rainiest year, the most blessed year!

In the oldest of the settlements, the mother of the settlements, abundance overflowed its banks. Mud to the neck. And it was easy and pleasant to wallow in abundance, to leap from stone to bank, and hop from bank to stone, amused and smiling lightly: Did you ever see a wanton like this, such a bully—ever in all your days?

Easy it was and pleasant, for the fields were already sown, sown correctly and in their appointed time, the harvest was growing prettily, and many were eager for it.

Pleasant it was and easy. For the ditches in the vineyard were open already . . . wide open . . . they stretched from tree to tree, ditch touched ditch . . . the price of almonds was higher than last year . . . new vines will be planted this year . . . grapes are paid for in advance . . . there are great preparations in the winepress . . . every one has his hands full of work.

Pleasant it was and easy. For there was so much water that it was impossible to get to the orange grove. One could only go out and stand far off by the acacia hedge, and from there gaze at the long, entangled, heavy-laden rows of greenage. Laden with abundant blessing, a green, ripening and yellowing. And while you are standing, as a thief might stand outside the fence, you take account, you reckon and set prices, you grow fantastic, exaggerate, and know that you exaggerate, and understand your folly. And you are satisfied and brimming with pleasure at this folly of yours.

Pleasant it was and easy. For this week a donkey sank in the swamp of the *hamrah*. Bells clanged and people gathered. Noise and tumult. The village folk rushed to the *hamrah*, some on foot, some horseback, some with rope, some with sticks. But they could not pull the donkey out. At last they harnessed a pair of mules and tied them to the donkey, jerked him out, dragged him through the whole village, pulled him from street to street singing and clamoring. People came out of their houses to whistle and hiss after them. Loafers beat on tins, trilled with their fingers on the lips, shrill feverish shrieks like the wailing lament of Arab women mourners.

Idle days they rode to the city to amuse themselves, one to the tailor or dressmaker, another to the theatre or movie. Anyone who owned a horse wore riding trousers. His legs encased in boots, a kafia on his head, and an abya on his shoulders. He and comrades his own age go down to the threshing floor, the one dry spot in the village, to sport with the horses. One remembers his friend in a neighboring village, puts double sacks on his saddle and gifts in the sacks, a branch loaded with oranges, some green and some ripe, branch and leaves and fruit together. In the evening he comes home with a gift to the house, honey, eggs and chickens that peep out of the sacks.

In the evening neighbor visits neighbor, housewife visits housewife, to sip tea, eat sweets and gossip.

The old men pass their time in the synagogue; one pondering over a holy book, another in secular talk.

And the village band, from its room in the council house, from early evening until late at night, booms through all the village with its great brass instruments. Out of satiety and pleasure, with childlike folly and innocent joy—boom boom—till midnight and later—boom boom—we are blessed this year, a wonder like this comes but once in seventy years.

Boom—boom—boom—

Slow moving as the waters of Siloam, abundance poured itself out over the face of the earth. Lovely in its order and pleasant in its season. Week after week, Sabbath after Sabbath, every Sabbath and every Wednesday. When Shevat comes the wells of Jerusalem are brimful of water, and every throat hoarse with praise and song. Every shoe and every sandal torn with dancing.

And the pasture floods over the face of the earth like a green river. Like the waters of early spring in western lands. Like the Nile at the end of summer. Wher-

ever grass could strike its root it climbed, sand, stone, mountain, valley, tree and roof.

The dew is still on the ground and the herd returns to the village to be shut up in the stalls a day and a night, until the morning of the morrow. Filled, glutted, every belly a barrel's width. All day and all night, they chew and ruminate. Until their jaws are tired and white foam, greenish foam dribbles from their mouths, weary of chewing, and paints all the ground about them green and white.

The calves suckle and do not empty the tits, not half, not a quarter, and they weary of sucking—they grow weary from too much sucking.

The flock are weary of carrying their fatted skins, and because of heaviness of their fleshy rumps the lambkins move lumberingly and lazily.

In the middle of Tebet a letter was sent from brother to brother—from Ain Hai, which is in Kfar Saba near Petach Tikwah, to Tel Adashim, which is in Emek Israel, saying:

"Cauliflower is plentiful here. We have so many that we could pave the streets with them. I talked it over with my wife Zipporah and she says perhaps it would be well to send you some, for who knows whether cauliflower has grown well with you this year."

And the man in Tel Adashim, which is in the Emek, answered his brother who is in Ain Hai, which is in Sharon:

"We have packed cauliflower in cans. We collected all the cans of Nazareth and Haifa, and it is impossible to get any more. And as for carrots, we have more than we can pull up, more than we can gather. I beg you to come to us. You were fond of *tzimmus*, and my wife Tobah will cook *tzimmus* for you as you liked it in the old days, as mother cooked it, may she rest in peace, for the Sabbath meal when we were still in our father's house."

And in the beginning of the month of Shevat a message was sent by word of mouth from Kfar Saba, which is near Petach Tikwah, through a worker going to Tel Aviv. By word of mouth, because the sender was not in the habit of writing. Nor had he the time, for he was alone at his work. And there was his vegetable garden and tree nursery of orange trees on which he must keep an eye, and the cowshed where the cows must be fastened, watered and milked.

The message was addressed to the house of the produce agent in Mercaz Mischari, Tel Aviv, who was to give it to a comrade who kept cows in Tel Nordia; and it was phrased in these words:

"The calves which were nearly dead at the end of last summer from lack of pasture in the fields will not die. Their skin is almost bursting with fat. And so I beg you to send your cattle to my pastures. For there is too much grass and the blessing of God is going to waste."

And a comrade of Magdel brought his old mother and young sister up to Eretz Israel from Motomashav, which is in the kingdom of Poland. He harnessed his horse and cart and drove to Tel Aviv himself to fetch them from the ship. Himself: first, because pennies are scarce among workers on the land and he hadn't the price of an auto; and, second, because he longed to show off; to boast, to strut before them like a child.

"Just look, what a driver! How handsomely he manages a horse!"

And they the whole way could not fill their eyes with looking, nor their hearts with marveling.

"See, see, what a driver. Look at the farmer, no evil eye upon him. . . . Look, look how sunburnt and how dirty he is! Look, how cracked his hands are, his dear hands."

And sister who had been a comrade of the *chalutz* in Poland laughed through her tears and wept in her laughter. She took the reins in her hands and learned how to drive the horse and then in the softest, gentlest voice she called to the horse, the big horse who was pulling the cart—my dove, my bird, my cat, my darling, my love. They got home late, tired from the journey, and overwrought with joy. And long they spoke and much they recounted, questioned and answered, until drowsiness fell upon them, and they slept.

And an old peasant, a man of Bertuvia in Shephelah, which is in Judah, returned at sunset from the fields, unyoked his oxen, watered them, put fodder before them, washed himself, prayed *mincha* and *maariv* peacefully and earnestly. And when he had refreshed himself with food, he sent to a neighbor for pen and ink. He tore an empty page from a notebook that belonged to his grandchild, mounted his glasses on his nose and sat down to write a letter to his son who lived in Nahalal, which is in the Emek, in a fine Yiddish seasoned here and there with bits of Russian. And this is the translation:

"First, I wish you and your wife and children peace and good health.

"Secondly, Mother, long life to her, asks how you are and how your wife and children are, may they be found worthy of long life and good health. Also I must tell you, my son, that the barley has come up beautifully this year, higher than a man's head. Perhaps you would lose nothing if you were to come to me, you and your horse and your wagon together to help us to reap our fields."

And the son who dwelt in Nahalal, which is in the Emek, returned from the fields to his house, set the yard and cowshed in order, and after he had washed and dressed, eaten and drunk, he turned his step to the council house. (Once there had been pen and ink in his house, but the pen rusted and the ink dried from the heat—and the boy was still in kindergarten, so there was no notebook to tear a piece of paper from.) And from the council house he wrote a letter to his father, who was in Bertuvia, in pure Hebrew—and this was its content:

"To my honored father and my mother who bore me—may you have long life. The barley and vetch have grown this year beyond all other years. We are tired of too much labor. Perhaps my father would consent to come to his son to help gather the fruit of his fields."

The letters met at the station Lydda and separated, one in one direction and other in another direction, this one to Bertuvia, which is in Shephelah, and that one to Nahalal, which is in the Emek.

And a Jew who dwelt in the settlement Hederah, a firmly planted Jew, broad-boned, a solid rich peasant, wrote to his daughter who was a shopkeeper in Jaffa, in Beneve Shalom:

"Lock the store and come, you, your husband and your children. There is plenty of work and plenty of food . . . milk and eggs and vegetables . . . more than we can eat . . . no one buys and no one sells!" . . .

And a farmer, a man of Ekron, met a former worker of his in a street of Tel Aviv. And they recognized one another—by the smell of the field and cowshed they knew one another. The smell clung to them and they carried it with them amid the sand and stone of the city. Both strong men, bent in stature, sunburnt faces. One in boots and the other in jacket, vest and *tsitsiyot*. They knew each other and rejoiced—they rejoiced whole-heartedly.

The plow had bent both their backs and made them equals.

"Do you know that in Mansorah each dunam gave two full sacks of wheat?"

"Do you know that with us in Ain Tivon the oats have grown higher than a man's head, so that when the watchman gets off his horse among the grain both horse and rider vanish?" . . .

And the comrades of Tel Hai wrote to their comrades in Tel Josef.

"Perhaps you can send us a few scythes. Our scythes broke this year. Each stalk of hay is thicker than a finger, and is almost impossible to cut."

And the comrades of Tel Josef, which is in the Emek, answered their comrades in Tel Hai, who dwell in the mountains of Upper Galilee.

"We have set up a carpenter to make handles for the scythes. Perhaps you are able to send us oak wood. For it is impossible to get any wood here except eucalyptus wood." . . .

And the writer of the story, who was shut up between the sand and stone of Tel Aviv, met a comrade of his, one day in Allenby Street, a comrade of many days gone by, a companion of the plow and scythe, broad-shouldered, sturdy and sunburnt. And he remembered his first month of work, that sweet, as it were, honeymoon of his working days, that bright singing month rose in his heart—horse, cow, and cowshed, plow, scythe and field, grass, sun and rain—earth—and sky—and God—

And the comrades rejoiced—rejoiced exceedingly—tears came to their eyes out of excessive joy. They questioned each other, told one another stories. Until the writer grew silent and his friend, the man of the colony, continued to recount, to relate joyously, out of his great joy.

"Beyond belief.

"Beyond conception.

"One year in seventy, one year in eighty, weary is the earth of great blessing, tired are the sowers of overwork, and every hand is heavy with overabundance."

The writer listens and is silent, tears choke in his throat, and his heart murmurs a prayer and a silent blessing.

"Blessed be the hands that have chosen hard labor for their lot.

"Blessed be ye in your houses, blessed in your gardens, blessed your garners and baking throughs, blessed your flocks and your herds, blessed your plows and your scythes—

"Even to the smallest weed of your field that grows by the wayside."

Translated by Edward Robbin.

Other works by Stavi: *Ba-arov yom: sipurim* (1952); *Geluyot u-setumot ba-lashon* (1960).

Hirsh Bloshtein

1895–1978

The Yiddish poet and short-story writer Hirsh Bloshtein was the son of a poor tailor in Kedainiai, Lithuania, but broke with traditional Judaism and embraced secularism and socialism. He taught in Jewish schools in Lithuania and Ukraine and in 1925 immigrated to Argentina. There he worked in left-wing Jewish schools, wrote for the communist press, and edited the radical literary monthly *Naye velt*. In 1931 he was arrested for his communist activity and deported to the Soviet Union. He survived the Holocaust in Kazakhstan and, unusually for Soviet literary figures, died a natural death.

In Opposite Directions
ca. 1930

They would run into each other twice a day: early in the morning, going to work; and in the evening, coming back. They would see one another on the same sidewalk, but they were headed in opposite directions—his factory was to the east and her office to the west. They would look at each other for just a moment, then pass by—hurriedly, so as not to punch into work late and lose half a day's pay.

They worked in the same places for about a year, so the fleeting moments of their mutual glances linked up to become hours. The hours spent looking were etched in their memories, and they had grown accustomed to each other. Deep in her being she held a picture of the tall, broad-shouldered, somewhat stooped young man with the black eyes and the thick, curly hair. As for him, he counted among his rare intimate relations the slim, blond girl with the lively grey eyes, which sparkled from under an elegant, pink hat. But neither of them knew the other's name, because they never exchanged a word, going as they did in opposite directions, dogged by their work. So he would quickly disappear to the east, and she to the west.

Occasionally he failed to see her, and he felt something missing then. A moment in his day would be gray and empty, yet that moment was perhaps his favorite time because of the secret pain it caused. Standing at his work on one of those lonely, bland days, he would think from time to time about how she must be sick, or how something bad had happened to her at home, or that she'd been fired from her job. In any case, the fleeting, meaningless moment stayed and caused him pain.

He tended to be a quiet young man, shy and retiring. He marveled at the boldness and impudence of the pals he ran with, who followed girls down the street and showered them with the cleverest, raciest pick-up lines and wisecracks. If he, Chaim, had possessed a mere tenth of their nerve, he could have stopped the slim, pretty girl long ago, and they would already have had a friendship going for who knows how long, since he had already liked her for a while now—a long while.

But he couldn't change the way he was: bashful, lacking in boldness. Only the night knew of his desire. He tossed and turned then in his hard, iron cot, with the blankets pulled over his head, while she gleamed in his dark life with her radiant hair and smiling eyes. She would never know about those nights, when his big, dark, hairy hands turn girlishly soft and white—and he kissed hers. She would never know that he even made up a name for her, the loveliest one he knew: his youngest sister's name, Rosie. That was what he called her, and she answered, with such a light, melodious voice.

She didn't know—and she never would—that he was looking for her. He never missed a lecture or show at a workers' organization, secretly hoping he might run into her. In such a place they were bound to meet someone whom they both knew and who could introduce each other. But soon a year had passed since he started seeking her, and she was nowhere to be found. She appeared only in the mad, yearning nights, when young blood glowed and rushed and merged with her eyes, her hair. And afterwards came two moments: one in the morning, one in the evening. They pricked sweetly at a distant, delicate corner of his soul and glimmered to a spark, which then faded.

A few weeks into the second year, on a spring day, two gray moments came: one in the morning and one in the evening. Next day the same thing. And the weeks worked their blunt pull on him. The spring turned gray and sad. The nights hurt with their yearning. His eyes sank ever deeper in his head and became ever bigger.

Chaim did not know where to look for her, and often he had the terrifying thought that she might have a lingering illness—or maybe she was dead?! But he kept going each day to the same sidewalk. He did this even when the downturn in his trade threw him out of work. At dawn he would run around looking for employment—and at the appointed hour, he would go to that sidewalk.

But she was never there.

One day, after a long period of fruitless job-hunting, he got lucky. He found work in a unionized shop at fairly good wages. But he still was not happy. The nights did not cease yearning, or tearfully gleaming in her glow.

Then came a Saturday, the day everyone gets off early and shop workers get their pay. Chaim went to the payroll office to get his envelope from the boss's son, who distributed the wages. And there she was, sitting next to him, as blond and slender as always, beautifully dressed—radiant.

Chaim felt something rip in his spirit, and a prickling, twisted feeling zigzagged through his hands and feet all the way to his heart, then out to the surface of his body in tiny, cold droplets. His feet trembled, and he avoided the eyes of his friends, who must have noticed he had gone pale.

It took him only a couple of moments to take his money, a couple of eternities, long, distraught moments. But in those two moments, Chaim met her eyes, and it seemed to him that she looked at him and turned red . . . It seemed also that she pulled her hand from the boss's son's hand—and on a finger of each one's fine, soft hand was a simple, shiny gold ring.

Chaim hurried from the payroll office and wandered off aimlessly, grieving and distressed as through betrayed. He walked with broad but shaky steps. A long chain fashioned from a year's worth of moments, two every day, was covered with deadly rust, cutting sharp and deep in his delicate soul—and it hurt him.

He decided he would never again go to that sidewalk where they once passed each other day, yet from the first were headed in opposite directions. It also was clear that he would never again work in that shop, and he searched for some excuse to give his friends about why he quit his job.

He stopped automatically at a large newsstand and bought a whole pile of papers, new and outdated—then quickly went home, where he locked himself into his dark little room and leafed through the pages with feverish fingers, looking for engagement and wedding announcements. His crazed heart yearned to know her name, the name of his first lover, whose voice he had never heard and would never hear.

Thus did fragile feeling entangle for a year on a piece of sidewalk in the big, rich-versus-poor, poor-versus-rich city. Two people had been headed in opposite directions, and one trod on the other's jumbled heart—wounding it, making it bleed.

Translated by Debbie Nathan.

Other works by Bloshtein: *Arbshulog, poeme* (1928); *Lider fun kamf* (1930); *Ich bin yung: lider un poemes* (1934).

Gertrud Kolmar

1894–1943

Gertrud Kolmar was the pseudonym of the German lyric poet and writer Gertrud Käthe Chodziesner. Kolmar came from a nonobservant Berlin family to whom she remained close, until her deportation to Auschwitz in 1943. Her poetry captures her feelings of alienation and isolation, as a woman and a Jew. In the 1930s, as the situation of Jews in Germany worsened, she turned increasingly to Jewish themes in her work and in 1940 began to study Hebrew, hoping to immigrate to Palestine. *The Jewish Mother* (the correct translation of the title) was her only novel.

A Jewish Mother from Berlin

1931

Part One, Chapter 2

Martha Jadassohn had come with her parents from a small West Poznanian town, named either Bobst or Meseritz, to Berlin where her father's only sister, a widow, was living alone. Martha was the youngest and only surviving child of the elderly couple, and since finishing her schooling, she had been keeping the modest household. Her aging mother still helped with the cooking; they had no other help. They lived quietly. Besides the aunt, they had spent their life in withdrawn, modest circumstances, always felt a little intimidated by the sprawling wilderness of the city. Neither of them was distrustful and they never thought of protecting their child from social contacts with young people. But

where should the daughter get to know other people? She lacked the opportunities others had to meet them at social gatherings or at the workplace. She always presented an impenetrable, aloof face, and not only when somebody tried to start a conversation with her in front of the store or in the hallway. Whether she was satisfied with her lot, with her work, nobody asked and nobody knew. Without many words she swept the rooms, worked at the sewing machine, passed her free time with a book, or went for two or three hours on solitary, far-flung walks. When the weather was nice in the summertime, she would sit with her parents on a bench in the park. Occasionally she would walk over to the train station and watch for a while the arriving and departing trains with a strange look in her eyes. This is how she lived in the last years of the decade of the twenties and she knew pitifully little of what people call experience.

As in other apartment buildings, a tenants' council had been formed in the building where the family lived. A meeting had been called to discuss above all else problems with the coal supply and the nightly gate closing time. Martha's father, who was already ailing then from the illness that was eventually to strangle him, was laid up in bed, but did not like the idea of having to forego his right to vote on the matter. And since the mother was at heart not adroit enough and too dawdling and fearful to speak up in front of a dozen people, or even finding herself in a position of having to contradict them, it was decided that the daughter should represent the family.

The meeting took place in the home of the wholesaler Wolg, an educated and apparently well-to-do man. The wholesaler's son, Friedrich Wolg, an engineer, had seen Martha Jadassohn before in passing but had hardly taken notice of her. On that day he really saw her for the first time as he listened to her speak, in her quiet, terse manner, yet determined and firm. The contrast with several of the other women who spoke excitedly all at the same time, moving from topic to topic and almost losing the evidence supporting their opinions in little anecdotes, made her appear in a favorable light. He even engaged her in a verbal duel, since he played the role of shield bearer for his father, and used this as an excuse to approach her the next day in front of the building. This was the first move and the rest unraveled like a ball of yarn whose beginning had been loosened by an invisible hand.

Old man Wolg took a hostile stand. His jovial, easy-going nature recoiled from the austere, reserved girl; he called her a wet blanket and cold. It also did not suit him that she was a Jewess, especially an impecunious Jewess. He warned his son that such a woman would eventually sap his freshness and vitality. He added that her severity—which the lover took for virginal shyness, immaculateness—would not die with the wedding and would prevent the wife from being a companion and friend to her husband. He might as well marry an antique statue.

"We are living in the twentieth century, not in Jacob's tent. She looks like someone out of the Old Testament. Her name should be Leah instead of Martha. You might think she is champagne on ice. I don't think so. Ice, yes: a big lump. Jerusalem at the North Pole. She is stronger than you, I can feel it by just looking at her. And if you should ever have a disagreement, she won't give an inch. Either you will bolt or she will break you to pieces. Without mercy." The warning had little effect.

Martha actually loved Friedrich in spite of herself. At first it seemed to her depraved even to consider a Christian. The parents asked no questions. They knew enough since the engineer had paid them several visits under the faintest of pretexts and had spent hours sitting around the table with mother and daughter. And then one morning the father called the girl over with a weak whisper; the mother listened with concern from the dark corner. He did not object. A co-religionist would have been preferable, certainly. But since he was on his sick bed, he had time to weigh things and there was much he saw now in a different light from before. Otherwise there was nothing wrong with the young man. And the Wolgs were rich and times were hard, and he would like to see his child well taken care of before his passing. One week later he died.

Hans Wolg considered this death a particular misfortune for his son, who, as he scolded in front of his wife, sneaked over there "every moment, to console the weeping bereaved." He changed his strategy now to gain by surreption and trickery what had been denied him in open battle. He knew that Friedrich was a sanguine type like himself, whose feelings were intense but of short duration. So he pulled a few strings and packed the fool off to England—for a few years, he hoped. There he would get to see and taste plenty of other ladies and the spark for this one would, for lack of nourishment, slowly but surely finally die. The calculation might have been right, but all too soon, after six months, Friedrich returned and seemed madder about her than ever. Although his promise to be faithful, made

at the moment of their painful parting, did not hold him to playing monk, to his father he made disparaging remarks about British beauties, about their blandness—what mush, milk porridge with raspberry syrup.

"If I want blue eyes and blond hair, all I have to do is look in the mirror."

He finally managed to ask his mother for a more favorable wind, and his father, who had just shown the iron determination of a weathervane, turned against his will, screeching, toward the undesirable side. Martha Jadassohn became Martha Wolg; she appeared calm and collected; Friedrich was madly in love and happy.

Disappointment followed soon, even though the young husband did not admit his error so he could give his father's warnings the lie. But he remarked very early to Martha with derision: "Actually I don't have a wife, only a lover." He spoke the truth. She lived with him only in a union of the night. Smiling he called her Vesuvius or Etna or Krakatoa, because her embrace resembled the eruptions of an apparently quiet, but secretly smoldering crater. In time, the erratic fluctuations between cold and heat tired, even plagued, him. And the woman he knew in the daytime depressed and bored him. He could forgive her for not understanding much of his work although she would listen and nod, what annoyed him was that she shared practically none of his interests. She did not like to go paddle boating with him, or sit on his motorcycle, and he was usually the only one listening to the radio that stood in the corner. When he went to the movies or a coffeehouse or visited friends, she always quickly found an excuse to stay home alone.

"Well, that's all quite convenient," he tried to persuade himself. "I couldn't wish for a more accommodating wife." Yet he did not want to feel that way. There was something peculiar, something strange, something . . . he searched for a name.

Maybe it was because she was of different blood, a Jewess. But she did not carry with her the practices and customs of her forebears. She did not observe Friday nights and never thought of going to the temple. But she did not abandon her faith. She did not wear it like a dress that could be washed or torn and be lightly tossed off. Rather with her it had become like a skin, vulnerable but incapable of being sloughed off, indissoluble. Friedrich had a sign of this; and it was this which led to their first brief spat.

They had gone into town shopping together. The pregnant woman stopped in front of a lingerie shop and looked for a moment at the tiny children's shirts and jackets. He nodded toward the window display: "This one, this would be a nice little dress if we have a girl, a baptismal dress . . ."

Awkwardly, she turned toward him in boundless amazement: "Baptismal dress? But our children will not be baptized."

He mumbled, "I thought . . ."

She replied calmly, "You promised me something, you know that."

He shrugged his shoulders: "Whether such a promise is binding is questionable . . . I read somewhere . . ."

Her voice was cold. "It doesn't matter what you read about it. If you don't want to keep your promise and incite the minister . . ." She interrupted herself. "It is useless to make threats if one does not know yet what one will do. But consider," she said softly, "that our child is still inside of me, in my womb and that you, once it is born, cannot take it with you to the factory, and if you take it from me, I will find it no matter where."

She walked beside him without saying another word. He continued to argue into the air a little while longer before beating his retreat, for she did not fend him off. She was victorious.

His parents were outraged, especially his father became quite outspoken. "A Jew . . . She should be glad if her brat receives a Christian upbringing."

Friedrich seemed very distressed. "I beg of you just one thing, don't fight with her, let her be, You don't know her. She is capable of killing the child; she is a Medea!"

"A vixen," the father grumbled. The mother looked at her son with deep pity and sighed.

Martha gave birth to the child and fell over it like a hungry she-wolf, as the in-laws remarked. It was her child, only hers. As if the lightness of the father had been battling with the darkness of the mother as it was coming into being, and as if her darkness had in the end demolished his light and devoured it, Ursula's eyes and hair were nocturnal, her skin yellowish, almost brown, and of an even deeper hue than the ivory tone of her mother's face. Her features likewise betrayed nothing of Friedrich Wolg. Of course, he found pleasure in the little creature, but his paternal pride was soon dampened since it was as if it banished him with tiny fists from Martha's life. His wife now often appeared to him like a savage he kept in a cage by force and whose only thought was to break free. Whenever he came near her, she held the child up against her breast, then she looked at him without saying a word, but with the strange, ominous glowering of an animal mother who trembles for her young. She never quarreled with him, she never complained. Most of the time she just pushed him unceremoniously away like a thing that was not needed just then. And if he tried to oppose her, insist on being accorded his due, then he would ram against a magic wall she erected around herself. The wall gave way, the blow landed in thin air, only his arm hurt, and she stood there untouched at the very spot where she had barricaded herself.

One day Martha happened to meet him in the company of a pretty young woman, an employee at the factory where he was working. He wanted to justify himself. "It is nothing, believe me." It really wasn't anything yet. Martha said in a bored, lazy tone: "Leave it be. I didn't complain, did I?" He continued his stammering; she wiped the crumbs off the table. Indifferently: "It's all right."

He could not bear this kind of behavior any longer. He did what his father had prophesied and fled. He escaped to America. He remained there almost a year, then he returned, gravely ill, and died. His parents were furious with the daughter-in-law who had driven him away; had he stayed in his homeland he would have, so they believed, lived a long life. And secretly they blamed her for his untimely death.

Martha's situation in the world was uncertain. She inherited nothing from her husband and very little from her mother, who had died. The elder Wolgs did not love her. But nobody would accuse them of letting their grandchild starve. And the eyes of strangers, who knew of Friedrich's marriage only as a happy one, needn't see, even now, that matters stood differently. Hans Wolg arranged an apprenticeship for the unskilled widow with Frau Hoffmann. And almost against expectations, Martha showed herself so willing and talented that after completion of her apprenticeship, the gentle old lady took her on as her partner. She had a special talent for photographing animals; she actually introduced animal photography to Lydia Hoffmann. A young Newfoundland, who just happened to accompany his master, started it all. Soon it became fashionable among the wealthy from the western part of the city to have their lap dogs, Angora cats, monkeys, and parrots photographed. Occasionally she would take the short walk from the studio to the zoo to take pictures of the sacred cows for a magazine. Her brittle bond with the Wolg family became ever more frayed and one day, without an audible sound, it just snapped completely. And Ursa hardly remembered her grandparents; what the mother offered her were worn, faded, unappealing little pictures, and she rarely asked about them.

Martha, who was then still unaware of how fate was to bend her, exchanged the expensive apartment in a new building for a cheap, smaller one. One room, a kitchen, and a pantry were enough for her even when her courage and purse swelled. An apartment of her own seemed a lofty possession, even one without many amenities, without steam heat, gas stove, electricity, and located "halfway out of the world," as Frau Hoffmann called it. Her immediate neighbors were Otto Lange, a clerk at the magistracy; Anna, his wife; Elschen, the daughter— a little girl with a pronounced limp—and Frau Beucker, the mother-in-law. And one day, Martha was locking her door and was about to bring her child, as usual, to the day care house, when Frau Beucker peered out from her cave and presented a wish. Since Ursa and Elschen were already good friends could she not stay with them? She, Frau Beucker, had time enough to take care of both children, and an extra spoonful of soup for lunch would not matter all that much, especially since the weather was so dismal today, just right for catching cold. From then on, Ursa was left every day in Frau Beucker's care, who also picked up in the kitchen and parlor, and received from Frau Wolg a weekly compensation for her labor of love.

Translated by Brigitte M. Goldstein.

Other works by Kolmar: *Gedichte* (1917); *Die Frau und die Tiere* (1938); *Dark Soliloquy: The Selected Poems of Gertrud Kolmar* (1975); *My Gaze Is Turned Inward: Letters, 1934–1943* (2004).

Moyshe Kulbak

1896–1937

Moyshe Kulbak is widely considered one of the most popular and important Yiddish writers of the early Soviet period. A teacher, poet, and novelist, Kulbak was a leader of Yiddish cultural organizations in all the cities he lived in, including Vilna, Berlin, and finally Minsk, then the capital of the Belorussian Soviet Socialist Republic. His work was firmly modernist in style and content, characterized by lyricism in his poetry, dynamism and reflection in his prose, and a sense of rootedness in the landscapes and experience

of everyday Lithuanian Jews throughout all his work. His novel *Zelmanyaner* is a masterful satire of Jewish life before, during, and after the Bolshevik Revolution, a text filled with insight and irony in its description of generational conflict and cultural adaptation. Kulbak was a victim of the particularly violent Stalinist Purges that liquidated much of the Soviet Yiddish intelligentsia in Minsk.

The Zelmenyaners: A Family Saga
1931

Part One

CHAPTER 5. ELECTRICITY

One day Bereh turned up in the yard. An unseasonably warm glow coated the world, glazing the storm windows with an unexpected spring sheen. He walked slowly down the dark footpath, followed by a worker of some kind. They surveyed the roofs, tapped the walls, and pointed at the sky.

A wave of unrest swept the yard.

"We're in for a new disaster!"

"What's he up to this time, the genius?"

Aunt Malkeleh took it as a sign to break out her primers and copy books and spread them on the table.

Bereh proceeded to have a look at all the rooms. He checked the walls and ceilings and went away.

At no time did he say a single word.

That evening it got around that he was planning to electrify the yard. They would all have to trade in their kerosene lamps for electric current.

At first no one knew what to make of it or realized how serious it was. Some even thought it a good thing. Hats and coats were donned, and all ran to Uncle Zishe to see what he had to say. Zishe proclaimed that things looked bad for two reasons:

1) No one knew what to do with electricity once you had it. 2) It wasn't for common folk like them.

"I'm all for it," Uncle Yuda declared, "as long as it's in someone else's house."

"Take my word for it, he'll be the death of us all!" Uncle Zishe told his beard as he paced back and forth in his room.

Only Uncle Itshe blinked and asked:

"What's the big deal? Doesn't the synagogue have electricity?"

Uncle Zishe stopped pacing, as if suddenly bolted to the floor. "Listen to the know-it-all!" he said to the womenfolk who were present. "The synagogue also has a prayer stand. Does that mean we need one in the yard?"

Bubbe Bashe took it the hardest. At first, thinking that Bereh was planning to dig a well in the yard, she remembered with a pang that this had been Reb Zelmele's great dream. It hadn't come to pass. Condemned to drink the water of strangers all his life, he had died with it unfulfilled.

Finally grasping the truth, however, she exclaimed with all her wits about her:

"Mark my words. No one is breaking down any walls around here as long as I'm alive!"

That night the elder Zelmenyaners assembled in the dark yard and waited for Bereh to come home. The sky was sprinkled with a few small stars. They stood wrapped in their scarves and kerchiefs, collars up, breathing heavily. It was close to midnight when Bereh turned into the yard from the street. At once they assailed him.

"Listen here, you bandit! What are you doing to us?"

"Why can't we live our lives with our old lamps?"

"You can have your electricity! We don't want it!"

"Get off the backs of us plain working folk, brother!"

[. . .]

CHAPTER 6. MORE ABOUT ELECTRICITY

Electricity won the day. Could Reb Zelmele have revisited his old home, he might have walked right by it thinking it was a government office building. Its long, narrow rooms flared each evening with a cold blaze that shone in the sickly gold windowpanes like a patient breathing through an oxygen mask.

There were rumors that here, on the outskirts of town, they were getting the electricity's dregs, second-class goods from the bottom of the boiler. This upset the Zelmenyaners greatly, as indeed it should have. After all, if you're going to give someone electricity, give him the best! It was even agreed upon that Aunt Malkaleh should go to Bereh and give him a talking-to. For once, however, she put her foot down. "Why does it always have to be me?" she wanted to know.

There followed a kind of electromania. Inspired by Bereh's exploits, the younger Zelmenyaners installed the light bulbs called "Lenin bulbs" in every room and scaled moldy walls and roofs to bang in nails and hang

wires as if they were building—pardon the comparison—a holiday sukkah. The yard was electrified to its foundations. Zelmenyaners ran around with hammers in their hands, screws in their pockets, and bits and pieces of cable. Uncle Itshe's son Falke presided over it all. Electricity shone in every eye.

In the black nights on the outskirts of town, whose kerosene-burning homes were soaked by the first rainstorms of spring, the yard was lit like a railroad station. Staring wide-eyed at its windows, the neighbors marveled to their children:

"Just look, darlings, what some people manage to make of themselves!"

Translated by Hillel Halkin.

Other works by Kulbak: *Meshiekh ben Efrayim* (1924); *Vilne* (1926); *Disner Tshayld-Harold* (1933).

Doiv Ber Levin

1904–1941

Born into a religious family in the town of Liadi, a center of the Chabad Hasidic movement, Doiv Ber Levin was a Russian-language writer of experimental prose and children's fiction, often on Jewish themes. A self-taught speaker of Russian, Levin was educated at the State Institute of Art History in Petrograd. He was also an active participant in the avant-garde group OBERIU as the collective's only writer of "pure prose." Levin spent much of the 1930s writing children's literature, which described the rapidly changing circumstances of Jewish life in the Soviet shtetl. Drafted into the Red Army during World War II, he was killed on the Leningrad front. While all of his manuscripts and personal archives were thought to be lost during the Siege of Leningrad, Levin has received renewed attention in recent years in Russia, where several of his works have been republished.

Cobblers' Street

1932

The heder was in the basement. It was a dark, damp room with a low ceiling. There were two windows on the ground level. In the middle of the room, there was a long wooden table covered with books, two long wooden benches, and an oven in the back. The sun entered this room very rarely, only on long summer days for a brief moment before the sunset, and so the white chalk walls were stained with black mold. The lamp hanging from the ceiling was so full of dead flies that it was difficult to discern whether it was a lamp or something else entirely. [. . .]

The rebbe was not yet old; he had a black beard, and he was thin and absurdly lanky. He had long arms, legs, a long nose and, most importantly—long teeth. They jutted out of his mouth so much that his mouth never closed. And so his mouth was always open. This gave the boys little joy, since the rebbe's breath stank.

Irme carefully opened the door and quickly sneaked into the heder, into a corner. He thought that the rebbe would not notice him right away, and he'd figure something out later. But the rebbe noticed him. He gave a nod, and the boys became quiet. They were all staring silently at Irme.

The rebbe beckoned to Irme with his index finger. Irme came closer, but not so close that the rebbe could reach him with his whip.

"Why, hello to you, Reb Irme," said the rebbe in a friendly voice as he extended his left hand, holding the whip in his right, "How are you feeling today?"

Irme decided not to shake the rebbe's hand but greeted him with equal friendliness.

"Thank you, Reb Yekhiel," said Irme. "It's just that my lower back hurts."

The boys snorted. The rebbe glared in their direction, and they instantly grew silent.

"It hurts?" he asked Irme with concern.

"Yes, it hurts," said Irme.

"Ay-ay-ay!" the rebbe exclaimed. "It really hurts, then?"

"It really hurts," said Irme.

"I see-ee-ee," said the rebbe and sighed.

"Ye-e-e-es," said Irme and also sighed.

The rebbe cracked the whip abruptly.

"I will break you in two, you little snot!"

The whip whistled through empty air. Irme anticipated the rebbe's movement and was already at the door. [. . .]

Chapter 6: An Evening Conversation

The sun was low in the sky. The sky turned deeper, darker. Twilight set in. Heat was rising from the ground, as from an oven. A light steamy mist floated over the field, and it seemed as if the field was smoldering and fuming.

Cobblers' Street was packed with people. Everyone poured out—to sit, to smoke, to stretch their back. Those who didn't manage to finish their work sat by the door and worked their sewing machines or drove the final nails into boots. [. . .] At the very bottom, in the basement, two sister-seamstresses, Libe and Neshe, sewed trousseaux for the wealthy brides of the shtetl. The young women sat by the window, and their needles flickered in their translucent fingers. The sisters sewed and sang in the thinnest of voices about a sweetheart who left for a faraway land, to America, who has forgotten about home and doesn't send letters. They sang and coughed silently, like two crones. The basement was dark, damp like a well, and there was a wretched smell of something sour, perhaps bedbugs, and the walls were covered with mold. [. . .]

At home, Irme didn't see anyone, only his youngest brother, the four-year-old Elye who was sleeping in his clothes on a bare cot by the window. Irme put a pillow under his head. The boy mumbled something indistinctly and angrily but didn't wake up. The room was dark. Irme bumped into a stool and toppled it over. Feeling the table with his hands, he found a top-crust of bread. He took the bread and went outside again. The street was more joyful, somehow.

Close to the house, his father, Meyer, was sitting on a log. Next to him, Simkhe the milliner and Nokhem the saddler were sitting. Nokhem was tall and skinny with a dark wrinkled face and a long moustache. He and Meyer were the same age, just over thirty, but he appeared older by at least a decade. Irme didn't like him: he was a bawler and a brawler. [. . .] They were talking loudly about something, arguing.

"What are they going on about?" thought Irme and, chewing the crust, drew closer so as to hear better.

When Irme came closer, Simkhe was talking. He spoke quietly and melodiously, as if praying.

" . . . That's how you always are, Nokhem," he said, "You make noise, raise a racket over the entire market. But why the noise, why all the racket, you don't even know yourself. Why am I saying this now? Because you should really think first, consider, and only then scream. But you should know, Nokhem, things that have been around for ages are not going to budge, no matter how loud you scream. God knows what he's doing. The holy scripture says. . . ."

"You won't quit with 'scripture' this, 'scripture' that!" Nokhem interrupted angrily. "I don't give a damn about your scripture! Here's some scripture for you: I am only thirty-four years old, and I've been working for twenty-three of those years. Twenty-three years flew by like one day! And what do I have? Fleas in my pocket and bugs in storage. That's it! 'Scripture, scripture.' . . ."

"Eh, Nokhem," Simkhe shook his head with disapproval. "There you go again. It's true. You're working. And I say you will work another twenty years. . . ."

"No way," gloomily muttered Nokhem. "I won't make it even five years. I'll croak before then."

"That, as you know, Nokhem, is impossible to know," said Simkhe. "We—what are we? We are clay vessels. The Supreme Master does with us what He wants. If He wants, He puts us on a shelf; if He wants, He breaks us on the floor. But this is what I mean: you will, as I was saying, work another twenty years, and will still be naked and barefoot, a parasite. I've been working not twenty but forty years, thank God. And what do I have to show for it? Everybody works."

"Everybody?" Nokhem narrowed his eyes with contempt. "Really now? Truly everybody? Only the simple-minded, naïve people like you, Reb Simkhe, think that everybody does. Everybody?! Does Fayvelke Rashall work? Does he do much at all? He walks through the yard all puffed up, saying 'Go on, make way!' then he clears his teeth, tells his clerk 'Hush!' and that's it. That's a real worker, may he burn in hell. And what about Mendl Sher? And Khayim Kazakov? The lot of them, what do they do exactly? Those low-lifes! I could break their necks! Bury them alive!"

"What are you talking about, Fayvl?" asked Simkhe. "Is that an example? He's a wealthy man, why should he work? He has a lot as it is. God provided for him."

"God provided for him. Pfft!" Nokhem spat and broke into a cough. After catching his breath, he spoke more quietly: "Ha! God provided for him! And where did God take it from exactly? From His own pocket, or what? Or did He transfer fifty thousand through His bank? God provided! We all know how He provides. We all know. So why doesn't He give me anything? God provided! They rob us fools and then say: 'What did we do wrong? God provided for us!' And what about us, the poor and barefoot, do we have a special account with God? It looks like He keeps forgetting about us, Reb Simkhe. You think our account got lost? Or maybe someone snatched it?"

"Don't blaspheme, Nokhem," Simkhe said sternly. "That's why He gives you nothing, because you are a blasphemer and a loudmouth."

"Really now!" Nokhem broke into a hoarse laugh, like an old dog. "Really, because I'm a blasphemer, He gives me nothing. That makes sense. That's righteous. I get it. What about you, though? What about you, Reb Simkhe? No doubt you are a pious person. First rate! In the morning—you're off to shul, in the evening—you're off to shul. Any chance you get, you go on about the scriptures. A holy person, a tsadik; you could be a warden in heaven. Nu, what about you? Did you get much from God? I don't seem to see any of your gold; it isn't jingling for some reason; there's no jingle-jangle. Are you tucking it away somewhere, Reb Simkhe? Full barrels under the floorboards I suppose?" Nokhem blinked slyly. "If so, Reb Simkhe, do me a favor and lend me a thousand until Wednesday, huh?"

"You, Nokhem, don't interfere in issues that are none of your business," Simkhe said. "I have my own account with God. He won't let me down, don't worry. Not here, and not there, either." [. . .]

"When the old rabbi was still alive," said Simkhe, "a person came to him. So this person came and said: 'Rabbi,' he said, 'I am a poor man. And I live,' he said, 'in great squalor. But I'm not angry with God. I serve him with all my heart. I go to shul, I fast, this and that, all of it.' He went on and on. 'Nu?' said the rabbi. 'Do I have a lot in heaven, rabbi?' 'Nu,' said the rabbi, 'What do you want?' 'Well I want to sell that lot,' said the man simply. 'My affairs, rabbi, are such that I might as well lay down and die. I have, praise God, seven children, and each one is smaller than the next. And so I thought: let me sell that lot, I thought.' 'Nu?' 'So do you think that perhaps one of your Hasids would buy it?' The man wasn't all there, clearly. Not the brightest, in other words. Nu, and the rabbi, may he rest in peace, that rabbi was a wise old man, nobody's fool. Any other rabbi would have stomped his feet and chased the man away, 'Get out, you so-and-so!' But this rabbi—nothing. He looked at him for a while and said, 'It's too late,' he said, 'To sell. You've lost that lot.' The man got scared and started crying, 'How? When?' 'Five minutes ago, when you said the word 'sell.'"

"An old fairy tale," grumbled Meyer.

He spoke for the first time this evening. Up to this point he had been sitting, smoking, listening, and not saying a word.

"What's the point of the story, Reb Simkhe?" Nokhem was confused. "Aah," he caught on. "So I also, it turns out, lost my lot? The hell with it, anyway. I can spare it."

He started coughing and coughed for a long time, completely hunched over, as if from a stomach ache. Then he got up.

"Time to go," he said in a hollow voice, "I have to get up early, with the sun. Oh man! This life of ours!" And, tall, hunched-over, he crossed the street to go home.

"He is a madcap," Osher said quietly. "I worry about him."

"What's to worry?" Meyer said. "He's a goner. That's clear."

"You see," said Simkhe, "He's got one foot in the grave, but he keeps raving and brawling."

"He's right!" Meyer gesticulated. "He's right, what can I say?" [. . .]

Translated by Alexandra Hoffman.

Other works by Levin: *Desiat' vagonov* (1931); *Fed'ka* (film; 1936).

Charles Reznikoff

1894–1976

Brooklyn-born Charles Reznikoff was an objectivist poet whose verse addressed the Jewish historical experience more than any other important American poet in the twentieth century. Although he trained as a lawyer, Reznikoff never practiced law and instead eked out a living doing various kinds of editorial work. Despite attracting favorable critical attention, Reznikoff labored in obscurity, self-publishing his work, until late in his life. His writings—both poetry and fiction—reflected a diasporic sensibility, which exacerbated his often troubled relationship with his wife, the Zionist activist Marie Syrkin, the daughter of Nachman Syrkin, founder of the Labor Zionist movement.

Meetings and Partings, Friends and Strangers
1932

Good-Bye Grandpa

I came to say good-bye. I was going away to the University of Missouri. My grandfather turned from the window at which he sat, looking across the lots at the parkway. To eyes used to the droshkies and sleighs, sleds, wagons and slow carts of the Ukrainian roads, the parkway was new, I suppose: its smooth surface—with orderly, swift automobiles and trucks, shining in the sun or under the streetlights—in a great sweep between rows of tall houses and brand-new little trees.

My grandfather knew Yiddish and Hebrew and a smattering of Russian, and I—except for the languages I had learned a little of at school—only English and a smattering of Yiddish. A man whose only study was Torah and Talmud, he had found when he came to this country that I had been brought up unable to recite a blessing or to read a word of Hebrew. So we could say little and had little to say to each other. Sick, his skin yellow, his eyes red and bleared, his hair still dark brown—for he had hardly any gray hair in his beard or on his head—I used to see him sitting at the window, reading a Hebrew book, or thinking about a sad, secret matter, or watching the automobiles and trucks along the parkway turn the curve.

As I came in, he rose with difficulty—he had been expecting me, it seems—stretched out his hands and blessed me in a loud voice—in Hebrew, of course, and I did not know what he was saying. Then he turned aside and burst into tears. "It is only for a little while, Grandpa," I said in my broken Yiddish. "I'll be back in June." (By June he had been dead seven months.)

He did not answer me. Perhaps he was in tears for other reasons. Perhaps because, in spite of all the learning I had acquired in school, I knew not a word of the sacred text and was now going out into the world with none of the accumulated wisdom of my people to guide me, with no prayers with which to talk to the God of my people, a soul—for it is not easy to be a Jew, or perhaps a man—doomed by his ignorance to stumble and blunder. Perhaps he wept because he alone of his family was true to the sacred—and so pleasant—ways of his fathers, and now he was about to die. Perhaps he wept because he was about to die. No, Achilles was a heathen; my grandfather would not weep because he was about to die.

Why My Friend Practiced Falling

I had a friend at school who practiced falling. After school we would go to a playground. There were boys at handball, though the ground was uneven and covered with pebbles—no one could tell how the ball would bounce. But each day, while the others played games, ran after each other, or swung on the bars and rings, my friend persisted at learning how to fall. He would work his way up the inclined ladder, higher and higher each time, and drop to the ground. The small clumsy body would drop heavily upon the hard-packed sand, pick itself up, and then the short arms—the body jerking—would work their way up the ladder again. The trick, he explained, was to land lightly, and not sting the soles of one's feet.

"Why learn how to fall?" I would ask him. "What good is it?"

"I don't know," he would answer and look puzzled. "I want to."

Once, when I was in his house, I stood at the window looking into the yard. My friend's father had a little store in front—a few bolts of cloth, a few dirty and broken paper boxes, a dusty showcase with pins and buttons, needles and thread. The yard was full of old wagons, the shafts in the air like masts. Along the back fence, almost as high as the second story, cats were walking gracefully, and now and then one jumped to the ground, landing lightly on its feet.

Why I Do Not Fast on the Day of Atonement

Until I was twenty-one I had never fasted on the Day of Atonement. I kept only the feasts. But that year—to meet the daughters of the congregation—I joined a synagogue in our neighborhood. And since everybody went to synagogue on the Day of Atonement, I thought it would not be nice for me not to go. That meant, it seemed to me, that I should fast because it would be hateful to sit, sated and belching, among the fasting worshipers. And it seemed to me that it might even be pleasant in that slight exaltation that comes from hunger to listen to the cantor and the choir chanting, to lose myself in the Hebrew of the prayers, to wrap myself in a silk prayer shawl and in meditation upon the Eternal forget myself. So I went to synagogue and fasted.

It was a warm day, as warm as a day in summer. About three o'clock I had gone down and up a depression, I no longer found the chanting and the prayers tiresome, my collar sticky, the air close, and, though my head ached a little, my spirit was nimble and joyous, conversing with the cherubim.

A member of the congregation greeted me. "How are you?" he asked. "You are really fasting?" he added surprised.

"How can you tell?"

"By your lips—they are dry and white. Come, let us go for a walk—a little walk. You will feel better."

"But I feel fine."

"Come, it is lovely outside. We will be back soon."

I was somewhat flattered at his attentions. We walked along the boulevard; the trees had on their holiday leaves of red and yellow. "How is it that a clever young man like you," began my companion, when we were a decent block or so from the synagogue, "carries so little insurance?"

I found my headache worse, excused myself, went home, and ate heartily. Since then I never fast: I am afraid that someone will sell me insurance, or who knows what, when I am weakened.

Sunday Afternoon

In the street one day Daniel met Rose who lived on the same block as he seven years before. He recognized her at once, but she did not know him. Of course. He had been fourteen and she had been a woman of twenty-four. In those days she would condescend to talk to him of the books he was reading; and he remembered a tall pale woman with deep blue eyes and a pleasant laugh. Now that he was a man she seemed not tall at all, in fact he was more than a head taller; she was thin, pale, and her eyes were a watery blue. But she spoke cheerfully as ever. He had tickets for a concert—Fritz Kreisler. Would she come? What was she doing? She was still a teacher. And now he was about to become a lawyer.

When he called for her, he was shown into the parlor: a small room with heavy furniture like a herd of pachyderms in a cage. He could hear Rose quarreling with her sister in an undertone. Rose had gone to the closet to get her coat. "Who took my rubbers?" she was saying. "Mine had my initial in them and you had no business to take them. It was not a mistake. You had no business to take them."

When they were in the street, he turned to the subway. "I can't ride in the subway," she said. Of course, he should have signaled a taxicab in the first place, but he did not have the money for it. The tickets had been more than he could afford.

"Shall we go by—?" and he looked at the elevated tracks a block away.

"That will do," she said. Luckily, she had a seat. As he held onto a strap in front of her, "I have no patience," she said, "with those girls—whenever we go out together—who want to sit in cheap seats. If they can't afford to sit in good seats, they ought not to go. I get dizzy when I am far from the stage, and if I don't enjoy myself, I'd rather not go."

"I hope," said Daniel, "that you will not be dizzy in our seats; they are in the balcony."

"As long as they are not in the gallery, they will do. Besides, this is music and not a play. But I do hope that we are not too far away; I should like to see what Fritz Kreisler looks like."

They certainly were not near Fritz Kreisler. They sat quietly and never turned in their seats or rustled a program, but Daniel acknowledged that he had not been more than mildly interested. As for Rose, she too had been somewhat disappointed. "I expected more," she said calmly, as if the disappointed did not matter much.

"Shall we have coffee?" Daniel asked, as they passed a place with many trays of pastry in the large windows.

"I am very particular about coffee," Rose said.

"I know nothing about it; we drink tea at home. But let's try this place; it looks good." His eye had caught the price of coffee on the menu pasted on one of the windows; it was only ten cents, and pastry would be fifteen to twenty.

They had their coffee. "How is the coffee?" Daniel asked.

"Mediocre, perfectly mediocre," she answered, a trace of vexation in her voice.

When he bought her home, her father and sister were about to have supper; there was a platter of smoked salmon, another of sliced meat, and a heap of boiled potatoes, smoking hot.

A large pot of coffee, no doubt excellent coffee such as Rose liked, was on the table. But no one asked Daniel to stay, and Rose was glad to have him go—at least, she said good-bye when he ventured to say it, quickly and cheerfully, without the mild protestation that Daniel expected.

Old Acquaintance

Once, when Daniel was in the gallery watching a play, he heard one of the girls behind him whisper, "There's Laura! She used to be Laura Stein. How pretty she still is!"

Daniel had known a Laura Stein years before—had been in love with her and he looked eagerly at the faces about him. There was a woman, somewhat like the girl he had known, in the second row. He knew that she had married and that she had a child.

How pretty Laura had been, especially when flushed with games or dancing. The girls, then, wore their hair coiled on the back of their heads like the statue of Diana. Some, who did not have hair enough for that, used to wind it about a contraption of wire called a "mouse-trap." Laura's would be sticking out of her hair after a game. She was the liveliest and, when she set herself going, ribbons, bands, pins, and hooks-and-eyes had a hard time of it. Once the placket of her skirt was open, and Daniel was furious at a boy for pointing at it, and tried not to see it.

Daniel greeted her, as she came up the aisle with her husband, when the play was ended. Yes, it was Laura, but the lithe body had become broad, and as she set down her quick little heels they sounded on the stairs and sidewalk. They walked to the corner. Would he come to see them any Sunday afternoon? He would. And the very next Sunday he did go.

Laura lived in a suburb where there were many large houses with broad lawns. But her house was one of a row of little wooden ones, unpainted, as alike as clothespins, set close together. Her street was narrow and the others were broad; it was unpaved, without trees or gardens. As Daniel walked up the rickety steps to the little porch, he could see thick black cobwebs in the corners and under the railing. As he looked at them and at a broken baby carriage on the porch, his heart failed him. Of course, their invitation had been merely a formality, and he turned away.

Delicatessen

I was in a delicatessen store. A boy of seven or eight came in, neither timid nor noisy like a schoolboy, but sedate. I supposed him to be in business—a newsboy who had sold his papers or an errand boy for one of the stores. He considered the meats on the counter and ordered his sandwich, gave the clerk a dime and was given cents in change. He counted this at a glance and slipped it carelessly into his pocket. As he chewed his sandwich, he eyed the bowl of pickles.

"How much," he asked, "for a small one?"

"Two cents," and the clerk dug his hand into the bowl.

"Too much. Haven't you any for a penny?"

"Two cents is the cheapest. I'll give you a good one, see!" And the clerk took out a pickle and held it up. I could smell the good smell of dill. The boy eyed it, shook his head, and went on chewing his sandwich.

A Cage

I was in a factory. There was a boy of three or four on a stool in a corner of the office, who smiled shyly at me and looked away. He had the stub of a pencil and a sheet of paper before him, but most of the time he was looking out of the window. There was only a row of buildings with shops in them to see, and all he could hear was the noise of the machines. "That is your little boy, I suppose," I said to the manufacturer.

"No, he is the child of one of the operators. He is too young to go to school, and she has no one with whom to leave him; so I let her bring him here." Later, I saw a woman dart into the office to steal a glance at the boy.

"When do you come here?" I asked him.

"Eight o'clock in the morning."

"And when do you go away?"

"Six o'clock." He smiled, his black eyes shining.

Next morning I had to go there again. The youngster was on his perch in the office. He had some empty spools before him to play with, but he was not playing.

A Peddler

I went to see my uncle, the jobber, and found one of his customers in a passionate discourse on some difficulty in the Talmud. "He is the son of a great rabbi," whispered my uncle to me. The discourse came to an end at last, and the son of the great rabbi turned to look at a heap of sweaters, the merits of which my uncle was proclaiming.

Walking down a street a week or so later, I was somewhat surprised to see, so far from any ghetto, a Jew carrying a bundle—he must have carried it a long way, for he was finding it heavy; with his derby on, he was no more than five feet tall; the sweat trickling from under the brim had soaked through the hatband and was soaking into his beard; his coat was too big for him, and for that matter so was his hat, and both had been well powdered by the dust of the street; his face was thin, the cheeks and lips pale, and his large black eyes were lost in thought. It was the discourser on the Talmud.

Other works by Reznikoff: *By the Waters of Manhattan* (1930); *In Memoriam: 1933* (1934); *Early History of a Sewing Machine Operator* (1936); *By the Well of Living and Seeing: New and Selected Poems, 1918–1973* (1974); *Holocaust* (1975).

Yehudah Yaari

1900–1982

The Hebrew short-story writer Yehudah Yaari was born into a Hasidic family in a Galician shtetl. Dur-

ing World War I, he moved to Tarnów and joined a Ha-Shomer ha-Tsa'ir group that moved to Palestine in 1920. He became a leading member of the labor brigade that built the Afula–Nazareth road and in 1923 was one of the founding members of Kibbutz Bet Alfa. He left the kibbutz two years later and began working in the National Library in Jerusalem. In the late 1920s he studied library science in the United States, and in the early 1930s he taught in Canada. On his return to Jerusalem, he worked for the National Library and then later served in the civil service and the diplomatic corps.

When the Candle Was Burning
1932

Father had been able to save a little from his earnings and felt that it would last till the end of the war—but he used that money to buy back those prayers shawls! So now we were penniless.

Father was at a loss. So long as the enemy was in the town he did not worry. Michal used to bring us various provisions and somehow we kept body and soul together. But now he knew that something had to be done. But he did not know what!

It was a long conversation. I did not hear all of it. I was very tired and the bed was soft and clean. I fell asleep . . .

I saw troops of Hussars riding along the road and Father walking about among the horses with a great bag in his hand, begging bread. The Hussars threw chunks of black Army bread into the bag till it was full. Father then stood in the middle of the road and divided the bread into two sacks. He put the smaller bag on my shoulder and took the larger one himself. A car came along and ran my father down, scattering the bread on the road. I hurried over to see whether he was still alive, and behold! his face had changed to that of a baby with aged features, with grown beard and wrinkled brow. I began to cry and felt I was choking. Suddenly Reb Zanvil-David stepped out from amongst the trees and, taking up the infant, began feeding it with a strange porridge. Then Father resumed his former appearance. He stood in the middle of the market-place and sang a sad Aramaic song. Reb Zanvil-David played Berele's violin and Peshe Friedman danced a wild dance. Cossacks assembled and stood by, laughing raucously. Father then went up to the Kosciusko Statue and began to call out: "I buy prayer shawls! Jewish prayer shawls! A crown for each shawl . . . !"

On walking the next morning I felt more tired than when I went to bed. I remembered my dream clearly: Father changed to a baby, then in the market-place singing in Aramaic. I felt sorry for him. I must help him over this bitter problem. I must do something . . . I must find work: apprenticeship, porterage, anything—anything to relieve Father of this worry!

I got up and prayed in a hurry. I ate and left the house without a word, fully resolved not to return before I had found work.

Troops of soldiers, infantry, cavalry and artillery were passing through the market-place, filling the air with their songs and making the earth tremble with their cannon and heavy motors. It was Wednesday, the pre-war market day. Only old men and old women drove into town in their wagons, with a few eggs, a hen, some butter. Now and then you could spot a city wagon filled with household goods and lean, emaciated fugitives returning to the town.

Some of the shops were open. The soldiers bought a few things. What could they have for sale there? Things that had been hidden away in cellars and garrets, apparently, and which the Cossacks had not looted.

My courage began to flag. What could I possibly find to do in all this confusion? How should I ever get work in this troubled, impoverished world? It was not such a simple thing to support a family, I could see that. I was in despair. I sat down at the foot of the Kosciusko Statue and watched the fugitives driving into town. Out of the din and confusion I heard someone calling to me from one of the wagons.

"Landau! Landau!"

A golden-haired youth with shorn earlocks and dressed like a young dandy jumped from the wagon. He ran excitedly towards me. I did not recognise him.

"You don't recognise me?" He said with a German Yiddish accent. "You don't know me? Paul! Paul Horowitz. . . ."

"Ah! Feivel the orphan! How are you, Feivel? But tell me: Why Paul all of a sudden?"

Feivel had been to Vienna, Prague, Budapest, and other large cities and had learned that Feivel becomes Paul in cosmopolitan lingo. He had become a man of the world. He sat down beside me at the foot of the statue and began to tell me at top speed of the world's wonders and of what he had heard and seen in the big cities. From time to time he tossed his head and winked knowingly; his thick lips glistened as if they had been smeared with oil. He spoke sneeringly of our small, backwoods town, which lacked life and bustle, and longingly of the great city which fulfils all your heart's desires.

So that was Feivel the Orphan, the fair-haired lad on whom we had lavished so much sympathy because he had no mother! I could not bear his effeminate face, his knowing winks, his sensuous, oily lips, and his Germanised Yiddish tongue. In fact, I hated him. I felt that our pity had been wasted. But I restrained my feelings because he could help me. I told him of my troubles.

"Why should you worry, you fool!" he exclaimed. "Why worry? You can earn a hell of a lot of money around here! Look at all the soldiers. Just sell each one of them *one* box of matches and you're rich. Yes, rich! This is a real goldmine, I tell you. That's why I came back. Do you suppose for a moment that I'd come back to this damned backwoods dump if it weren't for that? You can rake in a fortune here, I tell you!"

"But how?"

"Ach, you hick. I have to explain everything, have I? Take a tray and fill it with matches and cigarettes, candles and pictures and whatever you like. And you go out among the soldiers. When a soldier wants to buy something and says, 'How much?' you reply, 'As much as you're willing to give.' That's the important rule: *Never fix the price.* Get me? These men are on the way to the front and money means nothing to them. See? Come on. I'll show you how it's done."

"But Feivel, I haven't any money."

"I'll lend you money. I have enough. . . ."

I ran home and prepared a nice box and tacked a leather strap on to its sides to sling over my shoulders. The next morning I turned pedlar. We went about together so that Feivel could "show me the ropes," and in the afternoon we divided the territory between us, I took one side of the market and he the other.

"Cigarettes and matches. Pictures. Shoe-laces. Anything you like right here in this box. "How much?' 'Oh, as much as you like to give, sir.' Cigarettes . . . matches . . . shoe . . ."

It was a marvelous idea. The soldiers paid in paper notes. When I went home in the evening my pocket was loaded with money.

Thus I became the sole support of the family. Father hated the idea, but sullenly held his peace. Reb Zanvil-David would wake me at dawn for a lesson in Talmud. How I loved those early morning lessons of his! He taught me homiletics—entertaining legends: it was actually a story-telling hour.

Then I prayed hurriedly, took up my tray and went out. I learned to prattle in German, Hungarian, Czech; I became an excellent pedlar. My earnings grew and grew, even beyond a mere livelihood.

At dusk Feivel and I met at the statue and we sat down to count the profits. We tied the money in a stocking and then, stretched out on the bottom step of the statue, looked up at the stars and talked.

Those summer nights were hot and stuffy. We did not go to synagogue for Evening Prayer. Feivel taught me not to pray. He also taught me to smoke and to cut off my earlocks, and he instilled in me a longing for the big cities. I never before felt such a desire to see big cities. I loved our little town; I knew no other. It was my world. I loved its low houses, its people and even the puddles in its streets, which took on the brilliance of gold at sunset. I loved the Vistula and the windmill with its great wheel revolving against the horizon.

It was Feivel who taught me to despise our town. He never tired of telling me about the great cities, and I listened to his stories with bated breath. He also spoke of women, of a certain class of women. Feivel knew everything!

"In the great cities," he said knowingly, "there are special houses set apart for that purpose. You simply go in and pay the manageress a crown or two (it all depends upon the grade of house, you know) and choose any woman you fancy. . . ."

"Suppose the woman doesn't want you?"

"Fool! Suppose the woman doesn't want you!" Feivel guffawed at my naiveté. "What has that to do with it? She's not allowed to have any wants. Can merchandise say, 'I'll be sold to this person rather than that'? Understand?"

I did not understand. . . . Women, merchandise . . . sale. . . . Still, I said nothing. I did not want Feivel to think me a complete fool . . . .

We lay at the foot of the statue till late into the night and talked and talked. I became friends with Feivel. Though I still hated him, he attracted me.

On leaving him at night I would resolve not to meet him again, ashamed of having listened to him. But the next day, when it grew dark, I hurried to the statue. And it was I who began.

"Well, Feivel. Tell me something about Vienna. Tell me about those houses. Did you yourself go there . . . ?"

When I came home, Reb Zanvil-David was already asleep. My parents sat drowsing in the kitchen, awaiting my return.

I gave Father my earnings; Mother gave me supper. They did not speak to me, as though ashamed that I was supporting them. There were times, when I woke up in the middle of the night and overheard their whispers:

"Heshel, Heshel," Mother would say sadly. "We can't let the boy go on like this. No good will come of it. . . . Why don't you do something, Heshel?"

Father heaved a sigh, but said nothing. Summer passed and the Army left the town; and business grew slack. When Feivel and I met at dusk, at the foot of the statue, there were no earnings to be counted. Feivel was angry and sullen.

"Do you think I came here to loll about and tell you stories? I want to make money!" He stormed at me as if I were to blame for the change of fortune and I listened in cowed silence to his tirades. One night he proposed that we go over to the large city on the other side of the Vistula, where there were many soldiers. We could make a lot of money there, he said. I agreed readily. Now we'd have a look at the big city.

We got up early the next morning and crossed the Vistula. I said nothing to my parents. We decided to go to the first town across the river, and then take a train to the city itself, an hour and a half's ride. We intended to return at night.

As we were walking along the road by the river, happy and contented, we saw an officer staggering along and singing. He was drunk. Feivel ran towards him.

"Cigarettes for you, sir."

Drunkards as a rule were excellent customers. They always paid more than you asked. Feivel knew that and would not let this excellent opportunity slip by. The officer asked for cigarettes and matches.

"How much?" he asked drunkenly.

"As much as you'll give, sir," said Feivel with feigned politeness.

The officer guffawed and wept in turn, dribbling at the mouth.

"That's nice," he stammered. "Jesus! Mary! That's splendid!' 'As much as you like to give, sir!' ha! ha! ha!"

He took a fat wallet from his pocket and handed it to Feivel.

"Here, take this, you bastard, and get out of my sight."

Feivel took the wallet and ran off as fast as his legs could carry him.

"Come quickly!" he shouted to me. "We're rich, Yosef. Rich in a minute!"

I ran after him and caught up with him at the bridge. We looked about to see whether anyone was near and then divided the money between us. There were many ten and hundred crown notes in the wallet. We did not even stop to count the money, but divided it by sight. Feivel threw the empty wallet into the river.

I hurried home through the fields so as not to arouse suspicion. I hopped over the ploughed earth; my feet were light as feathers—I was so excited. I found Mother making the beds. Father was breakfasting in the kitchen. I laid the money before Mother.

"Here," I said, enthusiastically.

Mother's face turned white, as if I had placed a bomb in front of her.

"What's this? Where did you get so much money?"

"I found it," I replied and for some reason immediately believed it.

"You found it? Where?"

"I found it. Isn't that enough?" I cried, confused and angry. I thought she'd be overjoyed; instead she stood there sighing as if I had brought an instrument of destruction into the house.

"Heshel! Heshel!" Mother called out in the direction of the kitchen. "Come quickly! The boy has *found* money!"

Father came in. When he saw the notes lying on the bed his face went pale and his hands began to tremble.

"Where did you find that money?" he asked, frightened.

"Near Kosciusko? I pass by Kosciusko seven times a day and find nothing, and you have found money there?"

I became confused. I saw myself as vagabond, thief, liar. I began to cry.

"What of it!" I cried. "He was drunk and he himself gave it to us. Had I not taken my share, Feivel would have taken it all!"

"Feivel, Feivel," Mother groaned. "I always knew that this Feivel would lead him astray."

"Come, show me the drunkard!" Father said, restraining his anger.

"On the other side of the Vistula. . . . You won't find him now."

"You'll remember—now—not—to—*find*—any—more—money," cried Father, boxing my ears.

Then he tore the tray out of my hands and broke it to pieces.

"Enough! An end!" he stormed. "You're not going to earn any more money for us!"

I threw myself to the ground and burst out crying. This was the first time Father ever hit me. I felt desperate with shame at the disgrace. I wanted to die.

In the evening Father went to see my Uncle Naphtali Hayim, who dealt in skins and furs, and stayed till late. When he returned he informed us that he had become Uncle's partner.

That was the end of my business venture and my friendship with Feivel as well.

Translated by Menahem Hurwitz.

Other works by Yaari: *Prisoners of Hope: Ten Stories* (1945); *The Covenant: Ten Stories* (1965).

Arnold Zweig
1887-1968

The German-born novelist and writer Arnold Zweig is best known for his antiwar novel *The Case of Sergeant Grischa* (1927). A Zionist who was heavily influenced by Martin Buber, he wrote a romantic account of his encounter with East European Jewry, *The Eastern Jewish Countenance* (1920), which was illustrated by Hermann Struck. He was also influenced by the writings of Freud, with whom he corresponded for twelve years, and in 1927 published a psychological study of antisemitism, *Caliban oder Politik unter Leidenschaft*. After the Nazi takeover, he settled in Haifa, but, unable to master the Hebrew language and frustrated that Zionism failed to develop in a Buberian direction, he left the newly created State of Israel to settle in East Germany, where he was much feted.

De Vriendt Goes Home
1932

Chapter 4. A Blow at the Heart

De Vriendt shut the door, but stayed with his forehead pressed against it; the strength had gone out of him. This Englishman knew. He knew the nature of his relation to the boy Saûd. He might be ever so much a gentleman, and ever so much more a friend—this was ruin. The frightful affliction with which God had stricken him—it was now notorious. That he, Issac Josef de Vriendt, who contended so zealously for the spirit of the Torah, should be published abroad as a lover of boys, as a man to whom the ways of women were an abomination, as one that trembled under the wonderful gaze of a bright young lad, took him on his knee and let him embrace him and kiss him on the lips: that was the end.

He shuffled back into the room where his coins were, weak at the knees, bowed like an old man, flung himself on to the divan and buried his face in the arms. He did not dwell for an instant on the threat of which Irmin had spoken significantly enough. It was no matter. These clowns with their knives or pistols were not worth a thought. He, who lay there and groaned, strove with a much mightier foe of his secret hours and of his verse, who had placed him where he was and stricken him with this passion: he strove with God. Now, when it grew dark, since he had known the boy Saûd, he was emptied of the confident strength and purpose of his life, the boldness of his arguments, and the keenness of his fighting spirit. And what remained was a man possessed by a passion that was accursed, and contrary to his own will, a passion implanted in him from the beginning by a derisive Deity, against which he had fought with a superhuman and persistent fury, but which seemed to draw strength from the very struggle. There are psychological doctrines that maintain the existence in man of a resistant will that draws constant new vigour from the efforts of a man's true will, and thus frustrates them; but he, de Vriendt, knew better. It was the awful caprice of God, that had set upon him as a plaything. Of him, by set purpose, and of no other, had He made a plaything, and He delighted in the black and white of two conflicting worlds. By day, and to outward view, in all the strength of his mind and will he was the man of the Torah, nor was there in him any trace of hypocrisy; the faith transfigured him like his zeal for the word of the One creative God, who had chosen the people of Israel and this city of Jerusalem. And none the less He had merely created him so that there should be someone to curse God in Jerusalem, and shake his fists at Him, as soon as night fell. But thus had it been always. He always chose one of those most eager to serve Him, laid upon him the thumb-screws of his forbidding ordinances, and then transfixed him with the glowing iron of wild desires. He who lay here, by name Issac, was a worthy successor to the boy Issac who yonder, not a thousand yards away, had lain upon the stone of slaughter on the summit of Mount Moriah, to be sacrificed by the hand of his own father, Abraham, son of Terah—on the rock of Moriah, where the Moslems had erected that infamously splendid oc-

tagon building, faced with coloured tiles, and painted within like the peacock's tail, where the bare grey rock is worshipped under the marvelously vaulted dome, the only place in the world where the stone of the earth, the very earth itself is venerated as divine. What was to be done? At present only Irmin knew this secret, and the boy Saûd, who came, and gladly came, and came again, and drank in knowledge and paid for it with the radiance in his eyes and the grace of his body. Only a few of the most secret of his poems shared this knowledge: he only ventured to write of his struggle against God, hardly to give letter and verse to the reason for it. How the horrible vitality of life rolled onwards without pause, swept over all the barriers, contemned all commandments and laughed at every inhibition! That, that too was God. Why had He not let the world abide in the grave and simple fashion of the ancient times, when our forefathers, like the Bedouin of today, drove their sheep along the snow-flecked chains of Hebron, watered their camels in the springs of Hebron and Beersheba, when men were few, customs simple, and the word of Sinai could be followed. Why had He scattered millions and milliards upon the earth, and allowed it to become so populous, suffered the hellish accumulation of towns and giant cities, permitted mankind to multiply His work a thousandfold with daemonic machines, to portray in stone the ugliness of his life and to poison the guiltless earth, the grand immaculate sea, and even the living air, with their diseases, their turmoil, and their ant-like industry? If he, de Vriendt, took refuge in the desert, he would certainly be overtaken in a day or two by a tourist motor-bus; if he fled to the shores of the Dead Sea, he would be sure to find himself in a crowd of survey officials, with a light railway under construction to serve the factory to be erected below. And when he, thirsting for purity and the true fashion of human life, tried to secure the sanctity of the Sabbath in this land and the recognition of the Law, from his very self, from his own rebellious soul, burst forth this passion for a boy, at which the great teachers of the Talmud and all the Rabbis after them had shuddered with horror, and which they called the crime of Sodom and the loathsome sin of the accursed Emperor Hadrian. Yes, it was so, he could endure these two passions, he alone, the furious intensity of blessing and of cursing, Ebal and Garitsim, in his own breast; but only so long as no one knew it. Now there was one who shared his secret, one well disposed indeed, Irmin, but—he groaned, the sound seemed alien to that silent room with its walls covered with shelves of black folios—but Irmin must have got his knowledge from someone, from one of his agents, in fact; and the young man Mansur suspected or actually knew something. No, his life here must be broken off, like a tent blown away by the wind; he must not merely fly the city, but the country, and not only, as Irmin thought, for a few weeks' convalescence, but for ever. For more important than his own personal happiness was the struggle in which he was involved, more binding than his passion for this sacred and contentious city was the task of opposing the secularization of Jewry, and this was not confined to Palestine. He, Isaac Josef de Vriendt, could pursue his struggle wherever the guardians of the Torah were oppressed by the pretensions of the pagan Jews and the luke warmness of the Liberals, who transformed the faded creed of Protestantism, as the easiest way to dispose of God, into a philosophy. Everywhere, in England, America, Eastern Europe, he could carry on his work, where there would be none of these wonderful lads, true sons of Ishmael, with their nimble bodies and their nimble wits. There he could plunge into the asceticism of the Polish Rabbis, there it was easy to surrender happiness, because those folk did not know the varieties of happiness that flourished on the earth; there he could transmute that part of his nature into zeal for the cause, and beat a furious drum against the destroyers of holy things. It would indeed be a gloomy, dull, insensate task for that leaping heart of his, but he would gnash his teeth and tear that heart out and fling it in the face of the Creator: take it, I want it no more, I will no longer even hate Thee, I would be no more than a hollow ram's horn, to bellow forth Thy thunderous utterances, Thou crazy Creator of a world run mad, and of a marvelous garden of the spirit, called Torah, that is never fated to thrive upon this earth.

He gasped for a moment or two, and then collapsed; a surge of panic fear numbed him, from the chest to the knees. He must now do three things. First, he must only go out in the daytime; secondly, he must not see the boy Saûd again; thirdly, he must explain to his friend, the Rabbi Zadok Seligmann, that he proposed to take the next boat to Trieste. A recruiting campaign through the great Jewish communities of the East was indispensable, concluded by a congress in Vienna, a Sanhedrin of all the Rabbies between Helsingfors and Rome still loyal to the Law. There the claim of the Zionists to stand as representatives of the Jewish people would be explicitly denied and in a few pungent clauses the

real claims of what was really Jewry and their real representatives would be hammered into the League of Nations, the Governments, and above all the Mandatory Power. Failing other means, an alliance with the Liberals must bring about the fall of the Zionists; it must even be considered whether the most anti-Zionist group in the world, the Jewish section of the Communist Party in Russia, should not be invited to join the campaign against Imperialist Zionism, and its anti-Messianic heresies. This was a dreadful thought; it was an alliance with the devil himself, for this Jewish sect in Moscow was steadily and relentlessly destroying Jewry in the vast territories of the Soviet Union: they were abolishing the festivals, secularizing the Jewish schools, closing the institutes for teaching the Talmud (Yeshiboth), and transforming the synagogues into clubhouses for Jewish workmen. But their attack and their power were quite local and limited to Russian Jewry: Zionism attacked the spirit of world Jewry, and destroyed it, wherever it could make itself felt, throughout the world.

From the sea the sun poured a still burning radiance athwart Jerusalem and into the windows of the room where lay this solitary figure; heavily he roused himself. It would be good to leave this land, if only to feel the rain again, divine rain that fell from heaven. Well, he would dress and go and see Rabbi Zadok Seligmann, and discuss with him how the place of one de Vriendt could be filled in this country, as he had to travel to Europe on urgent business. Suddenly, there came another ring at the outer door.

It often happens that people start when they hear the buzz of the doorbell. That has nothing to do with their social gifts. On the street and in the café you can talk to them at any time, they are alert and responsive, and even show themselves quite talkative. But in their houses they spin themselves into an atmosphere of their own, which only their inmost character may breathe, and every intrusion from without has the effect of an almost physical shock.

De Vriendt crept softly out; but before he bent down to look through the grille, a sudden thrill took him, a thrill of happiness, he struck his hand to his forehead, and flung open the door.

There stood a boyish figure, with a red tarboosh on his head, white shirt, red girdle, and bare dark-brown legs emerging from white trousers. A book was clasped under his left arm. The boy solemnly raised his hand to the centre of his forehead in salutation, bowed as he did so, and said in Arabic: "Peace, Father of the book," and his dark eyes glittered roguishly in the half-light of the stairway. He entered, and the door closed behind him.

De Vriendt watched him as he slipped the flat shoes off his feet. Then he laid his arm round the slim shoulders and, taking great care to hide his emotion, led him affectionately into the western room. Of course he did not mention the fact that for the first time he had forgotten the appointed hour; or had Saûd realized what a menacing shade had suddenly appeared behind them, a third in their society? As his pulses throbbed, it seemed to him more and more impossible to set his mind upon escape. A choking sense of bliss rose from his heart into his throat as he watched the boy crouch on the divan with his legs tucked underneath him, open the book and lay it in front of him, with his brown hands on the table, and his eyes fixed expectantly and devotedly upon the teacher, his friend. To be able to speak, he had to moisten his dry throat. From a brown earthenware jug, in which the water was cooled by evaporation, he poured himself out a glassful. As he drank, he realized that he could not conceal from the boy what had happened. The boy was as much menaced as he was himself, and perhaps much more equal to the situation than a "Father of the Book." "You are very punctual, O Saûd," he began; "I must commend you."

"The praise of the teacher is like dew at evening," replied the boy, in the words of a proverb. "Now commend me also because I found the way hither, and because I have washed my hands and my nose is not dirty."

De Vriendt could not help laughing; once again he realized that he loved the lad for many gifts, but his gaiety was not the least of them.

"Indeed it was not easy to slip away this time," said Saûd. "My brother Mansur has surely denounced me to the sun and moon and stars, and my mother found a thousand things for me to do."

De Vriendt said lightly, "Do you think your brother Mansur knows where you go?"

Saûd uttered a contemptuous comparison between his eldest brother and a bug in springtime, which comes to life again and thinks itself the spring.

"I suppose you know that bugs bite in the dark," answered de Vriendt gravely; "they even bite Fathers of the Book, Europeans."

"Sometimes," answered the boy promptly; "but then they get into trouble, they make acquaintance with some evil stuff called petroleum."

"But suppose it is not a matter of a bug's bite, but a scorpion's? Listen to what has happened: Irmin Effendi was with me; he said my life was not safe, and he asked after your relations, the men of your blood."

The boy flung his body backwards, stretched out his fists and cried, "They want to take me away from you—Irmin and your friends. But I will not give you up."

De Vriendt shook his head. That was not what had happened. Men, who spoke in Arabic, one of them a man of good family, had said this and that one night. Perhaps he, Saûd, had been indiscreet?

The boy slid off the divan, sat on de Vriendt's knees and put his arms round his shoulders. He wept. By Allah and the prophets, he had never been indiscreet. He might have left the book about, the schoolbook with its owner's name written in Hebrew characters. This had been his error; he would dash his head against the wall.

De Vriendt held the slim body in his arms, kissed the tears from the boy's eyes, and soothed him. The fact that a human creature suffered so on his behalf filled him with a vague happiness, that seemed to emerge from the dimmest fastness of the past, undefined, and heavy-laden.

"There is no danger, sir, there is no shadow of a danger," stammered the boy. "We are many, a whole crowd of lads, some follow me of their own free will, for the others you shall give me a few piastres. We will find out what my brother Mansur is about. He shall not have been out of the house for an hour, without our knowing where and why. He is coward, I tell you, he will dare nothing if we frighten him a little. But you too must be sensible, sir, and not go out at night in the Old Town or hereabouts. Meanwhile, I will think of some ruse to mislead him. In two or three weeks he will have forgotten." Excited and eager, he looked at his friend out of his wide childish eyes, his small fists on the man's shoulders, and his body bent back. He was trying to belie himself, and he knew it. It was not so simple to avoid the menace, if the men of his family, the proud men of the Djellabi, had decided to step between him and this man.

Ah, pondered de Vriendt, wasn't it worth risking one's life, to be loved like this by a living soul? Life in rainy lands was good; but life was surely better in hot lands where men's emotions darted straight upon their object as the vultures plunge from the sky upon the dead camel by the wayside. For an instant he drew the boy's head towards him from which the tarboosh had fallen, put back his red cap, and said, "We must think of our lesson. Let us hear what you have remembered, and what you have been learning about the times when your fathers and my fathers lived in fellowship beyond the sea and achieved great things, in the cities of Granada, Cordoba, and Seville."

The boy Saûd, his legs crossed beneath him, again sat down on his divan with his hands flat upon the table. "Under the Caliph Abdurahman," he began and then broke off: "What did Irmin Effendi advise, O Father of the Book?"

De Vriendt reflected for a moment: should he speak to the boy only of a little journey, or reveal his plan to visit Europe, and an absence of months? He decided, and explained his latter purpose. But he added that, before doing anything, he would have to go out that evening and consult Rabbi Zadok.

The boy Saûd nodded: "But be careful and do not be drawn into a quarrel on the street, for that is a device of our people to work themselves into a fury. It is a good decision. It is wiser to avoid danger, even when it comes but from my brother." And he added, half-aloud, looking straight in front of him, "I will wait for you. What are three months in the friendship of friends? When the rains fall you will be back again. And you are not departing today or tomorrow for Jaffa, to go on board the *Vienna* or the *Carnaro*. I shall have forgotten nothing when you come back; I shall be able to draw your face in darkness on my closed eyelids."

Translated by Eric Sutton.

Other works by Zweig: *Ein Ritualmord in Ungarn* (1914); *Das neue Kanaan* (1925); *The Letters of Sigmund Freud and Arnold Zweig* (1987).

Shmuel Yosef Agnon

1887–1970

The Nobel laureate Shmuel Yosef Agnon (né Czaczkes) grew up in Buczacz, Galicia, memories of which haunted and fed his literary imagination throughout his life. He was educated at home, in both secular and religious subjects. He settled in Jaffa in 1908 and then lived in Berlin and Bad Homburg from 1913 to 1924, during which time the department store magnate Salman Schocken became his literary patron. In 1924, he once again left Europe and settled in Jerusalem, where he remained for the rest of his life. While his work is modernist in tone and content, its language is unlike that of other modern Hebrew masters. It relies on pre-modern Jewish idioms and phrases drawn from classical rabbinic texts. Its linguistic distinctiveness, along with the wealth of associations it evokes, renders the task of translating his work into modern European languages a daunting challenge.

A Whole Loaf
1933

1

I had not tasted anything all day long. I had made no preparations on Sabbath eve, so I had nothing to eat on the Sabbath. At that time I was on my own. My wife and children were abroad, and I had remained all by myself at home; the bother of attending to my food fell upon myself. If I did not prepare my meals or go to hotels and restaurants, I had to put up with hunger inside me. On that particular day, I had intended to eat at a hotel; but the sun had flamed like a furnace, so I decided it was better to go hungry than to walk about in that heat.

In all truth, my dwelling did not keep the heat from me either. The floor was as hot as glowing fire, the roof fevered like piercing fire, the walls simply burned like fire, and all the vessels simply sweated fire, so that it was like fire licking fire, fire of the room licking at the body, and the fire of the body licking against the fire of the room. But when a man is at home, he can soak himself in water if he likes, or take off his clothes when he wants to, so that they do not weigh on him.

Once the greater part of the day had passed, and the sun weakened, I rose and washed myself and dressed, and went off to eat. I was pleased to think that I would be sitting at a well-spread table with a clean tablecloth on it, and waiters and waitresses attending to me while I ate properly prepared food that I had not needed to exhaust myself about. For I was already tired of the poor food I used to prepare for myself at home.

The day was no longer hot, and a gentle breeze was blowing. The streets were filling up. From the Mahaneh Yehudah Quarter to the Jaffa Gate or nearby, the old men and women and the lads and girls were stretching their legs all the way. Round fur hats and caps and felt hats and turbans and tarbooshes shook and nodded, on and amid hairy and hairless heads. From time to time fresh faces joined them, coming from Rabbi Kook Street and from the Sukkat Shalom and Even Yisrael and Nahlat Shiva quarters, and from the Street of the

Prophets which people have the bad habit of calling the Street of the Consuls; as well as from all the other streets to which the authorities had not yet managed to give names. All day long they had been imprisoned in their homes by the heat. Now that day was past and the sun was losing its strength, they came out to glean a little of the atmosphere of Sabbath twilight which Jerusalem borrows from the Garden of Eden. I was borne along with them till I came to a solitary path.

2

While I was being carried along, an old man knocked at his window to draw my attention. I turned my head and saw Dr. Yekutiel Ne'eman standing at the window. I hurried over with great pleasure, for he is a great sage, and his words are pleasant. But when I came there, he had vanished. I stood looking into his house until he joined me and greeted me. I greeted him in return, and waited to hear some of those great thoughts we are accustomed to hearing from him.

Dr. Ne'eman asked me how my wife and children were. I sighed and answered, "You have reminded me of my trouble. They are still abroad and want to come back to the Land of Israel."

"If they want to come back," said he, "why don't they come?"

I sighed and said, "There's some delay."

"Verily the delay comes from a crooked way," said he, rhyming on my word. And he began to scold me. "There's some laziness about you," said he, "so that you have not devoted yourself to bringing them back; and the result for you is that your wife and children are wandering about without father or husband while you are without wife and children."

I looked down at the ground in shame and said nothing. Then I raised my head and turned my eyes to his mouth, in the hope that he would say something consoling. His lips were slightly open, and a kind of choked rebuke hung from them, while his fine, grayshot beard had creased and grown wavy, like the Great Sea when it rages. I regretted having brought his wrath down on me and causing him to bother about such trifles. So I took counsel with myself and began to talk about his book.

3

This was a book about which opinions were largely divided. There are some scholars who say that whatever is written in it as from the mouth of the Lord [. . .] was written by Yekutiel Ne'eman, who neither added nor took away anything from His words. And that is what Yekutiel Ne'eman declares. But there are some who say this is certainly not the case, and that Ne'eman wrote it all himself and ascribed his words to a certain Lord whom no man ever saw.

This is not the place to explain the nature of that book. Yet this I must add, that since it first became known the world has grown slightly better, since a few people have improved their behavior and somewhat changed their nature; and there are some who devote themselves body and soul to doing everything in the manner described there.

In order to make Dr. Ne'eman feel more pleased, I began proclaiming the virtues of his book and said, "Everybody admits that it is a great work and there is nothing like it." Then Yekutiel turned his face from me, let me be, and went his way. I stood eating my heart with grief and remorse for what I had said.

But Dr. Ne'eman did not remain annoyed with me for long. As I was about to go away, he returned with a packet of letters to be taken to the post office and sent by registered mail. I put the letters in my breast pocket and placed my hand on my heart as a promise that I would perform my mission faithfully.

4

On the way I passed the house of study and entered to recite the evening prayers. The sun had already set entirely, but the beadle had not yet kindled the light. In view of the mourning of Moses, the congregation did not engage in the study of the Torah, but sat discoursing and singing and taking their time.

Stars could already be seen outside, but complete darkness still held sway within the building. At length the beadle lit a light, and the congregation rose to recite the evening prayers. After the Havdalah ceremony, which brings the Sabbath day to a close, I rose to go to the post office.

All the grocery stores and other shops were open, and people crowded around the kiosks on every side. I also wished to cool myself with a glass of soda water, but since I was in a hurry to send off the letters, I kept my desire in check and did without drinking.

Hunger began to oppress me. I considered whether I should go and eat first. After starting, I changed my mind and said, Let me send off the letters and then I shall eat. On the way I thought to myself, If only

Ne'eman knew that I am hungry, he would urge me to eat first. I turned myself about and went toward the restaurant.

Before I had taken more than two or three steps, the power of imagination arrived. What it imagined! What did it not imagine! All of a sudden it brought a sickbed before me. There's a sick man somewhere, I told myself, and Dr. Ne'eman has been told about it and has written down a remedy for him; and now I have to hurry and take the letter containing it to the post office. So I got set to run to the post office.

In the middle of my running I stopped and thought, Is he the only doctor there is? And even if he is, does he promise that his remedy is going to help? And even if it does help, do I really have to put off my meal, when I haven't eaten anything at all the whole day long? My legs grew as heavy as stone. I did not go to eat because of the force of imagination, while I did not go to the post office because of my reasoning.

5

Since I was standing still, I had time to consider my affairs. I began to weigh what I ought to do first and what I ought to do later, and reached the decision to go to an eating place first, since I was hungry. I turned my face at once to the restaurant and marched off as quickly as I could before some other thought should strike me; for a man's thoughts are likely to delay his actions. And in order that my thoughts should not confuse me, I gave myself good counsel, picturing all the kinds of good food for which the restaurant was well known. I could already see myself sitting, eating and drinking and enjoying myself. The force of imagination helped me, producing more than an average man can eat or drink, and making good to my taste each article of food and drink. Undoubtedly the intention was for the best, but what pleasure does a hungry man have when he is shown all kinds of food and drink but is given no chance to enjoy them? Maybe he can find satisfaction from this in dream, but it is doubtful if he will do so when awake.

This being the case, I went back toward the restaurant, thinking over what I should eat and drink. At heart I was already happy to be sitting in a pleasant building at a spread table, among fine folk busy eating and drinking. Then maybe I would find a good acquaintance there, and we would spice our repast with pleasant conversation which satisfies the heart and does

not weigh on the soul; for I would have you know that Dr. Ne'eman had weighed somewhat on my heart.

Remembering Dr. Ne'eman, I remembered his letters. I began to feel afraid that I might be so carried away by my talk with my friend that I would not send the letters off. So I changed my mind and said, Let us go to the post office first and be done with the job, so that afterward we can sit comfortably and the letters will not keep on burdening my mind.

6

If only the ground had moved along under me, I would have done my mission at once. But the ground stood still, and the way to the post office is hard on the feet, because the ground is broken and uneven with heaps of earth and stones; while when you do get there the postal clerks are not in the habit of hurrying but keep you hanging about, and by the time they finish whatever it is they are doing, all the food will get cold and you will find no hot dishes, so that you are bound to remain hungry. But I gave no thought to this and went to the post office.

It is easy to understand the state of a man who has two courses in front of him: if he takes one, it seems to him that he has to follow the other, and if he takes the other, it seems to him that he ought to go along the first one. At length he takes the course that he ought to take. Now that I was going to the post office, I wondered that I could possibly have had any doubt for a while and wished to give my own trifling affairs precedence over the affairs of Dr. Ne'eman. And within a short while I found myself standing at the post office.

7

I was just about to enter when a carriage came along and I saw a man sitting in it. I stood and stared in astonishment: now, when as much as a horseshoe is not to be found in town, a man comes along in a two-horse carriage. And what was still more surprising, he was mocking the passersby and driving his horses along the pavement.

I raised my eyes and saw that he was Mr. Gressler. This Mr. Gressler had been the head of an agricultural school abroad, but there he used to ride a horse and here he drove a carriage. When he was abroad he used to joke with the peasants' daughters and the simple folk, and here in the Land of Israel he fooled about with anybody and everybody. Yet he was an intelligent and polite person, and although he was a fleshy fellow, his fleshiness was not noticed by reason of his wide learning.

This Mr. Gressler had something about him that attracted all who saw him. So it is not surprising that I was also affected. On this occasion Mr. Gressler sat leaning back in his carriage, the reins loose in his hand and dragging below the horses' legs, as he watched with pleasure while people passed on either side and returned to the place from which they had run, and jumped about in front of the horses, the dust of their feet mingling with the dust of the horses' hooves; all of them alike as cheerful as though Mr. Gressler were only out to please them.

This Mr. Gressler was my acquaintance, one of my special acquaintances. Since when have I known him? Possibly since the days I reached a maturity of knowledge. Nor do I exaggerate if I say that from the day I met him we have never ceased to have a liking for one another. Now, although all and sundry like him, I can say that he prefers me to all of them, since he has taken the trouble to show me all kinds of pleasures. When I used to tire of them he would amuse me with words of wisdom. Mr. Gressler is gifted with exceptional wisdom, of the kind that undermines all the wisdom you may have learned elsewhere. Never did he ask for any compensation, but he gives of his bounty and is happy to have people accept it. Ah, there were days when I was a lad and he went out of his way to divert me; until the night my house was burned down and all my possessions went up in flames.

The night my house burned, Mr. Gressler sat playing cards with my neighbor. This neighbor, an apostate Jew, was a dealer in textiles. He lived below with his wares, while I lived above with my books. From time to time my neighbor told me that there was no great demand for his goods, that all his textiles were like paper since they were made in wartime; now that the war was over, textiles were being made of proper wool and flax again, and nobody wanted to make a suit out of the substitute stuffs which wear through and tear as soon as they are put on, if he could get himself real material. "Are you insured?" Mr. Gressler asked him. "Insured I am," he answered. While they were talking Mr. Gressler lit a cigar and said, "Drop this match in this rubbish heap and collect your insurance money." He went and set his goods on fire, and the whole house was burned down. That apostate who was insured received the value of his goods, while I, who had not insured my possessions, came out of it in a very bad way. All that I had left after

the fire I spent on lawyers, because Mr. Gressler persuaded me to take action against the municipality for not saving my home and, what was more, making the fire worse. That night the firemen had had a party and grown drunk, filling their vessels with brandy and beer, and when they came to put the fire out, they made it burn even more.

For various reasons I kept my distance from Mr. Gressler after that, and it almost seemed to me that I was done with him for good and all, since I bore him a grudge for being the cause of my house burning down, and since I was devoting myself to Yekutiel Ne'eman's book. Those were the days when I was making myself ready to go up to the Land of Israel and neglected all worldly affairs; and since I was neglecting these worldly affairs, Mr. Gressler let me be. But when I set out for the Land of Israel the first person I ran across was Gressler, since he was traveling by the same ship as I was; save that I traveled on the bottom deck like poor folk do, while he traveled on the top deck like the rich.

I cannot say that I was very happy to see Mr. Gressler. On the contrary, I was very sad for fear he would remind me of my onetime deeds. So I pretended not to see him. He noticed this and did not bother me. Then it seemed to me that since our paths did not cross on board ship, they would do so even less on the land. But when the ship reached the port, my belongings were detained at the customs, and Mr. Gressler came and redeemed them. He also made things easier for me in my other affairs until we went up to Jerusalem.

Thenceforward we used to meet one another. Sometimes I visited him and sometimes he visited me, and I don't know who followed the other more. Particularly in those days when my wife was away from the country. I had nothing to do at that time, and he was always available. And when he came he used to spend most of the night with me. His was pleasant company, for he knew all that was going on and had the inside story even before the things happened. Sometimes my heart misgave me, but I disregarded it.

8

Seeing Mr. Gressler in front of the post office, I signaled and called him by name. He stopped his carriage and helped me up.

I forgot all about the letters and the hunger and went along with him. Or maybe I did not disregard the hunger and the letters, but I put them aside for a little while.

Before I had begun talking to him properly, Mr. Hophni came toward us. I asked Mr. Gressler to turn his horses to one side, because this Hophni is a bothersome fellow, and I am afraid to have too much to do with him. Ever since he invented a new mousetrap, it has been his habit to visit me two or three times a week, to tell me all that is being written about him and his invention. And I am a weak person, I am, who cannot bear to hear the same thing twice. It is true that the mice are a great nuisance, and the mousetrap can greatly correct the evil; but when this Hophni goes gnawing at your brains, it's quite likely that you would prefer the mice to the conversation of the trap-maker.

Mr. Gressler did not turn his horses away, but on the contrary ran the carriage up to Hophni and waved to him to get in. Why did Mr. Gressler think of doing this? Either it was in order to teach me that a man has to be patient, or because he wanted to have some fun. Now I was not at all patient at that time, nor was I in the mood for fun. I stood up, took the reins out of his hands, and turned the horses off in a different direction. Since I am not an expert in steering horses, the carriage turned over on me and Mr. Gressler, and we both rolled into the street. I yelled and shouted, "Take the reins and get me out of this!" But he pretended not to hear and rolled with me, laughing as though it amused him to roll about with me in the muck.

I began to fear that a motorcar might pass and crush our heads. I raised my voice higher, but it could not be heard because of Mr. Gressler's laughter. Woe was me, Mr. Gressler kept on laughing, as though he found pleasure in dusting himself with the dust of the horses' feet and fluttering between life and death. When my distress came to a head, an old carter came along and disentangled us. I rose from the ground and gathered my bones together and tried to stand. My legs were tired and my hands were strained and my bones were broken, and all of my body was full of wounds. With difficulty I pulled myself together and prepared to go off.

Although every part of me was aching, I did not forget my hunger. I entered the first hotel that came my way, and before entering the dining hall I cleaned off all the dirt and wiped my injuries and washed my face and hands.

This hotel has an excellent name throughout the town for its spacious rooms and fine arrangements and polite and quick service and good food and excellent wine and worthy guests. When I entered the dining hall, I found all the tables full, and fine folk sitting, eating and drinking and generally enjoying themselves. The light blinded my eyes and the scent of the good food confused me. I wanted to snatch something from the table in order to stay my heart. Nor is there anything surprising about that, as I had tasted nothing all day long. But when I saw how importantly and gravely everybody was sitting there, I did not have the courage to do it.

I took a chair and sat at a table and waited for the waiter to come. Meantime I took the bill of fare and read it once, twice, and a third time. How many good things there are which a hungry man can eat his fill of, and how long it seems to take until they are brought to him! From time to time I looked up and saw waiters and waitresses passing by, all of them dressed like distinguished people. I began to prepare my heart and soul for them, and started weighing how I should talk to them. Although we are one people, each one of us talks ten languages, and above all in the Land of Israel.

9

After an hour, or maybe a little less, a waiter arrived and bowed and asked, "What would you like, sir?" What would I like and what wouldn't I like! I showed him the bill of fare and told him to fetch me just anything. And in order that he should not think me the kind of boor who eats anything without selecting it, I added to him gravely, "But I want a whole loaf." The waiter nodded his head and said, "I shall fetch it for you at once, I shall fetch it for you at once."

I sat waiting until he came back with it. He returned carrying a serving dish with all kinds of good things. I jumped from my place and wanted to take something. He went and placed the food in front of somebody else, quietly arranged each thing separately in front of him, and chatted and laughed with him, noting on his list all kinds of drinks which the fellow was ordering for his repast. Meanwhile he turned his face toward me and said, "You want a whole loaf, don't you, sir? I'm bringing it at once."

Before long he came back with an even bigger tray than the first one. I understood that it was meant for me and told myself, That's the meaning of the saying: the longer the wait, the greater the reward. As I prepared to take something, the waiter said to me, "Excuse me, sir, I'm bringing you yours at once." And he arranged the food in front of a different guest most carefully, just as he had done before.

I kept myself under control and did not grab anything from others. And since I did not grab anything from others I told myself, just as I don't grab from others, so others won't grab my share. Nobody touches what's prepared for somebody else. Let's wait awhile and we'll get what's coming to us, just like all the other guests who came before me; for it's first come, first served.

The waiter returned. Or maybe it was another waiter and, because I was so hungry, I only thought it was the same one. I jumped from my chair in order to remind him of my presence. He came and stood and bowed to me as though mine were a new face. I began wondering who this waiter could be, a fresh fellow or the one from whom I had ordered my food; for if he were a fresh waiter, I would have to order afresh, and if it were the same one, all I had to do was to remind him. While I was thinking it over, he went his way. A little later he returned, bringing every kind of food and drink, all for the fellows sitting to the right or the left of me.

Meanwhile fresh guests came and sat down and ordered all kinds of food and drink. The waiters ran and brought their orders to them. I began to wonder why they were being served first when I had been there before them. Maybe because I had asked for a whole loaf and you could not get a whole loaf at present, so they were waiting till they could get one from the baker. I began to berate myself for asking for a whole loaf, when I would have been satisfied with even a small slice.

10

What is the use of feeling remorseful after the deed: While I was bothering my heart, I saw a child sitting holding white bread with saffron of the kind that my mother, peace be with her, used to bake us for Purim, and which I can still taste now. I would have given the world for just a mouthful from that bread. My heart was standing still with hunger, and my two eyes were set on that child eating and jumping and scattering crumbs about him.

Once again the waiter brought a full tray. Since I was sure he was bringing it for me, I sat quietly and importantly, like a person who is in no particular hurry about his food. Alas, he did not put the tray in front of me but placed it in front of somebody else.

I began to excuse the waiter with the idea that the baker had not yet brought the whole loaf, and wanted to tell him that I was prepared to do without it. But I could not get a word out of my mouth because of my hunger.

All of a sudden a clock began striking. I took my watch out of my pocket and saw that it was half-past ten. Half-past ten is just a time like any other, but in spite of this I began to shake and tremble. Maybe because I remembered the letters of Dr. Ne'eman which I had not yet sent off. I stood up hastily in order to take the letters to the post office. As I stood up, I bumped against the waiter fetching a tray full of dishes and glasses and flagons and all kinds of food and drink. The waiter staggered and dropped the tray, and everything on it fell, food and drink alike; and he also slipped and fell. The guests turned their heads and stared, some of them in alarm and some of them laughing.

The hotel keeper came and calmed me down and led me back to my place, and he asked me to wait a little while until they fetched me a different meal. From his words I understood that the food that had fallen from the waiter's hands had been intended for me, and now they were preparing me another meal.

I possessed my soul in patience and sat waiting. Meanwhile my spirit flew from place to place. Now it flew to the kitchen where they were preparing my meal, and now to the post office from which letters were being sent. By that time the post office doors were already closed, and even if I were to go there it would be no use; but the spirit flew about after its fashion, even to places that the body might not enter.

11

They did not fetch me another meal. Maybe because they had not yet had time to prepare it, or maybe because the waiters were busy making up the accounts of the guests. In any case, some of the diners rose from the table, picking their teeth and yawning on their full stomachs. As they went out, some of them stared at me in astonishment, while others paid me no attention, as though I did not exist. When the last of the guests had left, the attendant came in and turned out the lights, leaving just one light still burning faintly. I sat at a table full of bones and leavings and empty bottles and a dirty tablecloth, and waited for my meal, as the hotel keeper himself had asked me to sit down and wait for it.

While I was sitting there I suddenly began to wonder whether I had lost the letters on the way, while I had been rolling on the ground with Gressler. I felt in my pocket and saw that they were not lost; but they had become dirty with the muck and the mire and the wine.

Once again a clock struck. My eyes were weary and the lamp was smoking and black silence filled the room. In the silence came the sound of a key creaking in the lock, like the sound of a nail being hammered into the flesh. I knew that they had locked me into the room and forgotten about me, and I would not get out until they opened next day. I closed my eyes tight and made an effort to fall asleep.

I made an effort to fall asleep and closed my eyes tight. I heard a kind of rustling and saw that a mouse had jumped onto the table and was picking at the bones. Now, said I to myself, he's busy with the bones. Then he'll gnaw the tablecloth, then he'll gnaw the chair I'm sitting on, and then he'll gnaw at me. First he'll start on my shoes, then on my socks, then on my foot, then on my calf, then on my thigh, then on all my body. I turned my eyes to the wall and saw the clock. I waited for it to strike again and frighten the mouse, so that it would run away before it reached me. A cat came and I said, Here is my salvation. But the mouse paid no attention to the cat and the cat paid no attention to the mouse; and this one stood gnawing and that one stood chewing.

Meanwhile the lamp went out and the cats eyes shone with a greenish light that filled all the room. I shook and fell. The cat shivered and the mouse jumped and both of them stared at me in alarm, one from one side and the other from the other. Suddenly the sound of trotting hooves and carriage wheels was heard, and I knew that Mr. Gressler was coming back from his drive. I called him, but he did not answer me.

Mr. Gressler did not answer me, and I lay there dozing until I fell asleep. By the time day broke, I was awakened by the sound of cleaners, men and women, coming to clean the building. They saw me and stared at me in astonishment with their brooms in their hands. At length they began laughing and asked, "Who's this fellow lying here?" Then the waiter came and said, "This is the one who was asking for the whole loaf."

I took hold of my bones and rose from the floor. My clothes were dirty, my head was heavy on my shoulders, my legs were heavy under me, my lips were cracked, and my throat was dry, while my teeth were on edge with a hunger-sweat. I stood up and went out of the hotel into the street, and from the street into another until I reached my house. All the time my mind was set on the letters that Dr. Ne'eman had handed over for me to send off by post. But that day was Sunday, when the post office was closed for things that the clerk did not consider important.

After washing off the dirt I went out to get myself some food. I was all alone at that time. My wife and children were out of the country, and all the bother of my food fell on me alone.

Translated by I. M. Lask.

Other works by Agnon: *Days of Awe* (1948); *The Bridal Canopy* (1967); *In the Heart of the Seas* (1986); *Shira* (1989); *Only Yesterday* (2002); *A Simple Story* (2014).

Yehudah Burla

1886–1969

The Jerusalem-born Hebrew writer Yehudah Burla came from a rabbinic Sephardi family that had lived in the Land of Israel for three hundred years. He was educated at yeshivas and at a teachers' seminary in Jerusalem and worked as a teacher and administrator in Jewish schools in Palestine and in Damascus from 1908 to 1944, after which he held various civil service positions. During World War I, he was drafted into the Ottoman army and served as a translator for a German officer. His wartime experiences provided him with material for his early fiction. He was one of the first Hebrew writers to feature Sephardi and Middle Eastern Jews in his work, which was known for its "Eastern" color.

Battles

1933

I. The Way of a Man

It is often said that among the Gentiles there are men of noble lineage whose features and outward appearance show that nothing but the purest and most refined aristocratic blood flows in their veins. Perhaps this is true, and then again perhaps it is just talk, for blood is invisible to the eye, and nobody can examine or analyze it to determine whether it is noble, or just that of ordinary mortals. At the least, the tale is suspect. But on the other hand, where Jews are concerned, it is quite beyond doubt that there are men and women sprung from learned, pious stock, with the blood of the meek and the righteous in their veins, whose hearts are pure as the heavens themselves and whose souls are a perpetual abode of humility, peace and charity. For in their case, their virtues are evident and manifest to every eye, in thought and action, in speech and silence—throughout their life's journey on earth.

Thus it was clearly evident from the appearance of Mistress Reina Abouav and her husband, Master Gedaliah Abouav, that the two of them, both he and she, were descended from the stock of great rabbis, outstanding in learning and distinguished for humility—and the annals of both their lives and the tale of their actions bear indubitable witness to the sacred stream that flowed in their veins.

It is true the two were entirely different from one another; indeed it is doubtful if there was ever another couple of such absolute opposites as Master Gedaliah and his wife. Nevertheless, they were both known to all by their ways and their doings as kind and merciful folk, exemplary in the service of God and in the love of His Torah. Nor were their ways separate, but they followed a straight path together, in good days as in bad.

For all that, however, they were unlike in many respects. He Master Gedaliah, was a merry man fond of and always eager for a boisterous good time, while she, Mistress Reina, loved peace and quiet, and was never happier than when engaged in a quiet cosy talk. He would flare up quickly into a great rage, to the point of—for he was by nature subject to fainting. For instance, if anyone insulted him—a creditor, or just an irascible person, or someone who was stronger than he—and if Master Gedaliah could not give as good as he got, he would at once rush home and sit down cross-legged in a corner, still and silent as if his lips had stuck together, his head between his knees because of his great mortification, and thus he would fall into a prolonged coma, so that very often you would suddenly hear, among Master Gedaliah's neighbors, a frightened voice with tidings of disaster: "Master Gedaliah has passed out."

Mistress Reina, on the contrary, was slow to anger. Very seldom in her life had she been really angry. She was constantly dropping words of wisdom in censure of anger; for this was a fault she always taught herself to control and avoid.

Again, Master Gedaliah was hasty in his actions, and excitable by temperament, was unable to look ahead, while she was restrained, sober in her opinions. She was always quoting the Arab proverb:

"My word it was my servant, while in my mouth it stayed;
Escaped, it was the mistress, and I the captive maid."

But the difference that stamped all their lives was concerned with the knowledge of the Torah. For, in contrast to the usual situation, she was the learned one, while he was just an ordinary Jew, who was never considered a scholar. A simple man he was, knowing but little Scripture, Mishna, and Zohar. But just for that reason Master Gedaliah was all his life an enthusiastic devotee of the wise and learned, always eager to sit in on their gatherings; in this he was like a man who in the darkest night along a desolate road, runs through cold and wind towards a ray of light, yearning with every fibre of his being for rest, warmth and shelter.

Being a son of rabbis, of noble and exalted pedigree, Master Gedaliah was a decent and comely man, though he was low of stature. Ever since he had married Reina of the house of Najara, he had worn a fine black turban, as was the custom of men of good family in those days. He was very handsome: his face clear and bright; his beard reddish-yellow, like gold; his eyes blue and beautiful. And yet Mistress Reina used to tell her family from time to time that although he was handsome and she was never exactly a beauty, she had not loved him at first. In fact, she had felt no love for him for a whole year. The reason was, she explained, that she had wanted a learned husband, a man well-versed in the Torah. She had been most unhappy when they had presented him to her. Her father, the Rabbi, was dead, and she had felt that they had offered her an unlearned bridegroom only because she was an orphan. It could never have happened had her father been alive. Afterwards, however, little by little she had undergone a change of heart and come to love him, consoling herself with the thought that if she prayed to God perhaps she would bring forth wise sons.

So Mistress Reina had learned to love her husband and to honor and respect him as the law required; moreover, she came to realize that he had more virtues than failings.

Master Gedaliah had always shown particular prowess in his struggle against the evil impulse. All his life was no more than a single war, a series of battles—some great, some small, some hard and some easy—in all of which he had wrestled with himself, to conquer the evil impulse, and he had prevailed.

For whoever saw Master Gedaliah in the days of his youth, before the judgment fell upon him (as a result of the tragedy of his wife which we shall shortly relate), and whoever knew the strength and joy that was in him, as well as the humility and lowliness of spirit—would undoubtedly agree that his life was a turbulent spirit; his life was marked by light and darkness; desires and aversions wrestled within him, and his soul was a battlefield between the good instinct and the bad. At times he would dedicate himself to good deeds, learning and piety, and at others he would give full rein to his appetite for merriment, song and friendship. At such times, he would quote the words of the Torah: "Half for yourselves and half for the Lord!"

Everyone could clearly see how open was his soul, how frankly he gave himself to love and joy. Master Gedaliah's love was a great love—for earth and heaven, for man and the Almighty, for the sights of creation and for all God's creatures—for man and woman too, to put it quite plainly. But his love was pure, without any taint of sin, or guile. Of course he had been repeatedly tempted by his hot blood, but such was Master Gedaliah's valor that he would bear himself doughtily on such occasions—he would always manage to save his soul and after some slight or sinful thought, immediately recant his error, pouring out his heart in fasting and prayer and finding no repose until he had given to charity and thereafter purified himself in the ritual bath.

In general Gedaliah's qualities appeared in accordance with the order of the days of the week. On a Sunday, for instance, he would spend half the day in a listless mood, sad and silent, or simply weary and crushed—and not only in body (for everyone knows that all Jews are tired, more or less, on Sunday because of the numerous Sabbath foods), but also in spirit. His soul would be troubled and he would feel a load of regret because of what had taken place on the Sabbath, though he did not clearly understand the reason for his depression.

But the same Master Gedaliah seemed to be a completely different kind of person when the Sabbath came round. As he left the synagogue after the morning prayer, his face would appear to be bathed in light as if the radiance of the Sabbath morning had penetrated his very heart. He would go from house to house with a band of rhymesters, singers and cantors (for he held the hereditary post of synagogue warden) to fulfill certain obligations; the reading of *Idra Zuta* with a small group in the house of a mourner—rewarded by a gift of eggs—on some Sabbaths there were many mourners, and hence many eggs, and sometimes there were few. Afterwards they would come to the house of someone who on this Sabbath was celebrating a betrothal or a wedding or a circumcision. There the rhymesters would recite a chorus for a few moments, and receive in payment a titbit of some delicacy on the tip of the fork and a touch of perfume poured on the hands.

Once these "studies" and "visits" were ended, Master Gedaliah would turn homewards, accompanied by his son, little Shimon, and on his way he would go to the nearby courtyards and invite his neighbors to taste the oven-meats that he had on his table for the morning meal. For his kitchen was famous among all the neighbors and friends of the house of Abouav. Those who tasted of his Sabbath platter testified that there was nothing like it even in the homes of the rich and highborn. For Gedaliah would invent new savory hot dishes that no-one else had thought of, for example, spleens stuffed with rice, with tender pine-nuts and much spice; or thin noodles concealing a fat chicken or a goodly duck, like a silkworm wrapped in the threads of its cocoon; or lamb's breast, filled with stuffing flavored with all kinds of fragrant spices and soaked in oil—and other such novelties. Gedaliah would think up the idea, while his wife, Reina, an expert cook, would put it into practical effect. Thus neighbors were drawn to their home every week to partake of the Sabbath delicacies, richly seasoned with oil and spices.

When Master Gedaliah reached the door of his house, he would immediately lift up his voice, in joy and gladness, in the hymn: "Holy is the land of Israel" and continue with all the prescribed passages from the *Zohar* until the recital of the *kiddush* itself over the winecup.

During the meal itself, while the great dishes of oven-meats steamed, filling room and courtyard with their odor, and the members of the family were still eating and drinking the neighbors would already be coming in to have a taste. Immediately the sound of joy and laughter would fill the house. Some would praise the flavor of the delicacies, and some would marvel at their novelty.

Then Master Gedaliah could be seen entering more and more into his own Sabbath atmosphere. And here it is worth remembering that by this time Master Gedaliah had already managed to imbibe, according to law and custom, a goodly measure of liquid refreshment: first, the greater part of the *kiddush* cup; second, a little glass of brandy after the fish; third, a glass of brandy and water on eating the eggs from the oven and from the prior celebrations (for the better roasted and lighter the eggs, the tastier they were, and the more conducive to drinking); fourth, when eating meat dipped in fat, a glass of wine with the whole company was a matter of course.

At this stage Master Gedaliah would reach a kind of zenith and shower goodwill upon the company, with jesting and merriment, rhyme and song, and meanwhile he would favor the neighbors—men and women—with another titbit, another slice, of the delicacies on the table. Sometimes he would thrust three fingers into the corners of the dish like an artist knowing the secrets of his handiwork, bringing up some of the hidden treasures out of the depths, and bestow this wonderful morsel upon one of his favorite women neighbors, giving it to her affectionately straight from fingers to mouth. And when he was brimming over with delight from the meal and the praises of the neighbors, the end of the meal would bring with it the glass of the final benediction, which is also, by law, drunk mainly by the master of the feast.

After rising from the table, all the company would go out to the veranda or up to the roof and converse in the open air. Then Gedaliah would really be in his element. He would make the round of his guests, offering them from a paper bag in his hand, large, red, shiny apples, fresh, juicy pears, and all kinds of fruit, of the finest quality and highest price, not to be found at all in the Jewish quarter (for he would seek them in the distant Gentile districts, where Jews did not generally go)—all in honor of the Sabbath and in order to enjoy the praises of his guests.

And this is how he would wait on them:

Dressed in a light robe (without belt or girdle), its skirts flying in the wind, he would go to and fro presenting the fine fruit with affectionate, knightly gestures, like a generous host granting tokens of favor, especially to the handsome girls or young women among his neighbors. He would follow one, giving her a beautiful colored peach, big as an orange, and a moment later he would be seen walking by another, presenting her with some even more unusual fruit. And as Gedaliah rejoiced the hearts of his friends, he would consequently fill his own heart with joy. Thus he would continue, multiplying joy and gladness until it seemed as if the colors of the clothes of the pretty girl and women were mingling with the colors of the fruit, the apples, pears, sweet lemons and Yussuf Effendis, into one great galaxy of color; and the glowing faces and shining eyes of the beauties would be interwoven and intermingled with the rays of the Sabbath sun, filing the chambers of Master Gedaliah's heart and soul. And, thereupon, the alluring movements of the women's thighs, and breasts, would work powerfully on Gedaliah's mind, and in his

excitement, he would, for instance, accost one of the maidens (naturally, the most beautiful of them all), and bob up and down beside her, scraping with his foot, waving his arms, like a cock dropping beside a hen, and then he would caper after the girl emitting little chirps of delight. Or he would stand face to face with an attractive woman, bringing up from his throat a neighing sound just like a horse, exulting and scraping with his foot, and then drawing alarmingly close until there was scarcely a step between them—but as if by a miracle he would always manage to break away at the last minute and go back to some other matter.

At times like these, his wife, the wise and pious Reina, would observe his tricks from the side, calmly and tolerantly, or else she would pay no attention to them at all, for as the days went on she came to understand that such behavior was natural to him, a matter of temperament, and no cause for drastic steps or alarm. For him they were the fulfillment of the precept to rejoice on the Sabbath; in short the ways of a good and simple Jew not versed in the Torah . . .

Such was the way of Master Gedaliah in the morning hours of the Sabbath until he lay down for a long sleep, to fulfill the injunction: "Sleep on the Sabbath is a pleasure."

Now, if we tried to write down all the ways and customs of Master Gedaliah on the afternoon of the Sabbath until the end of the day, and all the more so if we wished to tell of his ways throughout the week, we would not have space enough to contain it all.

But it is worth while watching Gedaliah at a gathering of rhymesters and songsters on the Sabbath day. Whenever there happened to be a wedding Sabbath or a circumcision among his friends and acquaintances, Master Gedaliah would prepare himself from the eve of the holy day like a traveler equipping himself setting out on his journey, or like a commander planning his tactics and preparing everything necessary in good time.

First he would send to the house of the celebrant the *budjam* (a gift for the Sabbath midday meal: a large jar of wine together with sweetmeats and choice fruits), as is right and fitting. His fruit was famous, and the wine of the finest, so that the sages among the company would always find it incumbent to pronounce over it the special blessing: "Who art good and doest good." And when the company had drunk their fill of the wine provided by the generosity of the givers of the *budjam*, Gedaliah would sit down among the singers and become their patron and benefactor, bestowing upon them good things from his pockets, treasures of most excellent dainties and sweet-meats, with which he would encourage the singers, like one who pours oil upon a bonfire . . . He would be aroused to a particular state of ecstasy and enthusiasm if there was present a young man or boy gifted with a fine voice. To him he would pay particular attention, and every time the singer would bring forth a musical trill he would leave his place, jump and dance for joy, join in himself with tremendous enthusiasm and even go so far as to embrace and kiss the youthful singer before the eyes of the company; for the music would light a conflagration in Master Gedaliah's heart like a fire licking and devouring dry straw.

II. A Shoot from Rabbinical Stock

Mistress Reina Abouav's neighbors and acquaintances, with the exception of a few respected and familiars, were mostly simple women,—but all of them knew that her merits were due to her rabbinical heritage. Near neighbors and even distant ones would often submit questions to her connected with the dietary laws or other religious prohibitions—and she always gave a decision, but generally concluded by saying that so far as her memory went, that was the law according to the opinion of her sainted father, but heaven forbid that a woman should take upon herself the responsibility for a legal ruling—they should consult a sage.

And whenever the women heard her words of wisdom on one subject or another, they would praise her piety (naturally in her absence) saying: "That's what it is to come of good stock. And is it every woman who has her privileges! She is a daughter of the great luminary, Rabbi Shlomo Najara of Hebron, who was also rabbi of Alexandria, in Egypt, and won a great name there, like one of the ancient sages."

And when a woman stricken by fate came to Reina to relate her griefs, she would feel that it was a sister to whom she was pouring out her soul, for Mistress Reina would join her own tears, in sincere compassion, with those of her visitor. Not only that, but she would, as it were, sprinkle healing drops upon the wounded heart and sweet words of consolation, drawn from Holy Writ and from traditional lore and wisdom. And her words were like a gracious caress on the shoulder of her auditress, so that the women would say, as they gossiped with each other; "Sometimes a woman comes to Mistress Reina like a broken vessel beyond repair, and leaves her healed and refreshed."

You might therefore conclude that if Mistress Reina's heart was so generous, and her ways with her fellow creatures so gracious, it could only be because her own lot was pleasant and her path in life smooth.

But this was not so. Gedaliah, her husband, though not needy, had no stable livelihood; he lacked the security which comes from trade or property, and yet he lived all his life after the style of a man of means, and his house was wide open—especially to sages and scholars.

How could this be? There were three aspects of Gedaliah's husbandry: the first was, if you like, a matter of spiritual affirmation: he was always filled with trust in the Almighty: "Cast thy burden upon the Lord," he would say, "and the Lord will be merciful." Such faith, he declared, was a cure for half the troubles of life. Thus he depended most of his days upon the mercies of his Creator without knowing today what tomorrow would bring.

The second quality was more material, for Gedaliah in a sense subsisted from the "grace and favor" that he found in people's eyes; for he would borrow from one and pay a second, borrow from a third and pay a fourth, and so on. Hence he would say, by way of parable, that he existed in this world by changing tarbushes, taking off a tarbush from one man's head and putting it on another's—and so on and so forth.

And the third quality, which was the most substantial of the three, was the custodianship of the graves of the righteous. For he had in his charge the keys to several tombs, and was also in charge of the synagogue and the ritual baths. All these keys opened before him a small entry to the gates of material fortune. But as soon as he had a few pennies in his possession, he would immediately be filled with confidence and spend them in carefree fashion, quoting and fulfilling the words of the Scriptures: "Blessed be the Lord day by day." And then there would issue from his house, on Sabbaths and at the going out of the holy day, the sound of song and music, joy and merriment. And when the channels of plenty were closed—which happened many days in the year—and his pocket was like an empty well, he would go about sad and despondent by the roadside, or stay shrunken and shriveled at home, like a dry, empty wineskin whose liquor is exhausted. Then his world would be dark and he would castigate himself at length for his wastefulness and irresponsibility—until Heaven had mercy on him and he would once and again drag home on Thursdays and Fridays full baskets "in honor of the Sabbath."

And his wife, instead of coming forward to remind him of his days of distress, would welcome him with a pleasant smile and say to herself: "May God reward him for his generosity."

She behaved in this fashion because she realized that you cannot change a man's nature. His generosity was as natural to him as the beating of his heart. And besides, she knew that the way he fluctuated between depression and happiness was due to the absence of that one element—the Torah—which alone regulates the instincts and impulses of a man's heart.

But who would have expected it—for who can understand the secrets of God?—that such a thing would happen to this saintly woman!! Alas, Mistress Reina lost the sight of her eyes at the age of forty-five, after a few months' sickness, and she and her house were visited by grievous days, days of gloom and tribulation, and her last years were filled with bitterness and jealousy.

How could such a thing have been? How deep are the ways of God!

III. The Calamity

That day when Mistress Reina came home from hospital at sunset after the loss of her sight—led slowly by her two older daughters, with a white cloth covering her eyes—let not that bitter day be counted in the number of days.

As she set foot in the entrance to the large courtyard where she lived in the Old City, the evil tidings immediately spread throughout the neighborhood, and all the houses in the courtyard were at once emptied of their inhabitants: women stopped their work, boys and girls left their play, old and young hastened together—and all stood like mourners, each on the threshold of his house, grieving at the calamity, shaking their heads sadly as the blind woman felt about uncertainly for the ground under her feet, their eyes dropping a secret tear. At that hour of grief the people of the neighborhood felt as though they were witnessing an injustice that had been committed—if such a thing were possible—in Heaven in the light of day; they were struck dumb and their tongues cleaved to the roofs of their mouths. The grief and pain when the dead are brought to burial are nothing to the bringing of a blind man home. For unlike a living man led into darkness, the dead feel nothing and know nothing. The people's hearts were cleft in twain and they had to summon up all their strength to control themselves lest they should sin with their lips.

But when the house was reached and the mistress of the house was set down in a corner on a low cushion, the whole room, despite the many women standing and sitting, seemed to be completely empty, because all were choking back their sorrow and shame. Then a certain woman came in, called Sol de Nahmias, a former neighbor. As she approached the corner where Mistress Reina sat, she bent down and knelt at her feet, kissing her hands tenderly, at the same time wailing very quietly, and then she gave voice to her grief and astonishment, addressing the company in the following words:

"Is it true, good people, tell me, is this all not a dream, an evil dream? Has the light indeed departed from those eyes that used to illuminate all hearts with their goodness and compassion? Shall we see her no more going to and fro at home and is the street, shall we never again hear the sweetness of her voice? Which of us can enjoy the light of the world when she is thus pent up in a corner? Is the sight not enough to drive a person out for her senses? Who needed this sacrifice, O, you good people, tell me!"

Then bursting into tears, she ceased, and all the company wept with her, dumb and silent; no one could find a word to answer.

Mistress Reina sat still and submissive, her back bent and her head bowed, holding Sol's hands as she spoke and pressing them with love in silence.

And when her voice was stilled, Mistress Reina spoke—and her voice was quiet and kind and gracious as it had always been:

"Sister Sol, you have spoken freely as your heart moved you, and I did not interrupt you until you had ended, but, sister, let us not sin with our lips when the Lord chastens us. True, He, Blessed be His Name, will not inflict his punishment when we speak presumptuously—for it is from pain and anguish that we speak. And our sages said: 'A man is not judged by what he says in his hour of grief.' But Heaven forbid that we should question His actions, for what are we and what are our thoughts, our knowledge, our comprehension, that we should understand the ways and the deeds of God, His verdict and His righteousness? When our eyes are open, we walk like the blind; perhaps we shall be clear-sighted when our eyes are closed. Is this not possible, sisters? With our eyes we see everything, but do we understand in our hearts what we are seeing? How often we see clearly and do not understand, we look and do not know. How, then, shall we—Heaven forbid a thousand times—speak rebelliously when the

Almighty's rod falls upon our head? Is it not more fitting that we should give thanks to God who has chosen to visit His judgment upon us while we are still here, in this world?"

Thus Mistress Reina controlled her anguish and spoke consolingly to the hearts of those who saw her. And she continued at length to praise the deeds of God, and her voice grew more quiet, but she went on, as if speaking to herself: "And King David, of blessed memory, said: 'Such knowledge is too wonderful for me; it is high, I cannot attain it' (and she explained very thoroughly to her hearers, in Ladino, the meaning of the verse). I too must say: It is too wonderful for me, I cannot attain unto it. Why has this punishment been visited on me of all women? Why this stern and grievous penalty, which means . . . so much . . . degradation . . . shame . . . like an outcast dog . . . cast out from the world with shame and contempt . . . ? Whom have I shamed? Whose honor have I defamed?"

Meanwhile, Gedaliah, the master of the house, sat in the room full of people, and also after everyone had gone, in another corner at the opposite end of the room, like one put to shame, silent and still. His head was bowed between his knees and his eyes stared fixedly on the floor. In his deep dejection, he hardly heard what was being spoken, and the people of the house were anxious and disturbed, lest—Heaven forbid—his silence should end in a swoon. But though dejected and crushed by the hand of God, which had so stunned him, nevertheless he did not come to the point of swooning, for he was like her of whom it was said: "I sleep but my heart wakes." At the sight of the ruin of his house his heart was troubled even more than during his wife's sickness. And he toiled and wearied to compel himself to discover the reason for this punishment that had befallen his house. And since he was like one who beats upon the gates of heaven, he did not faint away, for he was busily enquiring: Why and wherefore has this castigation been inflicted? What does this finger of God signify? And, most inexplicable of all: Why had the fury of God fallen upon her? Why upon her? It would have been right and proper if God had poured out His wrath and indignation upon him; his eyes deserved darkness and blindness. It was his eyes that had wandered among the sights of this world. Beyond a doubt he had transgressed the commandment: "That ye go not astray after your heart and your eyes"—many times he had transgressed. His heart knew the bitterness of his soul. And how was it that she, the righteous

and saintly, had been condemned to degradation, while he had gone free?

Overcome by a sense of sin and guilt towards his partner, Gedaliah saw himself as a man sitting in filthy clothes next to another dressed in pure white. Like one suddenly overwhelmed by debts, who tries first of all to set his accounts in good order so Master Gedaliah was obsessed more and more with an urgent compulsion to lay bare all his accounts, the secrets of his heart, to make a full and complete confession—at least to himself—of all the sins he had committed with the glance of the eye and the enjoyment of forbidden sights.

Thus there rose up in his heart thoughts of repentance for all kinds of faults and transgressions in the past. And the more he examined his actions in days gone by, the more he called to mind many and various memories of his misdeeds.

Uppermost in his thought was one incident three or four years ago. On a Friday morning, having finished taking home all the things required for the Sabbath, he went in good spirits to the ritual baths and bathed in honor of the Sabbath. When he had finished and dressed himself, he saw from the dark entry, standing in the doorway, illuminated in the bright sunlight, the butcher's son, Nachman Russo, a lad who sang wonderfully well. The boy seemed to be waiting for someone, his face was ruddy and shining, and his merry, glowing eyes were for some reason—looking upwards like a dove, innocent and comely, waiting to fly up into the skies. Thus he saw him from the dark entry, but was himself not seen. And when he left the entrance and approached the doorway and came up to the lad, the other turned his shining face towards him, as if delighted to meet him. And he, as if pushed by the force of a hidden hand (the hand of the Evil One, no doubt) took hold of the boy's head and kissed him several times quickly and hastily, saying to him: "God be gracious to you, my son, God be gracious . . . be gracious to you . . ."

And the lad stood looking at him with wide open eyes . . .

Now surely this was a transgression of the command: "And ye shall not go astray . . ."

And now another occasion came to the surface—when he fell because of his neighbor, Mistress Zinbol. . . .

It was the New Moon of the month of Ellul, in the afternoon. He had been standing all day by the boiling vat preparing the liquor (it was two years ago that it happened). A sharp, pleasant odor, refreshing to body and soul, issued from the door of the cellar and spread all over the yard. The liquor was almost ready and he had been tasting and tasting its quality several times—merry and joyful that he had succeeded in making a brandy that literally made the heart sing. At that moment, in the twilight, his glance fell on a window in the second storey, in the neighboring yard, beside the stairs of the synagogue. There up above stood the widow Zinbol, polishing the window pane, and she did not notice him, occupied as she was with her work. As he raised his head he saw the gleam of her bare thighs—and in his lust he sought to look still more, bent over towards the stairs, and in his heedlessness his foot slipped and he fell from the top of the stairs to the bottom. This was a fall of the body after the fall of the soul—and although on the Monday fast of that week, as he lay bruised in bed, he tried to confess and atone for this unseemly act, nevertheless the power of his lust seemed to him until this moment greater than the power of repentance . . .

And again another incident . . . and still another . . . Painful memories awakened, stood there before him as they happened, and passed by in succession before Gedaliah's eyes as he sat still and silent, ashamed and confounded, staring fixedly on the ground.

IV. Trials

Since the disaster fell upon his house, Master Gedaliah forswore all contact with the affairs of this world. He would close his eyes, so that he should not see, and his ears, that he should not hear, abstaining from all converse with friends and acquaintances. In distress he bore his fate—and suffered too, from lack of livelihood—lowering his soul to the dust.

So Master Gedaliah passed the time, like a recluse, stricken by the hand of God. All alone he went on his way, morose and gloomy to his fellow men, confused and perplexed in himself. Every day he would spend long hours at prayer and linger in the synagogue. Ever since his heart was broken, he doubled and trebled the time he devoted to study, and each day would say: "I shall read three times eighteen chapters of the Mishna, corresponding to the numerical value of the word *hai*—life—and the five books of the Psalms, to invoke a perfect healing on my wife Reina, daughter of Esther." This burden he assumed, fasting regularly and rigorously every Monday and Thursday, and dedicating these fasts clearly and expressly to "a perfect healing for my wife, Reina, daughter of Esther."

Gedaliah was downcast in the secrecy of his soul, ashamed even to be seen by his fellow men. He felt that they were pointing at him: Behold the man from whom God has withheld his mercy.

Before his wife herself he was particularly ashamed. He felt that she surely knew and understood that it was on his account that all this sorrow had come upon her. Beyond a doubt these were the feelings she cherished in her heart, and right and truth were on her side. His heart knew the bitterness of her soul. Hence ever since she had lost the sight of her eyes Master Gedaliah lost his way to his wife in speech; his mouth found no words to utter—why should he trouble her ears with meaningless talk, if he did not dare to reveal his heart. And if he spoke without revealing to her all the secret thoughts of his soul, she would surely think that his heart was too foolish to understand and his soul bereft of all discernment. Should he make light of himself by speaking what was not in his heart, and be like a boor in her eyes, with no understanding in his spirit or feeling in his soul? So he found it best to be silent and avoided conversation with her, speaking only the simplest and most ordinary things, whilst his heart was a tomb for all his great compassion. Thus it was that Gedaliah was unwillingly sundered from his wife, as if he had lost the way to her heart—and he was sevenfold more lonely in his gloomy home.

And people said, seeing Gedaliah in his heartbreak, in his loneliness and separation from his friends: Indeed the hand of God has fallen upon the man. How he has altered and changed his ways! How he has lost the light of his days before his time, forgetting life and abandoning all that is good!

As for Gedaliah himself, his heart was heavy; he found it far from easy to eschew the pleasures of this world. Like plucking out a hook from the flesh, so it pained him to pluck out life and joy from his heart. Many times he sat, in the synagogue or a corner of his room, gloomy and silent—moved with compassion for himself. His heart ached with grief in his loneliness, especially when the sound of song and gladness from others' homes rose to his ears. In secret, none seeing, his eyes would brim with tears: Why had he been so doomed? How could he bear it all? Why and wherefore? Surely, He, the Blessed One, his Rock and Creator, had made him thus, as he was, with a heart yearning for life, thirsting for song and gladness, for love and affection—a creature of His hands. Previously Gedaliah had believed that God had cast his eyes upon him in love and favor. Hence he had always served the Lord in joy, pursuing good deeds and observing the Law, honoring and glorifying God both with his strength and worldly goods. With a whole heart and a willing soul he had always given their due to both Heaven and earth—"Half for yourself and half for the Lord"—but now his world had darkened. His wife had been cut off from the living, for a blind person is regarded as dead. And he, the husband of the afflicted one, was also as one defunct.

Heavily, the days flowed on; were it not for the few hours of satisfaction still remaining, when he could feast his soul on the blessing of song, who can tell whether Gedaliah would have endured. Apart from the soul-refreshing hour when the Torah was read with a trilling cadence every Sabbath by the well-skilled cantor, he still had one great moment, the hour before the dawn, when the *muezzin*—not to be compared, of course, with the cantor—would ascend to the minaret close to Master Gedaliah's synagogue, and sing eloquent praise of the Creator. Almost every night, summer and winter, Gedaliah would rise early, wash his hands, read the midnight service and hasten to the roof on the synagogue in the last watch of the night to listen attentively to the wonderful song. At that hour, in the mystic dusk before the dawn, above the quiet roofs, amid the fresh, cool breezes, Gedaliah would feel as if he had been transported to another world, where he could hear something of the music of the morning stars singing together. He would melt as he listened alone, his heart dilating and throbbing with yearning—and his soul revived and re-awakened.

When people noticed him sometimes rising alone before the dawn to stand on the roof of the synagogue they said: "God preserve his understanding! What is a man's spirit and what is it worth!" [. . .]

Translated by Misha Louvish.

Other works by Burla: *Beli kokhav* (1920); *Ishto hasenua* (1928); *Alilot akavya* (1939); *In Darkness Striving* (1968).

Samuel Eichelbaum

1894–1967

The son of Russian immigrants, Samuel Eichelbaum was a leading Argentine dramatist in the 1920s, 1930s, and 1940s, his plays a mainstay of the Buenos Aires theatrical season. He was raised amidst the Jewish agricultural colonies, which provided the inspiration for his early short fiction. "A Good Harvest" drew on his own family's experience: his father, who found the isolation of the colonies stultifying, burned two of his fields and moved the family to the capital. Eichelbaum's plays are known for their intense self-analysis and introspection, their probing of human motivation, and their searching for hidden motives behind even the most trivial acts. Several of his plays feature urban, middle-class Jewish characters.

A Good Harvest
1933

For four years now he had been working the two hundred acres of farm land they had given him when he arrived in Argentina from Russia. The Roschpina colony of Entre Ríos was the most cheerful one in the area, but this fact didn't affect his aversion to rural tasks. When he'd sailed for these lands, he'd agreed to accept the farm solely with the goal of getting to America and then later being able to dedicate himself to his trade. Never for a moment had he resigned himself to the idea of working the land. He didn't feel competent enough to do it, nor did he think the countryside was a suitable ambiance for his spirit. On the trip, because of unforeseen events he had to renounce, for the time being, his desire to settle in the city and dedicate his energies to mechanics, which was the trade that he loved as one loves his chosen work. It had been a trip so full of tragedy that it had totally exhausted him. Upon reaching port in Buenos Aires he no longer had any hopes, plans or desires. He never disagreed with his wife's suggestions, and she never dared to disagree with her mother.

So it was that Bernardo Drugova, to his mother-in-law's great and understandable surprise, without realizing it, turned into a bland and submissive son-in-law. When he didn't oppose his wife's desires, he indirectly obeyed his mother-in-law, since she always exercised total control over her daughter. He took possession of his farm with an indifference that was in visible contrast to the joy felt by other colonizers who had immigrated with him. Farm chores were completely alien to him, but because he had an extraordinary gift for learning manual labor, he very quickly became one of the most expert farmers in the area. Nevertheless, Drugova hated the land. When his wife gave him his first son, it reawakened in him more intensely than ever, his desire to live in the city. He expressed this to his wife and mother-in-law a number of times, and each time, he met with aggressive hostility from the old lady. Although his wife wasn't opposed exactly, neither did she share her husband's desires. Her attitude was one of indifference more from fear of her mother's anger, than from a desire to preserve the well-being she might enjoy where she happened to be. Drugova didn't pursue it. He didn't want to cause his mother-in-law's suffering, because of her age on the one hand, and her grumbling disposition on the other. He didn't believe that the stress that the move to Buenos Aires might cause the old woman would be a major and decisive factor in her health, as they wanted him to believe. Nevertheless, he sometimes thought, since both of them said this, it was better not to be too suspicious. Thus, Drugova rationalized and kept quiet. For the rest, the old woman knew how to argue skillfully when it came to upsetting her son-in-law's plans:

"Here you have bread and a roof," she would say, "nobly earned bread and an honorable roof. You have no reason whatsoever to reject the destiny you accepted when you started out."

"What would you do in the city? Work in your trade? Every city has a thousand men more competent than you in the same trade."

"It's important to think about the child," he would dare to argue. "We ought to give him a good education. I don't want him to be a laborer like me, ignorant like me."

"Educate him in what is good and honorable, which are the only things that matter. Let him learn to plow and sow the land and he will be good and honorable. Do you think, by chance, that he might become a rabbi? It would be a sin of vanity to aspire to that; a sin as great as if you aspired to make a scholar of him. Aspiring to grandeur is a sin unbecoming to poor people. My love as a grandmother is as great as your love as a father, but mine is sensible and humble. It doesn't need anything grandiose to nourish it. I don't demand anything from my grandson in order to love him."

The discussion would invariably come to an end, thanks to the discreet silence observed by Bernardo, who, although he felt violent sometimes, always managed to control himself.

For a long time, maybe a year, Drugova stopped talking about moving to Buenos Aires. To his wife and mother-in-law it seemed evident that he had abandoned the idea, a supposition doubly pleasing to them: because of the renunciation it implied in itself and the triumph it implied for them. Bernardo worked with such effort

that they thought he had completely adapted to his situation. Moreover, the harvest promised to be bountiful enough to complete the well-being which reigned on Drugova's farm, where three enormous stacks, two of wheat and one of oats, stood like hills of gold. The little one, meanwhile, had grown strong and beautiful. The color in his eyes had finally settled and whether it was so or not, the fact was that he seemed to look at the fields with utter indifference, as if his progenitor had transmitted to him his hatred of the land.

In Roschpina, the neighbours had already closed deals for the sale of their harvest. Drugova hadn't done so yet. His wife, on several occasions, suggested that he get on with the threshing, fearing that prices would suddenly suffer a strong drop as sometimes happened.

"I'm not saying you should be in a hurry to sell it, but I do think you should ready the harvest. You might get a really good offer on condition of immediate delivery, and you would be obliged to refuse it, hurting yourself."

Bernardo, a man of few words, answered such exemplary and sensible observations with silence, communicating the sense of having heeded the advice they always carried.

One morning, long before daybreak, Drugova awakened. He looked around, probably in search of some filter of light that would help him guess the time. He found everything dark and decided to get up. First he checked on his wife, who was in her usual deep sleep, her dark and muscular arms outstretched, her thick dark hair undone. Two minutes later, from the door of his tool shed, he pensively observed a tenuous and whitish-blue sky announcing good weather. A full moon, pure, limpid and transparent, adorned everything. Slowly he walked toward the fields. The farm dogs saw their master and followed him, although he tried in vain to stop them. Drugova reached the first shock of wheat, magnificent, unmovable like a house on strong and deep foundations, passed his rough hand over some stalks, as if he wanted to caress them, and felt the soft, pleasant moisture of the dew. Then, almost as if without thinking, he extracted a box of matches from one of his pockets, lit one and put it as far as he could under the stack which seemed to shudder at the threat from the insignificant little flame. When the man was sure that his intentions were being carried out, he directed his steps toward the next one, scarcely fifty meters from the first, and repeated the operation. When this was done, he noticed that the first stack of wheat was giving off a thick blackish smoke that thinned out disappearing entirely at a few meters.

Bernado started back in haste. Carefully, he undressed and got back into bed. About half an hour had passed when he heard the dogs barking furiously and immediately heard some knocking on one of the window shutters. It was Rogelio, a native servant from the neighboring farm, who had seen the smoke and then came at a gallop to give the warning.

"Don Bernardo, your wheat is on fire! They have set your wheat on fire!"

Drugova's wife woke with a start: "Bernardo, someone has set fire to our wheat."

"I heard," he replied in a dry tone of controlled violence, and started to get dressed while his wife jumped out of bed after thanking Rogelio.

When they went out to the patio, everything was already burned. Both stacks had turned into flames—unattractive because the dawn, which was just now breaking, took away any beauty that might have come from the fire. The woman observed the voracity of the flames; her eyes flooded with tears. As soon as Bernardo appeared, she said in a scarcely audible tone:

"By the time you get there with water, there won't even be a grain left!"

Beside the barn gate to the left, the squalid figure of the servant stood out.

"It seems to have been burning for a while. I rode bareback and came at a gallop as soon as I saw it." And after a silence he added, "How could it have happened, I wonder?"

In his fractured language, Drugova managed to say that this could not be an accident but rather an intentional act. Rogelio commented:

"Can there be Christians so mean spirited?"

A month later, with what he got from the oats (it was the only stack spared from the disaster), Drugova, his wife, his mother-in-law, and his little son, all moved to Buenos Aires.

Translated by Rita Gardiol.

Other works by Eichelbaum: *La mala sed* (1920); *Un hogar* (1923); *El judío Aarón* (1926); *Nadie la conoció nunca* (1926); *Tejido de madre* (1936).

Béla Illés

1895-1974

Béla Illés was a Hungarian communist who pioneered socialist realism in Hungarian literature. He served in the Habsburg army during World War I and partici-

pated in the communist revolution following the war. When the revolutionary regime was crushed, he fled to Vienna and then Carpathian Ukraine before finding refuge once again in Vienna. He was expelled in 1923 and went to Moscow, where he worked in various positions in the cultural bureaucracy until he returned to Budapest with the Russian army in 1945.

Carpathian Rhapsody
1933

In the Casino

At the time Iván Mihalkó called on me after my adventure in the forest to say that his father wanted to see me, I was not yet acquainted with Peméte, and had never heard the name of the bear-killer. Had Iván told me that Mihalkó, the blacksmith, wanted to see me, I would certainly not have been so quick to respond. But hearing that the message had been sent by Mihalkó the bear-killer, I was on my feet in an instant despite the aching pains in my bones. I was cured by the word "bear-killer."

"Géza, Géza! Have you forgotten that you ache all over?"

"Nothing hurts me now, Mother."

Fifteen minutes later I stood face to face with the bear-killer.

"Was the bear scared of you?"

The question was put by a man huge of stature and broad of shoulder. So this was Grigori Mihalkó! He was clean-shaven, and wore his brownish-blonde hair shoulder-length. So severe and clear-cut were his features that they appeared to have been carved from wood or stone. Two large, laughing eyes of cornflower-blue softened the severity of his face.

The bear-killer stood naked to his waist, grasping a big sledge-hammer. Motioning me to sit down with his hand holding the sledge-hammer, he promptly ignored me. His elder son, Elek, drew an iron rod from the fire. Grabbing one end of the rod in both hands with a wet sack, he supported the other end on the anvil. Under the blows of the bear-killer, a thousand sparks flew from the fiery iron rod. Muscles, which would have made a bear envious, twitched under the bear-killer's skin.

I sat on a tree-stump next to an old Jew crouching on a lower one. Holding his left hand to his face, the old Jew moaned grievously. He had a beard resembling the apostle's, and wore clothes like a beggar's.

"Do I have to wait long, Grigori?" pleaded the old Jew.

"Bring a bowl of water, Iván!" Grigori shouted to his younger son.

The bear-killer smith washed his hands with soap and water, drying them on his apron.

"If you kick, I'll kill you," he threatened the ancient Jew. "Iván, hold the pail, and if Isaac passes out, pour the water on his head. Open your jaw, Isaac."

Trembling with fear, the old Jew watched Mihalkó's movements and then spoke again.

"Wait, Grigori! Give me time to get my courage up."

"Open your mouth or I'll slay you."

The old man obeyed. "If you believe in God, Grigori—" he managed to say.

Encircling the thin, trembling body of the old man with his left arm, Mihalkó stuck his right hand into the old Jew's mouth. Before the old man had time to yell, the bear-killer held in his fingers the tooth he had pulled with his bare hands.

"You're as scared as a sick rabbit, Isaac," he snarled at the old man. "And you have teeth like an old horse's. Hurt, did it?"

"It didn't hurt," answered Isaac doubtfully. "May God repay your kindness."

Nodding his head, Mihalkó signified his satisfaction with the payment.

"I hope I didn't jerk a good tooth by mistake?"

"That would be hard to do," replied Isaac. "That was the last tooth, the only one on the left side."

"Well, everything's all right then. When is Rebecca coming home? Should've been here long ago."

"God knows where he's roving about," sighed Isaac.

"You've called on God a lot today, Isaac. You've got your sly old head set on some villainy, that's sure, and in the meantime you're getting your pigs. Better hurry or you'll be snivelling after them for nothing."

"Margaret's looking after 'em."

"Like the devil he is. Margaret chases every skirt he sees. This fly-killer is Peméte's swine-herd," Mihalkó said, turning to me.

"A Jew—a swine-herd," I was amazed.

"Why not?" demanded Isaac. "Four-legged pigs aren't anti-Semites."

"Ha, ha, ha," roared the bear-killer. "You hit the nail on the head, that time, Isaac. But anyway, you'd do well to hurry."

"Give me a wee tobacco for along the way, Grigori. My mouth hurts bad from your hand."

The apostle-bearded old man stuffed his clay pipe with Mihalkó's matches, then climbed to his feet, groaning.

"You stole a good hour of my time, Grigori, with this bit of a tooth-pulling. Well, coming out tonight?"

"Yes, if Rebecca comes home, bring him along."

"So, then, the bear was scared of you?" asked Grigori when old man Isaac had taken himself off.

"It didn't dream of being scared," I replied.

"So! But you were scared?"

"Scared out of my wits."

"Well done," exclaimed Mihalkó. "Not that you were scared, but that you admitted it. That's the very ticket. You've been going to school so far?"

"Yes."

"Did you study?"

"Yes, I did."

"If you studied, you ought to know how big this here Russia is. If you know, tell me."

I told him.

"You know that, I see. All right! Well, do you know this? How much bigger is Russia than Hungary?"

"Seventy-one times bigger," I reckoned quickly.

"I see you've been studying," said Mihalkó. "Now, do you know who Karl Marx was?"

So surprised was I at his question that I hesitated before answering.

"I know who he was: the founder of scientific socialism."

"Right! Now, tell me, do you know who János Fóti is?"

After Marx, János Fóti! I thought the bear-killer was joking, but Mihalkó's big blue eyes stared so earnestly, almost solemnly at me from his severe face that I replied to his question in all seriousness.

"By chance, I know. He's a socialist from Beregszász. I was living in Beregszász when he organized the brickyard strike. That was when I saw János Fóti."

"I see your head's screwed on right," said Mihalkó. "Just the same, if the bear that scared you had been a she-bear and not a he-bear, you wouldn't be sitting here in my house today. It would have been a pity to lose you. I hope you'll come here often. Sometime I'll take you along to hunt bears."

The smithy stood near the highway. The sound of a flute could be heard off the road, and then a tired, lazy voice singing,

Give me rags . . . rags . . .

All kinds of togs and duds,
For rags, I'll give satin-ribbons,
And for the kids, trombones.

"Ho, ho," bellowed Mihalkó. "Here comes Rebecca."

There hove into sight on the highway a thick-set, broad-shouldered, red-bearded Jew. The singing came from him. The singing Jew carried on his back a large green felt sack and, on his left arm, a checked umbrella.

"Over here! Over here, Rebecca."

A few minutes later Mihalko was wringing the right hand of the Jew with the pack.

"Any news, Rebecca?"

"Better if there wasn't."

"Iván," Mihalkó ordered his youngest son, "take your friend home."

By way of good-bye, the bear-killer held out his right hand which was as large as the paddle of a Danube canoe.

"Tell me, why does that red-beard have a woman's name?" I asked Iván on way home.

Iván looked around cautiously and though no one was near, he spoke in a whisper.

"Old man Schönfeld the swine-herd, gave both his son's girls' names so they wouldn't be called up for army service."

"And didn't they really call them up?"

"Of course they did. In fact, not only did they conscript the two boys—Rebecca and Margret—but the three girls, too, Deborah, Rosalie and Sarah. They only let the girls go home after three committees decided they were really girls. But it's forbidden to talk about it so Isaac won't be punished. He's sat enough—eight months."

"Why did the old man sit?" I asked.

"For usury."

"For usury? So your father's friend is an usurer?"

Iván looked at me as though he doubted my sanity. He didn't scold, merely set me right with gentle reproach.

"How can you say such a thing? Isaac an usurer? Or do you really think they lock up the usurers for usury in Hungary?"

"Naturally, that's what I think."

Iván's face betrayed his shame of my naivety.

"You know," he said after a brief pause, "old man Schönfeld was the first man to think of organizing and demanding a wage increase."

"Well, that isn't usury, is it?"

"You sure are from foreign parts," said Iván Mihalkó with a disappointing shake of his head.

Around the Shepherd's Fire

The next day, the bear-killer sent for me again in the afternoon. I found Hozelitz in the smithy with Mihalkó.

"Can you keep your mouth shut?" asked Mihalkó.

"I can."

"I won't ask if you can write. Tonight, when the first star comes out, Iván will call for you. Bring paper and a pencil along."

"You're a fool, Grigori," protested Hozelitz. "Why should we disturb the young gentleman's evening rest?"

"Don't start play-acting, Ábrahám. It was you who told me about the boy in the first place. 'Sound him out,' you said. Well, I sound him out so that there's not a bone left in his body?"

"I don't want you to make a fool of yourself, Grigori."

"You're a bloody wretch, Ábrahám and an uncommon one, at that. No matter what we take on, you always say, "Don't do something foolish, don't do something foolish." And then, when we succeed in doing what you thought was foolish, you still have something to say. Then you come with, 'We should've done it before.' Aren't you afraid we'll get fed up?"

"All I'm worrying about, Grigori, is that your head is weaker than your fists! You think with your fists. If you would start using your head to think, sooner or later you would wake up and see that if a man like you—who thinks he'll succeed at everything he does—is needed, then a man like me, who knows that nothing we begin will succeed—entirely—is also needed."

"It's a pity you didn't become a rabbi, Ábrahám."

"A pity," Hozelitz agreed. "If I were a rabbi, I would convert you and make you a church servant so you could throw out people who did not pay their congregation tax."

"I'll show you right off how I'd do it."

Picking up Hozelitz as though he were a child, Mihalkó swung him back and forth, pretending to get ready to toss him, then he set him down on the tree-stump.

"Now you know what to expect if you jabber too much."

After nightfall, Iván and I set out for the woods. It was pitch dark in the forest. Iván led me by the hand, but even so I would bump into a tree now and then.

"How do you know where to go?" I asked.

"I feel it," Iván answered.

An owl hooted overhead. As the trees thinned out, I caught sight in the distance of our goal: a shepherd's fire blazing in a clearing. Twelve or fourteen men were sitting round the fire—Hungarians, Ruthenians, Jews. All of them were puffing on their pipes. One of the men was the bear-killer.

"Sit down," Mihalkó told me, moving over to make room next to him on his sheepskin coat.

Nothing more said. A strange feeling of emotion came over me. A shepherd's fire in the Carpathian mountains . . .

For two hundred years these fires had been kindled, night after night. Two hundred years earlier they had lit up the way for the army of Rákóczi, the liberator. Now sitting around the campfire were the men who were seeking the path to liberation for themselves.

The shepherd's fire blazed skyward. The pungent odour of resin came from the burning pine branches. In the light of the flames, the dark background, the vast trackless Carpathian forests, seemed blacker than ever. In the midnight blue of the heavens, stars gleamed like a million shepherd's fires burning far off.

Swine-herd Isaac Schönfeld kicked off his moccasins, unwound his foot-cloths, and stretched out his bare feet towards the fire for warmth.

"Off there lies Russia, over there, the Great Hungarian Plain," explained Mihalkó, pointing with his pipe first to the northeast, then southwest.

"You've finally come alive," called Hozelitz.

He was speaking to Rebecca Schönfeld who at that moment came out of the forest.

Rebecca ignored him; he sat down on the ground next to his father, pulled a pipe and sack of tobacco out of his pocket, and filled the pipe. With a stick, he raked a glowing ember out of the fire, picked it up with his bare hand and lit his pipe.

Milhalkó commenced speaking when Rebecca blew out his first mouthful of smoke.

"We were told that the commissioner appointed to chase after usurers will be coming to Peméte a few days from now."

"Woe is me! Woe is me!" groaned Hozelitz.

"At Huszt," Mihalko continued, "the commissioner had Bertalan Hidvégi, the head of the wood-workers' union, locked up. The commissioner had Hidvégi arrested, but the examining judge released him a few days later. Hidvégi is Hungarian, and a Calvinist. And a Calvinist Hungarian can't be a Jewish usurer even if he is a trade union leader. This shows that the commissioner

isn't all powerful either. So you don't have to yell 'woe is me' right off the handle. We'll have to wait calmly and see what the commissioner wants of us. Calmly I said, not in idleness. I think the best thing to do would be to address a petition to the commissioner naming the real usurers."

"And what do you expect to get from that petition, Grigori?" questioned old man Schönfeld.

"Sometimes iron turns into gold," interposed swarthy Zoltán Megyeri before Mihalkó could answer. (Megyeri was, by the way, the only one here to wear a hat.)

"I've heard that plenty, but I've never seen it," objected Hozelitz.

"The commissioner knows very well who the usurer is here in Peméte. He usually lunches at her place."

"So," Mihalkó went on stubbornly, "now we'll draw up the petition."

There was a hush.

"You'll do the writing," Mihalkó told me. "As to writing, those of us who speak Hungarian know the Hebrew alphabet, those who know the Hungarian alphabet talk Ruthenian. Megyeri is ignorant of any alphabet. So, you'll write. Write down what I tell you. Did you bring paper and pencil? Good! Get set!"

Propping the thick note-book I had brought along on my knee, I wet the point of my pencil.

"Commissioner," Mihalkó began dictating in a loud voice.

"Write 'Mr. Commissioner,'" interrupted Megyeri.

"If you're writing 'Mr.' then write 'Honourable,' too," interjected Hozelitz.

"All right," agreed Mihalkó. "Let it be, 'Honourable Mr. Commissoner. You are looking for usurers. There are more than enough here in Sub-Carpathia. And there are some in Peméte, too—blast them on the spot.'"

"That's not necessary," Hozelitz objected. "Blast them, blast them all! The sooner the better; I wish they would blast, with all my heart. But you don't have to put that in."

"So don't write it," Mihalkó conceded. "So that the Honourable Commissioner should not waste his time—"

"His valuable time" said Hozelitz.

"His valuable time," Mihalkó dictated, "we are telling you—"

"We are telling Your Worship—"

"We are telling Your Worship where he can find the den of the bear Your Worship is hunting—"

"Is pleased to hunt—"

"Let it be, 'pleased to hunt.' 'The usurer of our village'—write it down, Bálint—'the blood-sucker of our village is Mrs. Náthán Scheiner, the same filthy strumpet with whom Your Worship dined when you last visited our village.'"

"When you last pleased to honour our village with your visit."

"Shut up!" Mihalkó bawled at Hozelitz. "Mrs. Náthán Scheiner," Mihalkó dictated, shouting in his rage, "the damn bitch, is the lowest usurer there ever was. Everybody knows that, Mr. Commissioner, except you. If a poor man at Peméte complains to that skunk Scheiner that he's starving, he can't feed his children—Scheiner sends him to his wife, and that mean woman lends the wretch three or four florins; and she collects three kreutzer interest a week for every florin she lends. Figure out, Mr. Commissioner, how much that adds up to in interest."

"We have to figure that out for ourselves," Megyeri said.

"156 per cent," I told them.

"Are you sure?" asked Mihalkó.

"Sure," Rebecca replied for me.

"Now, you see," Mihalkó threw at Hozelitz. "And you objected to the boy."

"I only have objections to you, Grigori."

"Don't quarrel. You can do anything, but you mustn't quarrel," whined old Schönfeld.

"Well, go on writing, Bálint. Write this: 'the filthy swine is squeezing 156 per cent interest out of the miserable Peméte villagers. She is feeding Your Worship on their blood.'"

"That's not necessary," protested Megyeri.

"It is!" bellowed Mihalkó. "It is necessary."

The dictation, allowing time for the bickering, took a good hour. And in ten minutes I copied the letter Mihalkó had dictated, in indelible ink on the two sides of a page torn out of an exercise-book.

"Now the question is who should sign it?" inquired Hozelitz after I had read aloud the final text of the petition.

"It should be sent unsigned," was Rebecca's opinion.

"Hog-wash! The commissioner knows everything we have written. We are only writing to him to show that we aren't blind, either; and so that later he won't say he didn't arrest Mrs. Scheiner because he didn't know what she was. The signers are witnesses against the commissioner," explained Hozelitz.

"We need a hundred signatures," Mihalkó said.

"The chief constable's jail will be a tight squeeze for a hundred men," faltered old Schönfeld. "We won't have room to sit, even. How'll we sleep?"

"A hundred signatures," repeated Mihalkó. "The Hungarians don't have to be afraid of signing; a Hungarian can't be a Jewish usurer. The Ruthenians aren't scared—they are used to jail. The Jews don't have to sign it."

"Hold on there, Grigori," snapped Hozelitz. "You are seeing the Jews like that prophet Dudics painted them: as scurvy, cowardly dogs. You should be ashamed, Grigori! I'll be the first to sign the petition, Isaac the second. Do you want to, Isaac?"

"Want to or not, I'll sign," said old Schönfeld.

The men sitting round the fire, with the exception of Mihalkó's son and myself, wrote down their names in a row on the page of the exercise-book. Megyeri and Isaac Schönfeld merely scratched three crosses each, and I wrote their names alongside the crosses.

Mihalkó took charge of the petition.

Rebecca threw fresh pine-boughs on the fire, stirring up a spray of sparks. For a few seconds, the fire sputtered and hissed its protest against the wet wood, then shot up in flames.

"I could do with a glass of wine," siged Megyeri.

"Or a swig of brandy," mused Mihalkó.

"I can think of plenty of things I could do with," added Hozelitz.

Commissioner Ákos Szemere rode into Peméte in style in a buggy drawn by two beautiful grey horses. A Hungarian gentleman of the old school, Szemere wore a moustache, whiskers and top-boots. He was a warm-hearted man, friendly to everyone, and would cordially return the greeting of even the shabbiest Jewish or Ruthenian woodcutter when they met in the street. He distributed kreutzer to the children, inquiring about their studies. He stopped the oldsters, too, listening patiently to their worries and complaints, and sighing as they sighed.

The commissioner stayed with manager Köbl. He lunched at Mrs. Scheiner's home, and spent his evenings in the company of the chief constable, drinking wine and playing cards.

Commissioner Szemere received Mihalkó bearing the Peméte workers' petition in Köbl's house. Shaking hands with the bear-killer, he promised that he would carefully study the Peméte workers' complaint. Next day, he called on Mihalkó.

He came on foot, trailed by a servant dressed in hussar uniform; the servant carried the commissioner's meerschaum pipe in his hand and, under his arm, a walnut box containing tobacco.

When his lordship had settled down comfortably on one of the tree-stumps in the smithy, his hussar filled the huge meerschaum pipe. The commissioner examined the pipe to make sure that it drew well, then the hussar rolled up a piece of newspaper to make a spill, lit it and handed it to his high and mighty lord, who held it to his pipe. Szemere started talking only when a thick column of smoke began to rise from the pipe.

Mihalkó thought that the commissioner had called to discuss the petition, but he was mistaken. Szemere was not interested for the moment in usurers; he wanted to know all about bears. He catechized Mihalkó closely about how to find the bear's tracks, how to overtake it, and how he (Mihalkó) was able to creep within knife's length of the deuced beast without the bear reaching the hunter. Mihalkó patiently answered the lord's questions, but he was not satisfied. He asked the bear-killer to demonstrate on the hussar how he would break out of the bear's embrace. And to please the commissioner, the bear-killer blacksmith played at bear-hunting. The hussar was the bear, Mihalkó the hunter. But after breaking the two feather-dusters—one on the hussar's throat and the other with a jab to the side—which served as the knife, Mihalkó grew bored with the game.

"What does Your Excellency think about the petition?"

"Ha, ha, my good man! Not so fast! Do you want me to make up my mind hastily in such an important matter? Or, before I have a chance to form an opinion, to talk drivel just for the sake of saying something? There is more than one way to kill a cat, my friend! Just as the bear-hunt has its own order of things, so the prosecution of usurers has to take place according to the rules. You are an expert at bear-hunting; but the prosecution of usurers is in my line. Just as I do not doubt that you will get the bear you've tracked down, you may rest assured that I do not feed goose-liver pate to the usurers crossing my path."

The commissioner's voice was loud, but not angry. As he got up to go, he held out his hand to the bear-killer.

Commissioner Szemere stayed for three more days in Pemóte, then left by buggy for Mezőlaborc. The day after he left, the gendarmes arrested eleven Peméte workers—nine Jews and two Ruthenians. Old man Schön-feld and Hozelitz were among the arrested men. Ten days later, the two Ruthenians were released. Six weeks later, seven Jews were also set free. Schönfeld sat in jail, however, for four months; Hozelitz, for almost six.

Mihalkó supplied game to the families who had been deprived of their bread-winners. Náthán Scheiner provided words of comfort and advice to the women bewailing the loss of their husbands.

"How often have I told those men to come to their senses," Scheiner declared, "that upright Jews have no business acting up with those knife-throwing Hungarians and brandy-swilling Ruthenian peasants? What kind of a Jewish brain does a man have if he can't understand that the terrible blacksmith, that Mihalkó, is the lackey of the infamous prophet Dudics? Does a decent Jew need that man who got together with that rascally, murderous traitor Megyeri and sent some kind of writing, reviling king and God, to his Honour the Commissioner? I am very, very sorry for you and the children, but as for your husband . . . he looked for trouble!"

A vast emptiness surrounded Mihalkó and Megyeri. The Jews began avoiding them on the street, and not a single Jew, except for Rebecca, would put his feet in the smithy.

But that was only half the trouble. The real danger was that the Hungarians would refuse to listen any longer to Zoltán Megyeri. Following Szemere's visit, manager Köbl had given fifteen Hungarians a wage increase of twelve kreutzer per day. Megyeri got the Hungarians together, attempting to convince them to accept the wage increase only if the Jews and Ruthenians employed on the same jobs would be given more pay, too.

Seeing that not a single man who had been given the wage increase was inclined to approve his recommendation, Megyeri proposed that the twelve kreutzer should be donated to support the prisoners' families. As Megyeri was declaiming about solidarity, someone hit him on the head with a club from behind, knocking him out. He went around with bandaged head for three weeks.

Then, when the rumour spread among the Ruthenians that they were not getting a wage increase because they had associated with the Jews, Mihalkó and Megyeri were completely isolated.

On my advice, the bear-killer wrote to the Woodworkers' Union in Budapest. To put it more precisely, I wrote the letter and it was signed by Mihalkó and Megyeri. Ten days later an answer arrived.

The union wrote that they considered the Peméte organization non-existent since Peméte had never sent in a single kreutzer in trade union fees.

I wrote to Fülöp Szevella about the "strange and sad" situation at Peméte. Uncle Fülöp wrote exhaustively in reply.

Your report, Géza, son, is not about the Peméte situation—it is about the status of the suppressed nationalities in Hungary, and of the agricultural and forest workers who make up the bulk of the people.

When I read the long letter telling about how the reactionaries were isolating the workers' socialist movement from the rebellions of the dispossessed farmhands and wood-workers on the counts' estates, and how much the rulers were gaining by doing it—there were only three of us sitting round the shepherd's fire; Mihalkó, Megyeri and I. I finished reading the letter and sat there in silence with my two companions.

A strange fire gleamed in Megyeri's deep-set black eyes. I had a feeling that he could have cheerfully killed someone. Mihalkó sat with head bowed.

Sitting between the two dour men, I thought of Fülöp Szevella, my uncle, who was a stranger among the gentry and who, it appeared, could not blend entirely with the workers' vast multitude, either. He knew where the trouble lay, but could not help. There are people who remain alien at all times and at all places. How ghastly!

I trembled. Almost as though in search of help, I took hold of the bear-killer's arm. Mihalkó looked at me in wonder.

"Don't be afraid, Géza," he said quietly. "No matter what happens, we'll strike the final blow."

Neither of us said any more. Slowly the fire at our feet turned to glowing embers, then even that was blanketed with ashes among which a bright red fire-brand glimmered here and there.

Hozelitz came home with the first snow-fall.

"We'll begin again," he told Mihalkó at their first meeting. "I heard that the factory manager had cut wages on September 1st. So we'll start from the bottom up. And if they should smash us for the hundredth time, we'll start again for the hundredth and first time. Isn't that so, Grigori?"

Translated by Grace Blair Gardos.

Other works by Illés: *Doktor Utrius Pál honvéd baka hátrahagyoyy irásai* (1917); *Eg a Tisza* (1957).

Abraham Vysotsky

1883-1949

A novelist in the Russian language, Abraham Vysotsky was born in the town of Zhornishche (in present-day Ukraine). Living for a time in Biysk, Siberia, he immigrated to Palestine in the winter of 1919–1920. Although Vysotsky was fluent in Hebrew, his literary career was carried out entirely in Russian, a rare choice for a member of the literary community in Palestine at the time. While considered a minor writer, Vysotsky is included by critics within the work of both the Third Aliyah and the prerevolutionary wave of Russian literature "in emigration." His novels were often works of historical fiction, concerning the lives of Jews in Palestine and elsewhere. Many of his works were translated into other European languages and into Hebrew.

Tel Aviv

1933

Avigdor walked beyond the city limits of Tel Aviv into the endless stretch of sand. He had never seen such sand. He walked among the sand dunes, as in a forest, seeing nothing except the glaring sands. A great stillness reigned there. One could hear the rustling of each grain of sand in the soft sea breeze.

Avigdor had not been alone for a very long time. Long months of camp life, always among his comrades, had become extremely painful to Avigdor. Now, alone in this peaceful stillness, his thoughts and feelings suddenly were stripped. He felt a keen, intoxicating joy listening to the rustle of the sands of Palestine. Words of an old forgotten song stirred his memory.

The sands glowed in the sun like a fiery carpet. His feet burned in his shoes, but everything seemed pleasant—even this heat and the glare of the flaming sands! He raised his eyes and beheld a blue desert which also burned like fire. Avigdor suddenly thought of himself as of a turtle which has a yellow shield below and a blue one above. . . . He smiled and hummed a tune which was like the sun, the sky, the sands of Palestine.

He came upon many stakes along the sand dunes with numbers on them. Evidently, he was not following Tabachnik's directions, because the numbers ran along the eighties.

"*Ein davar*" (never mind), he suddenly thought in Hebrew, "That's all right. One can't always follow the right direction!"

As far as the eye could see—hills, hills, whipped up by the heavy winds on the sand. On one of the remote hills he suddenly noticed a tree. The background of yellow sands made it look as if it had been freshly painted with bright green paint. It was a large, old shady tree. Under it stood a stake with the figure "48" on it. Avigdor burst into joyous laughter.

"Papa's land," he exclaimed and sat down between two large roots. For a moment images of his loved ones crowded about him. His father, so like him in spirit, with his broad, good-natured smile, his little sister, Rose, and before them all, his mother stretching her arms towards him and weeping. Apart from them stood the girl he loved. She was shy, did not have courage to step upon their soil . . .

"Come, beloved," sang his soul, while he lay down flat, his heart next to the ground. Thus he lay for quite a while, paying no attention to the excitement his appearance created.

Two ancient chameleons flew from him and up the tree, having turned the color of the bark. From there they observed the dangerous arrival. A black beetle was rolling a dry flower along the road, forming a complicated design on the sand. It suddenly stopped, scrutinized the strange animal which lay on the ground, but finding him motionless, decided to roll its burden back.

Above the tree hovered a feathered broad-beaked hunter, watching and waiting.

The sea breeze dried Avigdor's perspiration-soaked shirt while he lay on the ground. He rose, stood up on the hill, and, for the first time, looked about at the view. It seemed to him that at the horizon, the sky lay on the sand. He saw the sea, which was bluer than the sky. It played with the rolling white breakers, while in the distance a white sail fluttered. The sea was so sudden and so beautiful and its breath was so cool, refreshing and invigorating!

He turned about and beheld another miracle. Another sea, but a motionless one, which lifted its waves into the sky.

Avigdor did not at first realize what mountains these were, till it dawned upon him—the Hills of Judea! They seemed to lie behind a transparent blue curtain which vibrated continually. And beyond that curtain slumbered all the legendary happenings of this ancient land.

Avigdor stood, his body tense, his eyes wide open and sparkling. He was now more than twenty years old—he was two thousand years old, he has seen all, understood and remembered everything.

Close by, beyond the yellow dunes, lay the green orchards and gardens of Jaffa. Arab houses with flat roofs were plainly seen, throaty voices were audible. Every now and then one could distinguish little people in gowns and red fezzes. "This," reflected Avigdor, "was the new, unknown world of the desert, of revenge, and murder."

An object came from that direction, rolling along the sand. Avigdor finally distinguished a dog, running queerly, sideways, its ears to the ground. The animal ran straight at Avigdor, evidently not seeing him. Avigdor was seized with apprehension, as if he were seeing all this in a dream. Often in his childhood he would dream of just such dogs—with ears of a donkey, with shaggy, worn fur, a grinning, drooling mouth, and tearing, half-blind eyes. The animal noticed Avigdor, raised its head with only one eye, and uttered a sound that resembled a cough, laughing, and wheezing at the same time. Avigdor shuddered and, as he always did in his dreams, bent down for a stone. The dog scampered away in its queer one-sided way.

Avigdor suddenly yearned to return to town, to be among people. Around the barbed wire that surrounded Tel Aviv, a woman was chasing a chicken. She finally caught the playful chicken and was swearing under her breath.

"I hope you burst, accursed thing! Think of chasing after her way out here! Only three days ago the Arabs murdered a young *halutz* right around this spot!"

On the next day all five came to the little spot that belonged to Sorokino. They came in a noisy group and filled the sands with laughter and merriment. They soon quieted down. The young fellows spoke nostalgically of their respective families and made plans—someday all five families should meet under this tree; then their imagination stretched to all the Jews of Sorokino, and finally, to the Jews of the entire world. Their eyes lit up, their voices sounded stronger, and they were making all kinds of resolutions. . . . And right here, on the bit of Sorokino land, they resolved to write letters home.

"God knows, whether this letter will ever reach you, but I want you to know that I am happy here." Thus, Menasha concluded his letter. He finished and raised his childish, clouded eyes to the clear, high sky.

"They say that these trees are terribly old!" mused Isaak slowly, "Perhaps a thousand years or more!"

The five scrutinized the tree silently. The Sergeant gazed about idly. He wrote no letters—he had no one to write to. He remarked: "How can this lot be worked? The sand will cover it again."

Translated by Rose Wissotzky-Orlans.

Other works by Vysotsky: *Zelenoe plamia* (1928); *Subbota i voskresen'e* (1929).

Mark Egart
1901–1956

Born in Krivoy Rog [Kryvyi Rih], Ukraine, Mark Egart (pseudonym of Mordechai Moiseevich Boguslavskii) was a writer of fiction and nonfiction in the Russian language. Egart joined the Zionist youth group He-Ḥaluts at an early age and trained with them in Poland before moving to Palestine in 1923. Overcome by illness, hunger, and the dire economic situation of Jewish life there, as well as by ongoing conflicts with the local Arab population, Egart returned to the Soviet Union three years later. There he established himself as writer, joining the Moscow-based proletarian group Vagranka. His most significant work of this period was the autobiographical novel about young Jewish settlers in Palestine, entitled *Opalennaia zemlia* (Scorched Earth). He also produced sketches, novels, and other works on topics such as collectivization and the everyday lives of Soviet workers, and held various positions in the Soviet literary establishment. After serving in the Red Army, Egart spent the postwar period writing books for young adults.

Scorched Earth
1933–1934; followed by a corrected edition in 1937

I

. . . An empty street. An unfamiliar shack. A tightly shut gate. And hanging over the gate, over the dead street, over us all—a Cossack cap with a raspberry-colored band. A trail of smoke from an alley and—silence. No shouts, no gun-shots, no ringing of broken windows, just a cruel silence and a wayward Cossack forelock over us all.

I was four years old when the Cossacks raided Gnilopol.

Three years later, life assailed me a second time. At that time, I was living with my grandfather who worked as a weighman at the village sugar factory. A thick pine forest surrounded the factory. Cheerful rosy-cheeked maidens sang as they packed sacks with powdered sugar and sewed them up with long chrome needles. A currant bush grew by a window; poplars surrounded the weighman's booth. And in the midst of all this—Grandpa himself, my mother's father, a tall, heavy-set, and strong old man who intimidated even hot-headed porters.

In the winter, Grandpa would take me to the factory and show me how sugar was made. I saw hot copper pots with boiling syrup being carried on workers' shoulders. I couldn't comprehend how they managed to hold on to these piping hot containers. But Grandpa explained that people are resilient and can become accustomed to things. First they get hurt; then their wounds heal, and people get used to it.

"Lazar," my grandfather would say to me as I sat on his tall, bench-like knees. Shaking his thick finger, deformed from constantly dealing with weights, he would continue, "We are not allowed to have land. We are Jews, keep that in mind, Lazar. . . ."

I found out later that Grandpa had to have a special document because otherwise Jews were not allowed to reside in the village. Every holiday a sergeant showed up at Grandpa's house, took a drink and a bribe. Grandpa worked from dawn to dusk, and at night he stayed up and recorded the weighed sugar. And when he finished writing, he enjoyed singing Psalms.

Whenever I awoke, I would see him pacing around the small room, his fingers stuck in the armholes of his jacket. It seemed to me that he was holding an eternal dialogue with someone, probably with God. Grandpa's voice was awkward, heavy like the rest of him, but he sang his prayers with an unexpectedly delicate longing, and his dove-colored face which was overgrown with white hair, expressed a constant displeasure. It seemed that Grandpa did not approve of his God.

He worked as a weighman for thirty years. He outlived two of his bosses, weighing and reweighing others' property. And he was kicked out anyway. He was evicted within twenty-four hours; all his belongings were loaded on a wagon, and in the middle of the day, they took us out of the factory.

That's how I came back to Gnilopol.

Grandpa didn't last long. He wasn't accustomed to being without work, and no one would give an old man a job here. Grandpa had lived in the village his entire life, among muzhiks [peasants], in the free air, and he couldn't get used to the shtetl. He stopped singing

Psalms, stopped praying, and would sit on the stoop, bored, for days on end. Occasionally, he would call me to him, inspect my pale face, and ask: "Are you studying? . . . Make sure to study. Your grandfather is illiterate. He was kicked out. . . ." He would sigh loudly and whisper, no longer paying any attention to me. "We aren't allowed on the land, the tsar himself decided so. . . ."

Grandpa died soon thereafter.

Everywhere in the shtetl, there was oily mud, yellow like the leather that our furriers were producing. Puddles remained in the market square throughout the year. Over Gnilopol hung a perpetual smell of rot.

My parents lived on Panskaya Street. It was called Panskaya because most of it belonged to the landowner, Pan Stativa. Once a month, the pan's assistant showed up and collected rent from the resident carpenters, cobblers, tailors, and furriers. That day was the busiest and most restless on our street. Beginning in the morning hours, children were already running out to the edge of town on the look-out for the assistant's carriage. When the assistant was in a good mood, he would immediately sit down for a drink and snack prepared for him. In those instances, we managed to get an extension on the rent. More often than not though, the counterman was ill-disposed and unyielding. He summoned the parish-elder, issued decrees, and, through the parish government, charged the debtors with anything he could.

Our neighbor, Tovii Senderei, was the most talented in getting along with the pan's assistant. Tovii used to be a carpenter in Stativa's neighborhood and completed all kinds of repairs for the assistant, and so he stopped most often at our courtyard. Sometimes the pan's little son, Deniska, accompanied him. In those instances, we surrounded the carriage, and with a mixture of curiosity and mistrust, inspected the boy in a velvet jacket. He remained quiet, even timid. We couldn't believe that this is the son of the very same Stativa, in front of whom everyone on Panskaya Street trembled and who had the ability to kick us all out.

Only Tovii wasn't afraid of the pan's son or of the pan's assistant. In Gnilopol, Tovii was nicknamed "Jack of all Trades." He got this name because he socialized with muzhiks, liked to drink, and cursed. Tovii drank in a manner that inspired the admiration of Stativa's assistant, but he also knew his trade well, so being his friend was both fun and useful. His friend at the time was his neighbor and fellow carpenter—Opanas Jaundice. People said that there were no two people on our street who were closer than those two. But later, no greater enemies could be found.

It all started over an apparent trifle. Opanas Jaundice wanted to tear out two boards from the fence that separated his yard from ours, in order to have access to the street. No one in our courtyard liked this idea. It didn't appeal to Tovii either since his shack was located right next to the fence. He brought a dozen nails from his shop and solidly nailed the boards back into place.

Opanas observed his neighbor's work through his shop window and quietly hummed a tune. Having finished polishing a board, he took off his apron and slowly approached the fence. As he was walking, he was humming in the same quiet voice, and when he reached the fence, he stopped singing and leaned on the fence with all his weight. The rotten wood groaned under him, but the fence wouldn't budge. At that point, Opanas took up an axe.

Tovii Senderei was still young and hot-headed at the time. He also grabbed an axe.

The neighbors gathered because of the commotion. The first to appear was my sworn enemy—Jaundice's son, Mikolka. Mikolka and I shared a long-standing animosity. He was stronger than I and could topple me so that both of my shoulder blades touched the ground, but I still wouldn't surrender. Even then, as a little boy, I wouldn't surrender and fought, bit, pinched, threw dirt on Mikolka, and left, beaten-up, scratched, but unvanquished. I saw that even though I was weaker than he was, he still respected me, while he mocked Kopl and Ezra. Red-haired, short-legged, freckled Kopl Farfel and bigheaded Ezra, Senderei's youngest son, were in my circle. We also had with us Isachka Pikelnyi, the son of a wood-exporter from Oak Balk. Isachka was also pugnacious and didn't surrender.

"Jews are being attacked! . . ." yelled Mikolka and quickly started gathering stones, hurrying to take part in the attack. Broken glass rang out festively. My sister Rokhka squealed; women started wailing; and the beggar-fool Kutska stuck her head through the gate and whined: "Good Jewish women, Kutska is hungry, Kutska is hungry. . . . Spare something for good Kutska."

Mikolka was hurling rocks with increasing cheer and speed. Crowds were running down the street. The church bell was ringing. A thick, copper voice was floating over the shtetl: "Attack . . . Attack . . . Attack. . . ."

"Quiet . . ." my father was hissing, even though we were quiet. "Jews, be quiet. . . ."

My father was the best *melamed* in Gnilopol. Experts would say that he could have been a famous rabbi—a light unto Israel.

He sat down with a page of Talmud, swaying like a pendulum. His yarmulke stuck to his sweaty bald spot, a patched-up vest was screeching on his neck like a yoke. He was swaying, loudly mumbling, so as not to hear the noise of the fight:

" . . . Rabbi Akiva has said . . . aahh. . . . What did Rabbi Akiva say? . . ." [. . .]

I liked being in Senderei's shop. My father would send my sister to fetch me, but I would chase her away. Then my mother would come, obedient and timid, but I didn't want to obey her either. However, when the *melamed* himself appeared, I got what I deserved. Father would take me by the ear and drag me to heder through the entire yard while the other children looked on and laughed. In the evenings, when no one could hear, he would hit me with a ruler and say:

"A Jewish boy must obey, a Jewish boy mustn't be a *sheigetz*."

But I remained a *sheigetz* and kept running away to Senderei's shop.

I would sit for hours in a corner, breathing in the tart smell of resinous boards and glue, bathing in the gentle foam of shavings. Sometimes Tovii would scold me for neglecting my studies, but I could see in his grey and cheerful eyes that he understood me and sympathized. Occasionally, Tovii would give me a small job—to clean the shavings or cook the glue, and he even showed me how to use a jointer, a jack-plane to secure a board to a bench.

I was just a small child, but Tovii would say that even small children must work. Tovii couldn't stand idlers and paupers, and in Gnilopol, there were more paupers than anywhere else, or so it seemed to me. Of all the shtetl's professions, the pauper profession was considered the most numerous and organized. They even had their own elder—Yukl Goz, a cheerful, pimply Jew who liked to philosophize.

"Our life," Yukl Goz would say, "is but a child's shirt, short and bedraggled." While saying this, Yukl winked meaningfully and pointedly to himself. [. . .]

But Tovii was especially pleasant on Friday evenings, when, having finished praying in the Craftsmen's Synagogue, all washed and combed, he would sit on the stoop while waiting for dinner. We knew then that it was time for stories about Solomon the Wise, about King David—handsome, adventurous and playful—about the ten tribes of Israel, who are considered to be dead but who are living happily on the other side of the Sambatyon River. Our brothers live in a wonderful land where the sun always shines, where fig and carob trees are just as commonplace as elderberry and acacia are here, where all Jews till the land, cultivate grapes, and a king from the house of David is ruling over them, just as cheerful, adventurous, and playful as the original David. For six days and six nights, the mighty Sambatyon rages, hurling enormous stones and drowning anyone who dares to come near it. Only on the seventh night, when the Sabbath queen descends on the earth, does it calm down. No one has ever crossed the bewitched river, and no one has penetrated the magical kingdom. The Jews live happily there and remember their brothers who are in *golus* [exile, diaspora].

That's how Tovii the carpenter would tell it in the early evening on the stoop. We listened and wanted to cross Sambatyon like those daredevils who perished. Night descended upon us, stars fell silently from the sky. Tovii, patting his Sabbath beard, would say that stars fall into the Sambatyon and turn into stones. As he spoke, there was indestructible joy on his strong muscular face. In those moments, I loved him more than I loved my father, much more.

In the summer, father curtained the windows from the sun, and the heder was hot like the baths. In the winter, he caulked the windows with grey dirty cotton. The students' desks and his desk always stood with their backs to the light, and I have never seen even one ray of sun fall on his wrinkled face that was rancid with ancient wisdom. I have never seen a smile, a cheerful glance, or even heard a joke from father.

I saw two people who were like two halves of one world: Sholom-Hersh Dayan—*melamed*, and Tovii Senderei—carpenter. And God knows that, with all my soul, I was attracted to the carpenter, to labor, to healthy, real life.

I didn't want to go back to the heder, didn't want to know what Rashi had said, what the good, old Rabbi Akiva had thought, and on what question the entire great Sanhedrin of Jewish wise men was deliberating.

When I turned thirteen and, from the height of the synagogue's *bimah*, I was pronounced an adult, I was proud. Aloud, I was repeating the legally prescribed prayers, but in my heart, I was saying: "Lord, I came out of a generation of *melameds*, yeshiva students, and wise men, and I alone will be responsible to you for my life. And so you should know that I don't want to grow bald and slouch over Talmud pages. I will live differently, and you will see, Lord, that my life will be better."

That is how I prayed in my heart on the day of my adulthood in the Craftsmen's Synagogue on Panskaya Street, and my friends and contemporaries—Ezra Senderei and Kopl Red-Head—were praying next to me. In the evening we drank for the first time with Ezra's father, Tovii, and for the first time, we sang and danced, all four of us as equals; and as with equals, the carpenter was clinking his glass with ours and promising a happy life.

I remembered that night the hot high Ukrainian sky and bright stars. The wind was rocking the stars; they were falling like joyful rain into the dirty Sambatyon River. Kids were singing on the other side of the fence, and a harmonica was accompanying them. That night, life seemed glorious. And I myself, having just now emerged out of the shtetl's shell, was a brave, proud young man, who believed he could handle anything.

II

But life twisted me, just like it bent, mashed, pressed everyone around, as it twisted cheerful Tovii and his enemy, Opanas Jaundice.

In the old days, after finishing work, neighbors would come out and sit on the wide, mud-covered stoops to relax and wait for dinner. Neighbors exchanged greetings, collectively cursed the wood-merchant Nekhlin, and complained about customers who didn't understand or value real work. Occasionally, Jaundice would approach Tovii and, flaring the hairy nostrils of his nose, breathed in the smell of Senderei's polish. Nowhere could you find such a polish, such a gentle shine, as the one Tovii applied to crude containers.

"What can I say, Tovii is a great master even if he's a Jew."

Tovii would raise his thick, braid-like eyebrows in surprise, scratch his thin, rough beard and begin to protest. But Tovii's voice was insincere. Deep in his heart he probably believed, just as I did, that there is no nation more capable and wise than the Jews. [. . .]

Then the water-carrier and Opanas Jaundice the carpenter got drunk. They walked arm in arm down our street, and Jaundice mumbled: "I'm a water-carrier? . . . Go on then . . . and you are a stinker . . . Jew-face. . . ." Drunk, he invaded Senderei's shop and announced

that, from now on, he would never show his face here again. "One little bench," Jaundice screamed, advancing on his neighbor, "what are you worried about!"

After sleeping it off and sobering up, he may have forgotten about his prank, but Tovii Senderei did not forget and didn't want to have anything further to do with the offender. Uriah Nekhlin also didn't want anything to do with him. Out of vexation, Opanas Jaundice started drinking even more. He drank, roughhoused, and yelled that Jews were taking everyone's jobs. And the more he drank, the less work he had. And Tovii, to spite Jaundice, ordered a sign, which stated in shiny letters "Tovii Senderei—CARPENTER," and hung the sign over the gate.

Jaundice's yard opened into a dirty, dark alley, and our yard faced the street. This accented Tovii's superiority. Jaundice would come out of the alley and stand in front of the festive sign for a long time, building up his anger to a fever pitch, and, once riled up, would head to the water carrier, Garkusha. It was Garkusha who advised him to pave a road through the hated neighbor's yard.

Jaundice would then pointedly pace in front of Tovii's windows. On the gate, facing the street, there were now two signs: "Tovii Senderei—CARPENTER" and "Afanasii Jaundice, BETTER CARPENTER." That's what Opanas ordered from the sign-maker. He hung the sign above his competitor's with his own hands.

The signs hung, but work was becoming more scarce. Recently, a furniture store had appeared in the shtetl that imported fancy, Warsaw furniture for the local villagers. Later, the store started to supply the mining camps with large orders of plank-beds, tables, window frames, and doors, ready-made somewhere thousands of miles away. To top it all off, the store opened a credit line, which lured away the stingy villagers who had been the main customers of Jaundice and Senderei.

Time went by. The two competitors' signs faded. The formerly festive letters faded and lost their color. Work became more and more scarce. The pan's assistant appeared punctually, but there wasn't anything with which to treat him. Tovii's eldest son and assistant, Zalman, was taken away to the army. Work was so scarce that Tovii sent off even the younger one, Ezra, to the red-headed bookbinder, Farfel. Minor repairs and dowry chests, which the Warsaw storekeepers didn't carry, was all that remained for the carpenters. They would sit on the stoops more and more frequently, sighing and cursing, not the crook Nekhlin but the owners of the store and their stingy customers. Both were faring poorly, but their animosity didn't die down. On the contrary, Jaundice insisted even more firmly that the Jews were taking everyone's jobs: at the market—there they are; beyond the forest—there they are again; a store appears—again it's them; and there is no place for a Christian. [. . .]

I could read Garkusha's mind by seeing his eyes, his lowered, bull-like head. I saw how he, Jaundice, a drunkard, and the parish bell ringer, the one who rang the alarm during the fight and who always tried to get a free drink, how they were all observing the Jews that were passing by, their eyes squinting with impatience, greed and anger, as if their clothes were being torn off their bodies along with their skin.

I saw these former and future pogromists who thought of themselves as masters of the land, and the whole country seemed to me to be a bull-like head, heavily lowered as before a blow. On days like these, I didn't have the patience to listen to father's nasal mumbling, which reminded me of a lamb's bleating as it is led to slaughter. Even the *melamed*'s eyes, soured and red behind his glasses, were squinting lamb-like, as if he were afraid to turn around to see the cruel and severe sun of the masters of the land.

When my brother Danka was born and had to have a bris, father didn't have the courage to arrange a festive ceremony as was customary. The bris was done so quickly that you would think that it was a crime. Like a criminal, Father kept running out into the yard to make sure that no one was looking.

"Jewish life," he lectured Mother, who was insulted on both her own and her newborn's behalf, "Jewish life, Russian customs, and Kiev's Purishkevich.[1] . . . It's better if it's quiet. . . ."

It truly was quiet. The guests dispersed quietly; Mother was sighing quietly; and very quietly, Danka was sobbing. He was only eight days old but already had a sense of Jewish grace. Granted, Danka, just like me, didn't resemble his *melamed*-father or his obedient mother, but rather, his grandfather the toiling weighman who couldn't do it in the shtetl.

One day, Tovii Senderei asked me to read a letter he received from his brother, a baker in America. The baker wrote that he was living, "may all Jews have such a life—thank God. Work is plentiful, and Tovii wouldn't go idle either. Additionally, all are equal here, if there's money, every person is his own master. There

is no Pan Stativa here, no Pale of Settlement, Cossacks, pogroms—in America Jews live happily."

He wasn't the first baker to write in such a manner from Boston. I read his letters to Tovii; Tovii took them from me and looked at length at the foreign envelopes and stamps on which presidents were represented—serious, wise people. He looked at the presidents as if wanting to ask them about the foreign, enviable life that his brother was promising. I knew that in the evening, when Ezra returned from the bindery, that he would make him read these letters again and again. He would listen, anxiously yet joyfully, seeing his youngest son reading with such ease, unlike his illiterate father. Ezra should study [. . .]; that way he would become a real person. But there is no way for the son of a carpenter to progress. No progress and no money. And so Ezra will stay at the bindery and bind books that will be read by others.

I imagine Tovii tossing in bed at night, and his wife, Zlata, whispering out loud what the stubborn carpenter thinks in his heart. That's their longstanding custom: whatever Tovii thinks, Zlata says. She whispers and sobs into her pillow. "She's a mother," thinks Tovii; "her pain is greater. She didn't have any bright days; the eldest son breaks his back in the army, her youngest perishes in the basement of a bindery, and neither of them has a future. And in America, or so my brother writes, Jews live happily. . . ."

Then they will start counting together all those who have left overseas. Two brothers and the daughter of the binder Farfel; Salganik the tailor with his family; the Safronchik brothers and another Safronchik, the one who used to play at weddings, also left; then Kukuy the cripple and his wife; Ḥayim Poprytkin, and Todresh Gorelik. They count and recount in an anxious whisper, and they begin to imagine that all of Gnilopol has left for America. . . .

I can imagine their confused and gloomy faces so well, their sleepless eyes; I can see their thoughts, and the feeling is unbearable. I leave my books that the carpenter envies and go outside to sit on the stoop. Soon, Ezra and Kopl, whose sister left for America, will come. She's not doing that well; she writes that in America, life is also tough if you don't have any money.

"We have nowhere to go," I tell my friends.

We begin to discuss how good it would be if Jews were to return to the Holy Land. It would be our land, and no one would dare to touch us there. We would till the land, we would have vineyards, fig, date, carob trees, and even etrogs, which no one has in our shtetl aside from Nekhlin the rich man. In Palestine, each person would have his own etrog. But God is angry at us, and we are scattered all over the world; we don't have a corner to call our own anywhere. . . .

A warm night is splashing overhead. Stars are laughing at us. Dogs are barking in Jaundice's yard. And in the middle of the street, the Cossack, Ostap Garkusha, is striding. His shadow—shaggy and scary—sneaks through the fence and approaches us.

"Hey, pogromists," I want to yell, "do your thing, burn, beat us, so that we don't stink up your life. Beat us, pogromists! . . ." [. . .]

V

War!

Torn from their rotting roots as if by wind, people wandered from place to place with all of their worldly possessions that could fit into one basket, one parcel, one bundle of holy books and candle-holders—a noisy convoy from every corner of the blessed Pale.

I saw them wallowing, dirty, and crowded on the floor of our synagogue where they were placed by the Gnilopol community. I was looking at these feeble, pale-faced, and slouching people; at the unkempt children crawling in dirt; and at their mothers, bareheaded, loud, and pathetic; and all of us—our entire ancient nation—it seemed to me, were crawling and dying helplessly under the heels of foreign horses.

Jews were dying on the front lines, rotting on hospital cots; Jewish crutches were making no less noise than others', and yet we were considered traitors. Newspapers announced this, corrupt generals implied this, and, of course, Ostap Garkusha yelled this for everyone on Panskaya Street to hear. He, who hadn't been fit for war in years, was still healthy enough to be a pogromist. He and Jaundice, whose firstborn was killed on the German front, and the parish bell ringer—the familiar gang—would get drunk, rough-house, and vow to settle the score.

More and more often, tsarist military decrees were hung over the parish office. "Mobilization," "Additional Investigation," "Admissions Commission" became the most important words. Uriah Nekhlin and his family were given a deferment since he was wise enough to open a war-carriage plant at the right time, fulfilling the army's needs. His son Borenka, with his new Christian name Boris Orestovich, came to Gnilopol for the deferment.

"Protectors of the fatherland" now scurried to us from big cities, even from the capital itself, suddenly attracted to mining work. Engineers and foremen made a good living from "national defense." But young men from Panskaya Street didn't get a deferment from the front line. [. . .]

But Noyekh Pikelnyi, Issachka's Bundist brother, didn't want to support the fatherland on the front. He didn't give a damn that the Germans took over all of Poland or that [General] Brusilov was being pushed out from the Carpathian Mountains, that they were attacking on all fronts, that you could hear the bones crunch. Noyekh saw that the forest business was going well; Nekhlin was getting richer. "Let Nekhlin go and support the fatherland," the Bundist would yell. He was angry, slighted by people and by the God of little people, while Zalman Senderei, strong-bodied like his father but silent and quiet in character like his younger brother Ezra, obeyed resignedly.

Noyekh was a Bundist, a Social Democrat. That is, as far as we were concerned, a person who had forgotten his people. On one question I nevertheless agreed with the Bundist: Jews have no reason to go to the front. We are strangers here, we have been attacked and will continue to be attacked here, so why should we enter a stranger's quarrel? [. . .]

Our entire street was observing with impatience and sympathy the new "Egyptian plagues"—Noyekh and Zalman's self-deprivation of food and sleep in order to escape the front. Farfel, the bookbinder, advised everyone to drink strong tea "for the heart," while the cantor, Yoineh Immortal, the one who was so happy when Beilis was released, insistently suggested that one should pay attention to the "teeth." In the past, the cantor used to swallow egg yolks, which provided the tearful passion to his voice, and spoke only in a whisper to protect his voice. Now he had nothing to protect: he yanked out ten of his front teeth, received a "white ticket," a pardon from the army and ruined his voice.

A white ticket! . . . Zalman Senderei widened his sleepless, suffering eyes, but he didn't have the energy to be jealous. "What can I say, Yoineh Immortal is a fortunate man; no wonder no one in his family died younger than a hundred years old. That's how he got such a proud family name. . . ."

Neighbors and their wives would gather on Senderei's porch, entertaining the sleepy "defenders." However late I would come from my lessons, there was always light in Senderei's shack, and I could hear conversations. On the porch, wrinkled and desiccated and ruffled up like a sparrow, sat the stubborn Zalman who didn't want to go to war.

Tovii didn't take part in the "Egyptian plagues." Grey and bent over, though still of a joyful nature, he kept silent, letting his bustling wife mix castor oil into the dough.

"She's a mother," Tovii would say; "her pain is greater."

"Eh, Reb Tovii, Reb Tovii," my father shook his head, and he inflected the word *Reb* with the kind of scorn that a learned *melamed* may feel toward an illiterate carpenter. "I look at you, Reb Carpenter, and you haven't changed at all. . . . A Jew must change, a Jew must. . . ."

And here father, out of habit, indulged in a lengthy discourse about what a Jew should and shouldn't do, what themes he shouldn't talk about, what thoughts he shouldn't have. . . . Everything was clear-cut for Gnilopol's Talmudist. But Tovii was not a learned Talmudist. He saw that his son was fading away with everyone's consent.

In the end, Noyekh Pikelnyi couldn't stand it. He got drunk with the miners, binged, and slept off all the days of his suffering. Then, he went to the Commission and left for the front.

Noyekh returned from the front without an arm.

But Zalman Senderei obediently stood the test. He was wheeled to the Commission in a wagon, and the Commission was obliged to give him six months to recover. Six months later, the Commission itself had disappeared, and red flags were fluttering over Gnilopol.

That's how the "defenders" entered the revolution. One with gastritis and the other without an arm. They marched side by side from the first demonstration that our street had ever witnessed. Carpenters, shoemakers, furriers, and market vendors poured onto the stoops to gawk at the song-hollering and flag-carrying soldiers and miners. They were sober; they didn't assault market storerooms like they used to as part of the festivities. We had never seen them like this. Even Kutska the fool, who would appear at all gatherings, was now silent and didn't bother the passersby.

Ostap Garkusha stood by the fence and observed the demonstrators. Fat and greying, like Gogol's [Taras] Bulba, who once roared with the gentle carelessness of shtetl-dwellers, Garkusha was wearing enormous boots and striped, faded, patched, Cossack trousers, and a threadbare, though dashingly tilted army cap—spread

his powerful legs and stood, letting his still thick Cossack forelock onto his eyes, which were swimming with hatred. He towered over our squatting street like a severe guard, like a master, who observes everything silently, preparing to turn around and beat everyone into the ground.

The villagers, having descended into the mines during the war, began dividing the land. We got freedom! . . . Who wants to mine in a tight stall, knee-deep in cold water? Who wants to feed lice and eat iron rye in rotten barracks that have been smoked-through like a sea-roach? We got freedom! . . . You won't be able to chase us into a ditch at the front any longer. Go ahead, try and catch us—na-na-na-na! [. . .]

The pan's assistant escaped from the hellishly mad muzhiks by coming to Gnilopol, and our Jews protected him from their just revenge for an entire month. They weren't hiding him because they pitied him but because the shtetl lived, like my father, cautiously: who knows what tomorrow will bring—today I hide him, tomorrow he will hide me. A good deed doesn't go to waste. A cowardly hope of the weak. A good deed didn't go to waste for the pan's assistant. Oh no! . . .

The miners were astir and were electing a council. A miner was sitting in the parish government; the new police commissioner was Semka Mayofis, otherwise known as Semka "Fingerless"; Gnilopol's butcher and Noyekh Pikelnyi and Mikolka Jaundice were making a noise at the Oak Balk. That same Mikolka, who used to fight with me, was now sitting on the miners' council and was a "party man."

The demonstration had passed, the flags had fluttered, orators had yelled their fill, and Ezra Senderei and Kopl Farfel went back to cooking stinky glue. Tovii loitered looking for work, and I hurried to all my classes, which seemed to have multiplied. The Pale was abolished, the *numerus clausus* was canceled, and everybody was busy making up for lost time. Only Isachka Pikelnyi was left without work since Uriah Nekhlin was firing his office workers. Gnilopol's plutocrat was scratching his merchant's beard and looking at the slogan hanging above his desk: "Labor is a Holy Cause."

Nowadays, nobody was laboring, and everyone, absolutely everyone, was devouring his business while singing stupid songs like the one that Isachka Pikelnyi started singing as he was being fired. Uriah grumbled at his old mother, yelled at his innocent niece and, having vented, went to the lodge where he was hosting Deniska, the son of Stativa, who was killed by muzhiks.

Deniska volunteered for the army and managed to earn an ensign's rank and a cross. He should have run when the soldiers turned on the "nobility," but he couldn't find his estate, couldn't find his father, and didn't know where to turn. Then Deniska remembered a Christian-convert fellow soldier who sent letters to Gnilopol. Uriah welcomed his friend's son and housed him at the lodge. Uriah was probably reasoning in the same way as the shtetl politicians: a good deed doesn't go to waste.

Soon Boris, who became a cadet under Kerensky, also returned. In their idleness, the officers played cards for days on end, exhausted Nekhlin's wine and, once drunk, Denis would sit down at the piano and sing. Occasionally he stood at the window and looked out on our street, which only recently had belonged to his father and bowed down to him. Now it was named Freedom Street, where no one wanted anything to do with the pan. In an unbuttoned officer's coat, with insignia torn off, he stood, bowing his eighteen-year-old head, and his glance, a familiar pogromist glance, was full of anger and the promise of revenge.

The old men in the synagogue argued again, even more vehemently, and my father proclaimed for the thousandth time what a Jew should and shouldn't do in times of revolution. "We have nothing to do here, we are strangers in this festivity and in this fight," he kept telling his audience.

But his audience, just like his students, was becoming more and more scarce. The festivities and the fight came to our street as well, and the main fighter was the armless Noyekh Pikelnyi. "A workers' government will solve everything," Noyekh roared, having now become a Bolshevik; "Jews need to support the workers' government."

We laughed and didn't believe the invalid who was slighted by people and God. We have been assaulted for too long, and we saw Ostap Garkusha and his company too often. We saw the yellow Haidamak pins appearing more and more often in the villages, promising to settle the score with the Russians and the Jews. We read the "Universals" of the Ukrainian Nationalists and heard of Symon Petliura. We saw how this damned pot, formerly known as "Mother Russia," was coming to a boil, and, therefore, didn't believe that anyone would care about us. Instead of a red banner, we displayed a white and blue one; instead of the "The Internationale," we sang "Hatikvah"; instead of trying to get elected to the Workers' Council, we were collecting money for the National Fund. We went from house to house and told of our old-new homeland, agitated, recruited supporters, and felt that we, unlike the hollering Noyekh, were pursuing a truly Jewish path.

Formerly, we were lonely. Not that long ago, the shtetl's wise men, like my father, had laughed at us, but now we were becoming more and more numerous. Now, the most respectable Gnilopolers were becoming Zionists. Our rabbi and Uriah Nekhlin himself became Zionists. Even Potagaylo, the pharmacist, who previously was too afraid to hire a Jewish tutor, Potagaylo, the Christian convert, admitted while beating his chest that it was the tsarist regime, may it be forgotten, that had made him convert.

The Craftsmen Synagogue, where refugees had stayed not that long ago, was painted by us in nationalist colors. At the *bimah*, we erected a portrait of Herzl, decorated with ribbons and greens, and our rabbi, who at one time didn't dare to curse Nekhlin's progeny, was now reading the text of the famous declaration that returned to us our thousands-year-old homeland, to Gnilopolers. He held on to the last issue of *Rassvet* as if it were a tsarist declaration. I listened to his anxious and joyfully trembling voice and looked at the Gnilopolers, packed tightly into the synagogue as if it were Yom Kippur. The young men wore two-colored bows in their lapels. All of Gnilopol, along with the entire Jewish nation that was dispersed around the whole world, was listening to the happy news. I've never experienced such a joyous feeling of pride as in that hour.

Spring arrived late that year. The snow delayed its departure. In one night, the frail swamp bristled and gushed towards Gnilopol, breaking the ice. The shtetl was knee-deep in cold spring water. Flooded houses stared pathetically with their crooked windows, preparing to collapse. It seemed to me that life itself was bristling and breaking ice, to finally tear off its hateful, shabby rags.

We were shtetl guys, but we believed in our future, and we believed that our life would be unlike that of our fathers.

A different fate awaited us. But, in this fate was reflected, perhaps, the fate of our homeless, ever-dying in the cursed Pale nation. [. . .]

XVII

In the morning, the strike started, and at night, the guests arrived. Four people entered our barracks. The broad blades of spears glimmered in the night like extinguished candles. A sergeant with a bandaged cheek (he was really beaten up by porters), two border patrols, and a civilian were interested in our documents.

They were feeling our mattresses, went into nooks, tapped on the damp wooden walls and, it seemed, tried to sniff the air, which was concealing danger and guile. Like hounds that had lost their trail, the border patrols were stomping around in our barracks and, like hounds who caught the smell of an animal again, they rushed to the divider, behind which stood Dora's bed.

Ezra Senderei was standing by the divider.

"There is a girl there," Ezra said.

"A-ah. . . ." the sergeant groaned with anger, touching the dressing on his cheek. "This pan with the glasses looks very familiar. This pan will have to take a walk. . . ."

The sergeant pushed Ezra aside and tried to poke his head into the divider. But Ezra wouldn't surrender. He was taller than the short, paunchy sergeant, and grabbed him with his arms. For a moment, they wrestled quietly, and the border patrols stomped around helplessly and awkwardly, not wanting to insult their superior. Then they grabbed Ezra while the sergeant and the civilian went behind the divider where Dora, having had the time to get dressed, was waiting.

All this happened so quickly and was so unexpected that, by the time I got my bearings and rushed to help, Ezra was already being led away. I yelled that I would complain to the Palestinian Committee.

The sergeant was straightening his moustache and laughing: they will arrest the committee as well, when they get the chance. If he could have his way, he would arrest all the Jews, give them two weeks' time, and—off to Palestine, away from Poland! That's what he and every Pole would do.

With these words, the border patrols left, taking Ezra with them.

They held him for two days and, with the help of the Palestinian Committee's intercession, sent him to Warsaw, not having bothered the rest of us only because the committee promised to send us away from Devendzin by the end of the month.

That same day I was summoned by the committee.

The chairman screamed at me, and I had to take it and remain quiet. I only mentioned that the committee's money would not disappear; we would return it as soon as we could.

"If all the Russians would have returned that which they took, we could have bought up all of Devendzin

. . ." the chairman laughed wickedly. "Yes, yes, all of Devendzin and then some," he yelled, becoming irritated by the fact that I was silent and that this was very clearly a lie.

When I left, I was pale and angry with humiliation and because I couldn't throw his money into his face.

I didn't know that Yodidyo Kipnis had visited him before me. Having been fired a few days prior, Yodidyo was running around town looking for support. No one wanted to fight with the wealthy baker, and the Devendzin rabbi yelled at him and threw him out. Then, Yodidyo went to the barber shop.

The barber, making a meager living in this Hasidic town, thought that he had misheard at first. But Yodidyo, decisively and desperately, like a swimmer jumping from up high, threw his arms up and fell, rather than sat, into the chair.

An hour later he came to the chairman of the Palestinian Committee, clean-shaven. A flat cloth cap clung to the top of his head, funny and forlorn, and Yodidyo himself seemed naked. This was unheard of. Yodidyo knew that there would be no mercy for him. In any case, now the committee would not be able to refuse him money, the committee would have to send him out of Devendzin. That's what the naïve pastry-deliverer thought, but he was wrong.

"The committee has enough worries already; Yodidyo will have to wait," the chairman announced, tapping his Adam's apple with gall and carefully looking at the shaved young man, as if he were standing before him with no trousers on.

After this, Yodidyo had no other choice but to come to us. He lived with us all these days, helping with organizing and cleaning, working with such dedication that one would think that it was he who was leaving. Perhaps, at times, he did imagine exactly that, and then, coming to his senses, would sit in the corner. Perhaps because he shaved, or for some other reason, Yodidyo seemed taller now, as tall as his friend Zelig Slusch. His gypsy, swarthy face became even darker and appeared completely child-like. His full lips were bulging, like his sister's, and his dark, slanted eyes looked on with sadness. Yodidyo looked like he was sixteen or seventeen, not older.

He was afraid to come out of the barracks. But the fame of his performance had already spread throughout Devendzin. Little boys, on their way home from heder, stopped by our windows to stalk Yodidyo. With impatience and passion, they clung to the glass, trying to make out the heretic and, having spotted him, yelled and spat in exactly the same manner that Yodidyo's uncle had yelled and spat while excommunicating his nephew.

Kopl and I would go outside to chase away the god-fearing hooligans, but the small zealots did not back down. They were leading an actual siege on the barracks, throwing rocks and covering us with dirt. Kopl, worrying about Binka, who was left alone with the enraged relatives, volunteered to go get her. I saw with what humiliation he was chased out from the house. . . .

Late at night, having waited for everyone to fall asleep, Binka came running. She fell onto Dora's shoulder and cried with despair:

"Take me with you! . . . Take me!"

There was something in her sobbing that reminded me of Christina's crying. Just as before, everyone was standing around her with bowed heads. Just like then, we were embarrassed to look Binka in the eyes and, just like then, everyone knew that they couldn't help her.

Our last night.

Zelig Slusch comes over. The baker had to fire him and hire a Pole. Zelig is working as a porter at the train station. He lives from hand to mouth, this Devendzin giant, who is denied a piece of bread by the republic, since no one really needs porters at this small station.

Nyakha Lyam the bath attendant comes too. He is also unemployed, since the baths are closed. Kuntsya is now supporting the family single-handedly. On Fridays, Kuntsya goes to wealthy families, washes floors, polishes the candlesticks, and, if she's lucky, helps in the kitchen. Poor Nyakha fears her more than ever.

The last one to come is Yodidyo Kipnis. He was wandering the whole day looking for work. But no one wants to help him. The same story every day. But he doesn't despond. The committee allowed him to move into our barracks along with his sister. At least now they will have a nook of their own.

"Yes, yes, a nook of one's own is the most important thing," Nyakha readily agrees and taps Yodidyo's knee encouragingly, "A Jew mustn't despond; a Jew has his Jewish God on high. . . ."

At this point, Nyakha feels a pinch from his wife sitting next to him and stops in mid-sentence. Rigid Kuntsya cannot forgive Yodidyo's shaved cheeks. She doesn't look in his direction and makes clear her disapproval. Yodidyo is used to this tone. All of Devendzin

looks at him with Kuntsya's eyes. But he doesn't care anymore.

"A Jewish god?" Yodidyo says mockingly. "Who knows, maybe his ears are plugged so he doesn't hear what is happening with the Jews in Devendzin?"

"Shut up!" small Nyakha becomes frightened.

Yodidyo no longer hears him. He jumps up and yells, it's unclear at whom:

"A fat wreck. . . . He's seventy, and they say—that's what God commands. . . . Where are you, all-knowing and all-merciful? . . ." demands Yodidyo, raising his arms, shaking with anger and sorrow, to the barrack's low ceiling. "All-merciful God, you are quiet, your ears are plugged. . . . Reb Shmelts conducts judgment and punishment in your name, crooks and plutocrats are your children. . . . Delight in them and kiss them, my God, kiss them! . . ."

In such a way, Yodidyo Kipnis is blaspheming in a frenzy of anger, exiled due to pride and for daring to question divine mercy.

The frightened Nyakha Lyam is long gone, urged on by his wife. Zelig Slusch also left, having sullenly listened to the end of his friend's speech. Only Binka remains. She has been silent throughout the evening. She has been generally silent since the time she found out about the match with old man Shmelts. It seems as if, having been frightened once, the girl doesn't have the power for more. She eats, drinks, sleeps, obediently helps Dora with housekeeping, but doesn't leave the barracks. She is even afraid to come to the window and constantly clings to the corner.

Kopl Farfel is the only one who knows how to talk with her. Kopl sings to her all the songs he knows. He sings so well and so sadly, like he hasn't done since the time we used to pray, and when he sings, even the old men on the other side of the wall, in the study house, drone more quietly. Kopl has the funny hope that it might be possible to add Binka's name to his passport. Of course, nothing will come of this. That is why he sings so sadly now and spends all his free time with a girl who reminds him of Rokhka.

I stride slowly along the square, facing the train station for the last time, past the factory of canned fish, past the caving-in house of study, and further, along the train tracks. A green fog swirls over the roads. It resembles the smoke of a smoke-house and passersby disappear into the fog, just like smokers in smoke. Someone is singing:

How he was killed
By the Russian Bolsheviks . . .

The familiar song draws nearer, then farther, and all of a sudden, is right next to me. Christina is standing in front of me. Her unhandsome face is unskillfully made up. On her lips is an uncertain smile:

"Doesn't the pan want to treat a girl to a bottle of beer and so on? . . ."

Christina bends forward and recognizes me. . . .

Night descends on the small town, and candles are lit in the old house of study. The church bell rings hushed and pleasant in the fog.

Silence.

The extinguished tar cookers by the train-station are silent, no movement is heard in storage, in the vast courtyards of the tar factory. Lights blink intermittently. And only the strikers, like sentinels, march stubbornly and gloomily through the fog.

NOTE

1. [Antisemitic—Trans.]

Translated by Alexandra Hoffman.

Other works by Egart: *Marusia Zhuraleva* (1938); *Bukhta tumanov* (1956).

Vasily Grossman

1905–1964

Vasily Grossman was born in Berdichev, Ukraine, to an assimilated Jewish family. He attended university in Moscow and worked as a chemist; however, he became a writer, often exploring Jews and social issues. During World War II he served as a front-line newspaper correspondent. He was also a member of the Jewish Anti-Fascist Committee, and contributed, with Ilya Ehrenburg, to *Chernaia kniga* (The Black Book), outlining Russian anti-Jewish policies. After the war, Grossman continued not to be shy about expressing his views on Soviet antisemitism, and he refused to be censored.

In the Town of Berdichev

1934

Vavilova's face was dark and weather-beaten, and it was odd to see it blush.

"Why are you laughing?" she said finally. "It's all so stupid."

Kozyrev took the paper from the table, looked at it, and, shaking his head, burst out laughing again.

"No, it's just too ridiculous," he said through his laughter. "Application for leave . . . from the commissar of the First Battalion . . . for forty days for reasons of pregnancy." Then he turned serious. "So what should I do? Who's going to take your place? Perelmuter from the Divisional Political Section?"

"Perelmuter's a sound Communist," said Vavilova.

"You're all sound Communists," said Kozyrev. Lowering his voice, as though he were talking about something shameful, he asked, "Is it due soon, Klavdiya?"

"Yes," said Vavilova. She took off her sheepskin hat and wiped the sweat from her brow.

"I'd have got rid of it," she said in her deep voice, "but I wasn't quick enough. You know what it was like—down by Grubeshov there were three whole months when I was hardly out of the saddle. And when I got to the hospital, the doctor said no." She screwed up her nose, as if about to cry. "I even threatened the bastard with my Mauser," she went on, "but he still wouldn't do anything. He said it was too late."

She left the room. Kozyrev went on staring at her application. "Well, well, well," he said to himself. "Who'd have thought it? She hardly seems like a women at all. Always with her Mauser, always in leather trousers. She's led the battalion into the attack any number of times. She doesn't even have the voice of a woman . . . But it seems you can't fight Nature . . ."

And for some reason he felt hurt and a little sad.

He wrote on the application, "The bearer . . ." And he sat there and frowned, irresolutely circling his pen nib over the paper. How should he word it? Eventually he went on: "to be granted forty days of leave from the present date. . ." He stopped to think, added, "for reasons of health," then inserted the word "female," and then, with an oath, deleted the word "female."

"Fine comrades *they* make!" he said, and called his orderly. "Heard about our Vavilova?" he asked loudly and angrily. "Who'd have thought it!"

"Yes," said the orderly. He shook his head and spat.

Together they damned Vavilova and all other women. After a few dirty jokes and a little laughter, Kozyrev called for his chief of staff and said to him, "You must go around tomorrow, I suppose. Find out where she wants to have it—in a hospital or in a billet—and make sure everything's generally all right."

The two men then sat there till morning, poring over the one-inch-to-a mile map and jabbing their fingers at it. The Poles were advancing.

A room was requisitioned for Vavilova. The little house was in the Yatki—as the marketplace was called—and it belonged to Haim-Abram Leibovich-Magazanik, known to his neighbors and even his own wife as Haim Tuter, that is Haim the Tatar.

Vavilova's arrival caused an uproar. She was brought there by a clerk from the Communal Department, a thin boy wearing a leather jacket and a pointed Budyonny helmet. Magazanik cursed him in Yiddish; the clerk shrugged his shoulders and said nothing.

Magazanik then switched to Russian. "The cheek of these snotty little bastards!" he shouted to Vavilova, apparently expecting her to share his indignation. "Whose clever idea was this? As if there weren't a single bourgeois left in the whole town! As if there weren't a single room left for the Soviet authorities except where Magazanik lives! As if there weren't a spare room anywhere except one belonging to a worker with seven children! What about Litvak the grocer? What about Khodorov the cloth maker? What about Ashkenazy, our number-one millionaire?"

Magazanik's children were standing around them in a circle—seven curly-headed angels in ragged clothes, all watching Vavilova through eyes black as night. She was as big as a house, she was twice the height of their father. All this was frightening and funny and very interesting indeed.

In the end Magazanik was pushed out of the way, and Vavilova went through to her room.

From the sideboard, from the chairs with gaping holes and sagging seats, from bedclothes now as flat and dark and flaccid as the breasts of the old women who had once received these blankets as part of their wedding dowries, there came such an overpowering smell of human life that Vavilova found herself taking a deep breath, as if about to dive deep into a pond.

That night she was unable to sleep. Behind the partition wall—as if they formed a complete orchestra, with everything from high-pitched flutes and violins to the low drone of the double bass—the Magazanik family was snoring. The heaviness of the summer night, the dense smells—everything seemed to be stifling her.

There was nothing the room did not smell of.

Paraffin, garlic, sweat, fried goose fat, unwashed linen—the smell of human life, of human habitation.

Now and then she touched her swollen, ripening belly; the living being there inside her was kicking and moving about.

For many months, honorably and obstinately, she had struggled against this being. She had jumped down heavily from her horse. During voluntary working Saturdays in the towns she had heaved huge pine logs about with silent fury. In villages she had drunk every kind of herbal portion and infusion. In bathhouses, she had scalded herself until she broke out in blisters. And she had demanded so much iodine from the regimental pharmacy that the medical assistant had been on the point of penning a complaint to the brigade medical department.

But the child had obstinately gone on growing, making it hard for her to move, making it hard for her to ride. She had felt nauseous. She had vomited. She had felt dragged down, dragged toward the earth.

At first she had blamed everything on *him*—on the sad, taciturn man who had proved stronger than her and had found a way through her thick leather jacket and the coarse cloth of her tunic and into her woman's heart. She had remembered him at the head of his men, leading them at a run across a small and terrifyingly simple wooden bridge. There had been a burst of Polish machine-gun fire—and it was as if he had vanished. An empty greatcoat had flung up its arms, fallen, and then hung there over the stream.

She had galloped over him on her maddened stallion and, behind her, as if pushing her on, the battalion had hurtled forward.

What had remained was *it*. It, now, was to blame for everything. And Vavilova was lying there defeated, while *it* kicked its little hoofs victoriously. It was living inside her.

Before Magazanik went out in the morning, when his wife was serving him breakfast and at the same time trying to drive away the flies, the children, and the cat, he said quietly, with a sideways glance at the wall of the requisitioned room, "Give her some tea—damn her!"

It was as though he were bathing in the sunlit pillars of dust, in all the smells and sounds—the cries of the children, the mewing of the cat, the muttering of the samovar. He had no wish to go off to the workshop. He loved his wife, his children, and his old mother; he loved his home.

Sighing, he went on his way, and there remained in the house only women and children.

The cauldron of the Yatki went on bubbling all through the day. Peasant men traded birch logs as white as chalk; peasant women rustled strings of onions; old Jewish women sat above downy hillocks of geese tied together by their legs. Every now and then a seller would pluck from one of these splendid white flowers a living petal with a snaking, twisting neck—and the buyer would blow on the tender down between its legs and feel the fat that showed yellow beneath the soft warm skin.

Dark-legged lasses in colorful kerchiefs carried tall red pots brimming with wild strawberries; as if about to run away, they cast frightened looks at the buyers. People on carts sold golden, sweating balls of butter wrapped in plump burdock leaves.

A blind beggar with the white beard of a wizard was stretching out his hands and weeping tragically and imploringly, but no one was touched by his terrible grief. Everyone passed by differently. One woman, tearing the very smallest onion off her string, threw it into the old man's tin bowl. He felt it, stopped praying, and said angrily, "May your children be as generous to you in your old age!" And he again began intoning a prayer as ancient as the Jewish nation.

People bought and sold, poked and prodded, raising their eyes as if expecting someone from the tender blue sky to offer them counsel: Should they buy the pike or might they be better off with a carp? And all the time they went on cursing, screeching, scolding one another, and laughing.

Vavilova tidied and swept her room. She put away her greatcoat, her sheepskin hat, and her riding boots. The noise outside was making her head thump, while inside the apartment the little Tuters were all shouting and screaming, and she felt as though she were asleep and dreaming somebody else's bad dream.

In the evening, when he came back home from work, Magazanik stopped in the doorway. He was astounded: his wife, Beila, was sitting at the table—and beside her was a large woman in an ample dress, with loose slippers on her bare feet and a bright-colored kerchief around her head. The two women were laughing quietly, talking to each other, raising and lowering their large broad hands as they sorted through a heap of tiny undershirts.

Beila had gone into Vavilova's room during the afternoon. Vavilova had been standing by the window, and Beila's sharp feminine eye had made out the swollen belly partly concealed by Vavilova's height.

"Begging your pardon," Beila had said resolutely, "but it seems to me that you're pregnant.

And Beila had begun fussing around her, waving her hands about, laughing and lamenting.

"Children," she said, "children—do you have any idea what misery they bring with them?" And she squeezed the youngest of the Tuters against her bosom. "Children are such a grief, such a calamity, such neverending trouble. Every day they want to eat, and not a week passes by but one of them gets a rash and another gets a boil or comes down with a fever. And Doctor Baraban—may God grant him health—expects ten pounds of the best flour for every visit he makes."

She stroked little Sonya's head. "And every one of my lot is still living. Not one of them's going to die."

Vavilova had turned out to know nothing at all; she did not understand anything, nor did she know how to do anything. She had immediately subordinated herself to Beila's great knowledge. She had listened, and she had asked questions, and Beila, laughing with pleasure at the ignorance of this woman commissar, had told her everything she needed to know.

How to feed a baby; how to wash and powder a baby; how to stop a baby crying at night; how many diapers and babies' shirts she was going to need; the way newborn babies can scream and scream until they're quite beside themselves; the way they turn blue and your heart almost bursts from fear that your child is about to die; the best way to cure the runs; what causes diaper rash; how one day a teaspoon will make a knocking sound against a child's gums and you know that it's started to teethe.

A complex world with its own laws and customs, its own joys and sorrows.

It was a world about which Vavilova knew nothing—and Beila indulgently, like an elder sister, had initiated her into it.

"Get out from under our feet!" she had yelled at the children. "Out you go into the yard—quick march!" The moment they were alone in the room, Beila had lowered her voice to a mysterious whisper and begun telling Vavilova about giving birth. Oh no, childbirth was no simple matter—far from it. And like an old soldier talking to a new recruit, Beila had told Vavilova about the great joys and torments of labor.

"Childbirth," she had said. "You think it's child's play, like war. Bang, bang—and there's an end to it. No, I'm sorry, but that's not how it is at all."

Vavilova had listened to her. This was the first time in all the months of her pregnancy that she had met someone who spoke of the unfortunate accident that had befallen her as if it were a happy event, as if it were the most important and necessary thing in her life.

Discussions, now including Magazanik, continued into the evening. There was no time to lose. Immediately after supper, Magazanik took a candle, went up into the attic, and with much clattering brought down a metal cradle and a little tub for bathing the new person.

"Have no fears, comrade Commissar," he said. He was laughing and his eyes were shining. "You're joining a thriving business."

"Shut your mouth, you rascal!" said his wife. "No wonder they call you an ignorant Tatar."

That night Vavilova lay in her bed. The dense smells no longer felt stifling, as they had during the previous night. She was used to them now; she was not even aware of them. She no longer wanted to have to think about anything.

It seemed to her that there were horses nearby and that she could hear them neighing. She glimpsed a long row of horses' heads; the horses were all chestnut and each had a white blaze on its forehead. The horses were constantly moving, nodding, snorting, baring their teeth. She remembered the battalion; she remembered Kirpichov, the political officer of the Second Company. There was a lull in the fighting at present. Who would give the soldiers their political talks? Who would tell them about the July days? The quartermaster should be hauled over the coals for this delay in the issue of boots. Once they had boots, the soldiers could make themselves footcloths. There were a lot of malcontents in the second company, especially that curly-headed fellow who was always singing songs about the Don. Vavilova yawned and closed her eyes. The battalion had gone somewhere far, far away, into the pink corridor of the dawn, between damp ricks of hay. And her thoughts about it were somehow unreal.

It gave an impatient push with its little hoofs. Vavilova opened her eyes and sat up in bed.

"A boy or a girl?" she asked out loud.

And all of a sudden her heart felt large and warm. Her heartbeats were loud and resonant.

"A boy or a girl?"

In the afternoon she went into labor.

"Oy!" she screamed hoarsely, sounding more like a peasant woman than a commissar. The pain was sharp, and it penetrated everywhere.

Beila helped her back to her bed. Little Syoma ran off merrily to fetch the midwife.

Vavilova was clutching Beila's hand. She was speaking quickly and quietly: "It's started, Beila. I'd thought it would be another ten days. It's started, Beila."

Then the pains stopped, and she thought she'd been wrong to send for the midwife.

But half an hour later the pains began again. Vavilova's tan now seemed separate from her, like a mask; underneath it her face had gone white. She lay there with her teeth clenched. It was as if she were thinking about something tormenting and shameful, as if, any minute now, she would jump up and scream, "What have I done! What have I gone and done!" And then, in her despair, she would hide her face in her hands.

The children kept peeping into the room. Their blind grandmother was by the stove, boiling a large saucepan of water. Alarmed by the look of anguish on Vavilova's face, Beila kept looking toward the street door. At last the midwife arrived. Her name was Rosalia Samoilovna. She was a stocky woman with a red face and close cropped hair. Soon the whole house was filled by her piercing, cantankerous voice. She shouted at Beila, at the children, at the old grandmother. Everyone began bustling about. The Primus stove in the kitchen began to hum. The children began dragging the table and chairs out of the room. Looking as if she were trying to put out a fire, Beila was hurriedly mopping the floor. Rosalia Samoilovna was driving the flies away with the towel. Vavilova watched her and for a moment thought they were in the divisional headquarters and that the army commander had just arrived. He too was stocky, red-faced, and cantankerous, and he used to show up at times when the Poles had suddenly broken through the front line, when everyone was reading communiqués, whispering, and exchanging anxious looks as though a dead body or someone mortally ill were lying in the room with them. And the army commander would slash through this web of mystery and silence. He would curse, laugh, and shout out orders: What did he care about supply trains that had been cut off or entire regiments that had been surrounded?

Vavilova subordinated herself to Rosalia Samoilovna's powerful voice. She answered her questions; she turns onto her back or her side; she did everything she was told. Now and then her mind clouded. The walls and the ceiling lost their outlines; they were breaking up and moving in on her like waves. The midwife's loud voice would bring her back to herself. Once again she would see Rosalia Samoiloyna's red, sweating face and the ends of the white kerchief tied over her hair. Her mind was empty of thoughts. She wanted to howl like a wolf; she wanted to bite the pillow. Her bones were cracking and breaking apart. Her forehead was covered by a sticky, sickly sweat. But she did not cry out; she just ground her teeth and, convulsively jerking her head, gasped in air.

Sometimes the pain went away, as if it had never been there at all, and she would look around in amazement, listening to the noise of the market, astonished by a glass on a stool or a picture on the wall.

When the child, desperate for life, once again began fighting its way out, she felt only terror of the pain to come but also an uncertain joy: there was no getting away from this, so let it be quick.

Rosalia Samoilovna said quietly to Beila, "If you think I'd wish it upon myself to be having my first child at the age of thirty-six, then you're wrong, Beila."

Vavilova had not been able to make out the words, but it frightened her that Rosalia Samoilovna was speaking so quietly.

"What?" she asked. "Am I going to die?"

She did not hear Rosalia Samoilovna's anwer. As for Beila, she was looking pale and lost. Standing in the doorway, shrugging her shoulders, she was saying, "Oy, oy, who needs all this? Who needs all this suffering? She doesn't need it. Nor does the child. Nor does the father, drat him. Not does God in his heaven. Whose clever idea was it to torment us like this?"

The birth took many hours.

When he got back from work, Magazanik sat on the front steps, as anxious as if it were not Vavilova but his own Beila who was giving birth. The twilight thickened; lights appeared in the windows. Jews were coming back from the synagogue, their prayer garments rolled up under their arms. In the moonlight the empty marketplace and the little streets and houses seemed beautiful and mysterious. Red Army men in riding breeches, their spurs jingling, were walking along the brick pavements. Young girls were nibbling sunflower seeds, laughing as they looked at the soldiers. One of them was gabbling: "And I was eating sweets and throwing the wrappers at him . . ."

"Yes," Magazanik said to himself. "It's like in the old tale . . . So little work to do in the house that she had to go and buy herself a clutch of piglets. So few cares of my own that I have to have a whole partisan brigade giving birth in my house." All of a sudden he pricked up his ears and stood up. Inside the house he had heard a hoarse male voice. The oaths and curses this voice was shouting were so foul that Magazanik could only shake his head and spit. The voice was Vavilova's. Crazed

with pain, and in the last throes of labor, she was wrestling with God, with woman's accursed lot.

"Yes," said Magazanik. "You can tell it's a commissar giving birth. The strongest words I've ever heard from my own dear Beila are 'Oy, Mama! Oy, Mama! Oy, dearest Mama of mine!' "

Rosalia Samoilovna smacked the newborn on its damp, wrinkled bottom and declared, "It's a boy!"

"What did I say!" cried Beila. Half opening the door, she cried out triumphantly, "Haim, children, it's a boy!"

And the entire family clustered in the doorway, excitedly talking to Beila. Even the blind grandmother had managed to find her way over to her son and was smiling at the great miracle. She was moving her lips; her head was shaking and trembling as she ran her numb hands over her black kerchief. She was smiling and whispering something no one could hear. The children were pushing her back from the door, but she was pressing forward, craning her neck. She wanted to hear the voice of ever-victorious life.

Vavilova was looking at the baby. She was astonished that this insignificant ball of red-and-blue flesh could have caused her such suffering.

She had imagined that her baby would be large, snub-nosed, and freckled, that he would have a shock of red hair and that he would immediately be getting up to mischief, struggling to get somewhere, calling out in a piercing voice. Instead, he was as puny as an oat stalk that had grown in a cellar. His head wouldn't stay upright; his bent little legs looked quite withered as they twitched about; his pale blue eyes seemed quite blind and his squeals were barely audible. If you opened the door too suddenly, he might be extinguished—like the thin, bent little candle that Beila had placed above the edge of the cupboard.

And although the room was as hot as a bathhouse, she stretched out her arms and said, "But he's cold—give him to me!" The little person was chirping, moving his head from side to side. Vavilova watched him through narrowed eyes, barely daring to move. "Eat, eat, my little son," she said, and she began to cry. "My son, my little son," she murmured—and the tears welled up in her eyes and, one after another, ran down her tanned cheeks until they disappeared into the pillow.

She remembered *him*, the taciturn one, and she felt a sharp maternal ache—a deep pity for both father and son. For the first time, she wept for the man who had died in combat near Korosten: never would this man see his own son.

And this little one, this helpless one, had been born without a father. Afraid he might die of cold, she covered him with the blanket.

Or maybe she was weeping for some other reason. Rosalia Samoilovna, at least, seemed to think so. After lighting a cigarette and letting the smoke out through the little ventilation pane, she said, "Let her cry, let her cry. It calms the nerves better than any bromide. All my mothers cry after giving birth."

Two days after the birth, Vavilova got up from her bed. Her strength was returning to her; she walked about a lot and helped Beila with the housework. When there was no one around, she quietly sang songs to the little person. This little person was now called Alyosha, Alyoshenka, Alyosha . . .

"You wouldn't believe it," Beila said to her husband. "That Russian woman's gone off her head. She's already rushed to the doctor with him three times. I can't so much as open a door in the house: he might catch a cold, or he's got a fever, or we might wake him up. In a word, she's turned into a good Jewish mother."

"When do you expect?" replied Magazanik. "Is a woman going to turn into a man just because she wears a pair of leather breeches?"

And he shrugged his shoulders and closed his eyes.

A week later, Kozyrev and his chief of staff came to visit Vavilova. They smelled of leather, tobacco, and horse sweat. Alyosha was sleeping in his cradle, protected from the flies by a length of gauze. Creaking deafeningly, like a pair of brand-new leather boots, the two men approached the cradle and looked at the sleeper's thin little face. It was twitching. The movements it made—although no more than little movements of skin—imparted to it a whole range of different expressions: sorrow, anger, and then a smile.

The soldiers exchanged glances.

"Yes," said Kozyrev.

"No doubt about it," said the chief of staff.

And they sat down on two chairs and began to talk. The Poles had gone on the offensive. Our forces were retreating. Temporarily, of course. The Fourteenth Army was regrouping at Zhmerinka. Divisions were coming up from the Urals. The Ukraine would soon be ours. In a month or so there would be a breakthrough, but right now the Poles were causing trouble.

Kozyrev swore.

"Sh!" said Valilova. "Don't shout or you'll wake him."

"Yes, we've been given a bloody nose," said the chief of staff.

"You do talk in a silly way," said Vavilova. In a pained voice she added, "I wish you'd stop smoking. You're puffing away like a stream engine."

The soldiers suddenly began to feel bored. Kozyrev yawned. The chief of staff looked at his watch and said. "It's time we were on our way to Bald Hill. We don't want to be late."

"I wonder where that gold watch came from," Vavilova thought crossly.

"Well, Klavdiya, we must say goodbye to you!" said Kozyrev. He got to his feet and went on: "I've given orders for you to be delivered a sack of flour, some sugar, and some fatback. A cart will come around later today."

The two men went out into the street. The little Magazaniks were all standing around the horses. Kozyrev grunted heavily as he clambered up. The chief of staff clicked his tongue and leaped into the saddle.

When they got to the corner, the two men abruptly, as though by prior agreement, pulled on the reins and stopped.

"Yes," said Kozyrev.

"No doubt about it," said the chief of staff. They burst into laughter. Whipping their horses, they galloped off to Bald Hill.

The two-wheeled cart arrived in the evening. After dragging the provisions inside, Magazanik went into Vavilova's room and said in a conspiratorial whisper, "What do you make of this, comrade Vavilova? We've got news—the brother-in-law of Tsesarsky the cobbler has just come to the workshop." He looked around and, as if apologizing for something, said in a tone of disbelief, "The Poles are in Chudnov, and Chuddnov's only twenty-five miles away."

Beila came in. She had overheard some of this, and she said resolutely, "There's no two ways about it— the Poles will be here tomorrow. Or maybe it'll be the Austrians or the Galicians. Anyway, whoever it is, you can stay here with us. And they've brought you enough food—may the Lord be praised—for the next three months."

Vavilova said nothing. For once in her life she did not know what to do.

"Beila," she began, and fell silent.

"I'm not afraid," said Beila. "Why would I be afraid? I can manage five like Alyosha—no trouble at all. But whoever heard of a mother abandoning a ten-day-old baby?"

All through the night there were noises outside the window: the neighing of horses, the knocking of wheels, loud exclamations, angry voices. The supply carts were moving from Shepetovka to Kazatin.

Vavilova sat by the cradle. Her child was asleep. She looked at his little yellow face. Really, nothing very much was going to happen. Kozyrev had said that they would be back in a month. That was exactly the length of time she was expecting to be on leave. But what if she were cut off for longer? No, that didn't frighten her, either.

Once Alyosha was a bit stronger, they'd find their way across the front line.

Who was going to harm them—a peasant woman with a babe in arms? And Vavilova imagined herself walking through the countryside early on a summer's morning. She had a colored kerchief on her head, and Alyosha was looking all around and stretching out his little hands. How good it all felt! In a thin voice she began to sing, "Sleep, my little son, sleep!" And, as she was rocking the cradle, she dozed off.

In the morning the market was as busy as ever. The people, though, seemed especially excited. Some of them, watching the unbroken chain of supply carts, were laughing joyfully. But then the carts came to an end. Now there were only people. Standing by the town gates were just ordinary townsfolk—the "civilian population" of decrees issued by commandants. Everybody was looking around all the time, exchanging excited whispers. Apparently the Poles had already taken Pyatka, a shtetl only ten miles away. Magazanik had not gone out to work. Instead, he was sitting in Vavilova's room, philosophizing for all he was worth.

An armored car rumbled past in the direction of the railway station. It was covered in a thick layer of dust—as if the steel had gone gray from exhaustion and too many sleepless nights.

"To be honest with you," Magazanik was saying, "this is the best time of all for us townsfolk. One lot has left—and the next has yet to arrive. No requisitions, no 'voluntary contributions,' no pogroms."

"It's only in the daytime that he's so smart," said Beila. "At night, when there are bandits on every street and the whole town's in uproar, he sits there looking like death. All he can do is shake with terror."

"Don't interrupt," Magazanik said crossly, "when I'm talking to someone."

Every now and then he would slip out to the street and come back with the latest news. The Revolutionary Committee had been evacuated during the night, the district Party Committee had gone next, and the military headquarters had left in the morning. The station was empty. The last army train had already gone.

Vavilova heard shouts from the street. An airplane in the sky! She went to the window. The plane was high up, but she could see the white-and-red roundels on its wings. It was a Polish reconnaissance plane. It made a circle over the town and flew off toward the station. And then, from the direction of Bald Hill, cannons began firing.

The first sound they heard was that of the shells; they howled by like a whirlwind. Next came the long sigh of the cannons. And then, a few seconds later, from beyond the level crossing—a joyful peal of explosions. It was the Bolsheviks—they were trying to slow the Polish advance. Soon the Poles were responding in kind; shells began to land in the town.

The air was torn by deafening explosions. Bricks were crumbling. Smoke and dust were dancing over the flattened wall of a building. The streets were silent, severe, and deserted—now no more substantial than sketches. The quiet after each shell burst was terrifying. And from high in a cloudless sky the sun shone gaily down on a town that was like a spread-eagled corpse.

The townsfolk were all in their cellars and basements. Their eyes closed, barely conscious, they were holding their breath or letting out low moans of fear.

Everyone, even the little children, knew that this bombardment was what is known as an "artillery preparation" and that there would be another forty or fifty explosions before the soldiers entered the town. And then—as everyone knew—it would become unbelievably quiet until, all of a sudden, clattering along the broad street from the level crossing, a reconnaissance patrol galloped up. And, dying of fear and curiosity, everyone would be peeping out from behind their gates, peering through gaps in shutters and curtains. Drenched in sweat, they would begin to tiptoe out to the street.

The patrol would enter the main square. The horses would prance and snort; the riders would call out to one another in marvelously simple human language, and their leader, delighted by the humility of this conquered town now lying flat on its back, would yell out in a drunken voice, fire a revolver shot into the maw of the silence, and get his horse to rear.

And then, pouring in from all sides, would come cavalry and infantry. From one house to another would rush tired dusty men in blue greatcoats—thrifty peasants, good-natured enough yet capable of murder and greedy for the town's hens, boots, and towels.

Everybody knew all this, because the town had already changed hands fourteen times. It had been held by Petlyura, by Denikin, by the Bolsheviks, by Galicians and Poles, by Tyutyunik's brigands and Marusya's brigands, and by the crazy Ninth Regiment that was a law unto itself. And it was the same story each time.

"They're singing!" shouted Magazanik. "They're singing!"

And, forgetting his fear, he ran out onto the front steps. Vavilova followed him. After the stuffiness of the dark room, it was a joy to breathe in the light and warmth of the summer day. She had been feeling the same about the Poles as she had felt about the pains of labor: they were bound to come, so let them come quick. If the explosions scared her, it was only because she was afraid they would wake Alyosha; the whistling shells troubled her no more than flies—she just brushed them aside.

"Hush now, hush now," she had sung over the cradle. "Don't go waking Alyosha."

She was trying not to think. Everything after all, had been decided. In a month's time, either the Bolsheviks would be back or she and Alyosha would cross the front line to join them.

"What on earth's going on? said Magazanik. "Look at that!"

Marching along the broad empty street, toward the level crossing from which the Poles should be about to appear, was a column of young Bolshevik cadets. They were wearing white canvas trousers and tunics.

"Ma-ay the re-ed banner embo-ody the workers' ide-e-als," they sang, drawing out the words almost mournfully.

They were marching toward the Poles.

Why? Whatever for?

Vavilova gazed at them. And suddenly it came back to her: Red Square, vast as ever, and several thousand workers who had volunteered for the front, thronging around a wooden platform that had been knocked together in a hurry. A bald man, gesticulating with his cloth cap, was addressing them. Vavilova was standing not far from him.

She was so agitated that she could not take in half of what he said, even though, apart from not quite being able to roll his r's, he had a clear voice. The people standing beside her were almost gasping as they listened. An old man in a padded jacket was crying.

Just what had happened to her on that square, beneath the dark walls, she did not know. Once, at night, she had wanted to talk about it to *him*, to her taciturn

one. She had felt he would understand. But she had been unable to get the words out . . . And as the men made their way from the square to the Bryansk Station, *this* was the song they had been singing.

Looking at the faces of the singing cadets, she lived through once again what she had lived through two years before.

The Magazaniks saw a woman in a sheepskin hat and a greatcoat running down the street after the cadets, slipping a cartridge clip into her large gray Mauser as she ran.

Not taking his eyes off her, Magazanik said, "Once there were people like that in the Bund. Real human beings, Beila. Call us human beings? No, we're just manure."

Alyosha had woken up. He was crying and kicking about, trying to kick off his swaddling clothes. Coming back to herself, Beila said to her husband, "Listen, the baby's woken up. You'd better light the Primus—we must heat up some milk."

The cadets disappeared around a turn in the road.

Translated by Robert and Elizabeth Chandler.

Other works by Grossman: *Stepan Kol'chugin* (1936–1941); *Za pravoe delo* (1943–1952); *Zhizn i sud'ba* (1953–1960).

Žak Konfino

1892–1975

A physician, writer, and translator, Žak Konfino wrote popular stories and novels about Sephardic Jewish life in the Balkans in the early twentieth century. Born in the southern Serbian town of Leskovac and educated in Vienna, Konfino did not begin writing until he was in his forties. He participated actively in both world wars, serving in the Serbian army in the first conflict and as medical assistant and military doctor in both wars. He was briefly imprisoned in an Italian prison camp during World War II. His stories, travelogues, and articles on medicine and other topics were widely published in journals and magazines aimed at both general and Jewish audiences, and were translated into numerous languages.

A Newspaper Report about Us
1934

Did you know that *The Jewish Voice* almost became a defendant in a trial concerning the Press Act?

My fellow community members wanted to sue it.

Never have my fellow community members ever sued anyone, nor can they think of an inconvenience greater than having to deal with a court; that they considered, regardless of all that, resorting to a lawsuit means only that they were not having it easy. And against whom, can you imagine? Against *The Jewish Voice* of ours!

It happened like this.

Two handsome young men came to our town one week and told us to gather round, because they wanted, so they told us, to give us a lecture on Zionism.

It is nice of those youths to come and lecture us—so we thought, and we sort of felt pleased. Truth be told, we did not attend the lecture because we don't much understand those lectures. But we did send our children. So that people have someone to lecture. And we sort of thought, it is good for our children to hear something about Jewishness before they reach school age. And, moreover, elementary school students went too, and the few Gymnasium students that we have. Finally, several of us too, several of the eighteen adult members of our religious community. The *hakham*, for example, and so on. I think this is not so bad from our side.

The children later told us that those young men spoke very beautifully. About Palestine and so forth. And how it was a great thing, so they said, that we were Jewish . . .

True: it is a great thing. But it only great when you don't do what they did afterwards.

It was true luck that Hajim Hajon was there to respond, to say at least something. He told them the story about the parliamentary candidate who, campaigning before the election in some village or other, promised the peasants everything, even a new bridge. Surely you know that story: "We will, brothers, even build a new bridge for you."—"And what do we need a bridge for," the peasants asked, "since there is no river in the village?"—"No worries at all," the candidate replied, "we will work on that, too!"

We also don't have a river here, Hajim Hajon told them, and we have no idea what he wanted to say with that. The main thing is that at least he said something, because otherwise the young men would bring this up later as well, that none of the eighteen adult members of our religious community found it necessary to respond.

Those young men went for lunch at the *hakham*'s afterwards; then we walked them around town, and, in general, we hosted them and welcomed them as is

becoming us as well as them. I think this is not so bad from our side.

Barely a week later *The Jewish Voice* published an article about us and our town. Written by those same young men. About how we are, so they said, *materially brought to ruin.*

Now, please answer me, as I ask you: is this Zionism? Let's say that we are, for example, broke: does this have to be publicized? All those industrial plants and factories of ours, well not ours, but, for example, in our town, and they write that we are materially ruined? Do they know, those young gentlemen, that we have several seriously eligible bachelors, and what will people say now, across Yugoslavia, that is, our Jews and women with a dowry, about the fact that we are materially ruined? Do those gentlemen, those orators, think that, what with the crisis and the current monetary policies, we will go to Switzerland to get married?!

But that's how it is when people are only focused on publishing something in a newspaper; and what will happen afterwards, that the question does not concern them in the least. And there you have it: enlist in the Zionist camp now!

Ultimately, never mind what they wrote: they are young and green, they can't be expected to fully appreciate everything. But how could *The Jewish Voice* of ours publish it? *The Jewish Voice* should know if it all adds up: they first say that it's a great thing that we are Jewish, and then they report that we are materially in ruin!

—So, if it's come to that, we wrote to *The Jewish Voice*—then at least publish this as well, this piece of ours. Because whether it is a great thing or not, we are Jews, and here's the kind of Jews we are. So let that be known. And if they came to teach us, let them learn themselves—from us! That's why we demand that this too be known:

So, there used to live here, in the earlier years, before the current crisis, a tax payer, a Jew. We had no idea where he had come from. His job took him to our city, and so he found himself here. We had not even properly gotten to know him. Neither did he mingle with us: you know, we are simple people, while he is a civil servant, and so he did not appreciate our company.

One day, however, he came to us and told us about his misfortune. Or not a misfortune, but rather bad luck. He was in charge of the state coffers, and he ended up spending a few thousands more. In other words, jail time seemed to be in the cards. He started explaining to us what it will look like when it's announced that a Jew was arrested for embezzling state funds. The one and only Jewish civil servant we have known. He started explaining that to us, like we didn't know it ourselves, without his explanations. For it would be completely different, of course, if he was an ordinary merchant. But he was a civil servant. So it was clear: there will be shame for all Jews. So what else could we do? Everyone contributed something, we emptied the synagogue's safe, and so the man was saved. And there was also a little more than he needed, so since the summer was extremely hot, he sent his wife to a spa. As is becoming a civil servant. We said nothing: silence. We thought, he had more than enough, so better to send his wife to a spa than to gamble it away. Because such monetary surplus is usually gambled away. So it means that he took care about his honor, after all. And, let's say, ours.

However, when, after several years, that same civil servant was transferred to Belgrade, and a stunningly similar misfortune happened to befall him, do you think that the Belgraders did anything to save our man, a Jew, so to speak? Not a single thing! They let him go down the drain. They let a Jew go to prison! Ten thousand Belgrade Jews allowed that to happen!

And now those young gentlemen come here to teach us about Zionism!

There is much more to be said, but never mind. However, we are upset and, let's say, we feel insulted. Because they saw themselves how we also saved that other Jew, the waiter, I don't remember where he was from, who spent his travel expense allocation, which we had given him the previous day, on drinking because the inn singers swindled him, and now he was going to kill himself because he thought we were not even going to look at him, let alone help him again. But we thought it was not right for a Jew to kill himself for 100 dinars, and so [we helped].

So none of those things matter, and only one thing is important: that we are materially brought to ruin!

For this reason, this is what we wrote to *The Jewish Voice:*

"We ask and demand that you let everyone know, that is, all such orators as well as prospective ones, that no one is welcome to come to our town and tell us that we should be good Jews and Zionists. Because whatever we are like, it's our business. So let them not come because we will break their heads. Publish exactly this: we will break their heads. And concerning the fact that we are materially brought to ruin, publish that we are not. Because if you are good Jews, it would behoove you to report that we are sound financially. Because it is not right for a Jew to destroy another Jew's credit in front of the wide world. If you are afraid, do not report anything: neither that we are, nor that we are not, materially brought to ruin. At least until these bachelors of ours get married. And the economic crisis should also pass until then."

This is how and what my fellow community members wrote to *The Jewish Voice,* and then they threatened: "Now it is up to you, and we are ready to sue you in accordance with the Press Act. Even though you are Jews and Zionists!"

And then *The Jewish Voice* had no other way out, and so it published everything, as we demanded.

Translated by Emil Kerenji.

Other works by Konfino: *Moji opštinari* (1934); *Humoreske* (1941); *100 godina—90 groša* (1952); *Moje jedinče* (1952); *Požuri doktore!* (1972).

Henry Roth

1905–1995

Born in Galicia, the American novelist Henry Roth was brought to New York by his parents when he was eighteen months old. He graduated from the City College of New York in 1928 and lived with and was supported by a Protestant English professor, Eda Lou Walton, for ten years while he wrote his masterpiece, the novel *Call It Sleep*. Although it was well received at the time, the novel and the author were soon forgotten. It was rediscovered in the 1960s and widely recognized as a modernist masterpiece, both a distinguished proletarian novel and a powerful portrait of the terror of family life as seen by a child. It is notable for its sensitivity to the bilingualism of immigrant Jews and its ability to render this into English. After its publication, Roth wrote and published little until very late in his life.

Call It Sleep
1934

VII

Another week had passed. The two men had just gone off together. With something of an annoyed laugh, his mother went to the door and stood fingering the catch of the lock. Finally she lifted it. The hidden tongue sprang into its groove.

"Oh, what nonsense!" she unlocked it again, looked up at the light and then at the windows.

David felt himself growing uneasy. Why did Thursdays have to roll around so soon? He was beginning to hate them as much as he did Sundays.

"Why must they make proof of everything before they're satisfied?" Her lips formed and unformed a frown. "Well, there's nothing to do but go. I'll wash those dishes later." She opened the door and turned out the light.

Bewildered, David followed her into the cold, gas-lit hallway.

"We're going upstairs to Mrs. Mink." She cast a hurried look over the banister. "You can play with your friend Yussie."

David wondered why she needed to bring that up. He hadn't said anything about wanting to play with Yussie. In fact, he didn't even feel like it. Why didn't she just say she was running away, instead of making him feel guilty. He knew whom she was looking for when she looked over the banister.

His mother knocked at the door. It was opened. Mrs. Mink stood on the threshold. At the sight of his mother, she beamed with pleasure.

"Hollo, Mrs. Schearl! Hollo! Hollo! Comm een!" She scratched her lustreless, black hair excitedly.

"I hope you don't find my coming here untimely," his mother smiled apologetically.

"No," as I live!' Mrs. Mink lapsed into Yiddish. "You're wholly welcome! A guest—the rarest I have!" She dragged a chair forward. "Do sit down."

Mrs. Mink was a flat-breasted woman with a sallow skin and small features. She had narrow shoulders and meager arms, and David always wondered when he saw her how the thin skin on her throat managed to hold back the heavy, bulging veins.

"I thought I would never have the pleasure of seeing you in my house," she continued. "It was only the other day that I was telling our landlady—Look, Mrs. Schearl and I are neighbors, but we know nothing of each other. I dare not ask her up into my house. I'm afraid to. She looks so proud."

"I, proud?"

"Yes, not proud, noble! You always walk with your head in the air—so! And even when you go to market, you dress like a lady. I've watched you often from the window, and I've said to my man—Come here! Look,

that's her! Do you see how tall she is! He is not home now, my picture of a spouse, he works late in the jewelry store. I know he will regret missing you."

David found himself quickly tiring of Mrs. Mink's rapid stream of words, and looking about saw that Annie was observing him. Yussie was nowhere to be seen. He tugged his mother's hand, and when she bent over, asked for him.

"Yussie?" Mrs. Mink interrupted herself long enough to say. "He's asleep."

"Don't wake him," said his mother.

"That's all right. I've got to send him to the delicatessen for some bread soon. Yussele!" she called.

His only answer was a resentful yawn.

"He's coming soon," she said reassuringly.

In a few minutes, Yussie came out. One of his stockings had fallen, and he trod on it, shuffling sleepily. He blinked, eyed David's mother suspiciously a moment, and then sidled over to David, "W'y's yuh mudder hea?"

"She jost came."

"W'y'd she comm?"

"I donno."

At this point Annie hobbled over. "Pull yuh stockin' op, yuh slob!"

Obediently Yussie hoisted up his stocking. David could not help noticing how stiff and bare the white stocking hung behind the brace on Annie's own leg.

"So yuh gonna stay by us?" asked Yussie eagerly.

"Yea."

"H'ray! C'mon inna fron'room." He grabbed David's arm. "I godda—"

But David had stopped. "I am goin' inna fron' room, mama."

Turning from the chattering Mrs. Mink, David's mother smiled at him in slight distress and nodded.

"Waid'll I show yuh wod we god," Yussie dragged him into the frontroom.

While Yussie babbled on excitedly, David stared about him. He had never been in Yussie's front room before: Annie had barred the way as if it were inviolable ground. Now he saw a room which was illuminated by a gas lamp overhead and crowded with dark and portly furniture. In the middle of the floor stood a round glass topped table and about it chairs of the same dark stain. A china closet hugged one wall, a bureau another, a dressing table a third, cabinets clogged the corners. All were bulky, all rested on the same kind of scrolled and finical paw. On the wall space above the furniture hung two pairs of yellowed portraits, two busts of wrinkled women with unnatural masses of black hair, and two busts of old men who wore ringlets under their skull caps and beards on their chins. With an expression of bleak hostility in their flat faces, they looked down at David. Barring the way to the window squatted a swollen purple plush chair, embroidered with agitated parrots of various hues. A large vapid doll with gold curls and a violet dress sat on the glass top of a cabinet. After his own roomy frontroom with its few sticks of furniture, David not only felt bewildered, he felt oddly warm.

"It's inna closet in my modder's bedroom." Yussie continued. "Jost wait, I'll show yuh."

He disappeared into the darkness of the adjoining bedroom. David heard him open a door, rummage about for a minute. When he returned, he bore in his hand a curious steel cage.

"Yuh know wat dis's fuh?" he held it up to David's eyes.

David examined it more closely, "No. Wot d'yuh do wit' it?"

"It c'n catch rats, dot's wot yuh do wit' it. See dis little door? De rat gizz in like dot." He opened a thin metal door at the front of the cage. "Foist yuh put sompin ove' hea, and on 'iz liddle hook. An' nen nuh rat gizzin. Dey uz zuh big rat inna house, yuh could hear him at night, so my fodder bought dis, an' my mudder put in schmaltz f'om de meat, and nuh rat comes in, an' inna mawningk, I look unner by de woshtob, an'ooh—he wuz dere, runnin' dis way like dot." Yussie waved the cage about excitedly, "An I calls my fodder an'he gets op f'om de bed an' he fills op de woshtob and eeh! duh rat giz all aroun' in it, in nuh watuh giz all aroun'. An' nen he stops. An nen my fodder takes it out and he put it in nuh bag and trew it out f'om de winner. Boof! he fell inna guttah. Ooh wotta rat he wuz. My mudder wuz runnin' aroun', an aroun' an after, my fodder kept on spittin' in nuh sink. Kcha!"

David backed away in disgust.

"See, I tol' yuh I had sumtin tuh show yuh. See, like dot it closes." He snapped the little, metal door. "We didn't hea' it, cause ev'ybody wuz sleepin'. Rats on'y come out innuh da'k, w'en yuh can't see 'em, and yuh know w'ea dey comin' f'om, dey comin' f'om de cellah. Dot's w'ea dey live innuh cellah—all rats."

The cellar! That explained it. That moment of fear when he turned the bottom landing before he went out into the street. He would be doubly terrified now.

"Wotta yuh doin?" They started at the intruding voice. It was Annie coming in. Her face was writhed back in disgust.

"Eee! Yuh stoopid lummox! Put it away. I'll call mama!"

"Aaa, lemme alone."

"Yuh gonna put it away?" she squealed.

"Aa, shit on you," muttered Yussie sullenly. "Can't do nuttin'" Nevertheless, he carried the cage back to the bedroom.

"W'y d'yuh let 'im show it tuh yuh fuh?" she demanded angrily of David. "Such a dope!"

"I didn' know wot it wuz," he slammered.

"Yuh didn' know wot it wuz? Yurra lummox too!"

"Now g'wan." Yussie returned from the bedroom. "Leave us alone."

"I will not," she snapped. "Dis is my frontroom."

"He don' wanna play witchoo. He's my frien!"

"So who wants him!"

"So don' butt in."

"Pooh!" She plumped herself in a chair. The steel brace clicked disagreeably against the wood.

David wished she could wear long pants like a man.

"Comm on ove' by de winder," Yussie guided him through a defile in the furniture. "We mus' be a fireman. We c'n put out de fire inna house." He indicated the bureau. "Yuh wanna?"

"Awrigh'."

"An' we c'n slide down duh pipe an' we c'n have a fiuh-ingine, an' nen I'll be duh drivuh. Yuh wanna?"

"Yea."

"Den let's make fiuh hats. Waid, I'll get some paper inna kitchen." He ran off.

Annie slid off the chair and came over."Wot class yuh in?"

"1A."

"I'm in 4A," she said loftily. "I skipped a'reddy. An' now I'm duh sma'test one in my class."

David was impressed.

"My teacher's name is Miss McCardy. She's duh bes' teacher inna whole school. She gave me A. A. A."

By this time Yussie had returned bearing several sheets of newspaper.

"Wotta ya gonna do?" she demanded.

"Wotta you care!" he defied her. "We' gonna be fiuhmen."

"Yuh can't!"

"No?" Yussie inquired angrily, "Why can' we?"

"Cause yuh can't, dat's w'y! Cause yu'll scratch op all de foinichuh."

"We won' scratch nuttin'!" stormed Yussie whirling the newspaper about in frustration. "We gonna play."

"Yuh can't!"

"We will!"

"I'll give yuh in a minute," she advanced threateningly.

"Aa! Wodda yuh wan' us tuh play?"

"Yuh c'n play lottos."

"I don' wanna play lottos," he whined.

"Den don' play nuttin!" she said with finality.

A large bubble of saliva swelled from Yussie's lips as he squeezed his face down to blubber. "I'll tell mama on you!"

"Tell! She'll give yuh a smack!" She whirled threateningly on David. "Wadda *you* wanna play?"

"I don' know," he drew back.

"Doncha know no games?" she fumed.

"I—I know tag an' I know, I know hide an' gussee'."

Yussie revived. "Let's play hide an' gussee'."

"No!"

"You too!" he coaxed desperately. "C'mon, you too."

Annie thought it over.

"C'mon I'll be it!" And immediately, he leaned his face against the edge of a bureau and began counting. "G'wan hide!" he broke off.

"Wait!" shrilled Annie, hopping off. "Count twenny!"

David scurried behind the arm chair.

He was found last and accordingly was "it" next. In a little while the game grew very exciting. Since David was somewhat unfamiliar with the arrangement of the house, it chanced that several times he hid with Yussie when Annie was it and with Annie when Yussie was it. They had crouched together in barricaded corners and behind the bedroom door.

However, just as the game was reaching its greatest pitch, Mrs. Mink's voice suddenly called out from the kitchen.

"Yussele! Yussele, my treasure, come here!"

"Aa!" from somewhere came Yussie's exasperated bleat. David, who was "it" at the time, stopped counting and turned around.

"Yussie!" Mrs. Mink cried again, but this time shriller.

"Can't do nuttin'," complained Yussie, crawling out from under the bureau. "Waddayuh want?" he bellowed.

"Come here. I want you to go down stairs for a minute."

Annie, evidently aware that the game was over for the time being, came out of the adjoining bedroom. "He has to go down?"

"Yea," diffidently. "Fuh bread."

"Den we can't play."

"No. I'm gonna go back tuh my modder."

"Stay hea," she commanded, "We gonna play. Waid'll Yussie comes back."

The voices from the kitchen indicated that Yussie had been persuaded. He reappeared, dressed in coat and hat. "I'm goin' down," he announced, and went out again. An uncomfortable pause ensued.

"We can't play till he comes back," David reminded her.

"Yes, we can."

"Wot?"

"Wotcha want."

"Yoh know wot."

"Wot?"

"Yuh know," she said mysteriously.

That was the game then. David congratulated himself on having discovered its rules so quickly.

"Yea, I know," he answered in the same tone of mystery.

"Yea?" she peered at him eagerly.

"Yea!" he peered at her in the same way.

"Yuh wanna?"

"Yea!"

"Yuh wanna den?"

"Yea, I wanna." It was the easiest game he had ever played. Annie was not so frightening after all.

"W'ea?"

"W'ea?" he repeated.

"In the bedroom," she whispered.

But she was really going!

"C'mon," she motioned, tittering.

He followed. This was puzzling.

She shut the door: he stood bewildered in the gloom.

"C'mon," she took his hand. "I'll show yuh."

He could hear her groping in the dark. The sound of an unseen door opening. The closet door.

"In hea," she whispered.

What was she going to do? His heart began to race.

She drew him in, shut the door. Darkness, immense and stale, the reek of moth balls threading it.

Her breathing in the narrow space was loud as a gust, swooping down and down again. His heart throbbed in his ears. She moved toward him, nudged him gently with the iron slat of her brace. He was frightened. Before the pressure of her body, he retreated slightly. Something rolled beneath his feet. What? He knew instantly, and recoiled in disgust—the trap!

"Sh!" she warned. "Take me aroun'." She groped for his hands.

He put his arms about her.

"Now let's kiss."

His lips touched hers, a muddy spot in vast darkness.

"How d'*you* play bad?" she asked.

"Bad? I don' know," he quavered.

"Yuh wan' me to show how I?"

He was silent, terrified.

"Yuh must ask me," she said. "G'wan ask me."

"Wot?"

"Yuh must say, Yuh wanna play bad? Say it!"

He trembled. "Yuh wanna play bad?

"Now, *you* said it," she whispered. "Don' forget, you said it."

By the emphasis of her words, David knew he had crossed some awful threshold.

"Will yuh tell?"

"No," he answered weakly. The guilt was his.

"Yuh swear?"

"I swear."

"Yuh know w'ea babies comm from?"

"N-no."

"From de knish."

–*Knish*?

"Between de legs. Who puts id in is de poppa. De poppa's god de petzel. Yaw de poppa." She giggled stealthily and took his hand. He could feel her guiding it under her dress, then through a pocket-like flap. Her skin under his palm. Revolted, he drew back.

"Yuh must!" she insisted, tugging his hand. "Yu hast me!"

"No!"

"Put yuh han' in my knish," she coaxed. "Jus' once."

"No!"

"I'll hol' yuh petzel." She reached down.

"No!" His flesh was crawling.

"Den take me 'round again."

"No! No! Lemme oud!" he pushed her away.

"Waid. Yussie'll t'ink we're hidin'."

"No! I don' wanna!" He had raised his voice to a shout.

"So go!" she gave him an angry push.

But David had already opened the door and was out.

She grabbed him as he crossed the bedroom. "If you tell!" she whispered venomously. "W'ea yuh goin'?"

"I'm goin tuh my mamma!"

"Stay hea! I'll kill yuh, yuh go inside!" She shook him.

He wanted to cry.

"An' don' cry," she warned fiercely, and then strove desperately to engage him, "Stay hea an' I'll tell yuh a story. I'll let you play fiuhman. Yuh c'n have a hat. Yuh c'n climb on de foinichuh. Stay hea!"

He stood still, watching her rigidly, half hypnotized by her fierce, frightened eyes. The outer door was opened. Yussie's voice in the kitchen.

A moment later, he came in, breathlessly stripping off his coat.

"I god a penny," he crowed.

"Yuh c'n play fiuhman, if yuh wan'," she said severely.

"No foolin'? Yeh? H'ray! C'mon, Davy!"

But David held back. "I don't wanna play."

"C'mon," Yussie grabbed a sheet of newspaper and thrust it into his hands. "We mus' make a hat."

"G'wan make a hat," commanded Annie.

Cowed and almost sniffling, David began folding the paper into a hat.

He played listlessly, one eye always on Annie who watched his every move. Yussie was disgusted with him.

"David!" his mother's voice calling him.

Deliverance at last! With a cry of relief, he tore off the fireman's hat, ran down the frontroom stairs into the kitchen. His mother was standing; she seemed about to leave. He pressed close to her side.

"We must go now," she said smiling down at him. "Say good night to your friends."

"Good night," he mumbled.

"Please don't hurry off," said Mrs. Mink. "It's been such a pleasure to have you here."

"I really must go. It's past his bed time."

David was in the van stealthily tugging his mother toward the door.

"This hour I have been in heaven," said Mrs. Mink. "You must come often! I am never busy."

"Many thanks."

They hurried down the drafty stairs.

"I heard you playing in the frontroom," she said. "You must have enjoyed your visit."

She unlocked the door, lit the gas lamp.

"Dear God! The room has grown cold." And picking up the poker, she crouched before the stove, shook down the dull embers behind the grate. "I'm glad you enjoyed yourself. At least one of us has skimmed a little pleasure out of this evening! What folly! And that Mrs. Mink. If I had known she talked so much, drays could not have dragged me up there!" She lifted the coal scuttle, shook some coal vehemently into the stove. "Her tongue spun like a bobbin on a sewing machine—and she sewed nothing. It's unbelievable! I began to see motes before my eyes." She shook her head impatiently and put down the coal scuttle. "My son, do you know your mother's a fool? But you're tired, aren't you? Let me put you to bed."

Kneeling down before him, she began unbuttoning his shoes. When she had pulled his stockings off, she lifted his legs, examined them a moment, then kissed each one. "Praise God, your body is sound! How I pity that poor child upstairs!"

But she didn't know as he knew how the whole world could break into a thousand little pieces, all buzzing, all whining, and no one hearing them and no one seeing them except himself.

Other works by Roth: *Shifting Landscape: A Composite* (1987); *Mercy of a Rude Stream*, 4 vols. (1994–1998).

Bruno Schulz

1892–1942

Bruno Schulz is widely considered one of the most imaginative prose stylists in the Polish language in the twentieth century. Born in Drohobych, then in Galicia in the Austrian Empire (in present-day Ukraine), Schulz produced short stories as well as translations, articles, paintings, and other works of art suffused with a distinctive style of magical realism that remains beloved by readers in Poland, Ukraine, and elsewhere. For his contributions he was awarded the prestigious Golden Laurel by the Polish Academy of Literature in 1938. Eschewing the big city, Schulz lived for most of his life in his native town, away from the literary establishment. He was imprisoned by the Nazis in the Drohobych ghetto during World War II, and while he initially received special treatment from a Gestapo officer who admired his work, Schulz was killed by a rival officer while walking home from the "Aryan" part of town with a loaf of bread. Many of his works, including short stories and an unfinished novel, were lost. While his oeuvre is quite modest in quantity, Schulz is a revered figure with a vibrant legacy in contemporary Jewish literature and the arts across languages and cultures.

Cinnamon Shops
1934

At the time of the shortest, sleepy winter days, edged on both sides with the furry dusk of mornings and evenings, when the city reached out ever deeper into the labyrinth of winter nights, and was shaken reluctantly into consciousness by the short dawn, my father was already lost, sold and surrendered to the other sphere.

His face and head became overgrown with a wild and recalcitrant shock of grey hair, bristling in irregular tufts and spikes, shooting out from warts, from his eyebrows, from the openings of his nostrils and giving him the appearance of an old ill-tempered fox.

His sense of smell and his hearing sharpened extraordinarily and one could see from the expression of his tense silent face that through the intermediary of these two senses he remained in permanent contact with the unseen world of mouseholes, dark corners, chimney vents and dusty spaces under the floor.

He was a vigilant and attentive observer, a prying fellow-conspirator, of the rustlings, the nightly creakings, the secret gnawing life of the floor. He was so engrossed in it that he became completely submerged in an inaccessible sphere and one which he did not even attempt to discuss with us.

He often used to flip his fingers and laugh softly to himself when the manifestations of the unseen became too absurd: he then exchanged knowing looks with our cat which, also initiated in these mysteries, would lift its cynical cold striped face, closing the slanting chinks of its eyes with an air of indifference and boredom.

It sometimes happened that, during a meal, my father would suddenly put aside his knife and fork and, with his napkin still tied around his neck, would rise from the table with a feline movement, tiptoe to the door of the adjoining room and peer through the key-hole with the utmost caution. Then, with a bashful smile, he would return to the table slightly embarrassed, murmuring and whispering indistinctly in tune with the interior monologue that wholly preoccupied him.

To provide some distraction for him and to tear him away from these morbid speculations, my mother would force him to go out for a walk in the evenings. He went in silence, without protest but also without enthusiasm, distrait and absent in spirit. Once we even went all together to the theatre.

We found ourselves again in that large, badly lit, dirty hall, full of somnolent human chatter and aimless confusion. But when we had made our way through the crowd, there emerged before us an enormous pale blue curtain, like the sky of another firmament. Large, painted pink masks, with puffed up cheeks floated in a huge expanse of canvas. The artificial sky spread out in both directions, swelling with the powerful breath of pathos and of great gestures, with the atmosphere of that fictitious floodlit world created on the echoing scaffoldings of the stage. The tremor sailing across the large area of that sky, the breath of the vast canvas which made the masks revive and grow, revealed the illusory character of that firmament, caused that vibration of reality which, in metaphysical moments, we experience as the glimmer of revelation.

The masks fluttered their red eyelids, their coloured lips whispered voicelessly and I knew that the moment was imminent when the tension of mystery would reach its zenith and the swollen skies of the curtain would really burst open to reveal incredible and dazzling events.

But I was not allowed to experience that moment, because in the meantime my father had begun to betray a certain anxiety. He was feeling in all his pockets and at last declared that he had left behind at home a wallet containing money and certain most important documents.

After a short conference with my mother, during which Adela's honesty was submitted to a hasty assessment, it was suggested that I should go home to look for the wallet. According to my mother, there was still plenty of time before the curtain rose and, fleet-footed as I was, I had every chance of returning in time.

I stepped into a winter night bright from the illuminations of the sky. It was one of those clear nights when the starry firmament is so wide and spreads so far that it seems to be divided and broken up into a mass of separate skies, sufficient for a whole month of winter nights and providing silver and painted globes to cover all the nightly phenomena, adventures, occurrences and carnivals. [...]

Having taken a few steps, I realized that I was not wearing my overcoat. I wanted to turn back, but after a moment that seemed to me an unnecessary waste of time, especially as the night was not cold at all; on the contrary, I could feel waves of an unseasonal warmth, like breezes of a spring night. The snow shrank into a white fluff, into a harmless fleece smelling sweetly of violets. Similar white fluffs were sailing across the sky on which the moon was doubled and trebled, showing all its phases and positions at once.

On that night the sky laid bare its internal construction in many sections which, like quasi-anatomical exhibits showed the spirals and whorls of light, the pale green solids of darkness, the plasma of space, the tissue of dreams.

On such a night, it was impossible to walk along Rampart Street or any other of the dark streets which are the obverse, the lining as it were, of the four sides of Market Square, and not to remember that at that late hour the strange and most attractive shops were sometimes open, the shops which on ordinary days one tended to overlook. I used to call them cinnamon shops because of the dark panelling of their walls.

These truly noble shops, open late night, have always been the objects of my ardent interest. Dimly lit, their dark and solemn interiors were redolent of the smell of paint, varnish and incense; of the aroma of distant countries and rare commodities. You could find in them Bengal lights, magic boxes, the stamps of long forgotten countries, Chinese transfers, indigo, calaphony from Malabar, the eggs of exotic insects, parrots, toucans, live salamanders and basilisks, mandrake roots, mechanical toys from Nuremberg, homunculi in jars, microscopes, binoculars and most especially strange and rare books, old folio volumes full of astonishing engravings and amazing stories.

I remember those old dignified merchants who served their customers with downcast eyes, in discreet silence, and who were full of wisdom and tolerance for their customers' most secret whims. But most of all, I remember a bookshop in which I once glanced at some rare and forbidden pamphlets, the publications of secret societies lifting the veil on tantalizing and unknown mysteries.

I so rarely had the occasion to visit these shops—especially with a small but sufficient amount of money in my pocket—that I could not forgo the opportunity I had now, in spite of the important mission entrusted to me. [...]

Lent wings by my desire to visit the cinnamon shops, I turned into a street I knew and ran rather than walked, anxious not to lose my way. I passed three or four streets, but still there was no sign of the turning I wanted. What is more, the appearance of the street was different from what I had expected. Nor was there any sign of the shops. I was in a street of houses with no doors and of which the tightly shut windows were blind from reflected moonlight. On the other side of those houses—I thought—must run the street from which they were accessible. I was walking faster now, rather disturbed, beginning to give up the idea of visiting the cinnamon shops. All I wanted now was to get out of there quickly into some part of the city I knew better. I reached the end of the street, unsure where it would lead me. I found myself in a broad, sparsely built avenue, very long and straight. I felt on me the breath of a wide open space. Close to the pavement or in the midst of their gardens, picturesque villas stood there, the private houses of the rich. In the gaps between them were parks and walls of orchards. The whole area looked like Lesznianska Street in its lower and rarely visited part. The moonlight filtered through a thousand feathery clouds like silver scales on the sky. It was pale and bright as daylight—only the parks and gardens stood black in that silvery landscape.

Looking more closely at one of the buildings, I realized that what I saw was the back of the high school which I had never seen from that side. I was just approaching the gate which, to my surprise, was open; the entrance hall was lit. I walked in and found myself on the red carpet of the passage. I hoped to be able to slip through unobserved and come out through the front gate, thus taking a splendid shortcut.

I remembered that at that late hour there might be, in Professor Arendt's classroom, one of the voluntary classes which in winter were always held in the late evenings and to which we all flocked, fired by the enthusiasm for art which that excellent teacher had awakened in us.

A small group of industrious pupils was almost lost in the large dark hall on whose walls the enormous shadows of our heads broke abruptly, thrown by the light of two small candle s set in bottles.

To be truthful, we did not draw very much during these classes and the Professor was not very exacting. Some boys brought cushions from home and stretched themselves out on forms for a short nap. Only the most diligent of us gathered around the candle in the golden circle of its light.

We usually had to wait a long while for the Professor's arrival, filling the time with sleepy conversation. At last the door from his room would open and he would enter—short, bearded, given to esoteric smiles and discreet silences and exuding an aroma of secrecy. He shut the door of his study carefully behind him: through it for a brief moment we could see over his head a crowd of plaster shadows, the classical fragments of suffering Niobides, Danaids and Tantalides, the whole sad and sterile Olympus, wilting for years on end in that plaster-cast museum. The light in his room was opaque even in daytime, thick from the dreams of plaster-cast heads, from empty looks, ashen profiles and meditations dissolving into nothingness. We liked to listen sometimes in front of that door—listen to the silence laden with the sighs and whispers of the crumbling gods withering in the boredom and monotony of their twilight.

The Professor walked with great dignity and unction up and down among the half-empty forms in which, in small groups, we were drawing amidst the grey reflections of a winter night. Everything was quiet and cosy. Some of my classmates were asleep. The candles were burning low in their bottles. The Professor delved into a deep bookcase, full of old folios, unfashionable engravings, woodcuts and prints. He showed us, with his esoteric gestures, old lithographs of night landscapes, of tree clumps in moonlight, of avenues in wintry parks outlined black on the white moonlit background. [...]

These nightly drawing sessions held a secret charm for me, so that now I could not forgo the opportunity of looking for a moment into the art room. I decided however that I would not stop for more than a little while. But walking up the back stairs, their wood resounding under my steps, I realized that I was in a wing of the school building completely unknown to me. [...]

I faced all that magnificence with admiration and awe, guessing that my nightly escapade had brought me unexpectedly into the Headmaster's wing, to his private apartment. I stood there with a beating heart, rooted to the spot by curiosity, ready to escape at the slightest noise. How would I justify, if surprised, that nocturnal visit, that impudent prying? In one of those deep plush armchairs there might sit, unobserved and still, the young daughter of the Headmaster. She might lift her eyes to mine—black, Sybilline, quiet eyes, the gaze of which none could hold. But to retreat halfway, not having carried through the plan I had, would be cowardly. Besides, deep silence reigned in those magnificent interiors, lit by the hazy light of an undefined hour. Through the arcades of the passage, I saw on the far side of the drawing room a large glass door leading to the terrace. It was so still everywhere that I felt suddenly emboldened. It did not strike me as too risky to walk down the short steps leading to the level of the drawing room, to take a few quick steps across the large costly carpet and to find myself on the terrace from which I could get back without any difficulty to the familiar street.

This is what I did. When I found myself on the parquet floor under the potted palms that reached up to the frieze of the ceiling. I noticed that now I really was on neutral ground, because the drawing room did not have a front wall. It was a kind of large loggia, connected by a few steps with a city square, an enclosed part of the square, because some of the garden furniture stood directly on the pavement. I ran down the short flight of stone steps and found myself at street level once more.

The constellations in the sky stood steeply on their heads, all the stars had made an about turn, but the moon, buried under the featherbed of clouds which were lit by its unseen presence, seemed still to have before her an endless journey and, absorbed in her complicated heavenly procedures, did not think of dawn.

A few horse-drawn cabs loomed black in the street, half-broken and loose-jointed like crippled, dozing crabs or cockroaches. A driver leaned down towards me from his high box. He had a small, red, kindly face. 'Shall we go, master?' he asked. The cab shook in all the joints and ligatures of its many-limbed body and made a start on its light wheels.

But who would entrust oneself on such a night to the whims of an unpredictable cabby? Amidst the click of the axles, amidst the thud of the box and the roof, I could not agree with him on my destination. He nodded indulgently at everything I said and sang to himself. We drove in a circle around the city.

In front of an inn stood a group of cabbies who waved friendly hands to him. He answered gaily and then, without stopping the carriage, he threw the reins on my knees, jumped down from the box and joined the group of his colleagues. The horse, an old, wise cab-horse, looked round cursorily and went on in a monotonous regular trot. In fact, that horse inspired confidence—it seemed smarter than its driver. But I myself could not drive so I had to rely on the horse's will. We turned into a suburban street, bordered on both sides by gardens. As we advanced, these gardens slowly changed into parks with tall trees and the parks in turn into forests.

I shall never forget that luminous journey on that brightest of winter nights. The coloured map of the heavens expanded into an immense dome, on which there loomed fantastic lands, oceans and seas, marked with the lines of stellar currents and eddies, with the brilliant streaks of heavenly geography. The air became light to breathe and shimmered like silver gauze. One could smell violets. From under the white woolly lambskin of snow, trembling anemones appeared with a speck of moonlight in each delicate cup. The whole forest seemed to be illuminated by thousands of lights and by the stars falling in profusion from the December sky. The air pulsated with a secret spring, with the matchless purity of snow and violets. We entered a hilly landscape. The lines of hills, bristling with the bare spikes of trees, rose like sighs of bliss. I saw on these happy slopes groups of wanderers, gathering among the moss and the bushes the fallen stars which now were damp from snow. The road became steep, the horse began to slip on it and pulled the creaking cab only with an effort. I was happy. My lungs soaked up the blissful spring in the air, the freshness of snow and stars. Before the horse's breast the rampart of white snowy foam grew higher and higher, and it could hardly wade through that pure fresh mass. At last we stopped. I got out of the cab. The horse was panting, hanging its head. I hugged its head to my breast and saw that there were tears in its large eyes. I noticed a round wound on its belly. 'Why did not you tell me?' I whispered, crying. 'My dearest, I did it for you,' the horse said and became very small, like a wooden toy. I left him and felt wonderfully light and happy. I was debating whether to wait for the small local train which passed through here or to walk back to the city. I began to walk down a steep path, winding like a serpent amidst the forest; at first in a light, elastic step; later, passing into a brisk, happy run which became gradually faster, until it resembled a gliding descent on skis. I could regulate my speed at will and change course by light movements of my body.

On the outskirts of the city, I slowed this triumphal run and changed it into a sedate walk. The moon still rode high in the sky. The transformations of the sky, the metamorphoses of its multiple domes into ever more complicated configurations were endless. Like a silver astrolabe the sky disclosed on that magic night its internal mechanisms and showed in infinite evolutions the mathematics of its cogs and wheels.

In the market square I met some people enjoying a walk. All of them, enchanted by the displays of that night, walked with uplifted faces, silvery from the magic of the sky. I completely stopped worrying about father's wallet. My father, absorbed by his manias, had probably forgotten its loss by now, and as for my mother, I did not much care.

On such a night, unique in the year, one has happy thoughts and inspirations, one feels touched by the divine finger of poetry. Full of ideas and projects, I wanted to walk towards my home, but met some school friends with books under their arms. They were on their way to school already, having been wakened by the brightness of that night that would not end.

We went for a walk all together along a steeply falling street, pervaded by the scent of violets; uncertain whether it was the magic of the night which lay like silver on the snow or whether it was the light of dawn. . . .

Translated by Celina Wieniewska.

Other works by Schulz: *Sanatorium under the Sign of the Hourglass* (1978).

Mihail Sebastian

1907–1945

Mihail Sebastian was born Iosef Hechter in Brăila, Romania, and studied in Bucharest and Paris. Sebastian wrote for multiple periodicals on topics ranging from the literary to the social, in addition to being a novelist and a playwright. The novel *De două mii de ani* (For Two Thousand Years) is his most famous work, dealing with the interwar Jewish European experience. The novel was published in 1934 with a foreword by Nae Ionescu, his former mentor who by that time had become a spokesman for antisemitism, which has made the novel controversial. While he had spent his life writing as a Romanian and a Jew, and always in the Romanian language, he was confined to the Jewish cultural sphere under Ion Antonescu's regime. Sebastian died in Bucharest within a year of the end of Antonescu's reign, leaving behind a journal chronicling his experiences from 1935 to 1944.

For Two Thousand Years
1934

2

The university was closed the day before yesterday, 9 December, in anticipation of the 10th. Quiet days, however: the occasional scuffle and an unremarkable street demonstration.

In any case, things have settled down. I've re-read, from the green notebook, the page from this day last year.

How young I was! Someday I'll manage to accept hurt without it affecting my personal calm in the slightest. Perhaps this is the only way to be strong. Anyhow, probably many blows lie in store for me.

I ask myself if fleeing from the dorms and my fellow students, even for this rough sort of life I lead, was in fact an act of courage or one of cowardice.

I ask myself if I have the right, for the sake of my solitude, to laugh at the cheap heroism of Marcel Winder, who still today luxuriates in enumerating the beatings he gets. Though he goes off at the mouth and I restrain myself, the fact remains that he's the one facing adversity while I turn my back on it. My way might be more elegant, but is it fair?

And don't forget Liebovici Isodor, still out there on the front line, patient and silent, inexpressive, without illusions or vanity.

A visit to the dorms. Black, black misery. Nothing has changed here.

The same stoves, either cold or smoking, the same long rooms with their cracked cement, the same people. A few new faces—first-year boys.

Liova is gone. He died over the summer. He was somehow made for death, that boy, and seems to me to have fulfilled his destiny through tuberculosis in the same way others fulfil theirs by writing a book, building a house or completing their work. I talked to our old dormmates from last year about him. Nobody had much to say.

"He had these yellow boots, nearly new, that he left here when he went away," said Ianchelevici Șapsă. "But they're no good: too small."

Liova, poor boy, your death did not even do that small good.

This building, despite being warmly called a "shelter" is strangely apathetic, horribly icy . . . And yet several hundred young people live here. And only one room is alive, bustling, and breathing passion: 'the social issues room'. That's what they call it, with irony, because Winkler, the old medical student, has his bed here. Winkler has been kept from his exams by Zionism and by S.T. Haim, a mathematics student at the polytechnic and a fiercely argumentative Marxist.

The pair of them quarrel endlessly.

"I'm going to report you both," shouts Ionel Bercovici, despairing of ever getting to the end of a page on constitutional law.

"Idiot," replies S.T.H. (who is referred to by his initials, for some reason), "you want us to hold back the march of history until you've passed your exam?"

Neither Winkler nor S.T.H. can have a very good opinion of me. They regard me as an outsider. At any event, they felt I was a fence-sitter, someone who observed in passing, neutrally. I listened quietly in a corner to their confused disagreement without intervening, enduring stubbornly the hard, flashing glances they shot at me over their shoulders.

"Dilettantes, that's what you are," shouts S.T.H., "dilettantes in all you do, in all you feel or think you feel. Dilettantes in love, when you think you're making love, dilettantes in science when you dabble in science, dilettantes in poverty, when you live in poverty. Nothing is seen through to its conclusion. Nothing heroic. Nothing unto the death. Everything for a cautious, compromised life. And you call yourself a Zionist, but you haven't a clue if there really is a land called Zion. I don't believe in it, you do. So why don't you actually go there, set foot on that land? You sit here agitating, which consists in cutting out receipts for membership fees for ten thousand people as smart as you are, and they too reduce a drama to a membership card."

"And you?" asks Winkler, ever calm.

"Me? I'm here, where I should be. Wherever I am, that's where I should be, because I'm serving the revolution. By the simple fact that I exist, the simplest fact that I think. My every word is a protest, my every silence is a shout rising above your receipt-books and your smile . . ."

And he suddenly turns to me, pointing an accusatory finger, putting an end to my quiet corner, because my reserve clearly irritates him and because, in the end, he can't stand the presence of an additional person who is neither friend nor foe—who is simply paying attention. S.T.H. needs an audience, an adversary, to feel he's up against something.

Now, having issued the challenge, he waits for me to take it up, his eyes flashing cold fire. Fire "from the head," I'm sure, and not from the heart. He's tense as a folded razor, trembling in anticipation of being unsheathed. But I meet his gaze, and return it, though I feel it burning, and keep quiet. I let the silence grow, until it must shatter under its own weight.

He awaits a gesture, a sign, the start of a reply, something that will let him explode without being silly, but I'm determined not to help him out in any way, and all his violence, all his fury, is vain, useless.

But S.T.H. does not lose the match. Anybody else in his situation would have, but not him. He shakes off a lingering frown, passes his hand over his head, steps towards me and, in a tone that is surprisingly melodious and friendly after his previous vehemence, says:

"Won't you join me at the pictures this evening?"

S.T. Haim, my good friend, how well we play our roles, and how sadly.

I took my leave of S.T.H. last night and at seven-thirty this morning he was knocking on my door (when did he sleep? when did he get up?) so that I'd see the message he'd slipped under it . . . Then I heard him stomping down the stairs.

I wish to disturb you. Your complacency horrifies me. Montaigne, of whom you spoke last night, is heresy. Stendhal, a frivolity. If that's all it takes for you to sleep peacefully, all the worse for you. I wish you long, dark periods of insomnia.

"I wish to disturb you." If he's taken that from Gide, he's ridiculous. If he came up with it himself, he's doubly so.

S.T. Haim, charged by destiny to summon me to my duty! S.T Haim, called to shake me up and to remind me of the tragedies I've run from, Montaigne under my arm!

The messianic impulse and psychological insight are incompatible. S.T.H. is a missionary with no notion of what is going on in the people around him.

He wishes to disturb me. And I'd like to find a stone on which to lay my head.

Had I a sense of mission like his, I would do my best to bring calm to the situations and consciences around me. And most of all to that of S.T.H., who is a weary lunatic, a child under the spell of illusions.

"S.T. Haim," I would say to him, "you're worn out. Stop, sit still for an hour. Look around. Touch this and observe that it's a bit of stone. Hold this in your hand and know it's a piece of wood. Look, a horse, a table, a hat.

"Believe in these things, live with them, get used to regarding them normally, without looking for shimmering phantoms in them. Return to these sure, simple things, resign yourself to living with them, with their low horizons, in their modest families. And look around, entrust yourself to the seasons, to hunger, to thirst: life will get along fine with you, as it calmly does with a tree, or an animal."

But who will say these same things to me? And who will teach me how to teach the others?

Let's presume that the hostility of anti-Semites is, in the end, endurable. But how do we proceed with our own, internal, conflict?

One day—who knows—we may make peace with the anti-Semites. But when will we make peace with ourselves?

It's not easy to spend days or weeks running from yourself, but it can be done. You get into mathematics and Marxism like S.T.H., become a Zionist like Winkler, read books as I do, chase women. Or play chess, or else beat your head against a wall. But one day, in a careless moment, your own heart will be revealed to itself, as though you had turned a corner and collided with a creditor you had sought to avoid. You behold yourself and perceive your vain evasions in this prison without walls, doors or bars—this prison that is your life.

You can never be vigilant enough. Some are better at pretending than others. Some keep it up for years, others for just a few hours! It ends for all in an inevitable reversion to sadness, like returning to the earth.

For some reason, after so many years, last night I was remembering my grandfather on my mother's side. I see him at his work-table, among thousands of springs, screws, cogs, and the faces and hands of watches. I see him leaning over them, a watchmaker's monocle clamped as always in the socket of his right eye, an exacting master casting spells with his long-fingered hands over the world of mechanical wonders he ruled, putting it in motion.

On that monstrous table, which as a child I was forbidden to go near (a missing cog meant the onset of chaos), he organized tiny autonomous worlds, tiny abstract entities from those minuscule dots of metal, which came together as a precise, strict, ordered harmony of hundreds of rhythmic voices in fine, ticking music. Under the glass of every watch-face lay a planet with its own discrete life, indifferent to what went on beyond it, and the glass seemed specially made to separate it from that "beyond."

Though I sensed he was restless, the old man was truly enviable for the peace he enjoyed among the metal beings his hand created. He lived under their spell for hours, days, years. Yet his craft was surely also an escape, a refuge. And perhaps he ran from himself, and was in terror that he would never encounter his true self.

And so, in the evening, when darkness fell and he had risen suddenly from the workbench over which he had sat silently all day, there was no pause, no restful smile on the face [of] that gentle man. He was always hurrying. Why was he hurrying? Where was he hurrying to?

He would get his hat and coat and walking stick, say something in passing and hurry into the street, leaving the door open, and to the synagogue across the road. There he would rush about with the same harried air, shaking hands here and there, and finally come to a stop before his prayer stand. There he would recover his composure, leaning over an open book, as tensed and silent as he was before the tiny wheels of a clock. Many times I watched him there, reading. He seemed immersed in confecting more tiny mechanisms, and the letters in the book—terribly small—looked like more tiny parts to be organized by his eye, to be called forth from nothingness, from stillness. At home were clocks, here were ideas, and both were abstract, cold and exact, subject to the will of a man trying to forget himself. Did he succeed? I don't know. His face was at times illuminated from beyond, in expectation of what—or despairing of what—I am unable to say.

At least sixty years of life and twenty of death separate us. Even more—many more. He lived in the Middle Ages and I live today. We are separated by centuries. I don't read the books he read or believe the things he believed in, I am surrounded by different people and have other preoccupations. And yet today I feel I am his grandson, his direct descendant, heir to his incurable melancholy.

Why do we, who rebel against ourselves so often, for so many reasons, never revolt against our taste for catastrophe, against our kinship with pain?

There is an eternal amity between us and the fact of suffering, and more than once, in my most lamentable moments, I have been surprised to recognize the mark of pride in this suffering, the indulging of a vague vanity. There is perhaps something tragic in this, but to the same degree it also shows an inclination for theatricality. Indeed, in the very hour when I am deeply sad I sense, subconsciously, the metaphysical tenor of my soul taking the stage.

Perhaps I'm bad to think this way, but I will never be sufficiently tough with myself, will never strike myself hard enough.

I would criticize anti-Semitism above all, were it to permit me to judge it, for its lack of imagination: 'freemasonry, usury, ritual killing'.

Is that all? How paltry!

The most basic Jewish conscience, the most commonplace Jewish intelligence, will find within itself much graver sins, an immeasurably deeper darkness, incomparably more shattering catastrophes.

All they have to use against us are stones, and sometimes guns. In our eternal struggle with ourselves, we have a subtle, slow-working but irremediable vitriol in our own hearts.

I can well understand why a renegade Jew is more ferocious than any other kind of renegade. The harder he tries to shake his shadow, the tighter it sticks. Even in disowning his race, the very fact of his apostasy is a Judaic act, as we all, inwardly, renounce ourselves a thousand times, yet always go back home, with the willfulness of one who desires to be God himself.

I'm certainly not a believer and the matter doesn't concern me, doesn't really trouble me.

I don't attempt to be rigorous in this regard and acknowledge quite frankly the inconsistencies. I can know, or say, that God does not exist, and recall with pleasure the physics and chemistry textbooks from school that gave him no place in the Universe. That doesn't prevent me from praying when I receive bad news or wish to avert it. It's a familiar God, to whom I offer up sacrifices from time to time, under a cult of rules established by me and—I believe—corroborated by him. I suggest typhus for myself, instead of a flu He was thinking of sending to somebody dear to me. I indicate certain ways in which I would prefer him to smite me or show me mercy. Anyway, I cede to him much more than I retain, as what I give him comes from myself, but what I retain belongs to the others, the very few others, that I love.

And I doubt our conversation troubles him, as He doesn't quite see it as a transaction and is aware of the good intentions with which I approach him.

All the same . . . Sometimes I feel there is something more, beyond that: the God with whom I have seen old men in synagogues struggling, the God for whom I beat my breast, long ago, as a child, that God whose singularity I proclaimed every morning, reciting my prayers.

"God is one, and there is only one God."

Does not "God is one" mean that God is alone? Alone like us, perhaps, who receive our loneliness from him and for him bear it.

This clarifies so many things and obscures so many more . . .

Translated by Philip Ó Ceallaigh.

Other works by Sebastian: *Femei* (1933); *Cum am devenit huligan* (1935); *Orașul cu salcâmi* (1935); *Jocul de-a vacanța* (1938); *Corespondența lui Marcel Proust* (1939); *Accidentul* (1940); *Steaua fără nume* (1944); *Ultima oră* (1946).

Moyshe Altman

1890–1981

A Yiddish writer, journalist, and playwright, Moyshe Altman was born in Lipkan, Bessarabia, received his education in traditional Jewish and Russian schools, and worked for the Yiddish Culture Federation of Romania. He spent time in Argentina and then moved to Bucharest and Kishinev. He spent the years of World War II in Central Asia and was arrested in 1949 for his Zionist activities. Returning to Chernivtsi in 1955, Altman continued to write in Yiddish throughout his life.

The Vienna Coach
1935

The Little Leyviks

The antiquarian who spends his time amid his old things may well have his moments of despair. He probably asks himself more than once: "What is the use of all these antiques, while life around us is in turmoil and spits out, like a volcano, a constant stream of new things?" The antiquarian must have a lot of love for his old pieces of paper and this love can save him at difficult moments. But how difficult must it be for someone who wishes to be not just an antiquarian, but to bring back to life long-gone generations? That ambition is without a doubt a sign of sickness, of a serious psychological flaw.

And yet I will tell the story of Basye Leyvis.

Today there is no more to tell about Basye than there are ashes from a cigar. But if a woman like Basye Leyvis could undertake something that only the great would dare to do, then perhaps we can learn something from it.

Basye was descended from a family that people called the Leyviklekh, "the Little Leyviks." From what time that name dated is hard to say. No pedigree has survived, and the tradition of the family was based on relatively recent events, such as a prayer house erected by a member of the family. It was said about this occurrence that he had literally built the prayer house himself. He did not look just look on while others did the building, but personally brought the water, clay, and sand and painted the walls. Further it was told about another member of the Leyviklekh that he once encountered the prophet Elijah and that Elijah said to him: "Nosn, you ought to go home and marry off your youngest daughter." So Nosn—that was his name—understood that he was going to die soon and went home and married off his youngest daughter. A week later he was dead, though he was not very old and quite robust.

Similar stories can be heard from old families in quite a few small towns.

Why they were called "The Little Leyviks" cannot be explained from these stories. But one thing is certain: it was a large family with many branches, among the oldest in the region. There were no rich men among the Leyviklekh until Mekhel, about whom we will speak later. Nor were there any great merchants or big shots. They were ordinary, middling people. Since there were so many branches to the family, they were a varied lot—some were poor, others well off, still others once prospered but had fallen on hard times. So where did their attitude and determination come from? Their great self-confidence and arrogance toward the public, toward the rich and the community leaders? They had no respect for the rabbi, for the tax collector, for the moneylender and not even for the authorities. And one of them had a big lawsuit with the authorities and had to flee. Some say that he was Leyvik, the first of the Leyviklekh. [. . .]

Basye, who was known as Basye Leyvis, was descended from the main branch of the Leyviklekh, from the branch that claimed as its ancestor that Leyvik who had to flee from the authorities and left traces of himself in old and famous Jewish cities, for example Stanislav and Budapest. In her family, the one in which she had her roots, letters and marriage contracts, allegedly written by that Leyvik in his own hand, were handed down from father to son. From these documents it could be seen that this Leyvik was a master of calligraphy. It was

conjectured that this artistry of his caused him to be driven from his home. He supposedly forged the signatures and documents of very important people.

But there were other things said about Leyvik. People said that he was a great singer with a powerful voice. When he reached for the high notes, he could be heard for miles around.

It seems he was a restless sort, who could not stay in one place, could not live with anyone, did not remain long in one city and was a wanderer all his life.

That, in short, is what we know about the Leyviklekh. In addition, old people in that region knew that they were devoted Hasidim. But in Basye's family, Hasidism resided in the female line. The males were merchants, learned men, busy people. The Hasidism was inherited by the daughters.

And so it was with Basye.

The Vienna Coach

1

Who knows? It may be that if Mekhel had not been such a villain. . . . Or maybe it happened like that so that nothing would change in the order of the world.

And yet, who can say whether the woman might not have prevailed if it had not been for the Vienna coach.

Mekhel, the same Mekhel who to spite the other rich men lived simply and whose wife got rid of the old house when he had gone away for a week and only then did he build the new house with its drawing rooms and all its surroundings, that Mekhel ordered a coach with four Hungarian horses in harnesses with silver blinkers, like the highest dignitaries, and when the coach arrived and the horses were harnessed the whole town ran to look. Mekhel strolled around the courtyard, making fun of the poor people, and the poor people stared at the coachman and his boy who were having trouble managing the horses who could not stand still and kept pawing at the ground with their front hooves. In the meantime Kheve the maid went outside to have a look and the old mother likewise wanted to have a look. When Mekhel saw her he began to mock her and said to her, as if in a joke, but so that everyone outside could hear: "Mama, would you like to go for a ride?"

The whole crowd burst out laughing and she felt deeply shamed. She burst out: "After I'm dead!"

What is a word? Nothing. A straw in the wind. But a word that arrives suddenly, unasked for, on its own, an uninvited thought which splits the mind like a bolt of lightning, who knows the force of such a word and such a thought?

A healthy young man walks into a shop to order cloth for a garment for himself, or for someone close to him, a healthy young man whose life is going well. You might ask: what can a young and healthy man, who is able to get cloth for a garment for himself or a person close to him, have on his mind? And suddenly something like a flame leaps from his mind. . . . But I do not want to say what it is. And the result is that the garment is not worn by the person for whom the cloth was cut. That person. . . . But can paper convey a sigh that comes from concealed depths? How can you trust paper, when you are disappointed in living friends?

What had she said, Basye? Did she say it, or did she only imagine it?

She stowed herself away on top of the stove and seldom climbed down—on Fridays only to wash herself in honor of the Sabbath. She blessed the Sabbath candles on the stove. She pretended not to notice if anyone came into the kitchen. If her son came in, she covered herself and pretended to be asleep. She did not even answer her daughter-in-law, the simple, honest woman, when she spoke to her.

2

It was on a Sunday. Monday Gitl arrived, took Mekhel aside and told him that all was not well with mother.

Meanwhile word got around in the town that the old woman was nearing the end and people started drinking in all the taverns on credit. Mekhel was informed by his people that the town had placed watchmen to make sure that the corpse was not taken to one of the poor sons, but to Mekhel. And that they would not take less than twenty thousand from him.

Mekhel thought it over and his closest adviser apparently gave him a hint: the coach. . . .

So Mekhel had the closed Vienna coach harnessed with his four Hungarian horses with their silver blinkers and rode out to the estate ostensibly to see his dying mother but stopped off at the government offices.

On the night of Sunday to Monday Basye had dreams, as always. She imagined that she was on her way to her eldest son's wedding. It's winter, all the in-laws and relatives are sitting in sleighs, but she has been lost along the way. She sees the sleighs ride away and she wants to scream, but cannot. Then she dreams that she is in the courtyard of her old home. She wants to go into the house. The house is lit up and she gropes along the walls but cannot find the door.

At dawn she woke up and called by name one of her older uncles and a brother whom she had not seen for some sixty years, and fell asleep again. It wasn't until Monday evening that she fully woke up and called for Gitl:

"Daughter, please, give me a drink."

Afterwards, she asked who was there. She was told that present are Nosn, the oldest son and Yankl the melamed, a poor teacher in a traditional school, and Shoel. Also Velvl, the oldest grandson, Shoel and Gitl's oldest son, who happened to have come to visit his parents. So she requested that all of them should gather and then said: "This night is the last."

And fell asleep again.

Meanwhile Gitl was very tired, so she lay down for a bit and fell asleep. So did the oldest son and the grandson. Yankl sat poring over a religious book and said what it was his duty to say. Only Reb Shoel was awake. He watched as she opened her eyes, looked at him, recognized him and made a gesture like someone who is saying good-bye. And—that was that. No more Basye Leyvis. Reb Shoel uttered: "*Borekh dayen emes*— Blessed is the True Judge."

And everyone awoke.

In the same night, at Mekhel's request, Basye's body was carried in the closed Vienna coach, with the four Hungarian horses, with the silver blinkers. She was accompanied by her poor son, the *melamed*, and the oldest grandson, Gitl's oldest son. The route they followed was known only to the coachman. They rode over fields and ridges and at dawn, when they arrived in the distant town where Basye had been born, Jews, Christians, and noblemen ran outside and raised their hats, thinking it was the governor passing by. But when the carriage stopped at Basye Leyvis's house, people surmised what had happened.

The whole town gathered for her funeral. And although some of her children had already scattered across the world, she had a very big funeral.

And afterwards?

Afterwards Basye Leyvis's household fell into such ruin that it is painful to relate. The best of them met with violent ends that fill you with horror. There remained only a small number, and even these few kept each other at arm's length, worse than strangers. They were degraded and were trampled on even by all the others who were degraded. Even Mekhel, who had been the luckiest, became senile before his time. May all the enemies of the Jews have the kind of old age he had and have as much pleasure as he had from his children.

It follows from all this, that one must not aim for more than the whole world. The proof—Basye Leyvis.

Translated by Solon Beinfeld.

Other works by Altman: *Blendenish* (1926); *Medrash Pinkhes* (1936); *Shmeterlingen* (1939).

Pinkhes Berniker

1908–1956

Pinkhes Berniker was born in Belorussia, the son of a town rabbi. He received both a traditional religious education and a modern Hebrew education. In 1925, he immigrated to Cuba, where he worked as a teacher in the Havana Jewish school. He began at this time to publish stories and articles in Yiddish newspapers. In 1931, he moved to the United States, first to Rochester, New York, where he directed a Talmud Torah, and then to Hartford, Connecticut, where he taught at a Conservative synagogue.

Jesús

1935

He didn't take it seriously the first few times his roommates suggested that he start peddling images of Jesus, of *Yoshke*, as he preferred to call him. He thought they were kidding. How could they be serious? Were they fools? What could they mean? How could they possibly think that he should shlep the *goyish* icons through the streets of Havana? What was he, a boy, a young lad, who knew nothing of the world? How could they imagine that he—a middle-aged Jew with a beard and side curls, who had been ordained as a rabbi, who had devoted all the days of his life to Torah and to divine service—could all of a sudden peddle icons and spread word of Jesus of Nazareth? No, even they couldn't be serious about that! So he thought, and didn't even try to answer them. He just sighed quietly, wiped the sweat off his face, and sat without moving, sure that they wouldn't bring up such a notion again.

Later he realized he'd been mistaken. Those roommates of his had been very serious. Not daring to propose the idea outright, they had begun by alluding to it, joking about it. He had remained silent and, contrary to their expectations, hadn't jumped up from his seat as though he had been scorched. So they had begun to broach the subject directly, insisting that he not even try another livelihood, even if one presented itself. He, of all people, was in just the right position to turn the greatest profit from peddling the "gods." No one else could approach his success.

"For every god you sell, you'll clear a thousand percent profit." "And the Cubans love to buy gods." "Especially from you, Rabbi Joseph, who look so much like the bastard, pardon the comparison." "You'll see how eager they'll be to buy from you." "And they'll pay whatever you ask." "Listen to me, Rabbi Joseph, just try it! You'll see! They'll sacrifice everything they have for you! People who don't even need a god will buy one from you!" Thus his roommates urged him to become a god peddler. They couldn't stand to see him half starved, in total distress, bereft of the slightest prospects. And they really did believe that selling the gods would solve his problems.

The more persistent they became, the more pensive he grew. He didn't answer them, for what could he say? Could he cut out his heart and show them how it bled, how every word they uttered made a sharp incision in it, tearing at it painfully? How could they understand what he felt, if they didn't know how he'd been trained, what his position had been in the old country? He was consumed with self-pity. The world had stuck out its long, ugly tongue at him. Rabbi Joseph, so diligent a pupil that he'd been hailed as the prodigy from Eyshishok, was now supposed to spread tidings of Jesus of Nazareth throughout the world?!

He couldn't resign himself to his lot. Every day, in the blue, tropical dawn, he dragged himself through the narrow streets of Old Havana, offering his labor to one Jewish-owned factory after another, promising to do whatever it would take to earn a pittance. He was rejected everywhere. How could they let a venerably bearded Jew work in a factory? Who would dare holler at him? How could they prod him, ordering him around as necessary? "How could someone like you work in a factory?" "In the Talmudic academy of Volozhin, did they teach shoemaking?" "Rabbi, you're too noble to work here." They looked at him with pity, not knowing how to help.

"Why? Wasn't the great Rabbi Yokhannan a shoemaker?" he asked, pleading for mercy.

"That was then, this is now."

"And what about now? Wouldn't Rabbi Yokhanan still need to eat?" That was what he wanted to cry out, but he couldn't. He was already too discouraged. The unanimous rejections tortured him more than the constant hunger. And the charity, the sympathy, offered by all became harder to bear. It wouldn't have humiliated him had it not been for the presence, in a faraway Lithuanian town, of a wife and three small children who needed to eat. "Send some money, at least for bread." Thus his wife had written to him in a recent letter. And the word *bread* had swelled up and grown blurry from the teardrop that had fallen on it from the eye of a helpless mother.

Joseph recalled the words from *The Ethics of the Fathers*. "If I am not for me, who will be for me?"

"I must harden myself. I must find work!" He called out these words, forcing himself onto the street. Pale, thin, with a despairing mien, he posted himself at a factory door, glancing around helplessly, hoping to catch sight of the owner. From among the workers, a middle-aged Jew ran up to the door and pressed a few pennies into his palm. Joseph froze. His eyes popped out of his head; his mouth gaped open. The couple of cents fell from his hand. Like a madman, he ran from the factory. Late that night, when his roommates returned, he pulled himself off his cot, stared at them momentarily, and said, "Children, tomorrow you will help me sell the gods." They wanted to ask him what had happened, but, glimpsing the pain in his eyes, they could not move their tongues.

Binding both packages of gods together, he left between them a length of rope to place on his neck, thereby lightening the load. He had only to hold on to the packages with his hands, lest they bump into his sides and stomach.

The uppermost image on his right side portrayed Mother Mary cuddling the newborn child, and the one on his left showed Jesus already grown. Between the two images he himself looked like the Son of God. His eyes were larger than life, and his face was paler than ever. Deep, superhuman suffering shone forth from him, a reflection of the pain visited on Jesus of Nazareth as he was led to the cross.

The day was burning hot. Pearls of sweat shone on his mild, pale face, and his clothes stuck to his tortured body. He stopped for a while, disentangling his nightmarish thoughts, slowly removing the rope from his neck, straightening his back wracked with pain, and scraping away the sweat that bit into his burning face. He wiped tears from the corner of one eye.

He saw, far off, the low wooden cabins in the next village. In the surrounding silence, from time to time, there came the cries of the village children. Feeling a bit more cheerful, he slowly loaded his body with the two packages of gods. Trembling, he strode onward, onward. He was noticed first by the lean, pale children playing in the street. They immediately stopped their games and stiffened in amazement. The tropical fire in their black eyes burst forth as they caught sight of him. Never had they seen such a man.

"*¡Mamá, mamá, un Jesús viene!* A Jesus is coming!" Each started running home. "*¡Mira! ¡Mira!*" The children's voices rang through the village.

From windows and doors along the road women leaned their heads out, murmuring excitedly to one another: "*¡Santa María!*" "*¡Qué milagro!*" "*¡Dios mío!*" They all whispered in astonishment, unable to turn their straining eyes away from the extraordinary man.

Joseph approached one of the houses and pointed to the image of Jesus, mutely suggesting that they buy a god from him. But the hot-blooded tropical women thought he was indicating how closely the image resembled him. Filled with awe, they gestured that he should enter. "*¡Entre, señor!*" said each one separately, with rare submissiveness. He entered the house, took the burden off his neck, and seated himself on the rocking chair they offered him. Looking at no one, he began untying the gods. No one in the household dared to sit. Along with some neighbors who had sneaked in, they encircled him and devoured him with their wide-open eyes.

"*¿Tienes hijo?* Do you have a son?" a young *shiksa* asked, trembling.

"I have two," he answered.

"And are they as handsome as you?" asked another girl excitedly.

"I myself don't know."

"*¡Mira, él mismo tampoco sabe!* He himself doesn't know!" A strange shame overtook the girls. They looked at each other momentarily, then burst into embarrassed laughter: "Ha ha ha! Ha ha ha!" Their hoarse guffaws echoed through the modest home.

"What's going on?" asked the mothers, glancing unkindly toward the man.

"Nothing!" said the girls, embracing each other, then repeating ecstatically, "*¡El mismo tampoco sabe! ¡El mismo tampoco sabe!* Ha ha ha! Ha ha ha!" Their suffocating laughter resonated as each tucked herself more closely into her girlfriend's body.

"And what's your name?" One of the girls tore herself from her friend's embrace.

"José."

"What?" asked several of the women in unison.

"José."

"José-Jesús!"

The village women began to murmur, winking more than speaking.

One of the *shiksas* was unable to restrain herself: "And what's your son's name?"

"Juan."

"Juan, Juan," the *shiksas* began to repeat, drooling. Embarrassed, they pushed each other into the next room, wildly, bizarrely.

There was a momentary silence. Those watching were still under the spell of what had taken place. Joseph, however, was out of patience. "*Nu, ¿compran?* Are you going to buy or not?" he asked, raising his eyes, filled with the sorrow of the world. He could say no more in Spanish, but no more was necessary. Every woman purchased a god from him by paying an initial installment—from which he already cleared a handsome profit—and promising the rest later.

Home he went, with only the rope. All the gods had been sold. He had never felt so light, so unencumbered. He had no packages to carry, and a hope had arisen within him that he would be forever free from hunger and want.

Later he himself was astonished at how he had changed, at how indifferently he could contemplate Jesus' beard. He went to a Cuban barber and had his blond beard trimmed in the likeness of Jesus.

"Your mother must have been very pious!" said the barber to him, with great conviction.

"How can you tell?"

"When she conceived you, she couldn't have stepped away from the image of Jesus."

"Perhaps." Joseph was delighted.

How could he act this way? He didn't know. The Christian women, his customers in the villages all around, waited for him as Jews await the Messiah. They worshipped him, and he earned from them more than he could ever have dreamed.

They had no idea who he was. He never told them he was a Jew, and he still wondered how he could deny his Jewish background. He learned a little Spanish,

especially verses from the New Testament, and spoke with the peasant women like a true *santo*, a saint. Once, when a customer asked him, "*¿Qué eres tú?* What are you?" he rolled his eyes to the heavens and started to say, drawing out his words, "What difference does it make who I am? All are God's children."

"And the *judíos*? The Jews?" asked the women, unable to restrain themselves.

"The *judíos* are also God's children. They're just the sinful ones. They crucified our *señor Jesús*, but they are still God's children. *Jesús* himself has forgiven them." He ended with a pious sigh.

"And do you yourself love the *judíos*?"

"Certainly."

"*¿De veras?* Really?"

"*¿Y qué?* What of it?" He put on a wounded expression and soon conceded, "My love for them isn't as deep as for the Christians, but I do love them. A sinner can be brought back to the righteous path through love, as our *señor Jesús* said."

"*¡Tiene razón!* He's right!"

"*¡Y bien que sí!* And how!"

"*¡Es un verdadero santo!* He's a true saint!" All the women drank in his words.

"Have you yourself seen a real Jew?" Their curiosity couldn't be sated.

"Yes, I have."

"Where?"

"There, in Europe."

"What did he look like?"

"Just like me."

"Really?!"

"Yes, indeed."

"*¡Si él lo dice, debe ser verdad!* If he says it, it must be true." The peasant women winked at each other, and their faces grew intensely serious, as if in a moment of great exaltation. Joseph fell silent, engrossed in his thoughts. He let the peasant women examine some sample gods, for now he simply took orders, which he filled by mail. In the meantime, he took stock of his situation, how much money he had in the bank, how much he was owed, and how many more thousands he would earn in the coming year if business improved by just fifty percent. "Who needs to worry?" A smile lit up his face as he felt these words in his heart: "I give thanks and praise to Thee, almighty God, who hast given Jesus unto the world."

A new god peddler showed up in the same area. Day in and day out he dragged himself from one village to the next, stopping at every home. He scraped the scalding sweat off his face and neck as he knocked, trembling, on the hospitable Cuban doors.

"*¡Compran algo?* Will you buy something?" he asked, gesturing broadly. Solidly built mothers and passionate, well-formed daughters looked at him with pity, comforting him and caressing him with the softness of the Spanish tongue and the gentleness of their big, velvety eyes. They gladly offered him a handout but shook their heads at his gods. "I'm sorry." He got the same answer almost everywhere.

"*¡Compra y no lamentes!* Buy and don't be sorry!"

"You're right!" answered the women, with a slight smile. He stood with his distressed face and heavy heart, looking at the peasant women, unable to understand why they were so stubborn.

A few children gathered around him. They stared at his earnest face, carefully touched the frames of the unveiled images, and began playing with them. "Tell your mother to buy a *santo!*" he said, caressing one of the children. The child stopped laughing. His glance passed from the god merchant to his mother. It was hard for him to grasp what was happening.

"How sweet you are," said the mother, affectionately embracing her now serious child.

"I have a child just like him in the old country," said the god merchant, about to burst into tears.

"*¡Mira, parece una mujer!* He's acting just like a woman!" The peasants were astonished to see the shiny tears forming in the corners of his eyes.

"Should a man cry?" "And he's supposed to be the breadwinner for a wife and children!" "How funny!" A few girls, unable to restrain themselves, laughed in his face. Ashamed, he glanced at their widely smiling eyes, felt his own helplessness, and went away. His feet had grown heavier and his grasp of events slighter. Nonetheless, arming himself with courage, he went from village to village. He knocked on every door and humbly showed his wares: "*¡Compren!* Buy something! If you help me, God will help you. And I sell very cheap!"

But he seldom came across a customer interested in his low prices. Almost everyone was waiting for the *santo*, the holy peddler, who bore a great likeness to God Himself. They dismissed the new god merchant out of hand: "I don't need any." "I'm sorry." "We've already bought some from someone else." He already knew all their answers by heart.

"Are gods the only thing to peddle?" Such was the bitter question he asked his fellow immigrants every day.

"Do you know of something better? Food isn't about to fly into your mouth. And what are you going to do with the gods you've already bought?"

"*¡Hay que trabajar!* You've got to work!" exclaimed one of his countrymen, eager to show off his Spanish.

"But my work is in vain!"

"Right now your work is in vain, but it will pay off in time," said his friends, trying to console him.

"In time, in time!" he muttered nervously, not knowing at whom.

It had grown dark in the middle of the day. The clear, tropical sky had suddenly clouded over. Waves of heat rose from the ground, and the air became closer and denser. At any moment buckets of rain could fall. *Campesinos*, riding into town, became uneasy lest the storm catch up with them. So they pushed back their gritty straw hats, their *tijanas*, fastened the palm-leaf baskets full of fowl on one side of their saddles; secured the cans of milk on the other side; and urged the horses on with all their might. "*¡Pronto!* Faster! *¡Pronto!*" "Soon there'll be a deluge!" "You'll get soaked with all your gods in the middle of the field." The riders took pity on the poor foot traveler as they dug their spurs ever more deeply into the sides of their horses. But he scarcely moved his feet, hammering his steps out heavily. It was already past noon, and he hadn't sold a single god.

Arriving at the next village, soaked to the bone, he caught sight of an open door leading into a home full of people. Sneaking in, he put down his pack of gods in a corner behind the door. As he started removing his wet clothes from his even wetter body, he heard a woman speaking: "Here's five dollars; send me a *San Antonio* like that next week." "And send me a *Jesus by the Well.*" "I'll take a *San Pablo*. Take three dollars in the meantime, and I'll pay the rest later." "Make sure you don't forget to send me a *Santa Maria*." "And I want a *Mother with the Son*." The women shouted over each other.

He could hardly believe his ears. He thought he was dreaming one of his sweet nightly dreams, in which he saw himself amid circles of peasant women ripping his godly wares out of his hands. He had believed that such good fortune was possible only in a dream, but here it was happening for real. "What can this be?" He wondered why he hadn't yet looked into the opposite corner of the room, and he took a few steps toward it.

He stopped in his tracks, stupefied. All his limbs began to shake. He tried to hide his surprise, for never had he seen a man who looked so much like Jesus. "So that's it!" he murmured to himself, as he watched Joseph rolling his eyes from time to time toward heaven, blessing the peasant women as a *rebbe* blesses his Hasidim. "Aha!" He was astonished at the reverence the village women bestowed on the stranger. "No, no, I could never become such a showman!" He stepped off to one side to keep Joseph from noticing him.

His last bit of hope had run out. "*Y tú, ¿de dónde vienes?* And where have you come from?" The peasant women were surprised to see the new god peddler, after Joseph had left.

"From Santo Domingo."

"You've just gotten here?"

"No, I'm just about to leave."

"Did you see our *Jesusito?*"

"You mean the *vendedor,* the seller of the gods?"

"Yes. Doesn't he look just like Jesus?" asked the peasant women, offended.

"Like Jesus? But he's a *judío,* a Jew!" These words came flying out of his mouth with unusual force.

"*¡Mentira! ¡Mentira!* That's a lie! You yourself are the *judío,* and a dirty one at that!" cried the peasant women in unison, pale with emotion.

"*¡Palabra de honor!* I give you my word of honor that he's a *judío!*" The new peddler couldn't restrain himself when he realized what a terrible impression the word *judío* made on them. But his claims were all in vain. The village women still didn't believe him. He couldn't make them understand. "*¡No, no puede ser!* No, it can't be." "*¡Vamos, vete de aquí!* Come on! Get out of here!" They couldn't stand to hear his words any longer.

He fell silent and left the house, but not the village. He sought out some young men and bought them a round of drinks. As he sipped black coffee by the white marble table, he told them that the god peddler with the face like Jesus', who overcharged their mothers for the pictures they bought from him, was a Jew, a descendant of the ones who had crucified Jesus.

"*¡No hable boberías!* Don't talk nonsense!" "*¿Cómo es posible?* How can that be?" "*¡No me lo diga!* Don't tell me." The young men didn't want to believe him. As their stubbornness grew, so did his. Finally, he told them of the first Jewish commandment. He left twenty-five dollars with the owner of the café and swore that the money was theirs if he had been lying to them. The cash had the right effect. It was as though the young men had been touched by fire. The blood rushed to their faces, and they drank themselves into a stupor.

Joseph hadn't yet arrived at the first house in the village when a lad ran across his path. "*¡Oiga!* Listen sir, my mother wants to buy something." The boy breathed with difficulty, hardly able to utter these words.

"*¡Bendito eres, hijito!* Blessed art thou, my son!" Such was Joseph's gentle answer.

"*¡Por aquí es más cerca!* This way is shorter!" said the little *goy* as he strode over the field, with Joseph trailing behind him.

Soon they were far, very far, from the village. The boy had already pointed out that "right over there" was their house. Although Joseph saw no house "over there," he still suspected nothing, assuming that his eyes were not as keen as the little *goy's*

"*Oiga, santo, ¿tú eres judío?* Listen, Your Holiness, are you a Jew?" The earth had suddenly brought forth, before Joseph's eyes, a robust young Cuban. Joseph gazed in surprise. For once his quick tongue failed him. When he finally could say something, it was too late. He was already splayed on the ground, with several *goyim* pinning down his legs; one held his head and two his arms. He screamed bloody murder, thrashed with his feet, pulled with all his might, but to no avail. They were stronger and did what they had to.

When they found out that he was indeed a Jew, they left him lying there, half naked in the middle of the field. Every one of them spat in his face, hollered "*¡Judío!*" and ran to the village to tell of this wondrous thing.

The village women refused to believe even their own children. And for a long, long time they wouldn't patronize the new god merchant, for they hoped that *Jesús* would come back. But Joseph never returned.

Translated by Alan Astro.

Other works by Berniker: *Shtile lebns: dertseylungen* (1935).

Simon Blumenfeld

1907–2005

The novelist and journalist Simon Blumenfeld was born and raised in the East End of London. He was closely associated with his fellow East End writers Willy Goldman and the brothers Barnet and Emanuel Litvinoff. His first novel, *Jew Boy* (1935), was a harsh semiautobiographical portrait of a young Jewish man seeking to free himself from poverty and familial suffocation in London's immigrant quarter. After World

War II, Blumenfeld entered the world of show business and sports journalism and began to publish Western novels using various pseudonyms.

Jew Boy
1935

Chapter VIII

Olive liked her new job very much. She had never before tasted such rich, well-cooked food in her life. She put on weight. She was contented.

There wasn't too much work; just cleaning the shop in the morning, running a couple of errands during the day, making the beds and helping Mrs. Bercovitch keep the rooms tidy.

Dave's mother was a plump, rosy-faced middle-aged woman, very naive and good-tempered. She had never had a daughter so she rather enjoyed having Olive about the house. She treated her as a companion, someone to talk to; asked her advice and discussed almost everything that cropped up, with her.

At first, Mrs. Bercovitch had been worried about Dave. He was the only child and not used to strange women and she didn't want him to get into trouble, especially with a "shiksah." But Dave took not the slightest notice of Olive. When his mother was about, he wouldn't even look at her. Mrs. Bercovitch was reassured.

Mr. Bercovitch was a dear. He reminded Olive of fat, bald-headed little Spilliken of the "Dot and Carrie" strip; the same tubby figure, black eyebrows and wisp of a moustache. He was easy to handle. The first two days she answered "Yes, sir," promptly when he called, but she soon took her cue from the missus, and learned to bully him in an amiable, motherly way. Mr. Bercovitch didn't mind. So long as they let him alone, outside with his groceries, the women could do what they liked in the house, providing his meals were done to time.

That morning, Olive and Mrs. Bercovitch had got up at six. They had scrubbed the shutters till there was not a fleck of dust on them, cleaned the windows, whitened the doorstep, and heaped the gas stove with pots full of savoury food. They were busy as ants all day long, getting ready for the crown of the year, the eve of the Black Fast. Olive wonderd how Mr. Bercovitch would manage all day without his food. At sundown they had eaten an enormous meal and gone to the synagogue. It was "Kol Nidrei" night, explained Mrs. Bercovitch. Jews were forbidden to eat or drink anything from that hour until sundown the following day.

This Black Fast business gave her a queer feeling, frightened her a little. She couldn't explain it, really, but it seemed as though things were happening up in the heavens. With millions and millions of Jews praying and fasting this same night, all over the world, something was bound to be going on . . . .

She even felt religious herself. Sorry she'd missed mass on Sunday, and the Sunday before that. She'd go more regularly in future. After all, she wasn't worse than the Jews. She also had her duty to God and the Virgin Mary. She crossed herself surreptitiously. There was such a peculiar holy atmosphere about the place, as though the sacrament of the wine and the wafers were going on all the time, in a deeper, intenser form, like a much more incomprehensible mystery.

She was up very early the next morning, although there was nothing to do. The house was spotless. The scullery looked like the inside of a kitchen cabinet, newly painted with white enamel. All the food was outside in the safe. She recalled her instructions. When the sun was down low at the end of the day, she had to put the soup on the stove, the roast in the oven. On the table, the decanter of spirit and kummel, one Dutch and one pickled herring, green olives, bread and the horseradish sauce. Yes, she had it all pat. She knew where everything had to go.

She heard them stirring upstairs. They'd soon be down. She hurried to put on the kettle for tea. Then she remembered; they wouldn't drink anything. She turned out the light. Somehow she didn't feel like having any breakfast herself. It seemed sacrilege to eat on a day like this in a Jewish house. She felt, if she did, the food would choke her.

She heard Mr. Bercovitch coming down the stairs, his comical heavy wide tread, and behind, the softer footsteps of the missus. They were dressed all ready for going out. Mr. Bercovitch wore his frock coat and high hat, Mrs. Bercovitch her new black satin coat trimmed with ermine; it looked very nice finished. Olive had been with her to the tailor's for fitting. Both carried prayer books, and Mr. Bercovitch hugged under his arm an embroidered velvet bag in which was his silken praying shawl.

They stood in the kitchen ready to leave for the synagogue, waiting for Dave to come down. Mr. Bercovitch fidgeted impatiently and looked at the clock. Time didn't stand still. He went to the foot of the stairs and poked his chin in the air. "Davey! Davey! Come on—it's getting late."

There was no reply. At once Mrs. Bercovitch became alarmed. Mrs. Bercovitch always expected the worst.

"P-perhaps there's something wrong," she stammered. "I'll go up and see."

She ran up the stairs straight into Dave's room. He was in bed, lying quite still, his eyes open. Her heart thumping from the climb, beat more violently. He "taki" looked ill, the boy! She half-fell across the foot of the bed, and stared anxiously in his eyes. "What's the matter, Davey, boy?" she whisperd huskily, reaching for his hand to feel the pulse.

He sat up and passed his free hand wearily across his brow.

"I'm all right, Ma," he said. "Just a headache. I feel a bit weakish."

"Shall I get a doctor?"

She stood up, panting, ready to fly, to shout, to cry; she felt feverishly strong and heroic, she could tear walls down with her fingers. She bent over him again, so he could almost hear the tumult in her breast.

"Well?" she asked anxiously.

He gave her a reassuring smile and patted her hand.

"It isn't as bad as that," he said. "I'll be all right in an hour or so. I'll come to 'shool' in the afternoon."

"Are you sure?" she replied. "Sure you'll be all right?"

"Sure, Ma. Sure. It's only a bit of a headache, really. I'll be feeling first class in the afternoon."

Mr. Bercovitch was shouting again. She'd gone up to fetch Dave down, and now she'd got lost herself. Women were a funny lot! What was she doing up there all this while? At this rate, they'd get to "shool" in time to go home. It wasn't nice for a man in his position to be late on Yom Kippur. "Hy! Come on, up there!" he bawled.

At last Dave persuaded her to leave the room. She went out reluctantly, feeling as though she were betraying him, a load on her heart. As soon as the door shut, Dave settled down to sleep again.

He woke up at half-past ten and stretched himself lazily. He felt very much at ease. No one could deny he was much better off in bed than cooped up in a stuffy synagogue. He'd have something to eat, and then he'd manage to fast comfortably till the evening.

"Olive!" he shouted. "Olive!"

The girl came running up the stairs. She'd been warned he wasn't too well, maybe he was feeling queer again. She burst into the room.

"Yes," she answered breathlessly.

"Fetch me up a cup of tea," he said.

She stopped, breathing heavily, and stared at him in bewilderment. She couldn't believe he'd said tea. He looked all right, not delirious or anything . . .

"Tea?" she said.

He nodded, "That's right."

"But you mustn't have tea!"

"All right—cocoa, coffee—anything you've got."

"But, Dave," don't you know what day it is, to-day? It's the Black Fast!"

"I know all about that," he said impatiently, "but I want my cup of tea. Besides," he grinned slyly, "I'm an invalid."

Invalid! She glared at him angrily. It was disgusting. He was no more an invalid than she was . . . and make him tea! To-day! The Black Fast! She had quite enough sins on her conscience already.

"Well?"

"*Must* you have tea this morning?" she asked, fidgeting uneasily.

He answered sharply; he was losing his temper. "Yes. I must."

"Then make it yourself," she retorted angrily. "I won't!" She slammed the door behind her and went down to the kitchen. Dave jumped out of bed and threw on his clothes hurriedly. What the hell was she wriggling about for? What difference would a cup of tea make to her? For the life of him he couldn't understand what was going on in her mind. He followed her downstairs into the kitchen. She had her back to him and refused to say a word. He lit the stove himself, and waited for the kettle to boil.

The tea went down extra well. The old people were praying all day, in any case—they'd have to put in a word or two for him. Olive had been pottering about in the yard. She had no particular tasks, but she wanted to keep out of his way. She came into the kitchen for a moment and put the pail in the corner.

Dave fixed his eyes on her. She was getting more attractive than ever. Her figure was filling out; she was blossoming. Even under the stiff, gaily flowered cretonne overall, he could appreciate the full soft curves. It was the chance of a lifetime! Apart from himself and Olive, there was not a soul in the house. Not very often that both his parents went out and left him alone with her.

Olive turned round to go to the door. She guessed what he was thinking by the way he stared at her. She turned red. This would just about put the lid on! Any other time she didn't mind, but she couldn't bear to let him touch her to-day. The idea was revolting—made her feel sick!

She hurried towards the yard, but he jumped up, blocking the doorway, and caught her wrists. He smiled at her.

"Where's the fire?" he said.

She turned her head away, refusing to answer. He pulled her closer to him and put one arm round her waist, and bent over her, to kiss her. With her free hand she smacked his face. Some invalid! His grin broadened. He pressed his face against her cheek and kissed her lustfully.

"Let me go!"

He laughed. This was funny! Playing religious! She'd never made a fuss before. Coquetry! Some new stunt to work him up. . . . The girl squirmed in his arms. She was terrified. Sixteen million Jews, praying and fasting. Looking on angrily. . . . To-day! . . . Why today? . . . Her head whirled. Everything went black before her eyes. She gripped Dave tightly, trying to keep him off, but she felt herself growing weaker while he seemed to tower over her like a laughing giant, covering her face and neck with hot, wet kisses. . . .

Chapter IX

Up in the women's gallery, Mrs. Bercovitch cried softly. She kept making her way to the rails and looking over, but the seat next her husband was vacant. Always vacant. She had nothing to say to the women this morning; she even wished she had been taught Hebrew so she'd be able to read the prayers. She would have prayed and prayed and prayed. Almighty Jehovah in His loving-kindness would have been bound to incline an ear to her supplications in His own holy tongue.

For the fifth time she looked down into the body of the synagogue. Through a greyish fog, she saw the tinkling golden ornaments on the scroll of the law. Before the ark, the richly embroidered veil presented by the Ladies' Society. The cantor in his white robes on the raised dais and the male congregation swaying on the floor all round him. Bobbing skull caps, the constant movement of praying shawls fluttering like striped flags. Someone going out, someone coming in, never still, like ripples on the sea.

The beadle slapped his open palm on the prayer book three times. A hushed silence. Then the cantor's sweet nasal tenor rose upwards, pianissimo, with all the tiddly-bits, trilling fancy cadenzas like an overpaid opera-star. His last note hung in the air, till it was cut short by a roar of responses. The thin ragged contraltos of the choir-boys struggled through the noise with the first verse of a psalm, and the congregation joined in, the throbbing basses of the men chanting mournful incantations.

Everything, everything as it was every year, but no Dave. She couldn't bear it any longer. He might be lying in agony, crying for her, and she was selfishly standing here. The Almighty would forgive her if she didn't stay this once. She put on her coat and went down into the street. The clean air hit her in the face. For a moment she felt weak and faint. She leaned against the wall and someone passed her smelling salts. She sniffed and felt a little better. She started to walk sharply to escape the little nagging demon in her brain. Why hadn't she gone before? She should have left the synagogue an hour ago. Maybe it was too late; Oh, God! No! NO! NO! The suspense was twisting her mind. She never knew it was such a distance to the house. Her lips moved all the while, but no sound came from them. She was praying silently.

". . . Preserve him, O Lord. Preserve my Davey. Make him well again, O Lord. If someone must suffer, let me suffer for him. Let me be ill for him. Good God! Dear God . . . !"

The side door was open. A bad sign. It made her break into a cold sweat. There was something strange about the house. She'd felt that way before, the day she'd come home to find her father dead. And the side door had been open too. She burst into the kitchen almost demented, making straight for the stairs. She stopped. She must be seeing things. Dave! Out of bed? Dressed? It couldn't be! Yet it was so. And he was bending over Olive . . . what was happening here? What was going on? . . .

Her head swam, she felt giddy. She clutched the dresser to save herself from falling. What was going on here? . . . Olive was crying bitterly in the corner. Her overall lay on the floor. One shoulder strap from her slip had been torn off and hung down loosely. There were red marks like scratches across her chest. Now Mrs. Bercovitch understood. The young whore! They were all alike, these servant girls. She'd trusted her, cherished her, treated her like her own daughter, and now she did this. Servants! They were ruination in a house!

"Olive," she said, "what's this?"

The girl raised a moist flushed face. "But, Mrs. Bercovitch . . . !" she exclaimed piteously.

Mrs. Bercovitch silenced her with a look. "I'll speak to you later," she said. She moved to the door. Dave ran after her and plucked at her sleeve. "But listen, Mother . . . Mother," he begged.

"Don't call me Mother," she snapped at him.

She was in a white rage. She had never been so near hating him before. She almost felt she could whip the life out of him. That was what he deserved, the miserable little cheat. His touch contaminated her. And on such a holy day—Ach!—she shook herself free and rushed outside.

Dave hurried to the synagogue. He'd try and get the old man in a good mood. He wouldn't budge from his side all day. And perhaps his mother wouldn't tell; he'd have to get round her somehow. Pacify her. He kept glancing up at the gallery, hoping she'd look down like she always did, but she only came to the rail once, and as soon as she saw he was there, she went back to her seat and sat there like a statue.

She sat still, biting her lips, growing hot and cold as she thought of what had happened. She paid no more attention to the service. She scarcely heard a word of the sustained chattering all round her. She hardly knew what to do about it. Olive would have to go, of course, but what could she do about Dave? Disgraceful! Disgraceful! And on Yom Kippur too! Her cheeks burned as she thought of the shameful scene.

"Tekeeoooh," sung the cantor.

The ram's horn squeezed out a piercing howl, "EE-ee-ee-e!"

"Tekeeoooh!"

EE-ee-ee-e! EE-ee-ee-e!

"Tekeeoooh Gedaile!"

A last triumphant screech and the fast was over. Sundown, already! She was not at all grateful. She got up from her seat, kissed her neighbours, wished them long life and a prosperous year, listened half-heartedly to their greetings and pushed her way to the stairs.

Her husband and Dave were waiting for her in the street. She stared coldly at Dave, but he turned his head hastily to avoid her eyes. Mr. Bercovitch first shook her hand, then kissed her effusively. He was beaming. He stroked his stomach gently, patting it lovingly in anticipation. There were rumblings down in the emptiness, but he enjoyed the discomfort.

He walked home at a more leisured pace than usual, stretching out the time, so that when he did get to the house, the food would be still more welcome. First he'd have a good long wash and rinse his mouth. Then a schnapps. Then a couple of olives and some herring, then a plate of steaming hot soup. Then he'd have a little rest, and after that the roast chicken, and the stewed fruit and finish up with a couple of glasses of lemon tea.

By the time he reached the door, he was famished. The wash and rinse could wait. Now, his tongue was hanging out for a schnapps. Just the tiniest drop of spirit and kummel to save his life, and maybe while he was about it, an olive and a piece of herring. Only he'd have to do it on the sly. His wife hated to see him picking from the plates. He rolled the saliva on his tongue, and swallowed it, moistening his throat. Smiling happily, he walked straight into the dining room.

It was empty. His face dropped. He looked round. No one in the room, nothing on the table. He couldn't understand it; had she gone off her head, the girl? Not a drop of kummel, no herring, no hot soup, nothing to eat at all, and here he was starving. Absolutely starving! It was his wife's fault. This was her lovely management; and for twenty-four hours he'd looked forward to this moment. It was an outrage! He had to slave to keep a family week after week, year after year, to be treated like this! It was enough to make a man burst! He turned to his wife for an explanation, his fat baby face swollen with anger, so vexed he could hardly speak, the tears starting out of his eyes.

Other works by Blumenfeld: *Phineas Kahn: Portrait of an Immigrant* (1937).

Celia Dropkin
1887–1956

The Yiddish poet Celia Dropkin was born Zipporah Levine in Bobruisk, Belorussia, where she received both a religious and secular education. While continuing her studies in Kiev, she met the Hebrew writer Uri Nissan Gnessin, who encouraged her literary ambition. In 1909, she married a Bund activist, who fled to the United States the following year to escape government prosecution. She joined him in New York, where she lived for the rest of her life, in 1912. In the 1920s and 1930s, her poems, whose explicit sexuality was shocking at the time, appeared in avant-garde Yiddish periodicals. By undermining conventions, her work expanded the range of themes that were thought appropriate for female writers.

A Dancer
1935

At home they called her "dummy" and other names like that because she was always so quiet and still, never stirring when she was called. When she was nine years old, she went to school and began calling herself Gysia. She remained silent, motionless and without expression during her first years at school. The school mistress, who suffered from migraines and couldn't stand classroom noise, praised Gysia to the skies for her ability to be still.

One May, when Gysia was twelve years old, her quiet demeanor snapped. She had been sitting at home at the big wooden table, studying for her examinations. The distant scent of lilac drifted through the open window when the dressmaker arrived to measure Gysia for a new brown school-dress.

When the dressmaker left, Gysia remained standing at the full-length mirror. She was in no hurry to get dressed. Gysia saw herself in the mirror in the white, ruffled slip, her thin, bare white arms and dainty feet, and suddenly she leaped into a wild gallop around the table. She looked like a colt one chases but can't catch. Sparks flew from her eyes which had been so dull and expressionless. With strange impetuosity, she spun and whirled round the table. The house virtually shook and the crystal drops of the chandelier tinkled melodiously. No-one was at home but the servant girl, who stood at the door open-mouthed, her eyes fearful. She had never seen Gysia like this.

Another year went by and two round little mounds appeared on Gysia's chest. The white petticoat with the embroidered camisole no longer fit and a new one which laced in the front had to be made. Gysia couldn't resist looking down to catch a glimpse at the beautiful, curving rise under her blouse. Changing blouses and watching how the fresh folds of cloth laid themselves over her shapely length was a special joy to Gysia, a joy that made her move as if to a musical beat. At the same time, she would admire her dainty feet.

At school, during recess, Gysia would often burst into peals of laughter. Once the schoolmistress reproached her angrily, saying, "I didn't expect this from you!"

When Gysia turned sixteen she was taken to Warsaw. There, for the first time, she bought the kind of shoes she really wanted, not like the ones her mother usually bought. These were dainty shoes, red in colour. The salesman told her that an actress, a dancer, had left them behind and he was selling them now at half price. They were perfect for Gysia and suited her highly arched, well-turned feet (although she did get a corn on the small toe of her left foot). In Warsaw, Gysia saw an opera, "Carmen," for the first time. From that time on and for many years thereafter, in moments of joy and blood-tingling excitement, she would raise her hands and feet, just as Carmen had done. The Carmen who appeared on stage was a stout prima donna. Gysia felt she could dance the role of Carmen better.

At eighteen, Gysia married the tall and handsome young man who had fallen in love with her when she danced in the red shoes at her sister's wedding. Gysia wanted to have a child just like her sister, who had come home to her parents to give birth. Soon afterwards, Gysia's husband left for America. When she was left behind in that Polish *shtetl*, alone with a baby at her breast, she suddenly sensed that she had neglected something unique about which neither her husband nor anyone else would want to know. She felt this even more strongly after she weaned the child.

Gysia's body was agile, young and slender, her legs slim and lively. It was not of her body she was now thinking but of a melody within herself singing to the rhythm of her body and to the summer life around her; summer in that small Polish *shtetl* where woods and fields were only a few steps from her street. Clouds danced in circles overhead, trees bent their green shoots over her and grasses curled at her feet.

Gysia felt the dance of nature all around her, felt the dancer within her awaken. More than once she tried to express her longings to the rhythm of dance. When no-one was around she was rhythmic and expressive. However, she knew that to become a dancer you had to study. So Gysia began to dream that instead of travelling to her husband in America, she'd leave the child with her parents and run off to Warsaw and enroll in dance school. She would pay for these lessons with the money her husband sent her for the fare to America. . . . But Gysia did not do this. The child's father was waiting for them in America. So there she went.

All, all was over the moment Gysia's feet touched the ground in New York! Her husband worked hard to earn a living for her and their child while she toiled to raise, nourish and build a home for the family. But that struggle, together with the alien bit of sky between the tall buildings, clipped Gysia's wings. She became pregnant with a second child, then a third. With every pregnancy she became rounder at the hips and shoulders. A pair of thick blue veins bulged here and there through the white skin of her legs. She stopped admiring her body, didn't even want to look at it any more, not even through the transparent crystal green of the water in which she bathed.

Gysia's years dragged on, sometimes better, sometimes worse, with growing children, four in all. At thirty-nine, Gysia's body was already quite heavy; the skin on her face beginning to sag. Only the eyes retained the same opaque sheen. At celebrations Gysia rarely danced, but she didn't take her eyes off the young feet gliding by on the floor. Several times in her life, Gysia had attended recitals by famous dancers. Her pleasure at seeing these dancers bordered on ecstasy, yet she didn't envy them. It never occurred to her to imagine how she'd feel if she were to lift herself up ever so lightly off the ground and spin like a top. Though she lived in a world of house, husband and children, her heart would sometimes beat strangely when she saw people dancing; would beat as if in premonition, as if trying to recall something . . . something dear to her.

The momentary pleasure of watching dancers and couples gliding by did not raise for a moment the curtain on that strange magic that sleep brought her. Whenever she saw dancers and dancing couples, she tried to recall this magic, but without success. She wouldn't have called it a dream because it was repeated time and again so naturally, as though she had come to a familiar house and discovered a well-remembered object there. This magic was a world unto itself and didn't want to reveal itself to drab reality.

Gysia was never able to remember this strange dream, which she kept dreaming again and again. She used to wake up feeling she had not dreamt at all. It was magic but this magic was so natural to her, so easy, so pleasant. It was a very simple matter. Gysia would lightly, oh so lightly, like a feather, lift one foot after the other. Faster than a gliding bird, she would soar and hold a position, a dancer frozen in a pose. It was no trick. She did it so simply, so easily, just like a bird. Sometimes she saw herself surrounded by her women friends who were also trying to do the same thing but, unfortunately, they didn't know how. She, Gysia, did it almost without being aware; felt a strange spirituality,

a sweet serenity pervade her. No effort, no ecstasy, no superfluous joy—she felt like a bird lifting herself over a field of corn or over a tall forest.

In her magic, Gysia was nevertheless human. She understood with human intelligence that she was accomplishing something with this ability to lift herself at will ever higher than an ordinary person, even though it was so easy. Soaring into the air for several moments was no more to Gysia than smoking a cigarette was to her neighbour. A lot easier. Gysia didn't even have to spread her arms like a bird with outstretched wings when it takes off, or like a dancer before a leap. She simply took off again and again and yet again. So easily, so gracefully, so effortlessly. Her entire body felt beautiful, in harmony; the movements of her legs like Anna Pavlova's, her entire being swaying in rhythm like Isadora Duncan.

She was dressed as always when she finished her housework. A simple black or blue silk dress. Gysia remembered that the last time, she had worn the blue crêpe with the white ruffles. She had been with her friends and wanted to demonstrate her artistry, had wondered why no-one present could do the same. She was filled with quiet, good-natured pride.

It was a magical world that had separated itself from the real world and kept itself hidden and secret, the proof being that Gysia could never recall the dream when she awoke. Other dreams she did manage to remember, but nothing about that magical lifting off from the earth could she consider merely a dream. It was so real to her, so strangely real, that when her magic world suddenly revealed itself to the cold light of day, Gysia did not turn a hair in wonder. She simply could not think of it as a dream.

Gysia was now alert. It was just past the evening meal and she was clearing away the dishes, when she stopped to glance at the newspaper lying on the table. Her eye was caught by a headline about a famous dancer who had just died. She immediately began to read it. It said that he simply floated in the air whenever he danced. Gysia was wearing the blue crêpe dress with white ruffles. For the first time when awake, she was suddenly able to remember that it was in this very dress that she had lifted herself several feet off the ground. For the very first time, she was able to recall that she could float through the air.

Gysia wondered why the newspaper was making such a fuss about this dancer. Was dancing in the air such an art? How many times had she herself done the very same thing? She simply lifted herself upward! The newspaper was silent about this; no tickets were sold to see her perform. With a mocking smile she tossed the newspaper aside, quietly rose from her chair and slowly went into the kitchen to be alone. She stretched, stretched again, tried to lift both feet. Why couldn't she do it? What had happened to her? She became frightened. Her heart beat strangely. Her feet spun in the air, begging her heavy body for help. She wouldn't believe that she was incapable of doing it.

She went into the living-room. Her husband was reading the newspaper. "Have you read it yet?" Gysia asked him, making an effort to remain calm.

"What?" he asked, not raising his eyes from the newspaper.

"Such a trifle they consider art," she added scornfully, "see for yourself. . . ."

She lifted herself up and lunged forward. Her husband's face was hidden by the newspaper but he heard the dull thud and threw down the paper. He saw Gysia, strange, lost, her pale face covered in beads of sweat; she looked so drawn, so different.

"What happened?" he asked anxiously.

"I can't understand it," she replied disconsolately. "I can't do it any more."

"What do you want to do? Who asks you to work so hard?" her husband asked angrily.

"You don't understand. I used to be able to do it."

"What's the matter with you? Should I call the doctor?"

Gysia sensed terrible danger. She began to understand with shuddering clarity that she was confusing reality with dream, but this awareness lasted but a moment. Just as earlier she had been unable to remember her dream, now she could not remember reality. With her husband again asked anxiously, "What's the matter with you?" she answered with a conspiratorial expression, "Probably something I dreamt" but she knew it was far from a dream. She really was a great dancer, but tragedy had overtaken her. She was cursed, she could no longer do it. Her husband wouldn't possibly understand; she would tell him nothing. Even if she had dreamt it, he didn't want to understand and he said, "How can a person dream such things working around the house? You were talking to me just now. You just asked me something." He noticed that she became terribly upset by his words.

"Go on, go to sleep, maybe you'll sleep off all these dreams after all," he said in a worried voice. He heaved a deep sigh as she went off to her room. "All we need is more troubles!"

Gysia took it into her head that she had to regain the art of soaring into the air. "I'm too heavy," she thought to herself, "that's why I can't dance through the air any more." She virtually stopped eating and went about in a gloomy state. When no-one else was around she would try to glide off a bench. Each time she fell forward clumsily, bruising herself. Once, she was even laid up for an entire week with a sprained ankle. She had seen a stranger whom her husband called "doctor" near her several times already. This person tried to engage her in conversation but she stubbornly remained silent. She dared not talk about her great artistry which was now cursed. Once her daughter saw her standing on the window-ledge facing into the room. She stood there like some mournful bird wanting to warm itself and fly into the room. Although the window was closed, her daughter screamed in terror. From that time on, Gysia was carefully watched.

Many months have now passed since Gysia entered the sanatorium. The curse of being unable to dance, to soar, has been lifted from her. Quietly she floats with a benign smile on her parched lips. Her body, unnaturally thin, seems to float in the air. Impetuously, she tears herself from the spot and barely lifts her feet. She raises her head in ecstasy as a smile plays on her withered lips.

Translated by Shirley Kumove.

Other works by Dropkin: *In hesyn vint* (1935).

Vladimir Jabotinsky
1880–1940

While Vladimir (Zev) Jabotinsky is best known as the founding father of the right-wing Revisionist movement in Zionism, he was also a prolific novelist, journalist, poet, and essayist in several languages. Born into a middle-class, russified family in Odessa, the young Jabotinsky attended Russian schools and studied law in Rome and Berne. He worked as a journalist for Russian newspapers. He became a Zionist activist in 1903 and during World War I was instrumental in the formation of a Jewish fighting unit in the British army. His antisocialist, maximalist Zionism brought him into conflict with the Labor Zionist movement.

The Five
1935

Along Deribasov Street

This episode occurred on Deribasov Street, about two years after the beginning of our story.

At that time our editorial office was located at the upper end of the street, in the passageway next to Cathedral Square. Every day on my way to work I would walk the entire length of the street, the queen of streets in the whole world. It's impossible to prove by argument why it was the queen of streets: almost all the houses along both sides, as I recall, had two stories; the architecture was, for the most part, unexceptional, without any important monuments. But such things are not proven by argument; every honorific is a mirage—once it's attached and holds without coming unstuck, the bearer is considered worthy of it, and that's that. At least in those years, I, for one, could never simply pass along Deribasov Street as if it were the most natural thing in the world, without failing to realize where I was: as soon as my foot touched that sacred ground, I was immediately overcome with an awareness, as if some special event had transpired or some privilege had been bestowed on me. I straightened up involuntarily and checked to see if my necktie had come loose; I'm sure I wasn't the only one who did so.

The queen's maids of honor, the intersecting streets along the path of my pilgrimage, each had their own faces. I usually began my walk from the lower end, the corner of Pushkin Street, an important street, majestically sleepy, with no shops on that block; for some reason even the large hotel on the corner didn't stick out, didn't create a commotion; once, having lied and told others that I was going out of town, I spent a whole month in that hotel, dining on the terrace, and not one acquaintance ever walked by. I don't know who inhabited the splendid houses nearby, but it seemed that grand, classical antiquity was living out its last days on this section of Pushkin Street, where grain traders were still called merchants and mixed both Greek and Italian phrases into their conversations.

The next corner was Richelieu Street; the first thing that announced its special face were the tables of the moneychangers, right there on the sidewalks under the acacias. One could marvel at all the gold under glass on these tables and at the banknotes from all planets in the solar system; the street-side banker with his black mustache, sitting on a wicker chair, wearing a bowler hat or a felt hat perched on the back of his head, would tear himself away from his foreign newspaper and serve you or cheat you swiftly, speaking any language imaginable. Thus have you made the acquaintance of the upper thoroughfare of Black Sea trade. As I crossed it, I'd always cast an envious glance to the left, where from both sides glittered gilded signs of banking officers, unattainable stores, and Olympian barbershops where they could shave a man's face to an azure tint.

It was here, one wintry day at about four o'clock in the afternoon, that I witnessed a strange scene: the policeman on duty, directing carriage traffic at this crucial intersection, had gone off somewhere for a minute or so; his place was suddenly taken by two young men, one wearing a student's overcoat, the other, a skillfully sewn sheepskin jacket and a tall Caucasian fur cap. Staggering and clumsily leaning against each other, before the eyes of the astonished population, they headed for the middle of the intersection; conscientiously and thoughtfully, with keen eyes, they determined the exact midpoint, moved a little to the right, then a little back, until they wound up in the geometrical center; they bowed to each other, leaned their backs up against each other for support, and each, placing two fingers in his mouth, filled the surroundings with a whistle of indescribable purity and power. Hearing the familiar signal, all carriages and cabs from the north, south, east, and west automatically slowed their pace, cursing audibly, and searching for the policeman who'd issued such a peremptory sound. Seeing in his place this inexplicable dyad, they were all taken aback and stopped completely. The young man in the fur cap, although somewhat unsteady in his articulation, roared in an awesome bass voice with a great range, "Come on, you bums, why'd you stop?" And, in fact, they began moving again according to his command; both friends, gesticulating with their white gloves, started directing traffic any which way they liked. The bass voice coming from under the fur cap seemed somewhat familiar; but by now the policeman came rushing toward them from wherever he'd been, his fierce eyes bulging, obviously prepared to drag them both away and punish them—when suddenly, some five paces away from these usurpers, the expression on his face became benevolent, even sympathetic: he realized they were soused, and, obviously, it touched a fraternal string in his Russian heart. It was impossible to make out what he said to them, but undoubtedly it was something tender like: "Don't worry, my dear sirs, I'll take over from here." And the two of them, bowing imposingly to him, staggered away arm in arm in my direction. When they drew near, the one in the fur cap—now I definitely recognized Serezha—leaned up against my shoulder and, in the same voice, murmured to me confidentially:

"Take us somewhere outside the gates: the second bell's just rung and I have to heave . . ."

Then came Catherine Street: a mishmash, neither one thing nor the other; it had pretensions of wealth, flaunted tall, dandified houses in yesterday's styles, and for some reason "hereabouts" in the evening the main flow of pedestrians would pour into Deribasov Street and a boulevard nearby. A little farther along on the right, noisy as the sea at a massif, filled to overflowing with seated customers, surrounded by those waiting to get in, one could see the trading terraces of the cafés Robin and Fankoni. But at the same time "hereabouts" nannies also brought their charges to the nursery tucked away under the precipice of the boulevard itself; shop assistants and messengers, both with packages and without, scurried between the town and the port; and port folk themselves, wearing peaked caps pushed to one side, ladies in white kerchiefs who often, rather than dragging themselves through the plebian "gullies" and "slopes" assigned to this social class, preferred to ascend the heights proudly right from the harbor, climbing all one hundred and ninety-eight granite steps of the famous flight of stairs (one of the eight wonders of the world)—and from above, past the statue of the duke in a Roman toga, to encroach immediately on civilization and to scatter the sidewalks of Catherine Street with a stream of sunflower seed husks. This wasn't merely the intersection of two streets but a microcosm and symbol of democracy—of bourgeois efficiency and aimless loitering, of rags and high fashion, of the staid middle class and the down-and-outs. . . . There was only one person I never expected to meet on this corner—but did: my porter Khoma.

For the past several weeks, every Sunday, I encountered Khoma on Deribasov Street: very prim and proper, wearing a dark blue shirt and white apron just laundered and pressed, his beard neatly groomed. The first time our eyes met there, I was surprised: what was he doing here, at the other end of the world, far from his own courtyard? He wasn't carrying a folder—that means, he wasn't heading to the police station to register new residents, and he wasn't returning from there; besides, this corner wasn't even on the way to or from

the station. Was he out for a stroll, like everyone else? That couldn't possibly be, according to the very nature of things; besides, he wasn't moving at all, just standing in the entryway of a house with the look of a citizen who knew his place, and it was precisely there, where he stood. It was only the following Sunday that I noticed he wasn't alone: behind him, in the shadow of the entryway, I caught sight of a few more white aprons. This time, as it happens, Shtrok, our police reporter, was with me, a man who knew everything: he explained it all.

"You really don't know? It's all because of the expected demonstration; they've summoned brawny porters from all over town to lend the police a hand."

I would travel the block between Catherine Street and Harbor Street with a sense of gastronomic enthusiasm (even though I'd just had dinner), most often crossing over to the sidewalk on the right side of the street. There in the huge and squat Wagner house, in the depths of its deserted courtyard, sat the old Bruns Tavern, where at midnight, after the theater, heavenly angels using a magical recipe from paradise, created in the kitchen ambrosia in the form of sausages and potato salad, while Ganymede and Hebe themselves (I confuse demonological cycles, but such appreciative enthusiasm doesn't follow any rules), drew some March beer from the keg behind the partition. Here, at Bruns Tavern, on one such night, for a reason that will be explained at another time, Marko suddenly pushed away a plate of sausages he'd been served, and announced to me that from then on he would adopt a strictly kosher diet.

. . . The hand itches to render similar praise to remaining corners: Krasnyi Lane, with its tiny houses only ten feet wide, the last bastion of semi-Turkish Aegean Hellenism in the city which at one time was called Khadzhi-bei; quiet Harbor Street, where it was quite useless for cabbies to turn in; Cathedral Square, where Deribasov Street ended and the indistinct flavour of the poorer districts nearby—Moldavanka, Slobodka-Romanovka, Peresyp—just as if two different cities met here and, without merging, merely abutted each other outwardly. But it's impossible to yield to these temptations endlessly: the main thing's been achieved—we've arrived at the corner of Deribasov Street and Cathedral Square, where it all began and where, a minute later, it all ended.

I didn't even see it, but suddenly my colleague Shtrok ran into the editorial office, called everyone over, and communicated the news in a half-whisper: a "demon-stration" had just taken place. There were almost a hundred of them, all young people, mostly Jews, about a third, young women; one red banner, and a police officer we knew swore that it had the slogan "Down with Autocracy" (in the genitive case) embroidered on it. They'd proceeded only some twenty paces when from all sides a horde of policemen and porters fell upon them; women's cries could be heard; there was a scuffle and some panic; Cossacks appeared and began to disperse the crowd, clearing the sidewalks with their horses' hoofs and whips. Then they chased the demonstrators to the neighboring police station; the gates were closed and soldiers stood guard so no one could even pass by; people throughout the city were frightened, their faces downcast, and everyone whispered: "They're beating them to death, one after another . . ."

At about three o'clock the editorial assistant called me into his office; he was the single Russian Orthodox in the entire establishment, except for the typesetters, but his name was Abram:

"A lady's come to see you."

This lady turned out to be Anna Mikhailovna Milgrom. It was the first time I ever witnessed genuine human grief up close; it was worse than grief—you grieve about something that's already happened and has passed. But she looked as if a rusty nail had been driven into her head; it was still embedded and there was nothing she could do about it. It hadn't "passed," but was occurring then, taking place at that very moment, just around the corner, almost before her very eyes; she was sitting there on a leather armchair, and although it wouldn't help, it would've been embarrassing for her to scream.

"Lika was there!"

I said nothing. I asked Abram not to admit anyone; I closed the door, and stood next to her. She sat there, both of us silent and thinking; all of a sudden I, too, felt the same rusty nail being driven into my head. Whatever I tried to think, every half minute I kept coming back to that rusty nail. That must be why they say, "to pound a nail in." One thought kept hammering away: how that summer at the dacha I'd held Lika by the arm, merely to help her climb back onto the steep path up the cliff, and how she pulled away; and how, passing someone in the hallway, she always kept to one side, so that, God forbid, her puff sleeve might not touch someone. She was a sensitive person in all the nerves of her skin, down to the threads of her clothes. And now, these de-

scendants of our gorilla forebears were beating her with their hairy paws. Anna Mikhailovna sat there in that office for about an hour without saying anything at all and then she got up and left.

I heard a few details at home later that evening from our maid Motrya; she'd been told by Khoma, an eyewitness and participant. When the gates were closed, he'd done some work on the contingent of male demonstrators; the bones of both his fists were still aching as a result; they chased them into the fire brigade stable, brought them out one at a time, and then carried them away. It was different with the young women: you couldn't treat them the same way; the police station's not a tavern. They dealt with the young women delicately, said Khoma, paternally, without offending their modesty—in the sense that no one else was present at the time, except for the officials. He, that is, Khoma, offered his services, but the superintendent wouldn't allow it; the door to that room was closed tight, and only city police were allowed inside to do that work. [. . .]

Broad Jewish Natures

It had become dark and uncomfortable in Anna Mikhailovna's house. Ignats Albertovich had begun to stoop noticeably; he said that it was written somewhere in the Midrash—or, perhaps it was in the sayings of the old Volynian sages: man has two mothers. The first is his birth mother and the second, mother earth. When he's little, he listens to his first mother's voice, but she's taller than he is, so he has to lift his head up; at the approach of old age, his second mother begins talking to him, and the man has to lean over to hear her whisper. Anna Mikhailovna, on the other hand, didn't attempt to explain away the increase in her gray hair. It was gloomy in the house and they entertained only older guests; even Nyura and Nyuta appeared infrequently—Serezha, now without Marusya, stopped gathering his friends; after supper, around ten o'clock, he'd set off alone, while the staid Torik sat in his own room poring over his books.

Ignats Albertovich's business affairs also began to deteriorate. Whether it was because the padishah closed the Dardenelles too frequently, or because the towns of Kherson, after dredging the Dnepr "inlets," and Nikolaev, at the wide estuary, had begun to overtake the arid Odessa, or because of some other reason—Quarantine harbor began to be noticeably deserted, the boats on the Platonov and Androsov piers were fewer, and the prosperous hubbub of brokers at the stock exchange and on the sidewalk in front of the cafés Robin and Fankoni (the illegal but genuine stock exchange that everyone referred to as "Greek"), if it hadn't actually fallen silent, it had begun to sound anxious. At Ignats Albertovich's table in the evening Abram Moiseevich and Boris Mavrikievich would argue even more fractiously; the older brother was especially irritated by the new phrase "state of the market" which "Beiresh" would find in the lead article of my newspaper and pronounce in his own way, something like "stamark"; while he himself, the older brother, blamed the "banks" for all their misfortune.

"Hey, young man!" he'd say to me. "You should've seen what was happening on the Dnepr some thirty years ago, when there were only two rulers all the way from the rapids to our grain elevator: one was Webster-Kovalenko, and the other, even more important, was the "Russian Company." The Jew Ionya, the main buyer for "Ropit," would travel up from Kherson on a paddle-wheel steamboat; black beard, gold-frame eyeglasses, and a belly to match. He makes his way, like a tzaddik among Hassidim, with a retinue of some fifty people—bookkeepers, brokers, assayers, and miscellaneous scroungers. They serve tea all along the way, and sometimes even a glass of vodka with a spice cake; they play cards until three in the morning—and do you know, they would lose up to five hundred rubles; I myself have known some idiots who even paid to enter the game! The landings go by—Bolshaya Lepetikha, Malaya, Berislav, Kakhovka, Nikopol, up to Aleksandovsk. Three hours before Ionya arrives at each pier, even the governor himself couldn't push his way through the crowd: agents, brokers, secondhand dealers, horses pulling carts, ox-cart drivers, the whole square is piled with sacks, wagons, and oxen in the back. What do you think—Ionya didn't sleep all night, so he's tired? As soon as he sees the pier, he shouts to the sailor: "Yurka, over here—swing it! He shoves his own head under the spout, Yurka starts to pump water, and splashes half the Dnepr onto his bald pate, and once again Ionya's ready, even for a wedding. He stands on deck and shouts from afar: "How goes it, Stavro Lefterevich, how're you? I see you've put on some weight; this summer let's go to Marienbad together." "Hey, Kurolapchenko, what did I hear in Kakhovka, you've given birth to another daughter? Your seventh? Christen her Sofiya—it's time to make 'sofas!'" "Shalom aleichem, Monsieur Grobokopatel; hurry up, you numskull, you! Open up that shop!" He had a kind word for each person; they stood there and laughed, ready to kiss his hand. . . . That was the Dnepr then, but now, excuse me. And it's all because of the banks."

"But what do the banks have to do with it?"

"They began loaning money to every Tom, Dick, and Harry instead of 'Ropit' and Webster-Kovalenko, a bunch of small fry—'Mr. Exporter,' but he wears pants with a fringe, his uncle's pants at that. They themselves have nothing to eat, and the larger companies are also left with neither water nor air. It's time to die, Ignats Albertovich; but, you, Beiresh, should please die first."

In general, it became uncomfortable in Odessa. I had trouble recognizing our city, which only a short while ago had been so free and easy and good-natured. Now it was swept by malice that, they say, had previously never affected our mild southern metropolis, created over the course of centuries through the harmonious and loving efforts of four peaceful races. They'd always quarreled and cursed each other as rogues or idiots, and had sometimes even fought; but in all my memory there'd never been any authentic, ferocious hostility. Now all this had changed. The first sign of benevolence among men had disappeared—that is, the southern custom of considering the street as your home. Nowadays we walked the streets with caution, hurried along at night, and drew closer to the shadows . . .

The issue, however, was no longer limited to a mere tribal feud. Two years ago, when we all read about the first heroic raids from the underground on convoys of government gold, no one suspected to what extent the system of financial, nonmonetary transactions was gradually being democratized. Now it was referred to in Odessa by the shorthand of "ex" and had been adapted simply and openly for the replenishment of the raiders' personal benefit. At first, they would send a threatening letter or flash a revolver and mention some unnamed "party"; but soon they ceased doing that and merely began plundering openly. As for the breadth of their appetite, they were distinguished by their Spartan modesty: although there were a few attempts to extort large sums of money from a particular frightened wealthy individual, the usual type of "ex" took the form of a visit by two men to a grocery store and the confiscation of the morning's proceeds to the tune of two rubles plus change. The most curious thing of all was that this "ex" raged in our city only among Jews: Jews were its objects, rich and poor, and, as the victims swore, all of the them, without exception, were also its subjects. "They thrash the Jewish population with two whips," recorded my colleague at the newspaper with melancholy, the feuilletonist who wrote about serious themes: at night, with foreign swine, truncheons, and during the day, our own swine.

Our Abram, a worker at the newspaper, reported that a student by the name of Viktor Ignatievich, was asking to see me.

In general, Torik rarely visited anyone, and that was the very first time he'd come to see me. I realized that it must be important and told Abram not to let anyone else into the reception room. As it turned out, it was no laughing matter, though at first it was a bit amusing. Torik related it systematically, all the events and discoveries in chronological order, one after another, without jumping ahead; nor did I have to urge him on: he was a very sound, well-organized young man.

An "ex" had taken place yesterday at Abram Moiseevich's. Two young men showed up, one belonging to the common people, the other, better "educated"; they brandished a document with a stamp as well as two "pistols with large cylinders," and demanded five thousand rubles—if not, Abram Moiseevich would die. He looked at them, thought for a moment, and asked:

"How did you know I was back in town? I just returned from Marienbad yesterday."

The youths proudly explained that the committee knows everything: that was the system of shadowing now in place.

He thought for a bit, suddenly burst out laughing, and then said to them:

"Listen, you young men: how'd you like to get fifteen thousand rubles instead of five? Go to my brother Beiresh, show him your guns, and get ten from him. Then come back to me: if you show me his ten, I'll turn over my five to you then."

Their eyes bulged; of course they suspected he'd send for the police. They thanked him for his advice and agreed to go to "Beiresh," but he still had to pay up on the spot, now.

"Hey," he replied, "when people treat you with respect, don't behave like kikes. My word is good. Every banker in Odessa would hand over fifty thousand rubles on my say-so without a receipt, and here are two snivelers. Get out of here or else, do as I say! Your pistols? I don't give a damn about 'em. I'm not afraid of no bombs (Torik related the most characteristic parts of the story with grammatical fidelity to the original). And

if you do me this favor with regard to Beiresh, then your 'yes' is worth five thousand rubles: please go."

They conferred in a whisper in the corner and decided that they needed to confer with members of their "committee" by telephone. The one who belonged to the common people led Abram away to another room and locked the heavy door behind them, while the more educated one stayed behind to use the telephone. Ten minutes later he called them back and told them the committee's decision: they'd agreed, but while he went to see Beiresh, the other one would have to stay here in the room with Abram.

"Fine," said Abram Moiseevich. "Does he smoke cigars? I brought back some excellent ones."

So the member of the common people remained behind with Abram Moiseevich for two hours, they smoked cigars, and gradually got to chatting amicably. He said that he wasn't really a swindler but a decent fellow and a good Jew; he'd participated in the self-defense of 1905, had even contributed an entire militia unit, and then, after the manifesto, had worked diligently during the month of October. (I stopped smiling as he told this part of the story: something foul had begun to emerge as I listened.) In a word, the more educated one returned after two hours and displayed the ten thousand rubles; Abram Moiseevich opened his safe immediately and calmly extracted a packet of bills, counted out five thousand right in front of them, thought a bit, and added another thousand; then he put the rest of his money away—it never occurred to them to interfere—and he locked his safe.

"Good-bye and good luck," he said to them. "You'll end up in Siberia, but you've made me happy."

Right after this Abram Moiseevich summoned Torik and shared the following reflections with him. In the first place, it was very odd that they'd come to see him only one day after his arrival from Marienbad: who could've informed them? In the second place, they hadn't even asked for "Beiresh's" address: and he, too, had moved into a new apartment only a week ago. In the third place, his conversation partner, the member of the common people, bragging about his own exploits and relaying how he'd been praised by the organizers of the self-defense leagues, happened to say that his name was Motya—and Abram Moiseevich had heard that name somewhere before. Finally, when they were whispering in the corner, it seemed to him that he'd heard one more name.

"Serezha?!"

"Not exactly, even worse: 'Sirozhka.' The clues were flimsy, as you can see; but Abram Moiseevich believed in his own intuition. 'I'm an old horse thief,' he said, 'and for that reason alone, when a mare's taken away, I can sniff out who's taken it.' He'd stake his own life that the educated fellow hadn't called the committee at all but had called the number 9-62."

Torik himself had conducted a small inquiry at home. He didn't find Serezha there but carefully interrogated the maid. She said that around eleven in the morning Sergei Ignatievich had been called to the telephone, that he'd sent her out of his father's study where she'd been dusting, and he'd locked the door.

Torik related this story to me in such a way that I became interested unwittingly, even though I had better things to think about. He told it with just the right amount of anguish needed and the right amount of humor possible, given the level of anguish. He said not one accusatory word against his own brother: it was as if he were talking about a person who was ill, who had to be treated but not judged. And he'd come to see me because, in Marusya's absence, for Serezha I was the only one who could . . .

Translated by Michael R. Katz.

Other works by Jabotinsky: *A Pocket Edition of Several Stories, Mostly Reactionary* (1925); *Samson the Nazirite* (1930); *The War and the Jew* (1942).

Betty Miller

1910-1965

The English novelist Betty Miller was born in Cork but moved to London in 1922, after spending two years with her mother's family in Sweden. *Farewell Leicester Square* was her only work to focus on Jewish life in England. Completed in 1935, it was rejected by Victor Gollancz, a radical assimilationist, who had already published two of her novels, largely, it seems, because the novel was "too Jewish" for him. It was not published until 1941. She was married to Emanuel Miller, a distinguished psychiatrist.

Farewell Leicester Square

1935

"Alec," she said meekly, "you're wearing out my carpet."

He stopped. "Pardon?"

"Why the Man of Destiny act?" she asked.

He stared at her uncomprehending.

She put her hand on his arm and shook him. "Oh, come, wake up, lad. . . ." She smiled at him: her hand still on his arm. "The question is, what are you going to have to drink? If it's alcohol, you'll find the all and sundry in that cabinet over there." She released him. "Alternatively," she said, "I could boil up a kettle and produce a nice strong brew of tea. Does that say anything to you?"

The mood vanished. He was himself again. He smiled: his dark live eyes upon her face. "Now you're talking," he said. "Tea—of course!"

"And biscuits?" she said.

"And biscuits."

"What about a savoury sandwich?"

"A savoury sandwich—certainly."

"Anything else?" She smiled back, provocatively.

"Anything else," he said, "that you like to offer me. . . ."

While she was busy in what was, apparently, a small kitchenette off the main room, he permitted himself, for the first time, to examine the canvases piled up against the walls. He always avoided, if he could, considering a work in the presence of the artist, for, although all artists beg for candour, it is, in actual fact, the last thing that they can tolerate: and he knew too well what really lay beneath the casual-seeming exterior: the painful craving for praise: hunger of the exhibitionist child. . . . Moreover, the administration of this praise, in the guise of considered criticism, was an exhausting and often a thankless job. It was not enough to praise: one had to praise the right thing: disfavour fell at once if one admired that which the artist had decided to discard: or a work done a few years ago and already established, instead of the newly executed one. Since the latter, in turn, was liable to fall into disfavour once the heat of creation had cooled, it was important, even then, not to commit oneself too finally, for it would, under the new order of things, be a ticklish task to erase, diplomatically reverse, the old judgment: it being a recognized fact that an artist, however mild in everyday life, becomes a terrifying Nero when holding court with his own Art.

He picked up one or two canvases and examined them closely. They were of that type of modern work which makes little demand on technical ability; and has become, therefore, a happy hunting ground for those who can conceal in it both lack of originality and uncertainty of draughtsmanship. The effect aimed at, he realized, was a child-like simplicity of perception. He distrusted both the intention and the effect. The cult of infantilism had no appeal for him. He looked at the canvas he had in his hand: the distorted outlines, the deliberately naïve perspective, the bulbous legs, over-simplified face. "School of Truby King," he thought. He put it away gently, its face to the wall. He was both disappointed and relieved to discover that the artistic impulse in Catherine Nicolls was merely a derived one. Without roots, it might, in time, even, be gently extracted from her system. . . .

In the darkness, nested in some invisible steeple, a church clock gave forth its sudden ringing wail—emphasizing their solitude: the smallness of the hour. They each listened to it: to this tongue speaking impersonally out of the night: but neither of them stirred. The sound died away and left their intimacy undisturbed. Behind the bars of the stove, the coals glowed brazen; transparent with heat. Their faces, as they lounged on the cushions Catherine had spread for them on the floor, were illumined: a deep steady radiance enclosed them both.

Catherine stirred. She bent over the tray that lay between them, a dumpy brown tea-pot presiding over the cups. "I should think this must have brewed by now," she said. She put her hand on the sleek flank of the pot. "How do you take yours?" she asked.

He smiled. Abstractedly he gazed up at the ceiling. Without moving he remarked. "It always strikes me as a portentous moment when a woman asks a man for the first time how he takes his tea. . . ."

"Tut, tut," she said deprecatingly. "What a very romantic disposition you have."

Her manner was a little too easy: he was not deceived. Propped up on one elbow, he turned to look across at her. She diverted his attention to the tea-pot. "Medium," he said in response to her gesture. "And two sugars: that's perfect." He accepted the cup from her and set it down on the floor by him. She poured another for herself; sitting upright to do so, her legs curved under her. Lit by the fire, hair made a startling aura about her sharp pallid face. He thought: she looks like some old painting: a martyr saint. But it was only the hair, the pallor, that gave that effect: for the expression was wrong. Neither exaltation nor serenity informed that face. Here and there it was, already, faintly lined: the insidious, frittering effect of time, or dissatisfaction. . . .

He said, his eyes still upon her, speaking softly, "I wonder what you're really doing in this place."

"What do you mean? I live here."

"No," he said. "Not the real you." He explained: "I see you otherwise."

"How mysterious. How do you see me? A Rossetti model, living in a sort of junk-shop, surrounded with peacocks and pearls and corals?"

"By no means," he said, stirring his tea. "I see you in a spacious respectable house. Preferably double-fronted. With a large garden and a greenhouse. . . . Two maids, probably very neat in their uniform. A nursery at the top of the house. And a desk in the corner of a room somewhere, where you do all your house-keeping accounts and make out the menus for the week."

She raised her eyebrows. "How too, too suburb!"

He put away his cup. "Catherine," he said soberly, "don't be Noel Coward. It doesn't suit you."

She flushed at that. The rare colour transformed her face momentarily: she looked young and angry. He understood what he had done. He had shown her that he realized exactly to what extent she was posing: to a woman, whose emotions, pretensions, are intimately bound up in her pose, this is always the unpardonable brutality. . . . He got up suddenly; on the pretext of fetching a cigarette from his coat. Opening his case, he slipped one between his lips. There was a momentary silence as he scraped a match. She did not look round. He came back towards her: and stood prodding the mantelpiece with the charred end of the match. "I'm sorry," he said. "But I want to talk to you about real things."

"Oh, no, Alec." She was, now, formidably composed. "Not at this hour of the night. Not after all that tea." She looked at him maliciously. "Too, too Chekhov!"

Abruptly (but not entirely without memory of the countless actors who had performed this gesture under his direction), he ground out the unused cigarette. Left it splayed in the ashtray. . . . In a movement, he was beside her. She turned startled: but all he did was to take her hand with extreme gentleness. "No Catherine; please don't" he said. "You and I don't have to talk to each other like people in a third-rate modern comedy."

She did not relent. "Film Director Slates Snappy Dialogue," she said.

"Catherine." He spoke pleadingly.

"Alec?" She looked innocent.

"You know I—that I. . . ."

"Yes, Alec?"

He was silent, looking down at her hand imprisoned between his fingers. "Catherine," he said at last. Be a nice girl. . . . I know it's your feminine due, but don't force me into the ridiculous position of having to declare myself in words."

"Declare what?" she asked. "You speak as if I were a Customs official."

"That's not funny," he said. "It's merely tiresome."

"Oh, well, if we're going to quarrel, I'd like to have my hand back." She tried to withdraw it. His grasp tightened with violence. She was unable to disengage herself. She gave up the attempt and looked at him evenly. "So what?" she said.

She expected what came next. She was pulled roughly against him: held relentlessly at an angle that produced excruciating discomfort. She experienced the brusque infliction of his mouth, quick, seeking tongue: her cheek burned against the hard bristles of his face. In the midst of this, she had time to register once again the disheartening fact that all kisses taste alike. Her sense of his personality, far from being intensified, was diminished by proximity: blurred, put out of focus; in the blind anonymity of a kiss he was momentarily lost to her. . . .

He released her. His hair was disordered: he tried to smooth it back: his hand was shaking. She looked at him curiously: seeing him, for the first time, altered, as others had been altered, at such moment; the calm, superficial personality of social occasions surprisingly belied. . . . As always, she experienced two things: that smug feminine satisfaction which takes pride in being able to effect this: and a childish fear of the resulting consequences. . . . A certain regret, too. Something had gone. Something which hitherto had been intact between them, and, as such, of unique, of incalculable value, had lost its quality.

"Catherine," he murmured at last. His voice sounded strange after that impersonal silence. "You're not angry?"

"Angry?" She smiled a little. She leant back against the cushions, one elbow crooked under her. She continued to smile; looking up at him. He came close. "Catherine." He took her hand again. "You know, don't you what I feel about you? . . . " He lifted her hand to his mouth and she felt the warm pressure of his lips against her palm. His dark eyes were upon her: his warm living breath within her palm. A faint exquisite shudder ran through her. Her lids drooped. "Catherine?" She shut her eyes; and nodded. . . .

There was an unexpected pause. A sudden blankness. Alec's expression underwent a change. He stared

at her, incredulously; not understanding, at first; not wanting to understand. Then realization broke on him: the full implication of her gesture. His jaw dropped: he looked foolish, like a man who has, gratuitously, been slapped in the face.

She opened her eyes. A little surprised. He had permitted himself to miss his cue. . . . She found herself disinclined, in the circumstances, to act as prompter: with her, apathy was always quick to set in. . . . She waited, but with a certain amount of indifference, now, for the initiative to come from him.

He did not move. The first raging disappointment died out of him. There was nothing for him to say. She had been ready to surrender to him. Because of that, he was abased: made nothing of. Defeated by the light worthless victory she offered him. . . .

She sat up suddenly. Her manner changed. She looked at him with concern. "What's the matter, Alec? . . ."

He averted his face; as if he were ashamed. "Oh, nothing," he said.

"Don't be silly." Her voice was half sharp, half kindly. "Come on. What is it, now? Tell me."

He shook his head: and she reached out suddenly and tugged at his elbow. "For goodness sake Alec!"

He shrugged his shoulders. Then he said huskily, "Just that one of us made a slight mistake, that's all."

"A mistake?" Her eyebrows contracted.

"Yes." His eye met hers for a brief moment. The look in them explained much to her. "You see, I wanted to marry you."

"Oh!" She stared at him. He fancied that she drew back a little. "Marriage" she said. Her voice was hard. She would not let him realize how startled, how deeply moved she was. . . .

He said bitterly, "Does it amaze you so much that I should even have thought of that?"

"No, of course not." She tried to justify herself. "It's only that I've never considered marriage. Never thought of it."

"Not with me, at any rate."

"Not with anyone." She corrected him quickly. "Please don't flatter yourself by imagining that I discriminate specially against you." He made no reply to this. There was a look on his face that she did not then wholly understand: but with which she was about to become familiar. He had accepted his own defeat. And now he was clinging to it: forbidding her to wrest it from him or mitigate its effect. . . . "Don't be absurd," she said impatiently. "Do you think I don't mean what I say? I've never thought of myself as a married woman: as a wife; as a Mrs. Somebody-or-Other. . . ."

"As a Mrs Alexander Joseph Berman. Obviously, that would be out of the question."

So that was it! Light dawned on her. It was not her he was despising, but himself. She had misread the whole situation. "Alec!" she exclaimed: and her voice was incredulous. "You don't for a moment think that I could have anything to do with such an absurd prejudice!"

He shrugged his shoulders. He was carefully noncommittal. "The prejudice happens to be a very widespread one," he said.

"But Alec! *Darling*! Don't be absurd. It means nothing, nothing whatever to me." The sincerity in her voice was unmistakable.

He looked at her, then: and, seeing her candid eyes, his expression altered a little. "I suppose I ought to be grateful to you for feeling that," he said. "But I don't want to be grateful. . . . I don't want to have to feel grateful for being accepted."

"But why on earth should you?" she said.

He did not answer for a moment. When he spoke again it was in a new, a curiously elaborate manner: as if they had touched, now, on a subject which he found difficult to discuss naturally. "You see, Catherine," he said, "I'm afraid you can't possibly have the remotest idea of what it means to be born a Jew."

"Is it so different to being born an Englishman?"

"It shouldn't be. But it is. Very different."

"I can only repeat that I feel no difference between us that matters."

"But *I* feel it," he said violently. He got up abruptly and began to pace up and down the room. He was deeply agitated. "Let me try to explain," he said at last. "Look." He stopped in front her. "You've never, have you, Catherine, felt intensely gratified, happy, if someone happened to mistake you for other than what you are? Have you?"

"No, of course not." She was slightly at a loss.

"You've never had to. . . . You don't know, either, what it feels like to walk about on earth that doesn't belong to you, speak a language which isn't really yours (although you know no other): live every second of your life among people who at best tolerate you: be dependent for life itself upon those people. . . . You haven't—you can't possibly have—the slightest conception of the perpetual uneasiness in which a Jew lives—the terrifying lack of security: the sense that all one has yearned

and striven for (the every-day happiness which any human being is entitled to) is entirely at the mercy of politicians, is challenged by every hostile word, look, gesture. . . . The sense that everything, Catherine, that a Jew builds, is built upon quicksands. . . ."

"Wait a moment, Alec." She interrupted him. "What you say may be true in general—I don't know. I can't pretend to know, as you say. . . . But we're concerned now with a particular case: you yourself, Alec. And after all—you live in England. . . . Don't forget that."

"Forget it? The country I was born in? Catherine, my dear, I'm so little likely to forget, that (unlike my ancestors who wept when they remembered Zion) you'd find me sitting on the banks of a river in Zion weeping when I remembered Babylon. . . ." He gave a short laugh. "So you see, if I'm pushed out, I shall be doubly disinherited," he said.

"Since at the moment," she began patiently, "there seems to be absolutely no prospect of that happening. . . ."

"I know." This time it was he who interrupted her: quickly. "I'm one of the lucky ones. Do you think I don't know it? Treasure my momentary good fortune: tremble for it? . . . the fact that I'm allowed for a while to live more or less as other people. . . ." He paused. "Even then, Catherine," he said, "I don't think you quite realize the peculiar sort of psychological existence the *lucky* ones lead. The way one's mind and emotions are continually worked on. . . ." He began to pace up and down the room again. "I can give you some trivial examples," he said. He walked up and down without looking at her. "You, for instance," he said, "have never faced the moral dilemma of inclining, say, to a particular political party; at the same time knowing it expedient, for the safety of your fellow Jews, to uphold, instead, a more socially popular one."

"No," she said, "and I can't see you doing it either."

"Don't idealize me," he said. "Don't miscalculate what the force of circumstance can do to one. . . ."

He stopped. "Say a vacancy occurs at the studios," he began again after a moment. "Some candidates come up for the job; Jewish and otherwise. I have the casting vote. Well, in those circumstances, merit should be the only criterion. On the other hand, my own job is safer, myself less conspicuous if I'm not too surrounded by others of my kind. . . ."

"But what you say applies to all of us!" she cried at once. "In one way or another, we're all in the same boat: we're all guilty of hammering on the fingers of those who try to climb in and threaten our own security. . . ."

"Something that doesn't apply to all," he said, is fear—a very special type of low-grade fear that's always there, behind every situation. You don't know that—you can't. The walking in the street and wondering what the content is of the glances you receive. . . . The way a Jew lowers his voice to pronounce the word Jew. . . . You don't know the sixth sense which tells you that the man behind the counter, the boy who sells you a newspaper at the corner, has sized you up; the fact that even such a momentary relationship is qualified. You don't know the constant sense of inferiority. Before even the most inferior of your race, before anyone who really belongs. . . . One's gratitude if a bus-conductor, a waiter, a navvy, seem to accept one naturally."

"You don't feel that in the company of cultivated people."

"People who say that their best friends are Jews?" He gave a sad, wry smile. "That's another thing," he said. "You've never had the experience of warning people who seemed about to become friendly with you that you were Jewish: warning them in time, so that they could, if necessary, withdraw their overtures of friendship without too much difficulty or embarrassment."

Catherine was silent.

Alec said, staring before him, "You've never had the experience of hearing your own race casually vilified; and allowing the remark to pass . . . smiling even. . . . Degraded, again and again, not by the insult, but by your own reaction to it."

Catherine did not know what to say. She made an effort. "Oh, but it *isn't* as bad as all that, Alec. . . . As I said before—this is England."

He looked at her. "Yes. The concentration camp is only *spiritual*, here."

Catherine rose. She went towards him, as he stood there, and took both his hands: forcing him to look at her. "Alec," she said "don't be offended at what I'm going to say. Are you sure that the concentration camp isn't something subjective—that it doesn't exist largely in your own mind?"

He said incredulously: "Good Lord, do you think we *want* to be in it? That it's a sort of masochist's pleasure-resort? . . ." He controlled himself. "No," he said bitterly, "it's circumstance that has made us what we are. Not our own choice."

"You don't have to accept circumstance," she said. Her hands were still tightly locked in his.

"I don't accept it. My life is one long struggle to overcome it. To prove that it can be overcome."

"What do you want, then, Alec?" she asked.

"I want a chance to be *allowed* to be normal. To be *allowed* to be as other men."

"But, my darling," she said softly, "to me you are as other men. More than other men, perhaps. You diminish yourself by insisting on this difference."

He gripped her hands more fiercely. "Oh Catherine, I wish you loved me. That would make all the difference. That would make me whole. I'd belong then: like the others. I wouldn't be outside, any more, if I only had that." His face was entirely altered: all that was trivial and sensual seemed to have faded from it; leaving it like a mask that expressed, not individual anguish, but an impersonal sorrow, inbred through generations.

She went very white. Her hands were still imprisoned in his. She made no effort to withdraw from him: resist that claim. The situation was stronger than her: it was as if she were compelled to play her part in it. She heard herself say, "How do you know that I don't love you, Alec?" And, having spoken the words, she became aware of an exquisite sense of irresponsibility; of gladness: some deep tension released at last in this, her first surrender. Doubt vanished in that new emotion: in the answering emotion she saw in his face. "Catherine!" She saw his exalted look; she was unaware that tears glittered in her own eyes. They stood there, holding each others' hands: like two creatures suddenly and miraculously freed of barriers: sharing a brief, a unique moment in which they discovered themselves united in an unbelievable and healing simplicity.

Other works by Miller: *The Mere Living* (1933); *Sunday* (1934); *Portrait of the Bride* (1935); *On the Side of the Angels* (1945); *Robert Browning: A Portrait* (1952).

Clifford Odets

1906–1963

The American playwright and screenwriter Clifford Odets was the son of East European immigrants. He was raised in New York City and began his theatrical career, first as an actor, there. A member of the Communist Party from 1930, his plays of that decade, for which he is best known, portrayed working-class Jewish families coping with the material and emotional stresses of the Great Depression. They were notable for capturing the explosive energy and distinctive rhythms of the speech of second-generation New York

Jews. He also wrote screenplays for films and television and lived in Hollywood from 1942 to 1948 and from 1955 to his death. He was called to testify before the House Un-American Activities Committee in 1952 and cited for contempt when he refused to cooperate.

Awake and Sing!
1935

Act II

SCENE 1

One year later, a Sunday afternoon. The front room. JACOB *is giving his son* MORDECAI [UNCLE MORTY] *a haircut, newspapers spread around the base of the chair.* MOE *is reading a newspaper, leg propped on a chair.* RALPH *in another chair, is spasmodically reading a paper.* UNCLE MORTY *reads colored jokes. Silence, then* BESSIE *enters.*

BESSIE: Dinner's in half an hour, Morty.

MORTY [*Still reading jokes.*]: I got time.

BESSIE: A duck. Don't get hair on the rug, Pop. [*Goes to the window and pulls down shade.*] What's the matter the shade's up to the ceiling?

JACOB [*Pulling it up again.*]: Since when do I give a haircut in the dark? [*He mimics her tone.*]

BESSIE: When you're finished, pull it down. I like my house to look respectable. Ralphie, bring up two bottles seltzer from Weiss.

RALPH: I'm reading the paper.

BESSIE: Uncle Morty likes a little seltzer.

RALPH: I'm expecting a phone call.

BESSIE: Noo, if it comes you'll be back. What's the matter? [*Gives him money from apron pocket.*] Take down the old bottles.

RALPH [*To* JACOB]: Get that call if it comes. Say I'll be right back. [JACOB *nods assent.*]:

MORTY [*Giving change from vest.*]: Get grandpa some cigarettes.

RALPH: Okay. [*Exits.*]

JACOB: What's new in the paper, Moe?

MOE: Still jumping off the high buildings like flies—the big shots who lost all their cocoanuts. Pfft!

JACOB: Suicides?

MOE: Plenty can't take it—good in the break, but can't take the whip in the stretch.

MORTY [*Without looking up.*]: I saw it happen Monday in my building. My hair stood up how they shov-

eled him together—like a pancake—a bankrupt manufacturer.

MOE: No brains.

MORTY: Enough . . . all over the sidewalk.

JACOB: If someone said five, ten years ago I couldn't make for myself a living. I wouldn't believe—

MORTY: Duck for dinner?

BESSIE: The best Long Island duck.

MORTY: I like goose.

BESSIE: A duck is just like a goose, only better.

MORTY: I like a goose.

BESSIE: The next time you'll be for Sunday dinner I'll make a goose.

MORTY [*Sniffs deeply.*]: Smells good. I'm a great boy for smells.

BESSIE: Ain't you ashamed? Once in a blue moon he should come to an only sister's house.

MORTY: Bessie, leave me live.

BESSIE: You should be ashamed!

MORTY: Quack quack!

BESSIE: No, better to lay around Mecca Temple playing cards with the Masons.

MORTY [*With good nature.*]: Bessie, don't you see Pop's giving me a haircut?

BESSIE: You don't need no haircut. Look, two hairs he took off.

MORTY: Pop likes to give me a haircut. If I said no he don't forget for a year, do you, Pop? An old man's like that.

JACOB: I still do an A-1 job.

MORTY [*Winking.*]: Pop cuts hair to fit the face, don't you, Pop?

JACOB: For sure, Morty. To each face a different haircut. Custom-built, no ready-made. A round face needs special—

BESSIE [*Cutting him short.*]: A Graduate from the B.M.T. [*Going.*] Don't forget the shade. [*The phone rings. She beats* JACOB *to it.*] Hello? Who is it, please? . . . Who is it please? . . . Miss Hirsch? No, he ain't here. . . . No, I couldn't say when. [*Hangs up sharply.*]

JACOB: For Ralph?

BESSIE: A wrong number. [JACOB *looks at her and goes back to his job.*]

JACOB: Excuse me!

BESSIE [*To* MORTY]: Ralphie took another cut down the place yesterday.

MORTY: Business is bad. I saw his boss Harry Glicksman Thursday. I bought some velvets . . . they're coming in again.

BESSIE: Do something for Ralphie down there.

MORTY: What can I do? I mentioned it to Glicksman. He told me they squeezed out half the people. . . . [MYRON *enters dressed in apron*.]

BESSIE: What's gonna be the end? Myron's working only three days a week now.

MYRON: It's conditions.

BESSIE: Hennie's married with a baby . . . money just don't come in. I never saw conditions should be so bad.

MORTY: Times'll change.

MOE: The only thing'll change is my underwear.

MORTY: These last few years I got my share of gray hairs. [*Still reading jokes without having looked up once.*] Ha, ha ha—Popeye the sailor ate spinach and knocked out four bums.

MYRON: I'll tell you the way I see it. The country needs a great man now—a regular Teddy Roosevelt.

MOE: What this country needs is a good five-cent earthquake.

JACOB: So long labor lives it should increase private gain—

BESSIE [*To* JACOB.]: Listen, Poppa, go talk on the street corner. The government'll give you free board the rest of your life.

MORTY: I'm surprised. Don't I send a five-dollar check for Pop every week?

BESSIE: You could afford a couple more and not miss it.

MORTY: Tell me jokes. Business is so rotten I could just as soon lay all day in the Turkish bath.

MYRON: Why'd I come in here? [*Puzzled, he exits.*]

MORTY [*To* MOE]: I hear the bootleggers still do business, Moe.

MOE: Wake up! I kissed bootlegging bye-bye two years back.

MORTY: For a fact? What kind of racket is it now?

MOE: If I told you, you'd know something. [HENNIE *comes from bedroom.*]

HENNIE: Where's Sam?

BESSIE: Sam? In the kitchen.

HENNIE [*Calls.*]: Sam. Come take the diaper.

MORTY: How's the Mickey Louse? Ha, ha, ha. . . .

HENNIE: Sleeping.

MORTY: Ah, that's life to a baby. He sleeps—gets it in the mouth—sleeps some more. To raise a family nowadays you must be a damn fool.

BESSIE: Never mind, never mind, a woman who don't raise a family—a girl—should jump overboard.

What's she good for? [*To* MOE—*to change the subject.*] Your leg bothers you bad?

MOE: It's okay, sweetheart.

BESSIE [*To* MORTY.]: It hurts him every time it's cold out. He's got four legs in the closet.

MORTY: Four wooden legs?

MOE: Three.

MORTY: What's the big idea?

MOE: Why not? Uncle Sam gives them out free.

MORTY: Say, maybe if Uncle Sam gave out less legs we could balance the budget.

JACOB: Or not have a war so they wouldn't have to give out legs.

MORTY: Shame on you, Pop. Everybody knows war is necessary.

MOE: Don't make me laugh. Ask me—the first time you pick up a dead one in the trench—then you learn war ain't so damn necessary.

MORTY: Say, you should kick. The rest of your life Uncle Sam pays you ninety a month. Look, not a worry in the world.

MOE: Don't make me laugh. Uncle Sam can take his *seventy* bucks and—[*Finishes with a gesture.*] Nothing good hurts. [*He rubs his stump.*]

HENNIE: Use a crutch, Axelrod. Give the stump a rest.

MOE: Mind your business, Feinschreiber.

BESSIE: It's a sensible idea.

MOE: Who asked you?

BESSIE: Look, he's ashamed.

MOE: So's your Aunt Fanny.

BESSIE [*Naïvely.*]: Who's got an Aunt Fanny? [*She cleans a rubber plant's leaves with her apron.*]

MORTY: It's a joke!

MOE: I don't want my paper creased before I read it. I want it fresh. Fifty times I said that.

BESSIE: Don't get so excited for a five-cent paper—our star boarder.

MOE: And I don't want no one using my razor either. Get it straight. I'm not buying ten blades a week for the Berger family. [*Furious, he limps out.*]

BESSIE: Maybe I'm using his razor too.

HENNIE: Proud!

BESSIE: You need luck with plants. I didn't clean off the leaves in a month.

MORTY: You keep the house like a pin and I like your cooking. Any time Myron fires you, come to me, Bessie. I'll let the butler go and you'll be my housekeeper. I don't like Japs so much—sneaky.

BESSIE: Say, you can't tell. Maybe any day I'm coming to stay. [HENNIE *exits.*]

JACOB: Finished.

MORTY: How much, Ed. Pinaud? [*Disengages self from chair.*]

JACOB: Five cents.

MORTY: Still five cents for a haircut to fit the face?

JACOB: Prices don't change by me. [*Takes a dollar.*] I can't change—

MORTY: Keep it. Buy yourself a Packard. Ha, ha, ha.

JACOB: [*Taking large envelope from pocket.*] Please, you'll keep this for me. Put it away.

MORTY: What is it?

JACOB: My insurance policy. I don't like it should lay around where something could happen.

MORTY: What could happen?

JACOB: Who knows, robbers, fire . . . they took next door. Fifty dollars from O'Reilly.

MORTY: Say, lucky a Berger didn't lose it.

JACOB: Put it downtown in the safe. Bessie don't have to know.

MORTY: It's made out to Bessie?

JACOB: No, to Ralph.

MORTY: To Ralph?

JACOB: He don't know. Some day he'll get three thousand.

MORTY: You got good years ahead.

JACOB: Behind. [RALPH *enters.*]

RALPH: Cigarettes. Did a call come?

JACOB: A few minutes. She don't let me answer it.

RALPH: Did Mom say I was coming back?

JACOB: No. [MORTY *is back at new jokes.*]

RALPH: She starting that stuff again? [BESSIE *enters.*] A call come for me?

BESSIE [*Waters pot from milk bottle.*]: A wrong number.

JACOB: Don't say a lie, Bessie.

RALPH: Blanche said she'd call me at two—was it her?

BESSIE: I said a wrong number.

RALPH: Please, Mom, if it was her tell me.

BESSIE: You call me a liar next. You got no shame—to start a scene in front of Uncle Morty. Once in a blue moon he comes—

RALPH: What's the shame? If my girl calls, I wanna know it.

BESSIE: You made enough mish mosh with her until now.

MORTY: I'm surprised, Bessie. For the love of Mike tell him yes or no.

BESSIE: I didn't tell him? No!

MORTY [*To* RALPH.]: No! [RALPH *goes to a window and looks out.*]

BESSIE: Morty, I didn't say before—he runs around steady with a girl.

MORTY: Terrible. Should he run around with a foxie-woxie?

BESSIE: A girl with no parents.

MORTY: An orphan?

BESSIE: I could die from shame. A year already he runs around with her. He brought her once for supper. Believe me, she didn't come again, no!

RALPH: Don't think I didn't ask her.

BESSIE: You hear? You raise them and what's in the end for all your trouble?

JACOB: When you'll lay in a grave, no more trouble. [*Exits.*]

MORTY: Quack quack!

BESSIE: A girl like that he wants to marry. A skinny consumptive-looking . . . six months already she's not working—taking charity from an aunt. You should see her. In a year she's dead on his hands.

RALPH: You'd cut her throat if you could.

BESSIE: That's right! Before she'd ruin a nice boy's life I would first go to prison. Miss Nobody should step in the picture and I'll stand by with my mouth shut.

RALPH: Miss Nobody! Who am I? Al Jolson?

BESSIE: Fix your tie!

RALPH: I'll take care of my own life.

BESSIE: You'll take care? Excuse my expression, you can't even wipe your nose yet! He'll take care!

MORTY [*To* BESSIE.]: I'm surprised. Don't worry so much, Bessie. When it's time to settle down he won't marry a poor girl, will you? In the long run common sense is thicker than love. I'm a great boy for live and let live.

BESSIE: Sure, it's easy to say. In the meantime he eats out my heart. You know I'm not strong.

MORTY: I know . . . a pussy cat . . . ha, ha, ha.

BESSIE: You got money and money talks. But without the dollar who sleeps at night?

RALPH: I been working for years, bringing in money here—putting it in your hand like a kid. All right, I can't get my teeth fixed. All right, that a new suit's like trying to buy the Chrysler Building. You never in your life bought me a pair of skates even—things I died for when I was a kid. I don't care about that stuff, see. Only just remember I pay some of the bills around here, just a few . . . and if my girl calls me on the phone I'll talk to her any time I please. [*He exits.* HENNIE *applauds.*]

BESSIE: Don't be so smart, Miss America! [*To* MORTY.]: He didn't have skates! But when he got sick, a twelve-year-old boy, who called a big specialist for the last $25 in the house? Skates!

JACOB [*Just in. Adjusts window shade.*]: It looks like snow today.

MORTY: It's about time—winter.

BESSIE: Poppa here could talk like Samuel Webster, too, but it's just talk. He should try to buy a two-cent pickle in the Burland Market without money.

MORTY: I'm getting an appetite.

BESSIE: Right away we'll eat. I made chopped liver for you.

MORTY: My specialty!

BESSIE: Ralph should only be a success like you, Morty. I should only live to see the day when he rides up to the door in a big car with a chauffeur and a radio. I could die happy, believe me.

MORTY: Success she says. She should see how we spend thousands of dollars making up a winter line and winter don't come—summer in January. Can you beat it?

JACOB: Don't live, just make success.

MORTY: Chopped liver—ha!

JACOB: Ha! [*Exits.*]

MORTY: When they start arguing, I don't hear. Suddenly I'm deaf. I'm a great boy for the practical side. [*He looks over to* HENNIE, *who sits rubbing her hands with lotion.*]

HENNIE: Hands like a raw potato.

MORTY: What's the matter? You don't look so well . . . no pep.

HENNIE: I'm swell.

MORTY: You used to be such a pretty girl.

HENNIE: Maybe I got the blues. You can't tell.

MORTY: You could stand a new dress.

HENNIE: That's not all I could stand.

MORTY: Come down to the place tomorrow and pick out a couple from the "eleven-eighty" line. Only don't sing me the blues.

HENNIE: Thanks. I need some new clothes.

MORTY: I got two thousand pieces of merchandise waiting in the stock room for winter.

HENNIE: I never had anything from life. Sam don't help.

MORTY: He's crazy about the kid.

HENNIE: Crazy is right. Twenty-one a week he brings in—a nigger don't have it so hard. I wore my fingers off on an Underwood for six years. For what? Now I wash baby diapers. Sure, I'm crazy about the kid too. But half the night the kid's up. Try to sleep. You don't know how it is, Uncle Morty.

MORTY: No, I don't know. I was born yesterday. Ha, ha, ha. Some day I'll leave you a little nest egg. You like eggs? Ha?

HENNIE: When? When I'm dead and buried?

MORTY: No, when *I'm* dead and buried. Ha, ha, ha.

HENNIE: You should know what I'm thinking.

MORTY: Ha, ha, ha, I know. [MYRON *enters.*]

MYRON: I never take a drink. I'm just surprised at myself, I—

MORTY: I got a pain. Maybe I'm hungry.

MYRON: Come inside, Morty. Bessie's got some schnapps.

MORTY: I'll take a drink. Yesterday I missed the Turkish bath.

MYRON: I get so bitter when I take a drink, it just surprises me.

MORTY: Look how fat. Say, you live once. . . . Quack, quack. [*Both exit.* MOE *stands silently in the doorway.*]

SAM [*Entering.*]: I'll make Leon's bottle now!

HENNIE: No, let him sleep, Sam. Take away the diaper. [*He does. Exits.*]

MOE: [*Advancing into the room.*] That your husband?

HENNIE: Don't you know?

MOE: Maybe he's a nurse you hired for the kid—it looks it—how he tends it. A guy comes howling to your old lady every time you look cock-eyed. Does he sleep with you?

HENNIE: Don't be so wise!

MOE [*Indicating newspaper.*]: Here's a dame strangled her hubby with wire. Claimed she didn't like him. Why don't you brain Sam with an axe some night?

HENNIE: Why don't you lay an egg, Axelrod?

MOE: I laid a few in my day, Feinschreiber. Hard-boiled ones too.

HENNIE: Yeah?

MOE: Yeah. You wanna know what I see when I look in your eyes?

HENNIE: No.

MOE: Ted Lewis playing the clarinet—some of those high crazy notes! Christ, you coulda had a guy with some guts instead of a cluck stands around boilin' baby nipples.

HENNIE: Meaning you?

MOE: Meaning me, sweetheart.

HENNIE: Think you're pretty good.

MOE: You'd know if I slept with you again.

HENNIE: I'll smack your face in a minute.

MOE: You do and I'll break your arm. [*Holds up paper.*] Take a look. [*Reads.*] "Ten-day luxury cruise to Havana." That's the stuff you coulda had. Put up at ritzy hotels, frenchie soap, champagne. Now you're tied down to "Snake-Eye" here. What for? What's it get you? . . . A 2 × 4 flat on 108th Street . . . a pain in the bustle it gets you.

HENNIE: What's it to you?

MOE: I know you from the old days. How you like to spend it! What I mean! Lizard-skin shoes, perfume behind the ears. . . . You're in a mess, Paradise! Paradise—that's a hot one—yah, crazy to eat a knish at your own wedding.

HENNIE: I get it—you're jealous. You can't get me.

MOE: Don't make me laugh.

HENNIE: Kid Jailbird's been trying to make me for years. You'd give your other leg. I'm hooked? Maybe, but you're in the same boat. Only it's worse for you. I don't give a damn no more, but you gotta yen makes you—

MOE: Don't make me laugh.

HENNIE: Compared to you I'm sittin' on top of the world.

MOE: You're losing your looks. A dame don't stay young forever.

HENNIE: You're a liar. I'm only twenty-four.

MOE: When you comin' home to stay?

HENNIE: Wouldn't you like to know?

MOE: I'll get you again.

HENNIE: Think so?

MOE: Sure, whatever goes up comes down. You're easy—you remember—two for a nickel—a pushover! [*Suddenly she slaps him. They both seem stunned.*] What's the idea?

HENNIE: Go on . . . break my arm.

MOE [*As if saying "I love you."*]: Listen, lousy.

HENNIE: Go on, do something!

MOE: Listen—

HENNIE: You're so damn tough!

MOE: You like me. [*He takes her.*]

HENNIE: Take your hand off! [*Pushes him away.*] Come around when it's a flood again and they put you in the ark with the animals. Not even then—if you was the last man!

MOE: Baby, if you had a dog I'd love the dog.

HENNIE: Gorilla! [*Exits.* RALPH *enters.*]

RALPH: Were you here before?

MOE [*Sits.*]: What?

RALPH: When the call came for me?

MOE: What?

RALPH: The call came. [JACOB *enters.*]

MOE [*Rubbing his leg.*]: No.

JACOB: Don't worry, Ralphie, she'll call back.

RALPH: Maybe not. I think somethin's the matter.

JACOB: What?

RALPH: I don't know. I took her home from the movie last night. She asked me what I'd think if she went away.

JACOB: Don't worry, she'll call again.

RALPH: Maybe not, if Mom insulted her. She gets it on both ends, the poor kid. Lived in an orphan asylum most of her life. They shove her around like an empty freight train.

JACOB: After dinner go see her.

RALPH: Twice they kicked me down the stairs.

JACOB: Life should have some dignity.

RALPH: Every time I go near the place I get heart failure. The uncle drives a bus. You oughta see him—like Babe Ruth.

MOE: Use your brains. Stop acting like a kid who still wets the bed. Hire a room somewhere—a club room for two members.

RALPH: Not that kind of proposition, Moe.

MOE: Don't be a bush leaguer all your life.

RALPH: Cut it out!

MOE [*On a sudden upsurge of emotion.*]: Ever sleep with one? Look at 'im blush.

RALPH: You don't know her.

MOE: I seen her—the kind no one sees undressed till the undertaker works on her.

RALPH: Why give me the needles all the time? What'd I ever do to you?

MOE: Not a thing. You're a nice kid. But grow up! In life there's two kinds—the men that's sure of themselves and the ones who ain't! It's time you quit being a selling plater and got in the first class.

JACOB: And you, Axelrod?

MOE [*To* JACOB.]: Scratch your whiskers! [*To* RALPH.] Get independent. Get what-it-takes and be yourself. Do what you like.

RALPH: Got a suggestion?

[MORTY *enters, eating.*]

MOE: Sure, pick out a racket. Shake down the cocoanuts. See what that does.

MORTY: We know what it does—puts a pudding on your nose! Sing Sing! Easy money's against the law. Against the law don't win. A racket is illegitimate, no?

MOE: It's all a racket—from horse racing down. Marriage, politics, big business—everybody plays cops and robbers. You, you're a racketeer yourself.

MORTY: Who? Me? Personally I manufacture dresses.

MOE: Horse feathers!

MORTY: [*Seriously.*] Don't make such remarks to me without proof. I'm a great one for proof. That's why I made a success in business. Proof—put up or shut up, like a game of cards. I heard this remark before—a rich man's a crook who steals from the poor. Personally, I don't like it. It's a big lie!

MOE: If you don't like it, buy yourself a fife and drum—and go fight your own war.

MORTY: Sweatshop talk. Every Jew and Wop in the shop eats my bread and behind my back says, "a sonofabitch." I started from a poor boy who worked on an ice wagon for two dollars a week. Pop's right here—he'll tell you. I made it honest. In the whole industry nobody's got a better name.

JACOB: It's an exception, such success.

MORTY: Ralph can't do the same thing?

JACOB: No, Morty, I don't think. In a house like this he don't realize even the possibilities of life. Economics comes down like a ton of coal on the head.

MOE: Red rover, red rover, let Jacob come over!

JACOB: In my day the propaganda was for God. Now it's for success. A boy don't turn around without having shoved in him he should make success.

MORTY: Pop, you're a comedian, a regular Charlie Chaplin.

JACOB: He dreams all night of fortunes. Why not? Don't it say in the movies he should have a personal steamship, pyjamas for fifty dollars a pair and a toilet like a monument? But in the morning he wakes up and for ten dollars he can't fix the teeth. And millions more worse off in the mills of the South—starvation wages. The blood from the worker's heart. [MORTY *laughs loud and long.*] Laugh, laugh . . . tomorrow not.

MORTY: A real, a real Boob McNutt you're getting to be.

JACOB: Laugh, my son. . . .

MORTY: Here is the North, Pop.

JACOB: North, south, it's one country.

MORTY: The country's all right. A duck quacks in every pot!

JACOB: You never heard how they shoot down men and women which ask a better wage? Kentucky 1932?

MORTY: That's a pile of chopped liver, Pop.

[BESSIE *and others enter.*]

JACOB: Pittsburgh, Passaic, Illinois—slavery—it begins where success begins in a competitive system.

[MORTY *howls with delight.*]

MORTY: Oh Pop, what are you bothering? Why? Tell me why? Ha ha ha. I bought you a phonograph . . . stick to Caruso.

BESSIE: He's starting up again.

MORTY: Don't bother with Kentucky. It's full of moonshiners.

JACOB: Sure, sure—

MORTY: You don't know practical affairs. Stay home and cut hair to fit the face.

JACOB: It says in the Bible how the Red Sea opened and the Egyptians went in and the sea rolled over them. [*Quotes two lines of Hebrew.*] In this boy's life a Red Sea will happen again. I see it!

MORTY: I'm getting sore, Pop, with all this sweatshop talk.

BESSIE: He don't stop a minute. The whole day, like a phonograph.

MORTY: I'm surprised. Without a rich man you don't have a roof over your head. You don't know it?

MYRON: Now you can't bite the hand that feeds you.

RALPH: Let him alone—he's right!

BESSIE: Another county heard from.

RALPH: It's the truth. It's—

MORTY: Keep quiet, snotnose!

JACOB: For sure, charity, a bone for an old dog. But in Russia an old man don't take charity so his eyes turn black in his head. In Russia they got Marx.

MORTY [*Scoffingly.*]: Who's Marx?

MOE: An outfielder for the Yanks. [MORTY *howls with delight.*]

MORTY: Ha ha ha, it's better than the jokes. I'm telling you. This is Uncle Sam's country. Put it in your pipe and smoke it.

BESSIE: Russia, he says! Read the papers.

SAM: Here is opportunity.

MYRON: People can't believe in God in Russia. The papers tell the truth, they do.

JACOB: So you believe in God . . . you got something for it? You! You worked for all the capitalists. You harvested the fruit from your labor? You got God! But the past comforts you? The present smiles on you, yes? It promises you the future something? Did you found a piece of earth where you could live like a human being and die with the sun on your face? Tell me, yes, tell me. I would like to know myself. But on these questions, on this theme—the struggle for existence—you can't make an answer. The answer I see in your face . . . the answer is your mouth can't talk. In this dark corner you sit and you die. But abolish private property!

BESSIE [Settling the issue.]: Noo, go fight City Hall!

MORTY: He's drunk!

JACOB: I'm studying from books a whole lifetime.

MORTY: That's what it is—he's drunk. What the hell does all that mean?

JACOB: If you don't know, why should I tell you.

MORTY [Triumphant at last.]: You see? Hear him? Like all those nuts, don't know what they're saying.

JACOB: I know, I know.

MORTY: Like Boob McNutt you know! Don't go in the park, Pop—the squirrels'll get you. Ha, ha, ha. . . .

BESSIE: Save your appetite, Morty. [To MYRON.] Don't drop the duck.

MYRON: We're ready to eat, Momma.

MORTY: (To JACOB.) Shame on you. It's your second childhood.

(Now they file out, MYRON first with the duck, the others behind him.)

BESSIE: Come eat. We had enough for one day. [Exits.]

MORTY: Ha, ha, ha. Quack, quack. [Exits.]

[JACOB sits there trembling and deeply humiliated. MOE approaches him and thumbs the old man's nose in the direction of the dining room.]

MOE: Give 'em five. [Takes his hand away.] They got you pasted on the wall like a picture, Jake. [He limps out to seat himself at the table in the next room.]

JACOB: Go eat, boychick. [RALPH comes to him.] He gives me eat, so I'll climb in a needle. One time I saw an old horse in summer . . . he wore a straw hat . . . the ears stuck out on top. An old horse for hire. Give me back my young days . . . give me fresh blood . . . arms . . . give me—[The telephone rings. Quickly RALPH goes to it. JACOB pulls the curtains and stands there, a sentry on guard.]

RALPH: Hello? . . . Yeah, I went to the store and came right back, right after you called. [Looks at JACOB.]

JACOB: Speak, speak. Don't be afraid they'll hear.

RALPH: I'm sorry if Mom said something. You know how excitable Mom is . . . Sure! What? . . . Sure, I'm listening. . . . Put on the radio, Jake. [JACOB does so. Music comes in and up, a tango, grating with an insistent nostalgic pulse. Under the cover of the music RALPH speaks more freely.] Yes . . . yes . . . What's the matter? Why're you crying? What happened? [To JACOB.] She's putting her uncle on. Yes? . . . Listen, Mr. Hirsch, what're you trying to do? What's the big idea? Honest to God. I'm in no mood for joking! Lemme talk to her! Gimme Blanche! [Waits.] Blanche? What's this? Is this a joke? Is that true? I'm coming right down! I know, but—You wanna do that? . . . I know, but—I'm coming down . . . tonight! Nine o'clock . . . sure . . . sure . . . sure. . . . [Hangs up.]

JACOB: What happened?

MORTY [Enters.]: Listen, Pop. I'm surprised you didn't—[He howls, shakes his head in mock despair, exits.]

JACOB: Boychick, what?

RALPH: I don't get it straight. [To JACOB.] She's leaving . . .

JACOB: Where?

RALPH: Out West—To Cleveland.

JACOB: Cleveland?

RALPH: . . . In a week or two. Can you picture it? It's a put-up job. But they can't get away with that.

JACOB: We'll find something.

RALPH: Sure, the angels of heaven'll come down on her uncle's cab and whisper in his ear.

JACOB: Come eat. . . . We'll find something.

RALPH: I'm meeting her tonight, but I know—[BESSIE throws open the curtain between the two rooms and enters.]

BESSIE: Maybe we'll serve you for a special blue plate supper in the garden?

JACOB: All right, all right. [BESSIE goes over to the window, levels the shade and on her way out, clicks off the radio.]

MORTY [Within.]: Leave the music, Bessie. [She clicks it on again, looks at them, exits.]

RALPH: I know . . .

JACOB: Don't cry, boychick. [Goes over to RALPH.] Why should you make like this? Tell me why you should cry, just tell me. . . . [JACOB takes RALPH in his arms

*and both, trying to keep back the tears, trying fearfully
not to be heard by the others in the dining room, begin
crying.*] You mustn't cry. . . . .

[*The tango twists on. Inside, the clatter of dishes and
the clash of cutlery sound.* MORTY *begins to howl with
laughter.*]

CURTAIN

Other works by Odets: *Till the Day I Die* (1935);
Waiting for Lefty (1935); *Paradise Lost* (1936); *Golden
Boy* (1937).

Yehoshua Perle

1888–1943

Yehoshua Perle was a popular Yiddish-language writer
whose novels portrayed all classes of Jewish society
in interwar Poland. While never a favorite of literary
critics, Perle wrote works that were beloved by the
Yiddish-speaking public and therefore reached a wide
audience. While imprisoned in the Warsaw ghetto
during World War II, Perle produced an important
diary of events entitled *Khurbn Varshe* that details,
among other events, the collaboration of Jews with the
Nazis and their allies. He was killed in Auschwitz.

Everyday Jews: Scenes from a Vanished Life
1935

Chapter Sixteen

The question arises: How did my mother, who, with
her first husband, the *feldsher*, resided in spacious
rooms, with brass handles on the doors, come to be
with Father, a village Jew who lived in a place known as
the New Mill, a good judge of hay, who feasted on sour
milk and sour cream from large earthenware bowls,
who liked to bathe in the local river and sleep in the
forest under a pine tree? How did these two people ever
get together?

The story goes as follows.

Before Mother and Father decided to marry, neither
was aware of the exact number of children each had
had with their first spouses. In drawing up the marriage contract, they forgot to note the names of all the
orphaned children. It had been mentioned that there
were several such, but that they were already grown

and not dependent on either their father or mother for
support.

The wedding canopy was set up and a repast prepared for the guests. The bridegroom returned home,
and then Mother packed all her belongings into a trunk,
left her few pieces of jewelry with Aunt Miriam, and
went out by herself to the New Mill, where Father had
lived with his first wife. When mother arrived, her eyes
fell upon a large, dark room with an earthen floor, many
clay pots strewn about in the corners, two broken windowpanes stuffed with pillows, and four grown girls,
dark-skinned, bedraggled, dressed in loose cotton
blouses, hiding behind the headboards and staring in
wonder at the new wife their father had brought home
from town.

When Mother saw all this, her young face shriveled up like a fig. She didn't remove her head scarf, she
didn't take off her coat, but just stood there.

"Is this the farm that you told me you owned?" she
asked.

"Yes, this is the farm," Father replied.

"And who are the girls?"

"My daughters."

"All four of them?"

"All four, may they remain in good health."

"But you only spoke of two."

"Well, what does it matter? A person says things . . ."

Mother felt a pressure on her heart. She couldn't
speak. What good would speaking do? If she hadn't
been ashamed to do so, she would have fainted right
there and then.

However, she pulled herself together and said, "No,
Reb Leyzer! That's not what we agreed upon. You keep
your daughters, and all the best to you, but I will not be
your wife."

"What do you mean? What about our marriage
ceremony?"

"We'll get a divorce, Reb Leyzer!"

And with that, Mother and her trunk returned to
town.

She went straight to Aunt Miriam, her younger sister,
crying and lamenting, "Miriam, dear heart, what did
you want from me? Why did you talk me into this marriage? He's a pauper! There are four girls in the house,
like four hunks of wood. What am I to do with four
girls?"

Aunt Miriam knew that Father had four daughters
at home. She also knew that Reb Leyzer of the New
Mill was nothing but a pauper, that the "farm" cited as

an inducement in the marriage negotiation was nothing more than one room with an earthen floor and the clay pots for the sour milk. On the other hand, Mother was a widow and Reb Leyzer didn't ask for any dowry. Besides, she was left with children of her own, from her first husband, may he rest in peace. So why all the complaints?

"Why shouldn't I complain?" Mother insisted. "After the spacious rooms I had with my first husband, I should now go live in a single dark room with an earthen floor?"

Aunt Miriam's heart went out to her, and whoever heard about what happened felt sorry for the young, pretty Frimet. But it was a lost cause. What use would it be to complain? [. . .]

What could Mother do? She didn't want to become a laughingstock among respectable people. She wept, complained some more, and finally let herself be persuaded. But she refused to return to the New Mill.

"Let him move into town," Mother said. "He's a pauper, no matter what. So he'll be a pauper in town."

Before long, Father said goodbye to his clay pots, to the meadows and to the forest, and moved into town together with his four dark-skinned, bedraggled daughters.

Four such daughters couldn't sit on their father's impoverished shoulders forever. It was time to start thinking in practical terms about them. Bit by bit, Mother took it upon herself to see that they were provided for.

Ite, the youngest, became a cook for rich families in Warsaw. Once in a while, on holidays, she would come home to visit her father, always bringing gifts.

Khane-Sore, the eldest, tall, swarthy, and with a pair of big, strong hands, Mother married off to a butcher in a nearby village. She had nothing to complain about. Things went well for her. Wolf, her husband, a short man with a dark, pinched face, loved his wife. In due course, she bore him three daughters and four sons—may they live and be healthy—all like their mother, dark-skinned, green-eyed, quiet, and with abundant hair.

Khane-Sore herself came into town only once in a blue moon. She would come to buy a dress for a daughter and at the same time use the occasion both to drop in on her father and to practice her silence.

Father and his eldest daughter, both tall and proud, like spreading, deeply rooted poplars, would sit facing one another and looking into each other's eyes. They sat in silence, broken only by a brief exchange.

"How are you, Father?"
"How should I be?"
"What's new?"
"Not much. Wolf?"
"Fine."
"And the children?"
"God be praised."

That was all. They continued looking at each other. Once more, silence. Then she was gone, not to be seen again for another year, or two years, or five years. [. . .]

But Khane-Sore was Father's only married daughter. After her came Beyle, also big and tall, with long narrow hands and a wide, square chin. Beyle didn't have her sister Khane-Sore's prodigious calm. She spoke in broken-off, curt sentences. Every little thing made her cheeks break out in red spots.

Beyle looked at the world through quick, restless eyes. Strangers might have thought her malicious, but nothing was further from the truth. She would gladly have given away her last shirt. She was known by all for her good works. So worthy a woman, people said, couldn't easily be found, even if one went out searching with lit candles.

Beyle, however, had one great fault. She couldn't sit still for a moment. Cut her into bits and pieces and somehow she would find a way to get up and go. She was constantly on the move, to Warsaw, to Lodz, to some small town, anywhere, so long as she didn't have to stay in any one place for too long.

Sometimes, she would stop at an inn somewhere to get warm. If she liked the place and the people, she would hire herself out and stay a while.

At the inn, she would milk the cows, cook huge potfuls of food for Jews and for passing travelers, and set down pans of potatoes and mash for the cows' feed. She also knew how to work a spindle, to knit, to sew, and to mend clothes. She even knew how to banter with the sons of wealthy landowners, who rode by the inn on their splendidly outfitted horses.

Beyle knew how to do everything—except how to do some good for herself. The years passed. Beyle grew wider in girth, and still she remained unmarried, unable to find her match.

Only once, however, in one of the inns, did an opportunity seem to present itself. It happened in the person of a dark-skinned Jew who was passing through, a stocky man with a pair of eyes black as coal, wearing a hooded coat. A chat revealed that this Jew's wife had unfortunately died in childbirth.

Beyle handed him a large bowl of grits and gave him milk to drink, straight from the cow. One word led to another, and she was emboldened to ask him some questions. What did he do for a living? Did he have children? Where did he live?

He told her he had no children, that he lived on the other side of the Pilica River, that he made a good living, and that it was only through God's will that he remained a widower.

Beyle listened in silence. The red spots welled up on her cheeks. The dark-skinned Jew was staying overnight at the inn. Beyle slept in a tiny room elsewhere in the house. In the same little room, high on a ledge, hens were dreaming away. The door had no lock. Who needed one? What was there to steal?

Beyle was lying in bed, thinking about the dark-skinned Jew. She wanted to fall asleep, for she had to be up at dawn to milk the cows and to prepare breakfast for the passersby. But the Jew's black eyes kept her awake.

The hours slowly passed. Soon the sleeping hens would be stirring.

Just then Beyle became aware of something tickling her face. She could have sworn that a hen had slid from its perch and scratched her face with its leg or its wing.

"Shoo, shoo!" Beyle called out to the hen.

But suddenly it became obvious that this was no hen. The room was pitch-black. Nevertheless, Beyle could make out a pair of big, wide-open eyes looking at her.

She felt her heart constricting. A hot shudder rippled through her entire body. She knew instantly who it was.

"Reb Jew, what is this?" she asked in a very soft voice.

"What do you think?"

"What are you doing here, Reb Jew?"

"What should I be doing? Nothing. My wife—it shouldn't happen to us—has been taken from me."

"So you come crawling to strange women?"

"God forbid! Who said so? Only that . . ."

His hands burned even hotter than his eyes.

Again, Beyle said softly, "Please, Reb Jew, leave."

"Why? I don't mean any harm, Beyleshi. God forbid!" He called her Beyleshi . . .

"What kind of Beyleshi am I to you?"

"If you love someone, you stretch out the name."

"Since when do you love me?"

"From the very first moment I laid eyes on you."

"And are you ready to set up the wedding canopy?"

"Why not? We can do that, too."

"When?"

"Soon."

There was a sudden tumult in the tiny room. The hens, shaken from their dreaming, began to flap their wings and flew onto Beyle's and the dark Jew's heads. Beyle leaped up, slapped him across the face, yanked open the wooden door, and screamed out into the night.

"You fornicator! You should rot in hell! Is this what you want from me!?"

Lamps were quickly lit throughout the inn. Jews in feather-strewn caps hastily performed the morning ritual of the washing of the hands. Women in nightcaps, coats thrown over their shoulders, ran out barefoot.

"Woe is me," they cried, pinching their cheeks. "And a Jew, yet! Whoever heard of such a thing . . ."

The noise woke up the children, who started to cry. A dog barked furiously. The black-bearded Jew with the burning eyes vanished into the night, leaving behind his hooded coat.

Beyle sent the garment home to her father with Yarme the coachman. He would have something to wear for the winter as he made his rounds of the villages.

Yarme the coachman told everybody the whole story, from beginning to end. Beyle herself had asked him to do so. She wanted everybody back home to know that, even though she often stayed away overnight, she would never shame her father in his old age.

In fact, she never did. When the time came, she married in accordance with the laws of Moses and Israel.

Beyle was her own matchmaker. The man she married was also a widower, but not dark-skinned and with no burning eyes, like that person at the inn. He was a big, strapping man with a thick blond beard like the Russian Tsar's, Alexander III. [. . .]

Beyle and her husband lived on the outskirts of town, far away, almost at the edge of Skarszew. At night the winds howled across Beyle's roof. Wagons rumbled past, coming and going to and from town. The driver's shouts could be heard through the windows. Beyle cooked large pots of grits for herself and her husband. For the Sabbath she prepared the special *tsholent* with derma.

Her husband Wolf drove his horse and wagon to the fairs and markets. In between trips he shod horses. They eked out a living, they managed. And every year, in the middle of the night, you could hear the cries of the new being that Beyle had brought into the world.

The more children they had, the harder it became to support them. Beyle rented out an alcove and began baking poppy-seed rolls for sale to young wagon-drivers. But she never complained. After all, this is what she wanted.

Sometimes, when Beyle came by to wish us a happy holiday, Mother would ask her how she was getting on. Once Beyle let slip that, when all the children were asleep, her mind sometimes turned to the dark-skinned Jew with the burning eyes. She could still visualize the scene. She didn't know what to make of it. But after a night of such recollection, she could barely feel her heart beating. Everything went wrong. The grits failed. The young wagon-drivers turned up their noses at the poppy-seed rolls. She quarreled with the woman who rented the alcove.

Translated by Maier Deshell and Margaret Birstein.

Other works by Perle: *Nayn a zeyger in der fri* (1920); *Yidn fun a gants yor* (1937); *Khurbn Varshe* (1942/1952).

Isaac Bashevis Singer

Satan in Goray
1935

Part I

6. REB MORDECAI JOSEPH

It was Rabbi Benish's practice to say his afternoon and evening prayers by himself in his study. When the news reached his ears he hurried to the prayer house. But it was already empty. Everyone had hurried home after the legate's sermon to discuss the news in the midst of the family. A few people accompanied the legate to the inn; others went to the house of Reb Mordecai Joseph. They had to rub Mordecai Joseph with snow for a long time, to prick him with needles and pinch him hard before he was himself again. On his broken bench bed he lay, dressed in all his garments; leaning back on both elbows, he related that in his trance Sabbatai Zevi had come to him and cried: "Mordecai Joseph, the son of Chanina the Priest, be not of humble heart! Thou shalt yet offer up the priestly sacrifices!" Men and women jostled one another in the narrow, unfloored room; there was no candle, and Mordecai Joseph's wife heaped several dry twigs on the tripod and lit them. The flame crackled and hissed, red shadows danced on the irregular whitewashed walls, and the rafters loomed low. In a corner, on a pile of rags, sat Mordecai Joseph's only daughter, a monstrosity with a water-swollen head

and calf's eyes. Mordecai Joseph's wet beard shone in the reflection of the glowing coals like molten gold, and his green eyeballs burned like a wolf's as he divulged the mysteries he had seen in his trance. His cadence was that of a dying man speaking his last words to those nearest him.

"A great light shall descend on the world! Thousands and thousands times greater than the sun! It shall blind the eyes of the wicked and the scoffers! Only the chosen shall escape!"

That night Rabbi Benish could not sleep.

The shutters were barred, and thick candles burned in the two bent brass candlesticks. The old man paced back and forth with heavy tread, stopping from time to time to cock his ears, as though listening for a scratching in the walls. The wind tore at the roof, and sighed. Branches crackled with the frost, the long-drawn-out howls of dogs filled the air. There was silence and then the howling began again. Rabbi Benish took book after book out of the chest, studied their titles and leafed through the pages searching for omens of the coming of the Messiah. His high forehead wrinkled, for the passages were contradictory. From time to time Rabbi Benish would sit down at the table and press a key to his forehead so as not to doze off; nevertheless, he would soon be snoring heavily. Then he would lift his head up with a start, a crooked mark between his eyes. He paced back and forth, running into objects in dark corners, and his magnified shadow crept along the rafters, slid along the walls, and quivered as though engaged in a ghostly wrangle. Although the oven was glowing, a cold breeze stirred in the room. In the early morning, when Grunam the Beadle came to put more wood in the oven, Rabbi Benish looked at him as though he were a stranger.

"Go, bring the legate to me!" he commanded.

The legate was still sleeping in the inn, and Grunam had to waken him. It was early, and stars were still sparkling in the sky. Handfuls of dry salt-like snow fell across their faces. Rabbi Benish put on his outercoat and stepped over the threshold of the house to welcome the legate; putting up his beaver collar and crossing his arms, he thrust his hands up his sleeves. It was bitter cold and Rabbi Benish kept turning around, stamping his feet to keep warm. Somewhere from behind the snow hills, as huge as sand dunes, a man rose into view, windblown, dipped out of sight, and then emerged again, like a swimmer. Rabbi Benish glanced at the early morning sky. Fixing his gaze inwardly, he cried, "Master of the Universe, help us!"

No one ever learned what Rabbi Benish said that morning, nor what the legate replied. But one thing soon became common knowledge: the legate rode away with no farewells from Goray, in the same sleigh in which he had arrived. It was late afternoon when the news spread that the legate had disappeared. It was Grunam the Beadle who imparted the information, with a stealthy smile in his left eye. Reb Mordecai Joseph blanched. He gathered immediately who was responsible for the legate's departure, and his nostrils dilated with anger.

"Benish is to blame!" he screamed, and lifted his crutch threateningly. "Benish has driven him off!"

For many years Reb Mordecai Joseph had been the rabbi's enemy. He hated him for his learning, envied him his fame, and never missed an opportunity to speak evil of him. At the yearly Passover wrangle he would incite the people to break Rabbi Benish's windowpanes, crying that the rabbi had only his own reputation in mind and gave no thought to the town. The thing that chiefly vexed Reb Mordecai Joseph was that Rabbi Benish forbade the study of the cabala; in defiance Reb Mordecai Joseph called the rabbi by his first name. And now Reb Mordecai Joseph hammered on his lectern, inciting controversy.

"Benish is a heretic!" he shouted. "A transgressor against the Lord of Israel!"

An old householder who was one of the rabbi's disciples ran over to Mordecai Joseph and struck him twice. The blood streamed from Mordecai Joseph's nose. Several young people jumped up and grabbed their belts. The cantor pounded on the stand, and commanded them not to interrupt the prayers, but he was ignored. Men wearing the large black phylacteries on their heads, and with the broad phylactery thongs wound around their arms, milled about, pushing one another. A tall, black-complexioned man, whose head almost reached the ceiling, began to waver like a tree in the wind, and cried: "Sacrilege! Blood in the study house! Woe!"

"Benish is a heretic!" roared Mordecai Joseph.

Holding on to his crutch he bent over and hopped forward with insane speed.

"May he be torn from the earth . . . root and all!"

Drops of blood shimmered on his fire-red beard; his low forehead, parchment-yellow, was furrowed. Reb Senderel of Zhilkov, an ancient foe of the rabbi, suddenly screamed: "Rabbi Benish cannot oppose the world! He has always been a man of little faith!"

"Apostate!" someone shouted, it was hard to tell whether referring to the rabbi or his opponents.

"Disrupter!"

"Sinner that leadeth the multitude to sin!"

"The world's aflame!" Mordecai Joseph kept pounding with his fists. "Benish, the dog, denies the Messiah!"

"Sabbatai Zevi is a false Messiah!" a high, boyish voice cried out.

Everyone looked around. It was Chanina, the charity scholar, a young divorced man and a stranger, who sat in Goray studying and lived off the community. He was one of Rabbi Benish's brilliant students—tall, overgrown, nearsighted, with a long, pale face and a chin sprouting with yellow hair. His coat was always unfastened, his vest open, showing a thin, hairy chest. Now he stood there, bent over his study stand, his near-blind eyes blinking, waiting with a silly smile for someone to come and argue with him, so that he could show how learned he was. Mordecai Joseph, who bore Chanina a grudge on account of the many folios of the Talmud he knew by heart and because he was always mixing in where he had no right, suddenly sprang at Chanina with that agility the lame display when they flare up and forget their defect.

"You, too!" he screamed. "Take him, men!"

Several young men ran over to Chanina, grabbed hold of his shirt and began to drag him off. Chanina opened his mouth, shouted, tried to tear himself loose from their grip, twisted his long neck back and forth, and flailed about him with his arms, like a drowning man. His coat was torn, his skull cap fell off. Two long, tousled earlocks dangled from his shaven scalp. He tried to defend himself, but the charity students were quick to hold his head, punching him with their weak hands as they helped carry him, as though they were kneading dough. Mordecai Joseph himself proudly helped carry Chanina by the legs, spitting into his face and pinching him viciously. Soon Chanina was lying on the table. They lifted his coat tail. Mordecai Joseph was the first to do the honors.

"Let this be in place of me!" he cried, in the words of the Yom Kippur scapegoat ritual. He rolled up his sleeves, and gave Chanina so hard a blow that the unlucky youth burst all at once into tears, like a school boy, and whimpered.

"Let this be instead of me!" Mordecai Joseph exclaimed with a sigh and again struck Chanina.

"Let this fowl go to his death!" someone cried responsively, and a hail of blows fell on the idle scholar. Chanina gave a hoarse cry and began to gasp.

When they took him from the table, his face was blue and his mouth clenched. A boy immediately fetched a vessel of water and poured it over Chanina, drenching him from head to foot. The young man jerked spasmodically and remained full length on the ground. There was a terrified silence in the study house. The one woman who happened to be in the women's gallery pulled at the grate and sobbed. Mordecai Joseph limped back, beating the floor with his crutch, and his face behind the thicket of his beard was chalk-white.

"Thus rotteth the name of the wicked!" he said. "Now he shall know that there is a God who rules the world!" [. . .]

9. Reb Itche Mates, the Packman

A packman came to Goray with a full sack of holy scripts and fringed vests, phylacteries and skull caps for pregnant women and oval bone amulets for children, mezuzahs and prayer sashes. Packmen are notoriously short-tempered and suffer no one to touch their merchandise who is disinclined to purchase. Gingerly, one at a time, the young men approached the packman, stared curiously at the store of goods which he spread out on the table, ran their fingers along the books, and turned the leaves with silent caution, so as not to arouse his wrath. But apparently this was a courteous packman. Putting his hands up his sleeves, he allowed the boys to riffle through the books as much as they pleased. A packman comes from the great world, and usually brings with him all sorts of news. People sidled over to him and asked: "What do they call you, stranger?"

"Itche Mates."

"Well, Reb Itche Mates, what's happening in the world?"

"Praised be God."

"Is there talk of help for the Jews?"

"Certainly, everywhere, blessed be God."

"Perhaps you have letters with you and tracts, Reb Itche Mates?"

Reb Itche Mates said nothing, as though he hadn't heard, and they understood at once that these were matters one did not discuss openly. So, murmuring under their breath, they said, "Are you staying here awhile, Reb Itche Mates?"

He was a short man, with a round, straw-colored beard, and appeared to be about forty years old. His dilapidated hat, from which large patches of fur were missing, was pulled down over his damp, rheumy eyes; his thin nose was red with catarrh. He was wearing a long patched coat which reached to the ground. A red kerchief was wound about his loins. The young men rummaged through his books, ripping the uncut pages, and doing all sorts of damage, but the packman made no objection. Mischievous boys played with the embroidered fringed vests and tried on the gilded skull caps. They even dug down deep in the packman's sack and discovered a Book of Esther scroll cased in a wooden tube, a ram's horn, and a small bag containing white, chalky soil from the Land of Israel. Very few people bought, everyone handled the merchandise and seemed to be conspiring to enrage the packman. But he stood woodenly in front of his goods. When they recited the Holy, Holy, Holy, his straw mustaches quivered almost imperceptibly. When asked anything's price he capped his hand to his ear as though he were hard of hearing, thought for a long time, avoiding his questioner's face.

"What does it matter?" he would finally say in a low hoarse voice. "Give as much as you can." And he extended a tin coin box, as though he wasn't really a packman but was collecting money for some holy purpose.

Levi, the rabbi's son, invited him for supper, for in his controversy with his father Levi lent his silent support to the Sabbatai Zevi sect. Gathered together were members of the inner circle; all the cabalists apparently sensed that the packman had something of interest to tell. Reb Mordecai Joseph, Rabbi Benish's foe, was amongst them. Nechele, Levi's wife, closed the shutters and stuffed the keyhole so that Ozer's children would not be able to carry on their customary spying. Everyone sat around the table. Nechele offered them onion flatcakes, and set drinks on the table. Reb Itche Mates took only a morsel of bread, which he swallowed whole, but he bade those about him to feast their fill and drink hearty. Perceiving at once that Reb Itche Mates was one of the chosen, they did as he bade. Their foreheads became moist, and their eyes shone with the hope of great times to come. Reb Itche Mates unbuttoned his jacket and drew from the inner pocket a letter written on parchment in Aramaic, in a scribe's script, and with crownlets on the letters like a Torah scroll. The letter was from Abraham Ha-ychini and Samuel Primo, who resided in the Land of Israel. Hundreds of rabbis had put their signatures to this letter, most of them Sephardim with exotic names reminiscent of the Talmudic masters. It became so quiet that Ozer's boys, who were lurking outside the door, heard not even a whisper. The wick in the shard crackled and sputtered, long shadows trembled on the walls, shook back and forth, merged. The well-born Nechele stood beside the oven where she burnt kindling. Her thin cheeks were flaming hot; she glanced sidelong at the men, and absorbed every word.

Reb Itche Mates sat hunched up, speaking almost in a whisper, divulging mysteries of mysteries: only a few holy sparks still burned among the husks of being. The powers of darkness clung to these, knowing that their existence depended on them. Sabbatai Zevi, God's ally, was battling these powers; it was he who was conducting the sacred sparks back to their primal source. The holy kingdom would be revealed when the last spark was returned whence it had come. Then the ritual ceremonies would no longer hold. Bodies would become pure spirit. From the World of Emanations and from under the Throne of Glory new souls would descend. There would be no more eating and drinking. Instead of being fruitful and multiplying, beings would unite in combinations of holy letters. The Talmud wouldn't be studied. Of the Bible only the secret essence would remain. Each day would last a year, and the radiance of the holy spirit would fill all space. Cherubim and Ophanim would chant the praise of the Almighty and He Himself would instruct the righteous. Their delight would be boundless.

Reb Itche Mates' speech abounded in homilies and parables from the Torah and Midrash. He was familiar with the names of angels and seraphim, and quoted at length passages from the Book of Transmigrations and Raziel; all the mansions in heaven were known to him, every detail of the supreme hierarchy. There could be no doubt that here was a most holy, truly one of the elect. The decision was that all should keep silent and that Itche Mates should spend the night at the home of Reb Godel Chasid, who sat opposite. In the morning they would see what was to be done. Reb Godel Chasid took the packman by the hand and led him to his house. He offered him his own bed, but Reb Itche Mates preferred to sleep on the bench near the oven. Reb Godel Chasid gave his guest a sheepskin cover and a pillow and retired to the alcove that served as his bedroom. But he could not sleep. All night long there came from behind the stove a bee-like drone. Reb Itche Mates was busy at Torah and, although there was no window in the room, he was surrounded by light as though the moon shone upon him. Before daybreak Reb Itche Mates rose, poured water on his hands, and sought to steal away to the study house. But Reb Godel Chasid had not undressed. He took Reb Itche Mates by the arm

and whispered confidentially, "I saw everything, Reb Itche Mates."

"Ah but what was there to see?" murmured Reb Itche Mates, bowing his head. "'Silence is seemly for the wise.'"

In the study house Reb Itche Mates spread out his wares and again waited for buyers. After the morning prayers he set his sack in a corner and went from house to house through Goray, examining the mezuzahs, as is the way of packmen, who are generally scribes as well. Whenever he found an error in a mezuzah, he corrected it on the spot with a goose quill, accepted a penny from the householder, and left.

So it went until he came to Rechele's house. The mezuzah on Rechele's doorpost was an old one, covered with a white mold. Reb Itche Mates took a tong from his pocket, pulled out the nails that held the sign to the lintel, unrolled the scroll, and went over to the window for light in which to see whether any of the letters had blurred. It turned out that the word God had been completely erased, and that the right crown was missing from the letter "s" of the name Shaddai. His hands began to tremble, and he said with sternness, "Who lives here?"

"My father lives here—Reb Eleazar Babad," replied Rechele.

"Reb Eleazar Babad," said Reb Itche Mates, and he rubbed his forehead as though attempting to recall something. "Isn't he the head of the community?"

"No longer," Rechele said. "Now he's a rag picker." And she burst into high-pitched laughter.

That a Jewish girl should laugh so unrestrainedly was something new to Reb Itche Mates, and he glanced at her out of the corner of his wide-set eyes, browless and cool green, like those of a fish. Rechele's long braids were undone, like a witch's, full of feathers and straw. One half of her face was red, as though she had been lying on it, the other half was white. She was barefoot, and wore a torn red dress, through which parts of her body shone. In her left hand she held an earthen pot, in her right a straw whisk with ashes in it. Through her disheveled hair a pair of frantic eyes smiled madly at him. It occurred to Itche Mates that there was more here than met the eye.

"Are you a married woman, or a maiden?"

"A maiden," answered Rechele brazenly. "Like Jeptha's daughter, a sacrifice to God!"

The mezuzah fell out of Reb Itche Mates' hand. Never in his whole life, not since he had first stood on his feet, had he heard such talk. His flesh crawled as though he had been touched by icy fingers. He wanted to run away from such sacrilege, but then it came to him that this would not be right. So he sat down on a box and took out a ruler and a bottle of ink. He sharpened his goose quill with a piece of glass, dipped it in the ink, and—wiped it again on his skull cap.

"These are not proper things to say," he told Rechele after some hesitation. "The Blessed Name does not require human sacrifices. A Jewish girl should have a husband and heed the Law."

"Nobody wants me!" Rechele said, and limped so close to him that the female smell of her body overcame him. "Unless Satan will have me!"

She burst into sharp laughter which ended in a gasp. Large gleaming tears fell from her eyes. The pot slipped from her hands and broke into shards. Reb Itche Mates sought to reply, but his tongue had become heavy and dry. The cupboard, the walls, the floor swayed. He began to write, but his hand shook and a drop of ink blotted the parchment. So Reb Itche Mates lowered his head, wrinkled his forehead, and suddenly grasped the secret. For a while, he studied his pale fingernails, and then he muttered to himself:

"This is from Heaven." [. . .]

Part 2

6. A Wedding on a Dung-Hill

Reb Mordecai Joseph and Reb Itche Mates departed, and their wanderings took them to far places, bearing the good tidings. In Goray some believed that they had already passed the Polish borders and were now somewhere in Germany, or Bohemia. Others thought that the emissaries had embarked for Stamboul to see the Messiah. Now the affairs of Goray town were managed by Reb Gedaliya. His new rulings disagreed with the practices cited in the Shulchan Aruch, but the few learned men who remained pretended neither to see nor hear what was happening, for the common people believed in Reb Gedaliya. As for Reb Gedaliya, he settled Rechele in his house, and he lived with her under one roof although she was a matron. He had a room painted white for her, and he hung the walls with guardian amulets, and placed a Holy Ark and Torah there. Rechele was dressed in white satin; her face was hidden by a veil. During the week she could be seen by no one except Chinkele the Pious who served her. But on the Sabbath ten women from the sect gathered in her room to make a prayer quorum, as though they were men—for thus Reb Gedaliya had bidden. A woman cantor stood before the lectern chanting the Sabbath prayers. Then the scroll was taken from the Ark and Reb Gedaliya chanted the proper melody. Moreover, he permitted seven women to be called up to the lectern to read for the Sabbath, and after each reading he ordered a benediction of thanks to be offered in the name of Sabbatai Zevi and Rechele the prophetess.

His was a great name in Goray and in all of the surrounding countryside. Housewives gave him a tithe of their chickens, eggs, butter, and honey. A special poll tax had been laid by him on the rich. From every calf he slaughtered he put aside for himself not only the tripe and the milt, as the custom is, but all of the under-parts as well—these he cleaned, though it is not the practice to do so nowadays. He did not need these for himself, no, not Reb Gedaliya—but for the poor and hungry. Sabbath afternoons he held the midday feast in the study house, and every household sent him pudding, seasoned according to his taste. Men and women sat at the table on benches, or clustered about it, and Reb Gedaliya sang new Sabbath hymns, served portions of calf's foot jelly himself, and gave each person a cup of wine. The wine was red and smelled of ginger, onycha, and saffron. Reb Gedaliya hinted that it tasted like the wine reserved for the righteous to drink in the Garden of Eden.

Remarkable things were done by Reb Gedaliya, and his kindness was renowned. He was extremely charitable and would rise from bed in the middle of night to tend to the sick. Though an important man, he would roll up his sleeves when it was necessary, to massage men and women alike with aqua vitae and turpentine. He jested with the ill, forcing them to laugh and forget their pains. For children he imitated the mooing of cows and the twittering of birds. Stammerers began to speak properly under his guidance. The melancholy laughed heartily after he had spent some time with them. Adept at sleight of hand and hocus-pocus, he could turn a kerchief into a hare. His elbows bound with a sash, he would blow, freeing them once more—and then produce the sash from beneath the shirt of the person who had bound him! An expert at solving complex puzzles, he could write a row of words that might be read from top to bottom as well as the usual Hebrew right to left. He showed housewives who came to visit him how to put up new kinds of preserves, taught girls how to work on canvas and embroider. In the late afternoon he bathed in the river and instructed the young men how to swim and tread water. Afterward they all said their afternoon prayers at the riverbank, under the open sky. Once, when in good spirits, he gathered a few lusty young fellows who were boarding at their in-laws and went to the other side of the hill to scare the women bathing there. Chaos ensued. The more agile women sprang screaming into the water. Those who were large and slow-moving were so confused that they remained transfixed. Uncovered before the eyes of the men, they were publicly shamed. There was much jesting and frivolity that evening. Nevertheless, this was not taken amiss in Reb Gedaliya, for he was already known for his unconventional ways. Only a few hidden foes spoke out against him, with no attempt to disguise their irritation.

They whispered unpleasant things about him. They said that since becoming the slaughterer of Goray he had never once found any beast to be unclean and unfit to be eaten—this in order to win the favor of the butchers. Whenever the question arose, he ruled the beast clean, and he had abandoned all the laws of purity. He permitted the women to go to the bathhouse and then to bed with their husbands soon after menstruation; according to him, they did not have to keep the additional seven days of abstinence. He explained to young matrons ways to enflame their husbands, and whispered in their ears that, ever since Sabbatai Zevi had been revealed, the commandment against adultery was void. It was rumored that young men were exchanging wives, and everyone knew that Nechele, the wife of Levi, received men in her house and sat up past midnight with them, singing prurient songs. A servant girl who had been sent to look through the keyhole was said to have seen Nechele unhooking her blouse and offering the visitors her breasts to press and the nipples to be kissed. Of Levi it was said that he had forced Glicke, his brother Ozer's daughter, to lie with him, and that he had paid Ozer three Polish gold coins as requital money, that the sin might not be discovered. The young men who studied together in the study house were up to all kinds of evil. They would climb into the women's gallery in the middle of the day, committing pederasty with one another, and sodomy—with the goats. Evenings they went to the bathhouse and, through a hole they had bored in the wall, watched the women purifying themselves. Other young scholars even went off to observe the women tending to their bodily needs. . . .

There were few old householders in Goray, and no one heeded their grumbling. Reb Gedaliya bribed some with rich gifts. Others were warned that, if they rebelled against his rule, he would place them under a ban, or have them arrested and bound to the post in the study house anteroom. He also presented himself before the lord of Goray; speaking a fluent Polish, he gained the lord's promise to take him under his protection and punish those who tried to overthrow him.

Goray, that small town at the edge of the world, was altered. No one recognized it any longer.

Ever since the advent of Reb Gedaliya and since the miracle of the prophetess, the town had prospered. From Yanov, Bilgoray, Krasnistav, Turbin, Tishevitz, and other settlements, people came to visit the holy pair. The water in which Rechele washed her body had restoring powers, Reb Gedaliya proclaimed, and a barrel of it stood in the anteroom of his house. The dispirited who wandered from place to place in search of a cure came to Goray. They gathered before the porch of Reb Gedaliya's house: young women whose hiccuping was like the barking of dogs; barren women who yearned for a blessing that might unlock their wombs; monstrosities, with reptile outlines on their bodies; paralytics and epileptics. Chinkele the Pious stood at the door and let them in one by one. Many of the visitors had to wait at the Goray inns for a long time before being admitted to Reb Gedaliya's house, so they might receive from him amulets and pieces of magical amber and salves to be smeared on the disturbed part of the body and pills to be swallowed. He licked the faces of sickly children, massaged arthritic women, and had them spend the night in his house. Daily the number who came to the miracle worker increased. They shopped in Goray, and slept on the bare floor in the homes of the townsfolk, avidly listening to the amazing tales concerning Rechele the prophetess. Everywhere, they sat on benches in front of the houses. Their kerchiefs were pulled down over their eyes; their hands clutched baskets of food; between their breasts hung pouches containing the copper coins that were to buy them health. The young were bashful, and would say nothing. But the older women knitted stockings and recounted with relish their sicknesses and the cures they had been given by various magicians and miracle workers. Those whose menstrual flow had stopped prematurely were advised to eat the foreskin of a circumcised infant. Those who wished to please their husbands were told to have their men drink the water in which their breasts had been washed; those with the falling sickness were told to cut the nails of their hands and feet and have the nails kneaded into a lump of dough and thrown to a dog. At times older women would tease the young barren ones, shocking them with their lewd talk.

And then, finally, men also began to arrive in the town. There were beggars and vagabonds; there were ascetics, and there were husbands trying to get the signatures of a hundred rabbis for a writ of remarriage; a yeshiva student was seeking a master to teach him cabala; a penitent was tormenting himself by putting peas in his shoes. A convert from Amsterdam also came, a man who had taken a vow of silence as well as a bandsman who walked around blindfolded, so as not to perceive women, and a barefoot jester who asked for alms and recited obscene rhymes. These lived by begging from the pilgrims, slept in the poorhouse or, when that was full, any corner they could find. Evil often transpired secretly. Once two wandering beggars who had come to Goray decided to marry, and married they were by some mischief makers on a dung-hill.

Translated by Jacob Sloan.

Nehemiah Levinsky

1901–1957

Not much is known about the South African Yiddish writer Nehemiah Levinsky. He lived in Bloemfontein and participated in the Yiddish cultural life of the town, even attempting to publish a Yiddish journal there in the 1930s. He was not a prolific writer. His stories were collected in a posthumously published volume *Der regn hot farshpetikt* (1959). The focus of his writing was the interplay between immigrant Jews and South African blacks and the poisonous impact of segregation on everyone.

Changed His Name
ca. 1935

Johannes pushed his cart laden with fruit and vegetables. He pushed with difficulty for his route lay uphill. Automobiles rushed past him, hooting insolently, demanding the road. Awkwardly he turned his cart aside to allow the empty cars to travel up the hill. They flew wildly past, leaving clouds of yellow dust behind them.

Johannes had chosen a hard way of earning a living: in the morning before sunrise he would leave his home, pushing his little cart to the market. There were days when he would buy his fruit and vegetables quickly and, laden, would set off to take his goods to his customers. But there were also days when he could buy nothing at the market, and he had to go to the wholesalers. There he had to pay more and wait until someone glanced at him. There he had to stand to one side and wait until they had loaded the heavy trucks. The big customers did not have to ask to be helped or to be allocated a box of apples, a few sacks of oranges and some vegetables. He, Johannes, had to load himself and be thankful for everything given him, and all because of his name—Mokatlane, the name of a black man, which in his birthplace meant to plough, to sow, to dig and to build. There, all were human beings, those whose bodies were black, brown, tan, almost yellowish, like Johannes. Even light-brown, just like the owner of the café past which he was now dragging his little cart. There in the café stood a white man who, Johannes often thought, was not much whiter than himself: the same yellow-brown skin and black eyes, thick lips and even crinkly hair. But his name sounded different and he found himself numbered among those lucky ones who have everything, who are blessed with the choicest that our land has to offer. He, Mokatlane, had to sweat pushing his little cart and struggle to seek out his buyers. The other, the white man, stood in the beautifully clean, cheerful shop and awaited his customers.

Mokatlane heaved a heavy sigh. When he reached the top of the rise, he stopped to catch his breath. He straightened himself and wiped the sweat from his face. Here a light breeze blew which caressed and cooled his brow. After a few seconds' rest he started pushing his cart again. Here, near the café, he was not allowed to set himself up: the police had warned him several times that he was not permitted to trade in its vicinity. In the past he had a few customers, two doors away from the shop, who used to buy fruit from him. The owner of the café had reported him to the police, and since then he no longer called at that house.

. . . He pushes his cart on. He is travelling downhill, so he has to hold it back, braking it so that it does not topple over from the impetus. He sweats and pants. In the middle of the road, a white woman stops him. She buys a few shillings' worth of vegetables, having previously examined every bundle thoroughly; she weighs a head of cabbage in her hand and rummages for a heavier one; she selects several large bananas and pays for everything. Johannes tries to persuade her to buy more but she refuses, shaking her head. When she leaves, he counts the money, takes out two pennies and puts them in a little purse hanging from a string round his neck. This is money he is saving. In the days when he carried his fruit around in two big baskets, he used to save his pennies to buy a pushcart. Now that he has the cart, it is more difficult for him to save because he is married. His Jenny is a light-brown girl with thin lips and a narrow nose. Before her marriage she used to work in a clothing factory; now she helps to maintain the household by doing washing for white people. It is hard work. She is fortunate that her old mother looks after the four children who were born during the six years of her marriage. The eldest is now five years old and looks like his mother, but has a lighter skin . . .

In a flash a big truck roared past him and stopped suddenly with a screech and grating of brakes. Johannes saw how a small boy, unaware of the vehicle, chased after his ball and barely escaped from under the wheels. His heart thumped heavily with fright and then relief as the child got away unhurt. His Jimmy looked just like that and the same thing might have happened to him. Jimmy also played with a ball all day in the street. He pushed his cart more vigorously, as if to push away evil thoughts. When Jimmy turned six, he would send him to school. There he would not be in danger from speeding motor-vehicles; there he would become educated and have a better future than his father. Several customers stopped him, handled his goods and haggled briskly, and although he sold his goods far more cheaply than usual, he did not forget to deduct the pennies towards his son's education. In this way he went from street to street, stopped before houses at which he had customers, went into the back yards and knocked at the back doors. In some houses the black maid or cook would offer him a pot of tea or give him something to eat. Seldom did any of the white housewives speak to him or show any interest in his family. Often he would buy old clothing and shoes for his children from his customers. Once or twice a housewife made him a gift of an old garment. And late in the evening he would reach home with his half-empty cart.

In a remote lane of the big city stood the old building whose sagging, flat roof, made of corrugated iron and held down by rocks, looked like a cankered mound covered in giant warts. The windows peered out of broken frames with panes which wore huge cardboard patches, like cataracts on sightless eyes. It was in this building that Johannes had his home—a room as small and crowded as

a matchbox. There he lived with his wife, four children and Jenny's mother. Since the room was too small for everyone, they spent the greater part of the day outside. His wife and mother-in-law used to sit on a step at dusk and, by the glow of a nearby streetlight, patch old clothing. All four children lived in the street, played and fought with crowds of other dirty, tattered youngsters.

His children always met Johannes with a joyful clamour and with shining eyes, groping for fruit with their little hands. Johannes always had fruit for his children: somewhat damaged, it was true, but still better than that which the other children received. The neighbouring children would surround the cart, hoping to get a rotten pear or apple. Johannes would always distribute some; the rest he would put into bags and take up to the room.

After washing and eating, Johannes would sit down to count the day's takings. Presently he counted the savings in the little bag: "Only two shillings and six pennies." He would sadly shake his head, but soon added, turning to his wife, "Never mind, little by little I'll save up enough to buy the boy new clothes and schoolbooks." And as if to confirm his words, he would lift his ragged little urchin high into the air and announce proudly, as if he were stating a fact, "That's how tall you'll be, Jimmy, and you'll be an educated man." Jimmy liked being lifted like this and he shrieked loudly, "Let me ride on you, Daddy." Johannes shook his head. "Educated boys don't ride on people," he said. "If you do well at school, you'll get a bicycle to ride." Father and son were both overjoyed at the prospect.

The year passed. The school term started. Johannes rose very early that morning, washed, put on a clean shirt and dressed Jimmy in his new clothes. After breakfast he took his son by the hand, sat him in the delivery cart, and took him off to a school for coloured children. In the school yard there were already many mothers and fathers waiting for the principal of the school to register their children. Johannes patiently prepared to wait. When his turn came, he went with Jimmy to the office and asked the teacher to enrol his son as a pupil. The teacher cast a sympathetic glance at father and son, pulled out a printed form from a drawer and asked Johannes whether he could fill in the answers. Johannes replied shyly that all he had learnt was to count and add, but he could neither read nor write. The official took up his pen, ready to fill in the form for him.

"Your name, please," he asked.

"Johannes Mokatlane."

The teacher shook his head.

"We don't take any black children. Our school is only for coloureds."

"And what am I, then, and what's Jimmy?" Johannes asked. "Just look at us—we're almost white."

The teacher kept on repeating his name. "Mokatlane! No, this is not the name of a coloured. You'd better apply to a school for blacks—perhaps they will enrol your son."

Johannes wanted to argue and plead, but he soon realised that this would be of no avail; the teacher would not listen to him.

Deeply depressed, he went out into the road, sat his son back in the cart, and again pushed him through the city streets. Soon he came to a school for black children. But he turned his head away and resolutely pushed his cart in order to pass the place more quickly. He soon stopped, however, wheeled his cart round and entered the black school. Again he had a long wait until he got to the principal. This one only had to hear his request to tell him immediately that they had no place in their school for coloured children. "But I'm not coloured," a desperate Johannes protested, "my name is Johannes Mokatlane."

"Yes, that's a fine name for a black person," the teacher retorted, "but your son is almost white. He'll be unhappy in this school. Being half-white, he certainly won't fit in with our black children." Johannes again trundled out the cart in which Jimmy was sitting. That day's load seemed heavier to him than ever before. Late in the afternoon he brought Jimmy home.

2

When people sometimes told Hymie that he did not look Jewish he would smile with satisfaction. In his youth, his parents had given him a Jewish education: sent him to *cheder*, solemnised his *barmitzvah* in grand style, sent him regularly to synagogue services on Friday nights and Saturday mornings. All this, however, failed to make Hymie a good Jew. In the bank where he went to work as soon as he had matriculated, he found himself in a non-Jewish environment: the entire staff there was Gentile. He became friendly with some of them, started going with them to dances and other entertainments, played tennis and cricket with them and almost never came into contact with Jews. His parents called him Chaim; to his friends he was Kenneth. His father shrugged his shoulders when he heard this new name.

He explained to his son that he bore the name Chaim in memory of a pious grandfather, a deeply learned man. But his son countered that in the bank the name Chaim was a handicap. It was bad enough to have an outlandish surname like Babentchinsky. With two such Jewish names, one could get no promotion. So he stuck to the name Kenneth; only when his parents chatted about their son between themselves did he remain Chaim.

When Kenneth met Evelyn he became a guest in her home. He spent all his free time there. Evelyn was beautiful, slim, with a mane of black hair and blue eyes. He had met her at a dance and had immediately fallen in love with her. He thought of marriage, but not of the grief it would cause his parents. The girl, however, did not want to marry a Jew. She was an Aryan, brought up in the Roman Catholic faith, and devout. She told Kenneth openly that although she loved him and gladly went out with him, she would never renounce her religion and could therefore not marry him. Kenneth was deeply depressed by this declaration. His first thought was to tell her that he would change his faith and convert to Roman Catholicism. He did not say this, however, because he realised that a quick and easy change of persuasion would not satisfy Evelyn.

Months passed, and Kenneth still courted Evelyn, spent all his free time with her, and discussed their mutual problems. Eventually she consented to marry him on condition that their children would be brought up as Roman Catholics. Kenneth did not make a great display of their wedding: they went to the magistrate's office and took out a licence. Afterwards they gave a dinner in a good hotel to which they invited a few friends and acquaintances. Kenneth's parents did not attend.

For a few months the young couple lived in a small apartment. It was more convenient for them. They both worked—he in the bank, she as a stenographer. Some time later Kenneth bought a house. Evelyn gave up her job: she had decided to run the household. She saw to the furnishing, cleaned and polished, hung up pictures and curtains, and went to the market twice a week to buy fruit and vegetables.

One day, Johannes Mokatlane knocked at the kitchen door and offered his goods. Evelyn was satisfied with his prices, and asked him to come more regularly to save her the trips to the market. On one occasion she noticed how he deducted a few pennies from the money she paid him, and put them away in a special little purse which hung round his neck. She asked him why he did this.

"This is to pay for the studies of my eldest son. My Jimmy must be able to read and write and have better luck than his father."

And every time Johannes would come, he would have something to tell her. Once he came a day late. He apologised profusely for the delay: it was the result of his having tried to place his Jimmy in a school. They would not accept him in one school because he had the name of a black, and in a second because of his colour. He recounted this with tears in his eyes and waited to hear her response. Evelyn kept a long silence, not knowing what to say to him. Although born and bred in this country, she knew little of the hardships that her black and brown fellow-countrymen had to endure in order to get education. Suddenly she remembered:

"I'll speak to our parish priest—he'll surely be able to get Jimmy a place in a mission school."

Johannes joyfully thanked her, but soon, with accustomed doubt, he asked, "But, madam, surely there they only take in children of your religion?"

"Yes," Evelyn said, "but Jimmy is still young, and he will surely become a Catholic."

Johannes shook his head.

"My Jimmy," he said, "won't turn Catholic. We don't change our religion. Thanks, madam, for your kindness," and he pushed his cart out of the yard.

Some time later, Mokatlane came to Babentchinsky's yard cheerful and happy. Evelyn noticed this and wanted to know the reason for his good mood. Johannes took out of a pocket a folded page of the Government Gazette and gave it to her. On it were printed announcements of changes of name. Evelyn read:

"I, Johannes Mokatlane, a coloured dealer in fruit and vegetables, apply to the Government to change my name Mokatlane to the name of my father Matthew, who was a white man. I wish to change my present name because it sounds like the name of a black man, for which reason I cannot enrol my children in a school for coloureds. Secondly, because of his light complexion, my son will not be accepted in a school for blacks."

Evelyn looked at Mokatlane in astonishment. She glanced at the announcements again, and noticed the following:

"I, Kenneth (Chaim) Babentchinsky, a bank employee, wish to change my name to Bell, firstly because I do not belong to the Jewish community; secondly my wife is a Christian and my present name causes her unpleasantness."

Evelyn looked at the page of announcements and at the radiant Mokatlane, and turned red with agitation.

Translated by Woolf Levick and Joseph Sherman.

Sh. Horonczyk
1899–1939

The Yiddish novelist Sh. (Shimen) Horonczyk grew up in a Hasidic family in and around Kalisz, Poland, and lived in Łódź during World War I. In the 1930s he moved to France and Belgium, later settling in Warsaw. At the start of World War II, Horonczyk fled Warsaw and committed suicide in the town of Kałuszyn. Horonczyk's despondent writings about World War I characterize the decline of Polish Jewish values under the German occupation, and his works from the 1920s and 1930s realistically describe the dire situations of working-class Jews.

God's Trial
1936

I. Avraham-Yisroel, the Forest-Writer's Son Comes to Town

When the forest-writer Avraham-Yisroel moved from the woods into the city, he had his own wife, three daughters, and two sons. He also had some meager savings but had no idea about the kind of work he might undertake. In his youth, immediately after he married, Avraham-Yisroel longed powerfully for city life and to be a part of the Jewish community. He wanted to visit the Kotsker Rebbe, not by himself from the woods as an innkeeper, but with other Jews "in the multitude." He had been orphaned, and was full of sorrow and lonely in his wooden forest hut. However, he made a living and lived without envy. His young wife was happy and had no greater desires for herself. She was small and had a double hunchback, one hump in the front and the other in the back. Having very plain features as well, she had no use for city life. When her husband, with his longing for urban life, stared out the window beyond the forest to the market that led to the town, she understood what he meant and grudgingly spoke out:

"What don't you like about living here? You forget that you are already, may God spare you, a father.

We need a 'living,' and, without flour there are no dumplings!"

This short, inaccurate saying was a sincere recomposition of the lines "If there is no flour, there is no Torah." [. . .]

Now, eighteen years later, when forest life seemed to end and Avraham-Yisroel had to move to the city, the "dream-locale" no longer enticed him. It can be compared to someone who has lived his whole life in poverty and, in old age, becomes rich when he cannot enjoy his new-found riches. Or, it was like a barren woman who becomes prosperous on the doorstep of old age, when her breasts are already withering.

Avraham-Yisroel's faraway dream had already become "stale." The Kotsker Rebbe was no longer alive. He yearned for the abandoned forest, as if it were some relative. The narrow apartment in the city was always full of children's wailings and curses from the mother. Avraham-Yisroel had become a man burdened with many children. He had both boys and girls and . . . a little money saved. His beard was still brown, very slightly threaded with silver hair. He felt as lonely among the city people as he had among the trees in the forest. [. . .]

Raisel, Avraham-Yisroel's wife, had actually taken the move to the city quite differently. She had erased the eighteen years of living in the country from her memory, as if in one day. She immediately felt as comfortable as if she had never lived in the forest, but only in the city right from the beginning. She bought a pack of white wool right away and sat down by the wheel. She wanted to knit socks for "her man" for Yom Kippur. She knit many pairs, to last the whole year. When chatting with the womenfolk, she fit right in, as if she had always taken part in their chatter. Her voice resounded out of an open window as she joined in the choir of women singing out the holy words sung usually by Jewish children.

"Blessed be He, and Blessed be His Name, Amen!" Babbling on, they muttered, "In the merit of small children, merciful Father!"

Be that as it may, inside of her, the poisonous worm did not stop nagging. She had three daughters, and the oldest, Masha, was already seventeen years old. Masha, herself, had a small hunchback, a face with a red nose that was always moist, and a voice with a nasal drawl.

Her second daughter, Rana, was a glutton who ate straight out of the pots and was lazy. The whole day she sat like a "doll." She did absolutely nothing, and constantly fought with her sisters and told lies all day long. She didn't utter a word of truth. She had earned herself the nickname of "glutton-liar."

The third daughter, Hannah, the youngest at age fourteen, was crazy. Her one hand did not know what her other hand was doing. Her mouth did not know what it was saying, as long as it was "wagging." The two boys . . . forget it! One requires money for such daughters. Without money, no personable match will ever be found, and, he, Avraham-Yisroel, did not seem to care. As every day went by, his money dwindled and he, did he care? No way!

"For heaven's sake, Avraham-Yisroel! Why do you forgo everything and do nothing! We are eating up all our earnings. We will become beggars, it should happen to my enemies." With these words, his wife accosted him of an evening when he returned from the prayer house and sat down to browse a book by candlelight. She stands before him with her hands on her tightly bound, aproned stomach. She starts scratching her head quickly and nervously under her headscarf, out of a lack of patience.

She yells, "A person is a murderer to his own wife and children!"

"What do you want me to do? What work should I put my mind to?"

"A store!" Again, she screams out, repeating what she had said yesterday and the day before. [. . .]

2

The Sabbath passed by somberly. His wife had refused to give him a shirt for the Sabbath. He had always been accustomed to donning a clean shirt for the holy day.

"Go do some business. Go do something." She pushes him.

Avraham-Yisroel will not take her words seriously. However, for this specific reason, he had found work in a forge in the Kotsk district. Without having changed his shirt, he goes and sleeps in the prayer house, on the bench in his weekday shirt. However, this does not make him happy. No, he is not feeling any happiness at all. He is forced to eat at a strange Sabbath table, like a guest. This actually does not bother him as much as wearing a dirty shirt does. Nonetheless, the day must not pass without some kind of happy feeling. In the evening, the people who have been all day at prayer seem worn out, sitting around the prayer-house table. They are like melancholy horses standing around an empty corral. [. . .]

There were three eligible girls in the house. They were not pretty or accomplished. There were, besides those three, two sons in a yeshiva, somewhere. Those sons again had to stop eating from the charity of others ["essn teg"] and start taking care of themselves because they could not get any more care packages from home. Avraham-Yisroel was six years older and more fatigued than when he had emerged from the forest. He had no money, no means of maintaining the house.

9. Raisel's Life's Goal

A hard life had begun for Avraham-Yisroel's household. In the narrow, half-dark little store, near the marketplace in Shlomo-Yakov's house it was humid from the oils and salves. The girls continuously struck their elbows while serving customers and constantly got into each other's hair. They cursed and teased each other. It was tight and cluttered in the little store. With a careless move, a cup of varnish had spilled. In addition, a dipper of cod liver oil was turned over and then it was much ado about nothing! For Heaven's sake! The whole family worked in the little store, from morning until late at night, and, in order to make the Sabbath, they had to borrow from the store. Nonetheless, there was no money to pay the rent.

The landlord of their house was a nouveau-riche dealer in old clothes. He was short, stocky, and had a neatly trimmed, black-gray beard. He was topped off with a hat with a glossy band around it and bore a lacquered visor. Since he had become rich and had bought this house, he would walk with mincing steps as if he were walking on soft eggs. The landlord always came of an evening when Avraham-Yisroel was at home; not having been invited in, he nevertheless spread himself out in a chair by the table and turned with a boorish smile.

"Reb Avraham-Yisroel Hassid, you do know what the holy Torah, it should have long life, says when one does not pay the rent on time?" [. . .]

She, Raisel, looked yellow like a lemon, skinny and dried out, like a three-year-old esrog. She was now only a hunchback. From the front and the back, her two humps had grown. They got higher, and she, in that same measure, got more bent-over and smaller. The only thing that kept her alive at this point was not con-

cern for her husband and children. What kept her alive now, giving her strength and energy and "feeding" her, as oil feeds fire, was nothing other than hatred. Hatred toward Meir Rafalovitch's house in which she had the fervent hope to live long enough to gain revenge on him. [. . .]

Many years passed. The store expanded and became a hardware business, with oils and paints. Time moved on. Middle-aged people moved into old age. The old died. Different new things came up in the world and in the village. However, the family's hatred of Rafalovitch and their longing for revenge did not lessen, not by a hair's breadth. At every meal Hannah would spout her curses. Her mother answered with some religious counter-curse, like a silent prayer. Masha became a bride. A match was formulated for her, not for the family's sake.

Raisel remembered well and did not forget for a moment that the household had been broken because of Rafalovitch. They had not been able to make a required match for Hannah at the time. The youngest daughter, Hannah, had to marry a widower. Hatred again flamed up with every look at the groom and thereafter at the son-in-law's blind-cataracted eye. It flamed at his deafness, his stammering, and his inability to contribute to Torah conversations. She had not wanted to marry him, crying, and once even throwing a chair, thereby expressing her protest. Nonetheless, she married the widower. Added to this fiery hatred toward Rafalovitch was another flame.

When Avraham-Yisroel passed away, at the gravesite, when fragments were laid upon his eyes, Raisel could not hold back but yelled into the grave, "Remember, Avraham-Yisroel, carry forward my grievance to the Heavenly Court." [. . .]

The town was aware of Raisel's curses and it was said that Rafalovitch became richer and happier all because of Raisel's, Avraham-Yisroel's wife's curses.

Every curse becomes a blessing for Rafalovitch when she uttered them. However, Raisel still kept hoping. She hoped and became ever more certain that she would, that she had to live to see Rafalovitch's downfall.

10. Stronger than Death

I, the narrator of this specific event, am the son of Baruch, the grandson of Avraham-Yisroel and his wife, Raisel. When I remember my early childhood, my grandfather was no longer alive and my grandmother

lived with my Aunt Hannah and her husband Yitsḥak.
[. . .]

As I think back to that time, in the entrance to the town, near the town park, across the street, displayed in front with acacias and spread-out branches from the chestnut trees, stood a two-story house with large windows and an entrance door carved out of oak wood. The lock was shiny and glossy and the short little brass sign was highly buffed and shone as bright as a mirror. The only thing written on it in Polish was "Marian Rafalowicz [the Polish spelling]." I have very few clear memories from those quiet days. However, I do remember that rich, quiet house. It so happened that I passed by that place. I stood and looked at the rich building with its rare flowerpots adorning the windows. I tried to imagine the kind of extraordinarily beautiful and rich life that was proceeding behind those finely polished window panes. I tried with longing to see something.

Once a coach came out and stopped in front of the house. A person in a military uniform emerged. He must have been someone of high rank, because a Cossack sitting next to the coachman jumped down. This Cossack had an earring in one ear. Hurriedly, he opened the door and stood at full length, straight as a string. In the street, the Jews moved off to the side, placing their forelocks behind their ears. However, when this man, all-embossed in red military uniform started walking to the house and opened the door, he was faced with someone dressed in civil garb, coming from within the house. He had a moderate, white beard, no hat. He greeted the military man by shaking his hand and they began speaking in an ordinary way.

Even in my young mind, it became clear that the man in civilian garb held himself as not less important than the proud general. In the heder, where I learned, I found out from the boys that this man, without a hat and with a white beard, was called Meir Rafalovitch. He was very rich, a millionaire. The most important thing was, he is a Jew. This made us all proud. The rich Marian or Meir Rafalovitch who speaks with generals and talks as if with his own people is a Jew. [. . .]

Rafalovitch employed half the town. People were ready to jump into a fire for him and they encircled his name with rays of grandeur.

What of Rafalovitch's enemies? He probably did have enemies. No person is free of enemies, and Rafalovitch, with all his fancy deeds, surely had some. However, he did not have overt enemies. Most people kissed up to him, each in his own way. Every person needed

something from him; each person was dependent upon him and everyone was terrified of him.

But . . .

In the marketplace in a small store, from where smells of oils and paints would emanate in the half-darkness, among the rusted iron and tools, there would wander a very bent hunchbacked old woman with sunken cheeks and eyes dimmed from cataracts. She was old and always carried a torn tobacco handkerchief in her apron pocket. From time to time, her weakened eyesight would be jolted back to seeing clearly after she sniffed her tobacco handkerchief. [. . .]

This same old woman, half-beaten, was Rafalovitch's overt blood-enemy. Her entire present life was justified by her hatred to Rafalovitch. [. . .]

One evening in summer, my little brother, Aunt Hannah's children, and I were playing in the sand in the courtyard. Suddenly, the maid appeared.

"Children, inside. Grandmother is calling you!" Naturally, we did not feel like abandoning our game to go inside. Soon, grandmother herself came out. So we had no choice. We had to abandon building our mud palace and go inside. Inside, an inquiry was held. Each grandchild was questioned separately: "Did you say your prayers?"

"Are you obeying your parents?"

"Are you running around?"

Only after all this, of course the answers all being satisfying ones, did we get a *nosh*, a cookie or a fruit.

"Say a blessing," Grandmother reminded us.

Grandmother is now especially pressing us to listen to what she tells us. We kick each other, understanding what she means. When she tells us to go into our alcove and sit down on the coffer, my cousin Aaron-Leib, Hannah's son, gives me a pinch on my arm.

"Again she is starting her 'song.'" Grandmother indeed opens her mouth and says, "When your Grandfather, may he rest in peace, came from the forest into the town. . . ." She rests for awhile, before coming to the most important part of her story.

"So the 'predator,' the evil Rafalovitch started stealing himself into our hearts and the little money that we had saved up, like a thief, a robber, he came in, in the darkest night, into a home that was full."

Now, the "song" that she was "singing" was not known to us and we no longer had great respect for Grandmother, and since the story was boring and long-winded, we started behaving wildly. We pushed out, backwards, and laughed. Grandmother whose cataract-eyes were staring out at us, recognized, finally, that her story held no interest for us. She resented this and started annoying us. [. . .]

11. *In the Depths*

Meir Rafalovitch lived a rich and famous life. A third of the town made their living from his generosity. Another third were employed in his business, earning meager salaries. The third portion lived from his "people," salespeople and craftsmen. One always feared saying a bad word against Rafalovitch, almost as if he were the king. "Walls have ears" and one can pay dearly with one's job if one says a word against him. Just as the big, rich, fully leafed tree did not realize that somewhere in its roots a worm was gnawing away; so, too, does the rich and fortunate Rafalovitch not realize that there, in the corner of the marketplace, in the narrow, orderly dark store, stocked full of short pieces of iron, paints, and oils, is an old shrunken and bent-over woman. She has already lived her life and her skin is like dried bark as she walks, bent over, almost in half.

However, she is not yet thinking of dying. She still has a goal in her life. She does not want to leave this life until she has achieved that goal. It consists of living to see Rafalovitch's downfall. She wants to see him and his household in the same situation that she had been in, twenty-five years ago. That was the time he had subjected her husband to poverty.

Yes, this is her goal and she is sure that she will live to see it. It does not even occur to her that this is a dreadful sin. The opposite! She knows that, by herself, she is too weak. With God's help, she wants to live to see this. She hopes and waits. An old woman, half-deaf, she sits the day through in her house. She goes nowhere. However, she is up to date with everything that is happening in and around Rafalovitch. No one knows how she is apprised of everything, but she knows. [. . .]

The old woman lived in this way. She had already made her calculations. She lived like someone who was already gone. However, she still had one thing to take care of. After that, she could go off to the cemetery. She existed as a forgotten watchwoman who has remained behind to stand guard for just one thing. Thus, nothing bothered her, neither someone's deeds making him happy nor those bringing on sadness. When she was forty years old, her older son, Simcha Binem, died. She went to the neighboring town, went to the funeral, rent her garments, sat shiva, and then continued living.

Four years later, the second and last son, Baruch, died. He left a young widow with little children. So the old mother stood as if struck dumb by the grave and again allowed herself to rend her clothes. However, when the grave-digger put the last board over the coffin, she cried out with a raspy, old shaky voice: "My son! Let me attain my goal first, and then I will come and join you."

Rafalovitch at that time had bought a coach on rubber wheels for his own use. This was the town's first coach with rubber wheels. And, as he passed through the town, the streets filled with people who came to view the novelty. It was a new world that a Jew allows himself in the diaspora.

12. *Unraveling the Goal*

One by one, clangs were heard. Rafalovitch, the rich and greatly honored Jew, the pride of the village Jews, was not doing well. It seemed that his businesses were failing, going from bad to worse. It seemed that he was heading toward bankruptcy. Rafalovitch was going down. However, his behavior did not, under any circumstances, hint at a downturn in his fortunes. He seldom showed up by foot but always traveled in his coach with the rubber wheels. If he ever did go somewhere on foot, he would not be alone but was always surrounded by a group of people, with sons, grandsons, and his own "people." His house was always the richest and widest in the district. With regard to philanthropy, Rafalovitch was never too generous with his money. Nonetheless, the rumors stretched further, those stubborn rumors. Rafalovitch's businesses were not going well. [. . .]

Shortly after this, superintendent elections took place, and the Hasidim no longer chose Rafalovitch as their superintendent [*dozor*—Polish]. In the prayer house, another power was rising. The younger generation were mostly smart, "kept" [living with brides' parents] sons-in-law and young merchants who only recently had become aware of Rafalovitch and his powers. They looked grudgingly at the very proud Rafalovitch and his family, who wore ironed collars and were just Hasidic enough to come for an hour on the Sabbath to the prayer house. The young Hasidim would probably not do anything by themselves. Now, however, they had many elders on their side. Rafalovitch lost, and, in his stead, yes, it is true, as it would appear, story-wise, Avraham-Yisroel's son-in-law, Yitsḥak, who was Aunt

Hannah's husband and was pretty well-to-do, now became superintendent. This silent kill-joy nevertheless had brains enough to buy someone's favor, with small loans from his Hasidim. Since he was not cold and hard, he sometimes did a favor.

Yitsḥak, Avraham-Yisroel's son-in-law, became superintendent instead of Rafalovitch. In the city and the district, this news was most engaging for some time, overshadowing all the news from *Ha-Tsefirah* and dominating local gossip. [. . .]

How Rafalovitch felt about this was not known. Apparently he had other concerns than the fact that he was rejected from the position of superintendent. Rafalovitch commented, "They took someone, a store person with hands full of pitch [because Yitsḥak dealt with these kinds of materials] and made him a superintendent in my place."

Grandmother, however, did not wish to believe the whole story at first. She thought that they were trying to fool her, that her son-in-law, Yitsḥak, the "Zolenesher kasha miller," the "snuggler," the "ear-worm" (all of the names she would call him), became superintendent in place of Meir Rafalovitch. A grandchild who told this news to Grandmother was almost cursed by her. But then, she realized that this was not a joke but really was the truth. Her son-in-law Yitsḥak had really become superintendent in Rafalovitch's place. [. . .]

Not long after this, Grandmother, as was usual in recent years, fainted. We thought that her end was near. After the midday meal, mother asked me to go to Aunt Hannah to see how Grandmother was doing. When I got there, my heart told me that it was "after everything." This was the feeling, I had. In the house, a cousin, Mirel, Aunt Rana's daughter, sat opposite me.

"What's new?" I asked. "How is Grandmother?"

"Grandmother?" she repeated. "Not too bad. She is better." Laughingly, she said, "As always, some old man appeared to her in a dream and offered a small flask for her to smell. So she woke up and is feeling more cheerful."

"She probably has lost her mind," I said.

"Go on, you little fool," Mirel, my cousin, went on. "As always, she is waiting for Rafalovitch's downfall. Now after Uncle Yitsḥak's becoming superintendent, she is almost ready . . . I am telling you."

And Rafalovitch kept on going and Grandmother returned to her shrunken state, as if she feared that Satan might pull a joke on her. Suddenly, word got around that the army was leaving our city, and . . . the military did leave. All this was done before the gossipers had settled among themselves whether the military was leaving and only border guards were staying or the opposite was to happen. Only a small number of soldiers remained. For our town, this was bad. The streets emptied. Storekeepers began complaining. Contractors and other suppliers were wandering around like lost souls. Rafalovitch's properties emptied out. The barracks were silent and accursed. Everything emptied out around Rafalovitch. There was a silence all around, where before there had been life and noise. The military and officials moved out. Solitude spread, and this solitude also affected Rafalovitch and his household. Now everything grew topsy-turvy, as if someone were rolling downhill. No one saw Rafalovitch traveling in his coach with the rubber wheels. He did not appear at all. No one saw him anywhere, neither him nor his sons.

Yankel Hecht, Rafalovitch's former "man," who had recently met good fortune with a little money and a lot of impertinence, sued Rafalovitch over a sum owed to him, or something else. Yankel Hecht ran around, his little hat tucked up and with his colored necktie around the rubber collar. He walked around mischievously with his little walking-stick and boasted that he, Hecht, would bring the "big boss" down on his backside before everyone. And . . . one lovely morning, a commission came and sealed up the soap factory. [. . .]

A few weeks passed and the news became stale. They stopped talking about it as if this were agreed upon, that Rafalovitch was no longer Rafalovitch and was no longer worth talking about. No news items would come out of discussing it further.

After this, on the way to heder, I passed Aunt Hannah's store and I went in for a while, as usual. There were a few people there. Grandmother was sitting as if moved by something. All the others were silently looking at Yankel Hecht in his colored necktie, filled with "naches," leaning on his mischievous little stick, swearing loudly, as he usually did.

"Reb Avraham-Yisroel's widow, I should only continue to be a father to my children for many days longer as I swear today 'he' came with Meir the potato-seller from Viershev for forty groschen. But he was ashamed and got off on the walkway."

Grandmother sat with tears running down her face. From her old, shaky lips came a quiet murmur: "This is God's justice, God's justice!" she repeated. Shortly after this, Grandmother died. This was a unique kind of passing of a human being. She fell asleep on the

Sabbath by the table, calmly and happily sleeping, like a little hen.

Translated by Ruth Bryl Shochat.

Other works by Horonczyk: *Feldblume* (1921); *Farplonterte vegn oder tsvishn di khurves fun yidishn lebn* (1924); *In geroysh fun mashinen* (1928); *1905* (1929); *Baym shvel* (1935); *Geklibene shrift* (1950).

Rokhl Korn

1898–1982

From her earliest publications in Yiddish, the poet Rokhl Korn was applauded by critics for her forceful use of natural imagery, tight control over language, and alarming directness in style—all of which were rare qualities in Yiddish literature at the time. Born on a farming estate in Sucha Gora, Eastern Galicia, Korn was active promoting Yiddish culture in this region where Polish was generally considered the language of status and creativity among Jews. After a period of wandering and dislocation in Moscow, Soviet Central Asia, and Scandinavia during and after World War II, Korn settled in Montreal, becoming one of that city's leading Yiddish cultural figures in the postwar era. Her verse in this later period retained the qualities of her earlier work, but was also suffused with themes of pain, loss, suffering, and loneliness.

Earth
1936

IX

Mordecai walked home from the village on the path that bordered the forest. All the talk of the elders in the village chief's house had intoxicated him more than the strongest whiskey. Under his heavy shadows he crept out of the forest, and, like the hands of a blind man, touched a different part of the meadow each time. The forest that just a few minutes before had risen like a green wave of tree tops was now bending to reveal the naked wounds of its chopped-down trunks, and the first frost silvered the beds of sprouting winter wheat. Soon, Mordecai thought, his sweat-soaked field would belong to him, he would own it all. He wouldn't have to work his horses to death in order to make the earth yield enough for both him and the squire. A good thing he hadn't tried to marry off his daughter. If he had given her a dowry he wouldn't have been able to buy even an inch of land. He would have had to leave this place, to rattle his bones once more on the broken-down cart, delivering cans of milk to the villagers. Someone else would have taken his place and sown the fields that he had ploughed and manured with so much effort.

By the time Mordecai reached his house the lamp was already lit. Bailtsche was just raking some baked potatoes out of the coals and blowing on them as she tossed them from hand to hand.

"Why so late?" she asked without raising her eyes from the fire.

Mordecai seated himself opposite the open kitchen door. The reflection of the fire licked his boots like the red tongue of a dog. He answered her in his thick heavy voice: "The squire's wife wants to sell the field. She sent the steward to the village."

Ita was sitting at the table behind the lamp plucking chickens. She sat quietly without talking. That afternoon when no one was in the house she had searched for the white handkerchief. She had found it under Bailtsche's pillow. All four corners were knotted around some folded diapers and lace-trimmed undershirts. She had held the undershirts in her hands, staring at them, while a cold dread crawled up her back. Lace, she thought, where does she get the money to buy lace? He must surely give it to her. He . . . and Ita suddenly remembered how her father had refused to give her mother the money to buy shoelaces for the children. In order to buy them her mother had secretly had to sell a few eggs to the village shop.

The diapers burned her hands and still she could not put them down. The unknown, someone else's secret, that had intruded so suddenly into her life sent the blood to her throat, to her large mouth, to her lumpy cheeks. Now Ita began to observe Bailtsche closely, to notice her slow movements, her freckled face. She would have liked to insinuate herself inside the serene smile that momentarily flared Bailtsche's nostrils as she looked into Mordecai's eyes with the confidence of a wife who knows she is loved.

"Well, that's good—it means we can leave here soon, so let her sell it," Bailtsche said.

"What are you saying? I intend to buy the field myself."

"If you want to buy it, then buy. I won't stay here in the middle of the forest in times like these. A person can be killed here without even a rooster crowing."

Ita read uncertainty in her father's face, an uncertainty that she did not recognize. Her father, who had worked so hard in order to have his own piece of land in his old age, was now ready to ruin everything for Bailtsche's sake. Bailtsche, the intruder, the lazybones who didn't even know how to hold a spade or a hoe! Ita's face, with its white eyelashes, trembled.

She rose from the bench, her eyes narrowed into slits: "Father, don't listen to anyone, and buy! If you have the money, then don't wait until someone else buys. It will be your own, and wherever you step, it will be your own—"

Bailtsche bent her head as if to avoid an impending blow. Suddenly she felt that the ugly stepdaughter wanted to chain her to the twenty-acre field forever, wanted to enslave her to the land just as she herself was enslaved, just as Mordecai was, just as the tree on the roadside was. And she burst into helpless childish crying.

"So I'll go away by myself."

Now Ita could no longer contain herself: "If you find it so awful here, go on! No one is forcing you to stay. Go back where you came from—be a housemaid!"

Mordecai banged his stick against the bench and said in Polish, "That's my business!"

For him to speak Polish was the sign of deepest anger. It was a thousand times worse than his smile.

"With the money I'll do what I like, and the devil take all of you!"

Ita's head bent still lower and the veins on her neck tightened and throbbed with envy and hatred.

X

From early morning on the jays and crows chattered wildly. Their restlessness foretold snow. The wind lay coiled and tense along the valleys like an animal ready to spring. Later it spiraled into the air, knocking off the dried leaves still left on the trees from the summer.

It pulled the clouds together like balls of cotton wool, trying to stuff them into the space that separates sky and earth. In this the wind succeeded, for soon only a narrow crack between heaven and earth remained—a crack into which the short winter day now crawled to die.

Three men came riding out of the forest dragging several cows tied together with rope. The first to spot them was Bailtsche. "They look like men from the squire's estate."

Ita stepped outside and returned with a blanched face and ashen lips.

"Father, the Russians are here again, and they've taken our cows."

Mordecai fastened the belt of his trousers. "They have nothing to take from me. I'm not one of your squires, and you women, be quiet!"

They heard the horses on the icy ground beside the well. Two Russian soldiers dismounted and banged on the door with their rifle butts while their three companions guarded the cows who pawed the ground anxiously and, sensing the closeness of the barn, made yearning, homesick noises.

The house seemed to grow smaller. It filled up with the smell of cowhide, sweat, and a vague dull fear.

Mordecai greeted them. "Good evening! I suppose you're lost, eh? Not surprising in this drizzly fog."

One of the soldiers, with a fresh bluish sabre cut along one side of his face, burst into loud laughter. "Just look at him, the clever little Jew! No, we're not lost, sweetheart, in fact we've come especially to pay you a visit, and it's our commander who sent us."

The whiskers of the other Cossack danced for joy.

"In that case, please sit."

"No, you'd better lead us to the stable."

Mordecai's body stiffened.

"Are you coming or should we kick you over there with our boots?"

Ita got up from the bench and threw on her mother's old jacket. "Come on, father!"

Her eyes were still and their blue-grey nakedness was reminiscent of the frozen little rivers in winter, but her hands trembled as they buttoned the torn jacket. She went ahead, and the Cossacks followed to make sure that no one was hiding. The door to the house remained open behind them.

Bailtsche cowered on the bench. The sharp cold from outside poured a thick white mist which crept closer and closer to her fear-paralysed legs. She couldn't move. Suddenly her ears were assaulted by a knotted tangle of voices. She wiped the film from one of the panes and pressed her face to the window. The two soldiers on horseback were now beside the stable and holding a rope tied to her two finest cows. Mordecai kept pulling on the rope, until one of the soldiers took the rope end and whipped it across his hands. The blow raised a thick purple welt but Mordecai did not let go of the cows. The strain outlined the veins in his neck and forehead.

"These are my cows, my livelihood! I won't give them up. Go to the squire—he has stables full of cattle!"

The soldiers took down their rifles and for a second the metal gleamed thin and sharp as knives.

"For the last time, are you going to let go of the cows or not?"

Mordecai paled. Pearly drops of sweat rolled down his face, but he stood his ground. "Kill me if you like, but I won't give them up. They're mine."

Bailtsche watched Ita run forward and seize the soldier's arm. Then a red fog veiled her eyes and hid everything.

Neither did she hear it when the raw healthy laughter of the soldier shattered the strained and breathless silence like a bullet.

"Look at him—this little Jew, this nothing, is opposing the Russian might! If it wanted to, the Russian might could pulverize him, squash him under its heel like a worm, right now, on the spot!"

He laughed as heartily as a child. His laughter was like fresh water rinsing his throat.

And maybe he too would have looked and felt powerless if in his home he had been confronted by German soldiers?

"Well, come along with us to our commander—maybe if you beg and plead he'll let you keep one of your cows. I'll tell him you're a poor Jew. I can't do any more than that. I was ordered to bring the cows, and that's that."

When Mordecai came into the house to fetch his sheepskin coat, Bailtsche was still sitting where he had left her, her arms and legs stiff and lifeless.

"Bailtsche, what's wrong, Bailtsche?"

She didn't answer. Her lips were pressed tight.

Mordecai called Ita in. "Rub her chest and temples with snow."

He himself poured water into her mouth, forcing it between her clenched teeth, until she opened her eyes.

"Bailtsche, darling, do you feel better now?"

She saw that Mordecai was dressed for travel in his sheepskin and that the flaps of his cap were pulled down over his ears; her fingers clutched his arm.

"Where are you going, Mordecai?"

"I'll be back soon. I'm just going to get my cows, that's all."

"Don't go Mordecai, don't go! I beg you, wait til tomorrow morning."

"By tomorrow all that will be left is their hides."

"I'm so afraid, so afraid—" Her voice was full of tears.

"Go on, don't be silly. Don't act like a child. You won't be alone, Ita is here." He ran out quickly and kept running on the path through the orchard to catch up with the soldiers who had his cows.

XI

The two women were alone in the house. The lamp threw a patchwork of light over the uneven plastered wall. It was so quiet that you could hear the lamp's wick buzzing as the oil burned.

The wind was howling outside, and it seemed to Ita that she could hear someone crying. She opened her eyes wide and all her senses were on the alert as if to penetrate the surrounding darkness. Soon it began to snow and the hard white grains bounced off the window panes with a glassy ring. Ita's eyes could not break through that thick white blanket, but she could hear a long, drawn-out-wailing. She threw on her jacket and went out, carrying the stable lantern.

She returned with a small calf in her arms. When she put it down the calf stood uncertainly on the threshold blinking its round white-ringed eyes. Only when Ita approached the kitchen did the calf follow her on its helpless, splayed-out legs, beginning to wail all over again. Its lonely, orphaned call reached out across the distant fields to the footsteps of the mother cow, footsteps that had long since been covered over by the snow.

Ita lifted a pot of warm whey from the stove and offered it to the calf. But the calf wouldn't touch it and kept tossing its head back. Then Ita dipped her hand into the liquid and put her fingers into the calf's mouth. The calf nuzzled the spread-out fingers and began to suck vigorously. Ita patted its soft trembling body with one hand and laid her head against its warm side. Suddenly a wild inhuman cry broke the silence. It came from Bailtsche. She lay curled up on the bed. The shawl that she had seized to warm her shivering body had slipped down and was hanging from the edge of the bed like the broken wing of a bird. Her belly rose and fell with short jerky movements; it breathed by itself like a separate creature. Ita sat with her hands folded in her empty lap as if to rest them before they were forced to scrub the small white diapers and the dark blood from Bailtsche's sheets.

Bailtsche's broken cries stabbed Ita like so many knives while her hands patted her own narrow hips with vindictive pleasure.

Actually this giving birth was really Ita's. It was here on this bed that she should now have been lying, that she should have been giving birth to her child. And maybe the dark-haired bridegroom from the next village would have been standing beside her . . . but she wouldn't have been shrieking and carrying on like Bailtsche, that intruder. She would have accepted each new pain with joy, knowing it was bringing the ripened fruit closer to the edge of the opening womb. She would have dug her fingernails into the hard wooden frame of the bed and smiled. Just then her head fell to one side and landed on the table, rousing her from her trance.

Bailtsche was now lying stretched out taut as a violin string, with her legs pushing with all her strength against the foot of the bed, readying herself for the next onslaught of pain.

Her tense belly had dropped like a sack with the child's heavings. From time to time the child seemed to be seized by a fit of unexpected shivering. Bailtsche lay there with her eyes wide open, listening to her body, waiting for the next pains which came with merciless regularity, burrowing into her back and thighs, sharp, pointed, and drawn-out.

"Ita, come closer, I want to tell you something."

And when Ita bent over the bed with suppressed disgust, Bailtsche whispered in an ingratiating tone: "I beg you—take the lantern and go to the village. Call—you know who to call—the baby is coming too soon—maybe because of what happened."

Ita sensed the strange woman's shame. It ran through her mind that she should have felt the shame before, with her father. They used to kiss even in the daytime, enough to make people talk. That was all very well, Bailtsche had taken her mother's jewellery, had eaten up the family's hard-earned savings. She had bought lace to trim baby shirts, but when it came to her, Ita, they had refused to let her marry because they didn't want to give a dowry. And now everything would really fall apart. Because of Bailtsche, her father wouldn't buy the plot of land from the squire, he would move to town instead, and spend his old age playing the fool with a gaggle of children. Yes, yes, and she, Ita would have to go into service, to take the place of Bailtsche, just as Bailtsche had taken hers.

She answered her stepmother with a whisper, full of an odd tenderness. "Go yourself, auntie. I won't."

Only then, when Bailtsche looked into her stepdaugher's eyes did the meaning of those words become clear to her. There wasn't a hint of compassion in those eyes. Bailtsche's body was now covered in a cold sweat. With her last bit of strength she got off the bed, but her legs, filled with pain like two brimming buckets, gave way. She crawled to Ita on all fours: "Ita darling, I beg you to go—I can't bear it any longer; go get old Hanka, Ita take pity on me, Ita, it's tearing me apart, I wish I was dead—oh mother!"

She began to kiss Ita's feet feverishly. Only when Bailtsche's next pains came was Ita able to free herself. She grabbed a shawl and went out of the house.

Bailtsche was left all alone in the half-darkened room. A new fear inserted itself between her ribs, and dissolving, spread slowly through her whole body. Her heart wept and she was nauseated by the smell of manure that rose from Ita's barn-soaked boots. She dragged herself to the door. The cold icy air embraced her shivering body. She took a handful of snow and began to eat it greedily. Supporting herself against the wall, she slowly got up. Along her legs she felt a hot sticky flow, and when she looked down she saw that the snow at her feet was red.

It had stopped snowing, and from under the knotted clouds a pale stained moon swam out. Ita was nowhere to be seen. She began to call Ita's name. Her voice fell into the surrounding white silence and was drowned. Suddenly her eye fell on footsteps in the freshly fallen snow along the length of the orchard. The footsteps were black and definite. Bailtsche's knees grew weak with unexpected hope. It meant that Ita had gone for help after all! Her eyes followed the footsteps to the crossroads by the river. Then they opened wide, and grew dark with primitive pain. At the crossroads the footsteps were thick, all in one place, as if the person who had walked there had thought better of it, stopped, hesitated, and returned. From the crossroads the footsteps led in one direction—back into the forest. And now she could see Ita walking fast, almost running. The winds filled her shawl, spreading it open like black wings that carried her high, high into the air.

"Ita, Ita!"

Bailtsche called despairingly. She choked on her own voice. The veins in her throat were tight almost to bursting. For a second she imagined that Ita could hear her, that she had stopped to look back. . . .

But soon Ita's head sunk down into her shoulders and she diappeared among the trees. Only her footsteps were left to darken the endless white of the fields.

Bailtsche's knees gave way. She lay with her eyes closed. From time to time her blood reddened the snow beneath her.

Translated by Miriam Waddington.

Other works by Korn: *Dorf* (1928); *Royter mon* (1937); *Generations: Selected Poems* (1982); *Paper Roses* (1985).

Esther Singer Kreitman
1891–1954

Esther Singer Kreitman was born in Bilgoraj, Poland, the sister of the highly acclaimed Yiddish writers Israel Joshua and Isaac Bashevis Singer. Growing up in an abusive home, she never received a formal education and entered into an unhappy marriage with a diamond cutter from Antwerp in 1912. In 1926 she left her marriage and ultimately settled in London, where she published novels in Yiddish, worked as a translator, and managed the journal *Loshn un lebn*.

The Dance of the Demons
1936

Chapter XIII

Meanwhile Reb Zalman, all undeterred, was arranging a match for Deborah, and one evening he arrived with a brand new proposal, one that was—in these hard modern times—almost too good to be true.

"I have a remarkable story to tell you, Reb Avram Ber, of the strange workings of Providence," said Reb Zalman, beside himself with excitement at the strange workings of Providence. "But before I begin, Reb Avram Ber, do you know Reb Baruch Laib, the principal of the Berishlitz *yeshiva*?"

"I should say so," replied Reb Avram Ber. "Everybody knows Reb Baruch Laib!"

"And tell me, did you ever make, the acquaintance of his son?"

"Let me see now . . . I did meet him once in R——. He was going away to Belgium, I believe, and he came down with his father specially to say good-bye to the *Tsadik*. That's right, and I invited him to dinner. Yes, I know the young man you mean."

"Aha, now you just listen to this funny prank of Providence! Here you are, Reb Avram Ber, with a daugh-

ter on your hands, who is, shall we say, an up-to-date young lady, one of those modern young ladies who insists on having a husband dressed up in the new-fangled European style. You, for your part, would not dream, of course, of considering any such suitor in a new-fangled get-up. And for this reason all our proposals have been foredoomed to failure. Here you are, just about beginning to lose heart. So what must happen? Well it so happens that the other night Reb Baruch Laib drops in for a chat. We get talking about one thing and another, and suddenly it comes to me in a flash—just like that. The funny part about it is that I fancy Reb Baruch Laib was thinking on similar lines himself. Anyhow, guess what I did, Reb Avram Ber? I suggested a marriage between your daughter and his son. How's that for a brainwave? It's the old, old story of satisfying the wolf and saving the lamb, so to speak. Ha, ha, ha! Really, I must say that Providence weaves a very cunning net. I suppose you know that the town of Antwerp boasts of one of the most deeply religious Jewish communities in the world? "

"Well, I have heard something to that effect."

"No, but I beg you not to take it from hearsay! You take it from *me*! There is more true religion to be found in Antwerp than anywhere else. Here in Warsaw a great deal of wickedness is hidden away under orthodox gaberdines. Now in Antwerp, where everybody dresses in the modem style—after all, it's a foreign country, and when in Rome one must do as the Romans do—as I say, whereas they dress differently, at heart they're more orthodox and infinitely stricter than most of the people here. They are Jews in the best sense of the word, and Antwerp is a thoroughgoing Jewish city if ever there was one. Everybody there studies the Talmud. The place is full of synagogues and *hassidical* circles—in a word, a replica of Warsaw! Take Reb Baruch Laib's son! He devotes several hours to the Talmud in an *hassidical* circle every evening as soon as he's finished his day's work."

"What's that? Do you mean to tell me he's a working man?"

"A working man, if you please! You don't imagine he's a tailor or a cobbler or something low-down like that! Allow me to inform you that by profession he is nothing more nor less than a diamond-cutter!"

"What?!" Reb Avram Ber was left almost breathless.

"That's it, a diamond-cutter! I need hardly tell you, therefore, that he does not exactly have to struggle to make a living. How goes the old tag? The man who chops the wood gets the splinters. And believe me, the man who cuts great diamonds gets the little diamonds. Besides, it's a gentle art, a noble profession. I must make a confession to you, Reb Avram Ber—I envy you greatly. I only wish Reb Baruch Laib had chosen to marry into my family. But no, Providence would have it otherwise! What Reb Baruch Laib has set his heart on, is marrying into your family. He has heard say that you have a really fine daughter, good-looking and clever. And maybe you, Reb Avram Ber, will guess who it was imparted this knowledge to him. . . ." Here Reb Zalman smiled a significant smile. "The point is, Reb Baruch Laib is anxious to give to his son a wife who will be a good influence, who will help to keep his son the same as he's always been—a pious, upright and honourable Jew. That's the idea! After all, a girl that springs from such good stock as yours, Reb Avram Ber, is bound to set a shining example to any young man. . . ."

Reb Avram Ber's hand reached for his beard. It was all very odd. But who could tell? Maybe there was something in it! The ways of Providence were inscrutable. At any rate, he would call in Raizela. She found the proposal quite reasonable.

"But does he know that we have no dowry to offer?"

"That's a detail, which you need not worry about! I have already made it clear to Reb Baruch Laib what an honour it would be for his son to marry into your family. I'll even go a step further and say that, with a little management, I'll induce Reb Baruch Laib to provide the dowry himself. In fact, I'll go a step further than that, and make him bear the wedding expenses and all. You leave that to me. Once my mind's made up, nothing can stop me. I don't believe in delay, and to-morrow morning, please God, we shall write a letter to the young man asking him if he is willing to be married, and if his answer is yes, if only he gives his consent, then the whole thing will be almost too good to be true!"

The young man in far-away Belgium readily gave his consent. And why not? What could be better than marriage on such terms? Here was his father beseeching him to accept a fine dowry, wedding gifts, financial support after the wedding, and whatnot, with a wife thrown into the bargain! Better still, his father was accompanying the offer with a handsome remittance. And the girl was good-looking, too, because he remembered having seen her in R—. Not at all bad! He would have been a dolt to turn the proposal down. No, he would never do such a silly thing as that. He was going to be a bridegroom! It was a soft job. He liked soft jobs. He

hated hard work, and, above all, he hated looking for work!

When they approached Deborah on the subject, she considered it as a means of escape. If she could go abroad, then she would be able to live her own life. She would be under no more obligations as the daughter of an orthodox Rabbi, everything would be left behind, all her ties with the past would be severed. The past would be dead. So frantic was her impatience, so feverish her condition, that she failed to see any alternative to the dramatic gesture of giving herself away to a man whom she had never set eyes on—at least she could not remember him—an utter stranger about whom she knew nothing. She was conscious of only one thing: she must run away. And when Reb Zalman talked and talked, until she could bear to listen no longer, she said "Yes."

Her consent obtained, Reb Avram Ber waxed jubilant. Raizela was less effusive than he; she well concealed her satisfaction. But Deborah was the more deeply pained by her mother's attitude. It showed plainly enough that Raizela would feel no pangs at parting with her. It showed plainly enough that her mother was eager to see the back of her. Well, that being so, there was only one thing left for her to do, and that was to clear out! She had been given notice to quit! Did that really mean that her mother would never care to see her again, would never miss her? Yes, that was what it meant. It could mean nothing else, and her sense of surprise was even greater than her grief. She was a pariah. Simon wanted to have nothing to do with her. Her parents were quite willing, nay happy, to send her away to a distant land. The party had unceremoniously kicked her out. And she, poor fool, had been deluding herself all along that, despite all appearances, Simon was not really indifferent to her, that there was a mistake somewhere, that her parents loved her, that her mother's habit of preaching at her was prompted by motherly affection. [. . .]

She would go away and get married. As a means of escape from a home which was only a home in name, and which she hated like poison, as a last resort of getting away from parents who were eager to disown her, a marriage of convenience was surely no worse than the cowardice of dying by her own hand! As for the man whom she was going to marry, he did not matter at all! Why, not even her father had flinched. She could almost hear them all shouting at her, "Get out! We don't want you here!" And even her father did not care a damn. That her father loved her dearly, was something she had never doubted. Now she saw the hard truth: she was all alone in the world. She began to weep and sob in a loud voice.

Raizela came running in from the bedroom as fast as her feeble legs would carry her.

"What is the matter, Deborah?"

For the moment Deborah really hated her mother. She wished for nothing better than to make her suffer. She did not trouble to reply, and finally when Raizela had repeated her question many times over and had become quite alarmed, Deborah calmly declared that she was not crying and would her mother oblige by leaving the room. Raizela gaped at her. She had never known Deborah to address her in this manner. She became furious, and without a word trudged back to her bedroom.

"It's too bad," she said to Reb Avram Ber, who had joined her to discover the reason for Deborah's sudden outburst. "That precious daughter of ours is doing her best to kill me. I shall be very glad to see this marriage through, and have her go away—in peace (she added)."

"Of course you'll be glad, for it's a wonderful match, for which the Lord be praised! It's a very serious matter nowadays, finding a husband for a girl without a dowry."

"What's more, she picks and chooses. No one's good enough for her."

"Yes, thank God, she has not disgraced us by running off with a freethinker, or doing something of that sort!" Reb Avram Ber rejoiced. "And at the same time she'll be marrying a man dressed in the modern style, just as she has her heart on doing. Reb Zalman tells me that this young man in Antwerp is as good a Jew as you could wish for, godfearing and a Talmudist. He's well off and will make a splendid husband. The Lord be praised!"

A few days later the family received a formal visit from a short, tubby woman wearing on her huge bust a jacket of black cloth trimmed with innumerable silk ribbons and with a very broad, prosperous-looking shawl of fine lace on her head. Behind her, and overlooking her, came a tall, lean, red-faced woman, likewise wearing a black jacket with silk ribbons, although her trimmings were far fewer and less glossy, and her shawl was narrow and rather mean-looking. And trotting along at their side like a puppy, came yet another woman in a black jacket; but she was very skinny and tiny indeed, and she had no silk trimmings to boast of at all. The

shawl on her head was as narrow as a thread, and her pinched little nose was even narrower still. She had watery little eyes, a pitiful little mouth with wrinkles and a pitiful little chin with more wrinkles. These three ladies were Deborah's prospective mother-in-law, the mother-in-law's sister and the sister's sister-in-law respectively, and they had all come to inspect Deborah.

The sitting-room had been tidied up for the occasion. Raizela was wearing her black gown. The skin over her cheekbones was flushed. Deborah's face was glowing with fever. And the big paraffin lamp diffused its mellow light over her with a radiance such as befitted a young, innocent bride. [. . .]

Deborah passed muster. Some days later an engagement party was held.

Deborah's prospective father-in-law was a big, fat man with a very long and fiery red beard, and with a shiny forehead and beefy face in which his eyes were scarcely visible, lost in a tangle of fluffy side-whiskers, jutting eyebrows and puffy lumps of flesh. All through the ceremony he did nothing but stare at the bride-to-be. The more he saw of her, the more he wanted to see, and he had his eyes glued on her to the very end. On the other hand, his wife, who once again was unable to get the best part of herself on to the chair, had her eyes glued on *him* to the very end.

When they presented Deborah with a long, golden chain and hung it round her neck, she shivered at the touch of the cold metal and at the thought that the most vicious of dogs might safely be tied up with a chain such as this. She made no attempt to follow the flow of talk at the table, nor did she pay any heed to the shower of congratulations and blessings which fell all round her. Her thoughts all moved in one narrow channel: she was taking revenge on her parents, on Simon and on herself. Fully persuaded though she was that Simon cared for her not in the least, she experienced a perverse pleasure in this mean trick she was playing on him. At the height of the celebrations, however, when a plate was smashed to pieces on the floor and everybody began screaming, "*Mazal tov, mazal tov!*" a gloomy cloud, so dark and horrible, settled upon her, that even the guests suddenly noticed it for all their rejoicings. Everybody began to ask what was wrong: was she, God forbid, ill, or did she feel faint, or would she have a glass of water, or take a sip of brandy? And they begged her not to hide the truth from them. She reassured them that there was nothing the matter with her, but the deathly pallor of her face and the expression in her eyes belied her tongue.

At last the party dispersed. At last even Reb Zalman had taken his leave. And now the lamps were being put out. Deborah lay in her bed, fixedly gazing at the darkness enshrouding her. Her mind was a blank. She was incapable of thought, incapable of feeling. She had no regrets. She was not fully conscious of what had happened that evening. Already a clock somewhere in the distance was striking five. All things about her dwindled, growing smaller and smaller till they faded out of sight. She fell asleep. In the morning, as soon as he was awake, Reb Avram Ber hastened in with beaming face to renew his congratulations.

"*Mazal tov*, Deborah! May this be the beginning for you of a long, long life of happiness! Listen, Deborah, I cherish you in my heart now more than ever before. The Lord be praised for His graciousness! Well, Deborah, why don't you say something? Aren't you happy?"

She remained silent.

He brought a jug of water into her bedroom and slithered an enamel basin over the floor up to her bedside.

"Come, Deborah, hold out your hands and I'll pour the water for you."

"But what do I want to wash my hands in bed for? Can't I do that when I get up?"

"Don't you see, I want you to have breakfast in bed. I believe you were feeling rather faint last night."

He gave her a piece of honey cake which had been left over from the engagement party, and he brought her a glass of tea in bed. Deborah looked at the cake and winced, as if its sweetness were poisonous and its honeyed aroma stank in her nostrils.

"I can't touch it, papa, I just can't. Take it away and leave me alone."

"What's the matter with you, Deborah ? Don't you feel well?"

"Of course I'm feeling well, I feel splendid! And now let me go to sleep again, please! No, I don't want any tea either. No, I want nothing. Nothing at all." [. . .]

It was two o'clock in the afternoon when Deborah got out bed. She moved noiselessly about the home, clearing up the mess of last night's party. Her face was extraordinarily pale, and her eyes were in mourning, sparkling with gloom and despair.

From that day onwards she felt like a stranger in the house—a superfluous stranger. Her father, her mother, her brother—she regarded them all as acquaintances who were accommodating her as an unwanted guest and were looking forward to the hour of her departure. She began to look forward to it herself. That sense of resignation, oppressive and bewildering, never took leave of her no matter where she went or what she did. She was bowed down under her burden of ponderous thoughts, of weird and hideous notions, which from that morning onwards harrowed her brain without cease, distorted her vision, poisoned the blood in her veins. A thousand times over and over again she reasoned with herself— she could easily break off the engagement; and a thousand times over and over again she refused to listen to reason. If her parents wished to see the back of her, she must not miss this opportunity of quitting. It was only bare self-respect. There was but one alternative, and that was for her to find a way of earning her own living. But how? What was she to do? She had never been taught a trade. She was a useless ornament. Stubbornly, and with ever-growing bitterness, she let things slide. [. . .]

In the family circle they began to treat her with rather more deference, as if she were an independent person. Everybody tried to show her greater consideration, and her mother in particular was anxious to see her always well dressed. Her prospective father-in-law lavished many costly presents on her, but both he and his gifts left her quite cold. This peculiar attitude puzzled him and hurt his pride. His own womenfolk in particular were greatly astonished. Deborah's unmaidenly conduct formed an everlasting topic of conversation with them.

"What a queer girl!" they murmured. "She's very clever and all that, but so unreasonable. I was a good girl in my time, to be sure, but I wasn't above taking a present if it was offered to me. Why, she's such a funny creature, she won't even put her jewellery on. She just doesn't seem to care a hang whether she gets a present or not. . . ."

"She's shamming, that's what it is. You stop giving her presents, and then I bet she'll come begging for them. You take my tip," said the long-legged sister-in-law to Reb Baruch Laib.

Translated by Maurice Carr.

Other works by Kreitman: *Brilyantn* (1944); *Yikhes* (1949).

1076 FICTION AND DRAMA

Moyshe Kulbak

Boitre
1936

Cast of Characters [included in this excerpt]

Arn-Volf—*parnes khoydesh* (chairman of the *kahal*,
the community council)
Beyle—his wife
Stere—his daughter
Rabbi
First and Second *Dayen* (judges of the *bes din*, the
communal religious court)
Yekhiel Malve (moneylender)
Kalmen Giteles
Ziml—scribe
Bontshe Kot—*khaper* (catcher of army recruits to fill
the community quota)
Boitre
Lemele Put
Melke
Klezmers (musicians of the community band), includ-
ing Berl the Bass Player
Yishuvniks (village Jews)
Yerakhmiel the Coachman
Village Jews, Poor People

SCENE ONE

[*A meeting of the kahal at the house of the parnes khoydesh.*] [. . .]
Seated at the table: THE RABBI, THE FIRST DAYEN, YEKH-
IEL MALVE, KALMEN GITELES, ZISL THE SCRIBE. *On
a chair in the background:* BONTSHE KOT. *Looking
through the window from outside:* YERAKHMIEL THE
COACHMAN
YERAKHMIEL [*through the window*]: Reb Kalmen, what
road should I take when I deliver the chickens? The
black highway or the way through the Kreve Wood?
God be praised, they are both insecure—what else?
KALMEN GITELES [*looks into a religious text*]: Well, get
going, you fool. Go! It might as well be through the
Kreve Wood.
YERAKHMIEL: In the Kreve Wood the *yishuvniks*, the
Jews from the village, are wandering around. The
screams from the women and children reach to high
heaven. Listen, gentlemen, from what people are saying, this is just the beginning. They say that, God forbid, there will be no Jews left in the village, not one.

FIRST *Dayen*: Evil pogroms.
RABBI: And where is Reb Arn-Volf?
ZIML THE SCRIBE: There he sits, over there [*points to
the door with his goose-quill*]. With the assessor since
noon. [. . .]
YEKHIEL MALVE: Difficult times these days. What high
prices! I can't afford even a small wagon-load of
wood. *Dayen*, do you have a pinch of snuff?
KALMEN GITELES: A man who won't spend the money
for his own snuff? Upon my word, it turns my stomach, Reb Yekhiel.
YEKHIEL MALVE [. . .] Well, what's happening with the
trousseau for Arn-Volf's daughter? Has it really disappeared? The wagons attacked and robbed? Whom
do they suspect? Is it really the *yishuvniks*?
SECOND *Dayen*: They say that the *yishuvniks* do it out
of grief, hunger, poverty. But there's also an opinion
that it's the bandit Boitre, God help us, who is trying
to get even with the town.
FIRST *Dayen*: Boitre the bandit? Is he really a Jew?
SECOND *Dayen*: For our sins, a draft-dodger, and according to what people say, he's even from a good
family, more's the pity. Practically a grandson of the
Gaon of Vilna, a prodigy of the Volozhin Yeshiva.
KALMEN GITELES [*looks up from his book*]: What are you
talking about, *Dayen*? Gaon, shmaon! It's Yisroel the
coachman's son. Two years ago I had him drafted
into the army. There he sits, Bontshe the Recruit-
Nabber. I had no end of trouble with him. Had to
have him nabbed several times. [. . .]
KALMEN GITELES [*quietly to the bes din and to* YEKHIEL
MALVE, *the sexton*]: We come here and sit down at
our meetings like robots. We talk, but there's no one
to talk to. The *kahal* should not get involved. You'll
see, it will end badly. At that time, it was Arn-Volf
who insisted on having him drafted, not I. So who is
responsible here? [. . .]
KALMEN GITELES: Look, the boy was already a bandit
in his mother's belly [*looks around*]. And the girl,
Arn-Volf's Sterele . . . [*whispers*]
FIRST DAYEN: Is that true?
KALMEN GITELES: What did you think, that the daughter of the head of the Community, the *Parnes Khoydesh,* is going to remain an old maid for no reason?
That it is no concern of the *kahal*? Why should a
whole Jewish community be dragged into a misfortune, when it is Arn-Volf's own affair? It's already
impossible to ship any merchandise out of the city.
[. . .]

[*In the adjoining room the voice of woman is heard singing a Polish song*]. That's Sterke [*the* RABBI *and the* DAYENS *cover their ears*].

RABBI: "The voice of a woman . . ." It is not proper, not proper.

KALMEN GITELES: Take her to the courtyard, out there with the aristocratic ladies and such forbidden things.

[*The singing stops*]

YEKHIEL MALVE: What nonsense. And the *yishuvniks*, Kalmen? Are they really saying it's the *yishuvniks* that are committing robberies there?

KALMEN GITELES: And you, Yekhiel, think that because you're a moneylender and don't ship merchandise, that you're exempt from it all? Wait, they'll be after your promissory notes and your pawns as well!

YEKHIEL MALVE: Reb Kalmen, the whole town knows that he was handed over to the army on account of one of your geese as well. I'm not responsible. What harm do I do to anybody? [. . .]

[ARN-VOLF *goes over to the table, sets himself down with dignity in the chair of the parnes khoydesh.*]

ARN-VOLF: Nobody takes anything away from Arn-Volf! Nobody grabs anything from him! There's no higher Jewish authority. But the fact that a Jewish girl will now have to get married in a way that's not fitting for the daughter of a good family . . . [*ironically*] I suppose I deserve it. I insist that the *kahal* proclaim that the *yishuvniks* driven from the villages are not to be allowed into the town. Those wretches, once they became homeless, cast off all their Judaism—and busy themselves only with theft and robbery. They lead a dissolute life, they get drunk. Not only that, but they carry various diseases, fevers, scarlatina—may God spare us—with which they have been punished by God. Let it be thus. And the *kahal* will also not be silent regarding that Boitre fellow. Bontshe! The assessor will have the keeper of the keys accompany you. You then will travel the region from settlement to settlement to find out who he is and where he is. They say he keeps himself somewhere in a carpenter's workshop. The *kahal* cannot tolerate the influence of ruffians. And without fail, gentlemen, the wedding of the daughter of Arn-Volf the *parnes khoydesh* will not be delayed. The future in-laws are already on their way [*sighs*]. Because of the problems facing many of us, the evil decrees that cause Jews to lose their livelihoods, the wedding will be celebrated as the *parnes-khoydesh* decrees. There will be no barrels of liquor

in the streets. There will be no tables prepared for the poor, in order not to provoke, God forbid, the hostility of the few decent *yishuvniks*, who have been driven out of their homes and are, alas, wandering around the fields and forests. That is how it will be. I ask if the *kahal* is in agreement with my opinion.

YEKHIEL MALVE: The *kahal* is in agreement. [. . .]

ARN-VOLF: What other matters are before the *kahal*?

ZIML THE SCRIBE: The baker's apprentices came with a petition to the *kahal* that they wish to form a *khevre* [association]. They say they do not wish to be ranked with the riff-raff and sent off to serve in the army.

ARN-VOLF: Baker's apprentices in a *khevre*? It's not a trade. All the women can do it. What is the opinion of the *kahal*?

YEKHIEL MALVE: The *kahal* agrees.

KALMEN GITELES: The *kahal* agrees.

RABBI [*Bends over to the* DAYENS. *They converse quietly among themselves.*]: The *bes din* has deliberated and is in agreement with the opinion of the *parnes khoydesh*.

ZIML THE SCRIBE: They said that in case they do not get a *khevre* they will go over to Boitre, like Lemele Put.

ARN-VOLF: What, is there no more law or morality?

ZIML THE SCRIBE: In addition they said that the *parnes khoydesh* is mistaken if he thinks he will be giving away his daughter in marriage to the son of the Mohylna Rabbi. . . .

ARN-VOLF: Beggars, good-for-nothings—what kind of talk is that?

ZIML THE SCRIBE: That's what they said. And when I asked them "why?" they said "you'll soon see why." [. . .]

ARN-VOLF: [. . .] Rabbi, you are an honest man and scholar of the Torah, explain it to me. How many Jews earn their livelihood from my olive press, how many do I give employment in my brewery, my mill, and my flax business? Why do people hate me? Why does the town want to take revenge against me of all people? Tell me, Rabbi, why do they spread the rumor that my Sterke, an honest Jewish girl, was involved with Khayimke Boitre? I'll have them arrested, I'll make it a town of widows and orphans! I'll have them whipped till the blood flows. [. . .]

KALMEN GITELES: Reb Arn-Volf, in my opinion you're right. But, you see . . . the *kahal* after all can't . . . it can't, how shall I put it . . . can't be expected to. . . . You'll see, it will all end badly! [. . .]

[*All exit.* ARN-VOLF *remains alone, sits down at the table with his head in his hands.* BEYLE, *his wife, quietly enters at stage right and stands behind his chair.*]

BEYLE: Arn-Volf?

ARN-VOLF: It's not good! Not good!

BEYLE: What are we supposed to do with her? With Stere? She says she won't immerse herself in the *mikve*. She refuses. And when I started talking! Talking about the future bridegroom—what distinguished lineage, what a fine mind—she answered, I can hardly bring myself to say it, that she would strangle him.

ARN-VOLF: What? [*jumps up*]

BEYLE: What can I do? I'm only her stepmother. A *dybbuk* has entered into that girl.

ARN-VOLF: Where is she? What kind of talk is that? Beyle, call her! Sterke!

[BEYLE *goes to the door and calls her in.*]

BEYLE: Sterke, Sterkele. Your father is calling you!

[STERE *enters, wrapped in a shawl.*]

ARN-VOLF: Come here, Stere. Sit down. I want to ask your advice.

STERE [*sits down*]: Well?

ARN-VOLF: There's a world of mothers with children, not a *parnes-khoydesh* world, just simple people. They marry off their children on time, at eight years of age, at eleven, at fourteen! So I ask you, why have I been cursed? Doesn't it bother you that you're now an old maid?

STERE: I wanted to get married on time.

ARN-VOLF [*interrupts her*]: I've heard that already! Foolishness! I committed a great sin! I'm only human. Well and good, you had a fiancé, a fine man, a man of learning, a man of property. . . . But you have a father who is a murderer and he killed him. I have sinned. But Khayimke is no more. He died in the military, he's dead!

STERE: And who is Boitre?

BEYLE: Shh . . . Don't talk so loud . . . Shh . . .

STERE: It's good that Boitre carried off the trousseau. I'll dress in rags. I'll spit in his face, that fine bridegroom, with his sidelocks, his high Adam's apple. He's just like Yekhiel Malve and his promissory notes. It all smells of axle-grease and brandy. Oh no, I won't cut my hair! Never . . . Who can help me? God? I could have been born somewhere else. I could have been born among the Zelichowickis, not even a Jewish girl. And who is Boitre? Who is he? A robber? For justice! Such a man has already been written about, but you don't know it. You know nothing.

ARN-VOLF: You impudent girl! Khayimke Boitre is a murderer!

BEYLE: I told you, Arn-Volf, that nothing good will come out of those teachers, from learning German, from those books she reads.

STERE: I will run away! I will run wherever my eyes take me.

[BOITRE *appears in an open window.* STERE *stands with her face to the window, trembles.*]

STERE: Oh!

BEYLE: What is it, daughter?

[STERE *looks nervously at the window.* ARN-VOLF *and* BEYLE *also turn towards the window, but* BOITRE *has disappeared. They do not understand what has happened.*]

Curtain

[. . .]

[*In the Kreve Forest*]

YERAKHMIEL [*enters in holiday dress and with a whip in his hand*]: I've brought a wagon full of poor people and there are women and children as well. All hell has broken loose. The black highway is full of people. *Mazel tov*, bridegroom! [*kisses* BOITRE]. *Mazel tov*, bride. What, you're all going to Volhynia? Really? Right after the wedding, all of you to Volhynia? Well, why not? The poor will become peasants. Enough of slaving away! Why not? I'm coming too. Yes, Yerakhmiel Balegole [coachman] too. Why not? A country of our own. What else?

BOITRE: Sit, Yerakhmiel, sit down.

YERAKHMIEL: Ay, if your father Yisroel were alive, he'd be proud. What an honor! The son of a simple coachman. Are you really leading the common people to Volhynia? So, a king, a true monarch! I can understand it. We've labored long enough for the rich. We've had it up to here. Let the poor man do something for himself, too. Why not? As the prophet says—a wolf with a wolf and a sheep with a sheep.

KALMEN GITELES [*to the members of the bes din*]: My such a great scholar! A coachman the son of a coachman.

YERAKHMIEL: *Lechayim*, Jews, to life! An end to our troubles! What's the matter? Let there be joy! We'll do a dance [*tucks up his coat, dances*].

Let's sing the *Koza*! Jews, it's the messianic age! *Prideh koza do voza*! [Ukrainian, lit., "The goat will come to the cart," a song and saying meaning "your turn will come; we'll get you yet."]

ALL: *Pride koza do voza! Pride koza do voza!* [. . .]

[*The sound of drums is heard in the forest. The people grow silent.*]

MELKE [*runs in*]: The whole forest is surrounded by troops. It's impossible to get out of the forest.

STERE: Ay, he was the one who got us surrounded. He did it! [*to her father*] I will go to the magistrate and tell him that you hid people from the tax officials, hid soldiers, I'll say you steal Zelichowicki's brandy. He is not devout! Do not believe him! He once counted money on the Sabbath eve and lit candles!

ARN-VOLF: The *kahal* has no idea what this is about. Do not believe her. The young lout must have spread malicious rumors. The magistrate is a drunkard and a quarrelsome person and he doesn't care a whit about *kahal* matters.

BOITRE [*puts* STERE *in her seat.*]: Let it be! I'll do it myself! [. . .]

VOICE FROM THE FOREST: Khayim! Run away, Khayim! The magistrate and two hundred soldiers are coming here!

[*The* kahal *and Bes Din jump up from their seats. The poor at their table are terribly frightened.* BOITRE *remains seated as if nothing had happened.* STERE *falls to the table and weeps.*]

HAIRY POOR MAN: Oy, we'll all be arrested!

ARN-VOLF [*regains his previous appearance*]: What did you think, Khayimke—that the world is chaos, without rules? What did you think, you lowlife—that you will stomp on our traditional Jewish ways? *Kahal* is *kahal*, and you, my daughter, come with me now! I will forgive you. Do not shame me in front of people, daughter.

[*Stere jumps to her father, wants to throw herself at him.*]

BOITRE [*takes her and sits her down next to him*]: Let me do it.

RABBI [*to* BOITRE]: Sinful Jew, you thought to yourself: "there is no law and there is no judge." Wait, they will be flogging your hide. Do you know that even in hell there is no place for you. Jews, by the will of God and of this holy community, I decree that whoever has even a spark of Jewishness in his heart must at once avoid being in his presence [*all are silent*].

LEMELE PUT [*rushes in*]: Khayimke, run away!

BOITRE [*to* LEMELE]: Wait, Reb Arn-Volf, we still have to perform the marriage ceremony!

ARN-VOLF: In hell they'll perform the marriage ceremony for you and the Queen of Sheba!

[BOITRE *stands up. Everyone moves away from him. He comes forward, takes the* RABBI *and the* FIRST DAYEN *by the collar and stands them next to the table where he sits with* STERE.]

FIRST DAYEN: Help, robbers!

BOITRE: Perform the ceremony.

ARN-VOLF [*enraged*]: Disappear, you murderer! My daughter is no bride for you! Open the doors, you'll all be arrested! You'll be put in chains!

BOITRE [*takes* STERE's *hand, puts a ring on her fingers and says in Hebrew*]: *Harei at mekudeshet . . .* By this ring thou art consecrated unto me according to the laws of Moses and Israel.

ARN-VOLF: Ay, beat him! What has he done? Ay!

[*No one makes a move.* BOITRE *and* STERE *sit calmly as if nothing had happened. Everything is quiet for a while, a motionless pause. The drums are heard at the foot of the nearby hill.*]

A VOICE FROM THE FOREST: Khayim, they're coming! Here they come!

BOITRE [*to* LEMELE PUT]: Can we get out?

LEMELE PUT: No.

BOITRE: Burn the woods! Set the edge of the forest on fire!

LEMELE PUT [*turns away, takes a candle and sets a barrel of tar on fire. No one notices.*] [. . .]

A VOICE: Oh, there's a fire!

SECOND VOICE: They've set a fire!

THIRD VOICE: A raging fire! A raging fire! [. . .]

A VOICE: Where is Arn-Volf? Let's finish him off!

[*The crowd flings itself at* ARN-VOLF. LEMELE PUT, STERE *and* BOITRE *run to the hill.*]

STERE: Come quickly, quickly, run away!

BOITRE: Yes! [*he clasps* STERE *in his arms and leaps up the hill with her*]

[*A shot is heard.* STERE *falls.* BOITRE *bends over her.*]

LEMELE PUT: Come down, they're shooting here! Come down!

BOITRE: I'll take her with me.

LEMELE PUT: Come!

[*Shooting is heard.*]

[BOITRE, *lifting* STERE *in his arms, falls down together with her. He tries to lift her up, but he can't.*]

Translated by Solon Beinfeld.

Zalman Shneour

Newspapers
1936

I

Once upon a time, in the "good old days"—some ten or twenty years ago, let's say—the people in Shklov still did not know what newspapers really were like. Their sole source of news was a solitary issue of the *Hamelitz* (Hebrew daily), to which the apothecary subscribed. Willy-nilly the Jews in the little town had to quaff from this dubious source. Lacking an *ethrog* (citron), one pronounces a benediction over a potato.

Passing through so many Shklovian hands, the shop-worn news of the *Hamelitz* became rather thoroughly provincialized. When the Prince of Wales paid a visit to Marienbad, the people in Shklov already knew, for a certainty, that he had been overpowered by a hankering for Jewish stuffed fish, for which the kosher restaurants of Marienbad are celebrated. When Tolstoi began familiarizing himself with Hebrew legends, Shklov immediately ferreted out the fact that the Count had already reached the Talmudic tractate *Berachoth* and that, any day now, he was going to embrace the Jewish faith. When Rothschild was all set to make a loan to the Turks, the little town of Shklov grasped that what the financier had in view was to buy back Palestine. All the charts of the General Military Staff and all the political situations were adumbrated point by point by the politicos of Shklov as clearly as if they had everything in the palms of their hands. Each finger represented a sovereign state; each line on their palms, a fortress-guarded river. Between the afternoon prayer service of *mincha* and the evening prayer of *maariv* sundry beards, gray and rumpled, bent over the geographic palm of the moderator of the forum; there, by the gray light dribbling in through the window, did they search for national frontiers and the destinies of sovereign states. But, at the very height of the debate, with the twinkling of the first little star against the somber sky and the glimmering of the first small lamp in the impoverished synagogue in the backwoods of Lithuania, there would come the abrupt slam on the reading stand at the pulpit and the voice of the cantor soared up from the altar and diffused itself with a strange sadness:

"And He, the Merciful One, shall forgive us our trangressions and shall not destroy us—"

The sovereign states dissipated like smoke; the fish of the Prince of Wales lost its Jewish tang, the millions of Rothschild lost their value. The politicos, who had been so heated in their debate, began to chime in with the cantor, their voices sounding ever so rapt in the semidarkness:

"Help us, O Lord! The King of Heaven will respond to us in the hour we call upon Him—"

And then there arose a hero, a man with but one hand, who dwelt in the neglected little town of Shklov. He had been a cobbler but, having lost a hand, had been forced to give up his trade. Now he put forth, as it were, the palm of his remaining hand (the right one) and, like Peter the Great, broke a window through into Europe, letting a veritable torrent of newspapers rush into the little town. Thenceforth the newspapers passed from the keeping of isolated individuals and became common property. The desiccated hands of the synagogue politicos lost their geographical value; they were unable to withstand the competition of the maps that were printed in the newspapers in connection with each important political event.

However, although the reading of Yiddish newspapers had now become a necessity in Shklov, the reading of newspapers in the Russian language still remained a luxury, a caste mark of the intelligentsia, a symbol of importance tantamount, for instance, to stopping the Inspector of Police on the street for a chat. You could even read a Russian newspaper upside down, if you liked—it did not really matter.

Then, from the day Russian newspapers costing a kopeck appeared in Shklov, this luxury became a cheap one. Uncle Uri, too, God be thanked, could allow himself such a pleasure, and that not merely on account of public prestige, but also for the sake of being able, once every two weeks or so, to share with Aunt Feiga some conversation about the things they were writing about in the papers. Uncle Uri, now, was one man who surely knew how to handle a Russian newspaper. After all, he had once lived for half a year in Moscow—from whence he had been expelled.

II

But before Uncle Uri sits down to the perusal of his newspaper, you must be introduced to the man who sells the papers, and told just how he came to be like one of the family at the home of Uncle Uri.

There was, in Shklov, a Jewish shoemaker; they called him Mutteh—a naive little Jew he was, and a cobbler. One day he happened to run a rusty awl into his left hand; his hand became all swollen; he went with it from doctor to doctor until—may this never befall any Jew!—it was cut off for him. And this man, this Mutteh, came home from the county hospital without a left hand. All through that day he sat there by his neglected cobbler's bench without a word, and with glazed eyes stared at his battered lasts. The awl was there, so was the waxed thread, so were the hammer and pegs, and when it came to holes in Jewish soles, there was no shortage of them either—but as for a left hand, it was no longer there. All that remained was to seek relief from the community or to go begging from door to door.

But then, the Lord actually sends the cure before the affliction—and, even so, He had created newspapers before Mutteh had lost his hand. The wide, swishing waves of newsprint had been surging for a number of years from the centers of government into the towns and settlements. Locust swarms of inky words had come flying, bearing everywhere an echo of world-wide sensations, the hum of great cities, the nervous buzzing of recent days—but into Shklov itself they had as yet been unable to penetrate; they had always been forced to bypass Shklov's traditions, its little houses of wood, and its boggy roads, and had veered off. Things had gone on like that until one-winged Mutteh got up from his battered, dusty cobbler's bench and diverted the paper torrent into the tiny town.

One fine day the people suddenly beheld Mutteh, with his childlike blue eyes, and his snippy little beard, gray and rumpled, carrying some sort of a square bundle under his half-amputated arm. The bundle was wrapped up in a red bandanna. Come now, what could a Jew like Mutteh be distributing?

Quietly, like a beggar, he dropped in at every house and offered for sale a paper—written in Russian or Yiddish. The newspapers were, truth to tell, as much in keeping with Mutteh's appearance as a rifle in the hands of a *melamed*, but what can you do when you know the Jew, and he has a hand missing? You take his newspaper and give him a copper for it. The newspaper itself lies around for a day or two until you get a chance to look it over.

That's how, little by little, the people in the town began getting used to the printed sheets, and if Mutteh failed to show up they actually missed him and, as time went by, his clients would have a bone to pick with him when he did appear at last!

"What's all this, Mutteh? Wherever did you disappear to yesterday? Why, we're right up to the point in

the serial where they're dragging the girl to the sultan's harem!"

Thus did Mutteh's popularity increase from day to day; his beggarly peddling had turned into a mission, into a spiritual need for the little town, and his old, patched, sheepskin coat was now replaced by a new overcoat with a velvet collar. No longer did Mutteh conceal his newspapers in a bandanna, as if they were contraband; he took to distributing them openly and with pride, and dropped in at all the best homes with all the free-and-easy airs of a marriage broker. He called out his wares in the street: "Fellow Jews, buy a *Friend* to bring home, or get a bit of *Life*, or buy a *Day*, or a *Northie*—" the last being a coined contraction, peculiar to Mutteh, of the *Northwestern Region*. And, from time to time, he himself took a look at the "ink spots."

By now Mutteh was a hero. God alone knows where he got the combination of a pair of dandified, narrow trousers and a cap embroidered with the reddish bands of a clerk in some unknown branch of the government. To Mutteh's taste this was the most appropriate get up for a Jewish newsdealer. The little town at once accepted this mixed attire: if a newsdealer dressed that way, it followed that that was the way for a newsdealer to dress.

Exactly at five in the afternoon, after the delivery of the mail, the housewives would already be looking out of their windows to see if Mutteh was coming with the folded newspapers under the stump of his left arm. When he did arrive, he was met halfway. The common folk bought the Yiddish papers and paid cash, while the home owners bought the Russian ones, and on credit.

When Mutteh dropped in at the home of Uncle Uri, Auntie Feiga would come out to meet him, buy her kopeck paper and then place it on the bureau. There these Russian papers would accumulate, without being looked at for weeks at a time. Auntie Feiga herself was content to hear the most important news from the dealer:

"Well, Reb Mutteh, what's the latest?"

By this time Mutteh had got used to relieving his steady customers from the extra work of actually reading the papers. Before setting out on his deliveries, he would skim the cream of the news, which he would then impart to his clients.

"Well, now, in Warsaw, it says here, a mother and three children had their throats cut and in the morning, it says here, they were found dead—"

Ever since Mutteh had begun selling papers, a score or so of Russian words had battered their way into his head, and he was using them in season and out. With his "It says here" he was trying to express himself in really high-class style, but just who or what was actually saying all these things was something no one could possibly make out. However, Auntie Feiga felt certain that, when it comes to reporting the news in the papers, that was the way one should express oneself.

"*Oy*, may woe pass me by!" Auntie Feiga moans, after Mutteh has told her the newest item. She shakes her head and props up her cheek with two fingers.

"And in Riga, it says here—" Mutteh the newsdealer proceeds to throw a still greater scare into her, making a decisive sweep with the stump of his arm—"in Riga they're figuring on marching out with red 'symphonies' on the nineteenth of August—that's what them 'Soshalists' are figuring. So it says here, if they do march, they'll be ground to dust and powder—"

"They shouldn't go butting in where they don't belong." Auntie Feiga doesn't lose her presence of mind. "Hear anything about the war?"

"China is rioting—there's a republic coming. So, it says here, if they're met up with, blood will flow in the streets, it says here—"

"Where is that?" Auntie Feiga becomes frightened.

"In China," says Mutteh, with a nod in the direction of China.

"What a world this is, to be sure," says Auntie Feiga and takes her fingers away from her cheek. Just what has gotten into China to be acting up like this is something she cannot grasp, but she goes on standing there, just the same, ready to fulfill her duty of absorbing the latest news. As for Mutteh, he goes right on with his speech, and makes sure his client is supplied with all the necessary data:

"And in Moscow, it says here, twenty Jewish merchants of the Second Guild were put out of the city, so if they should come back, it says here, why—" At this point Mutteh makes an exceedingly wide sweep with his stump and words fail him. However, Auntie Feiga has grasped on her own what sort of a catastrophe there would be if these twenty merchants of the Second Guild should come back to Moscow; she sighs deeply and repeatedly, half out of pity, half for the looks of the thing.

Having dished out his portion of news, Mutteh takes off his cap with its trimming of some unknown governmental department, says goodby, kisses the tiny scroll on the lintel of the door, and makes his exit. A minute or so later, you can hear his assured voice piping at another door:

"So it says here, if, it says here—" and the tale begins all over again.

The sheets of the *Kopeck Gazette* lie on the bureau, accumulating from day to day, and assuring the whole household of a supply of paper and stoppers for the bottles of Sabbath wine, and yet there always remains a plentiful store of it. Should Auntie Feiga, in a huffy mood, notice this growing heap of newspapers, she will start yelling at the children:

"You rascals, you loafers. At first they give you no rest: 'Buy a paper, mamma—mamma, buy a paper!'—so's you might think that the only thing they do is read newspapers. But nothing of the sort! Just a lot of money thrown out of the window. There, tomorrow I'll stop buying the papers."

On the morrow, however, Mutteh arrives with a bundle of fresh newspapers, redolent of ink, says hello in his broken Russian, and launches into a recital of the news—dealing with Samara, with Berlin, with the Duma, and with Japan. All you hear is "If, it says here," and "It says here that, without fail." Auntie Feiga's wrath dissipates like smoke, and another newssheet, practically fresh off the press, is lying on top of the others on the bureau.

III

At midnight, in a great city, the linotypes clatter and the rotary presses rumble; metal pours through the matrices, enormous rolls of newsprint revolve. Workers in the graphic trades, men and women, sweating and covered with graphite dust, their eyes bloodshot and sleepy, are exerting their last strength by tinted electric bulbs—and all this to the end that Uncle Uri may have a fresh newssheet lying on his bureau and be able to throw a condescending squint at it from a distance. True, at times he will tap the pile of newspapers and say to himself: "I ought to read these"—only to settle down to his Mishna or his Hasidic *Holy Sayings*.

But, just the same, the one fine day comes at last, and Uncle Uri gets up from his postprandial siesta in an especially exalted spiritual mood—for the sole purpose of reading the Russian newspapers. One bearded cheek is rumpled and reddened, while the beard on the other is bristling: one can easily tell which side he has been sleeping on. He rinses his mouth, tossing his head quite energetically as he does so, then calls out in a reinvigorated voice:

"Feiga, get the samovar going!"

The samovar is lighted and, until it warms up, Uncle Uri leans on the ledges of the small window.

"Feiga, my wife," he sings out, "give me something from over there, a newspaper or something."

Auntie Feiga walks up to the bureau, fully prepared to help her husband in such an impulsive spiritual undertaking. The children's schoolbooks and notebooks are on top of the newspapers; Auntie Feiga thrusts two fingers into the pile: which newssheet she draws out will be the one that gets read. The date on the paper makes no difference—nor does the month, for that matter.

"There!" Auntie Feiga brings the paper over to Uncle Uri. "So you've gotten around to reading the papers at last."

"I can tell *you* have lots of time," Uncle Uri remarks in a tone implying that he himself is actually occupied day and night. At the same time, he saddles his nose with spectacles, making them jut out in a way that is somehow oddly strained, solemn. . . . His squinting eyes behind the old-fashioned lenses become large and profound: it's actually frightening merely to look at them.

Uncle Uri begins with the name of the masthead, then plunges into the terms of subscription—by the year, half-year, month—and makes certain calculations:

"Feiga," he shouts to his wife in the kitchen, "how much do you pay for the paper? A kopeck a day? Well, look here: you can subscribe for a whole year for three roubles. So what kind of a bargain are we getting? We'd be better off subscribing. There, Zhama gets it that way every day from St. Petersburg, with his address all in print: 'To Mr.——.' Looks impressive."

"So go ahead and subscribe," Feiga's voice answers from the kitchen.

"If God grants me health I, with God's help, will subscribe, so's to get the paper directly from St. Peterburg."

Having made this promise, Uncle Uri now buckles down to the job. As far as actual reading is concerned, Uncle Uri does read, but only the headlines in their bold type—this comes easiest of all to him. As for the tiny Russian characters that are strewn like black poppy seed under these headlines, well, he's afraid even to make a start on them. During his annual attendance at the fair at Nizhni Novgorod, Uncle Uri usually reads a goodish number of shop signs; the newspaper headlines have very much the same look to him as those soiled notices: there you have Furs, Fish, Machinery, Sugar; here you have Bombs, Scandal, Murder, Wars. Whatever the headlines fail to state fully he supplements from his own imagination.

Uncle Uri reads the heading of the leading editorial—two words from the text, and the third his own, in explanation:

"'We have no de-sire to en-en-dure, endure, hun-hun-ger, hunger.' That means, 'We have no desire to endure hunger.' You hear that, Feiga?" he shouts to his wife in the kitchen.

"I hear you," Auntie Feiga answers and pauses for a moment in the doorway of the dining room, where Uncle Uri is reading the papers.

"'We have no desire to endure hunger!'" proclaims Uncle Uri and looks at her from behind his old-fashioned spectacles with those frightening, magnified eyes. "Let there be an end to hunger! They have sucked our blood long enough! That's well written, and the man is right."

"'Bomb dis-dis-covered in Nizhini Nov-gorod,'" Uncle Uri reads the second headline. "'Bomb discovered in Nizhni Novgorod.' You hear that, Feiga?" he immediately shouts to his spouse, who is busy with the samovar. "There, they've started throwing bombs again in Nizhni. And who do you think they'll pick on? The Jews at the fair, of course. . . . Lord, have mercy on us!"

Auntie Feiga's faint sigh reaches him from the kitchen, as a sign that she has heard the news.

Uncle Uri reads on:

"'Ri-riot-ing in To-ky-o.' There you are! They're rioting again. You hear that, Feiga? Great riots in Tokyo. They're fighting, killing—the whole world is turning upside down there. God knows how this will end. Yes, sir!"

The news concerning the riots in Tokyo Auntie Feiga has already heard from Mutteh the newsdealer, a considerable while back. Just the same, she willingly listens to it a second time and rejoices because her old husband (not to sin before God) understands, among other things, how to read Russian; he's all right; one can rely on him.

As for Uncle Uri, he plunges still deeper into his newspaper:

"'Dis-dis-sens-sions, dissensions among Allies!' Allies—that means the members of the Black Hundreds, that's what it means! You hear that, Feiga?"

"What's that about the Allies?" Feiga questions him from the kitchen.

"Dis-sensions. The devil alone can make out what they have scribbled there. What a nasty word! Where's our Talmudist? Doing his lessons? There, ask him now what dis-sen-sions means—let's see what he knows—"

"He doesn't know," Auntie Feiga reports back a minute or so later. "He looked it up, he searched for it, he mumbled something—and he doesn't know."

"What's that? He doesn't know either? What's he studying for, in that case? Why, we pay his teacher three roubles a month, I think—we pay him, all right. It's just money thrown out!"

"It's money thrown out," Auntie Feiga concurs. But Uncle Uri chases away the fiasco of the news about dissensions with another headline:

"'Gran-gran-diose, grandiose scan-dal in the Duma. . . .' There, Feiga, you hear that? There's another scandal in the Duma already. If they write that, it's a grandiose scandal then, sure enough, it must be a scandal on a big scale—it's not just a small one. The foes of Israel there are again turning the world upside down. It must be that Pureshkevich again for sure—may his name and his memory be erased! Help, police! Whatever does he want from us, that *goy*? Pestering us like that—"

Auntie Feiga brings the samovar to the table and steeps the tea, but Uncle Uri is still reading the headlines out loud. From them he passes on to the advertisements, and he shares everything with his wife:

"You hear, Feiga? They're looking for servants. A great find—they have to go looking for them, yet. Listen to this, Feiga—there are doctors begging for people to come to them for treatment—there, look for yourself! And yet our miserable second-class doctor is dissatisfied when you give him fifteen kopecks—you've got to hand him twenty kopecks, without fail, otherwise it's lowering his dignity! There, Zhama's daughter, of all people, wants to go away to study toothjerking. Yes, yes, she'll be about as lucky as a tabby cat. You can see for yourself, dentists are as plentiful as dogs here. Let's see—boarding houses . . . theaters . . . face powder. There's nothing worth while hearing here and nothing worth seeing—"

Suddenly Uncle Uri's eye is arrested by the cut of a boot with Finest Footwear bold lettered on the sole; and he shouts to Auntie Feiga:

"Feiga, Feiga—how much did we pay for the children's shoes, now? Four roubles a pair? An awful bargain: you can have a pair for three roubles, according to this. You're a fine manager, when you have the money—"

"What are you picking on me for, now?" Auntie Feiga snarls back at him. "You feel like an accountant, maybe? There, you wanted tea, didn't you? So drink your tea! You've done enough reading!"

Uncle Uri, in a temper, throws the Russian paper aside.

"It's no use talking to you! Better pour me a glass of tea."

Auntie Feiga pours an overflowing glass of tea for Uncle Uri, and hands him some raspberry jam to quiet his nerves which have become frazzled from reading the paper. She replaces the paper on the bureau. On the morrow, and the day after, many more papers will be added to it—there will be plenty of paper for bottle stoppers. And—who knows—a couple of weeks later, when Uncle Uri sits down again to read a paper, Auntie Feiga's two fingers may pull out the very same one which he had read and forgotten, and Uncle Uri will read the headlines all over again, one after the other. He will begin with the leading editorial: "We have no desire to endure hunger," read about the sizable scandal in the Duma, and will keep on telling Auntie Feiga all the news until, among the advertisements, he stumbles upon the cut of a boot; that's where he'll stop, mildly surprised and a little dissatisfied, and hurl the paper to the floor:

"There, it's always the same thing, day after day! There's nothing worth while hearing here, nothing worth seeing. Feiga, you'd better pour me a glass of tea!"

Just the same, if the Russian writers, pressmen, and compositors only knew how closely Uncle Uri studied their paper, they would perform their heavy labors still more sedulously and with a greater will, amid the foggy, insomniac nights of St. Petersburg. . . .

Translated by Moshe Spiegel.

Israel Joshua Singer

The Brothers Ashkenazi
1936

Part One: Birth

Two

The Lodz merchant and community head, Abraham Hersh Ashkenazi, known as Abraham Hersh Danziger for his frequent trips to Danzig, sat over a Tractate Zebahim, brooding and tugging at his long and thick black beard.

He wasn't worried about making a living. Even after decades of exclusion from Wilki and the Weavers'

Guild a sizable Jewish community had managed to flourish in Lodz, complete with its own rabbi, assistant rabbis, ritual slaughterers, ritual bath, synagogues, and cemetery.

The reason the Jews prospered was that the German weavers produced a very inferior cloth that was disdained by the rich and the discriminating, who demanded the soft wools, fine silks, gleaming satins and velvets from abroad. To fill this need, the wealthier Jews took wagons and, later, the first trains to Danzig and Leipzig, while those less affluent conspired with border guards to smuggle in fabrics from Germany. At the same time barefoot Jewish peddlers and runners fanned out across sandy country lanes to buy wool from the peasants to sell to Lodz merchants, who in turn shipped it abroad to be spun into yarn. The peasants, who used to leave their sheep filthy and unshorn, now bathed them in streams to render the fleece white and clean. Speculators and leaseholders bought up entire future yields of flocks on landed estates.

The German master weavers of Lodz vilified the Jews for importing foreign goods from Germany at the expense of the local industry. They also resented the fact that Jewish merchants issued cotton to the poor German weavers, thus bringing down the price of the finished goods. These cotton merchants weren't able to obtain credit at the banks, as were their German competitors, and they lacked the cash with which to pay the weavers. They therefore issued their own scrip to the weavers when they delivered the finished goods on Friday evenings, and the Jewish tailors, cobblers, and shopkeepers accepted the scrip in lieu of money.

When the German master weavers complained, the authorities outlawed the practice. They also sent a representative to England to buy up cotton, thus pushing the Jews out of business. But the cotton ended up being stolen by government officials. The authorities generally found it easier to accept bribes from the Jews, who continued issuing the scrip and doing business as usual.

Among the most respectable and affluent citizens of Lodz was Abraham Hersh Ashkenazi, who traveled to Danzig on buying trips several times a year. He had just returned from such a journey which had proved even more profitable that usual. He had fine presents for his wife and daughters and a handsome silver cup that he was saving to present to the Rabbi of Warka, whose disciple he was.

Things at home were going along splendidly, and Abraham Hersh was delighted. But as a leader of the community, a position he held despite his youth and as the result of his wealth, scholarship, and piety, he was disturbed by a number of problems that had cropped up during his absence.

First, funds were needed to provide Passover products for the town's poor, not only the beggars but also those who worked but hadn't managed to save up enough from a year's toil to buy the necessary matzos, wine, eggs, meat, and cooking fat for the holiday. Upon his return, Abraham Hersh had taken his red kerchief and, accompanied by several other community leaders, had solicited the affluent households. It hadn't sufficed, and the poor had stormed the communal house, demanding their due.

Second, there were Jewish prisoners to be ransomed. Throughout Poland, the tsar's Cossacks were fighting the Polish gentry, who sought to restore a Polish king to the throne, and loyal Jewish leaseholders were engaged in smuggling gunpowder to their Polish masters hiding in the forests.

Just recently, a group of Jews had been caught smuggling a quantity of gunpowder in barrels of apples. At first, the Cossacks had found nothing by poking their lances into the barrels, but as they started appropriating the apples, they found the powder. Some of the Jews were hanged on the spot, others were thrown into prison. Those who were executed had to be given decent Jewish burials. Those in prison had to be ransomed or at least provided with matzos for the holiday.

Third, a group of newly rich, enlightened Jews who were anxious to shed the yoke of Jewishness had petitioned the government to allow them to put up a modern school where their children could learn the ways of the gentile. There were rumors that they also planned to build a German type of temple with an organ and a cantor who chanted like a priest. Although the authorities were slow to respond to this request, the parvenu Jews were tossing money about freely, and everyone knew what money could accomplish; Abraham Hersh and the other traditionalists considered such a temple far worse than a church since only Christians and converts attended the latter, while the former was liable to entice the poorer Jews away from the path of righteousness, which was the first step toward apostasy.

Fourth, Jewish runners who roamed the countryside buying up wool, hides, and hog bristles learned that a wayward Lodz youth, Naftali the Convert, who more than once had been driven from the synagogue courtyard for flouting the laws of Jewishness, had apprenticed himself to a German weaver, for whom he worked on the Sabbath and with whom he ate pork.

Abraham Hersh sent for the youth and warned that he would turn him over to the authorities for conscription, but the fellow remained recalcitrant. The authorities refused to conscript him despite the community's pleas, and this helped encourage other Jewish youths to make overtures to the gentiles. One, Mendel Flederbaum, who employed several gentile weavers, learned the trade from his workers and applied to the gentile guild to accept him as a master weaver. He was helped in this by the authorities after he had shaved his beard, renounced the traditional garb, and learned to speak and write Russian.

Following this, several others of shaky faith got the urge to emulate the renegades. At this time an epidemic swept the town, and children died of the scarlet fever. This was seen as a clear sign of God's punishment upon Lodz for the sins of its heretics.

Another thorn in Abraham Hersh's side was his wife's objections to his visiting his rabbi on the holiday. He was accustomed to going to Warka not only on Rosh Hashanah, Yom Kippur, and Shevuot but also on Passover, despite his wife's annual complaints that she would be forced to celebrate the Seder at her father's, the assistant rabbi of Ozorkow, like some widow, God forbid.

Not that Abraham Hersh was one to be moved by female tears. A woman was only a woman, after all. But this time things were somewhat different. His wife was due at any time now, and since the child kicked on her right side she expected a boy.

"I'll kill myself if you're not here for the circumcision! I'll never endure the shame of it . . ." she bleated.

Nor were the roads to Warka safe, people warned him. The Cossacks were scouring the countryside and harassing travelers. Innocent people had been flogged and even hanged.

But Abraham Hersh had urgent reasons to go. On his last visit he had mentioned that his wife was pregnant, to which the rabbi had commented, "Your generations shall be men of wealth."

This had disturbed Abraham Hersh, and he had quickly said, "I would prefer them to be God-fearing men, Rabbi.

But the rabbi hadn't responded, and Abraham Hersh hadn't pressed the issue. Still, the remark had sounded ominous, and Abraham Hersh was anxious to resolve it before it was too late.

The dangers of the road didn't concern him at all—he was accustomed to dealing with such things. The only thing that held him back was leaving his wife alone during the labor and delivery, and later, at the circumcision if, with God's help, the baby turned out to be a boy.

But there were other considerations. A number of impoverished Warka Hasidim were looking forward to a trip at his expense, and they would jeer at him for letting a woman dissuade him. It wasn't fair to deprive Jews of a holiday at their rabbi's table. Besides, how would it look if he presented the rabbi the silver Elijah's cup on Shevuot instead of on Passover? . . .

Had his wife been a sensible person instead of a woman, she would have urged him to go and resolve the question of their child's future with the rabbi. But he, being a man, couldn't allow her tears to sway him.

He went to the closet, got down the large leather valise that he always took with him to Danzig, and packed his phylacteries, prayer shawl, a satin gabardine, some shirts, the silver cup, and some holy books to study along the way. Being a good Warka Hasid, he remembered to include several bottles of Passover aquavit and sent the maid, Sarah Leah, for the coachman.

Belly jutting, his wife erupted with her usual complaints, but Abraham Hersh didn't even blink an eye. He kissed the doorpost amulet, and as he already stood on the threshold, he wished her an easy delivery. He suddenly reminded himself.

"If, with God's help, it's a boy, he is to be named Simha Bunem after the Przysucha Rabbi, blessed be his memory. That's the way I want it, you hear?" he shouted into the room.

THREE

Mistress Ashkenazi hadn't been wrong—the signs presaging the birth of a boy proved true. But instead of one son there were two.

After a night of anguish which coincided with the first Seder, a child was born at dawn. The neighbor women in attendance slapped the infant's rump to make it cry and held it up to the lamp.

"Congratulations, it's a boy!" they announced to the mother.

But she didn't stop screaming. The women stroked her sweating face. "Enough already. It's all over."

Sarah Leah, who was an experienced midwife, saw that it was far from over. "Grab hold of the headboard, mistress darling," she advised. "It'll make things easier."

After a number of minutes another infant emerged, a big, heavy baby that needed no slap to make it bawl.

Sarah Leah took it and held it to the light. "Another boy! A real buster this time, the evil eye spare him."

The women found two different colored ribbons to tie around the boys' wrists, but it wasn't necessary since only a fool could have mistaken the two. The elder was slight, scrawny, with sparse fair hair over a narrow skull, while the younger was long and robust with a huge head of black curly hair. The elder piped in a shrill wail, while the younger bellowed like a bullock.

"One just like the mistress and the other a spitting image of the master," Sarah Leah said, handing the cleansed, dressed infants to their mother, who quickly clasped the elder twin to her breast.

"Hush, don't carry on so," she chided the younger twin, who howled as if out of jealousy.

She sprayed a few drops of milk into the mouths of the boys to teach them how to suckle. The younger took to the nipple without a sound, but the elder could only scream in frustration.

For the whole eight days preceding the circumcision the mother fretted against her mound of pillows about the problem of naming the babies. She had mentioned to her husband that if it turned out a boy, she would have liked to name it after her grandfather Jacob Meir, the Rabbi of Wodzislaw, but Abraham Hersh wouldn't hear of it. He insisted it be called Simha Bunem after the Przysucha Rabbi.

"You can name girls after whomever you want, but the boys belong to me," he told her.

Now that he was away, the responsibility lay upon her. Having had twins, she had the latitude of apportioning four names, but for all that, she was uneasy. She knew how unreasonable her husband could be, and she knew that whatever she decided would displease him— he wouldn't tolerate even one name from her side of the family.

Women advised her to send a messenger to her husband asking him to come home, but she wouldn't. She was furious with him. She hadn't enjoyed a happy moment since their wedding. He was either away on business or at his rabbi's. When he was home, he was either with his Hasidic cronies at the studyhouse or poring over the books in his study.

Not that she demanded much. She herself came from a Hasidic family, her own father behaved no differently, and she knew that a learned Jew had nothing to say to a female, who wasn't even allowed to make her presence known in her own home when strange men came to call. That was the woman's lot, and she accepted it. Each morning she thanked God for having created her a female according to His will. Still, she chafed under the conditions.

True, she was well-off and fecund, providing her husband with a child each year, and bright, healthy children at that, for which she was envied. He brought her gifts from Danzig—a Turkish shawl or a piece of jewelry—but he paid no attention to her. They couldn't even share a Sabbath meal together since he always brought some pauper home and she was forced to eat in the kitchen with the maid after a single sip of the benediction wine and a slice of the ceremonial Sabbath loaf.

Nor could they go anywhere together since neither was allowed to mix with the opposite sex. On the rare occasions when they visited relatives, he always walked in front while she followed a few paces behind. The moment they entered the house, they quickly parted, each to his own gender. On Sabbaths, he lingered so long at the services that she almost fainted from hunger until the meal could be served.

But what irked her most was the air of superiority he adopted toward her. He never asked her advice, never reported how his business affairs were going, never confided in her when he was troubled. He would open his heavy purse and dole out the money she needed for household expenses, and that was the extent of their relationship. He never even addressed her by name but called her "thou" in the manner of the fanatics. When he came home from a trip, he never told her about it but merely kissed the doorpost amulet and grunted, "How are things in the house?" while he held out her present. If she took it from his hand, it was a sign that she was available for marital relations. If not, he only glanced at her darkly and went off to his Hasidim to hear news of their rabbi.

She feared him, his brooding silences, his booming chant as he studied the Gemara, his burly masculinity, his grim face. She didn't ask much—a kind word or a loving smile as compensation for her empty existence that was little better than a servant's, but even this he denied her. If he loved her in his own fashion, he showed it only in their bed, as the Law prescribed. Otherwise, he was quite rigid about a woman's role in life. She was to bear children, rear them, observe the laws of Jewishness, run a household, and obey her husband blindly. If his friends chose to drop in for a late get-together, he expected her to serve them refreshments regardless of the hour. "Woman," he shouted into the kitchen, where she had to sit with the maid, "whip up a mess of groats for us men!" And she had to stay up preparing the food.

He was away on all holidays, even on Passover when the humblest Jewish women joined their husbands and families at the table, while she had to be alone like some widow, God forbid. All these indignities she had borne in silence, but this time he had gone too far. She had begged and pleaded with him to be with her for the birth, but as usual he had ignored her, and a sense of deep outrage, built up over years of gray unfulfilled existence, consumed her. She disregarded the women's advice and determined not to send a messenger after him. Actually she wasn't all that sure that he would heed her plea.

All the female pride that her husband had so long trampled underfoot now emerged full-blown. She lay in her bed, cordoned off with sheets and draped with amulets to guard against the the evil forces. Responding with firm "amens" to the traditional prayers recited by heder boys on the other side of the sheets, bolstered by a sense of pride in her maternal accomplishments, she took it upon herself to arrange for the circumcision. Issuing orders like any imperious male, she decided on the names she would give her sons in defiance of her husband's wishes. She didn't feel bold enough to cross him completely, and she effected a kind of compromise. She named the elder twin Simha after the Przysucha Rabbi, but added Meir after her grandfather, and gave the remaining two names to the younger—Jacob Bunem.

The moment Abraham Hersh returned from Warka, he asked to see his newborn son. He was amazed to learn that there were two, and he gazed in bewilderment at the tightly swaddled infants.

"Which is the older?" he asked brusquely.

"The smaller one," his wife said, lowering her eyes under his burning gaze.

"What's he called?"

"Simha."

"Just one name?"

"No. Meir, too. After my grandfather, the Wodzislaw Rabbi, blessed be his memory," she whispered, trembling at her audacity.

"Here, take him!" Abraham Hersh growled.

Sarah Leah brought the other infant.

"Go to your daddy, Jacob Bunem," she crooned with sly innocence.

Abraham Hersh glared at the infant, who looked back at him with open, shining eyes, and some of his anger

dissipated. The knowledge that both of the Przysucha's Rabbi's names had been used mollified him somewhat, but the fact that they had been joined with that of some worthless nobody was hard to swallow.

"The image of the master . . . a shining light, may the evil eye spare him," Sarah Leah said.

"Pshaw! Take him away," the father growled in a fit of pique.

Eyes tearing, the mother clapped a son to each breast. "Suck, Meir darling, she urged the older, omitting the child's other name that her husband had forced upon her, but he only clamped his gums around her nipple and held it in a fierce grip.

She screamed in pain, and Sarah Leah came running. She plucked the infant from the breast and regarded him angrily, "Rascal, a baby mustn't pinch his mother's breast. Nurse like Jacob Bunem . . . so. . . ."

The baby emitted a howl of such indignation that Abraham Hersh shouted from his study, "Close the door! How can a man concentrate in all this tumult?"

He gathered scant joy from his sons' birth. He envisioned the time when he would present them to his rabbi and his shame would become public knowledge. He tried saying their names aloud, but they rang false to him. He wouldn't forgive his wife for defiling the rabbi's name, and he didn't go in to see her, even though she was still not fully recovered. To muffle the disgrace, he threw himself into his work. He no longer planned to go to Danzig since there was sufficient local business to keep him busy.

The town of Lodz grew from day to day. The first Jews to be granted the right to open weaving workshops had achieved this by adopting gentile ways and toadying to the authorities. But inevitably, ordinary observant Jews followed suit. The Russian officials who descended upon the country following the suppression of the Polish uprising were most eager for the bribes and gifts of Jews who sought permission to live and do business in prohibited areas, and soon Jewish looms clacked away in the old section of Lodz, even though the Germans still barred Jews from their guild.

At first, the Jews confined themselves to their own quarter. Seemingly overnight the houses already standing sprouted additional stories, annexes, wings, extensions, ells, attics, and garrets to accommodate the flow of newcomers converging upon Lodz from surrounding areas. Lacking legitimate sanction and permits, the construction was effected at night and proceeded helter-skelter, without order or plan. Buildings came down; buildings went up; buildings emerged slanted, top-heavy, leaning this way or that—all symmetry sacrificed to expediency There was no time to do otherwise as the town grew by leaps and bounds. .

Gradually the Jews began to spill out of their congested area into Wilki, which was officially closed to them. The first to stick a toe inside the restricted area were the more affluent, audacious Jews; presently the more timorous followed.

Then, like a torrent overflowing its banks, the Jews smashed down all barriers set up to exclude them. Thousands of rural leaseholders and innkeepers who had been dependent on the Polish nobility were now forced to seek their livelihoods in towns and cities. They opened dry goods stores by the hundred, but since the liberated serfs were starving, there were no customers, and the Jews turned to weaving. They set up their wooden handlooms wherever they could, but mostly they flocked to the city of Lodz. Having endured the irrational cruelty of their blueblooded former masters, they wouldn't be turned back by mere bans or decrees fashioned against them; they opened their workshops just as the German immigrants had done before them. [. . .]

Gradually young Jewish men, both married and single, began to learn the trade. Down the sandy roads leading to Lodz, fathers accompanied by sons who had no heads for books walked barefoot and waved sticks to keep off the village dogs. On the outskirts of town they put on their boots and admonished their sons before apprenticing them for three years to Jewish master weavers.

"Act like an adult, obey your employer, be kind to God and man, be honest and respectful, and you will reap the benefits of this world and the world to come."

They dug down deep into the pockets of their sheepskins and took out purses, from which they drew the greasy, hard-earned bills with which to pay the master weavers for agreeing to feed and board their sons while they taught them their trade.

The skullcapped youths stood before the looms with ritual garments dangling over grimy trousers, lint clinging to curly thatches and sprouting beards, fingers deftly weaving wool and cotton cloth or ladies' kerchiefs from dawn to midnight. As they worked, they chanted cantorial pieces, trilling and quavering over selected passages. The bosses passed to and fro, making sure nothing was stolen, checking the output and prodding the worker who paused to wipe his brow or roll a cigarette.

The bosses' wives and daughters peeled potatoes, fried onions, and stirred soups in huge kettles while apprentices wound yarn onto spools, rocking cradles with their feet.

In the marketplaces Jews bought and sold piece goods and remnants. Ragpickers brought in all kinds of waste, which they sold to dealers, who reclaimed it into reusable material. Women and girls wound thread onto red wooden bobbins. Hosiers knitted coarse colorful stockings for women. Wherever one turned, machines clacked and clattered, accompanied by the tailors' cantorial chants and the seamstresses' love ballads.

Eventually the city grew too congested to contain its rapidly growing population. As the wealthy and enterprising lease-holder Solomon David Preiss, who had made his fortune importing wheat and rye to Prussia, lay awake one night, it suddenly struck him that a suburb might be built on the infertile flats of Baluty, the Kanarski brothers' estate just outside the city. The land was too sandy even to pasture livestock, and the only people living on it were the liberated serfs who had nowhere else to go. [. . .]

Six

Abraham Hersh enrolled his twin sons in separate Hebrew schools.

Although they were but minutes apart in age, they were years apart in intellect. Jacob Bunem was normal for his age, an average student who showed no exceptional promise. He learned his lessons by sheer effort and by rote so that he could display his progress when his father examined him after his Sabbath nap.

"Well, so be it," Abraham Hersh grunted, not overly gratified by the boy's efforts. "Tell your mother to give you a piece of fruit and try to do better next time."

Jacob Bunem saw that he had disappointed his father, and a shadow fell over his merry face, but only for an instant. As soon as his mother served him his cookies and prune stew, he reverted to his normal self. He even felt like laughing for no reason whatever.

It was different with Simha Meir. He was a prodigy, and when his teacher failed to keep up with him, the father took him out of heder, the elementary Hebrew school, and turned him over to Baruch Wolf of Leczyca who taught boys of confirmation age and even older—youths already engaged to be married.

Every Sabbath Baruch Wolf came to Abraham Hersh's house to test his pupil. He drank gallons of blazing tea, poured from a stone jug kept warm by a wrapping of rags, and tried to trip up Simha Meir with tricky questions and pitfalls that the youngster easily parried. Baruch Wolf sweated rivers from the hot tea and from the boy's scholarship.

"Reb Abraham Hersh," he whispered in the father's ear in a tone the youngster easily heard, "you're raising a genius, a prodigy!"

Abraham Hersh was delighted, but he wouldn't allow himself to show it. "See to it he's God-fearing, Reb Baruch Wolf," he adjoined the teacher. "A decent Jew."

He never forgot what the Warka Rabbi had predicted, that his seed would be men of wealth, without adding that they would be God-fearing Jews as well. He was uneasy about this, more so about Simha Meir than Jacob Bunem. The very fact that the boy was such a genius frightened him. He showed traits that made the father apprehensive. He wanted to know everything; he stuck his nose everywhere; he was inquisitive, demanding, restless. Abraham Hersh knew that all prodigies tended to be this way, but this didn't reassure him. He knew that it was more important to obey God than to be a good student, better to be dull but pious than learned and lax in one's faith

And he sent Simha Meir into the kitchen for his Sabbath treat while he had another word with the teacher. "Don't forget to make the benediction," he cautioned his son. "And don't rush through it—recite every word clearly!"

He turned to Baruch Wolf with a sigh. "Don't spare the rod with the boy; he needs a firm hand."

He had enrolled Simha Meir with Baruch Wolf of Leczyca for a reason. His wife had been strongly opposed to it since the teacher was known throughout Lodz as a martinet who maimed his pupils even as he pounded the learning into them. Also, he kept them at it for hours, from early dawn until late at night. On Thursdays they got no sleep at all but studied through the night until morning. Nor did he teach them the Gemara and exegesis alone, but commentaries as well—those of others and, even more important, his own.

But as usual, Abraham Hersh disregarded what a woman said. He was anxious that the boy be broken to the yoke of Jewishness, and no one was better at this than Baruch Wolf of Leczyca.

Although the teacher was nearly seventy, his powers were far from waning. He was lean, rangy; his fingers were like pincers, and his face was slightly twisted as a result of a chill suffered during a freezing journey on foot from Leczyca to his rabbi in Kotzk. This had

caused the right side of his face to be somewhat elevated so that one pointed brow tilted up and the other down; one side of a mustache jutted up with abandon, while the other drooped angrily.

And Baruch Wolf's brain was as twisted as his face. He never taught his pupils the legends found in the Gemara since he considered these fit only for women. The Scriptures, the Pentateuch, and the lighthearted treatises dealing with customs and holidays he regarded as fluff. He preferred the more solemn treatises concerning business, promissory notes, reparations, contamination and purity, both in the land of Israel and outside it. That, and ritual slaughter, and questions dealing with the conduct of priests, the burnt offerings of cattle and sheep, and the rendering of fat and tallow constituted his curriculum. [...]

For hours the youths wandered through the streets of Lodz. They raced down side streets and alleys, exulting in their freedom. They visited marketplaces where peasants milled among wagons, horses, cattle, swine, poultry, sacks of grain. Jewish housewives in bonnets over shaved skulls wandered among the wagons. They tested the chickens by blowing into their behinds, even poked their fingers inside their cloacas to see if they were carrying eggs. Jews slapped gentile palms to seal bargains, haggled, chewed kernels of grain.

From there the boys headed for construction sites where masons slaked lime and toted bricks in hods. Lodz was still growing street by street, and new stores, bazaars, and warehouses were always going up.

They proceeded to Balut with its narrow alleyways where from all sides, looms and sewing machines clacked and the songs of the workers filled the air. They bought sticky almonds in tiny stores thick with flies, as well as all kinds of cloying cookies and candies.

Simha Meir collected the groschens from the boys and entered the shop of the Turk with the red skullcap to buy a slice of raisin bread. The boys hesitated to taste it since it was probably not kosher, but Simha Meir had no such compunctions, and he chewed with relish. Each raisin he found sparked a light in his darting eyes.

They proceeded to the cropped fields where goats grazed. They stretched out on the grass and played cards. As always, Simha Meir won all the money.

The day was long, but for the boys it was never long enough. They crawled over the sand flats where dragoons drilled while noncoms pounded their legs with their scabbards. They assembled in the marketplaces where the town crier beat his drum and reported all manner of official tidings: who had been the victim of a burglary, who had lost a pig, who had been sentenced to prison, whose candlesticks or bedding were being sold in lieu of taxes.

Finally, they entered the red-light district—a narrow street where only recently brothels had sprung up. Prior to that, people had gathered here from all over to fulfill their natural functions under the open sky. Now small flimsy shacks with slanted attics and low windows stood here. If someone came to urinate or defecate out of old habit, the pimps and brothel owners would beat him up.

The brothels were staffed by cheap whores to accommodate soldiers and peasants who had left wives behind to work in the city. They also serviced the young Jewish journeymen who manned the city's handlooms.

The boys knew that this street was out of bounds to them, and this very fact drew them here. They ran through the narrow little street, stole covert glances at the bedraggled Jewish and gentile wenches sitting on the thresholds, cracking seeds. Not that they had any intentions of coming close to these girls, God forbid. Still they loved to hear the girls' entreaties: "Come on in, boys, you'll enjoy it. . . ."

And they raced home at dusk in time to say the afternoon prayers, when across the poorly paved streets, lamplighters, dressed all in black and carrying long poles, lit the streetlights scattered sparsely through the city. It was miraculous the way the lamplighters used their long poles to hook the ropes holding the lamps, pull them down, and ignite them with their torches. The boys looked on enraptured as the men cleaned the sooty chimneys, poured out kerosene from their cans, turned the wicks, and hauled the lamps back into place with the ropes.

"A good week!" the boys exclaimed in Yiddish when the lanterns were lit. "A good week!"

The lamplighter was vexed. He thought that the Yids were making fun of him and chased after them. He seized the slowest and hauled him to the top of a lamppost.

The boys fled, the skirts of their gabardines and the fringes of their ritual garments fluttering behind them.

"Bah!" they hooted at the pursuing lamplighter. "Angel of Death!"

And in the midst of the teenaged youths raced the flushed, tiny ten-year-old Simha Meir.

At home, he would find Jacob Bunem down on all fours, giving his sisters piggyback rides. Little Dinele

was there, too. She no longer lived nearby, but she still came to visit her girlfriends and, more important, Jacob Bunem. Although he was already a big boy, he enjoyed playing with his sisters. He ignored the fact that it didn't behoove a boy his age to be with girls. He would get down on all fours when his mother wasn't looking and play the horse. He would tell all his sisters and Dinele to climb on his back, and he would gallop across the floor, supporting the whole crew. He would even rear like a real horse until the girls squealed in fear. Dinele would tighten her plump little arms around his neck to keep from falling and cling to him, laughing till tears came. Jacob Bunem gamboled with enthusiasm and whinnied like a colt.

"Jacob Bunem," Dinele asked, "are you afraid of a lion?"

"No," Jacob Bunem said resolutely.

When Simha Meir came in and saw his brother with the girls, he would try to shame him. "Jackass, I'll tell Father. . . . Dunce, you'll forget all your lessons!"

Jacob Bunem blushed. He was mortified to be called a dunce before Dinele, especially since it happened to be true. "'You'll hang by your tongue in the other world, tattletale!" he warned Simha Meir.

But he was afraid to have their father find out, and he dickered with his brother, offering him anything he wanted if he would only keep silent. But Simha Meir wouldn't be bribed with mere objects, and he offered to play cards with Jacob Bunem. Naturally he quickly won all of his brother's cash, while his sisters, and Dinele most of all, glared at him and chanted as they once had in the courtyard:

Simha Meir is a liar,
Watch him jump into the fire. . . . [. . .]

Part Three: Cobwebs

SIXTY-SEVEN

For the entire seven days of mourning that Max [formerly Simha Meir] Ashkenazi observed for his brother, his brain never ceased churning. He had been taken directly from the funeral to Gertrud's house, where father and daughter now sat in the living room with mirrors draped and chandeliers covered with crepe and mourned their loss together.

On the first day of mourning Max Ashkenazi took no food or drink. Dinele brought him milk to keep up his strength, but he wouldn't accept it. He only drew on his cigars and dropped the ashes on his unshod feet. He spoke to no one and read from the Book of Job:

Let the day perish wherein I was born,
And the night wherein it was said:
"A man-child is brought forth"
. . . Let them curse it that curse the day,
Who are ready to rouse up their mourning.

Gertrud leaned over the book and gazed at the Hebrew letters that she couldn't make out but that managed to reflect her sorrow. Max didn't comfort her. He had nothing to say to the daughter to whom he had brought only misery. The only time he had crossed her threshold was after a tragedy. He had brought only death to those who had forgiven him and sought to save him.

He buried his eyes in the book to avoid facing those he had wronged all his life. His present wife sat beside him and with her heavy, half-paralyzed hand tried to comfort him, but he ignored her as well.

"Is there not a time of service to man upon earth?" he read. "And are not his days like the days of a hireling? . . ."

On the second day of mourning people came to commiserate with Max Ashkenazi. They forgot whatever wrongs he had done them in the past and came to him, the former King of Lodz, now demoted to a tiny bench instead of a throne. They brought him news of the city, but he had no urge to listen. What did he care about such things? His life was forfeit. He was old, spent, broken. He had planned a new life in the bosom of his family, but God had deemed it otherwise. At the threshold of this new life He had driven him off like a leprous dog trying to enter a house. . . .

Apparently he was fated to bring only grief to those he loved. As one sowed, so did one reap. No, there was no place for him in the world. His fate was sealed. Somehow he would live out the few years left him. How much longer could he last, after all? Why even think of starting anew? He had never had any great needs. He certainly needed nothing now. A crust of bread, clothes on his back, a place to lay his head. The sages were right. There was no difference between man and beast. Each bore his own burden. Man struggled and strained until he fell in his tracks, whereupon the others trod over him, later to fall themselves.

On the third day of mourning Max Ashkenazi ceased brooding on the folly of life and considered such things as duty, obligation. He dared not renounce his responsi-

bilities. Even if he himself required nothing, there were others to consider—Gertrud, Little Privehle, Dinele, Ignatz, his elderly wife. . . . He couldn't leave them to fate. He had to be their protector, their provider. He had to take himself in hand and use his remaining powers to maintain them in comfort and security. In olden days when a man died, it fell upon his brother to care for his family. This was a good custom. It honored the life of the deceased.

No, the House of Ashkenazi couldn't be permitted to topple. He, Max, would see to that. He would restore it and correct all his past wrongs . . . pay back his loved ones for all the misfortunes he had heaped upon them.

He listened now to the visitors who came to pay condolence calls and paid attention to their comments regarding the state of business in the city. He still took no part in their discussions, but he listened. Not that he had any more interest in a country which had treated him so abominably and so viciously murdered his flesh and blood. No money on earth could tempt him to remain in a place where a Jew was considered something less than dirt, something to be squashed underfoot like vermin. He would go to the Land of Israel, as his Zionist friends advised. He no longer considered them wild-eyed visionaries for wanting to transform Jewish merchants into peasants. He realized that it was he who had been wrong. Why build factories and mansions so that others could snatch them away at will? He would liquidate everything at whatever cost and take the entire family to the Jewish homeland. He would sit in his vineyard among his own kind and fear no one. His life would be secure, serene. He would eat the bread of his own fields, drink the milk of his own cows. The moment he concluded the period of mourning, he would flee from those who thirsted for Jewish blood.

His visitors praised his decision. "Words of wisdom," they said. "If you lead the way, Mr. Ashkenazi, half of Lodz will follow. . . ."

On the fourth day of mourning Max Ashkenazi abandoned his plan to plant vineyards and work the land. This was a task for young people who knew no other skills, but it hardly befitted a man his age to become a peasant. What good could come of it? The earnings were minimal. You needed the cooperation of heaven. You based your livelihood on the sun, the wind, the rain, every whim of nature. You also needed physical strength. Didn't God say, "In the sweat of thy face shalt thou eat thy bread"? He, Ashkenazi, no longer had the strength for this. . . .

Besides, it behooved every man to do what he knew best. No, tilling the soil in the Land of Israel wouldn't benefit him or the Jews. He could contribute more by creating something big there. He would transport his factories there. He had done it before; he could do it again. . . . A nation couldn't exist on only what it grew. The wealth of a nation lay in its industry, and he, Ashkenazi, would establish an industry there, just as he had in Lodz and later in Russia. He would put up factories in the Holy Land. He would provide jobs for thousands of Jews and sell the goods they produced throughout the world, thus bringing valuable capital into the country. Instead of being King of Lodz, he would be King of Israel. . . .

Such an effort was certainly worthwhile. He would show the gentiles what Jews were capable of. What had Lodz itself been but an empty village not too long ago? People with energy had transformed it into a world-renowned center of industry and trade. Now it was time to do something for Jews, as Jacob said to Laban: "And now when shall I provide for mine own house also?"

On the fifth day of mourning Max Ashkenazi's fervor to expedite his new plan cooled somewhat, to be replaced by calm, studied reflection. A man was a fool to fly off half-cocked, to act on the spur of the moment. A man of reason considered carefully before taking such an important step. Better to test the water ten times than plunge in recklessly once. To establish an industry in the Land of the Ancestors was surely a noble gesture, a boon for Jewishness, but to build castles in the air was plainly stupid. It wasn't that difficult to put up one factory or many. The main thing was to have an outlet for the goods these factories produced. Such markets had to be created. True, Lodz, too, had once been a sandy waste, but it had been part of a country that desperately needed goods. The Russian Empire had a population in the hundreds of millions. And what was Israel? A land of penniless Arabs who dressed in rags and didn't need textiles. Nor would it be easy to compete with the English. One Englishman could outsell ten Jews. As for the Jews who lived in the Land of Israel, they were few in number and scholars for the main part. With Jews, generally, it was good to enjoy a Sabbath meal, but not to do business.

And what about the water there? Was it the right kind for scouring the goods? There were all kinds of other obstacles, too. It was easy enough to launch an enterprise; it was quite a problem to sustain it. All in all, the effort presented enormous difficulties. Israel was a land that subsisted on charity, on donations from abroad. If things turned out badly there, the Jews themselves would turn on him.

On the sixth day of mourning Max Ashkenazi listened intently to the merchants and manufacturers who came to him. They all were eager to know if he would be reopening his factory, when he would be doing this and what kinds of goods he planned to produce. The world had begun to recover from the effects of the war. Along with the first swallows of spring the traveling salesmen, buyers, and commission agents had made their appearance in Lodz. New markets had opened up in the neighboring agrarian nations, and all eyes were on Max Ashkenazi, the former King of Lodz. Like children playing follow-the-leader, the merchants and manufacturers looked to him to show the way. "If you take the first step, we'll go along," they told him.

On the seventh and last day of mourning Max Ashkenazi rose from his bench and began to pace through his daughter's living room.

He'd be damned if he'd give in! Just because they, the Poles, wanted to push him out he would spite them and stay. A plague take them! He had slaved to build his fortune while they caroused with their cards and their women. He had sacrificed his personal happiness, and now they thought they could simply walk in and gather the fruits of his labor? . . . He'd be damned if he'd hand it all over to them on a silver platter! There was no such thing as getting something for nothing in this world. . . .

If only Jacob Bunem had understood. . . . They could now be working hand in hand to become the masters of Lodz. But Jacob Bunem had chosen the gentile way. For "honor" he had sacrificed his life. What nonsense! If a pack of mad dogs attacked a man, was there any reason for the victim to feel degraded? Dogs were stronger than man, but they remained dogs, and man remained a man. The Jews of old had had the right idea. They held the gentile in such deep contempt that his insults and derision meant less to them than the bite of a mosquito.

No, it didn't pay to give up one's life for such foolishness. The strength of Israel lay not in physical force, but in intellectual superiority, in reason. Since time immemorial, gentiles had persecuted, mocked, and oppressed the Jew, and he had been forced to keep silent because he was in exile, because he was a helpless minority, a lamb among wolves. Could the lamb then oppose the wolf? . . .

Had Jews adopted the gentile's ways, they would have already long since vanished from the face of the earth. But the Jews had perceived that theirs had to be a different course, and it was this perception that had lent them the moral strength to endure and to accumulate the only kind of force the gentiles respected—intellectual and economic power.

This was the strength of the Jew and his revenge against the gentile. Not with the sword, not with the gun, but with reason would the Jew overcome. It was written: "The voice is Jacob's voice, but the hands are the hands of Esau." The Jew lived by his reason; the gentile, by his fists. For hundreds of years Jews had danced to the gentiles' tune because they were too few to resist. In times of danger the Jew was obliged not to sacrifice his life, but to appease the wild beast in order to survive and persevere.

If only Jacob Bunem had realized this! The humiliation that the bully imposed upon his weaker victim dishonored not the victim, but the tormentor. How did the saying in the Ethics of the Fathers go? "Those that drown others shalt themselves be drowned."

He had begged Jacob Bunem not to resist since it was sheer folly to fight against hopeless odds. The wild beast had to be turned away with reason and cunning. But his brother had always been headstrong. He had let his blood, rather than his reason, guide him. And blood was the way of the gentile.

Ashkenazi's eyes misted over. It hadn't been fated that he and his brother work together, but he would defend what was his with fang and claw. He would again be King of Lodz. Much as they loathed him, they would be forced to doff their caps to him and await his pleasure. He would show them who was master of Lodz. . . .

A Jew's weapon was money. Money was his sword, his shield. And he would use this weapon to pay his enemies back for his degradation and for his brother's murder. But to do this, he would have to keep his head. One rash, irrational act of temper, and the battle was lost, and he, Max Ashkenazi, wasn't about to give his enemies an advantage.

On the eighth day following the period of mourning Max Ashkenazi shaved, put on a fresh suit, and went out to reconquer the city that had once been his. [. . .]

SEVENTY-ONE

The paper chain holding Lodz together burst into a million pieces. The poorly printed marks were taken out of circulation to be replaced by silver guilders complete with the inevitable reliefs of Poland's saviors.

Along with the worthless marks also vanished all the work in the city, all hustle and bustle, all trade, the whole paper existence.

The warehouses were saturated with goods for which there were no buyers. The stores no longer sold a groschen's worth of merchandise. The jammed sidewalks grew deserted. In the cafés and restaurants waiters stood around swatting idly at flies. The agents, brokers, moneychangers, commission men, and traveling salesmen sat at tables, scribbling away, but they didn't order so much as a cup of coffee. They only chain-smoked, lighting their cigarettes with million-mark notes.

Lodz had come full circle. The speculators, profiteers, idlers, and various dreamers and hangers-on had managed to land on their feet, while solid businessmen, shrewd investors, insiders, and so-called experts ended up stuck with mounds of the worthless marks.

Just as Max had predicted, representatives of foreign wool and cotton suppliers came to demand payment for their raw goods. But all their customers had to offer were excuses. A rash of bankruptcies erupted. The courts and lawyers worked overtime. The musty, dim offices of notaries filled with husbands putting all their worldly goods in their wives' names.

All factories stood idle. Not a wisp of smoke rose from the sooty chimneys. Workers by the thousands milled in the streets. Huge mobs lined up before labor exchanges, waiting for announcement of jobs that never materialized. Help was needed in France to dig coal and the men surged forward to sign up. Agents of shipping lines tantalized the people with tales of life in the Americas and urged them to buy tickets and emigrate. Elegant flimflam artists posed as foreign consuls and issued counterfeit visas and passports on the spot. Anti-Semitic agitators vilified Jews for conspiring to ship good Christians out of the country in order to take over Poland for themselves. Priests and monks took up collections for the construction of a new church in the city. Revolutionaries issued proclamations urging a revolt of the oppressed. Secret agents, policemen, patriotic housewives, and students set upon these agitators and hustled them off, beaten and bloody, to the police stations.

"Hang the Trotskyites!" they bellowed. "Send them back to Palestine!"

In Balut, malnourished children peered out from behind grimy windows at the deserted streets. Secondhand clothes dealers walked about with empty sacks, their gloomy eyes cast heavenward but bereft of all hope. Real and pretend cripples crawled and slithered through courtyards, parroting beggars' laments.

The people of Balut had nothing more to hope for. The mills had already destroyed their livelihoods even before the collapse. The Polish and German workers wouldn't allow them into the factories, not even into those owned by Jews. They couldn't collect workmen's compensation since Magistrate Panczewski bent the law so that only employees of large factories were eligible for such payment.

Young and healthy Jewish youths applied at the labor exchanges for the filthiest jobs—digging sewers and building roads—but even this the gentiles denied them. "Beat it, Moshes!" they hooted. "Starve to death!"

All that was left them was charity and the soup kitchens set up by the Jewish community. The storekeepers dozed the days away without taking in so much as a groschen.

All the activity now centered on the railroad stations. Men, women, and children carrying bundles of bedding and Sabbath candelabra filled all the wagons as Jewish Lodz raced to escape. Wives went to their husbands in America, fathers to their children, children to their parents. Farmers anxious to go back to the land emigrated to Argentina.

Jewish boys and girls carrying military knapsacks and blue and white flags set out to colonize Palestine. They sang their Hebrew songs and danced their horas. Those who came to see them off shouted, "Next year in Jerusalem!"

Affluent Jews, accompanied by their bejeweled wives and daughters, took trains to Italian ports; from there they would sail on luxury liners to Palestine. They weren't going there to till the soil and dry the marshes like the pioneers, but to buy and develop real estate, build plants and factories, and restore their fortunes.

Lodz was in a crisis. You couldn't earn a groschen in a city glutted with goods for years to come. Like hyenas, tax collectors descended upon the city to grab what they could for the national treasury. The only people seen in the deserted streets were soldiers and civilian officials in gorgeous uniforms replete with braid and insignia. They confiscated machinery from cellars, stripped bedding from beds, removed food from shops, and took everything away to be sold for taxes. Jewish housewives trailed after the wagons, lamenting as if hearses were removing their loved ones to their final rest.

Business establishments were sealed; jewelry was plucked from women's necks and wrists; men's watches and wallets were seized. The wealthier Jews fled the city, salvaging whatever they could in order to resettle in the Land of Israel and build a new Poland, a new Piotrkow Street in the Land of the Ancestors, in North or South America.

The city gentiles stood before the gates of their houses, watching the exodus of Jews from the land their ancestors had occupied for a millennium. They didn't know whether to cheer or mourn.

Peasants shielded their eyes to watch the crowded trains rush by. Their wives listened to the exotic songs chanted by the Jewish pioneers, and their flaxen-haired children ran out from behind thatched fences with their dogs to scream and bark at the trains and hurl rocks at the windows.

Lodz was like a limb torn from a body that no longer sustained it. It quivered momentarily in its death throes as maggots crawled over it, draining its remaining juices.

And as the city succumbed, so did its king, Max Ashkenazi. Without the smoky air to breathe, without the hum of machinery to lull him, he languished. He lay awake nights, reviewing his life. The images of those he had known and wronged passed before his eyes—his parents, his in-laws, but especially Jacob Bunem. He could see the trickle of blood run down into the beard and congeal there, and his own blood chilled. He put on his robe and slippers and wandered through the palace. He went to the window and looked out at the deserted factory, at the stacks looking like huge extended tongues thrust into the sky.

He went to the bookcase and glanced over the books. He stopped where the Jewish holy volumes were kept somewhat out of sight and took down a worn copy of the Scriptures. He took it back to bed and switched on his night lamp. He leafed through the pages, scanning the moralistic exhortations in Ecclesiastes and Proverbs. They no longer struck him as preposterous ravings of fatuous dotards but as observations rife with truth and perception. He came to a folded page. It was the Book of Job, which he had been reading during the period of mourning for his brother. Eagerly he began to read half aloud;

So Satan went forth from the presence of the Lord, and smote Job with sore boils from the sole of his foot even unto his crown. And he took him a potsherd to scrape himself therewith; and he sat among the ashes. . . . Now when Job's three friends heard of all this evil that was come upon him, they came every one from his own place, Eliphaz the Temanite, and Bildad the Shuhite, and Zophar the Naamathite; and they made an appointment together to come to bemoan him and to comfort him. And when they lifted up their eyes afar off, and knew him not, they lifted up their voice, and wept; and they rent every one his mantle, and threw dust upon their heads toward heaven. So they sat down with him upon the ground seven days and seven nights, and none spoke a word unto him; for they saw that his grief was very great. After this opened Job his mouth and cursed his day—

From the adjoining rooms the clocks tolled the hour. Max Ashkenazi put down the book to listen. Just then he felt his chest tighten as if gripped by steel pincers. He cried and reached for the bellpull, but by the time the servant came his master was already dead. His head had fallen upon the opened Bible, and his fingers still clutched the cord.

Translated by Joseph Singer.

Shmuel Yosef Agnon

The Sense of Smell
1937

1. The Excellence of the Holy Tongue

The holy tongue is a language like no other. All other tongues exist only by agreement, each nation having agreed upon its language. But the holy tongue is the one in which the Torah was given, the one through which the blessed Holy One created His world. Angels and seraphim and holy beings praise Him in the holy tongue. And when He comes to praise Israel, He also does so in the holy tongue, as it is written: "Behold thou art beautiful, my beloved, behold thou art beautiful." What language does Scripture speak? Surely the holy tongue. And when He longs to hear the prayers of Israel, what language is it that He longs to hear? The holy tongue, as He says: "Let me hear your voice for your voice is sweet." What voice is sweet to Him? The voice of Jacob, praying in the holy tongue. By the holy tongue He will one day rebuild Jerusalem and return the exiles to her midst. By the holy tongue He heals the mourners of Zion, their hearts broken by the destruction, and He binds up their wounds. Thus it is written: "The Lord

builds Jerusalem, gathering the scattered of Israel; He heals the brokenhearted and binds up their wounds." For this reason all Israel should take care with their language, keeping it clear and precise, especially in these last generations so close to redemption, so that our righteous Messiah (may he be revealed speedily, in our own day!) will understand our language and we will understand his.

2. Against the Scholars of Our Generation Who Write in Every Language Except the Holy Tongue

But someone might object and say: "Is it possible to speak a language that has not been spoken for more than a thousand years?" as some stupid folk among the Jews have said. "Even most of the scholars in our generation cannot stand up to it, and they either make a mess of their language, even in the most simple things, or else they write in every other language except the holy tongue." Whoever says this hasn't paid attention to the most important fact. Even though speech passed from the lips, it never passed out of writing, and it is there for anyone who seeks it. How is this? A person reads Torah or studies Mishnah or learns Gemara and immediately all those treasures of the holy tongue that the blessed Holy One has stored up for His beloved are revealed to him. This is especially true on the Sabbath, when we are given an extra soul that understands the holy tongue just as well as do the angels.

Then why do certain scholars make such a mess of their language? Because they put worldly matters first and words of Torah second. If they would make Torah their basis, the Torah would come to their aid. As for those who write in every other language but not in the holy tongue, even a Gentile who writes in the holy tongue is more beloved than they, so long as he does not write words of folly. You can know this from the case of Balaam the Wicked. No man did such evil as the one who suggested that the daughters of Moab go whoring, by which one hundred fifty-eight thousand and six hundred of Israel were destroyed. But because he spoke in the holy tongue and in praise of Israel, he merited to have a section of the Torah called by his name, and to have all Israel open their prayers each morning with the verse "How goodly," which Balaam spoke in praise of Israel.

And if you should say, "But do we not find that some of our early sages composed a portion of their books in Arabic?" the early sages are different, because the people of their generations were made weary by exile and were far from Messiah's light. Therefore their sages wrote them letters of consolation in their own language, the same way you pacify a child in whatever language he understands. The language of Ishmael is also different, since the Land of Israel has been given over into their hands. Why was the Land of Israel entrusted to Ishmael? Because he had managed to wrest it from the hands of Edom. It remains entrusted to Ishmael until all the exiles are gathered and God returns it to their hands.

3. The Secret of Writing Stories

For love of our language and affection for the holy, I darken my countenance with constant study of Torah and starve myself over the words of our sages. These I store up in my belly so that they together will be present to my lips. If the Temple were still standing, I would be up there on the platform among my singing brothers, reciting each day the song that the Levites sang in the Temple. But since the Temple remains destroyed and we have no priests at service or Levites at song, instead I study Torah, the Prophets and the Writings, Mishnah, laws and legends, supplementary treatises and fine points of Torah and the works of the scribes. When I look at their words and see that of all the delights we possessed in ancient times there remains only this memory, my heart fills up with grief. That grief makes my heart tremble, and it is out of that trembling that I write stories, like one exiled from his father's palace who makes himself a little hut and sits there telling of the glory of his father's house.

4. All That Happened to the Author Because of a Certain Grammarian and All the Sufferings and Woe That Came upon the Author

Since I just mentioned a hut, let me say something about one. It once happened that I had written a story about a sukkah, a festival hut. Using colloquial language, I wrote, "The sukkah smells." A certain grammarian rose up against me, stuck his pen into me, and wrote, "You cannot say: 'The sukkah smells.' Only a person smells the aroma of the sukkah." I was worried that perhaps I had strayed from proper usage and done harm to the beauty of the language. I went and looked in reference books but found no support for my usage. Most of the books either tell you what you already know or else tell you nothing at all. I went to the scholars of

our time, and they did not know what to answer me. Scholars know everything except that particular thing you are looking for. Then I happened upon a certain Jerusalem scholar, and he brought support for my words from the book called Perfect Treatise by an early sage named Moses Taku, of blessed memory. I was somewhat consoled, but not completely. I still wanted further support. When I ran into people who were experts in the holy tongue, I would ask them, "Perhaps you have heard whether it is permitted to write: 'The sukkah smells.'" Some permitted while others forbade. Neither gave any reasons for their opinions, but just stated them, like a person who sticks his thumb out at someone and says, "Well that's my view," or someone who licks his lips and says, "That's my feeling." That being the case, I went to erase those two words against which the grammarian had raised a protest. But when I started to do so, the sukkah came and its aroma rose up before me until I really saw that it was smelling. I left the words as they were.

5. The Righteous from Paradise Come to the Author's Aid

Once somebody came to ask me a favor. In the course of the conversation he revealed to me that he was a descendant of Rabbi Jacob of Lissa. I put aside all my other concerns and did him great honor. I took the trouble to offer him some honey cake and a glass of whiskey. I fulfilled his request gladly, out of respect for his learned ancestor whose Torah we study and out of whose prayer book we pray.

After I'd accompanied him on his way, I ran into a certain scholar who was carrying a book under his arm. I asked him, "What's that you've got there? Isn't that the prayer book of the Sage of Lissa?" He smiled and said to me, "Sometimes you get so clever that you forget a simple custom of prayer and you have to look it up in a prayer book." I said to him, "It shows a special quality of that true sage, one who had already written novellae and commentaries known for both sharp insight and breadth of learning, that he would take the trouble to briefly lay out the laws of prayer and other matters in such an accessible way. His is a book that anyone can use to find the law and its sources, written right there with the prayers themselves. Our holy rabbis have left us lots of prayer books, filled with directions and commentaries both hidden and revealed, with matters grammatical or sagacious, with permutations of letters, secrets, and allegories, all to arouse the hearts of worshipers as they enter the King's palace. But if not for my respect for our early teachers, I would say that the prayer book of the Sage of Lissa is better than them all. In many of those prayer books the light is so bright that most people can't use them, while this one appeals to any eye."

While I was talking, my own heart was aroused and I started to tell of some things that happened to that sage whose teachings had spread throughout the scattered communities of Jews, who in turn followed his rulings. I told of some of his good qualities, things I had heard from reliable sources and had found in books.

Finally we parted from one another, he with his prayer book and I with my thoughts. I went home and lay down on my bed to sleep a sweet sleep. Since I had done a Jew a favor and had gone to bed after telling tales of the righteous, my sleep was a good one.

I heard someone trying to awaken me. I was feeling lazy and I didn't get up. On the second try I awoke, and I saw an old man standing before me. The prayer book *Way of Life* lay open in his hand; his eyes shone and his face bore a special radiance. Even though I had never seen a picture of Rabbi Jacob of Lissa, I recognized him right off. It wasn't that he looked like any of the members of his family. The great among Israel just don't look like their relatives, because their Torah gives their faces a special glow.

When a person darkens his face over study of Torah, the blessed Holy One gives him that radiant glow and makes his face shine.

While I was still staring, the prayer book closed, the old man disappeared, and I realized it had been a dream. But even though I knew that, I said: There must be something to this. I washed my hands, got out of bed, and walked over to the bookcase. I picked up the prayer book *Way of Life*. In it I noticed a slip of paper serving as some sort of marker. I opened up to that place and there I read: "One uses lots of flowers that smell sweet to make the holiday joyous." It seemed that I had once been reading that page and had put the slip of paper there as a marker.

I thought to myself. He wouldn't have used such language on his own, without some authority in Torah. In any case, I took the prayer book *Pillars of Heaven*, by his uncle the sage Javetz, of blessed memory, and there I found the same expression. I was glad that I hadn't failed in my words and had done no harm to our holy tongue. If these two great pillars of the universe wrote

this way, it must indeed be proper. The grammarian who had shot off his mouth at me would one day have to pay his due.

6. Reciting Psalms. How Rashi, of Blessed Memory, Interprets for the Author a Verse from the Psalms and Lights up His Spirit

It was hardly worth going back to bed, since most of the night had passed, but it wasn't yet time for morning prayers. I got up and took a Book of Psalms. Reciting psalms is good anytime, but especially early in the morning when the soul is still pure and the lips are not yet defiled by wicked chatter. I sat and read a few psalms; some I understood on my own, and the rest were explained to me by Rashi, of blessed memory, until I'd completed the first book of the Psalter. My soul still wanted to say more. I did its bidding and read psalm after psalm, until I got to the Psalm for the Chief Musician upon Lilies. This is a song in praise of the sages' disciples, those who are soft as lilies and pleasant as lilies, so that they come to love their learning.

That was a beautiful hour of psalm-saying. The lamp on the table was lit, crowning with light every word, every letter, every vowel point, every musical notation. Opposite it there was a window open, facing the south. Outside, the predawn breezes blew, but they didn't put out the lamp or even challenge its wick. The breezes danced about the trees and shrubs in the garden, and there wafted in a sweet fragrance of laurel and dew, smelling something like wild honey or perfume.

The light from the lamp had begun to pale. It seems that the night was over. It may be that God hangs up the sun in the sky at that hour for the sake of those simple folk who don't know the whole morning prayer by heart but who recite it out of the prayer book.

A sound was heard from the treetops, the voice of a bird reciting her song. Such a voice could interrupt a person's studies. But I didn't get up from my book to listen to the bird's voice, even though it was both sweet to the ear and attractive to the heart. I said: Here I am reciting the Psalms. Should I interrupt these to listen to the talk of birds?

Soon another voice was to be heard, even more attractive than the first. One bird had gotten jealous of another and had decided to outdo her in song. Or maybe she wasn't jealous and hadn't even noticed the other. She was aroused on her own to sing before her Creator, and her voice was just sweeter than the other bird's. In the end they made peace with one another, and each bird seemed to complement the other one's melodies. They sang new songs, the likes of which no ear had ever heard. Melodies and voices like these certainly could keep a man from studying, but I made as though I didn't hear. There is nothing especially wondrous or praiseworthy about this, because the psalm played itself like an instrument of many strings. A Song of Love, next to which all other songs are as nothing. I followed after its every word with melody.

"My heart overfloweth with a goodly matter . . . My tongue is the pen of a ready scribe; . . . ride on in behalf of truth, humility, and righteousness; let thy right hand teach thee awesome things." I understood as much as I could, and the rest was explained to me by Rashi, of blessed memory. When I got to the verse "Myrrh and aloes and cassia are all thy garments," I did not know what it meant. I looked in Rashi's commentary and there I read: "All thy garments smell like fragrant spices. And its meaning is that all your betrayals and foul deeds will be forgiven and will smell sweet before Me." My mind was eased, like a person smelling flowers that smell.

7. To Conclude with Praise as We Opened with Praise

Come and see how great is this holy tongue! For the sake of a single word a holy man troubled himself to come out of the Academy on High in the Garden of Eden, bringing his book before me, causing me to rise up at night to recite the Psalms, so that I might find something I'd been seeking for many days.

Translated by Arthur Green.

Meyer Levin

1905–1981

The child of East European immigrants, the novelist and journalist Meyer Levin was born and raised in Chicago, the setting for his masterpiece *The Old Bunch* (1937), a realistic novel about young Jews in the Jazz Age and during the Great Depression. While his earliest fiction was not concerned with Jewish themes, his writing from the early 1930s on was passionately engaged with the trials and tribulations of contemporary Jewry. He was an outspoken critic of the dejudaized version of Anne Frank's diary that was presented on Broadway and later filmed by Hollywood and

described the troubles he encountered thereby in *The Fanatic* (1964).

The Old Bunch
1937

"It was my fault, Sammy. I aggravate you when you're tired," she said, sitting up and drawing his head to her. "I shouldn't even have mentioned Ev. We ought to go to your family this year. It's only right."

"Oh, it doesn't matter, they probably won't even notice we're missing. We can go there for the second night, anyway. They're used to having us come then."

"Of course!" she exclaimed. The second night was a *seder*, too!

"C-o-n-
S-t-a-n-t-i-n . . ."

the radio was going, as they entered. Thelma was dancing with Manny Kassell, and there was a strange couple dancing. Ev, who looked ravishing in a flowing white gown that completely concealed her condition—though there was nothing as yet to conceal—came rushing toward them.

"Oh, darling, look at me! Does it show?" she whispered quite audibly, to Lil.

"It doesn't show a bit!" Lil whispered back.

"She just wanted an excuse to wear that gown," Phil remarked, with a loving proud sophisticated kidding glance at his wife.

"Oh, it's cute," Lil said. "It's darling."

"Oh, Jackie! Isn't he cute!" Ev swooped.

"Say hello to Aunt Ev, Jackie."

"Hi, toots," Jackie said, and they all roared.

Phil introduced them to the strangers, Mr. and Mrs. McIlwain, who were dying to see a Jewish Passover ceremony.

The maid passed around cocktails, and little caviar canapés on matzoth.

"Aren't they wonderful!" Mrs. McIlwain cried, examining the canapés. "Passover or no Passover, I think that's an awfully smart way to serve caviar."

"They're awfully cute," Lil agreed.

"Darling, you must tell me where to buy this—what do you call it?" Mrs. McIlwain said.

"Matt-zote," Ev carefully mispronounced the word, and giggled.

"Say, this don't taste like bathtub gin to me," Manny comically complained of his drink.

"That's real prescription stuff," Phil admitted. "I'm afraid you'll have to put up with it, as Ev has been using our bathtub lately."

They laughed.

"One of the saddest things about Prohibition," McIlwain said, "is we don't know good liquor when we get it. I always used my old man as a tester-in-chief. Boy, he used to sozzle the real stuff!"

They looked at him, envious of his being the son of a real drunken Irishman.

"Well, Sam, I hear you have deserted the sinking ship," Phil remarked.

"Yah, with the rest of the rats," Sam caught him up.

"Oh," Phil laughed appreciatively. "Well, I guess Big Bill is through, in this town."

"I don't know," Sam said. "He's still mayor."

"He must be kind of lonesome, in the city hall these days." McIlwain referred to the defeat of Thompson's candidates.

"Anyway, he might as well get out," Phil said. "His pals've grabbed everything there was to be grabbed."

"I guess that's so," Sam agreed. "They've about scraped the bottom of the till."

"I hear he has presidential aspirations," McIlwain remarked.

"With him, it's a case of I do choose to run," Manny cracked.

"Will you men stop talking politics!" Ev laughed, and steered them into the dining room.

"Oh, Ev, it's just too cute for words!" Lil screamed, seeing the table. In the center was a layer cake, and atop it was a doll in a flowing robe, with a long white cotton batting beard stuck to its cherubic chin. Moses!

"Do you get it?" Thelma tittered. "What's it supposed to be?"

"Moses on the Mountain?" Mrs. McIlwain ventured.

"Uh-uh."

"I got it! If you can't eat bread, eat cake!" Manny roared.

"No fair, you knew!" Ev cried.

They all laughed, and Ev modestly said: "It was Phil's idea."

The place cards were the cleverest things! Each card was a cut-out of a biblical character, only Ev had fixed devilish little short skirts over the long gowns of the women characters, and put derby hats on the men. But the most comical thing she had done was to get pictures of movie stars and paste their faces on the biblical figures.

"Who is this supposed to be?" Lil screeched, and they all piled around a picture of Adolphe Menjou, in a silk hat, on the body of an Egyptian taskmaster who wielded a whip.

First they thought it was McIlwain because he was a gentile (get it, Egyptian) and, besides, he was an engineer; but it turned out to be Manny Kassell on account of his Menjou mustache, and the whip was because he was a dentist. Next to him was a picture of Lillian Gish as Queen Esther playing a harp, and naturally that was Thelma, on account of the harp. Phil and Ev were Doug Fairbanks and Mary Pickford, the perfect couple, as Samson and Delilah! Sam was Groucho Marx as Adam, and Lil was Vilma Banky as Eve, and Jackie was Jackie Cooper as David. Immediately, he yelled: "Mother, I wanna slingshot!"

"Hush, Jackie, mother will buy you one tomorrow."

"Naw, I wan' it now!"

"Where on earth did you get all those pictures of the movie stars?" Lil said, trying to ignore him.

"Oh, Phil has a friend in Lubliner and Trinz," Ev said, "and he got them out of their advertising department, special."

"Wanna!" Jackie tugged at Lil.

"Look, Jackie," Phil said, and picked up the favor on Jackie's plate. It unfolded into an Indian headdress. "Nize beby," he quoted Milt Gross.

Jackie stopped bawling and put the paper feathers on his head. "Yay, I'm an Indian!" he yelled, happily.

"You know, Phil really has a way with children," Ev said. "I guess he'll make a good papa after all."

The others were discovering their favors. On each plate was a comical hat of the sort worn at New Year's parties.

"You see, good Jews always wear skull caps or some kind of hat at the table on Passover," Ev explained to the Gentiles.

"Don't get the idea this is a real service," Phil said. "We just decided to do this our own way for a change."

The McIlwains put on their hats. Mr. McIlwain had drawn a red-white-and-blue fez with a tassel on the top. His young, round, pink-massaged face beamed good will. Sam's hat was yellow and green, and shaped like an overseas cap. Manny had a dunce cap! The girls had hats, too.

"You know who would appreciate this? Alvin Fox!" Thelma exclaimed. "Remember he trained to be a rabbi and gave it up."

"I was going to ask him," Ev said, "but they just went to Europe on a late honeymoon."

"He married a Gentile girl," Thelma said to the Mc-Ilwains, beaming.

"He was ruining the business putting out those modernistic chairs," Phil laughed, "so the old man said it was cheaper to send him to Europe."

They all laughed good-naturedly.

Now the wine went around. Phil had secured some real Chianti, with the straw basket around the bottle.

"Just like a regular *seder!*" Lil cried as the maid served the first dish, consisting of hardboiled eggs cut up in salt water.

"What do you call this?" Mrs. McIlwain inquired.

"*Charokis,*" Ev promptly responded, anglicizing the word beyond recognition.

"How did you ever know about all this stuff?" Lil said, awed. "My mother used to make a kind of a *seder* but I would never dream of trying it myself!"

"Kid, you'll never guess where I got the directions," Ev said. "There was a complete Passover menu in Prudence Penny's column!"

"No!"

"I'll prove it to you!" And Ev produced the clipping. "I just gave it to the girl and told her to follow it religiously."

"Religiously, that's good," Manny repeated.

"What kind of bread would you like, rye or white?" Phil jested, passing the plate of matzoth.

"I'm really going to eat this, it's good for you, I'm on a diet!" Ev said. "My gynecologist said it was the best thing."

The maid brought in a plate of hot biscuits, which most of them accepted, though the McIlwains insisted on eating matzoth.

"Isn't there supposed to be a glass of wine for somebody?" Lil prompted.

"Oh, yah! *Eli hanoveh!*" Thelma supplied.

"What's that?"

"Elijah," Phil translated.

"Yah. That's cute," Lil said. "You're supposed to fill a glass with wine, and Elijah comes and drinks it up."

"How about giving Elijah a real treat, for a change?" Phil said, and filled a glass with gin. "There you are, old boy old boy! Open the door for Elijah!"

"Who is Elijah?" Jackie said.

"He comes and drinks it up," Lil explained.

"When?"

"Right away. You can't see him. He's invisible."

"Aw." Jackie watched her face. "You're kidding me."

"It's a fact," Lil said. "He goes into every house, and drinks the wine."

"Yah? Then I bet he gets pie-eyed!" Jackie piped.

They roared.

"Isn't he the cutest thing!"

Ev leaned intimately to Phil.

"Oh, Lil, make him ask the four questions!" suggested Thelma.

"That's right, that's what he's here for!"

Philip explained to the McIlwains. "Of course we're not doing this in proper order or anything, but at a real *seder* they follow the *Haggada,* that's a sort of book of procedure, and the youngest son of the house asks the traditional four questions, and the head of the household, usually the grandfather, reads the responses."

"Surprise!" Ev said, and produced a *Haggada,* printed in both Hebrew and English. This curiosity was passed around, everybody explaining to the Mc-Ilwains that the Hebrew was read backwards instead of up and down, like Chinese. They studied the booklet respectfully.

"Oh, you know what I want to sing!" Thelma cried. "*Chad gad yo!* We always used to sing that when I was a kid!" She turned the pages. "One kid, one kid for two *zusim!*" she began. The wine was affecting her noticeably, her cheeks were flaming. "*Chad gad yo! Chad gad yo!*"

"Doesn't that come at the end of the meal?" Ev said.

"What's the difference!"

Manny began to sing with her: "*Chad gad yo! Chad gad yo!*"

The maid brought in an immense, sugar-baked ham. Squeals and titters.

Manny picked up a curled streamer that lay near his plate and blew noisily. The red crape paper shot across the table, and dropped over Sam's ear.

"The four questions, the four questions!" Lil insisted.

"All right, you read them for Jackie, and Phil will answer them!" Ev said.

"Now, Jackie, look." Lil showed him the lines in the book.

"You say what I say—ready?"

Jackie nodded eagerly.

"Why . . ."

"Why."

"Is this night . . ."

"Is 'is night."

"Different . . ."

"Diffrunt."

Sam heard his son piping and, glancing across at the book in Lil's hand, suddenly remembered the Hebrew words: "*Mah nishtanoh halaylah hazeh . . . ?*" as he had used to say them, awed, and the grave answering intonation of his grandfather.

"From all other nights?"

"Fmallothnights." Jackie stuck out his hand, for a reward.

"Because this is April 4," Phil answered, "and every other night is another night."

Their guffaws rattled the glassware.

Sam got up.

"You'll have to excuse me," he managed to mumble, as he made for the door.

Lil rushed after him. "What's the matter, are you sick?" Her first look at him was worried. Then: "Are you crazy? Disgracing me before my best friends!"

Ev rushed up to them.

"This is the end!" Lil sputtered hotly, collapsing in tears into Evelyn's arms.

In Sam's mind, these words were flashing, as though he were reading them on an electric sign, on and off, on and off: "This is where I get off. This is where I get off."

Other works by Levin: *The New Bridge* (1933); *My Father's House* (1947); *In Search* (1950); *Compulsion* (1956); *The Obsession* (1973).

Ivan Olbracht

1882-1952

The Czech novelist, journalist, and screen writer Ivan Olbracht was the son of a Catholic writer and a mother who converted out of Judaism. Olbracht studied law in Berlin and Prague but became a journalist and fiction writer. He was active in the Communist Party and was highly critical of his government's policies. His expulsion from the party led him to live in rural areas, and his works delve into psychological analyses of persons living in the countryside.

Julie and the Miracle
1937

People like to get something for their money, doing business is entertainment as well, and indeed there would be precious little fun to be got out of life in Po-

lana if it were not so. It is equally entertaining for the seller, too; doing business without the entertainment may be a way of making money, but it just isn't business.

And so, in the village shop that smelt of the eastern regions of the country, not to mention vinegar, paraffin and printed cottons, Sura Fuchs was whiling away the time with Myter Mazucha, a Ruthenian peasant who, in the course of an hour and a half, had inspected and tapped all the scythes she had, and was now running his thumb along the edge of three carefully selected ones to see how sharp they were, and glumly tapping the best of those three best with his knuckle, as if trying to beat out of it those last fifty hallers which it seemed Sura was not going to knock off the price. Meanwhile Sura's father, Solomon Fuchs, was whiling away his time with a Ruthenian girl who was buying a kerchief, and with the three women who had come to help her buy it; he was taking red, green and yellow kerchiefs from the shelves, some of them sewn with spangles, some without; he would unfold them, shake them out, and hold them up to the light to show how the colours gleamed. On the general public's side of the counter was Baynish Zisovich, helping him to commend the quality and low price of his wares, but because Solomon Fuchs had asked twenty-five crowns for the red one with yellow roses and silver spangles, and the women had offered ten, and because so far they had only got to twenty-two crowns fifty and Baynish Zisovich could see it was going to last a long time, leaving him little chance of a proper talk with Solomon, he went over to Sura.

"Weigh me out four kilos of flour, Sura," he gave his order.

"For cash, mind, Baynish," Sura answered.

"Ts!" replied Baynish with an offended toss of the head, for such low suspicion was beneath contempt.

Sura put a paper bag on the scales accordingly, and using a mug scooped the maize flour out of a chest. [. . .]

Baynish Zisovich leaned against the counter, scratching his chin through his chestnut beard, and thinking, while Sura weighed out a bag of cattle salt for some woman: "Well, I haven't got it . . . Vampires! Bloodsuckers! A black year on you, pig-heads! I'd fling the five crown note down at your feet if I'd got it. I haven't got it, and so that's that!" Baynish was not thinking the way you do when vague notions drift through your mind; his thoughts were clad in definite words and the "I haven't got it" was thought very loud and as it were in capital letters. "I haven't got it, I haven't, I haven't . . .

What am I to do? The wife's waiting at home for that flour."

So he went towards the door where Solomon was standing with the three women and said to him in Yiddish: "Won't you let me have four kilos of flour on credit, Solly?"

"No."

"Don't you know I've got eight children?"

"That's none of my doing," replied Solomon Fuchs coldly and he shook out the red kerchief with the yellow flowers in front of the women.

"I know that, but do you realise they've had nothing to eat since yesterday?"

"It's no good, Baynish. You've been eighty crowns in debt to me for the last two years . . ."

"Don't I work it off hauling for you with my horse?"

"Hauling for me with your horse, that's a good one! You do twenty crowns' worth of work and go off with twenty-five crowns' worth of goods!"

"That's a good one, that is—as if anybody ever gave me anything for nothing!"

"And your debt doesn't get any smaller. What's the use of talking, Baynish?" and Solomon Fuchs turned back to the women. "All right, then, for the sake of good will . . ." and back he led them to the counter again, ". . . I'll say twenty."

Baynish was leaning against the counter, thinking again: "Just suppose—and there's no harm in imagining a thing like that—just suppose I'd got a hundred crown note in my pocket, right now. Would I break into it just because of this mangy dog? Once you break into a nice green hundred crown note like that instead of putting it away untouched, it's just as if you hadn't got a hundred crowns any more. Women are on to money like demons: We need maize and potatoes and we've got to have white bread for *shabos* and under those rags she's wearing Hanele hasn't even got a shift and what are you going to do about boots for the winter . . . and goodness only knows what else." Baynish sighed. "Oy, oyoyoy . . . perhaps I'd break into it after all. Of course I'd break into it." And he said to himself: "Well, I haven't got it . . . Yoy! What a lot of money! A hundred crowns! Wherever would a poor carter get all that money these days?"

The business with those women looked as though it were going to last a long time; they were ready to run out again, they weren't offering more than thirteen yet, and Fuchs was only at nineteen-fifty, and so Baynish tried Solomon once more:

"You know, Solly, it really is serious. The children honestly haven't had anything to eat. It's only a trifle, five crowns, and I'll work it off . . ."

"No."

"Have pity on my family, Solly!"

That was too much; Solomon Fuchs couldn't bear such strong language. He began shouting. He'd had enough, the same thing happened twice a week, week in, week out, and started all over again whenever it was a question of Baynish working off a debt. He didn't steal, either, and that was the end of it, and he wouldn't listen to another word, and: "Not another haller, ever, not even if you stand on your head for it!"

Baynish was hurt to the depths of his soul. He stayed by the counter for a little while, cursing gently in his friendly soul, and when there were several customers in the shop at once and nobody was taking any notice of him, he slipped quietly into the empty tap-room and from there into the kitchen.

Here, with her sleeves tucked up above her elbows and cutting into the plump flesh, Mrs. Fuchs was just rolling out noodles. She turned irritably to see who had come in. Her eyes, which people feared, did not exactly stab him right through at one go, but for a while they pricked him all over from head to foot.

"*Gut morgn!* I say, Esther," said Baynish quickly and as if quite unconcerned, "do you happen to have a bit of bread about? Just for a bite, I simply haven't had a moment today . . ."

"Ts!" Esther tossed her head angrily. "Why don't you go and buy some in the shop?"

"I was just telling you, I only want to have a bite."

Baynish Zisovich sat down on a low stool by the stove, thus showing his willingness to wait, and began to entertain Esther with gossip about the wedding of Khava Davidovich and Mendl Rosenthal in Pribuy. What the bride had worn, how young Gleizer, in a black coat, big stiff collar, and white cotton gloves, had looked like a poor Czech teacher laid out ready for his coffin, and how stout Malke Hergot's sister in America had sent her an old yellow dance frock embroidered with an enormous red wool rose, which fitted her so tight it was nearly bursting at the seams, and how the rose came just on her bosom and the end of the stem started just at the crotch. "Khee!" Esther squealed, Baynish laughed heartily, Esther brushed her floury hands on her fat belly and went to cut Baynish a slice of white bread.

"What are you making for dinner?" Baynish sniffed the air.

"Dinner! What am I making for dinner? What's it to do with you what I'm making for dinner?" Esther snapped.

That was a false step, and so Baynish went on retailing the wedding gossip; the way Miss Vilkovich had done her hair up she looked like the Tower of Babylon, and Izzy Hershkovich had on yellow shoes the size of boats, and old Rosenthal's nose was twitching all the time; Baynish kept breaking off bits of bread and eating it, and when Esther's eyes were safely on her noodles he stuffed a biggish piece into his pocket. When she showed signs of interest with a couple of high-pitched "Khees!" Baynish got up to go, imparting the last bit of gossip from the door and adding as if by the way:

"You know, Esther, they don't want to let me have four kilos of maize on credit, out there in the shop. Just tell Sura . . ."

He had prodded a wasps' nest. Esther banged the rolling-pin down on the board. Then she began to yell, arms akimbo.

"Come, now, don't take on so . . ." Baynish beat a hasty retreat.

Esther was going strong by now. Did people think they stole, or what? Week in, week out, they never saw a penny, let me have this and let me have that, every day the same old song: let me have this and wait for your money. Solly didn't know where to turn, he had to pay for maize, he had to pay for goods, he had to pay the bank, he had to pay his taxes, and the whole village living and clothing themselves at his expense, she'd be going barefoot before long, and poor Sura had to cry her eyes out before she got a single rag for her back . . .

Baynish had gone.

Not through the tap-room and the shop, though; he went out through the back yard. [. . .]

When Baynish had the village behind him and was drawing nearer home, and rounding a bend in the path saw the rags hanging on the fence round his cottage and his wife's red petticoat among them, and the pot upturned on a stake in the fence, the gnawing at his vitals changed to something that was no longer just hunger.

"Have you got it?" his wife asked before he had even shut the door.

"No," he replied timidly, and turned his head away not to see the angry tears in his wife's eyes.

He turned to his first-born, to the ten-year-old boy standing by the table murmuring something from a Hebrew book, his black almond-shaped eyes gazing wisely at his father. And Baynish's fear of his wife's reproachful face was amply compensated for by his pride in those eyes, King Solomon's own could not have been more beautiful, his pride in that face softer than lamb's fleece, and in those golden side-curls gleaming in the sun.

There were many children, though, in that room with its mud floor, and they could not be ignored.

"Now, children," said Baynish solemnly, lifting his forefinger, "Father has brought you something. Something really good. There isn't much of it, of course, because you must never have too much of a good thing, but it's something that is good for you, and ever . . ." Baynish smacked his lips and brought the tip of his thumb to the tip of his forefinger ". . . ever so nice . . . Now, Mother, cut it up in pretty rings for our little ones . . . two nice radishes and a lovely little onion . . ." then, because Mother would not dream of doing it, and because Mother was angrily tugging the bits of washing down from the pole over the stove and throwing them to the end of the bench, Baynish Zisovich did it all himself . . . "and now a pinch of salt . . . and it's all set out nicely for good children . . . and for the very littlest ones Daddy has brought a bit of white bread, as white as new snow and as sweet as sugar . . . and that's a dinner the President himself won't be eating today . . ."

Then Baynish Zisovich called Khaimek, his firstborn, out into the passage.

He sat down on an old sauerkraut barrel and took the boy between his knees.

How beautiful art thou, Joseph, son of Jacob! And Baynish Zisovich felt that if he were to gaze a little longer into the dark depths of those eyes, and if he were to stroke the fair, almost flaxen locks once more, and if that lovely mouth were to smile at him so wisely longer than was seemly, then the soft wave coursing down his spine would turn into something he could not allow himself to wish for just now. And so he said with the affectionate severity proper to a father:

"Khaimek, you had three potatoes for breakfast."

"Only two," replied the boy.

"That doesn't make any difference, two or three. Look, Father is hungry, too, but we must leave the bit of food we have got for the littlest ones . . ."

The boy gazed at his father with his almond-shaped eyes and nodded eagerly, as though to say he thought exactly the same, and as though to drive away as hastily as possible even the shadow of suspicion that he might have thought otherwise.

". . . because we two are not *goyim* who think of nothing but food, we are Jews, and our thoughts must be turned to higher things, because we are not to be brought low by such trifles as a moment's hunger, and because we know that the Eternal One has never let a Jew die of hunger, and that he will send us something before the day is out." [. . .]

No, the Lord sent no manna raining down that day, and not even one tiny little quail before night came. The Lord God worked his miracle the day after, towards midday, when Baynish Zisovich was right at the other end of the village.

The moment he saw those two tourists, the gentleman in check cloth that must have cost at least sixty crowns a yard, and the nice plump lady who seemed to Baynish to walk with a slight limp, he knew the good Lord had sent them to him. As He sent the ram to Abraham. That they might be sacrificed instead of his children. Baynish's mind at once started working feverishly.

God's purpose was clear. If God's purpose is clear, everything is clear. Then it only remains for man to be guided by it and do all he can to carry it out. The Lord had sent these two to him. But God does not, and indeed cannot, take care of the details. That's man's business, and it is his responsibility to contrive to rearrange things around him so that the Lord's will can be carried out.

He waited for them on the road, and since the Law did not allow him to take his hat off, he stood there respectfully and said in a deferential but not a beggar's voice:

"Excuse me, Your Honour, but as there is a God in Heaven, my children have had nothing to eat since yesterday . . ."

The gentleman looked him over from head to foot with cold eyes, and asked:

"Is there a decent horse anywhere in the village?"

"A decent horse?" Baynish repeated the words. So that was it; the lady could go no further. She must have hurt her foot or twisted her ankle. Baynish's mind was hard at work. And his fantasy began to work feverishly, too. High above was the will of God, the one fixed point in space, as hard as diamond and as bright. Down below was the world, which had not lost its normal appearance, but seemed to have acquired softer contours, as though it was of wax and could be shaped to need. Baynish's hands were at work shaping it. His fingers were still feverishly active when he asked, the words covering up what his fingers were doing: "A decent horse?" Then, with a broad sweep of his arm as if to show the job was finished: "There's only one decent horse in the village. Mordkhe Wolf's horse."

"I know," said the gentleman, "a twenty-year-old hack, blind and lame."

"Hm." Baynish smiled politely at the joke. "It's a seven-year-old, Your Honour. Mordkhe Wolf paid fourteen hundred for it. You will be very lucky indeed if he's got it at home, though, because there's not a single horse in the village today. They're all up on the high pastures or else they're in Pribuy, carting stone for the road."

"Now wait a minute: is the horse at home or isn't it?"

"I think . . ."

"No thinking! Is it—or is it not?"

"Well, I expect it is."

"There you are, you see." The gentleman laughed. "How far is it to this Mordkhe of yours?"

"How far? It's not at all far. Just a step."

"What do you call a step?"

"If Your Honour is going towards the town, it's in that direction. Just a step. It depends how slow the lady walks."

"So you've noticed that too, have you? A quarter of an hour?"

"A quarter of an hour."

"Hm. That means half an hour."

"Half an hour?" Baynish gave an injured smile.

"We could go on like this for ever." Then he spoke to the lady in a foreign tongue, French, maybe, and it looked to Baynish as though things were turning out well, and then the gentleman said: "Now just you listen to me." He glanced at his watch. "I'm giving you twenty minutes. Then I'll pay. If it takes half a minute over the twenty you'll get nothing. Agreed? Or don't you want it?"

"Haven't I said so, Your Honour? Would the lady like to wait here?—Mordkhe Wolf would bring the horse for her to ride."

"No. The lady would not like to wait here. The lady is very anxious to set eyes on that Arab steed first."

Baynish took the tourists' rucksacks from them— God in Heaven, they were heavy!—and set off towards home at a trot.

"Give them our best regards!" the gentleman called after him.

Baynish slowed down to their pace. He was thinking hard: how much should he ask for the horse? He enquired:

"How long have you been staying in these parts, Your Honour?"

"Long enough not to let myself be taken in by you and Mordkhe!" the gentleman laughed.

"I might be able to get two horses. I'll go and ask . . ."

"No, you won't. We haven't finished hiring one yet. What do people here pay for a horse and a man, for the day?"

"Well, now, what do people here pay for a horse and a man, for the day? It's not always the same, what people pay for a horse and a man for the day!"

"I know that well enough!' the gentleman shook an admonishing finger at Baynish and laughed.

"This one is a very fine horse, too," said Baynish, and thought to himself: Hm, this is a clever *goy*. He's in a good temper, though, he's laughing, and so is the lady, that's all to the good. "The horse will fly like a swallow with the lady on her back, if the lady likes, and if the lady doesn't like it, she'll carry her at a walk, like a lamb. And the way that horse climbs hills! Yuy! It's like a cat! What do people pay for a horse and a man for the day? How can I know what Mordkhe's going to ask?"

In truth: doing business is not only the making of money. Business is entertainment as well. And often very exciting entertainment. For it is a question of nothing less than the opportunity to reshape the world over and over again. It is a mistake to believe that the world is what it appears to our senses, something fixed and outside us, independent of what we do. It is nothing of the kind. The world is what we ourselves make it. Even a moment of time is what we make it. And so are things, and people.

Baynish Zisovich was hurrying home. Dragging a lady and gentleman behind him. God performs only the miracle. The rest is man's to think out. [. . .]

When they came in sight of the red rag on the fence round Baynish's cottage and the upturned pot stuck there, Baynish said in a very reproachful, injured tone:

"Well, and here we are in no time."

He ran into the passage and called into the room so loud that they could hear him out on the road: "Is Mord-khe Wolf at home? . . . Is the horse at home?" And added softly to his wife: "Twenty-five crowns." Then he ran out again.

"Hurrah!" he shouted happily. "The horse is at home, I'm glad about that. Mordkhe's not at home himself, though. I'll go with you instead. His wife's coming at once. In five minutes the lady will be nice and comfortable on horseback."

Royza stood at the door with her hands hidden under her apron.

"Now listen, Royza," Baynish explained to her slowly. "This lady and gentleman here would like to hire your horse, the lady's hurt her foot. What does Mordkhe usually ask for it?"

"Twenty-five crowns," replied Royza obediently without showing the slightest interest.

"Wha-a-at?" the gentleman was just going to lose his temper again but instead he made an abrupt gesture and turned away. "Get on with the job, saddle the thing."

Now Baynish carried the wooden saddle out of the dark stable—how ever does a horse manage to get inside?—and took as much time over it as he could. But sooner or later the critical moment had to be faced: now he was leading his Julie out. Over the threshold he managed to hide her behind his own body, but it was no good; it had to be: Julie appeared in the light of day, the whole of her, a fact Baynish could not talk away with his smiling "Here we are, now, just a minute and everything'll be ready for the lady." And when the irascible gentleman saw the finest horse in the whole village, the steed that would soon be off with the lady as fleet as a swallow—slightly larger than a goat, swollen like a football, dirty, knock-kneed, twenty years old if a day, with cataract on the right eye and sores on its neck where the bags of damp cheese carried down from the high pastures had rubbed it raw, all his wrath dissolved in laughter. Laughter which was angry only at the start, and soon changed into a hearty shout, peal after peal of merry and very loud laughter that made him throw his head about and jerked his body from side to side. The lady was gurgling like a dove, too, and infected by each other their laughter know no bounds and they did not know when to stop. Julie stood there indifferent, her head hanging and knees knocking as though she was ready to kneel down, dozing with her good eye as she waited for them to saddle her. Baynish was a little offended.

"It's a very good horse, though, I know it well."

"We'll see about that," the irascible gentleman tried in vain to save his face by speaking sternly. "The District Hetman will give your Mordkhe what for, asking twenty-five crowns for a tottering wreck like this."

"Will you get on the creature?" he asked his wife.

Wiping her eyes she gave him an answer in French which could not mean anything, but what else was she to do?

The gentleman shook his head in cheerful astonishment: "As if I didn't know these scoundrels through and through! And still you fall for it every time."

Baynish Zisovkh brought some old torn petticoats belonging to his wife, and stuffed them under the saddle on the horse's back; to make the lady comfortable he laid old sacks flat on the saddle. The pregnant woman stood looking on, motionless and indifferent. Ten-year-old Khaim, wearing a solemn expression and giving not the slightest hint that he was dealing with his own father, brought him odd bits of string and chain from inside the cottage, and started fastening them together. The lady was talking French again. Once more it sounded cheerful and friendly. God's will was nearing fulfilment and Baynish felt he might already take part of his earnings.

And so while Khaimek was tying a big awkward knot in a frayed strip of webbing to join it to a bit of chain and thus make a stirrup, Baynish went respectfully up to the anti-Semitic gentleman:

"Excuse me, Your Honour, and don't be angry, but I've had nothing to eat since yesterday morning, and neither have my children, as God is my witness. Let me have something in advance; I'll look after you properly and we'll settle things with Mordkhe all right. I'd only like to buy some bread for the journey."

The pretty lady was settling something with her husband, and said to Baynish: "Open that rucksack!" When Baynish had carried out her order she added: "That's bread on top."

It really was, wrapped in a white napkin, and not a trace of pork to be seen. In such circumstances it is permitted to take uncut bread from a *goy*. Baynish thanked her, polite but not servile, cut the bread in two and gave the bigger piece to his wife, saying:

"Take this to my wife, will you, please, Royza? She's to give it to the children."

Khaimek gazed at the bread with his beautiful eyes.

Then the gentleman gave Baynish an advance of ten crowns as well.

"Take this to my wife, too, Royza."

They were ready to set out.

Only the anti-Semitic gentleman, perhaps ashamed of the way he had started shouting, perhaps even a little affected by the poverty of the village, had something else to add, smiling as he spoke:

"And now, you rogue, just tell me how much Mordkhe will have to pay you for fobbing a stupid *goy* off with this piece of carrion!"

Baynish was breaking off bits of bread and his mouth busy with chewing broadened into a happy smile: "Of course, Your Honour, he'll have to let me have something."

"As if I didn't know you through and through, you rascally lot!"

They rode up into the mountains, up a steep hillside, in order to reach the road down in the next valley, and follow it down to the nearest town. Spavined old Julie got into her stride, she was in no hurry, but plodded steadily on with the lady on her back and the rucksacks in front of the saddle; the plump lady was no circus rider, anyway, and was glad to be sitting down at all. Fleecy clouds floated overhead in the sky, the steep slope ahead of them lay in the shadow, but the rest of the landscape, the mountains on both sides and the deep valley behind them with the stream at the bottom, were flooded with bright sunshine, and the stream gleamed and sparkled. Every now and again the lady reined Julie in, turned to look back at the valley, and sighed: "God, how beautiful it is!" and the word "God" came out with such feeling that it sounded as though she desperately needed Him at that very moment. The irascible gentleman smiled at her indulgently. [...]

"God, how beautiful it is!" the pretty lady sighed and turned back to look as she sat on Julie.

"That's nothing, lady," Baynish smiled at her. "There's far better to come!" and he thought of the streets in the town, of the shop-windows piled with goods, of chests of gold and silver and precious stones, of Khaimek's eyes and of all the really beautiful things he would like to show this kind *goy* woman.

"What's the name of that cone-shaped hill?"

"That hill? The cone-shaped one? Let me see, that's *Amhorets*." He called it the "Ignorant One."

"And that one over there?"

"That one over there?"

Of course Baynish did not know the name of a single one of those hills; such foolishness could interest only *goyim*, and anyway, it was not of the least significance what they were called (as if a pile of earth and rock with nothing to consecrate it deserved a name at all!), but why shouldn't he make the lady happy, when that made him happy too? And so while the plump lady took a notebook with a gold pencil out of the breast pocket of her hiker's jacket—she really was nicely built, that lady!—and wrote down all he said, Baynish Zisovich went on inventing names: *Cickes* (the Dugs) and *Toches* (the Arse), the *Shames' Wife, Mikvah* (the Bath-house), *Ganev* (the Thief), *Kovetny* (the Lickerous One), *Tole* (the Thief on the Cross), Greater *Minhorets* and Lesser *Minhorets* (the Pagan Heretics), Greater *Kelev* and

Lesser *Kelev* (the Dogs), and if need be he would go on inventing names for another three weeks.

"What strange names," commented the pretty lady.

"Oh, yes, the names are very interesting in these parts" replied the anti-Semitic gentleman. "Round here the Slav element came into contact with the Rumanian, while the original settlers were Tartars."

"Aren't there bandits in these hills?" the lady enquired.

Baynish could not be sure; was she asking because she was afraid there were? Or did she want to hear stories about them? He was in a quandary. And then the world was at once arranged to fit in with his wishes, so that there were no longer any bandits about at all, and you could safely carry open loads of pearls and diamonds on Julie's back; but not so long ago the place had been full of the villains, committing horrible crimes, murder, arson and robbery, holding up travellers, "Oyoyoy, dreadful, it was!"

He accompanied those *goyim* not for one day, but for four. The gentleman called him Baynish and familiarly said "thou"; the lady said "you" and called him Mr. Baynish; they not only paid him twenty-five crowns a day, but gave him another five for his food; if he had been able to eat *treyfe* they would have stuffed him with food from morning till night; the anti-Semitic gentleman promised him an old suit and the pretty lady said his wife should have a coat and the children shoes, and Baynish had got their address in his pocket, so that he could remind them in case they forgot.

The miracle had been accomplished. The fervour passed. The burning bush in which the Lord had appeared to him in the desert had burned out, and the desert again appeared in the sober light of every day. The contours had hardened like wax which has grown cold and can no longer be shaped. Until the Lord speak His will again.

Blessed be His name!

Translated by Iris Unwin.

Other works by Olbracht: *Obrazy ze soudobého Ruska* (1920–1921); *Zamřížované zrcadl* (1930); *Nikola Šuhaj, loupežník* (1933); *Marijka nevěrnice* (1934); *Hory a staletí* (1935); *Golet v údolí* (1937).

Károly Pap

1897-1945

The novelist and short-story writer Károly Pap was the son of the Reform rabbi of Sopron, Hungary. He served in the Austro-Hungarian army in World War I and then joined Béla Kun's Red Army. When the communist regime collapsed in 1919, Pap was jailed for eighteen months. He then lived abroad until 1925. His great novel, *Azarel* (1937), was a roman à clef that probed the successes and failures of Jewish acculturation and integration in Hungary. It scandalized many Jews because of its harsh depiction of the protagonist's father, a rabbi. He continued to write during the war years and his two dramas, *Batséba* (1940) and *Mózes* (1943–1944), were performed in the Budapest Jewish community theater. In 1944, he was sent to a compulsory labor camp, from which he was deported to Buchenwald and then Bergen-Belsen.

Azarel

1937

Saturday is the worst of the week. Whenever I touch anything on this day, straightway there comes a voice: Don't do that, today it's a sin.

"Sin?" I ask.

Says Mother: "Sin is that for which the Good Lord punishes man. That which is forbidden."

"If the Lord is good," I ask, "why does he punish people?"

"Because you mustn't sin," replies Mother.

"But if he's good," I press on, "why doesn't he let me do anything I want?"

"Well . . ." says Mother, but turns to Father. "Hey, you speak to him! He's always got a question."

At which Father says, "Be satisfied with what we tell you. You mustn't sin. And that's that. When you're bigger you'll learn the rest."

I think: "When you're bigger . . ." I don't get it. Instead of saying, "We can't explain this," they say, "When you're bigger . . ." It seems this is the best excuse to say no more.

Soon Mother adds: "A rabbi's child has got to pay more heed to Saturdays than others have to."

Such words only stir me to ask more questions. My father's a rabbi—that much, I know. But why him of all people? He ministers to the Jews, seeing as how we're Jewish—I know this too. But why are we Jewish, after all? When there are so many people who are not? A lot more than us. And they get to do anything they like, even on Saturdays.

Father replies that they have their own holiday, Sunday.

Very well, I think, Sunday; but that doesn't make Saturday a great holiday. Ernuskó and Oluska like it better than the other days, because they don't have to go to school, but it only bothers me.

Early in the morning I can hardly wait for Father to head out to synagogue, and I plop down on the floor in my nightshirt. And I watch the fire in the stove. Never was it as lovely all week long, through the six days up to today, never as golden, burning with such frightful rage, never as beguiling, exhilarating, as on this day, when one mustn't touch it one bit.

I crouch down before it, stand, then crouch down again, sighing angrily, bent on sighing Saturday clear away!

Never have I wanted to poke at the fire, to throw something in, as much as I do now. Yet I only watch the wood that Lidi has set beside the stove when we were still fast asleep. For Lidi it's okay; she's Christian.

This much is certain: This wood was never wood to the extent that it is now, so far as I see it. At other times it was just dumb, and even when it burned it stayed dumb. Although I'm not in the habit of looking at it for long, only for a bit, just now the whole spectacle promises to be far more interesting—if I have the guts to look. How gladly I'd watch it through to the end, until a whole piece of wood burns away.

But I don't have the guts.

Am I afraid of God? Maybe. Afraid of Father? That I am. And of Mother? Were she to so much as see me by the fire, she'd yell at once: "Get away from there! That's caught your fancy on Saturday of all days?"

Yes, that's how it is. Yet more exasperating is this: even the *sound* of the crackling flames is more intriguing today. The fire is almost talking, which so many times before I would certainly have wanted it to do, but in vain.

"For the past six days," says the fire, "you haven't even noticed me, isn't that right? And if you did, I was nothing but a dumb fire. Someone you couldn't play with because I started burning right away. But now you'd gladly play with me, huh? Except that I won't play with you, not today. . . . My name is forbidden. . . . Then again . . . whoop! Just take a look at how I can dance, how I burn this way and that!"

Indeed, if I crouch down really well and watch, the flames shoot up so high and so helter-skelter every which way that you wouldn't believe it.

And how the fire hisses! Just like when Lidi combs Oluska's hair, and Oluska jerks her huge, unbound head of hair this way and that, prompting Lidi to grum-

ble: "Oh, stay put! I can't comb you like this. I'll tell Madam about you."

To which Oluska replies: "Don't pull so hard, or *I'll* tell Mother!"

Lidi: "Go ahead. I'm not afraid."

Finally Oluska tears herself away and runs through the flat in search of Mother, her big head of hair streaming, tousled this way and that behind her, exactly like this fire, only that the fire's hair is not black, but red. And the breeze grumbles at the fire just like Lidi does at Oluska: "Oh, will you stay put already?"

I'd like to ask someone: Who combs the fire? I'd prefer to ask Oluska, but she's sleeping in the study, and to get there I've got to pass through Mother's bedroom; so Mother would no doubt wake up and immediately smell trouble.

Ernuskó is still asleep. Should I wake him up? Finally I do.

"Ernuskó," I say, "who combs the fire?"

He ponders the matter seriously, good student that he is, and only then does he speak.

"No one. You can't comb the fire. It's not a girl."

After a good laugh, I say, "And if it can be combed all the same?

I press my point: "And who is the fire's *Lidi?*"

He offers no reply. "You see," I remark, "you're a good student, and still you don't know!"

Angry at my gibes, he is even less inclined to speak. I try to calm him down.

"Don't be angry, Ernuskó," I say. "The fire's Lidi is the breeze. So it's the breeze that angrily combs the fire's red hair. And the fire jerks this way and that just like Oluska does."

"Asinine," he remarks seriously. "Is this why you woke me up?"

"All right," I say, "now you've gotten back at me, so come on. Let's see how angry the Good Lord gets if we fiddle with the fire on Saturday."

He shakes his head. "Just so we get Mother and Father all upset?"

"No, not them! The Good Lord! Mom and Dad won't find out. Come on."

"Not me," he says. "Why should I?"

"Okay," I reply, "then I'll do it alone."

I'm still a bit scared. Then I quickly toss a piece of wood on the fire nonetheless. And I wait to see how the Good Lord will show his anger.

Meanwhile, though, I'm scared anyway. I keep my eyes peeled. And watch Ernuskó too.

"Hey," I say to him, "I've already done it."

"What do I care."

Then I throw on another piece of wood. And suddenly another. But by then I'm scared. Maybe the Good Lord has already gotten angry? I don't know, but to be on the safe side I don't touch the fire anymore. Having lost my courage, I leave the stove.

It's not just the fire that tempts me more on this day of the week than on others. Mother's drawers and little boxes are suddenly imbued with all sorts of temptations that I've otherwise gotten bored of long ago.

Just like the fire, all of them shed their everyday dumbness; their noiseless, motionless presence, which has caused me so much suffering all week, is now transformed; the objects I've come to disdain, hold in contempt, and grow tired of now become tempting playthings once again, as they must have been when I first saw them. The drawers in the sewing table invite me to open them, and as for what's inside them, well, only now are the scissors truly scissors; and the needles are really needles, sparkling, more primed than ever for pricking; and the thread on the sundry spools is practically begging to be torn; the chalk is ready and waiting to be written with, as surely as is Oluska's slate pencil or Ernuskó's lead pencil and quill at the bottom of the large closet. And while Mother is still asleep, I hastily test God's fury on them all.

Before long I hear Mother's voice, then Oluska pops in half dressed, followed by Mother in her robe. Soon it will be time to wash up and get dressed; today we will all don our "best," for we are going to synagogue. Mother does not go to the market, since she can't even touch money, not today; nor will Father go teach after coming home from synagogue, but stay home instead. Seeing that we'll all be in the flat until it's time to leave for synagogue, time passes faster. I listen through the door as Father, in the big room, practices his sermon; or else I spy on Mother as she struggles away before the mirror while trying to put on her corset. First she tries it herself, then Oluska helps, followed by Lidi; but neither manages the job. Mother, her face all red, whimpers away. As tight as it is around her, the corset still doesn't clasp, so finally she calls Father. How she can walk about in a corset so tight is beyond me. Not even Father likes it being so tight, but Mother points out that every "respectable" woman wears them like this. One of the clasps among the many suddenly pops off, at which Mother sighs.

"Oh dear God, do be careful, all of you, it's Saturday you know. This isn't a sin, is it, Papa?"

Father replies seriously.

"It's all right, it popped off by itself."

The problems go beyond the corset. Mother's shoes are awfully tight as well, so she tries on two or three other pairs, only to find that one is tight here, the other there. Every Friday she has her corn removed, mostly, but she never dares to have as much removed as she should. Lidi and then Father help with her shoes, too, and by the time she manages to pull on a pair, once again she is all red and "dizzy," with a headache coming on full force. Then she puts her hair "in order." Since today is Saturday, she cannot use the curling iron, and so she only kind of frizzes it with the "cold iron" before sticking rollers into her hair, mushrooming it up and inserting a whole bunch of hairpins. I watch her fixedly. So strange is the spectacle that I can't help but laugh.

"What's so funny?" asks Mother.

"Nothing."

What else can I say?

"Nothing?" she asks, adding, "Only little donkeys laugh at nothing."

In that case, I'll tell her. "I'm laughing because what you're doing to yourself, Mother, is all so strange." I point to the rollers, the hairpins, the curling iron, the corset, the shoes.

"Hey, Father," calls Mother, "this child is making fun of how I'm dressing."

Father smiles. "Shoo him away."

"Why shouldn't I laugh?" I say. "I mean, how would *I* look with all this stuff?"

And I too begin sticking the pins and the rollers in my hair, and frizzing with the curling iron. Now Mother really does shoo me away.

"That's enough. Scram."

Still laughing, I step over to Oluska, who happens to be standing before the other mirror having her hair combed by Lidi. At least now I can ask her the question too. "Who combs the fire's red hair?"

She can't answer either. Oluska also shoos me away.

A few minutes later, Mother having barely finished, the little bell in the maid's room rings. Ölschein, the beadle of the synagogue, has pressed the buzzer in the courtyard.

This means that the synagogue is already getting packed. We can be off. Father stays behind a bit; for he will go alone. The three of us, however, go with Mother. Mother goes down the stairs circumspectly—so much so that I want nothing more than to laugh again.

Having passed through the little courtyard, then the big one, already we find ourselves at the synagogue. Here, behind the large door, the older students and men are on the ground floor; but we must go upstairs with Mother.

One step, two, then another. Though Mother goes slowly, I'm already upstairs and take a quick look down.

So many people, such a big room! Here, too, everyone sits on benches, like Ernuskó and Oluska in school.

We sit upstairs on both sides of Mother, behind metal grating. Further on I see more little boys and girls with their mothers, also behind the grating.

Ernuskó brought along his prayer book. Though he already recites the Hebrew text almost fluently, he doesn't quite understand it. To himself he softly pronounces it letter by letter. The two of us, Oluska and I, are more excited than he. My big sister's little pigtail jiggles to and fro as she keeps turning to whisper away with Mother. The others are whispering, too, as if a breeze were passing over the benches. Pressed right up against the grating, I only stare downward.

Though happy, I am afraid of the yawning depth beneath me. Nervous and red-faced, I shrink back repeatedly from the grating. After a deep breath I muster up my courage and make another go of it, gaping at the abyss.

In no time, I see Father step in through the big door downstairs! He proceeds between the benches slowly and silently, just like he does in our room when he thinks we're all asleep. He goes up a tiny set of stairs to the pulpit. What a big, dark, red velvety curtain I see there! Not to mention something golden up top, and those huge golden columns! All those burning candles left and right! They are much longer than the ones Mother lights at home on Friday nights. And right above the spot where Father comes to a stop, a lantern burns, some sort of red lantern.

"What's that, Mother, that red lantern? Why isn't it brighter?"

"That's the eternal flame. It's not supposed to burn any brighter; it's always got to burn just like that."

"And what's that big red curtain?"

"That's the altar curtain."

If it's really a curtain, why then, I think, there's got to be a window behind it too, like at home. But Mother says that behind it is the Holy Ark. I give a puzzled look. A closet, she adds, a holy closet.

I don't get it. Closet? Closet? Holy closet? No doubt there are clothes in the closet, maybe a robe, yes, maybe

Father will change again beside that closet. At home he dresses in front of the closet too. I share my theory with Mother.

She smiles.

"Don't make fun of me," I protest. "Tell me instead: isn't there a robe in there?"

"No," says Mother, "that's where the holy books are kept. Now be quiet. *Shh!* The service is about to begin!"

Father has already passed the velvet curtain. Now he is standing at his bench to the right of the pulpit. He looks up, and singing voices suddenly ring out. Says Mother: Those are the older students. Then music, booming, and again the singing. Now only one voice sings, robust and deep, then it's as if the singing voices were carrying on a dialogue.

"What are they telling each other?"

Mother leans close to me and whispers in my ear: "They're singing to the glory of God, but quiet now. . . . *Shh . . .*"

"Glory?"

She waves a hand and nods, *yes, yes*, but . . . *shh . . . shh!*

God, I've got that much. But *glory?* That only swirls about in my head.

"What's his glory'?"

Mother waves her hand again and whispers, "I'll tell you at home—at home."

I turn to Ernuskó, for he looks as if he knows.

"Ernuskó, do you know what his 'glory' is?"

"I know too," Oluska rustles, "it's because he created everything!"

Ernuskó counts on his fingers: "In six days . . ."

All right, I think, but why isn't Father singing yet?

I don't like this one bit. Singing is something to be proud of, but he just stands there with his head drooping way down low, like we do before him when we're ashamed. Is he ashamed of himself too? Perhaps because he is not allowed to sing? A fleeting sense of suspicion passes through me: maybe he's not even the rabbi?

Mother only smiles when I say this. But Oluska is all-out mad: How can I even think such a thing? Ernuskó gives me a serious look. "Of course he's not ashamed," Mother now says, "he's just praying to himself. The rabbi doesn't sing, only the cantor and the choir do. The rabbi prays and then preaches; he teaches."

Relieved, I think: Oh, how dumb I am! And here I thought he wasn't the rabbi!

They're still singing. And I ask: "Is this the 'glory of God,' too?"

"Yes, this too is the glory of God. They sing it in different ways, from serious to cheerful, as necessary. But . . . *shh* . . . *shh* . . . I'd like to pray!"

Again I am at a loss. How can the glory of God be cheerful and all that? As I see it, the glory of God can only be along the lines of Father's expression—solemn. Surely not cheerful.

At this Mother laughs again. I say no more.

Father just keeps standing there like before. I've never heard so much singing. When it's cheerful I want to jump about, but that's not allowed; and when it's really sad and slow, hushed and deep, then I want to cry, but that's not allowed either. When it blares I am afraid: I clutch the grating and shut my eyes over and over again, but this is cowardly and so makes me ashamed.

By now the singing has given way to murmurs and whispers. All at once everyone falls silent. Then a deep, lone voice begins a song, which, says Mother yet again, is still about the glory of God.

Before long, Father and the cantor go over to the big dark curtain before that closet Mother calls the "Holy Ark." The cantor draws back the curtain, revealing a mysterious light. Something is there. Now Mother is singing too. Meanwhile two old men covered in prayer shawls, even their heads, go from the pews down below up to where Father and the cantor stand, and they stand on either side of the Holy Ark. According to Mother, they see to it that no trouble befalls the holy books, for that would be a big sin indeed, even bigger than when someone writes, tears anything apart, pokes at a fire, or argues, on a Saturday. . . .

Father is the first to reach inside that large chest. The cantor now falls silent and the two old men step even closer to the Holy Ark. All are watching to see how Father removes the holy books. My eyes open wide. I am awaiting a book that I've seen at home pretty often: big, black, old. That which Father now takes from the Holy Ark is completely different. Suddenly I cry out: "That's not even a book, Mother! What is it?"

Alarmed, Mother turns to me with a finger on her lips: "*Shh!* . . ." A bunch of people look up at us. Even Father glances up. In my fright I try cowering behind Mother as best I can. Oluska is furious, Ernuskó stares at the floor. Slowly I come out from behind Mother, ever so warily pressing my face back up against the grating. Just now Father hands the cantor that which he removed from the Holy Ark. Again my eyes open wide, and I whisper: "It's a doll! Mother, it's a doll!"

That's just how I see it, too. It's wearing a skirt, like Oluska's doll, only the whole thing is much bigger, and its head is shining, even sparkling, strong; the cantor holds it the very same way that Oluska rocks her doll.

Mother lets me flounder about for a while. I keep repeating: "It *is* a doll! Are they trying to put it to sleep?"

Ernuskó offers no opinion. Only Oluska shakes her head: If Mother says it's a book, then it's a book, and not a doll.

Now the cantor starts off with the doll, Father just behind him. The two old men, still completely covered with prayer shawls, go behind Father. The cantor begins singing to the doll as they go down the steps and in front of the benches. By now, everyone in the benches has gotten on their prayer shawls, with which they now touch the doll as the cantor extends it their way. And so they proceed. I only stare. But I'm none too happy that it's not Father who leads the way, not him who carries the doll. Then they return the doll; not to the Holy Ark, however, but to the table before it. Everyone below sits back down, as does Mother. She whispers: "It's only from this far that it looks like a doll. Because it's written on a scroll." Mother draws a scroll in the air with her fingers. "True, you might say it's wearing clothes," she continues, "clothes of silk, embroidered with gold. Those aren't real clothes, though, but exist just to make the holy book more beautiful. As for what you see as a head, that's a big, lovely, silver crown, and that's there too so it will shine and be as beautiful as can be. When it comes down to it, though, it's really the holy book, with nothing but letters inside. In a moment you'll all see it. Just look! See?"

Again my eyes open wide as the two old men undress the doll as it lies there on the table. Just like we undress Oluska's doll.

Father helps them. The cantor meanwhile sings.

After they've removed the doll's velvet costume, one of the old men picks it up. Now I don't see a thing. No doubt they're removing her blouse, I figure.

Soon she'll be naked, and she'll scream!

But no. Now I can see it all again. They place the doll between the candles. Mother points, whispers.

"So, do you all see the scroll now? See it? Just pay attention! Now they'll open it up, and inside you'll see a bunch of letters! Just look!"

Ernuskó sees it already, and nods. Oluska nods too. The images of book and doll are still jumbled in my mind. I don't understand what a scroll is, and I certainly can't see any letters from my vantage point. Nor can I see the doll anymore, for it is completely obscured by Father, the cantor, and the two old men in prayer shawls. In vain Mother tells me that they'll now start reading from the holy book; for I only stare suspiciously downward, maybe Mother and them are secretly thinking the same, yes, Father and the cantor and the two old men are playing doll after all, and everything that Mother said, she said only so we'd all stay nice and quiet.

Ernuskó and Oluska sure aren't any help. They always want to be better than me. They only stare downward with expressions I can't figure out. They don't answer when I whisper to them. Mother now opens up another prayer book, and reads. With a wary smile I whisper to her: "Sure they're not playing doll?"

Mother chuckles to herself and says with a wave of the hand: "Can't you hear them? They're reading it already!"

Once more I look through the grating. The cantor is singing again. I've got to face it after all: he *is* singing what he reads, and this doll *is* the holy book. So now I badger Mother thus: "And what are they reading?"

"Something different every day."

"And today?"

"Maybe about Abraham, our forefather."

"Forefather? That's Grandpa," I think—and say. Mother smiles at this too. "No, no. This Abraham lived a much longer time ago. Before even our grandfather's grandfather. You'll find out when, once you too study the holy book."

This new round of singing is not the same as before. It makes me neither sad, nor happy, nor does it frighten me. For a while I listen, paying attention; I want something else to happen, but nothing does—nothing, but that this monotonous singing puts me slowly to sleep.

There's a surprise in store when Mother nudges me awake.

"Listen!" she says excitedly. "Your father is talking. He's praying for the homeland and the king."

Again I press myself to the grating. I don't know much about the king. One time Mother showed me his picture. He had *two* beards—not like Father. He lives far away in a great big palace, and God created him, just like Father, to take care that everyone keeps the Ten Commandments throughout the whole land. The *homeland.* I know even less about "home." Home: our flat and the courtyard. Mother says we'll find out the rest later on, but for now let's just pay attention.

Again Father is standing before the open Holy Ark, looking up with his hands clasped together on his chest. His voice is now completely different, like when he talks to us at home. But I just love it. Only a few of his words fix themselves in my head. The others fly right away, and I cannot hold them back.

All I hear is Father saying, in a more powerful voice: ". . . our sovereign, Francis Joseph, emperor of the monarchy and king of our country, our homeland, Hungary . . ."

Utter silence in the congregation. Everyone is watching my father. Being really proud of this, I smile. Everyone should know: I am his son.

All at once I see Father in the pulpit. Not even now do I understand what he's saying, but that's all right. It's enough for me that *he* is talking, that he is talking from so *high,* and that this high pulpit is so velvety, yes, its velvet hanging reaches all the way to the floor and is embroidered with gold just like the dress of the holy book. Even where Father rests a hand—all velvet. There, in the heart of the pulpit, as I stare and listen, Father grows ever larger! Especially when he stretches out his arms now and again, taking with them the arms of his gown, like giant wings, and he lets his surging voice resound, I am so proud to belong to him that I shudder with exhilaration, almost like I do when a military bugle sounds. I want to stomp about and shout—but this must not be done. I only sit there, my hands trembling with feverish pride, my feet pitter-pattering hard against the tile floor. Oh, Father, go ahead and shout, I think—shout, please do! Even louder! Louder! Spread out those wings more often, do, and while you're at it, don't forget to raise your hands up higher and higher, more and more! But when he suddenly drops his voice, I like that too. I find myself repeating some of his words at a whisper to myself, but then my blood freezes all at once: utter silence. Father bows his head. Thinking that he's forgotten his lines, like when Oluska sometimes trips up on one of the many lessons she must learn by rote, my breath stops in fear and shame; and only when Father finally resumes do I dare begin breathing, slowly, once again. Oh yes, he knows just what he's saying! All of you down there are sitting and listening to my father! None of you are rabbis, like my father! *You* don't even budge! *You* aren't even allowed to cough, not when *he's* talking, my father. Why, you can't so much as whisper, for my father will look up immediately, fix his eyes on the direction the coughing came from—and silence anew! *Nothing* may disturb him! Haughtily I turn my head about, and when my father locks his eyes on the direction of some whispering, I do too, with uncompromising wrath.

Now his voice grows louder. I am surprised to see that the whole congregation stands up at once. My father's voice resounds throughout the synagogue one last time, he spreads his arms wide once again, then he clasps his hands and looks up: "So be it, amen," he says, then bows and slowly descends from on high. . . .

There is silence in his wake. These final words and gestures, and not least the utter silence that follows, make me want to stand up on the bench and cry out: "So be it, amen, I'm his son! I'll be like him too! No matter how little, how bad I am, I'll be like that all the same!" I'd gladly shout all this—but I do not dare. Instead I only look conspicuously about and show myself, but no sooner do I begin than shame compels more stealthy glances here and there, while I think: See me, everyone? See me? Hmm? You do, don't you, and you *know* that I'm his son!

The silence continues. "Now we've really got to be quiet," Mother whispers. "This is the main prayer, we mustn't even whisper this, no, we've got to say it completely to ourselves." But this is the last thing on my mind just now. I'm thinking of Father. My satiated sense of pride in this great silence sees me warm up to him. I forgive him for all of his prohibitions, his stern discipline, interrogations, unexpected appearances, the whole of his dominion at home; I forgive him for my getting everything I have, from him. I watch only him as he stands facing the wall, and amid the profound silence all my thoughts of forgiveness slowly become repentance and ardent devotion. I regret never having loved him as much as do Ernuskó and Oluska, and soon I begin softly crying to myself. But I am ashamed of this too, and so I crawl underneath the bench as if to adjust my stockings, and there I snivel away.

Translated by Paul Olchváry.

Other works by Pap: *Pap Károly művei* (1998–2000).

José Rabinovich

1903–1977

Born in Białystok, the short-story writer José Rabinovich immigrated to Buenos Aires in 1924. He worked first as a typesetter and later owned a printing press. He began writing, in Yiddish, before his emigration, but after some time in Argentina he switched to Spanish. Many of his early stories were subsequently translated and published in Spanish. His stories feature poverty-stricken, downtrodden Jews who often suffer extreme degradation and debasement, especially during World War I and the turmoil that followed it. Even his fiction about East European Jews who have settled in Argentina highlights the disappointments of everyday life. He also wrote poetry and dramatic works.

A Man and His Parrot
1937

It is barely six in the morning and the stars are still out, but Manuel has to get up.

It isn't a job that wakes him. That obligation used to get him right to his feet, but now? Now just getting dressed is drudgery. His pants, his shoes—they resist when he puts them on. His hands have become so powerless that they can hardly drag his clothes on. He and his clothes are mutual enemies. His feet, like an old man's, don't want to walk—they balk. He can't stop yawning. What is he yawning about? Maybe he didn't get enough sleep? On the contrary, he slept too much. If only someone would knock on the door and say "Manuel, time for work!"

He is itching to do something so his hands will turn back into hands. So his body will be hard and strong. So he will stop yawning. So he will be a real man! But since nobody comes to his door or into his heart, Manuel moves like a phantom, with his socks in one hand and a shoe in the other. In his hands his clothes look like rags. His hands, too.

Manuel gets up to make maté for Matilda. He rolls the bitterness inside his mouth and catches it in his throat, unable to swallow, but unable to spit it out either. And the harsh taste refuses to stay in his throat. It goes all through his body and is concentrated around his heart. What a life!

Matilda needs a maté brought to her in bed and put in her hand to drink. His wife deserves this: after all, she is supporting them. It would be so good if he didn't have to do this. His excuse is that she is not sustaining only them but also another life inside her. In such a case, a man should take care of his wife. He dotes on her a bit more to make it easier for her to carry the burden he put in her body.

But ever since he became the housewife and she the breadwinner—even though she still seems like the same old Matilda—something has been piercing him like cats' claws, destroying him. It's a good thing to serve one's wife a maté in bed. It's an honor for the wife and no disgrace for the husband. But the terrible thing is that his wife knew this is only a duty he is forced to carry out because she brings home the rent money. Too, she buys him socks on the street, and she—not he—instructs that money be taken from the box on the table to shop for what they need. That is why it's no good, bringing his wife a maté in bed. Still, he knows Matilda isn't that kind of woman. She cares about him. She doesn't mind going to work, or even that he is unemployed. She doesn't think the things he imagines that she thinks. But she *could* be thinking them. After all, any woman would, and besides, Manuel is forcing her to think that way. It is thus no surprise that his clothes look like rags in his hands when he gets dressed at six o'clock to bring his wife a maté in bed.

The stars are still in the sky, and it is still dark outside. It is winter. If it were summer it would already be light by now, bright and pleasant, and he would not have to turn on the electricity in the kitchen. Matilda can make maté in the dark. Manuel can't, even though he would rather be in the dark. In the dark, the work doesn't seem so distasteful.

There's maté, and sugar too, but no coffee to sprinkle in. What a numbskull he is—they were out of coffee yesterday, too. And she can't drink maté without it. Or maybe she can, but she claims she can't. She usually says that everything he does is fine. But it seems to him that she really feels just the opposite, yet doesn't want him to feel bad that he's the housewife. So she says she can't drink maté without coffee so that he will be encouraged to learn how to run the house.

He sneaks into the kitchen on tiptoe so their parrot won't see him. Damned parrot! They've put up with so much from each other; they've had a longstanding, bitter war. Who will be the victor? Who will survive? Manuel, of course. After all, he has more years left to live than the parrot. Still, the parrot has given Manuel so much heartache, so much real anguish, that he is letting it die of thirst. As long as the parrot screams "Master!" Manuel will not put water in the cage.

The parrot is just another problem. He would let it scream if there were no neighbors in courtyard—would let the bird yell "Master!" until it exploded, and who would care? If no one else could hear, Manuel would not be taking it to heart.

Of course he would not feel happy about being mocked. After all, how can anyone be happy who peels potatoes, lights the stove, stokes the fire, cracks eggs, washes dishes and who also hears—screaming right over his head—"Master! Master!"? It's O.K. when the parrot screeches once then takes a break.

But as soon as it notices Manuel it starts up and will not stop. More than once, Manuel has been so enraged that he has felt like throwing a plate at the parrot's head. He is sure that his neighbors are quietly quaking with laughter. And that even Matilda is laughing. Back before he was unemployed, she never laughed when the crazy parrot screeched "Master! Master!" until it got hoarse. That is because Manuel was the breadwinner then. He liked it that the parrot recognized him. Back then, everyone enjoyed the shrieking, even though there really was no reason to laugh. And now, since he has become unemployed, even Matilda has begun to snicker when the parrot starts in with its cheery screech. The more the bird screeches, the more his wife's snicker reveals its teeth. But would she laugh if she knew about the relentless, bitter war being waged so stubbornly and silently by Manuel, so he won't have to listen anymore—and by the parrot, so Manuel will put a drop of water in its bowl? Would Matilda laugh then?

What is more, if Manuel thought it was merely in the bird's nature to scream, the same way a rooster has it in him to crow, maybe he wouldn't care. The neighbors wouldn't laugh either. But everyone *sees* and hears how hard it is for the bird, who shrieks "Master!" as tragically as if someone were cutting its throat. The parrot's labored cry to Manuel whenever he goes into the kitchen provokes laughter from wives in the other kitchens—so much laughter that the women could explode from it.

When the bird lets out its mocking fury, Manuel would just as well heave the whole thing, parrot and cage, out the window, and do it so hard that even the Messiah, were He to come, could not revive the bird. But that would be then end of Manuel, too, because people would run after him through the streets, as though he were a madman. Better to quietly carry the parrot out and get rid of it. But people would discover that trick, too.

The parrot has already been without water for three days. Manuel gives it seeds and little pieces of stale bread, but he wouldn't be feeding the bird either if he weren't scared about being seen starving it. So he merely denies it drink. They can see from outside the cage if the parrot has food or not. But no one can see the tin water bowl.

Matilda drinks her maté and leaves for work. Manuel gives her a hug, just as he should. His situation demands it. He receives instructions on what to cook for lunch. He listens, smiling. His situation demands it.

The parrot notices him and starts choking, screeching. "Master!" Manuel gives an involuntary glance at the sky, which is gloomy and on the verge of rain. Something about its appearance presses down on that place, the one in both beast and man, where anguish lies hidden. He goes back in the room, starts making the bed, and notices tiny infant's undershirts beneath the pillows. Matilda had been sewing them before she went to sleep and left them there. Tiny shirts. Manuel starts thinking. He cannot see anything in front of his eyes. Later, when he is again able to see, he rushes to give the parrot a drink of water.

Translated by Debbie Nathan.

Other works by Rabinovich: *Cabizbayos* (1943); *Tercera clase* (1944); *Pan duro* (1953); *Cuentos de pico y pala* (1971).

Delmore Schwartz

1913-1966

The poet, critic, and short-story writer Delmore Schwartz was born and raised in New York City, the son of Romanian immigrants. He attended the University of Wisconsin, New York University, and Harvard, where he taught composition from 1940 to 1947. He later held brief visiting appointments at other universities. From 1943 to 1955 he was an editor of *Partisan Review*. At his death he was teaching at Syracuse University. His personal life was unhappy and chaotic and he descended into alcoholism and madness and died prematurely from a heart attack. His short stories offer critical portraits of his parents' generation and of his own circle of New York intellectuals.

In Dreams Begin Responsibilities
1937

I

I think it is the year 1909. I feel as if I were in a motion picture theatre, the long arm of light crossing the darkness and spinning, my eyes fixed on the screen. This is a silent picture as if an old Biograph one, in which the actors are dressed in ridiculously old-fashioned clothes, and one flash succeeds another with sudden

jumps. The actors too seem to jump about and walk too fast. The shots themselves are full of dots and rays, as if it were raining when the picture was photographed. The light is bad.

It is Sunday afternoon, June 12th, 1909, and my father is walking down the quiet streets of Brooklyn on his way to visit my mother. His clothes are newly pressed and his tie is too tight in his high collar. He jingles the coins in his pockets, thinking of the witty things he will say. I feel as if I had by now relaxed entirely in the soft darkness of the theatre; the organist peals out the obvious and approximate emotions on which the audience rocks unknowingly. I am anonymous, and I have forgotten myself. It is always so when one goes to the movies, it is, as they say, a drug.

My father walks from street to street of trees, lawns and houses, once in a while coming to an avenue on which a streetcar skates and gnaws, slowly progressing. The conductor, who has a handle-bar mustache helps a young lady wearing a hat like a bowl with feathers on to the car. She lifts her long skirts slightly as she mounts the steps. He leisurely makes change and rings his bell. It is obviously Sunday, for everyone is wearing Sunday clothes, and the streetcar's noises emphasize the quiet of the holiday. Is not Brooklyn the City of Churches? The shops are closed and their shades drawn, but for an occasional stationery store or drug-store with great green balls in the window.

My father has chosen to take this long walk because he likes to walk and think. He thinks about himself in the future and so arrives at the place he is to visit in a state of mild exaltation. He pays no attention to the houses he is passing, in which the Sunday dinner is being eaten, nor to the many trees which patrol each street, now coming to their full leafage and the time when they will room the whole street in cool shadow. An occasional carriage passes, the horse's hooves falling like stones in the quiet afternoon, and once in a while an automobile, looking like an enormous upholstered sofa, puffs and passes.

My father thinks of my mother, of how nice it will be to introduce her to his family. But he is not yet sure that he wants to marry her, and once in a while he becomes panicky about the bond already established. He reassures himself by thinking of the big men he admires who are married: William Randolph Hearst, and William Howard Taft, who has just become President of the United States.

My father arrives at my mother's house. He has come too early and so is suddenly embarrassed. My aunt, my mother's sister, answers the loud bell with her napkin in her hand, for the family is still at dinner. As my father enters, my grandfather rises from the table and shakes hands with him. My mother has run upstairs to tidy herself. My grandmother asks my father if he has had dinner, and tells him that Rose will be downstairs soon. My grandfather opens the conversation by remarking on the mild June weather. My father sits uncomfortably near the table, holding his hat in his hand. My grandmother tells my aunt to take my father's hat. My uncle, twelve years old, runs into the house, his hair tousled. He shouts a greeting to my father, who has often given him a nickel, and then runs upstairs. It is evident that the respect in which my father is held in this household is tempered by a good deal of mirth. He is impressive, yet he is very awkward.

II

Finally my mother comes downstairs, all dressed up, and my father being engaged in conversation with my grandfather becomes uneasy, not knowing whether to greet my mother or continue the conversation. He gets up from the chair clumsily and says "hello" gruffly. My grandfather watches, examining their congruence, such as it is, with a critical eye, and meanwhile rubbing his bearded cheek roughly, as he always does when he reflects. He is worried; he is afraid that my father will not make a good husband for his oldest daughter. At this point something happens to the film, just as my father is saying something funny to my mother; I am awakened to myself and my unhappiness just as my interest was rising. The audience begins to clap impatiently. Then the trouble is cared for but the film has been returned to a portion just shown, and once more I see my grandfather rubbing his bearded cheek and pondering my father's character. It is difficult to get back into the picture once more and forget myself, but as my mother giggles at my father's words, the darkness drowns me.

My father and mother depart from the house, my father shaking hands with my mother once more, out of some unknown uneasiness. I stir uneasily also, slouched in the hard chair of the theatre. Where is the older uncle, my mother's older brother? He is studying in his bedroom upstairs, studying for his final examination at the College of the City of New York, having been dead of rapid pneumonia for the last twenty-one years. My mother and father walk down the same quiet streets once more. My mother is holding my father's arm and telling him of the novel which she has been reading; and my father utters judgments of the characters as the plot is made clear to him. This is a habit which he very much enjoys, for he feels the utmost superiority and confidence when he approves and condemns the behavior of other people. At times he feels moved to utter a brief "Ugh"—whenever the story becomes what he would call sugary. This tribute is paid to his manliness. My mother feels satisfied by the interest which she has awakened; she is showing my father how intelligent she is, and how interesting.

They reach the avenue, and the streetcar leisurely arrives. They are going to Coney Island this afternoon, although my mother considers that such pleasures are inferior. She has made up her mind to indulge only in a walk on the boardwalk and a pleasant dinner, avoiding the riotous amusements as being beneath the dignity of so dignified a couple.

My father tells my mother how much money he has made in the past week, exaggerating an amount which need not have been exaggerated. But my father has always felt that actualities somehow fall short. Suddenly I begin to weep. The determined old lady who sits next to me in the theatre is annoyed and looks at me with an angry face, and being intimidated, I stop. I drag out my handkerchief and dry my face, licking the drop which has fallen near my lips. Meanwhile I have missed something, for here are my mother and father alighting at the last stop, Coney Island.

III

They walk toward the boardwalk, and my father commands my mother to inhale the pungent air from the sea. They both breathe in deeply, both of them laughing as they do so. They have in common a great interest in health, although my father is strong and husky, my mother frail. Their minds are full of theories of what is good to eat and not good to eat, and sometimes they engage in heated discussions of the subject, the whole matter ending in my father's announcement, made with a scornful bluster, that you have to die sooner or later anyway. On the boardwalk's flagpole, the American flag is pulsing in an intermittent wind from the sea.

My father and mother go to the rail of the boardwalk and look down on the beach where a good many bathers are casually walking about. A few are in the surf. A peanut whistle pierces the air with its pleasant and active whine, and my father goes to buy peanuts. My mother remains at the rail and stares at the ocean. The ocean seems merry to her; it pointedly sparkles and again and again the pony waves are released. She notices the children digging in the wet sand, and the bathing costumes of the girls who are her own age. My father returns with the peanuts. Overhead the sun's lightning strikes and strikes, but neither of them are at all aware of it. The boardwalk is full of people dressed in their Sunday clothes and idly strolling. The tide does not reach as far as the boardwalk, and the strollers would feel no danger if it did. My mother and father lean on the rail of the boardwalk and absently stare at the ocean. The ocean is becoming rough; the waves come in slowly, tugging strength from far back. The moment before they somersault, the moment when they arch their backs so beautifully, showing green and white veins amid the black, that moment is intolerable. They finally crack, dashing fiercely upon the sand, actually driving, full force downward, against the sand, bouncing upward and forward, and at last petering out into a small stream which races up the beach and then is recalled. My parents gaze absentmindedly at the ocean, scarcely interested in its harshness. The sun overhead does not disturb them. But I stare at the terrible sun which breaks up sight, and the fatal, merciless, passionate ocean, I forget my parents. I stare fascinated and finally, shocked by the indifference of my father and mother, I burst out weeping once more. The old lady next to me pats me on the shoulder and says "There, there, all of this is only a movie, young man, only a movie," but I look up once more at the terrifying sun and the terrifying ocean, and being unable to control my tears, I get up and go to the men's room, stumbling over the feet of the other people seated in my row.

IV

When I return, feeling as if I had awakened in the morning sick for lack of sleep, several hours have apparently passed and my parents are riding on the merry-go-round. My father is on a black horse, my mother on a white one, and they seem to be making an eternal circuit for the single purpose of snatching the nickel rings which are attached to the arm of one of the posts. A hand-organ is playing; it is one with the ceaseless circling of the merry-go-round.

For a moment it seems that they will never get off the merry-go-round because it will never stop. I feel like one who looks down on the avenue from the 50th story of a building. But at length they do get off; even the music of the hand-organ has ceased for a moment. My father has acquired ten rings, my mother only two, although it was my mother who really wanted them.

They walk on along the boardwalk as the afternoon descends by imperceptible degrees into the incredible violet of dusk. Everything fades into a relaxed glow, even the ceaseless murmuring from the beach, and the revolutions of the merry-go-round. They look for a place to have dinner. My father suggests the best one on the boardwalk and my mother demurs, in accordance with her principles.

However they do go to the best place, asking for a table near the window, so that they can look out on the boardwalk and the mobile ocean. My father feels omnipotent as he places a quarter in the waiter's hand as he asks for a table. The place is crowded and here too there is music, this time from a kind of string trio. My father orders dinner with a fine confidence.

As the dinner is eaten, my father tells of his plans for the future, and my mother shows with expressive face how interested she is, and how impressed. My father becomes exultant. He is lifted up by the waltz that is being played, and his own future begins to intoxicate him. My father tells my mother that he is going to expand his business, for there is a great deal of money to be made. He wants to settle down. After all, he is twenty-nine, he has lived by himself since he was thirteen, he is making more and more money, and he is envious of his married friends when he visits them in the cozy security of their homes, surrounded, it seems, by the calm domestic pleasures, and by delightful children, and then, as the waltz reaches the moment when all the dancers swing madly, then, then with awful daring, then he asks my mother to marry him, although awkwardly enough and puzzled, even in his excitement, at how he had arrived at the proposal, and she, to make the whole business worse, begins to cry, and my father looks nervously about, not knowing at all what to do now, and my mother says: "It's all I've wanted from the moment I saw you," sobbing, and he finds all of this very difficult, scarcely to his taste, scarcely as he had thought it would be, on his long walks over Brooklyn Bridge in the revery of a fine cigar, and it was then that I stood up in the theatre and shouted: "Don't do it. It's not too late to change your minds, both of you. Nothing good will come of it, only remorse, hatred, scandal, and two children whose characters are monstrous." The whole audience turned to look at me, annoyed, the usher came hurrying down the aisle flashing his searchlight, and the old lady next to me tugged me down into my seat, saying: "Be quiet. You'll be put out, and you paid thirty-five cents to come in." And so I shut my eyes because I could not bear to see what was happening. I sat there quietly.

V

But after awhile I begin to take brief glimpses, and at length I watch again with thirsty interest, like a child who wants to maintain his sulk although offered the bribe of candy. My parents are now having their picture taken in a photographer's booth along the boardwalk. The place is shadowed in the mauve light which is apparently necessary. The camera is set to the side on its tripod and looks like a Martian man. The photographer is instructing my parents in how to pose. My father has his arm over my mother's shoulder, and both of them smile emphatically. The photographer brings my mother a bouquet of flowers to hold in her hand but she holds it at the wrong angle. Then the photographer covers himself with the black cloth which drapes the camera and all that one sees of him is one protruding arm and his hand which clutches the rubber ball which he will squeeze when the picture is finally taken. But he is not satisfied with their appearance. He feels with certainty that somehow there is something wrong in their pose. Again and again he issues from his hidden place with new directions. Each suggestion merely makes matters worse. My father is becoming impatient. They try a seated pose. The photographer explains that he has pride, he is not interested in all of this for the money, he wants to make beautiful pictures. My father says: "Hurry up, will you? We haven't got all night." But the photographer only scurries about apologetically, and issues new directions. The photographer charms me. I approve of him with all my heart, for I know just how he feels, and as he criticizes each revised pose according to some unknown idea of rightness, I become quite hopeful. But then my father says angrily: "Come on, you've had enough time, we're not going to wait any longer." And the photographer, sighing unhappily, goes back under his black covering, holds out his hand, says: "One, two, three, Now!," and the picture is taken, with my father's smile turned to a grimace and my mother's bright and false. It takes a few minutes for the picture to be developed and as my parents sit in the curious light they become quite depressed.

VI

They have passed a fortune-teller's booth, and my mother wishes to go in, but my father does not. They begin to argue about it. My mother becomes stubborn, my father once more impatient, and then they begin to quarrel, and what my father would like to do is walk off and leave my mother there, but he knows that that would never do. My mother refuses to budge. She is near to tears, but she feels an uncontrollable desire to hear what the palm-reader will say. My father consents angrily, and they both go into a booth which is in a way like the photographer's, since it is draped in black cloth and its light is shadowed. The place is too warm, and my father keeps saying this is all nonsense, pointing to the crystal ball on the table. The fortune-teller, a fat, short woman, garbed in what is supposed to be Oriental robes, comes into the room from the back and greets them, speaking with an accent. But suddenly my father feels that the whole thing is intolerable; he tugs at my mother's arm, but my mother refuses to budge. And then, in terrible anger, my father lets go of my mother's arm and strides out, leaving my mother stunned. She moves to go after my father, but the fortune-teller holds her arm tightly and begs her not to do so, and I in my seat am shocked more than can ever be said, for I feel as if I were walking a tight-rope a hundred feet over a circus-audience and suddenly the rope is showing signs of breaking, and I get up from my seat and begin to shout once more the first words I can think of to communicate my terrible fear and once more the usher comes hurrying down the aisle flashing his searchlight, and the old lady pleads with me, and the shocked audience has turned to stare at me, and I keep shouting: "What are they doing? Don't they know what they are doing? Why doesn't my mother go after my father? If she does not do that, what will she do? Doesn't my father know what he is doing?"—But the usher has seized my arm and is dragging me away, and as he does so, he says: "What are *you* doing? Don't you know that you can't do whatever you want to do? Why should a young man like you, with your whole life before you, get hysterical like this? Why don't you *think* of what you're doing? You can't act like this even if other people aren't around! You will be sorry if you do not do what you should do, you can't carry on like this, it is not right, you will find that out soon enough, everything you do matters too much," and he said that dragging me through the lobby of the theatre into the cold light, and I woke up into the bleak winter morning of my 21st birthday, the windowsill shining with its lip of snow, and the morning already begun.

Other works by Schwartz: *The World Is a Wedding and Other Stories* (1948); *Vaudeville for a Princess and Other Poems* (1950); *Selected Poems, 1938–1958* (1967); *Selected Essays* (1970).

Yoysef Smolazh

1906–1942

The Yiddish poet and prose writer Yoysef Smolazh was born to a poor family in Chmielnik, Poland, and received a traditional heder education and worked as a destitute tailor. Smolazh's literary talent was discovered by prominent Yiddish author I. M. Veisenberg, who secured Smolazh's reputation as a skilled poet and writer. Smolazh's poetry and stories were published in dozens of periodicals and journals in Poland and Latin America. After the publication of his first book, *Heym un fremd* (Home and Abroad), in 1937, he moved to Warsaw. He was murdered in Treblinka.

The Open Grave
1937

Crowds of people had been gathering since dawn at the morgue next to the city hospital. Drowsy, shivering, in damp gray clothes, they warmed themselves by huddling in one another's breath. Their faces were remote and gloomy, their lips pressed together in harsh sorrow, their eyes blinked naively and awkwardly. A damp autumn fog shrouded these people, isolating them from the rest of the city.

Now and then, however, the faded yellow light of a municipal streetcar flickered in the distance. A grating shriek shook them up, reminding them that living creatures were bustling on the other side of the fog. But they, virtually cast out on a wild steppe, stood there, silent, melancholy, motionless.

Somewhat later, new people tore through the foggy cloud. The air grew freer, the light vaster, and the fog evaporated like steam.

A red-hot strip cut the horizon more sharply, pouring like blood into the blue, cadaverous day.

The sleepy people, who, in their damp gray clothes, had come to pick up their dead relatives, breathed more easily with the arrival of the day, shaking courage into their cold, drowsy legs, peering at the growing crowd—God help us!

A Jewish woman wrapped in a blanket flung her arms apart and yelled in a dry, hoarse voice: "Why are we standing like wooden poles? Today's a Friday in winter. We won't be able to bury the dead! What an awful business!" She sobbed more vehemently. "My son set out a week ago . . . to save our home and his poor mother . . . Then he tried to hang himself. And then peasants cut him down, untied the noose—his face was blue, he was scarcely breathing, his head was twisting every which way! He kept gasping: 'Leave me alone! I don't wanna live! I don't wanna live!' My poor son! Your wish came true!"

The woman began shaking, writhing, she collapsed, bending and buckling. The throng was petrified.

Two men pulled her to her feet and kept her standing. Her head thrashed about as if she'd been slaughtered. Her face was flooded with tears, her entire body was sobbing, her heart was pounding recklessly, and in a staccato voice she bellowed: 'You dogs! Why don't you say something? Five suicides—six young men starved to death, and my son—" She burst into wild laughter. "And my son was the twelfth—is that a tiny number?" Her eyes flashed insanely. "Like in the epidemic—epidemic—epidemic!"

Two strong orderlies in blue scrubs took her into the hospital waiting room. A young doctor, clad in a white smock with a stiff, shiny collar, earnestly listened to her heart and then mumbled: "An attack of nerves."

The people in the crowd grew agitated; some of them were listening closely to a tall, red-haired young man with lean, drawn cheeks. Spraying saliva through his bared yellow teeth, he proclaimed that the dead were better off, they had already gotten across. "But we," he asked hopelessly, "what are we gonna do? This winter we'll be escorting a lot more people to the cemetery."

An old, bowed Gentile with a gray, tobacco-stained mustache opened the brown, rusty door to the morgue. At first the people shoved their way in, but a short while later they jumped back in disgust.

The long, narrow room, resembling a dark corridor, had thick walls, a high, black, vaulted ceiling, and tiny barred windows. The day seeping through the panes was heavy, overcast. The floor gave off a darkness like black, wind-tousled hair. The corners shuddered in mysterious terror. The blankness emitted the coolness of the damp smell of corpses. And corpses, covered with black rags, were laid out from one end of the room to the door. Tags stuck out between the crooked yellow toes, bearing the names of the dead. The bowed Gentile pulled out the tags and read the names aloud as if deafened by the noise:

"Moshek Shtein, thirty-two years old! Stefan Volotshuk, twenty-eight years old! Antonyova Kraftshik, nineteen years old!"

The crowd trembled. Nineteen . . . But the bowed Gentile's voice grew calmer, as if he were handing out mail parcels.

The hospital plaza resounded with the clattering of horses' hooves. And then came several black wagons drawn by horses with sad, lowered heads. A soft lament rose from the crowd. The corpses were carried out, and some of the people moved on.

A long, gray throng moved through the frosty autumn day, trudging across the slightly frozen earth. Their faces were drawn and gloomy, their lips narrow and sullen, their eyes moist and dark and submerged in an ocean of sorrow. Straight, stiff male backs in ragged jackets stuck out of the throng. Prematurely aged women with thin, feeble legs kept colliding with one another.

No bells were ringing, no Catholic priests in long cassocks were singing prayers of comfort, no Jewish women were naming the good angels that were to welcome the dead. Just a silent throng with grim, bony faces shuffled wearily through the noisy, clamorous streets.

The hospital plaza was completely deserted by now. The heavily charged air weighed down on me. The sun was soaking dimly in the dark clouds, floating tediously from one to the other.

In the morgue two corpses were left—homeless strangers perhaps. I uncovered one face. A pupil wedged inside out in a torn corner of an eye glared angrily at me. The head lay flung to the side. Filthy stickiness darkened the twisted yellow features. I gazed at the face for several minutes. Suddenly I shuddered. Then I stared hard. Yes, someone I knew. I pulled out the tag and I read: Sorre Rozen. My eyes darkened with memories that were struggling in my mind. Yes, Sorre Rozen, the girl with the flaming cheeks, the quiet girl with the modest smile in the corners of her mouth. Our paths had constantly crossed in the workers' homes; she had always worn a black apron on her slight figure, and she usually had a verse by Bovshover, the anarchist poet, on her dry lips:

"How can I, brothers, sing for joy?"

I looked around—there was no one here . . . I wanted to shriek: "Sorre, I never knew that you were this lonely. I never knew why your eyes were so sad."

It was almost dusk; a black wagon drove by, accompanied by a grinding streetcar and a peasant dozing on a wagonload of coal. I sat with a Jewish graveyard worker on the coachbox. Surprised looks drilled into my back. I wanted to shriek: "What indifference! A human being has died! A human being!"

The graveyard workers grumbled at me: "Hey, listen, why are you so late?"

I tried to point out that this was a homeless girl, a stranger.

"Fine!" they snapped. "Forget it!"

Three short, fat women with dark faces and warty chins, trudged out from the ritual cleansing house.

"Where's the shroud? Where's a candle? What a world!" they sighed heavily.

I stood there dumbfounded. What was this? Sorre Rozen . . . A girl had worked in a factory, then lost her job, gone hungry, and now—a tag on her toes: Sorre Rozen, twenty-five years old. And that was that!

I carried her on my shoulder. An old Jew slogged ahead of me. The wind whistled in his beard. His mouth shook out a grumbling Psalm Ninety-one, which is traditionally recited at Jewish funerals: "He that dwelleth in the secret place of the most High shall abide under the shadow of the Almighty . . ."

We halted at the end of the field, next to a brick barrier. A cavernous shout came from a grave: "Beryl, is this the last one already?"

"Yeah, thank God! The last one!"

I stood at the open grave. The corpse had been cleansed and it was shining. The shroud lent it a delicate charm. A human being had been purified . . . The sun blazed up, igniting the horizon. The mound of dug-up soil was aflame.

Suddenly a huge mob of people emerged before my eyes. They hurried like a wall toward the open grave. I recognized them—these were the people in the damp gray clothes. Forming a circle, they gaped down into the open grave. Then I heard a loud wailing: "People! Why are you silent? Can't you see that the graveyard is shut down, nailed up? We've been wandering through it since daybreak like cursed souls and we can't find a way out!"

The wailing grew louder: "We're trapped in the graveyard! We're doomed! The open grave is devouring us!"

I looked around. The woman in the blanket was writhing convulsively, pouring her words like sparks on the cold, mute mob.

The graveyard trees rustled eerily. The wailing grew softer, more profound. The western sky gazed like a blind man. Dark and cold, like lead. The night slid nimbly from the trees and settled like a huge black cat on the freshly dug grave.

Translated by Joachim Neugroschel.

Other works by Smolazh: *Heym un fremd* (1937).

Jerome Weidman

1913–1998

The son of immigrants, the prolific writer Jerome Weidman was born, raised, and educated in New York City. His work portrays the rough underside of business and often features ambitious young immigrants on the make, who, while clawing their way to success, lose their humanity. In addition to being a successful novelist and short-story writer, Weidman also made his mark on Broadway and in Hollywood. He wrote the book for the award-winning musical *Fiorello!* (1959) and for the musical adaptation (1962) of his early novel *I Can Get It for You Wholesale*, as well as the screenplay for *The Eddie Cantor Story* (1963).

I Can Get It for You Wholesale
1937

XIX

I entered the restaurant five minutes late on purpose, but Babushkin was already there. He was at the small table I'd reserved way over in the corner, hunched over the menu because he was scared of the waiter that stood a little way off and kept looking at him.

Everything he did was so in keeping with the way I'd figured him out, that it looked like a gag. But he wasn't playing dumb. He wasn't that good an actor.

I came late because I knew he'd be there ahead of me. He was the type that was always on time for appointments. That was a good sign. When a guy can manage to hit the time of an appointment right on the nose, the chances are he's been devoting quite a bit of time to reminding himself that he should be there, which means that his mind isn't exactly what you'd call a beehive, which means that he's at least a couple of notches lower than a genius, which means he was right up my alley. Another thing I'd decided on was that he wasn't exactly

a lion tamer, and here a waiter had him buffaloed, just by looking at him. If I had any doubts about him, this clinched it.

"Hello, there, Meyer," I said, shoving out my hand and giving him a healthy shot of the old personality smile, grade A.

"Hello, Mr. Bogen," he said, getting up to take my hand.

"Stay right where you are," I said, pushing him back into his chair and taking one that faced him, with my back to the wall. That's my Chicago training, you know. Keep the whole room in front of me. "Sorry to be late, but I couldn't help it. They had me tied up on the phone till just a couple of minutes ago. I came down as soon as I could."

"That's all right," he said, "I know how those things are."

Maybe I had a genius on my hands after all. He knew how those things were!

"How's the missus?" I asked.

"She's all right, thanks."

"One of these days," I said, "I'll have to invite her up to my house to try some of my mother's blintzes. You ought to hear the bawling out my mother gave me for not inviting her up the other night when you were there. She was so sore I thought she was going to hit me with a frying pan or something. They were all right, those blintzes, weren't they?"

"Yeah," he said.

"I guess your wife'll like them, too," I said. "What's a good night during the week for her? I mean, there's no rush, but any time you have a free night, just let me know."

"Well, I don't know—"

"All right, then, I'll tell you what I'll do. I'll let *you* know, and then, if it's not okay, why, we can change it for some other night."

"All right," he said.

"Don't forget, now," I said.

"I won't," he said.

Well, at least that made one of us who wouldn't.

"And the baby?" I said. "How's the baby?"

"All right," he said. "A little cold it had, but my wife she took it to the doctor and he gave her some kind of oil she should rub on, but now it's all right."

"Only one you got?" I said. "Just one, right?"

"Yeah," he said, "just one."

"Well," I said, with a laugh, "just wait till we get going good, then you'll be able to afford to have another dozen if you want to."

"Yeah," he said.

Well, that was enough of *that*. No sense in ruining my appetite completely. I picked up the menu and put it down again.

"I wonder what's keeping Mr. Ast?" I said, looking at my watch. "It's almost a quarter after two already."

"He's probably tied up with a customer, I guess," Babushkin said. Sure, either that, or it was because I'd told him the appointment was for later. But Babushkin didn't have to know that. There were going to be a lot of things that Babushkin wouldn't have to know about. "You know how it is with salesmen," he said.

He was taking a hell of a lot for granted. That made two things I knew how they were.

"You bet," I said, laughing. "I'm practically in the same boat myself." I picked up the menu again. "I'll tell you what. There's no sense in our waiting for Mr. Ast. We don't know how long he'll be. And while I don't know about you, Meyer, I know *I'm* nearly starved. Suppose we order, and when he comes, he can catch up."

"All right," he said.

"Waiter," I called, but I didn't really have to. He was practically sitting on my neck from the minute I'd drifted in.

I took my time about the order, making it sound complicated, and when I finished the waiter turned to Babushkin. He looked at the menu for a few seconds, rubbing his face a little like he had a toothache. Then he looked up and said, "Uh—I'll—I'll take the same."

Just a make-it-two guy. Every time I met him he showed more qualifications for the job of being my partner.

He didn't look very happy, and when the waiter brought the fruit cup and put it down in front of him, he picked up his spoon and went to work on it without a change of expression. I let him fiddle around with the cherry on top, until he got it onto the spoon and carried it to his mouth. Then I said:

"Well, what did your wife say about that proposition we were talking about the other night up at my house?"

He swallowed the cherry and began to talk to the plate of fruit in front of him.

"Well, she said it was a good idea, Bogen," he said slowly. "Only one thing she said—I hope you don't think there's anything personal in this, Bogen—she only said a man has to be very careful of the men he goes into business with. I mean, she said you can't pick your boss when you go to work for somebody, but, well, she said you ought to pick your partner pretty carefully when you go into business."

So far that looked like his only drawback as a partner—his wife. Was I glad I didn't act on that brainstorm I'd had about meeting her!

"She's perfectly right, too," I said as the waiter changed the plates in front of us. "Why do you think I went all over Seventh Avenue with a fine-tooth comb before I decided you were the best designer and factory man there was? If I wanted to rush this thing, hell, I could have picked up any one of a hundred dopes who know a little something about designing and cutting and things like that. But like your wife said, I knew that when you're going into business with a man, the thing to do is be very careful and pick him like, hell, I don't know, like you were picking an eye to put in your head."

I dipped my spoon into the plate, but I didn't carry it to my mouth. I'd rather have the soup get cold than Babushkin.

"That's just what Teddy Ast told me the first time we even talked about it," I said. "I said what we need more than anything else, Teddy, is a corker of a factory man. I don't care so much about the other things, I said, if any of the other things aren't so okay it isn't so bad. But a factory man, that has to be absolutely the top, I said. And he agreed with me right away. 'Get Babushkin of Pulbetkal,' he said to me, just like that, without even batting an eye, that's what he said."

He nodded slowly. Maybe he was finally beginning to realize himself that he was a good factory man.

"So what do you say, Meyer?" I said, leaning across the table toward him, and looking serious. "When Ast shows up, do we tell him we're in?"

"All right," he said, "all right."

I didn't have time to let out the sigh of relief that I should have let out. And I didn't waste any time complimenting myself, either. Because this was nothing. This was easy. The hard part was yet to come. I just leaned back in my chair and let my joints ease up a little. But in a moment they tensed up again. Because as I leaned back I saw two things. The clock on the restaurant wall, and that said twenty-five to three. And Teddy Ast, dressed to kill, bouncing across the restaurant toward us.

There were times when, seeing him as I did just then, my feelings toward Teddy Ast amounted almost to admiration. With all the handicaps of a body shaped like a toothpick and a face that had about as much distinction in it as a spoonful of mashed potatoes, he was still a snappy number. He was wearing a draped herringbone topcoat with a fly front and a gray velvet collar, tab shirt with a black knitted tie, peg-top pants, suede shoes, and a brown pork-pie hat with a black band and a tricky little feather stuck into it. I took it all in at a glance and filed it away for future reference.

"Here comes Mr. Ast now," Babushkin said. But I didn't have time to be astonished at the fact that he should have noticed something all by himself. I was too busy reminding myself that for the next few minutes I would be talking to Teddy Ast and not to Meyer Babushkin.

"Yeah," I said, "That's him all right."

Right about—*face*!

"Hello, Bogen," he said, nodding briskly, and, "Hello, Babushkin."

He slipped out of his coat and handed it to the waiter with his hat. The suit was a pepper-pot tweed, rough and shaggy-looking, but double-breasted. I marked that down on my list, too.

"Hello, there, Ast," I said. You have to put the "there" in. You can't say "Hello, Ast." It sounds dopey. "How's the boy?"

"Pretty good," he said, studying the menu. "Can't kick. Say, waiter," he said, tossing the menu down. "Just bring me a tongue on rye and a glass of beer. But the bread has to be thin, remember, and I don't want any of that lungy stuff on the tongue. Tell him to cut all that stuff away, understand?"

The waiter nodded. They were all doing it. I guess it was an epidemic.

"Okay, then," he said, dismissing him. "Step on it. I'm in a hurry."

Then he turned to us and rubbed his skinny hands.

"Well, gentlemen? What's the good word?"

"Pussy," I said, and grinned. "That's always the good word, isn't it?"

"Right, my friend," he said, jerking his face into a smile. "You getting much?"

I shrugged my shoulders and ducked my head and gave an imitation of a Seventh Avenue grease ball.

"End iff I go around makink complaindts, so it'll help me maybe?"

He laughed and showed his teeth. They weren't so hot. They were even and strong-looking, but they were yellow and sloped inward, so that his mouth looked like that of an old man, without teeth, sucked in.

"Well," he said, "any time you run short, just call on Uncle Teddy, and I'll get you fixed up."

He was going to get *me* fixed up!

"That's a promise?" I said.

"A promise," he said.

The waiter brought the sandwich and set it before him. He dug in. I lit a cigarette and watched him. Babushkin just looked worried.

"Did you ever hear about the way they catch fish up in Alaska?" I asked.

He pushed the food into a corner of his mouth, and said, "Not since I stopped wearing diapers, I didn't hear it."

"No, this one is new," I said.

He washed down the lump of food with a swallow of beer.

"They're all new," he said.

A wise guy. Well, that was all right. He was sure of himself. I liked them that way.

"I know," I said. "But this one is new."

"Yeah," he said. "Like my girl friend."

"See, it's this way," I said. "First they cut a hole in the *ice*. Then they—"

"Yeah," he said, taking another bite of the sandwich and examining it to see how much damage he'd done. "Try again, Bogen," he said.

"Well," I said, "they can't *all* be new."

"No," he said, "but they don't have to be *that* old."

He swallowed some beer and attacked the sandwich again.

"How about the he-virgin and the nurse?" I said. "Hear that one?"

"Probably," he said.

But when I finished and said, "Get it?" he squinted his eye and slopped chewing for a second.

"No," he said.

That was the wise guy that knew all of them. They were *all* new!

"Lemme explain," I said, and did.

"Oh, yeah, sure!" he said. "That's right."

Yeah, sure, that's right! He knew it all the time!

"Not bad, eh?" I said, laughing.

He finished the sandwich and lit a cigarette.

"Say, that's pretty good, you know?"

No, I didn't know. He was telling me.

"When you get to the gag line," I said, "You have to get the break in when you say the second 'cheap.' Like this: 'Cheap is *chea*-eap!'"

"Cheap is cheap," he said to himself, memorizing the words. "That one's pretty good, all right. Wait'll I tell that to a couple of the buyers. They'll die laughing when—say, that reminds me." He looked from me to

Babushkin and then back at me. "I hate to rush out on you like this, gentlemen, but I've got a couple of important buyers coming in, and, well, you know how those things are—"

"Sure," I said, "we know."

What the hell, I figured, Babushkin might have known, too. Maybe I wasn't lying when I spoke for both of us.

"So how do we stand, gentlemen?" he asked.

"We stand okay," I said. "It all depends on you now. Mr. Babushkin here and I, we're all set. We've got our money ready, both of us, and we're all set. Any time you say okay, all we have to do is make an appointment to go down to the lawyer and we're all set to go. We're just waiting to hear from you."

"Then you don't have to wait any longer," he said, spreading his skinny ringers out like a fan. "I'm all set any time you are. My money is ready now."

"Then we're all set?" I looked at Babushkin, who nodded, and then at Ast, who jerked his head up and down. "Fine. Let's see. To-day is Monday. Suppose we make it for Wednesday? Wednesday all right with you? All right, then. Wednesday at Golig's office. I don't know exactly what time, but I'll call you both up to let you know. Then it's Wednesday at Golig's office?"

They nodded. Ast stood up and shoved his arms into the sleeves of his coat that the waiter was holding for him. I got up, too, and Babushkin followed.

"How's my old friend Mr. Schmul of Toney Frocks?" I asked.

"You know Schmul?" Ast said, surprised.

"Do I know him?" I laughed. "I've been trying to forget him for over a year. I *worked* for the punk."

"You *worked* for him?"

"Sure."

"When?"

"About a year ago."

"A *year* ago? That's funny. I've been with him over two years already, and I don't remember you."

"That's because you never go into the back," I said with a laugh. "No salesman ever goes into the back."

"What do you mean, in the back?"

I figured I might as well give him a little jolt. It might shake a little of the cocksureness out of him and make him realize that he wasn't dealing with a schmoogie.

"I was one of his shipping clerks," I said.

He stared at me. It isn't every shipping clerk that can dig up ten thousand bucks with which to go into the dress business.

"You mean that?"

"I sure do," I said.

"A *year* ago?"

"You bet."

I bent down for the check, but I could feel the look of surprise he had trained on me, and I fumbled a little with the tip on purpose to give him a chance to recover. I didn't want him to get sore or anything. I just wanted him to think about it.

On the sidewalk, in front of the restaurant, we stopped.

"Which way you headed?" I asked.

"This way," they both said, pointing down.

"I'm going up," I said. I wasn't, but I said it anyway. No anticlimaxes for me. "Then it's Wednesday at Golig's office. I'll call you both up and give you the exact time. Okay?"

"Okay," they said, and walked off together.

I laughed a little to myself as I saw them go down the block, and I hoped they wouldn't get themselves run over or killed. They didn't know it, but they were worth their weight in—well, no, not even *they* were that valuable, but they were worth a lot to me. Two men make a dress business. A designer and a salesman. I was neither, but that didn't stop me. I took it easy. I picked and chose. And out of all of Seventh Avenue, I picked them. I hoped they would have brains enough to feel properly honored.

I grinned when I thought of what Pulvermacher's face would look like when he found out I'd taken away his factory man. But when I thought of that son of a bitch Schmul, and what *his* face would look like when he found that Toney Frocks, Inc. had lost the services of Theodore (Teddy to his pals and partners) Ast to me, I laughed out loud. A couple of people looked at me, but I didn't care. Meal or no meal, this called for a drink.

I went into Schrafft's for a soda.

When I got out I felt pretty good. I walked down Broadway slowly, whistling a little and window-shopping. A black and white tie in Gillette's window looked good to me, so I went in and bought it. On the corner of Thirty-Eighth Street I saw a women's accessory shop and I remembered that I'd promised Mother a purse to go with her new brown suit. I went in and bought her a good large one, the kind she liked. As I turned to leave the shop, a blue bag in a stand on the counter struck my eye.

It was made of soft blue suede, with a white leather border and two large white metal stars, one in each corner, for ornaments. Looking at it reminded me of Ruthie, and the dress she had worn to Totem Manor over the week-end. For a moment I couldn't think what the bag she had carried had looked like. And this one, aside from the color that matched her dress, seemed to have been made for her. Before I knew it, I had put my hand out and touched it, squeezing the soft sides gently.

"Did you want to see this purse?" the salesgirl said, moving down the counter toward me.

"Why, yes," I said. "Sure, you can wrap it up for me."

It was not until I reached the street and had walked half a block or so that I began to feel sore. It wasn't the money. It was just the feeling that I must have been going soft in the head. What the hell was the sense of buying things for a dame when you knew you weren't going to get anything back in exchange? What was I all of a sudden, Santa Claus? Where the hell did I get off playing around with a kike broad like that, anyway? Go buy her eight dollar purses! What the God damn hell for? Because my own mother had introduced her to me? The hell with that crap. If I was going around buying gifts, at least I ought to know enough to buy them for people who knew what was expected of them in return. A dame like Miss Marmelstein, for instance. She wasn't making any of the members of the Harvard faculty worry about their jobs. But she was smart enough to know that if I gave her a purse it wasn't because I all of a sudden thought it would be a good idea for her to have something that would match the color of her eyes.

I stopped walking and looked at my watch. Five-thirty. She *should* have been there yet. She'd been hanging around till after six for over a week. But it would be just my luck for her to skip out early this one night when I didn't want her to. Suddenly I began to walk quickly, and soon I was almost running.

I burst into the office breathlessly, and stopped short. She looked up at me from behind the switchboard in surprise.

"Why, Mr, Bogen!" she said. "What in the world—?"

I felt relieved and after I'd had a second or so to catch my breath I said, "I'm in a terrible hurry to get some very important letters out, Miss Marmelstein. I hope you don't mind staying a little later to-night."

"Why, of course not, Mr. Bogen," she said, smiling quickly. That was a dame for you! "I'm not doing anything special to-night, anyway."

It began to look like she did special things very seldom. Well, I'd see what I could arrange for her. After all, it wouldn't make any difference after to-night. But she didn't have to know about that.

"I'll tell you," I said, scratching my chin and looking at my watch. "It'll take me about a half hour or so to get my papers in shape before I'll be ready to dictate. I'll tell you what you do. You go down and have a bite, or go out and buy yourself a new brassiere or something. And say you get back here about six-thirty. That'll give me plenty of time."

She was all smiles.

"Okay," she said, and got up quickly.

"By the way," I said, holding out the package with the blue and white purse in it, "Here's a little trinket I picked up for you during the day."

She took it quickly and tore the wrapper off.

"Oh, Mr. Bogen, how am I ever going to thank you?"

I'll give you one guess, sister.

"That's all right," I said. "Just don't disappoint me. Six-thirty to-night."

"Don't worry," she said, "I won't."

As though I didn't know that.

"I'll be all ready by the time you get back," I said.

"That'll be good," she said.

Good my eye. This was going to be lots better than just plain good. This was going to be my swan song.

I went into my private office and began to clean out my desk and put the things I wanted to take with me aside. When I finished, my watch said twenty after six. Which meant I had ten minutes to think about how Miss Marmelstein was going to look on the couch in my private office as she performed her last official act as a salaried employee of the departing president of the Needle Trades Delivery Service, Inc.

Other works by Weidman: *What's in It for Me?* (1938); *The Enemy Camp* (1958); *My Father Sits in the Dark and Other Selected Stories* (1961); *The Center of the Action* (1969).

Shmuel Yosef Agnon

A Guest for the Night
1938

Chapter One. I Came to My Home Town

On the eve of the Day of Atonement, in the afternoon, I changed from the express to the local train that runs to my home town. The Jews who had traveled with me got out and went their way, while Gentile townsfolk, men and women, made their way in. The wheels rolled sluggishly between hills and mountains, valleys and gorges; at every station the train stopped and lingered, let out people and baggage, and started up again. After two hours, signs of Szibucz sprouted from both sides of the road. I put my hand to my heart. My hand throbbed against my heart, just as my heart throbbed under my hand. The townsfolk put out their pipes and shoved them into their leggings, got up to collect their baggage, and sat down again; the women elbowed their way to the window, crying "Rubberovitch," and laughed. The train whistled and puffed, whistled again, then sprawled to rest opposite the station.

Along came the dispatcher called "Rubberovitch"; his left arm had been lost in the war; the new one they gave him was made of rubber. He stood erect, waving the flag in his hand, and called: "Szibucz!" It was many years since I had heard the name of Szibucz coming from the lips of a man of my town. Only he who is born there and bred there and lives there knows how to pronounce every single letter of that name. After Rubberovitch had got the name of Szibucz out of his mouth, he licked his mustache as if he had been munching sweetmeats, carefully scrutinized the passengers stepping down, stroked his rubber arm, and made ready to send off the train.

I picked up my two valises and walked to the back of the station yard, looking for a carriage to take me into town. The yard lay in the sun; the smell of pitch and steam mingled with that of grass and plants, the odor of railway stations in small towns. I looked this way and that, but found no carriage. This is the eve of the Day of Atonement, I said to myself, time already for the Afternoon Service, so the coachmen are not going out on the road: if you want to get to town you will have to use your feet.

It takes an ordinary man a half hour to walk to the center of town; carrying baggage, it takes a quarter of an hour more. I took an hour and a half: every house, every ruin, every heap of rubbish caught my eye and held me. Of the large houses of two, three, or four storeys, nothing was left except the site. Even the King's Well, from which Sobieski, King of Poland, had drunk when he returned victorious from war, had its steps broken, its commemorative tablet cracked; the golden letters of his name were faded, and sprouted mosses red as blood, as if the Angel of Death had wiped his knife on them. There were no boys and girls standing on streetcorners, there was no singing, no laughter; and the well spouted water, pouring it into the street, as water is poured in the neighborhood of the dying. Every place was changed—

even the spaces between the houses. Nothing was as I had seen it when I was little, nor as it had been shown to me in a dream shortly before my return. But the odor of Szibucz had not yet evaporated—the odor of millet boiled in honey, which never leaves the town from the day after Passover until the end of November, when the snow falls, covering all.

The streets stood empty, and the market too. The town was already resting from its everyday labors, and the shops were locked; surely at that moment the men were reciting the Afternoon Service and the women preparing the final meal before the fast. Except for the noise of the ground echoing my footsteps, there was no sound.

I paid no attention to the echo from the ground, and walked on, wondering where I could put down my baggage and find lodging. Looking up, I saw a group of men standing around. I went up to them and asked, "Where can I find a hotel here?" They looked at my two bags and the clothes I was wearing, and did not answer. I asked again, "What hotel can I stay in here?" One of them spat out a shred of tobacco from his lips, rubbed his neck a little, stared at me and said: "'D'you think there are so many hotels here that you can choose the one you want? Of all the places in town, only two are left." Another said to him: "In any case, the divorcee's is not the right place for this gentleman." "Why?" "D'you hear?" said the second to his fellows. "He asks why. All right, if he wants to go there, no one will stop him." He folded his arms and turned his head away from me, as if to say: From now on I wash my hands of you.

Another spoke up. "I'll explain. When this poor woman came back after the war, she found nothing but the house her father had left. So she set to work and made it into a hotel, for her and her four daughters to earn a living. But when business got worse, she stopped being too careful about her guests, and the house became a rendezvous for sinners. Reb Hayim's wife she was—and he such a scholar, a good man, fit to be the rabbi of the town—and now what has become of her!" "And where is Reb Hayim?" I asked. "Where's Reb Hayim? He's a prisoner of the Russians. They took him and carried him away to the other end of Russia, and we don't know whether he's alive or dead, for we've heard nothing from him all these years, except for the time when he sent his wife a bill of divorce, so that she wouldn't remain tied all her life to a missing man."

I picked up my two bags and asked, "So where *can* one stay?" "Where? Daniel Bach will show you. He's going home and he lives next door."

While he was still speaking, a man came up and said, "You mentioned my name, so here I am. Come with me, sir, and I will show you your hotel."

Daniel Bach was tall and lean, his head small, his hair chestnut, and his beard short, not pointed, not blunt; a kind of smile hung on his lips, spreading into his sunken cheeks; and his right leg was wooden. I walked along keeping pace, so as not to distress him by too long steps. Daniel Bach noticed this. "If you are worrying about me, sir," he said, "you needn't, because I walk like any other man. In fact, this man-made leg is better than the other, which is the work of God. It doesn't have to worry about rheumatism, and beats the other for walking." "Does it come from the war?" I asked. "Oh no," said he, "but the rheumatism in the other I got from the war." Then I said, "If that's the case, then permit me to ask, sir, were you injured in the pogroms?" He smiled and replied: "From the pogroms I came out sound in body. And the hooligans should thank their stars they got out of my hands alive. So where did I get this leg? From the same source as all the other troubles; from things Jews have to do for a living. Hatach, 'the cutter,' the angel in charge of livelihoods, did not find me right with two legs, so he cut one off and made me stand on the other. How did it happen? But you have reached your hotel, and I my house, and you have to hurry for the final meal. I wish you a full atonement." I took his hand and said to him, "The same to you, sir." Bach smiled and said: "If you mean me, it's a wasted greeting, for I don't believe the Day of Atonement has any power to make things better or make them worse." Said I, "If it does not atone for those that do not repent, it atones for those that do." "I'm a skeptic," he replied, "I don't believe in the power of repentance." "Repentance and the Day of Atonement atone for half," said I, "and the troubles of the rest of the year for the other half." "I've already told you I'm a skeptic," retorted Daniel Bach, "and I don't believe the Almighty cares about the welfare of His creatures. But why should I be clever with you at dusk on the eve of the Holy Day? I wish you a full atonement."

Chapter Two. The Eve of the Day of Atonement

The people of the hotel received me as an untimely guest, for they had already finished the Closing Meal and were about to go to synagogue, and they were afraid I might detain them. "Don't worry," I told them, "I won't trouble you much, all I ask is a place to sleep." The innkeeper looked outside, and looked at me. Then he looked at the food left over from the meal, and looked at me again. I saw that he was considering whether it was still light enough to eat before the beginning of the fast at sunset. I too considered whether it was permissible for me to eat, for we are enjoined to add to the sacred at the expense of the secular, and to begin the fast before dark. I said to him, "There is no time to sit down to a meal," opened my bag, took out my festival prayer book and my prayer shawl, and went to the Great Synagogue.

In my childhood I thought that there was no bigger building in the world than the Great Synagogue, but now its area had dwindled and its height shrunk, for to eyes that have seen temples and mansions the synagogue appears even smaller than it is.

There was not a man I knew in the synagogue. Most of the worshippers were recent arrivals, who occupied the honorable places by the eastern wall and left the others empty. Some of them had risen and were walking about, either to show their proprietorship or because they did not feel comfortable in their places. The radiance that is wont to shine on the heads of the sacred congregation on the Eve of Atonement did not shine on their heads, and their prayer shawls shed no light. In the past, when everyone would come to pray and each would bring a candle, in addition to those that burned in the candelabra, the synagogue was brightly lit, but now that the candelabra had been plundered in the war and not all came to pray, the candles were few and the light was scanty. In the past, when the prayer shawls were adorned with collars of silver, the light used to gleam from them upon the heads of the worshippers, but now that the adornments had been carried off the light was diminished.

The cantor did not draw out the prayers—or perhaps he did, but that was my first prayer in my home town, and it was Atonement Eve, when the whole world stands in prayer, so I wanted to draw out the prayers even more and it seemed to me as if the cantor were cutting them shorter all the time. After he had ended the service, all the worshippers surrounded the Ark and recited the mourners' Kaddish. There was not a man there who did not say Kaddish.

After the service they did not recite psalms, nor did they chant the Song of Unity or the Song of Glory, but locked the synagogue and went home.

I walked to the river and stood there on the bridge, just as my father, of blessed memory, used to do on Atonement Eves; he used to stand on the bridge over the river because the odor of the water mitigates thirst and leads men to repentance; for as this water, which now meets your eye, was not here before this moment and will not be here afterwards, so this day, which was given us to repent of our sins, was not yet in the world before and will never be in the world again, and if you do not use it for repentance you have wasted it.

The water comes and the water goes; as it comes, so it goes, and an odor of purity rises from it. It seems as if nothing has changed since the day I stood here with Father, of blessed memory, and nothing will change here until the end of all the generations. Along came a group of boys and girls with cigarettes in their mouths. No doubt they had come from the feast they had held that night, as they do every year on Atonement Eve, to show that they are not in awe of the Day of Atonement. The stars were fixed in the firmament and their light gleamed on the river; the lights of the cigarettes moved among them. At the same time my shadow fell on the bridge and lay flat before the young people. Sometimes it mingled with their shadows and sometimes it was alone, quivering all the time as if it felt the trampling feet of the passers-by. I turned my eyes away and looked up at the sky, to see if that hand had appeared of which the children tell: they say that on Atonement Eve a little cloud, like a hand, rises in the firmament, for at that time the Almighty stretches out His hand to receive the repentant.

A young woman passed by and lit a cigarette. A young man passed by and said, "Look out or you'll burn your mustache!"

Startled, she dropped the cigarette from her mouth. The young man bent down and picked it up. Before he could put it in his mouth or the girl's, another came up, snatched the cigarette from his hand, took the girl by the arm, and disappeared with her.

The bridge began to empty of passers-by. Some of them went to the town and some turned toward the wood behind the slaughterhouse on the bank of the Stripa beside the oaks. I looked down at the river again. A fine odor rose from the water. I breathed in deeply and savored the air.

The well in the old market at the center of town could be heard again. Some little distance away was the gurgling of the King's Well, and the water of the Stripa also added its voice—not the water I had seen at first, for that had already gone, but fresh water, which had taken its place. The moon shone from the river and the stars began to dwindle. I said to myself: The time has come for sleep.

I went back to my hotel and found it closed. I was sorry I had not taken a key with me, for I had promised the people that I would not trouble them much, and now I had to rouse them from their sleep. Had I known that the *klois* still existed I should have gone there, for there the people would be awake all night singing hymns and psalms, and some would be studying all night long the talmudic tractates of *Yoma*, treating of the Day of Atonement itself, and *Keritot*, which deals with grave offenses.

I put out my hand to the door, as one puts out his hand when he does not expect it to open, but as I touched it the door opened. My host knew that his guest was outside, and he had not locked the door in his face.

I entered on tiptoe so as not to disturb the sleepers. If I had not worn my boots when I went out, they would not have heard my footsteps. But the streets of the town are dirty and I am fastidious, so I wore my boots, and when I came in they sensed my entrance and turned in their sleep.

A memorial light burned on the table in the middle of the dining room, and a prayer shawl and a prayer book lay there. The smell of warm povidl, which had been put away in the oven, sweetened the air of the house. For many years I had not felt its taste or come across its smell—that smell of ripe plums in the oven, which brings back the memory of days gone by, when Mother, may she rest in peace, would spread the sweet povidl on my bread. But this was not the time to think of such things, although the Torah has not forbidden the enjoyment of odors on the Day of Atonement. My host came out of his room and showed me my bed, leaving the door open so that I could undress in the candlelight. I closed the door behind him and went to bed.

The memorial candle shone into my room. Or perhaps it did not, and it only seemed to me that it shone. I said to myself; This night I shall know no sleep. Rubberovitch's hand or Bach's foot will come to terrify me. But as soon as I lay down on my bed, sleep overcame me, and I slept. And it is almost certain that I did not dream.

Translated by Misha Louvish.

Louis Golding

I Slept with a Murderer
1938

I slept with a murderer every night of my life for two years. The murderer is dead now. He died some weeks ago in Chicago. That is why I am free to tell the tale.

I was a small boy at that time. I must have been ten or eleven years old. We lived in a poor street in Manchester, which was blocked by a wire factory from the pitchy waters of the river Irwell. My father made his living by teaching Hebrew to small boys. One of these boys was named Benny.

Benny was alone in the world excepting for his mother. I never quite made up my mind what the two lived on. I think there was a father somewhere in America, who sent along a few dollars from time to time. Benny's mother couldn't do anything, she was so delicate. She died soon after.

The consequence was that Benny came to live with us, although we were pretty crowded already, and my mother had as much as she could do looking after the rest of us.

We put up a bed for Benny in the lodger's room on the first floor, though there wasn't much room left, what with the lodger and the bed and the table already in it. (The lodger wasn't really a lodger. He was just another down-and-out, a sort of elder Benny. That was the way my father and mother helped themselves out with the rent.) I had a tiny attic all to myself on the top floor.

When Benny lived with us I began to realize he was a strange boy, quite unlike all the other boys I knew. He was extraordinarily refined and delicate in all his perceptions. He would stand at a florist's shop window and stare at one single bloom for half an hour at a time.

If a woman came to the house wearing a silk frock, it would give him intense pleasure to be allowed to pass the soft texture between his fingers or against his cheek. In other words, the boy had an acute sense of beauty. I was fairly sensitive myself in those days, but compared with Benny I was a lump of wood.

Benny had been living with us getting on for a year, when my father one day announced that a young cousin of his named Mottel was coming over from Russia to Manchester. He would, of course, live with us. That went without saying.

My father announced the news, and my mother received it with so much excitement and pleasure that there was obviously something very special about this cousin Mottel.

I myself didn't feel too well disposed towards any more cousins from Russia. The place was littered with them.

"What's he like?" I asked, rather surlily.

"What's he like?" my father repeated. He lifted his hands, but words failed him. He turned to my mother.

"What's he like, he wants to know!" Then he found the word for it. "He's—he's beautiful!" he said.

"Yes," my mother corroborated. "He's beautiful!"

They went on night after night about how beautiful cousin Mottel was. There seemed to be no other word for it than that—beautiful. I've a vivid recollection of the picture of Mottel that built itself up in my mind, and a pretty shrewd one of the picture that must have built itself up in Benny's.

I had seen my first musical comedy lately—I think it was *Floradora*. There was a beautiful young man in it, tall and slim with wavy hair and dimpled cheeks. The girls in the chorus swooned when he came lolloping on to the stage in mauve flannels. That was how beautiful I thought Mottel was going to be.

Benny had saved up his weekly halfpennies and bought a book off a barrow. It had photographs of Greek statues in it. Benny studied them, and marvelled and worshipped. Benny's Mottel was like an early Apollo.

Then Mottel arrived. He wasn't a bit like a musical comedy star or a Greek statue. He was squat and dark and a bit bandy-legged. The hair on his skull was like black wire. There was still more hair on his cheeks and chin, which wasn't a beard, yet wasn't quite not a beard. He wasn't at all fair to outward view. He was, in fact, ugly.

Yet even in the first five minutes, after I had got over my first shock of disappointment, I began to have an inkling of what my father and mother meant when they said he was beautiful. To begin with, he had beautiful eyes, even though they were a bit watery. Or, if they were not quite beautiful, they were tender and had a sort of dewy glint in them. And though his face was rather awful, there was something charming in the set of his mouth. Again, it was a kind mouth—really almost a beautiful mouth.

But I realized almost immediately that his face or his body hadn't anything to do with it at all, when my parents called him beautiful. It was something else, something I'd have to find out.

And I did find out, before many weeks had gone by.

Mottel was a very learned and pious person, and to old-fashioned Jews, that is the very pinnacle of beauty. It doesn't occur to them even to see the body when the soul is full of learning and piety. And I must say Mottel was really very nice about his virtues. He didn't thrust them down your throat, as some people not half so learned and pious do.

I quite liked Mottel, even though I'd have preferred it if he'd been a little easier on the eye. There was another reason why I got over the shock quite soon. I saw the joke of it. It really was quite funny.

But little Benny never got over the shock of it. He had no sense of humour at all. I turned from Mottel's face to Benny's the very moment I could catch my breath after the vision burst on me. I saw Benny's eyes distended with horror. There was a glaze on them. His face was as pale as a candle.

And then another expression came into Benny's eyes—an expression of implacable hatred. I realized he would never forgive Mottel for betraying the lovely Greek ideal he had built up in his imagination. He would never forgive Mottel for being so ugly. Poor Mottel! Poor Benny!

Benny was not an articulate boy. I don't think anybody but me had an inkling of the way Benny detested Mottel, least of all Mottel himself. Mottel was so full of kindness, he couldn't begin to conceive how anybody hated anybody.

But there they were, sleeping a few feet away from each other night after night, month after month, with just a tiny table between them. (The earlier lodger kindly went next door to make room for Mottel.) It was a nightmare for poor Benny. Once or twice I saw Mottel pat Benny kindly on the back, up in their room or down in the kitchen. Benny winced as if something cold and horrible had touched him, like a toad or an adder.

Even if Mottel could have seen it, he wouldn't have realized what it meant when Benny shook all over at his touch, like a leaf. But Mottel couldn't see it. He had weak eyes. He washed them with lotion after lotion, but it didn't seem to make them any better. It was a pity, because, as I said before, they were quite beautiful eyes.

Mottel had been living with us for about a year when my cousin Hilda got married. It was rather a grand wedding, for cousin Hilda's young man was in business for himself, and, besides, he lived in Dalston, in London, which was particularly grand.

I don't quite know how my father managed it, but there were new suits for both Benny and me. It didn't run to a new suit for Mottel. He got his Saturday one pressed.

We went along in full strength to cousin Hilda's wedding. She was married from her own house. The festivities went on hour after hour; it was fine.

You never saw such fried fish and ducklings and chickens and wine as they had at cousin Hilda's wed-

ding. Mottel got just a little bit muzzy as the evening went on, partly because he wasn't used to so much drink, partly because it is really a good deed to show how happy you are when a good Jewish boy and girl get married to each other.

I must confess it didn't suit Mottel to get muzzy. His lips protruded more and more, and they were just a little damp. And there was something parboiled about his face, too.

A pious Jew isn't allowed to shave, but he'd put some powder on his face that morning, which seemed to have destroyed the hair-roots for life. He really looked better with a bit of a screen round his cheeks and chin.

Now and again my eyes fell on Benny. Benny didn't look at the bride or the bridegroom or me, or anybody but Mottel. He stared at him in fascinated loathing. He got paler and paler as the evening went on, his eyes larger and larger.

He lifted a glass to his lips as if to appease his sickness, but the glass slid between his fingers to the floor. I saw beads of sweat running down his forehead on to his face. I went over to him.

"Benny," I said. "What's wrong? Let me take you out into the open air."

"I'm going home," he said faintly. "Will you get the key from Uncle?" (He meant my father.)

"You'll be all right, Benny," I assured him. "All you want is a bit of fresh air."

"I want to go home," he said. He said it in such a tone I knew he meant it. "I want to go to bed."

"All right," I agreed. "I'll go with you."

"No, no!" he shrieked. His face was white with fury. His eyes were quite strange.

"All right," I said quietly. "I'll get the key for you."

So Benny went off home alone. The rest of us didn't go back till a few hours later. Mottel wasn't at all a pleasant sight. He got to bed somehow.

Benny and I had to go to school as usual next morning. The gentleman we knew as the "School Board" wouldn't have excused us school merely because we'd been to a strenuous wedding the day before.

When we got back at midday we found a crowd in front of the house. There was also a bucket of water and a cup for you to wash your hands in over the pavement's edge. That meant someone was dead in the house. My heart jumped like a stabbing pin. "Mottel!" I heard them say. "Mottel! Poor Mottel! A saint in Israel!"

Poor Mottel had been so muzzy when he came in the night before, he had poisoned himself. He always had a glass of water on the table by his bedside, which he drank off last thing.

On the shelf above his head he kept his bottle of eye-lotion: a fearsome blue bottle it was, marked "Poison" very clearly. He had been so drunk he poured the lotion into his glass of water and drained it. He was dead, anyhow.

The next few days were a trance of horror which I prefer not to recall, not until that culminating last moment in which Benny was so strangely involved. Benny, whose existence had been as completely obliterated from my mind during those few days as if he'd been a raindrop fallen into a gutter.

They lifted the coffin-lid to let us have a last look at Mottel before he was wiped out for ever. I tried to turn my head away, but I could not. I tried to shut my eyes, but I could not. Mottel easily and proudly commanded me to look at him. I looked.

A transformation had come over him. No, that is not right. The essential Mottel lay there revealed, the most beautiful thing I have ever set eyes on. His skin had the quality of marble, the loveliest smile of which the mortal mouth is capable lay on his lips. He had dignity, delicacy, serenity: he was more beautiful than any pagan Apollo.

My eyes turned from the dead face to a living face separated from me by the width of the coffin. I saw the beauty of dead Mottel impressed upon the eyes of the living Benny, as the sun is impressed upon a mountain tarn. His eyes were wild with beauty.

Then Benny turned towards me as if he had heard me call him. I looked into his eyes. I saw the glory go out of them and the desolation of a charnel-house extinguish them. I saw his lips quiver, his body shake. He broke down into a lugubrious howling, such as a lonely animal might make in an empty house.

They took him away, whispering: "Poor Benny. He is such a delicate boy." He was a delicate enough boy, but I knew as surely as I knew that my heart beat, that Benny was Mottel's murderer.

It was considered unwise for Benny to sleep any longer in the room where Mottel had died. There was no place for him anywhere else in the house, so he came to sleep in my bed up in the attic. I slept with him every night for two years, knowing he was a murderer. But I did not feel afraid—at least, not very often.

Meir Corona
1891–1965

The Yiddish novelist and short-story writer Meir Corona was born in Siedlce, Poland. He was ordained as a rabbi and worked in Palestine for five years as a laborer before moving to Mexico City in the mid-1920s.

Quite a Bank
1939

There's a stale, sour stench: a miscellany of heaped-up vegetables and fruits, cheese, fried fish, sweaty bodies, thighs, urine, and belching drunks. The smell sneaks harsh but titillating into the nose on a cold spring day. On this street the apartment complex is located.

A dank, dirty corridor leads to the first courtyard, home to a soda factory. Past the gate and the toilet for the entire building, a hallway leads to the second courtyard. There, a dark, narrow, twisting staircase takes you to the door of the bank. It has no sign, and none is needed. Even without one, many of Mexico's Jewish merchants and factory owners already know about the bank.

Its proprietors are two partners with capital worth half a million pesos. But their partnership is not based on the bank or the capital. Each one works separately, with his own capital for his own clients—arranging discounts, drawing up promissory notes, making loans, and so forth.

The partners also have different ways of keeping their books. One does the accounting in Hebrew, in a long, narrow book. He has a single book for all the customers, with each customer taking up two pages. The page for expenditures reads *Nosatti*—"I have given"—and the page for receipts bears the inscription *Qibbalti*—"I have received."

The other partner prefers a Germanized Yiddish, transcribed in Hebrew letters. He uses a separate notebook for each client. The pages for expenditures read *Hinaustragen*—"carry out"—and those for receipts are titled *Einnehmen*—"take in."

One afternoon, the shoe wholesalers Baumholtz and Langer knocked on the door and walked into the "bank"—a large, rectangular room that apparently once had been whitewashed. The shoe dealers looked around, amazed by the furnishings. In one corner of the room stood two little iron beds, arranged at a ninety-degree angle, like the Hebrew letter *daled*. On the wall over one bed hung a portrait of the kindly old Austrian

Kaiser Franz Josef; over the second bed was a picture of the stern old rabbi from Kovno, *reb* Isaac Elhanan Spector. Both pictures clearly showed the effects of houseflies that, apparently without the least respect for the Kaiser's medals or the rabbi's learned visage, had for years enjoyed free run of the place.

Opposite the intersecting beds, in a second corner, stood a wardrobe that looked ancient and second-hand. By the window between the wardrobe and beds stood a small, white table with a newspaper spread on it, and on top of that two and a half rolls and a sliced herring. Around the little table were three simple, white chairs. Two had all four legs, and one had three. Its fourth leg had fallen off and been replaced by a box underneath.

Once inside, the two shoe dealers found only one partner, the Germanic bookkeeper—a tall, blonde, broad-shouldered young man. He was sitting on one of the little beds with a shoe off and his pants leg rolled up, soaking his foot in a bowl of water.

"Good day, Mr. Fishman. So Mr. Tannenbaum isn't here?"

"Good day to you, men! Tannenbaum is here, surely. He just stepped out for a minute to buy something. Have a seat while you wait. He'll be right back."

They sat down and armed themselves with patience. One took a newspaper from his pocket to read. The other had Yehoyesh's Yiddish translation of the Bible, which had just arrived from the States. He opened it and glanced at it. Then they heard hard, slow, heavy steps on the stairway, matched by the rhythmic beating of a stick. Tannenbaum came in. He was a slightly hunchbacked man whose hair was already gray, and who leaned on a thick cane in his right hand. In his left hand he was carrying a seltzer bottle. With a smiling, happy face he turned to the visitors and panted to them in a hoarse voice, "Ah, welcome! Nice to meet you, esteemed guests! What's the good word, fellows?"

And without waiting for a reply, he turned to his partner: "Just look, Fishman, at the bargain I picked up. You hardly ever find anything like this. Take a look!" He lifted the bottle and showed "the little tube of the siphon inside. It reaches all the way to the bottom so you don't waste a drop!"

Then, he turned back to the guests: "What are you reading? Is it good?"

He took the book in hand and opened it to the title page: "Ah! The Bible in Yiddish! The Talmud says that when Onkelos translated the Torah into Aramaic, there was an earthquake that covered four hundred square miles. You can find that in the tractate *Megillah*."

"As far as I'm concerned," Langer answered, "the *entire earth* can quake, as long as I can read the Bible in my own language."

"But let's get to the point," Baumholtz interrupted him. "We came to get a loan from you, Herr Tannenbaum—two thousand pesos on two promissory notes. I will sign one of them, and Langer will co-sign; Langer will sign the other, and I'll be the co-signer."

The old man looked fixedly at both shoe dealers and measured them up, as though trying to read from their faces whether or not it paid to do this kind of business with them. Finally, he smiled shyly and answered: "You know where the Talmud speaks of carrying things on the Sabbath? It mentions 'two kinds that are actually four.' In this case, it seems that two are actually one!"

Langer interrupted him: "That's why we've come not about the Talmud, but for promissory notes. And we didn't come on the Sabbath, but during the work week."

"Especially during the work week, I like every promissory note to have a separate co-signer. As for the rate, you probably know that these days I won't take less than three percent."

Then, in order to sidetrack the conversation, he turned to Langer: "Please tell me, Herr Langer, since you are such an avid reader, if perhaps you could find me Droyanov's *Treasury of Parables and Proverbs*. I've been looking for that book for such a long time. I simply have to read it. In exchange, I could lend you one of my books."

The shoe dealers glanced at each other. They were not about to be tricked into changing the subject. With open contempt, they answered, "We'll make a separate visit to discuss literature. Right now, we're here for money."

In the end, they settled things—both the promissory notes and the interest rate.

Then Langer and Baumholtz hurried out, holding their noses in the reeking courtyard. They were scarcely two blocks away when they realized someone was calling them. They looked around and saw old Tannenbaum running after them, yelling, panting, and waving.

"Oy! Baumholtz, this means trouble!" said Langer. "I'm afraid the old moneybags has gotten cold feet."

"Oy! This is terrible!" echoed Baumholtz, in a frankly terrified voice. "Now what do we do?"

When Tannenbaum caught up and managed to stop gasping long enough to catch his breath, he called out: "Gentlemen, listen! I made a mistake! The passage isn't in the tractate *Megillah*, but in *Hagigah*!"

Translated by Debbie Nathan.

Other works by Corona: *Heymishe mentshn* (1939); *Tsaytn* (1943); *In shtrom fun leben* (1951).

Shmuel Halkin

1897–1960

Shmuel Halkin was a leading Soviet Yiddish poet during the interwar period. His verse was characterized by his attention to neoclassical forms anchored by sophisticated philosophical and biblical allusions. Halkin also worked closely with the Moscow State Yiddish Theatre, producing acclaimed translations, including *Kenig Lir* (*King Lear*, 1935), and adaptations of plays by Avrom Goldfaden, such as *Bar Kochba* (1937). A member of the Jewish Anti-Fascist Committee, Halkin was sent to a prison in northern Russia after the repression of Soviet Yiddish culture in 1948. A poetic memoir of his experiences in the camp was later published in Israel.

Bar Kochba

1939

Act II

SCENE 2

YOUNG MAN: Tell us, Bar Kochba, the words to use
When we return to our homes
And tell of meeting you.
BAR KOCHBA: For taking of the people's land,
For stealing of the people's wealth,
For towns and villages destroyed,
For all these, the sword must punish.
OLD MAN: If earlier I could not decide
You now have given my old hands
New certitude, for which your name be blessed . . .
YOUNG MAN: In towns and villages I will call for revenge.
Come, old man, it is a shame to waste time.
We have to leave the city this very day.
OLD MAN: Go from here in peace, but remember:
Bring war to wherever you come.
[*They bid farewell and the wanderers move away.*]

PNINA: The whole land is agitated:
One stands for peace, another for war.
BAR KOCHBA: And you, where do you stand?
PNINA [*bows her head*]: I stand . . . with you.
[*She embraces him.*]
My heart whispers to my reason
To go with you hand in hand.
BAR KOCHBA: For now you cannot go with me,
I must remain unnoticed.
I am returning to the mountains,
You will leave the forest alone . . .
PNINA [*leads him to their trees*]: Our trees stand together.
When, my beloved, will you make my heart rejoice?
BAR KOCHBA: When in the land not one Roman remains
Then these trees will be united.
PNINA: I will be the happiest among women,
In the forest we will build our *huppah*.
BAR KOCHBA: The people will, with dance and song,
From these trees make *huppah*-poles.
[BAR KOCHBA *moves away.* PNINA *accompanies him.* ANTONIUS *and several slaves appear.* ANTONIUS *looks at the trees.*]
ANTONIUS: Let a new axle be made at once
From the finest tree in the forest!
[MENASHE *arrives.*]
MENASHE: What's the matter?
ANTONIUS: The chariot in which the emperor's daughter is riding
Climbed over a stone
And broke an axle.
MENASHE [*pointing to* BAR KOCHBA'S *tree*]: I am from around here, and with eyes closed
I will show you a kind of tree
That will not break or bend.
ANTONIUS [*to his slaves*]: A fine tree, chop it down!
PNINA [*turns around, sees what is happening and embraces the tree*]: Chop down the tree together with my hands!
[*The slaves remain standing, perplexed.*]
ANTONIUS: What are you standing around for like sheep?
Are you dull or are the axes dull?
You see a girl . . . and you lose your nerve.
[*A slave pushes her aside.* PNINA *falls to the ground. The sounds of axe blows are heard.*
PNINA *jumps up, runs to* ANTONIUS *and falls to her knees before him.*]
PNINA: My lord, it all depends on you,
I beg you—quick, make it stop, forbid it!
ANTONIUS: What has happened here, explain . . .

[Pnina *weeps.* Antonius *turns to* Menashe.]
What injustice are they committing—explain it to me.
Menashe [*seriously*]: They are chopping down the tree
    of her intended . . .
[Menashe *exits.*]
[*A spark of hope arises in* Pnina's *heart.*]
Antonius [*bursts out laughing*]: The whole beautiful
    forest that grows here
Was waiting to become an axle in a Roman chariot . . .
Pnina [*jumps up*]: The whole beautiful forest that
    grows here
Was waiting to see how a Roman axle breaks . . .
Antonius: Bind her hands for these words!
Throw her into the fortress!
[*Two slaves grasp her by the hands.*]
Pnina [*shouts at the top of her voice*]: Bar Kochba!
[Bruria *comes running up. No one notices her.*]
Antonius: You call to Bar Kochba for help! If your
    intended
Comes to plead for you—
We will release you!
Pnina: Bar Kochba! [*All leave.*]
[Bruria *appears.*]
Bruria: Brothers! Fathers! Come here quickly! Come
    here!
[*Several people come running, among them* Uziel *and*
    Hillel.]
Pnina has just been tied up and taken away.
Uziel: Where to?
Bruria: Who knows where?
Bar Kochba's tree has been chopped down!
Hillel: By whom?
Bruria: Rome!
Man: How long will they trample upon us?
Uziel: Maybe it would be better to try persuasion?
Maybe with peaceful pleading we can make things better?
Hillel: Uziel, that's too laughable . . .
[*Suddenly pulls out a short sword*]
Let this do the pleading—it has a sharp tongue
And its message doesn't have to be spelled out.
[Bar Kochba *arrives.* Hillel *wants to tell him
    something.*]
Bar Kochba: I already know everything.
[*He goes over to the fallen tree.*]
All at once my youth has been destroyed . . .
Well, Eliezer, are you satisfied now?
I will remind you of this again, Eliezer.
And Rome, I will demand payment for this all my life.
Uziel: Why have you punished us like this, God!

Our daughters are disgraced.
Hillel: What do you propose to do, Bar Kochba, tell us.
Bar Kochba: Let today be the last day.
Someone: We will go to Rufus and demand
That he free her.
[*The sound of a trumpet is heard.*]
Hillel: He comes here.
We must fight to the last drop of blood in our veins.
Bar Kochba: In the meantime, hide your weapons.
[Rufus *arrives, along with several Romans.*]
Rufus: I have ordered that for the next two or three
    days,
None of you may appear on the road.
Make a detour of a mile around this forest.
Bar Kochba: First of all, I demand that she be freed—
The one whom you with force
Took away from here. Bring her here.
Rufus: To demand such a thing from me!
Who gave you the right, as a slave,
To stand and speak so impudently
To me, upon whom your life depends?
Bar Kochba: My life gives me the right, not you.
If even Emperor Hadrian stood here,
I would speak no differently to him.
Rufus: What are you waiting for? Take him!
[Bar Kochba *is attacked. He gets ready to resist.* Hillel
    and the others try to intervene.]
Bar Kochba: I alone! You would only hamper me now.
[*One of the Roman soldiers takes on* Bar Kochba *with
    a sword.* Bar Kochba *seizes the sword from him and
    breaks it on his knee.*]
Thus will Rome be broken!
Rufus: Throw a rope over him! Lead him in chains!
Bar Kochba: Ask them first to move me from this spot.
Rufus: You'll end your life in the arena, in the lion's
    mouth.
Bar Kochba: Bar Kochba will not surrender to you!
[*He tears the rope, frees himself and runs away. The oth-
    ers follow him.*]
Rufus: Bar Kochba, you will not run far.
Your country cannot serve you
As a hiding place. My hand will find you
Wherever in the land you hide.

Scene 2

[*At the city gate. On stage the Elders, the leaders of the
    city.* Eliezer *and* Menashe *arrive.*]
Eliezer [*to the assembly of the Elders*]: I have called you
    together, in order to tell you:

We will no longer bear Bar Kochba's sins on our heads.
Akiva is coming. It must be decided today
That if that disturber of peace will not listen to us,
And revolts against Rome—we will be justified
Before God . . .
MENASHE: And we will do no evil against the people.
ELIEZER: If we, the Elders, will declare in Rome:
We do not mean to struggle against Roman rule . . .
MENASHE: And not the whole nation is against the emperor, only a part,
And we will send men to go from cave to cave
To find their arms and send them to Rome ourselves.
With empty hands they will not dare to move.
ELIEZER: In this way we free the people from fear . . .
ONE OF THE ELDERS: And those who lead them astray
We will shun as we would lepers . . .
ANOTHER OF THE ELDERS: It's not too late—we must take timely precautions
Against bloodshed, misery and tears . . .
[Music is heard.]
ELIEZER: Akiva is coming—the matter must be settled today.
[A song is sung as a greeting to AKIVA.]
Ask each road, each highway
Ask each woodland bough
Ask each stone upon the road:
How does Akiva now?
Ask the spring and brook: did he
Drink their water clear?
Ask the cool and shady place
If he rested here.
[Surrounded left and right with friends, AKIVA arrives.]
AKIVA: Peace to you—both near and far!
Peace to you—from this day forth . . .
[All rise.]
ELIEZER: Peace to you, Rabbi Akiva,
Peace to you and to us all . . .
ALL: Peace.
[They make room for him at the forefront.]
ELIEZER: Take your place.
[AKIVA remains standing.]
AKIVA: A long time since I've been in my city
And seen my fellow city-dwellers
Allow me the honor of greeting you . . .
[Bows before the people. All greet him.]
ALL: Rabbi Akiva! Rabbi Akiva!
AKIVA: I hurried to arrive before the gate is locked . . .
And now I want to know, so tell me, good people:
Did the rains fall here at their appointed time?

Did the sower eat the bread made from his grain?
Did the planter have the joy of his vineyard?
Did the flocks multiply in the valley?
Was their wool soft and thick?
Did the workers in the city have
Bread enough for themselves and their children?
Were their hands filled with work?
Did sons and daughters pair off like doves?
[Those who greeted him move more closely together.]
ELIEZER: Akiva, not in vain did you hurry here:
Your coming must seize the sword from the hands
Of those who wish to fatten the soil with our blood.
YEHOYSHUA: With whose blood?
ELIEZER [To YEHOYSHUA]: With yours.
MENASHE [Points to AKIVA]: And with his.
AKIVA: What is happening with you here? Explain.
ELIEZER: What could be worse . . .
Yesterday there came to my house
Senator Lucius, who sternly declared:
"Eliezer, I warn you for the last time, remember
That the arms that your people hide
Will fall first upon your old head . . ."
ELISHA: And what did you say?
ELIEZER: What should I say?
I will not bear the guilt for that.
HILLEL [to YEHOYSHUA]: Ay . . . for me it's easy to bear arms,
But for him it's hard to bear guilt alone.
AKIVA: Why is there no peace among you?
Where there is no peace, there is no blessing . . .
ELIEZER [points to the Elders]: The head must always take first place
And what the head decides, the hands must do.
[points to the crowd]
ELISHA: But these hands were able to choose
[points to AKIVA]
A head that wants the same thing as the hands . . .
AKIVA: Rabbi Eliezer, in this world we have lived long.
It's time we knew that we must listen to the demands
Of those who can recognize a friend a mile away
And love to the quick and to the quick they hate . . .
ELIEZER: Hatred of a person is—half a punishment.
Therefore, when God punishes—he punishes to the end.
Rome has been provoked, the Torah will be in even more jeopardy.
The nation is sick—Bar Kochba knows the wound . . .
ELISHA: The nation is sick—Bar Kochba wants to heal it!

UZIEL: He wants no more children dying in caves.

HILLEL: He wants the peasant to breathe more easily.

YEHOYSHUA: And no more old people dying in the flames.

AKIVA: The Torah is in jeopardy? Perhaps, but you are deluded:

You think that Rome will lend it a hand?

Or do you not wish to understand, or cannot grasp

That when there is no nation—for whom is the Torah?

[takes a pot from UZIEL]

The people are like this pot:

When it is whole, each drop is safe within it . . .

[flings the pot to the ground—it shatters]

Do you wish the people to be likened to this? [. . .]

Act IV

SCENE 2

[Dawn in BAR KOCHBA's camp. On the ground, sleeping warriors. On the side, armor and pitchers of water. UZIEL stands watch at BAR KOCHBA's tent. BAR KOCHBA sits not far from the tent, singing.]

BAR KOCHBA: The sun will rise and glow

On us, as on our foe.

What brings to us this day?

O watchman, can you say?

Watchman, what of the night?

Watchman, what of the night?

If you know, then you must say

What will befall us this day.

They won the mountain fight—

Our heroes sleep tonight.

The foe they drove away

But what will bring the day?

Watchman, what of the night?

Watchman, what of the night?

If you know, you must say

And quickly: what of the day?

[a moment of silence]

Well, Uziel, what has the night brought us?

UZIEL: I looked to the west

I looked to the north.

Quiet—nothing has happened.

BAR KOCHBA: Too quiet . . . My ear is used to blows.

I live with the sound of steel on steel.

With it I arise, and with it I go to sleep.

You say nothing has happened?

UZIEL: No . . . I looked to the west,

I looked to the south

On the whole road

Corpses lie around

Many are our enemy's losses.

BAR KOCHBA: Our losses also were not few,

We too left many heroes on the road.

Death has settled deep within us . . .

UZIEL: But at least the city remained ours.

Since they drove us from the fortress

Everything has gone downhill.

City after city they retake . . .

BAR KOCHBA [sings sadly]: To the valley I came down to you,

From my cave over mountain and field.

Let me hear, O beloved, your voice,

Only then will my longing be healed.

[He moves close to UZIEL.]

Uziel, do you think she is alive?

UZIEL: Who?

BAR KOCHBA: You don't know who?

UZIEL: Bar Kochba, listen:

This very night

As I was standing guard

Not dozing, just lost in thought

Suddenly there came to mind—

You know who?

BAR KOCHBA: Who?

UZIEL: You and Pnina.

BAR KOCHBA: Tell me, did you see her up close?

What was she wearing?

UZIEL: The finest holiday dress,

And I accompanied you both the whole way

On my trumpet

That I brought from home

Kneaded from the best red clay . . .

BAR KOCHBA: Nevertheless, you should have left us alone.

UZIEL: I awoke—heard a loud groan.

I saw—you were turning over from left to right,

As if someone were tormenting you in your sleep . . .

BAR KOCHBA: Why am I punished like this?

No, something has happened to her.

I too saw her this night.

Someone was standing over me.

I hardly understood her words,

I only heard desperation in her voice:

Bar Kochba! Repay him for everything!

I wanted to strangle him—but it was a dream . . .

UZIEL: Watchman, what of the night?

Watchman, what of the night?

[*Shadows appear on the road.* BAR KOCHBA *reaches for his weapons.* UZIEL *moves at once toward the shadows.* NACHMONI *arrives.* BAR KOCHBA *goes to meet him.*]

NACHMONI: We have brought prisoners to you.
We captured them on the road tonight.

BAR KOCHBA: Bring them to me.

NACHMONI: They begged us to spare their lives.
They asked for you.
They are unarmed.

[*Exits.* ELISHA *arrives with two captives, a Parthian and a Syrian.*]

SYRIAN: Is someone here Bar Kochba?

UZIEL: He.

SYRIAN: Our lives are now in your hands.
We have been living in this land for a long time,
We were born and have grown old here.
And now you expel us with force?
An order came to us from you:
We are all chased from our fields
And driven from our homes.
Whoever is not a Jew shall not remain in the land.
Had you ordered us to be killed,
It would have been easier for us!

BAR KOCHBA: I will have your tongues cut out!
You have chosen the wrong path:
You lie, I never wrote such a thing . . .

[*to* UZIEL]
For now take them away and lock them up.

[*They are led away.*]
Then without delay
Bring Yoysi, tell him Bar Kochba calls.

[UZIEL *exits.*]

BAR KOCHBA: Elisha, what do you think?
Have we driven the enemy away for long?
There is little food left.

ELISHA: We will certainly be able to leave the city,
But I do not know if the road will be free to return.
There's little water, too . . . I've heard, people say,
We have to surrender before it's too late.

BAR KOCHBA: Who says it?

ELISHA: He won't be talking any more now.

BAR KOCHBA: Tell me who?

ELISHA: Even you would find it hard to bring him back to life.

[BAR KOCHBA *remains sitting silently.* ELISHA *waits for a moment and continues.*]

It's the rainy season, and look, the sun is shining mercilessly.

But do not fear, we could have a downpour even today,
That would fill the pits with water,
Even fill to overflowing.

[YOYSI *arrives, armed.*]

YOYSI: You sent someone to wake me. What has happened?

BAR KOCHBA: Are you still sleepy?

YOYSI: I am not fully rested. They say prisoners have been brought.
You want to judge them, I have heard.
The enemy delivers us to the sword,
We should do the same to him. I think
The judgment is not even needed.

BAR KOCHBA: I'm planning to judge not them—but you . . .

[YOYSI *interrupts him with an impudent laugh.*]

YOYSI: Why? I am free of sin.

BAR KOCHBA: Like a newborn child,
But still you deserve the death penalty.

YOYSI: I?

BAR KOCHBA: You!
Did you ever hear me give an order
That every non-Jew must leave the land
On which he and his grandfathers live?
Who gave you the right to say that?
You made use of Bar Kochba's name . . .
Whom did you want to benefit thereby?
Do you, Yoysi, know what that means?
In times like these, when side by side,
Not only Jews fight in my cause,
But also Greeks, Syrians, who are unhappy
With Rome and now do battle alongside us.
For such an order
You would never leave from here alive,
Though you have rendered great service until today.
Do you not understand it, Yoysi?
The Syrian and the Parthian and the Greek—
They want to be free of Rome just as I do.
We all have the same goal . . .

YOYSI: No—spilling blood is what I want
For myself, so the land can be free
For Jews alone. And if as a result
The Greek must lose his fields
And the Syrian return to Syria,
It's unfortunate, but let the Greek know
That I am the master in the land
And that their fate lies in our hands.

BAR KOCHBA: Whoever helps to free the land—the land is his.

[*to* UZIEL]

Bring them in . . .

[*Women arrive, among them* ROKHL *and* BRURIA.]

ROKHL: Daughters of mine, daughters tormented and
     driven out,

You have perished, mourned by no one.

Sisters of mine, scattered around the world

Today you mourn for Pnina, tomorrow another awaits
     your tears.

Suckling babes, torn from their mothers' breast,

A sister, whom a brother will never see again.

Children of mine, homeless and lost . . .

God, pour your wrath upon our enemies . . .

BRURIA: No, Pnina, I will not mourn for you.

No, no one sees my tears.

My tears have been dried out

Even before they are born

By the wrath that burns in my heart.

UZIEL: Repay, Bar Kochba, for the lost generations,

Repay, for all those who are tormented and held
     captive,

Repay, for all those born into slavery,

Repay, Bar Kochba, for everything.

[RABBI AKIVA *arrives.*]

BAR KOCHBA: Rabbi Akiva, your understanding is as
     clear as the sky,

Your heart is pure and you have been blessed with long
     life,

You have moved mountains with your wisdom

And you know the depths of the sea . . .

Rabbi Akiva, I ask, I demand, consolation of you . . .

AKIVA: Your pain is deeper than the sea,

Your power is stronger than the mountains.

I am blessed with long life,

But I am no more than a man . . .

BAR KOCHBA: The grief, the pain have blurred my
     vision,

What do you see, Rabbi . . .

AKIVA: When the people become a true nation,

You will be ranked among its heroes.

Now arise, my son

And summon here

Your battalions

And all those who have remained in the city,

Both young and old.

Let no one remain in his house.

I proclaim excommunication on Menashe

And on those who follow his advice.

Let all of them be cut off from the nation.

[BAR KOCHBA *gives a silent order to* UZIEL. UZIEL *and
     the women exit. After a brief silence* BAR KOCHBA
     continues.]

I always boasted

And always said with pride:

I have never yet carried out a death sentence,

Or proclaimed an excommunication,

But now I am pleased that before I die

I can cleanse the evil among the Jews.

JEWISH SOLDIER [*arrives and turns to* BAR KOCHBA]: I
     went out early this morning to change the guard,

I see Eliezer moving in the distance.

I recognized him at once.

I admitted him into the city

But kept him firmly in my grasp.

BAR KOCHBA: Bring him in.

[*The soldier exits.* HILLEL, ELISHA *and* YEHOYSHUA
     arrive.]

ELISHA: Why did you send for us, Rabbi?

We are preparing for battle . . .

AKIVA: You will soon return

To you sword and spear, to bow and arrow.

But for now, I would like you to hear out . . .

[ELIEZER *enters, accompanied by* UZIEL *and the soldier.
     Gradually, the soldiers assemble.*]

An old, pious man, as filled with Torah

As a pomegranate is filled with seeds. But his guilt

Is great, because he wished to be

With those who spill the blood of our people.

At night he left the city and went to the enemy.

Elisha, Hillel, Yehoyshua, be judges today!

[*They seat themselves in a half circle.*]

BAR KOCHBA: See, Eliezer. The enemy would have de-
     capitated all these men,

And Eliezer was in the lion's mouth, and is alive.

ELISHA: What did you promise them?

ELIEZER: My child is there . . .

BAR KOCHBA: Was there . . . where is she now?

ELIEZER: If you were there in her place, my child would
     be alive.

BAR KOCHBA: But you cursed your child . . .

What other excuses do you have?

You have always served the enemy faithfully.

You killed your child yourself.

ELISHA: You became Severus' right hand.

YEHOYSHUA: We lost a great deal, a great deal, because
     of you.

AKIVA: What did you do there?

ELIEZER: I wandered about

From village to village, from town to town,
Preaching God's commandment
And not war. I did what you should have done
And did not do.

YEHOYSHUA: You sharpened a sword against us.

ELIEZER: Jews live not only where Bar Kochba rules.
The Torah must be upheld everywhere.
Not everyone looks askance at the Elders.
That is where I have just come from.

ELISHA: Tell us, did you see Menashe there?

ELIEZER: I saw him.

ELISHA: And did he ask you about the *din*, the religious law?

ELIEZER: The *din* placed itself on Menashe's side.

AKIVA: The *beth din*, the religious Court—not the *din* itself.

BAR KOCHBA: If Menashe also likes that law,
Then I do not like the law.
[*unsheathes his sword*]

ELIEZER: If you could say such a thing,
May God knock it out of your hands.

[BAR KOCHBA *rushes at* ELIEZER. AKIVA *calms* BAR KOCHBA.]

AKIVA: Your hands must remain clean.
He stands before his judges.
[*after a short consultation with the judges*]

ELISHA: In wartime, whoever speaks out against
His people, even for the sake of God and his Torah,
His punishment is—death by the sword!

[*A sound of shofars—ram's horns—is heard.* AKIVA *stands apart.*]

AKIVA: Accursed man, Menashe! A curse upon you!
Let the curse enter your body and blood!
May your door be open for your enemy
And may snakes enter your house.
And may the same fate befall those that obey you!

VOICES: Amen, amen.

[*shofars*]

AKIVA: Accursed Menashe!
May your gold and silver be for strangers,
May your sheep and cattle be for wild beasts.
May your name be a curse among your people,
May death find you wherever you may be!
[*He turns to* ELIEZER.]
Let that be your fate as well, Eliezer . . .
[*an oppressive silence*]

ELIEZER: Akiva!
You excommunicate old Eliezer?

AKIVA: Let death be his punishment!

VOICES: Amen, A-a-amen!

[*Shofars. All those who stood around* ELIEZER *hastily move away from him.* ELIEZER *turns around and starts to leave. When he stands opposite* YOYSI, YOYSI *covers his face with the edge of his robe. At* BAR KOCHBA's *silent command, two soldiers accompany* ELIEZER *into the distance.*]

AKIVA [*pointing to the departing* ELIEZER]: We must lose the man who loses his way to the people
And tries with his hand to shade himself from their light.
There is no greater punishment than the people's wrath
And no greater happiness than the people's love.

YOYSI [*approaching* AKIVA]: Crown of the nation! I did not go in Menashe's ways,
Nor did Eliezer capture me
With his words. I did not listen to his advice,
Yet nevertheless I am sinful and deserving of punishment.
I distorted Bar Kochba's straightforward way.
Decide what punishment you wish for me.
But if the way of penance is still open for me,
I beg you not to punish me with excommunication.
When my people go to battle, I cannot remain alone.
[*to* BAR KOCHBA]
Allow me to go with Elisha.

BAR KOCHBA: You will have to remain here. You will be with me.
Your sin is not yet expiated.

AKIVA: If his words come from the depths of his heart
Perhaps his sins should be forgiven?

ELISHA: It is not Yoysi who speaks—it is the fear inside him,
That he will share the fate of him that left not long ago.
He will wobble more than once along the way.

NACHMONI [*cries out*]: Oh look! The sun has gone behind the clouds!
There will be a heavy rain!
[*All raise their heads. A thunderclap is heard.*]

AKIVA: Go Yoysi, go my child.
Accept your punishment.
You will have to atone for your sins.

[*The sound of a trumpet is heard.* YOYSI *falls to the ground and kisses the border of* AKIVA's *robe, then rises.* YOYSI *and* AKIVA *depart in opposite directions.*]

BAR KOCHBA: Make ready your battalions!

YEHOYSHUA: First battalion!

VOICES: Ready!

ELISHA: Second battalion!

VOICES: Ready!

HILLEL [*to* KUSI]: And you, Kusi, will carry the flag!

KUSI [*takes the flag and kisses it and says as if in prayer*]:
I have not dishonored it till now
And will not dishonor it in the future!

[*Leaves.* BAR KOCHBA *is alone.* NACHMONI *arrives.*]

NACHMONI: I too will go. I have grown taller.
I reach your shoulder now, Bar Kochba.
Until today I helped others fight
It is time for me to fight myself.

BAR KOCHBA [*hands him a sword*]: You must hold it
dear.

[NACHMONI *holds the sword at both ends, as if swearing
by it.*]

NACHMONI: In this sword lies our freedom!

[BAR KOCHBA *kisses* NACHMONI. *He leaves last. It grows
dark. From a cave under the earth* MENASHE *crawls
out.*]

MENASHE: Of all the crooked paths, this is the
straightest.
They have already left. Antonius—over here!

[*From the cave* ANTONIUS *crawls out, followed by more
Romans. Roman troops arrive from all sides.* AN-
TONIUS *silently gives an order and the troops disap-
pear.* ANTONIUS *follows them.* MENASHE *encounters*
ZAGIR.]

MENASHE [*perplexed*]: What are you doing here, with
the enemy?

ZAGIR: I did not come here of my own free will . . .

MENASHE: Quiet. Where is Bar Kochba, do you know?

ZAGIR: He is not in the city.

MENASHE: And who is here instead of Bar Kochba?

ZAGIR: Some kind of young men. No reason to be afraid.
The older ones are elsewhere.

MENASHE: Are you telling the truth or joking with me?
You're playing with fire.

[BAR KOCHBA *arrives.*]

BAR KOCHBA: A guest! Are you here alone? Who showed
you the way here?

MENASHE [*pointing to* ZAGIR]: She.

BAR KOCHBA: You are lying. Do you still have your wits
about you or are you already mad?
Do you think your cup of sins is not yet full?

[ZAGIR *leaves.*]

MENASHE [*fearfully*]: You ask who?
It was shame that led me here—
The shame of having been a tool in the enemy's hand.
It was my own free will that brought me here to serve
you,

If you will only grant me my life.
This road was easy for me to find.
I bring you live greetings from Pnina.

BAR KOCHBA [*beside himself*]: Live greetings from
someone who is already dead?!

[BAR KOCHBA *stabs him.* MENASHE *falls.*]

I am ashamed that my blood is red like yours,
That a mother once bore you.
A thousand deaths will not erase your treason.

MENASHE [*dying*]: It is not hard for me to give up my
life.
But who . . .

[*dies*]

BAR KOCHBA: The people!

[*From all sides Jewish fighters emerge. After them, with
a complete wall of armor, Roman troops. A battle
takes place.* ANTONIUS *arrives. The troops stand still
as if paralyzed.*]

ANTONIUS [*falling upon* BAR KOCHBA *with his sword*]:
My sword, cut off the heads of all the slaves!

BAR KOCHBA: A slave, as soon as he takes a sword in his
hand, is no longer a slave.

[*A struggle takes places between* BAR KOCHBA *and*
ANTONIUS. *Finally,* ANTONIUS *falls down, badly
wounded.*]

ANTONIUS: Rome! You have . . .

BAR KOCHBA: Begun well, but you will end badly.

[ANTONIUS *dies. On both sides—dead bodies. For a moment,* BAR KOCHBA *is on the stage alone. More Romans
arrive.* BAR KOCHBA *kills one of them, takes away his
sword and battles with two swords.* BAR KOCHBA *is
wounded. Battalions of Jewish fighters arrive.* UZIEL
carries the dead NACHMONI, *lays him down in front of*
BAR KOCHBA.]

UZIEL: My God! Why did you begrudge me my joy?
You did not protect my child!

BAR KOCHBA: Do not weep. Your child belongs to all
of us!

[BAR KOCHBA *bends down and kisses* NACHMONI.]

For whoever is destined to die
For the freedom of his people—lives forever.

[*A trumpet is heard.*]

To battle! To battle! The battle is not yet over!

CURTAIN

Translated by Solon Beinfeld.

Other works by Halkin: *Vey un mut* (1929); *Kontakt*
(1935); *Lider* (1939); *Mayn oytser* (1966).

Itzik Manger

1901–1969

Itzik Manger was born Isidor Helfer in Czernowitz (now Chernivtsi, Ukraine), attended a heder, and did not finish his gymnasium studies. During World War I, his family moved to Iaşi, Romania, where Manger began writing Yiddish verse. Later he lived in Bucharest, where he wrote journalism and lectured on folklore. His literary career began in the early 1920s, under the mentorship of Eliezer Shteynberg. Manger arrived in Warsaw in 1928, and spent a prolific decade there, writing and reciting poetry, composing lyrics for cabaret and film, writing and staging plays, as well as publishing multiple collections and periodicals, including two modernist revisions of Jewish biblical folklore: *Khumesh lider* and *Megile lider*. He left Poland for Paris in 1938, then to New York in 1951, and finally settled in Israel in 1958.

The Book of Paradise
1939

9. A Terrible Tale of the Messiah-Ox

Pisherl woke up. He was delighted when, on coming into the workroom, he discovered I was there. He ran up and embraced me as if we hadn't seen each other in years.

"Have you been here long, Shmuel-Aba?"

"I've been waiting for more than an hour. Praise God, you've had a good sleep."

We went over to the open window and looked out. There, in the meadow, the Messiah-Ox was grazing. The three barefoot angels who looked after him were playing cards.

I said to my friend, "The Messiah-Ox gets fatter every year. By the time the Messiah comes, he'll be too fat to move."

Pisherl was silent. We saw the angel Khasya walking across the Eden meadow. She was in her ninth month, and she took a walk every evening to get a bit of fresh air. "Pisherl, why is she wearing a red apron?" I asked my friend, "If the Messiah-Ox sees it, God forbid, there may be an accident."

"You're right. That's right," said Pisherl. And both of us began to signal to her, waving our hands, motioning to the pregnant angel to turn back, in God's name, while there was still time. But the angel Khasya didn't

understand our signals. She went peacefully on, getting closer to the place where the Messiah-Ox was grazing. The Messiah-Ox saw the red apron and his eyes lighted up. We thought that at any moment he would fling himself at her.

But we were mistaken. He did not take kindly to the red apron, it is true, but to our great surprise, he kept his peace. Evidently, it occurred to him that he was no ordinary ox. He was, indeed, the Messiah-Ox, for whom it was not fitting to fly into a rage over a piece of red cloth, like a common bull. Nevertheless, it was fated that a calamity should happen.

The angel Khasya was by no means overly bright. One might say that there was more beast in her than in the Messiah-Ox. When she was quite close, only a few paces from the grazing animal, she stopped to watch his pleasant cud-chewing. She stood for a while, admiring his appetite. The three barefoot angels were quarreling over their cards. One argued this way, the other that way, and the third disagreed with the other two. They were so engrossed by their quarrel that they did not notice that the pregnant angel went up to the Messiah-Ox and patted his neck.

"Let her . . . ," thought the Messiah-Ox. "Let her pat as much as her heart desires. If she'd only take off the red apron, all would be well." But, as Pisherl's mother, the angel Hannah-Deborah, says, "A fool brings trouble." The pregnant angel did not appreciate the Messiah-Ox's great forbearance. She patted and patted him. Suddenly she whispered in his ear, "The Messiah is coming."

The Messiah-Ox's entire huge body shuddered. "The Messiah is coming!" That meant that at any minute they would come to slaughter him. His body would be cut into pieces of meat. The meat would be cooked and the zaddikim would devour his flesh appreciatively: "Ah . . . ah . . . a true taste of Eden." It made the ox wild. "The Messiah is coming . . . danger near . . . time to run . . . escape . . . escape from the slaughter knife."

The Messiah-Ox did not know (what is an ox supposed to know?) that this was just the pregnant angel Khasya's idea of a joke; there was still plenty of time left for him to graze on the Eden meadow before the Messiah was due to come. Suddenly, he bent his head, and catching the pregnant angel up on his horns, he began to run wildly.

My friend Pisherl and I set up a shout; we shouted with all of our strength. "The Messiah-Ox is running away; the Messiah-Ox is running away."

The three cowherds jumped up and started to whistle at the ox, and to chase him. The angel Khasya, quivering on his horns, set up such a yowling that young and old ran to see what had happened. They asked each other, "What is it, eh? What happened?"

"The Messiah-Ox hooked a pregnant angel on his horns and ran off."

"Let's chase him."

"Let's catch him. Let's bring him back."

"To hell with the angel. The Messiah-Ox is more important. What will the zaddikim do without the Messiah-Ox if the Messiah should come?"

Now a real chase began. Angels, young and old—anyone with wings—flew after the Messiah-Ox. The enraged animal ran like a thousand devils. No doubt the image of the knife that would slaughter him was before his eyes. He was running away from the great feast of his flesh that the Messiah would make for the zaddikim. The pregnant angel twitched on his horns and waved her arms about, screaming and fainting at intervals, only to rouse herself to scream again.

We chased the Messiah-Ox. Before us flew the three cowherds; behind us, the angels, with or without beards. My friend Pisherl and I were the only children in pursuit. Some of the angels grew tired. They lost themselves in the crowd, panting, wiping the sweat from their wings, and finally they flew home.

"He's strong as iron, that Messiah-Ox."

"Did you ever see such running? Faster than the fastest Eden rabbit."

"The stupid female really scared him; she ought to be put in the courtyard of the synagogue and whipped until she promises never to play such practical jokes again."

That's the sort of thing the angels who returned to their homes were saying. Meanwhile, the Messiah-Ox continued to run away. We pursued him.

That Messiah-Ox did considerable damage in his flight. He ran across gardens, over newly sown fields where he trod down everything. He knocked over a couple of little angels who were playing ring-around-the-rosy. An old angel who was standing at the edge of a village playing a barrel organ was dealt such a blow that he turned several somersaults in the air before he fell in a dead faint from which he was revived only after the greatest difficulties.

"Pisherl! Do you see? He's heading westward, toward the border of the Christian Eden."

"I see, Shmuel-Aba. I see. May you live to tell me better news." It was beginning to get dark. The chase after the Messiah-Ox became more intense. If he was to be caught, it would have to be soon.

That was what we thought. But the Messiah-Ox had other ideas.

The pregnant angel quivering on his horns had no more strength left even to shriek. She was hoarse as a frog; her groans could barely be heard.

The Messiah-Ox's three cowherds were white as chalk. What would happen to them if, God forbid, the Messiah-Ox should cross the border into the Christian Eden? And by all indications, that was already happening. The bells of the Orthodox church were ringing, "Ding-dong. Ding-dong."

The leaps and dashes of the Messiah-Ox were so fierce that he was soon afoam with sweat. The border was very close. Already the Christian border guards, blond angels with blue eyes, could be seen. They wore huge boots and stood leaning on their pikes.

"Pisherl, what's going to happen?"

"A disaster," groaned my friend Pisherl. "A disaster, Shmuel-Aba."

The Messiah-Ox, the pregnant angel on his horns, crossed the border. Some of the Christian border guards tried to stop him, but he plunged on. Our angels, that is, the Jewish angels, drew up at the border. They could pursue the Messiah-Ox no farther. Or, to put it better, the Christian angels would have forbidden the pursuit.

Sad and shamefaced, we descended. We had no idea what to do, but stood looking after the Messiah-Ox as he disappeared in the distant fields.

An angel said, "Maybe they've caught him."

"What if they have," another angel retorted. "What good will it do us?"

"They're just as likely, God forbid, to make non-Kosher beef of him," a third angel observed.

"Our Messiah-Ox, God be praised, is fat enough. They can certainly make a feast of him."

"Our zaddikim are going to be left with their tongues hanging out. They've spent a lifetime sharpening their teeth and now what—no Messiah-Ox."

"Bite your tongue," said the angel Henzl angrily.

"Where do you get that 'no Messiah-Ox'? He's here, all right. And how! All he's done is cross over into the Christian Eden—we have to see about getting him back." The angel Henzl smoothed his wispy beard importantly while he tried to think of some means of freeing the Messiah-Ox.

"What's to be done, Reb Henzl?" asked a short angel with a dense beard. "Advise us, Reb Henzl."

The angel Henzl made no reply. He went up to the Christian border guards and began to talk with them, partly in their language, partly in Yiddish, and partly with expressive gestures. "Our Messiah-Ox," the angel Henzl said, "crossed . . . made escape . . . your paradise."

"What?" asked the angel Vassil, the squadron leader of the Christian border guard.

"Our Messiah-Ox . . . to your paradise," said the angel Henzl once more; then he made signs to indicate someone running. The Christian border guard burst into laughter. He gave his mustaches a twitch and said fiercely, "Beat it, filthy Jew."

The angel Henzl shuddered. We stood around him, our wings lowered, as if we were lost. From the fields of the Christian Eden, we heard the sound of a "hurrah" and then laughter. Evidently some of the Christian angels had succeeded in catching the Messiah-Ox. We stood on our side of the border listening to the Christians' joy. Our hearts beat like crazy watches. The angel Hillel, the street sweeper, sighed deeply. It was a sigh that could have been heard over a seven-mile radius.

The three barefoot cowherds stood about, looking as if they had been whipped. What were they to say when they were finally brought up on the carpet? ("So that's how you watched the Messiah-Ox, bastards." And the zaddikim would spit full in their faces—and they would be right, too. They just *had* to play cards, and while they played, the disaster happened.)

The laughter in the fields of the Christian Eden grew louder. "They're leading the Messiah-Ox toward the Christian stables. They're going to put that pious, Kosher animal near the same trough where they feed their pigs. Woe to them!"

The angel Henzl said, as if to no one in particular, "From bad to worse. They may even slaughter the Messiah-Ox with a non-Kosher knife. What will the holy zaddikim say? How will the Great Feast look without the Messiah-Ox? Angels! Help. What's to be done? Suggest something."

"Suggest something! Easier said than done." [. . .]

"Now *they* have the Messiah-Ox, and we have a fig for our pains, Pisherl."

"Then we'll have to do without the Messiah-Ox, Shmuel-Aba. When the Messiah comes, we can eat the Leviathan. The flesh of the Leviathan is tastier than that of the Messiah-Ox."

The angel Henzl, who was listening to our conversation, flared up. Beside himself with rage, he delivered a speech that was continually interrupted by his swallowing the wrong way; but he went on.

"So, the punks are ready to leave the Messiah-Ox in the Christian Eden! Who says we'll leave the Messiah-Ox to 'them'? Have we herded him these thousands of years only to let them make a feast of him? Haven't they pigs enough over there? Do we have to leave them the Messiah-Ox as well? Let there be chaos; let there be darkness, do you hear? Let there be darkness, but let the Messiah-Ox be returned to us."

My friend Pisherl and I were frightened. We began to stammer, to apologize. "Don't be angry, Reb Henzl. We meant no harm, God forbid. We only wanted . . . we only said . . . you understand, Reb Henzl."

But the angel Henzl is difficult to calm once he gets worked up. He loomed above the fire and talked and talked, droning on like a mill. None of us understood a word.

Suddenly, with a flap of his wings, he extinguished the fire that had been flickering in the field and cried at the top of his voice, "Angels, up! Why are you crouched like crones before a fire? Let's rouse all of Eden. Let's make an uproar. Let us confront our disaster. Woe unto me, that I have lived to see this day."

We got up, spread our wings, and flew. The angel Henzl went before us; his wings flapping fearfully, he shouted, "Like hell we'll let them have the Messiah-Ox. The Messiah-Ox is ours. We'll bring him back to our Eden by fair means—or foul."

10. The Turmoil over the Flight of the Messiah-Ox

The news that the Messiah-Ox had escaped set all Eden in a dither. One bird told another; one wind told another. In the morning, as we were coming back home, we found crowds of zaddikim already in the streets. They were disturbed, gesticulating, unable to believe that it had really happened.

"Escaped . . . really . . . the Messiah-Ox?" the rabbi of Apt asked the rabbi of Lublin. "It can't be. Such a thing was never heard of."

The white head of the rabbi of Lublin trembled. One could see he was vexed. "The very birds are calling the news on the housetops and you go on with your, 'It's not possible.'"

The rabbi of Apt was tenacious. "Maybe it's only a dream, and all of this anxiety is for nothing."

The rabbi of Lublin shook his head. "A dream . . . a dream. . . . If only it *were* a dream."

"No doubt they'll bring him back," said the rabbi of Apt, trying to console himself. "What do the saints in the Christian Eden need the Messiah-Ox for? They prefer pig meat, and they have pigs in plenty."

The rabbi of Lublin accepted a pinch of snuff from the rabbi of Apt. He sniffed deeply, then sneezed aloud.

"You sneezed on the truth," said the rabbi of Apt, though he did not believe it himself. [. . .]

We saw a cluster of people. In the middle stood the rabbi of Sadgura. His beard was disheveled; his eyes glittered. He was literally giving off sparks. "Where are they, the scoundrels? Where are the cowherds? They ought to be punished as they deserve. The little bastards ought to have their wings broken. They ought to be driven out of Eden; they, and their wives, and their children, and their children's children." The zaddikim nodded their heads, agreeing with his bitter words.

We saw the rabbi of Horodenka, running breathlessly. His gabardine was unpinned and he had lost a slipper on the way. Now, he ran up to the crowd, panting, "What a calamity! What a grief! What will I do with the gold fork and knife I bought especially for the Great Feast? What a calamity!" The rabbi of Horodenka was a small man with a long beard. One could say without exaggeration that his beard reached to his knees. Pisherl could contain himself no longer and burst out laughing.

"Don't laugh, Pisherl," I said. "It's a sin."

"How can I help laughing? Just look at the little rabbi. One slipper on, the other off. God be praised, what an appetite he has." Our luck was that the zaddikim were so engrossed in their discussion that none of them heard Pisherl's sly remarks.

"What's to be done? What's to be done?" the rabbi of Sadgura said, wringing his hands. "What sort of Great Feast can it possibly be without the Messiah-Ox?"

"We ought to cry woe . . . cry woe in the streets," the rabbi of Horodenka said heatedly. "Only think, such a thing has never happened before."

"This must be Satan's meddling," said the rabbi of Sadgura. "Where did the beast get the sense to think of running away?"

"Right. Right," the rabbi of Horodenka cried. "It's the work of Satan. Satan, may his name be cursed, has sneaked into Eden."

"We ought to inspect the *mezuzahs*," the rabbi of Zalishtchik suggested from the midst of the crowd. "Maybe a mezuzah has been defiled and that's the source of the whole calamity."

"Come," whispered Pisherl in my ear. "Let's leave these Galicians. Let them quarrel to their heart's content about spoiled *mezuzahs*. Let us fly on."

"Where, Pisherl?"

"I thought we might fly over and hear what the holy patriarchs have to say about the escape of the Messiah-Ox."

We left the crowd of Galician rabbis and flew in the direction of the Three Patriarchs' Allée, where the patriarchs lived in their villas. On the way there, we passed a number of zaddikim standing around in smaller or larger clusters. As we flew, we heard occasional words, "Messiah-Ox . . . escaped . . . cowherds . . . card-playing . . . to the Christian paradise . . . they must be punished . . . have their wings broken . . . what will the Messiah say?"

"The Messiah-Ox pulled off a real stunt, Pisherl. The zaddikim are at their wits' end. The Maggid of Kozienice has even forgotten to wear his fringed garment. . . ."

"And the grandfather of Shpola, Shmuel-Aba, has torn whole handfuls out of his beard; and how he beat his fists against his head, crying, 'My God, Jews. My God. What will we do if, God forbid, the Messiah should choose to come today?'"

"Tell me, Pisherl, where do these zaddikim get their remarkable appetites?"

"You ask funny questions. Don't you know that the zaddikim don't work? They never so much as put their hands in cold water. They go about all day long with nothing to do but to breathe the air; and it's said that the air is a great inducer of appetite."

We started down the Elijah-the-Prophet Boulevard. The morning sun covered the roofs with gold. The boulevard was empty. The richer angels were still asleep, and those zaddikim who lived on the boulevard had gone to consult with the others about the calamity.

Shmaya, the policeman in the green uniform, stood at the corner, yawning, his wings drooping. He had his truncheon in his hand as usual, but this time he didn't know what to do with it. My friend Pisherl and I had a moment of pity for him. He stood so alone, so lost with nobody before whom to be important. We flew over his head, made several loop-the-loops hand in hand, and sang a little song that Pisherl had invented after the policeman had turned in his report about us and the goat:

Shmaya, Shmaya, po-lice-man
With his stick stuck in his hand,

Stands upon the boulevard;
Like a dummy, like a fool
Wears a uniform of green.
Entirely green, his uniform . . .
Thinks he's great, thinks he's swell.
Come and see, O come and see,
You and him and her and me,
Come snicker at the likes of him.

Shmaya the policeman turned red as a beet. When he spotted us, he waved his stick and, foaming at the mouth, started after us, his wings outspread. But we were lucky. Just at that moment, Elijah the Prophet, who was taking his first stroll of the day on his boulevard, made his appearance. "Shmaya, where are you flying, hah? Why are you so excited, Shmaya?"

Shmaya folded his wings again. It appeared that he was ashamed to tell Elijah that we had sung a satirical song at him. He saluted the old prophet with a smile. "Good morning, Reb Elijah. Have you heard, Reb Elijah, the Messiah-Ox has run off. All the zaddikim in Eden are terribly upset about it, and you, Reb Elijah, are strolling about as if nothing had happened."

"I know. I know the Messiah-Ox has escaped and that the zaddikim are all agog. Let them, let them boil away. They have something to stew about. They are fortunate in having sound teeth, God be praised, while I," and here the old prophet showed his gums, "as it turns out, have nothing with which to chew my portion of the Messiah-Ox."

We left the old prophet talking to the cop and flew on in the direction of the Three Patriarchs' Allée. "Do you know what I think, Shmuel Aba?"

"How should I know what you think, Pisherl?"

"I think there must be considerable confusion among the patriarchs. I'm curious to see the patriarch Isaac. He's a great gourmand, our patriarch Isaac. He'd give you almost anything you can think of for a piece of good meat."

"How do you know that, Pisherl?"

Pisherl showed his astonishment. "Shmuel-Aba, have you forgotten what we learned in school? It's written clearly in the Bible that the patriarch Isaac loved Esau better because he regularly brought his father a portion of the meat from his hunting expeditions." Pisherl thought for a while. "And second, Shmuel-Aba, . . . second, I myself saw how, one evening, when Isaac came to the meadow where the Messiah-Ox was grazing . . . how he brought with him a piece of chalk . . ."

"What was the chalk for, Pisherl?"

"He made a mark on the Messiah-Ox's right side, to designate which piece was to be his at the coming of the Messiah."

"But the patriarch Isaac is blind. How could he have known where to make the mark?"

"Leave it to him, Shmuel-Aba," replied Pisherl. "Blind as he is, he tapped about with his finger and found the fat spot. Then he made his mark." [. . .]

No sooner had we left the Baal-Shem Alley and turned right than we recognized a familiar street. It was the Street of the Lovers of Israel. Here there lived Reb Moishe Leib of Sasov, Reb Velvl of Zbarazh, and Reb Levi Yitskhok of Berdichev. These zaddikim own small properties here. Behind every house, there's a cherry orchard. It's clear that they are not the richest of the zaddikim; there are a great many who are much richer; still, things are not too bad for them. They have no anxieties about making a living. They spend their days praying that God will have pity on the children of Israel and make room for them in Eden.

We looked down and saw a man of middle height, wearing a simple gabardine and, though it was really a warm day, his fur hat. He stood in the middle of the street, his head raised to the clouds, his arms lifted to the heavens. He was whispering.

"It's the rabbi of Berdichev," my friend Pisherl said in my ear, "Reb Levi Yitskhok of Berdichev. No doubt, he's talking things over with the Almighty. In the hour of calamity, he always stands in the middle of the street with his Sabbath clothes on and weeps and pleads with God."

"Let's find out what Reb Levi Yitskhok is saying to God, Pisherl."

"All right, Shmuel-Aba," my friend agreed. "We'll drop down and listen to one of his prayers in Yiddish. But remember, we won't stay too long."

"Only one prayer, Pisherl. I want to hear one prayer and no more. We settled down quietly a few paces from the rabbi of Berdichev and listened. The rabbi of Berdichev stood, as I've said, with his arms outstretched to the heavens. He was pleading, and his pleas would have moved a stone:

A good morning to you, O Lord of the Universe.
I, Levi Yitskhok of Berdichev,
Have come to you with a plea.
Where is justice, O Lord of the Universe,
And why do you plague your zaddikim, O Lord of
    the Universe?
Is it true that they followed in your ways?

You'll have to agree that they did . . . oh, yes.
Is it true that they obeyed your laws?

Once again, oh, yes.
Did you not promise them Eden?
Once again, Yes.
And the Messiah-Ox and the Leviathan?
And the red Messiah wine?
Once more, the answer is yes.

So where is the Messiah-Ox,
Father in Heaven?
Escaped to the Christians,
Father in Heaven.
Then bring him back to us again,
Father in Heaven,
Don't make a mockery of the Great Feast,
Father in Heaven.

I don't plead on my account,
Father beloved,
But for your zaddikim,
Father most faithful.

The rabbi of Berdichev waved back and forth, like a reed bent by the wind. There were tears in his voice, real tears.

"The rabbi of Berdichev must be a good man, Pisherl."

"A very good man, Shmuel-Aba. But let's keep going." [. . .]

We flew off. Below us, the patriarchs looked like three dots. "Quickly, quickly," Pisherl urged, and we flew to the Great Synagogue.

At the synagogue, there were already a number of the zaddikim. Naphthali, the caretaker of the synagogue, a man with a hump and a goat's beard, had flown from one villa to another, informing the zaddikim that the patriarchs Abraham, Isaac, and Jacob were calling together a council. The zaddikim had needed no urging to attend. Each one took a walking stick in hand and went at once. [. . .]

The synagogue filled up. There was no longer even standing room, and yet more and more late zaddikim pressed in. They pushed and shoved, elbowing each other, treading on each other's corns, until finally they got in. The air was so thick that we—my friend Pisherl and I—could hardly breathe. "What good is all this going to do us?" I asked Pisherl.

"Shhh-Shmuel-Aba." Pisherl put his hand over my mouth. "They'll hear us and throw us out."

Abraham, the oldest of the patriarchs, appeared on the podium. With the thumb of his right hand stuck in his waistband, he waved his left hand over the heads of the audience. "A great disaster has befallen us, friends," he began. "The Messiah-Ox has escaped; and not merely escaped as occasionally happens with an ox, but he's run off to the Christian Eden. Now, where did the Messiah-Ox get the intelligence to escape?—that's a question that cannot be answered at this time, my friends.

"At this time, we need to consider . . . to investigate . . . to find an idea that will help us bring him back, back to his place in the Jewish Eden." The audience set up a commotion. A man with a grizzled beard began thrusting about with his elbows, pushing closer and closer to the podium.

"I have a parable," he cried. "Friends, I have a parable just suited to this occasion—a precious parable, with a golden moral. Once upon a time, there was a king who had three—"

"No need for parables, Preacher of Dubno," cried voices in the audience. "We need advice, not parables." But the Dubno preacher was stubborn. He shouted everyone down and pushed his way, with all his force, toward the podium.

"You will regret it, gentlemen. It's a precious parable. The moral is a golden moral. Once there was a king—" The preacher of Dubno might have succeeded in telling his parable if a drum roll had not been heard at the door.

A Zaddik cried out, "King Solomon has driven up. He's just getting out of his carriage." For a moment the synagogue grew still, then the buzzing began again.

"King Solomon . . . the wisest man . . . he has the brains of a prime minister . . . fool . . . a king is greater . . . the king is a lord, and a minister is no more than a servant." Quarrels broke out. There were cries of "oaf," "fool," and other such nicknames. Suddenly, the voice of the synagogue caretaker was heard at the back. "Make way for King Solomon."

King Solomon thrust his way toward the podium at once. He was sweating like a beaver and wiping his forehead with a silk handkerchief.

The synagogue grew hushed. Solomon's tall, broadshouldered figure, his fox-red beard, his sharp, intelligent eyes commanded respect. He spoke softly, unhurriedly. "As soon as I heard the full story, I wasted no time, but sent a letter off to the Christian saints . . . if you know what I mean . . . I wrote to them about this and that and how much would they want for the return of the Messiah-Ox . . . if you know what I mean. We are ready to do business, I wrote . . . though we can do without the Messiah-Ox . . . he's not so very necessary to us and—"

At this point, the patriarch Isaac could contain himself no longer. He leaped from his seat and cried, "What do you mean we don't need him? We *need* him. Without the Messiah-Ox . . . where does he get off writing 'them' that we can do without the Messiah-Ox?"

King Solomon smiled wisely and reassured the outraged Isaac. "It's only a manner of speaking, if you know what I mean, Reb Isaac. One mustn't let them know that the Messiah-Ox is the apple of our eye. If they knew, they would ask for his weight in gold . . . if you know what I mean." Putting his finger to his forehead, he added slyly, "That's diplomacy, Reb Isaac. Diplomacy. One needs to understand it . . . if you know what I mean."

All the zaddikim nodded, agreeing that King Solomon was right, that he was indeed a wise man—if you turned Eden upside-down, you wouldn't find his match.

"So . . . I . . . if you know what I mean," continued Solomon, "so I wrote a letter inquiring how much they wanted. I sent the letter off with one of my postal pigeons. I estimate that we'll have a reply on the morning of the day after tomorrow."

A commotion began down below. "Where does he get off writing without our knowledge? We might at least have been informed of the contents of the letter. After all, we have a small stake in the matter. . . ."

King Solomon always hated back talk. Drawing himself up to his full height, his beard flaming, his eyes ablaze, he roared, "Attention!" with the voice of a lion.

The zaddikim stopped in their tracks, like soldiers before their commanding officer. There was not so much as the flicker of an eyelid. They stood this way for some fifteen minutes until King Solomon said, "Enough. Now you can go home. And when I get a reply from the Christian Eden, I'll let you know." He stepped down from the podium and pushed his way through the crowd. Outside, his gilded coach was waiting.

No sooner was Solomon gone than a dispute broke out. It was argued that King Solomon ought to have consulted with the zaddikim. Wise though he might be, he was, after all, only one man, and they were numerous. And though the zaddikim might not be as wise as he, still, their numbers counted for something.

"He's always behaved like this. He's always done just what he wanted, and paid about as much attention to us as to the cat. . . ."

"Pfooh! Pfooh! Jews, you're talking against a king . . . against a king," cried a small Zaddik with a sparse beard.

A way was made for the holy patriarchs. They left the synagogue and went home. "Then we may expect an answer on the morning of the day after tomorrow," said the patriarch Isaac.

The patriarch Abraham comforted him, "Don't worry. The reply will be favorable."

"May your wish pass from your mouth to God's ear, Father. And amen," sighed the patriarch Isaac. The patriarchs continued on their way.

Translated by Leonard Wolf.

Other works by Manger: *Shtern afn dakh* (1929); *Getseylte verter* (1929–1930); *Lamtern in vint* (1933); *Khumesh-lider* (1935); *Felker zingen* (1936); *Megile-lider* (1936); *Demerung in shpigl* (1937); *Velvl Zbarzher shraybt briv tsu malkele der sheyner* (1937); *Noente geshtaltn* (1938); *Di vunderlekhe lebns-bashraybung fun Shmuel-Abe Abervo* (1939); *Lid un balade* (1952); *Shriftn in prose* (1980).

Der Nister

1884–1950

Born in Berdichev (in present-day Ukraine), Der Nister ("The Hidden One," pseudonym of Pinkhes Kahanovitsh) is considered one of the most stylistically distinctive Yiddish writers of the twentieth century. An associate of the so-called Kiev gruppe ("The Kiev Group") and Kultur-lige (Culture League), Der Nister is remembered for his short prose that wove together mystical themes, modernist symbolist technique, and fantastical fairytale landscapes, overlain with richly biblical language. After a short stint in Berlin, he settled in the Soviet Union in 1926 where his esoteric and often irrational stories met with displeasure from the ideological establishment. In the late 1930s, Der Nister changed direction stylistically and produced *Di mishpokhe Mashber*, an expansive historical novel of his hometown. A member of the Jewish Anti-Fascist Committee, Der Nister was a victim of the postwar liquidation of Soviet Yiddish culture and died in a prison hospital in 1950.

The Family Mashber
1939

I. The Town N.

The city of N. is built in three rings. First ring: the marketplace at the very center. Second: surrounding the market, the great city proper with its many houses, streets, byways, back streets where most of the populace lives. Third: suburbs.

Should a stranger find himself in N. for the first time, he would at once be drawn, willy-nilly, to the city's center. That's where the hubbub is, the seething, the essential essence, the heart and pulse of the city.

His nose would be assailed immediately by smells: the smell of half-raw, rough or fine leather of all kinds; the acrid sweetness of baked goods; of groceries; of the salt smell of various dried fish; smells of kerosene, pitch, machine oil; of cooking and lubricating oils; of the smell of new paper. Of scruffy, shabby, dusty humid things: down-at-heels shoes; old clothes; worn-out brass; rusted iron—and anything else that refuses to be useless; that is, determined, via this petty buying and selling to serve someone, somehow.

There in the marketplace are shop after shop, squeezed narrowly together like boxes on a shelf. If one doesn't have a shop in the upper district, then he owns a warehouse in the lower. If he doesn't own a warehouse, then he has at least a covered booth outside a shop. If no booth, then he spreads his goods out on the ground, or depending on what he sells, holds his wares in his hands.

There, in the marketplace, it's a permanent fair. Wagons from nearby (or from distant) settlements arrive to pick up goods, and wagons from the railway depot endlessly discharge their loads—everything fresh, everything new.

Packing and unpacking!

Jewish tenant farmers, village merchants, come in from Andrushivkeh, Paradek, Yampole. They come from Zvill and Korets and even from the more distant Polesia. In summer, they wear their light coats and hoods. In winter, cloaks or fur coats with well-worn collars. They come to buy goods for cash or on credit. Some are decent and honorable—others are something else: their scheme is to buy on credit, then sell at a profit, then buy on credit again—then declare themselves bankrupt.

Wagons arrive empty and leave fully packed, covered with sacks, tarpaulins, rags—all of them tied down with cords. The wagons drive off at evening; others arrive at dawn.

"*Sholom aleichem.*" A storekeeper hurries down the steps of his shop to greet a newly arrived old customer, to lead him from the wagon directly into his shop lest some other merchant get at him. "*Sholom aleichem*, and how are things in Andrushivkeh?" he says with a show of familiarity, then he gets right to business. "Ah, it's good you're here. I have just what you're looking for. A marvelous this . . . a splendid that . . ."

Rival storekeepers endeavor to strike up conversations with one's customer, to entice him away from his usual shop. They inveigle him in by offering lower prices or better credit terms. Often enough this can lead to real battles. Shopkeepers against shopkeepers, clerks against clerks. Only the porters and errand boys, who occasionally earn something from one or another of the shops, keep aloof, refusing to mix in, to choose sides.

Sometimes it's the market women who quarrel. Then women's cries are heard. Blows are exchanged.

But that happens rarely. For the most part, everyone is much too busy. Morning and night, there's work to be done to meet the needs of hordes of customers—and there's enough profit for all.

Clerks do the heavy work: weighing, measuring, carrying things out, setting them in place and so on. The shopkeepers do the bargaining: the persuading, cajoling, displaying of goods, arriving at prices.

It is, as has been said, a permanent fair. Wholesale and retail. In the more successful shops, the owners carry home bundles of hundred- and fifty-ruble notes. The less successful tradesmen take home coins in their linen pouches and not much paper money. But they make a greater racket than their richer competitors. Endless contentions, quarrels, shouts, cries. They fight over a groschen or a pound of soap, over the sale of a little starch, the price of a dried fish. And curse each other unsparingly with the same vehemence over small matters as over large:

"Break a bone!"

"Go to hell . . ."

"Drop dead."

"See you at your funeral."

But they make up quickly, too. The stallkeepers drink tea frequently with each other; they dart into each other's booths to arrange a free loan, to borrow a weight for a scale. They club together the money needed to take advantage of an opportune bargain offered by a Gentile. Or they play tricks on each other, or shout to each other across five stalls, across ten. Everyone shouting at once.

That's how it is normally on market days. On special days, the crowding is more intense. There's a greater press of wagons, of unharnessed horses munching hay. Those still harnessed have their noses deep in their feed bags. Colts nuzzle between the legs of mares. A stallion whinnies, making a horsey racket that resounds throughout the market. And along with the horses and people—dirt, filth. In winter, snow that is not snow. In winter and summer, cow flops, horse piss, puddles of kerosene, hay, straw, barrel hoops, barrels, boxes—rarely cleared away.

During important market days, like those during Lent, there's hardly room to move. A mob of varicolored peasant pelts; brown coats, yellow furs; men's coarse-haired beaver jackets; headscarfs, neckcloths, hats, fur caps, felt boots, knitted leggings for landowners and peasants, for men and women.

Well-to-do folk coming to town shop seriously. The poor search for some trifle or other—something that might easily enough be bought at home But the yearning to come to town is great. The hunger to wander about the shops, to haggle over baubles. To haggle! To spend as mach time as possible over a purchase. For the sheer pleasure of buying.

Those with money move about prudently. They know what they want and where to look for it. The shopkeepers make them welcome, greet them courteously, respectfully. Throughout the bargaining sessions, they take great pains to be accommodating, to keep them from leaving the shop. Naturally, given the press of the crowds, the poorer customers are not very welcome. They are instantly recognizable as they wander confusedly about, their eyes searching every shelf and corner of the shop. It's clear that they have more enthusiasm than cash and are therefore greeted with suspicion or driven away. Their diffident poverty-stricken questions are not answered, and if a shopkeeper notices that one of his clerks is spending too long with such a customer he passes his clerk a note: "Don't waste time on this one. Can't you see what he wants, the damn thief?"

And, during the Great Market days, thefts are not infrequent. Occasionally it is a peasant who steals something from a shopkeeper, but more usually it is the other way around. There are certain specialists, well known in the market, who weigh with ten-pound weights instead of half a *pood* (twenty pounds): It's done quickly,

skillfully. On the scale and off! And the peasant has no inkling of what's happened. Until later, when he comes back complaining bitterly. But then, those specialists, those *half-pooders* as they are called, don't recognize their customer. Often slaps are exchanged, blows. Until the red-faced, drunken policeman, the *buddoshnik*, meddles in the matter, blows his whistle and parts the combatants, and hauls off to jail precisely the one who ought not to be hauled off.

Or it may happen that a peasant slips some trifle into his breast pocket. If he's caught, he's tried unceremoniously on the spot. The shop clerk strikes the blows. If the clerks in the nearby shops get wind of the matter (and if they have the time), they too get into the action. Bringing with them whatever implements are available, they lend a hand at the beating. Male peasants are struck around the head and neck, a woman, whether old or young, is hardly beaten at all. But she is disgraced. Her shawl and babushka are torn off and she is made to stand, disheveled and ashamed, exposed to the scorn of the entire marketplace.

However, such things happen rarely. Now and then. For the most part, customers buy and are satisfied with their purchases, and sellers are pleased with their gains. Everyone's busy, everyone glows.

Whatever the weather—wind, frost, snow, blizzard—no one pays the slightest attention. The market goes on. Profit warms the merchants.

In the course of those busy days, people eat very little. Whatever was eaten in the morning at home before leaving for the market suffices until evening, until dark, until, red-faced, swollen, exhausted, one gets home.

One ignores everything. Trembling hands, freezing faces, noses, ears. Blows are overlooked, and splinters. Never mind. In the evening at home where it's warm, the splinters can be removed.

All of this takes place in the "Rough Market," but similar things happen in the "Noble Market" on a parallel street. There, too, there's no way to get through the press of wagons, though there are no peasants here and generally no retail buyers. Only wholesale.

There, the important cloth merchants and the major ready-made shoe and clothing dealers are. Dealers in all sorts of goods from Lodz, Warsaw, and Bialystok. From distant Polish towns and from others as far away as White Russia.

There, the customers are landowners, rich nobility, prosperous small-town Jews. There, the clerks are more neatly dressed. There, too, customers are received and treated differently. There, flattery and chicanery are of a higher order. There the shopkeepers move about before their shops in skunk coats, forming little clusters in which they carry on serious business conversations, while inside the shops, the sly-tongued, persuasive chief clerks bustle about displaying their goods so skillfully that it is a rare customer who can escape them.

Outside, the shopkeepers talk endlessly about the money market, exchange rates, bankruptcies, trips to Lodz or Kharkov, of rising or falling prices. Inside the windowless shops, where the only light filters in from the street door, there is a perpetual half-light, even by day. The customers stand at counters behind which the clerks display yard goods: linens, woolens, silks, cottons with English, German, Russian labels. Lying labels, false seals. And in the course of displaying and measuring the goods and persuading the buyers, one does—what one does. As the clerks put it, "You steal the suckers blind."

In the Noble Market there is the same busyness during the Great Market days described above. Here, too, wagons are packed, boxes torn open, goods are moved. Porters carrying loads in bump into clerks carrying bundles out of the shops. Shelves are emptied, cash registers filled. These are good days for the shopkeepers, who beam at the flow of money. Good days for the clerks to whom the customers "give a little something." And of course they get a commission on their sales. These are good days for the brokers, for the middlemen who, for a fee, introduce new customers, or who, for a fee, serve as consultants to regular customers in making their deals.

During those Great Market days, the shopkeepers, their wives and even their children are all in the shops. No matter how many employees one has, they are not enough. So one brings in family members. Those who can do real tasks, do them. Others who can only look on serve as lookouts. But no one thinks of leaving the shop, of going home until evening, until night, until very late when the shops are locked and chained, when the shutters, with an iron shriek, are lowered. Then, the contented shopkeepers, their cashboxes full, are accompanied home by their clerks and the members of their family.

And that's how it is in the market before the winter holidays. A little less noisy, but the market always is and remains the market, with its deals, its money hunger, its devotion to profit. And once in it, one is entirely swallowed up by it and becomes unable to understand or to welcome anyone who is not part of it. There's no time

for such intruders. And in the eternally established organization of the market, no place for them.

So true is this that if, rarely, some nonmarket person—a clergyman or a child—should appear there (one does not count people who are merely passing through), their presence would be felt as a violation. Children are immediately shooed away by their parents: "What are you doing here? Get on home." A synagogue caretaker, or a cantor, may show up, but only to go from shop to shop to remind someone of a mourning anniversary, or to call shopkeepers to a circumcision or a wedding. But such an intruder must not linger. He must perform his errand quickly and leave. Because he is superfluous.

Even habitually insolent beggars, perpetual tramps, rarely receive alms in the market, but are turned away everywhere with the same sullen phrase: "Go. Go in good health. We don't give in the market. At home." Even the town's mad folk avoid the market, as if they knew that there was no place and no one to care for them there.

Market people are an earnest folk, worrying constantly. Those who don't have much money worry about where to get it. How to borrow a little. Those who have money worry about where to get it, how to borrow more. The prosperous merchants do their business with brokers and rack their brains for the means to pay them, and struggling shopkeepers worry about the weekly ruble they need to pay the interest to the loan sharks. But everyone is busy, heads whirring over profit when there *is* profit, or when there is none, over ways and means to meet expenses.

The clerks are less serious. More carefree. Since their time is not their own, they can be frivolous. The young ones who even at the busiest times are given to practical jokes turn especially silly when there is little to do. This is particularly true in the summer before the harvest, when the market quiets down and hardly anyone from the nearby villages (never mind those from the outlying districts) comes to town. Then, whole days go by with nothing to do.

Except hang around outdoors taking the sun, or cooling off inside the shops or cellars. And when things get particularly dreary, one thanks God for the occasional groschen in the till with which one can slip off to a nearby soda water shop for a drink and a snack. And when things get truly boring, one is grateful to the crazy noblewoman, the Panyi Akoto, notorious throughout the town, if suddenly she shows up in her old-fashioned cloak (from the time of King Sobieski) with its tassels and fringes, her hat with its many ribbons, beads and dangling baubles.

The clerks rush to greet her, as if they meant to welcome her into their shops. One of the clerks outdistances the others and speaking to her in the most respectful, sidelong manner, as one does to the rich—says, "What does *kometz tsaddik* spell?"

"*Tso?*"

The clerks crack up because the Hebrew letters *kometz tsaddik* actually spell *Tso*, "What" in Russian. And so they have trapped her in their joke, and they laugh, pinch each other, go berserk until their game ends with a crowd gathering, outrage, shouting, swearing, and the cursing of Jews and Gentiles until even the older clerks, even the shopkeepers are involved.

Or another time the clerks may entice the feebleminded Monish in from a nearby street. Monish, whose blond Jesus-beard frames the deep pallor of his face, is a sickly, gentle, usually silent boy who stutters.

The clerks press him into a corner where he is promised anything he wants if he will only answer, for the thousandth time, the question which, a thousand times before, they have put to him.

"Monish, why do you want to get married?"

"Three reasons," he says, smiling.

"What are they?"

"To c . . . c . . . cuddle. To k . . . k . . . kiss. And to t . . . t . . . tickle."

"And nothing more?"

"Wh . . . wh . . . what else is there?"

Thus the market in its off-season. The shops are opened just for the sake of appearances. There is a weary wait each day for the sun to move across the sky. Then lock-up time and home, only to return the next day for another round of wasted time. To stand in the doorway expecting no customers—because there are none.

And so pass the several weeks of the dead season before harvest-time.

Those who belong, those who are part of the market—shopkeepers, brokers, merchants who derive their livelihood from it, as their parents and grandparents derived theirs—have neither the time nor the inclination to wonder about its composition, or to doubt its permanence. [. . .]

Should a stranger come to the market, and should he stay for a while, he would very soon get a whiff of dissolution, the first hint that very soon the full stink of death would rise from the whole shebang: the buying and selling, the hullaballoo of wheeling and dealing, the entire giddiness of all those whirling there.

And especially if he came at night when the market, together with its main and side streets, was asleep, its shops barred, its booths and stalls closed down, its rows of dark warehouses behind heavy iron gates—locked and chained. And if he were to see the bored, yawning night watchmen sitting or standing about in clusters, or singly on various street comers, looking like dark, fur-clad manifestations of the wandering god Mercury, who, long delayed, has finally arrived here out of ancient times. If a stranger did show up, we say, and if he saw all this, if he was not already a prophet, he would not in truth become one. And yet, if he were a man with somewhat refined sensibilities, he would feel grief at his heart; he would sense that the thresholds on which the night watchmen sat were already mourning thresholds, that the sealed doors, chains and locks would never be replaced, and that to enlarge the picture, to frame it truly, one would need to hang a death lamp to burn quietly here in the middle of the market to be a memorial to the place itself.

That then is the market section of the city of N. The first ring. The second section: the city itself.

If on that same night a stranger leaving the market had turned toward the nearest houses, what would first catch his eye would be a series of one-, two- or many-storyed structures built in an old-fashioned way, and in a crazy style. Or better, in no style at all. He would know at once that these were not residences, but were destined for some other purpose. And if at first glance he was not able to tell that purpose, a second look would make everything clear. They were built by the religious community of the city of N. for their God and according to His requirements. He is a wandering and an exiled God, and does not ask much of them: no columns or airy spaces, no superfluous cleanliness. No exterior decor. Only that the guttering light of an economical kerosene lamp should reveal itself through a filthy window at night, that there be silence, and that a wounded spirit may rest on the threshold of the place, in its windows and on its roof. And that an old, somewhat slovenly bachelor sexton—a not particularly diligent servant of God—sleep in one of the buildings; and in others, let whole groups of homeless beggars lie sleeping on benches, on mountains of rags. Looking themselves like mountains of rags as they snore away there. And in other buildings, on the other hand, let all twelve of the windows that tradition requires in that God's structures be ablaze at midnight with the light of candles and burning lamps; and let there frequently be heard the warm singing of boyish voices which, as they study His laws and His commandments, serve Him, and are so accounted, as sacrifices such as in the days of His glory He received—and to which for a long time now He has been unaccustomed.

Here you have such a building. [. . .]

It is called the Open Synagogue.

Why?

In its builder's will more than a hundred years ago, it was specified in writing that the synagogue door must never close. Neither by day nor night, not in summer or in winter. Never. So long as the building remains standing—till the coming of the Messiah, it is hoped.

And so its door is always open to the town's inhabitants who come to say their prayers and to study there. Open also to those who in summer come in to cool off, and to those who in winter come to warm themselves. Open also to dealers, shopkeepers, porters and others who slip away from the empty tumult of the market so that they may breathe a bit of consoling air. It is a refuge for those poor wanderers for whom it is a pausing point in their arrivals or departures. Wanderers who sometimes stay for weeks, or even months. And nobody, according to the terms of the will, may prevent them.

In that synagogue, prayers are said from early morning to well past midday. Sometimes there are full quorums of ten men, at other times people pray alone. At night there is Torah study to which middle-aged and elderly men come in the evening, and who go home after their studies. Late at night there are sleepless young people.

It is rare then that one finds the Open Synagogue empty. The door swings in and out. Is never closed. [. . .]

Then the synagogue is brightly lighted. A lamp from the ceiling or from one of the wall brackets hangs above each of the young scholars' heads. Those sitting in the farther corners hold candles above the books they are studying. The accumulated light iluminates not only the synagogue, but it also spills out-of-doors. And a pious passerby, or an inhabitant looking out of one of the nearby low houses, seeing the synagogue so brightly lighted on all sides might get the feeling that he was looking at a lighthouse set in the midst of the city's darkness. The sense that the lighted synagogue is the sleepy town's brilliant representative before heaven, and heaven's directors.

Especially if a pious passerby hears the young voices shouting or humming the famished, ascetic, yearning melodies brought here from the mullah and dervish schools of the godforsaken distant East. These young people, who have voluntarily immured themselves here, utter ecstatic yells, and express by means of those melodies their discontent with corporeality. Creating, we say again, the feeling in a pious passerby that he is watching young victims sacrificing themselves for somebody else's sins.

There you have one synagogue.

And here is another one nearby. The "hotheaded" synagogue, so called because hotheads, half-mad, fanatically pious Hasidic sects like the Kotzkers, the Karliners pray there, wildly climbing the walls, running about cooling their interior religious fervor with the sounds of their own voices.

Facing the "hotheaded" synagogue, the "cold" one.

A building in which, even if you enter it in summer, a cold breeze chills your bones. This, too, is a two-story building. Again, with shops on the first level. On the second story, the synagogue itself.

Highly polished railings, which over the years have been rubbed by many hands holding to them on the way up, lead to a vestibule like a cold-storage vault, then there are several steps up to the synagogue's entryway.

A high, broken ceiling divided into five parts. Beneath the fifth, the middle section, the Torah-reading podium on tall pillars. Chandeliers suspended from ropes make one think that neither the candles in their sockets nor the gas in the lamps could illuminate or warm anything.

Those praying are cold, those studying are dry—Lithuanians. A sense of withered life, an emptiness, emanates from their songs, their prayers. They are called the Ibn-Ezraniks, after the early medieval Spanish poet and philosopher whose rational spirit has found a place like a chilly, abandoned nest among this thicket of synagogues.

If it were not for the synagogue furnishings—the Torah-reading pulpit, the Ark of the Covenant, the podiums, bookcases and books—both the interior and the exterior of this building would be easily taken for some sort of burial structure, or tomb.

Now for the "old one."

The oldest synagogue of all.

As you approach it, you notice how dilapidated the entryway is, worn away by dark and unhappy generations over centuries. If you go in, you sense at once that all those centuries have left behind their despised and desolate breath.

The path to the door, and all along the facade of the building, is paved with flat, well-trodden river stones that have worn thin.

An iron door, broad as a gate and studded with huge round-headed nails, can be opened with a long, old-fashioned, very heavy key—an ancient masterwork with short, chiseled teeth whose like it would be hard to find anywhere. It is a key that needs to be turned several times in its keyhole, and no one except the synagogue's regular sexton knows how to put the key into its proper position.

Inside the gate you come to the synagogue vestibule. Dark, poorly illuminated by an exterior light, and even less by the light that filters through the varicolored panes of glass high up in the second door that leads to the synagogue. [. . .]

It is true that in the days of which we speak, the community of workers who lived on the outskirts were not highly regarded by the town and that they lived isolated from it. But there will be times later, much later than those of which we speak, when the town will press an attentive ear to just these places. It will be from there, from those very swamps of poverty, that it will feel the current of an overthrowing, an extremely refreshing, wind. And it will be there, to those huts and ruins, to those poorest of workers, to those patch tailors and laborers—it will be to them that the finest youth of the town will come with trembling hearts to hear unusual news and to participate in historically pleasing events. Better educated and wiser heads than those of the inhabitants will bow before them at the low doorways and thresholds of their hovels because in the course of bringing knowledge to them, in the course of teaching them, they will themselves carry away a new knowledge.

It will be there that the first small circles will form for whom, in the course of time, the sense of the narrowness of the walls that enclose them will grow, and they will begin to gather out-of-doors—though still only in small groups. Then as they feel their strength and spirit ripening, they will (and the town will remember it as the beginning of an era) gather into a great mass—not quite bold yet, because not used to taking such steps—but still, in disciplined ranks, heading toward the town.

The evening will conceal them in darkness, and out of the concealment a humming, like the sound of distant floodwaters, will rise.

The calm, bourgeois householders accustomed to a lassitude sanctified by generations, will, when they hear the sound, step out to see: a strange human wave, with a flag at its head that has never been seen before, singing a song no one has ever heard before. Then, greatly frightened, the bourgeois householders will not know whether it is a plague advancing, or some other visitation with its roots in earth or in hell.

Averting their eyes from the sight, they will, like brood hens clucking for their young in time of danger, hurry their children indoors under the safe wings of their own roofs, under the generations-old eaves, and will lock the doors behind them, and will put the chains firmly on the latches.

That will happen much later. [. . .]

III. Luzi among His Own

At that time, among the numerous rich and noisy Hasidic sects in the town of N., there was also a small and not much respected group of Bratslavers.

They numbered not much more than one and a half or two prayer quorums—fifteen or twenty men. They were, for the most part, poor workingmen, but they were all of a type whose like had never been seen before. Given their small numbers and their poverty, they did not have—and did not dream of having—a synagogue of their own. They were, moreover, a severely persecuted sect. Sometimes they rented a place, but more usually they pleaded for and were given permission to say their early morning prayers in the synagogues of others.

Sometimes a young artisan who spoke with a musical lilt came to the sect from a distant part of Poland. He brought with him a skimpy pack of things from home as well as a sack of tools. He wanted to linger with them for a while so that he could study their teachings, their habits and their mode of life.

He was warmly welcomed and befriended. At first when he was still unable to support himself, he was helped out of the community funds—because, as they put it, money "is neither mine nor yours, but God's." Later, when he could look after himself, he shared his earnings with the others and contributed to the support of those poorer than himself.

On the other hand there were times when some rich man joined the sect. It was clear from his clothing and his demeanor that he was a prosperous man, one who was used to important business affairs, to an expensive home. He was, in short, a man who could take his ease. He stayed with them for a certain while and treated the members of the sect as if they were his own relatives. Any money he had left over after he had met his immediate expenses, he shared with them. Nor was it ever observed that the one who gave was prideful in his giving, or that the taker ever felt humiliated. Such was their custom, always. Among them money passed from hand to hand, from wallet to wallet. But it was rare, very rare, that money from a rich man fell into their hands. For the most part the general purse was empty, and it was that emptiness which members of the sect usually shared.

Many of the Bratslavers, grown fanatically religious, had abandoned their trades. Their wives, influenced by their pious husbands, did not ask them for money. And their emaciated, dejected children, condemned to anemia, made no demands either, knowing full well that there was nothing to be got from their parents.

For the most part, the members of the sect lived on prayers and fasting. They did not, as other people did, occupy their time with daily tasks. Their days were spent in prayer, and their nights lying on the graves of the town's holy men. As for doing something for the world or for themselves or for their families—they ignored all that to a criminal degree.

Some of them stand before us now:

First, Avreml, known as the Three Yard Tailor. Still young. In his late twenties. Smooth cheeks, sparse, colorless hair on his chin. A complexion so pale that it actually looked green—like pus under an abscess.

He is tall, withered, thin. He has given up his craft and occupies himself with books that are beyond his understanding. But chiefly he devotes himself to pious prayers and with spending his nights in the cemetery. A chill emanates from his mouth, and his breath is bad—the result of his fasts, of hunger.

"Ah! Ah!" He is often ecstatic at prayer, and, in the midst of a discussion, is sometimes overwhelmed by religious fervor.

"Avreml." Thus his wife sometimes wakes him out of his trance in the synagogue where he spends his evenings. "Avreml, the children have had nothing to eat all day. Have you got something?"

And Avreml has. A long, folded wallet with many compartments, segment after segment; and as he unfolds it, unwinds it, there is in the very last segment a six-kopeck piece. Though sometimes that last segment is empty.

His wife stands somberly by. She wants to leave but cannot. Wants to stay, but sees no point in it. And her husband is tall, withered, with a green complexion, the Three Yard Tailor with a sparse beard. And she sees that waiting is useless, that he is preoccupied. She sees, in the declining light of day or by the light of a candle that has been lighted before evening prayers, that he is already far from her world, absorbed in his book.

Second:

Moyshe-Menakhem, the dyer. Middle-aged, of middle stature, with a very black beard, and black brows and eyes. His right side warped above his left so that standing, walking or running, he moves a bit crookedly. He has a sewn harelip, but the edges of the wound have not healed so that his upper jaw shows through. And this is why he always sucks air as he speaks, and if he says something once, it seems to him that he has not finished and he sucks air and repeats his words again. He is an energetic fellow, inwardly mercurial, always in restless, feverish motion, never able to stand still

Menakhem, when he was not stupefied by piety, found tone to practice his craft—dyeing.

Winter or summer he might be seen alone beside the river rinsing or beating a bundle of dyed clothing. He was never dressed appropriately for his work, but wore, instead, his usual gabardine even as he did his work. But one could tell that his mind was elsewhere. Even in winter in the coldest weather, when as often happened he interrupted his washing and went away for a while, it was not, as it would have been with anyone else, to warm his frozen and stiffened hands—but rather because he had gone to think through some important consideration, some exalted, pious thought that had occurred to him.

And therefore he was frequently robbed. In summer in the fenced meadows beside the river where he did his washing, on those occasions when he went off with his bundle and turned his attention to his beloved book, *The Duties of the Heart*, and particularly to that chapter of the work that he specially loved, "The Gate of Hope," thieves, then knowing that he was preoccupied, stole up behind him and filched some customer's shirt or dress at the very moment that Moyshe-Menakhem, immersed in hope, was furthest from any worldly concerns.

And it goes without saying that Moyshe-Menakhem had, then, to pay for the loss. Since such thefts had lately been very frequent, he would very soon reach the point at which he would be without customers—and therefore without an income. And then his wife, too, would come to beg him for something, the way Avreml's wife did. Like her, Moyshe-Menakhem's wife would leave with empty hands.

Third:

Sholem, the porter. A huge man with a chest and shoulders of legendary proportions, with a milk-pale complexion and an ash-gray beard. His porter's garb— a coarse canvas apron with a hole cut in it for his head— had dangling corners bound with rope in front and in back. Because he was so tall, his apron was twice the size of any apron worn by the other market porters.

His arms and legs were in proportion to his size. Before he became a member of the sect, there were fabulous tales in the marketplace concerning his great strength: it was said that he had lifted a nobleman's enormous horse by its forelegs, that he could climb or descend a staircase carrying, entirely unaided, a hogshead of sugar weighing a thousand pounds, and that he could devour all the contents of Zekhariah's food shop, swallowing up the good things meant to last all the porters in the market for an entire day—all the shop's dumplings, chopped liver, gizzards, crackling and goose legs. And that he could drink up the Jordan River.

Whenever there was heavy work, he was the first to be called. Everyone bragged about him, clustered around him and was eager to work in his company.

Then without warning he was stricken with piety. No one quite knew how it was that he came to choose the Bratslaver sect. Perhaps because among them everyone was warmly welcomed and treated as an equal. Or perhaps because the sect had no living rabbi at its head. A relationship with a living rabbi would have troubled him. The formal routine of visiting a rabbi was alien to Sholem: the careful coming in, the greeting, would all have seemed strange to the porter. Among the Bratslaver, he was spared all of that.

Whatever his reasons for choosing them, he was completely altered when he became a member of the sect. He did not know what to do with his enormous bulk and was ashamed of it. He kept his hands folded in his apron, his eyes lowered. He tried to stand shorter than he was, to contract his shoulders. And little by little he succeeded. His eyes lost their natural luster and he acquired a melancholy look. His shoulders seemed yearning to be covered with a gabardine. And when he dressed for the Sabbath, he seemed to have shrunk to only half his usual size. And if the other market porters chanced to see him, they laughed. At other times of the week, they poked fun at him as they went by: "Sholem, what's going on in the Bratslaver's world beyond?"

And it was reaching the point at which very soon there would be no more legends told about Sholem, and as they disappeared, so, too, would his income. [. . .]

And here is one more of their number.

Yankl the shoemaker, who formerly had led a charmed life. To whom the whole town used to throng with orders for shoes. Mountains of completed shoes for adults and boots for children were piled high on his workbench. And then there were the shoes and boots in progress. He employed more than a dozen workingmen, sturdy young fellows from distant Lithuania, who, working for him, never had a slack moment—not even in the interval days of a holiday. All year long, every day, including the days before festivals, they worked late into the night and sometimes all night long.

Other shoemakers envied Yankl. As for himself, he was a quiet, modest, simple man who had no idea why he was so lucky, nor how to appreciate or safeguard it.

And indeed he did not properly appreciate it. He did not think highly of himself, was in no way boastful. Because his shoemaker's success, his workingman's achievement in *this* world, gave him no special pleasure. He did not pursue wealth, was rarely grateful to his customers and frequently confused their shoe sizes, offering large shoes to customers with small feet, or narrow shoes to people with wide feet. He got finally so confused that the book in which he wrote his orders became absolutely useless.

And the reason for all this was that Yankl was afflicted with a grief so great that neither his prosperity nor the abundance of his money gave him any relief. Yankl had no children and he passionately wanted them. At least one boy who would be able to say Kaddish, mourning for him after his death.

It was for this reason that he had made gifts to various wonder rabbis, that he bought talismans from various female conjurors and finally consulted a doctor. But nothing did any good.

But what did help—when, once, his good fortune exceeded all his expectations—was the year of the eclipse of the sun, a time when, as everyone knows, barren women can conceive. And Yankl's wife conceived—and gave birth.

The whole town was delighted by his good fortune— as it was for all those who were similarly blessed—although among the shoemakers, no doubt because of jealousy, a certain slander was current. It was said that in addition to the good he had received from the eclipse, he had also had some help from a young journeyman shoemaker from Pinsk, a handsome giant of a man with disheveled hair, who worked for him.

Whatever the truth of the matter might be, Yankl was made so giddy with happiness that that year it seemed that he worked entirely without using a measure. Long, short, wide, narrow—he got the piles of shoes on his bench so confused that even the most faithful of his customers went away displeased or angry because he did not get their shoes done on time or because they were ill made. In that year his customers had a revulsion of feeling, and many of them (along with his luck) left him to go to other shoemakers.

And with each succeeding year, things got worse and worse. The disheveled Lithuanian youths who worked for him left him one by one to work for more respected shoemakers. His customers were gone, his workbench empty. Even during his prosperity, Yankl had forgotten the secrets of his craft. Little by little he lost his skill until at last he could do nothing.

And thus we find him, still bearing the name Yankl Eclipse, now one of "them." A member of the sect described above. And poor like all of them. Modest and very pious. And even more naive than before, with eyes gleaming because of the miracle that had happened to him, that had so fulfilled his utmost hope that he had no need of anything else. Anything more would be superfluous happiness.

And here, now, is the chief of the sect: the one who has lived through more trials than any of them, who is truly worthy to be their leader, because of the various transmigrations of spirit he has experienced, or because of the struggles he lived through in his frequent waverings between belief and unbelief.

And the marks of that struggle could be seen in his physique. His upper body seemed always to be quarreling with the lower. He walked quickly, distractedly, pushing his head and upper body before him as if he meant to part them from the rest of him.

And there were signs of struggle in his face too. Though he was middle-aged, with a complexion solid and browned as leather, it was already deeply plowed with wrinkles. The hair of his beard, the color of dull brass, was prickly and hacked sharply off at the edges, like thatch. He gave off a powerful smell of cheap tobacco which he smoked, rolled in coarse cigarette paper—inhaling deeply, passionately, sucking the smoke so deeply into his belly that the tears came to his eyes.

Always distracted, he rarely looked anyone in the eyes. He kept his head lowered, but when he raised it one saw eyes as dark as smoked amber that frequently had a troubled look. When his eyes cleared, they took on a look of intelligence that was at once ironic and even teasing. The wrinkles at his temples and around his eyes were signs of much suffering, but in his head and forehead one saw signs of stubborn vigor, a readiness—if it should be necessary—to endure suffering once more.

His name is Mikhl Bukyer.

Now he is a primary-school teacher. There was a time when he was the author of various essays which now he disavows, rejecting them utterly to the point that he does not even want to recall them . . . they are so distant from anything that now concerns him.

In the days when he wrote those essays he had been so far gone that once on a Sabbath in the synagogue where he had gone to pray, he had had the audacity to say openly to a group of Jews sitting around him that when the Bible says that Moses went up to God in heaven, it does not literally mean that he walked there in his boots, but that he went there in spirit. And for saying so, he was immediately slapped in the face twice by an old graybeard Jew—not a particularly learned man, but a fanatically pious one. "One slap," the old man said, "is for Moses' first boot, the next one is for the second boot."

In those days he was so far gone that he had looked into the kinds of books which true believers avoid as they would the fire; though in fact such books have their place among other holy works, and have in fact been written by certain very great Jews *The Sefer ha-Kuzari* (Rabbi Judah ha-Levi), *The Guide of the Perplexed* (Rabbi Moses ben Maimon) and so on.

He was so far gone that his mind was constantly filled with such thoughts as, The universe may be anarchic. It has neither creator nor master. It has always existed. And if it has been created, it is not necessarily the work of one being. And from there he came to the point of denying the very foundations of the ancestral faith of his people, foundations that had been established for all eternity.

He had by then separated himself from the community, and the community from him. And things had come to such a pass that he had the choice of starving to death or of changing his faith.

But finally he mastered himself. And so it seemed to him, heaven, too, helped him to free himself from those thoughts and to redeem his soul.

He had, as has been said, a very changeable nature, and he changed from one extreme to another: from the profoundest belief to the outer reaches of unbelief. And the struggle had begun when he was still very young. He was some sixteen years old, still living in Buki, his village, when on a Thursday night he crept up to his mother's chest of drawers where the linen was kept. He took a shirt from a drawer, and with that . . . with a single shirt and the sack containing his tefillin, he started off toward Sadigure on foot. And the following morning, Friday, when he got to the nearby town, he went, as everyone does on the day before the Sabbath, he went to the bathhouse and there discovered that in the haste of his leaving, he had mistakenly taken one of his mother's shirts.

Then later he was arrested and beaten by gendarmes for trying to cross the Austrian border without a passport. He dragged himself home, sick and coughing. He was cared for for a long while, and given goats' milk to drink. Thanks to his natural vigor, his wounded lungs healed, and his parents, because of their son's miraculous recovery, borrowed or pawned everything they could to furnish him with a passport and expense money so that he might be sent to the Sadigure rebbe toward whom in his youthful thirst he had been drawn.

Later on his convictions changed again and he returned to his original faith, but fearful lest he be overtaken by the great disaster of unbelief, he refused to look into those dangerous books and would not permit so much as a phrase from one of them anywhere near him. For a considerable time he moved about among the holy men of his generation, trying to find one to whom he might be able to bind himself until having searched among the living holy men, he came at last to "them." To the Bratslavers. [. . .]

He devoted himself to his new beliefs with a special ardor, stronger and more diligent than that of people who had believed for a much longer time and who had had no doubts. He took on himself exceptional duties. For instance, in winter in the extremest cold, he went at dawn to bathe in holes cut in the ice. On Fridays when he trimmed his fingernails, he kept his eyes averted from his fingers so that his scissors drew blood. And he took on himself other penances of body and of soul such as people in those days assumed. [. . .]

And the sect was composed of such as these who have been described and of others like them. Avoided by the community, they were a persecuted group that acquired converts only rarely, though, as has been said,

sometimes a poor young artisan from outer Poland, carrying his sack of tools, came to them, or, also rarely, a rich man who after some interior crisis turned away from his wealth and left his family, his prosperity and his business and chose to come to *them*, the poorest and the most rejected of all.

And it was to them, to this sect, that Luzi had come.

It was in the Living Synagogue ("Living," because no one wanted to refer to a synagogue as "Dead"), which was built at the entrance to the old cemetery in the center of town, and whose windows looked out over the field in which the tombstones lay, half buried in the grass . . . it was in the Living Synagogue that the sect had paid for (or begged) permission for their prayer quorum to gather.

And it was there that they were already gathered very early on a Saturday morning, when the sun had just risen and the town was still pleasantly sleeping. All of them had been to the ritual bath, and their heads and beards were still damp and uncombed; they were pale from a whole week of poor nourishment (nor was what they had on the Sabbath any better or more pleasing). They all wore their one vaguely black Sabbath caftan, faded from its original hue and frayed from long years of use. [. . .]

Then there began the usual tumult of prayer. Some stood fixed where they were, others ran about from place to place as if they meant to climb the air, as if they wanted to separate themselves from their bodies. Some seemed to see ladders before them up which, with trembling hands and feet, they meant to climb. Still others plunged forward toward great expanses which only the synagogue walls prevented them from reaching. The consequence of so much plunging and climbing was that the synagogue was soon filled with cries of yearning. Cries like those of Avreml, the tall, withered tailor, from whose mouth a cold breath constantly emanated and who at his prayers, though he was weak and helpless, managed to summon up a last bit of warmth to cry "Ah! Ah!" as if he were screwing up his courage even as he was giving himself up to delight. Menakhem the dyer ran about like a caged beast, sucking back with his split lips the words he uttered because it seemed to him he had not put sufficient life into them the first time. Some of the congregants clapped their hands, others stamped their feet. Still others tossed their heads and screamed as if they were being slaughtered, and those who had neither voice nor strength stood facing a wall and vibrated in silent ecstasy. Some shook only half of their bodies, others their whole selves. All of them were impassioned as they uttered one or another exalted passage of praise:

Sing, with God, oh, saints, the praises due to the
    righteous
Favor us, O Lord, for our hopes are in Thee.

And so on.

All twelve of the windows facing on the cemetery were open. The newly ascending sun, now low in the sky, sent its first stripe of sunlight from the edge of the eastern horizon. The town was still sleeping the last sleep of the night and here, in the Living Synagogue, the little community was already raising its exalted, wildly rapturous sectarian Sabbath song. They were ecstatic with themselves and with the knowledge that they were, as always, the first to sound God's praises on this Sabbath dawn. And they were especially exalted today, when among them they had such a notable new adherent, one from whom, in the midst of their prayers, they had not taken their eyes because he had inspired them with courage and a desire to praise.

So they had watched him standing there, when his face was turned toward the open window that looked out on the cemetery and later when he turned to face the praying congregation making its mad movements.

And Luzi, too, was in a good mood—because he had left his comfortable bed at his rich brother's house and had come here to join this ill-dressed congregation whose members must have found it very easy to rise from their mean beds and who, so early in the morning, were capable of so much exaltation.

It had been long since he had had the taste of such prayers in his mouth, and the overflow of sheer delight he experienced made him catch his breath. He turned to face the open window and sent his heartfelt words outdoors. And then so he could unite himself again with this congregation, so that he could experience that joy again, he turned to face them in the interior of the synagogue, and stood that way throughout the course of their prayers, which lasted a considerable while.

Then the prayers came to an end and all of the congregants, some still wearing their prayer shawls, others without them, wished each other "A good Sabbath." And then excitedly they gathered around Luzi.

"A good Sabbath. A good Sabbath," he returned their greetings. [. . .]

So the sexton restrained himself and waited. Then still standing on the threshold, he saw, when the dance had come to a stop, how everyone formed a circle around Luzi, and he heard someone ask, "Well, and who will take Luzi home as his guest for the Sabbath?"

"I will," Mikhl Bukyer called first, before any of the others.

And on that Sabbath, Luzi was Mikhl Bukyer's guest for the entire day: for the meal in the morning, for the brief nap following the meal, for the short Sabbath conversation after the nap, and so on until it was time for early evening prayers when Mikhl brought Luzi back to the same synagogue where Mikhl served as a preacher to the small sect. [. . .]

The month of Elul came. And in that month it was the practice of the members of the sect to go off by twos to some place of isolation and recount to each other all that had happened to them in the course of the year, and each one confessed the other.

And here, then, one evening, well after the evening prayers, when everyone had left the Living Synagogue, two people still remained: Mikhl Bukyer and Luzi.

Luzi, at the east wall, sat on a bench before a podium while Mikhl stood before him in the attitude one takes standing before a teacher, or a spiritual guide, or a director of one's conscience. As if he was prepared, with great meekness, to open every drawer within himself which all year long he had kept closed, so that Luzi might have the opportunity to search among them, turning everything over, digging deeply so that he might reveal what needed to be revealed and judged.

The entire synagogue was dark except for the hanging lamp that feebly illuminated the place where the two of whom we are speaking stood at the east wall. Nevertheless, had anyone standing at a distance, even from as far away as the west wall, looked toward Mikhl, he would have seen the redness of his eyelids, reddened as they always were when he studied the Book of Job and was exalted by Job's grief and suffering. And now Mikhl was moved even more: he wept, and one could see tears running down his hard cheeks and into his dull-yellow beard.

And Luzi stern before him. He had, in the role of inquirer and judge, looked deeply into the exposed soul of the guilty one. He had stood silently by and listened, seeming to require of Mikhl ever greater revelations.

And Mikhl, standing there before Luzi, continued his confession.

He had a flaw. He had been touched by a heavy hand. Despite all his efforts, all of his struggles, since then and now, he had not yet recovered all of his former faith. It was a curse. He had been stricken somewhere in the innermost depths of his being. He felt as if strange winds were blowing in the structure of his self, as if very soon and violently, they would open its doors and shutters, creating such havoc as would leave him helpless to control whatever had been his own. Then he would be flung into the depths from those heights that had cost him so much pain and struggle to reach. And he would become like a dog on a chain dragged here and there according to the needs or the will of some unknown power.

It was an unhappy struggle. Lord, what had he not tried in the way of mortification of the flesh and of the spirit. And all to no avail.

He confessed that he had not been able to master a single human passion. On the contrary, they had mastered, defeated, imprisoned him. For example, bodily passion in him was intensified as he grew older. When he walked in the streets, he had to keep his eyes on the ground in order to avoid meeting—to avoid seeing—temptation, and just the same forbidden sights seemed to leap out at him as if from underground, and as a result, he saw—and sinned. It had reached the point that he found himself seeing only nakedness before him so that he trembled and was confused in the midst of his prayers and studies.

And the same was true of the other passions—for example, money, honor, envy, hatred and so on.

But worst of all was his tendency for denial—a tendency that in him was a passion and which had various consequences for him. Sometimes he found himself emptied, as if every bit of spirit had fled from him and he looked at his surroundings with indifference, and as if all the threads that bound him to the world and that ordered the world had suddenly snapped and he found himself walking in the void. Or, on the other hand, he felt sometimes as if a wild madman possessed him and made him frightful, excitable, and pushed him to want to spoil or to destroy everything, to break all bonds.

All of this, without mentioning the "trivia." For example, on the Sabbath when he stood before a lighted candle, his impulse was to blow it out. Or worse: when he was alone in the synagogue, he was seized with an impulse to run up to the Holy of Holies and tear down its curtain and (God forbid) to dash the Torahs to the ground. And worse, much worse. He could hardly bring himself to let his mouth form the words—but it had actually happened that he had held a knife to his own throat desiring to cut himself off both from this world and the next. Evidently out of a fear of denial, but the truth was that this was the greatest of all forms of denial.

Translated by Leonard Wolf.

Other works by Der Nister: *Mayselekh in ferzn* (1918/1919); *Gedakht* (1922/1923).

POETRY

In the interwar period, Jews wrote poetry to express their inner emotional states, to address public issues, and to explore complex sentiments and elusive perceptions. They wrote in a variety of styles, some experimental and pathbreaking, others more conventional and less daring. When they wrote in Hebrew and Yiddish, their choice of language evoked associations and references embedded in previous Jewish texts and traditions—even if they saw themselves as avant-garde artists. Some poets wrote in more than one language (Hebrew and Yiddish, for example), and some, like writers of fiction, wrote in languages that were not the language of the land in which they were living (Hebrew in the United States and Austria, Yiddish in Germany and the United States, and German in the Land of Israel, for example). This was a consequence of the unsettled nature of Jewish cultural life in the 1920s and 1930s. Jewish writers were often on the move, fleeing tyranny and seeking refuge, while the Yiddish and Hebrew languages were locked in competition, neither having yet outstripped the other. East European immigrants in North and South America and elsewhere still constituted a receptive audience for Yiddish writers, regardless of where they lived.

Alter Brody

1895-1979

The American poet Alter Brody was born in Ukraine and brought to the United States at age eight. He was educated in New York City public schools and rapidly became conversant in American culture and literature. At a young age he began contributing to well-known literary and public affairs magazines and attracted attention for his poetry. In the 1920s, however, his literary output diminished as he was drawn into political activism, specifically writing articles in praise of the Soviet Union. In 1934, he announced his intention to publish a wide-ranging anthology of Yiddish literature in English translation, but it never appeared. In the end, he disappeared from the literary scene and little is known of his later life.

A Family Album

1918

1

Worn and torn by many fingers
It stands on the bedroom dresser,
Resting back against its single cardboard buttress,
(There were two)
The gilt clasp that bound it, loose and broken,
The beautiful Madonna on its cover, faded and
    pencil-marked,
And the coarse wood of its back showing through its
    velvet lining.

2

I remember the time that my sister Pauline bought it
    for the house
(300 Cherry Street, fourth floor, right-hand side,
    front)
Thirteen years ago,
With the proceeds of her first week at the factory.
It was beautiful then,
The golden-haired, grave-eyed Madonna that
    adorned it,
Her blue eyes were ever so much bluer and clearer,
    and so sweetly pensive,

Her golden hair fell forward over her bare breast,
Brighter and yellower than gold,
And there were no black pencil marks across the
    pure white of her brow
Or the delicate pink of her cheeks.
She was beautiful . . .
And my father,
I remember my father didn't like that album,
And murmured against the open-bosomed female
    on its cover,
"It is sinful to have such a picture in a Jewish
    home!"
But I,
I loved that album because of its glorious, golden-
    haired Madonna.
And when I was left alone in the house
I would stand in the parlor for hours
And gaze into her ecstatic face
Half reverently, half tenderly.
And sometimes,
When I was doubly certain of being alone,
I would drag a chair up to the mantelpiece
And get on top of it,
And, timidly extending my hand,
Touch with my trembling fingers the yellow threads
    of her hair as they lay across her breast,
Or the soft slope of her breast into her loose robe.
And once, I remember,
Ashamed of my feelings, yet unable to repress them,
I drew the picture closer to my face.
And pressed my lips passionately on that white
    bosom—
My first kiss . . .

3

Somehow I never cared to open the gilt clasp of the
    album
And look through the photographs that were col-
    lecting there:
Photographs brought here from Russia,
Photographs taken here at various times,
Grandfathers, grandmothers, aunts, uncles, cousins,
Sisters and sisters-in-law, brothers and
    brothers-in-law;

Photographs of some of the many boarders that
    always occupied our bedrooms
(The family usually slept on folding beds in the
    kitchen and parlor
Together with some other boarders);
Boarders-in-law; sweethearts, wives, husbands of
    the boarders;
Group pictures: family pictures, shop pictures,
    school pictures.
Somehow I never cared to open the gilt clasp of the
    album
And look through that strange kaleidoscope of Life.
But now,
As I find myself turning its heavy cardboard pages,
Turning them meditatively back and forth,
My brain loosens like the gilt clasp of the album,
Unburdening itself of its locked memories,
Page after page, picture after picture,
Until the miscellaneous photographs take to them-
    selves color and meaning,
Standing forth out of their places like a series of
    paintings;
As if a Master-Artist had gone over them with his
    brush,
Revealing in them things I did not see in the
    originals,
Solving in Art that which baffled me in Life.
And all the while as I go through the album, sup-
    porting the cover with my hand,
The yellow-haired Madonna gazes at me from under
    my fingers,
Sadly, reproachfully.

4

Poor, warm-hearted, soft-headed, hard-fisted Uncle
    Isaac
In his jaunty coat and flannel shirt,
Stiff and handsome and mustached,
Standing as if he were in evening dress—
His head thrown backward, his eyes fixed forward
Conscious of the cleanliness of his face and hands,
Fresh washed from a day's grime at the coal cellar.
When I look at his bold, blank face
My mind tears through the dense years,
Along the crazy alley of his life,
Back to a Lithuanian village on a twig of the Vistula.
Kartúshkiya-Beróza (what a sweet name—
Beróza is the Russian for birch trees)

And from a background of a dusty road meandering
    between high, green banks of foliage
I feel two black eyes looking at me strangely,
Two black passion-pregnant eyes
Nestling in a little dark face.

5

Every Saturday afternoon in the summertime
When the town was like a green bazaar
With the houses half-hidden under leaves and the
    lanes drifting blindly between the dense shade
    trees
After the many-coursed Sabbath dinner and the
    long synagogue services that preceded it
Mother took the four of us over to Grandpa's
A few houses up the lane
Where the aunts and the uncles and the cousins and
    the nephews and the nieces
In silk and in flannel and in satin and in linen,
Every face shining with a Sabbath newness,
Gathered on the porch for the family promenade:
Up to the lane and across the Gentile quarter and
    around the Bishop's orchard;
Through the Polish Road past the Tombs of
    the Rebels to the haunted red chapel at the
    crossroads—
And back again by cross cuts through the cornfields,
With the level yellow plain mellowing mystically
    around us in the soft sunshine,
And the sunset fading behind us like the Sabbath,
At twilight—just before the evening service—
Every Saturday afternoon, in summertime.

6

They rise in my brain with mysterious insistence
The blurred images of those Sabbath walks—
Poignantly, painfully, vaguely beautiful,
Half obliterated under the cavalcade of the years,
They lurk in the wayside of my mind and ambush
    me unawares—
Like little children they steal behind me unawares
    and blindfold me with intangible fingers
Asking me to guess who it is:
Across a wide city street a patch of pavement like a
    slab of gold;
A flash of sunlight on a flying wheel—
And I am left wondering, wondering where I have
    seen sunlight before?

By a holiday-thronged park walk, a trio of huge trees
    thrust their great, brown arms through uplifted
    hillocks of green leaves—
And I stand staring at them penetratively;
Trying to assure myself that they were real,
And not something that had swum up in my mind
From a summer that has withered years ago—
In the beaches by the wayside on the Polish Road,
Isled among the birch woods,
As you come out of Kartúshkiya-Beróza.
On my bed, within the padded prison-walls of sleep,
    lurching through a night of dreams;
I am awakened by a shrill wide-spreading trium-
    phant outburst of incessant twittering—
Under my window in the park,
Catching like fire from tree to tree, from throat to
    throat
Until the whole green square seems ablaze with joy,
As if each growing leaf had suddenly found
    tongue—
And I raise myself in my bed, dreamily, on my
    elbows
Listening with startled attentiveness to a sweet,
    clear twittering in my brain
As of a hundred populous treetops vying with the
    pebble-tuned waters of a brook
Gurgling timidly across a wide road.
In a hallway among a party of girls and young men
    tripping downstairs for an outing on a Sunday
    morning,
The coarse, keen pungency of satin from some girl's
    new shirtwaist,
Though my nose into my brain pierces like a
    rapier—
And suddenly I am standing on a sunny country
    porch with whitewashed wooden columns,
All dressed up for a Sabbath walk,
In a red satin blouse with a lacquered, black belt
With my mother in her blue silk Sabbath dress and
    grandmother with a black lace shawl around her
    head
With my sisters and my brother and portly Uncle
    Zalman with his fat, red-bearded face
And my grandfather stooping in his shining black
    capote with his grizzled beard and earlocks and
    thoughtful, tiny eyes
And poor Aunt Bunya who died of her first
    childbirth, with her roguish-eyed young
    husband

And smooth-shaven, mustached Uncle Isaac half-
    leaning, half-sitting on the banister with his little
    girl clamped playfully between his knees
And his wife Rebecca, with black eyes and pursed
    up scornful lips standing haughtily aloof
And my cousins Basha and Miriam and little Nach-
    man clutching at Uncle Zalman's trousers
And their mother, smiling, big-hearted, big-bo-
    somed Aunt Golda, offering me a piece of tart
As I am staring absently sideways
Into the little dark face rimmed lovingly between
    Uncle Isaac's coarse hands.

Other works by Brody: *A Family Album and Other Poems* (1918); *Lamentations: Four Folk-Plays of the American Jew* (1928).

Alter Brody

Ghetto Twilight
1918

An infinite weariness comes into the faces of the old
    tenements,
As they stand massed together on the block,
Tall and thoughtful silent,
In the enveloping twilight.
Pensively,
They eye each other across the street,
Through their dim windows—
With a sad recognizing stare,
Watching the red glow fading in the distance,
At the end of the street,
Behind the black church spires;
Watching the vague sky lowering overhead,
Purple with clouds of colored smoke
From the extinguished sunset;
Watching the tired faces coming home from work,
Like dry-breasted hags
Welcoming their children to their withered arms.

Alter Brody

Lamentations
1918

In a dingy kitchen
Facing a Ghetto backyard

An old woman is chanting Jeremiah's Lamentations,
Quaveringly,
Out of a Hebrew Bible.

The gaslight flares and falls . . .

This night,
Two thousand years ago,
Jerusalem fell and the Temple was burned.
Tonight
This white-haired Jewess
Sits in her kitchen and chants—by the banks of the
    Hudson—
The Lament of the Prophet.

The gaslight flares and falls . . .

Nearby,
Locked in her room,
Her daughter lies on a bed convulsively sobbing.
Her face is dug in the pillows;
Her shoulders heave with her sobs—
The bits of a photograph lie on the dresser . . .

Moyshe-Leyb Halpern

1886-1932

The American Yiddish poet Moyshe-Leyb Halpern
was born in Galicia and immigrated to New York City
in 1908, where he remained for most of his life, living
in great poverty. In New York, he was associated with
Di Yunge, although his work transcended the high
aestheticism of the group. It was planted firmly in
the boisterousness of immigrant life and voiced the
longings and disappointments of confused newcomers trying to make sense of America. While Halpern's
poetry articulated a sense of alienation from America,
it did not indulge in, but firmly rejected, the nostalgic
move to idealize East European Jewish life. Indeed, it
was often brutally hostile to the shtetl.

Ghingeli

1919

Oh, Ghingeli, my bleeding heart,
Who is this guy who dreams in snow
And drags his feet like a pair of logs
In the middle of the street at night?

It is the rascal Moyshe-Leyb,
Who will freeze to death someday,

Having fantasies of flowers,
Of blossoms in the spring;
And while lying in the snow
And not stirring anymore,
In his dreams he will still
Stroll through cornfields.

Dreams the rascal Moyshe-Leyb,
Sings the watchman dum-dee-dee,
Answers the bum ah-choo,
Barks the dog bow-wow,
Mews the cat me-ow.

Oh, Ghingeli, my bleeding heart,
Who, in the snow, plods to and fro,
And thinks he sits by a fireplace
In the middle of the street at night?

It is the rascal Moyshe-Leyb
Who is too lazy to think.

He freezes in the snow and sees
A palace, closed every wing,
And, guarded by the sentries,
He is himself the King,
And all his years are passing by
Like setting suns at evening.

Yearns the rascal Moyshe-Leyb,
Sings the watchman dum-dee-dee,
Answers the bum ah-choo,
Barks the dog bow-wow,
Mews the cat me-ow.

Oh, Ghingeli, my bleeding heart,
Who cuts threefold on himself
And hops in snow by streetlamp-light
In the middle of the street at night?

It is the rascal Moyshe-Leyb
Who stops in snow for a dance—
To keep his feet from freezing
Completely, in the trance;
He sees the snowflakes on his clothes
Like blossoms in sunshine breathe,
And girls with hair let loose
Adorned with fire-wreaths.

Dances the rascal Moyshe-Leyb,
Sings the watchman dum-dee-dee,
Answers the bum ah-choo,
Barks the dog bow-wow,
Mews the cat me-ow.

Oh, Ghingeli, my bleeding heart,
Is there a rooster around?
Who was it crowing in the city
In the middle of the street at night?

It is the rascal Moyshe-Leyb
Who has no worry, no care,
And because he thinks the day
Has hidden itself somewhere,
And because he thinks the last
Rooster has been strangled,
He crows himself and says
Good-Morning to himself.

Crows the rascal Moyshe-Leyb,
Sings the watchman dum-dee-dee,
Answers the bum ah-choo,
Barks the dog bow-wow,
Mews the cat me-ow.

Translated by Benjamin Harshav and Barbara Harshav.

Other works by Halpern: *In nyu york* (1919); *Di gold-ene pave* (1924).

Moyshe-Leyb Halpern

In the Golden Land
1919

Would you, mama, believe if I told
That everything here is changed into gold,
That gold is made from iron and blood,
Day and night, from iron and blood?

—My son, from a mother you cannot hide—
A mother can see, mother is at your side.
I can feel from here, you have not enough bread—
In the Golden Land you aren't properly fed.

—Mama, oh mama, can you not see
That here they throw bread in the sea,
Because, when too bountiful is the earth,
It begins to lose its golden worth?

—I don't know, my son, but my heart cries:
Your face looks dark as the night's skies,
Your eyelids close, your head on your chest,
Like the eyes of a man dying for rest.

—Mama, oh mama, haven't you heard
Of trains racing under the earth,

That drag us from bed at break of dawn
And late at night bring us back home.

—I don't know, my son, but my heart is wrung:
I sent you away healthy and young—
It seems it was just yesterday!
And I want to see you like that today.

—Why do you, mama, sap the blood of my heart?
Can you not feel how it pulls me apart?
Why are you crying? Do you see at all
What I see here—a high and dark wall?

Why shouldn't I cry, my son? You see:
You've forgotten God and forgotten me.
Now your own life is a wall that will stand
Blocking your way in the Golden Land.

—Mama, you're right. We're divided in pain.
A golden chain . . . and an iron chain . . .
A golden throne—in heaven for thee,
In the Golden Land—a gallows for me.

Translated by Benjamin Harshav and Barbara Harshav.

Moyshe-Leyb Halpern

Memento Mori
1919

And if Moyshe-Leyb, the poet, tells
That he saw Death on the high waves—
Just as he sees himself in a mirror,
And it was in the morning, around ten—
Will they believe Moyshe-Leyb?

And if Moyshe-Leyb greeted Death from afar
With a wave of his hand, and asked how
    things are?
Just when thousands of people were
In the water, madly enjoying life—
Will they believe Moyshe-Leyb?

And if Moyshe-Leyb, tears in his eyes,
Swears that he was drawn to Death,
As a man is drawn at dusk in desire
To the window of a woman he adores—
Will they believe Moyshe-Leyb?

And if Moyshe-Leyb paints Death for them
Not gray and not dark, but dazzling and colorful,
As he appeared, around ten in the morning,

Doing full.

Far away, between sky and waves—
Will they believe Moyshe-Leyb?

Translated by Benjamin Harshav and Barbara Harshav.

Moyshe-Leyb Halpern

My Restlessness Is of a Wolf
1919

My restlessness is of a wolf, and of a bear my rest,
Riot shouts in me, and boredom listens.
I am not what I want, I am not what I think,
I am the magician and I'm the magic-trick.
I am an ancient riddle that ponders on its own,
Swifter than the wind, bound tightly to a stone.
I am the summer sun, I am the winter cold,
I am the rich dandy, spendthrift with gold.
I am the strolling guy, hat cocked to a side,
Who steals his own time, whistling with pride.
I am the fiddle, the bass and the flute
Of three old musicians who play in the street.
I am the children's dance and, on moonlit strand,
I am the fool longing for a far blue land.
And, as I walk past a tumble-down house,
I am its emptiness peering out.
Now, outside my door, I am myself the fear,
The open grave waiting for me in the field.
Now I am a candle for a dead soul,
A useless old picture on dusty gray walls.
Now I am the heart—the sadness in eye's glow—
That longed for me a hundred years ago.
Now I am the night that makes me weary soon,
The thick night-fog, the quiet evening-tune.
The star above my head, lost in night's dark cloak,
The rustle of a tree, a clanging bell, smoke.—

Translated by Benjamin Harshav and Barbara Harshav.

Dovid Hofshteyn

1889–1952

Dovid Hofshteyn was one of the premier Yiddish poets of the Soviet Union during the interwar period. An early adopter of the Bolshevik cause, Hofshteyn crafted verse noted for the clarity of its imagery, use of structure and form, and adoption of trends from earlier traditions of Russian, West European, and Hebrew

poetry. After publicly supporting the Hebrew language and moving to Palestine for a short time in the mid-1920s, Hofshteyn returned to the Soviet Union as a politically suspect but highly regarded poet. Given his history of "anti-Soviet activities," he was the first member of the Jewish Anti-Fascist Committee to be arrested by the Soviet authorities during the postwar repressions of Jewish culture; he was executed alongside other members of the Soviet Yiddish intelligentsia on August 12, 1952. The Dovid Hofshteyn Prize for Yiddish Literature was established in his name in Tel Aviv in 1987.

Procession
1919

We're striding in your front ranks,
marching mankind—
with the cool and with the fervid,
with the proud and the courageous—
step after step!
On his high gibbet, the old god
swings and swings.
Patched with air, the old red flag
still flutters and flutters.
Not one step back!

Sticks awakening scatter
buckshot on taut drums,
cymbals buffet brightness into drifting air,
and far into the distance shining trumpets
hurl their blare.

Today I, too, am a piece of clanging brass.
I leap across
hushed and velvet places,
I wake the weary,
and drown with my resounding laughter
the signs of those who languish.
Not one step back!

Translated by Robert Friend.

Other works by Hofshteyn: *Lider un poemes* (1977).

Leyb Kvitko

1890–1952

Born in the town of Holoskovo, near Odessa, Leyb Kvitko was a Soviet Yiddish poet of significant standing and lasting popularity. Praised for his early verse that combined the demands of modernism with the traditions of East European Jewish folksong, he was a member of the Kultur-lige (Culture League) literary group in Kiev and, like many of this circle, spent much of the 1920s in Berlin. Kvitko fell from favor a few years after his return to the Soviet Union when he published a critical caricature of Moyshe Litvakov, the editor of the Communist Party organ *Der emes* (The Truth), and was subsequently limited to writing children's poetry. His children's verse was, in turn, translated into Russian and became beloved by millions of Soviet readers for generations. A member of the Jewish Anti-Fascist Committee, Kvitko was executed alongside other Soviet Yiddish intellectuals on August 12, 1952.

Day Grows Darker
1919

> Day grows darker
> And darker.
> Mobs are advancing on the town,
> Mobs clotted with blood,
> Made remorseless by killing children,
> Lustfully they advance,
> To rip off heads,
> Feeble, melancholy heads.
> They are after mine as well,
> My head that is so young,
> And my heart,
> That has cradled in itself the joy of love.
>
> . . . A desolate survivor
> Will count the slaughtered.
> My dead name he will inscribe
> In tiny letters with the others
> In a long list.
> Ah, may he not forget at least
> To record in that long list
> What age I was!
> May he at least mention
> That my heart was very young,
> And my will to live as strong as fear itself,
> As strong and mad
> As my last day.

Translated by Heather Valencia.

Other works by Kvitko: *Lidelekh* (1917); *1919* (1923); *Gerangl* (1929); *Tsvey khaveyrim* (1933); *Gezang fun mayn gemit* (1947).

Peretz Markish

The Rinsed Fences . . .
1919

> The rinsed fences dry themselves in the wind.
> The kneaded black earth turns softer under my feet.
> Soaked soil, tousled and wanton wind,
> What more can I want from you today?
> It seems to me that I've seen you
> For the very first time in the world,
> And I, a child,
> Own you completely today.
>
> Red cattle, their bottoms smeared,
> Their udders swollen,
> Lie down in the mud-black dale.
> And in my hushed heart there lies
> A young delight
> In the warm silent morning,
> In last year's withered hay,
> In the unharnessed horses.
>
> I want to hug all the cows,
> To lie on the ground with them,
> And bellow along with them.

Translated by Leonard Wolf.

Saul Tschernikovsky
1875-1943

Considered one of the great Hebrew poets of the modern period, Saul Tschernikovsky was born in a small Ukrainian village. He attended a modern Hebrew school and at age ten entered a Russian school. At fourteen he was sent to Odessa, where he studied ancient and modern languages. In the 1890s, he was attracted to Zionist and Hebrew literary circles and published his first poems. He studied medicine in Heidelberg and Lausanne and then practiced in Kharkov and Kiev. During World War I, he served as an army doctor. He found it difficult to make a living as a physician in Russia after the revolution and in 1922 left for Istanbul, then Berlin, migrating to Mandate Palestine in 1931. Although known in particular for his nature poetry, Tschernikovsky also translated many works of world literature into Hebrew, including Homer, Shakespeare, Goethe, Heine, Byron, Shelley, and Pushkin.

To the Sun
1919

1

Hyacinth and mallow was I to God: lifelong
Only this pure sun fills, for each, the earth,
And an angel urges: "Bud, child, and bring forth
Among the biting thorns, your festive song."

The damp field suckled me: the smell, so near,
Of crumbled clods, rose to my head: did he
Not have a father and a priest in the city
That he fetched me to be his prophet here?

Shall the sap of the silver fir seem less in my eyes
Than your holy oil: gold on the head? There rise
Odours from pears and the fields that once I kept:

Are these less than the phials of Sheba where spike-
nard slept?
Slowly I bowed, honouring you without fear,
Like a golden stalk in the heavy-headed wheat.

As I stood between those who live and those who die
(Terrible craft!) a scalpel sharp in my hand,
Some wept for joy, and some swore at me, and
I drew the last light from the strange dying eye.

To the powerful thunder of cannon rolled over this
place,
And the single light that in my deep tunnel glows,
I incised the last line, I rubbed out all those
Alive: so a jewel is torn from its onyx case. [. . .]

15

I was to my god like a hyacinth, or a violet,
Like a bright sheaf of gold in the heavy wild corn;
And he brought me warm mists on a cold
mountain morn,
Symphonies of light and shade, blue, calm and
scarlet.

I grasped the time's sorrow, heard the songs men
create—
Voices shedding light, in alien darkness crying:
Between the living and those already dying,
Had I come too early or was my creator late?

Still in my heart sleeps dew that falls on Edom's sod,
High on the holy mount, home of the primal god,
For my heart murmurs songs to sun and Orion.

When pods burst, fruit ripen, and leaves of saplings
sprout,
A dead world's idols grab me, and there's no way
out—
Or a last statue from the age of the lion?

*Translated by Dom Moraes (Sonnet 1) and Richard Flantz
(Sonnet 15).*

Other works by Tschernikovsky: *Shirim* (1966);
Mivḥar shirim (2015).

Dovid Hofshteyn

Poem
ca. 1919

On Russian fields, in the twilights of winter!
Where can one be lonelier, Where can one be
lonelier?

The doddering horse, the squeaking sleigh,
the path under snow—that is my way.

Below, in a corner of the pale horizon,
still dying, the stripes of a sad fallen sun.

There, in the distance, a white wilderness,
where houses lie scattered, ten or less,
and—there—sleeps a shack, sunk deep in the snows.

A house like the others—but larger, its windows . . .
And in that house, to which many roads run,
I am the eldest of all of the children. . . .

And my world is narrow, my circle is small:
in two weeks I've gone once into town—if at all.

To long in the silence of space and of fields,
of pathways and byways that snow has
concealed. . . .

To carry the hidden sorrowing
of seeds that wait and wait for planting. . . .

On Russian fields, in the twilights of winter!
Where can one be lonelier, where can one be
lonelier?

Translated by Alan Mandelbaum.

Dovid Hofshteyn

Song of My Indifference
ca. 1919

For some the now is good enough—
and that is fine for them!
But what shall I do
when I always
see before me
phosphorescent questions flashing:
Where?
Where to?

I am ready tired
of hovering,
of flickering,
of swimming,
of soaking in strange seas.
Would that my own could tempt me!

Well, once upon my land,
in a green,
a valley corner,
in Galilee—
there was a Jewish mother
who had a child,
and from that child
there grew a man with sheepish, trusting
    eyes . . .
Whose business is it?

How long,
against the hollow of heaven,
above the cloistered steeples,
will golden stripes crisscross?

How long
will fugitive eyes
flash before me
at each of my weary,
each of my bloody steps?

And there was
a second man,
a darker man
who jingled—
within the blind,
within the hungry bosom—
thirty pieces of silver . . .
Now be cursed,
all you who exploit!

Chase
and scatter yourselves,
each against the other,
all of you whisper
about eternal
brimstone hail,
about eternal wandering.

Learn
to lift your heads!
See:
from the dust
of worldly markets
there is made
a mountain.

In a broad northern land,
within the capital
(for years they trembled,
fenced in by the thorns
of a Jewish shop)
in Moscow,
beside the believing Kremlin,
that lion-like bust—
Marx!

Listen!
From the breast
wrapped up in ancient fear,
from shivering, chattering, Jewish teeth,
is torn a voice, a tempest—
it speaks
across the broad Russian land—
Leib Bronstein. . . .

My great indifference!
There's nothing here for you,
nothing for anyone!
There's no one here who knows
my hatred, my hot hatred.

My love, my pure love!
One call I've always heeded—
mute, I've carried it
a thousand days:
above the gray head
of my people,
to be
a youthful radiance!

The gray head
of my people!

Like all heads, a head
that has its share of lice.

My great indifference,
There's nothing here for you,
and no one knows
my hatred, my hot hatred,
my love, my pure love!

And where?
And who—
are the people?
Shopkeepers?
What do they handle?
All the same!
A devil take your father's father
with his rags or linens.

Ah, the earnest
shopkeepers
who once
had given the world
Heinrich Heine!

No!
This is the way it goes—
fanatic,
stubborn pedants—
great-grandfathers
of Albert Einstein!
Farther there,
deeper there,
out of the black rubble of excommunication,
blooms at times
in white, in gleaming garments
striped with roses,
the polisher of limpid lenses,
Baruch Spinoza!

You secure peoples
Of masters and hangmen,
I am already sick—
remembering
the way you guard
my far, lost steps
upon your silent, gilded cemeteries,
in cities of the dead,
in dead cities!

Fugitives,
disgraced,
with quivering bodies,

with children and with women,
rip away the last borders,
the last chains.

With old, with longing arms,
I've gathered up myself
in all your crevices,
in layers of dust, for you—I dig graves . . .
together with the sharp, the heartfelt gaze
of Lev Shestov,
prepare yourselves—all of you—
for the blade of the slaughter,
the radiant
end!

Translated by Allen Mandelbaum.

Dovid Hofshteyn

Red Blossoms
1920

On this ancient trunk
With hanging branches, gray flax
I'm a young branch.
To grow: my sole passion.
Green shoot
rising
high
to the bright,
I'll bring red blossoms
to argue:
World, I'm right!
From this old trunk of mine
I'll tap
strength from aged sap.
I suckle old wine—
and when night leaves
this cold space,
in its place, with the first
unfolding rays—
from this old trunk,
its ancient rust,
my young crown, drunk,
will greet the sun!

Translated by Zackary Sholem Berger.

Else Lasker-Schüler

God, Hear . . .
1920

The night draws in around my eyes
Its ring of haze.
My pulse has sent my blood into a blaze
Though all about me a gray coldness lies.

O God, that I by living day
Should dream I'm dead,
Drink it in water, choke on it in my bread.
There's no measure of my grief your scale can
  weigh.

God, hear . . . in your own favorite color blue
I sang the song of the roof of your sky—
Yet, in your endless breath, I could not wake the
  day.
With its dull scar my heart's almost ashamed to
  come to you.

Where will I end?—O God!! For into the stars,
Also into the moon I looked, into your fruitful vale.
Even in the very berry the red wine grows stale . . .
And everywhere—the bitterness—at the core.

Translated by Robert P. Newton.

Peretz Markish

Hey, Women . . .
1920

Hey, women, spotted with typhus and riddled with
  rakes of fingers
Across autumn heads of woe,
Are you fruitful? Do you multiply? How many times
  each?
In whorehouses? On floors?
In the stable? In train stations?
In culverts, like bitches?
How many times, each?
In a moment, a train, like a coffin, will go into the
  earth—
Up on the roof! Lift your feet, like smokestacks,
Tie your shirts to foamy skies
And breathe the hot street-corner midnights—
And from each of you let there be born—a Jesus
To be gobbled on feast days
And not for the gallows, and not for crucifixions.

Hey, whores of discarded children,
Beat it!
Suck your own udders . . .
Milk them; choke on them.
Gnaw them away
from the body's gaunt walls—
Three echelons
Of swollen bastards—
No one knows where
They were muddied,
Nailed down—

Hey, human mothers! Thou shalt not roast them . . .
Thou shalt not fry them.

Translated by Leonard Wolf.

Peretz Markish

Out of Frayed Sackcloth . . .
1920

Out of frayed sackcloth—breasts of filthy cataracts,
Like raw potatoes, branched with rooted blue veins.
What shall we trade? Salt? How much do you want?
There's a dead child's hat still here.

In the marketplace, a surveyor dozes like a white
  skull—
A homeless dog sniffs him as he would an old
  cadaver.
What shall we trade? Bread? How much do you
  bid?
A pack of dogs in the street tears a heap of rusted
  brains to bits

And birds in the air flap like scattered black hats—
A disheveled tuft of wind keeps trying them on—
Is there a deal? Wind! What do you bid for a
  windmill?
There, across foothills, they aimlessly quarrel over
  eagles' wings.
Making a trade? Wind? What do you bid?

Translated by Leonard Wolf.

Julian Tuwim
1894–1953

Julian Tuwim was born into an assimilated Jewish
family in Łódź. He studied law and philosophy in
Warsaw, where he played an integral role in Pol-

ish modernist literary circles. In addition to writing poetry for children and adults, Tuwim was a lyricist, translator, and dramatist, active in the poetic group Skamander. Tuwim wrote exclusively in Polish and stressed his allegiance to Poland while downplaying his attachment to Judaism; in prewar years he was vilified by antisemites and tried to distance himself from Jewish culture. He lived in the United States during World War II and after the war returned to Poland, where he expressed deep sympathy for Jews who were killed in the Holocaust.

A Prayer
1920

I pray Thee O Lord
From all my heart,
O Lord! I pray to Thee.
With fervor and zeal,
For the sufferings of the humiliated,
For the uncertainty of those who wait;
For the non-return of the dead;
For the helplessness of the dying;
For the sadness of the misunderstood,
For those who request in vain;
For all those abused, scorned and disdained;
For the silly, the wicked, the miserable;
For those who hurry in pain
To the nearest physician;
Those who return from work
With trembling and anguished hearts to their
    homes;
For those who are roughly treated and pushed aside,
For those who are hissed on the stage;
For all who are clumsy, ugly, tiresome and dull,
For the weak, the beaten, the oppressed,
For those who cannot find rest
During long sleepless nights;
For those who are afraid of Death,
For those who wait in pharmacies;
For those who have missed the train;
—For all the inhabitants of our earth
And all their pains and troubles,
Their worries, sufferings, disappointments,
All their griefs, afflictions, sorrows,
Longings, failures, defeats;
For everything which is not joy,
Comfort, happiness, bliss— . . .
Let these shine forever upon them
With tender love and brightness,
I pray Thee O Lord most fervently—

I pray Thee O Lord from the depth of my heart.

Translated by Wanda Dynowska.

Other works by Tuwim: *Czyhanie na Boga* (1918); *Słowa we krwi* (1936); *Treść gorejąca* (1936); *Loko-motywa* (1938); *My, Żydzi Polscy* (1944); *Kwiaty polskie* (1949).

Aaron Zeitlin

After Havdoleh
ca. 1920

" . . . And all those who are on the left side go and wan-
    der in the world and seek to dress themselves in the
    body."—From *Zohar Beraishit*

When the Havdoleh candle is extinguished,
In Gehenna, the old fire ignites
A full, new week.
From abysmal crevices, black and narrow,
Swim the multitudes-from-the-left, topsy-turvy,
And again it's the weekdays, and again it's exile,
And again it's sorrow.

Hear how the black troops murmur!
They rage like storms on oceans.
And out of Gehenna, the sick soul
Of an evil man implores—
The raging is deaf to his pleas.
In gigantic waves, the impurity pours,
The armies of the Other God surge dreadfully,
And there's panic and there's riot,
As if cities were collapsing,
And shrieks reach up
To the heart of the heavens. In dark incantations
Understood by only the abysses of evil,
The demons call, "Tremble, world! Woe onto you!"
Thus they want bodies,
Thus they seek clothing—

*Translated by Kathryn Hellerstein; quotation from Zohar
translated by David Stern.*

Jacob Glatstein

1919
1921

Lately, there's no trace left
Of Yankl, son of Yitskhok,

But for a tiny round dot
That rolls crazily through the streets
With hooked-on, clumsy limbs.
The lord-above surrounded
The whole world with heaven-blue
And there is no escape.
Everywhere "Extras!" fall from above
And squash my watery head.
And someone's long tongue
Has stained my glasses for good with a smear of red,
And red, red, red.
You see:
One of these days something will explode in my head,
Ignite there with a dull crash
And leave behind a heap of dirty ashes.
And I,
The tiny dot,
Will spin in ether for eternities,
Wrapped in red veils.

Translated by Kathryn Hellerstein and Benjamin Harshav.

Peretz Markish

The Mound
1921

After you, the killed of the Ukraine;
After you, butchered
In a mound in Gorodishche,
The Dnieper town . . .
Kaddish

No! Heavenly tallow, don't lick my gummy beards.
Out of my mouth's brown streams of pitch
Sob a brown leaven of blood and sawdust.
No. Don't touch the vomit on the earth's black thigh.

Away. I stink. Frogs crawl on me.
Looking for mother-father here? Seeking a friend?
They're here. They're here, but taint the air with stink.
Away. Awkwardly they delouse themselves with
     hands like warped brass.

From top to bottom, a mound of filthy wash.
Claw, crazed wind. Take what you want; take it.
Before you, the church sits like a polecat beside a
     heap of strangled fowl.

Ah, black thigh. Ah, blazing blood. Out, shirttails!
     To the dance; to the dance.

We're laid out here. All. All. A mound. The whole
town.

                              11 Tishrei 5681

* * *

As one of the dead, I'll enter
The day of blood and honey.
My first doves will be
Dead spies upon the land.
Doves. Doves. Uphill.

It is my fate that hangs
Upon the bloody moon,
Her gleams, mere vowel signs.
Bellies, bellies to the dust—
Sleep is for dawn.

A mad town expires on my heart.
Street corners creep from my shoulders.
Ah, thou kid of the ascending sun,
Traded for two gulden,
I'm at your circumcision feast again.

Ah, you, my blind fathers,
How many bloated wombs,
How many debaucheries have borne me?
Then why am I afraid to take
A step into the ripped world?

Hey, boundaries of the earth! Spread.
The mill wheel turns from Nile to Dnieper now.
You, with spiked eyes,
Leap, mound, wild fever,
Over threshold, over ditches.

Blind Samson, blinded hero,
Hair's sprouting on your head again.
Leap upon a bow; on firebrands.
Make the distance tremble
And topple all the world.

* * *

Sunk to the loins in silence, the town sits
Like an upturned empty wagon in a marsh.
Ah, if only one would come
To say something.

Ah, grief and woe. The sunset, like a weeping hawk
Sits on the blind roof of an entreating palm.
Ah, Almightiest of the world,

Open—open up your starry title page.
  Hineni, he'oni. Unworthy, here I stand.

I yearn to merge with you in prayer
And yet my heart, my lips are moved
Only to blasphemies and curses.

Ah, my prayer-exhausted,
Tenfold dishonored hands turn.
Take them; take them.

Caress them, lick them, as a dog
Licks its scabby, suppurating hide.
I pledge them to you.

I've built you a new ark
In the middle of the marketplace.
A black mound, like a blotch.
Seat yourself upon its buxom roof
Like an old raven on a dungheap.

Take my heart, my prayer-exhausted heart,
And all such rubbish. Take it
And peck, peck what the chariot of twenty genera-
    tions brought.
I pledge it to you.

A wander-stick rolls about
Waiting for your steps that follow
Cain's unscrewed right legs.
I cool a capful
Of sanctifying blood
From Abel's throat for you.

You, whom noise diminishes,
A black wagon full of mud-smeared
Sleeping passengers pulls up
And something, something stirs.

Ah, sucked from my eyes, streams of pitch
To cleanse the dead. Take them, take them.
A black wagon with mud-smeared, sleeping
    passengers
More being driven there, more being driven, still
    being . . .

Come! cross yourself and count them.
A shekel a head,
A shekel a head,
And thrust them—as always—
Thrust them from you.
I pledge them to you.
I pledge them to you.

* * *

Go slow. Pilgrim winds, from rocky lands and wild,
Will you now tread the brass and scarlet snows
Of the mound's head?
Store food for a millennium and, wrapped in el-
    ephant hides,
Sanctify your wings with blood. I myself will guide
    you.

Here, like cliffs of hacked bellies,
Wells lurk around you.
Wild bones, gummed with a black hoof,
Protrude like giant horns,
Two thousand years of a fierce blizzard wandering
    in a well,
And still not yet arrived at the unsated depth.

Go slow. The mound climbs to lick the sky up like a
    plate of cloudy calf's-foot jelly,
To suck dry the hollow, scraped bone of the world.
Any moment now, red madness gushes to seas and
    distances.

Ah, pilgrim winds, you will yet tread upon my
    father's prayer shawl.
Though dead, there, on the mound, he delouses my
    sleeping mother.
Go slow! After me, step by step. After me.

Fluttering ribbons, beads,
Buttons and tubs
At fairs and marketplaces
Seethe.

At Sunday market stalls,
Joy flickers on all faces;
Each wagon heaped to the skies with wares,
Peddlers dance while dickering.
It's Yom Kippur's-end. Quickly. A ducat more or
    less.
Beggars on *banduras* pray for all,
And with false yardsticks measure
Ripped Torah parchments scrap by scrap.

"Hey, ribbons, beads, buttons and tubs!
use them in good health."
An idiot pig, somewhere in a culvert,
Wets the holy Ten Commandments
As on a piece of smeared and foaming rag.

* * *

From the heights, mouths like sheaves
Reach up to withered udders—
Clouded, sealed.
Will heaven yield a drop?

And skies, like blue tin teapots bent,
Or naked bakers bending.
Will they trickle at least once?

With hairs curled like twisted wires,
A jostled wheel quarrels.
Will there be the slightest puff of wind?

And sunsets chew the cud of trodden grass
Like tiny bones of childish hands.
Will there be no wondrous sign at last?

* * *

Ah, generation after generation will come
And go, in bread and salt,
In exhausted vexations,
And will pause, perhaps,
To count and caress their *groschens*
Beside the extinguished crow-shine
Of the Ark.

And, should sunshine
Ever again be desired,
Then, in the course of a meal
Of worldly radiance,
The outdoors will turn foul;
Thresholds will weep
And, in the midst of the world
A specter will swim into view,
Scratch its back on the sun,
And blaspheme:

"Brothers and sisters, I itch; I stink."

Shattered windowpanes are darkened with smoke;
On seaside hills, eyes protrude—
A wonder, a wonder. A miracle. A solar eclipse!

The day's sun is obscured with blood and pus,
With the cadaverous Mound, with a Babel of
    corpses.

And the Mound—a filthy cloud—blasphemes:
"Who'll cleanse me for death?
And who will console me?
And out of what deluge
Will a straying Ark

Bring me doves
To this City of Death?"

Ah, wind of the desert,
You will stay faithful to me.
Prometheus, perhaps, will kiss me from a cliff.
    Pass on; pass on.
    My head will not offer the Ark any respite,
    Nor desert cattle drink at my heart.

    "In thy blood live!
    In thy blood live."

* * *

It's a milky night, like moon-flesh set in a pitcher.
Oh, black cats, don't be afraid of my restless
    tapping—
I will utter the Sovereign Mound's decree:
It flings the Ten Commandments back at Mount
    Sinai.

Its thirsty mouth, a swill of grief that seethes
With black marrow, fumes like a glowing crater.
Hey, markets and mountain, I call you to oath with
    my song.
The Mound spatters Mount Sinai's Commandments
    with blood.

Two birds circle its mouth; they speak; they
    conjure.
From on high, they wind its tongue like a blazing
    scroll
And place on its brow a crown of frothing stars.

Ah, Mount Sinai! In the upturned bowl of sky, lick
    blue mud,
Humbly, humbly as a cat licks up its midnight prayers.
Into your face, the Sovereign Mound spits back the
    Ten commandments.

Translated by Leonard Wolf.

Salim Yitshak Nissim

1877–1950

A poet from Baghdad, Salim Yitshak Nissim was a Hebrew-language teacher and writer influenced by medieval Hebrew poetic conventions and moralistic genres. One of the contributors to the Hebrew- and Arabic-language journal *Yeshurun* (1921), Nissim called on Jews to honor their heritage while also adapting to cultural and political life in the diaspora.

Daughter of Babylon
1921

Return to your ancient past
Aid your sister with education and culture
And people of Israel will once more be a nation.

Awake, daughter of Babylon, mother of knowledge
Take up in your hand the pen of literature
Cast ignorance behind you
And be a source of great redemption to your people.

Undo the cuffs, release the binds,
Those tethers of dormant beliefs,
Gather lilies and flowers
From the field of the patriarchs' land.

Show [your] strength in knowledge of languages
    and the sciences
But turn not away from the Prophets
Open the Book of Chronicles
And know the greatness of Israel amongst the nations.

Exiled daughter of Babylon
Abandon not the language of [our] parents,
Teach your language, Hebrew,
Lest you be scorned amongst the nations.

Take *Yeshurun* in hand [or: Take Israel by the hand]
And become a blooming bud
With the courage of Yehoshua Bin Nun.
Find yourself spiritual repose.

NOTE
Words in brackets appear in the original translation.

Translated by Lital Levy.

Other works by Nissim: *Derekh tovim* (1938).

Abraham Shlonsky
1900-1973

The Hebrew poet and translator Abraham Shlonsky
was born in a Ukrainian village and sent to study at the
Herzliyah Hebrew Gymnasium in Tel Aviv when he
was thirteen. He returned to Ukraine when war broke
out in 1914. In 1921 his entire family settled in Mandate
Palestine. Shlonsky became a manual laborer, paving
roads, working on construction sites, and eventually
laboring on the land (he helped to establish Kibbutz
Ein Harod in the Jezreel Valley). He was associated
with the group of younger poets who rebelled against
the poetry of Bialik and his generation. His poetry is
characterized by its linguistic inventiveness and its
sophisticated wordplay. He was known for his many
translations of world literature, especially the Russian
classics, and for his children's poetry and plays.

Late Adar
1921

Like the golden bangles on the arms of a Bedouin
    woman, the hills of Gilboa bind their bracelets
    about the valley of Jezreel in the golden hours of
    late Adar evenings. Then do the women go down
    to the spring to draw water, and the anemones are
    like bangles around their feet.

Please lower your jar, now, so that we may drink the
    cool flowing waters of the spring, and they will be
    like spiced wine on our tongues.

For Adar has come down to expire of luxuriance as
    the Bedouins of the tribe of Asra die of love.
Then we became the sunset skies of the evening in
    late Adar.

Translated by T. Carmi.

Other works by Shlonsky: *Kitvei Avraham Shlonsky*,
10 vols. (1972–1973).

Moyshe Kulbak

Ten Commandments
1922

My grandfather's kinsman, a Jew who tamed bears,
Performed in the market towns;
By day his beast was confined in chains;
At night, they danced under the stars.

Nicknamed "Ten Commandments," the man was
    bald,
With long bony hands to his knees;
He was hunch-backed and scruffy and sweaty and old
And he stank of fur like a beast.

Traveling the roads with his bear at night,
The man led, the bear followed behind.
If a shoeless peasant chanced to walk by,
The bear grumbled and rattled his chain.

The burial society washed off the blood
Of "Ten"'s wives who all died in great pain,
For he stripped them naked and lashed them by night

Till their grief was heard by the town.

His thirteenth wife, who passed for a witch in
    Lithuania,
A year after their marriage bore him a daughter;
For years, he drained his wife's strength, then the
    witch
Too was laid out on a stretcher.

"Ten Commandments" he was, a man who tamed
    bears
And performed in the market towns;
By day his beast was confined in chains;
At night they danced under the stars.

Translated by Leonard Wolf.

Aharon Kushnirov
1890–1949

Aharon (Arn) Kushnirov was a prolific Soviet Yiddish poet, prose writer, playwright, literary translator, and editor. Born in Boyarka, Ukraine, and active in the Yiddish literary scene in Kiev, Kushnirov first wrote poetry that was full of youthful vigor and a desire for a revolutionary mass culture. The editor of influential literary journals throughout the interwar period and early postwar years—including the Moscow-based *Der shtrom*, the Minsk-based *Der shtern*, and the Moscow literary almanacs *Sovetish* and *Heymland*—Kushnirov was attracted to proletarian writing and culture, and enthusiastically participated in its production. Some of his most memorable works in this regard include the play *Hirsh Lekert* (1928), later translated into Russian by Eduard Bagritsky, and his writing on the settlement of Birobidzhan and other new industrial centers. A member of the Jewish Anti-Fascist Committee, Kushnirov was a victim of the repression of Soviet Yiddish culture and was killed in September 1949.

Memorial for the Dead
1922

    A Gift to Hofshteyn

1

Die, this scream of mine. Die—anyway
you're inaudible in the heavens.
Night got the best of the new moon

like a knife at the earth's throat.

Quiet will soon be choked
with a panicked howling
but night won't stop killing
but no one will come to aid.

Before whom then does one fall
to ask for mercy for oneself and you
when terrified stars hide
in river's steel folds.

2

[. . .]
I know, I'll no longer hear
any name or word . . .
Only a voice in Ramah is heard
Rachel weeping for her children . . .

How many weary beginnings
are set aglow by pain
on roads again pockmarked
with traces of your steps.

3

I won't hang my harp on the trees,
music for every wind . . .
Even in a dream I no longer possess
that milk-and-honey land.

A mouse scratches in my soul:
a tune from father, or grandpa.
But the door of my own Shabbes
Workaday bolted shut with a star.

Grind me—grind me like a seed,
millstones of all time,
if only thus the Morning Star,
like an apple, turned ripe.
[. . .]

5

So nights, besiege—besiege!—me,
from the front, on sides and nape,
And, winds, to left and right
Shake me. Like a pendulum.

I know that my last shout
shooting up to the dark skies,
like a stone hurled in a pond,

will aspire to the pitchblack.

[. . .]
But I will not extinguish my light,
Not throw open the gates for you.

* * *

You blue regions all in flame!
Stretched out in the world on the blade of dreams—
On the gray spool of your pathways
I wrapped up all my days.

And who will unloose someone's pain
and what can still my feelings
for the wild boil of your snows
which cooled my brain's very blood.

I waited with all my heart and might
for your banners' bright call
but you crossed my stubbornness
with soft fingers of a hatchet . . .

Not that sunrise should crown
your sky edge—not my yearning
when my unguarded dwelling
daubed your nights with conflagration.

But heart awakens to anthems' flourish
Every word's abud with praise;
For the mild sound of your heavens
dripping through my sternness' verse.

Translated by Zackary Sholem Berger.

Other works by Kushnirov: *Vent* (1921); *Geklibene lider* (1975).

H. Leivick

With the Holy Poem
1922

With the holy poem
clenched between my teeth,
I set forth alone
from that wolf-cave, my home,
to roam
street after street
like a wolf
with his solitary bone.

There is prey enough in the street
to sate wolf-hate, wolf-lust.

Sweet is the blood
that steams and drips
from flesh,
but sweeter the dry dust
that has settled on clamped lips.

Struggle in the streets.
from hoarse throats—the call.
Let me for once become
all deadly tooth and claw,
and come
to tear and gnaw.
Instead, I hunch into myself,
my head between my feet.

Back to my cave.
A lump on a cot. Alone.
But far from asleep,
as tireless of holding in my teeth
the holy poem
as the wolf
his solitary bone.

Translated by Robert Friend.

Esther Raab
1894–1981

Esther Raab was the first modern woman Hebrew poet born in the Land of Israel. Her religiously observant parents were among the founders of Petah Tikvah, where she was raised and educated. Although her father forbade her to attend the local secondary school because it was coeducational, she was widely read in Hebrew, French, and German literature. Her economically hard-pressed parents sent her in 1921 to live with relatives in Cairo, where she married. She and her husband returned and settled in Tel Aviv several years later. Her poetry is noted for its detailed evocation of the landscape of the Land of Israel.

Before Your Shining, Full Eyes
1922

Before your shining, full eyes
How good it is to live;
Before their light every limb is taut
Like a eucalyptus after a storm are you:
Tired, strong and still moving in the wind
My head will reach to your chest,

And your eyes above
Will distill warmth over me.

Translated by Anne Lapidus Lerner.

Other works by Raab: *Kol ha-shirim* (1994); *Thistles: Selected Poems of Esther Raab* (2002).

Antoni Słonimski
1895-1976

Raised Catholic in an assimilated Jewish family from Warsaw, Antoni Słonimski was a Polish poet, journalist, playwright, translator, and literary activist. The grandson of prominent religious thinker and writer rabbi Chaim Zelig Słonimski, he was a cofounder of the Skamander group of experimental poets and a frequent contributor to several periodicals, writing regular columns and reviews on theater, arts, and social satire. Słonimski spent World War II in exile in Paris and London, and served for several years in senior positions at UNESCO and the Polish Cultural Institute. Upon returning to Poland in the early 1950s, he was a leading member of the intelligentsia and head of the Union of Polish Writers, serving as a voice of criticism and liberalization. Although a victim of the wave of antisemitism that overtook Poland in 1968, Słonimski decided to stay in Poland. He was killed in an automobile accident in Warsaw.

Conversation with a Countryman
1922

An old Jew asked me near the Jaffa Gate:
"Is the Saxon Garden still there? The same as ever?

Is there a fountain? At the entrance from Czysta
    Street
In the old days confectioners had a shop there with
    water."

Everything is the way it was: the fountain and
    kiosks.
And Prince Poniatowski is still standing there."

"Poniatowski! The Polish army, as they used to say
    . . .
I don't know how it is now; it used to be good
    before.

I'm a little weak. But when I'm better

I want to travel; I'd like to live in Warsaw.

I even have a buyer here. As soon as I sell
    everything,
Maybe I'll have enough . . . But my son won't give
    me anything.

He's very educated; Levi's his name, too.
When I talk about Poland, he doesn't know a thing.

I talk to him, explain things as best I can:
'Warsaw's there after all!' He doesn't understand."

Translated by Harold B. Segel.

Other works by Słonimski: *Sonety* (1918); *Droga na Wschód* (1924); *Torpeda czasu* (1924); *Murzyn warszawski* (1928); *Dwa końce świata* (1937).

Antoni Słonimski

Jerusalem
1922

See the Mount of Olives and the Greek monastery.
Minarets and cupolas abound,
Squares of yellow houses like honeycomb.

The valley of Josephat, white, dry fields—
There in the dell, where it is azure and quiet,
Immobile, deep in the very depths, lies
The dead and sultry sea, golden Jericho.

That tree you see, that's the tree of Judah.
And those huge stones there—are Roman.
And there, where a red juniper shrub appears on the
    road,
Christ revealed himself to holy Magdalene.

You see this line of carriage, cars, and coaches?
Like a white road amid swirling dust, pious
    tourists
Travel to where far among the palm leaves
Sleeps the tiny earthen town of Nazareth.

And in this wild garden—here it's best—
I often sit a while, and leave with sadness;
Grass smells at noon, when sleep glues the eyes
    together;
Like in a village in Poland, flies buzz in Jerusalem.

Translated by Harold B. Segel.

Hillel Bavli

1893–1961

The American Hebrew poet Hillel Bavli was born in Lithuania and came to the United States in 1912. He received both a traditional religious education and a modern maskilic education. In the United States, he taught Hebrew in several cities on the East Coast. In 1917, he began teaching Hebrew language and literature at the Teachers Institute of the Jewish Theological Seminary, where he remained until his death. He was a central participant in the major Hebraist projects in the United States and worked to create bridges with Hebrew writers in the Land of Israel. He was known in particular for his lyric poetry.

Tefillah

1923

Oh my God, my God,
Mighty One of my existence,
have mercy on Your lost son
who has wandered from the ancestral path
and, exiled to cold and unfamiliar climes,
sought to be close to You,
but has not yet found You.

I know
that You are far beyond me,
elevated above my ken,
are You, my God.
Yet this I know too:
Somewhere,
in the hidden places,
You sit, waiting eternally
for the last of Your servants,
who strives,
faithfully,
to come into Your gates.

Favor me and have mercy on me,
Lord of the Winds,
and rip the veil from my eyes
so that I may see the shadows of Your glory!
For lost am I, wandering
in a vast and
alien land
and I know naught.
Like a sharp eyed spider,
I struggle in the web of darkness
I have woven for myself;

I flail, I scout out the path,
I seek escape,
but there is no escape.

Oh, my God, my God,
extend Your hand to me
and let Your mercy guide me.

Translated by Alan Mintz.

Other works by Bavli: *Shirim* (1938); *The Growth of Modern Hebrew Literature* (1939); *Aderet ha-shanim* (1955).

Uri Zvi Greenberg

In the Kingdom of the Cross

1923

[. . .]
The forest's black and dense; it grows out of the
    flatlands.
Such depths of grief, such terror out of Europe.
Dark and wild, dark and wild, the trees have heads
    of sorrow;
From their branches hang the bloody dead—still
    wounded.
All the faces of the heavenly dead are silver,
And the oil that moons pour out on minds is golden;
And if a voice shouts, "Pain!" the sound's a stone in
    water
And the sound of bodies praying—tears falling in a
    chasm.

I am the owl of that sad wood, the accusing-bird of
    Europe.
In the valleys of grief and fear, in blind midnights
    under crosses,
I want to raise a brother's plea to the Arab folk of
    Asia:
Poor though we may be, come lead us to the desert.
But my sheep are fearful, for the half moon is
    descending
Like a scythe against our throats.
So I, heart-of-the-world, complain at random. Oh,
    terror, and oh, Europe!
In the land of grief, its throats outstretched, the
    lamb lies,
And I wound-of-the-world, in Europe, spit blood
    upon the crosses—

(In the land of grief old men tremble, and the young
    whose heads are made of water.)

In the abyss, beneath the trees, two thousand years
    of burning silence,
The sort of poison the abyss accumulates.
Endured two thousand years—of silence and of
    blood, and no mouth ever spat against the poison.
And *I don't know what's wrong.*
Though there are books in which the Gentiles'
    murders have been written,
But there's nothing written there about our answers
    to the murders.

That forest of grief has grown; the trees are crowned
    with sorrow,
Dark and wild, and when the moon peers down,
    what terror.
And if a voice shouts, "Pain!" the sound's a stone in
    water.
And the bleeding of the dead's like dewdrops to the
    ocean.

Kingdom of the cross! Great Europe!

* * *

In the land of grief upon a sun-day, a black feast day
    in your honor,
I'll open up that forest and I'll show you all the trees
    where hang
My decaying dead.
Kingdom of the cross, be pleased.
Look and see my valleys:
The shepherds in a circle round the emptied wells;
Dead shepherds with their lambs' heads on their
    knees.

It has been long since there was water in those wells
    instead
Of execration.

* * *

[. . .]
Dress me in a broad Arab *abaya*, and toss a *tales*
    over my shoulder,
And the extinguished East flames up in my poor
    blood.
Take back the frock coat, the tie, and the patent-
    leather shoes
I bought in Europe.

Set me on a horse and command it to race with me
    to the desert.

Yield me my sands again. Farewell to the boule-
    vards. Let me have my sands of the desert.
There is such a people of naked bodies, bronzed
    youth under sun-brands.
(There is no bell there that hangs over heads. Only
    the planets.)
When one of those bronze young men opens his
    mouth in the spacious desert
And glows with love (at the time when the planets
    appear) and shouts his love to the planets,
There's an answering gush of blue-bloody water
    there at the seam of the desert:

                    LOVE

Translated by Leonard Wolf.

Shmuel Halkin

Russia
1923

Russia! If my faith in you were any less great
I might have said something different.
I might have complained: You have led us astray,
And seduced us young wandering gypsies.

Precious to us is each blow of your hand,
Though frightfully painful to bear.
Yet no matter how great the hurt or the shame,
We have come to you to declare:

To where could the oceans implore us
To go now, to what distant shores,
When glad Russian streets are before us?
To the end of our lives we are yours.

Until now we followed, unpledged to you,
Our wild birthright's star far and wide.
But now we have fallen in step with you,
Though of your kisses we die.

Translated by Hillel Halkin.

Moyshe-Leyb Halpern

In the Subway
1923

Daybreak.
Worn out from a night with wine
And womanly beauty,

I travel homeward.
While he, as if molded
from dirty clay and typhus-stained yellowness,
Travels the world, giving of his labor.
We sway, the two of us
In this house of iron.
Which carries us on tiny wheels.
Miles upon miles through the ground, a bleak portal
Beneath stones and earth.
We look at each other.
I—my eyes glazed over with sleep, through glasses,
And he—with tiny slits where eyes should be,
They evoke for me a bathhouse for women
Where once I stole (through the tiniest crack)
A peak inside.

We sway like this, the two of us.
I see him (as on a movie screen)
Yanking a horse from its stall,
Putting on a harness.
And riding above
An overfilled wagon,
I see a hunchbacked little man, sitting.
I ask him through the window:
—Dear father.
Where are you traveling, in this rain, at break of
    day?
He answers me: To the fair, my son.
To the fair.
I listen as the wheels begin to creak and rattle,
I am shouting, my nose pressed against the glass:
Go in peace, dear father.
He answers: Be well, my son.
His voice is muffled, as by a wall in the rain.
It seems my father is disguised
As a bear.
And I growl: Grrrrrrr!

We sway like this, the two of us.
He—the village with horse and stall,
And I—the town near the village
With a shul, a bath, and a tiny hammer
Which calls on shutters at break of day
Announcing the time to serve God.
He looks over my shoes,
Regretting, perhaps, the calf
He once sold
To buy his way here.
I look over the tiny bag
He clutches in his lap.

I hear my own voice
Praying faster and faster
So I may eat the wild strawberries with cream
Which stand waiting for me.
I glimpse a piece of pig's-meat
Crawling out of his bag
Crawling into my Shema Yisroel, as I recite,
And also a slice of cheese, which stinks,
And a stale piece of bread.
They rouse—as from a nightmare,
The Shmoneh Esrey
Which cowers in a corner and weeps.
The pig's-meat tilts wildly
Shouting into the prayers a song
Which I heard during a visit to the opera—
My prayers stretch apart
Like Jesus on the cross
And they begin their great lament: "My Lord, my
    Lord, why . . ."
Into their hands they take
The bread and the stinking cheese.
And all let out a howl in a chorus of hoarse voices
Like a pair of drunken peasants
Singing the Marseillaise and other songs of land and
    kin—
I realize that my veins are bursting.
A hand as hard and cold as iron
Hurls me upon a roof, where I stagger.
I listen below
As the bread, the cheese,
My Shema Yisroel, the pig's-meat,
And the Shmoneh Esrey
All make a big commotion, hunting down a ladder
So I can return to the world below—
But no such ladder is found.
I laugh from these heights
Until my tongue falls from my mouth in terror.
They think I've become a ghost
Doing devilish tricks like a circus clown
And each one down below is just as fearful
As I above.
Between earth and clouds.
They squeeze themselves into corners,
Each alone, and they cry
Like me, up here,
Between earth and clouds.

Translated by Julian Levinson.

Leyb Kvitko

Day and Night
1923

Day and night—
Shivering, we wait in bitter day
For moonlit night,
For the caressing moon.

Quivering, we wait in angry night—
For the sunlit day,
For the warming sun.

Day and night—
We must loom large within their eyes,
They bother with us so.

Small is what we are, so small—
Fear drags us to the earth,
As if we were fear's very own.

Where, then, we small ones,
Can we hide?
Where can we hide our full-grown grief?
Our grief?
Our love?
Our secrets?

Day and night—
We must loom large within their eyes,
They bother with us so.

Translated by Allen Mandelbaum and Harold Rabinowitz.

Leyb Kvitko

We're Laughing Our Heads Off
1923

We're laughing our heads off:
None of us wears a top-hat
We just go around with heads—or without heads—
But the Rabbi of Uman
Holds up a mirror to the sun.

We laugh our heads off
When a gang comes in,
When we run away like mice,
When only the rabbi in his top-hat,
His nose touching his clasped hands,
Knocked and knocks on the door marked "Danger";
When, with melancholy eyes,

He runs off to the Christians, the big cheeses,
Begging and grovelling like a dog.—
Hidden in our holes,
We put all our hope in him.

We laugh our heads off,
When he—the only one in a top-hat,
The only Jew in the street—
Takes those few good Christians
To the gang,
To wheedle a reprieve for us today,
Begging them to spare our life.

We laugh our heads off
When they tell him to stay outside,
To wait alone, to wait and wait
While danger stares him in the face.

When those riders see him,
First they trample his top-hat,
Then they flay him with their whips,
Just for fun!

When he's late and doesn't reappear,
And we are dying to know:—
Will they leave us in peace today,
Or are they going to begin at once?

From the holes and crevices,
Our young eyes are burning:
Probably he'll manage to wheedle a reprieve.
We're laughing our heads off:—
None of us wears a top-hat—
With heads—or without heads—we go around.—
But the Rabbi of Uman
Holds up a mirror to the sun.

Translated by Heather Valencia.

H. Leivick

Here Lives the Jewish People
1923

The towering life of the towering city
Is burning in white fires.
And in the streets of the Jewish East side
The whiteness of the fires burns even whiter.

I like to stroll in the burning frenzy of the Jewish
     East Side,
Squeezing through the crammed stands and
     pushcarts,

Breathing the smell and saltiness
Of a hot naked life.
And whenever, in the whiteness, before my eyes
    emerge
Bearded Jews, covered from head to toe
With long hanging gowns for girls and women;
Men or women with sick birds,
Looking up with craving, begging eyes
For a buyer, to offer him a lucky ticket;
Jews in wheelchairs,
Blind cripples, sunk deep in their own shoulders,
Who can see with their shoulders the color and size
Of a flung coin—
Then a hidden nostalgia awakens in me,
A nostalgia buried since childhood:
To be transformed into the limping beggar
Who used to hop from street to street in my
    hometown
(Luria was his name)
And knock with his crutch on sidewalks and
    thresholds.
Who knows, whether in this wheelchair before my
    eyes
Does not sit the beggar of my childhood nostalgia
Watching my amazement through blind eyelids?—
Then the world had no towers,
Yet was white as now,
Fiery and white as now.

I walk for hours in the streets of the Jewish East Side
And imagine in the fiery whiteness before my eyes
Fantastic gates, soaring columns,
Rising from all the dilapidated stands
Upward, to the far and empty New York sky.
Gates—on all their cornices
Glowing, sparkling signs, inscribed:
Here lives the Jewish people.
[. . .]
Silence. Midnight.
My childhood nostalgia cries in me.

Translated by Benjamin Harshav and Barbara Harshav.

H. Leivick

Unsatiated Passions
1923

Unsatiated passions want to be satiated,
Arms wish to be tired,

Lips look for merging,
Fingers long for cracking,
Green fires in the eyes are greening greener,
Like eyes of wolves in frozen fields,
Green eyes in frozen fields.

Where is he who should quell the passions?
Why doesn't he come? Why doesn't he come?
He promised, or didn't he promise?—
He did promise, he did promise.
Strained eyes—like pointed knives,
Strained eyes cut through all the windowpanes,
Strained eyes roam over the roads:
He who should come—why doesn't he come?
He did promise, he did promise.

Curtains in rooms—like wings torn apart,
Like torn-apart wings of slaughtered birds—
And the day is still bright, and the day is still gay—
Why doesn't it set? Why doesn't it set?
Thin fingers grow thinner,
Thin fingers freeze in freezing fields—
White beds—like freezing fields—
Blue fingers in freezing fields.

Translated by Benjamin Harshav and Barbara Harshav.

Esther Raab

My Heart Is with Your Dews, Homeland
1923

My heart is with your dews, homeland,
At night, above fields of nettles
And to the scent of cypresses and wet thistle
A hidden wing shall I spread out.
Soft sand-cradles are your roads
Spread out between fences of acacias,
As though across pure silk
Forever shall I move on them
Gripped by an unresolved spell,
And transparent skies whisper
Over darkness of a frozen sea of trees.

Translated by Anne Lapidus Lerner.

Esther Raab

Upon Your Nakedness a White Day Celebrates
1923

Upon your nakedness a white day celebrates,
You who are [so] poor and so rich,
A wall of mountains has frozen,
Transparent like a deceptive vision,
Attached to the horizon.
Noon. The vastnesses of your fields ignite
And your marrow totally revels and rises
Facing the white sky,
Like an endless screen
Stretched and trembling.
In the plain
A hill rises like a round breast
And its head a white grave covers;
And in the rubble of harvested fields
A lonely thornbush lies.
And it is when the eye tires
Of the streams of deceptive light
And is immersed in the green of the bluish
    thornbush,
As if in a pool of cool water.
You who are so poor with your reddening furrows
In the gold of the distance
With the ground of the wadis dry, white—
    How beautiful you are!

Translated by Anne Lapidus Lerner.

Zalman Shneour

Vilna
1923

Vilna, my great matriarch, an established Jewish
    city,
Jerusalem of the Exile, an ancient nation's consola-
    tion in the north!
This [poem] is your patched kerchief, like the roof
    of the old synagogue,
More exalted in the eyes of your great-grandchil-
    dren than gilded towers;
With your worn-out apron, embroidered with lions
    and crowns,
Looking like a *parokhet*,[1] you have wiped their tears
    more than once;

With your famous Purim honey-cookies and the
    Pesaḥ confiture
You have sweetened their troubles and entertained
    them with the eloquence of your authors.
Even those who drew your water were drawn from
    the source of great Torah scholars,
Every wall was suffused with tradition, with the
    fragrance of Shabbat cookery;
The Vilia [River, Neris in Lithuanian] warbles the
    tunes of "the Little Householder" on its bank;
The lindens will rhyme the visions of Mikhel the
    poet in their whispered prayer;
And Eliahu Hagaon and Montefiore, the
    philanthropist,
Greet you with mercy as you pass every Jewish
    threshold.

I remember your kindness from when I was young,
    the love of the daughters of your Jews,
Walking and dreaming with them in the shadow of
    your sown hills;
And the shooting of the cannon falling from your
    mountain at noon,
A thunderous, self-important, and encouraging
    sound: Be strong, citizens!
The day is long yet and the life struggle lasts until
    evening . . .
And that gloomy and wonderful tree on the tomb of
    the convert,
Whose figure is that of a huge mourner, thrusting
    out his hands to clap them;
In a moment it will release its sigh and wrap itself in
    increasing pain.
The Strashun Library—a great and petrified brain,
    which collected
The thoughts of a scattered and scattering nation,
    making them one;
Like the bones in the Valley of Ezekiel it raises them
    in hosts and makes them live.
The minds that gave birth to them are already ex-
    tinct, and it moves on and camps on its own
Preserving the thought of an eternal people, in the
    language of God.

I remember the figure of your leaders, with hand-
    some beards and high foreheads,
Pale majesty from the generation of the learned still
    gleams on their tranquil faces,
They listen and nod their bald heads at the great
    and secret things

That hasty Jewish lads prophesy about the future of
  the Russian peasant.
And your beggars who pull at the hems of every new
  face,
As if he were a rich uncle returning from distant
  places, plotting
To deprive them of their estate, and they protest and
  demand by right:
May everyone passing by in the street judge, and
  heaven and earth bear witness . . .
And your smelly and tasty apples, when autumn
  comes, which are sold
With cries of victory, like the preserved wine of
  Spain.
And boiled beans and chickpeas, yellow sold from
  baskets in the alleys,
And you might believe—"It's a boy," the faithful city
  will not cease celebrating,
And everyone who wishes will approach and taste
  from the ceremonial meal for a farthing.
And the steamboat is remembered fondly, laboring
And striving in the current of the Vilia and stopping
  at a sandbank every time;
Clamoring with Jews longing for their wives in sum-
  mer homes,
And the Sabbath eve is approaching, hot and
  steamy. Time is pressing . . .
The captain sends an angry, scolding face from his
  seat on high:
Sit, merciful ones, and don't get excited, lest my
  boat keel over onto its side!

[. . .] I loved Troki, a marvelous town, behind your
  mountains,
Seven great rivers around it, in which you can look
  and never be sated with its beauty;
There the Karaites—our lowly step-brothers,
Jews and not Jews. With their bulging and strange
  eyes
They look and do not recognize us . . .
They are Ruth to their daughters, Moabite and
  tanned, but they will not go
After the sons of Boaz and his grandsons. Hebrew
  prayers are on their lips,
And their black eyes ambush the sons of the locals.
Sometimes you go to hear their prayer in their pure
  synagogue:
Prolonged singing like weeping, until departure of
  the sorrowful soul,

Sucking, and monotonous and the dying accent of a
  Yemenite;
The voice of a limb torn from the people of the
  Lord, it quivers in pain,
It can neither live nor die, and how will it be
  cured?
But an idea flashes like lightning and ancient beauty
  straightens you:
If this withered limb yearns—how deep is the life in
  the body?
If this snipped off twig blossoms—the vine will not
  hope in vain.

In the morning light, the light of Lithuania, gray
  and green, I sometimes roam
In the twisting city alleys to see Jewish lads;
I watch them as they hurry to their heder, with soft
  faces and sad eyes.
From devastating poverty delicacy still looks out
  with bluish veins—
Sons of a king from the land of Judah, who were
  captured among yellowish gentiles,
They are pale and thin and sick like date
  seedlings,
Uprooted from their homeland and planted in the
  swamps of Polesia.[2]
Fearful, they rush to the heder, where their soul will
  seek, unwittingly,
The spark of the Galilean sun, which is as if hidden
  among the black letters:
They will hear something like the whisper of
  sheaves when they page through the book,
And they will smell the fragrance of the sea and the
  mountains in forgotten tales.

I pitied the old Jews, when they meet on wandering
  paths
And against their will they bare their good and
  miserable head, as they pass
Ostra-Brama,[3] the holy place of the proud gentiles.
Their neck bends and a bitter, hidden insult ferments in their depressed heart,
As if they were passing between the columns of
  shame. . . . Every day they go past,
And the mocking gaze of the ruling Catholics accompanies them from a distance,
And the enemy's holy place frightens them and stabs
  them from the height of the gate
With shining alien silver and the horror of gilded
  statues.

And when a storm of emotion overcomes you, and
  you flee to your dark room,
And there waking nights await you and dreams af-
  flict your sleep;
With a cross in his hand the legislator dances . . .
  Jews weep,
And the tablets of testimony collapse like mountains
  on panicked nations . . .
With the fogs of morning you go out like a sick man
  arising from his fever,
And the night visions evaporate like the vapor of
  wine, wavering before you in space.
And you are drawn to the iron tracks that cross the
  heart of this city,
The paths twist and wink in their cold laughter until
  there is no afterward;
Tu-tu . . . the train whistles in the distance full of
  steam and hidden motions.
How attractive the sound is, sucking you in, sucking
  till you weep tears of pity:
—Why are you bent over, young man, and what are
  you looking for in this remote city?—
In whose throat is the height of charity, and the
  whip of cruel policemen in her hand,
The honor of the Torah floats above her head, the
  shame of servitude beneath her.
Your brothers here are happy with their lot and the
  sigh of pleasures—their sigh,
They warm themselves in the mud of their heritage, praying with their mouths for the
  redeemer,
And fearing his advent in their hearts, lest he come
  and truly shock them.
Rise, you, and tear the veil of lies from the Jerusalem
  of Exile,
And if your soul rises to the occasion—flee, flee,
  young man, do not tarry! [. . .]

The urge to travel quivered within you and bore you
  up and your imagination
As a sea-wind bears a light sailboat;
You returned to wander in the streets and were like
  a stranger in your own eyes,
A passerby. . . . And the city—a great hotel, and its
  inhabitants, servants,
But there everything is good, everything is exalted. . . . And you didn't know where "there" is.
Suddenly something will meet you, coming in the
  wind to make your nostrils quiver:

Breathe in! . . . The smell of fish, peppery and hot,
  the gefilte fish of Sabbath,
Or the prayer shawls of elder worshipers, with black
  and white stripes,
Flickering in the window of a synagogue; or a Jewish tailor, listen,
Sounding the melodies of Yom Kippur, and the sewing machine hums beneath him.
And a kind of wave of old traditions floods you,
  stimulating and pleasant,
And a voice of darkness comes from your abyss and
  drips on your pain like oil:
Why this rush to wander and graze on visions in
  foreign parts!
You will not find, you will never find what you
  neglected here among us;
Your eyes are to the distant stars and happiness rolls
  at your feet.
Marry a woman, in your youth, marry a Hebrew
  woman as is ordained,
She will have your mother's deep eyes, a hidden fire
  with sweet weariness—
This, the intoxication of the ancient Light of the
  East, will not fade, until now . . .
And you, too, will be rooted on the soft and indul-
  gent rot of your forefathers.
And you know that this fertilizing rot is good for the
  healthy separation
From mighty boulders and the storms and the cur-
  rents tumbling into chasms.
Like a coral on the floor of the sea, everyone is on
  his brother, and everyone on his fathers,
Yes this nation will grow and yes, you, too, will rise
  and flourish,
And you will climb to unknown heights, reddish
  and solid,
Until you go out into the air of the world and are
  revealed to those avid for precious things;
Sit here, here you will grow . . . Do not flee! . . .

[. . .] How shall I pity you, old and crushed
  mother, poor, storm-tossed!
Who tore your broad apron, who bared your head,
  good woman?
Tangled gray hair peeks out and rises like smoke
From beneath your wig, pushed to the side over
  your ear with an insult,—
And the color of the sky whitens, and reddens with
  the burning of villages.

You shared in the prayer for Jerusalem, and you will
 also share in her fate:
Horrors of death and battle enveloped you, with
 their blood the wounded muddied
The waters of the Vilia, which play and make
 pebbles speak;
Legions swept over you, trampled you, and cannon
 carriages, and their stumbling horses,
Whinnied over their troughs in your houses of
 study;
And the weeping of refugees and the tumult with
 shouts of pillage
Overcame the music of psalms and those who studied Mishnayot with love.
Who could believe that you would see your orphans
 wrap themselves in hunger
And you would not slice bread for them or comfort
 them in your bosom?
And who prophesied, that you, so charitable, would
 withhold your mercy
From old people and children who freeze in the
 streets before your eyes?
Indeed sometimes in your poverty and hunger you
 appeared to be evil from a distance,
Their eyes brought your grandchildren down, and
 you and they too were ashamed.

I did not like comforters and comfort before their
 time,
I am not a man of peace; but this great sorrow of
 yours overcame me.
Thus I will pray in a whisper when I fear to hear
 your moan:
"Who will send a consoler to you, grandmother, an
 emissary from the land of peace,
And will go up to the top of the mountain of the
 temple, when the morning reddens towers,
And prophesy to the beauty of your valleys in a new,
 strong voice, and will cry out:
Be comforted, be comforted my people, and you,
 motherly city, be comforted!
Put a new kerchief on your head, tighten your waxed
 apron,
This is the dress of a heroic woman. . . . And mix
 the Purim sweets
And bake all the holiday cakes so famous in
 Lithuania,
And be a support for the hearts of your rejected
 ones—from far and near,

Who return to deal kindly with your dust and to
 wash their feet in your river.
Tell the owners of musical instruments to fix broken
 strings
Polish cymbals and drums, repair whistles.
Give an order to the multitude of beadles to open all
 the synagogues
Spread out embroidered curtains, put a long wick in
 the Eternal Light,
And let the pure raise their voices and trill:
 Welcome!
Let the chestnut trees clap hands on your moun-
 tains, and the dew,
Like tears among the wrinkles on your face—valleys
 and hills—let them glow,
See, your sons and grandsons who return, how
 many and different they are:
With long beards and with shaven side-locks, but
 your hidden grace
Will shine in all their eyelashes, and the milk of
 your wisdom on their lip;
In the sanctuary of the old synagogue, decorated
 with ancient carvings,
They will declaim their public prayer, the song of a
 new dawn,
And new hopes will ring in it for you and for all your
 seed forever!"

NOTES
1. [The curtain on the Holy Ark.—Eds.]
2. [A Belarusian-Ukrainian forest and marsh area.—Eds.]
3. [The Gate of Dawn, a city gate of Vilna.—Eds.]

Translated by Jeffrey M. Green.

Yisroel Shtern

1894–1942

Born in poverty in the shtetl of Ostrolenka, Poland,
Yisroel Shtern was a Yiddish poet and journalist.
Shtern maintained a religious lifestyle from youth into
adulthood, attending prominent yeshivas in Slobodka
and Łomża. After a brief stint in Vienna, Shtern settled
in Warsaw, where he associated with the local *musar*
movement and with Breslov Hasidism. In Warsaw, he
published articles and poetry in a wide variety of modernist literary journals and in a range of Bundist and
Zionist newspapers. His poetry was noted for its melancholy, gloom, and existential dread as it dealt with
themes of death, economic distress, and, paradoxi-

cally, the ultimate redemption of mankind. Shtern's *Shpitol lider* (Hospital Poems), published in a Warsaw journal in 1923, drew particular praise for its vision of illness, deep religious faith, and the slow passage of time. Shtern figures prominently in the Warsaw ghetto memoirs of Rokhl Oyerbakh, who describes how the poet continued to write even under most despairing conditions. He was murdered at the Treblinka death camp.

Springtime in the Hospital
1923

I

Is it any wonder that the sick are so pure and tender,
gazing across vast distances, seeing things that no
    one else does,
staying up at night, and smiling in the darkness,
as they caress their beds with the joy of having
    solved a mystery?

Is it any wonder that the sick arise from napping
rich and perfumed (like a seed awakening from
    sleep in spring),
lie fresh in quiet wards, and listen when a fly knocks
on their headboards, and someone calls them by
    name?

Is it any wonder that the sick accept their
    consecration
and wait the days out gladly, as one separates a tithe
. . .—
Is it any wonder—when the Ineffable walks in the
    hospital air,
as once His Spirit moved upon the waters of
    creation!

II

Where does the love come from, that goes like a
    doctor
from bed to bed, to incline an ear and listen
while the ward awakens like a frightened city
as cries go up from every gate?

And where does the love come from that hangs like a
    lamp
that rouses each lone dreamer from his sleep
until everyone is sitting up, white shapes in
    stillness,

looking—thinking—when suddenly—a sob takes
    hold?

And if the sick are close to one another
like the separate rays from one great source of grace,
is this not because, in this coarse and coarsened
    world,
they possess the finest city of them all?

III

For a city looks its best in the final, bloody clots
of day, as the shop doors fold up like quiet hands.
The market opens tenderly in darkness; for the first
    time it looks upwards.
In the sky someone lies faint in a bed of white and
    burns.

Sidewalks hide their faces and go their secret ways.
Whoever walks feels sick at heart and scrapes along
    the speechless walls,
mothers with fearful fingers test their young for
    fever,
and buildings hang their heads. The city mourns,
    lost in a foreign land,

looks for home, looks there, there where mountains
    grow in blood,
and thinks, for Day it's all right, far above, but I'm
    still in the Valley.

But what do you know, when days flow by like water
    in the twilight—
What do you know out on the street what a day
    means in the hospital?

IV

What do you know of how the early mornings
    sprout, grow upwards, bloom
into shape, and shine sadly red, like a rosy rash?
Do you see the night's beginning cling to the healthy
    face
of the mountains and grow large, as a cyst swells on
    the cheek?

What do you know out on the street of how the sun
    tastes
and how the miracle of spring looks when a knife
    strolls
deep within you (as one strolls through heavy-laden
    orchards—

handfuls of red cherries) and eagerly rips ulcers out?

What do you know out on the street of nights when blood
pours freely as a king through every gate of skin,
and the sky lies in the window, blue as spleen, already spent,
and the moon stands still—great death's white mask?

V

What do you know out on the street, what a day is in the hospital?
Sick, you must not go too far, you take your walks— inside yourself,
as in a garden. Worked over like a garden bed. All the trees
storm-damaged, overturned, stones under every step.

The days were strewn as by a peasant's ample fist,
and the sower sang, "The soil is ours, free like the plants
we'll grow!" The plough sinks deep in body and soul—why then have dogs
dragged the days out once again while bones grow in the fields?

You sit yourself on the remainder of the day as on a tree stump.
You look into the darkness: who's at fault? That's it—the caretaker's gone.
You fall exhausted in your sickbed . . . when your minder wakes you to drink tea:
Hey sleepyhead—where are you? You say: alone, here in the garden.

VI

Here the forms of loneliness all smell like hay, like grass in evening shadows.
Here the people live and grow as blue as trees when sunlight dies.
Here tired strangers come like winds across the fields at twilight
and go like the songs of peasants as they tie up the final sheaves . . .

Here hearts bend down and fall like days at sunset.
Yet, here the sunset's beautiful, and one falls in satin darkness.

Everyone turns into distance, every person is a stillness,
and the stillness hurts so much: here it's always time for prayers at end of day.—

They always pray, the ones who face the end. From there
white sadness flows into the world as from the early stars.
It turns so cold, uncertain: where? Who? Then someone writes
in golden letters on a cloud: Come! You will belong to me!—

VII

And while the day's red youth runs out and stains
the borders of the west, his rosy body dies painfully,
the distance holds its breath and listens to his burning will and testament—
the beds begin to tremble—"Someone there is calling us—but who?"

While the final hour burns out across the emptiness of the horizon,
the veins turn blue in the slender hands of streams and mountains:
Everyone takes it to heart as the night comes for her inheritance—
The sick wander half-asleep, ". . . someone's coming . . . who is it asks for us?"

And while the heiress-night is homesick and lingers in an avenue of trees,
or runs, madly drumming on the windowpanes, to grip the walls of houses,
the world outside dons sack-cloth, no one can go on without the day,—
and the eyes of the sick turn over: "Prepare to leave . . . to whom?"

VIII

As they run through ample tracts of heaven—for where else do stars run?—
those lamenting carry news—"You tender and endangered ones,
you've known me a long time; imagined me at length on your last shore,
you're all my mirrors, but the face is always mine.

You've looked on stones and dust, reflected back the
    rat-race,
the smooth surface laughing along with the rush of
    spaces;
but once the haste had faded, a sadness used to veil
    your quiet glass,
and you backed into the polished abyss.

You stood by the walls, looking back,—into your-
    selves—into your own
reflecting depths, and from your silence streamed
    forth
sorrow on to everything—so you hurt me,
you're all my mirrors, I your final form."

IX

One lies there, listening: something's moving be-
    tween the steps and the hospital roof.
One tries to go along, as darkly and as lightly as a
    star moves,
for example, stolen out of time, and time lags far
    behind.
(Here the bodies are washed with gasoline like rusty
    watches . . .)

Time bends down, listens: someone in the long
    ward hovers over her,
kindly visits the sick who cough, who cry, who spit,
the high ceiling grows yet higher, white walls wait:
    it's going to happen.
The doors are shut like the eyes of someone gripped
    by a mighty thought.

The night sits in concealment, knowing she's the
    last,
now and then out of the dark rises a heavy head, to
    look towards the door:
it's not my wife yet—not my child yet—where are
    they—it's so late—
the one who moves in silence calls: it's time—to
    come to me.

X

I've seen, poor brothers, your poor way,
You've gone, like winter goes through fields,
Your arms hanging heavy like the ice-covered
    branches,
and I've gone after you, like winter goes through
    fields.

The day hurt white and far: you were snow-covered
    villages,
the night howled deep within itself—a homeless
    dog.
While I, a stranger passing through your fields,
    bloomed with them;
stones grew up over me, and like your grass
    I froze.

And as the first mild hour arrives like the first
    swallow,
the second glitters in a small, white bed, and the
    third has brightly sounded:
I'm rich—I'm no more poor than you:
Now I'm radiance, now I'm sadness, I'm springtime
    in the hospital.

Translated by Jon Levitow.

Other works by Shtern: *Lider un eseyen* (1955).

David Vogel

I Saw My Father Drowning
1923

I saw my father drowning
In surging days.
His weak hand gave a last white flutter
In the distance—
And he was gone.

I kept on alone
Along the shore,
A boy still,
With small, thin legs,
And have grown as far as this.

And now I am my father,
And all those waves
Have broken over me,
And left my soul numb.

But all I held dear
Have gone into the wilderness
And I can stretch out a hand to no one.

I am happy to rest
In the black cradle of night,
Under the sky's canopy,
Studded with silver.

Translated by A. C. Jacobs.

David Vogel

When Night Draws Near
1923

When night draws near your window, come to him
naked.

Softly will he ripple and darken round your still
beauty, touching the tips of your breasts.

I shall stand with him there, a stray wanderer, and
silently we shall yearn: come into our dark.

And let your two eyes travel before us to light the
way for me and my friend.

Translated by T. Carmi.

David Vogel

With Gentle Fingers
1923

With gentle fingers
The rain is softly
Playing sad melodies
On the black instrument of night.

We are sitting in the darkness,
Each in his own house
(The children have fallen asleep)
Listening quietly to the rain
Telling our sorrow.

For we have no more words.
Our feet have been leadened
By day.
There is no dancing
Left in them.

Translated by A. C. Jacobs.

Izi Charik

1898-1937

Izi Charik was one the foremost Soviet Yiddish poets
of his generation, noted for his ardent, if sometimes
ambivalent, revolutionary zeal and ability to create
dynamic verse in a wide variety of poetic styles. Rising
to prominence at an early age, Charik edited many
Soviet Yiddish literary journals in Moscow and Minsk,
produced several widely read collections of poetry,
and rapidly climbed the ranks in the Communist
Party leadership in the Belorussian Soviet Socialist
Republic. By the late 1930s, many of Charik's works
were integrated into the Yiddish-language schools in
Belorussia, and the writer had achieved a kind of ce-
lebrity status among certain sections of the republic's
Yiddish-speaking youth. At the same time, in 1937,
Charik fell victim to the region's particularly brutal
Stalinist purges.

Shtetl
1924

1

A visitor came to the *shtetl*,
A stranger, with unrest in his step . . .
No-one recognized his unrest. No-one asked him:
"Stranger, are you weary?"

Across the blue sky the evening drew its curtain.
The stillness wept for someone who was lost.
Shops had long since closed, and there was no-one
Taking the road for home . . .

Till late at night the stranger walked alone
Around the deserted streets, until he came
To the last shabby dwelling of the *shtetl*.
He neither begged: "Let me in!" nor even paused.

He heard, and then could hear no more
The *shtetl* lying in despair behind the fence . . .
"Good!" he said: "Let it burn!"
He hardened his heart, and walked away.

Until dawn he heard the hot winds moaning
Full of fire, lamenting with the *shtetl* . . .
The stranger looked back one last time.
He walked away. And morning came.

2

Blown by the wind, a lingering pall of smoke
Covers my *shtetl*. O, how long,
How long, must I implore you?
Shtetl, disappear.

Dying you lie there still upon the road,
Between blue highways, and you can't depart.
Alas for all those aged ancestors
Who did not stop the beating of your heart,

But left you waiting, silent, there!
Oh, that a heavy wheel would rumble over you
Churning you up, crushing your ailing heart,
Turning and grinding . . .

I know: your days are numbered, and each day
Is raw and red with suffering.
Were I a believer, I would carve
A crucifix, to guard you as you die.

3

A harmonica plays in a courtyard somewhere,
Then fades behind cold walls,—
I long to remember what once was—
 But cannot recall.

Shtetl, *shtetl*, silent, mournful,
All your roofs abandoned and alone,
Sometimes, when I stand on the very highest wall,
The sound of your dry weeping reaches me.

When I first left your streets behind,
My fiery youth I held still in my hands,
I believed that you must never be forgotten,
But should always follow me to foreign lands.

Clutching my whole life in my arms,
Behind the cart, I shuffled on my way.
The city took me up to its highest storeys,
Led me to the window. Told me: "Stay!"

It's good to stand remembering by the window,
Then calmly to dismiss you from the scene . . .
Hearing the harmonica still playing;
Fading away, as though it had never been.

4

Night of all blue nights,
Restless like all nights, and still.
This night's raw pain I cannot vanquish—
 Ethereal, I rise up, and float away.

A sky. A lunatic moon
Trembles with fear and struggles violently.
My heart is torn. It speaks. Like a thousand flutter-
 ing flags
My yearning struggles to break free.

On such a night I cannot come to rest;
I am pulled upwards, lost and alone I spin,
Mother, mother, see, your son is mad,

Watch your blue son whirling in the wind . . .

I crane my neck, with thirsty eyes I peer,
And staring down I try to see:
There once were *shtetls* nestling here
In quiet rest, with peaceful bread and salt.

I helped to destroy them every one,
Set them ablaze and sent them up in smoke . . .
Now I hear the trembling of the stars,
As I am carried upwards through the air.

Translated by Heather Valencia.

Other works by Charik: *Af der erd* (1926); *Mit layb un lebn* (1928); *Kaylekhdike vokhn* (1929).

Jacob Israël de Haan
1881–1924

The Dutch-born poet, novelist, and journalist Jacob Israël de Haan was raised in a traditional Jewish home but abandoned Orthodox practice as a young man. In 1904, while teaching at an elementary school in Amsterdam, he published *Pijpelijntjes*, an autobiographical novel about a homosexual affair between two students. In 1907, he married a non-Jewish woman, but the marriage was platonic and they separated in 1919 without ever divorcing. Before this, however, he found his way back to Orthodoxy, and religious themes became prominent in his poetry. He joined the Mizrachi movement and settled in Jerusalem in 1919, but soon cast his lot with the ultra-Orthodox, anti-Zionist Agudah, for which he became a prominent spokesman. He was assassinated by secular Zionists in 1924, the first political murder in the Yishuv. Arnold Zweig published a novel, *De Vriendt Goes Home*, in 1932, based on his life.

All Is God's
1924

Man has separated lust and sorrow.
But God holds them together like day and night.
I know lust. I know intense suffering.
I praise God's one name.

Translated by David Soeterndorp.

Other works by de Haan: *Pathologieën* (1908); *Kwatrijnen* (1924); *Verzamelde gedichten*, 2 vols. (1952).

Jacob Israël de Haan

God's Gifts
1924

My most pious songs have I written
On rising from my sinful bed.
God has given me a wealth of sins,
And God alone has saved me from my sins.

Translated by David Soeterndorp.

Jacob Israël de Haan

Unity
1924

When God's holy law is read out
Do you think I forget one bold lust?
And enjoying each lust with fearing,
Do you think I know not God's law?

Translated by David Soeterndorp.

Alter-Sholem Kacyzne

Midos
1924

A Jewish Wedding
Deep in fields the klezmers can be heard
Driving horses foaming at the mouth,
Relatives, both poor and rich, arrive
To Reb Sane's daughter's wedding feast. [. . .]

But from a room where children's laughter reigns,
There suddenly is heard a scream of fear:
Shloymeles and Moysheles come running
Wide-eyed, to their trembling fathers' arms.

"Tell us what has happened, children dear!
Don't all scream at once, let Yankl speak":
"Daddy, Moyshe-Hersh, Reb Dovid's boy, he—
Fell down from the bench like he was dead!"

Reb Dovid runs in quickly and then soon
A noisy crowd is pressing at the door.
Attempts are made to help the fainted boy,
It seems, alas, he cannot be revived. [. . .]

Before the lifeless body Dovid asks:
"Am I now punished for my sinful deeds?"

The crowd moves back to show him its respect
When Khaye-Hindele enters at the door.

Painfully she drags her feet along.
The burden of her age—a hundred years.
"Jews, be still! I say: it's no one's sin.
The story is both beautiful and strange!

Dovid, take the boy out to the street
And never cross the threshold here again!
The rest of you go back to wedding-dance:
The riddle of my words will soon be clear.

Why stand you there in silence—go, be gay!
All is well—the stricken lad is safe.
For you Reb Sane's house brings joy and luck.
For Dovid from Opatow? Hear me out! [. . .]

This house is for Opatowers a curse,
Since many years ago there dwelt in here,
Reb Motele, the martyr of Opatow
A wealthy man, both generous and wise. [. . .]

Then livelihood was plentiful for Jews.
But how can Jewish comfort last for long?
A blood-libel arose one evil spring:
A peasant's little boy had disappeared.

'You seek the little boy with flaxen hair?
I saw two Jews who whispered right nearby . . .'
The libel-devil, hairy, ugly beast,
Lurks in lofts and stables once again!

At Sunday market: see his naked dance!
See him leap to tavern and to church!
Peasants will not plow their lands this year—
They'll take revenge upon the Yids instead.

At Motele's at midnight Jews convene.
The wealthy man speaks calmly, like a father:
'If I do not erase this libel soon,
My name is not Reb Motl of Opatow!'

His young white horses carry him at dawn,
In sable coat and snow-white flowing beard,
Swiftly to the Duke, who called him friend,
And often turned to Motye for advice.

The Duke sends down his footmen—'See who's
      there.'
Hears: 'Motele, the rich man from Opatow'
And bellows down: 'You murderer, you Jew!
Leave my threshold or I'll have you flogged!'
      [. . .]

The aged intercessor bows his head,
His hand, in search of something firm to hold,
Blindly grasps a stinging-nettle branch;
He pulls it down to make it whip his face.

Two young white horses quietly plod on,
An old Jew in the coach tears out his hair.
His red and swollen eyes seek any help
That might yet come from off some village path.

'Gentlemen who drink there in the inn:
To innocents you must not raise your knives!
Pan Motye throws his fortune to you now!
See his golden ducats freely flow!'

'Let Motye's ducats fall like golden rain,
They grew in soil he watered with our blood!
Christians, Maciej asks you, do we dare,
Sacrifice more children to the Jews?'

All eyes are turned to Motye as he stands
Poised upon his wagon at his porch.
His brows are dark, his mouth is strangely still.
His finger makes the sign: there is a God!

'Please, Reb Motye, save us from the knife!
Save us from the peasants' Easter wrath!'
From beneath his brows comes the reply:
'My shoulders will protect you like a wall!'

Passover and Easter—the same day!
Jews are at a loss—what shall we do?
The streets now show no sign of Jewish life.
The peasants crowd the market, filled with hate.

The church-bells ring a summons to the town,
Announcing that the violence may start.
Peasants walk the streets with daggers drawn,
To massacre the Jews to the last man.

In cellars and in attics full of dust
Already sensing knives against their throats,
Jews lie in wait like calves before the kill,
They do not cry or weep or even pray.

'Hand us now the murderer, you Jews!
Can't you see—for you the game is lost!
We'll give him what he's owed, then we'll go home,
If not—then all of you will have to pay!'

Reb Motele stands at his open door.
His shining face inspires awe and dread:
'You do not find the murderer you seek?
The murderer was I—I killed the boy!'

Then Maciej blinks his tiny eyes and smiles
And laughs his raucous laugh like drums of tin:
'Pan Motele, I thought so all along—
Come inside the house and meet your fate!'

Then winks Maciej to this one and to that,
And shapes his face into an evil smile.
Together he and Motele go in,
Alone he comes outside with bloody knife.

The peasant mob is suddenly afraid
And silently departs, as if midweek.
Beside his bloody bed Reb Motye's kin
Wail and tear their faces with their nails.

'Cover up my bloody entrails, torn apart . . .
Depart this house and let me die alone.
These walls, who see it all, shall be a curse
Upon Opatow's children for all time!'

And then at last Reb Motye's eyes were closed,
His face a death-mask paler than the sheets. . . .
Women! Do not weep—there is a God!
Jews still live and dance at weddings too!

Let the klezmers play the saddest tunes,
For Jewish tears are remedies that heal.
And let the martyr's ancient curse redeem
Bride and groom from sorrow in their lives."

Translated by Solon Beinfeld.

Izi Charik

Bread
1925

My steps are set down stiffly
on tired, empty paths.
This morning a little town of Jews
called me "Anti-Semite!"

All of them in wrinkles and in rags
out there pointing at me:
"Him! That guy! We know him—and his parents!
He's estranged from us completely!

"You feel like going up to him and saying
'Listen, buddy, there's such blight
If you depressed all of us
You'd be well within your rights.

You can't live here—can't die, in this shtetl.

You've been here before yourself.
Tell us—who will be our savior?
Who will keep our heads in check?'"

I looked at them—dead and empty,
nothing but beards, beards, beards, all dead.
I said, "Enough emptiness, settledness!
From the earth, to the earth—if not, then. . . ."

The town began heatedly shouting.
Every step and word—a slashing stroke.
I don't know why a town of Jews
called me Anti-Semite.

Translated by Zackary Sholem Berger.

Alter-Sholem Kacyzne

Screams in Ukraine
1925

How can it be told in simple, quiet words?
How can you gloss over the sharp outcry
So that people will listen to it and be silent,
With mute eyes, even without a sigh?
Without a sigh, since every sigh is empty,
An empty stalk in a field full of sorrows.

Today the sun will rise and tomorrow it will shine
And peer into the window of Reb Nokhemke.
It will look elsewhere too, where gloom strides on
    velvet,
Where mute stillness reigns, after screams in
    Ukraine.
After screams in Ukraine the family grows sparser,
Reb Nokhem remains alone—and with him, his
    daughter Brokhe.

They see each other seldom, they live like strangers.
She sits in her little room and combs her long hair.
He only knocks at her door, with fear and caution,
To ask for a clean shirt to go to the bathhouse.
"You needn't be angry, a Jew must remember—
As long as a spark still glows—you must keep clean!"

The father's eyes are red, from poring over sacred
    texts,
Hers are pale from darting to the ceiling.
They exude chaos and a bright emptiness.
Her father's words make them darken, like empty
    graves—

Two empty graves where dogs have dragged away
    the bodies,
Hands and feet torn off and carried off the devil
    knows where.

If some ordinary man had spoken and not her quiet
    father,
Brokhe would have rushed at him with her
    grievance.
Brokhe would have reawakened the screams in
    Ukraine:
"Tell me! What is the use of the world when your
    soul is in rags,
Patched till the grave with a big yellow lie!"
Her father's eyes are red, and Brokhe remained
    silent.

Silent, hidden in her humpbacked anger.
She can no longer go out to nearby places.
The glances of the everyday housewives stab her:
"How can a girl not feel shame for her calamity?
A calamity, for us all—it missed no one!
But the world is the world—you find a way. . . ."

A doctor from America, a specialist, a smooth talker,
Rummaged in attics and crawled into cellars,
Persuaded her father, while Brokhe was hiding.
She won't, she insists, join the transport to Warsaw,
"To Warsaw with girls crammed like geese in the
    rail-cars?
No, doctor, no! A girl without shame is undeserving
    of pity!"

In Warsaw stands a house some seven stories high,
With ninety-nine rooms, with seven hundred beds.
And the girls with the numbers and matrons with
    the tags—
They are picked out like worm-eaten peas,
Selected and noted and written down:
Here is your place—here's a cot and a number.

Dozens of doctors, thank God all are Jews.
White coats, bald pates and eyeglasses glisten.
Bellowing as at slaughter, weeping as on the Day of
    Atonement—
Jewish blood is flowing from the glossy pincers,
The glossy pincers in the maidenly entrails
Where the fruit of Ukrainian seed is ripped out.

Your Jewishness be praised, your learned sincerity,
Your skills be praised for making what is impure
    kosher,

We are used to blood, so let it run, no matter,
As long as the burned-in sign can be washed out
The burned-in stigma that tarnishes our honor.
Our honor is lost, but we can live without it.

Who is fated to live can live without it.
The pain is transient and the shame is forgettable.
But there are souls who wander in the alleys,
And drag their hunchbacked bodies like trash-bins.
The bodies are superfluous, the honor is broken . . .
Reb Nokhem sits in silence. In the other
    room—Brokhe.

What does the sad father seek in his prayer book?
Why does he sway like a graveyard tree in the wind?
A chant on the fifth note, a sigh at the octave,
But the chant coils smoothly and without
    interruption
Smooth and unending like the walls of a deep well.
It falls and falls and falls and finds no bottom.

The clock finished coughing and struck twelve
    o'clock.
The lamp flares up and rejoices in its dying.
Only then does the door to Brokhe's room open,
Her hair let down, her eyes glowing wolf-like.
Her eyes glow wolf-like at her studying father.
Does he feel her steps? Will he hear her coming?

Her father did sense her. He turned to the side,
Fixing his tearless eyes on Brokhe.
He kissed the prayer book, bent back a page
And prepared himself for the tragedy whose time
    has come.
Timely and expected, its arrival has sounded.
The wine has fermented in its goatskin sack.

Brokhe came in, wearing her nightclothes
With fires in the window-eyes of her skull.
And Brokhe spoke up: "Oh father, let me die.
With earth and spade put out the fire of my shame.
The fire of my shame, and the rage of my anger."
And Nokhem murmured: "You are right, my
    daughter!"

And Nokhem murmured—the weak and sickly old
    man
Lowered his head and dipped it into the Psalms.

So how can it be told in words, simple and quiet?
How the young day grew frightened from the
    murmurs,

Frightened from the sounds of mouths bursting
    open:
"Reb Nokhem's daughter has hanged herself from a
    sheet!"

The sun shines today and tomorrow it will shine.
From the past resound eerily the screams in
    Ukraine!

Translated by Solon Beinfeld.

Dovid Knut

1900–1955

A native of Kishinev (Chişinău, in present-day Moldova), Dovid Knut (pseudonym of David Mironovich Fiksman) was a poet, short-story writer, and journalist in the Russian language. Knut spent most of his life in Paris, working as a cultural activist and writer among other odd jobs in that city. There he published five collections of poetry that were well received by critics—including one sympathetic, if critical, review by Vladimir Nabokov—and noted for their biblical imagery and vibrant use of language in the "southern" Russian Jewish idiom. Knut also published numerous short stories about Jewish life in Bessarabia in Russian émigré journals. Increasingly attracted to Zionism and other Jewish affairs, Knut attempted to move to Palestine in the late 1930s but was drafted into the French Army at the beginning of World War II, during which time he also played a leading role in the French Resistance. After the war, Knut was an integral part of the early documentation of the Holocaust in France. Knut moved to Israel in 1949.

I, Dovid-Ari ben Meir
1925

I,
Dovid-Ari ben Meir,
Son-of-Meir-Enlightener-of-Darkness,[1]
Born by the foothills of Ivanos,[2]
In a plenteous land of plenteous hominy,
Of sheep cheese and sharp *caccocavallo.*[3]
In a land of forests and strong-loined bulls,
Of bubbling wines and bronzy breasted women;
Where midst the steppes and ruddy fields of corn
Still roam the smoky fires
Of gypsies making camp;

I,
Dovid-Ari ben Meir,
The boy who soothed the angry Saul with song,
Who gave
The rebel line of Israel
A star's six points as shield;

I,
Dovid-Ari,
Whose sling and stone
Brought bellowing oaths from the dying Goliath—
The one whose steps sent tremors through the
    hills—
I've come into your camp to learn your songs
But soon, I'll tell you
Mine.

I see it all:
The deserts of Canaan,
The sands and date trees of parched Palestine,
The guttural moan of Arab camel trains,
The cedars of Lebanon, and bored ancient walls
Of my Holy Yerushalaim.

And the awesome hour:
The crack, crumble, and roar of Sinai,
When fire and thunder sundered the Heavens,
And in the cauldron of wrathful clouds
Arose the knotted eye of Adonai-The-Lord
Staring in anger through the haze
At the lost creatures in the sand.

I see it all: the grieving Babylon rivers,
The creaking of carts, the tinkling of cymbals,
The smoke and stench of father's grocery—
Its quince, halvah, garlic, and tobacco sheaves—
Where I guarded from roving Moldavian fingers
The moldy half-moon cakes, fish, dried and salted.

I,
Dovid-Ari ben Meir,
Whose wine has wandered some thousands of years,
Stop now at this crossing in the sands
To sing you, brothers, my song—
My heavy burden of love and longing—

The blessed burden of my millennia.

NOTES

1. The editor [of the edition from which this poem is taken] is indebted to Vladimir Khazan's commentary in his two-volume edition of David Knut's works (Jerusalem, 1997–98). Knut simultaneously offers a literal translation and interpretation of the Hebrew "ben Meir," which literally means "son of Meir," but the word "Meir" means "he who enlightens/illuminates." Given that later in the poem Knut identifies himself with the future King David soothing King Saul with music and song (cf. I Kings 16) and slaying Goliath (cf. I Kings 17), the name "Ari," which in Hebrew means "lion," should not be overlooked.

2. The Ivanus (Ivanos) is one of the left tributaries of the Reut, a river in Moldova and itself a right tributary of the Dniester; Orgeev [today, Orhei, Moldova—Eds.], Knut's native town, is located in the Ivanus (Ivanos) valley.

3. *Cacciocavallo* (from the Italian for "horse muzzle")—type of hard cheese; Knut uses a Russian corruption, *kachkaval*.

Translated by Ruth Rischin.

Other works by Knut: *Moikh tysyachiletii* (1925); *Vtoraya kniga stikhov* (1928); *Izbrannye stikhi* (1949).

Rakhel (Rachel Bluwstein)
1890–1931

Rakhel (she is known by her first name alone) was among the first women in the Land of Israel to write modern Hebrew poetry. She was born into a wealthy merchant family in Ukraine that was both observant and receptive to secular currents. She and her sister traveled to Ottoman Palestine for what was supposed to be a short trip before visiting Italy, where they intended to study painting. Captivated by what they saw, they remained. She settled first in Reḥovot, where she worked in the orchards, and later at Kevutsat Kinneret, where she studied in a women's agricultural school. She was in France, continuing her studies in agronomy, when the war broke out, and she was able to return to Palestine only in 1919. She joined Kevutsat Deganyah and began to publish her poetry. When she was diagnosed with tuberculosis, she was forced to leave and lived a peripatetic life until her early death. Her poems are known for their unencumbered and straightforward style, their brevity, and lyricism. Many of them have been set to music and have become part of Israeli culture.

Aftergrowth
1925

Behold I have not plowed nor have I planted,
I have not prayed for the rain.
And suddenly, see! My fields have grown
Sun-blessed grain instead of thistle.

Is it the aftergrowth of ancient produce,
Grains of joy, cut then?

That have visited me during the days of distress
Burst forth, risen up in me in a mysterious way.

Flourish, grow, fields of wonder,
Flourish, grow and ripen quick!
I remember the words of comfort:
Eat *safiah* and also *sahish*.

Translated by Miryam Segal.

Other works by Rakhel: *Flowers of Perhaps: Selected Poems of Ra'hel* (1994).

I. J. Schwartz
1885–1971

The American Yiddish poet I. J. Schwartz was born in the province of Kovno, Lithuania. He received a traditional Jewish education but also immersed himself in the new modern Hebrew literature. In 1908, he immigrated to the United States. He settled first in New York City, where he earned a living as a Hebrew teacher, but in 1918 he, his wife, and daughter moved to Lexington, Kentucky, where he operated a millinery shop until 1929. There he wrote his 260-page verse epic *Kentucky*. Set in the post–Civil War period, it describes the natural beauty of the bluegrass region and the growth of Lexington and tells the story of an immigrant from Lithuania who starts as a peddler and becomes a successful merchant. In 1929, Schwartz returned to New York. He also translated Hebrew poetry into Yiddish.

Kentucky
1925

One

A. AFTER THE CIVIL WAR
Wide, open, free lay the land,
Extending to far horizons.
The sandy red tract stretches
Far and strange and lonely,
Bordered by low wild plants
And unknown herbs
With broad leaves. Free stretches of land
Not yet turned by the plow,
Untended thick succulent grass,
And humid woods here and there,

One tree grows into the next,
And root entwines with root.
From all this throbs, hot and strange,
An unknown tropical essence,
Of blossoming and decay.
Overhead, arched the sky, undulating and pink,
The evening sky of the south.
The whole landscape appears
Illuminated, bound
By red trees and rose colored plains.
From the blue eastern horizon,
Facing the burning west,
Across the red tract, the wanderer
Came with the pack on his shoulders.

Tramp, tramp, tramp, tramp, in the soft red sand.
Baked in flour-white dust
The tall bony figure bent
From head to foot—from the old bowler hat
To the hard, dried up boots.
The red, pointed beard bleached by the sun,
The eyes strained and bloodshot,
A world of worry in their red depths.
Tramp, tramp, tramp, tramp, in the soft red sand.

So came the Jew from afar into the unfamiliar,
His feet sore, his heart heavy,
A pack on his back, a stick in his hand,
Into the new, the free and enormous land.

The night set in—blue, wondrous.
At first colors merged,
Violet with blue and red.
Finally, one color engulfed the world:
A deep thick blue. Only in the west,
On distant black hills,
One dark red strip burned. And first stars,
Near and red, winked to one another.
With the onset of the Southern night
A great freshness arose:
The earth's luscious moisture
And warm odors
Filled the blue, cool air.
It was like water for the thirsty,
Like strong wine for the weary.

He kept going and going and going.
Suddenly at the bend in the road
The village appeared before him.
From the blue quiet darkness of the wood and field
Sound, song, and red fires

Burst forth suddenly, unexpectedly.
People spilled out from all the low huts,
Kith and kin, around the fires
In the middle of the street:
Clapping on brass and tin, and whistling,
Strumming on banjoes and singing,
Dancing strange wild dances,
Every muscle of half-naked bodies shaking.
Wild, in the red glow of the fires,
The black faces gleamed
With eyes red and heavy.
The fiery home brew
Went the hot rounds from mouth to mouth.
Heavy Negro women with red earrings,
Rolling and swaying, hoarse and hot,
Slapped themselves on their hips, laughing.
Naked children, with heads of black wool,
Jumped over fires
Like wild, young forest monkeys,
And kicked clouds of dust—
Up to the black and reddened sky.
Big black dogs barked,
And fat cats ran around in circles.

Through the reddish-black haze, the Jew
Passed with his heavy pack.
It seemed strangely familiar to him,
Known from old times:
As if he, himself, many years before,
Lived through the same.
So he went through the red dust.
Strange dogs barked,
Black children called,
Heavy women laughed,
And red eyes followed him—
Until the red wild camp was behind.
He was on the black field where
The old low farm houses stretched.
Letting down the pack from his shoulders,
He knocked on the nearest door.

From the house came a commotion.
The heavy bolt was loosened,
The door opened carefully,
And in the black void of the door
A tall, white, masculine figure
Appeared, with the black barrel of a gun
Extended in front of him, and a voice,
A hoarse sleepy voice, hissed:
"Who are you?"

"A Jew, who seeks a place to rest his head.
I am worn out and weary from my journey."
"How do you happen to be here?"
"I carry my business on my back. Night fell.
I am tired. My feet are sore. Let me in.
I'll give your wife a gift from my pack."
The barrel of the gun lowered,
The voice spoke out more softly: "Wait."
Then a figure in white came out,
A burning lantern in his hand.
Raising the light up to the Jew's eyes, he looked him
    over
From top to bottom and barked: "Come."
He led him into the barn,
Pointed out a pile of hay,
And said with feeling: "Don't smoke.
You may send the barn up in flames
Together with your pack and with the cows.
Take care." He slipped out of the barn.
And locked the door after him.

B. A Night of Dreams

The stall was fragrant
It smelled of dry warm hay
And the sweaty odor of horses and cows.
The cow sleepily chewed its cud,
And the horse snorted, switching its tail.
Crickets chirped into the night—
Long drawn out monotones—stopped,
Listened a moment to the stillness,
And again chirped into the night.
From far was heard another song,
The sleepy beat of a banjo.
A luminous late moon ascended,
And through the open windows near the roof
The moonlight settled into small white boxes;
Wherever a box of moonlight fell
Onto the hay where the Jew was lying,
Each stalk of hay shone in relief
And looked like a strip of silver.
Fresh breezes moved around,
Blew in the Jew's face and on his hands and feet.
As if his body were submerged
In fresh, cool waters,
His limbs relaxed,
Stretched out slumbering, oblivious,
And fell into a deep sleep.
The night stretched into eternity,

With pieces of broken suns,
With shreds of red, blue, and green stars
Floating in a chaotic sky
Of blue liquid.
From the bluish pale liquid
Thick greenish-red beams
Converged, forming
Rainbow rungs of a ladder
Whose top hung on nothing.
On the ladder were small black demons
With red, flashing, sharp eyes;
Up—down, up—down, they clambered.
Their bending, airy, thin limbs
Radiated from the black and blue liquid.
Reeling, turning quickly on the ladder,
Sticking out their long red tongues,
In a fit of loud wild screaming,
They badgered him and pulled his coat.
And then it dissipated.
A darkness settled on the world:
Thick, heavy, distinct, like black glass,
With red stars fitted into the blackness.
Suddenly out of the darkness
A forest appears,
A cold forest of gleaming guns
Advancing on him from every side
Blocking his path.
All his muscles strain,
The heart in his breast stops.
Suddenly, light and free and floating,
He lifts himself, swimming in the air.
His body dissolves—just a wave of his hand,
A movement of his foot, he swims, he swims,
And with his hand touches red stars
And pieces of pale cooled suns.
Through the long confusion of the night,
In the background of his weary mind,
His grief did not leave him for a moment,
His yearning homeward for his wife and child.
Every muscle craved sleep
As a thirsty man craved water.
Muted roars clamored to escape
From his constricted and anguished heart.
As a child complains to his father,
He complained to the Lord
Of all the worlds; he cried his heart out.
He recited Psalms with heart and soul,
With every bone, with his very marrow;
And he heard the melody,

The old solemn melody of Psalms.
Quietly, his tears flowed,
Escaping from tightly shut eyes.
Stubborn, fervent, the prayer struggled out,
The old prayer of Father Jacob
When he came to the alien land:
"Give us bread to eat, and a garment to put on,"
For him, for her, for his pale children.
As the blue morning approached,
And birds began to call,
His pained heart quieted.
He saw himself in a green field
Bathed in a tremendous light
It sprouts, it greens, it blossoms, it pours forth bread
With the powers of the first seven days.
And see! He has taken hold in the soil,
In the blackish, rich, wild earth.
He feels as if he drives roots into the earth
And the roots suckle the earth.
A tree, an oak, spreads wide
Its fresh young branches, covered with green,
Soft, fragrant leaves.
Birds twittering and nesting.
Fresh breezes blow on him.
Over him hangs a cool round sun
Which strokes and caresses him with thin rays.
Greenish-blue in the morning light,
He remains quietly in the hay.
He opens his eyes wide,
His heart beating loud with excitement.
From his heart a song comes out,
A prayer to the Lord:
"God of Abraham,
Of Isaac and of Jacob,
Who hast led Your servant
Here, and will lead me further,
It is probably Your will and Your wish,
To plant me in the wilderness,
To make known Your name among the nations.
Do not hide Your face from Your servant,
Lead me through danger and suffering and darkness
As long ago You led
Your chosen people for all of forty years
To the wished for and promised land. Amen."

C. MORNING

The farmer threw open the door of the barn
And into the cool stall burst

The reddish light of the rising sun.
Into the stranger's eyes flashed
The new, unfamiliar, fresh world:
Blue skies and thick grass,
Distant woods under a green leafy crown,
Nearby fruit trees covered with dew,
White-washed walls of the house
Bathed in green up to its windows.
Quietly the woman of the house approached
In a yellow straw hat with a wide brim;
From her open tanned face and gentle eyes
She glanced at him.
Wearing a white cotton house dress
She sat down to milk the cow.
The white frothy streams
Sang and danced as they squirted
Against the bottom of the shining pail.
The air smelled of warmth and abundance.
The farmer led him to the well;
And when the stranger washed
In the cold, clear water, the daughter
Approached him with a
Coarse white homespun towel.
The little ones, fingers in their mouths,
Their blond hair uncombed,
Timidly followed him with their blue eyes.
They shifted positions like geese on little brown
    legs,
Pinched one another, pushed each other,
Until the farmer chased them away
And invited the stranger to his table.
Thanking him, the Jew explained
That first he must pray, he must praise God.

He wrapped himself in his prayer shawl,
A large one with black stripes,
Put on the little four-cornered boxes
With hanging black straps.
Man and wife and child stood motionless,
Astonished and amazed. The strange man
Turned his face to the wall,
Closed his eyes, and with fervor
Rocked, rocked his bony body.
Afterwards he washed his hands again,
Intoned a short prayer—
And only then began to break his bread.
He didn't touch the meat.
He sat with his hat on,
And dipped black bread into the milk.

The farmer found his tongue.
He marveled at all the amazing things
Which he had seen for the first time.
He had, he said, traveled the world over
And had never seen and never heard such things.
The garment with the stripes he could
    understand,
But what are those boxes with the straps for?
And do all Jews pray exactly as he does?
At that the Jew smiled quietly.
A pious Jew, he explained, ought to do
As is written in the Old Testament,
As God commanded Moses, His servant.
The farmer, still marveling,
Insisted that he had never,
Until that day, heard of such things.
After the meal was over,
When the Jew closed his eyes
And again began to murmur quietly,
The farmer gave his wife a wink:
A pious man, he keeps on praying.

After the initial surprise had passed,
Everyone felt more at ease.
The farmer expansive, cheerful, lit
His short black pipe, and the Jew
Beginning to talk, unburdened himself.
He came, he said, from hell, from a city
Where people do not live, but fall under the yoke.
He suffered in that big, wild city.
He was a tailor fifteen hours a day,
Confined in a narrow hole
Without a drop of air, without a bit of sunshine.
His flesh started to shrivel
And every bone in his body sensed death.
His heart began to grieve
For himself, for the years of his youth.
And he, living, grieved
For his orphans
Whom he had not seen for years
While wandering in search of bread.
So, with a pack, he set out on the road.
Here, at least, he has the open sky,
The world is wide, and people good;
A Jew does not get lost, as they can see.
Quietly, sedately, the farmer kept on puffing,
Covering himself with curtains of smoke,
Putting a word in here and there,
While his wife wiped her eyes.

"That's all," said the stranger, "A Jew lives with
    trust."
He believes that God will not abandon him either.
And what does he desire: riches? money?
He wants only to reach the shore
And know that this is the place of refuge
God had destined for him. He is tired.
His every limb craves rest,
A roof of his own, a corner of his own.
He yearns to work in the sweat of his brow.
Does he look for more than a piece of bread?
He has wandered the length and breadth
Of the great new world. The land is rich,
It is fresh and young. The people are rough
But beneath their shells beat
Good hearts with compassion for strangers.
He saw how Jews,
Settling among Christian neighbors,
Engaged in selling products of the land.
They buy a skin, a bundle of wool, furs
Metals—plentiful here—they trade.
They work diligently and make a living.
The farmer sat quietly and thought,
Looked into the Jew's weary face,
Slowly stood up from his seat,
Knocked the gray ash from his pipe,
And patted him upon the back:
"Don't leave now, Jew.
I am going to meet with neighbors today;
We'll talk things over, then we'll see."
From the threshold the farmer called to his wife:
"Do not let the Jew budge from this place."

D. The End of the Pack

As the day drew to a close
And the slanted red rays fell,
The neighbors gathered.
Stout farmers arrived
With coarse calloused hands,
Ruddy faces and necks.
All wore baggy white pants,
Shirts unbuttoned, open on the chest,
Wide, straw hats on their heads.
The only one who was distinctive
Was the tall thin pastor
Dressed in black, every button
Fastened up to his neck. Behind the men
Came the quiet devout women

With thin drawn lips;
Reserved and hushed, only their eyes
Spoke eagerly and quickly,
Sliding from one face to the next.
They sat down on the porch,
The men separate and the women separate.
Immediately there rose,
From each man a puff of smoke.
(But no smoke came from the thin pastor.)
The hostess brought from the cellar
A heavy crock of cold apple cider
Bubbling up to the black rim.
She went around with eyes averted
Serving the smoking guests.

The Jew, stranger that he was, sat quietly.
Alien, he sat among the unfamiliar crowd.
Shyly, from the corner of his eyes, he looked
At the heavy bodies and necks,
As oaks rooted in the soil,
He felt helpless and weak
He sat forlorn, preoccupied,
His head down, his neck bent,
Not daring to raise his eyes.
Softly, the host started
To speak: "Neighbors"
"I told all of you about the Jew.
Here he sits, a stranger among us.
What can we do for him?" At this the pastor,
Quiet and sedate, spoke out:
"First, let's hear from the Jew,
And then we'll see." They agreed
And they all grunted "Right, right."
So the Jew told his story anew.
Above all else, they were touched by the sorrow
Crying out from his eyes,
By the frequent sigh which accompanied
The foreign pronunciation, the strange intonation
Of familiar words. The sorrow
Of the lonely, homeless man was
In every tone, in each unintelligible word.
And when the Jew stopped talking
Everyone sat quietly a while, their heads
Bent in the red evening light,
Heart talking mutely to heart.
Although they appeared hard as iron,
Their hearts still responded to suffering
For they, themselves, in early childhood,
Had known the taste of loneliness and sorrow.

They heard from fathers and from old grandfathers,
The first pioneers, of the life and death
Battle with the red man,
Of sleeping with a gun in hand for fear
Of sudden fires and tomahawks.
The sorrow of the lonely stranger
Touched the brave, silent hearts.

Now the thin pastor stood up,
Stroked his pale, high forehead,
And clearly, slowly, started to talk.
He began with the patriarchs:
With Abraham, Isaac, and Jacob,
He told of Joseph in the alien country,
Of the prophet Moses with the Ten
     Commandments,
Of old King David with the Psalms,
Until he came to the son of God,
The lord, Jesus Christ. "Because of that,"
He concluded,
"Open your door to the stranger who knocks."

One of the neighbors began,
Old Tompkins, with the face of a lion,
Hair, brow, and beard gray:
"My old barn and the house by the pond
Are standing empty, neglected. Let the Jew
Move in there and do business
I won't charge him any money for it.
Later, if he can, let him buy it.
I'll sell it cheap."
     "Good, that's good,"
The host thanked him kindly.
"But what do we do about the old place
That is in danger of collapsing?
We'll kill our Jew yet,"
He quipped.
     "I'll give lumber,
As much as is need to fix up the house,"
The lumber merchant said.
"We'll fix the house and the barn,"
They spoke up from every corner.
"But we need money to carry on a business,"
The host persisted.
"If I sell the merchandise in my pack,
I'll have enough," put in the Jew.
"Fine, Fine, a good idea, no need for a better one.
Hey, mother, let's have the pack over here."
And in reply, the pack appeared at once
And was unpacked

Onto the white world crept
Blue, red, pink, green
Knitted jackets for women,
Dresses of the most flaming silk,
Tablecloths with blue and red squares
And heavy, thick golden fringes,
Striped colored shirts for the men,
Pipes of golden amber,
And heavy silver watches like onions,
Long strings of glass beads
In gaudy rainbow colors,
White silvery pocket knives
With green tinged steel blades,
Sea-shells, mother-of-pearl, bone,
Green and pink playthings for the children,
All kinds of beads and eyeglasses.
And over this, as if suddenly on fire
A large, red, sun flamed.
The people squinted
And protected their eyes from the flames.
They looked at each other astonished,
Dazzled by the scream of colors.
Later they smiled into their whiskers.
Their wives continued to sit quietly,
Like geese, they craned their necks from afar,
Their eyes blazed.
"Hey, women, now it's your turn. Come
Show your stuff." So the women,
Sedate and quiet, came over,
At first with restrained movements,
But soon, as if they were at a fair,
They became more animated and cheerful,
Their eyes bright, as if on fire,
Their voices lively,
Their hands working deftly
As each one made a pile for herself.
The hostess was flushed,
Bustling, running among the customers,
Coming often over to the Jew
To ask the price of an article:
"Tell me only what the thing cost you,
And I'll set the price for them, myself."
The Jew sat ashamed
Among the smoking, joking men.

It got darker.
The excitement and merriment
Set with the sun.
The women, quiet once more,

Retired again to their corner.
The faces became earnest,
They got up, began to yawn,
And quietly prepared to leave,
The men led the way, smoking their pipes,
The women walked behind with their new linens.
The men slapped the Jew on the back:
"What is your name?"
     "Joshua."
"Fine name.
From now on we'll call you Josh."
And they withdrew into the night.

E. IN THE NEW LAND OF CANAAN

On a fresh, clear, summer day
The loud banging of iron reverberated.
The spacious yard was full of scrap:
Pieces of old, rusty iron,
Thousands of dusty old bottles
Which sparkled silver and green
In the glare of the hot summer sun.
A dozen hens pecked in the yard,
And the aristocratic rooster with spurs
Proudly ordered them around.
The old barn was strewn
With rags, with paper, with horse bones.
The sharp smell of wet, bloody, salted
Hides assaulted the nose.
And a cloud of flies buzzed.
At the entrance to the yard, the old shack,
Propped up by slanting railroad ties,
Looked young with its sparkling windows,
And smoke blowing from its new chimney.
In the shadow of the old barn
Were two bent figures:
A big black man knelt,
Half naked, his body glistening, his red tongue
Clenched between his teeth.
He gripped a piece of iron in his hands;
The Jew hit the iron,
Swung the heavy hammer and banged,
And every time the hammer fell
And struck the gray iron,
The Negro jumped back
Without taking his heavy red eyes
From the hammer flying in the air.
The Jew's face was tanned
His tapered bronze beard blackened

By dust. For all that, his eyes
Had acquired a new radiance.
His tall, pale, silent wife,
Wearing her dark wig, often
Ran out of the house to look for
Little Yankele. Now he is perched
On the high pile of iron,
Not knowing how to climb down,
And now he takes a walk on the narrow beams
Of the high, old barn; he jumps into the wool
Turning somersaults. He could break his neck.
And often she finds him, of all places, on the neck
Of the tall, stout, glistening Negro.
He sits on the Negro's shoulders, and drives
     him on,
He kicks him with his small brown feet,
And jabbers in a strange tongue.
The Negro dances and runs around the yard,
And jumps, his black feet like iron,
On glass bottles and sharp metal.
The mother's heart sinks, she trembles,
Lest that wild black man, forgive the thought,
     should,
God forbid, hurt her child.
Her husband watches this scene
But remembering another time in the barn,
He stands and looks in wonder and amazement
And sees in everything the hand of God.

Translated by Gertrude W. Dubrovsky.

Other works by Schwartz: *Yunge yorn* (1952).

André Spire
1868–1966

The French poet and Zionist activist André Spire was
born into a well-to-do industrial family in Nancy. He
was a high-ranking civil servant in Paris when the
Dreyfus affair and the discovery of a Jewish working
class, especially in London's East End, converted him
into a passionate champion of Zionism and a Jewish
cultural renaissance. He retired from the civil service
and from public life more generally in 1926 and henceforth devoted himself almost exclusively to literary
activities. When the Germans conquered France, he
took refuge in New York, returning to Paris at the end
of the war.

Abischag

1925

King David was old, advanced in years. Though covered in bedclothes, he could not get warm. They searched the land of Israel for a beautiful young woman and found Abischag the Shunammite, who was brought to the king. She tended to the king and served him.

—*First Book of Kings*

Abischag, sweet servant,
Buzzing round me like a bee,
Bringing blankets to warm me
And hot stones for my bed,
Graceful child, grave child,
Bearing dishes and goblets
Like a priest before the altar,
Your gaze is distant. Your eyes dream.
Let your gaze fall upon the old king.

I'm cold. I'm alone.
My guards in the antechamber,
My Gibborim, my Heroes,
Full of wine and swill,
Play cards on barrel drums.

Fat Yoav, writing his memoirs,
Dictates the story of our wars
To beardless commanders
Who claim that in our stead
They would have conquered at less cost.

Troops of young prophets,
In high places and low,
Come up with new techniques
And claim their rhythms beat my psalms
For capturing the Lord's spirit.

The Concubines, heavily made up,
Count their rubies and their sapphires,
The Queens, under the terebinth,
Gathered round the fountain,
Knit and natter, swapping
Recipes for sweets.

And Bathsheba, the beloved,
Dreams only of my end,
That the Messiah may come,
And, Solomon, her son, first of all.

Abischag, sweet servant,
Chaste young woman, shepherdess,
Whom my servants found

Leading your goats to the springs,
Let your bright eyes smile.

I'll tell you of my youth,
And of the holy oil with which, in Bethlehem,
The prophet Samuel anointed my blond curls;

Of my sheep, my dogs, my battles
With the bears and the lions,
King Saul, his spear, his tent,
The clever tricks I played on him.

So many years spent fearing,
Promising, yet not keeping,
Racing with my rear in the saddle,
From Jericho to Damascus;

Putting to the sword
The tribes of my enemies,
Razing their citadels,
Forcing the Lord, in the Ark,
To follow at my oxen's pace,
Past the windows of my wife,
In my city, Jerusalem!

So many years of songs and dances,
Slaughtered oxen, feasts!
Ten Queens, twenty Concubines,
A hundred victories, a hundred and fifty psalms,
Sons, daughters, a kingdom
That reaches from Dan to Beersheba!

Abischag, maiden, woman,
Prepare the wine and honey.
The evening breeze stirs my harp,
Which calmed both Saul and God,
And rattles the thongs
Of my sling, whence a single stone
Shot straight to the soul
Of that Philistine Goliath.
My eyes are laughing, my palms rise,
Poems spring up from my lips,
God's no longer turned from me!

Abischag, take down my harp.
Dance. I'll sing of your eyes,
Your arched eyebrows, your temples, your tresses,
Your sandals clicking on the tiles,
Your veil, your tunic floating
On the warm bulb of your hips,
Your figure, straight and supple
As the trunk of a poplar,

Your mouth, red anemone,
Your hands, silky and radiant
As the blue flower of wild flax
That joyful youths and maidens
Pluck from hillsides in the spring!

Abischag, Abischag, you're weeping!

Translated by Michele McKay Aynesworth.

Other works by Spire: *Les juifs et la guerre* (1917); *Quelques juifs et demi-juifs*, 2 vols. (1928); *Poèmes juifs* (1959).

Malka Lee
1904–1976

Malka Lee (pseudonym of Malka Leopold Rappaport) was a prolific and beloved Yiddish poet whose verse captured the feelings and experiences of a generation of Jewish immigrants to the United States. She was born in the Galician shtetl of Monastrikh (in present-day Ukraine) and immigrated to New York in 1921. Lee's poetry revolved around themes such as memory of the Old Country, the trials of life in the New World, the pain and guilt of witnessing the Holocaust from a distance, a renewed attachment to America, and the birth of the State of Israel. In addition to several collections of poetry, she also wrote prose fiction, children's literature, and fables. In 1965, she received the Hayim Greenberg Award of Pioneer Women of America.

Buy Cigarettes!
1925–1926

Cigarettes! Cigarettes!
My voice rings through the streets
With eyes overcast, cloudy—
Buy! Buy! Buy!
Hunting foxes—Cossacks ride—
With horseshoes like scythes—
And cut down sounds like sheaves:
Buy! Buy! Cigarettes!

Cossack and horse dance in a circle,
So I jump into the whirl,
Stroke the horsehide with quiet fear,
The way I stroke my grandfather's tefillin—
My eyes beg, beg—
Buy! Buy! Cigarettes!

Then comes a Cossack with lion-eyes,
Scalds my body as with spears—
Pierces through my flesh with knives—
Through the dress that covers me
He gulps, he gulps—nakedness . . .
Peels off my skin—
Limbs flaming, limbs red.
People—streets—in a whirl—
And, I, naked—in a circle
And my eyes beg, beg,
Buy! Buy! Cigarettes!

Then the Cossack wrings out laughter,
The way that laundry's wrung out
In the river:—
Ach, you pretty little thing
You are still such a little thing!!

Translated by Kathryn Hellerstein.

Other works by Lee: *Lider* (1932); *Kines fun undzer tsayt* (1945); *Durkh kindershe oygn* (1955); *In likht fun doyres* (1961); *Mayselekh far Yoselen* (1969).

Izi Charik

Pass On, You Lonely Grandfathers . . .
1926

Pass on, pass on, you lonely grandfathers,
With frightened beards covered with snow,
In the last sorrow, in the final grief
You're still here, the final witnesses.
Pass on, pass on, you lonely grandfathers!

Then woe and grief to your entire *shtetl*,
Trampled down with pain and poverty,
It's been so long you've had to smile and beg
For every famished morsel of your bread.
Then woe and grief to your entire *shtetl*.

Tired and fearful, do you look about you
And feel a frightened trembling in your knees?
Who knows, who knows whether these sons
Will still survive, these sons, as Jews?
There is a frightened trembling in your knees.

And we, the ones still calling you "Grandfather,"
Knowing we may not call you that for long—
We ascending, like the sound first heard,
The sound first heard of an oncoming joy,

We, the ones still calling you "Grandfather."

It's good to peer into your lonely eyes
When the sorrow of your beards is strange. . . .
We—I and he and they—it is our fate,
It is our fate never to bow again.
Pass on, pass on, you lonely eyes.

Translated by Leonard Wolf.

Jacob Glatstein

Abishag
1926

Abishag. Little, young, warm Abishag.
Shout into the street: King David is not yet dead.
But King David wants to sleep and they won't let him.
Adoniyahu with his gang shout my crown off my
    gray head.
The fat Bathsheba blesses me with eternal life and
    watches my last words with a sly smile.

Sleep, my king. The night is still. We are all your
    slaves.

Abishag. Little village girl, Abishag.
Throw my crown into the street—whoever wants,
    may catch it.
My dead might wails in my every finger.
Only over you I reign in my kingly, disgusting old age.
King David has lost all his servants. Just one maid-
    servant left.

Doze, my king. The night is dead. We are all your
    slaves.

Abishag. Little, sad Abishag.
A small kitten thrown into the cage of an old, tooth-
    less lion.
It befell my old age to expire in the lap of your
    lamenting young years.
My victorious wars are but puddles of blood in my
    memory.
And how long has it been since maidens praised me
    in their songs.

Rest, my king. The night is still. We are all your
    slaves.

Abishag. Little, sweet Abishag.
Fear is straying through all my limbs

Wandering through puddles of blood, can you reach
    the paths of God?
At the crossroads, will the soft songs of my pious
    hours come to my defense?
Abishag, you know that songs are more real than sins.

Dream, my king. The night is dead. We are all your
    slaves.

Abishag. Little, young, warm Abishag.
Shout into the street: King David is not yet dead.
But King David wants to die and they won't let him.
Throw out my crown—whoever wants may catch it.
Adoniyahu or Solomon over the people, and I over
    you in the last days of my disgusting old age.

Sleep, my king, it will soon be dawn. We are all your
    slaves.

Translated by Kathryn Hellerstein and Benjamin Harshav.

Uri Zvi Greenberg

My Brothers, the Sidelock-Jews
1926

And if there I lied to my brothers the sidelock-Jews
    in their wrathful basis and their indignation
    against us, the unbelievers,
Outsiders to the disgrace of Judaism in its deep
    pain, more like the gentiles with scented locks.
Who smoke cigars on Friday nights, in order to
    spoil the lungs of our Hebrew God—
Surely here, from afar, in days of the Hebrew clari-
    fication on land of the race and the Jerusalemite
    god-head.
God lives, I will not lie to my brothers the
    sidelock-Jews!
And as I love the breathing stones in my Land: *rocks
    of the mute gold* of our dead kingdom
And "gold-my-gold" I'll call the sand here; gold-my-
    gold in the Jewish *hamsin,*
And just as I favor all the ruins in Sion and I'll
    find also my happiness in this struggle in the
    wilderness,
All the more so I love the *living parts-of-gold*: my
    brothers the sidelock-Jews in *tallit-*and-*tefillin.*
In mink-hats of Sabbath and holiday in remem-
    brance of crowns and in overgowns of silk and of
    satin with the dull sheen

Of a sword of ancient silver . . .
And thus I'll see them from far off, as they walk in
Europe: *fabulous ambassadors of the kingdom of
the East.*
The NO-to-Christian-Europe takes on a splendor of
fire from the eyes of the adults
And from the eyes of the children, who walk in their
tracks with a warmth of lambs and their narrow
mouth is no more than a knife-slit——
And if at their oy-like exultation I once jeered because well I knew a ninth symphony in the world
And lighter is their lamentation in a rhythm of blood
and of tears than the gentile funeral-march of
Chopin—
Now I catch the depth of their oy-like exultation:
it's the song of the whole man from generation to
generation of the pain,
This heart-cutting song rises from my fingertips and
the leanness shines in my flesh as I sing it——
Now I hate like them the Latin script, the Cyrillic
script.
In those letters were written the terrible-de-
crees, they call placards on the walls of the
thoroughfares!
(And so what if in those letters I envisioned the vision of the superior man of Nietzsche!)
Now the cut of the Jewish soul opens in me, and I
continue upon myself the holiness of father's Jewish house,
Which is in time of slaughter *the only house in the
world.*

Translated by Harold Schimmel.

Peretz Markish

Old Women
1926

I

Aged woolen women, like old *siddurim*—moldy,
mossy
Bound in coarse canvas;
Pointless bellies dangling after them like empty
sacks,
Dried-out breasts, like horseradish roots, swaying
back and forth.

"God willing, till a hundred"—lost in thought over
beds, lonely and gray
Constantly counting days and the wash of their long
dead husbands rocked to sleep;
That's how they remember *yortsaytn*,[1] the end of
man and ancestral graves,
measuring wicks and laying grass on the stones of
the righteous.

They need to be no more than footstools for their
husbands in heaven,
Every sound resounds in their cold stomachs like in
empty graves,
And the quivering of voices is stilled in them;

But when they pack their noses with sharp spicy
tobacco
sneezing suddenly with a ringing screech,
they wipe off their chins and voice an oath: "May
you grow—God in Heaven."

II

It's daytime too early in the lonely beds of old
women,
they wake up in winter, nighttime, in long, coarse
shirts,
and with a candle in their hand which doesn't want
to burn, weeping,
they turn around and around, like awoken witches,
strange.

What are they looking for, the old women, in the
plank beds and sleeping chambers?
They seek white garments and gloaming shadows.
. . .
They dress up in white, like white cemetery
brides,
and lie down again—to drowse away the night. . . .

In the morning they walk in markets with straw
baskets,
At every stand they taste the fruit with cold gums
and spit it back out in thin streams of saliva.

And when they come—they ask about letters from
Russia and America,
they wash the dried-out edges of their hands, like
desert nomads,
and masticate the words with used up gums—"I
thank thee, God"

III

Sometimes, when their people go off, they stay by
    themselves
left alone at home to watch the house and look after
    the little children.
They hiccup then through all rooms, big and small.
    . . .
and someone makes answer to them from under
    deaf, cool walls

They love that time when no one is at home.
They pray a little by heart, they drowse a little, lean-
    ing on sticks,
and when they wake up in the middle of a day-
    dream, a dream of screaming,
they get angry for no good reason at the bare walls
    . . .

Then the noise of little children—the stampeding
    and the racket
no longer gets to their dried-out earlobes.
There flows from them a dull rushing of long, long
    life.

But when they get sad—they lure a child with a
    piece of sugar
put spectacles on the sharp edges of their nose
start loosening them with their nails, like aged
    monkeys.

IV

Their arms dangle after them, heavy and ashen;
lying down at times in their white nightgowns,
they like to stretch out, like cats on warm hatbrims,
and drive off flies with round, smooth sticks . . .

And flies are always hanging around them,
    half-dead,
Green, weeping and dusty,
and old women rest, as if they are resting into a
    distance.
In which old women must soon, laboring, rise . . .

And when they open their mouths
and start yawning from weariness
it is dark . . .

with the creak of a warped seesaw
their gums appear with rotten toothstumps
crumbled, child-size tombstones. . . .

V

Sometimes a buzzing memory flies through their old
    heads—
like a fly in winter from one end of the roofbeam to
    the other—
they grimace with a green smile
and exhale something over the years, as on snowy
    paths, windblown . . .

Their mouths get musty—they let out a bony moan
The gums with the yellow stumps are wobbly;
they like to cook themselves a little something
so no one gets in their way mucking about in the
    kitchen;

When no one is watching, they shut them with a
    loud smack,
gumming the gaping gnawing stumps
which are growing back in the bone, like kids' tomb-
    stones sunken into the plots.

Before that they try the one wraggling remaining tooth
sticking out in their mouth, a rusted nail in an old
    shoe,
to see if it's wobbly—and then eat fast. They eat up
    fast.

VI

They are grumpy. They bang away with a stick to
    accompany their talk.
They get up early to try the doorknobs, pouring out
water for the cows and crumbs for the chickens
driving away the demons with a broom and the
    merit of the foremothers.

Their kerchiefs get loose and bare, their nails black
    as pitch—like wicks,
They smell of valerian and lampblack at dawn;
"And in a hundred years, oy, they'll intercede for
    laboring women in Gan Eydn,
and make little shirts, for good luck, for little pauper
    kids. . . ."

The year's white burden, like old lambswool hides,
falls apart, feathery, disintegrating
A distant white path

of purified candles and swaddling clothes.
They listen with their thin mouths into the white
    distance—

"If only the holy mothers of Gan Eydn will come to
    meet them"

* * *

It's a long way to any settlement—the town is
    boarded up . . .
The lonely heaped-up houses sleep,
like someone's lost frozen shovels.

Someone passed through. Someone fled . . .

Snowy frozen wires weep
on frosty furlongs, frosty miles:
Someone passed through, someone trod
over roofs. Over mouths. . . .

Over patchwork fields an old windmill,
nearly dead, struggled with a wind—
grumbling and groaning. What's the problem,
    windmill?
Winds are free, loyal and greedy . . .

The windmill asks the mileposts
for some sort of hut. Civilization.
"Who passed through? Who found something?
Snow and storms blow over, wipe out!"

The winds answer with the snowed over wires:
"Any settlement is far away. The town is hidden."
"Someone passed through. Someone trod
over roofs. Over mouths."

NOTE
1. [Anniversaries of people's deaths.—Eds.]

Translated by Zackary Sholem Berger.

Esther Raab

My Palms Are Raised toward You
1926

My palms are raised toward you,
To the little light
Which I still have in your eyes,
And you—sharpen your teeth
For the softness of my yellow flesh;
And were this flesh to be thrown upon the field
And would a vulture circle above it—
Still my palms are raised toward you,
To the little light
Which I still have in your eyes.

Translated by Anne Lapidus Lerner.

Rakhel (Rachel Bluwstein)

To My Land
1926

I have not sung to you, my land,
And I have not glorified your name
With acts of valor,
With booty of battles;
My hands have planted just a tree
On the quiet Jordan shores,
My legs have trodden down just a path
Over the fields.
Indeed it is very meager—
I know that, mother,
Indeed it is very meager
Your daughter's offering;
Just a cry of joy
On a day when the light shines,
Just a secret sob
For your suffering.

Translated by Miryam Segal.

Julian Tuwim

Jewboy
1926

He sings in the courtyard, clad in rags
A small, poor chap, a crazed Jew.

People drive him away, God has muddled his wits
Ages and exile have confused his tongue

He wails and he dances, weeps and laments
That he is lost, is dependent on alms.

The gent on the first floor looks down on the
    madman
Look my poor brother at your sad brother.

How did we come to this? How did we lose
    ourselves
In the vast world, strange and hostile to us?

You on the first floor, your unhinged brother
With his burning head dances through the
    world

The first floor gent fancies himself a poet
he wraps up his heart, like a coin, in paper

And throws it out from the window, so that it will
    break
And be trampled and cease to be

And we will both go on our way
A path sad and crazed

And we will never find peace or rest
Singing Jews, lost Jews.

Translated by Antony Polonsky.

Aaron Zeitlin

Yosef de la Reina
1926-1927

Ten on a Mountain
    A mountain in the desert.
    On the desert mountain—
    Nine,
    Nine tall men.
    There must be something here—
    The Nine want something here—
    And the tenth man?

    He stands at the head of them all
    All are ready.
    De la Reina—readier.

    In the desert was revealed
    The Torah, our bride.
    He clothed her in fire
    And in the desert
    Spoke his words. [. . .]

    De la Reina has brought to a desert
    His little congregation.
    Taller than the nine tall men,
    Whiter than the nine white
    Holy mystics,
    He stands, the head of the ten-man *minyan*
    It is of all matters, the ultimate matter—
    The matter of The End.

    His hands are snow:
    Such whiteness annihilates
    Demons.
    The phylacteries—a chariot.
    Harnessed in the chariot is *shel-rosh*, the
        headpiece.
    Shel-rosh wishes to fly off,

Wants to pull the chariot—
But nothing happens.
As if someone had commanded: do not go!

The expectant *shel-rosh* stands there.
The Ten stand
Like the empty hats of beggars,
Into which no one throws a coin,

Nothing happened!
In the desert it is burning daylight.
But in the heavenly palaces it is dark,
Nothing to see!
De la Reina's *shel-rosh* is ready
To jump, to sing: Day!
But only dark midnights
Loom over the heavens
The light—still locked shut.
The worlds are dozing.

Their bodies made holy
By mortification
Their faces
Turned upward,

With holy formulas
The Nine
Call over and over:
"Redeemer, break the walls!"
De la Reina's urgent directives
Fly like high moons
From divine sphere to sphere.
They reach the middle pillar
Which holds up the universe.

Who can resist the power
Of such a holy man?

But nothing happens.
The heavenly beings
Do not budge in the least.

The lands of the high spheres,
Awaken and show themselves.
They shake their bright crowns,
Wink—and are gone,
Disappearing like distant ships.
The voiceless dogs of Egypt come running,
Filthy great dogs of Egypt
Run hellishly, flamingly,
Like red torches,
Bark out every savagery.

Suddenly—gone! Vanished!
Nothing. Silence.
The desert has put on a mountain
The mountain has put on the Nine and de la
   Reina.
The prayer-shawls weep.
He does not come.

Sands come alive,
Crawl to them on all fours,
Look on imploringly: "If not you—
Then who?"
Their rumbling seethes,
No answer comes;
They shrivel up—
And return
To their death-sleep.

Scorpions arise.
Begin to glitter like mirrors:
"If you will not throw open bolts—
Then who?"
They crawl back somewhere—
The Messiah does not come.

What will be, de la Reina?
Only a Jew can bring him,
A Jew like you,
Like your disciples.
When will God make full
The void in his worlds?

Suddenly—a woman!
High on her camel like a bride,
Lilith comes riding.

Lilith on the Other Side

Lilith has built herself a mountain,
The mountain of her desires,
Opposite the mountain of the Ten.
Her mountain looks like a camel,
Hung with carpets of Damascus.
A mountain that draws near,
A mountain that draws back—
A mountain that is a traveler.

In limpid nakedness
She stands on the mountain
And dazzles with her great feet
And slowly starts to shake

Her breasts—
Long, narrow-necked flasks of skin.

Her hips are cheeks,
Rounded, washed.
Her hips are cool as springs.
Black grow the shrubs of her hair—
Her hairs have mouths.
They seethe like poisons.
The hotter they seethe,
The cooler her hips,
The cooler her breasts.

With green fingers,
Lilith waves her hand:
Fire, menstrual blood,
Clamor and rage!
The roar of incest,
Like the roar of beasts!
And simultaneously—
A thin sound, thinner
Than waters
That sing in the dark.

How stiff, how straight
Is de la Reina!
His feet are chained to the mountain.

He is at once
A prison and a prisoner in shackles.

His head is turned aside and raised upward
He does not move at all.
He is a mountain upon a mountain.
The Nine, armored in their prayer-shawls,
Do not move.
They stand there below.
But soon they open the corks
Of tall concealed casks of wine.
Letters flutter out; the spears of incantations
Insert themselves into crowns.
Letters of the holy Name
Pull themselves together
And do dances.
Heavenly bodies
Roll high over all.

Good news is proclaimed
In all the Creator's worlds:
Soon, very soon!
The crocodiles of the demon-world,

POETRY 1926–1927   1215

That sleep in black rivers,
Quickly awaken.
They stare with fright:
What is happening here?

Happy is this generation!
Very soon! Any moment!

But Lilith's face
Is half yearning, half mockery.
Her ring does a dance in her ear,
She sings:
"De la Reina, be my husband!
My blood, my contamination,
My monthly impurity—
Subjugate them, de la Reina,
And I will become pure!
My lord,
My confession—
Hear it!

Whom
Do I need more than you?
Where
Should impurity go if not to sanctity?"

(The Nine—to themselves: Debauched
        woman!
Mouth without shame!)

"Yosef, you forget the essential:
You forget me, the impure one.
Are you not my greatest hope?
You, so holy—
Are you not my healing?"
The womb of the she-demon
Yearns from time immemorial
For holy semen.

The tree of de la Reina's spine
Wobbles at the sound of her song of praise,
The *shel-rosh* commands from above:
Straight!
The tree, full of piety,
Straightens itself.

Shh! A cup of water from Creation!
In a great glass,
Full of blue Creation-water
And lightning flashes like crooked swords,
Sits an embryo, wet and swollen,

An unborn child.

Under the clouds,
The cup swims
Like a little boat, like a little fish,
And de la Reina extend his arms
As if to present a pillow
To the unformed child.

Beaming, the tall Nine
Look on:
The Messiah—the Messiah!

The Unborn Messiah

Two mountains: on one—the Ten
On the one opposite—Lilith
And under the clouds—the child in the cup of
        Creation
In the flashing cup.

The Sign will soon appear
In the water amid the lighting flashes,
Sits the embryo—
And one flash says quickly to the other:
The Sign comes soon!

Says de la Reina: It is joy for me!
Here comes to me.
Here comes to us, the Messiah!
Revelation of revelations!
The child of everyone's joy
The Beloved Child
Comes to us unborn!
We Ten, the holiest *minyan*,
Will strengthen our incantations
And give him a face.
He comes from the glass of Creation
In form and image.

And the disciples answer:
In form and image!
Stronger, stronger the incantations—
Soon
He will receive the purest of bodies,
The most glorious Divine Measurements.

Lilith interjects: "Dreams!"

De la Reina says: Disciples,
You chosen individuals!
We will reach with our spells of holy letters,

Both the ten divine spheres of points of light
And the ten divine spheres of linked light,

And with the Child gladden
Both the depths of darkness below
And the supreme chariot above.
We will bring forth the Child
Without the womb of a woman,
Without the impure blood of a woman,
Without seed, without sin,
Without the evil side!
Like a snake is man's desire,
And the womb is—a snake!
The snake is in Eve herself.
Can the thing that is ill and evil,
Bear the Redeemer, the ultimate remedy?
Messiah, you do not need to be born:
We will form you and free you
With incantations, garments, prayers,
Without the transmigration of souls
Through blood and womb.

Lilith hears all this—
And laughs. [. . .]

The Fall

De la Reina throws off his phylacteries,
De la Reina tears away his prayer-shawl
De la Reina tears off his garment.

In haste,
The circle gathers its coattails
Stands up and strides away.

The disciples say nothing.
Is it from amazement or fright?

Dusk settles brown
Over the desert.
Lilith, my crown,
Says de la Reina,
Now I undress,
Now I lie at your feet,
Come,
Embrace,
Stab through me like a spear!
I have no choice,
But transgression.
How can I rise to sanctity, if God
Created you to be unclean?
I can only become unclean like you—nothing more!

I have ceased to be spirit:
I am body, nakedness, refuse . . .
To no avail the mortifications, the prayers,
I am smaller than small, smaller than small,
I stand ready for the marriage. Do not weep!
You wished for me to be your husband.
Lowest lowliness alone remains for me.
The summits said: This far and no further!
The heights laughed at me,
The Messiah was but my imagination.
The heights do not let me go further,
So ignite, Lilith, my pyre,
And I will go to the fire.
Devour my beard, guzzle my body!
Seat me,
On the bare coals of your knees
And scald!
Cover me with hair
And if I die
Do not awaken me to life!
Shame! Transgression!
Shame!

The Nine tremble.
The eldest says to de la Reina:
Let my mouth be like the ram's horn of
    excommunication!
Let my words stone you to death!
Be erased from God's book!
A stench goes forth from your heretical words
As if from carrion.
Unclean vessel—
We depart!
The sweat pours from his inflamed face.
He goes off. The rest follow.
The shadows of their long prayer-shawls
Tremble over the sand like spears.

De la Reina mocks them: "What heroes!
You stone me to death!
Holy men, I still have Lilith."

But Lilith weeps.

The Death of de la Reina

"Lilith why do you weep?
Why do you stand alone on your mountain,
Why do you not come near,
Why do your breasts cloud over,
Why do you wring your hands?"

Thus asks de la Reina.
And she answers: "For nothing
Did I exchange my foolish demon for you!
There's no lack of bodies that Lilith has sinned
    with.
What do you give me? Sin?
We will not give birth to the Messiah!
Our child would have been a gnome,
Would have been a polecat!

Do not beg!
You will not fill in my chasm.
Nor will you heal my wound.
You cannot raise me.
You want me to share my abyss with you.
I once had such a yearning,
But I lost it—
We will not give birth to the Messiah!

To whom shall I go?
To Ashmodai, that old sinner,
Forever rehashing his worn-out sins?
To the onanists?
To the gnomelike rabble?
You!
Why do you not pluck out your eyes?
In vain you hoped, in vain you expected—
You deceived.
My love is becoming hard like hate.
For my pain—here, take death.
Die!"

And she jumps up and attacks him,
Chokes with her hands, her feet, her hair.
The cold ball of the moon
Looks on at the wrestling pair.

He gurgles out a "Shma":
Shh.
De la Reina lies motionless. [. . .]

The End

    The heart of old Ashmodai
    Could bear the grief no longer. [. . .]
    Seeing his Lilith weeping
    Over the death of de la Reina
    And—leaning on his stick
    With enfeebled hands—
    He asks submissively:
    Lilith, why do you weep!

She does not want to look.
He sees only her back.
Her back shines—it is like a knife in his heart.
The knife of knives!

Have you anyone better?
Come back, I forgive you your erring!
If you become my Lilith again.
I will become iron!
I feel it—
Be my wife again!

Quickly she turns her head
And with sharp accents
Cuts into him: I remain!

On his face—the pain of death throes.
Then Matronita, the Divine presence as Woman.
Sends out her hand from a cloud.
Her face can no longer be seen.
Five silver birds
Caress Lilith's neck:
A mother's voice speaks:

"Daughter, I know
That your blood roars wildly.
I know the pains of your loins.
A second de la Reina,
A strong de la Reina,
Will come in the days of the End,
And he, only he,
Will fulfill your desire
And kill you through copulation.
The Redeemer's father must be
As strong as you imagine him, daughter!
His son, to bring redemption
To the enslaved world,
To give it salvation and restoration,
Must inherit
His father's audacity of holiness
And his mother's knowledge of impurity
And also her weariness of impurity.
He will come, your husband
And you will bear the child for him, daughter—
And you will be redeemed
And will perish. . . ."

Lilith seats herself in widowhood
And her word is steel:

For the true man,
Whose holiness will be might,

Whose light will be stronger
Than all of my night,
Who will bring out my son
And destroy my night,
Who with my death will make me bright,
For him, lord of all lords,
For his fatherly seed
Will I wait for generations,
And even if he tarries—
I will wait!

Translated by Solon Beinfeld.

Jacob Fichman

1881–1958

Born in Belz, Bessarabia, the Hebrew poet, critic,
and editor Jacob Fichman received both a secular and
religious education. In 1901, he moved to Odessa,
joining its lively circle of writers. Two years later he
began dividing his time between Odessa and Warsaw.
In 1912, he settled in the Land of Israel but returned to
Europe for periodic visits. He edited Hebrew journals,
including the prestigious *Moznayim*, the journal of
the Hebrew Writers Association, from 1936 to 1942.
Fichman distinguished himself in a variety of genres:
children's literature, textbooks, literary essays, and
poetry, including sonnets, idylls, ballads, and narrative poems. His poetry bridged the romantic tone of
Bialik's generation and the modernist outlook of the
following generation.

Ruth
1927

On these night fields of pure silence
My feet tread, light and sure, as upon
A homeland's holy soil from the day
My star led me here.
How loving are the night's wings! My eye
Discerns every bush here, each rock, each clod of
    earth,
And like a good and faithful hand it guides me.
Only a few days have I been here, and like a seed
Stricken by no frost, the strange land
Has received me with love;
Every touch of my feet on this earth
Is a holy covenant with the new homeland.
As if everything I knew and loved,

From the days of my much-riddled childhood
Till today, always pointed to this calm land
Where I found my soul.
From its silence the face of God shone white
    for me.
No longer will I fear the cruel hand of fate,
Nor will I be frightened of the gods' blows;
My soul is quiet, secure here. It believed.
Here it forgot and felt good. Be silent for me
You, good earth, and like my heart
Full of love, flourish, please, in your fields,
And drape yourself in white fringes, signs of
    grace,
For God has not forgotten the orphans of the land!
Oh, flourish, please, you gracious earth,
That slowly, here in your bosom, will bear me
We know not whither—and in the paths of the
    night
We will always remember all your abundant
    mercy!

Translated by Jeffrey M. Green.

Other works by Fichman: *Kitvei Yaakov Fichman*
(1959).

Shmuel Halkin

Transformation
1927

1

Year after year, that cruel monster in the heart
growing, sense of guardedness expanding.

Year after year—generations' blessing
gouged like a needle into the body.

I have wrenched it with irons, bent it out of
    shape—
grimly-soberly weighed it on the scale.

What's needed remains. What's not is destroyed.
But the sacrifice is for all that not granted.

Confess. Confess. And utter these words:
Rebirth from aleph is your fate.

Bow very deeply, and move your lips:
You are right. You are blessed, iron sieves

For selection rough, strict and clear—
for descent, for destruction. For rebirth.

3

Sisters and brothers in far-off lands,
it's hard to address you from here.

Sand is the same in a thousand locales,
but the grains here are—somehow—a different sort.

Burning and bloodying, a different sand.
Glows, scorches, tortures—for the greater good.

In cities of terror—New Yorks and Chicagos—
was there ever a thing that consumed you with fear?

Did you ever find joy, somewhere on the plains,
In the towering rise of golden wheat?

In cities of terror, peopled by millions,
Did you ever taste the poison of love

an elixir which embitters and sweetens at once,
which chases you down? You can't wall yourself in!

Are you acquainted, my brothers, with this kind of
     pain:
suffering, praising itself as reward!

Brothers, did you see a person there
under your blessing? Under your curse?

Happy brothers in far-off lands,
I would not change my fate for yours.

Thanking the flames of purification:
do you know this kind of happiness, brothers?

Sand is the same in a thousand locales,
but the grains here are—somehow—a different sort.

Burning and bloodying, a different sand.
Glows, scorches, tortures—for the greater good.

Translated by Zackary Sholem Berger.

Moyshe-Leyb Halpern

He Who Calls Himself Leader
1927

No one can order his face in advance
And you shouldn't throw a stone at a dog
Showing its howling muzzle to the night sky.

But when I think about it,
Losing myself in sadness, in this night-cafe
Fogged up in smoke,
And they point out a man across the room,
And tell me who he is,
And when I look at him
And he, with every fold and wrinkle of his face,
Reminds me of the undertaker back home, how he
     rejoiced
When they lit candles
At the head of my dead little brother—
And when the crookedness of his right eye,
Which strikes me suddenly, is almost as cold
As a hidden murder that wakes you up at night—
Am I not allowed then to feel pain,
Like a wound bleeding in my gut,
That he, of all people, insists that we blindly believe
He was chosen for leadership in life?
What does leadership mean?
It means a wind singing in spring!
It means, for sure, a pillar of light leading the way
Through a wilderness of stones and thorns.
It means a wind singing in spring,
Urging on the crying sick bird Hope
To spread its white wings
When we must cross mountains reaching to the
     clouds.
And what is the light in the leader's eye?
It is but a spark of his image, the chosen image.
One spark can perform the miracle
Of shining like a rainbow in the night.
But even if the man who sits across from me
Did not remind me, with his talk, of an angry fly
Buzzing around a pile of shit in the street—
And even if, while hearing his voice, I could stop
     thinking
That it is the evil of a human tongue, which braids
     words
Into a rope for a brother in the night—
Would it be any easier for me
To imagine him in the white robe of a leader?
Oh, what grief—
What an evil ghost play
In the night!
If a child, awakened from sleep,
Saw him, clad in white, in the night—
He would think: a corpse is running into the
     synagogue

In its shroud, and would comfort himself, perhaps,
That there is an early hour
When the cock chases the dead
Back to their peace, their cursed peace in the night.
Let my blood not poison me for this—
I've never seen a corpse walking around.
But to this, my breath dies in me from terror
When I remember the Negro woman in white in the
    night.
A step away from me, she stopped me.
I searched in the dark
For a hand, a human face, an eye,
And what I saw was a snowman with no head,
A white figure in a field at night
To scare away the hungry birds.
I didn't even hear her breathe.
Only the smell of her flesh—
Like sulphur-acid on rotting meat—
Brought me to my senses.
I remember, as if it were right now,
How heavily my head dropped.
From her, however, I could walk away in the night,
To cry quietly for myself
And for the darkness, which leads poverty
To trade for pennies
Its longing, the holiest in life.
But here, in this night-cafe
Fogged up in smoke,
Here is my resting place—
Here I've got friends—
And I have no place else to go.

Translated by Benjamin Harshav and Barbara Harshav.

Yitshak Lamdan

1899–1954

Hebrew-language poet, editor, translator, and essayist
Yitshak Lamdan was born in Mlinov (in present-day
Ukraine) and received both a religious and a secular
education. Lamdan was a committed communist in his
youth and volunteered for the Red Army during the
revolution, but soon left Europe for Palestine, where
he settled in 1920. In 1927, he published the influential
epic poem in Hebrew entitled *Metzada* (Massada, in
this translation), drawing parallels between the ancient
Jews of Masada and current Zionism. An established
literary presence in the State of Israel, Lamdan was the
editor of the literary monthly *Gilyonot* and a mem-

ber of the central committee of the Hebrew Writers
Association. From 1954 to 1983, the Lamdan Prize
was given in his memory to the best works of Hebrew
literature for children and youth.

Massada
1927

Myths Told Me

On an autumn night, on a bed of sorrows, far from
    home and shattered hearth,
My mother died;
A last tear froze in her eyes as she gasped a dying
    blessing
To me, her son, setting forth for far-off alien fields of
    battle,
An army kitbag weighing down my back . . .
On grave-studded pain-packed Ukrainian roads
My soft-eyed innocent brother fell,
And did not find a Jewish grave.
My father alone remained by the doorpost rising
    from the ashes of ruins,
Weeping a lonely prayer on the ravaged scroll of
    God.
And I—
Girding my disintegrating soul
With final words of courage
Fled at midnight to a ship of exiles
To ascend Massada.

Myths told me:
There the last banner of revolt is raised,
Calling to heaven and earth, to God and man:
"Reparation!"
And on tables of rock stubborn nails
Scratch a message of consolation;
There a breast of dissent is bared, roaring
Against a hostile fate of generations:
"Strife!
Me or you!
Here battle will pass the last judgment
On life!"

Myths told me:
Among Massada's walls walk prophets
Prophesying redemption,
And in the tents among the paths are Levites,
Singing "To the Chief Musician"
And the echo of tomorrow answers them:

"Amen, Selah!"
There, from the summit of the wall, flowers of
    priesthood
Raise arms of compassion
To the wretched sky of orphaned night,
Praying that its flawed moon wax full and bright . . .

Myths told me:
Over the heads of the fighters
A spirit has descended, weeping in atonement,
And through the curtain of the future a great eye of
    dawn looks out
And watches over Massada.

Tender Offering

And who are you ascending here so gay,
With dewdrops on your head?
—Not dewdrops—they are tears
A loving father and mother shed
On the head of their only son
As he went away
My mother sobbed and my father wept
"Where will you go, and you still so tender,
So tender and soft?"
And I hardened my heart
"And what of it?
A tender offering shall be accepted!"
And I went
And so I ascend in joy,
And though there be tears on my head—
I am happy and rejoice!
I know, my father and mother weep bitterly now
Into the palms of trembling hands,
And I love them, I love them so . . .
But the myth of Massada is so lovely
And the wall of wonders so alluring—
If father and mother knew the myth
They would not weep that their only son
Is gone towards it! . . .

The Hands of Israel

And who are you, ascending with your hands
    outspread?
—Not mine! They are the hands of Israel, that em-
    brace everything,
And everything tumbles out of their embrace,
And they hang like empty pails
Over the world's overflowing wells . . .

Ah, these hands, the first to raise the banner of any
    revelation,
And the last to gain its solace,—
Are lately raised towards Massada's walls—
To embrace!
I charge you, hands of Israel, if from here too you
    return empty—
Then fumble in empty space!
I charge you to grasp Massada's walls,
To grasp them unrelenting!
Or else—may these hands be cut off from whose
    embrace
Everything tumbles,
Whose grasp grips nothing!

The First Fruits

With song and drums, laden with all goodly things,
    let us ascend the wall.
Bringing as gifts hands filled with hearts golden in
    dreams,
Bearing pitchers of youth flowering with blood that
    sings,
And early clusters of life in baskets of love—
All as an offering to the battle and sacred to
    Massada!
O wall! Open up the gates of your empty crypts
And store the crops of our lives for the years of
    battle,
For still Massada's fields lie barren and
    sword-battered,
And who knows how much longer the battle and
    siege may last!
So till the good years come, and rains fall in their
    seasons,
And dew drops down each night on unfortified
    earth,
Until the scythe of victory reaps the blessings of the
    field securely—
Accept the first fruits of our lives, to feed your hun-
    gry fighters,
And the wells of our youth—for those who thirst!

Prayer

As for those who escaped foreign gallows and
    ascended the wall—
Guide their steps, O God, lest they stumble,
    or fall,
For they are feeble still, and weary.

And for those whose suns have grown dark in the
  world's seven heavens—
Grant, O God, the grace of Massada's last sun,
For if this too grows dark—where then shall they
  turn?
And to those who burst the swaddling banners of
  seventy nations—
Give O God a shirt to warm them and cover them,
In their trembling beaten nakedness . . .
As for those whose mother's milk has not yet dried
  upon their lips
And on whose cheeks the warm caress of father's
  hand still flutters—
Ease, O God, their orphanhood, be their father and
  their guard,
Lend their tender arms the strength to hold a heavy
  shield,
Soften Massada's hard rocks as pillows for their
  weary heads!
And for those who in tears have sown here the seed
  of soul and dreams—
Let not the seed be struck by the hail of grief, nor
  dried by sudden drought,
Command, O God, many rains of solace, many
  nourishing dews of night,
Till it grow to reap reparation!
As for those who breached the wall and came with
  ashes of destruction on their heads
And mourning sackcloth round their hips, to win
  consolation in this battle—
Lend them perseverance, God, when consolation is
  long in coming!
And to those on whom the nation's spirit has laid
  the riddle of its fate,
The task of providing solutions, of leading it to open
  gates—
Give strength, O God, and courage, to bear this
  heavy burden
Up to the border that in a last vision the afflicted
  spirit saw! . . .
Weary, weary are Massada's sons, the suffering of
  these few is heavy
And those who survived many battles, baring
  breasts to every arrow,
Have one more battle to survive, this long and stubborn battle
For this single strip of land—
Feast their spirits, God, extinguish not the flames of
  revolt

They brought as holy Sabbath candles to the wall
At the twilight of the worlds.
As night descends upon the wall—do not let the
  fires die!
From darkening horizons loneliness rises and
  threatens,
Satiety walks among the paths, whispering in every
  ear,
And weary ears incline, absorb the steady whisper
  . . .
Yesterday's memories weaken arms, and heads,
  always erect
And leaning forwards, are bent back in weariness;
Vain dreams spread dread and deep confusion
  among the fighters,
The sickle of misery reaps, and many, many are the
  fallen.
Spare them, O God, for the battle—why must these
  despairs come too
Upon Massada and its fighters?
Why should all the stars burn out when on the wall
  the fires die,
And one star alone remain—Israel's
  nightmare-star?—
Blazing seventyfold in ghastly light, sowing terror,
  its rays
Piercing the cracks in the walls, lighting up the
  chaos outside,
Ah, again and again the chaos———
How long will the emaciated hand of a nation
Fumble with blind fingers on the locks of
  salvation?
O God, look, the hand is stretched forth,
Between sea and wasteland it is stretched forth,
In its palm a last dream grown meagre from nights
  of restless wandering:
MASSADA!
To the numbered dead upon the wall this dream
  and its solution are given
If this time too you have no mercy, God, and the
  dream is not accepted,
And this time too the sacrifice of those who solved it
  is not respected
God, guard Massada!

Translated by Richard Flantz.

Other works by Lamdan: *Ba-Ritmah ha-meshuleshet*
(1930); *Mi-sefer ḥayamim* (1940); *Ma'aleh akravim*
(1945); *Otzar shel mazalot* (1950).

Kadya Molodovsky

1894–1975

The Yiddish poet Kadya Molodovsky was born in a small town in Belorussia, the daughter of a *maskil* who ensured that she received a broad Hebrew and secular education. She taught in Jewish schools and children's homes in Poland and Russia, both before and after World War I. In 1935, she settled in the United States. In her poetry, she was sensitive to the tension between the status of women in traditional Jewish life and her position as a creative writer. Her poetry also voiced the plight of impoverished Jewish workers, both men and women, and their children, whom she knew well as a teacher in Warsaw. She also wrote children's poetry.

Fallen Leaves
1927

I

> Words forsaken—fallen leaves,
> Let the wind scatter you,
> And let me forget you.
> I will remain like a wintry tree
> Behind closed eyes, still
> And silent.
> Both the night will cradle me, *ay-lu*,
> And the dark will cradle me, *ay-lu*.
> But these arms of mine, these white arms
> Will awaken, aroused,
> Still wanting to hug a warm body,
> A faithful body.
> These arms of mine, these white arms.

Translated by Kathryn Hellerstein.

Other works by Molodovsky: *Paper Bridges: Selected Poems of Kadya Molodowsky* (1999).

Kadya Molodovsky

Women-Poems I, II, VI
1927

I

> The women of our family will come to me in dreams
>   at night and say:

> Modestly we carried a pure blood across
>   generations,
> Bringing it to you like well-guarded wine from the
>   kosher
> Cellars of our hearts.
> And one woman will say:
> I am an abandoned wife, left when my cheeks
> Were two ruddy apples still fixed on the tree,
> And I clenched my white teeth throughout lonely
>   nights of waiting.
> And I will go meet these grandmothers, saying:
> Like winds of the autumn, your lives'
> Withered melodies chase after me.
> And you come to meet me
> Only where streets are in darkness,
> And where only shadows lie:
> And why should this blood without blemish
> Be my conscience, like a silken thread
> Bound upon my brain,
> And my life, a page plucked from a holy book,
> The first line torn?

II

> I will come to the one
> Who first brought me woman's delight,
> And say: Husband,
> I trusted someone else with my quiet gaze,
> And one night laid my head down near him.
> Now I bring my sorrow
> Like bees stinging around my heart,
> And have no honey to soothe the hurt.
> And when my husband takes me by the braid,
> I will drop to my knees
> And remain on the doorsill like the petrifaction of
>   Sodom.
> I will raise my hands to my head
> As my mother used to, blessing the candles,
> But my fingers will stand up like ten numbered sins.
>   [. . .]

VI

> For poor brides who were servant girls,
> Mother Sarah draws forth from dim barrels
> Pitchers of sparkling wine.
> To these so destined, Mother Sarah
> Carries a full pitcher with both hands.
> And for those so destined, Mother Sarah's
> Tear falls into the tiny goblet.

And for streetwalkers
Dreaming of white wedding shoes,
Mother Sarah bears pure honey
In small saucers
To their tired mouths.
For high-born brides now poor,
Who blush to bring patched underclothes
Before their mothers-in-law,
Mother Rebecca leads camels
Laden with white linen
And when darkness spreads before their feet,
And all the camels kneel on the ground to rest,
Mother Rebecca measures linen ell by ell
From her rings to her golden bracelet.
For those whose eyes are tired
From watching the neighborhood children,
And whose hands are thin from yearning
For a small, soft body
And for the rocking of a cradle,
Mother Rachel brings healing leaves
Discovered on distant mountains,
And comforts them with a quiet word:
At any hour, God may open the sealed womb.
To those who cry at night in solitary beds,
And have no one to share their sorrow,
Who talk to themselves with parched lips,
To them comes Mother Leah, quietly,
Shielding both eyes with her pale hands.

Translated by Kathryn Hellerstein.

Elizaveta Polonskaya

1890–1969

Born in Warsaw, Elizaveta Polonskaya was a Russian Jewish poet, translator, and journalist, and the only female member of the literary group known as the Serapion Brothers. After fleeing the 1905 pogroms in Poland, she spent much of her youth in St. Petersburg and was active in underground socialist politics, before leaving to study medicine at the Sorbonne. Polonskaya returned to Russia after the revolution, where her literary career began in earnest. Close to luminaries such as Lev Lunts and Ilya Ehrenburg, she produced verse rich in biblical and Jewish themes and female sexuality. In the 1930s, Polonskaya worked as a writer and journalist full-time, as well as being a translator of English and a children's writer, crafting prose sketches and poems in line with the Soviet Union's ideological literary guidelines. Aware of the sometimes violent repressions of her friends and colleagues, she produced almost no original verse in the postwar era.

Encounter

1927

Morning flew by in the usual way,
Up and down streets, it raced,
Unwinding the spring of an ongoing watch
That the night would wind up again.

A coat was fastened over the chest
With a clasp and a little chain,
Then a voice from the gut: "*tayer yiddish kind,*
Give to a beggar, Jewish daughter."

From under her rags she studies me
With a tender, cunning old face,
A sentinel's eye and a hookish nose,
And a black wig, parted smooth.

An ancient, yellowish hand
Grabs my sleeve, and the words
Of a language I don't comprehend
Sound out, seizing my heart.

And there I stop, I cannot go on,
Though I know—I shouldn't, I shouldn't
And drop a small coin in her open palm
And lift a thirsty heart to her face.

"Old woman, how did you, half-blind,
Pick me out among these strangers?
After all, your muttering is odd to me,
After all, I'm like them, the same as those—
Dull, alien, strange."

"Daughter, dear, there are things about us
That no one can mistake.
Our girls have the saddest eyes,
And a slow, languorous walk.

And they don't laugh like the others—
Openly in their simplicity—
But beam behind clouds as the moon does,
Their sadness alive in their smiles.

Even if you lose your faith and kin,
A yid iz immer a yid![1]
And thus my blood sings in your veins,"
She says in her alien tongue.

That morning flew by in the usual way,
Up and down streets, it raced,

Unwinding the spring of an ongoing watch
That the night would wind up again.

NOTE

1. Polonskaya's (imperfectly fictional?) old Jewish lady living in Moscow uses a Germanism, *immer* (always), in place of a Yiddish equivalent.

Translated by Larissa Szporluk.

Other works by Polonskaya: *Pod kamenym dozhdem* (1923); *Poezdka na Ural* (1927); *Upriamyi kalendar'* (1929); *Kamskaia tetrad'* (1945); *Na svoikh plechakh* (1948).

Rakhel (Rachel Bluwstein)

Rahel
1927

Behold her blood flows in my blood,
Behold her voice within me sings—
Rahel the herder of Laban's sheep,
Rahel—mother's mother.

And so the house is too constricting for me
And the city—alien,
For her shawl would flutter
In the desert winds;

And so I'll stick to my path
With much confidence,
For preserved in my legs are memories
From then, from then!

Translated by Miryam Segal.

Charles Reznikoff

Building Boom
1927

The avenue of willows leads nowhere:
it begins at the blank wall of a new apartment house
and ends in the middle of a lot for sale.
Papers and cans are thrown about the trees.
The disorder does not touch the flowing branches;
but the trees have become small among the new
    houses,
and will be cut down;
their beauty cannot save them.

How difficult for me is Hebrew:
even the Hebrew for *mother*, for *bread*, for *sun*

is foreign. How far have I been exiled, Zion.

I have learnt the Hebrew blessing before eating
    bread,
is there no blessing before reading Hebrew?

My thoughts have become like the ancient Hebrew
in two tenses only, past and future—
I was and I shall be with you.

God saw Adam in a town
without flowers and trees and fields to look upon,
and so gave him Eve
to be all these.
There is no furniture for a room
like a beautiful woman.

The sun shone into the bare, wet tree;
it became a pyramid of criss-cross lights,
and in each corner the light nested.

After I had worked all day at what I earn my living,
I was tired. Now my own work has lost another day,
I thought, but began slowly,
and slowly my strength came back to me.
Surely, the tide comes in twice a day.

Abraham Shlonsky

Toil
1927

Dress me, good mother, in a glorious robe of many
    colours, and at dawn lead me to [my] toil.

My land is wrapped in light as in a prayer shawl.
    The houses stand forth like frontlets; and the
    roads paved by hand, stream down like phylac-
    tery straps.

Here the lovely city says the morning prayer to its
    Creator. And among the creators is your son
    Abraham, a road-building bard of Israel.

And in the evening twilight, father will return from
    his travails, and, like a prayer, will whisper joy-
    fully: "My dear son Abraham, skin, sinews and
    bones—hallelujah."

Dress me, good mother, in a glorious robe of many
    colours, and at dawn lead me to toil.

Translated by T. Carmi.

Uri Zvi Greenberg

With My God the Blacksmith
1928

In all revelations my days flare like chapters of
    prophecy.
Mass of metal, my flesh between them awaits the fire.
Above looms my God the blacksmith, hammering
    terribly.
Each wound carved in me by Time splits into a
    fissure,
Sparking out inward fire in flashes of memory.

My fate controls me, till day has sunk in the west.
When this battered mass, thrown back on the bed,
    lies still,
With a gaping wound for a mouth, which none has
    dressed.
Naked I say to my God: Thou has wrought Thy
    will.
Now it is night: of Thy goodness, let us rest.

Translated by Dom Moraes.

Malka Lee

Red Evenings
1928

1

Into its own gold, the evening melted.
Bullet laughed midair across to bullet.
Colossal city fought with city, giants—
The sky disintegrated in red fragments.

Hatless, soldiers fly across the city,
Trampling through the fields, they crush like wheels,
Shrapnel tears the cliffs away from mountains—
Above abandoned market squares, night caws . . .

From the houses—through the cracks—the eyes of
    mothers,
Fingers clenching, tearing out tufts of hair.
If only our wombs could swallow back our
    daughters,
But paralyzed, dead watchmen, we guard them here.

There's the cellar, like a water-swollen belly.
The last of the food pulverized, submerged—

Shall we wrap ourselves around in prayer-shawls
And hide in the cemetery with the corpses?

2

In soft hay, in the attic, lie the marriageable girls—
They've hidden up there from the threat of rape,
The hay prickles—irritates their untouched
    bodies—
Let them come take us as their wives!

Armed with his sword, a soldier lies,
The girls' cold fear stares down at the ground,
Glances drown as in a muddy well—
Whose bridegroom has arrived here now?

Days and nights, buried deep in the hay,
Their female-crying shudders in their flesh,
Hey, Soldier! Throw down your gun,
Come to us on this exhausted bed.

Translated by Kathryn Hellerstein.

Miklós Radnóti

1909–1944

Miklós Radnóti is widely recognized as one of the greatest Hungarian poets of the twentieth century. He came from a highly acculturated Budapest family and received no Jewish education or introduction to Jewish ritual. He remained indifferent to Jewish affairs his entire life, assertively proclaiming his freedom from Jewish particularism. He and his wife converted to Catholicism in 1943 in a desperate effort to save themselves from further persecution. His poems, while more or less bereft of Jewish content, foretell and then record the savagery of the Nazi years. While serving in a forced labor battalion during the war because he was Jewish, according to Hungarian and Nazi racial laws, he was shot dead by his Hungarian guards.

"And Cain Spoke unto Abel His Brother"
1928

(Genesis 4:8)
for D.G., my uncle

Abel, brother, yesterday the primal crime awoke me:
I had murdered your snow-white dreams and
    damned I was urging myself
endlessly on down the night-darkening avenues of
    vainendeavor,

between rows of icy and dolorous trees toward the
    morning.

My sun-fragrant lands were weeping mistily after
    me,
my body in exile threw gasping onto my face the
    spotlight, the wounds,
the midnight woundings, the red roses of repen-
    tance; I implored
you, begged to purge the curse in the grand clasp of
    reunion.

You were the saint; oblation's burnt worship wafted
    over your birth;
but at mine, on the ancient day of my being, the
    gravid sky
bellowed aloud: with murderous weight I ripped my
    life
like the first leaf from the bitter, the sighing, curse-
    bearing tree.

And so I became Cain; on my rounded chest arose
    the sun
and my knees' weariness brought on the dusk of
    evening: that was when
I killed, that was when you scattered after me those
    your wordarrows,
wordhounds of your pain, and felled before my
    footsteps my night-gauntlet's guardians,
the icy and dolorous trees.

I stumbled, my flesh gashed open on the stumbling-
    blocks, and
I fell, and started to run again, blackly, biblically:
I am Cain, and yesterday the primal crime awoke
    me,
I am Cain, and you my brother Abel!

Translated by Zsuzannah Ozsváth and Frederick Turner.

Other works by Radnóti: *Miklós Radnóti: The Complete Poetry in Hungarian and English* (2014).

Itzik Feffer

1900–1952

Born to a working-class family in Ukraine, Itsik Feffer
joined the Communist Party as a teenager and rapidly
rose in the ranks of Soviet Union's first generation
of Yiddish-speaking intelligentsia. Feffer promoted
the use of *proste reyd*, or simple speech, in his liter-

ary works, a style that strove for simplicity and broad
comprehensibility for the mass of readers against
the more avant-garde and experimental trends of the
time. Feffer was fiercely loyal to the Soviet regime and
its ideology, crafting verse in praise of the state and
conforming strictly to the tenets of socialist realism, a
fact that drew significant literary and political criticism
from Yiddish literati in the West. Feffer served as an
informant for the NKVD on the Jewish Anti-Fascist
Committee, reporting on the activities of its members.
Despite his loyalty, he was executed for "nationalism"
and "anti-Soviet activities" alongside other members of
the committee on August 12, 1952.

Blooming Dungheaps
1929

Saturday evening—time for *havdoleh*.
No *havdoleh*, or candle. A blossoming moon.
Moon-streets and alleys are scorched with dust,
Scattered with strolling girls.

Girls in tulle, and their stockings too.
English coats—English shoes on their feet.
Mayakovsky and Blok they've read.
But not Arke, Izi, or me.

Tomorrow's Sunday. Fathers get ready:
A big market day in the town.
Girls and their Blok over shtetl mudpiles.
Moonlit streets with dust tamped down.

        * * *

Every home is ready for new poems
And every stone—for a new gaze.
Alive and tired
I go back home.

A turbid stream, like Bialik's cloudy tears.
An old man sits and sips weepy Frug.
Pioneers stroll on Holosravkeve
The Communist Youth sings on market day

Little streets recite contemporary poems;
My father sits, reading the Moscow *Emes*.
The day rings with golden coins and sun.
He dreams of a colony near Odessa.

        * * *

Who cares that I was circumcised
and they made—as Jews do—a bris.

The field winds scorched
my drowsy pale feet.

Jews are still dreaming of cholent here.
But the guys yearn for smoke and flame.
Eight years on the fields and valleys
Under the sea-blue sky.

They know me as good and quiet.
And honest. That's precious little, say some.
After all, I'm no market trader
Neither have I laid tefillin.

So what, then, that I'm circumcised
and they celebrated, like Jews, a bris.
Those field winds scorched
my pale drowsy feet.

Translated by Zackary Sholem Berger.

Other works by Feffer: *Proste reyd* (1925); *Bliendike mistn* (1929); *Birobidzhaner lider* (1939); *Roytarmeyish* (1943).

Itzik Feffer

I've Never Been Lost
1929

In all my short, happy life, I've never
Been lost, nor forgotten the way I came,
I laugh to myself when I remember
That I carry some famous rabbi's name.

The name that my grandfather wanted for me
Was the Holy Reb Itzikel of Skvira's,
That I might lay *tefillin* and wear a *tallis*
And do my singing of prayers and *zmires*,

That I might be the richest man in town,
And my wife's housekeeping be the best,
So days and nights gave way to each other,
And each year came to follow the rest.

The sun has blessedly bronzed my body,
My life is all battles and songs of fame;
It really breaks me up to remember
That I carry some famous rabbi's name.

Translated by John Hollander.

Jacob Fichman

Midnight
1929

A late crescent drips, its blood still red,
And the tranquil grasses of the night
Bend their small heads, one upon another,
Slumbering, arm beneath cheek,
In its peaceful light.
A weary wanderer kneels in a field's straits.
A horse in the meadow raises its head in surprise.

Then one stretches his arm over the world,
And everything congeals beneath him, unmoving.
A marvelous, strange light, like reddish copper,
Hangs over the dimmed earth.
A star falls from its chariot, and on its resting place
A sea-lion mutely licks its flippers.
Then no nursling will cry out, and the bud on its
    branch
Will contain its breath—
Only chaos, like a wild beast, from its lair
Will contend with the end of the world, will spread
    its jaws.
And at that hour, one can neither rise nor sink.

There is one hour. No one awaits it.
For it is the hour of the last watch,
Like hippos on the river the darkness will weigh,
And nature, unseen by its master,
Crouches without power upon the couch of night.
No eye watches at this hour and its misery
When yesterday, stricken, is gathered unto its
    ancestors.

Then the fruit ripens on the tree, and like a man
    forest
The vision of the world will bloom at the head of its
    bed.

Translated by Jeffrey M. Green.

Jacob Glatstein

Autobiography
1929

Yesterday, I dumped on my son the following story:
That my father was a cyclops and, of course, had
    one eye,

That my fifteen brothers wanted to devour me,
So, I barely got myself out of their clutches
And started rolling all over the world.
Rolling, I grew up in two days,
But I wouldn't go back to my father's house.
So, I went to Tsefania and learned *sprechen* Jewish,
I got myself circumcised and became a Yid.
So, I started selling flax, wax, esrogs with bitten-off
    tips,
And earned water for kasha.
Till I met an old princess
Who willed me an estate and died.
So, I became a landowner
And began guzzling and gorging.
And when I saw I was getting fat,
I made up my mind and got married.
After the marriage, my estate burned down.
So, I became a poor newspaper writer.

To my father, the cyclops, I sometimes write a letter,
But to my fifteen brothers—the finger.

Translated by Benjamin Harshav and Barbara Harshav.

Moyshe Kulbak

Grandfather Dying
1929

Gray as a dove, toward evening, my grandfather
    came from the pasture;
He made up his bed and said a prayer of confession,
Then inwardly bade his farewell to the world
And closed his eyes, utterly exhausted.

My uncles came in and gathered around at his
    bedside;
Bowing their shaggy heads they stood about, silent;
Something clutched at their hearts that left them all
    wordless—
Clutched at their hearts and kept them from
    sighing.

Then slowly my grandfather opened his eyes, and a
    smile
Spread over his face; he sat up, though it cost him
    much trouble;
And here's what he said to his sons: "You, my
    Ortsheh,
You've been the family keystone;

First in the field and the last one to sit at the table.
    The earth opened warmly to you and your
    plowshare.
May your seed, like the earth, be forever as fresh
    and as fertile.

And you, Rakhmiel, who is like you in the meadow?
Your scythe in the field was an outburst of fire.
You are known to the birds in the air; to the snakes
    in their marshes.
May my blessing rest on your barn; and blessed be
    your stable.

You, Schmulye, river man; who in the world is like
    you?
Eternally wet; and always a lash at your shoulders;
Smelling of fish scales, and smells of the scum of the
    river,
Blessed shall you be on the shore,
And blessed on the water."

It was evening; the glimmer of red at the window
Cast in the darkness, a tinge of light on my grandpa;
My uncles were still; and silent, too, was my father.
And caught every word of his blessing.

Then Grandfather said his goodbyes and gathered
    his limbs together;
He closed his wide eyes one more time, now and
    forever.
The watchers looked on and regarded his muted
    body;
There was nothing to see; and no tear was shed by
    my uncles.

A bird in the forest sang to the night of its sorrows;
The last bit of torch in the hut still gleamed in its
    socket.
My uncles formed a small band round my grandfa-
    ther's pillow,
Their heavy, their shaggy heads drooped on their
    shoulders.

Translated by Leonard Wolf.

Moyshe Kulbak

Summer
1929

Today, the world was unfurled once more and
    renewed.

The teeming earth, the whispering green, the swell-
　　ing bud.
Everything shook, as the tense body of a virgin
Becoming a joyful wife might be shaken.

And I, like a cat, lay in the middle of a field
Where light spurted and glistened and glowed.
One eye smeared by the sun, the other eye shut;
Silently laughing, silently feeling delight.
Across fields and valleys and woods, mile after mile,
I ramble: gleaming and hard, like steel.

Translated by Leonard Wolf.

Moyshe Kulbak

Vilna
1929

1

Someone in a *tales* is walking your rooftops.
Only he is stirring in the city by night.
He listens. Old gray veins quicken—sound
Through courtyard and synagogue like a hoarse,
　　dusty heart.
You are a psalm, spelled in clay and in iron.
Each stone a prayer; a hymn every wall,
As the moon, rippling into ancient lanes,
Glints in a naked and ugly-cold splendor.
Your joy is sadness—joy of deep basses
In chorus. The feasts are funerals.
Your consolation is poverty: clear, translucent—
Like summer mist on the edges of the city.
You are a dark amulet set in Lithuania.
Old gray writing—mossy, peeling.
Each stone a book; parchment every wall.
Pages turn, secretly open in the night,
As, on the old synagogue, a frozen water carrier,
Small beard tilted, stands counting the stars.

2

Only I am stirring in the city by night.
No sound. Houses are rigid—bales of rag.
A tallow candle flutters, dripping,
Where a cabalist sits, tangled into his garret,
Like a spider, drawing the gray thread of his life.
"Is there anyone in the cold emptiness?

In our deafness—can we hear the lost cries?"
Raziel is standing before him; he gleams in the
　　darkness.
The wings an old, faded parchment.
The eyes—pits filled with sand and with cobweb.
"There is no one. Only sorrow is left."
The candle drips. Stupefied, the weak man listens.
He suckles the darkness out of the angel's sockets.
The garrets breathe—lungs of
The hunchbacked creature who is drowsing in the
　　hills.
O city! You are the dream of a cabalist,
Gray, drifting in the universe—cobweb in the early
　　autumn.

3

You are a psalm, spelled in clay and in iron.
The letters fading. They wander—stray.
Stiff men are like sticks; women, like loaves of bread.
The shoulders pressed. Cold, secretive beards.
Long eyes that rock, like rowboats on a lake—
At night, late, over a silver herring,
They beat their breasts. "God, we are sinful . . .
　　sinful."
The moon's white eye, bulging through the tiny
　　panes,
Silvers the rags that hang on the line,
Children in beds—yellow, slippery worms,
Girls half undressed, their bodies like boards—
These gloomy men are narrow like your streets.
The brow mute—a rigid wall of a synagogue yard.
The eyebrows mossy: like a roof above your ruins.
You are a psalm inscribed upon the fields.
A raven, I sing to you by the flow of the moon.
No sun has ever risen in Lithuania.

4

Your joy is sorrow—joy of deep basses
In chorus. The quiet Maytime is somber.
Saplings grow from the mortar. Grasses push from
　　the wall.
Sluggishly, a gray blossom crawls out of the old tree.
The cold nettle has risen through mud.
Dung and rigid walls are sleeping in their damp.
It may happen by night that a breeze blows stone
　　and rooftop dry,
And a vision, moonbeam and drops of water,

Flows through the silver, tremulously dreaming
     streets.
It is the Viliya, cool, mistily arising,
Fresh and baby-naked, with long, riverlike hands,
That has come into the town. Blind windows are
     grimacing.
Arching bridges are crooked on their walls.
No door will open. No head will move
To meet the Viliya in her skinny, blue nakedness.
The bearded walls marvel—the hills around you.
And silence. Silence.

5

You are a dark amulet set in Lithuania.
Figures smolder faintly in the restless stone.
Lucid white sages of a distant radiance,
Small, hard bones that were polished by toil.
The red tunic of the steely bundist.
The blue student who listens to gray Bergelson—
Yiddish is the homely crown of the oak leaf
Over the gates, sacred and profane, into the city.
Gray Yiddish is the light that twinkles in the
     window.
Like a wayfarer who breaks his journey beside an
     old well,
I sit and listen to the rough voice of Yiddish.
Is that the reason why my blood is so turbulent?
I am the city: the thousand narrow doors into the
     universe,
Roof over roof, to the muddy-cold blue.
I am the black flame, hungry, licking at these walls—
That glows in the eyes of the Litvak in an alien land.
I am the grayness! I am the black flame! I am the
     city!

6

And, on the old synagogue, a frozen water carrier,
Small beard tilted, stands counting the stars.

Translated by Nathan Halper.

Anna Margolin
1887–1952

Although she published only one collection of poetry
in her lifetime, Anna Margolin (pseudonym of Rosa
Lebensboym) is widely considered one of the most important Yiddish writers of twentieth-century America.

A native of Brest (Brisk, in Yiddish, present-day
Belarus), Margolin lived in Warsaw, Western Europe,
and Palestine before settling permanently in New York
in 1914. There she began a successful career writing
for the Yiddish press and was a firmly established
member of the city's Yiddish intellectual circles. Her
poetry is modernist in style and tone, rooted in European and American intellectual traditions, and often
incorporates themes of love, loss, and alienation from
a woman's perspective. She belonged to no one literary
group or political party.

Once I Was Young
1929

Once I was young, hung out
in doorways, listening to Socrates.
My closest pal, my lover
Had the finest chest in Athens.

Then came Caesar, and a world
glittering with marble—I
the last to go. For my bride,
I picked out my proud sister.

At the late-night bashes, soused
and feeling fine, I'd hear
about the Nazareth weakling
and the exploits of the Jews.

Translated by Marcia Falk.

Other works by Margolin: *Lider* (1929).

Aharon Sason
1877–1962

Born in Baghdad, Aharon Sason was instrumental in
organizing the Zionist movement in Iraq after World
War I. He established a modern Jewish school, Pardes
Ha-Yeladim, in Baghdad, which employed the *ivrit-
be-ivrit* method for teaching Hebrew. In the late 1920s,
the Iraqi authorities began restricting his Zionist
activities and, after the 1936 Arab riots in Mandate
Palestine, they arrested him, charging him with advo-
cating Zionism. He was acquitted and fled to Palestine,
fearing for his safety. His poetry was didactic, a tool
for national revival, and not noted for its aesthetic
sophistication.

The National Movement
1929

Arise, shine, for thy light is come,
Shake thyself from the dust
Unlock the lock on your neck
Be saved from your enemy.

Awaken, get out of thy exile
Rise up from your degradation
Wake up from your sleep
Wake up from your deep slumber.

Awaken, return to your homeland
Don't sleep upon your bed
Don't drag your exile
Because your redemption is in your hands.

Awaken, see your friends
Most of whom returned to your cities
Sowing, planting your mountains
Building, paving your roads.

Awaken, perform your duty
Do not be a recluse of your community
Hurry up and do your fair share
Participate in your revival.

Awaken, research your history
Is there any faith in your prisoners
Do they look for your welfare
Or plunder your delights?

Awaken, speak your own language
Plant your plants, sow your garden
Clear the earth of stones, construct your edifice
Teach your children your culture.

Awaken, live in your country
A shelter, sanctuary, your life resort
The dawn arose, your buds bloomed
The moon shone on your pioneer.

Translated by Lev Hakak.

Other works by Sason: *Shirei tehiyah* (1924).

Julian Tuwim

To the Common Man
1929

When they begin to plaster the walls
With freshly printed proclamations,

When black print sounds alarm
Calling "To the People" and "To Soldiers"
And ruffians and adolescents
Are taken in by their recurring lies
And believe that you should start firing cannons
Murder, poison, burn and plunder
When they start clawing at the Fatherland
In a thousand variations.
Deceive with colored emblems,
With "history's right" incite to action
For expansion, glory, border,
Forefathers, fathers and the flag,
For heroes and for victims;
When the bishop, pastor, rabbi
Goes out to bless your rifle,
Because the Lord has whispered to him
"One must fight for Fatherland";
When the clamor of daily headlines
Has grown bitchy and brutish
And a horde of howling hags tosses
Flowers upon the "little soldiers."—
—O my unlearned friend,
My kin of this or any other land!
You'll know it's the kings, the bulging
Lords who toll the bells for danger,
You'll know it's for the birds, mere fraud,
When they command you "Shoulder weapon!"
It means that somewhere they have struck oil
Which will bring them riches:
That something has gone wrong in the banks they
    own
That they scent cash somewhere
Or that those bloated rascals have now thought up
A higher duty on cotton.
Throw down your rifle on the pavement!
The blood is yours, and the oil theirs!
And from one capital city to another
Cry out in defence of your hard-earned bread:
"Gentlemen—peddle your lies somewhere else!"

Translated by Antony Polonsky.

Aaron Zeitlin

Self-Portrait
1929

When the cool, colorful, gentile Sundays come,
both sit—Valenti, the watchman from my courtyard

and his pock-marked, redmouthed, piggish old lady
back-to-back on a wooden bench.
Both of them gaze away a whole Sunday afternoon
and don't get bored. They are realists.

And they do what? They stare silently, and relax.
They look at dogs, at a kid with a bagel,
At smoke, impoverished city birds,
at fragments of cloud that hold out
their glass hats—asking for donations—
at buttons in sand and a rabbi with earlocks.

And when I, newsman and kabbalist combined,
Me, the contradiction of anxiety and insight,
(the child of my people after all, a nation pairing
ash of reportage with emanation's glimmer)
when I run home on Sunday, half-eagle, half-worm
with a bunch of newspapers under my arm,
with hatred for my day, tortured blood
and the frozen waiting for a crystalline minute—
I meet out front the watchman Valenti with his wife
sitting out front and staring, half awake,
enjoying their *confirmation* of things.
I shoot them a look of envy and contempt,
and the thought runs through my head, "I couldn't
    do that!"
not even in another life, no I just couldn't,
I, Aharon—in the vulgate, Arik—paradox of the
    darling shekhina,
Abstract but sane, ideologico-artistic sectarian,
He who writes his verse for nothing and no one,
Not even for the sake of Holy Art (™),
but for the stern service
of his *own* commanding God,
me, kabbalists' grandson.

And at night,
At night, in my dream, the radiant *Crown*
bends, lost in thought, to the lips of the *Kingdom*:
And Reb Moshe Cordovero sings to the *Exalted
    Mother*,
Frank strolls, dressed in red, with the beautiful
    Avatshe,
Till my great-grandfather, the Lyubavitcher *khazn*,
starts chanting a *kol-nidre* of generations hence,
ending at the cave of the Ba'al-Shem,
among seventy-two dancing letters of the *Name*,
and among angels, scaling high walls,
holding shofars to their mouth and sounding the
    End . . .

A week later it's Sunday. Sunday again,
and there they sit, my watchman and his pock-
    marked wife,
back to back on a wooden bench,
staring gray-eyed at what's there,
enjoying themselves.

Translated by Zackary Sholem Berger.

Mani Leib
1883-1953

Mani Leib was the pen name of the American Yiddish poet Mani Leib Brahinsky. Born in Nizhyn, Ukraine, he ended his formal education at age eleven, when he was apprenticed to a bootmaker. While still in his teens, he was twice arrested for revolutionary activities. He emigrated in 1905, spent a year in England, and settled in New York in 1906. He worked throughout his life as a shoemaker. A central figure in the avant-garde Di Yunge, he was known for his "sound poems," verse that used alliteration, cadence, repetition, and sibilance to great effect.

I Am the Knight
1920s

I am the knight of yearned-for blue
On God's rosy, holy ways.
My yearning is white like milk and dew
And sweet as the honey-rain.

My armor, my sword—my word and my blood.
My sign—the green of cedar;
The lofty sky—my hat of blue,
The sun, my golden feather.

Translated by Solon Beinfeld.

Other works by Mani Leib: *Lider un baladn* (1955); *Sonetn* (1962).

Mani Leib

The Machine
1920s

The machine, the tool.
Walls without bricks—my cage.

My hands' holy blood
Drips from the walls.

But the blood of my soul
Drips beyond the threshold

Both out there and in here
Drips the blood of my hour.

Translated by Solon Beinfeld.

Mani Leib

You, My Master
1920s

You, my master, my hidden enemy! I see you hidden
In the wind that is around all, in all, everywhere:
In my uneasy sleep, in my dark fear at morning,
In my labors by day, in my bread and my salt.

Come out with your eyes and look sharply into
    mine:
Let our eyes cross—an arrow and a sword.
Whose knees will tremble—let him bow in sadness
With his honest blood on the bloody earth.

Come out, I am ready, and my arrow is sharpened:
I am here—an accursed pillar toward the sun.

Translated by Solon Beinfeld.

Izi Charik

Poem
1930

Who cares if eternity won't know me,
if no one ever watches my footsteps—
but now, right now, when hearts are burning,
I come with fists in my song.

Of course I'd like to sing myself away,
to cry out all my hurting with the wind—
but, though I would not find that hard, I cannot,
when life bears down too much on everyone.

The stars are not—till now—my enemies,
and I can keep my peace with all the winds,
but when I am ablaze I must not listen
to the air that, rustling, lingers over me.

Who cares if eternity won't know me,
if no one ever watches my footsteps—
but now, right now, when hearts are burning,

I must come with my song!

Translated by Allen Mandelbaum.

Moyshe-Leyb Halpern

In Central Park
1930

Who is to blame that I don't see your tree,
Garden in snow, my garden in snow.
Who is to blame that I don't see your tree—
When a woman goes out for a stroll in your snow,
Her bosom rising and bouncing so,
As on choppy waves in the sea
A boat with two pirates who row
And shout that they are two pirates who row—
Garden in snow, my garden in snow.

Who is to blame that there is no deer,
Garden in snow, my garden in snow.
Who is to blame that there is no deer—
When a priest who should be good as a child
Is running after his hat gone wild
In the wind, and shouting: Hey, Ho, and Oh dear!
And the hat, in its damn whirlblow,
Heeds him not, in its damn whirlblow—
Garden in snow, my garden in snow.

Who is to blame that I'm a stranger to you,
Garden in snow, my garden in snow.
Who is to blame that I'm a stranger to you—
When I wear a scarf and a cap at a slant,
Things that no one would wear in this land,
And I still have a beard that the wind blows
Like a woman seeking an egg in the straw
For her sick child, an egg in the straw—
Garden in snow, my garden in snow.

Translated by Benjamin Harshav and Barbara Harshav.

Aharon Kushnirov

A Letter to Feffer
1930

From other friends—poets, creators,
who are dear to me always,
I step away today,
Feffer,

and turn to you!

The battles still rage
on our literary planet
but it's time to consider
the creative meteor.

Our grand totals are considerable.
We have beautiful bottom lines
but a fair bit falls out
on our walking together.

[. . .]
Battles erupting
Right here
Still important
Right here
to shout out
with the best poem:
Down with neutral poetry!
Get out!
Out of the ranks—
Everything wanting to blur the battle!
We're strongly aligned
with every sense and mettle.

Heart's flame
and eyes' blade
for harsh attack, starting now
against those who bend right
and those who fold left!

From the point of view
of battles
resounding on our
planet, Feffer,
you must consider
the creative meteor.

The poem is worth no more than zero
when it isn't given full power—
packed with powder inside
and steel armor without!

The breath of our age
should smash every barrier,
sitting firm in the saddle
of the sharpest edged form.
Poet's meaning shouldn't
be hidden
but revealed
for bright exchanges

with close hearts
at a distance.

This poem, which millions
must take in thirstily
should rise, able
to overcome its mean.

No, this isn't the same
polishing and caressing
that any esthetic cat can do.

Both "turbulence"
and "blossoming junk"
can be proud of their craft.
But we don't need jewelers—
we need metal workers!

We need to grip the poem
while racing through entire weeks
to walk
in the steps
at the pace of our great age.

We demand
in the surefire name of victory
—ours and everyone's—
a poem:
a brick for construction
a poem:
a slogan for banners!

—*July 1930, Black Sea*
Translated by Zackary Sholem Berger.

Esther Raab

Holy Grandmothers in Jerusalem
1930

Holy grandmothers in Jerusalem,
May your virtue protect me.
The smell of blossoms and blooming orchards
I suckled with my mother's milk.
Feet soft as hands, fumbling
In the torrid sand,
And tousled eucalypti
Laden with bees and hornets
Whispered a lullaby to me.
Seven times shall I steep myself

Into the Mediterranean
To prepare for King David, my beloved,
And I shall go up to him, with glorious dignity,
To the mountains of Jerusalem;
I shall sit with Deborah under the date-tree,
Have coffee with her and talk
About war and defence.
Holy grandmothers in Jerusalem,
May your virtue protect me.
I can feel the smell of your garments,
The aroma of Sabbath-candles and naphthaline.

Translated by Abraham Birman.

Miklós Radnóti

Portrait
1930

This is what *he* must have looked like,
Christ in the autumn, like me with my
twenty-two summers: still beardless,
blond, and the girls couldn't help it,
dreamed of him night after night!

Translated by Zsuzannah Ozsváth and Frederick Turner.

Shimon Ginsburg
1890–1944

The American Hebrew poet Shimon Ginsburg was
born in Ukraine and received a traditional heder
education and then a secular education. He first attracted attention as a promising young Hebrew poet in
Odessa, then the capital of Hebrew letters, where he
lived from 1909 to 1912. Leaving for New York in 1912,
he studied at Columbia University and the University
of Saskatchewan before completing a doctorate at
Dropsie College. He worked in Hebrew education and
took part in American Hebraist projects. He immigrated to Palestine in 1933, finding work as an editor.
He returned to the United States in the late 1930s
to raise funds for literary institutions in the Land of
Israel. His poetry was unsparing in its portrayal of the
coarseness and ignorance of immigrant Jewish life in
the United States.

In Praise of the Hebraists in America
1931

Like a sparse string of lights, scattered but
    connected
belonging to a strange and darkly snowy train
    station
that suddenly pops up among the winter fields,
forgotten somewhere between New York and
    Cleveland,
I have imagined you, Hebraists in the expanses of
    America.

No one knows who planted your seed, a holy seed,
    here in this land
or who is the lost father and the lost mother who left
    you
on your own here in this winter night of snow and
    stars.
Yet—I swear by this vastness—the warmth of your
    breath
will dispel its secret melancholy
and light up and sweeten the darkness of the night.

Alien to your brethren, to yourselves and your fami-
    lies and misunderstood by your children,
you keep a holy compact with Peretz Smolenskin
and you carry this covenant with you at your peril
    through the din of life,
and through the forty-nine gates of impurity you
    bear it like the song of Eden.
As you march to your own lights on the road of life,
with a psalm or Bialik singing hidden in your souls,
the Potomac River will give heed to you and the
    Mississippi will look on astonished:
For passing before them is something surpassingly
    handsome
and sad and exalted,
which has no match and will remain unique forever.

John, the Yankee shopkeeper, settled among his
    people,
sits in his easy chair blowing smoke rings with his
    pipe
and, confused, listens to the barking
of Hitler giving his blessings to the slaughter,
and, sorting things out in his mind, he hesitates to
    take a stand.
Yet when one of you happens to pass by him,
with the light in your eyes and your modest gait,

John, with a radiant look, suddenly directs
the smoke of his pipe aloft,
like one who has intuitively sensed the presence of a
    figure drawn from the same ancient sources from
    which his own ancestors drank.

But you, alike men of action and princes of dreams,
John's complacency is not for you,
and not for you either is the frozen majesty of these
    fields
or the Lord of the Forest's great wintry tranquility.
Every day and every night, whether at work or
    leisure,
The horrid curse of Exile and the cry of your breth-
    ren from the corners of the earth mortally wound
    you,
like the venomous bite of the snake that darts out
    from its lair to pursue its prey.
Answering you are the frustrated dream of
    redemption
and the messianic vision that hangs arrested on the
    brink of the abyss.

Then will come the sound of the beating wings of
    an eagle, screeching, wounded, proud, above the
    Judean Hills.
You stand there momentarily dazed, as if you
    yourselves were eagle offspring, though far
    removed,
and your soul goes out to his wondrous sign
given to the generation and the world, and, behold,
    it is again hidden away.

Your heart drips blood with your brethren caught in
    the grip of Cain/Haman, your oppressor,
yet in your eye, that reservoir of pent-up tears,
there will forever shine, trembling and divine,
the sun-drenched prophetic dream.

Translated by Alan Mintz.

Other works by Ginsburg: *Shirim u-foemot* (1931).

Aharon Kushnirov

Friends of My Age!
1931

Friends of my age,
My happy generation,

We strode, pained-pleased,
Through the wreckage of whole worlds.

Before the living and the dead
fell on our portion
Inherited old skins
of ourselves—and others' wrappings.

The tracks on our path
are covered with smoke
while our eyes—are bright
with the gleam of those days.

And only for spun silver
in the storm of the tousled peruque—
the gleam of great winds
of crude storms.

Friends of my age,
my alert, proud generation,
we founded in the depths
pillars of new worlds.

The pillars of new worlds:
we raise them up up high!
And the days run after us
to dust off the freshness of bricks.

We won't always guard
Against that happy race
Sometimes won't even bother
To carve names on those bricks

But all founded thresholds
from our great buildings
will proudly tell out
the wonders of loyal hands.

How weariness did not break us
at start or at sum
and the wind of these ages
strengthened, did not shake us.

In the storm we were the axis
around which worlds were upended.
Comrades of my generation,
deployed at the last frontiers.

Ready for new challenges
Prepared for the new call
mightier whirling the Earth—
We don't lack breath!

Translated by Zackary Sholem Berger.

Osip Mandelstam

Poem No. 228
1931

A Jewish musiker,
Alex Herzovitch,
wound his Schubert around and around
like diamonds.

Morning to night, happy, oh happy,
he ground out that same old
sonata, ground it by rote, ground it
to a crunch.

Well Alex Herzovitch,
it's dark on the street . . .
Stop it, my Alex Scherzo-vitch,
who's listening, who cares, why bother? . . .

Let some *bella ragazza*
chase her Schubert from a tiny
sleigh, flying
on crackling snow.

For us, with our dove of music,
death's no very big deal,
we die, we hang on a peg
like a crow-skin coat.

It's all wound up, wound up, my
Alex Rare-tsevitch . . .

Translated by Burton Raffel and Alla Buragos.

Gertrud Kolmar

The Jewish Woman
1932

I am a stranger.

Since no one dares approach me
I would be girded with towers
That wear their steep and stone-gray caps
Aloft in clouds.

The brazen key you will not find
That locks the musty stair. It spirals skyward
As a serpent lifts its scaly head
Into the light.

Oh these walls decay like cliffs
That streams have washed a thousand years;

And birds with raw and wrinkled craws
Lie burrowed deep in caves.

Inside the halls of sifting sand
Crouch lizards hiding speckled breasts—
An expedition I would mount
Into my ancient land.

Perhaps somewhere I can unearth
The buried Ur of the Chaldeans,
The idol Dagon, Hebrew tents,
Or the horn of Jericho.

What once blew down the haughty walls
Now lies in twisted ruin underground;
And yet I once drew breath
To sound its note.

Eternal worlds will echo back my call.
And when I bend my neck
The shaking earth will wreck
Its cities: I am greatest. I am all.

Translated by Henry A. Smith.

Gertrud Kolmar

The Woman Poet
1932

You hold me now completely in your hands

My heart beats like a frightened little bird's
Against your palm. Take heed! You do not think
A person lives within the page you thumb.
To you this book is paper, cloth, and ink,

Some binding thread and glue, and thus is dumb,
And cannot touch you (though the gaze be great
That seeks you from the printed marks inside),
And is an object with an object's fate.

And yet it has been veiled like a bride,
Adorned with gems, made ready to be loved,
Who asks you bashfully to change your mind,
To wake yourself, and feel, and to be moved.

But still she trembles, whispering to the wind:
"This shall not be." And smiles as if she knew
Yet she must hope. A woman always tries,
her very life is but a single "You . . ."

With her black flowers and her painted eyes,
With silver chains and silks of spangled blue.

She knew more beauty when a child and free,
But now forgets the better words she knew.

A man is so much cleverer than us,
Conversing with himself of truth and lie,
Of death and spring and iron-work and time
But I say "you" and always "you and I."

This book is but a girl's dress in rhyme,
Which can be rich and red, or poor and pale,
Which may be wrinkled, but with gentle hands,
And only may be torn by loving nails.

So then, to tell my story, here I stand
The dress's tint, though bleached in bitter lye,
Has not all washed away. It still is real.
I call then with a thin, ethereal cry.

You hear me speak. But do you hear me feel?

Translated by Henry A. Smith.

Else Lasker-Schüler

Departure
1932

> The rain cleaned off the steep facade of houses;
> I write upon the white and stony sheet
> And feel how my tired hand so softly rouses
> From love poems that always, sweetly, were a cheat.
>
> I wake in the stormy night, on high waves of the sea!
> Perhaps I have slipped from my angel's loving hand;
> I cheated the world, and the world has cheated me;
> I buried the corpse with the seashells in the sand.
>
> We all look up to a *single* heaven, begrudge each
>   other land?
> Why has God drawn away with lightning toward
>   the East,
> By the image of His human being outmanned?
>
> I wake in the stormy night, on high waves of the sea!
> What bound me to the Day of Rest when His cre-
>   ation ceased
> Has flown, like a late eagle-army, into this dark
>   unsteadily.

Translated by Robert P. Newton.

Joseph Leftwich

1892–1984

Joseph Leftwich was born in Holland to Polish parents, who settled in the East End of London in 1897. He left school at age fourteen and, after working in the baking, furniture, and fur trades, became a journalist. He wrote for Yiddish, Hebrew, and English newspapers, composed verse in Yiddish and English, and wrote a valuable memoir of Israel Zangwill, whom he knew well. Leftwich was one of the "Whitechapel Boys," a group of aspiring writers and artists in the East End in the years just before World War I. The group included John Rodker, Isaac Rosenberg, Stephen Winsten, Mark Gertler, and David Bomberg. His most important contributions to Jewish culture were his anthologies of Yiddish literature, which introduced to English-speaking readers a body of literature that was otherwise inaccessible to them.

Zangwill
1932

> Someone gathered rich apples, rich corn,
> Grown of your heart and your brain,
> And in me, as a loft, has stored
> Some of the fruit and grain.
>
> The loft smells sweet with its store:
> The corn for making bread,
> And apples for cider to drink.
> And the floor for a weary head.
>
> Though your fields grow no more grain,
> And your trees no more apples bear,
> Your ripe corn still stands high,
> And many reapers are reaping there.

Other works by Leftwich: *The Golden Peacock: An Anthology of Yiddish Verse* (1939); *Yisroel: The First Jewish Omnibus* (1945); *The Way We Think: Jewish Essays at Mid-Century* (1969).

Mani Leib

I Am . . .
1932

> I am Mani Leyb, whose name is sung—
> In Brownsville, Yehupets, and farther, they
>   know it:

Among cobblers, a splendid cobbler; among
Poetical circles, a splendid poet.

A boy straining over the cobbler's last
On moonlit nights . . . like a command,
Some hymn struck at my heart, and fast
The awl fell from my trembling hand.

Gracious, the first Muse came to meet
The cobbler with a kiss, and, young,
I tasted the Word that comes in a sweet
Shuddering first to the speechless tongue.

And my tongue flowed like a limpid stream,
My song rose as from some other place;
My world's doors opened onto dream,
My labor, my bread, were sweet with grace.

And all of the others, the shoemaker boys,
Thought that my singing was simply grand:
For their bitter hearts, my poems were joys.
Their source? They could never understand.

For despair in their working day's vacuity
They mocked me, spat at me a good deal,
And gave me the title, in perpetuity,
Of Purple Patchmaker, Poet and Heel.

Farewell then, brothers, I must depart:
Your cobbler's bench is not for me.
With songs in my breast, the Muse in my heart,
I went among poets, a poet to be.

When I came, then, among their company,
Newly fledged from out my shell,
They lauded and they laureled me,
Making me one of their number as well.

O Poets, inspired and pale, and free
As all the winged singers of the air,
We sang of beauties wild to see
Like happy beggars at a fair.

We sang, and the echoing world resounded.
From pole to pole chained hearts were hurled,
While we gagged on hunger, our sick chests
    pounded:
More than one of us left this world.

And God, who feedeth even the worm—
Was not quite lavish with his grace,
So I crept back, threadbare and infirm,
To sweat for bread at my working place.

But blessed be, Muse, for your bounties still,
Though your granaries will yield no bread—
At my bench, with a pure and lasting will,
I'll serve you solely until I am dead.

In Brownsville, Yehupets, beyond them, even,
My name shall ever be known, O Muse.
And I'm not a cobbler who writes, thank heaven,
But a poet who makes shoes.

Translated by John Hollander.

Eliezer Shteynbarg

1880–1932

Born in the shtetl of Lipkany (Lipkon, in Yiddish),
Bessarabia (present-day Lipcani, Moldova), Eliezer
Shteynbarg was an educator and writer, famous for
his original fables. Ostensibly written for children,
Shteynbarg's fables were masterfully crafted with an
eye toward a sophisticated adult reader, incorporating
playful yet shrewd social commentary on Jewish life in
Eastern Europe. Seamlessly weaving together religious
and secular themes and language, the fables were
praised as uniquely Jewish texts that nevertheless drew
on a broader European tradition of modern fabulists,
including Jean de La Fontaine and Ivan Krylov. A
dedicated pedagogue and cultural activist, Shteynbarg
played a leading role in Romanian Jewish cultural life
throughout the interwar period. He died in Czernowitz (present-day Chernivtsi, Ukraine).

The Horse and the Whip
1932

"May an unforeseen disaster
Overtake your worthy master,
The wagoner, Reb Benjamin,
And strike at you along with him."
The horse was saying
to the whip and neighing,
"Did you ever
Hear of such a thing? I never . . .
Tell me why I'm always beaten.
And for nothing, too! You think it's fun to drag this
    dray?
Remember, first of all, I haven't even eaten
Half a barley grain today
Not to mention oats! Poor
Me! But go talk to a whip, a boor!

If your hide felt this stinging tanning
You'd stop that fanning
Flogging, flaying
What again . . . ? I'll raise a rumpus on the streets by
    neighing . . ."

"Shut up." The whipstick crackles its long tongue
It's true, that draggin' this here wagon,
And to top it off, on an empty stomach, naggin'
Well, it's possible to pop a lung
But when I whip, you see—
Just between . . . um . . . you and me—
It's not 'cause you don't want to drag
The wagon. They ought to chop your head for this.
You ass! Your horse-sense went amiss!
You let yourself be harnessed—nag!"

Translated by Curt Leviant.

Other works by Shteynbarg: *Mesholim*, vol. 1 (1932),
vol. 2 (1956); *The Jewish Book of Fables* (2003).

David Saliman Tsemah
1902–1981

The Hebrew poet David Saliman Tsemah was born
and educated in Baghdad, where he studied at both
a school of the Alliance Israélite Universelle and a
modern yeshiva. He worked as a dealer in books and
manuscripts, a rabbi, and a *mohel*. He wrote poetry
(much of it in medieval Hebrew meter) and published
scholarly articles on medieval Spanish Hebrew poetry.
He also published Judeo-Arabic collections of fables,
proverbs, and poems. He visited Mandate Palestine
twice: in 1932, when he became friendly with Bialik,
and in 1935, when he worked with David Yellin on an
edition of the work of the medieval Spanish mystic
Todros Abulafia. In 1949, when the status of Iraqi
Jewry deteriorated, he settled in Israel. He was the
first poet of Mizrahi origin to protest the treatment of
immigrants from Arab lands.

Jeshurun
1932

Jeshurun sings when they see him
Tender beauty in her youth
She plays and her violin is on her bosom
And its singing brings gladness to the heart of the
    gloomy

An unadorned graceful gazelle
Embellished with a variety of fragrances
And it was nourished among the Arabs and from
    them
With nose-rings
And four bracelets on her arms
And a string of pearls beautifies her corpse
And bells are upon the skirts of her fur
Ring the name of the sages.

Translated by Lev Hakak.

H. Leivick

Sanatorium
1932–1936

Gate, open
doorsill, creep near.
Room, I'm here;
back to the cell.

Fire in my flesh.
snow on my skull.
My shoulder heaves
a sack of grief.

Good-bye. Good-bye.
Hand. Eye.
Burning lip
charred by good-bye.

Parted from whom?
From whom fled?
Let the riddle slip
unsaid.

The circling plain
is fire and flame:
fiery snow
on the hills.

Look—this open door
and gate. Guess.
Hospital? Prison?
some monkish place?

Colorado! I throw
my sack of despair
on your fiery floor
of snow.

Translated by Cynthia Ozick.

H. Leivick

Song of the Yellow Patch
1932-1936

How does it look, the yellow patch
With a red or black Star-of-David
On the arm of a Jew in Naziland—
Against the white ground of a December snow?
How would it look, a yellow patch
With a red or black Star-of-David
On the arms of my wife and my sons,
On my own arm—
On the white ground of a New York snow?
Truly—
The question gnaws like a gnat in my brain.
The question eats at my heart like a worm.

And why should we escape with mere words?
Why not share in full unity
And wear on our own arms
The destined yellow patch with the Star-of-David
Openly, in New York as in Berlin,
In Paris, in London, in Moscow as in Vienna?
Truly—
The question gnaws like a gnat in my brain,
The question eats at my heart like a worm.

Today the first snow descended,
Children are gliding on sleds in the park,
The air is filled with clamor of joy—
Like the children, I love the white snow,
And I have a special love for the month of
    December.

(Somewhere far, somewhere far away
lies a prisoner, lies alone.)

O dear God, God of Abraham, of Isaac and of
    Jacob,
Scold me not for this love of mine—
Scold me for something else—
Scold me for not kneading
This wonderful snow of New York into a Moses,
For not building a Mount Sinai of snow,
As I used to in my childhood.—

(Somewhere wanders a man,
Deeply covered in snow.)

Scold me for not really wearing
The six-towered Star-of-David

And the infinite circle of the yellow patch—
To hearten the sons of Israel in Hangman's-Land
And to praise and raise our arm
With the pride of our ancestral emblem
In all the lands of the wide world
Truly—
The question gnaws like a gnat in my brain,
The question eats at heart like a worm.

(Somewhere far, somewhere far away
Lies the land, the forbidden land.)

Translated by Benjamin Harshav and Barbara Harshav.

Uri Zvi Greenberg

King Shabtai Tsvi
1933

. . . Shabtai Tsvi lived, in fact, by the grace of the
    Turkish Sultan—a Moslem like all his
    courtiers,
and fell (as was the custom) face down on a divan
    each day, to bow and pray toward Mecca—
upon his head not David's gold crown but a Turkish
    fez with a tassel—
false Messiah!
cursed by the pious among the Jews, derided by
    even the foolish.
But it was not sanctity, it was this mockery, that
    Shabtai Tsvi desired.

From Istanbul in Turkey to the Polish towns on the
    Visla,
as far as the River Bug and the Carpathian Moun-
    tains, as far as world-famed Cracow,
and from there to the Rhine and farther, wherever
    Jews are living
his name is mocked, and every boy in *kheder* an
    authority on his story—
Much bitterness on their lips. For the apostate
    hankered
for the gold of every treasure,
the crown of every Caesar.

Do you twig the devil's game?
If it were possible to cut up this apostate
into little slices, it would be worth the trouble!
To throw them to the street dogs and season them
    in salt.

Among the Jews each spider weaves all of this into
    its web,
and every Jewish eye beholds smoke rise, sparks fly
    from Turkey.
Shabtai's set fire to our faith's foundations—may His
    mercy preserve us—*ai! ai! ai!*

At morning and evening prayer Jews grimace their
    tiger-pain angrily, bitterly,
but no one knows the secret of his great suffering
as he lies on his Turkish bed at night, utterly divided:
half of him Messiah, the other a second Mohammed;
and between him and the people a curved knife
    looming.

And just as they cannot see him, eating gall and
    drinking poison as he sits at a Turkish table,
so they cannot know the secret of his weeping, head
    buried in a pillow,
the intensity of his horror!
No, no one knows the wound-woe of this Messiah,
    this newly-become effendi, as from afar
his people's poisoned glare falls on him in Turkey.
(The mockery survives in Jewish books—may he rot
    and putrefy!)

No, no one saw how he'd rise in the night and hold
    in his two hands
his uncrowned head-of-a-king, as if it were not a
    head but a sort of metal—seared,
and champ the scream within his mouth:

"Once my Messiah-body gave off the fragrance of
    balm; now it
throws off the smell of a body rotting
alive! a horror as if encrusted with the heads of pins!
I had set aflame like forests the sorrows of genera-
    tions. In the Slav lands
all the Jews celebrated—in sable hats and silken
    coats made pilgrimages to Turkey.
And those who didn't go—their eyes followed after,
followed those privileged to go to the King Messiah,
    he who would soon take over
the Turkish crown. And every night Jews dreamed
that the great hurts, the great needs, like little fish
    were swimming in clear streams of joy;
that figs were growing, dates were growing, and
    breads as well, breads, too;
that the mountains were all dissolving; that there
    were lying on either side the world-path
radiant stones, all gold!"

But the Jew's dark destiny did not wish it so.
There waited instead for Shabtai Tsvi a Turkish fez
    with a tassel—
and when Shabtai Tsvi-Mohammed-Effendi died,
    and the Moslems
buried him as their rituals required,
not one Jew tore his jacket cloth, or the cloth of the
    Ark in mourning.
The every opposite! Oh, Jews, rejoice, rejoice! Satan
    is his mourner!
Nor did the Jews inquire among the Moslems
regarding the blue-brown bruises everywhere upon
    him,
because, when he had been called throughout his
    days and nights Mohammed and Effendi,
his hands had pinched like dough the flesh of his
    body.

Once more among the Jews every table has grown
    sad.
Once more—anxiety and anguish, like a sea with its
    fish;
and curses and prayers in the morning and curses
    and prayers at night.
And thirsty cattle once more by the closed
    well-mouth.
Nor did there appear one Jew to redeem that
    wretched body
from Turkish hands, to cover with a *tales*
that folk-mocked Messiah—to cover him and flee.

How great then is the distance between Istanbul
    and Jaffa? He could have placed the dead man on
    a raft,
entrusted all to the current (just as the Jews once
    trusted Lithuanian waters),
with birds following after,
and like the waves beneath them, the clouds rolling
    above them—
that for cortège for a dead man on a raft, a folk-
    derided Messiah.
But there was no such Jew in Turkey.
Nor can any man in these parts realize
with what a shout of joy King Shabtai Tsvi
    descended
into the fire of hell, his own fire!

Translated by Robert Friend.

Antoni Słonimski

Two Fatherlands
1933

O, if through thy eyes, like through sea waves,
My love could sail like a ship,
Long ago with full sails I would have boldly
Struck to your heart, like to the Holy Land.

If you light up for me in Heaven like a morning star,
In the blue and on the earth and in the heart it is
      quiet.
Thou Plain of Sharon and Rose of Jericho,
Thou art my snowy Lebanon, my dark-haired
      mistress.

I would abandon, like Judean sands and deserts,
Sad northern countries and fertile black earth.
I would give away the sea, to drown in the depths of
      thy eyes,
For one kiss I would give away two homelands.

Translated by Lizy Mostowski.

César Tiempo
1906–1980

César Tiempo was the pen name of the Argentine
poet, playwright, and screenwriter Israel Zeitlin, who
was born in Ekaterinoslav (today, Dnipro), Ukraine,
and brought to Buenos Aires as an infant. A prominent
figure in Argentine literary circles, he wrote more than
three dozen screenplays for the Argentine cinema. His
plays and poetry feature Jewish characters and Jewish
themes and were often concerned with the downtrodden and the exploited of society. He was also a vocal
critic of Argentine antisemitism.

Dirge for a Bar That Has Closed Down
1933

The slow and green river that winds through
the blanched street of the Jewish Quarter
kept watch over your agony.
From my old table
I used to see him
approach your windows with
restless eyes. And as he wandered away beaten,
his responsory was a lamentation
on the winding streets of Callao and Corrientes.

Your unexpected departure
changed the course of the routine
lives of those bourgeois with their hesitant
and improbable fancies;
of those bourgeois who at the same hour
and with the same unction every day
abdicate the counters of their clothes stores
and, passing the sceptre to their wives,
enter with uncovered heads
at midafternoon—flashing
a smile—through the same familiar doorway
and with the same bland gestures
join the gesticulating circle
which, seated in a corner, struggles
—with its Russian tea and its philately—
to preserve the Wailing Wall
(While the implacable daughters
attached to the complicit nuptial telephone
and shaking the wires with guttural r's
begin to arrange charming rendezvous
in the lobby of the "Etual"
—adventures with insipid endings,
with episodes in your Family
Room, whose gravest folly
is to break each other's heart,
passionately, more or less,
or parsimoniously,
but with no harm intended . . .)

They too were forced to emigrate,
those youths addicted to drink
Who hailed Castelar as a co-religionist
along with Maimonides and Gabirol;
some: steadfast Zionists
who between "cubano" and "san martín"
before the dulled mirrors
declaim in precise terms
and cast their eyes like nets for the woman playing
      the violin;
and the others: experts on the Hebraica
with the pomposity of asses,
who know nothing of Mosaic Law
and break all the Commandments
Upon whom the University
bestows a title and the leisure
to give us performances
of their unfolding vanity.

And the friends whose scattering
you caused. Even now

their passionate dreams and wholesome happiness
gleam in your lounge.

And my stunted novel
a bit vulgar—a bit wistful
with the most beautiful girl in it
whom no one ever knew.

Bar that shattered my final scheme,
now that I see you from the viewpoint of
my loneliness, lost in this swarming city,
I think that if you had not closed down,
I might have prevailed.

The slow and green river that winds through
that blanched street of a Jewish quarter
kept watch over your agony.

From my old table
I used to see him
approach your windows with
restless eyes. And as he wandered away, beaten,
his responsory was a lamentation
On the winding streets of Callao and Corrientes.

Translated by Antonio J. Dajer.

Other works by Tiempo: *Libro para la pausa del sábado* (1930); *El teatro soy yo* (1933); *Sabatión argentino* (1933); *Pan criollo* (1938); *Sábadomingo* (1938).

César Tiempo

Freckled Childhood
1933

I certainly had an obscure childhood
but intensely my own,
a childhood which wanted to be dashing
but had the features of a caricature.

Yes, a caricature. For example:
that absurd love for Sophie,
the rabbi's wife whom I saw
every night, profaning the temple.

(To think that Tolstoi was the sentimental
bridge that almost united us
that Passover afternoon
I read "Resurrection," languishing.)

And this precocious, burning fever for Mariadela
—her father my namesake and matchmaker—

Where can I find four mad phrases
and an ending worthy of a novel?

Translated by Shepherd Bliss and Roberta Kalechofsky.

César Tiempo

Romance of the Gambler's Girls
1933

Reb Menashe Dorogofsky
what beautiful girls you have!
the brunette enchants me,
also, the red-head.

The trampled plants of our century
spring again from their feet
the curve of the Hebrew sky
which claimed my faith.
—the feast of Tabernacles of my life
new tablets of the law—
Adonai stretched out this bridge
with the figure of a woman
between my harsh dreams
and the dreams of Israel.

Sparkle of their laughs
and honey rose of their skin
are mirrored by the anxious water
of the world when it sees them
as golden as God commands
here and in Jerusalem.
The girls of this gambler
seem like the daughter of a king.

Reb Menashe Dorogofsky
what beautiful girls you have!
which will I choose
for a nuptial feast
if the brunette is made of roses
and the red-head of honey?

I would take them both
and the dowries which you give with them,
and with my tricks
I will know how to keep them;
for in hunting my fortune,
my verses are my decoy:
we will live with the happiness of the refrain:
"There are not two without three."
Restocking the branches
of the blonde trunk of Sem.

Thread of gold, thread of silver,
Reb Menashe, now you see it:
thread of gold: your daughters,
and of silver a well—what do you say!

Translated by Shepherd Bliss and Roberta Kalechofsky.

César Tiempo

A Series of Verses to the Venerable Ancient Whose Portrait Hangs in the Window of a Lottery Agency
1933

The Avenida de Mayo
glows with a virginal light beneath the Sabbath sky.

That light strikes
the window pane that displays your portrait:
Laban amidst a flock of gaily colored lottery
tickets, green, blue, and purple.

The skullcap, the flowing beard and the patriarchal
eyebrows give you a holy countenance
that beckons the unsuspecting sheep that wander
among the musical squabbles of the
asthmatic klaxons.

Why, with that haloed prophet's head,
to reveal the mystery of the coveted number
must be easier for you than it was for Jehovah
to create you from a bit of reverie and
another bit of clay.

Your sons and your servants
sell miracle bread:
tickets for a quick spin among the clouds
with its share of loops and crash landings.

They compete with their Creator
even during the sacred serenity of the Sabbath,
and you preside with that fathomless smile
and those Talmudic whiskers over their worldly
    needs.

With the mortal wisdom of the returning voyager,
Your gaze that wandered through the starless night
now regards who knows from what lofty perch
the snake dance of the final sin.

Now in the Gehenna where golden and bloody fag-
    gots of flame
crackle and burn

your soul will be scourged by somber angels,
deaf to your cries.

No passerby will know, seeing your kindly eyes,
the agony which mercilessly consumes you from
    within
while the impetuous waves of traffic surge on
beneath a sky that is bursting open, crystalline,
    restless.

Israelite! You who lead
another reprobate life
beyond the shallow glare of your windowpane,
I alone understand you!

Ah, if you would only show me the secret number
I would abandon myself with you over the mouth of
    hell
to pass a consecrated Sabbath of idleness
that would gladden the sleepless sea of your dead
    Sabbaths

Translated by Antonio J. Dajer.

César Tiempo

Verses to a Dictionary and to the Neckerchiefs (Worn by the Gauchos)
1933

With you, it is not impossible to define
creatures and things with the simplicity
of the fish whose scales streak the sea with blue and
    gold,
Or of the sea itself that swells with the gracefulness
    of the fishes.

Not even with that propriety,
constricted, harsh, tight, rigid
with which we quote you when the truth requires;
and what could be truer than truth itself?

We look for a precise definition
and we see that silken tongue is a scarf
worn by the ostentatious gauchos of our land,
a fluttering caricature of the heart

And the blue smile of that breast strap
and the clinging summer of the blouse
and the bright mullion that illuminates
the face of whoever wears it;

Multicolored and varied like

Laban's flock, the ranks of
neckerchiefs display their colors to the world,
their polychromed and shimmering shield.

They come from a simple, elemental world
where forms have a common root.
They know the profound language of shade
and like their masters, their destiny is mortal.

They lack the inner brilliance of precious stones
but not of the epicarp (is not color also a fruit?)
and like sorrow, they gather at the throat,
for not in vain is man their creator.

Flabby lexicon! Etymology and flimsy
semantics: your definition fails to persuade:
we want it as clear as our romantic
and wild happiness at being heedless and alive!

Translated by Antonio J. Dajer.

David Saliman Tsemah

For the Sixtieth Jubilee of the Poet Chaim Nahman Bialik

1933

Yeshurun sings, when in him it sees a delicate
   beauty in the bloom of her youth[1]
playing the lyre in her bosom's embrace, her song
   gladdening the sorrowful heart.
A charming doe[2] [even] without kohl or rouge, perfumed[3] with all kinds of fragrances,
she was cultivated amongst the Arabs, and from
   them she is adorned with nose-rings
and [with] four bracelets on her arms and a mother-
   of-pearl necklace[4] that embellishes the body.
On the hems of her cloak bells tinkle the names of
   the sages [i.e., great rabbis].
She is an orphan, and yet her father indeed lives, and
   she was born to him without labor pains or blood!
I had heard her sing long ago, and understood this
   as the song of orphans,
[and so] I asked her: "Whose are you, delicate
   one, whose daughter from amongst the holy and
   exalted?"
She answered me: "I am the daughter whose forefathers' hand turned the rock into water.
I will bring a sacrifice in celebration of the festival of
   the prophet of poetry[5] to honor him with a perfect
   offering,[6]

he who raised me from my youth of loathsome dust,
   moth and worm.
I am the daughter whose forefathers were prophets,
   and to whose glory nights and days are enslaved."
And with her right eye she winked to show me two
   wise men.
I saw them with their lips moving to the song of their
   daughter, which was in the mouths of all people.
Upon seeing them, I recognized them, and they
   were Gabirol with ibn 'Ezra, the giants[7]
and before me was a book in the hands of their
   daughter, filled with all kinds of precious pearls
   and diamonds
and I looked at it and the book written by Hayyim[8]
   and it was very beautiful, even if not ancient,
striking sparks of fire with the poems[9] and electrify-
   ing the flow of blood in its listeners' veins.
Verily, he is unique in his generation, a knight of
   poetry, and his virtues are great!
the sins of Time[10] waxed great when it destroyed
   the language of my people and it [the language]
   became full of sin[11]
until he came and revived their language, so that
   Time's guilt was removed.[12]
And therefore his parents called him Hayyim [life]:
   because he completely rejuvenated the language
   of Torah.
Sages may be harsh at times, he is a mild, righteous,
   and blameless man,
everyone's darling, friend to all, so that his virtues
   are inscribed in the heart of time.[13]
I'll congratulate him on the festival of his sixtieth
   [birthday], and in my eyes a whole world of congratulations would be too small for him.

NOTES
1. [Literally, "in the days of youth."—Trans.]
2. [Literally, "a charming ibex."—Trans.]
3. [*Me'uteret be-khol miney besamim*: *me'uteret* is a loan word from the Arabic *'itr* (fragrance or perfume).—Trans.]
4. [*Haruz dar*: literally, a mother-of-pearl bead; probably a necklace made of beads.—Trans.]
5. [Puns with "the festival on which we bring poetry." —Trans.]
6. [Literally, "bring to his splendor a whole [perfect] of-fering." The term "shelamim" refers to a sacrifice often trans-lated as a "peace offering" or "whole offering," often used in celebration.—Trans.]
7. [Literally, "rams" or "wild ox."—Trans.]
8. [Puns with "dedicated to life."—Trans.]
9. [Alternatively, "hews flames of fire out of songs."—Trans.]
10. [In medieval Hebrew and Arabic, "time" also connotes "fate" or "destiny."—Trans.]

11. [I.e., Time was filled with blame.—Trans.]

12. [I.e., "time" has ruined Hebrew, but Bialik has rebuilt what time ruined.—Trans.]

13. [Literally "the days." This use of *yamim* (days) is a personification of time (used invoked in the sense of fate); in medieval Hebrew and Arabic, saying someone's virtues were inscribed on your heart was a term of affection. Here, the speaker's affection for Bialik is inscribed not on his own heart, but on the heart time, as if to say that time itself has recognized his virtues and embraced him.—Trans.]

Translated by Lital Levy.

Eduard Bagritsky
1895-1934

Born in Odessa into a mostly assimilated Jewish family, Eduard Bagritsky (pseudonym of Eduard Godelevich Dziubin) was a renowned and sometimes controversial Soviet Jewish poet in the Russian language. Bagritsky began publishing poetry in 1913 in local literary journals in Odessa. After a stint in law enforcement and in the Red Army during the revolutionary years, in 1925 Bagritsky settled in Moscow, where he was much admired in the literary scene. His unsentimental style and direct treatment of difficult themes, such as violence, sexuality, and interethnic strife, drew ire and disapproval from critics in Russian nationalist circles. Bagritsky also worked as a translator, rendering Soviet Yiddish poets, such as Itzik Feffer and Peretz Markish, into Russian. Although Bagritsky was given an official funeral at the time of his untimely death in 1934, his works—which dealt with Jewish themes in only a few poems—were later spitefully critiqued by antisemitic intellectuals as evidence of Jewish infiltration and degradation of Russian cultural life.

February
1933-1934

[. . .]
I never loved properly . . .
A little Judaic boy,
I was the only one around
To shiver in the steppe wind at night.

Like a sleepwalker, I walked along tram tracks
To silent summer cottages, where in the
    underbrush
Of gooseberry or wild blackberry bushes
Grass snakes rustle and vipers hiss,
And in the thickets, where you can't sneak in,
A bird with a scarlet head darts about,

Her song is thin as a pin;
They've nicknamed her "Bull's eye." . . .

How did it happen, that born to a Hebrew,
And circumcised on the seventh day,
I became a fowler—I really don't know!

I loved Brehm better than Mayne Reid!
My hands trembled with passion
When I opened the book at random—
Birds would leap out at me from chance pages
Looking like letters of foreign alphabets,
Sabers and trumpets, globes and rhombuses.

I imagine the archer once paused
Above the blackness of our dwelling,
Above the notorious Jewish smoke
Of goosefat cracklings, above the cramming
Of tedious prayers, bearded faces
In family pictures. . . . [. . .]

I evaded the front: I tried everything. . . .
How many crumpled rubles
Escaped from my hands to the clerks'!
I bought my sergeants vodka,
I bribed them with cigarettes and salt pork. . . .
I roamed from ward to ward
Coughing in a paroxysm of pleurisy,
Puffing and gasping,
Spitting into bottles, drinking medicine,
Standing naked and unshaved
Under stethoscopes of all the doctors. . . .

When I was lucky enough by truth
Or lie—who can remember?—
To get a leave pass,
I would shine my boots,
Straighten my blouse, and sharply
Walk to the boulevard, where an oriole sang
In the treetops, its voice like baked clay,
Where above the sand of the path
A green dress swayed
Like a slender strand of smoke. . . .

Again I dragged on behind her,
Dying of love, swearing, stumbling into benches. . . .
She would go into a movie theater,
Into the rattling darkness, the tremble
Of green light in a square frame,
Where a woman beside a fireplace
Wrung her alabaster hands,
And a man in a granite vest
Was shooting from a silent revolver. . . .

I knew the faces of all her admirers,
I knew their habits, smiles, gestures,
How their steps slowed down, when on purpose
With chest, hips or palms
They would feel through a dainty cover
The anxious tenderness of a girl's skin. . . .

I knew it all . . .

  Birds flew away. . .
Grass withered . . .

  Stars collapsed . . .
The girl walked around the world,
Picking flowers, lowering her eyes . . .
Autumn . . .

  The air is soaked with rain,
Autumn . . .

  Rage, hurt and anguish!
I'll go up to her today.

    I'll stand
Before her.

  I won't let her turn away.
Enough of this hustle.

    Be strong!
Take yourself in hand.

    Stop dawdling!
The kiosk is boarded up . . .

      Pigeons fuss
Around the town hall clock.

      Soon it'll be four.
She appeared an hour earlier;
A hat in her hands . . .

    Her coppery hair—
Translucent in the chilly sun—
Streaming down her cheeks . . .

    Silence.

      And the voice
Of a tomtit, lost in this world . . .
I must go up to her.

  I must
Certainly go up to her.

  I must
Really go up to her.

  Don't think,
Just go after her.

    Enough gibbering! . . .
But my legs didn't move,

As if made of stone.

  My body
As if chained to the bench. . .
Couldn't get up. . . .

  Idler! Loser!

The girl had already approached the square,
And in the dark gray circle of museums
Her dress, flying in the wind,
Looked thinner and greener. . . .

I tore myself from the bench
With such effort, as if I had been
Bolted to it.

      And not turning back
Rushed after her toward the square.
All the things I used to read at night—
Sick, hungry, half-dressed—
Birds with non-Russian names,
People from an unknown planet,
World where they play tennis,
Drink orangeade and kiss women—
All that was now moving before me,
Dressed in a woolen dress,
Flaming with copper locks,
Swinging a striped satchel,
Heels running over cobblestones. . . .

I'll put my hand on her shoulder,
"Look at me!

      I am your misfortune!
I'm dooming you to the torment
Of incredible nightingale passion!
Wait!"

  But there, around the corner.
Twenty steps away her dress shows green . . .
I am catching up with her.

    A little farther on
And we shall stride abreast. . . .

I salute her as my superior,
What shall I tell her? My tongue
Mumbles some nonsense,

      "Will you . . .
Don't run away . . .

    May I
Walk you home? I was in the trenches! . . ."

She is wordless.

  Not even a look

In my direction.

    Her steps gets faster.
I run beside her, like a beggar,
Bowing respectfully.

    How on earth
Can I be her equal!

    Like a madman
I mumble some ridiculous phrases. . . .

And suddenly a halt.

    Silently
She turns her head—I see
Her copper hair, her blue-green eyes
And a purplish vein on her temple,
Pulsating with anger.
"Go away. Now." And her hand
Points to the intersection. . . .

    There he is—
Placed to guard the order—
He stands in my way like a kingdom
Of cords, shiny badges, medals,
Squeezed into high boots,
And covered on top by his hat,
Around which whirl in a yellow
And unbearably torturous halo
Doves from the Holy Scriptures,
And clouds, twisted like snails;
Paunchy, beaming with greasy sweat,
A policeman,

    from the early morning pumped
With vodka and stuffed with pork fat. . . . [. . .]

I stayed in the area. . . .

    I worked
As deputy commissar.

    At first
I spent many nights in damp sentry boxes;
I watched the world, passing by me,
Alien and dimly lit by crooked streetlamps,
Full of strange and unknown monsters
Oozing from thick fumes. . . .

I tried to be ubiquitous. . . .

    In a gig
I churned rural roads, searching
For horse thieves.

    In the middle of night
I rushed out in a motorboat
Into the gulf, curved like a black horn

Around rocks and sand dunes.
I broke into thieves' lodgings
Reeking of overfried fish.
I appeared, like the angel of death,
With a torchlight and a revolver, surrounded
By four sailors from the battleship
(Still young and happy. Still rosy-cheeked.
Sleepy after a night of reckless fun.
Cocked caps. Unbuttoned pea jackets.
Carbines under their arms. Wind in their eyes.).

My Judaic pride sang,
Like a string stretched to its limit. . . .
I would've given much for my forefather
In a long caftan and fox fedora,
From under which fell gray spirals
Of earlocks and clouds of dandruff
Flushing over his square beard,
For that ancestor to recognize his descendant
In this huge fellow, rising, like a tower,
Over flying lights and bayonets,
From a truck, shaking off midnight. . . .

Translated by Maxim D. Shrayer.

    Other works by Bagritsky: *Iugo-Zapad* (1928); *Duma pro Opanasa* (1932); *Izbrannye stikhi* (1932); *Pobediteli* (1932); *Posledniaia noch'* (1932).

Izi Charik

Stalinstan
1934

    Stalinstan,
    Stalinstan,
Who is present and on hand

    From the Party,
    From the Union?

Who was on his way
Somewhere else today,
When a chain of men caught him
And then brought him
To everyone's delight
To be here tonight?

Quieter. Hearts are now speaking.
Quieter, quieter.
We hear:
Hel-lo!

Hel-lo!
Hel-lo!
In this exalted hour
The region is coming alive!

—Vitebsk!
—And Orsha!
—Dubrovna!
—And Shklov!
—Zahorie!
—Zapolie!
—Kapulie!
Villages deep in sleep of straw,
Towns that limp on ruined crutches:
Be ready!
The highest
Moment
Is arriving.
Hot electric blood will flow
Hot vitality will glow.
Be ready!
"We're ready!"
And—
The minute explodes. . . .

And Vitebsk to Moscow:
"Long live the kilowatt!"
And Moscow to Vitebsk:
"Long live the kilowatt!"
Vitebsk to Orsha:
"Do you hear, brigadier?"
Orsha to Vitebsk:
"Loud and clear, brigadier!"

And shtetl and village:
"The lights are on here!"
"Do you hear, brigadier?"
"The lights are on here!"

And all together:
"Five-year plan in four years!"

Translated by Solon Beinfeld.

Moyshe-Leyb Halpern

Salute
1934

There are things in this country too—
And if they find no streetlamp pole,
There will be a tree—and that means clearly

That a Negro over twenty years old
May hate all things which spire
To hold a man for his hanging.
But the one whose death I saw
Was not even fifteen years old.

The white old maid was not sweet at all.
The rusty lock on an old valise—
Her nose and jaw. And the arms and legs,
I tell you—rather than touch skin-to-skin
Such a smudge—better death.

You are you,—she pointed at him.
And you will hang for me, she said.
It's true—in death-fear he nastily laughed;
But she laughed too, and brought the tar,
And inspected the tree above her head.
And the joy of the crowd at the first smoke,
I swear—from a mad-house on fire
You would not hear such a scream.

And the first spoon of tar at his heart
Was hot upon hot, and black upon black.
And the eyes were not lightning, but white bulging
    out.
And the body—tearing out of the skin,
As if it wished to undress its death.

But not only did they loop a rope
Around the neck of this piece of cattle,
The flag of the republic too
Was raised on high—
And the sky was blue—it didn't care—
And the wind rejoiced with the flag in the air,
And I—a beaten dog—said not a word.
Took no part—a partner to murder.

You don't have to swallow a sty of pigs
In order to vomit your green bile,
The priest will take care of that, that well of
    wisdom—
If blackness, he says, is a blunder of God,
Then it's sinful to let it mix with white.

And I tell you—it is not the groan of a branch,
Not the rope with the whole paraphernalia,
Not the feather flown in the wind,
Too late to stick to the body—
It's you, the sinking sorrow of the world,
Standing there at a distance, safe,
Hands through your pockets, on your groin,
Composing a poem for the world and yourself.

Better go, wake up the *klezmer* Chopin,
Let him pour something strong, if he can,
A rain of tones, for everyone to see
That a goy too has a mood of *Kol-Nidre*
When to spilled blood you need music.

Translated by Benjamin Harshav and Barbara Harshav.

Charles Reznikoff

Russia: Anno 1905
1934

A Young Jew. The weed of their hatred
which has grown so tall
now turns towards us
many heads,
many pointed petals and leaves;
what did they whisper to each other before the
      ikons,
and smile at over the glasses of vodka,
the spies and gendarmes, Cossacks and police,
that a crowd of ragged strangers burst into the street
leaving crooked shields of David in every pane of
      glass
and a Jew here and there in the gutter
clubbed to death for his coat like an animal for its
      skin,
the open mouth toothless, the beard stiffened with
      blood—
away, Jew, away!
obey the ancient summons, hurry out of this land!

Republic,
garrisoned by the waves;
every man welcome if distressed by lord or king;
and learning free to all as the streets and highways,
free as the light of street lamps,
piped into every house as the sweet water;
nation whose founders were not leaders of legions or
      regiments,
or masters of the long ships of war, of bowmen or
      artillery,
but farmers, who spoke of liberty and justice for all
and planted these abstractions in the soil
to send their seed
by every current of wind and water
to the despotisms of the earth;
your name

is like the cool wind
in a summer day
under the tyranny of the sun;
like a warm room
when, against the tyranny of the wind,
one has come a long way
on frozen ruts and clods;
the oblongs of your buildings in the west—
smooth brightness of electric light
on the white stone
and the motor cars gliding along your crowded
      streets—
are as the triangles of Egypt were,
and the semicircles of the arches of Rome;
how great you have become, United States!

Or to the land of rock and sand, mountain and
      marsh,
where the sun still woos Delilah
and the night entraps Samson,
Palestine—
and your speech shall be Hebrew;
what the mother has spun,
the daughter shall weave;
where the father has cleared away the stones,
the son shall sow and reap;
and lives will not burn singly
in single candlesticks—
how much better to live
where his fathers have lived,
than to be going about from land to land—
wasting one's life in beginnings;
how pleasant it is
for the body to sweat in the sun,
to be cool in the wind,
from dawn until twilight,
starlight to starlight;
how much better to live in the tip of the flame,
the blue blaze of sunshine,
than creep about in corners,
safe in cracks—
dribble away your days in pennies.
In that air
salty with the deeds of heroes and the speech of
      prophets,
as when one has left the streets and come to the
plunging and orderly sea, the green water
tumbling into yellow sand and rushing foam,
and rising in incessant waves—

upon your hills, Judah,
in your streets and narrow places
upon your cobblestones, Jerusalem!

Yet like the worm in horseradish
for whom there is no sweeter root,
should I, setting my wits against this icy
   circumstance,
make, like the Eskimo, my home of it?
The dust of this Russia,
breathed these many years,
is stored in my bones,
stains the skull and cortex of my brain—
the chameleon in us
that willy-nilly
takes the color where we lie.
Should I, like Abraham become the Hebrew,
leave Ur of the Chaldees, the accident of place,
and go to other pastures, from well to well;
or, the Jew, stay,
others buzzing on the window panes of heaven,
flatten myself
against the ground
at the sound of a boot;
as others choose the thistle or the edelweiss,
take the reed, knowing that the grey hairs of
   murderers
sometimes go bloody to the grave,
that the wicked die even as the good.
Or, a Russian,
the heat by day, the same frost at night,
the same enemies in microbes and in stars,
say,
These are my people,
Russian and Ukrainian, Cossack and Tartar, my
   brothers—
even Ishmael and Esau;
know myself a stitch, a nail, a word
printed in its place, a bulb screwed in its socket;
alight by the same current as the others
in the letters of this sign—*Russia.*
Or better still,
there is no Russia;
there is no peoples, only man!

Stay or go;
be still the shining piston
moving heavy wheels;
the propeller
before whom ocean and the heavens divide:

the steamer seen from the land
moves slowly
but leaves a tide
that washes shore and banks;
the airplane from the ground—
an insect crawling
but filling all the heavens with its drone;
a small cloud
raining its sound
from the wide sky.

Abraham Shlonsky

Three Old Women
1934

In the grey evening, beside the white house, three
   old ladies sit, gazing straight ahead. And stillness
   all around. As if the eagle had suddenly frozen in
   flight. Three old ladies sit beside the house.

And someone, silently, above their heads, knits a
   blue stocking in the old style. A golden skein un-
   ravels on the horizon. Three old ladies suddenly
   saw a child.

Three old ladies woke with a start and sighed: "Poor
   thing . . . an orphan, probably. . ." And then went
   over. Patted him on the cheek. The child looked,
   and burst into tears.

And then night came, like a baffling child. Three
   old ladies slipped away into the white house. And
   stillness all around. Only a kind of humiliation
   still circled like an eagle above the wooden
   bench, empty now, beside the house.

Translated by T. Carmi.

Julian Tuwim

About St. P.
1934

Spitting poison and frothing at the mouth
He spits, snorts and splutters
And writes that I am a butcher
A yid and bolshevik
Jewboy, bacillus
A baboon and a Skamandrite

That I sell out the Fatherland
That I deform the Polish language
That I provoke and profane
And the Devil knows what else.

And to think that from all
The fine activity
Of this gentleman—from the spittle
Wheezing, screaming, scribbling,
Spewing, kicking and wailing
On which he has lost half his life
From the books and articles
From the words, sentences and titles
From the review, from the sneering paragraphs
In a word from that whole
Journalistic mess
Will remain . . . one poem
And that will be—mine, not his.
Indeed *this* very poem . . . O stern revenge
Inspired by a Jewish God.
Here is a phrase, a few words with which I toy
To immortalize my enemy.

Translated by Antony Polonsky.

Kurt Wolfskehl

1869–1948

Born in Darmstadt, Germany, into a banking family,
the poet Karl Wolfskehl was the sole Jewish member
of the circle that worshiped the charismatic lyric
poet Stefan George. The circle, which included
outspoken ultranationalists, met at Wolfskehl's
Munich house from 1899 to 1932. When Hitler came
to power, Wolfskehl moved to Italy, but in 1938
he settled permanently in New Zealand. After he
left Germany, Jewish themes became central to his
work.

Lord, I Want to Return

1934

Lord, I want to return to your word,
Lord, I want to pour out my wine,
Lord, I want to go, to go to you,
Lord, I do not know what should be done,
I am alone.

I am alone in empty air,
In terror of myself, alone at heart,
All my gay balloons are wan and slack,

All my wisdom chaff and spray,
I am poor. Come back!

Lean as to my fathers, Lord, or dart
Down to me your ray,
Once you guarded even those
Who transgressed your laws.

Sign to us as flame or cloud,
Summon us to wander through wastes,
Lord, have you not held us dear?
Why has our survival been allowed?

Has the false day flown?
Has night split behind us?
All the stars are dull and drowned,
Call us, we call to you to come.
Even before the cocks crow
Your messengers draw close—
Closer without a sound.

Translated by Carol North Valhope and Ernst Morwitz.

Other works by Wolfskehl: *Gesammelte Dichtungen*
(1903); *Saul* (1905); *An die Deutschen* (1947).

Kurt Wolfskehl

To Be Said at the Seder

1934

Over and over, when the wayside dust had grayed
    us,
And we came and knocked at another's door,
He threatened us with his fist and gainsaid us:
This is not your place! Move on!
Over and over.

Over and over, when as helpers and sages
We worked and toiled in the other's ranks,
They put up with us for a time, and then shut us
From halls and from houses, and offered no thanks.

Over and over, when we sat with the others,
Forgot ourselves and shared their songs of joy,
Our wine was tinged with lye, and we shrank from
The icy look in a hostile eye.

Over and over, when we believed and trusted,
And built by the abyss, above our head
The roof cracked open, the old cliff tottered:
No place can be your home! is what was said,
Over and over.

Over and over, in the vise of torture,
We scream to the Lord to give us peace,
Can your word not at last find nurture
In us, and bear promised fruit?

Translated by Carol North Valhope and Ernst Morwitz.

Kurt Wolfskehl

The Voice
1934

Over and over, yes, over and over,
I shook the pinions of my anger,
Again and again you broke faith with me,
And I stormed at your crop of iniquity.

But over and over, and over and over,
Your songs are carried heavenward, I gather
The scattered people of Israel,
They shall not fall prey to other pale.

Over and over, now, and over and over,
I call the abandoned hosts of my people
To my Pesah hour in the dusk of the tent,
Strike and spare, true to my covenant,
Pace before you again and again,
As a cloud by day, by night as fire,
A pillar of fire!

Translated by Carol North Valhope and Ernst Morwitz.

Kurt Wolfskehl

Yom HaKippurim
1934

Do you know who turns and returns?
Do you know the meaning of Atonement?
Do you know who watched for you by night,
Late, and in the early morning light?
Do you know who verges on Atonement?
Do you know who flung Himself ajar,
When what foe—do you remember—
Ventured to lay siege upon your heart?
Do you know how He exists and where?
Do you know the thralldom of Atonement?
Do you know that sometimes He forgets?
Do you know the hour of Atonement?
Do you know what course the Pilot sets?
Do you know where you will find Atonement?
Do you know who spurs you to Atonement?

Clears for you the only trail, and plans
Covenant again and yet again,
Do you know who hankers for Atonement?
Do you know who ploughs the world and sows
Silently His seed within the furrows?
Unfathomed, unnamed—
Do you know? Do you weep?

Translated by Carol North Valhope and Ernst Morwitz.

Celia Dropkin

The Circus Lady
1935

I am a circus lady
And dance among the daggers
Set in the arena
With their points erect.
My swaying, lissome body
Avoids a death-by-falling,
Touching, barely touching the dagger blades.

Holding their breaths, the people are staring at my
    dancing,
And someone sends a prayer to God for me.
Before my eyes, the dagger points
Gleam fiery, in a circle,
And no one knows how the falling calls to me.

I grow tired, dancing between you,
Daggers of cold steel.
I want my blood to heat you through and through.
You, unsheathed points,
I want to fall on you.

Translated by Kathryn Hellerstein.

Itzik Manger

Itzik's Midrash
1935

Eve Brings Adam the Apple

The first man, Adam, lies in the grass,
And spits at a passing cloud,
Humbly, the cloud says, "Adam,
Please, would you cut that out."

But Adam sticks out his tongue
And says to the cloud, "Too bad,"

Then spits a slender stream of spit
And says, "There's more of that."

Wiping the spittle with his sleeve
The cloud grumbles angrily,
"That's what comes of nothing to do,
And lying about all day."

The first man, Adam, laughs and laughs,
His teeth make a fine display
Just as Mother Eve comes back
From her walk in the apple allée.

"Where have you been, oh Eve, my wife,
My dear, where have you been?"
"Strolling about in the plum allée
And chatting with the wind."

"You haven't been to the plum allée,
It's a lie; you've not been there.
Your body smells of ripe apples
And there's apple smell in your hair."

It's true, I've been in the apple allée—
What a poor memory I have;
You've guessed it at once, my dear husband,
God bless you, my darling love."

"What did you do in the apple allée,
My dear, where have you been?"
"I was chatting with the serpent
About a blessed-sin."

The apple trembles in her hand,
Gleaming scarlet red,
Foreshadowing, as she holds it,
Twilight and passion and death.

The first man, Adam, is puzzled by
The sweetness in her voice.
And he simply cannot understand
Her strange new loveliness.

Trembling, he puts his hand out—
"Stop, Adam. You're making me blush."
The night extinguishes their shapes—
H, U, S, H spells "Hush."

Abraham Scolds Lot

Lot—it's disgusting—it's got to be said—
You and your nightly carouse—
Yesterday, in the Golden Hart . . .
What a terrible scandal that was.

Manger the tailor can do such things,
But it simply won't do for you.
You've a couple of daughters to raise, you're rich—
Knock wood—and besides, you're a Jew.

You've cattle and sheep and flocks of goats—
Take my advice—fear God.
Already, a swilling Gentile is said
To be "As drunk as Lot."

I know how it is, on a Friday night,
To drink a cup or two
Of wine with the fish, while the Sabbath lights
Shed their holy glow.

But how can one go on drinking
Day in, day out—like you?
It's all right for Havrillah, the Sabbath-goy,
But certainly not for a Jew.

Consider what will be said one day—
That the Patriarch Abraham's kin
Was worse than a convert—steeped in wine
And other kinds of sin.

They're saying already—Listen to me!
My God, don't you care what they think?
And you're a father . . . the matchmaker
Avoids your house like a stink.

Even the humblest tailor's lad
Considers himself too fine
To marry your daughters—Shall their braids
Turn gray—for the sake of wine?

Lot—it's disgusting—it's got to be said—
You and your nightly carouse—
Yesterday, in the Golden Hart . . .
What a terrible scandal that was.

Manger the tailor can do such things,
But it simply won't do for you.
You've a couple of daughters to raise, you're rich—
Praise God!—and besides, you're a Jew.

Lot's Daughters

Lot's daughters sit in the kitchen
Whispering among themselves.
One of them plucks a new-killed goose,
The other one mends a dress.

The first one says, "A week ago
It was my fortieth year.

Today when I looked in the mirror,
I saw my first gray hair.

Father carouses in taverns
And the years pass swiftly by.
My bridal shoes in the closet
Lie waiting, hopelessly."

The second lets her needle drop
And sits engrossed in thought.
"Sister," she says, "my bedclothes
At night grow feverish hot."

She says, her breathing parched, "I dreamed
A blue-clad soldier came
And slept all night between my breasts . . .
It was a lovely dream.

And then he left the dream and me—
He does not reappear—
As if no troops were garrisoned
Among us any more."

The first one says, "Now listen,
Because I have a plan.
If bridegrooms will not come to us—
A father is also a man."

Her cheeks are flushed, her breath is hot,
Her voice unsteady, dim:
"Sister, on this very night
I mean to lie with him.

Tomorrow, you. Why should we wait?
Our father is drunk as Lot.
And mother, in that cursed town
Of Sodom turned to salt."

They're both inflamed. Around their lamp
Beats a tardy butterfly . . .
"Sister, get ready. Our father comes
Stumbling heavily." [. . .]

Jacob Studies "The Selling of Joseph" with His Sons

"What makes you all so silent,
Reuben, my oldest son":
"Our Purim play, dear father,
Is ready to begin."

"Come, put on your silken shirt,
Joseph, my best-loved son.
Your brothers need to sell you
To strangers once again.

When they throw you in the pit,
Weep, but not for long.
It's not the first time that you act
This play out, my dear son.

But when you pass your mother's grave
That stands beside the way,
Be sure you shed a real tear
And softly, gently say

That gladly would old Jacob serve
Another seventh year
If once before his death he might
Again caress her hair.

By now, you know the rest by heart—
Your exits, cues, and bows.
Again, in Pharaoh's dream there graze
His seven fattened cows.

Unriddle his dreams without a fault,
As truly as before;
And don't forget, in Heaven's name,
To send me a sack of flour.

And one thing more, in Heaven's name,
Be virtuous, my dear . . .
Look out for the wiles of Pharaoh's wife,
For she is young and fair.

Hey, now, my sons, why do you stand
Without a word to say?"
"Because, Father Jacob, you yourself
Have spoiled the Purim play."

Translated by Leonard Wolf.

Kadya Molodovsky

My Day
1935

My day—
Is punctured like a sieve,
And ridiculed like a whim.
May winter whiteness blossom,
May autumns turn gray,
May summers whistle—
Become nightingales.
When a rye-wind
Would have twisted my heart,
Intoxicated it,

Transformed it into summer—
Here, at the end of the street,
Three women stretched out their fists to me
From three wasted rooms,
As from sinking ships,
Pale,
Boney,
Sexless
Fists of poverty,
And swore at me:
May my life be miserable
In my summers, in my winters,
In the north and the south.
And I can escape nowhere.
The roads are busy, busy.
Here stand the Kulbak-like bronze youths,
With paper flowers,
With rubber dolls.
The youths, who can turn a city upside down,
Build railroads
And sow gardens and train tracks.
They deal with the-devil-knows-what—
With my heart and with paper pledges.
Their voice
Is decision,
Mockery,
And bloody menace,
And such is my day.
Punctured like a sieve.
And ridiculed like a whim.

Translated by Kathryn Hellerstein.

Melekh Ravitch

1893–1976

Modernist Yiddish poet, essayist, and cultural icon
Melekh Ravitch (b. Zekharye-Khone Bergner) was
born in Radymno, Poland. He served in the Austro-
Hungarian army during World War I and moved to
Warsaw in 1921, where he and the poets Uri Zvi Greenberg and Peretz Markish established the expressionist
literary group called Di Khalyastre. From 1924 to 1934
Ravitch was the executive secretary of the Association
of Jewish Writers and Journalists in Warsaw, at the renowned address of 13 Tłomackie Street. He ultimately
settled in Montreal.

Tropic Nightmare in Singapore
1935

Seven continents, seven seas,
and two and forty years—
and torrid equatorial nights
filled with nightmare fears.

Open eyes, naked heart.
And draining blood from me,
mosquitoes buzzing, buzzing, buzz
their nightmare melody.

Over seven continents, seven seas,
on fire-wind wings, dreams soar,
and in these soaring dreams
I am a child once more.

Across seven continents, seven seas
I see my village marketplace
and great throngs at a fair,
while mosquitoes all night long
buzz, buzz their buzzing song.

Across seven continents, seven seas—
a marketplace, a fair,
and their arms upon a windowsill,
my parents gazing on a train
winding a little hill.

And now the two old people go—
having gazed all day—
where from the kitchen they can see
the graveyard far away.

And my nightmares toss in a dance
of delirium and dread,
and suddenly, sharp, like a lightning flash
the notion enters my head

that the seven continents are dreams,
and dreams the seven seas,
and my forty-two years as well
mere fantasies.

Momma smiles. Poppa breaks into laughter:
"Though continent and sea
may appear mere dreams to you,
Our home is reality.

From one side of the house
you can see a hill and a train,
and always from the other side
the graveyard, sun or rain.

There our forefathers lie,
four generations or more.
We must rest, we must rest, my son,
after forty-two years are done
after tropics and Singapore."

Momma says, "You really believe—
I can read it clear in your face—
that the world out there is something more
than our little marketplace.

Well, out through the window go
your continents, if you please,
and into the kitchen pail
I pour your seven seas.

Sit down at my feet, little fool,
rest your head on my lap, my son.
The whole thing was only a dream,
and now the dream is gone.

Take these seven groschen instead;
buy a fresh apple and feel,
biting into the flesh,
the meaning of the real.

And help me to light the lamp
and see that the stove is lit,
and take off your shoes
from your tired feet, and sit.

And get rid of the thoughts in your head,
the buzz, buzz, buzz of ideas,
and toss from your shoulders at last
the burden of years.

And lie down in that cot again,
your childhood cot, my dear.
See, here's a screen in front of the lamp
to protect your eyes from the glare.

Ephraim, you must be tired.
So go to sleep as well,
and I shall croon our child a song
that has this tale to tell:

  Once there was story.
  Hardly happy, it could not sing,
  and the story had its beginning
  with a Jewish singer, a king.

  Over seven continents and oceans
  he wandered in every weather,
  finally returning
  to his old mother and father.

And tears from his eyes kept flowing
and all delight was drowned,
for on continent and ocean
the world was not to be found.

For on continent and ocean,
wherever he was blown,
the king, the singer, always
found himself alone.

From continent and ocean,
he returned to his piece of earth,
asking his old mother
why she had given him birth.

And his mother lamenting,
while tears ran down her face,
locked the king, the singer,
like a child in her embrace.

(The lamp began to flicker,
its glass shade turning black . . .)
I had to give birth to you, my child,
so that death would take you back.

***

Once there was a story.
Hardly happy, it could not sing,
and the story had its beginning
with a Jewish singer, a king.

Translated by Robert Friend.

Other works by Ravitch: *Af der shvel* (1912); *Nakete lider* (1921); *Di fir zaytn fun mayn velt* (1929); *Kontinentn un okeanen* (1937); *Di lider fun mayne lider* (1954); *Dos mayse-bukh fun mayn lebn* (1962–1975).

Nathan Alterman

1910–1970

The Hebrew poet Nathan Alterman was born in Warsaw and moved to Tel Aviv with his parents when he was fifteen. He continued his education at the Herzliyah Hebrew Gymnasium and at the Sorbonne but the following year decided to switch to agronomy and moved to Nancy. In 1932, he returned to Tel Aviv and began working at the Mikveh Yisrael agricultural school but soon decided to earn his living in journalism while devoting himself to poetry. He wrote both lyrical and political poetry. During the last years of the Mandate, the nationalist political verse that he published in his newspaper column, at first in *Haaretz* and then in *Davar*, attracted a wide readership and at times was censored by the British. He also wrote children's books and plays and translated Shakespeare, Racine, and Molière into Hebrew.

The Killers of the Fields
1936

In ascetic silence, in stony skirts,
God's handmaid falls on her face—
Flash of an empty night, a forlorn desert waste,
Shards of sunset upon the rocks.

This land. Trodden, just like this, by a wandering
  sadness,
Trailing in her thunders, calling her: "Where art
  thou?"
Speak to her, tell her of things that are other,
Tell her of fields that are learning to smile.

For it was your arms that held up her slumped
  head,
For it was you who injected her bloodstream with
  youth,
As she drank in the dew with noisy lips
And bore a tractor in her heart.

In the nights an oil of sky-blue anoints her,
And in a flutter of her lashes the grain creeps up . . .
Stars quiver like some fat candle.
Down the air
A garden
Pours.

Then out of the far-off villages,
On the hills, like massive-jawed raptors—
At a desert crawl, more primal than any law,
They descend,
The killers of the fields.

The skies have congealed. Red Capricorn is
  plumed.
The wind comes, soft and submissive.
In the night the grain fields of Jezreel are ablaze . . .
Splendid are the nights in Canaan.

Splendid. Broad and boundless.
Eternity wings over desert and home.
The hermits' mountains, now so dark and high,
Are cloaked by a moon in abbayas.

Only the threshing-floor decks itself out in sudden
  fire
And shadows are thrown without saddle or shout.
And the strange night tears off its veil
While the land looks on—

For destiny of old has not let go, no he hasn't,
For amid her quietude and the songs of her tents
He's been holding her neck in a lock since Vespasian
And brandishing his whip.

Translated by Lewis Glinert.

Other works by Alterman: *Selected Poems* (1978); *Little Tel Aviv* (1981).

Chaim Grade
1910–1982

A novelist and poet, Chaim Grade is considered one of the giants of Yiddish literature, particularly in the postwar period. Born in Vilna, Grade was educated in the yeshivas of the moralist *musar* movement that emphasized extreme ethical piety and harsh introspection. Although he left this milieu at age twenty-two, the religious ideology of his early years left an undeniable imprint on his later work. A member of the literary group Yung-Vilne, Grade achieved quick success as a poet with a distinctive, prophetic voice and as an award-winning novelist. After the war, Grade settled in the United States, where he published his most famous works, both poetry and novels. These explored themes such as survival and guilt, rage and remembrance, the sacred and the profane, and the failure of both secularism and religion to respond adequately to the Holocaust. He is perhaps best remembered for his later works—novel-length portrayals of Vilna Jewry, richly described in all its complexity and color.

Lullaby
1936

Hush little baby. Forty-six years now
the night has rocked itself in my empty cradle
Now a gray head is rocked to sleep with the same
  tune:
Standing at the cradle's head
No angel with two white wings—
The blond son rocks his gray mother to sleep
and one teardrop after another

he lets his tears fall with her together.

Hush little baby. Mother lies here for the umpteenth
day.
And since the doctor doesn't visit a pauper woman,
her son waits for the last, messianic hope:
God Himself to visit the sickbed.

Hush little baby. Mother's drying out like a swatch
of scorched earth—
and her son does—what?
His eyes hang open, overflowing with tears.
His blood rushes like rain.
The son, teary-eyed, can only water
her fevered countenance
to make her gray head on these sheets—shine
like a candle.

Hush little baby—Mother can't sleep,
She cries out from her doze, like a bird from a ruin:
My child, I saw you running, bleeding
And your blind face asked—where to?
You trampled on your brothers at the crossroads
your lost brothers
running, and bleeding, like you,
not knowing where to.

Hush little baby—The song of beginnings, about
raisins and almonds
Blood and wandering—the song of ending.
Only God knows how long more your children will
wander
like poor sheep
to be traded by the peoples of the world—
sleep my mother, sleep.

Translated by Zackary Sholem Berger.

Other works by Grade: *Yo* (1936); *Musernikes* (1939);
Der mames tsavoe (1949); *Der mames shabosim* (1955);
Tsemakh Atlas (1967); *Der shtumer minyen* (1976).

Chaim Grade

The Weeping of Generations
1936

I

On the white garments of my great-grandfather
the cross of the middle ages flames anew.

My great-grandfather sits at the seder,
holding a staff from a wild almond tree
to rouse the forefathers.
Not three matzos but three moons glimmer on a tray:
the bottom one black, the middle red
and the top one—light, that bright Paschal light.
My great-grandfather senses danger, death—
a child in the cellar—
a green serpent unwinds its way
out of the kiddush goblet,
the flame of its eye sockets
setting the drink alight.
My great-grandfather drinks the flaming cup,
feeling the forefathers on guard
but nearby, locked up
the barefoot monk.

II

I see my grandfather, Napoleon's soldier
lost in dark windstorms
the dream of liberation that he had
he buried with his horse in the snow.
Isolated, the last grenadier
fled from the cold North.
Chased by a polar bear—Siberia:
"Let Russia sleep, as she has slept till now
Accustomed to heavy bells and the lash.
Let Russia fear, as she had feared till now
And bleed to death in the snow."

My grandfather near Moscow, the French soldier
and patriot
singing the Marseillaise under a ring of cannons
hearing the hurricane whistle
drumming on his kettle drum
the guillotine march

III

Hands,
A pair of bright, quiet hands
unfold, and prayers flutter out of them like doves
Prophetic, the hands:
They are wrung. They can no more praise
Two iron fists
Smash the walls—
My father's hands.

My father loved the tumultuous Matron of kabbalah,
thereafter—the Princess of Haskalah,

and at last he condemned Mendelssohn and the
    Zohar both,
leaving only his hatred to the religious bigots.
Sadness devoured him,
since he lived only with the past and with graves,
like the worm dwells in the dead;
He was a teacher in wealthy houses,
had a wife and children,
But in him ran the blood of a conspirator
An arsonist.
A giant—he wept with the embarrassed tears of a child,
A philosopher—he wasted in drink the best years of
    his life,
He was only an omen of everything he should have
    become
and did not.

IV

My great-grandfather, who perished a martyr,
weeps as he stands at the foot of my bed, in flames:
"Did I die in a pyre,
so that the barefoot monk in his cell would be happy
that my grandson can't die for his cause?
That's not what I meant, my grandson.
I didn't mean that."

My grandfather, world-liberator, murdered soldier,
    frozen to death,
Gets up from the snow and looks at me, astonished:
"Why did I yoke myself to a cannon,
trudging along near Moscow after my dream and
    Napoleon,
so that you'd be scared of a gun and a flag?
That's not what I meant, my grandson.
I didn't mean that."

My father, who extinguished like a wind all *yortsayt*
    candles in the *shtibl*,
Caresses me with his gray head and weeps,
"This is why I was in exile in my own house,
Suffering, rejected like the philosopher of
    Amsterdam,
So that you would regret smashing boundaries?
That's not what I meant, my son.
I didn't mean that."

V

My great-grandfathers, my grandfathers
and my father, crouched over and bent down,

tortured, humble clan,
smile at me, love in their eyes.
One of my ancestors, tall and covered in snow,
spreads out his arms like thin branches:
"Grandson, a Jew must go to his Akedah,
Silently. . . ."

The dead congregation shakes like a forest in the
    wind:
"This is new, that we're poisoning wells,
That we're chased from our homes,
And all while our homes are up in flames.
New, to dig our own graves—
to hang our father and mother. . . .
The walls and windows are witness,
The blood and marrow-spattered pillows,
That our property is easy to pillage,
And our blood easy to wipe away.
Witness can bear our raped women,
Babies torn away in pregnancy,
Our shamed, crippled bodies,
And clothes, too, will bear witness:
We can make kiddush on our own bodies
as on challah or wine,
can reuse ourselves, like lambs or trees
for the axe or flames,
like food for animals,
nothing shocks us now.
None of this is new."
I lift myself up in bed on my elbows
and try to say like a dying man,
"The enemies claim that we have pushed them
    back . . ."

"Pushed them BACK?"
The whole dead congregation is shocked,
and my tall, slender, grandfather, covered with
    snow,
exchanges terrified, astonished looks
with the assembly of the departed. . . .
But my father is no longer standing so bent over,
broken down like the other old men,
an angry joy burns in his eyes
and his face flares with pained triumph:
"So you didn't let yourself be slaughtered for His
    name?
Your life is not just holy, but dear to you?
You didn't whisper Amen under their cleavers?
You didn't walk into the fires with song?
Even if you assume the sternest punishment,

You have nothing to complain about, my son!
You have nothing to be ashamed about!"

I take my father by the hand
and bury my inflamed face in him:
"Father, this is our pain and shame:
how can we overcome the punishment
for fighting our enemies?
Like always, we ran away, you know.
Like always: ran away."

VI

Many dreams tortured me and my heart
bled from terror. My will trembled,
till a grimace of a smile twisted my mouth,
and I entertained dark dreams,
swore in the night,
with tongue, head and body:
"Don't lose yourself in the night like a wind in
   the corn,
If you sink, fly head first
down into the abyss!
If you scream, stay numb!
Let no one say that I screamed
secretly in my sleep."

Then my father came in a night of storms,
tore off my cover
and smacked me in the face,
but I had, after all, sworn to stay mute.

He spoke: "You burning thorn,
you covered your hot body
in the very same sheet
that covered your mother as she birthed you
that smelled like my dead body.
You burning lustful thorn
tangling your limbs in my cover,
My lust carries the guilt for your birth,
And my lustfulness rose again in you—
you disobedient son, you rebel,
since I'm buried, let me be buried.
When one hides an invalid Torah, parts erased,
one shouldn't use its mantle either.
Go hunch up like a hill in a field
and let the yellow grass grow.
How can you bear your face in the world
leaving my suffering unredeemed?
Your ancestors demand an accounting:
What is your calling and what is your promise?

Answer the witnessing generations.
If you birth is mere coincidence, it is murder."

Thus did my wrathful father whip me with the
   covers,
as I lay naked and trembling.
So sworn, I could say nothing to him,
like a felled forest, no longer even able to mourn
the whirlwind.

Translated by Zackary Sholem Berger.

Miklós Radnóti

Just Walk On, Condemned to Die
1936

Just walk on, condemned to die!
in woods where winds and catscreams wail,
sentence in darkened lines
shall fall upon the pines;
hunchbacked with fear the road turns pale.

Just shrivel up, you autumn leaves!
shrivel, most hideous of worlds!
cold hisses from the sky;
on grasses rusted dry
the shadow of the wild geese falls.

O poet, live as clean as those
hilldwellers in their windblown snows,
O live as free of sin
as baby Jesus in
an ikon where the candle glows,

as hard as the great wolf who goes
wounded and bleeding through the snows.

Translated by Zsuzannah Ozsváth and Frederick Turner.

Saul Tschernikovsky

Eagle, Eagle!
1936

Eagle! Eagle on your hilltops, eagle flying o'er your
   hills!
Slow and buoyant—it seems a moment—only floating as it wills;
Floating, sailing through blue seas, hearing notes of
   sung delight

Filling heavens as it hovers, circling mute in burning light.

Eagle! Eagle on your hilltops, eagle flying o'er your hills!
Straight of back and heavy-bodied, broad of wing with blackest quills;
Flying tense (a speeding arrow), orbits spinning high and round,
Seeking traces of its quarry in dust and crannies on the ground.

Eagle! Eagle on your hilltops, eagle flying o'er your hills!
Fleeting, falling, sweeping wonder, wings not wavering as it spills:
For a moment freezing; then—the slightest motion of its wings,
Just a tremor, then of a sudden, up into a cloud it springs.

Eagle! Eagle on your hilltops, eagle flying o'er your hills!
Slow and buoyant—so it seems—a moment floats just as it wills . . .
Earth, the eagle's on your hilltops—o'er your surface casting shade,
With mighty wings it passes over, caressing hills that God has made . . .

Translated by Richard Flantz.

Aaron Zeitlin

Bottoms
1936

I

To be or not to be—that's not the question.
Sense or nonsense—that's *my* obsession.
For too long, Divine reckoning
has shredded human thinking.

The sum total of justice is a round number:
bright moon on bloody valleys.
But like tortured children
Digits are weeping.

To be or not to be? That's not the question.
Sense or nonsense—*that's* my obsession.

I want an ungodly reckoning
for tears of the Godless.

II

But he is surely here, Horatio!
He exists, you philosopher-fool.
Right here, though, my pain starts, Horatio.
He has no end. So where is it?

Where in him lies the bar to my unhappiness?
Carcass of a horse in a ditch,
Soul's conflagration on a cliff—
It must be all the same to the Ain-Sof?

Such a pain wasn't even dreamed
by your philosophers, Philosopher:
The pain of Searching is child's play
compared to belief in the Ain-Sof.

My belief is a volcano, Horatio.
My spirit lies, a slaughtered chicken (still alive)
in its own blood—and waits for mercy.
Mercy is the only hope which I hope for.

I wait for mercy. But *His* mercy
is God, not human—and for my poor substance
his mercy is punishment. Pure fire.
Where is man, where failure, in the Ain-Sof?

III

Perhaps he is not the Great Lord
that the philosophers made him out to be?
Maybe he is as long-suffering as people?
Perhaps he has no such power?

Maybe every night, like a tired beggar,
he knocks on the worlds' door?

IV

When did such a night fall?
When is that time ripe?
Perhaps he stands, asking like me,
in the night when the screaming Satan foams at the mouth.
The murderer stands on one side of night,
he and I—on the other side.

When did such a night fall?
For him and me—it's night together!

When did a generation thus generate?
The murderer says DEATH to both of us!

V

The eternal questions, Horatio, the eternal
    questions
were my daily questions.
My 24-7 questions—
I didn't find any answers in the stomach.

I sought answers in myself, and I found them.
I divined them in myself.
But now, now when in giant size
the towering shadow rises every higher
from his criminal Excellence—
the answers bleed like evening suns,
answers shamefaced
to be found.

VI

Jewish Ophelia, you won't give birth for me
to the new Jew, the redeemed, the Savior.
How can I provide redemption for you, when I
    wander
angrily in the great world of Esau—
An unredeemed Jew in the world without repair?

Wait! I know where I should send you.
Jewish Ophelia, I know your pain—
and I have advice for you, sister. Go
with that terrible suffering of the Jewish woman
and let yourself be violated by a soldier
as Miriam, Jesus' mother, did long ago—
so the melodrama will be over.

Jewish Ophelia, go and birth
a new mixed-blood bastard god
to the boor, the murderous youth, the ass's son!
And let your son enchant him anew,
poison his blood once again, which yearns for the
    forest
with the abandoned remains of Jewishness,
with Jewish dream and Jewish violence,
to God the Father. Who art in Heaven.

I can't sing a Song of Songs to you.
I can only ask in my final pain:
Go now and get pregnant from a swine!
Go to my murderer—become a Miriam!

VII

On the other hand, what do I care about Ophelia?
What are women? A cynical people, is all.
They birth the man—and devour him.
Eternal shame game of She and Him!

No mercy in them. Gleaming deception
at 20 or at 60. Dead-end earth.
The same thing binds them together
with wolf and blood, with Hitler and with sword.

VIII

Women and doctors are cynical.
They see us naked.
See us naked, physiological-clinical.
Even more cynical, the athlete Death.
He lets fall on our nakedness
A fist like a nightstick
and drops us to the ground:
Finished!

The woman, doctor, and Death—those three!
The cynical trio!
There must be an eye
which sees us even more naked
So naked that even nakedness itself
falls from us—and we become
substance, form, cover.

I pray to that eye.

Merciful eye,
see me,
glimpse that nakedness of mine
unseen by woman
by doctor
by Death.

Let that nakedness of mine
become from NOTHING—substance (I'll stand there
    flayed)!
nothingness shines through it,
that nothingness which is eternally
born and forever disappears.

That whose children
stand blindly
before his abyss
which the Indians call
Om

and the Kabbalist
Ayin

IX

I seek Man in God—
I seek Infinity—End.

––––––––––––

Suddenly my hands dangle
like dead branches.

Perhaps humanity has succeeded
in breaking through eternity,
but not the suffering person
and not the singing person
but
the shooter
the rejoicer

X

I stop
in the middle of the Trashy Kingdom
(The life of my people is trashy)—
and around me, on the most mundane of days
is the twilight of an old castle
I stand and ask
in the gloaming of the hours:
And how (do you see,
barely sensed, unknown
Vis-à-vis)
How, in your overtheres
How is it that in my heres
Insanity inheres?

I ask—and my people
(shopkeepers, reincarnated prophets)
does not know my Elsinore
doesn't see
my anxious
my querulous twilight.
Standing as it does in its store, advertising its
    wares
between the pogroms.
Before me, though
an abyss opens up in the street
and I ask the depths:
Just why (if you please)
do in the overtheres
just like the rightheres
Hitle the Hitlers?

And why do the devourers devour the Angel of Israel
and in eternity itself
blood sprays from the knife?

Then I know your being, O Eternity.
But, Eternity, have they not
broken your locks—the pillagers?

—Summer, 1936
Translated by Zackary Sholem Berger.

Aaron Zeitlin

A Trip in the Opposite Direction
1936

It's one in the morning. I'm writing this poem
in a train station.
What does poetry have to do with trains?
I came here unexpectedly
traveling the wrong way.
Telling the story is risky:
I was supposed to catch the train to Warsaw.
And—not to my glory—
I boarded instead the train to Kalish.
Now I'm in the Kalish central station
(next train 4 AM),
angry and annoyed enough
to slap myself silly.

At first
(I could barely control myself)
I looked up at the big clock
Above the cafeteria
Counted the minutes
Dreamed of bed.

After that
I put on a tragic face (such a schlimazel!)
almost like Dr. Herzl
on the bridge in Basel.

And then
I stuck my nose in the paper
and said to myself—basically
this is a meaningless episode
and there's no point
in making a giant deal
from such things
(yet somehow I didn't

feel like reading).
Then I sank my gaze
into the dark windows of the terminal
seeking concealed connections
between me and this unpleasant tale.
And then it came, as a revelation:
if I traveled
in the wrong direction
and I got to Kalish,
even in this mindless tale—
as in every senselessness—is some sense.
If I hadn't
been where I was supposed to be,
perhaps it's a hint from starry heights:
Dear friend of mine,
Turn back, while there's still time!
A hint from overhead:
"No comfort for you
because you're going
THE WRONG WAY!"

You just have to take the hint,
Be awake to the signal—
And suddenly it's obvious, that leap
to the Kalish terminal.

I finished my tea a long time ago,
it's almost 2 AM,
the gentile cafeteria lady is napping,
the electric lights are dimming,
and through my brain
fevered poems race in full gallop

disappearing
down the night-highway to the unknown.

I think again:
Facts are simulacra
imitating the superficial
but they link up to each other in the depths:
a whole generation, lost with Arn Tseitlin
going in reverse.
No, not one generation, but all of those
which led to him
and created him—
he who sits at the cafeteria table
and stares through black windowpanes.
They are now lost with him together
since: is he not their very
unsuccessful extract?
(A symbol—every fact!)

Is no one here besides me,
the passenger
who got lost?
Everyone's with me, I mean—and everything.
Everything which composes me, the person:
Forest and God,
pains and breezes,
dream and anger,
Sinai Desert,
Warsaw,
My grandpa Reb Avrom,
my zeyde Orlik-Leyzer.

But how do I know that I'm lost?
Just because I'm laughed at
by the internal schoolteacher, my mind
who points out
that I have no business at all in Kalish?
I'm probably supposed to be here tonight
because it was a thought
in the profoundly concealed head—
Head of all heads—
the thoughts of Homo sapiens
being telepathic reflections
from his heavenly thoughts
metaphysical.

But as if nothing had happened
my mind asks again, deliberately obtuse:
Why, again, are you in the Kalish terminal?
I answer it with a question:
What am I doing in this world at all?
Something deep brought me here
something deep will take me back.
The same thing which brought me here
will bring me back—back . . .

And by the way, dear mind, sir,
I'm doing the exact same thing
which I've been doing for years now in the world:
I make a poem
and wait—and make a poem and wait, for that train
which will take me back to the city
that I came from.

I argue with my mind,
and as the gentile cafeteria lady wakes up for a bit
I order from her again
a glass of tea
not really because I want to drink it
as much as because

the tea wants to be ordered.
And I say this to myself:
"The world is coming to you
needing the same thing,
and you
to the world.
So you two are both settled,
My dear Jew,
what more do you need?"

But someone else answers in me and says,
"Certainly, you're all very smart
but the truth is, I'm tired
and it's enough. I've done my part.
When does the train come?
When will it take me away?
When can I rest—is what I say?"

"Ridiculous!"
—interrupts the cafeteria clock,
sternly pointing with a firm hand—
"Listen to the idiot talk!
He says he can't wait?
That's his fate.
The train must come, understand?
Not a minute sooner or later!
What's he talking about?"

Then the other one in me, while he objects, is tired
    now
sees that the clock is correct,
and quietly obeys
with all the other I's in me—the attendant fray.

The electric lights yawn
and so does the gentile cafeteria lady
(not so musical, natch,
the cafeteria lady's yawns
in Kalish)
and there lies my poem
written out, on the table:
a report—my voyage
the wrong way.

Translated by Zackary Sholem Berger.

Benjamin Fondane

1898–1944

The poet and essayist Benjamin Fondane was born
Benjamin Wechsler in Iași, Romania. When he began
writing in local Zionist periodicals, he adopted the pen
name Fundoianu, which he later Gallicized to Fondane
when he settled in Paris in 1923 and began writing in
French. In Paris, he worked at an insurance company
and for Paramount Pictures as a screenwriter while
establishing himself as an avant-garde poet and exis-
tentialist philosopher. His poetry was deeply imbued
with Hebrew imagery. In 1944, he was arrested and
imprisoned in Drancy and then deported to Auschwitz, where he was murdered.

X-Rays
1937

I

Work, tradesmen, shops, the town is there
with old maids polished down by emptiness
on haberdashers' threshold where the antique sun
brushes off jewels dusty with being looked at.

Dressed up for Sunday, O doll with no navel,
you try out one by one your tools of reverie:
ribbons, combs, creams, rosaries, glass trinkets,
used witches' brooms.

Jews emerged from hunger's pure studies
dance a minuet of supply and demand
clothed in ancient prayers—
they capture the client by means of magic.

Peasants will come smelling of hay
from that far-off star-soaked land
to buy dizziness, noise, long illnesses,
tools of prime necessity, of course!

Peasants in embroidered shirts, a feather in their
    hats
purer than a pitcher of cold water
scared as a doe strayed into a drawing room
of trampling the glass sidewalks with their clogs.

Will they hurry away and down a brandy
to turn their hearts' clock hands back to noon
two steps from the church where the painted
    wooden Christ
crumbles in dust to redeem the rotten?

Children have leaped onto the wooden horses
itching acutely from the music,
in a world that turns,
that turns without knowing why.

Sarah, for thirty years you've been marking time
and your sex spins on itself like a noisemaker,
such strange mathematics, life
that still-undeciphered language.

Somewhere, sailors, smelling of seaweed,
drink in the port bars, with women's
buttocks on their heavy knees—they've known
the storms which lash the cape of solitudes.

Life isn't here, is it there, then?
Is there something that will quench the thirst—
that young thirst which overturns hearts—
our old maids' hearts?

II

It was at the flea market that I found you again
face of anguish—
greased like an old machine
a sewing machine, a coffee grinder.

Fountain of youth where furniture and umbrellas
which saw service for a thousand years
regain their virgin smiles,
straighten their twisted springs.

The same furniture and the same umbrellas,
the same used, threadbare Jews
go back into the circulation
of blood, objects, fate.

Human lives gnawed on like old coins
go back into the great numismatic current
—where will they find rest?
here they are imprinted with new features.

Are they things I had already seen in childhood
or in a past life?
The century passes, or perhaps a shower of trains—
who has time to give names to the faces?

Perhaps we are all the same everywhere
time is perhaps the same—
it's because of that that nothing changes
that only *change* grows old.

The gods prayed to with the same hieroglyphics
no longer kiss us with the kisses of their mouth;
our cries up like old nails
no longer penetrate the Eternal.

It's been a long time since words lost their meaning
such a long time—

and there they are, for heaven's sake, ripening

on the threshold of time to come—
of great events now *past*.

III

On Friday, the Turkish bath received us
with its wooden tiers, as in ancient theaters,
where old men sat, heat-struck, asleep
with the open eyes of dwarf crocodiles.

A chorus of Jews, steaming like hot soup,
moved from one side of the stage to the other,
ready to go into a trance
as soon as the god rose to the oracle's mouths.

Confusing show of moving snapshots,
of bodiless arms, faceless bodies, bellies,
of wrinkled, flabby feet from whose toes protruded
the delicate, aggressive jewels of corns.

Damp penises hung down along thin thighs
patriarchs' penises on which oaths were sworn
long ago, when sky-swaddled Jehovah
drove the long herd of Jews through the desert.

An acrid odor of dream and sweat floated
through that aquarium where limp meat
projected viscous shimmering flickers
the limbs of some bygone sea creature.

A sort of voluptuous, pure anguish
ran down backs and splashed over loins,
avid to preserve, in the folds of flesh,
that glandular, obscure, and uterine joy.

IV

To Line

No doubt hell passed that way, but in the evening
there was a sudden storm burst of prayers.
Crowds rushed into the cinema of synagogues,
visions of fire splattered the darkness.

The divine knife grinder sharpened spirits,
Vertigo! There you are, apocalyptic cattle,
risen from time's depths, racing along the rock
    face
slavering after the choir of underground angels.

Anger, you arose from the ancient parchment
purer than ever. The road, before your enormous

eye, recoiled. From the huge, extinguished crater
a distant tear dripped down my cheek.

The rattle of voices twirled in milky
candlelight. Someone was hiding time.
The stars emerged timidly from heaven's
bread box and Saturday crossed the border.

Saturday entered the blessed houses
breaking down no doors, and took a sip
from the full glasses . . . While the cows calved.
The Spirit counted the miserable on earth
and shook the clusters of dead among the living.
Ships were subject to those odd nauseas
which bring your guts to your teeth.
                              But fish,
golden-eyed, glittered among grandmother's
silverware.
          A hostile water clock
marked, as my heart did, time as it flowed away
flowed away, and which has never returned—
and will not return till Judgment Day.

Translated by Marilyn Hacker.

Other works by Fondane: *Le mal des fantômes* (1980);
*Entre Jérusalem et Athènes: Benjamin Fondane à la re-
cherché du Judaïsme* (2009); *Existential Monday: Philosophical Essays* (2016).

Jacob Glatstein

We the Wordproletariat
1937

Night. In the darkest places sparkle traces
Of words. Loaded ships with ideo-glyphs
Sail away. And you, armored in silence and wisdom,
Unwrap word from sense.

Mementos—rain-veiled horizon,
Flickering return, barely recalled:
A book, a face, a smile, a yawn.

The cursed night has got into your bones.

Soften up, cover up, forget.
Don't make a miracle of a trouser button.

Wordproletarian. Airplanes leave land
Full of understands.
And you in your vest of Sesames and Ali-Babas.
Don't you hear how yokes sigh?

Iron girders lie on your words.
Gnash them, curse them with disaster.
Where are your laughters, where are your groans?

The cursed night has got into your bones.

Your palm dates under your windows.
A stone and Here-Lies.
The in-between times have brought you to the
     absolute
Graves of individuals, masses, Jews, races—
Archives.
Now whole collectives sing,
Stratospheres, stars, even buildings, stones.

The cursed night has got into your bones.
The sky, the blue hazard, went out.
You still sit and seek the shadows of a word
And scrape the mold off meanings.
Words take on sadder and purer tones.

The cursed night has got into your bones.

Translated by Benjamin Harshav and Barbara Harshav.

Chaim Grade

A Child
1937

I have a friend, a teacher, with shaggy hair black as
     pitch.
He has a child (his wife is still a child too)
and when he comes home, difficult and gloomy,
she runs to meet him, like a quivering wave:
"The boy laughed today, you know,
and then cried,
furrowed his brow, thought, thought
but I didn't understand what he wants.
He can entertain himself with his laughter
is attracted to the boy in the mirror
He has your eyes! He'll be bad."
And Mom and Dad bend over the crib,
one across from the other, trees over a brook,
interlinked,
the little one drums his little feet on his belly
and is drawn to his mother.

My friend is a night reporter
his blond head wavy like a field of rye
all he needs to do is to drive a tractor
snore while submerged in a haystack—

he just needs to sit down on the turnpike
a rock between his knees
take a hammer—and bang! split it in two!
Such a stubborn, daring youth
should have heaved the whole day in labor—
but he's a night editor.

Like fire, he grabs telegrams,
He listens to the nightly world through telegrams,
His head flames in the darkness—a solar
    eclipse—
He aims cannon mouths at the dawn
When he strides home from the editorial offices
he gasps and waves his hands:
on page 2 or 3, the home editors,
on the front page, Europe is burning.
When he gets closer to home, his steps get softer
and when he opens the door
the last telegram wire snaps in his head.
The clock lectures him: it's four already
and you left her at seven PM.
left her alone since seven.
He gets upset at himself
since he can't walk any softer
disturbing the rising life in the womb.

In the soft carpeted room
in the dull, pale shine
of the watery blue shimmer
his wife tangles him up like a pallid plant.

He runs his fingers through her velvet hair;
You, girl, will give birth to—a boy
She is angry, even her earlobe turns red,
sticks out her tongue,
"I want a girl."

What about me, what can I entertain my wife with,
how can I quiet her pain,
when she caresses and kisses a girl,
a doll in a pink dress?
My wife, the angel
Has prepared for little children
crowns of ringlets, bells,
they won't be born, like fawns,
with shoes and stockings;
a child needs a cradle.
It's no little thing, that its mother can sing the lullaby
of the white goat
and that in the bedroom it shouldn't get wet, God
    forbid—

let's grab each other's hands and leap
with the kids on the street.
I will rock the evening to sleep
with a fatherly tune.
Then I will stay in your arms
like heaven's blue in the river—
and loneliness itself will rock over us
to and fro
like a willow
like a willow.

Translated by Zackary Sholem Berger.

H. Leivick

A Stubborn Back—and Nothing More
1937

Come, let us hide ourselves in caves,
in stony crevices, in graves
where stretched full length on the hard ground
we lie, backs up and faces down.

We shall not record, we shall not say
why we've immured ourselves this way.
No notch in a wall, our stony page,
shall mark the historic year or age.

We shall not leave behind as clue
one thread of ourselves—not the lace of a shoe.
No one shall find, hard though he look,
one shred of a dress, one page of a book.

Whether he search by night or by day,
no one shall find a trace of our clay.
But if someone should, let his find be poor:
a stubborn back—and nothing more.

Let him stand wondering, mouth agape,
why we fled to a cave for our escape,
what the last words of our distress
in these depths of stoniness.

And let him seek and still not find
if conscience here were undermined.
if the tormented heart grew faint
and blood and courage suffered taint;

If we were tortured by a fiend,
or maybe by someone just and kind;
by ax, by bullet, by lynching herd
or maybe by a casual word.

If he asks our bones mixed one with the other:
Are you the bones of a foe or a brother,
the answer will come: horror struck dumb
and from his own mouth white bubbles of foam.

Long will he stare—not comprehending—
till he turn—eyes bulging, arms extending—
to flee in his fear and consternation
from generation to generation.

The greater his fear, the faster his flight,
running till history flounder in night,
while we go on lying as heretofore:
a stubborn back and nothing more.

Translated by Robert Friend.

A. Leyeles

Bolted Room
1937

Dark, bolted room.
Thick air soaked with fear and danger.
Fabius Lind—eye to eye
With a bewildering woman.
Fabius Lind is small and trembling,
The woman is big and growing—and pouring out
Odors of a heavy body.
Smells of stable,
Of summer afternoons in the thick of a forest.
Powerful hips and powerful legs.
Fabius Lind is scared and feels so deadly good.
The odors enfold him,

Take away his will—
He doesn't need to need to exist.

He and the woman and the fear and the goodness
    are one.
And he is enormously alone.

Translated by Benjamin Harshav and Barbara Harshav.

A. Leyeles

An Encounter
1937

For two minutes we gazed at each other
In curious silence.
When politeness nudged me in the shoulder,

I introduced myself:
A man, the crown of creation.
The grasshopper
Was not overwhelmed.
He kept on gazing with careful, glimmering eyes.
Even when I proudly showed him the airplane
That just then buzzed by
Over our heads,
He did not lose his dignity.
Offended, I fixed him with my eye
And examined without ceremony
His finely wrought red legs,
His strong wings,
His manly mustaches.
He didn't like my impertinence, the trickster of
    grass.
With condescending indifference,
He turned to me his gracious ass
And hopped away—
With a leap
More beautiful, elegant, surer
Than my airplane.

If I live another hundred years
I shall probably have the necessary machine to hear
His great-, million times great-grandson's
Devastating laughter.

Translated by Benjamin Harshav and Barbara Harshav.

A. Leyeles

Fabius Lind Is Riding the Wind
1937

I

Fabius Lind clings to the flowing mane
Of young spring,
Galloping on the free highways of desire.
Voluptuous desert-winds around him,
Voluptuous desert-winds inside him.
Fabius Lind surrenders to the frivolous mane
And ponders
And dreams.

II

Fabius Lind has long since understood
That assorted young males,

Unbelievably younger than himself,
Will multiply daringly around him.
Damned if he knows
When so many days had time
To muster like armies of watchmen
Behind his unsuspecting proud back.
Damned he understands
Why all these strange witnesses should not retreat
Into unwanted yesterdays, before-yesterdays,
    five-years-ago—
At a mere wave of his young arm.
But why so many new males?
And why do insolent teeth bite off pieces of his joy
At the sight of the new Ophelias?

III

Fabius Lind's heart is full of tenderness
For the latest feminine fashions.
His lips mutter pious odes to the refined rhythm
Of not-overgrown vibrant hips,
And his happy eye glides lovingly
Over the taut curves of sincerely walking legs.
But the new "he"s
Impertinently obstruct the open view.
And Fabius Lind is not a Shaman-hunter,
Not a he-gorilla.
He isn't even a rival or a fighter.
He is a gentleman
Of the restrained, civilized city New York
Who wanders at times in the exciting-poisoning
    paths
Of Freud's dream-interpretation.
And though he's not ashamed,
Nor appeased,
Still the great seer and understander from Vienna
Allows him a good-natured smile.
And if light waves of sadness
Lap the shores of his smile—
Nobody will see it.

IV

Fabius Lind has ridden quite a distance
On his obedient horse.
Ever thirstier, he clings to the frivolous mane,
And hurries—
Hurries, hurries, hurries—
To ever newer and newer calls.

Translated by Benjamin Harshav and Barbara Harshav.

A. Leyeles

Fabius Lind's Days
1937

Fabius Lind's days are running out in blood.
Red serpents of failures empty his veins.
In his head—white muddy stains. Confusion.
And a heavy load on his heart.
He could have . . .
He could have . . .
Gray spiderwebs of melancholy
Cover his mind, veil his eyes
And a strange taut bow
Aims at the tip of his nose.
Fabius Lind, sunk in contemplation,
In talking, in reading, tightens—
Out of sheer being lost—
The noose around his neck.

Why can't Fabius Lind hold on to
The coattails of these times
And stride in the rows of all the marchers?
Why can't he swing back to his childhood playground
And bring his flutes to play
The song of calm?
Why is he so indifferent at funerals,
So nervous at a birth?
Why can't he grab the two whores—
    death and life
And let himself go in a holy-foolish dance?

Whom does he ask?
No one. Just himself.
If he could brain-out an answer,
He would not have asked.

In these days of straight rails, Fabius Lind
Is not awake.
He strays for hours, for days,
And dreams of pure isn'ts.
A time that isn't,
A land that isn't,
People that aren't,
A Fabius Lind who doesn't exist.
He could have . . .
He could have . . .
Yes, yes, he could have!

The desire, the thought, flies away on an
    uninvited wind

And comes back in a ball of smoke.
The calculating mind has never served Fabius
     Lind.

Translated by Benjamin Harshav and Barbara Harshav.

A. Leyeles

Fabius Lind's Diary: February 7 and 17
1937

February 7

I inherited naive open-heartedness
From generations of small-town Polish Jews,
And sharp talk
From hot-bathed women in my clan.
A blind June-night mixed it all
And sent me out—
With no regard for symmetry.

My counterpart weighs me carefully
On the scales of his experience with world and man.
My voice calls back—intimate and straight.
By the rule of half to the wall and half to the river,
He forgives me my intimacy.
And the straightness—like a steel ruler:
Cuts and divides.

My counterparts grow rarer and rarer.
And the rust on my door-knob—
Not just the oxygen in the air.
Luckily, from time to time
I can enjoy a joke with myself. [. . .]

February 17

Fabius Lind's kingdom—
A few fenced crates.
As to a permanent, identical incantation,
The crates open up to let his days out—
From one house with a number
To another house with a number.
All over him, noises of the big city.

Wheels, rails above,
Rails, wheels below, in deep tunnels.

When Fabius Lind undresses the noises,
He is left with crumbs of color, spots of sound,
A composite mask of unrest and confusion.

Sometimes a clearing flashes, it has the image
Of a dreamed-up Notre-Dame,
Of a well-planned Empire-State,
Of a hydro-electrical power-station on the
     Dnieper—
Once upon a time.
Once upon a time.

The once-upon-a-times are stabbed blind by the
     jagged wreckage
Falling on his head. His head in the midst
Of crush and downfall. And he himself on a side, on
     the brink.
Then he is wrapped in night's profusion,
All seems to him imagining, delusion,
Tricks and masks of death.

Translated by Benjamin Harshav and Barbara Harshav.

A. Leyeles

The Madonna in the Subway
1937

Across from me in the subway sat the madonna
Crossing her legs,
Bending over a tabloid.
She read about a cashier-girl who jumped into the
     water
When her bridegroom left her with a rising belly.
The madonna put lipstick on her mouth
And went on biting into the burning coal
Of tragedy.
She stroked her snakeskin shoe,
And proceeded to lament the drowning death
Of the cashier-girl.

My gaze tick-tocked.
The madonna's eyelids heard,
And two longish caves turned to me
Their suede depth, their intimate mystery.
And I perceived the words of the madonna,
The words which she spoke to me alone
In the subway:
In Galilee, once upon a time in Galilee,
The carpenters, the shoemakers, the tailors,
The fishermen, the moneylenders, the thieves
Needed a savior and a God.
Then I opened my virgin loins
And in a dark hour received in my womb

The needy seed of one whose name I still don't know.
A soldier, a stranger, an angry man, a slave of a Caesar,
A fisherman, hands calloused from pulling his nets,
Or just a bum who happened to whisper: my God!
All I can tell you is, I got pregnant.
Oh, there are nights when the spirit slices into your
    guts
Like a vulture's beak,
Embraces you like a serpent.
There are black, open hearted nights, that sense
The claim of virgin loins.
It was the spirit of God,
Because soldiers and fishermen and bums
Demanded a savior, a God.

The madonna powdered her nose and chin
(Her nose was noble and thin)
And spoke again:
From that far dazzle
And bright call,
From this near sorrow
In the heavy body—
Painters and poets dream up
My portraits, age after age.
From the old sprouting spring
In fields, in forests,
Hands stretch out: bestow on us!
Eyes pray
Through the warp and the woof of the year.
In the choking air
Of streets, in subways—
People still long for the miracle,
Though they don't believe in its birth.
Oh, one day I shall strip off the webs
Which enfold me, tie me,
I shall quench your thirst
With my nakedness.
You hear:
It will be like that great destiny
Then, in Galilee.

The madonna spoke much more,
Long and hot and fast.
But I—I no longer perceived.
In the pious flutter, I felt the coming
Of open-hearted moons and suns,
And I sensed God's spirit move in me
Like a hare, like a serpent, like a bird.

Translated by Benjamin Harshav and Barbara Harshav.

A. Leyeles

Moscow Night, End of December 1934
1937

It's hard to be clever these nights,
And useless to be modern.
Useless to smile knowingly and observe with
    melancholy
The language bastardisms of history:
"The government of the Republic is delivered into
    the hands of the Emperor."

A nasty old moon crawls in my window
And chokes me with a cold hand.
She coughs, she foams over me:
Who do you think you are
That you want to straighten the accounts of the
    world,
To rage when a childish toy of yours is broken.
The other day I saw a Palestinian bum and rebel
Growl: Justice, love,
And call for help to some daddy here in the sky.
Yesterday a crowd of yours made fools of
    themselves
Around a stone broad with a torch in her raised arm
And stormed, clamored in excitement:
Brotherhood, Equality, Reason!
And today you stare at me from a rumpled pillow
With fiery-dry eyes demanding an answer:
Why has an icon of yours fallen out of its frame,
And the frame itself is speckled with Abel's warm
    shudder?
Maybe you'd like to ask—even higher—the stars?
Go on, perceive (as you idiot poets like to say) their
    singing—
What do you hear?
But listen well.

I listened, I perceived,
I wanted to scream my last, and greatest scream
For me and for the whole creation.
But the hag's hand was on my neck,
The hag's chill in my throat.

Who said that pity is not a foundation of the
    world?
Right then the calendar
Gave the old witch a lewd wink
And she left with him, just like that.

My throat relaxed.
But my tongue is dumb.
Dumber.

Translated by Benjamin Harshav and Barbara Harshav.

Kadya Molodovsky

Alphabet Letters
1937

In the Bronx, in Brooklyn and in New York City,
My cousins all have stores.
Seven cousins with seven stores, like
    commandments.
Business people with long lists of going bankrupt.
And my family-name stares at me from their signs
With a gaze that's wild and foreign.
The flaming *mem* (of Moses and of Marx)
Skips on one green foot.
The *alef* winks glossily at the street below.
The *lamed* loops a knot like a gallows.
And the alphabet shrieks in the city's iron uproar:
—Bankrupt, bankrupt and bankrupt some more.
But beneath the sign, my Uncle Mikhl and Aunt
    Sore
Have gotten fat—evil eye, stay away—*keyn ayen
    hore.*
She—a blue silk barrel,
And he—a gray steel spring.
And their children—Julie, Beatrice, Max and
    Carolyn—
Proudly wear letter like stars on short sleeves and
    long,
For the card clubs and Boy Scout troops to which
    they belong.

Translated by Kathryn Hellerstein.

Kadya Molodovsky

A White Poet
1937

For H. Leyvik

New York.
A white poet stood on the hundred-and-fourth floor.
The sky and an iron city
Engaged in a conversation.
A thirsty "forever" marched on

In bewildered
Disorganization.

New York lit up green
And red,
With a dazzle of sun.
New York sank into thought
All the way to its far, noisy end.

A white poet stood on the hundred-and-fourth floor.
The sky and an iron city
Engaged in a conversation.
The barefoot built New York,
Blacks, Italians, Ukrainians, Chinese, Poles, and we
    Jews.
—I am the one who painted the highest floor here,
I am the one who pasted the wallpaper here,
It's absolutely true,
Here's proof: the bricklayer from Novidvor
Fell from the tenth floor here.

Here, all the peoples had their say,
All sang out their song.
A Black man died from a blow to the head.
A Ukrainian choked his falcon.
A Jew and a Czech led a strike.
A Chinese man withered and wept for a letter.
Now all stand—
In gray jackets of relief
On the foreign street.
Mister Joe interrupted words of a poet:
—Max, jazz!
And two hundred feet dazzled—
Blacks, Italians, Ukrainians, Chinese, a Jew and a
    Greek.
And danced out a sunny day
And starlight,
A luminous haven,
And the firmament in its first trembling happiness
Of creation.

A white poet stood on the hundred and fourth floor.
The sky and an iron city
Engaged in a conversation.
It's a dream—
It is not the truth
That my house is overgrown with grass and thorns,
And an entire New York City street
Has forgotten the last letter of the alphabet.

New York is all light.
There are no shadows.

A dream is a head on a stone, fast asleep,
Wrapped snugly in the hours of night.

It's a dream—a white dove
Seeking a mountaintop and a leaf,
That came back poisoned
From murder, betrayal, and grief.

The poet choked on his own words:
—Here is the crowbar, the ax,
The Empire State Building should return to clay,
Back to rocky stone.
I'm going down . . .
I'm going . . . I'm going to do this alone.

New York is all light,
It is sunny white,
It is sky-green—
Mister Joe interrupted the words of the poet:
—Max, my machine!

A white poet stood on the hundred and fourth floor.
The sky and an iron city
Engaged in a conversation.

Translated by Kathryn Hellerstein.

Miklós Radnóti

And Thus, Perhaps, I Will Reflect . . . ?
1937

I lived, but as for *living* I was shiftless in my life,
knew always I'd be buried here when all was done,
that year layers itself upon year, clod on clod, stone
    on stone,
that in the chill and wormy dark the body swells,
and cold, too, lies the fathom-deep and naked bone.
That up there scurrying time is ransacking my
    poems,
that down, down, down, my mortal heaviness must
    drive;
all this I knew. But tell me—did the work survive?

Translated by Zsuzannah Ozsváth and Frederick Turner.

J. L. Teller

1912–1972

Yehuda (Judd) Leyb Teller was born in Tarnopol,
Galicia, and was brought to New York City in 1921. He
studied in Hebrew day schools and then at City College and Columbia University, from which he received
a doctorate in psychology. He worked as a journalist
and was employed by several Jewish political and communal organizations. Versatile and prolific, he wrote
essays and poems in Yiddish and Hebrew and books
on Jewish history and contemporary Jewish affairs in
English. As a Yiddish poet, he was close to the American objectivists and the Yiddish Introspectivists.

Jud' Süss Oppenheimer on His First Visit with Professor Sigmund Freud
1937

That's you—the Eternal Jew.
Of Esau's lullaby, of Gentile legend.
And I am your nephew—Jud' Süss Oppenheimer.
You, seer, who can see far, see clear, see through,
You may say that I—am not I,
That one who craves feasts and shikses
Is not Jew Süss.

I am not the mirror-surface of a river,
Languid between bushy shores.
Springs emerge from me,
Water plants and worms.

My pedigree: traders in wheat and barley,
Who would slyly slip
Extra weights onto the scales.
I know why.
But you don't want to judge between good and bad.
You want to understand.

Scholars, who encircled themselves with barbed
    wire:
Like prisoners in a jail-yard,
They hopped with shackled feet
In a ring of Don'ts.
Midday. The sun seared their eyes.

Flatterers: they carried the Holy Torah
In processions to the Bishop,
Raked the dust with their beards,
And retreated backward,
Facing him who wore the cross.

They all were gentle shadow-men
Of the Gamzu-tribe.

And I am Gamzu's grandson.
He was a timid Jew—
And now he fires revolts in my dream,
Uses my voice for his profanities,

Wants to collect his pound of flesh.

In blue hours with a Gentile daughter,
He conjures up for me my violated sister
(Kishenev, Proskurov, Brisk),
And my limbs rage to rape.

I fear the unfinished syllable,
Things I have not sensed.

The dream gnaws at me, as the sea at the land.
You, who see clear, see through,
Take me like grains of barley in your fist,
Hold me like an egg against the light.

They say that at night
You mix herbs in a brew.
That's you—the Eternal Jew.
I am Jud Süss Oppenheimer,
Your nephew.
Gamzu was my grandfather.

You, interpreter of dreams.
Pull a stalk out of me.
Taste me
Like barley at the fair.

Translated by Benjamin Harshav and Barbara Harshav.

Other works by Teller: *Miniaturn* (1934); *Lider fun
der tsayt* (1940); *Durkh yidishn gemit* (1975).

Nathan Alterman

Beyond Melody
1938

With a violin in the alley grandfather and son
    disappeared.
Again the night was closed. Oh, speak, please
    speak!
I who grew up with all your stones,
I knew—like confession, they too would break.

Stones like tears in the lashes of the world.
How shall I set out to wipe them with a silken cloth?
Over the last song that opposite them trembles,
Silence circles like an eagle.

At times from the night we open amazed eyes,
With wisdom and folly slow, slow we shall smile.
Mother's greyness looks at our lives,
The silence of rooms where there is no child.

And we shall go out to pale roads we abandoned,
They stand erect with a cloud and a song,
They shall go rocking us in their bosom—
They shall go tall, go tender and strong.

Go and tell them
The well is filled,
The forest burns in its sovereign mantle.
But deaf and alone
Our field is tilled
By our petty, abashed pain.

It has no deliverer, it has no flags.
Dressed in mourning silence guards its cradles.
Like its big brothers it lives alone,
Like the end, the autumn, the heart.

It shines like light in mother's forgiveness,
In wisdom's and folly's bashful quiet—
On the lips of thresholds thirsty and wide
Its smile is stoned at our feet.

Translated by Ruth Finer Mintz.

Nathan Alterman

Moon
1938

An old sight too has its moment of birth.
A birdless sky
Strange and set apart.
Facing your widow on the moonlit night stands
A city plunged in crickets' tears.

And when you see a road still watching for a
    wayfarer
And the moon
Is on the cypress spear,
You say: "My God, are all these things still out
    there?
May one whisper them a greeting?"

From their pools the waters gaze upon us.
The tree is at rest
In a flush of catkin blossoms.
Never shall the sorrow of Your great playthings
Be plucked from me, O our God.

Translated by Lewis Glinert.

Nathan Alterman

Red Riding-Hood
1938

When our wild day is wiped like a tear
From cities and forest, from month and year,
Red Ridinghood walks on the road,
To pick a wild flower in the wood.

And following her is a duck and a cow,
Hobbling on a cane is a cat—
Like a tale that was lost, like a song long ago,
Like a smile that is old and forgot.

In the distance stand the coming years,
In vain our bewilderments increase,
A naked moon sucks on its thumb
As in father's lap, at the first.

And we are silent. A grassy earth
Flutters in lashes of green . . .
We closed our eyes—And suddenly look
The tree's crown is already dark.

Translated by Ruth Finer Mintz.

Jacob Glatstein

Good Night, World
1938

Good night, wide world.
Big, stinking world.
Not you, but I, slam the gate.
In my long robe,
With my flaming, yellow patch,
With my proud gait,
At my own command—
I return to the ghetto.
Wipe out, stamp out all the alien traces.
I grovel in your dirt,
Hail, hail, hail,
Humpbacked Jewish life.
A ban, world, on your unclean cultures.
Though all is desolate,
I roll in your dust,
Gloomy Jewish life.

Piggish German, hostile Polack,
Sly Amalek, land of guzzling and gorging.

Flabby democracy, with your cold
Compresses of sympathy.
Good night, world of electrical insolence.
Back to my kerosene, tallow shadow,
Eternal October, wee little stars,
To my crooked alleys, hunchbacked street-lamp,
My stray pages, my Twenty-Four-Books,
My Talmud, to the puzzling
Questions, to the bright Hebrew-Yiddish,
To law, to deep meaning, to duty, to right.
World, I stride with joy to the quiet ghetto-light.

Good night. I grant you, world,
All my liberators.
Take the Jesusmarxes, choke on their courage.
Drop dead on a drop of our baptized blood.
And I believe that even though he tarries,
Day after day rises my waiting.
Surely, green leaves will rustle
On our withered tree.
I do not need consolation.
I go back to my four walls,
From Wagner's pagan music—to tune, to humming.
I kiss you, tangled Jewish life.
It cries in me, the joy of coming.

Translated by Benjamin Harshav and Barbara Harshav.

Saul Tschernikovsky

Three Donkeys
1939

Three donkeys from Beersheba, so they say,
Plodded slowly down the road to Dan one day.
One brown, one black, one white, they went their way.

The three passed by a minaret, and there
The black one crouched, hearing the call to prayer.
The three passed by a monastery in line
And there the brown one knelt before the shrine.
The three passed by a holy ruin: it's said
The white one halted there, and bowed its head.

There is a sword upon the black one's back,
A crucifix upon the brown one's back,
A golden rug upon the white one's back.

Save for the golden rug its back is bare.
Soon in our time Messiah will ride there.

Translated by Dom Moraes.

Aaron Zeitlin

The Nest Disappears
1939

*(Written at the end of 1939 in Havana—with thoughts
    about Poland)*

Our poor nest eternally atremble
in the wind.
What will happen now, in bloody storm,
mayn kind?
Now, in bloody storm . . . ?

The tree will fall, fall
mayn kind.
And our nest—in the storm—will be lost,
mayn kind.
Our nest, from the storm, will be gone.

I see new nests on young trees
mayn kind.
But our nest (wait and dream no longer)
is disappearing.
The old nest—disappearing.

Somewhere, sure, there must be a land
mayn kind
Where disappeared nests can be found
mayn kind
but the old nest's disappearing.

Sometime we will, after pain, transformation,
mayn kind,
rejoice in the land where the lost is returned,
mayn kind.
But our old nest has disappeared.

Translated by Zackary Sholem Berger.

Mani Leib

Sing More Softly
1930s

Let no one cross my threshold,
Nor disturb my silence;
I no longer wish to hear
The noise of people and speech

From them I crawled away
In tears, into my corner,

To listen at last in quiet
To the song of my own life.

Sing softly, song of my life,
Muted like the kernel,
That sings of its genesis
In sunny songs of seed.

Translated by Solon Beinfeld.

Chaim Grade

Fall in Vilna
Date Unknown

Yom Kippur, when the narrow alleys of the *shulhoyf*
cradle the small *shtibls*, pious and scared,
householders hurry with their *taleisim*
and old men shuffle along in their socks—
I feel the narrow ghetto even more keenly
my yearning burns like autumn gold.

I wander through the alleys of neighboring Antokol
and up on the Three Holy Crosses mountain.
Down there, the city, as if its eye were shaken
Is covered by a film. Tears flow from her face.
The ancient ruins of the castle mountain
glow in piled-up leaves.

The trees cry nakedly, as if someone barefoot
smashed a step into broken glass.

The Bernadine Park flames in yellow
the church with its pointy spire
is thinner than a quiver of sunshine.
But the entrance is muddy in fall.
A beggar at the door looks me over sternly,
The Catholics consider me with surprise,
seeing how the autumn hangs upon me
and that my eyes are—a Jew's.

A stabbing: the sunset drips from domes,
crucified on Orthodox cathedrals.
Bells though ring out the echoes
of narrow Jewish *davening* streets.
I hear the struggles with their last ounce
of energy—the *daveners*. Head in ark. Wailing.
The cover flutters, pulled aside.
The day wanes. And there is no more mercy.

At his podium, the rabbi contains the scrum.
Narrow as a candle, pale from fasting,

he walks along with a cheerful song,
as if he bore a box of jewels,
and the crowd bent low before him
wishing to join itself to him in flame,
like a bow breaking on the last string,
they tear heaven with their last strength
and I jump up . . .

The night city fires up happily.
I rush home—that's our house, shuttered.
I run into the women's section—empty.
In the men's section—and I'm bathed in sweat.

In the empty *shtibl*, lit by the Eternal Light,
there where for years upon years
my father sat, my mother stands, quiet in regret,
eyes closed, face tired gray.
She looks at me, and with her slender hand
caresses me. Her moist gaze brightens.
Her lips tremble. Shadows of the candelabrum
tremble on the wall.
She whispers an unfinished prayer
as if she redeemed my gloomy silence:
"Now I'm asking forgiveness from your father,
that you, my son, have not taken his place."

Translated by Zackary Sholem Berger.

Chaim Grade

My Mother
Date Unknown

The cheeks collapsed and the eyes half-shut,
My mother listens as her knees sigh:
The whole morning under the winter sky
She ran about to every market.
So let us now at the gate of the wall
Sleep through the night . . .
And her hand cries:
A bird too gets exhausted from fluttering about
As its wings rise and fall . . .
And her head sinks down—
But my mother flicks the daydream off,
Like a tree shaking off the rain.

Her face smolders, a fire pot,
Her hands measure, weigh;
She pleads, she calls,
Till again she dozes with eyes half-shut;

Her hand taps at the freezing air
And stays there, stretched-out.

Just like
A shadow on the snow,
She sways back and forth the whole day long,
Until late at night;
She rocks herself like the pointer of her scale,
To the left, to the right.
Hunched-up, one large hump,
She rots in the snow flurries,
Like the apples in her basket—
And sleeps . . .

Her cheeks glow like coals,
Her neck is whipped by the sleet.
Wrapped up in wind and snow
My mother sleeps standing on her feet.
And when the market snores like a grisly black hound,
She gathers her baskets,
Like a beggar his pennies,
And the market's red eye is put out.
But right at the threshold her steps start to weep:
Wasted hope!
Worn out, she stumbles through the hut
And sleeps.

The lantern hiccups in her hand,
Choking with smoky tears.
She rocks at the wall
As in front of a grave,
And sleeps.

The ax lurks in her hand,
Above her twisted fingers,
And the fiery tongues of the little stove
Menace her wrinkled cheeks—
And she sleeps.
She forgets to take out her hands:
They are freezing in the kneading bowl.
Her thin shoulder shakes,
She washes, she trembles with eyes cast down,
And she sleeps.

When at last she takes the pot between her knees,
The spoon to her mouth,
Again her hand falls down,
Exhausted and slow
She falls asleep—
My mother sleeps . . .

Translated by Florence Victor.

Avrom Reisen

1876–1953

Born in Koidanov (in present-day Belarus), Avrom Reisen was a celebrated Yiddish writer, poet, editor, and literary activist. Admired by early Yiddish writers such as I. L. Peretz and Sholem Aleichem, Reisen frequently published poems and short stories in Yiddish periodicals and journals in Eastern Europe and the United States. After briefly serving in the tsarist army, he settled in Warsaw, where he founded the Tsentral publishing house and edited special collections and journals of Yiddish literature. Reisen moved to New York in 1911 and immediately became part of the Yiddish literary, cultural, and political scene, publishing in all the major Yiddish periodicals and issuing his collected works in some dozen volumes. A lifelong supporter of socialism and workers' politics, Reisen is remembered for his mastery of the short story, which depicted all strata of Jewish life with emphasis on everyday working people and immigrants. His poetry was noted for its simplicity, and many of his poems were set to music.

The New World
Date Unknown

A new world being made—one hears
In childhood that it has begun;
Then comes the passage of the years—
Is it not yet fully done?

The new world being made—always,
From childhood on—and on the day
They finally set the door in place,
All the walls have turned to gray.

The roof is hung—but as they start,
The pillars gradually give out;
It all begins to fall apart,
And so, once more, they rush about,

Calling to build it up again
And work, a true, united folk!
A spark is struck nearby, and then
All the world goes up in smoke.

Translated by John Hollander.

Other works by Reisen: *Tsayt lider* (1902); *Ertseylungen un bilder* (1903); *Epizodn fun mayn lebn* (1929).

Avrom Reisen

O Quickly, Messiah
Date Unknown

O quickly, Messiah, come quickly at last,
The world is engirdled with serpents, in vast
Poisonous circles of famine and care,
Terror and torment, decay and despair;
The earth has denied men the nurture they need—
O Messiah, come now on your silvery steed.

O quickly, Messiah, come; we are yet bound
In slavery's chains, wrapped round and around;
Humanity's blood lies in rust on the sword,
With no room in the world for the blood that has
    poured
Out from under the knout, from the wounds that
    still bleed—
O Messiah, come now on your silvery steed.

Translated by John Hollander.

Aaron Zeitlin

Summer 1937
Date Unknown

For my child, today, it is so easy
to make the awful discovery, that people kill
and are killed: both things and people
speak the language of the red angel.
My child asks me: *Why are people being murdered,*
    father?
And receives no answer. With lackluster eyes
I look above to the sun of summer.
A leaf on the table. A bloody number.
Through every line corpses wander.
Who will bury them? Who will give them their
    rites?

A glance up to the sun of summer,
a glance down to the bloody number.
My gaze falls on some long article—
And Bialik's verse comes to me, familiar and novel:
"The sun shone, the slaughterer slaughtered"
and the writer braided his flowery language
    together.

Over the radio some singer trills on
about her heartache. (What horror, poor girl!)
I decide to ease her suffering—
and shut her mouth with the radio.
Silence. The sun's silence. Hum of flies.
So long as artistic creation has been muted,
"sacred" art, the paid-for lie.

Listen, with a racket, a wild bird
soars against the sun:
A military aircraft,
singing its steel music.

Music of war, music of blood,
music of the new Genghis Khan.

Now flown by—and again an idyllic song
of vernal, peaceful flies.
As if it were prison, I sit in the summer light.
Sun and slaughter. Summer and demise.
I look to the sun as if through bars.
And my little one goes on: *You know I'm asking you,*
     father!
Why are people being murdered, father?

Translated by Maia Evrona.

Musical Selections

Arranged alphabetically by composers' names and then chronologically, this list of musical selections indicates the countries most associated with a particular composer or songwriter. Borders shifted frequently as a result of the vast political changes in Europe. Many states, among them Belarus, Lithuania, Latvia, parts of Poland, and Ukraine, became part of the Soviet Union in 1939–1941. This list retains the names of those states to give the reader a sense of geographical placement.

Cantorial

Chagy, Berele (1892–1954)
Latvia/South Africa/United
　States
V'lirisholayim irḥa, 1920

Hershman, Mordechai
　(1888–1940)
Ukraine/United States
Yismaḥ Moshe, 1927

Kwartin, Zawel (1874–1952)
Russia/United States
Tiher Rabi Yishmael, 1928

Machtenberg's Male Choir
　featuring Herbert Slotnick
United States
Areshes s'fosenu, 1927

Pinchik, Pierre (1900–1971)
Ukraine/United States
Rozo d'shabbos, 1928

Roitman, David (1884–1943)
Russia/United States
Unesane sokef, 1925

Rosenblatt, Yossele (1882–1933)
Ukraine/United States
Hineni heoni mima'as, 1927

Shlisky, Yosef (1894–1955)
Poland/Canada/United States
Ana b'khoaḥ, 1924
*Tikanta shabbos/Uveyom ha-
　shabbos*, 1927

Classical

Achron, Joseph (1886–1943)
Poland/Russia/United States
The Golem, suite for chamber
　orchestra, 1932
Sabbath Eve Service, choral
　work, 1932

Adler, Hugo Chaim (1894–1955)
Belgium/Germany/United States
Licht und Volk, cantata, 1928
Hiob, oratorio, 1932
Balak und Bilam, cantata,
　1934

Ben-Haim, Paul (1897–1984)
Germany/Palestine
Yoram, oratorio, 1933
String Quartet, Op. 21, 1937
Variations on a Hebrew Melody,
　piano, violin, and cello, 1939

Binder, Abraham Wolf
　(1895–1966)
United States
Two Hasidic Melodies, string
　quartet, 1934

Bloch, Ernest (1880–1959)
Switzerland/United States
Baal Shem, suite for violin and
　piano, 1923
From Jewish Life, piano and
　cello, 1924
Méditation hébraïque, piano
　and cello, 1924
*America: An Epic Rhapsody in
　Three Parts for Orchestra*,
　1926
Avodat ha-kodesh, choral work,
　1933

Boskovich, Alexander
　(1907–1964)
Romania/Hungary/United
　States
Sharsheret zahav (**Golden
　Chain**), orchestral suite,
　1937

Castelnuovo-Tedesco, Mario
　(1895–1968)
Italy/United States
Le danze del re David, piano
　suite, 1925
I profeti, violin concerto,
　1933

Chajes, Julius (1910–1985)
Poland/Austria/United States
Psalm 142, mixed chorus and
    organ, 1937
Hebrew Suite, orchestra, 1939

Copland, Aaron (1900–1990)
United States
Four Motets, unaccompanied
    mixed voices, 1921
Vitebsk, trio for violin, cello, and
    piano, 1929

Dessau, Paul (1894–1979)
Germany
Hagadah shel pesaḥ, oratorio,
    1936

Krein, Alexandr Abramovich
    (1883–1951)
Russia
Kaddish, symphonic cantata,
    1922
Suite dansée, piano, 1928
Zagmuk, opera, 1930
Birobidjan, symphonic poem,
    1935

Krein, Grigory Abramovich
    (1879–1955)
Russia
Hebrew Rhapsody, clarinet and
    orchestra, 1926

Lavry, Marc (1903–1967)
Latvia/Germany/Palestine
Emek, symphonic poem, 1937

Lazarus, Daniel (1898–1964)
France
Symphonie avec hymne juive,
    mixed choir with orchestra,
    1933

Milhaud, Darius (1892–1974)
France
Esther de Carpentras, opera
    buffa, 1925

*Six chants populaires
    hébraïques, Op. 86*, voice and
    piano or orchestra, 1925
La Reine de Saba, string quartet,
    1939

Milner, Moshe (Mikhail Moise
    Arnoldovich) (1886–1953)
Russia
*Vokal suite oyf "Tsen peretz's
    kinder lider,"* voice and piano,
    1919
*Di himlen brenen/Nebesa
    pylaiut*, opera, 1923
*Omrachennaya svadba/Di
    farshterte khasene*, quartet,
    1930

Pergament, Moses (1893–1977)
Finland/Sweden
Adon olam, mixed choir with
    accompaniment, 1927
Rapsodia ebraica, orchestral
    work, 1935

Rosowsky, Solomon (1878–1962)
Latvia/Russia/Palestine/United
    States
*Rhapsodie: Récitatif et danse
    hassidique*, cello and piano,
    1934

Saminsky, Lazare (1882–1959)
Russia/United States
Conte hébraïque, piano, 1919
Danse rituelle du Sabbath,
    piano, 1919
Sabbath Eve Service, choral work,
    1926
Sabbath Morning Service, choral
    work, 1926–1929
The Daughter of Jeptha, opera-
    ballet, 1929
*Jerusalem, City of Solomon and
    Christ*, symphony, 1932

Schalit, Heinrich (1886–1976)
Austria/Germany/United States

Eine Freitagsabend Liturgie,
    1932

Schoenberg, Arnold (1874–1951)
Austria/United States
Der Jakobsleiter, oratorio, 1926
Moses und Aron, opera, 1932

Stutschewsky, Joachim (1891–1982)
Russia/Palestine
Eli, Eli, Lama Asavtanu?, cello
    and piano, 1923
Méditation hébraïque, cello and
    piano, 1924
Fier jüdische Tanzstucke, piano,
    1929
Kinah, cello and piano, 1933
Méditation chassidique, cello and
    piano, 1933

Veprik, Alexander Moiseyevich
    (1899–1958)
Poland/Russia
Kaddish, voice and piano, 1925
Jewish Songs, voice and piano,
    1926
Dances and Songs of the Ghetto,
    orchestral, 1927

Weill, Kurt (1900–1950)
Germany/United States
The Eternal Road, opera-
    oratorio, 1937

Weinberg, Jacob (1879–1956)
Russia/United States
Heḥaluts (The Pioneers of
    Israel), opera, 1924
Berceuse Palestinienne, pastoral
    miniature, 1928
Shabbat ba-aretz, liturgical, 1934

Klezmer

Abe Schwartz Orchestra
    (Abe Schwartz, 1881–1963)
Romania/United States
Aleh in einem, 1920

Art Shryer Orchestra
United States
Dem rebns tanz, 1929

Boyberiker Kapelye, and Beresh
  Katz (composer)
United States
Di Boyberiker khaseneh, **Parts 1
  and 2**, 1927

Brandwein, Naftule (1884–1963)
Poland/United States
Der heiser, 1924
Freylekhs/Shpil es nokh a mol,
  1925

Cherniavsky, Joseph (1894–1959)
Ukraine/United States
Kale bazetzns un a freylekhs,
  1923

Jewish Folk Ensemble of the
  Belorussian SSR (dir. N. P.
  Klaus), Isaak Davydovich
  Kharik (composer)
Soviet Union
*Freylekhs/Birobidzhaner
  freylekhs*, 1936

State Ensemble of Jewish Folk
  Music of the Ukrainian SSR
  (dir. Solomon Fayntuch), and
  Mark Isakovich Rabinovich
  (composer)
Soviet Union
Dobranotsh & Freylekhs, 1937

Tarras, Dave (1895–1989)
Ukraine/United States
Dem Trisker rebns hosid, 1925

Concert

Alterman, Natan (1910–1970),
  and Daniel Samburski
  (1909–1977)
Poland/Palestine
Shir moledet/Shir boker, 1934

The Barry Sisters (Minnie
  Bagelman, 1923–1976; and Clara
  Bagelman, 1920–2014), with
  Ziggy Elman Orchestra; lyrics
  by Yakov Jadow
United States
Bublitchki baygelekh, 1939

Druker, Sofia Iurevna (1907–1984),
  and Belorussian State Choir;
  words by Sholem Aleichem
Russia
Shlof mayn kind, shlof keseyder,
  1936

Dunaevskii, Isaak (1900–1955)
Russia
Rybatskaia, 1936

Ellstein, Abe (1907–1963),
  and Solomon Smulevitz
  (1868–1943)
Russia/United States
A brivele der mamen, 1938

Fleishman, Janet (1907–1957), and
  Herman Yablokoff (1903–1981)
United States
Ver hot aza yingele, 1933

Gebirtig, Mordechai (1877–1942)
Poland
Hulyet, hulyet kinderlekh, 1924
Kinder yorn, 1932
Reyzele, 1936
Es brent, 1938

Iaunzem, Irma Petrovna
  (1897–1975)
Russia
Makhtaynisteh mayne, 1927

Kipnis, Menakhem (1878–1942)
Russia
Katarina moloditsa poydi suda,
  1918
A khazendl oyf shabes, 1918
Yoshke fort avek, 1918

Lebedeff, Aaron (1873–1960)
Russia/Poland/United States
*What Can You Mach? Es iz
  Amerike!*, 1925
Odessa mama, 1932

Lefkowitch, Henry (1891–1951),
  and Abe Ellstein (1907–1963)
United States
A zemerl (Lomir ale zingn),
  1927

Leivick, H. (Leivick Halpern;
  1888–1962)
Russia/United States
Ergets vayt, 1936

Low, Leo (1878–1960)
United States
Din toyre mit got (words by
  Levi Yitzhok Derbarmdiger),
  1927
A khazndl oyf shabes (with Al
  Jolson), 1932

Moscow State Yiddish Theater,
  and Lev M. Pulver (1883–1970)
Russia
Freylekhs, 1929

Moskowitz, Abraham (1883–1963)
United States
Vie iz dos geseleh, 1922

Olshanetsky, Alexander
  (1892–1946), and Isa Kremer
  (1887–1956)
United States
Mayn shtetele Belz, 1930

Oysher, Moishe (1906–1958)
In mayn shtetl/Bay dem shtetl
  (lyrics by Zalman Rosental),
  1925
Grine bleter, 1937
Dos keshenever shtikele, 1938
Unter beymer (music by
  Alexander Olshanetsky), 1939

Oysher, Moishe, and Florence
    Weiss (dates unknown)
Russia/Canada/United States
Hasidic in America, 1938

Papernikov, Joseph (1897–1993)
Poland/Palestine
Zol zayn, 1928

Peterburski, Jerzy (Jerzy
    Melodysta; 1895–1979)
Poland/Austria/Argentina
***Tango milonga ("Oh, Donna
    Clara")***, 1929

Pulver, Lev M. (1883–1970), and
    Shlomo Mikhoels (1890–1948)
Russia
Nit shimile/Nign on verter, 1937

Schwartz, Maurice (1889–1960)
Poland/United States
Histendiger ḥazn, 1929

Secunda, Sholom (1894–1974)
United States
Zmires/Melave Malka (lyrics by
    Jacob Jacobs), 1937

Shulman, Zinovii Zalman
    (1904–1976)
Soviet Union
Varnitchkes, 1939

Utesov, Leonid (Leyzer Veysbain;
    1895–1982)
Soviet Union
Bublichki/Bubliki (lyrics by
    Jakow Jadow), 1926

Limonichki, 1937
Uncle Elya (Diadia Elya), 1939

Yablokoff, Herman (1903–1981)
Belarus/United States
Papirosn, 1932

Yiddish National Arbeiter Farband
    Choir
United States
Fregt di velt an alte kashyeh, 1927

Unknown (folk song)
Lithuania
Az ikh vel zogn lekho doydi, 1938

Film Selections

1920
Wegener, Paul, and Carl Boese
Der Golem: Wie er in die Welt kam (The Golem: How He Came into the World)
Germany, Silent

1924
Breslauer, H. K.
Die Stadt ohne Juden (The City without Jews)
Austria, German

1925
Granovsky, Alexander
Yidishe glikn (Jewish Luck / Menakhem Mendl / Yevreiskoye Schastye)
Soviet Union, Silent

1927
Crosland, Alan
The Jazz Singer
United States, English

1932
Goldin, Sidney M., and Aubrey Scotto
Uncle Moses
United States, Yiddish

1932
Milman, Rashel, Mark Milman, and Boris Shpis
Nosn Beker fort aheym (Nosn Becker Journeys Home)
Soviet Union, Yiddish, Russian

1935
Ford, Aleksander
Mir kumen on (We're Coming! We're on the Way!)
Poland, English, Yiddish

1936
Green, Joseph, and Jan Nowina-Przybylski
Yidl mitn fidl (Yidl with His Fiddle)
Poland, Yiddish

1936
Korsh-Sablin, Vladimir
Seekers of Happiness (Birobidzhan, A Greater Happiness)
Soviet Union, Russian

1937
Turkow, Zygmund
Di freylekhe kabtsonim (The Jolly Paupers)
Poland, Yiddish

1937
Ulmer, Edgar G., and Jacob Ben-Ami
Grine felder (Green Fields)
United States, Yiddish

1937
Waszynski, Michal
Der dibuk (The Dybbuk)
Poland, Yiddish

1938
Goskind, Yitshak
A Day in Warsaw
Poland, Yiddish

1938
Green, Joseph
A brivele der mamen (A Letter to Mama)
Poland, Yiddish

Green, Joseph
Mamele (Mama)
Poland, Yiddish

1938
Ulmer, Edgar G.
Yankl der shmid (The Singing Blacksmith)
Poland and United States, Yiddish

1939
Berne, Joseph
Mirele Efros
United States, Yiddish

1939
Felt, Henry, and Edgar G. Ulmer
*The Light Ahead (Fishke der
    krumer / Fishke the Lame)*
United States, Yiddish

1939
Schwartz, Maurice
*Tevye der milkhiker (Tevye the
    Dairyman)*
Poland, Yiddish

1939
Seiden, Joseph
Kol Nidre
United States, Yiddish

Credits

Shmuel Yosef Agnon, "The Sense of Smell," trans. Arthur Green, and "A Whole Loaf," trans. I. M. Lask, excerpts from *A Book That Was Lost and Other Stories*, ed. Alan Mintz and Anne Golomb Hoffman (New York: Schocken Books, 1995), pp. 139–46, 355–69. Copyright © 1995 by Schocken Books. Used by permission of Schocken Books, an imprint of the Knopf Doubleday Publishing Group, a division of Random House LLC. All rights reserved. Any third party use of this material, outside of this publication, is prohibited. Interested parties must apply directly to Random House LLC for permission; excerpt from *A Guest for the Night*, trans. Misha Louvish (New York: Schocken Books, 1968), pp. 1–8. Copyright © 1968 and copyright renewed 1996 by Schocken Books, Inc. Used by permission of Schocken Books, an imprint of the Knopf Doubleday Publishing Group, a division of Random House LLC. All rights reserved.

Agudas Yisrael, *Manifesto* (1918).

Hillel Alexandrov, "Di yidishe bafelkerung in di shtet un shtetlekh fun vaysrusland" [The Jewish Population of the Cities and Towns of Belorussia], *Tseitshrift*, vols. 2–3 (Minsk: Institut far Vayruslendisher Kultur, 1928), unnumbered first page, and pp. 314–15, 317, 320–21, 324, 333, 335, 337, 339.

Mordechai Alpersohn, "Memoirs of a Jewish Colonist," from *Yiddish South of the Border*, ed. and trans. Alan Astro (Albuquerque: University of New Mexico Press, 2003), pp. 17–23. Copyright © 2003 University of New Mexico Press, 2003. Used by permission of the publisher.

Viktor Alter, "The Source of Our Belief," from *Henryk Erlich and Victor Adler: Two Heroes and Martyrs for Jewish Socialism*, trans. Samuel Portnoy (Hoboken, N.J.: KTAV, 1990), pp. 312–15. Used with permission of the publisher.

Nathan Alterman, "Red Riding-Hood" and "Beyond Melody," from *Modern Hebrew Poetry: A Bilingual Anthology*, ed. and trans. Ruth Finer Mintz (Berkeley: University of California Press, 1968), pp. 204, 206, 208, 210. © Nathan Alterman and ACUM. English translation copyright © 1966 by the Regents of the University of California. Used by permission of University of California Press and of ACUM; "Moon" and "The Killers of the Fields," trans. Lewis Glinert, from http://www.poetryinternationalweb.net/pi/site/poem/item/3435/auto/Moon and http://www.poetryinternationalweb.net/pi/site/poem/item/3439/auto/The-Killers-of-the-Fields. © Nathan Alterman and ACUM. Translation © Lewis Glinert. Used with permission of the author's estate and the translator.

Moshe Altman, from *Di viner karete* [The Vienna Coach] (Bucharest: Sholem Aleichem, 1935), pp. 5–8, 26–28, 40–43. Used with permission of the author's estate.

Anonymous, "The Voice of Yeshurun to the Hebrews," from *The Emergence of Modern Hebrew Creativity in Babylon, 1735–1950*, ed. and trans. Lev Hakak (West Lafayette, Ind.: Purdue University Press, 2009),

Pinkhes Berniker, "Jesús," from *Yiddish South of the Border*, ed. and trans. Alan Astro (Albuquerque: University of New Mexico Press, 2003), pp. 137–48. Copyright © 2003 University of New Mexico Press, 2003. Used by permission of the publisher.

Peretz (Friedrich) Bernstein, "Antisemitism as a Group Phenomenon: An Essay in the Sociology of Judaeophobia," from *Rebirth: A Book of Modern Jewish Thought*, ed. and trans. Ludwig Lewisohn (New York: Harper & Brothers, 1935), pp. 174–83. Used with permission of the author's estate and the translator's estate.

Elias Bickerman, excerpt from *From Ezra to the Last of the Maccabees*, trans. Moses Hadas (New York: Schocken, 1962), pp. 153–65. Copyright © 1947, 1962 by Schocken Books Inc. Copyright © 1949 by Louis Finkelstein. Used by permission of Schocken Books, an imprint of the Knopf Doubleday Publishing Group, a division of Random House LLC. All rights reserved.

Elisheva Bikhovsky, "Mikreh tafel" [An Unimportant Incident], from *Malkah la-Ivrim* (Tel Aviv: Babel/Tarmil, 2002), pp. 78–101. Used with permission of the author's estate.

Fishl Bimko, "Farn prizyv" [Before Conscription], from *Antologye fun der Yidisher proze in Poyln tsvishn beyde velt-milkhomes*, ed. Aaron Zeitlin and J. J. Trunk (New York: CYCO, 1946), pp. 89–100. Used with permission of the author's estate.

Solomon Birnbaum, "Judaism and Yiddish," from *The Way We Think: A Collection of Essays from the Yiddish*, vol. 2, ed. Joseph Leftwich, trans. Irene R. Birnbaum (South Brunswick, N.J.: Thomas Yoseloff, 1969), pp. 513–18. Used with permission of The Nathan & Solomon Birnbaum Archives, Toronto, and the editor's estate.

Hirsh Bloshtein, "In Opposite Directions," from *Yiddish South of the Border*, ed. Alan Astro, trans. Debbie Nathan (Albuquerque: University of New Mexico Press, 2003), pp. 36–40. Copyright © 2003 University of New Mexico Press, 2003. Used by permission of the publisher.

Simon Blumenfeld, from *Jew Boy* (London: Lawrence & Wishart, 1986), pp. 65–76. Used with permission of the publisher.

Boris D. Bogen, from *Born a Jew* (New York: Macmillan, 1930), pp. 171–80, 320–29, 335–39, 345–54.

Saul Borovoi, from *Evreiskaya zemledel'skaya kolonizatsia v staroi Rossii* [Jewish Agricultural Colonization in Old Russia] (Moscow: Sabashnikov, 1928), pp. 3, 122–27, 136–37.

Louis D. Brandeis, "Efficiency in Public Service," from *Brandeis on Zionism: A Collection of Addresses and Statements*, by Louis D. Brandeis (Washington, D.C.: Zionist Organization of America, 1942), pp. 116–25.

Yosef Haim Brenner, from *Breakdown and Bereavement*, trans. Hillel Halkin under the auspices of Institute for Translation of Hebrew Literature (ITHL) (Cornell University Press, 1971), pp. 5–26. Used with permission and with thanks to the Institute for the Translation of Hebrew Literature, for their generous support.

Alter Brody, "A Family Album," "Lamentations," and "Ghetto Twilight," from *A Family Album and Other Poems* (New York: B. W. Huebsch, 1918), pp. 18–24, 36, 39. Used with permission of the author's estate.

Rokhl Brokhes, "The Zogerin," from *Found Treasures: Stories by Yiddish Women Writers*, ed. Frieda Forman, Ethel Raicus, and Sarah Silberstein Swartz, trans. Shirley Kumove (Toronto: Second Story Press, 1994), pp. 85–90. Used with permission of the translator.

Martin Buber, "Herut: On Youth and Religion," excerpts from *On Judaism*, ed. Nahum N. Glatzer, trans. Eva Jospe (New York: Schocken Books, 1967), pp. 149–74. Translation copyright © 1967 by Schocken Books, a division of Random House LLC. Used by permission of Schocken Books, an imprint of the Knopf Doubleday Publishing Group, a division of Random House LLC. All rights reserved.

Naum Abramovich Bukhbinder, excerpts from *Di geshikhte fun der yidisher arbiter-bavegung in Rusland* [A History of the Jewish Labor Movement in Russia] (Vilna: Tomor, 1931), pp. 7–49.

Yehuda Burla, "Battles," trans. Misha Louvish, from *Hebrew Short Stories*, ed. S. Y. Penueli and A. Ukhmani (Jerusalem: Institute for the Translation of Hebrew Literature, 1965), pp. 134–49. © Yehuda Burla and ACUM. English Copyright © The Institute for the Translation of Hebrew Literature. Used with permission of the Institute for the Translation of Hebrew Literature and ACUM.

Julius Guttmann, "The Basic Ideas of Biblical Religion," from *Philosophies of Judaism: The History of Jewish Philosophy from Biblical Times to Franz Rosenzweig*, trans. David W. Silverman (New York: Schocken Books, 1973), pp. 3–18; Northvale, N.J.: Jason Aronson edition, 1989), pp. 3–18. Used with permission of Jason Aronson and the translator.

Shmuel Halkin, "Farvandlung" [Transformation], from *A shpigl oyf a shteyn: antologye poezye un proze fun tsvelf farshnitene yidishe shraybers in Ratn-Farband*, eds. Chone Shmeruk, Benjamin Harshav, Abraham Sutzkever, and Mendel Piekarz (Tel Aviv: Farlag Di goldene keyt / Farlag Y.L. Perets, 1964), pp. 587–90; from *Bar Kochba* (Moscow: Der Emes, 1939), pp. 37–48, 101–28. Both used with permission of the author's estate; "Russia," trans. Hillel Halkin, from *The Penguin Book of Modern Yiddish Verse*, ed. Irving Howe, Ruth Wisse, and Chone Shmeruk (New York: Viking, 1987), pp. 512, 514. Copyright © 1987 by Irving Howe, Ruth Wisse, and Chone Shmeruk. Used by permission of Viking Penguin, a division of Penguin Group (USA) LLC, and by permission of the author's estate.

Moyshe-Leyb Halpern, "In the Subway," trans. Julian Levinson, from Julian Levinson, "Moyshe-Leyb Halpern: A Modernist Yiddish Poet in New York," *Tikkun*, vol. 18, no. 2 (2003), p. 63. Copyright © 2003, Tikkun Magazine. All rights reserved. Republished by permission of the copyrightholder, and the present publisher, Duke University Press. www.dukepress.edu; "Memento Mori," "Ghingeli," "My Restlessness Is of a Wolf," "In the Golden Land," and "He Who Calls Himself Leader," from *American Yiddish Poetry: A Bilingual Anthology*, ed. Benjamin Harshav and Barbara Harshav, trans. Kathryn Hellerstein (Berkeley: University of California Press, 1986), pp. 393, 397–401, 405, 447–51. Used with permission of the author's estate and the translator; "Salute" and "In Central Park," from *American Yiddish Poetry: A Bilingual Anthology*, ed. and trans. Benjamin and Barbara Harshav, pp. 431–33, 465. Copyright © 1986, 2007 Benjamin and Barbara Harshav. All rights reserved. Reprinted with the permission of Stanford University Press, www.sup.org, and the author's estate.

Avigdor Hameiri, from *The Great Madness*, trans. Yael Lotan (Haifa: Or-Ron, 1984), pp. 8–14. Used with permission of the author's estate and the translator's estate.

Lajos Hatvany, from *Bondy Jr.*, trans. Hannah Waller (New York: Alfred A. Knopf, 1931), pp. 93–101. Used with permission of the author's estate.

Hayyim Hazaz, "Revolutionary Chapters," from *The Literature of Destruction: Jewish Responses to Catastrophe*, ed. David G. Roskies, trans. Jeffrey M. Green (Philadelphia: Jewish Publication Society, 1988), pp. 313–15, 317–323. Copyright © 1989 by the Jewish Publication Society. Reprinted by permission of the University of Nebraska Press.

Tuvia Heilikman, from *Geshichte fun der gezelshaftlicher bavegung fun di Idn in Poiln un Rusland* [History of the Social Movement of Jews in Poland and Russia] (Moscow: Tsentraler farlag far di felker fun FSSR, 1926), pp. 3–12. Used with permission of the author's estate.

Isaac Herzog, "The Ban Pronounced against Greek Wisdom" (originally published in *The Jewish Forum*, vol. xii, no. 3 [March 1929]), from *Judaism: Law & Ethics—Essays* by the Late Chief Rabbi Dr. Isaac Herzog, selected by Chaim Herzog (London/Jerusalem/New York: The Soncino Press, 1974), pp. 181–91. Copyright Sarah Herzog, 1974. Used with permission of the author's estate.

Abraham Joshua Heschel, "The Meaning of Repentance," from *Moral Grandeur and Spiritual Audacity*, ed. Susannah Heschel (New York: Farrar, Straus, & Giroux, 1996), pp. 68–70. Copyright © 1996 Sylvia Heschel. Reprinted by permission of Farrar, Straus and Giroux, LLC.

Peretz Hirshbein, from *Tsvai Shtet* [Two Cities] (New York and Los Angeles: Peretz Hirshbein, 1951), pp. 68–77, 79–87. Used with permission of the author's estate.

Morris Hoffman, "Adoons's Jealousy," from *From a Land Far Off: South African Yiddish Stories in English Translation*, ed. Joseph Sherman, trans. Woolf Levick and Joseph Sherman (Cape Town: Jewish Publications South Africa, 1987), pp. 30–32. Used with permission of the publisher, and the estates of the translators. In memory of Joseph Sherman, unique in stature, who dedicated his talents to the survival of Yiddish literature in translation.

Dovid Hofshteyn, "Procession," trans. Robert Friend, from *The Penguin Book of Modern Yiddish Verse*, ed. Irving Howe, Ruth Wisse, and Chone Shmeruk (New York: Viking Press, 1987), pp. 268, 270. Copyright © 1987 by Irving Howe, Ruth Wisse, and Chone Shmeruk. Used by permission of Viking Penguin, a division of Penguin Group (USA) LLC; "Poem" and "Song of My Indifference," from *A Treasury of Yiddish Poetry*, ed. Irving Howe and Eliezer Greenberg, trans. Allen Mandelbaum (New York: Holt, Rinehart and Winston, 1969), pp. 173–79. Used with permission of the author's estate and the translator's estate; "Royte blitn" [Red Blossoms], from *A shpigl oyf a shteyn: antologye poezye un proze fun tsvelf farshnitene yidishe shraybers in Ratn-Farband*, eds. Chone Shmeruk, Benjamin Harshav, Abraham Sutzkever, and Mendel Piekarz (Tel Aviv: Farlag Di goldene keyt / Farlag Y.L. Perets, 1964), p. 238. Used with permission of the author's estate.

Sh. Horonczyk, "Gots mishpet" [God's Trial], from *Antologye fun der Yidisher proze in Poyln tsvishn beyde velt-milkhomes*, ed. Aaron Zeitlin and J. J. Trunk (New York: CYCO, 1946), pp. 147–208. First published in the novel *Shtarke Mentshn* (Warsaw: Farlag Kultur-Lige, 1936).

David Horowitz, "Avodateinu ha-tarbutit" [Our Cultural Work], *Ha-poel ha-tsair*, vol. 15 (12 June 1922), p. 30. Used with permission of the author's estate.

Béla Illés, from *Carpathian Rhapsody*, vol. 1, trans. Grace Blair Gardos (Budapest: Corvina, 1963), pp. 253–66. Used with permission of the publisher.

Vladimir Jabotinsky, "Along Deribasov Street" and "Broad Jewish Natures," reprinted from *The Five: A Novel of Jewish Life in Turn-of-the-Century Odessa*, trans. Michael R. Katz (Ithaca: Cornell University Press, 2005), pp. 56–61, 136–41. Copyright © 2005 by Cornell University. Used by permission of the publisher, Cornell University Press.

Leo Jung, "The Rambam in True Perspective," from *Crumbs and Character: Sermons, Addresses, and Essays* (New York: The Night and Day Press, 1942), pp. 53–57. Used with permission of the author's estate.

Alter-Sholem Kacyzne, "Kolos oif Ukraine" [Screams in Ukraine], from *Gezamelte Shriftn* (Tel Aviv: Y. L. Peretz Publishing House, 1967), pp. 255–58; "Shayke," from *Antologye fun der Yidisher proze in Poyln tsvishn beyde velt-milkhomes*, ed. Aaron Zeitlin and J. J. Trunk (New York: CYCO, 1946), pp. 551–56; "Midos," from *Gezamelte shriftn* (Tel Aviv: Y. L. Peretz Publishing House, 1967), pp. 223, 225–30; "The Duke," from *Landmark Yiddish Plays: A Critical Anthology*, ed. and trans. Joel Berkowitz and Jeremy Dauber (Albany: State University of New York Press, 2006), pp. 295–301. © 2006, State University of New York. All rights reserved. Reprinted by permission of the publisher.

Max Kadushin, from *Organic Thinking: A Study in Rabbinic Thought* (New York: Bloch Publishing, 1976), pp. 1–15. Used with permission of the publisher.

Franz Kafka, excerpt from *Letter to His Father*, trans. Ernst Kaiser and Eithne Wilkins (New York: Schocken Books, 1966), pp. 75–101. Copyright © 1953, 1954, 1966 by Schocken Books, a division of Random House LLC. Used by permission of Schocken Books, an imprint of the Knopf Doubleday Publishing Group, a division of Random House LLC. All rights reserved.

Efraim Kaganovsky, "Lokator numer 88" [Tenant Number 88], from *Antologye fun der Yidisher proze in Poyln tsvishn beyde velt-milkhomes*, ed. Aaron Zeitlin and J. J. Trunk (New York: CYCO, 1946), pp. 535–43. Used with permission of the author's estate, in memory of Ephraim Kaganovskii of Warsaw, author, journalist, and painter.

Gustave Kahn, "One Yom Kippur," trans. Glenn Swiadon, *Yale French Studies*, vol. 85 (1994) pp. 62–66. First published in French as "Un jour de Kippour," from *Contes juifs* (Paris: Grasset-Fasquelle, 1977 [orig. ed. 1925]), pp. 127–36. Used with permission of *Yale French Studies*.

Horace M. Kallen, "'Americanization' and the Cultural Prospect," from *Culture and Democracy in the United States: Studies in the Group Psychology of the American Peoples* (New York: Boni and Liveright, 1924), pp. 126–31, 136–38. Used with permission of the author's estate.

Mordecai M. Kaplan, "Toward a Reconstruction of Judaism," *Menorah Journal*, vol. 13, no. 2 (April 1927), pp. 113–30. Used with permission of the author's estate.

Berl Katznelson, "Al inyanei ha-sha'a" [On Matters of the Hour], from *Kitvei B. Katznelson*, vol. 4 (Tel Aviv: Miflagat Poalei Erets-Yisrael, 1944–1950), pp. 284–95. "On the Question of Languages," trans. Barbara Har-

Verlag Berlin. Used by permission of the publishers; "The Wonder-Making Rabbi of Barcelona," from *The German-Jewish Dialogue: An Anthology of Literary Texts*, ed. and trans. Ritchie Robertson (Oxford: Oxford University Press, 1999), pp. 225–32. Used by permission of Oxford University Press, USA. Includes the poem "Pablo," from Else Lasker-Schüler, *Your Diamond Dreams Cut Open My Arteries: Poems by Else Lasker-Schüler*, trans. Robert P. Newton (Chapel Hill: University of North Carolina Press, 1982), p. 201. English translation copyright © 1983 by the University of North Carolina Press. Used by permission of the publisher.

Dante A. Lattes, from *Apologia dell'ebraismo* [Apology for Judaism] (Palermo: La Zisa, 2011), pp. 79–83. Used with permission of the author's estate.

Malka Lee, "Roite farnachtn" [Red Evenings], from *Yidishe dichterins: antologie*, ed. Ezra Korman (Chicago: L. M. Shtein, 1928), pp. 250–53. Used with permission of Yvette Marrin and Joseph Rappaport; "Koift papirosn" [Buy Cigarettes!], trans. Kathryn Hellerstein, from Kathryn Hellerstein, "Against 'Girl Songs': Gender and Sex in a Yiddish Modernist Journal," *Yiddish Studies Today*, vol. 1 (2012), pp. 86–87. © Düsseldorf University Press, Düsseldorf, 2012. Used with permission of Yvette Marrin and Joseph Rappaport, Düsseldorf University Press, and Kathryn Hellerstein.

Joseph Leftwich, "Zangwill," from *Along the Years: Poems, 1911–1937* (London: Robert Anscombe, 1937), p. 52. Used with permission of the author's estate.

Leibush Lehrer, from *Yidishkayt un andere problemen* [Jewishness (*Yidishkayt*) and Other Problems] (New York: Matones, 1940), pp. 13–15, 23–27, 30–32, 40, 46–48, 51–53, 57, 63, 65, 68–69, 83, 88–89, 93. Used with permission of the author's estate.

Mani Leib, "I Am . . ." trans. John Hollander, from *A Treasury of Yiddish Poetry*, ed. Irving Howe and Eliezer Greenberg (New York: Holt, Rinehart and Winston, 1969), pp. 87–88. Used with permission of the author's estate and the translator's estate; "Du, mayn har" [You, My Master], "Di mashin" [The Machine], "Ikh bin der riter" [I Am the Knight], and "Zing shtiler" [Sing More Softly], from *Lider un baladn*, vol. 1 (New York: CYCO-Bicher Ferlag, 1955), pp. 71, 87, 99, 199. Used with permission of the author's estate.

H. Leivick, "Sanatorium," from *A Treasury of Yiddish Poetry*, ed. Irving Howe and Eliezer Greenberg, trans. Cynthia Ozick (New York: Holt, Rinehart and Winston, 1969), p. 123. Used with permission of the translator and the author's estate; "Unsatiated Passions," "Here Lives the Jewish People," and "Song of the Yellow Patch," from *American Yiddish Poetry: A Bilingual Anthology*, ed. and trans. Benjamin and Barbara Harshav, pp. 688–91, 695–97, 745–47. Copyright © 1986, 2007 Benjamin and Barbara Harshav. All rights reserved. Reprinted with the permission of Stanford University Press, www.sup.org, and the author's estate; "With the Holy Poem" and "A Stubborn Back—and Nothing More," trans. Robert Friend, from *The Penguin Book of Modern Yiddish Verse*, ed. Irving Howe, Ruth Wisse, and Chone Shmeruk (New York: Viking Press, 1987), pp. 230–36. Copyright © 1987 by Irving Howe, Ruth Wisse, and Chone Shmeruk. Used by permission of Viking Penguin, a division of Penguin Group (USA) LLC., and by permission of the author's estate; *The Golem*, from *The Great Jewish Plays*, ed. and trans. Joseph C. Landis (New York: Horizon Press, 1966, 1972), pp. 224–33, 260–64. Used with permission of the author's estate and the translator's estate. Dr. Landis was Prof. Emeritus at Queens College, CUNY.

Theodor Lessing, "Jewish Self-Hatred," from *The Weimar Republic Sourcebook*, ed. Anton Kaes, Martin Jay, and Edward Dimendberg, trans. Don Reneau (Oakland: University of California Press, 1994), pp. 268–71. Copyright © 1994 by the Regents of the University of California. Used with permission of the publisher.

"Letters to the Central Committee of the Alliance Israélite Universelle from Tangier, Morocco, from Sousse, Tunisia, and from Tunis, Tunisia, 1920–1938," from *Images of Sephardi and Eastern Jewries in Transition: The Teachers of the Alliance Israélite*, ed. and trans. Aron Rodrigue (Seattle: University of Washington Press, 1993), pp. 102, 121–24, 218–20, 252–56. Used with permission of the publisher.

Doiv Ber Levin, "Vechernyi razgovor" [Evening Conversation], from *Uiltsa sapozhnikov* [Cobblers' Street] (Moscow and Leningrad: Ogiz and Molodaya gvardia, 1932), pp. 14–16, 54–59.

Meyer Levin, from *The Old Bunch* (New York: The Citadel Press, 1937), pp. 479–85. Used with permission of the author's estate.

Nehemiah Levinsky, "Changed His Name," from *From a Land Far Off: South African Yiddish Stories in England Translation*, ed. Joseph Sherman, trans. Woolf Levick and Joseph Sherman (Cape Town: Jewish Publications South Africa, 1987), pp. 101–6. Used with permission of the publisher and the estates of the translators. In memory of Joseph Sherman, unique in stature, who dedicated his talents to the survival of Yiddish literature in translation.

Sarah Lévy, from *My Beloved France*, trans. Glenn Swiadon, *Yale French Studies,* vol. 85 (1994), pp. 67–72. Used with permission of Yale French Studies.

Ludwig Lewisohn, from *The Island Within* (New York: Harper & Brothers, 1928), pp. 220–26, 273–89.

A. [Aaron Glanz] Leyeles, "Fabius Lind's Days," "Fabius Lind's Diary: February 7 and 17," "Bolted Room," "An Encounter," "Moscow Night," "End of December 1934," "Fabius Lind Is Riding the Wind," and "The Madonna in the Subway," from *American Yiddish Poetry: A Bilingual Anthology*, ed. and trans. Benjamin and Barbara Harshav, pp. 137–39, 145–65. Copyright © 1986, 2007 Benjamin and Barbara Harshav. All rights reserved. Reprinted with the permission of Stanford University Press, www.sup.org.

Chaim Lieberman, from *In tol fun toyt* [In the Valley of Death] (New York: H. Lieberman, 1938), pp. 3–9, 12–15, 18, 20, 23–25, 30–31, 36. Copyright © 1938 H. Lieberman.

Leo Löwenthal, "Heinrich Heine," from *Critical Theory and Frankfurt Theorists: Lectures, Correspondence, Conversations*, trans. Donald Reneau (New Brunswick, N.J.: Transaction Publishers, 1988), pp. 18–23. Reproduced with permission of Transaction Books in the format *Republish in other published product* via Copyright Clearance Center. This selection includes Heinrich Heine, "The New Israelite Hospital in Hamburg," from *The Complete Poems of Heinrich Heine*, trans. Hal Draper (Boston: Suhrkamp / Insel Publishers Boston, Inc., 1982), pp. 398–99. Used with permission of the publisher.

Armand Lunel, "Nicolo-Peccavi, or The Dreyfus Affair at Carpentras," trans. Michael T. Ward, *Yale French Studies*, vol. 85 (1994), pp. 73–80. Used with permission of Yale French Studies.

Lev Lunts, "The Homeland," from *In the Wilderness: The Prose of Lev Lunts*, ed. and trans. Gary Kern (Las Cruces, N.M.: Xenos Books, 2014), pp. 27–41. Used with permission of the publisher.

Osip Mandelstam, "Poem No. 228," from *The Complete Poetry of Osip Emilevich Mandelstam*, trans. Burton Raffel and Alla Burago, intro. and notes by Sidney Monas (Albany: State University of New York Press, 1973), p. 191. ©1973, State University of New York. All rights reserved. Reprinted by permission of the publisher; from *The Noise of Time*, trans. Clarence Brown (New York: Penguin Books, 1965; London: Penguin Books, 1993), pp. 88–94. Used with permission of the translator.

Itzik Manger, "A Terrible Tale of the Messiah-Ox" and "The Turmoil over the Flight of the Messiah-Ox," from *The Book of Paradise*, trans. Leonard Wolf (New York: Hill and Wang, 1965), pp. 123–49, 151–55. English translation copyright © 1995 by Itzik Manger. Reprinted by permission of Farrar, Straus and Giroux, LLC; "Jacob Studies 'The Selling of Joseph' with His Sons," trans. Leonard Wolf, from *The Penguin Book of Modern Yiddish Verse*, ed. Irving Howe, Ruth Wisse, and Chone Shmeruk (New York: Viking Press, 1987), pp. 570, 572. Copyright © 1987 by Irving Howe, Ruth Wisse, and Chone Shmeruk. Used by permission of Viking Penguin, a division of Penguin Group (USA) LLC, and with permission of B'nai Jeshurun Synagogue for the Estate of Itzik Manger; "Itzik's Midrash," from *The World According to Itzik: Selected Poetry and Prose*, trans. Leonard Wolf (New Haven, Conn.: Yale University Press, 2002), pp. 7–11. Used with permission of the publisher and the author's estate.

Anna Margolin [Rosa Lebensboym], "Once I Was Young," trans. Marcia Falk, from *The Penguin Book of Modern Yiddish Verse*, ed. Irving Howe, Ruth R. Wisse, and Khone Shmeruk (New York: Viking Press, 1987), p. 218. Copyright © 1987 by Irving Howe, Ruth Wisse, and Khone Shmeruk. Used by permission of Viking Penguin, a division of Penguin Group (USA) LLC.

Osher Margolis, from *Geshichte fun Yidn in Rusland: etudin un dokumentn* [History of the Jews in Russia: Studies and Documents], vol. 1 (Moscow: Tsentraler felker-ferlag fun FSSR, 1930), pp. 268–71, 290–95, 319–21, 335–41. Includes excerpts from Pauline Wengeroff, *Memoiren einer Grossmutter, Bilder aus der Kulturgeschichte der Juden Russlands im 19 Jahrhundert*, vol. 1 (1908; republished with vol. 2, 1910). Also contains a poem "Folks lider vegn rekruchina" attributed to [Saul] Ginzburg and [P.] Marek, *Evreiskie narodnye pesnii v Rosii* (St. Petersburg, 1901), no. 44 and 50.

Peretz Markish, "Ziknus" [Old Women], from *A shpigl oyf a shteyn: antologye poezye un proze fun tsvelf farshnitene yidishe shraybers in Ratn-Farband*, eds. Chone Shmeruk, Benjamin Harshav, Abraham Sutzkever, and Mendel Piekarz (Tel Aviv: Farlag Di goldene keyt / Farlag Y.L. Perets, 1964), pp. 457–60. Used with permission of the author's estate; "The Rinsed Fences . . . ," "Hey, Women . . . ," "Out of Frayed Sackcloth . . . ," and "The Mound," trans Leonard Wolf, from *The Penguin Book of Modern Yiddish Verse*, ed. Irving Howe, Ruth Wisse, and Chone Shmeruk (New York: Viking, 1987), 348–66. Copyright © 1987 by Irving Howe, Ruth Wisse, and Chone Shmeruk. Used by permission of Viking Penguin, a division of Penguin Group (USA) LLC; "The Workers Club," from *From Revolution to Repression: Soviet Yiddish Writing 1917–1952*, ed. Joseph Sherman, trans. Joseph Sherman and Aleksandra Geller (Nottingham: Five Leaves Publications, 2012), pp. 91–99, 104–9, 113–14, 116–18, 122–23, 125–28, 130–35. Used with permission of the publisher and the author's estate.

Rodion Markovits, from *Siberian Garrison*, trans. George Halasz (New York: Horace Liveright, 1929), pp. 289–99. Translation Copyright © 1929 by Horace Liveright, Inc. Copyright renewed 1956 by Liveright Publishing Corporation. Used by permission of Liveright Publishing Corporation.

Julius Martov, from *Zapiski sotsial-demokrata* [Notes of a Social Democrat] (Berlin, St. Petersburg, and Moscow: Z. I. Grzhebin, 1922), pp. 196–201.I.

Zvi Hirsch Masliansky, from *Memoirs: An Account of My Life and Travels*, trans. Isaac Schwartz and Zviah Nardi (Jerusalem: Ariel Publishing House, 2009), excerpts from pp. 15–20, 23–25, 27–28, 31–36, 106–10, 130–35, 184–88, 192–93, 196, 238–47, 250–51, 262–65, 267–69. Used with permission of Zviah Nardi and Marshall Weinberg.

Jacob Mazeh, "Lunacharskii ve-ha-ivrit" [Lunacharsky and Hebrew] and "Siah im Gorkii" [A Conversation with Gorky], from *Zihronot*, 4 vols. (Tel Aviv: Yalkut, 1936), vol. 4: pp. 7–14, 15–23.

Vladimir Medem, excerpts from *My Life*, trans. Samuel A. Portnoy in Samuel A. Portnoy, "The Life and Soul of a Legendary Jewish Socialist," *Yiddish*, vol. 1, no. 3 (Winter 1973–1976), pp. 22–23, 25–30, 32, 42–46. Used with permission of the family of Samuel A. Portnoy.

Beinish Michalevich [Yosef Izbicki], "Erev Bund" [Pioneers], from *Roiter pinkes* (Warsaw: Kultur-lige, 1921), pp. 35–37.

Betty Miller, from *Farewell Leicester Square* (London: Persephone Books, 2000), pp. 133–46. Used with permission of the publisher.

Dovid Mitzmacher, "Shmateh-klayber" [Rag Pickers], from *Antologye fun der Yidisher proze in Poyln tsvishn beyde velt-milkhomes*, ed. Aaron Zeitlin and J. J. Trunk (New York: CYCO, 1946), pp. 389–96.

Kadya Molodovsky, "Women-Poems I, II, VI," "My Day," "A White Poet," and "Alphabet Letters," from *Paper Bridges: Selected Poems of Kadya Molodowsky*, ed. and trans. Kathryn Hellerstein (Detroit: Wayne State University Press, 1999), pp. 69, 71, 79–81, 311–13, 337–41, 347. Copyright © 1999 Wayne State University Press. Reprinted with the permission of Wayne State University Press; from "Fallen Leaves I," from *Paper Bridges: Selected Poems of Kadya Molodowsky*, ed. and trans. Kathryn Hellerstein (Detroit: Wayne State University Press, 1999), p. 87. Copyright © 1999 Wayne State University Press. Originally published as "Opgeshite bleter," *Yidishe dichterins: antologie*, ed. E. Korman (Chicago: L. M. Shtein, 1928).

Irène Némirovsky, from *David Golder*, trans. Sylvia Stuart (New York: Horace Liveright, 1930), pp. 7–22. Copyright 1930 by Horace Liveright Inc. Copyright renewed 1957 by Liveright Publishing Corp. First published in French as *David Golder* (Paris: Grasset & Fasquelle, 1929). © 1929, Grasset & Fasquelle, Paris. Used by permission of Liveright Publishing Corporation and Éditions Grasset & Fasquelle.

Moshe Zvi Neriah, "Khomrai sha'ah" [Issues of the Hour], from *Jewish Solidarity Tested: Religious Zionism in Eretz-Israel Confronts the Holocaust, 1939–1949*, ed. Hava Eshkoli Wagman (Ramat Gan: Bar-Ilan University Press, Religious Zionist Archives, Bar-Ilan University, 2012), pp. 92–93. Used with permission of the publisher.

Elimelech Neufeld, "Mikotser yakhas u-mikotser ruakh" [From Lack of Concern and from Lack of Feeling], from *Jewish Solidarity Tested: Religious Zionism in Eretz-Israel Confronts the Holocaust, 1939–1949*, ed. Hava Eshkoli Wagman (Ramat Gan: Bar-Ilan University Press, Religious Zionist Archives, Bar-Ilan University, 2012), p. 100. Used with permission of the publisher.

Sh. Niger [Samuel Charney], "Tsvayter briv fun Nu York kayn Varshe" [Second Letter from New York to Warsaw], *Globus*, vol. 6 (1933), pp. 10–11. Used with permission of the author's estate; "About Yiddish Literature," from *The Way We Think: A Collection of Essays from the Yiddish*, vol. 2, ed. and trans. Joseph Leftwich (South Brunswick, N.J.: Thomas Yoseloff, 1969), pp. 631–34. Used with permission of the author's estate and the translator's estate. This selection includes two stanzas from a poem by Itzik Feffer. Used with permission of the poet's estate.

N. M. Nikolskii, from *Dos uralte folk Yisroel* [The Ancient People of Israel], trans. from Yiddish to Russian by A. Rozental (Moscow: Tsentraler Idisher komisariat, 1920), pp. 3–7. Used with permission of the author's estate.

Salim Yitshak Nissim, "Daughter of Babylon," trans. Lital Levy, from Lital Levy, "Reorienting Hebrew Literary History: The View from the East," *Prooftexts*, vol. 29, no. 2 (2009), pp. 150–51. Used with permission of Indiana University Press.

Der Nister [Pinye Kahanowitz], from *The Family Mashber*, trans. Leonard Wolf (New York: Summit Books, 1987), pp. 35–45, 58, 100–11, 116–17. Used with permission of the translator.

Hersh David Nomberg, "Dos rebishe ayniki" [The Rebbe's Grandson], from *Antologye fun der Yidisher proze in Poyln tsvishn beyde velt-milkhomes*, ed. Aaron Zeitlin and J. J. Trunk (New York: CYCO, 1946), pp. 397–404. Originally published in Yiddish in *Varshever shriftn* (Warsaw: Literatn-klub baym fareyn fun yidishe literatn un zhurnalistn in Varshe, 1926–27).

Clifford Odets, excerpt from *Awake and Sing!* from *Waiting for Lefty and Other Plays* (New York: Grove Press, 1994), pp. 59–75. Copyright © 1933, 1935 by Clifford Odets. Copyright © renewed 1961, 1962 by Clifford Odets. Used by permission of Grove/Atlantic, Inc. and Creative Artists Agency. Any third party use of this material, outside of this publication, is prohibited.

Ivan Olbracht [Kamil Zeman], excerpts from "Julie and the Miracle," from *The Bitter and the Sweet*, trans. Iris Unwin (New York: Crown, 1967), pp. 7–8, 10–13, 20–21, 24–27, 29–35. Translation copyright © 1964 by Iris Urwin. Originally published in Czechoslovakia as *Golet v údolí*. Used by permission of Crown Books, an imprint of the Crown Publishing Group, a division of Penguin Random House LLC, and by permission of Dilia Literary Agency. All rights reserved. Any third party use of this material, outside of this publication, is prohibited. Interested parties must apply directly to Penguin Random House LLC for permission.

Joseph Opatoshu, "Brothers," from *Jewish American Literature: A Norton Anthology*, ed. Jules Chametzky, trans. Kathryn Hellerstein (New York: W.W. Norton, 2001), pp. 254–57. Used with permission of the author's estate and the translator; "Vos iz Yidishkayt?" from *Yidish un Yidishkayt* [Yiddish and Jewishness] (Toronto: Gershn Pomerantz, 1949), pp. 36–43. Used with permission of Dan Opatoshu.

Mendel Osherovich, from *Vi mentshn lebn in Sovet-Rusland* [How People Live in the Soviet Union] (New York, 1933), from pp. 94–102, 112–29, 287–97, 372–74.

Y. Osherovich, "Di shtetlech fun V.S.S.R. in rekonstruktivn period" [The Shtetls of the Belorussian Soviet Socialist Republic in the Period of Reconstruction], from *Tsum fuftsnt yortag fun der Oktyaber-revolyutsye: historisher zamlbukh* (Minsk: Belorussian Academy of Sciences, 1932), pp. 28–41.

Károly Pap, from *Azarel*, trans. Paul Olchváry (South Royalton, Vt.: Steerforth Press, 2001), pp. 73–87. Reprinted by permission of Steerforth Press, LLC.

Bertha Pappenheim, "Die Jüdische Frau" [The Jewish Woman], from *Literarische und publizistische Text*, eds. Lena Kugler and Albrechte Koschorke (Vienna: Turia & Kant, 2002), pp. 87–99. Used with permission of the author's estate.

Yehoshua Perle, from *Everyday Jews: Scenes from a Vanished Life*, ed. David Roskies, trans. Maier Deshell and Margaret Birstein (New Haven, Conn.: Yale University Press, 2007), pp. 174–81. Used with permission of the publisher.

César Tiempo [Israel Zeitlin], "Dirge for a Bar that Has Closed Down," "A Series of Verses to the Venerable Ancient Whose Portrait Hangs in the Window of a Lottery Agency," and "Verses to a Dictionary and to the Neckerchiefs (Worn by the Gauchos)," trans. Antonio J. Dajer; "Freckled Childhood" and "Romance of the Gambler's Girls," trans. Shepherd Bliss and Roberta Kalechofsky, from *Echad: An Anthology of Latin American Jewish Writings*, eds. Robert and Roberta Kalechofsky, published by Roberta Kalechofsky (Marblehead, Mass.: Micah Publications, 1960), pp. 36–44. Used with permission of the publisher.

Leon Trotsky, from *My Life* (New York: Charles Scribner's Sons, 1930), pp. 84–87. Used with permission of the author's estate.

Saul Tschernikovsky, "To the Sun I" [Sonnet 15], trans. Richard Flantz, "To the Sun II" [Sonnet 1], trans. Dom Moraes, "Eagle, Eagle!," trans. Richard Flantz, and "Three Donkeys," trans. Dom Moraes, from *Anthology of Modern Hebrew Poetry*, ed. S. Y. Penueli and A. Ukhmani (Jerusalem: Israel Universities Press, 1966). English Copyright © The Institute for the Translation of Hebrew Literature. Used with permission of the Institute for the Translation of Hebrew Literature.

David Saliman Tsemah, "For the Sixtieth Jubilee of the Poet Hayyim Nahman Bialik," trans. Lital Levy from Lital Levy, *Poetic Trespass: Writing between Hebrew and Arabic in Israel/Palestine* (Princeton, N.J.: Princeton University Press, 2014), pp. 74–75. An updated translation appears in Lital Levy, "'From Baghdad to Bialik with Love'—A Reappropriation of Modern Hebrew Poetry, 1933," *Comparative Literature Studies*, vol. 42, no. 3 (2005), pp. 135–36. Used with permission of the Princeton University Press, Pennsylvania State University Press, and the author's estate; "Jeshurun," from *The Emergence of Modern Hebrew Creativity in Babylon, 1735–1950*, ed. and trans. Lev Hakak (West Lafayette, Ind.: Purdue University Press, 2009), p. 113. Used with permission of the publisher and the author's estate.

Kurt Tucholsky, "Herr Wendriner Makes a Phone Call," from *What If—? Satirical Writings of Kurt Tucholsky*, trans. Harry Zohn and Karl F. Ross (New York: Funk & Wagnalls, 1967), pp. 23–25. Used with permission of the author's estate.

Julian Tuwim, "A Prayer," from *The Scarlet Muse: An Anthology of Polish Poems*, ed. Umadevi [Wanda Dynowska] and Harischandra B. Bhatt (Bombay: N. M. Tripathi, 1944), p. 67. Original text of poems by Julian Tuwim © Fundacja im. Juliana Tuwima i Ireny Tuwim, Warsaw, Poland, 2006. Used with permission of the author's estate and the publisher; "To the Common Man," "Jewboy," "About St. P.," from "Julian Tuwim (1894–1953): Anthology," ed. and trans. Antony Polonsky, from www.aapjstudies.org/116. Original text of poems by Julian Tuwim © Fundacja im. Juliana Tuwima i Ireny Tuwim, Warsaw, Poland, 2006. Used with permission of the author's estate and the translator.

Ben-Zion Hai Uziel, "Women's Rights in Elections to Public Institutions," from *The Jewish Political Tradition, vol. 2, Membership*, ed. Michael Walzer, Menachem Lorberbaum, and Noam J. Zohar, trans. unknown (New Haven, Conn.: Yale University Press, 2003), pp. 202–8. Translated from Piske Uziel (Jerusalem: Mossad Harav Kook, 1977). Used with permission of the publishers.

H. Uziel, Z. Galuska, Dr. Saul Mezan, Issac Alcalay, Moritz Levy, and Moshe David Gaon, "Is There a Need for a World Sephardi Federation? A Debate by Jewish Delegates in Vienna," trans. Yehuda Sharim, from *Sephardi Lives: A Documentary History, 1700–1950*, eds. Julia Phillips Cohen and Sarah Abrevaya Stein (Stanford, Calif.: Stanford University Press, 2014), pp. 244–48. Copyright © 2015 by the Board of Trustees of the Leland Stanford Jr. University. All rights reserved. Used with the permission of Stanford University Press, www.sup.org. Originally published in Hebrew as *Protocols of the World Sephardi Federation in Vienna, 1925*, The Sephardi Community Archives, Jerusalem City Hall (Jerusalem), File 1268.

M. Veinger, "Vegn Yidishe dialektn" [On Yiddish Dialects], from *Tseitschrift*, vols. 2–3 (Minsk: Institut far Vayruslendisher Kultur, 1928), pp. 613–19, 629–34.

I. M. Veisenberg, "A hayser shabes-tog" [A Hot Shabbat Day], from *Antologye fun der Yidisher proze in Poyln tsvishn beyde velt-milkhomes*, ed. Aaron Zeitlin and J. J. Trunk (New York: CYCO, 1946), pp. 247–60.

Shmuel Veisenberg, "Di yidishe familie-nemen in Ukraine" [Jewish Family Names in Ukraine], from *Filologishe shriftn*, vol. 3 (Vilna: YIVO, 1929), pp. 311–66.

Meir Viner, "Di rol fun shprakh-folklor in der Yidisher literature" [The Role of Linguistic Folklore in Yiddish Literature], from *Shriftn* (Kiev: Kultur-Lige, 1928), pp. 73–91, 102–4.

Mark Vishniak, from *Doktor Veitsman* (Paris: Imp. S.N.I.E., 1939), pp. 10–13.

David Vogel, "When Night Draws Near," from *The Penguin Book of Hebrew Verse*, ed. and trans. T. Carmi (New York: Viking Press, 1981; London: Allen Lane, 1981), p. 525. Copyright © the Estate of David Vogel. English translation copyright © T. Carmi, 1981. Published by arrangement with The Institute for the Translation of Hebrew Literature and by permission of Penguin Books Ltd; "With Gentle Fingers" and "I Saw My Father Drowning," from *The Dark Gate: Selected Poems of David Vogel*, trans. A. C. Jacobs (London: The Menard Press, 1978), pp. 16, 18. Copyright © the Estate of David Vogel. English translation copyright © The Institute for The Translation of Hebrew Literature. Published by arrangement with The Institute for the Translation of Hebrew Literature, and with The Estate of A. C. Jacobs; from *Married Life*, trans. Dalya Bilu (New York: Grove Press, 1989), pp. 45–53. Copyright © the Estate of David Vogel. Worldwide English translation copyright © The Institute for The Translation of Hebrew Literature. Published by arrangement with The Institute for the Translation of Hebrew Literature.

Abraham Vysotsky, from *Tel Aviv*, trans. Rose Wissotzky-Orlans (n.p.), pp. 28–31. Used with permission of the estate of the author and the translator, who is the daughter of the author.

Ojzer Warszawski, from *Smugglers*, trans. Golda Werman (Jerusalem: Gefen, 2008), pp. 3–7, 10–14, 35–37, 70–72, 106–10, 167–72. Used with permission of the translator.

Elhanan Wasserman, "Halukat ha-tekufot ve-hishtalshelut ha-dorot" [Periodization of the Eras and the Evolution of the Generations], from *Kovetz maamarim ve-igrot*, vol. 2 (Jerusalem: Yeshivat Or Elkhanan, 1999), pp. 81, 82–85; "Tractate: The Onset of the Messiah," from *Wrestling with God: Jewish Theological Responses during and after the Holocaust*, ed. Steven Katz, Shlomo Biderman, and Gershon Greenberg (New York: Oxford University Press, 2007), pp. 30–36. By permission of Oxford University Press, USA; from *Da'as torah: A balaychtigung fun yetztign idishn matsev al pi da'as torah* [The Opinion of the Torah: Illuminating the Present Jewish Condition According to the Light of the Torah] (New York: Le-hasig etsel Young Israel Council, 1936), pp. 1–24. Includes verses from Jewish Publication Society, *Tanakh: The Holy Scriptures* (Philadelphia: Jewish Publication Society, 1985). Copyright 1985 by the Jewish Publication Society, Philadelphia. Reprinted with permission of University of Nebraska Press.

Jakob Wassermann, from *My Life as German and Jew*, trans. Sally Neumark Brainin (New York: Coward-McCann, 1933), pp. 4–25. Used with permission of the author's estate.

Jerome Weidman, from *I Can Get It for You Wholesale* (New York: Simon and Schuster, 1937), pp. 180–92. Copyright © 1937, 1964 by Jerome Weidman. Used by permission of Brandt & Hochman Literary Agents, Inc.

Yehiel Yaakov Weinberg, "Derashah le-rosh ha-shanah bishvil ha-av ha-ivri" [Rosh Hashanah Sermon for the Jewish Father], from *Lifrakim* (Bilgoraj: Hovevei ha-agadah ve-ha-drush be-varshah, 1937), pp. 30–34. Used with permission of the author's estate.

Bernard D. Weinryb, "Kalkalah yehudit" [The Jewish Economy], *Moznayim*, vol. 8 (1938), pp. 336–44. Used with permission of the author's estate.

Felix Weltsch, from *Antisemitismus als Volkerhysterie* [Antisemitism as Folk Hysteria] (Prague: Barissia, 1931), pp. 7–15. Used with permission of the author's estate.

Robert Weltsch, "Unser Nationalismus: Eine Chanukkah-Betrachtung" [Our Nationalism: A Hanukkah Reflection], *Jüdische Rundschau*, nos. 97–98 (11 December 1925), pp. 805–6. Used with permission of the author's estate.

Stephen S. Wise, "Five Mournful Years for Jewry," from *As I See It* (New York: Jewish Opinion Publishing Corp., 1944), pp. 97–102. Used with permission of the author's estate.

Oskar Yeshayahu Wolfsberg, "Koiches fun yerideh un koiches fun aliyeh" [Powers of Descent and Powers of Ascent], from *Oyfn shedveg* (Paris, 1939), pp. 88–98.

Karl Wolfskehl, "Lord, I Want to Return," "To Be Said at the Seder," "The Voice," and "Yom HaKippurim," from *1933: A Poem Sequence*, trans. Carol North Valhope [pseud. Olga Marx] and Ernst Morwitz (New York: Schocken Books, 1947), pp. 11, 35, 37, 47. Used with permission of the author's estate and the estate of Ernst Marcus Morwitz.

The World Convention of YIVO (Yiddish Scientific Institute) upon the Tenth Anniversary of Its Founding, edited for our volume by Zvi Gitelman, from *Altveltlekher tsuzamenfor fun yidishn visnshaftlichn insitut: tsum tenyorikn yoiivl fun YIVO* (Vilna, 1936), pp. 109–26. Courtesy of YIVO Institute for Jewish Research, New York.

Yehudah Yaari, from *When the Candle Was Burning*, trans. Menahem Hurwitz (London: Victor Gollancz, a division of The Orion Publishing Group, 1947), pp. 40–47. Originally published in Hebrew as *Ka-or yahel*. Used with permission of the author's estate.

Anzia Yezierska, "Children of Loneliness," from *Children of Loneliness*, ed. Joyce Antler (New York/London: Funk & Wagnalls, 1923) pp. 101–22. Used with permission of the author's estate;

Semyon Yushkevich, from *Dud'ka* [Dudka] (Berlin: Grani, 1922), pp. 21–29.

David Zaslavskii, "Tsu der geshichte fun Bund in Kiev" [On the History of the Bund in Kiev], from *Roiter pinkes* (Warsaw: Kultur-lige, 1921), pp. 70–73.

Aaron Zeitlin, "Zumer 1937" [Summer 1937], "Autoportret" [Self-Portrait], "Reize in a furkerter richtug" [A Trip in the Opposite Direction], "Dnoen" [Bottoms], "Di nest farshvindet" [The Nest Disappears], and "Noch havdoleh" [After Havdaleh], from *Gezamelte lider* (New York: Farlag Matones, 1947), vol. 1: pp. 187–88, vol 2: pp. 448–53, 460–67, 535–36, vol. 3: pp. 322–23; "Yosef dela Rena," *Varshever shriftn* (1926–1927), pp. 31–32; "Fliglman oif links" [Fligman on the Left], *Globus*, vol. 4 (1932), pp. 62–63.

Elchonon Zeitlin, "Mit Spektorn" [With Spektor], from *Antologye fun der Yidisher proze in Poyln tsvishn beyde velt-milkhomes*, ed. Aaron Zeitlin and J. J. Trunk (New York: CYCO, 1946), pp. 497–508.

Hillel Zeitlin, "Tsiyyun le-ayarah" [Memorial to a Shtetl], from *Al gevul shenei olamot* (Tel Aviv: Yavneh, 1997), pp. 15–44, 49–50, 53–56, 58–59, 113–26, 158–62, 257–62.

Yaakov Zerubavel, "Der grindings period fun Y.S.P.A.P. Poalei Zion" [The Beginnings of the Jewish Social Democratic Workers Party, Po'ale Tsiyon], from *Roiter pinkes: tsu der geshikhte fun der yiddisher arbiter bavegung un soltsialistishe shtremvayer bei yidn* (Warsaw, 1921), pp. 134–36. Used with approval from the author's family.

Hayim Zhitlowsky, "What Is Jewish Secular Culture?," from *The Way We Think: A Collection of Essays from the Yiddish*, vol. 1, ed. and trans. Joseph Leftwich (South Brunswick, N.J.: Thomas Yoseloff, 1969), pp. 91–98. Used with permission of the translator's estate.

Abraham J. Zhitnik, from *Di idn in Sovet-rusland* [The Jews of Soviet Russia] (Cleveland: Independent Press, 1925), pp. 8–18. Used with permission of the author's estate.

Arnold Zweig, from *De Vriendt Goes Home*, English language trans. Eric Sutton (New York: The Viking Press, 1933). Copyright 1933, renewed © 1961, by the Viking Press, Inc. Used by permission of Viking Books, an imprint of Penguin Publishing Group, a division of Penguin Random House LLC.

Stefan Zweig, "Mendel the Bibliophile" from *Collected Stories of Stefan Zweig*, trans. Anthea Bell (London: Pushkin Press, 2013), pp. 591–600, 602–18. Used with permission of the publisher.

Index of Authors and Artists

Biographical information about each author or artist appears at the beginning of the person's first selection. The reader may search by subject in the web-based version of *The Posen Library of Jewish Culture and Civilization.*